THE EMC MASTERPIECE SERIES

Literature and the Language Arts

GRADES 6–12

Discovering Literature
Grade 6

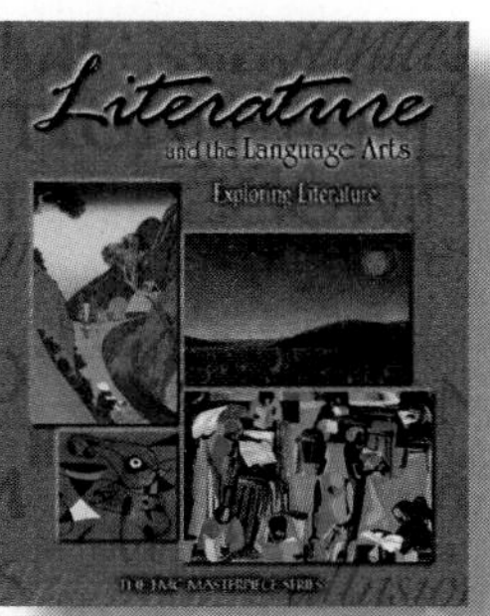

Exploring Literature
Grade 7

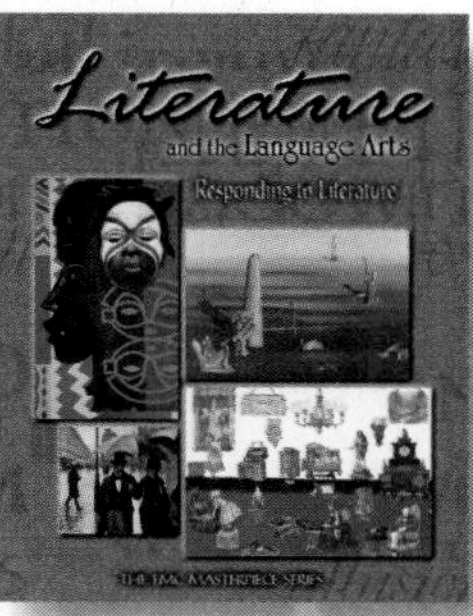

Responding to Literature
Grade 8

Experiencing Literature
Grade 9

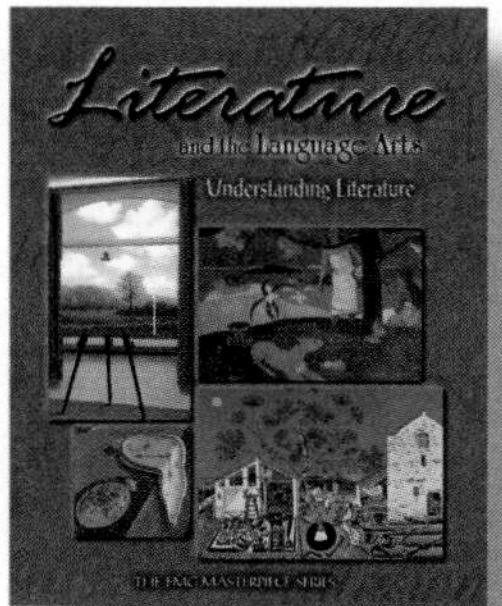

Understanding Literature
Grade 10

The American Tradition
Grade 11

The British Tradition
Grade 12

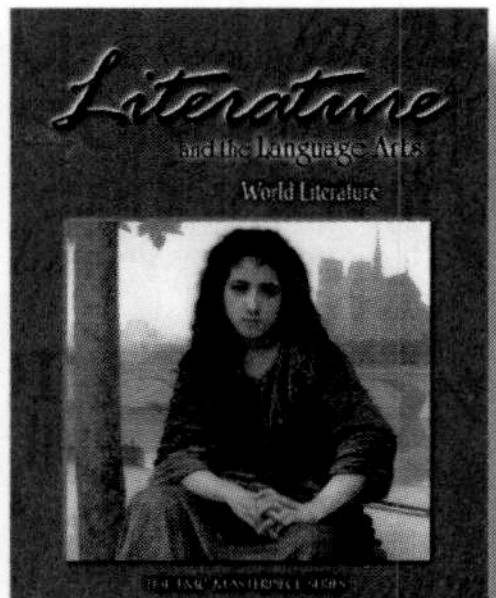

World Literature

Imagine the Possibilities...

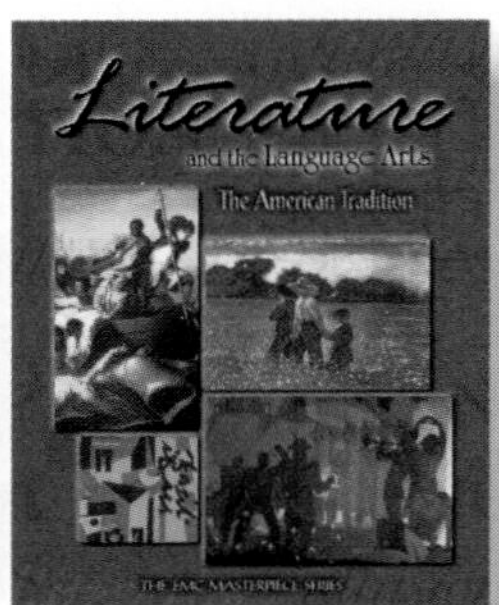

Literature and the Language Arts

GRADES 6–12

HIGH SCHOOL PROGRAM SAMPLER

Why Choose *The EMC Masterpiece Series*?

1. Quality of literature
2. Diversity of literature selections
3. Reading strategies that provide access for all students
4. Direct writing instruction integrated with grammar development
5. In-depth coverage of language arts skills
6. Comprehensive support materials

Six Reasons to Choose *The EMC Masterpiece Series*

Clockwise from left: William Faulkner, Sandra Cisneros, Seamus Heaney

1. Quality of Literature

The EMC Masterpiece Series:

- Provides you and your students with **a comprehensive collection of classic literary works** as well as compelling **contemporary and multicultural selections**.

Award-Winning Authors:

- William Faulkner, "Darl" from *As I Lay Dying*
- Seamus Heaney, "Follower"
- Sandra Cisneros, "A Smart Cookie"
- Doris Lessing, "A Sunrise on the Veld"
- Eudora Welty, "A Worn Path"
- Gabriel Garcia Marquez, "A Very Old Man with Enormous Wings"

Clockwise from left: Amy Tan, Langston Hughes, Pat Mora

2. Diversity of Literature Selections

- **Expands students' imaginative abilities and sympathies** by exposing them to points of view and cultural experiences unlike their own.
- Provides selections representative of the **cultural and ethnic diversity** of our literary heritage.
- Contains an unequaled representation of works by **authors from various cultural backgrounds.**

Diversity of Literature:

- Pat Mora, "Gentle Communion"
- Langston Hughes, "Thank You, M'am"
- Amy Tan, "Rules of the Game"
- Garrett Hongo, "The Legend"
- Julia Alvarez, "A White Woman of Color"
- Li-Young Lee, "A Story"

3. Reading Strategies Provide Access for All Students

The EMC Masterpiece Series:

- Provides step-by-step study strategies to ensure the careful development of student understanding.
- Features a **reader response** emphasis that motivates students through high-interest affective and cognitive activities to relate literature to students' experiences, followed by teacher-directed activities to ensure cultural transmission.

The EMC Masterpiece Series helps students before, during, and after their reading of the selection with its **Guided Reading** program.

Before Reading

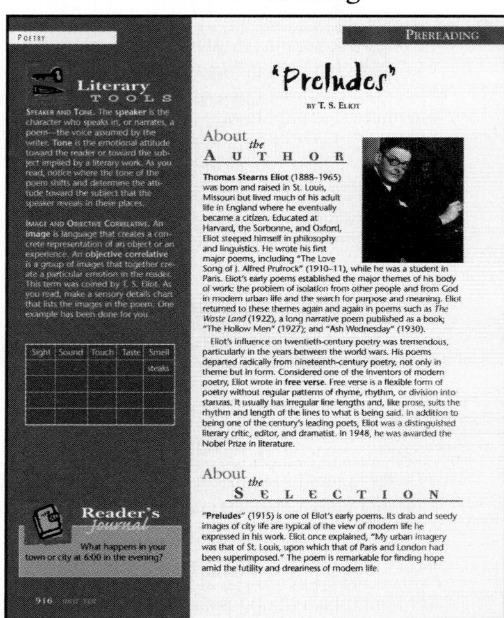

POETRY

PREREADING

Literary Tools

SPEAKER AND TONE. The **speaker** is the character who speaks in, or narrates, a poem—the voice assumed by the writer. **Tone** is the emotional attitude toward the reader or toward the subject implied by a literary work. As you read, notice where the tone of the poem shifts and determine the attitude toward the subject that the speaker reveals in these places.

IMAGE AND OBJECTIVE CORRELATIVE. An **image** is language that creates a concrete representation of an object or an experience. An **objective correlative** is a group of images that together create a particular emotion in the reader. This term was coined by T. S. Eliot. As you read, make a sensory details chart that lists the images in the poem. One example has been done for you.

Sight	Sound	Touch	Taste	Smell
				steaks

Reader's Journal

What happens in your town or city at 6:00 in the evening?

916 UNIT TEN

"Preludes"

BY T. S. ELIOT

About the Author

Thomas Stearns Eliot (1888–1965) was born and raised in St. Louis, Missouri but lived much of his adult life in England where he eventually became a citizen. Educated at Harvard, the Sorbonne, and Oxford, Eliot steeped himself in philosophy and linguistics. He wrote his first major poems, including "The Love Song of J. Alfred Prufrock" (1910–11), while he was a student in Paris. Eliot's early poems established the major themes of his body of work: the problem of isolation from other people and from God in modern urban life and the search for purpose and meaning. Eliot returned to these themes again and again in poems such as *The Waste Land* (1922), a long narrative poem published as a book; "The Hollow Men" (1927); and "Ash Wednesday" (1930).

Eliot's influence on twentieth-century poetry was tremendous, particularly in the years between the world wars. His poems departed radically from nineteenth-century poetry, not only in theme but in form. Considered one of the inventors of modern poetry, Eliot wrote in **free verse**. Free verse is a flexible form of poetry without regular patterns of rhyme, rhythm, or division into stanzas. It usually has irregular line lengths and, like prose, suits the rhythm and length of the lines to what is being said. In addition to being one of the century's leading poets, Eliot was a distinguished literary critic, editor, and dramatist. In 1948, he was awarded the Nobel Prize in literature.

About the Selection

"Preludes" (1915) is one of Eliot's early poems. Its drab and seedy images of city life are typical of the view of modern life he expressed in his work. Eliot once explained, "My urban imagery was that of St. Louis, upon which that of Paris and London had been superimposed." The poem is remarkable for finding hope amid the futility and dreariness of modern life.

During Reading

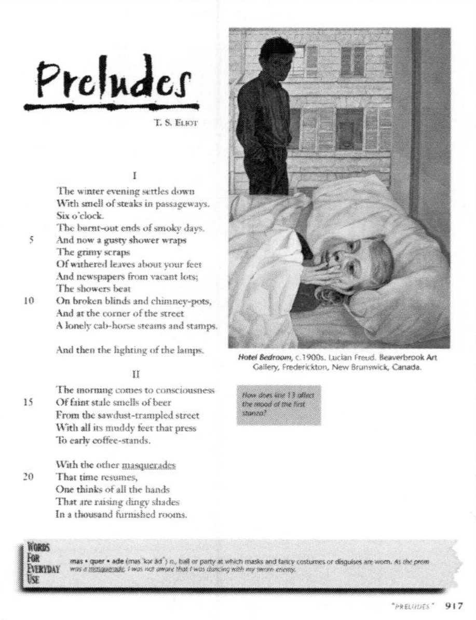

Preludes

T. S. ELIOT

I

The winter evening settles down
With smell of steaks in passageways.
Six o'clock.
The burnt-out ends of smoky days.
And now a gusty shower wraps
The grimy scraps
Of withered leaves about your feet
And newspapers from vacant lots;
The showers beat
On broken blinds and chimney-pots,
And at the corner of the street
A lonely cab-horse steams and stamps.

And then the lighting of the lamps.

II

The morning comes to consciousness
Of faint stale smells of beer
From the sawdust-trampled street
With all its muddy feet that press
To early coffee-stands.

With the other masquerades
That time resumes,
One thinks of all the hands
That are raising dingy shades
In a thousand furnished rooms.

Hotel Bedroom, c.1900s. Lucian Freud. Beaverbrook Art Gallery, Frederickton, New Brunswick, Canada.

How does line 13 affect the mood of the first stanza?

WORDS FOR EVERYDAY USE

mas • quer • ade (mas´kər ād´) *n.*, ball or party at which masks and fancy costumes or disguises are worn. *As the prom was a masquerade, I was not aware that I was dancing with my sworn enemy.*

"PRELUDES" 917

- **About the Author** provides contextual information about the author's life and the period in which he or she lived.
- **About the Selection** provides keys to comprehension of the selection; this covers literary movements, genres, techniques, or themes, depending upon the demands of the selection and its place in literary history.
- **Literary Tools** introduces literary techniques or concepts that will help the reader under-stand the selection. The same concepts are reinforced in the Understanding Literature section of the Post-Reading materials.
- A **Graphic Organizer** or other visual literacy piece is provided for visual learners.
- **Reader's Journal** activities help create the anticipatory set by relating the literature to students' experiences.
- **Guided Reading Questions** help students gather facts about the selection that will help in their response to higher-level thinking skills.
- **Words for Everyday Use** provide pronunciations, parts of speech, definitions, and contextual sentences for vocabulary underlined in the selection.
- **Footnotes** explain obscure references, unusual usage, and terms meant to enter students' passive vocabularies.
- **Art Notes** provide historical, cultural, or artistic information about fine art.

- **Respond to the Selection** activities relate the literature to students' lives.
- **Investigate, Inquire, and Imagine** questions base literature interpretation on textual evidence.
    - **Recall** questions address comprehension. **Interpret** questions use facts from the Recall question as a basis for valid interpretation.
    - **Analyze** questions ask readers to classify, compare and contrast, and identify relationships between ideas. **Synthesize** questions ask readers to integrate, restructure, predict, elaborate, and summarize.
    - **Evaluate** questions ask students to appraise, assess, critique, and justify certain aspects of a selection. **Extend** questions allow readers to try out their understanding in different situations.
    - **Perspective** questions encourage students to look for and value alternative perspectives. **Empathy** questions ask the student to demonstrate understanding of another person's worldview.
- **Understanding Literature** questions reinforce the literary concepts and techniques that were introduced on the Prereading page in the Literary Tools feature.
- **Writer's Journal** includes three quick-writing prompts that are graded as simple, moderate, and challenging.

After Reading

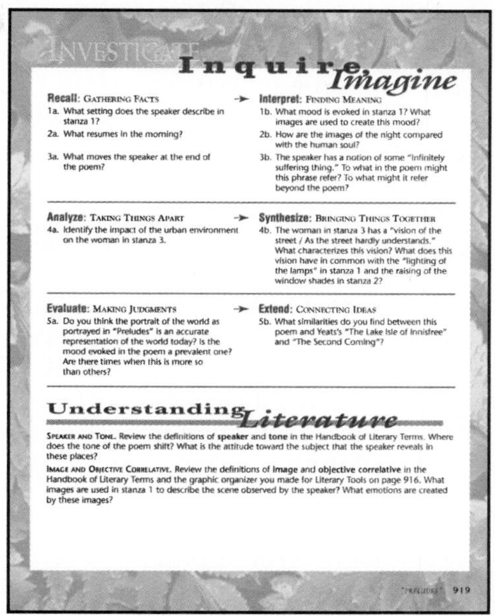

INVESTIGATE Inquire Imagine

Recall: GATHERING FACTS → **Interpret:** FINDING MEANING

1a. What setting does the speaker describe in stanza 1?

1b. What mood is evoked in stanza 1? What images are used to create this mood?

2a. What resumes in the morning?

2b. How are the images of the night compared with the human soul?

3a. What moves the speaker at the end of the poem?

3b. The speaker has a notion of some "infinitely suffering thing." To what in the poem might this phrase refer? To what might it refer beyond the poem?

Analyze: TAKING THINGS APART → **Synthesize:** BRINGING THINGS TOGETHER

4a. Identify the impact of the urban environment on the woman in stanza 3.

4b. The woman in stanza 3 has a "vision of the street / As the street hardly understands." What characterizes this vision? What does this vision have in common with the "lighting of the lamps" in stanza 1 and the raising of the window shades in stanza 2?

Evaluate: MAKING JUDGMENTS → **Extend:** CONNECTING IDEAS

5a. Do you think the portrait of the world as portrayed in "Preludes" is an accurate representation of the world today? Is the mood evoked in the poem a prevalent one? Are there times when this is more so than others?

5b. What similarities do you find between this poem and Yeats's "The Lake Isle of Innisfree" and "The Second Coming"?

Understanding Literature

SPEAKER AND TONE. Review the definitions of **speaker** and **tone** in the Handbook of Literary Terms. Where does the tone of the poem shift? What is the attitude toward the subject that the speaker reveals in these places?

IMAGE AND OBJECTIVE CORRELATIVE. Review the definitions of **image** and **objective correlative** in the Handbook of Literary Terms and the graphic organizer you made for Literary Tools on page 916. What images are used in stanza 1 to describe the scene observed by the speaker? What emotions are created by these images?

"PRELUDES" 919

- **Integrating the Language Arts** provides integrated activities in the following language arts areas, tying language arts instruction to the literature selection:
    - Language, Grammar, and Style
    - Speaking and Listening
    - Study and Research
    - Applied English
    - Collaborative Learning
    - Media Literacy
    - Vocabulary Development
    - Critical Thinking

4. Direct Writing Instruction Integrated with Grammar Development

The **Guided Writing Program** provides direct writing instruction for each literature unit and pairs the writing process with an **Integrated Language, Grammar, and Style** lesson. The Guided Writing lesson includes professional and student models, graphic organizers, questions that allow students to link their reading experience to the writing assignment, and an integrated grammar lesson. Additional support is provided by:

Writer's Resource. This ancillary provides general and mode-specific writing rubrics, student-friendly checklists, student models for each assignment, graphic organizers, and student handouts.

Electronic Guided Writing Software. The Guided Writing Software provides extended lessons that deliver print content and extensions electronically.

5. In-Depth Coverage of Language Arts Skills

Language Arts Survey

The **Language Arts Survey** in *The EMC Masterpiece Series* has the most extensive language arts skills coverage of any program. The coverage of English skills is so comprehensive that an additional English skills textbook is not necessary. The Language Arts Survey sections may be taught as separate units, using the student textbook and ancillary worksheets, or may be taught in conjunction with study of the literature.

Language Arts Survey: Writing

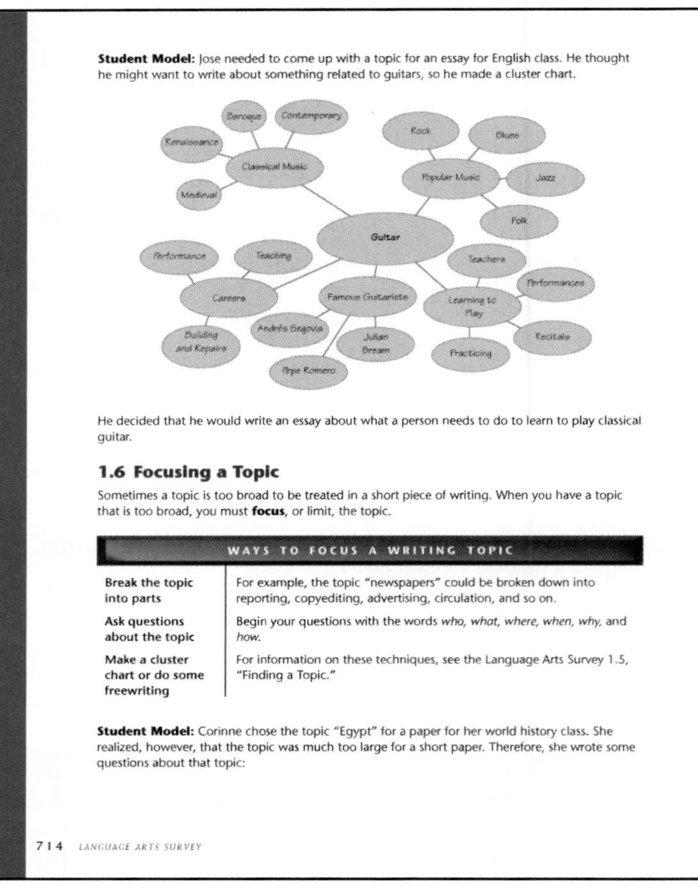

Student Model: Jose needed to come up with a topic for an essay for English class. He thought he might want to write about something related to guitars, so he made a cluster chart.

He decided that he would write an essay about what a person needs to do to learn to play classical guitar.

1.6 Focusing a Topic

Sometimes a topic is too broad to be treated in a short piece of writing. When you have a topic that is too broad, you must **focus**, or limit, the topic.

WAYS TO FOCUS A WRITING TOPIC	
Break the topic into parts	For example, the topic "newspapers" could be broken down into reporting, copyediting, advertising, circulation, and so on.
Ask questions about the topic	Begin your questions with the words *who, what, where, when, why,* and *how.*
Make a cluster chart or do some freewriting	For information on these techniques, see the Language Arts Survey 1.5, "Finding a Topic."

Student Model: Corinne chose the topic "Egypt" for a paper for her world history class. She realized, however, that the topic was much too large for a short paper. Therefore, she wrote some questions about that topic:

714 *LANGUAGE ARTS SURVEY*

There are six sections in the Language Arts Survey:

1. The **Reading Resource** surveys and enhances the reading process.
2. The **Writing Resource** surveys the entire process of writing. It includes computer-assisted composition and portfolio writing.
3. The **Language, Grammar, and Style Resource** surveys key concepts in grammar, usage, mechanics, spelling, vocabulary development, and language variety. Grammar, usage, and mechanics instruction focuses on editing and proofreading applications.
4. The **Speaking and Listening Resource** surveys verbal and nonverbal communication, active listening, interpersonal communication, discussion, public speaking, and oral interpretation.
5. The **Study and Research Resource** surveys thinking, reading, research, and test-taking skills, including skills for taking standardized tests.
6. The **Applied English Resource** surveys applications of English skills to the world of work.

6. Comprehensive Support Materials

Literature and the Language Arts

HIGH SCHOOL PROGRAM

Supplementary and Multimedia Components

The EMC Masterpiece Series provides a wide array of ancillary tools to offer teachers many options to help students connect with the literature.

Each level in the high school program includes the following materials:

- Pupil's Edition with Language Arts Survey
- Annotated Teacher's Edition
- Annotated Teacher's Edition on CD-ROM (with links to Language Arts Survey and ancillaries)
- Teacher's Resource Kit
  - Program Manager with Scope and Sequence / Lesson Planning Guide
  - Parent and Community Involvement Handbook
  - 12 Unit Resource Books
    - Guided Reading Resource (Selection Worksheets and Graphic Organizers for Reader's Toolbox / Literary Tools, Post-Reading, and Understanding Literature)
    - Vocabulary SkillBuilders / Daily Oral Language Activities
    - Selection Check Tests and Selection Tests
    - Unit Tests
    - Answer Keys
    - Reading Logs
    - Research Journal
    - Language, Grammar and Style; Speaking and Listening; Study and Research; and Applied English worksheets related to unit
  - Guided Reading Resource
  - Guided Writing Resource
  - Language, Grammar, and Style Resource
  - Speaking and Listening Resource
  - Study and Research Resource
  - Applied English Resource
  - Transparency and Visual Literacy Resource
  - Assessment Resource

Additional components:

- Guided Writing Interactive Software
- Test Generator
- Audio Library on Audiocassette and Audio CD
- Electronic Library on CD-ROM
- Access Edition Supplemental Novels and Plays
- Assessment Manuals for Access Editions

TEACHER'S RESOURCE KIT

The Teacher's Resource Kit for each level includes the following components:

Program Manager
The Program Manager provides thorough scope and sequence charts and clear, simple, ready-to-use lesson plans. Timed activities allow for a variety of approaches and scheduling options (including block scheduling) tailored to your classroom needs.

Parent and Community Involvement Handbook
The Parent and Community Involvement Handbook, featuring an introductory letter to parents written in both Spanish and English, helps parents assist their children with their studies through study log blackline masters, parent guides, activity lists, suggested reading lists, and additional resource references.

Unit Resource Books with ancillary materials for each unit:
Unit Resource Books pull together ancillary materials from a variety of sources that are used in each unit. They include the following:

- Guided Reading Resource
- Vocabulary Skillbuilders/Daily Oral Language
- Selection Check Tests and Selection Tests
- Unit Tests
- Answer Keys
- Reading Logs
- Research Journal
- Integrated Language Arts Worksheets

Assessment Resource
The Assessment Resource provides blackline master materials for:

- Unit study guides and tests, including vocabulary worksheets
- Selection check tests and comprehensive tests
- Language arts study guides, pre-tests, and post-tests
- Worksheets and forms for portfolio assessment
- Answer keys

Resource Workbooks
The Resource workbooks contain blackline masters of exercises keyed to the Language Arts Survey sections of the student textbooks. They provide additional skill exercises in these language arts subject areas:

- Reading
- Writing
- Language, Grammar, and Style
- Speaking and Listening
- Study and Research
- Applied English

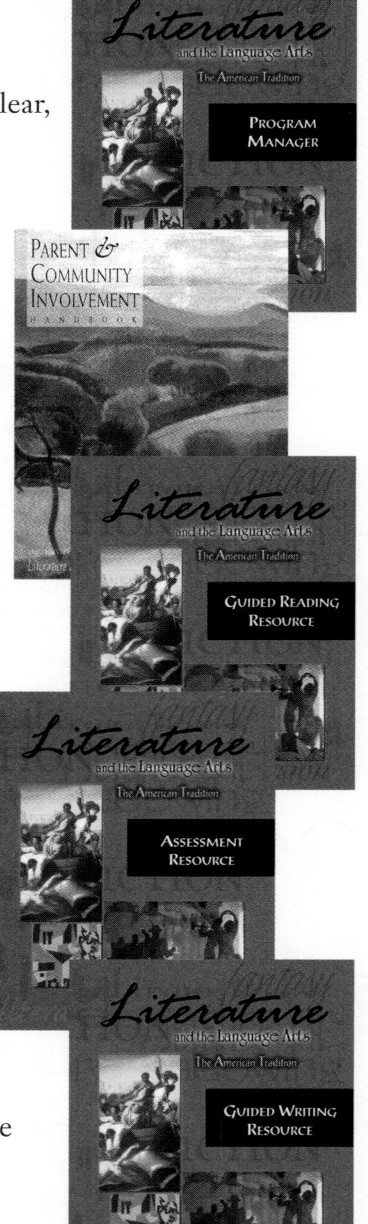

ADDITIONAL COMPONENTS FOR EACH LEVEL INCLUDE:

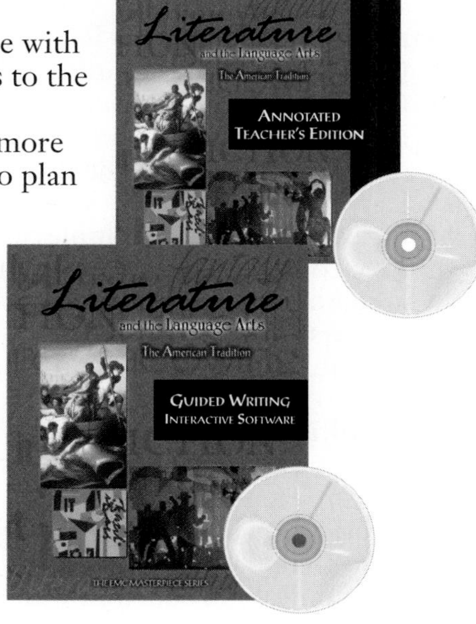

Annotated Teacher's Edition on CD-ROM

- Annotated Teacher's Edition on CD-ROM, compatible with Macintosh and Windows systems, provides easy access to the selections.
- Teachers can view on screen or print selections into a more portable form instead of carrying the textbook home to plan classes.
- Teachers can preview blackline masters from Resource workbooks and other supplemental materials via hyperlinks.

Guided Writing Interactive Software

The Guided Writing Interactive Software builds on the Guided Writing and Integrated Language, Grammar, and Style lessons in the textbook. The "writer-friendly" word processor includes:

- Capacity for self-, peer, and teacher evaluation notes
- Spelling and grammar utilities
- Hypertext links providing help specific to the writing task
- Printable graphic organizers, checklists, and student handouts
- Portfolio management system for teachers
- Windows and Macintosh compatibility

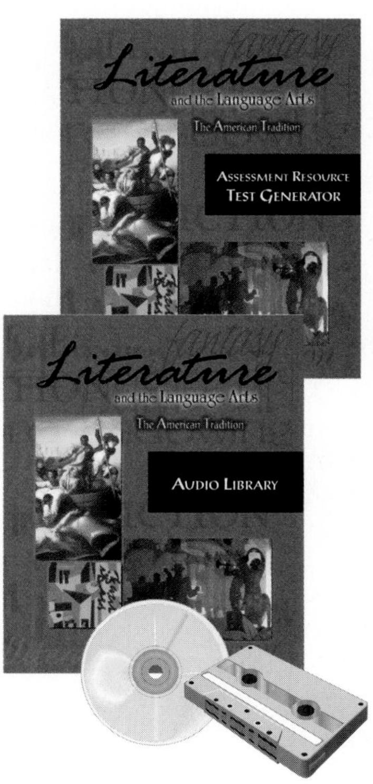

Assessment Resource Test Generator

The Assessment Resource is available in electronic form, running on Windows and Macintosh formats. Teachers can generate customized true/false, multiple choice, short answer, and essay tests based on literature selections in each unit.

Audio Library on Audiocassette and Audio CD

- Includes 10 to 12 hours of audio recordings for each grade level in the program.
- Features authentic, dramatic interpretations by professional actors and academic scholars with a balance of multicultural male and female voices.
- Readings are geared toward English language and auditory learners.
- Available on audiocassette and audio compact disc.
- Accompanying Audio Library Booklet describes each performance and offers creative ideas on how to use the audio component selection in the classroom.

OTHER SUPPLEMENTARY MATERIALS

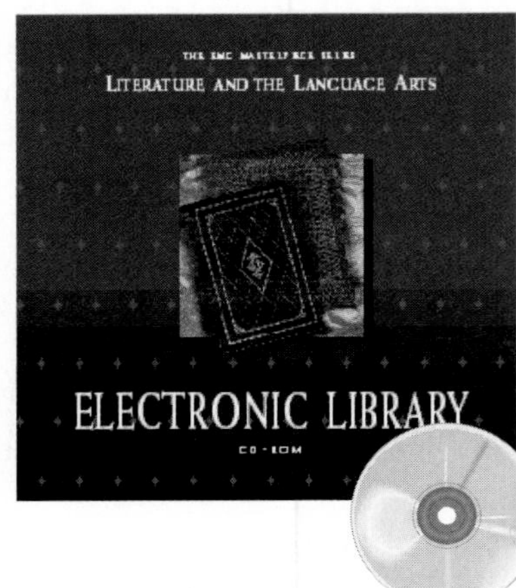

Electronic Library on CD-ROM

- Over 20,000 pages of literary classics
- Contains 120 long selections, including epic poems, novels, plays, nonfiction, and verse; as well as 194 short selections, which include poetry and excerpts.
- Can view on screen or print out individual selections instead of carrying multiple texts home to plan classes.
- Electronic Library Guide provides teaching suggestions, enrichment activities, and Guided Reading blackline masters.
- Available for Windows and Macintosh.

Access Editions

Each **Access Edition** contains the following materials:

- The complete literary work
- A historical introduction including an explanation of literary or philosophical movements relevant to the work
- A biographical introduction with a time line of the author's life
- Art, including explanatory illustrations, maps, genealogies and plot diagrams, as appropriate to the text
- Study apparatus for each chapter or section, including:
    - Guided Reading Questions
    - Words for Everyday Use entries for point-of-use vocabulary development
    - Footnotes
    - Responding to the Selection questions
    - Reviewing the Selection questions (with recalling, interpreting, and higher-level questions to assure your students a close and accessible reading of the text)
    - Understanding Literature questions
- A list of topics for creative writing, critical writing, and research projects
- A glossary of Words for Everyday Use
- A Handbook of Literary Terms

Contents

Overview

ORGANIZATION OF THE TEXT

Textbooks presenting surveys of British literature often begin with selections from the Aglo-Saxon period, thus confronting students at the beginning of the course with some of the most challenging work. The editors and authors of this text believe that before beginning a survey of British literature, students should review basic literary types and techniques in connection with readily accessible, high-interest selections. *Literature and the Language Arts: The British Tradition* has been designed to offer just such review of literary concepts in preparation for the historical survey that follows.

The text is organized into three parts:

Part One: Understanding Literature consists of a single unit that reviews the five genres of literature—the oral tradition, poetry, fiction, drama, and nonfiction—and provides an overview of the writing process. The unit is divided into five sections. Each section presents a model work in a particular literary genre. A brief introduction at the beginning of each section gives a history and taxonomy of the genre. This is followed by a thorough presentation of terminology and techniques of particular relevance to that genre. The model selections in each section contain passages set in blue ink and keyed to marginal notes that identify characteristics and techniques typical of works in that genre. Thus the model fictional piece contains highlighted passages identifying such elements as setting, character, theme, and the components of the plot. The selections in Unit 1 include ample reader response and teacher-assisted activities that integrate language arts skill development with the teaching of literature. Each selection also includes a Words for Everyday Use feature to help students develop their active vocabulary.

Unit 1 also presents the first of 12 end-of-unit Guided Writing lessons, thus setting the stage for direct writing instruction that will continue through the course of study. Each Guided Writing lesson includes a professional or student model and close look at the steps of the writing process: prewriting, drafting, evaluating, revising, publishing and presenting, and reflecting.

The unit concludes with a Unit Review that offers a review of vocabulary and literary terms and a feature that allows students to reflect on and synthesize their reading experience.

Part Two: The English Tradition presents British literature using a historical approach (to use other approaches such as theme or genre based, see the notes on page T22 of this *Annotated Teacher's Edition*). Units 2–12 begin with historical essays covering major social, political, and intellectual trends associated with the literature of each period from the Anglo-Saxon Era to the Contemporary Era. The "Echoes" page that follows each unit introduction offers intriguing quotations chosen to foster discussion and broaden awareness of that time period.

The selections within each unit have been chosen carefully to meet a number of criteria:

- To provide students with engaging, stimulating reading experiences
- To provide outstanding representative examples of each period
- To provide examples of the major genres of literature in each period
- To provoke interesting discussions of significant themes
- To represent major writers in the American literary tradition
- To represent significant literary contributions by women and writers of diverse ethnic backgrounds

Following most of the units are **Selections for Additional Reading.** These selections are not accompanied by the usual teaching apparatus, since they are intended for independent reading and enrichment activities. Students can use these selections for research when preparing critical papers on literary movements or trends. Beginning with the Middle Ages, each unit also includes **Multicultural Extensions**, literature from outside Britian linked thematically to developments in British literature.

In addition to the literature selections, early units include sections on the **Development of the English Language**. These sections cover the delevopment of the language from its origins through the emergence of Modern English.

Each unit teaches English vocabulary with **Words for Everyday Use** and concludes with a Unit Review that offers a review of vocabulary and literary terms and Reflecting on Your Reading questions for discussion or writing.

Part Three: **The Language Arts Survey** offers comprehensive instruction in the complete range of language arts skills, including Reading; Writing; Language, Grammar, and Style; Speaking and Listening; Study and Research; and Applied English. (Each lesson in the Language Arts Survey is keyed to a worksheet in one of the Resource Books in the Teacher's Resource Kit.) The **Handbook of Literary Terms** defines and provides examples of terms for literary movements and schools of thought, literary techniques, and genres of literature. The **Glossary** collects all the Words for Everyday Use and provides both pronunciations and definitions. The text ends with **indexes** of titles and authors, skills, Internet sites, and fine art.

The Oral Tradition

ArtNote

Part One: Understanding ***Literature*** *reviews basic literary genres and techniques in connection with readily accessible, high-interest selections. This part of the text prepares students for the historical survey to come.*

Nonfiction

Drama

Poetry

Fiction

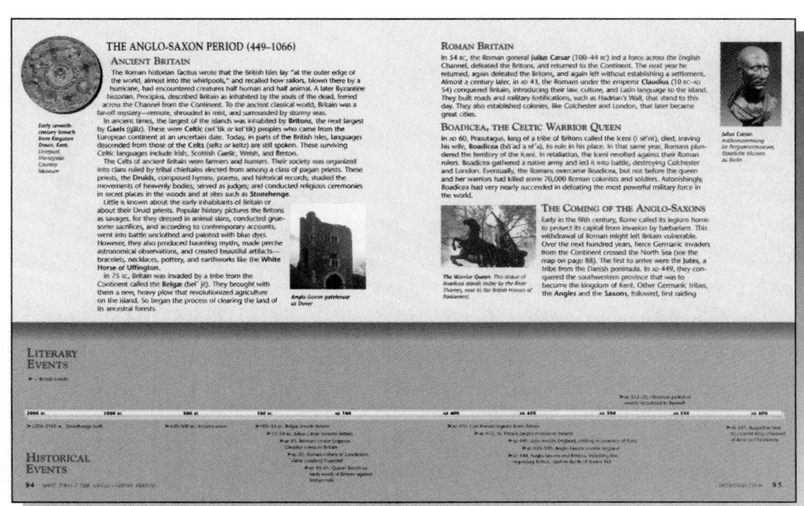
THE ANGLO-SAXON PERIOD (449–1066)

ANCIENT BRITAIN

ROMAN BRITAIN

BOADICEA, THE CELTIC WARRIOR QUEEN

THE COMING OF THE ANGLO-SAXONS

LITERARY EVENTS

HISTORICAL EVENTS

Part Two: The Englih Tradition *surveys British literature from the Anglo-Saxon Era to the present. Time lines in the introduction provide a spatial representation of key literary and historical events and developments.*

Part Three contains

- *A comprehensive **Language Arts Survey**. The Language Arts Survey contains the following 6 parts:*

  *(1) The **Reading Resource** shows students how to strategize and improve their reading abilities. It emphasizes adapting reading strategies depending on purpose: reading for experience (literature), reading to learn (textbooks and nonfiction), and reading for information (Internet materials, reference works, and visuals). It also includes a section on vocabulary development. The Reading Resource is used in Post-Reading activities and is referenced in the Individual Learning Strategies feature in the Annotated Teacher's Edition.*

  *(2) The **Writing Resource** provides an overview of the writing process and then takes students step by step through that process. The Writing Resource is used in Post-Reading activities and extensively in the Guided Writing lessons at the end of each of the twelve literature units.*

  *(3) The **Language, Grammar, and Style Resource** provides a Language Handbook, Grammar Handbook, and Style Handbook to help students master their use of the English language. The Language Handbook explores appropriate uses of English, including choices regarding formal and informal English; register, tone, and voice; irony, sarcasm, and rudeness; and dialects. The Grammar Handbook has been designed with the understanding that the basic unit of English meaning is the English sentence and takes a sentence-based approach in its instruction and all integrated grammar exercises. The Style Handbook is a capitalization, punctuation, and spelling reference.*

  *(4) The **Speaking and Listening Resource** provides instruction in the power of communication, listening skills, communicating with others, communication styles and cultural barriers, and public speaking. The Speaking and Listening Resource is used in Post-Reading activities and in the Guided Writing lessons.*

  *(5) The **Study and Research Resource** includes sections on thinking skills, study skills, research skills, and test-taking skills. It is used extensively in Post-Reading activities and in Guided Writing lessons. Particular attention is given to conducting research online and evaluating the reliability of Internet sources.*

  *(6) The **Applied English Resource** includes instruction on applications of English skills to the world of work. Topics include following and giving directions, writing step-by-step procedures, writing business letters, memos, proposals, résumés, and public service announcements, and displaying effective visual information. These and other topics are integrated in the Post-Reading activities throughout the textbook.*

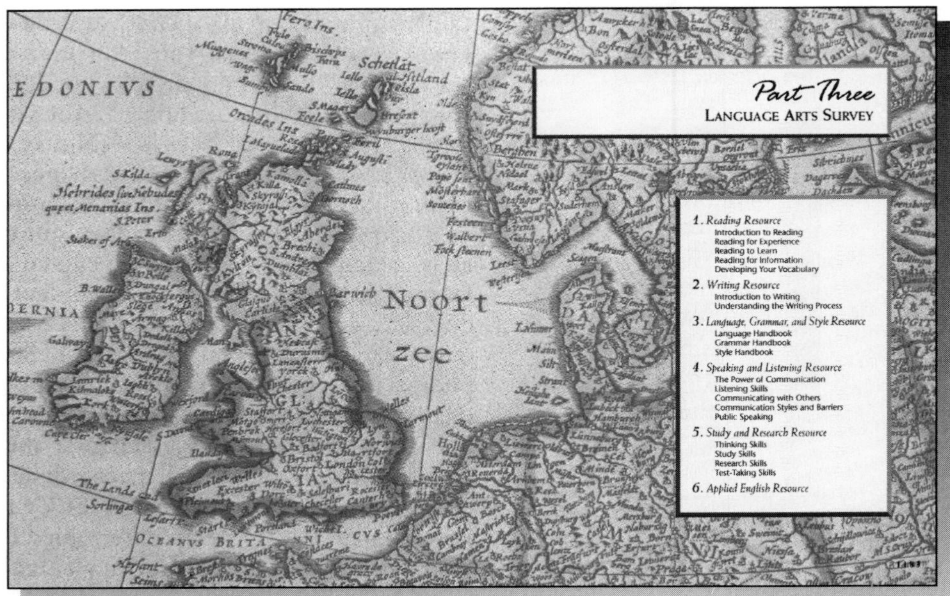

- *A thorough **Handbook of Literary Terms***
- *A **Glossary** of Words for Everyday Use*
- ***Indexes** of Titles and Authors, Skills, Internet Sites and Fine Art*

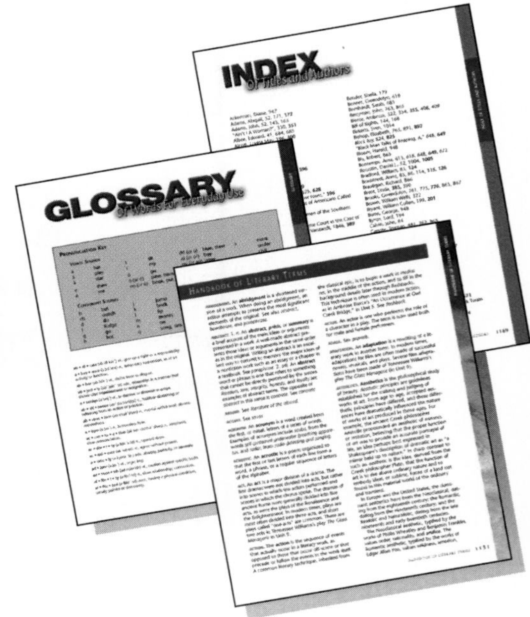

INDEX
of Titles and Authors
GLOSSARY
of Words for Everyday Use
Handbook of Literary Terms

Lesson Design and Teaching Strategies

Literature Instruction

Each lesson in *Literature and the Language Arts* contains materials for two phases of instruction, the Reader Response phase and the Teacher-Assisted phase.

The Reader Response Phase. Cognitive theory and common sense tell us that learning is more likely to occur when students are first provided with a context for what they are to learn. Each lesson in this book begins with a **Prereading** page that provides essential information about the author and the selection. The precise content of the entries **About the Author** and **About the Selection** varies according to the demands of the work to be read. If basic comprehension of the work requires understanding of a historical allusion, then that allusion is explained. If comprehension requires understanding of a literary technique, then that technique is described. In addition, the Prereading page provides information about the author and selection designed to arouse student interest. Each Prereading page also contains a **Literary Tools** box which introduces literary techniques or concepts that will help the reader understand the selection. The same concepts are reinforced in the Understanding Literature section of the Post-Reading material.

The Prereading page also includes a **Reader's Journal** activity that raises a central theme from the selection and asks the student to relate that theme to his or her own life. If, for example, a selection presents a character who fails to exhibit courage, the student might be asked to write about a time when he or she acted courageously or wanted to act coura-

Sample Prereading Page

Literary Tools *introduces literary techniques or concepts that will help the reader understand the selection.*

A Graphic Organizer *is provided in Prereading or Post-Reading for visual learners.*

Reader's Journal *activities help create the anticipatory set by relating the literature to students' own lives.*

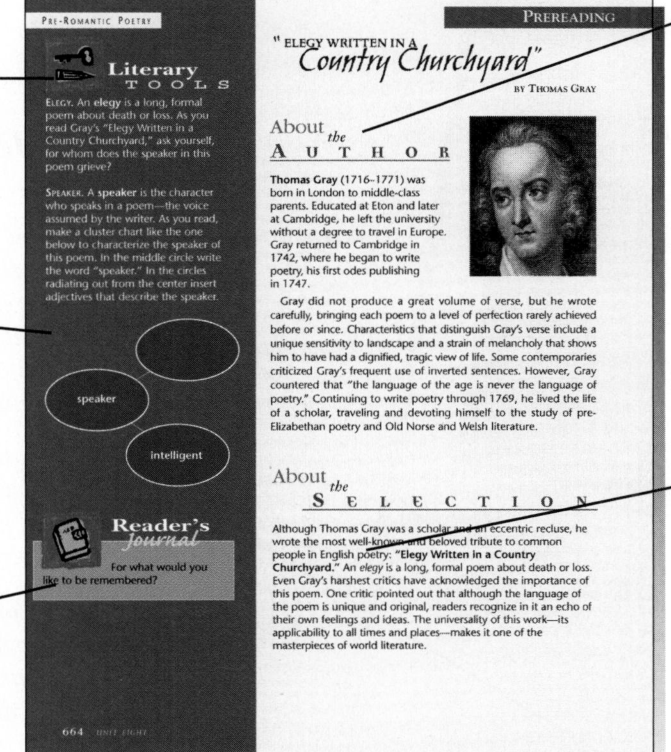

PRE-ROMANTIC POETRY

PREREADING

"ELEGY WRITTEN IN A Country Churchyard"

BY THOMAS GRAY

Literary TOOLS

ELEGY. An **elegy** is a long, formal poem about death or loss. As you read Gray's "Elegy Written in a Country Churchyard," ask yourself, for whom does the speaker in this poem grieve?

SPEAKER. A **speaker** is the character who speaks in a poem—the voice assumed by the writer. As you read, make a cluster chart like the one below to characterize the speaker of this poem. In the middle circle write the word "speaker." In the circles radiating out from the center insert adjectives that describe the speaker.

Reader's Journal

For what would you like to be remembered?

About *the* AUTHOR

Thomas Gray (1716–1771) was born in London to middle-class parents. Educated at Eton and later at Cambridge, he left the university without a degree to travel in Europe. Gray returned to Cambridge in 1742, where he began to write poetry, his first odes publishing in 1747.

Gray did not produce a great volume of verse, but he wrote carefully, bringing each poem to a level of perfection rarely achieved before or since. Characteristics that distinguish Gray's verse include a unique sensitivity to landscape and a strain of melancholy that shows him to have had a dignified, tragic view of life. Some contemporaries criticized Gray's frequent use of inverted sentences. However, Gray countered that "the language of the age is never the language of poetry." Continuing to write poetry through 1769, he lived the life of a scholar, traveling and devoting himself to the study of pre-Elizabethan poetry and Old Norse and Welsh literature.

About *the* SELECTION

Although Thomas Gray was a scholar and an eccentric recluse, he wrote the most well-known and beloved tribute to common people in English poetry: **"Elegy Written in a Country Churchyard."** An *elegy* is a long, formal poem about death or loss. Even Gray's harshest critics have acknowledged the importance of this poem. One critic pointed out that although the language of the poem is unique and original, readers recognize in it an echo of their own feelings and ideas. The universality of this work—its applicability to all times and places—makes it one of the masterpieces of world literature.

664 UNIT EIGHT

About the Author *provides contextual information about the author's life and the period in which he or she lived.*

About the Selection *provides keys to comprehension of the selection; this covers literary movements, genres, techniques, or themes, depending upon the demands of the selection and its place in literary history.*

geously but could not. After completing this exercise, students will be thinking of courage in terms of their own lives and will be more likely to relate personally to the selection and become emotionally invested in it. Emotional investment in the work is key to the reading of literature, and that is why the Reader's Journal activities are primarily affective in nature. Responses to these Reader's Journal activities can be made on the **Selection Worksheets** found in the **Unit Resource Books,** or they can be made in the student's notebook.

Once the student begins reading the selection, he or she can then take advantage of the **Guided Reading Questions** that appear in the margins. These questions are designed to bring to the student's attention key passages in the selection and issues raised by those passages. Like a guide taking a tourist through Oxford or Cambridge and pointing out important or interesting landmarks, these questions take the student through the selection, ensuring that the most important or interesting aspects of the selection will not be missed. (It would be wonderful if every student could have his or her own private guide to literature. These questions provide the next best thing.) The student can answer these questions on the Selection Worksheets or in his or her notebook.

After reading the selection, students can meet in small collaborative learning groups to share responses to the Reader's Journal activity and Guided Reading Questions. In these groups, students can also discuss the questions raised in the **Respond to the Selection** feature that follows the selection. Again, this is an affective-response prompt designed to connect the student emotionally to the literature.

These three components of the instructional apparatus, the Reader's Journal activity, the Guided Reading questions, and the Respond to the Selection activity, connect the student to the selection, guide him or her through it, and then make it possible for the student to share his or her responses with others. Together, these activities ensure that once the teacher-assisted phase of the instruction begins, the student will have a wealth of responses to share in discussions with the whole class.

Additional teaching suggestions for the Reader's Journal and Respond to the Selection activities are provided in the Annotated Teacher's Edition. Answers to Guided Reading Questions appear on the corresponding page of the Annotated Teacher's Edition.

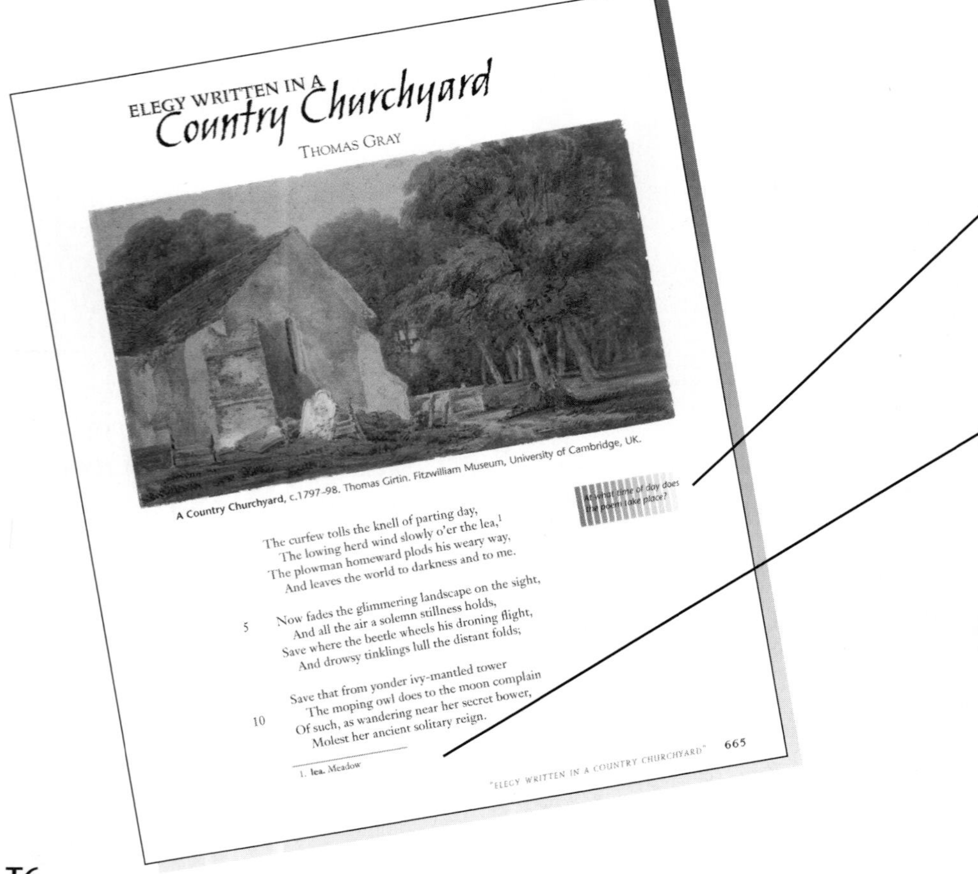

ELEGY WRITTEN IN A Country Churchyard

THOMAS GRAY

A Country Churchyard, c.1797–98. Thomas Girtin. Fitzwilliam Museum, University of Cambridge, UK.

At what time of day does the poem take place?

The curfew tolls the knell of parting day,
The lowing herd wind slowly o'er the lea,[1]
The plowman homeward plods his weary way,
And leaves the world to darkness and to me.

Now fades the glimmering landscape on the sight,
And all the air a solemn stillness holds,
Save where the beetle wheels his droning flight,
And drowsy tinklings lull the distant folds;

Save that from yonder ivy-mantled tower
The moping owl does to the moon complain
Of such, as wandering near her secret bower,
Molest her ancient solitary reign.

1. **lea.** Meadow

"ELEGY WRITTEN IN A COUNTRY CHURCHYARD" 665

Sample Selection Page

Guided Reading Questions *guide students through the selection and help them to recognize and understand important ideas and key points. The questions help all students reach a basic understanding of the selection.*

Footnotes *explain obscure references, unusual usages, and terms meant to enter students' passive vocabularies and are defined separately from active vocabulary.*

The ***Words for Everyday Use*** *feature (not shown), included in selections at point of use, defines and gives pronunciations for difficult terms meant to enter students' active vocabularies, and includes a contextual sentence to increase vocabulary development.*

The Teacher-Assisted Phase. The **Investigate, Inquire, Imagine** questions that follow the Respond to the Selection feature are designed to take the student through the selection step by step, building upon his or her responses and refining them through questions of successive complexity. These questions are paired to complement each other and increase in complexity and sophistication to develop higher-level thinking skills. The most basic pairing, **Recall/Interpret**, is followed by **Analyze/Synthesize**, and may conclude with either an **Evaluate/Extend** or **Perspective/Empathy** pairing.

These question sets are structured to develop different levels of cognitive thinking skills, based on *Bloom's Taxonomy of Educational Objectives*. Bloom's taxonomy has been the most widely employed system for labeling and understanding levels of cognitive processing used in test construction since its publication in 1956. It is commonly used in variously modified forms by many educational test developers. The primary categories of cognitive thinking levels in Bloom's taxonomy include the following six levels:

1. Knowledge: involves the recall of specifics, methods, and processes
2. Comprehension: represents the lowest level of understanding
3. Application: uses abstractions in particular and concrete situations
4. Analysis: breaks down communication into its elements or parts
5. Synthesis: brings together elements and parts to form a whole
6. Evaluation: makes judgments about the value of material and methods

The questions in Investigate, Inquire, Imagine take the students through these six levels of the cognitive domain, as well as taking them a step further by developing their appreciation of other perspectives and empathy for others.

- Recall questions ensure that students remember the basic key facts from the selections (knowledge).
- Interpret questions use facts from Recall questions as a basis for valid interpretation (comprehension).
- Analyze questions ask readers to classify, compare and contrast, and identify relationships between ideas (analysis).
- Synthesize questions are linked to Analyze questions and ask readers to integrate, restructure, predict, elaborate, and summarize (synthesis).
- Evaluate questions ask students to appraise, assess, critique, and make judgments about certain aspects of a selection (evaluation).
- Extend questions are paired with Evaluate questions, and allow readers to try out their understanding in a different context that may link to a student's own experience, to a contemporary real world situation, or to another literary or artistic work (application).
- Perspective questions develop insight and self-knowledge by encouraging students to look for and value alternative perspectives.
- Empathy questions complement Perspective questions and facilitate knowledge of others by asking students to demonstrate understanding of another person's worldview. See table below.

Because students are frequently unfamiliar with literary terminology and its applications, such terminology does not appear in the questions for Investigate, Inquire, Imagine. Literary terminology and techniques are covered in the next part of the instructional apparatus, which is called **Understanding Literature.** Reinforcing the terms defined in the Literary Tools feature on the Prereading page, each Understanding Literature activity begins with a boldfaced term that identifies a literary movement, genre, or technique. The term is followed by its definition and by one or more questions that apply the concept to the selection. Having responded to the selection and having reviewed it in detail, the student can now learn some of the technical details about how the selection worked to achieve its effects. Students needing or desiring additional information about a term introduced in the Literary Tools and Understanding Literature sections can refer to the discussion of that term in the **Handbook of Literary Terms** at the back of the book.

Approaches to the teacher-assisted phase of the literature instruction can vary, depending on your teaching style and the needs of your students. Some teachers will prefer to have students answer the Investigate, Inquire, Imagine and Understanding Literature questions individually or in small groups and will then hold whole-class discussions of these questions. Others will prefer to treat these questions as prompts for whole-class, teacher-directed discussions. Another alternative, especially appropriate in advanced classes, is to assign students to lead small group or whole-class discussions of these questions.

Inquire, Investigate, Imagine	Bloom's Taxonomy
Recall	Knowledge
Interpret	Comprehension
Analyze	Analysis
Synthesize	Synthesis
Evaluate	Evaluation
Extend	Application
Alternate Question Set	
Perspective	Insight and self-knowledge
Empathy	Knowledge of others

Gains in Critical Thinking

Instruction in Other Language Arts Skills: An Integrated Approach

It has been shown that a student may demonstrate knowledge in a classroom but be unable to use that knowledge in "real-life" situations. Grammar, usage, mechanics, spelling, and vocabulary skills have traditionally been taught in isolation as independent skills but, just as instruction in the separate concepts of physiology does not make us healthier, neither does instruction in the abstract concepts of speech or grammar make us speak or write better (Hillocks; Braddock). Skills must be taught in ways that enable students to "transfer" them to real contexts, i.e., to use them in their lives. The transferability of knowledge is a function of meaningfulness (Prawat). Teachers can promote meaningfulness by providing (1) a wide variety of examples, (2) practice in a wide variety of contexts, (3) an explanation of the value or uses of the lesson, (4) an advance organizer at the beginning of the lesson, and (5) reviews. These five tasks have served as guideposts in the planning and writing of *Literature and the Language Arts.*

The exercises in this text are organized so that instruction in essential skills—reading; writing; language, grammar and style; speaking and listening; media literacy; study and research; critical thinking;

Sample Post-Reading Page

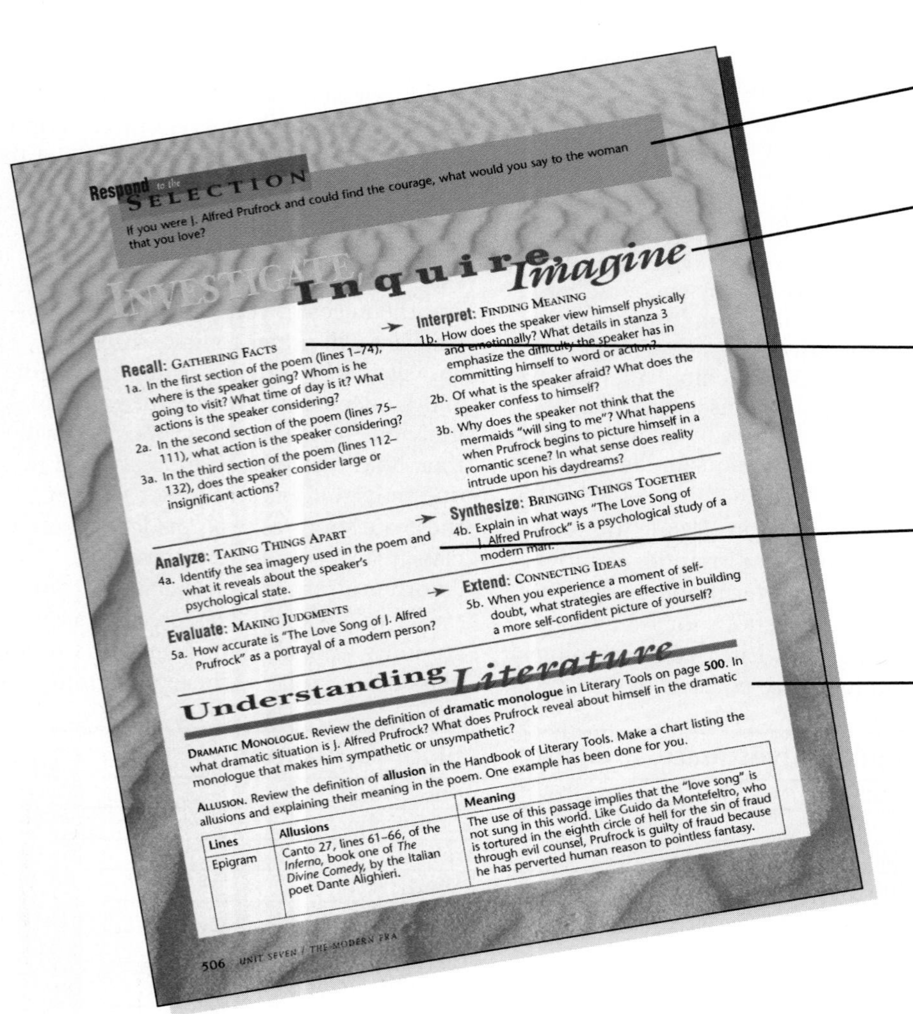

Respond to the **SELECTION**

If you were J. Alfred Prufrock and could find the courage, what would you say to the woman that you love?

INVESTIGATE Inquire Imagine

Recall: GATHERING FACTS

1a. In the first section of the poem (lines 1–74), where is the speaker going? Whom is he going to visit? What time of day is it? What actions is the speaker considering?

2a. In the second section of the poem (lines 75–111), what action is the speaker considering?

3a. In the third section of the poem (lines 112–132), does the speaker consider large or insignificant actions?

Interpret: FINDING MEANING

1b. How does the speaker view himself physically and emotionally? What details in stanza 3 emphasize the difficulty the speaker has in committing himself to word or action?

2b. Of what is the speaker afraid? What does the speaker confess to himself?

3b. Why does the speaker not think that the mermaids "will sing to me"? What happens when Prufrock begins to picture himself in a romantic scene? In what sense does reality intrude upon his daydreams?

Analyze: TAKING THINGS APART

4a. Identify the sea imagery used in the poem and what it reveals about the speaker's psychological state.

Synthesize: BRINGING THINGS TOGETHER

4b. Explain in what ways "The Love Song of J. Alfred Prufrock" is a psychological study of a modern man.

Evaluate: MAKING JUDGMENTS

5a. How accurate is "The Love Song of J. Alfred Prufrock" as a portrayal of a modern person?

Extend: CONNECTING IDEAS

5b. When you experience a moment of self-doubt, what strategies are effective in building a more self-confident picture of yourself?

Understanding Literature

DRAMATIC MONOLOGUE. Review the definition of **dramatic monologue** in Literary Tools on page **500**. In what dramatic situation is J. Alfred Prufrock? What does Prufrock reveal about himself in the dramatic monologue that makes him sympathetic or unsympathetic?

ALLUSION. Review the definition of **allusion** in the Handbook of Literary Tools. Make a chart listing the allusions and explaining their meaning in the poem. One example has been done for you.

Lines	Allusions	Meaning
Epigram	Canto 27, lines 61–66, of the *Inferno*, book one of *The Divine Comedy*, by the Italian poet Dante Alighieri.	The use of this passage implies that the "love song" is not sung in this world. Like Guido da Montefeltro, who is tortured in the eighth circle of hell for the sin of fraud through evil counsel, Prufrock is guilty of fraud because he has perverted human reason to pointless fantasy.

506 UNIT SEVEN / THE MODERN ERA

Respond to the Selection *is a* ***reader response*** *activity designed to elicit an affective response to the selection.*

Investigate, Inquire, Imagine *takes students through the work step by step, building from their individual responses a complete interpretation of the selection.*

Recall *questions address comprehension of key facts from the selection.* ***Interpret*** *questions, keyed to the Recall questions by arrows, evoke interpretations based on evidence from the selection.*

Paired questions such as ***Analyze / Synthesize, Evaluate / Extend****, and* ***Perspective / Empathy*** *lead students to higher-level thinking.*

Understanding Literature *questions reinforce the Literary Tools introduced in Prereading and provide selection-related study of literary movements, genres, and techniques.*

test-taking; vocabulary development; and applied English—develops in the context of activities integrated with the study of literature. The connection to engaging literature can provide motivation and context for teaching these practical skills.

The **Writer's Journal** activities in the Post-Reading section of the lesson use the selection as a springboard for creative and critical quick-writing assignments. Several **Integrating the Language Arts** activities follow the Writer's Journal. These help students develp proficiency in language arts areas, including language, grammar, and style; speaking and listening; study and research; applied English; collaborative learning; media literacy; vocabulary development; and critical thinking.

A typical skills activity asks students to read a section of the Language Arts Survey and then complete an exercise. The exercises relate to the work of literature that students have just studied. For example, a Study and Research activity following the excerpt from Virginia Woolf's *A Room of One's Own* refers students to the Language Arts Survey 5.20, "Using Reference Works" and then asks them to find information about the Bloomsbury Group, Woolf's circle of Cambridge-educated friends, and write a short report to share with the class. The Speaking and Listening activity in the Integrating the Language Arts section for "Heat" by Jean Rhys asks students to review the Language Arts Survey 4.2, "Active versus Passive Listening," and 4.14, "Conducting an Interview." Then students are to interview classmates, friends, or family about an event and compare the different versions they hear of the same event from different people.

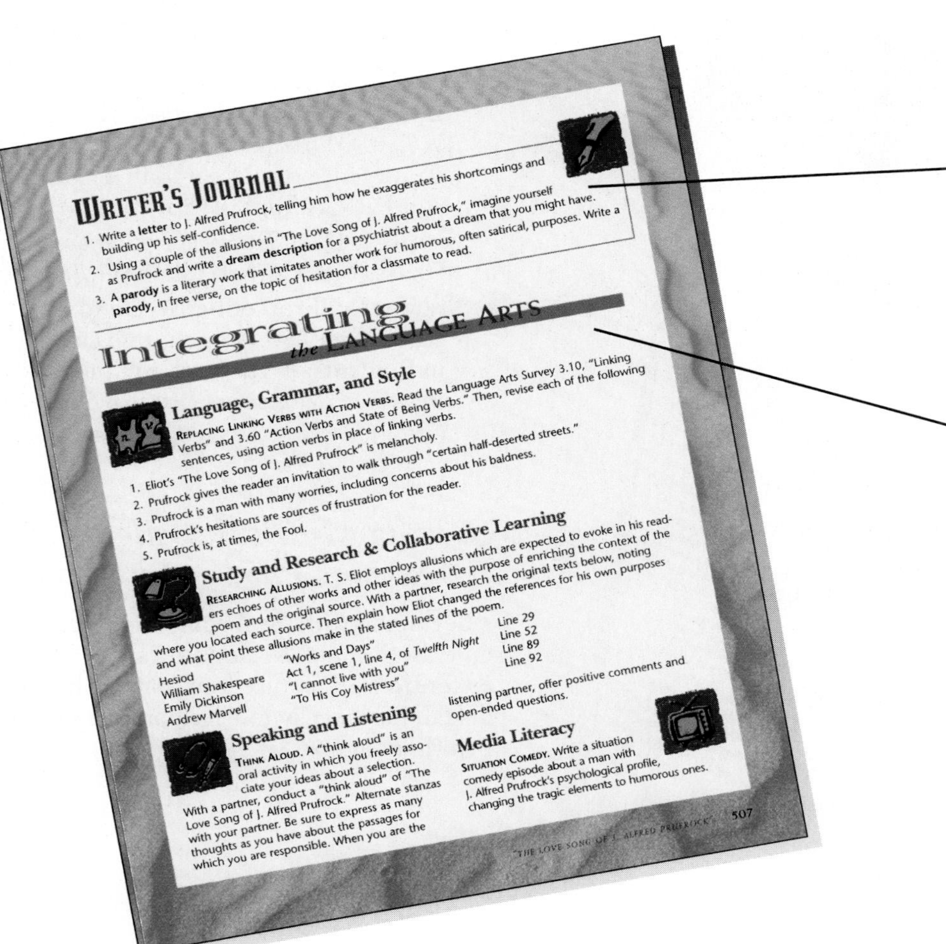

WRITER'S JOURNAL

1. Write a **letter** to J. Alfred Prufrock, telling him how he exaggerates his shortcomings and building up his self-confidence.
2. Using a couple of the allusions in "The Love Song of J. Alfred Prufrock," imagine yourself as Prufrock and write a **dream description** for a psychiatrist about a dream that you might have.
3. A **parody** is a literary work that imitates another work for humorous, often satirical, purposes. Write a **parody**, in free verse, on the topic of hesitation for a classmate to read.

Integrating the LANGUAGE ARTS

Language, Grammar, and Style

REPLACING LINKING VERBS WITH ACTION VERBS. Read the Language Arts Survey 3.10, "Linking Verbs" and 3.60 "Action Verbs and State of Being Verbs." Then, revise each of the following sentences, using action verbs in place of linking verbs.

1. Eliot's "The Love Song of J. Alfred Prufrock" is melancholy.
2. Prufrock gives the reader an invitation to walk through "certain half-deserted streets."
3. Prufrock is a man with many worries, including concerns about his baldness.
4. Prufrock's hesitations are sources of frustration for the reader.
5. Prufrock is, at times, the Fool.

Study and Research & Collaborative Learning

RESEARCHING ALLUSIONS. T. S. Eliot employs allusions which are expected to evoke in his readers echoes of other works and other ideas with the purpose of enriching the context of the poem and the original source. With a partner, research the original texts below, noting where you located each source. Then explain how Eliot changed the references for his own purposes and what point these allusions make in the stated lines of the poem.

Hesiod	"Works and Days"	Line 29
William Shakespeare	Act 1, scene 1, line 4, of *Twelfth Night*	Line 52
Emily Dickinson	"I cannot live with you"	Line 89
Andrew Marvell	"To His Coy Mistress"	Line 92

Speaking and Listening

THINK ALOUD. A "think aloud" is an oral activity in which you freely associate your ideas about a selection. With a partner, conduct a "think aloud" of "The Love Song of J. Alfred Prufrock." Alternate stanzas with your partner. Be sure to express as many thoughts as you have about the passages for which you are responsible. When you are the listening partner, offer positive comments and open-ended questions.

Media Literacy

SITUATION COMEDY. Write a situation comedy episode about a man with J. Alfred Prufrock's psychological profile, changing the tragic elements to humorous ones.

"THE LOVE SONG OF J. ALFRED PRUFROCK" 507

Sample Post-Reading Page

***Writer's Journal** activities use the selection as a springboard for engaging writing assignments that require both creative and critical thinking skills. Every literary selection includes three writing prompts that are graded as simple, moderate, and challenging.*

***Integrating the Language Arts** activities provide integrated activities in language arts areas, including language, grammar, and style; speaking and listening; study and research; applied English; collaborative learning; media literacy; vocabulary development; and critical thinking.*

The **Language Arts Survey** at the back of the book provides a comprehensive overview of the complete range of language arts skills. The survey is divided into six sections, as follows:

- Reading Resource
- Writing Resource
- Language, Grammar, and Style Resource
- Speaking and Listening Resource
- Study and Research Resource
- Applied English Resource

Students are asked to refer to these sections when doing writing or language arts skills activities. Teachers wishing to give their students additional practice in any of these skills areas will find, for each lesson in the Language Arts Survey, a corresponding worksheet in one of the **Resource Books** found in the Teacher's Resource Kit. Teachers wishing to present whole units related to specific language arts skills can have students work through parts of the Language Arts Survey, doing the activities found in the Resource Books.

Modern Poetry

Multicultural Extensions

St. Lucia

MAP OF THE NEW WORLD

Derek Walcott

I *Archipelagoes*[1]

At the end of this sentence, rain will begin.
At the rain's edge, a sail.

Slowly the sail will lose sight of islands;
into a mist will go the belief in harbours
of an entire race.

The ten-years war is finished.
Helen's hair, a grey cloud.
Troy, a white ashpit
by the drizzling sea.

The drizzle tightens like the strings of a harp.
A man with clouded eyes picks up the rain
and plucks the first line of the *Odyssey*.[2] ■

In what way does the opening sentence actually carry out, or perform, what it describes?

What feelings are created in you by this description of the ruin of Helen and of Troy?

Who is the man with clouded eyes? What is he doing?

1. ***Archipelagoes.*** Seas with many islands in them
2. ***Odyssey.*** References to Homer's *Odyssey*, an ancient Greek epic poem about the wanderings of Odysseus after the fall of Troy in the Trojan War

"MAP OF THE NEW WORLD" 977

Partial Bibliography

Ausubel, D. *Educational Psychology.* 2nd ed. New York: Holt, 1978.

Bloom, B., et al. *Taxonomy of Educational Objectives, Handbook I, Cognitive Domain*, New York, NY: David McKay Company, Inc., 1956.

Braddock, R., R. Lloyd-Jones, and L. Schoer. *Research in Written Composition.* Champaign, IL: NCTE, 1963.

Bruner, J. *Toward a Theory of Instruction.* New York: Norton, 1966.

Eggen, P., and D. Kauchak. *Educational Psychology: Classroom Connections.* 2nd ed. New York: Merrill, 1994.

Eisner, E. *The Educational Imagination.* 2nd ed. New York: Macmillan, 1985.

Hillocks, G., Jr. *Research on Written Composition: New Directions for Teaching.* Urbana, IL: Natl. Conference on Research in English and ERIC/CRCS, 1986.

Novak, J. D. *A Theory of Education.* Ithaca, NY: Cornell UP, 1984.

Prawat, R. "Promoting Access to Knowledge, Strategy, and Disposition in Students: A Research Synthesis." *Review of Educational Research* 59 (1989): 1–41.

Sample Multicultural Extensions Page

Beginning with the Middle Ages, each unit also includes **Multicultural Extensions**, literature from outside Britian linked thematically to developments in British literature.

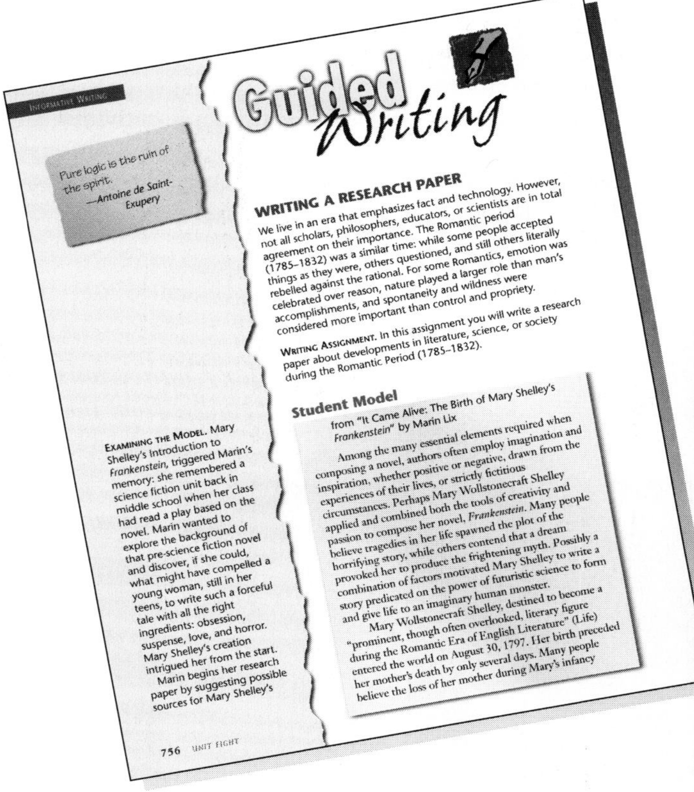

INFORMATIVE WRITING

Guided Writing

Pure logic is the ruin of the spirit.
—Antoine de Saint-Exupery

WRITING A RESEARCH PAPER

We live in an era that emphasizes fact and technology. However, not all scholars, philosophers, educators, or scientists are in total agreement on their importance. The Romantic period (1785–1832) was a similar time: while some people accepted things as they were, others questioned, and still others literally rebelled against the rational. For some Romantics, emotion was celebrated over reason, nature played a larger role than man's accomplishments, and spontaneity and wildness were considered more important than control and propriety.

WRITING ASSIGNMENT. In this assignment you will write a research paper about developments in literature, science, or society during the Romantic Period (1785–1832).

Student Model

from "It Came Alive: The Birth of Mary Shelley's *Frankenstein*" by Marin Lix

Among the many essential elements required when composing a novel, authors often employ imagination and inspiration, whether positive or negative, drawn from the experiences of their lives, or strictly fictitious circumstances. Perhaps Mary Wollstonecraft Shelley applied and combined both the tools of creativity and passion to compose her novel, *Frankenstein*. Many people believe tragedies in her life spawned the plot of the horrifying story, while others contend that a dream provoked her to produce the frightening myth. Possibly a combination of factors motivated Mary Shelley to write a story predicated on the power of futuristic science to form and give life to an imaginary human monster.

Mary Wollstonecraft Shelley, destined to become a "prominent, though often overlooked, literary figure during the Romantic Era of English Literature" (Life) entered the world on August 30, 1797. Her birth preceded her mother's death by only several days. Many people believe the loss of her mother during Mary's infancy

EXAMINING THE MODEL. Mary Shelley's Introduction to *Frankenstein*, triggered Marin's memory: she remembered a science fiction unit back in middle school when her class had read a play based on the novel. Marin wanted to explore the background of that pre-science fiction novel and discover, if she could, what might have compelled a young woman, still in her teens, to write such a forceful tale with all the right ingredients: obsession, suspense, love, and horror. Mary Shelley's creation intrigued her from the start. Marin begins her research paper by suggesting possible sources for Mary Shelley's

756 UNIT EIGHT

Guided Writing *lessons at the end of each unit of the student edition provide direct writing instruction that covers a variety of purposes and different approaches to the writing process. Each Guided Writing lesson includes integrated Language, Grammar, and Style instruction to teach key language arts concepts in the context of writing.*

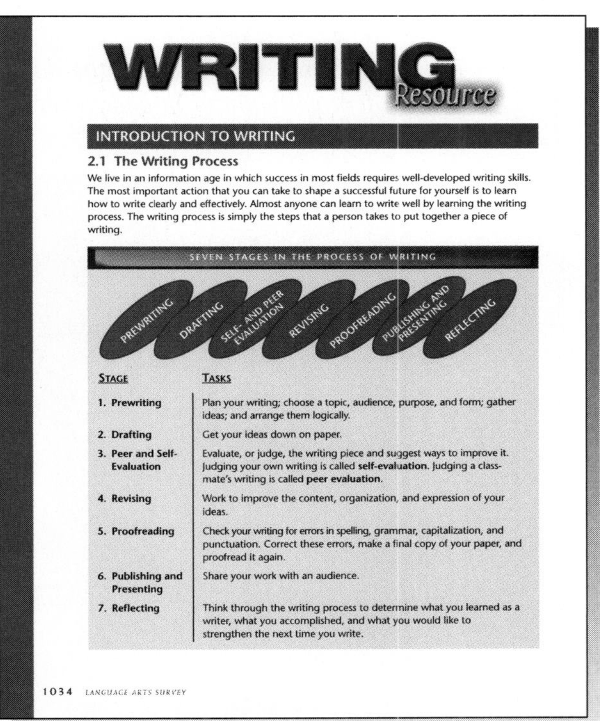

WRITING Resource

INTRODUCTION TO WRITING

2.1 The Writing Process

We live in an information age in which success in most fields requires well-developed writing skills. The most important action that you can take to shape a successful future for yourself is to learn how to write clearly and effectively. Almost anyone can learn to write well by learning the writing process. The writing process is simply the steps that a person takes to put together a piece of writing.

STAGE	TASKS
1. Prewriting	Plan your writing; choose a topic, audience, purpose, and form; gather ideas; and arrange them logically.
2. Drafting	Get your ideas down on paper.
3. Peer and Self-Evaluation	Evaluate, or judge, the writing piece and suggest ways to improve it. Judging your own writing is called **self-evaluation.** Judging a classmate's writing is called **peer evaluation.**
4. Revising	Work to improve the content, organization, and expression of your ideas.
5. Proofreading	Check your writing for errors in spelling, grammar, capitalization, and punctuation. Correct these errors, make a final copy of your paper, and proofread it again.
6. Publishing and Presenting	Share your work with an audience.
7. Reflecting	Think through the writing process to determine what you learned as a writer, what you accomplished, and what you would like to strengthen the next time you write.

1034 LANGUAGE ARTS SURVEY

The Writing Resource in the ***Language Arts Survey*** *at the end of the student edition provides a comprehensive overview of the complete range of language arts skills.*

Literature and the Language Arts — The American Tradition — PROGRAM MANAGER

Literature and the Language Arts — The American Tradition — GUIDED READING RESOURCE

Literature and the Language Arts — The American Tradition — ASSESSMENT RESOURCE

Literature and the Language Arts — The American Tradition — GUIDED WRITING RESOURCE

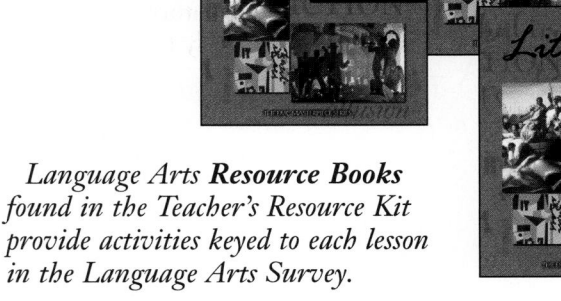

Language Arts ***Resource Books*** *found in the Teacher's Resource Kit provide activities keyed to each lesson in the Language Arts Survey.*

Annotated Teacher's Edition

The ***Annotated Teacher's Edition*** is designed to be as "teacher-friendly" as possible. Answers for exercises are usually provided on the same pages as the exercises themselves. All items are color-coded:

- white backgrounds: answers to student edition questions, exercises, and selection check tests
- green backgrounds: supplementary notes and background information
- pink backgrounds: cross-curricular connections and activities, and quotes
- blue backgrounds: additional resources and questions and activities

Sample Unit Opening Pages

*The **Unit Skills Outline** lists the skills taught in the student edition and in additional activities in this Annotated Teacher's Edition.*

***Cross-Curricular Connections** lists the cross-curricular activities from the unit.*

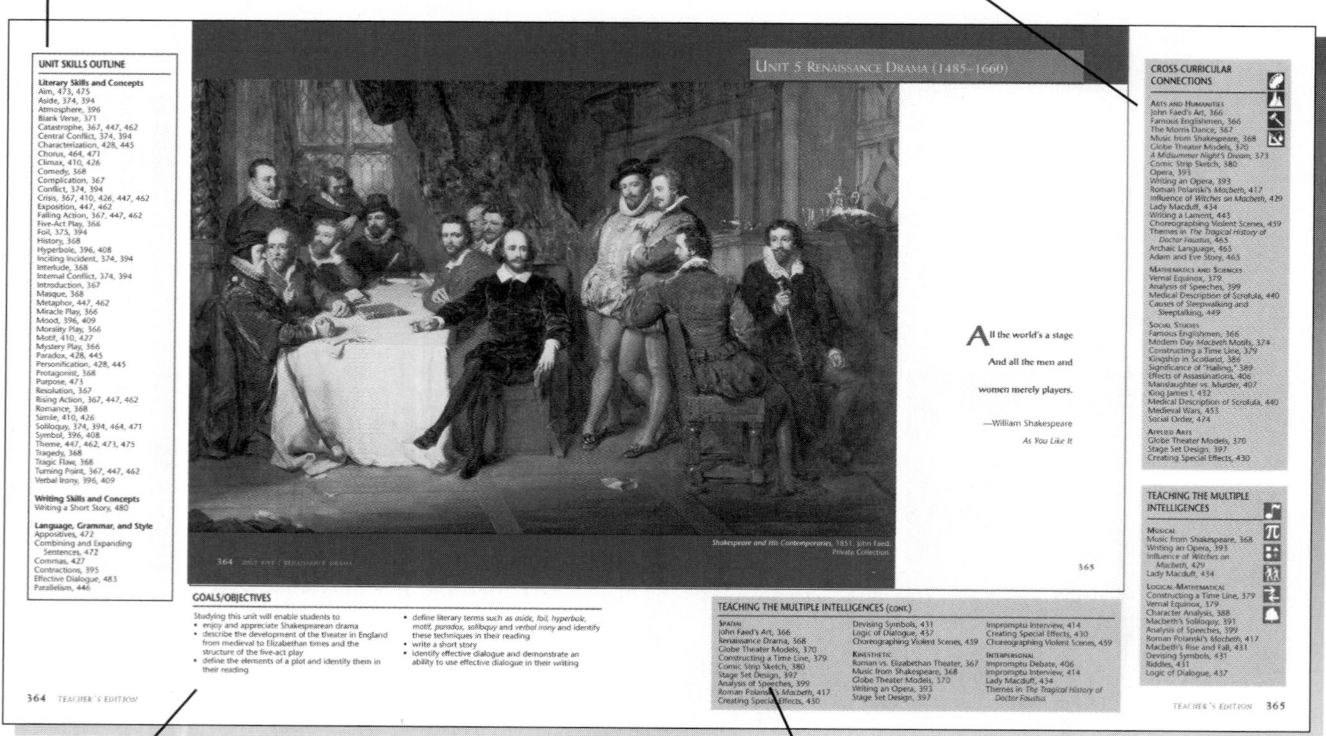

*A list of **Goals/Objectives** helps you plan overall intended learning outcomes for the unit. Affective goals are consistent with the philosophy of the program and its emphasis on reader involvement. Cognitive goals encompass content, literary technique, interpretation in historical context, and concepts taught in the Guided Writing lesson at the end of the unit.*

***Teaching the Multiple Intelligences** lists activities from the unit that call for the exercise of students' multiple intelligences.*

Sample Unit Review Pages

Additional Resources *notes identify assessment materials for the unit and study guides and worksheets for student review and practice.*

Vocabulary Development *provides an activity for students to use to reinforce vocabulary acquisition as they prepare for the unit test. Additional vocabulary development work is available in the Vocabulary Resource, which is part of the Teacher's Resource Kit.*

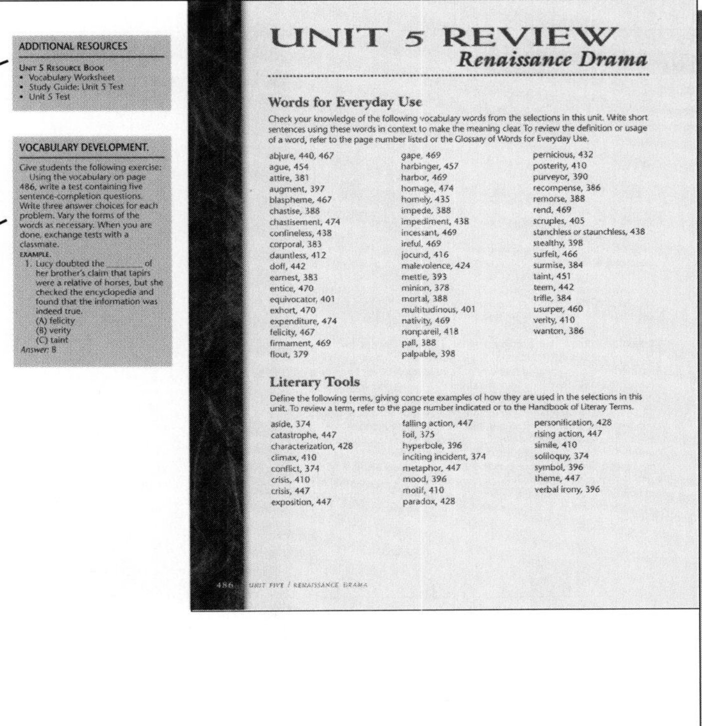

ADDITIONAL RESOURCES

UNIT 5 RESOURCE BOOK
- Vocabulary Worksheet
- Study Guide: Unit 5 Test
- Unit 5 Test

VOCABULARY DEVELOPMENT.

Give students the following exercise: Using the vocabulary on page 486, write a test containing five sentence-completion questions. Write three answer choices for each problem. Vary the forms of the words as necessary. When you are done, exchange tests with a classmate.

EXAMPLE.

1. Lucy doubted the ________ of her brother's claim that tapirs were a relative of horses, but she checked the encyclopedia and found that the information was indeed true.
   (A) felicity
   (B) verity
   (C) taint

Answer: B

UNIT 5 REVIEW
Renaissance Drama

Words for Everyday Use

Check your knowledge of the following vocabulary words from the selections in this unit. Write short sentences using these words in context to make the meaning clear. To review the definition or usage of a word, refer to the page number listed or the Glossary of Words for Everyday Use.

abjure, 440, 467
ague, 454
attire, 381
augment, 397
blaspheme, 467
chastise, 388
chastisement, 474
confineless, 438
corporal, 383
dauntless, 412
doff, 442
earnest, 383
entice, 470
equivocator, 401
exhort, 470
expenditure, 474
felicity, 467
firmament, 469
flout, 379
gape, 469
harbinger, 457
harbor, 469
homage, 474
homely, 435
impede, 388
impediment, 438
incessant, 469
ireful, 469
jocund, 416
malevolence, 424
mettle, 393
minion, 378
mortal, 388
multitudinous, 401
nativity, 469
nonpareil, 418
pall, 388
palpable, 398
pernicious, 432
posterity, 410
purveyor, 390
recompense, 386
remorse, 388
rend, 469
scruples, 405
stanchless or staunchless, 438
stealthy, 398
surfeit, 466
surmise, 384
taint, 451
teem, 442
trifle, 384
usurper, 460
verity, 410
wanton, 386

Literary Tools

Define the following terms, giving concrete examples of how they are used in the selections in this unit. To review a term, refer to the page number indicated or to the Handbook of Literary Terms.

aside, 374
catastrophe, 447
characterization, 428
climax, 410
conflict, 374
crisis, 410
crisis, 447
exposition, 447
falling action, 447
foil, 375
hyperbole, 396
inciting incident, 374
metaphor, 447
mood, 396
motif, 410
paradox, 428
personification, 428
rising action, 447
simile, 410
soliloquy, 374
symbol, 396
theme, 447
verbal irony, 396

486 UNIT FIVE / RENAISSANCE DRAMA

486 TEACHER'S EDITION

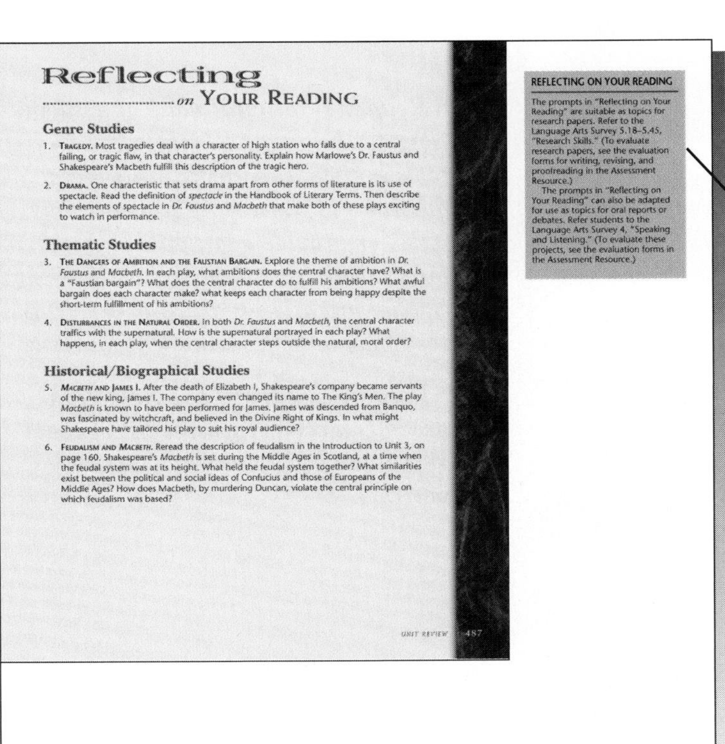

Reflecting on YOUR READING

Genre Studies

1. TRAGEDY. Most tragedies deal with a character of high station who falls due to a central failing, or tragic flaw, in that character's personality. Explain how Marlowe's Dr. Faustus and Shakespeare's Macbeth fulfill this description of the tragic hero.
2. DRAMA. One characteristic that sets drama apart from other forms of literature is its use of spectacle. Read the definition of *spectacle* in the Handbook of Literary Terms. Then describe the elements of spectacle in *Dr. Faustus* and *Macbeth* that make both of these plays exciting to watch in performance.

Thematic Studies

3. THE DANGERS OF AMBITION AND THE FAUSTIAN BARGAIN. Explore the theme of ambition in *Dr. Faustus* and *Macbeth*. In each play, what ambitions does the central character have? What is a "Faustian bargain"? What does the central character do to fulfill his ambitions? What awful bargain does each character make? what keeps each character from being happy despite the short-term fulfillment of his ambitions?
4. DISTURBANCES IN THE NATURAL ORDER. In both *Dr. Faustus* and *Macbeth*, the central character traffics with the supernatural. How is the supernatural portrayed in each play? What happens, in each play, when the central character steps outside the natural, moral order?

Historical/Biographical Studies

5. *MACBETH* AND JAMES I. After the death of Elizabeth I, Shakespeare's company became servants of the new king, James I. The company even changed its name to The King's Men. The play *Macbeth* is known to have been performed for James. James was descended from Banquo, was fascinated by witchcraft, and believed in the Divine Right of Kings. In what might Shakespeare have tailored his play to suit his royal audience?
6. FEUDALISM AND *MACBETH*. Reread the description of feudalism in the Introduction to Unit 3, on page 160. Shakespeare's *Macbeth* is set during the Middle Ages in Scotland, at a time when the feudal system was at its height. What held the feudal system together? What similarities exist between the political and social ideas of Confucius and those of Europeans of the Middle Ages? How does Macbeth, by murdering Duncan, violate the central principle on which feudalism was based?

UNIT REVIEW 487

REFLECTING ON YOUR READING

The prompts in "Reflecting on Your Reading" are suitable as topics for research papers. Refer to the Language Arts Survey 5.18–5.45, "Research Skills." (To evaluate research papers, see the evaluation forms for writing, revising, and proofreading in the Assessment Resource.)

The prompts in "Reflecting on Your Reading" can also be adapted for use as topics for oral reports or debates. Refer students to the Language Arts Survey 4, "Speaking and Listening." (To evaluate these projects, see the evaluation forms in the Assessment Resource.)

TEACHER'S EDITION 487

Reflecting on Your Reading *questions extend the ideas presented throughout the unit. These questions, which are appropriate prompts for writing, research, or discussion, cover genres, themes, and historical and biographical issues and allow students to synthesize the material from the unit.*

Sample Prereading Page

PREREADING

NOVEL EXCERPT

FROM

Ooronoko

BY APHRA BEHN

About the Author

Aphra Behn (1640–1689) is today honored as a great literary pioneer. The first woman in England to earn her living as a writer, she became one of the finest dramatists of her day and wrote what is arguably the first English novel. Her life, like her work, was interesting and unusual. As a child, she traveled with her foster family to the West Indies. While living in Suriname, she participated in a slave rebellion. On returning to England, she married, but her husband soon died. To earn money, she became a spy in Antwerp, Belgium, for King Charles II. When she was poorly paid for her spying, she ended up in debtor's prison. To rectify her situation, Behn began writing to earn money. This was an unusual motive for women writers in her day, for most were aristocrats who wrote for pleasure, not for pay. Over the next several years, Behn would write fourteen plays, many of which were favorably received in London. The fortunes of London theaters declined around 1680, and with them Behn's income. Still resourceful, she began writing fiction, and though she died poor, she left behind a rich legacy not just in her writings, but also in the ambitious, adventurous, and inspiring life she had lived.

About the Selection

Written just a year before Behn died, ***Oroonoko, or the Royal Slave,*** combines elements of autobiography, travel narrative, and fictional prose. Drawing on her own experiences in Suriname, Behn tells in this short novel the story of an African prince, Oroonoko, who is deceived by an Englishman and sold into slavery. Oroonoko falls in love with Imoinda, the daughter of one of the king's generals. Unfortunately, the king loves Imoinda as well. He chooses her as his own by bestowing upon her a royal veil. When he learns that Oroonoko has secretly visited Imoinda, he is very angry. Imoinda tells the king a lie to save her life. As a result, the king decides she is not fit for him or for Oroonoko, so he has her sold into slavery. In the meantime, Oroonoko is away at battle. This selection picks up upon Oroonoko's return from battle. Behn's book, with its noble hero, did much to turn British public opinion against the slave trade, which was outlawed in all British colonies in 1833.

Literary Tools

NOVEL. A **novel** is a long work of prose fiction. *Oroonoko* is considered to be one of the, if not *the*, first British novel. Novels usually have subplots in addition to their main plot. Furthermore, novels often realistically portray the interior psychological states of characters. Note the changes that Oroonoko undergoes in this selection.

CHARACTERIZATION. **Characterization** is the use of literary techniques to create a character. Writers use three major techniques to create characters—direct description, in which the writer through a narrator or other character comments directly on the character; portrayal of character's behavior, in which the writer presents the actions or speech of the character allowing the reader to draw his or her own conclusions; and representations of internal states, in which the writer reveals a character's private thoughts and emotions. As you read, keep a chart to show how Behn creates the character of Oroonoko.

Direct Description	Behavior	Internal States
beloved like a deity		

Reader's Journal

Write about a time when somebody deceived you. What did the deception cost you? How did you react to it?

APHRA BEHN 607

ADDITIONAL RESOURCES

UNIT 7 RESOURCE BOOK
- Selection Worksheet 7.6
- Selection Check Test 4.7.13
- Selection Test 4.7.14
- Language, Grammar, and Style Resource 3.94

GRAPHIC ORGANIZER

Students might include the following in their graphic organizers.

DIRECT DESCRIPTION
beloved like a deity
extremely civilized
generous

BEHAVIOR
decides not to eat, to die, so he won't have to endure slavery
never violated his word in his life
believes captain will keep his word
tells captain it was worth his suffering to understand the captain and the gods by which he swears

Quotables

"All women together ought to let flowers fall upon the tomb of Aphra Behn, for it was she who earned them the right to speak their minds."

—Virginia Woolf

READER'S JOURNAL

Students might brainstorm a list of emotions that they felt before they realized the deception and a list of those they felt afterward.

VOCABULARY FROM THE SELECTION

asseveration
ignominiously
repose

GOALS/OBJECTIVES

Studying this lesson will enable students to
- empathize with a main character in a novel
- describe Aphra Behn's literary accomplishments and explain the historical significance of her writings
- define *novel* and identify the elements of a novel in literature they read
- define *characterization* and identify the major techniques of characterization as used in their reading
- edit for errors in capitalization
- evaluate a film for its portrayals of race

TEACHER'S EDITION 607

Additional Resources *notes identify materials from the Teacher's Resource Kit to use in teaching the selection: worksheets from the Reader's Guide and from the Language Arts Resource Books, and selection check tests and tests from the Assessment Resource.*

*Color-coded **icons** identify at a glance **cross-curricular** activities (brown), **multiple intelligences** activities (green), and **SCANS** activities (blue). A key to these icons is provided on page T29 of this Annotated Teacher's Edition.*

Reader's Journal *notes give suggestions for helping students relate the topic to their experience, anticipate questions or difficulties students may have, or provide additional prompts for students who have trouble starting. Special attention is given to problems that may arise from student diversity.*

Vocabulary from the Selection *provides a comprehensive list of the Words for Everyday Use from the selection.*

*A list of **Goals/Objectives** helps you plan intended learning outcomes for the selection. Affective goals are consistent with the philosophy of the program and its emphasis on reader involvement. Cognitive goals encompass content, literary technique, interpretation of the selection in historical context, and language arts skills taught in the student text.*

Sample Selection Page

Answers to Guided Reading Questions *are keyed to questions in the student edition.*

The ***Art Note*** *feature provides a visual literacy component that connects fine art to the literature studied.*

Individual Learning Strategies *provide additional lesson plans for individual instruction in the following areas:*

- ***Motivation*** *strategies encourage students to take an interest in the selection and relate it to their own lives.*
- ***Reading Proficiency*** *activities focus on developing reading skills and present reading strategies to help students with reading difficulties.*
- ***English Language Learning*** *activities provide support for students whose native language is not English, including* ***Additional Vocabulary*** *to help you offer instruction before students encounter difficulty in reading.*
- ***Special Needs*** *activities offer assistance in planning instruction for students with learning disabilities and mentally challenged students to help them succeed in your classroom.*
- ***Enrichment*** *activities to challenge students with special academic gifts and talents and provide opportunities for independent study and self-guided research.*

ANSWER TO GUIDED READING QUESTION

1. Oroonoko has a genial business relationship with the European slave traders; he sells them slaves. The Europeans consider Prince Oroonoko to be more civilized than any of his predecessors.

ART NOTE

Joseph Turner painted *Slave Ship* in 1840, almost two hundred years after Behn wrote her story. During that time, however, the activities of slave traders had changed little. Turner's painting illustrates the common practice of pitching enslaved humans overboard, which was done either because of epidemics or to avoid unrest. In this case, because of an approaching typhoon, they are throwing overboard the dead and the dying. Have students discuss their reactions to the painting. What mood does the painting evoke? What connections do students make between this scene and the scene they imagine on the English captain's ship?

INDIVIDUAL LEARNING STRATEGIES

Motivation
Students can write about or discuss the opposition that Behn might have faced as a woman, as a writer, and as an outspoken opponent of slavery.

Reading Proficiency
Read through the selection once as a class, and then have them form partners in order to summarize each paragraph and answer the Guided Reading and Recall questions.

English Language Learning
Explain that the selection contains some uncommon contractions, such as *'em* for *them* and *'twas* for it *was*. This might be a good time to review contractions with students. Remind them that the apostrophe takes the place of dropped letters. Share with students the following additional vocabulary.
oblige—compel
indignity—affront; disgrace
circumventing—surrounding with evils
cognizance—perception; observation

608 *TEACHER'S EDITION*

Slave Ship, 1840. Joseph Mallord Turner. Museum of Fine Arts, Boston.

FROM

Oroonoko

APHRA BEHN

Oroonoko was no sooner returned from this last conquest, and received at court with all the joy and magnificence that could be expressed to a young victor, who was not only returned triumphant but beloved like a deity, when there arrived in the port an English ship.

This person had often before been in these countries and was very well known to Oroonoko, with whom he had trafficked for slaves, and had used to do the same with his predecessors.[1]

This commander was a man of a finer sort of address and conversation, better bred and more engaging than most of that sort of men are, so that he seemed rather never to have been bred out of a court than almost all his life at sea. This captain therefore was always better received at court than most of the traders to those countries were; and especially by Oroonoko, who was more civilized, according to the European mode, than any other had been, and took more delight in the white nations, and above all men of parts and wit. To this captain he sold abundance of his slaves, and for the favor and esteem he had for him, made him many presents, and obliged him to stay at court as long as possibly he could. Which the captain seemed to take as a very great honor done him, entertaining the Prince every day with globes and maps, and mathematical discourses and instruments; eating, drinking, hunting, and living with him with so much familiarity that it was not to be doubted but he had gained very greatly upon the heart of this gallant young man. And the captain, in return of all these mighty favors, besought[2] the Prince to honor his vessel with his presence, some day or other, to dinner, before he should set sail; which he condescended to accept, and appointed his day. The captain, on his part, failed not to have all things in a readiness, in the most magnificent order he could possibly. And the day being come, the captain in his boat, richly adorned with carpets and velvet cushions, rowed to the shore to receive the Prince, with another longboat where was placed all his music and trumpets, with which Oroonoko was extremely delighted; who met him on the shore attended by his French governor, Jamoan Aboan, and about a hundred of the noblest of the youths of the court. And after they had first carried the

At the beginning of the selection, what sort of relationship does Oroonoko have with the European slave traders?

1. **This . . . predecessors.** Throughout the history of Africa and the Middle East, the selling of war captives into slavery was common.
2. **besought.** Asked earnestly

608 *UNIT SEVEN / THE RESTORATION AND THE EIGHTEENTH CENTURY*

INDIVIDUAL LEARNING STRATEGIES (CONT.)

Special Needs
Ask students to create a story map listing the main events in this excerpt. They should also note the state of mind of Oroonoko as it changes throughout the story.

Enrichment
Students may wish to research the history of slavery in the British West Indies. For what purpose were slaves transported there? For how long was slavery legal in the West Indies, and how did it finally become abolished?

Internet Resources *(not shown) connect you with a wealth of online resources that provide additional information on authors and literary selections, links to related readings, and Internet activities.*

Historical, Literary, and Bibliography Notes *(not shown) provide additional information to enhance the reading of the selections.*

Cross-Curricular Connections and Activities *(not shown) are supplementary activities that involve knowledge, skills, research, and resources from disciplines other than language arts.*

Cross-references *(not shown) to additional instruction, worksheets, and assessment materials are provided throughout the annotations.*

Sample Selection Post-Reading Page

Answers to Inquire, Investigate, Imagine *give sample responses to Recall/Interpret, Analyze/Synthesize, Evaluate/Extend, and Perspective/Empathy question sets.*

ANSWERS FOR INVESTIGATE, INQUIRE, IMAGINE

RECALL
1a. Oroonoko is described as "a young victor," who was "beloved like a deity" by his people. He has recently returned from a conquest.
2a. The captain of the ship entertains Oroonoko "with globes and maps, and mathematical discourses and instruments; eating, drinking, hunting, and living with him."
3a. Oroonoko and his fellow captives show their nobility and their spirit by their quiet determination to refuse food. The captain feels compelled to release Oroonoko from his fetters because he knows that all the slaves, following Oroonoko's refusal to eat, will die and, therefore, be of no profit to him.

INTERPRET
1b. The adoration given Oroonoko and the description "young victor" establish him as a heroic character.
2b. Oroonoko might think that the captain is a friend because the captain seems to enjoy Oroonoko's company and to treat him as an equal.
3b. Oroonoko possesses both honesty and integrity, unlike the captain who believes he needs to be honest only with people who share his beliefs. The captain lies to gain an advantage over Oroonoko; unfortunately, Oroonoko believes the captain's lies because he himself would never be so dishonest.

ANALYZE
4a. Behn presents the Africans as noble, honest, trusting people. The slave traders are portrayed as unscrupulous, conniving liars who do and say what they have to in order to capture slaves.

SYNTHESIZE
4b. Oroonoko's naiveté and trust of the captain made him easy prey. He judges the captain by his own standards of behavior.

EVALUATE
5a. *Responses will vary.* Students may say that Behn is not completely objective, but that her intent is to portray Oroonoko as a heroic figure.

EXTEND
Responses will vary. Possible responses are given.
5b. Students may say that Behn views the Africans as a primitive people, still innocent and untouched by the corruption that Behn sees in the "civilized" people of Europe.

INVESTIGATE **Inquire** *Imagine*

Recall: GATHERING FACTS → **Interpret:** FINDING MEANING

1a. How is Oroonoko described in the first paragraph of the selection? From what has he recently returned?
1b. What information given at the beginning of the selection establishes Oroonoko as a heroic character?

2a. With what does the captain of the ship entertain Oroonoko in the third paragraph of the selection?
2b. What reason might Oroonoko have at the beginning of the selection to think that the English captain is a friend?

3a. What actions on the part of Oroonoko and his fellow captives show their nobility and their spirit? Why does the captain feel compelled to release Oroonoko from his fetters?
3b. How do the captain and Oroonoko differ with respect to their honesty and integrity? How do the negotiations over freeing Oroonoko from his fetters demonstrate this difference?

Analyze: TAKING THINGS APART → **Synthesize:** BRINGING THINGS TOGETHER

4a. Identify the main characteristic Behn presents of the Africans and of the slave traders.
4b. Explain the role their differences had in Oroonoko's capture.

Evaluate: MAKING JUDGMENTS → **Extend:** CONNECTING IDEAS

5a. Judge whether Behn is objective in her portrayal of the captain and of Oroonoko.
5b. Earlier in the novel, Behn writes, "And these People represented to me an absolute *Idea* of the first State of Innocence, before *Man* knew how to sin." How does Behn view the African people?

Understanding ***Literature***

NOVEL. Review the definition for **novel** in the Handbook of Literary Terms. One characteristic that sets novels apart from earlier types of prose fiction is their realistic portrayals of the interior psychological states of characters. What does Oroonoko learn about the differences between his values and those of the captain? In what sense does Oroonoko lose a certain innocence about the world?

CHARACTERIZATION. Review the definition for **characterization** and the graphic organizer you made for Literary Tools in the Prereading for this selection. Briefly describe the character of Oroonoko, using information you learn from all three techniques of characterization.

ANSWERS TO UNDERSTANDING LITERATURE

NOVEL. In the beginning of the selection, Oroonoko naturally believes that others share his values; he accepts the English captain at face value and never suspects his intentions. By the end of the selection, Oroonoko realizes that not everyone functions within his system of honor. Whereas Oroonoko's values are unconditional and applicable to all people, the captain's values are relative. Oroonoko loses a certain sense of innocence about the world because he discovers that not all people are honorable and that his responses must now always be guarded.
NOTE: Students should examine the characters' words as well as their actions for clues about changes in their psychological states.

CHARACTERIZATION. Oroonoko is a highly respected, heroic figure. He is a popular leader. He is honest and true to his word and he expects others to be the same.

Answers to Understanding Literature *provides possible answers for these discussion questions.*

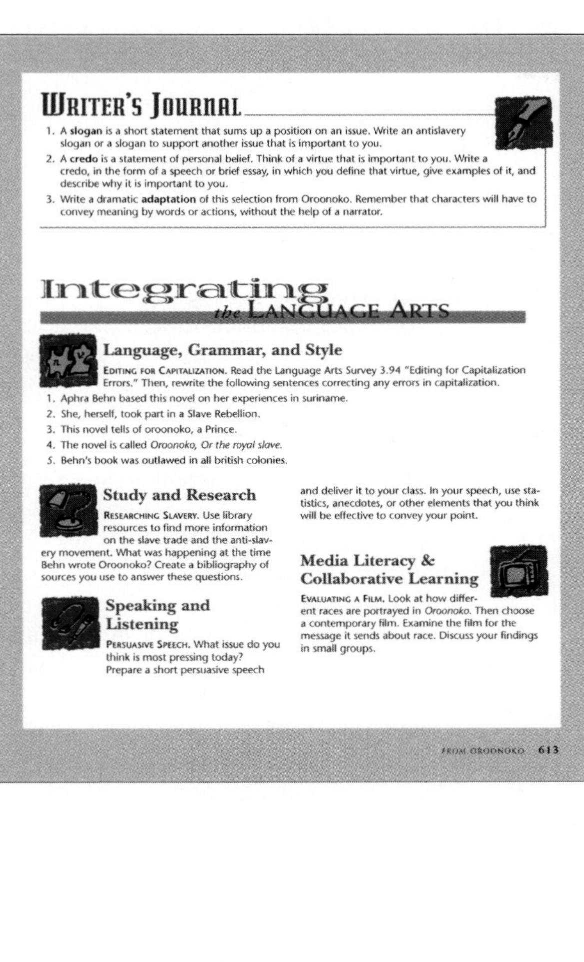

Writer's Journal

1. A **slogan** is a short statement that sums up a position on an issue. Write an antislavery slogan or a slogan to support another issue that is important to you.
2. A **credo** is a statement of personal belief. Think of a virtue that is important to you. Write a credo, in the form of a speech or brief essay, in which you define that virtue, give examples of it, and describe why it is important to you.
3. Write a dramatic **adaptation** of this selection from Oroonoko. Remember that characters will have to convey meaning by words or actions, without the help of a narrator.

Integrating *the* Language Arts

Language, Grammar, and Style

EDITING FOR CAPITALIZATION. Read the Language Arts Survey 3.94 "Editing for Capitalization Errors." Then, rewrite the following sentences correcting any errors in capitalization.

1. Aphra Behn based this novel on her experiences in suriname.
2. She, herself, took part in a Slave Rebellion.
3. This novel tells of oroonoko, a Prince.
4. The novel is called *Oroonoko, Or the royal slave.*
5. Behn's book was outlawed in all british colonies.

Study and Research

RESEARCHING SLAVERY. Use library resources to find more information on the slave trade and the anti-slavery movement. What was happening at the time Behn wrote Oroonoko? Create a bibliography of sources you use to answer these questions.

Speaking and Listening

PERSUASIVE SPEECH. What issue do you think is most pressing today? Prepare a short persuasive speech and deliver it to your class. In your speech, use statistics, anecdotes, or other elements that you think will be effective to convey your point.

Media Literacy & Collaborative Learning

EVALUATING A FILM. Look at how different races are portrayed in *Oroonoko*. Then choose a contemporary film. Examine the film for the message it sends about race. Discuss your findings in small groups.

FROM OROONOKO 613

ANSWERS TO INTEGRATING THE LANGUAGE ARTS

Language, Grammar, and Style

1. Aphra Behn based this novel on her experiences in Suriname.
2. She, herself, took part in a slave rebellion.
3. This novel tells of Oroonoko, a prince.
4. The novel is called *Oroonoko, or The Royal Slave.*
5. Behn's book was outlawed in all British colonies.

Study and Research
Students can focus on the slave-trade and anti-slavery movements in different countries.

Speaking and Listening
Students can work in pairs to practice their speeches. Partners can critique each other's speeches before the final presentation.

Evaluating Films
Students might also consider how different genders or ages are portrayed in the film they chose.

TEACHER'S EDITION 613

Sample Selection Post-Reading Page

Answers to Integrating the Language Arts *provide model answers for Language Grammar, and Style, Speaking and Listening, Critical Thinking, Study and Research, Media Literacy, Collaborative Learning, Vocabulary, and Applied English activities.*

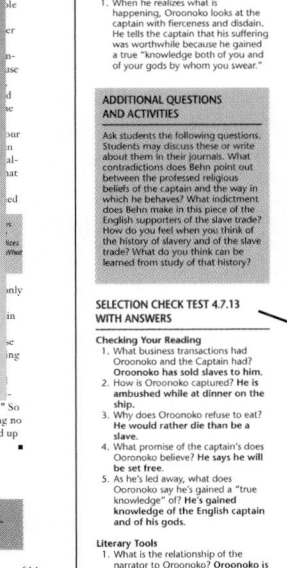

river of Surinam, a colony belonging to the King of England, and where they were to deliver some part of their slaves. There the merchants and gentlemen of the country going on board to demand those lots of slaves they

esty in the next world we shall touch upon." So he nimbly leaped into the boat, and showing no more concern, suffered himself to be rowed up the river with his seventeen companions. ■

Respond *to the* Selection

After reading this piece, how do you feel toward its main character, Oroonoko? toward the captain of the ship?

FROM OROONOKO 611

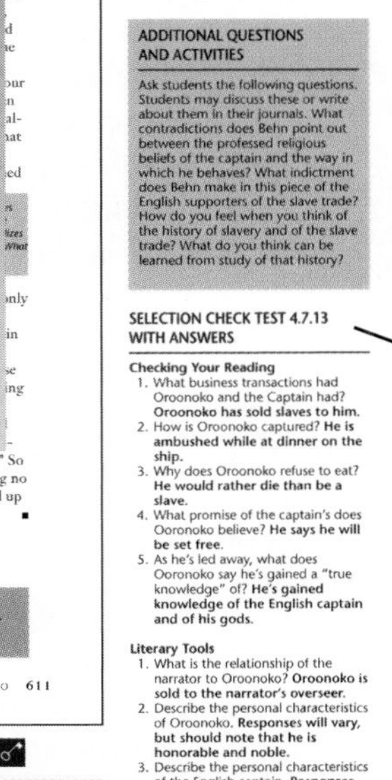

ANSWER TO GUIDED READING QUESTION

1. When he realizes what is happening, Oroonoko looks at the captain with fierceness and disdain. He tells the captain that his suffering was worthwhile because he gained a true "knowledge both of you and of your gods by whom you swear."

ADDITIONAL QUESTIONS AND ACTIVITIES

Ask students the following questions. Students may discuss these or write about them in their journals. What contradictions does Behn point out between the professed religious beliefs of the captain and the way in which he behaves? What indictment does Behn make in this piece of the English supporters of the slave trade? How do you feel when you think of the history of slavery and of the slave trade? What do you think can be learned from study of that history?

SELECTION CHECK TEST 4.7.13 WITH ANSWERS

Checking Your Reading

1. What business transactions had Oroonoko and the Captain had? **Oroonoko has sold slaves to him.**
2. How is Oroonoko captured? **He is ambushed while at dinner on the ship.**
3. Why does Oroonoko refuse to eat? **He would rather die than be a slave.**
4. What promise of the captain's does Oroonoko believe? **He says he will be set free.**
5. As he's led away, what does Oroonoko say he's gained a "true knowledge" of? **He's gained knowledge of the English captain and of his gods.**

Literary Tools

1. What is the relationship of the narrator to Oroonoko? **Oroonoko is sold to the narrator's overseer.**
2. Describe the personal characteristics of Oroonoko. **Responses will vary, but should note that he is honorable and noble.**
3. Describe the personal characteristics of the English captain. **Responses will vary, but should note that he is deceitful and dishonorable.**

RESPOND TO THE SELECTION

Students might work in pairs to role play an meeting between the captain and Oroonoko years after this selection takes place. Each character should speak about the selling of Oroonoko into slavery.

TEACHER'S EDITION 611

Selection Check Test with Answers *includes the questions with answers and appears on or near the last page of each selection. You can photocopy the test from the Assessment Resource and distribute it, or you can present the questions orally.*

Notes on the ***Respond to the Selection*** *questions help you help students relate the topic to their experience, anticipate questions or difficulties students might have, or suggest alternative formats (such as large or small group discussion or role playing). These notes give special attention to concerns of diversity.*

Using Literature and the Language Arts *for Writing Instruction*

Recent Advances in the Theory of Writing Instruction

One of the most exciting things that has happened in English education in the past few years is that a new model of writing instruction that respects the student's voice and effort has emerged. That model is the process and portfolio approach. Process and portfolio instruction breaks individual acts of writing and the overall business of learning to write into manageable steps, with guidance and feedback at each step. When students are given writing assignments today, they no longer have to figure out on their own how to get from the assignment to the completed piece of writing. Instead, they are trained in techniques for prewriting, drafting, evaluating their drafts by themselves and with peers, revising, and publishing. They are also given opportunities to reflect on this process. Writing portfolios and evaluation forms are used to track development of pieces of writing over time. Assessment has been expanded from simple marking of papers to include self-evaluation, peer evaluation, and a variety of approaches that avoid turning teachers into copyeditors. The result of these changes in writing instruction has been that student writing has improved dramatically in recent years.

Literature and the Language Arts contains comprehensive materials for integrated instruction in the writing process and for the management of writing portfolios. Through its **Guided Writing** program, students experience direct writing instruction that is integrated with the study of literature as well as with other key language arts areas, especially language, grammar, and style.

The **Writer's Journal** activities following each selection use the literature as a springboard for engaging quick-writing assignments that require both creative and critical thinking skills. Every literary selection includes three writing prompts that are graded 1) simple, 2) moderate, and 3) challenging.

Pre-testing and Assessment

Before beginning instruction in the writing process, you may wish to have students take the Writing Skills Comprehensive Test 3.1 in the Assessment Resource Book contained in the Teacher's Resource Kit. This test is designed to assess students' familiarity with basic writing concepts and skills. The test may be used to assess which techniques and skills students need to focus on during the course, or it may be used at the end of the course to assess students' understanding of basic writing skills and concepts. Beyond this, however, assessing individual pieces of student writing is the most critical step to knowing each student's strengths and weaknesses. See "Process for Writing Assignments," "Using Writing Portfolios," and "Assessing Student Writing" below.

The Guided Writing Program

Literature and the Language Arts offers complete, direct writing instruction that integrates the writing process with the study of literature and the development of other key language arts skills. At the end of each of twelve literature units, a Guided Writing lesson provides direct, step-by-step instruction in the process of writing. This lesson is integrated with the following:

(1) the literature in the unit
(2) a Language, Grammar, and Style lesson that teaches key concepts in the context of writing
(3) the Language Arts Survey in the textbook
(4) the Resource Books in the Teacher's Resource Kit
(5) the Guided Writing software that provides extended lessons and a writer-friendly word processor that allows self-, peer, and teacher evaluation comments to be delivered electronically.

Before starting the actual assignment, students are asked to consider the mode and purpose of the writing they are about to do, and to adapt their skills accordingly. The Language Arts Survey 2.3, "Identifying Your Purpose," outlines and explains the purpose of the following modes: expository/informative, imaginative, narrative, personal/expressive, and persuasive/argumentative. Many writing assignments work with a combination of modes.

The writing assignment ties directly to the literature unit studied, frequently using a passage from literature in that unit as a Professional Model that students are invited to examine as they prepare themselves to write. In some cases, a Student Model introduces the writing assignment. At other times, a Student Model appears later in the lesson to show the stages of drafting and revision.

As students enter the Prewriting stage, they are asked to consider voice, audience, and strategy in the Finding Your Voice, Identifying Your Audience, and Writing with a Plan sections. A Student Model Graphic Organizer shows prewriting work especially helpful to visual learners; from here students enter the Drafting stage, where they are coached through the process of organizing their words and getting them down on paper. From here, students are

shown a Student Model in draft form that contains self- and peer evaluation comments. A student-friendly evaluation checklist provides a rubric for students to use in the Self- and Peer Evaluation stage. Students are then led through the Revising, Proofreading, Publishing and Presenting, and Reflecting stages.

While the Guided Writing lesson takes students through these stages, it reminds them that writing is a continuing cycle and that they may need to go back to a previous stage before proceeding to the next step. It also shows how Reflecting, while always useful to bring closure to a writing assignment, can be done at any stage and at several times throughout the writing process. (For more information, see the Language Arts Survey 2.1, "The Writing Process," on page 1194 of this textbook.)

Students are also introduced to a key Language, Grammar, and Style concept within the Guided Writing lesson. Designed with the idea that grammar is best taught in the context of writing rather than in isolation, the Language, Grammar, and Style lesson offers solid instruction by helping students to 1) identify correct grammatical usage in the Professional Model, 2) revise incorrect grammatical usage in the Student Model and examples, and 3) demonstrate correct grammatical usage in their own work. Throughout this lesson, students can refer to the Language, Grammar, and Style Resource of the Language Arts Survey for additional support.

The Language Arts Survey further integrates language arts instruction with the Guided Writing lesson. Section 2 of the Language Arts Survey, the Writing Resource, begins on page 1194 and surveys the entire writing process from prewriting through drafting, self- and peer evaluation, revising, proofreading, publishing and presenting, and reflecting on the process. This section of the Survey is divided into fifty lessons. Additional practice activities for each lesson in the Language Arts Survey can be found in the Guided Writing Resource Book in the Teacher's Resource Kit. Other Language Arts Survey sections offer similar support, especially Section 3, the Language, Grammar, and Style Resource, and Section 5, the Study and Research Resource. Section 1, the Reading Resource, is frequently referenced in the Individual Learning Strategies feature of the Annotated Teacher's Edition as a way to offer students struggling with reading proficiency extra help as they work through the lessons. Section 3, the Speaking and Listening Resource, provides direct instruction for writing assignments that require oral communication; and Section 6, the Applied English Resource, provides direct instruction in technical writing and school-to-work applications.

Corresponding Resource Books in the Teacher's Resource Kit provide blackline masters with exercises keyed to each numbered section of the Language Arts Survey. This offers teachers a way to make sure students are mastering basic concepts.

Finally, the Guided Writing Interactive Software provides extended lessons and a writer-friendly word processor that allows self-, peer, and teacher evaluation comments to be delivered electronically. While the print lessons do not depend on software for students to complete the assignments, the electronic version of the Guided Writing program provides printable worksheets, graphic organizers, checklists, and student models to use as handouts; spelling and grammar utilities; Hypertext links providing help specific to the writing task; and a portfolio management system for teachers. The Guided Writing Interactive Software is compatible with Windows and Macintosh computers.

Note: Teachers who wish to do so can teach the Guided Writing program as a separate composition course by using the Guided Writing lessons at the end of each of the twelve literature units, the Writing Resource in the Language Arts Survey in its entirety, the Guided Writing Resource Books, and the Guided Writing Interactive Software.

Process for Writing Assignments

The editors and authors recommend the sequence of activities in the chart on page T20 for the writing assignments at the end of each unit. Steps 1–11 may be repeated for each writing assignment. Then, periodically, step 12 should also be completed.

Using Writing Portfolios

The student's **Writing Portfolio** is a folder in which he or she stores drafts and finished pieces of writing. You can ask your students to keep a portfolio to enable you and the students to assess their progress over time. Portfolios show students' capabilities and progress better than any test or single writing assignment can.

You may wish to ask your students to keep **comprehensive portfolios** that contain all the writing that they do for class, along with Writing Summary Forms and/or evaluation forms for each piece of writing. Alternatively, you can ask your students to keep **selected portfolios** that contain pieces of writing chosen by the students as representative of their best work. Students should be encouraged to choose for their selected portfolios pieces that show the various skills they have developed and the various types of writing that they have done (informative, persuasive, creative, etc.).

When students place works in their portfolios, make sure that they attach their notes and drafts behind the finished works so that you will be able to see at a glance how each piece of writing was developed. Also have students attach to their works any evaluation forms they have used.

From time to time, you will want to do a comprehensive evaluation of the students' portfolios. A Comprehensive Evaluation Form: Teacher in the Assessment Resource, has been provided for this purpose. You should also have each student do his or her own comprehensive evaluation using the Comprehensive Evaluation Form: Student in the Assessment Resource. Once these evaluations are complete, you can meet in a conference with each student to discuss his or her progress, provide praise for work well done, and make plans for improvement in the future.

PROCESS FOR WRITING ASSIGNMENTS

1. WHOLE CLASS: Study of the literature selection in the student edition textbook, along with its corresponding instructional apparatus
2. TEACHER: Introduction of the writing prompt from the student text
3. STUDENT: Prewriting (with reference to any applicable prewriting lessons in the Writing Resource section of the Language Arts Survey, pages 1195–1206 of the student text)
4. STUDENT: Drafting (with reference to the drafting lesson in the Writing Resource section of the Language Arts Survey, pages 1207–1208 of the student text)
5. STUDENT: Sharing of draft with one or more peers
6. STUDENT and PEER(S): Evaluation of the draft and conferencing with one another and with the teacher if necessary (with reference to the Analytic Scale for Evaluation from the Annotated Teacher's Edition and/or the general evaluation forms and revision checklists in the Assessment Resource)
7. STUDENT: Revising (with reference to the Revision and Proofreading Checklists in the Assessment Resource, and to the revision section of the Writing Resource section of the Language Arts Survey on pages 1209–1210 of the student text)
8. STUDENT: Proofreading and preparation of the final manuscript (with reference to the Revising and Proofreading Checklists in the Assessment Resource, and to the proofreading and manuscript preparation sections of the Writing Resource section of the Language Arts Survey, pages 1210–1212 of the student text) and completion of the Writing Summary Form in the Assessment Resource
9. STUDENT and PEER(S): Publishing and/or presenting of and reflecting about the completed draft (with reference to the lessons on publishing, presenting, and reflecting in the Writing Resource section of the Language Arts Survey, pages 1212–1213 of the student text)
10. STUDENT and TEACHER: Assessment and/or conferencing with regard to the completed work
11. STUDENT: Decision as to whether to place the completed work in the student's Writing Portfolio
12. STUDENT and TEACHER: Evaluate the student's Writing Portfolio (using the Comprehensive Portfolio Evaluation Form: Teacher and the Comprehensive Portfolio Evaluation Form: Student in the Assessment Resource) and hold a teacher-student conference to discuss the evaluation and to set goals for future writing improvement.

Assessing Student Writing

(For a more complete treatment of assessment, see the introduction to the Guided Writing and Assessment Resource Books in the Teacher's Resource Kit.)

Assessment of student writing should not have as its primary purpose meting out rewards or punishments. Instead, assessment should be seen as a development tool allowing the teacher and the student, working in collaboration, to monitor the student's progress toward achieving his or her goals.

Approaches to assessment vary. Two common approaches to assessing writing are analytic evaluation and holistic evaluation.

Analytic Evaluation. An analytic evaluation of a piece of writing begins with an analysis of the several features or qualities desired in the writing. These desired features or qualities are then used as standards or criteria against which the piece is compared. The evaluator merely goes down the list of criteria, giving the piece of writing a score for each criterion. A summary evaluation of the writing is obtained by combining these several scores.

Analytic evaluation is particularly valuable for formative evaluation. A general judgment of a student's work may be daunting, especially for students who do not do as well as they expect to do. Likewise, students who perform well, if given general comments about the writing, find in such general judgments little specific guidance telling them what they might do to write better. An analytic

evaluation can show students exactly what their strengths and weaknesses are and where they should concentrate their efforts.

Analytic evaluation is valuable as a measure of either progress or achievement. To evaluate progress, you can evaluate the student's progress in each area by comparing the current work with previous similar writing assignments. To measure raw achievement, you can compare the student's product against some imagined ideal. Of course, in either case you must make sure that your students are aware of the criteria on which they are being graded.

The Analytic Evaluation Scales provided in the Assessment Resource include lists of appropriate criteria for analytic evaluation, along with simple procedures for scoring. In addition, a general Writing Evaluation Form: Analytic Scale is provided in the Assessment Resource.

Holistic Evaluation. Holistic evaluation of a piece of writing calls for an overall judgment. Holistic evaluation is most useful as a measure of achievement. It is difficult to score holistic evaluations according to a student's progress. To do a holistic evaluation, simply look over the general analytic criteria and then assign a score that reflects how well the student met those criteria taken as a whole.

Holistic evaluation takes less time than analytic evaluation and in most cases results in the same score. The saved time can be used to make encouraging written comments to the student, pointing out features of the writing that you admire and features of the writing that you would like to see improve in the student's future work. A general Writing Evaluation Form: Holistic Response is provided in the Assessment Resource.

Grading. Some teachers prefer to grade each writing assignment. Others feel that grading selected assignments chosen by the teacher and student to reflect the student's best work provides a more realistic assessment of the student's optimal capabilities. If the latter option is chosen, you may wish to provide credit for completion of assignments that are not graded.

Marking Student Papers. A student who receives from a teacher a returned paper covered with corrections in red ink is not likely to be encouraged to do more and better writing. Furthermore, such marking of student papers is enormously time consuming and discourages frequent writing practice. A more encouraging approach is to mark one or two consistent problems and to mark three or four successes in each paper or, better yet, to allow students and their peers to do such marking and then to review these evaluations in conferences. Such marking can be done in conjunction with the completion of evaluation forms and/or analytic scales.

Reports and Research Papers

Literature and the Language Arts contains complete materials for instruction in the preparation of reports and research papers. The Research Skills section of the Study and Research Resource in the Language Arts Survey, pages 1036–1048 of the student text, contains a complete overview of research procedures, from using the library to documenting print and internet sources. The Reflecting on Your Reading questions that appear at the end of each Unit Review make excellent topics for extended reports or research papers. Further instruction on preparing longer papers can be found in the sections on organizing ideas, outlining, and drafting in the Writing Resource in the Language Arts Survey, pages 969–975 of the student text. These sections of the Language Arts Survey are accompanied by worksheets in the corresponding Resource Books in the Teacher's Resource Kit.

Remedial Exercises in Specific Writing Skills

As you evaluate your students' writing, you will discover consistent areas of weakness. One student may have trouble making transitions, another may consistently use serial commas incorrectly, and another may rely too heavily on the passive voice. The Language Arts Survey in the student edition and the accompanying Resource Book worksheets provide ample activities for remediation of particular recurring problems. Most of the instruction and activities in the Writing and Language, Grammar, and Style sections of the Language Arts Survey are useful for this purpose. Thus, if a student has a tendency to write sentence fragments, you can have him or her read the Language Arts Survey 3.33, "Correcting Sentence Fragments," on page 991 of the student text. That student can then do corresponding worksheet 3.33 in the Language, Grammar, and Style Resource Book. If a student has problems writing paragraphs, you can have him or her read the Language Arts Survey 2.24, "Writing Paragraphs," and do corresponding worksheet 2.24 in the Writing Resource Book. Thus, the Language Arts Survey and the Resource Books can be used to individualize your writing instruction and to target it to remediation of particular writing problems encountered by your students.

Instructional Options

Approaches to *Literature and the Language Arts*

Literature and the Language Arts contains a number of features that allow you the flexibility to organize your instruction to best suit you and your district's requirements. The following chart offers some tips for using your chosen approach to the text.

Features of the Program, by Approach

Historical Approach

- The Unit Introductions for units 2–12 tie literary developments to influential intellectual currents and political events, providing historical contexts for the selections.
- About the Author and About the Selection prereading notes provide additional historical background and context.
- Time lines in the introduction of the units provide a spatial representation of key literary and historical events and developments.

Thematic Approach

- The Thematic Organization chart on pages T32–T36 lists all the selections in the book under forty-seven major themes.
- Thematic Currents notes in the *Annotated Teacher's Edition* identify major themes for each unit.
- Writer's Journal prompts following selections ask students to explore and develop their thoughts about thematic topics.
- Reflecting on Your Reading questions in the Unit Review help students explore thematic relations among selections.

Writing Approach

- Writer's Journal activities following each selection use the literature as a springboard for engaging writing assignments that require both creative and critical thinking skills.
- Guided Writing lessons at the end of each unit provide direct instruction that integrates the writing process with the study of literature and the development of other language arts skills.
- The Selections by Genre pages beginning on page T37 list all the selections in the book under five genres of writing. Use the chart to find examples of the types of writing you wish to teach.
- The Language Arts Survey Writing Resource provides instruction in all phases of writing, editing, and proofreading, student and peer evaluation, publishing and presenting, and reflecting on the writing process.
- The *Writing Resource* book provides guided exercises in all writing phases. These worksheets are keyed to the instructional text in the Language Arts Survey.

Genre Approach

- Unit 1 provides an overview of the five literary genres with example selections.
- The Selections by Genre pages beginning on page T37 list all the selections in the book by genres. Use the chart to find examples of the types of literature you wish to teach. The selections are arranged in chronological order to help your class trace the historical development of the several genres.
- Unit Introductions and About the Selection prereading notes help your class trace the historical development of the major genres of literature in English.
- Thematic Currents notes in the *Annotated Teacher's Edition* identify two to four major literary concepts or techniques for each unit.
- The Language Arts Survey, Writing Resource, provides instruction in techniques that are characteristic of the various genres of writing.
- Questions for Understanding Literature following selections help students understand the use of literary techniques.
- Reflecting on Your Reading questions in the Unit Review relate matters of genre and literary technique to thematic issues.

Skills Approach

- The Language Arts Survey, following Unit 12, provides instruction in the range of language arts skills and concepts, including reading, writing, language, grammar and style, speaking and listening, study and research, and applied English.
- Use the Scope and Sequence Charts in the *Program Manager* to locate additional exercises in specific language arts skills.
- The Resource Books in the Teacher's Resource Kit provide guided exercises in the range of language arts skills: reading, writing, language, grammar and style, speaking and listening, study and research, applied English, critical thinking, and testing. These worksheets are coordinated with the instructional text in the Language Arts Survey.
- The *Assessment Resource* contains tests, study guides, and evaluation forms for language arts skills in reading, writing, language, grammar and style, speaking and listening, study and research, applied English, critical thinking, and testing. These materials are coordinated with the instructional text in the Language Arts Survey and with the worksheets in the Resource Books.
- The *Assessment Resource* also contains comprehensive pretests, post-tests, study guides, and analytic evaluation forms for skills in reading literature, and for skills in reading, writing, language, grammar and style, speaking and listening, study and research, applied English, critical thinking, and testing.

Teaching to Develop Students' Multiple Intelligences and to Accommodate Diverse Learning Styles

Activities using multiple intelligences are identified by green icons. See the legend on page T29.

Use the techniques in the chart at right to teach and encourage students with diverse intellectual strengths and learning styles and to help all students use and develop the full range of their abilities.

Teaching English Language Learners

Use the techniques in the chart at right to facilitate learning and participation for students whose native language is not English.

Teaching Students with Diverse Cultural Backgrounds

Use the techniques in the chart at right to facilitate learning and participation for students with diverse cultural backgrounds.

TEACHING MULTIPLE INTELLIGENCES

- Use multiple modes of expression: e.g., read selections aloud; read questions aloud; use visual aids—charts, graphs, tables, or other graphics, art, and films; play songs; and perform demonstrations.
- Encourage students to use multiple modes of expression, including nonverbal expressions and performances such as drawing, painting, collage, sculpture, dance and choreography, acting and oral interpretation, photography, filmmaking, video production, and musicianship and singing.
- Ask students to read aloud.
- Precede written work with a related oral activity.
- Teach students to use graphic aids for understanding and for studying.
- Facilitate group work.
- Use cooperative learning.
- Allow students ample thinking time.

TEACHING ENGLISH LANGUAGE LEARNERS

- Ask students to read aloud.
- Precede written work with a related oral activity.
- Use cooperative learning.
- Allow ample thinking time.
- When using small groups, pair with English-proficient students.
- Provide ample opportunity for nongraded, even nonevaluated, writing in English.
- Use multiple modes of expression: e.g., read selections aloud; read questions aloud; use visual aids—charts, graphs, tables, or other graphics, art, and films; play songs; and perform demonstrations.
- Encourage students to use multiple modes of expression, including nonverbal expressions and performances such as drawing, painting, collage, sculpture, dance and choreography, acting and oral interpretation, photography, filmmaking, video production, and musicianship and singing.

TEACHING STUDENTS WITH DIVERSE CULTURAL BACKGROUNDS

- Encourage discussion of cultural differences; invite students to share contrasting experiences; invite them to discuss events and characters from the selections that strike them as odd. Rely on students for your cultural information; be aware that you are liable to overlook differences unless you can take a different point of view.
- Use multiple modes of expression: e.g., read selections aloud; read questions aloud; use visual aids—charts, graphs, tables, or other graphics, art, and films; play songs; and perform demonstrations.
- Encourage students to use multiple modes of expression, including nonverbal expressions and performances such as drawing, painting, collage, sculpture, dance and choreography, acting and oral interpretation, photography, filmmaking, video production, and musicianship and singing.
- Precede written work with a related oral activity.
- Use cooperative learning.
- Allow ample thinking time.
- When using small groups, pair with English-proficient students.
- Preview/explain culturally loaded terms and names.
- Discuss idioms and word origins.
- Discuss topics with universal appeal and relevance—for instance, independence versus family ties, independence versus friendship, or identity.
- Discuss literature from both an "insider" and an "outsider" perspective.

Teaching Students with Special Needs

Students with special needs may include student with learning disabilities or students who are mentally challenged. Learning disabilities are physical conditions that make it difficult to complete certain types of tasks. Students with learning disabilities are often highly intelligent but lack specific abilities; for instance, one person may lack the ability to discriminate certain sounds, while another person may be able to discriminate among sounds but be unable to remember certain auditory messages. Mentally challenged students are often eager to learn but need lessons adapted to make learning meaningful to them. Use the techniques in the chart at right to help students with special needs succeed in your classroom.

Teaching Students with Special Needs

- Discover the particular effects of each individual's disability and try to fill gaps.
- Allow ample thinking time.
- Seat students in front.
- Repeat important ideas frequently.
- Summarize and check students' bearings frequently.
- Monitor progress frequently.
- On larger projects, provide step-by-step guidance.
- Precede written work with a related oral activity.
- Use cooperative learning.
- Use multiple modes of expression: e.g., read selections aloud; read questions aloud; use visual aids—charts, graphs, tables, or other graphics, art, and films; play songs; and perform demonstrations.
- Encourage students to use multiple modes of expression, including nonverbal expressions and performances such as drawing, painting, collage, sculpture, dance and choreography, acting and oral interpretation, photography, filmmaking, video production, and musicianship and singing.

Teaching Students with Special Academic Gifts and Talents

Just as students who work below grade level may lose interest because tasks are too difficult, students with special academic gifts and talents may lose interest because they complete work quickly or because they are not sufficiently challenged.

Activities involving other curricular areas are identified by red icons. See the legend on page T29.

Teaching Students with Special Academic Gifts and Talents

- Encourage students to use multiple modes of expression, including nonverbal expressions and performances such as drawing, painting, collage, sculpture, dance and choreography, acting and oral interpretation, photography, filmmaking, video production, and musicianship and singing.
- Use cooperative learning.
- Allow ample thinking time.
- Involve students in the planning, preparation, and presentation or conduct of lessons.
- Provide or encourage extension activities once mastery is demonstrated.
- Provide or encourage self-guided activities and independent research.

> "[C]hildren come to school with misconceptions about outside ethnic groups and with a white bias. However, . . . students' racial attitudes can be modified and made more democratic and . . . the racial attitudes of young children are much more easily modified than the attitudes of older students and adults. . . . If we are to help students acquire the attitudes needed to survive in a multicultural and diverse world, we must start early. . . .
>
> "A school experience that is multicultural includes content, examples, and realistic images of diverse racial and ethnic groups. Cooperative learning activities in which students from diverse groups work to attain shared goals is also a feature of the school, as well as simulated images of ethnic groups that present them in positive and realistic ways. Also essential within such a school are adults who model the attitudes and behaviors they are trying to teach. Actions speak much louder than words."
>
> —James A. Banks
> "Multicultural Education:
> Historical Development, Dimensions, and Practice"
> *Review of Research in Education*
> 19 (1993): 37–38

Achieving Gender Equity

Sexism cannot be combatted subtly (Sadker and Sadker 123). In addition to using the techniques listed at right, make a directed effort to combat gender stereotypes and to treat all students as valued learners.

ACHIEVING GENDER EQUITY

Facts: Boys call out answers eight times as frequently as do girls (Sadker and Sadker 43). Boys receive more evaluative feedback—both positive and negative (Sadker, Sadker, and Klein 300; Sadker and Sadker 55).

Responses:
- Make a special effort to call on girls and to give them specific feedback, both positive and negative. (Note: If you give more than one-third of your attention to girls you may be accused of favoring girls; see Sadker and Sadker 266–267.)
- When intervening in student-student interactions, concentrate on raising girls' confidence rather than criticizing boys' behavior.

Fact: Exposure to gender-biased materials appears to increase gender stereotypes (Sadker, Sadker, and Klein 279; Sadker and Sadker 73–75, 128–135, 266).

Responses:
- Be aware of biases in literature and point them out.
- When appropriate, provide historical context for stereotyping by explaining older attitudes and practices.
- Provide direct lessons about gender stereotypes and gender-related communication styles.

Facts: Girls are more likely than boys to attribute their successes to luck and less likely than boys to attribute their successes to ability (Sadker, Sadker, and Klein 303). Girls are more likely than boys to attribute their failures to lack of ability and less likely than boys to attribute their failures to lack of effort (303). Teachers are more likely to comment on girls' appearance and the neatness of their work, and more likely to comment on the intellectual qualities of boys' work (Sadker and Sadker 57).

Responses:
- Make an effort to avoid commenting on students', especially girls', appearance.
- Make an effort to attribute all success to effort and ability.
- Make an effort to rebut forcefully students' self-deprecating comments.

Facts: Girls have lower expectations of success (Sadker, Sadker, and Klein 302) and are more likely to display signs of "learned helplessness" (303). Teachers are more likely to help boys solve their own problems, but to solve problems for girls (Sadker and Sadker 81–83).

Responses:
- Fear of being "too tough" on girls is patronizing and hinders them from developing independence and confidence. Don't be afraid to criticize girls' work and don't let them off easy (Holt; Sizer).
- Make an effort to rebut forcefully students' self-deprecating comments.

Teaching Students to Work Cooperatively

Prepare your students for work in cooperative learning groups by teaching them how to listen actively, how to participate fully in discussions, and how to give one another positive feedback. Refer students to the lessons on listening, interpersonal communication, and discussion, sections 4.1–4.13 of the Language Arts Survey.

Uses for Small Groups. Use these task and project ideas to direct the work of collaborative learning groups.

- brainstorming
- peer tutorial sessions
- learning partners for practice or review and for all stages of the writing process
- inquiry-based concept learning
- multimedia and community-based projects
- topical symposia
- panel discussions
- mock jury trials
- role playing
- dramatizations
- simulations
- reader's theater

Teaching Students to Work Cooperatively

PREPARING STUDENTS FOR SMALL GROUP WORK

Participation

- Review/preteach vocabulary and cultural concepts for nonnative speakers.
- Begin with a nongraded, fun, get-to-know-one-another activity.
- Take steps to ensure that group members know each other's names.
- Assign tasks that call on multiple intelligences.
- Ask questions that call for personal response and interpretation.
- Value interpretations that differ from your own.
- Have students determine the wording of their topics or questions.
- Don't talk too much.
- Model tentativeness and openness.
- Model courtesy and respect for all.
- Respond only holistically and orally to early drafts and initial products.
- Avoid judging early drafts; discuss ideas rather than expression.
- Discuss anonymous samples.
- Praise students for taking risks.
- Require (only) positive feedback from peers.
- Use joint grading for group work: (1) everyone in the group receives the average among the group; (2) everyone receives the lowest grade among the group; (3) a final product is graded and everyone receives that grade.

Leadership

- Ask students to conduct lessons.
- Rotate leadership assignments in groups.
- Appoint two group leaders—one to learn from the other.
- Model and give direct instruction and practice in asking questions.
- Model and give direct instruction and practice in reporting a summary.
- Model and give direct instruction and practice in involving nonparticipants.
- Model and give direct instruction and practice in restraining dominators.
- Model and give direct instruction and practice in providing positive feedback.
- Model and give direct instruction and practice in providing constructive feedback.

Listening/Discussing

- Model, explain, and encourage attentive listening, eye contact, and not interrupting.
- Give practice in paraphrasing students' words and your own.
- Ask students to identify good speaking and listening habits and skills.
- Ask students to evaluate group processes and their roles in their groups (use *Assessment Resource* forms 7.13, 7.14, 7.22).

FORMING GROUPS

- Groups should contain a maximum of six students for a complex task, a maximum of four otherwise.
- For peer writing groups, two may be the ideal size. Require periodically that students change partners.
- In the prewriting stage, it can be helpful to match those who share a primary language other than English.
- Working groups should contain students of varied abilities.
- Allow groups to vary their seating arrangements (suggest possibilities).

GUIDING AND MONITORING

- Give specific tasks.
- Explain criteria for success.
- Assign roles in groups, or assign groups to distribute roles.
- When assigning roles in groups, divide responsibilities to assure interdependence and cooperation. One workable division of responsibilities includes (1) a discussion leader/facilitator; (2) a recorder; (3) a reporter; (4) a materials manager.
- Specify desired behaviors (see "Preparing Students for Small Group Work," above).
- Monitor group interactions and advise when appropriate.
- Intervene to diffuse conflict and to foster collaborative skills.
- When intervening in group work, ask a question rather than giving advice directly.
- If multiple groups have the same problem, interrupt the process and clarify or reteach.

CLOSURE AND ASSESSMENT

- Ask for sharing of a product.
- Both students and teacher should assess the quality of the product. Assessment can be among the entire class or only within groups.
- Both students and teacher should assess the quality of the group processes and communication.

Planning for Conferences and Portfolio Evaluation

As a teacher you have a number of distinguishable evaluative roles as outlined in the charts at right. Of course, you will not take on all of these roles at once. Make sure that students know which role to expect *before* they receive feedback.

References

Herman, J., P. Aschbacher, and L. Winters. *A Practical Guide to Alternative Assessment.* Alexandria, VA: ASCD, 1992.

Eggen, P., and D. Kauchak. *Educational Psychology.* 2nd ed. New York: Merrill, 1994.

Gardner, H. *Frames of Mind: The Theory of Multiple Intelligences.* New York: Basic, 1985.

———. *The Unschooled Mind: How Children Think and How Schools Should Teach.* New York: Basic, 1991.

Holt, J. *How Children Learn.* New York: Putnam, 1967.

Ohrlich, D., et al. *Teaching Strategies.* 4th ed. Lexington, MA: Heath, 1994.

Sadker, M., and D. Sadker. *Failing at Fairness.* New York: Scribner's, 1993.

Sadker, M., D. Sadker, and S. Klein. "The Issue of Gender in Elementary and Secondary Education." *Review of Research in Education* 17 (1991): 269–334.

Sizer, T. *Horace's Compromise.* Boston: Houghton, 1984.

Slavin, R. *Cooperative Learning: Theory, Research, and Practice.* Englewood Cliffs, NJ: Prentice, 1990.

———. *Educational Psychology.* 3rd ed. Englewood Cliffs, NJ: Prentice, 1991.

Understanding the Roles of Evaluators

ROLE	FUNCTION
AUDIENCE	to listen to ideas, to challenge, to question, to enlarge perspective
PROOFREADER	to correct grammar, usage, and mechanics
GRADER	to judge against external, more or less objective, and more or less arbitrary standards
ADVISOR	to prod for problem soutions, to encourage, to give suggestions, to remind of objectives

ROLE	TEACHING TIPS
AUDIENCE	Act exclusively as an audience when you read and comment on drafts. Comments on drafts should avoid direct criticism and should aim at raising students' excitement about further writing and revising.
PROOFREADER	Overemphasis on proofreading and points of grammar, usage, and mechanics can drain students' interest in and enthusiasm for writing as well as their self-confidence. Use proofreading as a peer function, and allow students to learn from reading and proofreading each other's papers.
GRADER	Avoiding grading as much as possible allows both you and students to concentrate on clear and honest expression and to preserve intrinsic motivation.
ADVISOR	Because the advising function requires one-on-one interchange, you should reserve for it as much of the precious evaluation time as you can.

Conducting Conferences

- Examine the portfolio before conferencing with the student. Make sure it contains all required material, including the student's evaluations of each piece of writing and of the portfolio as a whole (*See the Writing Resource and Assessment Resource Book for evaluation forms*).
- Evaluate the portfolio before conferencing. Complete the portfolio evaluation form, making special note of any discrepancies between your evaluaiton and the student's.
- Do not attempt to discuss all aspects of the portfolio or the student's class performance. Choose two or three broad, major points and one or two specific problems to focus on in the conference.
- As an alternative to conferencing, you may sometimes complete and hand to students a Portfolio Evaluation Form and additional writing evaluation forms in the *Assessment Resource*. You will still need to allow time for students to respond to and ask questions about their evaluations, and to hold conferences with students who need special help or encouragement.
- To allow ample class time for conferences, you must assign sufficient work that students can do independently to keep them busy on conference days. Thus, you must establish the writing process and the peer groups early in the term.
- In addition, to allow yourself ample time to evaluate portfolios you must involve students in ongoing self- and peer evaluation.

Additional Resources for Language Arts Teachers

TEACHING LITERATURE

Applebee, A. N. *Tradition and Reform in the Teaching of English: A History.* Urbana, IL: NCTE, 1974.

Atwell, N. *In the Middle: Writing, Reading, and Learning with Adolescents.* Portsmouth, NH: Heinemann, 1987.

Beach, R., and J. Marshall. *Teaching Literature in the Secondary School.* Orlando, FL: Harcourt, 1991.

Becoming a Nation of Readers: The Report of the Commission on Reading. Washington, DC: NIE, 1984.

Buck, C., ed. *The Bloomsbury Guide to Women's Literature.* New York: Prentice, 1992.

Bushman, J., and K. Bushman. *Using Young Adult Literature in the Classroom.* New York: Macmillan, 1992.

Cooper, C. R., ed. *Researching Response to Literature and the Teaching of Literature.* Norwood, NJ: Ablex, 1988.

Farrell, E. J., and J. Squire, eds. *Transactions with Literature: A Fifty-Year Perspective.* Urbana, IL: NCTE, 1990.

Flood, J., et al., eds. *Handbook of Research on Teaching the English Language Arts.* New York: Macmillan, 1991.

Glazer, S. *Reading Comprehension: Self-monitoring Strategies That Create Independent Readers.* New York: Scholastic, 1992.

Langer, J. A., ed. *Literature Instruction: A Focus on Student Response.* Urbana, IL: NCTE, 1992.

Lee, C., and T. Gura. *Oral Interpretation.* 8th ed. Boston: Houghton, 1992.

Marzano, R. *Cultivating Thinking English and the Language Arts.* Urbana, IL: NCTE, 1991.

Newell, G. E., and R. K. Durst. *Exploring Texts: The Roles of Discussion and Writing in the Teaching and Learning of Literature.* Norwood, MA: Christopher-Gorden, 1993.

Probst, R. E. *Response and Analysis: Teaching Literature in Junior and Senior High School.* Portsmouth, NH: Boynton/Cook, 1988.

Rosenblatt, L. *Literature as Exploration.* 4th ed. New York: MLA, 1983.

———. *The Reader, the Text, the Poem: The Transactional Theory of the Literary Work.* Carbondale, IL: Southern Illinois UP, 1978.

Wagner, B. J., and M. Larson. *Situations: A Casebook of Virtual Realities for the English Teacher.* Portsmouth, NH: Boynton/Cook, 1994.

Widdowson, P., ed. *Re-reading English.* London: Routledge, 1982.

TEACHING WRITING

Bogel, F. V., and K. K. Gottschalk, eds. *Teaching Prose.* New York: Norton, 1988.

Dellinger, D. G. *Out of the Heart: How to Design Writing Assignments for High School Courses.* Berkeley, CA: Bay Area Writing Project.

Elbow, P. *Writing with Power: Techniques for Mastering the Writing Process.* New York: Oxford UP, 1981.

Flower, L. S. *Problem-Solving Strategies in Writing.* 2nd ed. Orlando, FL: Harcourt, 1985.

Fulwiler, T., ed. *The Journal Book.* Portsmouth, NH: Heinemann, 1987.

Handa, C., ed. *Computers and Community: Teaching Composition in the Twenty-First Century.* Portsmouth, NH: Boynton/Cook, 1990.

Harris, M. *Teaching One-to-One: The Writing Conference.* Urbana, IL: NCTE, 1986.

Hawisher, G. E. "Research and Recommendations for Computers and Composition." *Critical Perspectives on Computers and Composition Instruction.* Ed. G. E. Hawisher and C. L. Selfe. New York: Teacher's Coll. P, 1989: 44–69.

Irmscher, W. *Teaching Expository Writing.* New York: Holt, 1979.

Kirby, D., and T. Liner. *Inside Out: Developmental Strategies for Teaching Writing.* Upper Montclair, NJ: Boynton/Cook, 1981.

Langer, J. A., and A. N. Applebee. *How Writing Shapes Thinking: A Study of Teaching and Learning.* NCTE Research Rept. No. 22. Urbana, IL: NCTE, 1987.

Lindemann, E. *A Rhetoric for Writing Teachers.* New York: Oxford UP, 1982.

Moffett, J., and B. J. Wagner. *Student-Centered Language Arts, K–12.* 4th ed. Portsmouth, NH: Boynton/Cook, 1992.

Murray, D. *Write to Learn.* New York: Holt, 1984.

Rodrigues, D., and R. Rodrigues. *Teaching Writing with Word Processors, Grades 1–13.* Urbana, IL: NCTE, 1987.

Romano, T. *Clearing the Way: Working with Teenage Writers.* Portsmouth, NH: Heinemann, 1987.

Ross, M., D. Brackett, and A. Maxon. *Assessment and Management of Mainstreamed Hearing-Impaired Children.* Austin, TX: Pro-Ed, 1991.

Shaughnessy, M. *Errors and Expectations.* New York: Oxford UP, 1977.

Spear, K. *Sharing Writing.* Upper Montclair, NJ: Boynton/Cook, 1988.

Tate, G., and E. Corbett, eds. *The Writing Teacher's Sourcebook.* New York: Oxford UP, 1981.

Weaver, Constance. *Grammar for Teachers.* Urbana, IL: NCTE, 1979.

TEACHING GRAMMAR

Elley, W. B., et al. "The Role of Grammar in a Secondary School English Curriculum." *Research in the Teaching of English* 10 (1976): 5–21.

Hillocks, G., Jr. *Research on Written Composition.* Urbana, IL: Natl. Conference on Research in English and ERIC/CRCS, 1986.

TEACHING THINKING SKILLS

Ausubel, D. P. *Educational Psychology.* 2nd ed. New York: Holt, 1978.

Chance, P. *Thinking in the Classroom: A Survey of Programs.* New York: Teacher's Coll. P, 1986.

Costa, A. L. *Developing Minds: A Resource Book for Teaching Thinking.* Rev. ed. 2 Vols. Alexandria, VA: ASCD, 1991.

Gardner, H. *The Unschooled Mind.* New York: Basic, 1991.

Horton, S. *Thinking through Writing.* Baltimore: Johns Hopkins UP, 1982.

Lazear, D. G. *Teaching for Multiple Intelligences.* Fastback No. 342. Bloomington, IN: Phi Delta Kappa Educ. Foundation, 1992.

Nickerson, R. S., D. N. Perkins, and E. E. Smith. *The Teaching of Thinking.* Hillsdale, NJ: Erlbaum, 1985.

Novak, J. D., and D. B. Gowin. *Learning How to Learn.* New York: Cambridge UP, 1984.

Pressley, M., et al. *Cognitive Strategy Instruction That Really Improves Children's Academic Performance.* Cambridge, MA: Brookline, 1990.

Resnick, L. B. *Education and Learning to Think.* Washington, DC: Natl. Academy P, 1987.

Resnick, L. B., and L. E. Klopfer, eds. *Toward the Thinking Curriculum: Current Cognitive Research.* Alexandria, VA: ASCD, 1989.

Rogoff, B. *Apprenticeship in Thinking.* New York: Cambridge UP, 1989.

Sternberg, R. J. "How Can We Teach Intelligence?" *Educational Leadership* 42 (1984): 38–50.

Sternberg, R. J., and T. I. Lubart. "Creating Creative Minds." *Phi Delta Kappan* 72 (1991): 608–614.

Sternberg, R. J., and R. Wagner. *Practical Intelligence.* New York: Cambridge UP, 1985.

ASSESSMENT

California Assessment Program. *The California Assessment Program: A Position Paper on Testing and Instruction.* Sacramento, CA: CAP, 1990.

Cambourne, B., and J. Turbil. "Assessment in Whole-Language Classrooms: Theory into Practice." *Elementary School Journal* 90 (1991): 337–349.

García, G. E., and P. D. Pearson. "Assessment and Diversity." *Review of Research in Education* 20 (1994): 337–391.

Gronlund, N. E., and R. L. Linn. *Measurement and Evaluation in Teaching.* 6th ed. New York: Macmillan, 1990.

Herman, J. L., P. R. Aschbacher, and L. Winters. *A Practical Guide to Alternative Assessment.* Alexandria, VA: ASCD, 1992.

Johnston, P. H. *Constructive Evaluation of Literate Activity.* White Plains, NY: Longman, 1992.

Smith, M. A., and M. Ylvisaker, eds. *Teacher's Voices: Portfolios in the Classroom.* Berkeley, CA: Natl. Writing Project, 1994.

Wolf, D., et al. "To Use Their Minds Well: Investigating New Forms of Student Assessment." *Review of Research in Education* 17 (1991): 31–74.

Yancey, K. B., ed. *Portfolios in the Writing Classroom.* Urbana, IL: NCTE, 1992

TEACHING SPECIAL POPULATIONS

Banks, J., and C. M. Banks, eds. *Multicultural Education: Issues and Perspectives.* 2nd ed. Boston: Allyn, 1993.

Brooks, C., ed. *Tapping Potential: English and the Language Arts for the Black Learner.* Urbana, IL: NCTE, 1985.

Cummins, J. *Empowering Minority Students.* Sacramento, CA: CA Assoc. for Bilingual Education, 1989.

Farr, M., and H. Daniels. *Language Diversity and Writing Instruction.* New York: ERIC Clearinghouse on Urban Education/Columbia UP, 1986.

Garcia, E. E. "Language, Culture, and Education." *Review of Research in Education* 19 (1993): 51–98.

Haberman, M. "The Pedagogy of Poverty versus Good Teaching." *Phi Delta Kappan* (1991): 290–294.

Hernandez, H. *Multicultural Education: A Teacher's Guide to Content and Process.* Columbus, OH: Merrill, 1989.

Kronick, D. *New Approaches to Learning Disabilities.* Philadelphia, PA: Grune & Stratton, 1988.

Marik, R. *Special Education Students Write: Classroom Activities and Assignments.* Berkeley, CA: Bay Area Writing Project, 1982.

Shade, B. J. *Culture, Style, and the Educative Process.* Springfield, IL: Charles Thomas, 1989.

Slavin, R., N. Karweit, and N. Madden, eds. *Effective Programs for Students at Risk.* Boston: Allyn, 1989.

West, W. W. *Teaching the Gifted and Talented in the English Classroom.* Washington, DC: NEA, 1980.

GENDER ISSUES

Brown, L. M., and C. Gilligan. *Meeting at the Crossroads: Women's Psychology and Girls' Development.* Cambridge: Harvard UP, 1992.

Gilbert, P. *Gender, Literacy, and the Classroom.* Carlton South, Victoria: Austral. Reading Assn., 1989.

Sadker, M., and D. Sadker. *Failing at Fairness: How Schools Cheat Girls.* New York: Scribner's, 1994.

Sadker, M., D. Sadker, and S. Klein. "The Issue of Gender in Elementary and Secondary Education." *Review of Research in Education* 17 (1991): 269–334.

Wellesley College Center for Research on Women. *How Schools Shortchange Girls: The AAUW Report.* Washington, DC: American Assn. of Univ. Women, 1992.

TEACHING HIGH SCHOOL-AGE STUDENTS

Applebee, A. N. *The Child's Concept of Story: Ages Two to Seventeen.* Chicago: U of Chicago P, 1978.

Flavell, J. *Cognitive Development.* 2nd ed. Englewood Cliffs, NJ: Prentice, 1985.

Kohlberg, L. "Education for Justice: A Modern Statement of the Platonic View." *Five Lectures on Moral Education.* Ed. N. F. Sizer and T. R. Sizer. Cambridge: Harvard UP, 1970.

KEY TO ICONS

Cross-curriculum Icons

 Arts and Humanities

 Mathematics and Sciences

 Social Studies

 Applied Arts

Multiple Intelligence Icons

 **Musical Intelligence**
Ability to produce and to appreciate forms of musical expression

 **Logical-Mathematical Intelligence**
Ability to reason and to discern logical or numerical patterns

 **Spatial Intelligence**
Ability to configure space to pose and solve problems

 **Kinesthetic Intelligence**
Ability to use the body effectively to solve problems

 **Interpersonal/ Intrapersonal Intelligence**
Ability to respond to the needs of others, self

 **Naturalist Intelligence**
Ability to respond to surrounding environment

SCANS Icons

 **Managing Resources**
Identifies, organizes, plans, allocates time, money, materials, space, human resources

 **Interpersonal Skills**
Works with others as member of team

 **Information Skills**
Acquires, evaluates, organizes, maintains, interprets, communicates, and processes information

 **Systems Skills**
Understands complex interrelationships

 **Technology Skills**
Selects, applies, and maintains appropriate technology to perform tasks and solve problems

 **Basic Skills**
Reads, writes, performs arithmetic and mathematical operations, and listens and speaks well

 **Thinking Skills**
Thinks creatively, makes decisions, solves problems, visualizes, knows how to learn, and reasons

 **Personal Qualities**
Displays responsibility, self-esteem, sociability, self-management, and integrity and honesty

Literature and the Language Arts, The British Tradition

Overview of Special Features

Art Notes

Selections for Additional Reading

Unit Reviews

Language Arts Survey

Thematic Organization Chart

The chart on these pages lists forty-seven common literary themes and identifies the selections in this book that deal with these themes. Choose the themes you wish to teach in your course, and use the chart to identify selections that deal with those themes.

	AGE	ALIENATION	ART AND ARTISTRY	BEAUTY	BIRTH	CONFUSION	COURAGE AND FEAR	DEATH	DISCOVERING AND LEARNING	DIVERSITY AND PLURALISM	DRAMA AND ACTING	EXILE	FAITH	FAMILY	FREEDOM	FRIENDSHIP	THE FUTURE	GIVING	GOD	GREED AND AMBITION	GROWTH/GROWING UP	HERO/HEROISM	HOME AND COUNTRY	HONESTY	HOPE	IDENTITY	IMAGINATION	INDEPENDENCE	JUSTICE	KNOWLEDGE/WISDOM	LAW AND CUSTOM	LEADERSHIP AND AUTHORITY	LOSS AND REMEMBRANCE	LOVE	NATURE	ORDER/DISORDER	PARENTS AND CHILDREN	PEACE	PRIDE AND VANITY	RELIGION	SCIENCE	STRUGGLE	TECHNOLOGY	TRUTH/REALITY	WAR	WORK	WRITING AND BOOKS
UNIT 1																																															
“Robin Hood and Allen a Dale,” 6																						•						•	•		•	•															
“The Naming of Cats,” 22																										•	•																				
“The Rocking-Horse Winner,” 32														•						•										•							•							•			
The Rising of the Moon, 51						•	•																•						•		•	•				•											
Speech to the Troops at Tilbury, 66							•															•	•									•										•				•	
UNIT 2																																															
“The Conversion of King Edwin,” 90								•					•						•																					•				•			
“The Story of Cædmon,” including “Cædmon’s Hymn,” 95			•										•						•																					•							•
“The Wife’s Lament,” 101		•										•		•									•										•	•	•												
Anglo-Saxon Riddles, 107																																											•		•		•
from *Beowulf*, 112							•	•														•	•																						•		
from “The Seafarer,” 144		•										•	•																				•		•					•						•	
“Wulf and Eadwacer,” 144													•																				•	•													
UNIT 3																																															
“Sir Patrick Spens,” 168							•	•														•										•			•												
“The Great Silkie of Shule Skerrie,” 171					•			•																						•							•										
“Ubi Sunt Qui ante Nos Fuerunt?” 175								•					•																				•						•	•							
“I Sing of a Maiden,” 179				•	•														•																•		•			•							
“The Honeysuckle: Chevrefoil,” 182			•																															•	•												
from *Sir Gawain and the Green Knight*, 187							•									•					•	•		•																							
from *Le Morte d’Arthur*, 200					•																•	•				•						•					•							•			
from *The Book of Margery Kempe*, 211		•	•						•					•												•		•	•	•	•											•				•	•
from *The Canterbury Tales*,																																															
“The Prologue,” 216			•										•			•				•				•											•					•							
from “The Pardoner’s Tale,” 236								•	•											•				•					•		•					•				•		•					
from *Everyman*, 243	•					•	•	•	•				•						•	•										•									•	•				•			
from *The Ingenious Hidalgo Don Quixote*, 254			•			•	•	•					•			•						•					•							•	•												
“Western Wind,” 262																																															•
“I am of Ireland,” 262																							•									•	•									•					
“The Bonny Earl of Murray” 262																						•	•						•																		
“The Twa Corbies,” 262								•								•																	•	•													
“Bonny Barbara Allan,” 262				•				•																									•				•										
“The Wife of Usher’s Well,” 262							•	•						•																		•		•		•						•		•	•		
UNIT 4																																															
“Whoso List to Hunt,” 288																																•	•	•													
Sonnet 31 (“With how sad steps . . .”), 292																																	•	•	•												
from *The Færie Queene*, 296							•						•						•			•																		•					•		

	AGE	ALIENATION	ART AND ARTISTRY	BEAUTY	BIRTH	CONFUSION	COURAGE AND FEAR	DEATH	DISCOVERING AND LEARNING	DIVERSITY AND PLURALISM	DRAMA AND ACTING	EXILE	FAITH	FAMILY	FREEDOM	FRIENDSHIP	THE FUTURE	GIVING	GOD	GREED AND AMBITION	GROWTH/GROWING UP	HERO/HEROISM	HOME AND COUNTRY	HONESTY	HOPE	IDENTITY	IMAGINATION	INDEPENDENCE	JUSTICE	KNOWLEDGE/WISDOM	LAW AND CUSTOM	LEADERSHIP AND AUTHORITY	LOSS AND REMEMBRANCE	LOVE	NATURE	ORDER/DISORDER	PARENTS AND CHILDREN	PEACE	PRIDE AND VANITY	RELIGION	SCIENCE	STRUGGLE	TECHNOLOGY	TRUTH/REALITY	WAR	WORK	WRITING AND BOOKS
“The Passionate Shepherd to His Love,” 301				●																			●											●	●												
“The Nymph’s Reply to the Shepherd,” 306	●							●																											●	●												
“The Doubt of Future Foes,” 310							●																●													●											
“When Thou Must Home to Shades of Underground,” 314				●				●																										●	●													
Sonnet 18 (“Shall I compare thee . . .”), 318			●					●																											●	●												●
Sonnet 29 (“When, in disgrace . . .”), 321		●																																	●													
Sonnet 130 (“My mistress’ eyes . . .”), 323				●																				●											●													
“Song, to Celia,” 326				●				●																											●													
from Ecclesiastes, Chapter 3, 330					●			●					●																	●					●					●							
from *Utopia, Book 2* “The Geography of Utopia,” 334 “Their Gold and Silver,” 337																		●												●	●	●				●		●								●	
from the *Canzoniere*, 342 Sonnet 1, 343 Sonnet 47, 344 Sonnet 54, 345																					●									●			●	●													
Sonnet 75 (“One day I wrote her name . . .”), 348								●																											●													
Sonnet 30 (“When to the sessions . . .”), 348																●																		●	●													
Sonnet 73 (“That time of year . . .”), 348								●																										●	●													
Eve’s Apology in Defense of Women, 348					●										●				●											●		●	●	●						●							
“Jack and Joan,” 349													●	●									●											●					●								
“A Litany in Time of Plague,” 350				●			●						●						●	●																			●	●							
Psalm 23, 350							●	●					●						●																												
Matthew 13, The Parable of the Sower, 350													●					●	●																												
1 Corinthians 13, 351																																															
UNIT 5																																															
The Tragedy of Macbeth, 374		●				●	●	●			●			●						●		●	●							●			●			●	●			●			●		●	●		
from . . . *Doctor Faustus*, 464								●			●								●	●										●									●	●							
from *The Analects*, 474														●																●	●	●															
from *The Tragedy of Hamlet, Prince of Denmark*																																															
(“And these few precepts . . .”), 477																														●							●										
(“To be, or not to be . . .”), 477						●	●																			●																●					
(“Speak the speech, I pray you . . .”), 477			●							●																																					
from *The Tragedy of King Richard the Second*																																															
(“Methinks I am a prophet . . .”), 478								●		●													●								●							●						●		
(“Let’s talk of graves . . .”), 479								●																								●							●								
from *The Merchant of Venice* (“The quality of mercy . . .”), 479													●						●										●		●									●							
from *The Tempest* (“Our revels now are ended...”), 479			●								●																●																	●			
UNIT 6																																															
Song (“Go and catch a falling star . . .”), 496				●																				●																							
Holy Sonnet 10 (“Death, be not proud . . .”), 500								●																																							

Selection	AGE	ALIENATION	ART AND ARTISTRY	BEAUTY	BIRTH	CONFUSION	COURAGE AND FEAR	DEATH	DISCOVERING AND LEARNING	DIVERSITY AND PLURALISM	DRAMA AND ACTING	EXILE	FAITH	FAMILY	FREEDOM	FRIENDSHIP	THE FUTURE	GIVING	GOD	GREED AND AMBITION	GROWTH/GROWING UP	HERO/HEROISM	HOME AND COUNTRY	HONESTY	HOPE	IDENTITY	IMAGINATION	INDEPENDENCE	JUSTICE	KNOWLEDGE/WISDOM	LAW AND CUSTOM	LEADERSHIP AND AUTHORITY	LOSS AND REMEMBRANCE	LOVE	NATURE	ORDER/DISORDER	PARENTS AND CHILDREN	PEACE	PRIDE AND VANITY	RELIGION	SCIENCE	STRUGGLE	TECHNOLOGY	TRUTH/REALITY	WAR	WORK	WRITING AND BOOKS
from Meditation 17 ("Perchance he for whom this bell tolls . . ."), 502													●						●																					●							
"Easter Wings," 507													●						●																					●							
from *Paradise Lost*, 511													●						●	●										●									●	●		●					
"On His Blindness," 521													●						●																					●							
from *The Pilgrim's Progress*, 524													●						●			●																	●	●		●					
"To Althea, from Prison," 533							●																											●													
"To His Coy Mistress," 538				●				●																										●													
from *The Rubáiyát*, 544								●					●																					●					●	●							
"The Indifferent," 550				●																														●													
from *Areopagitica*, 550																							●																								●
Sonnet 77 ("In this strange labyrinth . . ."), 550						●																												●													
"To Mrs. M. A. at Parting," 551								●								●																	●														
"The Garden," 551				●																														●	●												
Song ("Why so pale and wan . . ."), 552																														●				●													
"Corinna's Going A-Maying," 552				●			●																											●	●												
"To Lucasta, Going to the Wars," 552																						●												●											●		
UNIT 7																																															
"The Introduction," 572		●								●																●				●	●									●							
"A Song for St. Cecilia's Day," 578			●										●						●																					●							
"Pressed by the Moon, Mute Arbitress of Tides," 584																																			●							●					
from *The Diary of Samuel Pepys*, 588							●	●															●													●											
from *Gulliver's Travels*																																															
from "A Voyage to Lilliput," 598								●															●							●	●								●								
from "A Voyage to Brobdingnag," 602																							●						●	●	●											●			●		
from *Oroonoko*, 607							●			●										●									●		●																
Couplets from *An Essay on Criticism*, 614																														●											●						●
from *A Dictionary of the English Language*, 619			●																								●																				●
"A Brief to Free a Slave," 623										●													●						●		●																
from *The Life of Samuel Johnson, LL. D.*, 627																●																							●								●
from *Candide*, 634																							●							●																	
"To All Writing Ladies," 642										●													●							●												●					●
"Epigram on Milton," 642																							●										●														●
"Love Armed," 642																																●		●											●		
from *An Essay on Man*, 643	●																																			●				●							
"The Lover: A Ballad," 643																●																		●													
"A Modest Proposal," 643																							●														●					●		●			
from *The Spectator*, No. 62, 647																														●				●													
"A Short Song of Congratulation," 648	●																				●																		●								
UNIT 8																																															
"Elegy Written in a Country Churchyard," 664								●															●										●		●				●								
"Auld Lang Syne," 673																●					●		●										●														

Selection	AGE	ALIENATION	ART AND ARTISTRY	BEAUTY	BIRTH	CONFUSION	COURAGE AND FEAR	DEATH	DISCOVERING AND LEARNING	DIVERSITY AND PLURALISM	DRAMA AND ACTING	EXILE	FAITH	FAMILY	FREEDOM	FRIENDSHIP	THE FUTURE	GIVING	GOD	GREED AND AMBITION	GROWTH/GROWING UP	HERO/HEROISM	HOME AND COUNTRY	HONESTY	HOPE	IDENTITY	IMAGINATION	INDEPENDENCE	JUSTICE	KNOWLEDGE/WISDOM	LAW AND CUSTOM	LEADERSHIP AND AUTHORITY	LOSS AND REMEMBRANCE	LOVE	NATURE	ORDER/DISORDER	PARENTS AND CHILDREN	PEACE	PRIDE AND VANITY	RELIGION	SCIENCE	STRUGGLE	TECHNOLOGY	TRUTH/REALITY	WAR	WORK	WRITING AND BOOKS
"John Anderson, My Jo," 676	●							●								●																		●													
"The Lamb," 680													●						●																●					●							
"The Tyger," 682													●						●																●					●							
"London," 685		●						●															●																								
from Preface to *Lyrical Ballads*, 689			●	●																																											●
"The world is too much with us . . . ," 694				●																													●		●												
"Lines Composed a Few Miles above Tintern Abbey," 696				●									●																				●		●			●									
"Kubla Khan," 704				●																												●			●												
"Ozymandias," 710								●								●				●										●		●															
"Ode to the West Wind," 714																																			●												
"She Walks in Beauty," 720				●																															●			●									
from *Childe Harold's Pilgrimage*, 724				●																		●													●												
"When I Have Fears," 728			●				●	●																										●													●
"Ode on a Grecian Urn," 731			●	●																																								●			
from *A Vindication of the Rights of Woman*, 736										●													●		●	●				●																	
from the Introduction to *Frankenstein*, 742			●																															●							●		●				●
Poems from *The Narrow Road to the Deep North and Other Travel Sketches*, 749																●																			●												
"She Dwelt among the Untrodden Ways," 753		●		●				●																									●														
"Dirce," 753								●																																							
"The Harp That Once through Tara's Halls," 753								●							●																		●														
"Casabianca," 753							●	●														●															●								●		
from "Macbeth," 754			●																																												●
UNIT 9																																															
"The Lady of Shalott," 784			●					●																										●	●												
"Ulysses," 789							●							●								●	●			●		●																			
from *In Memoriam*, 789								●					●			●			●														●	●	●					●							●
"My Last Duchess," 799			●	●				●																										●													
"Andrea del Sarto," 803			●																							●				●				●								●				●	
"Dover Beach," 813													●																						●												
"The Man He Killed," 819								●								●							●																						●		
"Channel Firing," 821																			●				●																	●					●		
"The Darkling Thrush," 824																							●		●										●												
Sonnet 43 ("How do I love thee . . ."), 828																																		●													
"Pied Beauty," 832				●															●																●												
"God's Grandeur," 835																			●																●												
"Spring and Fall: To a Young Child," 837				●				●													●									●																	
"Promises Like Pie-Crust," 840																●																		●													
"A Birthday," 843					●																													●	●												
"To an Athlete Dying Young," 847								●																									●														

Selection	AGE	ALIENATION	ART AND ARTISTRY	BEAUTY	BIRTH	CONFUSION	COURAGE AND FEAR	DEATH	DISCOVERING AND LEARNING	DIVERSITY AND PLURALISM	DRAMA AND ACTING	EXILE	FAITH	FAMILY	FREEDOM	FRIENDSHIP	THE FUTURE	GIVING	GOD	GREED AND AMBITION	GROWTH/GROWING UP	HERO/HEROISM	HOME AND COUNTRY	HONESTY	HOPE	IDENTITY	IMAGINATION	INDEPENDENCE	JUSTICE	KNOWLEDGE/WISDOM	LAW AND CUSTOM	LEADERSHIP AND AUTHORITY	LOSS AND REMEMBRANCE	LOVE	NATURE	ORDER/DISORDER	PARENTS AND CHILDREN	PEACE	PRIDE AND VANITY	RELIGION	SCIENCE	STRUGGLE	TECHNOLOGY	TRUTH/REALITY	WAR	WORK	WRITING AND BOOKS
"The Signalman," 850																																																
from *Through the Looking Glass*, 863																							•	•																					•			
from *Madame Bovary*, 873	•																									•		•						•	•								•						
"Flower in the Crannied Wall," 882																				•																•													
"When I Was One-and-Twenty," 882	•								•																	•								•														
"Loveliest of Trees," 882	•																																		•													
"The Night Is Darkening," 882																								•												•													
from *The Subjection of Women*, 882										•													•																									
"The Slave Ship," 883			•							•																																				
UNIT 10																																																
"The Lake Isle of Innisfree," 906				•																														•													
"Adam's Curse," 909			•																														•	•												•
"The Second Coming," 912																								•												•					•							
"Preludes," 916		•																					•																									
"Snake," 921				•																										•	•				•													
"The Soldier," 928		•																					•																						•		
"Dulce et Decorum Est," 932								•														•																							•		
"Rough," 937		•																			•																•									•		
"Do Not Go Gentle into That Good Night," 941							•	•																														•						•						
"Who's Who," 945																											•								•														•	
"Musée des Beaux Arts," 948		•	•																																												
"Not Waving but Drowning," 952		•						•																																						
"Thistles," 956								•																											•							•							
"Follower," 960	•																																	•			•										•	
"A Call," 963									•																								•	•				•											
"Bread," 966								•										•		•																											
"Naked Girl and Mirror," 971																						•																										
"Map of the New World," 977			•																																											
UNIT 11																																																
from *A Room of One's Own*, 993			•					•	•	•	•																																				•
from *A Portrait of the Artist . . .*, 1000		•																•		•		•																									
"Shooting an Elephant," 1010																								•						•		•	•																	
"The Garden-Party," 1019								•						•									•																•		•									
"The Lagoon," 1033							•	•							•		•																			•	•								•					
"Heat," 1047						•		•																				•							•		•								•					
"A Sunrise on the Veld," 1051		•					•	•												•					•		•		•					•								•					
"Red Dress—1946," 1061							•		•						•		•						•			•		•		•		•								•									
from *Angela's Ashes*, 1073									•						•						•						•		•									•							•				•	
from *Nectar in a Sieve*, 1082							•			•				•	•				•						•			•								•	•			•	•	•	•						•					
UNIT 12																																																
Pygmalion, 1110									•	•						•											•		•		•	•																	
"The Story of Pygmalion," 1167			•	•																														•													

Selections by Genre

These pages list all the selections in this book, organized by genre. Choose the genres you wish to teach in your course, and use the list to identify selections that represent those genres.

THE ORAL TRADITION

FROM UNIT 1

FROM UNIT 3

FROM UNIT 12

POETRY

FROM UNIT 1

FROM UNIT 2

FROM UNIT 3

FROM UNIT 4

FROM UNIT 5

FROM UNIT 6

FROM UNIT 7

FROM UNIT 8

FROM UNIT 9

FICTION

DRAMA

NONFICTION

Literature

and the Language Arts

THE EMC MASTERPIECE SERIES

SECOND EDITION

EMCParadigm Publishing Saint Paul, Minnesota

Staff Credits

Editorial

Laurie Skiba
Editor

Brenda Owens
Associate Editor

Lori Ann Coleman
Associate Editor

Diana Moen
Associate Editor

Jennifer Joline Anderson
Assistant Editor

Gia Marie Garbinsky
Assistant Editor

Janice Johnson
Curriculum Specialist

Paul Spencer
Art and Photo Researcher

Chris Bohen
Editorial Assistant

Katherine S. Link
Editorial Assistant

Design

Shelley Clubb
Production Manager

C. Vern Johnson
Senior Designer

Jennifer Wreisner
Senior Designer

Michelle Lewis
Design Specialist

Julie L. Hansen
Design Specialist

Bill Connell
Design Specialist

Joan D'Onofrio
Art Researcher

Cover Credits

Cover Designer: C. Vern Johnson

Interior with a Table **[Detail]**, 1921. Vanessa Bell.

Saint George and the Dragon **[Detail]**, c.1460. Paolo Uccello.

London Bridge **[Detail]**, 1906. Andre Derain.

William Shakespeare **[Detail]**, 1598. French Artist.

ISBN 0-8219-2193-2 (Student Edition) ISBN 0-8219-2194-0 (Annotated Teacher's Edition)
©2001 by EMC Corporation

All rights reserved. No part of this publication may be adapted, reproduced, stored in a retrieval system, or transmitted in any form or by any means, electronic, mechanical, photocopying, recording, or otherwise without permission from the publisher.

Published by EMC/Paradigm Publishing
875 Montreal Way
St. Paul, Minnesota 55102
800-328-1452
www.emcp.com
E-mail: educate@emcp.com

Printed in the United States of America.
10 9 8 7 6 5 4 3 2 1 XXX 06 05 04 03 02 01

Literature
and the Language Arts

SECOND EDITION

REDWOOD LEVEL
DISCOVERING LITERATURE

WILLOW LEVEL
UNDERSTANDING LITERATURE

CEDAR LEVEL
EXPLORING LITERATURE

PINE LEVEL
THE AMERICAN TRADITION

OAK LEVEL
RESPONDING TO LITERATURE

MAPLE LEVEL
THE BRITISH TRADITION

BIRCH LEVEL
EXPERIENCING LITERATURE

CYPRESS LEVEL
WORLD LITERATURE

Consultants and Writers

Senior Consultant
Dr. Edmund J. Farrell
Emeritus Professor of English Education
University of Texas at Austin
Austin, Texas

Gwendolyn Alexander
Educational Consultant
Washington, DC

Amy Bergstrom
Instructor
English Education Department
University of Minnesota
Duluth, Minnesota

Diana Blythe
Senior Content Manager
Humanities Software,
a division of Advantage Learning Systems, Inc.
Hood River, Oregon

Cherie Boen
National Board Certified Teacher
Educational Consultant
Minneapolis, Minnesota

Gloria Canson
English Instructor
Roosevelt High School
Portland, Oregon

Linda Christopherson
Educational Writer
Charlotte, North Carolina

Mary Curfman
Language Arts Supervisor
Department of Curriculum and Professional Development
Clark County Schools
Las Vegas, Nevada

Deanna and Roger Hebbert
Educational Writers
Longmont, Colorado

Sara Hyry
Freelance Education Writer
Easthampton, Massachusetts

Christina Kolb
Educational Writer
Newton, Massachusetts

Sharon Kremer
English Department Chair
A. O. Calhoun Middle School
Denton, Texas

Jon Madian
Senior Instructional Designer
Humanities Software,
a division of Advantage Learning Systems, Inc.
Hood River, Oregon

Beverly Martin
Managing Editor
Humanities Software,
a division of Advantage Learning Systems, Inc.
Hood River, Oregon

Danielle Martin
Educational Writer
Brooklyn, New York

Kristi McGee
Educational Writer
Brooklyn, New York

Margaret Palmer
English Department Chair
Samuel Clemens High School
Shertz, Texas

David Rathbun
English Instructor
South High School
Minneapolis, Minnesota

Carol Satz
Clinician
Center for Reading and Writing
Rider University
Lawrenceville, New Jersey

Eric Schneider
English Instructor
Patrick Henry High School
Minneapolis, Minnesota

Elnora Shields
Educational Consultant
Durham, North Carolina

Dr. Jane S. Shoaf
Educational Consultant
Edenton, North Carolina

Kendra Sisserson
Research Associate
University of Chicago
Chicago, Illinois

James W. Swanson
Educational Consultant
Minneapolis, Minnesota

Anita Usmiani
Language Arts Supervisor
Hamilton Township School District
Hamilton, New Jersey

Hope Vasholz
Teacher of English
Hammond High School
Columbia, Maryland

Dr. Gary Wiener
Language Arts Chair
Brighton High School
Rochester, New York

TABLE OF CONTENTS

The Idlers, c.1916–18. Maurice Prendergast.

v

Saint George and the Dragon, c.1460. Paolo Uccello.

vi

vii

London Bridge, 1906. Andre Derain.

viii

ix

Rest on the Flight to Egypt, 1874. Luc Olivier Merson.

x

xi

xii

xiii

 xiv

To the Student

Features of Your Textbook

A Guide for Reading

When you open your *EMC Masterpiece Series* textbook, you will find great literature, both classic and contemporary, by a wide variety of authors. You will also find useful step-by-step study strategies for each selection, helpful background information, and activities that allow you to relate the literature to your own experiences and share your point of view.

The **Guided Reading** program in this *EMC Masterpiece Series* book gives you tips before, during, and after you read each selection. Read on for a description of the features you will find in your textbook.

- **About the Author** and **About the Selection** give you background information you'll find helpful in reading the literature selection.
- **Literary Tools** points out and explains literary concepts and techniques that are used in the selection.
- **Guided Reading Questions** within the selection help you check your understanding of the reading.
- **Words for Everyday Use** includes the definition and pronunciation for new vocabulary. A sample sentence demonstrates the use of the word in context.
- **Footnotes** explain unfamiliar terms or unusual words.
- **Art Notes** provide information about the history, culture, or artistic technique of the fine art throughout the textbook and foster critical viewing of the art.
- **Respond to the Selection** allows you to relate the literature to your own experiences.
- **Investigate, Inquire, and Imagine** contains questions you need to perfect your understanding of the reading, from basic recalling and interpreting questions to ones that ask you to analyze, synthesize, evaluate, and extend your ideas. Some questions also ask you to look at a specific point of view, or examine a different perspective.
- **Understanding Literature** follows up on the literary techniques introduced in Literary Tools and asks you questions to further your understanding.
- **Writer's Journal** gives you three quick-writing options to help you build writing skills.
- **Integrating the Language Arts** contains creative activities that tie literature to other language arts areas such as grammar, vocabulary development, public speaking, study and research, collaborative learning, media literacy, and applied English.

A Guide for Writing

At the end of each unit of your textbook you will find a **Guided Writing** activity that takes you through the steps of the writing process. The lesson includes models from professional writers and students. Also included are graphic organizers, questions to get you thinking, and an **Integrated Language, Grammar, and Style** lesson to help you brush up on grammar points.

A Guide for Language Arts Skills

The **Language Arts Survey** in the back of your textbook is your resource for information about how to use the English language effectively. It includes tips on what you need to know to write, speak, and read effectively. There are six sections in the Language Arts Survey: the **Reading Resource**, the **Writing Resource**, the **Language, Grammar, and Style Resource**, the **Speaking and Listening Resource**, the **Study and Research Resource**, and the **Applied English Resource**. Do you need to correct a passive sentence? include an Internet site in a research paper? interview someone in the community? write a résumé? It's all here for you.

xv

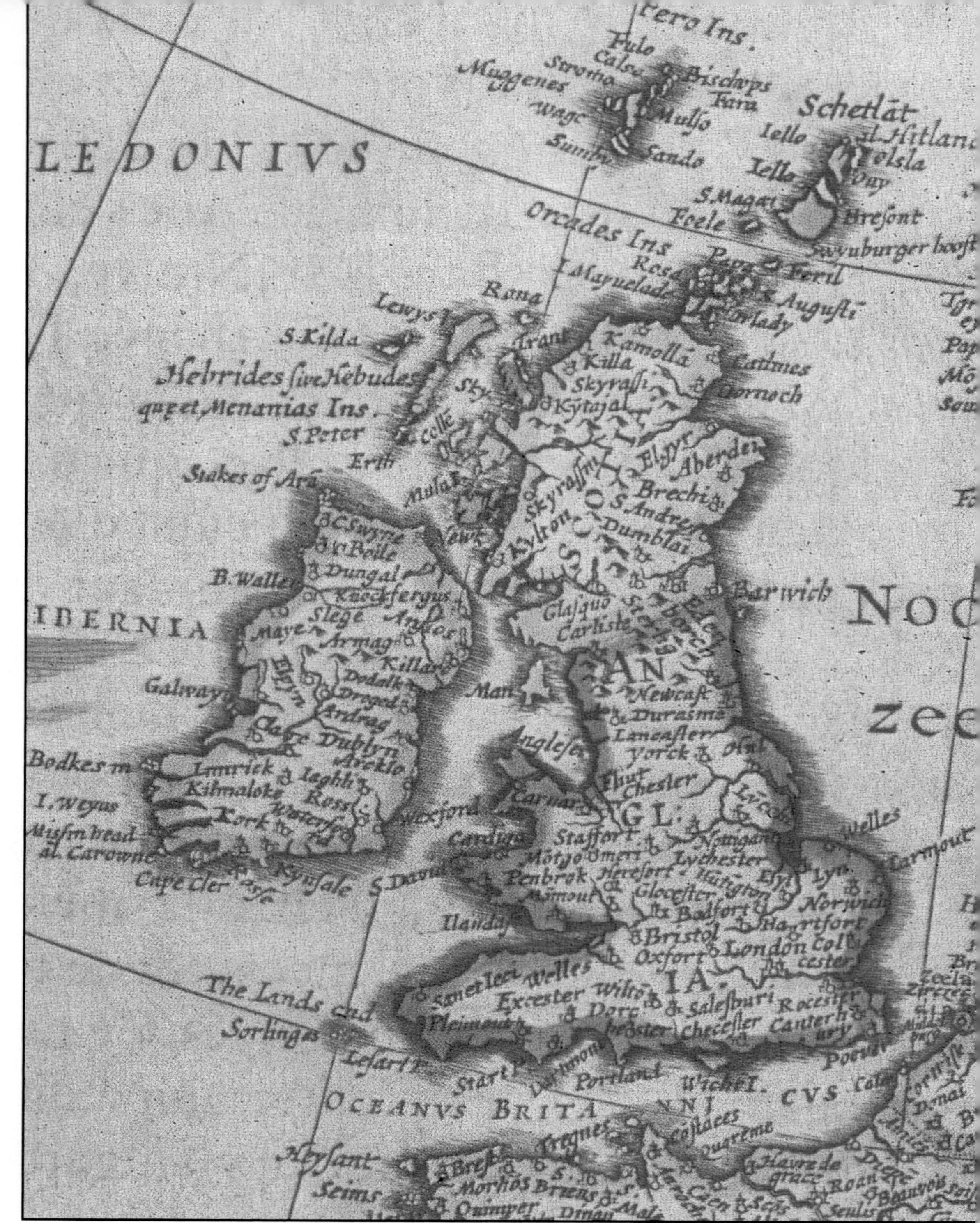

LEDONIVS
Schetlāt
Orcades Ins
Hebrides sive Hebudes
quæ et Menanias Ins.
S.Kilda
S.Peter
IBERNIA
Galway
Dublyn
Kork
Man
Anglesey
Barwich
Newcast
Yorck
Chester
Bristol
Oxfort
London
Norwich
Excester
The Lands end
Sorlingas
OCEANVS BRITA
CVS
Heysant
Noo
zee

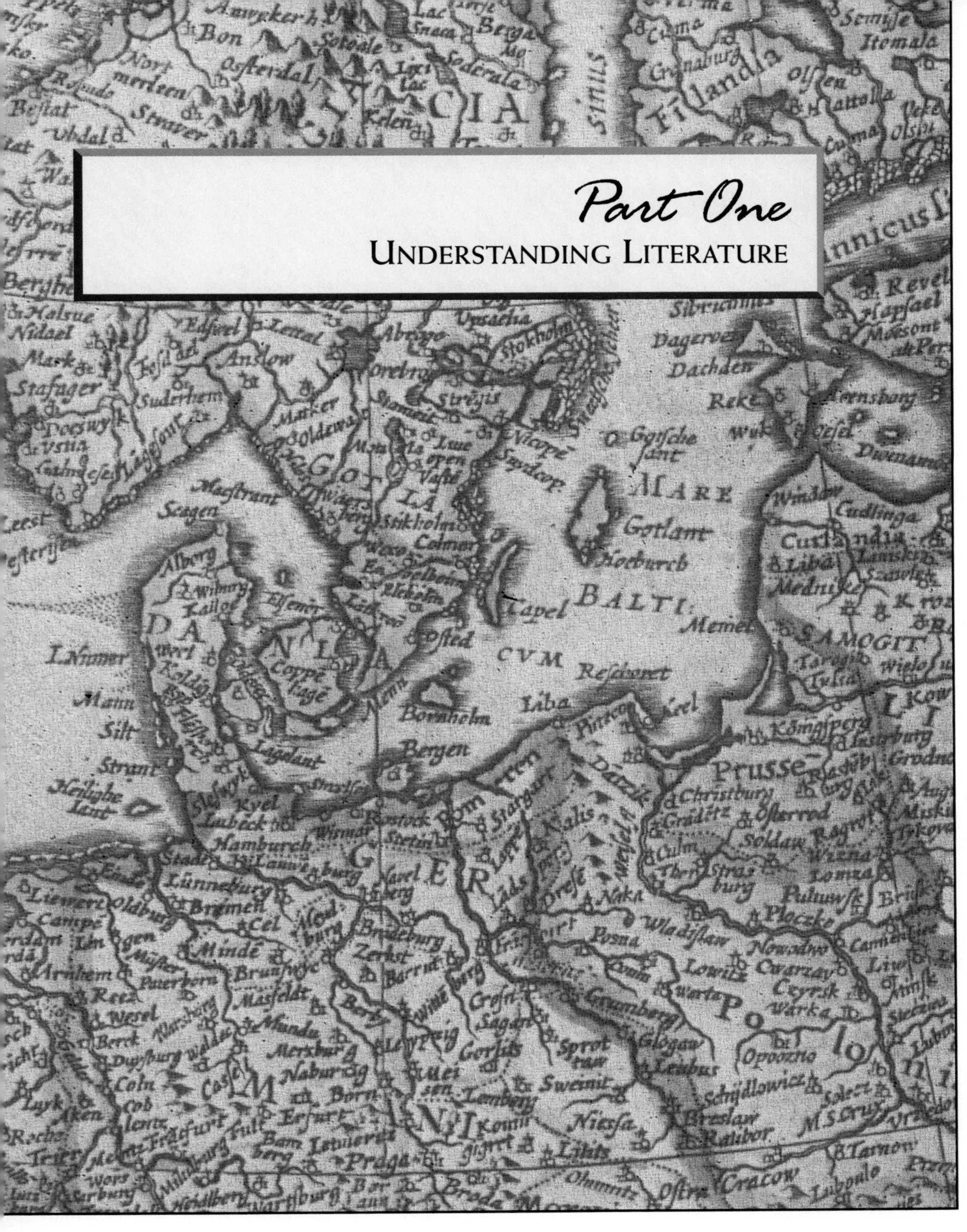

Part One
UNDERSTANDING LITERATURE

UNIT SKILLS OUTLINE

Literary Skills and Concepts

(Continued on page 4)

GOALS/OBJECTIVES

Studying this unit will enable students to

- appreciate each of the major genres of literature
- name and describe major elements and literary techniques of each of the genres of literature
- identify how the elements and literary techniques employed in each of the main genres applies to a specific literary work
- write a book review
- identify and use elements of a paragraph

Unit 1 Genres and Techniques of Literature

Salisbury Cathedral: from the Meadows. John Constable, 1834. Private Collection.

The poet's eye, in a fine frenzy rolling,
Doth glance from heaven to earth,
from earth to heaven;
And as imagination bodies forth
The forms of things unknown, the poet's pen
Turns them to shapes, and gives to airy nothing
A local habitation and a name.

—William Shakespeare
"A Midsummer Night's Dream"

3

CROSS-CURRICULAR CONNECTIONS

Arts and Humanities
Various Versions of Robin Hood, 7
Foxfire, 8
Retelling Robin Hood Story, 8
Genres of Poetry, 15
Samuel Palmer's Painting, 28
Horses and Racing, 33
Ellen Terry, 48
Play Performance, 51
Blocking Diagrams for Plays, 52
Irish Landscapes, 53
Famous Irish Writers, 57
Spanish Armada, 63
Elizabeth Film, 65

Mathematics and Sciences
TK for 20th Century Lit
Freudian Criticism, 923
World Hunger Organizations, 967
Animals as Pets, 22
Domestic Cats, 24
Financial Budgets, 36
Savings and Interest, 40
Finding Slope of Stage, 49

Social Studies
TK for 20th Century Lit
Judith Wright in Australia, 972
Horses and Racing, 33
Animal Protection Organizations, 36
Ellen Terry, 48
Irish Language, 55
Irish Nationalism, 56
Spanish Armada, 63
Elizabeth Film, 65

Applied Arts
Foxfire, 8
Retelling Robin Hood Story, 8
Poetry Bulletin Board, 16
Horses and Racing, 33
Money Management, 35
Financial Budgets, 36
Finding Slope of Stage, 49
Play Performance, 51
Properties of a Stage, 52

TEACHING THE MULTIPLE INTELLIGENCES

Musical
Retelling Robin Hood Story, 8
Meter in Poetry, 17
Folk Songs, 58

Logical-Mathematical
Domestic Cats, 24
Financial Budgets, 36
Financial Advisors, 37
Savings and Interest, 40

Spatial
Various Versions of Robin Hood, 7

TEACHING THE MULTIPLE INTELLIGENCES (CONT.)

Retelling Robin Hood Story, 8
Poetry Bulletin Board, 16
Animals as Pets, 22
Samuel Palmer's Painting, 28
Ellen Terry, 48
Properties of a Stage, 52
Irish Landscapes, 53
Spanish Armada, 63

Kinesthetic
Retelling Robin Hood Story, 8
Poetry Bulletin Board, 16
Play Performance, 51
Blocking Diagrams for Plays, 52

Intra/Interpersonal
Various Versions of Robin Hood, 7
Foxfire, 8
Effects of Gambling, 32
Money Management, 35
Animal Protection Organizations, 36
Interpersonal Relationships, 38

Naturalist
Domestic Cats, 24

ADDITIONAL RESOURCES

UNIT 1 RESOURCE BOOK
- Selection Check Test 4.1.1
- Selection Test 4.1.2

ADDITIONAL QUESTIONS AND ACTIVITIES

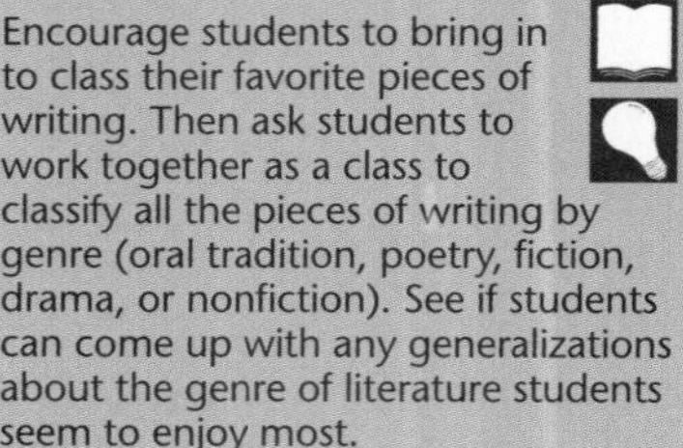

Encourage students to bring in to class their favorite pieces of writing. Then ask students to work together as a class to classify all the pieces of writing by genre (oral tradition, poetry, fiction, drama, or nonfiction). See if students can come up with any generalizations about the genre of literature students seem to enjoy most.

UNIT SKILLS OUTLINE (CONT. FROM PAGE 2)

The Oral Tradition

People love to hear and tell stories. Stories help us to explore who we are, who other people are, what our past experiences mean, and what the future might hold. In our stories we not only pose our questions but express our hopes and sorrows, our disappointments and expectations. Storytelling is one of the most ancient of human impulses, and it is out of this impulse that literature was born.

Storytelling existed long before people started writing things down. When writing was first invented over five thousand years ago by people living in what is now Iraq and Iran, storytelling was already very, very old. The earliest stories that have come down to us from the times before writing are **myths**—stories that explain where things come from, how the world took the form that it has today. Myths grew out of human curiosity—the desire to understand how things came to be as they are. "The Story of Pygmalion," in Unit 12 of this text, is an example of a myth.

In addition to myths, early people told stories about remarkable people in their clans or tribes. These stories, known as **legends**, dealt with heroes and leaders, people who had had exceptional experiences. The *Beowulf* story, on page 00 of this text, is such a legend, elaborated and made more fanciful over time. Other types of stories that survive from ancient days include **fables**, stories with animal characters that tell morals; **parables**, brief stories with human characters that tell morals; **tall tales**, stories with many fanciful, exaggerated elements; and **ballads**, songs that tell stories. English literature is particularly rich in such songs. Examples in this text include "Robin Hood and Allen a Dale," on the following pages, and "The Great Silkie of Shule Skerrie," in Unit 3.

As a child, you may have played the game called "gossip" or "telephone." If you haven't played the game, here's how it works: One person whispers something to another person and asks him or her to "pass it along." The second person whispers to the third, and so on, until the statement has been passed through many people. Inevitably, because people are fallible and don't always listen carefully or remember precisely, the statement gets changed from one person to the next. That's what happened to the first stories that people told. One person told a story. Someone else repeated it, often adding some exciting or interesting material because no one wants to tell a boring story. In this way the story was passed from generation to generation, becoming ever more fanciful and interesting. That's why so many early myths and legends are full of bizarre or unusual events that wouldn't occur in real life.

After writing was invented, people started setting down the stories that they knew or had heard from traditional storytellers. Consequently, many, many stories have come down to us from the time before writing. These early stories, passed by word of mouth from person to person, often over hundreds or even thousands of years, are known collectively as the **oral tradition.**

ArtNote

Title page of Contes de ma mère l'oye. Charles Perrault, 1695. **Charles Perrault** (1628–1703) is credited with authoring and illustrating *Contes de ma mère l'oye* (*Tales of Mother Goose*—1695) for his children's entertainment. However, there is some evidence that his son Pierre is the true author. One or both of these Perraults reworked French folk tales such as "Puss in Boots," "Little Red Riding Hood," and "The Sleeping Beauty" into the classics we know today.

UNIT SKILLS OUTLINE (CONT.)

Title page of ***Contes de ma mère l'oye.*** 1695. Charles Perrault. The Pierpont Morgan Library, New York.

SELECTION CHECK TEST 4.4.1 WITH ANSWERS

Checking Your Reading

Match each literary term with the most specific description. You may not use every letter, and you may use some letters more than once.

1. invented about 5,000 years ago by people living in what is now Iraq and Iran **F**
2. grew out of people's desire to understand how things came to be as they are **A**
3. the earliest stories **A**
4. brief stories with human characters that illustrate morals **D**
5. brief stories with animal characters that illustrate morals **G**

a. myth
b. tall tale
c. legend
d. parable
e. ballad
f. writing
g. fable

True or False

1. Stories are often distorted as they are passed along orally. **True**
2. Legends are generally based on real people. **True**
3. Tall tales are often set to music. **False**
4. Storytelling existed long before writing was invented. **True**
5. "Robin Hood and Allen a Dale" is an example of a myth. **False**

ADDITIONAL RESOURCES

UNIT 1 RESOURCE BOOK

- Selection Worksheet 1.1
- Selection Check Test 4.1.3
- Selection Test 4.1.4
- Language, Grammar, and Style Resource 3.1–3.5
- Speaking and Listening Resource 4.2–4.9

ANSWERS TO LITERARY TOOLS

Sequence:
Robin Hood sees a happy young man
Robin sees the young man, now sad
Little John brings man—Allen—to Robin
Robin asks Allen for money
Allen tells Robin of his bride taken by a knight
Allen offers to be Robin's servant for his help
Robin goes to church with men
Robin puts bishop's coat on Little John
Little John marries Allen and his bride

READER'S JOURNAL

As an alternate activity, encourage students to write about other stories they have heard about someone who tries to separate two people who love each other.

VOCABULARY FROM THE SELECTION

guile

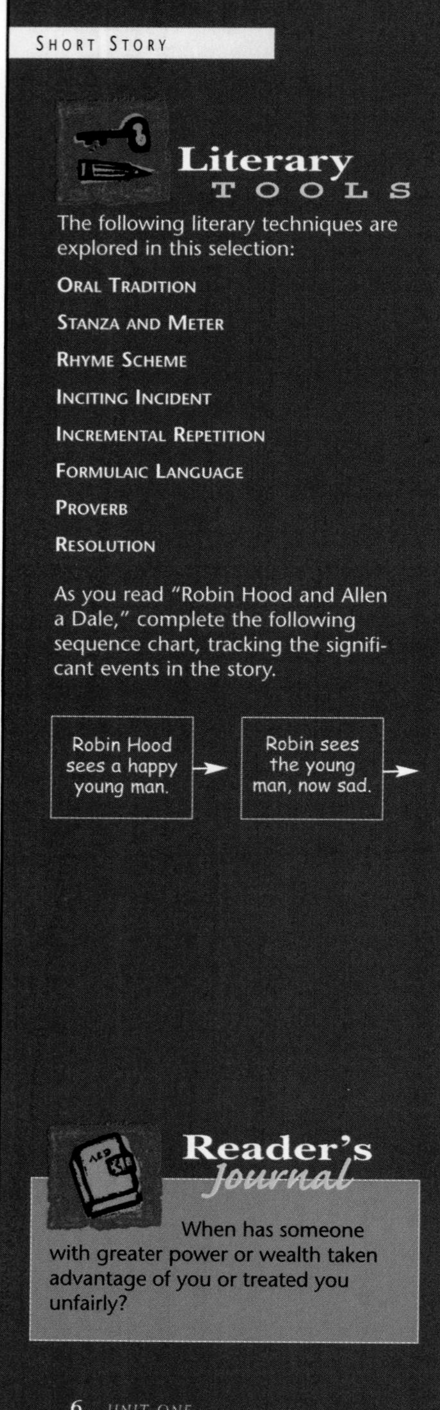

SHORT STORY

Literary TOOLS

The following literary techniques are explored in this selection:

ORAL TRADITION
STANZA AND METER
RHYME SCHEME
INCITING INCIDENT
INCREMENTAL REPETITION
FORMULAIC LANGUAGE
PROVERB
RESOLUTION

As you read "Robin Hood and Allen a Dale," complete the following sequence chart, tracking the significant events in the story.

Robin Hood sees a happy young man. → Robin sees the young man, now sad. →

Reader's Journal

When has someone with greater power or wealth taken advantage of you or treated you unfairly?

"Robin Hood and Allen a Dale"

ANONYMOUS

About the SELECTION

"Robin Hood and Allen a Dale" is a ballad which was passed from generation to generation, its author now unknown. No one knows for certain when the legend of Robin Hood first developed, although the legendary outlaw hero is mentioned in the poem *Piers Plowman* as early as 1377. It is quite likely that the legend is much older. In fact, it may have developed out of ancient Druidic or Teutonic rituals related to fertility gods, for Robin Hood in the ballads is invariably dressed in green and associated with the "greenwood," or forest. Through many centuries, down to our own, Robin Hood and various figures associated with him were central characters in May festivals celebrating the coming of spring, and, again, this practice may be a survival from ancient religious rituals that are now lost.

By historical times, Robin Hood had become transmuted in the oral tradition into the outlaw hero familiar to most children in English-speaking countries. In the early thirteenth century, the heir apparent to the English throne, Richard the Lion-Hearted, went on a Crusade to the Holy Land. On his return from the Crusade, he was captured and held captive by the Holy Roman Emperor. During the period of Richard's absence, his brother John ruled England. John was a terrible king who taxed his subjects heavily. Many of the Robin Hood stories and ballads are associated with this time. They tell of an outlaw, loyal to King Richard, who robs the wealthy to give to the poor. The historical record shows many outlaws in England throughout the Middle Ages who identified themselves with the Robin Hood of legend, but it is unknown whether there was, indeed, any single historical original on whom the legend is based.

GOALS/OBJECTIVES

Studying this lesson will enable students to

- enjoy an amusing verse narrative from the oral tradition
- briefly explain the significance of the Robin Hood legend
- define *stanza, meter, rhyme scheme, inciting incident, incremental repetition, formulaic language, proverb,* and *resolution* and point to the use of these techniques in "Robin Hood and Allen a Dale"
- identify and use modern English
- compare and contrast oral traditions

Robin Hood and ALLEN A DALE

ANONYMOUS

Come listen to me, you gallants so free,
All you that love mirth for to hear,
And I will you tell of a bold outlaw,
That lived in Nottinghamshire.

As Robin Hood in the forest stood,
All under the greenwood tree,
There was he aware of a brave young man,
As fine as fine might be.

The youngster was clothed in scarlet red,
In scarlet fine and gay,
And he did frisk it over the plain,
and chanted a roundelay.[1]

As Robin Hood next morning stood,
Among the leaves so gay,
There did he spy the same young man
Come drooping along the way.

The scarlet he wore the day before,
It was clean cast away;
And every step he fetched a sigh,
"Alack and a well a day!"

Then stepped forth brave Little John,
And Nick the miller's son,

What sort of person is Robin Hood?

ORAL TRADITION

Oral tradition is the passing of a work from one person to another by word of mouth rather than through writing.

STANZA AND METER

A ballad is divided into a four-line stanza known as a quatrain. In a ballad, the first and third lines are tetrameter (that is, they each have four feet). The second and fourth lines are trimeter (that is, they each have three feet).

1. **roundelay.** A joyful song

ANSWER TO GUIDED READING QUESTION

1. Robin Hood is an outlaw.

INDIVIDUAL LEARNING STRATEGIES

MOTIVATION
Show students the 1922 silent film *Robin Hood,* starring Douglas Fairbanks; *The Adventures of Robin Hood* (1938), starring Errol Flynn; the Disney version of *Robin Hood* (1973); *Robin Hood: Prince of Thieves* (1991), starring Kevin Costner; Mel Brooks's film *Robin Hood: Men in Tights,* which satirizes the film adaptation in which Costner starred. Encourage students to discuss the similarities and differences they see in the Robin Hood legend portrayed in these films (students will note the biggest differences in Brooks' satirical look at Robin Hood). Who do they believe plays the best Robin Hood?

READING PROFICIENCY
Encourage students to become part of the oral tradition by listening to the recording in the Audio Library before they read the ballad on their own. Students should listen to the ballad and imagine its action rather than following along in their books as they listen. Students should then go back and read the ballad on their own. Ask them to discuss whether they enjoyed listening to the ballad more or reading it independently. How were the experiences different?

ENGLISH LANGUAGE LEARNING
Explain the differences in word order between modern English and the English of the medieval ballad. In the ballad, sometimes a preposition is placed after its object, as in line 29, "And when he came bold Robin before." Sometimes the compliment is placed before the verb, as in line 3, "I will you tell." In addition, the verb sometimes comes before the subject, as in line 43, "'By the faith of my body,' then said the young man."

SPECIAL NEEDS
Students may find some of the medieval language and word order challenging. Share the information in the English Language Learning (above) with them, and tell them to pay close attention to footnotes as they read. Have them concentrate on responding to the Guided Reading questions and filling out the

(Continued on page 8)

ANSWER TO GUIDED READING QUESTION

1. Allen cannot marry because a wealthy, old knight has stolen his bride.

ADDITIONAL QUESTIONS AND ACTIVITIES

- Students may be interested in seeing or hearing about *Foxfire*, a magazine that depicts and describes an oral culture, including its legends, myths, parables, remedies, skills, and crafts. It is produced by a group of students in Georgia.
- Museums and libraries often have storytelling sessions. Ask students to research to find such offerings in your area. Have interested students attend these sessions and report to the class on the kinds of stories that were told and on the storytellers' techniques.
- Students interested in performing community service might volunteer to read or tell stories for children at nearby hospitals or libraries. Students should discuss with hospital officials or library program directors what stories would be appropriate, and why. Have students practice their storytelling in class before their public performance.

INDIVIDUAL LEARNING STRATEGIES (CONT.)

sequence chart (page 6) so that they grasp the basic action of this ballad.

ENRICHMENT
Robin Hood's legend has survived for centuries because it is always being retold. Encourage students to retell the Robin Hood story in their own way in a medium of their choosing. Students might work together to create their own video retelling of the story using a camcorder; they might work together or individually to write their own songs, short stories, or poems about Robin Hood; or they might represent the story visually in a mural, painting, or pantomime.

Sketch of Robin Hood.
Richard Dadd, 1852.
Yale Center for British Art.

Which made the young man bend his bow,
When as he saw them come.

"Stand off, stand off," the young man said,
"What is your will with me?"
"You must come before our master straight,
Under yon greenwood tree."

And when he came bold Robin before,
Robin asked him courteously,
"O hast thou any money to spare
For my merry men and me?"

"I have no money," the young man said,
"But five shillings and a ring;
And that I have kept this seven long years,
To have it at my wedding.

"Yesterday I should have married a maid,
But she is now from me tane,[2]
And chosen to be an old knight's delight,
Whereby my poor heart is slain."

RHYME SCHEME

A rhyme scheme is a pattern of rhymes in a poem. In traditional ballads, the rhyme scheme is abcb. *In other words, the second and the fourth lines rhyme.*

INCITING INCIDENT

Like most narratives, a ballad relates a plot, a series of causally connected events. In a plot, the event that sets in motion the central conflict, or struggle, is called the inciting incident.

Why will Allen not marry?

2. **tane.** Taken

"What is thy name?" then said Robin Hood,
"Come tell me, without any fail."
"By the faith of my body," then said the young man,
"My name it is Allen a Dale."

"What wilt thou give me," said Robin Hood,
"In ready gold or fee,
To help thee to thy true love again,
And deliver her unto thee?"

"I have no money," then quoth the young man,
"No ready gold nor fee,
But I will swear upon a book
Thy true servant for to be."

"How many miles is it to thy true love?
Come tell me without any guile."
"By the faith of my body," then said the young man,
"It is but five little mile."

Then Robin he hastened over the plain,
He did neither stint nor lin,[3]
Until he came unto the church
Where Allen should keep his wedding.

"What dost thou do here?" the bishop he said,
"I prithee now tell to me."
"I am a bold harper," quoth Robin Hood,
"And the best in the north country."

"O welcome, O welcome," the bishop he said,
"That music best pleaseth me";
"You shall have no music," quoth Robin Hood,
"Till the bride and the bridegroom I see."

With that came in a wealthy knight,
Which was both grave and old,
And after him a finikin[4] lass,
Did shine like glistering[5] gold.

What does Allen promise in return for Robin's help?

How does Robin talk his way into the church?

INCREMENTAL REPETITION

Ballads often make use of incremental repetition, the reuse of a line with some slight variation that advances the action.

FORMULAIC LANGUAGE

Works in the oral tradition often make use of formulaic language, words or phrases that are used again and again in various works. The formulas bold harper *and* bold outlaw *were often used to refer to Robin Hood.*

3. **stint nor lin.** Stop nor cease
4. **finikin.** Well-dressed, fine
5. **glistering.** Shining or sparkling

WORDS FOR EVERYDAY USE

guile (gīl) *n.*, slyness. *"This tricky new play will prove that guile is greater than brawn," said the quarterback.*

ANSWERS TO GUIDED READING QUESTIONS

1. Allen promises to be Robin's loyal servant in return for Robin's help in getting his bride back.
2. Robin tells the bishop he is a harper and the bishop thinks he is there to play for the wedding.

LITERARY NOTE

A few themes predominate in English ballads: stories of historical events ("Sir Patrick Spens," "The Bonny Earl of Murray," the Robin Hood ballads); stories of tragic love ("Bonny Barbara Allan"); and stories of the supernatural ("Tam Lin," "The Wife of Usher's Well").

LITERARY TECHNIQUE

BALLAD STANZA. Most ballads are written in **ballad stanza.** This is a quatrain, or four-line stanza, with alternating tetrameter (four-foot) and trimeter (three-foot) lines rhyming *abcb*. However, some ballads vary from this meter, as can be seen in these lines from "The Three Ravens":

There were three ravens sat on a tree.
Down a down, hay down, hay down.
There were three ravens sat on a tree.
Down a down, hay down, hay down.
There were three ravens sat on a tree.
They were as black as they might be.
With a down, derry, derry, derry, down down.

ANSWERS TO GUIDED READING QUESTIONS

1. Twenty-four of Robin's band of men have come with him.
2. Little John performed the marriage ceremony.

SELECTION CHECK TEST 4.1.3 WITH ANSWERS

Checking Your Reading

1. How is the young man acting the first time Robin sees him? **He is acting joyful.**
2. Why is the young man sad the next day? **His fiancée was taken to marry a knight.**
3. What does the young man promise if Robin helps him? **He promises to be faithful.**
4. Who comes to the church when Robin blows his horn? **His bowmen do.**
5. Who performs the ceremony? **Little John performs the ceremony.**

Literary Tools

Fill in the blanks using the letter for each of the following terms. You may use some choices more than once.

1. "Robin Hood and Allen a Dale" is an example of this type of literary work **G**
2. the conclusion of a central conflict in a literary work **A**
3. the passing of a work from one person to the next by word of mouth **D**
4. in this type of literary work, the pattern of rhymes is usually *abcb* **G**
5. the overall rhythmical pattern of a poem **C**

a. resolution
b. stanza
c. meter
d. oral transmission
e. inciting incident
f. repetition
g. ballad

"This is no fit match," quoth bold Robin Hood,
"That you do seem to make here;
For since we are come unto the church,
The bride she shall choose her own dear."

Then Robin Hood put his horn to his mouth,
And blew blasts two or three;
When four and twenty bowmen bold
Come leaping over the lee.[6]

Who had come with Robin?

And when they came into the churchyard,
Marching all in a row,
The first man was Allen a Dale,
To give bold Robin his bow.

"This is thy true love," Robin he said,
"Young Allen, as I hear say;
And you shall be married at this same time,
Before we depart away."

"That shall not be," the bishop he said,
"For thy word shall not stand;
They shall be three times asked in the church,[7]
As the law is of our land."

Robin Hood pulled off the bishop's coat,
And put it upon Little John;
"By the faith of my body," then Robin said,
"This cloth doth make thee a man."

PROVERB ➤ ➤ ➤
A proverb is a traditional saying. This is an ironic use, within the ballad, of a proverb.

When Little John went into the choir,
The people began for to laugh;
He asked them seven times in the church,
Lest three times should not be enough.

Who performed the marriage ceremony?

"Who gives me this maid," then said Little John;
Quoth Robin, "That do I,
And he that doth take her from Allen a Dale
Full dearly[8] he shall her buy."

RESOLUTION ➤ ➤ ➤
In a plot, the resolution is the event that ends the central conflict.

And thus having ended this merry wedding,
The bride looked as fresh as a queen,
And so they returned to the merry greenwood,
Among the leaves so green. ■

6. **lee.** Sheltered, hidden place
7. **three . . . church.** Intended marriages had to be announced three Sundays in a row.
8. **dearly.** At great cost

Respond to the SELECTION

Do you find the Robin Hood character in this ballad attractive? Why, or why not?

INVESTIGATE, Inquire, Imagine

Recall: GATHERING FACTS → **Interpret:** FINDING MEANING

1a. What associates of Robin's are mentioned by name in the ballad? How many of Robin's associates show up at the church near the end of the ballad?

1b. How do Robin and his associates earn their living?

2a. Who is the "youngster" dressed in scarlet mentioned in the third stanza?

2b. How does the mood of the youngster dressed in scarlet change from the first day to the next? What causes this change in mood?

3a. What deal does Allen a Dale strike with Robin Hood? How does Robin fulfill his part of the bargain? What warning does Robin make to the assembled crowd at the end of the ballad?

3b. What indication does the ballad give that Robin administers justice even though he lives outside the law?

Analyze: TAKING THINGS APART → **Synthesize:** BRINGING THINGS TOGETHER

4a. Whom was Allen a Dale's beloved being forced to marry? Compare this character to the character of Allen, based on the descriptions of each given in the ballad.

4b. What attitude toward the upper class is exhibited in this ballad? Why might those who popularized this ballad, the common people of the Middle Ages, have such an attitude?

Evaluate: MAKING JUDGMENTS → **Extend:** CONNECTING IDEAS

5a. Was Robin Hood justified in stealing the bride away from the knight and setting Little John up as bishop to perform the wedding? Why or why not?

5b. What can we learn about the customs and values of medieval England by reading this ballad? What modern outlaw heroes can you recall from popular film, television, and print? What conclusions can you draw from these individuals about our modern values? Have our values changed?

Understanding Literature

ORAL TRADITION. Review the definition of **oral tradition** in the Handbook of Literary Terms. Songs, stories and poems survive in the oral tradition because people find them valuable enough to be retold again and again. What phrase in the ballad indicates an assumption that the ballad will be performed orally, rather than read from print?

RESPOND TO THE SELECTION

Encourage students to explore which of Robin Hood's qualities make him attractive or unappealing.

ANSWERS FOR INVESTIGATE, INQUIRE AND IMAGINE

RECALL

1a. The ballad mentions Little John, Nick the miller's son, and Allen a Dale. Twenty-four of Robin's followers show up at the church.

2a. The "youngster" is Allen a Dale.

3a. Allen promises his loyalty in exchange for Robin's help. Robin prevents the wedding of Allen's fiancée and the knight by storming the church with twenty-four of his men. He designates one of them, Little John, to perform a marriage ceremony between Allen and his fiancée. He warns those in attendance that anyone who tries to steal Allen's wife will pay dearly.

INTERPRET

1b. They appear to earn their living through robbery.

2b. At first Allen seems happy and carefree, but on his return he is "drooping" and downtrodden. His mood has changed because his fiancée is forced to marry another.

3b. Robin helps Allen even though Allen cannot pay anything, apparently because Allen and his beloved have been treated unfairly by those with wealth and power. Robin also complains that a bishop would perform a wedding when the bride has not agreed to the marriage.

ANALYZE

4a. Allen a Dale's beloved is being forced to marry a knight who is described as "old" (line 32), "wealthy" (line 69), "grave and old" (line 70). Allen, on the other hand, is described as "a brave young man / As fine as fine can be" (lines 7–8) and as having no money (line 33). The knight seems able to buy or coerce people, including the bishop, to get what he wants. Allen, however, is brave, honest and loyal, promising to be Robin's servant in exchange for his help.

SYNTHESIZE

4b. The ballad exhibits an attitude of distrust towards the aristocracy and a belief that the upper class could be viciously selfish. Poor people of the time may have had such an attitude toward the aristocracy because their poor living conditions,

ANSWERS FOR INVESTIGATE, INQUIRE AND IMAGINE (CONT.)

high taxes, and indentured servitude were in stark contrast to the wealth of the nobles, who often exploited the poor.

EVALUATE

5a. *Responses will vary.*

EXTEND

5b. Taking Robin Hood as an exemplary character, one can surmise that the medieval English valued compassion, loyalty, justice, strength, and a sense of humor. Students may name Rambo, the Lone Ranger, and others as modern outlaws. Common values to all of these stories are justice, compassion, bravery, loyalty, and a sense of humor.

Answers to Understanding Literature can be found on page 12.

ANSWERS FOR UNDERSTANDING LITERATURE

Oral Tradition. The opening phrase, "Come listen to me, you gallants so free /…And I will you tell of a bold outlaw / That lived in Nottinghamshire" (lines 1–4), indicates that the ballad is being heard rather than read.

Stanza and Meter.
As Robin Hood next morning stood,
Among the leaves so gay,
There did he spy the same young man
Come drooping along the way.

Rhyme Scheme. The rhyme scheme is *aabccb.*

Inciting Incident. The inciting incident takes place when Allen tells Robin that a knight has stolen his bride.

Incremental repetition. The phrases repeated between Robin and Allen are "I have no money," (lines 33 and 49) and "no ready gold nor fee" (lines 46 and 50).

Proverb. The proverb used in line 96 is "clothes do not make the man." It is used ironically here to mean the opposite—that by putting the bishop's robe on Little John, Robin has "made" him into a bishop.

Resolution. The resolution is the marriage of Allen and his bride.

ANSWERS TO INTEGRATING THE LANGUAGE ARTS

Language, Grammar, and Style
Responses will vary.
Come listen to me everyone,
All of you who love to hear a good story!
And I will tell you about a bold outlaw
Who lived in Nottinghamshire.

As Robin Hood stood in the forest
Under a greenwood tree,
He noticed a brave young man
Who was as happy and fit as he could be.

(Continued on page 13)

Stanza and Meter. Review the definition of **meter** in the Handbook of Literary Terms. Copy the fourth stanza of this ballad on a sheet of paper and then read it aloud to yourself several times. How many feet are there in each of the four lines? On your paper, mark the stresses you hear as you read.

⌣ / ⌣ / ⌣ / ⌣ /
As Rob|in Hood|next morn|ing stood

Note that some of the lines in the ballad are irregular.

Rhyme Scheme. Review the definition of **rhyme scheme** in the Handbook of Literary Terms. What is the rhyme scheme of the following:

Little Miss Muffett
Sat on a tuffet,
Eating her curds and whey;
When along came a spider,
Who sat down beside her
And frightened Miss Muffett away.

Inciting Incident. The **inciting incident** is the event that sets in motion the central conflict in a plot. What is the inciting incident in "Robin Hood and Allen a Dale?"

Incremental repetition. **Incremental repetition** is often used in oral transmission to advance the action and to make the ballad or story more easily memorable. What phrases are repeated between Robin and Allen in this ballad?

Proverb. A **proverb** is a traditional saying. What traditional saying is used ironically in line 96? In what way is this ironic?

Resolution. In a plot, the **resolution** is the event that ends the central conflict. What is the resolution of "Robin Hood and Allen a Dale?"

Writer's Journal

1. Imagine that you are the Sheriff of Nottinghamshire and have been ordered by the knight to arrest Robin Hood and Little John for the crime of stealing his bride and impersonating a bishop. Write a **wanted poster** for the two outlaws.
2. A *motto* is a brief sentence or phrase that expresses the principles or ideals of a person or group. Imagine that you are Robin Hood and write a **motto** which, in a few catchy words, expresses the ideals of your band of "Merry Men."
3. Write a **ballad** of your own, describing some current event or school happening. You should use the traditional abcb rhyme scheme and make your ballad at least five stanzas.

Integrating the Language Arts

Language, Grammar, and Style

Modern English. Review the Language Handbook in the Language Arts Survey 3.1–3.5. Modern English is quite different from the English spoken by the common folk of medieval England and even more different from that of the medieval ballad in this selection. Take the following stanzas from the ballad and rewrite them in modern English. You will find that keeping the rhyme scheme and meter is nearly impossible, but do attempt to maintain the meaning of the original.

Come listen to me, you gallants so free,
   All you that love mirth for to hear,
And I will you tell of a bold outlaw,
   That lived in Nottinghamshire.

As Robin Hood in the forest stood,
   All under the greenwood tree,
There was he aware of a brave young man,
   As fine as fine might be.

Media Literacy

Setting Ballads to Music. Much of the music used in familiar children's songs fits the meter of this ballad, as does much popular Celtic music. Using your own collection or that available at your public library, find music you feel is appropriate and set this ballad to music. Using the music you have chosen, you may wish to perform the ballad for your class. If you play a musical instrument, you may wish to have another student join you for a performance of words and music.

Speaking and Listening & Collaborative Learning

Playing "Gossip." Review the Language Arts Survey 4.2–4.9, "Listening Skills" and "Communicating with Others." The following activity will require the involvement of the entire class. Play a version of the old children's game "telephone," or "gossip." Instead of passing a story from one person to another individually, divide the class into groups of three. Each group should choose one member as bard to relate the story to the next group. You or one member of the class begins the activity by reading a brief story to one group. (The story should be written down so it can be compared word-for-word with the story produced at the end of the activity.) The story may or may not be in verse. No one is permitted to take notes during the activity. The bard then retells the story to the small group, with the others offering corrections or improvements. When everyone agrees on a version, the bard tells it to the next group. The process is repeated for each group. After agreeing on its version, the last group writes down the story, and the class as a whole can compare it with the original.

Study and Research

Comparing Oral Traditions. Working in small groups, use library resources to research and compare the American oral tradition to the British oral tradition. You may utilize books such as Stith Thompson's classic, *Motifs of the Folktale,* or Joseph Campbell's survey of world mythologies, *The Masks of God.* Try to find two or three themes, characters, or stories that recur in both countries' oral traditions and share your group's findings with the class.

ANSWERS TO INTEGRATING THE LANGUAGE ARTS
(CONT. FROM PAGE 12)

Media Literacy
Encourage students to explore different types of music, not just the type traditionally associated with ballads. For example, students might adapt "Robin Hood and Allen a Dale," as a hip-hop, reggae, country and western, heavy metal, or any other genre of music they find interesting.

Speaking and Listening & Collaborative Learning
Encourage students to keep the "story" they tell to a paragraph or less. A poem might be well suited for this activity because rhyme and rhythm may serve as mnemonic devices to students. Remind students that they should really choose a simple anecdote to tell rather than a complete story because even most short short stories will be too long for this activity to be successful.

Study and Research
Refer students to the Language Arts Survey 5.19 "How to Locate Library Materials" for information on how library materials are organized so that they can find appropriate sources. If school or local library resources are limited, you may wish to place select books on reserve.

ADDITIONAL RESOURCES

Unit 1 Resource Book
- Selection Check Test 4.1.5
- Selection Test 4.1.6

ADDITIONAL QUESTIONS AND ACTIVITIES

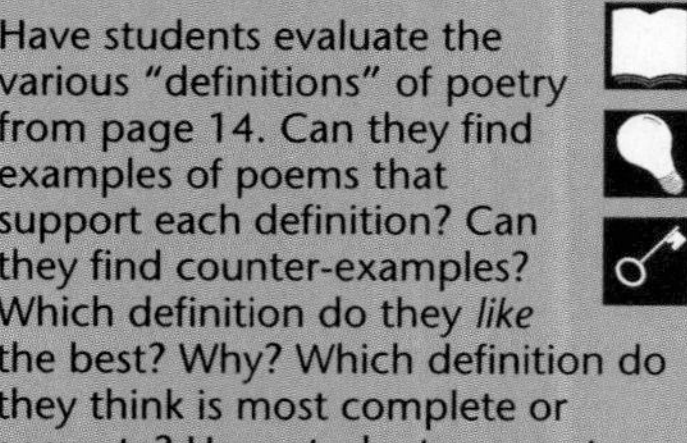

Have students evaluate the various "definitions" of poetry from page 14. Can they find examples of poems that support each definition? Can they find counter-examples? Which definition do they *like* the best? Why? Which definition do they think is most complete or accurate? Have students present their ideas to the class in an oral report.

Poetry

Today, the most common type of story, the kind that you find in a magazine or a newspaper, is told in **prose,** a type of writing similar to ordinary speech. However, the earliest stories that survive into our time are not told in prose. They are told in **poetry.** *Poetry* is notoriously difficult to define. Many individuals throughout history have tried to define it and failed. However, there is one element that most poems have in common: they use language in special ways. When early people told their stories, they wanted them to be memorable. In fact, if a story wasn't memorable, it wouldn't, by definition, be passed along; consequently, people used special techniques to make the language of their stories beautiful and interesting. These special techniques developed into the amazing collection of language tricks, or literary techniques, that writers use today to keep readers interested.

The earliest poems were **narratives.** That is, they told stories. Common types of oral narrative poems include **ballads**—short, simple stories told in song—and **epics**—long verse stories about heroes and gods complex enough to portray the ways of life, values, and beliefs of an entire culture. Soon, composers of verse discovered that poems could be used not only to tell stories, but also simply to express personal feelings. Thus **lyric poems** were born. A lyric poem is highly musical verse that expresses a speaker's feelings. Later poets invented a kind of hybrid form called the **dramatic poem** that presents the speech of one or more characters at a moment of crisis. Dramatic poems often tell or imply stories, as narrative poems do. They also express emotions, often using musical language, as lyric poems do.

Famous Definitions of Poetry

Poetry is . . .

"a representing, counterfeiting, or figuring forth: to speak metaphorically, a moving picture with this end: to teach and delight."

—Sir Philip Sidney

"emotion recollected in tranquility."

—William Wordsworth

"the record of the best and happiest moments of the happiest and best minds."

—Percy Bysshe Shelley

"at bottom a criticism of life."

—Matthew Arnold

"speech framed . . . to be heard for its own sake and interest even over and above its interest of meaning."

—Gerard Manley Hopkins

"the rhythmic, inevitably narrative, movement from an overclothed blindness to a naked vision."

—Dylan Thomas

"the clear expression of mixed feelings."

—W. H. Auden

When Apples were Golden and Songs were Sweet, c.1800s. John Melhuish Strudwick. Manchester City Art Gallery, UK.

LITERARY NOTE

Inform interested students that there are other types, or genres, of poetry that are subcategories of the three main types. Examples found in this textbook include the following:

Ballads
"Robin Hood and Allen a Dale," page 6

Sonnets
"Whoso List to Hunt," page 288
"When in disgrace with fortune," page 321

Elegiac Lyric
"The Wife's Lament," page 101
"To an Athlete Dying Young," page 847

Free Verse
"Snake," page 921

Dramatic Monologue
"Andrea del Sarto," page 803

ADDITIONAL QUESTIONS AND ACTIVITIES

Have students decorate a bulletin board or make a poster with examples of the three main types of poetry (narrative, lyric, and dramatic). Students should clearly label each poem to show its type. Students might choose examples from this textbook or from poetry collections in your school or community library.

Elements of Poetry

Types of Poetry

Narrative Poetry. A **narrative poem** is one that tells a story. Types of narrative poetry include **ballads** and **epics.**

Ballad. A **ballad** is a simple narrative poem, usually meant to be sung. The ballads of England and the United States usually are divided into four-line parts, or **stanzas,** that rhyme *abcb.* Examples of ballads include "Sir Patrick Spens" and "The Great Silkie of Shule Skerrie" on pages 136 and 139 of this text.

Epic. An **epic** is a long story, often told in verse, involving heroes and gods. Grand in length and scope, an epic provides a portrait of an entire culture, of the legends, beliefs, values, laws, arts, and ways of life of a people. Examples of epics include *Beowulf,* in Unit 2, and *Paradise Lost,* in Unit 6 of this text.

Lyric Poetry. A **lyric poem** is a highly musical verse that expresses the emotions of a speaker. There are many, many types of lyric poems. Among the most common are these:

Sonnet. A **sonnet** is a fourteen-line poem that follows one of a number of different rhyme schemes. Many sonnets deal with the subject of love. Examples include "Whoso List to Hunt" and Shakespeare's Sonnet 18, in Unit 4.

Ode. An **ode** is a lofty lyric poem on a serious theme. (Some odes follow a particular pattern of stanzas developed from Greek drama.) Examples of odes include "Ode to the West Wind," "Ode on a Grecian Urn," and "Ode: Intimations of Immortality," in Unit 8.

Free Verse Lyric. A **free verse lyric** follows no regular pattern of rhythm, rhyme, or meter. Examples include "Dover Beach," in Unit 9, and "Map of the New World," in Unit 10.

Elegiac Lyric. An **elegiac lyric** expresses a speaker's feelings of loss, often a loss through death of a loved one or friend. Examples of elegiac lyrics include "The Wife's Lament," in Unit 2, and *In Memoriam,* in Unit 9.

Dramatic Poetry. A **dramatic poem** is a verse that relies heavily on dramatic elements such as **monologue** (speech by a single character) or **dialogue** (conversation involving two or more characters). Often, dramatic poems are narratives as well. In other words, they often tell stories. Types of dramatic poems include the **dramatic monologue** and the **soliloquy.**

LITERARY TECHNIQUE

METER. The **meter** of a poem is its rhythmical pattern. Ask students to write down the lyrics to their favorite songs and describe the meter and stanza form. You may want to demonstrate how to find the meter using a popular song.

Dramatic Monologue. A **dramatic monologue** is a poem that presents the speech of a single character in a dramatic situation, often a moment of crisis or self-revelation. The speech is one side of an imagined conversation. "Ulysses" and "My Last Duchess," in Unit 9, are examples of dramatic monologues.

Soliloquy. A **soliloquy** is a speech from a play, often in verse, delivered by a lone character. The speech reveals the character's thoughts and feelings. A soliloquy from William Shakespeare's *Hamlet* can be found on page 477.

TECHNIQUES OF POETRY: METER AND STANZA FORM

Metrical vs. Free Verse. Metrical verse follows a set rhythmical pattern. **Free verse,** or ***vers libre,*** does not. Instead, it follows the rhythms of ordinary speech.

Meter. The **meter** of a poem is its rhythmical pattern. English verse usually is described as being made up of rhythmical units called **feet.** A **foot** is made up of some combination of **weakly stressed** (⌣) and **strongly stressed** (/) syllables, as follows:

TYPE OF FOOT	PATTERN	EXAMPLE
iamb, or **iambic foot**	⌣ /	⌣ / afraid
trochee, or **trochaic foot**	/ ⌣	/ ⌣ freedom
anapest, or **anapestic foot**	⌣ ⌣ /	⌣ ⌣ / in a flash
dactyl, or **dactylic foot**	/ ⌣ ⌣	/ ⌣ ⌣ feverish
spondee, or **spondaic foot**	/ /	/ / baseball

Some writers on meter also use the term **pyrrhee,** or **pyrrhic foot,** to describe a foot with two weak stresses, as follows:

anapest				**pyrrhee**	
⌣	⌣	/	|	⌣	⌣
un	be	liev	|	a	ble

LITERARY TECHNIQUE

FOOT. A **foot** is made up of some combination of weakly stressed and strongly stressed syllables.

- Ask students to analyze the meters of their own names. *Robert*, for example is a trochee; *Camille* is an iamb. You might also ask students to think of their own words or phrases to exemplify each type of metrical foot.
- Explain that the most common meters in English verse are iambic pentameter and iambic tetrameter. The former contains five iambs, and the latter contains four. Provide the following examples on a chalkboard or whiteboard:

  Is this the face that launched a thousand ships?
(iambic pentameter)

  That age is best which is the first
(iambic tetrameter)

The following terms are used to describe the number of feet in a line of poetry:

TERM	NUMBER OF FEET	EXAMPLE
monometer	one foot	And I Shall fly Away
dimeter	two feet	After | autumn Comes the | winter
trimeter	three feet	In the | midst of | mourning
tetrameter	four feet	O sad | dle up | my milk | white steed
pentameter	five feet	That time | of year | thou may'st | in me | behold
hexameter or Alexandrine	six feet	A per | fect knight | he was, | that all | could plain | ly see

A complete description of the meter of a line includes both the term for the type of foot that predominates in the line and the term for the number of feet in the line. The most common English meters are **iambic tetrameter** and **iambic pentameter.**

Stanza Form. A **stanza** is a group of lines in a poem. The following are some common types of stanza:

COUPLET *(two-line)*

For thy sweet love rememberèd such wealth brings
That then I scorn to change my state with kings.
—William Shakespeare, Sonnet 29

TRIPLET OR TERCET *(three-line)*

As thus with thee in prayer in my sore need.
Oh! lift me as a wave, a leaf, a cloud!
I fall upon the thorns of life! I bleed!
—Percy Bysshe Shelley, "Ode to the West Wind"

QUATRAIN
(four-line)

Thy voice is on the rolling air
    I hear thee where the waters run;
    Thou standest in the rising sun,
And in the setting thou art fair.

—Alfred, Lord Tennyson, *In Memoriam*

QUINTAIN
(five-line)

In summertime on Bredon
    The bells they sound so clear;
Round both the shires they ring them
    In steeples far and near,
A happy noise to hear.

—A. E. Housman, "Bredon Hill"

SESTET
(six-line)

O, young Lochnivar is come out of the west,
Through all the wide Border his steed was the best;
And save his good broadsword he weapons had none,
He rode all unarm'd, and he rode all alone.
So faithful in love, and so dauntless in war.
There never was knight like the young Lochnivar.

—Sir Walter Scott, "Lochnivar"

HEPTASTICH
(seven-line)

The flower that smiles today
    Tomorrow dies;
All that we wish to stay
    Tempts and then flies;
What is this world's delight?
Lightning, that mocks the night,
    Brief even as bright.

—Percy Bysshe Shelley, "Mutability"

OCTAVE
(eight-line)

Labor is blossoming or dancing where
The body is not bruised to pleasure soul,
Nor beauty born out of its own despair,
Nor blear-eyed wisdom out of midnight oil.
O chestnut tree, great-rooted blossomer,
Are you the leaf, the blossom, or the bole?
O body swayed to music, O brightening glance,
How can we know the dancer from the dance?

—William Butler Yeats, "Among School Children"

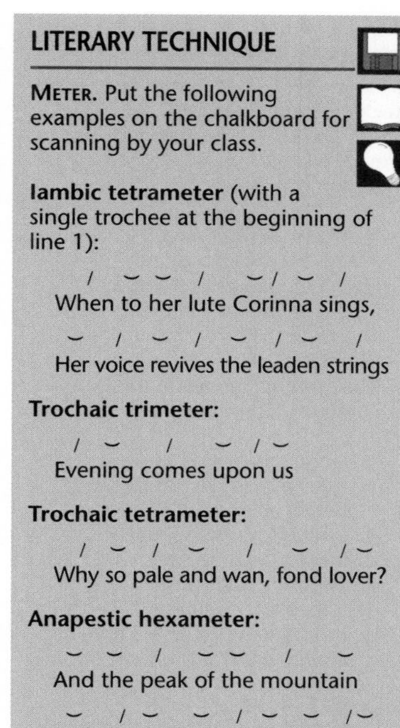

LITERARY TECHNIQUE

Meter. Put the following examples on the chalkboard for scanning by your class.

Iambic tetrameter (with a single trochee at the beginning of line 1):

When to her lute Corinna sings,
Her voice revives the leaden strings

Trochaic trimeter:

Evening comes upon us

Trochaic tetrameter:

Why so pale and wan, fond lover?

Anapestic hexameter:

And the peak of the mountain
was apples, the hugest that ever
were seen

Dactylic dimeter (with a final trochee):

Half a league, half a league
Half a league, onward

SELECTION CHECK TEST 4.1.5 WITH ANSWERS

Checking Your Reading
Choose the BEST conclusion for each sentence beginning. You may use each conclusion only once.

1. "Language tricks" that keep readers interested are also called… **D**
2. Epics help us understand… **B**
3. Lyric poems express… **F**
4. The earliest stories that survive today are… **E**
5. Most poems have one thing in common. They use… **A**

a. language in special ways.
b. the ways of life, values, and beliefs of an entire culture.
c. similar to ordinary speech.
d. literary techniques.
e. narrative poems.
f. a speaker's feelings.
g. the speech of one or more characters at a moment of crisis.

Elements of Poetry
True or False

1. A figure of speech is a word or phrase that has more than a literal meaning. **T**
2. The line "She sells seashells by the seashore" includes alliteration. **T**
3. A sonnet has no regular rhythm or rhyme scheme. **F**
4. Personification is the use of exaggeration to make an effect. **F**
5. Soliloquy is a conversation between two people that creates a conflict. **F**

Multiple Choice

1. The phrase "You may think at first I'm as mad as a hatter" illustrates
   a. antithesis
   b. personification
   c. simile
   d. metonymy

2. The line "maggie and millie and molly and may" illustrates
   a. personification
   b. alliteration
   c. elegiac lyric
   d. metonymy

3. A writer uses _____ to emphasize that two ideas are equally valuable.
   a. repetition
   b. synecdoche
   c. simile
   d. parallelism

Continued on page 21

Techniques of Poetry: Sound*

Rhythm. The **rhythm** is the pattern of beats or stresses in a poem. A regular rhythmic pattern is called a **meter.**

Rhyme. Rhyme is the repetition of sounds at the ends of words. The following are some types of rhyme:

> **End Rhyme. End rhyme** is the use of rhyming words at the ends of lines.
>
> **Internal Rhyme. Internal rhyme** is the use of rhyming words within lines.
>
> **Slant Rhyme. Slant rhyme** is the use of rhyming sounds that are similar but not identical, as in *rave* and *rove* or *rot* and *rock.*

Alliteration. Alliteration is the repetition of initial consonant sounds, as in *Peter Piper picked a peck of pickled peppers.*

Assonance. Assonance is the repetition of vowel sounds in stressed syllables with different consonant sounds, as in *praised* and *plains.*

Consonance. Consonance is the use in stressed syllables of identical final consonants preceded by different vowel sounds, as in *wind* and *wound.* This technique is also known as **half-rhyme** or **slant rhyme.**

Onomatopoeia. Onomatopoeia is the use of words or phrases that sound like the things to which they refer. Examples include the words *meow, clink, boom,* and *mumble.*

Techniques of Poetry: Meaning*

Image. An **image** is language that creates a concrete representation of an object or an experience. A group of images that together create a given emotion in a reader or listener is called an **objective correlative.**

Figure of Speech. A **figure of speech,** or **trope,** is an expression that has more than a literal meaning. The following are examples of common figures of speech:

> **Hyperbole.** A **hyperbole** is an exaggeration made for rhetorical effect.
>
> **Metaphor.** A **metaphor** is a figure of speech in which one thing is spoken or written about as if it were another. This figure of speech invites the reader to make a comparison between the two things: the writer's actual subject, the **tenor** of the metaphor, and another thing to which the subject is likened, the **vehicle** of the metaphor. In the metaphor "My love is a red, red rose," the tenor is the love. The vehicle is the rose. **Personifications** and **similes** are types of metaphor.

*Note: These techniques are commonly but not exclusively used in poetry.

Metonymy. Metonymy is the naming of an object associated with a thing in place of the name of the thing itself. Speaking of *the crown* when one means *the king* or *the queen* is an example.

Personification. Personification is a figure of speech in which an idea, animal, or object is described as if it were a person. "The wind sang its sad, sad song" is an example.

Simile. A **simile** is a comparison using *like* or *as*. "My love is like a red, red rose" is a simile.

Synaesthesia. Synaesthesia is a figure of speech that combines in a single expression images related to two or more different senses, as in *the singing light.*

Synecdoche. A **synecdoche** is a figure of speech in which the name of part of something is used in place of the name of the whole or vice versa, as in *hired hands* for *laborers.*

Understatement. An **understatement** is an ironic expression in which something of importance is spoken of as though it were not important.

Rhetorical Techniques. A **rhetorical technique** is an extraordinary but literal use of language to achieve a particular effect. Common rhetorical techniques used in poetry include the following:

Antithesis. An **antithesis** is a rhetorical technique in which words, phrases, or ideas are strongly contrasted, often by repeating a grammatical structure. An example is Pope's "To err is human, to forgive divine."

Apostrophe. An **apostrophe** is a rhetorical technique in which an object or person is directly addressed, as in Shelley's "O wild West Wind, thou breath of Autumn's being."

Catalog. A **catalog** is a list of people or things, as in the list of pagan gods in lines 374–505 of Book 1 of Milton's *Paradise Lost.*

Chiasmus. A **chiasmus** is a rhetorical technique in which the order of occurrence of words or phrases is reversed, as in the line "We can weather changes, but we can't change the weather."

Parallelism. Parallelism is a rhetorical technique in which a writer emphasizes the equal value or weight of two or more ideas by expressing them in the same grammatical form, as in the phrase "with hope, with joy, and with love."

Repetition. Repetition is the writer's conscious reuse of a sound, word, phrase, sentence, or other element, as in the sentence "*Do* as I say, not as I *do.*"

Rhetorical Question. A **rhetorical question** is one asked for effect but not meant to be answered because the answer is clear from the context, as in Christina Rossetti's lines "Who has seen the wind? Neither you nor I."

SELECTION CHECK TEST 4.1.5 WITH ANSWERS (CONT. FROM PAGE 20)

4. What is illustrated in the following lines?
   "The name that no human research can discover
   But THE CAT HIMSELF KNOWS, and will never confess"
   a. personification
   b. apostrophe
   c. metaphor
   d. synecdoche

5. The line, "and he in his brilliant stupidity…" illustrates
   a. parallelism
   b. antithesis
   c. metaphor
   d. apostrophe

Techniques of Poetry

1. Mark the stressed and unstressed syllables in the following lines:

When you notice a cat in profound
  meditation,
The reason, I tell you, is always the same:
His mind is engaged in a rapt
  contemplation
At the thought, at the thought, at the
  thought of his name:

2. What is the rhyme scheme of these lines? **The rhyme scheme is abab.**

3. How many feet are in each line? **Each line has four feet.**

ADDITIONAL RESOURCES

UNIT 1 RESOURCE BOOK
- Selection Worksheet 1.2
- Selection Check Test 4.1.7
- Selection Test 4.1.8
- Language, Grammar, and Style Resource 3.35
- Speaking and Listening Resource 4.19

VOCABULARY FROM THE SELECTION

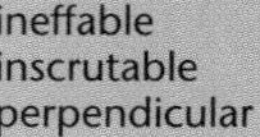

ineffable	profound
inscrutable	quorum
perpendicular	rapt

READER'S JOURNAL

Students might also list the characteristics they would use to describe another type of pet, such as a cat, rabbit, chinchilla, hamster, gerbil, parakeet, goldfish, or iguana.

INDIVIDUAL LEARNING STRATEGIES

MOTIVATION
Students may be interested in holding a class discussion about which creatures make good pets and which don't. You might create a large pro and con chart on the board and list the pros and cons of each type of pet that students suggest as they respond. Encourage your class to identify which pets, according to their own responses, seem to be the best.

READING PROFICIENCY
Read the poem aloud for students in a lively manner, emphasizing the use of literary techniques as appropriate. Then ask students to work in pairs and take turns reading the poem aloud to each other. Each pair can then work together to jot down written responses to the Guided Reading questions and the Investigate, Inquire, and Imagine section.

ENGLISH LANGUAGE LEARNING
Point out that even in verse, the primary unit of organization is the sentence. When students are

Continued on page 23

Literary TOOLS

RHYME SCHEME. *Rhyme* is the repetition of sounds at the ends of words. A **rhyme scheme** is a pattern of end rhymes or rhymes at the end of lines of verse.

ALLITERATION. **Alliteration** is the repetition of initial consonant sounds.

METER. The **meter** of a poem is its rhythmical pattern.

PERSONIFICATION. **Personification** is a figure of speech in which an idea, animal, or thing is described as if it were a person.

PARALLELISM. **Parallelism** is a rhetorical technique in which a writer emphasizes the equal value or weight of two or more ideas by expressing them in the same grammatical form.

ASSONANCE. **Assonance** is the repetition of vowel sounds in stressed syllables with different consonant sounds.

REPETITION. **Repetition** is the writer's conscious reuse of a sound, word, phrase, sentence, or other element.

Reader's Journal

What characteristics would you list to describe cats?

"The Naming of CATS"

BY T. S. ELIOT

About the AUTHOR

Thomas Stearns Eliot (1888–1965) was born and raised in St. Louis, Missouri, but lived much of his adult life in England and eventually became an English citizen. Educated at Harvard, the Sorbonne, and Oxford, Eliot steeped himself in philosophy and linguistics. He wrote his first major poems, including "The Love Song of J. Alfred Prufrock" (1910–11), while he was a student in Paris. Eliot's early poems established the major themes of his body of work: the problem of isolation from other people and from God in modern urban life and the search for purpose and meaning. Eliot returned to these themes again and again in poems such as *The Waste Land* (1922), a long narrative poem published as a book; "The Hollow Men" (1927); and "Ash Wednesday" (1930).

Eliot's influence on twentieth-century poetry was tremendous, particularly in the years between the world wars. His poems departed radically from nineteenth-century poetry, not only in theme but in form. Considered one of the inventors of modern poetry, Eliot wrote poetry which consisted of a series of images without a narrator's voice to connect or make sense of them. The reader is left to absorb the images and, through their cumulative effect, sense the idea the poet is trying to convey. Many of Eliot's major poems, including *The Waste Land* and *The Love Song of J. Alfred Prufrock,* develop through their images the theme of the decay of culture and society in the modern world through their images. In addition to being one of the century's leading poets, Eliot was a distinguished literary critic, editor, and dramatist. In 1948, he was awarded the Nobel Prize in literature.

About the SELECTION

"The Naming of Cats" is taken from Eliot's *Old Possum's Book of Practical Cats,* first published in 1939 (available in paperback from Harcourt, 1982). Some of the cats mentioned in the book include Mungojerrie; Rumpelteazer; Jennyanydots; Bustopher Jones, the cat about town; and Macavity, the mystery cat.

A musical play, *Cats,* based on the *Old Possum* poems set to music by Andrew Lloyd Webber (1948–), has had great success with audiences in the United States and in Great Britain. Recordings are available on CD and audiocassette.

GOALS/OBJECTIVES

Studying this lesson will enable students to
- have a nonthreatening, pleasant experience reading a humorous lyric poem
- identify T. S. Eliot as one of the early twentieth century's most well-known poets
- recall some famous definitions of poetry and describe some characteristics of poetry
- define *rhyme scheme, alliteration, meter, personification, parallelism, assonance,* and *repetition* and recognize the use of these techniques in a poem
- distinguish between techniques relating to meter, stanza form, sound, and meaning
- name and define the three main genres of poetry (narrative, lyric, and dramatic) and classify poems according to these genres
- edit sentences to reduce wordiness
- prepare and oral interpretation

The Naming of Cats

T. S. Eliot

The Naming of Cats is a difficult matter,
  It isn't just one of your holiday games;
You may think at first I'm as mad as a hatter[1]
When I tell you, a cat must have THREE DIFFERENT NAMES.
First of all, there's the name that the family use daily,
  Such as Peter, Augustus, Alonzo or James,
Such as Victor or Jonathan, George or Bill Bailey—
  All of them sensible everyday names.
There are fancier names if you think they sound sweeter,
  Some for the gentlemen, some for the dames:
Such as Plato, Admetus, Electra, Demeter[2]—
  But all of them sensible everyday names.
But I tell you, a cat needs a name that's particular,
  A name that's peculiar, and more dignified,
Else how can he keep up his tail perpendicular,
  Or spread out his whiskers, or cherish his pride?
Of names of this kind, I can give you a quorum,
  Such as Munkustrap, Quaxo, or Coricopat,
Such as Bombalurina, or else Jellylorum—
  Names that never belong to more than one cat.
But above and beyond there's still one name left over,
  And that is the name that you never guess;
The name that no human research can discover—
  But THE CAT HIMSELF KNOWS, and will never confess.

What helps a cat keep his tail up and his pride intact?

Rhyme Scheme
The poem follows the rhyme scheme abab.

Alliteration
The repeated b *sound is an example of alliteration.*

Meter
The poem is written in anapestic tetrameter with many variations.

Personification
Here human qualities are attributed to the cat.

Parallelism
These are parallel phrases, each made up of the word never *and a verb.*

1. **mad as a hatter.** This widely known **simile** may have originated from a disease common among hat makers caused by mercury used in the production of felt.
2. **Plato . . . Demeter.** Names of figures from Greek mythology and history.

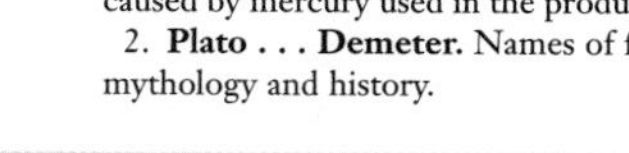

per • pen • dic • u • lar (pʉr´pən dik´yo͞o lər) *adj.,* exactly upright. *The townspeople of Pisa eventually got used to the idea that buildings need not be perpendicular.*

quo • rum (kwôr´əm) *n.,* a select group or company. *Dedication enabled her to join the quorum of those who have completed a marathon.*

ANSWERS TO GUIDED READING QUESTIONS

1. A name that is "peculiar and more dignified" than the name the family uses, one that no other cat has, helps a cat keep his tail up and his pride intact.

INDIVIDUAL LEARNING STRATEGIES (CONT. FROM PAGE 22)

reading poetry, they should pause according to the punctuation marks rather than at the end of every line.

Special Needs
This is a good poem to use to introduce special needs students to poetry as it will be easy for them to comprehend (with the exception of some vocabulary terms that are treated as Words for Everyday Use or footnotes) and they may find the subject matter engaging. Encourage them to become actively involved in the class discussion of the Investigate, Inquire, and Imagine questions. Make sure that special needs students review all the background information on poetic technique before they read the selection and respond to the Understanding Literature questions because special needs students may have some difficulty comprehending some of the more complex literary techniques used in poetry.

Enrichment
Encourage students to write personal essays about people, pets, objects, or activities that they have named. Ask them to briefly describe what or whom they have named, explain why they chose the name they did, and explore the significance of this name to them. Tell students that they can focus on one name they chose, or they can explore the patterns in the names they have chosen for different people, pets, objects, or activities.

ANSWERS TO GUIDED READING QUESTIONS

1. When cats seem lost in thought, they are pondering the name that only they know.

CROSS-CURRICULAR ACTIVITIES

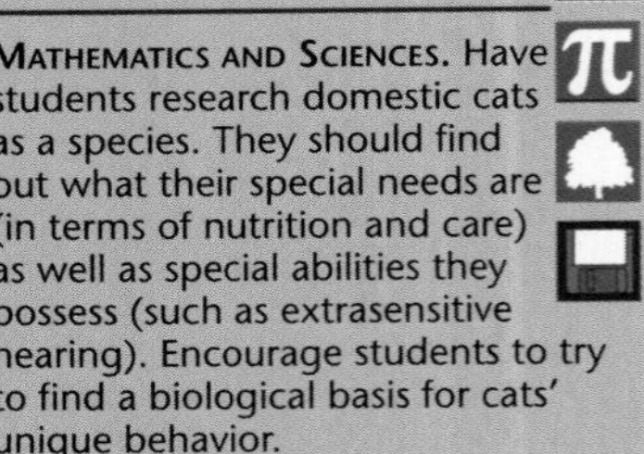

Mathematics and Sciences. Have students research domestic cats as a species. They should find out what their special needs are (in terms of nutrition and care) as well as special abilities they possess (such as extrasensitive hearing). Encourage students to try to find a biological basis for cats' unique behavior.

SELECTION CHECK TEST 4.1.7 WITH ANSWERS

Checking Your Reading

1. How many names does a cat have? **Each cat has three names.**
2. What kind of names are Peter, Augustus, George, and Bill Bailey? **These are sensible everyday names.**
3. How many cats share the names Coricopat, Bombalurina, or Jellylorum? **These names belong to only one cat.**
4. What can "no human research" discover? **No human can know a cat's third name.**
5. Of what are cats in meditation thinking? **They are thinking of their third names.**

Vocabulary in Context
Sentence Completion
Fill in each blank with the most appropriate word from the following Words for Everyday Use. You may have to change the tense of the word.

perpendicular quorum rapt
ineffable inscrutable

1. We needed a **quorum** of officers to vote, so we waited for Butch to arrive.
2. Burke felt **ineffable** grief when his dog died.
3. The jury filed back in, but their **inscrutable** expressions told me nothing.
4. We raised the mast until it was **perpendicular**, then tightened the screws to hold it.
5. We followed the countdown, then stared with **rapt** attention as the rocket lifted off.

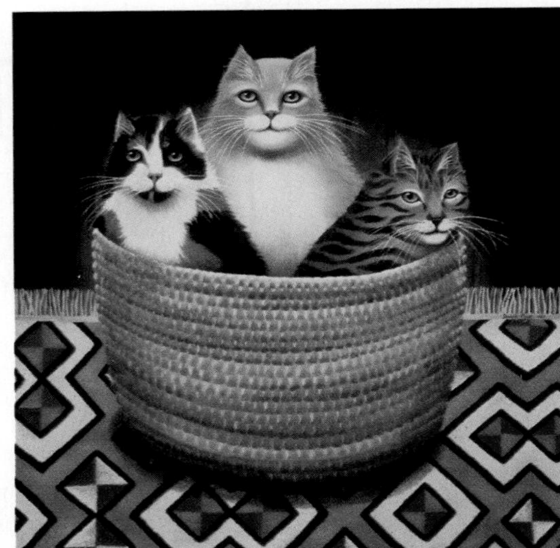

Tom, Dick and Harry, c.1980s.
Derold Page. Private Collection.

Assonance

The repeated long a sounds in line 27 are an example of assonance.

Repetition

The repetition of the phrase in line 28 mirrors the idea being described—thinking and thinking and thinking about something.

When you notice a cat in profound meditation,
The reason, I tell you, is always the same:
His mind is engaged in a rapt contemplation
Of the thought, of the thought, of the thought of his name:
His ineffable effable
Effanineffable[3]
Deep and inscrutable singular Name. ■

What is it that cats ponder when they seem lost in thought?

3. **Effanineffable.** A nonsense word.

Words for Everyday Use

pro • found (prō found′) *adj.,* very deep or intense. *A profound pleasure overcame Branford as he hit upon the solution to the physics problem he had been struggling with all week.*

rapt (rapt) *adj.,* deeply absorbed; engrossed. *Pouring over an art book, Julia was rapt in attention.*

in • ef • fa • ble (in ef′ə bəl) *adj.,* incapable of being expressed or described adequately; inexpressible. *Joan's ineffable excitement about getting front-row seats for the Lizard Babies concert was unacceptable to her mother, who demanded, "Well? Say something!"*

in • scru • ta • ble (in skro͞ot′ə bəl) *adj.,* completely obscure or mysterious. *Geoff concluded that if millions of Romans had mastered Latin, it need not remain inscrutable to him.*

Respond to the Selection

If you could choose an unusual, creative "secret name" for yourself, like one of Eliot's cats, what would it be? Why?

SELECTION CHECK TEST 4.1.7 WITH ANSWERS (CONT.)

Literary Tools
Sentence Completion
Fill in the blanks using the following terms. You may not use every term, and you may use some terms more than once. Choose the word that best completes each sentence.

rhyme scheme alliteration meter personification
parallelism assonance repetition

1. **Alliteration** is the repetition of vowel sounds in stressed syllables with different consonant sounds.
2. A writer might use **parallelism** to stress the equal value of two or more ideas.
3. The **rhyme scheme** of a poem is the pattern of rhymes at the ends of its lines.
4. The overall rhythmic pattern of a poem is its **meter**.
5. **Personification** allows a writer to speak of non-human things as if they were human.

INVESTIGATE, Inquire, Imagine

Recall: GATHERING FACTS → **Interpret:** FINDING MEANING

1a. How does the speaker characterize the naming of cats in line 1?

1b. What makes the naming of cats a difficult matter?

2a. According to the speaker, what three kinds of names should a cat have?

2b. What purpose is served by each of the first two kinds of names that a cat should have?

Analyze: TAKING THINGS APART → **Synthesize:** BRINGING THINGS TOGETHER

3a. Identify the characteristics of cats as described in "The Naming of Cats."

3b. What characteristics do actual cats have that might have led the speaker to suggest, humorously, each of the three kinds of names?

Evaluate: MAKING JUDGMENTS → **Extend:** CONNECTING IDEAS

4a. Evaluate T.S. Eliot's personal feelings toward cats.

4b. Cats tend to evoke strong feelings in most people, who either like them a great deal or dislike them strongly. Why do you think this is so? Is there something about cats themselves that gives rise to this?

Understanding Literature

RHYME SCHEME. Review the definition for **rhyme scheme** in the Handbook of Literary Terms. In this poem Eliot uses some amusing, unusual rhymes. Find examples in the poem. Are such rhymes better than rhymes of the *moon/June, sun/run* variety? Explain.

ALLITERATION AND ASSONANCE. Review the definitions for **alliteration** and **assonance** in the Handbook of Literary Terms. What is the effect of alliteration and assonance in this poem? Why do you think that Eliot uses these techniques in this poem?

METER. The **meter** of a poem is its rhythmical pattern. This poem is composed in **anapestic tetrameter,** with variations. An **anapest** is a foot made up of two weakly stressed syllables followed by one strongly stressed syllable. A **tetrameter** line is one with four strong stresses. Write the first four lines of the poem on a sheet of paper. Then scan the lines, marking the weakly stressed and strongly stressed syllables. Finally, divide the lines into feet. What variations from strict use of anapests can you find in the first four lines? Are all the lines of the poem tetrameter?

PERSONIFICATION. **Personification** is a figure of speech in which an idea, animal, or thing is described as if it were a person. What human qualities are attributed to cats in this poem? What actual qualities or actions of cats might lead people to attribute such qualities to them? What is the source of the humor of the poem?

PARALLELISM. Review the definition for **parallelism** in the Handbook of Literary Terms. What does the use of "never guess" and "never confess" in the poem imply about the relationship between cats and humans?

REPETITION. Review the definition for **repetition** in the Handbook of Literary Terms. What is the effect of the repetitions used in lines 28–30?

RESPOND TO THE SELECTION

If students have difficulty thinking of a "secret name" for themselves, have them begin by listing things about themselves that they alone know in their journals. Encourage students to share their "secret names" with you, but to share the reasons behind them only if they are comfortable doing so.

ANSWERS FOR INVESTIGATE, INQUIRE AND IMAGINE

RECALL

1a. Naming cats is described as difficult.

2a. A cat should have a sensible, common name; a peculiar name; and a secret name.

INTERPRET

1b. Naming cats is difficult because cats must have three very different types of names.

2b. The sensible name is for everyday and family use. The peculiar name is to support the cat's sense of dignity and individuality. The cat's secret name helps a cat retain his aura of mystery.

ANALYZE

3a. "The Naming of Cats" describes cats as proud, dignified, individualistic, thoughtful, and private.

SYNTHESIZE

3b. The fact that cats are part of human families and take part in everyday issues such as eating, sleeping, and being let in and out of the house makes them good candidates for having a common name to reflect this part of their lives. The peculiar name for cats reflects their unusual behavior, playfulness, and mercurial mood shifts. The third, secret name for cats reflects the fact that cats can act in a self-absorbed, mysterious manner.

EVALUATE

4a. *Responses will vary.* We may assume that he is at least intrigued by cats because he describes them as having more complex thoughts and desires than we may imagine. He probably also likes cats for that reason.

EXTEND

4b. *Responses will vary.* Cats tend to be unpredictable, sometimes affectionate and sometimes aloof, which leads many to think they are

ANSWERS FOR INVESTIGATE, INQUIRE AND IMAGINE (CONT.)

arrogant and not very loving. Dogs tend to be more reliable companions. Over many centuries, cats have been associated with evil and superstition as well, which may give rise to negative feelings. The fact that they can maneuver well in the dark is unsettling to some. Those who like cats appreciate their independence and playfulness as well as their affectionate side.

Answers to Understanding Literature can be found on page 26.

ANSWERS FOR UNDERSTANDING LITERATURE

Rhyme. Some examples of unusual rhymes are "sweeter/Demeter" and "particular/perpendicular." Rhymes often are more interesting when they are polysyllabic or near rhymes, as these pose greater challenges to the poet.

Alliteration and Assonance. *Responses will vary.* These techniques are two ways of creating a rhythm of sounds, in a sense. The poem is about unusual names and, hence, unusual sounds, so the use of alliteration and assonance adds to the texture of the poem.

Meter. The first four lines of the poem marked for stress and divided into feet appear as:

The Naming of Cats is a difficult matter,
It isn't just one of your holiday games;
You may think at first I'm as mad as a hatter
When I tell you, a cat must have
three different names.

The lines are all in tetrameter. They contain some iambic feet and some extra weakly stressed syllables.

Personification. Cats are called "gentlemen" and "dames" (line 10); they are spoken of as having dignity (lines 14–15) and pride (lines 15–16); as knowing their own names and having an identity (line 24); and as engaging in "profound meditation" (line 25) and "rapt contemplation" (line 27). Cats might appear dignified and prideful or intelligent and contemplative because they are ignorant of or disinterested in human affairs. Some might find the poem amusing because it implies that instead of being intelligent, cats are stupidly aware only of themselves.

Parallelism. The parallelism gives equal weight or importance to the fact that humans cannot guess the cat's secret name and that the cat will never tell. Of course, the cat cannot tell as it does not speak, but this bit of personification along with the parallelism implies that the relationship between cats and humans is a standoff between equals.

Repetition. The repetition of the phrase, "the thought," mirrors the idea being described—thinking and thinking and thinking about something. Lines 28–30, which also include the repetition of variations of "ineffable," creates the impression of rhythmically slipping into a trance, like the trance into which the cat has slipped, in contemplation of his secret name.

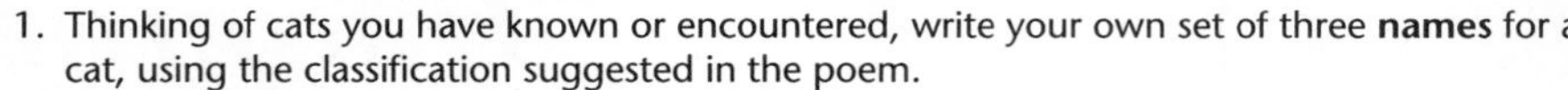

Writer's Journal

1. Thinking of cats you have known or encountered, write your own set of three **names** for a cat, using the classification suggested in the poem.
2. Imagine that you are a pet store owner who finds him or herself with an enormous over-supply of cats for sale. As a lover of cats, you agree with Eliot on the importance of names to cats and on the qualities of cats implied in the poem. Write an **advertisement** for a special sale, one to sell your excess cats to people who will truly appreciate their unique qualities and give them the treatment they deserve.
3. Eliot's poem might be seen as a tribute, of sorts, to cats and some of their idiosyncrasies. Imagine that you are a lover of some other sort of pet (dogs, snakes, mice, birds, etc.). Using an *abab* rhyme scheme and anapestic tetrameter meter, write your own **poem** about your favorite pet and some of its special qualities.

Integrating *the* Language Arts

Language, Grammar, and Style

Reducing Wordiness. After reading the Language Arts Survey 3.35 "Correcting Wordy Sentences," rewrite the sentences below, trying to use as few words as necessary to communicate each idea.

1. Tia went to the library with the intention of trying to find a book about T. S. Eliot, who was a man who wrote poetry in verse.
2. She was particularly interested in becoming familiar with his book that he named *Old Possum's Book of Practical Cats.*
3. Eliot's book of verse, which was intended for children, is the book on which the musical *Cats* was based.
4. This play, which is a musical, premiered in London in the year of 1981.
5. The musical then debuted in New York City in the following year, which was 1982, and the musical was an immediate smash hit with the public.

Speaking and Listening

Oral Interpretation. Review the Language Arts Survey 4.19, "Oral Interpretation of Poetry" and prepare an oral interpretation of "The Naming of Cats." Doing an oral interpretation implies more than simply reading aloud. To create the desired effect you should consider the pitch, pacing, tone, gestures and other elements of the interpretation as well. You will want to rehearse your interpretation before a mirror several times until you are satisfied, and then deliver it for your class. If several of you do this exercise independently, you will notice that you have made different choices on such things as pacing and gestures and that this has given each presentation a different effect. As a group, evaluate the effects of the various interpretations on the experience of the poem.

Study and Research

Researching Cats. Using library resources, research the history of the domestic cat, which begins with the ancient Egyptians, around 2500 BC. Are you able to trace the roots of the suspicion and antagonism toward cats that some people feel today? Share your findings with the class.

INTEGRATING THE LANGUAGE ARTS

Language, Grammar, and Style

1. Tia went to the library to find a book about the poet T. S. Eliot.
2. She was particularly interested in his Old Possum's Book of Practical Cats.
3. The musical Cats was based on Eliot's book of children's verse.
4. This musical premiered in London in 1981.
5. It debuted in New York City the following year and was an immediate hit.

Speaking and Listening

You might encourage your class to vote on which oral presentation were the most effective and then to analyze what these speakers did to make their presentations effective.

Study and Research

Especially encourage students to compare and contrast attitudes about cats in ancient Egypt and in medieval Europe during the Spanish Inquisition and the witchcraft trials for a startling contrast.

Fiction

Fiction is prose writing that tells an imaginative story. The most common classification of fiction is by length. Book-length works of fiction are **novels.** Short works of fiction are **short stories.** Fictions of intermediate length are sometimes called **novellas.**

The Origins of Fiction

Fiction developed from various kinds of stories told in the oral tradition, including myths, legends, and fables. The earliest stories were told in poetry, perhaps because rhythmic verse and a stock "poetic language" made them easy to memorize. Early examples of prose fiction from Europe include Petronius's *Satyricon* and Apuleius's *The Golden Ass,* Roman works of the first and second centuries. In the eleventh century in Japan, Lady Murasaki Shikibu wrote the first novel, *The Tale of Genji,* which tells of the life and loves of a Japanese prince. In Europe, early and influential works of fiction include Boccaccio's *Decameron,* a collection of short prose tales written in the mid-fourteenth century, and Cervantes's *Don Quixote,* a satire of medieval romance tales written in the early seventeenth century (see Unit 3).

The Novel

In England, fiction was an outgrowth of various kinds of nonfictional writing, including autobiographies, biographies, travel sketches, journals, and letters. Arguably the first full-fledged novel in English was Aphra Behn's *Oroonoko, or the Royal Slave,* published in 1688. (See selection on page 521). *Oroonoko,* a sympathetic account of the life of an enslaved African, contains elements of autobiography, biography, and travelogue, as do other early novels such as Daniel Defoe's *Robinson Crusoe* (1719) and *Moll Flanders* (1722). These were followed by Samuel Richardson's *Pamela* (1740) and *Clarissa* (1747–8), both moral tales told in letters. Important novelists from the British Isles since that time include Henry Fielding, Mary Shelley, Jane Austen, William Thackeray, George Eliot, Charles Dickens, Charlotte and Emily Brontë, Thomas Hardy, Joseph Conrad, James Joyce, E. M. Forster, George Orwell, Virginia Woolf, and D. H. Lawrence.

The Short Story

The word *novel* comes from the Italian *novella,* meaning "story," and was first applied to short works like those found in the *Decameron*. Although the writing of short, original fictional tales in Europe dates at least as far back as Boccaccio, the development of the short story as we know it today was a nineteenth-century phenomenon. The first great modern short-story writers emerged in the United States, France, and Germany. Among the best of these pioneering writers of short stories were Washington Irving, Nathaniel Hawthorne, Edgar Allan Poe, and Guy de Maupassant. The American Edgar Allan Poe described the short story as a brief imaginative fiction that can be read in one sitting and that creates a single dominant impression. In England and her former colonies, the short story came of age in the twentieth century with such great practitioners of the form as Virginia Woolf, James Joyce, D. H. Lawrence, Katherine Mansfield, Jean Rhys, and Alice Munro.

ArtNote

A Shoreham Garden.

Samuel Palmer, c.1829. **Samuel Palmer** (1805–1881) exhibited his paintings by the age of fourteen. In 1824, Palmer met William Blake, who encouraged Palmer's developing mysticism. Palmer was deeply religious and had intense emotions about nature. His recognition as an artist rests on his ability to display this intensity of feeling. Palmer was a leader of the Shoreham Ancients, a short-lived utopian community of artists who fled the city to pursue simplicity in living.

ADDITIONAL RESOURCES

Unit 1 Resource Book
- Selection Check Test 4.1.9
- Selection Test 4.1.10

LITERARY TECHNIQUE

Short Stories. The Oral Tradition. Medieval minstrels could recite astonishing numbers of songs from memory. Invite students to think about how this was possible. Have students read or listen to a passage from an encyclopedia or a newspaper. Then have them read or listen to a popular song lyric of similar length. Then ask them to recite each from memory. Discuss with them which they were better able to remember and why that might be.

ADDITIONAL QUESTIONS AND ACTIVITIES

Ask students to share a brief story about the person in Samuel Palmer's painting. Tell students to focus on questions such as the following: What is the woman doing in the garden? How did she get there? What is she thinking and feeling about her situation? about the garden? Use the discussion to exemplify such elements of fiction as character and characterization, setting and mood, plot and conflict, and theme.

Elements of Fiction

CHARACTER

A **character** is a person (or sometimes an animal) who figures in the action of a story. The following are some useful terms for describing characters:

A **protagonist,** or main character, is the central figure in a story.

An **antagonist** is a character who is pitted against a protagonist.

A **major character** is one with a significant role in the action of a story. A **minor character** is one who plays a lesser role. Because of limitations of length and focus, most short stories have, at most, one or two major characters.

A **one-dimensional character, flat character,** or **caricature** is one who exhibits a single dominant quality, or **character trait.**

A **three-dimensional, full,** or **rounded character** is one who exhibits the complexity of traits associated with actual human beings.

A **static character** is one who does not change during the course of the story.

A **dynamic character** is one who does change during the course of the story.

A **stock character** is one found again and again in different literary works. Examples of stock characters include the mad scientist and the absent-minded professor.

A **motivation** is a force that drives a character to act in a certain way.

CHARACTERIZATION

Characterization is the use of literary techniques to create a character. Three major techniques of characterization used by fiction writers include

1. direct description by a narrator or character,
2. portrayal of a character's words and behavior, and
3. representations of a character's internal states.

A Shoreham Garden. c.1829. Samuel Palmer. Courtesy of the Trustees of the Victoria and Albert Museum, London.

Quotables

"When I want to read a novel, I write one."

—Benjamin Disraeli

"There is power in a story. It testifies to the worth, the significance of an individual. For a short while all the strength and all the radiance of the world is brought to bear upon a few human figures."

—Saul Bellow

(Continued on page 30)

SELECTION CHECK TEST 4.1.9 WITH ANSWERS

Checking Your Reading

1. What is the most common classification of fiction? **The most common classification of fiction is by length.**
2. What is a book-length piece of fiction called? **It is called a novel.**
3. In England, fiction began as an outgrowth of what? **It grew from nonfiction.**
4. What does the Italian word novella mean? **It means "story."**
5. During what century did the short story really develop in America? **It developed in the nineteenth century.**

Elements of Fiction: Characterization, Setting, Mood, and Conflict
Choose the best conclusion for each sentence beginning. You may use each conclusion only once.

1. A stock character… **D**
2. The protagonist… **C**
3. Creating characters… **B**
4. Motivation… **G**
5. Understanding a story's setting… **A**

a. can help the reader grasp the social, political, psychological, or moral conditions that affect the characters.
b. requires literary techniques such as direct description, portrayal of behavior, and representation of characters' internal states.
c. is generally involved in the central conflict of the work.
d. can be found again and again in different literary works.
e. changes during the course of the story.
f. struggles against the main character of a story.
g. works as a force to move a character to think, feel, or behave in a certain way.
h. is the emotion created in the reader by a literary work.

Setting and Mood

The **setting** is the time and place in which a story occurs, together with all the details used to create a sense of a particular time and place. The **mood** is the emotion created in the reader by descriptions of the setting, of characters, and of events. In fiction, setting is most often revealed by means of description of such elements as landscape, scenery, buildings, furniture, clothing, weather, and seasons. It also can be revealed by how characters talk and behave. In its widest sense, setting includes the general social, political, moral, and psychological conditions in which characters find themselves.

Conflict

A **conflict** is a struggle between two forces in a literary work. A plot involves the introduction, development, and, usually, the resolution, or ending, of a conflict. One side of the central conflict in a work of fiction usually is taken by the main character. That character may struggle against another character, against the forces of nature, against society or social norms, against fate, or against some element within himself or herself. A struggle that takes place between a character and some outside force is called an **external conflict.** A struggle that takes place within a character is called an **internal conflict.**

Plot

A **plot** is a series of causally connected events in a literary work. The novelist E. M. Forster explained, famously, that if the king dies and then the queen dies, that is a story, but if the king dies and then the queen dies of grief, that is a plot. A typical plot involves the following elements:

The **exposition,** or **introduction,** sets the tone and mood, introduces the characters and the setting, and provides necessary background information.

The **inciting incident** is the event that introduces the central conflict.

The **rising action,** or **complication,** develops the conflict to a high point of intensity.

The **climax** is the high point of interest or suspense.

The **crisis,** or **turning point,** often the same event as the climax, is the point in the plot where something decisive happens to determine the future course of events and the eventual working out of the conflict.

The **falling action** is all the events that follow the climax and precede the resolution.

The **resolution** is the point at which the central conflict is ended, or resolved.

The **dénouement** is any material that follows the resolution and that ties up loose ends.

SELECTION CHECK TEST 4.1.9 WITH ANSWERS (CONT.)

Elements of Fiction: Plot
Short Answer

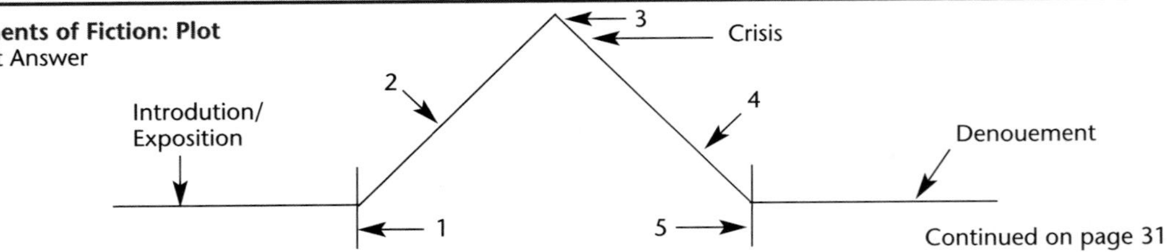

Continued on page 31

Plots are often illustrated using the following diagram, known as "Freytag's Pyramid" for its creator, Gustav Freytag:

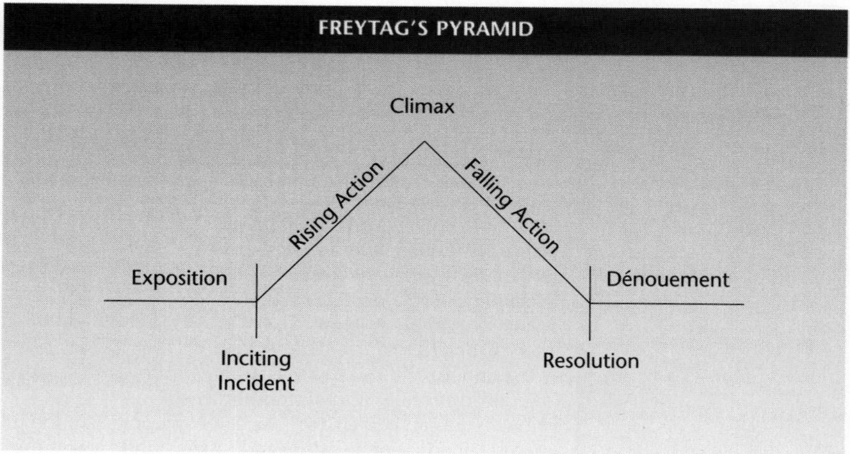

THEME

A **theme** is a central idea in a literary work. A long work such as a novel may deal with several interrelated themes.

> *"If one . . . thinks of the novel as a whole, it would seem to be a creation owning a certain looking-glass likeness to life . . . [I]t is a structure leaving a shape on the mind's eye."*
>
> *—Virginia Woolf*

SELECTION CHECK TEST 4.1.9 WITH ANSWERS (CONT. FROM PAGE 30)

Identify each element, and tell what occurs in a work of fiction at that point. A few are given as examples.

Element
What the element contributes to the plot

Introduction/Exposition
Sets the tone and mood, introduces the characters and the setting and provides background information.

1. **Inciting Incident**
   The event that introduces the central conflict

2. **Rising Action/Complication**
   Develops the conflict to a high point of intensity

3. **Climax**
   High point of interest or suspense

Crisis
Something decisive happens to determine the future course of events and eventual working out of conflict

4. **Falling Action**
   Events that follow the climax, leading toward a resolution of the central conflict

5. **Resolution**
   The central conflict is resolved, or concluded

Denouement
Follows the resolution and ties up loose ends.

ADDITIONAL RESOURCES

Unit 1 Resource Book
- Selection Worksheet 1.3
- Selection Check Test 4.1.11
- Selection Test 4.1.12
- Writing Resource 2.21
- Language, Grammar, and Style Resource 3.87

VOCABULARY FROM THE SELECTION

career	obscure
parry	stealth
remonstrate	uncanny

READER'S JOURNAL

Encourage students to explore aspects other than wealth or material success. Possibilities include being rich in friendship, in the support of one's family, in intellectual pursuits, in having a fulfilling career, or in finding true love.

INDIVIDUAL LEARNING STRATEGIES

Motivation
Encourage students to hold a class discussion on whether gambling should be universally legalized. Encourage students to explore the economic benefits gambling can bring to a state or group, the impact of casinos (both positive and negative) on a community, the way gambling can affect individuals and families (through addiction and bankruptcy, for example), and any moral or ethical issues.

Reading Proficiency
Students may be less likely to become bogged down by unfamiliar Briticisms if they hear the first few paragraphs of the story read aloud in class. Such a reading will raise their interest and make the text seem more accessible.

English Language Learning
Students who are used to hearing and reading only American English may need help with some of the Briticisms in the short story. Some British idioms to share with

Continued on page 33

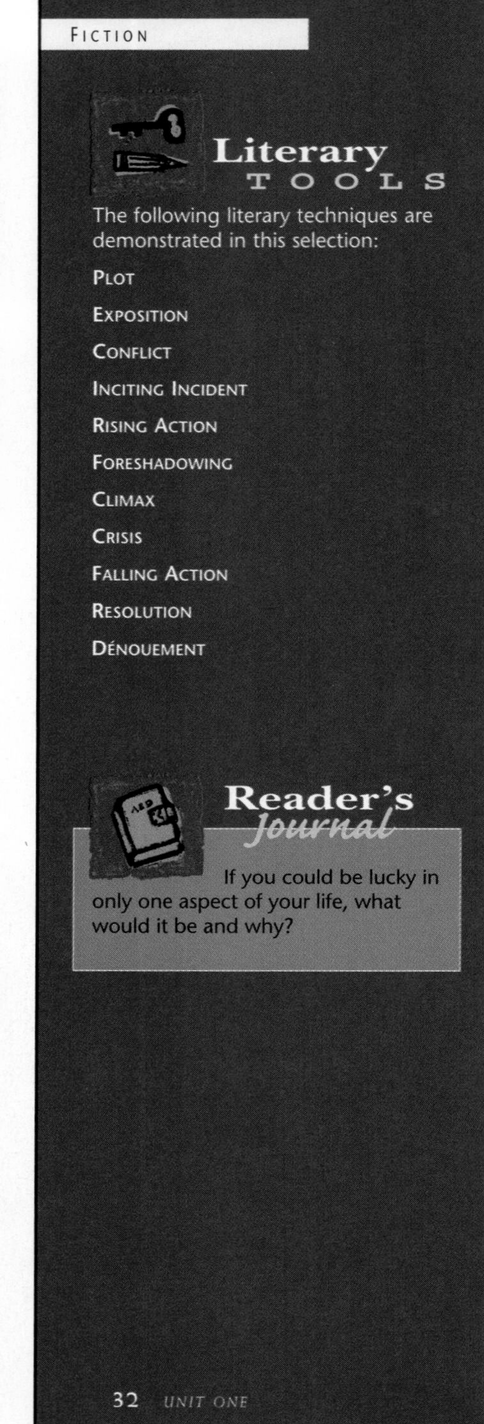

Literary Tools

The following literary techniques are demonstrated in this selection:

- Plot
- Exposition
- Conflict
- Inciting Incident
- Rising Action
- Foreshadowing
- Climax
- Crisis
- Falling Action
- Resolution
- Dénouement

Reader's Journal

If you could be lucky in only one aspect of your life, what would it be and why?

"The Rocking-Horse Winner"

by D. H. Lawrence

About the Author

David Herbert Lawrence (1885–1930) led a restless, colorful, controversial life. Born in Nottinghamshire, he was the son of a rough coal miner and a genteel mother. Lawrence's mother longed to have her children rise above their working-class origins, and the young boy identified strongly with his mother. However, as an adult, Lawrence came to appreciate the primitive natural integrity of his father and others of his class as opposed to the smothering conventional aspirations of his mother and other members of the higher social classes. In 1909, Lawrence published his first poems and in the following year a novel. He taught school for a while but gave this up after meeting Frieda von Richthofen, a German woman whom he married. Lawrence's first major novel, the autobiographical *Sons and Lovers,* was finished shortly thereafter. The novel deals with a boy's attempt to break away from a domineering mother and to establish his own identity.

Lawrence contracted tuberculosis, always fatal in those days, shortly after his mother's death from cancer and was acutely aware that his life would be short. He seems to have spent his brief life resisting the bounds of conventional society's expectations in order to live fully, and his fiction often explores the struggle of a character to escape the spiritual death of the modern world and live a full, exuberant life. Lawrence died at the age of 44 from tuberculosis.

About the Selection

In **"The Rocking-Horse Winner,"** a small boy finds a way to ease his poor family's money problems, hoping thereby to please his cold and distant mother. Though the story seems quite realistic in many ways, it contains elements of the supernatural as well. This form is often called **magical realism**. In magical realist tales, fantastic elements are treated as though they are relatively normal or ordinary. The term is most often used to describe works by certain Latin American authors of the twentieth century but applies quite well to Lawrence's story.

GOALS/OBJECTIVES

Studying this lesson will enable students to
- empathize with a main character in a short story
- explain D. H. Lawrence's literary contributions
- define the basic elements of fiction, including *character, characterization, setting, plot, mood,* and *theme* and identify these in a work of fiction
- identify all the elements of a plot in a work of fiction including *exposition, inciting incident, rising action, climax, crisis, falling action, resolution,* and *denouement*
- define *conflict* and *foreshadowing* and identify the use of these techniques in fiction
- use commas properly
- hold a class debate
- research an author

The Rocking-Horse Winner

BY D. H. LAWRENCE

Carousel Horse with Lowered Head, 1914. Charles Carmel. Museum of American Folk Art, New York.

There was a woman who was beautiful, who started with all the advantages, yet she had no luck. She married for love, and the love turned to dust. She had bonny[1] children, yet she felt—they had been thrust upon her, and she could not love them. They looked at her coldly, as if they were finding fault with her. And hurriedly she felt she must cover up some fault in herself. Yet what it was that she must cover up she never knew. Nevertheless, when her children were present she always felt the center of her heart go hard. This troubled her, and in her manner she was all the more gentle and anxious for her children, as if she loved them very much. Only she herself knew that at the centre of her heart was a hard little place that could not feel love, no, not for anybody. Everybody else said of her: "She is such a good mother. She adores her children." Only she herself, and her children themselves, knew it was not so. They read it in each other's eyes.

What secret did the woman have?

There were a boy and two little girls. They lived in a pleasant house, with a garden, and they had discreet servants, and felt themselves superior to anyone in the neighborhood.

Although they lived in style, they felt always an anxiety in the house. There was never enough money. The mother had a small income, and the father had a small income, but not nearly enough for the social position which they had to keep up. The father went into town to some office. But though he had good prospects, these prospects never materialized. There was always the grinding sense of the shortage of money, though the style was always kept up.

What caused the anxiety in the house?

At last the mother said: "I will see if *I* can't make something." But she did not know where to begin. She racked her brains, and tried this thing and the other,

CONFLICT

A conflict is a struggle between two forces, with one side of the conflict usually being taken by the main character.

EXPOSITION

The exposition introduces the central characters and their basic situation.

1. **bonny.** Attractive; healthy; robust (Scottish)

ANSWERS TO GUIDED READING QUESTIONS

1. The woman's secret was that she did not love her children and, in fact, could not love anyone.
2. The anxiety in the house was due to the fact that there was never enough money.

INDIVIDUAL LEARNING STRATEGIES (cont. from page 32)

your students are provided below. Others are defined in the footnotes.
in full tilt—at full speed
spinning yarns—telling fanciful tales

SPECIAL NEEDS
You may wish to ask them to create and fill out a plot pyramid as they read and to jot down their responses to Guided Reading Questions. Check their comprehension with the Selection Check Test.

ENRICHMENT
Inform students that as long as people have ridden horses, they have raced them. Encourage students to work in groups to explore different aspects of horses and racing. Students can focus on historical or cultural events, such as the Spanish reintroduction of horses to the Americas and its effect on native populations, horse and chariot racing in classical Greece and Rome, the reintroduction of the Przewalski horse back to its Mongolian homeland, and the rules of modern American horse racing. Students might also explore images of horses and racing in art. Horses figure in the earliest human art—cave drawings—and horses and racing have also inspired classical artists of Greece and Rome as well as more recent artists, such as Impressionist Edgar Degas. Each group should prepare a brief oral report on its findings, using visual and multimedia aids as necessary.

ANSWERS TO GUIDED READING QUESTIONS

1. Mother says the family is poor because the father has no luck, and luck is what causes you to have money.

LITERARY TECHNIQUE

Characterization. Read the entry on *characterization* in the Handbook of Literary Terms. In the first paragraph, what method of characterization does the author use? Ask students to find other instances in the story of these methods of characterization.

Answer

The narrator comments directly on the characters and depicts their internal states.

Setting and Mood. What elements of the story help to establish the setting? What elements of the story help to establish the mood?

Answers

The setting is an upper-class or upper-middle-class ("They lived in a pleasant house, with a garden, and they had discreet servants") suburban neighborhood ("The father went into town"). An ominous mood is created by details describing the relationships and emotional states of the characters ("They looked at her wildly"; "finding fault"; "felt the center of her heart go hard"; "they . . . felt themselves superior") and by details describing the conflict ("they felt always an anxiety. . . . There was never enough money").

but could not find anything successful. The failure made deep lines come into her face. Her children were growing up; they would have to go to school. There must be more money; there must be more money. The father, who was always very handsome and expensive in his tastes, seemed as if he never *would* be able to do anything worth doing. And the mother, who had a great belief in herself, did not succeed any better, and her tastes were just as expensive.

And so the house came to be haunted by the unspoken phrase: There must be more money! There must be more money! The children could hear it all the time, though nobody said it aloud. They heard it at Christmas, when the expensive and splendid toys filled the nursery. Behind the shining modern rocking-horse, behind the smart doll's house, a voice would start whispering: "*There must be more money! There must be more money!*" And the children would stop playing, to listen for a moment. They would look into each other's eyes, to see if they had all heard. And each one saw in the eyes of the other two that they too had heard. "There *must* be more money! There *must* be more money!"

It came whispering from the springs of the still-swaying rocking-horse, and even the horse, bending his wooden, champing head, heard it. The big doll, sitting so pink and smirking in her new pram,[2] could hear it quite plainly, and seemed to be smirking all the more self-consciously because of it. The foolish puppy, too, that took the place of the teddybear, he was looking so extraordinarily foolish for no other reason but that he heard the secret whisper all over the house: "There *must* be more money!"

Yet nobody ever said it aloud. The whisper was everywhere, and therefore no one spoke it. Just as no one ever says: "We are breathing!" in spite of the fact that breath is coming and going all the time.

"Mother," said the boy Paul one day, "why don't we keep a car of our own? Why do we always use uncle's, or else a taxi?"

"Because we're the poor members of the family," said the mother.

"But why *are* we, mother?"

What reason does Mother give for the family's poverty?

"Well—I suppose," she said slowly and bitterly, "it's because your father has no luck."

The boy was silent for some time.

"Is luck money, mother?" he asked, rather timidly.

"No, Paul. Not quite. It's what causes you to have money."

"Oh!" said Paul vaguely. "I thought when Uncle Oscar said *filthy lucker*, it meant money."

"*Filthy lucre* does mean money," said the mother. "But it's lucre, not luck."

"Oh!" said the boy. "Then what *is* luck, mother?"

"It's what causes you to have money. If you're lucky you have money. That's why it's better to be born lucky than rich. If you're rich, you may lose your money. But if you're lucky, you will always get more money."

"Oh! Will you? And is father not lucky?"

"Very unlucky, I should say," she said bitterly.

The boy watched her with unsure eyes.

"Why?" he asked.

"I don't know. Nobody ever knows why one person is lucky and another unlucky."

"Don't they? Nobody at all? Does *nobody* know?"

2. **pram.** A shortened version of perambulator, a British word for baby carriage

"Perhaps God. But He never tells."

"He ought to, then. And aren't you lucky either, mother?"

"I can't be, if I married an unlucky husband."

"But by yourself, aren't you?"

"I used to think I was, before I married. Now I think I am very unlucky indeed."

"Why?"

"Well—never mind! Perhaps I'm not really," she said.

The child looked at her to see if she meant it. But he saw, by the lines of her mouth, that she was only trying to hide something from him.

"Well, anyhow," he said stoutly, "I'm a lucky person."

What does Paul tell his mother?

"Why?" said his mother, with a sudden laugh.

He stared at her. He didn't even know why he had said it.

"God told me," he asserted, brazening it out.[3]

"I hope He did, dear!" she said, again with a laugh, but rather bitter.

"He did, mother!"

"Excellent!" said the mother, using one of her husband's exclamations.

The boy saw she did not believe him; or rather, that she paid no attention to his assertion. This angered him somewhere, and made him want to compel her attention.

He went off by himself, vaguely, in a childish way, seeking for the clue to "luck." Absorbed, taking no heed of other people, he went about with a sort of stealth, seeking inwardly for luck. He wanted luck, he wanted it, he wanted it.

When the two girls were playing dolls in the nursery, he would sit on his big rocking-horse, charging madly into space, with a frenzy that made the little girls peer at him uneasily. Wildly the horse careered, the waving dark hair of the boy tossed, his eyes had a strange glare in them. The little girls dared not speak to him.

When he had ridden to the end of his mad little journey, he climbed down and stood in front of his rocking-horse, staring fixedly into its lowered face. Its red mouth was slightly open, its big eye was wide and glassy-bright.

"Now!" he would silently command the snorting steed. "Now, take me to where there is luck! Now take me!"

And he would slash the horse on the neck with the little whip he had asked Uncle Oscar for. He *knew* the horse could take him to where there was luck, if only he forced it. So he would mount again and start on his furious ride, hoping at last to get there. He knew he could get there.

Where does Paul go on his horse?

INCITING INCIDENT

The inciting incident is the event that introduces the central conflict.

RISING ACTION

The rising action develops the conflict to a high point of intensity.

"You'll break your horse, Paul!" said the nurse.

"He's always riding like that! I wish he'd leave off!" said his elder sister Joan.

But he only glared down on them in silence. Nurse gave him up. She could make nothing of him. Anyhow, he was growing beyond her.

One day his mother and his Uncle Oscar came in when he was on one of his furious rides. He did not speak to them.

3. **brazening it out.** Acting boldly, without shame

WORDS FOR EVERYDAY USE

stealth (stelth) *n.*, act of proceeding secretly or imperceptibly. *The government moves by stealth to gather information on enemies of the state.*

ca • reer (kə rir´) *vi.*, move at full speed. *The sled careered down the ice-covered hill, but the three sisters dove off before hitting the trees.*

ANSWERS TO GUIDED READING QUESTIONS

1. Paul tells his mother that he is lucky.
2. Paul goes to where the luck is.

ADDITIONAL QUESTIONS AND ACTIVITIES

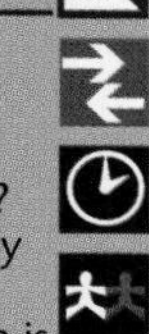

- Ask students what enables people to get money. How much is due to luck? What other factors are important? Why do people in this family think that they do not have enough money? How much is enough?
- Ask students what it means to be a good money manager. Why do some people never seem to have enough money, while others with the same amount of money are able to live comfortably? Ask students whether they are able to manage their money well. Some students may have suggestions to offer others for managing their money. Ask students what plans they have for their futures. How much do they think they need to earn in order to live comfortably?
- Ask students whether the mother in the story takes responsibility for her actions. Ask whether the father takes responsibility. In general, is it right to hold people responsible for what happens to them? When would it be right to hold someone responsible for what happens to him or her? When would it be wrong?

CROSS-CURRICULAR ACTIVITIES

Social Studies. The Society for the Prevention of Cruelty to Animals and other animal protection organizations have investigated training practices at racetracks and at stables. Students may want to contact a nearby racetrack; a state regulatory agency; the Thoroughbred Racing Association (420 Fair Hill Dr., Elkton, MD 21921); or the Jockey Club (380 Madison Ave., New York, NY 10017) for information on the treatment of racehorses.

CROSS-CURRICULAR ACTIVITIES

Mathematics and Sciences. "The Rocking-Horse Winner" deals with a family that is having financial difficulties. One way to avoid financial difficulties is to make regular budgets and to live within them. Have students prepare monthly budgets for a hypothetical family of four, tracking income and expenditures for housing, food, clothing, transportation, child care, insurance, utilities, and entertainment.

"Hallo, you young jockey! Riding a winner?" said his uncle.

"Aren't you growing too big for a rocking-horse? You're not a very little boy any longer, you know," said his mother.

But Paul only gave a blue glare from his big, rather close set eyes. He would speak to nobody when he was in full tilt. His mother watched him with an anxious expression on her face.

At last he suddenly stopped forcing his horse into the mechanical gallop and slid down.

"Well, I got there!" he announced fiercely, his blue eyes still flaring, and his sturdy long legs straddling apart.

"Where did you get to?" asked his mother.

"Where I wanted to go," he flared back at her.

"That's right, son!" said Uncle Oscar. "Don't you stop till you get there. What's the horse's name?"

"He doesn't have a name," said the boy.

"Gets on without, all right?" asked the uncle.

"Well, he has different names. He was called Sansovino last week."

"Sansovino, eh? Won the Ascot.[4] How did you know this name?"

"He always talks about horse-races with Bassett," said Joan.

The uncle was delighted to find that his small nephew was posted with all the racing news. Bassett, the young gardener who had been wounded in the left foot in the war and had got his present job through Oscar Cresswell, whose batman[5] he had been, was a perfect blade of the "turf."[6] He lived in the racing events, and the small boy lived with him.

Oscar Cresswell got it all from Bassett.

"Master Paul comes and asks me, so I can't do more than tell him, sir," said Bassett, his face terribly serious, as if he were speaking of religious matters.

"And does he ever put anything on a horse he fancies?"

"Well—I don't want to give him away—he's a young sport, a fine sport, sir. Would you mind asking him himself? He sort of takes a pleasure in it, and perhaps he'd feel I was giving him away, sir, if you don't mind."

Bassett was serious as a church.

The uncle went back to his nephew and took him off for a ride in the car.

"Say, Paul, old man, do you ever put anything on a horse?" the uncle asked.

The boy watched the handsome man closely.

"Why, do you think I oughtn't to?" he parried.

"Not a bit of it! I thought perhaps you might give me a tip for the Lincoln."

The car sped on into the country, going down to Uncle Oscar's place in Hampshire.

"Honor bright?"[7] said the nephew.

"Honor bright, son!" said the uncle.

"Well, then, Daffodil."

"Daffodil! I doubt it, sonny. What about Mirza?"

"I only know the winner," said the boy. "That's Daffodil."

4. **Ascot.** A prestigious horse race
5. **batman.** Orderly for a military officer
6. **turf.** The sport of horse racing
7. **honor bright.** A saying meaning, "on my honor" or "on your honor"

Words for Everyday Use

par • ry (par´ē) *vt.*, reply in a clever or evasive way. *When Rona interviewed for a job as a legal assistant, she tried to parry questions about relevant experience, since she had none.*

"Daffodil, eh?"

There was a pause. Daffodil was an obscure horse comparatively.

"Uncle!"

"Yes, son?"

"You won't let it go any further, will you? I promised Bassett."

What sort of horse does Paul predict will win?

"Bassett be damned, old man! What's he got to do with it?"

"We're partners. We've been partners from the first. Uncle, he lent me my first five shillings, which I lost. I promised him, honor bright, it was only between me and him; only you gave me that ten-shilling note I started winning with, so I thought you were lucky. You won't let it go any further, will you?"

What secret are the boy and Bassett keeping?

The boy gazed at his uncle from those big, hot, blue eyes, set rather close together. The uncle stirred and laughed uneasily.

"Right you are, son! I'll keep your tip private. Daffodil, eh? How much are you putting on him?"

"All except twenty pounds," said the boy. "I keep that in reserve."

The uncle thought it a good joke.

"You keep twenty pounds in reserve, do you, you young romancer? What are you betting, then?"

"I'm betting three hundred," said the boy gravely. "But it's between you and me, Uncle Oscar! Honor bright?"

The uncle burst into a roar of laughter. "It's between you and me all right, you young Nat Gould,"[8] he said, laughing. "But where's your three hundred?"

"Bassett keeps it for me. We're partners."

"You are, are you! And what is Bassett putting on Daffodil?"

"He won't go quite as high as I do, I expect. Perhaps he'll go a hundred and fifty."

"What, pennies?" laughed the uncle.

"Pounds," said the child, with a surprised look at his uncle. "Bassett keeps a bigger reserve than I do."

Between wonder and amusement Uncle Oscar was silent. He pursued the matter no further, but he determined to take his nephew with him to the Lincoln races.

"Now, son," he said, "I'm putting twenty on Mirza, and I'll put five on for you on any horse you fancy. What's your pick?"

"Daffodil, uncle."

"No, not the fiver on Daffodil!"

"I should if it was my own fiver," said the child.

"Good! Good! Right you are! A fiver for me and a fiver for you on Daffodil."

The child had never been to a race-meeting before, and his eyes were blue fire. He pursed his mouth tight and watched. A Frenchman just in front had put his money on Lancelot. Wild with excitement, he flayed his arms up and down, yelling *"Lancelot! Lancelot!"* in his French accent.

Daffodil came in first, Lancelot second, Mirza third. The child, flushed and with eyes blazing, was curiously serene. His uncle brought him four five-pound notes, four to one.

What was the outcome of the race?

"What am I to do with these?" he cried, waving them before the boy's eyes.

8. **Nat Gould.** An authority on horse racing

Words For Everyday Use

ob • scure (äb skyür') *adj.*, relatively unknown; not prominent or famous. *The actor was obscure until his part in the hit movie.*

ANSWERS TO GUIDED READING QUESTIONS

1. Paul predicts that an obscure, or unknown, horse will win.
2. The boy and Bassett are keeping secret the fact that they are betting on the horse races.
3. The horse Paul predicted, Daffodil, won.

ADDITIONAL QUESTIONS AND ACTIVITIES

Financial advisors caution people not to invest more money in the stock market than they can afford to lose. Ask students why financial advisors might give this advice. How would this advice pertain to betting on horses, too?

LITERARY TECHNIQUE

Dead Metaphor. A **dead metaphor** is one that has been used so widely that people no longer think of its metaphorical meaning when using it. In the sentence "The uncle burst into a roar of laugher," "roar of laughter" is a dead metaphor comparing loud laughter to the equally loud roar of a lion. See the entry on *dead metaphor* in the Handbook of Literary Terms.

ANSWERS TO GUIDED READING QUESTIONS

1. Bassett says "It's as if he had it from heaven."
2. When Paul is "sure," he says "Then we go strong, for all we're worth." When he does not have any idea, he says, "Then we're careful, because we mostly go down."

ADDITIONAL QUESTIONS AND ACTIVITIES

- Ask students to compare how Bussett and Oscar Cresswell feel about Paul. Do they both like him? Do they both care about him? Do they both love him? Do they take him seriously? Do they take his problems seriously? Do they try to help him?
- Ask students to compare how Paul feels about Bassett and Uncle Oscar and to consider how Paul treats the people around him generally.

"I suppose we'll talk to Bassett," said the boy. "I expect I have fifteen hundred now; and twenty in reserve; and this twenty."

His uncle studied him for some moments.

"Look here, son!" he said. "You're not serious about Bassett and that fifteen hundred, are you?"

"Yes, I am. But it's between you and me, uncle. Honor bright?"

"Honor bright all right, son! But I must talk to Bassett."

"If you'd like to be a partner, uncle, with Bassett and me, we could all be partners. Only, you'd have to promise, honor bright, uncle, not to let it go beyond us three. Bassett and I are lucky, and you must be lucky, because it was your ten shillings I started winning with. . . ."

Uncle Oscar took both Bassett and Paul into Richmond Park for an afternoon, and there they talked.

"It's like this, you see, sir," Bassett said. "Master Paul would get me talking about racing events, spinning yarns, you know, sir. And he was always keen on knowing if I'd made or if I'd lost. It's about a year since, now, that I put five shillings on Blush of Dawn for him: and we lost. Then the luck turned, with that ten shillings he had from you: that we put on Singhalese. And since that time, it's been pretty steady all things considering. What do you say, Master Paul?"

"We're all right when we're sure," said Paul. "It's when we're not quite sure that we go down."

"Oh, but we're careful then," said Bassett.

"But when are you *sure?*" smiled Uncle Oscar.

"It's Master Paul, sir," said Bassett in a secret, religious voice. "It's as if he had it from heaven. Like Daffodil, now, for the Lincoln. That was as sure as eggs."

How does Bassett explain Paul's intuition about horse race winners?

"Did you put anything on Daffodil?" asked Oscar Cresswell.

"Yes, sir. I made my bit."

"And my nephew?"

Bassett was obstinately silent, looking at Paul.

"I made twelve hundred, didn't I, Bassett? I told uncle I was putting three hundred on Daffodil."

"That's right," said Bassett, nodding.

"But where's the money?" asked the uncle.

"I keep it safe locked up, sir. Master Paul he can have it any minute he likes to ask for it."

"What, fifteen hundred pounds?"

"And twenty! And *forty,* that is, with the twenty he made on the course."

"It's amazing!" said the uncle.

"If Master Paul offers you to be partners, sir, I would, if I were you: if you'll excuse me," said Bassett.

Oscar Cresswell thought about it.

"I'll see the money," he said.

They drove home again, and, sure enough, Bassett came round to the garden-house with fifteen hundred pounds in notes. The twenty pounds reserve was left with Joe Glee, in the Turf Commission deposit.

"You see, it's all right, uncle, when I'm *sure!* Then we go strong, for all we're worth. Don't we, Bassett?"

"We do that, Master Paul."

"And when are you sure?" said the uncle, laughing.

"Oh, well, sometimes I'm *absolutely* sure, like about Daffodil," said the boy; "and sometimes I have an idea; and sometimes I haven't even an idea, have I, Bassett? Then we're careful, because we mostly go down."

How does Paul decide which races to bet on carefully and which to bet on strongly?

"You do, do you! And when you're sure, like about Daffodil, what makes you sure, sonny?"

"Oh, well, I don't know," said the boy uneasily. "I'm sure, you know, uncle; that's all."

"It's as if he had it from heaven, sir," Bassett reiterated.

"I should say so!" said the uncle.

But he became a partner. And when the Leger was coming on Paul was "sure" about Lively Spark, which was a quite inconsiderable horse. The boy insisted on putting a thousand on the horse, Bassett went for five hundred, and Oscar Cresswell two hundred. Lively Spark came in first, and the betting had been ten to one against him. Paul had made ten thousand.

"You see," he said, "I was absolutely sure of him."

Even Oscar Cresswell had cleared two thousand.

"Look here, son," he said, "this sort of thing makes me nervous."

"It needn't, uncle! Perhaps I shan't be sure again for a long time."

"But what are you going to do with your money?" asked the uncle.

"Of course," said the boy, "I started it for mother. She said she had no luck, because father is unlucky, so I thought if *I* was lucky, it might stop whispering."

Why did Paul start gambling on the horse races?

"What might stop whispering?"

"Our house. I *hate* our house for whispering."

"What does it whisper?"

"Why—why"—the boy fidgeted—"why, I don't know. But it's always short of money, you know, uncle."

"I know it, son, I know it."

"You know people send mother writs,[9] don't you, uncle?"

"I'm afraid I do," said the uncle.

"And then the house whispers, like people laughing at you behind your back. It's awful, that is! I thought if I was lucky—"

To what does Paul compare the house's whispering?

"You might stop it," added the uncle.

The boy watched him with big blue eyes, that had an uncanny cold fire in them, and he said never a word.

"Well, then!" said the uncle. "What are we doing?"

"I shouldn't like mother to know I was lucky," said the boy.

"Why not, son?"

"She'd stop me."

"I don't think she would."

"Oh!"—and the boy writhed in an odd way— "I *don't* want her to know, uncle."

"All right, son! We'll manage it without her knowing."

They managed it very easily. Paul, at the other's suggestion, handed over five thousand pounds to his uncle, who deposited it with the family lawyer, who was then to inform Paul's mother that a relative had put five thousand pounds into his hands, which sum was to be paid out a thousand pounds at a time, on the mother's birthday, for the next five years.

"So she'll have a birthday present of a thousand pounds for five successive years," said Uncle Oscar. "I hope it won't make it all the harder for her later."

9. **writs.** Legal notices

WORDS FOR EVERYDAY USE

un • can • ny (ən ka′ nē) *adj.*, seeming to have an supernatural or mysterious character or origin. *The mountain guide had an uncanny sense of direction.*

ANSWERS TO GUIDED READING QUESTIONS

1. Paul started gambling to help his mother and to stop the house from whispering that there must be more money.
2. Paul compares the house's whispering to "people laughing at you behind your back."

LITERARY TECHNIQUE

CHARACTERIZATION. Writers use three major techniques to create characters: direct description, portrayals of behavior, and representations of internal states. Portrayals of behavior can be of the characters' own behavior or of other characters' behavior toward them. Ask students the following questions:

1. Which technique(s) does the author use to create Paul's character?
2. What does the reader learn about Paul on this page?
3. What technique(s) does the author use to create the mother's character?
4. What does the reader learn about the mother on this page?

Answers

1. Paul's character is created by portrayal of behavior (dialogue and description).
2. The reader learns that Paul is aware of the pressure to have more money and is disturbed by it, that he wants to please his mother, that he feels he needs to keep secrets from her, and that he is anxious about how she feels about him.
3. The mother's character is created by portrayal of behavior and by representation of internal states.
4. The reader learns that she is difficult to satisfy, that she is prideful, and that she has both practical and emotional difficulties with money.

ANSWERS TO GUIDED READING QUESTIONS

1. When mother touched the money, the voices in the house grew much louder and "went mad, like a chorus of frogs on a spring evening."

CROSS-CURRICULAR ACTIVITIES

Mathematics and Sciences. One benefit of having savings is that they can earn interest. Ask students to calculate how much interest Paul's mother could have earned if she had received one thousand per year instead of taking the whole five thousand at once. They may assume an interest rate of 10 percent and may calculate the amounts in dollars rather than in pounds if that is easier for them.

Answer

Assuming an interest rate of 10 percent per year and that Paul's mother took one thousand immediately, deposited the other four thousand, and took one thousand annually, her account would look like this at the end of each year:

End of first year:
4,000 x 1.10 = 4,400

End of second year:
3,400 x 1.10 = 3,740

End of third year:
2,740 x 1.10 = 3,014

End of fourth year:
2,014 x 1.10 = 2,215.40

End of fifth year:
1,215.40 x 10 = 1,336.94

Paul's mother had her birthday in November. The house had been "whispering" worse than ever lately, and, even in spite of his luck, Paul could not bear up against it. He was very anxious to see the effect of the birthday letter, telling his mother about the thousand pounds.

When there were no visitors, Paul now took his meals with his parents, as he was beyond the nursery control. His mother went into town nearly every day. She had discovered that she had an odd knack of sketching furs and dress materials, so she worked secretly in the studio of a friend who was the chief "artist" for the leading drapers. She drew the figures of ladies in furs and ladies in silk and sequins for the newspaper advertisements. This young woman artist earned several thousand pounds a year, but Paul's mother only made several hundreds, and she was again dissatisfied. She so wanted to be first in something, and she did not succeed, even in making sketches for drapery advertisements.

She was down to breakfast on the morning of her birthday. Paul watched her face as she read her letters. He knew the lawyer's letter. As his mother read it, her face hardened and became more expressionless. Then a cold, determined look came on her mouth. She hid the letter under the pile of others, and said not a word about it.

"Didn't you have anything nice in the post for your birthday, mother?" said Paul.

"Quite moderately nice," she said, her voice cold and absent.

She went away to town without saying more.

But in the afternoon Uncle Oscar appeared. He said Paul's mother had had a long interview with the lawyer, asking if the whole five thousand could not be advanced at once, as she was in debt.

"What do you think, uncle?" said the boy.

"I leave it to you, son."

"Oh, let her have it, then! We can get some more with the other," said the boy.

"A bird in the hand is worth two in the bush, laddie!" said Uncle Oscar.

"But I'm sure to *know* for the Grand National; or the Lincolnshire; or else the Derby. I'm sure to know for *one* of them," said Paul.

So Uncle Oscar signed the agreement, and Paul's mother touched the whole five thousand. Then something very curious happened. The voices in the house suddenly went mad, like a chorus of frogs on a spring evening. There were certain new furnishings, and Paul had a tutor. He was *really* going to Eton, his father's school, in the following autumn. There were flowers in the winter, and a blossoming of the luxury Paul's mother had been used to. And yet the voices in the house, behind the sprays of mimosa and almond blossom, and from under the piles of iridescent cushions, simply trilled and screamed in a sort of ecstasy: "There *must* be more money! Oh-h-h; there *must* be more money. Oh, now, now-w! Now-w-w—there *must* be more money!—more than ever! More than ever!"

What happened when mother got the whole five thousand pounds?

It frightened Paul terribly. He studied away at his Latin and Greek with his tutor. But his intense hours were spent with Bassett. The Grand National had gone by: he had not "known," and had lost a hundred pounds. Summer was at hand. He was in agony for the Lincoln. But even for the Lincoln he didn't "know," and he lost fifty pounds. He became wild-eyed and strange, as if something were going to explode in him.

"Let it alone, son! Don't you bother about it!" urged Uncle Oscar. But it was as if the boy couldn't really hear what his uncle was saying.

"I've got to know for the Derby! I've got to know for the Derby!" the child reiterated, his big blue eyes blazing with a sort of madness.

His mother noticed how overwrought he was.

"You'd better go to the seaside. Wouldn't you like to go now to the seaside, instead of waiting? I think you'd better," she said, looking down at him anxiously, her heart curiously heavy because of him.

But the child lifted his uncanny blue eyes.

"I couldn't possibly go before the Derby, mother!" he said. "I couldn't possibly!"

"Why not?" she said, her voice becoming heavy when she was opposed. "Why not? You can still go from the seaside to see the Derby with your Uncle Oscar, if that's what you wish. No need for you to wait here. Besides, I think you care too much about these races. It's a bad sign. My family has been a gambling family, and you won't know till you grow up how much damage it has done. But it has done damage. I shall have to send Bassett away, and ask Uncle Oscar not to talk racing to you, unless you promise to be reasonable about it: go away to the seaside and forget it. You're all nerves!"

What vice has troubled the family, according to Mother?

"I'll do what you like, mother, so long as you don't send me away till after the Derby," the boy said.

"Send you away from where? Just from this house?"

"Yes," he said, gazing at her.

"Why, you curious child, what makes you care about this house so much, suddenly? I never knew you loved it."

He gazed at her without speaking. He had a secret within a secret, something he had not divulged, even to Bassett or to his Uncle Oscar.

But his mother, after standing undecided and a little bit sullen for some moments, said:

"Very well, then! Don't go to the seaside till after the Derby, if you don't wish it. But promise me you won't let your nerves go to pieces. Promise you won't think so much about horse-racing and *events*, as you call them!"

"Oh no," said the boy casually. "I won't think much about them, mother. You needn't worry. I wouldn't worry, mother, if I were you."

"If you were me and I were you," said his mother, "I wonder what we *should* do!"

"But you know you needn't worry, mother, don't you?" the boy repeated.

"I should be awfully glad to know it," she said wearily.

"Oh, well, you *can*, you know. I mean, you *ought* to know you needn't worry," he insisted.

"Ought I? Then I'll see about it," she said. Paul's secret of secrets was his wooden horse, that which had no name. Since he was emancipated from a nurse and a nursery-governess, he had had his rocking-horse removed to his own bedroom at the top of the house.

What was Paul's "secret of secrets"?

"Surely you're too big for a rocking-horse!" his mother had <u>remonstrated</u>.

"Well, you see, mother, till I can have a *real* horse, I like to have *some* sort of animal about," had been his quaint answer.

WORDS FOR EVERYDAY USE

re • mon • strate (ri män´ strāt) *vt.*, say in protest or object. *He <u>remonstrated</u> that the shoes were uncomfortable, but his mother would hear none of it.*

ANSWERS TO GUIDED READING QUESTIONS

1. Mother says that gambling has caused a great deal of damage to the family.
2. Paul's "secret of secrets" was that he was still riding his rocking horse.

ADDITIONAL QUESTIONS AND ACTIVITIES

Even though he is no longer a toddler, Paul still rides his rocking-horse and considers this his "secret of secrets." Encourage students to write in their journals about the childish habit that they found it difficult to let go of. Why did this habit means so much to them? Have them explain whether this habit became their "secret of secrets."

ANSWERS TO GUIDED READING QUESTIONS

1. Mother saw Paul furiously riding his rocking horse, in a frenzy.
2. Paul fell off the horse in a feverish fit.

ADDITIONAL QUESTIONS AND ACTIVITIES

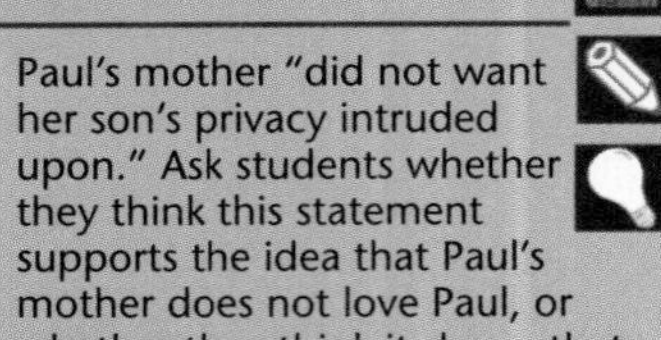

- Paul's mother "did not want her son's privacy intruded upon." Ask students whether they think this statement supports the idea that Paul's mother does not love Paul, or whether they think it shows that she does love him.
- Explain to students that some people believe that there is a fundamental right to privacy. The word *privacy* does not appear in the United States Constitution, but courts have interpreted the due process clause of that document to mean that a right to privacy does exist, though the exact nature of this right remains controversial. Discuss with students their own feelings about privacy. Do they believe that privacy is a fundamental right, like free speech? Why, or why not?

"Do you feel he keeps you company?" she laughed.

"Oh yes! He's very good, he always keeps me company, when I'm there," said Paul.

So the horse, rather shabby, stood in an arrested prance in the boy's bedroom.

The Derby was drawing near, and the boy grew more and more tense. He hardly heard what was spoken to him, he was very frail, and his eyes were really uncanny. His mother had sudden strange seizures of uneasiness about him. Sometimes, for half an hour, she would feel a sudden anxiety about him that was almost anguish. She wanted to rush to him at once, and know he was safe.

FORESHADOWING
An event or description that hints at something that will occur later in the story is called foreshadowing.

Two nights before the Derby, she was at a big party in town, when one of her rushes of anxiety about her boy, her first-born, gripped her heart till she could hardly speak. She fought with the feeling, might and main, for she believed in common sense. But it was too strong. She had to leave the dance and go downstairs to telephone to the country. The children's nursery-governess was terribly surprised and startled at being rung up in the night.

"Are the children all right, Miss Wilmot?"

CRISIS
The crisis, or turning point, is the point in the plot where something decisive happens to determine the future course of events and the resolution of the conflict.

"Oh yes, they are quite all right."

"Master Paul? Is he all right?"

"He went to bed as right as a trivet.[10] Shall I run up and look at him?"

"No," said Paul's mother reluctantly. "No! Don't trouble. It's all right. Don't sit up. We shall be home fairly soon." She did not want her son's privacy intruded upon.

CLIMAX
The climax presents the high point of interest or suspense in the story.

"Very good," said the governess.

It was about one o'clock when Paul's mother and father drove up to their house. All was still. Paul's mother went to her room and slipped off her white fur cloak. She had told her maid not to wait up for her. She heard her husband downstairs, mixing a whisky and soda.

And then, because of the strange anxiety at her heart, she stole upstairs to her son's room. Noiselessly she went along the upper corridor. Was there a faint noise? What was it?

She stood, with arrested muscles, outside his door, listening. There was a strange, heavy, and yet not loud noise. Her heart stood still. It was a soundless noise, yet rushing and powerful. Something huge, in violent, hushed motion. What was it? What in God's name was it? She ought to know. She felt that she knew the noise. She knew what it was.

Yet she could not place it. She couldn't say what it was. And on and on it went, like a madness.

Softly, frozen with anxiety and fear, she turned the door handle.

The room was dark. Yet in the space near the window, she heard and saw something plunging to and fro. She gazed in fear and amazement.

Then suddenly she switched on the light, and saw her son, in his green pajamas, madly surging on the rocking-horse. The blaze of light suddenly lit him up, as he urged the wooden horse, and lit her up, as she stood, blonde, in her dress of pale green and crystal, in the doorway.

What did Mother discover when she entered Paul's room?

"Paul!" she cried. "Whatever are you doing?"

"It's Malabar!" he screamed in a powerful, strange voice. "It's Malabar!"

His eyes blazed at her for one strange and senseless second,

What happened to Paul after he shouted the winner's name?

10. **trivet.** Metal stand with short feet for use under a hot dish at table.

as he ceased urging his wooden horse. Then he fell with a crash to the ground, and she, all her tormented motherhood flooding upon her, rushed to gather him up.

But he was unconscious, and unconscious he remained, with some brain-fever. He talked and tossed, and his mother sat stonily by his side.

"Malabar! It's Malabar! Bassett, Bassett, I *know!* It's Malabar!"

So the child cried, trying to get up and urge the rocking-horse that gave him his inspiration.

"What does he mean by Malabar?" asked the heart-frozen mother.

"I don't know," said the father stonily.

"What does he mean by Malabar?" she asked her brother Oscar.

"It's one of the horses running for the Derby," was the answer.

And, in spite of himself, Oscar Cresswell spoke to Bassett, and himself put a thousand on Malabar: at fourteen to one.

The third day of the illness was critical: they were waiting for a change. The boy, with his rather long, curly hair, was tossing ceaselessly on the pillow. He neither slept nor regained consciousness, and his eyes were like blue stones. His mother sat, feeling her heart had gone, turned actually into a stone.

In the evening, Oscar Cresswell did not come, but Bassett sent a message, saying could he come up for one moment, just one moment? Paul's mother was very angry at the intrusion, but on second thoughts she agreed. The boy was the same. Perhaps Bassett might bring him to consciousness.

The gardener, a shortish fellow with a little brown moustache and sharp little brown eyes, tiptoed into the room, touched his imaginary cap to Paul's mother, and stole to the bedside, staring with glittering, smallish eyes at the tossing, dying child.

"Master Paul!" he whispered. "Master Paul! Malabar came in first all right, a clean win. I did as you told me. You've made over seventy thousand pounds, you have; you've got over eighty thousand. Malabar came in all right, Master Paul."

"Malabar! Malabar! Did I say Malabar, mother? Did I say Malabar? Do you think I'm lucky, mother? I knew Malabar, didn't I? Over eighty thousand pounds! I call that lucky, don't you, mother? Over eighty thousand pounds! I knew, didn't I know I knew? Malabar came in all right. If I ride my horse till I'm sure, then I tell you, Bassett, you can go as high as you like. Did you go for all you were worth, Bassett?"

"I went a thousand on it, Master Paul."

"I never told you, mother, that if I can ride my horse, and *get there*, then I'm absolutely sure—oh, absolutely! Mother, did I ever tell you? I *am* lucky!"

> What is Paul's last statement?

"No, you never did," said his mother.

But the boy died in the night.

And even as he lay dead, his mother heard her brother's voice saying to her: "My God, Hester, you're eighty-odd thousand to the good, and a poor devil of a son to the bad. But, poor devil, he's best gone out of a life where he rides his rocking-horse to find a winner." ■

DÉNOUEMENT
The dénouement presents material left unresolved by the ending of the central conflict. It may also present a commentary on or analysis of the events of the story.

FALLING ACTION
The falling action includes all the events that follow the crisis.

RESOLUTION
At this point in the story, the central conflict is ended, or resolved.

ANSWERS TO GUIDED READING QUESTIONS

1. Paul says to his mother, "I am lucky!"

SELECTION CHECK TEST 4.1.11 WITH ANSWERS

Checking Your Reading

1. What is Paul's mother like? **She is cold and distant.**
2. What unspoken phrase haunts the house? **There must be more money!**
3. What secret knowledge does Paul have? **He knows which horse will win.**
4. What birthday present does Paul arrange for his mother? **He arranges for her to receive $1,000 a year on her birthday for five years.**
5. Why does Paul's mother call home during the party? **She is concerned for him.**

Vocabulary in Context

Fill in each blank with the most appropriate word from these Words for Everyday Use. You may have to change the tense of the word.

stealth remonstrate career parry obscure uncanny

1. My uncle always **parries** when my aunt asks what he wants to do for vacation.
2. The Amazing Kreskin has an **uncanny** ability to predict the future.
3. That gallery specializes in the work of **obscure** artists.
4. The 3-D movie made it seem like I was in the car **careering** through the race course.
5. As soon as his mom's light went out, Ray moved with **stealth** to turn the TV back on.

Literary Tools

Fill in the blanks using the following terms. You may not use every term, and you may use some terms more than once. Make the most specific choice for each statement.

conflict foreshadowing climax crisis resolution denouement exposition

1. The **exposition** introduces the central characters, the setting, and the situation.
2. The **denouement** presents material left unresolved after the central struggle is over.

SELECTION CHECK TEST 4.1.11 WITH ANSWERS (CONT.)

3. The **conflict** is the struggle at the center of the work.
4. The use of **foreshadowing** gives hints about what is to come in the story.
5. The **inciting incident** introduces the central struggle.

RESPOND TO THE SELECTION

Students may suggest that this story presents several clear morals: people shouldn't become obsessed with money; money doesn't buy happiness; and children need unconditional love and support and should not be forced to take on adult burdens.

ANSWERS FOR INVESTIGATE, INQUIRE AND IMAGINE

Recall

1a. The house is haunted by the phrase, "There must be more money!"

2a. Paul learns the winning horse by riding his rocking-horse. To gain this knowledge, he must become obsessed with horse-betting.

3a. When the mother learns that she is to receive an annual sum, she asks for the whole amount immediately and spends it all.

Interpret

1b. The family may have too little money because the parents are not accomplished at anything (page 000: "[The mother] racked her brains . . . but could not find anything successful . . . The father . . . seemed as if he never would be able to do anything worth doing"); or because they gamble (page 000: "My family has been a gambling family, and you won't know until you grow up how much damage it has done"); or because they are overly concerned with keeping up appearances (page 000: "The father . . . was always very handsome and expensive in his tastes . . . and her tastes were just as expensive").

2b. To get to where the luck is, Paul must ride himself into a frenzied trance. Doing so eventually kills him.

3b. The real problem may be that the parents have expensive tastes, that one or both of them have a gambling problem, or that they are incapable of being happy with what they have.

Analyze

4a. Paul keeps his betting partnership with Bassett and Uncle Oliver secret from his mother and he keeps the method of learning the winners—by riding his rocking horse—secret even from Bassett and Oliver. Paul is also desperate to keep secret from

Continued on page 45

Respond *to the* SELECTION

What do you think would be the moral of this story?

INVESTIGATE, Inquire, *Imagine*

Recall: GATHERING FACTS →

1a. What "unspoken phrase" does the house come "to be haunted by"?

2a. How does Paul come to know that a horse will win a particular race? What does he have to do to gain this knowledge?

3a. What happens as a result of Paul's winning the ten thousand and arranging to have half of it sent to his mother?

Interpret: FINDING MEANING

1b. Why do the mother and father in this story have too little money? What hints are provided in the story to explain their continual need for money?

2b. What is the cost, to Paul, of getting to where the luck is?

3b. Receiving the five thousand pounds does not solve Paul's mother's problem. What point is Lawrence making here? What is the real problem in the household?

Analyze: TAKING THINGS APART →

4a. The images of whispering and keeping secrets run throughout "The Rocking Horse Winner." Identify the secrets kept by the Mother and by Paul in this story.

Synthesize: BRINGING THINGS TOGETHER

4b. How would you characterize Paul's relationship with his mother? He says he does the horse betting for his mother. Why would a small child want so desperately to get more money? Paul's frenzied rides on his rocking horse are examples of the use of magical realism in this story. In magical realism, fantastical or supernatural elements are treated as though they are realistic and often symbolize something else. What do you think Paul's rides symbolize?

Evaluate: MAKING JUDGMENTS →

5a. Paul believes that he is lucky, while his mother says that she and her husband are poor because they are not lucky. Evaluate these ideas about luck. Do you agree that Paul is lucky? Why, or why not? Do you agree that having enough money is a matter of luck? Why, or why not? What role does luck play in an individual's success or happiness?

Extend: CONNECTING IDEAS

5b. Paul's mother, like D.H. Lawrence's mother, struggled to keep up appearances and live in a style that required more money than the family had. Our modern phrase, "keeping up with the Joneses" would indicate that this struggle is still a problem in our society. In what ways have you seen this kind of struggle cause harm?

Understanding *Literature*

Conflict. Review the definition of **conflict** in the Handbook of Literary Terms. What is the central conflict in "The Rocking Horse Winner?" Is it an internal conflict or an external conflict?

Plot. Review the definitions of **plot** and its elements in the Handbook of Literary Terms. Then draw the following diagram, called a Freytag's Pyramid, and identify the elements of the plot of "The Rocking-Horse Winner."

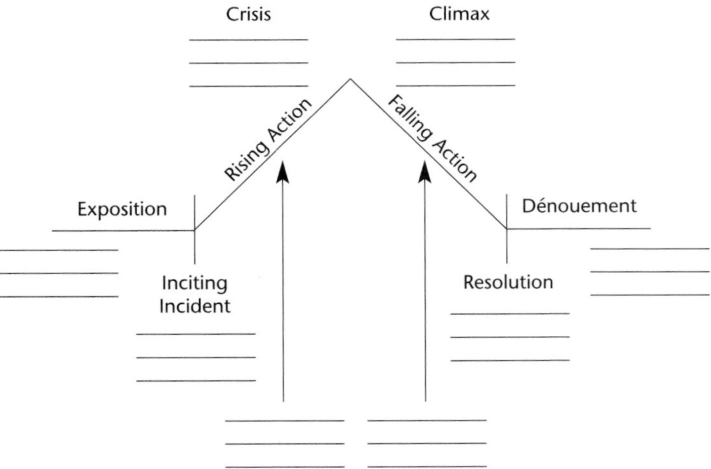

Foreshadowing. Review the definition of **foreshadowing** in the Handbook of Literary Terms. In addition to the passage in which we learn of Paul's frailty and his mother's uneasiness about him, there are other descriptive passages about Paul that foreshadow his final, crazed ride and his destruction. What are some of those descriptive passages?

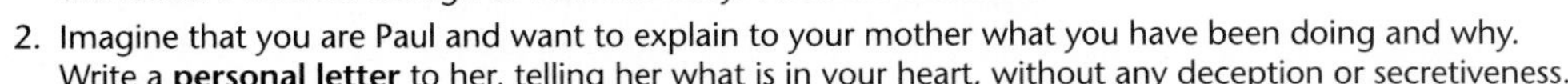

Writer's Journal

1. Imagine that you are a newspaper editor. In a local race, an unknown horse named "Daffodil" has won. One of your reporters has written a story about the race, and you must write the headline, a few short words that convey the main subject and that engage the reader's interest enough to read the story. Write the **headline**.
2. Imagine that you are Paul and want to explain to your mother what you have been doing and why. Write a **personal letter** to her, telling her what is in your heart, without any deception or secretiveness.
3. Imagine you are a newspaper reporter assigned to write an account of the strange death of young Paul. As the reporter, you have interviewed Bassett, Uncle Oliver, and the boy's mother. From having read "The Rocking-Horse Winner," infer what they might have been willing to tell you. Then write your **newspaper article** about the death of Paul.

Answers for Understanding Literature

Conflict. The central conflict involves the fact that the family does not have enough money to live in style. The struggle to keep up the style of living caused anxiety in house. Paul's conflict is a struggle to get luck and, thereby, get money and stop the whispering and anxiety in the house.

Plot. Exposition: Pages 31–32 relate facts about the family's money problems, their lack of communication, and the secret whispering.
Inciting incident: Paul questions his mother about their money problems and luck (page 32).
Rising action: Paul attempts to find luck; Uncle Oscar discovers that Paul has been wagering on horse races;

Continued on page 46

Answers for Investigate, Inquire and Imagine
(cont. from page 44)

his mother the fact that he is the one who has given her the 5,000 pounds. His mother keeps secret the fact that her heart is cold and that she cannot love anyone. She senses that her children know this, but she does her best to act anxious and concerned for them to keep up appearances and look like a good mother to those around her. She is also keeping secret from the society around her the true nature of her financial condition. Her desperate struggle for more money is necessary to continue to live beyond her means and not let others know they are poor.

Synthesize

4b. The relationship between the two is distant and cold, fraught with deceptions and secrets. Student responses will vary as to what Paul's rides may symbolize. One possibility is that his desperate efforts to get "luck" and money symbolize his desperate need to please his cold mother, gain her love, and put an end to the terrible anxiety in the household.

Evaluate

5a. Paul may be said to be lucky because he is able to predict the winners of races, but he is also quite unlucky in having a family so troubled by obsession with getting more money and in having a mother who cannot love him. He dies as a result of his desperate struggle to get more money. His mother and father seem to be more accurately described as greedy and lacking ambition and industriousness than unlucky. They seem to drift in and out of attempts to earn money while they furiously spend all that they have and more. Student responses on the role luck plays in an individual's success and happiness will vary. Many will believe that hard work and persistence are more important. As we see in the story, Paul's luck does not bring him happiness.

Extend

5b. *Responses will vary.*

ANSWERS FOR UNDERSTANDING LITERATURE (CONT. FROM PAGE 45)

they conspire; using Paul's winnings, they arrange for money to be paid to Paul's mother.
Climax: Paul discovers the name of the Derby winner and screams, "It's Malabar! It's Malabar!"
Crisis: Paul collapses off the horse.
Falling action: Paul's mother asks what he means; Oscar bets on Malabar; Paul's illness progresses.
Resolution: Bassett reports that Paul has won over seventy thousand pounds sterling.
Dénouement: Paul proudly tells his mother that he is lucky, and she does not recall their earlier conversation; Paul dies; Oscar says that Paul is better off.

FORESHADOWING. There are many descriptions of Paul's eyes which foreshadow a descent into a kind of madness and ultimate destruction: p. 33: "his eyes had a strange glare in them"; p. 33: "a blue glare from his big, rather close set eyes"; p. 35: "His eyes were blue with fire"; p. 35 "eyes blazing"; p. 37: "big blue eyes, that had an uncanny cold fire in them"; p. 38: "He became wild-eyed and strange, as if something were going to explode . . . in him"; p. 38: "his big blue eyes blazing with a sort of madness."

ANSWERS TO INTEGRATING THE LANGUAGE ARTS

Language, Grammar and Style

1. Wanting to please his mother, Paul rode his rocking horse frantically to get to where the luck is.
2. Paul's last big win, Malabar, earned him over seventy thousand pounds.
3. Hester spent huge sums of money on clothing, furniture, jewelry, and parties.
4. Bassett enjoyed his day at the track, consuming huge quantities of fish and chips, popcorn, and beer.
5. Paul's mother was dreadfully afraid of having to give up her lavish lifestyle, and Paul wanted very much to ease her anxiety and please her.

Speaking and Listening
Refer students to the Language Arts Survey 4.21, "Participating in a Debate." Remind students that regardless of their personal opinions, they should do their best to support their position. Remind them that this exercise is an opportunity to research a controversial issue and argue one position rather than a forum for personal expression.

Integrating *the* Language Arts

Language, Grammar, and Style

COMMA USAGE. Review Language Arts Survey 3.87, "Commas." Then insert appropriate commas in the following sentences.

1. Wanting to please his mother Paul rode his rocking horse frantically to get to where the luck is.
2. Paul's last big win Malabar earned him over seventy thousand pounds.
3. Hester spent huge sums of money on clothing furniture jewelry and parties.
4. Bassett enjoyed his day at the track consuming huge quantities of fish and chips popcorn and beer.
5. Paul's mother was dreadfully afraid of having to give up her lavish lifestyle and Paul wanted very much to ease her anxiety and please her.

Speaking and Listening

DEBATE. Many states have established lotteries instead of raising taxes. Some people believe that state-sponsored lotteries are bad because low-income people spend money they cannot afford on the extremely unlikely chance that they might become rich. Others think that lotteries are good because they keep down taxes and give everyone a chance to achieve "the American dream." Working in two teams of three students each, debate the following proposition: *States should end their lotteries.* Each team should take either a pro or con position and research the facts available to support their position, using library or internet resources, interviews with sociologists, government officials, or other experts. For your position, you may wish to include moral grounds that cannot be traced to fact, but you should identify these arguments as such. In preparation for the actual debate, you may find it helpful to prepare a Pro and Con Chart outlining your arguments and those you believe your opponent will make. See Language Arts Survey 2.21, "Pro and Con Charts," for reference.

Study and Research

RESEARCHING AN AUTHOR. Research the life of D.H. Lawrence, with particular attention to his childhood and his relationship with his mother. You will find much written about Lawrence in the library. What was his childhood like? How might his childhood have influenced his writing of this story? Share your findings with your class.

ANSWERS TO INTEGRATING THE LANGUAGE ARTS (CONT.)

Study and Research
Inform students that a great place to start is general encyclopedias and literary encyclopedias as well as the Internet. Students should, however, branch out to examine deeper sources such as biographies.

Drama

A **drama** is a performance of a story by actors who take the parts of the characters. The origins of drama are mysterious, though in cultures around the globe, early peoples often enacted scenes as part of rites or celebrations having to do with hunting, warfare, religion, or passage from one stage of life into another.

In the Western world, drama originated in ancient Greece. The earliest Greek dramas may have arisen as ritual enactments of sacrifices made to the gods. In fact, the Greek word *tragoidia,* from which our word *tragedy* derives, meant "song of the goats." According to one theory, people in ancient Greece would come together to sacrifice an animal to win a god's favor. Eventually, that sacrifice developed into an elaborate ritual involving one actor, the priest, and a chorus with whom the priest interacted. In the fifth century BC, the Greek playwright Aeschylus added a second actor, and drama as we know it was born. Drama became another vehicle, like poetry, for telling stories. In classical times, dramas were performed in open- air amphitheaters, or **arena stages.**

Early Greek dramas were of two major kinds: comedy and tragedy. A **comedy,** in its original sense, was any work with a happy ending. The term is widely used today to refer to any humorous work, especially one prepared for the stage or the screen. A **tragedy** initially was a drama that told the story of the fall of a person of high status.

The earliest English drama, that of the Middle Ages, can be divided into three kinds: **mystery plays** presented stories from the Bible; **miracle plays** told stories from the lives of saints; **morality plays** presented stories containing abstract virtues and vices as characters. These plays were commonly performed on wagons, with the audience gathered around.

With the coming of the Renaissance and the rebirth of classical learning, playwrights in England began to create five-act plays based on Roman models. The latter half of the sixteenth century and the beginning of the seventeenth saw the greatest flowering of theatrical invention in English history, the period of **Elizabethan and Jacobean Drama.** William Shakespeare, Christopher Marlowe, and Ben Jonson were among the many talented playwrights of the time. A play of this period typically was produced on a **thrust stage,** which jutted into an area open to the sky.

The highlight of eighteenth-century drama was the so-called **Restoration Comedy,** which dealt satirically with social mores. Early-to-mid-nineteenth-century theater tended toward **melodrama,** which presented exaggerated and sentimental characters and scenes. The late nineteenth century saw the emergence of **Realist Theater,** with its social and political commentary and profound explorations of the psychology of characters. In the nineteenth and twentieth centuries, the **proscenium stage,** or **picture stage,** with three walls and a removed "fourth wall," replaced the thrust stage in most Western theater.

ADDITIONAL RESOURCES

UNIT 1 RESOURCE BOOK
- Selection Check Test 4.1.13
- Selection Test 4.1.14

ART NOTE

(Alice) Ellen Terry (1847–1928) was one of the most popular British stage performers of the last quarter of the nineteenth century. She is also noted for a magnificent series of letters to the playwright Bernard Shaw (a biography of Shaw appears on page 986). She was trained as an actress by her parents and began performing professionally at the age of nine. She gave notable performances in the major Shakespearean roles. Terry was knighted in 1925. Her former home is now the Ellen Terry Memorial Museum. She is the subject of many biographies, including *Bernhardt, Terry, Duse: The Actress in Her Time* (1988).

John Singer Sargent's (1856–1925) portraits of noted personalities and of American and European aristocrats serve as a visual record of the Edwardian age. His first Parisian exhibit caused a scandal, so he moved to London, where his work was also poorly regarded, earning him an award for worst painting of the year. Then, in 1887, he achieved his first popular success since his school days. He is today regarded as one of the finest painters of the early Modern Era.

Ellen Terry as Lady Macbeth. 1889. John Singer Sargent. Tate Gallery, London.

Elements of Drama

The Playwright and the Script

Playwright. The author of a play is the **playwright.** The relationship between a playwright and the play is more tenuous than that of an ordinary author to his or her text. Novelists or poets have enormous control over the form in which their work will be presented to its audience, the reader. Playwrights, in contrast, must depend upon the interpretations given their work by producers, directors, set designers, actors, and other persons involved in producing the work for the stage. The playwright's art is collaborative.

Script. A **script** is the written work from which a drama is produced. It contains stage directions and dialogue and may be divided into acts and scenes.

Stage Directions. **Stage directions** are notes provided by the playwright to describe how something should be presented or performed on the stage. Stage directions often describe elements of the **spectacle,** such as lighting, music, sound effects, costumes, properties, and set design. They also may describe entrances and exits, the movements of characters, facial expressions, gestures, body language, tone of voice, or other elements related to the acting of the play. Sometimes, especially in reading versions of plays, stage directions provide historical or background information. Stage directions usually are printed in italics and enclosed in brackets or parentheses. In stage directions, the parts of the stage are often described using the terms *up, down, right, left,* and *center,* which describe stage areas from the point of view of the actors.

Stage Areas

Up Right	Up Center	Up Left
Right Center	Center	Left Center
Down Right	Down Center	Down Left

Dialogue. **Dialogue** is the term used to describe the speech of actors in a play. The dialogue usually consists of the characters' names and the words and other utterances spoken by the actors. The dialogue of a play may contain **monologues,** or long speeches given by actors. A speech given by a lone character on stage is called a **soliloquy.** A statement intended to be heard by the audience or by a single other character but not by other characters on the stage is called an **aside.**

Literary Technique

Stage Directions. The stage directions *up* and *down* are used because some stages are "raked." In other words, they actually slope down toward the audience, allowing more of the audience a better view.

Cross-Curricular Activities

Applied Arts. If your school has a stage or if there is a stage nearby, challenge students to determine the absolute slope of the stage, the absolute slope of the floor, and their relative slope (angle of incidence). What other features unique of stage or auditorium design and construction can they notice?

For background, students might refer to the introduction to Unit 5, which describes the development of English theater through the Elizabethan Age.

SELECTION CHECK TEST 4.1.13 WITH ANSWERS

Checking Your Reading

1. What were the two major kinds of Greek drama? **They were tragedy and comedy.**
2. Where were dramas performed in classical times? **They were performed in open-air amphitheaters, also called arena stages.**
3. What kinds of stories did mystery plays portray? **They portrayed Biblical stories.**
4. What is a melodrama? **It is a play with exaggerated characters and scenes.**
5. What does a proscenium stage look like? **It is a modern stage, with three walls.**

Elements of Drama: The Playwright and the Script
True or False

1. An actor who moves toward the audience is walking upstage. **F**
2. Stage directions may describe gestures, costumes, or background information. **T**
3. Plays may be divided into acts, which may be divided into scenes. **T**
4. A playwright has more control over his work than a novelist or a poet. **F**
5. A character alone on a stage may deliver a soliloquy. **T**

Elements of Drama: The Spectacle
Match each element with the items it includes.

1. properties **C**
2. spectacle **F**
3. sound effects **D**
4. script **G**
5. set **B**

a. an arch around a removed "fourth wall"
b. walls, furniture, painted backdrops
c. books, gavels, swords, handbags
d. thunder, ringing telephone, howling dogs, gunfire
e. up center, down right, up left
f. lights, curtains, costumes, makeup, set, actors
g. stage directions, dialogue, acts, scenes

Acts and Scenes. An **act** is a major division of a drama. Plays of the Elizabethan and Jacobean periods in English drama usually are divided into **five acts.** In the modern era, **three-act** and **one-act plays** are quite common. The acts may be divided into scenes. Typically, a **scene** begins with the entrance of one or more characters and ends with the exit of one or more characters. The time and place of acts or scenes may change from one to the next.

The Spectacle

Spectacle. The **spectacle** is all the elements of the drama presented to the senses of the audience—the lights, sets, curtains, costumes, make-up, music, sound effects, properties, and movements of the actors, including any special movement such as pantomime or dance. Spectacle is one major feature that differentiates dramatic from nondramatic works. The following chart describes common parts of the spectacle.

ELEMENT OF SPECTACLE	DESCRIPTION
Stage	This is the area in which the action is performed. An **arena stage,** or **theater in the round,** is one in which the audience stands or sits around a circular or semicircular open space. A **thrust stage** is one that extends into the audience, which is situated on three sides of the playing area. A **proscenium,** or **picture stage,** is one that has an arch around an opening that acts as a removed "fourth wall."
Set	The set is everything placed upon the stage to give the impression of a particular setting, or time and place. Sets often include walls, furnishings, and painted backdrops.
Properties	Properties are items that can be carried on and off the stage by actors or manipulated by actors during scenes. Examples of properties include swords, torches, and umbrellas.
Sound Effects	These are sounds introduced to create mood or to indicate the presence of something. Common sound effects include rain, ringing telephones, and police sirens.
Blocking	This is the act of determining how actors will move on a stage. Blocking is almost always done by the director of the play.

"The Rising of the Moon"

BY LADY AUGUSTA GREGORY

About the Author

The literary career of **Lady Augusta Gregory** (1852–1932) began in 1892 when her husband died. Prior to that time she had been a patron of Irish literature, subsidizing writers such as W. B. Yeats, John Synge, and James Joyce. Wanting to revive the Irish literary heritage, which had been in a torpor since the English conquest, she did so in a number of ways. With Yeats and Edward Martyn Lady Gregory founded the Abbey Theatre, a spur to the Irish national movement. She also collected traditional Celtic tales and folklore in such works as *Cuchulain of Muirthemne* and *Gods and Fighting Men.* Perhaps most importantly, with her own dramatic writings she founded modern Irish dialect literature. Productions of her plays drew capacity audiences. Lady Gregory lived to see the establishment of the Irish Free State in 1922.

About the Selection

"The Rising of the Moon" was a ballad popular with Irish rebel nationalists. Part of the ballad is sung on page 53. Written in 1907, this one-act play reflects the time when all of Ireland was under British rule, with the Irish Nationalist Movement struggling for independence. Today, most of Ireland is independent though Northern Ireland remains part of the United Kingdom and is occupied by the British. However, the Catholic minority in Northern Ireland continues to seek independence from England and wants to join the Irish Free State. Peace talks have long been underway and people are anxious to find a solution that will put an end to this 500-year-old conflict.

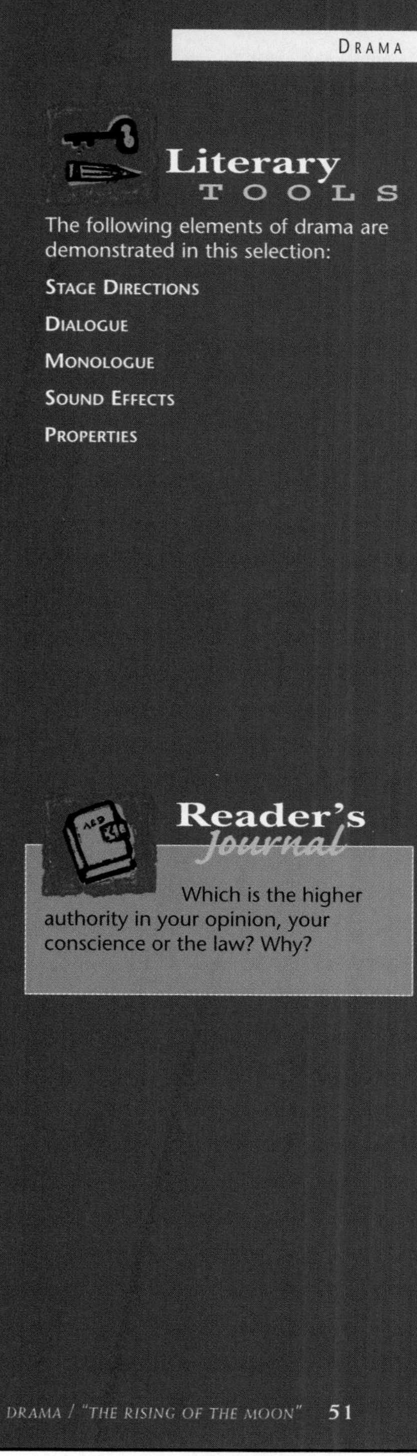

Literary Tools

The following elements of drama are demonstrated in this selection:

STAGE DIRECTIONS

DIALOGUE

MONOLOGUE

SOUND EFFECTS

PROPERTIES

Reader's Journal

Which is the higher authority in your opinion, your conscience or the law? Why?

ADDITIONAL RESOURCES

UNIT 1 RESOURCE BOOK
- Selection Worksheet 1.4
- Selection Check Test 4.1.15
- Selection Test 4.1.16
- Language, Grammar, and Style Resource 3.5

INDIVIDUAL LEARNING STRATEGIES

MOTIVATION
Encourage students to put on a class performance of "The Rising of the Moon." They can begin planning the performance by assigning students to the roles of director, actors, set designer, properties manager, costume designer, stage manager, and so forth just as they begin the selection to peak their interest. After students complete the lessons and activities involved with the selection, encourage them to rehearse their version of the play and deliver it for another English class.

READING PROFICIENCY
Play the Audio Library selection to help students understand the play. Some students may have extra trouble reading a play because of unfamiliarity with dramatic conventions. Carefully explain stage directions and dialogue to these students. Then have them read or study the play in groups of four, with each person taking the part of one character.

ENGLISH LANGUAGE LEARNING
This play is written in a dialect of Irish English. Point out to students nonstandard expressions and explain that these expressions do not exemplify standard English. One recurring regionalism in the story is the use of *It's* to begin a sentence—e.g., "It's he makes" (He makes); "It's little chance we'd have" (We'd have little chance). Explain that students should ignore this word if they have trouble understanding a sentence.

Continued on page 52

GOALS/OBJECTIVES

Studying this lesson will enable students to
- appreciate a drama that is read rather than witnessed on stage or in film
- briefly explain who Lady Augustus Gregory was and summarize her place in the dramatic tradition
- name and describe the main elements of drama (playwright, script, stage directions, dialogue, stage, set, properties, sound effects, and blocking)
- research the Irish Nationalist movement
- rewrite dialect into the dialect of another place and time
- use a map to locate places in Ireland

READER'S JOURNAL

Encourage students to discuss nonviolent and positive ways of effecting change when their conscience and the law differs.

ANSWERS TO GUIDED READING QUESTIONS

1. It is important to watch the flight of steps because they lead down to the water, where a boat could pick up the escaping fugitive.
2. One hundred pounds is the reward.

CROSS-CURRICULAR ACTIVITIES

Applied Arts. Have students identify the properties carried onto the stage at the beginning of the play (a pastepot and a bundle of placards). You may wish to have students design sets for the play by working on a stage diagram like the one provided on page 46.

VOCABULARY FROM THE SELECTION

quay

INDIVIDUAL LEARNING STRATEGIES (cont. from page 51)

Encourage students to ask about any words or expressions they do not understand.

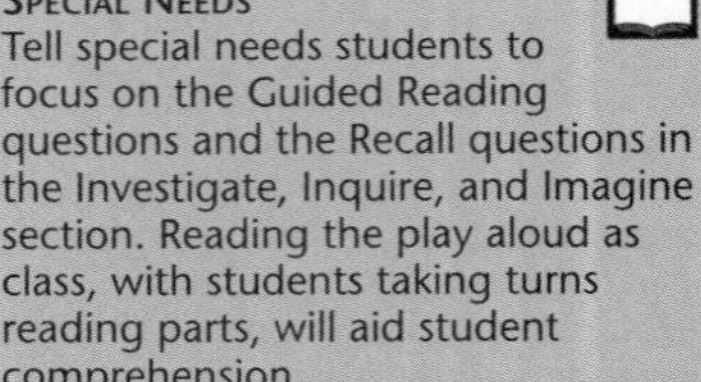

Special Needs
Tell special needs students to focus on the Guided Reading questions and the Recall questions in the Investigate, Inquire, and Imagine section. Reading the play aloud as class, with students taking turns reading parts, will aid student comprehension.

Enrichment
Have students prepare blocking diagrams for the play. Students interested in another treatment in drama of the Irish nationalist movement might read W. B. Yeats's *Cathleen Ni Houlihan.* In Yeats's play, a beautiful woman, symbolizing, perhaps, the attractiveness of patriotism and glory, goes from door to door luring young men to join the rebellion. However, the woman turns out to be a hag, symbolizing, perhaps, the actual consequences of going to war.

The Rising of the Moon

LADY AUGUSTA GREGORY

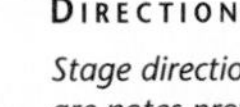

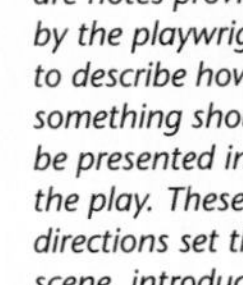

STAGE DIRECTIONS
Stage directions are notes provided by the playwright to describe how something should be presented in the play. These directions set the scene, introduce the characters, and describe the characters' actions.

DIALOGUE
The names of the characters are given, followed by the words that they speak.

PERSONS

SERGEANT.
POLICEMAN X.
POLICEMAN B.
A RAGGED MAN.

SCENE

Side of a quay in a seaport town. Some posts and chains. A large barrel. Enter three policemen. Moonlight.

(**SERGEANT,** *who is older than the others, crosses the stage to right and looks down steps. The others put down a pastepot and unroll a bundle of placards.*)

POLICEMAN B. I think this would be a good place to put up a notice. (*He points to barrel.*)

POLICEMAN X. Better ask him. (*calls to* **SERGEANT**) Will this be a good place for a placard?

(*no answer*)

POLICEMAN B. Will we put up a notice here on the barrel?

(*no answer*)

SERGEANT. There's a flight of steps here that leads to the water. This is a place that should be minded well. If he got down here, his friends might have a boat to meet him; they might send it in here from outside.

Why is the flight of steps an important place to watch?

POLICEMAN B. Would the barrel be a good place to put a notice up?

SERGEANT. It might; you can put it there.

(*They paste the notice up.*)

SERGEANT. (*reading it*) Dark hair—dark eyes, smooth face, height five feet five—there's not much to take hold of in that—It's a pity I had no chance of seeing him before he broke out of gaol.[1] They say he's a wonder, that it's he makes all the plans for the whole organization. There isn't another man in Ireland would have broken gaol the way he did. He must have some friends among the gaolers.

POLICEMAN B. A hundred pounds is little enough for the Government to offer for him. You may be

What is the reward if the fugitive is caught?

1. **gaol.** British spelling of *jail*

WORDS FOR EVERYDAY USE
quay (kē) *n.,* wharf. *The fishing boat docked at the quay to unload two tons of fish.*

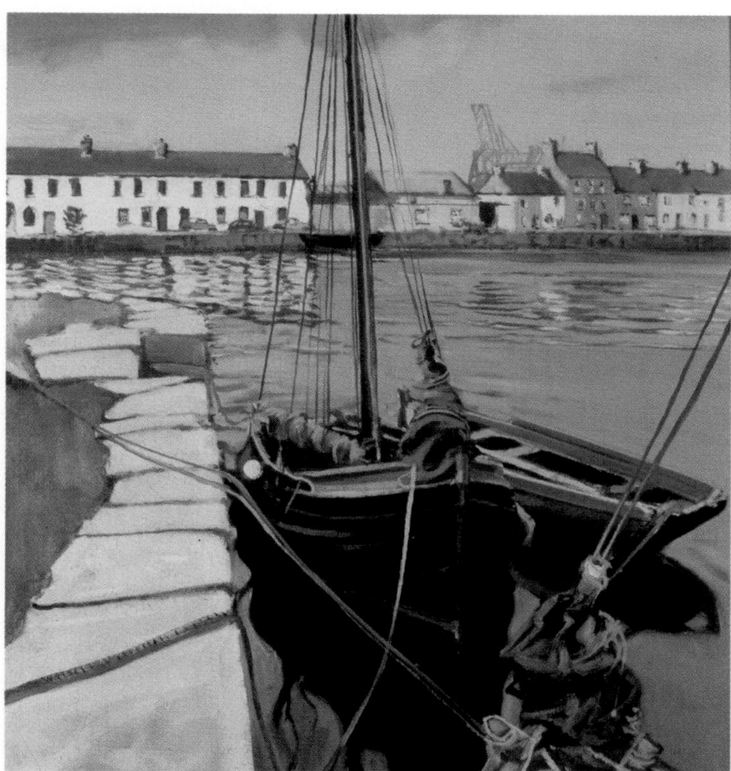

Long Walk from Claddagh, Galway, c.1900s. Cecil Maguire. Taylor Gallery, London.

sure any man in the force that takes him will get promotion.

SERGEANT. I'll mind this place myself. I wouldn't wonder at all if he came this way. He might come slipping along there (*points to side of quay*), and his friends might be waiting for him there (*points down steps*), and once he got away it's little chance we'd have of finding him; it's maybe under a load of kelp he'd be in a fishing boat, and not one to help a married man that wants it to the reward.

POLICEMAN X. And if we get him itself, nothing but abuse on our heads for it from the people, and maybe from our own relations.

SERGEANT. Well, we have to do our duty in the force. Haven't we the whole country depending on us to keep law and order? It's those that are down would be up and those that are up would be down, if it wasn't for us. Well, hurry on, you have plenty of other places to placard yet, and come back here then to me. You can take the lantern. Don't be too long now. It's very lonesome here with nothing but the moon.

What would happen to the social order if not for the police?

POLICEMAN B. It's a pity we can't stop with you. The Government should have

ANSWER TO GUIDED READING QUESTION

1. According to the Sergeant, those that are up would be down and those that are down would be up if it were not for the police.

CROSS-CURRICULAR ACTIVITIES

ARTS AND HUMANITIES. Encourage students to find images of the Irish landscape. Students might find such works in art books featuring the works of landscape painters or they might search for photographs (a good source would be magazines or brochures advertising travel in Ireland). Have students share the images they find with others in the class, so students will be able to visualize the land for which Irish Nationalists and the British clashed.

ANSWER TO GUIDED READING QUESTION

1. The man wants to go down the steps.

LITERARY TECHNIQUE

Dialect. A **dialect** is a version of a language spoken by the people of a particular place, time, or social group. Have students identify the dialectical elements of the Man's speech, beginning with "I'll just sit on the top" and ending with "that's a lovely song." Students might identify these elements by doing a line-by-line translation into their own dialect or into standard English.

BIBLIOGRAPHIC NOTE

Works by Lady Augusta Gregory

Gregory, Augusta. *Collected Plays.* Ed. Ann Saddlemyer. 1970.

Gods and Fighting Men: The Story of the Tuatha de Danaan and of the Fianna of Ireland. Ed. T. R. Henn and C. Smythe. 1903, *Lady Gregory's Journals.* Ed. T. R. Henn and C. Smythe. 1946, *Seventy Years: Being the Autobiography of Lady Gregory.* Ed. Colin Smythe. 1974.

Additional Readings

Coxhead, Elizabeth. *Daughters of Erin: Five Women of the Irish Renascence.* 1965, *J. M. Synge and Lady Gregory.* 1962, *Lady Gregory: A Literary Portrait.* 1966.

Hopper, Edward. *Lady Isabella Persse Gregory.* 1976.

Mikhail, E. H. *Lady Gregory: An Annotated Bibliography of Criticism.* 1982, *Lady Gregory: Interviews and Recollections.* 1977.

brought more police into the town, with *him* in gaol, and at assize[2] time too. Well, good luck to your watch.

(*They go out.*)

Sergeant. (*walks up and down once or twice and looks at placard*) A hundred pounds and promotion sure. There must be a great deal of spending in a hundred pounds. It's a pity some honest man not to be better of that.[3]

(**A Ragged Man** *appears at left and tries to slip past.* **Sergeant** *suddenly turns.*)

Sergeant. Where are you going?

Man. I'm a poor ballad-singer, your honor. I thought to sell some of these (*holds out bundle of ballads*) to the sailors.

(*He goes on.*)

Sergeant. Stop! Didn't I tell you to stop? You can't go on there.

Man. Oh, very well. It's a hard thing to be poor. All the world's against the poor!

Sergeant. Who are you?

Man. You'd be as wise as myself if I told you, but I don't mind. I'm one Jimmy Walsh, a ballad-singer.

Sergeant. Jimmy Walsh? I don't know that name.

Man. Ah, sure, they know it well enough in Ennis.[4] Were you ever in Ennis, sergeant?

Sergeant. What brought you here?

Man. Sure, it's to the assizes I came, thinking I might make a few shillings here or there. It's in the one train with the judges I came.

Sergeant. Well, if you came so far, you may as well go farther, for you'll walk out of this.

Man. I will, I will; I'll just go on where I was going.

Where does the man want to go?

(*goes towards steps*)

Sergeant. Come back from those steps; no one has leave to pass down them tonight.

Man. I'll just sit on the top of the steps till I see will some sailor buy a ballad off me that would give me my supper. They do be late going back to the ship. It's often I saw them in Cork[5] carried down the quay in a hand-cart.

Sergeant. Move on, I tell you. I won't have any one lingering about the quay tonight.

Man. Well, I'll go. It's the poor have the hard life! Maybe yourself might like one, sergeant. Here's a good sheet now. (*turns one over*) "Content and a pipe"—that's not much. "The Peeler and the goat"—you wouldn't like that. "Johnny Hart"—that's a lovely song.

Sergeant. Move on.

Man. Ah, wait till you hear it. (*sings*)

There was a rich farmer's daughter
 lived near the town of Ross;
She courted a Highland soldier, his
 name was Johnny Hart;
Says the mother to her daughter, "I'll
 go distracted mad
If you marry that Highland soldier
 dressed up in Highland plaid."

Sergeant. Stop that noise.

(**Man** *wraps up his ballads and shuffles towards the steps.*)

Sergeant. Where are you going?

Man. Sure you told me to be going, and I am going.

Sergeant. Don't be a fool. I didn't tell you to go that way; I told you to go back to the town.

2. **assize.** Periodic court sessions held in each county
3. It's a pity some honest man doesn't benefit from the money.
4. **Ennis.** A town in County Clare, Ireland
5. **Cork.** A county in southern Ireland

MAN. Back to the town, is it?

SERGEANT. (*taking him by the shoulder and shoving him before him*) Here, I'll show you the way. Be off with you. What are you stopping for?

MAN. (*who has been keeping his eye on the notice, points to it*) I think I know what you're waiting for, Sergeant.

SERGEANT. What's that to you?

MAN. And I know well the man you're waiting for—I know him well—I'll be going.

(*He shuffles on.*)

SERGEANT. You know him? Come back here. What sort is he?

Why does the Sergeant call the man back?

MAN. Come back is it, sergeant? Do you want to have me killed?

SERGEANT. Why do you say that?

MAN. Never mind. I'm going. I wouldn't be in your shoes if the reward was ten times as much. (*goes on off stage to left*) Not if it was ten times as much.

SERGEANT. (*rushing after him*) Come back here, come back. (*drags him back*) What sort is he? Where did you see him?

MAN. I saw him in my own place, in the County Clare. I tell you you wouldn't like to be looking at him. You'd be afraid to be in the one place with him. There isn't a weapon he doesn't know the use of, and as to strength, his muscles are as hard as that board (*slaps barrel*).

SERGEANT. Is he as bad as that?

MAN. He is then.

SERGEANT. Do you tell me so?

MAN. There was a poor man in our place, a sergeant from Ballyvaughan.[6]—It was with a lump of stone he did it.

SERGEANT. I never heard of that.

MAN. And you wouldn't, sergeant. It's not everything that happens gets into the papers. And there was a policeman in plain clothes, too. . . . It is in Limerick he was. . . . It was after the time of the attack on the police barrack at Kilmallock[7]. . . Moonlight . . . just like this . . . waterside. . . . Nothing was known for certain.

SERGEANT. Do you say so? It's a terrible county to belong to.

MAN. That's so, indeed! You might be standing there, looking out that way, thinking you saw him coming up this side of the quay (*points*), and he might be coming up this other side (*points*), and he'd be on you before you knew where you were.

> "There isn't a weapon he doesn't know the use of, and as to strength, his muscles are as hard as that board."

SERGEANT. It's a whole troop of police they ought to put here to stop a man like that.

MAN. But if you'd like me to stop with you, I could be looking down this side. I could be sitting up here on this barrel.

Why does the sergeant allow the man to stay?

SERGEANT. And you know him well, too?

MAN. I'd know him a mile off, sergeant.

SERGEANT. But you wouldn't want to share the reward?

MAN. Is it a poor man like me, that has to be going the roads and singing in fairs,

---

6. **Ballyvaughan.** Another town in County Clare
7. **Limerick . . . Kilmallock.** Kilmallock is a town in the county of Limerick.

ANSWERS TO GUIDED READING QUESTIONS

1. The Sergeant calls the man back because the man says he knows the fugitive.
2. The Sergeant allows the man to stay because he will help the Sergeant spot the fugitive but does not want to share the reward.

CROSS-CURRICULAR CONNECTIONS

HISTORY. In the early nineteenth century, many in the Irish nationalist movement tried to revive the Irish language, which was then spoken only in isolated rural areas. Modern Irish is now spoken primarily in western and southern Ireland and is taught for its historical and cultural value in Irish schools. See Hindley, Reg. *The Death of the Irish Language.* 1990; and O'Rahilly, T. F. *Irish Dialects: Past and Present.* 1988.

ANSWERS TO GUIDED READING QUESTIONS

1. According to the Sergeant, police have a hard life being out at night, in danger, and receiving abuse from the common people rather than thanks. He says they have no choice but to obey their orders.
2. Granuaile (Ireland) is bound with iron bands in the man's song.

CROSS-CURRICULAR CONNECTIONS

HISTORY. The ballad singer uses the word *Granuaile* because, during their rule over/occupation of Ireland, the English enacted laws prohibiting nationalism to the extent of forbidding the use of the word *Ireland.*

BIBLIOGRAPHIC NOTE

Writers of the Irish Revival

Ferguson, Samuel. *Lays of the Western Gael.* 1865.
Hyde, Douglas. *Love Songs of Connacht.* 1893.
O'Casey, Sean. *Juno and the Paycock.* 1925,
The Plough and the Stars. 1926,
The Shadow of a Gunman. 1925.
O'Grady, Standish. *History of Ireland.* 1880.
Synge, John Millington. *The Aran Islands.* 1907, *The Playboy of the Western World.* 1907, *Riders to the Sea.* 1904.

Also see the sections on Shaw (pages 986–1056) and Yeats (pages 840–851).

to have the name on him that he took a reward? But you don't want me. I'll be safer in the town.

SERGEANT. Well, you can stop.

MAN. (*getting up on barrel*) All right, sergeant. I wonder, now, you're not tired out, sergeant, walking up and down the way you are.

SERGEANT. If I'm tired I'm used to it.

MAN. You might have hard work before you tonight yet. Take it easy while you can. There's plenty of room up here on the barrel, and you see farther when you're higher up.

SERGEANT. Maybe so. (*Gets up beside him on barrel, facing right. They sit back to back, looking different ways.*) You made me feel a bit queer with the way you talked.

MAN. Give me a match, sergeant. (*He gives it, and Man lights pipe.*) Take a draw yourself? It'll quiet you. Wait now till I give you a light, but you needn't turn round. Don't take your eye off the quay for the life of you.

What hardships do police suffer, according to the sergeant?

SERGEANT. Never fear, I won't. (*Lights pipe. They both smoke.*) Indeed it's a hard thing to be in the force, out at night and no thanks for it, for all the danger we're in. And it's little we get but abuse from the people, and no choice but to obey our orders, and never asked when a man is sent into danger, if you are a married man with a family.

MAN. (*sings*)—

As through the hills I walked to view
the hills and shamrock plain,
I stood awhile where nature smiles to
view the rocks and streams,
On a matron fair I fixed my eyes
beneath a fertile vale,
And she sang her song: it was on the
wrong of poor old Granuaile.[8]

SERGEANT. Stop that; that's no song to be singing in these times.

MAN. Ah, sergeant, I was only singing to keep my heart up. It sinks when I think of him. To think of us two sitting here, and he creeping up the quay, maybe, to get to us.

SERGEANT. Are you keeping a good lookout?

MAN. I am; and for no reward too. Amn't I the foolish man? But when I saw a man in trouble, I never could help trying to get him out of it. What's that? Did something hit me? (*rubs his heart*)

SERGEANT. (*patting him on the shoulder*) You will get your reward in heaven.

MAN. I know that, I know that, sergeant, but life is precious.

SERGEANT. Well, you can sing if it gives you more courage.

MAN. (*sings*)—

Her head was bare, her hands and feet
with iron bands were bound,
Her pensive strain and plaintive wail
mingles with the evening gale,
And the song she
sang with
mournful air,
I am old
Granuaile.
Her lips so sweet that monarchs
kissed . . .

Who is bound with iron bands, in the man's song?

SERGEANT. That's not it . . . "Her gown she wore was stained with gore. . . ." That's it—you missed that.

MAN. You're right, sergeant, so it is; I missed it. (*repeats line*) But to think of a

8. **Granuaile.** A name for Ireland

man like you knowing a song like that.

SERGEANT. There's many a thing a man might know and might not have any wish for.

MAN. Now, I daresay, sergeant, in your youth, you used to be sitting up on a wall, the way you are sitting up on this barrel now, and the other lads beside you, and you singing "Granuaile"? . . .

SERGEANT. I did then.

What does the sergeant acknowledge doing in his youth?

MAN. And the "Shan Van Vocht"? . . .

SERGEANT. I did then.

MAN. And the "Green on the Cape"?

SERGEANT. That was one of them.

MAN. And maybe the man you are watching for tonight used to be sitting on the wall, when he was young, and singing those same songs. . . . It's a queer world. . . .

SERGEANT. Whisht! . . . I think I see something coming. . . . It's only a dog.

MAN. And isn't it a queer world? . . . Maybe it's one of the boys you used to be singing with that time you will be arresting today or tomorrow, and sending into the dock. . . .

SERGEANT. That's true indeed.

MAN. And maybe one night, after you had been singing, if the other boys had told you some plan they had, some plan to free the country, you might have joined with them . . . and maybe it is you might be in trouble now.

What might the sergeant have done if his friends had suggested it?

SERGEANT. Well, who knows but I might? I had a great spirit in those days.

MAN. It's a queer world, sergeant, and it's little any mother knows when she sees her child creeping on the floor what might happen to it before it has gone through its life, or who will be who in the end.

SERGEANT. That's a queer thought now, and a true thought. Wait now till I think it out. . . . If it wasn't for the sense I have, and for my wife and family, and for me joining the force the time I did, it might be myself now would be after breaking gaol and hiding in the dark, and it might be him that's hiding in the dark and that got out of gaol would be sitting up here where I am on this barrel. . . . And it might be myself would be creeping up trying to make my escape from himself, and it might be himself would be keeping the law, and myself would be breaking it, and myself would be trying to put a bullet in his head, or to take up a lump of stone the way you said he did . . . no, that myself did. . . . Oh! (*gasps . . . after a pause*) What's that? (*grasps man's arm*)

MAN. (*jumps off barrel and listens, looking out over water*) It's nothing, sergeant.

SERGEANT. I thought it might be a boat. I had a notion there might be friends of his coming about the quays with a boat.

MAN. Sergeant, I am thinking it was with

> "And maybe the man you are watching for tonight used to be sitting on the wall, when he was young, and singing those same songs. . . ."

MONOLOGUE

A monologue is an extended speech by one character. This speech illuminates what the sergeant is thinking.

ANSWERS TO GUIDED READING QUESTIONS

1. The Sergeant acknowledges singing nationalist songs, popular with the rebels.
2. The Sergeant says he might have joined in some plan to free Ireland, if his band of friends had gotten involved in one.

LITERARY NOTE

Famous Irish writers in English include William Congreve, author of *The Way of the World*; Jonathan Swift, author of *Gulliver's Travels*; Oliver Goldsmith, author of *The Vicar of Wakefield;* and Oscar Wilde, author of *The Importance of Being Ernest.* Other notable Irish writers include George Farquhar, Maria Edgeworth, Samuel Ferguson, William Allingham, Thomas Moore, W. B. Yeats, John Millington Synge, Sean O'Casey, James Joyce, and Samuel Beckett.

ANSWERS TO GUIDED READING QUESTIONS

1. The people are on one side of the struggle and the law is on the other.
2. The Sergeant and the man hear a whistle from below, at the water.
3. The Sergeant hides the hat and wig worn by the man.

Quotables

"Can we not build up a national literature which shall be none the less Irish in spirit from being English in language?"

—W. B. Yeats

LITERARY TECHNIQUE

Folk Song. A **folk song** is a song composed anonymously and passed from person to person without being recorded or written down for some time. The title of this play comes from the folk song "The Rising of the Moon," two verses of which are sung in the play by the rebel leader. You may wish to locate a recording of this song to play for your students. An excellent recording of this and other songs of Irish Rebellion was done by Tommy Makem and the Clancy Brothers.

the people you were, and not with the law you were, when you were a young man.

Sergeant. Well, if I was foolish then; that time's gone.

Properties
Items like the hat and the wig, ones that are manipulated by actors during scenes, are called properties.

Who is on each side of the struggle?

Man. Maybe, sergeant, it comes into your head sometimes, in spite of your belt and your tunic, that it might have been as well for you to have followed Granuaile.

Sergeant. It's no business of yours what I think.

Man. Maybe, sergeant, you'll be on the side of the country yet.

Sergeant. (*gets off barrel*) Don't talk to me like that. I have my duties and I know them. (*looks round*) That was a boat; I hear the oars. (*Goes to the steps and looks down.*)

Man. (*sings*)—

O, then, tell me, Shawn O'Farrell,
 Where the gathering is to be.
In the old spot by the river
 Right well known to you and me!

Sergeant. Stop that! Stop that, I tell you!

Man. (*sings louder*)—

One word more, for signal token,
 Whistle up the marching tune,
With your pike upon your shoulder,
 At the Rising of the Moon.

Sergeant. If you don't stop that, I'll arrest you.

Sound Effects
Sound effects can indicate the presence of something, in this case the man's friend.

(*A whistle from below answers, repeating the air.*)

What do the sergeant and the man hear?

Sergeant. That's a signal. (*stands between him and steps*) You must not pass this way. . . . Step farther back. . . . Who are you? You are no ballad-singer.

Man. You needn't ask who I am; that placard will tell you. (*points to placard*)

Sergeant. You are the man I am looking for.

Man. (*Takes off hat and wig.* **Sergeant** *seizes them.*) I am. There's a hundred pounds on my head. There is a friend of mine below in a boat. He knows a safe place to bring me to.

> "If he makes his escape it won't be unknown he'll make it."

Sergeant. (*looking still at hat and wig*) It's a pity! It's a pity. You deceived me. You deceived me well.

Man. I am a friend of Granuaile. There is a hundred pounds on my head.

Sergeant. It's a pity, it's a pity!

Man. Will you let me pass, or must I make you let me?

Sergeant. I am in the force. I will not let you pass.

Man. I thought to do it with my tongue. (*puts hand in breast*) What is that?

(*voice of* **Policeman X** *outside*). Here, this is where we left him.

Sergeant. It's my comrades coming.

Man. You won't betray me . . . the friend of Granuaile. (*slips behind barrel*)

(*voice of* **Policeman B**). That was the last of the placards.

Policeman X. (*as they come in*) If he makes his escape it won't be unknown he'll make it.

What does the sergeant hide from his officers?

(**Sergeant** *puts hat and wig behind his back.*)

Policeman B. Did any one come this way?

SERGEANT. (*after a pause*) No one.

POLICEMAN B. No one at all?

SERGEANT. No one at all.

POLICEMAN B. We had no orders to go back to the station; we can stop along with you.

SERGEANT. I don't want you. There is nothing for you to do here.

POLICEMAN B. You bade us to come back here and keep watch with you.

SERGEANT. I'd sooner be alone. Would any man come this way and you making all that talk? It is better the place to be quiet.

POLICEMAN B. Well, we'll leave you the lantern anyhow.

(*hands it to him*)

SERGEANT. I don't want it. Bring it with you.

POLICEMAN B. You might want it. There are clouds coming up and you have the darkness of the night before you yet. I'll leave it over here on the barrel. (*goes to barrel*)

SERGEANT. Bring it with you I tell you. No more talk.

POLICEMAN B. Well, I thought it might be a comfort to you. I often think when I have it in my hand and can be flashing it about into every dark corner (*doing so*) that it's the same as being beside the fire at home, and the bits of bogwood blazing up now and again.

(*flashes it about, now on the barrel, now on* **SERGEANT**)

SERGEANT. (*furious*) Be off the two of you, yourselves and your lantern!

(*They go out.* **MAN** *comes from behind barrel. He and* **SERGEANT** *stand looking at one another.*)

SERGEANT. What are you waiting for?

MAN. For my hat, of course, and my wig. You wouldn't wish me to get my death of cold? (**SERGEANT** *gives them.*)

MAN. (*going towards steps*) Well, good-night, comrade, and thank you. You did me a good turn tonight, and I'm obliged to you. Maybe I'll be able to do as much for you when the small rise up and the big fall down . . . when we all change places at the Rising (*waves his hand and disappears*) of the Moon.

When will the man return the sergeant's favor?

SERGEANT. (*turning his back to audience and reading placard*) A hundred pounds reward! A hundred pounds! (*turns towards audience*) I wonder, now, am I as great a fool as I think I am?

Curtain. ■

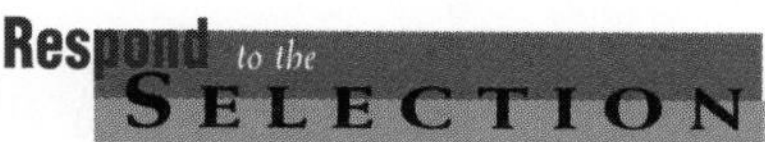

If you were the sergeant, what would you have done?

ANSWER TO GUIDED READING QUESTION

1. The man says he will "do as much for you when the small rise up and the big fall down…when we all change places at the Rising of the Moon."

SELECTION CHECK TEST 4.1.15 WITH ANSWERS

Checking Your Reading

1. Why are the policemen at the quay? **They are looking for a man who escaped jail.**
2. What does the ragged man want to sell to sailors? **He wants to sell ballads.**
3. What does the ragged man offer to help the Sergeant do? **He offers to help watch.**
4. What is the signal from the men in the boat? **The signal is a whistle.**
5. What happens to the ragged man? **He escapes.**

Literary Tools

Sentence Completion

Fill in the blanks using the following terms. You may not use every term, and you may use some terms more than once. Make the most specific choice for each statement.

dialogue properties plot
stage directions characters
sound effects monologue

1. Horns, bird calls, sirens, and whistles are examples of **sound effects**.
2. **Stage directions** are notes provided by the playwright to describe how something should be presented in a play.
3. In this play, the hat and wig are examples of **properties**.
4. An extended speech by one character is called **monologue**.
5. **Stage directions** set the scene, introduce the characters, and describe the characters' actions.

RESPOND TO THE SELECTION

Imagine students to write a journal entry about what might motivate a person to make a choice other than the one they themselves might make.

ANSWERS FOR INVESTIGATE, INQUIRE AND IMAGINE

Recall

1a. The police are putting up wanted posters. They discuss the wanted man, how to catch him, and the reward that is offered.

2a. A "Ragged Man" appears and claims to be a singer. He convinces the Sergeant to let him stay by saying he knows the wanted man and that the wanted man is dangerous.

3a. He suggest that if circumstances had been different, they might be in each other's situation.

Interpret

1b. The wanted man has escaped from prison, but we are not told why he was imprisoned. He is probably a political prisoner. The police are willing to catch him, but they are not happy about it because he is popular with the public and perhaps because they have nationalist sympathies.

2b. He poses as a singer so that he can sing to warn his comrades of the presence of the police. The songs indicate his nationalism as well as a general interest in culture and political conflict.

3b. The Sergeant imagines that he might have been a wanted criminal or perhaps a rebel nationalist. This makes him more sympathetic to the Ragged Man and more willing to help him.

Analyze

4a. The title of the play comes from the ballad of the same name, popular with Irish nationalist rebels. Part of the ballad is sung on page 56. On page 53, the Sergeant refers to the moon as his only companion. The Ragged Man's last line is "When we all change places at the Rising of the Moon." The changing of the moon's phases symbolizes a time of change. On page 59, one of the policemen offers to leave the Sergeant a lantern because "clouds are coming up and you have the darkness of the night before you," indicating the lack of moonlight. The Sergeant refuses the lantern. The moonlight represents light and clarity, the ability to see what is true, as opposed to the darkness of confusion or oppression.

Synthesize

4b. This is an appropriate title for the play because it deals with revolution and political change, as well as the change in a man's heart. The changing of the moon phases is a familiar symbol for many kinds of change, including changing political philosophies. The light of the moon is an appropriate symbol for a

INVESTIGATE

Inquire, Imagine

Recall: Gathering Facts → **Interpret:** Finding Meaning

1a. What are the police doing as the play opens? What do they discuss as they work?

1b. Why is the man on the placard wanted? Do the police want to catch the man? Why or why not?

2a. Who appears as the Sergeant is keeping watch? What does he claim to be? How does the Ragged Man convince the Sergeant to let him stay?

2b. Why is the man posing as a ballad singer? What do his songs reveal?

3a. What does the Ragged Man say about the Sergeant's and his own past and present lives?

3b. What does the Sergeant think his life might have been like? How does this thinking affect the Sergeant's actions at the end of the play?

Analyze: Taking Things Apart → **Synthesize:** Bringing Things Together

4a. What is the source of the play's title? What other references to the moon are made in the play? What other meanings might the moonlight have?

4b. Why is this an appropriate title for the play? Why does the sergeant refuse the lantern offered by Policeman B at the end of the play?

Evaluate: Making Judgments → **Extend:** Connecting Ideas

5a. Evaluate the sergeant's decision to let the man go. With what conflicting feelings does the sergeant struggle? On what basis does he decide to let him go? Was he right to do so? Why or why not?

5b. Both this play and the ballad, "Robin Hood and Allen a Dale" deal with outlaws who struggle against an authority they see as unjust. The literature of our own country, too, is full of tales of an underdog who triumphs over those in power. Why do you think stories of underdogs who win, or who get away, are popular?

Understanding Literature

Stage Directions. Review the definition for **stage directions** in the Elements of Drama on page 49. What purpose do stage directions serve for a reader? Look at the stage notes at the beginning of *The Rising of the Moon.* What purpose do these stage directions serve?

Monologue. Review the definition of **monologue** in the Handbook of Literary Terms. Monologues are one way in which a playwright develops a character and reveals his or her inner thoughts. What revelation does the sergeant come to in this monologue?

Sound Effects. Review the definition for **sound effects** in the Elements of Drama on page 49. What does the audience of this play immediately know when they hear the whistle on page 58? In reading a play,

ANSWERS FOR INVESTIGATE, INQUIRE AND IMAGINE (cont.)

movement whose members believe their ideals represent truth and freedom as opposed to the darkness of oppression. On a surface level, the Sergeant refuses the lantern because he does not want the policemen to see the fugitive he has decided to help. On a symbolic level, the Sergeant refuses the lantern because he has decided to embrace the "light" offered by the Ragged Man and his revolution and does not need artificial light.

Evaluate

5a. The Sergeant is divided between his duty on the one hand, and his sympathy for the fugitive man on the other. The Sergeant may also resent his duty as an officer of the law, given that he gets abuse from the citizens rather than gratitude for taking on the danger of his job (p. 51). In the end, he decides to let the man go, largely because he

Continued on page 61

one is unable to hear the sound effects which would be used in a stage production. How does a reader of a play know what the sound effects would be?

PROPERTIES. Review the definition for **properties** in Elements of Drama. In addition to the wig and the hat, what significant property is used in this play?

WRITER'S JOURNAL

1. Imagine that you are the police officer responsible for writing wanted posters in this seaport town. Write a **wanted poster** for the fugitive man. You will have to imagine what the charge against him might be, given what you know about his role in the nationalist movement. How will you describe him? What will you say to impress upon those who read the poster, the importance of his capture?
2. When this play was first staged, Ireland was still under British rule. Advertising it may have been a tricky affair. You would want to attract those sympathetic to the cause without arousing the anger of the officials. Imagine that you are the manager of the Abbey Theatre, and write a **playbill** to announce the upcoming production.
3. What might have happened if the two policemen had, in fact, seen the Ragged Man and noticed that the sergeant was trying to hide the wig and hat? If the two policemen had reported their sergeant's attempt to aid the fugitive, he would have been called upon to explain his actions. Imagine that you are the sergeant, and write a brief **report** to your superior, defending your actions that night on the quay.

Integrating *the* LANGUAGE ARTS

Study and Research

RESEARCHING THE IRISH NATIONALIST MOVEMENT. Research the Irish Nationalist movement up through today. When did it begin? What was the impetus for it? What were the circumstances behind the establishment of the free Republic of Ireland and the retention of Northern Ireland by the United Kingdom? What is the nature of the continuing conflict there today? Do you think Northern Ireland should be returned to Irish rule or remain a part of the UK? Why? Prepare a report for your teacher.

Language, Grammar, and Style & Speaking and Listening

REWRITING A DIALECT. Review Language Arts Survey 3.5, "Dialects of English." This play is written in an Irish dialect, clearly linking it with the Irish Nationalist movement. However, aside from this and the songs, little else identifies the play with Ireland and, in fact, one could change the dialect and recast the play as one about two men caught up in the struggle for independence in South Africa or India. Working with a partner, read the dialogue between the sergeant and Policeman B on pages 52–53, and rewrite the dialect as if the play were taking place in America or, if you wish, in some other country. Then read your rewrite aloud for the class.

Study and Research

USING A MAP. Locate Ireland on a world map and note its relation to England. Then locate the places mentioned in the play, including Ennis, Cork, County Clare, County Limerick, and Kilmallock.

ANSWERS FOR INVESTIGATE, INQUIRE AND IMAGINE (CONT. FROM PAGE 60)

recognizes that he and the man are not so different and that, given slightly different circumstances, he might have joined the rebel movement, too. Responses will vary as to whether or not this was the right decision.

EXTEND

5b. *Responses will vary.* One possibility is the fact that we can each imagine ourselves in a powerless situation and we can therefore identify with the underdog. The United States is, itself, a nation founded in a revolution against a power seen as unjust, making Americans particularly sympathetic to underdogs.

ANSWERS FOR UNDERSTANDING LITERATURE

STAGE DIRECTIONS. Stage directions help the reader imagine or visualize the action. Sometimes they fill in plot elements that are not stated or implied by the dialogue. The stage notes at the beginning of the play establish the setting.

MONOLOGUE. The Sergeant realizes that, but for a few decisions he made in his youth, he might have gone down the same path as the Ragged Man and become a rebel himself. He begins to look at the man quite differently and this leads to his ultimately letting the man go.

SOUND EFFECTS. The audience immediately knows that the man is the fugitive on the wanted poster when they hear the whistle—a signal from a fellow rebel below at the water. The reader of a play cannot hear the sound effects but sees directions for them in the stage directions and can imagine them.

PROPERTIES. The lantern plays a significant role in the play.

ANSWERS TO INTEGRATING THE LANGUAGE ARTS

Study and Research
Refer students to the Language Arts Survey 5.19, "How to Locate Library Materials." Inform students that good sources include encyclopedias and books on Irish history; however, for the most up-to-date information on political turmoil in Ireland, students should delve into periodicals of recent newspaper and newsmagazine articles. Students might also use the Internet as a tool to find both historical and current information on the situation in Ireland.

ANSWERS TO INTEGRATING THE LANGUAGE ARTS (CONT.)

Language, Grammar, and Style
Students will find it easiest to translate the dialect into that of their own place and social group. Encourage them to do so. Interested students might try to experiment translating the dialect into a dialect other than their own for extra credit.

Study and Research
If a history teacher in your school teaches a world history class, you might have him or her come to your class for a period, if possible, as a guest lecturer. He or she can tell the students some basic background information on the geography, culture, and history of Ireland.

ADDITIONAL RESOURCES

UNIT 1 RESOURCE BOOK
- Selection Check Test 4.1.17
- Selection Test 4.1.18

Nonfiction

Nonfiction is writing that deals with actual events, people, places, things, and ideas. The roots of nonfiction lie in oral accounts of actual occurrences among pre-literate peoples. Actual events—the deeds of heroes, major events in the history of a clan or a tribe—would be retold, often with embellishments that melded the actual with the legendary or mythological. After the invention of writing, such accounts of the histories of peoples, of their heroes and leaders, their trials and accomplishments, were written down, becoming the earliest **histories.** In much early historical writing, such as that of the Greek historian Herodotus, accounts of actual historical personages appear side by side with accounts of fabulous beasts, mythical lands, and magical transformations. In early writing, myth, history, and biography were one.

The first great historian in England was the Venerable Bede, a monk who lived in Northumbria from AD 673 to 735 (see page 88). An important nonfiction work from the Old English period is the *Anglo-Saxon Chronicle,* begun in 891, a year-by-year account of English history from the beginnings of the Anglo-Saxon settlement.

Of importance to historians are the many kinds of nonfiction, such as **speeches, contracts, constitutions, laws,** and **political tracts,** that provide a record of political life. A fine example of a political speech is Queen Elizabeth's Speech to the Troops at Tilbury, on page 67. Examples of political writing in this text include the selections from John Milton's *Areopagitica* (Unit 6), Mary Wollstonecraft's *A Vindication of the Rights of Woman* (Unit 8), and John Stuart Mill's *The Subjection of Women* (Unit 9).

Since the beginning of writing, people have recorded parts of their own lives or of the lives of others. These **autobiographies** and **biographies** are among the most important types of nonfiction. The first full-fledged autobiography in English is generally held to be *The Book of Margery Kempe,* written in the mid-fifteenth century (Unit 3). The first of the great modern biographies is James Boswell's *The Life of Samuel Johnson, LL.D.,* published in 1788 (Unit 7).

Other important types of nonfiction that provide information about people's lives include their **letters, diaries,** and **journals.** Examples of journal writing in this text include selections from *The Diary of Samuel Pepys* (Unit 7) and from *The Grasmere Journals* of Dorothy Wordsworth (Unit 8).

Related to letters, diaries, and journals by the personal nature of their content, **essays** are among the most important of the types of nonfiction represented in the English literary tradition. The word *essay* comes from a French word meaning "a trial or attempt." An essay presents a short but not exhaustive treatment of a subject from the perspective of the author. Examples of essay writing in this text include selections by Joseph Addison (Unit 7), William Wordsworth (Unit 8), William Hazlitt (Unit 8), John Ruskin (Unit 9), and Virginia Woolf (Unit 11).

The Launching of English Ships Against the Spanish Armada. [Detail], English artist. National Maritime Museum, Greenwich.

ArtNote

The Launching of English Ships Against the Spanish Armada [Detail]. English artist.
The ships depicted in the painting are English galleons, long, lean ships that rode low in the water for extra stability. They would bear up to twenty-eight powerful cannons along each side. When the English engaged the Spanish Armada in 1588, the two sides each had about the same number of warships. The Spanish were better prepared for the traditional tactics of ramming, boarding, and hand-to-hand fighting. However, the English ships were faster and had more effective cannons. Numerous Spanish ships were sunk before they could get close enough to board the English ships. The few Spanish ships that survived after the fighting were forced to flee to the North Sea and to sail around Scotland in order to return home.

CROSS-CURRICULAR ACTIVITIES

HISTORY. Students can research the intent of the Spanish Armada and depict their own vision of it by writing a news report, drawing or painting a battle scene, creating a map, or using some other form of expression. Sources for research include Graham, Winston, *The Spanish Armada,* 1972, and Martin, Colin, and Geoffrey Parker, *The Spanish Armada,* 1988.

CROSS-CURRICULAR CONNECTION

HISTORY. The Spanish Armada was launched against England by Philip II of Spain, who was angered by English piracy and by English aid given to rebels against Spanish authority in the Low Countries. The Spanish planned to use their fleet to protect an invasion force from the continent. Students might find it interesting to speculate about the differences that would have occurred in the subsequent course of world history had the Spanish plan succeeded.

Purpose and Organization in Nonfiction

THE PURPOSES OF WRITING

Purpose. A writer's **purpose**, or **aim**, is what he or she wants to accomplish. All writing, including nonfiction, is generally produced with some overall purpose in mind. The following chart classifies modes, or categories, of prose writing by purpose.

MODE OF WRITING	PURPOSE	EXAMPLE
expository / informative	to inform	news article, research report
imaginative	to entertain, enrich, enlighten, and/or use an artistic medium such as fiction, poetry, or creative nonfiction, to share a perspective	poem, short story, humorous essay
narrative	to share a story about an event, often to make a point	biography, family history
personal / expressive	to reflect	diary entry, personal letter
persuasive / argumentative	to persuade readers or listeners to respond in some way, such as to agree with a position, change a view on an issue, reach an agreement, or perform an action	editorial, petition

Note that a written work can have more than one purpose. For example, a nonfiction work may start with a brief story, or narrative, to introduce the topic or to make a point. It may then incorporate imaginative writing, provide information, express a personal reaction to that information, and strive to persuade the reader to adopt the writer's view. The emerging form known as "creative nonfiction" in fact combines purposes and aims in new ways.

For more information, consult the Language Arts Survey 2.3, "Identifying Your Purpose."

ADDITIONAL QUESTIONS AND ACTIVITIES

Have students write five paragraphs, each with one of the five purposes. Encourage advanced students to write each of these paragraphs on the same topic.

SELECTION CHECK TEST 4.1.17 WITH ANSWERS

Checking Your Reading

1. How does nonfiction differ from other types of literature considered so far? **Nonfiction explores actual people, places, things, events, and ideas with the idea of being true to the original occurrences.**
2. How did nonfiction begin? **It began when preliterate people told of actual events.**
3. What is the difference between autobiography and biography? **Biography is written by another person and autobiography is written by the subject himself or herself.**
4. What type of nonfiction comes from the French word for "a trial or attempt" and is a short treatment of a subject from the author's perspective? **This is an essay.**

Purposes and Organization in Nonfiction: The Purposes of Writing

1. What is the writer's aim? **A writer's aim is the goal he or she wants to achieve.**
2. What is a writer's purpose when he or she uses the imaginative mode? **Imaginative mode is used to entertain, enrich, enlighten, and/or share a unique perspective.**
3. News articles and research reports are examples of what mode? **They are examples of the expository/informative mode.**
4. Why might a writer use several modes in one piece of writing? ***Responses will vary.***
5. If a writer's purpose were to reflect on a significant event in his or her life, what mode would he or she use? **The personal/expressive mode is used for reflection.**

Purposes and Organization in Nonfiction: Types of Writing

Match the first part of each sentence with its best fitting conclusion. You may use some choices more than once and you may not use every choice.

a. usually uses chronological order as a method of organization

SELECTION CHECK TEST 4.1.17 WITH ANSWERS (CONT.)

b. places subjects into categories according to their characteristics.
c. presents words in quotation marks.
d. often uses spatial order as a means of organization.
e. presents the steps in a process or gives directions how to do something.
f. presents facts or opinions, and can be organized in many ways
g. breaks something into its parts and shows how the parts are related.

1. Description… **D**
2. Analysis… **G**
3. Exposition… **F**
4. Narration… **A**
5. Classification order… **B**

Types of Writing

A writer may structure, or organize, a piece of writing in different ways in order to communicate more clearly. The following chart describes types of writing commonly used in nonfiction and explains how these types are typically structured.

TYPE OF WRITING	DESCRIPTION AND ORGANIZATION
Narration	As with the narrative mode, this method tells a story or describes events using time, or **chronological order,** as a way of organization.
Dialogue	This method presents words as they were actually spoken by people. Quotation marks are usually used to set off direct speech.
Description	This method portrays a character, an object, or a scene. Descriptions make use of sensory details—words and phrases that describe how things look, sound, smell, taste, or feel. Descriptive writing frequently uses **spatial order** as a way of organization.
Exposition	This method presents facts or opinions in an organized manner. There are many ways to organize exposition. Among the most common are the following: **Analysis** breaks something into its parts and shows how the parts are related. **Classification Order** involves placing subjects into categories, or classes, according to their properties or characteristics. These groups are then presented, one-by-one, in some reasonable order. **Comparison and Contrast Order** organizes details about the similarities and differences between two subjects in one of two ways. In the first, characteristics of one subject are presented, followed by the characteristics of a second subject. In the second, both subjects are compared and contrasted with regard to one characteristic, then with regard to a second characteristic, and so on. **Process / How-to** writing presents the steps in a process or gives the reader directions on how to do something.

INDIVIDUAL LEARNING STRATEGIES

Note: The selection Speech to the Troops at Tilbury begins on page 66.

Motivation
Show students a brief portion of the film *Elizabeth*, released in 1998 and starring Cate Blanchett as Queen Elizabeth I. The film vividly portrays the political intrigue of Elizabeth's court. The film, however, is rated R, so choose carefully the scene you show to your students. You might, for example, simply show just a scene in which Elizabeth delivers a speech.

Reading Proficiency
Students will find the piece much more stirring if they hear it delivered dramatically, rather than just reading it on their own. Play the Audio Library selection or find a student whocan practice and deliver Speech to the Troops at Tilbury to your class.

English Language Learning
Inform students that in England, kings and queens often spoke about themselves in the plural, using the "royal we." Tell students that, in part, this unusual use of language stemmed from the fact that a monarch was viewed as more than just an individual but as the representative of England and all its people.

Special Needs
Students may have trouble with the speech's long, compound-complex sentences. Tell them that despite the speech's length, there are only five sentences in it. Have special needs students work in pairs with a student who can help them summarize the main idea in each sentence.

Enrichment
Encourage interested students to write an essay on why nonfiction is not defined simply as "writing that tells the truth." Tell students that their essays should answer questions such as the following: What types of nonfiction would such a definition leave out? In what circumstances might a nonfiction writer not be completely factual? To what extent is truth subjective, and how does this affect the nonfiction writer?

ADDITIONAL RESOURCES

Unit 1 Resource Book
- Selection Worksheet 1.5
- Selection Check Test 4.1.19
- Selection Test 4.1.20

VOCABULARY FROM THE SELECTION

concord
treachery

See page 65 for the Individual Learning Strategies for this selection.

READER'S JOURNAL

As an alternate activity, encourage students to recalls what speech they have heard in their own lives that they remember the most. What made this speech memorable?

NONFICTION

Aim. A writer's **aim** is his or her purpose, or goal. All writing, including nonfiction, is generally produced with some overall purpose in mind. As you read Elizabeth I's speech, try to determine what her main aim is.

Mode. A **mode** is a form of writing. One common classification system, based on purpose or aim, divides types of writing into five modes: expository/informative, imaginative, narrative, personal/expressive, and persuasive/argumentative. What mode of writing does Queen Elizabeth I's speech to her troops fall under?

Description. **Description** portrays a character, an object, or a scene. Descriptions make use of sensory details—words and phrases that describe how things look, sound, smell, taste, or feel. Notice how Queen Elizabeth I uses description in her speech.

Exposition. **Exposition** is writing that presents facts or opinions in an organized manner. What method of organization does Queen Elizabeth use in this speech?

Parallelism. **Parallelism** is a rhetorical technique in which a writer emphasizes the equal value or weight of two or more ideas by expressing them in the same grammatical form. Look for an example of parallelism in this speech.

Reader's Journal

How do you prepare yourself for stressful or frightening situations?

SPEECH TO THE TROOPS AT TILBURY

BY QUEEN ELIZABETH I

About the Author

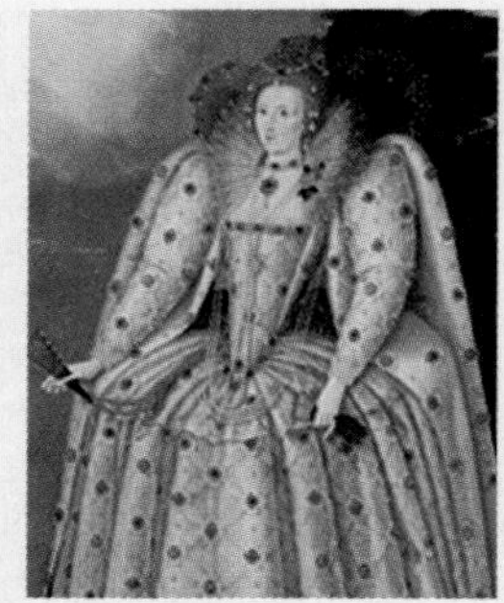

Queen Elizabeth I (1533-1603), daughter of Henry VIII and Anne Boleyn, was perhaps the greatest monarch in all of English history. Her long reign, from 1558–1603, is known as the Elizabethan Age. Elizabeth used her navy to explore and colonize foreign lands and sent Sir Walter Raleigh to establish the colony of "Virginia" in North America. With Elizabeth's secret support and blessing, the pirate, Sir Francis Drake, preyed on Spanish ships and colonies for treasure, helping to finance the growth of the greatest power in Europe. Elizabeth's reign was unprecedented in many respects: forty-five years of stable government and internal peace, the flourishing of English art, drama and literature, the exploration of the world by her adventurous nobles, and the domination of the seas by her much feared navy. Not least was the fact that she commanded such power and respect and ruled so capably as a single woman in an era when women's power, usually slight, was normally derived through their husbands. She was, and still is, known by the people of England as "Good Queen Bess."

About the Selection

Prince Phillip of Spain, enraged by the continuing raids on his ships and colonies by Drake and the English, decided in 1588 to attack England with his mighty fleet, the Spanish Armada. The English navy prepared for sea battle while Elizabeth's lords assembled an army of 4000 at Tilbury to fend off the possible invasion by 30,000 men of the Armada and 16,000 troops from Spain's ally, Parma. Elizabeth insisted on going to Tilbury, against the urgent advice of her ministers who feared for her safety. This speech to the troops, made on the morning of August 9, 1588, would become one of the most famous of her reign. After hearing it, the Earl of Leiceister said her words "had so inflamed the hearts of her good subjects, as I think the weakest among them is able to match the proudest Spaniard that dares land in England." The English navy, led by Sir Francis Drake and Lord Charles Howard, defeated the Armada, and the invasion was avoided.

GOALS/OBJECTIVES

Studying this lesson will enable students to
- be moved by a stirring speech delivered by a great leader at a time of crisis
- identify Queen Elizabeth I and briefly explain her significance
- define *nonfiction* and name and describe the types of nonfiction
- describe the main purposes of writing (expository/informative, imaginative, personal/expressive, and persuasive/argumentative) and identify examples of these purposes in their reading
- define *mode, description, exposition*, and *parallelism* and point out examples of these techniques in a nonfiction speech
- research some famous speeches
- research Queen Elizabeth I

Speech to the Troops at Tilbury, *August, 1588*

My loving people,

We[1] have been persuaded by some that are careful of our safety, to take heed how we commit our selves to armed multitudes, for fear of treachery; but I assure you I do not desire to live to distrust my faithful and loving people. Let tyrants fear. I have always so behaved myself that, under God, I have placed my chiefest strength and safeguard in the loyal hearts and goodwill of my subjects; and therefore I am come amongst you, as you see, at this time, not for my recreation and disport,[2] but being resolved, in the midst and heat of the battle, to live or die amongst you all; to lay down for my God, and for my kingdom, and my people, my honor and my blood, even in the dust. I know I have the body but of a weak and feeble woman; but I have the heart and stomach of a king, and of a king of England too, and think foul scorn that Parma[3] or Spain, or any prince of Europe, should dare to invade the borders of my realm; to which rather than any dishonor shall grow by me, I myself will take up arms, I myself will be your general, judge, and rewarder of every one of your virtues in the field. I know already, for your forwardness you have deserved rewards and crowns;[4] and We do assure you in the word of a prince, they shall be duly paid you. In the mean time, my lieutenant general shall be in my stead, than whom never prince commanded a more noble or worthy subject; not doubting but by your obedience to my general, by your concord in the camp, and your valor in the field, we shall shortly have a famous victory over those enemies of my God, of my kingdom, and of my people. ■

What would Elizabeth do, rather than be dishonored by allowing Spain or Parma to invade her kingdom?

Aim

Queen Elizabeth nowhere in this speech specifically expresses her purpose, or aim. However, the purpose can be inferred from statements such as this.

1. **We.** It is customary for a monarch to refer to him or herself as "We" rather than "I." This is known as the "royal We."
2. **disport.** Fun
3. **Parma.** Parma had allied with Spain and was expected in the invasion.
4. **crowns.** British coins

Words for Everyday Use

treach • er • y (trech´ ər ē) *n.,* treason. *A wise and benevolent ruler has no need to fear treachery.*

con • cord (kän´ kôrd) *n.,* agreement; harmony. *Please lay down your weapons and let us come to a concord.*

Respond *to the* Selection

If you were among the troops listening to her speech, how would you react to Elizabeth's presence and what she says?

ANSWERS TO GUIDED READING QUESTIONS

1. Elizabeth says that she would take up arms and fight along with her troops before allowing any foreign prince to invade her realm.

SELECTION CHECK TEST 4.4.19 WITH ANSWERS

Checking Your Reading

1. Whom does Elizabeth claim she will not distrust? **She will not distrust her faithful and loving people.**
2. Who should fear? **Tyrants should fear.**
3. Although she has a weak body, Elizabeth has the heart and stomach of a what? **She has the heart and stomach of a king.**
4. Who will represent her on the battlefield? **He lieutenant general will represent her.**
5. What does Elizabeth expect to occur shortly? **She expects a victory.**

Literary Tools

Fill in the blanks using the following terms. You may not use every term, and you may use some terms more than once. Make the most specific choice for each statement.

purpose mode description exposition parallelism expository/informative imaginative narrative personal/expressive persuasive/argumentative

1. **Description** employs sensory details to portray characters, objects, and scenes.
2. All writing is generally produced with some overall **purpose** in mind.
3. The primary aim of "Speech to the Troops at Tilbury" is **persuasive/argumentative**.
4. **Parallelism** is a rhetorical technique in which a writer emphasizes the equal value or weight of two or more ideas by expressing them in the same grammatical form.
5. Another word for *aim* is **purpose**.

RESPOND TO THE SELECTION

Encourage students to imagine themselves on a battlefield facing hundred of enemies armed with swords and spears. Ask them whether the speech is rousing enough to encourage them despite the very real danger they face.

ANSWERS FOR INVESTIGATE, INQUIRE AND IMAGINE

RECALL

1a. The queen has been advised to avoid crowds for fear of traitors.

2a. Elizabeth says that she is determined to die for honor and for her people if necessary and that despite her "weak" body she has the spirit of a king.

INTERPRET

1b. She does not fear her subjects because she trusts them and because they love her.

2b. Her outward appearance is weak, but her inner resolve is strong.

ANALYZE

3a. Elizabeth tells her troops that they will be paid and that they will claim a famous victory. She also tells them that she would, herself, take up arms and fight with them if need be to preserve England and her honor.

SYNTHESIZE

3b. *Responses will vary.* One possibility is that the troops, seeing that the queen was willing to put her own life in jeopardy, would conclude that their cause was a truly important one, worthy of their best efforts.

EVALUATE

4a. Elizabeth appeals to the pride of the troops, suggesting that to allow a foreign power to invade is to be dishonored. She also figuratively raises them to noble status by saying that she is asking them to fight a battle she, herself, is willing to fight. By placing herself on the same plane as the troops, even if only in a speech, she earns their loyalty and love and makes them feel superior. The speech seems to have been quite effective.

EXTEND

4b. *Responses will vary.* She might have appealed to greed, reminding the troops that if they defeated the Armada, there would be more pirate raids to join and more loot to be had. She might have appealed to fear of what the Spaniards would do if they won. She might have simply used her power to order them to obey and fight well. The fact that she placed herself on their level to engage their love and loyalty reveals that she had a shrewd understanding of human nature, that she was more interested in the best outcome for England than in her own personal comfort, and that she was a brave woman. She seems to be bold, determined, and shrewd.

Investigate, Inquire, Imagine

Recall: GATHERING FACTS → **Interpret:** FINDING MEANING

1a. What have some people advised the queen not to do?

2a. What does Queen Elizabeth tell the assembled troops about herself?

3. Why does the queen not fear being among her subjects?

4. What contrast does Queen Elizabeth draw between her outward appearance and her inner resolve?

Analyze: TAKING THINGS APART → **Synthesize:** BRINGING THINGS TOGETHER

3a. Elizabeth is speaking to her troops before they go into battle. What reasons does she give them for fighting? What does she say to strengthen their resolve?

3b. Why might her vow to join the fray if necessary, "to live or die amongst you all; to lay down for my God, and for my kingdom, and my people, my honor and my blood, even in the dust" have strengthened the will and passion of the troops for a victory?

Evaluate: MAKING JUDGMENTS → **Extend:** CONNECTING IDEAS

4a. Evaluate this speech as a motivational one. What is the tone of the speech? To what values or emotions does Elizabeth appeal? Given the purpose of this speech, how effective do think it is?

4b. To what other emotions might she have appealed? Based on this speech, what adjectives would you choose to describe her?

Understanding Literature

AIM. Review the definition of **aim** in the Handbook of Literary Terms. What do you think was Queen Elizabeth I's main aim in this speech? Does the speech seem to accomplish this purpose? Explain.

MODE. Review the definition of **mode** in the Handbook of Literary Terms. Review the Mode of Writing chart on page 64. Based on Queen Elizabeth's principal purpose, what mode of writing did she use? What kind of a response is the Queen trying to elicit from her audience?

DESCRIPTION. Review the definition of **description** in the Handbook of Literary Terms or in Literary Tools on page 66. In what part of her speech does Queen Elizabeth use description?

EXPOSITION. Review in the chart on page 65 the types of organization used in **exposition.** In what part of Elizabeth's speech does she use the type of exposition known as *comparison and contrast*? What contrast does she make? Why does she do so?

PARALLELISM. Review the definition of **parallelism** in the Handbook of Literary Terms. At what point in this speech does Elizabeth use parallelism? For what purpose?

Answers to Understanding Literature can be found on page 69.

Writer's Journal

1. Imagine you are Queen Elizabeth preparing to leave for Tilbury. What concerns would be uppermost in your mind? Write a **journal entry** that Queen Elizabeth might have written on this occasion.
2. Since there were no telephones, computers, or fax lines in Elizabethan times, heralds carried news of far off battles back to London and the court. If you were a court herald and witnessed the speech given by Elizabeth, what account would you give to the court on your return? Write a **news account** to be read at court, describing the events on the battlefield at Tilbury on August 9, 1588.
3. Think of something that you wish to encourage or promote. Such as a victory in a school football game, a decision you want your parents to make, or an important choice a friend is considering. Write a brief **persuasive paragraph** designed to influence someone to do or not do a particular thing. Before you write, consider how you will persuade your reader, what emotions or values you will appeal to, and what reasons you will give.

Integrating *the* Language Arts

Language, Grammar, and Style & Media Literacy

Identifying Modes of Writing. Review page 64 on Purpose and Mode in Nonfiction. Then scan a newspaper or magazine to find examples of expressive writing, expository writing and persuasive writing. You may also be able to find examples of literary writing. Share your findings and classification with your class.

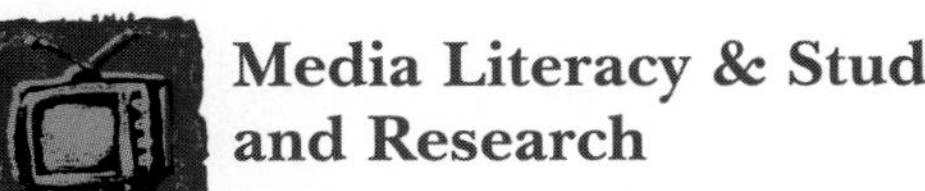

Media Literacy & Study and Research

Researching Speeches. Throughout history, leaders have given speeches on the eve of a conflict to stiffen the resolve and courage of their followers. The speech in Act 3, scene 1 of Shakespeare's *Henry V* is a classic military example. In non-military settings, some memorable examples include Martin Luther King's speech in Memphis the night before he was assassinated, as well as Knute Rockne's "win one for the Gipper" speech to the Notre Dame football team. Research some of these famous inspirational speeches and compare them to this one. To what kinds of emotions do these other leaders appeal? Are they as effective as Elizabeth? Why, or why not?

Study and Research

Researching Queen Elizabeth I. Research the life and reign of Elizabeth I. Prepare a report for your teacher on her accomplishments and the nature of life in Elizabethan England. You may find her a more interesting historical figure if you are able to find information about her personal life as well as her official actions. The recent biography by Alison Weir, *The Life of Elizabeth I,* is an excellent resource on both. Alternatively, you may choose to research the Spanish Armada under Phillip of Spain and the battles between the Armada and England.

ANSWERS FOR UNDERSTANDING LITERATURE

Purpose. Elizabeth's purpose was to arouse the loyalty of her troops and to persuade them to fight hard in the battle to come. Answers will vary, but students may say that the speech does accomplish its purpose, for in it Elizabeth appeals to her troops by demonstration her own courage as an example.

Mode. Since Elizabeth's purpose is to persuade her troops to rally to fight against the oncoming invasion, she uses the persuasive/argumentative mode. She is attempting to appeal to her troop's sense of patriotism and valor.

Description. Near the middle of the speech, Elizabeth uses descriptions of herself and of her lieutenant general.

Exposition. She uses comparison and contrast to explain her reasons for coming before the crowd. She contrasts a frivolous reason with her true reason to show her seriousness.

Parallelism. Elizabeth uses parallelism at the end of her speech to show what she cares about: Her God, her kingdom, and her people.

INTEGRATING THE LANGUAGE ARTS

Language, Grammar, and Style
You might also encourage students to examine some of their own favorite pieces of writing and to classify them by mode.

Media Literacy & Study and Research
Other speeches students might explore are Abraham's Lincoln's Gettysburg Address, Peggy Noonan's "Challenger Disaster" speech (delivered by Ronald Reagan), and John F. Kennedy's Inaugural Address.

Study and Research
Tell students that they should prepare brief research reports (under three pages), but they should prepare a bibliography, document their sources carefully, and use endnotes. Refer them to the Language Arts Survey section on Documenting Sources, 5.36–5.45.

LESSON OVERVIEW

GUIDED WRITING *Software*

See the Guided Writing Software for an extended version of this lesson that includes printable graphic organizers, extensive student models and student-friendly checklists, and self-, peer, and teacher evaluation features.

INDIVIDUAL LEARNING STRATEGIES

MOTIVATION
Ask students where they have seen reviews of books and hold a class discussion on how useful they have been to students.

READING PROFICIENCY
Point out the subheads in the Guided Writing lesson and ask students to speculate and predict what each section will be about.

ENGLISH LANGUAGE LEARNING
Have students review a book written in their native language and then translate that review into English. Then have them share both

Continued on page 71

Guided Writing

"Let us dare to read, think, speak, and write....Let every sluice of knowledge be opened and set a-flowing."
—John Adams

WRITING A BOOK REVIEW

Thumbs up or thumbs down? What you think about a movie, a book, or a painting starts with a gut feeling. But almost no one will let you stop there. Whenever you say, "It was a great movie," or "What an awful painting," your listener will invariably say, "What do you mean?" and that's when you start to analyze or explain your opinion or even vigorously defend it.

WRITING ASSIGNMENT. Write a review of a British short story or novel. In this lesson you will use your natural tendency to evaluate in order to state an opinion and support it with details from the book.

EXAMINING THE MODEL. Notice how the opening of this book review draws the reader in with a biographical tidbit about McCourt and a snapshot of the reviewer's opinion. How would you describe the reviewer's evaluation of *Angela's Ashes* ? Which sentence in the opening paragraph would you say is the thesis, or main idea of this review?

What other books does Michiko Kakutani compare to *Angela's Ashes*? And what does this comparison tell you about Frank McCourt's book?

A book reviewer doesn't waste the reader's time with windy analysis or drawn-out plot summaries. That's the quickest way to lose a reader. Reviewers typically start out with an intriguing fact, description, or story and then

continued on page 71

Professional Model

"Generous Memories of a Poor, Painful Childhood"
By Michiko Kakutani

from book review of *Angela's Ashes* by Frank McCourt. Published in the *New York Times Book Review,* September 17, 1996 © 2000, The New York Times Company.

Frank McCourt, who taught writing for many years in the New York public school system, waited more than four decades to tell the story of his childhood. It's been well worth the wait. With *Angela's Ashes*, he has used the storytelling gifts he inherited from his father to write a book that redeems the pain of his early years with wit and compassion and grace. He has written a book that stands with *The Liar's Club* by Mary Karr and Andre Aciman's *Out of Egypt* as a classic modern memoir.

There is not a trace of bitterness or resentment in *Angela's Ashes*, though there is plenty a less generous writer might well be judgmental about. Indeed Mr. McCourt's childhood is, as he has said, "an epic of woe." Besides a father who drank away the family's meager food money and a mother who was reduced to begging, there were three siblings who died in infancy from illness. The McCourts were too poor to afford sheets or blankets for their flea-infested bed, too poor to buy new shoes for the children, too poor to get milk for the new baby. A boiled egg was considered a luxury, a bit of discarded apple peel a coveted treat....

In the end, of course, Mr. McCourt's memoir is not just the story of his family's struggles, but the story of his own sentimental education: his discovery of poetry and girls, and his efforts to come to terms with God and death and faith. By 11, he's the chief breadwinner for the family. By 15, he's lost his first girlfriend to tuberculosis. By 19, he's saved enough money to make his escape to the States.

The reader of this stunning memoir can only hope that Mr. McCourt will set down the story of his subsequent adventures in America in another book. *Angela's Ashes* is so good it deserves a sequel.

Prewriting

Finding Your Voice. Book reviews should reflect a real voice, full of conviction. You will want to use language that is straightforward and strong. Depending on your message, you can use humor, but let it reflect a genuine opinion. Let your ear and your meaning guide you.

When you read the final draft of the student model for this lesson, look at the word choices that Tasha Samuels made. Even though she was writing for other students, she decided to change the word *slap* to *scold* in her review because she felt *slap* was too silly for the point she was trying to make.

Identifying Your Audience. Here's an opportunity to write reviews for your peers as well as teachers and other readers. Assume that your reader is an intelligent person who has not read the book you are reviewing but will be bored by ordinary observations. Tell your reader the kind of information you would want to know if you had picked up the book in the library and were wondering whether to read it or not.

Writing with a Plan. A book review is not a book report. You are not merely summarizing the story line. In a review, you judge a novel based on the answers to questions that ask *how* and *why.* How has the author developed the character? Why has the author included images of light and dark? In a review, you ask what the author was trying to do and then evaluate the effort.

Choose a British short story or novel that you have read recently and one that you have some feelings about. Next, ask and answer questions that will help you generate ideas.

Copy the graphic organizer on page 72 onto your own paper and write as many responses as you can.

Tasha Samuels, a 12th grade student, began her graphic organizer as follows:

move on to a strong statement of evaluation. They take a stand and then prove or show the reader why they hold that stand.

What are several points that Michiko Kakutani makes to show that McCourt's book is a "classic modern memoir"? Are these examples convincing? Based on the details Kakutani includes, do you think the book sounds interesting? Would you want to read it?

Read an excerpt from *Angela's Ashes* in Unit 11.

Individual Learning Strategies (cont. from page 70)

the native language and English review to the class. This activity is an excellent way to introduce issues in translation and the richness of a different language.

Special Needs
Pair students with an advanced student who can help them complete the Graphic Organizer on page 72. Encourage students to refer back to their completed Graphic Organizer to help them write their book review.

Enrichment
Refer students to the Language Arts Survey 2.47, "Publishing and Presenting Your Work." Then have them brainstorm some unique ways in which they can present or publish their finished book review.

Prewriting

Finding Your Voice
For more information on voice, refer students to the Language Arts Survey 3.3, "Register, Tone, and Voice."

Identifying Your Audience
Students will find a chart, "Thinking about Your Audience" in the Language Arts Survey 2.4, "Identifying Your Audience" to help them focus on the audience that has been suggested to them on page 71.

Writing with a Plan
Refer students to the Language Arts Survey 5.11, "Evaluating." Reinforce to students that a book review requires them to make a judgment on a piece of work. Therefore, they will need to be critical of both the content and style of the book.

STUDENT MODEL—GRAPHIC ORGANIZER

See the Guided Writing Resource for a blackline master of the Graphic Organizer for this lesson.

Drafting

Encourage students to use their completed Graphic Organizer to help them get started on writing their draft. For additional help, refer students to the Language Arts Survey 2.31–2.35, "Drafting."

"Purpose and craftsmanship—end and means—these are the keys to your judgment in all the arts."
—Marya Mannes

Student Model—Graphic Organizer

Jude the Obscure by Thomas Hardy, published in 1896

What are the most surprising, remarkable or memorable qualities of this story or novel? Write your first and strongest impressions.

the tone, the sadness, symbolism, Jude's conflict between love and learning, the social criticism about class structure, the light and dark imagery

What are the strengths and weaknesses of the story or novel? How do elements such as character, motivation, plot, conflict, setting, and style add to or take away from its effectiveness?

strengths are that you really understand character motivation and what Jude is thinking and feeling — because Hardy adds so many descriptions and symbols that show us.

weakness is in the plot — that Jude has so much bad luck it's almost unbelievable, but in the end doesn't take away that much from the book because we understand and like him so well

Which elements of the story or novel do you think would or would not appeal to a reader? Tell why.

I think teenagers would identify with Jude's yearnings to get away from home and make a better life for himself. They would understand his passion for Sue and his depression when he can't be with her. Some people might not like all the trouble Jude has.

Write two or three possible thesis statements for your review. These should clearly state your opinion of the work and possibly include reasons for your evaluation.

I like the way the novel shows you personal human mistakes like falling love with the wrong person alongside big universal problems like poverty.

Jude loves two women who represent two different desires: physical love and spiritual love.

Hardy has created a character so human you care about him — even though he has the worst luck of anybody you ever knew.

Circle the thesis statement you think has the most promise. Now list below at least three ideas, examples, or reasons that support your opinion.

You understand Jude's desires
—from the things he says he wants
—from descriptions
—from the symbols

Drafting

Use your prewriting notes to write a quick first draft. Begin your review with a sentence that makes your reader want to know more. You may include interesting bits of biographical information about the author, compelling moments from the work, or even a quirky comparison to a sport, food, or animal.

State your opinion in the thesis—usually placed toward the end of the introductory paragraph. In the body of the review, support your opinion with an analysis of the work's literary elements. If you quote directly from the work, remember to use quotation marks.

Conclude your review with a strong statement of your evaluation. Try to end with an intriguing sentence.

One last note: all professional reviews are written in the present tense—what is called, in this case, the literary present. This is because the characters are considered to be existing now — no matter how old the book or how long ago you read it. So use words like *is* and *are* rather than *was* or *were*.

Student Model—Draft

Jude the Obscure: A Book Review
by Tasha Samuels ← Boring title

Jude Fawley must be the unluckiest character to ever walk across the pages [Good image!] of a novel. Yet Thomas Hardy's protagonist in *Jude the Obscure* pulls [Good verb!] the reader along with him through one bad situation after another all the way to the bitter end. If you liked the 1996 movie [version], you'll like the novel [When was it written?]. The book is more of the same trouble, but is written so well that you understand and feel for [slang] the desires that motivate Jude.

Jude is a working class country boy unlucky in love [and work] [Isn't he unlucky in more areas than love?]. He is tricked into marriage before he is ready, then abandoned by his wife. He falls in love with his cousin whom he can't marry. Unable to stay away from each other, Jude and his cousin live together and have

What a Review Should Avoid

The American writer John Updike recommends that reviewers take care not to blame an author for not achieving what he or she did not attempt to do. If you find the selection you are reviewing lacking, try to understand why and cite successful examples of similar books to explain your reasons.

Language, Grammar, and Style

Effective Paragraphs
In this lesson, students will be asked to do the following:

- Identify the Elements of a Paragraph
- Revise Ineffective Paragraphs
- Use Effective Paragraphs

Introducing the Skill. Explain to students that this lesson will show students how to distinguish paragraph breaks and the importance of paragraphs in written works.

Previewing the Skill. Refer students to the Language Arts Survey 2.26, "Writing Main Ideas and Supporting Details" and 2.33, "Drafting Body Paragraphs" for more information on effective paragraphs.

Practicing the Skill. For additional practice, ask students to exchange their drafts with another classmate. Then have them identify the topic sentence, the main ideas, and the supporting statements of each paragraph. Also have them suggest paragraph breaks if one paragraph covers too much information or too many ideas.

Language, Grammar, and Style

Effective Paragraphs

Identifying the Elements of a Paragraph. Paragraphs represent units of thought. They discuss one idea in a composition and help the reader organize and understand the writer's thinking. Imagine how intimidating a full page of text would be without the spacing or indentation offered by paragraphs. Paragraphs offer the reader a visual break in the text.

Paragraphs can be long or short, but they usually follow two patterns: general to specific and specific to general. In expository compositions where you are trying to explain something, the general-to-specific pattern is used most often.

In this pattern, the opening sentence states the general topic of the paragraph, then narrows that topic to one main idea and gives three or more illustrations or supports to prove or explain the main idea. The topic and main idea can be combined in one sentence or can occupy separate sentences. Review the Language Arts Survey 2.24, "Writing Paragraphs."

General Topic Sentence with Main Idea
Read this example of a general-to-specific paragraph from the professional model.

continued on page 75

children out of wedlock. The children die. The cousin leaves him.

This ¶ is not well developed

And while all this is going on, Jude is pining to go to university. But he is poor and in 19th century England, that means he is ~~locked out~~ from a higher education. *excluded from*

Sometimes you want to ~~slap~~ *scold* Jude for his bad choices and you can't believe how his plans fall apart. And yet you stay with the book, not because you like what happens to Jude but because he is so human that you care what happens to him.

Move this ¶ – it would be a good conclusion

~~Everywhere in the book~~, Hardy plants symbols and descriptions that show us Jude's predicament. For example, the walls of the university become a symbol of Jude's thwarted desire to go to school. Jude works as a stonemason on the crumbling walls of the university, repairing the old rotten stones, but that's as close as he will get to school. The university is built on the set rules of social classes, a society which allows no class mobility and which tells the laboring class to stay down ~~and accepts only the rich within its walls~~. *redundant & a bit off topic*

Move this to the underdeveloped 3rd paragraph

Hardy's descriptions are always related to the character's desires and moods. You can see how much Jude loves his cousin Sue by his perceptions of the landscape: "The oppressive strength of his affection for Sue showed itself on the morrow and the following days yet more clearly. He could no longer endure the light of the Melchester lamps; the sunshine was drab paint; and the blue sky as zinc." *Good quote* *Move all to under-developed 3rd paragraph.*

The book is sad, but it is not a ~~downer~~ *e*. It holds your interest and moves your heart. *This ¶ could be replaced by the 4th ¶*

Self-and Peer Evaluation

After you write your rough draft, complete a self-evaluation of your piece. If time allows, have one or two other students give you peer evaluations.

- Does the first sentence of the review make you want to read on? If not, what changes would make it more compelling?
- Does the opening paragraph contain a thesis statement? Does the thesis include an evaluation of the work? What is the opinion stated in the thesis? Is it clear?
- How does each paragraph in the body of the paper support the writer's opinion of the work?
- Would this work's review benefit from the addition of biographical information about the author? If so, where would it be appropriate?
- If the review is lacking comparisons to similar works, are there any works that come to mind as good examples? Where could they be mentioned?
- Does the review contain excessive plot summary? How and where could more critical analysis be included?
- Does each paragraph contain a general topic and one main idea? Identify these sentences. Which, if any, are unclear or unrelated to the rest of the paragraph?
- Does each paragraph include sufficient and appropriate illustrations to explain the topic/main ideas? Do some paragraphs need more or different illustrations?
- Is the review careful not to reveal the ending of the work or give away suspenseful moments?

EXAMPLE

"In the end, of course, Mr. McCourt's memoir is not just the story of his family's struggles, but the story of his own sentimental education: his discovery of poetry and girls, and his efforts to come to terms with God and death and faith. By 11, he's the chief breadwinner for the family. By 15, he's lost his first girlfriend to tuberculosis. By 19, he's saved enough money to make his escape to the States."

Note how the opening sentence combines the general topic "story of his family's struggles" with the main idea of a "sentimental education." The reader wonders how McCourt came to terms with "God and death and faith." What are the specific illustrations or examples that Michiko Kakutani includes to explain that education?

General Topic Sentence/ Main Idea Sentence

In the following paragraph from the professional model, the general topic and main idea are placed in separate sentences.

EXAMPLE

"There is not a trace of bitterness or resentment in *Angela's Ashes*, though there is plenty a less generous writer might well be judgmental about. Indeed Mr. McCourt's

continued on page 76

Self- and Peer Evaluation

Have students use the questions on this page for self- and peer evaluation. Remind students that comments from classmates can be helpful and can help them to identify weaknesses and strengths in their writing. A blackline master of the checklist is available in the Guided Writing Resource.

Revising and Proofreading

Remind students that revising includes adding or expanding, cutting or condensing, replacing and moving text. Have students read the Language Arts Survey 2.41, "Revising." Also encourage students to use common proofreader's symbols found in the Language Arts Survey 2.44, "Using Proofreader's Marks."

childhood is, as he has said, "an epic of woe." Besides a father who drank away the family's meager food money and a mother who was reduced to begging, there were three siblings who died in infancy from illness. The McCourts were too poor to afford sheets or blankets for their flea-infested bed, too poor to buy new shoes for the children, too poor to get milk for the new baby. A boiled egg was considered a luxury, a bit of discarded apple peel a coveted treat...."

The paragraph opens with a general statement about how the book is lacking bitterness when McCourt had every reason to be bitter. The next sentence limits the paragraph to the main idea that McCourt's childhood was "an epic of woe." The reader wonders what this means. How was McCourt's life woeful? What are the examples Kakutani uses to explain?

Revising Ineffective Paragraphs. Find a paragraph from the rough draft of the student model that does not have a topic, main idea, or adequate illustrations. Now find the same material reworked into a clear, complete paragraph in the final draft. What changes did Tasha make when she revised?

continued on page 77

Revising and Proofreading

Review your self- and peer evaluations and revise your writing according to these comments. Is your opinion of the work clearly stated in your opening paragraph? Have you kept the plot summary to a minimum and used your skills of critical analysis to explain the strengths and weaknesses of the work?

When you are satisfied with your draft, revise it for errors in spelling, grammar, punctuation, capitalization and other details.

Student Model—Revised

Jude the Obscure:
Meeting a Memorable Character
by Tasha Samuels

Jude Fawley must be the unluckiest character to ever walk across the pages of a novel. Yet Thomas Hardy's protagonist in Jude the Obscure pulls the reader along with him through one bad situation after another, all the way to the bitter end. If you liked the 1996 movie version, you'll like the 1896 novel. The book is more of the same trouble, but is written so well that you can't help but feel empathy for Jude.

Jude is a working-class country boy unlucky in love and work. He is tricked into marriage before he is ready, then abandoned by his wife. He falls in love with his cousin whom he can't marry. Unable to stay away from each other, Jude and his cousin live together and have children out of wedlock. The children die. The cousin leaves him. And as if that isn't bad enough, Jude is pining to go to university, but can't because he is poor.

We can sympathize with Jude's situation because we understand it. In nearly every description in the novel, Hardy shows us Jude's desires and moods. You can see how much Jude loves his cousin Sue by his perceptions of the landscape: "The oppressive strength of his affection for Sue showed itself on the morrow and the following days yet more clearly. He could no longer endure the light of the Melchester lamps; the sunshine was drab paint; and the blue sky as zinc."

Hardy also develops Jude's character by planting symbols that show us his predicament. For example, the walls of the university become a symbol for Jude's thwarted desire to go to school. Jude works as a stonemason on the crumbling walls of the university, repairing the old rotten stones, but that's as close as he will get. The 19th century society that Jude lives in was built on ancient rules that allow no class mobility and tell the laborers to stay down.

Sometimes you can't believe how Jude's plans fall apart and you want to scold him for his bad choices. Yet you stay with the book, not because you like what happens to Jude but because he is so human that you care what happens to him.

Publishing and Presenting

Consider publishing your review online. Two websites that publish teen writing are The 21st Century at www.TeenInk.com and Writes of Passage at http://www.writes.org/index.html. Or your class might want to put together a literary review for your school library. Photocopy and bind all of the reviews in a book to be shared with other students and teachers in your school.

Reflecting

Learning to analyze and judge literature is a skill you can use your entire life. Where else might you use this process and how might it benefit you? What were new insights from your critical analysis that you gained about the work, the author, or about your own life?

Without topic sentences, the reader is stuck guessing what the writer meant. They are a guide, a focus, a plan for the paragraph. Good writers almost always include them.

USING EFFECTIVE PARAGRAPHS. Read over your literary review and examine your paragraphs. Check to see if your paragraphs have topic sentences, main ideas, and supporting statements. Add in any missing parts to your paragraphs and be sure that each paragraph discusses one main idea and only one. Break apart any paragraphs that try to cover too much.

Publishing and Presenting

Students may consider creating a TV production for their school TV station that focuses only on reviewing books, similar to the style of the movie review program Roger Ebert & the Movies.

Reflecting

Ask students to answer these questions in their journals. Then have them refer back to the comments they made and the things they learned through this activity (analyzing and being critical of literature) as they continue to read and analyze the literature in this textbook.

ADDITIONAL RESOURCES

Unit 1 Resource Book
- Vocabulary Worksheet
- Study Guide: Unit 1 Test
- Unit 1Test

VOCABULARY DEVELOPMENT

Give students the following exercises. Read the Language Arts Survey 1.16, "Using Context Clues to Estimate Word Meaning." Then choose fifteen words from the list on page 78 that you would like to incorporate into your everyday vocabulary. Write a sentence containing a context clue for each word. Use more than one type of context clue in your sentence.

EXAMPLE
guile, *n.*, slyness
Sentence with context clue using restatement:
Donald was so sly that he knew exactly how to use guile to trick his sister into doing his chores.

UNIT 1 REVIEW
Genres and Techniques of Literature

Words for Everyday Use

Check your knowledge of the following vocabulary words from the selections in this unit. Write short sentences using these words in context to make the meaning clear. To review the definition or usage of a word, refer to the page number listed or the Glossary of Words for Everyday Use.

career, 35
concord, 67
guile, 9
ineffable, 24
inscrutable, 24
obscure, 37
parry, 36
perpendicular, 23
profound, 24
quay, 52
quorum, 23
rapt, 24
remonstrate, 41
stealth, 35
treachery, 67
uncanny, 39

Literary Tools

Define the following terms, giving concrete examples of how they are used in the selections in this unit. To review a term, refer to the page number indicated or to the Handbook of Literary Terms.

aim, 67
alliteration, 20, 23
assonance, 20, 24
climax, 42
conflict, 33
crisis, 42
dénouement, 43
description, 66
dialogue, 52
exposition, 33
falling action, 43
foreshadowing, 42
formulaic language, 9
inciting incident, 8, 35
incremental repetition, 9
meter, 7, 23
monologue, 57
oral tradition, 7
parallelism, 23
personification, 23
properties, 58
proverb, 10
repetition, 24
resolution, 10, 43
rhyme scheme, 8, 23
rising action, 35
sound effects, 58
stage directions, 52
stanza and meter, 7

Reflecting *on* Your Reading

The Oral Tradition

1. **Ballads and the Oral Tradition.** What characteristics does "Robin Hood and Allen a Dale" have that are common to all folk ballads? What subjects did the composers of ballads relate? What characteristics might have caused "Robin Hood and Allen a Dale" to survive in the oral tradition?

Poetry

2. **Lyric Poetry.** What characteristics make "The Naming of Cats" a lyric poem? How do lyric poems differ from narrative and dramatic ones? What special poetic devices—devices of sound, figurative language, and rhetorical techniques—are used in "The Naming of Cats"?

Fiction

3. **Short Story Structure.** Into what parts is a typical plot divided? What events in "The Rocking-Horse Winner" correspond to these parts?

Drama

4. **The Spectacle in Drama.** Imagine that you will be directing a production of *The Rising of the Moon.* Make a complete list, with descriptions, of the following elements of the spectacle in your production: the stage set, the lighting, the properties, the sound effects, and the costumes.

Nonfiction

5. **The Rhetoric of a Speech.** A speech often has as its purpose persuading an audience—moving them to adopt some point of view or to take some course of action. The art of moving an audience to thought, feeling, or action is called rhetoric. What techniques does Queen Elizabeth I use in her Speech to the Troops at Tilbury to move her audience? What purpose does she want to achieve? What makes a good speech? Is this a good speech by your criteria?

REFLECTING ON YOUR READING

The prompts in "Reflecting on Your Reading" are suitable as topics for research papers. Refer to the Language Arts Survey 5.18–5.45, "Research Skills." (To evaluate research papers, see the evaluation forms for writing, revising, and proofreading in the Assessment Resource.)

The prompts in "Reflecting on Your Reading" can also be adapted for use as topics for oral reports or debates. Refer students to the Language Arts Survey 4, Speaking and Listening. (To evaluate these projects, see the evaluation forms in the Assessment Resource.)

LEDONIVS
Schetlãt
Orcades Ins
S.Kilda
Hebrides sive Hebudes
Aberden
S.Andre
Dumblai
Barwick
IBERNIA
Galway
Glasquo
Carlisle
Newcast
Dublyn
Kork
Wexford
Kynsale
Cape Cler
Man
Anglesey
Lancaster
Yorck
Chester
Stafford
Norwich
Penbrok
Glocester
Bristol
Oxfort
London
Excester
Salesburi
The Lands end
Sorlinges
Portland
OCEANVS BRITA
Heysant
Brest
Quimper
Paris

Part Two
THE ENGLISH TRADITION

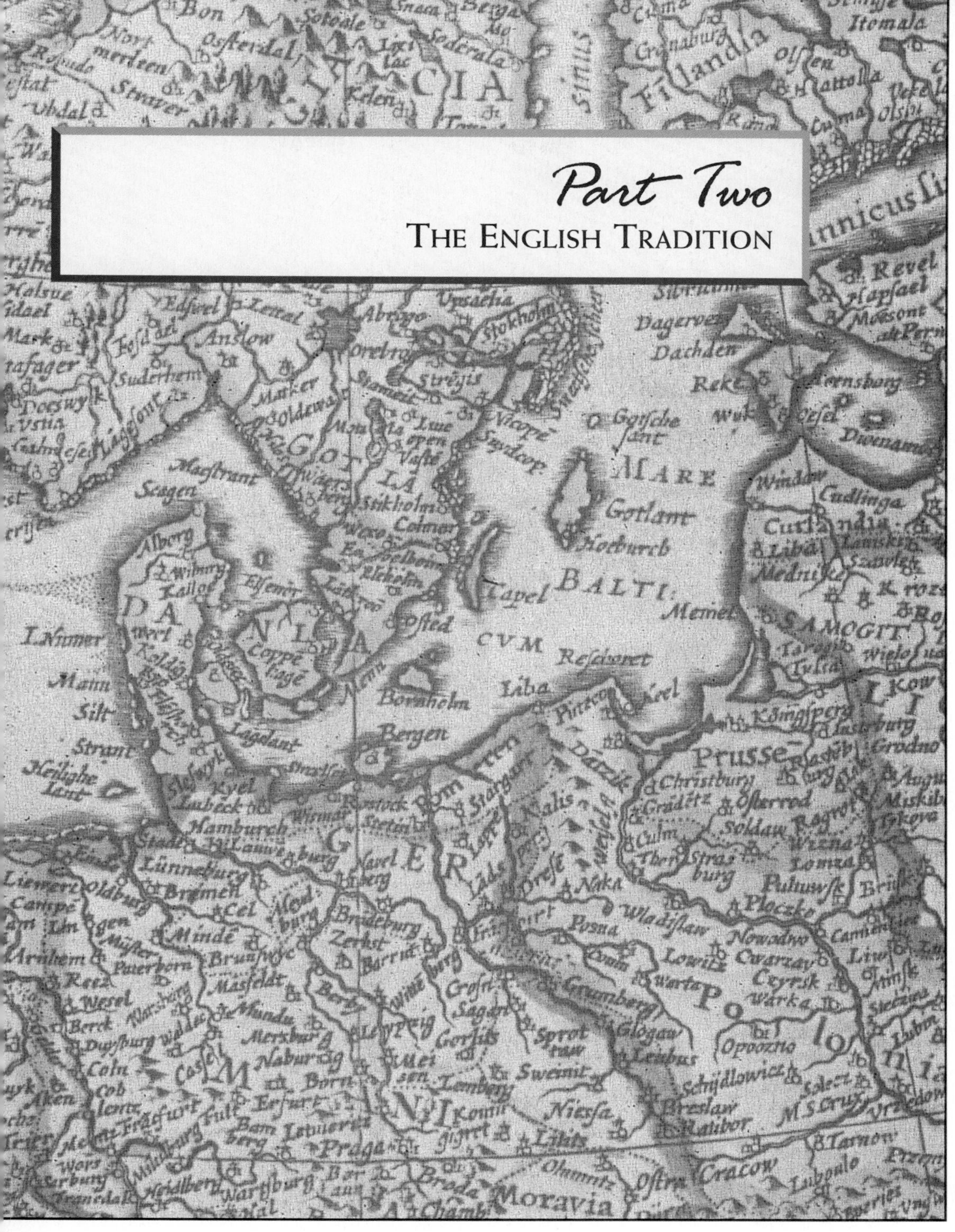

UNIT SKILLS OUTLINE

Literary Skills and Concepts

Writing Skills and Concepts

Language, Grammar, and Style

King Ælla's Messengers before Ragnar Lodbroke's Sons. J. A. Malmström, 1857. Norrköping Art Museum, Sweden

82 *UNIT TWO / THE ANGLO-SAXON PERIOD*

GOALS/OBJECTIVES

Studying this unit will enable students to
- interpret and appreciate Anglo-Saxon literature
- summarize the history of pre-Christian England and its literature
- name the sources and tell the history of Old English
- relate themes common in Anglo-Saxon literature to characteristics of Anglo-Saxon society
- describe the achievements of Boadicea, Bede, and Alfred
- describe and explain the influence of Christianity on Anglo-Saxon literature and culture
- identify and give examples of the major characteristics of Anglo-Saxon verse

You each have something divine in your soul, namely Reason and Memory and a discerning will to make choices in life.

—Alfred the Great
King of the West Saxons

CROSS-CURRICULAR CONNECTIONS

Arts and Humanities
Anglo-Saxon Research, 89
Art about Cain, 127
Frithiof's Saga, 102
Researching Scops, 113

Mathematics and Sciences
Physics of Singing Swords, 123
Stonehenge, 84

Social Studies
Achievements of Alfred, 87
Alfred the Great, 83
Anglo-Saxon Research, 89
Barbarians, 85
Celtic Religion, 89
Discussion about Sharing Stories, 86
Exploring the Historical Beowulf, 115
Geography of the Geats, 115
King Edwin, 90
Linguistics Research, 146
Mapping the Language Tree, 147
Researching History of Christianity in England, 91
Researching the *Exeter Book,* 108
Researching Scops, 113
Researching Weaponry, 112
Saint Hild of Whitby, 98
Separation of Church and State, 91
Slavery in Anglo-Saxon England, 86
Stonehenge, 84

Applied Arts
Constructing a Family Tree, 114
Researching Weaponry, 112

TEACHING THE MULTIPLE INTELLIGENCES

Musical
Artistic Portrayal of Loneliness, 102
Old English Verse, 115

Logical-Mathematical
Internet Riddle Research, 108
Linguistics Research, 146
Physics of Singing Swords, 123
Separation of Church and State, 91
Work with Riddles, 108

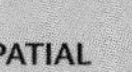

Spatial
Art about Cain, 127
Artistic Portrayal of Loneliness, 102
Constructing a Family Tree, 114
*Frithiof's Saga,*102
Geography of the Geats, 115
Mapping the Language Tree, 147
Researching Weaponry, 112

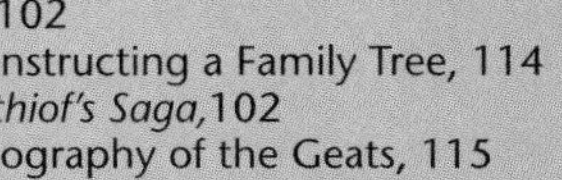

Kinesthetic
Artistic Portrayal of Loneliness, 102
Diagramming the Banished Wife's Home, 102

TEACHING THE MULTIPLE INTELLIGENCES (cont.)

Researching Weaponry, 112

Interpersonal
Artistic Portrayal of Loneliness, 102
Constructing a Family Tree, 114
Creativity Factors, 96
Discussing the Practice of Boasting, 110
Discussing the Banished Wife, 102
Exploring the Historical Beowulf, 115
Interviewing Elders about Language, 145
Linguistics Research, 146
Old English Verse, 115
Researching Weaponry, 112
Separation of Church and State, 91

ADDITIONAL RESOURCES

UNIT 2 RESOURCE BOOK
- Selection Check Test 4.2.1
- Selection Test 4.2.2

ADDITIONAL QUESTIONS AND ACTIVITIES

Ask students why they think one should study English history in a course on English Literature.

CROSS-CURRICULAR CONNECTIONS

HISTORY. Have students research Stonehenge to learn details about its construction and possible uses. The structure pre-dates the appearance in Britain of the Druids, so it was not originally built by them as a temple. Attempts have been made to interpret the structure as an ancient astronomical observatory. However, this idea also remains controversial.

BIBLIIOGRAPHIC NOTE

The following are some excellent sources of additional information on Old English language, history, and literature.

Baugh, A. C. ed. *A Literary History of England.* 1967

Blair, P. Hunter. *An Introduction to Anglo-Saxon England.* 1956.

Brodeur, A. G. *The Art of Beowulf.* 1959

Garmonsway, G. N., trans. *The Anglo-Saxon Chronicle.* 1955

Sherley-Price, L., trans. *A History of The English Church and People.* 1968

Shippey, T. A. *Old English Verse.* 1972.

Stanley, E. G., ed. *Continuations and Beginnings: Studies in Old English Literature.* 1966.

Stenton, F. M. *Anglo-Saxon England.* 3rd ed. 1971

Whitlock, Dorothy. *The Beginnings of English Society.* 1952

Wrenn, C. L. *A Study of Old English Literature.* 1967.

THE ANGLO-SAXON PERIOD (449–1066)

ANCIENT BRITAIN

Early seventh-century brooch from Kingston Down, Kent. *Liverpool, Merseyside Country Museum*

The Roman historian Tacitus wrote that the British Isles lay "at the outer edge of the world, almost into the whirlpools," and recalled how sailors, blown there by a hurricane, had encountered creatures half human and half animal. A later Byzantine historian, Procipius, described Britain as inhabited by the souls of the dead, ferried across the Channel from the Continent. To the ancient classical world, Britain was a far-off mystery—remote, shrouded in mist, and surrounded by stormy seas.

In ancient times, the largest of the islands was inhabited by **Britons**, the next largest by **Gaels** (gālz). These were **Celtic** (sel´tik *or* kel´tik) peoples who came from the European continent at an uncertain date. Today, in parts of the British Isles, languages descended from those of the **Celts** (seltz *or* keltz) are still spoken. These surviving Celtic languages include Irish, Scottish Gaelic, Welsh, and Breton.

The Celts of ancient Britain were farmers and hunters. Their society was organized into clans ruled by tribal chieftains elected from among a class of pagan priests. These priests, the **Druids**, composed hymns, poems, and historical records; studied the movements of heavenly bodies; served as judges; and conducted religious ceremonies in secret places in the woods and at sites such as **Stonehenge**.

Anglo-Saxon gatehouse at Dover

Little is known about the early inhabitants of Britain or about their Druid priests. Popular history pictures the Britons as savages, for they dressed in animal skins, conducted gruesome sacrifices, and according to contemporary accounts, went into battle unclothed and painted with blue dyes. However, they also produced haunting myths, made precise astronomical observations, and created beautiful artifacts—bracelets, necklaces, pottery, and earthworks like the **White Horse of Uffington.**

In 75 BC, Britain was invaded by a tribe from the Continent called the **Belgæ** (bel´ jē). They brought with them a new, heavy plow that revolutionized agriculture on the island. So began the process of clearing the land of its ancestral forests.

LITERARY EVENTS

➤ = British Events

2000 BC — 1000 BC — 500 BC — 100 BC — AD 100

HISTORICAL EVENTS

- ➤2200–2100 BC. Stonehenge built
- ➤600–500 BC. Britains arrive
- ➤100–55 BC. Belgæ invade Britain
- ➤55–54 BC. Julius Cæsar invades Britain
- ➤AD 43. Romans under Emperor Claudius conquer Britain
- ➤AD 50. Roman colony of Londinium (later London) founded
- ➤AD 60–61. Queen Boadicea leads revolt of Britons against Roman rule

THEMATIC CURRENTS

Use the following selections to explore these themes with your students.

SEPARATION
- "The Wife's Lament," 101
- from *Beowulf,* 113
- from "The Seafarer," 144
- "Wulf and Eadwacer," 144

RELIGION
- "The Conversion of King Edwin," 90
- "The Story of Cædmon," including "Cædmon's Hymn," 95
- from *Beowulf,* 113

STRUGGLE
- Anglo-Saxon Riddles, 107
- "The Wife's Lament," 101
- from *Beowulf,* 113
- "Wulf and Eadwacer," 144

Roman Britain

In 54 BC, the Roman general **Julius Cæsar** (100–44 BC) led a force across the English Channel, defeated the Britons, and returned to the Continent. The next year he returned, again defeated the Britons, and again left without establishing a settlement. Almost a century later, in AD 43, the Romans under the emperor **Claudius** (10 BC–AD 54) conquered Britain, introducing their law, culture, and Latin language to the island. They built roads and military fortifications, such as Hadrian's Wall, that stand to this day. They also established colonies, like Colchester and London, that later became great cities.

Julius Cæsar. *Antikensammlung im Pergamonmuseum, Staatliche Museen zu Berlin*

Boadicea, the Celtic Warrior Queen

In AD 60, Prasutagus, king of a tribe of Britons called the Iceni (ī sē′nī), died, leaving his wife, **Boadicea** (bō´ad ə sē´ə), to rule in his place. In that same year, Romans plundered the territory of the Iceni. In retaliation, the Iceni revolted against their Roman rulers. Boadicea gathered a native army and led it into battle, destroying Colchester and London. Eventually, the Romans overcame Boadicea, but not before the queen and her warriors had killed some 70,000 Roman colonists and soldiers. Astonishingly, Boadicea had very nearly succeeded in defeating the most powerful military force in the world.

The Warrior Queen. *This statue of Boadicea stands today by the River Thames, next to the British Houses of Parliament.*

The Coming of the Anglo-Saxons

Early in the fifth century, Rome called its legions home to protect its capital from invasion by barbarians. This withdrawal of Roman might left Britain vulnerable. Over the next hundred years, fierce Germanic invaders from the Continent crossed the North Sea (see the map on page 88). The first to arrive were the **Jutes**, a tribe from the Danish peninsula. In AD 449, they conquered the southwestern province that was to become the kingdom of Kent. Other Germanic tribes, the **Angles** and the **Saxons**, followed, first raiding

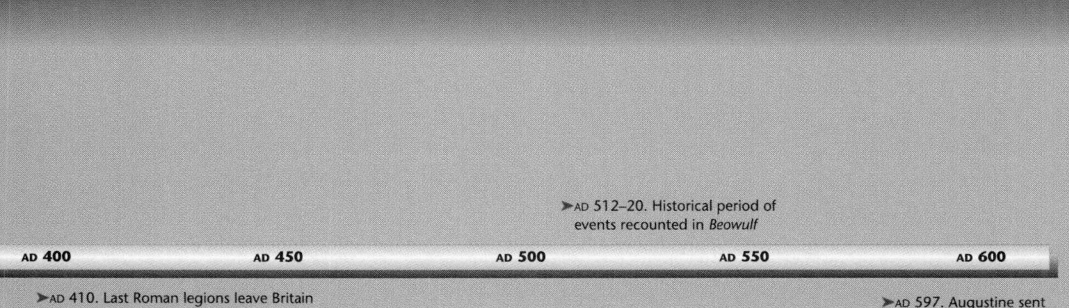
AD 512–20. Historical period of events recounted in *Beowulf*
AD 400
AD 450
AD 500
AD 550
AD 600
AD 410. Last Roman legions leave Britain
AD 432. St. Patrick begins mission in Ireland
AD 449. Jutes invade England, settling in province of Kent
AD 450–500. Anglo-Saxons invade England
AD 449. Anglo-Saxons and Britons, including the legendary Arthur, clash in Battle of Badon Hill
AD 597. Augustine sent to convert King Ethelbert of Kent to Christianity

HISTORICAL NOTE

The term *barbarian* has multiple meanings. In Classical times it meant "alien" or "foreigner." Thus, the Greek historian Herodotus (*circa* 485–*circa* 425 BC) used it to refer to Persians and all non-Greeks. Because Herodotus is widely read and because of certain impolite and gruesome practices of the ancient Persians, the word has taken on the additional meanings of "uncivilized," "primitive," "brutal," and "savage."

According to different versions of the story, Boadicea (or Boudicca), upon her army's defeat, either killed herself with poison or died of shock.

HISTORICAL NOTE

Alfred the Great (849–899) became king of Wessex, one of the seven Anglo-Saxon kingdoms, in 871. His military exploits contained Danish invaders to the northern part of England and thus made possible the emergence of England as a nation. His commitment to learning did much to further the creation of a native English literature. Alfred subsidized the creation of works in the Old English language and himself translated many Latin works into Old English. These works included Boethius's *Consolation of Philosophy* and, some believe, the *Ecclesiastical History* of the Venerable Bede.

LITERARY CURRENTS

Use the following selections to explore these lconcepts and techniques with your students.

Expository Writing
- "The Conversion of King Edwin," 90
- "The Story of Cædmon," including "Cædmon's Hymn," 95

Anglo-Saxon Verse
- "The Story of Cædmon," including "Cædmon's Hymn," 95
- from *Beowulf,* 113

Lyric Poem
- "The Story of Cædmon," including Cædmon's Hymn, 95
- "The Wife's Lament," 101
- from "The Seafarer," 144
- "Wulf and Eadwacer," 144

ADDITION RESOURCES

Unit 2 Resource Book
- Selection Check Test 4.2.1
- Selection Test 4.2.2

ADDITIONAL QUESTIONS AND ACTIVITIES

Have students discuss times in their lives when they have shared stories in group settings. Many students have had the experience of sharing stories around a campfire. Point out that when young people today do this, they are engaging in an ancient practice, a form of entertainment that predated television by many millennia.

HISTORICAL NOTE

Slavery was the rule in Anglo-Saxon England. Most farms were worked by slaves. Men could become slaves by going too far into debt, or they could be sentenced to slavery as punishment for a crime. A man could sell his wife and children as slaves to pay off a debt (wives had no similar right). Any children born to a slave were the property of the owner. Slaves had no rights at all. They could be killed or tortured at will and had no standing in courts of law.

We know that Anglo-Saxon men engaged in war and trades. What was life like for Anglo-Saxon women? In what ways was it similar to or different from the lives of Anglo-Saxon men? What differences can be inferred from the literature selections in this unit?

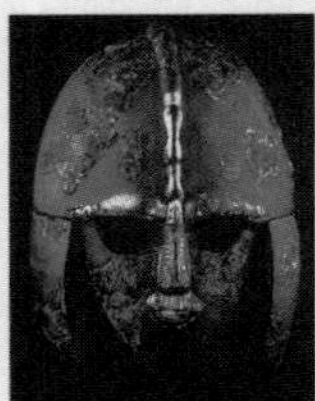

Sutton Hoo helmet.
British Museum

along the eastern coast of Britain, then establishing outposts, and finally conquering much of the country. The Angles established three kingdoms in the northern and midland sections of the island—Northumbria, Mercia, and East Anglia. The Saxons established three kingdoms in the south—Wessex (West Saxony), Essex (East Saxony), and Sussex (South Saxony). From the name of one of these tribes come the modern words *England* (*Angle-lond*) and *English* (*Angle-isc*).

Anglo-Saxon Culture

The warlike, seafaring Anglo-Saxons brought to Britain legends about ancient Germanic heroes and kings. Some of these legends, like the later heroic epic *Beowulf*, told of giants, demons, sea monsters, trolls, and fire-breathing dragons. Warriors were celebrated in heroic **lays**, or songs, sung at feasts by a minstrel called a **gleeman** or **scop** (shôp, skōp, *or* skäp), literally, a "shaper." Kings would entertain friends, retainers, and visitors at feasts held in great mead halls, so called for the **mead**, or wine made from fermented honey, that the warriors drank. The scop recited verse based on the exploits of great warriors of the tribe's past, often adding fanciful details about impossible feats of courage and strength. These lays were performed to the accompaniment of a **harp**, or lyre. Such orally composed songs not only provided entertainment but also embodied the heroic ideals of the people and kept alive their history.

Anglo-Saxon society was organized into a class of warriors called **earls** or **thanes**, a class of freemen called **churls**, and a class of slaves called **thralls**. The king depended for protection on his earls and for guidance on a council of wise elders, the ***Witenagemot***. Anglo-Saxon justice was simple and crude. A wrong done to one's kin required redress in kind or a payment of treasure, the ***wergild***, or "man-money." Blood feuds, invasions, and desire for land or treasure led to frequent warfare.

Life among the Anglo-Saxons was harsh and unpredictable. Death from disease, famine, battle wounds, or storms at sea could come at any time, depending upon the whims of the goddess ***Wyrd*** (würd), or "fate." If a person were courageous and not fated to die, then he might survive. As the legendary hero

Golden Horns.
The National Museum, Copenhagen

Literary Events

➤ = British Events

➤AD 731. Bede completes *Ecclesiastical History of the English People*

➤AD 700–750. *Beowulf* composed orally in kingdom of Northumbria or Mercia

➤AD 658–80. "Cædmon's Hymn" composed

AD 650 — AD 700 — AD 750 — AD 800 — AD 850

➤AD 664. Church of England organized at Council of Whitby

➤AD 673–735. The Venerable Bede

➤AD 750–825. Cynewulf, author of religious poetry and possibly of riddles

➤AD 790–878. Danes (Vikings) invade England

➤AD 849. King Alfred the Great born

Historical Events

Beowulf says in the poem that bears his name, "Fate often saves an undoomed man if his courage is good."

The Anglo-Saxons believed their kings to be descended from divinities such as ***Tiu***, god of war; ***Woden***, king of the gods; ***Thor***, god of thunder and the sky; and ***Freia***, goddess of the home. The names of these gods survive, today, in our names for days of the week: *Tuesday* (*Tiwesdœg*), *Wednesday* (*Wodnesdœg*), *Thursday* (*þuresdœg*), and *Friday* (*Frigedœg*).

Monasteries. *Reconstruction of stained glass window from Jarrow, birthplace of the Venerable Bede* *(see page 90)*

The Coming of Christianity

Christianity first reached Britain during the Roman occupation. In the fifth century, neighboring Ireland had been converted to Christianity by the renowned **St. Patrick** (*circa* AD 385–*circa* 461), and soon thereafter Christian immigrants from Ireland crossed into Scotland and northern England. However, the conversion of the whole of England to Christianity came after the arrival of **Augustine** (d. AD 604), sent by Pope Gregory the Great in AD 597 to convert King Ethelbert of Kent.

The coming of Christianity to England meant the establishment of **monasteries**, centers of religious retreat and learning where **scribes** produced books by hand, writing on vellum parchment made of calves' or sheep's skin. Many of these books were religious works, such as saints' lives and collections of sermons, but some were copies of the oral literature of the common people. To the labors of the monks and to a great king named Alfred we owe the survival of Anglo-Saxon literature in written form.

Alfred the Great

In the eighth and ninth centuries, the **Danes**, or **Vikings**, invaded Anglo-Saxon England. Arriving from Scandinavia in longboats, they plundered monasteries, burnt cities and towns, and conquered much of the island, including three of what were then the four major Anglo-Saxon kingdoms: **Northumbria, Mercia,** and **East Anglia.** England may well have become a Danish nation if not for **Alfred the Great,** ruler of the fourth major kingdom, **Wessex.** In AD 878, Alfred, whose epilepsy did not prevent him from becoming a great warrior, defeated the Danes and unified southern and central England under his command, so earning the title of **bretwalda**, or "King of Britain." Alfred forced the Danes to accept a treaty confining them to an area of northern and eastern England called the **Danelaw**. King Alfred's daughter Ethelfled ruled

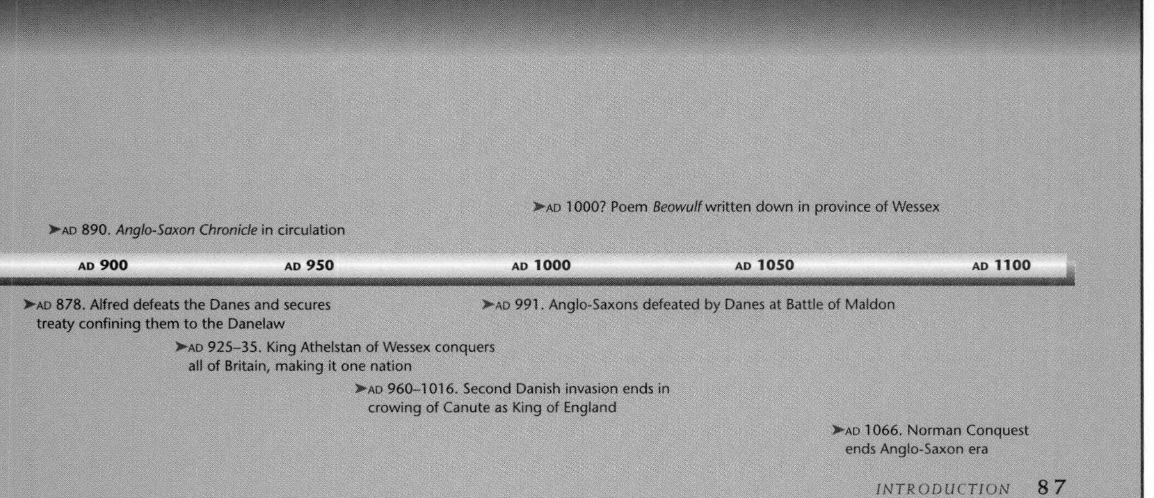

➤AD 1000? Poem *Beowulf* written down in province of Wessex
➤AD 890. *Anglo-Saxon Chronicle* in circulation
AD 900
AD 950
AD 1000
AD 1050
AD 1100
➤AD 878. Alfred defeats the Danes and secures treaty confining them to the Danelaw
➤AD 991. Anglo-Saxons defeated by Danes at Battle of Maldon
➤AD 925–35. King Athelstan of Wessex conquers all of Britain, making it one nation
➤AD 960–1016. Second Danish invasion ends in crowing of Canute as King of England
➤AD 1066. Norman Conquest ends Anglo-Saxon era

HISTORICAL NOTE

The following is a list of kings of England during the Old English period.

802–839	Egbert, King of Wessex
839–858	Ethelwulf
858–860	Ethelbald
860–866	Ethelbert
866–871	Ethelred I
871–899	Alfred the Great
899–924	Edward the Elder
924–940	Athelstan the Glorious
940–946	Edmund I
946–955	Edred
955–959	Edwy the Fair
959–975	Edgar the Peaceful
975–978	Edward the Martyr
978–1016	Ethelred II the Unready
1016–1016	Edmund II
1016–1035	Canute the Dane
1035–1040	Harold I
1040–1042	Hardecanute
1042–1066	Edward the Confessor
1066–1066	Harold II (died in the Norman Conquest

BIOGRAPHICAL NOTE

Alfred devoted much of his energies not only to defending against military attacks, but also to preventing them by diplomacy and by establishing strong defenses. Nevertheless, his greatest accomplishments are probably in the realm of culture and education. During the peace from AD 878 to 885, Alfred invited scholars from parts of Britain and the Continent to visit him, and he learned Latin. By 887, he was translating to English those Latin works which he believed "most necessary for all men to know." These included Bede's *Ecclesiastical History* (see page 91), Orosius's *7 Books of Histories Against the Pagans,* Augustine of Hippo's *Soliloquies,* and Boethius's *Consolation of Philosophy,* as well as a manual for priests for the training of parishioners. *Alfred the Great: Asser's Life of King Alfred and Other Contemporary Sources,* ed. and trans. by S. Keynes and M. Lapidge (1983), is a new translation of an AD 893 biography.

SELECTION CHECK TEST 4.2.1 WITH ANSWERS

Checking Your Reading

Britain before the Anglo-Saxons. Choose the best answer to complete each of the following sentences about the history of Britain.

1. Ireland was converted to Catholicism by
   a. Julius Caesar
   b. Pope Gregory
   c. St. Patrick
   d. Alfred the Great
2. Who nearly defeated the Romans in battle?
   a. Augustine
   b. Claudius
   c. Boadicea
   d. St. Patrick
3. To the ancient classical world, Britain…
   a. was mysterious and dangerous.
   b. was the promised land that everyone wished to reach.
   c. was too cold and rocky to settle.
   d. was the land where their gods and goddesses lived.
3. To practice their religious beliefs, the ancient people of Britain…
   a. memorized the Bible because they could not read.
   b. built monasteries out of granite.
   c. built temples of gold to gods and goddesses.
   d. worshipped at Stonehenge and in forests.
4. The Belgæ
   a. drove the Romans from Britain.
   b. brought plows to Britain.
   c. were pagan priests.
   d. built Stonehenge.
5. The Druids
   a. built roads and forts.
   b. were spirits who inhabited forests and rivers.
   c. were judges, artists, historians, and religious leaders.
   d. were half human and half animal.

Put the following hierarchy of classes in ancient Britain order, from HIGHEST RANKING to LOWEST RANKING. Put a (1) by the highest and a (5) by the lowest.

_3_ earl, or thane
_1_ Woden
_5_ thrall
_4_ churl
_2_ king

Mercia as regent and queen, built cities, and captured other cities from the Danes.

After securing the future of the English nation, Alfred turned his attention to education and learning. A pious king, he believed that the strength of his country depended on the spread of education and of the Christian faith. Therefore, he conceived a plan to rebuild the monasteries destroyed by the Vikings and to

> render into the language that we all understand [English] some of those books that are most necessary for all to know and bring it to pass that the freeborn youth of England will devote themselves to learning until they can read English.

Alfred sponsored the translation of many books into the Old English language, including works of history, philosophy, and religion. He also sponsored the writing of a year-by-year account of English history up to his time, the *Anglo-Saxon Chronicle*. The *Chronicle*, along with Bede's *Ecclesiastical History*, is among our most valuable sources of information about the period.

THE END OF THE ANGLO-SAXON ERA

Between AD 925 and AD 939, King Athelstan of the West Saxons conquered the rest of the island of Britain, making it one nation. The Anglo-Saxon peace, however, was not to last. In AD 960, another wave of Danish invasions began, culminating in AD 1016 with the crowning of Canute, a Dane, as king. Thereafter, the country passed briefly back into English control. However, a new threat awaited the Anglo-Saxons. In AD 1066, a Norman duke, William the Conqueror, crossed the English Channel and defeated the English king Harold at the Battle of Hastings, bringing the Anglo-Saxon era to a close.

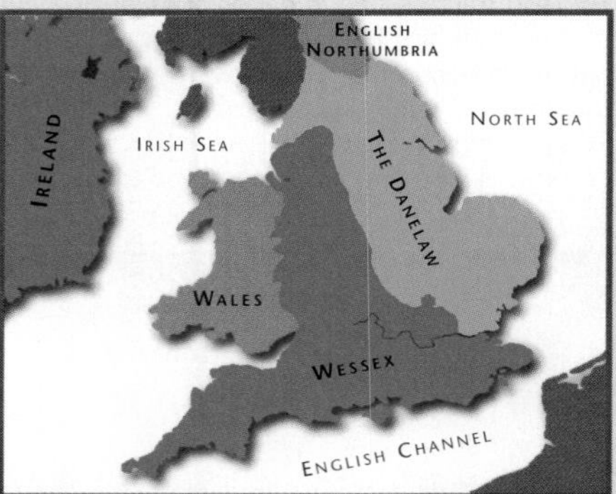

***Britain circa** AD 886 (above), showing Wessex and the Danelaw*

***Britain circa** AD 800 (left), showing the seven Anglo-Saxon kingdoms*

Anglo-Saxon Culture. Fill in the blanks using the following terms.

scop mead Wyrd Angles
Danes Saxons Witenagemot

1. The **Saxons** had three kingdoms (Wessex, Essex and Sussex) in southern Britain.
2. Life was harsh and unpredictable, subject to the whims of the goddess **Wyrd**, or fate.
3. Kings would entertain in great halls named for **mead**, a wine made from honey.
4. The council of elders, or **Witenagemot**, advised the king.
5. Alfred defeated the **Danes**, united southern and central England, and believed in education and Christianity.

Several groups held power over Britain prior to the year 1066. Order the following groups from the earliest to the latest rulers. Put a (1) by the earliest group (449 or earlier) and a (5) by the latest.

_4_ Danes
_5_ bretwalda, King of Britain
_2_ Romans
_1_ Celts

ECHOES

Ancient and Anglo-Saxon England

[Boadicea] was very tall, the glance of her eye most fierce, her voice harsh. A mass of red hair fell to her hips. Around her neck hung a necklace of gold. She wore a multi-colored tunic fastened by a brooch. She was terrifying to look upon.

—from an account by the Roman historian Dio Cassius

Hale be thou, earth, mother of men,
Be thou with growing things in God's embrace,
Filled with food for the good of men

—from "Æcerbot," an Anglo-Saxon spell or charm

Therefore I sing   and recite a tale
Before many men   in the mead-hall gathered
.
.
.
With clear voice   for our victorious leader
Raise up a song   to the sound of the harp.

—from "Widsith," an Anglo-Saxon poem that tells the story of a minstrel, or scop

Fate often saves an undoomed man if his courage is good.

—from *Beowulf*

HISTORICAL NOTE

Celts in pre-Christian Britain worshipped the *eorpan modor* (Mother Earth), regarded as the creator of life and of fertility. Some students may be interested in researching and reporting on the pre-Christian religions of Britain.

ADDITIONAL QUESTIONS AND ACTIVITIES

Students can discuss the idea of fate. Do they think individuals control their own fate, or do they think fate is determined by outside forces? How do they interpret the quotation from *Beowulf* at left? Do they agree with it?

ADDITIONAL QUESTIONS AND ACTIVITIES

Research Anglo-Saxon England. The following topics are suitable for research reports on early Britain and Anglo-Saxon England:

1. Stonehenge
2. Cæsar's Invasion of Britain
3. Boadicea's Revolt against Roman Rule
4. The Anglo-Saxon Invasion
5. The Origins of English
6. Anglo-Saxon Social and Political Structures
7. Women in Anglo-Saxon England
8. The Life and Works of Alfred the Great
9. The Influence of Christianity on Anglo-Saxon Literature
10. The Anglo-Saxon Heroic Ideal

ADDITIONAL RESOURCES

Unit 2 Resource Book
- Selection Worksheet 2.1
- Selection Check Test 4.2.3
- Selection Test 4.2.4
- Language, Grammar, and Style Resource 3.34
- Speaking and Listening Resource 4.15, 4.18

READER'S JOURNAL

Students may write about changes they made to their religious beliefs, their political beliefs, beliefs about how to conduct their lives, or assumptions about other people. Ask students whether they find changing their beliefs to be difficult or easy. What kind of reasons would inspire them to change their beliefs?

VOCABULARY FROM THE SELECTION

adversity	efficacious
diligently	precept
ecclesiastical	temporal

HISTORICAL NOTE

From AD 616 to 632, Edwin was king of Northumbria and was recognized across England as overlord. Edwin married the princess Aethelburth of Kent, a Christian. She was responsible for bringing Paulinus to Northumbria because she wanted to convert Edwin and his subjects. In 632, Northumbria was invaded by the united armies of King Cadwallon of Gwynedd and King Penda of Mercia. Edwin was killed and his army defeated. Aethelburth and Paulinus fled, and Christianity was suppressed for a time.

Literary Tools

Allegory. An **allegory** is a work in which each element *symbolizes*, or represents, something else. As you read, try to determine what part of this historical writing presents an allegory.

Aim. A writer's **aim** is his or her purpose, or goal. People may write with the following aims:

- to inform (expository/informational writing)
- to entertain, enrich, enlighten, and/or use an artistic medium, such as fiction or poetry, to share a perspective (imaginative writing)
- to make a point by sharing a story about an event (narrative writing)
- to reflect (personal/expressive writing)
- to persuade readers or listeners to respond in some way (persuasive/argumentative writing)

Copy the following cluster chart onto your own paper. As you read, try to determine with what aims Bede wrote "The Conversion of King Edwin."

AIM

Reader's Journal

Write about a time when someone persuaded you to change a belief.

"The Conversion of King Edwin"

from *Ecclesiastical History of the English People*

BY SAINT BEDE THE VENERABLE

About the Author

Saint Bede the Venerable (AD 672– or 673–735) was born in Jarrow, in the kingdom of Northumbria. He entered the Monastery of St. Peter in nearby Wearmouth at the age of seven. At nineteen, he was ordained a deacon; at thirty, a priest. Like other monastics of his time, Bede wrote in Latin. He traveled very little, but his fame spread throughout Europe due to his writings on subjects as varied as history, poetry, grammar, mathematics, science, the scriptures, and lives of the saints. Bede's histories make fascinating reading not only for the light that they shed on the distant Anglo-Saxon past but also for their engaging accounts of miraculous and legendary events. In his histories, Bede introduced the practice of dating events from the birth of Christ (i.e., from AD 0, where AD is an abbreviation for the Latin *Anno Domini,* meaning "the year of our Lord"). This method of dating was adopted throughout Europe and is still in use today. Bede was canonized (made a saint of the Roman Catholic Church) in 1899, eleven hundred years after his death.

About the Selection

Most notable among Bede's works is the *Historia Ecclesiastica Gentis Anglorum,* or ***Ecclesiastical History of the English People.*** Bede's five-book Latin history of the Church in England covers the period from Cæsar's invasion of Britain (55–54 BC) to his own time (the history was finished around AD 731). King Alfred considered the book important enough to have it translated into Old English, the language of the common people. **"The Conversion of King Edwin"** comes from Book II of Bede's history and relates the process by which Christian missionaries converted the Anglo-Saxon kings. The selection shows the dramatic contrast between the Anglo-Saxons' grim view of the afterlife and the positive alternative offered by the missionaries.

GOALS/OBJECTIVES

Studying this lesson will enable students to
- empathize with Edwin's uncertainties about the afterlife
- describe Bede's accomplishments and explain the historical significance of Bede's writings
- describe some key differences between Anglo-Saxon paganism and Christianity
- explain what an allegory is and recognize allegories as they encounter them in their reading
- recognize and correct run-ons
- deliver a persuasive speech

The Conversion of King Edwin

from *Ecclesiastical History of the English People*

BY SAINT BEDE THE VENERABLE

At this time the nation of the Northumbrians, that is, the nation of the Angles that live on the north side of the river Humber, with their king, Edwin, received the faith through the preaching of Paulinus.[1] This Edwin, as a reward of his receiving the faith, and as an earnest of his share in the heavenly kingdom, received an increase of that which he enjoyed on earth, for he reduced under his dominion all the borders of Britain that were provinces either of the aforesaid nation, or of the Britons, a thing which no British king had ever done before. . . .

According to Bede, what reward does Edwin receive for converting to Christianity?

For some time he delayed to receive the word of God at the preaching of Paulinus, and used to sit several hours alone, and seriously to ponder with himself what he was to do, and what religion he was to follow. Then the man of God came to him, laid his right hand on his head, and asked whether he knew that sign.[2] The king in a trembling condition, was ready to fall down at his feet, but he raised him up, and in a familiar manner said to him, "Behold, by the help of God you have escaped the hands of the enemies whom you feared. Behold you have of His gift obtained the kingdom which you desired. Take heed not to delay that which you promised to perform; embrace the faith, and keep the precepts of Him who, delivering you from temporal adversity, has raised you to the honor of a temporal kingdom; and if, from this time forward, you shall be obedient to His will, which through me He signifies to you, He will not only deliver you from the everlasting torments of the wicked, but also make you partaker[3] with Him of His eternal kingdom in Heaven."

1. **Paulinus.** Pope Gregory I sent Paulinus as a missionary to Northumbria in AD 601.
2. **that sign.** The laying on of hands is a ceremony for transmitting spiritual grace to the recipient.
3. **partaker.** One who takes part or shares in something

Words for Everyday Use

ec • cle • si • as • ti • cal (e klē´ zē as´ ti kəl) *adj.*, having to do with the church. *The cardinal needed his ecclesiastical robes for the service on Sunday.*

pre • cept (prē´ sept) *n.*, commandment or direction meant as a rule of action or conduct. *My mother made her rule about finishing all our homework before watching television a precept in our house.*

tem • po • ral (tem´ pə rəl) *adj.*, lasting only for a time, limited; of this world, not spiritual. *The minister said that solving our temporal troubles is less importand than caring for our immortal souls.*

ad • ver • si • ty (ad vʉr´ sə tē) *n.*, misfortune, trouble. *Do you admire someone who deals with adversity by working harder instead of giving in?*

ADDITIONAL QUESTIONS AND ACTIVITIES

As an additional activity, students imagine that they are research assistants for an Anglo-Saxon scholar and that they have been asked to visit the library to find books with information about Saint Bede the Venerable. Refer them to the Language Arts Survey 5.19, "How to Locate Library Materials." For each book, students should list the title, the author's name, the year of publication, the call number, and the kind of information given. You may want to combine this activity with a lesson on proper bibliography form. Refer students to the Language Arts Survey 5.40, "Making Bibliographies and Bibliography Cards."

ANSWERS TO GUIDED READING QUESTION

1. Edwin receives an increase of that which he had on earth (an enlarged domain).

INDIVIDUAL LEARNING STRATEGIES

MOTIVATION
Have students discuss or write about the ways in which a political leader's religion can be significant for his or her country. This can be linked to current events. Ask them to discuss their feelings on the separation between church and state. How much should a leader's religious beliefs affect the way he or she conducts political business?

READING PROFICIENCY
Have students answer all of the Guided Reading questions and summarize in their own words each paragraph of the selection.

ENGLISH LANGUAGE LEARNING
Explain to students that Old English and Modern English are different and separate languages and that students are not expected to know or to learn Old English. Share with them the following additional idioms and vocabulary:

shed light on—reveal information that helps one to understand something
fair weather—good weather
earnest—something given as a pledge or token
aforesaid—mentioned before
partaker—one who participates
confer—speak with
verily—truly
hitherto—until now
forward—help or advance
exhortation—urging
emerge—come into view

SPECIAL NEEDS
Consider taking some time to help students complete the cluster chart on page 90. Ask them to summarize what King Edwin and his people expect from their religion—why did they convert?

ENRICHMENT
Interested students may research the history of Christianity in England. In the Unit Introduction, students learned that Christianity was introduced during the Roman occupation. Ask them to research what changes King Henry VIII made to religion in England, and what conflict later ensued between Catholic and Protestant rulers of England.

ANSWERS TO GUIDED READING QUESTION

1. The counselor compares life to the flight of a sparrow.
2. The priest rejects the old gods because his faith in them has not brought him wealth or influence.

SELECTION CHECK TEST 4.2.3 WITH ANSWERS

Checking Your Reading

1. Who brought Christianity to Edwin? **Paulinus, a Catholic priest and missionary, brought Christianity to Edwin.**
2. What political success of Edwin's is described as a reward for "receiving the faith"? **Edwin expanded his kingdom and this is seen as a reward for his conversion.**
3. With whom did Edwin consult before converting, and why? **He consulted his wise men, hoping they would agree to be converted also.**
4. Why had Coifi expected to be more prosperous and favored? **He was the most devout worshipper of their gods.**
5. With what is the sparrow's short flight through a warm room compared? **It is compared to a man's life.**

Vocabulary in Context

Fill each blank with the most appropriate word from the Words for Everyday Use from "The Conversion of King Edwin." You may have to change the tense of the word.

ecclesiastical temporal adversity
precept diligently efficacious

1. Often, we don't know the extent of our strength until we face **adversity**.
2. When Sondra toured Mexico, she was amazed by its **ecclesiastical** architecture, especially by the gorgeous, ornate cathedral in Guanajuato.
3. We tried several methods before we finally found the most **efficacious** one.
4. People who live in the north take every advantage of summer's **temporal** pleasures.
5. The scribes toiled **diligently**, often ruining their eyesight with years of careful work.

Literary Tools

1. What type of writing is this selection: imaginative, narrative, or expressive? **It is a narrative.**
2. What is the main means of organization used in this piece? **It is chronological.**
3. What is an allegory? **An allegory is a symbolic story.**
4. How is allegory used in this piece? **The description of a sparrow's flight is an allegory of a person's life.**
5. What is one of the aims of this selection? ***Responses will vary.* Students may name one of the aims they listed in their graphic organizer; i.e., to inform; to make a point; or to persuade.**

RESPONDING TO THE SELECTION

Ask students to consider whether the arguments advanced by Edwin's counselors seem reasonable to them. Do they feel that Edwin had reason to forsake his old beliefs and embrace these new ones? Why, or why

---

The king, hearing these words, answered, that he was both willing and bound to receive the faith which he taught; but that he would confer about it with his principal friends and counselors, to the end that if they also were of his opinion, they might all together be cleansed in Christ the Fountain of Life. Paulinus consenting, the king did as he said; for, holding a council with the wise men,[4] he asked of every one in particular what he thought of the new doctrine, and the new worship that was preached. To which the chief of his own priests, Coifi, immediately answered, "O king, consider what this is which is now preached to us; for I verily declare to you, that the religion which we have hitherto professed has, as far as I can learn, no virtue in it. For none of your people has applied himself more diligently to the worship of our gods than I; and yet there are many who receive greater favors from you, and are more preferred than I, and are more prosperous in all their undertakings. Now if the gods were good for any thing, they would rather forward me, who have been more careful to serve them. It remains, therefore, that if upon examination you find those new doctrines, which are now preached to us, better and more efficacious, we immediately receive them without any delay."

A page from the Grimbald Gospels. British Library, London.

What is the king's chief priest, Coifi's, reason rejecting the old gods?

Another of the king's chief men, approving of his words and exhortations, presently added: "The present life of man, O king, seems to me, in comparison to that time which is unknown to us, like to the swift flight of a sparrow through the room wherein you sit at supper in winter, with your commanders and ministers, and a good fire in the midst, whilst the storms of rain and snow prevail abroad; the sparrow, flying in at one door, and immediately out at another, whilst he is within, is safe from the wintry storm; but after a short space of fair weather, he immediately vanishes out of your sight, into the dark winter from which he had emerged. So this life of man appears for a short space, but of what went before, or what is to follow, we are utterly ignorant. If, therefore, this new doctrine contains something more certain, it seems justly to deserve to be followed." The other elders and king's counselors, by Divine inspiration, spoke to the same effect. ■

To what does the wise counselor compare life as the Anglo-Saxons knew it?

4. **wise men.** These wise men are the Anglo-Saxon *Witenagemot*, or council of elders. From the Old English *witen*, "to know," comes our modern word *wit*.

WORDS FOR EVERYDAY USE

dil • i • gent • ly (dil´ ə jənt lē) *adv.*, with great care and attention. *We all worked diligently throughout the day, and the project was completed on time.*

ef • fi • ca • cious (ef´ i kā´ shəs) *adj.*, effective, producing the desired result. *The doctors looked for the most efficacious remedy, without regard for cost.*

Respond *to the* SELECTION

If you were one of Edwin's counselors, what advice would you give him about the decision he is trying to make?

INVESTIGATE, Inquire, Imagine

Recall: GATHERING FACTS → **Interpret:** FINDING MEANING

1a. Who is Paulinus? What does he say has happened to King Edwin recently? What does Paulinus say he wants Edwin to do?

1b. Explain what Paulinus is asking King Edwin to do. To what does Paulinus attribute recent events in Edwin's life? Explain what makes Paulinus's request persuasive.

2a. What are Coifi's reasons for wanting to reject the old religion?

2b. What do Coifi's reasons for wishing to abandon the old religion reveal about the type of person he is? Explain whether his reasons are good ones. Are his reasons selfish or selfless?

3a. To what does another of the king's advisors compare the swift flight of a sparrow through a room?

3b. In what way are the two things being compared alike? What view of life and the afterlife is presented in this comparison?

Analyze: TAKING THINGS APART → **Synthesize:** BRINGING THINGS TOGETHER

4a. What details about the old Germanic religion are presented in this historical writing? What details about Christianity are presented? In what ways are the two religions similar? In what way do the two religions seem to differ?

4b. Based on the differences between the two religions presented in this historical account, why might the new religion have been appealing to the king's advisors and the king?

Perspective: LOOKING AT OTHER VIEWS → **Empathy:** SEEING FROM INSIDE

5a. Explain what you believe the king's chief priest Coifi saw as the purpose of religion. Why might he have felt this way? Explain how his views are similar to or different from your own.

5b. Explain why the decision Edwin makes in the selection might have been difficult for him. Why might he have felt the need to call together his advisors and friends before making such a decision?

Understanding Literature

ALLEGORY. Review the definition for **allegory** in the Handbook of Literary Terms. The last paragraph of this historical account contains an allegory comparing human life to the flight of a sparrow. The allegory mentions a sparrow, a dining room with a door, supper, winter storms, commanders and ministers, a fire, and our sight. What do these elements of the allegory represent in the human world?

AIM. Review the definition for **aim** in Literary Tools on page 90. Explain what you think the aim or aims of Bede were when writing "The Conversion of King Edwin." Based on the selection, how can you tell that Bede was a Christian? How might his purpose have been different if he were not a Christian?

ANSWERS TO INVESTIGATE, INQUIRE, AND IMAGINE

RECALL

1a. Paulinus is a Catholic priest and missionary. He says Edwin recently escaped his enemies, obtained the kingdom he desired; he wants Edwin to fulfill his promise and embrace the faith.

2a. Coifi thinks the old religion is ineffectual because even though he is the chief priest, he has attained little wealth, influence, or power.

3a. The flight of a sparrow through a room is compared to human life.

INTERPRET

1b. Paulinus is asking Edwin to convert to Christianity. Paulinus attributes these fortunate events to God's help. Paulinus's argument is persuasive because he points out that the Christian God has already done much for Edwin and because he reminds Edwin of his promise to convert.

2b. Coifi's reasons reveal that he is greedy, power-hungry, and bitter about not gaining the status he desires. He is mainly concerned about what a religion can "get" for its practitioners. Most students will say that his reasons are selfish.

3b. Both human life and the flight are brief, both humans and the sparrow are witnesses to company and feasting, and nobody knows what happens to the sparrow before or after its flight just as nobody knows what happens to human souls before birth and after death. Human life is short, but joyous when filled with companions and feasting. The afterlife is unknown and possibly threatening.

ANALYZE

4a. The two religions are similar in that they both have priests and in that priests of both religions seem to expect that the God (or gods) of their religion should be able to do something to increase the wealth, influence, or power of individual humans. Differences are that the Christian God seems more inclined to act on the behalf of humans and the certainty about an afterlife, while the Germanic religion had more remote gods and anxiety about the afterlife.

SYNTHESIZE

4b. They may have been attracted to the new religion because they think it offers more spiritual certainty and more worldly advantage.

PERSPECTIVE

5a. Coifi believes that the purpose of religion is worldly success. He might feel this way because life in his time and place was harsh, so he felt that religion was purposeless unless it bettered humans' worldly lives in some way. Responses will vary.

EMPATHY

5b. Students may say that Edwin wanted to make sure he would have the support of the most influential people in his kingdom before changing his religion (and that of his people) because he might have been deposed or even killed if his decision to adopt Christianity had proved unpopular.

Answers to Understanding Literature can be found on page 94.

ANSWERS TO UNDERSTANDING LITERATURE

Allegory. The sparrow symbolizes human life; its brief flight in the dining room represents our short life on earth; the people and comforts in the room symbolize the pleasures of our lives on earth; sight symbolizes our knowledge and so the room also symbolizes the limits of human knowledge; the winter storms outside symbolize the unknown periods before and after our lives.

Aim. Students may say that Bede's aims were to inform his audience about a historical event and to persuade his readers about the value of Christianity. Students should be able to tell that Bede was a Christian because his piece is one-sided and pro-Christian. If Bede had been a practitioner of the old Germanic religion, his purpose might have also been to inform and persuade, but he may have tried to persuade his audience that Edwin's decision to convert to Christianity was wrong.

ANSWERS TO INTEGRATING THE LANGUAGE ARTS

Language, Grammar, and Style

1. Bede's history of Britain was not the first. It was partly based on *On the Fall of Britain,* by Welsh writer Gildas, in AD 550.
2. According to stories told by early Welsh historians, one of the soldiers who fought against the Anglo-Saxons was named Arthur. Such stories gave rise to legends about King Arthur and the knights of the Round Table.
3. The early Germanic peoples, including the Anglo-Saxons, used alphabetic characters called runes to write inscriptions on stones. The runic alphabet is known as futhark.
4. The treasure of Sutton Hoo was found in 1939. At Sutton Hoo, a seventh-century Anglo-Saxon king had been buried with a large number of jewels, coins, weapons, and tools. He was entombed in a ninety-foot-long ship that had been hauled to the top of a one-hundred-foot-high cliff.
5. Our knowledge of the Anglo-Saxons comes from many sources. These sources include inscriptions, histories, literature, and archaeological finds like Sutton Hoo.

- Additional practice is provided in the Language, Grammar, and Style Resource Book 3.34.

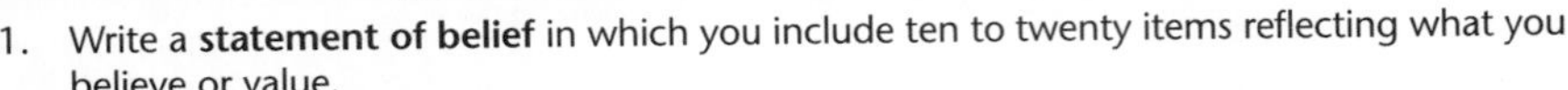

Writer's Journal

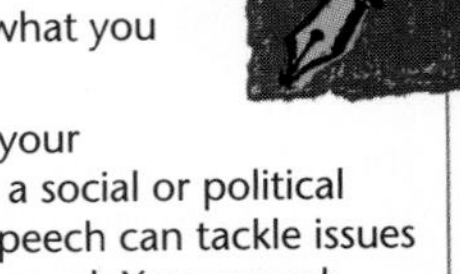

1. Write a **statement of belief** in which you include ten to twenty items reflecting what you believe or value.
2. Write a **persuasive speech** in which you try to convince your audience to adopt your viewpoint and respond in some way. Your speech can express your viewpoint on a social or political issues and provide compelling reasons for others to share your opinion, or your speech can tackle issues such as who is the best sports hero of all time and how this person should be honored. Your speech should clearly state your position and provide arguments or reasons to support your opinion, as well as some call to action.
3. Write an **allegorical paragraph**. Each element in your allegory should represent something about your chosen topic. For example, if you are comparing working hard to accomplish something to climbing a tall mountain, the sharp rocks on the mountain might represent some of the unexpected obstacles in your way. Topics include working hard to accomplish something, saying goodbye to a friend or loved one, or developing your own skills, interests, and talents.

Integrating *the* Language Arts

Language, Grammar, and Style

Correcting Run-ons. Read the Language Arts Survey 3.34, "Correcting Sentence Run-ons." Then revise the sentences below by changing punctuation and capitalization and adding words as necessary.

1. Bede's history of Britain was not the first, it was partly based on *On the Fall of Britain*, written by Gildas, a Welshman, in AD 550.
2. According to stories told by early Welsh historians, one of the soldiers who fought against the Anglo-Saxons was named Arthur such stories gave rise to legends about King Arthur and the knights of the round table.
3. The early Germanic peoples, including the Anglo-Saxons, used alphabetic characters called runes to write inscriptions on stones, the runic alphabet is known as futhark.
4. The treasure of Sutton Hoo was found in 1939, at Sutton Hoo a seventh-century Anglo-Saxon king had been buried with a large number of jewels, coins, weapons, and tools he was entombed in a ninety-foot-long ship that had been hauled to the top of a one-hundred-foot-high cliff.
5. Our knowledge of the Anglo-Saxons comes from many sources these sources include inscriptions, histories, literature, and archeological finds like Sutton Hoo.

Speaking and Listening

Delivering a Speech. If you have not already done so, complete the Writer's Journal activity above, writing a persuasive speech. Then review the Language Arts Survey 4.15 and 4.18, "Giving a Speech" and "Guidelines for Giving a Speech." Perfect your speech by delivering it in front of your mirror and then in front of friends or family members. Follow the tips in the Language Arts Survey to make your delivery effective. On a day appointed by your teacher, deliver your persuasive speech to your classmates. Remember to use your tone of voice, pitch, eye contact, facial expression, and gestures to help persuade your audience to adopt your point of view.

"The Story of Cædmon"

from *Ecclesiastical History of the English People*

BY SAINT BEDE THE VENERABLE

About the AUTHOR

Saint Bede the Venerable (see About the Author, page 90) tells in Book IV of his *Ecclesiastical History* the story of an Anglo-Saxon poet named **Cædmon**. Excluding self-descriptions in poems of the period, Bede's "Story of Cædmon" provides the only biographical information we have about an early Anglo-Saxon poet. It also contains, embedded in the story, "Cædmon's Hymn" the earliest Old English poem that has survived. Little is known of Cædmon other than the miraculous story that Bede recounts. According to Bede, Cædmon was an illiterate cowherd and keeper of horses with no training as a singer of tales, or *scop*. One night after having listened to others sing at an entertainment, Cædmon went to sleep in his stable. A figure appeared to him in a dream and demanded that he sing about the creation of the world. Cædmon suddenly found himself able to compose beautiful poetry. The next day, he sang his hymn to Hild, the Abbess of the Monastery of Whitby, and to some "learned men." They all agreed that Cædmon had received a divine gift, a miraculous inspiration. Cædmon went on to compose many long poems on religious subjects. Among the surviving poems commonly attributed to Cædmon are a number of Old English Christian epics that retell stories from the Bible. These epics include *Genesis, Exodus, Daniel, Azariah, Judith,* and *Christ and Satan.*

About the SELECTION

"The Story of Cædmon" is an excellent example of an early **miracle tale** of the kind usually found in saints' lives. Another interesting aspect of the selection is that it shows, at the very dawn of English literature, the important role played by women. It was a woman, Hild, founder of Whitby Abbey, who made possible the literary career of the first English writer whose name has come down to us.

Reader's Journal

What song lyrics mean the most to you? What appeals to you about these lyrics?

Literary TOOLS

STRESS AND CAESURA. Stress, or **accent,** is the level of emphasis given to a syllable. Syllables are generally described as being strongly or weakly stressed, (accented or unaccented). A **caesura** is a major pause in a line of poetry. Most Old English poetry follows a special verse form that relies on rhythmic techniques, including stress and caesura, rather than rhyme. The typical Old English verse is composed of lines that have four strong stresses, or beats. In the middle of the line is a pause, or caesura. As you read aloud the sample lines of Old English in "Cædmon's Hymn," listen for patterns in each line of two strong stresses, a pause, and two strong stresses. When reading these lines, bear in mind that *sc* in Old English is pronounced as *sh*, and the character þ (called a *thorn*) has the sound of the modern *th*.

ALLITERATION. Alliteration is the repetition of initial consonant sounds. Old English verse uses alliteration extensively. Often the first three strongly stressed syllables use alliteration, beginning with the same consonant sound. Read through the lines below, noting examples of alliteration (which are underlined), strongly stressed syllables (which are marked with a slash), and caesuras (indicated by a break in the line).

Oft Scyld Scefing
Often Scyld Scef's son

sceaþena þreatum
from bands of robbers,

Monegum mægþum
from many tribes

meodo-setla ofteah
their mead-benches dragged away.

ADDITIONAL RESOURCES

UNIT 2 RESOURCE BOOK
- Selection Worksheet 2.2
- Selection Check Test 4.2.5
- Selection Test 4.2.6
- Reading Resource 1.17
- Writing Resource 2.22
- Speaking and Listening Resource 4.14

READER'S JOURNAL

Ask students to recall a time when an especially apt song came on the radio. Students may write about how certain music can affect one's mood.

VOCABULARY FROM THE SELECTION

agency
literal
secular

GOALS/OBJECTIVES

Studying this lesson will enable students to
- empathize with Cædmon's feelings of inadequacy and his sudden awareness of an unknown talent
- describe the life of Cædmon and his literary accomplishments
- define the terms *stress, cæsura,* and *alliteration* and give examples from their reading
- recognize and correct errors in the capitalization of words that name sacred beings and writings
- use a dictionary to check the etymology of words

ANSWERS TO GUIDED READING QUESTIONS

1. Cædmon does not sing at feasts because he has never learned any songs.
2. Cædmon dreamt that someone asked him to sing a song about the Creation.

INDIVIDUAL LEARNING STRATEGIES

MOTIVATION
Students can discuss or write about what inspires them to be creative. How much does inspiration depend on learning and study and how much on **ineffable** (nonsensory and unexplainable) factors?

READING PROFICIENCY
Play the audiotape recording of "Cædmon's Hymn" and discuss the poem's alliteration, stress, and cæsuras (discussed in Literary Tools on page 95).

ENGLISH LANGUAGE LEARNING
Share with students the following idioms and additional vocabulary:
all the same—nevertheless, anyway
sacred history—history as told in the Old and New Testaments
brother—monk
contempt—dislike and disrespect
expound—tell; explain; relate
commission—assign as a task or duty

SPECIAL NEEDS
Ask students to examine the painting on page 98, and then describe what sort of person they think Cædmon was. Ask them if they can think of any other characters from fairy tales or literature who came from humble origins and earned fame through their virtuous nature.

ENRICHMENT
Students can research other creation stories and compare them to the creation story told in "Cædmon's Hymn." Alternatively, students might find a book about the lives of Christian saints and compare one of the stories in that book to the story of Cædmon.

The Story of Cædmon

from *Ecclesiastical History of the English People*

BY SAINT BEDE THE VENERABLE

Heavenly grace had especially singled out a certain one of the brothers in the monastery ruled by this abbess,[1] for he used to compose devout and religious songs. Whatever he learned of holy Scripture with the aid of interpreters, he quickly turned into the sweetest and most moving poetry in his own language, that is to say English. It often happened that his songs kindled a contempt for this world and a longing for the life of Heaven in the hearts of many men. Indeed, after him others among the English people tried to compose religious poetry, but no one could equal him because he was not taught the art of song by men or by human agency but received this gift through heavenly grace. Therefore, he was never able to compose any vain and idle songs but only such as dealt with religion and were proper for his religious tongue to utter. As a matter of fact, he had lived in the secular estate until he was well advanced in age without learning any songs. Therefore, at feasts, when it was decided to have a good time by taking turns singing, whenever he would see the harp[2] getting close to his place, he got up in the middle of the meal and went home.

What doesn't Cædmon do at feasts? Why not?

Once when he left the feast like this, he went to the cattle shed, which he had been assigned the duty of guarding that night. And after he had stretched himself out and gone to sleep, he dreamed that someone was standing at his side and greeted him, calling out his name. "Cædmon," he said, "sing me something."

What did Cædmon dream?

And he replied, "I don't know how to sing; that is why I left the feast to come here—because I cannot sing."

"All the same," said the one who was speaking to him, "you have to sing for me."

"What must I sing?" he said.

And he said, "Sing about the Creation."

At this, Cædmon immediately began to sing verses in praise of God the Creator, which he had never heard before and of which the sense is this:

1. **abbess.** Hild, or Hilda, founded the Monastery of Whitby, a religious community that included both men and women. An abbess is the head of such a community, which is called an abbey.
2. **singing . . . harp.** In Anglo-Saxon times, poetry was performed aloud to the accompaniment of a harp.

WORDS FOR EVERYDAY USE

a • gen • cy (ā´jən sē) *n.*, force or power. *Was it the agency of a meteor that ended the age of the dinosaurs?*
sec • u • lar (sek´yə lər) *adj.*, of the world; not sacred or religious. *Hild gave up her secular concerns and worldly possessions in exchange for a monastic life.*

[Cædmon's Hymn]

Nu sculon herigean *Now we must praise*	heofonrices Weard *heaven-kingdom's Guardian,*
Meotodes meahte *the Measurer's might*	and his modgeþanc *and his mind-plans,*
weorc Wuldor-Fæder *the work of the Glory-Father,*	swa he wundra gehwæs *when he of all wonders,*
ece Drihten *eternal Lord,*	or onstealde *the beginning established.*
He ærest sceop *He first created*	ielda bearnum *for men's sons*
heofon to hrofe *heaven as a roof,*	halig Scyppend *holy Creator;*
ða middańgeard *then middle-earth*	moncynnes Weard *mankind's Guardian,*
ece Drihten *eternal Lord,*	æfter teode *afterward made—*
firum foldan *for men earth,*	Frea ælmihtig *Master almighty.*

How many different names for God can you find in Cædmon's hymn about the creation?

This is the general sense but not the exact order of the words[3] that he sang in his sleep; for it is impossible to make a literal translation, no matter how well-written, of poetry into another language without losing some of the beauty and dignity. When he woke up, he remembered everything that he had sung in his sleep, and to this he soon added, in the same poetic measure,[4] more verses praising God.

What does Bede say it is impossible to do?

The next morning he went to the reeve,[5] who was his foreman, and told him about the gift he had received. He was taken to the abbess and ordered to tell his dream and to recite his song to an audience of the most learned men so that they might judge what

3. **the general sense . . . words.** Bede is referring to his Latin version of the poem, not printed here.
4. **measure.** As used here the word means "rhythm" or "poetic form."
5. **reeve.** A person who oversees farms

WORDS FOR EVERYDAY USE

lit • er • al (lit' ər əl) *adj.*, word-for-word; true to the actual or original meaning. *Some jokes are funny because of the difference between the literal and the common meanings of a phrase: "He said 'I'd sure like a bite,' so I bit him."*

ANSWERS TO GUIDED READING QUESTIONS

1. Cædmon uses seven names for God: "heaven-kingdom's Guardian,""the Measurer," "the Glory-Father," "eternal Lord," "holy Creator," "mankind's Guardian," and "Master almighty."
2. Bede says it is impossible to translate poetry literally without losing some of its beauty and dignity.

SELECTION CHECK TEST 4.2.5 WITH ANSWERS

Checking Your Reading

1. What did Cædmon's poetry kindle in the hearts of many men? **It kindled contempt for this world and a longing for heaven in the hearts of many men.**
2. What songs was Cædmon unable to compose? **He could not compose idle songs.**
3. What had Cædmon always done when his turn to sing neared? **He had gone home.**
4. What was "Cædmon's Hymn" (his first song) about? **It was about the Creation.**
5. What did Cædmon learn under Hilda's orders? **He learned the sacred history.**

Vocabulary in Context

Fill each blank with the most appropriate word from the Words for Everyday Use. You may have to change the tense of the word.

agency secular literal

1. Many learned to read to study the Bible, but they also enjoyed **secular** texts.
2. The new equipment gave us the **agency** to compete with established companies.
3. Mark struggled to come up with **literal** translations of the business terminology.

Literary Tools

Fill in the blanks using the following terms.

cæsura stress alliteration miracle tale translation scop poem

1. This selection is an example of the **miracle tale**, works which usually told of saints' lives.
2. According to Bede, a figure in a dream prompted Cædmon to become a(n) **scop**.
3. Many Old English poetry was arranged in lines with four **stresses** each.
4. Bede was responsible for the **translation** of "Cædmon's Hymn" into Latin.
5. The repetition of sounds at the

ANSWER TO GUIDED READING QUESTION

1. Hild provides Cædmon with food and lodging at the abbey, which frees him from his work as a cowherd so he can write poetry. She also has him educated.

RESPONDING TO THE SELECTION

How do students think Cædmon felt when he discovered his gift for composing poetry? Have students work alone or with a partner to identify abilities they have as well as

BIOGRAPHICAL NOTE

Saint Hild of Whitby (614–680) was one of the first abbesses of Anglo-Saxon England and the founder of Streaneshalch, which is now called Whitby Abbey. In 654 or 655, Ælfflaed, the daughter of King Oswiu, was placed in her care. Hild also received from the king land on which she built her abbey.

the nature of that vision was and where it came from. It was evident to all of them that he had been granted the heavenly grace of God. Then they expounded some bit of sacred story or teaching to him, and instructed him to turn it into poetry if he could. He agreed and went away. And when he came back the next morning, he gave back what had been commissioned to him in the finest verse.

What important role does Abbess Hild play in Cædmon's life?

Therefore, the abbess, who cherished the grace of God in this man, instructed him to give up secular life and to take monastic vows. And when she and all those subject to her had received him into the community of brothers, she gave orders that he be taught the whole sequence of sacred history. He remembered everything that he was able to learn by listening, and turning it over in his mind like a clean beast[6] that chews the cud, he converted it into sweetest song, which sounded so delightful that he made his teachers, in their turn, his listeners. ■

6. **clean beast.** In the Old Testament, and in ancient Hebrew law, "clean beasts" are those, like cattle, that have cloven hooves and that regurgitate and chew again plants that they have eaten.

Inspiration of Cædmon. c.1900. Lexden L. Pocock. Cheltenham Art Gallery & Museums, UK.

Respond *to the* SELECTION

If you woke one morning and discovered you could suddenly compose beautiful poetry, what would you do with your newfound talent? With whom would you share it? What would you write poems about?

INVESTIGATE, Inquire, Imagine

Recall: GATHERING FACTS →

1a. What would Cædmon do when it was his turn to sing at a feast before he received his gift? What is Cædmon doing when he composes his first song? Who urges him to compose a song and what does this person say the song should be about?

Interpret: FINDING MEANING

1b. Why would Cædmon do this at feasts before he received his gift? What explanation do you think Bede might have for the "someone" who appears and urges Cædmon to sing? Why does the way in which Cædmon gains his poetic ability make him an unequaled poet, according to Bede?

2a. What is Cædmon's first hymn about? To whom or what does Cædmon give many names in this hymn? What are some of these names?

2b. Explain why this subject was a fitting first subject for a religious poet. What do the names Cædmon attributes to this being or thing indicate about its nature?

3a. What do the abbess and her learned men do when they hear of Cædmon's talent? What test do they give him? What does the abbess then instruct Cædmon to do?

3b. Why do the abbess and the learned men give Cædmon a test? In what way does Cædmon's gift alter his life?

Analyze: TAKING THINGS APART →

4a. Why do you think Cædmon only composed religious poetry? In what way are spiritual matters portrayed in this account? In what way is the Church and its leaders portrayed?

Synthesize: BRINGING THINGS TOGETHER

4b. Based on what you have read in this account, how would you describe Bede's spiritual views? How did he regard religion and the Church?

Evaluate: MAKING JUDGMENTS →

5a. Explain whether you think Cædmon's hymn is evidence of great talent. What do you like or dislike about the poem?

Extend: CONNECTING IDEAS

5b. What are your own criteria for evaluating a work of literature? How do you distinguish a great work from an average one or a bad one?

Understanding Literature

STRESS AND CAESURA. Review the definitions for **stress** and **caesura** in Literary Tools on page 95. In the second and third lines of Old English in "Cædmon's Hymn," what syllables are strongly stressed and where does the caesura fall? You will find the explanation and example of Old English poetry you were given on the Prereading page helpful in determining where stress and caesura fall.

ALLITERATION. Review the definition for **alliteration** in Literary Tools on page 95. Identify the examples of alliteration that occur in lines 2 and 3 of the Old English version of "Cædmon's Hymn." Explain whether the modern English translation of these lines is able to maintain the same pattern of alliteration.

ANSWERS TO INVESTIGATE, INQUIRE, AND IMAGINE

RECALL

1a. Cædmon would leave before his turn to sing came. Cædmon is asleep and dreaming in a cattle shed when he composes his first song. Someone appears to Cædmon in his dream, possible a divine messenger, and asks him to sing about creation.

2a. Cædmon's first hymn is about creation. Cædmon gives many descriptive names in honor of God, the Creator, including "heaven-kingdom's Guardian," "the Measurer," "Glory-Father," "eternal Lord," "holy Creator," "mankind's Guardian," and "Master almighty."

3a. They have Cædmon tell his dream and sing his hymn to them and then they tell him another sacred story and ask him to turn it into poetry. When Cædmon successfully turns this new story into beautiful verse, the abbess instructs Cædmon to take monastic vows, so he can be taught sacred history and turn it into poetry.

INTERPRET

1b. Cædmon would leave before it was his turn because he never learned any songs, so he could not entertain others with his singing. Bede might see the "someone" as a heavenly messenger, and angel, or even God Himself inspiring Cædmon with poetic ability. According to Bede, Cædmon is an unequaled poet because he received the gift of poetic ability through "heavenly grace."

2b. Students might point out that creation is a fitting subject for Cædmon because a new talent is just being created within him; also creation is the first act at the Bible's beginning, and so a fitting one for a religious poet's first poem. The many names Cædmon attributes to God indicate that God was viewed as all-powerful and as worthy of praise. Many of the names also indicate that God has a role in protecting and guarding humans.

3b. They give Cædmon a test to see if his claims of divinely given ability are legitimate. Cædmon is given an opportunity to study religion and use his creative talent as a result of his gift, and he gives up his life as a simple cowherd.

ANALYZE

4a. Cædmon only composed religious poetry because his gift was divinely given and because he only studied sacred history. Students may note that Bede portrays the spiritual very positively and as if divine events are

ANSWERS TO INVESTIGATE, INQUIRE, AND IMAGINE (CONT.)

a matter of fact. Church leaders are portrayed as devout, wise, and encouraging of creative talent.

SYNTHESIZE

4b. Students may say that Bede seems to be a very devout person and a true believer in his religion. He seems to be an enthusiastic supporter of his religion and the Church.

EVALUATE

5a. *Responses will vary.*

EXTEND

5b. *Responses will vary.*

Answers to Understanding Literature can be found on page 100.

ANSWERS TO UNDERSTANDING LITERATURE

Stress and Cæsura. Students should copy lines 2 and 3 onto their own paper, marking the stressed syllables with a / and the cæsuras with a ||, as shown:

```
 /          /      /           /    /
Meotodes meahte || and his modge_anc
  /        /                  /
weorc Wuldor-Fæder || swa he wundra
     /
gehwæs
```

Remind students that there should be only four strongly stressed syllables in each line. They should be able to find the first three accented syllables of each line by looking for where similar consonant sounds fall. Students should note that the cæsuras are marked by a gap in the middle of each line on p. 97.

Alliteration. Students should note the alliteration of m sounds in line 2 and the w sounds in line 3, as shown:

Meotodes **m**eahte || and his **m**odge_anc
weorc **W**uldor-Fæder || swa he **w**undra
gehwæs

Students may note that the translation maintains some of the alliteration, but not all.

ANSWERS TO INTEGRATING THE LANGUAGE ARTS

Language, Grammar, and Style

1. Judaism; Torah
2. Muslim; Koran
3. Christian; Bible; Old Testament; New Testament
4. Vedas; gods; Vishnu, Indra
5. psalm; Book of Psalms

Study and Research

Responses will vary. Possible responses are given.

Line 1: **"Nu"**— now, [OE *nu*]; **"heofon"**— heaven [OE *hefen, heofon*]; **"Weard"**— ward [OE *weard,* akin to OG *warta,* act of watching]
Line 2: **"meahte"**— might [OE *miht*]
Line 3: **"weorc"**— work [OE *weorc*]; **"wundra"**— wonder [OE *wundor*]
Line 6: **"hrofe"**— roof [OE *hrof*]; **"halig"**— holy [OE *halig*]
Line 7: **"middang"**— middle [OE *middel*]; **"eard"**— earth [OE *eorthe*]; **"moncynnes"**— mankind (man [OE *man, mann, mon, monn*], kind [OE *gecynd*])
Line 8: **"æfter"**— after [OE *æfter*]
Line 9: **"ælmihtig"**— almighty [OE *ælmihtig*]

WRITER'S JOURNAL

1. Imagine that you lived in Cædmon's day and that you must deliver a eulogy at his funeral, celebrating his life and his work. Write a **eulogy** for Cædmon, expressing the type of person he was, praising his talent, and explaining the contribution he made and why he will be missed. Base the details of your eulogy on what you learned about Cædmon in Bede's account.
2. Cædmon's career as a poet began with a vivid dream. Write a **dream report** describing a vivid dream that you have had. You might began by keeping a notebook and a pen by your bed and jotting down what you remember of a vivid dream as soon as you wake up in the morning.
3. Write **song lyrics** that express your beliefs about social or political issues, or about friendship, love, growth, or struggle.

Integrating *the* LANGUAGE ARTS

Language, Grammar, and Style

Capitalization of Sacred Beings and Writings. With few exceptions, the names of religions, sacred beings, and writings are capitalized. For example, if you are referring to God (the Christian deity), *God* would be capitalized as it is the name of a sacred being, but if you are referring to the word *god* in general, as " Zeus was one of the Greek gods," you would lowercase *god.* Similarly, names of sacred writings are capitalized (the Bible, Upanishads, Saint Paul's Epistles); however, if a term that refers to a sacred writing can be used in a general sense ("Early novels were often based on epistles, or letters."), the term should appear in lowercase letters. Choose the correct word from the terms in parentheses below.

1. The sacred book of those who practice (judaism, Judaism) is the (Torah, torah).
2. The (muslim, Muslim) family read daily from the (koran, Koran).
3. The (christian, Christian) (Bible, bible) is made up of two parts: the (old testament, Old Testament) and the (New Testament, new testament).
4. Hindu writings known as the (Vedas, vedas) attribute creation to different (Gods, gods), including (vishnu, Vishnu) and (indra, Indra).
5. The Sunday school students read his favorite (Psalm, psalm) from the (Book of Psalms, book of psalms).

Speaking and Listening

Interviewing. Imagine that you have traveled back in time to interview Cædmon. Read the Language Arts Survey 2.22, "Interviewing," and then prepare your interview questions. After you have written your questions, read the Language Arts Survey 4.14, "Conducting an Interview," and pair up with a partner. Each of you should take turns role-playing the interviewer and Cædmon. When you are the interviewer, ask the questions you prepared. When you are Cædmon, use what you learned about him from Bede's account as well as your own imagination to respond. Then write your own version of "The Story of Cædmon.

Study and Research

Using a Dictionary. Many modern English words originated in Old English. The part of a dictionary entry that tells you about a word's origin is known as an **etymology**. Refer to the Language Arts Survey 1.17, "Using a Dictionary." Then review the Old English words in "Cædmon's Hymn," searching for words that remind you of modern English words. Check the etymology in a dictionary to verify each word's origins.

"The Wife's Lament"

ANONYMOUS

About the AUTHOR

The author of "The Wife's Lament" is unknown. It is one of the literary works contained in the Exeter Book, a collection of poems written in Old English and one of the few manuscripts that have survived from the Anglo-Saxon period. Two of the poems in the Exeter book are attributed to a poet named Cynewulf, but no other authors are mentioned for the other poems. Scholars can tell that one person compiled the poems in the Exeter Book, but this person almost certainly served as just a scribe, not the author.

In the Anglo-Saxon period (AD 449–1066), books were all copied and illustrated by hand, one by one. Monks played an important role in preserving the literature of this period by laboriously copying books by hand and housing them in their monasteries. Despite the work of scribes like the one who copied the Exeter Book, much of this literature has been lost. Invasions, war, disasters, and the passing of time have destroyed all but a few of the manuscripts of this period.

"The Wife's Lament" is unusual for its day. It was one of the very few Anglo-Saxon poems to explore a woman's point of view. Another such poem is "Wulf and Eadwacer" (see Selections for Additional Reading on page 144).

About the SELECTION

Many people have debated whether **"The Wife's Lament"** is secular (focusing on worldly things) or whether it explores Christian themes. It is hard to say, as the details of the plot in the poem are sketchy. Some have suggested that the poem was based on a story that would have been known to Anglo-Saxon readers or listeners.

"The Wife's Lament" does explore a fear that Anglo-Saxons explore repeatedly in their literature—exile. Early Anglo-Saxons lived in small, closely knit groups. Many of the people in a group would be blood relatives. Life was harsh enough as part of a group, but someone who was cut off from the group or made an outcast would have a hard time surviving. Old English poems often celebrate ties to family, ruler, and community and emphasize how terrible it is to be exiled from these important parts of life.

Literary TOOLS

ELEGIAC LYRIC. A **lyric** is a short, musical poem that tells the emotions of a speaker. An **elegiac lyric** is a kind of lyric that expresses grief over death or loss. As you read, try to determine for what the speaker is expressing grief.

APHORISM. An **aphorism** is a short saying or pointed statement. Anglo-Saxons often summed up an important idea from a poem in an aphorism. As you read, try to identify the aphorism.

Reader's Journal

How would it feel to be a stranger, alone, in a faraway land? What would you miss about home?

ADDITIONAL RESOURCES

UNIT 2 RESOURCE BOOK
- Selection Worksheet 2.3
- Selection Check Test 4.2.7
- Selection Test 4.2.8

READER'S JOURNAL

Suggest that students think of the many different people they see each day in their families, clubs, teams, school, religious organizations, and neighborhoods.

VOCABULARY FROM THE SELECTION

asunder	garrison
blithe	hovel
dreary	whorled

HISTORICAL NOTE

Virginia Woolf, in *A Room of One's Own,* writes: "I would venture to guess that Anon, who wrote so many poems without signing them, was often a woman."

LITERARY NOTE

Lines 15–26 may be difficult for students because they seem to introduce another person. Scholars still debate whether this is actually a second person. It can be argued that these lines do not chronologically follow lines 6–14 but are rather a return to the past to explain the relationship between the speaker and her husband. Ask students if they think the "husbandly man" the speaker refers to is more likely her husband or another lover.

GOALS/OBJECTIVES

Studying this lesson will enable students to
- empathize with the speaker's feeling of loneliness, loss, and isolation
- define the terms *elegaic lyric* and *aphorism* and give examples from their reading
- write a humorous limerick
- define *kenning,* an imaginative compound word, and invent kennings
- write a personal letter

ART NOTE

In *Frithiof's Saga,* by Esaias Tegnér (Swedish, 1782–1846), Ingeborg is the princess courted and won by the Viking Frithiof. Tegnér was a classical scholar who attempted to revive the Old Icelandic saga form. J. August Malmström (1829–1901) illustrated the 1888 edition of *Frithiof's Saga.*

INDIVIDUAL LEARNING STRATEGIES

MOTIVATION
The early Anglo-Saxons lived in small, closely knit groups, the members of which were generally related by blood. Ask students to compare this sort of society to the present-day society with which they are familiar. How near to or how far from their relatives do students live? Where do students plan to live after leaving high school or after marrying? In what ways might the wife's story have been different if she had lived in a community more like theirs?

READING PROFICIENCY
The story told in the poem may be difficult for some students to untangle because it is not told chronologically. Explain that the story is not told in sequence, and work with the group to help them infer the order of events.

ENGLISH LANGUAGE LEARNING
Share with students the following additional vocabulary:
smote (past tense of smite)—kill
brooding—troubles, worrying
bearing—mood
longing—desire and loneliness
garrison—fortress
blithe—carefree

SPECIAL NEEDS
You may wish to read the selection aloud to students with a lot of expression, conveying the emotional highs and lows of the speaker.

ENRICHMENT
Ask student to work in groups to depict loneliness. Their depiction might be in the form of a group performance before the class, or they might produce a work of music or visual art. Encourage them to be as

The Wife's Lament

Ingeborg's Lament. J. A. Malmström.
University College, London, Scandinavian Library

ADDITIONAL QUESTIONS AND ACTIVITIES

Ask students to draw, diagram, or describe the banished wife's home from two or three different perspectives. Where are the grove, oak, valleys, and brambles in relation to each other? Where is the entrance?

"A lazy person often puts off making decisions, / Lets opportunities slip, and so dies alone."—*Old English gnomic*
Do students think the husband is happy? Has he let his opportunities slip? What mistakes has the husband made? Will he die alone?
Will the wife die alone? Has she let her opportunities slip? Has the wife made mistakes?

I tell this story about me, in my sorrow,
I sing the fate of my voyaging self. I may say that
whatever hardship I lived through since I grew up—
new griefs and old—in those days it was not worse than now.
Always I grieve in the pain of my torment.

> *What is the subject of the speaker's song? What does she say about her present feelings?*

First my lord went away from his people
over the tossing waves. I felt cold care in the dark before dawn,[1]
wondering where my lord of the lands might be.
Then I left on a journey to seek and serve him—
a friendless wanderer in my terrible need.
That man's kinsmen began to plot
with secret scheming to split us both apart,
so that we two—widely asunder in the world—
lived most wretchedly. And longing smote me.

> *What did the speaker's "lord" do? What did the speaker do?*

> *What does the speaker say her lord's kinsmen did?*

My lord called to me to take up my hard dwelling here.
I had few loved ones in this country,
few devoted friends. For this my mind mourns.
Then I found myself a most husbandly man,
but a man with hard luck, brooding in his heart;
he hid his moods, his murderous thoughts,
yet seemed blithe in his bearing. Very often we boasted that
none but death alone would drive us apart—
not anything else! All that is whorled backward, changed;
now it's as if it never had been,
the loving friendship the both of us had. Far and near I must
suffer the feud[2] of my dearly loved man.
They forced me to live in a grove of wood
under an oak tree in an earth hovel.
Old is this den of earth. I am stabbed with longing.

> *What did the speaker and her beloved used to boast? What has happened to that boast?*

---

1. **cold care . . . dark before dawn.** The translator is imitating the alliteration of the original Anglo-Saxon verse.
2. **feud.** Disdain, hatred

Words for Everyday Use

a • sun • der (ə sun´dər) *adv.*, apart; separate. *The log was split asunder by one powerful blow of the axe.*

blithe (blīth) *adj.*, cheerful; carefree. *Derwood-MacHeath Senior remained blithe throughout the award ceremony, despite his son's uncouth and frequent belches.*

whorled (hwôrld) *adj.*, coiled. *The natural oils in her skin left a whorled smudge on the mirror.*

hov • el (huv´əl) *n.*, a shed or hut. *Relief workers spent weeks replacing the hovels with wood-framed houses.*

Answers to Guided Reading Questions

1. The speaker's subject is her "voyaging self." She says she is experiencing worse hardship now than ever before in her life and that she "grieve[s] in the pain of [her] torment."
2. The speaker's "lord" went away from his people on a journey across the "tossing waves." The speaker, concerned about where her lord might be, left on a journey to find him.
3. She says they plotted to separate her from her lord.
4. They used to boast that only death could drive them apart. The speaker says that their boast has "whorled backward," changed so much that it seems as if their loving friendship never existed at all.

Selection Check Test 4.5.7 with Answers

Checking Your Reading

1. Where did the speaker's husband go? **He went away on a ship.**
2. Who plotted against the wife? **Her husband's kinsmen plotted against her.**
3. What did the speaker's beloved hide from her? **He hid his moods, his murderous thoughts.**
4. Where is the wife living now? **She is alone, in exile.**
5. How does she feel about her husband now? **Responses will vary. She misses him; she is bitter but also lonely and worried about him.**

Vocabulary in Context

Fill each blank with the most appropriate word. You may have to change the tense of the word.

asunder hovel blithe
whorled dreary

1. Mrs. Watson thought she would dislike retirement, but she felt **blithe** and relaxed.
2. I held my breath as the movie's heroine disappeared inside the abandoned **hovel**.
3. The hurricane-force winds tore the buildings awnings **asunder**.

Literary Tools

1. What is a lyric? **A lyric is a short, musical poem that tells the emotions of the speaker.**
2. What is an elegaic lyric? **An elegaic lyric is a kind of lyric that expresses grief over death or loss.**
3. What is an aphorism? **An aphorism is a short saying or pointed statement.**
4. Name an aphorism from "The Wife's Lament." **Unhappy is anyone who must longingly wait for a lover.**

ANSWERS TO GUIDED READING QUESTIONS

1. She lives in an earth den covered with brambles under an oak tree in a grove of wood. Around her are dark valleys and high hills.
2. She imagines him sitting under a stone cliff covered with frost in a storm, with water flowing around him. She says he suffers "great sorrow of heart."

RESPOND TO THE SELECTION

Students may also write about or discuss what they might do in a similar situation to that of the wife. Would they be as accepting as she was? Did she have any options?

ANSWERS TO INVESTIGATE, INQUIRE, AND IMAGINE (CONT. FROM PAGE 105)

ANALYZE

4a. The speaker expresses concern and worry (lines 7–8); determination to reunite with the beloved (line 9); loneliness and longing (lines 10–14); resentment and betrayal (lines 18–21); bitterness, sorrow, and regret (lines 21–26); loneliness, longing, and sorrow (lines 27–41); sympathy and understanding for the beloved's emotional state (lines 41–46); concern and empathy (lines 47–53).

SYNTHESIZE

4b. The speaker seems to have forgiven her beloved enough to feel concern and sympathy for what he is undergoing, rather than just focusing on her own hardships. The speaker feels mixed emotions about the broken romantic relationship; on the one hand, she feels hurt and betrayed and experiences self-pity; on the other, she is concerned about her beloved's condition. Students may suggest that she is experiencing mixed emotions because she is trying to come to terms with her relationship's end under such difficult circumstances, alone and friendless.

EVALUATE

5a. Students may say that the speaker allows her emotions and imagination to color some of her husband's

---

What is the place like where the speaker lives?

The valleys are dark, the hills rise high,
bitterly sharp is my <u>garrison</u> overgrown with brambles,
a joyless stronghold. Here very often what seizes me fiercely
is the want of my husband! There are friends on earth,
lovers living who lie clasped in their bed,
while I walk alone in the hours before daybreak
under the oak tree, throughout this earth cave
where I must remain the summerlong day,
where I can weep the sorrows
of my many hardships, because I never can
find sweet rest for that heart's grief of mine—
not for all of that longing laid on me in this life.

Always must the young be troubled in mood,
with thoughts harsh in their hearts, yet at the same time
seem blithe in bearing despite a care-burdened breast
and a swarm of sorrows. The young man must rely on himself
for all he gets of the world's joy. He must be a far-flung outlaw
in a distant country.

Where does the speaker imagine her "loved friend"? What does she say he suffers?

So my loved friend sits
under a stone cliff crusted with frost in the storm—
my lover <u>dreary</u> in spirit. Water flows all around him
in his bleak dwelling. That friend of mine suffers
great sorrow of heart. Too often he remembers
a more blissful house. Unhappy is anyone
who must longingly wait for a lover. ■

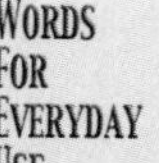

WORDS FOR EVERYDAY USE

gar • ri • son (gā' ri sən) *n.,* fortified place; military post or station. *Although cannons thundered outside, the soldiers felt safe in their secure <u>garrison</u>.*

drear • y (dri' rē) *adj.,* gloomy; cheerless. *The castles halls were <u>dreary</u> passages—long, dark, and without adornment.*

Respond *to the* SELECTION

Imagine that you befriended the speaker of this poem? What might you say to her about her situation? What advice would you give?

ANSWERS TO INVESTIGATE, INQUIRE, AND IMAGINE (CONT.)

actions and situation, probably because she is under great emotional duress. Students may say that the speaker is separated from her beloved, so she may be imagining a fate for her beloved and attributing to him emotions of regret that he may not feel.

EXTEND

5b. Responses will vary, but students should describe either a time when they let emotion alter perception or came up with an imaginative ending for unresolved events.

Investigate, Inquire, Imagine

Recall: Gathering Facts →

1a. What did the speaker's "lord" do in lines 6–7? What did the speaker then do? What did the lord's kinsmen do?

2a. In lines 18–21, what does the speaker's beloved hide from her? What is his "bearing" toward her like? What did the two used to boast? What has happened to their "loving friendship"?

3a. Where do the lord and his kinsmen force the speaker to live? To what does the speaker contrast her situation in lines 32–33? What does the speaker say about her former beloved's situation in lines 46–47? Where does the speaker say her beloved is in the last stanza?

Interpret: Finding Meaning

1b. How does the speaker feel about this person she calls her "lord"? What signs are there in the second stanza that the lord felt the same way about the speaker? Why might the kinsmen have acted as they did?

2b. Explain whether it seems as if the kinsmen have succeeded in separating the speaker from her beloved. How does the speaker feel about their "boast" now?

3b. In what way is the speaker's situation different from that of the "friends on earth"? According to the speaker, in what way is her beloved's situation similar to her own, both physically and emotionally?

Analyze: Taking Things Apart →

4a. Identify the different emotions the speaker expresses toward or about her beloved in this poem.

Synthesize: Bringing Things Together

4b. What do the speaker's feelings reveal about her as a person? about the way she is coping with a broken romantic relationship?

Evaluate: Making Judgments →

5a. Explain whether you think the speaker judges her beloved's actions and situation, both past and present, accurately and fairly or whether she allows her emotions and imagination to make up some of the details.

Extend: Connecting Ideas

5b. Describe a time in your own life when strong emotions altered your perception of events.

Understanding Literature

Elegiac Lyric. Review the definition for **elegaic lyric** in Literary Tools on page 101. For what does the speaker of "The Wife's Lament" express grief?

Aphorism. Review the definition for **aphorism** in Literary Tools on page 101. Identify the aphorism that appears at the poem's end. Explain how this aphorism relates to some of the feelings expressed in the poem.

ANSWERS TO INVESTIGATE, INQUIRE, AND IMAGINE

Recall

1a. The speaker's "lord" journeyed away from his people across the tossing waves. The speaker left on a journey to find him and serve him. The speaker's beloved's kinsmen began plotting against the couple to split them apart.

2a. He hides "murderous thoughts" beneath a cheerful bearing. They used to boast that "none but death alone would drive [them] apart." Their loving friendship is "now . . . as if it never had been."

3a. They force her to live far from others in an earth den covered with brambles. She compares her situation to that of living lovers lying clasped in bed. She says her former beloved must rely on himself "for all he gets of the world's joy." She says he must be an outlaw in a distant country. The speaker imagines her beloved sitting under a frost-covered stone cliff in a storm with water flowing all around him.

Interpret

1b. The speaker seems to love this person deeply, feeling wretched without him and willing to undergo a perilous journey to seek him out. The lord may have felt the same way about the speaker because she says that he also lived "wretchedly" when they were asunder. Students may suggest that the kinsmen might not have approved of the speaker because of her social rank or her fortune.

2b. Students may say that the kinsmen of the speaker's beloved have succeeded in separating the speaker from him. They seem to have poisoned the beloved's attitude toward her and planted doubts in his mind. It seems they have succeeded in causing a "feud" between the couple. She feels that the notion that death alone would part them was a naïve boast, as now her beloved behaves as if they never felt such love.

3b. Unlike the "friends on earth" the speaker is alone and cannot take comfort in the presence of her beloved. Unlike the living lovers, she spends "the summerlong day" weeping. The speaker says that her beloved is an exile like her, physically separated from others by his surroundings. She says he too feels sorrow and remembers his former happiness with his beloved.

Continued on page 104

ANSWERS TO UNDERSTANDING LITERATURE

Elegiac Lyric. The speaker expresses grief over her exile (the loss of her home and friends) and the loss of her beloved's presence and affection.

Aphorism. The aphorism is "Unhappy is anyone who must longingly wait for a lover." Students should recognize that this aphorism sums up the speaker's feelings of unhappiness living apart from her beloved.

ANSWERS TO INTEGRATING THE LANGUAGE ARTS

Language, Grammar, and Style
Responses will vary. Possible responses are given.
1. love-shattered
2. whisper-mouthed
3. frozen diamond blaster
4. life rays
5. concrete ocean

WRITER'S JOURNAL

1. Write a **love letter** from the speaker of "The Wife's Lament" to her beloved, explaining what her life is like now and how she feels about her beloved.
2. Some of the saddest and most moving poems in literature have inspired humorous parodies. Write a humorous **limerick** parodying the story of "The Wife's Lament." A limerick is a form of light verse with five lines in which the first, second, and fifth lines rhyme.
3. Write a **short short story** based on some of the details of "The Wife's Lament," but set in the present day.

Integrating *the* LANGUAGE ARTS

Language, Grammar, and Style

COMPOUND WORDS AND USING COLORFUL LANGUAGE. Anglo-Saxon writing often makes use of an imaginative type of compound called a *kenning*. Kennings are almost word puzzles, or miniature riddles, used in place of common terms. For example, *whale-road* is a kenning the Anglo-Saxons sometimes used for *sea*. In "The Wife's Lament," the speaker uses the compound *summerlong* to imaginatively describe how long her days spent weeping seem to her. Try coming up with your own imaginative compounds to replace the common compound nouns listed below.

1. heartbroken
2. soft-spoken
3. snowstorm
4. sunshine
5. parking lot

Speaking and Listening & Collaborative Learning

PLANNING A CELEBRATION. "The Wife's Lament" is a poem about people's need for one another. Many holidays exist to celebrate particular relationships: Valentine's Day, Mother's Day, and even Secretary's Day. However, in Western countries today, there is no holiday dedicated specifically to celebrating friendship, although this is arguably one of the most important of all human relationships. In a group, plan a holiday for celebrating friendship. When would it be held? What would people do to celebrate it? Come up with creative ways of expressing the value and importance of friends.

Applied English

PERSONAL LETTER. Imagine that you are a friend of the woman in this poem. Write her a letter consoling her and advising her about what to do.

Anglo-Saxon RIDDLES

ANONYMOUS, TRANSLATED BY GEORGE K. ANDERSON

About the AUTHOR

As you learned on the Prereading page for "The Wife's Lament," Anglo-Saxon literature survives in manuscripts that monks hand-copied for posterity. Many manuscripts were destroyed during the two waves of Viking invasions during the Anglo-Saxon period. Many more were lost centuries later when Henry VIII of England broke with the Church of Rome and ordered the destruction of monasteries throughout England. Manuscripts were also lost or destroyed in other ways as the centuries passed. The Exeter Book, which contains "The Wife's Lament" (see page 102), is one of the most important surviving manuscripts of Old English verse. In addition to more traditional Anglo-Saxon poems, the Exeter Book contains ninety-five riddles. At one time people thought that a poet named Cynewulf wrote the riddles because he is the only named poet in the Exeter Book. Now it is generally believed that the riddles are the works of anonymous writers.

About the SELECTION

A **riddle** is a word game in which something is described in an unusual way and the reader or listener must figure out what that something is. Sometimes the clues in a riddle obscure the answer; at other times the answer is obvious. The more valuable aspect of riddles is their descriptive imagery, which often helps the reader see things in a new, vivid way. The riddles on the following pages show an interesting combination of light-hearted word play and a grim world view. As you read the riddles, look for clues to figure out what each one describes.

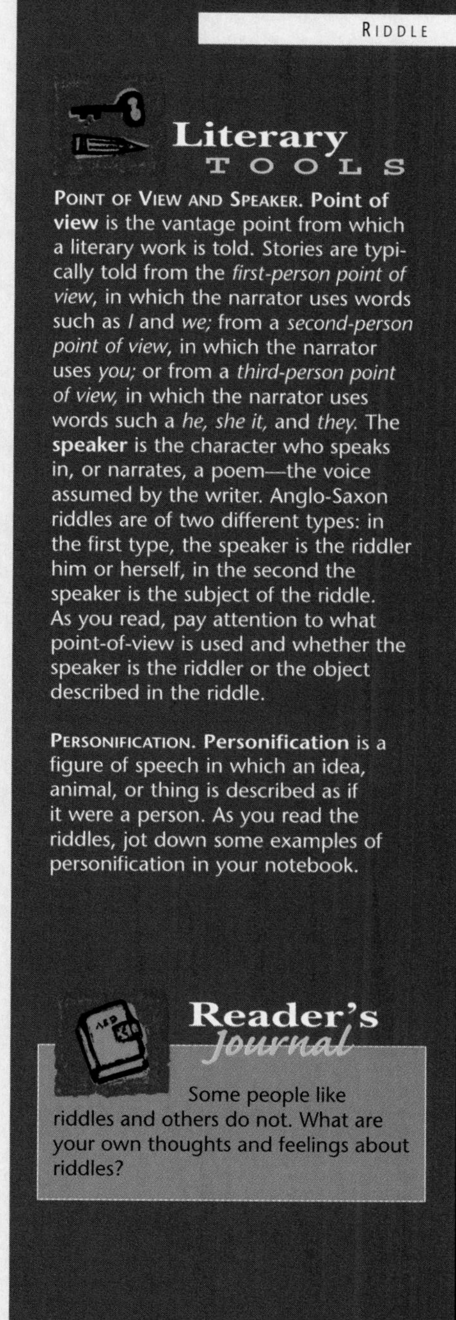

Literary TOOLS

POINT OF VIEW AND SPEAKER. Point of view is the vantage point from which a literary work is told. Stories are typically told from the *first-person point of view,* in which the narrator uses words such as *I* and *we;* from a *second-person point of view,* in which the narrator uses *you;* or from a *third-person point of view,* in which the narrator uses words such a *he, she it,* and *they.* The **speaker** is the character who speaks in, or narrates, a poem—the voice assumed by the writer. Anglo-Saxon riddles are of two different types: in the first type, the speaker is the riddler him or herself, in the second the speaker is the subject of the riddle. As you read, pay attention to what point-of-view is used and whether the speaker is the riddler or the object described in the riddle.

PERSONIFICATION. Personification is a figure of speech in which an idea, animal, or thing is described as if it were a person. As you read the riddles, jot down some examples of personification in your notebook.

Reader's *Journal*

Some people like riddles and others do not. What are your own thoughts and feelings about riddles?

ADDITIONAL RESOURCES

UNIT 2 RESOURCE BOOK
- Selection Worksheet 2.4
- Selection Check Test 4.2.9
- Selection Test 4.2.10
- Language, Grammar, and Style Resource 3.86

READER'S JOURNAL

Ask students to share some riddles they may know from childhood. For example, they may have heard the riddle of the Sphinx, which was: What has 4 legs in the morning and 2 in the afternoon and three at night? (Answer: a human—first they crawl, then walk, then use a cane.)

VOCABULARY FROM THE SELECTION

blithe	staunch
hacked	sully
quill	wrought
scourger	

GOALS/OBJECTIVES

Studying this lesson will enable students to
- appreciate the challenge of writing and solving Anglo-Saxon riddles
- define the terms *point of view, speaker,* and *personification* and identify examples in their reading
- proofread for errors in end marks
- write a résumé

INDIVIDUAL LEARNING STRATEGIES

Motivation
Ask students to solve the following commonly heard riddles: What runs but never walks, has a mouth but never talks, and has a bed but never sleeps? (Answer: a river.) A cowboy arrives into town on Sunday. He stays for 3 days and then leaves on Sunday. How is that possible? (Answer: the horse's name is Sunday.) Students may also enjoy the Internet Activity on this page.

Reading Proficiency
Go over with students the material in Literary Tools so they are aware that the speaker of each poem is a personified object. They should also answer all of the Guided Reading questions, to keep them aware of the details. Have students paraphrase each of the riddles in their own words.

English Language Learning
Share with students the following additional vocabulary:
dale—valley
down—open expanse of land
grovel—crawl
toil—work
feud—fighting, battle
adorned—decorated
penance—repentance or reparation for wrongdoing

Special Needs
Have students work in pairs to solve the riddles, brainstorming possible solutions. If students are having trouble solving Riddle 1, tell them to disregard the second sentence. (That sentence refers to bees that carry the honey. Since honey mead is not common these days, if students are able to simply guess that the answer is liquor, they are close enough!)

Enrichment
Invite students to research the *Exeter Book.* What does it contain besides riddles? When was it composed? When was it printed? Why wasn't it destroyed by Vikings or during the destruction of the monasteries? How was it constructed, and what materials were used? Where is the book now?

Anglo-Saxon RIDDLES

Frontispiece to the Gospel of Saint Matthew in the Book of Durrow. Trinity College, Dublin.

INTERNET RESOURCES

Students will enjoy searching the Internet for sites that contain riddles! They may enter the word *riddles* into any search engine. One good site to visit is **Just Riddles and More** at http://www.justriddlesandmore.com/riddles.html. This site contains all types of riddles and also allows students to submit their own riddles, such as the one they are asked to create in Writer's Journal on page 111. You may want to divide the class into groups and have each group visit a particular site. There, each group should select two or three riddles to share with the rest of the class.

Riddle 1

I am honored of men, searched for everywhere, brought from the groves and the mountain-heights, from the dales and the downs. Wings bear me in air, and carry me beneath the sheltering roof. Then men bathe me in a barrel. When I emerge, I am a binder and a scourger. I throw old men to the earth. Whoever foolishly wrestles me, sets his strength against mine, will soon find himself flat on his back, groveling on ground, without rule of mind, feet, or hands, though still strong in his speech. Tell me what I am called—I who fell men to the earth, dizzy with my blows.

What do wings do to the speaker? What do men do?

What does the speaker say will happen to any who "foolishly wrestle" with the speaker?

Riddle 2

I am lonely, hacked with steel, wounded by weapons; the toil of battle has wearied me, swords have worn me out. Often have I seen war, the rage of battle; nor do I hope for rest from strife before I die. Hammered swords have struck me; hard and sharp of edge, the wrought swords have bitten me; and even more deadly feud I shall endure. I can never find a leech[1] to heal my wounds with herbs, but only more mortal blows and deeper wounds each day and night.

What has "wounded" the speaker?

What has the speaker seen?

Riddle 3

A man of violence killed me, took away my earthly strength; then he plunged me in water, plucked me out, and set me in the sun. I lost my hair; the keen knife-edge cut me, scraped off my impurities. Then the quill of a bird spread drops upon me, sullied my surface. It drank deep in the ink, stepped again upon me; black was its track. A man then covered me with a binding, stretched a hide over me, adorned me with gold, decked me with the marvelous works of craftsmen, strengthened me with wire.

Thus made splendid with red and gold, may I live to make known the glory of God and never as a penance to man. If the children of men will employ me, they shall be more safe, more sure of success, more staunch in soul, blithe in heart, and wise in mind. They shall have in me a friend who will be dear and near to them, loyal and kind—a friend who will gladly labor to increase their joy and fame, who will cover them with his kindness, and clasp them with loving bonds. Find out what I am called—I who am useful to men, famous and holy. ■

What is the first thing that happens to the speaker?

What does the quill of a bird do to the speaker? What does a man then do?

What does the speaker say he or she will be to the "children of men"?

1. **leech.** A leech was a doctor, so called because he or she used leeches to draw blood in the belief that sickness was caused by impurities in the blood.

Words for Everyday Use

scourg • er (skurj´ər) *n.,* one who scourges, or flogs. *They hired a scourger to help age their "antiques."*

hacked (hakt) *adj.,* cut rudely, roughly, or irregularly. *Marjorie's hair looks hacked and untidy, but it's part of her costume for the seventies "punk" party.*

wrought (rôt) *adj.,* shaped by hammering or beating. *The handle of the poker was wrought to display a likeness of Mrs. O'Leary.*

quill (kwil) *n.,* stiff feather of a bird. *Veruca made a pen from the quill she found on the beach.*

sul • ly (sul´ē) *vt.,* soil or stain. *The waiter replaced the sullied table linens with clean ones before seating the next diners.*

staunch (stônch) *adj.,* strong. *Trinh's staunch belief that we would win never failed even when the rest of the team was in despair.*

blithe (blīth) *adj.,* cheerful; carefree. *The gloomy weather really dampened my spirits, but Igor was as blithe as ever.*

ANSWERS TO GUIDED READING QUESTIONS

1. Wings bear the speaker in the air, and men bathe the speaker in a barrel.
2. The speaker says people who do so will find themselves on their backs, groveling on the ground, without rule of their minds, feet, or hands, but still strong in their speech.
3. Weapons have wounded the speaker.
4. The speaker has seen war and the rage of battle.
5. A "man of violence" kills the speaker.
6. The quill of the bird covers the speaker with ink. A man then binds the speaker with hide and adorns the speaker with gold.
7. The speaker says he or she will be a dear, loyal, and kind friend to them.

ANSWERS TO RIDDLES

Riddle 1: mead (wine made from honey)
Riddle 2: a shield
Riddle 3: a tree that is made into a book

SELECTION CHECK TEST 4.2.9 WITH ANSWERS

Checking Your Reading

1. What does the subject of Riddle 1 do to men? **It makes them fall down, dizzy and without control of their mind, feet, or hands.**
2. What is the subject of Riddle 2? **It is a shield.**
3. How has the subject of Riddle 2 been wounded? **It has been wounded by weapons in war.**
4. What is the subject of Riddle 3? **It is a book (probably a religious one).**
5. What effect does the subject of Riddle 3 have on people? **Responses will vary, but the book describes itself as useful, loyal, kind – a friend to all who reads it.**

Vocabulary in Context

Fill each blank with the most appropriate word from the Words for Everyday Use from the Anglo-Saxon riddles. You may have to change the tense of the word.

scourger hacked wrought quill
sully staunch blithe

1. We built a **staunch** shelter in case the wind picked up during the night.
2. As spring wore on, we felt more **blithe** and excited about outdoor activities.
3. Jason **hacked** his and his girlfriend's initials into the wooden fence.
4. The museum curator arranged the **quills** to demonstrate how to identify each bird.

SELECTION CHECK TEST 4.2.9 WITH ANSWERS (CONT.)

5. The babysitter sighed as the twins dropped food and **sullied** the tablecloth.

Literary Tools

1. What is personification? **Personification is a figure or speech that describes something that is not human as if it were human.**
2. How is personification used in this selection? **Mead, a shield, and a book speak in the riddles.**
3. How were Anglo-Saxon manuscripts produced? **Monks wrote them by hand.**

RESPOND TO THE SELECTION

The objects featured in the riddles are each unique and important in different ways. Ask students to pick three objects in their lives about which to write.

ANSWERS TO INVESTIGATE, INQUIRE, AND IMAGINE

Recall

1a. It comes from forests, mountains, valleys, and plains carried by wings. Men bathe it in a barrel. When it comes out, it throws men to the earth and deprives them of the rule of their minds, hands, and feet.

2a. Hardships include going to war, having no hope of rest from strife, and being struck by swords. A doctor can never heal the speaker's wounds with herbs.

3a. Hardships include being killed, sapped of strength, and plunged into water; losing its hair; being sullied and stepped on by ink; and bound with hide. The speaker can help people to be safer, sure of success, courageous, happy, and wise. It will be a loyal friend and kind helper.

Interpret

1b. *Responses will vary.* The subject of the riddle is mead, but many may have never heard of this drink. Students may be able to gather that the subject is some sort of alcoholic beverage, but they may not know what type. At the very least, students should gather that the subject is dangerous to men. This may be a good opportunity for you to discuss the dangers of alcohol with their students, and point out that drinking alcoholic beverages is illegal at their age.

2b. The speaker is a shield.

3b. The speaker is a book. Reading books can fill the imagination, serve as a companion, introduce us to likable and admirable characters, and teach us.

Analyze

4a. Difficulties and hardships include problems with drinking too much, warfare, and the difficulty of instilling faith and knowledge in people.

Synthesize

4b. The riddles show the Anglo-Saxon love of feasting (and sometimes drinking to excess at feasts), the warfare that was part of Anglo-Saxon life, and the growing importance of books. The riddles show that while the Anglo-Saxons valued socializing, they realized the dangers of drinking too much; the Anglo-Saxons were preoccupied by war and fighting and valued valor in war; and the Anglo-Saxons values the knowledge, both religious and secular, that could be shared through books.

Perspective

5a. *Responses will vary.*

Empathy

5b. *Responses will vary.*

Respond *to the* Selection

Did you find it easy to solve these riddles? Which one or ones were hardest for you? What made this riddle, or these riddles, difficult to solve?

Investigate, Inquire, *Imagine*

Recall: Gathering Facts →

1a. Where does the thing described in the first riddle come from? What do men do to it? What does it do to men?

2a. What hardships does the speaker in the second riddle undergo? What can never ease the speaker's wounds?

3a. What hardships does the speaker of the third riddle undergo? What benefits does the speaker bring to people in its new condition?

Interpret: Finding Meaning

1b. What is the subject of the first riddle? (Hints: the wings in the riddle belong to bees, and honey is bathed "in a barrel.")

2b. What is the speaker of the second riddle?

3b. What is the speaker of the third riddle? How might the speaker bring about the benefits promised?

Analyze: Taking Things Apart →

4a. What difficulties and hardships in Anglo-Saxon life are mentioned in the three riddles?

Synthesize: Bringing Things Together

4b. Explain what different aspects of Anglo-Saxon life these riddles show you? What do these riddles reveal about Anglo-Saxon values?

Perspective: Looking at Other Views →

5a. Which perspective shared by the speakers of the riddles appealed the most to you? What did you enjoy about what this riddle revealed?

Empathy: Seeing from the Inside

5b. Explain whether, based on these riddles, you think you would have enjoyed living among the Anglo-Saxons.

Understanding *Literature*

Point of View and Speaker. Review the definitions for **point of view** and **speaker** in Literary Tools on page 107. Anglo-Saxon riddles are of two different types: in the first type, the speaker is the riddler him or herself, in the second the speaker is the subject of the riddle. What point-of-view is presented in each of the riddles? Who are the speakers in the riddles—the riddler or the subject if the riddle?

Personification. Review the definition for **personification** in the Handbook of Literary Tools. Each of the three riddles is an example of extended personification. What specific examples of personification can you find in each of the three riddles? Refer to the notes you tool when reading the riddles as a starting point.

Writer's Journal

1. Successful riddles use descriptive writing to help the reader figure out their object. Write a **descriptive paragraph** focusing on a setting—perhaps your room, your school cafeteria, or your locker. Appeal to sensory details, such as sight, sound, smell, taste, or touch and make your descriptive paragraph vivid enough so that someone who has never seen your setting before can imagine it clearly from your description.
2. Write an **advertising brochure** to describe a product that appeals to you, such as a stereo system, an item of clothing, a telescope, or anything else you find interesting. Include photographs or drawings in your brochure to make it appealing to a prospective customer.
3. Write your own **riddle**. Use vivid description to create a picture of your subject, but do not include so many details that the subject of your riddle is given away easily.

Integrating *the* Language Arts

Language, Grammar, and Style

Proofreading for Errors in End Marks. Read the Language Arts Survey, 3.85, "End Marks." Then, correct the errors in end marks by adding punctuation as necessary.

A Riddle

1. People talk with me Why do they never talk to me
2. When people call on me I never answer them, but they usually answer me when I call
3. If I'm busy I will let you know; if I'm not busy I will let you talk to someone else
4. I come in a box, but I give you the world How amazing
5. Now I ask, "Can you guess what I am"

Applied English

Writing a Résumé. Riddles provide much descriptive information about their subjects. One of the challenges of writing a résumé is to describe yourself and your achievements. (Unlike a riddle, however, a résumé should answer questions in the reader's mind rather than leave the reader wondering.) When writing a résumé, bear in mind that you are a product that you are trying to "sell" to potential employers. You should never stretch the truth, but you should take a close look at your own experiences—you may find that you have learned skills you never dreamed you were learning when you first undertook certain jobs or courses. For example, if you began your own neighborhood babysitting business, you have probably learned skills such as how to guide and instruct others, how to manage your own time by balancing school and your babysitting, how to create a realistic budget (by, for example, charging more to babysit a household of five children that a household with only one child), and how to behave professionally and responsibly both with employers and people under your supervision. Review the Language Arts Survey 6.8, "Writing a Résumé," and then follow the guidelines to create a résumé that both describes and sells you as a product.

ANSWERS TO INTEGRATING THE LANGUAGE ARTS

Language, Grammar, and Style

1. People talk with me. Why do they never talk to me?
2. When people call on me, I never answer them, but they usually answer me when I call.
3. If I'm busy, I will let you know; if I'm not busy, I will let you talk to someone else.
4. I come in a box, but I give you the world. How amazing!
5. Now I ask, "Can you guess what I am?"

(**Answer to Riddle:** telephone)

ANSWERS TO UNDERSTANDING LITERATURE

Point of View and Speaker. The riddles are told from the first-person point of view, and the speakers of the riddles are the subjects of the riddles.

Personification. Any mention of "I" or "me" in the riddles is an example of personification, because it implies that the object can identify itself. Some specific examples of personification are as follows: *Riddle 1:* "I throw old men to the earth"; *Riddle 2:* "I am lonely," and "Often have I seen war"; *Riddle 3:* "A man of great violence killed me," and "I live to make known the glory of God."

ADDITIONAL RESOURCES

UNIT 2 RESOURCE BOOK
- Selection Worksheet 2.5
- Selection Check Test 4.2.11
- Selection Test 4.2.12
- Language, Grammar, and Style Resource 3.53
- Speaking and Listening Resource 4.11, 4.13
- Study and Research Resource 5.49

VOCABULARY FROM THE SELECTION

avenge	infamous
billowing	lamenting
bog	moor
bolt	purge
brood	pyre
cower	relish
heaving	spoil
hoary	tribute

INDIVIDUAL LEARNING STRATEGIES

MOTIVATION

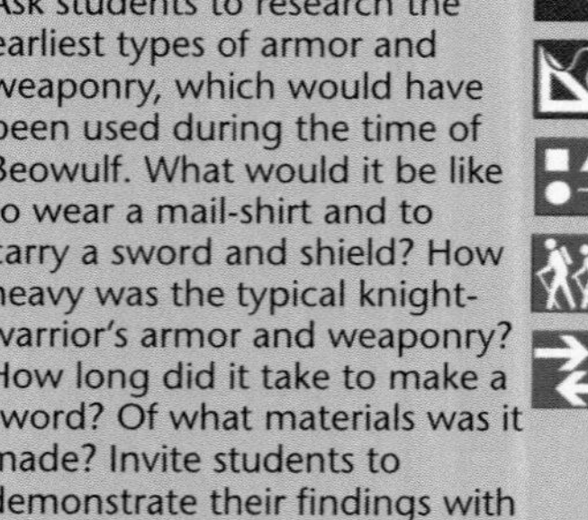

Ask students to research the earliest types of armor and weaponry, which would have been used during the time of Beowulf. What would it be like to wear a mail-shirt and to carry a sword and shield? How heavy was the typical knight-warrior's armor and weaponry? How long did it take to make a sword? Of what materials was it made? Invite students to demonstrate their findings with costumes, models, and visual aids.

READING PROFICIENCY

Instruct students to answer all of the Guided Reading questions and to summarize the action of the poem after each canto. In addition, play the Audio Library selection, especially the Old English prologue. Explain to students that they do not need to understand the Old English but that they should listen to get a sense of its sound and cadence.

ENGLISH LANGUAGE LEARNING

See the instruction for Reading Proficiency and Special Needs to help non-native speakers of English understand the action of the poem. English language learners may be at less of an advantage with *Beowulf* than with other selections since

Continued on page 113

PREREADING

FROM

BEOWULF

ANONYMOUS, VERSE TRANSLATION BY BURTON RAFFEL
INTERLINEAR TRANSLATION OF PROLOGUE BY ROBIN LAMB

About *the* SELECTION

Widely acknowledged at the greatest masterpiece of Anglo-Saxon literature, *Beowulf* was composed in Northumbria or West Mercia, which were kingdoms in the Northern part of present-day Great Britain, by an unknown singer of tales. Such singers were known as *gleemen* or *scops*. The poem probably dates from the early 700s, but it tells a story that is much older. The poem's characters are not Anglo-Saxon, but rather related Germanic people—Geats and Danes from Scandinavia. The hero of the poem, Beowulf, may be based on a historical figure, but no independent record of his existence survives.

Like most stories passed by word-of-mouth from generation to generation, *Beowulf* may contain a kernel of historical truth. Around this kernel a fabric of miraculous elaboration has been woven. For example, the real Beowulf, if he existed, may have been a great swimmer, but it is doubtful that he was able, as the poem says, to swim underwater for an entire day. In a manner typical of products of the oral tradition, the poem tells of many such fantastic feats and is filled with imaginary creatures such as trolls, giants, and dragons.

No one knows precisely when *Beowulf* was first written down. The poem survives in a West Saxon manuscript created in the late 900s by a monastic copyist, or scribe, who added to the original pre-Christian poem many references to stories from the Old Testament. The single existing manuscript of the poem contains many errors introduced by the scribe. To make matters worse, a fire damaged the manuscript in 1731. Nonetheless, the poem is fairly complete and remains the finest surviving example of the ancient Germanic heroic epic.

Beowulf was composed in the traditional Anglo-Saxon verse form described on page 95 and was chanted by the gleeman to the music of a harp. The poet's primary technique was *alliteration*, or the repetition of initial consonant sounds. This technique, combined with the pattern of four strong stresses per line and a pause, or *caesura*, in the middle of the line, gave the verse a formal, elevated quality appropriate for heroic tales.

The poem consists of a prologue and forty-three sections, known as cantos. The first three-fourths of the poem tells the story of Beowulf's heroic exploits as a young man, while the final portion of the poem tells of Beowulf as an aged king of the Geats. The parts of the poem presented here are perhaps the most famous parts of the epic—they deal with Beowulf's heroic confrontation with a monster named Grendel, his subsequent battle with Grendel's vengeful mother, and finally, as an aged king, his fatal battle with a dragon.

GOALS/OBJECTIVES

Studying this lesson will enable students to
- appreciate the classic Anglo-Saxon epic Beowulf and empathize with the difficulties of life in Anglo-Saxon times
- describe and identify characteristic features of Anglo-Saxon verse, including alliteration, kenning, compound words, caesura, and apposition
- gain a sense of the important role of gleemen, or scops, in conveying stories via the oral tradition
- retell the story of Beowulf and identify features it shares with other traditional tales and epics
- describe the Anglo-Saxon heroic ideal
- write a critical essay about Beowulf
- define and identify compound and collective nouns

The poem teaches a modern audience much about Anglo-Saxon ideals of heroism and kingship. A Germanic king of the period gathered around him a group of loyal retainers, known as earls or thanes, who shared his house and fought in his battles. A king earned his retainers' loyalty through generosity, by holding feasts in a mead hall and dispensing gifts, such as gold and silvers, armor, or weapons. A great king was liberal in dispensing gifts as well as courageous enough to protect his people, and even sacrifice himself for them if need be.

Germanic law required that the death of a family member, even if accidental, be paid for by the person responsible for the death. This payment was known as a *wergild*, literally "man-price." If a payment were not made, the family would avenge the death in battle to uphold their honor. As a result blood feuds and battles were common among Germanic tribes. Warfare also resulted from invasions to extend a tribe's land and plundering to gather treasures to give to warriors.

Life was harsh under such conditions. The likelihood of dying in battle was high, and great warriors were highly prized. A great warrior showed courage in the face of almost certain doom; upheld his honor by avenging friends, family members, and his king; and achieved fame through feats of strength and skill in battle. Beowulf embodies all these ancient Germanic heroic ideals.

Modern readers of *Beowulf* often remark on the sense of gloom that pervades the poem. Throughout the work, many references are made to the harshness of life and to the fickleness of **Wyrd**, or "fate." Although the excerpt you are about to read deals with three of Beowulf's brave exploits, you may note that the poem seems gloomy at times. Anglo-Saxons viewed their world with pessimism. They often described life as harsh and fate as fickle. The Anglo-Saxons believed that eventually everyone would meet his or her doom, and the most one could hope for was to do great deeds and live on after one's death in a gleeman's song.

The text of *Beowulf* given on the following pages begins with the Prologue reprinted in Old English with a word-for-word translation by Robin Lamb. Studying this Prologue will give you a sense of the sound of the original. The remaining selections from the text are given in a verse translation by Burton Raffel. The portions of the text not given in verse translation have been summarized. The summaries appear in italics.

Literary TOOLS

HEROIC EPIC. An **epic** is a long story, often told in verse, involving heroes and gods. Grand in length and scope, an epic provides a portrait of an entire culture, of the legends, beliefs, values, laws, arts, and ways of life of a people. A **heroic epic** is an epic that has a main purpose of telling the life story of a great hero. Some of the cultural values of the Anglo-Saxons are discussed in the About the Selection section. Review this section carefully, and as you read think about what else this heroic epic reveals about the Anglo-Saxons.

COMPOUND WORDS AND APPOSITION. **Compound words** are made up of two words joined together. The Old English language was rich in compound words. Many of these words were stock formulas for describing people and objects. For example, kings were often called *ring-givers.* Some of these stock formulas are known as *kennings,* metaphorical two-word replacements for nouns. An example is the use of *earth-hall* for *grave.* An **apposition** is a grammatical form in which a thing is renamed in a different word, phrase, or clause. Old English poets made extensive use of apposition to name and rename things. For example, Grendel is described as, "Till the monster stirred, that demon, that fiend, Grendel." As you read, jot down examples of compound words and appositions.

Reader's Journal

What makes a person a hero?

INDIVIDUAL LEARNING STRATEGIES (CONT. FROM PAGE 112)

other students may also rely heavily on summarizing the basic story as they go.

Share with non-native speakers of English the following additional vocabulary and idioms:

taking no lives—killing no one
when darkness had dropped—when night had come
gaped—looked with open mouths; be astonished
blunted—made dull
mail shirt—armor made of rings of metal
venom—poison

SPECIAL NEEDS
As someone reads the selection aloud, students may enjoy watching or participating in a pantomime of the actions described. Hearing the poem read aloud will also help them to understand its rhythmic pattern and sound techniques.

ENRICHMENT
Suggest that students research scops. They might consider such questions as these: When did scops exist? Where? How many were there? What were their lives like? How were they regarded by others in society? Why are there no scops now? People in what occupation are closest to scops today? (Students may suggest that actors, comedians, and storytellers today convey stories and things of importance to contemporary culture.)

READER'S JOURNAL

Students might think about examples of admirable persons from their lives as well as in popular books, songs, and films.

ADDITIONAL QUESTIONS AND ACTIVITIES

Before discussing the poem with students, prepare students to examine the genealogies on page 114 by having students briefly construct their own family trees. Then explain that Hrothgar and Beowulf the Geat are main characters in the story. As students read the chart, ask them what the relation is between these two characters. Also ask them to determine whether there is any relation between Beo, or Beowulf the Dane, and Beowulf of the Geats.

Answers

There is no kinship relation between Hrothgar of the Danes and Beowulf of the Geats. Likewise, there is no kinship relation between Beo (Beowulf the Dane) and Beowulf of the Geats.

Teaching Note: For instruction in reading charts, refer students to the Language Arts Survey 1.15, "Using Graphic Aids." Have students especially focus on the guidelines for Before Reading, During Reading, and After Reading.

CROSS-CURRICULAR ACTIVITIES

Geography. The Geats are believed to have lived in what is now southeastern Sweden. Have students locate Sweden on a map of northern Europe. What route would Beowulf and the Geats have taken to reach the Danes?

Tribes and Genealogies in *Beowulf*

A. Tribes Mentioned in *Beowulf*

1. **The Danes** (Also called Gar-Danes, Ring-Danes, Spear-Danes, and Scyldings)
2. **The Geats** (Also called Sea-Geats, War-Geats, and Weather-Geats)
3. **The Swedes**
4. **The Frisians** (or Jutes)
5. **The Heatho-Bards** (or Battle-Bards)

B. Genealogy and Descendants of the Danish King Hrothgar

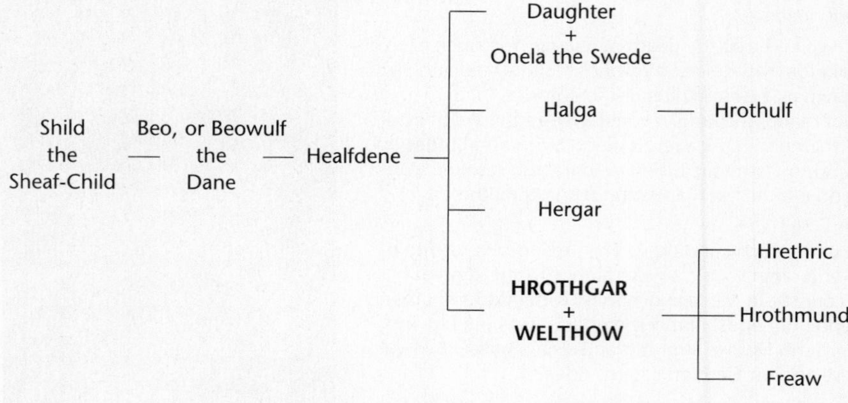

C. Genealogy of Beowulf of the Geats

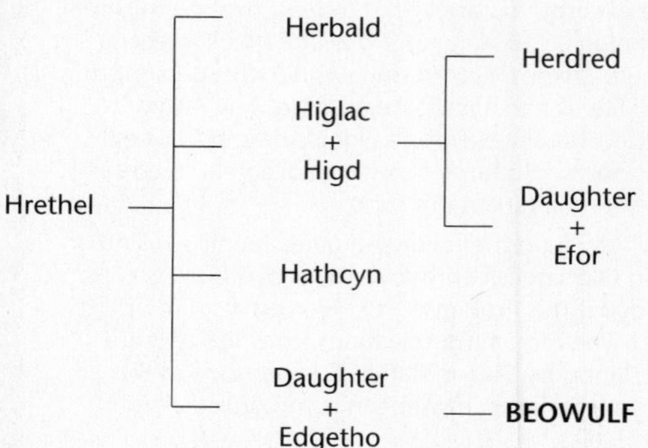

Anglo-Saxon belt buckle. The British Museum, London.

FROM

BEOWULF

ANONYMOUS, VERSE TRANSLATION BY BURTON RAFFEL
INTERLINEAR TRANSLATION OF PROLOGUE BY ROBIN LAMB

Prologue (lines 1-11), in Old English,
with an interlinear translation

Hwaet we Gar-Dena — in gear-dagum,
Yes, we of the Gar-Danes — in days of old,

þeod-cyninga, — þrym gefrunon:
The great kings' — renown have heard of,

Hu ða æþelingas — ellen fremendon.
How those princes — bravery displayed.

Oft Scyld Scefing — sceaþena þreatum
Often Scyld the Sheaf-child — from bands of robbers,

Monegum mægþum, — meodo-setla ofteah:
From many tribes, — their mead-benches dragged away,

egsode eorlas — sýððan ærest weárð
Inspired earls with fear, — after he first was

feasceaft funden: — he þæs frofre gebad,
Found helpless. — He thence looked for comfort,

Weox under wolcnum, — weorþmyntum þah,
Flourished under the clouds, — in dignities prospered,

Oðþœt him æghwylc — þara ymb-sittendra
Until him every one — of those sitting around

Ofer hron-rade — hyran scolde,
Over the whale-road — must obey,

Gomban gyldan: — þæt wæs god cyning.
[and] tribute pay. — That was a good king!

CROSS-CURRICULAR ACTIVITIES

HISTORY. Tell students that there is no independent source to confirm the existence of an historical Beowulf. An independent reference to one of Beowulf's uncles, Higlac (also spelled Hygelac), has enabled scholars to date the events told of and embellished in the poem.

Have students research how such a poem as *Beowulf* is dated. They may wish to use a research log to trace their steps and document their findings while using traditional and Internet sources.

ART NOTE

Anglo-Saxon art combined Celtic interlaced ornament and Germanic interlaced animal forms. Similar styles were also found among the nomadic tribes throughout Russia and Asia. The art of nomadic and migratory peoples tend toward small crafts that are functional and could be carried on the body.

LITERARY NOTE

Kennings are imaginative compounds. Examples of kennings in the poem include *whale-road* for "sea" and *ring-giver* for "king."

ADDITIONAL QUESTIONS AND ACTIVITIES

Encourage students to try to sound out the Old English verse on this page. Have them see how many words they can identify. Point out that the characters (þ) and (ð) are pronouns like *th*. To help with their pronunciation of Old English, have students listen to the Audio Library selection. Interested students can also consult a textbook such as *Bright's Old English Grammar and Reader.*

ANSWERS TO GUIDED READING QUESTIONS

1. Hrothgar decides to build a great hall for his band that will reach higher toward heaven than anything that had ever been built.
2. Hrothgar names his hall Herot, and he holds a feast there once the building is completed.

ADDITIONAL ACTIVITIES

Students might research and compare the use of the motif of a baby left in a basket in sources such as the legend of Scyld Scefing, the epic of Gilgamesh, and the story of Moses in the Bible. In what ways are the stories different? In what way are they similar? Why might this motif have been used?

Prologue (lines 1-11), in verse translation

Hear me! We've heard of Danish heroes,
Ancient kings and the glory they cut
For themselves, swinging mighty swords!
How Shild[1] made slaves of soldiers from every
Land, crowds of captives he'd beaten
Into terror; he'd traveled to Denmark alone,
An abandoned child, but changed his own fate,
Lived to be rich and much honored. He ruled
Lands on all sides: wherever the sea
Would take them his soldiers sailed, returned
With tribute and obedience. There was a brave
King!

. . .

Shild has a son and dies. He is laid to rest on a ship loaded with treasures and weapons, and the ship is then set adrift on the sea.

Canto 1

Shild's son rules; Shild's grandson rules; and then finally Shild's great-grandson attains the throne.

Then Hrothgar, taking the throne, led
The Danes to such glory that comrades and kinsmen
Swore by his sword, and young men swelled
His armies, and he thought of greatness and resolved
To build a hall that would hold his mighty
Band and reach higher toward Heaven than anything
That had ever been known to the sons of men.
And in that hall he'd divided the spoils
Of their victories, to old and young what they'd earned
In battle, but leaving the common pastures
Untouched, and taking no lives. The work
Was ordered, the timbers tied and shaped
By the hosts that Hrothgar ruled. It was quickly
Ready, that most beautiful of dwellings, built
As he'd wanted, and then he whose word was obeyed

What does Hrothgar decide to do?

What does Hrothgar name his hall? What does he do once the building is completed?

1. **Shild.** Shild's name can be translated literally as "Shild the Sheaf-Child." The name comes from a legend that he was found as a baby floating in a basket of reeds (as Moses was in the Old Testament). This legend is what the poet refers to when he calls Shild "an abandoned child."

WORDS FOR EVERYDAY USE

trib • ute (tri′ byo͞ot) *n.,* regular payment of money or goods made by one ruler or nation to another as acknowledgment of servitude, for protection from invasion, etc. *Ancient Egypt became a wealthy nation in part because of the tributes of gold and products it demanded from nations it conquered.*

spoil (spoil) *n.,* arms, money, or goods taken from a defeated foe; plunder. *The victors of a war often take spoils from the defeated.*

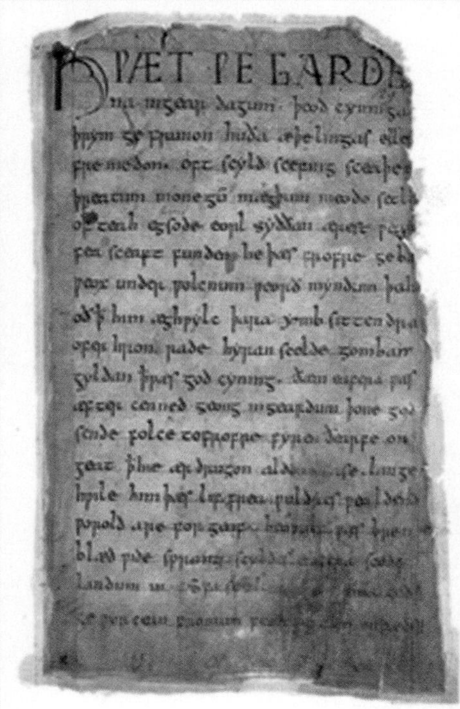

The first page of *Beowulf*. British Library, London.

All over the earth named it Herot.
His boast come true he commanded a banquet,
Opened out his treasure-full hands.
That towering place, gabled and huge,
Stood waiting for time to pass, for war
To begin, for flames to leap as high
As the feud that would light them, and for Herot to burn.
   A powerful monster, living down
In the darkness, growled in pain, impatient
As day after day the music rang
Loud in that hall[2], the harp's rejoicing
Call and the poet's clear songs, sung
Of the ancient beginnings of us all, recalling
The Almighty making the earth, shaping
These beautiful plains marked off by oceans,
Then proudly setting the sun and moon
To glow across the land and light it;
The corners of the earth were made lovely with trees

Who is impatient with the music coming from Herot?

2. **hall.** Herot

ANSWER TO GUIDED READING QUESTION

1. A powerful monster is impatient with the music coming from Herot.

ANSWERS TO GUIDED READING QUESTIONS

1. The monster's name is Grendel and it roams the moors.
2. Grendel's ancestor is Cain, who was punished for the crime of Abel's death.
3. Grendel kills thirty sleeping men.

And leaves, made quick with life, with each
Of the nations who now move on its face. And then
As now warriors sang of their pleasure:
So Hrothgar's men lived happy in his hall
Till the monster stirred, that demon, that fiend,
Grendel, who haunted the moors, the wild
Marshes, and made his home in a hell
Not hell but earth. He was spawned in that slime,
Conceived by a pair of those monsters born
Of Cain[3], murderous creatures banished
By God, punished forever for the crime
Of Abel's death. The Almighty drove
Those demons out, and their exile was bitter,
Shut away from men; they split
In a thousand forms of evil—spirits
And fiends, goblins, monsters, giants,
A brood forever opposing the Lord's
Will, and again and again defeated.

What is the monster's name? Where does it roam?

Who is Grendel's ancestor? For what crime did God punish Grendel's ancestor?

Canto 2

Grendel terrorizes Herot. Hrothgar and his councilors seek a plan to rid themselves of Grendel, but to no avail.

Then, when darkness had dropped, Grendel
Went up to Herot, wondering what the warriors
Would do in that hall when their drinking was done.
He found them sprawled in sleep, suspecting
Nothing, their dreams undisturbed. The monster's
Thoughts were as quick as his greed or his claws:
He slipped through the door and there in the silence
Snatched up thirty men, smashed them
Unknowing in their beds and ran out with their bodies,
The blood dripping behind him, back
To his lair, delighted with his night's slaughter.
At daybreak, with the sun's first light, they saw
How well he had worked, and in that gray morning
Broke their long feast with tears and laments
For the dead. Hrothgar, their lord, sat joyless

What does Grendel do when he comes to Herot?

3. **Of Cain.** The Christian copyist has made Grendel a descendant of Cain, the oldest son of Adam and Eve. According to Genesis 4, Cain killed his brother Abel and so was made an outcast, despised by others.

WORDS FOR EVERYDAY USE

moor (mo͞or) *n.,* tract of open, rolling wasteland, usually covered with heather and often marshy. *The vast moor attracted birds, which hunted for fish in the remote marshy area.*

brood (bro͞od) *n.,* offspring, or a family of offspring, of animals. *The mother hen sat on her nest until she hatched her brood.*

In Herot, a mighty prince mourning
The fate of his lost friends and companions,
Knowing by its tracks that some demon had torn
His followers apart. He wept, fearing
The beginning might not be the end. And that night
Grendel came again, so set
On murder that no crime could ever be enough,
No savage assault quench his lust
For evil. Then each warrior tried
To escape him, searched for rest in different
Beds, as far from Herot as they could find,
Seeing how Grendel hunted when they slept.
Distance was safety; the only survivors
Were those who fled him. Hate had triumphed.
So Grendel ruled, fought with the righteous,
One against many, and won; so Herot
Stood empty, and stayed deserted for years,
Twelve winters of grief for Hrothgar, king
Of the Danes, sorrow heaped at his door
By hell-forged hands.

Who are the only warriors who survive Grendel's attacks?

What are the effects of Grendel's attacks in Herot?

Cantos 3–5

Beowulf, the hero of this epic, hears of Grendel's deeds and vows revenge. He has a ship built to carry him and his followers to Hrothgar's aid. After a sea-journey, Beowulf and his men are challenged by one of Hrothgar's men who overlooks the coast. Beowulf asks to be taken to see Hrothgar, king of the Danes. On being told of this, Hrothgar remembers having known Beowulf as a child. He asks that Beowulf be brought to him, and then Wulfgar, a servant of Hrothgar, shows Beowulf in.

Canto 6

. . .

Then Wulfgar went to the door and addressed
The waiting seafarers with soldier's words:
"My lord, the great king of the Danes[4], commands me
To tell you that he knows of your noble birth
And that having come to him from over the open
Sea you have come bravely and are welcome.
Now go to him as you are, in your armor and helmets,
But leave your battle-shields here, and your spears,
Let them lie waiting for the promises your words
May make."

What does Wulfgar ask Beowulf and his companions to do with their weapons before they approach the king?

4. **the great king of the danes.** Hrothgar

ANSWERS TO GUIDED READING QUESTIONS

1. The only warriors who survive Grendel's attacks are those who flee.
2. Herot is deserted for twelve years because of Grendel's attacks.
3. Wulfgar asks Beowulf and his companions to leave their weapons behind when they approach the king.

ANSWERS TO GUIDED READING QUESTIONS

1. Beowulf's people believe he should go help the Danes because they have witnessed his great strength.
2. Beowulf has killed five giants and chased their race from the earth. He also swam out into the ocean at night to kill monsters one by one.
3. Beowulf's request is that he be allowed to purge the evil from Hrothgar's hall.
4. Beowulf plans to attack Grendel with his bare hands.

Beowulf arose, with his men
Around him, ordering a few to remain
With their weapons, leading the others quickly
Along under Herot's steep roof into Hrothgar's
Presence. Standing on that prince's own hearth,
Helmeted, the silvery metal of his mail shirt
Gleaming with a smith's high art, he greeted
The Danes' great lord:
"Hail, Hrothgar!
Higlac[5] is my cousin and my king; the days
Of my youth have been filled with glory. Now Grendel's
Name has echoed in our land: sailors
Have brought us stories of Herot, the best
Of all mead-halls, deserted and useless when the moon
Hangs in skies the sun had lit,
Light and life fleeing together.
My people have said, the wisest, most knowing
And best of them, that my duty was to go to the Danes'
Great king. They have seen my strength for themselves,
Have watched me rise from the darkness of war,
Dripping with my enemies' blood. I drove
Five great giants into chains, chased
All of that race from the earth. I swam
In the blackness of night, hunting monsters
Out of the ocean, and killing them one
By one; death was my errand and the fate
They had earned. Now Grendel and I are called
Together, and I've come. Grant me, then,
Lord and protector of this noble place,
A single request! I have come so far,
O shelterer of warriors and your people's loved friend,
That this one favor you should not refuse me—
That I, alone and with the help of my men,
May purge all evil from this hall. I have heard,
Too, that the monster's scorn of men
Is so great that he needs no weapons and fears none.
Nor will I. My lord Higlac
Might think less of me if I let my sword
Go where my feet were afraid to, if I hid

According to Beowulf's people, why should he go to the Danes?

What great deeds have won Beowulf fame?

What is Beowulf's request?

With what weapon does Beowulf plan to attack Grendel?

5. **Higlac.** Higlac, king of the Geats, was Beowulf's feudal lord and uncle. The term *cousin* refers generally to any relative.

WORDS FOR EVERYDAY USE

purge (pərj) *vt.,* cleanse or rid of impurities, foreign matter, or undesirable elements. *Roland bought some bottom-dwelling fish to purge his aquarium of algae.*

Behind some broad linden[6] shield: my hands
Alone shall fight for me, struggle for life
Against the monster. God must decide
Who will be given to death's cold grip."

Beowulf plans to confront Grendel in the hall. He asks Hrothgar to return his armor to Beowulf's king, Higlac, if he dies in the confrontation.

Cantos 7–10

One of Hrothgar's thanes, or pledged warriors, named Unferth challenges Beowulf, doubting that he can best Grendel. Beowulf answers the challenge by telling a story about a mighty feat he performed as a boy, a swimming match against a man named Brecca. Beowulf tells how he encountered sea monsters while swimming and was dragged to the sea floor by one of them. He managed to escape and killed nine of the sea monsters. Beowulf then points out that no such brave tales are told about Unferth and accuses him of murdering his own brothers. Hrothgar is pleased by the tales and Beowulf's boldness of spirit. Hrothgar's wife then serves mead to the guests and thanks God for Beowulf's assistance. Hrothgar and his men retire for the night, leaving Beowulf and his men to face Grendel in the hall.

Canto 11

Out from the marsh, from the foot of misty
Hills and bogs, bearing God's hatred,
Grendel came, hoping to kill
Anyone he could trap on this trip to high Herot.
He moved quickly through the cloudy night,
Up from his swampland, sliding silently
Toward that gold-shining hall. He had visited Hrothgar's
Home before, knew the way—
But never, before nor after that night,
Found Herot defended so firmly, his reception
So harsh. He journeyed, forever joyless,
Straight to the door, then snapped it open,
Tore its iron fasteners with a touch
And rushed angrily over the threshold.

What words describe Grendel?

6. **linden.** A type of wood known for its strength

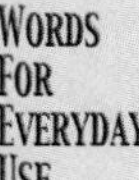

bog (bôg) *n.,* wet, spongy ground. *It is a dangerous to ride a horse across a bog because its hoof might get caught in the mulch and it might break a leg.*

ANSWER TO GUIDED READING QUESTION

1. Grendel is described as "forever joyless."

ANSWERS TO GUIDED READING QUESTIONS

1. Grendel intends to "tear the life" from the sleeping men.
2. Grendel kills and eats this Geat. Next, Grendel grabs Beowulf. Beowulf grabs onto Grendel with his powerful grip.

Expedition of Danish Soldiers, c.1150. Danish Artist. Nationalmuseet, Copenhagen.

He strode quickly across the inlaid
Floor, snarling and fierce: his eyes
Gleamed in the darkness, burned with a gruesome
Light. Then he stopped, seeing the hall
Crowded with sleeping warriors, stuffed
With rows of young soldiers resting together.
And his heart laughed, he relished the sight,
Intended to tear the life from those bodies
By morning; the monster's mind was hot
With the thought of food and the feasting his belly
Would soon know. But fate, that night, intended
Grendel to gnaw the broken bones
Of his last human supper. Human
Eyes were watching his evil steps,
Waiting to see his swift hard claws.
Grendel snatched at the first Geat[7]
He came to, ripped him apart, cut
His body to bits with powerful jaws,
Drank the blood from his veins and bolted
Him down, hands and feet; death
And Grendel's great teeth came together,

What does Grendel intend to do to the sleeping men?

What happens to the first Geat Grendel grabs? Whom does Grendel grab next? What happens when Grendel grabs this person?

7. **Geat.** Beowulf's people, who are ruled by Higlac, are known as the Geats.

WORDS FOR EVERYDAY USE

rel • ish (re′ lish) *vt.,* enjoy; like. *Renee relished Sunday afternoons because she had time to do whatever she wanted—read a novel, skate in the park, or get together with friends.*

bolt (bōlt) *vt.,* swallow (food) hurriedly; gulp down. *Our dog never seems to chew his dinner but just greedily bolts whatever we feed him.*

Snapping life shut. Then he stepped to another
Still body, clutched at Beowulf with his claws,
Grasped at a strong-hearted wakeful sleeper
—And was instantly seized himself, claws
Bent back as Beowulf leaned up on one arm.
  That shepherd of evil, guardian of crime,
Knew at once that nowhere on earth
Had he met a man whose hands were harder;
His mind was flooded with fear—but nothing
Could take his talons and himself from that tight
Hard grip. Grendel's one thought was to run
From Beowulf, flee back to his marsh and hide there:
This was a different Herot than the hall he had emptied.
But Higlac's follower[8] remembered his final
Boast and, standing erect, stopped
The monster's flight, fastened those claws
In his fists till they cracked, clutched Grendel
Closer. The infamous killer fought
For his freedom, wanting no flesh but retreat,
Desiring nothing but escape; his claws
Had been caught, he was trapped. That trip to Herot
Was a miserable journey for the writhing monster!
  The high hall rang, its roof boards swayed,
And Danes shook with terror. Down
The aisles the battle swept, angry
And wild. Herot trembled, wonderfully
Built to withstand the blows, the struggling
Great bodies beating at its beautiful walls;
Shaped and fastened with iron, inside
And out, artfully worked, the building
Stood firm. Its benches rattled, fell
To the floor, gold-covered boards grating
As Grendel and Beowulf battled across them.
Hrothgar's wise men had fashioned Herot
To stand forever; only fire,
They had planned, could shatter what such skill had put
Together, swallow in hot flames such splendor
Of ivory and iron and wood. Suddenly
The sounds changed, the Danes started

What does Grendel know? How does Grendel feel about the situation? What does he want to do?

What is the effect of the battle on Herot, Hrothgar's hall?

---

8. **Higlac's follower.** Beowulf

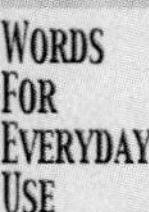

in • fa • mous (in' fə məs) *adj.*, having a very bad reputation; notorious; in disgrace or dishonor. *Jesse James was an infamous outlaw of the nineteenth century in the American West.*

ANSWERS TO GUIDED READING QUESTIONS

1. Grendel knows he has never met a man with harder hands. Grendel is filled with fear and wants to run away to his marsh to hide.
2. Hrothgar's hall rings with noise and sways but stands firm.

CROSS-CURRICULAR ACTIVITIES

SCIENCE. Students can investigate why a sword makes a "singing" noise when it is swung quickly through the air. Does the shape of the blade affect the sound? Would a cylindrical or rectangular object make a similar noise? Does the sharpness of the blade affect the sound? How? Does the length affect the sound? How? Does the material of which the object is made affect the sound? How? Does varying the speed affect the sound? How?

ANSWERS TO GUIDED READING QUESTIONS

1. Beowulf's men jump from their beds, grab their weapons, and attack Grendel, but their weapons cannot hurt Grendel because of a spell on Grendel.
2. Grendel learns what it means to feud with Almighty God.
3. Beowulf snaps off Grendel's arm. Grendel flees to his den at the bottom of the marsh to die.

In new terror, cowering in their beds as the terrible
Screams of the Almighty's enemy sang
In the darkness, the horrible shrieks of pain
And defeat, the tears torn out of Grendel's
Taut throat, hell's captive caught in the arms
Of him who of all the men on earth
Was the strongest.

Canto 12

That mighty protector of men
Meant to hold the monster till its life
Leaped out, knowing the fiend was no use
To anyone in Denmark. All of Beowulf's
Band had jumped from their beds, ancestral
Swords raised and ready, determined
To protect their prince if they could. Their courage
Was great but all wasted: they could hack at Grendel
From every side, trying to open
A path for his evil soul, but their points
Could not hurt him, the sharpest and hardest iron
Could not scratch at his skin, for that sin-stained demon
Had bewitched all men's weapons, laid spells
That blunted every mortal man's blade.
And yet his time had come, his days
Were over, his death near; down
To hell he would go, swept groaning and helpless
To the waiting hands of still worse fiends.
Now he discovered—once the afflictor
Of men, tormentor of their days—what it meant
To feud with Almighty God: Grendel
Saw that his strength was deserting him, his claws
Bound fast, Higlac's brave follower tearing at
His hands. The monster's hatred rose higher,
But his power had gone. He twisted in pain,
And the bleeding sinews deep in his shoulder
Snapped, muscle and bone split
And broke. The battle was over, Beowulf
Had been granted new glory: Grendel escaped,
But wounded as he was could flee to his den,
His miserable hole at the bottom of the marsh,

What do Beowulf's men do to help? What frustrates their efforts to help Beowulf?

What does Grendel learn?

What happens to Grendel's arm? What will become of Grendel?

WORDS FOR EVERYDAY USE

cow • er (cou′ ər) *vi.,* shrink and tremble, as from fear or cold. *When we brought our new kitten home, it was terrified and ran under the bed to cower.*

Only to die, to wait for the end
Of all his days. And after that bloody
Combat the Danes laughed with delight.
He who had come to them from across the sea,
Bold and strong-minded, had driven affliction
Off, purged Herot clean. He was happy,
Now, with that night's fierce work; the Danes
Had been served as he'd boasted he'd serve them; Beowulf,
A prince of the Geats, had killed Grendel,
Ended the grief, the sorrow, the suffering
Forced on Hrothgar's helpless people
By a bloodthirsty fiend. No Dane doubted
The victory, for the proof, hanging high
From the rafters where Beowulf had hung it, was the monster's
Arm, claw and shoulder and all.

What does Beowulf do to prove his victory over Grendel?

Canto 13

And then, in the morning, crowds surrounded
Herot, warriors coming to that hall
From faraway lands, princes and leaders
Of men hurrying to behold the monster's
Great staggering tracks. They gaped with no sense
Of sorrow, felt no regret for his suffering,
Went tracing his bloody footprints, his beaten
And lonely flight, to the edge of the lake
Where he'd dragged his corpselike way, doomed
And already weary of his vanishing life.
The water was bloody, steaming and boiling
In horrible pounding waves, heat
Sucked from his magic veins; but the swirling
Surf had covered his death, hidden
Deep in murky darkness his miserable
End, as hell opened to receive him.
Then old and young rejoiced, turned back
From that happy pilgrimage, mounted their hard-hooved
Horses, high-spirited stallions, and rode them
Slowly toward Herot again, retelling
Beowulf's bravery as they jogged along.
And over and over they swore that nowhere
On earth or under the spreading sky
Or between the seas, neither south nor north,
Was there a warrior worthier to rule over men. . . .

How do the Danes feel about what has happened to Grendel?

What do the Danes say about Beowulf?

ANSWERS TO GUIDED READING QUESTIONS

1. Beowulf hangs Grendel's arm from the rafters of Herot.
2. The Danes feel no sorrow or regret for Grendel's suffering.
3. The Danes tell each other about Beowulf's bravery and swear that nowhere is a man worthier to rule over men.

ADDITIONAL QUESTIONS AND ACTIVITIES

Ask students how they feel about boasting. Is it ever appropriate? Is it ever inappropriate? Do they tend to like people who boast? Do they feel comfortable boasting themselves? If not, do they ever wish they were comfortable with it? Why, or why not?

Do students find Beowulf's boasting appropriate? Why, or why not? Does part of their answer depend on what Beowulf's contemporaries would have expected?

ANSWER TO GUIDED READING QUESTION

1. Grendel's mother still lives.

Cantos 14–18

People gather from far and wide to praise Beowulf's mighty deed. Hrothgar promises to treat Beowulf, thereafter, as his own son, then commands that Herot be cleaned and decorated with golden tapestries in preparation for a feast. Beowulf's victory is rewarded by gifts of armor, horses, and weapons.

Beowulf's warriors receive gifts from Hrothgar, and the man whom Grendel killed is honored. The entertainment continues.

The scop finishes his song. Then Queen Welthow gives Beowulf presents—a corselet, rings, and a collar. After the feast, Hrothgar's thanes lie down to sleep in the hall, their armor beside them.

Canto 19

. . .

And now it was known that a monster had died
But a monster still lived, and meant revenge.
She'd brooded on her loss, misery had brewed
In her heart, that female horror, Grendel's
Mother, living in the murky cold lake
Assigned her since Cain had killed his only
Brother, slain his father's son
With an angry sword. God drove him off,
Outlawed him to the dry and barren desert,
And branded him with a murderer's mark. And he bore
A race of fiends accursed like their father;
So Grendel was drawn to Herot, an outcast
Come to meet the man who awaited him.
He'd snatched at Beowulf's arm, but that prince
Remembered God's grace and the strength He'd given him
And relied on the Lord for all the help,
The comfort and support he would need. He killed
The monster, as God had meant him to do,
Tore the fiend apart and forced him
To run as rapidly as he could toward death's
Cold waiting hands. His mother's sad heart,
And her greed, drove her from her den on the dangerous
Pathway of revenge[9]. . . .

What monster still lives?

9. **Pathway of revenge.** Germanic custom required that the kin of a slain person avenge the death.

Cain's Punishment, c.1800s. James Tissot. French Jewish Museum, New York.

Seeking vengeance, Grendel's mother kills Hrothgar's closest friend and advisor and takes the severed arm of her son back to the fen. Because Beowulf is not present, she is able to do as she wishes. Hrothgar summons Beowulf for help.

Cantos 20-21

Hrothgar tells Beowulf of the loss of his trusted friend Aeschere, and of the murderous mother of Grendel:

"I've heard that my people, peasants working
In the fields, have seen a pair of such fiends
Wandering in the moors and marshes, giant
Monsters living in those desert lands.
And they've said to my wise men that, as well as they could see,
One of the devils was a female creature.
The other, they say, walked through the wilderness
Like a man—but mightier than any man.
They were frightened, and they fled, hoping to find help
In Herot. They named the huge one Grendel:
If he had a father no one knew him,
Or whether there'd been others before these two,
Hidden evil before hidden evil.
They live in secret places, windy
Cliffs, wolf-dens where water pours
From the rocks, then runs underground, where mist

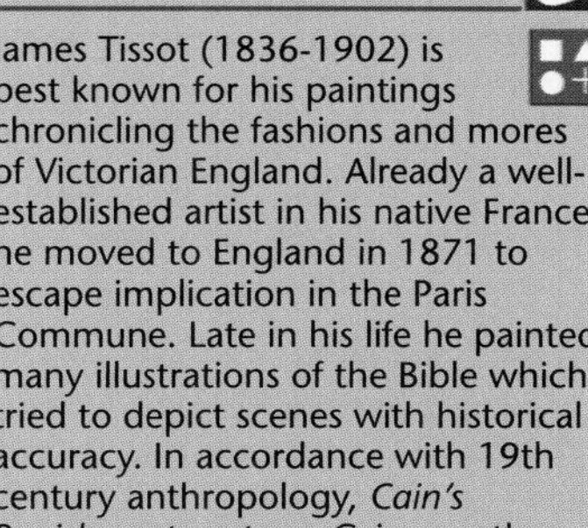

ART NOTE

James Tissot (1836-1902) is best known for his paintings chronicling the fashions and mores of Victorian England. Already a well-established artist in his native France, he moved to England in 1871 to escape implication in the Paris Commune. Late in his life he painted many illustrations of the Bible which tried to depict scenes with historical accuracy. In accordance with 19th century anthropology, *Cain's Punishment* portrays Cain as rather like a caveman.

ANSWERS TO GUIDED READING QUESTIONS

1. These monsters live in a lake so deep that "No one knows its bottom."
2. Hrothgar asks Beowulf to save the Geats from Grendel's mother.

Steams like black clouds, and the groves of trees
Growing out over their lake are all covered
With frozen spray, and wind down snakelike
Roots that reach as far as the water
And help keep it dark. At night that lake
Burns like a torch. No one knows its bottom,
No wisdom reaches such depths. A deer,
Hunted through the woods by packs of hounds,
A stag with great horns, though driven through the forest
From faraway places, prefers to die
On those shores, refuses to save its life
In that water. It isn't far, nor is it
A pleasant spot! When the wind stirs
And storms, waves splash toward the sky,
As dark as the air, as black as the rain
That the heavens weep. Our only help,
Again, lies with you. Grendel's mother
Is hidden in her terrible home, in a place
You've not seen. Seek it, if you dare! Save us,
Once more, and again twisted gold,
Heaped-up ancient treasure, will reward you
For the battle you win!"

Where do these monsters live?

What does Hrothgar ask of Beowulf?

. . .

Beowulf agrees to fight Grendel's maker, "this lady monster," and to avenge the death of Aeschere. Hrothgar and his men lead Beowulf to the water under which is Grendel's mother's cave. The water is filled with sea serpents and boils with blood. Beowulf dons a helmet and mail shirt, and borrows from one of Hrothgar's men the sword named Hrunting.

Canto 22

. . . As his words ended
He leaped into the lake, would not wait for anyone's
Answer; the heaving water covered him
Over. For hours he sank through the waves;
At last he saw the mud of the bottom.[10]
And all at once the greedy she-wolf

10. **For hours . . . bottom.** Such impossible feats are a common element, or *motif*, in folklore.

WORDS FOR EVERYDAY USE

heav • ing (hē′ viŋ) *vt.,* to cause to swell or rise; to rise and fall rhythmically. *When my little brother saw the heaving ocean, he was terrified by the rolling waves.*

Who'd ruled those waters for half a hundred
Years discovered him, saw that a creature
From above had come to explore the bottom
Of her wet world. She welcomed him in her claws,
Clutched at him savagely but could not harm him,
Tried to work her fingers through the tight
Ring-woven mail on his breast, but tore
And scratched in vain. Then she carried him, armor
And sword and all, to her home; he struggled
To free his weapon, and failed. The fight
Brought other monsters swimming to see
Her catch, a host of sea beasts who beat at
His mail shirt, stabbing with tusks and teeth
As they followed along. Then he realized, suddenly,
That she'd brought him into someone's battle-hall,
And there the water's heat could not hurt him,
Nor anything in the lake attack him through
The building's high-arching roof. A brilliant
Light burned all around him, the lake
Itself like a fiery flame.
Then he saw
The mighty water witch[11], and swung his sword,
His ring-marked blade, straight at her head;
The iron sang its fierce song,
Sang Beowulf's strength. But her guest
Discovered that no sword could slice her evil
Skin, that Hrunting could not hurt her, was useless
Now when he needed it. They wrestled, she ripped
And tore and clawed at him, bit holes in his helmet,
And that too failed him; for the first time in years
Of being worn to war it would earn no glory;
It was the last time anyone would wear it. But Beowulf
Longed only for fame, leaped back
Into battle. He tossed his sword aside,
Angry; the steel-edged blade lay where
He'd dropped it. If weapons were useless he'd use
His hands, the strength in his fingers. So fame
Comes to the men who mean to win it
And care about nothing else! He raised
His arms and seized her by the shoulder; anger
Doubled his strength, he threw her to the floor.
She fell, Grendel's fierce mother, and the Geats'
Proud prince was ready to leap on her. But she rose

What does Beowulf discover about the sword Hrunting?

11. **mighty water witch.** Grendel's mother

ANSWER TO GUIDED READING QUESTION

1. Beowulf discovers that all swords, including Hrunting, cannot harm Grendel's mother.

ANSWER TO GUIDED READING QUESTION

1. Beowulf's mail shirt saves him from Grendel's mother's sword.

At once and repaid him with her clutching claws,
Wildly tearing at him. He was weary, that best
And strongest of soldiers; his feet stumbled
And in an instant she had him down, held helpless.
Squatting with her weight on his stomach, she drew
A dagger, brown with dried blood, and prepared
To avenge her only son. But he was stretched
On his back, and her stabbing blade was blunted
By the woven mail shirt he wore on his chest.
The hammered links held; the point
Could not touch him. He'd have traveled to the bottom of the earth,
Edgetho's son[12], and died there, if that shining
Woven metal had not helped—and Holy
God, who sent him victory, gave judgment
For truth and right, Ruler of the Heavens,
Once Beowulf was back on his feet and fighting.

What saves Beowulf from Grendel's mother's sword?

Canto 23

Then he saw, hanging on the wall, a heavy
Sword, hammered by giants[13], strong
And blessed with their magic, the best of all weapons
But so massive that no ordinary man could lift
Its carved and decorated length. He drew it
From its scabbard[14], broke the chain on its hilt,
And then, savage, now, angry
And desperate, lifted it high over his head
And struck with all the strength he had left,
Caught her in the neck and cut it through,
Broke bones and all. Her body fell
To the floor, lifeless, the sword was wet
With her blood, and Beowulf rejoiced at the sight.
The brilliant light shone, suddenly,
As though burning in that hall, and as bright as Heaven's
Own candle,[15] lit in the sky. He looked
At her home, then following along the wall
Went walking, his hands tight on the sword,

12. **Edgetho's son.** Beowulf
13. **giants.** *Beowulf* contains many references to giants. Some echo Genesis 6:3, "In those days there were giants on the earth."
14. **scabbard.** Sheath for a sword
15. **Heaven's / Own candle.** The sun

WORDS FOR EVERYDAY USE

a • venge (ə venj') *vt.*, to take vengeance for or on behalf of someone else. *The angry soldiers sought to avenge the death of their comrade.*

His heart still angry. He was hunting another
Dead monster, and took his weapons with him
For final revenge against Grendel's vicious
Attacks, his nighttime raids, over
And over, coming to Herot when Hrothgar's
Men slept, killing them in their beds,
Eating some on the spot, fifteen
Or more, and running to his loathsome moor
With another such sickening meal waiting
In his pouch. But Beowulf repaid him for those visits,
Found him lying dead in his corner,
Armless, exactly as that fierce fighter
Had sent him out from Herot, then struck off
His head with a single swift blow. The body
Jerked for the last time, then lay still.

Who else does Beowulf want to hunt? What does he do for final revenge?

The men waiting on the shore see the water turn red and fear for Beowulf.

After the blade of Beowulf's sword melts, Beowulf swims to shore with the jeweled hilt and Grendel's head. He is greeted with much rejoicing. Beowulf presents Grendel's head to Hrothgar.

Cantos 24-30

Beowulf tells Hrothgar of his adventure and gives the king the hilt of Grendel's mother's sword, which is decorated with ancient runic[16] *letters describing the war of the giants before Noah's flood. Beowulf returns the sword Hrunting to Hunferth. Graciously, he says nothing about how the sword had failed him. Then Beowulf and his men set sail for the land of the Geats, their home.*

Once home, Beowulf recounts his adventures and the gifts that he received in the land of the Danes.

Canto 31

. . .

Afterwards, in the time when Higlac was dead
And Herdred, his son, who'd ruled the Geats
After his father, had followed him into darkness—
Killed in battle with the Swedes, who smashed

16. **runic.** Characteristic of runes, letters in an alphabet used by the Germanic peoples from about the 3rd to the 13th centuries AD

ANSWER TO GUIDED READING QUESTION

1. Beowulf wants to hunt down the dead Grendel. He finds Grendel's body and cuts off Grendel's head as final revenge.

ANSWERS TO GUIDED READING QUESTIONS

1. Beowulf rules for "fifty winters" in Geatland when a dragon begins to terrorize the Geats.
2. The beast is angered when a man steals a gem-studded cup from its treasure.

Anglo-Saxon brooch. British Museum, London.

His shield, cut through the soldiers surrounding
Their king—then, when Higd's one son
Was gone, Beowulf ruled in Geatland,
Took the throne he'd refused, once,
And held it long and well. He was old
With years and wisdom, fifty winters
A king, when a dragon awoke from its darkness
And dreams and brought terror to his people. The beast
Had slept in a huge stone tower, with a hidden
Path beneath; a man stumbled on
The entrance, went in, discovered the ancient
Treasure, the pagan jewels and gold
The dragon had been guarding, and dazzled and greedy
Stole a gem-studded cup, and fled.
But now the dragon hid nothing, neither
The theft nor itself; it swept through the darkness,
And all Geatland knew its anger.

When and for how long does Beowulf rule in Geatland? What begins to terrorize the Geats?

What angers this beast?

Cantos 32-34

Furious at the theft of the cup, the dragon begins attacking the countryside and setting fire to buildings by night. Having made up his mind to fight the dragon, Beowulf and some companions go to view the monster in his lair. Sitting some distance from the dragon, the companions listen to Beowulf tell of other battles and of other warriors slain.

Canto 35

. . .

And Beowulf uttered his final boast:
"I've never known fear; as a youth I fought
In endless battles. I am old, now,
But I will fight again, seek fame still,
If the dragon hiding in his tower dares
To face me."
Then he said farewell to his followers,
Each in his turn, for the last time:
"I'd use no sword, no weapon, if this beast
Could be killed without it, crushed to death
Like Grendel, gripped in my hands and torn
Limb from limb. But his breath will be burning
Hot, poison will pour from his tongue.
I feel no shame, with shield and sword
And armor, against this monster: when he comes to me
I mean to stand, not run from his shooting
Flames, stand till fate decides
Which of us wins. My heart is firm,
My hands calm: I need no hot
Words. Wait for me close by, my friends.
We shall see, soon, who will survive
This bloody battle, stand when the fighting
Is done. No one else could do
What I mean to, here, no man but me
Could hope to defeat this monster. No one
Could try. And this dragon's treasure, his gold
And everything hidden in that tower, will be mine
Or war will sweep me to a bitter death!"
Then Beowulf rose, still brave, still strong,
And with his shield at his side, and a mail shirt on his breast,
Strode calmly, confidently, toward the tower, under
The rocky cliffs: no coward could have walked there!
And then he who'd endured dozens of desperate
Battles, who'd stood boldly while swords and shields
Clashed, the best of kings, saw
Huge stone arches and felt the heat
Of the dragon's breath, flooding down

What does Beowulf say about using a weapon?

How does Beowulf judge himself as a warrior? What does he vow about the treasure?

ANSWERS TO GUIDED READING QUESTIONS

1. Beowulf says he'd use no weapon if he could kill the monster without one. Because of the dragon's fiery breath, however, he will need to fight with shield, sword, and armor.
2. Beowulf declares that no man but he could defeat the monster. He vows to defeat the dragon and gain the treasure.

ANSWER TO GUIDED READING QUESTION

1. Beowulf's shield begins to melt. Fate is against Beowulf for the first time.

Through the hidden entrance, too hot for anyone
To stand, a streaming current of fire
And smoke that blocked all passage. And the Geats'
Lord and leader, angry, lowered
His sword and roared out a battle cry,
A call so loud and clear that it reached through
The hoary rock, hung in the dragon's
Ear. The beast rose, angry,
Knowing a man had come—and then nothing
But war could have followed. Its breath came first,
A steaming cloud pouring from the stone,
Then the earth itself shook. Beowulf
Swung his shield into place, held it
In front of him, facing the entrance. The dragon
Coiled and uncoiled, its heart urging it
Into battle. Beowulf's ancient sword
Was waiting, unsheathed, his sharp and gleaming
Blade. The beast came closer; both of them
Were ready, each set on slaughter. The Geats'
Great prince stood firm, unmoving, prepared
Behind his high shield, waiting in his shining
Armor. The monster came quickly toward him,
Pouring out fire and smoke, hurrying
To its fate. Flames beat at the iron
Shield, and for a time it held, protected
Beowulf as he'd planned; then it began to melt,
And for the first time in his life that famous prince
Fought with fate against him, with glory
Denied him. He knew it, but he raised his sword
And struck at the dragon's scaly hide.
The ancient blade broke, bit into
The monster's skin, drew blood, but cracked
And failed him before it went deep enough, helped him
Less than he needed. The dragon leaped
With pain, thrashed and beat at him, spouting
Murderous flames, spreading them everywhere.
And the Geats' ring-giver did not boast of glorious
Victories in other wars: his weapon
Had failed him, deserted him, now when he needed it
Most, that excellent sword. Edgetho's

What happens to Beowulf's shield? What is against Beowulf for the first time?

WORDS FOR EVERYDAY USE

hoar • y (hōr′ ē), *adj.*, gray or white with age; extremely old; ancient. *When they found the frostbite victim, her skin was so hoary it made her look as if she were a very old woman.*

Famous son[17] stared at death,
Unwilling to leave this world, to exchange it
For a dwelling in some distant place—a journey
Into darkness that all men must make, as death
Ends their few brief hours on earth.
Quickly, the dragon came at him, encouraged
As Beowulf fell back; its breath flared,
And he suffered, wrapped around in swirling
Flames—a king, before, but now
A beaten warrior. None of his comrades
Came to him, helped him, his brave and noble
Followers; they ran for their lives, fled
Deep in a wood. And only one of them
Remained, stood there, miserable, remembering,
As a good man must, what kinship should mean.

All must make what journey?

How do Beowulf's comrades respond?

Canto 36

His name was Wiglaf, he was Wexstan's son
And a good soldier; his family had been Swedish,
Once. Watching Beowulf, he could see
How his king was suffering, burning. Remembering
Everything his lord and cousin had given him,
Armor and gold and the great estates
Wexstan's family enjoyed, Wiglaf's
Mind was made up; he raised his yellow
Shield and drew his sword . . .
Then he ran to his king, crying encouragement
As he drove through the dragon's deadly fumes:
"Beloved Beowulf, remember how you boasted,
Once, that nothing in the world would ever
Destroy your fame: fight to keep it,
Now, be strong and brave, my noble
King, protecting life and fame
Together. My sword will fight at your side!"
The dragon heard him, the man-hating monster,
And was angry; shining with surging flames
It came for him, anxious to return his visit.
Waves of fire swept at his shield
And the edge began to burn. His mail shirt
Could not help him, but before his hands dropped
The blazing wood Wiglaf jumped
Behind Beowulf's shield; his own was burned
To ashes. Then the famous old hero, remembering

Who remains with Beowulf? What does he do?

How does Wiglaf protect himself?

17. **Edgetho's / Famous son.** Beowulf

ANSWERS TO GUIDED READING QUESTIONS

1. All must make a journey into darkness as they die.
2. Beowulf's followers run for their lives, fleeing deep into a wood.
3. Wiglaf, Wexstan's son, remains with Beowulf. He runs to Beowulf and says he will fight at his side.
4. Wiglaf protects himself by jumping behind Beowulf's shield as his own shield burns to ashes.

ANSWERS TO GUIDED READING QUESTIONS

1. Beowulf's sword Nagling, breaks into pieces because of Beowulf's strength.
2. The dragon dies as Beowulf cuts the beast in half.
3. Beowulf begins to die from the dragon's venomous wounds.

Days of glory, lifted what was left
Of Nagling, his ancient sword, and swung it
With all his strength, smashed the gray
Blade into the beast's head. But then Nagling
Broke to pieces, as iron always
Had in Beowulf's hands. His arms
Were too strong, the hardest blade could not help him,
The most wonderfully worked. He carried them to war
But fate had decreed that the Geats' great king
Would be no better for any weapon.
Then the monster charged again, vomiting
Fire, wild with pain, rushed out
Fierce and dreadful, its fear forgotten.
Watching for its chance it drove its tusks
Into Beowulf's neck; he staggered, the blood
Came flooding forth, fell like rain.

What happens to Beowulf's sword?

Canto 37

And then when Beowulf needed him most
Wiglaf showed his courage, his strength
And skill, and the boldness he was born with. Ignoring
The dragon's head, he helped his lord
By striking lower down. The sword
Sank in; his hand was burned, but the shining
Blade had done its work, the dragon's
Belching flames began to flicker
And die away. And Beowulf drew
His battle-sharp dagger: the blood-stained old king
Still knew what he was doing. Quickly, he cut
The beast in half, slit it apart.
It fell, their courage had killed it, two noble
Cousins had joined in the dragon's death.
Yet what they did all men must do
When the time comes! But the triumph was the last
Beowulf would ever earn, the end
Of greatness and life together. The wound
In his neck began to swell and grow;
He could feel something stirring, burning
In his veins, a stinging venom, and knew
The beast's fangs had left it. He fumbled
Along the wall, found a slab
Of stone, and dropped down; above him he saw
Huge stone arches and heavy posts,
Holding up the roof of that giant hall.

What happens to the dragon?

What happens to Beowulf?

Then Wiglaf's gentle hands bathed
The blood-stained prince, his glorious lord,
Weary of war, and loosened his helmet.
  Beowulf spoke, in spite of the swollen,
Livid wound, knowing he'd unwound
His string of days on earth, seen
As much as God would grant him; all worldly
Pleasure was gone, as life would go,
Soon:
        "I'd leave my armor to my son,
Now, if God had given me an heir,
A child born of my body, his life
Created from mine. I've worn this crown
For fifty winters: no neighboring people
Have tried to threaten the Geats, sent soldiers
Against us or talked of terror. My days
Have gone by as fate willed, waiting
For its word to be spoken, ruling as well
As I knew how, swearing no unholy oaths,
Seeking no lying wars. I can leave
This life happy; I can die, here,
Knowing the Lord of all life has never
Watched me wash my sword in blood
Born of my own family. Beloved
Wiglaf, go, quickly, find
The dragon's treasure: we've taken its life,
But its gold is ours, too. Hurry,
Bring me ancient silver, precious
Jewels, shining armor and gems,
Before I die. Death will be softer,
Leaving life and this people I've ruled
So long, if I look at this last of all prizes."

What does Beowulf know?

Beowulf makes what request of Wiglaf?

Canto 38

. . .

  Then Wiglaf went back, anxious
To return while Beowulf was alive, to bring him
Treasure they'd won together. He ran,
Hoping his wounded king, weak
And dying, had not left the world too soon.
Then he brought their treasure to Beowulf, and found
His famous king bloody, gasping
For breath. But Wiglaf sprinkled water
Over his lord, until the words

ANSWERS TO GUIDED READING QUESTIONS

1. Beowulf knows that he is dying and that all worldly pleasure has gone for him.
2. He requests that Wiglaf bring back the dragon's treasure so he can see it before he dies.

ANSWER TO GUIDED READING QUESTION

1. Beowulf says that he sold his life "well" for the treasure. He instructs Wiglaf to lead his people and to build him a tomb high at the water's edge.

Deep in his breast broke through and were heard.
Beholding the treasure he spoke, haltingly:
"For this, this gold, these jewels, I thank
Our Father in heaven, Ruler of the Earth—
For all of this, that His grace has given me,
Allowed me to bring to my people while breath
Still came to my lips. I sold my life
For this treasure, and I sold it well. Take
What I leave, Wiglaf, lead my people,
Help them; my time is gone. Have
The brave Geats build me a tomb,
When the funeral flames have burned me, and build it
Here, at the water's edge, high
On this spit of land, so sailors can see
This tower, and remember my name, and call it
Beowulf's tower, and boats in the darkness
And mist, crossing the sea, will know it."
Then that brave king gave the golden
Necklace from around his throat to Wiglaf,
Gave him his gold-covered helmet, and his rings,
And his mail shirt, and ordered him to use them well:
"You're the last of all our far-flung family.
Fate has swept our race away,
Taken warriors in their strength and led them
To the death that was waiting. And now I follow them."
The old man's mouth was silent, spoke
No more, had said as much as it could;
He would sleep in the fire, soon. His soul
Left his flesh, flew to glory.

How does Beowulf regard his sacrifice for the treasure? What does he tell Wiglaf to do?

The men who had fled to the forest return and are reproved by Wiglaf. Wiglaf then sends a messenger to tell of Beowulf's death.

The men go to the dragon's lair, where they see the bodies of the beast and of their king. Wiglaf and seven others load a cart with the dragon's treasure.

Canto 43

The people prepare a large pyre and mourn Beowulf. They build a memorial to him and remember his great deeds.

WORDS FOR EVERYDAY USE

pyre (pīr'), *n.*, a combustible heap for burning a dead body as a funeral rite. *The flames from the pyre were so bright that people from miles away knew when the emperor's funeral had begun.*

Saxon font relief, Toller Frantrum Church, Dorset, UK.

A huge heap of wood was ready,
Hung around with helmets, and battle
Shields, and shining mail shirts, all
As Beowulf had asked. The bearers brought
Their beloved lord, their glorious king,
And weeping laid him high on the wood.
Then the warriors began to kindle that greatest
Of funeral fires; smoke rose
Above the flames, black and thick,
And while the wind blew and the fire
Roared they wept, and Beowulf's body
Crumbled and was gone. The Geats stayed,
Moaning their sorrow, lamenting their lord;
A gnarled old woman, hair wound
Tight and gray on her head, groaned
A song of misery, of infinite sadness
And days of mourning, of fear and sorrow
To come, slaughter and terror and captivity.

What happens to Beowulf's body?

WORDS FOR EVERYDAY USE

la • ment • ing (lə ment′iŋ), *vt.,* to mourn aloud; wail; to express sorrow, mourning, or regret, often in a demonstrative way. *My brother moaned and cursed, lamenting in grief when my parents took his video game privileges away.*

ANSWER TO GUIDED READING QUESTION

1. Beowulf's body is burned in a funeral pyre as the Geats mourn his death.

ANSWERS TO GUIDED READING QUESTIONS

1. The Geats bury the treasure Beowulf and Wiglaf had won from the dragon so it is "forever hidden and useless to men."
2. The speaker says that all should praise their own lords with the same warmth and love that the Geats expressed for Beowulf.

RESPOND TO THE SELECTION

Encourage students to give concrete examples that support their opinions. You might also want to encourage them to connect these characters with persons they know in real life or with characters from television shows, movies, or books.

SELECTION CHECK TEST 4.2.3 WITH ANSWERS

Checking Your Reading

1. Why does Beowulf come to Hrothgar's castle? **He wants to kill Grendel.**
2. Why is Beowulf given a hero's banquet? **He defeated Grendel.**
3. Who comes to Heorot, seeking vengeance? **Grendel's mother seeks vengeance.**
4. What two things does Beowulf give to Hrothgar when he returns from the underwater cave? **He gives him Grendel's head and the jeweled sword hilt.**
5. What do most of Beowulf's men do when the dragon attacks? **They hide.**

Vocabulary in Context
Fill each blank with the most appropriate word from the Words for Everyday Use.

remorse perpetual savor
wretched hale moor resound

1. We'd looked forward to camping, but because of the cold rain the trip was **wretched**.
2. On the third day of vacation, Lottie toured the **moors** that surrounded the castle.
3. Norbert is in **perpetual** motion; no one knows where all his energy comes from.
4. Thomas had cancer as a child, but now he's a **hale** adult who lives life to the fullest.
5. Lucy tore a page from the school's encyclopedia, and has felt **remorse** ever since.

And Heaven swallowed the billowing smoke.
  Then the Geats built the tower, as Beowulf
Had asked, strong and tall, so sailors
Could find it from far and wide; working
For ten long days they made his monument,
Sealed his ashes in walls as straight
And high as wise and willing hands
Could raise them. And the riches he and Wiglaf
Had won from the dragon, rings, necklaces,
Ancient, hammered armor—all
The treasures they'd taken were left there, too,
Silver and jewels buried in the sandy
Ground, back in the earth, again
And forever hidden and useless to men.
And then twelve of the bravest Geats
Rode their horses around the tower,
Telling their sorrow, telling stories
Of their dead king and his greatness, his glory,
Praising him for heroic deeds, for a life
As noble as his name. So should all men
Raise up words for their lords, warm
With love, when their shield and protector leaves
His body behind, sends his soul
On high. And so Beowulf's followers
Rode, mourning their beloved leader,
Crying that no better king had ever
Lived, no prince so mild, no man
So open to his people, so deserving of praise. ■

What happens to the jewels Beowulf and Wiglaf had won from the dragon?

According to the speaker, what should all do?

WORDS FOR EVERYDAY USE

bil • low • ing (bi' lō wiŋ), *adj.*, rising and rolling in waves or surges. *The billowing sails made a wavelike motion in the wind.*

Respond to the SELECTION

With what character or characters in Beowulf do you feel most sympathy? Which do you admire the most? Which do you dislike?

SELECTION CHECK TEST 4.2.3 WITH ANSWERS (CONT.)

Literary Tools
Fill in the blanks using the following terms. You may not use every term, and you may use some terms more than once.

scop scribe heroic epic cantos alliteration
kennings cæsura

1. *Beowulf* consists of a prologue and 43 **cantos**.
2. The poem survives in a manuscript recorded by a West Saxon **scribe**.
3. **Heroic epics** are long stories that tell the life stories of great heroes.
4. *Battle-flasher, life-house,* and *earth-hall* are examples of **kennings**.
5. The **cæsura** in the middle of a line helped give Anglo-Saxon verse a formal, elevated quality.

INVESTIGATE, Inquire, Imagine

Recall: GATHERING FACTS →

1a. Who is Hrothgar? What does he build for his people? Whom does the feasting at this place disturb? From whom is this creature descended? What has the Almighty done to the descendents of this person, and how does this creature behave? What is the result of this creature's actions on Herot?

2a. For what purpose does Beowulf come to the land of the Danes? What does Beowulf say about his own courage and strength? What does Beowulf request of Hrothgar and others to help him fight Grendel, Grendel's mother, and the dragon?

3a. What is the end result of Beowulf's three battles in this selection? In what ways does Beowulf exhibit strength throughout his life?

Interpret: FINDING MEANING

1b. What signs are there that Hrothgar is a good king? How do you think Grendel feels about his situation? about Hrothgar's building? Why might Grendel react as he does, growling in pain and impatience?

2b. What desires do you think motivate Beowulf to travel across the sea to help Hrothgar? Explain whether Beowulf seems able and equipped to carry out his missions to fight Grendel, Grendel's mother, and the dragon.

3b. How do the Danes regard Beowulf throughout the selection? In what ways do they judge him to be heroic?

Analyze: TAKING THINGS APART →

4a. Some biblical references in this epic include references to the story of Cain and more direct references to the Christian God, often referred to in this translation of the poem as the "Almighty." Explain what role both Grendel and Beowulf play in terms of these biblical references.

Synthesize: BRINGING THINGS TOGETHER

4b. How does the poet—and perhaps the Christian scribe who copied and embellished this epic—use the Bible to explain Grendel's evil actions? Why do you think biblical events were used in the retelling of this epic? In what way do the biblical elements help to tie the story together and give it greater meaning?

Evaluate: MAKING JUDGMENTS →

5a. Which of Beowulf's qualities and deeds classify him as a hero, according to ancient Germanic values?

Extend: CONNECTING IDEAS

5b. Based on your own contemporary standards, explain whether Beowulf is a hero.

Understanding Literature

HEROIC EPIC. An **epic** is a long story, often told in verse, involving heroes and gods. Grand in length and scope, an epic provides a portrait of an entire culture, of the legends, beliefs, values, laws, arts, and ways of life of a people. A **heroic epic** is an epic that has a main purpose of telling the life story of a great hero. What have you learned from reading this poem about the beliefs and ways of life of the ancient Germanic peoples? How was their society organized? What did they do for entertainment? What struggles did they face in life? For them, what made a great person? What aspects of their world do you admire or dislike? Why?

COMPOUND WORDS AND APPOSITION. Compound words are made up of two words joined together. The Old English language was rich in compound words. Many of these words were stock formulas for

ANSWERS TO INVESTIGATE, INQUIRE, AND IMAGINE

RECALL

1a. Hrothgar is the king of the Danes. He builds Herot, an enormous hall, for his people. The feasting at Herot disturbs the monster Grendel who lives in the moors and marshes. Grendel is descended from Cain, who slew his brother Abel. The Almighty exiled the descendents of Cain from men. Grendel comes to Herot in the night and kills thirty sleeping warriors. He then kills the Danes at Herot night after night.

2a. Beowulf comes to the land of the Danes to help Hrothgar defeat Grendel and to earn honor for himself. Beowulf tells of some remarkable exploits of strength and courage—killing giants and sea monsters out in the ocean. Beowulf asks Hrothgar to be allowed to kill the monsters alone with his own men and with his bare hands whenever possible.

3a. In the battle against Grendel, Beowulf severs the monster's arm and Grendel goes off to die. In the battle against Grendel's mother, Beowulf kills her and finds Grendel's dead body. He then severs Grendel's head as final revenge. In Beowulf's final battle, he kills the dragon but dies from the venomous wounds he suffers. In all three battles, the Danes celebrate Beowulf as a brave warrior-hero.

INTERPRET

1b. Hrothgar leads the Danes to glory in battle and then builds a hall for his people in which to feast them and divide the spoils of war. Grendel may feel bitter about his role as an exile and jealous of the world of men, which he is made painfully and noisily aware of once Hrothgar builds Herot. Grendel might resent the humans their companionship and happiness because he is doomed by his birth to be an exile.

2b. Beowulf's loyalty, desire for fame, and sense of duty to someone he knew as a boy inspire Beowulf to help Hrothgar, king of the Danes. Students may say that Beowulf's skill, bravery, honor, and desire for fame make his especially suited to battle the monsters.

3b. The Danes feel relief and joy when he saves them from the monsters. They honor Beowulf by making him their king and celebrate his fifty-year tenure. Students may note that the Danes mourn him deeply when he dies, following his instructions to build a tower honoring him; they also bury the treasures he and

Continued on page 142

ANSWERS TO UNDERSTANDING LITERATURE

HEROIC EPIC. The ancient Germanic peoples believed in the supernatural and in fate. They were religious, but there may have been a shift from more ancient religions to Christianity. They valued strength and courage and put their trust in warrior leaders. They seems to attach themselves to a leader or king who would feast them and provide for them in return for their loyalty and help in battle. The Germanic peoples clearly enjoyed feasting, but also expected to face many battles and armed conflicts in their life. To them, a great person was one who was strong, courageous, generous, loyal, and who could defeat his enemies. *Responses will vary.*

Answers to Understanding Literature are continued on page 142.

ANSWERS TO INVESTIGATE, INQUIRE, AND IMAGINE (CONT. FROM PAGE 141)

Wiglaf recovered from the dragon so that they are "forever hidden and useless to men." The selection ends with the Dane's "mourning their beloved leader, / Crying that no better king had ever / Lived..."

ANALYZE

4a. Students should note that Grendel is described as part of the cursed race of Cain, despised by God, and Beowulf is described as God's champion against this monster.

SYNTHESIZE

4b. Students should note that as the poet makes Grendel descended from an cursed race of monsters descended from Cain, he or she explains why Grendel commits such antisocial acts of great evil. Students might suggest that the poet was attempting to give some Christian value to a pagan story. Students might say that the Biblical references help to explain why Grendel behaves with such malice, as well as give the story greater meaning by creating an allegory about the power of God and the struggle Christians face against evil.

EVALUATE

5a. Students might point out that Beowulf's past valorous deeds, slaying giants and sea monsters, make him a hero before he comes to help the Danes. His courage and daring in confronting Grendel and Grendel's mother barehanded, and his willingness to succumb to death in confronting the dragon also reveal heroic qualities.

EXTEND

5b. *Responses will vary.*

ANSWERS TO UNDERSTANDING LITERATURE (CONT. FROM PAGE 141)

COMPOUND WORDS AND APPOSITION. Students' kennings, or imaginative compounds, will vary, but they should provide at least one for Beowulf and one for Grendel. Listing such compounds on the board as students come up with them might encourage students to list even more. The apposition is unusual because both shepherds and guardians are usually associated with good rather than with evil and crime. There are numerous examples of apposition students might list. Students should note that these examples provide them with many descriptive epithets for characters and many informative descriptions for places. The appositions help present different aspects of people and things.

describing people and objects. Some of theses stock formulas are known as *kennings,* metaphorical two-word replacement for nouns. While this translation of *Beowulf* does not capture many of the unusual compounds of the poem, it does capture more common ones, such as *hell-forged* and *blood-thirsty* (used to describe Grendel) and *strong-hearted* and *strong-minded* (used to describe Beowulf). What are some original kennings you might use to describe both the monster and the hero in this Germanic epic? An **apposition** is a grammatical form in which a thing is renamed in a different word, phrase, or clause. Old English poets made extensive use of apposition to name and rename things. One example of apposition in the poem refers to Grendel as "That shepherd of evil, guardian of crime." What makes this apposition unusual? How do people typically think of guardians and shepherds? What are some other examples of apposition from the poem? What do the appositions add to the poem?

WRITER'S JOURNAL

1. Write a **menu** imaginatively describing foods and beverages that might be served at an ancient Germanic feast. You do not have to limit your descriptions to ordinary food items, but can base some of them on supernatural elements of the poem, *Beowulf.* For example, one item served might be "Fresh filet of sea monster, our catch of the day—freshly strangled off the coastline by a hero of local renown—served with fresh sea salt and lemon, an unusual dish for the adventurer in you."
2. Write a **script** for a brief scene in an adventure movie about Beowulf. How might you update some of the dialogue and action in your chosen scene to appeal to a contemporary audience?
3. In a critical essay, a writer presents an argument in support of a particular interpretation of a work of literature. Draft a **critical essay** on one of the following thesis statements, or main ideas, or come up with your own thesis about *Beowulf:*
   - Beowulf perfectly embodies the Germanic heroic ideal.
   - Hrothgar is an example of a once great Germanic king who is past his prime and whose power is beginning to wane.
   - Grendel is a more sympathetic character than many of his actions may lead the reader initially to believe.

Integrating *the* LANGUAGE ARTS

Language, Grammar, and Style

SUBJECT-VERB AGREEMENT IN COMPOUND SUBJECTS AND COLLECTIVE NOUNS. Read the Language Arts Survey 3.28, "Compound Subjects," and 3.53, "Collective Nouns." Copy the following sentences onto your own paper, writing in the correct tense of the verb in parentheses. Then, underline the subject (or subjects) of each verb and tell whether the subject is compound or whether it is a collective noun.

1. The ancient Germanic people (was/were) often at war amongst themselves.
2. Many poems and histories of the period (describe/describes) these people's battles.
3. The Welsh historian Gildas (is/are) credited with writing a stirring account of a battle that took place on Badon Hill, in the English countryside.
4. In the story, the Britons and the Anglo-Saxon tribe (is/are) at war, because the Anglo-Saxon tribe (is/are) invading England.
5. Today, the community of historians (disagree/disagrees) as to whether this story was the source of the legend of King Arthur.

ANSWERS TO INTEGRATING THE LANGUAGE ARTS

Language, Grammar and Style

1. The ancient Germanic people **were** often at war amongst themselves. (collective noun)
2. Many poems and histories **describe** these people's battles. (compound subject)
3. The Welsh historian Gildas **is** credited with writing a stirring account of a battle that took place on Badon Hill, in the English countryside. (subject is not compound nor collective)
4. In the story, the Britons and the Anglo-Saxon tribe **are** at war, because the Anglo-Saxon tribe is invading England. (compound subject; collective noun)
5. Today, the community of historians **disagree** as to whether this story was the source of the legend of King Arthur. (collective noun; members are acting individually)

Continued on page 143

Study and Research Skills

Working with Analogy Questions. Analogy questions often appear on standardized tests. They ask you to find the relationship between a given pair of words and then to recognize a similar relationship between another pair of words. In an analogy question, the symbols : and :: mean "is to" and "as," respectively. For more information, read the Language Arts Survey 5.49, "Analogy Questions." Then read the analogy questions based on Beowulf below. Choose the letter of the best answer for each numbered example.

1. Beowulf : Grendel ::
   a. master : servant
   b. enemy : villain
   c. hero : villain
   d. hero : victor
2. Beowulf : strength ::
   a. sprinter: slowness
   b. thief: stealth
   c. hero: cowardice
   d. singer: song
3. Beowulf: barehanded ::
   a. warrior: plunder
   b. king : hall
   c. archer : arrow
   d. Grendel: joylessness
4. Hrothgar : Herot
   a. baseball player : outfield
   b. architect: building
   c. worker: office
   d. Webmaster : computer
5. Hrothgar : Danes
   a. Russian : European
   b. Beowulf : Danes
   c. Anglo-Saxon : Scandinavians
   d. President : United States citizens

Speaking and Listening & Collaborative Learning

Conducting a Survey. An epic poem communicates the values of a people. Find out about the values of people around you by surveying and discussing people's beliefs and attitudes. Before you begin, read the Language Arts Survey 4.11, "Being Considerate of Other Cultures and Communication Styles," and 4.13, "Guidelines for Discussion." Then work as a class to come up with a list of questions that will tell you what people care about, what they would be willing to struggle for, and so on. Possible questions for your survey include:

- What do you like to do in your free time?
- Of all the things that you have done, what are you proudest of?
- What do you want to be remembered for in the future?

Then choose a random sample of people and ask them your questions. You may want to divide your sample into two groups (men and women, perhaps, or young people and older people) and compare the results that you obtain from these groups. As a class, discuss the responses you gathered and your reactions to and thoughts about them.

Answers to Integrating the Language Arts

(Cont. from page 142)

Study and Research Skills

1. Beowulf : Grendel ::
   a. master : servant
   b. enemy : villain
   c. hero : villain
   d. hero : victor
2. Beowulf : strength ::
   a. sprinter: slowness
   b. thief: stealth
   c. hero: cowardice
   d. singer: song
3. Beowulf: barehanded ::
   a. warrior: plunder
   b. king : hall
   c. archer : arrow
   d. Grendel: joylessness
4. Hrothgar : Herot
   a. baseball player : outfield
   b. architect: building
   c. worker: office
   d. Webmaster : computer
5. Hrothgar : Danes
   a. Russian : European
   b. Beowulf : Danes
   c. Anglo-Saxon : Scandinavian
   d. President : United States citizens

Speaking and Listening and Collaborative Learning
For additional practice with these skills, provide students with the exercises and handouts in the Teacher's Resource Kit, Speaking and Listening Resource Book 4.11, "Being Considerate of Other Cultures and Communication Styles," and 4.13, "Guidelines for Discussion."

FROM "THE SEAFARER"

About the Selection. "The Seafarer" probably was composed in the eighth century by a sailor. It shows extensive familiarity with the weather and wildlife as they would have been experienced by a seafarer of the North Sea. It was formerly believed that the poem represents a dialogue between a disillusioned old salt and an enthusiastic young mariner, but a more likely interpretation is that the poem presents the conflicting feelings of a sailor who loves the sea but hates the hardships of sea life.

"WULF AND EADWACER"

About the Selection. The song **"Wulf and Eadwacer"** appears in the *Exeter Book,* which was compiled in the tenth century. The *Exeter Book* also contains "The Wife's Lament" (page 88) and Anglo-Saxon Riddles (page 94). Like the speaker in "The Wife's Lament," the speaker in "Wulf and Eadwacer" mourns the loss of her beloved who has gone on an extended journey, perhaps never to return. Also as in "The Wife's Lament," the speaker accepts this separation as something beyond her power to remedy and feels no hope. One interpretation of the song sees the speaker addressing her legal husband Eadwacer in line 16, and her listeners in lines 1–13. In this interpretation, the speaker and Wulf have been separated by Eadwacer. A second interpretation is that the whole song is an appeal to Eadwacer for help. As you discuss the poem with students, ask them to whom they think *us* in lines 3 and 8 refers.

from "The Seafarer," Anonymous, translated by George K. Anderson

I can sing a true song about myself; I can tell of my journeys, how in troublous days I often endured hours of hardship, how I lived to feel bitterness of heart in the wretched quarters of my ship while the waves rolled high. Often have I stood my narrow night-watch in the prow of the boat, when it knocked against the rocky cliffs. Stiff with cold were my feet bound fast by frost's icy claws; there cares seethed hot about my heart, and hunger within rent the courage of the seaweary.

No man so happy as to enjoy the land can know how I, careworn, dwelt on the wintry ice-cold waves, paths of exile for me deprived of my kinsmen. Icicles hung from me; hail lashed me in showers. There I heard naught but the howling sea, the icy waves, at times the song of the wild swan. I had for my delight the cry of the gannet; for me the scream of the sea-gull rather than the laughter of men; the singing of the sea-mew rather than the drinking of mead. Storms beat upon the stone cliffs; there icy-feathered birds gave them a stern answer; full often screamed the dewy-feathered eagle. No protecting lord was there to console the heart of the needy man. He who dwells in the city, who has the joy of living, proud and flushed with wine, feels little hardship, such as I many a time had to endure on the ocean wastes. The shadow of night lowered; it snowed from the north; frost bound the earth; hail, the coldest of grains, showered upon the land.

Still, for all that, desires agitate my heart, to try myself the high streams, the sport of the salt waves; always I am urged on to fare forth, to seek far hence the home of alien peoples. Yet there is no man on earth so proud, nor so good of gifts, nor in youth so active, nor in his deeds so brave, nor to his Lord so faithful that he does not have sorrow in the time of his seafaring—whatever the Fate the Lord may send him. Not for him the harp, nor the giving of rings, nor the love of a woman, nor the pleasures of the world, nor aught else but the rolling of the waves—ever he will have longing who sets out on the sea.

The groves take on their blossoms; the towns and meadows grow fair; the earth revives; all things urge on the mind of the eager-hearted to the journey, to depart far over the flood-ways. Yet the cuckoo, guardian of the summer, sings a warning with its mournful voice, bodes bitter sorrow in its breast-hoard. No man living in comfort can know what they endure who lay their paths of exile far and wide!

So now my thoughts go roaming; my spirit is with the sea-flood beyond the home of the whale; it hovers afar over the folds of earth; it returns to me yearning and greedy; the solitary flier cries out; it drives me irresistibly on the whale-road over the waves of the sea. . . .

"Wulf and Eadwacer," Anonymous, translated by Marcelle Thiébaux

For my clan he would be like a gift of booty—
they will waste him if he crosses their path.
With us it isn't like that.

Wulf is on one island, I on another—
his island is made fast, girded by fens.
Fierce men are on that island.
They will waste him if he crosses their path.
With us it isn't like that.

I yearned for Wulf in his harried wandering.
When the weather poured rain I sat here in tears.
When the brash fighter folded me in the branches
of his arms,
I felt pleasure, yes, but I felt loathing too.

Wulf, my Wulf, to think about you
made me faint with sickness, for you seldom came.
It was my mood of mourning, not want of food.
Do you hear, Eadwacer? Wulf carries our forlorn
whelp to the wood.
Men can easily wrench apart what has never been
wedded—
our story together.

The Development of the English Language:

Origins

LANGUAGE CHANGE

The chances are that you know some words that are unfamiliar to people who are older than you. In every generation, the language changes. Over time, these changes accumulate until an entirely new language emerges. Look at the samples of Old English on pages 97 and 115. A thousand years ago, that's what the English language looked like. Today, because of the accumulated changes in the language, it is impossible to read Old English without special training. However, it is still possible to make out many words. For example, the sentence

We sungeon monige songas.

is quite similar to

We sang many songs.[1]

Compare the following words:

MODERN ENGLISH	OLD ENGLISH
come	cuman
fiend	feond
folk	folc
heaven	heofon
holy	halig
king	cyning
love	lufu
mind	mynd
see	seon
sit	sittan
work	weorc
what	hwæt

1. See Cassidy, F. G., and Richard N. Ringler, eds. *Bright's Old English Grammar and Reader* (New York: Holt, 1971), p. 24.

ADDITIONAL QUESTIONS AND ACTIVITIES

Have students interview older people they know and ask them about words that were introduced to the language when they were young persons. Students can also share with them current adolescent dialect.

TEACHING NOTE: For instruction in interview, refer students to the Language Arts Survey 4.14, "Conducting an Interview." For practice in interviewing skills, refer students to the Speaking and Listening Resource Book 4.14, "Conducting an Interview."

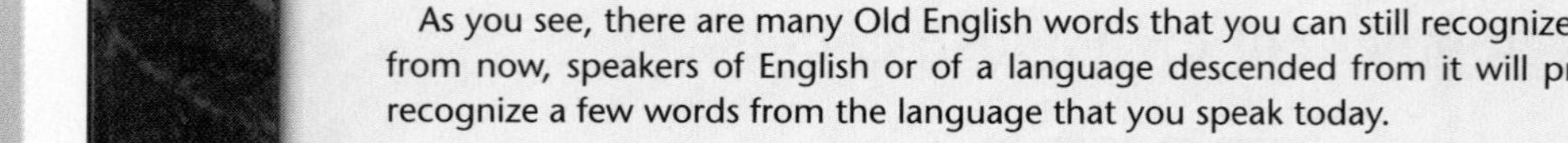

As you see, there are many Old English words that you can still recognize. A thousand years from now, speakers of English or of a language descended from it will probably be able to recognize a few words from the language that you speak today.

LANGUAGE FAMILIES

English belongs to the **Indo-European** family of languages. These languages developed from a long-dead language known as **Proto-Indo-European,** which was probably spoken by a people called the Kurgans who lived in the steppe region of southern Russia around 4000 BC. From there the language spread east and west to India and to Europe, slowly developing into many different but related languages. The common ancestry of these languages can be seen by comparing similar words found in them. Consider the following examples:

INDO-EUROPEAN WORDS FOR *FATHER*	
Sanskrit	piter
Classical Greek	pater
Latin	pater
Gothic	fadar
Old Irish	athir
French	père
Spanish	padre
Italian	padre
Portuguese	pai
English	father
German	Vater

Such similarities between words, combined with knowledge of how speech sounds change over time, enable linguists (people who study language) to reconstruct languages that no longer exist. All the words on the list above probably come from a common Proto-Indo-European word, pəter.

The relationships of the Indo-European languages can be seen quite clearly by looking at a language tree:

CROSS-CURRICULAR ACTIVITIES

SOCIAL STUDIES. Ask students how linguists might have discovered the existence of Proto-Indo-European and the Kurgans. What kinds of evidence might be available to those who study linguistic change? Interested students might research these questions and present their findings to the class.

SELECTED INDO-EUROPEAN LANGUAGES

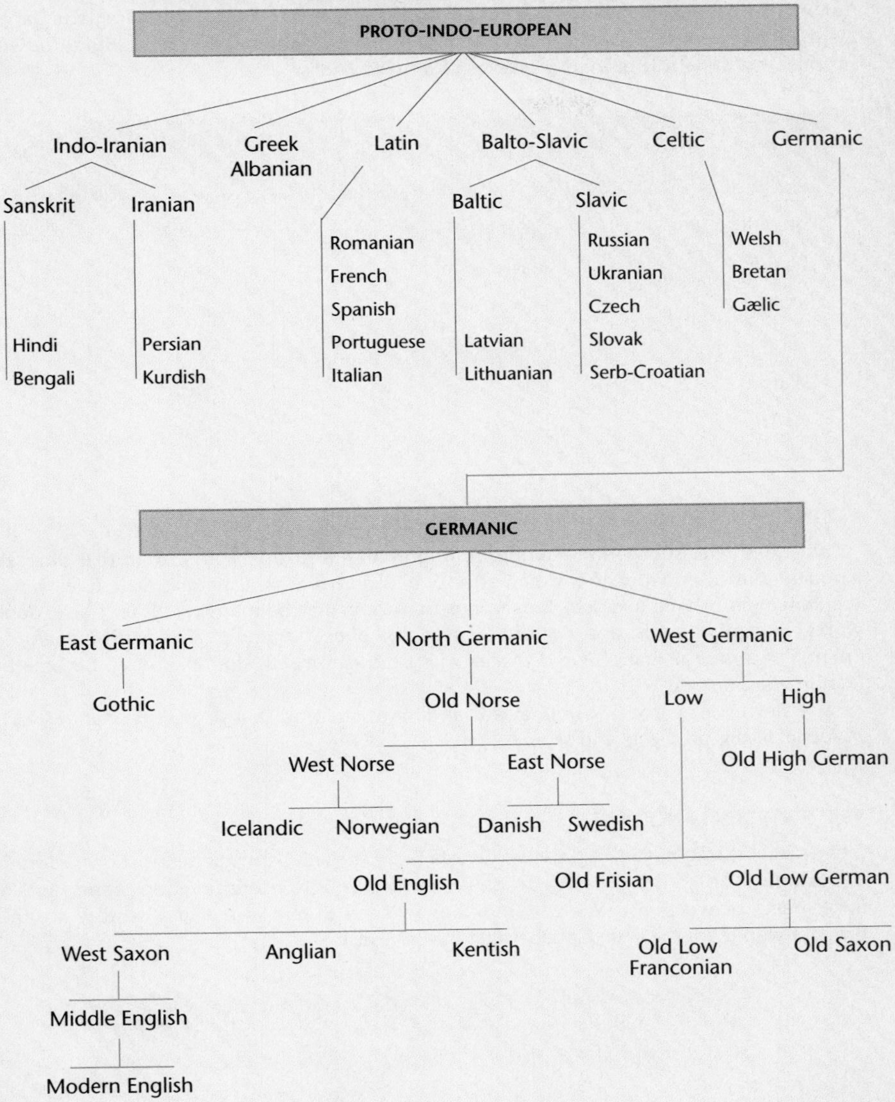

PROTO-INDO-EUROPEAN

- Indo-Iranian
  - Sanskrit
    - Hindi
    - Bengali
  - Iranian
    - Persian
    - Kurdish
- Greek
- Albanian
- Latin
  - Romanian
  - French
  - Spanish
  - Portuguese
  - Italian
- Balto-Slavic
  - Baltic
    - Latvian
    - Lithuanian
  - Slavic
    - Russian
    - Ukranian
    - Czech
    - Slovak
    - Serb-Croatian
- Celtic
  - Welsh
  - Bretan
  - Gælic
- Germanic

GERMANIC

- East Germanic
  - Gothic
- North Germanic
  - Old Norse
    - West Norse
      - Icelandic
      - Norwegian
    - East Norse
      - Danish
      - Swedish
- West Germanic
  - Low
    - Old English
      - West Saxon
        - Middle English
          - Modern English
      - Anglian
      - Kentish
    - Old Frisian
    - Old Low German
      - Old Low Franconian
      - Old Saxon
  - High
    - Old High German

CROSS-CURRICULAR ACTIVITIES

SOCIAL STUDIES. Have students plot the language tree on a world map, showing the areas where ancient languages were spoken and where modern languages currently are spoken. What can they conclude about how language changes?

ADDITIONAL QUESTIONS AND ACTIVITIES

Have students research the etymologies of other Modern English words. Show them how to trace etymology using an Oxford English dictionary if possible. For basic work with dictionaries, refer them to the Language Arts Survey 1.17, "Using a Dictionary."

THE EMERGENCE OF ENGLISH

When the Anglo-Saxons invaded England in the fifth century, they brought with them their West Germanic dialects, which are today collectively known as **Old English,** or **Anglo-Saxon.** The English language, descended from Old English, is related to modern Danish, German, Norwegian, Icelandic, and Dutch. Here are some interesting **etymologies,** or word histories, of Modern English terms derived from Old English:

OLD ENGLISH WORD	MEANING OF OLD ENGLISH WORD	MODERN ENGLISH WORD
dæge's eage	day's eye	daisy
hlaf-dige	loaf kneader	lady
hlaf-ward	loaf guardian	lord
wita	wise person	wit
Wyrd	fate	weird
wyrm	dragon	worm

EARLY BORROWINGS FROM OTHER LANGUAGES

Old English was spoken in Britain from roughly AD 450 to AD 1100. During that time, the language borrowed words from the native Celtic and from the Latin and Danish spoken by the Roman and Viking invaders. Borrowings from Latin include many words for trade, public works, religious figures, and institutions, such as *abbot* and *port.* The Latin *moneta,* for "mint," became the English word *money.* The Latin *dies malus,* for "bad day," became the English word *dismal.*

Early borrowings from Scandinavian languages such as Danish include *outlaw, knife, husband, fellow, take, egg,* and *sky.*

THE WRITTEN LANGUAGE

In its earliest stages, Old English was written in an ancient Germanic script known as **runic,** or **futhark.** This script is known to us primarily through inscriptions on stones and on implements or weapons. When the Romans invaded Britain in the first century AD, they brought with them the Latin alphabet that we use today.

THE FIRST SIX LETTERS OF THE RUNIC ALPHABET
ᚠᚢᚦᚨᚱᚲ
f u th a r k

CREATING A NARRATIVE POEM

Epic clashes between foes are the bedrock of stories we tell and retell. Much of the literature you enjoy, the computer games you've played, the movies you've seen, focus on the classic struggle between good and evil, and sometimes, the dilemma in defining each of them. In Old English storytelling, heroes were traditionally delineated in recognizable forms, and villains were obvious.

How would a hero of the 21st century behave, and what monsters would that hero face? Where do we draw the line between monster and hero? How convincingly can you create a narrative poem about a contemporary figure?

WRITING ASSIGNMENT. In this lesson, you will create a narrative poem in the Anglo-Saxon style of *Beowulf.*

A **narrative poem** is one that tells a story. One type of narrative poetry is the epic. An **epic** is a long story, often told in verse, involving heroes and gods. Grand in length and scope, an epic such as *Beowulf* provides a portrait of an entire culture, of the legends, beliefs, values, laws, arts, and ways of life of a people.

Professional Model

from *Beowulf,* translated by Burton Raffel, page 117

…A powerful monster, living down
In the darkness, growled in pain, impatient
As day after day the music rang
Loud in that hall, the harp's rejoicing
Call and the poet's clear songs, sung
Of the ancient beginnings of us all, recalling
The Almighty making the earth, shaping
These beautiful plains marked off by oceans,
Then proudly setting the sun and moon
To glow across the land and light it;
The corners of the earth were made lovely with trees
And leaves, made quick with life, with each
Of the nations who now move on its face. And then
As now warriors sang of their pleasure:
So Hrothgar's men lived happy in his hall
Till the monster stirred, that demon, that fiend,
Grendel, who haunted the moors, the wild
Marshes, and made his home in a hell
Not hell but earth.

EXAMINING THE MODEL. *Beowulf* sounds archaic in language and phrasing, even when a translation brings it forward into our vernacular. Long phrases and sentences, with a minimum of full stops in semicolons or periods, are the rule. Notice the alliteration in "*s*ongs, *s*ung" or in "So Hrothgar's men lived *h*appy in *h*is *h*all." There is also often a break, or a pause, in the middle of the lines in the poem—the lines don't often end at the right edge, but rather midway through the next line.

These kinds of peculiarities make Anglo-Saxon poetry an adventure to read, and a fun challenge to mimic.

LESSON OVERVIEW

GUIDED WRITING *Software*

See the Guided Writing Software for an extended version of this lesson that includes printable graphic organizers, extensive student models and student-friendly checklists, and self-, peer, and teacher evaluation features.

Examining the Model

Read or have a student read aloud this selection from Beowulf, or another selection from the epic (pages 116–140). Then work through Examining the Model, pointing out the examples of archaic language and phrasing, alliteration, and breaks, or cæsuras. This is an excellent opportunity to reinforce the ideas of meter and alliteration in Anglo-Saxon poetry.

INDIVIDUAL LEARNING STRATEGIES

MOTIVATION
You may wish to play the Audio Library recording on the prologue from *Beowulf* as read in the original Old English. Have students listen for the alliteration and phrasing as well as the mood and expression. If your students enjoy performing, have them form small groups or pairs and prepare oral readings of selections from this unit. Encourage them to alternate lines or paragraphs, or to work together collaboratively to introduce and perform the selections.

READING PROFICIENCY
Encourage students to read the Professional Model, Revised Student Model, and their own poem aloud to get a sense of how the language sounds as they work through the lesson. Refer them to the Language arts Survey 1.6, "Reading Silently versus Reading Out Loud."

ENGLISH LANGUAGE LEARNING
See strategies for Reading Proficiency above that will also benefit students who are English language learners. You may also want non-native speakers to write their narrative poem first in their own language and then to translate it into English. You may suggest that students read both versions of the poem to the class. This activity can be an excellent way to introduce issues in translation and the richness of a different culture's language.

SPECIAL NEEDS
Students with special needs may need help identifying and creating meter in poetry. Have them pair with another student who can help them "hear" the beats in a line and imitate the meter in their own writing.

ENRICHMENT
Students may wish to work their poems collaboratively into a performance piece or to prepare their work for publication. For additional ways to enrich the lesson, see the Language Arts Survey 2.47, "Publishing and Presenting Your Work" and 4.14, "Oral Interpretation."

FINDING YOUR VOICE. Play with elevated language when you write a narrative poem. Elevated language is achieved with vocabulary as well as with sentence structure, using phrases such as *living down in darkness*, and complex sentences such as

> *A powerful monster living down In the darkness growled... As day after day the music rang...*[which was]... *the harp's... Call and the poet's...songs.*

Notice for how many lines the poet carries the reader (from line 1), with further description, before coming to the stop of a semicolon (at line 10).

Writing an Anglo-Saxon narrative poem will stretch the vocal chords of your innate writing voice. Your social vocabulary, your college essay vocabulary, or your research report vocabulary may not suffice. Welcome the opportunity to delve into a thesaurus and expand your knowledge of words to use in alliteration. The voice you develop may ring of Beowulf—or an anguished Grendel.

Assonance is the repetition of vowel sounds in stressed syllables with different consonant sounds, as in *praised* and *plains.*

Alliteration is the repetition of initial consonent sounds.

Prewriting

WRITING WITH A PLAN. The structure of an Anglo-Saxon narrative poem is rigid in four different aspects. Your poem should be written to conform to these four characteristics.

First, each line of the poem has four accented syllables.

...A powerful monster living down
In the darkness, growled in pain, impatient
As day after day the music rang
Loud in that hall, the harp's rejoicing

Second, most of the lines, at least in the original Old English, use **alliteration** for three words, partially as a mnemonic tool to help the storyteller remember his lines.

Then, when *d*arkness had *d*ropped, Grendel
Went up to Herot, *w*ondering *w*hat the *w*arriors
Would *d*o in that hall when their *d*rinking was *d*one.
He found them *s*prawled in *s*leep, *s*uspecting
Nothing, their *d*reams undisturbed.

Third, Anglo-Saxon narrative poetry uses a **caesura**, a break in many of the lines, often after the first two alliterated words, generally identified by a comma. This created a pause that allowed the teller to recall the tale.

Went up to Herot, wondering what the warriors

And, notice also:

He found them sprawled in sleep, suspecting

Fourth, the vivid language of this narrative form is accomplished through highly metaphorical phrases used to describe simple things. This is known as **kenning**. In some translations of the poem, the sea is described as *whale-path* and the sun as *the candle of the skies. Beowulf*, "bee-wolf," is a kenning for "bear."

The language of the narrative poem is thickly descriptive. The listeners needed to *see* the action, as well as the background for and gory results of the action. The very act of using alliteration with so much of the poem allowed free play with descriptions as the composers searched their minds for a third word to use in each line, and then built what they had to say around it.

The melodic qualities of the narrative poem were also enhanced by **assonance**, the repetition of vowel sounds in stressed syllables that end with different consonant sounds.

...A p*ow*erful monster, living d*ow*n
in the darkness, gr*ow*led in pain, impatient

Prewriting

FINDING YOUR VOICE. Students should also read over Beowulf until they can unconsciously imitate the voice used in the poem. Refer students to the Language Arts Survey 2.12, "Freewriting," to help them work toward the right voice for their narrative poem. This can also lead to a focused freewrite that can be used in the drafting stage.

WRITING WITH A PLAN. Students may write the basic framework of their poems, going back to work in sound techniques such as alliteration, assonance, and accented syllables later. They should also substitute imaginative kennings for more conventional names of things and feelings.

In this example, the *ow* sound repeats with several different consonant sounds: *p-*, *d-*, and *gr-*.

Keep assonance in the back of your mind as you select vocabulary and phrasing.

In addition to the uncommon structural elements of an Anglo-Saxon narrative poem, the subject matter itself deserves your attention. What approach will you take to an epic hero and the demons he/she faces?

Traits of the Epic Hero of 1000 AD

- Struggles entail great suffering.
- Exhibits awesome courage in the face of doom.
- Honor lies in avenging friends, family, or king.
- Feats of strength and skill in battle bring fame.
- Aspires to everlasting fame in song.

An Anglo-Saxon narrative poem like Beowulf is over 3,200 lines. For this assignment, try for a more direct narrative by writing a portion of an epic.

Developing the plot line for your narrative poem will help you determine the traits you will develop in your hero. Try to focus on one aspect of an epic, such as:

- describing the basic situation at the beginning of the story
- developing the conflict between a group and their demon
- writing the climactic scene of a battle between hero and foe
- resolving the story as the hero or the monster dies.

Another prewriting technique is to chart the attributes of the hero-protagonist and the monster-antagonist.

Candi was drawn to the plight of Grendel in her poem, particularly his final hours. She filled in the following graphic organizer to help her brainstorm details.

Student Model—Graphic Organizer

HERO-PROTAGONIST Beowolf	MONSTER-ANTAGONIST Grendel
PERSONALITY (self-confidence, self-esteem, reaction to friends/family, what does he/she most want, what does he/she most value) Beowulf has self-confidence, but he does not feel he accomplishes feats by himself. He feels that God helps him.	PERSONALITY (self-confidence, self-esteem, reaction to friends/family, what does he/she most want, what does he/she most value) Grendel does not have a lot of self-confidence. He is basically rejected because of his family background.

continued

Identifying Your Audience. Performing a narrative poem in front of an audience is the best method for determining if it speaks to this century. Consider whether your appeal will be to your immediate classmates, who have studied Old English literature, or to an unexposed group of students, who will need a common connection that you must develop. For example, targeting a hero/ monster relationship that evokes *Star Wars* or *Matrix* characters would help develop that connection for people unfamiliar with Anglo-Saxon literature.

Identifying your Audience. Students should keep in mind that their piece must have a dramatic appeal; it should be something that could be told with exaggerated expression in front of a large group of people or around a campfire.

GRAPHIC ORGANIZER

See the Guided Writing Resource for a blackline master of the Graphic Organizer for this lesson.

BIOGRAPHIC NOTE

You may be interested in consulting the following works for more ideas about teaching poetry:

Lehman, David, ed. *Ecstatic Occasions, Expedient Forms: 85 Leading Contemporary Poets Select & Comment on their Poems.* Ann Arbor: University of Michigan Press, 1996.

Padgett, Ron, ed. *Handbook of Poetic Forms.* New York: Teachers & Writers Collaborative, 1987.

Tsujimoto, Joseph I. Teaching Poetry Writing to Adolescents. NCTE/ERIC, 1988.

Drafting

Encourage students to use their completed Graphic Organizer to help them get started on writing their draft and to make sure they reflect the attributes listed in their narrative poem. For additional help, refer students to the Language Arts Survey 2.31–2.35, "Drafting."

Self- and Peer Evaluation

Have students use the checklist on pages 152–153 for self- and peer evaluation. The checklist is intended to act as a student-friendly rubric that should help students identify specific evidence of writing strengths and areas needing improvement. Make sure students provide concrete suggestions for improvement or specific evidence of the effectiveness of the narrative poem and its use of meter. Encourage students to evaluate their peer's poem by reading it out loud outside of class. See the Guided Writing Resource located in the Teacher's Resource Kit for a blackline master of the self- and peer evaluation checklist.

"Trochee trips from long to short;
From long to short in solemn sort
Slow Spondee stalks; strong foot! yet ill able
Ever to come up with Dactyl trisyllable.
Iambics march from short to long—
With a leap and a bound the swift Anapests throng."
—*Samuel Taylor Coleridge*

Language, Grammar, and Style

Working with Meter in Poetry

Identifying Meter. The meter of a poem is its rhythmical pattern. English verse usually is described as being made up of rhythmical units called **feet**. A **foot** is made up of some combination of **weakly stressed** (˘) **and strongly stressed** (/) syllables, as follows:

iamb, or iambic foot

˘ /
afraid

trochee, or trochaic foot

/ ˘
freedom

anapest, or anapestic foot

˘ ˘ /
in a flash

continued on page 153

HERO- PROTAGONIST Beowulf	MONSTER - ANTAGONIST Grendel
APPEARANCE (size, age, experience, first impressions made on strangers, physical movements, speaking ability and voice quality) Beowulf is large and muscular. He is young. Probably mid-20s. He is brave.	APPEARANCE (size, age, experience, first impressions made on strangers, physical movements, speaking ability and voice quality) Grendel isn't described in much detail physically. We know he is a horrible monster and his presence frightens strangers.
STATURE IN SOCIETY (sources of wealth and/or fame, social class) Beowulf is well known for his heroic exploits. It doesn't say specifically, but you get the idea that he is from a family of wealth and stature.	STATURE IN SOCIETY (sources of wealth and/or fame, social class) He is not a part of society. He is on the outside, but he is well-known and feared.
SKILLS AND TALENTS (education/training background, special combat abilities/magical qualities, special negotiation abilities) None that we know of.	SKILLS AND TALENTS (education/training background, special combat abilities/magical qualities, special negotiation abilities) Grendel has a spell so no sword can slay him.

Drafting

Once you've identified attributes of your hero and an antagonist, you may decide to write a portion of the continuing saga that explains one of these characters, or a portion that shows the protagonist and antagonist in conflict. The choice is yours.

Remember to include the four structural aspects of the Anglo-Saxon narrative. Pay attention to meter and keep your beat as consistent as possible.

Self- and Peer Evaluation

Follow this checklist as you evaluate your own work and the work of your peers.

- Where have you accomplished **four stressed beats** per line?
- Have you been able establish a steady meter throughout much of the poem that can be identified as **iambic, trochaic, dactylic**, or **anapestic**?
- Where do you maintain **alliteration** of 3 words in most of your lines?
- Where do you retain a pause, a **caesura**, in your lines?

- Where do you include **kenning** in your poem?
- Where can you spot instances of **assonance**?
- What about this narrative is most interesting?

Student Model—Draft

Grendel
By Candi Wilson

Lo, gather the guards of God's forsaken
He alone, aloof; ostracized from all
Rage boiled, revealed and wretched
A son in his halls, whom hell sent
Stumbled in stupor o'er Satan's path
Trail red life, lost limb
Earth quiet in fear quaking and
quivering
Slow crawled he the wretched one
Blood boiled and breaking the crust

Life takes him o'er whale-road
Dance the wave of death and doom
The demon drifts downward to rest
His house stood badged with blood
Sorrow filled the monster skull
Savage crimes of the series stalker
He cursed by birth, punished of God
Sprung of Cain never the chance
Seed of evil on the darkest day
Tormented kin on walks of silence
Jealous of the flesh and he
Followed his fate
Curled in stillness yet the thoughts
move
Peace at last: Free of Fate!

dactyl, or dactylic foot

feverish

spondee, or spondaic foot

baseball

The following terms are used to describe the number of feet in a line of poetry:

monometer	one foot
dimeter	two feet
trimeter	three feet
tetrameter	four feet
pentameter	five feet
hexameter	six feet

A complete description of the meter of a line includes both the term for the type of foot that predominates in the line and the term for the number of feet in the line. Although the most common English meters are iambic tetrameter and iambic pentameter, trochaic tetrameter and anapestic tetrameter seem to dominate in this translation of *Beowolf*:

. . . The Al**migh**ty **drove**
Those **de**mons **out**, and their
exile was **bit**ter, (anapestic feet)
Shut a**way** from **men**; they
split (iambic feet)
Into a **thou**sand **forms** of
evil—**spir**its (trochaic feet)
And **fiends**, **gob**lins,
monsters, **gi**ants, (trochaic feet)

continued on page 154

Language, Grammar, and Style

Working with Meter in Poetry
Lesson Overview
In this lesson, students will be asked to do the following:
- Identify Meter in a Poem, 152
- Fix Irregular Meter, 154
- Demonstrate Ability to Use Regular Meter, 155

Introducing the Skill. Tell students that understanding meter can make their poems more musical and create a greater impact on readers and on themselves.

Previewing the Skill. You may want to refer students to Unit 1, page 16, "Elements of Poetry," as you begin the lesson. Refer them to *Macbeth* in Unit 5 for examples of iambic pentameter.

Practicing the Skill. Students should work in pairs, reading the sample lines on page 153 aloud to each other, paying attention to where the stressed syllables naturally fall. Together, they should come up with a short list of words and phrases that demonstrate each type of poetic foot. Next, they should compose a line of poetry for each type of meter: monometer, dimeter, trimeter, tetrameter, pentameter, and hexameter.

Student Model—Draft

Have students mark the meter for the second stanza of Candi's poem.

Revising and Proofreading

Point out that revising a poem can be a lengthy process and that many published poets might work on a poem for a year or more. Also let students know that several false starts can occur before a poet can find the right voice, topic, or form to make a truly workable poem. Encourage them to continue working on their poems or to start new ones after this assignment is completed.

A handout of the proofreading checklist in the Language Arts Survey is available in the Teacher's Resource Kit, Writing Resource Book 2.45. Encourage students to use common proofreader's symbols, which are found in the Language Arts Survey 2.44, "Using Proofreader's Marks."

Student Model—Revised

Have students compare the Student Model—Draft on page 153 with the final version presented on page 154. What other ways would they strengthen the writing? Are there any parts of the first draft that seem stronger than the final draft? Tell students that one poetic choice they might make is to go back to their original draft and rework things a different way or realize they liked an earlier passage better than a later draft.

A simple way to remember metric foot patterns is to associate them with the names of people.

Two-syllable first names, with a strong stress on the first syllable, are *trochaic:*

/ ˘ / ˘ / ˘
Bob-by, **Sar**-ah, **Hel**-en

Two-syllable first names, with a weak stress on the first syllable are *iambic*, and are rather rare:

˘ / ˘ /
Ma-**rie**, Na-**nette**

Another common rhythm pattern in names, this time with three syllables, is *dactylic*, which starts with a strong stress, followed by two weaker stresses:

/ ˘ ˘ / ˘ ˘
Frank-en-stein, **Ang**-e-la

The reverse of the dactyl is the *anapestic foot*, with two weakly stressed syllables, followed by a strongly stressed syllable:

˘ ˘ / ˘ ˘ /
Chev-ro-**let** Ra-pha-**el**

Fixing Irregular Meter. Evaluate the following lines from Candi's draft for regular rhythm or meter. In cases where she needs more stressed syllables to fill out a line, suggest how she can either reword or add words to the line. In spots where she needs fewer syllables, suggest where she could cut.

Candi wanted to focus on alliteration and four stressed beats per line in her first draft.

˘ / ˘ / ˘
Rage **boiled**, re**vealed** and

continued on page 289

Revising and Proofreading

You may need to work through several drafts of your narrative poem, strengthening both its meter and storyline. Continue reshaping your lines, marking the stresses of your syllables and experimenting with such poetic devices as alliteration, assonance, caesura, and kenning. Work toward a polished revision as if it is a puzzle with many elements to piece together before it is complete.

Student Model—Revised

Candi's completely revised Anglo-Saxon narrative poem has reached a higher level of rhythm and sound:

The Final Day of Grendel
by Candi Wilson

Lo, gather the guards of God's forsaken
He alone and aloof; ostracized by all,
His rage had boiled: revealed and
wretched.
A son in his halls, whom hell hath sent
Stumbled in stupor o'er Satan's path
A trail of life bled red, lost limb.
Earth quiet in fear, quakes and quivers
Slow crawled he, the wretched one
Blood boiled and broke the crust.

Weeps blood trails o'er the whale-road
Dances the crests of death and doom
The demon drifts downward to rest.
His barren house, badged with blood
Sorrow filling the monster skull
With savage crimes of the serial
stalker.
He cursed by birth, punished of God
Sprung of Cain, never a chance.
Seed of evil on the darkest day
Tormenting kin on walkways of silence.
Jealous of flesh, he followed his fate.
Curled now in silence, serene in
thought,
Peace at last: Free of Fate!

Publishing and Presenting

The scope and boldness of Anglo-Saxon narrative poetry commands a bold setting. Performing your poems for each other might occasion a classroom outside on a day the weather cooperates. Videotaped presentations of costumed readers, with the appropriate musical accompaniment, could also make the fruits of your labors fun to reveal—or consider a medieval banquet.

Reflecting

Our perception of a contemporary hero in the movies, literature, and movies differs from that of our Anglo-Saxon progenitors. Do we have heroes today, and if so, who are they? Consider the traits of a hero described in this lesson and try to apply them to the heroes of your generation. Do they fit?

Is your definition of the term "hero" broader or more narrow than the Beowulf model? Is there a spiritual component to contemporary heroes? Do we revere notoriety or humility? Do we appreciate strength of character or physical strength? Do we value humanitarian lives or celebrity lives more?

Could a group of five individuals in your classroom agree on a definition of "honor"? Where do we draw the line between what is honorable and what is not?

/ ˘
wretched
(only 3 stresses in the line)
˘ / ˘ ˘ / ˘ /
A **son** in his **halls**, whom **hell**
/
sent
(no pattern of stresses)
/ ˘ ˘ / ˘ ˘
Stumbled in **stu**por o'er
/ ˘ /
Satan's **path**
/ ˘ / ˘ /
Trail red **life**, lost **limb**
(only 3 stresses in the line)

Using Regular Meter. Read your poem with a critical ear to determine its meter. Add or delete syllables where you can to make the poem read more smoothly and rhythmically.

"It is a cherishable irony that a language that succeeded almost by stealth, treated for centuries as the second-rate tongue of peasants, should one day become the most important and successful language in the world."
—*Bill Bryson*

Publishing and Presenting

Refer students to the Language Arts Survey 2.49, "Sharing Your Work with Others," and 4.19, "Oral Interpretation," for ideas on how to present their poems to an audience.

Reflecting

You may want to have students write about the questions presented in Reflecting and submit them when they turn in their narrative poems. The questions are also an excellent source of review for the terms and themes covered in Unit 2.

ADDITIONAL RESOURCES

UNIT 2 RESOURCE BOOK

- Vocabulary Worksheet
- Study Guide: Unit 2 Test
- Unit 2 Test

VOCABULARY DEVELOPMENT

Give students the following exercises.

- Choose twenty words from the list on page 156. For each word, write a sentence that relates to something you have read in this unit. The vocabulary word need not have appeared in the selection to which you refer.
  EXAMPLE
  Jeannette cowered in her seat, hoping the teacher wouldn't call on her for the answer.

- Read the Language Arts Survey 5.4, "Classifying." Then devise a scheme for classifying the vocabulary words from the list on page 156, and classify the words. Your system should be based on the meanings of the terms (rather than on their spelling, part of speech, etc.). Try to use as few categories as you can.
  EXAMPLES
  places: bog, moor
  things that have to do with religion: ecclesiastical, precept
  troubles: adversity, remorse

UNIT 2 REVIEW
The Anglo-Saxon Period

Words for Everyday Use

Check your knowledge of the following vocabulary words from the selections in this unit. Write short sentences using these words in context to make the meaning clear. To review the definition or usage of a word, refer to the page number listed or the Glossary of Words for Everyday Use.

adversity, 91
agency, 96
asunder, 103
avenge, 130
billowing, 140
blithe, 109
bog, 121
bolt, 122
brood, 118
cower, 124
diligently, 91
dreary, 104
ecclesiastical, 91
efficacious, 92
garrison, 104
hacked, 109
heaving, 128
hoary, 134
hovel, 103
infamous, 123
lamenting, 139
literal, 93
moor, 118
precept, 91
purge, 120
pyre, 138
quill, 109
relish, 122
scourger, 109
secular, 92
spoil, 116
staunch, 109
sully, 109
temporal, 91
tribute, 116
whorled, 103
wrought, 109

Literary Tools

Define the following terms, giving concrete examples of how they are used in the selections in this unit. To review a term, refer to the page number indicated or to the Handbook of Literary Terms.

aim, 90
allegory, 90
alliteration, 95, 150
anapest, 152
aphorism, 101
apposition, 113
assonance, 150
caesura, 95, 150
compound word, 113
dactyl, 153
elegiac lyric, 101
epic, 113
first-person point of view, 107
heroic epic, 113
iamb, 152
kenning, 113, 150
meter, 152
narrative poem, 149
personification, 107
point of view, 107
second-person point of view, 107
spondee, 153
stress, 95
third-person point of view, 107
trochee, 152

Reflecting on Your Reading

Genre Studies

1. **Poetic Devices.** The gleeman, or scop, remembered epic tales well enough to recite them to an Anglo-Saxon audience; they were eventually written down, allowing us to know them today. What poetic devices allowed the gleeman to remember long epic poems? How did these poetic devices aid in memorizing this literature?

2. **Heroic Epic.** What is a heroic epic? How does the poem *Beowulf* meet that definition? What makes the poem an epic? How does the character Beowulf meet the Anglo-Saxon ideal of the hero?

Thematic Studies

3. **The Treatment of Outcasts.** Explore the theme of the outcast in "The Wife's Lament" and in *Beowulf.* How do the treatments of outcasts differ in the two poems? Which poem is sympathetic toward outcasts? Which is not? Provide evidence from the texts to support your views.

4. **Heroes versus Monsters.** Some critics have compared Beowulf to the monsters he kills. In what ways are the monsters and Beowulf similar? In what way is any great hero like a monster? Do you agree with Beowulf's people that if all "world-kings" he is "the mildest of men and the gentlest, kindest to his people, and most eager for fame"? Explain your response.

Historical / Biographical Studies

5. **Kinship in Society.** Describe the structure of early Anglo-Saxon society and the importance of kinship in that society. Support your points with examples from "The Wife's Lament" and *Beowulf.*

6. **The Influence of Christianity.** The pre-Christian Anglo-Saxon world view was essentially grim and fatalistic. In what way do you think the introduction of Christianity changed the fabric of Anglo-Saxon society? Using specific examples from "The Conversion of King Edwin," "Cædmon's Hymn," the Anglo-Saxon riddles, and *Beowulf*, describe Anglo-Saxon values and perspectives both before and after the introduction of Christianity.

Reflecting on Your Reading

The prompts in "Reflecting on Your Reading" are suitable as topics for research papers. Refer to the Language Arts Survey 5.18–5.45, "Research Skills." (To evaluate research papers, see the evaluation forms for writing, revising, and proofreading in the Assessment Resource.)

The prompts in "Reflecting on Your Reading" can also be adapted for use as topics for oral reports or debates. Refer students to the Language Arts Survey 4, "Speaking and Listening." (To evaluate these projects, see the evaluation forms in the Assessment Resource.)

UNIT SKILLS OUTLINE

Literary Skills and Concepts
Arthurian Romance, 187, 197
Autobiography, 211, 214
Ballad, 168, 173
Characterization, 216, 241
Chivalry, 187, 197
Folk Tale, 199, 209
Frame Tale, 216, 241
Medieval Romance, 254, 260
Mood/Atmosphere, 168, 173
Morality Play, 243, 252
Motif, 199, 209
Naïve Allegory, 243, 252
Point of View, 211, 214
Rhyme Scheme, 168, 173
Romance and Courtly Love, 182, 185, 199, 209, 254, 260
Simile, 175, 180
Theme, 175, 180

Writing Skills and Concepts
Personal Letter, 186
Identifying Personality Traits, 198
Expository Writing, 215
Letter of Recommendation, 253
Writing a Forward, 261
Writing a Parable, 268

Language, Grammar, and Style
The Parts of Speech, 174
Identifying Nonstandard Language, 181
Contractions in Sentences, 186
Identifying Gerunds, 198
Combining Sentences, 210
Avoiding Double Negatives, 215
Reducing Wordiness, 242
Using Proper Capitalization, 253

CROSS-CURRICULAR CONNECTIONS

Arts and Humanities
Chaucer Quote, 159
Thomas a Becket, 161
Romance Heroes, 164
The Lion in Winter, 164
The Grail Legend, 165
Middle English Language, 166
William Langland and Adreas Capellanus, 167
Cathedral Photographs, 176
Persian Love Poems, 179
Lais or Rap Poems, 183
Tristan und Isolde, 184
The Gawain Legend, 189
Chivalry, 190
Adventure in Romance Literature, 191
Depictions of Knights, 193
Morgan le Fay, 195
Arthurian Legend Figures, 200

Continued on page 159

158 *UNIT THREE / THE MEDIEVAL PERIOD*

GOALS/OBJECTIVES

Studying this unit will enable sutdent to
- interpret and appreciate medieval literature
- explain the social organization of medieval English society, with particular reference to feudalism and the church, using examples from The Canterbury Tales and other works
- identify and explain he main characteristics of ballads, medieval romances, frame tales, and morality plays
- write a parable
- demonstrate the ability to use correct verb tense

Saint George and the Dragon, c.1460. Paolo Uccello. The National Gallery, London.

There was a Knight, a most distinguished man,
Who from the day on which he first began
To ride abroad had followed chivalry,
Truth, honor, generousness and courtesy.

—Geoffrey Chaucer

CROSS-CURRICULAR CONNECTIONS (CONT. FROM PAGE 158)

TEACHING THE MULTIPLE INTELLIGENCES

TEACHING THE MULTIPLE INTELLIGENCES (CONT.)

ADDITIONAL RESOURCES

UNIT 3 RESOURCE BOOK
- Selection Check Test 4.3.1
- Selection Test 4.3.2

CROSS-CURRICULAR ACTIVITIES

GEOGRAPHY. Ask students to identify England and Normandy on the map. Students can consult an atlas to determine the narrowest passage across the English Channel between the two.

CROSS-CURRICULAR CONNECTION

HISTORY. The following is a list of kings of England during the Medieval Period:

Norman Kings
1066–1087 William I (the Conqueror)
1087–1100 William II
1100–1135 Henry I

Blois King
1135–1154 Stephen

Plantagenet Kings
1154–1189 Henry II
1189–1199 Richard I (the Lion-Hearted)
1199–1216 John Lackland
1216–1272 Henry III
1272–1307 Edward I
1307–1327 Edward II
1327–1377 Edward III
1377–1399 Richard II

Lancaster Kings
1399–1413 Henry IV
1413–1422 Henry V
1422–1461 Henry VI
1470–1471 Henry VI, reinstated

York Kings
1461–1470 Edward IV
1471–1483 Edward IV, reinstated
1483–1483 Edward V
1483–1485 Richard III

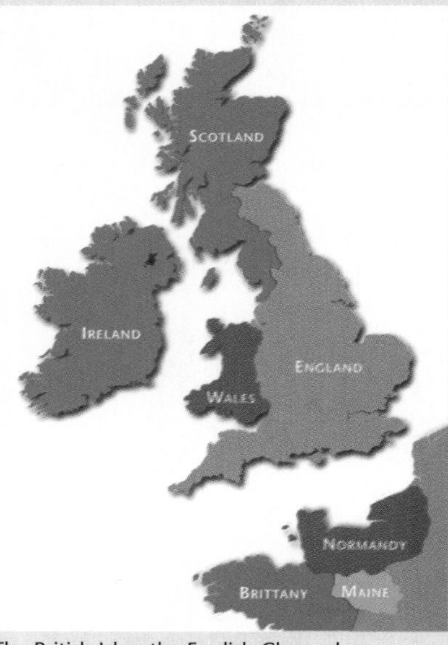

The British Isles, the English Channel, and France.

THE MEDIEVAL PERIOD (1066–1485)

THE NORMAN CONQUEST OF ENGLAND

When in 878 Alfred the Great defeated the Danes and confined them to the north of England, they looked for other lands to conquer. Some of these Danes invaded northern France, settling in an area that came to be known as the land of the north men, or **Normandy**. The Normans adopted the French language and developed a sophisticated culture.

In 1066, the English king, Edward the Confessor, died, and the Anglo-Saxon Witanagemot, or council of elders, chose Harold II as king. However, **Duke William of Normandy** (*circa* 1028–1087), cousin to Edward the Confessor, claimed with some justification that Edward had promised the English throne to him. With the support of the church, Duke William invaded England in September of 1066 and defeated Harold at the **Battle of Hastings.** In four years of bloody fighting that followed the Battle of Hastings, the Normans killed most of the native English nobility, subjugated the rest of the populace, and divided the country into estates, or **fiefdoms,** ruled by French-speaking barons loyal to **William the Conqueror.** The **Norman Conquest** brought the era of the Anglo-Saxons to a close and ushered in the **Medieval Period** of English history.

ANGLO-NORMAN LITERATURE

The effect of the Norman Conquest on the English language and on English literature was, as one scholar has put it, "shattering." For two hundred years following the Conquest, English became a lower-class language in England—one spoken almost exclusively by the poor and powerless. The language of the court, of the noble classes, and of almost all the non-Latin literature produced on the island was Norman French. The production of literature in the English language came to a near standstill. Some monks continued to produce works in English, and the illiterate,

LITERARY EVENTS

➤ = British Events

- 1076–1142. French philosopher Abélard
- ➤1086–1127. William X, Duke of Aquitaine, first of the great troubadour poets to produce works on romance themes
- ➤1137. Geoffrey of Monmouth's *History of the Kings of Britain* written
- 1140–91. Greatest of French romance writers, Chrétien de Troyes

1050 — 1075 — 1100 — 1125 — 1150

HISTORICAL EVENTS

- ➤1058. Malcolm III of Scotland deposes the usurper Macbeth
- ➤1066. Battle of Hastings; Norman Conquest of England
- ➤1066–87. Reign in England of William the Conqueror
- 1090–1153. St. Bernard, founder of Benedictine monasteries
- 1095. First Crusade proclaimed
- 1099. Crusaders win Jerusalem
- ➤1100–35. Reign of Henry I of England
- 1110. University of Paris founded
- ➤1122–1204. Eleanor of Aquitaine
- ➤1154–89. Henry II, first of Plantagenet line of English kings

CROSS-CURRICULAR CONNECTION

HISTORY. Scholarly usage differs as to what this period should be called. Some scholars use the terms *Middle Ages* and *Medieval Period* interchangeably to refer to the entire period from the Anglo-Saxon invasion to the end of the fifteenth century. In this text, the term *Middle Ages* is used to refer to this larger period and *Medieval Period* is used to refer to the period following the Norman Conquest.

The Bayeux Tapestry, c.1000s.

English-speaking common people continued to compose their oral songs, but very little of this material survives today, for the monks' works in English were few, and the common people's songs were not written down (though a few survived to be recorded centuries later).

Most of the non-Latin literature produced in England between 1066 and roughly 1260 was written in Norman French and is therefore known as **Anglo-Norman literature.** This literature tends to be quite practical, in keeping with the no-nonsense character of the Norman people. Much of it consists of religious tracts and other works meant more for edification than for entertainment. However, the Normans did import from the Continent some French entertainment literature, including romances and fabliaux, which are

ArtNote

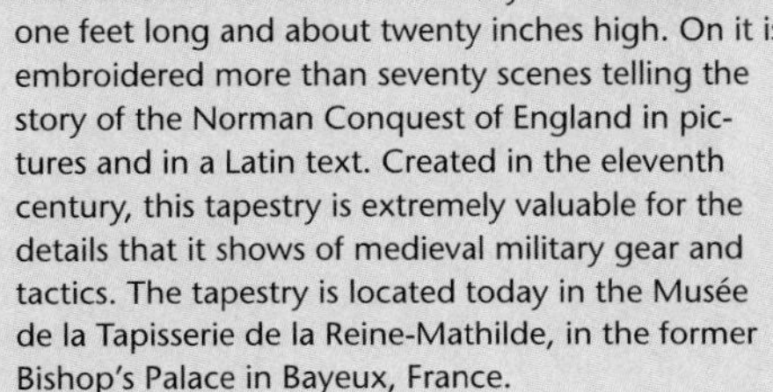

The Bayeux Tapestry is a piece of linen cloth two hundred and thirty-one feet long and about twenty inches high. On it is embroidered more than seventy scenes telling the story of the Norman Conquest of England in pictures and in a Latin text. Created in the eleventh century, this tapestry is extremely valuable for the details that it shows of medieval military gear and tactics. The tapestry is located today in the Musée de la Tapisserie de la Reine-Mathilde, in the former Bishop's Palace in Bayeux, France.

1265–1321. Dante, Italian poet

1225–74. St. Thomas Aquinas, philosopher

➤1214–92. Roger Bacon, English philosopher

➤1180. Birth of Marie de France

1175 — 1200 — 1225 — 1250 — 1275

➤*circa* 1167. Oxford University founded

➤1166. Murder of Archbishop of Canterbury Thomas à Becket

➤1189–99. Richard the Lion-hearted

➤1199–1216. King John of England

➤1209. Cambridge University founded

➤1215. King John signs Magna Carta

1244. Jerusalem captured by Moslems

1271–95. Asian travels of Marco Polo

➤1272–1307. Edward I King of England

CROSS-CURRICULAR CONNECTIONS

Humanities and History. Students might be interested in learning more about the life of Thomas à Becket, the "blissful martyr" whose tomb is the site of pilgrimage in Chaucer's *The Canterbury Tales.* Becket was born in London in 1118 to a middle-class merchant family. As a young man, he became a servant in the household of the powerful Archbishop Theobald. In 1154, Theobald made Becket archdeacon of Canterbury. Then, in 1155, King Henry II appointed Becket chancellor of England (the country's highest administrative post). As chancellor, Becket assisted Henry in his ongoing battle to wrest privileges from the church. When Theobald died, Henry hoped that the election of Thomas to the post of archbishop of Canterbury would solidify his control over the church in England. However, such was not to be the case. In a dramatic turnabout, Thomas, on assuming the post of archbishop, became a devout, crusading defender of church rights, opposing Henry on such matters as civil punishment for clerical offenders and the exemption of royal officials from excommunication. In 1170, Henry rashly and in anger said in front of a group of barons that he wished that someone would rid him of this meddlesome bishop. The barons, taking Henry literally, murdered Thomas inside the cathedral at Canterbury. Within days, Thomas's tomb became a site of pilgrimage and, in 1173, Thomas was canonized. This story is told grippingly in two modern plays, T. S. Eliot's *Murder in the Cathedral* and Jean Anouilh's *Becket.*

CROSS-CURRICULAR CONNECTION

Sociology. Point out that the organization of medieval society depended upon *vassalage*—the loyalty or obligation that a lesser member of the society owed to higher members in exchange for favors granted. For example, a knight might be granted property by a great lord—a duke, an earl, or a king. That knight would then owe obligations of loyalty to the lord. This loyalty would be recognized in a public act of *homage* in which the knight would kneel before the lord, the lord would take the knight's hands between his own, and the two would then exchange kisses on the cheeks.

When the peasant classes, or villeins, revolted, the nobility and upper classes regarded them with hostility and disdain, connotations that carry over to the modern use of the word *villain.*

described on page 164. An excellent example of Anglo-Norman literature is the selection from the **lais,** or songs, of **Marie de France** given in English translation on pages 182–184.

One important literary innovation introduced to England by the Normans was poetry written in rhymed stanzas. Almost overnight, rhymed stanzas replaced Anglo-Saxon alliterative verse as the primary form of poetry written in England.

From the time of the Conquest to 1202, Normandy remained part of England. After England lost Normandy, the influence of the French language in England rapidly declined. By the middle of the century, most English ties to France had been severed, and the upper classes in England began to adopt the native language. By the end of the century, English was again the primary language of both the lower and the upper classes.

The Organization of Medieval Society

William the Conqueror brought to England a system of political organization that we now refer to as **feudalism.** This was the system by which Europe was ruled throughout the Middle Ages. In feudal states, all land and all people ultimately belonged to the king, who granted large tracts of the land to members of the nobility, known as **barons.** The barons were bound in exchange to be loyal to the king, to raise armies to fight in his battles, and to pay taxes to support his court. In turn, the barons granted land to lesser nobles and required service and support from them. At the very bottom of the social order was a class of bondsmen, known as **peasants, villeins,** or **serfs,** who lived on and worked the nobles' land. The lot of the serfs was generally miserable. They were the property of their feudal lords and could not leave the land or even marry without permission. They lived on meager diets, suffered terribly from disease, and worked very hard only to turn over much of what they produced for the support of the lord's household. Occasionally, a serf could earn freedom by some exceptional service to his or her lord. Gradually, throughout the Medieval Period, the class of **freemen** grew to include many merchants, traders, laborers, and artisans.

In a feudal society, each person is bound by a system of loyalties, known as **vassalage,** to some person higher on the social hierarchy. Thus a serf might be the **vassal,** or servant, of a lesser nobleman who held the title of knight. The knight, in turn, might be the vassal of a duke, the duke the vassal of a powerful earl, and the earl

Literary Events

➤1386. Chaucer begins *The Canterbury Tales*

➤*circa* 1375. *Sir Gawain and the Green Knight* written

1341. Petrarch becomes Poet Laureate in Rome

1300 — 1325 — 1350 — 1375 — 1400

➤1337. Beginning of Hundred Years' War between England and France

➤1346. English defeat French in Battle of Crécy

➤1348. Beginning of Great Plague in England

➤1381. Peasants' Revolt in England

Historical Events

CROSS-CURRICULAR CONNECTION

History. William the Conqueror introduced feudalism to England by granting land to followers who had served him in the conquest. These men, numbering fewer than one hundred and eighty, became "tenants in chief," the great lords or barons of the land. In exchange for their land, they were required to provide soldiers to the king when necessary. At first these soldiers came from the households of the tenants in chief, but later they came from the households of knights who themselves were granted land by the great lords. William replaced the Anglo-Saxon *witan* with the *curia regis,* or king's court, made up of his barons. These courts met thrice annually, at Christmas, Easter, and Whitsuntide.

the vassal of the king. The king himself was considered a vassal of the Pope, the head of the Roman Catholic Church.

The Influence of the Church

At no time in the history of the West has the church been more influential than in the Medieval Period. Throughout this time, the Catholic Church, centered in faraway Rome (and for a time also in Avignon, France), had tremendous wealth and power both in the political and personal spheres. Vast resources went into the building of churches, first in the squat, towered, and turreted **Norman** or **Romanesque** style and later in the grand **Gothic** style of Canterbury Cathedral.

Canterbury Cathedral.

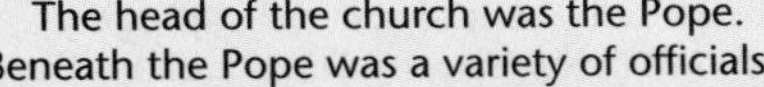

The head of the church was the Pope. Beneath the Pope was a variety of officials, from learned cardinals, archbishops, and bishops down to often semi-literate parish priests. In addition, the church was represented by religious orders of monks and nuns living in monastic houses. Many clerics served as government officials, and the church and crown often collaborated. However, in many ways medieval England was a house with two masters, and often political leaders and members of the clergy quarreled. Such a quarrel led in 1170 to the murder of Thomas à Becket, the Archbishop of Canterbury, by barons loyal to Henry II.

Much of medieval literature deals with religious subjects and themes. Surviving works include retellings of Biblical stories, biographies of saints, collections of sermons, tracts on the seven deadly sins and the seven cardinal virtues, and so on. A common theme of religious and quasi-religious literature was the *memento mori,* or "reminder of death": death comes soon and without warning. Therefore, you must prepare yourself for the life hereafter.

Another common theme was that of *contemptu mundi*, or "contempt for the world." An excellent exposition of these themes can be found in the medieval play

➤1476. William Caxton sets up first printing press in England
➤*circa* 1470. Sir Thomas Malory writes *Le Morte d'Arthur*
1453. Gutenberg prints Bible on first press using movable type in Germany
1425
1450
1475
1500
1428. Joan of Arc leads French to victory in Siege of Orleans
➤1453. Hundred Years' War ends
➤1455. Beginning of War of the Roses

CROSS-CURRICULAR ACTIVITIES

Arts and Science. One type of church-related literature common in the Middle Ages was the **bestiary.** A typical bestiary contained descriptions and pictures of fabulous or exotic beasts such as whales, lions, and unicorns. Each description would have an allegorical or symbolic meaning in addition to its literal one. Thus, a snake stripping off its skin might symbolize a human being stripping off sin through repentance or penitence.

An interesting assignment that combines writing and graphics skills is to prepare a class bestiary. Have students make a list of animals for the bestiary and then do some research in books of natural history. Zoology textbooks and field guides are excellent sources. For each animal, students should prepare a short written description of its appearance and behavior. The description should then be likened to some part of human life. For example, a modern bestiary might describe a bee colony falling apart at the death of the queen bee and liken that to a corporate office that falls apart when a manager resigns.

CROSS-CURRICULAR CONNECTION

Social Studies. Medieval people applied special magical significance to the numbers three and seven. The number three, associ-ated with the Holy Trinity, figured prominently in medieval charms and spells. Medieval theologians enumerated seven cardinal virtues—*prudence, temperance, fortitude, justice, faith, hope,* and *love*—and seven deadly sins—*pride, avarice, lechery, anger, gluttony, envy,* and *sloth*. Much of medieval literature can be understood as providing illustrations of, or warnings about, these virtues and vices. Discuss with students the effect that following virtues and avoiding sin might have on society. Why was this important in medieval times?

CROSS-CURRICULAR CONNECTION

History. After the collapse of the Roman Empire, Europe was plunged into barbarism. The Roman Catholic Church filled the void left by the collapse of the Empire, becoming the great unifying force of medieval civilization.

LITERARY/HISTORICAL NOTE

Medieval Attitudes toward Death. Point out that in the Middle Ages, a simple flu or accident could well be fatal. Children rarely lived to adulthood, and adults often found themselves healthy one day and fatally ill the next. Such conditions led to a widespread preoccupation with death that was reflected in medieval art and literature. The *memento mori* and *contemptu mundi* themes were expressions of the ever-present reality of death in the lives of medieval people.

One of the most common subjects in all of medieval art is the *Danse Macabre,* or Dance of Death, in which the figure of death, usually a skeleton dressed in a hooded robe, often carrying a scythe, is shown dancing with the living. The idea behind such art was that people should remember that death, although often disguised, is always present.

LITERARY NOTE

Literary historians often divide medieval romances by subject into those dealing with the matter of Britain, the matter of Rome, and the matter of France. Heroes in romances dealing with the matter of Britain included Guy of Warwic, Richard the Lion-Hearted, and such figures from the Arthurian legends as Lancelot and Gawain. Heroes in romances dealing with the matter of Rome included Alexander the Great and Æneas. Heroes in romances dealing with the matter of France included Roland and Charlemagne.

Alexander was not Roman but Macedonian, and Æneas's connection to Rome was mythological. However, in the Middle Ages, writers often lumped together stories from antiquity under the general rubric "Gesta Romanarum," or Roman stories.

CROSS-CURRICULAR CONNECTION

Social Studies. The stormy and fascinating story of the relationship of Henry II and Eleanor of Aquitaine is told dramatically in William Golding's play *The Lion in Winter,* which may be recommended to students interested in learning more about Eleanor, one of the most fascinating female political figures in all of European history.

Everyman, which describes how death comes when a person least expects it and how that person is then deserted by all worldly things, such as goods, beauty, strength, and even the five senses. In the end, worldly things are worthless. All that goes with a person to the grave is his or her good deeds, which are weighed on Judgment Day.

From the eleventh to the thirteenth century, the church sponsored a series of **Crusades,** or holy wars, to recapture Jerusalem from the Moslems. Christians from all over Europe participated in the Crusades and brought back with them Persian and Arabic stories and scholarship. Of considerable importance to the church and to the development of English literature was the influence on the Crusaders of Persian love poetry, with its many portraits of idealized women. This poetry influenced the development in Europe, beginning in the twelfth century, of passionate devotion to the Virgin Mary, mother of Christ, who was portrayed in both popular and religious literature as the ideal of perfect womanhood. An example of this literature of devotion to Mary is "I Sing of a Maiden," on page 179.

Geoffrey Chaucer

The devout people of the Medieval Period often went on journeys, or **pilgrimages,** to visit holy sites such as the burial places of saints. In ***The Canterbury Tales,*** perhaps the greatest work of the period, the court poet Geoffrey Chaucer describes a group of people taking such a pilgrimage to Canterbury, England, the site of the killing, or **martyrdom,** of St. Thomas. Chaucer has his pilgrims make up stories to entertain one another, and he tells us these stories, which include examples of many kinds of medieval literature, including knightly romances, pious moral tales, folk tales, and ribald stories of the kind known as **fabliaux.**

Romance Literature, Chivalry, and Courtly Love

The Crusades and devotion to the Virgin Mary influenced the development of a unique literature known as **romance,** which portrayed the standards of knightly conduct known as **chivalry.** The word comes from the French word for horse, *cheval,* and reflects the fact that knights fought on horseback, a necessary arrangement because their heavy suits of protective armor made movement on the ground difficult.

Today, we associate the word *romance* with love stories, and indeed love does play a major role in early romance literature. At root, however, medieval romances were stories of adventure. They dealt with the exploits of knights—their battles, crusades, tournaments, jousts—and, incidentally, the loves that inspired these. Typically, a romance would present a series of loosely connected adventures, each a **trial,** or test, of the knight's virtues—his loyalty, honesty, gentleness, faith, courtesy, skill, and courage. The trial might take the form of a **quest,** a journey to some far-off place to do some mighty deed. The most famous such quest was the search for the **Holy Grail,** the cup from which Christ offered communion at the Last Supper. Often the knight's trial or quest was undertaken to rescue or win the favor of a fair lady who was represented in unrealistically idealized terms as the worthy inspiration of great deeds. This idealization of women and of the knights' faithful service to them formed the core of courtly love, the code of behavior between women and their suitors known as **courtly love.** The ideas of courtly love originated in France and spread to England in the twelfth century under the patronage of the French-born queen of Henry II, **Eleanor of Aquitaine** (c.1122–1204).

The most famous and enduring of the English romances are those written about the legendary **King Arthur** and his **knights of the Round Table,** including Sir Gawain, Sir Lancelot, and Sir Galahad. Two samples from Arthurian romances are given in this unit—the selections from *Sir Gawain and the Green Knight,* on page 188, and from Sir Thomas Malory's compilation and retelling of the Arthur legends, *Le Morte d'Arthur,* on page 200.

SELECTION CHECK TEST 4.3.1 WITH ANSWERS (cont. from page 165)

5. How did John Wycliff help make it possible for common people to read the Bible? **He translated it into English.**

Match each of the following terms with its definition.

__B__ 1. "reminder of death"
__E__ 2. told stories from the lives of saints
__H__ 3. told of journeys to far-off lands to perform great deeds
__G__ 4. songs of the common people
__F__ 5. had virtues and vices as characters

a. *contemptu mundi*
b. *memento mori*
c. romances
d. mystery plays
e. miracle plays
f. morality plays
g. ballads
h. quests

ArtNote

Quest for the Holy Grail, c.1800s.

Sir Edward Coley Burne-Jones (1833–1898), one of the foremost painters of late nineteenth-century England, produced vivid, romantic paintings, often on medieval subjects and themes. In addition to this tapestry depicting a scene from the Grail legend, Burne-Jones painted such works as "Merlin and Nimue" and "The Beguiling of Merlin." A follower of the painter and poet Dante Gabriel Rossetti, Burne-Jones is associated with Rossetti's Pre-Raphaelite Brotherhood, which sought to return painting to an imagined purity that existed in the early days of the Italian Renaissance. He created many designs for the famous *Kelmscott Chaucer* published by his friend and fellow artist William Morris. He also contributed to the decorative arts, creating stained glass, reliefs, and decorations for musical instruments.

Quest for the Holy Grail, c.1800s.
Edward Burne-Jones. Birmingham City Museums.

The Ballads

Even during the period when Norman French was the official language of the court, common people continued to produce oral poetry and songs. Many songs of the common people, known as **ballads,** survived for hundreds of years, long enough to be printed after the invention of the printing press, or gathered by scholars from oral sources. The ballads were simple narratives in four-line stanzas that served as entertainment and as records of events that captured the popular imagination. Some ballads told fantastic tales of ghosts and demons. Some recorded important events, such as the death of a lord or the sinking of a ship. Others immortalized legendary outlaws such as **Robin Hood**. Many were simple tales of love or betrayal.

Medieval Drama

Medieval drama, initially performed in churches, had its origins in simple skits based on Bible stories and saints' lives. Gradually these moved out of the churches and were performed in town marketplaces and in the courtyards of roadhouses, or inns. Three types of drama developed in the period: **mystery plays,** which told stories from the Bible; **miracle plays,** which told stories from the lives of the saints; and **morality plays,** like *Everyman*, which represented abstract virtues and vices as characters.

Political Developments in the Medieval Period

Politically, the Medieval Period in England was one of enormous change. The feudal system introduced by William the Conqueror was solidified by his successors. Henry II, who reigned from 1154 to 1189, introduced a system of traveling judges whose rulings were to make up the **common law** that still provides the basis for the legal systems of England and the United States. Another innovation of the period was legislative government, in the form of a **Parliament,** or representative ruling body. After the

LITERARY NOTE

The Grail was the cup used by Jesus Christ at the Last Supper. According to medieval romances, this cup was brought to England by Joseph of Arimathea, one of Pontius Pilate's soldiers, and could only be found by a knight of exceptional purity. Many medieval romances tell stories of searches, or quests, undertaken to find the Grail. In some, the knight who attains the Grail is Percival. In Malory's *Le Morte d'Arthur,* it is Galahad, Percival, and Bors. One legend claims that the Grail was hidden by Joseph near a spring in Glaston-bury, England, which runs red because the Grail was the vessel containing Christ's blood. The Grail legend continues to fascinate artists. Can students think of any modern interpretations of this story?

SELECTION CHECK TEST 4.3.1 WITH ANSWERS

Social and Political Developments

1. Following the Norman Conquest, who spoke English in England? **Only the poor and the powerless spoke English.**
2. What was life like for the average serf in Medieval England? **Life was difficult for serfs, who lived in extreme poverty, worked hard, and had little freedom.**
3. What was chivalry? **Chivalry was the code of conduct followed by knights.**
4. What was the Peasants' Revolt about? **It was concerned with human rights.**
5. Who formed guilds? **Merchants and/or artisans formed guilds.**

Put the following hierarchy of classes in a feudal system in order, from HIGHEST RANKING to LOWEST RANKING. Put a (1) by the highest and a (5) by the lowest.

__3__ baron
__5__ peasant
__1__ pope
__2__ king
__4__ nobleman

Fill in the blanks using the following terms. You may not use every term, and you may use some terms more than once.

vassalage Crusades pilgrimage
courtly love chivalry Magna Carta
Black Death War of the Roses
Hundred Years' War Battle of Hastings

1. **Vassalage** is the system of loyalties in a feudal society.
2. The code of **courtly love** dictated behavior between women and their suitors.
3. Lancasters and Yorks fought for

SELECTION CHECK TEST 4.3.1 WITH ANSWERS (CONT.)

Continued on page 164

control of England in the **War of the Roses**.

4. The **Black Death** was responsible for the deaths of one-third of England's people.
5. The church supported William's invasion of England for the **Battle of Hastings**.

Literary Developments

1. Why is much English literature from 1066 to about 1260 called Anglo-Norman literature? **It was written in Norman French.**
2. What kind of literature did the Crusaders bring back to England? **Responses should include Persian or Arabic stories and poetry.**
3. Who was portrayed in much of the literature as the ideal of perfect womanhood? **The Virgin Mary was depicted as the ideal woman.**
4. How were medieval romances different from romances today? **Responses should note that medieval romances included love but centered around adventure.**

death of Henry II, his son John taxed the barons so heavily and made so many enemies that he was forced in 1215 to sign the **Magna Carta,** or "great charter," a document that limited the rights of the king, made him subject to the rulings of the baronial Parliament, and guaranteed trial by a jury of one's peers.

From 1339 to 1453, England fought the **Hundred Years' War** over possession of French lands. In 1346, England won a decisive victory at the **Battle of Crécy** by introducing to warfare the longbow, used to shoot the horses out from under the French. Having fallen to the ground in their heavy suits of armor, the French could not get up and flee. Most of the noblemen of France died in that single battle. For a time England held sway over the country. In the next century, however, thanks to the leadership of that astonishing warrior **Joan of Arc** (1412–1431), France was able to win back its territory. England retreated to its own boundaries.

The period also saw, in the **Peasants' Revolt** led by Jack Straw and Wat Tyler in 1381, the first stirrings of demands for individual liberty and human rights on the part of the common people. During this revolt, peasants armed with stones and farming tools marched on the city of London. Their rallying cry was,

> When Adam delved° and Eve span,° — *plowed, spun*
> Who was then a gentleman.

The revolt was brutally suppressed, and its leaders were executed. Challenges to authority were not taken lightly in the Middle Ages.

Social and Cultural Changes in the Medieval Period

Important social and cultural changes occurred during the Medieval Period. The founding of universities at Oxford and Cambridge promoted learning. Towns and cities grew around mills for the processing of wool into cloth. Merchants and artisans organized themselves into **guilds** responsible for training apprentices and for regulating business. A **middle class** of free merchants and tradespeople emerged. The crowding of people into towns made possible great markets and fairs but also increased the possibilities for spreading disease. In the mid-1300s, the bubonic plague, or **Black Death,** devastated England, killing one-third of its inhabitants.

Late in the fourteenth century, a religious reformer, **John Wycliff** (*circa* 1330–1384), finished the first complete translation of the Bible into English. For the first time, ordinary people could read and interpret the text on their own. This event set the stage for the Protestant Reformation.

An important figure in the spread of ideas of all kinds was **William Caxton** (1422–1491), who in 1476 introduced to England the new technology of printing from movable type. He printed much of the literature of his day, including *The Canterbury Tales* and *Le Morte d'Arthur.* For the first time, books were easily made in large quantities, and the subsequent spread of learning would change England forever, making the decline of the powerful aristocracy inevitable.

The End of the Medieval Period

From 1455 to 1485, England was torn by civil war between two noble houses. The House of Lancaster, whose crest bore a red rose, fought against the House of York, whose crest bore a white rose. The thirty-year **War of the Roses** ended with the defeat of Richard III of the House of Lancaster by Henry Tudor, who became King Henry VII.

BIBLIOGRAPHIC NOTE

The following are some excellent sources of additional information on Middle English language, history, and literature.

Chaucer's Major Poetry. Ed. A. C. Baugh. 1963.

Child, F. J. *The English and Scottish Popular Ballads.* 1882.

Donaldson, E. T. *Speaking of Chaucer.* 1970.

Emmerson, Richard, ed. *Approaches to Teaching Medieval Drama.* 1990.

A History of Private Life: Revelations of the Medieval World. Ed. Philippe Ariès and George Duby. Trans. Arthur Goldhammer. 1988.

Hodgart, M. J. C. *The Ballads.* 1950.

Howard, Donald. *Chaucer: His Life, His Work, His World.* 1987.

Huizinga, J. *The Waning of the Middle Ages.* 1924.

Lais of Marie de France, The. Trans. Glyn S. Burgess and Keith Busby. 1986.

Lewis, C. S. *The Allegory of Love.* 1964.

Loomis, R. S. *The Development of Arthurian Romance.* 1963.

Mehl, D. *The Middle English Romances of the Thirteenth and Fourteenth Centuries.* 1968.

Middle English Lyrics. Ed. M. S. Luria and R. L. Hoffman. 1974.

Power, Eileen. *Medieval People.* 1963.

The Riverside Chaucer. Ed. L. D. Benson et al. 1987.

Sir Gawain and the Green Knight. Ed. J. R. R. Tolkien and E. V. Gordon, 1925. Rev. Norman Davis. 1967.

Thiébaux, Marcelle. *The Writings of Medieval Women: An Anthology.* 1994.

Tuchman, Barbara. *A Distant Mirror.* 1978.

The Voice of the Middle Ages in Personal Letters, 1100–1500. Ed. Catherine Moriarty. 1989.

The Works of Sir Thomas Malory. Ed. Eugène Vinaver. 1967.

CROSS-CURRICULAR CONNECTION

History. The Peasants' Revolt began as a reaction to a poll tax instituted to finance war with France. Violence broke out in the southeastern portion of England and included attacks on landlords and tax collectors. Peasants from Essex and Kent marched on London, killed several royal officials, and met with the king. During one of these meetings, at which King Richard made many promises that he later failed to keep, the mayor of London attacked and killed the leader of the rebellion, Wat Tyler.

ECHOES

MEDIEVAL ENGLAND

Lo, yonder I see Everyman walking:
Full little he thinketh on my coming;

—Anonymous, spoken by the character Death in the play *Everyman*

There came to me reclining there a most curious dream
That I was in a wilderness, nowhere that I knew;
But as I looked into the east, up high toward the sun,
I saw a tower on a hill-top, trimly built,
A deep dale beneath, a dungeon tower in it,
With ditches deep and dark and dreadful to look at.
A fair field full of folk I found between them,
Of human beings of all sorts, the high and the low,
Working and wandering as the world requires.

—William Langland, *The Vision of Piers Plowman*

The life so short, the craft so hard to learn.

—Geoffrey Chaucer, *The Parliament of Fowls*

St. Paul himself, a saint of great discerning,
Says all things are written for our learning:
So take the grain and let the chaff be still.
And, gracious Father, if it be thy will
As saith my Savior, make us all good men,
And bring us to his heavenly bliss.
Amen.

—Geoffrey Chaucer, The Nun's Priest's Tale

A person who is the prey of love eats little and sleeps little. . . . Love can deny nothing to Love.

—Andreas Capellanus, *The Art of Courtly Love*

"Truly," said Sir Palomides, "as for Sir Lancelot, of his noble knighthood, courtesy, and prowess, and gentleness, I know not his peer; for this day," said Sir Palomides, "I did full uncourteously unto Sir Lancelot, and full unknightly, and full knightly and courteously he did to me again; for and he had been as ungentle to me as I was to him, this day I had won no worship. And therefore," said Palomides, "I shall be Sir Lancelot's knight whiles my life lasteth."

This talking was in the houses of kings. But all kings, lords, and knights, said, of clear knighthood, and of pure strength, of bounty, of courtesy, Sir Lancelot and Sir Tristram bare the prize above all knights that ever were in Arthur's days. And there were never knights in Arthur's days did half so many deeds as they did; as the book saith, no ten knights did not half the deeds that they did, and there was never knight in their days that required Sir Lancelot or Sir Tristram of any quest, so it were not to their shame, but they performed their desire.

—Sir Thomas Malory, *Le Morte d'Arthur*

Alas, that ever I did sin!
It is full merry in Heaven.

—Margery Kempe

Lancelot Mad with Love for Guinevere.
Bodleian Library, University of Oxford.

BIOGRAPHICAL NOTE

Little is known of **William Langland** (circa 1330–1387) except that he was the author of the great alliterative Middle English poem *The Vision of Piers Plowman.* The poem opens with a famous dream vision of a "fair field full of folk" which presents a portrait of English society at the time through Langland's satirical eyes. The hero of the poem, Piers Plow-man, is an idealized common man, a simple farmer whose humble virtues Langland contrasts with the corrupt excesses of members of the wealthy classes and of the clergy.

Andreas Capellanus is the Latin name of André le Chapelain, a twelfth-century French writer whose *The Art of Courtly Love* presented a thorough exposition of the ideals of love celebrated in medieval romances. Capellanus is believed to have served Marie, the daughter of Eleanor of Aquitaine, and to have written his famous book for her. See *courtly love* in the Handbook of Literary Terms.

ADDITIONAL QUESTIONS AND ACTIVITIES

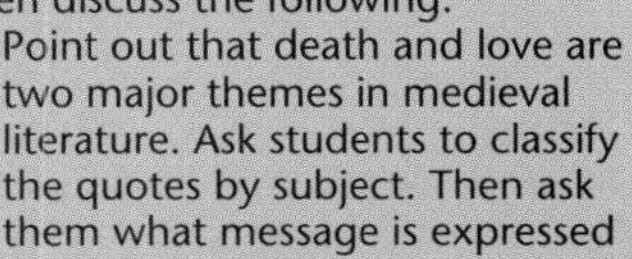

Have students examine the quotations on page 167 and then discuss the following:

- Point out that death and love are two major themes in medieval literature. Ask students to classify the quotes by subject. Then ask them what message is expressed about each subject.
- Ask students to comment on the qualities of a knight that they can discern from the quotation from *Le Morte d'Arthur.*

ADDITIONAL RESOURCES

UNIT 3 RESOURCE BOOK
- Selection Worksheet 3.1
- Selection Check Test 4.3.3
- Selection Test 4.3.4
- Language, Grammar, and Style Resource 3.7

READER'S JOURNAL

Students might consider whether sensational stories would have had more impact on people living in the Medieval Period than on people today, who are constantly bombarded with information from a variety of sources.

INDIVIDUAL LEARNING STRATEGIES

MOTIVATION
"The Great Silkie of Shule Skerrie" is a shape-shifter. Ask student to imagine a being that can transform. Have students draw pictures of the being in its different shapes. After students have read the selection, have them write a scene in which their shape-shifter creates or deals with a problem by changing shape.

READING PROFICIENCY
Both "Sir Patrick Spens" and "The Great Silkie of Shule Skerrie" present fairly straightforward narratives. However, some students may have trouble with the archaic language in the poems and with inversions such as "I'm sure was he" for "I'm sure he was." Inversions may be explained by paraphrases. Archaic forms are explained below and in the footnotes.

Archaic and Poetic Language
wi'—with
ere—before
e'er—ever
o'er—over
wee—little

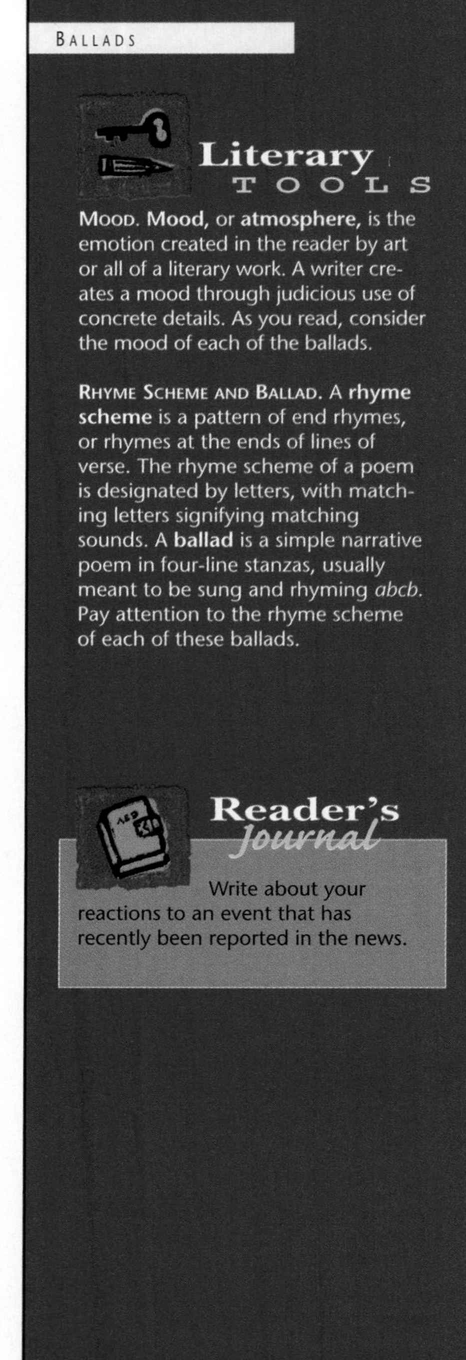

Literary TOOLS

MOOD. Mood, or **atmosphere,** is the emotion created in the reader by art or all of a literary work. A writer creates a mood through judicious use of concrete details. As you read, consider the mood of each of the ballads.

RHYME SCHEME AND BALLAD. A **rhyme scheme** is a pattern of end rhymes, or rhymes at the ends of lines of verse. The rhyme scheme of a poem is designated by letters, with matching letters signifying matching sounds. A **ballad** is a simple narrative poem in four-line stanzas, usually meant to be sung and rhyming *abcb.* Pay attention to the rhyme scheme of each of these ballads.

Reader's Journal

Write about your reactions to an event that has recently been reported in the news.

"Sir Patrick Spens"
"The Great Silkie of Shule Skerrie"

ANONYMOUS

About the AUTHORS

Like most ballads, **"Sir Patrick Spens"** and **"The Great Silkie of Shule Skerrie"** are not attributed to any one author. Medieval troubadours and common people passed such songs orally from generation to generation. Most of the ballads we know today were collected in the late nineteenth century from elderly women in rural areas. Many of these ballads were hundreds of years old, songs that mothers had sung to their children for centuries. Facts such as these led the English author Virginia Woolf to comment that "Anonymous was a woman."

About the SELECTIONS

"Sir Patrick Spens" is a perfect example of a popular English folk ballad. **Folk ballads** were composed orally and passed by word-of-mouth from generation to generation and functioned like sensational news reports. Traveling musicians would sing ballads telling about tragic or newsworthy events such as shipwrecks, hangings, robberies, and murders. "Sir Patrick Spens" tells of the shipwreck of a Scottish knight and his men, a story that may be based on an actual thirteenth-century tragedy. Although warned that the voyage would be dangerous, Sir Patrick Spens still undertook the journey from which no one returned.

"The Great Silkie of Shule Skerrie" was collected in 1852 from an elderly woman in the Shetland Islands off the far northern coast of England. Many ballads, such as this one, dealt with improbable or supernatural occurrences. This ballad is based on common Scandinavian folk tales about silkies, seal-like creatures who lived in the sea but could come to land and take human form. Legends about swan maidens, mermaids, and related creatures are among the common folk inheritance of the European nations.

GOALS/OBJECTIVES

Studying this lesson will enable students to
- empathize with the feelings of fear and loss of the main characters
- explain how ballads illustrate relationships between classes in medieval feudal society and explain how ballads were used to communicate during the Medieval Period
- define ballad and folk ballad and recognize distinguishing features of these forms, including rhyme scheme, stanza form, and typical subjects
- identify different parts of speech
- conduct research to find ballads

Sir Patrick Spens

Cantiga De Santa Maria #33, **[Detail]** c.1200s. Spanish artist. Biblioteca monasterio del Escorial, Madrid, Spain.

ANONYMOUS

The king sits in Dumferline town,
Drinking the blood-red wine:
"O where will I get a good sailor
To sail this ship of mine?"

Up and spoke an ancient knight,
Sat at the king's right knee:
"Sir Patrick Spens is the best sailor
That sails upon the sea."

The king has written a broad letter
And signed it wi' his hand,
And sent it to Sir Patrick Spens,
Was walking on the sand.

The first line that Sir Patrick read,
A loud laugh laughed he;
The next line that Sir Patrick read,
The tear blinded his eye.

"O who is this has done this deed,
This ill deed done to me,
To send me out this time o' the year,
To sail upon the sea?

"Make haste, make haste, my merry men all,
Our good ship sails the morn."
"O say not so, my master dear,
For I fear a deadly storm.

"Late late yestren I saw the new moon
Wi' the old moon in her arm,[1]
And I fear, I fear, my dear master,
That we will come to harm."

Why is one of the sailors afraid to begin the voyage? What sign did he see that made him afraid?

O our Scots nobles were right loath
To wet their cork-heeled shoes;
But long ere a' the play were played
Their hats they swam above.

O long, long may their ladies sit,
Wi' their fans into their hand,
Or e'er they see Sir Patrick Spens
Come sailing to the land.

O long, long may the ladies stand,
Wi' their gold combs in their hair,
Waiting for their own dear lords,
For they'll see them no more.

Half o'er, half o'er to Aberdour
It's fifty fathoms deep,
And there lies good Sir Patrick Spens,
Wi' the Scots lords at his feet. ■

1. **new moon . . . arm.** This natural phenomenon in which an outline of the old moon is seen filling out the crescent of the new moon was considered an omen of bad things to come.

ANSWER TO GUIDED READING QUESTION

1. The sailor believes there is a "deadly storm" on the way because he saw a faint outline of the old moon in the bright crescent of the new moon, which was considered a bad omen.

INDIVIDUAL LEARNING STRATEGIES (CONT.)

ENGLISH LANGUAGE LEARNING
Give students the idioms and the additional vocabulary words below:

IDIOMS
up and spoke—spoke up
make haste—hurry

ADDITIONAL VOCABULARY
ancient—old
fathom—distance of six feet
grumbly—discontented; unhappy

SPECIAL NEEDS
Students may find it helpful to listen to the selection using the Audio Library. Make sure students focus on the Guided Reading questions and the Recall questions in the Investigate, Inquire, and Imagine section.

ENRICHMENT
Encourage musically inclined students to try their hands (or voices) at setting these ballads to music.

SELECTION CHECK TEST 4.3.3 WITH ANSWERS

"SIR PATRICK SPENS"

1. What is Sir Patrick Spens' occupation? **He is a sailor.**
2. For what are the ladies waiting? **They wait for the sailors to come home.**

"THE GREAT SILKIE OF SHULE SKERRIE"

3. What does the maiden not know? **She doesn't know who her baby's father is.**
4. What does the visitor want from the maiden? **He wants her son.**
5. What does the visitor predict the maiden will do? **He says she'll marry.**

Literary Tools

1. What is mood? **Mood is the emotion created in the reader by a literary work.**
2. How many lines are in a stanza of a ballad? **There are four lines.**

RESPOND TO THE SELECTION

Ask students to consider the king's perspective. In the context of feudal values, what would he think of Sir Patrick's undertaking the voyage at the king's request? Would he think Sir Patrick acted foolishly or nobly? How would Sir Patrick's actions be viewed today? Why?

ANSWERS TO INVESTIGATE, INQUIRE, AND IMAGINE

RECALL

1a. The knight recommends Sir Patrick Spens because he is the best sailor who sails upon the seas. Sir Patrick laughs and then he cries.

2a. The sailor fears a deadly storm because he saw the new moon with the old moon in her arm.

3a. The ladies wait for the Scot sailors.

INTERPRET

1b. Sir Patrick is upset that somebody suggested he make such a dangerous voyage. The knight may have recommended Sir Patrick because he thought that if anyone could make such a voyage, Sir Patrick could. He may have recognized the danger and had ill will toward Sir Patrick.

2b. The sailor is superstitious.

3b. They will be waiting a long time because their lords are dead under the sea.

ANALYZE

4a. *Responses will vary.* Sir Patrick's own feelings that it is a dangerous time to sail. One of the sailors saw the new moon with the old moon in her arm, commonly believed to be a bad omen. The nobles were loath to sail.

SYNTHESIZE

4b. *Responses will vary.* Sir Patrick was fulfilling his duty to the king. As a knight he was expected to risk his life out of loyalty to his lord. He did not have much choice within the societal structures.

EVALUATE

5a. *Responses will vary.* The king was concerned about getting his ship where he wanted it. He did not seem to consider the risks or took the human lives at risk lightly.

Respond to the SELECTION

If you were the king in the ballad, how would you react to the death of Sir Patrick Spens?

INVESTIGATE, Inquire, Imagine

Recall: GATHERING FACTS →

1a. Why does the knight recommend Sir Patrick Spens? What is Sir Patrick's reaction when he reads the king's letter?

2a. What fear does one of Sir Patrick's men reveal in stanzas 6 and 7?

3a. Who is waiting for the Scot sailors in stanzas 9 and 20?

Interpret: FINDING MEANING

1b. How does Sir Patrick feel about the person who recommended him for the voyage? Why do you think the knight recommended Sir Patrick?

2b. What does this fear tell you about the sailor?

3b. Why will they be waiting a long, long time?

Analyze: TAKING THINGS APART →

4a. List the signs that suggest Sir Patrick Spens should not make this voyage.

Synthesize: BRINGING THINGS TOGETHER

4b. Explain whether Sir Patrick made a wise choice to make the trip. What do you think motivated him to undertake the voyage?

Evaluate: MAKING JUDGMENTS →

5a. Evaluate the king's motivation for ordering the voyage. Do you think he took the danger to the sailors seriously?

Extend: CONNECTING IDEAS

5b. Give some examples of things that motivate people to take risks.

ANSWERS TO INVESTIGATE, INQUIRE, AND IMAGINE (CONT.)

EXTEND

5b. *Responses will vary.* Some people are thrill-seekers who are motivated by the rush they get from taking risks. Others like to challenge themselves or want to prove themselves to others.

The Great Silkie of Shule Skerrie[1]

Anonymous

In Norway there sits a maid.
 "Bye-loo,[2] my baby," she begins.
"Little ken[3] I my bairn's[4] father,
 Far less the land that he steps in."

Then there rose at her bedside,
 And a grumbly guest, I'm sure was he:
Saying, "Here am I, thy bairn's father,
 Although that I be not <u>comely</u>."

Who came to the maid's bedside? What was he like in manner and appearance?

1. **Shule Skerrie.** A rockie isle off Scotland.
2. **Bye-loo.** Nonsense syllables used as filler. Here the maid is singing to her child.
3. **ken.** Know
4. **bairns.** A Scottish dialectical word for child.

Words For Everyday Use

come • ly (kum´ lē) *adj.*, attractive. *Which is more important in a mate: a <u>comely</u> face or a faithful heart?*

Reader's Journal

If you could change shapes, what would you become and why?

ANSWER TO GUIDED READING QUESTION

1. The father of her baby came to her bedside; he was comely in appearance and acted "grumbly," or annoyed.

READER'S JOURNAL

As an alternate activity, students might write about how they would feel if somebody they knew turned into a different being.

VOCABULARY FROM THE SELECTION

comely

ANSWER TO GUIDED READING QUESTION

1. She says that "It is not well."

RESPOND TO THE SELECTION

Students might also imagine that the Silkie has come to claim a sibling or a friend. How would they feel upon hearing the Silkie's news under those conditions?

S.O.S., c.1912 Evelyn de Morgan. The De Morgan Foundation, London.

I am a man upon the land,
  And I am a silkie[5] in the sea;
And when I'm far away from land,
  My dwelling is in Shule Skerrie."

"It is not well," quoth[6] the maiden fair;
  "It is not well, indeed," quoth she,
"That the Great Silkie of Shule Skerrie
  Should have got a child from me."

How does the maiden feel upon learning of her child's father?

Now he has taken a purse of gold,
  And he has put it upon her knee,
Saying, "Give to me my little young son,
  And take these up thy nurse's fee."

"And it shall come to pass on a summer's day,
  When the sun shines bright on every stone,
That I shall take my little wee son
  And teach him how to swim the foam."[7]

"And you shall marry a proud gunner,[8]
  And a proud gunner, I'm sure he'll be,
And the very first shot that e're he shoots,
  He'll shoot both my young son and me." ■

5. **Silkie.** Seal-like creature who takes on a human form on land
6. **quoth.** Said
7. **foam.** Refers to the sea
8. **gunner.** Harpooner

Respond *to the* SELECTION

If you were the mother in this ballad, how would you feel about what the silkie has to say?

INVESTIGATE, Inquire, Imagine

Recall: GATHERING FACTS → **Interpret:** FINDING MEANING

1a. What is the maid's lament in stanza 1?

1b. Why is the maid troubled?

2a. What does the Great Silkie reveal about himself in stanza 3?

2b. How do you think the maid feels about learning the identity of her child's father?

3a. What predictions does the Great Silkie make in stanzas 6 and 7?

3b. Contrast the predictions in stanza 6 with that in stanza 7.

Analyze: TAKING THINGS APART → **Synthesize:** BRINGING THINGS TOGETHER

4a. Identify both positive and negative information about the interaction between the human and the supernatural world.

4b. What does this ballad suggest about interactions between the human and the supernatural world?

Evaluate: MAKING JUDGMENTS → **Extend:** CONNECTING IDEAS

5a. In what way do circumstances affect the way in which you judge the gunner?

5b. Do you think people should take circumstances into consideration when judging others? Explain.

Understanding Literature

MOOD. Review the definition of **mood,** or **atmosphere,** in Literary Tools on page 168. A writer creates a mood through judicious use of concrete details. These ballads have similar moods. Describe the mood and identify three details from each ballad that help create that mood.

RHYME SCHEME AND BALLAD. Review the definition for **rhyme scheme** and **ballad** in the Handbook of Literary Terms. Use a chart to note the rhyme scheme of "The Great Silkie of Shule Skerrie." Write the last word of each line in the left column. Identify the rhyme of that line with a letter. The rhyme scheme of "Sir Patrick Spens" has been done for you.

"Sir Patrick Spens"	
Last word of line	**Rhyme**
town	*a*
wine	*b*
sailor	*c*
mine	*b*

"The Great Silkie of Shule Skerrie"	
Last word of line	**Rhyme**

ANSWERS TO INVESTIGATE, INQUIRE, AND IMAGINE

RECALL

1a. She laments the fact that she doesn't know her child's father.

2a. He says that he takes the form of a man when he is on land, but turns into a silkie when he is in the ocean.

3a. He promises that he will teach his son to swim in the ocean, and predicts that the maiden will someday marry a gunner who will kill both the Great Silkie and his son.

INTERPRET

1b. She is troubled by the fact that she doesn't know the father of her baby. Perhaps she knows that the Great Silkie is its father, but is sad that she and the silkie do not share the same world.

2b. The maid is probably not comforted by learning that the silkie is the father. She is probably distraught at the thought of giving up the child and distressed to hear the silkie's predictions.

3b. Stanza 6 paints a bright picture of the child's future, fulfilling his destiny as the child of a silkie by learning to "swim the foam." Stanza 7, which predicts the maiden will marry a gunner who will kill the father and son, is disturbing and tragic.

ANALYZE

4a. *Responses will vary.* The maiden and the Great Silkie have had a child together, but she is disgusted by the Great Silkie's strangeness, and her future husband will supposedly destroy the silkie and the child.

SYNTHESIZE

4b. *Responses will vary.* The relationship is both intimate and antagonistic. The tone of the ballad suggests that the tragic essence of the relationship is inevitable.

EVALUATE

5a. *Responses will vary.* It is easy to dislike the gunner for he will kill the son of the maid. This is especially distasteful, since he will be married to her at the time.

EXTEND

5b. *Responses will vary.* Some students may think that judgments and justice are black and white issues. Others may suggest that each case is unique and should be judged accordingly. Others may say that people should not judge others.

ANSWERS TO UNDERSTANDING LITERATURE

MOOD. Both have foreboding moods. The "blood red" wine, the bad omen, and Sir Patrick's tears upon reading the letter help create this mood in "Sir Patrick Spens." The grumbly silkie, the maid's cry that "it is not well," and especially the silkie's prediction create a foreboding mood in "The Great Silkie of Shule Skerrie."

RHYME SCHEME AND BALLAD.

maid *a*
begins *b*
father *c*
in *b*
The rhyme scheme is *abcb*.

ANSWERS TO INTEGRATING THE LANGUAGE ARTS

Language, Grammar, and Style

1. *medieval*—adj.
2. *for*—prep.
3. *tells*—v.
4. *drowning*—part.
5. *to be*—v. (inf.)
6. *mysteriously*—adv.
7. *They*—pron.
8. *and*—conj.
9. *go*—v.
10. *graves*—n.

Speaking and Listening

Students may choose to present an oral interpretation of a different version of one of these ballads. This can become a collaborative project if students work on the oral interpretations in small groups, with each student presenting a different stanza or a different voice within the ballad.

Writer's Journal

1. Write a **note** to the king about your feelings about the death of Sir Patrick Spens. Or write a note to the Great Silkie regarding your feelings about the anticipated death of the child.
2. Write a **tabloid report** about the Great Silkie. Describe the creature. In your story tell about the child and how it was taken from the maid by the Great Silkie.
3. Write a **eulogy** for Sir Patrick Spens. A eulogy is a speech usually given at a funeral that describes the deceased. The eulogy might describe key characteristics, major accomplishments, and the person's effect on others.

Integrating *the* Language Arts

Language, Grammar, and Style

The Parts of Speech. Read the Language Arts Survey 3.7, "Grammar Reference Chart—Parts of Speech Overview." Then identify the part of speech of each italicized word in the sentences below.

Many of the most popular of the [1] *medieval* ballads are ghost stories. "The Wife of Usher's Well," [2] *for* example, [3] *tells* the story of a mother whose three sons are killed, perhaps by [4] *drowning* at sea. The mother then wishes for her sons [5] to *be* resurrected. On the feast day of St. Martin, the sons [6] *mysteriously* appear at her door. [7] *They* feast with their mother that evening [8] *and* then [9] *go* to bed. However, they have to return to their [10] *graves* before the cock crows in the morning.

Study and Research

Other Versions of Ballads. Because ballads were passed orally, there are often many versions of any one ballad. Do some research in books of songs or poetry or on the Internet to find other versions of "Sir Patrick Spens" and "The Great Silkie of Shule Skerrie." Compare and contrast the different versions you find.

Collaborative Learning & Study and Research

Researching Shape Shifters. Working in small groups, brainstorm to develop a list of topics under which you might find information about shape shifters, such as Norway, Scandinavian folklore, folktales, etc. Then research these topics using the library or the Internet.

Speaking and Listening

Presenting a Ballad. Ballads were often passed as songs. Prepare an oral presentation of either "Sir Patrick Spens" or "The Great Silkie of Shule Skerrie." Vary your pace, volume, and tone to match the meaning of each stanza.

"Ubi Sunt Qui ante Nos Fuerunt?"[1]
"I Sing of a Maiden"

ANONYMOUS, TRANSLATED BY ROBIN LAMB

About the Authors

"Ubi Sunt Qui ante Nos Fuerunt?" and "I Sing of a Maiden" were both written anonymously. Although some medieval lyrics were secular, most were religious. Very few of these hymns were attributed to a specific author. Such literature existed many years before it was ever written down and was considered popular verse rather than the work of individual writers.

About the Selections

Because of the tremendous influence of the Catholic Church, the religious lyrics from the Medieval Period far outnumber the secular ones. Some religious lyrics, including **"Ubi Sunt Qui ante Nos Fuerunt,"** dwelt on the fear of death and the contemplation of heaven. As the selection's title demonstrates, many of these lyrics were originally written in Latin.

The religious lyric **"I Sing of a Maiden"** (*circa* 1400) celebrates the Virgin Mary. Such lyrics had their origins in France, where the veneration of the Virgin Mary developed into the code of courtly love. Poetry brought back to France with the Crusaders from Persia influenced the development of courtly love as well. "I Sing of a Maiden" also contains elements of secular lyrics that celebrate the coming of spring. The poet creates a symbolic comparison between the return of spring and the Virgin Birth.

The following selections are printed in the original Middle English alongside Modern English translations.

1. **Ubi . . . Fuerunt.** Latin for "Where are they who came before us?"

Literary Tools

THEME. A **theme** is the central idea in a literary work. Try to identify the theme as you read each lyric.

SIMILE. A **simile** is a comparison using *like* or *as.* It compares two things that have some feature or aspect in common. Look for a simile in one of the lyrics.

Reader's Journal

Explain whether you live your life based on your beliefs about the afterlife or if you live solely for the moment.

ADDITIONAL RESOURCES

UNIT 3 RESOURCE BOOK
"Ubi Sunt Qui ante Nos Fuerunt?"
"I Sing of a Maiden"
- Selection Worksheet 3.2
- Selection Check Test 4.3.5
- Selection Test 4.3.6
- Language, Grammar, and Style Resource 3.6

READER'S JOURNAL

Students may choose to write about a specific situation in which they made a decision based on their beliefs.

Students might use a sensory detail chart or cluster chart to jot down and organize their ideas.

INDIVIDUAL LEARNING STRATEGIES

MOTIVATION
"Ubi Sunt Qui Ante Nos Fuerunt?" asks "where are they who came before us?" The poem identifies some things that people in the past did. Ask students to imagine that somebody in the future is writing about the period of time in which they live. What activities or descriptions might that person use? Have students brainstorm ideas as a group.

READING PROFICIENCY
Several lines in the translation of "Ubi Sunt Qui ante Nos Fuerunt?" follow closely the word order of the original Middle English. Some students may need help interpreting sentences that are in inverted word order. Here are transpositions into normal word order of key lines from the poem:

line 1: Where are they that were before us?
line 8: They led their lives with gaming.
line 19: They took their paradise here.
line 24: They never come [back] from there.

ENGLISH LANGUAGE LEARNING
Give students the following idioms and additional vocabulary words listed below:

IDIOMS
in the twinkling of an eye—in a moment

Continued on page 176

GOALS/OBJECTIVES

Studying this lesson will enable students to
- experience the speaker's awareness of the inevitability of death
- explain the influence of the medieval church on early English lyric poetry
- explain the *memento mori* and *contemptu mundi* themes as used in medieval lyrics
- create dictionary entries in proper form
- identify nonstandard language

INDIVIDUAL LEARNING STRATEGIES

(CONT. FROM PAGE 175)

were lost—fell irretrievably into sin, with its inevitable punishment

ADDITIONAL VOCABULARY
bore—past tense of bear; carry
bower—bedroom
gaming—gambling
wailing—crying

SPECIAL NEEDS
Students will find it helpful to listen to the selection using the Audio Library. Make sure students focus on the Recall questions in the Investigate, Inquire, and Imagine section.

ENRICHMENT
Have students find photographs of medieval cathedrals such as Chartres or Notre Dame. (Such photos may be found in books on European travel, the Middle Ages, and the history of art or architecture. David MacCauley's *Cathedral* shows, in step-by-step drawings, how a medieval cathedral was constructed.) Ask students to describe the characteristics of the cathedral. Ask them to compare cathedral architecture to that of medieval castles.

LITERARY NOTE

Point out to students the following differences between the Middle English text and Modern English:

- **Word order.** The verb sometimes appeared at the end of the sentences, as in "biforen us weren."
- **Inflectional endings.** Modern English is simpler than Middle English in its inflectional system, having lost endings such as those that appear at the ends of the words *hound<u>es</u>, ladd<u>en</u>, havek<u>es</u>,* and *ber<u>en</u>.*
- **Double negatives.** The last line contains a double negative *ne . . . nevere,* that is nonstandard in Modern English.
- **Word change.** Most of the words in the poem are still found in Modern English, though with different spellings and pronunciations. A word that has disappeared from Modern English is *stoundes,* in line 18.

Young Women and Death, 1872. Pierre Puvis de Chavannes. Clark Institute, Williamstown, Massachusetts.

Ubi Sunt Qui ante Nos Fuerunt?

ANONYMOUS

RESPOND TO THE SELECTION

Students might discuss whether they fear death or whether they take the fact that they will someday die into consideration when they make decisions or choose what they do or say.

Were beth they that biforen us weren,
Houndes ladden and havekes beren,
And hadden feld and wode?
The riche levedies in here bour,
That wereden gold in here tressour,
With here brighte rode;

Eten and drounken, and maden hem glad;
Here lif was al with gamen y-lad;
Men kneleden hem biforen;
They beren hem wel swithe heye:
And in a twincling of an eye
Here soules weren forloren.

Were is that lawhing and that song,
That trayling and that proude gong,
Tho havekes and tho houndes?
Al that joye is went away,
That wele is comen to weylaway,
To manye harde stoundes.

Here paradis they nomen here,
And nou they lyen in helle y-fere;
The fyr hit brennes evere:
Long is ay, and long is o,
Long is wy, and long is wo;
Thennes ne cometh they nevere. ■

Where are they that were before us,
[Who] led hounds and bore hawks
And had fields and woods?
The rich ladies in their bowers,
That wore gold in their hair,
With their bright complexions;

Ate and drank, and made themselves glad;
Their lives were all with gaming led;
Men knelt before them;
They bore themselves so high:
But in a twinkling of an eye,
Their souls were lost forever.

Where is that laughing and that song,
That trailing of gowns and that proud walk,
Those hawks and those hounds?
All that joy has gone away,
Their wellness has come to wailing,
To many hard times.

Their paradise they took here,
And now they lie in hell together
The fire it burns forever:
Long is *a*, and long is *o*,
Long is *y* [why], and long is woe;
From there come they never. ■

How do you feel about the ideas about life and death expressed in this poem?

ANSWERS TO INVESTIGATE, INQUIRE, AND IMAGINE

RECALL

1a. The speaker asks, "Where are they that were before us?"
2a. They hunted, feasted, wore fine clothes, and gambled.
3a. In a twinkling of an eye, their souls were lost. They are now in hell.

INTERPRET

1b. He refers to people who have died.
2b. The people were probably nobles because they hunted, were rich, wore gold and trailing gowns, and ate and drank well.
3b. Their joy has gone away because they are now among the damned.

ANALYZE

4a. *Responses will vary.* The people were rich, wore gold, had bright complexions. They ate, drank, and were happy. They laughed and sang. Their happiness quickly turned to woe and wailing. They are in hell.

SYNTHESIZE

4b. *Responses will vary.* The poem suggests that death comes quickly and that it is important to prepare for the afterlife. During the Medieval Period, death was common due to disease and the life expectancy was much younger. Also the church stressed the importance of the afterlife. It is not surprising that the theme of death was common in the Medieval Period.

EVALUATE

5a. *Responses will vary.*These people provide a lesson, a warning, about what happens if one gives oneself over entirely to pleasure in this life, without thinking of the life to come.

EXTEND

5b. *Responses will vary.* Some students may not feel comfortable discussing their beliefs.

INVESTIGATE, Inquire, Imagine

Recall: GATHERING FACTS → **Interpret:** FINDING MEANING

1a. What question does the speaker ask in line 1?
1b. What does the author mean by the phrase "they that were before us"?

2a. What did these people do while they lived?
2b. What was the social status of these people? How do you know?

3a. What happened to these people? Where are they now?
3b. Why has "all that joy gone away"?

Analyze: TAKING THINGS APART → **Synthesize:** BRINGING THINGS TOGETHER

4a. What observations are made about these people during their lives? What observations are made about them during the afterlife?
4b. What connections between life and the afterlife does this poem suggest? Why might medieval audiences have been so concerned with death?

Evaluate: MAKING JUDGMENTS → **Extend:** CONNECTING IDEAS

5a. Why should the reader or listener take notice of these women and men?
5b. What current books or movies do you know of that deal with the afterlife? Which of these, if any do you identify with?

LITERARY NOTE

Explain that European soldiers on Crusade in the Holy Land gathered and then brought back to Europe, Persian love poems that idealized women. At the same time, possibly as a consequence, many Europeans began to devote more attention to the adoration of the Virgin Mary. The Persian idealization of women, combined with the adoration of the Virgin, led to the creation of a literature that death with idealized women pursued by knights attempting to show themselves worthy. This was the literature of romance, chivalry and courtly love.

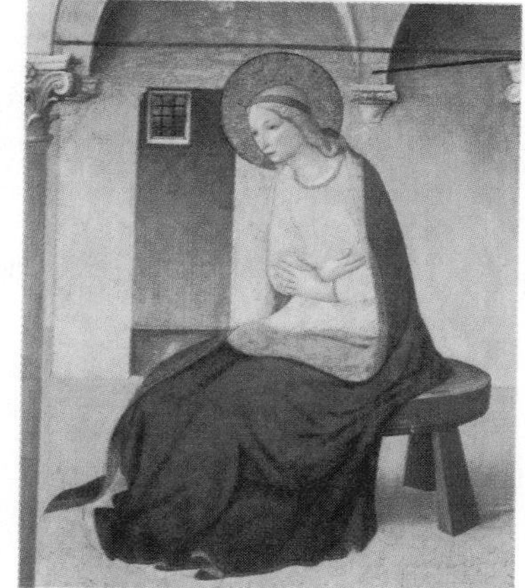

The Anunciation [Detail], c.1438–45. Fra Angelico.
Museo di San Marco dell'Angelico, Florence, Italy.

ANONYMOUS

I sing of a maiden
  That is makelees:
King of alle kinges
  To her sone she chees.

He cam also stille
  Ther his moder was
As dewe in Aprille
  That falleth on the gras.

He cam also stille
  To his modres bowr
As dewe in Aprille
  That falleth on the flowr.

He cam also stille
  Ther his moder lay
As dewe in Aprille
  That falleth on the spray.

Moder and maiden
  Was nevere noon but she:
Wel may swich a lady
  Godes moder be. ■

I sing of a maiden
  That is matchless:[1]
King of all kings
  As her son she chose.

He came as still
  Where his mother was
As dew in April
  That falls on the grass.

He came as still
  To his mother's bower
As dew in April
  That falls on the flower.

He came as still
  Where his mother lay
As dew in April
  That falls on the spray.

Mother and maiden
  Was never none but she:
Well may such a lady
  God's mother be. ■

1. **matchless.** The word is a pun meaning both "unequaled" and "without a mate, or match."

LITERARY NOTE

If you have a mixed group of students, some with Catholic backgrounds, then you may wish to place a Catholic student in each group who can serve as a resource for the other students. If there are no Catholic students in your class, you may have to provide some additional background information yourself. Explain that in many Christian belief systems and in Catholicism in particular, the Virgin Mary is said to have conceived the infant Jesus by divine intervention, not by the usual method. You may further wish to explain that in Catholicism, Mary plays the role of one who intercedes with God on behalf of the prayerful. A central prayer in Catholic observance is the "Ave Maria," or "Hail, Mary," the text of which is as follows: "Hail, Mary, full of grace, the Lord is with Thee. Blessèd art Thou among women, and blessèd is the fruit of Thy womb, Jesus. Holy Mary, mother of God, pray for us sinners, now and at the hour of our death." Mary is the embodiment of gentleness and grace. Because of its word choice and tone, "I Sing of a Maiden" brilliantly evokes those qualities and is widely considered to be the most beautiful of Middle English lyrics.

SELECTION CHECK TEST 4.3.5 WITH ANSWERS

"UBI SUNT QUI NOS FUERUN"

1. What kind of life have the ladies led? **They have led a life of pleasure.**
2. Who knelt before them? **Men knelt before them.**
3. Where are the ladies together now? **They are in hell.**

"I SING OF A MAIDEN"

4. What is the maiden described as being? **She is described as "matchless."**
5. Whose mother is she? **She is God's mother.**

Literary Tools

1. What is a theme? **A theme is a central idea in a literary work.**
2. What is a simile? **A simile is a comparison using "like" or "as."**
3. What might be a theme of "Ubi Sunt Qui Nos Fuerun"? **Responses will vary, but the poem warns that earthly lives built on pleasure may land one in hell.**

RESPOND TO THE SELECTION

Ask students to consider the tone of the poem as they think about the music that might be used with these lyrics.

ANSWERS TO INVESTIGATE, INQUIRE, AND IMAGINE

Recall

1a. The maiden is the Virgin Mary.

2a. The maiden's son is Jesus, the "King of all kings." The poet compares his coming to the coming of spring.

3a. She is also a mother.

Interpret

1b. She is matchless in the sense that she is unequaled ("Blessed art Thou among women") and in the sense that she conceived without a mate, or match.

2b. The comparison suggests that the son's coming is a renewal or rebirth. His coming is peaceful and painless.

3b. The woman is a maiden and a mother. She is also unique in that she is the mother of God.

Analyze

4a. *Responses will vary.* The son came as the dew in April "that falls on the grass," "That falls on the flower," "That falls on the spray."

Synthesize

4b. *Responses will vary.* The repetition emphasizes the gentleness of the son's coming. The changes suggest an upward progression, moving from the grass to the flower to the spray.

Evaluate

5a. *Responses will vary.* The speaker reveres the woman in the poem.

Extend

5b. *Responses will vary.* The reverential tone of the poem is consistent with a love poem. The subject, especially the first and last stanzas, focus very much on the religious theme of the poem.

ANSWERS TO UNDERSTANDING LITERATURE

Theme. The message, or theme, of the ubi sunt literature of the Middle Ages was to remind people that they should think about and prepare for the afterlife.

NOTE: Ask students to consider how the ubi sunt, memento mori, and

Respond to the SELECTION

What kind of music do you think would be used to sing this lyric?

INVESTIGATE, Inquire, Imagine

Recall: GATHERING FACTS

1a. Who is the maiden in the poem?

2a. Who is the maiden's son? To what does the poet compare His coming?

3a. What is the woman besides a maiden?

Interpret: FINDING MEANING

1b. How do the two meanings of the word *matchless* apply to the maiden?

2b. What does the the comparison suggest about the son's coming?

3b. What is unique about the woman in this lyric?

Analyze: TAKING THINGS APART

4a. Identify the repeated elements in this poem and the change that occurs with each repetition.

Synthesize: BRINGING THINGS TOGETHER

4b. What purpose does this repetition serve? Why do you think the changes occur in the order they do?

Evaluate: MAKING JUDGMENTS

5a. How does the speaker feel about the woman in this poem?

Extend: CONNECTING IDEAS

5b. Courtly love was a code of romantic love celebrated in medieval songs and romances in France and England. The woman of this code was idealized. Explain whether you think this poem is primarily a love poem or a religious poem.

Understanding Literature

Theme. Review the definition of **theme** in Literary Tools on page 175. Common themes in medieval literature included *contemptu mundi* (contempt for the world), which lamented that the world is fallen and full of woe, and *memento mori* (reminder of death), which warned that because death comes quickly and unexpectedly that it is important to prepare for the afterlife. What is the theme of "Ubi Sunt Qui ante Nos Fuerunt"?

Simile. Review the definition of **simile** in the Handbook of Literary Terms. A simile compares two things that have some feature or aspect in common. What similes are used in "I Sing of a Maiden"? What do the two things being compared have in common?

ANSWERS TO UNDERSTANDING LITERATURE (CONT.)

contemptu mundi themes are related. The ubi sunt serves as a memento mori, or reminder of death. The purpose of reminding people of death is to get them to feel contemptu mundi, or contempt for the world, so that they will place stock, instead, in the world after this one.

Simile. The poet compares the coming of Christ to the falling of dew in April and, by extension, to the coming of spring. The two subjects are treated in the poem with a kind of reverent expectation and awe. Both the coming of Christ and the coming of spring are times of renewal or opportunities for rebirth.

WRITER'S JOURNAL

1. Write a **descriptive paragraph** about spring. In your paragraph, use images to describe the season and your feelings about spring.
2. Write a **lyric poem** about your view of the world. The tone of the poem should reflect your feelings.
3. Explore either the *contemptu mundi* theme or the *momento mori* theme in a **personal essay.** Use examples from your own life to address the theme you choose.

Integrating *the* LANGUAGE ARTS

Language, Grammar, and Style

IDENTIFYING NONSTANDARD LANGUAGE. Language is constantly evolving. As you compared the Middle English version of the poems to the modern translations, you probably noticed many differences. You may have noticed that words you use differ from those used by older people. Make a list of words that you use that you think older people may not understand. Write a definition of each word. Then interview some older people to see what words they use that are not often used by your generation.

Vocabulary

DICTIONARY ENTRIES. Write entries for a Middle English–Modern English dictionary. Choose ten words from the Middle English version of the selection. Identify the part of speech and the Modern English counterpart for each word. When necessary, note how a word meaning has changed over time. Refer to the Language Arts Survey 3.6, "Identifying the Parts of Speech." You might also want to look at the *Oxford English Dictionary* or another reference work that lists comprehensive word histories. Remember to list entries in alphabetical order.

Speaking and Listening

WOMEN'S STUDIES. Many Medieval lyrics address idealized women. Examine some contemporary lyrics that address or talk about women. Prepare a speech to present your analysis of the view of women in songs today.

Study and Research

RESEARCHING THE MEDIEVAL PERIOD. Find sources that would help you better understand the Medieval Period. Make a bibliography that includes both printed and audio, video, or online sources. Include at least three sources that provide general background on the Medieval Period, two that have good coverage of the Crusades, and two that discuss Medieval literature.

ANSWERS TO INTEGRATING THE LANGUAGE ARTS

Language, Grammar, and Style
This may also be a good time to discuss formal and informal English. Point out to students that in social situations, slang has a place, but that in others, such as formal speeches, business letters, or interviews, standard English is preferable.

Study and Research
Refer students to the Language Arts Survey 5.40, "Making Bibliographies and Bibliography Cards," to help them with this activity.

ADDITIONAL RESOURCES

UNIT 3 RESOURCE BOOK
- Selection Worksheet 3.3
- Selection Check Test 4.3.7
- Selection Test 4.3.8
- Language, Grammar, and Style Resource 3.29

READER'S JOURNAL

Students may also wish to write about what they would be willing to do for someone they love.

INDIVIDUAL LEARNING STRATEGIES

MOTIVATION
Ask students to find stories about famous contemporary couples. After students have read the selection, they can compare the contemporary couple to Tristan and Iseult.

READING PROFICIENCY
Before students read this selection, point out the selection begins with the narrator's comments. The actual story begins in the second paragraph. It may also be helpful to review the relationship between King Mark, Tristan, and the Queen. Marie de France assumes her audience knows what she is talking about, so it is important that students understand the background of this story, which is presented in About the Selection.

ENGLISH LANGUAGE LEARNING
Give students the following additional vocabulary words:

ADDITIONAL VOCABULARY
recount—tell or tell again
embittered—made bitter, or angry and unhappy
pensive—thoughtful
melancholy—very sad
emerged—came out
enlaced —intermingled
escort—accompany
banish—throw out; exile

SPECIAL NEEDS
Students will find it helpful to listen to the selection using the Audio Library. Make sure students focus on the Guided Reading questions and the Recall questions in the Investigate, Inquire, and Imagine section.

Continued on page 183

Literary TOOLS

ROMANCE AND COURTLY LOVE. In medieval literature, **romance** is used to refer to stories about the adventures and loves of knights. **Courtly love** is a code of romantic love celebrated in songs and romances of the Medieval Period. According to the code, the lover knows himself or herself to be truly in love if he or she is overcome by extreme, transforming emotion. "The Honeysuckle: Chevrefoil" provides a good example of both romance and courtly love.

ArtNote

La Belle Isould at Joyous Gard is taken from a 1893 edition of Sir Thomas Malory's *Le Morte d'Arthur,* illustrated by Aubrey Vincent Beardsley (1872–1898). See the excerpt on page 200. Beardsley was the foremost English illustrator of the late 1800s and a leader in the Art for Art's Sake movement, which emphasized aestheticism as opposed to any political, social, moral, or practical value that art might have. The Arthurian legend has inspired artists and writers across the centuries. What aspects of Arthurian legend does Beardsley's illustration emphasize?

Reader's Journal

What does it mean to be faithful to somebody you love?

"The Honeysuckle: Chevrefoil"

BY MARIE DE FRANCE, TRANSLATED BY MARCELLE THIÉBAUX

About the AUTHOR

Marie de France (c.1200) was a French poet who had considerable influence over English writers. She spent most of her life at the English court. Some scholars believe she was the half-sister of Henry II of England, who was king during that time. She perfected the **Breton lai,** a type of narrative poem or song, and is probably responsible for its introduction in England. Many of Marie de France's lais had Celtic themes and included characters and storylines from the legends of King Arthur and his Knights of the Round Table.

About the SELECTION

"The Honeysuckle: Chevrefoil" is one of the fifteen Breton lais known to be written by Marie de France. It tells of an Arthurian knight, Tristan, and his love for a Celtic queen, Iseult. Their love is complicated by Iseult's marriage to Tristan's uncle, King Mark of Cornwall. As a young man in the service of his uncle, Tristan is asked to travel to Ireland to bring back Iseult, who is to be Mark's queen.

On the journey back to Cornwall, Tristan and Iseult fall in love because of a love potion that they unwittingly drink. Iseult is married to Mark, but at night her serving maid takes her place; in that way she remains faithful to Tristan. However, rumors of Tristan's love for the Queen reach Mark, who banishes him. This is the point at which Marie de France's lai begins. Although "The Honeysuckle: Chevrefoil" was originally written as a Breton lai, the following selection is a Modern English prose translation.

GOALS/OBJECTIVES

Studying this lesson will enable students to
- empathize with the love and longing of the main characters
- relate the principal events in the legend of Tristan and Iseult and recognize that the stories of these characters are told in many forms
- identify, define, and illustrate with examples the terms romance and courtly love
- use a dictionary to find definitions and build vocabulary
- demonstrate knowledge of the proper form of a personal letter

La Belle Isould at Joyous Gard, Aubrey Beardsley. Wellesley College Library.

The Honeysuckle: Chevrefoil

MARIE DE FRANCE, TRANSLATED BY MARCELLE THIÉBAUX

It pleases me very much, and I really wish to recount to you the true story of the "lai"[1] they call *Chevrefoil,* and why it was written and how it came about. Many people have told me the story and recounted it to me, and I have also found it written down. It's about Tristan and the Queen and their love which was so strong that they suffered greatly, and they both died on the same day because of it.

King Mark was embittered, outraged against his nephew, Tristan, and drove him from the land because of his love for the Queen. Tristan went back to his own country, to his birthplace in South Wales. He spent a year there, unable to return without risking death and ruin.

How is Tristan related to King Mark? Why does the king send Tristan away?

Don't be surprised. Anyone who loves most faithfully will grieve and grow pensive if he cannot have what he desires. Tristan grieved, he

1. **lai.** A lai, or lay, is a narrative poem or song.

LITERARY NOTE

The end of the story differs in the various sources. Some say that Tristan was killed by Mark. Others say that Iseult sailed to meet Tristan, sending word ahead that if she were alive and on the ship, the ship would have a white sail, but if she were dead, it would have a black sail. Incorrectly informed that the ship had a black sail, Tristan took his own life. On learning of her beloved's death, Iseult died of grief.

ANSWER TO GUIDED READING QUESTION

1. Tristan is King Mark's nephew. The king sends Tristan away because he is in love with the king's wife.

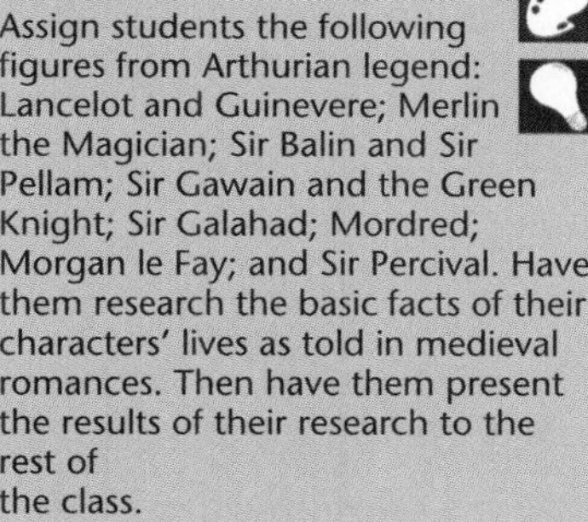

INDIVIDUAL LEARNING STRATEGIES

(CONT. FROM PAGE 182)

ENRICHMENT

Assign students the following figures from Arthurian legend: Lancelot and Guinevere; Merlin the Magician; Sir Balin and Sir Pellam; Sir Gawain and the Green Knight; Sir Galahad; Mordred; Morgan le Fay; and Sir Percival. Have them research the basic facts of their characters' lives as told in medieval romances. Then have them present the results of their research to the rest of the class.

ADDITIONAL QUESTIONS AND ACTIVITIES

Have students analyze "The Honeysuckle: Chevrefoil," dividing it into those parts that are narration and those that are lay proper.

Answer

Students should be able to recognize with very little prompting that this story is framed by a narrative voice. In the first paragraph, the narrator announces the name and subject of the story that she is going to tell. In the last paragraph, she repeats the name, adding the further information that Tristan himself was the original teller of the story.

LITERARY NOTE

Point out to students that Marie de France was reworking materials passed down from singer to singer and that she does not claim originality for her story. In fact, ideas about the originality of a tale were quite foreign to writers of the Middle Ages, who generally thought of stories as part of the common inheritance of all people. Oral storytelling was vital because few people could read.

ANSWERS TO GUIDED READING QUESTIONS

1. He carved his name on a hazel wand.
2. Their love is compared to honeysuckle that has grown around the hazelwood so that the two are intertwined and cannot be separated without resulting in the deaths of both.

SELECTION CHECK TEST 4.3.7 WITH ANSWERS

1. Why does King Mark banish Tristan? **Tristan is in love with the Queen.**
2. What does Tristan write on the hazel branch? **He writes his name on it.**
3. What does the Queen do when she sees the branch? **She stops in the road.**
4. Tristan goes to Wales to wait for what? **He goes to wait for the King's orders.**
5. What does Tristan compose when he gets home? **He writes a new lai.**

Literary Tools
Match each sentence beginning with the *best fitting* conclusion. You will not use any choices more than once.

A 1. Marie de France…
D 2. In medieval literature, romance …
G 3. The code of courtly love…
B 4. The Breton lai…
F 5. "The Honeysuckle: Chevrefoil" …

a. perfected the Breton lai.
b. is a type of narrative poem or song.
c. has had great influence over French poets.
d. refers to stories about adventures and loves of knights.
e. includes supernatural forces or creatures, like dragons.
f. provides a good example of both romance and courtly love.
g. says that a lover is truly in love if he or she is overcome by extreme emotion.

RESPOND TO THE SELECTION

Students may wish to compare these feelings to their own feelings upon being reunited with somebody they love. Students may think about a friend or family member in addition to or instead of a romantic love.

grew melancholy, and so he left his own country and went straight to Cornwall, where the Queen lived. He hid alone in the forest, for he did not want anyone to see him. At evening he emerged when it was time to seek lodging, and he stayed with peasants and poor people. He asked them for news of the King's doings. They told him they'd heard that the barons had been summoned to Tintagel where the King wished to hold court. Everyone would be in attendance for Pentecost.[2] There would be rejoicing and festivity, and the Queen would also be there.

Tristan heard this news with great joy. The Queen would not be able to journey to Tintagel without his seeing her pass by. The day the King set forth, Tristan returned to the wood by the road that he knew the royal company would have to take.

He split a hazel branch in half and whittled it on four sides to make it square. Having prepared the wood, he inscribed his name on it with his knife. If the Queen saw it (for this had happened once before and she had perceived it then), she would know that the hazel wand came from her beloved.

What sign did Tristan make to the Queen?

The sum of what he wrote and said was to tell her that he had been there a long time, he had waited and tarried in the hope of learning how he might see her, since he could not live without her.

For the two of them it was like the honeysuckle spiraling itself around the hazelwood, the two enlaced and grown completely together. Together they can live, but if anyone tries to tear them apart, the hazel swiftly dies and the honeysuckle too. "Sweet friend, so it is with us: neither you without me, nor me without you." *Bele amie, si est de nus—ne vus sanz mei, ne mei sanz vus!*

To what is their love compared? Why is their love like this?

The Queen rode on horseback along the road. She glanced at a hill slope and noticed the little branch and saw what it was. She recognized all the letters. She ordered the knights who escorted her, those who rode alongside with her, to stop. She wished to dismount and rest. They obeyed her command and she moved far away from her attendants. To her side she summoned her maidservant, Brenguein, who was very faithful.

At a short distance from the road she found in the forest the man she loved more than any living person, and they shared great joy. He felt at ease as he spoke, and she told him her desires. She let him know how he might become reconciled to the King and how unhappy the King was that he had banished Tristan because of the accusations against him. Then she had to leave, and she parted from her beloved. But when it was time to go, they both wept. Tristan returned to Wales to await his uncle's orders.

Because of the joy he had shared with his beloved when he saw her, and because of what he had written (for the Queen had said he should) and his desire to remember the words, Tristan—who was an excellent musician on the harp—composed a new "lai." Briefly I'll name it for you: The English call it *Goteleaf* and the French name it *Chevrefoil.* I have told you the truth of the "lai" I've recited for you. ■

2. **Pentecost.** A Christian festival seven weeks after Easter

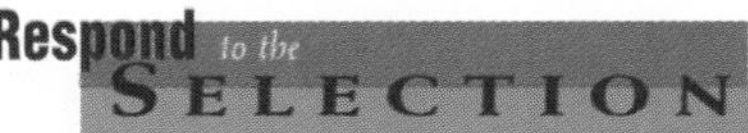

If you were Tristan, how would you feel about your reunion with the Queen?

CROSS-CURRICULAR ACTIVITIES

Arts and Humanities. The Tristan and Iseult story has been told many times in many different media. You may wish to have students create their own artworks based on the story. Possibilities include paintings or drawings of the characters, song lyrics, or dramatic adaptations. Students interested in learning more of the story may wish to read a translation of Gottfried von Strassburg's *Tristan und Isolde.* Some might also appreciate Richard Wagner's opera by the same name, which was based on von Strassburg's work.

INVESTIGATE

Inquire, Imagine

Recall: GATHERING FACTS → **Interpret:** FINDING MEANING

1a. Why are Tristan and the Queen separated? To what is their love compared?

1b. What does this comparison suggest about their love?

2a. Why does Tristan return to Cornwall?

2b. What do Tristan's actions reveal about his feelings for the Queen?

3a. How does the Queen discover that Tristan is waiting for her in the forest?

3b. Why might the Queen hope the Tristan is reconciled with the King?

Analyze: TAKING THINGS APART → **Synthesize:** BRINGING THINGS TOGETHER

4a. List signs of the love between Tristan and the Queen.

4b. Who do you think shows greater love—Tristan or the Queen?

Evaluate: MAKING JUDGMENTS → **Extend:** CONNECTING IDEAS

5a. Judge whether the love between Tristan and the Queen is honorable. Do you think their love is portrayed realistically or idealistically?

5b. What qualities do you think make a solid relationship?

Understanding Literature

ROMANCE AND COURTLY LOVE. Review the definitions for **romance** and **courtly love** in Literary Tools on page 182. According to the code, the lover knows himself or herself to be truly in love if he or she is overcome by extreme, transforming emotion. Read about other aspects of the code in the Handbook of Literary Terms. In a chart, note the ways in which Tristan and the Queen fit the code of courtly love.

Courtly Love in "The Honeysuckle: Chevrefoil"	
Tristan	**The Queen**
grows melancholy	subject of Tristan's great love

ANSWERS TO INVESTIGATE, INQUIRE, AND IMAGINE

RECALL

1a. The king banished Tristan when he learns of Tristan's love for the queen. Their love is compared to a honeysuckle wrapping itself around a hazelwood.

2a. He returns in hopes of seeing the Queen.

3a. The Queen sees the hazel wand on which Tristan has carved his name.

INTERPRET

1b. The comparison suggests that their lives are intertwined, that one cannot live without the other.

2b. Tristan's actions reveal that he loves the queen very deeply.

3b. The queen might hope that Tristan is reconciled with the king so that Tristan can return and be near her again.

ANALYZE

4a. *Responses will vary.* Tristan grew melancholy. He lived among the poor and hid in the forest in hopes of getting a chance to see the queen. He used a sign they had used before to let her know he was there. The queen stopped her party and entered the woods to see Tristan. They both wept upon parting.

SYNTHESIZE

4b. *Responses will vary.* Some may say that Tristan seems to be more upset by their separation. Both are happy to see one another and unhappy to part ways again.

EVALUATE

5a. *Responses will vary.* Students may say that Tristan and the queen really love each other and should be together. Others may say that the queen is married and should not be pursuing a relationship with Tristan. Tristan is also betraying his uncle through his actions. Their love is portrayed idealistically.

EXTEND

5b. *Responses will vary.* Some answers may include love, trust, understanding, and fidelity.

ANSWERS TO UNDERSTANDING LITERATURE

ROMANCE AND COURTLY LOVE

Courtly Love in "The Honeysuckle: Chevrefoil" Chart:

Tristan
grew melancholy
risked the king's wrath by returning
writes a lai about his love and the joy they shared together

The Queen
subject of Tristan's great love
wants to be with him
tries to help him reconcile with king

ANSWERS TO INTEGRATING THE LANGUAGE ARTS

Language, Grammar, and Style

1. Do not be surprised. SS: You; Verb: do not be
2. He hid alone in the forest, for he did not want anyone to see him. SS: he; Verb: hid, did not want
3. They told him they had heard that the barons had been summoned. SS: They; Verb: told, had heard
4. Briefly I will name it for you. SS: I; Verb: will name
5. I have told you the truth of the "lai" I have recited for you. SS: I; Verb: have told, have recited

Speaking and Listening

Refer students to the Language Arts Survey, 4.20, "Telling a Story" for advice on preparing a dramatic telling of a story. Students might practice in pairs and critique each other's work.

Vocabulary

beret—kind of hat
cafe—coffee shop
valet—employee who perfoms services such as taking care of clothes
hors d'oeurve—appetizer
tête-à-tête—literally "head-to-head," refers to a private conversation between two people

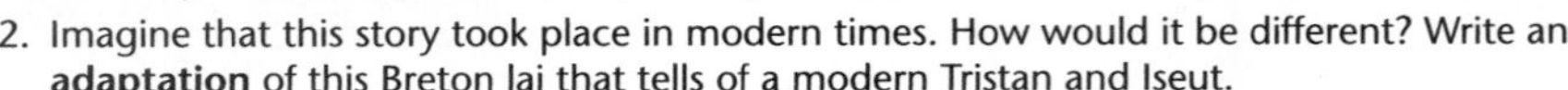

Writer's Journal

1. Write a **journal entry** from the Queen's point of view about her separation from Tristan.
2. Imagine that this story took place in modern times. How would it be different? Write an **adaptation** of this Breton lai that tells of a modern Tristan and Iseut.
3. Write your own **medieval romance.** Include a knight and an idealized woman. Show how they prove their love.

Integrating *the* Language Arts

Language, Grammar, and Style

Contractions in Sentences. Contractions combine two words by shortening and joining them with an apostrophe. When you are trying to determine subjects and verbs in a sentence, contractions need to be written out into the two words that they represent. After the contraction is written out, each word should be considered separately. Review the Language Arts Survey 3.29, "Working with Negatives and Contractions." In the following sentences, write out all contractions. Then identify the simple subject and verb.

1. Don't be surprised.
2. He hid alone in the forest, for he didn't want anyone to see him.
3. They told him they'd heard that the barons had been summoned.
4. Briefly I'll name it for you.
5. I have told you the truth of the "lai" I've recited for you.

Speaking and Listening

Story Tellers. Marie de France told a story that was familiar to her listeners. Choose a story that you think others will know. Prepare your own version of the story and present it in a dramatic manner to your classmates.

Applied English

Personal Letter. Review the form of the personal letter. Then write a personal letter from Tristan to King Mark asking for forgiveness and requesting permission to return to Tintagel.

Vocabulary

Defining Words with French Origins. Many words enter the English language from other languages. Use a dictionary to find the meaning of these words that are taken or adapted from French.

beret
cafe
valet
hors d'oeuvre
tête-à-tête

FROM

Sir Gawain and the Green Knight

BY THE PEARL POET, TRANSLATED BY Y. R. PONSOR

About the AUTHOR

Almost nothing is known about **The Pearl Poet.** The author's name comes from the first poem, *Pearl,* found with the *Sir Gawain* manuscript. The Pearl Poet is thought to have written four poems, *Pearl, Purity, Patience,* and *Sir Gawain and the Green Knight.* The poems were probably written around 1370, which would make the poet a contemporary of Geoffrey Chaucer. Although The Pearl Poet did not live in London, the center of England's cultural activities at the time, his narrative technique demonstrates a sophistication equal to that of his London peers.

About the SELECTION

Many medieval writings dealt with the legend of King Arthur and the knights of the Round Table. ***Sir Gawain and the Green Knight*** stands out from other writing of its time because it is the only story that interweaves two common plot devices—the beheading contest and the moral temptation of a knight by a lady. The following selection is a modern English prose translation; the original poem was written in a West Highland dialect, very different from that used in London and very difficult for modern readers to understand without special training.

Literary TOOLS

ARTHURIAN ROMANCE. **Arthurian romances** are stories of the exploits of the legendary King Arthur and his knights of the Round Table. Most romances involving the King Arthur legend center on a knight's adventures *or* his loves. Notice how *Sir Gawain and the Green Knight* combines the two plot types.

CHIVALRY. **Chivalry** was the code of conduct of the medieval knight. According to the code of chivalry, a knight was to be a perfect exemplar of such virtues as bravery, courage, courtesy, honesty, faith, and gentleness. As you read, keep a chart of ways in which the Green Knight honors the virtues of chivalry.

Virtue	Example
bravery	demonstrates in his challenge
courage	
courtesy	
honesty	
faith	
gentleness	

Reader's Journal

Write about a time when you attempted to do something that seemed impossible or frightening.

ADDITIONAL RESOURCES

UNIT 3 RESOURCE BOOK
- Selection Worksheet 3.4
- Selection Check Test 4.3.9
- Selection Test 4.3.10
- Language, Grammar, and Style Resource 3.80
- Study and Research Resource 5.50

READER'S JOURNAL

This activity and, indeed, the Gawain story itself provide excellent opportunities for discussing the foolhardiness of taking risks because of dares. Discuss the difference between taking a foolish dare and accepting a worthwhile challenge. Have students provide examples of each.

GRAPHIC ORGANIZER

courage—demonstrates in his challenge
courtesy—demonstrates as the host
honesty—does not demonstrate this virtue because he fails to Gawain who he really is
faith—does not demonstrate this virtue because he fails to Gawain who he really is
gentleness—demonstrates in the way he deals with Gawain when they meet again

GOALS/OBJECTIVES

Studying this lesson will enable students to
- empathize with Gawain's difficulties
- explain the code of chivalry and identify the virtues that are part of that code
- define Arthurian romance and give examples of the two main types of situations found in the plots of those romances
- identify gerunds
- answer synonym and antonym questions

INDIVIDUAL LEARNING STRATEGIES

MOTIVATION
Send students to the library to do research on knights—their armor, weapons, codes of conduct, methods of fighting, tournaments, and so on. Have them share with one another what they learn from their research. Of particular interest to students will be any photographs or illustrations that they can find illustrating the armor and weapons of knights.

READING PROFICIENCY
Students should read through the Prereading page before they begin the selection. Also have students look over the vocabulary words. For the words they don't know, ask them to read through the definition and come up with their own contextual sentence.

ENGLISH LANGUAGE LEARNING
Give students the following additional vocabulary words:

clutch—grip
unwary—unsuspecting; unaware
mirth—happiness
revel—a good time; a feast
celebrants—people who celebrate, or have a good time in honor of something
prowess—strength; power
bard—one who tells stories through song
apparition—something that comes unexpectedly; a ghost
tunic—loose article of clothing worn over the upper body
banish—throw out; exile
honed—sharpened
deem—think; believe

SPECIAL NEEDS
Students will benefit from listening to the selection using the Audio Library. Students should focus on Guided Reading questions and the Recall questions in the Investigate, Inquire, and Imagine section.

ENRICHMENT

After reading the selection, students can analyze the value system of chivalry and compare it to the value systems they see in the contemporary world.

Sir Gawain and the Green Knight

THE PEARL POET,
TRANSLATED BY Y. R. PONSOR

Sir Gawain Beheads the Green Knight, c.1300s. English artist. British Library, London.

CHAPTER 1

Winter lay upon the land. Cold held forest and field in its grim clutch, and in the night sky the stars glittered like gems. The wolf slid from shadow to shadow, stalking hapless prey, falling upon the unwary with death in his fangs. Deep in caverns, the great trolls and other monsters mumbled in uneasy sleep, seeking warmth. Over moor and fen[1] the mists rose and fell, and strange sounds troubled the chill silence.

But on the hill, lights gleamed in the castle. In the court of Camelot were gathered all the brothers-in-arms of the Table Round and their fair highborn ladies to celebrate the Christmas season. A full fifteen days it was then, a time of merriment and mirth and rich revel. Laughter rang loud through the halls, and all the music and delight that the mind of man might devise. With merrymaking and glee the company welcomed the New Year, exchanging gifts and calling out glad Noel.

On this New Year's day, fresh and crisp-cold, twice the usual number of celebrants crowded the great hall; and the most noble, the fairest, and most famous was Arthur himself, the most honorable man who ever ruled a court or led an army into battle. This king was a man of the greatest good will and generosity of soul, and it would be difficult to imagine a bolder company than that one gathered in the castle on the hill.

Among the group on the high dais, facing the great hall lined with tables of noble knights, was

1. **fen.** Marshy bog; swampy land

WORDS FOR EVERYDAY USE

hap • less (hap´lis) *adj.*, unfortunate; unlucky. *The hapless hockey player crashed into the goalie.*
da • is (dā´is) *n.*, raised platform. *The speakers at the conference sat on a dais at the front of the room.*

Guenevere, Arthur's wife, the comeliest maid, the gracious lady of the gleaming gray eyes. Her silken garments sparkled with rich jewels, and her golden hair shone as softly as her eyes. With her sat the young Gawain, with Agravaine the Stronghand on the other side; both were the king's nephews and worthy knights who had proved their prowess many times in test and trial. At the head of the table sat the chief of all bishops in Cornwall, the saintly Bedwin, and with him, Urien's son Iwain.

But Arthur, full of his own happiness and childlike in his joy, would not sit until all were served. For most of all he loved life, its joys and its adventures, and his eager brain and young blood would not allow him to lie abed or sit around lazily. And besides, he had taken upon himself a vow that on this special day of all days, he would not eat until a rare tale of ancestors and arms and high adventure were told, or some grand marvel might be devised, or a challenge of knights to join in jeopardy, jousting life for life as fortune might favor. So he stood before the high table, speaking of trifles and laughing at the noise and fine festival of his free men as the first course was announced with the crackling of trumpets, with drums and tuneful pipers. In the corner a bard awakened the lute and many a heart lifted with his touch upon the strings. Then came the platters piled high with fine food, venison and other meats, and great bowls of soup, and plenty of strong beer and fine red wine. And all drank and ate as much as they wanted.

Hardly had the first course been finished when the great hall door crashed open and in rode a terrifying knight. He must have been the hugest man on earth, so broad and thick from neck to waist, so long of leg and strong of arm that I half thought him a giant, except for his fine features of face. Everyone knows that giants are hideous to look upon, besides being fearful in size. At sight of him, all in the hall fell silent, struck dumb by this apparition. For this bold man, from toe to top, in clothes and in countenance, was bright green.

Who interrupted the feast? What was strange about this person?

Believe me: all garbed in green, this man, and all his trappings. He wore a tight coat with a heavy mantle adorned with ermine, the same fur lining the hood that had fallen from his head and lay upon his shoulders. Green were the stockings on his legs, and decorated with gold embroidery, and bright golden spurs on his feet, and shoes with upturned toes. His belt was set with gleaming jewels, all emerald green, and indeed they were scattered over all his array and that of his horse, the saddle and bridle and reins, all gaudy in gold and green. The trappings of the horse, the breast-cloth and bits and bridle, even the stirrups in which he stood, all were enameled and gleamed goldenly, and the green gems glittered like the eyes of a cat. The steed itself which he straddled was a great heavy horse, hard to hold; and it was the same green as the man who rode it.

Gloriously was this man outfitted in green, and the hair of his head as green as his horse. It fanned out full and fell to his shoulders, and he had a heavy beard which reached his chest. It gleamed green upon the leather tunic. Such a pair had never before been seen on earth, nor since that time! Everyone said he looked as bright as a flash of lightning, and, indeed, who could withstand his stroke! He wore neither helm nor hauberk[2]—no, no coat of mail did he wear, nor want!—and he carried no weapons,

2. **hauberk.** A tunic made of joined metal links

WORDS FOR EVERYDAY USE

come • li • est (kum´lē est) *adj.,* most attractive. *The comeliest of the heroines of Greek myth was Helen of Troy.*

coun • te • nance (kown´ tə nəns) *n.,* appearance. *When the police officer in the car behind us turned on his lights, my companion's countenance changed from joy to despair.*

ANSWER TO GUIDED READING QUESTION

1. The feast was interrupted by a knight on horseback. He was gigantic and green from toe to head.

LITERARY TECHNIQUE

TRANSLATION. Translation is the art of rendering speech into another language. Explain that this is a loose prose translation into Modern English of a Middle English poem. You may wish to have students compare this prose translation to the closer, line-by-line verse translation of *Sir Gawain and the Green Knight.* Trans. Brian Stone. New York: Penguin.

LITERARY NOTE

THE GAWAIN LEGEND. *Gawain* translator Brian Stone explains that Gawain may have been derived from a pre-Arthurian Welsh hero named Gwalchmai. Gawain was the hero of early versions of the Grail legend and was in early stories the owner of the sword Excalibur. Stories about the exploits of Gawain became quite popular in England. In one of these stories, Gawain marries a hag to save the life of King Arthur, only to have her become transformed into a beautiful woman. Gawain is one of the most written about figures in Arthurian legend; hence, his character is also one of the most fluid. He ranges, depending on the source, from a virtuous and perfect embodiment of chivalry to a somewhat philandering low comic character. In the story of the Green Knight, Gawain is portrayed at his most human, as his faults are fully revealed along with his strengths.

VOCABULARY FROM THE SELECTION

amiably	covenant	respite
beguile	dais	smite
betide	entreat	sunder
burnish	hapless	transgress
comeliest	intrigue	treachery
countenance	mortification	vanquish

ANSWERS TO GUIDED READING QUESTIONS

1. The knight carries a bough of holly and an ax. Student answers to the question about why he carries these objects will vary. Encourage them to speculate. The bough of holly, being green, is consistent with the rest of the knight's appearance. (Note: This knight and, indeed, the entire tale, probably owes its existence to fertility myths that preceded it. Explain to your students that in ancient days many peoples in Europe worshiped fertility gods associated with evergreens like the holly.) The presence of the ax suggests that the knight intends some violence.
2. The text says that green is a magic color. The people at the feast thought that he was a phantom or fey creature. (Note that the color green has associations with spring and the rebirth of the seasons, which was considered magical by early peoples. See the note on fertility myths above.)

LITERARY/HISTORICAL NOTE

Explain to your students that *Sir Gawain and the Green Knight* provides an excellent example of the code of chivalry by which knights lived. **Chivalry** was the code of conduct of the medieval knight. The word derives from the French cheval, for "horse," indicating the importance of this animal to the knight, who typically traveled and fought on horseback. According to the code of chivalry, a knight was to be a loyal servant to his lord or lady and a perfect exemplar of such virtues as bravery, courage, courtesy, honesty, faith, and gentleness. Medieval romances like *Sir Gawain and the Green Knight* typically present a series of tests (trials or quests) of these knightly virtues. In this story, Gawain fails in one small respect with regard to the virtue of keeping good faith. However, in other ways he proves himself to be an exemplar of knightly virtue.

What two things does the knight carry? Why might he have each of these things?

neither spear nor shield to smite or to save. But in his hand he carried a bough of holly, that branch which is greenest when all others are bare; and in his other hand an ax, heavy and horrid, a cruel weapon right out of a nightmare. The head measured at least an arm's length, and was of green steel worked with gold, the bit burnished bright, the broad edge honed to shear as closely as a sharp razor. The steel of the haft[3] which he held in his hand was wrapped with iron wire to its very end, graven with green in delicate design. A thong bound it about and fastened at the head where it was tasseled and braided with bright green.

This knight moved through the great hall's silent crowd right up the high table, and he feared no danger, greeted no one, but looked straight ahead. Then he reined in his horse and faced the room. He stared boldly at the knights, looking them up and down, and his voice thundered when he spoke.

"Where is the leader of this company? I would like to see him and to speak in courtesy with him, as the rules of chivalry require."

He waited and looked at them and considered who might among this company be the most renowned.

Everyone stared at him in wonder, marveling as to what his appearance might mean, how such a knight and such a horse might be such a strange color, green as growing grass, and glowing with enamel and gold. Everyone studied him as he sat there on his horse, and they walked cautiously around him with all the wonder in the world as to what he might do. Many strange things had they seen, but never any such as this. Possibly a phantom, or some fey[4] creature, they deemed him to be, for green is a magic color. But all of these brave knights feared to question him and, stunned at his voice, were dumbstruck. A heavy silence filled the royal chamber, and all those who had been chattering sat as if caught in a dream—some, I suppose, out of politeness, some out of uneasiness, and some in fear, but let another man decide which!

What was special about his color? What did it make the people think of him?

Then Arthur, standing before the dais, greeted him, and bowed courteously, for he was never rude, and said,

"Fair knight, welcome to this place. I am Arthur, the chief of this company. Alight and rest, I beg you, and whatsoever your will may be, we shall be glad to learn."

"No, God is my witness that to waste time in idle talk is not my errand," replied the knight. "But your fame, lord, is raised high, and through town and countryside you are regarded as the best and bravest ever to ride in battle gear, the noblest and the finest of the world's kind. You are all known to be valiant in dealing with all sorts of adventures, and your hall is known for courtliness. Many tales of this company have reached my ears, and that is what has brought me hither at this special time."

"You may see by this branch which I bear here that I have come in peace, seeking no trouble; for had I fared forth in a frame of mind to fight, I would have brought helm and hauberk,[5] and shield and bright-shining spear, and other weapons to wield also. But because I seek no strife, I am dressed as you see. But if you are as brave as everyone says, you will gladly grant me the game that I ask as a guest's right."

And Arthur answered, "Gentle knight, if you crave combat, you will not fail to find it here."

3. **haft.** Hilt of a knife
4. **fey.** Magical, enchanted
5. **hauberk.** Tunic of chain mail worn as defensive armor

WORDS FOR EVERYDAY USE

smite (smīt) *vt.,* inflict a heavy blow. *A sumo wrestler is not allowed to smite his opponents.*

bur • nish (bur´nish) *vt.,* make smooth and shiny by rubbing. *We had to burnish the silver before the wedding banquet.*

"No, I seek no contest, as I have told you, especially since I see on these benches only beardless children! If I were geared up for fighting and mounted on my high steed there is no man here who could match me." And he looked upon them with scorn. "I seek in this court only a Christmas game, for it is Yule and the New Year, and the time to exchange gifts. If there should be any in this hall who considers himself brave enough in heart, hot enough in blood, or quick enough of wit that he would dare exchange stroke for stroke with me, let him come forth. I will give him as my gift this fine heavy ax—heavy enough it is to do his will!—and I shall take the first blow as bare as here I sit. If any of these fine warriors may be so bold as to accept my challenge, let him step forth and seize this weapon. I quitclaim it forever, and he may keep it as his own, and I shall kneel before him and stand him a stroke. And then you will grant me the right to deal him an equal blow, though I will give him respite of a year and a day. Now let any man who so dares speak quickly."

What game does the knight suggest? Why is it likely that his plan will be accepted?

CHAPTER 2

If the people had been astonished at first, now they all, high and low throughout the hall, sat as if turned to stone. The knight on his steed twisted in the saddle, his red eyes flashing around the room, his green hair flying with each movement of his head. Then he sat still, staring at them and stroking his beard as the silence lengthened. When no one spoke, he stood in his stirrups and, shaking his fist above his head, he shouted at them.

"What is this? Is this Arthur's court and castle, of which the whole world sings praises? Where now is your pride? Where is your fighting spirit? Where now your fierceness and fame and all your fine words? Now is the reputation and glory of the Round Table overthrown by the mere words of one man, without a single blow being struck, because you are afraid to answer!"

Then the blood shot for shame into Arthur's face, and he turned as angry as a stormwind, as indeed did all of them. Men muttered and surged forward in anger, half-rising from their places, white with wrath. But Arthur held up his hand and sprang to face the green man.

"Sir, by heaven! Seek no further! As you in your own folly have asked, so shall it be! No man here is afraid of your boasts. Give me your ax, and with God's help, I shall break every bone in your body. I myself accept your challenge and will meet your terms."

The Green Knight laughed aloud and leaped lightly from his horse and landed before Arthur, taller by head and shoulders than any man in the court. The king seized the ax and gripped the handle tightly and waved it about, striking this way and that to test its feel. The knight calmly removed his mantle and then his short coat, no more dismayed by the threatening blows than if some man had brought him a glass of wine.

Then Gawain, who sat by the queen, called out, "I beseech you, uncle, to grant me a kindness. Let this contest be mine. Gentle lord, give me permission to leave this table and stand in your place there. If I may without discourtesy—if my liege[6] lady will not take it amiss—I would presume to counsel you before your royal court." He stood up and spoke clearly. "I think it is not seemly that such a challenge should be raised in this high chamber, much less that you yourself should so valiantly choose to answer it,

6. **liege.** One to whom loyalty is given

WORDS FOR EVERYDAY USE

res • pite (res´pit) *n.,* short interval of rest or delay. *The editors worked without respite until the project was done.*

ANSWER TO GUIDED READING QUESTION

1. The knight suggests that one of the assembled knights deal him a blow with the ax and that he will return the favor, dealing the knight an equal blow, in a year and a day. It is likely that the knight's plan will be accepted because he has challenged the courage of Arthur's knights. Also, one would expect that the blow dealt to the Green Knight would kill him, thereby saving the Green Knight's challenger from any possible harm.

LITERARY NOTE

Most medieval romances are little more than loosely connected episodes relating various adventures experienced by one or more knights. *Sir Gawain and the Green Knight* is exceptional in not being episodic but rather being a coherent, sustained narrative that works out a single story line.

In many medieval romances, the fact that the adventures are had by a single knight is one of the few connections between episodes. The adventures usually take the form of a trial of the knight's virtues—his courage, strength, bravery, faithfulness, and so on. Some adventures, like the one described in *Gawain,* involve challenges (often challenges to combat). Many involve trials, or quests, undertaken to find or accomplish something (to locate the Holy Grail, to slay a dragon, to rescue a maiden, for example).

ANSWER TO GUIDED READING QUESTION

1. Gawain says that he is the least brave and least intelligent of the company and that the only worthy thing about him is that he is of Arthur's blood. He makes this speech out of extreme modesty, a chivalric virtue.

ADDITIONAL QUESTIONS AND ACTIVITIES

Ask students why they think Gawain beseeches Arthur to let him respond to the challenge. What does this action say about Gawain? Ask students if they would stand in for a friend in the case of a challenge.

CROSS-CURRICULAR CONNECTION

ORAL TRADITION. Explain to your students that *Sir Gawain and the Green Knight* contains fantastic elements from the oral tradition. Chief among these is the Green Knight himself, a fertility figure with the fantastic ability to live even after his head has been cut off. Have students share stories that they know from the oral traditions in their communities. Many will know stories about fantastic creatures—ghosts, fairies, goblins, and monsters—stories that they heard as children.

while so many brave warriors remain on these benches. No better men can be found on any field of battle, nor any more skillful in arms. All men know that I am the least brave, and the feeblest of wit, and the least deserving to be of this company. In truth, it is only because I am your nephew that I am worthy at all; I know no bounty but your blood in my body. And since this business is so foolish and trivial, none of it should concern you at all.

What does Gawain say about himself? Why does he make this speech?

"So I ask: Let it come to me, and if I fail in its performance, then the fault is in me and no blame shall fall on this court."

Arthur moved from table to table consulting with his nobles, as is the custom in such cases, and all agreed that the king should retire from the contest and give Gawain the game.

Gawain turned and bowed to the gray-eyed Guenevere, and she smiled on him, and he came down from the dais and, kneeling before his king, he received the ax from Arthur's hands. And Arthur smiled affectionately upon him and raised his hand and asked God's blessing, praying that both Gawain's heart and his hand should be strong.

"Be careful, nephew," he said softly, "and set yourself for the stroke. If you direct it properly, I am sure that you will be able to bear the burden of the blow which he will later inflict." And Arthur removed himself and went and leaned against the edge of the dais and watched eagerly.

Gawain walked, ax in hand, to the Green Knight, who had been waiting patiently. He looked upon Gawain and he said, "Now, let us reaffirm our bargain before we go on. But first I would ask you, sir, what is your name?"

"I am Gawain," the young man said. "It is Gawain who gives you this blow, whatever may happen afterwards. One year from now, you may return the favor with whatever weapon you wish, asking leave of no one else."

"By God," shouted the other, "it pleases me greatly that I should receive this blow from your hands. You have rightly repeated the covenant which I made with your king —except that you must seek me, friend, wheresoever you think I may be found, pledging to come alone, and return to me such wages as you deal to me today before this court."

"And where shall I look for you? Where is your home? I know neither your kingdom nor your name, kith nor kin. Tell me your realm and name and I shall certainly find you. That I swear on my honor."

"No," said the green man, "nothing more is necessary now. But I promise that when I have taken your blow, if you strike squarely, then I will tell you how to find me so that you may fulfill our bargain."

Then he laughed.

"If I do not speak, then so much the better for you; you can stay in your own land and light no wayfarer's fires. But enough! Take up your weapon and let us see how you handle an ax!"

"Sir," said Gawain, "I will," and he stroked the edge of the ax.

The Green Knight knelt on the floor and bent his head and gathered his long, thick hair in one hand and drew it over the crown of his head. His bare neck shone whitely. Gawain set himself, left foot forward on the floor. He grasped the ax and lifted it aloft, and he brought it down like a lightning bolt upon the bare neck. The sharp steel sliced through the pale flesh and sundered the bones and sheared it in half, and the steel blade buried itself in the floor with a great ringing crash.

The fair head flew from the shoulders and rolled about near the tables, and some of the knights kicked at it with their feet, a grim, grisly game. Blood burst from the body, red gleaming on

WORDS FOR EVERYDAY USE

cov • e • nant (kuv´ə nənt) *n.*, binding agreement. *The kings made a covenant never again to take arms against one another.*

sun • der (sun´dər) *vt.*, break apart; separate. *The bolt of lightning sundered the tree, splitting its trunk in two.*

green. The knight did not falter or fall, but at once he sprang up on his strong legs and jumped into the crowd and snatched up his head by the hair and lifted it high for all to see. Then, striding to his horse, he caught up the reins, stepped into the stirrups and sat aloft, still holding his head high in one hand.

What happened after the knight was beheaded?

And they say that he sat in his saddle as though nothing whatever ailed him, headless though he was. He twisted from side to side, turning that hideous, still-bleeding body in the saddle. Those who watched in fear were even more horrified to see that he was about to speak.

He turned the grim face toward the high table, and the head lifted up its eyelids and looked at them. Then it looked at Gawain, and the mouth moved, and the lips spoke.

"Look to it, Gawain, that you do as you have sworn, and seek faithfully until you find me. All men know me as the knight of the Green Chapel. To the Green Chapel you must come, I charge you, to receive such a blow as you have dealt here to me today. You will find me if you try. If you fail to come, coward shall you be called by the whole world."

What must Gawain do?

With a quick movement he pulled his horse around and fled through the great door, still head-in-hand, and the fire from the hooves of his flint-shod steed flashed through the hall. What native land he would return to, none there knew, any more than they knew from whence he had come. In a moment a roar of astonishment filled the hall, and Arthur and Gawain burst into laughter at the strange event. All agreed that it had been a marvel among men.

Although Arthur, ever the wise king, had a great uneasiness in his heart, he did not let a hint of it be seen, but he spoke to his queen with courtly speech.

"Dearest lady, let not today dismay you. Often such a magic and wondrous event occurs at this season, along with the music of minstrels and the laughter of lovely ladies and brave knights."

And he touched her hand gently and gazed into her eyes. Then he sat back, looked around the room, and cried out, "Now at last I may address myself to my dinner, for I have certainly seen a marvel, I must admit."

He smiled at Gawain with love shining on his fair face and he said, "Hang up your ax, nephew, it has done its work for today." And it was placed on the wall above the high table where all might admire and wonder at the sight and the strange adventure. Then they sat down again at the tables, each to his place, king and knights, and the servants brought double portions of all the best dishes and with all manner of good will they passed the rest of the evening.

But be sure, Sir Gawain, that fear does not cause you to fail in this test, this challenge which you yourself have taken into your own hands!

Summary of Chapters 2–10: *True to his word, Gawain sets out after a year to find the Green Knight. Coming to the country where the Knight of the Green Chapel lives, Gawain finds lodging with a friendly lord. Each day the lord goes hunting, leaving his wife alone with Gawain. On the very first day, the wife of the lord approaches Gawain romantically. At the end of that day, the lord gives Gawain a deer and Gawain gives the lord a kiss, for the two have agreed beforehand to trade whatever they have gained during the day. At the end of the second day, the lord gives Gawain the head of a boar and Gawain gives the lord two kisses. On the third day, the lady gives Gawain a green scarf, saying that it will keep him from harm. At the end of that day, the lord gives Gawain a fox, and Gawain gives the lord three kisses. However, Gawain keeps the scarf. This is a violation of the code of chivalry, which requires a knight to keep faith, or be true to his word.*

The following day, Gawain keeps his promised appointment with the Green Knight. With a sharp blade, the Green Knight feigns a stroke in the direction of Gawain's neck. Gawain flinches, and the Green Knight reproves him for coward liness. When the

ANSWERS TO GUIDED READING QUESTIONS

1. The knight did not falter or fall. Instead, he sprang up, grabbed his head, and held it up for all to see. Then he climbed back on his horse, still holding the head up.
2. Gawain must find the knight in a year and a day at the Green Chapel and submit to a blow like that received by the Green Knight. Gawain, being an ordinary man, would be killed by such a blow.

CROSS-CURRICULAR ACTIVITIES

ARTS AND HUMANITIES. The descriptions of the knight are detailed and full of vivid colors. Students can create their own depictions of the knight before and after he was beheaded.

ADDITIONAL QUESTIONS AND ACTIVITIES

1. What is interesting about the scarf given to Gawain?
2. What does this color mean?
3. What do you think the significance of the scarf is?

Answers

1. The scarf is magic and will keep Gawain from harm.
2. The scarf is the color of the Green Knight.
3. Have students make predictions about the significance of the scarf. They should check their predictions as they read.

ANSWER TO GUIDED READING QUESTION

1. Gawain did not give the lord the green scarf that he received from the lord's wife, despite the promise that he made to the lord to exchange whatever the two had gained during each day.

LITERARY NOTE

Sir Gawain and the Green Knight was originally written in alliterative verse. While most of the alliteration has been lost in this prose translation, a fine example exists in the lines "Cursed be both cowardice and covetousness! In them is villainy and vice that destroys virtue!"

Green Knight tries again, Gawain does not flinch. However, the knight again stops short of dealing a blow to Gawain. On the third try, the Green Knight inflicts a scratch, but no more, on Gawain's neck.

CHAPTER 11

The Green Knight turned from him and leaned upon his ax, set the shaft to the ground and leaned upon the blade and looked at the lad who waited there. How steadfast, how fearless, and how bold he looked, how ready for battle! And he was pleased in his heart. He laughed with a ringing voice and spoke happily with the lad.

"Bold knight, upon this field of honor be not so fierce! No man here has used you dishonorably, nor treated you discourteously, but only as the decree at Arthur's court allowed. I owed you a stroke and you took it, so hold yourself well paid. I release you of any remnant of all other rights. If I had been more nimble, perhaps I could have wrought you a more harmful blow. First, I merely menaced you with a pretended blow and cut you with no cruel blade. That was for the agreement we made on that first night when you faithfully gave me the day's gains, as an honest man would. That second pretended blow was for the second day when you kissed my dear wife, which kisses you gave to me. And for both of those I offered you but two scant blows without scathe.[7] For an honorable man is true to his word and he needs fear no danger.

"But on the third day you failed in that honor, and therefore you took that tap on the neck."

He looked at Gawain steadily, and Gawain at him, still as stone. And the green man continued.

"It is my garment you wear, that green silken girdle. My own wife offered it to you, I know. Ah, I know all about those kisses and your character also, and the wooing of my wife! I wrought all this myself. I sent her to test you. Truly I think that you must be the most faultless man that ever walked the earth. As a pearl in purity is to white peas, so is Gawain in virtue to all famous knights. But you fell short a little there, sir; you failed in faith. But it was not for intrigue, nor for lawless lust either, but because you loved your life, and I cannot blame you for that."

Gawain still stood like one stunned, so aggrieved with embarrassment that he cried for anguish inside. All the blood of his body burned in his face and he shrank for shame as the green man talked. He took off his helm and held it in his hands. At last he spoke wrathfully.

How did Gawain fail in his honor?

"Cursed be both cowardice and covetousness! In them is villainy and vice that destroys virtue!" And he caught up the pentangle[8] and tore it loose and flung it roughly down. "Lo!—there is breaking of faith. Foul be its fall! I coveted my life and cowardice led me into fault for fear of your blow, made me forsake my nature, the generosity and loyalty that are a true knight's." And he bowed his head and wept bitterly. "Now am I false indeed and from fear have I fallen into treachery and deceit. Both bring only sorrow and shame. I confess to you, sir, here on this spot, that I have indeed been false to you in my conduct. If you will but allow me to regain your good will, I shall guard against its happening again."

Then the Green Knight laughed and said amiably: "I consider it entirely acquitted, any harm that I had. You have confessed freely and are aware of your failing and you have stood the sharp penance of my sword. I hold you cleansed

7. **scathe.** Injury or harm
8. **pentangle.** Helmet

WORDS FOR EVERYDAY USE

in •trigue (in trēg´) *n.,* plotting or scheming. *The spy's life was one of continual intrigue.*
treach • er • y (trech´ər ē) *n.,* betrayal of trust. *Telling the secrets of a friend is a form of treachery.*

of that fault and made as pure as if you had never transgressed since your birth. And I give you, sir, as a gift, that very scarf, as green as my own robe." He touched the silk at Gawain's waist lightly, and laid an arm across his shoulders.

"Sir Gawain, you may think upon this particular contest as you fare forth among the great and chivalrous knights of this world. Let this be the clear token of the adventure of the Green Chapel." Then he laughed and said merrily, "Now, you shall in this New Year come back again to my dwelling and we shall revel away the remainder of this festal time. With my wife, I promise, we shall certainly reconcile you, she who you thought was your keen enemy."

"No," said Gawain, and he took up his helm and looked sadly at the green man. "This has been a sorrowful journey. Good fortune betide you, and may He who ordains all honor grant it to you! And commend me to that gracious lady, your comely companion, and the other lady, both the honored ladies who so cunningly beguiled this knight with their tricks.

"It is no great marvel to be made a fool of or to be won to sorrow through the wiles of a woman; for so was Adam, the first man on earth beguiled; and Solomon by many and various women; and Samson also, Delilah dealt him his wyrd![9] David was deluded by Bathsheba and suffered much woe. All these men were brought to disaster by woman's wiles.

"It would be a great gain to love them and yet to believe them not. But no man can do that. For these were the noblest men of old, all blessed above other men and yet they were all beguiled by women with whom they had dealings. To find myself in that company I think must be excused." Then he shook off sad thoughts.

"But your girdle I will accept with a right good will, not for the bright gold, nor for its magic—" here Gawain blushed again—"nor for the silk or fringed sides, nay, not for worth nor worship nor noble works. But as a symbol of my transgression I shall keep it always with me, a reminder, when I ride in renown, of the fault and frailty of feeble flesh, how susceptible it is to the stains of evil. And when pride of prowess inflates me, the sight of this will humble my heart.

"But one request I make, if it does not displease you: Since you are the lord of that land where I stayed with such pleasure, thanks to you, will you tell me your name? Only that and no more?"

Why does Gawain keep the green girdle?

"That I shall, certainly," replied the green man. "I am called Bercilak de Hautdesert in this land. Through the power of Morgan le Fay;[10] who lives in my house and has the skill of magical lore, all of this has happened. Morgan, the beautiful, the mistress of Merlin—many men has she taken, for she has had love dealings with that excellent wizard who knows all the knights of your court. Morgan the goddess is also her name. There is none so high in power or pride that she cannot tame!

"She sent me in that manner to your royal court in order to test the pride of its men, to see if the reputation of the Round Table were true. She sent me in that strange way to take away your wits and to frighten the fair Guenevere, to make her die with fear at the sight of that man who spoke with his head in his hand before that

9. **wyrd.** Fate
10. **Morgan le Fay.** The fairy half-sister of King Arthur

WORDS FOR EVERYDAY USE

a • mi • a • bly (ā´ mē ə blē) *adv.*, in a pleasant and friendly manner. *The schoolboy amiably held the door for the principal.*
trans • gress (trans gres´) *vi.*, overstep or break a law. *After Jeremy transgressed, he felt guilty.*
be • tide (bē tīd) *vi.*, happen to. *The silly romance novel ended with the line, "May such happiness as I described herein betide all true men and women."*
be • guile (bē gīl´) *vt.*, mislead by tricking. *Did the deceptive advertisement beguile you into buying the product?*

ANSWER TO GUIDED READING QUESTION

1. Gawain keeps the green girdle, or scarf, as a reminder of his sin of covetousness. This reminder will keep him from becoming too proud. Pride was considered by medieval men and women to be one of the seven deadly sins.

LITERARY NOTE

In Arthurian legend, **Morgan le Fay** was Arthur's half-sister and the Queen of Avalon. Her attitude toward Arthur remains inconstant as she tries to kill him through her lover Sir Accolon, but later spirits him away to cure his wounds after his battle with Mordred. In this story, Morgan is responsible for the planning and undertaking of the Green Knight and his beheading game.

SELECTION CHECK TEST 4.3.9 WITH ANSWERS

1. What does Gawain do to the Green Knight? **He beheads him.**
2. What gift from the lord's wife does Gawain keep for himself? **He keeps a scarf.**
3. Whose magic created this scenario? **Morgan le Fay was responsible.**
4. What does Gawain regard the scar on his neck as a sign of? **He considers it a sign of his disloyalty to the Green Knight.**
5. What do the knights of the Round Table agree to wear? **They wear green scarves.**

Vocabulary in Context
Fill each blank with the most appropriate word from the Words for Everyday Use. You may have to change the tense of the word.

hapless respite sunder scathe
amiably transgress betide

1. The hostess gave the toast, asking that good fortune **betide** everyone present.
2. Marshall **amiably** gave up his seat to a woman standing on the bus.
3. Spring break offered a welcome **respite** from rising early every morning.
4. The chef expertly **sundered** the bread into smaller pieces before preparing the filling.
5. Our team's **hapless** catcher is forever getting hit with the ball.

SELECTION CHECK TEST 4.3.9 WITH ANSWERS (CONT.)

Literary Tools
1. What is *chivalry?* **Chivalry is the code of conduct of the medieval knight.**
2. What is an Arthurian Romance? **An Arthurian Romance is a story of the adventures of King Arthur and his knights of the Round Table.**
3. Name one virtue held by Gawain. Explain your choice. **Responses will vary.**

ANSWER TO GUIDED READING QUESTION

1. Morgan le Fay sent the Green Knight to test the knights of the Round Table to see if their reputation for chivalry was deserved, and to try to kill Guenevere from fright.

ANSWERS TO INVESTIGATE, INQUIRE, IMAGINE

Recall

1a. The Green Knight offers the challenge of an exchange of blows. Gawain accepts the challenge. The Green Knight's head is severed as a result.

2a. Gawain stays with the lord's wife while the lord goes out hunting. Gawain and the lord make a pact to share whatever each gets during the day.

3a. Gawain is nicked on the neck by the knight. Gawain realizes he has fallen prey to the sins of covetousness and cowardice. He keeps the green belt, or girdle, as a reminder of his weakness.

Interpret

1b. The Green Knight claims he seeks no contest, and he calls the knights "beardless children." He warns Gawain that if the agreement is not kept, Gawain shall be known the world over as a coward.

2b. Gawain's actions reveal that the knights' moral code values courage and despises covetousness. His actions also show how difficult it is to live a flawless life.

3b. Gawain wants to remember his meeting with the Green Knight so he will behave more virtuously in the future.

Analyze

4a. *Responses will vary.* The knight is green. He continues to live although his head is cut off. The lord Gawain encounters is really the knight.

Synthesize

4b. *Responses will vary.* These elements add to the romance and to the challenge Gawain faces. The magical elements are part of the legendary nature of these stories.

Evaluate

5a. *Responses will vary.* Gawain did judge himself too harshly because he had lived up to most of his ideals and he seemed to have learned from his mistake. Also, others were willing to forgive him for what he had done.

Table High. She took the form of that old one in my house, the ancient lady; she is in fact your aunt, the half-sister of Arthur, daughter of the Duchess of Tintagel, that lady upon whom the mighty Uther later fathered Arthur, who is your king.

Why did Morgan le Fay arrange this event?

"Therefore I entreat you, dear man, to come to your aunt and rejoice in my house. My court loves you, and I do as well, indeed, as any man under heaven."

But Gawain still refused. He would not under any conditions. So they embraced in friendship and saluted each other as fine princes and parted right there in the cold. Gawain, mounted on his fine horse, hastened homeward to Arthur's court and the Green Knight wended wheresoever he would.

Gawain rode then through many wild ways in the world on Gringolet. He had been given back his life, a fine gift indeed, and many a thought he gave to that strange event as he traveled. Sometimes he harbored in a house and sometimes out of doors. He had many adventures in the valley and he vanquished many, but I will not take time to tell all that in this tale.

The wound in his neck healed and he wore the green belt fastened like a baldric[11] at his side, tied under his left arm, the end in a knot, as token of the fact that he was guilty of sin. And thus at last he came to the court, did Gawain the good knight.

Happiness sped through those halls when it was learned that Gawain had returned. Everyone thought it was a fine thing, indeed, and somewhat unlooked for. The king kissed the knight and the queen did also, and many knights sought him out to salute him and make inquiry of his wayfaring fortune. And he told the wondrous tale and confessed everything that had happened, the adventure at the chapel, the good will of the green man, the love of the lady, and the silk that he wore. He showed them the scar that he bore on his neck, the sign of his shameful disloyalty to the green man. He suffered when he told them and groaned with grief and mortification, and the blood burned in his face for shame when he spoke of it.

"Lo, lord," said Gawain to Arthur, as he held forth the silk, "here is the band of blame which I bear like the scar on my neck. This is the offense and the loss, the cowardice and covetousness that caught me there. This is the symbol of falsity in which I was taken. I will wear it all my life, for no one may hide his misdeed, nor may he undo it. Once guilt has touched a man, he is never free of it again."

And the king comforted the knight and all the court laughed and lovingly agreed on the spot that each man of the Table Round should henceforth wear such a baldric, the slanting ribbon of bright green, for the sake of that beloved man, and they would wear it with delight. And so it came to be accorded as the renown of the court and always afterward anyone who wore it was especially honored.

So in Arthur's day this adventure occurred, as books of romance will witness. Many strange and curious wonders have happened in Britain since the days of Brutus whose race came from Troy. But surely this tale of Gawain and his contest with the Green Knight in a trial of honor and faith is one of the most wondrous. ■

11. **baldric.** A belt worn over the shoulder and chest to support a sword

Words for Everyday Use

en • treat (en trēt´) *vt.*, ask earnestly; beg. *"I entreat you," said the defense attorney, "to let this man return to his wife and children."*

van • quish (vaŋ´kwish) *vt.*, conquer or defeat in battle. *The Celtic warrior queen vanquished the enemy.*

mor • ti • fi • ca • tion (môr´tə fi kā´shən) *n.*, shame; humiliation. *When the diary entry was read aloud over the public address system, my mortification was complete.*

ANSWERS TO INVESTIGATE, INQUIRE, AND IMAGINE (cont.)

Extend

5b. *Responses will vary.* Students might identify a hero, or person they strive to emulate, or they might list specific qualities they have or rules they live by, such as being fair or doing unto others as you would have others do unto you.

Respond *to the* SELECTION

Do your agree with Sir Gawain's belief that "once guilt has touched a man, he is never free of it again"?

INVESTIGATE

Inquire, *Imagine*

Recall: GATHERING FACTS →

1a. What challenge does the Green Knight make? Who meets the challenge? What is the result?

2a. What happens to Gawain at the lord's castle?

3a. What is the result of Gawain's final meeting with the Green Knight? What object does Gawain keep as a reminder of the meeting?

Interpret: FINDING MEANING

1b. What words spoken by the Green Knight make his challenge seem more than a good-spirited contest?

2b. What do Gawain's actions at the castle reveal about the knights' moral code?

3b. Why does Gawain want to remember his meeting with the Green Knight?

Analyze: TAKING THINGS APART →

4a. Identify magical or supernatural elements in this selection.

Synthesize: BRINGING THINGS TOGETHER

4b. What do these elements add to the story? What would the effect be if they were replaced with more realistic elements?

Evaluate: MAKING JUDGMENTS →

5a. Do you think Sir Gawain judges himself too harshly after his final meeting with the Green Knight? Why, or why not?

Extend: CONNECTING IDEAS

5b. What ideals do you try to live up to?

Understanding *Literature*

ARTHURIAN ROMANCE. Review the definition for **Arthurian Romance** in the Handbook of Literary Terms. How are the plots of adventure and love in *Sir Gawain* interdependent? How are they typical of the romance genre?

CHIVALRY. Review the definition for **chivalry** in Literary Tools on page 187. How does the Green Knight adhere to the code of chivalry? How does he violate it? How does he use it to his advantage?

RESPOND TO THE SELECTION

Students should explain their responses and provide examples to support their beliefs. Ask students to think about forgiveness, punishment, and making up for a wrong done.

ANSWERS TO UNDERSTANDING LITERATURE

ARTHURIAN ROMANCE. In the story *Sir Gawain and the Green Knight,* Gawain's adventure leads him to love. Both his adventure and his love are involved in the test of his knightly virtues.

CHIVALRY. The Green Knight demonstrates bravery and courage in his challenge. He demonstrates courtesy as the host, and gentleness in his dealing with Gawain when they finally meet again. He does not uphold the virtue of honesty and faith because he fails to tell Gawain who he really is.

ANSWERS TO INTEGRATING THE LANGUAGE ARTS

Language, Grammar, and Style

1. Beheading
2. beheading, exchanging
3. Jousting
4. Riding, holding
5. Competing

Study and Research

1. c. pretty
2. a. contract
3. c. friendly
4. d. plead

Collaborative Learning

If students are interested in exploring Arthurian legend more deeply before creating their questions, they might seek other sources in the library, as well as reading the selection from *Le Morte d'Arthur* on page 200.

WRITER'S JOURNAL

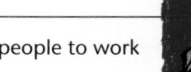

1. Challenges can create positive change. Write a **challenge** that encourages people to work toward some kind of change in your community.
2. Use vivid verbs, adjectives, and nouns to create **descriptive paragraph** about a knight.
3. Write your own **medieval romance** about the adventure of a knight. Use this adventure to show some of the knight's virtues.

Integrating *the* Language Arts

Language, Grammar, and Style

Identifying Gerunds. Read the Language Arts Survey 3.80, "Verbals: Participles, Gerunds, and Infinitives." Then underline the gerunds in the sentences below. If a sentence contains no gerund, write *None* after it.

1. Beheading is a common fate in medieval romances.
2. Sometimes beheading occurs as part of a contest that involves the exchanging of blows with an ax or sword.
3. Another popular contest, jousting, pitted knight against knight.
4. Riding on horseback wasn't easy for a man in a heavy suit of armor.
5. Competing in such contests was a form of entertainment as well as a preparation for battle.

Study and Research

Selecting Synonyms. Read the Language Arts Survey 5.56, "Answering Synonym and Antonym Questions." Then choose the best synonym for each of the following words:

1. comely
   - a. plain　　c. pretty
   - b. brilliant　　d. ugly
2. covenant
   - a. contract　　c. deal
   - b. oath　　d. breach
3. amiable
   - a. focused　　c. friendly
   - b. pleasing　　d. courageous
4. entreat
   - a. force　　c. ask
   - b. plead　　d. assist

Applied English

Identifying Personal Traits. Bravery, courage, courtesy, honesty, faith, and gentleness were characteristics expected of knights. Knowing your personal qualities is an important starting point for a job search. Brainstorm a list of your personal traits and values.

Collaborative Learning

Trivia Contest. Beheading contests are no longer in style, but you and your classmates can still challenge one another by holding a literary trivia contest. As a class, decide what topics the questions will cover. As a class, you should also decide how you will write the questions. Have each person write at least one question; be sure to include an answer for each question. As a class, decide the rules for the contest—the goal of the contest, how points are awarded, how disputes are resolved, and so on.

PREREADING

FROM *Le Morte d'Arthur*

BY SIR THOMAS MALORY

About the AUTHOR

Very little is known about **Sir Thomas Malory** (c.1405–1471). Although he seems to have led a quiet life in his younger years, he began having trouble with the law in 1451. He was arrested for attacking a religious house, then faced further charges for escaping from prison and for other crimes. By some accounts, Malory spent most of his life after 1451 in prison. During this time, the War of the Roses (1455–1485) raged in England, and Malory's involvement in an unsuccessful revolt against Edward IV landed him in prison again in 1468. Malory was definitely in prison when he completed the manuscript for ***Le Morte d'Arthur*** around 1469. He died two years later, while still in prison.

The Arthurian romances of thirteenth-century France greatly influenced Malory's work. He translated these prose narratives into English and used them as the basis of his romantic masterpiece, *Le Morte d'Arthur.* Unlike Chaucer and other English writers who wrote primarily narrative poetry, Malory was the first to master the narrative prose form.

About the SELECTION

By the time that Malory wrote ***Le Morte d'Arthur,*** romance literature had declined in popularity. Living at the end of what is now considered the Medieval Period, Malory wrote with a nostalgia not only for the Arthurian legends of romance and chivalry, but also for a time that celebrated them. Ironically, his book is the most complete and engaging retelling of the Arthurian legend.

The legend of Arthur has vague ties to a historical person. Arthur is supposed to have lived in fifth-century Britain, but a significant account of his history doesn't appear until the middle of the twelfth century. At that time, tales of his deeds as British king and of the members of his court were detailed. Although Malory's work is titled *The Death of Arthur* (the name given by its publisher in 1485), the majority of the book tells of the adventures of the individual knights of the Round Table. The massive work is divided into twenty-one books, and each book is divided into chapters.

The following excerpt is taken from the first book of *Le Morte d'Arthur* and relates the story of Arthur's birth and youth. The tale of Arthur's proof that he is the rightful heir to the throne has been retold many times in many ways.

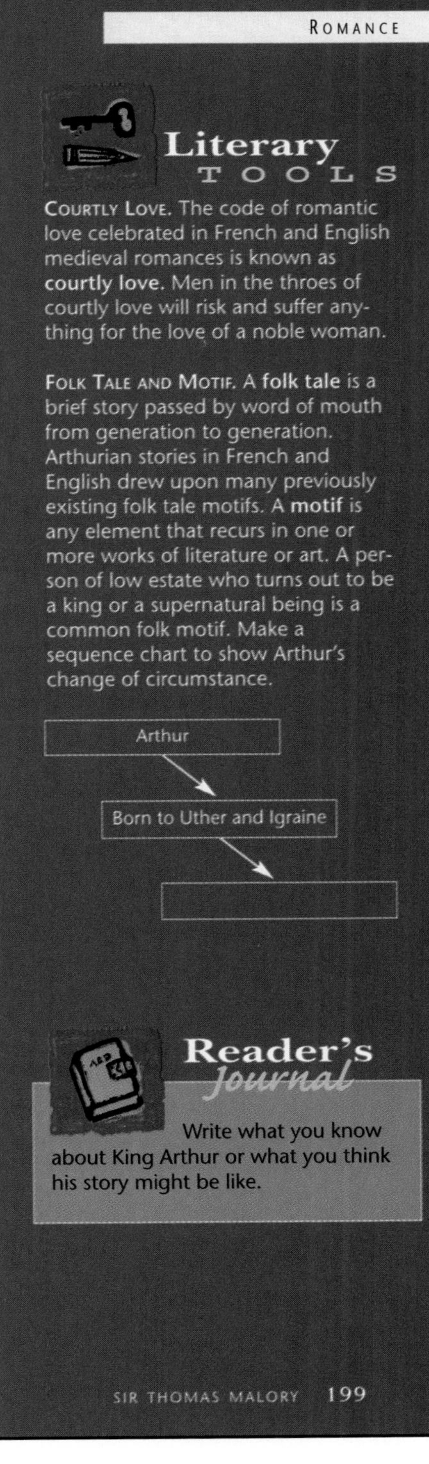

Literary TOOLS

COURTLY LOVE. The code of romantic love celebrated in French and English medieval romances is known as **courtly love.** Men in the throes of courtly love will risk and suffer anything for the love of a noble woman.

FOLK TALE AND MOTIF. A **folk tale** is a brief story passed by word of mouth from generation to generation. Arthurian stories in French and English drew upon many previously existing folk tale motifs. A **motif** is any element that recurs in one or more works of literature or art. A person of low estate who turns out to be a king or a supernatural being is a common folk motif. Make a sequence chart to show Arthur's change of circumstance.

Reader's Journal

Write what you know about King Arthur or what you think his story might be like.

ADDITIONAL RESOURCES

UNIT 3 RESOURCE BOOK
- Selection Worksheet 3.5
- Selection Check Test 4.3.11
- Selection Test 4.3.12
- Language, Grammar, and Style Resource 3.36

READER'S JOURNAL

Most students will have encountered Arthurian stories before. Have them share what they already know and note variations. Then point out that such variations in memory give rise to changes in texts as they are passed down in the oral tradition. If students are not familiar with King Arthur or the Knights of the Round Table, have them predict what Arthur might be like based on their knowledge of chivalry and courtly love.

GRAPHIC ORGANIZER

ARTHUR
- Born to Uther and Igraine
- Merlin receives Arthur at the back door and delivers him to Sir Ector
- Uther declares his son Arthur should be king upon his death
- Arthur pulls the sword from the stone
- Many lords want to king themselves, complain of Arthur's low blood and postpone making him king
- Arthur becomes king

GOALS/OBJECTIVES

Studying this lesson will enable students to
- empathize with Arthur, the main character
- explain how courtly love is expressed in the legend of Arthur and the knights of the Round Table
- identify a folk tale motif
- combine sentences using appositive phrases

INDIVIDUAL LEARNING STRATEGIES

MOTIVATION
Have students create a heroes mural. Have students identify personal heroes, either contemporary or from the past. Students can use photographs or their own artwork to depict their heroes.

READING PROFICIENCY
To help students understand this selection, spend a little time going over the introduction to each section which explains the main events of each chapter. Make sure students understand the language and syntax in these introductions to give them a clearer sense of what they should expect in each chapter.

ENGLISH LANGUAGE LEARNING
Point out the following vocabulary words to your students:
summons—call
betwixt—between
nourish—feed
remnant—what is left; remainder
estates—properties
anon—soon

SPECIAL NEEDS
Students should pay special attention to the Guided Reading questions and to the Recall questions in Investigate, Inquire, and Imagine.

ENRICHMENT
Have students do research in the library to find depictions of Merlin, Arthur, Guinevere, and other famous figures in Arthurian legend. Students should gather these materials and share them in class.

VOCABULARY FROM THE SELECTION

appurtenance
countenance
indignation
inter
necromancy
obeisance
postern
providence
usurp
wax
wroth

Le Morte d'Arthur

SIR THOMAS MALORY

FROM BOOK I CHAPTER 1

FIRST, HOW UTHER PENDRAGON SENT FOR THE DUKE OF CORNWALL AND IGRAINE HIS WIFE, AND OF THEIR DEPARTING SUDDENLY AGAIN

It befell in the days of Uther Pendragon, when he was king of all England, and so reigned, that there was a mighty duke in Cornwall that held war against him long time. And the duke was called the Duke of Tintagel. And so by means King Uther sent for this duke, charging him to bring his wife with him, for she was called a fair lady, and a passing[1] wise, and her name was called Igraine.

So when the duke and his wife were comen unto the king, by the means of great lords they were accorded both. The king liked and loved this lady well, and he made them great cheer out of measure, and desired to have lain by her. But she was a passing good woman, and would not assent unto the king. And then she told the duke her husband, and said, "I suppose that we were sent for that I should be dishonored, wherefore, husband, I counsel you that we depart from hence suddenly, that we may ride all night unto our own castle." And in like wise as she said so they departed, that neither the king nor none of his council were ware of their departing.

As soon as King Uther knew of their departing so suddenly, he was wonderly wroth. Then he called to him his privy council,[2] and told them of the sudden departing of the duke and his wife. Then they advised the king to send for the duke and his wife by a great charge: "And if he will not come at your summons, then may ye do your best, then have ye cause to make mighty war upon him."

1. **passing.** Exceedingly
2. **privy council.** The king's group of advisors

WORDS FOR EVERYDAY USE

wroth (rôth) *adj.*, angry. *When the display of balloons broke loose and floated to the ceiling, the store manager was terribly wroth.*

The Romance of King Arthur and His Knights of the Round Table. Wellesley College Library.

ArtNote

The Romance of King Arthur and His Knights of the Round Table. Wellesley College Library.

Discuss this illustration depicting the battle between Arthur and Mordred, Arthur's nemesis. Which figure is Arthur and which is Mordred? How can you tell? Who are the people to the left, and what are they doing? How does the artist depict the dead bodies? What might he be trying to show? Describe the sky. What effect does the sky have on the mood of the painting?

ADDITIONAL QUESTIONS AND ACTIVITIES

Have students discuss the idea that all events are controlled by destiny. This idea depends on the assumption that life is guided by outside forces. Students should in their discussion respect differences of belief on this matter.

INTERNET RESOURCES

Students can examine evidence that Arthur was a real king. Have them check www.britannia.com. This site offers a great deal of information about the period during which Arthur was believed to live as well as on Arthur himself. Students may find this a helpful resource as they work on other activities in this unit.

ANSWER TO GUIDED READING QUESTION

1. Merlin asks that the child of Igraine and Uther be delivered to him for nourishing.

LITERARY TECHNIQUE 

Foreshadowing. Foreshadowing is the act of presenting materials that hint at events to occur later in the story. At the end of the excerpt from Book 1, Chapter 1, Merlin says, "ride on your way, for I will not be long behind." Ask students to predict what events this might foreshadow. Ask what effect this use of foreshadowing has.

Answer

Since Merlin is a wizard, students may expect him to do some act of magic later on. The use of foreshadowing builds excitement and suspense by raising curiosity.

LITERARY NOTE 

Students may be familiar with **Merlin,** the magician who guided the fate of Uther and Arthur. His background is less widely known. He was the son of a devil and a virtuous maiden, but he was not evil as his father wished him to be. Merlin fell in love with Nimue, the Lady of the Lake, who appears later in this story.

ADDITIONAL QUESTIONS AND ACTIVITIES 

Encourage students to read actively. Ask them to make some predictions. They might try to answer the following questions:

- Why does Merlin help King Uther?
- Why does Merlin want the child delivered to him?
- How will Uther feel when Merlin comes for his child?

So that was done, and the messengers had their answers, and that was this shortly, that neither he nor his wife would not come at him. Then was the king wonderly wroth. And then the king sent him plain word again, and bad him be ready and stuff him and garnish him,[3] for within forty days would fetch him out of the biggest castle that he hath.

When the duke had this warning, anon he went and furnished and garnished two strong castles of his, of the which the one hight[4] Tintagel, and the other castle hight Terrabil. So his wife Dame Igraine he put in the Castle of Tintagel, and himself he put in the Castle of Terrabil, the which had many issues and posterns out. Then in all haste came Uther with a great host, and laid a siege about the Castle of Terrabil. And there he pitched many pavilions, and there was great war made on both parties, and much people slain.

Then for pure anger and for great love of fair Igraine the King Uther fell sick. So came to the King Uther Sir Ulfius, a noble knight, and asked the king why he was sick.

"I shall tell thee," said the king. "I am sick for anger and for love of fair Igraine that I may not be whole."

"Well, my lord," said Sir Ulfius, "I shall seek Merlin, and he shall do you remedy, that your heart shall be pleased."

So Ulfius departed, and by adventure he met Merlin in a beggar's array, and there Merlin asked Ulfius whom he sought. And he said he had little ado to tell him.

"Well," said Merlin, "I know whom thou seekest, for thou seekest Merlin; therefore seek no farther, for I am he, and if King Uther will well reward me, and be sworn unto me to fulfil my desire, that shall be his honor and profit more than mine, for I shall cause him to have all his desire."

"All this will I undertake," said Ulfius, "that there shall be nothing reasonable but thou shalt have thy desire."

"Well," said Merlin, "he shall have his intent and desire. And therefore," said Merlin, "ride on your way, for I will not be long behind."

FROM BOOK I CHAPTER 2

HOW UTHER PENDRAGON MADE WAR ON THE DUKE OF CORNWALL, AND HOW BY THE MEAN OF MERLIN HE LAY BY THE DUCHESS AND GAT[5] ARTHUR

Then Ulfius was glad, and rode on more than a pace till that he came to King Uther Pendragon, and told him he had met with Merlin.

"Where is he?" said the king.

"Sir," said Ulfius, "he will not dwell[6] long."

Therewithal Ulfius was ware where Merlin stood at the porch of the pavilion's door. And then Merlin was bound to come to the king. When King Uther saw him, he said he was welcome.

"Sir," said Merlin "I know all your heart every deal.[7] So ye will be sworn unto me as ye be a true king anointed, to fulfil my desire, ye shall have your desire."

What does Merlin ask in return for helping King Uther?

Then the king was sworn upon the four Evangelists.[8]

"Sir," said Merlin, "this is my desire: the first night that ye shall lie by Igraine ye shall get a child on her, and when that is born, that it shall

3. **stuff. . . him.** Prepare for a siege
4. **hight.** Called
5. **gat.** Begat, fathered
6. **dwell.** Delay
7. **deal.** Part
8. **four Evangelists.** The Gospels

WORDS FOR EVERYDAY USE

pos • tern (pōs ´tərn) *n.*, private rear entrance. *The servant was able to come and go through a secret postern behind the castle.*

be delivered to me for to nourish there as I will have it; for it shall be your worship,[9] and the child's avail as mickle[10] as the child is worth."

"I will well," said the king, "as thou wilt have it."

"Now make you ready," said Merlin, "this night ye shall lie with Igraine in the Castle of Tintagel, and ye shall be like the duke her husband, Ulfius shall be like Sir Brastias, a knight of the duke's, and I will be like a knight that hight Sir Jordans, a knight of the duke's. But wait[11] ye make not many questions with her nor her men, but say ye are diseased,[12] and so hie you to bed, and rise not on the morn till I come to you, for the Castle of Tintagel is but ten miles hence."

How does Merlin arrange for King Uther to lie with Igraine?

So this was done as they devised. But the Duke of Tintagel espied how the king rode from the siege of Terrabil, and therefore that night he issued out of the castle at a postern for to have distressed the king's host. And so, through his own issue, the duke himself was slain or-ever[13] the king came at the Castle of Tintagel.

So after the death of the duke, King Uther lay with Igraine more than three hours after his death, and begat on her that night Arthur; and, or day came, Merlin came to the king, and bad him make him ready, and so he kissed the lady Igraine and departed in all haste. But when the lady heard tell of the duke her husband, and by all record he was dead or-ever King Uther came to her, then she marvelled who that might be that lay with her in likeness of her lord; so she mourned privily and held her peace.

Then all the barons by one assent prayed the king of accord betwixt the lady Igraine and him; the king gave them leave, for fain would he have been accorded with her. So the king put all the trust in Ulfius to entreat[14] between them, so by the entreaty at the last the king and she met together.

"Now will we do well," said Ulfius. "Our king is a lusty knight and wifeless, and my lady Igraine is a passing fair lady; it were great joy unto us all, and it might please the king to make her his queen."

Unto that they all well accorded and moved it to the king. And anon, like a lusty knight, he assented thereto with good will, and so in all haste they were married in a morning with great mirth and joy.

And King Lot of Lothian and of Orkney then wedded Margawse that was Gawain's mother, and King Nentres of the land of Garlot wedded Elaine. All this was done at the request of King Uther. And the third sister Morgan le Fay was put to school in a nunnery, and there she learned so much that she was a great clerk of <u>necromancy</u>, and after she was wedded to King Uriens of the land of Gore, that was Sir Uwain's le Blanchemains father.

FROM BOOK I CHAPTER 3

OF THE BIRTH OF KING ARTHUR AND OF HIS NURTURE

Then Queen Igraine <u>waxed</u> daily greater and greater, so it befell after within half a year, as King Uther lay by his queen, he asked her, by the faith she ought to him, whose was the child within her body; then was she sore abashed to give answer.

9. **worship.** Honor
10. **mickle.** Much
11. **wait.** Take care
12. **diseased.** Tired
13. **or-ever.** Before
14. **entreat.** Negotiate

WORDS FOR EVERYDAY USE

nec • ro • man • cy (nek´rə man´sē) *n.*, black magic; sorcery. *The wizard's <u>necromancy</u> was held responsible for the mayor's being turned into a crow.*

wax (waks) *vi.*, grow gradually larger. *The crescent moon <u>waxes</u> daily until it becomes a full moon.*

ANSWER TO GUIDED READING QUESTION

1. Merlin makes Uther look like Igraine's husband.

LITERARY NOTE 

Morgana le Fay was an important force in Sir Gawain and the Green Knight. Here the source of her knowledge of sorcery is revealed. In some stories Morgan harms Arthur but later takes him away to cure his wounds after his final battle. Have students find stories about Morgana le Fay. Ask them is she is a sympathetic character.

ANSWER TO GUIDED READING QUESTION

1. King Uther tells her the story of the enchantment wrought by Merlin. Queen Igraine feels great joy on learning that Uther is the father.

LITERARY NOTE

The king says, "tell me the truth, and I shall love you the better, by the faith of my body." The oath was a key part of the code of chivalry. Ask students to find other examples of oaths in the selection. Then, have students explain the importance of oaths.

BIBLIOGRAPHIC NOTE

The Arthurian Legends have been widely retold. The follow is a brief list of adaptations. These and other versions may appeal to students.

Idylls of the King
by Alfred, Lord Tennyson
The Mists of Avalon
by Marian Zimmer Bradley
The Once and Future King
by T.H. White
Camelot
by Lerner and Loewe (musical)

"Dismay you not," said the king, "but tell me the truth, and I shall love you the better, by the faith of my body."

"Sir," said she, "I shall tell you the truth. The same night that my lord was dead, the hour of his death, as his knights record, there came into my castle of Tintagel a man like my lord in speech and in countenance, and two knights with him in likeness of his two knights Brastias and Jordans, and so I went unto bed with him as I ought to do with my lord, and the same night, as I shall answer unto God, this child was begotten upon me."

"That is truth," said the king, "as ye say; for it was I myself that came in the likeness, and therefore dismay you not, for I am father to the child;" and there he told her all the cause, how it was by Merlin's counsel. Then the queen made great joy when she knew who was the father of her child.

How does Igraine learn who fathered her child? How does she feel when she learns this?

Soon came Merlin unto the king, and said, "Sir, ye must purvey you for the nourishing of your child."

"As thou wilt," said the king, "be it."

"Well," said Merlin, "I know a lord of yours in this land, that is a passing true man and a faithful, and he shall have the nourishing of your child; and his name is Sir Ector, and he is a lord of fair livelihood in many parts in England and Wales; and this lord, Sir Ector, let him be sent for, for to come and speak with you, and desire him yourself, as he loveth you, that he will put his own child to nourishing to another woman, and that his wife nourish yours. And when the child is born let it be delivered to me at yonder privy postern unchristened."

So like as Merlin devised it was done. And when Sir Ector was come he made fiance[15] to the king for to nourish the child like as the king desired; and there the king granted Sir Ector great rewards. Then when the lady was delivered, the king commanded two knights and two ladies to take the child, bound in a cloth of gold, "and that ye deliver him to what poor man ye meet at the postern gate of the castle." So the child was delivered unto Merlin, and so he bare it forth unto Sir Ector, and made an holy man to christen him, and named him Arthur; and so Sir Ector's wife nourished him with her own pap.

FROM BOOK I CHAPTER 4

OF THE DEATH OF KING UTHER PENDRAGON

Then within two years King Uther fell sick of a great malady. And in the meanwhile his enemies usurped upon him, and did a great battle upon his men, and slew many of his people.

"Sir," said Merlin, "ye may not lie so as ye do, for ye must to the field though ye ride on an horse-litter; for ye shall never have the better of your enemies but if your person be there, and then shall ye have the victory."

So it was done as Merlin had devised, and they carried the king forth in an horse-litter with a great host toward his enemies. And at St. Albans there met with the king a great host of the north. And that day Sir Ulfius and Sir Brastias did great deeds of arms, and King Uther's men overcame the northern battle and slew many people, and put the remnant to flight. And then the king returned unto London, and made great joy of his victory.

And then he fell passing sore sick, so that three days and three nights he was speechless;

15. **fiance.** A promise

WORDS FOR EVERYDAY USE

coun • te • nance (koun´tə nəns) *n.*, appearance; facial features. *Her countenance displayed emotions that her words could not.*

u • surp (yo͞o zʉrp´) *vt.*, unlawfully seize a throne. *After Cromwell usurped Charles I's throne, he had that king tried and beheaded.*

wherefore all the barons made great sorrow, and asked Merlin what counsel were best.

"There is none other remedy," said Merlin, "but God will have his will. But look ye all, barons, be before King Uther to-morn, and God and I shall make him to speak."

So on the morn all the barons with Merlin came tofore the king; then Merlin said aloud unto King Uther, "Sir, shall I your son Arthur be king, after your days, of this realm with all the appurtenance?"

Then Uther Pendragon turned him, and said in hearing of them all, "I give him God's blessing and mine, and bid him pray for my soul, and righteously and worshipfully that he claim the crown upon forfeiture of my blessing." And therewith he yielded up the ghost, and then was he interred as longed to a king, wherefore the queen, fair Igraine, made great sorrow, and all the barons.

What arrangement did King Uther make for his succession?

FROM BOOK I CHAPTER 5

HOW ARTHUR WAS CHOSEN KING, AND OF WONDERS AND MARVELS OF A SWORD TAKEN OUT OF A STONE BY THE SAID ARTHUR

Then stood the realm in great jeopardy long while, for every lord that was mighty of men made him strong, and many weened[16] to have been king. Then Merlin went to the Archbishop of Canterbury, and counselled him for to send for all the lords of the realm, and all the gentlemen of arms, that they should to London come by Christmas, upon pain of cursing; and for this cause: that Jehu, that was born on that night, that He would of his great mercy show some miracle, as He was come to be king of mankind, for to show some miracle who should be rightwise king of this realm. So the Archbishop, by the advice of Merlin, sent for all the lords and gentlemen of arms that they should come by Christmas even unto London. And many of them made them clean of their life, that their prayer might be the more acceptable unto God.

What problem was there after Uther's death?

So in the greatest church of London (whether it were Paul's or not the French book maketh no mention) all the estates were long or day in the church for to pray. And when matins[17] and the first mass was done, there was seen in the churchyard, against the high altar, a great stone four square, like unto a marble stone, and in midst thereof was like an anvil of steel a foot on high, and therein stuck a fair sword naked by the point, and letters there were written in gold about the sword that saiden thus:—WHOSO PULLETH OUT THIS SWORD OF THIS STONE AND ANVIL, IS RIGHTWISE KING BORN OF ALL ENGLAND. Then the people marvelled, and told it to the Archbishop,

How is the king to be determined?

"I command," said the Archbishop, "that ye keep you within your church, and pray unto God still; that no man touch the sword till the high mass be all done."

So when all masses were done all the lords went to behold the stone and the sword. And when they saw the scripture, some assayed,[18] such as would have been king. But none might stir the sword nor move it.

"He is not here," said the Archbishop, "that shall achieve the sword, but doubt not God will

16. **weened.** Thought
17. **matins.** Morning prayers
18. **assayed.** Made an attempt

WORDS FOR EVERYDAY USE

ap • pur • te • nance (ə pʉrt´'n əns) *n.*, thing that belongs to another. *The computer and all of its appurtenances were sold at an auction.*

in • ter (in tʉr´) *vi.*, bury. *At the family cemetery, Jed's grandfather was interred.*

ANSWERS TO GUIDED READING QUESTIONS

1. Uther expressed the desire to have Arthur become king after him.
2. Many lords took this opportunity to become stronger to further their ambitions to be king.
3. The person who can pull the sword from the stone will become king.

LITERARY NOTE

Malory's references to the French book as in "whether it were Paul's or not the French book maketh no mention" (Book I, Chapter 5) are indications of Malory's source or sources. Many scholars believe that Malory actually drew on a number of French sources in which stories were intertwined. He simplified the narrative and focused on Arthur rather than on Sir Lancelot, the chief figure in the French stories.

ADDITIONAL QUESTIONS AND ACTIVITIES

1. Ask students what danger exists after Uther's death.
2. Why is the succession unclear?
3. What time is chosen to prove who the new king is? Why is this time chosen? What comparison is drawn?

Answers

1. Danger troubles the realm as many lords seek to become king.
2. The succession is unclear because Uther's son Arthur is unknown.
3. Christmastime is chosen to prove the right of the new king because at that time a miracle showed Jesus as the king of humankind and in his mercy he would give a sign showing the new king of Uther's realm.

ADDITIONAL QUESTIONS AND ACTIVITIES

In small groups student can brainstorm other ways of proving kingship. They may wish to consider the role magic plays in this test.

ANSWER TO GUIDED READING QUESTION

1. Arthur wants to get a sword for his brother, Sir Kay.

ADDITIONAL QUESTIONS AND ACTIVITIES

1. Why does Sir Kay claim he must be king?
2. How does Sir Ector learn that Arthur is the one who got the sword?
3. What proof does Sir Ector want?

Answers

1. When Arthur gives him the sword from the stone, Sir Kay goes to Sir Ector and says that since he has the sword he must be king of the land.
2. Sir Ector makes Sir Kay swear upon a book in the church how he got the sword.
3. Sir Ector asks Arthur to pull the sword from the stone, and Arthur is able to do it. When Sir Ector tries, he fails.

make him known. But this is my counsel," said the Archbishop, "that we let purvey[19] ten knights, men of good fame, and they to keep this sword."

So it was ordained, and then there was made a cry, that every man should assay that would, for to win the sword. And upon New Year's Day the barons let make a jousts and a tournament, that all knights that would joust or tourney there might play. And all this was ordained for to keep the lords together and the commons, for the Archbishop trusted that God would make him known that should win the sword.

So upon New Year's Day, when the service was done, the barons rode unto the field, some to joust and some to tourney, and so it happed that Sir Ector, that had great livelihood about London, rode unto the jousts, and with him rode Sir Kay his son, and young Arthur that was his nourished brother; and Sir Kay was made knight at All Hallowmass afore. So as they rode to the jousts-ward, Sir Kay had lost his sword, for he had left it at his father's lodging, and so he prayed young Arthur for to ride for his sword.

"I will well," said Arthur, and rode fast after the sword. And when he came home the lady and all were out to see the jousting.

Then was Arthur wroth, and said to himself, "I will ride to the churchyard, and take the sword with me that sticketh in the stone, for my brother Sir Kay shall not be without a sword this day." So when he came to the churchyard, Sir Arthur alit and tied his horse to the stile, and so he went to the tent, and found no knights there, for they were at jousting; and so he handled the sword by the handles, and lightly and fiercely pulled it out of the stone, and took his horse and rode his way until he came to his brother Sir Kay, and delivered him the sword.

Why does Arthur pull out the sword from the stone?

And as soon as Sir Kay saw the sword, he wist[20] well it was the sword of the stone, and so he rode to his father Sir Ector, and said; "Sir, lo here is the sword of the stone, wherefore I must be king of this land."

When Sir Ector beheld the sword, he returned again and came to the church, and there they alit all three, and went into the church. And anon he made Sir Kay to swear upon a book how he came to that sword.

"Sir," said Sir Kay, "by my brother Arthur, for he brought it to me."

"How gat ye this sword?" said Sir Ector to Arthur.

"Sir, I will tell you. When I came home for my brother's sword, I found nobody at home to deliver me his sword, and so I thought my brother Sir Kay should not be swordless, and so I came hither eagerly and pulled it out of the stone without any pain."

"Found ye any knights about this sword?" said Sir Ector.

"Nay," said Arthur.

"Now," said Sir Ector to Arthur, "I understand ye must be king of this land."

"Wherefore[21] I," said Arthur, "and for what cause?"

"Sir," said Ector, "for God will have it so, for there should never man have drawn out this sword, but he that shall be rightwise king of this land. Now let me see whether ye can put the sword there as it was, and pull it out again."

"That is no mastery," said Arthur, and so he put it in the stone; therewithal Sir Ector assayed to pull out the sword and failed.

FROM BOOK I CHAPTER 6

HOW KING ARTHUR PULLED OUT THE SWORD DIVERS TIMES

"Now assay," said Sir Ector unto Sir Kay. And anon he pulled at the sword with all his might, but it would not be.

"Now shall ye assay," said Sir Ector to Arthur.

19. **let purvey.** Appoint
20. **wist.** Knew
21. **Wherefore.** Why

"I will well," said Arthur, and pulled it out easily. And therewithal Sir Ector knelt down to the earth, and Sir Kay.

"Alas!" said Arthur, "my own dear father and brother, why kneel ye to me?"

"Nay, nay, my lord Arthur, it is not so, I was never your father nor of your blood, but I wot[22] well ye are of an higher blood than I weened ye were." And then Sir Ector told him all, how he was betaken[23] him for to nourish him, and by whose commandment, and by Merlin's deliverance. Then Arthur made great dole[24] when he understood that Sir Ector was not his father.

"Sir," said Ector unto Arthur, "will ye be my good and gracious lord when ye are king?"

"Else were I to blame," said Arthur, "for ye are the man in the world that I am most beholding to, and my good lady and mother your wife, that as well as her own hath fostered me and kept. And if ever it be God's will that I be king as ye say, ye shall desire of me what I may do, and I shall not fail you, God forbid I should fail you."

"Sir," said Sir Ector, "I will ask no more of you, but that ye will make my son, your foster brother, Sir Kay, seneschal[25] of all your lands."

"That shall be done," said Arthur, "and more, by the faith of my body, that never man shall have that office but he, while he and I live."

Therewithal they went unto the Archbishop, and told him how the sword was achieved, and by whom. And on Twelfthday all the barons came thither, and to assay to take the sword, who that would assay. But there afore them all, there might none take it out but Arthur; wherefore there were many lords wroth, and said it was great shame unto them all and the realm, to be over-governed with a boy of no high blood born, and so they fell out at that time, that it was put off till Candlemas,[26] and then all the barons should meet there again; but alway the ten knights were ordained to watch the sword day and night, and so they set a pavilion over the stone and the sword, and five always watched.

How did the lords feel about Arthur being king?

So at Candlemas many more great lords came thither for to have won the sword, but there might none prevail. And right as Arthur did at Christmas, he did at Candlemas, and pulled out the sword easily, whereof the barons were sore agrieved and put it off in delay till the high feast of Easter. And as Arthur sped before, so did he at Easter, yet there were some of the great lords had <u>indignation</u> that Arthur should be king, and put it off in a delay till the feast of Pentecost.[27] Then the Archbishop of Canterbury by Merlin's <u>providence</u> let purvey then of the best knights that they might get, and such knights as Uther Pendragon loved best and most trusted in his days. And such knights were put about Arthur as Sir Baudwin of Britain, Sir Kay, Sir Ulfius, Sir Brastias. All these with many other, were always about Arthur, day and night, till the feast of Pentecost.

FROM BOOK I CHAPTER 7

HOW KING ARTHUR WAS CROWNED, AND HOW HE MADE OFFICERS

And at the feast of Pentecost all manner of men assayed to pull at the sword that would assay, but none might prevail but Arthur, and pulled it out afore all the lords and commons that were there, wherefore all the commons

22. **wot.** Know
23. **betaken.** Assigned to care for
24. **dole.** Lamentation
25. **seneschal.** Steward
26. **Candlemas.** A church feast on February 2
27. **Pentecost.** The seventh Sunday after Easter

WORDS FOR EVERYDAY USE

in • dig • na • tion (in dig´nā shən) *n.*, anger or scorn. *The coach showed great <u>indignation</u> when she was charged with a technical foul and ejected from the playing area.*

prov • i • dence (präv´ə dəns) *n.*, benevolent guidance. *"Your <u>providence</u> has helped us to avoid disaster," the government minister said to the relief worker.*

ANSWER TO GUIDED READING QUESTION

1. The lords were unhappy that a boy who was not of noble blood should become king.

ADDITIONAL QUESTIONS AND ACTIVITIES

Students can discuss different ways people deal with fame and fortune. How might people treat their friends if they were suddenly to become rich or famous? Why might such changes in lifestyle cause changes in relationships?

SELECTION CHECK TEST 4.3.11 WITH ANSWERS

1. Who is Arthur's father? **His father is King Uther.**
2. To whom is Arthur given soon after his birth? **He is given to Merlin.**
3. What appears in the churchyard on Christmas? **A stone appears with a sword in it.**
4. What does Arthur learn about his family from Sir Ector? **He learns that Sir Ector, his wife, and Sir Kay are not his family.**
5. Name one thing Arthur accomplished as king. **Responses will vary. Arthur returned many lands to their rightful owners; he appointed his family and friends to high positions; he won Wales and Scotland to unite Britain.**

Vocabulary in Context
Fill each blank with the most appropriate word from these Words for Everyday Use. You may have to change the tense of the word.

postern countenance usurp
appurtenance indignation
providence obeisance

1. After his loss, Tyler tried not to let his disappointment show on his **<u>countenance</u>**.
2. While the boss was out sick, his assistant **<u>usurped</u>** many of his privileges.
3. After the coup, the citizens of the country were under the **<u>obeisance</u>** of the dictator.
4. The villagers rewarded the hero after his **<u>providence</u>** helped them avert disaster.
5. I sold my drum set, and the new owner loaded it and its **<u>appurtenances</u>** on a truck.

SELECTION CHECK TEST 4.3.11 WITH ANSWERS (CONT.)

Literary Tools

1. What is a folk tale? **A folk tale is a brief story that is passed by word of mouth from generation to generation.**
2. What is a motif? **A motif is a brief story that is passed by word of mouth from generation to generation.**
3. What is courtly love? **Courtly love is the code of love in medieval romance.**

ANSWER TO GUIDED READING QUESTION

1. At the feast of Pentecost, fifty days after Easter, after Arthur has pulled out the sword, the common people cry that it is God's will that Arthur be king. They threaten to slay anyone who opposes that view.

ANSWERS TO INVESTIGATE, INQUIRE, AND IMAGINE

RECALL

1a. Uther tricks Igraine into thinking he is her husband by disguising himself as her husband. As a result of the deception, Igraine sleeps with Uther and conceives Arthur.

2a. In his early years, Arthur is raised by Sir Ector and his wife. Arthur's royal background is revealed when he pulls the sword from the stone.

3a. Some men say Arthur is not really dead, but in another place. His tombstone reads: Here lies Arthur who was king and will be king again.

INTERPRET

1b. Igraine is saddened by her husband's death. When she learns what time he died, she wonders with whom she had slept.

2b. Merlin convinced Uther to declare Arthur his rightful heir. Merlin had Arthur raised in the family of Sir Ector, where he was safe and acquired the strengths that would serve him well as king. Merlin convinced the Archbishop of Canterbury that the next king would be identified miraculously by being able to remove a sword from a stone.

3b. The magical story about Arthur's beginning make it easier to believe that his death was magical as well. Arthur was a popular king; people want to believe that he will return.

ANALYZE

4a. *Responses will vary.* Merlin allowed Uther to be with Igraine so Arthur could be conceived. He chose where Arthur would be raised. He had Uther declare that Arthur was to succeed him. He set up the test that proved Arthur was the rightful king.

SYNTHESIZE

4b. *Responses will vary.* Merlin may have realized a strong leader was needed. He may have wanted to have behind the scenes control.

cried at once, "We will have Arthur unto our king; we will put him no more in delay, for we all see that it is God's will that he shall be our king, and who that holdeth against it, we will slay him." And therewithal they kneeled at once, both rich and poor, and cried Arthur mercy because they had delayed him so long. And Arthur forgave them, and took the sword between both his hands, and offered it upon the altar where the Archbishop was, and so was he made knight of the best man that was there.

When is Arthur accepted as king? What do the people say to show they accept him as king?

And so anon was the coronation made. And there was he sworn unto his lords and the commons for to be a true king, to stand with true justice from thenceforth the days of this life. Also then he made all lords that held of the crown to come in, and to do service as they ought to do. And many complaints were made unto Sir Arthur of great wrongs that were done since the death of King Uther, of many lands that were bereaved lords, knights, ladies, and gentlemen. Wherefore King Arthur made the lands to be given again unto them that ought them.[28] When this was done, that the king had stablished all the countries about London, then he let make Sir Kay Seneschal of England; and Sir Baudwin of Britain was made constable; and Sir Ulfius was made chamberlain; and Sir Brastias was made warden to wait upon the north from Trent forwards, for it was that time the most part the king's enemies. But within few years after, Arthur won all the north, Scotland, and all that were under their obeisance. Also Wales, a part of it, held against Arthur, but he overcame them all, as he did the remnant, through the noble prowess of himself and his knights of the Round Table.

◆ ◆ ◆

FROM BOOK XXI CHAPTER 7

OF THE OPINION OF SOME MEN OF THE DEATH OF KING ARTHUR; AND HOW QUEEN GUENEVER MADE HER A NUN IN ALMESBURY

Yet some men say in many parts of England that King Arthur is not dead, but had by the will of Our Lord Jesu into another place; and men say that he shall come again, and he shall win the holy cross. I will not say that it shall be so, but rather I will say, here in this world he changed his life. But many men say that there is written upon his tomb this verse: HIC IACET ARTHURUS, REX QUONDAM REXQUE FUTURUS.[29] ■

28. **ought them.** Owned them

29. **HIC . . . FUTURUS.** Here lies Arthur who was king and will be king again.

WORDS FOR EVERYDAY USE

o • bei • sance (ō bā´ səns) *n.*, authority; rule. *The newly crowned king showed he was under the obeisance of the church by bowing before the archbishop.*

ANSWERS TO INVESTIGATE, INQUIRE, AND IMAGINE (CONT.)

EVALUATE

5a. *Responses will vary.* Arthur is kind, thoughtful and faithful toward the people who cared for him. He was a fair and powerful leader.

EXTEND

5b. *Responses will vary.* Arthur and Gawain are both knights. They share the knightly virtues of honor to their lords. Both show success in their tests.

Respond *to the* SELECTION

Explain whether or not you think Arthur is an impressive legendary figure.

INVESTIGATE, Inquire, *Imagine*

Recall: GATHERING FACTS → **Interpret:** FINDING MEANING

1a. How does King Uther Pendragon trick Igraine? What is the result of this deception?

1b. Why is Igraine doubly distressed when she learns of the death of her husband?

2a. Under what circumstances does Arthur spend his early years of life? How is his royal heritage discovered?

2b. How have Merlin's actions prepared Arthur to assume the role of king?

3a. What do some men say about Arthur's death? What is written on his tomb?

3b. What might prompt such beliefs?

Analyze: TAKING THINGS APART → **Synthesize:** BRINGING THINGS TOGETHER

4a. List ways in which Merlin affected Arthur's life.

4b. Why do you think Merlin acted as he did?

Evaluate: MAKING JUDGMENTS → **Extend:** CONNECTING IDEAS

5a. What virtues does Arthur possess?

5b. Briefly compare Arthur to Gawain.

Understanding *Literature*

COURTLY LOVE. Review the definition of **courtly love** in Literary Tools on page 199. Men in the throes of courtly love will risk and suffer anything for the love of a noble woman. How does Uther Pendragon adhere to the code of courtly love?

FOLK TALE AND MOTIF. Review the definition of **folk tale** and **motif** in the Handbook of Literary Tools. Arthurian stories in French and English drew upon many previously existing folk tale motifs. A person of low estate who turns out to be a king or a supernatural being is a common folk motif. Explain how the motif is used in this selection. Why might this motif be popular?

RESPOND TO THE SELECTION

Students might respond by identifying the qualities or information about Arthur that make him an impressive figure. If they don't think he is an impressive legend, ask them to contrast him to someone they think is legendary.

ANSWERS TO UNDERSTANDING LITERATURE

COURTLY LOVE. Uther Pendragon's willingness to give his son Arthur to Merlin in return for spending one night with Igraine reflects his adherence to the code of courtly love.

FOLK TALE AND MOTIF. Arthur is brought to Sir Ector to be raised. Nobody knows that he is the son of the king until he pulls the sword from the stone. This motif gives many people the chance to believe that they could be transformed into something great.

ANSWERS TO INTEGRATING THE LANGUAGE ARTS

Language, Grammar, and Style
Responses will vary.

1. Arthur easily pulled the sword from the stone.
2. Many other great lords who desired to become king tried to pull the sword from the stone.
3. Crying out loudly, the common people insisted that Arthur be made king.
4. The great lords had to comply, although they weren't happy about it.
5. Thus Arthur became king with the help of Merlin.

Study and Research
Students might want to identify on their maps such places as Cornwall, Tintagel, Glastonbury, Colcester, and Cadbury Castle in Somerset.

Cornwall was the seat of King Mark and Queen Igraine. Tintagel is the place in Cornwall where Arthur was conceived. Some legends claim that Arthur and Guenever (Guinevere) were buried in Glastonbury, in Somerset. The site of Arthur's city, Camelot, has been variously placed at Colcester and at Cadbury Castle in Somerset.

Collaborative Learning
Some versions include the modern musical *Camelot,* the novel *The Mists of Avalon* by Marian Zimmer Bradley, the novel *The Once and Future King* by T.H. White, and the poetic series *Idylls of the King* by Tennyson. Many children's story or picture books use these stories as well.

Writer's Journal

1. Write a **thank you note** from Arthur to Sir Ector for raising him.
2. Write a **eulogy,** or speech of praise, for Arthur. Identify his accomplishments and virtues.
3. Arthur has been called the "once and future king." Write a **scene** in which Arthur returns and reveals himself.

Integrating *the* Language Arts

Language, Grammar, and Style

Combining Sentences. Read the Language Arts Survey 3.36, "Combining and Expanding Sentences." Then combine each pair of sentences below to create a single sentence. Follow the directions given in parentheses.

1. Arthur pulled the sword from the stone. He did so *easily.* (Add the italicized word.)
2. Many other great lords tried to pull the sword from the stone. They *desired to become king.* (Add the italicized words in a clause beginning with the word *who.*)
3. The common people insisted that Arthur be made king. They *cried out loudly* (Change *cried* to *crying* and add the phrase.)
4. The great lords had to comply. *They weren't happy about it.* (Add the second sentence as a subordinate clause beginning with the word *although.*)
5. Thus Arthur became king. He did so *with the help of Merlin.* (Add the italicized phrase.)

Study and Research

Map of Arthur's Britain. Although the location of Camelot, the site of King Arthur's court, has not been historically verified, many of the geographical locations mentioned in *Le Morte d'Arthur* did exist. For instance, Cornwall lay at the southwestern tip of England. Use a historical atlas to make your own map of fifth-century Britain. Use *Le Morte d'Arthur* or another Arthurian romance as a source for place names. Give your map a key that notes places where Arthur and other knights lived and fought.

Collaborative Learning

Discussing Arthur. The story of Arthur and the sword in the stone has been retold and depicted in movies, comics and other media. Find another version of the story. Discuss in small groups how the version you find is similar to or different from Malory's version.

FROM The Book of Margery Kempe

BY MARGERY KEMPE

About the AUTHOR

Margery Kempe (c.1373–1438) was born in King's Lynn, a busy port in Norfolk, England. At the age of twenty, she was married to John Kempe. After the extremely difficult birth of her first child, Kempe feared she might die and made her confession to a priest who criticized her harshly for what she confessed. These traumatic events led to a mental breakdown, from which she recovered when she had the first of her visions. Kempe became extremely devout, claiming to have personal visions of Jesus Christ and the Virgin Mary. Unlike other religious women of the time, who either entered convents or lived in reclusion, Kempe continued to live with her husband. She gave birth to fourteen children by the age of forty, at which time she took a vow of celibacy (to which her husband agreed) and began to make pilgrimages. Neighbors and fellow pilgrims criticized Kempe for her lifestyle and her loud, emotional displays, which included public sobbing and screaming. However, Kempe did win the support of some clergy and townspeople.

Like many women of her time, Kempe could neither read nor write. However, she had an extensive knowledge of the scriptures and other religious texts, having heard them from town clerics and traveling scholars. About the year 1433, Kempe dictated the two parts of her book to two different scribes; the second scribe, a priest, revised the entire text.

About the SELECTION

Although other people had written about themselves prior to the Medieval Period, ***The Book of Margery Kempe*** is the earliest surviving full-length autobiography in English. Unlike modern autobiographies, it does not relate a chronological story of a person's life. There is little sense of the passage of time throughout the book, although the events span approximately forty years. Instead, the book is Kempe's spiritual history. In the book's preface, Kempe states that she wrote the book to glorify God and to share her spiritual experiences. In doing so, however, she gives modern readers a glimpse into the life of an ordinary medieval woman.

Unlike most autobiographers who use a first-person voice, Kempe refers to herself throughout in the third person as "this creature," meaning one of God's creations. The following selection comes from the second chapter, in which Kempe relates events that followed her mental breakdown and eventually led to her decision to devote her life to God.

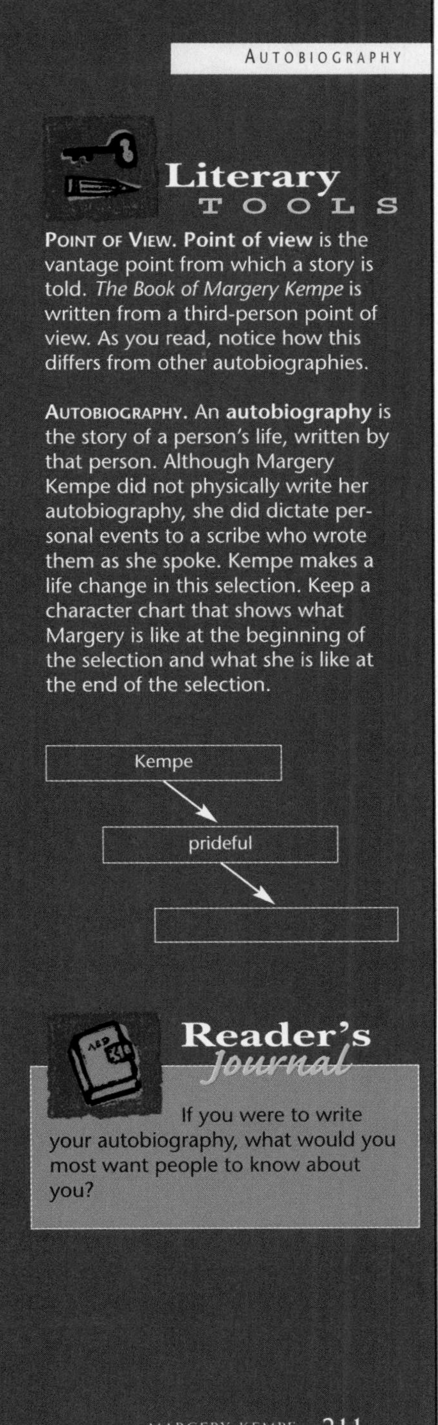

AUTOBIOGRAPHY

Literary TOOLS

POINT OF VIEW. Point of view is the vantage point from which a story is told. *The Book of Margery Kempe* is written from a third-person point of view. As you read, notice how this differs from other autobiographies.

AUTOBIOGRAPHY. An **autobiography** is the story of a person's life, written by that person. Although Margery Kempe did not physically write her autobiography, she did dictate personal events to a scribe who wrote them as she spoke. Kempe makes a life change in this selection. Keep a character chart that shows what Margery is like at the beginning of the selection and what she is like at the end of the selection.

Reader's Journal

If you were to write your autobiography, what would you most want people to know about you?

ADDITIONAL RESOURCES

UNIT 3 RESOURCE BOOK
- Selection Worksheet 3.6
- Selection Check Test 4.3.13
- Selection Test 4.3.14
- Language, Grammar, and Style Resource 3.29

GRAPHIC ORGANIZER ANSWERS

BEGINNING
proud
showy dresser
ignored advice
envious
wanted to be admired
greedy

END
asked forgiveness from her husband
said to be cursed
"punished" to make her lose her pride and vanity

READER'S JOURNAL

Suggest that students think about important people, places, and experiences in their lives. Ask them to describe any life-changing learning experiences that they have had. What do they believe is unique about their lives at this point in history?

VOCABULARY FROM THE SELECTION

cajole
ostentatious
vengeance

GOALS/OBJECTIVES

Studying this lesson will enable students to
- experience Kempe's determination and devotion to her undertakings
- describe the life and works of Margery Kempe and the events that led her to devote herself to a religious vocation
- describe the elements of autobiography and identify the point of view in a piece of writing
- write an explanation of a process
- present their ideas clearly and coherently in a debate

INDIVIDUAL LEARNING STRATEGIES

Motivation
In this selection, Margery Kempe begins a business. Ask students what kind of business they would want to have if they were to start their own business. Students might consider a business they could start now or one that they might like to start when they are older.

Reading Proficiency
Some students might have trouble following the sequence of events in the piece because of its formal language. You might want to have them read the piece slowly, stopping every few paragraphs to summarize the events described. Remind students that although the piece is written in the third person, using the pronoun *she* to refer to the central character, it is nonetheless an autobiography. Make sure that before reading the selection students are familiar with the information provided in the author biography.

English Language Learning
Point out the following words to your students.
alderman—senior member of a local council
prestigious—having the power to impress
lofty—noble
mortified—ashamed
amends—something done to make up for an injury
venture—a business undertaking in which there is a danger of loss as well as a chance for profit
enterprise—project; undertaking
marvel—wonderful thing; miracle
vanity—excessive pride or conceit

Special Needs
Students should pay special attention to the Guided Reading questions and to the Recall questions in Investigate, Inquire, and Imagine.

Enrichment
Ask students to research the period in which Margery Kempe lived, AD 1373–1438, to find out what opportunities were available for women. Excellent sources of information on this subject include Thiébaux, Marcelle, *The Writings of Medieval Women,* 1994, and Klapisch-Zuber, Christiane, ed. *Silences of the Middle Ages.* Vol. 2 of A History of Women. Ed. George Duby and Michelle Perrot. 1992.

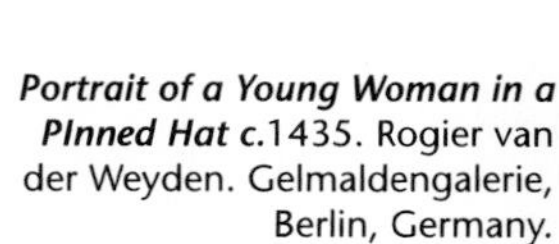

***Portrait of a Young Woman in a Plnned Hat c.*1435. Rogier van der Weyden. Gelmaldengalerie, Berlin, Germany.

FROM The Book of Margery Kempe

MARGERY KEMPE

3. Her Fanciful Clothing, Her Brewing and Horse Mill Ventures

And when this creature had through grace recovered her senses again, she believed she was bound to God and that she would be his servant. Still, she would not abandon her pride or the ostentatious style of dress that she was always used to before. She wouldn't follow her husband's advice or anyone else's. And yet she knew very well that people gossiped viciously about her, for she wore gold pipes on her head and her hoods with the tippets were dagged.[1] Her cloaks also were dagged and lined with many colors between the dags so that her outfit would draw people's stares and she would be more admired.

And when her husband told her to give up her pride, she answered sharply and shortly and said that she had come from an excellent family—he seemed an unlikely man to have married her, since her father had formerly been mayor of the

1. **gold . . . dagged.** She wore golden cylindrical hats decorated with hanging points.

Words for Everyday Use

os • ten • ta • tious (äs´tən tā´shəs) *adj.,* excessively showy. *The new mansion on the block is a bit ostentatious for Haley's tastes.*

town of N- and afterwards had been alderman of the prestigious Guild of the Trinity in N-. And therefore she maintained the lofty status of her kin, no matter what anyone said. She was very envious of her neighbors lest they dress as well as she did. Her whole desire was to have people admire her. She would not put up with criticism, or be content with the goods God had sent her, as her husband was, but always desired more and more.

What business did Kempe start? Why did she start this business?

And then out of pure greed and the wish to keep up her pride, she began to brew and was one of the greatest brewers in the town of N- for three or four years till she had lost a good deal of money, for she had never had any experience in brewing. For no matter how good her servants were and clever at brewing, yet things never went well with them. For even when the ale looked as splendid—standing under its head of froth—as anyone might see, suddenly the froth would sink down so that the ale was ruined, one brewing after another, and her servants were mortified and would not stay with her.

Then this creature thought how God had punished her already, and she refused to be warned, and now again she was punished with the loss of her goods, and then she gave up brewing and did it no more. Then she asked her husband's forgiveness for she had not followed his advice, and she said that her pride and sin had brought about her punishment and she would willingly make amends for her faults.

Yet she would not leave the world entirely, for now she thought of a new kind of housewifely venture. She had a horse mill. She got herself two good horses and a man to grind people's corn, and in this way she felt sure she could make her living. This enterprise did not last long, for a short time after the Eve of Corpus Christi,[2] the following marvel occurred. This man was in good health of body, with two horses that were lusty and in good condition, and up till now had drawn well in the mill. Now when the man took one of these horses and put him in the mill as he had done all along, this horse would not drag a load in the mill no matter what the man did. Sometimes he led him by the head, sometimes he beat him, and sometimes he cajoled him, but it was all useless because the horse would rather go backward than forward. Then this man set a pair of sharp spurs on his heels and rode on the horse's back to make him pull, but it was never any better.

When this man saw it was useless, then he put up the horse in the stable and fed him, and he ate well and freshly. Then he took the other horse and put him in the mill. And just as his fellow horse had done, so this one did, for he wouldn't pull despite anything the man did. And then this man quit his service and would no longer stay with this creature we have mentioned. As soon as the word got around the town of N- that no man or beast would work for that creature, then some people said she was cursed. Some said God took open vengeance on her. Some said one thing and some said another. And some wise men whose mind was more grounded in the love of our Lord said it was the high mercy of our Lord Jesus Christ that commanded and called her from the pride and vanity of the wretched world. ■

What problem did she have with her second venture?

What did people say about Kempe because of these failures? How did Kempe see the matter?

2. **Corpus Christi.** A Christian festival on the fifth Thursday or sixth Sunday after Easter

WORDS FOR EVERYDAY USE

ca • jole (kə jōl´) *vt.*, coax with flattery. *Gordon will try to cajole the bus driver to stop at his house, which isn't on the scheduled route.*

venge • ance (ven´jens) *n.*, revenge; retribution. *It often isn't healthy to seek vengeance for the wrongdoings of others.*

ANSWERS TO GUIDED READING QUESTIONS

1. Kempe started a brewery. The business was based on her pride and greed.
2. Kempe's second venture, a horse mill, was unsuccessful because both of her horses refused to cooperate and would not drag a load in the mill. The man she had hired to work at the mill quit because of the problems with the horses.
3. People said the Kempe must be cursed and the God must be getting her back for something. Kempe believed that the Lord was probably calling her "from the pride and vanity of the wretched world."

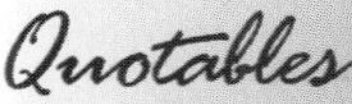

In God's sight we do not fall; in our own we do not stand.

—Julian of Norwich, Revelations of Divine Love

ADDITIONAL QUESTIONS AND ACTIVITIES

Share with students the quotation from Julian of Norwich, a mystic who was born about thirty years before Margery Kempe. Ask students how this quotation applies to Margery Kempe.

SELECTION CHECK TEST 4.3.13 WITH ANSWERS

Checking Your Reading

1. Who is "this creature"? **"This creature" is Margery Kempe.**
2. Whose orders will she not obey? **She won't obey anyone's orders.**
3. What does she reveal about her family? **They are highborn and wealthy.**
4. At what venture does she lose much money? **She loses money brewing.**
5. People said many things about her mill's failure. Name one. **Responses will vary.**

Literary Tools

1. This work is the earliest English example of what type of work? **It is the earliest example of autobiography in English.**
2. From what point of view is this selection told? **It is in third-person point of view.**
3. Why is this an unusual choice of point of view for this type of work? **This is an autobiography, and they are usually written in first person.**

RESPOND TO THE SELECTION

Students may want to decide if they agree with the conclusions to which the townspeople jumped. Some students might feel respect for Kempe and her attempts at starting these businesses. She was, after all, one of the first female entrepreneurs.

ANSWERS TO INVESTIGATE, INQUIRE, AND IMAGINE

Recall

1a. Kempe has a particularly showy, extravagant style of dress.

2a. Kempe's first business venture is a brewery. It fails because the ale never comes out right. Her servants become embarrassed and leave.

3a. After the brewery fails, Kemp starts a horse mill. This business fails because the horses will not cooperate.

Interpret

1b. Kempe believed that she was prideful because she was conscious of the fact that she came from a wealthy and politically important family. She was envious of her neighbors, always in search of admiration, unable to tolerate criticism, and "always desired more and more."

2b. After the brewery failed, Kempe believed that God was punishing her for having too much pride. She begged her husband for forgiveness and decided to "make amends for her faults."

3b. One can assume that Kempe did not give up easily, that she always wanted more, and that she often changed her mind.

Analyze

4a. *Responses will vary.* Towns were governed by mayors. Status was based on money and occupation. Businesses included brewing and milling. Religion was important.

Synthesize

4b. *Responses will vary.* Some students may get the impression from the description of the horse mill that medieval life was very labor intensive. Others might remark that the small town atmosphere encouraged gossip. Students may be able to relate to Kempe's desire to gain the admiration of others.

Respond *to the* Selection

Imagine that you are one of the townspeople mentioned in the selection. Write your response to Kempe's actions.

Investigate, Inquire, Imagine

Recall: Gathering Facts → **Interpret:** Finding Meaning

1a What outward signs point to Kempe's pride?

1b. Why does Kempe think she is prideful?

2a. What is the first business venture that Kempe undertakes? Why does it fail?

2b. How did this business failure affect Kempe's opinion of herself?

3a. What business does she start next? Why does it fail?

3b. What does Kempe's willingness to start another business say about her personality?

Analyze: Taking Things Apart → **Synthesize:** Bringing Things Together

4a. Identify elements revealed about everyday medieval life.

4b. What is your overall impression about medieval life?

Evaluate: Making Judgments → **Extend:** Connecting Ideas

5a. Summarize the religious beliefs of Kempe.

5b. Compare and contrast the religious theme in this selection with that expressed in the lyric poetry earlier in this unit.

Understanding Literature

Point of View. Review the definition of **point of view** in the Handbook of Literary Terms. How does the point of view affect the tone of the text? How would a first person point of view change the tone?

Autobiography. Review the definition of **autobiography** and the chart you made for Literary Tools on page 211. Kempe makes a life change in this selection. What do you learn about Kempe's life? Explain whether her life fits what you expected of the life of a medieval woman.

ANSWERS TO INVESTIGATE, INQUIRE, AND IMAGINE (cont.)

Evaluate

5a. *Responses will vary.* Kempe believed she would be a servant of God, but she had a difficult time giving up her worldly ways. After several trials, she believed she was being punished for these ways and tried to give up her greed and pride.

Extend

5b. *Responses will vary.* As in several other selections, religious beliefs guide the way of life. The idea of not focusing too much on the pleasures of this world is presented here as it was in "Ubi Sunt qui Ante Nos Feurunt." Death is not as closely connected in this selection.

Writer's Journal

1. Write a **notice** from Margery Kempe explaining why she is not starting a new business.
2. Choose an important event in your life. Write an **autobiographical essay** about this event and the effect it had on you.
3. Imagine that you had the chance to interview Margery Kempe for a television show. Write a **dialogue** for that interview.

Integrating *the* Language Arts

Language, Grammar, and Style

Avoiding Double Negatives. Negatives such as *not* and *never* frequently affect verbs, but they are not verbs themselves. They are adverbs, because they add to the meaning of the verb. The verb tells what the action is, and the negative indicates that the writer or speaker means the opposite of that. Using more than one negative in a sentence, or using a *double negative,* cancels out the meaning of the original negative used in the sentence. Review the Language Arts Survey 3.29, "Working with Negatives and Contractions" for examples.

In the following sentences, underline the negatives. If you find a double negative, change it so there is only one negative in each sentence. If the sentence is correct, write *Correct.*

1. Like many women of her time, Kempe couldn't neither read nor write.
2. Margery Kempe didn't never physically write her autobiography.
3. Kemp's autobiography does not relate a chronological story of a person's life.
4. There is not hardly any sense of the passage of time throughout the book.
5. Kemp didn't enter a convent nor live in reclusion neither.

Study and Research

Researching Medieval Women. Learn more about the lives of women during the Medieval Period. Use the Internet and print sources to learn either about typical daily life or about the lives of specific women. Discuss your findings in small groups.

Speaking and Listening

Debate. Hold a debate on pride. Can pride be a good thing, or does pride always go before a fall?

Applied English

Expository Writing. Writing that explains a process must be very clear and organized. A reader should be able to understand or perform an action after reading the text. Kempe's description of the horse mill incorporates expository elements; for example, she details how the horse should have performed in the mill. Think of a process that you perform every day, such as opening a computer file or taking the bus. Write a paragraph or two explaining the process for someone who has never done the activity. As you write, remember to use spatial and time order to detail the process. You might brainstorm by listing and numbering the steps of the process.

Answers to Integrating the Language Arts

Language, Grammar, and Style

1. couldn't, neither, nor: Like many women of her time, Kempe could neither read nor write.
2. didn't, never: Margery Kempe didn't ever physically write her autobiography.
3. does not: Correct
4. not, hardly: There is hardly any sense of the passage of time throughout the book.
5. didn't, nor, neither: Kempe didn't enter a convent or live in reclusion.

Study and Research

You might have students begin by making some predictions about what they will find. That is, they should note what they think life was like for a medieval woman and compare these ideas to their findings.

Applied English

Have pairs of students review each other's instructions for clarity, organization, and completeness. If the student reviewer has never performed the described action, he or she should note any questions they have about terminology, order of steps, etc. If the student has performed the action, he or she should imagine going through the instructions, step-by-step, as they are written and note any place where something is missing or unclear.

Answers to Understanding Literature

Point of View. The third-person point of view might make the judgments about the central character seem more objective. It also makes the piece seem more like a story.

Autobiography. Kempe was a greedy, proud, and vain woman. She tries to change to become more a servant of God. She was a business woman, who in this selection tried two different businesses. Kempe had a great deal of autonomy, which wasn't uncommon among medieval women.

ADDITIONAL RESOURCES

UNIT 3 RESOURCE BOOK

- "The Prologue"
- Selection Worksheet 3.7
- Selection Check Test 4.3.15
- Selection Test 4.3.16
- From "The Pardoner's Tale"
- Selection Worksheet 3.8
- Selection Check Test 4.3.17
- Selection Test 4.3.18

GRAPHIC ORGANIZER

Students might include following information about the Pardoner: yellow hair, smooth like flax; hair like rat tails; tried to be stylish; bulging eyes; carried fake relics; voice like a goat; no beard; told a good story; able to get lots of money from people.

VOCABULARY FROM THE SELECTION

absolution	personable
abstrusest	prating
accrue	prelate
ambling	prevarication
arbitrate	sanguine
asunder	saucy
cloister	scrupulosity
diligent	scurrility
duress	sedately
encumbered	seemly
felicity	sober
flax	solicitous
frugal	splay
fustian	stature
grisly	stile
guile	strife
heath	superfluity
hoary	sward
hostelry	tillage
lanyard	unworldly
mire	verity
miscreant	wanton
motley	wary
perdition	withal

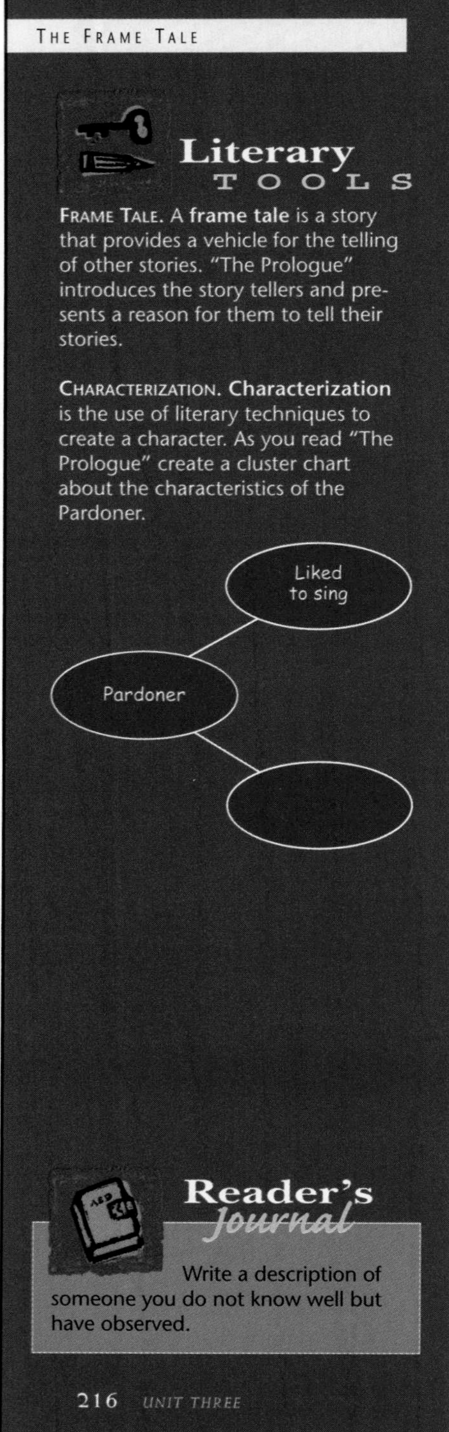

THE FRAME TALE

Literary TOOLS

FRAME TALE. A **frame tale** is a story that provides a vehicle for the telling of other stories. "The Prologue" introduces the story tellers and presents a reason for them to tell their stories.

CHARACTERIZATION. Characterization is the use of literary techniques to create a character. As you read "The Prologue" create a cluster chart about the characteristics of the Pardoner.

Reader's Journal

Write a description of someone you do not know well but have observed.

"THE PROLOGUE"

FROM "THE PARDONER'S TALE"

FROM *The Canterbury Tales*

BY GEOFFREY CHAUCER, TRANSLATED BY NEVILL COGHILL

About the AUTHOR

Geoffrey Chaucer (c.1342–1400), a public servant and a poet, was the most important writer of *Middle English.* As the son of a London wine merchant, he was a member of the growing middle class in England. Much of his life was spent in the company of royalty, however. By 1357, he had entered the service of Elizabeth, countess of Ulster, and had met John of Gaunt, who would become one of his chief patrons. Chaucer's favor with the aristocracy continued to grow. King Edward III contributed to his ransom after Chaucer was captured during an invasion of France in 1359. In 1367, he was granted a life pension by the king and subsequently returned to France and Italy on several diplomatic missions. For the rest of his life, he continued his civil work as a Controller of Customs, a justice of the peace, a member of Parliament, and a Clerk of the King's Works. In his old age, he was generously provided for by both Richard III and Henry IV. Despite all of his work as a public servant, Chaucer found time to write poetry.

Chaucer was widely read and educated on a variety of subjects. His first literary influences were the French allegorical poets, who were popular with the English aristocracy of the time. One of his first known works is "The Romaunt of the Rose," a translation of a French poem. *The Book of the Duchess,* one of his earliest original works, was written as an elegy for John of Gaunt's first wife. A diplomatic journey to Italy in 1372 put Chaucer in direct contact with the Italian Renaissance, giving him new ideas for subjects and forms for his own writing. Boccaccio served as a source for both *Troilus and Criseide* and for "The Knight's Tale" in *The Canterbury Tales,* considered the major literary achievement in Middle English. Chaucer wrote both poetry and prose on a wide range of subjects, drawing on his own broad reading and on his varied personal experience.

GOALS/OBJECTIVES

Studying this lesson will enable students to

- enjoy the variety of characters introduced in the selection
- explain the literary significance of Geoffrey Chaucer
- define frame tale and explain why *The Canterbury Tales* is an example of a frame tale
- rewrite sentences to reduce wordiness
- understand how to take multiple-choice tests

About the SELECTIONS

The Canterbury Tales is a *frame tale,* a story that itself provides a vehicle for the telling of other stories. The vehicle story of *The Canterbury Tales* is established in **"The Prologue,"** which introduces a diverse group of characters, including the narrator. *The Canterbury Tales* consists primarily of tales the characters share with each other to pass the time during their pilgrimage to Canterbury, the site of a shrine to *St. Thomas à Becket.* The characters, who represent various aspects of society, are introduced roughly in order of their rank in society. The descriptions of the characters are brief but vivid. The characters are further developed throughout *The Canterbury Tales,* by their discussions between the several tales as well as by the stories they tell. The interaction among the characters and the diversity of narrators and stories are all innovations that Chaucer made to the frame tale, which was already a popular form.

Chaucer planned for each pilgrim to tell four stories, but he never completed the project. Many stories are nonexistent, and others exist only as unfinished fragments. The order the poet intended for the tales is also unclear. Chaucer began work on *The Canterbury Tales* around 1386, but the stories were probably written over a long period of his life, and some may not originally have been intended to be included. **"The Pardoner's Tale"** is preceded by a prologue, in which the pardoner explains how he preaches against greed. Like many of Chaucer's stories, there were several possible sources for this story. The most likely direct source is one of the many collections of *exempla,* stories illustrating moral lessons, which were circulated throughout Europe and intended for use in sermons. The tale has many analogues in Latin, Italian, and German sources, but may be of non-European origin.

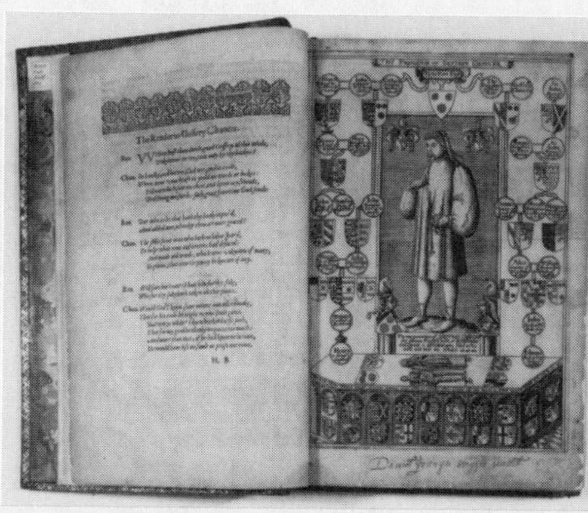

The Works of Our Ancient and Learned English Poet. London, 1598. Wellesley College Library, Special Collections.

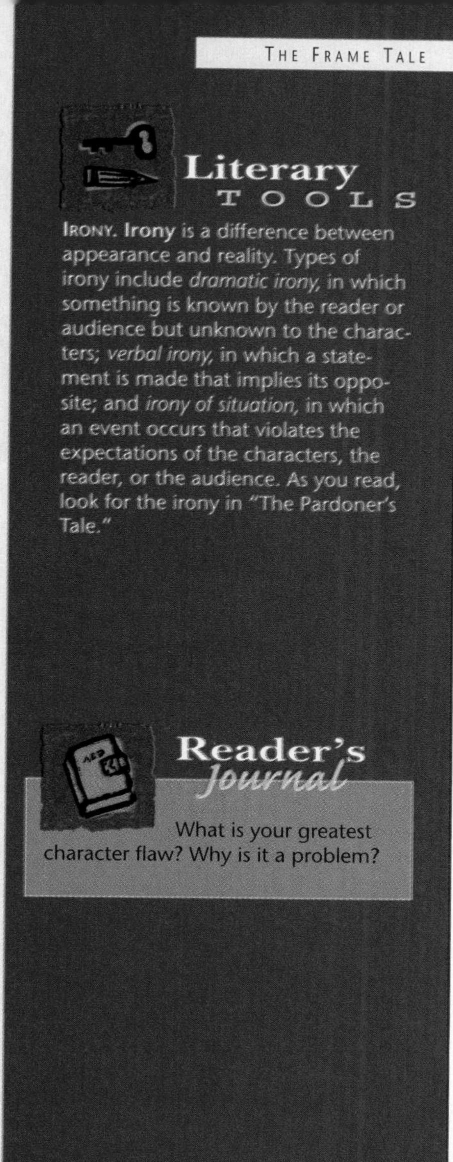

Literary TOOLS

IRONY. Irony is a difference between appearance and reality. Types of irony include *dramatic irony,* in which something is known by the reader or audience but unknown to the characters; *verbal irony,* in which a statement is made that implies its opposite; and *irony of situation,* in which an event occurs that violates the expectations of the characters, the reader, or the audience. As you read, look for the irony in "The Pardoner's Tale."

Reader's Journal

What is your greatest character flaw? Why is it a problem?

INDIVIDUAL LEARNING STRATEGIES (CONT.)

SPECIAL NEEDS
Students should stop after each pilgrim is introduced and identify three major characteristics of the character. They should pay special attention to the Recall questions in Investigate, Inquire, and Imagine.

ENRICHMENT
Students can read from other examples of frame tales, such as *A Thousand and One Nighs* and *Boccaccio's Decameron.* Students can discuss in groups the frame used in each case. Ask students if they think the frame is realistic or contrived? How are the stories in each frame tale connected?

READER'S JOURNAL

Students might begin by describing the individual's facial features, build and dress. Then, they can move on to any words, mannerisms, or actions they observed. Students may also wish to speculate about the person they observed: what do the person do for a job, where does he or she live, what does he or she do for fun, etc.

If students do not feel comfortable writing about their own flaw, ask them to think about what they consider to be a great character flaw in general. Students should still explain their response.

INDIVIDUAL LEARNING STRATEGIES

MOTIVATION
Have students create a contemporary frame tale. Have them brainstorm situations in which people might tell each other stories (for example being stuck inside a ski cabin during a blizzard). Then have each student contribute a story. Students can tell any kind of story they want. Some suggestions might be a favorite childhood memory, a story they have heard about a celebrity, a fairy tale they remember, or a story they have made up.

READING PROFICIENCY
Some students may be intimidated by the length of the selection. To deal with this problem, have students read and discuss each part of "The Prologue" separately. Begin with lines 1-42, and make sure your students understand the basic situation—that Chaucer is describing a group of medieval people from all walks of life who are going on a pilgrimage or religious journey, and decide to tell one another stories to pass the time. Before relating the stories, the narrator describes each of the people who will be telling them. These descriptions make up "The Prologue."

ENGLISH LANGUAGE LEARNING
There are many challenging vocabulary words in this selection. A list of words to review with your students appears in the margins by each section of "The Prologue."

ENGLISH LANGUAGE LEARNING

Introduction to "The Prologue"
drought—period without rain
engendering—birth; creation
exhale—breathe out
pilgrimage—a journey taken to a place with religious significance
hallowed—sacred; holy
sundry—many and varied
shire—community
wend—travel
fellowship—friendliness; community
array—dress

ADDITIONAL QUESTIONS AND ACTIVITIES

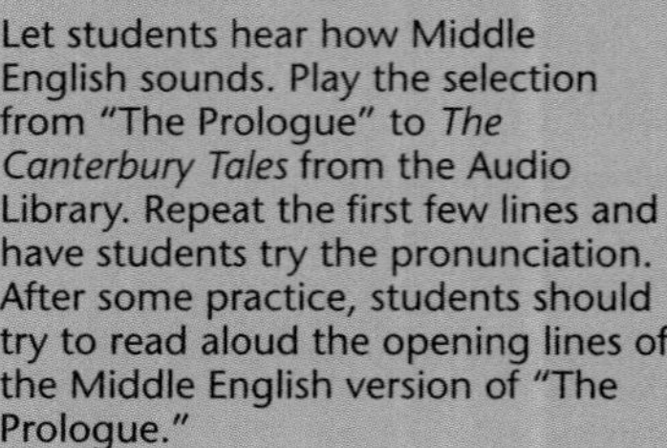

Let students hear how Middle English sounds. Play the selection from "The Prologue" to *The Canterbury Tales* from the Audio Library. Repeat the first few lines and have students try the pronunciation. After some practice, students should try to read aloud the opening lines of the Middle English version of "The Prologue."

ADDITIONAL QUESTIONS AND ACTIVITIES

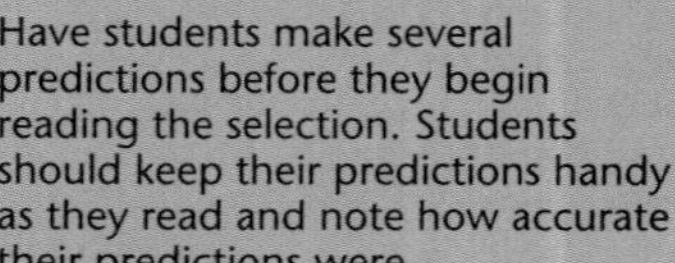

Have students make several predictions before they begin reading the selection. Students should keep their predictions handy as they read and note how accurate their predictions were.

FROM *The Canterbury Tales*

THE PROLOGUE

GEOFFREY CHAUCER, TRANSLATED BY NEVILL COGHILL

han that Aprill with his shoures soote[1]
The droghte of March hath perced to the roote,
And bathed every veyne in swich licour
Of which vertu engendred is the flour;
Whan Zephirus eek with his sweete breeth
Inspired hath in every holt and heeth
The tendre croppes, and the yonge sonne
Hath in the Ram his halve cours yronne,
And smale foweles maken melodye,
That slepen al the nyght with open ye
(So priketh hem nature in hir corages);
Thanne longen folk to goon on pilgrimages,
And palmeres for to seken straunge strondes,
To ferne halwes, kowthe in sondry londes;
And specially from every shires ende

hen in April the sweet showers fall
And pierce the drought of March to the root, and all
The veins are bathed in liquor of such power
As brings about the engendering of the flower,
When also Zephyrus[2] with his sweet breath
Exhales an air in every grove and heath
Upon the tender shoots, and the young sun
His half-course in the sign of the Ram has run,[3]
And the small fowl are making melody
That sleep away the night with open eye
(So nature pricks them and their heart engages)
Then people long to go on pilgrimages
And palmers long to seek the stranger strands[4]
Of far-off saints, hallowed in sundry lands,
And specially, from every shire's end

1. **Lines 1–26** are given here in the original Middle English (left column) and in a Modern English translation (right column). The rest of "The Prologue" follows in Modern English.

2. **Zephyrus.** The west wind

3. **young . . . run.** The sun has gone halfway through its course in Aries, the Ram, the first sign of the Zodiac in the solar year.

4. **palmers . . . strands.** Pilgrims want to visit faraway shrines.

WORDS FOR EVERYDAY USE

heath (hēth) *n.,* open wasteland. *Accustomed to the lush vegetation of her tropical home, the visitor to England was depressed by the barren heath.*

Title page of The Works of Geoffrey Chaucer. William Morris. Wellesley College Library.

Of Engelond to Caunterbury they wende,
The hooly blisful martir for to seke,
That hem hath holpen whan that they
were seeke.
Bifil that in that seson on a day,
In Southwerk at the Tabard as I lay
Redy to wenden on my pilgrymage
To Caunterbury with ful devout corage,
At nyght was come into that hostelrye
Wel nyne and twenty in a comaignye,
Of sondry folk, by aventure yfalle
In felaweshipe, and pilgrimes were they alle,

Of England, down to Canterbury they wend
To seek the holy blissful martyr,[5] quick
To give his help to them when they
were sick.
It happened in that season that one day
In Southwark,[6] at *The Tabard*, as I lay
Ready to go on pilgrimage and start
For Canterbury, most devout at heart,
At night there came into that hostelry
Some nine and twenty in a company
Of sundry folk happening then to fall
In fellowship, and they were pilgrims all

5. **holy . . . martyr.** Saint Thomas à Becket, who was killed in Canterbury Cathedral in 1170

6. **Southwark.** A suburb of London, located south of the River Thames and the site of the Tabard Inn

WORDS FOR EVERYDAY USE

hos • tel • ry (häs´təl rē) *n.*, lodging place. *After twenty hours of driving we were not picky about which hostelry we stopped at for the night.*

CROSS-CURRICULAR CONNECTION

Thomas à Becket (circa 1118–1170) served as the chancellor of England and as the Archbishop of Canterbury under the reign of Henry II. After being named archbishop, Becket amended his life style and became a truly devout follower of church law. This angered Henry, who thought that he would have greater control over the church by having Becket in this position. Quarreling between Henry and Becket intensified, and in 1170 four knights acted on the violent utterings of Henry and killed Becket in the cathedral. Within a few days of his death, his tomb became a popular pilgrimage destination.

ADDITIONAL QUESTIONS AND ACTIVITIES

Students can use an atlas to find the river Thames, Southwerk, and Canterbury. They can determine the distance between Southwerk and Canterbury. As other place names arise in "The Prologue," students can locate them on the map as well.

ART NOTE

William Morris (1834–1896) was noted for his design of furniture, fabrics, wallpaper, and stained glass windows. Morris's designs were so impressive that they gave birth to what is now known as the Arts and Crafts Movement. The elaborateness of Victorian design is due to Morris's impact, although it can also be said that Victorian taste was a reaction to the squalor brought on by the Industrial Revolution.

Quotables

"Unless people care about carrying on their business without making the world hideous, how can they care about Art?"

—William Morris

ENGLISH LANGUAGE LEARNING

The Knight
heathen—non-Christian
embark—set sail; leave on a journey
sovereign—kingly; royal
boorish—rude; awkward, ill-mannered
render—give
The Squire
moderate—average
agility—ease of movement
valiantly—bravely

ADDITIONAL QUESTIONS AND ACTIVITIES

Students can research what an inn or hostelry was like during Chaucer's time. They can then draw a picture or construct a model of a typical inn.

ADDITIONAL QUESTIONS AND ACTIVITIES

1. Which pilgrim is introduced first?
2. What word is used to describe him?
3. Who is traveling with the knight?

Answers

1. The knight is introduced first.
2. He is distinguished.
3. His son, a squire, is traveling with him.

That towards Canterbury meant to ride.
The rooms and stables of the inn were wide;
They made us easy, all was of the best.
And, briefly, when the sun had gone to rest,
I'd spoken to them all upon the trip
And was soon one with them in fellowship,
Pledged to rise early and to take the way
To Canterbury, as you heard me say.
But none the less, while I have time and space,
Before my story takes a further pace,
It seems a reasonable thing to say
What their condition was, the full array
Of each of them, as it appeared to me,
According to profession and degree,
And what apparel they were riding in;
And at a Knight I therefore will begin.

There was a *Knight*, a most distinguished man,
Who from the day on which he first began
To ride abroad had followed chivalry,
Truth, honor, generousness and courtesy.
He had done nobly in his sovereign's war
And ridden into battle, no man more,
As well in Christian as in heathen places,
And ever honored for his noble graces.
When we took Alexandria, he was there.
He often sat at table in the chair
Of honor, above all nations, when in Prussia.
In Lithuania he had ridden, and Russia,
No Christian man so often, of his rank.
When, in Granada, Algeciras sank
Under assault, he had been there, and in
North Africa, raiding Benamarin;
In Anatolia he had been as well
And fought when Ayas and Attalia[7] fell,
For all along the Mediterranean coast
He had embarked with many a noble host.
In fifteen mortal battles he had been
And jousted for our faith at Tramissene
Thrice in the lists,[8] and always killed his man.
This same distinguished knight had led the van
Once with the Bey of Balat, doing work
For him against another heathen Turk;
He was of sovereign value in all eyes.
And though so much distinguished, he was wise
And in his bearing modest as a maid.
He never yet a boorish thing had said
In all his life to any, come what might;
He was a true, a perfect gentle-knight.
Speaking of his equipment, he possessed
Fine horses, but he was not gaily dressed.
He wore a fustian tunic stained and dark
With smudges where his armor had left mark;
Just home from service, he had joined our ranks
To do his pilgrimage and render thanks.

He had his son with him, a fine young *Squire*,
A lover and cadet, a lad of fire
With locks as curly as if they had been pressed.
He was some twenty years of age, I guessed.
In stature he was of a moderate length,
With wonderful agility and strength.
He'd seen some service with the cavalry
In Flanders and Artois and Picardy

7. **Alexandria . . . Attalia.** Sites of battles in which the Knight fought against the Moslems, Moors, and northern enemies
8. **lists.** Arena for jousting tournaments

WORDS FOR EVERYDAY USE

fus • tian (fus´chən) *n.,* coarse cloth. *Natalie's simple fustian dress stood out sharply in the crowd of elaborate satin frocks.*

stat • ure (stach´ər) *n.,* height. *Judging by the stature of her parents, Winnifred will probably grow to over six feet tall.*

And had done valiantly in little space
Of time, in hope to win his lady's grace.
He was embroidered like a meadow bright
And full of freshest flowers, red and white.
Singing he was, or fluting all the day;
He was as fresh as is the month of May.
Short was his gown, the sleeves were long and wide;
He knew the way to sit a horse and ride.
He could make songs and poems and recite,
Knew how to joust and dance, to draw and write.
He loved so hotly that till dawn grew pale
He slept as little as a nightingale.
Courteous he was, lowly and serviceable,
And carved to serve his father at the table.

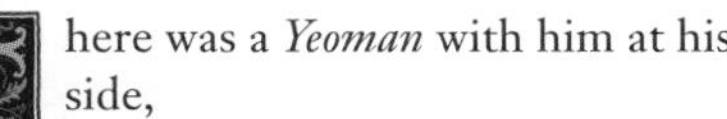
There was a *Yeoman* with him at his side,
No other servant; so he chose to ride.
This Yeoman wore a coat and hood of green,
And peacock-feathered arrows, bright and keen
And neatly sheathed, hung at his belt the while
—For he could dress his gear in yeoman style,
His arrows never drooped their feathers low—
And in his hand he bore a mighty bow.
His head was like a nut, his face was brown.
He knew the whole of woodcraft up and down.
A saucy brace was on his arm to ward
It from the bow-string, and a shield and sword
Hung at one side, and at the other slipped
A jaunty dirk,[9] spear-sharp and well-equipped.
A medal of St. Christopher[10] he wore
Of shining silver on his breast, and bore
A hunting-horn, well slung and burnished clean,
That dangled from a baldrick[11] of bright green.
He was a proper forester, I guess.

There also was a *Nun*, a Prioress,
Her way of smiling very simple and coy.
Her greatest oath was only "By St. Loy!"
And she was known as Madam Eglantyne.
And well she sang a service, with a fine
Intoning through her nose, as was most seemly,
And she spoke daintily in French, extremely,
After the school of Stratford-atte-Bowe;[12]
French in the Paris style she did not know.
At meat her manners were well taught withal;
No morsel from her lips did she let fall,
Nor dipped her fingers in the sauce too deep;
But she could carry a morsel up and keep
The smallest drop from falling on her breast.
For courtliness she had a special zest,
And she would wipe her upper lip so clean
That not a trace of grease was to be seen
Upon the cup when she had drunk; to eat,
She reached a hand sedately for the meat.
She certainly was very entertaining,

9. **dirk.** Dagger
10. **St. Christopher.** Patron saint of travelers
11. **baldrick.** Belt worn over one shoulder and across the chest
12. **Stratford-atte-Bowe.** Location of a convent school where French was taught, but not especially well

Words for Everyday Use

sau • cy (sô´ sē) *adj.*, stylish. *George's hat was outdated, but he thought it was stylish with its saucy feather.*

with • al (with ôl´) *adv.*, besides; nevertheless. *I have a headache but I am going to the party withal.*

se • date • ly (si dāt´lē) *adv.*, in a dignified manner. *Leon usually causes a commotion when he runs through the library, but today he walked through very sedately.*

ENGLISH LANGUAGE LEARNING

The Yeoman
jaunty—stylish; fashionable
burnish—shine

The Nun
intone—sing or recite like a chant
daintily—in a delicate or refined way
morsel—bit of food
zest—enjoyment; desire; gusto
counterfeit—fake

ADDITIONAL QUESTIONS AND ACTIVITIES

Chaucer creates very vivid portraits of the characters in words. Students can draw portraits of one or more of the pilgrims based on their descriptions in "The Prologue." Students may work together to illustrate this whole motley group.

ADDITIONAL QUESTIONS AND ACTIVITIES

1. To whom is the Yeoman a servant?
2. What color does the Yeoman wear?
3. What is the Nun's name?
4. What kind of manners does the Nun have? Do her actions seem genuine?

Answers

1. The Yeoman is servant to the Squire.
2. The Yeoman wears green.
3. The Nun is known as Madam Eglantyne.
4. The Nun seems to be careful with her manners. Her actions seemed to be "straining to counterfeit a courtly kind of grace."

ENGLISH LANGUAGE LEARNING 

The Monk
garnished—decorated
cunningly—in a crafty or clever way
prominent—projecting, sticking out
supple—flexible

ADDITIONAL QUESTIONS AND ACTIVITIES 

To check students' reading comprehension, ask the following questions:

1. What did the Monk like to do?
2. What did the church teach about hunting?
3. How did the Monk respond to church teaching?

Answers

1. The Monk liked to hunt.
2. The church said that hunters were not holy men.
3. Although the Monk was supposed to uphold the rules and beliefs of the church, he flagrantly violated them and lived a pleasurable life.

LITERARY TECHNIQUE 

Satire. Satire is humorous writing or speech intended to point our errors, falsehoods, or failings. Whom does Chaucer satirize? What failings does he point out?

Answer

Chaucer satirizes many of his characters, especially the church figures, such as the Nun, the Monk, and the Friar. He points out the Nun's overzealous manners, her oversentimentality, and her attention to her appearance. He shows that the monk does not lead the life prescribed by the church, nor does the Friar, who spends his time in taverns and in winning the attention of young women.

Pleasant and friendly in her ways, and straining
To counterfeit a courtly kind of grace,
A stately bearing fitting to her place,
And to seem dignified in all her dealings.
As for her sympathies and tender feelings,
She was so charitably solicitous
She used to weep if she but saw a mouse
Caught in a trap, if it were dead or bleeding.
And she had little dogs she would be feeding
With roasted flesh, or milk, or fine white bread.
And bitterly she wept if one were dead
Or someone took a stick and made it smart;
She was all sentiment and tender heart.
Her veil was gathered in a seemly way,
Her nose was elegant, her eyes glass-grey;
Her mouth was very small, but soft and red,
Her forehead, certainly, was fair of spread,
Almost a span across the brows, I own;
She was indeed by no means undergrown.
Her cloak, I noticed, had a graceful charm.
She wore a coral trinket on her arm,
A set of beads, the gaudies[13] tricked in green,
Whence hung a golden brooch of brightest sheen
On which there first was graven a crowned A,
And lower, *Amor vincit omnia.*[14]

Another Nun, the secretary at her cell,
Was riding with her, and three Priests as well.
A Monk there was, one of the finest sort
Who rode the country; hunting was his sport.
A manly man, to be an Abbot able;
Many a dainty horse he had in stable.
His bridle, when he rode, a man might hear
Jingling in a whistling wind as clear,
Aye, and as loud as does the chapel bell
Where my lord Monk was Prior of the cell.
The Rule of good St. Benet or St. Maur
As old and strict he tended to ignore;
He let go by the things of yesterday
And took the modern world's more spacious way.
He did not rate that text at a plucked hen
Which says that hunters are not holy men
And that a monk uncloistered is a mere
Fish out of water, flapping on the pier,
That is to say a monk out of his cloister.
That was a text he held not worth an oyster;
And I agreed and said his views were sound;
Was he to study till his head went round
Poring over books in cloisters? Must he toil
As Austin bade and till the very soil?
Was he to leave the world upon the shelf?
Let Austin have his labor to himself.
This Monk was therefore a good man to horse;
Greyhounds he had, as swift as birds, to course.
Hunting a hare or riding at a fence
Was all his fun, he spared for no expense.
I saw his sleeves were garnished at the hand
With fine gray fur, the finest in the land,
And on his hood, to fasten it at his chin

13. **gaudies.** Every eleventh bead in a rosary marks a special prayer and is called a gaudy.
14. ***Amor vincit omnia.*** Latin for "Love conquers all."

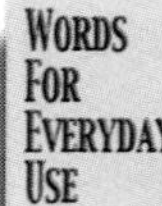

so • lic • i • tous (sə lis´ə təs) *adj.*, showing concern. *Nancy shows little concern for her own well-being, but she is extremely solicitous of others.*

seem • ly (sēm´lē) *adv.*, proper. *Beatrice usually dresses outrageously, but the outfit she wore to the wedding was quite seemly.*

clois • ter (klois´tər) *n.*, monastery. *The monk lives in a quiet cloister.*

He had a wrought-gold cunningly fashioned pin;
Into a lover's knot it seemed to pass.
His head was bald and shone like looking-glass;
So did his face, as if it had been greased.
He was a fat and <u>personable</u> priest;
His prominent eyeballs never seemed to settle.
They glittered like the flames beneath a kettle;
Supple his boots, his horse in fine condition.
He was a <u>prelate</u> fit for exhibition,
He was not pale like a tormented soul.
He liked a fat swan best, and roasted whole.
His palfrey[15] was as brown as is a berry.

There was a *Friar*, a <u>wanton</u> one and merry,
A Limiter,[16] a very festive fellow.
In all Four Orders[17] there was none so mellow,
So glib with gallant phrase and well-turned speech.
He'd fixed up many a marriage, giving each
Of his young women what he could afford her.
He was a noble pillar to his Order.
Highly beloved and intimate was he
With County folk within his boundary,
And city dames of honor and possessions;
For he was qualified to hear confessions,
Or so he said, with more than priestly scope;
He had a special license from the Pope.
Sweetly he heard his penitents at shrift[18]
With pleasant <u>absolution</u>, for a gift.
He was an easy man in penance-giving
Where he could hope to make a decent living;
It's a sure sign whenever gifts are given
To a poor Order that a man's well shriven,
And should he give enough he knew in <u>verity</u>
The penitent repented in sincerity.
For many a fellow is so hard of heart
He cannot weep, for all his inward smart.
Therefore instead of weeping and of prayer
One should give silver for a poor Friar's care.
He kept his tippet[19] stuffed with pins for curls,
And pocket-knives, to give to pretty girls.
And certainly his voice was gay and sturdy,
For he sang well and played the hurdy-gurdy.
At sing-songs he was champion of the hour.
His neck was whiter than a lily-flower
But strong enough to butt a bruiser down.
He knew the taverns well in every town
And every innkeeper and barmaid too
Better than lepers, beggars and that crew,
For in so eminent a man as he
It was not fitting with the dignity
Of his position, dealing with a scum
Of wretched lepers; nothing good can come
Of commerce with such slum-and-gutter dwellers,

15. **palfrey.** Horse
16. **Limiter.** A friar who could beg only in a limited, assigned area
17. **Four Orders.** There are four orders—Dominican, Franciscan, Carmelite, and Augustinian—whose friars all live by begging.
18. **shrift.** Confession to a priest
19. **tippet.** Long scarf worn by the clergy

WORDS FOR EVERYDAY USE

per • son • a • ble (pur´sən ə bəl) *adj.*, having a pleasant appearance and personality. *Lila hit it off immediately with her <u>personable</u> new neighbor.*
prel • ate (prel´it) *n.*, high-ranking member of the clergy. *The unambitious country priest has no desire to become a <u>prelate</u>.*
wan • ton (wän´tən) *adj.*, unrestrained; extravagant. *"Eat, drink, and be merry" is the motto of one of my <u>wanton</u> friends.*
ab • so • lu • tion (ab´sə lo͞o shən) *n.*, forgiveness. *I confessed my sins and asked for <u>absolution</u>.*
ver • i • ty (ver´ə tē) *n.*, truth. *Jim is such a liar he doesn't even know what <u>verity</u> is.*

ENGLISH LANGUAGE LEARNING

The Friar
festive—happy; merry
gallant—showy; stylish; noble
scope—range or limit
shriven—absolved through confession
eminent—well known; powerful; respected
wretched—in a terrible condition
commerce—dealings; interaction
victual—food
poaching—taking something from another's land or territory
farthing—coin

ADDITIONAL QUESTIONS AND ACTIVITIES

Students can research the hurdy-gurdy and bring in pictures and recordings of this instrument. Are any of the other pilgrims musically inclined? What instruments do they play? Which pilgrims are said to sing?

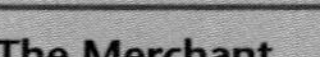

ENGLISH LANGUAGE LEARNING

The Merchant
beaver—made of beaver skin
harped—talked about continuously
exchanges—trading

The Cleric
preferment—promotion, advancement
secular—non-religious, worldly
philosopher—one who studies basic questions
lofty—high, important

ADDITIONAL QUESTIONS AND ACTIVITIES

1. What don't people know about the Merchant?
2. What is the only interest of the Oxford Cleric?

Answers

1. People do not know that the Merchant is in debt. They also do not know his name.
2. The Oxford Cleric only cares about studying or reading.

But only with the rich and victual-sellers.
But anywhere a profit might accrue
Courteous he was and lowly of service too.
Natural gifts like his were hard to match.
He was the finest beggar of his batch,
And, for his begging-district, paid a rent;
His brethren did no poaching where he went.
For though a widow mightn't have a shoe,
So pleasant was his holy how-d'ye-do
He got his farthing from her just the same
Before he left, and so his income came
To more than he laid out. And how he romped,
Just like a puppy! He was ever prompt
To arbitrate disputes on settling days
(For a small fee) in many helpful ways,
Not then appearing as your cloistered scholar
With threadbare habit hardly worth a dollar,
But much more like a Doctor or a Pope.
Of double-worsted was the semi-cope
Upon his shoulders, and the swelling fold
About him, like a bell about its mold
When it is casting, rounded out his dress.
He lisped a little out of wantonness
To make his English sweet upon his tongue.
When he had played his harp, or having sung,
His eyes would twinkle in his head as bright
As any star upon a frosty night.
This worthy's name was Hubert, it appeared.

here was a *Merchant* with a forking beard
And motley dress; high on his horse he sat,
Upon his head a Flemish beaver hat
And on his feet daintily buckled boots.
He told of his opinions and pursuits
In solemn tones, he harped on his increase
Of capital; there should be sea-police
(He thought) upon the Harwich-Holland ranges;[20]
He was expert at dabbling in exchanges.
This estimable Merchant so had set
His wits to work, none knew he was in debt,
He was so stately in administration,
In loans and bargains and negotiation.
He was an excellent fellow all the same;
To tell the truth I do not know his name.

n *Oxford Cleric*, still a student though,
One who had taken logic long ago,
Was there; his horse was thinner than a rake,
And he was not too fat, I undertake,
But had a hollow look, a sober stare;
The thread upon his overcoat was bare.
He had found no preferment in the church
And he was too unworldly to make search
For secular employment. By his bed
He preferred having twenty books in red
And black, of Aristotle's philosophy,
Than costly clothes, fiddle or psaltery.[21]
Though a philosopher, as I have told,
He had not found the stone for making gold.[22]
Whatever money from his friends he took
He spent on learning or another book
And prayed for them most earnestly, returning

20. **sea-police . . . ranges.** He wanted the sea to be well policed to guard his wool trade.
21. **psaltery.** A type of harp
22. **the stone . . . gold.** Imaginary stone sought by alchemists

WORDS FOR EVERYDAY USE

ac • crue (ə kro̅o̅) *vi.*, accumulate periodically. *I went to the bank to see how much interest my savings had accrued.*
ar • bi • trate (är´bə trāt´) *vt.*, settle a dispute. *We need an unbiased party to arbitrate this argument.*
mot • ley (mät´lē) *adj.*, multicolored. *Jim wore a motley tie-dyed shirt.*
so • ber (sō´bər) *adj.*, serious; grave. *Monica's smiling face turned sober when she heard about the catastrophe.*
un • world • ly (un wurld´lē) *adj.*, unsophisticated. *The unworldly traveler was easy prey for pickpockets.*

Thanks to them thus for paying for his learning.
His only care was study, and indeed
He never spoke a word more than was need,
Formal at that, respectful in the extreme,
Short, to the point, and lofty in his theme.
A tone of moral virtue filled his speech
And gladly would he learn, and gladly teach.

A *Sergeant at the Law* who paid his calls,
Wary and wise, for clients at St. Paul's[23]
There also was, of noted excellence.
Discreet he was, a man to reverence,
Or so he seemed, his sayings were so wise.
He often had been Justice of Assize
By letters patent,[24] and in full commission.
His fame and learning and his high position
Had won him many a robe and many a fee.
There was no such conveyancer[25] as he;
All was fee-simple[26] to his strong digestion,
Not one conveyance could be called in question.
Though there was nowhere one so busy as he,
He was less busy than he seemed to be.
He knew of every judgment, case and crime
Ever recorded since King William's time.
He could dictate defenses or draft deeds;
No one could pinch a comma from his screeds
And he knew every statute off by rote.
He wore a homely parti-colored coat,
Girt with a silken belt of pin-stripe stuff;
Of his appearance I have said enough.

There was a *Franklin*[27] with him, it appeared;
White as a daisy-petal was his beard.
A <u>sanguine</u> man, high-colored and benign,
He loved a morning sop of cake in wine.
He lived for pleasure and had always done,
For he was Epicurus'[28] very son,
In whose opinion sensual delight
Was the one true <u>felicity</u> in sight.
As noted as St. Julian was for bounty
He made his household free to all the County.
His bread, his ale were finest of the fine
And no one had a better stock of wine.
His house was never short of bake-meat pies,
Of fish and flesh, and these in such supplies
It positively snowed with meat and drink
And all the dainties that a man could think.
According to the seasons of the year
Changes of dish were ordered to appear.
He kept fat partridges in coops, beyond,
Many a bream and pike were in his pond.
Woe to the cook unless the sauce was hot
And sharp, or if he wasn't on the spot!
And in his hall a table stood arrayed
And ready all day long, with places laid.
As Justice at the Sessions none stood higher;
He often had been Member for the Shire.
A dagger and a little purse of silk
Hung at his girdle, white as morning milk.
As Sheriff he checked audit, every entry.
He was a model among landed gentry.

A *Haberdasher*, a *Dyer*, a *Carpenter*,
A *Weaver* and a *Carpet-maker* were
Among our ranks, all in the livery[29]

23. **St. Paul's.** The porch of St. Paul's Cathedral was a common meeting place for lawyers and their clients.
24. **letters patent.** Legal documents granting rights
25. **conveyancer.** Land speculator
26. **fee-simple.** Absolute and unrestricted
27. ***Franklin.*** A prosperous landowner of lower-class ancestry
28. **Epicurus'.** Of the Greek philosopher who taught that pleasure should be a large part of life
29. **livery.** Uniform.

ENGLISH LANGUAGE LEARNING

The Sergeant at the Law
discreet—careful about what one says or does
reverence—respect
conveyance—transfer of land
deed—a document showing land ownership
screeds—a long, boring piece of writing
rote—memory

The Franklin
benign—gentle; harmless
sensual—having to do with the senses (sight, sound, taste, touch, or smell)
bounty—generosity
dainties—delicate, fine foods
arrayed—organized
audit—financial accounting
gentry—land-owning people just below the nobility in social rank

The Haberdasher, Dyer, Carpenter, Weaver, and Carpet-maker
wrought—made
mantle—loose, sleeveless cloak or cape

WORDS FOR EVERYDAY USE

san • guine (saŋ´gwin) *adj.*, ruddy, red; happy. *Adrian's usually <u>sanguine</u> face paled after three days of illness.*

fe • lic • i • ty (fə lis´i tē) *n.*, happiness; bliss. *After the long, harsh winter, Bonnie found true <u>felicity</u> on her sun-filled cruise.*

ENGLISH LANGUAGE LEARNING

The Skipper
draft—drink
vintage—wine of a certain year or age
dispatch—efficiency or ease in doing a job
prudent—wise
tempest—storm

The Doctor
emerged—appeared; came out
ascendant—rising
malady—sickness
pestilences—outbreaks of disease

ADDITIONAL QUESTIONS AND ACTIVITIES

Students can research guilds or guild-fraternities to learn about the formation of guilds, the kinds of guilds, and how people became members of guilds. They can present their findings to the class.

CROSS-CURRICULAR ACTIVITIES

SOCIAL STUDIES. Students can locate Dartmouth, Bordeaux, Hull, Carthage, Gotland, and the Cape of Finisterre on a map.

Of one impressive guild-fraternity.
They were so trim and fresh their gear would pass
For new. Their knives were not tricked out[30] with brass
But wrought with purest silver, which avouches[31]
A like display on girdles and on pouches.
Each seemed a worthy burgess,[32] fit to grace
A guild-hall with a seat upon the dais.
Their wisdom would have justified a plan
To make each one of them an alderman;
They had the capital and revenue,
Besides their wives declared it was their due.
And if they did not think so, then they ought;
To be called *'Madam'* is a glorious thought,
And so is going to church and being seen
Having your mantle carried, like a queen.

They had a *Cook* with them who stood alone
For boiling chicken with a marrow-bone,
Sharp flavoring-powder and a spice for savor.
He could distinguish London ale by flavor,
And he could roast and seethe and broil and fry,
Make good thick soup and bake a tasty pie.
But what a pity—so it seemed to me,
That he should have an ulcer on his knee.
As for blancmange,[33] he made it with the best.

There was a *Skipper* hailing from far west;
He came from Dartmouth, so I understood.
He rode a farmer's horse as best he could,
In a woolen gown that reached his knee.
A dagger on a lanyard falling free
Hung from his neck under his arm and down.
The summer heat had tanned his color brown,
And certainly he was an excellent fellow.
Many a draft of vintage, red and yellow,
He'd drawn at Bordeaux, while the trader snored.
The nicer rules of conscience he ignored.
If, when he fought, the enemy vessel sank,
He sent his prisoners home; they walked the plank.
As for his skill in reckoning his tides,
Currents and many another risk besides,
Moons, harbors, pilots, he had such dispatch
That none from Hull to Carthage was his match.
Hardy he was, prudent in undertaking;
His beard in many a tempest had its shaking,
And he knew all the havens as they were
From Gottland to the Cape of Finisterre,
And every creek in Brittany and Spain;
The barge he owned was called *The Maudelayne.*

A *Doctor* too emerged as we proceeded;
No one alive could talk as well as he did
On points of medicine and of surgery,
For, being grounded in astronomy,[34]
He watched his patient closely for the hours
When, by his horoscope, he knew the powers

30. **tricked out.** Dressed up
31. **avouches.** Gives reason to expect
32. **burgess.** Citizen of a borough or town
33. **blancmange.** A bland, custard-like dessert
34. **astronomy.** Astrology

WORDS FOR EVERYDAY USE

lan • yard (lan´yərd) *n.*, cord worn around the neck. *Farley made the lanyard he wears around his neck at summer camp.*

Of favorable planets, then ascendant,
Worked on the images[35] for his dependent.
The cause of every malady you'd got
He knew, and whether dry, cold, moist or hot;[36]
He knew their seat, their humor and condition.
He was a perfect practicing physician.
These causes being known for what they were,
He gave the man his medicine then and there.
All his apothecaries[37] in a tribe
Were ready with the drugs he would prescribe
And each made money from the other's <u>guile</u>;
They had been friendly for a goodish while.
He was well-versed in Aesculapius too
And what Hippocrates and Rufus knew
And Dioscorides, now dead and gone,
Galen and Rhazes, Hali, Serapion,
Averroes, Avicenna, Constantine,
Scotch Bernard, John of Gaddesden, Gilbertine.[38]
In his own diet he observed some measure;
There were no <u>superfluities</u> for pleasure,
Only digestives, nutritives and such.
He did not read the Bible very much.
In blood-red garments, slashed with bluish gray
And lined with taffeta, he rode his way;
Yet he was rather close as to expenses
And kept the gold he won in pestilences.
Gold stimulates the heart, or so we're told.
He therefore had a special love of gold.

worthy *woman* from beside Bath city
Was with us, somewhat deaf, which was a pity.
In making cloth she showed so great a bent
She bettered those of Ypres and of Ghent.[39]
In all the parish not a dame dared stir
Toward the altar steps in front of her,
And if indeed they did, so wrath was she
As to be quite put out of charity.
Her kerchiefs were of finely woven ground;[40]
I dared have sworn they weighed a good ten pound,
The ones she wore on Sunday, on her head.
Her hose were of the finest scarlet red
And gartered tight; her shoes were soft and new.
Bold was her face, handsome, and red in hue.
A worthy woman all her life, what's more
She'd had five husbands, all at the church door,
Apart from other company in youth;
No need just now to speak of that, forsooth.
And she had thrice been to Jerusalem,
Seen many strange rivers and passed over them;
She'd been to Rome and also to Boulogne,
St. James of Compostella and Cologne,
And she was skilled in wandering by the way.
She had gap-teeth, set widely, truth to say.
Easily on an <u>ambling</u> horse she sat

35. **powers . . . images.** Effigies were made and used during the most influential hours according to the patient's horoscope.
36. **dry . . . hot.** It was believed that the human body was made up of four elements: earth, water, air, and fire. Earth was considered cold and dry; water, cold and wet; air, hot and moist; and fire, hot and dry. Disease, it was believed, was caused by an imbalance in these elements.
37. **apothecaries.** Pharmacists
38. **Aesculapius . . . Gilbertine.** Historic medical authorities
39. **Ypres . . . Ghent.** Flemish cities known for cloth-making
40. **ground.** Texture

WORDS FOR EVERYDAY USE

guile (gīl) *n.*, slyness and cunning. *Marissa's <u>guile</u> won out over the shrewd shopkeeper, and her scam was a success.*

su • per • flu • i • ty (so͞o´pər flo͞o´ə tē) *n.*, something unnecessary or extra. *The icing made the cake, but the decadent festoons and flower clusters were a <u>superfluity</u>.*

am • bling (am´bliŋ) *adj.*, in an easy and smooth manner. *After having to dash through his backyard on a rainy Thursday, Aaron was happy <u>ambling</u> about in the sun on Friday.*

ENGLISH LANGUAGE LEARNING

The Woman of Bath
parish—church district
charity—kindness toward others
forsooth—in truth
mischance—accident

ADDITIONAL QUESTIONS AND ACTIVITIES

Students can discuss how medieval medicine differs from modern medical practices. How would the Doctor's practices be viewed by modern standards?

ADDITIONAL QUESTIONS AND ACTIVITIES

Note that there were not very many women on the pilgrimage. Ask students why they think this is so. Students can research what life was like for women in Chaucer's time. Students might also compare the Woman of Bath to Margery Kempe.

INTERNET RESOURCES

For more information on Geoffrey Chaucer, his times, and his writings, students can try the following Internet sites:
www.unc.edu/depts/chaucer
www.siue.edu/CHAUCER/canterbury.htm

ENGLISH LANGUAGE LEARNING

The Parson

renown—fame
devoutly—with devotion, or steady religious feeling
adversity—difficulty
extort—to get by force or by illegal means
stave—a staff or cane
contemptuous—looking down upon
disdainful—showing distaste for
obstinate—stubborn
rebuke—blaming or scolding
pomp—fancy show or display

ADDITIONAL QUESTIONS AND ACTIVITIES

1. What is the parson rich in?
2. What kind of example does he set?
3. What didn't the parson seek?

Answers

1. The parson is rich in holy thought and work.
2. He sets and example of giving and living by the rules of the church.
3. He did not seek pomp or glory.

Well wimpled up,[41] and on her head a hat
As broad as is a buckler[42] or a shield;
She had a flowing mantle that concealed
Large hips, her heels spurred sharply under that.
In company she liked to laugh and chat
And knew the remedies for love's mis-chances,
An art in which she knew the oldest dances.

A holy-minded man of good renown
There was, and poor, the *Parson* to a town,
Yet he was rich in holy thought and work.
He also was a learned man, a clerk,
Who truly knew Christ's gospel and would preach it
Devoutly to parishioners, and teach it.
Benign and wonderfully diligent,
And patient when adversity was sent
(For so he proved in much adversity)
He hated cursing to extort a fee,
Nay rather he preferred beyond a doubt
Giving to poor parishioners round about
Both from church offerings and his property;
He could in little find sufficiency.
Wide was his parish, with houses far asunder,
Yet he neglected not in rain or thunder,
In sickness or in grief, to pay a call
On the remotest, whether great or small,
Upon his feet, and in his hand a stave.
This noble example to his sheep he gave
That first he wrought, and afterwards he taught;
And it was from the Gospel he had caught
Those words, and he would add this figure too,
That if gold rust, what then will iron do?
For if a priest be foul in whom we trust
No wonder that a common man should rust;
And shame it is to see—let priests take stock—
A shitten shepherd and a snowy flock.
The true example that a priest should give
Is one of cleanness, how the sheep should live.
He did not set his benefice[43] to hire
And leave his sheep encumbered in the mire
Or run to London to earn easy bread
By singing masses for the wealthy dead,
Or find some Brotherhood and get enrolled.
He stayed at home and watched over his fold
So that no wolf should make the sheep miscarry.
He was a shepherd and no mercenary.
Holy and virtuous he was, but then
Never contemptuous of sinful men,
Never disdainful, never too proud or fine,
But was discreet in teaching and benign.
His business was to show a fair behavior
And draw men thus to Heaven and their Savior,
Unless indeed a man were obstinate;
And such, whether of high or low estate,
He put to sharp rebuke, to say the least.
I think there never was a better priest.
He sought no pomp or glory in his dealings,

41. **wimpled up.** Medieval women commonly wrapped their heads and necks in a cloth called a *wimple.*
42. **buckler.** Small shield
43. **benefice.** Endowed office

WORDS FOR EVERYDAY USE

dil • i • gent (dil´ə jənt) *adj.*, hard-working; persevering. *Unlike Laura, who seldom does her homework or studies for tests, Lucy is a diligent student.*

a • sun • der (ə sun´dər) *adj.*, apart or separate in direction. *After sharing a room for many years, Lisa and her sister found it difficult to be so far asunder once Lisa had left for the navy.*

en • cum • bered (en kum´bərd) *part.*, held back. *The hikers were encumbered by heavy rains.*

mire (mīr) *n.*, soggy ground. *After heavy rain, the dirt road, once firm, turned into a track of impossible mire.*

No <u>scrupulosity</u> had spiced his feelings.
Christ and His Twelve Apostles and their lore
He taught, but followed it himself before.

here was a *Plowman* with him there, his brother;
Many a load of dung one time or other
He must have carted through the morning dew.
He was an honest worker, good and true,
Living in peace and perfect charity,
And, as the gospel bade him, so did he,
Loving God best with all his heart and mind
And then his neighbor as himself, repined
At no misfortune, slacked for no content,
For steadily about his work he went
To thrash his corn, to dig or to manure
Or make a ditch; and he would help the poor
For love of Christ and never take a penny
If he could help it, and, as prompt as any,
He paid his tithes in full when they were due
On what he owned, and on his earnings too.
He wore a tabard smock[44] and rode a mare.

here was a *Reeve*,[45] also a *Miller*, there,
A College *Manciple*[46] from the Inns of Court,
A papal *Pardoner*[47] and, in close consort,[48]
A Church-Court *Summoner*,[49] riding at a trot
And finally myself—that was the lot.

he *Miller* was a chap of sixteen stone,[50]
A great stout fellow big in brawn and bone.
He did well out of them, for he could go
And win the ram[51] at any wrestling show.
Broad, knotty and short-shouldered, he would boast
He could heave any door off hinge and post,
Or take a run and break it with his head.
His beard, like any sow or fox, was red
And broad as well, as though it were a spade;
And, at its very tip, his nose displayed
A wart on which there stood a tuft of hair
Red as the bristles in an old sow's ear.
His nostrils were as black as they were wide.
He had a sword and buckler at his side,
His mighty mouth was like a furnace door.
A wrangler[52] and buffoon, he had a store
Of tavern stories, filthy in the main.
His was a master-hand at stealing grain.
He felt it with his thumb and thus he knew
Its quality and took three times his due—[53]
A thumb of gold, by God, to gauge an oat!
He wore a hood of blue and a white coat.
He liked to play his bagpipes up and down
And that was how he brought us out of town.

he *Manciple* came from the Inner Temple;
All caterers might follow his example

44. **tabard smock.** Loose jacket, sometimes bearing a lord's crest
45. ***Reeve.*** The overseer of an estate
46. ***Manciple.*** Purchasing agent
47. ***Pardoner.*** A person with authority from the Pope to sell pardons and indulgences
48. **consort.** Partnership
49. ***Summoner.*** An employee of the ecclesiastical court who was paid to summon those who were suspected of breaking church law
50. **stone.** A unit of weight equal to fourteen pounds
51. **win the ram.** Rams were the usual prize at the popular wrestling tournaments.
52. **wrangler.** One who provokes arguments
53. **three . . . due.** Took for himself more than the lawful percentage

WORDS FOR EVERYDAY USE

scru • pu • los • i • ty (skro͞o pyo͞o lôs ´i tē) *n.*, moral worry or qualm. *Pickpockets at races and fairs hold no <u>scrupulosity</u> about taking what belongs to others.*

ENGLISH LANGUAGE LEARNING

The Plowman
repine—feel or express unhappiness
thrash—beat
tithes—payments made to a church

The Miller
brawn—muscles; strength
buckler—small, round shield
buffoon—clown

The Manciple
illiterate—unable to read
stewards—protectors; guardians

ADDITIONAL QUESTIONS AND ACTIVITIES

With which group of pilgrims does the narrator place himself?
Answer
He groups himself with the Reeve, the Miller, the Manciple, the Pardoner, and the Summoner.

ENGLISH LANGUAGE LEARNING 

The Reeve
choleric—quick-tempered
heath—area of open wasteland
cavalcade—a group riding or traveling one behind the other

In buying victuals; he was never rash
Whether he bought on credit or paid cash.
He used to watch the market most precisely
And got in first, and so he did quite nicely.
Now isn't it a marvel of God's grace
That an illiterate fellow can outpace
The wisdom of a heap of learned men?
His masters—he had more than thirty then—
All versed in the abstrusest legal knowledge,
Could have produced a dozen from their College
Fit to be stewards in land and rents and game
To any Peer in England you could name,
And show him how to live on what he had
Debt-free (unless of course the Peer were mad)
Or be as frugal as he might desire,
And make them fit to help about the Shire
In any legal case there was to try;
And yet this Manciple could wipe their eye.

he *Reeve* was old and choleric and thin;
His beard was shaven closely to the skin,
His shorn hair came abruptly to a stop
Above his ears, and he was docked[54] on top
Just like a priest in front; his legs were lean,
Like sticks they were, no calf was to be seen.
He kept his bins and garners[55] very trim;
No auditor could gain a point on him.
And he could judge by watching drought and rain
The yield he might expect from seed and grain.
His master's sheep, his animals and hens,
Pigs, horses, dairies, stores and cattle-pens
Were wholly trusted to his government,
He had been under contract to present
The accounts, right from his master's earliest years.
No one had ever caught him in arrears.
No bailiff, serf or herdsman dared to kick,
He knew their dodges, knew their every trick;
Feared like the plague he was, by those beneath.
He had a lovely dwelling on a heath,
Shadowed in green by trees above the sward.
A better hand at bargains than his lord,
He had grown rich and had a store of treasure
Well tucked away, yet out it came to pleasure
His lord with subtle loans or gifts of goods,
To earn his thanks and even coats and hoods.
When young he'd learnt a useful trade and still
He was a carpenter of first-rate skill.
The stallion-cob he rode at a slow trot
Was dapple-grey and bore the name of Scot.
He wore an overcoat of bluish shade
And rather long; he had a rusty blade
Slung at his side. He came, as I heard tell,
From Norfolk, near a place called Baldeswell.
His coat was tucked under his belt and splayed.
He rode the hindmost of our cavalcade.

here was a *Summoner* with us at that Inn,
His face on fire, like a cherubin,[56]

54. **docked.** Trimmed
55. **garners.** Granaries
56. **cherubin.** Cherubs are often depicted with red faces.

WORDS FOR EVERYDAY USE

ab • strus • est (ab stro͞os′ əst) *adj.*, most difficult to understand. *Because of the complex vocabulary the math teacher always used, many students found him the abstrusest of all their instructors.*
fru • gal (fro͞o′gəl) *adj.*, thrifty. *Unlike Gina, who spends her paycheck within a few days, Reneé is frugal with her money.*
sward (swôrd) *n.*, grass-covered soil. *After many days in the desert, the travelers reached more fertile land, a sward perfect for tillage.*
splay (splā) *vt.*, spread out. *Although the room was crowded, Frank splayed his legs across the sofa, refusing to let others have a seat.*

For he had carbuncles.[57] His eyes were narrow,
He was as hot and lecherous as a sparrow.
Black scabby brows he had, and a thin beard.
Children were afraid when he appeared.
No quicksilver, lead ointment, tartar creams,
No brimstone, no boracic, so it seems,
Could make a salve that had the power to bite,
Clean up or cure his whelks[58] of knobby white
Or purge the pimples sitting on his cheeks.
Garlic he loved, and onions too, and leeks,
And drinking strong red wine till all was hazy.
Then he would shout and jabber as if crazy,
And wouldn't speak a word except in Latin
When he was drunk, such tags as he was pat in;
He only had a few, say two or three,
That he had mugged up out of some decree;[59]
No wonder, for he heard them every day.
And, as you know, a man can teach a jay
To call out "Walter" better than the Pope.
But had you tried to test his wits and grope
For more, you'd have found nothing in the bag.
Then *"Questio quid juris"*[60] was his tag.
He was a noble varlet[61] and a kind one,
You'd meet none better if you went to find one.
Why, he'd allow—just for a quart of wine—
Any good lad to keep a concubine
A twelvemonth and dispense him altogether!
And he had finches of his own to feather:
And if he found some rascal with a maid
He would instruct him not to be afraid
In such a case of the Archdeacon's curse
(Unless the rascal's soul were in his purse)
For in his purse the punishment should be.
"Purse is the good Archdeacon's Hell," said he.
But well I know he lied in what he said;
A curse should put a guilty man in dread,
For curses kill, as shriving[62] brings, salvation.
We should beware of excommunication.
Thus, as he pleased, the man could bring <u>duress</u>
On any young fellow in the diocese.
He knew their secrets, they did what he said.
He wore a garland set upon his head
Large as the holly-bush upon a stake
Outside an ale-house, and he had a cake,
A round one, which it was his joke to wield
As if it were intended for a shield.

e and a gentle *Pardoner* rode together,
A bird from Charing Cross of the same feather,
Just back from visiting the Court of Rome.
He loudly sang *"Come hither, love, come home!"*
'The Summoner sang deep seconds to this song,
No trumpet ever sounded half so strong.
This Pardoner had hair as yellow as wax,
Hanging down smoothly like a hank of <u>flax</u>.
In driblets fell his locks behind his head

57; 58. **carbuncles; whelks.** Pus-filled boils
59. **he had . . . decree.** He had hurriedly studied when a new law required it.
60. ***Questio quid juris.*** A common phrase in ecclesiastical courts, Latin for "What point of law does this involve?"
61. **varlet.** Rascal
62. **shriving.** Confessing

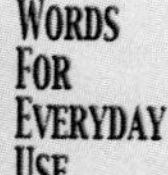

Words for Everyday Use

du • ress (do͞o res´) *n.*, constraint by threat. *After a lifetime of <u>duress</u> in a dark dungeon, the former prisoner rejoiced in the light of the outside world.*

flax (flaks) *adj.*, pale-yellow plant used to make linen. *The golden <u>flax</u> that the weavers spun into cloth always reminded Tim of his mother's blond hair.*

ENGLISH LANGUAGE LEARNING

The Summoner
lecherous—indecent
concubine—lover
diocese—area under the leadership of a bishop of the church
garland—ring of flowers, ivy, or other plants

The Pardoner
hank—a loop or coil
mode—fashion; manner
relic—object of religious devotion
ecclesiast—person of the church
Offertory—song sung in church during collection of money (the offering)

ADDITIONAL QUESTIONS AND ACTIVITIES

The description of the Summoner is especially pungent. To further explore this description students might make a sensory detail chart. For information on sensory detail charts refer them to the Language Arts Survey, 1.18.

ENGLISH LANGUAGE LEARNING

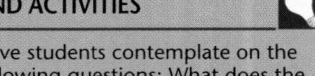

Conclusion of "The Prologue"
hostelry—inn; hotel
girth—distance around
burgess—citizen or freeman
entreaty—pleading; begging
unanimously—in complete agreement; all agreed
evensong—song sung or prayers said in the evening
matins—song sung or prayers said in the morning
decree—official decision or order

ADDITIONAL QUESTIONS AND ACTIVITIES

Have students contemplate on the following questions: What does the narrator ask of the reader? What reasons might each pilgrim have for undertaking this journey?

LITERARY NOTE

Students may be interested in the types of stories told by the pilgrims. The following list briefly outlines the twenty-four stories. Interaction between characters continues between and within the stories. Students may find it interesting that several of the tales are told to get the goat of other pilgrims or in retort to another story.

Knight—a courtly romance based on Boccaccio's Teseida
Miller—a humorous story of love and deception
Reeve—a fabliau in retort to the tale told by the Miller
Cook—a fragment of another fabliau
Sergeant at the Law—the story of the Christian Constance who is married to a sultan; a common story in medieval times
Woman of Bath—the story of the "loathly lady" is another tale of a knight's quest
Friar—a story of a summoner and the devil who agree to split whatever they are given
Summoner—a retort to the Friar's story in which a friar is to divide a deathbed legacy
Clerk—another story based on Boccaccio, this is the story of patient Griselda and her trials
Merchant—a story of a

Down to his shoulders which they overspread;
Thinly they fell, like rat-tails, one by one.
He wore no hood upon his head, for fun;
The hood inside his wallet[63] had been stowed,
He aimed at riding in the latest mode;
But for a little cap his head was bare
And he had bulging eye-balls, like a hare.
He'd sewed a holy relic on his cap;
His wallet lay before him on his lap,
Brimful of pardons come from Rome, all hot.
He had the same small voice a goat has got.
His chin no beard had harbored, nor would harbor,
Smoother than ever chin was left by barber.
I judge he was a gelding, or a mare.
As to his trade, from Berwick down to Ware
There was no pardoner of equal grace,
For in his trunk he had a pillow-case
Which he asserted was Our Lady's veil.
He said he had a gobbet[64] of the sail
Saint Peter had the time when he made bold
To walk the waves, till Jesu Christ took hold.
He had a cross of metal set with stones
And, in a glass, a rubble of pigs' bones.
And with these relics, any time he found
Some poor up-country parson to astound,
In one short day, in money down, he drew
More than the parson in a month or two,
And by his flatteries and prevarication
Made monkeys of the priest and congregation.
But still to do him justice first and last
In church he was a noble ecclesiast.
How well he read a lesson or told a story!
But best of all he sang an Offertory,
For well he knew that when that song was sung
He'd have to preach and tune his honey-tongue
And (well he could) win silver from the crowd.
That's why he sang so merrily and loud.

ow I have told you shortly, in a clause,
The rank, the array, the number and the cause
Of our assembly in this company
In Southwark, at that high-class hostelry
Known as *The Tabard*, close beside *The Bell.*
And now the time has come for me to tell
How we behaved that evening; I'll begin
After we had alighted at the Inn,
Then I'll report our journey, stage by stage,
All the remainder of our pilgrimage.
But first I beg of you, in courtesy,
Not to condemn me as unmannerly
If I speak plainly and with no concealings
And give account of all their words and dealings,
Using their very phrases as they fell.
For certainly, as you all know so well,
He who repeats a tale after a man
Is bound to say, as nearly as he can,
Each single word, if he remembers it,
However rudely spoken or unfit,
Or else the tale he tells will be untrue,
The things pretended and the phrases new.
He may not flinch although it were his brother,
He may as well say one word as another.
And Christ Himself spoke broad in Holy Writ,
Yet there is no scurrility in it,

63. **wallet.** Knapsack
64. **gobbet.** Bit, fragment

WORDS FOR EVERYDAY USE

pre • var • i • ca • tion (pri var´i kā shən) *n.,* lie. *Adam was so honest that everyone believed even his strangest tales, but everyone knew that John just liked to tell prevarications.*

scur • ril • i • ty (skə ril´ə tē) *n.,* coarseness or indecency of language. *Everyone in church was shocked when Tim stubbed his toe and used some scurrility in his speech.*

LITERARY NOTE (CONT.)

December/May, or in this case January/May, romance that is prone to infidelity
Squire—a king's daughter is given the gift of understanding the birds and a falcon tells her a story of desertion
Franklin—a story of lovers and magic which Chaucer claims is based on a Breton lai
Doctor—a daughter is killed by her father to save her from a corrupt judge
Pardoner—the tale of three rioters (This tale follows "The Prologue" in this text.)
Skipper—the tale of a woman who requests a loan from a priest who borrows the money from her merchant husband

And Plato says, for those with power to read,
"The word should be as cousin to the deed."
Further I beg you to forgive it me
If I neglect the order and degree
And what is due to rank in what I've planned.
I'm short of wit as you will understand.

ur *Host* gave us great welcome; everyone
Was given a place and supper was begun.
He served the finest victuals[65] you could think,
The wine was strong and we were glad to drink.
A very striking man our Host withal,
And fit to be a marshal in a hall.
His eyes were bright, his girth a little wide;
There is no finer burgess in Cheapside.[66]
Bold in his speech, yet wise and full of tact,
There was no manly attribute he lacked,
What's more he was a merry-hearted man.
After our meal he jokingly began
To talk of sport, and, among other things
After we'd settled up our reckonings,
He said as follows: "Truly, gentlemen,
You're very welcome and I can't think when
—Upon my word I'm telling you no lie—
I've seen a gathering here that looked so spry,
No, not this year, as in this tavern now.
I'd think you up some fun if I knew how.
And, as it happens, a thought has just occurred
To please you, costing nothing, on my word.
You're off to Canterbury—well, God speed!
Blessed St. Thomas answer to your need!
And I don't doubt, before the journey's done
You mean to while the time in tales and fun.
Indeed, there's little pleasure for your bones
Riding along and all as dumb as stones.
So let me then propose for your enjoyment,
Just as I said, a suitable employment.
And if my notion suits and you agree
And promise to submit yourselves to me
Playing your parts exactly as I say
Tomorrow as you ride along the way,
Then by my father's soul (and he is dead)
If you don't like it you can have my head!
Hold up your hands, and not another word."
Well, our opinion was not long deferred,
It seemed not worth a serious debate;
We all agreed to it at any rate
And bade him issue what commands he would.
"My lords," he said, 'now listen for your good,
And please don't treat my notion with disdain.
This is the point. I'll make it short and plain.
Each one of you shall help to make things slip
By telling two stories on the outward trip
To Canterbury, that's what I intend,
And, on the homeward way to journey's end
Another two, tales from the days of old;
And then the man whose story is best told,
That is to say who gives the fullest measure
Of good morality and general pleasure,
He shall be given a supper, paid by all,
Here in this tavern, in this very hall,
When we come back again from Canterbury.
And in the hope to keep you bright and merry
I'll go along with you myself and ride
All at my own expense and serve as guide.
I'll be the judge, and those who won't obey
Shall pay for what we spend upon the way.

65. **victuals.** Prepared foods
66. **Cheapside.** A section of London, the site of a marketplace in Chaucer's day

LITERARY NOTE

In the introduction to "The Prologue," Chaucer says that twenty-nine pilgrims arrive at the hostelry. Students might note that there are actually thirty-one pilgrims mentioned. Another pilgrim, the Canon's Yeoman, joins the pilgrimage and tells a tale. These inconsistencies may be due to the fact that the tales were written over a long period of time and were never finished.

ADDITIONAL QUESTIONS AND ACTIVITIES

1. Who is the last character introduced?
2. What is his role in the story?

Answers

1. The host is the last character introduced.
2. He suggests the idea of a story contest.

LITERARY NOTE (CONT. FROM PAGE 232)

Nun—a murder story about a child who continues to sing after death
Chaucer (two tales)—the tale of Sir Thopas, a parody of romances, followed by the story of Melibee about marriage
Monk—eight-lined stanzas relaying many tragedies of people falling from high positions
Nun's Priest—a mock heroic story of a fox and a cock
Second Nun—a story of the miracles and martyrdom of Cecilia
Canon's Yeoman—about the dishonesty of alchemists
Manciple—a fable about the tell-tale crow
Parson—a long tale about the seven deadly sins

SELECTION CHECK TEST 4.3.15 WITH ANSWERS

Checking Your Reading

1. Why are the pilgrims going to Canterbury? **They seek to honor Saint Thomas.**
2. What are the pilgrims using for transportation? **They ride horses.**
3. Where does the narrator meet the pilgrims? **They meet at an inn in Southwark.**
4. Who is of the lowest rank: the Merchant, the Squire, the Oxford Cleric, or the Plowman? **The Plowman is of the lowest rank.**
5. The host promises a few dinner to the pilgrim who does what? **He promises a free dinner to the pilgrim who tells the best tale.**

Vocabulary in Context

Fill each blank with the most appropriate word from the Words for Everyday Use from "The Prologue" of *The Canterbury Tales.*

stature saucy personable wanton asunder mire encumbered

1. Amra looked forward to wearing her **saucy** flapper dress to the costume party.
2. The staff held a **wanton** celebration after they completed the difficult project.
3. The toddlers raced to the playground to jump in the pen full of **motley** plastic balls.
4. Melissa realized that her political beliefs had grown **asunder** of her parents' views.
5. Chante enjoyed introducing her boyfriend to her friends, because everyone liked the **personable** fellow.

Literary Tools

Match each sentence beginning with the *best fitting* conclusion. You will not use any choices more than once.

__B__ 1. The characters in "The Prologue"…
__A__ 2. Dramatic irony occurs…
__F__ 3. A likely source of the Canterbury Tales is a collection of **exempla,** which
__C__ 4. The *Tales* contains much irony, including irony of situation, which occurs…
__G__ 5. "The Prologue"…

a. when something is known to the reader or audience but not the characters.
b. represent various aspects of society.
c. when something happens that goes against expectations.
d. are stories within a larger story.

Now if you all agree to what you've heard
Tell me at once without another word,
And I will make arrangements early for it."
Of course we all agreed, in fact we swore it
Delightedly, and made entreaty too
That he should act as he proposed to do,
Become our Governor in short, and be
Judge of our tales and general referee,
And set the supper at a certain price.
We promised to be ruled by his advice
Come high, come low; unanimously thus
We set him up in judgment over us.
More wine was fetched, the business being done;
We drank it off and up went everyone
To bed without a moment of delay.
Early next morning at the spring of day
Up rose our Host and roused us like a cock,
Gathering us together in a flock,
And off we rode at slightly faster pace
Than walking to St. Thomas' watering-place;[67]
And there our Host drew up, began to ease
His horse, and said, "Now, listen if you please,
My lords! Remember what you promised me.
If evensong and matins will agree
Let's see who shall be first to tell a tale.
And as I hope to drink good wine and ale
I'll be your judge. The rebel who disobeys,
However much the journey costs, he pays.
Now draw for cut and then we can depart;
The man who draws the shortest cut shall start.
"My Lord the Knight," he said, "step up to me
And draw your cut, for that is my decree.
And come you near, my Lady Prioress,
And you, Sir Cleric, drop your shamefastness,[68]
No studying now! A hand from every man!"
Immediately the draw for lots began
And to tell shortly how the matter went,
Whether by chance or fate or accident,
The truth is this, the cut fell to the Knight,[69]
Which everybody greeted with delight.
And tell his tale he must, as reason was
Because of our agreement and because
He too had sworn. What more is there to say?
For when this good man saw how matters lay,
Being by wisdom and obedience driven
To keep a promise he had freely given,
He said, "Since it's for me to start the game,
Why, welcome be the cut in God's good name!
Now let us ride, and listen to what I say."
And at the word we started on our way
And in a cheerful style he then began
At once to tell his tale, and thus it ran. ■

67. **St. Thomas' watering-place.** A brook crossed by the road to Canterbury two miles from London
68. **shamefastness.** Shyness
69. **Whether . . . Knight.** Chance, fate, and accident play a large role in the Knight's tale. It is fitting that he begin the storytelling for the same reason that he is described first, namely, because of his rank in society.

SELECTION CHECK TEST 4.3.15 WITH ANSWERS (CONT.)

e. when a statement is made that implies its opposite.
f. are stories illustrating moral lessons intended to be used in sermons.
g. presents the vehicle for the other stories in this frame tale.

Respond *to the* SELECTION

If your were part of this group, who would you want to befriend? avoid? Explain your choices.

INVESTIGATE, Inquire, *Imagine*

Recall: GATHERING FACTS →

1a. Which character is introduced first? What are his main characteristics?

2a. Which of the pilgrims are affiliated with the church?

3a. What did the Pardoner carry with him?

Interpret: FINDING MEANING

1b. Why is this character introduced first? What does he represent?

2b. What makes the Parson a "good man" of religion? How does he compare with the other religious figures on the trip?

3b. What is the narrator's opinion of the Pardoner?

Analyze: TAKING THINGS APART →

4a. What values are honored in "The Prologue"? What failings are pointed out?

Synthesize: BRINGING THINGS TOGETHER

4b. If you were to create a contemporary *Canterbury Tales,* what kinds of people would you include? What values and failings would you present?

Evaluate: MAKING JUDGMENTS →

5a. The narrator says that he is going to report the journey as it happens and is not to be held responsible for what he says. From his prologue, judge whether he does what he says he will do.

Extend: CONNECTING IDEAS

5b. In general do you think reporters are objective or do their personal beliefs or feelings shape their reports? Explain your answer.

RESPOND TO THE SELECTION

Students may wish to role play a meeting with one of Chaucer's characters. Students should take turns role playing the different pilgrims, drawing their character cues from Chaucer's descriptions.

ANSWERS TO INVESTIGATE, INQUIRE, AND IMAGINE

RECALL

1a. The knight is introduced first. He is courageous, honorable, wise, and loyal.

2a. The Nun, the Monk, the Friar, the Parson, the Pardoner, and the Summoner are affiliated with the church.

3a. The Pardoner carried false relics.

INTERPRET

1b. He is first because his is the highest ranking. He represents chivalric values.

2b. The Parson practices what he preaches. He lives by his priestly vows, and he cares for his parishioners more than for himself. He is in sharp contrast to the other church figures who think only of their own comfort and prosperity.

3b. The narrator does not care for the Pardoner. He thinks he is very good at what he does—getting money from people. The narrator presents the Pardoner as an unsavory, but not altogether unpleasant person.

ANALYZE

4a. *Responses will vary.* Courage, honor, wisdom, loyalty are honored. Hypocrisy, greed and self-indulgence are some of the failings pointed out.

SYNTHESIZE

4b. *Responses will vary.* Students might include more women. They might include sports stars, musicians, and actors because of the prominence of entertainment figures in modern society. Students might also include politicians and people who work in fields, such as computers, that did not exist in Chaucer's day. Some of the failings that might be included are dishonesty, hypocrisy, greed, and corruption. Students may notice that although characters might change, many human failings remain the same.

ANSWERS TO INVESTIGATE, INQUIRE, AND IMAGINE (CONT.)

EVALUATE

5a. *Responses will vary.* The narrator presents opinions by the way he describes the characters. His disclaimer is a way to avoid blame for what he may say.

EXTEND

5b. *Responses will vary.* Students may note that reports may be colored by the reporter's beliefs. Some reporting is also simply sensational, that is, it tries to effect a strong response from the audience.

INDIVIDUAL LEARNING STRATEGIES

MOTIVATION
The Pardoner uses his story to get money from others. Ask students to role play scenes in which they are trying to convince somebody to give them something or to do something for them. They should try different tactics based on the situation.

READING PROFICIENCY
Explain to students the Death is personified, or treated as a character, in this story.

ENGLISH LANGUAGE LEARNING
Give students the following additional vocabulary words:

Additional Vocabulary
spry—full of life
slain—past tense of slay, kill
privy—secret, sneaky
page—servant
vow—promise, oath

SPECIAL NEEDS
Students should pay special attention to the Recall questions in Investigate, Inquire, Imagine. Check student comprehension periodically.

ENRICHMENT

Students can share lesson tales they know. Students can compile these tales into a book.

THE PARDONER'S TALE

FROM *The Canterbury Tales*

GEOFFREY CHAUCER, TRANSLATED BY NEVILL COGHILL

It's of three rioters I have to tell
Who, long before the morning service bell,
Were sitting in a tavern for a drink.
And as they sat, they heard the hand-bell clink
Before a coffin going to the grave;
One of them called the little tavern-knave
And said "Go and find out at once—look spry!—
Whose corpse is in that coffin passing by;
And see you get the name correctly too."
"Sir," said the boy, "no need, I promise you;
Two hours before you came here I was told.
He was a friend of yours in days of old,
And suddenly, last night, the man was slain,
Upon his bench, face up, dead drunk again.
There came a privy thief, they call him Death,
Who kills us all round here, and in a breath
He speared him through the heart, he never stirred.
And then Death went his way without a word.
He's killed a thousand in the present plague,
And, sir, it doesn't do to be too vague
If you should meet him; you had best be wary.
Be on your guard with such an adversary,
Be primed to meet him everywhere you go,
That's what my mother said. It's all I know."
The publican joined in with, "By St. Mary,
What the child says is right; you'd best be wary,
This very year he killed, in a large village
A mile away, man, woman, serf at tillage,
Page in the household, children—all there were.
Yes, I imagine that he lives round there.
It's well to be prepared in these alarms,
He might do you dishonor." "Huh, God's arms!"
The rioter said, "Is he so fierce to meet?
I'll search for him, by Jesus, street by street.

WORDS FOR EVERYDAY USE

war • y (wer´ē) *adj.*, cautious. *He stopped at the crosswalk and looked both ways because he had always been told to be wary when crossing the street.*

till • age (til´ij) *n.*, land that is tilled for farming. *There are no rocks or tree stumps in Farmer Brown's land; it is good tillage for planting.*

Chaucer, the Knight and the Squire, c.1900s. Harry Mileham. Private Collection.

God's blessed bones! I'll register a vow!
Here chaps! The three of us together now,
Hold up your hands, like me, and we'll be brothers
In this affair, and each defend the others,
And we will kill this traitor Death, I say!
Away with him as he has made away
With all our friends. God's dignity! Tonight!"
They made their bargain, swore with appetite,
These three, to live and die for one another
As brother-born might swear to his born brother.
And up they started in their drunken rage
And made towards this village which the page
And publican had spoken of before.
Many and <u>grisly</u> were the oaths they swore,
Tearing Christ's blessed body to a shred;
"If we can only catch him, Death is dead!"
When they had gone not fully half a mile,
Just as they were about to cross a <u>stile</u>,
They came upon a very poor old man
Who humbly greeted them and thus began,
"God look to you, my lords, and give you quiet!"
To which the proudest of these men of riot
Gave back the answer, "What, old fool? Give place!
Why are you all wrapped up except your face?
Why live so long? Isn't it time to die?"
The old, old fellow looked him in the eye
And said, "Because I never yet have found,
Though I have walked to India, searching round
Village and city on my pilgrimage,
One who would change his youth to have my age.
And so my age is mine and must be still
Upon me, for such time as God may will.

WORDS FOR EVERYDAY USE

gris • ly (griz´lē) *adj.,* horrible; terrifying. *The violent murder scene in the horror movie was particularly <u>grisly</u>.*

stile (stīl) *n.,* steps used to climb over a wall. *If the steep stone wall did not have a <u>stile</u>, it would be an effective barrier.*

ADDITIONAL QUESTIONS AND ACTIVITIES

Have students review lines 689–734 of "The Prologue." Then, as they read "The Pardoner's Tale," they should compare the pardoner to the characters in his story.

LITERARY TECHNIQUE

Exemplum. An **exemplum** is a brief shorty or anecdote, common in the Middle Ages. An exemplum illustrates an idea or moral and was often told as part of a sermon.

ADDITIONAL QUESTIONS AND ACTIVITIES

Have students make wanted posters for the killer Death. They should include a picture, a physical description, and a list of crimes and accomplices.

LITERARY TECHNIQUE

FOLK TALE. A **folk tale** is a brief story passed by word-of-mouth from generation to generation. Why might this story have been passed down? To whom might it most appeal? What is its appeal?

Answers

The story was probably passed down to teach a lesson about greed. It is appealing because the moral is tied up in an interesting story and the characters seem to get what they deserve.

"Not even Death, alas, will take my life;
So, like a wretched prisoner at strife
Within himself, I walk alone and wait
About the earth, which is my mother's gate,
Knock-knocking with my staff from night to noon
And crying, 'Mother, open to me soon!
Look at me, mother, won't you let me in?
See how I wither, flesh and blood and skin!
Alas! When will these bones be laid to rest?
Mother, I would exchange—for that were best—
The wardrobe in my chamber, standing there
So long, for yours! Aye, for a shirt of hair
To wrap me in!' She has refused her grace,
Whence comes the pallor of my withered face
"But it dishonored you when you began
To speak so roughly, sir, to an old man,
Unless he had injured you in word or deed.
It says in holy writ, as you may read,
'Thou shalt rise up before the hoary head
And honor it.' And therefore be it said
'Do no more harm to an old man than you,
Being now young, would have another do
When you are old'—if you should live till then.
And so may God be with you, gentlemen,
For I must go whither I have to go."
"By God," the gambler said, "you shan't do so,
You don't get off so easy, by St. John!
I heard you mention, just a moment gone,
A certain traitor Death who singles out
And kills the fine young fellows hereabout.
And you're his spy, by God! You wait a bit.
Say where he is or you shall pay for it,
By God and by the Holy Sacrament!
I say you've joined together by consent
To kill us younger folk, you thieving swine!"
"Well, sirs," he said, "if it be your design
To find out Death, turn up this crooked way
Toward that grove, I left him there today
Under a tree, and there you'll find him waiting.
He isn't one to hide for all your prating.
You see that oak? He won't be far to find.
And God protect you that redeemed mankind,
Aye, and amend you!" Thus that ancient man.
At once the three young rioters began
To run, and reached the tree, and there they found
A pile of golden florins[1] on the ground,
New-coined, eight bushels of them as they thought.
No longer was it Death those fellows sought,
For they were all so thrilled to see the sight,
The florins were so beautiful and bright,
That down they sat beside the precious pile.
The wickedest spoke first after a while.
"Brothers," he said, "you listen to what I say.
I'm pretty sharp although I joke away.
It's clear that Fortune has bestowed this treasure
To let us live in jollity and pleasure.
Light come, light go! We'll spend it as we ought.
God's precious dignity! Who would have thought
This morning was to be our lucky day?
"If one could only get the gold away,
Back to my house, or else to yours, perhaps—
For as you know, the gold is ours, chaps—

1. **florins.** Gold coins

WORDS FOR EVERYDAY USE

strife (strīf) *n.*, conflict; struggle. *There seldom was peace between the two countries; they were in a constant state of bitter strife.*
hoar • y (hôr´ē) *adj.*, white- or gray-haired. *His beard had faded long ago from a lustrous black to a hoary gray.*
prat • ing (prāt´iŋ) *ger.*, chattering. *The teacher told Henry's parents that prating kept him from passing her course.*

We'd all be at the top of fortune, hey?
But certainly it can't be done by day.
People would call us robbers—a strong gang,
So our own property would make us hang.
No, we must bring this treasure back by night
Some prudent way, and keep it out of sight.
And so as a solution I propose
We draw for lots and see the way it goes;
The one who draws the longest, lucky man,
Shall run to town as quickly as he can
To fetch us bread and wine—but keep things dark—
While two remain in hiding here to mark
Our heap of treasure. If there's no delay,
When night comes down we'll carry it away,
All three of us, wherever we have planned."
He gathered lots and hid them in his hand
Bidding them draw for where the luck should fall.
It fell upon the youngest of them all,
And off he ran at once toward the town.
As soon as he had gone the first sat down
And thus began a parley with the other:
"You know that you can trust me as a brother;
Now let me tell you where your profit lies;
You know our friend has gone to get supplies
And here's a lot of gold that is to be
Divided equally amongst us three.
Nevertheless, if I could shape things thus
So that we shared it out—the two of us—
Wouldn't you take it as a friendly act?"
"But how?" the other said. "He knows the fact
That all the gold was left with me and you;
What can we tell him? What are we to do?"
"Is it a bargain," said the first, "or no?
For I can tell you in a word or so
What's to be done to bring the thing about."
"Trust me," the other said, "you needn't doubt
My word. I won't betray you, I'll be true."
"Well," said his friend, "you see that we are two,
And two are twice as powerful as one.
Now look; when he comes back, get up in fun
To have a wrestle; then, as you attack,
I'll up and put my dagger through his back
While you and he are struggling, as in game;
Then draw your dagger too and do the same.
Then all this money will be ours to spend,
Divided equally of course, dear friend.
Then we can gratify our lusts and fill
The day with dicing[2] at our own sweet will."
Thus these two <u>miscreants</u> agreed to slay
The third and youngest, as you heard me say.
The youngest, as he ran towards the town,
Kept turning over, rolling up and down
Within his heart the beauty of those bright
New florins, saying, "Lord, to think I might
Have all that treasure to myself alone!
Could there be anyone beneath the throne
Of God so happy as I then should be?"
And so the Fiend, our common enemy,
Was given power to put it in his thought
That there was always poison to be bought,
And that with poison he could kill his friends.
To men in such a state the Devil sends

2. **dicing.** Gambling

WORDS FOR EVERYDAY USE

mis • cre • ant (mis´ krē ənt) *n.,* evil person. *Because Rick performed so many malicious deeds and showed no sign of reforming, he was seen as the town's <u>miscreant</u>.*

SELECTION CHECK TEST 4.3.17 WITH ANSWERS

Checking Your Reading

1. Who has killed thousands in the village? **Death has killed thousands.**
2. How do the three rioters offend the old man? **They speak roughly to him.**
3. What do the three find under the tree? **They find money under the tree.**
4. How does the youngest plan to kill his friends? **He plans to poison them.**
5. What happens to the youngest? **His friends stab him.**

Vocabulary in Context

Fill each blank with the most appropriate word from these Words for Everyday Use from "The Pardoner's Tale." You may have to change the tense of the word.

wary tillage grisly stile strife hoary miscreant perdition

1. The priest's sermon warned of the dangers of **<u>perdition</u>.**
2. The old ape cradled his **<u>hoary</u>** head in his arms and napped.
3. Today's moviegoers seem to enjoy **<u>grisly</u>** thrillers more than earlier audiences did.
4. The novel's **<u>miscreant</u>** created many difficulties for the hero and the heroine.
5. Although Pru apologized, I was **<u>wary</u>** around her for quite a while.

Literary Tools

1. What is a frame tale? **It is a story that provides a vehicle for telling other stories.**
2. What is the frame tale for "The Pardoner's Tale"? **The frame tale is the story of the storytelling contest that takes place during the pilgrimage to Canterbury.**
3. What is ironic about the ending of "The Pardoner's Tale"? **The three rioters kill each other (students may note that they found Death under the tree after all).**

RESPOND TO THE SELECTION

Ask students to think about whether it is possible to overcome a serious flaw, whether people can change for the better.

Thoughts of this kind, and has a full permission
To lure them on to sorrow and perdition;
For this young man was utterly content
To kill them both and never to repent.
And on he ran, he had no thought to tarry,
Came to the town, found an apothecary
And said, "Sell me some poison if you will,
I have a lot of rats I want to kill
And there's a polecat too about my yard
That takes my chickens and it hits me hard;
But I'll get even, as is only right,
With vermin that destroy a man by night."
The chemist answered, "I've a preparation
Which you shall have, and by my soul's salvation
If any living creature eat or drink
A mouthful, ere he has the time to think,
Though he took less than makes a grain of wheat,
You'll see him fall down dying at your feet;
Yes, die he must, and in so short a while
You'd hardly have the time to walk a mile,
The poison is so strong, you understand."
This cursed fellow grabbed into his hand
The box of poison and away he ran
Into a neighboring street, and found a man
Who lent him three large bottles. He withdrew
And deftly poured poison into two.
He kept the third one clean, as well he might,
For his own drink, meaning to work all night
Stacking the gold and carrying it away.
And when this rioter, this devil's clay,
Had filled his bottles up with wine, all three,
Back to rejoin his comrades sauntered he.
Why make a sermon of it ? Why waste breath?
Exactly in the way they'd planned his death
They fell on him and slew him, two to one.
Then said the first of them when this was done,
"Now for a drink. Sit down and let's be merry,
For later on there'll be the corpse to bury."
And, as it happened, reaching for a sup,
He took a bottle full of poison up
And drank; and his companion, nothing loth,
Drank from it also, and they perished both.
There is, in Avicenna's long relation[3]
Concerning poison and its operation,
Trust me, no ghastlier section to transcend
What these two wretches suffered at their end.
Thus these two murderers received their due,
So did the treacherous young poisoner too. ■

3. **Avicenna's long relation.** A lengthy medical book by Avicenna, with a detailed chapter on poisons

WORDS FOR EVERYDAY USE

per • di • tion (pər dish´ən) *n.,* loss of soul. *The priest warned others against committing an act that could lead to perdition, thereby ruining their chances to experience heaven.*

Respond *to the* SELECTION

Explain whether you think anything could have saved the rioters.

INVESTIGATE, Inquire, Imagine

Recall: GATHERING FACTS → **Interpret:** FINDING MEANING

1a. What do the rioters agree to do?

1b. What prompts the rioters to make this pact?

2a. Who tells the rioters that Death is up the way under a tree? What do they find instead?

2b. What does the meeting with the old man show about the rioters? Whom or what might the old man represent?

3a. How did the first rioter die? How do the others die?

3b. What kills all three rioters?

Analyze: TAKING THINGS APART → **Synthesize:** BRINGING THINGS TOGETHER

4a. Identify the various ways in which the rioters show their greed.

4b. Why might the Pardoner choose a story on this theme?

Evaluate: MAKING JUDGMENTS → **Extend:** CONNECTING IDEAS

5a. Judge whether the rioters got what they deserved.

5b. What flaws, other than greed, lead people to act irrationally?

Understanding Literature

FRAME TALE. Review the definition of **frame tale** in The Handbook of Literary Terms. What is the basic story that provides the setting for *The Canterbury Tales*? In what way does the frame make it plausible for this variety of characters to tell stories?

CHARACTERIZATION. Review the definition of **characterization** in Literary Tools on page 216. What are the main characteristics of the Pardoner? In what way does the story he tells contribute to his characterization?

IRONY. Review the definition of **irony** in the Handbook of Literary Terms. What is the moral of the story told by the Pardoner? Why does the Pardoner tell this story? Why is it ironic that the Pardoner is telling this story?

WRITER'S JOURNAL

1. Write a brief **character sketch** about the person you wrote about in your Reader's Journal for "The Prologue." Embellish quirks or interesting features if you like. How do you feel about this person? Let your opinion show in your description.
2. Create an **interview** of one of the pilgrims. First write a set of questions. Then imagine how the pilgrim you have chosen would answer them.
3. Write a **tale** with a moral. You might choose a moral like "Pride goes before a fall" or "Greed is the root of all evil." Think of a situation that will support your moral, and use the situation as the center of your tale.

ANSWERS TO INVESTIGATE, INQUIRE, AND IMAGINE

RECALL

1a. The rioters agree to kill Death.

2a. The old man tells them that Death is just up the way under a tree. The rioters find a pile of gold coins.

3a. The first rioter is stabbed by the other two. The others are killed by the poison the first rioter had put in their drinks.

INTERPRET

1b. The rioters agree to kill Death because Death had killed their friend.

2b. The meeting with the old man sends the three rioters to Death and shows that the rioters do not respect Death. He might be Death disguised, or the Grim Reaper.

3b. Their own greed gets the better of them, which causes their death.

ANALYZE

4a. *Responses will vary.* The rioters lose sight of their original quest when they find the gold. They make a pact because they fear the gold will be taken from them. They kill each other, each hoping to have all the gold for himself.

SYNTHESIZE

4b. *Responses will vary.* The Pardoner benefits from pointing out that Greed is a deadly flaw when he asks people for money.

EVALUATE

5a. *Responses will vary.* Many students may say the greedy rioters did indeed get what they deserved, since they were trying to kill the others for their own gain. Others may feel that death is never a suitable punishment.

EXTEND

5b. *Responses will vary.* Students may list love, pride, envy, or others.

ANSWERS TO UNDERSTANDING LITERATURE

FRAME TALE. The pilgrimage brings together characters from many different stations in society, allowing for the diversity of the group. In every day life, it would probably be rare for all of these characters to socialize.

IRONY. It is ironic that such a greedy character tells a tale that moralizes against greed.

CHARACTERIZATION. The Pardoner is not very attractive. He has yellow hair, smooth like flax, and much like rat tails. His eyes bulge and he has a voice like a goat. He liked to be stylish. He carried fake relics, told a good story, and was able to get lots of money from people. His story shows his goal of trying to get money from others. It also shows his hypocrisy, since he is greedy himself.

ANSWERS TO INTEGRATING THE LANGUAGE ARTS

Language, Grammar, and Style
Responses will vary.

1. Geoffrey Chaucer was a talented writer who produced many works.
2. Chaucer is best known for his unfinished frame tale, *The Canterbury Tales.*
3. Chaucer drew his ideas for *The Canterbury Tales* from many sources including the writings of Boccaccio, religious works, and fables.
4. The pilgrims tell tales that represent their own characters. For example, the Knight tells a courtly tale, the low-life Miller tells a bawdy story, and the Pardoner gives an example of one of his sermons.
5. The variety of stories and narrators and the rich description of English society make *The Canterbury Tales* a masterpiece of English literature.

Study and Research

1. b
2. d
3. e
4. b
5. c

Speaking and Listening
Before students begin, lead a class discussion about what makes an oral story interesting. Remind them to keep these elements in mind as they prepare. Students may wish to use family stories, local tall tales, or stories of their own invention. Encourage them to use brief written notes to guide their performance.

Integrating *the* Language Arts

Language, Grammar, and Style

Reducing Wordiness. Read the Language Arts Survey 3.35, "Correcting Wordy Sentences." Then rewrite the following sentences to make them more concise and clear.

1. Geoffrey Chaucer was a talented, skilled writer who produced a large collection of well-written works.
2. Chaucer is probably best known for his stories within a story, *The Canterbury Tales*, which is an unfinished frame tale.
3. The stories for *The Canterbury Tales* are not all original creations of Chaucer, rather they are drawn from many sources, including love poems and other writings by Boccaccio, the lives of saints, and other religious works with which Chaucer was extremely familiar, and fables that were more commonly passed by word-of-mouth than by written words.
4. The tales are not randomly assigned, but are rather well chosen to fit the variety of characters. For example, the Knight tells a tale of courtly romance, the low-life Miller tells a bawdy story that is typical of his character, and the preaching Pardoner gives a sample of one of the sermons that he typically delivered as a preacher.
5. Because of the wide variety of stories and narrators, as well as the richness of its concise summation of English society in "The Prologue," *The Canterbury Tales*, even in its unfinished state, remains a masterpiece of English literature.

Study and Research

Multiple-choice Questions. Read the Language Arts Survey 5.49, "Multiple-Choice Questions." Then select the correct answers to the following:

1. Chaucer's *The Canterbury Tales*
   a. was written in Canterbury
   b. was written about a trip to Canterbury
   c. was found in Canterbury
   d. was set in Canterbury
   e. has nothing to do with Canterbury
2. The Pardoner tells a story about
   a. a tavern-knave
   b. a poor, old man
   c. two prisoners
   d. three rioters
   e. the devil
3. "The Pardoner's Tale" takes place during
   a. the winter
   b. the spring
   c. the summer
   d. the fall
   e. an unspecified season
4. The relics in the story are owned by
   a. the Knight
   b. the Pardoner
   c. an old man
   d. a young man
   e. Jesus
5. The sin that leads to the deaths at the end of the story is
   a. gluttony
   b. sloth
   c. greed
   d. envy
   e. despair

Speaking and Listening

Storytelling Contest. Hold a storytelling contest in class. You may choose a story you have written or one that you have read or heard. Consider adding details to make the story more appealing. Practice telling your story in a way that will interest the others in your group. Pay attention to your pace and loudness, your facial expressions, where you stand, how you move about, and your arm and hand movements.

Mock Trial. In a group of seven to ten students, hold a mock trial of Death and his accomplice, Greed, for the murder of the three rioters. Choose group members to assume the roles of judge, members of the jury, prosecutor, defendants, and defense lawyers. After the two sides present their cases, the jury should explain its decision.

FROM Everyman

ANONYMOUS

About the Author

No author is known for ***Everyman***. Although no manuscript of the play has ever been found, its first printing dates to about 1530. Most scholars believe that the play was first written in Flemish and then translated into English sometime after 1485.

About the Selection

A *morality play* is a type of medieval drama in which the characters are abstract caricatures of virtues, vices, and the like. Morality plays are like dramatized sermons—they deliver a clear religious message. ***Everyman*** is considered the finest known medieval morality play because of its lofty poetry, its unity, its consistent and clear allegorical message, and its engaging theatricality.

Literary Tools

MORALITY PLAY. A **morality play** is a type of medieval drama in which the characters are abstract caricatures of virtues, vices, and the like. Morality plays attempted to dramatize the Christian struggle to choose between good and evil, and ultimately, heaven and hell. As you read, try to identify the lessons taught in the play.

NAIVE ALLEGORY. An **allegory** is a work in which each element symbolizes, or represents, something else. In a **naive allegory,** characters, objects, places, and actions are personifications of abstraction such as Good Deeds, Beauty, Vanity, or the journey to the Celestial Kingdom. Keep a chart of characters Everyman meets and what the role of each is.

Character	Role
Death	To set Everyman on the pilgrimage to his judgment upon death

Reader's Journal

Explain whether you think people are held accountable after death for their actions while alive.

ADDITIONAL RESOURCES

UNIT 3 RESOURCE BOOK
- Selection Worksheet 3.9
- Selection Check Test 4.3.19
- Selection Test 4.3.20
- Language, Grammar, and Style Resource 3.99

GRAPHIC ORGANIZER ANSWERS

Character	Role
Death	To set Everyman on the pilgrimage to his judgment upon death
Beauty, Strength, Discretion, Five-wits	Show Everyman that these are fleeting
Good Deeds	Stays with Everyman
Knowledge	Let's Everyman know he has endured all he must
Angel	Comes to take Everyman to heaven

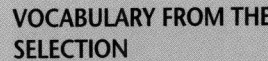

READER'S JOURNAL

If you ask students to discuss their answers, preface the discussion with comments about the importance of respecting the wide variety of beliefs that people hold on these matters.

VOCABULARY FROM THE SELECTION

amends
caitiff
proffer
respite
transitory

GOALS/OBJECTIVES

Studying this lesson will enable students to
- empathize with fear and losses Everyman experiences as he faces judgment and death
- recognize the essential characteristics and social purpose of medieval morality plays
- define *naive allegory*
- capitalize titles properly
- demonstrate the ability to format a business letter correctly

INDIVIDUAL LEARNING STRATEGIES

MOTIVATION
in this selection, Everyman prepares for his death. Ask students what they would like to do if they knew they only had short time to live. What legacy would they like to leave?

READING PROFICIENCY
Explain in advance the basic plot situation: Death comes to take Everyman. Everyman tries to get various characters (Strength, Beauty, etc.) to accompany him, but they refuse. In the end, only his good deeds go with him to the grave. Remind students that the characters in this play are mainly personified virtues. Review the cast of characters and make sure students understand the meaning of fellowship, kindred, knowledge, beauty, strength, and discretion. They should also understand the words kindred, cousin, goods, confession, and five-wits.

ENGLISH LANGUAGE LEARNING
Point out the following vocabulary words:
reverence—deep respect and awe
jollity—happiness; good times
reckoning—an account or judgment
prosperity—wealth; success
forsake—leave
pilgrimage—a journey to a holy place
tarrying—staying; delaying

SPECIAL NEEDS
Students will find the play easier to understand if it is performed aloud. You could play the selection from the Audio Library, or ask other students to take on different to roles.

ENRICHMENT
Have students review the selection and then prepare detailed descriptions and drawings of costumes and sets for a modern production of *Everyman*. Students can choose to do the play as a period piece, in medieval costume, or they can do it in modern costume with a modern set. (One famous production of Shakespeare's *The Taming of the Shrew* was set in Chicago in the 1920s and featured characters dressed as gangsters and flappers.) Ask students to consider how modernization of costumes and setting simultaneously throws into relief the archaic aspects of a play and, paradoxically, underscores its timelessness—the applicability of its ideas to life today.

FROM EVERYMAN

ANONYMOUS

CAST OF CHARACTERS

MESSENGER
GOD
DEATH
EVERYMAN
FELLOWSHIP
KINDRED
COUSIN
GOODS
GOOD DEEDS
KNOWLEDGE
CONFESSION
BEAUTY
STRENGTH
DISCRETION
FIVE-WITS
ANGEL
DOCTOR

HERE BEGINNETH A TREATISE HOW THE HIGH FATHER OF HEAVEN SENDETH DEATH TO SUMMON EVERY CREATURE TO COME AND GIVE ACCOUNT OF THEIR LIVES IN THIS WORLD, AND IS IN MANNER OF A MORAL PLAY

[*Enter* MESSENGER.]

MESSENGER. I pray you all give your audience,
And hear this matter with reverence,
By figure[1] a moral play.
The Summoning of Everyman called it is,
That of our lives and ending shows
How transitory we be all day.[2]
The matter is wonder precious,
But the intent of it is more gracious
And sweet to bear away.
The story saith: Man, in the beginning
Look well, and take good heed to the ending,
Be you never so gay.
You think sin in the beginning full sweet,
Which in the end causeth the soul to weep,
When the body lieth in clay.
Here shall you see how fellowship and jollity,
Both strength, pleasure, and beauty,
Will fade from thee as flower in May.
For ye shall hear how our Heaven-King
Calleth Everyman to a general reckoning.
Give audience and hear what he doth say.

[*Exit* MESSENGER.—*Enter* GOD.]

1. **figure.** Form
2. **all day.** Always

WORDS FOR EVERYDAY USE
tran • si • to • ry (tran´sə tôr´ē) *adj.*, temporary. *The birds' stay here is only transitory, for they will be heading south for the winter soon.*

ArtNote

Le Mort et Le Boucheron, c.1800s. Alphonse Legros. Corcoran Gallery of Art, Washington, D.C.

Alphonse Legros (1837–1911), a French-born British artist, revitalized the arts of drawing and painting in Britain. He is best known for his works on macabre and fantastic themes. What do you think he is depicting in this piece?

God. I perceive, here in my majesty,
How that all creatures be to me unkind,[3]
Living without dread in worldly prosperity.
Of ghostly[4] sight the people be so blind,
Drowned in sin, they know me not for their God.
In worldly riches is all their mind:
They fear not of my righteousness the sharp rod;
My law that I showed when I for them died
They forget clean, and shedding of my blood red.
I hanged between two,[5] it cannot be denied:
To get them life I suffered to be dead.
I healed their feet, with thorns hurt was my head.
I could do no more than I did, truly—
And now I see the people do clean forsake me.
They use the seven deadly sins damnable,
As pride, coveitise, wrath, and lechery[6]
Now in the world be made commendable.
And thus they leave of angels the heavenly company.
Every man liveth so after his own pleasure,
And yet of their life they be nothing sure.
I see the more that I them forbear,
The worse they be from year to year:
All that liveth appaireth[7] fast.
Therefore I will, in all the haste,
Have a reckoning of every man's person.
For, and[8] I leave the people thus alone
In their life and wicked tempests,
Verily they will become much worse than beasts;
For now one would by envy another up eat.
Charity do they all clean forgeet.
I hoped well that every man

3. **unkind.** Thoughtless
4. **ghostly.** Spiritual
5. **I . . . two.** Christ was crucified between two thieves.
6. **seven . . . lechery.** The seven deadly sins are pride, avarice, wrath, lechery, envy, gluttony, and sloth.
7. **appaireth.** Degenerates
8. **and.** If

ADDITIONAL QUESTIONS AND ACTIVITIES

Explain that predicting is one of the most common mental activities engaged by readers. A writer keeps a reader interested by raising questions in the reader's mind, by making the reader wonder what is going to happen next. As a reader reads, he or she continually guesses what is going to happen next. Reading on then becomes an opportunity to confirm or alter hypotheses that the reader has made. Have students predict how the characters will respond to Everyman's request to accompany him on his journey.

HISTORICAL/LITERARY NOTE

Explain that in the Middle Ages plays were typically produced on the backs of wagons in the courtyards of inns and in other public places. The audience would stand around the wagon stage on three or four sides. Sets were minimal, but costumes and properties were used. People would travel for days to see a play.

ADDITIONAL QUESTIONS AND ACTIVITIES

How does God feel towards people in the speech on page 245? What has caused these feelings?

Answer

God is upset that people do not honor God and live in sin, even though he gave his son to die for them.

ADDITIONAL QUESTIONS AND ACTIVITIES

Have students compare the character of Death in *Everyman* to the character of Death in "The Pardoner's Tale." Are the characters portrayed in a similar way? How are they different? How does the reaction of other characters in relation to Death differ between the two pieces? Why might the role of Death be so common in medieval times?

INTERNET RESOURCES

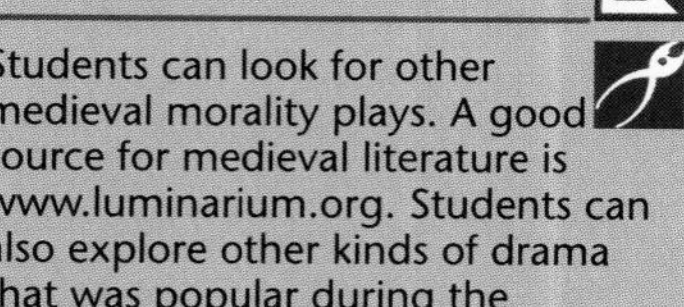

Students can look for other medieval morality plays. A good source for medieval literature is www.luminarium.org. Students can also explore other kinds of drama that was popular during the Medieval Period.

In my glory should make his mansion,
And thereto I had them all elect.[9]
But now I see, like traitors deject.[10]
They thank me not for the pleasure that I to[11] them meant,
Nor yet for their being that I them have lent.
I proffered the people great multitude of mercy,
And few there be that asketh it heartily.[12]
They be so cumbered[13] with worldly riches
That needs on them I must do justice—
On every man living without fear.
Where art thou, Death, thou mighty messenger?

[*Enter* DEATH.]

DEATH. Almighty God, I am here at your will,
Your commandment to fulfill.

GOD. Go thou to Everyman,
And show him, in my name,
A pilgrimage he must on him take,
Which he in no wise may escape;
And that he bring with him a sure reckoning
Without delay or any tarrying.

DEATH. Lord, I will in the world go run over all,
And cruelly out-search both great and small.

[*Exit* GOD.]

Everyman will I beset that liveth beastly
Out of God's laws, and dreadeth not folly.
He that loveth riches I will strike with my dart,
His sight to blind, and from heaven to depart—[14]
Except that Almsdeeds be his good friend—
In hell for to dwell, world without end.
Lo, yonder I see Everyman walking:
Full little he thinketh on my coming;
His mind is on fleshly lusts and his treasure,
And great pain it shall cause him to endure
Before the Lord, Heaven-King.

[*Enter* EVERYMAN.]

Everyman, stand still! Whither art thou going
Thus gaily? Hast thou thy Maker forgeet?[15]

EVERYMAN. Why askest thou?
Why wouldest thou weet?[16]

DEATH. Yea, sir, I will show you:
In great haste I am sent to thee
From God out of his majesty.

EVERYMAN. What! sent to me?

DEATH. Yea, certainly.
Though thou have forgot him here,
He thinketh on thee in the heavenly sphere,
As, ere we depart, thou shalt know.

EVERYMAN. What desireth God of me?

DEATH. That shall I show thee:
A reckoning he will needs have
Without any longer respite.

9. **elect.** Chosen
10. **deject.** Abased
11. **to.** For
12. **heartily.** Sincerely
13. **cumbered.** Encumbered
14. **depart.** Separate
15. **forgeet.** Forgotten
16. **weet.** Know

WORDS FOR EVERYDAY USE

prof • fer (präf´ər) *vt.*, offer. *The child proffered her hand, so I took it and led her across the street.*

res • pite (res´pit) *n.*, postponement; reprieve. *The players hoped for some respite from the jeers of the audience.*

EVERYMAN. To give a reckoning longer leisure I crave.
This blind[17] matter troubleth my wit.

DEATH. On thee thou must take a long journay:
Therefore thy book of count[18] with thee thou bring,
For turn again thou cannot by no way.
And look thou be sure of thy reckoning,
For before God thou shalt answer and shew
Thy many bad deeds and good but a few—
How thou hast spent thy life and in what wise,
Before the Chief Lord of Paradise.
Have ado that we were in that way,[19]
For weet thou well thou shalt make none attornay.[20]

EVERYMAN. Full unready I am such reckoning to give.
I know thee not. What messenger art thou?

DEATH. I am Death that no man dreadeth,
For every man I 'rest, and no man spareth;
For it is God's commandment
That all to me should be obedient.

EVERYMAN. O Death, thou comest when I had thee least in mind.
In thy power it lieth me to save:
Yet of my good[21] will I give thee, if thou will be kind,
Yea, a thousand pound shalt thou have—
And defer this matter till another day.

DEATH. Everyman, it may not be, by no way.
I set nought by gold, silver, nor riches,[22]
Nor by pope, emperor, king, duke, nor princes,
For, and[23] I would receive gifts great,
All the world I might get.
But my custom is clean contrary:
I give thee no respite. Come hence and not tarry!

EVERYMAN. Alas, shall I have no longer respite?
I may say Death giveth no warning.
To think on thee it maketh my heart sick,
For all unready is my book of reckoning.
But twelve year and I might have a biding,[24]
My counting-book I would make so clear
That my reckoning I should not need to fear.
Wherefore, Death, I pray thee, for God's mercy,
Spare me till I be provided of remedy.

DEATH. Thee availeth not to cry, weep, and pray;
But haste thee lightly[25] that thou were gone that journay
And prove[26] thy friends, if thou can.
For weet[27] thou well the tide[28] abideth no man,
And in the world each living creature
For Adam's sin must die of nature.[29]

EVERYMAN. Death, if I should this pilgrimage take
And my reckoning surely make,
Show me, for saint[30] charity,
Should I not come again shortly?

DEATH. No, Everyman. And thou be once there,
Thou mayst never more come here,
Trust me verily.

---

17. **blind.** Unexpected
18. **count.** Accounts
19. **Have . . . way.** Let's get started right away.
20. **shalt . . . attornay.** Nobody shall go in your place.
21. **good.** Goods
22. **I . . . riches.** Riches, gold, and silver mean nothing to me.
23. **and.** If
24. **But . . . biding.** If I could put this off for just twelve years
25. **lightly.** Quickly
26. **prove.** Test
27. **weet.** Know
28. **tide.** Time
29. **of nature.** Naturally
30. **saint.** Holy

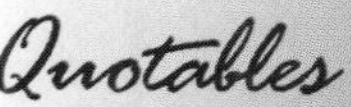

"Everyman, I will go with thee and be thy guide, In thy most need go by thy side."

—Knowledge in *Everyman*

ADDITIONAL QUESTIONS AND ANSWERS

Students can discuss why Knowledge might step forward to be Everyman's guide.

ADDITIONAL QUESTIONS AND ACTIVITIES

What request does Every man ask of Death? What is Death's response?

Answers

Everyman asks Death to give him one more day. Death says he kills people suddenly, without respite.

EVERYMAN. O gracious God in the high seat celestial,
Have mercy on me in this most need!
Shall I have company from this vale terrestrial
Of mine acquaintance that way me to lead?

DEATH. Yea, if any be so hardy
That would go with thee and bear thee company.
Hie[31] thee that thou were gone to God's magnificence,
Thy reckoning to give before his presence.
What, weenest[32] thou thy life is given thee,
And thy worldly goods also?

EVERYMAN. I had weened so, verily.

DEATH. Nay, nay, it was but lent thee.
For as soon as thou art go,
Another a while shall have it and then go therefro,
Even as thou hast done.
Everyman, thou art mad! Thou hast thy wits[33] five,
And here on earth will not amend thy live!
For suddenly I do come.

EVERYMAN. O wretched caitiff! Whither shall I flee
That I might 'scape this endless sorrow?
Now, gentle Death, spare me till tomorrow,
That I may amend me
With good advisement.[34]

DEATH. Nay, thereto I will not consent,
Nor no man will I respite,
But to the heart suddenly I shall smite,
Without any advisement.
And now out of thy sight I will me hie:
See thou make thee ready shortly,
For thou mayst say this is the day
That no man living may 'scape away.

[*Exit* DEATH.]

EVERYMAN. Alas, I may well weep with sighs deep:
Now have I no manner of company
To help me in my journey and me to keep[35]
And also my writing is full unready—
How shall I do now for to excuse me?
I would to God I had never be geet![36]
To my soul a full great profit it had be.
For now I fear pains huge and great.

◆ ◆ ◆

EVERYMAN. Alas, I am so faint I may not stand—
My limbs under me doth fold!
Friends, let us not turn again to this land,
Not for all the world's gold.
For into this cave must I creep
And turn to earth, and there to sleep.

BEAUTY. What, into this grave, alas?

EVERYMAN. Yea, there shall ye consume,[37] more and lass.[38]

BEAUTY. And what, should I smother here?

EVERYMAN. Yea, by my faith, and nevermore appear.
In this world live no more we shall,
But in heaven before the highest Lord of all.

---

31. **Hie.** Hasten
32. **weenest.** Suppose
33. **wits.** Senses
34. **advisement.** Preparation
35. **keep.** Guard
36. **never be geet.** Never been begotten; never been born
37. **consume.** Decay
38. **more and lass.** More and less

WORDS FOR EVERYDAY USE

cai • tiff (kāt´ if) *n.*, mean, cowardly person. *"The Joker speaks bravely, but he is actually a cowardly caitiff," said Batman.*

BEAUTY. I cross out all this! Adieu, by Saint John—
I take my tape in my lap and am gone.

EVERYMAN. What, Beauty, whither will ye?

BEAUTY. Peace, I am deaf—I look not behind me,
Not and thou wouldest give me all the gold in thy chest.

[*Exit* BEAUTY.]

EVERYMAN. Alas, whereto may I trust?
Beauty goeth fast away fro me—
She promised with me to live and die!

STRENGTH. Everyman, I will thee also forsake and deny.
Thy game liketh[39] me not at all.

EVERYMAN. Why then, ye will forsake me all?
Sweet Strength, tarry a little space.

STRENGTH. Nay, sir, by the rood of grace,
I will hie me from thee fast,
Though thou weep till thy heart tobrast.[40]

EVERYMAN. Ye would ever bide by me, ye said.

STRENGTH. Yea, I have you far enough conveyed![41]
Ye be old enough, I understand,
Your pilgrimage to take on hand:
I repent me that I hither came.

EVERYMAN. Strength, you to displease I am to blame,[42]
Yet promise is debt, this ye well wot.[43]

STRENGTH. In faith, I care not:
Thou art but a fool to complain;
You spend your speech and waste your brain.
Go, thrust thee into the ground.

[*Exit* STRENGTH.]

EVERYMAN. I had weened[44] surer I should you have found.
He that trusteth in his Strength
She him deceiveth at the length.
Both Strength and Beauty forsaketh me—
Yet they promised me fair and lovingly.

DISCRETION Everyman, I will after Strength be gone:
As for me, I will leave you alone.

EVERYMAN. Why Discretion, will ye forsake me?

DISCRETION Yea, in faith, I will go from thee.
For when Strength goeth before,
I follow after evermore.

EVERYMAN. Yet I pray thee, for the love of the Trinity,
Look in my grave once piteously.

DISCRETION Nay, so nigh will I not come.
Farewell everyone!

[*Exit* DISCRETION.]

EVERYMAN. O all thing faileth save God alone—
Beauty, Strength, and Discretion.
For when Death bloweth his blast
They all run fro me full fast.

FIVE-WITS. Everyman, my leave now of thee I take.
I will follow the other, for here I thee forsake.

EVERYMAN. Alas, then may I wail and weep,
For I took you for my best friend.

FIVE-WITS. I will no longer thee keep.[45]
Now farewell, and there an end!

39. **liketh.** Pleases
40. **tobrast.** Break
41. **conveyed.** Escorted
42. **you . . . blame.** I'm to blame for displeasing you.
43. **wot.** Know
44. **weened.** Supposed
45. **keep.** Watch over

ADDITIONAL QUESTIONS AND ACTIVITIES

What virtues appear to and then leave Everyman?
Answers
First beauty leaves him, then strength, then discretion an five wits.

ADDITIONAL QUESTIONS AND ACTIVITIES

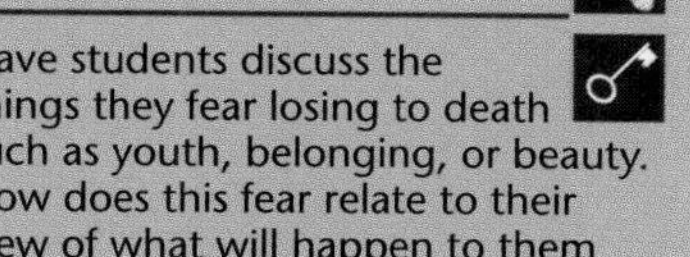

Have students discuss the things they fear losing to death such as youth, belonging, or beauty. How does this fear relate to their view of what will happen to them after death?

ADDITIONAL QUESTIONS AND ACTIVITIES

1. Who is last to leave Everyman?
2. Who stays with Everyman?
3. What welcome does the angel offer?

Answers

1. Knowledge is the last to leave Everyman.
2. Good Deeds stays with him.
3. The angel welcomes Everyman's soul to Heaven.

[*Exit* FIVE-WITS.]

EVERYMAN. O Jesu, help, all hath forsaken me!

GOOD DEEDS. Nay, Everyman, I will bide with thee:
I will not forsake thee indeed;
Thou shalt find me a good friend at need.

EVERYMAN. Gramercy, Good Deeds! Now may I true friends see.
They have forsaken me every one—
I loved them better than my Good Deeds alone.
Knowledge, will ye forsake me also?

KNOWLEDGE. Yea, Everyman, when ye to Death shall go,
But not yet, for no manner of danger.

EVERYMAN. Gramercy, Knowledge, with all my heart!

KNOWLEDGE. Nay, yet will I not from hence depart
Till I see where ye shall become.[46]

EVERYMAN. Methink, alas, that I must be gone
To make my reckoning and my debts pay,
For I see my time is nigh spent away.
Take example, all ye that this do hear or see,
How they that I best loved do forsake me,
Except my Good Deeds that bideth truly.

GOOD DEEDS. All earthly things is but vanity.
Beauty, Strength, and Discretion do man forsake,
Foolish friends and kinsmen that fair spake—
All fleeth save Good Deeds, and that am I.

EVERYMAN. Have mercy on me, God most mighty,
And stand by me, thou mother and maid, holy Mary!

GOOD DEEDS. Fear not: I will speak for thee.

EVERYMAN. Here I cry God mercy!

GOOD DEEDS. Short our end, and 'minish our pain.
Let us go, and never come again.

EVERYMAN. Into thy hands, Lord, my soul I commend:
Receive it, Lord, that it be not lost.
As thou me boughtest,[47] so me defend,
And save me from the fiend's boast,
That I may appear with that blessed host
That shall be saved at the day of doom.
In manus tuas, of mights most,
Forever *commendo spiritum meum*.[48]

[EVERYMAN *and* GOOD DEEDS *descend into the grave.*]

KNOWLEDGE. Now hath he suffered that we all shall endure,
The Good Deeds shall make all sure.
Now hath he made ending,
Methinketh that I hear angels sing
And make great joy and melody
Where Everyman's soul received shall be.

ANGEL. [*within*] Come, excellent elect[49] spouse to Jesu![50]
Here above thou shalt go
Because of thy singular virtue.
Now the soul is taken the body fro,
Thy reckoning is crystal clear:
Now shalt thou into the heavenly sphere—
Unto the which all ye shall come
That liveth well before the day of doom.

---

46. **Till . . . become.** Until I see what will become of you
47. **boughtest.** Redeemed
48. ***In . . . meum.*** Into your hands, Almighty One, I forever commend my spirit.
49. **elect.** Chosen
50. **spouse to Jesu.** The soul is often called the bride of Jesus.

[*Enter* DOCTOR.]

DOCTOR. This memorial[51] men may
have in mind:
Ye hearers, take it of worth, old and young,
And forsake Pride, for he deceiveth you in
the end.
And remember Beauty, Five-Wits,
Strength, and Discretion,
They all at the last do Everyman forsake,
Save his Good Deeds there doth he take—
But beware, for and they be small,
Before God he hath no help at all—
None excuse may be there for Everyman.
Alas, how shall he do than?[52]
For after death amends may no man make,
For then mercy and pity doth him forsake.
If his reckoning be not clear when he doth
come,
God will say, "*Ite, maledicti, in ignem
eternum!*"[53]
And he that hath his account whole and
sound,
High in heaven he shall be crowned,
Unto which place God bring us all thither,
That we may live body and soul togither.
Thereto help, the Trinity!
Amen, say ye, for saint charity. ■

51. **memorial.** Reminder
52. **than.** Then
53. ***Ite . . . eternum.*** Go, cursed one, into the everlasting fire.

WORDS FOR EVERYDAY USE

a • mends (ə mendz´) *n. pl.,* something done to make up for injury, loss, etc., that one has caused. *"I would like to make amends for the long hours that you have had to work," said the boss.*

Respond *to the* SELECTION

If you were to judge Everyman, what kind of person would you deem him to be?

SELECTION CHECK TEST 4.3.19 WITH ANSWERS

1. What is man's attitude toward God? **Man is thoughtless toward God.**
2. Who does God send to Everyman? **He sends Death.**
3. What had Beauty, Strength, and Discretion promised? **They had promised to stay.**
4. Who goes with Everyman to the grave? **Good Deeds goes with Everyman.**
5. What does the Doctor say we cannot do after death? **We cannot make amends.**

Vocabulary in Context
Fill each blank with the most appropriate word from these Words for Everyday Use from *Everyman*. You may have to change the tense of the word.

transitory proffer respite caitiff amends

1. The hurricane's eye offered only a brief **respite**.
2. In many dramas, the hero must defeat one or more **caitiffs** before the conclusion.
3. The team's elation was **transitory**; soon they focused on preparing for the next trial.

Literary Tools
1. What is a morality play? **A morality play is a type of medieval drama in which the characters are abstract caricatures of virtues, vices, etc.**
2. What is an allegory? **An allegory is a work in which each element symbolizes something else.**
3. Explain how a morality play is a type of allegory. **In an allegory, every element symbolizes something else and in a morality play, the characters symbolize virtues and vices.**

RESPOND TO THE SELECTION

Student responses about the character of Everyman will vary. However, they should be based on evidence from the play. For example, some students may point out that Everyman is a worldly fellow, as is shown by the fact that when death comes, his mind is on his goods and treasures.

ANSWERS TO INVESTIGATE, INQUIRE, AND IMAGINE

RECALL

1a. Everyman asks death for more time.
2a. Beauty, Strength, Discretion, and Knowledge desert Everyman. Good Deeds alone remains with him.
3a. Everyman goes to the heavenly sphere because he has Good Deeds to take with him to his reckoning.

INTERPRET

1b. Everyman is at first incredulous and then terrified as he talks to Death. He is totally unprepared for Death's coming because he has been living a worldly life. He has acted as though he were going to live forever.
2b. Everyman despairs over the loss of his companions because he fears that he will have to take his hard pilgrimage (to the general reckoning) all alone.
3b. Everyman's last speech shows that he is certain. He commends his spirit to God, echoing the words of Jesus on the cross, and asks God to receive that spirit and to save him from the fiend, or the devil.

ANALYZE

4a. *Responses will vary.* The play teaches that many things that are valued during this life, such as beauty, strength, and wits, will leave us. There is a "you can't take it with you" message. Because of this, it is important to do good deeds during this life, which will accompany us to a good afterlife.

SYNTHESIZE

4b. *Responses will vary.*

EVALUATE

5a. *Responses will vary.* Students may say that because of his good deeds, Everyman did indeed deserve to be saved.

EXTEND

5b. *Responses will vary.* Possible answers might include kindness, compassion, and help to others.

INVESTIGATE, Inquire, Imagine

Recall: GATHERING FACTS

1a. What does Everyman want from Death?
2a. Who deserts Everyman? Who stays with him?
3a. What is Everyman's fate? Why?

→ **Interpret:** FINDING MEANING

1b. What is Everyman's state of mind as he talks with Death? Why?
2b. Why does Everyman despair over the loss of his companions?
3b. What does Everyman's last speech show?

Analyze: TAKING THINGS APART

4a. What lessons does this play teach?

→ **Synthesize:** BRINGING THINGS TOGETHER

4b. This play is based on the religious assumption that people will be judged at the end of life. Explain whether the play is effective if you do not share that belief.

Evaluate: MAKING JUDGMENTS

5a. Evaluate whether Everyman deserved to be saved.

→ **Extend:** CONNECTING IDEAS

5b. What qualities do you think people should strive for in their lives?

Understanding Literature

MORALITY PLAY. Review the definition of **morality play** in Literary Tools on page 243. Morality plays are clearly didactic, or meant to teach a lesson. How is the message of *Everyman* didactic? How do specific characters contribute to a didactic tone?

NAIVE ALLEGORY. Review the definition of **naive allegory** in the Handbook of Literary Terms. Explain what makes *Everyman* a naive allegory.

ANSWERS TO UNDERSTANDING LITERATURE

MORALITY PLAY. *Everyman* is a specifically didactic play, because it was written with the purpose of conveying a moral. This moral is communicated directly by the Messenger, by the character God, by the Doctor, and indirectly by the action of the play (the desertion of Everyman by all but Good Deeds).

NAIVE ALLEGORY. *Everyman* is, a naive allegory, because each of the characters has a specific allegorical interpretation. The allegory is quite straightforward and is expressed in the characters' names.

Writer's Journal

1. Write **fortune cookie inserts** that make pronouncements about human nature, such as those expressed in *Everyman.*
2. Write a **sermon** or **persuasive speech** about an issue related to human nature or behavior about which you feel strongly. For example, you might write about being kind to others or about respecting differences.
3. Write a short **naive allegory.** First choose a purpose for your allegory. Then identify the objects, action, abstractions that will be personified.

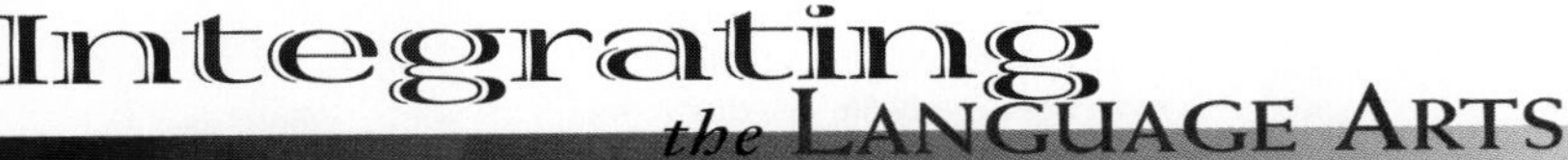

Integrating *the* Language Arts

Language, Grammar, and Style

Using Proper Capitalization. Read the Language Arts Survey 3.99, "Titles of Art Works and Literary Works." Then, revise the following sentences to correct errors in capitalization. If no corrections are needed, write *No Errors* after the sentence.

1. In addition to Everyman, other morality plays and another type of religious play, called the mystery play, were produced in the Medieval Period.
2. The morality play the Pride of life predates Everyman by almost a century.
3. Another morality play, The castle of perseverance, also appeared at the beginning of the fifteenth century.
4. Mystery plays, such as The York Play Of The Crucifixion, dramatized Biblical stories for the common people.
5. The Second shepherds' play, one of the mystery plays, uses comedy as well as drama to tell the story of Christ's birth.

Collaborative Learning & Speaking and Listening

Morality Play. As a class, perform part or all of this selection from *Everyman.* Assign character parts and read through the play as a group, with each person reading his or her lines aloud. Then discuss whether you would like to perform the play as a staged production or simply as a reading of the character parts. If you decide to perform the play, you might want to make masks or some form of costuming to represent each character. As you rehearse the play, talk with each other about the scene's dramatic interpretation. Decide what the characters are thinking and feeling and how their words relate to their body movements and facial expressions. When you are ready, perform your scene for the class.

Applied English

Letter of Recommendation. Review the format of a business letter. Then, write a letter of recommendation for Everyman to take with him to his judgment. Use proper business format for your letter.

Answers to Integrating the Language Arts

Language, Grammar, and Style

1. No errors.
2. The morality play *The Pride of Life* predates Everyman by almost a century.
3. Another morality play, *The Castle of Perseverance,* also appeared at the beginning of the fifteenth century.
4. Mystery plays, such as *The York Play of the Crucifixion,* dramatized biblical stories for the common people.
5. *The Second Shepherd's Play,* one of the mystery plays, uses comedy as well as drama to tell the story of Christ's birth.

Collaborative Learning & Speaking and Listening

An allegorical play like *Everyman* works very well when produced in a highly stylized manner. Masks and special costumes might be appropriate. An alternate possibility for student productions is to perform the play as puppet theater. Hand puppets representing the characters can easily be made from socks or pieces of felt decorated by sewing or by drawing with markers.

ADDITIONAL RESOURCES

Unit 3 Resource Book
- Selection Worksheet 3.10
- Selection Check Test 4.3.21
- Selection Test 4.3.22
- Study and Research Resource 5.19, 5.40

GRAPHIC ORGANIZER

idealizes a lady—loves lady from afar
longs for adventure—hopes to prove himself

READER'S JOURNAL

Students can discuss what appeals to them about the part they describe. For example, does the character have qualities they wish they had? Do they long for an exciting activity? Are they looking to enter a fantasy world?

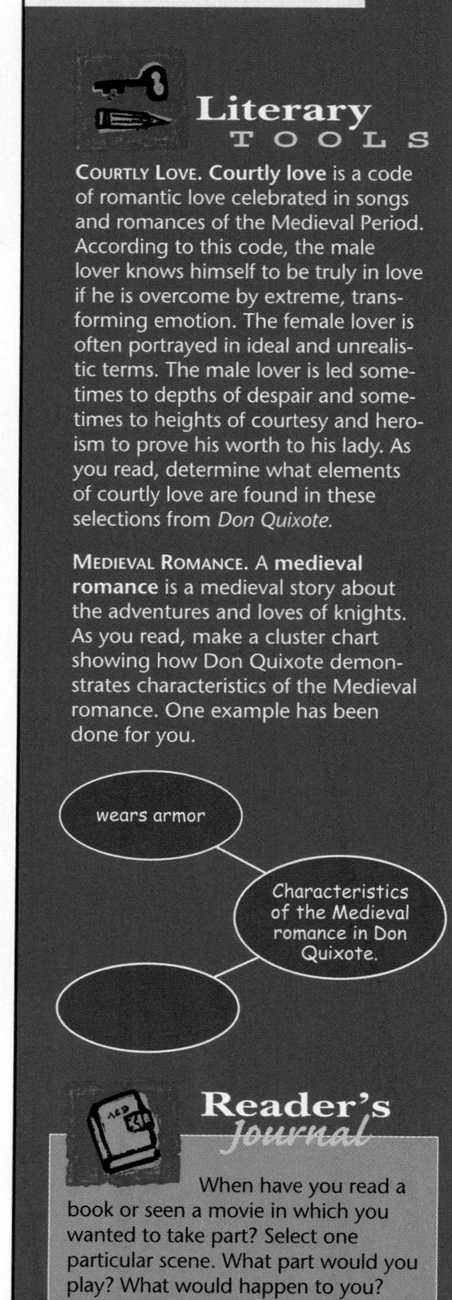

MULTICULTURAL EXTENSIONS

Literary TOOLS

Courtly Love. Courtly love is a code of romantic love celebrated in songs and romances of the Medieval Period. According to this code, the male lover knows himself to be truly in love if he is overcome by extreme, transforming emotion. The female lover is often portrayed in ideal and unrealistic terms. The male lover is led sometimes to depths of despair and sometimes to heights of courtesy and heroism to prove his worth to his lady. As you read, determine what elements of courtly love are found in these selections from *Don Quixote.*

Medieval Romance. A **medieval romance** is a medieval story about the adventures and loves of knights. As you read, make a cluster chart showing how Don Quixote demonstrates characteristics of the Medieval romance. One example has been done for you.

Reader's Journal

When have you read a book or seen a movie in which you wanted to take part? Select one particular scene. What part would you play? What would happen to you?

FROM *The Ingenious Hidalgo Don Quixote de la Mancha*

BY MIGUEL DE CERVANTES, TRANSLATED BY WALTER STARKIE

About the AUTHOR

Miguel de Cervantes (1547–1616), the most famous of all Spanish authors, was born near Madrid to a family of seven children. Little is known of his early life or education. His father combined the duties of a barber and surgeon, and his family traveled from town to town. In 1571, he fought bravely in a sea battle against the Turks and was severely wounded, losing the use of his left hand. In 1575, he was captured and sold into slavery in Algiers. There he remained for five years, until he was ransomed and returned to Spain in 1580. In 1584, he married Ana de Villafranca from the province of La Mancha, a woman eighteen years younger than he. The following year, he published his first novel, *La Galatea.* From 1582 to 1587, he wrote numerous plays. As a government officer, he helped raise provisions for the Spanish Armada launched against England during the reign of Queen Elizabeth (see page 254 of this text). The first part of his most famous work, *The Ingenious Hidalgo Don Quixote de la Mancha,* was published in 1605, the second part in 1615.

About the SELECTION

Don Quixote de la Mancha is a mock epic in which a deranged gentleman, having spent too much time reading romances about the adventures of knights in shining armor, decides to enter upon a life as a knight, enlisting as his unwilling companion a servant named Sancho Panza. This parody of medieval romance, with its absurd, comic, and tragic hero, has enjoyed enormous popularity throughout the ages and has inspired countless other works of literature, music, and art. The novel has also given to the English language the word *quixotic,* meaning "impractical" or "foolishly idealistic," as well as the phrase *to tilt at windmills,* meaning "to make a ludicrous effort."

GOALS/OBJECTIVES

Studying this lesson will enable students to
- experience amusement at the comic side of Don Quixote's character and empathize with the tragic side
- recognize the selection as a parody of romances
- define *courtly love* and give examples of it
- create a bibliography

FROM *The Ingenious Hidalgo Don Quixote de La Mancha*

MIGUEL DE CERVANTES SAAVEDRA, TRANSLATED BY WALTER STARKIE

FROM PART I, BOOK 1

THE QUALITY AND MANNER OF LIFE OF THAT FAMOUS GENTLEMAN DON QUIXOTE OF LA MANCHA

At a village of La Mancha, whose name I do not wish to remember, there lived a little while ago one of those gentlemen who are wont to keep a lance in the rack, an old buckler, a lean horse, and a swift greyhound. His stew had more beef than mutton in it and most nights he ate the remains salted and cold. Lentil soup on Fridays, "tripe and trouble"[1] on Saturdays and an occasional pigeon as an extra delicacy on Sundays, consumed three-quarters of his income. The remainder was spent on a jerkin[2] of fine puce, velvet breeches, and slippers of the same stuff for holidays, and a suit of good, honest homespun for week-days. His family consisted of a housekeeper about forty, a niece not yet twenty, and a lad who served him both in the field and at home and could saddle the horse or use the pruning-knife. Our gentleman was about fifty years of age, of a sturdy constitution, but wizened and gaunt-featured, an early riser and a devotee of the chase. They say that his surname was Quixada or Quesada (for on this point the authors who have written on this subject differ), but we may reasonably conjecture that his name was Quixana. This, however, has very little to do with our story: enough that in its telling we swerve not a jot from the truth. You must know that the above-mentioned gentleman in his leisure moments (which was most of the year) gave himself up with so much delight and gusto to reading books of chivalry that he almost entirely neglected the exercise of

1. **tripe and trouble.** Saturday's meal was light, semi-abstinence fare in memory of the defeat of the Moors.
2. **jerkin.** Hip-length usually sleeveless jacket.

INDIVIDUAL LEARNING STRATEGIES

MOTIVATION
Students can enact a comic scene from this selection or create a drawing or model that shows the famous windmill scene.

READING PROFICIENCY
Before having students read the selection, direct their attention to the discussion of parody in About the Selection. Then, as they read, have students look for ways in which Don Quixote's story parodies traditional medieval romances.

ENGLISH LANGUAGE LEARNING
Point out the following vocabulary words.
lance—long, pointed spear carried by a knight
buckler—a small, round shield
surname—last name; family name
conjecture—guess
domestic—having to do with the home
extravagant—exceptional; beyond the ordinary or the acceptable
arable—good for growing crops
immersed—submerged; completely involved
enchantment—magic spell
authentic—real
thwart—lying or extending across
cleft—split

SPECIAL NEEDS
Have students focus on the Guided Reading Questions and the Recall questions in the Investigate, Inquire, and Imagine sections.

ENRICHMENT
- Find a recording or film of the musical *Man of La Mancha* and share this with your students.
- Have students brainstorm a list of activities that might be described as quixotic or as tilting at windmills (i.e., activities that are absurd or doomed to failure).

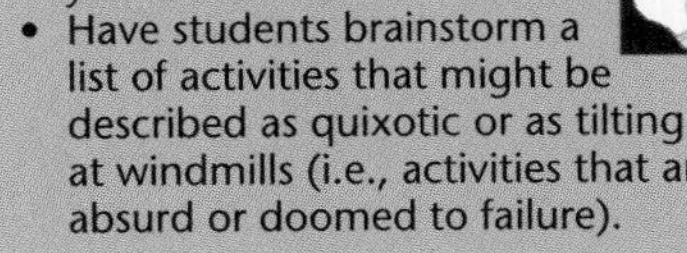

VOCABULARY FROM THE SELECTION

caitiff
phantasmagoria
sonorous

Don Quixote Fighting the Windmill. Gustave Doré.

the chase and even the management of his domestic affairs: indeed his craze for this kind of literature became so extravagant that he sold many acres of arable land to purchase books of knight-errantry, and he carried off to his house as many as he could possibly find. . . .

◆ ◆ ◆

In short, he so immersed himself in those romances that he spent whole days and nights over his books; and thus with little sleeping and much reading his brains dried up to such a degree that he lost the use of his reason. His imagination became filled with a host of fancies he had read in his books—enchantments, quarrels, battles, challenges, wounds, courtships, loves, tortures, and many other absurdities. So true did all this phantasmagoria from books appear to him that in his mind he accounted no history in the world more authentic. He would say that the Cid Ruy Diaz was a very gallant knight, but not to be compared with the Knight

WORDS FOR EVERYDAY USE

phan • tas • ma • go • ri • a (fan taz´mə gôr´ē ə) *n.*, rapidly changing series of imagined figures or events. *Brian's nightmare was filled with phantasmagoria—horned and winged creatures that were pursuing him through a cavern.*

of the Burning Sword, who with a single thwart blow cleft asunder a brace of hulking blustering giants. He was better pleased with Bernardo del Carpio, because at Roncesvalles he had slain Roland the Enchanted by availing himself of the stratagem Hercules had employed on Antaeus, the son of the Earth, whom he squeezed to death in his arms. He praised the giant Morgante, for he alone was courteous and well-bred among that monstrous brood puffed up with arrogance and insolence. Above all, he admired Rinaldo of Montalvan, especially when he saw him sallying out of his castle to plunder everyone that came his way; and, moreover, when, beyond the seas, he made off with the idol of Mahomet, which, as history says, was of solid gold. But he would have parted with his housekeeper and his niece into the bargain for the pleasure of rib-roasting the traitor Galalon.

At last, having lost his wits completely, he stumbled upon the oddest fancy that ever entered a madman's brain. He believed that it was necessary, both for his own honor and for the service of the state, that he should become knight-errant and roam through the world with his horse and armor in quest of adventures, and practice all that had been performed by the knights-errant of whom he had read. He would follow their life, redressing all manner of wrongs and exposing himself to continual dangers, and at last, after concluding his enterprises, he would win everlasting honor and renown. The poor gentleman saw himself in imagination already crowned Emperor of Trebizond by the valor of his arm. And thus, excited by these agreeable delusions, he hastened to put his plans into operation.

What did Quixana decide he must do?

The first thing he did was to furbish some rusty armor which had belonged to his great-grandfather and had lain moldering in a corner. He cleaned it and repaired it as best he could, but he found one great defect: instead of a complete helmet there was just the simple morion.[2] This want he ingeniously remedied by making a kind of visor out of pasteboard, and when it was fitted to the morion it looked like an entire helmet. It is true that, in order to test its strength and see if it was sword-proof, he drew his sword and gave it two strokes, the first of which instantly destroyed the result of a week's labor. It troubled him to see with what ease he had broken the helmet in pieces, so to protect it from such an accident, he remade it and fenced the inside with a few bars of iron in such a manner that he felt assured of its strength, and without making a second trial, he held it to be a most excellent visor. Then he went to see his steed, and although it had more cracks than a Spanish *real* and more faults than Gonela's jade which was all skin and bone, he thought that neither the Bucephalus of Alexander nor the Cid's Babieca could be compared with it. He spent four days deliberating over what name he would give the horse; for (as he said to himself) it was not right that the horse of so famous a knight should remain without a name, and so he endeavored to find one which would express what the animal had been before he had been the mount of a knight-errant, and what he now was. It was indeed reasonable that when the master changed his state, the horse should change his name too, and assume one pompous and high-sounding as suited the new order he was about to profess. So, after having devised, erased and blotted out many other names, he finally

2. **morion.** Crested helmet without a visor

Words For Everyday Use

so • no • rous (sə nôr´əs) *adj.*, having an impressive sound. *The* sonorous *horn of the tugboat warned the ferry boat pilot of its proximity.*

ANSWER TO GUIDED READING QUESTION

1. Quixana decided that he must become a knight and seek adventures in order to achieve fame.

ADDITIONAL QUESTIONS AND ACTIVITIES

How does Quixana prepare to be a knight-errant? What is humorous about these preparations?

Answer

Quixana prepares a suit of armor and a helmet with a visor and renames his horse. His preparations are comical because he makes his helmet himself out of pasteboard and cares not for the quality of his steed but only for its name.

ANSWERS TO GUIDED READING QUESTIONS

1. Dulcinea is a simple country girl named Aldonza Lorenzo. Quixote calls her Dulcinea because the name sounds like that of a princess or a lady of quality. (Note: the word dulce means "sweet."
2. Quixote intends to fight some giants. The are actually windmills.

ADDITIONAL QUESTIONS AND ACTIVITIES

How does Quixana prepare to be a knight-errant? What is humorous about these preparations?

Answer

Quixana prepares a suit of armor and a helmet with a visor and renames his horse. His preparations are comical because he makes his helmet himself out of pasteboard and cares not for the quality of his steed but only for its name.

determined to call the horse Rozinante—a name, in his opinion, lofty, sonorous and significant, for it explained that he had only been a "rocín" or hack before he had been raised to his present status of first of all the hacks in the world.

Now that he had given his horse a name so much to his satisfaction, he resolved to choose one for himself, and after seriously considering the matter for eight whole days he finally determined to call himself Don Quixote. Wherefore the authors of this most true story have deduced that his name must undoubtedly have been Quixano, and not Quesada, as others would have it. Then remembering that the valiant Amadis had not been content to call himself simply Amadis, but added thereto the name of his kingdom and native country to render it more illustrious, calling himself Amadis of Gaul, so he, like a good knight, also added the name of his province and called himself Don Quixote of La Mancha. In this way, he openly proclaimed his lineage and country, and at the same time he honored it by taking its name.

Now that his armor was scoured, his morion made into a helmet, his horse and himself new-named, he felt that nothing was wanting but a lady of whom to be enamored; for a knight-errant who was loveless was a tree without leaves and fruit—a body without soul. "If," said he, "for my sins or through my good fortune I encounter some giant—a usual occurrence to knight-errants—and bowling him over at the first onset, or cleaving him in twain, I finally vanquish and force him to surrender, would it not be better to have some lady to whom I may send him as a trophy? so that when he enters into her presence he may throw himself on his knees before her and in accents contrite and humble say: 'Madam, I am the giant Caraculiambro, Lord of the Island of Malindrania, whom the never-adequately-praised Don Quixote of La Mancha has overcome in single combat. He has commanded me to present myself before you, so that your highness may dispose of me as you wish.' " How glad was our knight when he had made these discourses to himself, but chiefly when he had found one whom he might call his lady! It happened that in a neighboring village there lived a good-looking country lass, with whom he had been in love, although it is understood that she never knew or cared a jot. She was called Aldonza Lorenzo, and it was to her that he thought fit to confide the sovereignty of his heart. He sought a name for her which would not vary too much from her own and yet would approach that of a princess or lady of quality: he resolved to call her Dulcinea del Toboso (she was a native of that town), a name in his opinion musical, uncommon and expressive, like the others which he had devised. . . .

Who is Dulcinea? Why does Don Quixote call her that?

◆ ◆ ◆

FROM PART I, BOOK 7

THE TERRIFYING AND UNPRECEDENTED ADVENTURE OF THE WINDMILLS, AND THE STUPENDOUS BATTLE BETWEEN THE GALLANT BISCAYAN AND THE PUISSANT MANCHEGAN

Just then they came in sight of thirty or forty windmills which rise from that plain, and as soon as Don Quixote saw them, he said to his squire: "Fortune is guiding our affairs better than we ourselves could have wished. Do you see over yonder, my friend Sancho Panza, thirty or more huge giants? I intend to do battle with them and slay them: with their spoils we shall begin to be rich, for this is a righteous war and the removal of so foul a brood from off the face of the earth is a service God will bless."

What foe does Don Quixote intend to fight? What is he really battling?

"What giants?" said Sancho, amazed.

"Those giants you see over there," replied his master, "with long arms: some of them have them well-nigh two leagues in length."

"Take care, sir," answered Sancho; "those over there are not giants but windmills, and those things which seem to be arms are their sails, which when they are whirled round by the wind turn the millstones."

"It is clear," answered Don Quixote, "that you are not experienced in adventures. Those are giants, and if you are afraid, turn aside and pray whilst I enter into fierce and unequal battle with them."

Uttering those words, he clapped spurs to Rozinante, without heeding the cries of his squire Sancho, who warned him that he was not going to attack giants but windmills. But so convinced was he that they were giants that he neither heard his squire's shouts nor did he notice what they were though he was very near them. Instead, he rushed on, shouting in a loud voice: "Fly not, cowards and vile caitiffs; one knight alone attacks you!" At that moment a slight breeze arose, and the great sails began to move. When Don Quixote saw this he shouted again: "Although ye flourish more arms than the giant Briareus, ye shall pay for your insolence!"

Saying this, and commending himself most devoutly to his Lady Dulcinea, whom he begged to help him in this peril, he covered himself with his buckler, couched his lance, charged at Rozinante's full gallop and rammed the first mill in his way. He ran his lance into the sail, but the wind twisted it with such violence that it shivered the spear to pieces, dragging him and his horse after it and rolling him over and over on the ground, sorely damaged.

Sancho Panza rushed up to his assistance as fast as his ass could gallop, and when he reached the knight he found that he was unable to move, such was the shock that Rozinante had given him in the fall.

"God help us!" said Sancho. "Did I not tell you, sir, to mind what you were doing, for those were only windmills! Nobody could have mistaken them unless he had windmills in his brains."

"Hold your peace, dear Sancho," answered Don Quixote; "for the things of war are, above all others, subject to continual change; especially as I am convinced that the magician Freston—the one who robbed me of my room and books—has changed those giants into windmills to deprive me of the glory of victory: such is the enmity he bears against me. But in the end his evil arts will be of little avail against my doughty sword."

"God settle it his own way," cried Sancho, as he helped his master to rise and remount Rozinante, who was well-nigh disjointed by his fall. ■

Words for Everyday Use

cai • tiff (kāt´if) *n.*, cowardly person. *The knight warned the caitiff that he would return if he tried to poach from the king's forest again.*

Respond *to the* Selection

Role-play a conversation in which, as Don Quixote's neighbors, you and a classmate discuss the changes he has made in his life. Be sure to share if you admire him or not, giving reasons for your opinion.

SELECTION CHECK TEST 4.3.23 WITH ANSWERS

Checking Your Reading

1. What did Quixana most like to do? **Quixana enjoyed reading books of chivalry.**
2. What did Quixana decide he must become? **He decided he must become a knight-errant.**
3. What did Quixana name his horse? **He named it Rozinante.**
4. Why does Don Quixote attempt to fight the windmills? **He thinks they are giants.**
5. Who advises Don Quixote not to fight the windmills? **Sancho Panza advises him not to fight the windmills.**

RESPOND TO THE SELECTION

One student might join in as Don Quixote. Students could show how they would react to his face. Would they be as honest and open as they were when he was not there?

ANSWERS TO INVESTIGATE, INQUIRE, AND IMAGINE

RECALL

1a. Quixana goes mad. He hopes to win honor as a knight-errant. He armors himself, makes a helmet, names his horse Rozinante and himself Don Quixote of La Mancha, and finds a lady to serve.

2a. He imagines they are giants.

3a. Sancho denies his master's assertion that the windmills are giants and warns Quixote against attacking them. Quixote charges the windmills on horseback, gets his lance caught in the windmill's sail, and is dragged after it, injuring himself. Sancho rushes to Quixote's assistance and tries to argue with Quixote about the nature of his adventure.

INTERPRET

1b. Don Quixote has an aggrandized attitude toward himself.

2b. Quixote can be seen either as a foolish madman or as a courageous and fanciful believer in the chivalric age. He is made both noble and ludicrous by his faith in the world described in books of chivalry and by his resulting attempts to make the most common occurrences into adventures.

3b. Sancho Panza has a much more realistic view of the world. It would be interesting to know what he thinks of Don Quixote and why he stays with him.

ANALYZE

4a. *Responses will vary. Possible responses are given.* Cervantes satirizes the lack of realism in the medieval romance, specifically the fantastic giants or monsters, the beautiful but remote lady, and the incredible exploits of the knight-errant.

SYNTHESIZE

4b. *Responses will vary. Possible responses are given.* Cervantes seems to object to the lack of realism in the medieval romance. He admires the imagination and values expressed in books of chivalry.

EVALUATE

5a. His manner is consistent. There is some logic behind his decision, but mostly it is guided by the romances he has read and the growing picture he has of himself as a knight-errant.

EXTEND

5b. *Responses will vary.*

INVESTIGATE, Inquire, Imagine

Recall: GATHERING FACTS ➤ **Interpret:** FINDING MEANING

1a. What happens to Quixana's mind as a result of reading too many medieval romances? What does he hope to accomplish by becoming a knight-errant? What preparations does he make for his new life?

1b. What is Don Quixote's attitude toward himself?

2a. What does Don Quixote imagine the windmills to be?

2b. Given Quixote's imaginings, what might you say about his character?

3a. How does Sancho Panzo react to his master's beliefs about the windmills? What happens in the battle of the windmills? What does Sancho do thereafter?

3b. How does Sancho Panza see the world differently from his master? What would be interesting to know about Sancho?

Analyze: TAKING THINGS APART ➤ **Synthesize:** BRINGING THINGS TOGETHER

4a. What elements of medieval romance literature does Cervantes satirize in these selections?

4b. Why do you think Cervantes chose to satirize medieval romances? What does Cervantes seem to admire about books of chivalry?

Evaluate: MAKING JUDGMENTS ➤ **Extend:** CONNECTING IDEAS

5a. Evaluate whether the manner in which Quixana chooses his new name is consistent with his other behaviors.

5b. Watch the 1972 movie *Man of La Mancha.* Is Don Quixote portrayed as Cervantes intended, or has his character been altered for the big screen? If so, how is Don Quixote different in the movie?

Understanding Literature

COURTLY LOVE. Review the definition for **courtly love i**n the Handbook of Literary Terms. What elements of courtly love are found in these selections from Don Quixote? Who is the object of Don Quixote's veneration? Why does he need to find such a lady before he sets out on his quests? What does he do immediately before entering into battle with the windmills?

MEDIEVAL ROMANCE. Review the definition for **medieval romance** in the Handbook of Literary Terms and the graphic organizer you made in Literary Tools on page 254. In what ways is Don Quixote similar to Arthur in Le Morte d'Arthur, to Tristan in "Chevrefoil," and to the Knight in "The Prologue" to *Chaucer's Canterbury Tales*?

ANSWERS TO UNDERSTANDING LITERATURE

COURTLY LOVE. Quixote idealizes his lady, loves her from afar, and longs for an adventure in order to send her a trophy to prove himself a chivalric hero. The object of his veneration is Aldonza Lorenzo, or Dulcinea del Toboso. He needs to find a lady due to the conventions of the medieval romance n which courtly love inspires all of a knight's adventures. He commends himself to his lady before entering battle.

MEDIEVAL ROMANCE. Quixote is similar to Arthur, Tristan, and Chaucer's knight in that he wears armor, carries a weapon, rides a horse, and searches for adventure. Like the heroes of medieval romance, Quixote practices the values of chivalry; he is always brave, courteous, and honorable.

Writer's Journal

1. Imagine you are Miguel de Cervantes. Write a **journal entry** about your idea for a novel based on medieval romances. What inspires you? Whom do you want to read your novel? What is your purpose in writing it?
2. Write a **paragraph** describing the ways in which *Don Quixote* satirizes medieval romances.
3. A *parody* is a literary work that imitates another work for humorous, often satirical, purposes. Write a **parody** of a heroic adventure in which you attempt to poke fun at your character's loyalty, honesty, courage, inventiveness, or other positive attribute. You might select a hero from a movie, cartoon, or comic strip.

Integrating *the* Language Arts

Media Literacy

Don Quixote Exhibit. Visit the Don Quixote de la Mancha Exhibit website at http://milton.mse.jhu.edu:8006/index.html. This site is a digital exhibit of translations and illustrations of Miguel de Cervantes's novel *Don Quixote de la Mancha.* The exhibit features the holdings of the George Peabody Library on the Johns Hopkins University campus. You may tour the exhibit station by station, viewing images, legends, and associated text at each of 35 stations, and read any or all of six chapters from the novel at this site. The exhibit can also be followed in a Spanish version. After viewing the site, access some of the Internet links listed and create your own exhibit of information that you find interesting about Don Quixote and present it to the class.

Study and Research

Creating a Bibliography. Create a bibliography of books about a topic of your choice pertaining to the medieval era, such as pilgrimages, cathedrals, weapons, food, or jousting tournaments. Read the Language Arts Survey 5.19, "Computerized and Card Catalogs," and 5.40, "Making Bibliographies and Bibliography Cards." Then use either a card or a computerized catalog to find works about medieval subjects. Compile a list of such sources, listing the titles, authors, and other necessary publication information.

Applied English & Study and Research

Writing a Forward. Read about how Cervantes affected writers that came after him. Then write a forward for a new edition of *Don Quixote* in which you discuss the influence the novel has had on other writers and periods of literature.

ANSWERS TO INTEGRATING THE LANGUAGE ARTS

Media Literacy
Refer students to the Language Arts Survey 5.35, "How to Understand Internet Sites" to help them with this activity.

"WESTERN WIND"

About the Selection. Nothing is known about the author or date of this poem. It is generally regarded as a masterpiece of "minimalist" poetry, using a few briefly stated images to evoke worlds of meaning. Ask students to find the images in the poem. Then ask what they can infer about the poet. What desire is expressed in the poem? What kind of life did the poet lead? Do they think the poet was a man or a woman? Why?

"I AM OF IRELAND"

About the Selection. In the Middle Ages, ancient works of literature and learning were preserved and studied in monasteries in the outskirts of Ireland (and elsewhere). Thus, Ireland is considered a "holy land."

"THE BONNY EARL OF MURRAY"

About the Selection. In 1592, the Earl of Murray, a popular Scottish noble, was murdered by Huntly. King James VI of Scotland had ordered Murray arrested for fomenting dissent among the people by supporting their calls for relief from poverty and indentured servitude. Huntly, the king's agent, killed him instead of arresting him.

"THE TWA CORBIES"

About the Selection. This poem expresses early medieval attitudes regarding the loneliness and eternity of death. The crows note that all the knight's former servants and friends, including his "lady," have deserted him. He once was a noble, but now he is food for scavengers, who will also use parts of him to repair their nest.

"BONNY BARBARA ALLAN"

About the Selection. The subject of this ballad is the death of Sir John Grehme caused by unrequited love for Barbara Allan.

Selections for Additional Reading: Medieval Literature

"Western Wind"
Anonymous

Westron wind, when will thou blow?
The small rain down can rain.
Christ, that my love were in my arms,
And I in my bed again.

"I Am of Ireland"
Anonymous

Ich am of Irlonde,
And of the holy londe
Of Irlonde.
Goode sire, praye ich thee,
For of[1] sainte charitee,
Com and dance with me
In Irlonde.

"The Bonny Earl of Murray"
Anonymous

Ye Highlands and ye Lawlands,
O where have you been?
They have slain the Earl of Murray,
And they laid him on the green.

"Now wae be to thee, Huntly,[2]
And wherefore did you sae?
I bade you bring him wi' you
But forbade you him to slay."

He was a braw[3] gallant,
And he rid at the ring;[4]
And the bonny Earl of Murray,
O he might have been a king.

He was a braw gallant,
And he played at the ba';
And the bonny Earl of Murray
Was the flower among them a'.

He was a braw gallant,
And he played at the glove;
And the bonny Earl of Murray,
O he was the queen's love.
O lang will his lady
Look o'er the Castle Down,
Ere she see the Earl of Murray
Come sounding through the town.

"The Twa Corbies"
Anonymous

As I was walking all alane,
I heard twa corbies making a mane;[5]
The tane unto the t'other say,
"Where sall we gang and dine to-day?"
"In behint yon auld fail dyke,[6]
I wot there lies a new slain knight;
And naebody kens that he lies there,
But his hawk, his hound, and lady fair.

"His hound is to the hunting gane,
His hawk to fetch the wild-fowl hame,
His lady's ta'en another mate,
So we may mak' our dinner sweet.

"Ye'll sit on his white hause-bane,[7]
And I'll pike out his bonny blue e'en;
Wi' ae lock o' his gowden hair
We'll theek our nest when it grows bare.

"Mony a ane for him makes mane,
But nane sall ken where he is gane;
O'er his white banes, when they are bare,
The wind sall blaw for evermair."

"Bonny Barbara Allan"
Anonymous

It was in and about the Martinmas[8] time,
When the green leaves were a-fallin';
That Sir John Graeme in the West Country
Fell in love with Barbara Allan.

He sent his man down through the town
To the place where she was dwelling':
"O haste and come to my master dear,
If you be Barbara Allan."
O gently, gently rose she up,
To the place where he was lyin',
And when she drew the curtain by:
"Young man, I think you're dyin'."

1. **For of.** For sake of
2. **Huntly.** In 1592, Huntly killed Murray though he was only supposed to arrest him.
3. **braw.** Brave
4. **rid . . . ring.** Knights tried to put their spears through a hanging ring.
5. **twa . . . mane.** Two crows making a moan
6. **fail dyke.** Wall of turf
7. **hause-bane.** Neck bone
8. **Martinmas.** The feast of St. Martin, November 11

"O it's I'm sick, and very, very sick,
And 'tis a' for Barbara Allan."
"O the better for me you shall never be,
Though your heart's blood were a-spillin'.

"O do you remember, young man," said she,
When you the cups were fillin',
That you made the healths go round and round,
And slighted Barbara Allan?"

He turned his face unto the wall,
And death with him was dealin':
"Adieu, adieu, my dear friends all,
And be kind to Barbara Allan."

And slowly, slowly rose she up,
And slowly, slowly left him;
And sighing said she could not stay,
Since death of life had reft[1] him.

She had not gone a mile but two,
When she heard the death-bell knellin',
And every stroke that the death-bell made,
It cried, "Woe to Barbara Allan!"

"O mother, mother, make my bed,
O make it soft and narrow:
Since my love died for me today,
I'll die for him tomorrow."

"The Wife of Usher's Well"
Anonymous

There lived a wife at Usher's Well,
And a wealthy wife was she;
She had three stout and stalwart sons,
And sent them o'er the sea.

They had not been a week from her
A week but barely one,
When word came to the carlin[2] wife
That her three sons were gone.

They had not been a week from her,
A week but barely three
When word came to the carlin wife
That her sons she'd never see.

"I wish the wind may never cease
Nor flashes in the flood,
Till my three sons come home to me,
In earthly flesh and blood."

It fell about the Martinmas,
When nights are long and mirk,[3]
The carlin's wife's three sons came hame,
And their hats were o' the birk.[4]

It neither grew in field nor ditch,
Nor yet in any furrow
But at the gates o' Paradise
That birk grew fair enough.

"Blow up the fire, my maidens,
Bring water from the well:
For a' my house shall feast this night,
Since my three sons are well."

And she has made to them a bed,
She's made it large and wide,
And she's ta'en her mantle her about,
Sat down at the bedside.

Up then crew the red, red cock,
And up and crew the gray.
The eldest to the youngest said,
"'Tis time we were away."

The cock he had not crowed but once,
And clapped his wings that day,
When the youngest to the eldest said,
"Brother, we must away.

"The cock doth crow, the day doth dawn,
The channerin'[5] worm doth chide:
If we be missed out o' our place,
A sore pain we must bide.

"Fare you well, my mother dear,
Farewell to barn and byre.[6]
And fare you well, the bonny lass
That kindles my mother's fire."

---

1. **reft.** Deprived
2. **carlin.** Old
3. **mirk.** Dark
4. **birk.** Birch
5. **channerin'.** Fretting
6. **byre.** Cattle house

"THE WIFE OF USHER'S WELL"

About the Selection. This ballad is believed to have come from people living near the Scottish border. It deals with the common subject of untimely death.

LITERARY NOTE

You may wish to review the form of a ballad with your students. Remind them of ballad rhyme scheme and use of refrain. Have them determine the rhyme scheme of "Bonny Barbara Allan" and "The Wife of Usher's Well." Can they find refrains in these poems? Refer them to the entry on ballad in the Handbook of Literary Terms.

LITERARY NOTE

Students interested in how Middle English was pronounced may refer to this chart:

1. Pronounce all consonants, including ones silent in Modern English, such as the *g* in *gnat* and the *k* in *knight*.
2. Pronounce an *h* or *gh* before a *t* as in the modern Scottish *loch*. (This is an approximation for some Middle English words.)
3. Pronounce all vowels, including final *e's*, which have the sound of the initial *a* in *afraid*.
4. Pronounce vowels as in modern Italian, French, or German. (Again, this is an approximation.) A rough guide is as follows:

PRONOUNCE . . .

long *a*	as in	father
long *e*	as in	they
long *i*	as in	machine
long *u*	as in	fool
long *o*	as in	boat
short *a*	as in	rock
short *e*	as in	bet
short *i*	as in	bit
short *u*	as in	bull
short *o*	as in	bought
ei and *ai*	as in	bay-ee
au and *aw*	as in	mouse

The Development of the English Language: Middle English

THE EMERGENCE OF MIDDLE ENGLISH

The Norman Conquest brought about profound changes in the English language. From 1066 to the mid-1200s, the aristocratic ruling class in England spoke Norman French almost exclusively. During this time, few French words entered English. However, from about 1260 to the late 1300s, most English aristocrats were bilingual, speaking both Norman French and English. When speaking and writing English, these aristocrats borrowed heavily from the pronunciation, grammar, and vocabulary of their native French. As a result, the English language underwent rapid change, developing into what is now known as **Middle English.**

The vast changes that occurred in the language can be seen by comparing the passages written near the beginning and near the end of the Medieval Period. The first passage below, written shortly after the Norman Conquest, can barely be read today without translation. The second passage, written in the 1300s, presents few difficulties to the modern reader.

ENGLISH LYRIC FROM THE EARLY 1100S

Merie sungen ðe muneches binnin Ely
Da Cnut ching reu ðer by.
Roweð, cnites, noer the land
And here we pes muneshes sæng.
[Translation: Merrily sang the monks with Ely
When Cnut the king rowed thereby.
Row, knights, nearer the land
And let us hear the monks' song.]

PASSAGE FROM CHAUCER'S *TROILUS AND CRESSIDA*

Go, lytle° booke, — *little*
And for ther is so greet diversitee° — *great diversity*
In English and in wryting° of our tonge,° — *writing, tongue*
So preye I god that noon miswryte° thee. — *no one miswrite*

WORDS BORROWED FROM FRENCH

The American poet Wallace Stevens once wrote that English and French are the same language. Stevens's comment was an exaggeration, but it contains a kernel of truth. As a result of borrowings from French that began in the Medieval Period, it is today almost impossible to write an English paragraph without using many words of French origin.

Since the Norman conquerors were the ruling class, one would expect that many of the words that they introduced would be related to their power and prestige, as the following chart demonstrates:

SOME WORDS BORROWED FROM FRENCH

Politics and Political Entities

assembly
baron
chancellor
city
constable
council
councilor
count
countess
county
crown
duchess
duke
empire
esquire
government
majesty
marquis
master
mayor
minister
mistress
nation
noble
palace
parliament
peer
prince
realm
reign
royal
scepter
sovereign
squire
throne
tyrant
village

Financial Matters

account
assets
balance
bargain
budget
customer
dues
estate
fine
heir
lease
merchant
price
property
purchase
receipt
revenue
tax
treasury
value

Power Relationships

allegiance
authority
bondage
command
homage
obey
oppress
power
servant
slave
subject
vassal

The Law

accuse
advocate
arrest
assault
assembly
attorney
bail
bailiff
banish
bill
burglary
condemn
convict
coroner
crime
decree
defendant
equity
evidence
exile
felony
fine
innocent
jail
judge
judgment
jury
just
justice
legal
libel
pardon
perjury
petition
plaintiff
plea
punishment
ransom
rebel
sentence
suit
summons
traitor
treason
trespass
verdict
warden

War

advance
arms
army
attack
besiege
conquer
defense
defend
lance
lieutenant
mail
peace
pursue
retreat
siege
surrender
vanquish
war

Manners

agreeable
bounty
calm
chivalry
courage
courteous
courtesy
dainty
dangerous
debonair
dignity
error
false
folly
frank
gentleness
gracious
honest
honor
loyalty
mean
mercy
nice
perfect
pity
pleasant
please
praise
pure
suffer
tender
valor

Religion

altar
angel
baptism
cardinal
cathedral
chapel
choir
clergy
cloister
communion
conscience
devotion
evangelist
faith
feat
grace
pew
preach
prophet
relic
saint
sermon

LITERARY NOTE

You may wish to share with your students the following lovely ballad in Middle English:

Lully, lulley, lully, lulley
The faucon hath borne my make away.
He bare him up; he bare him down;
He bare him into an orchard brown.
In that orchard there was an halle
That was hanged with purpill and pall!
And in that hall there was a bede,
It was hanged with gold so rede.
And in that bed there lithe a knight
His woundes bleding day and night.
By that bede side kneleth a may,
And she wepeth both night and day.
And by that bede side there stondeth a stone,
Corpus Christi written there on.

The lovely lyric "The Falcon Hath Borne My Mate Away" may be read as a mystical statement of the ever present death of Christ to believers (his mates). Purple and gold are associated with royalty. The may, or maid, might be the Virgin Mary. *Corpus Christi* is Latin for "the body of Christ."

ADDITIONAL QUESTIONS AND ACTIVITIES

To give students an idea what Middle English sounded like, play for them the opening to "The Prologue" to *The Canterbury Tales* on Track 7 of the audiocassette in the Teacher's Resource Kit. Students can follow along by looking at the text on page 218.

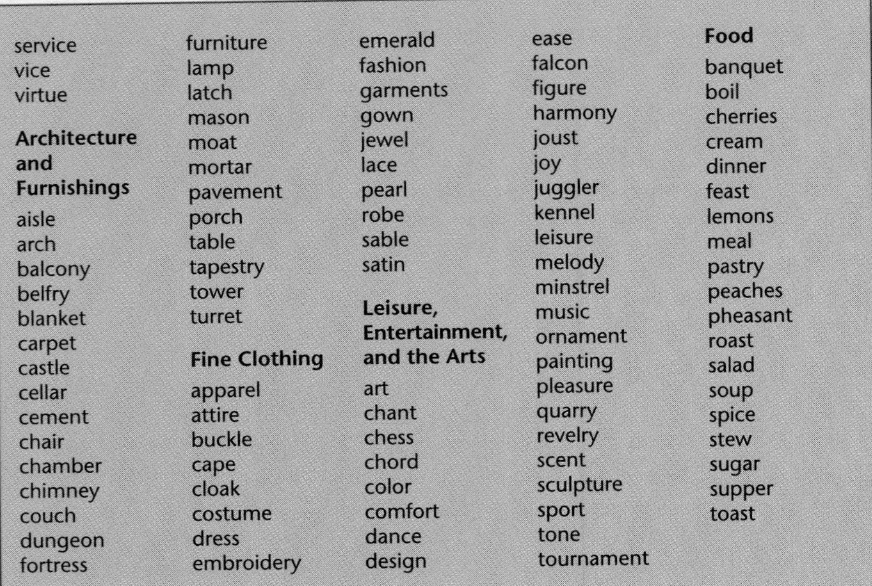

service
vice
virtue

Architecture and Furnishings

aisle
arch
balcony
belfry
blanket
carpet
castle
cellar
cement
chair
chamber
chimney
couch
dungeon
fortress
furniture
lamp
latch
mason
moat
mortar
pavement
porch
table
tapestry
tower
turret

Fine Clothing

apparel
attire
buckle
cape
cloak
costume
dress
embroidery
emerald
fashion
garments
gown
jewel
lace
pearl
robe
sable
satin

Leisure, Entertainment, and the Arts

art
chant
chess
chord
color
comfort
dance
design
ease
falcon
figure
harmony
joust
joy
juggler
kennel
leisure
melody
minstrel
music
ornament
painting
pleasure
quarry
revelry
scent
sculpture
sport
tone
tournament

Food

banquet
boil
cherries
cream
dinner
feast
lemons
meal
pastry
peaches
pheasant
roast
salad
soup
spice
stew
sugar
supper
toast

Fortunately for English writers and speakers, many native English words survived alongside their newer French counterparts, creating a wealth of choices between words that are more formal or less. The following chart shows some examples.

ORIGINS OF WORDS IN ENGLISH WITH RELATED MEANINGS

FROM OLD ENGLISH	FROM FRENCH
begin	commence
bloom	flower
buy	purchase
fight	battle
foe	enemy
folk	people
help	aid
hide	conceal
house	mansion
king	emperor
theft	burglary
weapons	arms
wedding	marriage
wish	desire

Notice that the French word often carries **connotations,** or associations, of formality or sophistication not carried by the corresponding English word. This is because the French-speaking Normans were the sophisticated ruling class. The distinction can be seen clearly in certain word pairs related to food. Native English people, made by the Normans into a subservient, lower class, had responsibility for caring for barnyard animals. Therefore, the terms that survived for describing these animals when alive were English in origin. However, the terms that were used to describe animals when killed and cooked were of French origin, for it was the French-speaking Normans who were wealthy enough to eat prepared meat.

ENGLISH WORDS FOR LIVE ANIMALS	FRENCH TERMS FOR PREPARED MEATS
pig, boar, swine	pork, bacon
cow, ox	beef, veal
deer	venison
sheep	mutton

OTHER CHANGES IN THE LANGUAGE

Changes in Pronunciation and Grammar. We have seen that Norman French greatly influenced the vocabulary of English, increasing the size and diversity of the word stock, or **lexicon.** French also influenced both the pronunciation and grammar of English. In the area of pronunciation, English became much less harsh and guttural. In the area of grammar, the use of English by aristocrats unfamiliar with its intricacies led to simplification. Grammatical endings, or **inflections,** that were common in Old English were dropped, and subjects generally began to appear before their verbs rather than vice versa, as was common in Old English.

Standardization. Throughout the Medieval Period, spoken and written English appeared in what Chaucer called a "greet diversitee" of forms, making it difficult for people of one part of England to communicate effectively with people from another part. Middle English was divided into five major dialects: Northern, East Midland, West Midland, Southeastern, and Southwestern. Within these major dialects areas, individual communities, speakers, and writers followed their own rules for pronunciation and spelling, making communication all the more difficult. Toward the end of the Medieval Period and during the early Renaissance, two forces conspired to change that situation by introducing regularities of pronunciation and spelling into the language. The first of these was the rise in prestige of the **East Midland dialect** spoken in London, the capital city. The second was the spread of printed works following the introduction of printing by Thomas Caxton in the late 1400s. Caxton printed his books in the East Midland dialect and regularized to some extent the spelling and vocabulary of the authors whose works he made available. The East Midland dialect of London and of Caxton developed into the **Modern English** spoken and written today.

ADDITIONAL QUESTIONS AND ACTIVITIES

Ask students to answer the following questions:

1. Why are English words used for animals, but French words used for prepared meats?
2. How did the Norman French influence English vocabulary?
3. Why was it difficult for the people of England to communicate effectively with each other during the Medieval Period?

Answers

1. Because native English people were responsible for taking care of barnyard animals, the words they used to described them survived. However, the words used to describe prepared meat are French because the French-speaking Normans were wealthy enough to eat prepared meat.
2. The Norman French increased the size and diversity of word stock, or lexicon.
3. There was a "greet diversitee" of dialects within England, making it difficult for one part of England to communicate with another part.

LESSON OVERVIEW

INDIVIDUAL LEARNING STRATEGIES

MOTIVATION
Ask students to bring photographs of childhood memories to class. Allow students to pass their pictures around the room and to share the story that is behind the photographs.

READING PROFICIENCY
Encourage students to read the Guided Writing lesson one section at a time, summarizing each section as they work through the lesson.

ENGLISH LANGUAGE LEARNING
As students read the Guided Writing lesson, have them keep notes in their reading of words or phrases they find difficult to understand, and to use context clues or help from the text to uncover meaning. It may also be helpful to pair them with another student who can review their completed Graphic Organizer and make sure it demonstrates understanding of the lesson.

SPECIAL NEEDS
Students with special needs should concentrate on completing the Graphic Organizer on page 270 and working their ideas into a parable. You may want them to pair up with another student who can help make sure they work their final draft into a story.

A **parable** is a very brief story told to teach a moral lesson.

WRITING A PARABLE

Emily was leafing through her grandparents' photo album on a rainy day in May. Each faded color picture provoked stories about her mother and her aunts and uncles, her family's movement from place to place, houses with histories, parades, trips, and holidays. And then there was a progression of Emily's baby smiles and Emily in each of her growing up stages.

Each of us has our private cashe of memories. We should move them out of the storage box of mental visions and into concrete images, on paper, so that we can pass them around alongside the photo albums and videotapes. We should record them. A Native American saying cautions: "They didn't tell their stories, and so they died."

WRITING ASSIGNMENT. Your assignment for this lesson is to write a family story in the form of a parable.

EXAMINING THE MODEL. In Chaucer's "The Pardoner's Tale," two men are possessed by greed. This classic parable demonstrates how a story about ordinary people can give its listeners something to think about.

Chaucer presents three friends—"rioters"—whose friendship is founded on drinking together. He shows us their commitment, all for one and one for all, in an inebriated show of loyalty. But in the plot line for this parable, complications arise rather quickly as the three berate and accost an old man. The characters reveal an increasingly ugly side of themselves. The old man directs them to the "Death" they are seeking.

continued on page 269

Professional Model

from "The Pardoner's Tale"
by Geoffrey Chaucer, page 236

They made their bargain, swore with appetite,
These three, to live and die for one another
As brother-born might swear to his born brother....

"Well, sirs," he said, "if it be your design
To find out Death, turn up this crooked way
Toward that grove, I left him there today
Under a tree, and there you'll find him
Waiting....

Why make a sermon of it? Why waste breath?
Exactly in the way they'd planned his death
They fell on him and slew him, two to one.
Then said the first of them when this was done,
"Now for a drink. Sit down and let's be merry,
For later on there'll be the corpse to bury."
And, as it happened, reaching for a sup,

INDIVIDUAL LEARNING STRATEGIES (CONT.)

ENRICHMENT
Allow students the opportunity to share their stories with elementary or middle school students by assigning a time for them to visit a class. In order for students to tell their story successfully, ask students to prepare by reading and following the tips in the Language Arts Survey 4.20, "Telling a Story."

> He took a bottle full of poison up
> And drank; and his companion, nothing loth,
> Drank from it also, and they perished both.

Prewriting

Finding Your Voice. In writing a parable, there is no better place to start than with your own family stories. Real people, rich territory for description of personalities and motives, populate family stories. You know these people. The voice of the parable will be the natural voice of your family. Then, as you approach the statement of a moral lesson, your own perspective, and your own voice, will evolve. This is your interpretative creation of events and situations that might not have had a "lesson" in them at all until you evoke it. You may be putting into words, for the first time, a principle your family considers worth preserving.

Identifying Your Audience. Since this may or may not end up as a historically accurate depiction of a family "myth," you might want to retain your classmates as your primary target audience. It is possible that you will, on the other hand, uncover an authentic family value—and your audience may indeed end up being your family. Be open to both options as you proceed.

Writing With a Plan. Freewrite—without stopping or editing your thoughts, words, sequences—a story from your family "history." Choose a story outside of your self, one that you've overheard older adults telling, or one that creeps out in bits and pieces when you're looking at home videos or photographs:

Freewrite for at least 15 minutes. When one story runs dry, move on to another one. Just keep writing. Do not be deterred by holes in your recollections or facts you don't have straight.

Now, look at one of the main characters in one of your story possibilities. Write four or five adjectives that describe the person as he or she behaved in the story.

Little brother *bold, innocent, curious, unaware, fond (of the old one)*

Choose one adjective that best fits this person as he acts in this story.

Little brother *curious*

Change it into its noun form. Write down the noun you've chosen followed by "is" and then complete the sentence to create a definition. That definition should grow out of the story you have written.

Curiosity is a blessing, for it reaches toward the truth.

They uncover a stash of gold. Ultimately the more nefarious side of their souls is revealed as they sabotage their brotherhood by plotting each other's deaths—and succeed. They indeed find the "Death" they so audaciously seek to destroy. They learn the lesson of this parable, "Greed is the root of all evil," the hard way.

Notice that this parable does not explicitly state the lesson it teaches. Nowhere in Chaucer's tale is there a mention of the word "greed." The actions of the characters teach by example. When a message is strongly delivered, there is an echo of the moral it teaches. Sometimes, however, the lesson is stated within the tale itself.

There are two fundamental elements of a parable:

(1) common people in easily identifiable situations, and
(2) a lesson is learned by the character(s), and thus taught to the reader.

"Freewriting helps you to think of topics to write about. Just keep writing, follow threads where they lead and you will get to ideas, experiences, feelings, or people that are just asking to be written about."
—Peter Elbow

Prewriting

Finding Your Voice
To make sure students represent the true "voice" of their family, suggest that they confer with their family about the tone, style, and voice of the family.

Identifying Your Audience
What style of writing intrigues you? With what style of words do you most identify? What method of storytelling draws you into the story most? Have students reflect on these questions to help them write to an audience of their peers and family members.

Writing with a Plan
This section provides freewriting as a way to gather ideas and organize their thoughts. For additional ideas, refer students to the Language Arts Survey 2.9-2.23, "Gathering Ideas."

GUIDED WRITING *Software*

See the Guided Writing Software for an extended version of this lesson that includes printable graphic organizers, extensive student models and student-friendly checklists, and self-, peer, and teacher evaluation features.

STUDENT MODEL—GRAPHIC ORGANIZER 

See the Guided Writing Resource 12.3 for a blackline master of the Graphic Organizer for this lesson.

That definition will undoubtedly be figurative and rich in imagery—a metaphor for what that attribute has come to mean in your family. The result may be a revelation about one of your family's long-held values, principles by which you all unconsciously live. In writing your parable, you will crystallize the story that demonstrates this principle.

You might need another technique for expanding your draft. Construct a graph of the adjectives you can find throughout your freewrite, a noun form for each, and metaphorical definitions.

As you consider nouns, avoid using the noun form that means "the one who…" because this form of the word narrows the definition to the personal—it doesn't allow generalization. For example, the adjective *adventurous* could become *adventurer*, which is limiting (an "adventurer is Uncle Bob," for example). A better noun for considering a message about shared values would be *adventure* because you can expand on action: "adventure is trying something no one's ever done before."

Laurie filled in the following graphic organizer as she found ideas in her very rough freewrite.

"There are as many solutions as there are human beings."
—George Tooker

Student Model—Graphic Organizer

Adjective	Noun	Definition
Active	Action	Action is continuing your course even with setbacks
Story idea: the time when Renee played soccer in the snow the day after she got her rejection letter on the scholarship		

Adjective	Noun	Definition
Calm	Calmness	Calmness is never reacting to the first emotion you feel, but instead pausing to think logically
Story idea: Grandpa sipping coffee while everyone spaced out about Susan running away from home and then calmly getting in the car and going to fetch her from the police station		

Adjective	Noun	Definition
Adventurous	Adventure	Adventure is being bold, unafraid of the unknown
Story idea: Grandpa and the bear (when we were camping in Yellowstone)		

There are many possibilities for parables centered in family stories, stories that are real.

Drafting

Armed with your freewrite and a graphic organizer that reflects your possibilities, decide on the best one to develop as a parable. Some story ideas that you've generated are undoubtedly tragic or represent extreme moments of panic or unhappiness, for all families have these experiences, and they spring to mind immediately. You might want to avoid those incidents of crisis. Parables work best when they focus on everyday dilemmas.

Student Model—Draft

Laurie chose to write about her grandfather and a bear. Her rough draft captured the details of the experience.

CAMPGROUND BEAR

"Let's find that bear," Grandpa whispered in my ear. I looked up at my mother to see if she heard, but she was busy putting together the meal we were going to cook over the campfire. I turned to face my grandfather with a big smile and wide eyes. *move to correct misplaced modifier*

"Do you think we could really find him?" I whispered back. *– good verb* Since I was the only granddaughter, my grandfather and I held a special bond. *Expand a bit?* I could be easily talked into going on his little escapades for which he was so famous.

We were camping at Yellowstone National Park. A park ranger came around warning everyone that there was a bear in the area, but that it probably wasn't mean.

A bear! Of all the sights and

Finding Parables in Family Stories

You may be surprised to see how a family story can become a parable. But think for a moment about the well-worn stories a family loves to tell. Almost always these stories reveal a deeply held value of the family. Telling and retelling the tales is a way the family has of passing along its values to next generations, of saying, "This is what it means to be a Smith." True, the lessons may be a good deal more subtle than in the "The Pardoner's Tale"—usually family members don't even examine the underlying lesson the stories teach. Yet retell them, they do. And the message, along with the story, is carried along. The lesson is not preachy, but is no less powerful.

Drafting

Encourage students to use their completed Graphic Organizer on page 270 to help them get started in drafting their ideas into a parable.

Self- and Peer Evaluation

Have students use the questions on this page for self- and peer evaluation. Remind students that comments from classmates can be helpful and can help them to identify weaknesses and produce a better piece through revision. By reflecting on reviewer comments and their own self-evaluations, they will be ready to go on to the next step: revision. A blackline mater is available of the self- and peer evaluation checklist in the Guided Writing Resource book.

Revising and Proofreading

A handout of the proofreading checklist in the Language Art Survey is available in the Teacher's Resource Kit, Guided Writing Resource Book. Encourage students critiquing their classmates' work to use common proofreader's symbols which are found in the Language Arts Survey 2.44, "Using Proofreader's Marks."

Self- and Peer Evaluation

The evaluation stage of your writing requires paying attention to the elements of a parable. As you look over your work, ask yourself these questions:

- Have you described a situation that reveals a bump in the road of a family, or a revelation about what is valuable in the use of time, the manifestations of affection, the humor or joys of interaction? The examples are endless, but they all share depth of feeling.
- Where in the parable have you demonstrated that depth of feeling?
- Has something happened in your parable that gives insight into principled behavior, what is considered worthy or desirable?
- State what that worthy or desirable behavior, that value, is.
- Where has the writer included dialogue in the narrative to bring the characters alive?
- Where has the writer used effective description?
- Where in the draft has the writer used the correct verb tense to indicate events completed in the past?

national monuments we ~~saw~~ over the past two weeks of our vacation, this was by far the best. *had seen*

After supper my Grandpa announced that he and I were going for a walk. *Dialog? What did he say? How did he say it?*

"Be careful, remember the bear," my dad said.

"Oh that bear's long gone by now," Grandpa said. For a minute my heart sank; I thought the bear would be gone. But when we were out of hearing distance from the others, Grandpa said, "I was just saying that so they wouldn't worry. Now let's go bear hunting."

We walked hand-in-hand through the dusty roads of the campground. I could smell the campfires and the roasting marshmallows. I could smell the sweet kerosene as people began firing up their lanterns to fight off the approaching darkness... *Excellent sensory detail*

Grandpa would stop and chat to people. "We're tracking a bear," he would say. *Expand more here*

You still need to make this a parable.

Revising and Proofreading

A review of Laurie's story indicated she should add more detail to make the piece more vivid, and add foreshadowing of her Grandpa's actions to maintain the excitement of a bear encounter. She also decided to add more dialogue. She added to the description of the stuffed bear in order to provide clearer contrast with the real bear, and included her thoughts.

Student Model—Revised

Campground Bear
by Laurie Higgins

"Let's find that bear," Grandpa whispered in my ear. I looked up at my mother to see if she had heard, but she was busy putting together the meal we were going to cook over the campfire. I turned with a big smile and wide eyes to face my grandfather.

"Do you think we could really find him?" I whispered back. Since I was the only granddaughter, my grandfather and I held a special bond. Maybe it was because he'd only had sons. Or maybe it was because I was a free spirit like he was. I could be easily talked into going on his little escapades for which he was so famous.

It all began when my parents and grandparents took my brother and me on vacation out west. One night we were staying at Yellowstone National Park.

When we entered the campground, we saw a cage-like contraption set back off the main drive. I remember it had caught my eye, because I twisted my neck just looking at it. The cage was a gray color and shaped like a tube. It was solid metal, but it had a wire door that was propped up by something. Inside the cage was what appeared to be a big chunk of meat. I forgot about it until that afternoon when a park ranger came up to our campsite.

"Folks," he said, "there's a bear in the park. He probably isn't mean, but we're just warning you not to leave any food or garbage out overnight because they sure can make a mess of things if they think there's food around.

"Oh!" he added, "you might want to keep the kids in sight, just in case."

Language, Grammar, and Style

Using Verb Tenses

Identifying Verb Tenses. Verbs carry the concept of time, called **tense**. The simple tenses indicate relatively simple time relationships. **Present tense** verbs show that something is happening now. **Past tense** verbs show that something happened before now, and **future tense** verbs show that something will happen in the future.

PRESENT TENSE
I hike
I am hiking

PAST TENSE
I hiked
I was hiking

FUTURE TENSE
I will hike
I will be hiking

The **perfect tenses** express past, present, and future, but they add information about actions that continued over a period of time and were completed in the past or will be completed in the present or future. All perfect tenses use some form of the helping verb *to have.*

PRESENT PERFECT
I have hiked
I have been hiking

PAST PERFECT
I had hiked
I had been hiking

continued on page 274

LANGUAGE, GRAMMAR, AND STYLE

Using Verb Tenses
In this lesson, students will be asked to do the following:
- Identify Verb Tenses
- Fix Faulty Verb Tense
- Use Verb Tense Correctly

Introducing the Skill
Explain to students that using verb tense correctly is extremely important in comprehending and understanding a piece of writing. When verb tenses are used incorrectly, readers are confused about the organization and time frame the story takes place. As students write their parables, remind them to use consistent verb tense.

Previewing the Skill
Ask students to identify the verb tenses that are used in the Student Model—Revised. What is the overall parable told in—present tense, past tense, or future tense? How do you know?

FUTURE PERFECT
I will have hiked
I will have been hiking

Fixing Faulty Verb Tense. As you write, make sure you use verb tenses in a way that will allow the reader to understand the time in which events have occurred. One problem can result when a writer uses inconsistent verb tense.

INCONSISTENT VERB TENSE
As I hiked over the mountains, I see a bear.

REVISED
As I hiked over the mountains, I saw a bear.

or
As I hike over the mountains, I see a bear.

Notice that the writer can make a choice to keep the action either in the present or past, but that the verbs must be consistent.

Another problem can occur when a writer fails to show a correct shift in tenses when one event precedes or comes after another.

LACKING CORRECT TENSE SHIFT
The bear followed the hikers for days when they reported him to the ranger.

REVISED
The bear had been following the hikers for days when they reported him to the ranger.

continued on page 275

A bear! That's what the trap was for. Through all the sights and national monuments we had seen over the past two weeks of our vacation, this was by far the best.

After supper my Grandpa said, "Let's take a walk, Sis."

"Be careful, remember the bear," my dad said.

"Oh, that bear's long gone by now," Grandpa said. "He ain't gonna stay around a bunch of people." For a minute my heart sank; I thought the bear would be gone. But when we were out of hearing distance from the others, Grandpa said, "I was just sayin' that so they wouldn't worry. Now let's go bear huntin'."

We walked hand-in-hand along the dusty roads of the campground. I could smell the campfires and the roasting marshmallows. I could smell the sweet kerosene as people began firing up their lanterns to fight off the approaching darkness. Groups were sitting at their tables playing cards or checkers. Some were just lounging around the campfire, laughing at old family stories, or making new ones to be told at future fireside gatherings. Grandpa would stop and chat with people. "We're trackin' a bear," he would say.

As we rounded a dark bend in the dirt road, I noticed that there seemed to be more trees. My heart raced because it looked like a place a bear would want to hang out. Sure enough—we heard a deep snort that caused both of us to freeze in our tracks. Grandpa squeezed my hand tightly. The brush in a small group of trees swayed!

Out stepped the bear. He had the shiniest black fur I had ever seen. He had a light brown nose and huge feet with curved claws coming out of them. He swung his head back and forth as he walked towards us. Grandpa picked me up and walked slowly backward. I think he knew the bear was harmless because he remained so calm. Just then we heard someone say, "Quick, in here!" It was a woman who was camped nearby. We scrambled inside. From her camper window, we watched the bear climb on picnic tables, dig through ashes, and turn over garbage cans. He disappeared into the thicket just as quickly as he had appeared.

When we returned to our campsite a few minutes later, everyone was getting ready for bed. "You didn't see that bear, did ya?" Dad asked.

"Nope," was Grandpa's only reply.

It was hard to keep it a secret. I ended up telling everyone the next morning. But I knew for that night it was just for Grandpa's and my dreams.

It has been years since that memorable night. I have had many wonderful times with my grandfather. When I go to the cemetery to visit him, my mind fills with happy thoughts. Even his headstone shows evidence of his adventurous life. His friends from his motorcycle club had a Harley-Davidson engraved on it. Many family stories involve Grandpa John. Whenever it thunders, the youngest will say, "There goes Grandpa John racing his Harley engine again."

My grandpa taught me that adventure is seeking the unknown. For an old man, adventure is a way to keep his life exciting. For a young girl, it's reaching out beyond the boundaries of imagination. And the best adventure of all is shared.

Publishing and Presenting

The people in your family can be awed by the writing you produce; they might even welcome copies of your parable as companions to your graduation picture.

You might also make a poster illustrating the lesson learned in your parable and post it in a display area with other posters by your classmates. These illustrated statements can be a powerful way to capture shared values within your school community.

Explain how you would fix these sentences from Laurie's early draft to indicate actions that had been completed before the main action in her story.

He disappeared into the thicket just as quickly as he has appeared.

My mom bought me the toy bear at a gift shop when I was five.

Of all the sights we saw over the past two weeks of our vacation, this was by far the best.

Using Verb Tense Correctly. Look at each sentence in your parable. Correct any verb tenses that do not accurately depict the passage of time. For more information, see the Language Arts Survey 3.62, "Properties of Verbs: Tense."

"Writers will happen in the best of families."
—*Rita Mae Brown*

Practicing the Skill
Ask students to exchange their drafts with a classmate. As they read, note parts that are confusing—especially having to do with the concept of time. Then using the techniques they learned to fix faulty verb tenses, correct sentences that use verb tense incorrectly.

Publishing and Presenting

Encourage students to organize a "Storytelling Recital" where family members and friends commune to hear the parables they wrote. To help students read their parables in an interesting and engaging manner, ask them to use the suggested tips in the Language Arts Survey 4.19, "Oral Interpretation." You may also suggest that students decorate the room and provide refreshments for this exciting event.

ADDITIONAL RESOURCES

UNIT 3 RESOURCE BOOK

- Vocabulary Worksheet Unit 3
- Study Guide: Unit 3 Test
- Unit 3 Test

VOCABULARY DEVELOPMENT

Give students the following exercise: Read the Language Arts Survey 5.51, "Sentence Completion Questions." Using the vocabulary words on page 276, write a test containing ten sentence-completions questions. Write their answer choices for each problem. Vary the forms of the words as necessary. When you are done, exchange tests with a partner.

EXAMPLE

1. The knight sought _____ at the hermit's retreat, because he had been _____ in engaging in battles with his fellows.

(A) absolution . . . wanton
(B) vengeance . . . personable
(C) indignation . . . saucy
Answer: A

UNIT 3 REVIEW
The Medieval Period

Words for Everyday Use

Check your knowledge of the following vocabulary words from the selections in this unit. Write short sentences using these words in context to make the meaning clear. To review the definition or usage of a word, refer to the page number listed or the Glossary of Words for Everyday Use.

absolution, 223
abstrusest, 230
accrue, 224
ambling, 227
amends, 251
amiably, 195
appurtenance, 205
arbitrate, 224
asunder, 228
beguile, 195
betide, 195
burnish, 190
caitiff, 248, 259
cajole, 213
cloister, 222
comeliest, 189
comely, 171
countenance, 171, 204
covenant, 192
dais, 188
diligent, 228
duress, 231
encumbered, 228
entreat, 196
felicity, 225
flax, 231
frugal, 230
fustian, 220
grisly, 237
guile, 227
hapless, 188
heath, 218
hoary, 238
hostelry, 219
indignation, 207
inter, 205
intrigue, 194
lanyard, 226
mire, 228
miscreant, 239
mortification, 196
motley, 224
necromancy, 203
obeisance, 208
ostentatious, 212
perdition, 240
personable, 223
phantasmagoria, 256
postern, 202
prating, 238
prelate, 223
prevarication, 232
proffer, 246
providence, 207
respite, 191, 246
sanguine, 225
saucy, 221
scrupulosity, 229
scurrility, 232
sedately, 221
seemly, 222
smite, 190
sober, 224
solicitous, 222
sonorous, 257
splay, 230
stature, 220
stile, 237
strife, 238
sunder, 192
superfluity, 227
sward, 230
tillage, 236
transgress, 195
transitory, 244
treachery, 194
unworldly, 224
usurp, 204
vanquish, 196
vengeance, 213
verity, 223
wanton, 223
wary, 236
wax, 203
withal, 221
wroth, 200

Literary Tools

Define the following terms, giving concrete examples of how they are used in the selections in this unit. To review a term, refer to the page number indicated or to the Handbook of Literary Terms.

Arthurian romance, 187
autobiography, 211
ballad, 168
characterization, 216
chivalry, 187
courtly love, 182, 199, 254
folk tale, 199
frame tale, 216
irony, 217
medieval romance, 254
mood, 168
morality play, 243
motif, 199
naive allegory, 243
point of view, 211
rhyme scheme, 168
romance, 182
simile, 175
theme, 175

Reflecting on Your Reading

Genre Studies

1. **Medieval Ballads.** What form does a ballad have? Why did people compose ballads? What purposes did they serve? Refer to the ballads in this unit and in the Selections for Additional Reading on pages 262–263. See also "Robin Hood and Allen-a-Dale" on page 7 in Unit 1.

2. **Medieval Romance.** What were the ideals of courtly love and chivalry? How do Tristan in "The Honeysuckle: Chevrefoil," Gawain in *Sir Gawain and the Green Knight,* and King Uther, Arthur, and his knights in *Le Morte d'Arthur* embody or fail to embody these ideals? Refer to the descriptions of *courtly love* and of *chivalry* in the Unit Introduction and in the Handbook of Literary Terms.

Thematic Studies

3. **The *Memento Mori* Theme.** What is the *memento mori* theme? How is it expressed in the play *Everyman* and in the lyric poem "Ubi Sunt Qui ante Nos Fuerunt"? Why might this have been a common theme in medieval literature? What does the widespread use of this theme in medieval literature tell us about the beliefs of medieval people in Europe?

Historical and Biographical Studies

4. **Medieval Women.** What ideals of womanhood were common in medieval England? How were these ideals influenced by adoration of the Virgin Mary and by romance literature? How did the ideals differ from the realities? Explore the lives of medieval English women. Refer to the following materials from the unit: "I Sing of a Maiden," "The Great Silkie," "The Honeysuckle: Chevrefoil," the selection from *The Book of Margery Kempe,* and the descriptions of women in "The Prologue" to Chaucer's *The Canterbury Tales.*

5. **Medieval English Poetry.** Consider the effect of the Norman invasion on the English poetry. What differences are there between medieval English poetry and Anglo-Saxon poetry? What changes or innovations occurred in English poetry as a result of the Norman Conquest? What old forms were abandoned? What new forms emerged? How did the form and content of poetry change?

6. **Medieval English Literature and the Church.** Much of medieval literature is didactic. In other words, it teaches moral lessons. What lessons are taught by "Ubi Sun Qui ante Nos Fuerunt?", *Everyman,* "The Prologue" to *The Canterbury Tales,* and "The Pardoner's Tale"? What teachings of the church are embodied in these selections?

REFLECTING ON YOUR READING

The prompts in the "Reflecting on Your Reading" section of the Unit Review are suitable topics for research papers. Refer to the Language Arts Survey 5.18-5.45, "Research Skills." (To evaluate research papers, see the evaluation forms for writing, revising, and proofreading in the Assessment Resource.)

The prompts can also be adapted for use as topics for oral reports or debates. Refer students to the Language Arts Survey 4, Speaking and Listening. (To evaluate these projects, see the evaluation forms in the Assessment Resource.)

UNIT SKILLS OUTLINE

Literary Skills and Concepts
Aim, 310, 312
Alliteration, 296, 299
Allusion, 314, 316
Ambiguity, 314, 316
Dactyl, 326, 328
Iambic Pentameter, 288, 290
Image, 293, 294, 306, 308
Irony, 334, 340
Lyric Poem, 301, 304
Metaphor, 288, 290, 306, 308, 310, 312, 326, 328
Parallelism, 330, 332
Pastoral Poem, 301, 304
Personification, 293, 294
Petrarchan Sonnet, 288, 290, 342, 346
Repetition with Variation, 330, 332
Shakespearean Sonnet, 318, 324
Source, 296, 299
Speaker, 318, 324
Theme, 342, 346
Utopia, 334, 340

Writing Skills and Concepts
Complaint Letter, 333
Constructing a Utopia, 355
Press Release, 300, 341

Language, Grammar, and Style
Agreement of Pronouns and Antecedents, 325
Building Sentences, 305
Commas, 309
Correcting Fragments and Run-Ons, 329
Double Negatives, 313
Identifying Adjectives, 317
Making Passive Sentences Active, 341
Personal Pronouns, 291
Precise and Colorful Language, 359
Split Infinitives, 333
Transitive and Intransitive Verbs, 300
Using a Thesaurus to Find Colorful Language, 295

GOALS/OBJECTIVES

Studying this unit will enable students to

- experience the personal feelings expressed in and typical of Renaissance lyrics
- explain how Renaissance ideas affected English literature
- describe the historical and literary importance of the Protestant Reformation and Counter- Reformation, Martin Luther, King Henry VIII, Queen Elizabeth I, and the King James Bible
- describe and identify sonnets, allegories, and pastoral poems
- describe the work and influence of several major Elizabethan poets

A Young Man Playing a Theorbo and a Young Woman Playing a Cittern, c.1630. Jan Miense Molenaer. National Gallery, London

In the little frame of [a person's] body there is a representation of the universal . . . a kind of participation of all the parts thereof; therefore was [a person] called microcosmos, or the little world.

—Sir Walter Raleigh

279

CROSS-CURRICULAR CONNECTIONS

TEACHING THE MULTIPLE INTELLIGENCES

TEACHING THE MULTIPLE INTELLIGENCES

ADDITIONAL RESOURCES

UNIT 4 RESOURCE BOOK
- Selection Check Test 4.4.1
- Selection Test 4.4.2

CROSS-CURRICULAR CONNECTION

One of the ancient Greek philosophers who had a tremendous influence on Renaissance thought was Aristotle (BC 384–322). Aristotle believed that the purpose of human life was to pursue happiness and that the way for an individual to achieve happiness was to exercise intellectual and moral virtues. He further believed that the proper function of a state was to allow its citizens to pursue the good life, although he thought that only a few people in any society were capable of living a truly good and virtuous life. His ideas that human happiness was attainable and that a government should facilitate the happiness of its citizens were in direct opposition to the medieval view of earthly life. Near the end of the Middle Ages, St. Thomas Aquinas (1224–1274) incorporated Aristotelian philosophy into his Christian theology. Interpreting Aristotle's idea that knowledge is gained by applying reason to human experience, Aquinas argued that God reveals truths not only through revelation, but also through reason and sense perception. Aquinas's thought remains to this day a pillar of Roman Catholic doctrine.

Henry VIII, c.1400s. Hans Holbein.
Walker Art Gallery, Liverpool.

THE ENGLISH RENAISSANCE (1485–1660)

THE RENAISSANCE

The word ***renaissance*** means, literally, a "rebirth." Historians use the word to refer to the period between the fifteenth and early seventeenth centuries when, influenced by a rebirth of interest in Greek and Latin learning, Europe was moving away from medieval habits of thought toward the modern. Medieval thought looked for happiness not in this life but in the next. People in the Middle Ages tended to think of earthly life as brief and of little value. Consequently, medieval literature is dominated by religious subjects and themes.

Typically, if a decision needed to be made, or if a question arose, a medieval man or woman would look to some authority. To Europeans of the Middle Ages, the Roman Catholic Church was the ultimate authority in all things. Lines of authority also dominated in the political sphere. The feudal lord had complete authority over the serfs living on his land. In turn, the lord looked to the higher authority of a greater noble or the king.

In sharp contrast, the writers and thinkers of ancient Greece and Rome often looked not to some authority but to individual conscience. The Greeks and Romans tended to place value on the arts and works of this world. Their literature was dominated by questions related to human life: what is the good life? what is a good state? Rediscovering the arts and literature of ancient Greece and Rome brought about, first in Italy and then in the rest of Europe, a renewed inter-

LITERARY EVENTS

➤ = British Events

1500. Desiderius Erasmus publishes *Adages*

➤ 1515. Thomas More publishes *Utopia*

1485 — 1490 — 1495 — 1500 — 1505 — 1510 — 1515

➤ 1485. Henry VII reigns (1485–1509)

1492. Christopher Columbus arrives in Americas

1504. Queen Isabella (Castile) dies after a thirty-year reign

1507. Leonardo da Vinci paints *Mona Lisa*

➤ 1509. Henry VII dies and is succeeded by his son, Henry VIII

1517. Martin Luther challenges the Roman Catholic Church

HISTORICAL EVENTS

est in human life on earth, as opposed to life after death. Therefore, the Renaissance devotion to the Greek and Latin classics has come to be known as **Humanism.**

This is not to say that the humanists were irreligious. Far from it. Much humanist philosophy was based on the idea that human beings were created in the image of God. The humanists saw each person as a little world, or *microcosmos,* complete in itself. They believed that human beings, sharing as they did in the divine, could perfect themselves and the institutions of this world. Out of this belief came a new emphasis on learning and the arts, as well as religious and political debates that led to the Protestant Reformation, the decline of feudalism, and the emergence of modern nationalism.

Key to these developments was the invention of printing. In 1453, Johannes Gutenberg set up the first printing press in Germany. Soon, presses appeared all over Europe, and people began to read and think for themselves, to challenge authority, and to change their institutions and their lives.

The Beginnings of the Tudor Dynasty

From 1455 to 1485, England was torn by civil war between two noble families, York and Lancaster. The Wars of the Roses ended with the defeat by Henry Tudor of Richard III. **Henry VII** ascended the throne, becoming the first monarch of the **Tudor Dynasty,** which ruled England until 1603.

Henry VII inherited a country exhausted by war. However, he proved to be a capable leader, one who rebuilt the nation's treasury, established a powerful central government, made profitable commercial treaties with other nations, and built a fleet of merchant ships that formed the basis for English power during the coming centuries. During Henry VII's reign, England began exploratory expeditions to the New World that led to the colonialization of North America.

Henry VII died in 1509, leaving the throne to his son, **Henry VIII,** one of the most important and colorful figures in English history. Well-educated, strong-willed, self-absorbed, and charismatic, Henry VIII further increased the power of the monarchy. His desire for a male heir to carry on his successes led to the most important event of his reign, the English break with the Church of Rome.

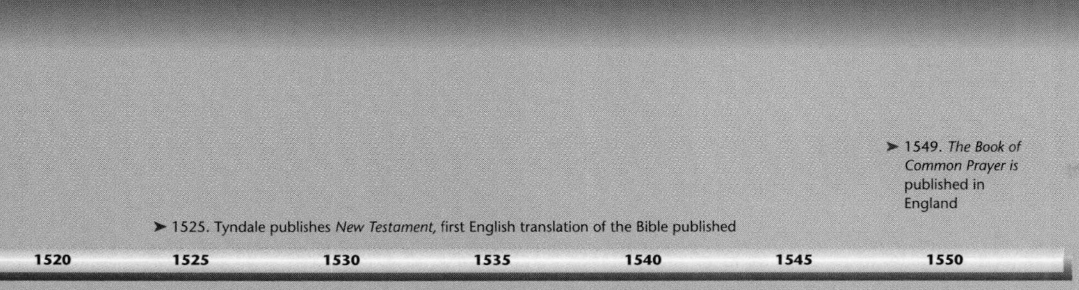

➤ 1549. *The Book of Common Prayer* is published in England

➤ 1525. Tyndale publishes *New Testament,* first English translation of the Bible published

1520 1525 1530 1535 1540 1545 1550

➤ 1534. Henry VIII breaks with Church of Rome

➤ 1536. Anne Boleyn is beheaded

1543. Nikolaus Copernicus defies the church and establishes the theory that the earth revolves around the sun

➤ 1547. Henry VIII dies and is succeeded by Edward VI

CROSS-CURRICULAR ACTIVITIES

Social Studies. Suggest that students research the history of the rise of nationalism in Europe. The division of the world into nation-states is something we take for granted today. However, the modern nation-state did not develop until the decline of feudalism cleared the way for it. What exactly did the concept of a "nation" mean to people during this transition period? How did the birth of nation-states change life for ordinary people?

Geography. Some students may wish to research the geographical borders of this period and then draw maps representing these borders. Have students compare their maps to a current map of Europe to note how the boundaries of various countries have changed.

BIOGRAPHICAL NOTE

The movable-type printing press was invented by Johannes Gutenberg (circa 1400–1468), the son of an aristocratic German family. During the 1430s and 1440s, Gutenberg worked secretly on his invention. He developed a new kind of printing press, a new metal alloy from which he molded type, a method for casting large quantities of type, and an oil-based ink. Gutenberg's first book, completed around 1455, was the Forty-two Line Bible (also called the Gutenberg Bible). As the name suggests, each column of text consisted of forty-two lines. Like other books of its time, Gutenberg's Bible had no page numbers. Gutenberg's second work was a Psalter, or collection of Psalms for use in church services. The Psalter (1457) was beautifully designed with colorful borders and initial letters, but Gutenberg did not receive credit for the innovative processes that made these possible. The name of Johann Fust, an investor who had won a lawsuit against Gutenberg in 1455, appeared on the book instead. During the rest of his career, Gutenberg printed grammar textbooks and letters of indulgence.

CROSS-CURRICULAR ACTIVITY

Applied Arts. To gain an appreciation for early bookmaking and the meticulous work it entailed, students can research details of the Gutenberg press or earlier machines and can then design their own models for setting type (using either wood or metal) and printing a line or a whole page. They might also think about ways to incorporate a second color in a fancy initial letter or border. Other students might use a computer to design and print a page from a favorite book. Students can make design decisions with regard to layout, type style, decorative elements, and illustrations. Others can use computers to create diagrams of the Gutenberg press to illustrate its parts and the functions of those parts.

Martin Luther fastening his 95 Theses to the door of All Saints Church.

The Protestant Reformation in England

In 1517, a German monk named **Martin Luther** nailed to the door of a church in Wittenburg, Germany, his so-called **"95 Theses,"** a list of objections to central beliefs and practices of the Roman Catholic Church. While preparing for his ordination as a priest, Luther had been struck by his own unworthiness to take the holy sacraments. He believed that because of the Original Sin of Adam in the Garden of Eden, people were fundamentally sinful and could not, through their works, become worthy of taking such sacraments as Holy Communion and Holy Orders. Instead, according to Luther, people had to depend on the grace of God, extended to them despite their sinfulness. Luther also objected to practices of the church such as the sale of indulgences, or pardons for sins. He challenged the authority of the Pope and of the church in general, claiming that religion was a matter of individual conscience to be worked out between each person and God without the intermediary of a priest. This belief led him to emphasize reading of the Holy Scriptures, which was made possible for ordinary men and women by the invention of printing and the translation of the Bible into the vernacular languages of Europe.

Luther's ideas spread throughout Europe, leading to a widespread, often bloody revolt against church authority known as the **Protestant Reformation.** A central figure in the Protestant Reformation was **John Calvin** of Switzerland, who took Luther's ideas about Original Sin a step further, teaching that all events were preordained by God, that God chose at the beginning of time which people would be saved, or among the **elect,** and which would be damned. This Calvinist doctrine, known as **predestination,** became the central belief of the **Puritan Movement** that was to have a strong effect on life in England and in the English colonies in North America.

Literary Events

➤ = British Events

➤1579. Edmund Spenser publishes *The Shepheardes Calender*

➤1588. Christop[her] Marlowe writes *The Tragical His[tory] of Doctor Faustu[s]*

1555 | 1560 | 1565 | 1570 | 1575 | 1580 | 1585

➤1553. Edward VI dies and is succeeded by Mary Tudor

➤1555. Mary reestablishes Catholicism and persecutes Protestants

➤1558. Elizabeth I becomes queen at Mary Tudor's death

➤1588. England defeats the Sp[anish] Armada

Historical Events

In England, the Protestant Reformation came about because of Henry VIII's inability to sire a son. Modern science has learned that it is the male who determines the gender of offspring. However, Henry had no way of knowing this. He was angered by the failure of his wife, Catherine, to produce a male heir, and he was attracted to a young woman of his court, Anne Boleyn. At that time, under church law, a divorce could be obtained only through annulment, a procedure by which the church determined that the original marriage was invalid for some reason, such as consanguinity, or closeness of blood relations. Henry VIII appealed to the Pope for an annulment of his marriage to Catherine. However, the Pope would not grant Henry's request. Furious, Henry broke with the Roman Church; asked Parliament to declare him Supreme Head of the new **Church of England,** or **Anglican Church;** received a divorce from an English church court; and married Anne, who gave him a female child, Elizabeth. Henry dismantled the Roman Catholic Church in England, seizing its land and wealth. He burned and pillaged the monasteries, in the process destroying many precious manuscripts. He even ordered the execution of his one-time friend **Sir Thomas More,** chancellor of England and author of *Utopia,* because More would not sign a document recognizing Henry as head of the church.

Anne Boleyn did not produce a male heir. In 1536, Anne was convicted of adultery and beheaded. Henry then married Jane Seymour, who bore him a son, Edward. When Henry died in 1547, this frail, sickly nine-year-old became King Edward VI. During Edward's reign, Protestantism spread throughout England, the Anglican creed was established, and the **Book of Common Prayer** was written. Edward died at the age of fifteen and was succeeded by his older sister, Mary I, child of Henry's first wife, the Spanish Catherine of Aragon.

Mary I and the Counter Reformation in England

Mary I, a staunch Catholic, attempted to restore the power and authority of the Roman Catholic Church in England. Historians call such attempts throughout Europe to undo the Protestant Reformation the **Counter Reformation.** Mary restored Roman Catholic practices to English church services, ordered the execution of many Protestants, made the Pope once again the head of the English church, and married her Roman Catholic cousin, the Spaniard Philip II. At the time, Spain was a powerful country, and the English people resented the marriage, not wanting England to

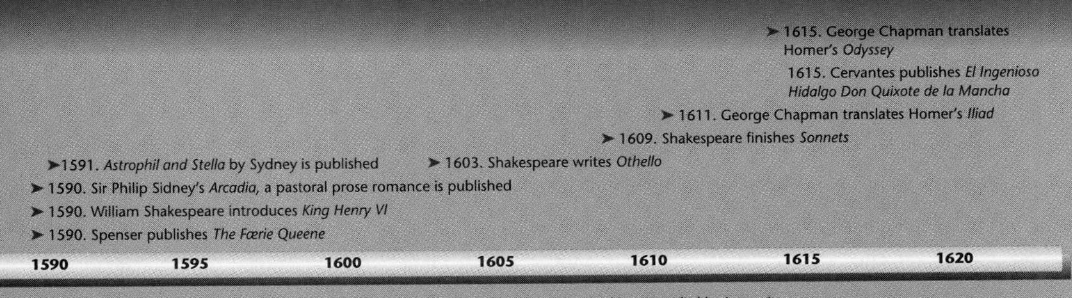
➤ 1615. George Chapman translates Homer's *Odyssey*
1615. Cervantes publishes *El Ingenioso Hidalgo Don Quixote de la Mancha*
➤ 1611. George Chapman translates Homer's *Iliad*
➤ 1609. Shakespeare finishes *Sonnets*
➤ 1591. *Astrophil and Stella* by Sydney is published
➤ 1603. Shakespeare writes *Othello*
➤ 1590. Sir Philip Sidney's *Arcadia,* a pastoral prose romance is published
➤ 1590. William Shakespeare introduces *King Henry VI*
➤ 1590. Spenser publishes *The Fœrie Queene*
1590
1595
1600
1605
1610
1615
1620
➤ 1603. Elizabeth I dies and is succeeded by James I
➤ 1607. Jamestown, Virginia is settled
➤ 1619. First African slaves arrive in the Virginia colony

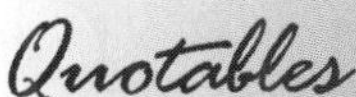

"This hath not offended the king."

—Sir Thomas More (spoken as he moved his beard aside while placing his head on the executioner's block)

BIOGRAPHICAL NOTE

Thomas More (1477–1535) is one of the most widely respected figures in English history. As a young man he studied Latin and logic, and in 1501 he entered the law profession. Despite the demands of his career, More continued to read widely and became a Humanist scholar. The most famous expression of his Humanist philosophy was his book Utopia, published in 1516. In it he described his vision of a perfect society ruled by reason. More was intimately involved in the education of his own children and other young people who joined his household. Most of these were girls, who received a then unusual opportunity for a classical education. More became a trusted advisor to King Henry VIII, who made him chancellor in 1529. More tried to resign his position two years later, realizing that he could never acknowledge a secular king as head of the Church of England. Because he did not accept Henry's divorce of his previous queen, More did not attend the coronation of Anne Boleyn in 1533, and the next year he refused to sign the Act of Succession. After spending over a year imprisoned in the Tower of London, More was convicted of treason and sentenced to death. He was canonized by the Roman Catholic Church in 1935.

BIOGRAPHICAL NOTE

Anne Boleyn was born around 1507. As a child she lived in France, but she returned to England and joined the court of Henry VIII in 1522. The teenager became the object of many courtiers' attentions, including those of the poet Sir Thomas Wyatt and the king himself. Henry became determined to marry her and finally did so in a secret ceremony in early 1533. Later that year, Anne gave birth to a daughter, Elizabeth. As queen, Anne fell out of favor at court. Henry tired of her as well, and when accusations of adultery surfaced, he had her thrown into the Tower of London. She was convicted and executed in 1536, partly as a result of maneuvering by Thomas Cromwell, who also played a part in the demise of Thomas More.

ART NOTE

Ask students to study the painting of Elizabeth I on this page. What mood does the artist's portrayal of the queen create? What details contribute to this mood? What do students think of her clothing? What impression would it have given to people in the sixteenth century? How do leaders in the United States and in other countries of the world dress today? What impressions are they trying to create through their clothing?

CROSS-CURRICULAR ACTIVITIES

You might show students brief portions of the film *Elizabeth*, released in 1998 and starring Cate Blanchett as Queen Elizabeth I. The film vividly portrays the political intrigue of Elizabeth's court. The film, however, is rated R, so you may want to choose carefully the scenes you show to your students.

Queen Elizabeth I (the "Ditchley" portrait).

ArtNote

Study the painting of Elizabeth I on this page. What mood does the artist's portrayal of the queen create? What details contribute to this mood? What do you think of her clothing? What impression would it have given to people in the sixteenth century? How do leaders in the United States and in other countries of the world dress today? What impressions are they trying to create through their clothing?

become a client state. Anti-Catholic and anti-Spanish feeling ran high in England, especially in the cities and towns. Mary I met this feeling with repression and brutality, earning for herself the nickname "Bloody Mary." She died in 1558.

THE ELIZABETHAN AGE

Perhaps the greatest monarch in all of English history was Mary's successor, **Elizabeth I,** daughter of Henry VIII and Anne Boleyn. One of the ironies of European history is that this child, unwanted by Henry, should have turned out to be so able a leader. Under Queen Elizabeth I, England grew to become the most powerful nation in Europe, and English literature reached what many people consider its zenith. Elizabeth's long reign, from 1558 to 1603, is known as the **Elizabethan Age.**

Elizabeth I was a true exemplar of the Renaissance person. Widely read in Latin, Greek, and various European languages, she gathered around her many of the finest writers of her time. Her court was a center of literary activity, and many of the greatest works of the period are dedicated to her. She herself wrote poetry and made Greek and Latin translations. Elizabeth was also a shrewd leader. Cleverly, she remained unmarried and played European states off against one another, leading each to hope for an alliance, through marriage, to the English throne. The

LITERARY EVENTS

➤ = British Events

➤ 1632. John Milton writes "On His Having Arrived at the Age of Twenty-Three"

➤ 1649. Richard Lovelace publishes *Lucasta*

➤ 1651. Thomas Hobbes writes *Leviathan*

1625 | 1630 | 1635 | 1640 | 1645 | 1650 | 1655

➤ 1625. James I dies. Charles I ascends the throne

➤ 1648. Charles I is executed

HISTORICAL EVENTS

The Launching of the English ships against the Spanish Armada. English Artist.
National Maritime Museum, Greenwich, England.

peace that resulted from this policy gave England an opportunity to build its navy, which became the foundation of English power for centuries to come. At home, Elizabeth quelled religious strife with a policy of moderation. She reestablished the monarch as head of the Church of England and ended the persecution of Protestants. She also tolerated Catholic beliefs and practices.

However, this policy of moderation did not please everyone. Throughout much of her reign, Elizabeth had to cope with Catholic plots against her. These plots sought to bring to power Mary Stuart, the exiled Queen of Scotland, who had fled to England after an uprising led by Protestants. Stuart, the Catholic great-granddaughter of Henry VII, stood next in line for the throne. Catholics, who did not accept as lawful Henry VIII's marriage to Anne Boleyn, and who therefore considered Elizabeth an illegitimate pretender, thought of Mary as the rightful Queen of England. Mary Stuart was imprisoned but allowed to live for nineteen years. Finally, however, the English Parliament ordered her execution for plotting to kill Elizabeth.

The execution of Mary Stuart infuriated Spain's king, Philip II, who already had cause to be upset with the English. For years, English pirates such as Sir Francis Drake had preyed on Spanish ships and colonies with the secret blessing and support of Queen Elizabeth. In 1588, Philip decided to attack England with a mighty fleet, the **Spanish Armada.** Fortunately for England, a storm wrecked part of the Spanish fleet, and in a battle in the English Channel, England's navy destroyed the rest of it. The destruction of the Spanish Armada made England the greatest power in Europe.

James I, First of the Stuart Kings

The death of the much-revered Queen Elizabeth in 1603 ended the Tudor Dynasty and brought to the throne the first of the Stuart kings, James VI of Scotland, who became **James I** of England. James was a Protestant, but he had Catholic sympathies and, like Elizabeth, detested the radical Protestants, who were called **Puritans** because they wished to "purify" the Church of England by removing all vestiges of Roman Catholic ritual. James I released Catholics from prison and tried to force all English men and women to adopt the rituals of the less radical Protestant high church. This

CROSS-CURRICULAR ACTIVITIES

Social Studies. Interested students may wish to research the defeat of the Spanish Armada. Specific topics include Spain's use of its navy for trade and war; piracy among the European colonial powers; the career of Sir Francis Drake; the design of Spanish and English ships; and the aftermath of the battle.

BIOGRAPHICAL NOTE

The life of **Francis Drake** (circa 1541–1596) was filled with adventure from the time of his youth. Some of his adventures were as horrifying as others were admirable. In his mid-twenties he participated in the slave trade in the West Indies. On an expedition in 1567, he narrowly escaped death in a Spanish attack near Mexico; the Spanish navy was to become his lifelong enemy. In 1570, he raided Spanish settlements in Panama, returning home with a rich booty of gold and silver. Competition with Spain was the impetus for his most famous expedition. Not to be outdone by Spaniard Ferdinand Magellan's accomplishment, Elizabeth I sent Drake to sail around the world for England. He did this between 1577 and 1580—alternately plundering, trading, and signing treaties along the way. He was knighted upon his return to England. Drake's role in the defeat of the Spanish Armada sealed his reputation as a naval hero.

SELECTION CHECK TEST 4.4.1 WITH ANSWERS

Social and Political Developments Changes in Thought
During the English Renaissance, people began to think differently about life, religion, politics, and authority than people during the Medieval years had. Write "M" by statements that describe the Medieval period, and "R" by statements that describe the Renaissance period.

_M_ 1. The Roman Catholic church is the ultimate authority in all things.
_R_ 2. People should examine their own consciences to make decisions.
_R_ 3. Human beings are created in God's image.
_R_ 4. People can improve themselves and their worlds.
_M_ 5. Earthly life is brief and of little value.

Key Terms
Fill in the blanks using the following terms. You may not use every term, and you may use some terms more than once.

_E_ 1. claims that all events were determined by God at the beginning of time
_D_ 2. list of objections to central beliefs and practices of the Catholic church
_C_ 3. "little world"
_B_ 4. "rebirth"
_A_ 5. devotion to the Greek and Latin classics that explored life on earth

a. humanism
b. renaissance
c. microcosmos
d. "95 theses"
e. predestination
f. Book of Common Prayer
g. Protestant Reformation
h. Divine Right of Kings

Key Figures
_B_ 1. argued that religion should be worked out between each person and God
_G_ 2. put to death for plotting against the life of Elizabeth I
_F_ 3. the first of the Stuart monarchs to take the English throne
_H_ 4. wished to purify the Church of England of Roman Catholic rituals
_A_ 5. founded the Church of England

a. Henry VIII
b. Martin Luther
c. Sir Thomas More

brought him into conflict with the House of Commons, which was dominated by Puritans, and led, after his death, to a revolution against the monarchy. The growing resentment in England against the monarchy was partially due to the arrogance of James I, who believed in the doctrine of the **Divine Right of Kings.** According to this doctrine, the monarch is divinely appointed by God. The monarch's will is God's will, and any challenge to regal authority is a challenge to God.

In 1620, a group of Puritans led by **William Bradford** sailed to North America and established the **Plymouth Colony.** However, this was not the first permanent English colony in North America. The first, called **Jamestown** after James I, had been established in 1607.

After the death of James I in 1625, his son **Charles I** became king. A revolution against the monarchy brought the Puritans to power for a while, but eventually the monarchy was restored under **Charles II.** (The story of this revolution and of the Restoration is told in the introduction to Unit 6.)

Nondramatic Literature During the English Renaissance

The early Tudor Period was not a great one in the history of English literature. The literature of that time tended to be backward-looking. Printers, following in the footsteps of Caxton, produced editions of works by authors of previous centuries, but few exceptional new works were written.

The reign of Henry VIII saw increased literary activity. Notable poets of the period included **Thomas Wyatt** and **Henry Howard, Earl of Surrey,** jointly credited for introducing to England the fourteen-line Italian verse form known as the **sonnet.** Surrey is also credited with introducing, in his translation from Latin of Virgil's epic poem the *Aeneid,* a new poetic form called **blank verse** (unrhymed verse in iambic pentameter). Blank verse became the medium of many of the greatest plays written during the latter part of the Renaissance.

The true flowering of literary creativity in the English Renaissance had to await the arrival on the scene of Queen Elizabeth. Elizabeth was a great patron of the arts, and under her, literature of all kinds flourished. The Elizabethan Age was remarkable for two kinds of literature: **lyric poetry** and **drama.** Great lyric poets of the period included courtiers such as **Sir Philip Sidney, Christopher Marlowe, Thomas Campion,** and **Ben Jonson,** and would-be courtiers such as **Edmund Spenser.** Sidney, Spenser, and **William Shakespeare** all produced outstanding **sonnet sequences,** or collections of related sonnets. Often, in this time, lyric poems were written for circulation among friends and acquaintances. Only later would some of these poems find their way into one of the numerous anthologies popular in the period. (For information about Elizabethan drama, see the introduction to Unit 5.)

The English Renaissance was also remarkable for its achievements in prose. Three works, in particular, stand out. **Sir Thomas More's** *Utopia* gave the world a new word (the book's title) and spawned a great deal of thinking about what society might be like if organized anew on different principles. Over the coming centuries, many utopian experiments in living would be founded on More's belief in the power of people to examine and remake the social order. **Francis Bacon's** *Novum Organum* promoted scientific thought and championed the idea that scientific principles should be developed through careful experimentation and unprejudiced inference. By far the greatest prose work of the period, however, was the **King James Bible,** a translation into English of the Hebrew and Greek scriptures. No work ever produced has had so profound an influence on the language, literature, and culture of England and the United States.

SELECTION CHECK TEST 4.4.1 WITH ANSWERS (CONT.)

d. Mary I, "Bloody Mary"
e. Elizabeth I
f. James I
g. Mary, Queen of Scotland
h. Puritans

Short Answer
1. What 1453 invention by Gutenberg helped people read and think for themselves? **This invention was the printing press.**
2. What does the doctrine of Original Sin say about ordinary people? **It says that all people are sinful.**

(Continued on page 287)

Echoes

Renaisssance England

Man hardly hath a richer thing than honest mirth.

—John Heywood (1497–1580)

[I]t is not my desire to live or to reign longer than my life and reign shall be for your good. And though you have had and may have many mightier and wiser princes sitting in this seat, yet you never had, nor shall have, any love you better.

—Elizabeth I (1533–1603), addressing the House of Commons in 1607

Go, little book: thyself present.

—Edmund Spenser (1552–1599)

Alas! so all things now do hold their peace,
Heaven and earth disturbèd[1] in no thing;
The beasts, the air, the birds their songs do cease,
The nightès chare[2] the stars about doth bring.
Calm is the sea, the waves work less and less;
So am not I, whom love, alas, doth wring,
Bringing before my face the great increase
Of my desires, whereat I weep and sing,
In joy and woe, as in a doubtful ease.
For my sweet thoughts sometime do pleasure bring,
But by and by the cause of my disease
Gives me a pang that inwardly doth sting,
When that I think what grief it is again
To live and lack the thing should rid my pain.

—Henry Howard, Earl of Surrey, "Alas! So All Things Now Do Hold Their Peace"

I love Rome, but London better; I favor Italy, but England more; I honor the Latin, but I worship the English. . . . I do not think that any language, be it whatsoever, is better able to utter all arguments, either with more pith or greater plainness, than our English tongue is.

—Richard Mulcaster (1530–1611)

Not marble, nor the gilded monuments of princes, shall outlive this powerful rhyme.

—William Shakespeare (1564–1616)

Wouldst thou hear what man can say
In a little? Reader, stay.
Underneath this stone doth lie
As much beauty as could die;
Which in life did harbor give
To more virtue than doth live.
If at all she had a fault,
Leave it buried in this vault.
One name was Elizabeth;
Th' other, let it sleep with death:
Fitter, where it died, to tell,
Than that it lived at all. Farewell!

—Ben Jonson, "Epitaph on Elizabeth, L. H."

1. **disturbèd.** The accent over the e means that the *-ed* should be pronounced as a separate syllable.
2. **chare.** Sweet

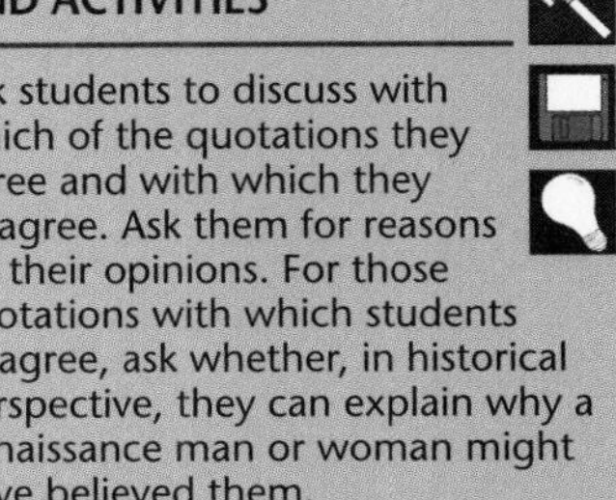

ADDITIONAL QUESTIONS AND ACTIVITIES

Ask students to discuss with which of the quotations they agree and with which they disagree. Ask them for reasons for their opinions. For those quotations with which students disagree, ask whether, in historical perspective, they can explain why a Renaissance man or woman might have believed them.

SELECTION CHECK TEST 4.4.1 WITH ANSWERS (CONT. FROM PAGE 286)

3. What did Henry VIII do when the pope refused to grant him an annulment from his wife, Catherine? **He broke from the Catholic Church.**
4. What was the goal of the Counter Reformation? **The Counter Reformation sought to reverse the Protestant Reformation.**
5. What was Elizabeth able to do to European countries by remaining unmarried? **She played them against one another because they each wanted to marry her and form an alliance to the English throne.**

Literary Developments

1. To whom is much of the great literature of the Renaissance dedicated? **Many of these works are dedicated to Elizabeth I.**
2. What two kinds of literature flourished during the Elizabethan Age? **Drama and lyric poetry flourished during the Elizabethan Age.**
3. What form of Italian verse was introduced to England by Wyatt and Howard? **These poets introduced the sonnet to England.**
4. What is the name for the unrhymed iambic pentameter that became the medium for many Renaissance plays? **This is called blank verse.**
5. What prose work has had a more profound influence on the language, literature, and culture of England and the United States than any other work ever printed? **This work is the King James Bible.**

ADDITIONAL RESOURCES

UNIT 4 RESOURCE BOOK

- Selection Worksheet 4.1
- Selection Check Test 4.4.3
- Selection Test 4.4.4
- Language, Grammar, and Style Resource 3.55

GRAPHIC ORGANIZER

/ / / /
Whoso list to hunt,
/ / /
I know where is an hind,
/ / / / /
But as for me, alas, I may no more.
/ / / / /
The vain travail hath wearied me so sore
/ / / / /
I am of them that farthest cometh behind.
/ / / / /
Yet may I, by no means, my wearied mind
/ / / / /
Draw from the deer, but as she fleeth afore,
/ / / /
Fainting I follow. I leave off therefore,
/ / / / /
Since in a net I seek to hold the wind.
/ / / / /
Who list her hunt, I put him out of doubt,
/ / / / /
As well as I, may spend his time in vain.
/ / / / /
And graven with diamonds in letters plain
/ / / / /
There is written, her fair neck round about,
/ /
"Noli me tangere, for Cæsar's I am,
/ / / /
And wild for to hold, though I seem tame."

READER'S JOURNAL

As an alternate activity, ask students to write about whether it is ever okay to stop trying to attain a goal? If so, when?

Literary TOOLS

METAPHOR. A **metaphor** is a figure of speech in which one thing is spoken or written about as though it were another. In this sonnet, the writer uses a metaphor to describe the object of the speaker's affections.

PETRARCHAN SONNET AND IAMBIC PENTAMETER. A **Petrarchan sonnet** is a lyric poem of fourteen lines, often in **iambic pentameter. Iambic pentameter** is a kind of meter, or rhythmic pattern, of five iambs, each iamb being one weakly stressed syllable followed by one strongly stressed syllable. The Petrarchan sonnet generally follows the rhyme scheme *abbaabba cdecde* (or *cdcdcd* or *cdedce*) and is divided into two parts: the first eight lines forming the **octave** and the last six forming the **sestet.** The theme of a sorrowful male and an unattainable female is typical in this type of sonnet. **Iambic pentameter** is a kind of meter or rhythmic pattern, of five iambs, each **iamb** being one weakly stressed syllable (⌣) followed by one strongly stressed syllable (/). Write each line of the poem and make a line over each stressed syllable.

⌣ / ⌣ / ⌣ / ⌣ / ⌣ /
But as for me, alas, I may no more.

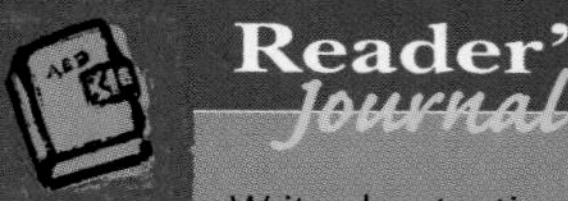

Reader's Journal

Write about a time when you couldn't get what you wanted.

"Whoso List to Hunt"

BY SIR THOMAS WYATT

About the AUTHOR

Sir Thomas Wyatt (1503–1542) was born in Kent at Allington Castle and studied at St. John's College, Cambridge. He was a courtier and diplomat for much of his life and served King Henry VIII as clerk and ambassador. This life was not a serene one, and Sir Thomas was twice arrested and imprisoned as a result of quarrels at court. He spent most of his adult life away from England and was interested in foreign, especially Italian, literature. Wyatt was influenced by the Italian-style sonnets, particularly those of the great fourteenth-century Italian poet Petrarch (see page 000). Along with Henry Howard, Earl of Surrey, he introduced the **Petrarchan sonnet** to England. Although Wyatt never published a collection of his own poems, ninety-seven of them appear in a book now referred to as *Tottel's Miscellany,* which was first published in 1557 by a printer named Richard Tottel.

About the SELECTION

Wyatt's "**Whoso List to Hunt**" is a superb example of a Petrarchan sonnet, both technically and thematically. The sonnet may have been written about Anne Boleyn. Wyatt grew up in the same household with Anne and fell deeply in love with her. He was devastated when Anne became the wife of Henry VIII, and Henry grew, quite naturally, suspicious of him. The reference in the poem to Cæsar may be read as meaning "any powerful man," such as King Henry.

GOALS/OBJECTIVES

Studying this unit will enable students to

- enjoy reading a Petrarchan sonnet
- describe the features of a Petrarchan sonnet
- define *metaphor* and recognize and interpret metaphors in a poem
- use personal pronouns correctly
- research Anne Boleyn and prepare a brief biography of her
- discuss songs, movies, and other works about love in a group

***After the Hunt*, c.1644.** Karel Dujardin. Michaelis Collection, Cape Town, South Africa.

Whoso List to Hunt

Sir Thomas Wyatt

Whoso list[1] to hunt, I know where is an hind,[2]
But as for me, alas, I may no more.
The vain travail hath wearied me so sore
I am of them that farthest cometh behind.
Yet may I, by no means, my wearied mind
Draw from the deer, but as she fleeth afore,
Fainting I follow. I leave off therefore,
Since in a net I seek to hold the wind.
Who list her hunt, I put him out of doubt,
As well as I, may spend his time in vain.
And graven with diamonds in letters plain
There is written, her fair neck round about,
"*Noli me tangere*, for Cæsar's I am,[3]
And wild for to hold, though I seem tame." ■

For what has the speaker been hunting?

Did the speaker attain his goal?

1. **list.** Desires
2. **hind.** Deer
3. ***Noli . . . tangere am.*** *Touch me not* is the imagined inscription on the collars of Cæsar's deer.

Words for Everyday Use

trav • ail (trə vāl´) *n.*, very hard work. *The marathon runner crossed the finish line and collapsed after more than four hours of athletic travail.*

grav • en (grāv´ ən) *vt.*, engraved. *Jean's parents gave her a ring graven with the date of her high school graduation.*

ANSWERS TO GUIDED READING QUESTIONS

1. The speaker has been hunting a hind, or deer.
2. No, the speaker does not attain his goal of catching the deer.

INDIVIDUAL LEARNING STRATEGIES

Motivation
Ask students to work in pairs to role play a conversation between the speaker and the woman he admires. Encourage them to portray the speaker's beloved as regretful that she cannot be with the speaker as being scornful and outraged by the speaker's declaration, and so forth.

English Language Learning
Explain that the author often uses words in a sequence different from the way people read, write, and speak English today. Examples include "Yet may I, by no means, my wearied mind/Draw from the deer," "her fair neck round about," and "Cæsar's I am."

Reading Proficiency
Read the poem aloud to students twice. The first time, ask them just to listen. The second time, ask students to follow along with the text of the poem as you read.

Special Needs
Work with students to help them restate the main ideas of the poem in a language they can understand and with which they are comfortable. If students have difficulty recasting the poem into their version of modern English, you might restate the first few lines for them.

Enrichment
The sonnet uses a hunter pursuing a deer as a metaphor for a man pursuing a romantic relationship with a woman. Students may wish to discuss or write about ways in which this metaphor does and does not work effectively.

SELECTION CHECK TEST 4.4.3 WITH ANSWERS

Checking Your Reading

1. What has the speaker been hunting? **He has been hunting deer (hind).**
2. What is the speaker's physical condition? **He is exhausted and "fainting."**
3. What has he sought to hold in a net? **He has sought to hold the wind in a net.**

SELECTION CHECK TEST 4.4.3 WITH ANSWERS (CONT.)

4. What does this creature wear around its neck? **A sign saying "touch me not."**
5. To whom does the creature belong? **The creature belongs to Caesar.**

Literary Tools

1. A Petrarchan sonnet has:
   a. eight lines
   b. four lines
   c. fourteen lines
   d. twelve lines
2. The theme of a sorrowful male and an unattainable female is common for:
   a. iambic pentameter
   b. metaphor
   c. Petrarchan sonnet
   d. octave

RESPOND TO THE SELECTION

Students may work as a class or in small groups to brainstorm a list of situations similar to that experienced by the speaker in "Whoso List to Hunt." You may want to prime the list with these suggestions:

- trying out for, but not making, an athletic team
- attempting to fit in with a particular group of friends who don't want to include you
- trying to write a poem or story but being unable to find the right words to express yourself
- studying for a math test but finding it impossible to comprehend certain concepts

ANSWERS FOR INVESTIGATE, INQUIRE AND IMAGINE

Recall

1a. The speaker knows where to find a hind.

2a. The speaker compares the hunt to catching the wind in a net.

3a. The inscription reads, "Noli me tangere, for Caesar's I am, and wild for to hold, though I seem tame."

Interpret

1b. The speaker is tired of the unsuccessful hunt.

2b. The comparison suggests that the hunt is impossible.

3b. The message of the inscription suggests that the object of the hunt is unattainable because it belongs to Caesar, but even if the hunt were successful, the hind is wild and impossible to tame.

Analyze

4a. Lines 1–8 express the difficulties the speaker has had with the hunt, yet his unwillingness to give up on it. Lines 9–14 offer advice to others about why the hunt is impossible.

Synthesize

4b. The octet shows the effects of the hunt on the speaker. The sestet emphasizes why his task is impossible.

Evaluate

5a. The hind supposedly belongs to Caesar, but it sounds as though the subject of this poem is very independent, based on the last line.

Extend

5b. *Responses will vary.* Students may say that the speaker is tiring of the hunt and would like to attain his goal. Whether or not the speaker enjoys the hunt, he seems unable to stop even though it seems to be causing him pain.

Respond to the SELECTION

Do you think the speaker should give up the hunt? Explain using an example of a time when you continued or stopped pursuing an unattainable goal.

Inquire, Imagine

Recall: Gathering Facts

1a. What does the speaker know where to find?

2a. To what task does the speaker compare this hunt?

3a. What is written on the collar around the deer's neck?

→ **Interpret:** Finding Meaning

1b. Why is the speaker willing to share this information with another hunter?

2b. What does this comparison suggest about the nature of this hunt?

3b. Why does this message mean the hunt will be unsuccessful?

Analyze: Taking Things Apart

4a. What is the main idea of lines 1–8? What is the main idea of lines 9–14?

→ **Synthesize:** Bringing Things Together

4b. How does the message of the sestet relate to the message of the octet?

Evaluate: Making Judgments

5a. Judge whether the hind belongs to anyone.

→ **Extend:** Connecting Ideas

5b. Do you think the hunter really wants the hind? Or, does he enjoy the hunt?

Understanding Literature

Metaphor. Review the definition for **metaphor** in the Handbook of Literary Terms. A hunting metaphor is used in this sonnet. What similarities exist between the woman and the deer? between the speaker and the hunter?

Petrarchan Sonnet and Iambic Pentameter. Review the definitions for **Petrarchan sonnet** and **iambic pentameter** in Literary Tools on page 288. After marking the stresses of the meter, identify the rhyme scheme in "Whoso List to Hunt." Does it completely follow the Petrarchan model?

ANSWERS FOR UNDERSTANDING LITERATURE

Metaphor. The woman is like a deer in that both flee to preserve their freedom, both are difficult to catch, and both are claimed by a powerful figure. The speaker is like a hunter in that both are pursuing something and both grow weary from the chase.

Petrarchan Sonnet and Iambic Pentameter. The rhyme scheme is abbaabba cddcee.

Writer's Journal

1. Write a **journal entry** from the speaker's point of view, or from your own point of view, about being disappointed in love.
2. Write a **dialogue** between the speaker of this sonnet and woman he loves and pursues. Remember the speaker's feelings as expressed in this sonnet when you create his lines.
3. Write a **sonnet**. You may choose a traditional or nontraditional subject and tone, but make sure your poem follows the meter and rhyme scheme of a sonnet.

Language, Grammar, and Style

Personal Pronouns. Read the Language Arts Survey 3.55, "Personal Pronouns." Then choose the correct pronoun in parentheses to complete each of the following sentences.

1. In Wyatt's sonnet, (who, whom) had the hunter tried to catch?
2. The speaker says that the hunt tired (he, him).
3. Will (they, them) who hunt the hind catch her?
4. (Whomever, Whoever) touches Cæsar's property will answer to Cæsar.
5. Of all of (us, we) hunters, I am the farthest behind the deer.

Speaking and Listening & Collaborative Learning

Discussion Groups. Think about songs, movies, or other works about love. How many of them are about unrequited love? How many of them have happy endings? Which do you prefer? Why? Discuss these questions with others in your class.

Study and Research

Researching Anne Boleyn. Some scholars believe this sonnet was written about Anne Boleyn. Research the life of Anne Boleyn and prepare a brief biography of her. If you do your research on the Internet, one site you will find helpful is at GeoCities http://www.geocities/CollegePark/2809/page11.html.

ANSWERS TO INTEGRATING THE LANGUAGE ARTS

Language, Grammar, and Style

1. whom
2. him
3. they
4. Whoever
5. us

Speaking and Listening & Collaborative Learning

Tell students to follow the guidelines for discussion in the Language Arts Survey 4.9, "Communicating in a Large Group," and 4.13, "Collaborative Learning and Communication."

Study and Research

Encourage students to research Anne Boleyn in encyclopedias, both hardbound and electronic; on the Internet; and in books on English history. Tell students that they should rely on more than one source of information when writing their brief biographies. Set a one-page limit for students, so they must choose what details are important to include.

ADDITIONAL RESOURCES

UNIT 4 RESOURCE BOOK
- Selection Worksheet 4.2
- Selection Check Test 4.4.5
- Selection Test 4.4.6
- Language, Grammar, and Style Resource 3.39
- Study and Research Resource 5.3

INDIVIDUAL LEARNING STRATEGIES

MOTIVATION
Encourage students to create an artistic creation capturing this poem. For example, they might paint a lover staring up at a full moon, or make a sculpture of the moon with a wan face. Display students' creations around the classroom.

ENGLISH LANGUAGE LEARNING
Remind students to watch for the unexpected word order that marks much Elizabethan poetry. In particular, point out that the object of a verb often precedes the verb, as in "That busy archer his sharp arrows tries."

READING PROFICIENCY
Students may have an easier time with both the language of the poem and interpreting the speaker's mood and feelings if they listen to a dramatic reading of the poem. Either play an audiocassette recording of such a reading or ask a student who is interested in theater to prepare a dramatic reading for your students.

SPECIAL NEEDS
Students may have difficulty with this poem. You may wish to tell students that in lines 3–6, the speaker wonders if Cupid causes love even in heaven and then says he can tell that the moon understands and feels sympathy for a lover's position. In lines 10–14, the speaker describes love on earth by asking the moon about love in heaven.

ENRICHMENT
Sidney uses the moon to represent inconstancy. Students may think of other objects or events in the natural world that can symbolize aspects of human relationships. Have them spend time outdoors reflecting on nature. When they have discovered a metaphor they like, they may write a poem or a paragraph describing the metaphor and its personal significance.

Sonnet 31
"With how sad steps . . ."

FROM ASTROPHIL AND STELLA

BY SIR PHILLIP SIDNEY

About the AUTHOR

Sir Philip Sidney (1554–1586) was a well-loved courtier, soldier, and poet, deeply mourned by the English people after his death in battle at the age of thirty-two. His father was Sir Henry Sidney, three times governor of Ireland. Philip Sidney attended Shrewsbury School, where he was admired for his grace and maturity, and then Oxford. His staunch Protestantism was reinforced by having witnessed massacres of Protestants in France in 1572.

After his travels, Sidney returned to England where he was a courtier and patron of the arts, and in particular of Edmund Spenser, who dedicated *The Shepheardes Calender* to him. Later, in disfavor with the queen, Sidney retired to Wilton and wrote his pastoral prose work, *The Countess of Pembroke's Arcadia,* as well as sonnets and literary criticism. In his "Defense of Poesy [Poetry]," Sidney argued that poets can actually improve upon nature by his creating worlds better than the real one. Sidney's argument shows clearly the English Renaissance faith in human abilities and esteem for poetic art.

In the cause of Protestantism, Sidney went to the Low Countries in 1585 as a volunteer in the war against Spain. There he died heroically. Sidney never published his work himself, though today it is considered to be among the most lovely and lyrical in the English language.

About the SELECTION

Sonnet 31 is part of the sonnet cycle *Astrophil and Stella,* which generally follows the sonnet conventions established by Petrarch. The rhyme scheme is Petrarchan: *abba abba cdcd ee.* So is the subject: unrequited, or unreturned, love. Petrarch addressed his poems to an unattainable woman named Laura. Sidney addressed his to Stella, whose name means "star." Sidney's speaker, Astrophil, or "star-lover," expresses many of the complex emotions of a person in love. Sidney used dialogue to express Astrophil's mental state, including everyday speech and internal conversations, or interior monologues.

Much of the best of Elizabethan literature was private work, circulated among people in the queen's court. One way to obtain favor with the queen and other powerful figures was to be amusing, or witty. Wittiness therefore became a central feature of literature of the period, which employs elaborate conceits and word play. In Sonnet 31, the speaker uses an exaggerated metaphor, personifying and addressing the moon. The moon has long been a symbol of faithlessness, or inconstancy, because its appearance changes throughout the month. In this poem, Astrophil asks the moon if in the heavenly sphere, as on Earth, constancy, or faithfulness, is considered lack of wit.

GOALS/OBJECTIVES

Studying this unit will enable students to
- empathize with a speaker's emotions
- define *image* and identify imagery in a poem
- define *personification* and recognize personification in their reading
- use a thesaurus to find colorful language
- research folk beliefs about the moon
- identify faulty arguments

Unrequited Love.
English Artist.

Sonnet 31
With how sad steps . . .

SIR PHILIP SIDNEY

With how sad steps, O Moon, thou climb'st the skies,
How silently, and with how <u>wan</u> a face!
What, may it be that even in heavenly place
That busy archer[1] his sharp arrows tries?
Sure, if that long-with-love-acquainted eyes
Can judge of Love, thou feel'st a Lover's case;
I read it in thy looks: thy <u>languished</u> grace,
To me that feel the like, thy state descries.[2]
Then even of fellowship, O Moon, tell me
Is constant *love* deemed there but want of wit?
Are beauties there as proud as here they be?
Do they above love to be loved, and yet
Those lovers <u>scorn</u> whom that *love* doth possess?
Do they call *virtue* there ungratefulness? ■

What feelings does the speaker attribute to the moon?

1. **That busy archer.** The *busy archer* is Cupid, the Roman god of love who is often pictured with a bow and arrow, which he uses to strike at people's hearts, causing them to feel love and, sometimes, love's sorrows.
2. **descry.** Shows clearly.

WORDS FOR EVERYDAY USE

wan (wän) *adj.*, pale, faint. *When he heard the shocking news, all the color drained out of Roderick's face, leaving it <u>wan</u> and ghostlike.*

lan • guished (lan´ gwisht) *adj.*, drooping, lacking vitality. *When I returned from vacation, the <u>languished</u> leaves of my house-plants seemed to cry out, "Water! Help!"*

scorn (skôrn) *vt.*, view with contempt. *If Jasmine wants to be a journalist, why does she <u>scorn</u> the idea of working on the school newspaper?*

Literary TOOLS

IMAGE. An **image** is language that creates a concrete representation of an object or an experience. Try to identify the main image in this poem as you read.

PERSONIFICATION. Personification is a figure of speech in which an idea, animal, or thing is described as if it were a person. The moon is personified in this selection. Keep track of human characteristics attributed to the moon.

Reader's *Journal*

Describe somebody you admire.

ANSWERS TO GUIDED READING QUESTIONS

1. The speaker attributes sadness to the moon.

SELECTION CHECK TEST 4.4.5 WITH ANSWERS

Checking Your Reading

1. Who or what is the speaker addressing? **The speaker addresses the moon.**
2. Whose "sharp arrows" does the speaker ask about? **He asks about Cupid.**
3. What condition does the speaker recognize? **He recognizes the moon's love, probably a painful love.**
4. What does he ask about the beauties in the heavens? **He asks if they are proud.**
5. The speaker asks if virtue is called what? **He asks if it is called ungratefulness.**

Vocabulary in Context
Fill each blank with the most appropriate word from the Words for Everyday Use. You may have to change the tense of the word.

wan languished descry scorn

1. Our **<u>languished</u>** comrades were all too happy for us to take over the difficult task.
2. Despite the governor's reassurances, the look on his face **<u>descried</u>** his concern.
3. Marcelle **<u>scorned</u>** poetry until he discovered the works of Pablo Neruda.

Literary Tools

1. What is personification? **Personification is the attribution of human characteristics to something that is not human.**
2. What is the central image in this poem? **The moon is the central image.**

READER'S JOURNAL

Suggest that students consider older people in their community, historical figures, or an imaginary person with qualities they admire as subjects for their dialogues.

VOCABULARY FROM THE SELECTION

descry
languished
scorn
wan

RESPOND TO THE SELECTION

Students may also consider these questions: Is it possible to have a sincere feeling that changes over time? What might cause these changes? What can people learn from their changing emotions and beliefs?

ANSWERS FOR INVESTIGATE, INQUIRE AND IMAGINE

RECALL

1a. He addresses the moon.

2a. The speaker asks, "Is constant love deemed there but want of wit? Are beauties there as proud as here they be?"

3a. In the speaker's experience, beauties love to be loved and scorn the lovers whose love they possess.

INTERPRET

1b. Perhaps the speaker chooses the moon as his confidant because he feels that others do not understand him or because the moon cannot judge him. Students may also suggest that imagining the moon as sympathetic character comforts him.

2b. The speaker feels rejected by proud beauties and finds constant love unappreciated.

3b. The speaker feels he has been treated unkindly by his beloved. His love has not been returned.

ANALYZE

4a. The moon appears to move sadly and to have a wan face.

SYNTHESIZE

4b. The speaker is not taking rejection well. The speaker may be expressing fresh feelings or he may be wallowing in self-pity.

EVALUATE

5a. The speaker's bitterness and his baring his soul to the moon rather than to another person suggest that he feels other people do not understand his pain.

EXTEND

5b. Sidney's speaker feels rejected, while Wyatt's feels hopeless. Neither is able to attain his beloved.

Respond *to the* SELECTION

What is constancy? Why is it important for people to be constant in their feelings? Discuss these questions with your classmates.

INVESTIGATE, Inquire, Imagine

Recall: GATHERING FACTS → **Interpret:** FINDING MEANING

1a. Who or what does the speaker address in line 1?

1b. Why do you think the speaker chooses such a confidant?

2a. What questions does the speaker ask in lines 10 and 11?

2b. What do you learn about the speaker's own experience from these questions?

3a. What, in the speaker's experience, do beauties do regarding love?

3b. How has the speaker been treated by his beloved?

Analyze: TAKING THINGS APART → **Synthesize:** BRINGING THINGS TOGETHER

4a. What signs show the moon's feelings?

4b. How do you think the speaker is acting in response to rejections?

Evaluate: MAKING JUDGMENTS → **Extend:** CONNECTING IDEAS

5a. Judge whether the speaker feels understood in his pain. Explain how you know.

5b. Compare and contrast the speaker of Sidney's Sonnet 31 with the speaker of Wyatt's "Whoso List to Hunt." Think about how they have been treated by the objects of their affection and their attitude toward love.

Understanding *Literature*

IMAGE. Review the definition for **image** in Literary Tools on page 293. What is the main image in this sonnet? Describe the image. How does the speaker react to this image?

PERSONIFICATION. Review the definition for **personification** in the Handbook of Literary Terms. The moon is personified in this selection. Describe the characteristics of the moon. What purpose does this personification have in this sonnet?

ANSWERS FOR UNDERSTANDING LITERATURE

IMAGE. The central image is of the moon climbing the night sky. The speaker described the moon as looking "wan: and says he can read the moon's emotional state from its "looks." He treats the moon as if it were a sympathetic friend.

PERSONIFICATION. In this sonnet, the moon is depicted as having human characteristics: It feels sad and takes slow steps across the sky. It also is described as if it were able to listen to the speaker. The poet uses personification to describe the speaker's emotions in an indirect and interesting way. The emotions that the speaker attributes to the moon are the ones that he is feeling.

WRITER'S JOURNAL

1. Images can relate to any of the five senses. Write five **images**, one for each sense, that share a common mood.
2. Imagine that the moon responds to the speaker. Write a **poem** or **paragraph** that answers the questions in the sonnet.
3. What is your definition of love? Write a **personal essay** that expresses your views on love.

Integrating *the* LANGUAGE ARTS

Language, Grammar, and Style

USING A THESAURUS TO FIND COLORFUL LANGUAGE. Rewrite the following passage using more colorful nouns, verbs, and modifiers. Use a thesaurus if you need help. Refer to the Language Arts Survey 3.39, "Adding Colorful Language to Sentences."

Cupid's arrow hit its mark. My heart hurts because my beloved doesn't know me. We walk the same streets and hear the same birds call. The white moon looks down upon us both as we sit under the same black sky. But she might as well be on the moon, for she thinks not of me.

Study and Research & Collaborative Learning

MOON RESEARCH. Working in two groups, learn more about the moon. One group should focus on symbolic meaning and folk beliefs about the moon. As explained in the introduction to this sonnet, the moon is often associated with fickleness. If you look at the ballad "Sir Patrick Spens," you will find a superstition related to the moon. What other beliefs have people held about the moon? Use the Internet and print sources in your library to find out more. The second group should learn about the moon from a scientific perspective. Some questions to ask are: What is the surface of the moon like? How far is the moon from the Earth? What causes the phases of the moon? How is the moon related to tides? Each group should share their findings with the other. Then together explore the traits that lend themselves to literary references.

Critical Thinking

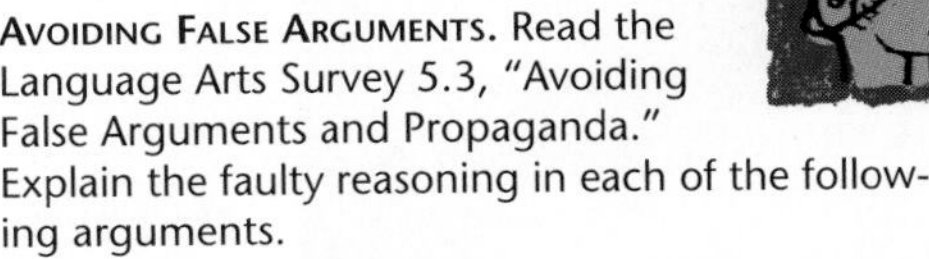

AVOIDING FALSE ARGUMENTS. Read the Language Arts Survey 5.3, "Avoiding False Arguments and Propaganda." Explain the faulty reasoning in each of the following arguments.

1. Everyone scorns love once they get it.
2. I love him because he is so lovable.
3. I dated a freshman once. Never again—they're too immature.
4. Nobody will ever love you because you're a loser.

ANSWERS TO INTEGRATING THE LANGUAGE ARS

Language, Grammar, and Style

USING A THESAURUS TO FIND COLORFUL LANGUAGE

Responses will vary. One possible response is given.

Cupid's arrow struck its mark. My heart throbs because my beloved doesn't know me. We stroll the same streets and hear the same birds chirp sweetly. The pearly moon gazes down upon us both as we sit under the same murky sky. But, she might as well be on the moon for she thinks not of me.

Study and Research

Note that the superstition about the moon in "Sir Patrick Spens" is that seeing the outline of the old moon in the crescent of the noon moon brings bad luck.

If your class size is too large to make dividing it in two effective for a research assignment, divide students into smaller groups of four or five. Assign groups the tasks of researching folk beliefs about the moon or researching scientific facts about the moon. Each group should then prepare and present and oral report on their assigned topic. Encourage them to use multimedia aids to make their reports more appealing to the rest of the class. For example, students who are researching scientific aspects of the moon might bring in photographs or videotape of the moon, while students who are researching folk beliefs might play a CD of a folk song about the moon.

Critical Thinking

AVOIDING FALSE ARGUMENTS

Explain the faulty reasoning in each of the following arguments.

1. over generalization
2. circular reasoning
3. stereotypes
4. name-calling

ADDITIONAL RESOURCES

Unit 4 Resource Book
- Selection Worksheet 4.3
- Selection Check Test 4.4.7
- Selection Test 4.4.8
- Language, Grammar, and Style Resource 3.61
- Applied English Resource 6.9

GRAPHIC ORGANIZER

Alliteration

P	pricking plaine
S	silver shielde
D	dints, deepe
W	wherein, wounds
M	markes, many
T	till, time
F	fierce, fitt
B	but, brest, bloudie, bore
D	deare, dying
S	sweete sake
H	hope, his helpe he had
S	seeme, solemne sad

READER'S JOURNAL

Explain that showing courage means risking something that you value and thus fear losing. When students write about their experiences, suggest that they consider what it was that they valued. Do they still value this thing or idea?

VOCABULARY FROM THE SELECTION

score
wield

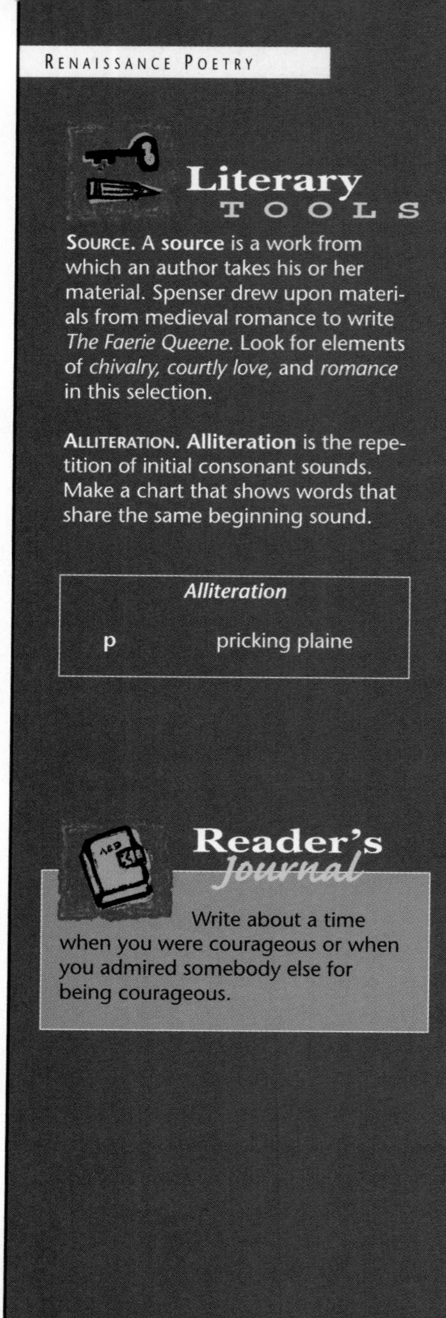

Literary Tools

Source. A **source** is a work from which an author takes his or her material. Spenser drew upon materials from medieval romance to write *The Faerie Queene.* Look for elements of *chivalry, courtly love,* and *romance* in this selection.

Alliteration. **Alliteration** is the repetition of initial consonant sounds. Make a chart that shows words that share the same beginning sound.

Alliteration	
p	pricking plaine

Reader's Journal

Write about a time when you were courageous or when you admired somebody else for being courageous.

from The Faerie Queene

by Edmund Spenser

About the Author

Edmund Spenser (1552–1599) has been called the greatest nondramatic poet of the Elizabethan Era. Born in London to a family of meager means, he attended Merchant Taylor's School and then Cambridge University. Later he became aide and secretary to several important men. In one of their households, he met courtier and poet Sir Philip Sidney, to whom he dedicated *The Shepheardes Calender,* a series of pastoral poems.

Spenser went to Ireland as aide to Lord Grey of Wilton, Lord Deputy of Ireland, and tried unsuccessfully for the rest of his life to return to England to live. Staunchly nationalistic and Protestant, he wrote an apology for British colonial repression of the Irish called *A View of the Present State of Ireland.* In the last decade of the 1500s, a bitter rebellion broke out in Ireland, and Spenser's castle was demolished. Spenser died while on a mission back to England and was buried in the Poets' Corner of Westminster Abbey.

About the Selection

This selection is from Spenser's masterpiece, ***The Fœrie Queene,*** a long, epic romance dedicated to Queen Elizabeth. *The Fœrie Queene* uses material from medieval romances to tell allegorical tales dealing with religion, politics, and other matters. Spenser's revival of medieval romance had considerable effect on later poets like Alfred, Lord Tennyson. In his epic romance, Spenser deliberately used archaic language in homage to Chaucer.

In this selection from *The Fœrie Queene,* the poet recounts the medieval story of the slaying of the dragon by St. George, the patron saint of England.

GOALS/OBJECTIVES

Studying this lesson will enable students to
- have a positive experience reading a Renaissance poem that draws on medieval romance
- identify elements of medieval romance
- define *alliteration* and point to examples of alliteration in a poem
- distinguish between transitive and intransitive verbs
- prepare and deliver a speech on courage
- write a press release

Port after Stormy Seas (from Spenser's 'Færie Queene'), 1905. Evelyn de Morgan. The De Morgan Foundation, London.

FROM

The Faerie Queen

EDMUND SPENSER

A Gentle Knight was pricking[1] on the plaine,
Ycladd[2] in mightie armes and silver shielde,
Wherein old dints of deepe wounds did remaine,
The cruell markes of many a bloudy fielde;
Yet armes till that time did he never wield:
His angry steede did chide his foming bitt,
As much disdayning to the curbe to yield:
Full jolly[3] knight he seemd, and faire did sitt,
As one for knightly giusts[4] and fierce encounters fitt.

What is the knight wearing?

1. **pricking.** Cantering
2. **Ycladd.** Dressed
3. **jolly.** Gallant
4. **giusts.** Jousts

WORDS FOR EVERYDAY USE

wield (wēld) *vt.,* handle and use a weapon or tool. *"Didn't you ever wield a hammer before?" Joe remarked cruelly as Liz nursed her throbbing thumb.*

ANSWERS TO GUIDED READING QUESTIONS

1. The knight is wearing armor and carrying a shield.

INDIVIDUAL LEARNING STRATEGIES

MOTIVATION
Students may especially enjoy researching the St. George and the dragon story for the Study and Research activity. You might encourage students to decorate the room with their own artistic representations of the St. George and the dragon story.

ENGLISH LANGUAGE LEARNING
Point out the following idioms:
the like—the same thing
right faithfull true—completely loyal and honest

READING PROFICIENCY
Remind students that Spenser uses many archaic spellings, but that the language of the poem is still modern English. Share with students the following definitions to help them decipher some unusual spellings and word choices:
armes—arms, or weapons
dints—dents
fielde—battlefield
steede—steed, horse
chide—show disapproval
curbe—bit—the part of a bridle that fits in a horse's mouth
remembrance—object that serves as a reminder
soveraine—of the highest kind
cheere—cheer; facial expression
dread—fear
bond—bound; going
puissance—strength

SPECIAL NEEDS
Students will have a difficult time with the antiquated spellings and word choices in this poem. Share with them the information in English Language Learning and Reading Proficiency above. Special needs students will also benefit from hearing the poem read aloud, as they won't have to be concerned about the unusual spellings when the poem is read aloud.

INDIVIDUAL LEARNING STRATEGIES (CONT.)

ENRICHMENT

Students can write about or discuss the idea of being faithful to a social superior. The feudal system of medieval Europe was founded on such duties and loyalties. Do students think there is any parallel in the modern world? If so, what are some examples?

ANSWERS TO GUIDED READING QUESTIONS

1. The knight wishes to go to battle to win the honor and grace of Gloriana, Queen of Faerie Land.

SELECTION CHECK TEST 4.4.7 WITH ANSWERS

Checking Your Reading

1. What evidence does the knight wear of his battles? He has dents in his armor.
2. Who does the knight remember with the Cross he wears? He remembers his lord.
3. How does the knight feel about this person? He loves him.
4. What does the knight crave most "of all earthly things"? He craves the affection of the Faerie Queen.
5. Who is the knight's foe? The knight's foe is the Dragon.

Literary Tools

In his poetry, Spenser drew upon materials from medieval literature like the concepts of chivalry, romance, and courtly love. Alliteration is common in poetry. Which of these elements is best illustrated in each of the following lines of poetry?

a. chivalry b. romance c. courtly love d. alliteration

__B__ 1 Upon a great adventure he was bond. (Discussion: romance dealt with the adventures of knights.)

__A__ 2. Right faithfull true he was in deede and word (Discussion: chivalry was the code by which knights lived, which included loyalty as a virtue.)

__D__ 3. But on his brest a bloudie Cross he bore, (Discussion: alliteration is the repetition of consonant sounds.)

RESPOND TO THE SELECTION

Students may begin by thinking about what "dragons" they might need to fight in their own lives. Such a dragon might be any person or institution that threatens them. A dragon might even exist within a person's own mind, in the form of a fear or prejudice.

But on his brest a bloudie Crosse he bore,
The deare remembrance of his dying Lord,
For whose sweete sake that glorious badge he wore,
And dead as living ever him adored:
Upon his shield the like was also scored,
For soveraine hope, which in his helpe he had:
Right faithfull true he was in deede and word,
But of his cheere did seeme too solemne sad;[5]
Yet nothing did he dread, but ever was ydrad.[6]
Upon a great adventure he was bond,
That greatest Gloriana to him gave,
That greatest Glorious Queen of Færie Lond,
To winne him worship,[7] and her grace to have,
Which of all earthly things he most did crave;
And ever as he rode, his hart did earne[8]
To prove his puissance[9] in battell brave
Upon his foe, and his new force to learne;
Upon his foe, a Dragon horrible and stearne. ■

Why does the knight wish to go to battle?

5. **solemne sad.** Grave; serious
6. **ydrad.** Dreaded
7. **worship.** Honor
8. **earne.** Yearn
9. **puissance.** Power

WORDS FOR EVERYDAY USE

score (skôr) *vt.,* mark with lines or notches. *Kim opened the little box carefully and found that it was* scored *inside with a beautiful design.*

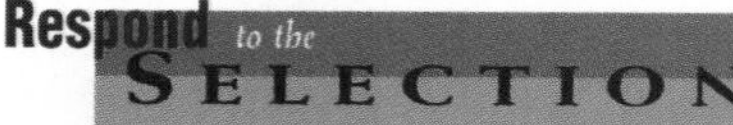

Respond to the SELECTION

Discuss with one or two peers what cause you might be willing to risk your life for.

Investigate, Inquire, Imagine

Recall: GATHERING FACTS → **Interpret:** FINDING MEANING

1a. What were the marks on the knight's shield?
2a. What was the symbol the knight wore on his chest?
3a. On what adventure was the knight sent? Who sent the knight on this mission?

1b. What does these signs suggest about the knight?
2b. How does this knight represent holiness?
3b. What does the knight hope to prove by this feat?

Analyze: TAKING THINGS APART → **Synthesize:** BRINGING THINGS TOGETHER

4a. What do you learn about the knight in each stanza?

4b. What does the knight hope to accomplish?

Evaluate: MAKING JUDGMENTS → **Extend:** CONNECTING IDEAS

5a. Evaluate the character of this knight.

5b. Compare this knight to the knight described by Chaucer in the prologue to *The Canterbury Tales.*

Understanding Literature

SOURCE. Review the definition of **source** in Literary Tools on page 296. To write *The Fœrie Queene,* Spenser drew upon materials from medieval romance. Read the definitions of *chivalry, courtly love,* and *romance* in the Handbook of Literary Terms and discuss the romance elements, or motifs, used by Spenser in the selection.

ALLITERATION. Review the definition for **alliteration** in the Handbook of Literary Terms and the chart you made for Literary Tools on page 296. What examples of alliteration did you find in the selection?

ANSWERS FOR INVESTIGATE, INQUIRE AND IMAGINE

RECALL

1a. There were dents on the shield from past battles.
2a. He wore a red cross on his chest.
3a. The knight was sent to kill a dragon by his queen, Gloriana, the "Glorious Queen of Faerie Lond."

INTERPRET

1b. They suggest he is battle worn.
2b. Then knight wears a bloody cross in remembrance of his Lord. He is faithful and true and believes his Lord helps him in his conquests.
3b. The knight hopes to gain glory for himself and win the approval of Gloriana.

ANALYZE

4a. Stanza 1 shows that the knight has been in many battles, is gallant, and is successful at jousts and other challenges. Stanza 2 shows that he is religious and honors the Lord. Stanza 3 shows that he does like earthly glory and hopes to win the grace and worship of Gloriana.

SYNTHESIZE

4b. The knight hopes to achieve success in killing the dragon. This will bring him honor and the approval of Gloriana. He will demonstrate his power and honor his Lord and his queen.

EVALUATE

5a. The knight is gallant, faithful, powerful, and honorable.

EXTEND

5b. Both knights seem to demonstrate the chivalric values.

ANSWERS FOR UNDERSTANDING LITERATURE

SOURCE. Romance elements include the glorification of the knight's skills in battle, the knight's steadfast loyalty, a magical creature such as a dragon, a solemn quest such as the mission to slay the dragon, and the knight's yearning for honor and glory through following the rules of chivalrous behavior.

ALLITERATION. Some examples of alliteration include the following:

"prickling plain," "silver shielde," "dints, deepe," "markes, many," "till, time," "fierce, fitt," "but, brest, bloudie, bore," "deare, dying," sweete sake," "hoe, his helpe he had," and "seeme, solemne sad."

ANSWERS TO INTEGRATING THE LANGUAGE ARTS

Language, Grammar, and Style
Responses will vary.
1. wielded (T)
2. bore (T)
3. appeared (I)
4. went (I)
5. craved (T)

Study and Research
Encourage students to work in groups of six so that more students can have access to school or local library materials, such as general encyclopedias and literary encyclopedias, that share the St. George legend. You may wish to expand this activity as indicated in the Motivation section of Individual Learning Strategies.

Speaking and Listening
Students responses to the Reader's Journal activity should provide a good starting point for the preparation of their speeches. Refer them to the Language Arts Survey 4.15, "Giving a Speech," for help in preparing and for some helpful delivery tips.

Applied English
Students will have to be imaginative if they choose the first option, but they should still make sure their press release contains pertinent information. If students choose the second choice, they can add a speaking and listening activity by interviewing somebody who was involved with the courageous act or witnessed it.

Writer's Journal

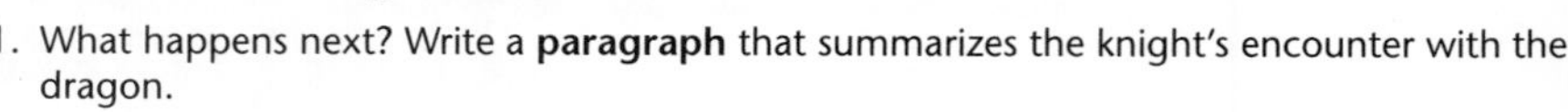

1. What happens next? Write a **paragraph** that summarizes the knight's encounter with the dragon.

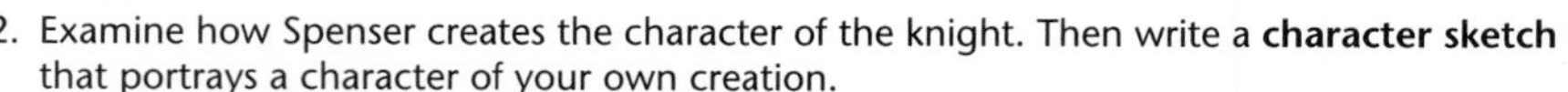

2. Examine how Spenser creates the character of the knight. Then write a **character sketch** that portrays a character of your own creation.
3. Write a **short story** about a courageous act. It might be an act, like slaying a dragon, that takes courage because of physical danger, or it may be an act in which someone courageously overcomes a fear.

Integrating *the* Language Arts

Language, Grammar, and Style

Transitive and Intransitive Verbs. Read the Language Arts Survey 3.61, "Transitive and Intransitive Verbs." Then complete the following sentences (which paraphrase lines from the selection), using either a transitive or an intransitive verb. Write *T* for *transitive* or *I* for *intransitive* at the end of the sentence.

1. Yet until that time, he never ______________ arms.
2. On his chest, he ______________ a bloody cross.
3. The cross ______________ on his shield.
4. He ______________ on a great adventure.
5. He ______________ the grace of the queen.

Study and Research

Understanding Sources. Learn more about the story that forms the background to this selection—St. George slaying the dragon. Find sources that tell this story or images of art that depict this tale. Write a summary of your findings.

Speaking and Listening

Speaking about Courage. Prepare and give a speech on courage to your classmates. Explain what courage means to you or try to encourage others to be courageous. Use examples from your own life or examples you have seen in others to illustrate your points.

Applied English

Writing a Press Release. Review the information in the Language Arts Survey 6.9, "Delivering a Press Release." Then write a press release about one of the following:

- the slaying of the dragon by the knight
- a courageous act performed by someone in your school or community

"The Passionate Shepherd to His Love"

BY CHRISTOPHER MARLOWE

About the AUTHOR

Christopher Marlowe (1564–1593) was a contemporary of Shakespeare's (born two months before him). He was the son of a shoemaker and received a scholarship to attend Cambridge, where he was granted a degree only after some controversy over his plan to go to Reims, the center of Catholic opposition to Queen Elizabeth and the Church of England. While at Cambridge, he wrote the famous play *Tamburlaine,* which dramatizes the adventures of a fourteenth-century Mongol chieftain and conqueror of much of the known world. He introduced to the English theater the use of **blank verse,** which was well-suited to projection from the stage.

Marlowe's life was a turbulent one. Only six years after his early success with *Tamburlaine,* he was killed by a dagger thrust in a brawl over a tavern bill. During the six years before his death, he wrote five more plays, including a sequel to *Tamburlaine,* two major tragedies, and a chronicle history play.

About the SELECTION

"The Passionate Shepherd to His Love" is a plea from the speaker to his beloved. The shepherd invites his beloved to come live with him. Several poets wrote responses to this lyric invitation. Marlowe wrote this poem in iambic tetrameter—a simple, natural meter—to give the poem a simplicity of expression that mirrors its subject.

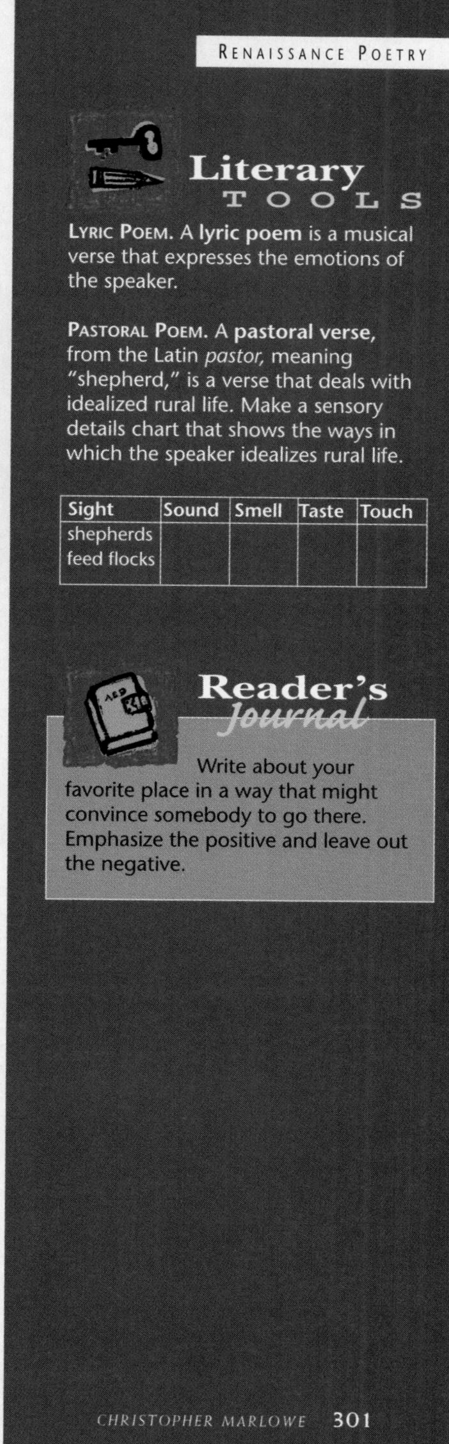

Literary TOOLS

LYRIC POEM. A **lyric poem** is a musical verse that expresses the emotions of the speaker.

PASTORAL POEM. A **pastoral verse,** from the Latin *pastor,* meaning "shepherd," is a verse that deals with idealized rural life. Make a sensory details chart that shows the ways in which the speaker idealizes rural life.

Sight	Sound	Smell	Taste	Touch
shepherds feed flocks				

Reader's Journal

Write about your favorite place in a way that might convince somebody to go there. Emphasize the positive and leave out the negative.

ADDITIONAL RESOURCES

UNIT 4 RESOURCE BOOK
- Selection Worksheet 4.4
- Selection Check Test 4.4.9
- Selection Test 4.4.10
- Language, Grammar, and Style Resource 3.17
- Study and Research Resource 5.4

GRAPHIC ORGANIZER

Sight
shepherds feed flocks
shallow rivers with waterfalls
pretty lambs
buckles of gold
coral clasps and amber studs
shepherd swains dancing

Sound
melodious birds singing madrigals
shepherd swains sing

Smell
beds of roses and fragrant posies

Touch
gown of wool
slippers against the cold

READER'S JOURNAL

Ask students to think of counter arguments that they might offer if somebody were to point out drawbacks to the place they choose.

VOCABULARY FROM THE SELECTION

madrigal
swain

GOALS/OBJECTIVES

Studying this lesson will enable students to
- enjoy reading a pastoral poem
- describe the characteristics of pastoral poetry and identify pastoral poems as they encounter them in their reading
- define *lyric poem* and identify the emotions of a speaker
- distinguish between declarative and imperative sentences
- create a classification scheme for poems they have read
- prepare and deliver a speech on land development

ANSWERS TO GUIDED READING QUESTIONS

1. The shepherd wants his beloved to move to the countryside and live with him. He promises that together they will enjoy the many pleasures of living amidst nature.

INDIVIDUAL LEARNING STRATEGIES

Enrichment
Ask students to imagine that they are trying to convince someone to move to their neighborhood. What would they tell the person about the neighborhood to make it seem like an attractive place to live? Students who have access to a video camera may want to make a narrated videotape showing favorite places and activities. Other students may present their neighborhoods through drama, artwork, poetry, or narrative writing.

English Language Learning
Point out to students the following words and expressions that are used in ways that might be unfamiliar to modern readers:
prove—learn by experiencing
steepy—high
posy—small bunch of flowers
move—persuade

Reading Proficiency
Students may benefit from hearing this poem read aloud. Play a recording of the poem from the Audio Library. Tell students to follow along with the text of the poem as they listen. Then tell students to go back and read the poem on their own.

Special Needs
Explain that Elizabethan poetry often uses word order that sounds unnatural to modern ears. Help students to locate the subject and the verb in each sentence of the poem. Then ask students to work in small groups to rewrite the lines as sentences using standard, contemporary word order.

Motivation
Students may enjoy working in pairs to prepare dramatic oral interpretations of this poem and the one that follows it, Raleigh's "The Nymph's Reply to the Shepherd." Encourage pairs of students to work together in preparing their presentations, and tell them to use their imaginations to capture different aspects and motivations of the shepherd and his beloved.

The Hireling Shepherd, c.1800s. William Holman Hunt. Manchester City Art Gallery.

CHRISTOPHER MARLOWE

Come live with me and be my love,
And we will all the pleasures prove
That valleys, groves, hills, and fields,
Woods, or steepy mountain yields.

And we will sit upon the rocks,
Seeing the shepherds feed their flocks,
By shallow rivers to whose falls
Melodious birds sing madrigals.

What does the shepherd want? What does he promise in the first stanza?

Words for Everyday Use

mad • ri •gal (má dri gəl) *n.*, song, often in several parts. *The group sang a lovely four-part madrigal written in the sixteenth century.*

And I will make thee beds of roses
And a thousand fragrant posies,
A cap of flowers, and a kirtle[1]
Embroidered all with leaves of myrtle;[2]

A gown made of the finest wool
Which from our pretty lambs we pull;
Fair lined slippers for the cold,
With buckles of the purest gold;

A belt of straw and ivy buds,
With coral clasps and amber studs:
And if these pleasures may thee move,
Come live with me, and be my love.

What gifts does the shepherd promise? Are his promises realistic?

The shepherds' swains shall dance and sing
For thy delight each May morning:
If these delights thy mind may move,
Then live with me and be my love. ■

1. **kirtle.** Woman's dress
2. **myrtle.** Type of plant with evergreen leaves and white or pink flowers

Words For Everyday Use

swain (swān) *n.*, country youth, especially a shepherd. *The speaker in this pastoral poem is a swain who appreciates the natural beauty around him as he tends his sheep.*

Respond *to the* Selection

Explain whether the life the speaker describes is appealing to you.

ArtNote

The Hireling Shepherd, c.1800s. William Holman Hunt.

William Holman Hunt (1827–1910) was one of three founding members of the Pre-Raphaelite Brotherhood in England. Like pastoral poets who idealized the simple, rustic life of the peasant, members of the Pre-Raphaelite Brotherhood had an exalted view of certain fifteenth-century painters who predated Raphael (1483–1520). They saw the pre-Raphaelites' style as being passionate and honest, with meticulous attention to detail. This detailed, realistic style is exemplified in *The Hireling Shepherd,* as is Hunt's desire to tell a rich story on the canvas. What aspects of the painting idealize the life of a shepherd?

ANSWERS TO GUIDED READING QUESTIONS

1. The shepherd promises to make his beloved such gifts as a bed of roses, an embroidered dress, a wool gown, beautiful slippers, and a belt. Some of these things are possible, although he mentions expensive and rare materials such as gold and coral, which most shepherds would not have.

RESPOND TO THE SELECTION

Ask students whether they think the shepherd has given a com-plete description of life in the countryside. Suggest that they assume the role of the beloved and create a list of questions to ask to round out the picture.

SELECTION CHECK TEST 4.4.9 WITH ANSWERS

Checking Your Reading

1. What does the speaker ask his love to do? **He asks his love to live with him.**
2. Where does the speaker say they will sit? **They will sit on rocks by rivers.**
3. What does the speaker promise to make of roses? **He promises beds of roses.**
4. What will he make a gown of? **He will make a gown of lambs' wool.**
5. What will the shepherds' swains do? **They will dance and sing.**

Literary Tools

1. What is a lyric poem? **A lyric poem is a musical verse that expresses emotions.**
2. What does the Latin word pastor mean in English? **It means *shepherd.***
3. What is a pastoral poem? **A pastoral poem idealizes rural life.**

ANSWERS FOR INVESTIGATE, INQUIRE AND IMAGINE

RECALL

1a. He refers to valleys, groves, hills, woods, and mountains.

2a. He promises gifts of flowers and handmade clothing.

3a. References to spring include singing birds (line 8), blooming flowers (lines 9–11), and mornings in May (line 22).

INTERPRET

1b. They delights the senses with their beauty.

2b. Perhaps he does not feel comfortable speaking directly about his feelings, or perhaps he thinks his beloved is the kind of person who will be impressed by gifts and signs of material riches.

3b. Spring is a metaphor for youth. It suggests that the love of the shepherd will live forever and that they will both be young and happy forever.

ANALYZE

4a. The shepherd promises his love beds of roses, fragrant posies, a cap, and a kirtle. He will give her a gown, slippers, and a belt. They will enjoy the beautiful countryside and be entertained by the local people.

SYNTHESIZE

4b. The shepherd may be nothing but a smooth talker. On the other hand, he may be sincerely enthusiastic about his future life with the woman he loves.

EVALUATE

5a. Some students may say that the shepherd's promise that they will enjoy nature together may be realistic, but that the promise of expensive gifts may not be realistic.

EXTEND

5b. The speaker of this poem has not yet attained his love, but he is very confident that he will, unlike the speaker of "Whoso List to Hunt," who is worn from his efforts to win his beloved.

INVESTIGATE, Inquire, Imagine

Recall: GATHERING FACTS

1a. To what elements of nature does Marlowe refer in the first stanza?

2a. What possessions will the speaker give to his beloved?

3a. What references are made to spring in the poem?

→ **Interpret:** FINDING MEANING

1b. How do these elements of nature give pleasure to people?

2b. Why might the speaker try to persuade his sweetheart with promises of gifts instead of with professions of his love?

3b. What is the significance of spring in this poem?

Analyze: TAKING THINGS APART

4a. What promises does the shepherd make to his beloved?

→ **Synthesize:** BRINGING THINGS TOGETHER

4b. How would you describe the character of the speaker?

Evaluate: MAKING JUDGMENTS

5a. Do you think the speaker's promises are realistic? Why or why not?

→ **Extend:** CONNECTING IDEAS

5b. Compare the speaker of this poem with speaker in "Whoso List to Hunt."

Understanding Literature

LYRIC POEM. Review the definition for **lyric poem** in the Literary Tools on page 301. What emotions does the speaker express?

PASTORAL POEM. Review the definition for **pastoral poem** in the Handbook of Literary Terms and the chart you made for Literary Tools on page 301. What idea does the shepherd hope to convey about pastoral life?

ANSWERS FOR UNDERSTANDING LITERATURE

LYRIC POEM. The speaker expresses his devotion and love for his beloved. He expresses delight in hopes of sharing that feeling with his beloved.

PASTORAL VERSE. The speaker hopes to suggest that life in the country is perfect and idyllic. He and his beloved will be very happy in this life, or so he would like her to think.

Writer's Journal

1. Choose a mood, such as joy, hope, fear, or sorrow. Then create a list of **images** that help create that mood in a reader.
2. Write a **pastoral poem** or a poem that idealizes a favorite place, even if it not rural.
3. Write a **poem** or **letter** in response to the shepherd. In your response, explain why you decided as you did.

Integrating *the* Language Arts

Language, Grammar, and Style

Building Sentences. Read the Language Arts Survey 3.17, "Functions of Sentences." Classify as either declarative or imperative each of the following lines from the poem. (Note: Some of the lines were not written by Marlowe as complete sentences, but they appear as complete sentences here. The brackets around periods indicate that they are not part of the original work.)

1. Come live with me and be my love[.]
2. And we will sit upon the rocks[.]
3. Melodious birds sing madrigals.
4. The shepherds' swains shall dance and sing[.]
5. Then live with me and be my love.

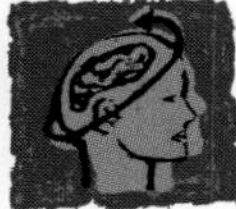

Critical Thinking

Classifying Poetry. Read the Language Arts Survey 5.4, *"Classifying."* Then flip through the poetry you have read so far. How might you classify these poems? Create your own headings. Undoubtedly, there will be some overlap. That is, some poems will fit into two or more categories. Be sure to include at least one example for each category that you create.

Speaking and Listening

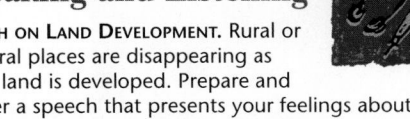

Speech on Land Development. Rural or pastoral places are disappearing as open land is developed. Prepare and deliver a speech that presents your feelings about this topic. Do you think it is important to save some open spaces? Do you think that a new school, mall, or housing area is more important?

ANSWERS TO INTEGRATING THE LANGUAGE ARTS

Language, Grammar, and Style
1. imperative
2. declarative
3. declarative
4. declarative
5. imperative

Critical Thinking
Possible categories include the following: poems about romantic love, poems about unrequited love, poems that use personification, poems dominated by sensory imagery, and poems that draw on earlier sources. You might also encourage students to classify some of the books they have read in the past year. If students tend to read mostly one genre, such as mysteries or science fiction, what subcategories can they devise to classify these books within this genre?

Speaking and Listening
Students might choose to speak about their feelings on this topic in general, or they might do some research and use specific examples of the fight for open space. Refer students to the Language Arts Survey 4.15, "Giving a Speech," for tips that will help them with their preparation and delivery.

ADDITIONAL RESOURCES

UNIT 4 RESOURCE BOOK
- Selection Worksheet 4.5
- Selection Check Test 4.4.11
- Selection Test 4.4.12
- Language, Grammar, and Style Resource 3.87
- Study and Research Resource 5.10

GRAPHIC ORGANIZER

See
flowers fade
fields yield to winter
gowns, etc., break and wither
Hear
Philomel has become dumb.
honeyed tongue
Touch
rocks grow cold

READER'S JOURNAL

You might suggest a specific issue (e.g., the condition of the environment by the year 3000, whether or not they believe in love at first sight) and ask students to write both cynical and hopeful thoughts about the topic.

VOCABULARY FROM THE SELECITON

wanton
gall

Literary TOOLS

METAPHOR. A **metaphor** is a figure of speech in which one thing is spoken or written about as if it were another. This figure of speech invites the reader to make a comparison between the two things. The two "things" involved are the writer's actual subject, the *tenor* of the metaphor, and another thing to which the subject is likened, the *vehicle* of the metaphor. Look for metaphors as you read this poem.

IMAGE. An **image** is a word or phrase that names something that can be seen, heard, felt, tasted, or smelled. Raleigh uses images that alter the images used in Marlowe's "The Passionate Shepherd to His Love." Use a sensory details chart to keep track of the images used by Raleigh.

See	
Hear	Philomel has become dumb.
Smell	
Taste	
Touch	

Reader's journal

Explain whether you think you are a cynical or an optimistic person.

"The Nymph's Reply to the Shepherd"

BY SIR WALTER RALEIGH

About the AUTHOR

Sir Walter Raleigh (1552–1618) led an astonishingly full and varied life as a soldier, explorer, courtier, philosopher, colonist, poet, student of science, and historian. His accomplishments included establishing the Roanoke colony in Virginia, importing the potato to Ireland, and introducing the poet Edmund Spenser to the English court. Raleigh was a favorite of Queen Elizabeth, and he was known at court for his flamboyant dress, his enthusiasm for life, and his quick temper. Among his literary works is "The Ocean to Cynthia," a five-hundred-line poem that exists only in fragments.

Raleigh did not find favor with Elizabeth's successor, King James, who sent him to the Tower of London, where he was imprisoned until his execution for treason in 1618. While incarcerated, Sir Raleigh wrote his long, unfinished *History of the World,* which begins with the creation of the world and breaks off at 168 BC.

About the SELECTION

Written in response to "The Passionate Shepherd to His Love," by Christopher Marlowe, this selection is a mirror image of Marlowe's poem in almost all its characteristics. **"The Nymph's Reply to the Shepherd,"** like Marlowe's piece, makes many references to nature; it also has the same rhyme scheme and meter of Marlowe's poem. There the resemblance ends because, as you will read, Raleigh's speaker is thoughtful and resigned, rather than passionate. This piece is one of Raleigh's best-known shorter poems.

GOALS/OBJECTIVES

Studying this unit will enable students to
- enjoy reading a poem written in response to another poem
- define *metaphor* and identify metaphors in a poem
- define *image* and identify imagery and classify it by the sense to which it appeals
- use commas properly
- compare and contrast two speakers
- interview others and classify their views
- write a persuasive essay

The Nymph's Reply to the Shepherd

SIR WALTER RALEIGH

If all the world and love were young,
And truth in every shepherd's tongue,
These pretty pleasures might me move
To live with thee and be thy love.

Time drives the flocks from field to fold
When rivers rage and rocks grow cold,
and Philomel[1] becometh dumb;
The rest complains of cares to come.
The flowers do fade, and wanton fields
To wayward winter reckoning yields;
A honey tongue, a heart of gall,
Is fancy's spring, but sorrow's fall.

What does the nymph believe comes of the "pretty pleasures" of the world and of love?

Thy gowns, thy shoes, thy beds of roses,
Thy cap, thy kirtle, and thy posies
Soon break, soon wither, soon forgotten—
In folly ripe, in reason rotten.

Thy belt of straw and ivy buds,
Thy coral clasps and amber studs,
All these in me no means can move
To come to thee and be thy love.

But could youth last and love still breed,
Had joys no date nor age no need,
Then these delights my mind might move
To live with thee and be thy love. ■

What would change the nymph's mind about living with the shepherd and being his love?

1. **Philomel.** A *philomel* is a nightingale, so called after Philomela, a character in Greek and Roman mythology who was changed into a nightingale by the gods.

WORDS FOR EVERYDAY USE

wan • ton (wän´ tən) *adj.*, luxuriant. *The lawn in front of the abandoned house had not been mowed for months, and wanton tufts of green grass reached out through the gate.*

gall (gôl) *n.*, bitterness. *How sad that the sweetness of their friendship was turned to gall by that silly argument!*

ANSWERS TO GUIDED READING QUESTIONS

1. The nymph believes that the "pretty pleasures" of the world and love fade with time.
2. She implies that if they could both stay young and in live forever, then she might consider living with the shepherd and being his love.

INDIVIDUAL LEARNING STRATEGIES

MOTIVATION
Students may especially enjoy the Speaking and Listening Activity as it presents them with a chance to become involved with the community. Encourage them to see the benefits of interacting with older members of the community.

ENGLISH LANGUAGE LEARNING
Point out to students that Raleigh uses a metaphor involving seasons in this poem. Discuss the symbolic meaning of the seasons used in this poem.

READING PROFICIENCY
Point out to students that Raleigh alludes to Marlowe's "The Passionate Shepherd to His Love" in this poem—in fact, his poem is a direct response to Marlowe's work.

SPECIAL NEEDS
Students may have difficulty understanding this poem unless they directly compare it to "A Passionate Shepherd to His Love." Have students create a chart with two columns. Have students list in the first column the arguments the shepherd presents to support his position that his beloved should live with him. Students should list one reason per stanza. Then, in the second column, students should list how the nymph responds to each of the shepherd's arguments. Pair special needs students with others in the class for additional help with this activity.

ENRICHMENT
Letters to the editor are often replies to what someone else has said or written. Interested students may locate such letters in a newspaper and analyze them in light of the following questions.

- What is the argument or point of view presented by each side?
- Has the writer of the response clearly understood the other side of the argument?

INDIVIDUAL LEARNING STRATEGIES (CONT.)

- Has the writer given a logical response to his or her opponent?
- Can you see any common ground between the two sides? What suggestions might you make to these people to bring about a reconciliation?

RESPOND TO THE SELECTION

Have students recall times in their own lives when they were very excited about something but a person they cared about showed no interest. How did they respond to the lack of interest? Were they able to overcome it?

SELECTION CHECK TEST 4.4.11 WITH ANSWERS

Checking Your Reading

1. The speaker might be moved if what were in every shepherd's tongue? **She might be moved if truth were in every shepherd's tongue – if she could believe him.**
2. What drives the flocks from field to fold? Time drives the flocks from field to fold.
3. What does the speaker say happens to gifts such as gowns, shoes, and roses? **She says they soon wither or break, and are forgotten.**
4. What effect to these gifts have on the speaker? **They do not move her.**
5. What might happen if "youth could last and love still breed"? **She might be moved to live with him and be his love.**

ANSWERS FOR INVESTIGATE, INQUIRE AND IMAGINE

Recall

1a. If youth and love were eternal and unchanging, then the nymph might consider the shepherd's offer.
2a. She says beautiful clothes and flowers can make a person happy only for a short time.
3a. She has been promised flowers, gowns, shoes, and other fancy articles of clothing.

Interpret

1b. She says that if there were "truth in every shepherd's tongue," she might decide to live with him; she implies that the shepherd is not being truthful.
2b. Some things that seem pleasurable will turn out to be trivial inducements when evaluated rationally. She means that only a fool would believe and be tempted by the things the shepherd has promised.
3b. She knows that these gifts could not give her lasting happiness.

Respond *to the* Selection

If you were the shepherd, how would you feel upon hearing the nymph's reply? Write about your response as though you were talking to a friend.

Investigate, Inquire, *Imagine*

Recall: Gathering Facts → **Interpret:** Finding Meaning

1a. What would cause the nymph to accept the shepherd's offer?
1b. What in the first stanza clues the reader about the nymph's attitude toward the shepherd?

2a. In the fourth stanza, what does the nymph say about beautiful clothes and flowers?
2b. Why might some things be "in folly ripe" but "in reason rotten"? What does the nymph mean by this?

3a. What material possessions have been promised to the nymph?
3b. Why is the nymph not persuaded by the idea of fancy gifts?

Analyze: Taking Things Apart → **Synthesize:** Bringing Things Together

4a. What attitude is expressed in stanza 1? What attitude is expressed in 6?
4b. Although the wording of the first and last stanzas is similar, the tone or attitude of the speaker is different. Explain how Raleigh creates the difference in tone.

Evaluate: Making Judgments → **Extend:** Connecting Ideas

5a. Would you say that the speaker in Sir Walter Raleigh's poem is idealistic and romantic? Explain your reasoning.
5b. Compare and contrast the attitude of the nymph to the attitude of the shepherd in Marlowe's poem.

Understanding *Literature*

Metaphor. Review the definition for **metaphor** in the Literary Tools on page 306. Identify two metaphors in this poem. How do these metaphors help to illustrate the poem's theme?

Image. Review the definition for **image** in the Handbook of Literary Terms and the sensory details chart you made for Literary Tools on page 306. Contrast three images as presented by Marlowe and by Raleigh.

ANSWERS FOR INVESTIGATE, INQUIRE AND IMAGINE (cont.)

Analyze

4a In stanza 1, the nymph seems disgusted with the shepherd. In stanza 6, she seems sad that the world is not the perfect place that the shepherd has imagined.

Synthesize

4b. In stanza 1, the nymph suggests that the shepherd is not truthful. She seems scornful of the "if" she suggests. The "if" suggests a possibility. By saying, "But could," she seems resigned to the fact that such dreams are not possible, yet she seems regretful that the world is not as simple and lovely as the shepherd says it is.

Continued on page 309

WRITER'S JOURNAL

1. Write a **note** to the shepherd. Share your sympathy or advice with him upon hearing what the nymph had to say.
2. Write a **scene** that leads up to the exchange between the shepherd and the nymph. Describe the scenery and what the two characters are doing before the shepherd speaks.
3. Brainstorm a list of symbols for love, such as roses or rings. Then, write a **summary** of a short story in which a symbol is used in both its traditional sense and in a cynical way.

Integrating *the* LANGUAGE ARTS

Language, Grammar, and Style

BUILDING SENTENCES. Read the Language Arts Survey 3.87, "Commas." Add commas as necessary in each of the following sentences.

1. Shepherds may use dogs flutes and prods to help them in their work.
2. A philomel is a nightingale but Philomela is the name of a woman from Greek mythology.
3. Sir Walter Raleigh was a poet historian and adventurer.
4. Raleigh was helped by Queen Elizabeth and he also had a friend in Prince Henry the son of Elizabeth's successor.
5. Gowns posies and belts of straw did not convince the nymph to come live with the shepherd.

Critical Thinking

COMPARING AND CONTRASTING. Read the Language Arts Survey 5.10, "Comparing and Contrasting." Make two columns on a piece of paper, one headed *Shepherd* and the other headed *Nymph.* To the left of the columns, write *Compare* and then under that, *Contrast.* Draw lines across your page starting under each of these two words. List the characteristics of each within the boxes of the matrix you have created with these four headings.

	Shepherd	Nymph
Compare		
Contrast		

Speaking and Listening

COMMUNITY ACTIVITY. Visit a nursing home with several of your classmates and interview some of the residents about their experiences in love. (Make sure to check with the nursing home staff first to make sure your questions are appropriate.) As a group, write down descriptions of each of the interviews and categorize individuals as representing either "nymph" attitudes or "shepherd" attitudes about love and romance.

Collaborative Learning

PERSUASION. With a group of your classmates, write a persuasive essay to an imaginary person in an attempt to convince him or her to move to a new place to be near you. First, list some of the advantages of the move. Next, anticipate the person's objections and respond to them. Finally, summarize your strongest arguments in a closing statement.

ANSWERS FOR UNDERSTANDING LITERATURE

METAPHOR. "Time drives the flocks" is a metaphor in which time is likened to a shepherd. This enforces the message of the march of time. The death of flowers and the fields yielding to winter are metaphors for the lost bloom of youth and love. Both metaphors illustrate the theme of the inevitability of time, growing old, and death depriving some of the joy of life.

IMAGE. The shepherd says they will sit on the rocks and watch the shepherds herd flocks while birds sing. The nymph replies that time will drive the flocks from the field, the rocks will grow cold and the birds will become mute. The shepherd offers beds of roses, fragrant posies, and a cap and kirtle embroidered with myrtle. The nymph says these things will break, wither, and be forgotten. The shepherd refers to May mornings as a sign of youth. The nymph replies that love and youth can't last.

ANSWERS TO INTEGRATING THE LANGUAGE ARTS

Language, Grammar, and Style

1. Shepherds may use dogs, flutes, and prods to help them in their work.
2. A philomel is a nightingale, but Philomela is the name of a woman from Greek mythology.
3. Sir Walter Raleigh was a poet, historian, and adventurer.
4. Raleigh was helped by Queen Elizabeth, and he also had a friend in Prince Henry, the son of Elizabeth's successor.
5. Gowns, posies, and belts of straw did not convince the nymph to come live with the shepherd.

Study and Research

Students might note that the poems are alike in that each is addressed to a particular person, uses imagery from nature, and presents an opinion about love. The poems are different in that one expresses a romantic view, while the other expresses a cynical view.

Speaking and Listening

Refer students to the Language Arts Survey 4.14, "Conducting an Interview," for help in preparing and for tips about conducting interviews. The Motivation section of Individual Learning Strategies also contains information that might help students to successfully complete this activity.

ANSWERS FOR INVESTIGATE, INQUIRE AND IMAGINE (CONT. FROM PAGE 308)

EVALUATE

5a. No; the knowledge that she must grow old someday and that love sometimes fades makes the nymph cynical.

EXTEND

5b. The shepherd in Marlowe's poem is idealistic, hopeful, and sure of himself. The nymph is equally sure in her response, but is cynical and sad.

ADDITIONAL RESOURCES

UNIT 4 RESOURCE BOOK

- Selection Worksheet 4.6
- Selection Check Test 4.4.13
- Selection Test 4.4.14
- Reading Resource 1.12
- Language, Grammar, and Style Resource 3.29
- Study and Research Resource 5.20

GRAPHIC ORGANIZER

AIM. Words included in the cluster chart might include "doubt of future foes," "snares," "falsehood now doth flow," "subjects faith doth ebb," "pride," "ambition blinds," "daughter of debate," "discord doth sow," and "poll their tops that seek such change."

READER'S JOURNAL

Encourage students to explore different examples of such times, such as when concern about a test on Monday makes them enjoy their weekends less.

As an alternate activity, you might ask students to write about how they would feel if they were a presidential candidate toward the other candidates.

VOCABULARY FROM THE SELECTION

brook
guile
shun

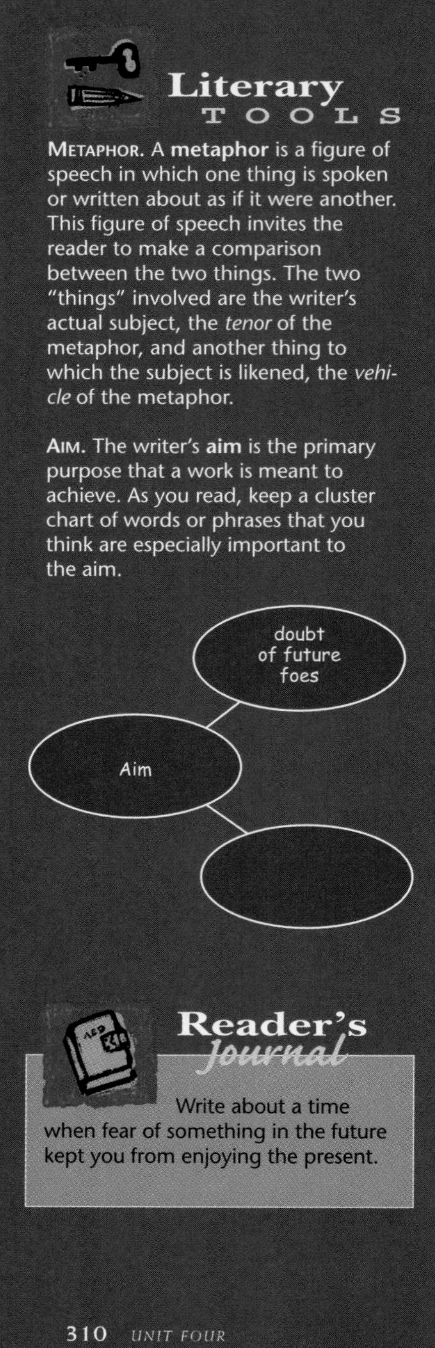

Literary TOOLS

METAPHOR. A **metaphor** is a figure of speech in which one thing is spoken or written about as if it were another. This figure of speech invites the reader to make a comparison between the two things. The two "things" involved are the writer's actual subject, the *tenor* of the metaphor, and another thing to which the subject is likened, the *vehicle* of the metaphor.

AIM. The writer's **aim** is the primary purpose that a work is meant to achieve. As you read, keep a cluster chart of words or phrases that you think are especially important to the aim.

Reader's Journal

Write about a time when fear of something in the future kept you from enjoying the present.

"The *Doubt* of Future Foes"

BY QUEEN ELIZABETH I

About the AUTHOR

Queen Elizabeth I (1533–1603) was so powerful a cultural influence that her time is now commonly referred to as the Elizabethan Era. She was the subject of many works of art, as well as the creator of some. She was well educated, in both Greek and Latin, and she read widely in the classics. Because Elizabeth was proud of these talents, she enjoyed displaying them in her speeches, poetry, and translations of biblical and classical prose and poetry. Her own poetry is about actual events from her life. Its **tone** is vigorous and somewhat moralistic, and much of it is written in **poulter's measure,** which makes use of alternating iambic hexameter and iambic heptameter couplets. For more information on Elizabeth and her reign, see the unit introduction (pages 284–285).

About the SELECTION

This poem describes Elizabeth's concerns about being overthrown and delivers a vow to defend herself and her court. Specifically, **"The Doubt of Future Foes"** concerns the queen's suspicion of her Roman Catholic cousin Mary Stuart, Queen of Scotland, who sought refuge in England from rebellious subjects. Elizabeth had good reason to "fear" Mary as a "future foe" because there were several Catholic conspiracies to put Mary on the throne of England. (See the unit introduction, page 285.)

GOALS/OBJECTIVES

Studying this unit will enable students to

- empathize with a speaker's feelings of betrayal and confidence
- analyze a poem to determine its aim
- identify and interpret metaphors in a poem
- recognize and correct double negatives
- research Elizabeth I and Mary, Queen of Scots
- develop critical questions when reading
- role play a conversation between historical figure

Portrait of Mary Stuart,
(1542–1587), c.1800s. French Artist.
Musée des Beaux-Arts, Blois, France.

The *Doubt* of Future Foes

Queen Elizabeth I

The doubt[1] of future foes exiles my present joy,
And wit me warns to shun such snares as threaten mine annoy.[2]
For falsehood now doth flow, and subject faith doth ebb,[3]
Which would not be, if reason ruled or wisdom weaved the web.
But clouds of toys[4] untried do cloak aspiring minds,
Which turn to rain of late repent, by course of changèd winds.
The top of hope supposed, the root of ruth[5] will be,
And fruitless all their graffèd[6] guiles, as shortly ye shall see.
The dazzled eyes with pride, which great ambition blinds,
Shall be unsealed by worthy wights[7] whose foresight falsehood finds.
The daughter of debate,[8] that eke discord doth sow
Shall reap no gain where former rule hath taught still peace to grow.
No foreign banished wight shall anchor in this port,
Our realm it brooks no stranger's force, let them elsewhere resort.
Our rusty sword with rest, shall first his edge employ
To poll[9] their tops that seek such change and gape for joy. ■

Who shall reap no gain from causing discord?

1. **doubt.** Fear
2. **threaten . . . annoy.** Threaten to harm me
3. **falsehood . . . ebb.** Falsehood is rising, and faith, or loyalty, is falling.
4. **toys.** Tricks
5. **ruth.** Sorrow
6. **graffèd.** Grafted; added or taken on
7. **wights.** People
8. **daughter of debate.** The *daughter of debate* was a name given to Mary Stuart because she was the center of many conspiracies.
9. **poll.** Cut off

Words for Everyday Use

shun (shun) *vt.,* keep away from; avoid. *Bill's doctor told him to limit his cholesterol; now he shuns fried foods.*
guile (gīl) *n.,* deception. *The babysitter wondered what clever guiles the children would use to avoid going to bed on time.*
brook (bro͞ok) *vt.,* put up with. *My sister will brook no interruptions when she is practicing her violin.*

ANSWERS TO GUIDED READING QUESTIONS

1. The "daughter of debate," Mary, Queen of Scots, shall reap no gain from causing discord.

INDIVIDUAL LEARNING STRATEGIES

Motivation
Students might especially enjoy the opportunity to role play the part of a historical character in the Speaking and Listening & Collaborative Learning activity. You may wish to provide students with some examples of historical enemies and let them choose from your list.

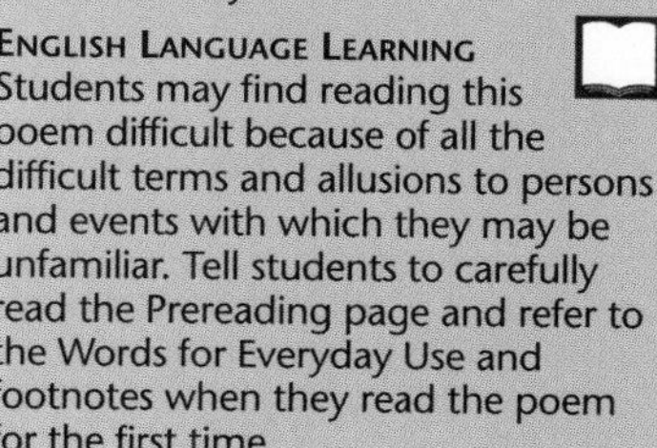

English Language Learning
Students may find reading this poem difficult because of all the difficult terms and allusions to persons and events with which they may be unfamiliar. Tell students to carefully read the Prereading page and refer to the Words for Everyday Use and footnotes when they read the poem for the first time.

Reading Proficiency
The poem contains many tricky vocabulary words and examples of word play. Advise students to read slowly, tackling one sentence at a time. Have them take notes as they read, translating each line into simpler English.

Special Needs
Students may have a very difficult time with this poem. Tell them to focus on responding to the Recall questions in the Investigate, Inquire, and Imagine section.

Enrichment
In research papers or oral reports, students can compare Elizabeth's attitudes toward her potential foes with those of Cæsar in Shakespeare's Julius Cæsar.

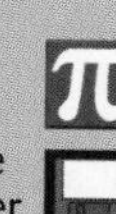

SELECTION CHECK TEST 4.4.13 WITH ANSWERS

Checking Your Reading

1. While loyalty ebbs, what is flowing? **Falsehood is flowing.**
2. Who is blinded by great ambition? **Those who plot against her are.**
3. Who is the "daughter of debate"? **This is her cousin, Mary Stuart.**
4. Why is Elizabeth concerned about this person? **There were many plots to overthrow Elizabeth and put Mary on the throne.**
5. What point does Elizabeth make to her enemies? **She warns them to stay away.**

Vocabulary in Context
Fill each blank with the most appropriate word from the Words for Everyday Use. You may have to change the tense of the word.

shun guile brook poll

Continued on page 312

RESPOND TO THE SELECTION

Students might refer to the poem or to the biographical information about Elizabeth when responding to this question.

ANSWERS FOR INVESTIGATE, INQUIRE AND IMAGINE

Recall

1a. Her own intelligence, or :wit," helps her to avoid these traps.
2a. Their loyalty to her is decreasing.
3a. She calls it a "port." She will not allow her opponents to seek shelter in England. She tells them to seek another "resort" in line 14.

Interpret

1b. Some of the people around her are planning "toys" or tricks to seize power from her and give the throne to Mary Stuart.
2b. She is confident that Mary will not succeed in planting discord in a country where the subjects are used to peace (lines 11 012); she believes she will regain her subjects' loyalty and keep the throne.
3b. Elizabeth thinks that Mary would bring only disorder and conflict to England. It seems a good idea to banish her enemies because they have already succeeded in turning some of her subjects against her.

Analyze

4a. She is intelligent, determined, and self-confident.

Synthesize

4b. Leaders have to be self-confident to inspire confidence in others and to have others follow. Determination is important for accomplishing goals. Intelligence is important for setting and meeting goals, finding solutions to problems, and addressing issues.

Evaluate

5a. *Responses will vary*. Students may say that because of possible treason, beheading is an acceptable punishment. Others may not agree with the death penalty for any reason.

Extend

5b. *Responses will vary.*

Respond *to the* Selection

How do you think Elizabeth would respond to a report of a plot against her?

Investigate, Inquire, Imagine

Recall: Gathering Facts → **Interpret: Finding Meaning**

1a. What warns the queen to avoid the "snares" that may harm her?
2a. According to line 3, how are the feelings of the queen's subjects changing?
3a. What does she call her kingdom in line 13? Will Elizabeth allow her opponents to seek shelter in England?

1b. What are some potential "snares" that may harm the queen?
2b. How do her subjects' feelings make the queen feel about the likelihood of maintaining her position?
3b. How does Elizabeth feel her kingdom would change under the would-be leaders? Is Elizabeth's decision about not allowing her opponents into the country a wise one? Why, or why not?

Analyze: Taking Things Apart → **Synthesize: Bringing Things Together**

4a. What traits of Elizabeth are displayed in this poem?

4b. Why are these traits important in a leader?

Evaluate: Making Judgments → **Extend: Connecting Ideas**

5a. Judge whether the actions Elizabeth describes in lines 15–16 are justified.

5b. Do you agree with what Elizabeth says in lines 15–16? Would your response be different if she were a male leader?

Understanding Literature

Metaphor. Review the definition for **metaphor** in the Handbook of Literary Terms. Look at line 3. What subtle metaphor is the queen using in reference to her situation? Does this metaphor help to illustrate the situation? How?

Aim. Review the definition for **aim** in Literary Tools on page 310. A piece might highlight a certain character, theme, or situation. What is this poem's primary purpose? Does it succeed? If so, how does the poem achieve its purpose?

SELECTION CHECK TEST 4.4.13 WITH ANSWERS (cont. from page 311)

1. Last spring, we **polled** the dead branches from the trees over our house.
2. Mariela **shuns** department stores because she is trying to save money.
3. The coach announced that he would **brook** no insubordination during training.

Literary Tools

1. In the metaphor, "No foreign banished wight shall anchor in this port," what is Elizabeth referring to with the word *port?* **She is referring to England.**
2. In the metaphor, "No foreign banished wight shall anchor in this port," what is the *vehicle* of the metaphor? **The vehicle is *port*.**
3. What is the primary aim of this poem? **Responses will vary. She vows to defend herself and her court, and warns conspirators not to try to overthrow her.**

WRITER'S JOURNAL

1. Write a **paragraph** that summarizes the ideas Elizabeth presents in this poem.
2. Choose a recent or ongoing national or world event. Write a **poem** that expresses your feelings about this event.
3. Imagine that you are either a supporter of the queen or one of her enemies. Write a **speech** to garner support for your side. In your speech, respond to, or address, the ideas Elizabeth presents in this poem.

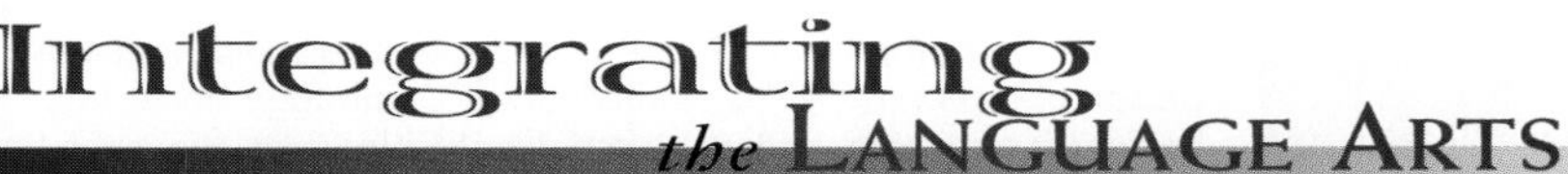

Language, Grammar, and Style

DOUBLE NEGATIVES. Read the Language Arts Survey 3.29, "Working with Negatives and Contractions." Correct the following sentences to avoid double negatives.

1. Queen Elizabeth I was not hardly a pushover.
2. She wouldn't never give up the throne easily.
3. Mary, Queen of Scots, did not have no chance of deceiving the queen of England.
4. Queen Elizabeth I didn't have no friends that she trusted absolutely.
5. None of her subjects never got away with betrayal neither.

Study and Research

RESEARCHING ELIZABETH AND MARY. Read the Language Arts Survey 5.20, "Using Reference Works." Find encyclopedia articles or books about Queen Elizabeth I and Mary, Queen of Scots. Make a brief list describing the major events of each queen's life.

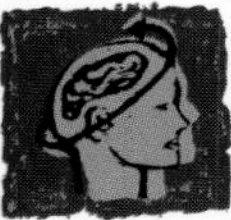

Critical Thinking

QUESTIONING. Read the Language Arts Survey 1.12, "Seeking Knowledge as an Active Reader." Then go to the encyclopedia articles and sources from the Research Skills activity above. Choose an encyclopedia entry or a chapter from a book. On a separate sheet of paper, write six questions to bear in mind as you read one of your sources. Keep the paper beside you as you read.

Speaking and Listening & Collaborative Learning

ROLE-PLAYING. With one of your classmates, choose two characters from history who have been known to be enemies and dramatize a conversation between them.

- Decide upon a setting and a conflict that will be the basis for your role play.
- Establish your character's basic personality and motivation.
- Write a loose dialogue from which you can ad lib.

ANSWERS FOR UNDERSTANDING LITERATURE

METAPHOR. The metaphor compares the loyalty and disloyalty of her subjects to ocean tides going in and out. Because the loyalties are constantly changing, the metaphor seems apt.

AIM. The aim of this poem is to describe the political situation Elisabeth is dealing with and to voice her determination to overcome her enemies. The poem succeeds through its unmistakable tone of determination and self-confidence.

INTEGRATING THE LANGUAGE ARTS

Language, Grammar, and Style

1. Queen Elizabeth I was not a pushover.
2. She would never give up the throne easily.
3. Mary, Queen of Scots, had no chance of deceiving the queen of England.
4. Queen Elizabeth I had no friends that she trusted absolutely.
5. None of her subjects ever got away with betrayal, either.

Study and Research

Students may also make an annotated bibliography of various types of reference works. To do this, they should write the title, author, and publication information for each work, followed by a brief description of the information the work contains.

Critical Thinking

Students should prepare six questions, the answers to which are worth knowing and could reasonably be expected to be found in the reference work.

Speaking and Listening & Collaborative Learning

Researching the characters for this role-playing activity is a good opportunity for students to practice the active reading technique. (See the Language Arts Survey 1.12, "Seeking Knowledge as an Active Reader.") Have students list questions about their characters' personalities and histories.

ADDITIONAL RESOURCES

Unit 4 Resource Book
- Selection Worksheet 4.7
- Selection Check Test 4.4.15
- Selection Test 4.4.16
- Language, Grammar, and Style Resource 3.7

READER'S JOURNAL

Students might begin by thinking about popular people they have known and then brainstorming a list of their personal qualities. Which of these qualities might make a person respected? Which might not?

VOCABULARY FROM THE SELECTION

beauteous

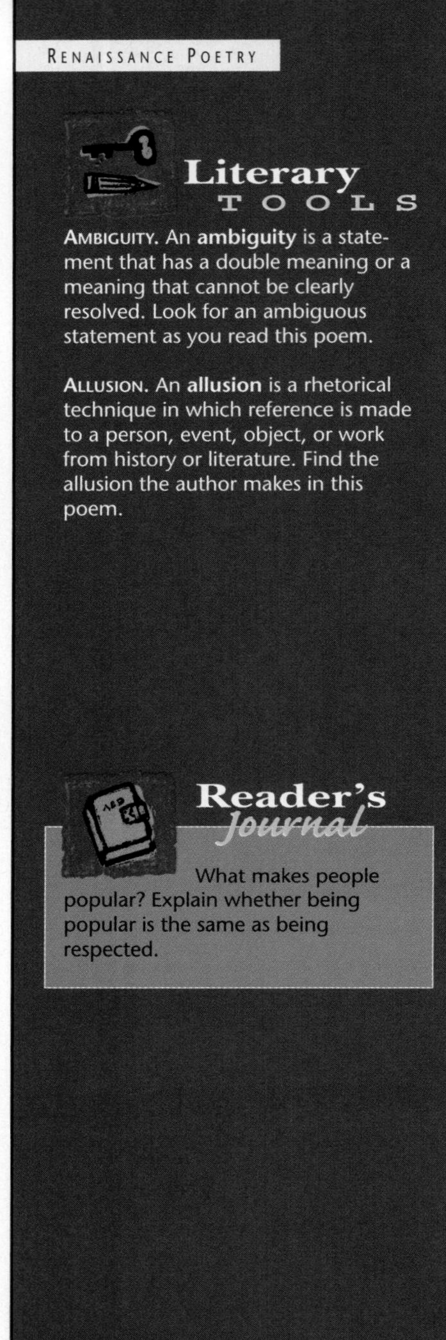

Literary TOOLS

Ambiguity. An **ambiguity** is a statement that has a double meaning or a meaning that cannot be clearly resolved. Look for an ambiguous statement as you read this poem.

Allusion. An **allusion** is a rhetorical technique in which reference is made to a person, event, object, or work from history or literature. Find the allusion the author makes in this poem.

Reader's Journal

What makes people popular? Explain whether being popular is the same as being respected.

"When Thou Must Home to Shades of Underground"

BY THOMAS CAMPION

About the AUTHOR

Thomas Campion (1567–1620) was a true Renaissance man—a person of broad scope. He studied law at Cambridge University, became a physician, and was a scholar of Latin verse. However, he was best known as a writer of songs, for which he composed both music and lyrics.

About the SELECTION

"When Thou Must Home to Shades of Underground" comes from Campion's *A Book of Airs,* published in 1601. The poem is addressed to a woman who has hurt the speaker deeply. He imagines this woman descending after death into the "underground"—the place to which the dead were said to go in Greek and Roman mythology. There the woman is met by the spirits of beautiful women from classical times who gather around to hear stories of masques, revels, and tournaments—stories about the carefree life of a popular, attractive woman of the upper classes.

GOALS/OBJECTIVES

Studying this lesson will enable students to
- experience the speaker's feelings of anguish and betrayal
- define *ambiguity* and identify and interpret ambiguity in a poem
- define *allusion* and identify and understand allusions in a poem
- identify adjectives and the words they modify
- research Iope and Helen and write a summary of their research
- use elements of public speaking to tell a story

Banquet, c.1600s.
Anthonie Palamendesz.

When Thou Must Home to Shades of Underground

Thomas Campion

When thou must home to shades of underground,
And there arrived, a new admired guest,
The <u>beauteous</u> spirits do engirt thee round,
White Iope, blithe Helen,[1] and the rest,
To hear the stories of thy finished love
From that smooth tongue whose music hell can move,

Then wilt thou speak of banqueting delights,
Of masques[2] and revels which sweet youth did make,
Of tourneys and great challenges of knights,
And all these triumphs for thy beauty's sake;
When thou hast told these honors done to thee,
Then tell, Oh tell, how thou didst murther me. ■

What sort of person is the woman addressed in this poem? What sort of life does she lead?

1. **White Iope, blithe Helen.** Spirits of women from Greek and Roman mythology famed for their beauty
2. **masques.** Masked balls, or dances

Words For Everyday Use

beau • te • ous (byōōt´ ē əs) *adj.*, beautiful. *<u>Beauteous</u> Helen of Troy is called "the face that launched a thousand ships" because the men who competed for her love started the Trojan War.*

ANSWER TO GUIDED READING QUESTION

1. She is beautiful and has a sweet voice. She enjoys parties and is sought after by many men.

INDIVIDUAL LEARNING STRATEGIES

Motivation
Campion was a well-known Renaissance writer of songs and music. Locate a CD that contains some examples of Campion's musical work. Once you have found such a CD, play it for students.

English Language Learning
Point out to students that some of the words in this poem are archaic or poetic forms of words. Share with students contemporary forms for these words as follows:
engirt—gather round
wilt—will
tourney—tournament, refers to a medieval sporting event in which knights compete to win the favor of a woman
murther—murder

Reading Proficiency
Have students work in pairs. One student should read a line aloud to the other. The listener should repeat back the line in his or her own words. Each student should take a turn reading a stanza.

Special Needs
Guide students to divide the poem into three meaningful parts after they read: stanza 1 describes what will happen when the woman first arrives in Hades, or the "underground"; the first four lines of stanza 2 tell what she will discuss with the other spirits; and the final couplet tells what the speaker thinks she should tell the other spirits. Then tell students to go back and reread the poem.

Enrichment
Interested students may draw or paint the scene that is described in this poem, depicting its interesting juxtaposition of life and death.

SELECTION CHECK TEST 4.4.15 WITH ANSWERS

Checking Your Reading

1. To what event does the title of this poem refer? **It refers to the woman's death.**
2. Who will sit around her? **Beautiful spirits will sit around her.**
3. What will the woman be asked to do? **She will be asked to tell stories.**
4. What is the woman's life like? **Responses will vary: she is beautiful and privileged, and she attends banquets, tournaments, dances, and revels.**
5. What does the speaker want her to tell? **He wants her to tell how she "murthered me."**

Literary Tools

1. What is an ambiguity? **An ambiguity is a statement that has a double meaning.**

(Continued on page 316)

SELECTION CHECK TEST 4.4.15 WITH ANSWERS (CONT.)

2. How is the last line of the poem an example of an ambiguity? **It claims that the woman "murthered" the speaker, which is not literal but refers to a broken heart.**
3. What is an allusion? **An allusion is a reference to a person, event, object, or work from history or literature.**

RESPOND TO THE SELECTION

Ask students to recall a situation in which they felt some other person was receiving undeserved praise. How did this make them feel? Did they take action? How do they feel about their decision to act or not to act now? Do they believe confronting the woman might help the speaker to feel better?

ANSWERS FOR INVESTIGATE, INQUIRE AND IMAGINE

RECALL

1a. The spirits of other beautiful women of the past will greet her.
2a. He calls it "smooth," and says that the sound of it would stir emotions even in hell.
3a. She tells them stories about all the parties and banquets she attended when she was alive and about all the men who competed for her favor.

INTERPRET

1b. Yes; they will all rush to surround the new arrival and hear her stories.
2b. It suggests that she knows how to use her charm to get what she wants out of people.
3b. She has led a life rich in excitement and glamour, but perhaps poor in sustaining meaningful relationships.

ANALYZE

4a. Others see the subject of the poem as a smooth storyteller; a beauty; a popular young woman who enjoyed banquets, masques, and revels.

SYNTHESIZE

4b. The speaker seems bitter and resentful toward the woman. He thinks she is heartless. He was probably once attracted to the qualities that others appreciate in her, but changed his mind when she "murdered" him, or dashed his romantic hopes.

Respond *to the* SELECTION

What might you say or do if you witnessed the subject of the poem bragging to a crowd of people at a banquet?

INVESTIGATE, Inquire, *Imagine*

Recall: GATHERING FACTS → **Interpret:** FINDING MEANING

1a. Who will greet the new arrival in the "underground"?
1b. Will others find the new arrival interesting? How do you know?

2a. How does the speaker describe the subject's speaking voice in line 6?
2b. What does line 6 suggest about the subject of the poem's interactions with others?

3a. What does the new arrival tell the spirits when they gather around her?
3b. What sort of life has the subject of the poem led?

Analyze: TAKING THINGS APART → **Synthesize:** BRINGING THINGS TOGETHER

4a. Identify words or phrases that show how others view the subject of this poem.
4b. How does the speaker see the subject of this poem? Why do these two views differ?

Evaluate: MAKING JUDGMENTS → **Extend:** CONNECTING IDEAS

5a. What is your opinion of the subject of this poem? Do you think the speaker has presented an objective portrait of her? Explain.
5b. Several of the poems in this unit deal with unsuccessful relationships. To which other subject of a poem do you think this subject is most similar? Explain your response.

Understanding *Literature*

AMBIGUITY. Review the definition for **ambiguity** in Literary Tools on page 314. Look at the last line of the poem. Did the subject of the poem actually hurt the speaker physically? How else is it possible to hurt a person?

ALLUSION. Review the definition for **allusion** in the Handbook of Literary Terms. Campion makes an allusion to Iope and Helen. What purpose does this allusion serve?

ANSWERS FOR INVESTIGATE, INQUIRE AND IMAGINE (CONT.)

EVALUATE

5a. *Responses will vary.* Students may say that the speaker's comment in the last line about what the subject did to him suggests that he may not be objective about this woman.

EXTEND

5b. *Responses will vary.* The speaker is cynical like the nymph in Raleigh's poem. The speaker is frustrated by the woman he pursued like the hunter in Wyatt's poem. The tone is less mournful than that of Sidney's poem.

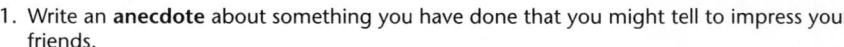

WRITER'S JOURNAL

1. Write an **anecdote** about something you have done that you might tell to impress your friends.
2. Write a **comparison-and-contrast essay** about the similarities and differences between popularity and admirability. You may wish to think about these questions: Are popular people always admirable? Are admirable people always popular?
3. Think about ways in which people can hurt each other emotionally. Write an **anecdote** about a person who is hurt emotionally and how he or she deals with this hurt.

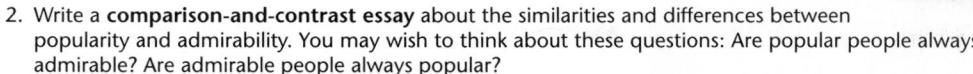

Integrating *the* LANGUAGE ARTS

Language, Grammar, and Style

IDENTIFYING ADJECTIVES. Review the parts of speech in the Language Arts Survey 3.7, "Grammar Reference Chart—Parts of Speech Overview." Then identify five adjectives and the words they modify in the poem.

Study and Research & Collaborative Learning

RESEARCHING HELEN. Using reference works, learn more about Helen, a famous woman from Greek mythology. Write a summary of the stories you learn about her. Then, in small groups, discuss whether you think she would get along with the subject of this poem.

Speaking and Listening

STORY TELLING. Take turns telling stories about things you have done. Each person should share one story about something that makes him or her proud. Think about using gestures, changes in pace and tone, and other verbal and nonverbal elements to make your story engaging. For more information, see the Language Arts Survey 4.20, "Telling a Story."

ANSWERS TO INTEGRATING THE LANGUAGE ARTS

Language, Grammar, and Style
Admired modifies guest. Beauteous modifies spirits. White modifies lope and blithe modifies Helen. Smooth modifies tongue. Sweet modifies youth.

Study and Research & Collaborative Learning
Students might also discuss how they think the speaker of the poem would get along with these women.

Speaking and Listening
If possible, try to make a videotape of students' storytelling. Share the tape with students, so they can evaluate whether their verbal and nonverbal elements of their deliveries were effective. You may wish to point out ways in which students might make improvements (e.g., by varying their tone more, by avoiding habitual nervous gestures, by making better eye contact, and so forth).

ANSWERS TO UNDERSTANDING LITERATURE

AMBIGUITY. It is possible that the speaker means the last line literally; however, because the poem is focused in the woman'' easy popularity and polished social skills, it seems more likely that she has somehow hurt him within the social realm. For example, she may have spurned his love publicly and embarrassed him.

ALLUSION. The allusion suggests that the subject of the poem is a great beauty like Helen and Iope.

ADDITIONAL RESOURCES

Unit 4 Resource Book

- Sonnet 18
- Sonnet 29
- Sonnet 130
- Selection Worksheet 4.8
- Selection Check Test 4.4.17
- Selection Test 4.4.18
- Language, Grammar, and Style Resource 3.45

GRAPHIC ORGANIZER

Speaker—Sonnet 18
idealizes beloved
thinks love is eternal
speakers of longevity of literature
Speaker—Sonnet 29
disgraced, outcast
wants what he doesn't have
content when thinks of beloved
Speaker—Sonnet 130
doesn't idealize beloved
in love despite "flaws"

READER'S JOURNAL

- Inform students that there are many different types of love and that they needn't choose a person for whom they feel romantic love. For example, they might choose to write about family members or best friends.
- Have students begin by brainstorming a list of specific traits possessed by the person they plan to write about.

VOCABULARY FROM THE SELECTION

temperate

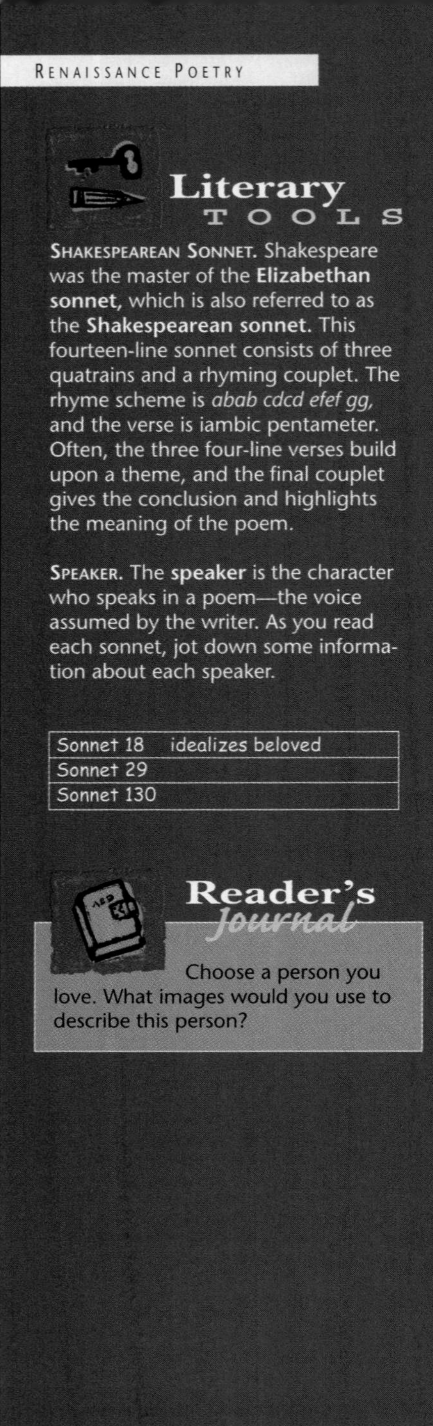

Literary Tools

Shakespearean Sonnet. Shakespeare was the master of the **Elizabethan sonnet,** which is also referred to as the **Shakespearean sonnet.** This fourteen-line sonnet consists of three quatrains and a rhyming couplet. The rhyme scheme is *abab cdcd efef gg,* and the verse is iambic pentameter. Often, the three four-line verses build upon a theme, and the final couplet gives the conclusion and highlights the meaning of the poem.

Speaker. The **speaker** is the character who speaks in a poem—the voice assumed by the writer. As you read each sonnet, jot down some information about each speaker.

Sonnet 18	idealizes beloved
Sonnet 29	
Sonnet 130	

Reader's Journal

Choose a person you love. What images would you use to describe this person?

Sonnet 18
Sonnet 29
Sonnet 130

by William Shakespeare

About the Author

William Shakespeare (1564–1616), the son of a prominent citizen, was born in Stratford-upon-Avon. Although he probably attended grammar school, he did not go to college. Very little is known about his youth. The first written record of his life, after his birth certificate, is the record of his marriage to Anne Hathaway in 1582. Within a few years of their marriage, a daughter and then twins (a boy and a girl) were born. The next written evidence of his life dates to 1592 and indicates that he was then an actor and playwright in London. By 1597, Shakespeare was a man of wealth and high social standing, since, in addition to his own theatrical success, his father had been granted a coat of arms. For more information on Shakespeare, see the introduction to Unit Five, page 371.

About the Selections

While Shakespeare is primarily revered for his brilliance as a playwright, he was also the most important lyric poet of his era. The sonnet sequence was a popular form in Elizabethan England. Shakespeare's sonnet sequence is made up of 154 numbered sonnets. There have been many theories about the autobiographical content of these sonnets, but none has been proven decisively. However, most people agree that there are three distinct phases in the sequence. Most of the sonnets refer to a handsome young man. In these poems, Shakespeare tries to advise the young man about making choices in life. Another set of sonnets is addressed to a rival poet. The third group is addressed to a mysterious woman, who is often referred to as the "dark lady."

GOALS/OBJECTIVES

Studying this unit will enable students to

- have a positive experience reading Shakespearean sonnets
- describe the characteristics of Elizabethan, or Shakespearean, sonnets
- identify and describe the speaker of a poem
- use pronouns that agree with their antecedents
- visualize a room
- hold a Shakespearean sonnet reading
- illustrate a sonnet

The Sonnet. William Mulready. The Victoria & Albert Museum, London.

Sonnet 18

William Shakespeare

Shall I compare thee to a summer's day?
Thou art more lovely and more temperate:
Rough winds do shake the darling buds of May,
And summer's lease hath all too short a date:
Sometime too hot the eye of heaven shines
And often is his gold complexion dimmed;
And every fair from fair sometimes declines,
By chance or nature's changing course untrimmed;[1]
But thy eternal summer shall not fade,
Nor lose possession of that fair thou ow'st,[2]
Nor shall death brag thou wander'st in his shade,
When in eternal lines to time thou grow'st:
So long as men can breathe, or eyes can see,
So long lives this, and this gives life to thee. ■

What, according to the speaker, "will not fade"?

1. **untrimmed.** Stripped of beauty
2. **ow'st.** Own

Words for Everyday Use

tem • per • ate (tem´ pər it) *adj.*, moderate. *We hoped the day of our picnic would be temperate; we didn't want to be either scorched by the sun or chilled by rain and wind.*

Answers to Guided Reading Questions

1. The speaker says his beloved's qualities that are like summer will not fade.

Individual Learning Strategies

Motivation
Students may enjoy illustrating Sonnet 130 in the Collaborative Learning activity. Encourage students to depict the woman described in the poem in various ways. Display students' illustrations in your classroom.

English Language Learning
Students may benefit from a discussion of metaphors people are compared to in English literature, such as a summer's day, the whiteness of snow, or the redness of roses. Encourage students to share any such common metaphors they can think of.

Reading Proficiency
Play recordings of readings of these poems from the Audio Library. The first time you play the recordings, tell students to close their eyes and try to picture what the speakers describe. Then play the recordings again and have students follow along with the text of the poems as they listen.

Special Needs
Tell students to focus on responding to the Guided Reading questions and the Recall questions in the Investigate, Inquire, and Imagine section as soon as they read each poem.

Enrichment
Ask students to investigate how standards of beauty differ over time and across cultures. What influences these ideals? They might also consider the question of what effects such standards have on individuals' self-esteem. What are some of the unrealistic standards of male and female beauty in our society?

RESPOND TO THE SELECTION

Students should formulate a clear statement of the poem's theme before they begin writing their letters. Have them work together in pairs to discuss the poem's main ideas before they begin writing.

ANSWERS FOR INVESTIGATE, INQUIRE AND IMAGINE

RECALL

1a. In the first line, the speaker asks, "Shall I compare thee to a summer's day?"

2a. The subjects "eternal summer" or beauty will last forever.

3a. The speaker thinks his beloved will live for as long as men can breathe, eyes can see, and "this" (the sonnet itself) lives.

INTERPRET

1b. A summer's day seems like something perfect and at its peak.

2b. That the subject's beauty will never fade may suggest that she possesses more than a physical beauty.

3b. The speaker has captured his beloved's beauty and preserved it for all time in the sonnet, so even when her physical beauty does fade it will live on in the sonnet.

ANALYZE

4a. The subject is more lovely and temperate than a summer's day. Unlike the beauty of summer, her beauty will not fade.

SYNTHESIZE

4b. The speaker suggests that the subject is perfect and that the subject is finer than the natural world. The speaker is also suggesting that by writing a sonnet he his giving the subject and her beauty a type of immortality.

EVALUATE

5a. Students may say that since they are reading about this beautiful women hundreds of years after the sonnet was written, that the poem continues to give life to her.

EXTEND

5b. *Responses will vary.* Students might point out memorials such as war memorials, the AIDS names quilt, and scholarships given in memory of someone. They might also mention stories that are passed on about people who have died, or traditions carried on by a new generation in memory of someone.

Respond *to the* SELECTION

If the speaker had chosen to write a personal letter instead of a poem, what might the letter have said?

INVESTIGATE, Inquire, *Imagine*

Recall: GATHERING FACTS ➤ **Interpret:** FINDING MEANING

1a. What is the speaker's opening question?

1b. Why might the speaker suggest a comparison such as the one in line 1?

2a. What shall not fade?

2b. In lines 5–10, do you think the speaker is referring only to physical beauty? Why, or why not?

3a. How long will the subject of this poem "live"?

3b. What has the speaker done with this sonnet?

Analyze: TAKING THINGS APART ➤ **Synthesize:** BRINGING THINGS TOGETHER

4a. List the ways in which the subject compares to a summer's day.

4b. What, overall, is the speaker saying about the subject of this sonnet?

Evaluate: MAKING JUDGMENTS ➤ **Extend:** CONNECTING IDEAS

5a. Judge whether the speaker speaks the truth in the couplet.

5b. In what other ways can people be immortalized?

Sonnet 29

William Shakespeare

When, in disgrace with Fortune and men's eyes,
I all alone beweep my outcast state,
And trouble deaf heaven with my bootless[1] cries,
And look upon myself and curse my fate,
Wishing me like to one more rich in hope,
Featured like him, like him with friends possessed,
Desiring this man's art and that man's scope,
With what I most enjoy contented least;
Yet in these thoughts myself almost despising,
Haply[2] I think on thee, and then my state
(Like to the lark at break of day arising
From sullen earth) sings hymns at heaven's gate;
For thy sweet love remembered such wealth brings
That then I scorn to change my state with kings. ■

How does the speaker's mood change in lines 9–14?

1. **bootless.** Useless
2. **Haply.** By chance or accident

Respond *to the* **Selection**

How would you feel if you were the object of the speaker's love?

ANSWERS TO GUIDED READING QUESTIONS

1. The speaker's mood changes from despairing to joyous when he remembers his relationship with his beloved.

RESPOND TO THE SELECTION

As an alternate topic, suggest that students discuss something that makes them happy when they are sad.

ANSWERS FOR INVESTIGATE, INQUIRE AND IMAGINE

RECALL

1a. The speaker is in disgrace with fortune and with men.
2a. He wishes he had the hopeful attitude, the handsome face, the popularity, the skill, and the range of abilities that other men he knows possess.
3a. The speaker's mood changes completely.

INTERPRET

1b. He is feeling lonely and friendless.
2b. No; he realizes that the love of the person he addresses is all he needs to feel happy.
3b. The reaction suggests that love has a very strong pull and that it is stronger than material wealth and popularity.

ANALYZE

4a. The speaker refers to people who are rich in hope, friends, ability, and scope.

SYNTHESIZE

4b. The speaker is rich in his love. This wealth overcomes everything the speaker is lacking.

EVALUATE

5a. *Responses will vary.* Students who believe in the transforming power of love or who have experienced sudden changes in mood may find it realistic. Others may think it is an overstatement of the power of love.

EXTEND

5b. *Responses will vary.*

SELECTION CHECK TEST 4.4.17 WITH ANSWERS

Checking Your Reading

SONNET 18

1. The speaker says the listener is "more lovely and more temperate" than what? **The listener is more lovely than a summer's day.**
2. What does the speaker say will never fade? **His love's beauty ("thy eternal summer") will not fade.**

SONNET 29

3. How does the speaker feel as the poem opens? **He feels depressed and unhappy.**
4. What changes his state of mind? **He thinks of "thy sweet love."**

SONNET 130

5. What image does the speaker paint of his mistress? She is not beautiful, melodious, or goddess-like.

INVESTIGATE

Inquire, *Imagine*

Recall: GATHERING FACTS →

1a. According to the opening lines, with whom is the speaker in disgrace?

2a. For what does the speaker wish in lines 5–7?

3a. What happens when the speaker thinks of the subject of this sonnet?

Interpret: FINDING MEANING

1b. What specific feelings do you think the speaker is experiencing in the opening lines?

2b. In the end, are the things for which the speaker wishes the key to his happiness? If not, what is?

3b. What does the speaker's reaction suggest about the power of love?

Analyze: TAKING THINGS APART →

4a. Identify the kinds of wealth identified in this sonnet.

Synthesize: BRINGING THINGS TOGETHER

4b. What kind of wealth does the speaker have? How does this kind of wealth compare with other kinds of wealth?

Evaluate: MAKING JUDGMENTS →

5a. Evaluate the speaker's change of mood. Explain whether you think it is realistic.

Extend: CONNECTING IDEAS

5b. What turns things around for you when you are in a bad mood?

SELECTION CHECK TEST 4.4.17 WITH ANSWERS (cont.)

Literary Tools

1. How many lines are in a Shakespearean sonnet? **It has 14 lines.**
2. What is the rhyme scheme for a Shakespearean sonnet? **It is abab cdcd efef gg.**
3. What is a rhyming couplet? **A rhyming couplet is two lines that rhyme.**

Sonnet 130

William Shakespeare

My mistress' eyes are nothing like the sun;
Coral is far more red than her lips' red;
If snow be white, why then her breasts are dun;[1]
If hairs be wires, black wires grow on her head.
I have seen roses damasked,[2] red and white,
But no such roses see I in her cheeks;
And in some perfumes is there more delight
Than in the breath that from my mistress reeks.[3]
I love to hear her speak, yet well I know
That music hath a far more pleasing sound;
I grant I never saw a goddess go;
My mistress, when she walks, treads on the ground.
  And yet, by heaven, I think my love as rare
  As any she belied with false compare. ■

What does the speaker realize about his beloved's voice? about her walk?

1. **dun.** Dark
2. **damasked.** Intermingled
3. **reeks.** flows; has an unpleasant odor

Words For Everyday Use

be • lie (bē lī) *vi.*, misrepresent. *Katya's carefree attitude belies her underlying determination.*

Respond to the Selection

For what would you like to be loved?

ANSWERS TO GUIDED READING QUESTIONS

1. He makes fun of the conventional but unrealistic images to which the characteristics of women are typically compared.

RESPOND TO THE SELECTION

Ask students to also discuss the differences between being worshipped, being admired, and being loved. Which of these feelings do they have for people in their own lives?

ANSWERS FOR INVESTIGATE, INQUIRE AND IMAGINE

Recall

1a. The woman's eyes are not like the sun, and her lips are far less red than coral.

2a. The woman's voice is less pleasing to the ear than music, but the speaker loves to hear it nonetheless.

3a. The speaker thinks his love is rare and as powerful as any misrepresented by "false compare."

Interpret

1b. All of these characteristics can be perceived with the five senses, suggesting that such characteristics gave little to do with real love, which goes beyond mere physical attraction.

2b. The speaker loves her mind and spirit, and for this reason he finds physical attributes such as her voice pleasing, regardless of their objective value.

3b. The speaker's love is based on true affection and appreciation of his beloved as a person. It is not based on physical beauty or stereotypical ideals.

Analyze

4a. The speaker's mistress does not have eyes like the sun, coral red lips, snow white skin, rosy cheeks, perfumed breath, a musical voice, or a gliding-on-air movement when she walks.

Synthesize

4b. The speaker points out these shortcomings to show the depths of his love—his love transcends physical beauty. He is able to see his beloved realistically yet loves her even more for her lack of perfection.

Evaluate

5a. Yes, the speaker loves his mistress. He is able to see beyond ideals and physical beauty.

Extend

5b. The woman in Sonnet 18 is highly idealized. She is finer than a summer's day. The woman in Sonnet 130 is not idealized at all.

Investigate, Inquire, Imagine

Recall: Gathering Facts →

1a. What does the speaker say about the woman's eyes and lips?

2a. How does the speaker feel about the woman's voice?

3a. What does the speaker think of his love?

Interpret: Finding Meaning

1b. What do all of the characteristics that the woman does not possess have in common?

2b. Why might the speaker still love to hear his beloved's voice?

3b. On what is the speaker's love based? On what is it not based?

Analyze: Taking Things Apart →

4a. What ideal characteristics does the speaker say his mistress does not have?

Synthesize: Bringing Things Together

4b. Why does the speaker point out the short-comings of his mistress in this regard?

Evaluate: Making Judgments →

5a. Does the speaker of the poem truly love the woman? Explain.

Extend: Connecting Ideas

5b. In what way does the description of the woman in sonnet 130 differ from the description of the woman in sonnet 18.

Understanding Literature

Shakespearean sonnet. A **Shakespearean** or **Elizabethan sonnet** is a fourteen-line poem, usually in iambic pentameter, that follows the rhyme scheme *abab cdcd efef gg.* The sonnet is broken into three quatrains and a final couplet. For each sonnet, identify the theme expressed by the three quatrains and the main idea that the couplet highlights.

Speaker. The **speaker** is the character who speaks in a poem—the voice assumed by the writer. Describe the speakers in Sonnets 18, 29, and 130. How are the speakers similar to one another? Do any of them seem to have a sense of humor? Do you find each of the speakers likable? Are they equally likable? Why, or why not?

WRITER'S JOURNAL

1. Write a **thank you note** for the things in your life that would make you "scorn to change [your] state with kings."
2. Write a **description** of someone you know. Use the technique of saying what the person is not like to show what he or she is like.
3. Write a **sonnet.** Choose any subject you like. Think about the main idea you want to express. Make sure this idea is clear in the final couplet. Use the other 12 lines to express your feelings further.

Integrating *the* LANGUAGE ARTS

Language, Grammar, and Style

AGREEMENT OF PRONOUNS AND ANTECEDENTS. Read the Language Arts Survey 3.45, "Getting Pronouns and Antecedents to Agree." Then complete each of the sentences below by adding the correct pronoun. Write your answers on your own paper.

1. The woman wore ______________ black hair in a French knot, as ______________ usually did.
2. The man who is the speaker changes ______________ attitude in the last lines of the poem.
3. Although the woman is not perfect, ______________ is loved by the speaker.
4. William Shakespeare and other lyric poets use ______________ imaginations.
5. Sara and I read Sonnet 130 aloud; then______________ wrote about it.

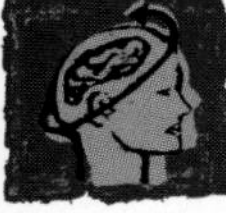

Critical Thinking

VISUALIZING. In order to create vivid images, Shakespeare had to be able to visualize and describe places and objects in clear detail. Improving your ability to visualize will help your creative writing. Try to visualize a room in your home or in your school. Make a list of twenty items in the room. Use reasoning to help you think of items you may have overlooked. Write an asterisk next to items on your list that you remembered through reasoning.

Speaking and Listening & Collaborative Learning

CIRCLE POETRY READING. As a group, select a favorite Shakespearean sonnet for each group member. (You don't necessarily need to use the foregoing sonnets.) Sitting in a circle, have each classmate read a poem. As you listen, try to hear and enjoy the meter and rhyme. As you read, try to read lines with feeling, as if you have climbed inside the speaker.

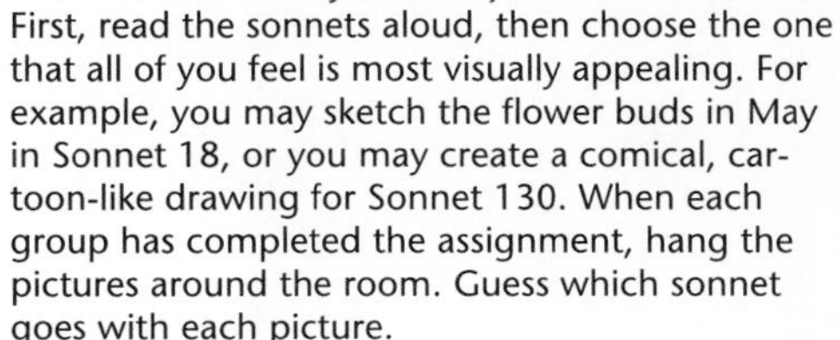

Collaborative Learning

ILLUSTRATING SONNETS. Form groups of three or four. As a group, illustrate one of the sonnets that you have just read. First, read the sonnets aloud, then choose the one that all of you feel is most visually appealing. For example, you may sketch the flower buds in May in Sonnet 18, or you may create a comical, cartoon-like drawing for Sonnet 130. When each group has completed the assignment, hang the pictures around the room. Guess which sonnet goes with each picture.

ANSWERS FOR UNDERSTANDING LITERATURE

ELIZABETHAN OR SHAKESPEAREAN SONNET. Sonnet 18—The quatrains build upon the theme that the woman is more perfect than a summer day. The couplet suggests that the woman will be immortalized by this sonnet and her beauty will live on forever.
Sonnet 29—The quatrains build on the theme that the speaker is distraught because of what he does not have, but upon thinking of his beloved his mood changes. The couplet underscores the idea that the speaker's beloved is his greatest wealth.
Sonnet 130—The quatrains point out the many ways in which the speaker's beloved fails to live up to the typical ideal mistress. The couplet points out that none of these things matter in a case of true love.

SPEAKER. The speaker in Sonnets 18 and 130 both refuse to use standard metaphors to describe their beloved, instead saying that the person has qualities that transcend time or the senses. Both speakers have a subtle sense of humor, especially the one in Sonnet 130. The speaker in Sonnet 29 seems highly emotional, drowning in self-doubt one moment and soaring in rapture the next. Students' opinions about how likable the various speakers are will vary.

ANSWERS TO INTEGRATING THE LANGUAGE ARTS

Language, Grammar, and Style

1. her; she
2. his
3. she
4. their
5. we

Critical Thinking
Students' lists will vary, but should contain twenty items. If students have trouble using reasoning to list items, share with them the following examples. If you were to try to remember objects in your kitchen, you might not remember everything in your refrigerator, but based on what you had for breakfast, you might be able to list milk, eggs, and orange marmalade. If you picked the janitor's closet, you might be able to use reasoning to list a brush, based on the fact that the janitor sweeps the halls, even if you don't remember seeing one there.

ANSWERS TO INTEGRATING THE LANGUAGE ARTS (CONT.)

Speaking and Listening/Collaborative Learning
Students with experience in drama may share their techniques for "getting inside" a character and projecting the character's feelings through spoken language.

Collaborative Learning
Have students photocopy the sonnet they wish to illustrate. They can then highlight sensory words and images they wish to incorporate into their illustrations. Remind students that when they work in groups, all group members must participate and contribute ideas. Students should not, for example, rely on the best artist in the group to carry out this project himself or herself.

ADDITIONAL RESOURCES

UNIT 4 RESOURCE BOOK

- Selection Worksheet 4.9
- Selection Check Test 4.4.19
- Selection Test 4.4.20
- Language, Grammar, and Style Resource 3.33-3.34
- Study and Research Resource 5.49

GRAPHIC ORGANIZER

And I will pledge with mine;
Or leave a kiss but in the cup,
And I'll not look for wine.
The thirst that from the soul doth rise
Doth ask a drink divine
But might I of Jove's nectar sup,
I would not change for thine.

READER'S JOURNAL

Write about a time when you attributed abilities or qualities to a person that person did not actually possess.

VOCABULARY FROM THE SELECTION

wither

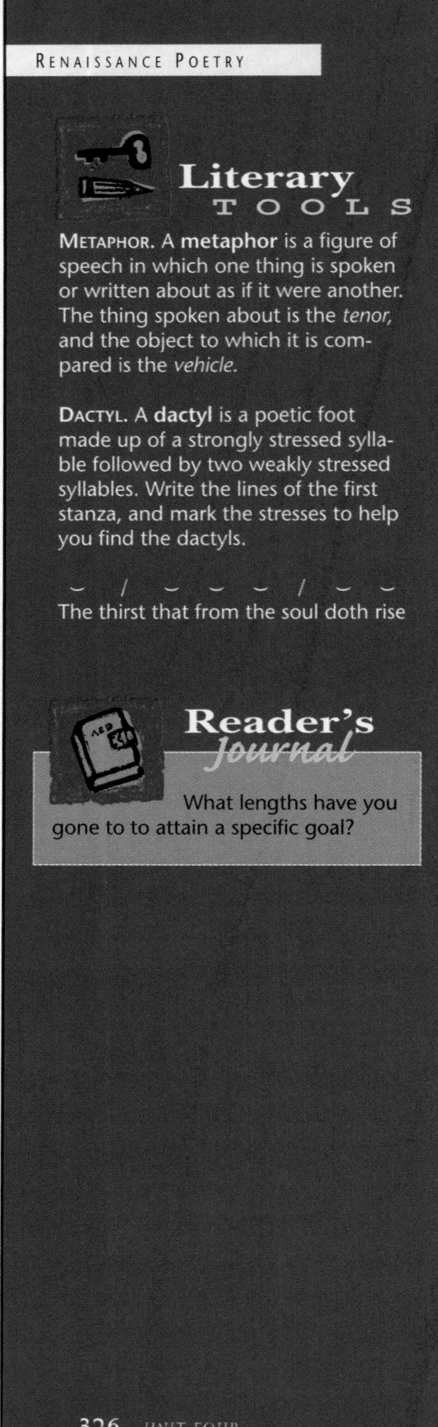

Literary TOOLS

METAPHOR. A **metaphor** is a figure of speech in which one thing is spoken or written about as if it were another. The thing spoken about is the *tenor,* and the object to which it is compared is the *vehicle.*

DACTYL. A **dactyl** is a poetic foot made up of a strongly stressed syllable followed by two weakly stressed syllables. Write the lines of the first stanza, and mark the stresses to help you find the dactyls.

˘ / ˘ ˘ ˘ / ˘ ˘
The thirst that from the soul doth rise

Reader's Journal

What lengths have you gone to to attain a specific goal?

"Song, to Celia"

BY BEN JONSON

About the AUTHOR

Ben Jonson (1572–1637) was born after the death of his father, a clergyman, and became the stepson of a master bricklayer. He was educated by the great classical scholar William Camden at Westminster School, worked for a short time by his stepfather's side, and then entered the army. He was a brave soldier in hand-to-hand combat at Flanders, where the Dutch and English were fighting the Spaniards. When he returned to England in 1594, he became a playwright and actor.

Jonson was not a mild-mannered man. He was nearly hanged for murder after killing another actor in a duel. Later he was jailed for insulting the Scottish nation. As he grew older, he calmed down considerably, and he became a father figure to London's literary circle. A favorite of the royal court, Jonson was made the first poet laureate in all but name by King James I. His followers became known as the Sons of Ben. Unlike other poets of his time, such as his friend William Shakespeare, Jonson was not meek about publicizing his poetry. Concerned about preserving his works for posterity, he personally oversaw their publication.

About the SELECTION

Like many English poems of this period, **"Song, to Celia"** is a lyric poem honoring a goddess-like and unattainable woman. Each of the two eight-line stanzas has its own individual rhyme scheme. Jonson uses a variety of meters in this poem, mainly iambic, but there are also many lines and phrases that begin on an accented syllable. Moreover, the poem's lines are not all the same length; they vary from three to five feet, with most of the odd lines being at least one foot longer than the even ones.

GOALS/OBJECTIVES

Studying this lesson will enable students to

- interpret and appreciate a love poem
- define dactyl and identify examples of this metrical foot in their reading
- define *metaphor* and identify a metaphor's tenor and vehicle
- correct sentence fragments and run-ons
- respond to analogy questions and create their own analogies
- prepare an oral interpretation
- role-play a conversation between a speaker and his beloved

Woman in a Garland of Flowers, 1658.
Daniel Seghers. Kunsthistorisches Museum, Vienna, Austria.

Song, to Celia

Ben Jonson

Drink to me only with thine eyes,
  And I will pledge with mine;
Or leave a kiss but in the cup,
  And I'll not look for wine.
The thirst that from the soul doth rise
  Doth ask a drink divine:
But might I of Jove's nectar[1] sup,
  I would not change for thine.

I sent thee late a rosy wreath,
  Not so much honoring thee,
As giving it a hope that there
  It could not withered be.
But thou thereon didst only breathe,
  And sent'st it back to me;
Since when it grows and smells, I swear,
  Not of itself, but thee. ■

Is the word wine used literally or symbolically?

What gift has the speaker bestowed upon Celia?

1. **Jove's nectar.** Jove is a Roman god, and nectar is the drink of the gods.

Words for Everyday Use

with • er (with´ ər) *vi.*, wilt and shrivel. *Because of the drought, most of the tomatoes withered on their vines.*

ANSWER TO GUIDED READING QUESTION

1. He sent her a wreath, or woven ring, of roses.

INDIVIDUAL LEARNING STRATEGIES

Motivation
Ask students to write their own toasts. Tell them to write the toast for a specific occasion that they can imagine, such as a friend's birthday party or a sibling's wedding.

English Language Learning
You may wish to list the archaic verb forms *doth, didst,* and *sent'st* and the pronouns *thine, thee,* and *thou* on the board with their modern equivalents. Also, explain that this poem is in the form of a toast, a short speech in which someone is honored or complimented.

Reading Proficiency
Have students read aloud this poem to each other. One student should read the poem aloud dramatically to the other. The second student should then deliver his or her reading. Ask students to think about whether their partner chose to emphasize parts of the poem in different ways than they did.

Special Needs
Ask students to discuss their ideas about the Investigate, Inquire, and Imagine questions in small groups before you discuss the questions as a class. Previewing the questions in this way may give special needs students the confidence and understanding necessary to participate actively in class discussion of these questions.

Enrichment
Students can work in small groups to create a short, one-act play based on "Song, to Celia." After all groups perform their plays, the class can discuss the various interpretations of the story.

SELECTION CHECK TEST 4.4.19 WITH ANSWERS

Checking Your Reading

1. What does the speaker ask Celia to leave in the cup? **He asks her to leave a kiss in the cup.**
2. What kind of a drink does the "thirst that from the soul doth rise" ask for? **It asks for a divine drink.**

SELECTION CHECK TEST 4.4.19 WITH ANSWERS (cont.)

3. What does the speaker send to Celia? **He sends her a rosy wreath.**
4. Why does he send it to her? **He hopes it will not wither if she cares for it.**
5. What does Celia do with it? **She breathes on it and sends it back.**

Literary Tools

1. In the metaphor, "The thirst that from the soul doth rise," what is the tenor? The tenor is longing, or desire for his love.
2. In the metaphor, "The thirst that from the soul doth rise," what is the *vehicle?* **The vehicle is** ***thirst,*** **as in a need to drink.**
3. Mark the stressed syllables in the following line, and circle the dactyl:

   Or leave a kiss but in the cup

RESPOND TO THE SELECTION

As an optional response, students might discuss or write about a return toast from Celia.

ANSWERS FOR INVESTIGATE, INQUIRE AND IMAGINE

Recall

1a. He asks her to drink to him with her eyes. He promises that he will pledge with his.

2a. He asks her to leave a kiss in the cup.

3a. He sends her a "rosy wreath; which she returns to him.

Interpret

1b He seems to have strong feelings for his beloved. The word pledge suggests that he may want to marry her.

2b. He wants the woman to return his romantic feelings; then he would not care about mundane things such as food and drink.

3b. Her response does not seem to have deterred him. He even puts a positive spin on the event, claiming that her breath on the roses has preserved and transformed them.

Analyze

4a. The speaker sent Celia a wreath, and she returned it. He keeps asking her for things she does not give him.

Synthesize

4b. The speaker and Celia do not seem to be in an amicable relationship. The speaker may be trying to get to know Celia; this "toast" may be the latest in a string of attempts to woo her, or they may have had a relationship in the past that she has decided to end.

Evaluate

5a. *Responses will vary.* Some students may say that Celia has clearly shown that she wants the speaker to stop his attentions and he should leave her alone. Others may say that if he feels as strongly as he seems to he should try to convince her of his love.

Extend

5b. *Responses will vary.* The speaker is like the hunter in the Wyatt poem in that he is unsuccessful in his pursuit. He is like the speaker in Sidney's sonnet and in Campion's poem in that he has been scorned.

Respond *to the* Selection

How would you feel if you were in the speaker's place? What advice would you offer the speaker?

Investigate, Inquire, *Imagine*

Recall: Gathering Facts

1a. What does the speaker ask his beloved to do in line 1? What does he promise to do?

2a. What does he ask her to leave in the cup?

3a. What does he give Celia? What does she do with the gift?

→ **Interpret:** Finding Meaning

1b. Judging from the first two lines, how strong do you think the speaker's feelings are for his beloved? What evidence do you have?

2b. What does the speaker really want? If he had this, why do you think he would not look for wine?

3b. Does her response to the gift change his feelings about pursuing the relationship? What makes you think so?

Analyze: Taking Things Apart

4a. Identify signs that this is not a working relationship.

→ **Synthesize:** Bringing Things Together

4b. Describe the relationship between Celia and the speaker. What do you think has happened between them?

Evaluate: Making Judgments

5a. Evaluate whether you think the speaker should continue to pursue Celia.

→ **Extend:** Connecting Ideas

5b. Identify similarities between the speaker of this poem and at least one other speaker in this unit.

Understanding *Literature*

Metaphor. Review the definition for **metaphor** in the Handbook of Literary Terms. What is the metaphor in the first stanza of this poem? What is the vehicle? What is the tenor? Explain why this metaphor works well.

Dactyl. Review the definition for **dactyl** in the Literary Tools on page 326. Identify the dactyls in this poem.

ANSWERS FOR UNDERSTANDING LITERATURE

Metaphor. In stanza 1, the poet uses a toast (the vehicle) as a metaphor for a declaration of love (the tenor). The metaphor works well because Jonson is able to approach it from several angles: the "pledge" with the eyes, the kiss as a substitute for wine, and the thirst in the speaker's soul.

Dactyl. Examples of dactyls in poem include line 2, "Drink to me," and line 10, "Not so much honoring."

WRITER'S JOURNAL

1. Write a **note** from Celia to the speaker, telling him how she feels.
2. Write a wedding **toast** to the speaker in this poem, assuming that he is finally marrying Celia. In your toast, mention all that he did to try to win the affection of his beloved.
3. Write a **lyric poem** about rejuvenation. You might want to mirror the meter used in the first stanza of this poem.

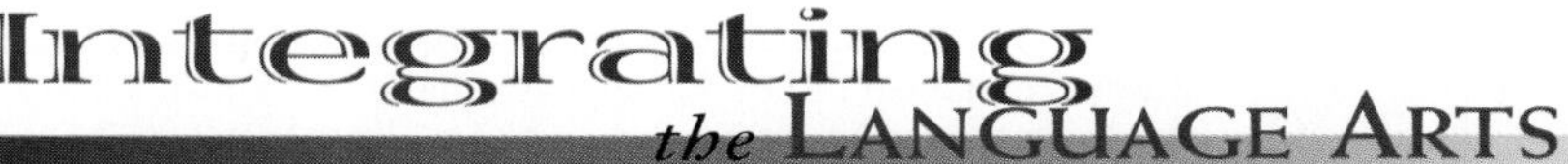

Language, Grammar, and Style

CORRECTING FRAGMENTS AND RUN-ONS. Review "Correcting Sentence Fragments" and "Correcting Sentence Run-ons" in the Language Arts Survey 3.33–3.34. Then correct the fragments and run-ons in the following examples.

1. Ben Jonson was influenced by the Roman poets he influenced many poets himself.
2. His followers were called the sons of Ben flourished in the seventeenth century.
3. Robert Herrick and Richard Lovelace, two of the sons of Ben.
4. These poets often called the cavalier poets as well.
5. Like many poets of this period.

Study and Research

MAKING ANALOGIES. Read the Language Arts Survey 5.49, "Analogy Questions." Write three analogies using words or ideas from this poem. Then choose the word that best completes the following analogies.

1. SADNESS : DESPONDENCY :: Love :
   a. Fatigue c. Ardor
   b. Remorse d. Fellowship
2. INFORMATION : RELATE :: Gift :
   a. Generate c. Accept
   b. Absolve d. Bestow
3. POEM : METER :: Song :
   a. Beat c. Lyrics
   b. Notes d. Vocals
4. THIRST : QUENCH :: Yearning :
   a. Longing c. Appease
   b. Optimism d. Covet
5. PURE : SULLIED :: Divine :
   a. Angelic c. Ethereal
   b. Diabolical d. Convoluted

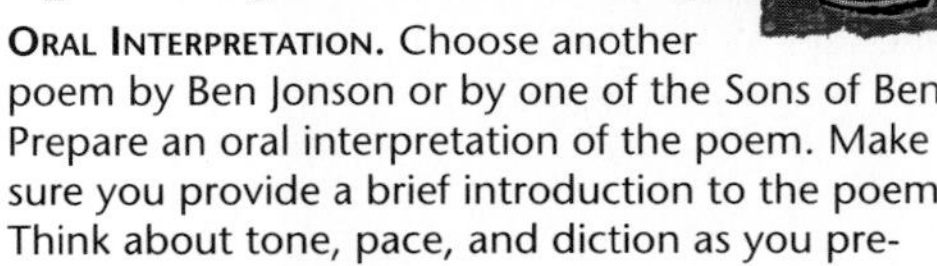

Study and Research & Speaking and Listening

ORAL INTERPRETATION. Choose another poem by Ben Jonson or by one of the Sons of Ben. Prepare an oral interpretation of the poem. Make sure you provide a brief introduction to the poem. Think about tone, pace, and diction as you prepare to deliver the poem orally.

Speaking and Listening & Collaborative Learning

ROLE-PLAY. Communication is important in relationships. Role-play a conversation between the speaker and Celia. A third student can act as a moderator between the two.

ANSWERS TO INTEGRATING THE LANGUAGE ARTS

Language, Grammar, and Style
Responses may vary. Possible responses are given.

1. Ben Jonson was influenced by the Roman poets. He influenced many poets himself.
2. His followers, the sons of Ben, flourished in the seventeenth century.
3. Robert Herrick and Richard Lovelace were two of the sons of Ben.
4. These poets are often called the cavalier poets, as well.
5. Like many poets of this period, Jonson wrote about love.

Study and Research
Students' analogies will vary.

1. c
2. d
3. a
4. c
5. b

Study and Research & Speaking and Listening
Refer students to the Language Arts Survey 4.19, "Oral Interpretation of Poetry," for tips that will help them with their preparation and delivery.

Speaking and Listening & Collaborative Learning
You might ask students to take turns playing the roles of speaker, Celia, and moderator.

ADDITIONAL RESOURCES

Unit 4 Resource Book
- Selection Worksheet 4.10
- Selection Check Test 4.4.21
- Selection Test 4.4.22
- Language, Grammar, and Style Resource 3.42

GRAPHIC ORGANIZER

Verse	First Pair	Second Pair
3	kill, heal	break down, build up
4	weep, laugh	mourn, dance
5	cast away, gather	embrace, refrain from embracing
6	get, lose	keep, cast away
7	rend, sew	keep silence, speak
8	love, hate	war, peace

READER'S JOURNAL

Ask students to consider what stages in their lives to which they are in a hurry to experience. Tell them to consider whether it is important to appreciate each stage of their life as they are in it or whether it is better to constantly look in anticipation toward the future.

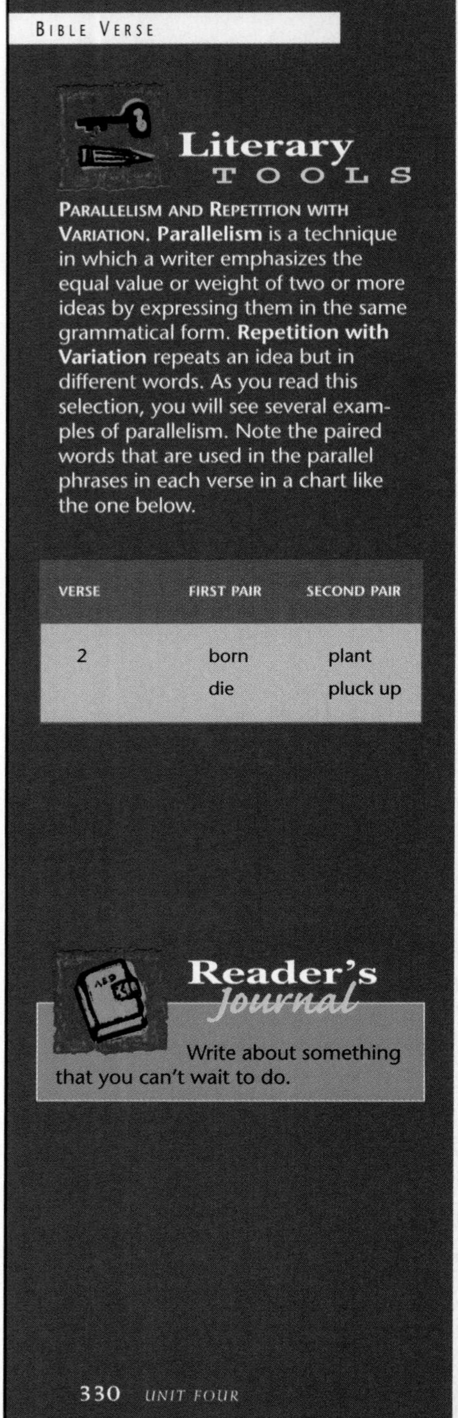

Bible Verse

Literary Tools

Parallelism and Repetition with Variation. Parallelism is a technique in which a writer emphasizes the equal value or weight of two or more ideas by expressing them in the same grammatical form. **Repetition with Variation** repeats an idea but in different words. As you read this selection, you will see several examples of parallelism. Note the paired words that are used in the parallel phrases in each verse in a chart like the one below.

VERSE	FIRST PAIR	SECOND PAIR
2	born	plant
	die	pluck up

Reader's Journal

Write about something that you can't wait to do.

FROM Ecclesiastes
Chapter 3, Verses 1–8
FROM The King James Bible

About the Selection

Chapter 3 of **Ecclesiastes** tells about the balance of give and take in the lives of human beings and suggests that every human activity has its proper season, or time.

The first of the great translators of the Bible into English was William Tyndale (1494–1536), who produced a version of the New Testament that was smuggled into England from Germany, where he had completed it. For his pains, Tyndale was hounded through various European cities and eventually imprisoned and put to death. After Henry VIII broke with Rome, however, Biblical translations met with official approval. The greatest of those produced in England was the King James Bible, or Authorized Version, which appeared in 1611, the work of fifty-four scholars appointed by the king.

For centuries, the simple, stately language of this book has influenced the content and rhythms of writing in the English language.

GOALS/OBJECTIVES

Studying this unit will enable students to
- appreciate a verse about balance in life
- text
- explain parallelism and recognize its use in literature
- define *repetition* with variation and point to examples of its use in their reading
- correct split infinitives
- hold a group discussion
- write a letter of complaint
- create a visual display

Spring, Summer, Autumn, Winter, c.1600s. Abel Grimmer.

FROM

Ecclesiastes

Chapter 3, Verses 1-8

To every *thing there is* a season, and a time to every
purpose under the heaven:
2 A time to be born, and a time to die; a time to plant,
and a time to pluck up *that which is* planted;
3 A time to kill, and a time to heal; a time to break
down, and a time to build up;
4 A time to weep, and a time to laugh; a time to mourn,
and a time to dance;
5 A time to cast away stones, and a time to gather
stones together; a time to embrace, and a time to refrain
from embracing;
6 A time to get, and a time to lose; a time to keep, and a
time to cast away;
7 A time to rend, and a time to sew; a time to keep
silence, and a time to speak;
8 A time to love, and a time to hate; a time of war, and
a time of peace. ■

When would be a good time to cast away stones?

WORDS FOR EVERYDAY USE

rend (rend) *vi.* tear. *Isn't that my favorite shirt that you're about to rend into rags?*

ANSWER TO GUIDED READING QUESTION

1. Clearing a field might be a good time to cast away stones.

INDIVIDUAL LEARNING STRATEGIES

MOTIVATION
Encourage students to work in groups of four to illustrate the line, "To every thing there is a season, and a time to every purpose under the heaven." Each group needs to decide what images might best represent each season. Each student then can choose a specific season and illustrate it.

ENGLISH LANGUAGE LEARNING
Point out that the Old and New Testaments were not originally written in English. They were written in Hebrew and Greek, respectively. If students are learning English as a second language, encourage them to read these verses from Ecclesiastes in their native language and to compare this translation verse-by-verse with the King James translation of the Bible.

READING PROFICIENCY
Point out that the paired words are often opposites or close to opposite. Have students try to determine the meaning of any words they do not know by comparing the meaning to that of the word with which it is paired.

SPECIAL NEEDS
After many of the selections in this unit, special needs students will find the verses from Ecclesiastes to be refreshingly straightforward and easy to understand. Encourage special needs students to involve themselves in the class discussion of the Investigate, Inquire, and Imagine questions.

ENRICHMENT
Students can discuss or research the teachings of various other religious or philosophical systems on the topic of death. What answers are given to the questions, "why are we here" and "why must we die?"

SELECTION CHECK TEST 4.4.21 WITH ANSWERS

Checking Your Reading

1. The opening line claims that to every thing there is a what? **There is a season.**
2. What action is opposed with mourning? **Dancing is opposed with mourning.**
3. Sometimes we gather stones, and sometimes we do what? **Sometimes we cast stones away.**
4. *Killing* and *healing* are juxtaposed with *breaking down* and *building up.* How are these two sets of things similar? **Responses will vary. Breaking down and building up can be seen as killing a society (by killing its members) or healing it.**
5. How does this poem suggest that agriculture was important to its authors? **It compares planting and plucking up with birth and death.**

Literary Tools

1. What is repeated throughout this poem? **"A time**

(Continued on page 332)

SELECTION CHECK TEST 4.4.21 WITH ANSWERS (CONT. FROM PAGE 331)

to..." is repeated throughout.

2. How is parallelism used in this poem? Every line in the poem is similar. **This emphasizes that all of the statements are equally important.**
3. How does the last stanza, dealing with love, hate, war, and peace, illustrate *repetition* with *variation?* ***War* and *hate* are related as are *love* and *peace; hate* is an emotion associated with war, and *love* is an emotion associated with *peace.***

RESPOND TO THE SELECTION

Encourage students to explore why it sometimes unclear when it is the right time to do something? Is it ever better to make the wrong choice than to take no action at all?

ANSWERS FOR INVESTIGATE, INQUIRE AND IMAGINE

1a. There is an appropriate season, or time, for everything.
2a. There is a time to be born, a time to die, a time to plant, and a time to pluck up that which is planted.
3a. There is a time to love, a time to hate, a time of war, and a time of peace.

INTERPRET

1b. For every activity, there is an appropriate time to do it or for it to happen.
2b. The first two times are parallel or similar to the second two times. Both sets are a beginning of life followed by and ending of life.
3b. Responses will vary. Some students may say that because there is a time for bad things as well as good, the message is not hopeful. Others may think that the balance, or the knowledge that there will be good, even if there is bad, is comforting or positive.

ANALYZE

4a. There is time to be born and die, plant and pluck up, kill and heal, break down and build up, weep and laugh, mourn and dance, cast away and gather, embrace and refrain from embracing, get and lose, keep and cast away, rend and sew, keep silence and speak, love and hate, and war and peace.

Respond *to the* SELECTION

If there is a time for everything, what do you think happens when something is done at the wrong time?

INVESTIGATE, Inquire, *Imagine*

Recall: GATHERING FACTS →

1a. For what are there appropriate seasons, or times, according to verse 1?
2a. According to verse 2, what is there a time for?
3a. What is there time for according to verse 8?

Interpret: FINDING MEANING

1b. In your own words, what is the main idea expressed by verse 1?
2b. In what way are the two sets of things similar?
3b. Explain whether this selection presents a positive or hopeful message.

Analyze: TAKING THINGS APART →

4a. List the things there is a time for according to this selection.

Synthesize: BRINGING THINGS TOGETHER

4b. Explain how these pairs of things are related.

Evaluate: MAKING JUDGMENTS →

5a. Do you agree that there is a time for everything? For example, do you think there is a time for hate or for war? Explain your response.

Extend: CONNECTING IDEAS

5b. What kinds of problems could people encounter if they ignored the advice given in this poem? Give specific examples of people acting at inappropriate times.

Understanding *Literature*

PARALLELISM AND REPETITION WITH VARIATION. Review the definition for **parallelism** and **repetition with variation** in the Literary Tools on page 330. The selection from Ecclesiastes makes extensive use of parallelism. It also makes use of repetition with variation. Consider the second verse. Notice that it is made up of four parallel phrases, each beginning with the words "a time." The second two phrases repeat with variation the ideas expressed in the first two phrases. How is planting similar to being born? How is dying similar to being plucked up? Review the chart you completed for Literary Tools. Discuss the similarities between the pairs in the rest of the poem.

ANSWERS FOR INVESTIGATE, INQUIRE AND IMAGINE (CONT.)

SYNTHESIZE

4b. Each pair is part of a cycle. For example, there is a time to break down and a time to build up, and again will come a time to break down.

EVALUATE

5a. *Responses will vary.*

EXTEND

5b. By doing or failing to do something at its proper time, some type of relationship or cycle will be destroyed. For example, blurting out a secret when it is "a time to keep silence" could ruin the trust between two people. On the other hand, saying nothing to defend a friend who is being put down by others could also destroy that trust.

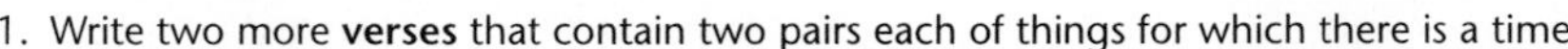

WRITER'S JOURNAL

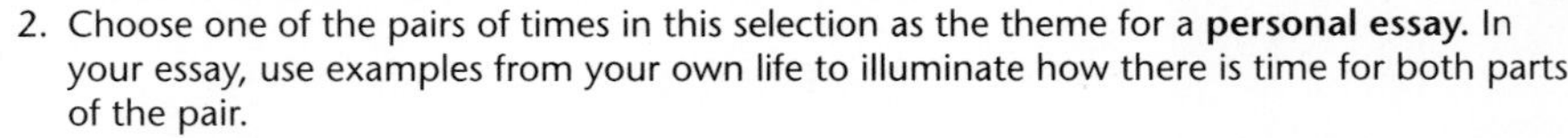

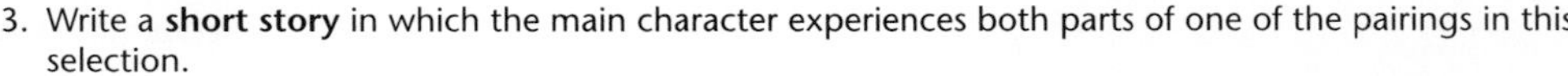

1. Write two more **verses** that contain two pairs each of things for which there is a time.
2. Choose one of the pairs of times in this selection as the theme for a **personal essay.** In your essay, use examples from your own life to illuminate how there is time for both parts of the pair.
3. Write a **short story** in which the main character experiences both parts of one of the pairings in this selection.

Integrating *the* LANGUAGE ARTS

Language, Grammar, and Style

SPLIT INFINITIVES. Read the Language Arts Survey 3.42, "Avoiding Split Infinitives." Then fix the split infinitives in the following sentences.

1. Because there is a time to die, there is also a time to sadly weep.
2. If you eat too quickly, there will be time to loudly moan.
3. To fully live, you must experience pain as well as joy.
4. If you want to beat the crowd, you have to quickly run.
5. There is no time like the present to begin to really be happy.

Speaking and Listening & Collaborative Learning

DISCUSSION. This passage is often read at funerals or memorial services. In small groups, discuss why this passage might be chosen for such occasions.

Applied English

COMPLAINT LETTER. There is a time to accept and a time to complain. Think about a time when you received poor service, got something you didn't order, or had a problem with an organization. Write a firm, but polite, letter of complaint. In your letter, detail the problem and what you would like to have happen.

Collaborative Learning

VISUAL DISPLAY. Discuss times when it would be appropriate for certain things to happen and times when it might be inappropriate for those same things to happen. You may want to create a poster or other visual display that shows your ideas.

ANSWERS FOR UNDERSTANDING LITERATURE

PARALLELISM AND REPETITION WITH VARIATION. Being planted is the way in which some plants begin their lives, just as being born is the way that people and animals begin their lives. A plant's life may end when it is plucked up; the life of a person or animal ends when it dies. Students may note, for example, that in verse 5 that casting down stones is similar to breaking down barriers between people, which is similar to embracing. On the other hand, gathering together stones to build a wall makes "embracing" impossible.

ANSWERS TO INTEGRATING THE LANGUAGE ARTS

Language, Grammar, and Style

1. Because there is a time to die, there is also a time to weep sadly.
2. If you eat too quickly, there will be time to moan loudly.
3. To live fully, you must experience pain as well as joy.
4. If you want to beat the crowd, you have to run quickly.
5. There is no time like the present to begin to be really happy.

Speaking and Listening & Collaborative Learning
If students have difficulty getting their discussion started, ask them what the verses says about death as a part of human life. What do they say about cycles in general?

Applied English
Remind students to use the proper format for a business letter. They will find information on this format in the Language Arts Survey, 6.5, "Writing a Business Letter."

Collaborative Learning
If students have trouble brainstorming such ideas, ask them to think about when it might be a bad time to plant (in the middle of a blizzard) and when it might be a good time to weep (a funeral). Ask them to come up with similar ideas for many of the times mentioned in the poem.

ADDITIONAL RESOURCES

UNIT 4 RESOURCE BOOK
- Selection Worksheet 4.11
- Selection Check Test 4.4.23
- Selection Test 4.4.24
- Language, Grammar, and Style Resource 3.37

GRAPHIC ORGANIZER

Ideal Element
no cities want to enlarge
everyone performs two years of farm duty for the good of everyone
they know how much food will be needed and they produce surplus, if areas are in need
they just ask for what they need
gold, silver, and jewels are looked down upon

Real Element
cities enlarge as more people move there, business grow, etc.
people begin careers based on their own interests or skills
some areas have abundance, other areas have shortages; during shortages items
may be expensive or difficult to acquire
gold, silver, and jewels are highly valued

READER'S JOURNAL

Students might begin by listing or discussing problems that they see in the world. Their descriptions can then be based on ways of eliminating such problems.

VOCABULARY FROM THE SELECTION

adage
contingency
crestfallen
fortified
indulgent
mettle
subdue
uncouth
vanquished

Literary TOOLS

IRONY. **Irony** is a difference between appearance and reality. Note how More uses irony in this selection.

UTOPIA. A **utopia** is an imaginary, idealized world. More was not the first to create such a world, but the name he chose is now used for any such site. As you read, observe the idealized elements of Utopia and compare them to how they really are or how you think they were in More's time.

Ideal Element	Real Element
language, laws, appearance, etc. the same in all cities	people speak different languages; some cities are well-kept, while others are rundown

Reader's Journal

What do you think a perfect world would be like? Describe such a place.

FROM *Utopia, Book 2*

"THE GEOGRAPHY OF UTOPIA THEIR GOLD AND SILVER"

BY THOMAS MORE

About the AUTHOR

Thomas More (1477–1535) is one of the most widely respected figures in English history. As a young man he studied Latin and logic, and in 1501 he entered the law profession. Despite the demands of his career, More continued to read widely and became a Humanist scholar. The most famous expression of his Humanist philosophy was his book *Utopia,* published in 1516. In it he described his vision of a perfect society ruled by reason. More was intimately involved in the education of his own children and other young people who joined his household. Most of these were girls, who received a then unusual opportunity for a classical education. More became a trusted advisor to King Henry VIII, who made him chancellor in 1529. Two years later More tried to resign his position, realizing that he could never acknowledge a secular king as head of the Church of England. Because he did not accept Henry's divorce of his previous queen, Catherine of Aragon, More did not attend the coronation of Anne Boleyn in 1533, and the next year he refused to sign the Act of Succession. After spending over a year imprisoned in the Tower of London, More was convicted of treason and sentenced to death. He was canonized by the Roman Catholic Church in 1935.

About the SELECTION

More chose the name ***Utopia,*** which comes from the Greek term for *Nowhere,* for the imaginary perfect world he creates. *Utopia* was published in 1516 in two parts. The first part analyzes the problems More saw in the England of his day. The second part describes the world run based on his Humanist views. The selection you are about to read from Book 2 describes the physical set-up of Utopia and some of its guiding principles.

GOALS/OBJECTIVES

Studying this lesson will enable students to
- appreciate an idealized world
- understand what a utopia is and how the word was coined
- define *irony* and identify irony in their reading
- make passive sentences active
- research cities
- write a press release
- understand how both utopias and dystopias critique society

Venice, c.1580. Egnazio Danti.

FROM *Utopia, Book 2*

THE GEOGRAPHY OF UTOPIA THEIR GOLD AND SILVER

THOMAS MORE

From *Book 2*

[The Geography of Utopia]

The island of Utopia is two hundred miles across in the middle part where it is widest, and is nowhere much narrower than this except toward the two ends. These ends, drawn toward one another in a five-hundred-mile circle, make the island crescent-shaped, like a new moon. Between the horns of the crescent, which are about eleven miles apart, the sea enters and spreads into a broad bay. Being sheltered from the wind by the surrounding land, the bay is never rough, but quiet and smooth instead, like a big lake. Thus, nearly the whole inner coast is one great harbor, across which ships pass in every direction, to the great advantage of the people. What with shallows on one side, and rocks on the other, entrance into the bay is very dangerous. Near midchannel, there is one rock that rises above the water, and so presents no danger in itself, on top of it a tower has been built, and there a garrison is kept. Since the other rocks lie under the water, they are very dangerous to navigation. The channels are known only to Utopians, so hardly any strangers enter the by without one of their pilots; and even they themselves could not enter safely if they did not direct their course by some landmarks on the coast. Should these landmarks be shifted about, the Utopians could lure to destruction an enemy fleet coming against them, however big it was.

INDIVIDUAL LEARNING STRATEGIES

Motivation
Generate a class discussion on students' own visions of a utopia. Ask them to consider what a perfect world would be like in terms of its geography, climate, political and social system, and the ways of life of its people.

English Language Learning
More's language is not particularly difficult, but he does borrow several words from ancient Greek. Many of these are names. Others, such as *phylarch* refer to the government of Utopia. It may be helpful to give an overview of these terms in addition to reviewing the vocabulary. Review the footnotes with students before they begin reading.

Reading Proficiency
Have students work in groups of four or five. Each group member should take turns reading paragraphs aloud as the other group members follow along in their texts. Tell students to try to read the lines in such a way that group members can imagine what the reader describes.

Special Needs
Tell students to read the Prereading page closely. Let them know that even though the selection reads as if More is describing the history and customs of a particular place accurately, in reality he is describing a country that he has imagined.

Enrichment
Interested students can read another section of *Utopia* and summarize what they learn about More's imaginary land to their classmates.

ANSWERS TO GUIDED READING QUESTIONS

1. Utophus cut a channel fifteen miles wide where their land joined the continent.
2. He put his soldiers to work so that the vanquished wouldn't feel that their labor was a disgrace.
3. People work on the farm for two years so that the labor is divided and so that there are always some people who know what they are doing.

CROSS-CURRICULAR ACTIVITIES

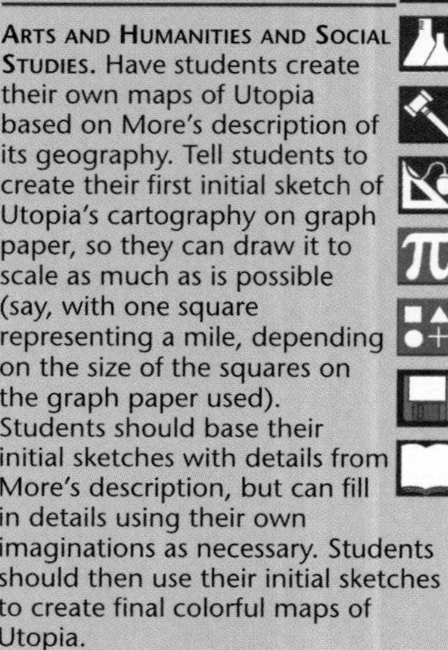

Arts and Humanities and Social Studies. Have students create their own maps of Utopia based on More's description of its geography. Tell students to create their first initial sketch of Utopia's cartography on graph paper, so they can draw it to scale as much as is possible (say, with one square representing a mile, depending on the size of the squares on the graph paper used). Students should base their initial sketches with details from More's description, but can fill in details using their own imaginations as necessary. Students should then use their initial sketches to create final colorful maps of Utopia.

LITERARY NOTE

The Greek philospher, Plato, created his own utopia in *The Republic.* Plato (427–347 BC) was the second of the three most renowned philosophers of ancient Greece. The first was his teacher, Socrates, and the third was Plato's student Aristotle. Plato's family had long been involved in Athenian politics. After Socrates was put to death, Plato became sickened by Athenian politics. He decided that the only just state would be one in which political power rests with philosophers. He describes his ideal leader as a philosopher-king. The ideal state he envisioned is described in *The Republic.*

On the outer side of the island, occasional harbors are to be found; but the coast is rugged by nature, and so well fortified that a few defenders could beat off the attack of a strong force. They say (and the appearance of the place confirms this) that their land was not always an island. But Utopus, who conquered the country and gave it his name (for it had previously been called Abraxa),[1] brought its rude, uncouth inhabitants to such a high level of culture and humanity that they now excel in that regard almost every other people. After subduing them at his first landing, he cut a channel fifteen miles wide where their land joined the continent, and caused the sea to flow around the country. He put not only the natives to work at this task, but all his own soldiers too, so that the vanquished would not think the labor a disgrace. With the work divided among so many hands, the project was finished quickly, and the neighboring peoples, who at first had laughed at his folly, were struck with wonder and terror at his success.

How did Utopia become an island?

Why did he put his soldiers to work?

There are fifty-four cities on the island, all spacious and magnificent, identical in language, customs, institutions, and laws. So far as the location permits, all of them are built on the same plan, and have the same appearance. The nearest are at last twenty-four miles apart, and the farthest are not so remote that a man cannot go on foot from one to the other in a day.

Once a year each city sends three of its old and experience citizens to Amaurot[2] to consider affairs of common interest to the island. Amaurot lies near the omphalos[3] of the land, so to speak, and convenient to every other district, so it acts as a capital. Every city has enough ground assigned to it so that at least ten miles of farm land are available in every direction, though where the cities are farther apart, their territories are more extensive. No city wants to enlarge its boundaries, for the inhabitants consider themselves good cultivators rather than landlords. At proper intervals all over the countryside they have built houses and furnished them with farm equipment. These houses are inhabited by citizens who come to the country by turns to occupy them. No rural house has fewer than forty men and women in it, besides two slaves. A master and mistress, serious and mature persons, are in charge of each household, and over every thirty households is placed a single phylarch.[4] Each year twenty persons from each rural household move back to the city after completing a two-year stint in the country. In their place, twenty others are sent out from town, to learn farm work from those who have already been in the country for a year, and who are better skilled in farming. They, in turn, will teach those who come the following year. If all were equally untrained in farm work and new to it, they might harm the crops out of ignorance. This custom of alternating farm workers is solemnly established so that no one will have to perform such heavy labor for more than two years; but many of them who take a natural pleasure in farm life ask to stay longer.

Why do people work on the farms for two years?

The farm workers till the soil, hew wood, and take their produce to the city by land or water, as is most convenient. They breed an enormous number of chickens by a most marvelous

1. **Abraxa.** Greek, meaning insignificant
2. **Amaurot.** Adapted from a Greek word meaning dark
3. **omphalos.** Center
4. **phylarch.** Head of a tribe

Words For Everyday Use

for • ti • fied (fȯr´ tə fīd) *part.*, strengthened. *The fortified steel of the battleship withstood the enemy's shelling.*

un • couth (un küth´) *adj.*, uncultured, crude. *My neighbor is so uncouth; she has no manners at all.*

sub • due (səb dü´) *vt.*, conquer. *Alan tried to subdue his fears.*

van • quished (van´ kwisht) *n.*, conquered people. *After battle, the vanquished were often forced into slavery.*

method. Men, not hens, hatch the eggs by keeping them in a warm place at an even temperature. As soon as they come out of the shell, the chicks recognize the men, follow them around, and are devoted to them instead of to their real mothers.

They raise very few horses, and these full of mettle, which they keep only to exercise the young men in the art of horsemanship. For the heavy work of plowing and hauling they use oxen, which they agree are inferior to horses over the short haul, but which can hold out longer under heavy burdens, are less subject to disease (as they suppose), and so can be kept with less cost and trouble. Moreover, when oxen are too old for work, they can be used for meat.

Grain they use only to make bread. They drink wine made of grapes, apple or pear cider, or simple water, which they sometimes mix with honey or licorice, of which they have plenty. Although they know very well, down to the last detail, how much food each city and its surrounding district will consume, they produce much more grain and cattle than they need for themselves, and share the surplus with their neighbors. Whatever goods the folk in the country need which cannot be produced there, they request of the town magistrates,[5] and since there is nothing to be paid or exchanged, they get what they want at once without any haggling. They generally go to town once a month in any case, to observe the holy days. When harvest time approaches, the phylarchs in the country notify the town-magistrates how many hands will be needed. Crews of harvesters come just when they're wanted, and in one day of good weather they can usually get in the whole crop.

What do the country folk do if they need something?

[Their gold and silver]

For these reasons,[6] therefore, they have accumulated a vast treasure, buy they do not keep it like a treasure. I'm really quite ashamed to tell you how they do keep it, because you probably won't believe me. I would not have believed it myself if someone had just told me about it; but I was there and saw it with my own eyes. As a general rule, the more different anything is from what people are used to, the harder it is to accept. But considering that all their other customs are so unlike ours, a sensible man will not be surprised that they treat gold and silver quite differently than we do. After all, they never do use money among themselves, but keep it only for a contingency that may or may not actually arise. So in the meanwhile they take care that no one shall overvalue gold and silver, of which money is made, beyond what the metals themselves deserve. Anyone can see, for example, that iron is far superior to either; men could not live without iron, by heaven, any more than without fire or water. But gold and silver have, by nature, no function with which we cannot easily dispense. Human folly has made them precious because they are rare. But in fact nature, like a most indulgent mother, has placed her best gifts out in the open, like air, water, and the earth itself; vain and unprofitable things she has hidden away in remote places.

Why are gold and silver considered precious outside of Utopia?

If in Utopia gold and silver were kept locked up in some tower, foolish heads among the common people might concoct a story that the prince

5. **magistrates.** Civil workers who administer the law
6. **these reasons.** More is referring to a section in which he explains that the Utopians, who hire mercenary soldiers for war, pay them very well, and enemies often desert to their side.

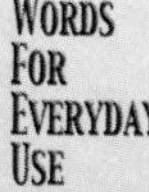

Words For Everyday Use

met • tle (me´ təl) *n.,* high quality. *Nora showed her mettle against the stiff competition.*

con • tin • gen • cy (kən tin´ jən(t) se) *n.,* occurrence that depends upon chance. *Because of a contingency the meeting was postponed.*

in • dul • gent (in dəl´ jənt) *adj.,* excessively kind or lenient. *Mrs. Morris is very strict, but Mr. Morris is quite indulgent.*

ANSWERS TO GUIDED READING QUESTIONS

1. They ask the town magistrates.
2. Gold and silver are considered precious because they are rare.

ADDITIONAL QUESTIONS AND ACTIVITIES

Encourage students to write personal essay examining their own attitudes about wealth. Give students the following questions to freewrite responses to in preparation for writing their essay:

- How important are money and material things to you?
- Could you be happy without money and material things?
- How could you live without money?
- Do you value people more for the money and goods they possess or for their internal qualities?
- How does media—television, movies, books, and music—shape your ideas about wealth?
- How might you incorporate your ideas and values about wealth into your future life as an adult?

ANSWERS TO GUIDED READING QUESTIONS

1. The Utopians use gold and silver for their humblest vessels and for the chains of slaves.
2. Utopian children are given jewels as play things. They see that they are babyish and give them up before they are adults.
3. The ambassadors thought they would impress the Utopians.

ADDITIONAL QUESTIONS AND ACTIVITIES

Students may be surprised to learn that slavery is a part of life in More's Utopian vision. Encourage students to discuss the slavery present in More's Utopia. Ask them the following questions to help spark a class discussion:

- What were your first thoughts or feelings on learning that slavery is present in More's Utopia?
- Why do you think More included slavery in his vision of Utopia? Was it to emulate ancient Greek society? Was it because slavery existed in More's own day and he was a product of his times? Was it for practical reasons? Was it due to a combination of these reasons or some other factor?
- If you could meet travel back in time and meet More, what might you tell him about twenty-first century attitudes toward slavery? (You might wish to point out to students that slavery still exists in certain countries, most notable Africa.)
- If you could work together with More as a co-author, how might you help update his vision of Utopia to account for more twenty-first century attitudes and ideals?

and senate[7] were out to cheat ordinary folk and get some advantage for themselves. The gold and silver might indeed be put into beautiful plateware and rich handiwork, but then in case of necessity the people would not want to give up such articles, on which they had begun to fix their hearts, only to melt them down for soldiers' pay. To avoid these problems they thought of a plan which conforms with their institutions as clearly as it contrasts with our own. Unless one has actually seen it working, their plan may seem incredible, because we prize gold so highly and are so careful about guarding it. With them it's just the other way. While they eat from china dishes and drink from glass cups, well made but inexpensive, their chamber pots and toilet bowls—all their humblest vessels, for use in common halls and even in private homes—are made of gold and silver. The chains and heavy fetters of slaves are also made of these metals. Finally, criminals who are to bear through life the mark of some disgraceful act are forced to wear golden ornaments on their ears, golden rings on their fingers, golden chains around their necks, even gold crowns in their heads. Thus they hold up gold and silver to scorn in every conceivable way. As a result, when they have to part with these metals, which other nations give up with as much agony as if they were being disemboweled, the Utopians feel it no more than the loss of a penny.

What do Utopians do with their gold and silver?

They pick up pearls by the seashore, diamonds and garnets in certain cliffs, but never go out of set purpose to look for them. If they happen to find some, they polish them and give them to the children who, when they are small, feel proud and pleased with such gaudy decorations. But after, when they grow a bit older and notice that only babies like such toys, they lay them aside. The parents don't have to say anything, they simply put those trifles away out of a shamefaced sense that they're no longer suitable, just as our children, when they grow up, put away they rattles, marbles, and dolls.

Why don't Utopians like jewels as adults?

Different customs, different feelings: I never saw the adage better illustrated than in the case of the Anemolian[8] ambassadors, who came to Amaurot while I was there. Because they came to discuss important business, the senate had assembled ahead of time, three citizens from each city. The ambassadors from nearby nations, who had visited Utopia before and knew the local customs, realized that fine clothing was not much respected in that land, silk was despised, and gold a badge of contempt; therefore they came in the very plainest of their clothes. But the Anemolians, who lived farther off and had fewer dealings with the Utopians, had heard only that they all dressed alike and very simply; so they took for granted that their hosts had nothing to wear that they didn't put on. Being themselves rather more proud than wise, they decided to dress as splendidly as the very gods, and dazzle the eyes of the poor Utopians with their gaudy garb.

Why did the ambassadors dress in such finery?

Consequently the three ambassadors made a grand entry with a suite of a hundred attendants, all in clothing of many colors, and most in silk. Being noblemen at home, the ambassadors were arrayed in cloth of gold, with heavy gold chains on their necks, gold jewels at their ears and on their fingers, and sparkling strings of pearls and gems on their

7. **prince and senate.** Households select an assembly. The assembly selects the senate, and the senate chooses a prince for life.
8. **Anemolian.** Refers to people from another country and means "windy people"

WORDS FOR EVERYDAY USE

ad • age (a´ dij) *n.*, old saying that is popularly believed to be true. *Like the adage says, you can't judge a book by its cover.*

caps. In fact, they were decked out in all the articles which in Utopia are used to punish slaves, shame wrongdoers, or pacify infants. It was a sight to see how they strutted when they compared their finery with the dress of the Utopians who had poured out into the street to see them pass. But it was just as funny to see how wide they fell of the mark, and how far they were from getting the consideration they expected. Except for a very few Utopians who for some special reason had visited foreign countries, all the onlookers considered this splendid pomp a mark of disgrace. They therefore bowed to the humblest servants as lords, and took the ambassadors, because of their golden chains, to be slaves, passing them by without any reverence at all. You might have seen children, who had themselves thrown away their pearls and gems, nudge their mother when they saw the ambassador's jeweled caps, and say:

Why did the Utopians bow to the servants of the ambassadors?

"Look at that big lummox, mother, who's still wearing pearls and jewels as if he were a little kid!"

But the mother, in all seriousness, would answer:

"Hush, my boy, I think he is one of the ambassador's fools."

Others found fault with the golden chains as useless because they were so flimsy any slave could break them, and so loose that he could easily shake them off and run away whenever he wanted.

But after the ambassadors had spent a couple of days among the Utopians, they learned of the immense amounts of gold which were as thoroughly despised there as they were prized at home. They saw too that more gold and silver went into making chains and fetters for a single runaway slave than into costuming all three of them. Somewhat crestfallen, then they put away all the finery in which they had strutted so arrogantly; but they saw the wisdom of doing so after they had talked with the Utopians enough to learn their customs and opinions. ■

What did the ambassadors learn?

Words for Everyday Use

crest • fal • len (krest´ fô lən) *adj.*, dejected, humbled. *Uldis was crestfallen when he did not make the team.*

Respond *to the* Selection

Would you want to live in Utopia? Why, or why not?

ANSWERS TO GUIDED READING QUESTIONS

1. The servants were dressed simply, so the Utopians thought they must be the important people.
2. The ambassadors learned that they had not impressed the Utopians with their finery. In fact, the opposite was true.

RESPOND TO THE SELECTION

If students would like to live in Utopia, ask them to describe what about it they would enjoy. If students wouldn't like to live in Utopia, ask them what changes they would make to make it a place they would like to live.

SELECTION CHECK TEST 4.4.23 WITH ANSWERS

Checking Your Reading

1. What has happened to the natives who were living here when Utopus conquered it? **They have become cultured and humane.**
2. What do farm workers and city dwellers do every two years? **They rotate.**
3. What to Utopians do with excess goods? **They share them with their neighbors. Their gold and silver.**
4. What kinds of things are made out of gold and silver? **Humble (chamber pots, toilet bowls) and disgraceful (criminals' ornaments) are made from gold and silver.**
5. What do the Utopians think of the gaudily dressed ambassadors? **They think they are slaves.**

Vocabulary in Context

Fill each blank with the most appropriate word from the Words for Everyday Use. You may have to change the tense of the word.

fortified uncouth subdue vanquished contingency indulgent adage

1. The children love to visit their **indulgent** grandparents, who have very few rules.
2. Joe was afraid he would seem **uncouth** at his first black-tie affair.
3. The gamekeepers **subdued** the injured puma so they could set his broken leg.

SELECTION CHECK TEST 4.4.23 WITH ANSWERS (CONT.)

4. Hordes of volunteers helped **fortify** the sea wall against the approaching storm.
5. I could tell by Jolene's **crestfallen** expression that things had not gone well.

Literary Tools

1. What is a utopia? **A utopia is an imaginary, idealized world.**
2. What is irony? **Irony is a difference between appearance and reality.**
3. Give one example of irony from the selection. **Responses will vary.**

ANSWERS FOR INVESTIGATE, INQUIRE AND IMAGINE

Recall

1a. The cities are all spacious and magnificent. They are the same in many ways.

2a. Farms are set up and everyone works on the farms for at least two years. They request the goods from the town magistrates.

3a. Utopians use gold and silver for their most common vessels. They also use them to chain and mark criminals and slaves. They give jewels to small children.

Interpret

1b. There do not seem to be problems in any of the cities. Also, because the cities are similar in so many ways, there is no competition or jealousy between them.

2b. There are always enough people to produce the food needed. Nobody is stuck doing a necessary job for a lifetime if they do not like it.

3b. Economic disparity is a problem. More recognized this. He chose to make useful things the valued things in Utopia rather than rare things.

Analyze

4a. Cities all have the same appearance. There is more than enough food for everybody, and it is distributed evenly. Gold, silver, and jewels are not valuable.

Synthesize

4b. Such a place does not exist and will not exist. More's creation points out some of the problems of the world he knew, but he suggests that his creation is not a realistic solution to solving such problems.

Evaluate

5a. *Responses will vary.* Students may have questions about aspects of Utopia that they have not read about or wonder how such a set-up actually works. Students may also point out that slavery exists in Utopia, and apparently crime does, too. Neither of these elements is ideal.

Extend

5b. *Responses will vary.* Students will probably say that a perfect society cannot exist. They may point out that it is possible to work towards a better society even if perfection or idealism is not a realistic goal.

INVESTIGATE

Inquire, Imagine

Recall: Gathering Facts → **Interpret:** Finding Meaning

1a. What are the fifty-four cities on the island like?

1b. Why might these characteristics be important?

2a. How do the Utopians grow the food they need? What happens if some people need goods?

2b. What problems does this system eliminate?

3a. What do Utopians do with gold and silver? What do they do with jewels?

3b. Why might More have felt these attitudes were important for Utopia?

Analyze: Taking Things Apart → **Synthesize:** Bringing Things Together

4a. Identify three ways in which Utopia differs from the world you know.

4b. Based on these differences, why do you think More chose a name that means "nowhere"?

Evaluate: Making Judgments → **Extend:** Connecting Ideas

5a. Judge whether the society described by More is ideal.

5b. Do you think an ideal society can exist? Explain your response.

Understanding Literature

Irony. Review the definition for **irony** in Literary Tools on page 334. More uses irony in this selection to highlight some of the problems in his own society. What is ironic about the way the ambassadors dress when they visit Utopia?

Utopia. Review the definition for **utopia** and the chart you made for Literary Tools on page 334. A utopia can be used to illuminate societal problems. What shortcomings do you think More saw in his society?

ANSWERS FOR UNDERSTANDING LITERATURE

Utopia. *Responses will vary.* Based on the elements More introduces in this selection, he seems to be critiquing wealth and a socioeconomic system based on useless commodities. He also points out that economic disparity and basic needs, such as food, not being met are problems.

Irony. The ambassadors make the assumption that their gaudy appearance, bejeweled and covered in gold and silks will impress the Utopians, when in fact the opposite is true and the ambassadors' appearance lowers the Utopians' opinion of the ambassadors.

Writer's Journal

1. Imagine that you are a visitor to Utopia. Write a **post card** home about what is most striking to you about the land, its people, or its customs.
2. Write an **editorial** about a problem you see in your community.
3. Create your own utopia. Write a **description** of the land, the government, and any other customs that make this place unique and ideal.

Integrating *the* Language Arts

Language, Grammar, and Style

Review "Making Passive Sentences Active" in the Language Arts Survey 3.37. Then rewrite the following sentences in the active voice.

1. Ancient Greek and Roman works were often read by the Humanists of the Renaissance.
2. Plato's *Republic* was read carefully by Thomas More.
3. More was influenced by the exploration of the New World.
4. Even though Plato's *Republic* came before *Utopia,* it is often referred to as a utopia.
5. *Utopia* was published by More in 1516.

Study and Research

Researching Cities. In Utopia, communities create surpluses to share with neighbors who may be in need. Everyone takes turns at farming because it is a necessary task. Using reference materials, find out about several cities in your state. What are their main industries? What professions do people hold? How does the wealth of one city compare to another?

Applied English

Press Release. Imagine that a planned community is being created. The community should be a utopia for the new residents. Write a press release about the community. Use your imagination to decide what will be special about this community.

Collaborative Learning & Speaking and Listening

Dystopia. The opposite of a utopia is a *dystopia,* or imaginary, horrible world. Dystopias, like utopias, are common in science fiction. Watch a sci-fi movie or read a science fiction novel or short story. Like utopias, dystopias can illuminate problems in our society. Discuss what the story you read or the movie you watched suggests about our society.

ANSWERS TO INTEGRATING THE LANGUAGE ARTS

Language, Grammar, and Style

1. The Humanists of the Renaissance often read ancient Greek and Roman works .
2. Thomas More was very interested in Plato's Republic.
3. This work and the exploration of the New World strongly influenced him when he wrote Utopia.
4. Plato's Republic is often referred to as a utopia, even though it came before Utopia.
5. More published Utopia in 1516.

Study and Research

Students might also research planned communities and try to answer the following questions: How is the community organized? What products, services, and other activities are available in the community? What are the goals of the community? How well are these goals met? How can/could people join the community.

Applied English

Refer students to the Language Arts Survey 6.9, "Delivering a Press Release," for more information on the form of a press release and for tips on preparing one.

Collaborative Learning & Speaking and Listening

Possible dystopias students might explore through science fiction are George Orwell's 1984 and the film by the same name, Anthony Burgess's A Clockwork Orange and Staley Kubrick's film adaptation of this novel, Alfred Bester's novel The Demolished Man, and William Gibson's novel Virtual Light. Be forewarned that dystopias portray negative, and sometimes very adult and disturbing, aspects of the world. You may want to excerpt potions of these works for students.

ADDITIONAL RESOURCES

Unit 4 Resource Book
From the Canzoniere

- Sonnet 1
- Sonnet 47
- Sonnet 54
- Selection Worksheet 4.12
- Selection Check Test 4.4.25
- Selection Test 4.4.26
- Study and Research Resource 5.35

GRAPHIC ORGANIZER

1 The speaker regrets the excessive love he devoted himself to in his youth. The speaker has learned how love can "sear," and seeks pardon for his "vain and empty" hopes of romance in his youth. The speaker is ashamed that now he is renowned for his feelings of romantic love, which he considers a vanity.
47 The speaker blesses the place and time where he first became the "prisoner" to his beloved's eyes. The speaker blesses the pain that entered his heart when he fell in love. The speaker blesses his expression of his love—his sighs, his tears and his sonnets. He also expresses hope that his thoughts will always be focused on his beloved.
54 The speaker says he is tired of wondering why he never grows tired of thinking of his beloved, even though doing so brings him sorrow. The speaker wonders why he still finds new ways to describe his beloved and why he still murmurs her name in the night. The speaker says that just as his limbs will grow stiff one day from his fruitless pursuit (his strength consumed), his poems to his beloved have consumed too much ink, which he blames on love rather than art.

READER'S JOURNAL

Encourage students to focus their journal responses on romantic love. You might wish to just review students' journal writing personally, rather than share students' views on love and spark a class discussion. Students might be too embarrassed or find it to difficult to reveal their thoughts on romantic love as a group.

MULTICULTURAL EXTENSIONS

Literary TOOLS

Petrarchan Sonnet. A **Petrarchan** sonnet is divided into two parts: an octave and a sestet. The rhyme scheme of the octave is *abbaabba.* The first quatrain presents the theme while the second quatrain develops it. The rhyme scheme of the sestet can be arranged *cdecdecdcdcd,* or *cdedce.* The first three lines exemplify or reflect on the theme while the last three lines bring the whole poem to a unified close.

Theme. A **theme** is a central idea in a literary work. As you read the selection, summarize the theme in each sonnet. What is the speaker saying about love? To help you find the theme of each sonnet, make a chart like the one below to organize your thoughts and to analyze the poem. Under each category, describe the theme, development, reflection of the theme, and the conclusion for each sonnet.

Theme	Development	Reflection of Theme and Conclusion
There are more important things than love.		

Reader's Journal

What are your thoughts about love? Is your view positive or negative? How do you know when you love someone?

FROM THE *Canzoniere*

Sonnet 1, translated by Thomas Bergin
Sonnet 47, translated by Francis Wrangham
Sonnet 54, translated by Thomas Bergin

BY PETRARCH

About the AUTHOR

Francesco Petrarca (1304–1374), known in English-speaking countries as **Petrarch,** is often considered the father both of Italian Humanism and of the European tradition of lyric poetry. Petrarch was born in Arezzo, Italy. His family moved to Avignon, France, in 1312, and there he received his early education. He studied at Montpellier, France, and in Bologna, Italy, but his real interest lay with literature. After his father died in 1326, Petrarch returned to Avignon and worked for an influential cardinal, a high official of the Catholic Church. In 1327, in the Church of St. Clare in Avignon, he met the woman named Laura for whom he developed a deep, unrequited love that was to inspire his great vernacular Italian sonnets and other poems. In subsequent years, Petrarch made a great name for himself as a classical scholar and vernacular poet. In 1340, he was invited by both Paris and Rome to be crowned as poet laureate. In 1348, the plague claimed the lives of several of his friends and of his beloved Laura. During the later part of his life, he collected his poems about Laura into a book, the *Canzoniere,* divided into works written during Laura's life and after her death. Today, Petrarch is remembered for two reasons. First, he helped to revive interest in the literature of ancient Italy and so gave impetus to the movement that we know as Humanism. Second, his highly personal, highly musical vernacular verse gave to Europe the model for lyric poetry down to our own day. Such poetry deals with the intensely felt emotions of an individual speaker.

About the SELECTIONS

The following sonnets from Petrarch's ***Canzoniere*** deal with love and unrequited love. A sonnet is a fourteen-line poem that follows one of a number of different rhyme schemes. The Petrarchan form of the sonnet is divided into two parts: an octave and a sestet. The sonnet form was introduced to England during the sixteenth century by Wyatt and Sidney, both admirers of Petrarch's work.

GOALS/OBJECTIVES

Studying this lesson will enable students to

- empathize with the mixed emotions expressed by the speaker in a sonnet cycle
- identify the characteristics of Petrarchan sonnets
- define *theme* and identify the theme of a poem
- research Petrarch's influence among his contemporaries
- create a music video

FROM THE

Canzoniere

PETRARCH

SONNET 1

O ye who in these scattered rhymes may hear
The echoes of the sighs that fed my heart
In errant youth, for I was then, in part
Another man from what I now appear,
If you have learned by proof how Love can sear,
Then for these varied verses where I chart
Its vain and empty hope and vainer smart
Pardon I may beseech, nay, Pity's tear.
For now I see how once my story spread
And I became a wonder to mankind
So in my heart I feel ashamed—alas,
That nought but shame my vanities have bred,
And penance, and the knowledge of clear mind
That earthly joys are dreams that swiftly pass. ■

How does the speaker now feel about the earlier part of his life?

ANSWERS TO GUIDED READING QUESTIONS

1. He feels foolish and ashamed for having wasted so much time in a vain and unrequited love, in part because he now feels that love is a shallow concern.

INDIVIDUAL LEARNING STRATEGIES

MOTIVATION
Students may especially enjoy the opportunity to create their own music video for the Media Literacy & Collaborative Learning Activity. Tell students to bear in mind, however, that a music video produced for the classroom should avoid foul language and graphic depiction of violence, substance abuse, or other adult themes.

ENGLISH LANGUAGE LEARNING
Point out that the Petrarchan poems presented here are translations from the original Italian. Tell students that one of the challenges of translating poetry is preserving meter and rhyme scheme. If there is a native Italian speaker/reader in school, encourage him or her to translate the Italian original literally, word-for-word. How does it differ from the translation presented in their textbooks?

READING PROFICIENCY
Encourage students to work in groups of three. Each group member should read all three poems. Each group member should dramatically read aloud one of the poems as the other students listen. Encourage students to discuss how hearing the poems read aloud helped them to better understand the poems.

SPECIAL NEEDS
Students may have difficulty understanding how the three poems are related. Tell them that all three poems have the same speaker, and the woman the speaker is talking about loving is the same in each. The differences in the speaker's attitude toward both his beloved and love itself stem from the fact that these sonnets are written on the same subject or theme over the course of many years.

INDIVIDUAL LEARNING STRATEGIES (CONT.)

ENRICHMENT
Students can explore the different meanings of the term *Humanism.* What does the term mean when applied to Petrarch or to Renaissance thought generally? What various meanings does the term have today? Students should find works by Humanists, by critics of Humanism, and by neutral parties.

ANSWER TO GUIDED READING QUESTION

1. He talks of a "blest" time and place where he first felt "oppressed," and of a "blest" pain or pang. The contradictory language reflects that love often brings mixed emotions of joy and sorrow.

BIOGRAPHICAL NOTE

Petrarch devoted nearly all of his life to secular literature, especially to reviving the works of Classical Rome. The sonnets presented here deal with Petrarch's unrequited love for a woman named Laura. Sonnet 1 was written after the rest of the sonnets and placed at the beginning of the *Canzoniere* introduction. As Sonnet 1 indicates, near the end of his life, Petrarch began to regret his lifelong obsession with Laura, which led, he says, to "empty hope and vainer smart." Sonnet 1 is thus a sort of retraction, written in old age, of the work that follows it. Literary history has not shared Petrarch's own assessment of his secular sonnets, which he calls in Sonnet 1 his "vanities." Quite the contrary, Petrarch's work has served from the Renaissance on as a model for the entire tradition of secular love poetry in Europe.

Lady with Book of Verse by Petrarch, c.1500s. Andrea del Sarto. Uffizi, Florence, Italy.

SONNET 47

Blest be the day, and blest the month, the year,
The spring, the hour, the very moment blest,
The lovely scene, the spot, where first oppressed
I sunk, of two bright eyes the prisoner:
And blest the first soft pang, to me most dear,
Which thrilled my heart, when Love became its guest;
And blest the bow, the shafts which pierced my brest.
And even the wounds, which bosomed thence I bear.
Blest too the strains which, poured through glade and grove,
Have made the woodlands echo with her name;
The sighs, the tears, the languishment, the love:
And blest those sonnets, sources of my fame;
And blest that thought—Oh! never to remove!
Which turns to her alone, from her alone which came. ■

What contradictory language does the speaker use when discussing the moment when he fell in love? Why would he use such contradictory language?

ADDITIONAL QUESTIONS AND ACTIVITIES

Ask students why unrequited love is such a common theme in poetry and is far more prevalent than the theme of satisfaction in love. Are we merely fascinated with the unattainable? Is pain and sadness more interesting to us than joy?

Ask students to bring in a sampling of current love songs. Do they have similar messages and images? Has the way we talk about love changed dramatically since Petrarch's time? Why, or why not?

SONNET 54

I grow a-weary of my wondering
Why my thoughts never weary, love, of you,
Why I consent to living as I do
Under the burden that my sorrows bring.
Why is it that, for all the songs I sing,
I still find words and numbers ever new
For your fair face and eyes—why all night through
'Tis still your name my lips go murmuring?
If, just as after many fruitless days
In your pursuit, for utter weariness
My limbs grow stiff, so likewise my poor lays
Have too much ink consumed (as I confess)
And filled too many pages with your praise,
'Tis not for fault of art but Love's excess. ■

Of what does the speaker never grow weary?

Respond *to the* **SELECTION**

Why do you think unrequited love is such a common theme in poetry and in song lyrics?

ANSWER TO GUIDED READING QUESTION

1. He never grows weary of thinking of his beloved.

RESPOND TO THE SELECTION

Encourage students to discuss or write about some of the emotions they have seen people in love show in films or on television, heard them show in song or music, or read about in literature. Draw their attention to common emotions such as joy, sadness, anger, and resignation.

SELECTION CHECK TEST 4.4.25 WITH ANSWERS

Checking Your Reading

SONNET 1

1. What did the speaker become once his story spread? **He is a wonder to mankind.**
2. What are earthly joys? **They are dreams that swiftly pass.**

SONNET 47

3. What event is the speaker recalling? **He is recalling falling in love.**

SONNET 54

4. Of what do the speaker's thoughts never weary? **They never weary of his love.**
5. With what has the speaker filled too many pages? **He has filled too many pages with praise for his love.**

Literary Tools

Match each sentence beginning with the *best fitting* conclusion. You will not use any choices more than once.

_A_ 1. The second quatrain of a Petrarchan sonnet…
_C_ 2. A theme…
_B_ 3. Every sonnet …
_G_ 4. The rhyme scheme of a sestet…
_E_ 5. An octave…

a. develops a theme.
b. has fourteen lines.
c. is a central idea in a literary work.
d. is *abab abab*.
e. has eight lines.
f. introduces a theme.
g. is *cdecde* or *cdcdcd* or *cdedce*.

ANSWERS TO INVESTIGATE, INQUIRE AND IMAGINE

RECALL

1a. The speaker is addressing his reader.

2a. The speaker blesses the place and time he fell in love; the pain love has made him feel in his heart; the sighs, tears, and poems that were a product of his love; and that part of him that thinks only of his beloved. Words such as wounds, tears, and languishment contradict the poem's overall message that love is something to treasure.

3a. The speaker wonders why he never grows tired of thinking of his beloved, living with the sorrow that his unrequited love brings him, finding new ways to describe his beloved, saying her name in the night, engaging in fruitless pursuit of her, or writing poems to praise her.

INTERPRET

1b. The speaker is more bitter about unrequited love. He has learned that unrequited love is fruitless and passes in time and that there are more important things.

2b. The speaker feels joy because he is so enraptured with his beloved, but he feels pain because she does not share the intensity of his feelings.

3b. The speaker's unrequited love consumes his every thought. He is obsessed and focuses all his energy toward attaining his beloved, which he realizes is impossible. Therefore, his love wearies him because it has become a compulsion he cannot give up.

ANALYZE

4a. The speaker was obsessed with his love and his beloved I his youth, but as an older person he has decided that love, especially unrequited love, is trivial and is embarrassed about the passion he showed in his youth.

SYNTHESIZE

4b. Petrarch is capable of feeling very strong emotions, is consumed by the emotion he is feeling at the moment, and is capable of growing and changing. He seems to be very passionate yet philosophical and analytical.

EVALUATE

5a. *Responses will vary.* Many students will not agree with the decision Petrarch made to cast aside love later in life (as revealed in Sonnet 1).

EXTEND

5b. *Responses will vary.* Many of the poems—those by Wyatt, Sidney, Campion, Jonson, and Petrarch—explore unrequited love, or love that

INVESTIGATE, Inquire, Imagine

Recall: GATHERING FACTS → Interpret: FINDING MEANING

1a. Whom is the speaker addressing in Sonnet 1?

1b. The speaker in Sonnet 1 claims to be different from the person he was "in errant youth." How is he different? What has he learned?

2a. What does the speaker bless in Sonnet 47? What words contradict the overall sentiment of the poem?

2b. Why does the speaker feel both joy and pain?

3a. About what does the speaker in Sonnet 54 wonder?

3b. Why has this become a burden to him?

Analyze: TAKING THINGS APART → Synthesize: BRINGING THINGS TOGETHER

4a. Describe the speaker based on his thoughts, feelings, and the decisions he makes that are reflected by the sonnets.

4b. How would you summarize Petrarch's personality and character? What kind of person would you describe him as?

Evaluate: MAKING JUDGMENTS → Extend: CONNECTING IDEAS

5a. How would you critique Petrarch's conclusions on love? Do you agree or disagree with him? Why, or why not?

5b. Review the lyric poems in this unit that deal with the subject of love. What different experiences of love are expressed in these poems? Of all the love poems in the unit, which can you identify with the most? Explain.

Understanding Literature

PETRARCHAN SONNET. Review the definition of a **Petrarchan sonnet** in the Literary Tools on page 342. In what ways is the Petrarchan sonnet different from the Shakespearean sonnet? How does the difference in form affect the way that the theme or message is portrayed?

THEME. Review the definition of **theme** in the Handbook of Literary Terms and the chart you made for Literary Tools on page 342. What similar theme is treated in Petrarch's sonnets and those by Wyatt and Sidney in this unit?

ANSWERS TO INVESTIGATE, INQUIRE AND IMAGINE (CONT.)

ends unhappily. Some (by Shakespeare, Jonson, Spenser, Marlowe, and Petrarch) express very romantic ideals about love, but others (Raleigh, Campion and Petrarch's sonnet 1) express more cynical attitudes toward love. Students may also note that some poems discuss love using conventional images (Marlowe, Jonson), while others use more unconventional images (most notable Shakespeare). Encourage students to explore the reasons behind why thy identified with a particular poem.

WRITER'S JOURNAL

1. Imagine you are Ann Landers or Dear Abby. Write an **advice column** addressing what Petrarch should do about his unrequited love for Laura.
2. Write your own **definition** of love. How does it compare with Petrarch's definition and attitude towards love? How does it compare with your classmates?
3. Write **song lyrics** consisting of 10–15 lines about unrequited love.

Integrating *the* LANGUAGE ARTS

Study and Research

INFLUENCES OF PETRARCH. The Petrarchan sonnet was introduced to England during the sixteenth century by Englishmen Wyatt and Sidney, both great admirers of Petrarch's work. Petrarch also had followers throughout Europe who established the sonnet tradition in their own countries. For example, Torquato Tasso and Luis de Camoes established the sonnet tradition in Portugal, and Pierre de Ronsard and Joachmín du Bellay established it in France. Research one of these poets and find information on how Petrarch influenced their writing style and content. Also find information on how Petrarch's work has affected the arts and literary culture of that country. A good place to start your research is to do an Internet search on one of the poets mentioned. Read the Language Arts Survey 5.35, "How to Understand Internet Web Sites," to help you in your search. Organize your information into a written report. In your written report, you may want to include some poems that the poet writes using the Petrarchan sonnet form.

Media Literacy & Collaborative Learning

MAKING A MUSIC VIDEO. Imagine you are competing for the MTV music video award. Get into groups of 6–10 people. Decide who will be the songwriters, performers, and producers in your group. Those who are the songwriters will write lyrics that address love using the Petrarchan sonnet form. Those who are the performers will put the lyrics to music and perform the song. Those that are the producers will be in charge of sound, lights, camera, staging, props, costumes, and other aspects of making a music video. After you have completed the music video, present it to the rest of the class. Then vote on which video receives the MTV music video award.

ANSWERS FOR UNDERSTANDING LITERATURE

PETRARCHAN SONNET. While a Shakespearean stanza can be broken up into three quatrains and a couplet, Petrarchan sonnets can be broken up into an octet and a sestet. While Shakespearean sonnets rhyme *abab cdcd efef gg,* Petrarchan sonnets rhyme *cdecde, cdcdcd,* or *cdedce.* Students may suggest that because of the rhyme scheme and arrangement of stanzas, a Shakespearean sonnet necessarily breaks a theme into smaller parts.

THEME. The similar theme treated is unrequited love.

ANSWERS TO INTEGRATING THE LANGUAGE ARTS

Study and Research
Inform students that other possible sources include literary encyclopedias, encyclopedias (both hardbound and electronic), books on the literature of a particular country, and biographies.

Media Literacy & Collaborative Learning
You may wish to follow some of the tips in the Motivation section of the Individual Learning Strategies box to make sure that this assignment is not too disruptive to your classroom.

ADDITIONAL QUESTIONS AND ACTIVITIES

Students may form small groups to discuss the following questions.

Sonnet 75

What are the rhyme scheme and meter of Spenser's Sonnet 75? Can it be called an Elizabethan or a Petrarchan sonnet? What is the theme? What other sonnet from the unit has a similar theme? Do you prefer one over the other, and if so, why?

Answers

Sonnet 75 is written in iambic pentameter with the rhyme scheme abab bcbc bdbd ee; it is neither Elizabethan nor Petrarchan. The theme is the immortality of literature (as opposed to the mortality of human flesh), the same as Shakespeare's Sonnet 18.

Sonnet 30

A session is a meeting of a court of justice. What conceit does Shakespeare use in the opening lines of Sonnet 30? What is the theme of Shakespeare's Sonnet 30?

Answers

In Sonnet 30, Shakespeare compares his thoughts about past sadnesses and regrets to a court of law, with each memory testifying as a witness. The theme is the value of friendship.

Sonnet 73

What are the major metaphors in Shakespeare's Sonnet 73? Do you find them effective?

Answers

In Sonnet 73, Shakespeare uses a tree in winter, nightfall, and a dying fire as metaphors for approaching the end of life.

SELECTIONS FOR ADDITIONAL READING: RENAISSANCE LITERATURE

Sonnet 75 ("One day I wrote her name . . .") from *Amoretti* by Edmund Spenser

One day I wrote her name upon the strand,° *beach*
But came the waves and washèd it away:
Agayne[1] I wrote it with a second hand,
But came the tyde, and made my paynes his pray.° *prey*
"Vayne man," sayd she, "that doest in vaine assay,° *attempt*
A mortall thing so to immortalize,
For I my selve shall lyke to this decay,
And eek my name bee wypèd out lykewize."° *also*
"Not so," quod° I, "let baser things devize,° *quoth/contrive*
To dy in dust, but you shall live by fame:
My verse your vertues rare shall eternize,
And in the heavens wryte your glorious name.
Where whenas death shall all the world subdew,
Our love shall live, and later life renew."

Sonnet 30 ("When to the sessions . . .") by William Shakespeare

When to the sessions of sweet silent thought
I summon up remembrance of things past,
I sigh the lack of many a thing I sought,
And with old woes new wail my dear time's waste:
Then can I drown an eye (unused to flow)
For precious friends hid in death's dateless night,
And weep afresh love's long since canceled woe,
And moan th' expense of many a vanished sight:
Then can I grieve at grievances foregone,
And heavily from woe to woe tell o'er
The sad account of fore-bemoanèd moan,
Which I new pay as if not paid before.
But if the while I think on thee, dear friend,
All losses are restored and sorrows end.

Sonnet 73 ("That time of year . . .") by William Shakespeare

That time of year thou mayst in me behold
When yellow leaves, or none, or few, do hang
Upon those boughs which shake against the cold,
Bare ruined choirs, where late the sweet birds sang.
In me thou seest the twilight of such day
As after sunset fadeth in the west;
Which by and by black night doth take away,
Death's second self that seals up all in rest.
In me thou seest the glowing of such fire,
That on the ashes of his youth doth lie,
As the deathbed whereon it must expire,
Consumed with that which it was nourished by.
This thou perceiv'st, which makes thy love more strong,
To love that well, which thou must leave ere long.

Eve's Apology in Defense of Women[2] from *Salve Deus Rex Judaeorum*[3] by Aemilia Lanyer

Now Pontius Pilate is to judge the cause
Of faultless Jesus, who before him stands,
Who neither hath offended prince, nor laws,
Although he now be brought in woeful bands.
O noble governor, make thou yet a pause,
Do not in innocent blood inbrue thy hands;
But hear the words of thy most worthy wife,[4]
Who sends to thee, to beg her Saviour's life.
Let barb'rous cruelty far depart from thee,
And in true justice take affliction's part;
Open thine eyes, that thou the truth may'st see.
Do not the thing that goes against thy heart,
Condemn not him that must thy Saviour be;
But view his holy life, his good desert.
Let not us women glory in men's fall.
Who had power given to overrule us all.

---

1. **Agayne.** Again; this is one example of Spenser's antiquated spellings.
2. **Eve's . . . Women.** A narrator offers Eve's apology for her actions in defense of all women in an impassioned address to Pilate, the Roman official who authorized Christ's crucifixion. Eve and Pilate's wife represent all women, and Pilate and Adam represent all men.
3. ***Salve . . . Judaeorum.*** A variation of the inscription on Christ's cross. It means "Hail, God, King of the Jews."
4. **But . . . wife.** Pilate's wife wrote him a letter asking him to spare Jesus because she had received a warning in a dream (Matthew 27:19).

EVE'S *APOLOGY IN DEFENSE OF WOMEN*

About the Selection. The word *apology* is most often used today to mean a statement of regret or an admission of error. In the title of Lanyer's poem, however, it means a formal defense, a carefully reasoned argument proclaiming someone's innocence. Lanyer argues that women's lowly social status, which had been justified by Eve's "guilt" in encouraging Adam to eat from the tree of knowledge, is not fair in light of the much greater sin committed by men's representative, Pontius Pilate.

Till now your indiscretion sets us free.
And makes our former fault much less appear;
Our mother Eve, who tasted of the tree,
Giving to Adam what she held most dear,
Was simply good, and had no power to see;[7]
The after-coming harm did not appear:
The subtle serpent that our sex betrayed
Before our fall so sure a plot had laid.
That undiscerning ignorance perceived
No guile or craft that was by him intended;
For had she known of what we were bereaved,[1]
To his request she had not condescended.
But she, poor soul, by cunning was deceived;
No hurt therein her harmless heart intended:
For she alleged God's word, which he denies,
That they should die, but even as gods be wise.

But surely Adam cannot be excused;
Her fault though great, yet he was most to blame;
What weakness offered, strength might have refused,
Being lord of all, the greater was his shame.
Although the serpent's craft had her abused,
God's holy word ought all his actions frame,
For he was lord and king of all the earth,
Before poor Eve had either life or breath,

Who being framed by God's eternal hand
The perfectest man that ever breathed on earth;
And from God's mouth received that strait command,
The breach whereof he knew was present death;
Yea, having power to rule both sea and land,
Yet with one apple won to lose that breath
Which God had breathed in his beauteous face,
Bringing us all in danger and disgrace.

And then to lay the fault on Patience' back,
That we (poor women) must endure it all.
We know right well he did discretion lack,
Being not persuaded thereunto at all.
If Eve did err, it was for knowledge sake;
The fruit being fair persuaded him to fall:
No subtle serpent's falsehood did betray him;
If he would eat it, who had power to stay him?
Not Eve, whose fault was only too much love,
Which made her give this present to her dear,
That what she tasted he likewise might prove,
Whereby his knowledge might become more clear;
He never sought her weakness to reprove
With those sharp words which he of God did hear;
Yet men will boast of knowledge, which he took
From Eve's fair hand, as from a learned book.

If any evil did in her remain,
Being made of him,[2] he was the ground of all.
If one of many worlds could lay a stain
Upon our sex, and work so great a fall
To wretched man by Satan's subtle train,
What will so foul a fault amongst you all?[3]
Her weakness did the serpent's words obey,
But you in malice God's dear Son betray,

Whom, if unjustly you condemn to die,
Her sin was small to what you do commit;
All mortal sins that do for vengeance cry
Are not to be compared unto it.
If many worlds would altogether try
By all their sins the wrath of God to get,
This sin of yours surmounts them all as far
As doth the sun another little star.

Then let us have our liberty again,
And challenge to yourselves no sovereignty.
You came not in the world without our pain,
Make that a bar against your cruelty;
Your fault being greater, why should you disdain
Our being your equals, free from tyranny?
If one weak woman simply did offend,
This sin of yours hath no excuse nor end,

To which, poor souls, we never gave consent.
Witness, thy wife, O Pilate, speaks for all,
Who did but dream, and yet a message sent
That thou shouldest have nothing to do at all
With that just man; which, if thy heart relent,
Why wilt thou be a reprobate with Saul[4]
To seek the death of him that is so good,
For thy soul's health to shed this dearest blood?

"Jack and Joan" by Thomas Campion

Jack and Joan they think no ill,
But loving live, and merry still;
Do their week-days' work, and pray
Devoutly on the holy day;
Skip and trip it on the green,
And help to choose the summer queen;
Lash out, at a country feast,
Their silver penny with the best.

1. **Our . . . see.** Eve, tempted by the serpent, ate the forbidden fruit. Genesis emphasizes Eve's knowledge that the fruit was forbidden and blames her action on pride and ambition.
2. **bereaved.** Deprived of eternal life; this along with suffering, work, and pain in childbirth were punishment for eating the forbidden fruit.
3. **made of him.** According to Genesis, Eve was created from Adam's rib.
4. **What . . . all?** How terrible a stain on all men can Pilate's condemnation of Jesus be?
7. **reprobate with Saul.** Damned like Saul, King of Israel, who wanted God's prophet-king, David, killed

ADDITIONAL QUESTIONS AND ACTIVITIES

"Jack and Joan"
What is the speaker's attitude toward the title characters? Based on this attitude, how would you classify the poem? How does the theme of "Jack and Joan" compare with that of Campion's other poem "When Thou Must Home to Shades of Underground" (page 276)? Do any other poems in the unit have a similar theme?

Answers
The speaker has an idealized view of Jack and Joan's simple country life; it is a pastoral poem. Like "When Thou Must Home to Shades of Underground," this poem expresses disdain for the superficiality and pettiness of life in a royal court; Spenser's Sonnet 31 also expresses this feeling.

"A LITANY IN TIME OF PLAGUE"

About the Author. The theme of **Thomas Nashe**'s (1567–1601) "A Litany in Time of Plague" is well suited to his life, which was cut short at about age thirty-three. He arrived in London around 1588 and became friends with the likes of Robert Greene and Christopher Marlowe. His bold, eccentric style of writing and sharp wit made him a talented pamphleteer; in the 1590s he engaged in verbal combat with another writer, Gabriel Harvey, exchanging a series of caustic, slanderous pamphlets. In 1599, the Archbishop of Canterbury put an end to this exchange by banning the further publication of any of the two writers' works. Other significant works by Nashe include the first English picaresque novel, entitled *The Unfortunate Traveler, or the Life of Jack Wilton* (1594), and *Christ's Tears Over Jerusalem* (1593), in which Nashe warned that a plague gripping London was a sign that the city's decadence could lead to the same destruction suffered by Jerusalem in biblical times.

Well can they judge of nappy ale,
And tell at large a winter tale;
Climb up to the apple loft
And turn the crabs till they be soft.
Tib is all the father's joy,
And little Tom the mother's boy.
All their pleasure is content;
And care, to pay their yearly rent.

Joan can call by name her cows
And deck her windows with green boughs;
She can wreaths and tutties make,
And trim with plums a bridal cake.
Jack knows what brings gain or loss,
And his long flail can stoutly toss,
Makes the hedge, which others break,
And ever thinks what he doth speak.

Now, you courtly dames and knights,
That study only strange delights,
Though you scorn the home-spun gray
And revel in your rich array,
Though your tongues dissemble deep
And can your heads from danger keep,
Yet, for all your pomp and train,
Securer lives the silly swain.

"A Litany in Time of Plague"
by Thomas Nashe

Adieu, farewell, earth's bliss;
This world uncertain is;
Fond are life's lustful joys;
Death proves them all but toys;
None from his darts can fly;
I am sick, I must die.
Lord, have mercy on us!

Rich men, trust not in wealth,
Gold cannot buy you health;
Physic himself must fade.
All things to end are made,
The plague full swift goes by;
I am sick, I must die.
Lord, have mercy on us!

Beauty is but a flower
Which wrinkles will devour;
Brightness falls from the air;
Queens have died young and fair;
dust hath closèd Helen's[1] eye.
I am sick, I must die.
Lord, have mercy on us!

Strength stoops unto the grave,
Worms feed on Hector brave;
Swords may not fight with fate,
Earth still holds ope her gate.
"Come, come!" the bells do cry.
I am sick, I must die.
Lord, have mercy on us.

Wit with his wantonness
Tasteth death's bitterness;
Hell's executioner
Hath no ears for to hear
What vain art can reply.
I am sick, I must die.
Lord, have mercy on us.

Haste, therefore, each degree,
To welcome destiny;
Heaven is our heritage,
Earth but a player's stage;
Mount we unto the sky.
I am sick, I must die.
Lord, have mercy on us.

Psalm 23 from The King James Bible

The LORD *is* my shepherd; I shall not want.
2 He maketh me to lie down in green pastures: he
leadeth me beside the still waters.
3 He restoreth my soul: he leadeth me in the
paths of righteousness for his name's sake.
4 Yea, though I walk through the valley of the
shadow of death, I will fear no evil: for thou *art* with
me; thy rod and thy staff they comfort me.
5 Thou preparest a table before me in the
presence of mine enemies: thou anointest my head
with oil; my cup runneth over.
6 Surely goodness and mercy shall follow me all
the days of my life: and I will dwell in the house of the
Lord for ever.

Matthew 13, The Parable of the Sower
from The King James Bible

1 The same day went Jesus out of the house, and
sat by the sea side.
2 And great multitudes were gathered together
unto him, so that he went into a ship, and sat; and the
whole multitude stood on the shore.

1. **Helen.** The reference is to Helen of Troy, who was known for her great beauty. Both she and Hector, a hero of the Trojan War, died despite their respective beauty and power.

3 And he spake many things unto them in parables, saying, Behold, a sower went forth to sow;

4 And when he sowed, some *seeds* fell by the way side, and the fowls came and devoured them up;

5 Some fell upon stony places, where they had not much earth: and forthwith they sprung up, because they had no deepness of earth:

6 And when the sun was up, they were scorched; and because they had no root, they withered away.

7 And some fell among thorns; and the thorns sprung up, and choked them:

8 But other fell into good ground, and brought forth fruit, some an hundredfold, some sixtyfold, some thirtyfold.

9 Who hath ears to hear, let him hear.

10 And the disciples came, and said unto him, Why speakest thou unto them in parables?

11 He answered and said unto them, Because it is given unto you to know the mysteries of the kingdom of heaven, but to them it is not given.

12 For whosoever hath, to him shall be given, and he shall have more abundance: but whosoever hath not, from him shall be taken away even that he hath.

13 Therefore speak I to them in parables: because they seeing see not; and hearing they hear not, neither do they understand.

14 And in them is fulfilled the prophecy of Esaias, which saith, By hearing ye shall hear, and shall not understand; and seeing ye shall see, and shall not perceive:

15 For this people's heart is waxed gross and *their* ears are dull of hearing, and their eyes they have closed; lest at any time they should see with *their* eyes, and hear with *their* ears, and should understand with *their* heart, and should be converted, and I should heal them.

16 But blessed *are* your eyes, for they see: and your ears, for they hear.

17 For verily I say unto you, That many prophets and righteous *men* have desired to see *those things* which ye see, and have not seen *them;* and to hear *those things* which ye hear, and have not heard *them.*

18 I Hear ye therefore the parable of the sower.

19 When any one heareth the word of the kingdom and understandeth *it* not, then cometh the wicked *one*, and catcheth away that which was sown in his heart. This is he which received seed by the way side.

20 But he that received the seed into stony places, the same is he that heareth the word, and anon with joy receiveth it;

21 Yet hath he not root in himself, but dureth for a while: for when tribulation or persecution ariseth because of the word, by and by he is offended.

22 He also that received seed among the thorns is he that heareth the word; and the care of this world, and the deceitfulness of riches, choke the word, and he becometh unfruitful.

23 But he that received seed into the good ground is he that heareth the word, and understandeth *it*; which also beareth fruit, and bringeth forth, some an hundredfold, some sixty, some thirty.

1 Corinthians 13 from The King James Bible

1 Though I speak with the tongues of men and of angels, and have not charity, I am become *as* sounding brass, or a tinkling cymbal.

2 And though I have *the gift of* prophecy, and understand all mysteries, and all knowledge; and though I have all faith, so that I could remove mountains, and have not charity, I am nothing.

3 And though I bestow all my goods to feed *the poor*, and though I give my body to be burned, and have not charity, it profiteth me nothing.

4 Charity suffereth long, *and* is kind; charity envieth not; charity vaunteth not itself, is not puffed up,

5 Doth not behave itself unseemly, seeketh not her own, is not easily provoked, thinketh no evil;

6 Rejoiceth not in iniquity, but rejoiceth in the truth;

7 Beareth all things, believeth all things, hopeth all things, endureth all things.

8 Charity never faileth: but whether *there be* prophecies, they shall fail; whether *there be* tongues, they shall cease; whether *there be* knowledge, it shall vanish away.

9 For we know in part, and we prophesy in part.

10 But when that which is perfect is come, then that which is in part shall be done away.

ADDITIONAL QUESTIONS AND ACTIVITIES

"A Litany in Time of Plague"

What is a litany? What kinds of items comprise the litany in Thomas Nashe's poem?

Answers

A litany is a prayer in which a leader makes a series of statements, each of which is followed by a response from the congregation. Nashe's "Litany" is a list of things that are temporary and subject to death, like human beings; the repeated lines "I am sick, I must die./Lord, have mercy on us!" are the response.

ADDITIONAL QUESTIONS AND ACTIVITIES

Psalm 23

Inform students that this psalm is often read at funerals. Encourage students to discuss why this might be so.

Matthew 13

Ask students to explain in what way the metaphor of planting is used in both Matthew 13 and Chapter 3 of Ecclesiastes.

Answer

In Matthew 13 sees is used as a metaphor for the word of God; in Ecclesiastes it is used as a metaphor for birth.

1 Corinthians 13

Inform students that this psalm is often read at weddings. Encourage students to discuss why this might be so.

ADDITIONAL QUESTIONS AND ACTIVITIES

Ask students the following questions:

1. How was the English language described during the early modern period by Richard Mulcaster?
2. During what time did Modern English emerge?
3. What is the most significant difference between Middle English and Modern English?

Answers

1. Mulcaster described the English language to be the most beautiful and expressive during the Middle Ages than any other time.
2. Modern English emerged between AD 1400 and 1600.
3. The changes in pronunciation of vowels, or the Great Vowel Shift, is the most significant difference between Middle English and Modern English.

The Development of the English Language: Modern English

In *The First Part of the Elementarie,* a treatise on education published in 1582, Richard Mulcaster wrote that "whatsoever shall become of the English state, the English tongue cannot prove fairer than it is at this day." Readers of Sidney, Spenser, Shakespeare, Marlowe, and the King James Bible tend to agree with Mulcaster that at no time has the English language been more beautiful or expressive than it was during the early modern period.

THE EMERGENCE OF MODERN ENGLISH

The version of English that we use today, known as **Modern English,** emerged in the two-hundred-year period from roughly 1400 to 1600. However, for convenience's sake, the Modern English period is often dated from the publication of Caxton's version of Malory's *Le Morte d'Arthur* in 1485. At that time, most of the changes in pronunciation, vocabulary, and grammar that transformed Middle English into Modern English were well underway.

THE GREAT VOWEL SHIFT

Perhaps the most important difference between Middle English and Modern English is in the sound of the language. Between 1400 and 1600 dramatic changes in pronunciation of vowels occurred. These changes are known collectively as the **Great Vowel Shift.** The positions of articulation in the mouth of all the long vowels except *i* and *u* were raised. Thus the word *name,* which was pronounced in Chaucer's day as *nah - muh,* became, in Modern English, *naym.* The word *bete,* pronounced *bay - tuh,* became *beet.* The long *i* and long *u* sounds became diphthongs, made of two vowels slurred together. Thus *re - dun,* became *ridden,* which has a vowel that combines *ah* and *ee.* The word *mus,* pronounced *moos,* became *mouse,* which has a vowel that combines *ah* and *oo.* Notice that in both *name* and *bete,* as in many other words, the final *–e* was pronounced in Middle English but became silent or was dropped altogether in Modern English.

GRAMMATICAL CHANGES

Throughout the Medieval Period, English gradually moved from being an **inflected language,** in which the grammatical roles of words are shown by word endings, to an **analytical language,** in which grammatical roles are shown by position in the sentence. In the early Modern Period, this change became fairly complete. An important change of this kind that occurred during this period was the introduction of *–s* as the standard sign of the plural. In Middle English, plurals had often been shown by the addition of *–en.* Thus the plural of *eye,* in Chaucer, is *yen,* and the plural of *pea* is *pesen.* In Modern English, most plurals, are formed with *–s,* but a few older plurals survive in words like *children, oxen,* and *brethren.* Other important grammatical changes that occurred during the early Modern Period include the introduction of new relative pronouns, prepositions, and conjunctions that increased the ability of English speakers to make precise logical distinctions and connections.

VOCABULARY AND THE NEW LEARNING

Of great importance to the development of the language that we use today was the introduction by scholars during the early Modern Period of thousands of new words from Latin and Greek. Professor George Lyman Kitteridge of Yale estimated that fully one-fourth of the words that appear in a standard Latin dictionary have been incorporated into English in some form. Many of these words were introduced as a result of humanist learning in the Renaissance. New Latin words that entered the language during the Renaissance include many terms related to literary study, including *accent, allusion, alphabet, anonymous, antithesis, critic, drama, elegy, epic, fiction, irony, lyric, metaphor, metrical, ode, phrase, poem, satire, simile, sonnet,* and *stanza.* Other new Latin and Greek words that date from the Renaissance are shown on the following chart; however, a complete listing of these words would fill many, many pages.

WORDS FROM LATIN AND GREEK INTRODUCED DURING THE EARLY MODERN PERIOD

adapt	conspicuous	erupt	idea	patriot
agile	crisis	excursion	impetus	precise
antipathy	criterion	exert	impression	premium
appropriate	cynic	exist	item	scene
area	decorum	exit	lexicon	scientific
arena	delirium	expensive	machine	skeleton
benefit	dexterity	explicit	malignant	squalor
catastrophe	disaster	external	meditate	system
chemist	emancipate	extinguish	method	theory
circus	energy	function	minor	vacuum
compatible	enormous	genius	numerous	
consolidate	enthusiasm	habitual	omen	

PURE VERSUS "INKHORN" ENGLISH

During the Renaissance, some writers and editors objected to the rapid influx of learned words from Latin and Greek, dubbing these "inkhorn" terms because scholars used quill pens and ink for writing. Sir John Cheke of Cambridge University wrote, for example, that "our tongue should be written clean and pure, unmixed and unmangled with borrowing of other tongues, wherein if we take not heed by time, ever borrowing and never paying, she shall be fain to keep her house as bankrupt." A brief glance at the list given on the preceding chart of loan words from Latin and Greek will suffice to show that our language was greatly enriched by the learned additions that occurred during Renaissance times. However, many writers and editors to this day would agree with Cheke that, in most writing, a simple word of Anglo-Saxon origin should be preferred over a more elaborate one derived from a classical language. In English one often has a choice between the two. One can write *way* instead of *method, home* instead of *domicile, put out* instead of *extinguish, go* instead of *exit,* and so on. Overuse of words of Latin or Greek origin can make writing or speech seem too formal or stilted. Fortunately for English speakers and writers, the first great translator of the Bible, Tyndale, preferred simple words of English origin, and much of his phrasing was adopted in the King James Bible, which became the standard text in English-speaking countries for centuries. The simple, Anglo-Saxon language of the King James Bible has dramatically influenced the shape of spoken and written English from that day to this.

ADDITIONAL QUESTIONS AND ACTIVITIES

Ask students the following questions:

1. From where did new Latin words come?
2. In what way is the style different between classical languages (such as Latin and Greek) different from pure Anglo-Saxon words?

Answers

1. Latin words came from humanists learning during the Renaissance.
2. Words from classical languages have a formal and stilted style, whereas Anglo-Saxon words are much simpler.

ADDITIONAL QUESTIONS AND ACTIVITIES

Ask students the following questions:

1. From what other countries did early Modern English borrow words?
2. How was spelling different during the early Modern Period compared to today?

Answers

1. Modern English borrowed words from France, Spain, and Italy.
2. Spelling during the early Modern English was not regularized. The spelling of words were strictly based on personal preference whereas today, there is a write and wrong way to spell words.

OTHER SOURCES OF NEW WORDS

In addition to borrowing from Latin and Greek, early Modern English borrowed heavily from other European languages, especially from French, Spanish, and Italian. From French came *battery, comrade, entrance, essay, mustache, pioneer, trophy,* and *vogue*. From Spanish came *apricot, bravado, cavalier, embargo, guitar,* and *tornado*. From Italian came *artichoke, balcony, bankrupt, cameo, fresco, pastel, piazza, porcelain,* and *traffic*. Some of these words, such as *pioneer, apricot, embargo,* and *traffic,* reflected the worldwide exploration and trade that began during the Renaissance. Other such words added because of exploration are listed in the following chart.

NEW WORDS IN EARLY MODERN ENGLISH RELATED TO EXPLORATION	
armada	llama
buffalo	maize
cacao reef	moccasin
canoe	savannah
caravan	sherry
chocolate	smuggle
coconut	tattoo
cruise	tomahawk
dock	tomato
flamingo	totem
galleon	yacht
harem	yam
hurricane	

PRINTING AND REGULARIZATION OF SPELLING

During the early Modern Period, as during the Middle Ages, spelling was largely a matter of personal preference. Most literature of the day was written by noble men and women for circulation among friends, and in this literature, as in the letters of the day, spelling varied widely. In fact, an educated person might well spell the same word several different ways in the same piece. An example of this variety can be seen in the spelling of Shakespeare's name. Existing signatures show the great poet and dramatist signing his name variously as *Shaksp, Shakspe, Shakspeare,* and *Shakspere*, but nowhere with the spelling that is commonly used today. As printing became widespread and books became more common, spelling tended to become regularized.

CONSTRUCTING A UTOPIA

How would you describe the perfect place? For centuries, great thinkers have tried to create an imaginary, idealized world where everyone could live happily and share in the wealth of the community. This is your chance to create that perfect world.

WRITING ASSIGNMENT. Your assignment is to create and describe your utopia, including its geography, laws, and customs. You will write as if you have been to this place and are describing it for a tourist book, talking directly to the reader and pointing out the many unique aspects of your utopia.

> "Imagination is more important than knowledge. Knowledge is limited. Imagination encircles the world."
> —*Albert Einstein*

Professional Model

from *Utopia, Book 1* by Thomas More, page 335

The island of Utopia is two hundred miles across in the middle part where it is widest, and is nowhere much narrower than this except toward the two ends. These ends, drawn toward one another in a five-hundred-mile circle, make the island crescent shaped, like a new moon. Between the horns of the crescent, which are about eleven miles apart, the sea enters and spreads into a broad bay. … Thus, nearly the whole inner coast is one great harbor, across which ships pass in every direction, to great advantage of the people…there are fifty-four cities on the island, all spacious and magnificent, identical in language, customs, institutions, and laws. So far as the location permits, all of them are built on the same plan, and have the same appearance. The nearest are at least twenty-four miles apart, and the farthest are not so remote that a man cannot go on foot from one to the other in a day. …they have accumulated a vast treasure, but they do not keep it like treasure. I'm really quite ashamed to tell you how they keep it, because you probably won't believe me. I would not have believed it myself if someone had just told me about it; but I was there, and saw it with my own eyes. … But considering that all their customs are so unlike ours, a sensible man will not be surprised that they treat gold and silver quite differently than we do…"

EXAMINING THE MODEL. Sir Thomas More's *Utopia* centers on community. He describes the government, the economy, and even the unusual way the people of Utopia hatch chickens. He begins with a detailed description of the geography of the island of Utopia. He explains what it looks like, where the cities are located. He draws a picture, a map of sorts, of his perfect world.

More then describes the laws and customs of its people. To illustrate these customs, he tells the story of three ambassadors who are noblemen from another country. They come to Utopia dressed in their finest silk clothes, with gold chains on their necks and jewelry on

continued on page 356

LESSON OVERVIEW

GUIDED WRITING *Software*

See the Guided Writing Software for an extended version of this lesson that includes printable graphic organizers, extensive student models and student-friendly checklists, and self-, peer, and teacher evaluation features.

INDIVIDUAL LEARNING STRATEGIES

MOTIVATION
To prompt students to imagine their utopia, ask students to recall their favorite part about More's utopia from what they read of *Utopia, Book 1.* What changes would they make in their own utopia?

READING PROFICIENCY
Have students summarize what they are being asked to do for each step of the assignment. Refer students to Language Arts Survey 5.17, "Taking Notes, Summarizing, and Outlining Information" to help them with this activity.

ENGLISH LANGUAGE LEARNING

See strategies for Reading Proficiency above that will also

INDIVIDUAL LEARNING STRATEGIES (CONT.)

benefit students who are English language learners. Also make sure students know and understand the definition of utopia.

SPECIAL NEEDS
Students may need this activity simplified. Change the writing assignment by asking students to describe their perfect place through story form instead of through the eyes of a tour guide.

ENRICHMENT
Students may want to take this activity a step further by constructing a model of their utopia. Make sure students have access to the utensils and tools from the art department to complete this activity.

Prewriting

Finding Your Voice
For more information on voice, have students review the Professional Model and/or reread *Utopia, Book I*. The more familiar they are with the voice More uses, the easier it will be to write in second-person point of view.

Identifying Your Audience
Remind students that they will need to use both formal and informal English in their writing to attract both their peers and adults. Refer students to the Language Arts Survey 3.2, "Formal and Informal English."

Writing with a Plan
Encourage students to focus on the questions that are asked to prompt imagination by asking them to answer each of the questions listed. Refer students to the Language Arts Survey 2.13, "Clustering" to help students complete their Graphic Organizer.

their fingers and ears. They think they are so well dressed compared to the humble Utopians. They don't realize that in Utopia, gold and silver are reserved for slaves and jewels are used as playthings for children, so when the Utopians see the ambassadors, they think they are fools. How does telling an anecdote like this help illustrate the customs and underlying principles of Utopia?

Prewriting

Finding Your Voice. More directly addresses the reader, using the second-person point of view. He writes that he has been to Utopia, stating that "I was there, I saw it with my own eyes." As you describe your utopia, write as though you have been there and truly believe that what you are describing is factual. Your voice will be one of a travel writer in a tourist book like *Let's Go, Utopia!* In those books, a writer visits a place and then writes about it for future visitors, describing the geography, laws, and customs much like More has done. Strive to make your voice engaging, not preachy, as you paint a concrete picture of your utopia.

Look at the two examples below to determine which has the more effective voice.

> There are fifty-four cities on this island, all spacious and magnificent, identical in language, customs, and laws.

or

> This is a wonderful place to live and you would love it.

Identifying Your Audience. Your audience is anyone interested in making a journey, albeit an imaginary one, to an ideal world. Your audience is also your class and teacher. Your class will be publishing a travel book, so plan to publish your maps and writing for your class as someone who has visited this ideal world.

Writing With a Plan. Like Thomas More, you may decide to describe what the land looks like before you detail the laws and customs of Utopia. The laws and customs you create, however, could determine the lay of the land. For example, do you favor an economy based on farming or fishing? If it's an agricultural society, you must have land to work with, but if fishing is the main source of income, then you want coastland. As a prewriting activity, draw a map of your utopia. It should include the locations of cities, mountains, and bodies of water. Think of it as a nation unto itself. It can border other countries or be an island or even be a planet or a space station.

Next, determine what values are important to you. On what principles will your society be based? How can all your citizens get along? In More's Utopia, the people rotate farming duties, living in communal housing and helping with harvesting. Does this kind of shared workload appeal to you? An attribute map can help you organize your thoughts. Cherie filled in the graphic organizer below to help her think of details to include in her utopia.

Student Model—Graphic Organizer

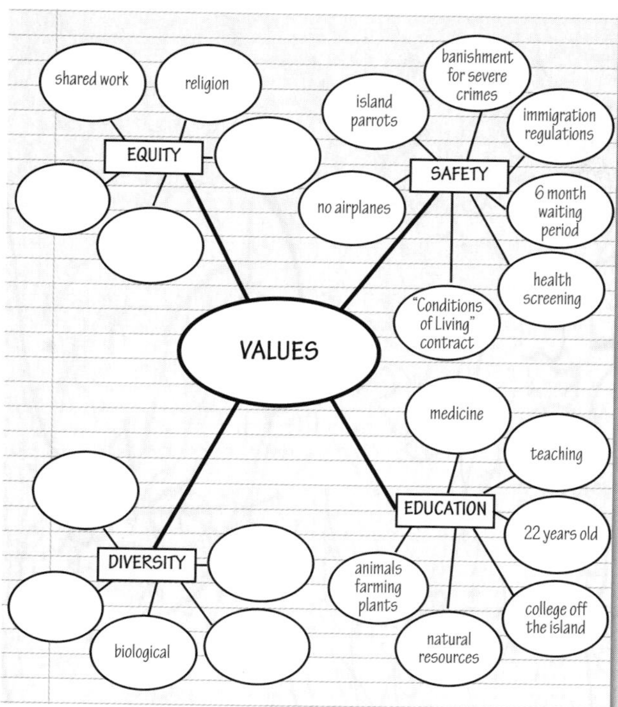

Student Model—Draft

The island of Adaven is a magnificent utopian island. The island's middle lies widthwise across the equator in the Atlantic Ocean. The shape of the island looks exactly like that of an artist's palette, *(– good description)* which makes up the harbor on the island, is at the top *(sense?)* part of the island facing north.

There are lots of different places *(Be specific-describe the places)* on the island. The harbor of the island is very calm and beautiful, an idyllic

Drafting

Don't focus on mechanics yet. Instead, get your ideas on paper. Focus on "painting a picture with words," helping the reader form a vision of your utopia. Keep your drawing and attribute map handy as you write. It might work best to follow the order that More followed. Write the description of the geography of your utopia from your drawing. Then, using your attribute map, describe the laws and customs of its people. Remember to write as if you have actually visited there. Write with confidence, provide clear descriptions, and consider adding humor. Include a story that helps illustrate the customs of the people, like More's story of the three ambassadors.

STUDENT MODEL—GRAPHIC ORGANIZER

See the Guided Writing Resource for a blackline master of the Graphic Organizer for this lesson.

Drafting

Encourage students to use their completed Graphic Organizer on page 357 to help them get started on their writing assignment. For additional help, refer students to the Language Arts Survey 2.31–2.35, "Drafting."

Self- and Peer Evaluation

Have students use the questions on this page for self- and peer evaluation. Remind students that comments from classmates can be helpful and can help them identify weaknesses and produce a better piece through revision. By reflecting on reviewer comments and their own self-evaluations, they will be ready to go on to the next step: revision. A blackline master is available of the self- and peer evaluation checklist in the Guided Writing Resource Book.

Self- and Peer Evaluation

After you finish your draft, complete a self-evaluation using the questions below:

- Where does the writing "paint a picture" of the place? Is the description detailed enough that the reader can envision what your utopia looks like?
- Where does the writer sound as though he or she has visited the utopia?
- Does the writing read like a travel book? Where does the writer use humor?
- Where does the writer directly address the reader, using the second person "you" point of view?
- How is the writing organized? How do the sections on geography, laws, and customs work together?
- Where is there an anecdote to illustrate the customs of the people of the utopia?
- Where are there examples of colorful language to make the writing lively?

place to go boating or swimming because the current isn't a ~~harm~~ *threat*. It is also the only place that cargo isn't shipped in. The island imports medical supplies and books. The only source of importing and exporting is the harbor. *How can this be? Don't these contradict?*

Anything that is brought to the island or that remotely comes near it is checked by the people of Adaven to protect the people from diseases, unwanted plant or animal species or humans. *Good specifics* There are people whose job is to patrol all around the island to make sure no unwanted objects, people, or things *unnecessary repetition* come in contact with the island. This is one thing the people of Adaven are very strict about.

When a person reaches the age of ~~22~~ *twenty-two*, the person is shipped off to the outside world to learn things to improve their minds and help their community. The people of Adaven are very well educated, so when they leave Adaven they go straight into college, maybe a little older than the rest of their peers, are able to have the college of their choice. *How can they automatically do that? Do they control outside colleges?* Some learn the ways of medicine, some learn more advanced ways of farming, some people learn to become teachers in Adaven. All Adavenians have been taught from an early age about farming, producing *work on parallelism here* plants, finding natural resources and the many uses for them and how animals are useful in their lives.

No Adavenian has wanted not to return to Adaven. They lead simple but more happy lives than we could ever hope to live. *this lacks support* All Adavenians are kind gentle, compatiotate, *sp* happy people who help each other. They help one another *Repetition* to the best of their abilities to form strong bonds of friendship. They like to do all kinds of things. They all respect one another.

Access to Adaven is very easy, but that does not necessarily mean that anyone can step foot on Adaven at any time. Besides the strict checking procedures, there are regulations to how many people can come to Adaven and when. There are no airplanes allowed so everything is brought by ships. There is a six-month waiting period for people who want to come or live in Adaven... *need an anecdote*

Revising and Proofreading

It is usually best to wait before revising to give yourself perspective about your work. Revise your piece according to your self- and peer evaluations. Make sure it contains all the required elements, like descriptions of geography, laws, customs, and, if possible, an anecdote to help illustrate your ideal world.

Finally, proofread your piece for errors in spelling, grammar, punctuation and capitalization, as always. See the Language Arts Survey 2.45 for a proofreading checklist.

Language, Grammar, and Style

Precise and Colorful Language

IDENTIFYING PRECISE AND COLORFUL LANGUAGE. Use colorful language to sentences to keep the writing lively. When you write, use words that tell your reader exactly what you mean. Precise and lively language makes your writing more interesting to read. Look at the examples below to see which creates a more colorful and lively picture.

EXAMPLES

The mob roared its approval.

The people made noise.

As Thomas More creates his utopia, he carefully describes the bay, helping the reader envision this place:

> Being sheltered from the wind by the surrounding land, the bay is never rough, but quiet and smooth instead, like a big lake.

More tells you what the bay is not, which is "never rough," and then tells you what it is, which is "quiet and smooth." He then uses the simile "like a big lake" to help paint the picture of this idyllic harbor.

Specific verbs help to create a clear picture in the reader's mind. Use precise verbs to tell exactly what you mean. If you find yourself needing a long list of adjectives, you probably haven't found the right verb.

continued on page 360

Language, Grammar, and Style

PRECISE AND COLORFUL LANGUAGE

In this lesson, students will be asked to the following:

- Identify Precise and Colorful Language
- Make Language More Precise and Colorful
- Use Precise and Colorful Language

INTRODUCING THE SKILL

Explain to students that precise and colorful language are essential in making a descriptive setting memorable and alive. Choosing the right language is a way to keep readers connected with a writer's work.

Revising and Proofreading

A handout of the proofreading checklist in the Language Arts Survey is available in the Teacher's Resource Kit, Writing Resource Book 2.45. Encourage students critiquing their classmates' work to use common proofreader's symbols, which are found in the Language Arts Survey 2.44, "Using Proofreader's Marks."

PREVIEWING THE SKILL
Refer students to the Language Arts Survey 3.39, "Adding Colorful Language to Sentences." This is the basis of the Language, Grammar, and Style lesson. You may also want to make sure students understand such basic concepts as verbs and modifiers. Refer those who need such review to the Language Arts Survey 3.59, "Expressers—Verbs," and 3.65, "Modifiers—Adverbs and Adjectives."

PRACTICING THE SKILL
For additional practice, have student work through the exercises in the Language, Grammar, and Style Resource Book 3.59, "Expressers—Verbs," and 3.65, "Modifiers—Adverbs and Adjectives," located in the Teacher's Resource Kit.

Compare these two sentences:

There was dirty water all over the place.

Black sludge oozed across the cement floor.

MAKING LANGUAGE MORE PRECISE AND COLORFUL. Notice the language in the following sentences from Cherie's student model:

The sand was flat.

They make lots of goods.

The weather is calm.

Improve each of these by adding strong verbs and a few carefully selected adjectives or adverbs.

USING PRECISE AND COLORFUL LANGUAGE. Search through your description of your utopia, looking for places where the writing is dull or colorless. Replace lazy, overused expressions. Find stronger, more interesting verbs and nouns to make your writing livelier. Go easy on modifiers. Try to create a video, a movie in the minds of your readers so they can experience your utopia.

Student Model—Revised

The island of Adaven is a magnificent utopian island. The island's middle lies widthwise across the equator in the Atlantic Ocean. The shape of the island exactly matches that of an artist's palette. The harbor on the island is at the top part of the island facing north.

Variety marks the ecosystems on the island. Tropical rain forests, jungles, deserts, wetlands, and bogs all combine to make Adaven diverse. Because of this, almost every type of animal and plant species thrives here.

The harbor of the island is placid and beautiful, an idyllic place to go boating or swimming because the current isn't a threat. The island imports only medical supplies and books. All else is produced on the island. The people of Adaven live well without televisions, radios, compact discs, magazines and the many other things we think we think essential. Adaven exports its natural resources. The only site of importing and exporting is the harbor.

To protect against diseases, unwanted plant or animal species or humans, the people of Adavan check anything that is brought to the island. Guards patrol all around the island to make sure no unwanted intruders come into contact with the island.

When a person reaches the age of twenty-two, he or she is shipped off to the outside world to learn things to improve his mind and help the community. The people of Adaven are very well educated, so when they leave Adaven, they go straight into college, maybe a little older than the rest of their peers, but ready to learn what good the outside world can provide. Some learn the ways of medicine, some learn more advanced ways of farming, and others learn to become teachers in Adaven. All Adavenians have been taught from an early age about farming, producing plants, finding natural resources and using both resources and animals.

No Adavenian has not wanted to return to Adaven. They lead simple but happy lives. All Adavenians are kind, gentle, compassionate, happy people who help each other and form strong bonds of friendship. They love to dance, make music, and laugh. A feeling of love and happiness emanates from the island.

To keep life so ideal, there are regulations as to how many people can come to Adaven and when. There are no airplanes allowed so ships bring everything. There is a six- month waiting period for people who want to visit or to immigrate to Adaven. This allows time for proper health screening and for people to look over and read the "Conditions of Living Contract." It states the ways of living in Adaven.

Once a famous baseball player wanted to retire on Adaven. He felt that, as a celebrity, he should receive preferential treatment. Although he said he was tired of being mobbed by fans, he was clearly disappointed when the Avedanians treated him as an equal—no better than anyone else. Within a week, he returned to Cincinnati...

Reflecting

How is your utopia different from Sir Thomas More's? Do the values expressed in your utopia contrast with More's values? As you wrote about your utopia, to what extent did you find yourself really wishing for such a place? What about your utopia and those of your peers appeals to you most? least?

Publishing and Presenting

Print a final draft of your piece. Together with your classmates, publish a *Let's Go, Utopia!* book with all your descriptions bound together. Use your prewriting drawings as illustrations. Someone could even design a cover. When you share your pieces, read as if you are trying to persuade tourists to visit your utopia.

"To invent, you need a good imagination and a pile of junk."

—Thomas Edison

Publishing and Presenting

Hold a *Let's Go, Utopia!* book party in the library for your entire school to attend. Include ways to promote your book through book signings, posters, memo distributions, and readings from the book. Ask your school if they would be willing to provide refreshments for this momentous occasion.

Reflecting

Ask students to answer the questions listed in their journals. You may even want to post these responses on the walls for the book party. Then have students tell their peers what they liked most about their utopia.

ADDITIONAL RESOURCES

Unit 4 Resource Book
- Vocabulary Worksheet
- Study Guide: Unit 4 Test
- Unit 4 Test

VOCABULARY DEVELOPMENT

Give students the following exercise: Identify at least eight words on page 362 with positive connotations, that is, that refer to positive experiences or things, and at least eight others with negative connotations or meanings. Then write ten sentences about the authors or selections in this unit, using five words from the "positive connotations" group and five words from the "negative connotations" group.

UNIT 4 REVIEW
The English Renaissance

Words for Everyday Use

Check your knowledge of the following vocabulary words from the selections in this unit. Write short sentences using these words in context to make the meaning clear. To review the definition or usage of a word, refer to the page number listed or the Glossary of Words for Everyday Use.

adage, 338
beauteous, 315
belie, 323
brook, 311
contingency, 337
crestfallen, 339
fortified, 336
gall, 307
graven, 289
guile, 311
indulgent, 337
languished, 293
madrigal, 302
mettle, 337
rend, 331
score, 298
scorn, 293
shun, 311
subdue, 336
swain, 303
temperate, 319
travail, 289
uncouth, 336
vanquished, 336
wan, 293
wanton, 307
wield, 297
wither, 327

Literary Tools

Define the following terms, giving concrete examples of how they are used in the selections in this unit. To review a term, refer to the page number indicated or to the Handbook of Literary Terms.

aim, 310
alliteration, 296
allusion, 314
ambiguity, 314
dactyl, 326
Elizabethan sonnet, 318
iambic pentameter, 288
image, 293, 306
irony, 334
lyric poem, 301
metaphor, 288, 306, 310, 326
parallelism, 330
pastoral poem, 301
Petrarchan sonnet, 288, 342
personification, 293
repetition with variation, 330
Shakespearian sonnet, 318
source, 296
speaker, 318
theme, 342
utopia, 334

Reflecting *on* YOUR READING

Genre Studies

1. **The Sonnet.** What are the essential characteristics of a sonnet? What subjects do sonnets typically treat? How do Petrarchan and Elizabethan sonnets differ? Refer to the sonnets in the unit, in the Selections for Additional Reading, and in the Multicultural Extensions on page 342.

2. **Pastoral Poetry.** Marlowe's "The Passionate Shepherd to His Love" and Psalm 23 from the Bible are both pastoral poems. What are the essential characteristics of a pastoral poem? Why would pastoral poetry emerge among people who lived in cities and towns? What longing is embodied in pastoral poetry?

Thematic Studies

3. **IDEALIZATION OF LOVE IN RENAISSANCE POETRY.** Idealized women and idealized love are common themes in Renaissance poetry. How are these themes expressed in Shakespeare's Sonnet 18 ("Shall I compare thee . . . ") and Marlowe's "The Passionate Shepherd to His Love"? What twist do Shakespeare and Ralegh put on this theme in Sonnet 130 ("My mistress' eyes . . . ") and "The Nymph's Reply to the Shepherd"? Explore the theme of idealized women and love by contrasting these sets of poems.

4. **UNREQUITED LOVE IN RENAISSANCE ENGLISH POETRY.** Many of the most famous Renaissance poems deal with the theme of unrequited, or unreturned, love. Explore this theme in the following works from the unit: "Whoso List to Hunt," Sidney's Sonnet 31, "The Nymph's Reply to the Shepherd," "When Thou Must Home to Shades of Underground," "Song, to Celia," Shakespeare's Sonnet 73 (in the Selections for Additional Reading, page 348), and the sonnets of Petrarch (in the Multicultural Extensions, page 342). Explain how each poem illustrates this theme.

Historical and Biographical Studies

5. **ELIZABETH I, MARY STUART, AND CATHOLICISM.** In "The Doubt of Future Foes" Queen Elizabeth expresses her fear of being overthrown. Explain the historical circumstances that created this fear and how specific lines of the poem are related to these events and historical figures. Refer to the Unit Introduction on page 284.

6. **RENAISSANCE LITERATURE AND THE EMERGENCE OF THE INDIVIDUAL.** The Renaissance saw the emergence of a new emphasis on the individual and on the value of life on earth, in sharp contrast to the emphasis in medieval literature on society and on the afterlife. Consider Marlowe's "The Passionate Shepherd to His Love" and Shakespeare's Sonnet 18 ("Shall I compare thee . . ."). How do these poems embody the new emphasis in literature on the personal lives of individuals?

REFLECTING ON YOUR READING

The prompts in the "Reflecting on Your Reading" are suitable as topics for research papers. Refer to the Language Arts Survey 5.18–5.45, "Research Skills." (To evaluate research papers, see the evaluation forms for writing, revising, and proofreading in the Assessment Resource.)

The prompts can also be adapted for use as topics for oral reports or debates. Refer students to the Language Arts Survey 4, "Speaking and Listening." (To evaluate these projects, see the evaluation forms in the Assessment Resource.)

UNIT SKILLS OUTLINE

GOALS/OBJECTIVES

Studying this unit will enable students to

- enjoy and appreciate Shakespearean drama
- describe the development of the theater in England from medieval to Elizabethan times and the structure of the five-act play
- define the elements of a plot and identify them in their reading
- define literary terms such as *aside, foil, hyperbole, motif, paradox, soliloquy* and *verbal irony* and identify these techniques in their reading
- write a short story
- identify effective dialogue and demonstrate an ability to use effective dialogue in their writing

Unit 5 Renaissance Drama (1485–1660)

Shakespeare and His Contemporaries, 1851. John Faed. Private Collection.

All the world's a stage

And all the men and

women merely players.

—William Shakespeare

As You Like It

365

CROSS-CURRICULAR CONNECTIONS

Arts and Humanities
John Faed's Art, 366
Famous Englishmen, 366
The Morris Dance, 367
Music from Shakespeare, 368
Globe Theater Models, 370
A Midsummer Night's Dream, 373
Comic Strip Sketch, 380
Opera, 393
Writing an Opera, 393
Roman Polanski's *Macbeth*, 417
Influence of *Witches on Macbeth*, 429
Lady Macduff, 434
Writing a Lament, 443
Choreographing Violent Scenes, 459
Themes in *The Tragical History of Doctor Faustus*, 465
Archaic Language, 465
Adam and Eve Story, 465

Mathematics and Sciences
Vernal Equinox, 379
Analysis of Speeches, 399
Medical Description of Scrofula, 440
Causes of Sleepwalking and Sleeptalking, 449

Social Studies
Famous Englishmen, 366
Modern Day *Macbeth* Motifs, 374
Constructing a Time Line, 379
Kingship in Scotland, 386
Significance of "Hailing," 389
Effects of Assassinations, 406
Manslaughter vs. Murder, 407
King James I, 432
Medical Description of Scrofula, 440
Medieval Wars, 453
Social Order, 474

Applied Arts
Globe Theater Models, 370
Stage Set Design, 397
Creating Special Effects, 430

TEACHING THE MULTIPLE INTELLIGENCES

Musical
Music from Shakespeare, 368
Writing an Opera, 393
Influence of *Witches on Macbeth*, 429
Lady Macduff, 434

Logical-Mathematical
Constructing a Time Line, 379
Vernal Equinox, 379
Character Analysis, 388
Macbeth's Soliloquy, 391
Analysis of Speeches, 399
Roman Polanski's *Macbeth*, 417
Macbeth's Rise and Fall, 431
Devising Symbols, 431
Riddles, 431
Logic of Dialogue, 437

TEACHING THE MULTIPLE INTELLIGENCES (cont.)

Spatial
John Faed's Art, 366
Renaissance Drama, 368
Globe Theater Models, 370
Constructing a Time Line, 379
Comic Strip Sketch, 380
Stage Set Design, 397
Analysis of Speeches, 399
Roman Polanski's *Macbeth*, 417
Creating Special Effects, 430
Devising Symbols, 431
Logic of Dialogue, 437
Choreographing Violent Scenes, 459

Kinesthetic
Roman vs. Elizabethan Theater, 367
Music from Shakespeare, 368
Globe Theater Models, 370
Writing an Opera, 393
Stage Set Design, 397
Impromptu Interview, 414
Creating Special Effects, 430
Choreographing Violent Scenes, 459

Interpersonal
Impromptu Debate, 406
Impromptu Interview, 414
Lady Macduff, 434
Themes in *The Tragical History of Doctor Faustus*

ADDITIONAL RESOURCES

Unit 5 Resource Book
- Selection Check Test 4.5.1
- Selection Test 4.5.2

ART NOTE

The painting *Shakespeare and His Contemporaries* by John Faed, shown on pages 364–65, is also known as Shakespeare and His Friends at the Mermaid Tavern. The Mermaid Tavern was a gathering place for a group of elite, scholarly men of the day who called themselves the Friday Street Club. The club, started by Sir Walter Raleigh, was named for the tavern's address, which was Friday Street. Shakespeare did know the owner of the Mermaid, William Johnson, through business, but it is unkown if Shakespeare actually attended the meetings. Nevertheless, Faed features the playwright at center, surrounded by famous writers and thinkers of his day. **Standing at left:** John Selden; Francis Beaumont; Sir Francis Bacon; and Thomas Carew. **Seated on left side of table:** Joshua Sylvester; William Camden; Thomas Sackville, the Earl of Dorset; and John Fletcher (wearing a hat). **Seated on right side of table:** Ben Jonson (at Shakespeare's shoulder); Samuel Daniel; John Donne (behind Shakespeare's head); and Shakespeare. **At far right:** standing are Sir Walter Raleigh and Henry Wriothesley, third Earl of Southampton; sitting on chair with back to us, Sir Robert Bruce Cotton; next to him, Thomas Dekker.

RENAISSANCE DRAMA (1485–1660)

The Dramatic Inheritance

Our word *holiday* is a compound of the words *holy* and *day*. Throughout the Middle Ages, on "holy days" in the calendar of the Roman Catholic Church, people would gather on village greens, in innyards, and at marketplaces for celebrations. Entertainments on these days included dancing, feasting, juggling, puppetry, animal shows, music, singing, archery contests, and plays. Plays were presented by traveling troupes of actors or by members of professional business associations called **guilds.** Almost always, these plays dealt with religious subjects. **Miracle plays** told fantastic stories from the lives of saints. **Mystery plays** told stories from the Bible. **Morality plays** told stories about virtues and vices through characters with names like "Good Deeds" and "Sloth." Although these plays were religious in nature, they occasionally depicted ordinary people and sometimes contained elements of coarse humor.

If you could travel back in time six or seven hundred years to a festival held in an English town such as Chester or Wakefield, you could find yourself a place in the crowd at a market or innyard and stay from sunup to sundown to watch play after play. The plays would make up a cycle telling a continuous story. The first play, for example, might tell about the creation of the world, the second about Noah and the flood, and so on. A patient English festival-goer could witness, in the course of a day, the entire history of the world as medieval people understood it. The plays would be presented on the backs of wagons. The first wagon would pull up. The actors would perform their play. Then they would move on, and a second wagon would take its place. In other words, instead of the audience going to the theater, the theater would come to the audience.

At the beginning of the Renaissance, theater was still being performed in the open air by guildsmen and by traveling troupes of actors. Performances were also held in schools and in halls in the great homes of noble men and women.

The Five-Act Play

One of the fruits of **Humanism,** that rebirth of classical learning during the fifteenth and sixteenth centuries, was the emergence in England of the **five-act play.** In six-

Elizabethan and Jacobean Theater

1553. Udall's *Ralph Roister Doister* and Stevenson's *Grammer Gurton's Needle,* first five-act plays in English

1562. First English tragedy, the *Tragedy of Gorboduc,* presented before Queen Elizabeth I

1564. Westminster boys' troupe presents Plautus's Latin play *Miles Gloriosus* for Queen Elizabeth I

1550 1555 1560 1565 1570

1564. Christopher Marlowe born

1564. William Shakespeare born

Marlowe and Shakespeare

CROSS-CURRICULAR ACTIVITIES

Arts and Humanities. Have students research one of the famous Englishmen depicted in Faed's painting to find biographical information, portraits, a bibliography of the person's published work, and a sample of that writing if available. Students can find poems by Raleigh and Jonson in Unit 4 and poems by John Donne in Unit 6. Other works can be found online.

The website of the **University of Toronto Libraries** maintains a page called "A Time-Line of English Poetry 651–2000," It can be found at http://www.library.utoronto.ca/utel/rp/timeline.html). This page contains biographical information and links to the works of many of Great Britain's poets.

teenth-century English schools, students typically studied a Latin curriculum. Included in students' reading lists were works by Roman playwrights—Plautus, Seneca, and Terence. In the mid-1500s, two schoolteachers, one a master at Christ's College, Cambridge, and the other headmaster of Eton and Westminster, wrote plays called, respectively, *Grammer Gurton's Needle* and *Ralph Roister Doister.* These comedies, written for performance by students, used the five-act structure common in Roman plays but dealt with English subjects and themes. Other playwrights during the reigns of Queen Elizabeth I (The Elizabethan Age) and King James I (The Jacobean Age) adopted the five-act structure, which divided up the action as explained in the chart below. The acts were divided into scenes that began and ended with characters entering or leaving the stage. (These scenes were not typically marked in printed editions of the plays. The scene markings given in the plays in this unit were added by later editors.)

STRUCTURE OF A TYPICAL FIVE-ACT PLAY

Act I	**Introduction**	Presents the setting and main characters Presents the inciting incident (the event that sets in motion the play's central conflict, or struggle)
Act II	**Rising Action, *or* Complication**	Develops the central conflict
Act III	**Crisis, *or* Turning Point**	Presents a decisive occurrence that determines the future course of events in the play
Act IV	**Falling Action**	Presents events that happen as a result of the crisis
Act V	**Resolution, *or* Catastrophe**	Presents the event that resolves, or ends, the central conflict (In a tragedy, this event is called the *catastrophe* because it marks the ultimate fall of the central character.)

1576. James Burbage erects first playhouse, the Theater

1575 1580 1585 1590 1595

1582. Marriage license issued to William Shakespeare and Anne Hathaway

1583. Shakespeare's daughter Susanna born

1585. Shakespeare's twins Judith and Hamnet born

1587. Marlowe writes first part of *Tamburlaine,* graduates from Cambridge

1592. Shakespeare's *Henry VI* presented at Rose Theater (perhaps first public performance of his work); Marlowe's *Faustus* written

1593. Christopher Marlowe killed in tavern; Shakespeare's *Venus and Adonis* published

1594. Shakespeare shareholder in theatrical company, The Lord Chamberlain's Men

CROSS-CURRICULAR CONNECTIONS

Dance & Theater. One of the faint links between the drama of ancient times and the Renaissance was the Morris dance. The Morris dance of England has parallels in cultures in the Middle East, India, and Central and South America and is believed to be related to religious rites thousands of years old. In these folk dances, the dancers—commonly wearing white clothing, with bells and ribbons on their arms and legs— acted out the ritual death and revival of a god represented as an animal. In England, the Morris dance featured characters such as a deer, a fool, a hunter, a woman, and a hobby horse. Most contem-porary Morris companies have abandoned the tradition of excluding women. The banter of these "mummers," as the dancers/actors were also called, may have evolved into the sophisticated wit in the dialogue of dramatists such as Shakespeare. The fools, jesters, and clowns so popular with that playwright (and with his audiences) may well be descended from the dancing fools of the Morris groups.

CROSS-CURRICULAR ACTIVITIES

Arts and Humanities

- Have students research descriptions of the dances mentioned above. Students can locate videotapes to use in class; some may wish to recreate the dances.
- If your school or another school nearby has a Latin department, you may wish to ask a teacher or student there to give a brief lecture on Roman theater, comparing it to Elizabethan theater.

ADDITIONAL QUESTIONS AND ACTIVITIES

Students can use a graphic organizer to organize characteristics of the different types of Renaissance drama. One possible organizer is a cluster diagram with six circles—one each for comedies, tragedies, histories, romances, interludes, and masques. Students can cluster characteristics of each drama near the appropriate head. They can also draw lines between the types likely to have links. Romances and masques are likely to be comedies, for instance; histories are often tragedies. Suggest students focus in particular on tragedy and comedy and add adjectives to their organizers that describe these two types. Tragedies, for instance, might be grand, solemn, or sad; comedies might be hopeful or funny. See the Language Arts Survey, 1.17, "Clustering."

CROSS-CURRICULAR ACTIVITIES

Musically inclined students may want to research and perform some of the songs from Shakespeare's plays for the class. References they may wish to consult are Naylor, Edward W. *Shakespeare and Music.* 1965; and Elson, Louis C. *Shakespeare in Music,* 1970.

TYPES OF RENAISSANCE DRAMA

The two most common types of drama during the English Renaissance were **comedies** and **tragedies.** The key difference between comedies and tragedies is that the former have happy endings and the latter have unhappy ones. (It is only a slight exaggeration to say that comedies end with wedding bells and tragedies with funeral bells.)

A comedy is typically lighthearted, though it may contain serious action and themes. Action in a comedy usually progresses from initial order to a humorous misunderstanding or confusion and back to order again. Stock elements of comedy include mistaken identities, puns and word play, and coarse or exaggerated characters.

A tragedy tells the story of the downfall of a person of high status. Often it celebrates the courage and dignity of a flawed **protagonist,** or main character, in the face of an inevitable doom. In Christopher Marlowe's *Tragical History of Doctor Faustus,* for example, the protagonist's major failing, or **tragic flaw,** is his willingness to do anything for knowledge and the power that knowledge brings. In William Shakespeare's *Macbeth,* the protagonist falls because of ambition and a desire not to be considered unmanly.

Other kinds of plays produced during the period included **histories**—plays about events from the past—and **romances**—plays that contained highly fantastic elements such as fairies and magical spells. Also popular were short plays called **interludes,** as well as elaborate entertainments, called **masques,** that featured acting, music, and dance.

THE POLITICAL CONDITIONS OF THEATER IN RENAISSANCE LONDON

In the late sixteenth century, London was a bustling city of perhaps 150,000 people, the mercantile, political, and artistic center of England. The city proper was ruled by a mayor and aldermen who frowned upon theater because it brought together large crowds of people, creating the potential for lawlessness and the spread of controversial ideas and disease. Many times during the period, London city officials or Parliament ordered the theaters closed, once because they objected to the political content of a play called the *Isle of Dogs,* and regularly because of outbreaks of plague. Parliament, which was dominated by Puritans, passed laws that made it possible for traveling actors and other performers to be arrested as vagabonds and cruelly punished. For protection,

ELIZABETHAN AND JACOBEAN THEATER

1599. The Globe Theater built

1597. Performance of *The Isle of Dogs* leads to temporary closing of all London theaters

1600 — 1605 — 1610 — 1615 — 1620

1596. Shakespeare's father, John, granted a coat of arms; Shakespeare's *Romeo and Juliet* performed; Shakespeare's son Hamnet dies

1597. Shakespeare purchases large Stratford home, New Place

1598. Marlowe's narrative poem *Hero and Leander* finished and published by his friend George Chapman

1598. Shakespeare listed as actor in play by Ben Jonson

1601? Shakespeare's *Hamlet* performed

1604. James I becomes king; Shakespeare's company becomes The King's Men

1605? Shakespeare's *Macbeth* performed

1608. Shakespeare's company purchases Blackfriars Theater

1609. Shakespeare's sonnets published

1613. Shakespeare's last play, *Henry VIII,* presented at the Globe; Globe burns down due to cannon firing

1616. Shakespeare dies

MARLOWE AND SHAKESPEARE

actors sought the patronage of members of the nobility. Actors would become, technically, servants of a famous lord and go by such names as The Lord Worcester's Men. Fortunately for actors and playwrights, Queen Elizabeth and other members of the nobility loved the theater and protected it. Elizabeth herself maintained two troupes of boy actors, connected to her royal chapels. In addition to these acting troupes made up of boys, London boasted several professional troupes made up of men. In those days, women did not act, and women's roles were played by men, a fact that further increased Puritan disapproval of the theaters. When the Puritans took control of England in 1642, theater was banned altogether.

The Globe
The Globe Theater.

The Renaissance Playhouse

In 1576, James Burbage built the first professional playhouse in England. Burbage located his playhouse, which he called simply "the Theater," just outside the northern boundaries of the City of London, where he could avoid control by city authorities. Another professional theater, the Curtain, was built nearby shortly thereafter. In 1598, Burbage and other members of his theater company, the Lord Chamberlain's Men, tore down the Theater and used its materials to build a new playhouse, **the Globe Theater,** south of the city on the banks of the river Thames. One of the shareholders in the Globe was William Shakespeare.

From contemporary drawings and descriptions and from evidence in plays, we can reconstruct what Shakespeare's Globe must have looked like. The building was octagonal, or eight-sided. The walls were covered with peaked, thatched roofs. The center of this "wooden O," as Shakespeare called it, was open to the air. The stage projected into the middle of this open space, and poorer theatergoers called "groundlings," who paid a penny apiece for admission, stood around three sides of the stage. Wealthier theatergoers could pay an additional penny or two and sit in one of the three tiers, or stories, of seats in the

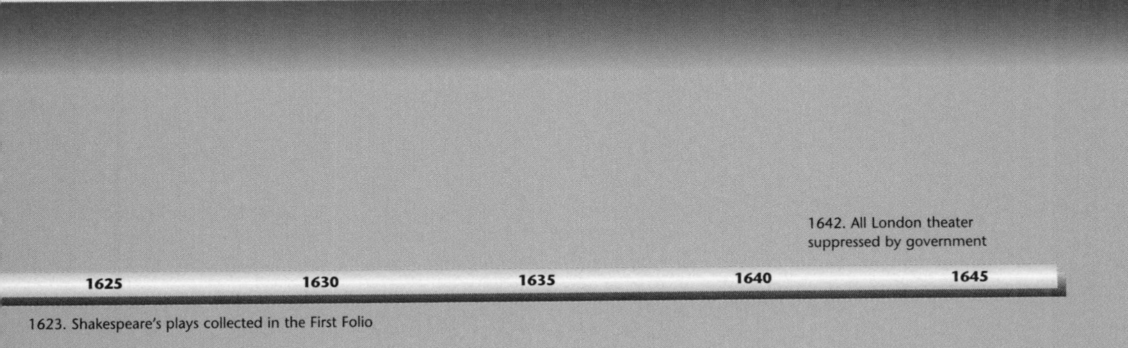
1642. All London theater suppressed by government
1625
1630
1635
1640
1645
1623. Shakespeare's plays collected in the First Folio

ADDITIONAL QUESTIONS AND ACTIVITIES

Students can participate in a collaborative guided imagery activity. After the students have read the introduction to the unit, have them close their eyes and imagine that they are in Renaissance London, walking through the streets on the way to the Globe Theater. Ask them to name things that they can imagine hearing (the cries of street merchants or crowds), seeing (old and young, rich and poor people; soldiers; horses; buildings), smelling (refuse, ditchwater, manure), touching (passersby, muddy streets), and tasting (coarse bread, fruits, cheeses) on their way. Then continue the activity by having students imagine that they have entered the Globe and are waiting for the play to start.

CROSS-CURRICULAR ACTIVITIES

THEATER. Students can form groups to build models of the Globe Theater. Models may be as sophisticated as skills will allow, from simple cardboard constructions to elaborate scale replicas made of wood. To help students build their models, direct student to http://www.GreatBuildings.com/models/Globe_Theater_mod.html. This website allows them to view a 3D model of the Globe Theater. It also provides information about the architectural structure of the theater that may help students with their construction.

walls of the theater. In many respects, the theater was similar to the medieval wagon stage pulled into the open courtyard of an inn, with the inn's balconies around it.

The stage itself was partially covered by a canopy supported by two large pillars. Trapdoors in the stage floor allowed for appearances by spirits or fairies and for the disappearance of bodies. Behind the stage, between the pillars, was an inner area called the "tiring house" that could be used for changing costumes and for indoor scenes such as throne rooms, bedchambers, and taverns. On either side of the stage were doors for entrances and exits. At the back of the tiring house was a door and stairway that led to a second-level playing area that could be used as a hilltop, a castle turret, or a balcony (perhaps for the famous balcony scene from *Romeo and Juliet*). On the third level, above this balcony area, was an area for musicians and sound-effects people. A cannon shot from this area during a performance of Shakespeare's *Henry VIII* in 1613 caused a fire that burned the Globe to the ground.

Because the playhouse was open to the air, plays were presented in the daytime, and there was little or no artificial lighting. Scenery in the modern sense was nonexistent, and very few properties were used, beyond an occasional table or chair. Audiences had to use their imaginations to create the scenes, and playwrights helped their audiences to do this by writing descriptions of scenes into their characters' speeches, as in these descriptions from Shakespeare's play *Macbeth:*

DUNCAN. This castle hath a pleasant seat. The air
Nimbly and sweetly recommends itself
Unto our gentle senses.

BANQUO. This guest of summer,
The temple-haunting martlet, does approve,
By his lov'd mansionry that the heaven's breath
Smells wooingly here; No jutty, frieze,
Buttress, nor coign of vantage, but this bird
Hath made his pendant bed and procreant cradle.
Where they most breed and haunt, I have observ'd
The air is delicate.

—act 1, scene 6

MACBETH. Now o'er the one half-world
Nature seems dead, and wicked dreams abuse
The curtain'd sleep; witchcraft celebrates
Pale Hecate's off'rings; and wither'd Murther,
Alarum'd by his sentinel, the wolf,
Whose howl's his watch, thus with his stealthy pace,
With Tarquin's ravishing strides, towards his design
Moves like a ghost. Thou sure and firm-set earth,
Hear not my steps, which way they walk, for fear
The very stones prate of my whereabout
And take the present horror from the time,
Which now suits with it.

—act 2, scene 1

The Renaissance Audience

If you go to a public entertainment today, you are likely to find certain types of people at certain types of shows—young people at rock concerts, middle-class businesspeople at musicals, the elite of a city at the ballet, the symphony, or the opera. Audiences at the Globe and similar theaters were more mixed, or heterogeneous. They included people from all stations of society: laboring people from the lower classes, middle-class merchants, members of Parliament, and lords and ladies. Pickpockets mingled among the noisy, raucous groundlings crowded around the stage. Noble men and women sat on cushioned seats in the first-tier balcony. The fanfare of trumpets that signaled the beginning of a play was heard by some twenty-five hundred people, a cross section of the Elizabethan world. That Shakespeare's plays have such universal appeal may be explained by this fact: they were written for everyone, from "the most able, to him that can but spell."[1]

William Shakespeare.
Courtesy the Dean and chaplaincy, Westminster Abbey

Marlowe and Shakespeare

The two greatest playwrights of the Elizabethan Age were Christopher Marlowe and William Shakespeare.

In 1587, **Christopher Marlowe** wrote *Tamburlaine,* the first of his great plays, the story of a prideful, doomed Mongol conqueror. In this play and in others produced during the following six years, Marlowe revolutionized English theater. Perhaps his most important innovation was his use of **blank verse**—unrhymed iambic pentameter. Other playwrights before him had employed this meter, but Marlowe raised it to great heights. Marlowe's blank verse was lofty and heroic while having, at the same time, the grace and naturalness of ordinary speech. Marlowe blended elements of the comic and the tragic, treated romantic themes, probed the psychology of his characters, and exhibited a consummate sense of what constituted an exciting and dramatic situation. Later playwrights, including Shakespeare, would owe him a great debt.

William Shakespeare may well be the greatest dramatist the world has ever known. Shakespeare became a shareholder with Richard Burbage, son of John Burbage, in a theater company known as The Lord Chamberlain's Men. In 1599, Burbage, Shakespeare, and others opened the Globe Theater, and in 1603 they bought the Blackfriars, a small, artificially lighted indoor theater for winter performances. Their company began performing regularly at the court of Queen Elizabeth. After the death of Elizabeth in 1603, Shakespeare's company became, officially, servants of King James I, and their name was changed to The King's Men.

Shakespeare did not personally prepare his plays for publication, and no official collection of them appeared until after his death. A collection of his sonnets, considered by critics to be among the best ever written in English, appeared in 1609. Many individual plays were published during his lifetime in unauthorized editions known as **Quartos.** Many of these quartos are quite unreliable. Some were probably based on actors' memories of the plays. Some were reprintings of so-called prompter's copies used in production of the plays. Some may have been based on final manuscript versions produced by the author. In 1623, seven years after Shakespeare's death, his

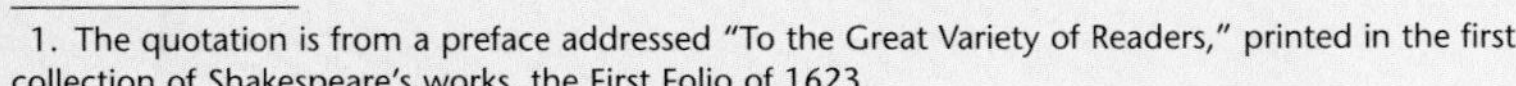

1. The quotation is from a preface addressed "To the Great Variety of Readers," printed in the first collection of Shakespeare's works, the First Folio of 1623.

Literary Technique

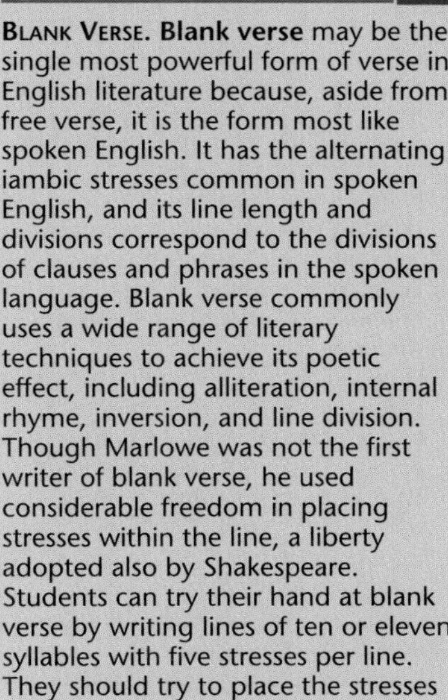

Blank Verse. Blank verse may be the single most powerful form of verse in English literature because, aside from free verse, it is the form most like spoken English. It has the alternating iambic stresses common in spoken English, and its line length and divisions correspond to the divisions of clauses and phrases in the spoken language. Blank verse commonly uses a wide range of literary techniques to achieve its poetic effect, including alliteration, internal rhyme, inversion, and line division. Though Marlowe was not the first writer of blank verse, he used considerable freedom in placing stresses within the line, a liberty adopted also by Shakespeare. Students can try their hand at blank verse by writing lines of ten or eleven syllables with five stresses per line. They should try to place the stresses on alternate syllables. For related information, see the Handbook of Literary Terms.

Biographical Note

That Shakespeare was the author of nearly all the plays associated with him is a widely accepted idea among scholars familiar with the details of Elizabethan literary history. In his own lifetime, some fifty people (including the illustrious Ben Jonson) testified to his authorship of many of the plays that now bear his name. Furthermore, many of the plays were published during Shakespeare's lifetime in quarto editions that bear his name. Nevertheless, since the 1900s, some scholars have claimed that Shakespeare was of too humble and ignorant parentage to have written such varied, brilliant, and learned verse. Various theories about the "true" author of the plays have been proposed. One of them alleges that Christopher Marlowe did not die in a tavern brawl, as is commonly believed, but lived, escaped to France, and paid Shakespeare to pretend that he was the author of the plays, which Marlowe in fact wrote. Another theory proposes the scholar Francis Bacon as the author. As "proof," the proponents of this theory point to the word *honorificabilitudinitatibus* found in *Love's Labour's Lost.* This nonsense word is an anagram, they claim, for the Latin *Hi ludi F. Baconis nati tuiti*

Biographical Note (cont.)

orbi—"These plays, the offspring of F. Bacon, are preserved for the world." Students may enjoy researching these and other claims about the authorship of the plays. Refer them to the Language Arts Survey, 5.3, "Avoiding False Arguments and Propaganda."

SELECTION CHECK TEST 4.5.1 WITH ANSWERS

Checking Your Reading

1. How were plays brought to and performed for people in small towns? **They were performed on the backs of wagons.**
2. Name one of the two reasons why London officials objected to the theater. **Theater-going crowds created the potential for lawlessness and the spread of diseases.**
3. How did Humanism help bring the five-act play to English theater? **Humanism was the rebirth of classical learning, which meant that English students studied a Latin curriculum. The five-act play was common in Roman plays.**
4. What did Puritans do to theater once they got control of England? **It was banned.**
5. What sorts of people would you be most likely to see at Renaissance plays? **All sorts of people attended Renaissance plays.**

TYPES OF RENAISSANCE DRAMA. Fill in the blanks using the following terms. You may not use every term, and you may use some terms more than once.

miracle play morality play history
romance interlude masque
tragedy

1. **Miracle plays** told fantastic stories from the lives of saints.
2. Audiences loved **masques,** elaborate entertainments with acting, music, and dance.
3. **Tragedies** told of the downfall of a person of high status.
4. **Romances** contained highly fantastic elements, like fairies and magic spells.
5. The protagonist of a **tragedy** was essentially good but had a fatal character flaw.

THE FIVE-ACT PLAY. The stages of a five-act play are similar to the stages in a short story plot. In the blanks below, fill in the names of stages and the actions that take place in each stage.

	STAGE	ACTION
ACT I	Introduction	Presents setting, main characters, inciting incident
Act II	Rising Action or Complication	**1. Develops the central conflict**
Act III	**2. Crisis or Turning Point**	Presents a decisive occurrence that determines the rest of the action in the play

Shakespeare's Birthplace.

friends and fellow actors John Heminge and Henry Condell published a collected edition of thirty-five of Shakespeare's plays. This collection is known to literary historians as the **First Folio.** In the centuries since 1623, and especially during the last century and a half, editors have worked diligently to compare the various early printed versions of Shakespeare's works to determine which version or versions of each play best represent Shakespeare's intent.

No brief summary can begin to catalog the many virtues of Shakespeare's work. He was a gifted observer of people, capable of creating unforgettable characters from all stations and walks of life. He used one of the largest vocabularies ever employed by an author, filling his plays with concrete details and with actual speech faithfully recalled. His plays probe the range of human experience. They are romantic in the sense that they are filled with passions rendered intensely. However, the plays rarely strain credibility or sink into sensationalism or sentimentality. Shakespeare's language tends to be dense, metaphorical, full of puns and word play, and yet natural, so that it comes "trippingly off the tongue" of an actor. A scene from Shakespeare tears across the stage, riveting and dramatic, and yet it bears close rereading, revealing in that rereading astonishing depth and complexity. Shakespeare used in his plays a combination of prose, rhymed poetry, and blank verse always appropriate to the character or scene at hand. His plays have given many, many phrases to the English language. They have filled audiences with laughter, pity, compassion, fear, terror, sadness, despair, suspense, and joy for over four hundred years. To begin to read Shakespeare is to enter a world, one might say the world, for his art is, as Hamlet says it should be, "a mirror held up to nature," to human nature. To read him well is to begin to understand others and ourselves. His art is, as Ben Jonson wrote, "not of an age, but for all time."

(Note: For a critical discussion of Shakespeare's *Macbeth,* see William Hazlitt's "Macbeth," included as a Selection for Additional Reading at the end of Unit 8: The Romantic Era.)

SELECTION CHECK TEST 4.5.1 WITH ANSWERS (CONT.)

Act IV	Falling Action	**3. Events that happen as a result of the crisis**
Act V	**4. Resolution or Catastrophe**	**5. The event that resolves the central conflict**

SHAKESPEARE AND MARLOWE. The Renaissance gave us two of the greatest playwrights of all time: William Shakespeare and Christopher Marlowe. Put an "S" by the statements that describe Shakespeare, and an "M" by those that describe Marlowe.

__S__ 1. Thirty-five of his plays were collected in what is known as the First Folio

Continued on page 373

Echoes

Renaissance Drama

Shakespeare on Theater

Jaques. All the world's a stage,
And all the men and women merely players;
They have their exits and their entrances,
And one man in his time plays many parts.

—As You Like It

Theseus. The Poet's eye, in a fine frenzy rolling,
Doth glance from heaven to earth, from earth to heaven;
And as imagination bodies forth
The forms of things unknown, the poet's pen
Turns them to shapes, and gives to aery nothing
A local habitation and a name.

—A Midsummer Night's Dream

Prologue.
O for a Muse of fire, that would ascend
The brightest heaven of invention!
A kingdom for a stage, princes to act,
And monarchs to behold the swelling scene!
Then should the warlike Harry, like himself,
Assume the port of Mars, and at his heels
(Leash'd in, like hounds) should famine, sword, and fire
Crouch for employment. But pardon, gentles all,
The flat unraised spirits that hath dar'd
On this unworthy scaffold to bring forth
So great an object. Can this cockpit hold
The vasty fields of France? Or may we cram
Within this wooden O the very casques
That did affright the air at Agincourt?
O, pardon! since a crooked figure may
Attest in little place a million,
And let us, ciphers to this great accompt,
On your imaginary forces work.
Suppose within the girdle of these walls
Are now confin'd two mighty monarchies,
Whose high, upreared, and abutting fronts
The perilous narrow ocean parts asunder.
Piece out our imperfections with your thoughts;
Into a thousand parts divide one man,
And make imaginary puissance;
Think, when we talk of horses, that you see them
Printing their proud hoofs i' th' receiving earth;
For 'tis your thoughts that now must deck our kings,
Carry them here and there, jumping o'er times,
Turning th' accomplishment of many years
Into an hour-glass: for the which supply,
Admit me Chorus to this history;
Who, Prologue-like, you humble patience pray,
Gently to hear, kindly to judge, our play.

—Henry V

***Shakespeare and His Contemporaries*, 1851.** John Faed. Private Collection.

ADDITIONAL QUESTIONS AND ACTIVITIES

Students can memorize one of the passages on page 373 to increase their comprehension of Shakespearean verse and to practice their memorization skills. You may wish to assign the shorter passages to students who find such activities challenging. Schedule a "recitation hour" either during class or at some other time.

LITERARY TECHNIQUE

Metaphor. Refer students to the entry on **metaphor** in the Handbook of Literary Terms, and explain that a metaphor is a description of one thing as if it were another. Work with students to identify metaphors in the three passages on page 373. Write the metaphors on the board as students suggest them. Some of the metaphors they may find include the world as a stage, actors as spirits, the stage as a cockpit (pit for cockfights), the theater as the letter O, actors as ciphers (numbers), theater walls as a girdle, and thoughts as costumes.

BIBLIOGRAPHIC NOTE

Of Shakespeare's plays, *A Midsummer Night's Dream* is one of the most accessible and interesting to high school students. You may wish to suggest that play for outside reading. Other plays by Shakespeare that your students might enjoy include *Julius Cæsar, Romeo and Juliet, The Tempest,* and *The Taming of the Shrew.*

SELECTION CHECK TEST 4.5.1 WITH ANSWERS (CONT. FROM PAGE 372)

__M__ 2. wrote Tamburlaine, the story of a Mongol conqueror
__S__ 3. His plays were published in unauthorized editions known as Quartos
__M__ 4. wrote The Tragical History of Doctor Faustus
__M__ 5. popularized blank verse
__S__ 6. was part owner of a theater company known as The Lord Chamberlain's Men
__S__ 7. turned to narrative poetry when theaters closed in 1593
__S__ 8. was known for his large vocabulary and works full of puns and word play

ADDITIONAL RESOURCES

UNIT 5 RESOURCE BOOK

- Selection Worksheet 5.1
- Selection Check Test 4.5.3
- Selection Test 4.5.4
- Speaking and Listening Resource 4.1

INDIVIDUAL LEARNING STRATEGIES

MOTIVATION
Encourage students by suggesting that this play is much like a murder thriller. Ask them to try to envision the action as if it were a film. Have students work in partners to rewrite the dialogue of one of the scenes using language they would hear in a modern thriller.

READING PROFICIENCY
Help students to understand the contractions used so frequently by Shakespeare by choosing several from the text and writing them on the board along with the uncontracted forms. Explain to them that in many cases, words were contracted in order to maintain the rhythm of ten beats per line (pentameter) Shakespeare used throughout much of the play. Students should also pay attention to the many footnotes used to clarify outdated usages of words. Students may also enjoy listening to the audiocassette recording of act 5 of *Macbeth,* which can be found in the *EMC Audio Library.*

ENGLISH LANGUAGE LEARNING
Ask students to read through each act by themselves, trying to get the gist of it. Then they should read through a second time, copying down words that obscure the meaning for them and that they cannot guess from the context. Share with them the Additional Vocabulary on page 376 of the teacher's edition. Students may also note confusing lines and discuss these as a class in order to reach an interpretation. Finally, the class should read the act aloud, going around the room taking turns.

SPECIAL NEEDS
Read over with students the tips on studying Shakespeare (in About the Selection on page 375). Explain that much of the language of *Macbeth* is poetry, and suggest that students watch for language that describes one thing as if it were something else. Also ask them to

Literary TOOLS

ASIDE. An **aside** is a statement made by a character in a play, intended to be heard by the audience but not by other characters on stage. The term may also be used to describe a statement made privately by one character to another so that other characters on the stage cannot hear it. In scene 3, Macbeth and Banquo use both kinds of asides. As you read, consider the meaning of the asides and what they reveal about the characters of the two men.

CONFLICT AND INCITING INCIDENT. The **central conflict** is the primary struggle dealt with in the plot of a story or play. A struggle that takes place within a character is called an **internal conflict.** The **inciting incident** is the event that introduces the central conflict. As you read act 1, determine the central conflict and the inciting incident.

SOLILOQUY. A **soliloquy** is a speech delivered by a lone character that reveals the speaker's thoughts and feelings. Scene 5 opens with Lady Macbeth's soliloquy. As you read it, consider what it reveals about her character.

The Tragedy of Macbeth

BY WILLIAM SHAKESPEARE

About *the* AUTHOR

William Shakepeare's mother, Mary Arden Shakespeare, was from a well-to-do, well-connected family. His father, John Shakespeare, was a prosperous glove maker and local politician. William's exact birthdate is unknown, but he was baptized in his hometown of Stratford-upon-Avon on April 26, 1564, and tradition has assigned him a birthdate of April 23, which was also the day of his death and the feast day of Saint George, England's patron saint. Shakespeare attended the Stratford grammar school, where he studied Latin and perhaps some Greek. At the age of eighteen, Shakespeare married an older woman, Anne Hathaway, who was with child. Altogether, William and Anne had three children, Susanna and the twins Hamnet and Judith. He may have worked for a while as a schoolteacher, for there are many references to teaching in his plays. By 1592, however, he was living in London and pursuing a life in the theater. Scholars have speculated that Shakespeare's marriage was unhappy, but he continued to provide for his family and to expand his holdings in Stratford while living in London. He retired to Stratford-upon-Avon at the end of his life.

By 1593, Shakespeare was a successful actor and playwright. His history plays *Henry VI, Parts 1, 2,* and *3,* and *Richard III* had established him as a significant force in London theater. In 1593, when an outbreak of the plague forced the closing of the theaters, Shakespeare turned to narrative poetry, producing *Venus and Adonis* followed by *The Rape of Lucrece,* both dedicated to a patron, the Earl of Southampton. When the theaters reopened, Shakespeare plunged back into his primary vocation, writing thirty-seven plays in less than twenty years, including *The Taming of the Shrew, A Midsummer Night's Dream, The Merchant of Venice, Twelfth Night, All's Well That Ends Well, Richard II, Romeo and Juliet, Julius Cæsar, Hamlet, Othello, King Lear, Macbeth, The Winter's Tale,* and *The Tempest.*

Shakespeare's final play, Henry VIII, was performed in London in 1613. At that time he was probably living again in Stratford in a large house called New Place that he had bought in 1597. When he died in 1616, survived by his wife and his two daughters, Shakespeare was a wealthy man. He was buried in the Holy Trinity Church in Stratford-upon-Avon, where his bones rest to this day. The stone over his grave reads: "Good frend for Jesus sake forbeare, / To digg the dust enclosèd heare! / Blest be the man that spares thes stones, / And curst be he that moves my bones."

INDIVIDUAL LEARNING STRATEGIES (CONT.)

determine a common meter used in the play by counting the number of beats, or syllables, per line. Beats will vary depending on how a student interprets the number of syllables, but they should recognize that most of the lines are ten beats long (meaning the meter is pentameter).

ENRICHMENT

Ask students to find modern examples of any

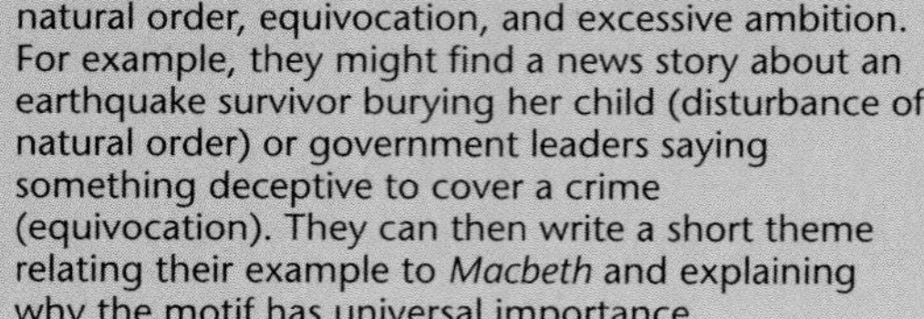

of the following motifs in *Macbeth:* disturbance of natural order, equivocation, and excessive ambition. For example, they might find a news story about an earthquake survivor burying her child (disturbance of natural order) or government leaders saying something deceptive to cover a crime (equivocation). They can then write a short theme relating their example to *Macbeth* and explaining why the motif has universal importance.

About *the* SELECTION

Sources. A **tragedy** is a drama that tells the story of the fall of a person of high status. Along with *Hamlet, Othello,* and *King Lear,* ***Macbeth*** is considered one of Shakespeare's greatest tragedies. Shakespeare used Holinshed's *Chronicles of England, Scotland, and Ireland* as the major source for his story. The *Chronicles* tell of the reign of a bloodthirsty, twelfth-century Scottish king named Macbeth. They also tell of the murder of the Scottish king Duff by Donwald. Shakespeare combined these two tales to create the storyline of his play for performance before King James I of England, who was descended from one of the characters in the play, Banquo. Shakespeare's dark tale of a man's ambition and treachery, written in 1605–1606, strikes a frighteningly familiar chord today, almost four centuries later.

Reading the Play. Shakespeare's *Macbeth* is a history, a chilling ghost story, and a psychological thriller. Few plays have ever matched it for sheer spectacle and suspense. As you read the play, remember that the script for a play is like a score for a piece of music. It comes alive when performed. To appreciate fully the experience of reading a play, you should visualize the scenes in your mind as they might appear on stage. Allow yourself to be drawn into the play's dark, disturbing atmosphere. Thrill to its many witches, ghosts, and other apparitions. Follow the murky descent of the central character into a horror of his own making.

Try not to be overwhelmed by Shakespeare's use of Elizabethan English. Read each scene through quickly to get the gist of it. Concentrate on seeing the scene in your mind and not on the details of the language. Then go back and read the scene carefully, using the footnotes. Soon you will find that you have grown accustomed to Shakespeare's English and can appreciate its sometimes spine-tingling, sometimes noble beauty.

One technique that will help you to grasp the themes, or main ideas, of the play is to look for and think about recurring elements, or **motifs.** These include references to ambition; to equivocation, or double-talk; to blood; to madness; to sickness; to foul weather; to manliness (or lack thereof); and to disturbances in the natural order. As you read the play, note these elements, and think about how they are related to one another. Also bear in mind that James I, for whom the play was performed by Shakespeare's company, The King's Men, was a staunch believer in demons and witches (about which he wrote a book) and in the Divine Right of Kings (the idea that kings gain their authority directly from God and, therefore, rule absolutely). To James, the overthrow or murder of a king would be an attack on the natural order of the universe.

Literary Tools continued

Foil. A **foil** is a character whose attributes, or characteristics, contrast with and therefore throw into relief the attributes of another character. In act 1, Banquo, King Duncan, and Lady Macbeth all serve as foils for Macbeth. As you read, notice the differences in character between Macbeth and these characters. Make a chart listing the characters who are foils to Macbeth on the left. List characteristics of these foils in the middle. On the right compare these characteristics to Macbeth. One example has been done for you.

Foils	Characteristics	Macbeth
Banquo	cautious about prophecy believes the witches are evil	eager to believe prophecy unconcerned about witches' morality

Reader's Journal

You have heard the saying, "The end justifies the means." What means would you be willing to use to achieve your goals?

GRAPHIC ORGANIZER

Students should list the following information in their charts. Duncan is open, honest, trusting, and grateful, whereas Macbeth is secretive, dishonest, untrustworthy, and ungrateful. Lady Macbeth is more ruthless about killing the king, whereas Macbeth has some scruples and reservations about committing murder.

VOCABULARY FROM THE SELECTION

Act 1

chastise
corporal
earnest
flout
gall
impede
mettle
minion
mortal
pall
peak
purveyor
recompense
remorse
surmise
trifle
wanton

READER'S JOURNAL

You might ask students to list several goals they have for their life and pick one to focus on. You might also hold a class discussion to reveal questionable means used by characters on TV and in films. Ask students to share how they would have used different means to achieve the same ends.

GOALS/OBJECTIVES

Studying this lesson will enable students to

- experience the suspense, horror, and catharsis of a Shakespearean tragedy
- recognize themes and motifs in a play
- define *aside, soliloquy, foil, symbol, hyperbole, verbal irony, mood, simile, metaphor, paradox,* and *personification* using examples from the play
- list and identify the elements of plot as they appear in the play
- review the use of contractions, edit for correct comma usage, edit sentences for parallelism
- design a stage set and present dramatic interpretations of scenes from *Macbeth*
- tape a television show based on the murder of Duncan in *Macbeth*

ADDITIONAL VOCABULARY

Students will find Shakespeare's vocabulary challenging, especially since much of it is no longer in colloquial use. Share with them the following vocabulary from act 1:

ere—before
heath—open wasteland
valor—bravery
furbished—fixed up; renovated
dismal—unpleasant
curb—restrain
deign—stoop down
disburse—pay out
dwindle—become smaller or weaker
pine—yearn, long for
tempest—storm
start—startle
trifles—insignificant amusements
rapt—enthralled
wrought—made
interim—time between
liege—lord
become—suit
purpose *(v.)*—intend
sway *(n.)*,—determining power
procreant—fruitful
undaunted—fearless

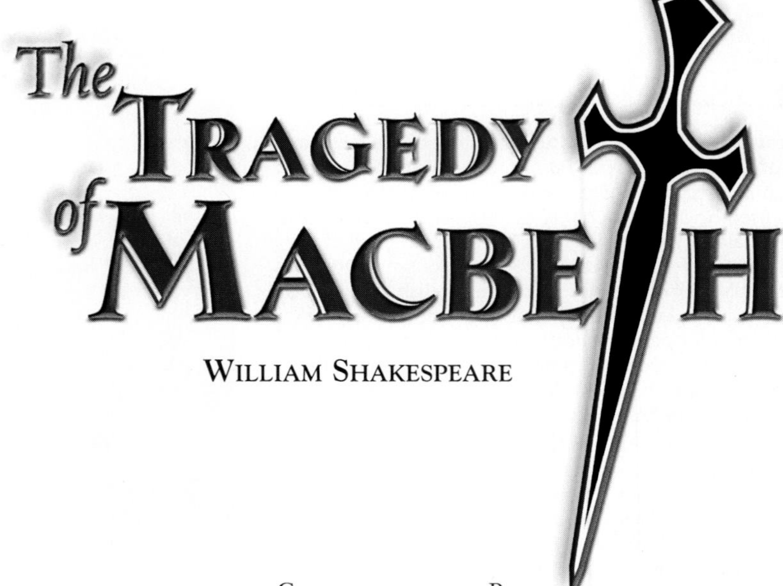

The Tragedy of Macbeth

WILLIAM SHAKESPEARE

CHARACTERS IN THE PLAY

DUNCAN, *King of Scotland*
MALCOLM, DONALBAIN — *Duncan's sons*
MACBETH, BANQUO — *Duncan's thanes, generals in his service*
MACDUFF, LENNOX, ROSSE, MENTETH, ANGUS, CATHNESS — *Scottish noblemen*
FLEANCE, *Banquo's son*
SIWARD, *Earl of Northumberland, leader of the English troops*
YOUNG SIWARD, *Siward's son*
SEYTON, *Macbeth's servant*
BOY, *Macduff's son*

ENGLISH DOCTOR
SCOTS DOCTOR
SERGEANT
PORTER, *or* GATEKEEPER
OLD MAN
Three MURDERERS

LADY MACBETH
LADY MACDUFF
GENTLEWOMAN, *Lady Macbeth's servant*
Three WITCHES, *the Weïrd Sisters*
Three other WITCHES
HECATE, *Queen of the Witches*
APPARITIONS

LORDS, GENTLEMEN, OFFICERS, SOLDIERS, ATTENDANTS, MESSENGERS *and* BANQUO'S GHOST

SCENES: Scotland and England

ACT 1

SCENE 1: an open place

Thunder and lightning. Enter three WITCHES.

1. WITCH. When shall we three meet again?
In thunder, lightning, or in rain?

2. WITCH. When the hurly-burly's[1] done,
When the battle's lost and won.

3. WITCH. That will be ere the set of sun.

1. WITCH. Where the place?

2. WITCH. Upon the heath.

3. WITCH. There to meet with Macbeth.

1. WITCH. I come, Graymalkin.[2]

2. WITCH. Paddock[3] calls.

3. WITCH. Anon.

ALL. Fair is foul, and foul is fair,
Hover through the fog and filthy air. *Exeunt.*

What parting pronouncement do the witches make?

SCENE 2: a camp in Scotland

Alarum[4] within. Enter KING *Duncan*, MALCOLM, DONALBAIN, LENNOX, *with* ATTENDANTS, *meeting a bleeding* SERGEANT.

DUNCAN. What bloody man is that? He can report,
As seemeth by his plight, of the revolt
The newest state.

MALCOLM. This is the sergeant,
Who like a good and hardy soldier fought
'Gainst my captivity. Hail, brave friend!
Say to the King the knowledge of the broil
As thou didst leave it.

SERGEANT. Doubtful it stood,
As two spent swimmers that do cling together
And choke their art.[5] The merciless Macdonwald
(Worthy to be a rebel, for to that
The multiplying villainies of nature
Do swarm upon him) from the Western Isles
Of kerns and gallowglasses[6] is supplied,
And Fortune, on his damned quarrel[7] smiling,

1. **hurly-burly.** Commotion of the battle
2. **Graymalkin.** Gray cat, the witch's familiar
3. **Paddock.** Toad, the second witch's familiar
4. **Alarum.** Trumpet call
5. **art.** Skill (in swimming)
6. **kerns and gallowglasses.** Kerns are lightly armed foot soldiers, and gallowglasses are heavily armed soldiers.
7. **quarrel.** Cause

ANSWER TO GUIDED READING QUESTION

1. The witches say, "Fair is foul, and foul is fair."

LITERARY TECHNIQUE

OXYMORON. Explain to students that an **oxymoron** is a combination of incongruous or contradictory words. Examples are *whispered shout* and *deadly assistance.* An oxymoron accurately expresses a conflict between elements of a thing or situation, however odd or surprising it may be. Though the witches do not use an oxymoron as such in the first scene, the phrase "fair foulness" would sum up the battle at the beginning of the play and its results: as war it is grim and foul, but because the "right" side wins, it is also fair or good. Similarly, the opening could be described as "foul fairness" because it is the fair starting point that leads to Macbeth's later "foul" actions. Students should be alert to situations in the play that can be described as oxymorons. For example, "foul fairness" describes the behavior of Macbeth and Lady Macbeth later in act I, when they treat Duncan well (with fairness) while plotting to kill him (and are thus foul).

ANSWER TO GUIDED READING QUESTION

1. Macbeth killed Macdonwald, cutting him from his navel to his jaw.

ADDITIONAL QUESTIONS AND ACTIVITIES

Most teenagers lack a time sense; they assume that anything that preceded them historically is passé and has little to offer them. The following exercise is recommended to get students to begin thinking of their place on the continuum of time: Run a piece of chalk across the chalkboard. Assume that the beginning of the line represents the beginning of time. Ask students when time began. Did it begin with the beginning of the universe? With the emergence of Homo sapiens and of human consciousness? Assume that the end of the time line is 1996. Ask students where on the line they would place Greek and Roman civilizations. Where would they place 1564–1616? Make the point that Shakespeare is a contemporary of theirs in time, that if the species endures and time continues, the time may come when students will study all of Western Civilization, from the Greeks through our time, from a single chapter in a history book.

Macbeth and the Three Witches, c.1700s. John Wootton. Rafael Valls Gallery, London.

Show'd like a rebel's whore. But all's too weak;
For brave Macbeth (well he deserves that name),
Disdaining Fortune, with his brandish'd steel,
Which smok'd with bloody execution,
(Like Valor's minion) carv'd out his passage
Till he fac'd the slave;
Which nev'r shook hands, nor bade farewell to him,
Till he unseam'd him from the nave to th' chops,[8]
Ant fix'd his head upon our battlements.

DUNCAN. O valiant cousin,[9] worthy gentleman!

What was the outcome when Macbeth met Macdonwald on the field of battle?

---

8. **unseam'd . . . chops.** Cut him from navel to jaw
9. **cousin.** General term for relative (Duncan and Macbeth were both grandsons of King Malcolm)

WORDS FOR EVERYDAY USE

min • ion (min´ yən) *n.,* favorite. *Rather than hiring unknowns, the politician filled all the local government offices with one minion after another.*

SERGEANT. As whence the sun gins his reflection[10]
Shipwracking storms and direful thunders break,
So from that spring whence comfort seem'd to come
Discomfort swells. Mark, King of Scotland, mark!
No sooner justice had, with valor arm'd,
Compell'd these skipping kerns to trust their heels,
But the Norweyan lord, surveying vantage,
With furbish'd arms and new supplies of men,
Began a fresh assault.

How did Macbeth and Banquo react to Norway's assault?

DUNCAN. Dismay'd not this
Our captains, Macbeth and Banquo?

SERGEANT Yes,
As sparrows eagles; or the hare the lion.
If I say sooth, I must report they were
As cannons overcharg'd with double cracks,[11] so they
Doubly redoubled strokes upon the foe.
Except they meant to bathe in reeking[12] wounds,
Or memorize another Golgotha,[13]
I cannot tell—
But I am faint, my gashes cry for help.

DUNCAN. So well thy words become thee as thy wounds,
They smack of honor both. Go get him surgeons.
Exit SERGEANT, *attended.*

Enter ROSSE *and* ANGUS.

Who comes here?

MALCOLM. The worthy Thane[14] of Rosse.

LENNOX. What a haste looks through his eyes! So should he look
That seems to speak things strange.

ROSSE. God save the king!

DUNCAN. Whence cam'st thou, worthy thane?

ROSSE. From Fife, great King,
Where the Norweyan banners flout the sky
And fan our people cold.
Norway himself, with terrible numbers,

10. **gins his reflection.** Begins turning back (at the vernal equinox)
11. **cracks.** Charges
12. **reeking.** Steaming
13. **memorize . . . Golgotha.** Make the place as memorable for slaughter as Golgotha, the place of skulls
14. **Thane.** Scottish title of nobility

WORDS FOR EVERYDAY USE

flout (flout) *vt.*, show scorn or contempt for. *The reckless driver managed to flout nearly every rule of the road before he skidded into a ditch.*

ANSWER TO GUIDED READING QUESTION

1. Macbeth and Banquo were not dismayed; they redoubled their assault.

CROSS-CURRICULAR ACTIVITIES

SCIENCE. Have students research the vernal equinox. They should explain what it is and find out what date it usually occurs. Students could create a diagram showing the sun's relative position to the earth as it approaches the vernal and autumnal equinoxes. After they have done this, ask them to explain the simile used by the Sergeant.

Answers

The vernal and autumnal equinoxes take place when the sun crosses the equator and day and night are everywhere of the same length. The vernal equinox occurs around March 21 and marks the first day of Spring on the Western calendar; the autumnal equinox occurs around September 23 and marks the first day of Fall.

ANSWERS TO GUIDED READING QUESTIONS

1. The Thane of Cawdor joined the enemy, Norway, but they were defeated.
2. Duncan sentences the Thane of Cawdor to death and awards his title to Macbeth.

CROSS-CURRICULAR ACTIVITIES

ARTS AND HUMANITIES. Explain to students that when illustrators draw the first version of a comic strip, they often sketch quickly the contents of each frame. A student who has drawing skills can stand at the chalkboard and do a rough sketch of four or five frames to illustrate scene 1 of *Macbeth.* Other students can contribute by suggesting what viewing angle might be used in each frame, how the contents should be cropped (for instance, as a close-up of one witch's face or as a view of all three witches), and how the lines of dialogue should be allocated to the various frames. Students can insert bits of dialogue in speech balloons in each frame. Discuss with students how graphic representation differs from dramatic representation.

What traitor joined Norway in his assault? What was the outcome of the battle?

Assisted by that most disloyal traitor,
The Thane of Cawdor, began a dismal conflict,
Till that Bellona's bridegroom, lapp'd in proof,[15]
Confronted him with self-comparisons,
Point against point, rebellious arm 'gainst arm,
Curbing his lavish spirit; and to conclude,
The victory fell on us.

DUNCAN. Great happiness!

ROSSE. That now
Sweno, the Norways' king, craves composition;
Nor would we deign him burial of his men
Till he disbursed at Saint Colme's inch[16]
Ten thousand dollars to our general use.

What judgment does Duncan pronounce on the traitor, Cawdor?

DUNCAN. No more that Thane of Cawdor shall deceive
Our bosom interest. Go pronounce his present[17] death,
And with his former title greet Macbeth.

ROSSE. I'll see it done.

DUNCAN. What he hath lost, noble Macbeth hath won.

Exeunt.

SCENE 3: a heath

Thunder. Enter the three WITCHES.

1. WITCH. Where hast thou been, sister?

2. WITCH. Killing swine.[18]

3. WITCH. Sister, where thou?

1. WITCH. A sailor's wife had chestnuts in her lap,
And mounch'd, and mounch'd, and mounch'd. "Give me!" quoth I.
"Aroint[19] thee, witch!" the rump-fed ronyon[20] cries.
Her husband's to Aleppo gone, master o' th' *Tiger*;[21]
But in a sieve I'll thither sail,
And, like a rat without a tail,
I'll do, I'll do, and I'll do.

2. WITCH. I'll give thee a wind.

1. WITCH. Th' art kind.

3. WITCH. And I another.

1. WITCH. I myself have all the other,

15. **Bellona's . . . proof.** Macbeth, who is paired with Bellona, goddess of war, is clad in tested armor.
16. **Saint Colme's inch.** A small island near Edinburgh, Scotland
17. **present.** Immediate
18. **killing swine.** It was commonly believed that witches killed domestic animals, especially pigs.
19. **Aroint.** Be gone
20. **rump-fed ronyon.** Fat, good-for-nothing creature
21. **Aleppo . . . *Tiger*.** Her husband went to Aleppo, a trading center in Syria, on a ship called the *Tiger.*

And the very ports they blow,
All the quarters that they know
I' th' shipman's card.[22]
I'll drain him dry as hay:
Sleep shall neither night nor day
Hang upon his penthouse lid;[23]
He shall live a man forbid;[24]
Weary sev'nnights, nine times nine,
Shall he dwindle, peak,[25] and pine;
Though his bark cannot be lost,
Yet it shall be tempest-toss'd.
Look what I have.

What will Witch 1 do to the sailor?

2. Witch. Show me, show me.

1. Witch. Here I have a pilot's thumb,
Wrack'd as homeward he did come.
Drum within.

3. Witch. A drum, a drum!
Macbeth doth come.

All. The weïrd[26] sisters, hand in hand,
Posters[27] of the sea and land,
Thus do go, about, about,
Thrice to thine, and thrice to mine,
And thrice again, to make up nine.
Peace, the charm's wound up.

Enter Macbeth *and* Banquo.

Macbeth. So foul and fair a day I have not seen.

Banquo. How far is't call'd to Forres? What are these
So wither'd and so wild in their attire,
That look not like th' inhabitants o' th' earth,
And yet are on't? Live you? or are you aught
That man may question? You seem to understand me,
By each at once her choppy[28] finger laying
Upon her skinny lips. You should be women,

What do the witches look like?

22. **shipman's card.** Compass or chart
23. **penthouse lid.** Eyelid
24. **forbid.** Under a curse
25. **peak.** Become peaked, or pale and sickly
26. **weïrd.** Destiny-serving, from the Old English *wyrd* or fate
27. **Posters.** Swift travellers
28. **choppy.** Chapped

Words for Everyday Use

at • tire (ə tīr′) *n.,* dress; clothing. *Greg detested parties that required formal attire; he felt unnatural in a suit and tie.*

ANSWERS TO GUIDED READING QUESTIONS

1. She will make him endure a bad storm.
2. The witches are withered and bearded creatures "That look not like th' inhabitants o' th' earth."

LITERARY NOTE

The poet and critic Dr. Samuel Johnson (1709–1784) had this comment about why belief in witchcraft was accepted in Shakespeare's London: "[King James had] not only examined in person a woman accused of witchcraft but had given a very formal account of the practices and illusions of evil spirits, the compacts of witches, the ceremonies used by them, the manner of detecting them, and the justice of punishing them, in his dialogues of *Daemonologie.* This book was, soon after his accession, reprinted at London, and as the ready way to gain King James's favor was to flatter his speculations, the system of *Daemonologie* was immediately adopted by all who desired either to gain preferment or not to lose it. Thus the doctrine of witchcraft was very powerfully inculcated; and as the greatest part of man-kind have no other reason for their opinions than that they are in fashion, it cannot be doubted but this persuasion made a rapid progress, since vanity and credulity co-operated in its favor."

ANSWERS TO GUIDED READING QUESTIONS

1. The witches call Macbeth the Thane of Glamis, the Thane of Cawdor, and King-to-be.
2. The witches tell Banquo he will father a line of kings but not be one himself.

And yet your beards forbid me to interpret
That you are so.

With what three titles do the witches greet Macbeth?

MACBETH. Speak, if you can: what are you?

1. WITCH. All hail, Macbeth, hail to thee, Thane of Glamis!

2. WITCH. All hail, Macbeth, hail to thee, Thane of Cawdor!

3. WITCH. All hail, Macbeth, that shalt be King hereafter!

BANQUO. Good sir, why do you start, and seem to fear
Things that do sound so fair?—I' th' name of truth,
Are ye fantastical,[29] or that indeed
Which outwardly ye show? My noble partner
You greet with present grace,[30] and great prediction
Of noble having and of royal hope,
That he seems rapt withal; to me you speak not.
If you can look into the seeds of time,
And say which grain will grow, and which will not,
Speak then to me, who neither beg nor fear
Your favors nor your hate.

1. WITCH. Hail!

2. WITCH. Hail!

3. WITCH. Hail!

1. WITCH. Lesser than Macbeth, and greater.

2. WITCH. Not so happy, yet much happier.

3. WITCH. Thou shalt get kings, though thou be none.
So all hail, Macbeth and Banquo!

What predictions do the witches make for Banquo?

1. WITCH. Banquo and Macbeth, all hail!

MACBETH. Stay, you imperfect[31] speakers, tell me more:
By Sinel's[32] death I know I am Thane of Glamis,
But how of Cawdor? The Thane of Cawdor lives
A prosperous gentleman; and to be king
Stands not within the prospect of belief,
No more than to be Cawdor. Say from whence
You owe this strange intelligence,[33] or why
Upon this blasted heath you stop our way
With such prophetic greeting? Speak, I charge you.

WITCHES *vanish.*

BANQUO. The earth hath bubbles, as the water has,

29. **fantastical.** Imaginary
30. **present grace.** By his present title; that is, Thane of Glamis
31. **imperfect.** Incomplete
32. **Sinel.** Macbeth's father
33. **owe this strange intelligence.** Possess this strange information

And these are of them. Whither are they vanish'd?

MACBETH. Into the air; and what seem'd corporal melted,
As breath into the wind. Would they had stay'd!

BANQUO. Were such things here as we do speak about?
Or have we eaten on the insane root[34]
That takes the reason prisoner?

MACBETH. Your children shall be kings.

BANQUO. You shall be king.

MACBETH. And Thane of Cawdor too; went it not so?

BANQUO. To th' self-same tune and words. Who's here?

Enter ROSSE *and* ANGUS.

ROSSE. The King hath happily receiv'd, Macbeth,
The news of thy success; and when he reads
Thy personal venture in the rebels' fight,
His wonders and his praises do contend
Which should be thine or his.[35] Silenc'd with that,
In viewing o'er the rest o' th' self-same day,
He finds thee in the stout Norweyan ranks,
Nothing afeard of what thyself didst make,
Strange images of death. As thick as tale
Came post with post,[36] and every one did bear
Thy praises in his kingdom's great defense,
And pour'd them down before him.

ANGUS. We are sent
To give thee from our royal master thanks,
Only to herald thee into his sight,
Not pay thee.

ROSSE. And for an earnest of a greater honor,
He bade me, from him, call thee Thane of Cawdor;
In which addition, hail, most worthy thane,
For it is thine.

BANQUO. What, can the devil speak true?

MACBETH. The Thane of Cawdor lives; why do you dress me
In borrowed robes?

Where do the witches go?

Which of the witches' predictions comes true immediately?

34. **insane root.** Insanity-causing root, probably hemlock or henbane

35. **His wonders . . . his.** Duncan is torn between amazement and admiration

36. **post with post.** Messenger after messenger

WORDS FOR EVERYDAY USE

cor • po • ral (kôr′ pə rəl) *adj.*, of the body; bodily. *The whipping of people for minor offenses was a common form of corporal punishment in colonial America.*

ear • nest (ʉr′nist) *n.*, something given or done as an indication or assurance of what is to come. *When we offered to buy the couple's house for $95,000, we gave them $2500 as an earnest.*

ANSWERS TO GUIDED READING QUESTIONS

1. The witches disappear into thin air.
2. Macbeth is named Thane of Cawdor.

ADDITIONAL QUESTIONS AND ACTIVITIES

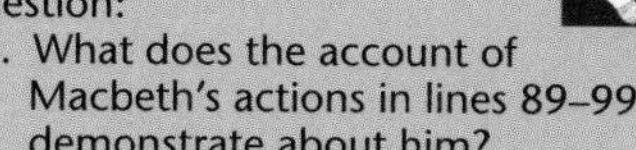

Ask students the following question:

1. What does the account of Macbeth's actions in lines 89–99 demonstrate about him?
2. If such a person hesitated to commit a crime, what would you conclude was the reason for his or her hesitation?

Answers

1. The account demonstrates that Macbeth is "Nothing afeard of . . . /Strange images of death" (lines 96–97), in other words, that he is brave.
2. One would have to conclude that when such a person shows hesitation to commit a crime, he or she does so as a result of moral scruples, not of cowardice.

ANSWER TO GUIDED READING QUESTION

1. Banquo tells Macbeth that sometimes the forces of darkness will trick humans by telling them minor truths to gain their faith and then betray them in larger things.

ANGUS. Who was the thane lives yet,
But under heavy judgment bears that life
Which he deserves to lose. Whether he was combin'd[37]
With those of Norway, or did line[38] the rebel
With hidden help and vantage, or that with both
He labor'd in his country's wrack,[39] I know not;
But treasons capital, confess'd and prov'd,
Have overthrown him.

MACBETH. [*Aside.*] Glamis, and Thane of Cawdor!
The greatest is behind.[40] [*To Rosse and Angus.*] Thanks for your pains.
[*Aside to Banquo.*] Do you not hope your children shall be kings,
When those that gave the Thane of Cawdor to me
Promis'd no less to them?

BANQUO. [*Aside to Macbeth.*] That, trusted home,[41]
Might yet enkindle you unto[42] the crown,
Besides the Thane of Cawdor. But 'tis strange;
And oftentimes, to win us to our harm,
The instruments of darkness tell us truths,
Win us with honest trifles, to betray 's
In deepest consequence.—
Cousins, a word, I pray you.

What warning does Banquo give to Macbeth?

MACBETH. [*Aside.*] Two truths are told,
As happy prologues to the swelling act
Of the imperial theme.[43]—I thank you, gentlemen.
[*Aside.*] This supernatural soliciting
Cannot be ill; cannot be good. If ill,
Why hath it given me earnest of success,
Commencing in a truth? I am Thane of Cawdor.
If good, why do I yield to that suggestion
Whose horrid image doth unfix my hair
And make my seated heart knock at my ribs,
Against the use of nature? Present fears
Are less than horrible imaginings:
My thought, whose murther[44] yet is but fantastical,
Shakes so my single state of man that function
Is smother'd in surmise, and nothing is
But what is not.

37. **combin'd.** Allied
38. **line.** Align with, support
39. **wrack.** Ruin
40. **behind.** Right behind it; yet to come
41. **home.** Completely
42. **enkindle you unto.** Cause you to hope for
43. **swelling . . . theme.** Grand idea that I will be king
44. **murther.** Murder

WORDS FOR EVERYDAY USE

tri • fle (trī´fəl) *n.*, something of little value or importance. *After the writer was made poet laureate, people expected great things of him, but his later poems were only trifles.*

sur • mise (sər mīz´) *n.*, guessing, imagined actions. *Although he did not know what was in the sealed locker, an intelligent surmise told him that the locker's contents must be very valuable.*

Banquo. Look how our partner's rapt.

Macbeth. [*Aside.*] If chance will have me king, why, chance may crown me
Without my stir.

Banquo. New honors come upon him,
Like our strange garments, cleave not to their mould
But with the aid of use.[45]

Macbeth. [*Aside.*] Come what come may,
Time and the hour runs through the roughest day.

Banquo. Worthy Macbeth, we stay upon your leisure.

Macbeth. Give me your favor;[46] my dull brain was wrought
With things forgotten. Kind gentlemen, your pains
Are regist'red where every day I turn
The leaf to read them. Let us toward the King.
[*Aside to Banquo.*] Think upon what hath chanc'd; and at more time,
The interim having weigh'd it, let us speak
Our free hearts each to other.

Banquo. Very gladly.

Macbeth. Till then, enough.—Come, friends. *Exeunt.*

SCENE 4: a room in the palace at Forres

Flourish. Enter King Duncan, Lennox, Malcolm, Donalbain, *and* Attendants.

Duncan. Is execution done on Cawdor? Are not
Those in commission[47] yet return'd?

Malcolm. My liege,
They are not yet come back. But I have spoke
With one that saw him die; who did report
That very frankly he confess'd his treasons,
Implor'd your Highness' pardon, and set forth
A deep repentance. Nothing in his life
Became him like the leaving it. He died
As one that had been studied in his death,
To throw away the dearest thing he ow'd,
As 'twere a careless trifle.

Duncan. There's no art
To find the mind's construction in the face:
He was a gentleman on whom I built
An absolute trust.

How had Duncan felt about the first Thane of Cawdor, before his betrayal?

45. **New honors . . . aid of use.** Banquo is saying that Macbeth needs to wear his new title a while before it will feel right, just as one needs to break in new clothes.

46. **favor.** Pardon

47. **in commission.** Delegated to oversee the execution

ANSWER TO GUIDED READING QUESTION

1. Duncan had trusted him absolutely.

ANSWER TO GUIDED READING QUESTION

1. Duncan declares his son, Malcolm, the Prince of Cumberland, to be his successor.

LITERARY TECHNIQUE

METAPHOR. A **metaphor** is a figure of speech in which one thing is written or spoken about as if it were another. Ask students to identify the two things being related in scene 4, lines 16–18. What metaphor does Duncan use in his next lines when addressing Macbeth and Banquo? How does Banquo reply, and what does his reply mean?

Answers

Recompense, or reward, is described as though it were a flying creature such as a bird. The next metaphor Duncan uses is one in which he compares Macbeth to a plant, which he will plant and work to help grow. Banquo responds that if he does grow, the harvest will belong to the King—meaning that in his gratitude, he will forever serve the King. Students may note that Macbeth does not say the same.

ADDITIONAL QUESTIONS AND ACTIVITIES

Students can imagine that they are Duncan's court poet. They can write a poem describing the heroic exploits of Macbeth, Duncan's noble gratitude to him, and Macbeth's winning the title of Thane of Cawdor. Other students can imagine they are court reporters and write a "news" story on what has taken place.

CROSS-CURRICULAR CONNECTION

HISTORY. In early Scotland, the kingship was not passed down automatically from father to son. The king was chosen according to an old Celtic tradition called "tanistry," which called for nobles to elect to the throne the most worthy kinsman of a deceased king. Thus Macbeth had hopes that he might legitimately attain the throne until Malcolm is declared the heir of the king in lines 35–42. Unless students understand the peculiar custom of tanistry, they will not understand why Macbeth reacts to the declaration as if it were not inevitable (lines 48–50).

Enter MACBETH, BANQUO, ROSSE, *and* ANGUS.

O worthiest cousin!
The sin of my ingratitude even now
Was heavy on me. Thou art so far before,
That swiftest wing of recompense is slow
To overtake thee. Would thou hadst less deserv'd,
That the proportion both of thanks and payment
Might have been mine![48] Only I have left to say,
More is thy due than more than all can pay.

MACBETH. The service and the loyalty I owe,
In doing it, pays itself. Your Highness' part
Is to receive our duties; and our duties
Are to your throne and state children and servants;
Which do but what they should, by doing every thing
Safe toward your love and honor.

DUNCAN. Welcome hither!
I have begun to plant thee, and will labor
To make thee full of growing. Noble Banquo,
That hast no less deserv'd, nor must be known
No less to have done so, let me infold thee
And hold thee to my heart.

BANQUO. There if I grow,
The harvest is your own.

DUNCAN. My plenteous joys,
Wanton in fullness, seek to hide themselves
In drops of sorrow. Sons, kinsmen, thanes,
And you whose places are the nearest, know
We will establish our estate upon
Our eldest, Malcolm, whom we name hereafter
The Prince of Cumberland; which honor must
Not unaccompanied invest him only,
But signs of nobleness, like stars, shall shine
On all deservers. From hence to Enverness,[49]
And bind us further to you.

Whom does Duncan declare his successor to the throne?

MACBETH. The rest is labor, which is not us'd for you.
I'll be myself the harbinger,[50] and make joyful
The hearing of my wife with your approach;

48. **Would . . . mine.** If you had been less deserving, I could have rewarded you as you deserve.

49. **Enverness.** Inverness, Macbeth's castle

50. **harbinger.** Something or someone that arrives before

WORDS FOR EVERYDAY USE

rec • om • pense (rek´əm pens´) *n.*, repayment; reward. *Carmen demanded recompense for all the extra hours she had worked.*

wan • ton (wän´ tən) *adj.*, undisciplined; unmanageable. *Although destined to grow into a disciplined racehorse, for now the wanton colt galloped about the pasture.*

So humbly take my leave.

DUNCAN. My worthy Cawdor!

MACBETH. [*Aside.*] The Prince of Cumberland! that is a step
On which I must fall down, or else o'erleap,
For in my way it lies. Stars, hide your fires,
Let not light see my black and deep desires;
The eye wink at the hand;[51] yet let that be
Which the eye fears, when it is done, to see.

Exit.

What stands in the way of Macbeth becoming king?

DUNCAN. True, worthy Banquo! he is full so valiant,
And in his commendations I am fed;
It is a banquet to me. Let's after him,
Whose care is gone before to bid us welcome:
It is a peerless kinsman.

Flourish. Exeunt.

SCENE 5: a room in MACBETH'S castle at Inverness

Enter MACBETH'S WIFE *alone with a letter.*

LADY MACBETH. [*Reads.*] "They met me in the day of success; and I have learn'd by the perfect'st report, they have more in them than mortal knowledge. When I burnt in desire to question them further, they made themselves air, into which they vanish'd. Whiles I stood rapt in the wonder of it, came missives[52] from the King, who all-hail'd me 'Thane of Cawdor,' by which title, before, these weïrd sisters saluted me, and referr'd me to the coming on of time with 'Hail, King that shalt be!' This have I thought good to deliver thee, my dearest partner of greatness, that thou mightst not lose the dues of rejoicing by being ignorant of what greatness is promis'd thee. Lay it to thy heart, and farewell."
Glamis thou art, and Cawdor, and shalt be
What thou art promis'd. Yet do I fear thy nature,
It is too full o' th' milk of human kindness
To catch the nearest way. Thou wouldst be great,
Art not without ambition, but without
The illness[53] should attend it. What thou wouldst highly,
That wouldst thou holily; wouldst not play false,
And yet wouldst wrongly win. Thou'ldst have, great Glamis
That which cries, "Thus thou must do," if thou have it;
And that which rather thou dost fear to do
Than wishest should be undone. Hie thee hither,

What does Lady Macbeth fear when she reads of the witches' prediction about Macbeth becoming king?

51. **The eye . . . hand.** Be blind to what the hand does
52. **missives.** Messengers
53. **illness.** Wickedness

ANSWERS TO GUIDED READING QUESTIONS

1. Malcolm, the Prince of Cumberland, stands in the way of Macbeth becoming king.
2. Lady Macbeth fears that her husband is too kind to do what he must to become king.

LITERARY TECHNIQUE

SYMBOL. A symbol is something that stands for or represents both itself and something else. When Macbeth says in scene 4, line 50, "Stars, hide your fires," what might the stars symbolize? Why would Macbeth want darkness?

Answers
Stars are traditional symbols of the eyes, or watchfulness, of heaven. Macbeth wants darkness to hide the deed that he is contemplating.

ANSWER TO GUIDED READING QUESTION

1. Lady Macbeth begs the spirits to "unsex" her—to make her more like a man, less moved by pity or remorse and more aggressive and cruel.

ADDITIONAL QUESTIONS AND ACTIVITIES

Students can list attributes of Macbeth and Lady Macbeth that they have learned about up to this point in the play. They should be able to support each characteristic they list with a reference to specific line numbers. After students have made their lists, have them save these lists to study the changes in Macbeth and Lady Macbeth that will have taken place by act 5.

Answers

They should observe that Macbeth is described as brave, noble, and loyal and that he demonstrates both ambitiousness and a loving attitude toward his wife. From his wife's distrust of his ability to act ruthlessly, students can infer that he has demonstrated kindness before this time. Lady Macbeth likewise shows ambition and an immoral willingness to become queen at all costs.

That I may pour my spirits in thine ear,
And chastise with the valor of my tongue
All that impedes thee from the golden round,
Which fate and metaphysical[54] aid doth seem
To have thee crown'd withal.

Enter MESSENGER.

What is your tidings?

MESSENGER. The King comes here tonight.

LADY MACBETH. Thou'rt mad to say it!
Is not thy master with him? who, were't so,
Would have inform'd for preparation.

MESSENGER. So please you, it is true; our thane is coming.
One of my fellows had the speed of him,
Who, almost dead for breath, had scarcely more
Than would make up his message.

LADY MACBETH. Give him tending,
He brings great news. *Exit* MESSENGER.
The raven himself is hoarse
That croaks the fatal entrance of Duncan
Under my battlements. Come, you spirits
That tend on mortal thoughts, unsex me here,
And fill me from the crown to the toe topful
Of direst cruelty! Make thick my blood,
Stop up th' access and passage to remorse,
That no compunctious visitings of nature[55]
Shake my fell[56] purpose, nor keep peace between
Th' effect and it! Come to my woman's breasts,
And take my milk for gall,[57] you murth'ring ministers,
Wherever in your sightless substances
You wait on nature's mischief! Come, thick night,
And pall thee in the dunnest smoke of hell,
That my keen knife see not the wound it makes,
Nor heaven peep through the blanket of the dark
To cry, "Hold, hold!"

What aid does Lady Macbeth beg from the spirits?

54. **metaphysical.** Supernatural
55. **compunctious . . . nature.** Natural feelings of pity
56. **fell.** Cruel
57. **gall.** Bile

WORDS FOR EVERYDAY USE

chas • tise (chas tīz´) *vt.,* scold or condemn sharply. *The grandmother chastised the child for chasing a ball into the road.*

im • pede (im pēd´) *vt.,* obstruct or delay. *The only thing that impedes us from happiness is our own negative thoughts.*

mor • tal (môr´təl) *adj.,* deadly. *Susan kissed the scrape on her daughter's arm and assured her it was not a mortal wound.*

re • morse (rē môrs´) *n.,* pity; compassion. *Because the defendant showed no remorse for the murder, the judge sentenced him to life in prison.*

pall (pôl) *vt.,* cloak in darkness. *Drawing the curtains palled the house, so they switched on the lights.*

Enter MACBETH.

Great Glamis! worthy Cawdor!
Greater than both, by the all-hail hereafter!
Thy letters have transported me beyond
This ignorant present, and I feel now
The future in the instant.

MACBETH. My dearest love,
Duncan comes here tonight.

LADY MACBETH. And when goes hence?

MACBETH. Tomorrow, as he purposes.

LADY MACBETH. O, never
Shall sun that morrow see!
Your face, my thane, is as a book, where men
May read strange matters. To beguile the time,[58]
Look like the time; bear welcome in your eye,
Your hand, your tongue; look like th' innocent flower,
But be the serpent under't. He that's coming
Must be provided for; and you shall put
This night's great business into my dispatch,[59]
Which shall to all our nights and days to come
Give solely sovereign sway and masterdom.

What advice does Lady Macbeth give to her husband?

MACBETH. We will speak further.

LADY MACBETH. Only look up clear:[60]
To alter favor ever is to fear.
Leave all the rest to me. *Exeunt.*

SCENE 6: in front of MACBETH'S castle

Hoboys and torches. Enter KING DUNCAN, MALCOLM, DONALBAIN, BANQUO, LENNOX, MACDUFF, ROSSE, ANGUS, *and* ATTENDANTS.

DUNCAN. This castle hath a pleasant seat,[61] the air
Nimbly and sweetly recommends itself
Unto our gentle senses.

What is the air like when Duncan arrives at Macbeth's castle?

BANQUO. This guest of summer,
The temple-haunting marlet,[62] does approve,
By his lov'd mansionry,[63] that the heaven's breath
Smells wooingly here; no jutty, frieze,
Buttress, nor coign of vantage,[64] but this bird
Hath made his pendant bed and procreant cradle.

58. **beguile the time.** Deceive everybody
59. **dispatch.** Management
60. **look up clear.** Seem innocent
61. **seat.** Location
62. **temple-haunting marlet.** A bird that nests around churches
63. **mansionry.** Nest
64. **no jutty . . . vantage.** No projecting structure or convenient corner

ANSWERS TO GUIDED READING QUESTIONS

1. Lady Macbeth tells her husband to look innocent and leave the rest to her.
2. The air is sweet and "delicate."

CROSS-CURRICULAR CONNECTION

SOCIAL STUDIES. In many cultures (both in the past and the present) the act of hailing someone is a critical component of social interaction. Hailing affirms the power structure, not only because inferiors thereby recognize their superiors, but also because inferiors thereby indicate that they are united in recognition of their superiors and pose no threat. Hailing also takes place between peers, indicating that one peer is acknowledging, not challenging, the status of another. Examples from *Macbeth* of this custom include the following: act 1, scene 2, line 65 ("with his [the Thane of Cawdor's] former title greet Macbeth"); the passage in act I, scene iii, lines 48–69, in which the witches hail Macbeth and Banquo repeatedly; act 1, scene 3, lines 105–106 ("He bade me, from him, call thee Thane of Cawdor;/In which addition, hail, most worthy thane"); and act I, scene v, lines 59-60, in which Lady Macbeth hails Macbeth as Glamis, Cawdor, and as the object of "the all-hail hereafter!" Compare the scene in act 5, scene 9, lines 22–25, where Macduff requests all present to all-hail the new king, Malcolm. Relics of this custom include the greeting students give the teacher in some schools and the title of the presidential anthem of the United States, "Hail to the Chief."

ADDITIONAL QUESTIONS AND ACTIVITIES

Students can study Macbeth's soliloquy in scene vii, lines 1–28, by outlining its structure. One possible outline is as follows:

Macbeth's Consideration of the Pros and Cons of Acting Immediately to Kill Duncan

I. Pro: Necessity for Quick Action ("'Twere well/It were done quickly")
II. Con: Assassination Will Have Consequences
Others may try to assassinate Macbeth ("We but teach/Bloody instructions")
III. Con: Morality Argues against Assassination
A. Macbeth is Duncan's "kinsman and his subject"
B. Macbeth is Duncan's host
IV. Con: Duncan Is a Good King
A. Duncan's virtues will only point up the heinousness of his murder
B. Pity for Duncan will provoke outrage against the assassin
V. Con: Duncan Has Not Offended Macbeth
("I have no spur . . . but only/Vaulting ambition")

Point out to students that when the speech is outlined, it becomes clear why Macbeth shortly afterward (line 31) says to Lady Macbeth, "We will proceed no further in this business." He sees more reasons not to commit the deed than to go ahead with it. See the Language Arts Survey, 5.1, "Making Decisions and Solving Problems."

Where they most breed and haunt, I have observ'd
The air is delicate.

Enter LADY MACBETH.

DUNCAN. See, see, our honor'd hostess!
The love that follows us sometime is our trouble,
Which still we thank as love. Herein I teach you
How you shall bid God 'ield us for your pains,
And thank us for your trouble.[65]

LADY MACBETH. All our service
In every point twice done, and then done double,
Were poor and single[66] business to contend
Against those honors deep and broad wherewith
Your Majesty loads our house. For those of old,
And the late dignities heap'd up to them,
We rest your ermites.[67]

DUNCAN. Where's the Thane of Cawdor?
We cours'd him at the heels, and had a purpose
To be his purveyor; but he rides well,
And his great love, sharp as his spur, hath holp[68] him
To his home before us. Fair and noble hostess,
We are your guest tonight.

LADY MACBETH. Your servants ever
Have theirs, themselves, and what is theirs, in compt,[69]
To make their audit at your Highness' pleasure,
Still[70] to return your own.

DUNCAN. Give me your hand.
Conduct me to mine host, we love him highly,
And shall continue our graces towards him.
By your leave, hostess. *Exeunt.*

SCENE 7: a room in MACBETH'S castle

Hoboys, torches. Enter a SEWER[71] *and divers* SERVANTS *with dishes and service over the stage. Then enter* MACBETH.

65. **The love . . . trouble.** Although my visit is an inconvenience to you, you should ask God to reward me for your pains because I came out of love for you.
66. **single.** Feeble
67. **We . . . ermites.** We shall be your hermits (that is, we shall always pray for you).
68. **holp.** Helped
69. **compt.** Trust
70. **Still.** Always
71. **Sewer.** Butler

WORDS FOR EVERYDAY USE

pur • vey • or (pər vā′ ər) *n.,* one who supplies or provides. *The purveyor of fine wines made frequent trips to France to select new wines for his stores.*

Macbeth. If it were done, when 'tis done, then 'twere well
It were done quickly. If th' assassination
Could trammel up the consequence, and catch
With his surcease, success;[72] that but this blow
Might be the be-all and the end-all—here,
But here, upon this bank and shoal of time,
We'ld jump the life to come. But in these cases
We still have judgment here, that we but teach
Bloody instructions, which, being taught, return
To plague th' inventor. This even-handed justice
Commends[73] th' ingredience of our poison'd chalice
To our own lips. He's here in double trust:
First, as I am his kinsman and his subject,
Strong both against the deed; then, as his host,
Who should against his murtherer shut the door,
Not bear the knife myself. Besides, this Duncan
Hath borne his faculties[74] so meek, hath been
So clear[75] in his great office, that his virtues
Will plead like angels, trumpet-tongu'd, against
The deep damnation of his taking-off;
And pity, like a naked new-born babe,
Striding the blast, or heaven's cherubin, hors'd
Upon the sightless couriers[76] of the air,
Shall blow the horrid deed in every eye,
That tears shall drown the wind. I have no spur
To prick the sides of my intent, but only
Vaulting ambition, which o'erleaps itself,
And falls on th' other—

For what two reasons does Duncan trust Macbeth to keep him safe?

What sole motivation does Macbeth have to kill Duncan?

Enter Lady Macbeth.

How now? what news?

Lady Macbeth. He has almost supp'd. Why have you left the chamber?

Macbeth. Hath he ask'd for me?

Lady Macbeth. Know you not he has?

Macbeth. We will proceed no further in this business:
He hath honor'd me of late, and I have bought[77]
Golden opinions from all sorts of people,
Which would be worn now in their newest gloss,
Not cast aside so soon.

What decision does Macbeth make?

Lady Macbeth. Was the hope drunk
Wherein you dress'd yourself? Hath it slept since?

72. **If . . . success.** If the assassination could be successful and without consequence
73. **Commends.** Offers
74. **faculties.** Royal powers
75. **clear.** Blameless
76. **sightless couriers.** Invisible messengers, the wind
77. **bought.** Earned

ANSWERS TO GUIDED READING QUESTIONS

1. Duncan trusts Macbeth because Macbeth is his kinsman and subject and because, as the host, Macbeth has an obligation to protect the king from harm.
2. Macbeth's "vaulting ambition" is the only "spur" to make him kill Duncan.
3. Macbeth decides he cannot kill the king.

ANSWERS TO GUIDED READING QUESTIONS

1. Lady Macbeth accuses her husband of being a coward.
2. Lady Macbeth says she would not hesitate to have "dash'd the brains out" of her own infant if she had sworn to do so.
3. Lady Macbeth proposes to drug the king's chamberlains with drink and then kill the king.

SELECTION CHECK TEST 4.5.3 WITH ANSWERS

Checking Your Reading

1. Why does Duncan make Macbeth the Thane of Cawdor? **The previous Cawdor has been accused of treason, and Macbeth was a war hero who defeated him.**
2. Who predicts that Macbeth will be king? **The witches (weird sisters) predict this.**
3. What is predicted for Banquo? **It is predicted that his children will be kings.**
4. Who visits the Macbeths? **King Duncan visits the Macbeths.**
5. What does Lady Macbeth suggest doing to the visitor? **She plans to murder him.**

Vocabulary in Context

Fill each blank with the most appropriate word from the Words for Everyday Use. You may have to change the tense of the word.

impede trifle surmise mettle
purveyor remorse recompense

1. Martin barely kept up during training, but on the job he proved he had **mettle**.
2. The children's possessions may seem like **trifles** to us, but they're important to them.
3. Lulu quickly attacked anyone who appeared to **impede** her success at the company.
4. After a long strike, workers were thrilled to receive the **recompense** they'd sought.
5. We could tell by his broad grin that Lawrence was the **purveyor** of good news.

Literary Tools

Fill in the blanks using the following terms.

motif oxymoron aside
inciting incident foil soliloquy
internal conflict

And wakes it now to look so green and pale
At what it did so freely? From this time
Such I account thy love. Art thou afeard
To be the same in thine own act and valor
As thou art in desire? Wouldst thou have that
Which thou esteem'st the ornament of life,[78]
And live a coward in thine own esteem,
Letting "I dare not" wait upon, "I would,"
Like the poor cat i' th' adage?[79]

Of what does Lady Macbeth accuse her husband?

MACBETH. Prithee peace!
I dare do all that may become a man;
Who dares do more is none.

LADY MACBETH. What beast was't then
That made you break[80] this enterprise to me?
When you durst do it, then you were a man;
And to be more than what you were, you would
Be so much more the man. Nor time, nor place,
Did then adhere,[81] and yet you would make both:
They have made themselves, and that their fitness now
Does unmake you. I have given suck, and know
How tender 'tis to love the babe that milks me;
I would, while it was smiling in my face,
Have pluck'd my nipple from his boneless gums,
And dash'd the brains out, had I so sworn as you
Have done to this.

What does Lady Macbeth vow she would do rather than break a promise?

MACBETH. If we should fail?

LADY MACBETH. We fail?
But[82] screw your courage to the sticking place,[83]
And we'll not fail. When Duncan is asleep
(Whereto the rather shall his day's hard journey
Soundly invite him), his two chamberlains
Will I with wine and wassail[84] so convince,
That memory, the warder of the brain,
Shall be a fume, and the receipt of reason
A limbeck[85] only. When in swinish sleep
Their drenched natures lies as in a death,
What cannot you and I perform upon
Th' unguarded Duncan? what not put upon
His spungy[86] officers, who shall bear the guilt
Of our great quell?[87]

What plan does Lady Macbeth propose?

78. **ornament of life.** The crown
79. **cat . . . adage.** Refers to an old saying about a cat who wants to eat fish without getting its paws wet
80. **break.** Broach
81. **Did then adhere.** Were then suitable
82. **But.** Only
83. **the sticking place.** The notch that holds the string of a crossbow
84. **wassail.** Carousing
85. **That . . . limbeck.** The fumes of wine would rise from the stomach and confuse the brain.
86. **spungy.** Spongy with drink, drunk
87. **quell.** Murder

SELECTION CHECK TEST 4.5.3 WITH ANSWERS (CONT.)

1. **Foils** contrast with and help us understand other important characters.
2. **Asides** are directed to audiences; other characters on stage are not meant to hear.
3. Scene 5 opens with Lady Macbeth, alone on stage, delivering her **soliloquy**.
4. Discussions of ambition, manliness, and madness set up several **motifs** in the play.
5. The Macbeths' plan becomes the **inciting incident** for the play's central conflict.

Jean Philippelafont and Maria Guleghing in the opera version of *Macbeth*, 1999.

MACBETH. Bring forth men-children only!
For thy undaunted <u>mettle</u> should compose
Nothing but males. Will it not be receiv'd,
When we have mark'd with blood those sleepy two
Of his own chamber, and us'd their very daggers,
That they have done't?

LADY MACBETH. Who dares receive it other,
As we shall make our griefs and clamor roar
Upon his death?

MACBETH. I am settled, and bend up
Each corporal agent to this terrible feat.
Away, and mock the time[88] with fairest show:
False face must hide what the false heart doth know.

Exeunt.

What does Macbeth decide?

88. **mock the time.** Deceive the world

WORDS FOR EVERYDAY USE

met • tle (met'l) *n.,* spirit, courage. *The long-distance runner won in part because of her superior strength but mostly because of her superior <u>mettle</u>.*

Respond *to the* SELECTION

Imagine that you, not Macbeth, were to write the letter that Lady Macbeth reads at the beginning of scene 3. What would your letter say?

RESPOND TO THE SELECTION

Remind students that Banquo, who also sees and hears the witches, responds very differently from Macbeth. In their letters, students may describe the same events as Macbeth but interpret them in some other way.

ANSWER TO GUIDED READING QUESTION

1. Macbeth changes his mind and decides to kill Duncan after all.

CROSS-CURRICULAR ACTIVITIES

OPERA. The opera version of *Macbeth* was composed in 1847 by famous Italian composer Giuseppe Verdi (1813–1901). Verdi wrote the opera early in his career and later, in 1865, he revised it. Verdi greatly admired the work of Shakespeare and wrote two other operas based on Shakespeare's plays: *Otello* (1887) and *Falstaff* (1893, based on *The Merry Wives of* Windsor). Verdi was a brilliant composer and greatly honored during his lifetime. His beautifully melodic works are performed throughout the world. *Macbeth* is considered one of his most expressive operas.

CROSS-CURRICULAR ACTIVITIES

MUSIC. Ask students to imagine they are writing an opera or musical based on *Macbeth*. Ask them to choose one of the scenes or speeches in act 1 and decide what musical accompaniment would be appropriate. What instruments would they use? What melody would reflect the mood of the scene? Musically inclined students should compose a song based on one of the scenes or speeches. They could write the sheet music, then perform the song on their own musical instrument and collaborate with another student who would do the singing. If your school computer lab is equipped with a sound card and a program like real audio, you might have students visit the site <u>http://www.boadicea.com/macbeth/index.html</u>. This site offers Times Education Supplements, including a rock opera version of *Macbeth,* for which it provides and sample audio clips. Students might enjoy listening to the audio clips and writing a review evaluating the music.

ANSWERS TO INVESTIGATE, INQUIRE, AND IMAGINE

RECALL

1a. Macbeth calls the battle "foul" and "fair." This echoes the witches' statement in scene 1, line 11.

2a. The witches predict that Macbeth will be Thane of Cawdor and King. They predict Banquo will be the father of kings. The first prediction comes true almost immediately when the title of Thane of Cawdor is awarded to Macbeth.

3a. She doubts Macbeth's ability to do what is necessary to become king. She decides to encourage him to pursue the crown.

INTERPRET

1b. By echoing the witches' line, Macbeth suggests that those things we judge fair may in fact be foul—that we have no moral guideposts in the world. This hints that, thought Macbeth appears as a hero now, we may judge him differently later.

2b. Banquo is less interested in what the witches have to say than Macbeth, who is eager to know what the witches know. Macbeth is more ambitious and more willing to act immorally than Banquo.

3b. Macbeth and Lady Macbeth disagree about the proposed assassination. Macbeth is reluctant to kill Duncan, and Lady Macbeth wants him to do so.

ANALYZE

4a. Macbeth is motivated by "vaulting ambition" and a desire to make the witches' prediction come true. His reasons for not killing Duncan include the fact that the king is his kinsman, his king, and his guest. Macbeth acknowledges that Duncan trusts him and has recently honored him for his loyalty and courage by naming him Thane of Cawdor. Duncan is a good king and his virtues will provoke outrage against whoever kills him. Besides, Macbeth has reason to believe the prediction might come true without any action on his part.

SYNTHESIZE

4b. Macbeth's ambition, impatience, and inability to endure the contempt of his wife could lead him to kill Duncan anyway.

EVALUATE

5a. Lady Macbeth attempts to shame Macbeth into killing Duncan by accusing him of being less than manly. To Lady Macbeth manliness calls for ruthlessness, unshakable determination, and a willingness to stop at nothing to realize the desired ambition. Responses will

INVESTIGATE, Inquire, Imagine

Recall: GATHERING FACTS → **Interpret:** FINDING MEANING

1a. How does Macbeth describe the day of the battle in his first statement in the play (scene 3, line 38)? What earlier line from the play is echoed by Macbeth in this statement?

1b. Why is line 38 from scene 3 ominous? What does it foreshadow, or hint, about Macbeth's future associations?

2a. What predictions do the witches make when talking to Macbeth and Banquo in scene 3? Which of these predictions comes true almost immediately?

2b. How do Macbeth and Banquo differ in their reactions to the witches' prophecies? What do these differences reveal about the two characters?

3a. How does Lady Macbeth react to her husband's letter? What does she make up her mind to do?

3b. Why do Macbeth and Lady Macbeth argue in scene 7? How do they differ in their feelings about the planned assassination of Duncan?

Analyze: TAKING THINGS APART → **Synthesize:** BRINGING THINGS TOGETHER

4a. What reasons does Macbeth have for killing Duncan? What reasons does he have for not killing the king?

4b. What character traits in Macbeth could lead him to kill Duncan anyway?

Evaluate: MAKING JUDGMENTS → **Extend:** CONNECTING IDEAS

5a. Evaluate the notion of manliness presented by Lady Macbeth and the technique she uses to get her husband to change his mind about killing Duncan.

5b. Discuss characteristics of manliness in popular culture. How do they compare with Lady Macbeth's notions of manliness?

Understanding Literature

ASIDE. Review the definition for **aside** in the Handbook of Literary Terms. What do Macbeth's and Banquo's asides in scene 3 reveal about their characters? Why are these asides necessary?

CONFLICT AND INCITING INCIDENT. Review the definitions for **central conflict**, **internal conflict**, and **inciting incident** in the Handbook of Literary Terms. What is Macbeth's internal conflict? What incident introduces the central conflict?

SOLILOQUY. Review the definition for **soliloquy** in the Handbook of Literary Terms. What does Lady Macbeth's soliloquy in scene 5 reveal about her character?

FOIL. Review the definition for **foil** in the Handbook of Literary Terms and the chart you made for Literary Tools on page 374. How do the foils for Macbeth—Banquo, King Duncan, and Lady Macbeth—contrast with Macbeth?

ANSWERS TO INVESTIGATE, INQUIRE, AND IMAGINE (CONT.)

vary, but students will probably say that Lady Macbeth's idea of manliness is wrong—that a "real man" does not act immorally— and that her technique of convincing Macbeth is manipulative.

EXTEND

5b. *Responses will vary.*

Answers to Understanding Literature can be found on page 395.

Writer's Journal

1. Review the letter written by Macbeth to his wife. Imagining you are Banquo, write a **letter** to your own wife in which you relate the battle and your encounter with the witches.
2. When Macbeth expresses doubts about the plan to kill Duncan, Lady Macbeth launches an emotional attack on his manhood. Imagining you are Macbeth, write a **rebuttal** to her words in scene 7, lines 35–78.
3. Imagine you are Duncan's court poet. Write a **poem** describing the heroic exploits of Macbeth, Duncan's noble gratitude, and Macbeth's winning of the title Thane of Cawdor.

Integrating *the* Language Arts

Language, Grammar, and Style

Contractions. A contraction is a shortened form of a word, formed by omitting one or more letters and combining the remaining letters with an apostrophe. For example, "He isn't" means "He is not." Rewrite the following sentences, spelling out the contractions.

1. I' th' shipman's card. (scene 3, line 17)
2. How far is't call'd to Forres? (scene 3, line 39)
3. If it were done, when 'tis done, then 'twere well. . . . (scene 7, line 1)
4. We'ld jump the life to come. (scene 7, line 7)
5. Striding the blast, or heaven's cherubin, hors'd. . . . (scene 7, line 22)

Collaborative Learning & Speaking and Listening

Dramatic Interpretation. Read the Language Arts Survey 4.1, "Verbal and Nonverbal Communication." Then, with several classmates, decide which elements of verbal and nonverbal communication you would use to present a scene of your choice from act 1. Finally, present your scene to the class.

Speaking and Listening & Collaborative Learning

Paraphrasing. Review Lady Macbeth's soliloquy in scene 5, lines 43–59. In your own words, paraphrase the soliloquy, being careful to preserve its meaning while using modern English. Then read your version to a classmate, being sure to use appropriate volume, melody, pitch, pace, tone, and enunciation.

Answers to Understanding Literature

Aside. The asides reveal Banquo's reservations about the value of the witches' prophecies and Macbeth's eager reception of the possibility that he may someday be king. Banquo is characterized by being cautious and prudent, whereas Macbeth is characterized by being ambitious and superstitious. The asides are necessary so that the audience can understand Banquo's thoughts (which Banquo would not express in the hearing of Rosse and Angus) and Macbeth's thoughts (which he would not express in the hearing of any of those present).

Conflict and Inciting Incident. Macbeth's internal conflict is between his desire to honor his obligations to Duncan and his ambition to be king at all costs. The inciting incident is the prophecy of the witches and the fact that part of it comes true almost immediately.

Soliloquy. Lady Macbeth's soliloquy shows her willingness to incite her husband to violence, which reveals that she values power more than morality. She is revealed as having "undaunted mettle," a description given later by Macbeth.

Foil. Banquo is cautious about accepting the witches' prophecy, whereas Macbeth is eager to believe it. Banquo believes the witches are malevolent, whereas Macbeth is concerned only with their message and not their morality. Duncan is honest, open, grateful, and trusting, whereas Macbeth is deceptive, secretive, ungrateful, and untrustworthy. Lady Macbeth is more ruthless, whereas Macbeth has scruples about murdering the king.

Answers to Integrating the Language Arts

Language, Grammar, and Style
Refer students to the Language Arts Survey 3.29, "Working with Negatives and Contractions," if they need a definition and some examples of contractions.

1. In the shipman's card.
2. How far is it called to Forres? (Meaning, "How far do they say it is to Forres?")
3. If it were done, when it is done, then it were well. . . .
4. We would jump the life to come.
5. Striding the blast, or heaven's cherubin, horsed. . . .

ADDITIONAL RESOURCES

UNIT 5 RESOURCE BOOK
- Selection Worksheet 5.2
- Selection Check Test 4.5.5
- Selection Test 4.5.6
- Speaking and Listening Resource 4.1

GRAPHIC ORGANIZER

Students should include the following details in their cluster charts.
owl shrieks; bell rings; voices are heard; chimneys are blown down; screams are heard in the air; the "feverish" earth shook, darkness during the day; owl killed a falcon; horses ate each other

VOCABULARY FROM THE SELECTION

augment	palpable
equivocator	scruples
multitudinous	stealthy

READER'S JOURNAL

Due to the personal nature of the question, students may want to keep their journal entries private.

Literary TOOLS

SYMBOL. A **symbol** is a thing that stands for or represents both itself and something else. As you read, try to figure out what the blood on his hands symbolizes to Macbeth.

HYPERBOLE. A **hyperbole** (hi pur' bə lē) is an exaggeration made for rhetorical effect. As you read, try to find an example of hyperbole in scene 2.

VERBAL IRONY. **Verbal irony** occurs when a statement is made that implies its opposite. As you read, try to find an example of verbal irony in scene 3.

MOOD. **Mood,** or **atmosphere,** is the emotion created in the reader by part or all of a literary work. As you read, make a cluster chart to list details from act 2 that create a horrific atmosphere. One example has been done for you.

HORRIFIC MOOD

dark night, no stars

Reader's Journal

Describe a time when you felt guilty. Was it for something you had done, or for something you had failed to do?

ACT 2

SCENE 1: open court within MACBETH'S castle

Enter BANQUO, *and* FLEANCE *with a torch before him.*

BANQUO. How goes the night, boy?

FLEANCE. The moon is down; I have not heard the clock.

BANQUO. And she goes down at twelve.

FLEANCE. I take't, 'tis later, sir.

BANQUO. Hold, take my sword. There's husbandry[1] in heaven,
Their candles are all out. Take thee that too.
Gives him his belt and dagger.
A heavy summons[2] lies like lead upon me,
And yet I would not sleep. Merciful powers,
Restrain in me the cursed thoughts that nature
Gives way to in repose!

Enter MACBETH, *and a* SERVANT *with a torch.*

Give me my sword.
Who's there?

MACBETH. A friend.

BANQUO. What, sir, not yet at rest? the King's a-bed.
He hath been in unusual pleasure, and
Sent forth great largess to your offices.[3]
This diamond he greets your wife withal,
By the name of most kind hostess, and shut up[4]
In measureless content.

MACBETH. Being unprepar'd,
Our will became the servant to defect,
Which else should free have wrought.[5]

BANQUO. All's well.
I dreamt last night of the three weïrd sisters:
To you they have show'd some truth.

MACBETH. I think not of them.
Yet when we can entreat an hour to serve,

1. **husbandry.** Thrift
2. **heavy summons.** Sleepiness
3. **largess . . . offices.** Gifts to your servants' quarters
4. **shut up.** Concluded
5. **Being . . . wrought.** Because we were not prepared, we were not able to entertain as fully as we would have liked.

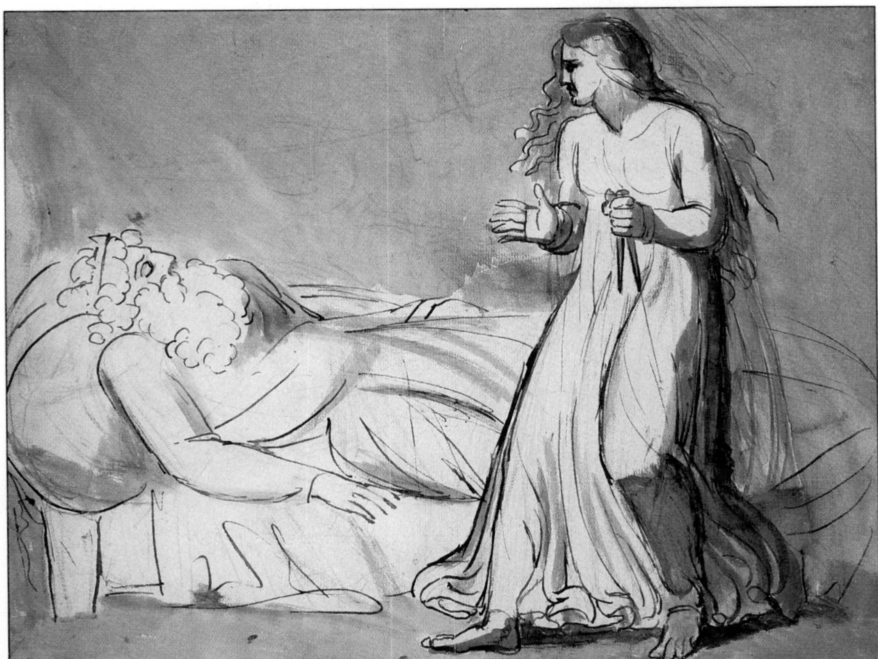

Lady Macbeth Approaching the Murdered Duncan, c.1800s. William Blake. Agnew & Sons, London.

We would spend it in some words upon that business,
If you would grant the time.

Banquo. At your kind'st leisure.

Macbeth. If you shall cleave to my consent, when 'tis,[6]
It shall make honor for you.

Banquo. So I lose none
In seeking to augment it, but still keep
My bosom franchis'd[7] and allegiance clear,
I shall be counsell'd.

Macbeth. Good repose the while!

Banquo. Thanks, sir; the like to you!

Exit Banquo *with* Fleance.

What two requests does Macbeth make of Banquo? How does Banquo respond?

6. **cleave . . . 'tis.** Support my cause when the time comes
7. **franchis'd.** Free from guilt

Words For Everyday Use

aug • ment (ôg ment') *vt.,* add to; supplement. *Joe augmented his income by playing saxophone in a jazz club.*

ANSWER TO GUIDED READING QUESTION

1. Macbeth asks Banquo to grant him the time to talk about the witches' predictions, and he asks Banquo to support him when the time comes. Banquo agrees to talk with Macbeth and to support him if he can do so with a clear and free conscience.

ADDITIONAL VOCABULARY

Act 2
hold—wait
entreat—plead
sentinel—guard
prate—speak
infirm—weak
grooms—servants
appalls—shocks
lechery—excessive indulgence in sexual activity
provoke—excite
mar—mark, scar, harm
requite—repay
renown—fame
amiss—wrong
breach—tear, opening
warrant—good reason
predominance—superiority in quality or quantity
minions—servants
adieu—goodbye

CROSS-CURRICULAR ACTIVITIES

Applied Arts. Have students design a stage set for a modern production of Act 2. The general setting is the castle of Macbeth at Inverness, Scotland. Sets should include the courtyard of the castle and a castle gate. Students will need to do research to find out how castles of the Norman era looked. They should also research the floor plan for a proscenium arch stage like the one used in the Globe Theater so that they can base their design on the type of stage Shakespeare would have used.

ANSWERS TO GUIDED READING QUESTIONS

1. Macbeth sees an illusion of a dagger.
2. Macbeth sees drops of blood on the dagger and its handle.

LITERARY NOTE

Point out to students that in Shakespeare's time, and for centuries afterward, the ringing of a church bell was an indication that someone had died. Thus the ringing of the bell following line 61 would have an ominous connotation. Scene 2, lines 3 and 4 (and the note there) are also worth pointing out. As Macbeth's crimes progress, Scotland will reach a point where the tolling of the death bell is so frequent that people will not even inquire for whom the bell tolls (act 4, scene 3, lines 170–171).

MACBETH. Go bid thy mistress, when my drink is ready,
She strike upon the bell. Get thee to bed.

Exit SERVANT.

Is this a dagger which I see before me,
The handle toward my hand? Come, let me clutch thee:
I have thee not, and yet I see thee still.
Art thou not, fatal vision, sensible[8]
To feeling as to sight? or art thou but
A dagger of the mind, a false creation,
Proceeding from the heat-oppressed brain?
I see thee yet, in form as palpable
As this which now I draw.
Thou marshal'st[9] me the way that I was going,
And such an instrument I was to use.
Mine eyes are made the fools o' th' other senses,
Or else worth all the rest. I see thee still;
And on thy blade and dudgeon[10] gouts of blood,
Which was not so before. There's no such thing:
It is the bloody business which informs[11]
Thus to mine eyes. Now o'er the one half world
Nature seems dead, and wicked dreams abuse[12]
The curtain'd sleep; witchcraft celebrates
Pale Hecate's off'rings;[13] and wither'd Murther,
Alarum'd by his sentinel, the wolf,
Whose howl's his watch, thus with his stealthy pace,
With Tarquin's[14] ravishing strides, towards his design
Moves like a ghost. Thou sure and firm-set earth,
Hear not my steps, which way they walk, for fear
The very stones prate of my whereabout,
And take the present horror from the time,
Which now suits with it. Whiles I threat, he lives:
Words to the heat of deeds too cold breath gives.

A bell rings.

I go, and it is done; the bell invites me.
Hear it not, Duncan, for it is a knell,
That summons thee to heaven or to hell.

Exit.

What does Macbeth see?

What does Macbeth see on the dagger and its handle?

8. **sensible.** Perceptible by the senses
9. **Thou marshal'st.** You lead
10. **dudgeon.** Handle of a dagger
11. **informs.** Takes shape
12. **abuse.** Deceive
13. **Hecate's off'rings.** Offerings to Hecate, goddess of witchcraft
14. **Tarquin.** Roman tyrant

WORDS FOR EVERYDAY USE

pal • pa • ble (pal´pə bəl) *adj.,* tangible. *His nervousness was palpable in the form of the sweat that ran down his back.*

stealth • y (stel´thē) *adj.,* furtive, sly. *The pickpocket was caught when a police officer noticed the stealthy motion of his hand toward a tourist's wallet.*

SCENE 2: open court within MACBETH'S castle

Enter LADY MACBETH.

LADY MACBETH. That which hath made them drunk hath made me bold;
What hath quench'd them hath given me fire. Hark! Peace!
It was the owl that shriek'd, the fatal bellman,
Which gives the stern'st good-night.[15] He is about it:
The doors are open; and the surfeited grooms[16]
Do mock their charge with snores. I have drugg'd their possets,[17]
That death and nature do contend about them,
Whether they live or die.

What has Lady Macbeth done?

MACBETH. [*Within.*] Who's there? What ho?

LADY MACBETH. Alack, I am afraid they have awak'd,
And 'tis not done; th' attempt, and not the deed,
Confounds[18] us. Hark! I laid their daggers ready,
He could not miss 'em. Had he not resembled
My father as he slept, I had done't.

Enter MACBETH.

My husband!

MACBETH. I have done the deed. Didst thou not hear a noise?

What has Macbeth done?

LADY MACBETH. I heard the owl scream and the crickets cry.
Did not you speak?

MACBETH. When?

LADY MACBETH. Now.

MACBETH. As I descended?

LADY MACBETH. Aye.

MACBETH. Hark! Who lies i' th' second chamber?

LADY MACBETH. Donalbain.

MACBETH. This is a sorry sight.
Looking on his hands.

LADY MACBETH. A foolish thought, to say a sorry sight.

MACBETH. There's one did laugh in 's sleep, and one cried, "Murther!"
That they did wake each other. I stood and heard them;
But they did say their prayers, and address'd them
Again to sleep.

LADY MACBETH. There are two[19] lodg'd together.

15. **owl . . . good-night.** The owl's cry was a sign of death, as was the midnight ringing of the bell outside of a prisoner's cell.
16. **surfeited grooms.** Overfed servants
17. **possets.** Bedtime drinks of wine and hot milk
18. **attempt . . . Confounds.** A failed attempt ruins us
19. **two.** The two are the grooms described in act 1, scene 7, line 75.

ANSWERS TO GUIDED READING QUESTIONS

1. Lady Macbeth has drugged the king's servants.
2. Macbeth has murdered Duncan.

CROSS-CURRICULAR ACTIVITIES

MATHEMATICS AND SCIENCES. In act 2, scene 2, lines 14–49, Shakespeare varies the lengths of the alternating speeches made by Macbeth and Lady Macbeth. At first, equally shocked and frightened, they both speak in short speeches. Then, as Macbeth begins to add horrific details in his description of what occurred, his speeches grow longer and longer. Lady Macbeth interjects only a line or two between his speeches, trying to stop him or reassure him. ("A foolish thought, to say a sorry sight… Consider it not so deeply… These deeds must not be thought/After these ways; so, it will make us mad.") When his tale of horror reaches a crescendo in the account of the phantom voice that cried "Sleep no more!" Lady Macbeth can only gasp feebly "What do you mean?" She then rises to the occasion, however, regaining control of herself and the situation in a lengthier speech. Have students use graphing skills to chart the length of the alternating speeches in this passage (according to number of words). The graph will clearly show the dramatic dynamics of this passage.

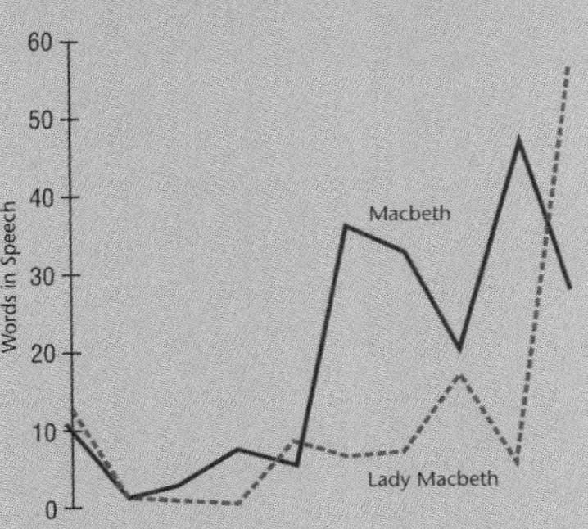

Speech Length in *Macbeth*, act 2, scene 2, lines 14–49

ANSWERS TO GUIDED READING QUESTIONS

1. The imagined voice says to Macbeth, "Macbeth does murther sleep."
2. Macbeth refuses to go back to the dead servants and smear them with blood, saying, "I am afraid to think what I have done. / Look on't again I dare not." Lady Macbeth says the dead are nothing to fear and that she will do the deed.
3. Macbeth is afraid he will not be able to wash all the blood off his hands.

LITERARY TECHNIQUE 

PUNS. A **pun** is a play on words, one that wittily exploits a double meaning. Scholars have counted at least a hundred puns in *Macbeth.* To encourage students to keep their eyes open for puns, write lines 52–54 on the board and ask students to try to find the pun in Lady Macbeth's words: ("If he do bleed, / I'll gild the faces of the grooms withal, / For it must seem their guilt [gilt].") Lady Macbeth is suggesting that guilt is something that can be painted on (like gilt, a thin layer of gold) as easily as it can be washed off ("A little water clears us of this deed," line 64). Students may also have missed the pun in line 60 of act 1, scene 7: "But screw your courage to the sticking place"—the sticking place suggesting not only its literal meaning, the trigger notch on a crossbow, but the place where Macbeth will stick the knife: Duncan's heart.

MACBETH. One cried, "God bless us!" and "Amen!" the other,
As they had seen me with these hangman's hands.
List'ning their fear, I could not say "Amen,"
When they did say "God bless us!"

LADY MACBETH. Consider it not so deeply.

MACBETH. But wherefore could not I pronounce "Amen"?
I had most need of blessing, and "Amen"
Stuck in my throat.

LADY MACBETH. These deeds must not be thought
After these ways; so, it will make us mad.

MACBETH. Methought I heard a voice cry, "Sleep no more!
Macbeth does murther sleep"—the innocent sleep,
Sleep that knits up the ravell'd sleave[20] of care,
The death of each day's life, sore labor's bath,
Balm of hurt minds, great nature's second course,[21]
Chief nourisher in life's feast.

What does the imagined voice say to Macbeth?

LADY MACBETH. What do you mean?

MACBETH. Still it cried, "Sleep no more!" to all the house;
"Glamis hath murther'd sleep, and therefore Cawdor
Shall sleep no more—Macbeth shall sleep no more."

LADY MACBETH. Who was it that thus cried? Why, worthy thane,
You do unbend[22] your noble strength, to think
So brain-sickly of things. Go get some water,
And wash this filthy witness[23] from your hand.
Why did you bring these daggers from the place?
They must lie there. Go carry them, and smear
The sleepy grooms with blood.

MACBETH. I'll go no more.
I am afraid to think what I have done;
Look on't again I dare not.

What does Macbeth refuse to do? Why? How does Lady Macbeth respond?

LADY MACBETH. Infirm of purpose!
Give me the daggers. The sleeping and the dead
Are but as pictures; 'tis the eye of childhood
That fears a painted devil. If he do bleed,
I'll gild[24] the faces of the grooms withal,
For it must seem their guilt. *Exit. Knock within.*

MACBETH. Whence is that knocking?
How is't with me, when every noise appalls me?
What hands are here? Hah! they pluck out mine eyes.

What is Macbeth afraid of?

20. **knits . . . sleave.** Straightens the tangled threads
21. **nature's second course.** Nature has two courses: food and sleep.
22. **unbend.** Relax
23. **witness.** Evidence
24. **gild.** Blood was often referred to as golden.

Will all great Neptune's ocean wash this blood
Clean from my hand? No; this my hand will rather
The multitudinous seas incarnadine,[25]
Making the green one red.

Enter LADY MACBETH.

LADY MACBETH. My hands are of your color; but I shame
To wear a heart so white. (*Knock.*) I hear a knocking
At the south entry. Retire we to our chamber.
A little water clears us of this deed;
How easy is it then! Your constancy
Hath left you unattended.[26] (*Knock.*) Hark, more knocking.
Get on your night-gown, lest occasion call us
And show us to be watchers.[27] Be not lost
So poorly in your thoughts.

MACBETH. To know my deed, 'twere best not know myself. *Knock.*
Wake Duncan with thy knocking! I would thou couldst! *Exeunt.*

SCENE 3: open court within MACBETH'S castle

Enter a PORTER. *Knocking within.*

PORTER. Here's a knocking indeed! If a man were porter of Hell Gate, he should have old[28] turning the key. (*Knock.*) Knock, knock, knock! Who's there, i' th' name of Belzebub?[29] Here's a farmer, that hang'd himself on th' expectation of plenty. Come in time! Have napkins enow about you, here you'll sweat for't. (*Knock.*) Knock, knock! Who's there, in th' other devil's name? Faith, here's an equivocator, that could swear in both the scales against either scale, who committed treason enough for God's sake, yet could not equivocate to heaven. O, come in, equivocator. (*Knock.*) Knock, knock knock! Who's there? Faith, here's an English tailor come hither for stealing out of a French hose.[30] Come in, tailor, here you may roast your goose.[31] (*Knock.*) Knock, knock! Never at quiet! What are you? But this place is too cold for hell. I'll devil-porter it no further. I had thought to have let in some of all professions that go the primrose way to th' everlasting bonfire. (*Knock.*) Anon, anon! [*Opens the gate.*] I pray you remember the porter.

25. **incarnadine.** To turn red
26. **constancy . . . unattended.** Firmness of purpose has abandoned you.
27. **watchers.** People who stay up late
28. **he should have old.** He would get tired of
29. **Belzebub.** Chief devil
30. **tailor . . . hose.** The tailor stole cloth while making French hose.
31. **roast your goose.** Heat your iron

WORDS FOR EVERYDAY USE

mul • ti • tu • di • nous (mul´tə to͞od´ nəs) *adj.*, very numerous. *His client's multitudinous troubles included homelessness and schizophrenia.*

e • quiv • o • ca • tor (ē kwiv´ə kā´tor) *n.*, one who speaks ambiguously. *In Shakespeare's time, an equivocator might be a religious heretic or a potential traitor who supported both sides in a political struggle.*

LITERARY TECHNIQUE

COMIC RELIEF. Writers sometimes insert into a serious work of fiction or drama a humorous scene that is said to provide **comic relief** because it relieves the seriousness or emotional intensity felt by the audience. Paradoxically, a scene introduced for comic relief can sometimes, because of the contrast it provides, increase the perceived intensity or seriousness of the action around it. Point out to students that the brief scene with the porter provides comic relief. Ask them how it can also be said to provide additional suspense. Point out that the porter's "game" of playing the porter of Hell's gate also ominously and ironically reflects what is going on in the scene: the castle has indeed become a Hell.

ADDITIONAL QUESTIONS AND ACTIVITIES

Teachers might be interested in reading to students or in duplicating for silent reading Thomas DeQuincey's famous short essay on "The Knocking at the Gate," which describes the profound effect on the audience that this scene evokes. It comes from DeQuincey's *Miscellaneous Essays,* 1851, and appears in many collections of famous essays.

ANSWER TO GUIDED READING QUESTION

1. Duncan told Macduff and Lennox to wake him up at a certain hour.

LITERARY TECHNIQUES

Motif. A **motif** is any element that recurs in one or more works of literature or art. You might point out to students that the porter's lines 20–25 echo one theme of Macbeth: equivocation, or double-dealing.

Paraphrase. A **paraphrase** is a restatement of a piece of writing in another form or in different words. To examine the richness and humor of the porter's speech, students can paraphrase the porter's soliloquy (lines 1–24) in Modern American English or in slang. You may wish to give as an example a paraphrase that explains the porter's comments in lines 41–45. The porter picks up on a pun of Macduff's and fires off several puns, all comparing his drinking bout metaphorically to a wrestling match. "Drink had me pinned down and had me by the throat; but I got him back for knocking me down; and (I think) I was too strong for him, though he knocked me off my legs sometimes; all the same I made a change of position that enabled him to throw him off [or throw him up]."

Enter Macduff *and* Lennox.

Macduff. Was it so late, friend, ere you went to bed,
That you do lie so late?

Porter. Faith, sir, we were carousing till the second cock;[32] and drink, sir, is a great provoker of three things.

Macduff. What three things does drink especially provoke?

Porter. Marry, sir, nose-painting, sleep, and urine. Lechery, sir, it provokes, and unprovokes: it provokes the desire, but it takes away the performance. Therefore much drink may be said to be an equivocator with lechery: it makes him, and it mars him; it sets him on, and it takes him off; it persuades him, and disheartens him; makes him stand to, and not stand to; in conclusion, equivocates him in a sleep, and giving him the lie, leaves him.

Macduff. I believe drink gave thee the lie[33] last night.

Porter. That it did, sir, i' the very throat on me; but I requited him for his lie, and (I think) being too strong for him, though he took up my legs sometime, yet I made a shift to cast[34] him.

Macduff. Is thy master stirring?

Enter Macbeth.

Our knocking has awak'd him; here he comes.

Lennox. Good morrow, noble sir.

Macbeth. Good morrow, both.

Macduff. Is the King stirring, worthy thane?

Macbeth. Not yet.

Macduff. He did command me to call timely on him,
I have almost slipp'd the hour.

Why have Macduff and Lennox come?

Macbeth. I'll bring you to him.

Macduff. I know this is a joyful trouble to you;
But yet 'tis one.

Macbeth. The labor we delight in physics pain.[35]
This is the door.

Macduff. I'll make so bold to call,
For 'tis my limited service.

Exit Macduff.

Lennox. Goes the King hence to-day?

Macbeth. He does; he did appoint so.

---

32. **second cock.** 3 A.M.
33. **gave thee the lie.** Knocked you out
34. **cast him.** Pun meaning both "throw him off," as in wrestling, and "throw him up," as in vomit him (the drink) up
35. **The labor . . . pain.** The work we enjoy cures the pain of labor.

LENNOX. The night has been unruly. Where we lay,
Our chimneys were blown down, and (as they say)
Lamentings heard i' th' air; strange screams of death,
And prophesying, with accents terrible,
Of dire combustion[36] and confus'd events
New hatch'd to th' woeful time. The obscure bird
Clamor'd the livelong night. Some say, the earth
Was feverous, and did shake.

What was the night like?

MACBETH. 'Twas a rough night.

LENNOX. My young remembrance cannot parallel
A fellow to it.

Enter MACDUFF.

MACDUFF. O horror, horror, horror! Tongue nor heart
Cannot conceive nor name thee!

MACBETH AND LENNOX. What's the matter?

MACDUFF. Confusion now hath made his masterpiece!
Most sacrilegious murther hath broke ope
The Lord's anointed temple,[37] and stole thence
The life o' th' building!

What does Macduff report?

MACBETH. What is't you say—the life?

LENNOX. Mean you his Majesty?

MACDUFF. Approach the chamber, and destroy your sight
With a new Gorgon.[38] Do not bid me speak;
See, and then speak yourselves.

Exeunt MACBETH *and* LENNOX.

Awake, awake!
Ring the alarum-bell! Murther and treason!
Banquo and Donalbain! Malcolm, awake!
Shake off this downy sleep, death's counterfeit,
And look on death itself! Up, up, and see
The great doom's image![39] Malcolm! Banquo!
As from your graves rise up, and walk like sprites,
To countenance this horror! Ring the bell.

Bell rings.

Enter LADY MACBETH.

LADY MACBETH. What's the business,
That such a hideous trumpet calls to parley
The sleepers of the house? Speak, speak!

36. **combustion.** Confusion
37. **Lord's anointed temple.** The body of the king
38. **Gorgon.** A mythological monster who turned to stone all who looked at it
39. **great doom's image.** Likeness of Doomsday

ANSWERS TO GUIDED READING QUESTIONS

1. The weather has been "unruly," blowing down chimneys. "Lamentings" and "strange screams" were heard in the air. The earth "Was feverous, and did shake."
2. Macduff reports that the king has been murdered.

ADDITIONAL QUESTIONS AND ACTIVITIES

The speech of Macduff in lines 62–68 wrings the motifs of sleep and death for all they are worth. "Awake, awake!" he cries, and "Shake off this downy sleep, death's counterfeit." He compares the sleeping Malcolm and Banquo to the dead and calls on them to walk "like sprites" to see the dead king. Motifs of sleep, sleeplessness, death, and weariness with life recur over and over in the play. Students can do research to find other passages in other plays by Shakespeare where sleep is mentioned, using either a library concordance of Shakespeare's works or an electronic search program on CD/ROM or another storage medium. If they need specific targets, they can look for instances of death as sleep, of sleep as death, and of magical sleep. They should write a paragraph presenting some examples and analyzing their results. The paragraph can begin, "In his works, Shakespeare uses the motif of sleep to. . ."

ANSWERS TO GUIDED READING QUESTIONS

1. Macduff calls her "gentle lady." He doesn't want to tell her what has happened because he fears it is too harsh for a woman's ears.
2. Lennox blames the king's servants.
3. Macbeth says he regrets his "fury," which prompted him to kill the servants.

LITERARY TECHNIQUE 

Irony. Irony is a difference between appearance and reality. Ask students what is ironic about Macduff's calling Lady Macbeth "gentle lady" and saying that the terrible news is not for her to hear.

Macduff. O gentle lady,
'Tis not for you to hear what I can speak:
The repetition in a woman's ear
Would murther as it fell.

What does Macduff call Lady Macbeth? Why doesn't he want to tell her what has happened?

Enter Banquo.

O Banquo, Banquo,
Our royal master's murther'd!

Lady Macbeth. Woe, alas!
What, in our house?

Banquo. Too cruel any where.
Dear Duff, I prithee contradict thyself,
And say, it is not so.

Enter Macbeth, Lennox, Rosse.

Macbeth. Had I but died an hour before this chance,
I had liv'd a blessed time; for from this instant
There's nothing serious in mortality:[40]
All is but toys:[41] renown and grace is dead,
The wine of life is drawn, and the mere lees[42]
Is left this vault to brag of.

Enter Malcolm *and* Donalbain.

Donalbain. What is amiss?

Macbeth. You are, and do not know't.
The spring, the head, the fountain of your blood
Is stopp'd, the very source of it is stopp'd.

Macduff. Your royal father's murther'd.

Malcolm. O, by whom?

Lennox. Those of his chamber, as it seem'd, had done't.
Their hands and faces were all badg'd[43] with blood;
So were their daggers, which unwip'd we found
Upon their pillows. They star'd and were distracted;
No man's life was to be trusted with them.

Whom does Lennox blame for Duncan's death?

Macbeth. O, yet I do repent me of my fury,
That I did kill them.

What does Macbeth say he regrets?

Macduff. Wherefore did you so?

Macbeth. Who can be wise, amaz'd, temp'rate, and furious,
Loyal, and neutral, in a moment? No man.
Th' expedition[44] of my violent love
Outrun the pauser, reason. Here lay Duncan,

40. **serious in mortality.** Worthwhile in human life
41. **toys.** Trifles
42. **lees.** Dregs
43. **badg'd.** Marked
44. **expedition.** Haste

His silver skin lac'd with his golden blood,
And his gash'd stabs look'd like a breach in nature
For ruin's wasteful entrance; there, the murtherers,
Steep'd in the colors of their trade, their daggers
Unmannerly breech'd with gore.[45] Who could refrain,
That had a heart to love, and in that heart
Courage to make 's love known?

Lady Macbeth. Help me hence, ho!

Macduff. Look to the lady.

Malcolm. [*Aside to* Donalbain.] Why do we hold our tongues,
That most may claim this argument for ours?

Donalbain. [*Aside to* Malcolm.] What should be spoken here, where our fate,
Hid in an auger-hole,[46] may rush and seize us?
Let's away,
Our tears are not yet brew'd.

Malcolm. [*Aside to* Donalbain.] Nor our strong sorrow
Upon the foot of motion.

Banquo. Look to the lady.

Lady Macbeth *is carried out.*

And when we have our naked frailties hid,[47]
That suffer in exposure, let us meet
And question this most bloody piece of work,
To know it further. Fears and scruples shake us.
In the great hand of God I stand, and thence
Against the undivulg'd pretense[48] I fight
Of treasonous malice.

What does Banquo suggest?

Macduff. And so do I.

All. So all.

Macbeth. Let's briefly put on manly readiness,
And meet i' th' hall together.

All. Well contented.

Exeunt all but Malcolm *and* Donalbain.

45. **breech'd with gore.** Covered with blood
46. **auger-hole.** A small hole, an unlikely hiding place
47. **naked frailties hid.** Gotten dressed
48. **undivulg'd pretense.** Secret purpose

Words for Everyday Use

scru • ples (skrōō′ pəlz) *n.*, doubts, qualms. *Although the smuggler did not hesitate to break the law, he had scruples about cheating his friends.*

ANSWER TO GUIDED READING QUESTION

1. Banquo suggests they get dressed and then meet to investigate the situation further.

SELECTION CHECK TEST 4.5.5 WITH ANSWERS

Checking Your Reading

1. Whom does Lady Macbeth smear with blood? **She smears Duncan's two servants.**
2. What does Lennox say about the night that has just passed? **It was wild and full of strange noises.**
3. Who does Macbeth admit to killing? **He admits to killing the two servants.**
4. What do Malcolm and Donalbain do? **They leave Scotland.**
5. Why has Macbeth gone to Scone? **He has gone to be crowned king.**

Vocabulary in Context

Fill each blank with the most appropriate word from the Words for Everyday Use. You may have to change the tense of the word.

augment palpable stealthy
multitudinous equivocator scruples

1. Bisha **augmented** her training schedule with a ten-mile run once a week.
2. The last day of school, the children listed the **multitudinous** delights awaiting them.
3. "Devon's such a(n) **equivocator** that I can never understand him," grumbled Lynn.
4. Despite Todd's **stealthy** tread, his dog heard him and came running with the leash.
5. The tension in the stadium was **palpabl**e as the two teams battled for the pennant.

Literary Tools

1. What internal struggle of Macbeth's forms a central conflict of this play? **He is conflicted between his loyalty to Duncan and his ambition to be king.**
2. How is this conflict developed in act 2? *Responses may vary.* **The Macbeths have killed Duncan; Malcolm and Donalbain flee; Macbeth is mad.**
3. Identify one symbol from act 2. **Responses will vary, but could include blood, the imaginary dagger, prophecy, or stormy weather.**
4. What is verbal irony? **Verbal irony is a statement that implies its opposite.**
5. What is hyperbole? **Hyperbole is an exaggeration made for effect.**

ANSWERS TO GUIDED READING QUESTIONS

1. Malcolm goes to England and Donalbain to Ireland to avoid being murdered themselves.
2. The sky is as dark as night, although it is daytime.
3. A falcon has been killed by an owl and Duncan's horses have eaten each other.

ADDITIONAL QUESTIONS AND ACTIVITIES

- Students can divide into two sides for a ten-minute impromptu debate on whether Malcolm and Donalbain should stay in Scotland or leave the country. Some of the points they may wish to raise in favor of leaving can be found in Malcolm and Donalbain's discussion of the matter. Points against Malcolm and Donalbain's leaving are that they will be under suspicion, they will not be able to assume control of the country, and they will not be able to discover readily who killed their father. Although this is not a central issue in the play, such a debate will help clarify for students the political situation in Scotland that results from the death of the king.
- Have students compare the death of a king to the assassination of a president. Is the resulting upheaval similar in the two situations? Relying on American government or history texts, have students outline the orderly succession that would take place. Discuss the political, social, and emotional impact an assassination could have.

MALCOLM. What will you do? Let's not consort with them;
To show an unfelt sorrow is an office
Which the false man does easy. I'll to England.

Where do Malcolm and Donalbain go?

DONALBAIN. To Ireland, I; our separated fortune
Shall keep us both the safer. Where we are,
There's daggers in men's smiles; the near in blood,
The nearer bloody.[49]

MALCOLM. This murtherous shaft that's shot
Hath not yet lighted,[50] and our safest way
Is to avoid the aim. Therefore to horse,
And let us not be dainty of leave-taking,
But shift away. There's warrant in that theft
Which steals itself,[51] when there's no mercy left.

Exeunt.

SCENE 4: outside MACBETH'S castle

Enter ROSSE *with an* OLD MAN.

OLD MAN. Threescore and ten I can remember well,
Within the volume of which time I have seen
Hours dreadful and things strange; but this sore[52] night
Hath trifled former knowings.

ROSSE. Ha, good father,
Thou seest the heavens, as troubled with man's act,
Threatens his bloody stage. By th' clock 'tis day,
And yet dark night strangles the travelling lamp.[53]
Is't night's predominance, or the day's shame,
That darkness does the face of earth entomb,
When living light should kiss it?

What is unusual about the sky?

OLD MAN. 'Tis unnatural,
Even like the deed that's done. On Tuesday last,
A falcon, tow'ring in her pride of place,
Was by a mousing owl hawk'd at, and kill'd.

ROSSE. And Duncan's horses (a thing most strange and certain),
Beauteous and swift, the minions of their race,
Turn'd wild in nature, broke their stalls, flung out,
Contending 'gainst obedience, as they would make
War with mankind.

What strange occurrences have taken place?

49. **the near . . . bloody.** The closer we are related to Duncan, the greater the danger of being murdered ourselves.
50. **lighted.** Hit its mark
51. **steals itself.** Sneaks away
52. **sore.** Dreadful
53. **travelling lamp.** The sun

Old Man. 'Tis said, they eat[54] each other.

Rosse. They did so—to th' amazement of mine eyes
That look'd upon't.

Enter Macduff.

Here comes the good Macduff.
How goes the world, sir, now?

Macduff. Why, see you not?

Rosse. Is't known who did this more than bloody deed?

Macduff. Those that Macbeth hath slain.

Rosse. Alas the day,
What good could they pretend?

Macduff. They were suborned.[55]
Malcolm and Donalbain, the King's two sons,
Are stol'n away and fled, which puts upon them
Suspicion of the deed.

What does Macduff suspect?

Rosse. 'Gainst nature still!
Thriftless ambition, that will ravin up[56]
Thine own live's means! Then 'tis most like
The sovereignty will fall upon Macbeth.

Macduff. He is already nam'd, and gone to Scone[57]
To be invested.

Who is now king?

Rosse. Where is Duncan's body?

Macduff. Carried to Colmekill,[58]
The sacred store-house of his predecessors
And guardian of their bones.

Rosse. Will you to Scone?

Macduff. No, cousin, I'll to Fife.[59]

Rosse. Well, I will thither.

Macduff. Well, may you see things well done there: adieu,
Lest our old robes sit easier than our new!

Rosse. Farewell, father.

Old Man. God's benison[60] go with you, and with those
That would make good of bad, and friends of foes!

Exeunt omnes.

54. **eat.** Ate (pronounced *et*)
55. **suborned.** Bribed
56. **ravin up.** Eat ravenously
57. **Scone.** Where Scottish kings were crowned
58. **Colmekill.** Where Scottish kings were buried
59. **Fife.** Macduff's castle
60. **benison.** Blessing

ANSWERS TO GUIDED READING QUESTIONS

1. Macduff suspects that Malcolm and Donalbain bribed the king's servants to kill their father and have fled out of guilt.
2. Macbeth is now king.

LITERARY TECHNIQUE

Juxtaposition. Explain to students that **juxtaposition** is the device of creating irony or some other effect by the significant proximity of ideas, images, or actions. In act 1, scene 4, lines 11–14, Duncan remarks of the previous Thane of Cawdor that "There's no art/To find the mind's construction in the face:/He was a gentleman on whom I built/An absolute trust." Immediately thereafter the new Thane of Cawdor, Macbeth, enters the scene—similarly trusted and similarly untrustworthy. Likewise, in act 1, scene 7, lines 25–28, Macbeth says he has "no spur" for his intention to assassinate Duncan but ambition, whereupon Lady Macbeth enters to spur him on. In act 2, scene 4, lines 28–30, Rosse exclaims: "Thriftless ambition, that will ravin up/Thine own live's means! Then 'tis most like/The sovereignty will fall upon Macbeth." The juxtaposition of ravining ambition and the sovereignty falling on Macbeth creates a sharp irony of which Rosse is perhaps unaware. Students can improve their ability to recognize irony by writing five pairs of sentences with juxtapositions like the example in this scene. Their examples may draw on characters or situations in the play.

CROSS-CURRICULAR ACTIVITIES

Law. Ask students to use a resource such as Black's Law Dictionary and look up the difference between manslaughter and murder. They may also find the distinction between murder in the first and second degrees. Of what crime is Macbeth guilty by the end of act 2? Of what might Lady Macbeth be charged?

Answer

Manslaughter is the unjustifiable, inexcusable, and intentional killing of a human being without deliberation, premeditation, and malice. Manslaughter may be committed in the heat of passion or while being

CROSS-CURRICULAR ACTIVITIES (cont.)

careless. Murder is the unlawful killing of a human being with malice of forethought, either express or implied. First degree murder includes murder by any kind of willful, deliberate, and premeditated killing, such as poisoning or lying in wait or killing which is committed in the perpetration of, or attempt to perpetrate, a felony (such as arson, rape, robbery, or burglary). Any other murder is deemed murder of the second degree. Macbeth would be charged with murder in the first degree and Lady Macbeth is guilty of aiding and abetting the murder and so might be tried as an accessory.

RESPOND TO THE SELECTION

You might make a list of students' suggestions on the board and have students vote for the solution they would choose.

ANSWERS TO INVESTIGATE, INQUIRE, AND IMAGINE

Recall

1a. Macbeth believes he sees a dagger. He attributes this illusion to a "heat-oppressed brain" and to the "bloody business" at hand.

2a. Macbeth believes he hears the voice say that Macbeth has murdered sleep and that Macbeth will never sleep again.

3a. They report that the day is as dark as night; that a falcon was killed by an owl; and that Duncan's horses turned wild, broke from their stalls, and ate each other.

Interpret

1b. Macbeth is confused, upset, and obsessed with the horror of what he plans; this is clear to the audience from the hallucination he has and from his long soliloquy on the horrors of the night.

2b. Macbeth, though he may become king, will be affected by his conscience for the great wrong he has done. He may go mad from the guilt or he may harden himself so he doesn't think about the murder.

3b. Macbeth's deed is unnatural because subjects are supposed to honor their kings, not kill them, and because Duncan is Macbeth's kinsman and guest. The consequence of the murder is to upset the natural order and to make someone king who should not be.

Analyze

4a. Macbeth is tormented with guilt and filled with horror at what he has done. He relates that he was unable to say the word "amen" and has heard voices saying "Macbeth does murther sleep!" Every noise rattles him and he despairs that he will never wash the blood from his hands.

Synthesize

4b. *Responses will vary.*

Evaluate

5a. Macbeth wishes his life could have ended before the murder. Rosse's lines, though aimed at Malcolm and Donalbain, could be applied to

Respond *to the* Selection

If you were Macbeth, how would you overcome your guilt?

Investigate, Inquire, Imagine

Recall: Gathering Facts

1a. What does Macbeth imagine that he sees in scene 1? To what does he attribute this illusion?

2a. In scene 2, Macbeth reports hearing a voice cry out. What does he think he hears the voice say about sleep?

3a. In scene 3, Lennox reports strange disturbances in nature on the night of Duncan's murder. In scene 4, Rosse and the Old Man likewise speak of disturbances. What are these disturbances?

Interpret: Finding Meaning

1b. What is Macbeth's state of mind immediately before the murder? How can you tell?

2b. What do you think might be the consequences for Macbeth of having committed this murder?

3b. In what sense is Macbeth's deed unnatural? What are the consequences of the murder on the natural order?

Analyze: Taking Things Apart →

4a. Analyze Macbeth's state of mind in scene 2, giving examples from the text to support your conclusion.

Synthesize: Bringing Things Together

4b. Given this state of mind, what do you predict for Macbeth as he takes the throne and attempts to rule Scotland?

Evaluate: Making Judgments →

5a. At the end of the act, Rosse says of Malcolm and Donalbain that "thriftless ambition" will devour greedily their "own live's means." Evaluate the truth of these lines when applied to Macbeth.

Extend: Connecting Ideas

5b. Do you believe that a person can be tempted to do something that is totally out of character? Can a good person be led down the wrong road? Explain.

Understanding Literature

Symbol. Review the definition for **symbol** in the Handbook of Literary Terms. Before murdering Duncan, Macbeth imagines that he sees a bloody dagger. After the murder, he laments that he will never be able to clean the blood from his hands. What does the blood symbolize?

Hyperbole. Review the definition for **hyperbole** in the Handbook of Literary Terms. After Macbeth murders Duncan, he laments, "Will all great Neptune's ocean wash this blood / Clean from my hand? No; this my hand will rather / The multitudinous seas incarnadine, / Making the green one red" (scene 2, lines 57–60). What exaggeration is being made? What effect does this hyperbole have?

ANSWERS TO INVESTIGATE, INQUIRE, AND IMAGINE (cont.)

Macbeth if one considers how Macbeth's ambition has only served to destroy the natural order of king and subject that previously gave Macbeth stability and peace of mind.

Extend

5b. *Responses will vary.*

Answers to Understanding Literature can be found on page 409.

Verbal Irony. Review the definition for **verbal irony** in the Handbook of Literary Terms. When Duncan's murder is discovered, Macbeth says to Banquo and Macduff, "Had I but died before this chance, / I had liv'd a blessed time; for from this instant / There's nothing serious in mortality" (scene 3, lines 79–81). What do Macbeth's words mean to his compatriots? What meaning do they have for Macbeth? What is ironic about the statement?

Mood. Review the definition for **mood** in the Handbook of Literary Terms and the cluster chart you made for Literary Tools on page 396. What kind of mood do these details create? What is the meaning of these details?

Writer's Journal

1. Write two **headlines** to summarize the crucial events in act 2. When writing your headlines, aim for active, descriptive phrases that immediately convey the events.
2. Imagine that you are Macbeth, newly named king, and write a **funeral elegy** for the murdered Duncan. In it you will want to honor the king and summarize his finest qualities. Consider also that his murder has caused apprehension and instability in the kingdom. What can you say to your subjects to restore a feeling of harmony in the kingdom?
3. Macbeth and Lady Macbeth are both involved in Duncan's murder. However, each reacts differently. Write a **comparison-and-contrast paragraph** about their roles in the murder and their reactions to it. Consider how each character acts and what each says, both in private and in public. For more information on writing a comparison-and-contrast paragraph, read the Language Arts Survey 2.27, "Choosing a Method of Organization."

Integrating the Language Arts

Collaborative Learning

Designing a Stage Set. Working with several classmates, design a stage set for a production of act 2, which takes place at Macbeth's castle in Inverness, Scotland. You will need to carefully consider the action that takes place in each scene to determine the set requirements. You will also find it useful to research castle architecture of the Norman era. Using drawings or models, share your set design with the class.

Speaking and Listening & Collaborative Learning

Dramatic Interpretation. Select a scene from act 2 that you want to interpret. Then read the Language Arts Survey 4.1, "Verbal and Nonverbal Communication." With several classmates, decide which elements of verbal and nonverbal communication you will use to present your scene. You may also want to select appropriate music for the opening of your scene. Finally, after rehearsing, present your dramatic interpretation to the class.

Media Literacy & Collaborative Learning

Taping a Television Show. Write a brief account of the murder as it might be described on a sensationalistic television program about unsolved mysteries. Include interviews with witnesses who were close to the action. Provide theories as to who committed the murder of Duncan. Then videotape your television show and show it to the class.

ANSWERS TO UNDERSTANDING LITERATURE

Symbol. The blood symbolizes Macbeth's guilt in killing Duncan.

Hyperbole. The exaggeration lies in the notion that the small quantity of blood on Macbeth's hand could actually stain a huge expanse of water (the sea) red. The effect of the hyperbole is to suggest the extent of Macbeth's horror at and remorse for what he has done.

Verbal Irony. To the other characters present in the scene, Macbeth's words suggest that he so grieved at what has happened that he would have preferred to die rather than to have seen such a terrible event. To Macbeth, his words may mean that he seriously regrets having taken the action he took and fears that life will become meaningless for him. The irony derives from the contrast between its apparent meaning to the characters who hear it and its actual meaning to Macbeth. They take is as a despairing expression of his love for the king, as he intends they should; but for him it also expresses his new despair and disgust with his own life.

Mood. The details create a horrific and frightening mood. Darkness in daytime, an owl killing a falcon, and horses eating each other reinforce the destruction of the natural order that Duncan's murder symbolizes.

ADDITIONAL RESOURCES

Unit 5 Resource Book

- Selection Worksheet 5.3
- Selection Check Test 4.5.7
- Selection Test 4.5.8
- Language, Grammar, and Style Resource 3.87
- Speaking and Listening Resource 4.1

ANSWER TO GUIDED READING QUESTION

1. Banquo suspects that Macbeth is guilty of foul play in the events that led to his becoming king.

GRAPHIC ORGANIZER

Students should include the following answers in their cluster charts.

- Macbeth hides from Banquo the fact that he considers killing Duncan.
- Macbeth pretends to be a loving host to Duncan.
- Macbeth is plagued by a vision of a bloody dagger.
- Macbeth deceives Banquo and Macduff with these words: "Had I but died an hour before this chance, / I had liv'd a blessed time; for from this instant / There's nothing serious in mortality."
- Macbeth and Lady Macbeth mask their murderous hearts (act 3, scene 2, lines 33–34).

READER'S JOURNAL

Due to the personal nature of the question, students may not want to share their answers. To change the question to a discussion question, ask, "When do some people feel panic and find it difficult to think clearly?"

Literary Tools

Simile. A **simile** is a comparison using *like* or *as*. As you read scene 4, look for the simile in which Macbeth compares himself to an element of nature.

Climax and Crisis. The **climax** is the point of highest interest and suspense in a literary work. The **crisis** is that point in the development of the conflict at which a decisive event occurs that causes the main character's situation to become better or worse. As you read act 3, identify the climax and the crisis.

Motif. A **motif** is any element that recurs in one or more works of literature or art. Motifs in *Macbeth* include ambition, deception, disturbances in nature, blood, madness, and sleep. As you read, make a cluster chart listing examples of deception in the play.

DECEPTION

Witches appear to be men but are women.

Reader's Journal

When have you felt panic and been unable to think clearly?

ACT 3

SCENE 1: a room in the palace at Forres

Enter BANQUO.

BANQUO. Thou hast it now: King, Cawdor, Glamis, all,
As the weïrd women promis'd, and I fear
Thou play'dst most foully for't; yet it was said
It should not stand in thy posterity,
But that myself should be the root and father
Of many kings. If there come truth from them—
As upon thee, Macbeth, their speeches shine[1]—
Why, by the verities on thee made good,
May they not be my oracles as well,
And set me up in hope? But hush, no more.

What does Banquo suspect?

Sennet[2] *sounded. Enter* MACBETH *as King*, LADY MACBETH *as Queen*, LENNOX, ROSSE, LORDS, *and* ATTENDANTS.

MACBETH. Here's our chief guest.

LADY MACBETH. If he had been forgotten,
It had been as a gap in our great feast,
And all-thing unbecoming.

MACBETH. To-night we hold a solemn supper, sir,
And I'll request your presence.

BANQUO. Let your Highness
Command upon me, to the which my duties
Are with a most indissoluble tie
For ever knit.

MACBETH. Ride you this afternoon?

BANQUO. Aye, my good lord.

MACBETH. We should have else desir'd your good advice
(Which still hath been both grave and prosperous)[3]
In this day's council; but we'll take tomorrow.
Is't far you ride?

BANQUO. As far, my lord, as will fill up the time
'Twixt this and supper. Go not my horse the better,

1. **shine.** Are fulfilled
2. **Sennet.** Trumpet call
3. **grave and prosperous.** Serious and profitable

Words for Everyday Use

pos • ter • i • ty (päs ter´ə tē) *n.*, succeeding generations. *The old general wrote his memoirs in the belief that posterity would thank him for his efforts.*

ver • i • ty (ver´ə tē) *n.*, truth. *That mothers love their children is an eternal verity.*

VOCABULARY FROM THE SELECTION

dauntless	nonpareil
jocund	posterity
malevolence	verity

Banquet Scene from Macbeth, c.1800s. Daniel Maclise. Guidhall Art Gallery, London.

I must become a borrower of the night[4]
For a dark hour or twain.

MACBETH. Fail not our feast.

BANQUO. My lord, I will not.

MACBETH. We hear our bloody cousins are bestow'd[5]
In England and in Ireland, not confessing
Their cruel parricide,[6] filling their hearers
With strange invention. But of that tomorrow,
When therewithal we shall have cause of state
Craving us jointly.[7] Hie you to horse; adieu,
Till you return at night. Goes Fleance with you?

BANQUO. Aye, my good lord. Our time does call upon 's.[8]

MACBETH. I wish your horses swift and sure of foot;
And so I do commend you to their backs.
Farewell. *Exit* BANQUO.
Let every man be master of his time
Till seven at night. To make society
The sweeter welcome, we will keep ourself
Till supper-time alone; while[9] then, God be with you!
Exeunt LORDS *with* LADY MACBETH *and others.*

4. **Go . . . night.** If my horse doesn't go faster, I will have to ride on at night.
5. **are bestow'd.** Living
6. **parricide.** Murder of a parent or other close relative
7. **Craving us jointly.** Requiring attention from both of us
8. **Our . . . upon 's.** Our business is urgent.
9. **while.** Until

ADDITIONAL QUESTIONS AND ACTIVITIES

After students have read through act III and know the fate of Banquo and the crisis Macbeth faces at the feast, reread with them the opening of the act (lines 11–39). Ask them to find examples of hypocrisy and irony.

Answer

Examples of hypocrisy are Macbeth's insistence that Banquo is his chief guest (line 11) and Lady Macbeth's comment that Banquo's absence would make a gap in the feast (lines 11–13). Examples of irony are the fact that Banquo will not leave a gap in the feast (there is no place for him; he takes Macbeth's seat) and the exchange between Macbeth and Banquo at line 28, "Fail not our feast."—"My lord, I will not," which proves to be fully correct: Banquo does not fail the feast, even after death.

ADDITIONAL VOCABULARY

oracles—predictors of the future
indissoluble—unbreakable
parricide—killing one's parent
chide—scold
rancor—spite, malice
execution—completion
buffet—blow, shock, bump
incensed—angered
sundry—various
abide—stay
assailable—vulnerable
apace—quickly
vouch—promise
infirmity—weakness
mockery—mimicry; cruel joking
spurn—reject
right—truly
valiant—brave
delinquent—one who neglects or flaunts duty or the law
exasperate—frustrate

ANSWERS TO GUIDED READING QUESTIONS

1. Macbeth wants security. He fears Banquo for his kingly nature.
2. Banquo's offspring will benefit from Macbeth's actions.

ADDITIONAL QUESTIONS AND ACTIVITIES

The brooding soliloquy in lines 47–71 of scene i ("To be thus is nothing . . .") is one of the most powerful in the play. Students can capture its poetic force by reciting it in unison, either as a class or in small groups. Students who have choral experience can be asked if they wish to volunteer to lead the groups.

ADDITIONAL QUESTIONS AND ACTIVITIES

Have students compare lines 63–71 of scene 1 with the soliloquy from Hamlet, act 3, scene 1, on page 477. Ask the following questions:

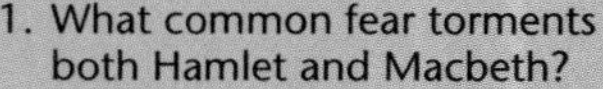

1. What common fear torments both Hamlet and Macbeth?
2. How do the conclusions of the two soliloquies differ?

Answers

1. They are both worried about what will happen to their souls after death. Macbeth feels that his soul will be "Given to the common enemy of man" (the devil); although he seems to have accepted this, he does not want it to happen on behalf of Banquo's posterity.
2. Hamlet comes to no decision; Macbeth concludes that he will proceed headlong on the same course.

Manent MACBETH *and a* SERVANT.

Sirrah, a word with you. Attend those men
Our pleasure?

SERVANT. They are, my lord, without the palace gate.

MACBETH. Bring them before us. *Exit* SERVANT.
To be thus[10] is nothing,
But to be safely thus. Our fears in Banquo
Stick deep, and in his royalty of nature[11]
Reigns that which would be fear'd. 'Tis much he dares,
And to that dauntless temper of his mind,
He hath a wisdom that doth guide his valor
To act in safety. There is none but he
Whose being I do fear; and under him
My Genius is rebuk'd, as it is said
Mark Antony's was by Caesar. He chid the sisters
When first they put the name of king upon me,
And bade them speak to him; then prophet-like
They hail'd him father to a line of kings.
Upon my head they plac'd a fruitless crown,
And put a barren sceptre in my gripe,[12]
Thence to be wrench'd with an unlineal hand,
No son of mine succeeding. If't be so,
For Banquo's issue have I fil'd[13] my mind,
For them the gracious Duncan have I murther'd,
Put rancors in the vessel of my peace
Only for them, and mine eternal jewel[14]
Given to the common enemy of man,
To make them kings—the seeds of Banquo kings!
Rather than so, come fate into the list,[15]
And champion me to th' utterance![16] Who's there?

What does Macbeth want? Whom does he fear and why?

Who will benefit from Macbeth's actions?

Enter SERVANT *and two* MURDERERS.

Now go to the door, and stay there till we call.
Exit SERVANT.

Was it not yesterday we spoke together?

MURDERERS. It was, so please your Highness.

10. **thus.** *i.e.,* King
11. **royalty of nature.** Natural kingliness
12. **gripe.** Grip
13. **fil'd.** Defiled
14. **eternal jewel.** Immortal soul
15. **list.** Arena for combat
16. **champion . . . utterance.** Fight me to the death

WORDS FOR EVERYDAY USE

daunt • less (dônt´ləs) *adj.,* fearless. *I would say that anyone who jumped a motorcycle over the Grand Canyon was either a fool or utterly dauntless, or perhaps both.*

MACBETH. Well then, now
Have you consider'd of my speeches?—know
That it was he in the times past which held you
So under fortune, which you thought had been
Our innocent self? This I made good[17] to you
In our last conference, pass'd in probation[18] with you:
How you were borne in hand, how cross'd, the instruments,
Who wrought with them, and all things else that might
To half a soul and to a notion craz'd[19]
Say, "Thus did Banquo."

1. MURDERER. You made it known to us.

MACBETH. I did so; and went further, which is now
Our point of second meeting. Do you find
Your patience so predominant in your nature
That you can let this go? Are you so gospell'd,[20]
To pray for this good man, and for his issue,
Whose heavy hand hath bow'd you to the grave,
And beggar'd yours for ever?

1. MURDERER. We are men, my liege.

MACBETH. Aye, in the catalogue ye go for men,
As hounds and greyhounds, mungrels, spaniels, curs,
Shoughs, water-rugs, and demi-wolves[21] are clipt[22]
All by the name of dogs; the valued file[23]
Distinguishes the swift, the slow, the subtle,
The house-keeper, the hunter, every one,
According to the gift which bounteous nature
Hath in him clos'd; whereby he does receive
Particular addition, from the bill
That writes them all alike: and so of men.
Now, if you have a station in the file,
Not i' th' worst rank of manhood, say't,
And I will put that business in your bosoms,
Whose execution takes your enemy off,
Grapples you to the heart and love of us,
Who wear our health but sickly in his life,
Which in his death were perfect.

2. MURDERER. I am one, my liege,
Whom the vile blows and buffets of the world
Hath so incens'd that I am reckless what
I do to spite the world.

Who is responsible for the murderers' misfortunes, according to Macbeth?

17. **made good.** Demonstrated
18. **pass'd in probation.** Reviewed and proved
19. **half . . . craz'd.** A half wit and crazed mind
20. **so gospell'd.** Such good followers of the Gospel
21. **Shoughs . . . demi-wolves.** Types of dogs
22. **clipt.** Called
23. **valued file.** List of the values of each

ANSWER TO GUIDED READING QUESTION

1. According to Macbeth, Banquo is responsible for the murderer's misfortunes and not Macbeth, as the murderers had thought.

ADDITIONAL QUESTIONS AND ACTIVITIES

Ask the following questions to promote discussion of the interview between Macbeth and the murderers:

1. How has Macbeth persuaded the murderers to hate Banquo?
2. What point is the first murderer making when he says, "We are men . . ." (line 90)?
3. Macbeth tells the murderers that they are counted as men, just as mongrels are categorized as dogs. He implies that they are valued more than they are due by being counted among a species containing better examples than they. Why does he say such an insulting thing to the murderers?
4. What kind of people are the murderers, by their own description (lines 107–113)?
5. At the end of his meeting with the murderers, Macbeth tells them that they must also kill Fleance. He then tells the murderers to take some time to make up their minds. How do the murderers respond?
6. What does the discussion with the murderers demonstrate about how the characters in the play use the notion of manliness?

Answers

1. Macbeth has told the murderers that the difficulties they have had in the past, for which they blamed Macbeth, were the fault of Banquo.
2. He is suggesting that they are only human and do not have enough saintly patience or religious belief not to loathe Banquo.
3. Macbeth is attempting to provoke the murderers into proving that they deserve to be called men because they are willing to strike back at the person who has injured them.
4. The first murderer is so angry at the world that he doesn't care what he does to make the world angry at him; the second murderer is so downtrodden that he has nothing to lose and everything to gain by taking a chance.
5. The murderers insist that they are resolved to kill Banquo and Fleance.
6. The notion of manliness is repeatedly used in the play to goad men into violent action.

ANSWER TO GUIDED READING QUESTION

1. Macbeth asks the murderers to kill Banquo and his son, Fleance.

ADDITIONAL QUESTIONS AND ACTIVITIES

Students can conduct impromptu "interviews" in which one student plays Macbeth and two others play the murderers. The student playing Macbeth should adhere to the general argument taken by Macbeth, which he or she can paraphrase; the other two students can each respond as they wish—either by playing the part of the murderers or reacting in their own characters to the request that they commit the crime. The purpose of the activity is to explore the situation and characters of the play more fully.

1. MURDERER. And I another,
So weary with disasters, tugg'd with fortune,
That I would set my life on any chance,
To mend it, or be rid on't.

MACBETH. Both of you
Know Banquo was your enemy.

MURDERERS. True, my lord.

MACBETH. So is he mine; and in such bloody distance,[24]
That every minute of his being thrusts
Against my near'st of life;[25] and though I could
With barefac'd power sweep him from my sight,
And bid my will avouch[26] it, yet I must not,
For certain friends that are both his and mine,
Whose loves I may not drop, but wail his fall[27]
Who I myself struck down. And thence it is
That I to your assistance do make love,
Masking the business from the common eye
For sundry weighty reasons.

2. MURDERER. We shall, my lord,
Perform what you command us.

1. MURDERER. Though our lives—

MACBETH. Your spirits shine through you. Within this hour, at most,
I will advise you where to plant yourselves,
Acquaint you with the perfect spy o' th' time,[28]
The moment on't, for't must be done tonight,
And something[29] from the palace; always thought
That I require a clearness: and with him—
To leave no rubs[30] nor botches in the work—
Fleance his son, that keeps him company,
Whose absence is no less material to me
Than is his father's, must embrace the fate
Of that dark hour. Resolve yourselves apart,[31]
I'll come to you anon.

What does Macbeth ask the murderers to do?

MURDERERS. We are resolv'd, my lord.

MACBETH. I'll call upon you straight; abide within.

Exeunt MURDERERS.

It is concluded: Banquo, thy soul's flight,
If it find heaven, must find it out tonight.

Exit.

---

24. **distance.** Hostilities
25. **near'st of life.** Life itself
26. **avouch.** Justify
27. **wail his fall.** Must seem to be lamenting his death
28. **perfect . . . time.** Precise moment
29. **something.** Some distance
30. **rubs.** Imperfections
31. **Resolve yourselves apart.** Go and make up your minds.

SCENE 2: another room in the palace

Enter MACBETH'S LADY *and a* SERVANT.

LADY MACBETH. Is Banquo gone from court?

SERVANT. Aye, madam, but returns again tonight.

LADY MACBETH. Say to the King, I would attend his leisure
For a few words.

SERVANT. Madam, I will. *Exit.*

LADY MACBETH. Nought's had, all's spent,
Where our desire is got without content;
'Tis safer to be that which we destroy
Than by destruction dwell in doubtful joy.

Enter MACBETH.

How now, my lord, why do you keep alone,
Of sorriest fancies your companions making,
Using those thoughts which should indeed have died
With them they think on? Things without all remedy
Should be without regard: what's done, is done.

MACBETH. We have scorch'd[32] the snake, not kill'd it;
She'll close[33] and be herself, whilest our poor malice
Remains in danger of her former tooth.[34]
But let the frame of things disjoint, both the worlds suffer,[35]
Ere we will eat our meal in fear, and sleep
In the affliction of these terrible dreams
That shake us nightly. Better be with the dead,
Whom we, to gain our peace, have sent to peace,
Than on the torture of the mind to lie
In restless ecstasy.[36] Duncan is in his grave;
After life's fitful fever he sleeps well.
Treason has done his worst; nor steel, nor poison,
Malice domestic, foreign levy, nothing,
Can touch him further.

LADY MACBETH. Come on;
Gentle my lord, sleek o'er your rugged looks,
Be bright and jovial among your guests tonight.

MACBETH. So shall I, love, and so, I pray, be you.
Let your remembrance apply to Banquo,
Present him eminence both with eye and tongue:
Unsafe the while, that we

What is preferable to "the torture of the mind"?

32. **scorch'd.** Lightly wounded
33. **close.** Heal
34. **our . . . tooth.** Despite our hatred our danger is the same as before.
35. **both . . . suffer.** Heaven and earth fall apart
36. **restless ecstasy.** Agitated frenzy

ANSWER TO GUIDED READING QUESTION

1. Death is preferable.

ADDITIONAL QUESTIONS AND ACTIVITIES

In scene 2, lines 18–19, Macbeth refers to "these terrible dreams / That shake us nightly." In lines 21–22 he speaks of lying by nights "on the torture of the mind… / In restless ecstasy." Students can write a dream report describing one of the dreams Macbeth or Lady Macbeth might have endured.

ANSWER TO GUIDED READING QUESTION

1. Macbeth and Lady Macbeth must wear masks to disguise their true feelings.

Must lave our honors in these flattering streams,[37]
And make our faces vizards[38] to our hearts,
Disguising what they are.

What must Macbeth and Lady Macbeth do?

LADY MACBETH. You must leave this.

MACBETH. O, full of scorpions is my mind, dear wife!
Thou know'st that Banquo and his Fleance lives.

LADY MACBETH. But in them nature's copy's not eterne.[39]

MACBETH. There's comfort yet, they are assailable.
Then be thou jocund; ere the bat hath flown
His cloister'd flight, ere to black Hecate's summons
The shard-borne[40] beetle with his drowsy hums
Hath rung night's yawning peal, there shall be done
A deed of dreadful note.

LADY MACBETH. What's to be done?

MACBETH. Be innocent of the knowledge, dearest chuck,[41]
Till thou applaud the deed. Come, seeling[42] night,
Scarf up the tender eye of pitiful day,
And with thy bloody and invisible hand
Cancel and tear to pieces that great bond[43]
Which keeps me pale! Light thickens, and the crow
Makes wing to th' rooky[44] wood;
Good things of day begin to droop and drowse,
Whiles night's black agents to their preys do rouse.
Thou marvel'st at my words, but hold thee still:
Things bad begun make strong themselves by ill.
So prithee go with me. *Exeunt.*

SCENE 3: a road leading to the palace

Enter three **MURDERERS.**

1. MURDERER. But who did bid thee join with us?

3. MURDERER. Macbeth.

2. MURDERER. He needs not our mistrust, since he delivers
Our offices,[45] and what we have to do,

37. **Unsafe . . . streams.** We are unsafe, so we must wash our honors in streams of flattery.
38. **vizards.** Masks
39. **in . . . eterne.** They are not eternal.
40. **shard-borne.** Carried on scaly wings
41. **chuck.** A term of endearment
42. **seeling.** Blinding
43. **great bond.** Promise made to Banquo by the witches
44. **rooky.** Gloomy
45. **offices.** Duties

WORDS FOR EVERYDAY USE

joc • und (jäk´ənd) *adj.*, cheerful, merry. *Santa Claus is known to be a jocund and merry old man.*

To the direction just.[46]

1. Murderer. Then stand with us.
The west yet glimmers with some streaks of day;
Now spurs the lated[47] traveller apace
To gain the timely inn, and near approaches
The subject of our watch.

3. Murderer. Hark, I hear horses.

Banquo. (*Within.*) Give us a light there, ho!

2. Murderer. Then 'tis he; the rest
That are within the note of expectation
Already are i' th' court.

1. Murderer. His horses go about.

3. Murderer. Almost a mile; but he does usually,
So all men do, from hence to th' palace gate
Make it their walk.

Enter Banquo, *and* Fleance *with a torch.*

2. Murderer. A light, a light!

3. Murderer. 'Tis he.

1. Murderer. Stand to't.

Banquo. It will be rain tonight.

1. Murderer. Let it come down.

They attack Banquo.

Banquo. O, treachery! Fly, good Fleance, fly, fly, fly!
Thou mayst revenge. O slave!

Banquo *dies.* Fleance *escapes.*

What are Banquo's last words?

3. Murderer. Who did strike out the light?

1. Murderer. Was't not the way?[48]

3. Murderer. There's but one down; the son is fled.

2. Murderer. We have lost
Best half of our affair.

1. Murderer. Well, let's away, and say how much is done. *Exeunt.*

Scene 4: a banquet room in the palace

Banquet prepar'd. Enter Macbeth, Lady Macbeth, Rosse, Lennox, Lords, *and* Attendants.

Macbeth. You know your own degrees,[49] sit down. At first
And last, the hearty welcome.

46. **To . . . just.** Exactly as Macbeth ordered
47. **lated.** Belated
48. **Was't not the way?.** Wasn't that the right thing to do?
49. **degrees.** Order of seating based on rank

ANSWER TO GUIDED READING QUESTION

1. Banquo tells his son, Fleance, to flee and avenge his death.

ADDITIONAL QUESTIONS AND ACTIVITIES

The appearance of the third murderer in scene 3 has led to much speculation on the part of critics. Some believe that the murderer must have been introduced in a short scene that was later cut when Shakespeare edited the script before it was performed for James I. No version of the script exists to verify this theory, however. Some directors have assigned the role of the third murderer to another existing character in the play to add intrigue to the plot. For example, view Roman Polanski's 1971 version of *Macbeth.* His interpretation of scene 3 and of act 4, scene 2, adds an entirely different twist to the plot and darkens the mood of the play. To spark discussion about scene 3, ask the following questions: Who is the third murderer? Why does he mysteriously appear at the beginning of scene 3, though he has never been referred to before? Is it possible that the third murderer is Macbeth in disguise? The third murderer is best acquainted with Banquo's habits (scene 3, lines 12–14) as Macbeth would be. The third murderer also positively identifies Banquo when he enters ("'Tis he," line 14) and the third murderer is the first to observe that Fleance has fled. Though Macbeth expresses surprise and disappointment when he is told that Fleance is still alive (scene 4, lines 20–22), might those lines be insincere? If the third murderer is not Macbeth, why does Shakespeare bring him in as a stranger to the others at the beginning of the scene? Could the third murderer be a symbolic representation of Macbeth without actually being Macbeth?

After discussing these questions, have students vote by show of hands as to whether they think the third murderer is Macbeth. Challenge adherents on both sides of the issue to justify their opinions.

Could the third murderer be an oversight on the playwright's part? Could he be a spy sent by Macbeth because of the latter's distrust of the men he has hired?

ANSWER TO GUIDED READING QUESTION

1. Macbeth feels imprisoned by "saucy doubts and fears."

Lords. Thanks to your Majesty.

Macbeth. Ourself will mingle with society,
And play the humble host.
Our hostess keeps her state,[50] but in best time
We will require her welcome.

Lady Macbeth. Pronounce it for me, sir, to all our friends,
For my heart speaks they are welcome.

Enter First Murderer *to the door.*

Macbeth. See, they encounter thee with their hearts' thanks.
Both sides are even; here I'll sit i' th' midst.
Be large in mirth;[51] anon we'll drink a measure[52]
The table round.— *Goes to the door.*
There's blood upon thy face.

Murderer. 'Tis Banquo's then.

Macbeth. 'Tis better thee without than he within.[53]
Is he dispatch'd?

Murderer. My lord, his throat is cut;
That I did for him.

Macbeth. Thou art the best o' th' cut-throats,
Yet he's good that did the like for Fleance.
If thou didst it, thou art the nonpareil.

Murderer. Most royal sir, Fleance is scap'd.

Macbeth. Then comes my fit again. I had else been perfect,
Whole as the marble, founded as the rock,
As broad and general[54] as the casing[55] air;
But now I am cabin'd, cribb'd, confin'd, bound in
To saucy doubts and fears. But Banquo's safe?[56]

How does Macbeth feel when he learns of Fleance's escape?

Murderer. Aye, my good lord; safe in a ditch he bides,
With twenty trenched gashes on his head,
The least a death to nature.

Macbeth. Thanks for that:
There the grown serpent lies; the worm[57] that's fled
Hath nature that in time will venom breed,

50. **state.** Seat
51. **large in mirth.** Very merry
52. **measure.** Large glass
53. **better . . . within.** Better on your face than in his body
54. **broad and general.** Free and unrestrained
55. **casing.** Surrounding
56. **safe.** No longer a threat
57. **worm.** The little serpent, Fleance

Words for Everyday Use

non • pa • reil (nän´pə rel´) *n.*, someone unequaled. *The widower would not marry again because his wife of sixty years had been a nonpareil, and he could find no other like her.*

No teeth for th' present. Get thee gone; tomorrow
We'll hear ourselves[58] again.

Exit MURDERER.

LADY MACBETH. My royal lord,
You do not give the cheer. The feast is sold
That is not often vouch'd, while 'tis a-making,
'Tis given with welcome.[59] To feed were best at home;
From thence, the sauce to meat is ceremony,
Meeting were bare without it.

Enter the GHOST OF BANQUO *and sits in* MACBETH'S *place.*

MACBETH. Sweet remembrancer!
Now good digestion wait on appetite,
And health on both!

LENNOX. May't please your Highness sit.

MACBETH. Here had we now our country's honor roof'd,[60]
Were the grac'd person of our Banquo present,
Who may I rather challenge for unkindness
Than pity for mischance.[61]

ROSSE. His absence, sir,
Lays blame upon his promise. Please't your Highness
To grace us with your royal company?

MACBETH. The table's full.

LENNOX. Here is a place reserv'd, sir.

MACBETH. Where?

LENNOX. Here, my good lord. What is't that moves your Highness?

MACBETH. Which of you have done this?

LORDS. What, my good lord?

MACBETH. Thou canst not say I did it, never shake
Thy gory locks at me.

What does Macbeth say to Banquo's ghost?

ROSSE. Gentlemen, rise, his Highness is not well.

LADY MACBETH. Sit, worthy friends; my lord is often thus,
And hath been from his youth. Pray you keep seat.
The fit is momentary, upon a thought[62]
He will again be well. If much you note him,
You shall offend him and extend his passion.
Feed, and regard him not.—Are you a man?

58. **hear ourselves.** Talk to each other
59. **The feast . . . welcome.** Unless the guests feel welcome, a feast is no better than a dinner one buys.
60. **roof'd.** Under one roof
61. **Who . . . mischance.** Who I hope is absent due to discourtesy and not due to an accident
62. **upon a thought.** Momentarily

ANSWER TO GUIDED READING QUESTION

1. Macbeth says Banquo can't prove he had anything to do with his death.

ADDITIONAL QUESTIONS AND ACTIVITIES

- One of the major motifs of *Macbeth* is hypocrisy—feigning to be what one is not. Sometimes this motif is described as the difference between being and seeming. Ask students to recall instances of hypocrisy in the play (act I, scene vii, lines 81–82; act III, scene ii, lines 27–34). Point out the extreme hypocrisy of Lady Macbeth and Macbeth at the beginning of act iii, scene iv as they act the genial hosts while being fully conscious that a murder is being committed on their behalf. Macbeth actually interrupts his participation in the feast to speak with the murderer, who comes to the door with Banquo's blood on his face. Ask students to describe their reactions to Macbeth's hypocrisy.
- Students can imagine that they are reporters on a television journalism program with only one chance to ask a question to expose Macbeth's hypocrisy. What would that question be?

ANSWERS TO GUIDED READING QUESTIONS

1. Lady Macbeth tells Macbeth that his fear is playing tricks on his mind.
2. Macbeth says he has a "strange infirmity."

ADDITIONAL QUESTIONS AND ACTIVITIES

Ask students the following questions:

1. Was the ghost really in the banquet hall, or was it just a figment of Macbeth's imagination?
2. Why was Macbeth the only one who saw the ghost?
3. What hallucination previously seen by Macbeth did Lady Macbeth refer to in her attempt to persuade him to stifle his fears?
4. The witches, like the ghost of Banquo, are also a vital supernatural element of the play. Is it likely that Shakespeare, who was not familiar with the concept of the subconscious mind, nevertheless intended the witches and the ghost as expressions of Macbeth's subconscious fears and motivations?
5. How else might Shakespeare have represented the subconscious if he did not resort to depicting supernatural beings like witches and ghosts?

Answers

1. *Responses will vary.* Macbeth, in line 141, refers to the ghost as self-deception ("self-abuse").
2. Responses may state that Macbeth was the only one who saw it because the ghost chose to appear only to him or because the ghost was only a figment of Macbeth's imagination.
3. Lady Macbeth refers to the "air-drawn dagger" seen by Macbeth before he murdered Duncan (act 2, scene 1, lines 33–49).
4. *Responses will vary.*
5. Shakespeare might have used other characters as representatives of the subconscious mind of the main character.

MACBETH. Aye, and a bold one, that dare look on that
Which might appall the devil.

LADY MACBETH. O proper stuff!
This is the very painting of your fear;
This is the air-drawn dagger which you said
Led you to Duncan. O, these flaws[63] and starts
(Impostors to true fear) would well become
A woman's story at a winter's fire,
Authoriz'd by her grandam. Shame itself,
Why do you make such faces? When all's done,
You look but on a stool.

What does Lady Macbeth tell her husband is responsible for his vision?

MACBETH. Prithee see there!
Behold! look! lo! how say you?
Why, what care I? if thou canst nod, speak too.
If charnel-houses[64] and our graves must send
Those that we bury back, our monuments
Shall be the maws of kites.[65] *Exit* GHOST.

LADY MACBETH. What? quite unmann'd in folly?

MACBETH. If I stand here, I saw him.

LADY MACBETH. Fie, for shame!

MACBETH. Blood hath been shed ere now, i' th' olden time,
Ere humane statute purg'd the gentle weal;[66]
Aye, and since too, murthers have been perform'd
Too terrible for the ear. The time has been,
That when the brains were out, the man would die,
And there an end; but now they rise again
With twenty mortal murthers on their crowns,[67]
And push us from our stools. This is more strange
Than such a murther is.

LADY MACBETH. My worthy lord,
Your noble friends do lack you.

MACBETH. I do forget.
Do not muse at me, my most worthy friends,
I have a strange infirmity, which is nothing
To those that know me. Come, love and health to all,
Then I'll sit down. Give me some wine, fill full.

What explanation does Macbeth give his guests for his odd behavior?

Enter GHOST.
I drink to th' general joy o' th' whole table,
And to our dear friend Banquo, whom we miss;
Would he were here! to all, and him, we thirst,

63. **flaws.** Emotional outbursts
64. **charnel-houses.** Storage spaces for human bones
65. **maws of kites.** Stomachs of birds of prey
66. **Ere . . . weal.** Before human laws cleansed and civilized the stat
67. **mortal . . . crowns.** Deadly wounds to the head

ADDITIONAL QUESTIONS AND ACTIVITIES

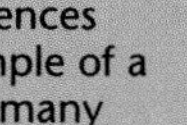

One reason that *Macbeth* has delighted audiences for centuries is that the play is a superb example of a horror story. Among the most horrific of the many horrors in the play is the appearance at the banquet, in Act III, of the ghost of Banquo. Prepare students for reading Act III by having them share some of their favorite horror stories, especially ones involving ghosts. Give students time to remember their stories and to jot down basic outlines of them before they tell the stories in class. You may wish to combine this activity with a lesson on the art of storytelling. Refer students to the information on storytelling in the Language Arts Survey, 4.20 "Telling a Story".

And all to all.

LORDS. Our duties, and the pledge.

MACBETH. Avaunt, and quit my sight! let the earth hide thee!
Thy bones are marrowless, thy blood is cold;
Thou hast no speculation in those eyes
Which thou dost glare with!

LADY MACBETH. Think of this, good peers,
But as a thing of custom. 'Tis no other;
Only it spoils the pleasure of the time.

MACBETH. What man dare, I dare.
Approach thou like the rugged Russian bear,
The arm'd rhinoceros, or th' Hyrcan[68] tiger,
Take any shape but that,[69] and my firm nerves
Shall never tremble. Or be alive again,
And dare me to the desert[70] with thy sword;
If trembling I inhabit then,[71] protest me
The baby of a girl. Hence, horrible shadow!
Unreal mock'ry, hence! *Exit* GHOST.
Why, so; being gone,
I am a man again. Pray you sit still.

LADY MACBETH. You have displac'd the mirth, broke the good meeting,
With most admir'd[72] disorder.

MACBETH. Can such things be,
And overcome us like a summer's cloud,
Without our special wonder? You make me strange
Even to the disposition that I owe,[73]
When now I think you can behold such sights,
And keep the natural ruby of your cheeks,
When mine is blanch'd with fear.

What does Lady Macbeth ask of Rosse and Lennox?

ROSSE. What sights, my lord?

LADY MACBETH. I pray you speak not. He grows worse and worse,
Question enrages him. At once, good night.
Stand not upon the order of your going,[74]
But go at once.

LENNOX. Good night, and better health
Attend his Majesty!

LADY MACBETH. A kind good night to all!
Exeunt LORDS *and* ATTENDANTS.

MACBETH. It will have blood, they say; blood will have blood.

68. **Hyrcan.** From Hyrcania, a desert near the Caspian Sea
69. **that.** The shape of Banquo
70. **Desert.** Deserted area where nobody would intervene
71. **If . . . then.** If I feel fear then
72. **admir'd.** Attention-getting
73. **You . . . owe.** You make me feel like a stranger to the courageous person I thought I was.
74. **Stand . . . going.** Dispense with formality as you leave.

ANSWER TO GUIDED READING QUESTION

1. Lady Macbeth asks Rosse and Lennox not to speak any more to Macbeth because questioning worsens his condition.

LITERARY TECHNIQUE

IDIOM. Remind students that an **idiom** is an expression with a figurative meaning. Such an expression is often absurd if taken literally. In lines 118–119, Lady Macbeth says, "Stand not upon the order of your going,/But go at once." Normally, the most important members of the nobility would depart first and the least important members would follow; they would "stand" or wait until the proper order of their ranks had been observed before they left the room. Lady Macbeth urges the nobles to disregard their customary order and leave immediately. Explain to students that this phrase of Shakespeare's has become an idiom in English. It is now possible to say to a single individual, "Stand not upon the order of your going, but go"—a use that would have been absurd in Shakespeare's time. Students may research Shakespeare in a dictionary of quotations and find at least three examples of idioms derived from Shakespeare's plays.

After seeing the large contribution of Shakespeare to the idioms of the English language, students may appreciate the remark of an unknown wit to the effect that Shakespeare was not very original; he took most of his material out of *Bartlett's Dictionary of Quotations.*

ADDITIONAL QUESTIONS AND ACTIVITIES

Explain to students that an oracle is a person who answers a question asked by a seeker at certain holy sites (also called oracles). The answer, often cryptic in form, is usually a prediction of the future or a revelatory statement about something unknown in the present or past. The answers given by oracles are often phrased in ambiguous or equivocating language. Point out that Macbeth's remarks in lines 121–125 suggest a fear that some supernatural power will reveal his crimes. Students can write an oracular statement that reveals Macbeth's murder of Duncan and Banquo. Encourage them to make the statement mysterious and equivocating. If any students are familiar with *Œdipus Rex,* they might comment on the use of oracles in that play.

ANSWERS TO GUIDED READING QUESTIONS

1. Macbeth knows that Macduff is not home because he has placed a spy in the home of each of his nobles. The next day he plans to visit the witches to know his fate.
2. Hecate accuses Macbeth of being "Spiteful and wrathful."

LITERARY TECHNIQUE

CHARACTERIZATION. Characterization is the use of literary techniques to create character. Remind students of the strength of Lady Macbeth's character earlier in the play. At times she seemed a stronger figure than Macbeth; now, however, Macbeth is beginning to harden and strengthen—"We are yet but young in deed," he says (scene 4, line 143), promising to accustom himself to crime. At this point, Lady Macbeth and he are about equal in mental stamina. Later, Lady Macbeth will break down in madness, and Macbeth will resolve to fight to the bitter end (act 5, scene 5, line 51). In that respect, Scene 4 is the crisis for Macbeth and Lady Macbeth, the point at which he determines to press on; all she does is attempt to persuade him to rest.

Stones have been known to move and trees to speak;
Augures and understood relations[75] have
By maggot-pies and choughs[76] and rooks brought forth
The secret'st man of blood. What is the night?

LADY MACBETH. Almost at odds with morning, which is which.

MACBETH. How say'st thou, that Macduff denies his person
At our great bidding?

LADY MACBETH. Did you send to him, sir?

MACBETH. I hear it by the way; but I will send.
There's not a one of them but in his house
I keep a servant fee'd.[77] I will tomorrow
(And betimes I will) to the weïrd sisters.
More shall they speak; for now I am bent to know,
By the worst means, the worst. For mine own good
All causes shall give way. I am in blood
Stepp'd in so far that, should I wade no more,
Returning were as tedious as go o'er.
Strange things I have in head, that will to hand,
Which must be acted ere they may be scann'd.[78]

How does Macbeth know that Macduff is not at home? Where does he plan to go the next day?

LADY MACBETH. You lack the season[79] of all natures, sleep.

MACBETH. Come, we'll to sleep. My strange and self-abuse[80]
Is the initiate fear that wants hard use:
We are yet but young in deed.[81] *Exeunt.*

SCENE 5: the heath

Thunder. Enter the three WITCHES, *meeting* HECATE.

1. WITCH. Why, how now, Hecate? you look angerly.

HECATE. Have I not reason, beldams[82] as you are?
Saucy and overbold, how did you dare
To trade and traffic with Macbeth
In riddles and affairs of death;
And I, the mistress of your charms,
The close contriver[83] of all harms,
Was never call'd to bear my part,
Or show the glory of our art?
And which is worse, all you have done
Hath been but for a wayward son,
Spiteful and wrathful, who (as others do)

What does Hecate think of Macbeth?

75. **Augures . . . relations.** Omens and the meanings associated with them
76. **maggot-pies and choughs.** Magpies and crows
77. **fee'd.** Paid as a spy
78. **ere . . . scann'd.** Before they can be properly examined
79. **season.** Preservative
80. **strange and self-abuse.** Strange self-delusion
81. **young in deed.** Inexperienced in crime
82. **beldams.** Hags
83. **close contriver.** Secret inventor

Loves for his own ends, not for you.
But make amends now. Get you gone,
And at the pit of Acheron[84]
Meet me i' th' morning; thither he
Will come to know his destiny.
Your vessels and your spells provide,
Your charms and every thing beside.
I am for th' air; this night I'll spend
Unto a dismal and a fatal end.
Great business must be wrought ere noon:
Upon the corner of the moon
There hangs a vap'rous drop profound,
I'll catch it ere it come to ground;
And that, distill'd by magic sleights,
Shall raise such artificial sprites
As by the strength of their illusion
Shall draw him on to his confusion.[85]
He shall spurn fate, scorn death, and bear
His hopes 'bove wisdom, grace, and fear;
And you all know, security[86]
Is mortals' chiefest enemy.

Music, and a song. Sing within: "Come away, come away, etc."

Hark, I am call'd; my little spirit, see,
Sits in a foggy cloud, and stays for me. *Exit.*

What will Macbeth spurn and scorn as he pursues his hopes? What does Hecate sugggest is Macbeth's worst enemy?

1. WITCH. Come, let's make haste, she'll soon be back again. *Exeunt.*

SCENE 6: a place in Scotland

Enter LENNOX *and another* LORD.

LENNOX. My former speeches have but hit your thoughts,
Which can interpret farther;[87] only I say
Things have been strangely borne.[88] The gracious Duncan
Was pitied of Macbeth; marry, he was dead.
And the right valiant Banquo walk'd too late,
Whom you may say (if't please you) Fleance kill'd,
For Fleance fled. Men must not walk too late.
Who cannot want the thought,[89] how monstrous
It was for Malcolm and for Donalbain
To kill their gracious father? Damned fact!
How it did grieve Macbeth! Did he not straight
In pious rage the two delinquents tear,

84. **pit of Acheron.** Place of a passage through the earth to Hell
85. **confusion.** Ruin
86. **security.** False sense of security; overconfidence
87. **interpret farther.** Draw more conclusions
88. **borne.** Handled
89. **Who . . . thought.** Who can help thinking

ANSWER TO GUIDED READING QUESTION

1. He will spurn fate and scorn death. She suggests his worst enemy is his overconfidence.

ADDITIONAL QUESTIONS AND ACTIVITIES

- Ask students what is striking or unusual about Hecate's speech. If they do not notice that it is in a shorter line of four iambic feet, in rhyming couplets, instead of in blank verse, have them read it out loud. Point out that most of the witches' speeches are in this verse form.
- Have students read lines 10–13, part of Hecate's speech to the three witches. Ask the following questions:
  1. Of what does Hecate accuse Macbeth?
  2. What other character in the play might accuse Macbeth of this fault (if he could)?
  3. Do you agree with Hecate's assessment of Macbeth's character?

Answers

1. She accuses him of ingratitude, of loving for his own ends.
2. Duncan would accuse Macbeth of ingratitude.
3. Responses will vary, but the charge of ingratitude can easily be supported.

LITERARY TECHNIQUE

VERBAL IRONY. Verbal irony occurs when a statement is made that implies its opposite. Ask students whether Lennox is speaking sincerely when he says that it was "monstrous" of Malcolm and Donalbain to have killed their father and that Macbeth was grieved by their crime. They should recognize that Lennox's speech is ironic, or sarcastic, as opposed to sincere.

LITERARY NOTE

Some critics believe that scene 5, as well as other scenes in which the witches appear, were not written by Shakespeare but by some other author, who added these scenes to increase the length of the play. As evidence they point out that these scenes are written in a different style than that of the rest of the play. Some directors have simply cut this scene altogether. Ask students if they think scene 5 "fits" with the rest of the play. Is it essential to the play or does it seem like "filler"? Could it be cut?

ANSWERS TO GUIDED READING QUESTIONS

1. He refers to Macbeth as a tyrant.
2. Macduff has gone to England to raise troops for Malcolm.

SELECTION CHECK TEST 4.5.7 WITH ANSWERS

Checking Your Reading

1. Why is Macbeth worried about the witches' prophecy? **They predicted that Banquo's son would be king.**
2. What plan does Macbeth not share with Lady Macbeth? **He does not tell her of his plans to kill Banquo and Fleance.**
3. Who escapes the murderers' attack? **Fleance escapes.**
4. What apparition does Macbeth see at the feast? **He sees Banquo's ghost.**
5. Where has Macduff gone? **He has gone to England.**

Vocabulary in Context

Fill each blank with the most appropriate word from the Words for Everyday Use. You may have to change the tense of the word.

posterity verity dauntless jocund nonpareil malevolence

1. The baseball team gave their **nonpareil** center fielder a hefty bonus.
2. Although smaller than others, Kat is a **dauntless** competitor and never backs down.
3. The reporter's research supported the **verity** of the statements the witness made.
4. The atmosphere at the art show was **jocund** as the judges announced the winners.
5. Pat knew that the damage was not accidental, but had been done with **malevolence**.

Literary Tools

1. What happens to the protagonist of a tragedy following the crisis? **His fortunes fall.**
2. What occurrence do you think is the turning point in Macbeth? **Responses will vary, but could include when Macbeth hires murderers to kill Duncan and Fleance, when Macbeth sees the ghost at the banquet, or when Macduff leaves for England to support Malcolm.**
3. A reversal is a sudden change in the fortunes of a character. Identify a reversal in Act 3. **Macbeth undergoes a reversal when he acts oddly at the feast.**

That were the slaves of drink and thralls[90] of sleep?
Was not that nobly done? Aye, and wisely too;
For 'twould have anger'd any heart alive
To hear the men deny't. So that, I say,
He has borne all things well, and I do think
That had he Duncan's sons under his key
(As, and't please heaven, he shall not), they should find
What 'twere to kill a father; so should Fleance.
But peace! for from broad words,[91] and 'cause he fail'd
His presence at the tyrant's feast, I hear
Macduff lives in disgrace. Sir, can you tell
Where he bestows himself?

In line 22, how does Lennox refer to Macbeth?

LORD. The son of Duncan
(From whom this tyrant holds the due of birth)[92]
Lives in the English court, and is receiv'd
Of the most pious Edward[93] with such grace
That the <u>malevolence</u> of fortune nothing
Takes from his high respect. Thither Macduff
Is gone to pray the holy king, upon his aid[94]
To wake Northumberland and warlike Siward,
That by the help of these (with Him above
To ratify the work) we may again
Give to our tables meat, sleep to our nights;
Free from our feasts and banquets bloody knives;[95]
Do faithful homage and receive free honors;
All which we pine for now. And this report
Hath so exasperate the King[96] that he
Prepares for some attempt of war.

Why has Macduff gone to the English court?

LENNOX. Sent he to Macduff?

LORD. He did; and with an absolute "Sir, not I,"
The cloudy[97] messenger turns me his back,
And hums, as who should say, "You'll rue the time
That clogs me with this answer."[98]

90. **thralls.** Slaves
91. **Broad words.** Outspokenness
92. **Holds . . . birth.** Withholds the birthright; i.e., the crown
93. **Edward.** King Edward the Confessor (1003?–1066), considered to be a very saintly person
94. **upon his aid.** On Malcolm's behalf
95. **Free . . . knives.** Restore order so that violence is not a common occurrence at banquets
96. **the King.** Macbeth
97. **cloudy.** Surly, scowling
98. **hums . . . answer.** Harrumphs as if to say, "You'll regret making me waste my time trying to get an answer." (The messenger probably realizes that Macduff won't answer.)

WORDS FOR EVERYDAY USE

ma • lev • o • lence (mə lev´ə lens) *n.*, malice, spitefulness. *The villain of the murder mystery displayed his <u>malevolence</u> through an evil glare and wicked laugh.*

SELECTION CHECK TEST 4.5.7 WITH ANSWERS (CONT.)

4. Choose one of the following motifs and cite one way the motif is used in this act: sleep, madness, blood, ambition, or the supernatural. **Responses will vary.**
5. Who delivers the opening soliloquy, worrying that Macbeth has "play'dst most foully" to be king? **Banquo delivers this soliloquy.**

John Gielgud as Macbeth, 1942.

Lennox. And that well might
Advise him to a caution, t' hold what distance
His wisdom can provide.[99] Some holy angel
Fly to the court of England, and unfold
His message ere he come, that a swift blessing
May soon return to this our suffering country
Under a hand accurs'd!

What does Lennox now think of the ruling "hand" of Macbeth?

Lord. I'll send my prayers with him.

Exeunt.

99. **Advise him . . . provide.** Warn him to keep as far out of Macbeth's way as he can

Respond *to the* Selection

What do you think of the role Lady Macbeth has played in the action so far? Do you agree with Macbeth that she is more courageous than he? Explain.

ANSWER TO GUIDED READING QUESTION

1. Lennox thinks that Macbeth's ruling hand is "accurs'd."

LITERARY TECHNIQUE

Reversal. Explain to students that a **reversal** is a sudden change in the fortunes of a character, for good or bad. In *Macbeth,* such a reversal seems to occur during the banquet scene, when Macbeth disgraces himself in front of the assembled nobles. From this point on (beginning in scene 6), the audience hears more and more about the disaffection of the nobility. Lennox is the spokesman who explains the reversal to the audience. Ask students this question: Why might Shakespeare have chosen to present the reversal in ironic terms?

Answer

Responses will vary. Certainly the irony lends life and depth to the reversal; Lennox's commentary is not simply a flat, moralistic pronouncement that Macbeth is a wicked man who ought to die. It is sophisticated, witty, and all the more scathing for its understatement.

RESPOND TO THE SELECTION

Students will probably say that Lady Macbeth has so far been cruel and ruthless. She has pushed Macbeth to commit his terrible acts and tried to encourage him to feel no remorse. They may say that she is not more courageous than Macbeth, but instead perhaps more immoral.

ANSWERS TO INVESTIGATE, INQUIRE, AND IMAGINE

RECALL
1a. Banquo is killed; Fleance escapes.
2a. Macbeth sees Banquo's ghost sitting in Macbeth's chair.
3a. Macbeth says he has waded into blood so deep that going back would be as tedious, or difficult, as going on through it. This statement suggests that Macbeth will continue to kill those in his way.

INTERPRET
1b. Macbeth regrets that Fleance was not killed but consoles himself with the fact that Fleance is still young and incapable of harming him.
2b. The ghost may be the product of Macbeth's guilty conscience.
3b. Macbeth reacts with displeasure and suspicion. He seems to have planned to destroy Macduff. *Responses will vary.*

ANALYZE
4a. Lady Macbeth's words recall Macbeth's description of the phantom voice in act 2 that cried "Sleep no more!" Macbeth is cursed with sleeplessness because his guilt keeps him awake. Lack of sleep makes it more difficult for Macbeth to deal with his guilt and with the stress of carrying on as an unrighteous king.

SYNTHESIZE
4b. Macbeth admits that he cannot turn back (scene 4, lines 135–137). The speech of Lennox at the end of the play indicates that the other Scottish lords have realized Macbeth is to blame for Duncan's death and that they will not allow Macbeth to stay on the throne. Macbeth's vision of Banquo's ghost testifies to his increasing bouts of madness. The ghost is a symbol of the guilt he feels and his resultant despair.

EVALUATE
5a. *Responses will vary.*

EXTEND
5b. *Responses will vary.*

INVESTIGATE, Inquire, Imagine

Recall: GATHERING FACTS

1a. What is the result of the murder plot against Banquo and his son?
2a. What does Macbeth see at the banquet which no one else sees?
3a. What indication does Macbeth give, at the end of scene 4, that he will continue to kill anyone who stands in his path?

→ Interpret: FINDING MEANING

1b. What is Macbeth's reaction to the news of the outcome of the murder plot?
2b. Why is Macbeth the only one who sees this?
3b. How does Macbeth react to the news that Macduff refused to come to the feast? What do you think Macbeth has planned for Macduff? What do you think will happen to Macduff in the next act?

Analyze: TAKING THINGS APART

4a. Lady Macbeth says to her husband, "You lack the season of all natures, sleep." What lines of Macbeth's from act 2, scene 2 does her statement recall? Why can't Macbeth sleep, and what consequences does sleeplessness have for him?

→ Synthesize: BRINGING THINGS TOGETHER

4b. What indications are there in this act that Macbeth is on a course from which he cannot turn? What indications are there that this course will bring him to complete madness or despair?

Evaluate: MAKING JUDGMENTS

5a. The word "weird" is derived from the Old English word "wyrd," which means fate. It has been suggested by some critics that the predictions of the "weïrd sisters" represent Macbeth's fate, which arises out of his character. The witches do not cause it, they merely report it. Other critics have pointed out that Shakespeare's audience would have believed in witches and black magic and therefore we should see the witches as representations of evil that cause Macbeth's downfall. Which interpretation seems right to you? Be sure to provide reasons for your evaluation.

→ Extend: CONNECTING IDEAS

5b. Macbeth admits that "vaulting ambition" is the reason for his killing Duncan. Besides ambition, what other characteristics can lead to a character's downfall? Describe the downfall of a TV or movie character or a character from fiction. To what character trait do you attribute the character's downfall?

Understanding Literature

SIMILE. Review the definition for **simile** in the Handbook of Literary Terms. In scene 4, lines 20–21, Macbeth says, "I had else been perfect, / Whole as the marble, founded as the rock." What things are being compared in this simile? What traits do they have in common? Why is Macbeth not, at this point in the play, like a rock?

CLIMAX AND CRISIS. Review the definitions for **climax** and **crisis** in the Handbook of Literary Terms. In a

ANSWERS TO UNDERSTANDING LITERATURE

SIMILE. Macbeth is comparing himself to marble and rock embedded in the earth. His point is that he does not have much in common with the strength or rootedness of the marble or the rock because Fleance is still alive, and Macbeth has no assurance that his own offspring will continue his royal line.

CLIMAX AND CRISIS. The key event in act 3 is the banquet scene, in which Macbeth learns that Fleance has escaped and Macbeth confronts the ghost of Banquo. This forms a crisis because Macbeth's peculiar behavior casts him in a bad light, beginning the disaffection that culminates in Lennox's ironic

(Continued on page 427)

traditional five-act tragedy, the climax occurs in act 3. The crisis and the climax are often the same event. The fortunes of the protagonist improve steadily until the crisis is reached. Then they start to decline. What event in this act is a major blow for Macbeth, a reversal of his fortunes that may well bring about his downfall? What is the point of highest interest or suspense? Support your answers with evidence from the play. Bear in mind that readers and critics disagree about the answers to these questions.

Motif. Review the definition for **motif** in Literary Tools on page 410 and the cluster chart you made for Literary Tools. Discuss the motifs of ambition, deception, disturbances in nature, blood, madness, and sleep. How are these motifs interrelated?

Writer's Journal

1. Imagine you are Macbeth, needing a murderer. Write a **classified ad** to recruit the right person for the job of killing Banquo and his son.
2. Imagine you are a reporter present at the banquet and you witnessed the king's hysterical imaginings. Write an **article** about Macbeth's mental health. How did the king embarrass himself? In your opinion, is he fit to rule the kingdom? Whom would you support to replace Macbeth as ruler?
3. Imagine you are Macbeth. Write a **letter of apology** to one of the Scottish lords at the banquet. Be sure to provide some plausible explanation for the strange and incriminating things you said.

Integrating the Language Arts

Language, Grammar, and Style

Editing for Commas. Read the Language Arts Survey 3.87, "Commas." Then revise the sentences below, adding or deleting commas as necessary.

1. Shakespeare wrote *Macbeth,* for a royal performance before James I England's king.
2. James I was one of the Stuarts of Scotland a line of kings descended from Banquo.
3. James's mother was Mary Queen of Scots and his father was Lord Darnley.
4. Shakespeare's emphasis on the supernatural may have been in honor of King James who had an interest in the subject.
5. The fact that the king's brother-in-law the king of Denmark also attended the performance, may have influenced Shakespeare's decision to eliminate the detail of Denmark's defeat from the opening scene.

Speaking and Listening

Dramatic Interpretation. Scene 4 of act 3 is one of the most powerful depictions of terror and madness in Western literature. With several classmates, choose roles to enact in scene 4. Then read the Language Arts Survey 4.1, "Verbal and Nonverbal Communication" and decide on verbal and nonverbal elements to use in interpreting your role. Finally, after rehearsing, interpret scene 4 for your class.

Study and Research

Studying Transitions to Power. In medieval Europe, the death of a monarch frequently set off civil war between factions vying for the throne, sometimes even when there was a clear, legitimate successor. Research a European king or queen's transition to power. Then give an oral report on your findings to a small group of your classmates.

Answers to Understanding Literature (cont. from page 426)

comments in the last scene. The scene is also a crisis because Fleance's being alive is key to Banquo's progeny inheriting the throne instead of Macbeth's and possibly because it shows the beginning of Macbeth's final descent into irrecoverable madness and withdrawal from the world. The climax, it can be argued, is the same as the crisis. Students might also argue that the crisis is Macbeth's decision to continue on his bloody career or Macduff's departure for England to seek aid in overthrowing Macbeth.

Motif. The rise to power of Macbeth and Lady Macbeth illustrates the motif of ambition. Deception occurs in the witches' appearance as men, Macbeth hiding from Banquo the fact that he considers killing Duncan, Macbeth pretending to be a loving host to Duncan, the illusion of the dagger, Macbeth deciving Banquo and Macduff with double entendre ("Had I but died an hour before this chance, / I had liv'd a blessed time; for from this instant / There's nothing serious in mortality"), and Macbeth and Lady Macbeth masking their murderous hearts (act 3, scene 2, lines 33–34). The sounds heard on the night Duncan is murdered, the shaking of the earth, and the madness of his horses are examples of disturbances in the natural world. Blood is frequently mentioned (act 2, scene 2, lines 43–47, 52–54, 57–62; act 3, scene 4, lines 13, 74, 134–137). Macbeth shows signs of madness when he imagines the dagger before him (act 2, scene 1, lines 33–43), and he feigns madness as an excuse for his reaction to Banquo's ghost (act 3, scene 4, lines 84–86.) The motif of sleep is repeated often: Duncan and the groom are murdered in their sleep, and Macbeth hears a voice saying that he shall sleep no more (act 2, scene 2, lines 32–40). These motifs are all intricately interrelated because the course taken by Macbeth to fulfill his ambition comes as a result of the witches' prophecies and leads into disruption of the natural order and bloody murder, which in turn lead to disturbed sleep and madness.

Answers to Integrating the Language Arts

Language, Grammar, and Style

1. Shakespeare wrote *Macbeth* for a royal performance before James I, England's king.
2. James I was one of the Stuarts of Scotland, a line of kings descended from Banquo.
3. James's mother was Mary Queen of Scots, and his father was Lord Darnley.
4. Shakespeare's emphasis on the supernatural may have been in honor of King James, who had an interest in the subject.
5. The fact that the king's brother-in-law, the king of Denmark, also attended the performance may have influenced Shakespeare's decision to eliminate the detail of Denmark's defeat from the opening scene.

ADDITIONAL RESOURCES

Unit 5 Resource Book
- Selection Worksheet 5.4
- Selection Check Test 4.5.9
- Selection Test 4.5.10
- Language, Grammar, and Style Resource 3.38

ANSWER TO GUIDED READING QUESTION

1. The witches are cooking a "charm of pow'rful trouble."

GRAPHIC ORGANIZER

Students should recognize that the method of characterization used for Lady Macduff is portrayal of her behavior. In their cluster charts, students might note that Lady Macduff displays a sense of humor in her bantering with her son; she shows she does not fully understand the politics of the times which have forced her husband to leave his home, yet she shows she is aware that her husband is participating in traitorous activities and that she does not approve of her husband's choice; she shows a cynical knowledge that the world is not always kind to the innocent in her lines "I am in this earthly world—where to do harm / Is often laudable, to good sometime / Accounted dangerous folly" (lines 72–74).

READER'S JOURNAL

Students should write about character traits or behaviors that support predictions about their lives.

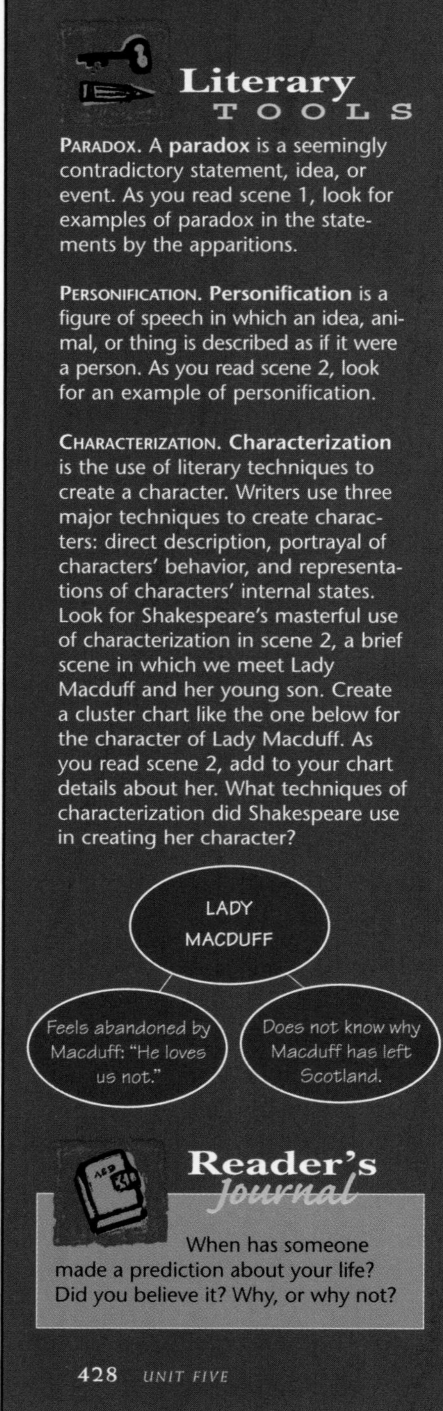

Literary TOOLS

Paradox. A **paradox** is a seemingly contradictory statement, idea, or event. As you read scene 1, look for examples of paradox in the statements by the apparitions.

Personification. **Personification** is a figure of speech in which an idea, animal, or thing is described as if it were a person. As you read scene 2, look for an example of personification.

Characterization. **Characterization** is the use of literary techniques to create a character. Writers use three major techniques to create characters: direct description, portrayal of characters' behavior, and representations of characters' internal states. Look for Shakespeare's masterful use of characterization in scene 2, a brief scene in which we meet Lady Macduff and her young son. Create a cluster chart like the one below for the character of Lady Macduff. As you read scene 2, add to your chart details about her. What techniques of characterization did Shakespeare use in creating her character?

Reader's Journal

When has someone made a prediction about your life? Did you believe it? Why, or why not?

ACT 4

SCENE 1: a cave

Thunder. Enter the three Witches.

1. Witch. Thrice the brinded[1] cat hath mew'd.

2. Witch. Thrice, and once the hedge-pig whin'd.

3. Witch. Harpier[2] cries, " 'Tis time, 'tis time."

1. Witch. Round about the cauldron go;
In the poison'd entrails throw;
Toad, that under cold stone
Days and nights has thirty-one
Swelt'red venom sleeping got,
Boil thou first i' th' charmed pot.

All. Double, double, toil and trouble;
Fire burn, and cauldron bubble.

2. Witch. Fillet of a fenny snake,[3]
In the cauldron boil and bake;
Eye of newt and toe of frog,
Wool of bat and tongue of dog,
Adder's fork and blind-worm's[4] sting,
Lizard's leg and howlet's[5] wing,
For a charm of pow'rful trouble,
Like a hell-broth boil and bubble.

What are the witches cooking?

All. Double, double, toil and trouble;
Fire burn, and cauldron bubble.

3. Witch. Scale of dragon, tooth of wolf,
Witch's mummy,[6] maw and gulf
Of the ravin'd salt-sea shark,[7]
Root of hemlock digg'd i' th' dark,
Liver of blaspheming Jew,[8]
Gall of goat, and slips of yew
Sliver'd in the moon's eclipse,
Nose of Turk and Tartar's lips,[9]

1. **brinded.** Brindled, striped
2. **Harpier.** The third witch's spirit
3. **fenny snake.** Swamp snake
4. **blind-worm.** Small legless lizard
5. **howlet.** Small owl
6. **Witch's mummy.** Medicinal substance made from parts of a mummy
7. **Maw . . . shark.** Stomach and gullet of the voracious shark
8. **Liver . . . Jew.** This line reflects anti-Semitic attitudes that existed in Shakespeare's England.
9. **Nose . . . lips.** This line reflects a similar prejudice against Turkish people and natives of Eastern Europe and Asia.

VOCABULARY FROM THE SELECTION

abjure	impediment
confineless	pernicious
doff	stanchless
homely	teem

The Witches in Macbeth, c.1941–42. Alexandre Gabriel Decamps. Wallace Collection, London.

Finger of birth-strangled babe
Ditch-deliver'd by a drab,
Make the gruel thick and slab.
Add thereto a tiger's chawdron,[10]
For th' ingredience of our cau'dron.

ALL. Double, double, toil and trouble;
Fire burn, and cauldron bubble.

2. WITCH. Cool it with a baboon's blood,
Then the charm is firm and good.

Enter HECATE *and the other three* WITCHES.

HECATE. O, well done! I commend your pains,
And every one shall share i' th' gains.
And now about the cauldron sing,
Like elves and fairies in a ring,
Enchanting all that you put in.

Music and a song: "Black spirits, etc." *Exeunt* HECATE *and singers.*

2. WITCH. By the pricking of my thumbs,

10. **chawdron.** Entrails

ADDITIONAL QUESTIONS AND ACTIVITIES

Have students read carefully the incantation at the beginning of act 4, scene 1, and list the ingredients named in it. Then ask them these questions:

1. What are the commonly held views about these ingredients?
2. How do the characteristics of the creatures named reflect on the magic of the witches and in turn on Macbeth?

Answers

1. Many of the creatures are reptiles, amphibians, and other "low" creatures often considered cold and repulsive (toad, snake, newt, frog, adder, blind-worm, lizard). A few are animals with a reputation for being dangerous (dragon, wolf, shark, tiger, baboon). Others are associated with darkness and horror (bat, howlet). The hemlock is known to be poisonous.
2. These characteristics suggest that the witches' magic, and Macbeth's indirect use of it, promotes repulsive, dangerous, and horrible acts.

ADDITIONAL VOCABULARY

Act 4
entrails—intestines
exploits—deeds, adventures
judicious—prudent
prattler—one who babbles
laudable—praiseworthy, honorable
redress—remedy
transpose—reverse
hoodwink—fool
verity—truth
credulous—trusting
rend—tear
pertain—have to do with

CROSS-CURRICULAR CONNECTIONS

ARTS AND HUMANITIES. Shakespeare frequently called for a certain song to be played or sung without giving more than the title or first line. Here and in Act 3, Scene 5, he specified two songs known from another play, *Witches,* by Thomas Middleton (1570?–1627). The first lines of the song "Black Spirits" are "Black spirits and white, red spirits and gray,/Mingle, mingle, mingle, you that mingle may!" Though Middleton also used the songs, it is not clear who composed them. Scholars believe that *Witches* was written after *Macbeth,* but that may only mean that Middleton took a hint from Shakespeare and borrowed from the same source.

CROSS-CURRICULAR ACTIVITIES

APPLIED ARTS. Have students imagine that they work for a company that produces special effects for movie directors. A famous director of films about creatures from outer space and dinosaurs is planning to do a new film version of *Macbeth* and wants special effects for the witches' scenes in act 4. Have students draw up plans for the special effects to be used in these scenes. Students may write descriptions, do illustrations, or both. You may wish to have students do some library research on special effects techniques currently used in the cinema, including claymation, animatronics, and 3-D computer graphics. However, it isn't necessary for students to know these technologies in order to do the activity: as special effects designers, they can simply describe the effects they want and depend upon technicians to carry out their ideas.

Something wicked this way comes. (*Knocking.*)
Open, locks,
Whoever knocks!

Enter MACBETH.

MACBETH. How now, you secret, black, and midnight hags?
What is't you do?

ALL. A deed without a name.

MACBETH. I conjure you, by that which you profess[11]
(How e'er you come to know it), answer me:
Though you untie the winds, and let them fight
Against the churches; though the yesty[12] waves
Confound[13] and swallow navigation up;
Though bladed corn be lodg'd,[14] and trees blown down;
Though castles topple on their warders' heads;
Though palaces and pyramids do slope
Their heads to their foundations; though the treasure
Of nature's germains[15] tumble all together,
Even till destruction sicken; answer me
To what I ask you.

1. WITCH. Speak.

2. WITCH. Demand.

3. WITCH. We'll answer.

1. WITCH. Say, if th' hadst rather hear it from our mouths,
Or from our masters'?

MACBETH. Call 'em; let me see 'em.

1. WITCH. Pour in sow's blood, that hath eaten
Her nine farrow;[16] grease that's sweaten
From the murderer's gibbet[17] throw
Into the flame.

ALL. Come high or low;
Thyself and office deftly show!

Thunder. FIRST APPARITION, *an* ARMED HEAD.[18]

MACBETH. Tell me, thou unknown power—

1. WITCH. He knows thy thought:
Hear his speech, but say thou nought.

1. APPARITION. Macbeth! Macbeth! Macbeth! beware Macduff,

11. **that . . . profess.** Your witchcraft
12. **yesty.** Foamy
13. **Confound.** Destroy
14. **bladed . . . lodg'd.** Ripe wheat is beaten down
15. **germains.** Seeds
16. **nine farrow.** Nine offspring
17. **gibbet.** Gallows where executed criminals were left hanging as a warning
18. **armed Head.** Signifies Macduff

Beware the Thane of Fife. Dismiss me. Enough. *He descends.*

Macbeth. What e'er thou art, for thy good caution, thanks;
Thou hast harp'd[19] my fear aright. But one word more—

What does the first apparition warn Macbeth?

1. Witch. He will not be commanded. Here's another,
More potent than the first.

Thunder. Second Apparition, *a* bloody Child.[20]

2. Apparition. Macbeth! Macbeth! Macbeth!

Macbeth. Had I three ears, I'ld hear thee.

2. Apparition. Be bloody, bold, and resolute: laugh to scorn
The pow'r of man; for none of woman born
Shall harm Macbeth. *Descends.*

What prophecy does the second apparition make?

Macbeth. Then live, Macduff; what need I fear of thee?
But yet I'll make assurance double sure,
And take a bond of fate:[21] thou shalt not live,
That I may tell pale-hearted fear it lies,
And sleep in spite of thunder.

Thunder. Third Apparition, *a* Child crowned, *with a tree in his hand.*[22]

What is this
That rises like the issue of a king,
And wears upon his baby-brow the round
And top of sovereignty?[23]

All. Listen, but speak not to't.

3. Apparition. Be lion-mettled, proud, and take no care
Who chafes, who frets, or where conspirers are:
Macbeth shall never vanquish'd be until
Great Birnan wood to high Dunsinane hill
Shall come against him. *Descends.*

What does the third apparition foresee?

Macbeth. That will never be.
Who can impress[24] the forest, bid the tree
Unfix his earth-bound root? Sweet bodements![25] good!
Rebellious dead, rise never till the wood
Of Birnan rise, and our high-plac'd Macbeth
Shall live the lease of nature,[26] pay his breath
To time and mortal custom.[27] Yet my heart
Throbs to know one thing: tell me, if your art
Can tell so much, shall Banquo's issue ever
Reign in this kingdom?

What does Macbeth want to know?

All. Seek to know no more.

19. **harp'd.** Hit upon
20. **bloody Child.** Signifies Macduff at birth
21. **bond of fate.** Force fate to keep the agreement to kill Macduff
22. **Child . . . hand.** Signifies Malcolm and foreshadows Malcolm's soldiers carrying boughs to Dunsinane
23. **round . . . sovereignty.** The crown
24. **impress.** Force into service
25. **bodements.** Prophecies
26. **lease of nature.** Natural life span
27. **mortal custom.** Natural death

ADDITIONAL QUESTIONS AND ACTIVITIES

- The statements of two of the apparitions, the second and third, read like riddles. If students have not read to the end of the play by the time of the discussion on this passage, ask them to try to "solve" the riddles. How could someone not be "of woman born"? How could a forest move?
- Students can write their own riddles based on a current event. For instance, they may wish to predict the outcome of an election or a trial.
- Have students share riddles they may remember from childhood or have found in books. When they have become familiar with the form of the riddle, students might try their hand at writing their own riddle.

ANSWERS TO GUIDED READING QUESTIONS

1. The first apparition warns Macbeth to beware of Macduff.
2. The second apparition tells Macbeth that "none of woman born / Shall harm Macbeth."
3. The third apparition foresees that "Macbeth shall never vanquish'd be until / Great Birnan wood to high Dunsinane hill / Shall come against him."
4. Macbeth wants to know if Banquo's descendents will reign over Scotland.

ADDITIONAL QUESTIONS AND ACTIVITIES

Use the accompanying graphic organizer to demonstrate the rise and fall of Macbeth's hopes as he listens to the apparitions in scene 1.

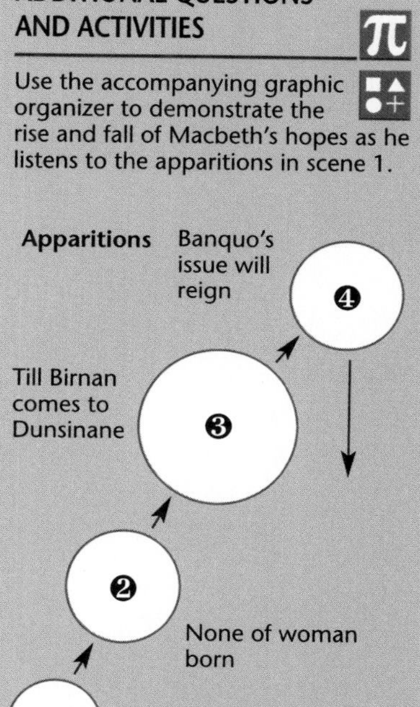

LITERARY TECHNIQUE

Symbol. A **symbol** is a thing that stands for or represents both itself and something else. Students can devise new symbols to represent each of the first three apparitions. The first, for instance, might be a tower carrying a sword, representing Fife, Macduff's castle; the second might be a man carrying an infant in his arms; the third might be a tree carrying a crown.

ANSWER TO GUIDED READING QUESTION

1. Macbeth learns that Banquo's descendants will rule Scotland.

CROSS-CURRICULAR CONNECTIONS

HISTORY. James I, who was king at the time Shakespeare wrote *Macbeth,* was a descendant of Banquo. The "twofold balls" symbolize the fact that he was crowned twice, once as King James VI of Scotland, and again when he became James I of England. As noted in the footnote, the "treble sceptres" symbolize Ireland, Scotland, and England, the three countries that were united under the rule of James I.

MACBETH. I will be satisfied. Deny me this,
And an eternal curse fall on you! Let me know.
Why sinks that cauldron? and what noise[28] is this? (*Hoboys.*)[29]

1. WITCH. Show!

2. WITCH. Show!

3. WITCH. Show!

ALL. Show his eyes, and grieve his heart;
Come like shadows, so depart.

A show of eight KINGS, *the eighth with a glass*[30] *in his hand, and* BANQUO *last.*

MACBETH. Thou art too like the spirit of Banquo; down!
Thy crown does sear mine eyeballs. And thy hair,
Thou other gold-bound brow, is like the first.
A third is like the former. Filthy hags,
Why do you show me this?—A fourth? Start, eyes!
What, will the line stretch out to th' crack of doom?
Another yet? A seventh? I'll see no more.
And yet the eighth appears, who bears a glass
Which shows me many more; and some I see
That twofold balls and treble sceptres[31] carry.
Horrible sight! Now I see 'tis true,
For the blood-bolter'd[32] Banquo smiles upon me,
And points at them for his. APPARITIONS *vanish.*
What? is this so?

What does Macbeth learn from the vision?

1. WITCH. Aye, sir, all this is so. But why
Stands Macbeth thus amazedly?
Come, sisters, cheer we up his sprites,[33]
And show the best of our delights.
I'll charm the air to give a sound,
While you perform your antic round;[34]
That this great king may kindly say
Our duties did his welcome pay.

Music. The WITCHES *dance and vanish.*

MACBETH. Where are they? Gone? Let this pernicious hour

28. **noise.** Music
29. **Hoboys.** Oboes
30. **show . . . glass.** A silent procession of eight kings, the last holding a mirror
31. **twofold . . . sceptres.** English coronation regalia. The treble sceptres also symbolize Ireland, Scotland, and England, united when James VI of Scotland became James I of England.
32. **blood-bolter'd.** Hair matted with blood
33. **sprites.** Spirits
34. **antic round.** Fantastic circular dance

WORDS FOR EVERYDAY USE

per • ni • cious (pər nish´əs) *adj.,* causing ruin and death. *The novelist disdainfully viewed his critics as pernicious foes of truth and art.*

Stand aye accursed in the calendar!
Come in, without there!

Enter LENNOX.

LENNOX. What's your Grace's will?

MACBETH. Saw you the weïrd sisters?

LENNOX. No, my lord.

MACBETH. Came they not by you?

LENNOX. No indeed, my lord.

MACBETH. Infected be the air whereon they ride,
And damn'd all those that trust them! I did hear
The galloping of horse. Who was't came by?

LENNOX. 'Tis two or three, my lord, that bring you word
Macduff is fled to England.

MACBETH. Fled to England!

LENNOX. Aye, my good lord.

MACBETH. [*Aside.*] Time, thou anticipat'st my dread exploits:
The flighty purpose never is o'ertook
Unless the deed go with it.[35] From this moment
The very firstlings[36] of my heart shall be
The firstlings of my hand. And even now,
To crown my thoughts with acts, be it thought and done:
The castle of Macduff I will surprise,
Seize upon Fife, give to th' edge o' th' sword
His wife, his babes, and all unfortunate souls
That trace[37] him in his line. No boasting like a fool;
This deed I'll do before this purpose cool.
But no more sights!—Where are these gentlemen?
Come bring me where they are. *Exeunt.*

What does Macbeth decide to do?

SCENE 2: MACDUFF'S castle in Fife

Enter MACDUFF'S WIFE, *her* SON, *and* ROSSE.

LADY MACDUFF. What had he done, to make him fly the land?

ROSSE. You must have patience, madam.

LADY MACDUFF. He had none;
His flight was madness. When our actions do not,
Our fears do make us traitors.

ROSSE. You know not
Whether it was his wisdom or his fear.

35. **flighty . . . it.** Purpose is always fleeing unless it is done immediately.

36. **firstlings.** First-born (first thoughts; impulses)

37. **trace.** Follow

ANSWER TO GUIDED READING QUESTION

1. Macbeth decides to kill Macduff's wife and children.

ANSWER TO GUIDED READING QUESTION

1. Lady Macduff is concerned that her son has no father.

LITERARY NOTE

Some scholars believe that line 23 should actually read "Each way and none" and that it was copied down incorrectly.

CROSS-CURRICULAR ACTIVITIES

Arts and Humanities. The forlorn loneliness of Lady Macduff is sketched at great length in scene ii. It creates a sense of her pathetic and helpless state and shows the new and dark depths to which Macbeth is sinking in murdering her and her children. Because the fear of abandonment is such a common human experience, nearly everyone can identify with her feelings to some extent. Students can work together in small groups to portray the abandonment of Lady Macduff in another artistic medium—mime, dance, or music, for instance. Students should also note the increasing infamy of Macbeth's deeds: from being personally involved in murdering Duncan, to hiring murderers to kill Banquo, to hiring murderers to kill innocent women and children. He successively, but unsuccessfully, attempts to distance himself from the murders for which he is responsible.

Lady Macduff. Wisdom? to leave his wife, to leave his babes,
His mansion and his titles,[38] in a place
From whence himself does fly? He loves us not,
He wants the natural touch;[39] for the poor wren,
The most diminutive of birds, will fight,
Her young ones in her nest, against the owl.
All is the fear, and nothing is the love;
As little is the wisdom, where the flight
So runs against all reason.

Rosse. My dearest coz,[40]
I pray you school[41] yourself. But for your husband,
He is noble, wise, judicious, and best knows
The fits o' th' season.[42] I dare not speak much further,
But cruel are the times when we are traitors,
And do not know ourselves;[43] when we hold rumor
From what we fear, yet know not what we fear,
But float upon a wild and violent sea
Each way, and move. I take my leave of you;
'Shall not be long but I'll be here again.
Things at the worst will cease, or else climb upward
To what they were before. My pretty cousin,
Blessing upon you!

Lady Macduff. Father'd he is, and yet he's fatherless.

What is Lady Macduff's concern?

Rosse. I am so much a fool, should I stay longer,
It would be my disgrace and your discomfort.
I take my leave at once. *Exit* Rosse.

Lady Macduff. Sirrah, your father's dead,
And what will you do now? How will you live?

Son. As birds do, mother.

Lady Macduff. What, with worms and flies?

Son. With what I get, I mean, and so do they.

Lady Macduff. Poor bird, thou'dst never fear the net nor lime,[44]
The pitfall nor the gin.[45]

Son. Why should I, mother? Poor birds they are not set for.
My father is not dead, for all your saying.

Lady Macduff. Yes, he is dead. How wilt thou do for a father?

Son. Nay, how will you do for a husband?

Lady Macduff. Why, I can buy me twenty at any market.

38. **titles.** Properties
39. **wants . . . touch.** Lacks natural feelings toward his family
40. **coz.** Cousin, kin
41. **school.** Control
42. **fits . . . season.** Disturbances of the time
43. **know ourselves.** Recognize ourselves as traitors
44. **lime.** Birdlime, used to catch birds
45. **gin.** Snare

SON. Then you'll buy 'em to sell[46] again.

LADY MACDUFF. Thou speak'st with all thy wit, and yet, i' faith,
With wit enough for thee.[47]

SON. Was my father a traitor, mother?

LADY MACDUFF. Aye, that he was.

SON. What is a traitor?

LADY MACDUFF. Why, one that swears and lies.

SON. And be all traitors that do so?

LADY MACDUFF. Every one that does so is a traitor, and must be hang'd.

SON. And must they all be hang'd that swear and lie?

LADY MACDUFF. Every one.

SON. Who must hang them?

LADY MACDUFF. Why, the honest men.

SON. Then the liars and swearers are fools; for there are liars and swearers enow[48] to beat the honest men and hang up them.

LADY MACDUFF. Now God help thee, poor monkey! But how wilt thou do for a father?

SON. If he were dead, you'ld weep for him; if you would not, it were a good sign that I should quickly have a new father.

LADY MACDUFF. Poor prattler, how thou talk'st!

Enter a MESSENGER.

MESSENGER. Bless you, fair dame! I am not to you known
Though in your state of honor I am perfect.[49]
I doubt[50] some danger does approach you nearly.
If you will take a homely man's advice,
Be not found here; hence with your little ones.
To fright you thus, methinks I am too savage;
To do worse to you were fell[51] cruelty,
Which is too nigh your person. Heaven preserve you!
I dare abide no longer. *Exit* MESSENGER.

What warning does the messenger bring?

LADY MACDUFF. Whither should I fly?
I have done no harm. But I remember now

46. **sell.** Betray
47. **With . . . thee.** You are clever for a child.
48. **enow.** Enough
49. **in . . . perfect.** I know you are an honored person.
50. **doubt.** Fear
51. **fell.** Savage

WORDS FOR EVERYDAY USE

home • ly (hōm′ lē) *adj.*, simple, unpretentious. *Though the house seemed sterile and bleak from the outside, inside it was made warm by comfortable, homely furnishings.*

ANSWER TO GUIDED READING QUESTION

1. The messenger tells Lady Macduff that she and her children should flee the castle.

ADDITIONAL QUESTIONS AND ACTIVITIES

Ask the following questions to probe the dynamics of scene 2:

1. In lines 22–26, Rosse tries to tell Lady Macduff he is leaving. What is her reaction? Why does she react in this way?
2. Study Rosse's final speech to Lady Macduff. What are Rosse's feelings about her? How can you tell? How does the reference to his feelings further the plot?
3. Why does Lady Macduff repeatedly say things to her son that seem cruel (e.g., telling him that Macduff is dead and that he is a traitor)?

Answers

1. Lady Macduff ignores Rosse's hint that he is leaving. She seems to be reluctant to see him go or is so preoccupied by Macduff's abandonment of her that she pays no attention.
2. Two possible interpretations of Rosse's comments are possible. One is that Rosse is attracted to Lady Macduff, so infatuated that if he stays longer he will disgrace himself and make her uncomfortable, presumably by making some advance that he should not make. Another common interpretation is that Rosse is so overcome with feelings for Lady Macbeth's plight that he fears breaking down in tears and thereby disgracing himself and causing her discomfort. The reference to Rosse's feelings explains why he feels driven to depart and is thus out of the way when the murderers arrive.
3. She seems to want someone to contradict her; her son senses this and readily offers witty contradictions.

ANSWERS TO GUIDED READING QUESTIONS

1. Lady Macduff and her son are killed by the murderers.
2. Malcolm worries that Macduff may betray him.

I am in this earthly world—where to do harm
Is often laudable, to do good sometime
Accounted dangerous folly. Why then, alas,
Do I put up that womanly defense,
To say I have done no harm?

Enter MURDERERS.

What are these faces?

1. MURDERER. Where is your husband?

LADY MACDUFF. I hope, in no place so unsanctified
Where such as thou mayst find him.

1. MURDERER. He's a traitor.

SON. Thou li'st, thou shag-ear'd villain!

1. MURDERER. What, you egg![52] *Stabbing him.*
Young fry of treachery!

SON. He has kill'd me, mother:
Run away, I pray you! [*Dies.*]

Exit LADY MACDUFF *crying* "Murther!" *and pursued by the* MURDERERS

What happens to Lady Macduff and her son?

SCENE 3: England, the king's palace

Enter MALCOLM *and* MACDUFF.

MALCOLM. Let us seek out some desolate shade, and there
Weep our sad bosoms empty.

MACDUFF. Let us rather
Hold fast the mortal sword, and like good men
Bestride our downfall birthdom.[53] Each new morn
New widows howl, new orphans cry, new sorrows
Strike heaven on the face, that it resounds
As if it felt with Scotland, and yell'd out
Like syllable of dolor.[54]

MALCOLM. What I believe, I'll wail,
What know, believe; and what I can redress,
As I shall find the time to friend,[55] I will
What you have spoke, it may be so perchance.
This tyrant, whose sole name blisters our tongues,
Was once thought honest;[56] you have lov'd him well;
He hath not touch'd you yet. I am young, but something
You may discern of him through me, and wisdom[57]

What possibility worries Malcolm?

52. **egg.** Traitor to be
53. **Bestride . . . birthdom.** Fight to protect our downfallen country
54. **Like . . . dolor.** A similar shout of pain
55. **to friend.** Favorable
56. **honest.** Honorable
57. **You . . . wisdom.** You may see a way to help yourself by betraying me; it is the worldly way.

To offer up a weak, poor, innocent lamb
T' appease an angry god.

MACDUFF. I am not treacherous.

MALCOLM. But Macbeth is.
A good and virtuous nature may recoil
In an imperial charge.[58] But I shall crave your pardon;
That which you are, my thoughts cannot transpose:
Angels are bright still, though the brightest[59] fell.
Though all things foul would wear the brows of grace,
Yet grace must still look so.[60]

MACDUFF. I have lost my hopes.

MALCOLM. Perchance even there where I did find my doubts.
Why in that rawness[61] left you wife and child,
Those precious motives,[62] those strong knots of love,
Without leave-taking? I pray you,
Let not my jealousies be your dishonors,
But mine own safeties.[63] You may be rightly just,
What ever I shall think.

What action of Macduff's causes Malcolm to suspect he may be in league with Macbeth?

MACDUFF. Bleed, bleed, poor country!
Great tyranny, lay thou thy basis sure,
For goodness dare not check thee; wear thou thy wrongs,
The title is affeer'd![64] Fare thee well, lord,
I would not be the villain that thou think'st
For the whole space that's in the tyrant's grasp,
And the rich East to boot.

MALCOLM. Be not offended;
I speak not as in absolute fear of you.
I think our country sinks beneath the yoke:
It weeps, it bleeds, and each new day a gash
Is added to her wounds. I think withal
There would be hands uplifted in my right;
And here from gracious England[65] have I offer
Of goodly thousands. But, for all this,
When I shall tread upon the tyrant's head,
Or wear it on my sword, yet my poor country
Shall have more vices than it had before,
More suffer, and more sundry ways than ever,
By him that shall succeed.

MACDUFF. What should he be?

58. **imperial charge.** Order from the king
59. **the brightest.** Lucifer
60. **Though . . . so.** Even if wickedness takes on the appearance of virtue, virtue must keep its appearance.
61. **rawness.** Unprotected state
62. **motives.** People who inspire your love and protection
63. **Let . . . safeties.** My suspicions are not meant to dishonor you, but rather to protect me.
64. **affeer'd.** Confirmed
65. **England.** The King of England, Edward the Confessor

ANSWER TO GUIDED READING QUESTION

1. Because Macduff left his wife and children alone in Scotland, suggesting he does not fear that Macbeth will harm them, Malcolm fears that Macduff is in league with Macbeth.

ADDITIONAL QUESTIONS AND ACTIVITIES

Students can create a diagram to indicate the logic of the dialogue between Malcolm and Macduff in scene 3, lines 1–37. (See accompanying sample diagram.)

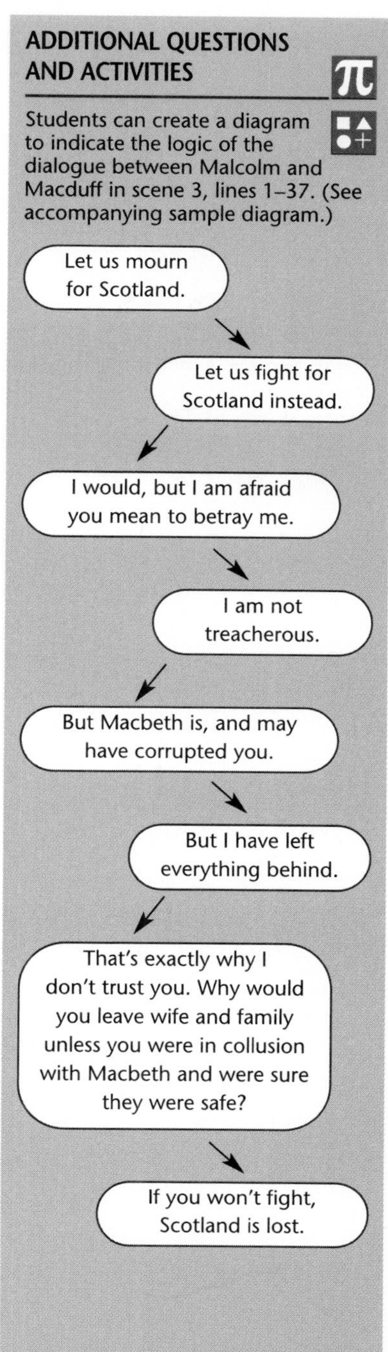

ANSWERS TO GUIDED READING QUESTIONS

1. Malcolm says his lustfulness will make him an unfit king.
2. Malcolm confesses that he is greedy.

ADDITIONAL QUESTIONS AND ACTIVITIES

The conversation between Malcolm and Macduff in lines 60–114 is a prolonged test of Macduff's character. Students can restate it in the form of a written test or questionnaire. It might begin with the following question: "Do you believe that a king who is prone to voluptuousness would be better than Macbeth?" Each separate speech of Malcolm in lines 60–99 should be represented by one question.

After students have composed their tests, each can trade with a partner and answer the test in the character of Macduff. Their answers should parallel the initial rationalizations and eventual despair and disgust of Macduff in his replies in lines 66–114.

MALCOLM. It is myself I mean; in whom I know
All the particulars of vice so grafted
That, when they shall be open'd, black Macbeth
Will seem as pure as snow, and the poor state
Esteem him as a lamb, being compar'd
With my confineless harms.

MACDUFF. Not in the legions
Of horrid hell can come a devil more damn'd
In evils to top Macbeth.

MALCOLM. I grant him bloody,
Luxurious,[66] avaricious, false, deceitful,
Sudden, malicious, smacking of every sin
That has a name; but there's no bottom, none,
In my voluptuousness. Your wives, your daughters,
Your matrons, and your maids could not fill up
The cestern of my lust, and my desire
All continent impediments would o'erbear
That did oppose my will. Better Macbeth
Than such an one to reign.

What weakness does Malcolm say will make him an unfit king?

MACDUFF. Boundless intemperance
In nature is a tyranny; it hath been
Th' untimely emptying of the happy throne,
And fall of many kings. But fear not yet
To take upon you what is yours. You may
Convey your pleasures in a spacious plenty,[67]
And yet seem cold,[68] the time you may so hoodwink.
We have willing dames enough; there cannot be
That vulture in you to devour so many
As will to greatness dedicate themselves,
Finding it so inclin'd.

MALCOLM. With this, there grows
In my most ill-compos'd affection[69] such
A stanchless avarice that, were I king,
I should cut off the nobles for their lands,
Desire his jewels, and this other's house,
And my more-having would be as a sauce

What other weakness does Malcolm confess to Macduff?

66. **Luxurious.** Lustful
67. **Convey . . . plenty.** Find plenty of space to indulge secretly in your pleasures
68. **cold.** Chaste
69. **ill-composed affection.** Immoral character

WORDS FOR EVERYDAY USE

con • fine • less (kən fīn´ləs) *adj.*, limitless. *Many astronomers believe that the universe, while not infinite, is confineless.*
im • ped • i • ment (im ped´ə mənt) *n.*, obstacle. *Jim's dyslexia was an impediment to his studying.*
stanch • less or **staunch • less** (stônch´ləs) *adj.*, unstoppable. *Environmentalists protested what they said was a stanchless flow of pollutants into the Mediterranean Sea.*

To make me hunger more, that I should forge
Quarrels unjust against the good and loyal,
Destroying them for wealth.

MACDUFF. This avarice
Sticks deeper, grows with more pernicious root
Than summer-seeming[70] lust; and it hath been
The sword of our slain kings. Yet do not fear,
Scotland hath foisons[71] to fill up your will
Of your mere own.[72] All these are portable,[73]
With other graces weigh'd.

MALCOLM. But I have none. The king-becoming graces,
As justice, verity, temp'rance, stableness,
Bounty, perseverance, mercy, lowliness,
Devotion, patience, courage, fortitude,
I have no relish of them, but abound
In the division of each several crime,
Acting it many ways. Nay, had I pow'r, I should
Pour the sweet milk of concord into hell,
Uproar the universal peace, confound
All unity on earth.

What kingly graces does Malcolm disavow?

MACDUFF. O Scotland, Scotland!

MALCOLM. If such a one be fit to govern, speak.
I am as I have spoken.

MACDUFF. Fit to govern?
No, not to live. O nation miserable!
With an untitled tyrant bloody-sceptred,
When shalt thou see thy wholesome days again,
Since that the truest issue of thy throne
By his own interdiction[74] stands accus'd,
And does blaspheme his breed?[75] Thy royal father
Was a most sainted king; the queen that bore thee,
Oft'ner upon her knees than on her feet,
Died every day she liv'd.[76] Fare thee well,
These evils thou repeat'st upon thyself
Hath banish'd me from Scotland. O my breast,
Thy hope ends here!

MALCOLM. Macduff, this noble passion,
Child of integrity, hath from my soul
Wip'd the black scruples,[77] reconcil'd my thoughts

70. **summer-seeming.** Lasting only for the summer or prime of life
71. **foisons.** Plenty
72. **mere own.** Royal property
73. **portable.** Bearable
74. **interdiction.** Legal restriction
75. **blaspheme his breed.** Slander his ancestors
76. **Died . . . liv'd.** Died to the world (prepared for heaven) every day, and so lived in a state of grace
77. **scruples.** Doubts

ANSWER TO GUIDED READING QUESTION

1. Malcolm disavows justice, verity, temperance, stableness, bounty, perseverance, mercy, lowliness, devotion, patience, courage, and fortitude.

LITERARY NOTE

Point out to students that in lines 91–94, Shakespeare lists the qualities that were considered important in a king, and that throughout scene 3, he also points out these qualities through antithesis, as Malcolm professes to hold the opposite of all the kingly graces. The definition of a good king is one of the themes of *Macbeth*.

LITERARY TECHNIQUE

IMAGERY. An **image** is language that creates a concrete representation of an object or experience. It is also a vivid mental picture created in the reader's mind by that language. Shakespeare enters so fully into the personalities of his characters that even the nuances of the imagery they use are apt. Ask students to examine the speech of Macbeth in act 2, scene 1, lines 49–61, and list some of the nouns, adjectives, adverbs, and verbs that form the images of the passage. (These include *dead, wicked dreams, abuse, witchcraft, pale, wither'd Murther, alarum'd, wolf, howl, stealthy, ravishing, ghost, stones, horror, heat of deeds,* and *cold breath.*) Then point out that Malcolm, even in detailing his fictitious appetites (lines 50–99), uses a very different vocabulary. Before beginning to describe himself as evil, he refers to himself as a weak, poor, innocent lamb. Then words and phrases such as *pure as snow, lamb, sweet milk of concord, universal peace,* and *unity* crop up in his speeches. He lists the "king-becoming graces" at great length (lines 92–93). Pose this question: What does Malcolm's choice of words say about him, in contrast to Macbeth's choice of words in the passage from act 2?

Answer

Malcolm's vocabulary gives away his essential goodness even when he is trying to deny it; Macbeth's shows a disturbed mind fixated on horrors.

ANSWERS TO GUIDED READING QUESTIONS

1. Malcolm confesses that he was lying about himself; he has not been lustful, nor has he perjured himself, been covetous, or broken his faith.
2. The King of England has the power to heal his sick subjects with his touch.

CROSS-CURRICULAR ACTIVITIES

MEDICINE. Students can research the medical description and basis of the ailment scrofula and the historical background of Edward the Confessor. Their findings can be summarized in a one-page report.

To thy good truth and honor. Devilish Macbeth
By many of these trains[78] hath sought to win me
Into his power, and modest wisdom plucks me
From over-credulous haste. But God above
Deal between thee and me! for even now
I put myself to thy direction, and
Unspeak mine own detraction; here <u>abjure</u>
The taints and blames I laid upon myself,
For strangers to my nature. I am yet
Unknown to woman, never was forsworn,
Scarcely have coveted what was mine own,
At no time broke my faith, would not betray
The devil to his fellow, and delight
No less in truth than life. My first false speaking
Was this upon myself. What I am truly
Is thine and my poor country's to command:
Whither indeed, before thy here-approach,
Old Siward, with ten thousand warlike men
Already at a point, was setting forth.
Now we'll together, and the chance of goodness
Be like our warranted quarrel![79] Why are you silent?

What does Malcolm confess to Macduff?

MACDUFF. Such welcome and unwelcome things at once
'Tis hard to reconcile.

Enter a DOCTOR.

MALCOLM. Well, more anon.—Comes the King forth, I pray you?

DOCTOR. Aye, sir; there are a crew of wretched souls
That stay his cure.[80] Their malady convinces
The great assay of art;[81] but at his touch,
Such sanctity hath heaven given his hand,
They presently amend.

What power does the King of England have?

MALCOLM. I thank you, doctor. *Exit* DOCTOR.

MACDUFF. What's the disease he means?

MALCOLM. 'Tis call'd the evil:[82]
A most miraculous work in this good king,
Which often, since my here-remain in England,

78. **trains.** Devices
79. **chance . . . quarrel.** May our luck be as good as our cause is just.
80. **stay his cure.** Wait for him to cure them
81. **convinces . . . art.** Defeats even the highest medical skill
82. **the evil.** Scrofula, tuberculosis of the lymph nodes, was thought to be cured by the touch of royalty.

WORDS FOR EVERYDAY USE

ab • jure (ab joor´) *vt.*, renounce. *After the time when Durfey put his lit pipe in his pocket and set his jacket on fire, he <u>abjured</u> smoking.*

I have seen him do. How he solicits heaven,
Himself best knows; but strangely-visited people,
All swoll'n and ulcerous, pitiful to the eye,
The mere despair of surgery, he cures,
Hanging a golden stamp[83] about their necks,
Put on with holy prayers, and 'tis spoken,
To the succeeding royalty he leaves
The healing benediction. With this strange virtue,
He hath a heavenly gift of prophecy,
And sundry blessings hang about his throne
That speak him full of grace.

Enter ROSSE.

MACDUFF. See who comes here.

MALCOLM. My countryman; but yet I know him not.

MACDUFF. My ever gentle[84] cousin, welcome hither.

MALCOLM. I know him now. Good God betimes remove
The means that makes us strangers![85]

ROSSE. Sir, amen.

MACDUFF. Stands Scotland where it did?

ROSSE. Alas, poor country,
Almost afraid to know itself! It cannot
Be call'd our mother, but our grave; where nothing,
But who knows nothing, is once seen to smile;
Where sighs, and groans, and shrieks that rent the air
Are made, not mark'd;[86] where violent sorrow seems
A modern ecstasy.[87] The dead man's knell
Is there scarce ask'd for who, and good men's lives
Expire before the flowers in their caps,
Dying or ere[88] they sicken.

According to Rosse, what is the present state of Scotland?

MACDUFF. O relation!
Too nice,[89] and yet too true.

MALCOLM. What's the newest grief?

ROSSE. That of an hour's age doth hiss the speaker;[90]

83. **stamp.** Coin
84. **gentle.** Noble
85. **betimes . . . strangers.** Soon remove Macbeth who has caused our separation
86. **mark'd.** Noticed
87. **modern ecstasy.** Common emotion
88. **or ere.** Before
89. **relation! / Too nice.** Tale all too accurate
90. **hiss the speaker.** Cause the speaker to be hissed for telling old news

ANSWER TO GUIDED READING QUESTION

1. Rosse says that "sighs, and groans, and shrieks" fill the air and are not even noticed.

ADDITIONAL QUESTIONS AND ACTIVITIES

Ask students the following questions:

1. How does the condition of England under Edward contrast with the condition of Scotland under Macbeth?
2. Why, do you suppose, might Shakespeare have introduced the material about Edward? How does it further the plot?

Answers

1. England under Edward is governed by someone with healing and other divinely given powers. Scotland is the home of men who expire "before the flowers in their caps," dying before they even pass through illness. In other words, England is relatively healthy, and Scotland absolutely sick.
2. Shakespeare may have introduced the material about Edward to emphasize the damage caused to Scotland by Macbeth. It furthers the plot by showing the deterioration of conditions there and providing more motivation for the invasion by Malcolm, Macduff, and Siward. Shakespeare was also probably trying to flatter James II, who believed that he, like Edward the Confessor, had the power to cure scrofula by touch.

ANSWERS TO GUIDED READING QUESTIONS

1. Rosse tries to hide from Macduff that his family is dead.
2. Malcolm tells Rosse that the King of England has promised ten thousand soldiers to help their cause.

ADDITIONAL QUESTIONS AND ACTIVITIES

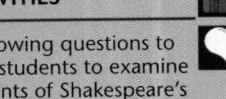

Ask the following questions to encourage students to examine the fine points of Shakespeare's dialogue in scene 3, lines 176–188:

1. Why does Rosse say "why" before saying "well" in line 177?
2. What does Rosse mean when he says Macduff's children were "well at peace when I did leave 'em"?
3. When Macduff asks Rosse for more details, apparently about his wife and children, how does Rosse react?
4. Why, do you suppose, does Rosse decide to tell Macduff about his family after avoiding doing so?

Answers

1. He is hesitating because he does not want to tell Macduff the truth; he seems surprised that he is able to say that Macduff's wife is well (that is, safe from further harm).
2. He means that they are dead.
3. Rosse changes the subject and begins talking about Scotland in general.
4. One might conjecture that he feels he has to tell Macduff sooner or later.

Each minute <u>teems</u> a new one.

MACDUFF. How does my wife?

ROSSE. Why, well.

MACDUFF. And all my children?

ROSSE. Well too.

MACDUFF. The tyrant has not batter'd at their peace?

ROSSE. No, they were well at peace when I did leave 'em.

What does Rosse try to hide from Macduff?

MACDUFF. Be not a niggard[91] of your speech; how goes't?

ROSSE. When I came hither to transport the tidings,
Which I have heavily[92] borne, there ran a rumor
Of many worthy fellows that were out,[93]
Which was to my belief witness'd the rather,[94]
For that I saw the tyrant's power[95] afoot.
Now is the time of help; your eye in Scotland
Would create soldiers, make our women fight,
To <u>doff</u> their dire distresses.

MALCOLM. Be't their comfort
We are coming thither. Gracious England hath
Lent us good Siward, and ten thousand men;
An older and a better soldier none
That Christendom gives out.

What comforting news does Malcolm give to Rosse?

ROSSE. Would I could answer
This comfort with the like! But I have words
That would be howl'd out in the desert air,
Where hearing should not latch[96] them.

MACDUFF. What concern they?
The general cause? or is it a fee-grief[97]
Due to some single breast?

ROSSE. No mind that's honest
But in it shares some woe, though the main part
Pertains to you alone.

MACDUFF. If it be mine,
Keep it not from me, quickly let me have it.

91. **niggard.** Stingy
92. **heavily.** Very sadly
93. **out.** Out in arms
94. **witness'd the rather.** Made more believable
95. **tyrant's power.** Armed forces
96. **latch.** Catch
97. **fee-grief . . . breast.** A private sorrow to be held by just one person

WORDS FOR EVERYDAY USE

teem (tēm) *vi.*, bring forth. *Though life spawns problems, it also <u>teems</u> its little joys.*

doff (dôf) *vt.*, take off, remove. *The gentleman <u>doffed</u> his cap to salute a passing lady.*

ROSSE. Let not your ears despise my tongue for ever,
Which shall possess them with the heaviest sound
That ever yet they heard.

MACDUFF. Humh! I guess at it.

ROSSE. Your castle is surpris'd; your wife, and babes,
Savagely slaughter'd. To relate the manner,
Were on the quarry[98] of these murther'd deer
To add the death of you.

MALCOLM. Merciful heaven!
What, man, ne'er pull your hat upon your brows;
Give sorrow words. The grief that does not speak
Whispers the o'er-fraught heart,[99] and bids it break.

MACDUFF. My children too?

ROSSE. Wife, children, servants, all
That could be found.

MACDUFF. And I must be from thence![100]
My wife kill'd too?

ROSSE. I have said.

MALCOLM. Be comforted.
Let's make us med'cines of our great revenge
To cure this deadly grief.

According to Malcolm, what will heal Macduff's grief?

MACDUFF. He has no children. All my pretty ones?
Did you say all? O hell-kite! All?
What, all my pretty chickens, and their dam,[101]
At one fell swoop?

MALCOLM. Dispute[102] it like a man.

MACDUFF. I shall do so;
But I must also feel it as a man:
I cannot but remember such things were,
That were most precious to me. Did heaven look on,
And would not take their part? Sinful Macduff,
They were all strook for thee! naught[103] that I am,
Not for their own demerits, but for mine,
Fell slaughter on their souls. Heaven rest them now!

Whom does Macduff blame for the deaths of his wife and children?

MALCOLM. Be this the whetstone of your sword, let grief
Convert to anger; blunt not the heart, enrage it.

MACDUFF. O, I could play the woman with mine eyes,

98. **quarry.** Heap of slaughtered bodies, like game from a hunting expedition
99. **Whispers the o'er-fraught heart.** Whispers to the overburdened heart
100. **from thence.** Away from there
101. **dam.** Mother
102. **Dispute.** Revenge
103. **naught.** Wicked

ANSWERS TO GUIDED READING QUESTIONS

1. Revenge, like medicine, will heal Macduff's grief.
2. Macduff blames himself for the deaths of his wife and children.

ADDITIONAL QUESTIONS AND ACTIVITIES

The words of Macduff in lines 217–227 make up one of the briefest and yet most powerful laments in English literature. (The American poet Anne Sexton chose them as the epigraph and title for her volume of poems *All My Pretty Ones.*) Students can write a lament expressing Macduff's sorrow for his wife and/or family, using whatever form of poetry or prose seems appropriate to them. They should assume that the lament is to be delivered at a memorial service attended by other nobles and family members. For inspiration, you may wish to read students the poem "On the Death of His Wife" by the Irish poet Muireadach O'Dalaigh (early 1200s), translated by Frank O'Connor in Montague, John, ed. *The Book of Irish Verse.* 1974.

My body's self deserts me now,
The half of me that was her own,
Since all I knew of brightness died
Half of me lingers, half is gone.

And braggart with my tongue! But, gentle heavens,
Cut short all intermission. Front to front[104]
Bring thou this fiend of Scotland and myself;
Within my sword's length set him; if he scape,
Heaven forgive him too!

MALCOLM. This tune goes manly.
Come go we to the King, our power is ready,
Our lack is nothing but our leave. Macbeth
Is ripe for shaking, and the pow'rs above
Put on their instruments.[105] Receive what cheer you may,
The night is long that never finds the day. *Exeunt.*

---

104. **Front to front.** Face to face
105. **Put . . . instruments.** Prepare for action by arming themselves

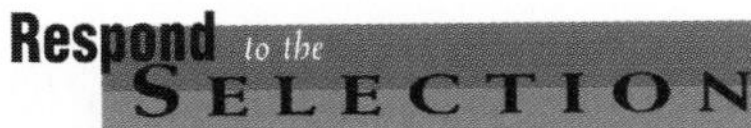

Imagine you are Macduff. What were you thinking when you left your family alone and unprotected in Scotland?

SELECTION CHECK TEST 4.5.9 WITH ANSWERS

Checking Your Reading

1. What does the second apparition, a child, assure Macbeth? **It assures him that "none of woman born" will harm him.**
2. Who is last in the apparition of a line of kings? **Banquo is last.**
3. What does Lady Macduff tell her son about Macduff? **She says he is a traitor.**
4. What does Malcolm say he is unworthy of? **He says he is unworthy to be king.**
5. What news does Rosse bring about Macduff's family? **They have been murdered.**

Vocabulary in Context

Fill each blank with the most appropriate word from the Words for Everyday Use. You may have to change the tense of the word.

pernicious homely impediment
staunchless abjure teem doff

1. Henry VIII **abjured** the Catholic Church and founded the Church of England.
2. Weather was an insurmountable **impediment** for many, but some made it to work.
3. The theaters and public houses were closed in fear of the **pernicious** virus.
4. Many students gave her gifts, but Ann's favorites were the **homely** handmade ones.
5. Bilkie and her friends gleefully **doffed** their coats and hats in the warm spring sun.

Literary Tools

1. What is a paradox? **A paradox is a contradictory statement, idea, or event.**
2. Give an example of paradox from Act 4. **Responses will vary.**
3. What is personification? **Personification is the attribution of human characteristics to something that is not human.**
4. What is characterization? **Characterization is the act of creating a character.**
5. In what unusual way does Shakespeare establish the character of Malcolm as a kingly person? **Shakespeare characterizes Malcolm by having him make many statements about himself that are the opposite of what is true of him. We learn his true character by first learning what he is not.**

RESPOND TO THE SELECTION

Do you think the fate of Macduff's family would have been different if he were there to protect them? Where do you think Macduff's responsibilities lie—to his country or to his family? Explain.

INVESTIGATE, Inquire, Imagine

Recall: GATHERING FACTS → **Interpret:** FINDING MEANING

1a. What apparitions do the witches show Macbeth and what do they tell him? What does Macbeth plan to do to Macduff?

1b. Given the apparitions and the explanations given by them, why does Macbeth decide upon this course of action?

2a. Why is Lady Macduff upset with her husband in scene 2? What does she say to her son regarding her husband?

2b. Why might Shakespeare have inserted an interchange between Lady Macduff and her son before their murder? How does having such an interchange affect the feelings of the audience about the outcome of scene 2?

3a. What falsehoods does Malcolm tell to Macduff in scene 3?

3b. Why does Malcolm mislead Macduff in scene 3? What does he accomplish by doing so?

Analyze: TAKING THINGS APART → **Synthesize:** BRINGING THINGS TOGETHER

4a. How does the condition of England under Edward, as described in this act, compare to Scotland under Macbeth?

4b. Why, do you suppose, did Shakespeare introduce material about England into the play? How does it further the plot? How does it relate to the theme of "natural order"?

Evaluate: MAKING JUDGMENTS → **Extend:** CONNECTING IDEAS

5a. Evaluate whether Macbeth has become more and more inured, or used to, doing evil. Use evidence from the play to support your opinion.

5b. Over the centuries, Macbeth has developed a reputation for being cursed. Veterans of the theater recount a series of mishaps and disasters, from scenery crashes and flat performances, to the death of the manager of the Old Vic Theatre in London and Laurence Olivier's twisted ankle on opening night in 1955. Superstitious actors refer to it as "The Scottish Play" rather than say its name. How would you account for these strange occurrences?

Understanding Literature

PARADOX. Review the definition for **paradox** in the Handbook of Literary Terms. Which statements made by the apparitions in scene 1 are paradoxes?

PERSONIFICATION. Review the definition for **personification** in the Handbook of Literary Terms. In scene 3, lines 39–41, what is personified? What human characteristics are attributed to this thing?

CHARACTERIZATION. Review the definition for **characterization** in the Handbook of Literary Terms. Reread scene 3. How does Shakespeare establish the characters of Malcolm and Macduff in this scene? What

ANSWERS TO INVESTIGATE, INQUIRE, AND IMAGINE

RECALL

1a. The witches show Macbeth apparitions of an armed head, a bloody child, a crowned child holding a tree, and eight kings, including Banquo. The first apparition indicates Macbeth should beware of Macduff; the second indicates that he will not be killed by anyone born of a woman; the third indicates that he will not be defeated until Birnan wood comes to Dunsinane; the last apparitions indicate that Banquo will father a line of kings. Macbeth plans to klll Macduff's family.

2a. Lady Macduff is upset because her husband has left her and her children to go to England. She tells her son that his father is a traitor.

3a. Malcolm tells Macduff that he would be a worse king than Macbeth. He tells him that his is sexually intemperate, greedy, and devoid of any good qualities.

INTERPRET

1b. His decision arises out of the fact that he does not fully trust the witches and their apparitions. He feels compelled to make doubly sure that he is secure, and for this reason he decides to kill Macduff's family.

2b. The interchange between Lady Macduff and her son points to their humanity and their helplessness. It promotes feelings of pity and shows Macbeth's crime to be all the more terrible.

3b. Malcolm is testing Macduff to see if he is an agent sent by Macbeth to suborn him. He determines that Macduff is a moral person whom he can trust.

ANALYZE

4a. England is healthy and whole while Scotland is sick and full of evil.

SYNTHESIZE

4b. The material on England provides a contrast by which we see just how far Scotland has fallen. All is well in England where the divinely anointed king is revered. In Scotland, where the rightful king has been murdered, there is chaos and darkness. An audience in Shakespeare's time would have shared the opinion that the murder of Duncan disrupted the natural order and led to chaos and darkness.

EVALUATE

5a. By the end of scene 1, Macbeth has determined that he will no longer hesitate to commit crimes. Gone are his indecisiveness and scruples. By

ANSWERS TO INVESTIGATE, INQUIRE, AND IMAGINE (CONT.)

murdering Macduff's innocent family, Macbeth reveals that he is callous, cruel and selfish.

EXTEND

5b. *Responses will vary.* A possible explanation is that people only think that more than the usual number of problems occur during productions of *Macbeth*. If the number of mishaps and disasters in *Macbeth* were compared to other productions, perhaps it could be proved that there is only a normal number of these occurrences. The focus of the play on evil and its prevailing aura of superstition may well have given rise to a greater susceptibility to superstition in *Macbeth* productions.

Answers to Understanding Literature can be found on page 446.

ANSWERS TO UNDERSTANDING LITERATURE

Paradox. The second apparition says that "none of woman born" will harm Macbeth, which is paradoxical because all of his enemies were seemingly born of a woman, including Macduff. The third apparition says that Macbeth need fear nothing until wood comes to Dunsinane, an event that seems impossible because forests are immobile.

Personification. Scotland is being personified. The abilities to weep and to bleed are attributed to the personified Scotland.

Characterization. As an alternative to the cluster charts, you may wish to have students fill out a Venn diagram highlighting the similarities between Macduff and Malcolm. Students' responses will vary, but they should recognize that both Malcolm and Macduff value the kingly virtues and detest kings such as Macbeth who do not possess these virtues and "Uproar the universal peace, confound / All unity on earth." Both men want to "heal" Scotland of the harm it has suffered under the tyrannical Macbeth.

ANSWERS TO INTEGRATING THE LANGUAGE ARTS

Language, Grammar, and Style

1. The apparitions reveal an armed head, a bloody child, a crowned child, and eight kings.
2. Macduff had left his family and had gone to England.
3. Rosse told Lady Macduff that her husband is gone, and then he left Fife.
4. Did Malcolm break his oath or covet the possessions of another?
5. King Edward is raising 10,000 soldiers and is prepared to aid Malcolm.

does Malcolm's plan to deceive Macduff reveal about him? Create a cluster chart like the one on the Prereading page for Malcolm and for Macduff, including the character traits of each man. What traits do the two men have in common? What do both men value the most, and what do they detest? Based on the characterization in scene 3, how closely does Malcolm fit the ideal of a king?

Writer's Journal

1. Create a wanted poster for Macbeth, including information about what crimes he has committed, why he should be arrested, where he can be found, and what reward is being offered. Use your imagination and descriptions from the play to make a sketch of him. As an alternative, create a **wanted poster** that Macbeth might have posted for Malcolm or Donalbain, including information about their alleged crimes and suspected whereabouts.
2. Imagine you are Malcolm. Write a **letter** to your brother in Ireland telling him about your plans to return to Scotland, how you have been received in England, and what you learned from your encounter with Macduff.
3. Write a **dramatic scene** in which Macbeth tells Lady Macbeth about the apparitions and about his plans to kill Macduff's family. Make sure your characterization of Macbeth and Lady Macbeth fits with their portrayals so far in the play.

Integrating *the* Language Arts

Language, Grammar, and Style

Achieving Parallelism. Read the Language Arts Survey 3.38, "Achieving Parallelism." Then rewrite the following sentences, using parallel structure.

1. The apparitions reveal an armed head, a child who is bloody, a crowned child, and eight kings.
2. Macduff left his family and had gone to England.
3. Rosse tells Lady Macduff that her husband is gone, and then he left Fife.
4. Did Malcolm break his oath or coveted the possessions of another?
5. King Edward is raising 10,000 soldiers and was prepared to aid Malcolm.

Media Literacy & Study and Research

Selecting Special Effects. Imagine that you are a famous movie director planning a new film version of Macbeth and you want special effects for the witches' scene in act 4. Write a description of the special effects you plan to use. Before you begin, you may wish to research special effects techniques, including claymation, animatronics, and 3-D computer graphics to understand what options are available to you.

Study and Research & Speaking and Listening

Researching Elizabethan Superstitions. Modern audiences have trouble taking the witches in *Macbeth* seriously, but Shakespeare's audience would have found them to be believable and frightening. Research superstitions in Elizabethan England, such as belief in witches. Then share your findings with the class.

ACT 5

SCENE 1: a castle at Dunsinane

Enter a DOCTOR OF PHYSIC *and a* WAITING-GENTLEWOMAN.

DOCTOR. I have two nights watch'd with you, but can perceive no truth in your report. When was it she last walk'd?

GENTLEWOMAN. Since his Majesty went into the field,[1] I have seen her rise from her bed, throw her nightgown upon her, unlock her closet, take forth paper, fold it, write upon't, read it, afterwards seal it, and again return to bed; yet all this while in a most fast sleep.

DOCTOR. A great perturbation in nature, to receive at once the benefit of sleep and do the effects of watching![2] In this slumb'ry agitation, besides her walking and other actual performances, what, at any time, have you heard her say?

GENTLEWOMAN. That, sir, which I will not report after her.

DOCTOR. You may to me, and 'tis most meet you should.

GENTLEWOMAN. Neither to you nor any one, having no witness to confirm my speech.

Enter LADY MACBETH *with a taper.*

What is Lady Macbeth doing?

Lo you, here she comes! This is her very guise,[3] and upon my life, fast asleep. Observe her, stand close.[4]

DOCTOR. How came she by that light?

GENTLEWOMAN. Why, it stood by her. She has light by her continually, 'tis her command.

DOCTOR. You see her eyes are open.

GENTLEWOMAN. Aye, but their sense are shut.

DOCTOR. What is it she does now? Look how she rubs her hands.

1. **went . . . field.** Went to battle
2. **do . . . watching.** Do activities one normally does awake
3. **her very guise.** Precisely what she has been doing
4. **close.** Hidden

Literary TOOLS

METAPHOR. A **metaphor** is a figure of speech in which one thing is spoken or written about as if it were another. Macbeth uses a metaphor in some famous lines spoken in scene 5. Look for the metaphor as you read.

THEME. A **theme** is a central idea in a literary work. As you read act 5, think about what the themes of the play are.

EXPOSITION, RISING ACTION, CRISIS, FALLING ACTION, AND CATASTROPHE. The exposition, rising action, crisis, falling action, and catastrophe are parts of a plot. The **exposition** sets the tone or mood, introduces the characters and the setting, and provides necessary background information. The **rising action** develops the conflict to a high point of intensity. The **crisis**, or **turning point**, is the point in the plot where something decisive happens to determine the future course of events and the eventual working out of the conflict. The crisis is often the same event as the **climax**, or high point of interest or suspense in the plot. The **falling action** is all the events that follow the climax. The **catastrophe**, in tragedy, is the event that marks the ultimate tragic fall of the central character. Often this event is the character's death.

Reader's Journal

What personal strength do you possess that could bring you success? What personal weakness do you possess that could prevent your success?

ADDITIONAL RESOURCES

UNIT 5 RESOURCE BOOK

- Selection Worksheet 5.5
- Selection Check Test 4.5.11
- Selection Test 4.5.12
- Speaking and Listening Resource 4.19

ANSWER TO GUIDED READING QUESTION

1. Lady Macbeth is walking in her sleep and rubbing her hands as if she were washing them.

READER'S JOURNAL

Due to the personal nature of these questions, students may prefer to keep their journal entries private. Students might begin by defining success and then answering the questions in light of their definition.

ADDITIONAL QUESTIONS AND ACTIVITIES

Have students pause between reading acts 4 and 5 to describe, in writing, how they would conclude the play. Remind students that their conclusions should resolve the major conflicts in the play (between Macduff and Macbeth, between Malcolm and Macbeth, and between Macbeth's ambition and his conscience). Ask students to share their conclusions in class, and have the class vote to decide on a favorite. Then ask students to discuss why they chose that conclusion over the others.

ANSWERS TO GUIDED READING QUESTIONS

1. Lady Macduff's murder is on Lady Macbeth's mind.
2. Lady Macbeth cannot eliminate the smell of blood from her hands; even "All the perfumes of Arabia" will not get the smell out.

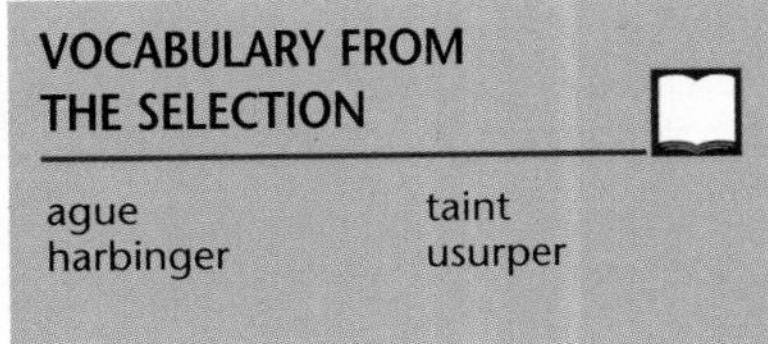

VOCABULARY FROM THE SELECTION

ague
harbinger
taint
usurper

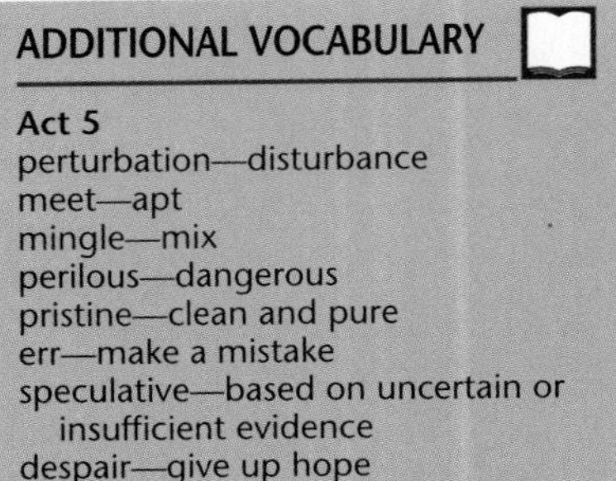

ADDITIONAL VOCABULARY

Act 5
perturbation—disturbance
meet—apt
mingle—mix
perilous—dangerous
pristine—clean and pure
err—make a mistake
speculative—based on uncertain or insufficient evidence
despair—give up hope

GENTLEWOMAN. It is an accustom'd action with her, to seem thus washing her hands. I have known her continue in this a quarter of an hour.

LADY MACBETH. Yet here's a spot.

DOCTOR. Hark, she speaks. I will set down what comes from her, to satisfy my remembrance the more strongly.

LADY MACBETH. Out, damn'd spot! out, I say! One—two—why then 'tis time to do't. Hell is murky. Fie, my lord, fie, a soldier, and afeard? What need we fear who knows it, when none can call our pow'r to accompt?[5] Yet who would have thought the old man to have had so much blood in him?

DOCTOR. Do you mark that?

LADY MACBETH. The Thane of Fife had a wife; where is she now? What, will these hands ne'er be clean? No more o' that, my lord, no more o' that; you mar all with this starting.[6]

Whose murder is on Lady Macbeth's mind?

DOCTOR. Go to, go to; you have known what you should not.

GENTLEWOMAN. She has spoke what she should not, I am sure of that; heaven knows what she has known.

LADY MACBETH. Here's the smell of the blood still. All the perfumes of Arabia will not sweeten this little hand. O, O, O!

What is Lady Macbeth unable to eliminate?

DOCTOR. What a sigh is there! The heart is sorely charg'd.[7]

GENTLEWOMAN. I would not have such a heart in my bosom for the dignity of the whole body.

DOCTOR. Well, well, well.

GENTLEWOMAN. Pray God it be, sir.

DOCTOR. This disease is beyond my practice; yet I have known those which have walk'd in their sleep who have died holily in their beds.

LADY MACBETH. Wash your hands, put on your nightgown, look not so pale. I tell you yet again, Banquo's buried; he cannot come out on 's grave.

DOCTOR. Even so?

LADY MACBETH. To bed, to bed; there's knocking at the gate. Come, come, come, come, give me your hand. What's done cannot be undone. To bed, to bed, to bed.

Exit LADY.

DOCTOR. Will she go now to bed?

GENTLEWOMAN. Directly.

DOCTOR. Foul whisp'rings are abroad. Unnatural deeds
Do breed unnatural troubles; infected minds

5. **call our pow'r to accompt.** Call to account anyone so powerful as we
6. **starting.** Sudden, startled movements
7. **charg'd.** Burdened

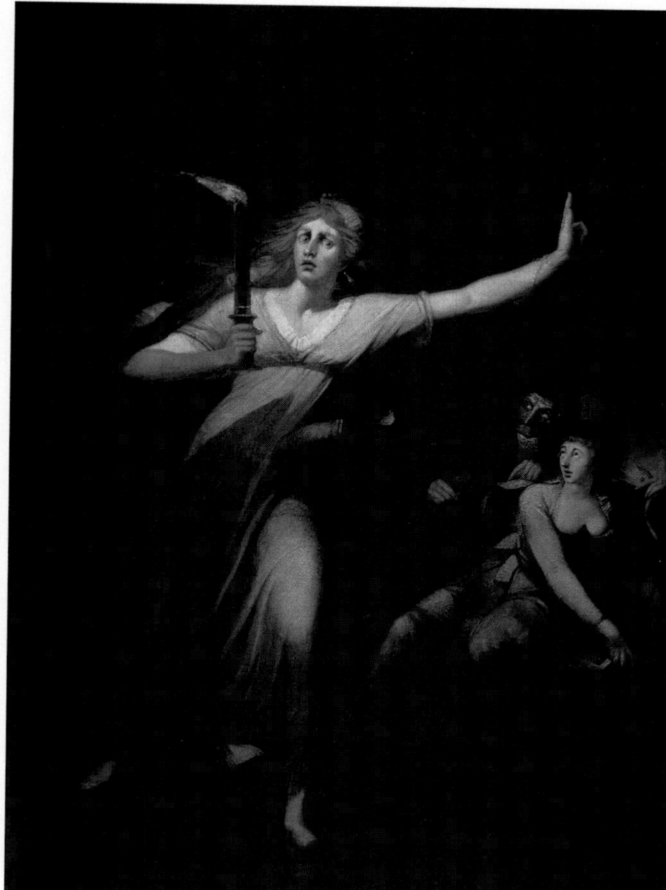

Lady Macbeth Sleepwalking, 1783. Henry Fuseli. Louvre, Paris.

To their deaf pillows will discharge their secrets.
More needs she the divine than the physician.
God, God, forgive us all! Look after her,
Remove from her the means of all annoyance,
And still keep eyes upon her. So good night.
My mind she has mated, and amaz'd my sight.[8]
I think, but dare not speak.

GENTLEWOMAN. Good night, good doctor. *Exeunt.*

Whose help does the doctor say Lady Macbeth needs?

8. **My . . . sight.** She has confused my mind and bewildered my sight.

ANSWER TO GUIDED READING QUESTION

1. The doctor says Lady Macbeth needs God's help.

CROSS-CURRICULAR CONNECTIONS

Psychology. Shakespeare made use of sleepwalking and sleeptalking to reveal the extent of Lady Macbeth's mental disturbance, but his depiction of these activities contravenes what modern science knows about them. Both activities take place during a type of sleep called non-rapid eye movement (NREM) sleep. Although sleeptalking and sleepwalking are popularly believed to be due to an enactment of the sleeper's dream, in fact NREM sleep is characteristically dreamless. Furthermore, instead of delivering prolonged, intelligent speeches of the kind delivered by Lady Macbeth, sleeptalkers generally mumble only sounds or a barely coherent sentence or two. Most sleepwalking occurs in children ages eleven to fourteen. All the same, anecdotal evidence suggests that sleepwalking and sleeptalking of the sort Shakespeare described are not out of the range of possibility. They may not be reproducible in the laboratory, but they are commonly reported. Students may be able to share stories about sleepwalking and sleeptalking from their own experience or from the experiences of family members.

LITERARY TECHNIQUE

Motif. A **motif** is any element that recurs in more than one way in a work of literature or art. Point out to students that the motif of hell can be found throughout Macbeth, especially associated with Macbeth and Lady Macbeth. "Come, thick night," says Lady Macbeth in act 1, "and pall thee in the dunnest smoke of hell" (scene v, lines 55–57). The porter scene (act 2, scene 3, lines 1–45) is based on a scene, common in the old mystery plays, in which the porter of hell's gate admitted sinning souls to everlasting torment. Certainly by that scene, Macbeth and Lady Macbeth have made their home a hell. By Act 5, scene 1, Lady Macbeth herself is wandering in a hell of her own making. "Hell is murky,"

LITERARY TECHNIQUE (cont.)

she mutters at line 43. Macbeth's attendant in scene iii is called Seyton, perhaps a pun on "Satan." (See also scene 7, line 7; scene viii, line 3.) The sleepwalking scene is remarkable as a nexus, or connecting point, for many of the motifs of the play. Ask students what other motifs can be found repeated in the sleepwalking scene.

ANSWER TO GUIDED READING QUESTION

1. Macbeth is dealing with constant revolts. His men obey out of fear rather than love.

ADDITIONAL QUESTIONS AND ACTIVITIES

Students can summarize the status of Scotland by writing a proclamation such as might have been issued by Malcolm or the forces of Lennox as they closed in on Dunsinane. Their proclamation should detail the crimes of Macbeth and Lady Macbeth and recapitulate what the speakers report in scene 2. The proclamation should rally people to Malcolm's side and urge those in Macbeth's forces to change sides.

SCENE 2: countryside near Dunsinane

Drum and Colors. Enter MENTETH, CATHNESS, ANGUS, LENNOX, SOLDIERS.

MENTETH. The English pow'r is near, led on by Malcolm,
His uncle Siward, and the good Macduff.
Revenges burn in them; for their dear causes
Would to the bleeding and the grim alarm[9]
Excite the mortified[10] man.

ANGUS. Near Birnan wood
Shall we well meet them; that way are they coming.

CATHNESS. Who knows if Donalbain be with his brother?

LENNOX. For certain, sir, he is not; I have a file[11]
Of all the gentry. There is Siward's son,
And many unrough[12] youths that even now
Protest their first of manhood.[13]

MENTETH. What does the tyrant?

CATHNESS. Great Dunsinane he strongly fortifies.
Some say he's mad; others that lesser hate him
Do call it valiant fury; but for certain
He cannot buckle his distemper'd cause
Within the belt of rule.[14]

ANGUS. Now does he feel
His secret murthers sticking on his hands;
Now minutely revolts[15] upbraid his faith-breach;
Those he commands move only in command,
Nothing in love. Now does he feel his title
Hang loose about him, like a giant's robe
Upon a dwarfish thief.

What problems is Macbeth having? Why do his men obey?

MENTETH. Who then shall blame
His pester'd senses to recoil and start,
When all that is within him does condemn
Itself for being there?

CATHNESS. Well, march we on
To give obedience where 'tis truly ow'd.
Meet we the med'cine of the sickly weal,[16]
And with him pour we, in our country's purge,
Each drop of us.

LENNOX. Or so much as it needs

---

9. **bleeding . . . alarm.** Bloody and horrible battle
10. **mortified.** Almost dead
11. **file.** List
12. **unrough.** Unbearded
13. **Protest . . . manhood.** Show their manhood for the first time
14. **He . . . rule.** He cannot confine his corrupt cause within self-control.
15. **minutely revolts.** New revolts every minute
16. **med'cine . . . weal.** Malcolm is the medicine that can cure the state.

To dew the sovereign flower[17] and drown the weeds.
Make we our march towards Birnan.

Exeunt marching.

SCENE 3: the castle at Dunsinane

Enter MACBETH, DOCTOR, *and* ATTENDANTS.

MACBETH. Bring me no more reports, let them fly all.
Till Birnan wood remove to Dunsinane
I cannot taint with fear. What's the boy Malcolm?
Was he not born of woman? The spirits that know
All mortal consequences[18] have pronounc'd me thus:
"Fear not, Macbeth, no man that's born of woman
Shall e'er have power upon thee." Then fly, false thanes,
And mingle with the English epicures![19]
The mind I sway[20] by, and the heart I bear,
Shall never sag with doubt, nor shake with fear.

Enter SERVANT.

The devil damn thee black,[21] thou cream-fac'd loon!
Where got'st thou that goose-look?

SERVANT. There is ten thousand—

MACBETH. Geese, villain?

SERVANT. Soldiers, sir.

MACBETH. Go prick thy face, and over-red thy fear,
Thou lily-liver'd boy. What soldiers, patch?[22]
Death of thy soul! those linen cheeks of thine
Are counsellors to fear. What soldiers, whey-face?

SERVANT. The English force, so please you.

MACBETH. Take thy face hence. [*Exit* SERVANT.]
Seyton!—I am sick at heart
When I behold—Seyton, I say!—This push[23]
Will cheer me ever, or disseat[24] me now.
I have liv'd long enough: my way of life

Why does Macbeth not fear Malcolm?

17. **sovereign flower.** Malcolm
18. **mortal consequences.** Human destinies
19. **epicures.** Those who like easy living, not soldiers
20. **sway.** Control myself
21. **devil . . . black.** Damned souls were said to turn black
22. **patch.** Fool
23. **push.** Surge of effort
24. **disseat.** Dethrone (with word-play on *cheer,* pronounced *chair*)

WORDS FOR EVERYDAY USE

taint (tānt) *vi.,* be infected. *The Shakespearean scholar looked in the refrigerator and exclaimed, "My goodness! Mold taints this cheese!"*

ANSWER TO GUIDED READING QUESTION

1. Macbeth does not fear Malcolm because he was "born of woman."

ADDITIONAL QUESTIONS AND ACTIVITIES

Ask the following questions to guide students in their reading of Scene 3:

1. With which characters does Macbeth interact in this scene?
2. How does Macbeth treat the servant? What emotion does the servant show that provokes Macbeth to react in this way?
3. What does Macbeth's intense reaction to the servant tell you about the emotions Macbeth is feeling?
4. Cite the lines Macbeth and Seyton exchange concerning the armor.
5. What does Macbeth's insistence on having the armor on and then his sudden change of intention suggest about his state of mind?
6. Macbeth suggests to the doctor that Scotland is diseased, infected with English troops. What lines in scene 2 does this statement echo? How is the perspective there different?

Answers

1. Macbeth interacts with a servant, with Seyton, and with the doctor.
2. Macbeth treats him with fury and contempt because he is pale with fear.
3. Macbeth is perhaps frightened of being afraid or is wound to a very tight pitch.
4. Macbeth: "Give me my armor" (line 33); Seyton: "'Tis not needed yet" (line 33); Macbeth: "I'll put it on" (line 34); "Give me mine armor" (line 36); "Come, put mine armor on" (line 48); "Come sir, dispatch" (line 50); "Pull't off, I say" (line 54); "Bring it after me" (line 58).
5. It suggests he is rattled and not thinking coherently.
6. Macbeth's words echo the words of Cathness (lines 27–29): "Meet we the med'cine of the sickly weal,/And with him pour we, in our country's purge,/Each drop of us." In scene 2, the speaker views Macbeth as the source of sickness, and Malcolm and his troops as healing medicine.

ANSWERS TO GUIDED READING QUESTIONS

1. Macbeth regrets that he will not have "honor, love, obedience, troops of friends" in his old age.
2. Macbeth asks the doctor to cure Lady Macbeth and to find a remedy for the presence of the English.

Is fall'n into the sear,[25] the yellow leaf,
And that which should accompany old age,
As honor, love, obedience, troops of friends,
I must not look to have; but in their stead,
Curses, not loud but deep, mouth-honor,[26] breath,
Which the poor heart would fain[27] deny, and dare not.
Seyton!

What does Macbeth realize he will never have? What will he have instead?

Enter SEYTON.

SEYTON. What's your gracious pleasure?

MACBETH. What news more?

SEYTON. All is confirm'd, my lord, which was reported.

MACBETH. I'll fight, till from my bones my flesh be hack'd.
Give me my armor.

SEYTON. 'Tis not needed yet.

MACBETH. I'll put it on.
Send out moe[28] horses, skirr[29] the country round,
Hang those that talk of fear. Give me mine armor.
How does your patient, doctor?

DOCTOR. Not so sick, my lord,
As she is troubled with thick-coming fancies,
That keep her from her rest.

MACBETH. Cure her of that.
Canst thou not minister to a mind diseas'd,
Pluck from the memory a rooted sorrow,
Raze out[30] the written troubles of the brain,
And with some sweet oblivious antidote[31]
Cleanse the stuff'd bosom of that perilous stuff
Which weighs upon the heart?

DOCTOR. Therein the patient
Must minister to himself.

MACBETH. Throw physic[32] to the dogs, I'll none of it.
Come, put mine armor on; give me my staff.
Seyton, send out. Doctor, the thanes fly from me.—
Come, sir, dispatch.—If thou couldst, doctor, cast
The water of my land, find her disease,[33]
And purge it to a sound and pristine health,
I would applaud thee to the very echo,

What does Macbeth request of the doctor?

25. **sear.** Dried and withered
26. **mouth-honor.** Honored in words but not in actions
27. **fain.** Gladly, eagerly
28. **moe.** More
29. **skirr.** Scour
30. **Raze out.** Erase
31. **oblivious antidote.** Medicine that causes forgetfulness
32. **physic.** Medical science
33. **cast . . . disease.** Diagnose the disease

That should applaud again.—Pull't off, I say.—
What rhubarb, cyme, or what purgative drug,
Would scour these English hence? Hear'st thou of them?

DOCTOR. Aye, my good lord; your royal preparation
Makes us hear something.

MACBETH. Bring it after me.—
I will not be afraid of death and bane,[34]
Till Birnan forest come to Dunsinane.

Exeunt all but the DOCTOR.

DOCTOR. Were I from Dunsinane away and clear,
Profit again should hardly draw me here.

Exit.

SCENE 4: countryside near Dunsinane

Drum and Colors. Enter MALCOLM, SIWARD, MACDUFF, SIWARD'S SON, MENTETH, CATHNESS, ANGUS, LENNOX, ROSSE, *and* SOLDIERS, *marching.*

MALCOLM. Cousins, I hope the days are near at hand
That chambers will be safe.

MENTETH. We doubt it nothing.

SIWARD. What wood is this before us?

MENTETH. The wood of Birnan.

MALCOLM. Let every soldier hew him down a bough,
And bear't before him, thereby shall we shadow
The numbers of our host,[35] and make discovery[36]
Err in report of us.

How will the English troops disguise their approach?

SOLDIERS. It shall be done.

SIWARD. We learn no other but the confident tyrant
Keeps still in Dunsinane, and will endure
Our setting down before't.[37]

MALCOLM. 'Tis his main hope;
For where there is advantage[38] to be given,
Both more and less[39] have given him the revolt,
And none serve with him but constrained things,
Whose hearts are absent too.

MACDUFF. Let our just censures
Attend the true event,[40] and put we on
Industrious soldiership.

34. **bane.** Destruction
35. **shadow . . . host.** Camouflage our numbers
36. **discovery.** The reports of scouts
37. **setting down before't.** Laying siege to
38. **advantage.** Opportunity
39. **more and less.** Nobles and common people
40. **Let . . . event.** Let our judgments wait for the actual event.

ANSWER TO GUIDED READING QUESTION

1. The English troops will carry tree branches in front of themselves.

CROSS-CURRICULAR CONNECTIONS

HISTORY. Students may benefit from a reminder of what war was like in medieval times. Most wars were fought by relatively small numbers of troops (the ten thousand mentioned in scene 3, line 13 would have been a huge army and was certainly intended by Shakespeare to be an impressive figure). A single battle frequently decided an entire campaign. In those days before cannons and firearms, a defending force, well-supplied and ensconced in a good position such as a castle, was very difficult to destroy. The only recourse an attacker might have would be to besiege or blockade the castle, preventing any supplies from reaching it; but such a siege might require a year or more to produce results. Furthermore, the difficulty of supplying a besieging army and of keeping it intact despite boredom and disease often proved overwhelming. Thus Macbeth says, "here [before the castle] let them lie/Till famine and the ague eat them up" (scene 5, lines 3–4). Fortunately for Malcolm, Macbeth has so little support that his own people surrender the castle to the approaching army (see scene vii, line 24, "This way, my lord, the castle's gently rend'red").

ANSWERS TO GUIDED READING QUESTIONS

1. Macbeth plans to make the English raise a siege against the castle until hunger and the ague conquer them.
2. Lady Macbeth is dead.

ADDITIONAL QUESTIONS AND ACTIVITIES

If students made lists of the attributes of Macbeth and Lady Macbeth while studying act 1, have them write new lists of attributes for these characters as they read act 5. Their lists should show the disintegration of personalities that has taken place as a result of Macbeth and Lady Macbeth's crimes.

SIWARD. The time approaches
That will with due decision make us know
What we shall say we have, and what we owe.
Thoughts speculative their unsure hopes relate,
But certain issue strokes must arbitrate,[41]
Towards which advance the war.

Exeunt marching.

SCENE 5: the castle at Dunsinane

Enter MACBETH, SEYTON, *and* SOLDIERS, *with Drum and Colors.*

MACBETH. Hang out our banners on the outward walls,
The cry is still, "They come!" Our castle's strength
Will laugh a siege to scorn; here let them lie
Till famine and the ague eat them up.
Were they not forc'd with those that should be ours,[42]
We might have met them dareful, beard to beard,
And beat them backward home.

What is Macbeth's strategy?

(*A cry within of women.*)
What is that noise?

SEYTON. It is the cry of women, my good lord. *Exit.*

MACBETH. I have almost forgot the taste of fears.
The time has been, my senses would have cool'd
To hear a night-shriek, and my fell of hair[43]
Would at a dismal treatise[44] rouse and stir
As life were in't. I have supp'd full with horrors;
Direness, familiar to my slaughterous thoughts,
Cannot once start me.[45]

Enter SEYTON.

Wherefore was that cry?

SEYTON. The Queen, my lord, is dead.

What news does Seyton bring?

MACBETH. She should have died hereafter;[46]
There would have been a time for such a word.
Tomorrow, and tomorrow, and tomorrow,

41. **Thoughts . . . arbitrate.** Talking about an event is just dealing with hopes; issues are only solved through action.
42. **forc'd . . . ours.** Reinforced with traitors from our side
43. **my . . . hair.** Hair on my skin
44. **treatise.** Story
45. **once start me.** Ever startle me
46. **should . . . hereafter.** Was bound to die eventually

WORDS FOR EVERYDAY USE

a • gue (ā´ gyo͞o´) *n.,* fever and chills. *Lord Byron complained of catching the ague after taking a long swim.*

Creeps in this petty pace from day to day,
To the last syllable of recorded time;
And all our yesterdays have lighted fools
The way to dusty death. Out, out, brief candle!
Life's but a walking shadow, a poor player,
That struts and frets his hour upon the stage,
And then is heard no more. It is a tale
Told by an idiot, full of sound and fury,
Signifying nothing.

Enter a MESSENGER.

Thou com'st to use thy tongue;
Thy story quickly.

MESSENGER. Gracious my lord,
I should report that which I say I saw,
But know not how to do't.

MACBETH. Well, say, sir.

MESSENGER. As I did stand my watch upon the hill,
I look'd toward Birnan, and anon methought
The wood began to move.

What news does the messenger bring?

MACBETH. Liar and slave!

MESSENGER. Let me endure your wrath, if't be not so.
Within this three mile may you see it coming;
I say, a moving grove.

MACBETH. If thou speak'st false,
Upon the next tree shall thou hang alive,
Till famine cling[47] thee; if thy speech be sooth,[48]
I care not if thou dost for me as much.
I pull in[49] resolution, and begin
To doubt th' equivocation of the fiend
That lies like truth. "Fear not, till Birnan wood
Do come to Dunsinane," and now a wood
Comes toward Dunsinane. Arm, arm, and out!
If this which he avouches[50] does appear,
There is nor flying hence, nor tarrying here.
I gin to be a-weary of the sun,
And wish th' estate o' th' world were now undone.
Ring the alarum-bell! Blow wind, come wrack,[51]
At least we'll die with harness[52] on our back.

What does Macbeth resolve?

Exeunt.

47. **cling.** Wither
48. **sooth.** Truth
49. **pull in.** Rein in
50. **avouches.** Affirms
51. **wrack.** Ruin
52. **harness.** Armor

ANSWERS TO GUIDED READING QUESTIONS

1. The messenger says that Birnan wood is moving.
2. Macbeth resolves to die fighting.

ADDITIONAL QUESTIONS AND ACTIVITIES

The speech of Macbeth in lines 19–28 is well known independently of the play itself. (The American writer William Faulkner [1897–1962] used the phrase "sound and fury" in the title of one of his novels.) The speech has been called the *ne plus ultra* as a statement of nihilism. Ask students the following questions:

1. What is Macbeth's view of life? Do you agree with it?
2. To what extent, do you think, is Macbeth's disgust with life a result of his own rejection of everything of value in life?
3. Even those who do not accept Macbeth's view of life find his statement deeply moving. Why, do you suppose, is this so?

Answers

1. Macbeth's view of life is that life signifies nothing (is without meaning). Responses to the second part of the question will vary.
2. Macbeth's disgust with life seems to stem immediately from his own decisions to disregard morality, friendship, gratitude, societal norms, and so on. Support for this view can be found in act 5, scene 3, where he regrets the loss of honor, love, obedience, and friends.
3. Nearly everyone has felt at one time or another that life is meaningless or has been concerned that it may prove to be. However, such commonplace temporary questioning is far from the pathological state of despair into which Macbeth sinks.

ART NOTE

The Death of Lady Macbeth.
Dante Gabriel Rossetti.

Dante Gabriel Rossetti (1828-1882), a British poet and painter born in London, England, was part of a talented, Anglo-Italian family. The son of an exiled Italian poet and politician, Rossetti enjoyed a childhood home that was often a gathering place for Italian exiles who discussed politics, art, and literature. He, his brother William, and his sister Christina wrote poetry and painted from childhood.

At twenty, Rossetti helped to found a group of writers, artists, and critics known as the Pre-Raphaelite Brotherhood, whose goals of simplicity, naturalness, and expressiveness in art and literature was modeled on the artwork produced in Italy before the Renaissance.

Rossetti's paintings are known for bright, glowing color and mystical beauty, and his poetry for its rich and unique imagery.

The Death of Lady Macbeth, 1828–82. Dante Gabriel Rossetti. Ashmolean Museum, Oxford, England.

SCENE 6: field at Dunsinane

Drum and Colors. Enter MALCOLM, SIWARD, MACDUFF, *and their army, with boughs.*

MALCOLM. Now near enough; your leavy[53] screens throw down,
And show like those you are.[54] You, worthy uncle,
Shall with my cousin, your right noble son,
Lead our first battle.[55] Worthy Macduff and we
Shall take upon 's what else remains to do,
According to our order.

SIWARD. Fare you well.
Do we but find the tyrant's power tonight,
Let us be beaten, if we cannot fight.

53. **leavy.** Leafy
54. **show . . . are.** Show yourselves as you are
55. **battle.** Battalion

MACDUFF. Make all our trumpets speak, give them all breath,
Those clamorous <u>harbingers</u> of blood and death.

Exeunt. Alarums continued.

SCENE 7: field at Dunsinane

Enter MACBETH.

MACBETH. They have tied me to a stake; I cannot fly,
But bear-like I must fight the course.[56] What's he
That was not born of woman? Such a one
Am I to fear, or none.

Enter YOUNG SIWARD.

YOUNG SIWARD. What is thy name?

MACBETH. Thou'lt be afraid to hear it.

YOUNG SIWARD. No; though thou call'st thyself a hotter name
Than any is in hell.

MACBETH. My name's Macbeth.

YOUNG SIWARD. The devil himself could not pronounce a title
More hateful to mine ear.

MACBETH. No; nor more fearful.

YOUNG SIWARD. Thou liest, abhorred tyrant, with my sword
I'll prove the lie thou speak'st.

Fight, and YOUNG SIWARD *slain.*

MACBETH. Thou wast born of woman.
But swords I smile at, weapons laugh to scorn,
Brandish'd by man that's of a woman born.

Exit.

Alarums. Enter MACDUFF.

MACDUFF. That way the noise is. Tyrant, show thy face!
If thou beest slain and with no stroke of mine,
My wife and children's ghosts will haunt me still.
I cannot strike at wretched kerns,[57] whose arms
Are hir'd to bear their staves;[58] either thou, Macbeth,

What is Macduff's mission? What does he say will happen if he does not fulfill it?

56. **bear-like . . . course.** It was a common sport to tie a bear to a stake and make it fight with dogs.
57. **kerns.** Foot soldiers
58. **staves.** Spears

WORDS FOR EVERYDAY USE

har • bin • ger (här´bin jər) *n.,* person or thing that comes before and hints at what is to follow. *The robin is often described as the <u>harbinger</u> of spring.*

ANSWER TO GUIDED READING QUESTION

1. Macduff's mission is to kill Macbeth himself. If he does not fulfill this mission, his wife and children's ghosts will continue to haunt him. He will fight Macbeth himself or put his sword away.

ADDITIONAL QUESTIONS AND ACTIVITIES

Ask these questions to help students understand the meaning of scene 7:

1. What motifs common elsewhere in the play also occur in scene 7?
2. What dramatic purpose does the killing of Young Siward serve?
3. How does Shakespeare emphasize the contrast between Macbeth and Malcolm in scene 7?

Answers

1. Hell and ghost motifs are common.
2. The killing of Young Siward extends the action and thus the suspense and suggests to the audience that Macbeth is invincible.
3. He shows Macbeth as the arrogant killer of a young, brave nobleman and shows Malcolm as so loved and appreciated that he achieves his goals gently and with little fighting.

ANSWERS TO GUIDED READING QUESTIONS

1. Some of Macbeth's troops have gone over to Malcolm's side.
2. Macduff tells Macbeth that he was ripped from his mother's womb.

ADDITIONAL QUESTIONS AND ACTIVITIES

Ask these questions to help students understand the meaning of scene 8:

1. In scene 8, how does Macbeth describe his reaction when Macduff tells him that he was not born of woman?
2. What is Macbeth's final comment about the witches? How might the same be said of the temptation to do evil?

Answers

1. He says that Maacduff has "cow'd" the "better part" of his manliness.
2. He says that they should not be believed because they equivocate, saying words that sound like promises but prove to be lies. The same might be said of the temptation to do evil in that temptation entices us with promises of satisfaction, clouding our better judgment and scruples which tell us to avoid committing wrongful acts because they will cause pain.

LITERARY NOTE

The text indicated in brackets at the end of scene 8 (*"Macduff carries off Macbeth's body"*) is not found in the Folio edition, but was added by a later editor who was trying to explain how Macduff could reenter later with Macbeth's severed head. (The stage directions in the Folio editions are sometimes corrupt, as if they had been hastily inserted by a printer or actor.) Instead of adding the line in brackets, some editors prefer to delete the stage direction that calls for Macduff and Macbeth to reenter; thus Macbeth is killed offstage, and Macduff does not reappear until scene ix. The latter version is often preferred by directors: it is very difficult to lug a "dead" actor off the stage without causing laughter; further, the audience will wonder where Macduff is taking the body and why. Ask students which version they prefer, and have them explain their reasoning.

Or else my sword with an unbattered edge
I sheathe again undeeded.[59] There thou shouldst be;
By this great clatter, one of greatest note
Seems bruited.[60] Let me find him, Fortune!
And more I beg not. *Exit. Alarums.*

Enter MALCOLM *and* SIWARD.

SIWARD. This way, my lord, the castle's gently rend'red:[61]
The tyrant's people on both sides do fight,
The noble thanes do bravely in the war,
The day almost itself professes yours,
And little is to do.

What have some of Macbeth's troops done?

MALCOLM. We have met with foes
That strike beside us.[62]

SIWARD. Enter, sir, the castle. *Exeunt. Alarum.*

SCENE 8: field at Dunsinane

Enter MACBETH.

MACBETH. Why should I play the Roman fool, and die
On mine own sword?[63] Whiles I see lives,[64] the gashes
Do better upon them.

Enter MACDUFF.

MACDUFF. Turn, hell-hound, turn!

MACBETH. Of all men else I have avoided thee.
But get thee back, my soul is too much charg'd
With blood of thine already.

MACDUFF. I have no words,
My voice is in my sword, thou bloodier villain
Than terms can give thee out!

Fight. Alarum.

MACBETH. Thou losest labor.
As easy mayst thou the intrenchant[65] air
With thy keen sword impress as make me bleed.
Let fall thy blade on vulnerable crests,
I bear a charmed life, which must not yield
To one of woman born.

What does Macduff reveal to Macbeth?

MACDUFF. Despair thy charm,
And let the angel whom thou still hast serv'd

59. **undeeded.** Unused
60. **bruited.** Announced
61. **castle's gently rend'red.** Surrendered easily
62. **strike beside us.** Fight on our side
63. **Roman fool . . . sword.** Commit suicide like a Roman soldier faced with defeat
64. **Whiles . . . lives.** As long as I see others alive
65. **intrenchant.** Incapable of being cut

Tell thee, Macduff was from his mother's womb
Untimely ripp'd.[66]

MACBETH. Accursed be that tongue that tells me so,
For it hath cow'd my better part of man!
And be these juggling fiends no more believ'd,
That palter[67] with us in a double sense,
That keep the word of promise to our ear,
And break it to our hope. I'll not fight with thee.

MACDUFF. Then yield thee, coward,
And live to be the show and gaze o' th' time!
We'll have thee, as our rarer monsters are,
Painted upon a pole,[68] and underwrit,
"Here may you see the tyrant."

What does Macduff say will happen to Macbeth if he refuses to fight?

MACBETH. I will not yield,
To kiss the ground before young Malcolm's feet,
And to be baited with the rabble's curse.
Though Birnan wood be come to Dunsinane,
And thou oppos'd, being of no woman born,
Yet I will try the last. Before my body
I throw my warlike shield. Lay on, Macduff,
And damn'd be him that first cries, "Hold, enough!"

Exeunt fighting. Alarums.

Enter fighting, and MACBETH *slain.* MACDUFF *carries off* MACBETH'S *body.*

SCENE 9: castle at Dunsinane

Retreat and flourish. Enter, with Drum and Colors, MALCOLM, SIWARD, ROSSE, THANES, *and* SOLDIERS.

MALCOLM. I would the friends we miss were safe arriv'd.

SIWARD. Some must go off;[69] and yet, by these I see,
So great a day as this is cheaply bought.[70]

MALCOLM. Macduff is missing, and your noble son.

ROSSE. Your son my lord, has paid a soldier's debt.
He only liv'd but till he was a man,
The which no sooner had his prowess confirm'd
In the unshrinking station where he fought,[71]
But like a man he died.

SIWARD. Then he is dead?

66. **Untimely ripp'd.** Delivered prematurely and by Caesarean section—not "of woman born" in the natural way
67. **palter.** Equivocate, speak deceitfully
68. **Painted . . . pole.** Portrait carried on a pole
69. **go off.** Die
70. **cheaply bought.** Marked with few casualties
71. **unshrinking . . . fought.** Spot from which he did not retreat

ANSWER TO GUIDED READING QUESTION

1. Macduff tells Macbeth that his portrait will be hung on a pole and paraded with the words "Here may you see the tyrant."

CROSS-CURRICULAR ACTIVITIES

ARTS AND HUMANITIES

- Explain to students that one of the basic conventions of drama, dating back to ancient times, is that violent and gory scenes "take place" offstage and are reported to the audience afterwards. Ask for two reasons why this convention might have developed.

Answer

(1) The audience will not be so shocked by the sight of violence and blood that it will lose track of the message of the drama, and (2) some violent acts are very difficult to stage realistically (such as the beheading that occurs at the end of Macbeth).

- Explain further that while some violent scenes in Shakespeare (such as the slaying of Duncan) take place offstage, some (such as the slaying of Macduff's son and the slaying of Young Siward) are enacted before the audience. Such sword fights and slayings require careful planning and choreography. To give students an appreciation of the difficulty of staging these scenes, have them form small groups and plan the choreography of the sword fight between Macbeth and Siward. (To avoid injuries, it is very important that they be forbidden to use props of any kind, including even paper or cardboard swords; imaginary swords are sufficient for amateur actors.) Emphasize that the actions of the players must be planned and repeated precisely. Some members of each group can be players, and others can be planners, critics, and directors.
- Instruct students that when they are acting out their scenes, all action must halt instantly if you say the word *freeze.* As the groups enact their choreographed scenes for the class as a whole, use the freeze technique if the action is becoming too rough. If freezing the action from time to time is not sufficient to keep it under control, tell students to act out the swordplay in slow motion.

ANSWERS TO GUIDED READING QUESTIONS

1. Macduff greets Malcolm with "Hail, King" and shows him Macbeth's head.
2. Lady Macbeth killed herself.

ADDITIONAL QUESTIONS AND ACTIVITIES

To prompt discussion of the end of the play, ask these questions:

1. How does Young Siward contrast with Macbeth?
2. How does the previous Thane of Cawdor's death, as described by Malcolm in act 1, scene 4, lines 3–11, compare with Macbeth's death?
3. What emotion does Malcolm express in the concluding two lines of the play? How does it compare to Duncan's behavior toward Macbeth in act 1? How does it contrast with Macbeth's actions in the play?

Answers

1. Young Siward acted bravely in a cause that was not his own, whereas Macbeth acted only in his own cause and did not behave nobly even in that endeavor.
2. Macbeth seems to cling to life more desperately than the previous Cawdor.
3. Malcolm expresses gratitude, an emotion that Duncan also conspicuously showed (see act 1, scene 6, lines 10–14) but that Macbeth conspicuously lacked in killing Duncan.

RESPOND TO THE SELECTION

Ask students to remember Macbeth's love for his wife, his doubts, his fears, his guilt, and his remorse which make him more human. The moral of the play is that everyone, even ordinary people who seem noble and good, must face a struggle between good and evil, but that ultimately one must heed the commandment "Thou shalt not kill."

ROSSE. Aye, and brought off the field. Your cause of sorrow
Must not be measur'd by his worth, for then
It hath no end.

SIWARD. Had he his hurts before?

ROSSE. Aye, on the front.

SIWARD. Why then, God's soldier be he!
Had I as many sons as I have hairs,
I would not wish them to a fairer death.
And so his knell is knoll'd.

MALCOLM. He's worth more sorrow,
And that I'll spend for him.

SIWARD. He's worth no more;
They say he parted well, and paid his score,
And so God be with him! Here comes newer comfort.

Enter MACDUFF *with* MACBETH'S *head.*

MACDUFF. Hail, King! for so thou art. Behold where stands
Th' usurper's cursed head: the time is free.[72]
I see thee compass'd with thy kingdom's pearl,[73]
That speak my salutation in their minds;
Whose voices I desire aloud with mine:
Hail, King of Scotland!

How does Macduff greet Malcolm?

ALL. Hail, King of Scotland! *Flourish.*

MALCOLM. We shall not spend a large expense of time
Before we reckon with your several loves,
And make us even with you.[74] My thanes and kinsmen,
Henceforth be earls, the first that ever Scotland
In such an honor nam'd. What's more to do,
Which would be planted newly with the time,
As calling home our exil'd friends abroad
That fled the snares of watchful tyranny,
Producing forth[75] the cruel ministers
Of this dead butcher and his fiend-like queen,
Who (as 'tis thought) by self and violent hands[76]
Took off her life; this, and what needful else

How did Lady Macbeth die?

72. **time is free.** Freedom reigns now
73. **compass'd . . . pearl.** Surrounded by the most noble in your realm
74. **make . . . you.** Reward as you deserve
75. **Producing forth.** Bringing forward to trial
76. **self . . . hands.** The violence of her own hands

WORDS FOR EVERYDAY USE

u • surp • er (yo̅o̅ sʉrp´ər) *n.*, one who assumes power without right. *After the election was shown to be illegal, the candidate who had originally lost the race took office, and the usurper went to jail.*

Poster for 1884 theater production of *Macbeth.*

That calls upon us, by the grace of Grace,
We will perform in measure, time, and place.
So thanks to all at once and to each one,
Whom we invite to see us crown'd at Scone.

Flourish. Exeunt omnes. ■

Respond *to the* Selection

What feelings do you have for Macbeth at the end of the play? What moral does his story provide?

SELECTION CHECK TEST 4.5.11 WITH ANSWERS

Checking Your Reading

1. What does the doctor observe Lady Macbeth doing? **He sees her sleepwalking.**
2. Why is Macbeth not afraid of the soldiers marching on his castle? **He thinks he is protected by the prophecy.**
3. What do Malcolm, Macduff, and their men do for camouflage? **They use tree branches for camouflage.**
4. What does Macduff say about his birth? **He was delivered by Caesarian, and therefore not "born."**
5. What does Macduff bring to Malcolm at the end of the play? **He brings Macbeth's head to Malcolm.**

Vocabulary in Context

Fill each blank with the most appropriate word from the Words for Everyday Use. You may have to change the tense of the word.

taint ague harbinger usurper

1. Neely won the election fairly, but her opponent referred to her as the "**usurper**."
2. The smile on Mr. Smith's face assured me that he was the **harbinger** of good news.
3. Residents were warned not to drink the water that was **tainted** with pesticides.

Literary Tools

Identify the key events from the play that make up each stage of the plot. Some are done for you.

	Stage	Action
Act I	Introduction	Macbeth is named a hero and given a title taken from a man named as a traitor; the Macbeth's ambition is revealed; the Macbeths plan to kill Duncan
Act II	Rising Action or Complication	1. Macbeth murders Duncan; Malcolm and Donalbain flee the country; Macbeth is made king
Act III	Crisis or Turning Point	2. Macbeth has Banquo murdered; Fleance escapes; Macbeth behaves strangely at feast
Act IV	Falling Action	The witches make more prophecies; Macduff'sfamily is killed; Malcolm and Macduff plan the attack on Macbeth
Act V	Resolution or Catastrophe	3. Lady Macbeth kills herself; the men march on Macbeth's castle; Macduff kills Macbeth

4. Identify one theme from the play. Be prepared to defend your choice. **Responses will vary.**
5. *Disorder* is a key motif in this play. Give an example of disorder from this play. **Responses will vary.**

ANSWERS TO INVESTIGATE, INQUIRE, AND IMAGINE

RECALL

1a. Lady Macbeth's gentlewoman and doctor observe her walking in her sleep. She appears to be continually rubbing her hands in an attempt to clean them. This recalls her statement to Macbeth in act 2, scene 2, lines 21–22 that "A little water clears us of this deed. / How easy it is then!"

2a. Macbeth is relying upon the words of the apparitions and assumes he is safe from harm since does he not believe there is a man not born of a woman and that Birnan wood will come to Dunsinane.

3a. Macbeth hears that Birnan wood is moving toward Dunsinane, and he realizes he is no longer safe.

INTERPRET

1b. Lady Macbeth's actions reveal that she is insane. She is feeling remorse for the crimes she committed. She might have been driven to her present state of mind by the murder of Lady Macduff and her children.

2b. Macbeth characterizes his way of life as dried, withered, and friendless. He is unhappy because he sees he will never have true friends or true honor.

3b. The witches equivocated with Macbeth by making him believe that he is invincible when he is not.

ANALYZE

4a. Malcolm is proclaimed king and makes his allies earls. He promises to call home all exiles who fled under Macbeth and to bring to trial Macbeth's officials.

SYNTHESIZE

4b. The murder of a king was sacrilegious because it was believed that kings were divinely anointed and answerable only to God. Thus, to take a king off the throne was to defy God. This play seems to say that regicide is an unnatural act that destroys the natural order and leads to chaos and disaster.

EVALUATE

Responses will vary.

5a. Act 2, scene 4, lines 28–29; act 3, scene 2, lines 4–7; and act 5, scene 3, lines 22–26 all concern the futility of pursuing ambition. Macbeth pays for the consequences of his actions, giving up honor, love, and friendship since he has violated them all.

EXTEND

5b. *Responses will vary.*

INVESTIGATE, Inquire, Imagine

Recall: GATHERING FACTS → Interpret: FINDING MEANING

1a. What do Lady Macbeth's gentlewoman and doctor observe her doing at the beginning of scene 1? What action does she continually perform? What statement of hers from act 2 does this recall?

1b. What do Lady Macbeth's actions reveal about her state of mind? What do you think she is feeling? What event might have driven her to this state?

2a. Why is Macbeth so confident at the beginning of scene 3?

2b. In lines 22–28 of scene 3, how does Macbeth characterize his life? Why is he so unhappy, despite his confidence?

3a. In scene 5, Macbeth receives bad news related to the witches' prophecies. What is this news? What does Macbeth realize?

3b. In what ways have the witches equivocated with Macbeth?

Analyze: TAKING THINGS APART → Synthesize: BRINGING THINGS TOGETHER

4a. What indications are given at the end of the play that order will be restored in Scotland?

4b. In act 2, Macduff says of Duncan's murder that "Most sacrilegious murder that broke open / The Lord's anointed temple and stole hence / The life o' the building." In what sense was the murder of a king sacrilegious? What is this play saying about the nature and effects of regicide?

Evaluate: MAKING JUDGMENTS → Extend: CONNECTING IDEAS

5a. Evaluate whether Shakespeare develops the theme that an immoral life is meaningless.

5b. Write a rebuttal to Macbeth's words in act 5, scene 5, lines 24–28.

Understanding Literature

METAPHOR. Review the definition for **metaphor** in the Handbook of Literary Terms. In scene 5, lines 26–28, Macbeth respond to the news of Lady Macbeth's death. What two things does he compare? What do they have in common? What does the metaphor tell you about Macbeth's view of life?

THEME. Review the definition for **theme** in the Handbook of Literary Terms. James I, king of England when Shakespeare wrote *Macbeth,* believed in the divine right of kings, the idea that a king was divinely appointed and his rule was part of the natural order of things. What recurring elements, or motifs, in this play deal with disturbances to the natural order? Give examples of psychological disorder, disorder in nature, disorder in the kingdom, and disordered (or equivocal) speech. What incident in the play brings about all of this disorder? What elements of Duncan's murder make it particularly unnatural? What theme do you think Shakespeare is expressing regarding the natural order?

A complex play like *Macbeth* has, of course, many themes. Another theme of the play is the consequences of ambition. What are the consequences of ambition for Macbeth? What are some other themes that you have noticed while reading the play?

ANSWERS TO UNDERSTANDING LITERATURE

METAPHOR. Macbeth compares life to "a tale / Told by an idiot, full of sound and fury, / Signifying nothing." In Macbeth's view, life and a tale are similar in that despite the fuss and bother of each, they ultimately mean nothing. The metaphor indicates that Macbeth sees no value in life.

Exposition, Rising Action, Crisis, Falling Action, Catastrophe. Review the definitions for **exposition, rising action, crisis, falling action,** and **catastrophe** in Literary Tools on page 447. Then, create a chart like the one on the right and list key events from *Macbeth* that contribute to the exposition, rising acton, crisis, falling action, and catastrophe. What tragic flaw in *Macbeth* leads to the catastrophe? In which acts do these points in the plot occur?

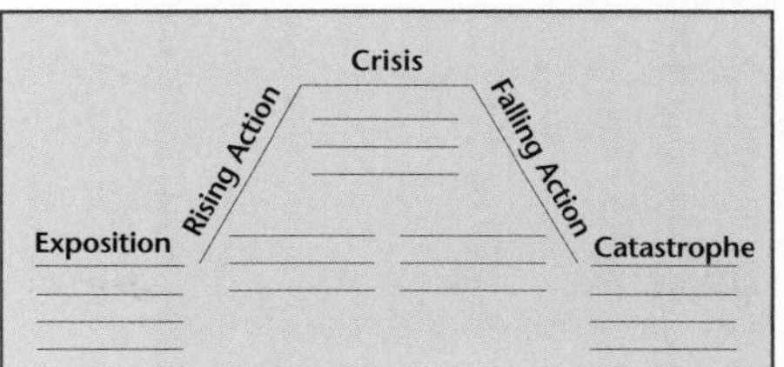

Writer's Journal

1. An obituary is a written notice of a person's death, listing the cause of death, survivors, and some biographical information. Write an **obituary** for Macbeth, Lady Macbeth, Banquo, or Duncan.
2. Imagine that you are Malcolm and you have just won the battle against Macbeth. Write a **proclamation** to your people detailing the outcome of the battle, the crimes of Macbeth and Lady Macbeth, and your plans to reunify Scotland. Use language to rally the people to your side.
3. There is more than one way to look at a piece of literature; that is, there is not necessarily a right or a wrong interpretation. However, a good expository essay about a piece of literature states its thesis, or main, idea, clearly, and then supports that thesis with solid, convincing evidence. Write an **expository essay** about one of the central themes of *Macbeth*. State your thesis, the idea that you wish to prove, and then present in a logical, organized manner evidence from the play to support your thesis.

Integrating the Language Arts

Study and Research & Speaking and Listening

Researching Warfare. The nature of war in medieval times, the setting for *Macbeth,* was different from war today. Research the weapons and tactics used in warfare during the Middle Ages. Then present your findings to the class.

Media Literacy & Study and Research

Researching Guy Fawkes Day. In 1605 a plan to blow up Parliament and the king was discovered. Since then, the British have celebrated Guy Fawkes Day. Research Guy Fawkes Day. What were the details of the plot? What would have happened if the plot succeeded? Who was Guy Fawkes? How is Guy Fawkes Day celebrated today? Find answers to these questions on the Internet and present your findings to the class.

Speaking and Listening

Oral Interpretation. Read the Language Arts Survey 4.19, "Oral Interpretation." Then choose a short speech from the play to memorize. For example, you might choose Macbeth's speech in act 5, scene 5, lines 17–28. Rehearse the speech that you have memorized and present it to a group of your classmates.

Answers to Understanding Literature

(cont. from page 462)

Theme. Recurring elements of the play that deal with disorder are these: the witches and their prophecies (disorder in language); horrific occurrences, such as the day of Duncan's death being as dark as night, the killing of a falcon by an owl, and the wildness of Duncan's horses (disorder in nature); murder, including the murder of the king and the murder of an innocent wife and her children (disorder in the kingdom); and sleeplessness and madness (psychological disorder). These motifs can be seen to be related to the central motif of ambition, for this disorder is all brought about by the assassination of Duncan. The murder of Duncan is particularly unnatural because it was done by his host shortly after that host had been honored for putting down a rebellion. Shakespeare believed that humankind (and human kingdoms) are intimately bound up with the natural world; the one reflects disorder in the other. The consequences of ambition for Macbeth are despair, loss of his wife, and death. Other themes in the play are the importance of one's relation to posterity, the inevitable failure of an attempt to use evil to one's own ends, the nature of evil, the misuse of political power, and the relationship between character and fate.

Exposition, Rising Action, Falling Action, Catastrophe. The exposition occurs in act 1. The rising action occurs in act 2. The crisis occurs in act 3. The falling action occurs in act 4. The catastrophe occurs in act 5. Students may list the following elements in their graphic organizers:
Exposition: Macbeth acts heroically. The witches foretell kingship for Macbeth. Duncan rewards Macbeth. Macbeth and Lady Macbeth debate murdering Duncan. Duncan arrives at Macbeth's castle. **Rising Action:** Macbeth kills Duncan. Macduff discovers the king's body. Macbeth kills the king's grooms. Malcolm and Donalbain flee. Macbeth is to be named king. **Crisis:** Macbeth has Banquo murdered. Banquo's ghost haunts Macbeth at the feast. Macbeth is publicly disgraced. Macduff travels to England to find support. **Falling Action:** Witches give ambiguous signs encouraging to Macbeth. Macbeth has Macduff's family murdered. Macduff joins forces with Malcolm in England. **Catastrophe:** Lady Macbeth goes mad and kills herself. The English army moves on Macbeth's stronghold. Signs foretold by the witches are fulfilled. Macduff kills Macbeth. Malcolm reestablishes order in Scotland.

ADDITIONAL RESOURCES

Unit 5 Resource Book

- Selection Worksheet 5.6
- Selection Check Test 4.5.13
- Selection Test 4.5.14
- Language, Grammar, and Style Resource 3.36, 3.77

GRAPHIC ORGANIZER

Responses will vary, but students might include the following information in their cluster charts: Leap up to God (line 65); Be saved by a drop of Christ's blood (lines 66–67); Have mountains and hills fall on him (line 72); Run into the earth (line 75); Ascend to heaven as a cloud (lines 79–83); Live in hell a thousand years and then be saved (lines 88–89); Change into "some brutish beast" (lines 94–95); Change into drops of water and fall into the ocean (lines 104–105).

READER'S JOURNAL

Because of the personal nature of this question, students may want to keep their entry private. Ask students to write about whether they wish they could take back what they did, and what they could have done to avoid the experience. What did they learn from the experience? Students who have difficulty thinking of an action they did and later regretted may be reminded that not to take an action is in a sense to take an action. Is there anything they did not do that they wish they had done? Would they like the chance to do it now?

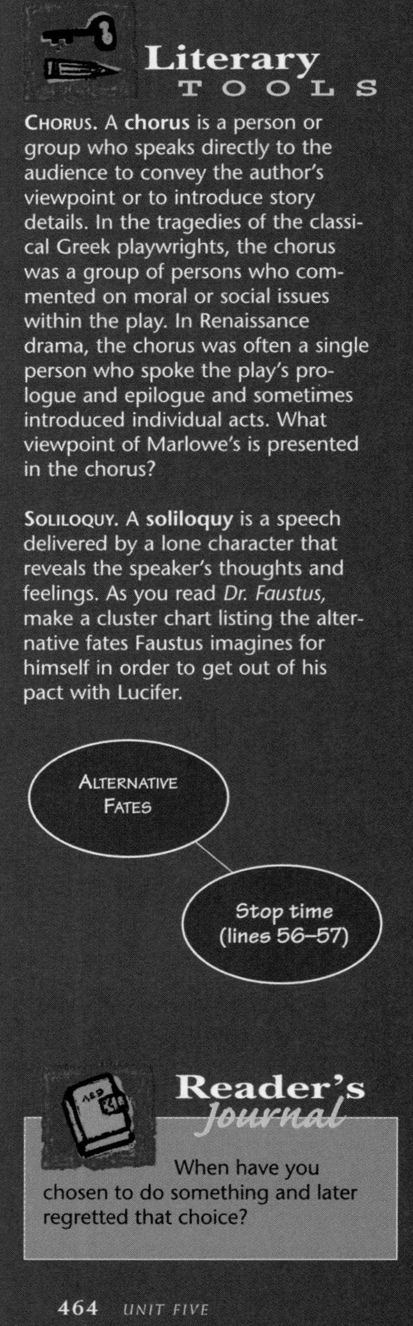

DRAMA

Literary TOOLS

Chorus. A **chorus** is a person or group who speaks directly to the audience to convey the author's viewpoint or to introduce story details. In the tragedies of the classical Greek playwrights, the chorus was a group of persons who commented on moral or social issues within the play. In Renaissance drama, the chorus was often a single person who spoke the play's prologue and epilogue and sometimes introduced individual acts. What viewpoint of Marlowe's is presented in the chorus?

Soliloquy. A **soliloquy** is a speech delivered by a lone character that reveals the speaker's thoughts and feelings. As you read *Dr. Faustus,* make a cluster chart listing the alternative fates Faustus imagines for himself in order to get out of his pact with Lucifer.

Reader's Journal

When have you chosen to do something and later regretted that choice?

FROM

The Tragical History of Doctor Faustus

BY CHRISTOPHER MARLOWE

The Tragicall History of the Life and Death of Doctor Faustus.

Written by Ch. Marklin.

LONDON, Printed for Iohn Wright, and are to be sold at his shop without Newgate, at the [illegible] Bible. 1616.

Frontispiece of another version of the Faust story, *The Tragicall History of the Life and Death of Doctor Faustus,* 1616. English Artist. Private Collection.

GOALS/OBJECTIVES

Studying this lesson will enable students to

- empathize with Faustus's torment and his regret
- compare and contrast Macbeth and Faustus as tragic figures
- define the literary terms *chorus* and *soliloquy* and recognize the use of these techniques in their reading
- write a treatment for a science fiction film
- practice combining sentences
- conduct a mock trial
- research the Faustian theme in other works of literature

About *the* AUTHOR

Christopher Marlowe was born in February, 1564, to a Canterbury shoemaker. He attended Cambridge University, took bachelor's and master's degrees, studied widely and deeply, and may have begun his studies with the intention of becoming an Anglican priest. The actual course of his life was to be quite different. Evidence suggests that, while still in school, Marlowe became a spy for the British government, and on graduation he immediately began a career in the theater. He wrote his first great play, *Tamburlaine,* in 1587, and continued producing plays over the next six years.

In 1593, Marlowe's friend and fellow dramatist Thomas Kyd, author of *The Spanish Tragedy,* was arrested and executed for treason. Some heretical, freethinking papers were found in Kyd's quarters, and Kyd implicated Marlowe in their production. Conservatives accused Marlowe of atheism, but the government interceded to protect him from prosecution, perhaps because Marlowe was still serving as a spy. Later that year, Marlowe was killed in a tavern brawl. Puritans slandered the dead playwright, calling him an impious and immoral man and pointing to the manner of his death as proof. However, given the tender sincerity of Marlowe's lyric poetry and the moral fervor of such works as *The Tragical History of Doctor Faustus,* one can hardly accept such charges against him. It is possible that Marlowe was murdered by the government because of embarrassment over the Kyd episode. At his death, Marlowe was only twenty-nine years old.

About *the* SELECTION

At the time Marlowe wrote ***The Tragical History of Doctor Faustus,*** translations of German Faust stories had already appeared in London, and the story of a man who sells his soul to the devil in exchange for magical powers was well known. Marlowe set his play in the German university town of Wittenberg at the end of the sixteenth century. Dr. Faustus, a brilliant scholar, makes a deal with the devil: Faustus will receive the powers of black magic and the services of the devil's servant, Mephastophilis, in exchange for his soul. Throughout the remainder of the play, Faustus agonizes over his decision, yearning for forgiveness but believing that ultimately he cannot be saved. This selection, which is the final scene of the play, begins as Faustus confesses his bargain to his fellow scholars.

The plot of the Faustus story derives originally from the story of Adam and Eve, who tasted the forbidden fruit of the tree of knowledge and so were cast out of Eden (see the selection from Milton's *Paradise Lost* in Unit 6). The influence of the Faustus story on later literature has been enormous. This tale has given rise over the years to thousands of similar stories about people who make "devil's bargains" in a quest for knowledge, power, beauty, fame, or fortune.

INDIVIDUAL LEARNING STRATEGIES

MOTIVATION
Students might be interested in discussing why the theme of selling one's soul to the devil has been such a popular one over the centuries. Point them to the Study and Research activity on page 472, where they can research other versions of the Faustus story.

READING PROFICIENCY
Point out the archaic word *thou,* which Faustus uses to address himself in his soliloquy. Explain that it is the old singular form of "you." Then point out the word *thy* and explain that it is the possessive of "thou," and that it can be translated as "your." Then ask students to notice the archaic forms verbs for "thou" which include *hast* and *wert,* and the forms for third person, which include *hath* and *doth.*

ENGLISH LANGUAGE LEARNING
Explain to students that the word *doctor,* as in the title of the play, does not mean a medical doctor but a person who has completed several years of study beyond the college level. Share with them the following additional vocabulary:

ail—trouble, bother
belike—apparently
perpetually—forever
headlong—recklessly
wanting—without

SPECIAL NEEDS
Have students pay special attention to the Guided Reading Questions and the Recall questions at the end of the selection.

ENRICHMENT
Students can study the story of Adam and Eve as literature (the Bible, Genesis 2:15–3:24). A general discussion could begin with asking: is knowledge good or bad? Is it good to a point and then bad? Is too little knowledge a dangerous thing, or is too much, or both? If knowledge does become dangerous at some point, how can one tell when it does so?

ANSWER TO GUIDED READING QUESTION

1. Faustus says "A surfeit of deadly sin" is the cause of his condition.

VOCABULARY FROM THE SELECTION

abjure
blaspheme
entice
exhort
felicity
firmament
gape
harbor
incessant
ireful
nativity
rend
surfeit

FROM

The Tragical History of Doctor Faustus

CHRISTOPHER MARLOWE

SCENE 13

[*Enter* FAUSTUS *with the* SCHOLARS.]

FAUSTUS. Ah, gentlemen!

1 SCHOLAR. What ails Faustus?

FAUSTUS. Ah, my sweet chamber-fellow, had I lived with thee, then had I lived still; but now I die eternally. Look, comes he not, comes he not?

2 SCHOLAR. What means Faustus?

3 SCHOLAR. Belike he is grown into some sickness, by being oversolitary.

1 SCHOLAR. If it be so, we'll have physicians to cure him; 'tis but a surfeit: never fear, man.

What does Faustus say is the cause of his condition?

FAUSTUS. A surfeit of deadly sin, that hath damned both body and soul.

2 SCHOLAR. Yet Faustus, look up to heaven; remember God's mercies are infinite.

FAUSTUS. But Faustus' offense can ne'er be pardoned! The serpent that tempted Eve[1] may be saved, but not Faustus. Ah gentlemen, hear me with patience, and tremble not at my speeches, though my heart pants and quivers to remember that I

1. **The serpent . . . Eve.** In the book of Genesis the serpent tempted Eve to eat from the tree of knowledge, bringing the first sin into the world.

WORDS FOR EVERYDAY USE

sur • feit (sur´ fit) *n.*, overabundance. *The politicians, claiming the nation had a* surfeit *of laws, passed new laws to abolish the old.*

have been a student here these thirty years—O would I had never seen Wittenberg,[2] never read book—and what wonders I have done, all Wittenberg can witness—yea, all the world; for which Faustus hath lost both Germany and the world—yea, heaven itself—heaven, the seat of God, the throne of the blessed, the kingdom of joy; and must remain in hell for ever—hell, ah, hell for ever! Sweet friends, what shall become of Faustus, being in hell for ever?

What does Faustus regret?

3 SCHOLAR. Yet Faustus, call on God.

FAUSTUS. On God, whom Faustus hath abjured? On God, whom Faustus hath blasphemed? Ah my God—I would weep, but the devil draws in my tears! gush forth blood, instead of tears—yea, life and soul! O, he stays my tongue! I would lift up my hands, but see, they hold them, they hold them!

ALL. Who, Faustus?

FAUSTUS. Lucifer and Mephastophilis![3] Ah gentlemen, I gave them my soul for my cunning.

What bargain did Faustus strike with Lucifer and Mephastophilis?

ALL. God forbid!

FAUSTUS. God forbade it indeed, but Faustus hath done it: for the vain pleasure of four-and-twenty years hath Faustus lost eternal joy and felicity. I writ them a bill with mine own blood, the date is expired, the time will come, and he will fetch me.

1 SCHOLAR. Why did not Faustus tell us of this before, that divines might have prayed for thee?

How do Faustus's colleagues feel about him?

FAUSTUS. Oft have I thought to have done so, but the devil threatened to tear me in pieces if I named God, to fetch both body and soul, if I once gave ear to divinity; and now 'tis too late. Gentlemen away, lest you perish with me!

2 SCHOLAR. O what shall we do to save Faustus?

3 SCHOLAR. God will strengthen me. I will stay with Faustus.

1 SCHOLAR. Tempt not God, sweet friend, but let us into the next room, and there pray for him.

FAUSTUS. Aye, pray for me, pray for me; and what noise soever ye hear, come not unto me, for nothing can rescue me.

---

2. **Wittenberg.** A famous university in Germany
3. **Lucifer and Mephastophilis.** Devils

WORDS FOR EVERYDAY USE

blas • pheme (blas' fēm) *vt.,* show contempt or irreverence for something sacred. *The young children were taught never to blaspheme God by using His name in vain.*

ab • jure (ab jo͞or') *vi.,* renounce, give up publicly. *The day he entered juvenile court, Monty solemnly abjured his habit of thoughtless vandalism and vowed to lead a better life.*

fel • lic • i • ty (fə lis' i tē) *n.,* happiness. *A peaceful garden, a summer morning, the music of birds—that, Horatio, is the highest felicity life has to offer.*

ANSWERS TO GUIDED READING QUESTIONS

1. Faustus regrets ever having seen Wittenberg or read a book, events which he believes led him to lose his chance of going to heaven.
2. Faustus exchanged his soul for knowledge.
3. The scholars care about Faustus enough to wish to save him.

LITERARY NOTE

The text of Marlowe's play is often very close to the text of his source, *The History of the Damnable Life and Deserved Death of Doctor John Faustus,* a translation of an older German work. Marlowe even preserves some of the errors of fact made by the translator. The similarity of the two works can be judged by comparing two passages. The source reads: "May it please your grace to understand that the year is divided into two circles over the whole world, that when with us it is winter, in the contrary circle it is not withstanding summer; for in India and Saba there falleth or setteth the sun so that it is so warm that they have twice a year fruit." Marlowe's text reads: "Please it your Grace, the year is divided into two circles over the whole world, so that when it is winter with us, in the contrary circle it is likewise summer with them, as in India, Saba, and such countries that lie far east, where they have fruit twice a year."

ANSWER TO GUIDED READING QUESTION

1. Faustus's colleagues still have hope for him; Faustus apparently has no hope ("nothing can rescue me," line 48).

ADDITIONAL QUESTIONS AND ACTIVITIES

Ask students to consider the following question as they read: To what extent is Faustus a symbol of the human race, in all its endeavors?

Dr. Faustus in his Study, c.1600s. Rembrandt van Rijn. Leeds Museums and Galleries, Leeds, U.K.

2 SCHOLAR. Pray thou, and we will pray, that God may have mercy upon thee.

Do Faustus's colleagues still have hope for him? Does Faustus have any hope for himself?

FAUSTUS. Gentlemen, farewell. If I live till morning, I'll visit you; if not, Faustus is gone to hell.

ALL. Faustus, farewell.

[*Exeunt* SCHOLARS.]

[*The clock strikes eleven.*]

FAUSTUS. Ah Faustus,
Now hast thou but one bare hour to live,
And then thou must be damned perpetually.
Stand still, you ever-moving spheres of heaven,
That time may cease, and midnight never come.
Fair Nature's eye, rise, rise again, and make
Perpetual day, or let this hour be but
A year, a month, a week, a natural day,

That Faustus may repent and save his soul.
O lente, lente currite noctis equi! [4]
The stars move still, time runs, the clock will strike,
The devil will come, and Faustus must be damned.
O, I'll leap up to my God! Who pulls me down?
See, see where Christ's blood streams in the firmament!
One drop would save my soul, half a drop: ah my Christ—
Ah, rend not my heart for naming of my Christ;
Yet will I call on him—O spare me, Lucifer!
Where is it now? 'Tis gone: and see where God
Stretcheth out his arm, and bends his ireful brows!
Mountains and hills, come, come and fall on me,
And hide me from the heavy wrath of God.
No, no?
Then will I headlong run into the earth:
Earth, gape! O no, it will not harbor me.
You stars that reigned at my nativity,
Whose influence hath allotted death and hell,
Now draw up Faustus like a foggy mist
Into the entails of yon laboring cloud,
That when you vomit forth into the air,
My limbs may issue from your smoky mouths,
So that my soul may but ascend to heaven.

[*The watch strikes.*]

Ah, half the hour is past: 'twill all be past anon.
O God, if thou wilt not have mercy on my soul,
Yet for Christ's sake, whose blood hath ransomed me,
Impose some end to my incessant pain:
Let Faustus live in hell a thousand years,
A hundred thousand, and at last be saved.
O, no end is limited to damned souls!
Why wert thou not a creature wanting soul?
Or why is this immortal that thou hast?
Ah, Pythagoras' *metempsychosis* [5]—were that true,

How does Faustus imagine God will judge him?

Whom is Faustus addressing?

4. ***O lente . . . equi.*** Slowly, slowly run, O horses of the night (Latin).

5. ***metempsychosis.*** Pythagoras's theory that souls pass from one body to another at death

WORDS FOR EVERYDAY USE

fir • ma • ment (fɘrm'ə mənt) *n.*, sky. *The stars in the firmament number in the billions.*

rend (rend) *vt.*, rip apart. *These new plastic bags are so tough you practically have to rend them with a chainsaw to get them open.*

ire • ful (īr'fəl) *adj.*, angry. *People with impairment of the amygdala, a region of the brain, are unable to distinguish an ireful glare from an affectionate glance.*

gape (gāp) *vi.*, open wide. *Holes gaped in the roads after the long winter had damaged the pavement.*

har • bor (här'bər) *vt.*, provide protection to. *The Gestapo punished families for harboring Jews in their homes.*

na • tiv • i • ty (nə tiv' ə tē) *n.*, birth. *In celebration of the hundredth anniversary of her nativity, Ms. Cosway took her first parachute jump.*

in • ces • sant (in ses'ənt) *adj.*, neverending. *The incessant blather of the television set soon drove Maxine out of the waiting area.*

ANSWERS TO GUIDED READING QUESTIONS

1. Faustus says that God is ireful and wrathful toward him, indicating that he believes God will judge him harshly.
2. Faustus addresses himself.

SELECTION CHECK TEST 4.5.13 WITH ANSWERS

Checking Your Reading

1. What do the scholars advise Faustus to do? **They advise him to call on God.**
2. What has Faustus promised? **He promised his soul to the devil.**
3. Why does Faustus fear midnight? **The devils will come for him at midnight.**
4. Why does Faustus wish to be turned into a beast? **They have no souls to be tortured in hell.**
5. What warning is issued at the end of the selection? **Responses will vary, but could include that we are warned to only wonder at "unlawful things," or not to wish for more than "heavenly power permits."**

Vocabulary in Context

Fill each blank with the most appropriate word from the Words for Everyday Use. You may have to change the tense of the word.

abjure harbor entice felicity
incessant rend surfeit

1. The children's **incessant** laughter helped Mrs. Perkins feel better.
2. The seamstress began work by **rending** old garments and sorting the materials.
3. The play was a classic tragedy, so we knew the characters' **felicity** would not last.
4. After their **surfeit** at the banquet, the twins decided to go for a long walk.
5. Grant knew he would regret it if he let his friends **entice** him to stay out too late.

Literary Tools

Choose the sentence ending that *best* fits each sentence beginning. You may not use any choice more than once.

__D__ 1. A soliloquy is…
__F__ 2. In Renaissance drama, the chorus is…
__A__ 3. A genre is…
__E__ 4. Playwrights use soliloquies to share…
__G__ 5. In Greek drama, the chorus is…

SELECTION CHECK TEST 4.5.13 WITH ANSWERS (CONT.)

a. a type or category of literary works.
b. delivered by the main character to the chorus.
c. spoken by the audience so that the actors can hear.
d. a speech delivered by a character alone on stage.
e. a character's thoughts, feelings, or motives with an audience.
f. a group of people who comment on moral or social issues in the play.
g. a single person who reads the prologue, epilogue, and sometimes introduces acts.

ANSWER TO GUIDED READING QUESTION

1. Faustus blames himself and Lucifer for his terrible life.

ADDITIONAL QUESTIONS AND ACTIVITIES

- Students can write an essay comparing and contrasting Macbeth and Faustus as tragic figures. Suggest they compare Macbeth's tragic flaw (his hunger for power) with Faustus's flaw (the hunger for knowledge) and that they contrast the different attitude of each man toward repentance.
- Read to students line 109, the last words of Faustus's final speech ("I'll burn my books—ah, Mephastophilis!"). Explain that in the sixteenth century books were considerably more rare and valuable than they are now. Ask the following questions to stimulate discussion:

1. Why did Marlowe choose these words as Faustus's last?
2. Throughout the play, Mephastophilis is Faustus's tempter, companion in crimes and travels, fellow trickster, and menacing guard. What is the effect of Faustus's calling his name as his last word in the play?

Answers

1. The offer to burn his books if he is left in peace is a shocking indication of the despair of Faustus. He has sought knowledge all his life and now is willing not only to renounce it but literally to burn and destroy it. Faustus's offer is virtually the most powerful one he could make in his situation.
2. He seems to call upon Mephastophilis for help, for pity, and yet also in acknowledgment that no help is possible from that spirit. His call is poignant and yet pointless.

This soul should fly from me, and I be changed
Unto some brutish beast:
All beasts are happy, for when they die,
Their souls are soon dissolved in elements;
But mine must live still[6] to be plagued in hell.
Cursed be the parents that engendered me:
No, Faustus, curse thy self, curse Lucifer,
That hath deprived thee of the joys of heaven.

Whom does Faustus blame for his terrible life?

[*The clock strikes twelve.*]

O it strikes, it strikes! Now body, turn to air,
Or Lucifer will bear thee quick[7] to hell.

[*Thunder and lightning.*]

O soul, be changed into little water drops,
And fall into the ocean, ne'er be found.
My God, my God, look not so fierce on me!

[*Enter* DEVILS.]

Adders and serpents, let me breathe awhile!
Ugly hell gape not! Come not, Lucifer!
I'll burn my books—ah, Mephastophilis!

[*Exeunt with him.*]

EPILOGUE

[*Enter* CHORUS.]

Cut is the branch that might have grown full straight,
And burnèd is Apollo's laurel bough,[8]
That sometime grew within this learned man.
Faustus is gone! Regard his hellish fall,
Whose fiendful fortune[9] may exhort the wise
Only to wonder at unlawful things:
Whose deepness doth entice such forward wits,
To practice more than heavenly power permits.

[*Exit.*]

Terminat hora diem, terminat author opus.[10] ■

6. **still.** Always
7. **quick.** Alive
8. **laurel bough.** The laurel bough is a conventional symbol of achievement, in this case, attainment of wisdom or learning.
9. **fiendful fortune.** Devilish fate
10. ***Terminat . . . opus.*** The hour ends the day, the author ends his work (Latin).

WORDS FOR EVERYDAY USE

ex • hort (eg zôrt´) *vt.,* warn, plead with. *The preacher exhorted the people of his impoverished congregation to give kindness freely to their neighbors.*

en • tice (en tīs´) *vt.,* tempt. *Mustafa enticed his cat down from the tree with tuna fish.*

Respond *to the* Selection

If you were one of the scholars who heard Dr. Faustus's explanation of his situation, how would you have responded to him?

Investigate, Inquire, *Imagine*

Recall: Gathering Facts

1a. What does Faustus tell the scholars he has done to himself? What do the scholars urge Faustus to do?

2a. Why does Faustus beg for the mountains and hills to fall upon him? What does Faustus want to be turned into?

3a. What will happen to Faustus now that "the date is expired" on his contract with the devil?

Interpret: Finding Meaning

1b. What attitudes do the scholars express toward Faustus and the sin which he confesses?

2b. How does Faustus feel about the decision that he made? Why does he want to be turned into something else?

3b. With whom does the blame lie for Faustus's situation?

Analyze: Taking Things Apart →

4a. What aspects of Faustus's personality make him a sympathetic character?

Synthesize: Bringing Things Together

4b. What do Faustus's thoughts and feelings tell you about his character?

Evaluate: Making Judgments →

5a. Evaluate Marlowe's attitude toward knowledge. Do you agree or disagree? Why?

Extend: Connecting Ideas

5b. With what modern technological and scientific advances would Marlowe probably find fault? How do these advances overstep the limits set on humans by God?

Understanding *Literature*

Chorus. Review the definition for **chorus** in Literary Tools on page 464. What function does the chorus at the end of the play serve? Is the chorus helpful? Is it necessary? Do you agree or disagree with the viewpoint expressed by the chorus?

Soliloquy. Review the definition for **soliloquy** in the Handbook of Literary Terms and the cluster chart you made for Literary Tools on page 464. What do the examples in your cluster chart reveal about Faustus? When Faustus recites his soliloquy, what is his state of mind? Which lines from the soliloquy help to shape your opinion? What is your opinion of Faustus? What is the advantage of presenting Faustus's state of mind in a soliloquy rather than a dialogue?

RESPOND TO THE SELECTION

You might suggest possible responses for students to choose from, such as empathy, derision, or condescension.

ANSWERS TO INVESTIGATE, INQUIRE, AND IMAGINE

Recall

1a. Faustus says he made a contract in blood with the devil to gain knowledge. The scholars tell him to pray and have faith in God.

2a. Faustus begs for the mountains and hills to fall upon him because he wants to hide from the wrath of God. Faustus wants to be turned into an animal.

3a. Faustus will be drawn down to hell to be tortured for eternity.

Interpret

1b. The scholars express sorrow and a willingness to ask God to pardon him.

2b. Faustus feels tormented by regret: "for the vain pleasure of four-and-twenty years hath Faustus lost eternal joy and felicity" (lines 33–35). Faustus wants to become an animal because he believes that animals do not endure eternity.

3b. The blame for Faustus's situation lies with himself and Lucifer.

Analyze

4a. Faustus's remorse and repentance make him a sympathetic character. He is capable of looking at his actions, examining them, and admitting wrongdoing.

Synthesize

4b. Now that his time on earth is finished, Faustus is humble and self-reflective.

Evaluate

5a. As expressed in the epilogue, Marlowe believes that the wise marvel at those things they cannot do or know, whereas the foolish investigate them and overstep the limits set on humans by God. Responses will vary.

Extend

Responses will vary.

5b. Students might mention genetic engineering, cloning, and space exploration, to name a few.

ANSWERS TO UNDERSTANDING LITERATURE

Chorus. The chorus explains the putative moral of the story. The chorus is necessary to demonstrate that Marlowe does not approve of Faustus's career. *Responses will vary. Possible responses are given.* One reason supporting the viewpoint of the chorus is that it does point out that Faustus pried into knowledge and was doomed; a reason for disagreeing with the chorus is that advances in science, for example, would never be made if people didn't risk destruction in the search for knowledge.

Soliloquy. Faustus's search for an alternative fate reveals his desperation; he is willing to do anything to avoid the wrath of God and eternal damnation. When

(Continued on page 472)

ANSWERS TO UNDERSTANDING LITERATURE (CONT. FROM PAGE 471)

Faustus recites his soliloquy, he feels despair and contrition. Most of the soliloquy expresses his fear and his wish that he could repent. *Responses will vary.* Faustus may be seen as an essentially good man who was tempted beyond his ability to resist. The soliloquy reveals his innermost feelings, enabling the reader to understand him and so to sympathize with him even while judging him. The soliloquy allows for unrestricted exposition of Faustus's feelings without distraction; however, a dialogue could also have been used effectively.

ANSWERS TO INTEGRATING THE LANGUAGE ARTS

Language, Grammar, and Style

1. The fictional character of Doctor Faustus was based on a real German magician named Georg Faust, who gained fame during the early 1500s.
2. *The History of the Damnable Life and Deserved Death of Doctor John Faustus* was an English translation of a German narrative that appeared in London in 1592.
3. Goethe, a German author and poet, wrote a two-part Faust play in the nineteenth century.
4. Unlike earlier versions of the tragic hero, Goethe's Faust is finally saved by angels.
5. Thomas Mann wrote a novel, *Doctor Faustus,* that was only loosely based on the Faust legend.

Sentences 3 and 5 use appositives.

Study and Research & Speaking and Listening

The **Internet site of the University of Texas at Brownsville and Texas Southmost College** contains a page with a link to Irving's story "The Devil and Tom Walker," along with a short quiz. Have students visit this page at http://unix.utb.edu/~783824/tomwalke.htm. Students may also be interested in viewing the 1941 movie *The Devil and Daniel Webster,* which is based on Stephen Vincent Benét's short story.

Speaking and Listening & Collaborative Learning

Students can consult a lawyer or judge in the community (perhaps a parent) willing to give a quick overview of trial procedures. Question each group before it begins its work to make sure its members understand what roles have been assigned to them. Emphasize the necessity of developing arguments ahead of time and anticipating the arguments that the other side will offer.

WRITER'S JOURNAL

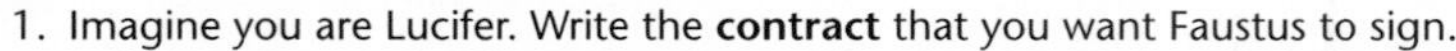

1. Imagine you are Lucifer. Write the **contract** that you want Faustus to sign.
2. Imagine you are Faustus and are writing to your colleagues from hell. Write a **memo** explaining what happened to you and giving advice so that your fellow scholars do not make the same mistakes you made.
3. Write a **treatment** for a science fiction film based on *The Tragical History of Doctor Faustus.* A treatment is a narrative that tells the storyline for a film. One possible approach would be to change the devils of Marlowe's play to aliens that give some of their power or knowledge to an earthling in exchange for giving up life on earth after a certain period of time expires.

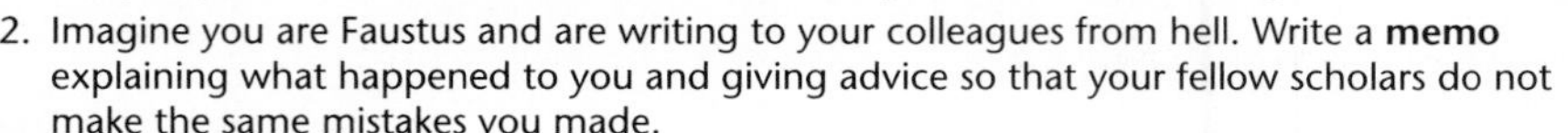

Integrating *the* Language Arts

Language, Grammar, and Style

COMBINING SENTENCES. Read the Language Arts Survey 3.36, "Combining and Expanding Sentences." Then revise the sentences below by combining their ideas. Then identify which of your sentences use appositives. Read about appositives in the Language Arts Survey 3.77.

1. Doctor Faustus was a fictional character. The character of Doctor Faustus was based on a real German magician named Georg Faust. Georg Faust gained fame during the early 1500s.
2. *The History of the Damnable Life and Deserved Death of Doctor John Faustus* was an English translation of a German narrative. The translation appeared in London in 1592.
3. A two-part Faust play was written by Goethe. Goethe was a German author and poet. Goethe wrote in the nineteenth century.
4. Goethe's Faust is unlike earlier versions of the tragic hero. Goethe's Faust is finally saved by angels.
5. Thomas Mann wrote *Doctor Faustus. Doctor Faustus* is a novel. Mann's novel was only loosely based on the Faust legend.

Study and Research & Speaking and Listening

RESEARCHING THE FAUST THEME. The theme of selling one's soul to the devil is common in Western art and literature. Research one of the following treatments of the Faust theme: Johann von Goethe's drama *Faust* (1790), Washington Irving's story "The Devil and Tom Walker" (1800), Stephen Vincent Benét's "The Devil and Daniel Webster" (1937), Thomas Mann's novel *Doktor Faustus* (1947), the film *Damn Yankees!* (1958), and the song "The Devil Went Down to Georgia" (1979), by the Charlie Daniels Band. As a class, discuss how each is similar and different from what you read of Marlowe's play.

Speaking and Listening & Collaborative Learning

MOCK TRIAL. Determine if the punishment Faustus receives is fair. Select a role, either Faustus, the defense attorney, the prosecuting attorney, or the judge. You may also want to present several witnesses. Then conduct a mock trial.

FROM

The Analects

BY CONFUCIUS, TRANSLATED BY ARTHUR WALEY

About the AUTHOR

Confucius (551–479 BC) is the Anglicized name of K'ung Ch'iu, the most famous teacher and philosopher in Chinese history. Through the ages, he has been referred to most commonly as K'ung-fu-tzu, or "Master K'ung." His presumed birthday, September 28, is celebrated in Taiwan as "Teacher's Day." Confucius was born in the state of Lu, now the Shantung province of China, probably to a poor, but noble, family. Orphaned at an early age and with few resources, he nonetheless devoted himself to education in the six practical arts (ritual, music, archery, charioteering, calligraphy, and arithmetic), as well as in classical history and poetry. He became the most learned man of his era, attracting thousands of students and a core group of devoted disciples. Renowned for his teachings, he believed that learning should serve the practical ends of public service. He himself served for a time as a government official in the state of Lu. At the age of 73, he died a revered sage.

About the SELECTION

The teachings of Confucius were collected by his disciples in the ***Lun-yü,*** or ***Analects.*** The word *analects* means "miscellaneous excerpts." Confucius lived in a time of great political and social unrest. His teachings stressed the moral order of the universe as reflected in the proper behavior and interrelations of people of various stations in life. Important themes in Confucian teaching include duty, loyalty, obligation, ritual, social norms, and action befitting one's place in society. For more than two thousand years, Confucius's teachings were the official basis for education in China. They permeate thought and codes of behavior throughout the Asian world.

Reader's Journal

What characteristics define a good leader?

MULTICULTURAL EXTENSIONS

Literary TOOLS

AIM. A writer's **aim** is his or her purpose, or goal. People may write with the following aims: to inform (expository/informational writing); to entertain, enrich, enlighten, and/or use an artistic medium, such as fiction or poetry, to share a perspective (imaginative writing); to make a point by sharing a story about an event (narrative writing); to reflect (personal/expressive writing); to persuade readers or listeners to respond in some way, such as to agree with a position, change a view on an issue, reach an agreement, or perform an action (persuasive/argumentative writing). As you read *The Analects,* decide which aim(s) Confucius had in mind.

THEME. A **theme** is a central idea in a literary work. As you read this selection, determine what themes are being covered. Create a chart like the one below. List each theme along the left-hand side of the chart, and on the right side, include quotes from the selection that fit that theme. One example is provided.

THEME	EXAMPLES
Duty	ruler must "attend strictly to business" (his duty) "young man's duty is to behave well to his parents"

ADDITIONAL RESOURCES

UNIT 5 RESOURCE BOOK
- Selection Worksheet 5.7
- Selection Check Test 4.5.15
- Selection Test 4.5.16
- Writing Resource 2.27
- Study and Research Resource 5.43

GRAPHIC ORGANIZER

Responses will vary. Students might include the following themes and examples in their charts:

loyalty— a man must be "faithful to his superiors"; a ruler can gain loyalty by governing by moral force and ritual

obligation—ruler must attend strictly to business; people must observe their promises

ritual—use the labor of the peasantry only at proper times of year; "keep order among them by ritual"

social norms—young men may study the polite arts

action befitting one's place in society—a ruler must show affection toward his people; a young man must behave well to parents and elders; a gentleman must be faithful to his superiors

READER'S JOURNAL

Students might consider leaders they have worked with at school or work. They might also consider public leaders such as the governor and president. As a class, you might compile a list of characteristics that define a good leader, using the list later to see if students' opinions differ from those of Confucius.

GOALS/OBJECTIVES

Studying this lesson will enable students to
- interpret and appreciate Confucius's philosophy
- define *aim* and identify the aim of a literary work
- identify themes and values in a literary work
- compare works of writing across cultures
- understand and apply the concepts and ideals of social order, duty, leadership
- write a comparison-contrast essay about the ideas of Confucius and Mao Tse-Tung
- create a book of analects

INDIVIDUAL LEARNING STRATEGIES

MOTIVATION
Have students brainstorm common adages they have heard that give advice. For example, "Don't count your chickens before they hatch." They should then interpret these sayings.

READING PROFICIENCY
Explain that the selection students are about to read is made up of the sayings of Confucius. The "Master" referred to at the beginning of each paragraph is Confucius. Explain also that "social order" means the degree of orderliness in society—how well people in a society work and live together, without crime, hunger, suffering, and other widespread problems.

ENGLISH LANGUAGE LEARNING
Point out to students that this selection is written in high style, and uses many formal words, such as "attends," "expenditure," "polite arts," amending," "moral force," "homage," and "chastisements." Provide students with the following definitions:
administer—govern, manage
punctual—on time
expenditure—spending
abroad—in other lands
frivolous—lacking seriousness
homage—honor
chastise—scold

SPECIAL NEEDS
Have students pay attention to the Recall questions in Postreading. Then they should work in partners and explain to each other in their own words what each excerpt in the selection means to them.

ENRICHMENT
Students can list any problems they see in the social order of the United States at this time. Discuss how these problems compare with the problems in social order described in this unit.

VOCABULARY FROM THE SELECTION

chastise
expenditure
homage

FROM *The Analects*

CONFUCIUS, TRANSLATED BY ARTHUR WALEY

BOOK I, SECTION 5

The Master said, A country of a thousand war-chariots cannot be administered unless the ruler attends strictly to business, punctually observes his promises, is economical in expenditure, shows affection toward his subjects in general, and uses the labor of the peasantry only at the proper times of year.

BOOK I, SECTION 6

The Master said, A young man's duty is to behave well to his parents at home and to his elders abroad, to be cautious in giving promises and punctual in keeping them, to have kindly feelings toward everyone, but seek the intimacy of the Good. If, when all that is done, he has any energy to spare, then let him study the polite arts.

BOOK I, SECTION 8

The Master said, If a gentleman is frivolous, he will lose the respect of his inferiors and lack firm ground on which to build his education. First and foremost, he must learn to be faithful to his superiors, to keep promises, to refuse the friendship of all who are not like him. And if he finds he has made a mistake, then he must not be afraid of admitting the fact and amending his ways.

BOOK II, SECTIONS 1–3

1. The Master said, He who rules by moral force is like the pole star, which remains in its place while all the lesser stars do homage to it.

2. The Master said, If out of the three hundred Songs I had to take one phrase to cover all my teaching, I would say, "Let there be no evil in your thoughts."

3. The Master said, Govern the people by regulations, keep order among them by chastisements, and they will flee from you, and lose all self-respect. Govern them by moral force, keep order among them by ritual, and they will keep their self-respect and come to you of their own accord. ■

What is the best way to govern people? Why is this way good for both the governed and the governing?

WORDS FOR EVERYDAY USE

ex • pen • di • ture (ik spen′ di chər) *n.,* disbursement of money. *In a successful business, income should exceed expenditures.*

hom • age (ä′ mij) *n.,* expression of high regard or tribute. *The Knights of the Round table paid homage to King Arthur.*

chas • tise • ment (chas′ tīz′ mənt) *n.,* punishment or censure. *A common chastisement during Puritan times was to put offenders in the stocks.*

Respond *to the* SELECTION

Which precept in this excerpt of *The Analects* do you choose to live by? Why?

INVESTIGATE, Inquire, *Imagine*

Recall: GATHERING FACTS

1a. According to Confucius, how should a ruler act?

2a. According to Confucius, what saying does Confucius say best sums up all of his teaching?

3a. According to Confucius, what methods of government do not work? What should government be based on?

Interpret: FINDING MEANING

1b. Why can't a ruler act in any way he or she chooses?

2b. Why is this the most important precept of his teaching?

3b. Why is chastisement ineffective in governing people?

Analyze: TAKING THINGS APART →

4a. According to Confucius, what should the relationship between a ruler and his subjects be like?

Synthesize: BRINGING THINGS TOGETHER

4b. What kind of a system of government does Confucius seem to promote?

Evaluate: MAKING JUDGMENTS →

5a. Evaluate the applicability of Confucius's sayings to society today.

Extend: CONNECTING IDEAS

5b. Does Duncan, as portrayed in Shakespeare's play *Macbeth,* meet Confucius's ideal of the perfect king? Explain. How does Macbeth fall short of the Confucian ideal? Both Macbeth and Doctor Faust violate the moral order that Confucius espouses. What are the consequences of these violations?

Understanding *Literature*

AIM. Review the definition for **aim** in the Handbook of Literary Terms. With what aim(s) did Confucius share the lessons that were collected in *The Analects*? To what audience did he address his teachings?

THEME. Review the definition for **theme** in Prereading on page 473. Through his teachings as recorded in this selection from *The Analects,* what theme does Confucius develop about the moral order of the universe? How did he believe this order could be expressed in society?

RESPOND TO THE SELECTION

It might be interesting to have the class rate the analects of Confucius in order of their importance. Students should give reasons for selecting a specific analect for their journal entry.

ANSWERS TO INVESTIGATE, INQUIRE, AND IMAGINE

RECALL

1a. A ruler must attend to business, keep promises, be economical, be affectionate to his or her subjects, and use peasant labor for his or her own purposes at the proper time of the year.

2a. The phrase that best sums up Confucius's teaching is, "Let there be no evil in your thoughts."

3a. Governing by regulations and keeping order by chastisement do not work. Government should be based on moral force and ritual.

INTERPRET

1b. A ruler must follow certain codes of behavior out of respect for his subjects and his position. A ruler needs to uphold the social order and be someone that others can look up to and respect.

2b. This is the most important precept of his teaching because with evil thoughts, peace and order cannot be established. If a ruler has evil thoughts, power will be abused. If the subjects have evil thoughts, they will not obey the ruler. The whole moral order of the kingdom is dependent on its members not having evil thoughts.

3b. If chastised the people may revolt and flee from their leader. This would disrupt the whole social order.

ANALYZE

4a. The ruler should treat his subjects with affection and the subjects should be loyal and faithful to their ruler.

SYNTHESIZE

4b. Confucius seems to promote a benevolent dictatorship.

EVALUATE

5a. *Responses will vary.*

EXTEND

5b. Duncan is the type of benevolent ruler that Confucius writes about. Duncan treats Macbeth with affection, rewarding his loyalty and courage and wishing he had more

Continued on page 476

ANSWERS TO UNDERSTANDING LITERATURE

AIM. *The Analects* were written for the purpose of teaching. In this light, Confucius's central aims were to inform people how to live and to persuade them to follow his precepts.

THEME. Confucius develops the theme that there is a moral order in the universe which must be reflected in society. People could express this order in society by observing their duties and obligations, keeping their promises, respecting their superiors, and purging evil from their thoughts. A ruler was bound to rule by moral force and keep order by ritual.

ANSWERS TO INVESTIGATE, INQUIRE, AND IMAGINE (CONT. FROM PAGE 475)

to give him. As Macbeth himself admits in act 1, scene 7, lines 16–18, "this Duncan / Hath born his faculties so meek, had been / So clear in his great office, that his virtues / Will plead like angels." Macbeth drives his subjects from him with his murderous cruelty. In murdering Duncan he is not being faithful to his superiors, which is a Confucian ideal. Although Macbeth realizes that he made a mistake, he makes no recompense: "I am in blood / Stepp'd in so far that, should I wade no more, / Returning were as tedious as go o'er." The consequences of violating the moral order are the sickening of the nation (act 4, scene 3, lines 164–173; act 5, scene 2, lines 27–28), his mental disintegration (act 3, scene 4, lines 85-87), the loss of all the consolations of old age (act 5, scene 3, lines 22–26), the loss of the loyalty of his subjects (act 5, scene 7, lines 25–28), the death of his wife, and his own eventual destruction. Doctor Faustus also violates the moral order by falling victim to an evil force which tempts away from being faithful to his superior—God. He breaks a promise to God by making a deal with the Devil. The consequences for him are being sent to eternal Hell.

ANSWERS TO INTEGRATING THE LANGUAGE ARTS

Study and Research
Assign a score from 1 to 25 for each grading criterion below. (For more detailed evaluation, see the evaluation forms for writing, revising, and proofreading, in the Assessment Resource.

Comparison-Contrast Essay

Content/Unity. The essay compares and contrasts precepts of Confucius with those of Mao Tse-tung.

Organization/Coherence. The essay uses one of these two methods: the characteristics of one subject are presented, followed by the characteristics of the second subject; or both subjects are compared and contrasted with regard to one quality, then with regard to a second quality, and so on.

Language/Style. The essay uses formal English.

Conventions. The essay avoids errors in spelling, grammar, usage, mechanics, and manuscript form.

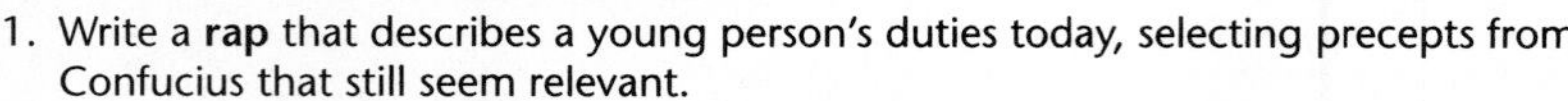

WRITER'S JOURNAL

1. Write a **rap** that describes a young person's duties today, selecting precepts from Confucius that still seem relevant.
2. Write a **code of conduct** for employers and employees based on precepts from *The Analects.*
3. Read Portia's speech from act 4, scene 1 of *The Merchant of Venice,* which appears in the Selections for Additional Reading on page 000. Then write a **paragraph** explaining what Confucius would agree and disagree with in the speech.

Integrating *the* Language Arts

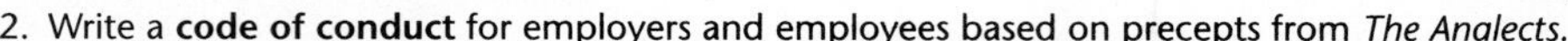

Study and Research

Comparison-Contrast Essay. During the Chinese Cultural Revolution of the twentieth century, citizens of China were encouraged to discard Confucian ideals and live by the precepts of the Chinese Communist Party, led by Chairman Mao Tse-tung. Research Mao's philosophy and write down some of his quotes that illustrate it. Then select one or two topics and write a comparison-contrast essay comparing Confucius's precepts with those of Mao Tse-tung. Before you begin, read about comparison-and-contrast order in the Language Arts Survey 2.27, "Choosing a Method of Organization." You may also find it useful to review how to quote a source; read the Language Arts Survey 5.43, "Paraphrasing, Summarizing, and Quoting."

Media Literacy

Creating a Book of Analects. Analects are passages collected from the works of one or more authors. Create your own book of analects by researching quotations from your favorite authors on topics of your choice such as music, love, work, society, and government. You may want to limit your sources to works from a certain literary movement such as Neoclassicism, Romanticism, or Post-Modernism. You can use the Internet to research quotations. One good online source is the Bartleby.com Internet site. It allows you to search, by quotation or keyword, the ninth edition of John Bartlett's *Familiar Quotations,* a collection of passages, phrases, and proverbs from ancient and modern literature. Visit the site at http://www.bartleby.com/99/.

Collaborative Learning & Study and Research

Chinese Banner. In their original form, *The Analects* are written in Chinese characters. Working with several classmates, select several key words from the selection. Then research how they are represented in Chinese characters. Work together to make a banner of these Chinese characters that summarizes for you the key ideas of Confucius's sayings.

Monologues and Soliloquies from

The Tragedy of Hamlet, Prince of Denmark by William Shakespeare

In the tragedy *Hamlet,* Hamlet's father, the king of Denmark, has recently died, and Hamlet's uncle, Claudius, has taken the throne. The ghost of Hamlet's father appears to Hamlet, accuses Claudius of murdering him, and asks Hamlet to seek revenge.

In the first selection, Polonius, an elderly government minister, is saying good-bye to his son, Laertes.

In the second selection, Hamlet is alone and thinking aloud about what makes people willing to face the many difficulties of life. The speech follows a conversation in which the king and the queen discuss their fears that Hamlet is deranged.

Hamlet persuades a group of actors to perform for King Claudius a play about regicide, to see if the king's reactions confirm his suspicions. In the third selection, Hamlet is giving the actors directions prior to the performance. Hamlet's speech to the actors provides superb advice about the craft of acting, advice that has stood the test of time and that was written by the greatest dramatist who ever lived.

FROM ACT 1, SCENE 3

POLONIUS. And these few precepts in thy memory
Look thou character.[1] Give thy thoughts no tongue,
Nor any unproportion'd thought his act.
Be thou familiar, but by no means vulgar:
Those friends thou hast, and their adoption tried,
Grapple them unto thy soul with hoops of steel,
But do not dull thy palm with entertainment
Of each new-hatch'd, unfledg'd courage. Beware
Of entrance to a quarrel, but being in,
Bear't that th' opposed may beware of thee.
Give every man thy ear, but few thy voice,
Take each man's censure, but reserve thy judgment.
Costly thy habit as thy purse can buy,
But not express'd in fancy, rich, not gaudy,
For the apparel oft proclaims the man,
And they in France of the best rank and station
[Are] of a most select and generous chief in that.
Neither a borrower nor a lender [be],
For [loan] oft loses both itself and friend,
And borrowing dulleth [th'] edge of husbandry.[2]
This above all: to thine own self be true,
And it must follow, as the night the day,
Thou canst not then false to any man.
Farewell, my blessing season this in thee!

FROM ACT 3, SCENE 1

HAMLET. To be, or not to be, that is the question:
Whether 'tis nobler in the mind to suffer
The slings and arrows of outrageous fortune,
Or to take arms against a sea of troubles,
And by opposing, end them. To die, to sleep—
No more, and by a sleep to say we end
The heart-ache and the thousand natural shocks
That flesh is heir to; 'tis a consummation
Devoutly to be wish'd. To die, to sleep—
To sleep, perchance to dream—ay, there's the rub,
For in that sleep of death what dreams may come,
When we have shuffled off this mortal coil,
Must give us pause; there's the respect
That makes calamity of so long life:
For who would bear the whips and scorns of time,
Th' oppressor's wrong, the proud man's contumely,
The pangs of despis'd love, the law's delay,
The insolence of office, and the spurns
That patient merit of th' unworthy takes,
When he himself might his quietus[3] make
With a bare bodkin;[4] who would fardels[5] bear,
To grunt and sweat under a weary life,
But that the dread of something after death,
The undiscover'd country, from whose bourn[6]
No traveller returns, puzzles the will,
And makes us rather bear those ills we have,
Than fly to others that we know not of?
Thus conscience does make cowards [of us all],
And thus the native hue of resolution
Is sicklied o'er with the pale cast of thought,
And enterprises of great pitch and moment
With this regard their currents turn awry,
And lose the name of action.

FROM ACT 3, SCENE 2

HAMLET. Speak the speech, I pray you, as I pronounc'd it to you, trippingly on the tongue, but if you mouth it, as many of our players do, I had as live[7] the town-crier spoke my lines. Nor do not saw the air too much with your hand, thus, but use all gently, for in the very torrent, tempest, and, as I may say, whirlwind of your passion, you must acquire and beget a temperance that

1. **character.** Inscribe
2. **husbandry.** Thrifty management, frugality
3. **quietus.** Release from an obligation
4. **bodkin.** Dagger
5. **fardels.** Burdens
6. **bourn.** Domain
7. **had as live.** Would prefer

ADDITIONAL QUESTIONS AND ACTIVITIES

Divide the class into four groups. Assign each group one of the plays from which selections have been taken. Each group will be responsible for a dramatic reading of the scene in which the selection appears. Students need not memorize or enact their parts, although they should stand at the front of the room and move about as necessary to convey the sense of the passage.

As an alternate activity, make each group responsible for answering any questions that may arise about the context of the selections as the passages are studied in class. This will require students to have a solid grasp of the plot and characters of their assigned play.

ADDITIONAL QUESTIONS AND ACTIVITIES

from *The Tragedy of Hamlet, Prince of Denmark,* act III, scene i. After students have read and studied the passage, point out the metaphor "to take arms against a sea of troubles" and explain that this is a mixed metaphor—something writers generally avoid. Note that Shakespeare is full of constructions and usages that contradict modern grammatical conventions, including double negatives and double comparisons, among other things. He lived and wrote in a time when the language was much more fluid—that is, before grammarians had begun making up rules about it. He also used strained grammar for special effects. The mixed metaphor in this passage may be one such instance, perhaps showing the turmoil of Hamlet's thought.

What words does Hamlet use to describe the misfortunes of life in the passage?

Answer

He uses "slings and arrows," line 3; "sea of troubles," line 4; "heart-ache," line 7; "thousand natural shocks," line 7; "calamity," line 14; and "whips and scorns," line 15.

LITERARY TECHNIQUE

CHARACTER. One way writers establish character is to determine what quality a person in their work will have and then repeatedly show that person acting out an idiosyncrasy that expresses the desired quality. In Hamlet's speech, for instance, Shakespeare shows him as brusque, direct, even slightly imperious, though these qualities are softened by his extremely lively intelligence. To bring out these qualities for students, draw their attention to a line or two of Hamlet's speech and ask them what kind of person someone would have to be to speak those words as Hamlet speaks them. Write down all suggestions on the blackboard, emphasizing with a star those the entire class agrees are best.

CROSS-CURRICULAR ACTIVITIES

GEOLOGY. In *The Tragedy of King Richard the Second,* act II, scene i, lines 13-18, John of Gaunt emphasizes that England is part of an island, and as such is partially protected from invasion. Students can research the geology of the British Isles to understand the physical history of the landform. You may want to ask the following questions: 1. How is England geologically related to Europe? 2. Were Britain and Europe ever connected? 3. How might Britain's isolation have affected its view of itself? of the outside world?

Answers

Britain and Europe are part of the same rock structure. They were connected by a land bridge until about 6000–5000 bc. Perhaps Britain's isolation has resulted in the feelings of patriotism and superiority found in Gaunt's speech.

may give it smoothness. O, it offends me to the soul to hear a robustious periwig-pated fellow tear a passion to totters, to very rags, to spleet[1] the ears of the groundlings,[2] who for the most part are capable of nothing but inexplicable dumb shows and noise. I would have such a fellow whipt for o'erdoing Termagant, it out-Herods Herod,[3] pray you avoid it.

[1] **PLAYER.** I warrant your honor.

HAMLET. Be not too tame neither, but let your own discretion be your tutor. Suit the action to the word, the word to the action, with this special observance, that you o'erstep not the modesty[4] of nature: for any thing so o'erdone is from the purpose of playing, whose end, both at the first and now, was and is, to hold as 'twere the mirror up to nature: to show virtue her feature, scorn her own image, and the very age and body of the time his form and pressure.[5] Now this overdone, or come tardy[6] off, though it makes the unskillful laugh, cannot but make the judicious grieve; the censure of which one must in your allowance o'erweigh a whole theatre of others. O, there be players that I have seen play—and heard others [praise], and that highly—not to speak it profanely,[7] that, neither having th' accent of Christians nor the gait of Christian, pagan, nor man, have so strutted and bellow'd that I have thought some of Nature's journeymen had made men, and not made them well, they imitated humanity so abominably.

[1] **PLAYER.** I hope we have reform'd that indifferently with us, [sir].

HAMLET. O, reform it altogether. And let those that play your clowns speak no more than is set down for them, for there be of them that will themselves laugh to set on some quantity of barren spectators to laugh too, though in the mean time some necessary question of the play be then to be considered. That's villainous, and shows a most pitiful ambition in the fool that uses it. Go make you ready. ■

The Tragedy of King Richard the Second by William Shakespeare

Shakespeare's *Richard the Second* tells of the fall of a king who rules arbitrarily, willfully, and selfishly, and yet is a person with whom many can sympathize. When Richard's uncle, John of Gaunt, dies, Richard unjustly confiscates Gaunt's estates to finance a campaign to put down a rebellion. Eventually Richard is deposed by Gaunt's son, the fiercely ambitious Bullingbrook (Bolingbroke), later King Henry IV.

In the first selection, John of Gaunt, near death from illness, has stated a desire to advise his nephew Richard, whom he views as a reckless youth. In the second selection, Richard, in the face of defeat by Bolingbroke, ponders how even the greatest among us must meet his or her end. Richard's claim that some kings are "haunted by the ghosts they have deposed" (line 158) often reminds readers of *Macbeth,* Shakespeare's tragedy about the downfall of another king.

FROM ACT 2, SCENE 1

GAUNT. Methinks I am a prophet new inspir'd,
And thus expiring do foretell of him:[8]
His rash fierce blaze of riot cannot last,
For violent fires soon burn out themselves;
Small show'rs last long, but sudden storms are short;
He tires betimes that spurs too fast betimes;
With eager feeding food doth choke the feeder;
Light vanity, insatiate cormorant,[9]
Consuming means, soon preys upon itself.
This royal throne of kings, this sceptred isle,
This earth of majesty, this seat of Mars,[10]
This other Eden, demi-paradise,
This fortress built by Nature for herself
Against infection and the hand of war,
This happy breed of men, this little world,
This precious stone set in the silver sea,
Which serves it in the office of a wall,
Or as [a] moat defensive to a house,
Against the envy of less happier lands;
This blessed plot, this earth, this realm, this England,
This nurse, this teeming womb of royal kings,
Fear'd by their breed, and famous by their birth,
Renowned for their deeds as far from home,
For Christian service and true chivalry,
As is the sepulchre in stubborn Jewry
Of the world's ransom, blessed Mary's Son;
This land of such dear souls, this dear dear land,
Dear for her reputation through the world,
Is now leas'd out—I die pronouncing it—
Like to a tenement or pelting farm.
England, bound in with the triumphant sea,
Whose rocky shore beats back the envious siege
Of wat'ry Neptune,[11] is now bound in with shame,
With inky blots and rotten parchment bonds;
That England, that was wont to conquer others,
Hath made a shameful conquest of itself.
Ah, would the scandal vanish with my life,
How happy then were my ensuing death!

---

1. **spleet.** Split
2. **groundlings.** Spectators who stood on the ground in the pit of the theater
3. **Termagant . . . Herod.** Both Termagant and Herod were noisy, violent characters in medieval drama.
4. **modesty.** Moderation
5. **pressure.** Exact image
6. **tardy.** Inadequately
7. **profanely.** Irreverently
8. **him.** Gaunt is referring to King Richard.
9. **cormorant.** A glutton
10. **Mars.** Roman god of war and protector of the nation
11. **Neptune.** Roman god of the sea

FROM ACT 3, SCENE 2

RICHARD. Let's talk of graves, of worms, and epitaphs,
Make dust our paper, and with rainy eyes
Write sorrow on the bosom of the earth.
Let's choose executors and talk of wills;
And yet not so, for what can we bequeath
Save our deposed bodies to the ground?
Our lands, our lives, and all are Bullingbrook's,[1]
And nothing can we call our own but death,
And that small model of the barren earth
Which serves as paste and cover to our bones.
For God's sake let us sit upon the ground
And tell sad stories of the death of kings:
How some have been depos'd, some slain in war,
Some haunted by the ghosts they have deposed,
Some poisoned by their wives, some sleeping kill'd,
All murthered—for within the hollow crown
That rounds the mortal temples of a king
Keeps Death his court, and there the antic sits,
Scoffing his state and grinning at his pomp,[2]
Allowing him a breath, a little scene,
To monarchize, be fear'd, and kill with looks,
Infusing him with self and vain conceit,
As if this flesh which walls about our life
Were brass impregnable; and humor'd thus,
Comes at the last and with a little pin
Bores thorough his castle wall, and farewell king!
Cover your heads, and mock not flesh and blood
With solemn reverence, throw away respect,
Tradition, form, and ceremonious duty,
For you have but mistook me all this while.
I live with bread like you, feel want,
Taste grief, need friends: subjected thus,
How can you say to me I am a king? ■

The Merchant of Venice by William Shakespeare

In *The Merchant of Venice,* Antonio, in order to help a friend, has borrowed money from a prosperous Venetian merchant named Shylock. Shylock agrees to the loan without interest, but holds as part of the bargain that if the loan cannot be repaid, he can "collect" on it by cutting a pound of flesh from Antonio's body. When the ships carrying Antonio's merchandise are lost at sea, Antonio is left bankrupt, and Shylock comes to close his part of the bargain. In the selection, Antonio's friend Portia tries to appeal to a better side of Shylock in order to save Antonio.

FROM ACT 4, SCENE 1

PORTIA. The quality of mercy is not strain'd,[3]
It droppeth as the gentle rain from heaven
Upon the place beneath. It is twice blest:
It blesseth him that gives and him that takes.
'Tis mightiest in the mightiest, it becomes
The throned monarch better than his crown.
His sceptre shows the force of temporal power,
The attribute to awe and majesty,
Wherein doth sit the dread and fear of kings;
But mercy is above this sceptred sway,
It is enthroned in the hearts of kings,
It is an attribute to God himself;
And earthly power doth then show likest God's
When mercy seasons justice. ■

The Tempest By William Shakespeare

The Tempest, a highly poetic work of fantasy, is thought to be the last play Shakespeare wrote before retiring to Stratford. In the play, the magician Prospero has been exiled to an enchanted island, home to many spirits and to the savage Caliban. Prospero is the rightful Duke of Milan, but his brother, Antonio, has usurped his rule. When a ship carrying Antonio passes the island, Prospero stirs up a storm, and Antonio and his party are capsized and washed ashore. Eventually, Caliban and Antonio plot to kill Prospero, who becomes aware of their scheme. In the selection, Prospero's speech closes an episode in which the spirits have been performing an entertainment, and Prospero, remembering the schemes against him, has called an end to the festivities.

FROM ACT 4, SCENE 1

PROSPERO. Our revels now are ended. These our actors
(As I foretold you) were all spirits, and
Are melted into air, into thin air,
And like the baseless fabric of this vision,
The cloud-capp'd tow'rs, the gorgeous palaces,
The solemn temples, the great globe itself,
Yea, all which it inherit, shall dissolve,
And like this insubstantial pageant faded
Leave not a rack[4] behind. We are such stuff
As dreams are made on; and our little life
Is rounded with a sleep. Sir, I am vex'd;
Bear with my weakness, my old brain is troubled.
Be not disturb'd with my infirmity.
If you be pleas'd, retire into my cell,
And there repose. A turn or two I'll walk
To still my beating mind. ■

1. **Bullingbrook.** Bulllingbrook or Bolingbroke is the surname of Henry, Duke of Herford, who later became King Henry IV.
2. **antic . . . pomp.** The antic is a jester who makes fun of the ceremonious regality of the king.
3. **strain'd.** Constrained, forced
4. **rack.** A wisp of cloud

LITERARY TECHNIQUE

SPEAKER. A **speaker** is the character who speaks in a poem—the voice assumed by the writer. Examine the passage from *The Merchant of Venice*, act IV, scene i. Though it was Shakespeare who wrote the lines here, he devised them for the character of Portia, and he chose words and phrases that are appropriate for her character: the ideas may or may not have been shared by Shakespeare himself. Look through the speech again to find evidence about the speaker's character. In particular, examine Portia's reasons for preferring mercy, the tone of her language, and the way in which she appeals to Shylock. Is she forceful? Does she show understanding? Does she seem to be merciful herself? What other qualities are shown in her speech?

Answer

Portia's very focus on mercy says something about her character. Furthermore, she prefers mercy apparently because it confers intangible blessings on both giver and receiver, because it is superior to the highest form of human power, and because it is a divine and not a temporal attribute—all of which argues for her disregard for material advantages in preference to spiritual ones. Her tone is gentle—she does not attack Shylock, but kindly encourages him to be kindly. She shows great understanding, intelligence, and ingenuity in stating her case, and demonstrates mercy in her own refusal to attack Shylock. Other qualities she demonstrates are a respect for temporal authority and a love of God.

To clarify how the character of the speaker is revealed in the speech, have students rephrase the speech as an attack, beginning, "Now listen here, Shylock, mercy is not something that you should have to be forced into. . . ."

LESSON OVERVIEW

GUIDED WRITING *Software*

See the Guided Writing Software for an extended version of this lesson that includes printable graphic organizers, extensive student models and student-friendly checklists, and self-, peer, and teacher evaluation features.

Examining the Model. In the Student Model that appears on this page and continues on page 484, writer Marie Wade focuses on the ambition of a controlling woman, quite a nasty character. Marie wanted to explore a relationship where the woman made all the decisions for her partner. And she had observed some of the details of poverty. It is in those details that she creates her main character and her surroundings:

crumpled stack of dirty jeans
pilled gray sweater
queen sized bed, the one someone had dropped on their porch two summers ago

As Marie developed this story, she chose wisely to cover a very brief moment in time. As the couple argues in the boyfriend's car, the reader realizes that it is the girl who is truly in the "driver's seat."

WRITING A SHORT STORY

William Shakespeare has created characters who say something to all centuries about enduring themes. His works have influenced artists from all disciplines as they explore similar themes in fiction, novel, music, and the visual arts.

Writing Assignment. In this lesson you will write a short story based on one of the themes Shakespeare explored in *Macbeth.*

Student Model

You Gotta Do Whatcha Gotta Do
by Marie Wade

"Some night my prince will come," she half-whispered, half-sung to herself. She bustled around her bedroom, flinging the pilled gray sweater over to the far corner onto the crumpled stack of dirty jeans, underarm-stained t-shirts, and gray undies she called her "wardrobe." She settled herself onto the queen-sized bed, the one someone had dropped on their porch two summers ago, and crossed her ankles, stretched out her legs, and folded her arms behind her head.

"Beth! Bethie! Hey, hey—are you up there?" Her mom's voice rose to the cracking edge it always reached when she stretched it too far.

Beth swung her legs off the edge of the bed. "Yeah, I hear you!" she shouted. Then to herself, "You gotta' get outta' this place—" She sang the familiar refrain in her mind. "You gotta do whatcha gotta do..."

Prewriting

Finding Your Voice. Shakespeare was more than just a great writer; he was also a first-class psychologist and student of human nature. Every word he wrote was of people talking, revealing themselves. What is it about written dialogue that is so effective when drawing a character? Many characters in *Macbeth* seem particularly vibrant because they often reveal insights that even they don't know about themselves when they speak.

The dialogue and voices of the characters in your short story will reveal their hopes and fears. To "get into" character, think of the facial expressions, the walk and the posture of your main character. Model her or him after someone you know. These aspects of the character are clues to his or her opinion of self and of the external world. Try impersonating that person. Think of the vocabulary your character uses. Getting that spoken communication down on paper isn't difficult if you listen to what the sounds are, and the phrasing patterns used. Listen especially for repetition.

In your story, the characters will do the talking. Their actions and words will reveal your theme with clarity if you show, rather than tell. You will want your main characters to sound like real, complex people with real hopes and fears.

Identifying Your Audience. We write primarily for ourselves and our peers in order to relate an angle on the chosen theme. Your audience doesn't have to end there, however. Do you want your older sister to understand, too? What about your network of adult contacts? While you write, keep your audience in mind, whether it is broad or narrow. Use language they'll understand and appreciate.

Writing With a Plan. Now that you've selected a character and a theme, you need to bring the two together, keeping your audience in mind. What situation will offer a chance to see your theme in action? This will be your Setting. Remember, something must happen to your characters in the setting, or it's not a short story.

First, Build a Setting. **Setting** is the time and location in which a story takes place. A short story cannot have the scope of *Macbeth*. Select a narrow time frame. It should be short—maybe as short as one hour, or even half an hour. As a writer, you decide how quickly the reader will move from scene to scene or thought to thought. Try to keep your characters in a handful of locations, or even better, one location. Consider where you would usually find your characters—in a mall? a basketball game? the cafeteria?

Next, build a conflict. A **conflict** is a struggle between two forces in a literary work. The conflict between your characters may not be as violent as Macbeth's with MacDuff, but it should matter. In the Student Model, Beth faces a conflict when Jason wants to back out of working so many hours. She convinces him

Types of Conflict

There are four different major categories of conflict:

- human against self
- human against human
- human against nature
- human against society

In the student model, the conflict is Beth against Jason manipulates him to her own selfish ends.

Individual Learning Strategies

Motivation
Ask students to tape record an everyday conversation with friends or family members. Students could then transcribe the tape onto paper, including all of the vocalizations such as "Hm," and "Uh-huh" that people naturally interject into their everyday speech. This activity could serve to make them aware of how people ordinarily talk and help them to create natural-sounding dialogue.

Reading Proficiency
Students might read over the main headings in this Guided Writing lesson and tell you what steps they will be taking as they write their short stories.

English Language Learning
See strategy for Reading Proficiency above that will also benefit students who are English language learners. They also might need to review the proper punctuation of dialogue in English. Refer them to the Language Arts Survey 3.92, "Quotation Marks."

Special Needs
Help students brainstorm ideas for their characters, setting, and plot. You may write down some of the good ideas on the board and students may select from these ideas and build their story around them.

Enrichment
Students may enjoy writing a character sketch of their character before they begin the story itself. Then, they should follow the suggestion on page 481, "Finding Your Voice," and enact the part of their chosen character. They may choose a partner and conduct an improvisational role-play based on their character and another person.

Prewriting

Identifying Your Audience
Encourage students to read the Language Arts Survey 2.4, "Identifying Your Audience," and to use the helpful chart "Thinking About Your Audience" included in this section.

Finding Your Voice
Ask students to read the Language Arts Survey 2.12, "Freewriting," to help them discover their voice, (or their character's voice!). They can also use this technique when trying to create a setting for their story.

Writing with a Plan
To help them gain good story ideas for this and future writing projects, suggest that students keep a small

(Continued on page 482)

Prewriting (CONT.)

notebook and write down observations and bits of dialogue they hear in everyday life. These little snippets can inspire a story! Refer them to the Language Arts Survey 2.11, "Keeping a Journal," for ideas on what kinds of information to record in their notebooks.

Students may benefit from using a sensory detail chart to help them intensify the imagery in their description of the setting. The Language Arts Survey 2.18, "Sensory Detail Charts," provides a useful example of such a chart. Ask students to close their eyes and visualize the setting of their story, noting descriptive details they can use in their story. Refer students to the Handbook of Literary Terms to review the definition for **conflict**.

STUDENT MODEL—GRAPHIC ORGANIZER

See the Guided Writing Resource for a blackline master of the Graphic Organizer for this lesson.

Finding a Theme

Refer students to the Handbook of Literary Terms to review the definition for **theme.**

Finding a Theme

Modeling the ideas in a play such as *Macbeth* requires attention to your own confrontations with a world that is not always pleasant. The themes in *Macbeth* revolve around the ugliness of a mature world. Delving into them will illuminate your own understandings of life as you know it.

The themes in *Macbeth* are many. Think about the play and the many plots and subplots you studied. Did the deception appeal to you, or the idea of order versus chaos? or the theme of blind ambition and its results? the rise of one person at the expense of another? Writing is a way to find out what you think; it is not necessary to fully understand a theme before you choose it. Your understanding will come as you develop your draft.

to continue by appealing to their future together, and he succumbs. She overcomes his objections and is secretly victorious. The conflict with Jason had to happen in order for the author to reveal, the story progresses, that Beth has a secret goal: to use Jason's money to leave him behind. This relates to the theme in Marie's graphic organizer below: Do whatever it takes to succeed.

You're ready to "fill in the blanks" and start to write. Copy the following graphic organizer onto your own paper. Then examine the aspects of the story you have been mulling over and work through the graphic organizer.

Marie, the student writer of "You Gotta Do Whatcha Gotta Do," completed the organizer in this way:

Student Model—Graphic Organizer

Short Story: "You Gotta Do Whatacha Gotta Do"	
Theme relate to blind ambition: do whatever it takes to succeed	**Main Characters** Beth—manipulative high school senior and Jason, her boyfriend
Setting couple in a car, both poor	**Time Frame** no more than one hour as Beth tries to get Jason to earn more money for her
Exposition	Girl in a poor home situation with a plan for running away together with boyfriend
Conflict	Boyfriend thinking he can't sustain another job
Rising Action	1. Boyfriend tries to persuade her that it's too much for him to handle 2. She feels increased tension but maintains her composure, uses his weaknesses against him
Climax	He believes her and agrees to work two jobs, for their future
Resolution	Reader knows she will take the cash and dump the boyfriend

Drafting

As you draft your story, use wide margins and leave room for those flashes of revision inspiration that will come later. If you are writing on a word processor, don't delete—just cut and paste your deletions to the bottom of the document. Then, when you decide you really *did* like that paragraph, it won't be gone.

On your first draft, try to write straight through without stopping or second-guessing yourself. The idea is just to get something down on paper. As you introduce the main character, write at least two paragraphs that describe his or her appearance and movements. Does he wear baggy jeans or dirty khakis? Is her hair long or would that just cover her tattoos? If it's too much, you can always tighten it later—for now, capture as much of the essence of the character as you can.

Self- and Peer Evaluation

Pair up with a classmate. Each of you should read your short story out loud to the other. Do not say anything while each person reads. When you're done, thank your classmate for listening to your draft. Repeat these steps with another classmate. Then go back and make notes on your draft about what you noticed while reading.

- Where does the dialogue sound stiff and unnatural? Where does it sound right? Do you need more or less description of how things are said?
- What is the theme of this story?
- Where in the story do you know what the theme is?
- Examine the nouns—where can they be made more specific?
- Where can adjectives be added to nouns to make descriptions more exact?
- Where are the characters' movements described to show how something is said?
- Where can you tell how other characters view the main character, and the other way around?
- How does setting contribute to the story? How much time elapses in the story? Is it enough time? Too much?
- Note where there should be indicators of full stops or pauses.
- Note grammatical mistakes.

Once you have one or two peer reviews, ask yourself these questions:

- Is this the theme you thought you were revealing?
- Is this the same spot you thought the theme emerged?
- Are your characters interacting as you thought they would?

Writing is about self-discovery; don't be alarmed if your readers find a different theme than you intended. The theme your work reveals might be truer to you than the theme you intended to write.

Language, Grammar, and Style

Effective Dialogue

Identifying Effective Dialogue. Dialogue should be true to sound, phrasing, pauses, and incompletes. Speakers jump around and follow tangents. Capturing the reality of dialogue means spelling words as they are said. It means using fragments, parenthetical comments, slang, jargon, and exclamations.

> "Beth! Bethie! Hey, *hey*, are you up there?"
>
> "You know that we've got a plan. You know that it's gonna take us where we wanna go."
>
> "I don't know. I don't think—I'm not sure I can do this—"

Combining sentences would change the pace of "You Gotta Do Whatcha Gotta Do" and take the story into a slower mode, defeating the writer's need to show Beth's quick resolution of problems, her simplistic tried-and-true methods for dealing with Jason's reluctance.

> She turned her head away and sighed, but he didn't notice, and he thankfully never did

does not capture the way she thinks as well as

continued on page 484

Language, Grammar, and Style

Effective Dialogue

Lesson Overview
In this lesson, students will be asked to do the following:

- Identify Effective Dialogue
- Fix Ineffective Dialogue
- Use Effective Dialogue

Introducing the Skill
Explain to students that authentic dialogue can make their characters come alive. They may also represent dialect and slang in their dialogues.

Drafting

Tell students to use their completed Graphic Organizer and the freewriting exercise they did for "Finding Your Voice" as a basis for their first drafts. Have students write a discovery draft in which they do not focus on spelling, grammar, usage, or mechanics. Students might benefit from reading the Language Arts Survey 2.31, "Drafting," and 2.36, "Writing Description, Dialogue, Narrative, and Exposition."

Remind students that there are three major techniques for creating a character: direct description, portrayal of characters' behavior, and representations of characters' internal states. Refer them to the complete definition of **characterization** in the Handbook of Literary Terms. Then ask them to identify details in the Student Model that represent different types of characterization.

Self- and Peer Evaluation

Have students use the questions on this page for self- and peer evaluation. Remind students that comments from classmates can be helpful and can help them to identify strengths and weaknesses in their writing. By reflecting on reviewer comments and their own self-evaluations, they will be ready to go on to the next step: revision. A blackline master of the checklist is available in the Guided Writing Resource.

Revising and Proofreading

Encourage students to experiment with their creative writing. A proofreading checklist can be found in the Language Arts Survey 2.45. A handout of this checklist is available in the Teacher's Resource Kit, Guided Writing Resource Book. Students critiquing their classmates' work might be interested in using common proofreader's symbols, which are found in the Language Arts Survey 2.44, "Using Proofreader's Marks."

Previewing the Skill
Have students read the Language Arts Survey 3.36, "Combining and Expanding Sentences." They can choose to use longer, rambling sentences to imitate dialogue, or short, clipped, incomplete sentences. Remind them that the length of their sentences contributes to the flow of the story and adds to characterization.

Practicing the Skill
For additional practice, have students work through the exercise in the following section of the Study and Research Resource located in the Teacher's Resource Kit: 3.36, "Combining and Expanding Sentences."

She turned her head away and sighed. He didn't notice. He, thankfully, never did.

Or, combining her bursts of revelation:

So he wanted her reaction and he wanted her to push him again, just like it always was and would probably always be with him.

This is less effective than:

So he wanted her reaction. He wanted her to push him again. This is the way it always was. It was probably the way it would always be with him.

Fixing Ineffective Dialogue. Rewrite the sentences in the first paragraph of this writer's piece as simple subject-verb sentences and notice the difference. Does the choppiness fit the exposition stage of the piece?

Try writing three lines of dialogue from your short story, or from the writer's model, the way that a parent or a scholar of British literature would say these lines.

Using Effective Dialogue. Examine the dialogue in your story. Where does the dialogue sound stiff and unnatural? Where does it sound most authentic? Work through your story by reading the conversations of your characters aloud, revising as you go.

Revising and Proofreading

As you begin to revise, consider your self- and peer evaluations. Decide what changes you would like to make. Make the dialogue sound like the people on whom they are based. If the theme was not evident to you or your peers, decide how you can make it more apparent. Here is an excerpt of Marie's revised draft.

Student Model—Revised

You Gotta Do Whatcha Gotta Do
[continued]
by Marie Wade

...She drew her shoulders in to protect her as she walked resolutely to Jason's '65 Mustang, grabbed the door handle and twisted it up with a bit of pressure on the upswing. It opened on the first try this time, and she curled herself into its stench of old crank case oil and sun-bleached greasy carpet.

He acknowledged her with a nod as she fumbled for the lipstick she kept tucked in the side of the seat. He turned to back out as she turned the rear view mirror so she could add some more color to her lips.

One sigh, and then: "Ok, did you get it?"

"Yeah, but Bethie, you know, I've been thinking. This is really hard for me. It's too much, maybe one job too many—"

She let him struggle, said nothing.

"I don't know. I'm not sure I can do this. I mean, what about my grades? Like, one job is nearly killing me—I never have time to study, I'm sleeping at the drive-up window half the time—and I only get to see you on my way to some job. I'm running crazy, Bethie." He paused. She refused to rise to his pathetic bait...

He wanted her reaction. He wanted her to push him again. It was probably the way it would always be with him.

"All right." She drew herself up, fingers still on the tendon in his neck.

"Let's say you don't take the job," and she raised her right hand as if it were the balance on a scale. "What then, hey? No escape. No Colorado. No music. No adventure. No chance to be free, to be ourselves." The last one always worked.

She rubbed his shoulder and he arched it, loosening the tension in the car. And she began to speak, slowly, confidently, soothingly.

"With this job, after just a few short months, we'll be home free." He listened again, she could tell, because his chin tipped up a bit. "You're right, it's tough. But you're strong and so am I. We can do anything."

He pulled into the lakeside park, glad to see it was empty, downshifted and rolled to a stop right at the water's edge. "Hey, babe, you know you keep me going."

"Of course I do." She smiled at him. He had no idea about Jim, the other guy, waiting for her in Miami.

"Yeah, I guess we can hold out a little bit longer," he said with confused resignation.

She placed her right hand on his hand on the steering wheel. She let it rest there. She waited. He curled his finger up over her forefinger.

"You and me are all that count," she said softly. "We need to get outta here. We can do it baby, I know we can."

Jason looked at her for one long minute. He could see what he thought was the future in her eyes. He exhaled, moved his gear into reverse with the old familiar grind, then catapulted forward.

Publishing and Presenting

Now that you've written something, let someone see it. Publish the stories from your class in a chapbook or an anthology. You may also want to check out the teen writing forums on the Internet. Perform your short story at a public open mike. If you have none in your neighborhood, consider setting up a performance evening at your school or an in-school coffee house. Whatever you choose to do, don't deprive your peers of your creation and your message. You have a unique voice and a fresh outlook on your theme.

Reflecting

For balance, whenever writers dwell in the dark shadows of human failings, it is wise to consider the goodness, the wisdom, and the beauty of humanity. Write some notes to yourself about three enriching, warm, and reinforcing events that you have experienced in the past week. The themes in those experiences deserve to be explored in stories as well.

Publishing and Presenting

If you intend to have students read or recount their stories, refer them to the Language Arts Survey 4.18, "Guidelines for Giving a Speech," and/or 4.20, "Telling a Story." Ask the editor of your school newspaper if he or she would be willing to publish (perhaps in a serial form) some of the stories written by your class.

Reflecting

Encourage students to write a journal entry that considers the questions listed in "Reflecting."

ADDITIONAL RESOURCES

Unit 5 Resource Book
- Vocabulary Worksheet
- Study Guide: Unit 5 Test
- Unit 5 Test

VOCABULARY DEVELOPMENT.

Give students the following exercise:
Using the vocabulary on page 486, write a test containing five sentence-completion questions. Write three answer choices for each problem. Vary the forms of the words as necessary. When you are done, exchange tests with a classmate.

EXAMPLE.

1. Lucy doubted the ________ of her brother's claim that tapirs were a relative of horses, but she checked the encyclopedia and found that the information was indeed true.
   (A) felicity
   (B) verity
   (C) taint

Answer: B

UNIT 5 REVIEW
Renaissance Drama

Words for Everyday Use

Check your knowledge of the following vocabulary words from the selections in this unit. Write short sentences using these words in context to make the meaning clear. To review the definition or usage of a word, refer to the page number listed or the Glossary of Words for Everyday Use.

abjure, 440, 467
ague, 454
attire, 381
augment, 397
blaspheme, 467
chastise, 388
chastisement, 474
confineless, 438
corporal, 383
dauntless, 412
doff, 442
earnest, 383
entice, 470
equivocator, 401
exhort, 470
expenditure, 474
felicity, 467
firmament, 469
flout, 379
gape, 469
harbinger, 457
harbor, 469
homage, 474
homely, 435
impede, 388
impediment, 438
incessant, 469
ireful, 469
jocund, 416
malevolence, 424
mettle, 393
minion, 378
mortal, 388
multitudinous, 401
nativity, 469
nonpareil, 418
pall, 388
palpable, 398
pernicious, 432
posterity, 410
purveyor, 390
recompense, 386
remorse, 388
rend, 469
scruples, 405
stanchless *or* staunchless, 438
stealthy, 398
surfeit, 466
surmise, 384
taint, 451
teem, 442
trifle, 384
usurper, 460
verity, 410
wanton, 386

Literary Tools

Define the following terms, giving concrete examples of how they are used in the selections in this unit. To review a term, refer to the page number indicated or to the Handbook of Literary Terms.

aside, 374
catastrophe, 447
characterization, 428
climax, 410
conflict, 374
crisis, 410
crisis, 447
exposition, 447
falling action, 447
foil, 375
hyperbole, 396
inciting incident, 374
metaphor, 447
mood, 396
motif, 410
paradox, 428
personification, 428
rising action, 447
simile, 410
soliloquy, 374
symbol, 396
theme, 447
verbal irony, 396

Reflecting on Your Reading

Genre Studies

1. **Tragedy.** Most tragedies deal with a character of high station who falls due to a central failing, or tragic flaw, in that character's personality. Explain how Marlowe's Dr. Faustus and Shakespeare's Macbeth fulfill this description of the tragic hero.

2. **Drama.** One characteristic that sets drama apart from other forms of literature is its use of spectacle. Read the definition of *spectacle* in the Handbook of Literary Terms. Then describe the elements of spectacle in *Dr. Faustus* and *Macbeth* that make both of these plays exciting to watch in performance.

Thematic Studies

3. **The Dangers of Ambition and the Faustian Bargain.** Explore the theme of ambition in *Dr. Faustus* and *Macbeth*. In each play, what ambitions does the central character have? What is a "Faustian bargain"? What does the central character do to fulfill his ambitions? What awful bargain does each character make? what keeps each character from being happy despite the short-term fulfillment of his ambitions?

4. **Disturbances in the Natural Order.** In both *Dr. Faustus* and *Macbeth,* the central character traffics with the supernatural. How is the supernatural portrayed in each play? What happens, in each play, when the central character steps outside the natural, moral order?

Historical/Biographical Studies

5. ***Macbeth* and James I.** After the death of Elizabeth I, Shakespeare's company became servants of the new king, James I. The company even changed its name to The King's Men. The play *Macbeth* is known to have been performed for James. James was descended from Banquo, was fascinated by witchcraft, and believed in the Divine Right of Kings. In what might Shakespeare have tailored his play to suit his royal audience?

6. **Feudalism and *Macbeth*.** Reread the description of feudalism in the Introduction to Unit 3, on page 160. Shakespeare's *Macbeth* is set during the Middle Ages in Scotland, at a time when the feudal system was at its height. What held the feudal system together? What similarities exist between the political and social ideas of Confucius and those of Europeans of the Middle Ages? How does Macbeth, by murdering Duncan, violate the central principle on which feudalism was based?

REFLECTING ON YOUR READING

The prompts in "Reflecting on Your Reading" are suitable as topics for research papers. Refer to the Language Arts Survey 5.18–5.45, "Research Skills." (To evaluate research papers, see the evaluation forms for writing, revising, and proofreading in the Assessment Resource.)

The prompts in "Reflecting on Your Reading" can also be adapted for use as topics for oral reports or debates. Refer students to the Language Arts Survey 4, "Speaking and Listening." (To evaluate these projects, see the evaluation forms in the Assessment Resource.)

GOALS/OBJECTIVES

Studying this unit will enable students to

- understand seventeenth-century values
- understand why the freedom, love, honor, and *carpe diem* themes were important to seventeenth-century writers
- name and describe the main characteristics of Metaphysical and Cavalier poetry
- define *hyperbole, metaphor, sonnet, rhyme scheme, paradox, personification, analogy, theme, concrete poem, speaker, epic hero, antihero, epic, Puritanism, allegory, image, simile, couplet, stanza, mood,* and the *carpe diem theme* and recognize the use of these techniques in the selection
- write a résumé and application letter
- identify specific action verbs and use them effectively

The Battle of Preston and Walton, August 17th, 1648, 1877. Charles Cattermole. Harris Museum and Art Gallery, Preston, UK.

So restless Cromwell
could not cease
In the inglorious arts of peace,
But through adventurous war
Urgéd his active star.

—Andrew Marvell,
"An Horatian Ode upon
Cromwell's Return from Ireland"

CROSS-CURRICULAR CONNECTIONS

TEACHING THE MULTIPLE INTELLIGENCES

ADDITIONAL RESOURCES

Unit 6 Resource Book

- Selection Check Test 4.6.1
- Selection Test 4.6.2

CROSS-CURRICULAR CONNECTIONS

History. Unlike the United States Congress, which was established by the Constitution in 1787, the English Parliament developed gradually over the course of many centuries. King John signed the *Magna Carta* in 1215, formalizing the principle of limited sovereignty. Under King Edward I, who reigned from 1272 to 1307, two royal advisory bodies were merged. The Norman *Magnum Concilium* was a group of feudal lords and church leaders serving the king, and the *Curia Regis* was a group of semiprofessional advisors. Both bodies met whenever the king called them together, and under Edward I the two often met jointly. In the early 1300s, the two bodies sometimes debated important issues. Parliament gradually developed the power to introduce legislation, called *bills,* which became acts of Parliament after they were approved by the monarch. By the reign of Henry VI, the approval of both houses of Parliament was needed to pass a law. During the period of the British Civil War, the balance of power between Parliament and the sovereign was seriously questioned, and much blood was spilled before the issue was resolved.

The Puritan Movement was very influential in all aspects of English life. Have students research other religious movements—both in Western and Eastern cultures—that had an impact on society.

ArtNote

Charles I on Horseback. Sir Anthony Van Dyck. Dutch painter Anthony Van Dyck came to the court of King Charles I in 1632. The king had a great appreciation for painting, and he and his family and many members of the court had their portraits painted by Van Dyck. *Charles I on Horseback* (c.1637) grandly depicts Charles I as a warrior knight. Clad in full armor and holding his commander's baton, the monarch wears around his neck a gold locket with an engraving of St. George, a symbol of knightly chivalry. The painting portrays Charles I as majestic and powerful—good propaganda for a ruler who was, in fact, a rather unimposing figure and who was struggling to enforce his firm belief in the divine right of kings in the face of increasing opposition from Parliament.

THE EARLY SEVENTEENTH CENTURY

The first quarter of the seventeenth century, the end of the reign of James I, was relatively peaceful. The second quarter was a period of turbulence such as England had not experienced since the days of the Viking invasions. During the period from 1625 to 1649, the unthinkable happened: the English people rose in revolt and beheaded their king.

The Early Years of Charles I

When James I died in 1625, his son Charles inherited the throne. **Charles I** had been a weak child, unable to walk before the age of seven and afflicted with a severe impediment of speech. However, he overcame these difficulties by engaging in sports and practicing elocution. A studious young man, Charles devoted himself to mathematics, music, art, theology, and languages.

Charles inherited his father's belief in the divine right of kings. This conviction was further increased by his marriage to Henrietta Maria, a French Catholic with absolutist views regarding royal prerogatives. Charles himself was an Anglican, but he sympathized with Catholic views and detested the Protestant **Puritans,** whom he considered extremists.

The Puritans received their name from the fact that they wished to "purify" the Anglican Church of vestiges of Roman Catholic ritual. They believed in the Calvinist doctrine of **predestination,** the idea that God had at the beginning of time determined which people would be saved, or among the **elect,** and which would not. The Puritan Movement was particularly strong in the cities of the south of England, especially in London. In the cities, Puritan members of the new, wealthy class of merchants, traders, and shopkeepers came increasingly to see their needs as opposed to those of

Literary Events

➤ = British Events

➤1632. William Prynne publishes *Histriomastix, the Player's Scourge*

➤1633. John Donne's *Poems* and George Herbert's *The Temple* published

➤1636. William Prynne publishes *News from Ipswich,* a Puritan denunciation of popes and bishops

➤1640. Donne's *Devotions upon Emergent Occasions* published

➤1642. Sir Thomas Browne publishes *Religio medici;* theaters in England closed; Richard Lovelace, imprisoned by Parliament, writes "To Althea from Prison"

➤1644. John Milton writes *Areopagitica*

1625 1630 1635 1640 1645

Historical Events

➤1625. James I dies; Charles I becomes king

➤1628. Parliament requires Charles to sign Petition of Right; thirty-nine articles of the Anglican creed made law of the land

➤1629. House of Commons passes laws making dissent from orthodox religious beliefs and collecting unauthorized taxes capital crimes; Charles threatens House with troops

1630. In North America, John Winthrop founds Boston

➤1632. William Laud, a staunch anti-Puritan, becomes Archbishop of Canterbury

1636. In North America, Roger Williams founds Rhode Island

➤1629–40. Charles reigns as absolute ruler, without convening Parliament

➤1638–40. First and Second Bishops' Wars with Scotland end in Charles's defeat

➤1640. Long Parliament convenes, sends Laud and Strafford to Tower

➤1641. Charles signs "Grand Remonstrance"

➤1641. Revolt occurs in Ireland

➤1642. Civil War begins

the hereditary landed aristocracy of the north, where Catholicism still flourished despite official discouragement.

In 1625, Charles called Parliament into session to raise money to meet the expenses of his government and of his ongoing war with Spain. The lower house of Parliament, the House of Commons, was dominated by wealthy Puritans. Parliament granted Charles less money than he wanted and put restrictions on his right to collect import and export duties. It also voted to meet annually thereafter to examine government expenses. Charles disbanded this session of Parliament but was soon forced by financial need to call another session. Parliament asked for the removal of Charles's Chancellor, Buckingham, who had gotten England involved in its disastrous war with Spain. Charles angrily dismissed this second Parliament without receiving the funds he needed. He then began a campaign to raise funds on his own, collecting taxes without Parliamentary consent and requiring the English people to make "loans" to the government. He also pressed many English men into involuntary military service.

In 1628, having spent the money from the "loans," Charles again called Parliament into session, demanding that it meet his requests. Parliament responded with its own demands, requiring the king to sign a Petition of Right forcing the king to receive Parliamentary consent to levy new taxes. Having no choice, Charles signed it. Shortly thereafter, Buckingham was murdered.

Charles I on Horseback. Sir Anthony Van Dyck. The National Gallery, London.

➤1667. Milton's *Paradise Lost* published

➤1660. Theaters in England are reopened

➤1649. Richard Lovelace publishes *Lucasta*

➤1648. Robert Herrick publishes collection of his work, *Hesperides* and *Noble Numbers*

➤1657. Andrew Marvell is appointed assistant to John Milton, the Commonwealth's blind Latin Secretary

1650 **1655** **1660** **1665** **1670**

➤1649. Charles I is executed; Commonwealth Period begins

➤1653. Oliver Cromwell becomes Lord Protector

➤1658. Cromwell dies

➤1660. Monarchy restored, Charles II becomes King

Quotables

"Never make a deference or apology before you be excused."

—King Charles I

"Not what they want but what is good for them."

—Oliver Cromwell

BIOGRAPHICAL NOTE

Oliver Cromwell (1599–1658) began his career in Parliament in 1628 when he was elected to represent his home district of Huntingdon. Cromwell was an outspoken advocate of church reform, favoring the abolition of bishops and the *Book of Common Prayer.* A skilled military leader, he quickly rose through the army ranks during the English Civil War. He was appointed commander in chief in 1650 and used his power to dissolve the ineffectual Rump Parliament. Less than a year later, Cromwell had his army officers draw up a new constitution, the Instrument of Government, naming himself lord protector. He remained in this position until his death in 1658, during which time he laid the groundwork for England's future empire by strengthening its army and navy and gaining control of Jamaica and Dunkirk. Cromwell also extended religious tolerance in England to Christian sects outside the Church of England and to Jews.

ADDITIONAL QUESTIONS AND ACTIVITIES

Have students role play to recreate the meeting between Charles and his council of nobles. Ask them to discuss what action they should take after the defeat by the Scots. Allow students time to research and brainstorm.

Parliament then turned its attention to religious matters, resolving to enforce a strictly Calvinist view and to punish Catholics and other nonconformists. Charles ordered Parliament to adjourn, but it refused to do so until threatened by the king's troops. Charles then put several of the leading Parliamentarians in prison.

For eleven years thereafter, Charles ruled as an absolute king, without calling Parliament into session, financing his government with new taxes collected without consent of the people. In 1632, he appointed **William Laud** Archbishop of Canterbury. Laud immediately angered the Puritans by sanctioning sports on Sundays and during the coming years had many Puritan leaders imprisoned, tortured, and executed. During this time, many Puritans and members of other nonconformist religious sects emigrated from England to North America.

The Scottish Revolt

Charles angered the Protestant Presbyterians of Scotland by attempting to enforce there the rituals approved by Archbishop Laud, which were known as "Laud's Canons." In St. Giles's Church in Edinburgh, Scotland, the bishop of Edinburgh attempted to conduct a service according to the new rules. A riot broke out, and a woman named **Jenny Geddes** threw a stool at the bishop. There followed the two so-called **Bishops' Wars** with Scotland. To raise money for the Second Bishops' War, Charles was forced to convene Parliament once again. Parliament struck a deal with the Scots, and Charles immediately disbanded it. He then headed toward Scotland with an army, but the Scots soundly defeated him, and he retreated to York. There, on advice from a council of nobles, Charles decided to call another session of Parliament in order to come to some agreement with his Parliamentary foes. This seemed to be the only way to avoid being caught between his rebellious subjects in Scotland and in the Puritan south.

Lord Cromwell, Wearing the Order of St. George.
School of Hans Holbein. Weston Park Foundation, UK.

Revolution and Civil War

When the so-called **Long Parliament** met in 1640, it imprisoned Laud, ordered the execution of the king's councilor Strafford, excluded bishops from the House of Lords, passed laws in support of Puritan religious beliefs, and made the king subject to Parliament in the levying of taxes and collection of duties. Then it passed a "Grand Remonstrance," requiring that the king's government appointees be approved by Parliament. Charles met this demand by going, himself, to the House of Commons with a troop of soldiers to arrest the Parliamentary ringleaders. They were not there. Parliament had moved to London's Guildhall, protected by armed citizens. Queen Henrietta left for France, and Charles fled to York with some loyal troops.

Parliament assembled a citizen army known to history as **Roundheads** because of the Puritans' habit of cutting their hair very short. These soldiers were met by royalist troops known as **Cavaliers,** long-haired, dandyish supporters of the king. The Puritan army, under the leadership of **Oliver Cromwell,** defeated the royalist forces. In 1646, the king surrendered to the Scots, who turned him over to the Parliamentary forces, but he soon escaped. In 1648, Charles made an agreement with the Scots to enforce Scottish Presbyterianism in England in exchange for troops to win back his throne. However, Cromwell defeated the Scots, recaptured the king, and took control of the House of Commons. In 1649, Cromwell's so-called **Rump Parliament** had Charles tried for the treasonous action of making war on Parliament. On January 30 of that year, astonished crowds watched as the executioner's ax fell.

The Commonwealth and The Protectorate

The era of Puritan rule in England, which lasted from 1649 to 1660, is known as the **Protestant Interregnum.** The Interregnum, from the Latin *inter* (between) and *regnum* (reign), is divided into two periods, the **Commonwealth** and the **Protectorate.** The Commonwealth lasted from 1649 to 1653. During this period, Cromwell and the radical Puritan Parliament instituted various forms of censorship, closing newspapers and outlawing "frivolous" entertainments such as theater and dancing. Cromwell faced rebellions in Scotland and in Ireland, as well as war with Spain and Holland. He also had to rule over a country deeply divided over the rightness of the execution of a lawful king. In 1653, Cromwell dissolved Parliament and initiated the Protectorate, declaring himself **"Lord Protector for Life,"** in effect making himself a dictator no different from an absolute monarch. When Cromwell died in 1658, his son took power, but he was unable to stem the tide of public opinion in favor of a restoration of the old monarchy, with its system of royal rule subject to certain limits imposed by a House of Lords and a House of Commons. The feelings of many English men and women of the time were reflected in these words by **Isaak Walton:**

The Execution of King Charles I. Ernest Crofts, 1890.
Bridgeman Art Library

> When I look back upon the ruin of families, the bloodshed, the decay of common honesty, and how the former piety and plain dealing of this now sinful nation is turned into cruelty and cunning, I praise God that he prevented me from being of that party which helped to bring in this Covenant and those sad confusions that have followed it.

A special session of Parliament convened and invited **Charles II,** in exile in France, to return as king. Thus the monarchy was restored, and this revolutionary period in English history came to an end.

Literature in the Early Seventeenth Century

For convenience, scholars and critics often place writers of the early seventeenth century into three groups:

The **Metaphysical poets,** including **John Donne** (1572?–1631) and **George Herbert** (1593–1633), wrote highly intellectual, often paradoxical verse using unusual metaphors, or **conceits,** drawn from astronomy, botany, zoology, theology, alchemy, medicine, cartography, law, and other sources. Metaphysical verse can be challenging to read, and it often strains the imagination, but the strain equally often yields rewards of insight.

The **Cavalier poets,** including **Richard Lovelace** (1618–1657), **Sir John Suckling** (1609–1642), and **Robert Herrick** (1591–1674), were members of the court of

CROSS-CURRICULAR CONNECTIONS

Sciences. Present to students the following lines as an example of *conceit.*

"Mark but this flea, and mark in this
How little that which thou deny'st me is;
It sucked me first, and now sucks thee,
And in this flea our two bloods mingled be."
—John Donne, "The Flea"

You might challenge students to draw on their work in science classes to develop a list of conceits or metaphors that a Metaphysical poet might use. Ask them to compare concepts or systems from the sciences to things in the social realm, such as relationships or institutions. Suggest that they save their lists for future writing.

CROSS-CURRICULAR CONNECTIONS

History. After Charles II was restored to the English throne in 1660, the term *Cavaliers* remained in use to describe those who supported a strong monarchy. This political faction was renamed the Tory party around 1679, when it supported the succession of Charles II's brother, the Roman Catholic prince who became King James II. The Tory party name was based on a rather unflattering nickname, *tory* being the word for an Irish bandit. The Tory party became the Conservative party in the nineteenth century. Members of the Conservative party today are sometimes called *Tories* by their political opponents.

CROSS-CURRICULAR CONNECTIONS

CIVICS. Ask students to discuss censorship. Does it still exist in the world? Where? Encourage interested students to research the results of censorship in another country or in the United States at an earlier time. Why is, or was, censorship practiced? Is, or was, it effective? Is censorship ever acceptable? under what circumstances, if any?

SELECTION CHECK TEST 4.6.1 WITH ANSWERS

Checking Your Reading

1. Why were the Puritans called Puritans? **They wished to purify the church of Roman Catholic ritual.**
2. According to predestination, who were the elect? **They were God's chosen.**
3. Why was Charles I forced to call Parliament into session? **He needed money.**
4. What happened to Charles I in 1649? **He was beheaded.**
5. How did the Puritans change English society when they took power? **They outlawed newspapers and entertainments, such as theater and dancing.**

Key Figures

D 1. threw a chair at a bishop
E 2. Commonwealth leader who declared himself "Lord Protector for Life"
G 3. soldiers who supported King Charles I
A 4. called from exile in France to lead the country
C 5. responsible for the war with Spain; murdered in 1628

a. Charles II
b. William Laud
c. Buckingham
d. Jenny Geddes
e. Oliver Cromwell
f. Roundheads
g. Cavaliers

Literary Developments
Writers and works of the early seventeenth century are often categorized into three groups. Identify each of the following as pertaining to the Metaphysical poets (M), Cavalier poets(C), or Puritans (P).

"Now night her course began" . . . from *Paradise Lost,* c.1800s. Gustave Doré.

Charles I—dashing, long-haired, well-dressed, well-spoken, well-educated young cavaliers. They wrote lyrics about subjects of interest to young men of the court—love, honor, and loyalty to their king. As poets, they considered themselves to be **Sons of Ben,** or followers of Ben Jonson, the gifted lyric poet and contemporary of William Shakespeare. The cavaliers sought, like Jonson, to produce lyrics that conveyed a sense of grace and ease. The writing of **Andrew Marvell** (1621–1678) shares features with that of both the Metaphysical and the Cavalier poets. "To His Coy Mistress," for example, is a lyric dealing with a typical Cavalier theme, enjoying love while there is still time to do so. However, the poem also makes use of numerous metaphysical conceits.

The Commonwealth period produced two great **Puritan** writers, **John Milton** (1608–1674) and **John Bunyan** (1628–1688). John Milton wrote numerous important political and religious tracts, including an eloquent argument against censorship, the ***Areopagitica.*** He is remembered primarily, however, as a poet of great power and genius, the composer of eloquent lyrics and sonnets and the great Christian epic poem ***Paradise Lost.*** Milton was one of the best-educated men of his time. John Bunyan, on the other hand, was poorly educated, having taught himself using a few religious tracts and the scriptures. Bunyan's masterpiece of Christian allegory, ***The Pilgrim's Progress,*** was, until the nineteenth century, the most widely read book in the English language after the Bible.

THE DRAMA IN THE EARLY SEVENTEENTH CENTURY

In the opening years of the seventeenth century, Shakespeare and Jonson were still producing works for the stage. These were arguably the greatest years in the history of the English theater (see Unit 5). However, Puritan London had no love for the theater. The solid merchants and businesspeople of London considered exhibitions on the stage to be lewd and, because they attracted crowds, an invitation to crime and disease. Puritan attitudes toward the theater are perhaps best illustrated by William Prynne's ***Histriomastix, the Player's Scourge,*** published in 1632. In this book, Prynne argues that drama is the work of the devil and that churches, not playhouses, are the proper schools for devout men and women. For entertainment, Prynne suggests that people remember that they can turn to nature and to "the comfort of friends, kindred, husbands, wives, children, possessions, wealth, and all other external blessings that God hath bestowed upon them." In 1642, when the Puritans came to power under Cromwell, they closed the theaters. English stages were silent until 1660, when the theaters were reopened after the restoration of the monarchy.

SELECTION CHECK TEST 4.6.1 WITH ANSWERS (CONT.)

C 1. members of the court of Charles I
M 2. wrote highly intellectual works that used unusual metaphors from many sources
C 3. often dealt with themes such as love, honor, or loyalty
C 4. modeled themselves after Ben Jonson, who wrote graceful lyric poetry
P 5. primarily produced political and religious works

ECHOES ECHOES ECHOES ECHOES ECHOES ECHOES

The Early Seventeenth Century

During the time men live without a common power [a king] to keep them all in awe . . . the life of man [is] solitary, poor, nasty, brutish, and short.

—Thomas Hobbes, *Leviathan*

Wise men say nothing in dangerous times. The lion . . . called the sheep to ask her if his breath smelled; she said Yes; he bit off her head for a fool. He called the wolf and asked him; he said No; he tore him to pieces for a flatterer. At last he called the fox and asked him. Why [said the fox], he had got a cold and could not smell.

—John Selden, *Table Talk*

Then let me take the right- or left-hand way;
Go forward, or stand still, or back retire;
I must these doubts endure without allay
Or help, but travail find for my best hire.
Yet that which most my troubled sense
doth move
Is to leave all, and take the thread of love.

—Lady Mary Wroth, *Sonnet 77*

Come, my Celia, let us prove,
While we can the sports of love; . . .
Suns that set may rise again;
But if once we lose this light,
'Tis with us perpetual night.

—Ben Jonson, *Volpone*

The human understanding is of its own nature prone to abstractions and gives a substance and reality to things which are fleeting.

—Francis Bacon, *Novum Organum*

Bless me in this life with but peace of my conscience, command of my affections, the love of Thyself and my dearest friends, and I shall be happy enough to pity Cæsar.

—Sir Thomas Browne, *Religio medici*

Where there is much desire to learn, there of necessity will be much arguing, much writing, many opinions; for opinion in good men is but knowledge in the making.

—John Milton, *Areopagitica*

It is too little to call man a little world; except God, man is a diminutive to nothing. Man consists of more pieces, more parts, than the world; than the world doth, nay than the world is. And if those pieces were extended and stretched out in man as they are in the world, man would be the giant and the world the dwarf; the world but the map, and the man the world.

—John Donne, *Meditation 4*

Nature doth nothing so great for great men
As when she's pleased to make them lords of truth:
Integrity of life is fame's best friend,
Which nobly, beyond death, shall crown the end.

—John Webster, Delia in *The Duchess of Malfi*

The Battle of Preston and Walton, August 17th, 1648, **1877** [Detail], Charles Cattermole.

ADDITIONAL QUESTIONS AND ACTIVITIES

- Have students summarize the concerns of seventeenth-century writers by classifying the poems by subject: politics, faith in God, love.
- Many of the quotations on this page are by highly respected writers of this period. Ask students to read and review one work by one of these writers.
- Have students choose one of the quotations on this page. In a personal essay, each student should reflect on the meaning of the quotation and its applicability to the world in the seventeenth century, or to the student's own experiences.

Song ("Go and catch a falling star . . .")
Holy Sonnet 10 ("Death, be not proud . . .")
FROM Meditation 17 ("Perchance he for whom this bell tolls . . .")

BY JOHN DONNE

About the AUTHOR

John Donne (1572–1631), born into an old Roman Catholic family, attended Oxford and Cambridge and studied law at Lincoln's Inn. Strong anti-Catholic feelings in England prohibited Donne from following many of the usual paths toward success. In his twenties, Donne survived on a small inheritance from his father and on charm, intelligence, and courtly favor. Donne's prospects for advancement seemed secure when, at the age of twenty-six, he was appointed secretary to a high official in the court of Queen Elizabeth I. In 1601, however, after Donne secretly married Anne More, a marriage opposed by her powerful father, he was fired from his position and imprisoned. In 1614, he converted to Anglicanism. The next year, he entered the ministry and became an Anglican priest. With his deep learning, dramatic wit, and metaphorical style, Donne at once established himself as a great preacher. Appointed dean of St. Paul's Cathedral in 1621, Donne became one of the most influential ministers in England. His private devotions were published in 1624, but his collected poems were not published until 1633, two years after his death. Donne's poetic style influenced other writers, including Herbert, Crashaw, and Marvell. That style, which came to be known as "Metaphysical," also greatly influenced a number of important twentieth-century poets.

About the SELECTIONS

Donne once described himself as a dual character—Jack Donne, the writer of ironic, worldly verse; and Dr. Donne, the writer of fervent religious poems. Whatever his character, Donne, in the intensely personal and immediate tone of his poetry, made a keen break from the decorative style of most Elizabethan verse. **Song ("Go and catch a falling star . . .")** is one of Donne's early love poems and shows his playful and worldly skepticism about finding true and faithful love. The selection also shows Donne's fondness for unusual comparisons and for diction that imitates ordinary speech. **Holy Sonnet 10 ("Death, be not proud . . .")** is among the most famous of Donne's later religious poems. The selection shows Donne's bold use of paradox, unexpected use of a traditional form, and refusal to accept conventional ideas about death. **Meditation 17 ("Perchance he for whom this bell tolls . . .")** is taken from ***Devotions upon Emergent Occasions,*** published in 1624, a series of meditations on the themes of sickness and mortality.

ADDITIONAL RESOURCES

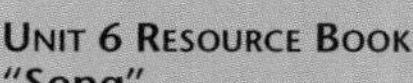

UNIT 6 RESOURCE BOOK

"Song"
- Selection Worksheet 6.1
- Selection Check Test 4.6.3
- Selection Test 4.6.4

"Holy Sonnet 10"
- Selection Worksheet 6.2
- Selection Check Test 4.6.5
- Selection Test 4.6.6

"Meditation 17"
- Selection Worksheet 6.3
- Selection Check Test 4.6.7
- Selection Test 4.6.8
- Language, Grammar, and Style Resource 3.10, 3.60
- Applied English Resource 6.5

INDIVIDUAL LEARNING STRATEGIES

MOTIVATION
Play a country song in which a lover has been untrue. Then ask students to answer the following questions: How does the singer feel? What had been the singer's hopes or expectations? Does the singer make a philosophical observation about his or her pain?

READING PROFICIENCY
Alert students to the archaic verbs and pronouns Donne uses in "Song," such as *beest, return'st, wilt, find'st, thee,* and *thou.*

ENGLISH LANGUAGE LEARNING
Point out to students the Western idea of the devil so that they understand line 4. Explain that befall means "happen to." Give meanings for the archaic words listed in Reading Proficiency.

SPECIAL NEEDS
Have students reread the last line by placing "to two, or three" after "False." Make sure students can answer the Guided Reading Questions and the Recall questions from the Investigate, Inquire, and Imagine section.

ENRICHMENT
Have students brainstorm the kinds of experiences the speaker might have had to give him such a cynical view of women's faithfulness. Discuss what it would take to change the speaker's view of women; students might dramatize such an event or write a short story to show how the speaker's views could change.

GOALS/OBJECTIVES

Studying this lesson will enable students to
- interpret and appreciate John Donne's ideas about love, religion, and death
- describe the literary contributions of Donne, both as an ironic poet and as a religious writer
- define *hyperbole, metaphor, sonnet, rhyme scheme, paradox, personification, analogy,* and *theme* and recognize the use of these techniques in the selections
- identify action and linking verbs
- research the Kübler-Ross's five stages of dying
- define Latin expressions
- use proper manuscript form for a business letter

Starry Night in the Rhone, 1888. Vincent Van Gogh. Musee D'Orsay, Paris.

Song

("Go and catch a falling star . . .")

JOHN DONNE

Go and catch a falling star,
  Get with child a mandrake root,
Tell me where all past years are,
  Or who <u>cleft</u> the Devil's foot,
Teach me to hear mermaids singing,[1]
Or to keep off envy's stinging,
    And find
    What wind
Serves to advance an honest mind.

What does the speaker tell the reader to do?

1. **Get with . . . singing.** Mandrake root is a forked root resembling the human body. The devil has been conventionally pictured as having goatlike hooves. *Mermaids singing* may refer to the sirens whose song led to destruction of all who heard it except Odysseus.

WORDS FOR EVERYDAY USE

cleft (kleft) *vt.,* divide; split. *The martial arts expert <u>cleft</u> the brick in two.*

Literary TOOLS

HYPERBOLE. A **hyperbole** is an exaggeration made for rhetorical effect. As you read "Song," look for an example of hyperbole.

METAPHOR. A **metaphor** is a figure of speech in which one thing is spoken or written about as if it were another. As you read, make a cluster chart listing the things in stanza 1 that the speaker compares to finding a mate who is true and fair. One example has been done for you.

Catch a falling star

Metaphors

Reader's Journal

What are the two most important qualities you would like to find in a mate?

ANSWER TO GUIDED READING QUESTION

1. The speaker lists seven impossible tasks for the reader: catch a falling star, impregnate a mandrake root, tell what happens to times past, tell who split the Devil's cloven foot, teach the speaker to hear the Sirens without perishing, learn how to avoid feeling envy, and explain what motivates a person to act honestly.

GRAPHIC ORGANIZER

Students should list the following tasks in their cluster charts: Impregnate a mandrake root; Tell where past years are; Tell who split the Devil's cloven foot; Teach how to hear the Sirens without perishing; Teach how to avoid feeling envy; Find the wind that advances an honest mind.

READER'S JOURNAL

Before students write their journal entry, you might make a class list of attributes and vote on them. It might be interesting to make a separate list for boys and girls and hold a discussion about gender differences.

VOCABULARY FROM THE SELECTION

cleft

ANSWER TO GUIDED READING QUESTION

1. He says she would have betrayed two or three people by that time.

SELECTION CHECK TEST 4.6.3 WITH ANSWERS

Checking Your Reading

1. What does the speaker want to hear? He wants to hear mermaids singing.
2. How long will the listener ride? **He will ride ten thousand days and nights.**
3. How will the listener age? **Age will turn his hair white.**
4. What two qualities cannot be found in a woman? **No woman is both true and fair.**
5. What will happen before the speaker reaches the woman? **She will prove false.**

Literary Tools

1. What is hyperbole? **Hyperbole is an exaggeration used for effect.**
2. Give one example of hyperbole from the selection. ***Responses will vary.***
3. How does the mood change in this poem from the first stanza to the last? **The first stanza is lighthearted and playful; the last is resigned and bitter.**

RESPONDING TO THE SELECTION

Students might begin by working in small groups to define what true and fair mean to them to see if they mean different things to different people. Is one of these qualities

If thou beest[2] born to strange sights,
Things invisible to see,
Ride ten thousand days and nights,
Till age snow white hairs on thee,
Thou, when thou return'st, wilt tell me
All strange wonders that befell thee,
And swear
No where
Lives a woman true, and fair.

If thou find'st one, let me know,
Such a pilgrimage were sweet;
Yet do not, I would not go,
Though at next door we might meet;
Though she were true when you met her,
And last till you write your letter,
Yet she
Will be
False, ere[3] I come, to two, or three. ■

What does the speaker say would be true of the woman by the time he met her?

2. **beest.** You have been
3. **ere.** Before

Respond to the SELECTION

If you could talk to the speaker of this poem, would you agree or disagree with him that it is impossible to find a mate both "true" and "fair"?

Inquire, Imagine

Recall: GATHERING FACTS →

1a. What task does the speaker tell the reader or listener to perform in line 1?

2a. What does the speaker predict that the reader or listener will "swear" after returning from the ride of "ten thousand days and nights"? What request does the speaker make in line 19?

3a. What prediction does the speaker make about the woman in the last stanza?

Interpret: FINDING MEANING

1b. What type of person is capable of such an act?

2b. How does the speaker contradict his own statement that "Such a pilgrimage were sweet"?

3b. What is the speaker's attitude toward the possibility of finding an ideal mate?

Analyze: TAKING THINGS APART →

4a. What adjectives best describe the speaker?

Synthesize: BRINGING THINGS TOGETHER

4b. What do you think the speaker's love life has been like up to now? Does the speaker understate or overstate his assessment of women?

Evaluate: MAKING JUDGMENTS →

5a. Explain whether the speaker judges women and love fairly and without bias.

Extend: CONNECTING IDEAS

5b. How does the speaker's view of women compare with the view of women in courtly love?

Understanding Literature

HYPERBOLE. Review the definition for **hyperbole** in the Handbook of Literary Terms. What exaggeration does the speaker in this poem make about finding a true and fair mate?

METAPHOR. Review the definition for **metaphor** and the cluster chart you made for Literary Tools on page 497. What, according to the speaker's perspective, do the things in stanza 1 have in common with finding a mate who is true and fair?

ANSWERS TO INVESTIGATE, INQUIRE, AND IMAGINE

RECALL

1a. The speaker tells the reader or listener to catch a falling star.

2a. The speaker predicts that the reader or listener will swear that no woman exists who is both true and fair. The speaker wishes to be informed if a true and fair woman is actually found.

3a. The speaker predicts that even if the woman were true and fair at the time when he heard about her, she would have become untrue by the time he went to meet her.

INTERPRET

1b. Only a heroic or mythic person is capable of catching a falling star.

2b. The rest of the stanza describes how the sweetness of discovering the woman turns sour when she becomes "false."

3b. He seems to think it is impossible.

ANALYZE

4a. The speaker is cynical, disillusioned, bitter, resigned, and arrogant.

SYNTHESIZE

4b. It appears that he has known a woman or women whom he thought were unfaithful, and he has concluded that all women are so. The speaker overstates his assessment of women with his prediction that a true and fair woman would have betrayed her lover two or three times by the time the speaker met her.

EVALUATE

Responses will vary.

5a. Most students will recognize that the speaker judges women harshly and is not optimistic about finding love in his life. He may be hampered by an ideal view of love and the lover.

EXTEND

5b. In courtly love women are idealized, faithful, and venerated. The speaker seems to want just such a woman, but he does not believe anyone will live up to his standard.

ANSWERS TO UNDERSTANDING LITERATURE

HYPERBOLE. The poem exaggerates the odds of finding such a mate by saying that a man could go on a pilgrimage searching for her and that any woman who at first seemed true would inevitably turn out to be false.

METAPHOR. All of the tasks in stanza 1 are impossible, as the speaker believes is finding a mate who is true and fair.

ANSWERS TO GUIDED READING QUESTIONS

1. Some have called death "mighty and dreadful."
2. The speaker is quite disrespectful and insulting when addressing death, making the point that death is not something to be feared but almost pitied.

SELECTION CHECK TEST 4.6.5 WITH ANSWERS

Checking Your Reading

1. What have some called Death? **Some have called it "mighty and dreadful."**
2. With what does Death dwell? **Death dwells with "poison, war, and sickness."**
3. What do "poppy and charms" do better than Death? **They induce sleep.**
4. What happens after "one short sleep"? **People wake to eternity.**
5. What will happen to death? **Death will die.**

Literary Tools

1. What is personified in this poem? **Death is personified in this poem.**
2. How many lines does a sonnet have? **A sonnet has 14 lines.**
3. What is a paradox? **A paradox is a contradictory statement, idea, or event.**

READER'S JOURNAL

Students should consider how death makes people feel and act.

GRAPHIC ORGANIZER

Students should include the following information in their cluster charts. Death is proud because it has power over human beings. (lines 1–3; line 12) Death itself will die. (line 14)

Literary
TOOLS

SONNET AND RHYME SCHEME. A **sonnet** is a fourteen-line poem, usually in iambic pentameter, that follows one of a number of different rhyme schemes. A **rhyme scheme** is a pattern of end rhymes, or rhymes at the ends of lines of verse. The rhyme scheme of a poem is designated by letters, with matching letters signifying matching sounds. Before you read the poem, figure out its rhyme scheme.

PARADOX. A **paradox** is a seemingly contradictory statement, idea, or event. As you read "Holy Sonnet 10," look for two examples of paradox.

PERSONIFICATION. **Personification** is a figure of speech in which an idea, animal, or thing is described as if it were a person. As you read, make a chart listing examples of how death is personified in the poem.

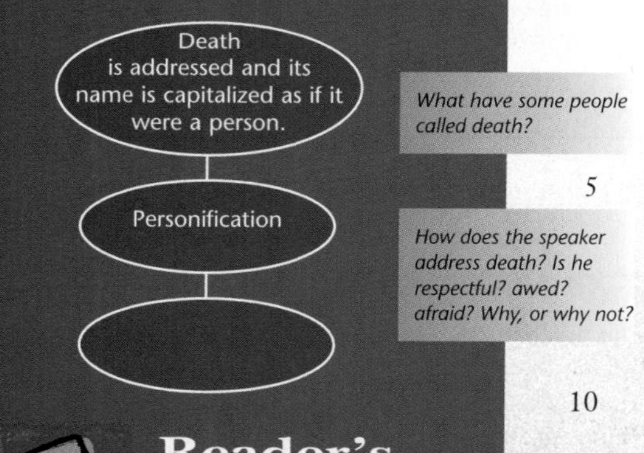
Death is addressed and its name is capitalized as if it were a person.
Personification

Reader's Journal

If death were a person, what characteristics would describe it?

Death on a Pale Horse, c.1800. William Blake.

Holy Sonnet 10

("Death, be not proud . . .")

JOHN DONNE

What have some people called death?

How does the speaker address death? Is he respectful? awed? afraid? Why, or why not?

Death, be not proud, though some have callèd[1] thee
Mighty and dreadful, for thou art not so;
For those whom thou think'st thou dost[2] overthrow
Die not, poor Death, nor yet canst thou kill me.
From rest and sleep, which but thy pictures be,
Much pleasure; then from thee much more must flow,
And soonest our best men with thee do go,
Rest of their bones, and soul's delivery.
Thou art slave to fate, chance, kings, and desperate men,
And dost with poison, war, and sickness dwell,
And poppy or charms can make us sleep as well
And better than thy stroke; why swell'st thou then?[3]
One short sleep past, we wake eternally
And death shall be no more;
Death, thou shalt die. ■

1. **callèd.** The accent on the *e* makes the *-ed* a separate syllable: *call-ed.*
2. **dost.** Do
3. **why swell'st thou then?** Why do you puff up with pride?

Respond *to the* SELECTION

What views expressed in the poem seem to reflect Donne's religious training?

RESPONDING TO THE SELECTION

You might ask students to reread About the Author on page 496 and provide background information

Inquire, Imagine

Recall: GATHERING FACTS → **Interpret:** FINDING MEANING

1a. What assertion about death does the speaker makes in lines 1-2?

1b. Who or what has the power to decide when death will happen?

2a. According to the speaker, to what is death a slave?

2b. Why might death be in the position of a slave to these things?

3a. What prediction does the speaker make in line 14 of the poem?

3b. What does line 14 indicate about the speaker's own religious beliefs?

Analyze: TAKING THINGS APART → **Synthesize:** BRINGING THINGS TOGETHER

4a. What tone does the speaker use in addressing death?

4b. How does the speaker feel about death?

Evaluate: MAKING JUDGMENTS → **Extend:** CONNECTING IDEAS

5a. What advice do you think the speaker would give to someone facing death?

5b. If you were the speaker, how would you paint death?

Understanding Literature

SONNET AND RHYME SCHEME. Review the definitions for **sonnet** and **rhyme scheme** in the Handbook of Literary Terms. Is "Holy Sonnet 10" an English, Elizabethan, or Shakespearean sonnet? What is its rhyme scheme?

PARADOX. Review the definition for **paradox** in the Handbook of Literary Terms. What is paradoxical about death in the selection?

PERSONIFICATION. Review the definition for **personification** in the Handbook of Literary Terms and the cluster chart you made for Literary Tools on page 500. Does the sonnet provide an example of limited or extended personification?

ANSWERS TO INVESTIGATE, INQUIRE, AND IMAGINE

RECALL

1a. The speaker says that death is not "Mighty" or "dreadful."

2a. Death is a slave to "fate, chance, kings, and desperate men."

3a. The speaker predicts that death itself will die.

INTERPRET

1b. Fate and human beings have the power to decide when death will happen.

2b. Death must wait upon decisions determined by fate or chance, which is a position of servitude. Death must also attend decisions made by kings, who can order wars and executions, as well as the decisions made by desperate men, who may kill others or themselves.

3b. The speaker holds the belief that people will enjoy eternal life after their deaths in the temporal world.

ANALYZE

4a. The speaker uses a scornful tone.

SYNTHESIZE

4b. By presenting death as a dependent, powerless lackey, the speaker shows he or she almost pities it.

PERSPECTIVE

5a. Since the speaker is not afraid of death, the speaker might tell a person facing death to greet it like a friend and welcome it into his or her home.

EMPATHY

Responses will vary.

5b. The speaker says that the "pictures" of death are "rest" and "sleep." The speaker might paint a person with a calm countenance and show the "soul's delivery" by painting a spirit leaving the dead person.

ANSWERS TO UNDERSTANDING LITERATURE

SONNET AND RHYME SCHEME. No, Holy Sonnet 10 is not an English, Elizabethan, or Shakespearean sonnet because it does not have the rhyme scheme *abab cdcd efef gg*. The rhyme scheme of the sonnet is *abba abbc beed cf*.

PARADOX. It is paradoxical that death brings pleasure (lines 5–6) and dies itself (line 14).

PERSONIFICATION. The sonnet provides an example of extended personification because death is personified throughout the poem.

ANSWER TO GUIDED READING QUESTION

1. The speaker describes the church as a living organism with a head and body.

GRAPHIC ORGANIZER

Students should include the following main ideas in their cluster charts.
The church has a head and a body. God is the author of us all and closes our chapters. Death unites humans with God. Affliction is a treasure because it brings us closer to God.

READER'S JOURNAL

Before students begin writing, you might hold a class discussion that addresses the following questions. In what ways are people necessarily connected to one another? What experiences do all people share? Why is it difficult for people to have happy, productive lives if they are not connected to others?

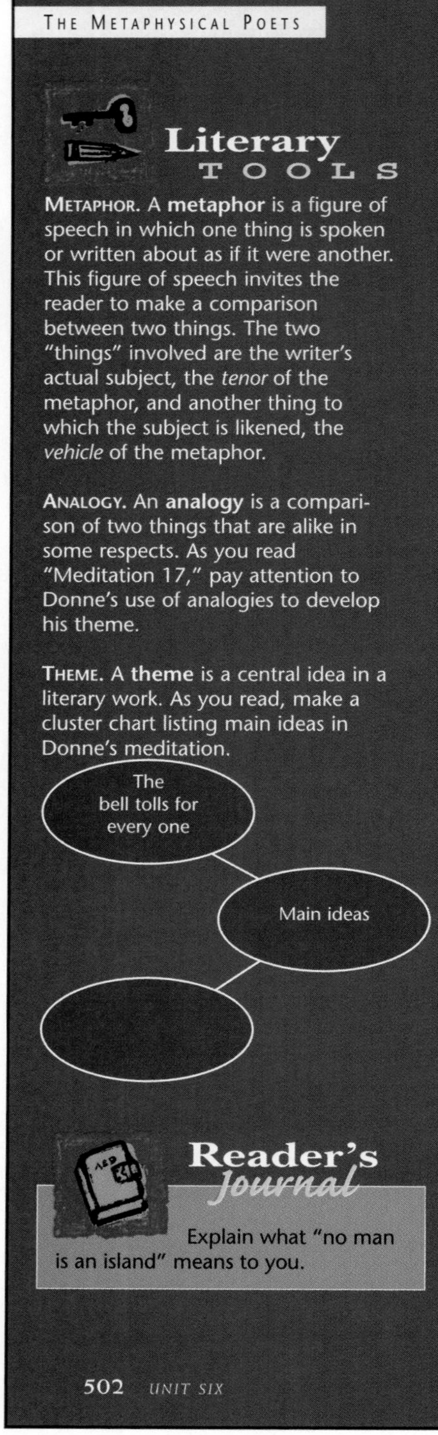

Literary TOOLS

METAPHOR. A **metaphor** is a figure of speech in which one thing is spoken or written about as if it were another. This figure of speech invites the reader to make a comparison between two things. The two "things" involved are the writer's actual subject, the *tenor* of the metaphor, and another thing to which the subject is likened, the *vehicle* of the metaphor.

ANALOGY. An **analogy** is a comparison of two things that are alike in some respects. As you read "Meditation 17," pay attention to Donne's use of analogies to develop his theme.

THEME. A **theme** is a central idea in a literary work. As you read, make a cluster chart listing main ideas in Donne's meditation.

Reader's Journal

Explain what "no man is an island" means to you.

Meditation 17

("Perchance he for whom this bell tolls . . .")

FROM *DEVOTIONS UPON EMERGENT OCCASIONS*

JOHN DONNE

Nunc lento sonitu dicunt, morieris.
Now this bell tolling softly for another, says to me, Thou must die.

Perchance he for whom this bell[1] tolls may be so ill as that he knows not it tolls for him; and perchance I may think myself so much better than I am, as that they who are about me and see my state may have caused it to toll for me, and I know not that. The church is catholic,[2] universal, so are all her actions; all that she does belongs to all. When she baptizes a child, that action concerns me; for that child is thereby connected to that head which is my head too, and ingrafted[3] into that body[4] whereof I am a member. And when she buries a man, that action concerns me: all mankind is of one author and is one volume; when one man dies, one chapter is not torn out of the book, but translated into a better language; and every chapter must be so translated. God employs several translators; some pieces are translated by age, some by sickness, some by war, some by justice; but God's hand is in every translation, and his hand shall bind up all our scattered leaves[5] again for that library where every book shall lie open to one another. As therefore the bell that rings to a sermon calls not upon the preacher only, but upon the congregation to come, so this bell calls us all; but how much more me, who am brought so near the door by this sickness. There was a contention as far as a suit[6] (in which piety

How does the speaker describe the church?

1. **bell.** A "passing" bell rung for the dying
2. **catholic.** Universal; all-embracing
3. **ingrafted.** Transplanted
4. **body.** The church
5. **leaves.** Pages
6. **contention . . . suit.** A controversy that resulted in a lawsuit

and dignity, religion and estimation,[7] were mingled) which of the religious orders should ring to prayers first in the morning; and it was determined that they should ring first that rose earliest. If we understand aright the dignity of this bell that tolls for our evening prayer, we would be glad to make it ours by rising early, in that application, that it might be ours as well as his whose indeed it is. The bell doth toll for him that thinks it doth; and though it <u>intermit</u> again, yet from that minute that that occasion <u>wrought</u> upon him, he is united to God. Who casts not up his eye to the sun when it rises? but who takes off his eye from a comet when that breaks out? Who bends not his ear to any bell which upon any occasion rings? but who can remove it from that bell which is passing a piece of himself out of this world? No man is an island, entire of itself; every man is a piece of the continent, a part of the main.[8] If a clod be washed away by the sea, Europe is the less, as well as if a <u>promontory</u> were, as well as if a manor of thy friend's or of thine own were. Any man's death diminishes me, because I am involved in mankind; and therefore never send to know for whom the bell tolls; it tolls for thee. Neither can we call this a begging of misery or a borrowing of misery, as though we were not miserable enough of ourselves but must fetch in more from the next house, in taking upon us the misery of our neighbors. Truly it were an excusable <u>covetousness</u> if we did; for affliction is a treasure, and scarce any man hath enough of it.

To what does the speaker compare the group, or body, of people that make up the church?

No man is an island, entire of itself . . .

No man hath affliction enough that is not matured and ripened by it, and made fit for God by that affliction. If a man carry treasure in bullion, or in a wedge of gold, and have none coined into current moneys, his treasure will not defray him as he travels. <u>Tribulation</u> is treasure in the nature of it, but it is not current money in the use of it, except we get nearer and nearer our home, heaven, by it. Another man may be sick too, and sick to death, and this affliction may lie in his bowels as gold in a mine and be of no use to him; but this bell that tells me of his affliction digs out and applies that gold to me, if by this consideration of another's danger I take mine own into contemplation and so secure myself by making my <u>recourse</u> to my God, who is our only security. ■

7. **estimation.** Self-esteem
8. **main.** Mainland

WORDS FOR EVERYDAY USE

in • ter • mit (in´ tər mit´) *vt.*, pause. *Lena hated to <u>intermit</u> her reading of Donne's meditations even to eat dinner.*

wrought (rôt) *adj.*, worked. *The enthusiastic young minister <u>wrought</u> quite a change in the formerly apathetic congregation.*

prom • on • to • ry (präm´ən tôr´ē) *n.*, peak of land that juts into water. *The ancient castle was built on a rocky <u>promontory</u> overlooking the sea on three sides.*

cov • et • ous • ness (kuv´ ət əs nis) *n.*, greed. *Paul struggled with feelings of <u>covetousness</u> as Charlie proudly showed off his new computer.*

trib • u • la • tion (trib´ yo͞o lā´shən) *n.*, deep sorrow, distress; suffering. *Second period always felt like a time of <u>tribulation</u> to Stephen, who hated math.*

re • course (rē´kôrs´) *n.*, turning to someone for help or protection. *Asking her father for the money she needed was Erin's only <u>recourse</u>.*

ANSWER TO GUIDED READING QUESTION

1. The church is like a continent, and each person is like a part of soil that forms the larger body of land.

SELECTION CHECK TEST 4.6.7 WITH ANSWERS

Checking Your Reading

1. Why might the person for whom the bell tolls not realize it is for him? **He is too ill.**
2. When a man dies, what happens to his "chapter"? **It is translated into a better language.**
3. How does "any man's death" affect the speaker? **It diminishes him.**
4. What does affliction do for us? **It makes us mature and/or ready for God.**
5. What is our only security? **God is our only security.**

Vocabulary in Context

Fill each blank with the most appropriate word from the Words for Everyday Use. You may have to change the tense of certain verbs.

intermit   wrought   promontory
covetousness   tribulation   recourse

1. The civil war brought **<u>tribulation</u>** to every citizen of the nation.
2. From the **<u>promontory</u>** we had a clear view of the sea.
3. The disease **<u>wrought</u>** great damage, leaving Fred permanently deaf.
4. When the tenants couldn't agree, they sought **<u>recourse</u>** with the homeowners' association.
5. Jack regretted the **<u>covetousness</u>** that led him to steal his friend's CD.

Literary Tools

Match the letter of each of the following types with the description of primary aim each one helps achieve.

a. expository/informational writing
b. narrative writing
c. imaginative writing
d. personal/expressive writing
e. persuasive/argumentative writing

<u>**D**</u> 1. to reflect
<u>**A**</u> 2. to share information
<u>**B**</u> 3. to tell a story, either true or invented, about an event or a sequence of events

4. What did Donne mean by the metaphor, "all of mankind is of one author and is one volume"? **All of mankind is a single unit, created by God.**
5. What might be a theme for this selection? **Responses will vary, but could include that death is universal, or that death is not an end but a transformation.**

RESPONDING TO THE SELECTION

The epigram says that the tolling bell is for all humanity, announcing everyone's death. This idea is reinforced throughout the meditation, most notably in the line,

ANSWERS TO INVESTIGATE, INQUIRE, AND IMAGINE

Recall

1a. The speaker says that the church is *catholic* and *universal.*
2a. The death of any other person diminishes the speaker.
3a. The speaker compares an affliction or tribulation to a treasure.

Interpret

1b. Baptism and burial—in which a person is welcomed into or ushered out of the worldly church—are rituals that support Donne's view that the church acts on behalf of all its people throughout the important stages of their lives.
2b. Since the individual is part of the whole, when the whole is diminished by a death, so is the individual diminished.
3b. The affliction, or treasure, means that "we get nearer and nearer our home, heaven, by it." Affliction is a treasure because it brings us nearer to God.

Analyze

4a. The speaker wants the reader to feel that he or she belongs to the mainland of humanity, to the church, and to heaven.

Synthesize

4b. The speaker probably wants the reader to feel fellowship and sympathy for all of humanity and to feel secure in the knowledge that God will protect him or her.

Evaluate

5a. *Responses will vary.*

Extend

Responses will vary.

5b. In "Holy Sonnet 10" death is demystified and portrayed as a powerless lackey who is to be pitied because he dies too. "Meditation 17" develops the idea that death is not to be feared because it brings people closer to heaven. In both poems death is reduced as a means to an end, eternal salvation in heaven with God.

Respond *to the* Selection

How is the image of the tolling bell in the epigram echoed in the meditation?

Investigate, Inquire, Imagine

Recall: Gathering Facts → **Interpret: Finding Meaning**

1a. What words does the speaker use to describe the church?
1b. What rituals of the church support the speaker's description?
2a. What "diminishes" the speaker?
2b. Why does the speaker experience a diminishment?
3a. To what does the speaker compare an affliction or tribulation?
3b. Why does the speaker see it in that way?

Analyze: Taking Things Apart → **Synthesize: Bringing Things Together**

4a. To what does the speaker want the reader to believe he or she belongs?
4b. What do you think the speaker wants the reader to feel after reading the meditation?

Evaluate: Making Judgments → **Extend: Connecting Ideas**

5a. Evaluate whether the speaker provides a convincing argument for not fearing death.
5b. Compare the view of death expressed in "Holy Sonnet 10" and "Meditation 17."

Understanding Literature

Metaphor. Review the definition for **metaphor** in the Handbook of Literary Terms. What metaphor does Donne use to express the interconnectedness of humans? What is the tenor? What is the vehicle?

Analogy. Review the definition for **analogy** in the Handbook of Literary Terms. What analogies does Donne use in "Meditation 17"? What point is he trying to make with each analogy?

Theme. Review the definition for **theme** and the cluster chart you made for Literary Tools on page 502. What is the theme of this selection?

ANSWERS TO UNDERSTANDING LITERATURE

Metaphor. The **metaphor** that expresses humans' interconnectedness is "every man is a piece of the continent, a part of the main." The tenor is "every man." The vehicle is "a piece of the continent, a part of the main."

Analogy. Donne makes the **analogy** between God and an author in order to show God's involvement in the process of human life. Chapters are the lives of believers that are torn out to make way for better translations; in other words, the temporal life is replaced by the eternal one. Donne also makes an analogy between affliction and treasure. The point of this analogy is to show how suffering brings the afflicted closer to God.

Theme. The **theme** is the universality and inevitability of death. The speaker believes that by confronting death, people can grow closer to God.

Writer's Journal

1. Imagine you are the speaker of "Song" and you have just met a woman whom you believe to be "true" and "fair." Write her a **love letter** expressing your hopes and fears as you enter the relationship.
2. Imagine you are John Donne and one of your parishioners has just died. Write a **sympathy card message** for the dead person's family that eases their grief and expresses your beliefs about death.
3. Write a **meditation** about a philosophical or religious topic. You might consider one of the following subjects.
   - Why do bad things happen to good people?
   - What is enlightenment, and how does one become enlightened?
   - What is sin, and how does one repent for a sinful life?

Integrating *the* Language Arts

Language, Grammar, and Style

Action and Linking Verbs. Read the Language Arts Survey 3.60, "Action Verbs and State of Being Verbs," and 3.10, "Linking Verbs." Then identify each action verb and each linking verb.

1. Perchance he for whom this bell tolls may be so ill as that he knows not it tolls for him.
2. God employs several translators; some pieces are translated by age, some by sickness, some by war, some by justice.
3. When she baptizes a child, that action concerns me; for that child is thereby connected to that head which is my head too, and ingrafted into that body whereof I am a member.
4. If a clod be washed away by the sea, Europe is the less, as well as if a promontory were, as well as if a manor of they friend's or of thine own were.
5. Any man's death diminishes me, because I am involved in mankind; and therefore never send to know for whom the bell tolls; it tolls for thee.

Vocabulary

Defining Latin Expressions. Donne begins his quote with an epigraph in Latin. Many Latin words and expressions are used in English. Write out definitions for the following Latin words and expressions. Then use each one in a sentence.

1. *ab ovo usque ad mala*
2. *ad infinitum*
3. *ad hoc*
4. *ad hominem*
5. *cogito, ergo sum*

Answers to Integrating the Language Arts

Language, Grammar, and Style

1. tolls-AV; may be-LV; knows-AV; tolls-AV
2. employs-AV; are-LV
3. baptizes-AV; concerns-AV; is-LV; is-LV; am-LV
4. be-LV; is-LV; were-LV; were-LV
5. diminishes-AV; am-LV; send-AV; to know-AV; tolls-AV; tolls-AV

Vocabulary

1. from egg to apples (from soup to nuts); from beginning to end
2. without end or limit
3. for the particular end or case at hand without consideration of wider application
4. appealing to feelings or prejudices rather than intellect
5. I think, therefore I am.

ANSWERS TO INTEGRATING THE LANGUAGE ARTS (CONT.)

Applied English
You might want students to correct the business letter in the computer lab. Students should make the following corrections.

111 East River Drive
Blefuscu, MO 00440
February 18, 2001

Scholarship Director
Department of History
University of Erewhon
989 Indiana Place
Erewhon, In 08440

Dear Scholarship Director:

Please consider me an applicant for the 2001-2002 "Young Historian" scholarship.

I am eighteen years old and a senior at West High School. My course of advanced study has included classes in English, World Literature, World History, and Ancient History.

Last summer I was employed by the Indiana State Historical Society as an exhibit intern. I worked with the exhibit designers, curators, and historians to create a traveling exhibit for grade school children on the history of the state of Indiana.

I will be happy to provide you with references who can tell about my qualifications for this scholarship and my enthusiasm for history. If you wish to see samples of my writing, I shall be happy to provide you with completed history papers.

I am available for a personal interview at your convenience. My telephone number is (555) 555-7128. I can be reached most evenings after 6 P.M.

Sincerely, Esme Rodriguez

Collaborative Learning & Study and Research

RESEARCHING THE STAGES OF DYING. In Holy Sonnet 10, Donne's position is that death is nothing of which to be frightened. Research one of the most important psychological studies on death of the late twentieth century, *On Death and Dying*, by Dr. Elisabeth Kübler-Ross. In the book the noted psychologist delineates the now-famous five stages of death: denial and isolation, anger, bargaining, depression, and acceptance. Working with a small group of your classmates, select a stage for each group member to research and present.

Applied English

WRITING A BUSINESS LETTER. Read the Language Arts Survey 6.5, "Writing a Business Letter." Then copy the following business letter onto your own paper, correcting its errors in manuscript form.

111 East River Drive
Blefuscu, MO, 00440

February 18, 2001

Scholarship Director
Department of History
University of Erewhon
989 Indiana Place
Erewhon, IN 08440
Dear Scholarship Director:

Please consider me an applicant for the 2001-2002 "Young Historian" scholarship.

I am eighteen years old and a senior at West High School. My course of advanced study has included classes in English, World Literature, World History, and Ancient History.

Last summer I was employed by the Indiana State Historical Society as an exhibit intern. I worked with the exhibit designers, curators, and historians to create a traveling exhibit for grade school children on the history of the state of Indiana.

I will be happy to provide you with references who can tell about my qualifications for this scholarship and my enthusiasm for history. If you wish to see samples of my writing, I shall be happy to provide you with completed history papers.

I am available for a personal interview at your convenience. My telephone number is (555) 555-7128. I can be reached most evenings after 6 P.M.

Sincerely,

Esme Rodriguez

"Easter Wings"

BY GEORGE HERBERT

About the AUTHOR

George Herbert (1593–1633) was born in Montgomery Castle, Wales, to Richard and Magdalen Herbert. After receiving his early education at home, Herbert attended Westminster School and Trinity College, Cambridge, where he took his degrees with distinction. At the age of twenty-seven, Herbert was elected public orator of Cambridge, a position fitting a young man of political ambition. Seven years later, however, Herbert resigned his position, turning from Parliament and politics to religion. He married Jane Danvers in 1629 and, one year later, after being ordained by the Anglican Church, he accepted a clerical appointment in Bermerton. Known as "Holy Mr. Herbert," he devoted himself to his rural Bermerton parish and wrote poetry. Like the Metaphysical poet John Donne, who was a friend of the aristocratic Herbert family, Herbert struggled with questions of spiritual emptiness. During his brief three years as a country rector, he finished writing a collection of 160 religious poems known as *The Temple*. Nearing his fortieth birthday and gravely ill with tuberculosis, Herbert gave the manuscript to a friend, Nicholas Ferrar. After Herbert's death in 1633, Ferrar published the first edition of *The Temple*, the major work upon which Herbert's reputation still stands.

About the SELECTION

The Temple is divided into three parts: "The Church-porch," "The Church," and "The Church Militant." The collection's dramatic range is powerful, including such different narrative voices and experiences as those of Christ in "The Sacrifice," a courtier in "The Pearl," and a storyteller in "The Pulley." "**Easter Wings**" comes from "The Church" section of *The Temple* and shows Herbert's mastery of ancient forms like the *concrete poem* or *carmen figuratum*. In a concrete poem, the shape of the poem is related to its content. Characteristic of the Metaphysical poets, Herbert made use of bold literary devices, particularly the device of *paradox*. Eighteenth-century critics called Herbert's use of shape "false wit." Other critics and readers, including those of our own time, are drawn to the combination of intellectual challenge and graceful plainness of language in Herbert's writing.

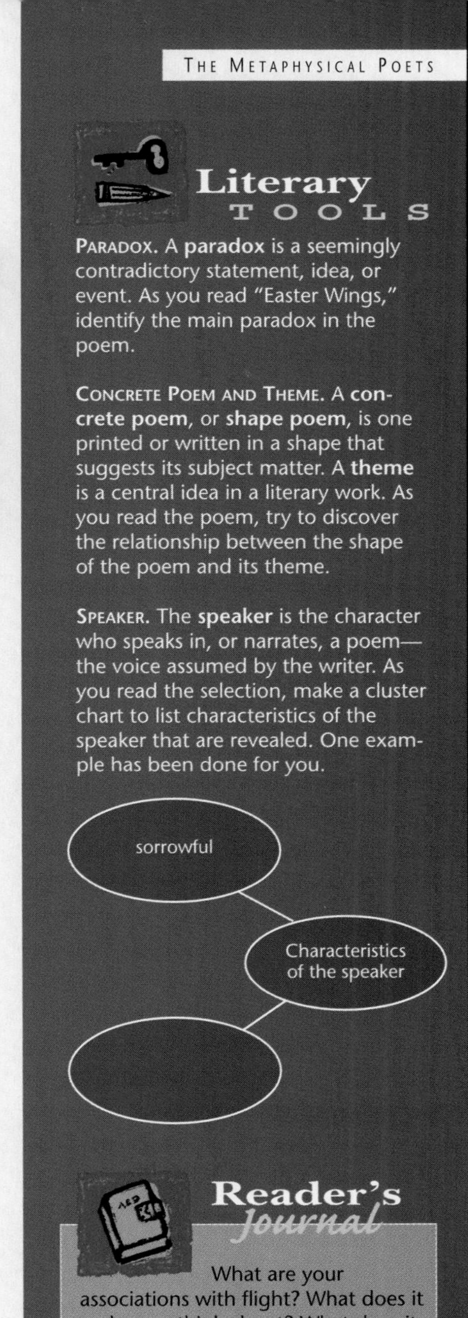

Literary TOOLS

PARADOX. A **paradox** is a seemingly contradictory statement, idea, or event. As you read "Easter Wings," identify the main paradox in the poem.

CONCRETE POEM AND THEME. A **concrete poem**, or **shape poem**, is one printed or written in a shape that suggests its subject matter. A **theme** is a central idea in a literary work. As you read the poem, try to discover the relationship between the shape of the poem and its theme.

SPEAKER. The **speaker** is the character who speaks in, or narrates, a poem—the voice assumed by the writer. As you read the selection, make a cluster chart to list characteristics of the speaker that are revealed. One example has been done for you.

Reader's Journal

What are your associations with flight? What does it make you think about? What does it make you feel?

ADDITIONAL RESOURCES

UNIT 6 RESOURCE BOOK
- Selection Worksheet 6.4
- Selection Check Test 4.6.9
- Selection Test 4.6.10
- Language, Grammar, and Style Resource 3.13, 3.14
- Speaking and Listening Resource 4.20
- Study and Research Resource 5.3

GRAPHIC ORGANIZER

Students should include the following characteristics in their cluster charts. The speaker is sick, ashamed, and thin.

READER'S JOURNAL

Artistically inclined students might draw a picture of what flight means to them.

GOALS/OBJECTIVES

Studying this lesson will enable students to
- appreciate the speaker's hopeful feelings
- identify George Herbert as one of the Metaphysical poets and describe his literary contributions
- define *paradox, concrete poem, theme,* and *speaker* and recognize the use of these techniques in the selection
- use proper syntax
- identify false arguments and propaganda
- tell a story

ANSWERS TO GUIDED READING QUESTIONS

1. Human beings foolishly lost the "wealth and store" that they enjoyed at the time of creation, eventually becoming "most poor."
2. The speaker has been similarly degraded, becoming sick and thin as he has grown older.

INDIVIDUAL LEARNING STRATEGIES

Motivation

Discuss with students what Easter means to Christians and the associations students have with the word *wings*.

Reading Proficiency

Point out that Herbert refers to the story of Adam and Eve in lines 1–5 and line 10 ("the fall"). The speaker feels that he, too, has "fallen" and he elaborates on this idea in stanza 2.

English Language Learning

Tell students the story of Adam and Eve so that they can appreciate the allusions in lines 1–5 and line 10.

Special Needs

Point out the following vocabulary words:
harmoniously—in a pleasing manner
affliction—pain; suffering
Be sure students know the answers to the Guided Reading Questions and the Recall questions in Investigate, Inquire, and Imagine.

Enrichment

You might have students read the story of Adam and Eve in the book of Genesis. This activity will also be useful for reading the excerpt from Milton's *Paradise Lost* in this unit.

"Easter Wings"

George Herbert

Lord, who createdst man in wealth and store,[1]
Though foolishly he lost the same,
Decaying more and more
Till he became
Most poor:[2]
With thee
O let me rise
As larks, harmoniously,
And sing this day thy victories:
Then shall the fall[3] further the flight in me.

My tender age in sorrow did begin:
And still with sicknesses and shame
Thou didst so punish sin,
That I became
Most thin.
With thee
Let me combine,
And feel this day thy victory;
For, if I imp[4] my wing on thine,
Affliction shall advance the flight in me. ■

According to the speaker, what happened to humankind?

What does the speaker say has happened to him?

1. **store.** Abundance
2. **Though foolishly . . . poor.** These lines refer to the story of Adam and Eve in the book of Genesis in the Bible. Adam and Eve lived a life of bliss in the Garden of Eden until they were expelled for their sin.
3. **fall.** Adam and Eve's, and any sinner's, fall from innocence and grace
4. **imp.** Graft

SELECTION CHECK TEST 4.6.9 WITH ANSWERS

Checking Your Reading

1. What has mankind lost? **He has lost the "wealth" that the Lord gave him.**
2. How did the speaker's "tender age" begin? **It began in sorrow.**
3. What happened to the speaker when the Lord punished his sin? **He grew thin.**
4. What does the speaker wish to feel "this day"? **He wants to feel the Lord's victory.**
5. What will the fall and affliction do for the speaker? **They will advance his flight.**

Literary Tools

1. What does the shape of the poem resemble? **It resembles a pair of wings.**
2. What do you think is the poem's theme? ***Responses will vary.***
3. What is a paradox? **A paradox is a contradictory statement, idea, or event.**

Respond *to the* SELECTION

According to the speaker, what purpose does affliction serve?

INVESTIGATE, Inquire, *Imagine*

Recall: GATHERING FACTS → **Interpret:** FINDING MEANING

1a. To whom is this poem addressed?

1b. What tone does the speaker use in his address?

2a. For what two things does the speaker ask?

2b. What emotions do you think the speaker would feel if his pleas were granted?

3a. What did humankind lose, and for what was humankind punished?

3b. What indications does the speaker give that he feels afflicted himself? Why does the speaker want divine help?

Analyze: TAKING THINGS APART → **Synthesize:** BRINGING THINGS TOGETHER

4a. Analyze the similarities between stanza 1 and stanza 2.

4b. Why is this poem called "Easter Wings"?

Evaluate: MAKING JUDGMENTS → **Extend:** CONNECTING IDEAS

5a. Evaluate whether the poem is a prayer.

5b. Compare Herbert's view of affliction with that expressed by Donne in "Meditation 17."

Understanding *Literature*

PARADOX. Review the definition for **paradox** in the Handbook of Literary Terms. What is the main paradox of "Easter Wings"?

CONCRETE POEM AND THEME. Review the definitions for **concrete poem** and **theme** in the Handbook of Literary Terms. What does the shape of the poem reveal about its theme?

SPEAKER. Review the definition for **speaker** and the cluster chart you made for Literary Tools on page 507. How does the speaker portray himself to God? What emotions does the speaker express in the poem?

RESPONDING TO THE SELECTION

What disappointments, frustrations, and problems in interpersonal relationships have you experienced? What have you learned from these experiences?

ANSWERS TO INVESTIGATE, INQUIRE, AND IMAGINE

RECALL

1a. The poem is addressed to the Lord, or God.

2a. The speaker wants to rise and sing with the Lord (stanza 1) and to combine with the Lord and share in His victory (stanza 2).

3a. Humankind lost the perfect life enjoyed by Adam and Eve in the Garden of Eden. People who came after them were punished for Adam and Eve's sin of disobeying God.

INTERPRET

1b. The tone is respectful, humble, adoring, and hopeful.

2b. The speaker would feel joyous, free, and victorious.

3b. The speaker's desire to participate in his Lord's victory suggests that by himself he feels defeated. He mentions "sorrow," "sicknesses and shame," and becoming "most thin" with the weight of sin upon him. The speaker feels despair at overcoming his sin without divine help.

ANALYZE

4a. Stanza 1 begins by describing the downfall of humankind; stanza 2 begins by describing the downfall of the speaker. The middle of stanza 1 describes the sinfulness and despair of humankind in general; the middle of stanza 2 describes the sinfulness and despair of the speaker. In the end of stanza 1 the speaker asks God to let him rise "As larks"; in the end of stanza 2 the speaker asks to fly up to heaven on God's wings.

SYNTHESIZE

4b. The speaker seeks his salvation in Easter, which commemorates Christ's dying for the sins of humanity, his victory over death. Easter gives the speaker wings, the ability to be saved and go to heaven.

EVALUATE

5a. The poem is a prayer because the speaker begins by addressing the Lord and in both stanzas concludes by making supplications. As in many prayers, there are references to the

ANSWERS TO INVESTIGATE, INQUIRE, AND IMAGINE (CONT.)

scriptures: Adam and Eve and Easter. The poem is also a hymn of praise to the Lord (line 9).

EXTEND

5b. In "Meditation 17" Donne likens affliction to a treasure because "we get nearer and nearer our home, heaven, by it." Herbert, in the last lines of stanza 2, states, "For, if I imp my wing on thine, / Affliction shall advance the flight in me." Herbert echoes Donne's meaning by stating that his flight toward heaven is advanced by affliction.

Answers to Understanding Literature can be found on page 510.

ANSWERS TO UNDERSTANDING LITERATURE

Paradox. The major paradox is the idea that the fall of humankind and the affliction experienced by the speaker actually serve to make his "flight" with the Lord more glorious. Perhaps the speaker feels that suffering during his worldly existence will help him to appreciate the freedom from affliction that he will know after death, when he will finally be joined with the Lord.

Concrete Poem and Theme. The tragedy of the fall and human suffering diminish the quality of human life; this diminishment is reflected in the dwindling lines in the first half of each stanza. However, the expanding lines in the second half of each stanza reflect the Christian doctrine of redemption or salvation through Jesus's suffering.

Speaker. The speaker portrays himself as a humble sinner, incapable of saving himself from sin, sickness, and death without help from the Lord. The speaker expresses both despair at his present state and joy and hope at the prospect of being joined with the Lord in victory over his afflictions.

ANSWERS TO INTEGRATING THE LANGUAGE ARTS

Language, Grammar, and Style

1. My tender age did begin in sorrow.
2. I think I know whose woods these are.
3. The branch that might have grown full straight is cut.
4. Macduff was ripp'd from his mother's womb untimely.
5. He had black scabby brows, and a thin beard.

Critical Thinking

1. bandwagon appeal
2. stereotype
3. spin
4. circular reasoning
5. loaded words

Speaking and Listening

Students might retell a story they have seen on TV or in a movie if they cannot think of an original story idea. Encourage students to develop the setting and motive for their stories.

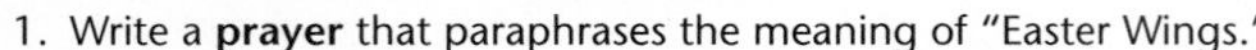

Writer's Journal

1. Write a **prayer** that paraphrases the meaning of "Easter Wings."
2. Write a **character sketch** of the speaker based on what you know about him from the poem.
3. Write a **concrete poem** that suggests its subject matter. You may chose to imitate the shape of Herbert's poem to express your own thoughts on flight.

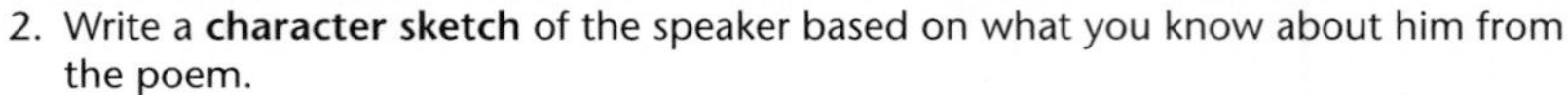

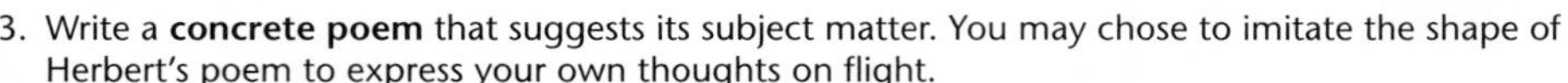

Integrating *the* Language Arts

Language, Grammar, and Style

Using Proper Syntax. Poets often use a different syntax from normal word order to underline an idea, make a line rhyme, or establish an intended meter. Rephrase the poets' lines below in order to express the ideas using normal syntax. Read the Language Arts Survey 3.13, "English Is a Syntactic Language," and 3.14, "The Importance of Syntax, or Word Order."

1. My tender age in sorrow did begin. (George Herbert)
2. Whose woods these are I think I know. (Robert Frost)
3. Cut is the branch that might have grown full straight. (Christopher Marlowe)
4. Macduff was from his mother's womb / Untimely ripp'd. (William Shakespeare)
5. Black scabby brows he had, and a thin beard. (Geoffrey Chaucer)

Critical Thinking

Identifying False Arguments and Propaganda. Religion is a topic about which many people have passionate views. However, sometimes these views are expressed using false arguments and propaganda. Read the Language Arts Survey 5.3, "Avoiding False Arguments and Propaganda." Then identify the type of false argument or propaganda in each sentence below.

1. If you join our religion, you will go straight to heaven.
2. Every Muslim knows the Koran from cover to cover.
3. Judaism is an insignificant religion because nobody in this town practices that religion.
4. My religion is the true one because my pastor tells us that all other religions are false.
5. People who practice that religion are dangerous, terrorist fanatics.

Speaking and Listening

Telling a Story. In "Easter Wings" George Herbert describes the speaker's shame. In a small group, tell a story in which a character is overwhelmed by feelings of shame. What causes the feelings? Is the shame evident or hidden? How does the character resolve his or her shame? Before you begin, you might find it helpful to read the Language Arts Survey 4.20, "Telling a Story."

FROM

Paradise Lost

"On His Blindness"

BY JOHN MILTON

About the AUTHOR

John Milton (1608–1674) was the eldest son of a self-made London businessman. Before entering Christ's College, Cambridge, Milton had mastered Latin, Greek, most modern European languages, and Hebrew. After graduating in 1632, Milton returned home and for the next six years followed his own rigorous reading program. In 1637, he wrote the elegy *Lycidas,* a contribution to a volume memorializing a college classmate. Throughout the next year, Milton traveled through Europe, returning home after hearing of looming troubles in England. The next twenty years, 1640–1660, were a period of controversy during which Milton devoted most of his energy to writing prose. He wrote a number of tracts, essays, and pamphlets, including his *Areopagitica,* a defense of unlicensed or uncensored printing. He also served in the position of Latin secretary to Oliver Cromwell, the leader of the Puritans who had taken over England. In 1651, at the age of forty-three, Milton went blind. The next year, his first wife died. In 1656, he married Katherine Woodcock, who died in childbirth two years later. In 1663, Milton married his third wife and returned to writing poetry. During the last fourteen years of his life, he published his three major poems, *Paradise Lost, Paradise Regained,* and *Samson Agonistes.* Milton's writings reveal the influences of two powerful and contrasting intellectual and social movements, the Renaissance and the Reformation. These two paradoxical sources of work place him within the tradition of Renaissance Christian Humanism.

About the SELECTION

The twelve-book epic poem ***Paradise Lost*** was published in 1667 and was immediately recognized as a masterpiece. "To justify the ways of God to men," Milton tells in the poem the story of Adam and Eve's fall. Milton published a sequel, *Paradise Regained,* in 1671. **"On His Blindness"** was published in 1655, four years after Milton lost his sight. In the selection, Milton eloquently alludes to events in the Bible, which he knew by heart.

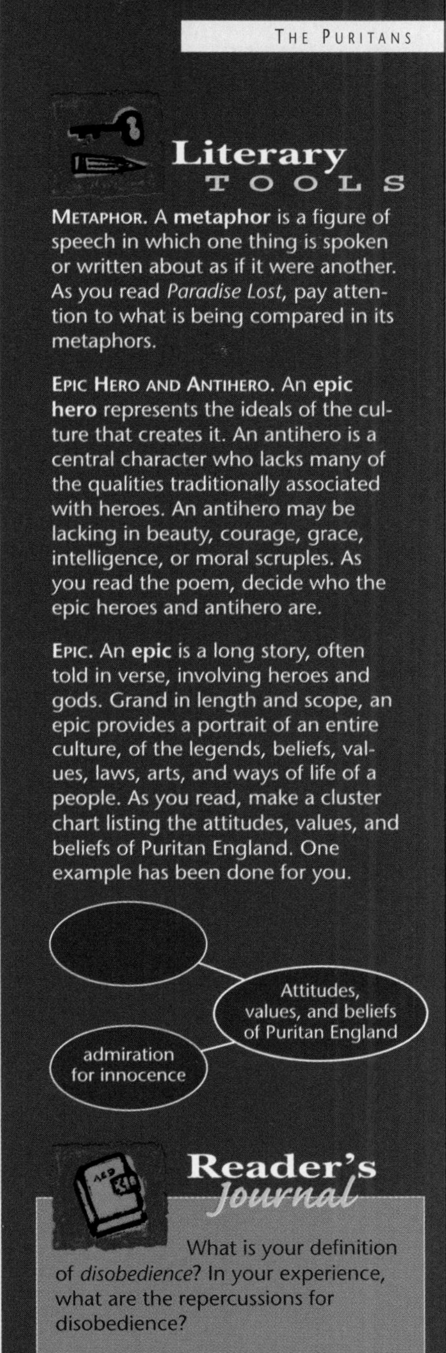

Literary TOOLS

METAPHOR. A **metaphor** is a figure of speech in which one thing is spoken or written about as if it were another. As you read *Paradise Lost,* pay attention to what is being compared in its metaphors.

EPIC HERO AND ANTIHERO. An **epic hero** represents the ideals of the culture that creates it. An antihero is a central character who lacks many of the qualities traditionally associated with heroes. An antihero may be lacking in beauty, courage, grace, intelligence, or moral scruples. As you read the poem, decide who the epic heroes and antihero are.

EPIC. An **epic** is a long story, often told in verse, involving heroes and gods. Grand in length and scope, an epic provides a portrait of an entire culture, of the legends, beliefs, values, laws, arts, and ways of life of a people. As you read, make a cluster chart listing the attitudes, values, and beliefs of Puritan England. One example has been done for you.

Reader's Journal

What is your definition of *disobedience*? In your experience, what are the repercussions for disobedience?

ADDITIONAL RESOURCES

UNIT 6 RESOURCE BOOK
- Selection Worksheet 6.5
- Selection Check Test 4.6.11
- Selection Test 4.6.12

"On His Blindness"
- Selection Worksheet 6.6
- Selection Check Test 4.6.13
- Selection Test 4.6.14
- Reading Resource 1.4, 1.20
- Study and Research Resource 5.4

VOCABULARY FROM THE SELECTION

baleful	invoke
coy	obdurate
dalliance	omnipotent
damask	perdition
dandle	proboscis
disheveled	ruminate
ethereal	sanctitude
exalt	sovereign
guile	zephyr
impious	

GRAPHIC ORGANIZER

Students should list the following details in their cluster charts: admiration for humility, admiration for obedience, disapproval for arrogance, belief in stereotypical gender roles (strong and authoritative men, soft and submissive women).

READER'S JOURNAL

Students might consider whether they think it is more important to obey rules or to follow one's own conscience. They should provide personal examples of repercussions they have known for their disobedience.

GOALS/OBJECTIVES

Studying this lesson will enable students to
- interpret and appreciate two views on the ways of God and the limits of human understanding
- describe the literary accomplishments of John Milton and explain how his work was influenced by the Renaissance and the Reformation
- define *metaphor, epic hero, antihero, epic, speaker, allusion, pun, sonnet,* and *rhyme scheme* and recognize the use of these techniques in the selections
- select synonyms
- classify
- apply reading techniques
- research a person with a disability

ANSWER TO GUIDED READING QUESTION

1. "Man's first disobedience," eating fruit from the tree of knowledge that God had instructed Adam and Eve to avoid, brought death and suffering into the world.

INDIVIDUAL LEARNING STRATEGIES

MOTIVATION
Ask students what they remember learning about American colonial Puritans. How did they live? How did they dress? What did they believe?

READING PROFICIENCY
Even proficient students will probably have some difficulty with the length and complexity of the sentences. Get them started reading by pointing out the poem opens with an imperative sentence. The main verb, *sing,* does not appear until line 6. Lines 1-5 are a prepositional phrase that modifies *sing.*

ENGLISH LANGUAGE LEARNING
Ask students what creation myths exist in their cultures. Have students share these stories with the class.

SPECIAL NEEDS
Xerox the poem for students and have them underline the subject and circle the verb for each sentence in the poem. Point out the following vocabulary words:

oracle—place where a deity is consulted, usually for a prophecy
illumine—light up
transgress—break a law or commandment
aspire—yearn
doleful—mournful; melancholy
deluge—flood; rain; rush
sublime—noble; majestic
suffice—be enough; adequate
compliant—yielding
gambol—skip; frolic
pine—yearn; desire

ENRICHMENT
Have students compare and contrast the depiction of Satan in the Genesis account with Milton's version. What details did Milton add to his story? The fall from grace and loss of innocence are common literary themes. Invite students to share other examples of this motif in modern and contemporary works with which they are familiar.

FROM

Paradise Lost

JOHN MILTON

Paradise Lost, c.1800s. Gustave Doré.

FROM BOOK 1

Of man's first disobedience, and the fruit
Of that forbidden tree whose mortal taste
Brought death into the world, and all our woe,
With loss of Eden, till one greater Man
Restore us, and regain the blissful seat,
Sing, Heavenly Muse,[1] that on the secret top
Of Oreb, or of Sinai,[2] didst inspire
That shepherd who first taught the chosen seed[3]
In the beginning how the heavens and earth
Rose out of Chaos: or, if Sion hill
Delight thee more, and Siloa's brook that flowed
Fast[4] by the oracle of God, I thence

What brought death and woe into the world?

1. **Heavenly Muse.** Ambiguous, referring both to Urania, Greek muse of astronomy, and to the Holy Spirit
2. **Oreb . . . Sinai.** Oreb, or Horeb, was the mountain on which God spoke to Moses from a burning bush. Sinai was the mountain on which Moses received the Ten Commandments.
3. **chosen seed.** The Jews
4. **Fast.** Close

Invoke thy aid to my adventurous song,
That with no middle flight intends to soar
Above th' Aonian mount,[5] while it pursues
Things unattempted yet in prose or rhyme.
And chiefly thou, O Spirit, that dost prefer
Before all temples th' upright heart and pure,
Instruct me, for thou know'st; thou from the first
Wast present, and with mighty wings outspread
Dovelike sat'st brooding on the vast abyss,
And mad'st it pregnant: what in me is dark
Illumine; what is low, raise and support;
That to the height of this great argument
I may assert Eternal Providence,
And justify the ways of God to men.
Say first (for Heaven hides nothing from thy view,
Nor the deep tract of Hell), say first what cause
Moved our grand[6] parents, in that happy state,
Favored of Heaven so highly, to fall off
From their Creator, and transgress his will
For one restraint, lords of the world besides?
Who first seduced them to that foul revolt?
Th' infernal serpent; he it was, whose guile,
Stirred up with envy and revenge, deceived
The mother of mankind, what time his pride
Had cast him out from Heaven, with all his host
Of rebel angels, by whose aid aspiring
To set himself in glory above his peers,
He trusted to have equaled the Most High,
If he opposed; and with ambitious aim
Against the throne and monarchy of God
Raised impious war in Heaven and battle proud,
With vain attempt. Him the Almighty Power
Hurled headlong flaming from th' ethereal sky
With hideous ruin and combustion down

What does the speaker wish to justify?

What did the "infernal serpent" do?

5. **Aonian mount.** The Aonian mount is Helicon, home of the Muses.
6. **grand.** First in importance as well as in time

WORDS FOR EVERYDAY USE

in • voke (in vōk´) *vt.*, ask solemnly for; beg for; implore. *After smashing the fender of his mother's new car, Kang was forced to invoke her mercy.*

im • pi • ous (im´pē əs) *adj.*, lacking respect or dutifulness. *After making an impious remark to his father, Ira was grounded for a week.*

e • the • re • al (ē thir´ē əl) *adj.*, not earthly; heavenly; celestial. *The dancer's airy costume transformed her from flesh and blood to an ethereal spirit floating about the stage.*

ANSWERS TO GUIDED READING QUESTIONS

1. The speaker intends to "justify the ways of God to men," or explain and elaborate for readers what happened in the Garden of Eden.
2. The serpent tricked Eve, "the mother of mankind," into disobeying God.

ADDITIONAL QUESTIONS AND ACTIVITIES

Ask students the following questions: What image of God's power in Heaven does Milton create in line 42? How does this image reflect the historical period in which Milton lived? Does the image work for you? What are some other ways you might imagine God's power?

Answers

The image is of God as an absolute monarch. Milton lived in a time when the absolute authority of English kings was being successfully challenged by Parliament, but the notion of complete power resting in the hands of one person was still viable in many people's minds. Students may think that the image is outdated. They might imagine God as resembling not so much an earthly monarch as an omnipresent force of nature, for example.

ANSWER TO GUIDED READING QUESTION

1. The "great furnace" of Hell is the new home of the rebellious angels. The lost archangel is horrified to compare this place to his former home, Heaven, but he is resigned to his fate.

LITERARY TECHNIQUE

CHARACTERIZATION. Characterization is the use of literary techniques to create a character. Milton's characterization of Satan is superbly complex and memorable. The former archangel fully appreciates the splendors of Heaven that he will never again be able to enjoy, and yet he defiantly says he prefers "to reign in Hell than serve in Heaven." You might ask students to discuss whether they have any sympathy for Satan and whether they think he deserves the fate to which God has condemned him. As they continue reading, students should try to be aware of how Milton reveals the facets of Satan's personality.

Have students list the aspects of Hell that are described in lines 60–72. What would Milton's Hell be like?

To bottomless perdition, there to dwell
In adamantine[7] chains and penal fire,
Who durst defy th' Omnipotent to arms.
Nine times the space that measures day and night
To mortal men, he with his horrid crew
Lay vanquished, rolling in the fiery gulf
Confounded though immortal. But his doom
Reserved him to more wrath; for now the thought
Both of lost happiness and lasting pain
Torments him; round he throws his baleful eyes,
That witnessed huge affliction and dismay,
Mixed with obdúrate pride and steadfast hate.
At once, as far as angels ken,[8] he views
The dismal situation waste and wild:
A dungeon horrible, on all sides round
As one great furnace flamed; yet from those flames
No light, but rather darkness visible
Served only to discover sights of woe,
Regions of sorrow, doleful shades, where peace
And rest can never dwell, hope never comes
That comes to all, but torture without end
Still urges,[9] and a fiery deluge, fed
With ever-burning sulphur unconsumed:
Such place Eternal Justice had prepared
For those rebellious; here their prison ordained
In utter darkness and their portion set
As far removed from God and light of Heaven
As from the center thrice to th' utmost pole.[10]

What type of place has been prepared "for those rebellious"?

◆ ◆ ◆

Said then the lost archangel, "this the seat
That we must change for Heaven? this mournful gloom

7. **adamantine.** Rigidly firm; unbreakable
8. **ken.** Can see
9. **urges.** Afflicts
10. **utmost pole.** Here the earth is the utmost pole in Milton's concept of the cosmos, which places Heaven at the center and Earth tacked on as an appendage.

WORDS FOR EVERYDAY USE

per • di • tion (pər dish´ən) *n.*, complete and irreparable loss; ruin. *What caused the once wealthy and powerful software baron to fall into such perdition?*

om • nip • o • tent (äm nip´ə tənt) *n.*, God; one having unlimited power. *Do you believe the Omnipotent watches over you?*

bale • ful (bāl´fəl) *adj.*, sorrowful; wretched. *Tamara surveyed the cafeteria's unappetizing selections with a baleful expression.*

ob • du •rate (äb´door it) *adj.*, stubborn; obstinate; inflexible. *Minh tried to negotiate a later curfew for Friday night, but her parents were obdurate.*

For that celestial light? Be it so, since he
Who now is sovereign can dispose and bid
What shall be right: farthest from him is best,
Whom reason hath equaled, force hath made supreme
Above his equals. Farewell, happy fields,
Where joy forever dwells! Hail, horrors! hail,
Infernal world! and thou, profoundest Hell,
Receive thy new possessor, one who brings
A mind not to be changed by place or time.
The mind is its own place, and in itself
Can make a Heaven of Hell, a Hell of Heaven.
What matter where, if I be still the same,
And what I should be, all but less than he
Whom thunder hath made greater? Here at least
We shall be free; th' Almighty hath not built
Here for his envy, will not drive us hence.
Here we may reign secure; and in my choice
To reign is worth ambition, though in Hell:
Better to reign in Hell than serve in Heaven . . ."

What is the lost archangel's first reaction to this place?

What does the lost archangel finally decide?

◆ ◆ ◆

FROM BOOK 4

◆ ◆ ◆

Beneath him with new wonder now he views
To all delight of human sense exposed
In narrow room Nature's whole wealth; yea more,
A Heaven on Earth; for blissful Paradise
Of God the garden was, by him in the east
Of Eden planted. . . .

◆ ◆ ◆

From this Assyrian garden, where the fiend
Saw undelighted all delight, all kind
Of living creatures, new to sight and strange.
Two of far nobler shape, erect and tall,
Godlike erect, native honor clad

WORDS FOR EVERYDAY USE

sov • er • eign (säv´rən) *adj.*, above or superior to all others; greatest; supreme. *Joe may be the worst basketball player in our class, but he is sovereign at the chess board.*

ANSWERS TO GUIDED READING QUESTIONS

1. The lost archangel, Satan, bids farewell to the "celestial light" of Heaven and greets the "horror" and "gloom" of Hell. Satan realizes that he has lost forever the happiness of Heaven due to his rebellious nature.
2. He concludes that he prefers Hell to Heaven, because in Hell he is free and in control rather than subject to God's power.

ANSWER TO GUIDED READING QUESTION

1. The Garden of Eden is a place of pure delight, inhabited by many newly created animals. The most interesting creatures are the two humans. They are most interesting because they resemble God.

ADDITIONAL QUESTIONS AND ACTIVITIES

Discuss with students the differences between Adam and Eve, and between men and women generally, as depicted by Milton in this poem. Lead them through the following questions:

1. How is Adam described? What does he do? The author uses Adam to represent men generally. How might the author characterize men generally?
2. How is Eve described? What does she do? The author uses Eve to represent women generally. How might the author characterize women generally?
3. What similarities and differences do you find between men and women as characterized in the poem?
4. Do you agree with this characterization of men? Why, or why not? Do you agree with this characterization of women? Why, or why not?
5. Do you think these views of men and women are common today?
6. What might it be like for a man to live in a society in which these views were universally shared? What might it be like for a woman to live in such a society?

In naked majesty, seemed lords of all,
And worthy seemed; for in their looks divine
The image of their glorious Maker shone,
Truth, wisdom, sanctitude severe and pure—
Severe, but in true filial freedom placed,
Whence true authority in men; though both
Not equal, as their sex not equal seemed;
For contemplation he and valor formed,
For softness she and sweet attractive grace;
He for God only, she for God in him.
His fair large front[11] and eye sublime declared
Absolute rule; and hyacinthine locks
Round from his parted forelock manly hung
Clustering, but not beneath his shoulders broad:
She, as a veil down to the slender waist,
Her unadornéd golden tresses wore
Disheveled, but in wanton ringlets waved
As the vine curls her tendrils, which implied
Subjection, but required with gentle sway,
And by her yielded, by him best received,
Yielded with coy submission, modest pride,
And sweet, reluctant, amorous delay.
Nor those mysterious parts were then concealed;
Then was not guilty shame. Dishonest shame
Of Nature's works, honor dishonorable,
Sin-bred, how have ye troubled all mankind
With shows instead, mere shows of seeming pure,
And banished from man's life his happiest life,
Simplicity and spotless innocence!
So passed they naked on, nor shunned the sight
Of God or angel, for they thought no ill;
So hand in hand they passed, the loveliest pair
That ever since in love's embraces met:
Adam the goodliest man of men since born
His sons; the fairest of her daughters Eve.

How is the Garden of Eden described? What two creatures are particularly interesting? Why?

11. **front.** Forehead

WORDS FOR EVERYDAY USE

sanc • ti • tude (saŋk´tə to͞od) *n.*, fact of being sacred or inviolable. *No one but the priestesses could enter the inner chamber; an intrusion by anyone else would violate the sanctitude of this holy place.*

fil • ial (fi' lē əl) *adj.*, of, relating to, or befitting a son or daughter. *Jeremy and Claudette thought it was their filial duty to plan a party for their father's fortieth birthday.*

di • shev • eled (di shev´əld) *adj.*, disarranged and untidy. *With his disheveled clothing and faraway gaze, Dr. Tanaka fit the image of the absent-minded professor.*

coy (koi) *adj.*, playful or evasive. *The coy kitten hid beneath the couch, venturing forth a lightning paw only when tempted with one of her favorite toys.*

Under a tuft of shade that on a green
Stood whispering soft, by a fresh fountain-side,
They sat them down, and after no more toil
Of their sweet gardening labor than sufficed
To recommend cool Zephyr,[12] and made ease
More easy, wholesome thirst and appetite
More grateful, to their supper fruits they fell,
Nectarine fruits which the compliant boughs
Yielded them, sidelong as they sat recline
On the soft downy bank damasked with flowers.
The savory pulp they chew, and in the rind
Still as they thirsted scoop the brimming stream;
Nor gentle purpose, nor endearing smiles
Wanted, nor youthful dalliance, as beseems
Fair couple linked in happy nuptial league,
Alone as they. About them frisking played
All beasts of th' earth, since wild, and of all chase[13]
In wood or wilderness, forest or den.
Sporting the lion ramped,[14] and in his paw
Dandled the kid, bears, tigers, ounces, pards,[15]
Gamboled before them; th' unwieldy elephant
To make them mirth used all his might, and wreathed
His lithe proboscis; close the serpent sly,
Insinuating,[16] wove with Gordian twine
His braided train,[17] and of his fatal guile
Gave proof unheeded. Others on the grass
Couched, and now filled with pasture gazing sat,
Or bedward ruminating; for the sun,
Declined, was hasting now with prone career

12. **Zephyr.** God of the west wind
13. **of all chase.** Of all places in woods or wilderness
14. **ramped.** Reared up
15. **ounces, pards.** Lynxes and leopards
16. **Insinuating.** Writhing
17. **braided train.** Knotted, like the Gordian Knot that was cut by Alexander the Great

Words for Everyday Use

dam • ask (dam´əsk) *vt.,* make a deep pink or rose. *The singer damasked her cheeks before going onstage.*

dal • li • ance (dal´yəns) *n.,* flirting; toying; trifling. *"I have no time for such dalliance! My term paper is due tomorrow," Haesun told her boyfriend when he suggested a movie.*

dan • dle (dan´dəl) *vt.,* swing up and down. *Jon felt like a human seesaw as he dandled the delighted toddler on his leg.*

pro • bos • cis (prō bäs´is) *n.,* an elephant's trunk; a long, flexible snout. *The elephant washed itself with a powerful stream of water from its proboscis.*

guile (gīl) *n.,* slyness and cunning in dealing with others. *The guile of used-car dealers is often joked about, but surely there are a few honest ones!*

ru • mi • nat • ing (ro͞o´mə nāt´ŋ) *part.,* chewing cud, as a cow does. *As she considered the question, Margaret chewed on her lip, reminding me of a cow ruminating.*

Cross-Curricular Activity

Social Studies. As the poem suggests, Eden was traditionally located in the ancient region of Assyria, in northern Mesopotamia. Genesis 2:10–14 describes Eden's location at the source of four rivers, two of which are the Tigris and Euphrates. Students might locate this area on a map of the Middle East; it is in present-day Iraq. Interested students might also find a map showing the ancient kingdoms and cities in this region and research some of the creation stories from these civilizations to compare them with the Genesis account. How do these other traditions explain the creation of the first humans? How did the various traditions influence one another?

You might encourage students to look at one of the most significant myths of the ancient Mesopotamean culture, the *Enuma elish.* You may also have students read *Inanna's Descent,* in which a rebellious goddess descends to the underworld, in order to examine counterparts of the Satan figure in other mythologies. Selections of both myths can be found in Jocobsen, Thorkild. *The Treasures of Darkness.* New Haven: Yale UP. 1976.

ANSWERS TO GUIDED READING QUESTIONS

1. Satan, in the form of a serpent or snake, is watching them.
2. Satan burns with envy at the pleasures Adam and Eve enjoy, but he plans to trick them into disobeying God's command to avoid the tree of knowledge.
3. Satan predicts that Adam and Eve will disobey God's command and eat from the tree of knowledge.

ADDITIONAL QUESTIONS AND ACTIVITIES

You may wish to encourage students to draw inferences from the text with questions such as the following:

1. What conflicting emotions on Satan's part are revealed in lines 358–368? Why do you think he feels this way?
2. What is Satan talking about in lines 512–513? What conversation has he overheard?
3. What is Satan planning in the passage that begins, "Knowledge forbidden?/Suspicious, reasonless" (lines 515–516)? How would you react to his argument if you were Adam or Eve?

Answers

1. Satan feels "wonder" and "could love" Adam and Eve because they are so beautiful and "Godlike." At the same time, he hates them because they are enjoying Paradise while he suffers. These conflicting emotions arise from his nature as a fallen archangel, once a "heavenly spirit" himself but now doomed to an eternity of pain and malevolence.
2. In lines 512–513, he refers to a conversation he has overheard between Adam and Eve, in which they discussed the tree of knowledge that God has forbidden them to eat from.
3. In line 515 he plans the argument he will use to convince them to disobey God's order, making them suspicious of God's intentions.

To th' ocean isles,[18] and in th' ascending scale
Of heaven the stars that usher evening rose:
When Satan, still in gaze as first he stood,
Scarce thus at length failed speech recovered sad:
"O Hell! what do mine eyes with grief behold?
Into our room of bliss thus high advanced
Creatures of other mold, Earth-born perhaps,
Not spirits, yet to heavenly spirits bright
Little inferior; whom my thoughts pursue
With wonder, and could love; so lively shines
In them divine resemblance, and such grace
The hand that formed them on their shape hath poured.
Ah! gentle pair, ye little think how nigh
Your change approaches, when all these delights
Will vanish, and deliver ye to woe,

Who is watching the new creatures?

◆ ◆ ◆

"Sight hateful, sight tormenting! thus these two
Imparadised in one another's arms,
The happier Eden, shall enjoy their fill
Of bliss on bliss, while I to Hell am thrust,
Where neither joy nor love, but fierce desire,
Among our other torments not the least,
Still unfulfilled with pain of longing pines.
Yet let me not forget what I have gained
From their own mouths: all is not theirs, it seems.
One fatal tree there stands, of knowledge called,
Forbidden them to taste. Knowledge forbidden?
Suspicious, reasonless. Why should their lord
Envy them that? Can it be sin to know,
Can it be death? and do they only stand
By ignorance, is that their happy state,
The proof of their obedience and their faith?
O fair foundation laid whereon to build
Their ruin! Hence I will excite their minds
With more desire to know, and to reject
Envious commands, invented with design
To keep them low whom knowledge might exalt

How does Satan feel about God's new creatures?

What does Satan predict will happen?

18. **ocean isles.** The Azores

WORDS FOR EVERYDAY USE

ex • alt (eg zôlt´) *vt.,* heighten or intensify the action or effect of. *Kevin was a good player but, not ready to exalt him to the position of team captain, I voted for Michael instead.*

CROSS-CURRICULAR CONNECTIONS

VEGETARIANISM. Students might be interested to note that in the Garden of Eden, neither humans nor any other animals ate meat. In Genesis 1:30, God declares, "And to every beast of the earth, and to every bird of the air, and to everything that creeps on the earth, everything that has the breath of life, I have given every green plant for food." The need to eat the flesh of animals in order to survive was considered a result of the Fall.

Teaching Note: Students might compare Genesis 9:2–3, in which God tells Noah that "the fear of you and the dread of you shall be upon every beast. . . . Every moving thing that lives shall be food for you; and as I gave you the green plants, I give you everything. " *The New Oxford Annotated Bible.* New York: Oxford UP. 1977.

Equal with gods. Aspiring to be such,
They taste and die; what likelier can ensue?
But first with narrow search I must walk round
This garden, and no corner leave unspied;
A chance but chance may lead where I may meet
Some wandering spirit of Heaven, by fountain side
Or in thick shade retired, from him to draw
What further would be learnt. Live while ye may,
Yet happy pair; enjoy, till I return,
Short pleasures, for long woes are to succeed." ■

Respond *to the* Selection

Imagine you are Adam or Eve before the serpent changed your life. Express your feelings about the topics of knowledge and temptation.

SELECTION CHECK TEST 4.6.11 WITH ANSWERS

Checking Your Reading

1. For what does Milton appeal to the Heavenly Muse? **He asks help writing his song.**
2. Who are "our grand parents"? **They are Adam and Eve.**
3. What does the archangel decide is better than serving in Heaven? **He decides that it is better to reign in Hell than serve in Heaven.**
4. What new creatures are described in Book 4? **Adam and Eve are described.**
5. What does Satan learn "from their own mouths"? **He learns of the forbidden tree.**

Vocabulary in Context

Fill each blank with the most appropriate word from the Words for Everyday Use. You may have to change the tense of certain verbs.

perdition disheveled coy exalt
damask dandle obdurate

1. Gerard thought Ann's **coy** glances meant she liked him.
2. After being out in the wind, Pietro fixed his **disheveled** appearance.
3. Diane **exalted** the new band in her column when she called it "the most popular band in town."
4. "Utter **perdition**," moaned the relief worker as she surveyed the wreckage.
5. The **obdurate** child refused to eat her dinner.

Literary Tools

1. What is an epic? **An epic is a long verse story that involves heroes and gods.**
2. What can we learn about a culture from an epic? **We learn values and ways of life.**
3. What does this epic suggest about the culture who produced it? **Responses will vary, but it suggests that the culture is Christian and believes in God, Heaven and Hell, Satan, and the downfalls of Satan and of Adam and Eve.**

   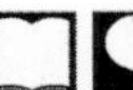 

RESPOND TO THE SELECTION

Suggest that students reread lines 515–526, in which Satan outlines the argument he will use to convince Adam and Eve to eat from the tree of knowledge. Do they believe that God's injunction against eating that fruit is an "envious command" (line 524)?

ANSWERS TO INVESTIGATE, INQUIRE, AND IMAGINE

RECALL

1a. The speaker says that the subject of the epic will be Adam and Eve's disobedience to God and the resultant death and woe it brought to humanity until Jesus restored humanity's "blissful seat."

2a. Satan, in his pride, sought to equal God in his power and raised a band of rebel angels to war against God, who cast them out of heaven and into hell. Satan says farewell to the light of heaven, hails the horrors of hell, says that the mind "Can make a Heaven of Hell" or "a Hell of Heaven."

3a. The phrases "Nature's whole wealth," "Heaven on Earth," and "blissful Paradise" describe the Garden of Eden. Satan predicts that Adam and Eve will eat the fruit from the tree of knowledge, and God will cast them out of paradise.

INTERPRET

1b. The speaker needs divine inspiration because he has a lofty and arduous goal in mind: to "justify the ways of God to men."

2b. Satan's pride, envy, ambition, disobedience, and persuasion are traits associated with his revolt against God. His moral turpitude, determination, envy, and persuasion are traits associated with his corruption of Adam and Eve.

3b. Satan's point of view is presented. He feels he could love humans because of their resemblance to God.

ANALYZE

4a. Satan and Adam and Eve went from knowing God's favor, from living in heaven or heaven on earth, to being chased from paradise.

SYNTHESIZE

4b. As he did with Satan when he rebelled, God will most likely exhibit anger when Adam and Eve rebel against him.

EVALUATE

Responses will vary.

5a. Students may say that examining Satan's actions and motivations is like learning "the ways of God" because Satan is the antithesis of God.

EXTEND

Responses will vary.

5b. Snakes seem to humans to be sneaky the way they slither in and out of hiding places. This characteristic of Satan is evident in *Paradise Lost* when he listens in on Adam and Eve's conversation without them knowing it. Foxes are also sneaky, but not being a reptile they are more appealing than snakes.

INVESTIGATE, Inquire, Imagine

Recall: GATHERING FACTS

1a. In lines 1–5, what does the speaker say the subject of the epic will be?

2a. What did Satan do to get cast out of heaven? What is his reaction to his new position?

3a. How is the Garden of Eden described in lines 205–210? What future does Satan predict for Adam and Eve?

→ **Interpret:** FINDING MEANING

1b. Why does the speaker need divine inspiration?

2b. What character traits does Satan possess? In which episodes are they evident?

3b. Whose point of view is presented in lines 356–535? What is his attitude toward the human creatures?

Analyze: TAKING THINGS APART

4a. What parallel experience exists between Satan and Adam and Eve?

→ **Synthesize:** BRINGING THINGS TOGETHER

4b. Based on his response to Satan's rebellion, what do you think will be God's emotional reaction to the rebellion of Adam and Eve?

Evaluate: MAKING JUDGMENTS

5a. Milton states that his purpose is to "justify the ways of God to men." In what you have read of *Paradise Lost,* is Milton successful? How is describing Satan's actions and motivations a part of this purpose? What do you learn about God's ways from the passages about Satan?

→ **Extend:** CONNECTING IDEAS

5b. What makes the snake an appropriate incarnation of the devil? Can you think of another animal that would work just as well?

Understanding Literature

METAPHOR. Review the definition for **metaphor** in the Handbook of Literary Terms. In the following two metaphors, what two things are being compared?

> "O Spirit, . . . thou from the first / Wast present, and with mighty wings outspread / Dovelike sat'st brooding on the vast abyss." (lines 17–21)
>
> Hell is "A dungeon horrible, on all sides round / As one great furnace flamed." (lines 61–62)

EPIC HERO AND ANTIHERO. Review the definitions for **epic hero** and **antihero** in the Handbook of Literary Terms. Who are the epic heroes and who is the antihero in *Paradise Lost*? What qualities do they exhibit?

EPIC. Review the definition for **epic** in the Handbook of Literary Terms and the cluster chart you made for Literary Tools on page 511. What supernatural characters are included in *Paradise Lost*? What attitudes, values, and beliefs does the poem portray?

ANSWERS TO UNDERSTANDING LITERATURE

Continued on page 521

METAPHOR. The first metaphor compares the Holy Spirit to a bird. Both have the power to create—either by brooding (laying an egg) or by making a universe out of an abyss. The second metaphor hell is compared to a horrible dungeon; both hell and a dungeon are dark and bleak, allowing only enough light to reveal "sights of woe."

EPIC HERO AND ANTIHERO. The epic heroes are Adam and Eve, who are portrayed as having divine qualities from being made in the image of God. Satan possesses heroic qualities such as great energy, self-confidence, and determination, but his excessive pride and envy, as well as his desire to thwart God's plan, make him an antihero.

EPIC. God and the fallen archangel, Satan, are two supernatural characters in the poem. *Paradise Lost* expresses the religious beliefs of its Puritan author and the historical context in which he lived. The poem

John Milton Composing Poetry, c.1800s. Leon Bortarel. Cider House Galleries, Bletchingley, UK.

On His Blindness

JOHN MILTON

When I consider how my light is spent
Ere half my days[1] in this dark world and wide,
And that one talent[2] which is death to hide
Lodged with me useless, though my soul more bent[3]
To serve therewith my Maker, and present
My true account, lest He returning chide;[4]
"Doth God exact day-labor, light denied?"
I fondly[5] ask. But Patience, to prevent
That murmur, soon replies, "God doth not need
Either man's work or his own gifts. Who best
Bear his mild yoke,[6] they serve him best. His state
Is kingly: thousands at his bidding speed,
And post[7] o'er land and ocean without rest;
They also serve who only stand and wait." ■

At what point in his life did the speaker go blind?

What is this speaker unable to do now?

1. **half my days.** Milton went blind when he was forty-three.
2. **one talent.** An allusion to Jesus's parable of the talents in which a servant was condemned for hiding a coin called a "talent." Milton's uses the word to mean both "coin" and "ability."
3. **bent.** Strongly inclined or determined
4. **chide.** Scold
5. **fondly.** Foolishly
6. **mild yoke.** An allusion to Jesus's words, "my yoke is easy"
7. **post.** Travel fast

Literary TOOLS

SPEAKER. The **speaker** is the character who speaks in, or narrates, a poem—the voice assumed by the writer. As you read "On His Blindness," look for the emotions the speaker expresses.

ALLUSION AND PUN. An **allusion** is a rhetorical technique in which reference is made to a person, event, object, or work from history or literature. A **pun** is a play on words, one that wittily exploits a double meaning. As you read, look for the reference that is both an allusion and a pun.

SONNET AND RHYME SCHEME. A **sonnet** is a fourteen-line poem, usually in iambic pentameter, that follows one of a number of different rhyme schemes. A **rhyme scheme** is a pattern of end rhymes, or rhymes at the ends of lines of verse. The rhyme scheme of a poem is designated by letters, with matching letters signifying matching sounds. As you read, make a chart of the words that rhyme and designate a letter to each group of rhyming words. The first quatrain has been done for you.

Rhyming Words	Designated Letter
spent, bent	*a*
wide, hide	*b*

Reader's Journal

Which sense would be the most difficult for you to lose? Why?

ANSWERS TO GUIDED READING QUESTIONS

1. According to the poem, the speaker went blind before he was halfway through his life.
2. The speaker is unable to do what he considers God's work.

SELECTION CHECK TEST 4.6.13 WITH ANSWERS

Checking Your Reading

1. What is "death to hide"? **Talent is death to hide.**
2. Who reassures the speaker? **Patience reassures the speaker.**
3. What does God not need from man? **God does not need man's work or gifts.**
4. How do people respond to God's bidding? **Thousands speed to do his bidding.**
5. Who also serves? **Those who stand and wait also serve.**

Literary Tools

Fill in the blanks using the following terms. You may not use every term, and you may use some terms more than once.

parable allusion
pun personification

1. **Parables** are brief stories told to make a point.
2. A writer uses **personification** when he or she assigns human qualities to something that is not human.
3. In this poem, Milton refers to the biblical **parable** in which a servant hides a coin.

GRAPHIC ORGANIZER

Students should fill in their chart as follows.

Rhyming Words	Designated Letter
spent, bent, present, prevent	*a*
wide, hide, chide, denied	*b*
need, speed	*c*
best, rest	*d*
state, wait	*e*

ANSWERS TO UNDERSTANDING LITERATURE (CONT. FROM PAGE 520)

conveys admiration for innocence, humility, and obedience, and disapproval for arrogance. It also expresses attitudes about the proper roles of men and women: Adam is portrayed as strong and authoritative, while Eve is soft and submissive.

READER'S JOURNAL

Students could begin by brainstorming a list of activities that require the use of each sense, and then identify what they would have to discontinue if they lost that sense.

RESPONDING TO THE SELECTION

Students should think of specific activities and go beyond the speaker's answer that he will "stand and wait."

ANSWERS TO INVESTIGATE, INQUIRE, AND IMAGINE

RECALL

1a. The speaker has lost his sight halfway through his life. The speaker is eager to serve God.

2a. The speaker asks whether God will punish him for not doing the work that he needs his sight to do.

3a. God does not need people's work or their "gifts."

INTERPRET

1b. The speaker may mean that the world is dark in its sinfulness. The speaker feels that writing is his way of serving God; he knows no other way to "present his true account" to God, or to show God his worth.

2b. The speaker has missed the point: God would not demand work if a person did not have the ability to produce it.

3b. Patience has shown the speaker that there are many ways to serve God, even without his sight. God will give him whatever talents he needs, such as patience for waiting.

ANALYZE

4a. The speaker is confronting the loss of his sight, which he fears will make him unable to serve God since he is no longer able to write.

SYNTHESIZE

4b. Patience assures the speaker that there is a way for everyone to serve God, even if it is a very different way than the person imagined.

PERSPECTIVE

5a. The poem is paradoxical because the speaker says that, in his blindness, he cannot write; yet he has written this poem.

EXTEND

5b. The speaker of "On His Blindness" recognizes that the world was dark before his blindness (line 2). He is most concerned with the state of his soul and his possibility for redemption. He wants to be supported by finding a way to serve God now that he is blind.

Respond to the SELECTION

If you were the speaker, how would you decide to serve God in your blindness?

INVESTIGATE, Inquire, Imagine

Recall: GATHERING FACTS → **Interpret:** FINDING MEANING

1a. What has the speaker lost? What is the speaker more eager to do now than ever?

1b. In what sense has the world always been dark? In what sense is losing his talent (the ability to write) like a death?

2a. What does the speaker "fondly ask"?

2b. What makes the speaker's question in line 7 a fond, or foolish, one?

3a. What, according to Patience, does God not need?

3b. What comfort can the speaker draw from Patience's closing remark?

Analyze: TAKING THINGS APART → **Synthesize:** BRINGING THINGS TOGETHER

4a. What crisis is the speaker confronting in this poem? What does he fear that he will no longer be able to do?

4b. Why, according to the poem, is his fear unjustified or unfounded?

Evaluate: MAKING JUDGMENTS → **Extend:** CONNECTING IDEAS

5a. Evaluate whether the poem is paradoxical.

5b. In *Paradise Lost*, Milton states, "what in me is dark / Illumine; what is low, raise and support." How are these lines echoed in "On His Blindness"?

Understanding Literature

SPEAKER. Review the definition for **speaker** in the Handbook of Literary Terms. Sometimes the speaker's voice is the same voice as the author; sometimes the speaker's voice is separate from the voice of the author. What do you think is the case for "On His Blindness"? What emotions does the speaker express in the poem?

ALLUSION AND PUN. Review the definitions for **allusion** and **pun** in the Handbook of Literary Terms. What allusion is made in line 3? Why is this also a pun? In what sense is the hiding of his talent a kind of death for the speaker?

SONNET AND RHYME SCHEME. Review the definitions for **sonnet** and **rhyme scheme** and the chart you made for Literary Tools on page 521. What is the rhyme scheme for this sonnet?

ANSWERS TO UNDERSTANDING LITERATURE

SPEAKER. Since Milton himself went blind in middle age, it is possible that the speaker's voice is the same as the author's voice. The speaker feels frustrated and frightened that he will no longer be able to serve God.

ALLUSION AND PUN. In line 3 an allusion is made to a New Testament parable in which a servant is condemned for hiding a coin called a "talent." This is a pun because *talent* has the additional meaning of "ability" or "skill." The loss of his talent for writing leaves the speaker, he at first thinks, without a way to "earn" eternal life.

SONNET AND RHYME SCHEME. The rhyme scheme of this sonnet is *abba abba cdec de.*

Writer's Journal

1. Imagine that you are one of the characters who disobeys God in *Paradise Lost*: Satan, Adam, or Eve. Write an **apology** to God giving reasons for your actions, apologizing for them convincingly, and asking for forgiveness.
2. A **parable**, like the story of the hidden talent, is a brief story told to teach a moral lesson. Write your own parable. You might choose to write your parable about someone who is physically challenged like the speaker in "On His Blindness."
3. In *Paradise Lost*, Milton states his intent is to pursue "Things unattempted yet in prose or rhyme." Write a **paragraph** in which you argue whether Milton achieves his lofty goal.

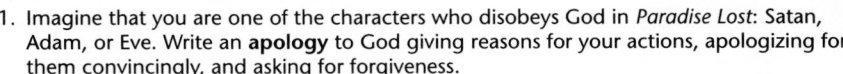

Integrating *the* Language Arts

Vocabulary

Using Synonyms. Read the Language Arts Survey 1.20, "Learning Synonyms, Antonyms, and Homonyms." Then read each of the following excerpts from Milton's essay on censorship, the *Areopagitica*. (See the complete excerpt in the Selections for Additional Reading on page 000.) Give a synonym for each underlined word.

1. Methinks I see in my mind a noble and <u>puissant</u> nation rousing herself like a strong man after sleep.
2. . . . while the whole noise of <u>timorous</u> and flocking birds, with those also that love the twilight, flutter about, . . .
3. . . . and in their envious <u>gabble</u> would <u>prognosticate</u> a year of sects and schisms.
4. And though all the winds of doctrine were let loose to play upon the earth, so Truth be in the field, we do <u>injuriously</u> by licensing and prohibiting to misdoubt her strength.
5. Believe it, Lords and Commons, they who <u>counsel</u> ye to such a suppressing do as good as <u>bid</u> ye <u>suppress</u> yourselves; and I will soon show how.

Collaborative Learning & Critical Thinking

Classifying. Read the Language Arts Survey 5.4, "Classifying." Then, with a classmate, identify a common class and at least two common features for each of the following sets of subjects.

1. Eleanor Roosevelt and Hillary Clinton
2. Mayan pyramids and Egyptian pyramids
3. personal computer and fax machine
4. aerobics and walking
5. John Milton and John Bunyan

Critical Thinking

Educating Your Imagination as an Active Reader. Read the Language Arts Survey 1.4, "Educating Your Imagination as an Active Read." Then select one of the Selections for Additional Reading that begins on page 550. Take notes as you read of the questions you ask yourself about the selection, the predictions you make as to what will happen next or what will be discussed next, and the summaries you make of the different stanzas, paragraphs, or sections.

Answers to Integrating the Language Arts

Vocabulary

1. powerful
2. timid
3. babbling; predict
4. harm
5. advise; tell; restrain or control

Critical Thinking

1. wives of United States presidents
   Both are women and married Democratic presidents.
2. monuments
   Both are pyramid-shaped and have religious significance to the cultures that built them.
3. machines
   Both are found in offices and are tools for manipulating information.
4. forms of exercise
   Both are cardiovascular activities and have special shoes designed for them.
5. English Puritan writers
   Both lived in England and wrote works with religious themes.

ADDITIONAL RESOURCES

UNIT 6 RESOURCE BOOK
- Selection Worksheet 6.7
- Selection Check Test 4.6.15
- Selection Test 4.6.16
- Reading Resource 1.24

VOCABULARY FROM THE SELECTION

contrive
incorruptible
undefiled

GRAPHIC ORGANIZER

Other allegorical elements include Christian, the great burden he carries on his back, Evangelist, the journey, the fair, and the Celestial City.

READER'S JOURNAL

Students' should reveal something they learned from the trip.

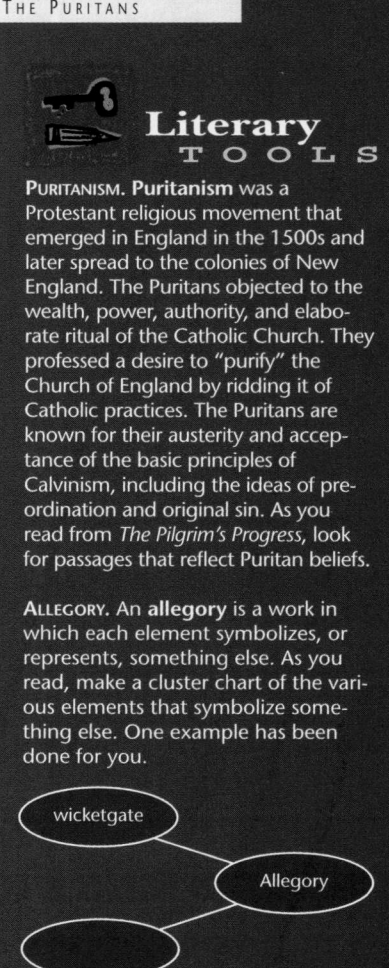

Literary TOOLS

PURITANISM. Puritanism was a Protestant religious movement that emerged in England in the 1500s and later spread to the colonies of New England. The Puritans objected to the wealth, power, authority, and elaborate ritual of the Catholic Church. They professed a desire to "purify" the Church of England by ridding it of Catholic practices. The Puritans are known for their austerity and acceptance of the basic principles of Calvinism, including the ideas of preordination and original sin. As you read from *The Pilgrim's Progress*, look for passages that reflect Puritan beliefs.

ALLEGORY. An **allegory** is a work in which each element symbolizes, or represents, something else. As you read, make a cluster chart of the various elements that symbolize something else. One example has been done for you.

wicketgate — Allegory — (blank)

Reader's Journal

Describe a journey you have taken (or would like to take) that meant more than what you saw or did. For example, maybe you took a trip and something made you realize you were no longer a child; that trip is always connected with losing your childhood innocence.

FROM *The Pilgrim's Progress*

BY JOHN BUNYAN

About the AUTHOR

John Bunyan (1628–1688), the son of a Bedfordshire tinker, received only a meager education before adopting his father's trade. From 1644 to 1646, Bunyan served in the Parliamentary army. After his marriage in 1648, he turned his thoughts to religion. Bunyan experienced a period of spiritual struggle, after which he converted in 1653 and joined the Baptist church at Bedford. Like many other men and women in his day, Bunyan answered the "call" to preach. The Anglican Church viewed the lay preachers as dissenters and sought to persecute and silence them. For his refusal to obey royal bans on nonconformist preaching, Bunyan was imprisoned from 1660 to 1672. While in prison, he wrote his spiritual autobiography, *Grace Abounding to the Chief of the Sinners*, which uses the details of his early life to reveal the purposes of divine Providence. After his release from prison, Bunyan became minister of the Bedford nonconformist church. Again imprisoned in 1675, he wrote *The Pilgrim's Progress*, his most celebrated work. Prompted by the success of his allegory, Bunyan published in 1684 Part II of *The Pilgrim's Progress*, but it never captured the popularity of Bunyan's original tale.

About the SELECTION

One of the most popular allegories in English literature, ***The Pilgrim's Progress*** tells the story of the life journey of a pilgrim named Christian. Bunyan modeled his writing style in *The Pilgrim's Progress* on the prose of the English Bible, enabling even the humblest reader to share the experiences of Christian and the travelers he meets. Once a household book, *The Pilgrim's Progress* gave many phrases to our language: "the slough of despond," "the house beautiful," "Mr. Worldly-Wiseman," and "Vanity Fair." As *The Pilgrim's Progress* opens, the speaker has a dream in which he sees Christian, who is weeping and wondering what to do.

GOALS/OBJECTIVES

Studying this lesson will enable students to
- empathize with the main character's struggles on his journey
- describe John Bunyan's literary accomplishments and the religious and historical context of *The Pilgrim's Progress*
- define *Puritanism* and *allegory* and recognize the use of these techniques in the selection
- explain the connotations of vocabulary from the selection
- research biblical references in *The Pilgrim's Progress*
- play a board game
- research the Puritan Interregnum

FROM *The*

Pilgrim's Progress

JOHN BUNYAN

From this World to That Which Is to Come: Delivered Under the Similitude[1] *of a Dream*

[Christian Sets out for the Celestial City]

As I walked through the wilderness of this world, I lighted on a certain place where was a Den, and I laid me down in that place to sleep; and, as I slept, I dreamed a dream. I dreamed, and behold I saw a man clothed with rags, standing in a certain place, with his face from his own house, a book in his hand, and a great burden upon his back (Isaiah lxiv.6; Luke xiv.33; Psalms xxxviii.4; Habakkuk ii.2; Acts xvi.31). I looked and saw him open the book and read therein; and, as he read, he wept, and trembled; and not being able longer to contain, he brake out with a lamentable cry, saying, "What shall I do?" (Acts ii.37).

In what frame of mind is Christian in the opening scene?

In this plight, therefore, he went home and refrained himself as long as he could, that his wife and children should not perceive his distress; but he could not be silent long, because that his trouble increased. Wherefore at length he brake his mind to his wife and children; and thus he began to talk to them. O my dear wife, said he, and you the children of my bowels, I your dear friend am in myself undone by reason of a burden that lieth hard upon me; moreover, I am for certain informed that this our city will be burned with fire from heaven, in which fearful overthrow both myself, with thee, my wife, and you, my sweet babes, shall miserably come to ruin, except (the which yet I see not) some way of escape can be found, whereby we may be delivered. At this his relations were sore amazed; not for that they believed that what he had said to them was true, but because they thought that some frenzy distemper[2] had got into his head; therefore, it drawing towards night, and they hoping that sleep might settle his brains, with all haste they got him to bed; but the night was as troublesome to him as the day; wherefore, instead of sleeping, he spent it in sighs and tears. So when the morning was come, they would know how he did. He told them, Worse and worse; he also set to talking to them again, but they began to be hardened. They also thought to drive away his distemper by harsh and surly carriages[3] to him: sometimes they would deride, sometimes they would chide, and sometimes they would quite neglect him. Wherefore he began to retire himself to his chamber, to pray for and pity them, and also to condole his own misery; he would also walk solitarily in the fields, sometimes reading, and sometimes praying; and thus for some days he spent his time.

Now I saw, upon a time, when he was walking in the fields, that he was (as he was wont[4]) read-

1. **Similitude.** Allegory
2. **frenzy distemper.** An illness causing madness
3. **carriages.** Behavior
4. **wont.** Accustomed

ANSWER TO GUIDED READING QUESTION

1. Christian is sad, frightened, and confused.

INDIVIDUAL LEARNING STRATEGIES

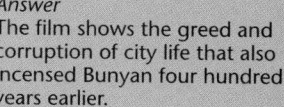

MOTIVATION
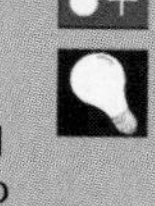
Show a segment of the film *Bonfire of the Vanities* to the class. Ask students to analyze how city life is depicted.
Answer
The film shows the greed and corruption of city life that also incensed Bunyan four hundred years earlier.

READING PROFICIENCY
Point out that Bunyan does not use quotation marks to signal when characters begin and stop talking. Ask students to identify what genre sets up dialogue as that on pages 527–528 between Christian, Obstinate, and Pliable.
Answer
Drama.

ENGLISH LANGUAGE LEARNING
Have students look up the words *pliable, obstinate,* and *vanity* in the dictionary before they begin reading. Ask them to write a contextualized sentence using each word.

SPECIAL NEEDS
Point out the following vocabulary words:
lamentable—sorrowful
surly—bad tempered; hostile; rude
obstinate—stubborn; immovable
pliable—flexible; ready to be persuaded
vanity—inflated pride in oneself

ENRICHMENT
Ask students to decide whether *The Pilgrim's Progress* should be considered a novel. Have them read the definition for *novel* in the Handbook of Literary Terms and review the background information on the novel in Unit 1.

ANSWER TO GUIDED READING QUESTION

1. Christian wants to be saved, but he does not know what to do or where to run in order to accomplish this.

LITERARY TECHNIQUE

ALLUSION. An **allusion** is a rhetorical technique in which reference is made to a person, event, object, or work from history or literature. Students will have noticed that Bunyan alludes to frequent biblical references in parentheses. You may wish to share the following passages with them and discuss how they support the allegory.

Regarding the burden on Christian's back, Bunyan lists several verses. One is Psalm 38:4: "For my iniquities [sins] have gone over my head; they weigh like a burden too heavy for me." Another is Luke 14:33: "So therefore, [Jesus said,] whoever of you does not renounce all that he has cannot be my disciple." Help students to understand that Christian's burden can be interpreted as both his own sin and the material possessions that tie him to the temporal world.

Regarding the wicketgate, Bunyan refers readers to Matthew 7:13–14: "[Jesus said,] 'Enter by the narrow gate; for the gate is wide and the way is easy, that leads to destruction, and those who enter by it are many. For the gate is narrow and the way is hard, that leads to life, and those who find it are few.'" You might ask students why Christian is unable to see the wicketgate that Evangelist points to across the wide field.

O the Roast Beef of Old England! William Hogarth, 1748–1749. Tate Gallery, London.

ing in this book, and greatly distressed in his mind; and as he read, he burst out, as he had done before, crying, "What shall I do to be saved?"

I saw also that he looked this way and that way, as if he would run; yet he stood still, because (as I perceived) he could not tell which way to go. I looked then, and saw a man named Evangelist[5] coming to him, who asked, Wherefore dost thou cry? (Job xxxiii.23). He answered, Sir, I perceive by the book in my hand that I am condemned to die, and after that to come to judgment (Hebrews ix.27), and I find that I am not willing to do the first (Job xvi.21), nor able to do the second (Ezekiel xxii.14). . . .

What problem is Christian faced with?

Then said Evangelist, Why not willing to die, since this life is attended with so many evils? The man answered, Because I fear that this burden that is upon my back will sink me lower than the grave, and I shall fall into Tophet[6] (Isaiah xxx.33). And, sir, if I be not fit to go to prison, I am not fit to go to judgment, and from thence to execution; and the thoughts of these things make me cry.

5. **Evangelist.** One who preaches the good news of the Christian Gospel
6. **Tophet.** A name for hell

Then said Evangelist, If this be thy condition, why standest thou still? He answered, Because I know not whither to go. Then he gave him a parchment roll, and there was written within, "Fly from the wrath to come" (Matthew iii.7).

The man therefore read it, and looking upon Evangelist very carefully,[7] said, Whither must I fly? Then said Evangelist, pointing with his finger over a very wide field, Do you see yonder wicketgate? (Matthew vii.13, 14.) The man said, No. Then said the other, Do you see yonder shining light? (Psalms cxix.105; II Peter i.19.) He said, I think I do. Then said Evangelist, Keep that light in your eye, and go up directly thereto; so shalt thou see the gate; at which when thou knockest it shall be told thee what thou shalt do.

How does Evangelist help Christian?

So I saw in my dream that the man began to run. Now, he had not run far from his own door, but his wife and children perceiving it, began to cry after him to return; but the man put his fingers in his ears, and ran on, crying, Life! life! eternal life! (Luke xiv.26.) So he looked not behind him, but fled towards the middle of the plain (Genesis xix.17).

The neighbors also came out to see him run (Jeremiah xx.10); and as he ran some mocked, others threatened, and some cried after him to return; and, among those that did so, there were two that resolved to fetch him back by force. The name of the one was Obstinate, and the name of the other Pliable. Now by this time the man was got a good distance from them; but, however, they were resolved to pursue him, which they did, and in a little time they overtook him. Then said the man, Neighbors, wherefore are ye come? They said, To persuade you to go back with us. But he said, That can by no means be; you dwell, said he, in the City of Destruction (the place also where I was born) I see it to be so; and, dying there, sooner or later, you will sink lower than the grave, into a place that burns with fire and brimstone;[8] be content, good neighbors, and go along with me.

Obstinate. What! said Obstinate, and leave our friends and our comforts behind us?

"All which you shall forsake is not worthy to be compared with a little of that which I am seeking to enjoy"

Christian. Yes, said Christian (for that was his name), because that ALL which you shall forsake is not worthy to be compared with a little of that which I am seeking to enjoy (II Corinthians v.17); and, if you will go along with me, and hold it, you shall fare as I myself; for there, where I go, is enough and to spare (Luke xv.17). Come away, and prove my words.

Obstinate. What are the things you seek, since you leave all the world to find them?

Christian. I seek an inheritance <u>incorruptible</u>, <u>undefiled</u>, and that fadeth not away (I Peter i.4), and it is laid up in heaven,

7. **carefully.** Sorrowfully
8. **brimstone.** Sulfer

Words for Everyday Use

in • cor • rupt • i • ble (in´kə rup´tə bəl) *adj.,* that cannot be contaminated or debased. *A dishonest businessman tried to bribe the mayor into giving his company the contract, but the mayor proved <u>incorruptible</u>.*

un • de • filed (un dē fīld´) *adj.,* uncorrupt; honorable. *The pristine forests in the national park are some of the few <u>undefiled</u> wilderness areas in this region.*

ANSWER TO GUIDED READING QUESTION

1. When Christian is confused about which way to go, Evangelist paints him toward a "shining light" in the distance.

ADDITIONAL QUESTIONS AND ACTIVITIES

You may wish to ask students the following questions:

1. Why are Obstinate and Pliable so named?
2. Which characteristic, obstinacy or pliability, do you think Bunyan thinks is more desirable? Why?

Answers

1. The character Obstinate is stubborn, and Christian is not able to convince him to join the journey to the wicketgate. Pliable, however, is more flexible and open-minded. He changes his mind about forcing Christian to return home and instead joins the pilgrimage. Since Obstinate does not respond to the "good news" of Evangelist and returns to the City of Destruction, he is not an admirable character.
2. Bunyan seems to value the open-mindedness or pliability that makes a person receptive to the Christian message.

ANSWER TO GUIDED READING QUESTION

1. Beelzebub, Apollyon, and Legion established the fair along the route to the Celestial City almost five thousand years ago, hoping to tempt pilgrims away from the path of righteousness.

and safe there (Hebrews xi.16), to be bestowed, at the time appointed, on them that diligently seek it. Read it so, if you will, in my book.

OBSTINATE. Tush! said Obstinate, away with your book; will you go back with us or no?

CHRISTIAN. No, not I, said the other, because I have laid my hand to the plow (Luke ix.62).

OBSTINATE. Come, then, neighbor Pliable, let us turn again, and go home without him; there is a company of these crazed-headed coxcombs, that, when they take a fancy[9] by the end, are wiser in their own eyes than seven men that can render a reason (Proverbs xxvi.16).

PLIABLE. Then said Pliable, Don't revile; if what the good Christian says is true, the things he looks after are better than ours; my heart inclines to go with my neighbor.

OBSTINATE. What! more fools still? Be ruled by me, go back; who knows whither such a brain-sick fellow will lead you? Go back, go back, and be wise.

CHRISTIAN. Nay, but do thou come with thy neighbor, Pliable; there are such things to be had which I spoke of, and many more glories besides. If you believe not me, read here in this book; and for the truth of what is expressed therein, behold, all is confirmed by the blood of Him that made it (Hebrews ix.17–22; xiii.20.).

PLIABLE. Well, neighbor Obstinate, said Pliable, I begin to come to a point, I intend to go along with this good man, and to cast in my lot with him: but, my good companion, do you know the way to this desired place?

CHRISTIAN. I am directed by a man, whose name is Evangelist, to speed me to a little gate that is before us, where we shall receive instructions about the way.

PLIABLE. Come, then, good neighbor, let us be going. Then they went both together.

[VANITY FAIR][10]

Then I saw in my dream, that when they were got out of the wilderness, they presently saw a town before them, and the name of that town is Vanity; and at the town there is a fair kept, called Vanity Fair; it is kept all the year long; it beareth the name of Vanity Fair because the town where it is kept is lighter than vanity; and also because all that is there sold, or that cometh thither, is vanity. As is the saying of the wise, "All that cometh is vanity" (Ecclesiastes i.2, 14; ii.11, 17; xi.8; Isaiah xl.17).

This fair is no new-erected business, but a thing of ancient standing; I will show you the original of it.

Almost five thousand years agone, there were pilgrims walking to the Celestial City, as these two honest persons are; and Beelzebub, Apollyon, and Legion,[11] with their companions, perceiving by the path that the pilgrims made, that their way to the city lay through this town of Vanity, they contrived here to set up a fair; a fair wherein should be sold all sorts of vanity, and that it should last all the year long. Therefore at this fair are all such merchandise sold, as houses, lands, trades, places, honors, preferments,[12] titles, countries, kingdoms, lusts, pleasures, and delights of all sorts, as whores, bawds, wives, husbands, children, masters, servants, lives, blood, bodies, souls, silver, gold, pearls, precious stones, and what not.

How did Vanity Fair begin?

9. **coxcombs . . . fancy.** Fools that become deluded
10. **Vanity Fair.** Fairs were an annual event in England. *Vanity* means "emptiness." Vanity Fair is an allegory of corruption of religious life through worldly attractions.
11. **Beelzebub . . . Legion.** Prince of Devils, the Destroyer, and the Unclean Spirit
12. **preferments.** Appointments to political or ecclesiastical positions

WORDS FOR EVERYDAY USE

re • vile (ri vīl′) *vt.,* subject to verbal abuse. *Mrs. Manning reviled the pickpocket who tried to steal her wallet.*
con • trive (kən trīv′) *vt.,* scheme. *Yolanda and Coretta contrived a brilliant plan to lure the unsuspecting Kimberly to her surprise birthday party.*

And, moreover, at this fair there is at all times to be seen jugglings, cheats, games, plays, fools, apes, knaves, and rogues, and that of every kind.

Here are to be seen, too, and that for nothing, thefts, murders, adulteries, false swearers, and that of a blood-red color.

And as in other fairs of less moment, there are the several rows and streets, under their proper names, where such and such wares are vended; so here likewise you have the proper places, rows, streets (viz., countries and kingdoms), where the wares of this fair are soonest to be found. Here is the Britain Row, the French Row, the Italian Row, the Spanish Row, the German Row, where several sorts of vanities are to be sold. But, as in other fairs, some one commodity is as the chief of all the fair, so the ware of Rome and her merchandise[13] is greatly promoted in this fair; only our English nation, with some others, have taken a dislike thereat.

Now, as I said, the way to the Celestial City lies just through this town where this lusty fair is kept; and he that will go to the City, and yet not go through this town, must needs "go out of the world" (I Corinthians v.10). The Prince of princes himself, when here, went through this town to his own country, and that upon a fair-day too,[14] yea, and as I think, it was Beelzebub, the chief lord of this fair, that invited him to buy of his vanities; yea, would have made him lord of the fair, would he but have done him reverence as he went through the town. (Matthew iv.8; Luke iv.5–7.) Yea, because he was such a person of honor, Beelzebub had him from street to street, and showed him all the kingdoms of the world in a little time, that he might, if possible, allure the Blessed One to cheapen[15] and buy some of his vanities; but he had no mind to the merchandise, and therefore left the town, without laying out so much as one farthing upon these vanities. This fair, therefore, is an ancient thing, of long standing, and a very great fair.

How did the fair affect the journey of the pilgrims?

"Turn away mine eyes from beholding vanity"

Now these pilgrims, as I said, must needs go through this fair. Well, so they did; but, behold, even as they entered into the fair, all the people in the fair were moved, and the town itself as it were in a hubbub about them; and that for several reasons: for

First, The pilgrims were clothed with such kind of raiment as was diverse from the raiment of any that traded in that fair. The people, therefore, of the fair, made a great gazing upon them: some said they were fools, some they were bedlams, and some they are outlandish[16] men. (I Corinthians ii.7, 8.)

13. **Rome . . . merchandise.** Refers to the temporal power of the Roman Catholic Church
14. **Prince . . . too.** Refers to the temptation of Jesus in the wilderness
15. **cheapen.** Ask the price
16. **bedlams . . . outlandish.** Bedlams were lunatics from an insane asylum in London and outlandish men were foreigners.

WORDS FOR EVERYDAY USE

rai • ment (rā′ mənt) *n.*, clothing; garments. *The queen wore red raiment for her coronation.*

ANSWER TO GUIDED READING QUESTION

1. Christian and Pliable had to pass through the Vanity Fair on their journey, since there is no way to avoid it.

ANSWER TO GUIDED READING QUESTION

1. The pilgrims are not interested in the vain material goods sold at the fair; they are interested only in reaching heaven.

LITERARY TECHNIQUE

Allusion. You may wish to point out Bunyan's allusion to the story of the Tower of Babel (Genesis 11:1–9), when he says that the merchants "from one end of the fair to the other . . . seemed barbarians [foreigners speaking different languages] each to the other." In the biblical story, the descendants of Noah worked together to build a tower that reached up to the heavens. God, upon seeing this display of arrogance, punished them by scattering them over the earth and confusing their language so that the various groups could no longer understand each other.

RESPONDING TO THE SELECTION

Students should note that the townspeople in Vanity Fair are painted in an unfavorable light.

SELECTION CHECK TEST 4.6.15 WITH ANSWERS

Checking Your Reading

1. What gives Christian the idea that he is in danger? **He reads it in a book.**
2. What do the others do as Christian runs to the gate? **They mock and threaten him.**
3. What kinds of things are sold at the fair? **Vanities and/or pleasures are sold there.**
4. What do the pilgrims offer to buy? **They offer to buy truth.**
5. What happens to the pilgrims at the fair? **They are beaten and caged.**

Literary Tools

This selection revolves around an allegory, in which the names of the characters and places serve as symbols. Match each character with his actions from the allegory.

Secondly, And as they wondered at their apparel, so they did likewise at their speech; for few could understand what they said, they naturally spoke the language of Canaan,[17] but they that kept the fair were the men of this world; so that, from one end of the fair to the other, they seemed barbarians each to the other.

Thirdly, But that which did not a little amuse the merchandisers was that these pilgrims set very light by all their wares; they cared not so much as to look upon them; and if they called upon them to buy, they would put their fingers in their ears, and cry, "Turn away mine eyes from beholding vanity," and look upwards, signifying that their trade and traffic was in heaven. (Psalms cxix.37; Philippians iii. 19, 20.)

Why didn't the pilgrims buy anything at the fair?

One chanced mockingly, beholding the carriages of the men, to say unto them, What will ye buy? But they, looking gravely upon him, said, "We buy the truth" (Proverbs xxiii.23). At that there was an occasion taken to despise the men the more; some mocking, some taunting, some speaking reproachfully, and some calling upon others to smite[18] them. At last things came to an hubbub and great stir in the fair, insomuch that all order was confounded. Now was word presently brought to the great one of the fair, who quickly came down, and deputed some of his most trusty friends to take these men into examination, about whom the fair was almost overturned. So the men were brought to examination; and they that sat upon them[19] asked them whence they came, whither they went, and what they did there, in such an unusual garb? The men told them that they were pilgrims and strangers in the world, and that they were going to their own country, which was the Heavenly Jerusalem (Hebrews xi.13–16); and that they had given no occasion to the men of the town, nor yet to the merchandisers, thus to abuse them, and to let[20] them in their journey, except it was for that, when one asked them what they would buy, they said they would buy the truth. But they that were appointed to examine them did not believe them to be any other than bedlams and mad, or else such as came to put all things into a confusion in the fair. Therefore they took them and beat them, and besmeared them with dirt, and then put them into the cage, that they might be made a spectacle to all the men of the fair. ■

17. **Canaan.** The Promised Land
18. **smite.** Strike sharply or heavily
19. **sat upon them.** Questioned and tried them
20. **let.** Hinder

Respond *to the* Selection

With whom do you identify more closely in this excerpt—the townspeople in Vanity Fair or the pilgrims? Explain.

SELECTION CHECK TEST 4.6.15 WITH ANSWERS (CONT.)

__D__ 1. joins Christian on his journey
__E__ 2. chief lord of the fair
__G__ 3. the town where the fair is held
__C__ 4. tries to convince Christian to return home
__B__ 5. advises Christian to run to the wicketgate

a. Apollyon
b. Evangelist
c. Obstinate
d. Pliable
e. Beelzebub
f. Canaan
g. Vanity

Investigate, Inquire, Imagine

Recall: Gathering Facts →

1a. What lament does Christian make in the first paragraph of the allegory?

2a. What directions does Evangelist give to Christian?

3a. What is the only other way to the Celestial City besides passing through the fair?

Interpret: Finding Meaning

1b. What troubles Christian at the beginning of the allegory?

2b. What will Christian be told at the wicketgate?

3b. What does the pilgrims' passage through the ancient fair symbolize?

Analyze: Taking Things Apart →

4a. In the seventeenth and eighteenth centuries nearly every home in England had a copy of *The Pilgrim's Progess.* One reason for its popularity is the Everyman quality of Christian. What circumstances in this allegory might cause the reader to feel empathy for him?

Synthesize: Bringing Things Together

4b. The outcome of Christian's journey is evident in the complete title of the allegory: *The Pilgrim's Progress From This World, to That Which is to Come: Delivered Under the Similitude of a Dream Wherein is Discovered, the Manner of His Setting Out, His Dangerous Journey; and Safe Arrival at the Desired Countrey.* What characteristics of Christian will help him reache his goal?

Evaluate: Making Judgments →

5a. Why do you think Christian agreed to go on his pilgrimage with Pliable?

Extend: Connecting Ideas

5b. If you were Christian, how would you describe the townspeople of Vanity Fair?

Understanding Literature

Puritanism. Review the definition for **Puritanism** in the Handbook of Literary Terms. What passages did you find that reflect Puritan beliefs or practices?

Allegory. Review the definition for **allegory** and the cluster chart you made for Literary Tools on page 524. What do Christian, the great burden he carries on his back, Evangelist, the journey, the fair, the wicketgate, and the Celestial City represent?

ANSWERS TO INVESTIGATE, INQUIRE, AND IMAGINE

Recall

1a. Looking up from his book (the Bible), Christian cries, "What shall I do?"

2a. Evangelist tells Christian to follow a shining light he sees in the distance, which will lead him to the wicketgate.

3a. The only other way is to "go out of the world," in other words, to die.

Interpret

1b. Christian knows that he is condemned to die if he cannot find the way to salvation.

2b. Christian will be told how to gain eternal life.

3b. The pilgrims' passage through the ancient fair represents the struggle to live a righteous life in the midst of a corrupt world.

Analyze

4a. Christian's unhappiness at the beginning of the story, his concern for his family even as they abuse him, and his simple, honest desire to live righteously help to make Christian a sympathetic character.

Synthesize

4b. Christian's honesty, single-mindedness, and tenacity will help ensure that he reaches his goal.

Perspective

5a. Pliable's interest in finding his spiritual inheritance infers he is a righteous man like Christian and makes a good traveling companion for him.

Empathy

5b. Christian might say that the townspeople of Vanity Fair are worldly, sinful, and punitive.

ANSWERS TO UNDERSTANDING LITERATURE

Puritanism. The Puritans' displeasure with the papacy in Rome is reflected in the passage where Bunyan states "the ware of Rome and her merchandise is greatly promoted in this fair; only our English nation, with some others, have taken a dislike thereat." Christian and Pliable wear the simple, unadorned garments that the Puritans preferred: "The pilgrims were clothed with such kind of raiment as was diverse from the raiment of any that traded in that fair." The Puritans believed in original sin, which Christian carries on his back as "a great burden."

ANSWERS TO UNDERSTANDING LITERATURE (cont.)

Allegory. Christian represents any man or woman who wants to live a good Christian life. Christian's burden is original sin, or the temptations of earthly life. Evangelist is a preacher of the Gospel, or a knowledgeable Christian who helps others find the way to salvation. Christian's journey symbolizes any sinner's passage through life and life's temptations on the way to salvation. Vanity Fair represents the corrupt world and all its temptations. The wicketgate is the narrow entrance into heaven, which few people get through. The Celestial City is redemption or heaven.

ANSWERS TO INTEGRATING THE LANGUAGE ARTS

Language, Grammar, and Style

1. *Evils* suggests a wicked threat or force; it is associated with immorality rather than mere misfortune.
2. *Obstinate* suggests firmly rooted stubbornness.
3. *Directed* implies a specific direction or route that should be taken.
4. *Pilgrims* suggests people on a moral or religious mission.
5. *Gravely* suggests that a weighty matter with dire consequences is being considered.

WRITER'S JOURNAL

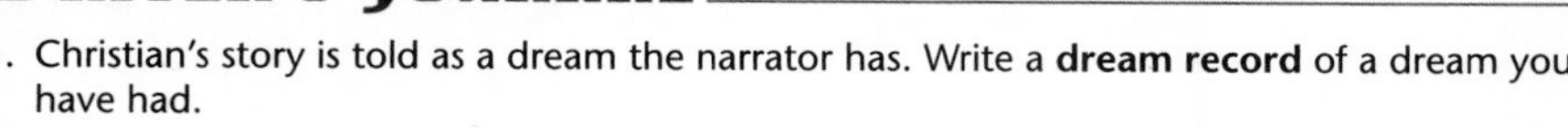

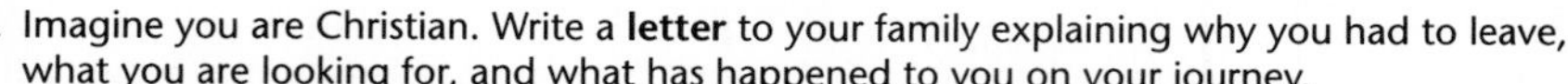

1. Christian's story is told as a dream the narrator has. Write a **dream record** of a dream you have had.
2. Imagine you are Christian. Write a **letter** to your family explaining why you had to leave, what you are looking for, and what has happened to you on your journey.
3. Write a **paragraph** retelling the pilgrims' experience in Vanity Fair from the perspective of one of the townspeople.

Integrating *the* Language Arts

Language, Grammar, and Style

Connotation. Read the Language Arts Survey 1.24, "Connotation and Denotation." Then, for each underlined word in the sentences below, explain the connotations the word has.

Example: I looked and saw him open the book and read therein; and, as he read, he wept and trembled; and not being able longer to contain, he brake out with a lamentable cry, saying, "What shall I do?" (Both *wept* and *lamentable* suggest deep sorrow or mourning.)

1. Then said Evangelist, Why not willing to die, since this life is attended with so many evils?
2. The name of the one was Obstinate, and the name of the other Pliable.
3. I am directed by a man, whose name is Evangelist, to speed me to a little gate that is before us, where we shall receive instructions about the way.
4. Now these pilgrims, as I said, must needs go through this fair.
5. But they, looking gravely upon him, said, "We buy the truth."

Study and Research & Collaborative Learning

Researching Biblical References. You probably noticed that Bunyan places biblical references throughout *The Pilgrim's Progress*. Working with several classmates, divide up these references from the Bible. Look up those that you are assigned. Then report back to your group, explaining how the biblical references tie into the passages that they reference.

Collaborative Learning

Board Game. In a group, plan an allegorical board game that presents a journey like that described in Bunyan's *The Pilgrim's Progress*. Design and lay out your game board, including on it places such as Vanity Fair and the Celestial City. You may wish to consult a full text of *The Pilgrim's Progress* to complete this activity, or you may use your own imagination to create places and experiences Christian might encounter next.

Study and Research

Researching the Puritan Interregnum. The English Puritans overthrew the monarchy and, under Oliver Cromwell, governed the country during what is known as the Commonwealth, or Puritan Interregnum, from 1642 to 1646. Research the life of Oliver Cromwell or the changes to British society brought about by the Interregnum. Then report to the class on your findings.

"To Althea, from Prison"

BY RICHARD LOVELACE

About *the* AUTHOR

Richard Lovelace (1618–1657) was born outside London, in Woolwich. The eldest son of an old and wealthy Kentish family, Lovelace was educated at Oxford. Young and handsome, the very model of a courtier with his cool demeanor and wit, he caught the admiration of King Charles and Queen Henrietta Maria, who visited Oxford in 1636 and immediately awarded him his master's degree. Lovelace then fought for the king in the civil wars against the Puritans and was wounded, imprisoned, and exiled. In 1648, after his return to England from Holland and France, Lovelace was imprisoned again. When he was released the following year, he was poor and had no means of supporting himself. Surviving on charity, Lovelace lived in squalor for the last ten years of his life. He published *Lucasta* in 1649. A collection of Lovelace's writings was published in 1659, two years after his death.

About *the* SELECTION

The most famous of Lovelace's poems, **"To Althea, from Prison,"** probably was written while Lovelace was imprisoned in 1642. Lovelace and Sir John Suckling are often paired as representative of the "Cavalier spirit," but while both their work and their lives share similarities, there are as many differences. While Suckling's verse is often flippant and lighthearted, Lovelace's verse is thoughtful and somber.

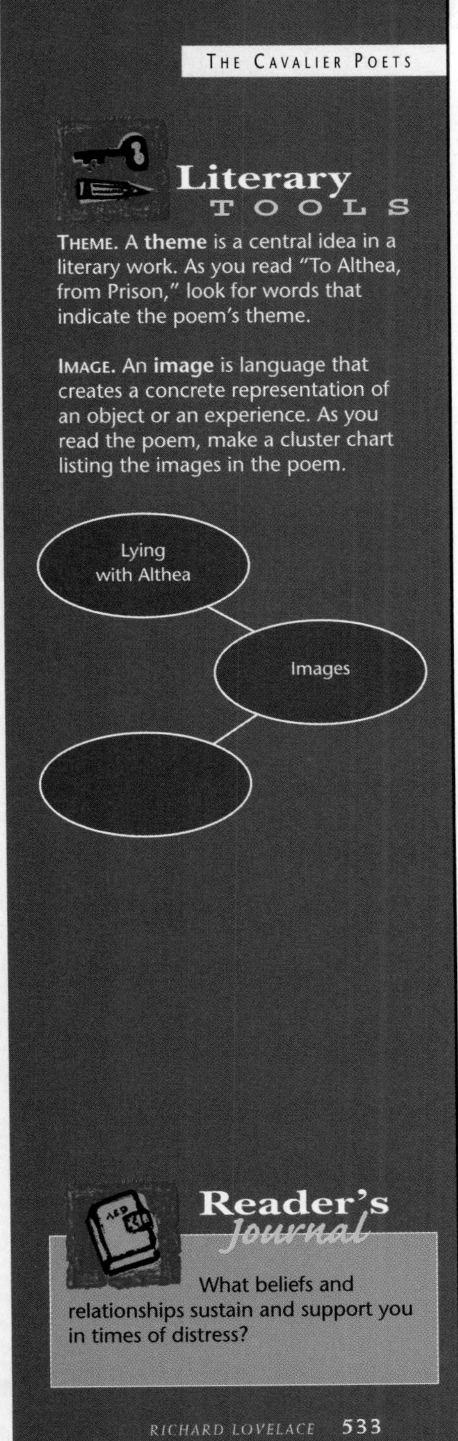

Literary TOOLS

THEME. A **theme** is a central idea in a literary work. As you read "To Althea, from Prison," look for words that indicate the poem's theme.

IMAGE. An **image** is language that creates a concrete representation of an object or an experience. As you read the poem, make a cluster chart listing the images in the poem.

Reader's Journal

What beliefs and relationships sustain and support you in times of distress?

ADDITIONAL RESOURCES 

UNIT 6 RESOURCE BOOK
- Selection Worksheet 6.8
- Selection Check Test 4.6.17
- Selection Test 4.6.18
- Language, Grammar, and Style Resource 3.51
- Study and Research Resource 5.49
- Applied English Resource 6.5

VOCABULARY FROM THE SELECTION 

fettered
hermitage
steep

GRAPHIC ORGANIZER 

Students should list the following images in their cluster charts: Drinking a toast with his loyal friends, Singing a song praising the king's qualities.

READER'S JOURNAL

Students unfamiliar with distress may write about what it would be like to be imprisoned.

GOALS/OBJECTIVES

Studying this lesson will enable students to
- interpret and appreciate the speaker's feelings about liberty and honor
- describe the literary accomplishments of Richard Lovelace
- define *theme* and *image* and recognize the use of these techniques in the selection
- identify common and proper nouns
- answer analogy questions
- participate in a letter-writing campaign
- research a famous prisoner
- make a time line of the English civil war

ANSWER TO GUIDED READING QUESTION

1. His beloved Althea visits him, and he feels free in his love for her, even though he is in prison.

INDIVIDUAL LEARNING STRATEGIES

Motivation
Ask students to brainstorm a list of words associated with freedom and imprisonment.

Reading Proficiency
Ask students to tell in which ways the speaker, since he is imprisoned, can be free.

English Language Learning
Have students make a list of the words Lovelace uses that are related to freedom and imprisonment.

Special Needs
Make sure students can answer the Guided Reading Questions and the Recall questions in Investigate, Inquire, and Imagine.

Enrichment
Have students studying a world language find a poem about freedom in that language and share it with several classmates. For example, Spanish students might select "Mujer" by Juana De Ibarbourou. French students might select "Page d'écriture" or "Quartier libre" by Jacques Prévert. German students might select "Das Lied von der Glocke" by Friedrich von Schiller. English Language Learners should be encouraged to find a poem in their language to share as well. Students should compare and contrast the different poems and decide on common perceptions about freedom around the world.

The Tower of London. London, England

To Althea, from Prison

RICHARD LOVELACE

When Love with unconfinèd wings
  Hovers within my gates,
And my divine Althea brings
  To whisper at the grates;
When I lie tangled in her hair
  And fettered to her eye,
The gods that wanton[1] in the air
  Know no such liberty.

Who visits the speaker in prison? How does he feel when she visits?

1. **wanton.** Frisk; play; frolic

Words for Everyday Use

fet • tered (fe′ tərd) *part.*, chained or shackled. *Prisoners of the chain gang were fettered by chains.*

CROSS-CURRICULAR ACTIVITY

Social Studies. William the Conqueror began building the Tower of London, shown on this page, in 1078. The large, many-towered complex was begun on foundations from the days of the Roman Empire, and it was expanded and redesigned over the centuries. In addition to housing some of the most eminent pris-oners in English history, the Tower of London also served at various times as a zoo, a national treasury, a royal residence, and a fortress. Interested students may research the history of the Tower of London and share their findings with the class in a historical drama, a presentation of a detailed map and other visual materials, or some other suitable format.

When flowing cups run swiftly round,
With no allaying Thames,[2]
Our careless heads with roses bound,
Our hearts with loyal flames;
When thirsty grief in wine we <u>steep</u>,
When healths[3] and draughts[4] go free,
Fishes that tipple[5] in the deep
Know no such liberty.

When, like committed linnets,[6] I
With shriller throat shall sing
The sweetness, mercy, majesty,
And glories of my king;
When I shall voice aloud how good
He is, how great should be,
Enlargèd winds, that curl the flood,
Know no such liberty.

According to the speaker, what are the positive qualities of the king?

Stone walls do not a prison make,
Nor iron bars a cage;
Minds innocent and quiet take
That for an <u>hermitage</u>.
If I have freedom in my love,
And in my soul am free,
Angels alone, that soar above,
Enjoy such liberty. ■

How is the speaker free?

2. **When . . . Thames.** When wine that has not been watered down is passed
3. **healths.** Toasts
4. **draughts.** Drinks
5. **tipple.** Drink
6. **committed linnets.** Caged finches

Words For Everyday Use

steep (stēp) *vt.*, soak; immerse. *Loretta planned to <u>steep</u> herself in American history during the week leading up to the exam.*

her •mit • age (hur´ mi tij) *n.*, secluded retreat. *A study cubicle in the remotest corner of the library was Kevin's <u>hermitage</u> during exam week.*

Respond *to the* Selection

What is a synonym for *quiet* in line 27? Would you agree with this assessment of your state of mind if you were a prisoner?

ANSWERS TO GUIDED READING QUESTIONS

1. The speaker is free in his love and in his political convictions; no one can imprison his emotions or his mind.
2. According to the speaker, the king is sweet, merciful, and majestic.

SELECTION CHECK TEST 4.6.17 WITH ANSWERS

Checking Your Reading

1. What do "gods that wanton in the air" not know? **They know no greater liberty than the speaker.**
2. What do the friends steep in their wine? **They steep their grief.**
3. What will the speaker sing? **He will sing God's praises.**
4. With what does the speaker compare prison? **He compares it with a hermitage.**
5. What does the speaker have in his love and in his soul? **He has freedom.**

Literary Tools

Fill in the blanks using the following terms.

repetition stanza theme personification metaphor narrative lyric

1. <u>**Repetition**</u> is the writer's conscious reuse of a sound, word, phrase, sentence, or other element.
2. A <u>**theme**</u> is a central idea in a literary work.
3. <u>**Lyric**</u> poetry is highly musical and expresses emotion.
4. Mark the stressed syllables in the following lines:

When **flow**ing **cups** run **swift**ly **round**,
With **no** allaying **Thames**,
Our **care**less **heads** with **ro**ses **bound**,
Our **hearts** with **loy**al **flames**:

5. What is the rhyme scheme of these four lines? **The rhyme scheme is *abab*.**

RESPOND TO THE SELECTION

"Untroubled" or "restful" are synonyms for *quiet*.

ANSWERS TO INVESTIGATE, INQUIRE, AND IMAGINE

RECALL

1a. Love's wings are "unconfinèd," or free.
2a. The speaker's voice will be shriller than that of a caged bird.
3a. "Stone walls" do not make a prison and "iron bars" do not make a cage.

INTERPRET

1b. The words *gates*, *grates*, and *fettered* suggest the speaker's imprisonment.
2b. The speaker feels loyal toward the king, about whose "sweetness, mercy, majesty, / And glories" he sings loudly.
3b. The entire stanza is about the freedom the speaker experiences; the last four lines especially express his feeling that he is as free as the "Angels . . . that soar above."

ANALYZE

4a. The speaker does not seem to be suffering mental anguish during his imprisonment. He feels that true liberty is a state of mind, so only the body can truly be imprisoned.

SYNTHESIZE

4b. Nothing threatens true liberty because no prison or external circumstance can take away the freedom of one's mind and soul.

EVALUATE

Responses will vary.

5a. In the sense that Althea is not with the speaker physically in prison, she is a figment of his imagination, a memory that sustains him. But, like the friends he also recalls in stanza 2, she most likely existed in reality and he probably had a relationship with her prior to his imprisonment.

EXTEND

5b. In "The Hurricane" Carter finds freedom in his appeals through the judicial system and in friendship with his Canadian friends who fight for his release. In "In the Name of the Father" Conlon finds freedom by fighting to clear his father's name and overturn his own conviction. The character of "The Jericho Mile" finds freedom by running.

INVESTIGATE, Inquire, Imagine

Recall: GATHERING FACTS →

1a. What kind of wings does the speaker describe Love as having?
2a. With what kind of voice will the speaker sing the "glories of [his] king"?
3a. What does not make a prison or a cage?

Interpret: FINDING MEANING

1b. What words in stanza 1 remind the reader of the speaker's imprisonment?
2b. How does the speaker feel towards his king?
3b. What lines in stanza 4 show that the speaker does not think of himself as imprisoned?

Analyze: TAKING THINGS APART →

4a. What is the speaker's state of mind in prison?

Synthesize: BRINGING THINGS TOGETHER

4b. What, if anything, threatens true liberty?

Evaluate: MAKING JUDGMENTS →

5a. Evaluate whether Althea is a real person or a figment of the poet's imagination.

Extend: CONNECTING IDEAS

5b. Watch a film about prison life, such as *The Hurricane, In the Name of the Father,* or *The Jericho Mile.* How does the imprisoned film character rise above his imprisonment to attain freedom in mind and soul?

Understanding Literature

THEME. Review the definition for **theme** in the Handbook of Literary Terms. What words suggest the poem's theme? What do you find to be the theme of the poem?

IMAGE. Review the definition for **image** in the Handbook of Literary Terms and the cluster chart you made for Literary Tools on page 533. What three images support the poem's theme?

WRITER'S JOURNAL

1. Examine the things in lines 7, 15, and 23 that "Know no such liberty." Then write a **list** adding other examples that Lovelace could use if he lengthened his poem.
2. Write a **recipe** for freedom, listing the essential ingredients and quantities needed. You may wish to incorporate some of Lovelace's ideas as a basis for your recipe.
3. Imagine you are the speaker and have been given the opportunity to speak in your own defense in court. Write a **speech** in favor of the Cavalier position. Explain why the Puritan point of view is wrong. You may want to reread on page 492 the discussion of the civil war fought between the Cavaliers and the Puritans.

ANSWERS TO UNDERSTANDING LITERATURE

THEME. Words related to freedom (*unconfinèd, wanton, liberty, careless,* and *soar*) and imprisonment (*fettered, bound, committed, prison, cage*) suggest the poem's theme. The theme of the poem is that true freedom resides in the mind and the soul and cannot be taken from an individual, even one in prison.

IMAGE. Images of the speaker enjoying the love of Althea, drinking toasts with his loyal friends, and singing the praises of his beloved king support the theme of freedom.

Integrating *the* Language Arts

Language, Grammar, and Style

Common and Proper Nouns. Read the Language Arts Survey 3.51, "Common Nouns and Proper Nouns." Then identify the common and proper nouns in the following sentences.

1. Lovelace was an English poet, soldier, and Royalist whose graceful lyrics and dashing career made him the prototype of the perfect Cavalier.
2. He was educated at Charterhouse and Oxford, where he earned an M.A. degree.
3. He took part in the expeditions to Scotland at the time of the rebellions against Charles I.
4. Lovelace was imprisoned in the Gatehouse for presenting a Royalist petition to a hostile House of Commons.
5. There he wrote "To Althea, from Prison," which contains the famous lines "Stone walls do not a prison make / Nor iron bars a cage."

Critical Thinking

Analogy Questions. Read the Language Arts Survey 5.52, "Answering Analogy Questions." Then choose the word that best completes the following analogies.

1. UNCONFINED : TRAPPED : : Unopened : _____
   a. Closure b. Closed c. Open d. blocked
2. FETTERED : CHAIN : : Released : _____
   a. Unlock b. Sky c. Key d. Locked
3. PRISONER : CELL : : Livestock : _____
   a. Pen b. Walls c. Grate d. Cage
4. HERMITAGE : MONK : : Prison: _____
   a. Resort b. Cell c. Judge d. Convict
5. FREEDOM : LIBERTY : : Soul: _____
   a. Love b. Innocence c. Spirit d. Nature

Applied English & Media Literacy

Letter-Writing Campaign. Write a letter to get someone out of prison who is falsely incarcerated. For a list of names and addresses to write to, access Amnesty International's Freedom Writers site at www.amnestyusa.org/group/aicasework/ fw.html. For a model of how to write a business letter, review the Language Arts Survey 6.5, "Writing a Business Letter."

Study and Research & Collaborative Learning

Researching a Famous Prisoner. Famous people who have been imprisoned include Saint Paul, Thomas More, Martin Luther King, Jr., Susan B. Anthony, Daw Aung, San Suu Kyi, and Nelson Mandela. Select a person to research. Find out the reason(s) for the person's imprisonment, the cause he or she was fighting for, and his or her accomplishments. Then share your research with several classmates.

Collaborative Learning & Study and Research

Making a Time Line. With a partner, make a time line of important events of the civil war between the Puritans and the Cavaliers, beginning with the establishment of the Long Parliament and ending with the execution of Charles I.

ANSWERS TO INTEGRATING THE LANGUAGE ARTS

Language, Grammar, and Style

1. Common Nouns: poet, soldier lyrics, career, prototype; Proper Nouns: Lovelace, Royalist, Cavalier
2. Common Nouns: degree; Proper Nouns: Charterhouse, Oxford
3. Common Nouns: expeditions, time, rebellions; Proper Nouns: Scotland, Charles I
4. Common Nouns: petition; Proper Nouns: Lovelace, Gatehouse, House of Commons
5. Common Nouns: prison, lines, walls, prison, bars, cage; Proper Nouns: Althea

Critical Thinking

1. b. Closed
2. c. Key
3. a. Pen
4. d. Convict
5. b. Spirit

ADDITIONAL RESOURCES

UNIT 6 RESOURCE BOOK
- Selection Worksheet 6.9
- Selection Check Test 4.6.19
- Selection Test 4.6.20
- Language, Grammar, and Style Resource 3.34
- Speaking and Listening Resource 4.19
- Study and Research Resource 5.50

VOCABULARY FROM THE SELECTION

coyness
languish
strife

GRAPHIC ORGANIZER

Students should complete their cluster chart with the following information.
Stanza 2: Life is too short to wait for love to blossom.
Stanza 3: Given the shortness of life, one should act quickly while there is still time.

READER'S JOURNAL

You might play the scene from the movie "The Dead Poets' Society" in which Robin Williams explains the *carpe diem* theme.

Literary TOOLS

METAPHOR AND SIMILE. A **metaphor** is a figure of speech in which one thing is spoken or written about as if it were another. A **simile** is a comparison using *like* or *as.* These figures of speech invite the reader to make a comparison between the two things being compared. The two "things" involved are the writer's actual subject, the *tenor* of the figure of speech, and another thing to which the subject is likened, the *vehicle* of the figure of speech. As you read "To His Coy Mistress," look for metaphors and similes and identify the tenor and vehicle for each one.

IMAGE. An **image** is language that creates a concrete representation of an object or an experience. As you read, look for an image in line 11.

COUPLET AND STANZA. A **couplet** is two lines of verse that usually rhyme. A **stanza** is a group of lines in a poem. As you read, make a cluster chart to describe what each stanza is about. One example has been done for you.

Stanza 1:
The speaker describes how the couple's love might unfold had they an eternity to spend together

Stanza

Reader's Journal

When have you tried to persuade someone to do something?

"To His Coy Mistress"

BY ANDREW MARVELL

About the AUTHOR

The rise of the reputation of **Andrew Marvell** (1621–1678) has been gradual but steady. Marvell, for the most part a reserved man, graduated from Cambridge and traveled for years before becoming a tutor to the daughter of the British General Sir Thomas Fairfax. Some of the poems written during this time reveal Marvell's sharp intellect and keen wit. His primary role in literary history would have been no more than that of secretary to the author John Milton had it not been for the publication of Marvell's poems, three years after his death, by a woman believed to be his housekeeper. At first, many of Marvell's verses appear light and satiric, but beneath this surface one finds serious observations and ideas and at times even an element of darkness. Another side of his character was revealed in public life, for besides writing poetry Marvell represented his hometown of Hull in the British Parliament. He worked diligently as a member of Parliament from 1659 until his death. His letters sent from the Halls of Parliament back to his constituents are noteworthy for their historical value.

Marvell is also considered a Metaphysical poet because of his preoccupation with death, physical love, and the intellect.

About the SELECTION

"To His Coy Mistress" has the whimsical quality that characterizes so much of Marvell's poetry. The poem is written in a fairly uncomplicated style, which fits Marvell's *carpe diem* theme. Lightheartedly, the speaker of the poem urges his beloved to "seize the day"—to make good use of the little time available in life by devoting that time to love. This lightheartedness is clouded by the dark shadows of passing time and even of oncoming death. Beneath the seeming lightness is a serious idea that we are left to ponder.

GOALS/OBJECTIVES

Studying this lesson will enable students to
- appreciate the *carpe diem* theme in a lyric poem
- describe Andrew Marvell's literary contributions
- define *metaphor, simile, image, couplet,* and *stanza* and recognize the use of these techniques in the selection
- correct sentence run-ons
- select antonyms
- research the British Parliament
- orally interpret "To His Coy Mistress"

First Whisper, c. 1800s. James Clarke Hook. Private Collection.

To His Coy Mistress

Andrew Marvell

Had we but world enough, and time,
This coyness, lady, were no crime.
We would sit down, and think which way
To walk, and pass our long love's day.
Thou by the Indian Ganges' side
Shouldst rubies find; I by the tide
Of Humber[1] would complain. I would
Love you ten years before the Flood,
And you should, if you please, refuse
Till the conversion of the Jews.[2]
My vegetable love should grow
Vaster than empires, and more slow;
An hundred years should go to praise
Thine eyes, and on thy forehead gaze;

1. **Ganges' . . . Humber.** The Ganges river in India is compared to the small, muddy Humber river, which flows past Hull, Marvell's hometown.
2. **the Flood . . . the Jews.** The Flood is an early occurrence in Biblical times, while the conversion of the Jews is supposed to occur just before the Last Judgment.

Words for Everyday Use

coy • ness (koi´nes) *n.,* playful evasiveness; pretense of shyness or bashfulness. *Elise could not tell whether Jason's behavior reflected true shyness or mere coyness.*

Individual Learning Strategies

Motivation
Play the segment of *Dead Poets Society* at the beginning of the film in which Robin Williams explains to his students the meaning of *carpe diem.*

Reading Proficiency
Write summaries of the 3 stanzas on the board, but out of order, and have students order them correctly in their notes after an initial reading of the poem.
Stanza 1: Discusses how a romance might progress if the couple had all the time in the world.
Stanza 2: Points out that people's lives are in fact very short and indicates what will happen if they wait too long to enjoy life's pleasures.
Stanza 3: Suggests how the speaker thinks people, in particular he and his mistress, should behave, given the shortness of life.

English Language Learning
Ask English Language Learners if children in their native cultures are taught to seize the day or defer enjoyment. Encourage students to share their personal experiences with the class.

Special Needs
Point out the following vocabulary words:
complain—formally state
vegetable—capable of growth
hue—color
strife—contention
Be sure students know the answers to the Guided Reading Questions and the Recall questions in Investigate, Inquire, and Imagine.

Enrichment
Encourage students to view the rest of *Dead Poets Society* and then describe the ways in which Robin Williams's students seize the day, based on what they learned in English class.

ANSWER TO GUIDED READING QUESTION

1. The speaker suggests that life should be vigorously enjoyed while it lasts.

SELECTION CHECK TEST 4.6.19 WITH ANSWERS

Checking Your Reading

1. What would not be a crime if time were limitless? **The speaker's mistress's coyness would not be a crime.**
2. What does the speaker say his mistress deserves? **She deserves to be wooed slowly and attentively.**
3. What is a "fine and private place"? **The grave is a fine and private place.**
4. What does the speaker want to do "while we may"? **He wants to "sport" (have fun).**
5. What does the speaker say they can do to the sun? **They can make him run.**

Literary Tools

1. Identify a metaphor used to suggest the passage of time. ***Responses will vary.***
2. What does the image of "amorous birds of prey" suggest? **It suggests that the speaker and his mistress can seize the moment and not give in to time, but enjoy what they have.**
3. What might be a theme of this poem? ***Responses will vary.***

Two hundred to adore each breast,
But thirty thousand to the rest;
An age at least to every part,
And the last age should show your heart.
For, lady, you deserve this state,[3]
Nor would I love at lower rate.
　But at my back I always hear
Time's wingèd chariot hurrying near;
And yonder all before us lie
Deserts of vast eternity.
Thy beauty shall no more be found,
Nor, in thy marble vault, shall sound
My echoing song; then worms shall try
That long-preserved virginity,
And your quaint honor turn to dust,
And into ashes all my lust:
The grave's a fine and private place,
But none, I think, do there embrace.
　Now therefore, while the youthful hue
Sits on thy skin like morning dew,
And while thy willing soul transpires[4]
At every pore with instant fires,[5]
Now let us sport us while we may,
And now, like amorous birds of prey,
Rather at once our time devour
Than languish in his slow-chapped[6] power.
Let us roll all our strength and all
Our sweetness up into one ball,
And tear our pleasures with rough strife
Through the iron gates of life:
Thus, though we cannot make our sun
Stand still, yet we will make him run.[7] ■

How does the speaker suggest dealing with the swift passage of time?

3. **state.** dignity
4. **transpires.** Breathes forth
5. **instant fires.** immediate enthusiasm
6. **slow-chapped.** Here the slow jaw belongs to Time, which is slowly chewing up the world.
7. **though . . . run.** Although we can't make time stand still, we can force it to race us.

WORDS FOR EVERYDAY USE

lan • guish (laŋ′ gwish) *vi.*, lose vigor or vitality. *The explorer languished in Brazil when fever sapped him of strength and energy.*

strife (strīf) *n.*, contention; act of striving or vying. *The strife between union members and the factory owners ended in a walkout.*

ANSWERS TO UNDERSTANDING LITERATURE (CONT. FROM PAGE 541)

COUPLET AND STANZA. The entire poem is comprised of couplets. The poem concludes with a closed couplet. The poem has a dialectical form, presenting a thesis, its antithesis, and a synthesis, or conclusion. The first stanza describes how the couple's love might unfold had they an eternity to spend together. The second explains that life is too short. The third says that given the shortness of life, one should act quickly while there is still time.

Respond to the Selection

What does the poem suggest as a way to handle the problem posed by time? Do you find the suggestion helpful?

Investigate, Inquire, Imagine

Recall: Gathering Facts → **Interpret:** Finding Meaning

1a. At the beginning of the poem, what quality does the speaker attribute to his mistress? What biblical allusions does the speaker use to express the longevity of his love?

1b. Why is this trait troublesome to the speaker? Why does the speaker feel he can't wait for a long time to have his love come to him?

2a. What is seen and heard at the beginning of the second stanza?

2b. Why does the speaker feel a sense of urgency?

3a. What actions are suggested in the last stanza?

3b. How does the speaker perceive time in the last stanza?

Analyze: Taking Things Apart → **Synthesize:** Bringing Things Together

4a. Identify the emotions that the speaker is appealing to.

4b. What is the speaker's main argument in the poem?

Evaluate: Making Judgments → **Extend:** Connecting Ideas

5a. Evaluate the progression of Marvell's argument. If stanza 1 and stanza 2 were transposed, would the argument be just as effective? Explain.

5b. What themes from other selections in this unit conflict with Marvell's?

Understanding Literature

Metaphor and Simile. Review the definitions for **metaphor** and **simile** in the Handbook of Literary Terms. What metaphors and similes does Marvell use in the poem? What are the tenor and vehicle for each figure of speech?

Image. Review the definition for **image** in Literary Tools in Prereading on page 538. What image is presented in line 11? How does this image reinforce the speaker's message in stanza 1?

Couplet and Stanza. Review the definitions for **couplet** and **stanza** and the cluster chart you made for Literary Tools on page 538. How are couplets used in the poem? With what type of couplet does the poem end? How is the poem's theme developed in the three stanzas?

RESPONDING TO THE SELECTION

Students might respond by taking into consideration the opportunity they missed that was discussed in the Reader's Journal. What prevented them from seizing the day? Did they make any resolution about how to respond to future opportunities?

ANSWERS TO INVESTIGATE, INQUIRE, AND IMAGINE

Recall

1a. The speaker accuses his mistress of coyness. The speaker says he would love her from before the Flood to the Last Judgment.

2a. The speaker hears the "wingèd chariot" of time behind him and sees "deserts of vast eternity" before him.

3a. In the last stanza, the speaker urges, "Now let us sport us while we may," imagines "devouring" time before it devours him and his love, and suggests that they "tear [their] pleasures . . . / Through the iron gates of life."

Interpret

1b. The mistress's coyness is troublesome because the speaker feels they are wasting precious time while she deliberates. Life is short, and they might be dead before she is ready to make a commitment.

2b. The speaker is keenly aware of the passage of time and the inevitability of death.

3b. Time is a mortal enemy who must be attacked, or an opponent in a race who must be challenged directly.

Analyze

4a. The speaker is appealing to the human fear of death and the human love of pleasure.

Synthesize

4b. The speaker's main argument is to take advantage of the pleasures life has to offer while there is still time.

Evaluate

5a. *Responses will vary.*

Extend

5b. The pilgrims' avoidance of worldly pleasures at Vanity Fair in *The Pilgrim's Progress* contrasts with the message of "To His Coy Mistress" because the pilgrims want to avoid all worldly temptations, including those of the flesh. In "On His Blindness" the speaker asks God for patience, which conflicts with the speaker of Marvell's poem asking for immediate gratification.

ANSWERS TO UNDERSTANDING LITERATURE

Metaphor and Simile. "Time's wingèd chariot" (line 22) is a metaphor. The tenor is "time" and the vehicle is the "wingèd chariot." "The youthful hue / Sits on thy skin like morning dew" (lines 33–34) presents a simile. The tenor is "youthful hue" and the vehicle is "morning dew." Another simile is visible in the comparison "like amorous birds of prey" (line 38). The tenor is the speaker and his mistress; the vehicle is "amorous birds of prey."

Image. The speaker presents an image of his "vegetable love" growing in line 11. A vegetable grows in stages, which reinforces the speaker's imagining how his love would unfold gradually if he had all the time in the world.

Continued on page 540

ANSWERS TO INTEGRATING THE LANGUAGE ARTS

Language, Grammar, and Style

1. Andrew Marvell's poems are more than fanciful verses because he makes serious points. The reader would miss some of the poems' value by overlooking these points.
2. The mistress in the poem does not show fondness for the speaker. It is not clear whether she feels any or not, since her feelings are left for the reader to imagine.
3. Marvell prevented the poet John Milton from going to prison. Without Marvell's help, Milton may well have been put to death.
4. It's easy to imagine that Andrew Marvell was a delightful tutor to Thomas Fairfax's daughter. His poems written at that time show a witty sense of humor and even some satire, though these qualities aren't immediately apparent in Marvell's character.
5. The Latin phrase *carpe diem* means "seize the day." Marvell's poem is one of the most famous statements in English of the *carpe diem* theme.

WRITER'S JOURNAL

1. Write a **letter** to a friend encouraging him or her to seize the day and not put off any longer an important goal or opportunity.
2. Imagine you are the coy mistress being addressed in the poem. Write a **letter** to the speaker telling him whether or not you agree with his argument.
3. Imagine you write an advice column and the speaker has just written you a letter stating that his girlfriend has rejected him. Write an **advice column** giving the speaker ideas about how he should proceed to try to win her back.

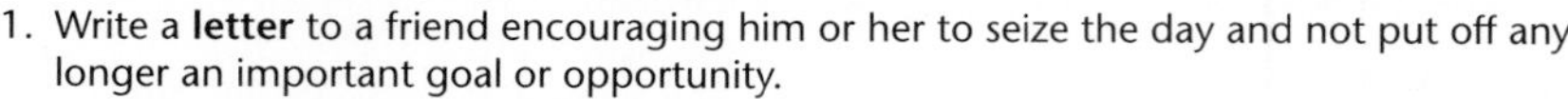
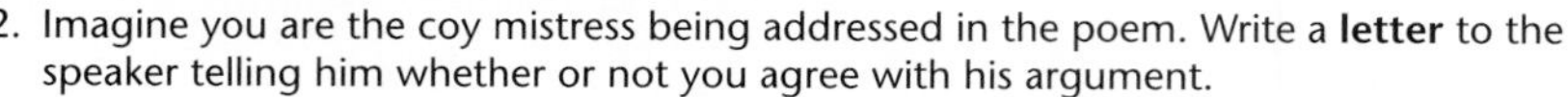

Integrating *the* Language Arts

Language, Grammar, and Style

Correcting Run-ons. Read the Language Arts Survey 3.34, "Correcting Sentence Run-ons." Then rewrite the following sentences, adding punctuation, removing words as necessary, and capitalizing words to create new sentences.

1. Andrew Marvell's poems are more than fanciful verses because he makes serious points, the reader would miss some of the poems' value by overlooking these points.
2. The mistress in the poem does not show fondness for the speaker, it is not clear whether she feels any or not, since her feelings are left for the reader to imagine.
3. Marvell prevented the poet John Milton from going to prison, without Marvell's help, Milton may well have been put to death.
4. It's easy to imagine that Andrew Marvell was a delightful tutor to Thomas Fairfax's daughter, his poems written at that time show a witty sense of humor and even some satire, though those qualities aren't immediately apparent in Marvell's character.
5. The Latin phrase *carpe diem* means "seize the day," Marvell's poem is one of the most famous statements in English of the *carpe diem* theme.

Study and Research & Collaborative Learning

Researching Parliament. Andrew Marvell served as a member of Parliament from 1659 until his death in 1678. Research a topic about the British Parliament. Possible topics include the origins of Parliament, the growth of sovereignty, the ascendancy of the Commons, the Reform Bill of 1832, the Representation of the People Acts in the twentieth century, the architecture of the Parliament buildings, and parliamentary law. After researching your chosen topic, present your findings to several classmates.

Speaking and Listening

Oral Interpretation. Choose two classmates to work with. Each student in your group should select a stanza from "To His Coy Mistress" to interpret orally. Decide what facial expressions, body language, and gestures to use in interpreting your section of the poem. In addition, decide on emotions you want to express, places to increase or decrease your pace, and places to raise or lower your volume. Then present your interpretation to the class. You may want to review the Language Arts Survey 4.19, "Oral Interpretation of Poetry" before you rehearse.

Media Literacy

FILM REVIEW. View the 1989 film *Dead Poet's Society,* written by Tom Schulman and starring Robin Williams as a brilliant young English professor, John Keating, in a posh private school on the East Coast. Set in 1959, the film takes place during the first Fall semester, a special time for a group of friends at the Welton Academy preparing to head off to the finest Universities in the world. Williams's character, Keating, encourages his students to seize the day, employing the *carpe diem* theme, and make their lives extraordinary. Through his example and encouragement, the students begin to exercise their individuality. Write a review of the film, analyzing the importance of the *carpe diem* theme to the development of the characters and the plot.

Critical Thinking

SELECTING ANTONYMS. Read the Language Arts Survey 5.56, "Answering Synonym and Antonym Questions." Then read the sentences below, and choose the word that means the *opposite* of the underlined word.

1. Andrew Marvell was a reserved man, though his poetry showed his humor and wit.
   a. quiet　　b. funny
   c. outgoing　　d. restrained
2. In many of Marvell's poems, his casual approach belies his serious message.
   a. reinforces　　b. disguises
   c. belittles　　d. underlies
3. In "To His Coy Mistress," the speaker explains why there is no time to be coy.
   a. evasive　　b. coquettish
   c. forthright　　d. hasty
4. According to the poem, we should take charge of time rather than languish under its power.
   a. submit　　b. flourish
   c. suffer　　d. express ourselves
5. The theme of this poem is that we should enjoy youth, beauty, love, and life now, because they are only temporal.
   a. short-lived　　b. quick
   c. eternal　　d. tempting

ANSWERS TO INTEGRATING THE LANGUAGE ARTS (CONT.)

Critical Thinking

1. c. outgoing
2. a. reinforces
3. c. forthright
4. b. flourish
5. c. eternal

ADDITIONAL RESOURCES

Unit 6 Resource Book
- Selection Worksheet 6.10
- Selection Check Test 4.6.21
- Selection Test 4.6.22
- Language, Grammar, and Style Resource 3.33
- Study and Research Resource 5.1

VOCABULARY FROM THE SELECTION

aureate
sans

GRAPHIC ORGANIZER

Students should list the following line in their graphic organizer: "Ah, my Beloved, fill the cup that clears/ Today of past Regrets and future Fears."

READER'S JOURNAL

Students might write a scene in the present tense in which they are enjoying a favorite activity.Studying this lesson will enable students to

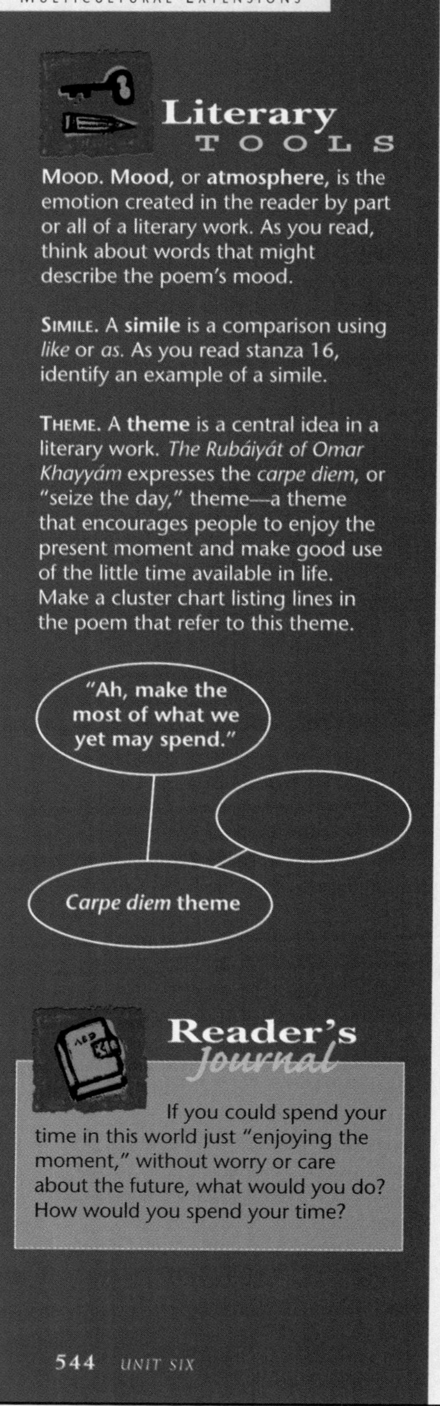

MULTICULTURAL EXTENSIONS

Literary TOOLS

Mood. **Mood,** or **atmosphere,** is the emotion created in the reader by part or all of a literary work. As you read, think about words that might describe the poem's mood.

Simile. A **simile** is a comparison using *like* or *as.* As you read stanza 16, identify an example of a simile.

Theme. A **theme** is a central idea in a literary work. *The Rubáiyát of Omar Khayyám* expresses the *carpe diem,* or "seize the day," theme—a theme that encourages people to enjoy the present moment and make good use of the little time available in life. Make a cluster chart listing lines in the poem that refer to this theme.

"Ah, make the most of what we yet may spend."
Carpe diem theme

Reader's Journal

If you could spend your time in this world just "enjoying the moment," without worry or care about the future, what would you do? How would you spend your time?

FROM "The Rubáiyát of Omar Khayyám"

BY OMAR KHAYYÁM,
TRANSLATED BY EDWARD FITZGERALD

About the AUTHOR

Omar Khayyám (AD 1048–1123). Omar Khayyám was born in Nishapur, Persia, on May 18, 1048. The name Khayyám means "tent maker," possibly indicating the profession of Omar's father. Khayyám's primary occupation was as a mathematician and astronomer, and his work in algebra became a standard text. He also mastered the subjects of philosophy, astronomy, law, medicine, and history.

About the SELECTION

The Rubáiyát is a compilation of roughly five hundred **epigrams,** or short, often witty sayings, presented in quatrains, or *ruba'i,* written throughout Khayyám's life. In his translation, FitzGerald modified the original ordering of the quatrains to increase their thematic coherence. In general, the epigrams, often satiric in tone, express a rebellious dissatisfaction with orthodox belief. Perhaps Khayyám's idea that one should try to get as much pleasure as possible from each passing moment is part of what attracted FitzGerald to the Persian writer's work.

While Khayyám rhymed each of the four lines in a quatrain, FitzGerald rhymed only the first, second, and fourth lines of each quatrain in his translation. The content of FitzGerald's translation mirrors his rhyme scheme, as each third line expresses an idea that is completed in the fourth. This combination defines the "FitzGerald stanza," which other English writers have adopted. The first edition of FitzGerald's *Rubáiyát,* containing only seventy-five quatrains, was published in 1859. The definitive fourth edition (1879) included 101 stanzas.

GOALS/OBJECTIVES

Studying this lesson will enable students to
- appreciate multicultural lyric poetry in translation
- understand the *carpe diem* theme in the poem and compare it to the same theme in works by seventeenth-century British authors
- describe the literary accomplishments of Edward FitzGerald and Omar Khayyám
- correct sentence fragments
- make decisions and solve problems

FROM *The Rubáiyát of Omar Khayyám*

OMAR KHAYYÁM, TRANSLATED BY EDWARD FITZGERALD

12

A Book of Verses underneath the bough,
A jug of Wine, a Loaf of Bread—and Thou
  Beside me singing in the Wilderness—
Oh, Wilderness were Paradise enow![1]

What four things would turn a wilderness into a paradise for the speaker of this poem?

13

Some for the Glories of This World; and some
Sigh for the Prophet's[2] Paradise to come;
  Ah, take the Cash, and let the Credit go,
Nor heed the rumble of a distant Drum!

Does the speaker think we should live for today or for tomorrow?

14

Look to the blowing Rose about us—"Lo,
Laughing," she says, "into the world I blow,
  At once the silken tassel of my purse
Tear, and its Treasure on the Garden throw."

15

And those who husbanded the Golden Grain,
And those who flung it into the winds like Rain,

1. **enow.** Enough
2. **Prophet's.** Mohammed's

ANSWERS TO GUIDED READING QUESTIONS

1. A book of poetry, a jug of wine, a loaf of bread, and the presence of the speaker's beloved would turn a wilderness into paradise.
2. The speaker says we should love for today: "take the Cash, and let the Credit go."

INDIVIDUAL LEARNING STRATEGIES

MOTIVATION
Ask students what image comes to mind when they picture "A jug of Wine, a Loaf of Bread—and Thou."

READING PROFICIENCY
Point out that each quatrain contains a separate idea. Ask students to find the quatrains that express the *carpe diem* theme.

ENGLISH LANGUAGE LEARNING
Point out the following vocabulary words and expressions.
tassel—decorative tuft of threads
husband—manage prudently and economically
prosper—succeed in an enterprise or activity
anon—soon
portal—door; entrance
pomp—show of magnificence
fledge—acquires independent activity

SPECIAL NEEDS
Explain that the numbered stanzas are separate pieces. There is some continuity of themes among them, but each can be understood on its own. Make sure students can answer the Guided Reading Questions and the Recall questions in Investigate, Inquire, and Imagine.

ENRICHMENT
One theme in "The Rubáiyát of Omar Khayyám is *carpe diem* or "seize the day." Ask students to analyze this theme by having them make a pro and con chart to weigh the advantages and disadvantages of "seizing the day."

ADDITIONAL QUESTIONS AND ACTIVITIES

In line 8, the speaker says we should not "heed the rumble of a distant Drum." What might this distant rumbling symbolize? Why should we ignore it? How does the attitude toward death expressed in *The Rubáiyát* compare with the attitude expressed in John Donne's Meditation 17 ("Perchance he for whom this bell tolls . . .")?
Answers
The distant rumbling might symbolize death. The speaker seems to think that since death is inevitable but distant, it makes sense to enjoy life while we can and not let a preoccupation with mortality spoil the time we have on earth. The speaker in Meditation 17, on the other hand, seems to think that it is appropriate to think about death and suffer at the thought, since this suffering brings us closer to God.

ANSWERS TO GUIDED READING QUESTIONS

1. All must die. People's hopes are either dashed, or they come true but provide only fleeting happiness.
2. The "Sleep" of the great hunter is actually death. His feats are of little significance, since the animal he once hunted now stamps on his grave.

LITERARY TECHNIQUE

Simile. A **simile** is a comparison using *like* or *as*. You might draw students' attention to the simile in stanza 16, in which prospered hopes are compared to "Snow upon the Desert's dusty Face." Ask them to describe the image this simile creates in their minds. How does this image support the poem's *carpe diem* theme?

Answer

The image of snow falling in the desert and immediately melting underscores the fleeting nature of life. Since life is so brief, the speaker is saying, people should enjoy it while it lasts and not fasten their hopes to impermanent things.

ADDITIONAL QUESTIONS AND ACTIVITIES

1. What is the speaker's attitude toward the ancient Caesar's death? What benefit does his death provide in the present?
2. What is the theme of stanza 19 and 20? How does it make you feel about the cycle of life and death?

Answers

1. The speaker seems grateful ti the Caesar, whose blood fertilized the earth and made possible the bloom of a beautiful rose that the speaker can appreciate in the present.
2. The theme of these stanzas might be stated: "The natural world is full of both death and sensual pleasures, the former making the latter possible." The cycle of life and death seems benevolent and beautiful as the poem describes it.

Rubáiyát of Omar Khayyám. Edmund Dulac.

Alike to no such <u>aureate</u> Earth are turned
As, buried once, Men want dug up again.

What do lines 13–16 suggest about life?

16

The Worldly Hope men set their Hearts upon
Turns Ashes—or it prospers; and anon,
Like Snow upon the Desert's dusty Face,
Lighting a little hour or two—is gone.

What is the common fate of all? What happens to people's hopes?

17

Think, in this battered Caravanserai[3]
Whose Portals are alternate Night and Day,
How Sultán after Sultán with his pomp
Abode his destined Hour, and went his way.

3. **Caravanserai.** Inn; here, metaphorically, the world

Words For Everyday Use

au • re • ate (ô´rē it) *adj.,* splendid or brilliant. *We were struck with awe watching the <u>aureate</u> sun rise over the surging sea.*

18

They say the Lion and the Lizard keep
The Courts where Jamshyd[4] gloried and drank deep;
and Bahrám,[5] that great Hunter—the Wild Ass
Stamps o'er his Head, but cannot break his Sleep.

Why cannot the great hunter be awakened? Of what significance are his feats now?

19

I sometimes think that never blows so red
The Rose as where some buried Caesar bled;
That every Hyacinth[6] the Garden wears
Dropped in her Lap from some once lovely Head.

20

And this reviving Herb whose tender Green
Fledges the River-Lip on which we lean—
Ah, lean upon it lightly! for who knows
From what once lovely Lip it springs unseen!

21

Ah, my Belovéd, fill the cup that clears
TODAY of past Regrets and future Fears:
Tomorrow!—Why, Tomorrow I may be
Myself with Yesterday's sev'n thousand Years.

What does the speaker want his beloved to do?

22

For some we loved, the loveliest and the best
That from his Vintage rolling Time hath pressed,
Have drunk their Cup a Round or two before,
And one by one crept silently to rest.

23

And we, that now make merry in the Room
They left, and Summer dresses in new bloom,
Ourselves must we beneath the Couch of Earth
Descend—ourselves to make a Couch—for whom?

24

Ah, make the most of what we yet may spend,
Before we too into the Dust descend;
Dust into Dust, and under Dust to lie,
Sans Wine, sans Song, sans Singer, and—sans End! ■

What does the speaker think we should do, given that we shall all die?

---

4. **Jamshyd.** In Persian myth, a king of the fairies who was forced to live a human life because he boasted of his immortality
5. **Bahrám.** King who was lost while hunting a wild donkey
6. **Hyacinth.** Plant of the lily family

WORDS FOR EVERYDAY USE

sans (sänz) *prep.*, without. *Louise was annoyed when she ordered her sandwich* sans *mayonnaise but then received a sandwich drenched in it.*

ANSWERS TO GUIDED READING QUESTIONS

1. The "Sleep" of the great hunter is actually death. His feats are of little significance, since the animal he once hunted now stamps on his grave.
2. The speaker wants his beloved to enjoy love and pleasures today—now.
3. Since death is inevitable and eternal, we should enjoy the pleasures of this world—such as wine and song—while we can.

SELECTION CHECK TEST 4.6.21 WITH ANSWERS

Checking Your Reading

1. What four things would turn the wilderness into paradise for the speaker? **A book of poetry, a jug of wine, a loaf of bread, and the speaker's beloved would turn wilderness into paradise.**
2. Does the speaker live for the "Glories of This World" or for the "Prophet's Paradise"? **The speaker lives for this world.**
3. To what are people's hopes compared? **People's hopes are compared to snow in the desert.**
4. What cup should we fill today? **We should fill the cup that erases past regrets and future fears.**
5. What does the speaker suggest we should do, given that we will all die? **We should make the most of the time we have.**

Literary Tools

1. What is mood? **Mood, or atmosphere, is the emotion created in the reader by part or all of a literary work.**
2. Is "Like Snow upon the Desert's dusty Face" an example of a metaphor or a simile? **It is a simile.**
3. What is the *carpe diem* theme? **The *carpe diem* theme tells people not to waste time but rather to enjoy themselves while they have a chance.**

CROSS-CURRICULAR ACTIVITY

BIOLOGY. Interested students might investigate to what extent stanzas 19 and 20 describe scientific truths. How do the bodies of dead plants and animals make life possible for later organisms?

RESPOND TO THE SELECTION

Students might begin by listing character traits the speaker seems to possess.

ANSWERS TO INVESTIGATE, INQUIRE, AND IMAGINE

Recall

1a. The speaker's recipe for happiness is a book of verses, a jug of wine, a loaf of bread, and good company, or "Thou."

2a. All people, including great sultans, must die.

3a. According to the speaker, great people who have died nourish hyacinths and herbs.

Interpret

1b. Intellectual stimulation, sustenance, and good company are everything the speaker needs to love a perfectly happy life.

2b. Earthly achievements, no matter how important, do not matter in that they do not prevent death. Many earthly achievements die when the people who accomplished them die.

3b. The speaker believes that life springs from death—that flowers grow from those who have died. These stanzas reveal the power of the natural world which can create life from death.

Analyze

4a. The speaker tells readers that they should do away with regrets and fears and that they should make the most of time on earth. The line in stanza 24, "Ah, make the most of what we yet may spend,/Before we too into the Dust descend," sums up the speaker's advice.

Synthesize

4b. *Responses will vary.* Some students may suggest that seeing others die and all their life's work abruptly end might encourage some people to embrace the *carpe diem* theme.

Evaluate

5a. *Responses will vary.*

Extend

5b. Students might suggest that both writers express the *carpe diem* theme and advocate enjoying life before one dies. Khayyám focuses on a broader range of ways to enjoy life, however, than does Marvell who focuses solely on love.

Respond *to the* SELECTION

What type of person do you imagine the speaker of this poem to be? Would you like to meet him? Why, or why not?

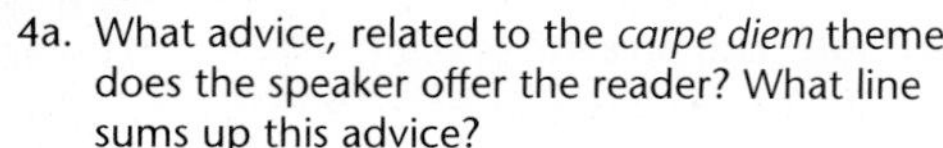

INVESTIGATE, Inquire, Imagine

Recall: GATHERING FACTS → **Interpret:** FINDING MEANING

1a. In stanza 12, what does the speaker describe as his recipe for happiness?

1b. Why are these things sufficient for the speaker to create a paradise on earth?

2a. What, according to stanzas 17 and 18, happens to all people, including great sultans?

2b. What do stanzas 17 and 18 say about the importance of earthly achievements?

3a. According to stanzas 19 and 20, what nourishes hyacinths and herbs?

3b. In stanzas 19 and 20, what is the speaker's attitude toward the cycle of life and death? What do these stanzas reveal about the natural world?

Analyze: TAKING THINGS APART → **Synthesize:** BRINGING THINGS TOGETHER

4a. What advice, related to the *carpe diem* theme, does the speaker offer the reader? What line sums up this advice?

4b. What experiences and events might inspire a person to embrace the *carpe diem* theme?

Evaluate: MAKING JUDGMENTS → **Extend:** CONNECTING IDEAS

5a. Explain whether the *carpe diem* philosophy is one that appeals to you. How might you seize the day in your own life?

5b. Compare and contrast Khayyám's views about time and pleasure to those Marvell expresses in "To His Coy Mistress."

Understanding Literature

Mood. **Mood,** or **atmosphere,** is the emotion created in the reader by part or all of a literary work. What is the general mood of the stanzas from *The Rubáiyát* that you have read? What words and phrases help create this mood? Explain if the mood is appropriate given this poem's subject.

Simile. A **simile** is a comparison using *like* or *as.* In stanza 16, what two things are being compared? In what way does this comparison support the poem's subject?

Theme. Review the definition of **theme** in Literary Tools on page 544. In addition to its expression in this Persian poem, the *carpe diem* theme is found in classical literature as well as English literature. Sum up in your own words the theme of this excerpt from *The Rubáiyát.*

ANSWERS TO UNDERSTANDING LITERATURE

Mood. Students might say that the mood is lighthearted , joyful, and positive. Phrases that describe simple pleasures, the natural world, and doing away with regrets contribute to this mood. For example, "Look to the blowing Rose about us—'Lo,/Laughing,' she says, 'into the world I blow,/At once the silken tassel of my purse/Tear, and its Treasure on the Garden throw.'" The mood is appropriate because the speaker is trying to convince readers to make the most of life on earth, to do away with regret and fear, and to seek happiness in simple pleasures.

Simile. The speaker compares humans' worldly hopes to snow "upon the Desert's dusty Face," which

Continued on page 549

Writer's Journal

1. Write a **proposal** for creating a new holiday to celebrate the *carpe diem* theme. Specify what people might do to celebrate this holiday.
2. Write a **dialogue** between two characters, one who supports the *carpe diem* mentality and one who devoutly believes that human life should be focused on living modestly, and attaining salvation.
3. A **tall tale** is a story, often lighthearted or humorous, that contains highly exaggerated, unrealistic elements. Write a tall tale about a character who takes the *carpe diem* mindset to a ridiculous extreme.

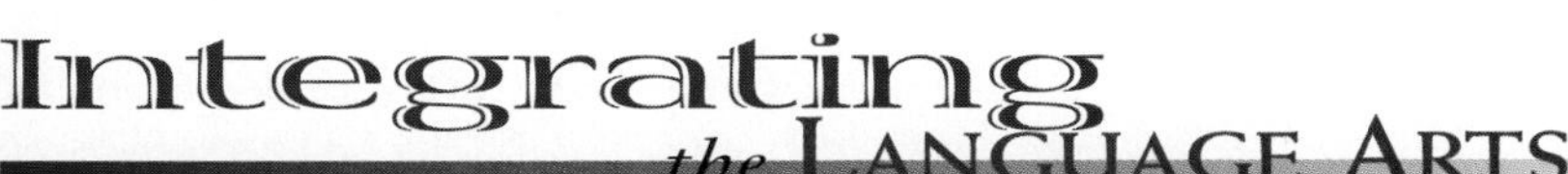

Language, Grammar, and Style

Correcting Sentence Fragments. Poets do not always follow all the rules of grammar and sentence structure. When you are writing prose, however, you should follow these rules. For example, a poet might write, "A Book of Verses underneath the bough, / A jug of Wine, a Loaf of Bread—and Thou / Beside me singing in the Wilderness—" If you were to write this as prose it might look like the following: "A book of verses underneath the bough, a jug of wine, a loaf of bread, and thou beside me singing in the wilderness." This is an example of a sentence fragment, not a complete sentence, because it does not express a complete thought. Review the Language Arts Survey 3.33, "Correcting Sentence Fragments." Then rewrite the following fragments below so that they form complete sentences.

1. Some the glories of this world, and some the paradise to come.
2. The worldly hope that men set their hearts upon.
3. So they could forget their cares.
4. Lived his destined hour and then passed away.
5. Where some buried Caesar bled.

Critical Thinking

Making Decisions and Solving Problems. Review the Language Arts Survey 5.1, "Making Decisions and Solving Problems." Then create a chart in which you weigh the pros and cons of always living for the moment and never worrying about the future. When you have completed your chart, study it and try to come up with a reasonable compromise for your own life. When is planning and thinking for the future important? When might worrying too much about the future stand in the way of enjoying the present moment? When might living too much in the moment cause problems? How might you achieve a balance in your life? Your completed assignment should include a pros and cons chart, as well as statements about what you learned from your chart.

ANSWERS TO INTEGRATING THE LANGUAGE ARTS

Language, Grammar, and Style
Responses will vary.

1. Some prefer the glories of this world, and some focus on the paradise to come.
2. The worldly hope that men set their hearts upon turns to ashes.
3. The speaker urges humans to live for today, so they could forget their cares.
4. Even the greatest sultan lived his destined hour and then passed away.
5. The rose is reddest where some buried Caesar bled.

ANSWERS TO UNDERSTANDING LITERATURE (CONT.)

"Lighting a little hour or two—is gone." Hope and snow in the dusty desert are being compared. These lines mean that humans' goals and hopes give them only momentary pleasure, but any accomplishment dies when people die. Hopes are as ephemeral as snow in a hot desert, lasting only a short while. The speaker is encouraging others to live for the moment because life on earth is fleeting, which is central to the *carpe diem* theme.

Theme. *Responses will vary.* The theme can be summarized as making the most of the present, seeking joy in simple pleasures, and doing away with regrets and fears.

"THE INDIFFERENT"
ABOUT THE AUTHOR. A biography of **Donne** appears on page 414.

FROM *AREOPAGITICA*
ABOUT THE AUTHOR. A biography of **Milton** appears on page 429.

ADDITIONAL QUESTIONS AND ACTIVITIES

Students may form small groups to discuss the following questions:

1. What is the theme of Donne's poem "The Indifferent"? What does the speaker want? Why will he never find it? Compare and contrast this poem with Donne's Song ("Go and catch a falling star . . .").
2. What is the subject of Milton's *Areopagitica?* What is the "noble and puissant nation"? In what way has the eagle's sight been "long-abused"? What does Milton say will be the outcome if "[Truth] and Falsehood grapple" openly?
3. What problem is faced by the speaker in Sonnet 77? Why can she not "turn back"? What is the "thread of love"? How will it help the speaker?

Answers

1. The theme of "The Indifferent" is women's faithlessness. The speaker wants to find a mate who is "true," but the goddess of love has declared that people who are foolish enough to love truly shall love only those who are untrue. This poem shares a common theme with Song ("Go and catch a falling star . . ."), but the language is more formal.
2. Milton's *Areopagitica* is about censorship. The "noble and puissant nation" is England, whose people have a long history of being blinded by the suppression of free speech and press. Milton says that Truth will inevitably win if she is allowed to compete openly with Falsehood.
3. The speaker in Sonnet 77 is confused about which direction to take in life. Turning back would be shameful and cowardly. The "thread of love" will guide her so she does not get lost in the "labyrinth" of life—as long as she is true to what she loves, she will not go wrong.

SELECTIONS FOR ADDITIONAL READING: THE EARLY SEVENTEENTH CENTURY

"The Indifferent"
by John Donne

I can love both fair and brown,
Her whom abundance melts, and her whom want betrays,
Her who loves loneness best, and her who masks and plays,
Her whom the country formed, and whom the town,
Her who believes, and her who tries,
Her who still weeps with spongy eyes,
And her who is dry cork, and never cries;
I can love her, and her, and you, and you,
I can love any, so she be not true.

Will no other vice content you?
Will it not serve your turn to do as did your mothers?
Or have you all old vices spent, and now would find out others?
Or doth a fear that men are true torment you?
O we are not, be not you so;
Let me, and do you, twenty know.
Rob me, but bind me not, and let me go.
Must I, who came to travail thorough[1] you,
Grow your fixed subject, because you are true?

Venus heard me sigh this song,
And by love's sweetest part, variety, she swore,
She heard not this till now; and that it should be so no more.
She went, examined, and returned ere long,
And said, Alas, some two or three
Poor heretics in love there be,
Which think to 'stablish dangerous constancy.
But I have told them, Since you will be true,
You shall be true to them who are false to you.

from *Areopagitica*[2]
by John Milton

Methinks I see in my mind a noble and puissant nation rousing herself like a strong man after sleep, and shaking her invincible locks: methinks I see her as an eagle mewing her mighty youth, and kindling her undazzled eyes at the full mid-day beam; purging and unscaling her long-abused sight at the fountain itself of heavenly radiance; while the whole noise of timorous and flocking birds, with those also that love the twilight, flutter about, amazed at what she means, and in their envious gabble would prognosticate a year of sects and schisms.

What should ye do then, should ye suppress all this flowery crop of knowledge and new light sprung up and yet springing daily in this city? Should ye set an oligarchy of twenty engrossers[3] over it, to bring a famine upon our minds again, when we shall know nothing but what is measured to us by their bushel? Believe it, Lords and Commons, they who counsel ye to such a suppressing do as good as bid ye suppress yourselves; and I will soon show how. [4]

◆ ◆ ◆

And now the time in special is by privilege to write and speak what may help to the further discussing of matters in agitation. The temple of Janus with his two controversial faces might now not unsignificantly be set open. And though all the winds of doctrine were let loose to play upon the earth, so Truth be in the field, we do injuriously by licensing and prohibiting to misdoubt her strength. Let her and Falsehood grapple; who ever knew Truth put to the worse in a free and open encounter?

Sonnet 77
by Lady Mary Wroth

In this strange labyrinth how shall I turn?
Ways are on all sides, while the way I miss:
If to the right hand, there in love I burn;
Let me go forward, therein danger is;
If to the left, suspicion hinders bliss,
Let me turn back, Shame cries I ought return,
Nor faint though crosses with my fortunes kiss;
Stand still is harder, although sure to mourn.
Then let me take the right- or left-hand way;
Go forward, or stand still, or back retire;
I must these doubts endure without allay
Or help, but travail find for my best hire.
Yet that which most my troubled sense doth move
Is to leave all, and take the thread of love.[5]

---

1. **thorough.** Through
2. ***Areopagitica.*** Pamphlet against censorship
3. **engrossers.** People who hoarded grain and sold it for high prices during famine
4. **Belzieve . . . how.** Milton argues that Parliament has created the inquisitive minds that censorship now tries to suppress.
5. **thread of love.** The reference is to the thread that Ariadne gave to Theseus so he would not get lost in the labyrinth at Crete.

SONNET 77
ABOUT THE AUTHOR. Lady Mary Wroth (*circa* 1586–*circa* 1651) spent much of her life in the royal courts of Elizabeth I and James I. She was born into a literary family; her father was Sir Robert Sidney, and she was the niece of poets Sir Philip Sidney and Mary, Countess of Pembroke. Among the courtiers who admired her was Ben Jonson, who dedicated his comic play *The Alchemist* to her. Lady Mary's only major work published in her lifetime was a dark and cynical romance entitled *The Countesse of Mountgomeries Urania* (1621), which she was forced to withdraw under charges of libel. Some of her poetry involving the main characters in *Urania* was published in or along with the romance. More was published in 1977 under the title *Pamphilia to Amphilanthus.*

"To Mrs. M. A.[1] at Parting"
by Katherine Philips

I have examined and do find,
Of all that favor me
There's none I grieve to leave behind
But only only thee.
To part with thee I needs must die,
Could parting separate thee and I.

But neither chance nor compliment
Did element our love:
'Twas sacred sympathy was lent
Us from the choir above.
(That friendship fortune did create,
Still fears a wound from time or fate.)

Our changed and mingled souls are grown
To such acquaintance now,
That if each would resume their own,
Alas! we know not how.
We have each other so engrossed
That each is in the union lost.

And thus we can no absence know,
Nor shall we be confined;
Our active souls will daily go
To learn each other's mind.
Nay, should we never meet to sense,
Our souls would hold intelligence.

Inspirèd with a flame divine,
I scorn to court a stay;[2]
For from that noble soul of thine
I ne'er can be away.
But I shall weep when thou dost grieve;
Nor can I die whilst thou dost live.

By my own temper I shall guess
At thy felicity,
And only like my happiness
Because it pleaseth thee.
Our hearts at any time will tell
If thou or I be sick or well.

All honor, sure, I must pretend,
All that is good or great:
She that would be Rosania's friend
Must be at least complete.
If I have any bravery,
'Tis cause I have so much of thee.

Thy leiger soul in me shall lie,
And all thy thoughts reveal;
Then back again with mine shall fly,
And thence to me shall steal.
Thus still to one another tend:
Such is the sacred name of friend.

Thus our twin souls in one shall grow,
And teach the world new love,
Redeem the age and sex, and show
A flame fate dares not move:
And courting death to be our friend,
Our lives, together too, shall end.

A dew shall dwell upon our tomb
Of such a quality
That fighting armies, thither come,
Shall reconcilèd be.
We'll ask no epitaph, but say:
ORINDA and ROSANIA.[3]

"The Garden"
by Andrew Marvell

How vainly men themselves amaze
To win the palm, the oak, or bays,
And their uncessant labors see
Crowned from some single herb or tree,
Whose short and narrow-vergèd shade
Does prudently their toils upbraid;
While all flowers and all trees do close
To weave the garlands of repose!

Fair Quiet, have I found thee here,
And Innocence, thy sister dear?
Mistaken long, I sought you then
In busy companies of men.
Your sacred plants, if here below,
Only among the plants will grow;
Society is all but rude,
To this delicious solitude.

No white nor red was ever seen
So amorous as this lovely green.
Fond lovers, cruel as their flame,
Cut in these trees their mistress' name:
Little, alas, they know or heed

1. **M. A.** Mary Aubrey, a member of Philips's literary circle of friends
2. **court a stay.** Postpone their parting
3. **Orinda and Rosania.** Pseudonyms for Philips and Aubrey

"TO MRS. M. A. AT PARTING"
ABOUT THE AUTHOR. Katherine Philips (1631–1664) and her husband, James, were the center of the so-called Society of Friendship, a group of literary-minded people who often gathered at their home in Wales. She and her friends each took a Neoclassical nickname; Philips herself was playfully known as "The Matchless Orinda." She wrote many poems about her friendships with women, along with other works exploring her Puritan faith and several plays. Most of her poetry was not published in her lifetime but rather circulated among her friends. When a collection of her poetry and plays was published after her death of smallpox at the age of thirty-three, her work was highly praised.

ADDITIONAL QUESTIONS AND ACTIVITIES

Students may discuss the following questions:

1. What is the theme of "To Mrs. M. A. at Parting"?
2. Why is it so difficult for the speaker to part from her friend? What comforts the speaker at this painful time?
3. Compare and contrast "To Mrs. M. A. at Parting" with some of the other poems about love that you have read in this unit.

Answers

1. The theme is friendship: the difficulty of parting from close friends and the ties that bind friends across time and distance.
2. The speaker has grown so close to her friend that "each is in the union lost" (line 18). She is comforted by the fact that she and her friend cannot really be parted because their hearts and minds will always be joined.
3. This poem is different from others in this unit because it deals with friendship rather than romantic love. The love between the two characters is mutual and is based on intellectual and spiritual closeness rather than romantic longing.

"THE GARDEN"
ABOUT THE AUTHOR. A biography of **Marvell** appears on page 457.

ADDITIONAL QUESTIONS AND ACTIVITIES

Students may discuss the following questions:

1. What is the attitude of the speaker in Andrew Marvell's poem toward the garden he describes?
2. What attitude does the speaker have toward women and relationships between men and women?

Answers

1. The speaker loves the garden for its quiet and innocence (lines 9–10), and he prefers it to socializing with other people.
2. The speaker has a cynical attitude toward romantic relationships, describing "Fond lovers" as "cruel as their flame" for carving their mistresses' names in the trunks of trees (lines 19–20) and saying that the "white [and] red" that symbolize romance were never so "amorous" as the green of the garden (lines 17–18). The speaker goes on to say that the truest paradise was the Garden of Eden before the creation of Eve, when Adam enjoyed both the beauty of nature and perfect solitude.

How far these beauties hers exceed!
Fair trees, wheresoe'er your barks I wound,
No name shall but your own be found.

When we have run our passion's heat,
Love hither makes his best retreat.
The gods, that mortal beauty chase,
Still in a tree did end their race:
Apollo hunted Daphne[1] so,
Only that she might laurel grow;
And Pan did after Syrinx[2] speed,
Not as a nymph, but for a reed.

What wondrous life in this I lead!
Ripe apples drop about my head;
The luscious clusters of the vine
Upon my mouth do crush their wine;
The nectarine and curious peach
Into my hands themselves do reach;
Stumbling on melons as I pass,
Insnared with flowers, I fall on grass.

Meanwhile the mind, from pleasure less,
Withdraws into its happiness;
The mind, that ocean where each kind
Does straight its own resemblance find;
Yet it creates, transcending these,
Far other worlds and other seas,
Annihilating all that's made
To a green thought in a green shade.

Here at the fountain's sliding foot,
Or at some fruit tree's mossy root,
Casting the body's vest aside,
My soul into the boughs does glide:
There like a bird it sits and sings,
Then whets and combs its silver wings,
And, till prepared for longer flight,
Waves in its plumes the various light.

Such was that happy garden-state,
While man there walked without a mate:
After a place so pure and sweet,
What other help could yet be meet!
But 'twas beyond a mortal's share
To wander solitary there:
Two paradises 'twere in one
To live in paradise alone.
How well the skillful gardener drew
Of flowers and herbs this dial new,
Where from above the milder sun
Does through a fragrant zodiac run;
And as it works, th' industrious bee
Computes its time as well as we!
How could such sweet and wholesome hours
Be reckoned but with herbs and flowers?

Song (*"Why so pale and wan . . ."*)
by Sir John Suckling

Why so pale and wan, fond lover?
Prithee,[3] why so pale?
Will, when looking well can't move her,
Looking ill prevail?
Prithee, why so pale?

Why so dull and mute, young sinner?
Prithee, why so mute?
Will, when speaking well can't win her,
Saying nothing do 't?
Prithee, why so mute?

Quit, quit, for shame; this will not move,
This cannot take her.
If of herself she will not love,
Nothing can make her:
The devil take her!

"Corinna's Going A-Maying"
by Robert Herrick

Get up! get up for shame! the blooming morn
Upon her wings presents the god unshorn.
See how Aurora throws her fair
Fresh-quilted colors through the air.
Get up, sweet slug-a-bed, and see
The dew bespangling herb and tree.
Each flower has wept and bowed toward the east
Above an hour since, yet you not dressed;
Nay, not so much as out of bed?
When all the birds have matins said,
And sung their thankful hymns, 'tis sin,
Nay, profanation to keep in,
Whenas a thousand virgins on this day
Spring, sooner than the lark, to fetch in May.

Rise, and put on your foliage, and be seen
To come forth, like the springtime, fresh and green,
And sweet as Flora. Take no care
For jewels for your gown or hair;
Fear not; the leaves will strew
Gems in abundance upon you;

1. **Apollo . . . Daphne.** In Greek mythology Daphne was transformed into a laurel tree to end Apollo's pursuit.
2. **Pan . . . Syrinx.** Syrinx was changed into a reed to escape Pan.
3. **prithee.** Please

SONG ("WHY SO PALE AND WAN . . .") ABOUT THE AUTHOR. Sir John Suckling (1609–1642) enrolled at Trinity College, Cambridge, at the age of fourteen but left without taking a degree. Suckling's father died one year later, and Suckling inherited vast estates. In many ways a model Cavalier, Suckling was known for his wit and extravagance. In 1638, he published a play, *Aglaura,* and a number of poems. In 1641, Suckling was implicated in a royalist plot against Parliamentary forces. England was headed toward civil war, and Suckling was pressed by Parliament to account for his actions. He fled to Paris and died a fugitive in France.

"CORINNA'S GOING A-MAYING" ABOUT THE AUTHOR. Robert Herrick (1591–1674) attended Cambridge University and was ordained in the Anglican Church in 1623. He enjoyed the literary society of London and was at first dismayed by his appointment to a rural congregation in Devonshire, but much of his poetry reveals the deep love he developed for the countryside. A Cavalier poet influenced by Ben Jonson and the Classical Latin poets, Herrick often wrote lyric verse on the *carpe diem* theme. One such poem, "To the Virgins, to Make Much of Time," became one of the most popular songs of the seventeenth century after William Lawes composed a tune for it. "Corinna's Going A-Maying" also expresses the *carpe diem* theme and displays Herrick's mastery of pastoral imagery.

Besides, the childhood of the day has kept,
Against you come, some orient pearls unwept;
Come and receive them while the light
Hangs on the dew-locks of the night,
And Titan on the eastern hill
Retires himself, or else stands still
Till you come forth. Wash, dress, be brief in praying:
Few beads are best when once we go a-Maying.

Come, my Corinna, come; and, coming, mark
How each field turns a street, each street a park
Made green and trimmed with trees; see how
Devotion gives each house a bough
Or branch: each porch, each door ere this,
An ark, a tabernacle is,
Made up of whitehorn neatly interwove,
As if here were those cooler shades of love.
Can such delights be in the street
And open fields, and we not see 't?
Come, we'll abroad; and let's obey
The proclamation made for May,
And sin no more, as we have done, by staying;
But, my Corinna, come, let's go a-Maying.

There's not a budding boy or girl this day
But is got up and gone to bring in May;
A deal of youth, ere this, is come
Back, and with whitehorn laden home.
Some have dispatched their cakes and cream
Before that we have left to dream;
And some have wept, and wooed, and plighted troth,
And chose their priest, ere we can cast off sloth.
Many a green-gown has been given,
Many a kiss, both odd and even;
Many a glance, too, has been sent
From out the eye, love's firmament;
Many a jest told of the keys betraying
This night, and locks picked; yet we're not a-
Maying.

Come, let us go while we are in our prime,
And tale the harmless folly of the time.
We shall grow old apace, and die
Before we know our liberty.
Our life is short, and our days run
As fast away as does the sun;
And, as a vapor or a drop of rain
Once lost, can ne'er be found again,
So when or you or I are made
A fable, song, or fleeting shade,
All love, all liking, all delight
Lies drowned with us in endless night.
Then while time serves, and we are but decaying,
Come, my Corinna, come, let's go a-Maying.

"To Lucasta, Going to the Wars"
by Richard Lovelace

Tell me not, sweet, I am unkind,
That from the nunnery
Of thy chaste breast and quiet mind
To war and arms I fly.

True, a new mistress now I chase,
The first foe in the field;
And with a stronger faith embrace
A sword, a horse, a shield.

Yet this inconstancy is such
As you too shall adore;
I could not love thee, dear, so much,
Loved I not honor more.

"Corinna's Going A-Maying"
About the Selection. The tradition of celebrating May Day, or May 1, has very ancient roots. Springtime fertility rites were a part of the cultures of pagan Rome and the ancient civilizations of India, Egypt, Europe, and Mexico. In medieval England, people danced around maypoles and enjoyed performances of morris dances, in which traditional stories were acted out in pantomime. The Christian celebration of Easter largely took the place of the ancient rites but retained some fertility symbols, such as brightly colored eggs.

ADDITIONAL QUESTIONS AND ACTIVITIES

Students may discuss the following questions:

1. What is the setting of "Corinna's Going A-Maying"? What does the speaker want Corinna to do? Why? What does he mean by "put on your foliage" in line 15? How does he want Corinna to dress herself, and why?
2. What theme is expressed in stanza 5? What other poems in this unit have a similar theme?
3. What situation is the speaker in "To Lucasta, Going to the Wars" facing? How has Lucasta responded to this situation? What does the speaker say to comfort her?

Answers

1. It is the month of May, and the speaker is eager to get outside and enjoy the celebration of spring. He wants Corinna to get out of bed and come with him. "Put on your foliage" means "get dressed"; he wants her to dress quickly and not worry about putting on jewelry because he's in a hurry and because she doesn't need fancy attire to go out and appreciate nature.
2. The stanza expresses the *carpe diem* theme, one also treated in Marvell's "To His Coy Mistress."
3. In "To Lucasta, Going to the Wars," the speaker is leaving his love to go to war. She is apparently upset at the prospect, and he tells her that she should not feel betrayed because their love is made possible by the same sense of honor that leads him to fight.

"To Lucasta, Going to the Wars"
About the Author. A biography of **Lovelace** appears on page 451.

LESSON OVERVIEW

GUIDED WRITING *Software*

See the Guided Writing Software for an extended version of this lesson that includes printable graphic organizers, extensive student models and student-friendly checklists, and self-, peer, and teacher evaluation features.

Examining the Model

Point out that Marvell's proposed three-month voyage to New York is humorous. Students may need to be reminded that their letters should be serious and, unlike Marvell, they should make themselves immediately available to their prospective employer.

"...I'd like to remind people that writing a résumé is truly hard work, and remind them not to take it personally when they run up against how tough it is. Just "hang in there," knowing that you'll be MUCH more clear about what you're aiming for and about what you've got to offer after you go through this process. The end product, your résumé, is a morale booster and a confidence builder, well worth all that sweat whether anybody else sees it or not."

—Yana Parker

WRITING A RÉSUMÉ AND APPLICATION LETTER

Often seventeenth-century writers had to find other work because they were not able to support themselves on their writing alone. If you can imagine an age before technology, you can visualize how different a job-hunter's quest was then compared to today: no word processing for résumés and cover letters, no faxing or cell phones to aid in the process. Handwritten letters of introduction, if they could be obtained from respected individuals, were more common. Showing up and hoping for an interview? Scary, but probably the most likely scenario.

Are you looking for a job? If not, chances are good that you soon will be. Whether it's a summer job or the beginning of a lifelong career, the best way to get hired is with a resume and cover letter. Some employers require only an application, but you will often be expected to have a resume. Your resume must be accompanied by a cover letter. Consider these necessary parts of your job-hunting tools.

WRITING ASSIGNMENT. Your assignment in this lesson is to write a cover letter and résumé.

EXAMINING THE MODEL. Andrew Marvell's cover letter is fictional, of course, crossing not only continents but centuries. The format, however, is the same for the letter you will write in this assignment.

Look at the form of Mr. Marvell's letter. The sample letter follows the block form, which means that each line begins at the left margin and paragraphs are separated by line spaces. For another example of a job application letter, see the Language Arts Survey 6.5.

Professional Model—Cover Letter

14 Donne Street
Winestead, Yorkshire, UK

September 4, 1670

Alice N. Wheeler
Recruiting Coordinator
BBB Corporation
55 Washington Street
New York, New York 10081

Dear Madam Wheeler:

I am writing due to my recently acquired knowledge, from a rather prescient friend, of the good works of BBB

Corporation; these accomplishments are such that I would like to be considered for the position of recorder and secretary. I am pleased to include among my vocations that of clerk, tutor, diplomat, and lifetime member of the British Parliament.

My education at Cambridge University, followed by extensive travel on the continent, has given me the proper background for any position in international relations or commerce. My work experience as tutor to Lord Fairfax's daughter and assistant to John Milton in the Latin secretaryship taught me the value of a work ethic. Both positions demanded much of me. Lord Fairfax has high expectations for his daughter and we would spend many long days reviewing Latin phrases. Mr. Milton's workday would begin at 4 a.m., when I would read the Bible to him in the original Hebrew. After contemplation, we would write and read until our 6 p.m. dinner, followed by a walk in the gardens, poetry reading, or musical interpretation. During this time, I penned many poems and sonnets in both English and Latin, strengthening my language abilities. My years as a clerk required excellent penmanship, and so I am proud of the fact that I consistently copied the required papers quickly, sometimes even finishing an entire one- page draft in less than two days.

I hope that the skills and experience described in my résumé suggest how I might be of service to your corporation. I would be honored to meet with you to discuss my possible contributions to BBB. If you wish to arrange an interview, please contact me at the above address. I will book steerage on the next available merchant vessel setting sail from a convenient harbor that would put me in New York not three months after receiving your letter.

Thank you for your kind consideration of this matter.

Sincerely yours,

Andrew Marvell

Writing a Cover Letter
A cover letter is your prospective employer's first impression of you, so use proper formal tone and avoid errors in spelling, grammar, usage, and mechanics. The format includes your address so employers know exactly how to contact you. Cover letters, as with any business letter, should bear the name and address of the company to which you are applying and should address by name the person responsible for hiring. If you don't know the person's name, "Dear Sir or Madam" or "To Whom It Concerns" is acceptable.

While a résumé serves as more of a generic advertisement for yourself, a cover letter is uniquely tailored to each job for which you are applying.

The first paragraph should be brief, perhaps two or three sentences. In the body of the application letter, be specific, refer to the résumé, and be as brief as you can while still covering your skills and abilities. Include an appropriate closing, such as "Sincerely," and sign the letter.

INDIVIDUAL LEARNING STRATEGIES

Motivation
Ask students to write a journal entry about where they expect to be working in five years and to list the skills and experiences they anticipate having by then. Some students may want to prepare a cover letter and résumé for their ideal job and this journal entry will help them write.

Reading Proficiency
Point out that the cover letter is anachronistic since corporations did not exist in New York in 1670.

English Language Learning
Ask students to share whether cover letters and résumés are common in their native countries.

Special Needs
Make sure students understand words such as *prescient, vocation, international relations,* and *steerage* used in the model cover letter.

Enrichment
Have students write a résumé for a famous person, leaving off the name and address. Put students in small groups and have them take turns reading the résumés. You may want to award points to the student who correctly guesses the famous person's identity. Award 30 points if the identity of the famous person is unmasked when the career objective is read, 25 points if the identity of the famous person is guessed when the educational background is read, 20 points if the identity is of the famous person is guessed when the work experience is read, and so on.

Prewriting

Finding Your Voice. Have students read the Language Arts Survey 3.3, "Register, Tone, and Voice."

Identifying Your Audience. Ask students to read the Language Arts Survey 2.4, "Identifying Your Audience." Encourage students to think about what they know about their prospective employer. For example, if the company values community involvement, students might want to list any volunteer work they have done.

Examining the Model. The professional model is a fictional résumé for Andrew Marvell. Again, the format is correct, but the content is only loosely based on his life.

Marvel's contact information is at the top of the résumé. You'll want to include your phone number and e-mail address if you have one.

The fictional Andew Marvell used heads for basic categories of information such as *career objective, education,* and *work experience.* The résumé contains action verbs: *speak, write,* and *demonstrate* specifically name his skill strengths. The résumé is scrupulously error free.

Finding Your Voice. Use a serious and sincere voice in your letter and résumé. Follow the conventions of style for these pieces to show your serious intent. Avoid being too casual or overly courteous.

Decide which of the following sentences shows a voice that is appropriate here:

> Please consider me for a clerk position in your store for this summer.
>
> I just found out you were looking, so I said to myself why not give it a shot!
>
> It has come to my attention that your excellent company, without a doubt the most outstanding in the field, might consider taking on some additional workers, and it occurs to me, humble as I am, you might please look at my résumé.

Professional Model—Résumé

Andrew Marvell
14 Donne Street
Winestead, Yorkshire, UK

Career Objective:
To become secretary to a private corporation

Education:
Cambridge University, Cambridge, UK
Graduated 1639
Major areas of study: Poetry, Latin, Hebrew
Grade Point Average: 3.9

Work Experience:

1662-1678	British Parliament Member
1657-1662	Assistant to John Milton Latin Secretaryship
1651-1657	Tutor Lord Fairfax's Estate
1647-1651	Clerk City of Winestead, Yorkshire

Skills:
Speak and write fluently in Latin and Hebrew
Declaim eloquently
Script with exemplary calligraphy skills
Demonstrate a strong poetic sensibility

Extracurricular Activities:
Published poet, well traveled throughout the continent, debate team, President of the Metaphysical Poets Society

References:
Available upon request

Prewriting

Identifying Your Audience. Both the résumé and cover letter are designed to help you get hired, so your audience will be a prospective employer. Your first goal is to stay in consideration, to avoid elimination at a glance. Never has attention to surface features been more important. Misspelled words or sloppy work can flag a résumé before its contents are seriously considered. A prospective employer will be impressed with your qualifications only if your letter and résumé make it through the first look.

Writing With a Plan. Your successful job application will include both a cover letter and résumé. Start by brainstorming a list of skills, considering jobs you have had. If you can't immediately list skills associated with a job, do this: Think what you did on the job hour by hour. Write those skills down, using your own paper, on the following Résumé Worksheet.

Use action verbs. A newspaper deliverer not only "delivers the paper," but also "maintains a budget," "collects payments," and "handles customer concerns." Think of the things you are good at, like baseball, or art, or working with children, and then brainstorm the skills you have in that area. Those are the kinds of skills you'll want to list on your résumé.

Student Model—Graphic Organizer

Résumé Worksheet

Job #1	The Taylor Lodge
Actions:	Hauled dimensional lumber
Actions:	Operated hammer
Actions:	Constructed framing
Actions:	
Actions:	

Job #1	The Taylor House
Actions:	Operated lawn mower
Actions:	Mowed yard
Actions:	
Actions:	
Job #1	The Cookie Connoisseur
Actions:	Operated cash register
Actions:	Baked cookies and handled sales
Actions:	
Actions:	

Skills Groups:

Technical Skills	**Construction Skills**
Operated cash register Operated lawn mower	Construction framing Operated hammer Hauled dimensional lumber
Sales skills	**Yard Maintenance skills**
Sold cookies	Mowed yard

Writing a Résumé

A résumé gives the reader a quick snapshot of your skills and abilities. It must include all your contact information—name, address, phone number, and e-mail address, if applicable—at the top of the first page in a format that is easy to read.

Use heads for basic categories of information such as career objective, education, work experience, skills, extracurricular activities, awards, and references. List your work experience with the most recent job first, and work backward. Organize these heads in whatever way you think makes you look best.

If you have little work experience, place it lower on the résumé. Any job can demonstrate good work habits and skills, so include babysitting, paper routes, yard work, and other jobs. You can also include volunteer work.

For references, you may list them or state that they are available upon request. Either way, you should have at least three people who are willing and able to discuss your job skills with a prospective employer. Ideally, use family friends or other adults who have known you for at least a few years. Always check with your references before you include them on a résumé. They should not be surprised if a potential employer calls them.

Proofread your résumé carefully. Double-check dates and other factual information. Keep your résumé looking neat, as it is a reflection of you.

GRAPHIC ORGANIZER 

See the Guided Writing Resource for a blackline master of the Graphic Organizer for this lesson.

Drafting

Encourage students to use their completed Graphic Organizer to help them make sure they are including the appropriate actions and skills in their résumés.

Drafting

To draft your cover letter and résumé, use the examples in this lesson, along with your completed **résumé worksheet.** Collect all necessary information, such as addresses for schools and jobs, dates you attended or were employed, and phone numbers for references. Use the phone book to call previous employers to find out if your supervisor is still working there or to get a zip code.

Student Model—Draft

March 7, 2000
Put your own address here
Pizza Pirate
1000 Arundel Street
Morehead City, North Carolina 28557

Dear Sir or Madam:

I am looking for employment as a cook or food handler with Pizza Pirate. I learned about this position from my friends Lisa Lee and Sarah O'Donnell who currently work for Pizza Pirate. *mention the resume here*

I am a dedicated and persevering person. I learned that from playing basketball and baseball. I can handle multiple priorities at the same time. I learned that while trying to ~~pass the basketball to a closely guarded forward while I was bringing the ball upcourt with two defenders trying to take it away from me~~. Nothing develops handling multiple priorities like ~~being a point guard in basketball~~. I'm sure I would prove a valuable asset to Pizza Pirate. *off track; tangent*

If you would like to interview me, please feel free to contact me at the above address or phone number. ~~I get out of school at 2:45 P.M. and am usually home by 3:15 P.M. Monday through Friday. I can be reached from 7:00 A.M. to 10:00 P.M. on Saturdays. On Sundays you may reach me between 1:00 P.M. and 10:00 P.M.~~ *Too wordy* *after school hours.*

Thank you very much for *your* ~~taking the time and~~ consideration ~~to read this letter and review my résumé~~. *Too humble*

Sincerely yours,
Jesse Taylor *leave more room for signature*

Jesse Taylor
868 Crow Hill Road
Beaufort, NC 28516
919-555-0130

Font is too large

OBJECTIVE: To gain an opportunity to apply my education learned in high school in private industry. *Wordy—too general*

STRENGTHS: Good people skills. ~~Great sense of humor~~. Very quick learner. *Efficient worker* *maybe not relevent to a job.*

EDUCATION:

- East Carteret High School
  Beaufort, North Carolina
  Diploma: June 2002
  Grade Point Average: 2.55

WORK EXPERIENCE:

- April 2000 - September 2000
  The Cookie Connoisseur
  Bak~~ing~~ed cookies and sales *—Split these two actions*
- Operated cash register
- March 2000 - October 2000
  The Taylor House *maintained large yard*
  Mowed yard (~~big yard~~—over 4 acres!)
  Operated and maintained lawn mower *and trimmer*
- June 1999
  The Taylor Lodge
  Did frame ~~Framing~~ construction
  Operated hammer
  Hauled dimensional lumber

SKILLS:

- Speak some Spanish *Action verb? Enjoys physical challenges*
- Very coordinated
- Skilled with a cash register *—Action verb?*
- Very comfortable with people *Relates well with people*

Self- and Peer Evaluation

The following checklists will help you determine if your cover letter and résumé are ready to use.

Cover Letter

- Where does the cover letter expand on items included in the résumé and tailor them to this job's requirements?
- Does the cover letter follow the correct form?
- Is the writing clear?
- Is the letter free of spelling, capitalization, grammar, and punctuation errors?

Résumé

- Is the contact information clearly stated at the top of the résumé? Is it correct?
- Does the résumé contain
  - a clearly stated job objective?
  - a skill assessment related to the job objective?
  - a listing of your work history?
  - a list of your education and training?
- Where have you used action verbs?
- What strengths does the résumé highlight? Are they easy to spot?
- Have you proofread carefully, especially for punctuation errors?
- Have you checked with your references?
- Does the résumé follow a standard one-page format?
- Are headings, subheadings, and text readable and clear?

Self- and Peer Evaluation

Have students use the checklists on this page. A blackline master is available of the self-evaluation checklist in the Guided Writing Resource 12.6. The checklist is intended to act as a student-friendly rubric that should help students identify specific evidence of writing strengths and areas needing improvement. If they have time, students should allow a classmate to read their cover letter and résumé. Peer reviewers may be interested in using proofreader's marks; have them read the Language Arts Survey 2.44, "Using Proofreader's Marks." A handout of the proofreading checklist is available in the Teacher's Resource Kit, Guided Writing Resource Book 2.45.

Language, Grammar, and Style

Action Verbs

Lesson Overview
In this lesson, students will be asked to do the following:

- identify specific action verbs
- use action verbs effectively

Introducing the Skill
You might find a quote that is memorable and have students identify the action verbs that make the thought come alive, for example, "I came, I saw, I conquered."

Previewing the Skill
Refer students to the Language Arts Survey 3.60, "Action Verbs and State of Being Verbs." You might also want students to review the Language Arts Survey 3.59, "Expressers—Verbs."

Practicing the Skill
For additional practice using action verbs, have students work through exercise 3.60 of the Language, Grammar, and Style Resource located in the Teacher's Resource Kit.

Student Model—Revision

Have students compare the Student Model—Draft on pages 558–559 with the final version presented on pages 560–561. Can they think of any other ways to strengthen the writing? Students might discuss whether or not Jesse should include his grade point average.

Language, Grammar, and Style

Action Verbs

Identifying Specific Action Verbs. A verb is either an **action verb** or a **state of being verb**. **Action verbs** refer to actions and to things you can do.

EXAMPLES
speak, write, demonstrate

State of being verbs indicate that something exists. They are all forms of the verb *to be*.

EXAMPLES
am, is, was, had been

Action verbs give your writing a sense of motion, of getting the job done. That is exactly what you want to convey to a prospective employer. State of being verbs lack action and can slow your writing to a crawl. Look at the difference between action and state of being verbs in a resume:

ACTION
Speak and write fluently in Latin and Hebrew

STATE OF BEING VERBS
am a student of Latin and Hebrew

Revising Verb Use. The following sentences from the student model use state of being verbs:

am very coordinated

was in a Spanish class

am comfortable with people

continued on page 561

Student Model—Revision

868 Crow Hill Road
Beaufort, North Carolina 28516

March 7, 2000

Pizza Pirate
1000 Arundel Street
Morehead City, North Carolina 28557

Dear Sir or Madam:

I am looking for employment as a cook or food handler with Pizza Pirate. As you can see from my attached résumé, I have experience baking and selling food products to the public. I learned about this position from my friends Lisa Lee and Sarah O'Donnell who currently work for Pizza Pirate.

I am a dedicated and persevering person. I learned from playing basketball and baseball that I can handle multiple priorities at the same time. Participating in sports after school and keeping up my grades and family life helped me to focus on what is important. I'm sure I would prove a valuable asset to Pizza Pirate.

I would like very much to meet with you and let you get to know me better. If you would like to interview me, please feel free to contact me at the above address or phone number after school hours.

Thank you very much for your consideration.

Sincerely yours,

Jesse Taylor

Jesse Taylor

Jesse Taylor
868 Crow Hill Road
Beaufort, North Carolina 28516
919-555-0130

OBJECTIVE: To gain employment working in the food industry

STRENGTHS: Good people skills. Efficient worker. Quick learner.

EDUCATION:
- East Carteret High School
  Beaufort, North Carolina
  Diploma: June 2002
  Grade Point Average: 2.55

WORK EXPERIENCE:
- April 2000 - September 2000
  The Cookie Connoisseur
  Baked cookies
  Sold over the counter
  Operated cash register
- March 2000 - October 2000
  The Taylor House
  Maintained large lawn
  Operated lawn mower and trimmer
  Trimmed trees
- June 1999
  The Taylor Lodge
  Did frame construction
  Operated hammer
  Hauled dimensional lumber

SKILLS:
- Speak some Spanish
- Enjoy physical challenges
- Relate well with people
- Skilled in use of cash register

EXTRACURRICULAR ACTIVITIES:
- Basketball
- Baseball
- Golf

REFERENCES: Available upon request

To energize these sentences, rewrite them using action verbs. Examine Jesse's revised student model to see how he strengthened his verbs.

Using Action Verbs Effectively. When writing to get a job, use action verbs. If possible, avoid state of being verbs entirely. Go through your cover letter and résumé, identifying state of being verbs and replacing them wherever possible with action verbs. Your employer will read your résumé and get a strong sense that you can get the job done!

Publishing and Presenting

You may want to share your cover letter and résumé with your classmates to get an idea what everyone else did, but ultimately these documents are to help you get a job. Save the résumé on a disk to update as needed. This résumé could be the one you use and reuse for some time to come. Whether you're currently job-hunting or not, save a copy for your portfolio.

Reflecting

Résumés and cover letters are advertisements for you, allowing you to list your strengths and experiences. Most people feel good after collecting this information and getting it down on paper. It can also serve as a road map of where you've been and where you'd like to go. Where would you like your résumé to take you?

Publishing and Presenting

If students choose to include their cover letter and résumé in a portfolio, they should review the Language Arts Survey 2.48, "Maintaining a Writing Portfolio."

INTERNET RESOURCES

For tips on how to format a résumé to be placed online, students can access **RecruitHound** at http://www.recruithound.com/resume_tips.htm.

ADDITIONAL RESOURCES

Unit 6 Resource Book
- Vocabulary Worksheet: Unit 6
- Study Guide: Unit 6 Test
- Unit 6 Test

VOCABULARY DEVELOPMENT

Give students the following exercise.

For ten words in the vocabulary list on page 562, write the part of speech and a brief definition. Then write a different form of the word, its part of speech, and a brief definition.

EXAMPLE
cleft—adj., divided; cleave—vt., to divide

UNIT 6 REVIEW
The Early Seventeenth Century

Words for Everyday Use

Check your knowledge of the following vocabulary words from the selections in this unit. Write short sentences using these words in context to make the meaning clear. To review the definition or usage of a word, refer to the page number listed or the Glossary of Words for Everyday Use.

aureate, 546
baleful, 514
cleft, 497
contrive, 528
covetousness, 503
coy, 516
coyness, 539
dalliance, 517
damask, 517
dandle, 517
disheveled, 516
ethereal, 513
exalt, 518
fettered, 534
filial, 516
guile, 517
hermitage, 535
impious, 513
incorruptible, 527
intermit, 503
invoke, 513
languish, 540
obdurate, 514
omnipotent, 514
perdition, 514
proboscis, 517
promontory, 503
raiment, 529
recourse, 503
revile, 528
ruminating, 517
sanctitude, 516
sans, 547
sovereign, 515
steep, 535
strife, 540
tribulation, 503
undefiled, 527
wrought, 503

Literary Tools

Define the following terms, giving concrete examples of how they are used in the selections in this unit. To review a term, refer to the page number indicated or to the Handbook of Literary Terms.

allegory, 524
allusion, 521
analogy, 502
antihero, 511
concrete poem, 507
couplet, 538
epic, 511
epic hero, 511
hyperbole, 497
image, 533, 538
metaphor, 497, 502, 511, 538
mood, 544
paradox, 500, 507
personification, 500
pun, 521
Puritanism, 524
rhyme scheme, 500, 521
simile, 538, 544
sonnet, 500, 521
stanza, 538
speaker, 507, 521
theme, 502, 507, 533, 544

Reflecting on YOUR READING

Genre Studies

1. **METAPHYSICAL POETRY.** Metaphysical poetry is characterized by elaborate, unusual comparisons called conceits. Find examples of conceits in the following Metaphysical poems from the unit: "Song", Holy Sonnet 10, "Easter Wings," and "To His Coy Mistress." (The last poem, like other works by Marvell, belongs to both the Metaphysical and the Cavalier schools.)

2. **Cavalier Poetry.** Who were the Cavaliers? What subjects did they write about? What literary form did they prefer? What meanings does the word *cavalier* have? (Consult a dictionary if necessary.) Of the Cavalier poets—Herrick, Suckling, and Lovelace—which was the most cavalier in the sense of "carefree"? Which wrote poetry that was quite serious and not at all cavalier in that sense?

3. **Allegory.** What is an allegory? How does an allegory work? In what ways is the medieval play *Everyman,* in Unit 3, similar to Bunyan's *The Pilgrim's Progress*?

4. **Epic Poetry.** An epic poem is grand in scope. What is the subject of Milton's epic *Paradise Lost*? What purpose did Milton have for writing the poem?

Thematic Studies

5. **The *Carpe Diem* Theme.** What do the words *carpe diem* mean? What poems in this unit and in the Selections for Additional Reading best illustrate the *carpe diem* theme? Who is being addressed in each of these poems, and what idea is being conveyed?

Historical and Biographical Studies

6. **Literature of the English Civil War.** The Puritans and the Cavaliers opposed one another in what great conflict? What differing attitudes and beliefs did the Puritans and the Cavaliers have? How are these differences reflected in the literature in this unit?

Reflecting on Your Reading

The prompts in "Reflecting on Your Reading" are suitable as topics for research papers. Refer to the Language Arts Survey 5.18–5.45, "Research Skills." (To evaluate research papers, see the evaluation forms for writing, revising, and proofreading in the Assessment Resource.)

The prompts in "Reflecting on Your Reading" can also be adapted for use as topics for oral reports or debates. Refer students to the Language Arts Survey 4, Speaking and Listening. (To evaluate these projects, see the evaluation forms in the Assessment Resource.)

UNIT SKILLS OUTLINE

Literary Skills and Concepts
Alliteration, 584, 586
Allusion, 572, 576, 578, 582
Anaphora, 584, 586
Anecdote, 627, 632
Argument, 619, 625
Assonance, 572, 576
Biography, 569
Characterization, 607, 612, 627, 632
Connotation, 619, 622
Consonance, 572, 576
Couplet, 614, 617
Critical Essay, 567
Denotation, 619, 622
Diction, 652
Epigram, 614, 617
Epistle, 567
Essay, 567
Fantasy, 599, 605
Heroic Couplet, 614
Historical Prose, 570
Irony, 599, 605, 634, 640
Journal, 588, 596
Mock Epic Poetry, 567
Mock Heroic Poetry, 567
Neoclassicists, 567
Novel, 567, 607, 612
Ode, 578, 582
Parody, 567
Point of View, 588, 596
Register, 652
Rhymed Couplet, 567
Romanticism, 570
Sarcasm, 654
Satire, 567, 599, 634, 640, 649
Slant Rhyme, 572, 576
Thesis, 619, 625
Tone, 653
Verbal Irony, 653

Writing Skills and Concepts
Prose Satire, 649

Language, Grammar, and Style
Avoiding Wordiness, 618
Capitalization, 613
Connotation and Denotation, 626
Correcting Sentence Fragments, 577
Editing for Punctuation Errors, 633
Formal English, 597
Register and Tone, 652
Subject/Verb Agreement, 583
Tone, 606, 652
Vivid Verbs, 587

GOALS/OBJECTIVES

Studying this unit will enable students to

- interpret British Enlightenment literature
- name and describe three major periods of British Enlightenment literature and their main practitioners
- describe the scientific principles behind the Enlightenment
- explain the significance of the Greek and Roman classics to Enlightenment writers
- describe the obstacles faced by women writers during the Restoration and Enlightenment
- define and identify satire and explain the significance of satire as a form of Enlightenment writing
- compose a prose satire
- identify register and tone and use them effectively in their writing

Unit 7 The Restoration and the Eighteenth Century (1660–1785)

Scene from the Beggar's Opera, c.1728–29. William Hogarth. Tate Gallery, London.

The general ORDER, since the whole began,

Is kept in Nature, and is kept in man. . . .

All Nature is but art, unknown to thee;

All chance, direction, which thou canst not see;

All discord, harmony not understood;

All partial evil, universal good:

And, spite of pride, in erring reason's spite,

One truth is clear: Whatever is, is RIGHT.

—Alexander Pope,
from *An Essay on Man*

CROSS-CURRICULAR CONNECTIONS

TEACHING THE MULTIPLE INTELLIGENCES

Continued on page 566

ADDITIONAL RESOURCES

Unit 7 Resource Book
- Selection Check Test 4.7.1
- Selection Test 4.7.2

HISTORICAL NOTE

England's constitutional monarchy was the exception in European politics. On the Continent, absolutist monarchs held sway from 1643 until 1789. France's Louis XIV, XV, and XVI are perhaps the best known examples. With the Glorious Revolution, a powerful Protestant minority assumed rule over the Roman Catholics in Scotland and in Ireland.

TEACHING THE MULTIPLE INTELLIGENCES

(CONT. FROM PAGE 565)

Art Note: *Slave Ship,* 608
Creating a Story Map, 608
Frederick the Great and the Franco-Prussian War, 638

Kinesthetic
Role Playing a Discussion, 573
Staging a Talk-Show Interview, 589
Writing a Satirical Skit, 598
Fable Skits, 615
Philosophical Debate, 635

Interpersonal/Intrapersonal
Comparing Quotations of Pope, Butler, and Hume, 571
Discussing Gender Equality, 573
Women's Rights Discussion, 573
Role Playing a Discussion, 573
Staging a Talk-Show Interview, 589
Discussing Journal and Novel Writing, 591
Discussing Crowd Behavior, 591
Finding Humor in Societal Problems, 598
Gulliver and Modern Politics, 601
Art Note: *Slave Ship,* 608
Opposition to Women Writers, 608
Aphorisms of Pope and Franklin, 615
Court Cases in the News, 620
Interviewing, 628
Discussing Biography Research, 629
Philosophical Debate, 635

Naturalist
Discussing Gender Equality, 573

ArtNote

A Scene from the Beggar's Opera, c.1728–29. Painter and engraver William Hogarth (1697–1764) gained great fame as a satirist of English society. Writer John Gay (1685–1732), a friend of Alexander Pope, was also well known for his satiric wit. In the painting on page 564, Hogarth illustrates a scene from *Gay's Beggar's Opera* (1728), which satirized political corruption and Italian opera. Such satire epitomizes the wit and intellectualism of eighteenth-century literature.

THE RESTORATION AND THE EIGHTEENTH CENTURY

The Monarchy Restored

The **Restoration** in England began in 1660 when **Charles II** became king, ending the Protestant Interregnum. With the monarchy restored and Parliament meeting again, an end to the political differences between Protestants and Catholics was also in sight.

James II succeeded Charles II in 1685. James, like his brother Charles, was Catholic. This fact precipitated what is known as the **Glorious Revolution.** Parliamentary leaders, leery of another Catholic ruler, applied pressure to James II, who abdicated the throne. **William and Mary,** staunch Protestants both, became joint monarchs in 1688. William and Mary ceded Parliament the right to levy taxes, along with other wide-ranging powers, and so moved the country toward a form of government known as **constitutional monarchy.**

Following the deaths of William and Mary, Anne, the sister of Mary, became queen. Among **Queen Anne's** achievements was the creation in 1707 of the nation of Great Britain, formed by the union of England and Scotland. Anne was succeeded by **George I** in 1714. George's prime minister, Robert Walpole, formed the cabinet system of ministers chosen from Parliament to aid the monarch.

Science, Philosophy, and Reason

Amid this political upheaval, philosophers, writers, and scientists were defining new ways of looking at the world in which they lived. By discovering the laws of motion and gravitation that governed the movements of heavenly and earthly bodies, **Sir Isaac Newton** had revealed an orderly, clockwork universe regulated by rational principles. This idea of a natural order discoverable by reason attracted many adherents. People came to believe that the human intellect could discover natural laws that would solve social, political, and economic problems. Because of this emphasis on the power of intellect over feeling, the period is sometimes called the **Enlightenment,** or **Age of Reason.**

Literary Events

➤ = British Events

1664. Jean Racine publishes his play *Phædra*
1664. Jean-Baptiste Poquelin Molière's play *Tartuffe* is first performed
➤1667. John Milton publishes *Paradise Lost*
➤1668. John Dryden is appointed Poet Laureate
➤1678. John Bunyan publishes *The Pilgrim's Progress*
➤1681. John Dryden publishes *Absalom and Achitophel*

1660 | 1665 | 1670 | 1675 | 1680

Historical Events

➤1660. Monarchy is restored under King Charles II
➤1660–1685. King Charles II reigns
1664. English take over town of Nieuw Amsterdam from Dutch and rename it New York
➤1666. Great Fire burns 80 percent of London
1667. Qing dynasty begins in China
1669. Rembrandt van Rijn dies
1672. Ann Bradstreet dies
➤1673. Test Act compels Anglicanism
➤1674. John Milton dies
➤1678. Popish Plot is uncovered; persecution of Catholics is renewed
1681. The dodo bird is hunted to extinction

THEMATIC CURRENTS

Use the following selections to explore these themes with your students.

Political and Social Commentary
- from *Gulliver's Travels,* 598
- from Oroonoko, 607
- "A Brief to Free a Slave," 619
- from *Candide,* 643
- "A Modest Proposal," 634

Reason
- "A Song for St. Cecilia's Day," 578
- Couplets from *An Essay on Criticism,* 615
- from *A Dictionary of the English Language,* 619
- from *The Life of Samuel Johnson, LL. D.,* 627
- from *The Spectator,* 647

Women Writers
- "The Introduction . . . ," 572
- "Pressed by the Moon . . . ," 584
- from *Oroonoko,* 607
- "To All Writing Ladies," 642
- "Love Armed," 642
- "The Lover . . . ," 643

Among the influential figures of the Enlightenment were the German philosopher and writer **Immanuel Kant** (1724–1804); the English doctor, philosopher, and writer **John Locke,** (1632–1704); and the Scottish philosopher and economist **Adam Smith** (1723–1790).

Kant's philosophy held that knowledge is a combination of sensation and understanding, a synthesis of sensual perception and the principles, or laws, of thought. Locke, who has been called the "founder of the analytic philosophy of mind," published the *Two Treatises of Government,* which disputed the divine right of kings and popularized the idea of **"natural rights."** The economist Smith, in his book *The Wealth of Nations,* proposed that even economics is governed by a system of natural laws that work in an ordered and rational way, if not interfered with by governments and monopolies.

Charles II, c.1600s. Philippe de Champaigne. Cleveland Museum of Art.

Neoclassical Literature

In their search for rationality and order, many writers of the Enlightenment rediscovered the classic works of the ancient Greeks and Romans and emulated them. For this reason, they are called **Neoclassicists.** The Neoclassical literature of the eighteenth century made use of classical forms and allusions and promoted ideals of harmony, tradition, and reason. Popular forms of Neoclassical writing included the **essay, rhymed couplets, satire, parody,** and the formal letter, or **epistle.** The first **novels** were also written during this period. The literature of the period is notable for its wittiness and its emphasis on social interactions.

There are three major divisions, or periods, of Enlightenment literature: the **Age of Dryden, the Age of Pope,** and **the Age of Johnson.** The Age of Dryden (1660–1700) began with the restoration of the monarchy and ended with the death of writer **John Dryden** (1631–1700). Dryden wrote many plays, poems, and essays. His satirical poem "Mac Flecknoe" appears to be an epic because of its grand scope and lofty language, but it actually ridicules its so-called "heroes." This satiric style is called **mock heroic** poetry or **mock epic** poetry. Dryden's series of essays on literary criticism, including *An Essay of Dramatic Poesy,* presaged a new type of writing, the **critical essay,** which attempts to evaluate works of literature.

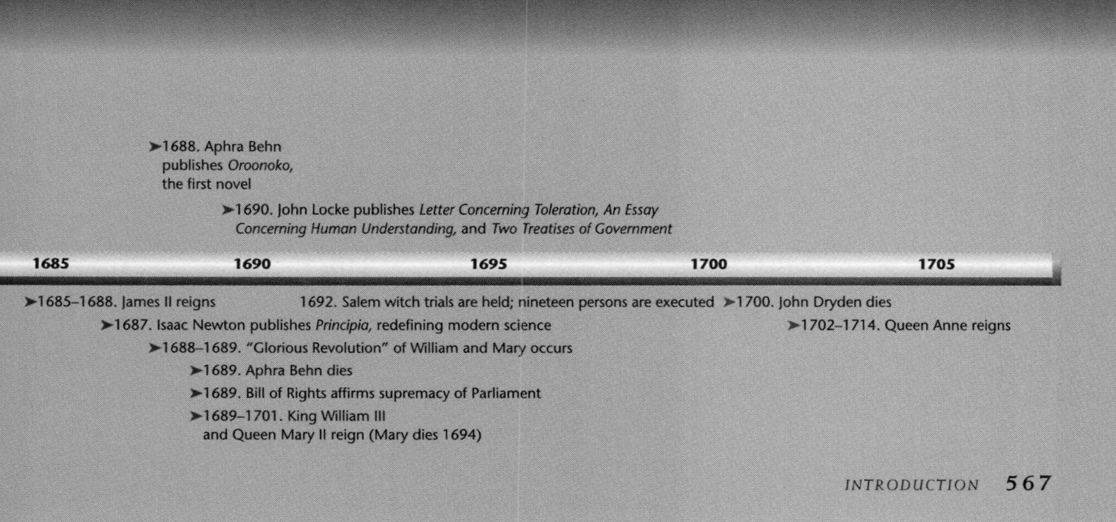

➤1688. Aphra Behn publishes *Oroonoko,* the first novel
➤1690. John Locke publishes *Letter Concerning Toleration, An Essay Concerning Human Understanding,* and *Two Treatises of Government*
1685
1690
1695
1700
1705
➤1685–1688. James II reigns
1692. Salem witch trials are held; nineteen persons are executed
➤1700. John Dryden dies
➤1687. Isaac Newton publishes *Principia,* redefining modern science
➤1702–1714. Queen Anne reigns
➤1688–1689. "Glorious Revolution" of William and Mary occurs
➤1689. Aphra Behn dies
➤1689. Bill of Rights affirms supremacy of Parliament
➤1689–1701. King William III and Queen Mary II reign (Mary dies 1694)

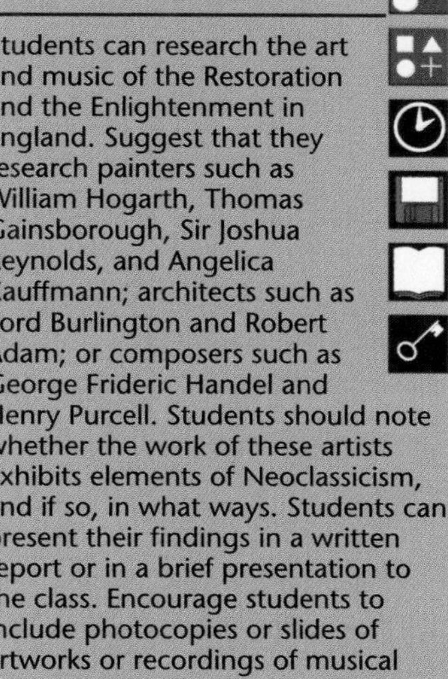

CROSS-CURRICULAR ACTIVITIES

Students can research the art and music of the Restoration and the Enlightenment in England. Suggest that they research painters such as William Hogarth, Thomas Gainsborough, Sir Joshua Reynolds, and Angelica Kauffmann; architects such as Lord Burlington and Robert Adam; or composers such as George Frideric Handel and Henry Purcell. Students should note whether the work of these artists exhibits elements of Neoclassicism, and if so, in what ways. Students can present their findings in a written report or in a brief presentation to the class. Encourage students to include photocopies or slides of artworks or recordings of musical compositions.

Quotables

"Two things fill the mind with awe, the more often and the more seriously reflection concentrates upon them: The starry heaven above me and the moral law within me."

—Immanuel Kant

"Here lies a great and mighty king whose promise none relies on;/He never said a foolish thing,/ Nor ever did a wise one."

—John Wilmot, Earl of Rochester

"This is very true: for my words are my own, and my actions are my ministers."

—King Charles II

LITERARY CURRENTS

Use the following selections to explore these techniques with your students.

Couplet
- Couplets from *An Essay on Criticism,* 615

Essay
- "To All Writing Ladies," 642
- "A Modest Proposal," 643
- from *The Spectator,* 647

Journal
- from *The Diary of Samuel Pepys,* 588
- from *The Life of Samuel Johnson, LL. D.,* 627

Irony
- "The Introduction," 572
- from *Gulliver's Travels,* 598
- from *A Dictionary of the English Language,* 619
- "A Modest Proposal," 643
- "A Short Song . . . ," 648

CROSS-CURRICULAR ACTIVITIES

APPLIED ARTS AND SCIENCES. Students can begin keeping a computer journal as a record of daily events. Encourage students to record personal as well as factual material. By the end of the unit, allow students the option of sharing their journals.

BIOGRAPHICAL NOTE

Aphra Behn was also a noted playwright of Restoration drama. Among her eighteen plays, the best are *The Rover* (1679) and *The Lucky Chance* (1686). In both plays the witty female protagonists must come to terms with the pitfalls of love and marriage.

Quotables

"Plots, true or false, are necessary things,

To raise up commonwealths and ruin kings."

—John Dryden

Queen Anne.

Drama made a comeback during this period. London theaters closed by the repressive Puritan government were reopened by Charles II. Refurbished and offering new forms of drama, the theaters became very popular with the middle and upper classes. Dryden's *All For Love,* a tragedy about Antony and Cleopatra, drew large audiences.

Today, many literary historians consider Dryden to have written the first modern prose. Other notable prose works of the time include **Samuel Pepys's** *Diary,* a journal of daily events in Pepys's life from 1660 to 1669, and **Aphra Behn's** *Oroonoko* (1688), a prose work about slavery in the West Indies. *Oroonoko* is one of the first (some argue *the* first) English **novels,** or extended works of prose fiction.

The Age of Pope (1700–1750), also called the **Augustan Age,** was the peak period of Neoclassicism. The work of **Alexander Pope** (1688–1744), an admired poet of his time, was representative of the style, employing wit, rationality, and balance in his poetry. Pope's *The Rape of the Lock,* is a mock epic that satirizes the "battle of the sexes." Pope's *An Essay on Criticism,* a long **verse essay** in **heroic couplets,** exerted tremendous influence on literary criticism, and many well-known aphorisms still in use today come from it.

Pope was a member of a salon society in London that included **Jonathan Swift, Joseph Addison,** and **Sir Richard Steele.** Swift's satire was pointed and sharp, in contrast to Pope's, which was less barbed but equally devastating. Swift's *Gulliver's Travels* is famous for its satirization of the European political and intellectual landscape. Addison and Steele collaborated on *The Tattler and The Spectator,* groundbreaking examples of that new literary medium, the **periodical**. The most talented literary figures of the day contributed reflective **essays** in literature, art, politics, and society to the periodicals. **Daniel Defoe** wrote a major work that vies

LITERARY EVENTS

➤ = British Events

➤1710. First English copyright law is passed

➤1711. Alexander Pope publishes *An Essay on Criticism*

➤1719. Daniel Defoe publishes *Robinson Crusoe*

➤1726. Jonathan Swift publishes *Gulliver's Travels*

1710 | 1715 | 1720 | 1725 | 1730

HISTORICAL EVENTS

➤1707. Act of Union unites Scotland and England, creating Great Britain

➤1714–1727. King George I reigns

1715. King Louis XIV (the Sun King) of France dies; the reign of King Louis XV of France begins

➤1727. Sir Isaac Newton dies

➤1727–1760. King George II reigns

➤1729. John and Charles Wesley found Methodism at Oxford

with Behn's for the title of first novel in the English language, *Robinson Crusoe* (1719).

The Restoration period is also called the **Augustan Age** because many writers openly imitated Greek and Roman literature. The term *Augustan* is a reference comparing King George I to Emperor Augustus Cæsar of Rome. Indeed, London was considered the center of the literary universe, much as ancient Rome was during the days of Augustus, Virgil, and Horace.

The Age of Johnson (1750–1798), named after **Samuel Johnson** (1709–1784), the most famous writer of his generation, bridges the span between the Enlightenment and the Romantic Age. During this time some writers began to move away from the ideals of Neoclassicism toward the freer, more emotional, more natural style of the Romantics.

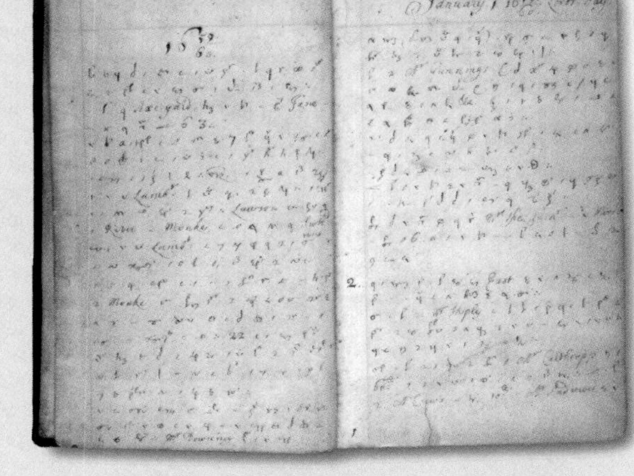
Samuel Pepys's Diary. Masters and Fellows, Magdalene College, Cambridge.

Johnson, master of many forms of writing, including poetry, literary criticism, and prose fiction, is most renowned for his *Dictionary of the English Language.* Published in 1755, this was the first authoritative, definitive dictionary of English. Nine years in the making, the dictionary contained over 40,000 words and 114,000 quotations.

Johnson started his own periodical, *The Rambler,* which contained essays, allegories, and literary criticism written primarily by himself. In his later years he was an eminent figure in literary circles and founded a literary club. In May of 1763, he met **James Boswell** (1740–1795), whose *Life of Samuel Johnson, LL. D.,* presented the actions and opinions of the great man. Boswell's book is considered the first great modern English **biography.**

1732. Benjamin Franklin publishes the first *Poor Richard's Almanack* and begins publishing *Philadelphia Zeitung,* the first foreign-language newspaper in the American colonies

➤1742. G. F. Handel's oratorio *Messiah* is performed

1751. Denis Diderot publishes Volume I of *Encyclopédie*

➤1755. Dr. Samuel Johnson completes his *Dictionary*

1735 | 1740 | 1745 | 1750 | 1755

1735–1753. Carl Linnaeus publishes a systematic classifications of plants, founds science of botany

1741. Antonio Vivaldi (composer) dies

➤1744. Alexander Pope dies

➤1745. Jonathan Swift dies

1750. Benjamin Frankin proves that lightning is an electrical phenomenon

1750. Johann Sebastian Bach (composer) dies

BIOGRAPHICAL NOTE

The term "bluestockings" was the label applied to a group of intellectual women who met in London in the latter part of the eighteenth century. Headed by critic and letter writer **Elizabeth Montagu** (1720–1800), these women met to discuss intellectual and social issues, including education and women's traditional role in society. Although most meetings were attended by women, some men, including Samuel Johnson and James Boswell, attended the discussions. The term "bluestocking" referred to inexpensive stockings worn by some members on informal occasions; the term was sometimes used derisively about any woman who dared to pursue intellectual activities.

LITERARY TECHNIQUE

During the late seventeenth century, British writers developed the **novel.** The novel can be seen as resulting, in part, from the rise of the bourgeoisie as a class. The novel neither borrowed from traditional sources for content nor celebrated kings. Rather, it celebrated the "common" man and woman. Various works qualify for the title "The First Novel," depending on how one defines the idea. Besides Behn, Defoe, and Swift, important early novelists include Samuel **Richardson** (1689–1761), **Henry Fielding** (1707–1754), **Tobias Smollett** (1721–1771), and **Laurence Sterne** (1713–1768).

CROSS-CURRICULAR ACTIVITIES

History. The Great Fire of London lasted from September 2 to September 5, 1666. It remains the worst fire in the history of London. More than thirteen thousand homes and many important civic buildings were burned. People fled from the city to the countryside and swarmed the river Thames.

- Have students investigate how the fire started, how it spread, and why it was so destructive.
- Have students research or reason about what life was like for Londoners during the next few months after the fire. Where did they live? How did they eat? What work did they do? As part of their research, students can investigate the results of fires or other disasters in other parts of the world for comparison. You might inform students that today governments provide disaster relief for communities that meet with misfortune. Some students may wish to consider what, if any, assistance was available to people after the Great Fire of London. How did people manage to rebuild the city?

SELECTION CHECK TEST 4.7.1 WITH ANSWERS

Checking Your Reading

Key Political Figures

G 1. saw knowledge as a combination of sensory perception and logical thought

F 2. described the universe as orderly and regulated by rational principles

A 3. Reopened London theaters that had been closed by the Puritan government

D 4. gave Parliament many powers, including the right to levy taxes

E 5. abdicated the throne, paving the way for the Glorious Revolution

a. Charles II
b. Queen Anne
c. Adam Smith
d. William and Mary
e. James II
f. Sir Isaac Newton
g. Immanuel Kant

Literary Developments

1. Why was this period of time known as the Age of Reason? **Responses**

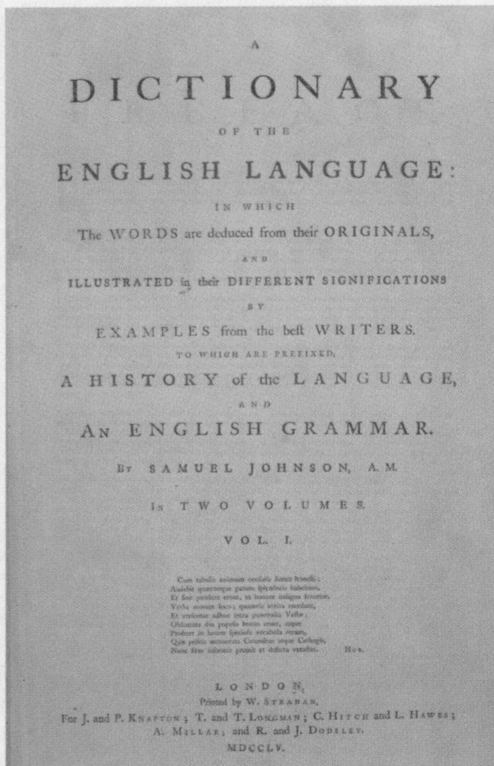
A

DICTIONARY

OF THE

ENGLISH LANGUAGE:

IN WHICH

The WORDS are deduced from their ORIGINALS,

AND

ILLUSTRATED in their DIFFERENT SIGNIFICATIONS

BY

EXAMPLES from the best WRITERS.

TO WHICH ARE PREFIXED,

A HISTORY of the LANGUAGE,

AND

AN ENGLISH GRAMMAR.

By SAMUEL JOHNSON, A.M.

In TWO VOLUMES.

VOL. I.

LONDON,
Printed by W. Strahan,
For J. and P. Knapton; T. and T. Longman; C. Hitch and L. Hawes;
A. Millar; and R. and J. Dodsley.
MDCCLV.

Title page of the English Dictionary by Dr. Samuel Johnson, 1755.

During the Restoration, theatrical productions flourished, with **Oliver Goldsmith's** *She Stoops to Conquer* and **Richard Sheridan's** *The School for Scandal* standing out among the most popular comedies. In other areas of literature, **Edward Gibbon's** *The Decline and Fall of the Roman Empire* was a landmark of **historical prose.** Other notable works of the period include the following novels: **Lawrence Sterne's** *Tristram Shandy* (1759), **Henry Fielding's** *Tom Jones* (1794), and **Tobias (George) Smollett's** *Humphry Clinker* (1771).

Toward the end of the Enlightenment, the progress achieved through the scientific and technological advances of the Industrial Revolution began to appear less positive. Many people were overworked in the new factories and mills. Social conditions in the cities and towns deteriorated, and the price of progress began to be questioned. In reaction to these changes, some philosophers and literary figures turned from the rational and orderly ideals of Neoclassicism to the intense, emotional ideals that would become **Romanticism.**

Literary Events

➤ = British Events

1759. Voltaire publishes *Candide*

1774. Johann Wolfgang von Goethe publishes *The Sorrows of Young Werther*

1781. Immanuel Kant publishes *Critique of Pure Reason*

➤1784. Charlotte Smith publishes the first of eleven editions of *Elegiac Sonnets and Other Essays*

1760 — 1765 — 1770 — 1775 — 1780 — 1785

Historical Events

➤1759. Georg Friedrich Handel, composer, dies

➤1760–1820. Reign of King George III

1762. Jean-Jacques Rousseau publishes *The Social Compact*

➤1769. James Watt patents steam engine

1770. Boston Massacre

➤1770. Thomas Gainsborough paints *The Blue Boy*

➤1774–1779. Joseph Priestly and Antoine Lavoisier discover oxygen

1775. American Revolutionary War begins

➤1776. Adam Smith publishes *The Wealth of Nations*

1778. Voltaire (François Marie Arouet) dies

➤1784. Samuel Johnson dies

1784. Phyllis Wheatley dies

SELECTION CHECK TEST 4.7.1 WITH ANSWERS (cont.)

will vary, but should suggest that there was an emphasis on the power of the intellect.

2. What literature did the Neoclassicists study and emulate? **They emulated ancient Greek and Roman literature.**
3. During the Augustan Age, what place was considered the center of the literary universe? **London was considered the center of the literary universe.**
4. What stylistic elements were favored by Neoclassicists (and exemplified by Pope)? **Neoclassicists favored wit, rationality, balance and eschewed stylistic flourishes.**
5. What negative effects of progress were evident by

Continued on page 571

Echoes

Eighteenth-Century England

Two things fill the mind with awe, the more often and the more seriously reflection concentrates upon them: The starry heaven above me and the moral law within me.

—Immanuel Kant

The rest to some faint meaning
make pretense,
But Sh—— never deviates into
sense.
Some beams of wit on other souls
may fall,
Strike thro', and make a lucid interval;
But Sh——'s genuine night admits no ray,
His rising fogs prevail upon the day.

—John Dryden, from "Mac Flecknoe" (writing about the poet Thomas Shadwell)

What makes all doctrines plain and clear?
About two hundred pounds a year.
And that which was prov'd true before,
Prove false again?—Two hundred more.

—Samuel Butler, from "Hudibras"

But let us strive to build us Tombs while we live, of Noble, Honourable, and good Actions, at least harmlesse;

That though our bodies dye,
Our Names may live to after memory.

—Margaret Cavendish

Reason is, and ought to be, the slave of the passions, and can never pretend to any other office than to serve and obey them.

—David Hume, *Treatise on: Human Nature*

Why did I write? What sin to me
unknown Dipped me in ink, my parents', or my own?

—Alexander Pope, from "Epistle to Dr. Arbuthnot"

A favor well bestowed is almost as great an honor to him who confers it as to him who receives it.

—Richard Steele, from *The Spectator*

Books, like men their authors, have no more than one way of coming into the world, but there are then thousand to go out of it, and return no more.

—Jonathan Swift, from *A Tale of a Tub*

Satire should, like a polished razor keen,
Wound with a touch that's scarcely felt or seen.

—Lady Mary Wortley Montagu, from *To the Imitator of the First Satire of Horace,* book II

Curiosity is one of the permanent and certain characteristics of a vigorous mind.

—Samuel Johnson, from *The Rambles*

If a man does not make new acquaintances as he advances through life, he will soon find himself left alone. A man, sir, should keep his friendship in constant repair.

—Samuel Johnson

A Scene from the Beggar's Opera **[Detail],**
William Hogarth.

SELECTION CHECK TEST 4.7.1 WITH ANSWERS (CONT. FROM PAGE 570)

the end of the Age of Reason? **Responses will vary, but could include that people were overworked in factories and mills or that the social conditions in towns were deteriorating.**

Literary Forms of the Age of Reason

<u>E</u> 1. *The Tattler, The Spectator,* and *The Rambler* are examples of this new medium

<u>G</u> 2. Boswell's *Life of Samuel Johnson, LL. D.* is the first modern-English example

<u>B</u> 3. satirized the gods and goddesses, grand scope, and lofty language of epics

<u>A</u> 4. these formal letters were popular during the Age of Reason

<u>C</u> 5. a type of writing that evaluates works of literature

a. epistle
b. mock heroic poetry
c. critical essay
d. novel
e. periodical
f. historical prose
g. biography

LITERARY TECHNIQUE

METAPHOR. A **metaphor** is a figure of speech in which one thing is spoken or written about as if it were another. Dryden used metaphor to satirize Shadwell.

1. What metaphor did Dryden use to describe wit or sense?
2. What metaphor describes Shadwell's lack of sense?

Answers

1. Dryden used the metaphor of sun or light for wit; the speaker describes sense as "beams of wit."
2. He used the metaphor of darkness or night to describe Shadwell's lack of sense; the speaker says that Shadwell's "genuine night admits no ray," or that Shadwell is incapable of perceiving wit.

ADDITIONAL QUESTIONS AND ACTIVITIES

Students in small groups can compare the ideas represented in the quotations from Pope, Butler, and Hume. Remind students of the importance of irony, wit, and reason in these writings. Students may want to create a comparison and contrast chart to analyze the quotations.

ADDITIONAL RESOURCES

UNIT 7 RESOURCE BOOK
- Selection Worksheet 7.1
- Selection Check Test 4.7.3
- Selection Test 4.7.4
- Language, Grammar, and Style Resource 3.33

GRAPHIC ORGANIZER

Word 1	Word 2	Assonance or Consonance
house	use	consonance
returned	mourned	consonance
join	refine	consonance
declare	war	consonance
prolong	gone	assonance
on	song	assonance

READER'S JOURNAL

Students should note whether these social customs are defined by age, gender, or other circumstances. Are there any social customs that students find personally limiting? How does it feel to want to do something that "just isn't done"?

VOCABULARY FROM THE SELECTION

debarred
diffusive
insipid
retired

Literary TOOLS

ALLUSION. An **allusion** is a a rhetorical technique in which reference is made to a person, event, object, or work from history or literature. As you read, note the Biblical allusions Finch makes in this selection.

SLANT RHYME, ASSONANCE, AND CONSONANCE. A **slant rhyme** is a substitution of assonance or consonance for true rhyme. **Assonance** is the repetition of vowel sounds in stressed syllables that end with different consonant sounds. **Consonance** is the use in stressed syllables of identical final consonants preceded by vowels with different sounds. Slant rhymes are also called half rhymes, near rhymes, or off rhymes. Keep a chart of the slant rhymes you find in this poem.

Word 1	Word 2	Assonance or Consonance
house	use	consonance

Reader's Journal

Write about a social custom or rule with which you disagree.

"The Introduction"

BY ANNE FINCH

About the AUTHOR

Anne Finch, Countess of Winchilsea (1661–1720), a perceptive and skilled poet, circulated much of her work in manuscript form before finally publishing a book in 1713. Her reluctance to make her literary talents widely known was due to the often hostile treatment of women writers in her day. Finch came from a family of staunch supporters of the Stuart king James II. Anne was wealthy and well-educated, and in 1683 she went to court to serve as a Maid of Honor to Mary Modena, Duchess of York. In 1684 she married Heneage Finch, another member of the court. When King James was exiled in the late 1680s, Anne, Heneage, and her family were themselves in political exile for a time. Then Heneage's distant cousin, the Earl of Winchilsea, died, leaving him an elegant estate. He and Anne were able to assume a life of luxury. Gradually becoming more open about her poetry, Anne wrote pieces that celebrated the beauty and pleasures of rural life. The countryside around Eastwell where the Finches lived represented to her a retreat from a world that she as a talented woman found quite limiting. Today, much of her work is difficult to find, as no complete collection exists. However, the works that have survived have been admired by many subsequent writers and critics, including William Wordsworth and Virginia Woolf.

About the SELECTION

"The Introduction" is the first selection in Finch's first and only book of poetry, *Miscellany Poems on Several Occasions, Written by a Lady,* published in 1713. This thoughtful poem expresses Finch's feelings about the lost opportunities of women in a world that treats them as mindless persons interested only in fashion, dances, and the like. In the poem, Finch comments on the experiences and ambitions of women through the ages by making Biblical references and by emphasizing the role that learned prejudices play in hindering the development of female potential.

GOALS/OBJECTIVES

Studying this lesson will enable students to
- empathize with a female perspective in the Enlightenment period
- describe Anne Finch's literary accomplishments and explain the historical significance of her poetry
- define *allusion, slant rhyme, assonance,* and *consonance* and recognize these techniques in a poem
- write an essay comparing the work of Anne Finch to that of Mary Wollstonecraft and Virginia Woolf
- correct sentence fragments
- answer sentence-completion questions on a test

Thalia, c.1700s. Daniel Gardner.

The Introduction

Anne Finch

Did I my lines intend for public view,
How many censures[1] would their faults pursue,
Some would, because such words they do affect,
Cry they're insipid, empty, uncorrect.
And many have attained, dull and untaught,
The name of wit only by finding fault.
True judges might condemn their want of wit,
And all might say they're by a woman writ.
Alas! a woman that attempts the pen
Such an intruder on the rights of men,
Such a presumptuous creature is esteemed,
The fault can by no virtue be redeemed.
They tell us we mistake our sex and way;

What must some people of Finch's day have thought of women poets? Why, according to these people, should women not write?

1. **censures.** Criticisms

Words For Everyday Use

in • sip • id (in sip´id) *adj.,* not exciting or interesting. *We left the theater in the middle of the insipid movie because we were bored.*

ANSWER TO GUIDED READING QUESTION

1. Some people thought a female poet was presumptuous to attempt a man's job. According to these people, a woman shouldn't write because it makes her less attractive and wastes her time ("cloud[s] [her] beauty and exhaust[s] [her] time," line 17).

INDIVIDUAL LEARNING STRATEGIES

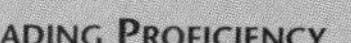

Motivation
Encourage students to discuss the status of gender equality today. Do they feel that gender bias still exists in schools, in the workplace, and elsewhere? What would they like to see changed in the attitudes of people in American society?

Reading Proficiency
Explain to students that the syntax, or word order, is often switched around in poetry. For example, if the first two lines of the poem were reordered to sound more like typical speech, they would read as follows: "[If] I did intend my lines for public view, / How many censures would pursue their faults[!]" Then, have the students break into pairs and read the poem aloud to each other, interpreting each line as they go. Also, review the footnotes with students before they read the poem.

English Language Learning
Encourage non-native students to enter a discussion of women's rights as suggested in the Motivation activity above. Students might be able to share information about the status of women in their native countries. Give students the following additional vocabulary:
intend—plan
pursue—seek
affect—influence
attain—gain through effort
condemn—convict
presumptuous—too bold
esteemed—valued highly
redeem—deliver from sin
enquire—seek information
excel—be better or greater than
convey—make known
refine—free from imperfection
prolong—lengthen or extend

INDIVIDUAL LEARNING STRATEGIES (cont.)

Special Needs
Ask students to create a cluster chart listing the arguments people have given to show why women should not write. Then, students in pairs or small groups can role play a discussion between Anne Finch and her contemporary critics, who might be men or women. Discussion should focus on the rights of women writers.

Enrichment
Students can research women writers who would support Finch's theory of "women that excelled of old." Encourage students to share their information in short reports to the class. Students may wish to research the lives and works of early women writers such as Margery Kempe, Queen Elizabeth I, or Aemilia Lanyer.

ANSWER TO GUIDED READING QUESTION

1. In the past, women have been viewed as possessing wit and poetry. They were viewed as being capable of more than simply the art of managing a house.

CROSS-CURRICULAR ACTIVITIES

History. As an alternative to the Enrichment activity on page 573, students may also examine the role of warrior women in history, such as Joan of Arc or Boadicea, as well as "women that excelled of old" in the mythologies or oral traditions of various cultures. Examples include the Greek goddess Athena, the African-American folk hero Annie Christmas, and the Chinese woman warrior Fa Mu Lan. As a third option, they may examine the tradition of the heroic woman in literature; some examples include Juliana and Judith in Old English literature and Bradamonte in Ludovico Ariosto's romance, *Orlando Furioso*.

SELECTION CHECK TEST 4.7.3 WITH ANSWERS

Checking Your Reading

1. What in a woman was thought to "cloud...beauty" and "exhaust...time"? **Intellectual accomplishment was thought to cloud a woman's beauty and be a waste of her time.**
2. How was David greeted when he returned from war? **He was treated as a hero.**
3. Who "[led] fainting Israel on"? **Deborah led Israel.**
4. Women are not nature's fools, but the fools of what? **Women are education's fools.**
5. What does the speaker say she was never meant to have? **She was never meant to have laurel leaves, or honors.**

Vocabulary in Context
Fill each blank with the most appropriate word from the *Words for Everyday Use* from "The Introduction." You may have to change the tense of the word.

debarred diffusive retired insipid

1. My cousin, an accountant, **retired** to a small cabin for a vacation after tax season.

Good breeding, fashion, dancing, dressing, play
Are the accomplishments we should desire;
To write, or read, or think, or to enquire
Would cloud our beauty, and exhaust our time,
And interrupt the conquests of our prime;[2]
Whilst the dull manage of a servile house[3]
Is held by some our utmost art, and use.
 Sure 'twas not ever[4] thus, nor are we told
Fables, of women that excelled of old;
To whom, by the diffusive hand of Heaven
Some share of wit and poetry was given.
On that glad day on which the Ark[5] returned,
The holy pledge for which the land had mourned,
The joyful tribes attend it on the way,
The Levites[6] do the sacred charge convey,
Whilst various instruments before it play;
Here holy virgins in the concert join,
The louder notes to soften and refine,
And with alternate verse complete the hymn divine.
Lo! the young poet,[7] after God's own heart,
By Him inspired, and taught the Muses' art,[8]
Returned from conquest, a bright chorus meets,
That sing his slain ten thousand in the streets.
In such loud numbers they his acts declare,
Proclaim the wonders of his early war,
That Saul[9] upon the vast applause does frown,
And feels its mighty thunder shake the crown.
What, can the threatened judgment now prolong?
Half of the kingdom is already gone;
The fairest half, whose influence guides the rest,

How have women been viewed in the past?

2. **prime.** Maturity
3. **servile house.** Home employing servants
4. **ever.** Always
5. **Ark.** Chest holding the Ten Commandments. Its return signifies the return of the Hebrews to the Temple in Jerusalem.
6. **Levites.** Jewish priestly class
7. **the young poet.** David, composer of psalms
8. **Muses' art.** In Greek mythology, the Muses inspired creative activity.
9. **Saul.** First king of Israel

Words for Everyday Use

dif • fu • sive (di fyo͞o´ siv) *adj.*, causing diffusion or scattering. *One of the science fair projects demonstrates the diffusive qualities of the prism.*

SELECTION CHECK TEST 4.7.3 WITH ANSWERS (cont.)

2. Jacqueline finds small talk **insipid**, and she avoids it whenever possible.
3. We were told that as students we were **debarred** from some parts of the courthouse.

Literary Tools
Fill in the blanks using the following terms. You may not use every term, and you may use some terms more than once.

allusion slant rhyme assonance consonance meter

1. The repetition of vowel sounds, with differing consonants, is known as **assonance**.
2. This poem includes a long biblical **allusion**.
3. Word pairs such as *house/use* and *declare/war* illustrate **slant rhyme**.

Have David's empire o'er their hearts confessed.
A woman[10] here leads fainting Israel on,
She fights, she wins, she triumphs with a song,
Devout, majestic, for the subject fit,
And far above her arms exalts her wit,
Then to the peaceful, shady palm withdraws,
And rules the rescued nation with her laws.
How are we fallen, fallen by mistaken rules?
And education's, more than nature's fools,
Debarred from all improvements of the mind,
And to be dull, expected and designed;[11]
And if some one would soar above the rest,
With warmer fancy and ambition pressed,[12]
So strong th' opposing faction still appears.
The hopes to thrive can ne'er outweigh the fears.
Be cautioned then my Muse, and still retired;
Nor be despised, aiming to be admired;
Conscious of wants, still with contracted wing,
To some few friends and to thy sorrows sing;
For groves of laurel[13] thou wert never meant;
Be dark enough thy shades, and be thou there content. ■

According to the speaker, what is the state of women's education in her time? What happens if a woman soars above the rest?

10. **A woman.** Deborah, an Israelite leader
11. **designed.** Required
12. **With . . . pressed.** Driven by stronger desire and ambition
13. **laurel.** The leaves of the laurel tree were used to bestow honors.

WORDS FOR EVERYDAY USE

de • barred (dē bärd) *part.*, kept from some right or privilege; excluded. *All reporters have been debarred from the courtroom.*

re • tired (ri tīrd´) *adj.*, withdrawn or apart from; secluded. *The hermit lives a retired existence in a remote mountain cabin.*

Respond *to the* SELECTION

Suppose you lived in Finch's day and were trying to talk someone into publishing this piece. What might you say to convince that person of the piece's value?

ANSWER TO GUIDED READING QUESTION

1. Women's education is severely limited, designed to keep the female mind "dull." If a woman soars above the rest, she is strongly opposed.

HISTORICAL NOTE

Finch's reference to her Muse (line 58) is typical of Neoclassical poetry, which sought to emulate ancient Greek and Roman literature. The nine Muses of Greek mythology were the daughters of Zeus and Mnemosyne, the goddess of memory. Each Muse was linked to a specific art, and poets often called upon a particular Muse for inspiration. (See the Handbook of Literary Terms for a complete definition of *Muse*.)

RESPOND TO THE SELECTION

As students consider their responses, they should think about the arguments they are likely to receive against publishing the piece. Students can roleplay this discussion in pairs.

ANSWERS TO INVESTIGATE, INQUIRE, IMAGINE

Recall

1a. Finch feels the general public would sharply criticize her poem.

2a. Society believes the "proper" activities of women are "fashion, dancing, dressing, play."

3a. The poet states that her Muse should not aim to be admired because she was never meant for groves of laurel, or praise.

Interpret

1b. People in Finch's world might believe that a woman poet is "presumptuous" because poetry was considered the occupation or pastime of educated men. Finch is certain she would get criticism for her work because she is a woman. Finch would probably be criticized by educated and sophisticated men, possibly by the successful writers of her time.

2b. The most a woman can achieve is to be admired for her beauty, good manners, graceful dancing, and her ability to manage a household. Her achievements are limited to physical appearance and domestic activities.

3b. The Muses and groves of laurel are significant to the poem because they call to mind the grand tradition of poetry and because they are traditionally associated with men.

Analyze

4a. As a woman poet, Finch faces the following arguments: women's writing is "insipid, empty, uncorrect"; a woman writer presumptuously intrudes on the rights of men; writing is not suited to a woman's sex and way; women should concern themselves with "good breeding, fashion, dancing, dressing, play"; reading, writing, and thinking cloud a women's beauty; women should busy themselves running a household. Finch counters that women throughout history have had powerful and important roles.

Synthesize

4b. The poem might disarm a reader who approached the book thinking women could not or should not write.

Evaluate

5a. *Responses will vary.* Some students may suggest that there are no differences. Others may have certain ideas about what each gender can or should do.

Extend

5b. Responses will vary.

INVESTIGATE, Inquire, *Imagine*

Recall: Gathering Facts

1a. How does Finch feel the general public would react to her poem?

Interpret: Finding Meaning

1b. Why might people in Finch's world believe that a woman poet is "presumptuous"? Why is Finch certain that she would get criticism for her work? Who do you think would criticize Finch?

2a. According to Finch, what does society believe are the "proper" activities of women?

2b. In the world Finch describes, what is the most a woman can achieve? To what aspects of life are her achievements limited?

3a. What does the poet state about her Muse and about groves of laurel?

3b. What significance do Muses and groves of laurel have in the poem?

Analyze: Taking Things Apart

4a. Analyze the poem to find the arguments Finch faces against women poets and her counter-argument, which forms the main idea of the poem.

Synthesize: Bringing Things Together

4b. Why might Finch have chosen this poem as the first in her published collection of poems?

Evaluate: Making Judgments

5a. Evaluate the idea that people are limited by their gender in what they can do.

Extend: Connecting Ideas

5b. Do you think barriers still exist based on gender? on race? on other criteria? Explain your response.

Understanding *Literature*

Allusion. Review the definition for **allusion** in the Handbook of Literary Terms. Identify two Biblical allusions in the selection. What point does Finch make by using these allusions?

Slant Rhyme, Assonance, and Consonance. Review the definition for **slant rhyme, assonance,** and **consonance** in Literary Tools in Prereading. Identify examples of slant rhymes in this poem. Why might Finch have chosen to vary the rhyme scheme in these places?

Writer's Journal

1. Write a **note** of support to Finch. In your note address the difficulties she mentions in this poem. Or, write a note of support to somebody you know who is trying to do something that defies convention.
2. This poem serves as an introduction to Finch's poetry collection. Write a prose **epilogue** for this volume. In your epilogue, you may wish to reiterate, in your own words, some of the main ideas expressed in Finch's poem. You may also refer to the volume as an example of what a woman can accomplish.

ANSWERS TO UNDERSTANDING LITERATURE

Allusion. Finch uses allusions to the holy virgins who played upon the return of the Ark and to Deborah, an Israelite leader, to show that in the past, women were not always resigned to looking pretty and keeping house.

Slant Rhyme, Assonance, and Consonance. Examples of slant rhyme in this poem include *house/use, Heaven/given, declare/war, prolong/gone,* and *on/song.* A poet might choose to vary rhyme scheme in order to emphasize a particular idea. The slant rhyme affects the tone by highlighting significant ideas. For instance, the slant rhyme of *house/use* in lines 19 and 20 signals the completion of an idea. It also signals the poet's dissatisfaction with the circumscribed life that women are supposed to lead, a life described in the preceding lines that end in perfect rhyme. Eliminating rhyme wouldn't make the poem have a completely different effect; its subject and argument would still be compelling.

Continued on page 577

3. Read Mary Wollstonecraft's *A Vindication of the Rights of Woman* in Unit 8 and Virginia Woolf's *A Room of One's Own* in Unit 11. These three women all wrote in different eras, yet they share similar ideas and concerns. Write a short **essay** comparing the theme of each selection.

Integrating *the* Language Arts

Language, Grammar, and Style

Correcting Sentence Fragments. Read the Language Arts Survey 3.33, "Correcting Sentence Fragments." Then make whatever changes are needed to convert the following fragments into complete sentences. Delete or add words or phrases if you wish.

1. Considering the disadvantages of being born into an aristocratic family
2. The pastoral beauty of the English countryside as a subject of Anne Finch's poems
3. That the literary efforts of women were not regarded as serious literature
4. Moving into a house in the countryside to escape the conventions of social life
5. Bitterness and depression that result from effort and excellence without acceptance

Vocabulary

Sentence Completion. Mary Astell, a contemporary of Anne Finch, also was concerned about the ways in which women might improve their lives. Below is a vocabulary exercise based on Astell's piece "A Serious Proposal to the Ladies." Choose the words that best complete each of the sentences below.

1. There is a sort of _____ indeed which is worse than the greatest _____.

   (A) sacrifice . . . pleasure
   (B) criminal . . . lawyer
   (C) trouble . . . pleasure
   (D) nightmare . . . dream
   (E) learning . . . ignorance

2. A woman may study plays and _____ all her days, and be a great deal more _____ but never a jot the wiser.

   (A) work . . . wise
   (B) puppetry . . . populous
   (C) stitchery . . . literate
   (D) romances . . . knowing
   (E) games . . . serious

3. Such a _____ as this serves only to instruct and put her forward in the practice of the greatest _____.

   (A) quest . . . uncertainty
   (B) frivolity . . . importance
   (C) occupation . . . uselessness
   (D) complication . . . art
   (E) knowledge . . . follies

4. Yet how can they justly _____ her who _____ or at least won't afford opportunity of better?

   (A) employ . . . suffer
   (B) accuse . . . reproach
   (C) blame . . . forbid
   (D) berate . . . can't
   (E) tolerate . . . daren't

5. A rational _____ will be employed; it will never be _____ in doing nothing.

   (A) person . . . useful
   (B) desire . . . idle
   (C) mind . . . satisfied
   (D) toleration . . . angry
   (E) defense . . . guilty

Collaborative Learning

Bill of Rights. What rights do you think the students in your school should have? Brainstorm a list of rights with your classmates. Then discuss each idea and decide as a group if it should be included or if it spawns other ideas. Make a final "Bill of Rights."

ANSWERS TO INTEGRATING THE LANGUAGE ARTS

Language, Grammar, and Style
Answers will vary. Possible answers are given.

1. Considering the disadvantages of being born into an aristocratic family, Anne Finch had a successful career.
2. The pastoral beauty of the English countryside was the subject of many of Anne Finch's poems.
3. The literary efforts of women were not regarded as serious literature.
4. Moving into an estate in the countryside enabled Anne Finch to escape the conventions of social life.
5. Anne Finch suffered the bitterness and depression that result from effort and excellence without acceptance.

Study and Research

1. E
2. D
3. E
4. D
5. C

FOR MORE PRACTICE

Problem. Because she anticipated public—, Mary Astell published her writings—.

(A) admiration . . . reluctantly
(B) censure . . . anonymously
(C) reviews . . . promptly
(D) indifference . . . posthumously
(E) humiliation . . . openly
Answer. B

Collaborative Learning
Remind students to address all types of freedom, even those that may seem small or trivial. Students should come to consensus on any issues that cause debate.

ANSWERS TO UNDERSTANDING LITERATURE (cont. from page 576)

(cont. from page 576)

NOTE: Explain that some rhymes that appear to be slant rhymes actually were considered perfect rhymes in Finch's day. For example, "fault" in *untaught/fault* (lines 5 and 6) was pronounced *fawt,* and "join" in *join/refine* (lines 30 and 31) was pronounced *jine.*

Meter. Generally, the poem is written in iambic pentameter, as in the initial four lines. When the meter varies, the change emphasizes an idea, word, or phrase, as in line 19: "Whilst the dull manage of a servile house." The stress on *dull* is immediately followed by the stress of the first syllable of *manage,* thus calling attention to the phrase.
NOTE: Students should make a written and spoken analysis of the poem to determine its meter. Encourage students to read the information about *scansion, meter* in the Handbook of Literary Terms.

ADDITIONAL RESOURCES

UNIT 7 RESOURCE BOOK
- Selection Worksheet 7.2
- Selection Check Test 4.7.5
- Selection Test 4.7.6
- Language, Grammar, and Style Resource 3.40

GRAPHIC ORGANIZER

Person or Thing Alluded To	Significance of this Person or Thing
Jubal	creator of lyre and pipe
Orpheus	entrances animals and trees with his music

READER'S JOURNAL

Students might share some of their favorite songs with each other and explain why they like the song.

VOCABULARY FROM THE SELECTION

celestial
disdainful
indignation
quell

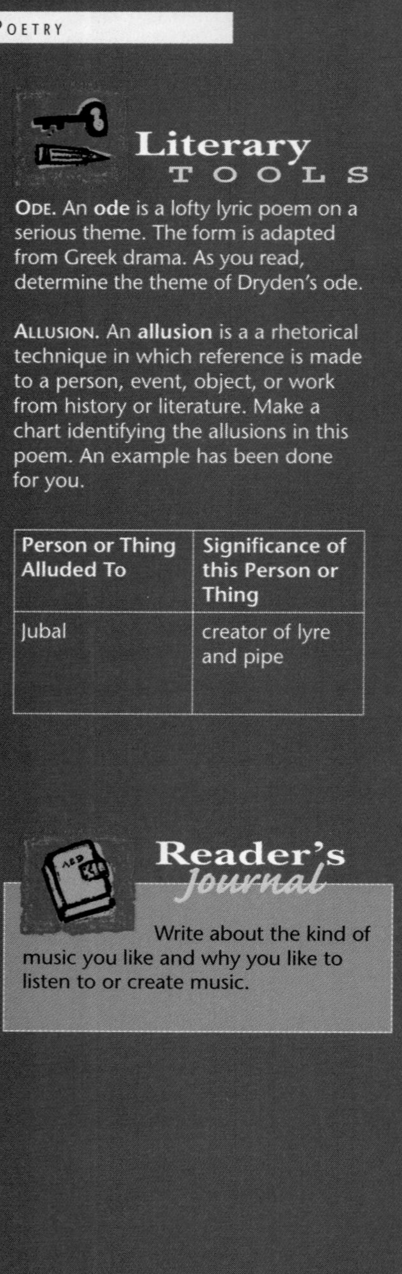

Literary TOOLS

ODE. An **ode** is a lofty lyric poem on a serious theme. The form is adapted from Greek drama. As you read, determine the theme of Dryden's ode.

ALLUSION. An **allusion** is a a rhetorical technique in which reference is made to a person, event, object, or work from history or literature. Make a chart identifying the allusions in this poem. An example has been done for you.

Person or Thing Alluded To	Significance of this Person or Thing
Jubal	creator of lyre and pipe

Reader's Journal

Write about the kind of music you like and why you like to listen to or create music.

"A Song for St. Cecilia's Day"

BY JOHN DRYDEN

About the AUTHOR

John Dryden (1631–1700) was the monumental literary figure of his time. His works, which span the range of drama, epic poetry, lyric poetry, satire, essay, and translation, serve as a record of the ideas and spirit of the seventeenth century. While the work of some poets reveals intimate personal feelings, Dryden's concerned issues of public moment, including on occasion the commemoration of public events. Dryden's best works, perhaps, are his satirical verses, including *Absolom and Achitophel.* Dryden's verse established him as a major literary figure, and his public support for King Charles I contributed to his being named poet laureate in 1668. Dryden wrote prose essays and is widely regarded as the first "modern" prose writer, insofar as he developed a style that was clear, precise, and dignified but at the same time lyrical. In addition to the early and highly regarded *Essay of Dramatic Poesy* (1668), Dryden wrote criticism that he published as prefaces to his many well-received dramas.

With the Glorious Revolution came the Anglican monarchy, and Dryden lost his post as laureate. Replaced by Thomas Shadwell, whom he had satirized in "Mac Flecknoe" (1682), he wrote a few more plays but took primarily to literary translation and commentary. Written near the end of his life, *Fables, Ancient and Modern* includes Dryden's translations of Ovid, Boccaccio, and Chaucer.

About the SELECTION

"A Song for St. Cecilia's Day" celebrates St. Cecilia, a Roman noble martyred *circa* AD 230. Her feast day is November 22. In addition to evangelizing and performing miracles, she is believed to have invented the organ, a musical instrument whose power and versatility was utterly beyond comparison until the development of electronic synthesizers and amplifiers in the present century; hence, she is the patron saint of music and musicians. In Dryden's time, St. Cecilia's feast day was a religious holiday in celebration of music. This poem was set to music by G. B. Draghi and performed at the St. Cecilia's Day festival of 1687, but **G. F. Handel's** (1685–1759) later setting is now used almost exclusively.

GOALS/OBJECTIVES

Studying this lesson will enable students to
- have a positive experience reading a highly musical lyric
- describe Dryden's literary accomplishments and explain the historical significance of his writings
- name the characteristics of an *ode* and identify the theme of an ode
- define *allusion* and identify and interpret allusions they encounter in their reading
- verify subject-verb agreement in their writing
- create a multimedia presentation and a press release

The Lute Player, c.1610. Orazio Gentileschi. National Gallery of Art, Washington, DC.

A Song for St. Cecilia's Day[1]

JOHN DRYDEN

From harmony, from heavenly harmony
This universal frame began:
When Nature underneath a heap
Of jarring atoms lay,
And could not heave her head,
The tuneful voice was heard from high:
"Arise, ye more than dead."
Then cold, and hot, and moist, and dry,[2]
In order to their stations leap,
And Music's power obey.
From harmony, from heavenly harmony
This universal frame began:
From harmony to harmony

What was the source of this "universal frame"?

To what original ordering of things does the speaker compare that most orderly of art forms, music?

1. **St. Cecilia's Day.** November 22, the feast day of St. Cecilia, the patron saint of music
2. **Nature . . . dry.** Nature was created out of the jarring elements of earth, fire, water, and air or "cold," "hot," "moist," and "dry."

ANSWERS TO GUIDED READING QUESTIONS

1. The "universal frame" began from "heavenly harmony."
2. The speaker compares music to the ordering of the elements.

INDIVIDUAL LEARNING STRATEGIES

Motivation
Bring or ask students to bring the instruments mentioned in the poem. (You will need a recording of organ music.) Have someone play each instrument, and then, as a group, discuss the words and images in the poem and list additional related words. Help students distinguish the meanings of these words.

Reading Proficiency
Read through the poem with students once, pointing out footnotes. Then students should read silently to themselves and make notes about the poem as they read. Have students pause at the end of each stanza and summarize the stanza's main ideas.

English Language Learning
Share with students the following additional vocabulary:
universal frame—frame or structure of the universe
jarring—crashing into each other
dirge—funeral hymn
proclaim—announce
lays—poems or songs, popular during medieval times

Special Needs
Ask students to create a graphic organizer or chart in which they list along one side the musical instruments and along the other side, the adjectives used to describe the sounds of the instruments. For example, the trumpet has a "loud clangor" and "shrill notes." Point out to students that this poem spans from the Creation to the biblical Last Judgment Day: Dryden writes that heavenly music created humans, then humans created music, and that someday when humans live no longer on earth, music will "untune the sky" or destroy the world.

Enrichment
Refer students to the Historical Note on page 580. Ask them to research another poet laureate of England or one from the United States. They should prepare biographical information and select one poem to discuss in a brief report. They may be able to find this information on the Internet.

LITERARY TECHNIQUE

Refrain. A refrain is a line or group of lines repeated in a poem or song. Have students identify the refrains in the first fifteen lines of the poem. What are the effects of these refrains? Do they emphasize a point? In what way are they musical?

ANSWER TO GUIDED READING QUESTION

1. The trumpet, drum, flute, and violin are mentioned. Each conveys a different strong emotion. The effect of the trumpet is alarm. The effect of the drum is a call to action. The effect of the flute is woe and longing. The effect of the violin is a jumble of intense emotion, the "Depth of pains, and height of passion."

HISTORICAL NOTE

England has had seventeen poet laureates since Dryden, including William Wordsworth; Alfred, Lord Tennyson; and Ted Hughes, the current poet laureate. However, in the more than three hundred years since the office was established, a woman has never been appointed. In the United States, however, Mona Van Duyn became the first woman to receive the title of poet laureate in 1992. She was succeeded by another woman, Rita Dove, in 1993.

CROSS-CURRICULAR ACTIVITIES

Music. Students can research musical terms to describe the different effects and sounds of the instruments in the poem. For example, they might use the terms *piano, staccato,* or *arpeggio.* The school music teacher might be able to help them with this information and even demonstrate some of the terms on an instrument.

HISTORICAL NOTE

Dryden's theme of harmony and order was a common theme of the Enlightenment. Dryden balanced the passion of music with the ordering element of harmony.

Through all the compass of the notes it ran,
The diapason[3] closing full in man.

What passion cannot Music raise and quell!
When Jubal[4] struck the corded shell,
His listening brethren stood around,
And, wondering, on their faces fell
To worship that celestial sound.
Less than a god they thought there could not dwell
Within the hollow of that shell
That spoke so sweetly and so well.
What passion cannot Music raise and quell!

The trumpet's loud clangor
Excites us to arms,
With shrill notes of anger,
And mortal alarms.
The double double double beat
Of the thundering drum
Cries: "Hark! the foes come;
Charge, charge, 'tis too late to retreat."

The soft complaining flute
In dying notes discovers
The woes of hopeless lovers,
Whose dirge is whispered by the warbling lute.

Sharp violins proclaim
Their jealous pangs, and desperation,
Fury, frantic indignation,
Depth of pains, and height of passion,
For the fair, disdainful dame.

But O! what art can teach,
What human voice can reach,
The sacred organ's praise?

What musical instruments are mentioned in these lines? How are they different from one another? What effect does each one have on listeners?

3. **diapason.** The whole range of notes in the musical scale
4. **Jubal.** The Book of Genesis credits Jubal with the invention of the lyre and the pipe.

WORDS FOR EVERYDAY USE

quell (kwel) *vt.*, subdue. *Has the army's offensive maneuver quelled the enemy attack?*
ce • les • tial (sə les´chəl) *adj.*, heavenly, divine. *The painting depicts a celestial scene filled with cherubs and angels.*
in • dig • na • tion (in´dig nā´ shən) *n.*, anger, scorn. *Customer-relations representatives are often the target of customers' indignation.*
dis • dain • ful (dis dān´ fəl) *adj.*, proud, aloof. *Her sarcastic tone revealed her disdainful attitude toward the idea.*

Quotables

"Music has charms to soothe a savage breast,

To soften rocks, or bend a knotted oak."

—William Congreve

Notes inspiring holy love,
Notes that wing their heavenly ways
To mend the choirs above.
Orpheus[5] could lead the savage race;
And trees unrooted left their place,
Sequacious[6] of the lyre;
But bright Cecilia raised the wonder higher:
When to her organ vocal breath was given,
An angel heard, and straight appeared,
Mistaking earth for heaven.

Who mistook earth for heaven? Why was this mistake made?

GRAND CHORUS

As from the power of sacred lays
The spheres began to move,
And sung the great Creator's praise[7]
To all the blest above;
So, when the last and dreadful hour
This crumbling pageant shall devour,
The trumpet shall be heard on high,
The dead shall live, the living die,
And Music shall untune the sky. ■

What, according to the speaker, begins and ends with music?

5. **Orpheus.** Legend has it that the poet Orpheus played the lyre so wonderfully that the animals were tamed, and even rocks and trees followed him.
6. **sequacious.** Following
7. **power . . . praise.** The idea that sacred songs put the stars and planets into motion

Respond *to the* SELECTION

What happens to you when you feel or perceive disharmony? What kinds of harmony do you value most? Why do you think harmony is important to people?

ANSWERS TO GUIDED READING QUESTIONS

1. An angel mistook earth for heaven. The mistake was made because the angel heard Cecilia's organ and thought such a sound could only come from heaven.
2. The world begins and ends with music.

SELECTION CHECK TEST 4.7.5 WITH ANSWERS

Checking Your Reading

1. What once lay beneath "a heap of jarring atoms"? **Nature lay there.**
2. What do the people think must live in Jubal's shell? **They think a god lives there.**
3. What kind of sound does the flute produce? **It's soft, melancholy, and woeful.**
4. What mistake does an angel make as Cecilia plays? **The angel mistakes earth for heaven.**
5. Who will "untune the sky" at the last "dreadful hour"? **Music will untune the sky.**

Vocabulary in Context

Fill each blank with the most appropriate word from the Words for Everyday Use from "A Song for St. Cecilia's Day." You may have to change the tense of the word.

quell celestial indignation disdainful

1. The results from the poll **quelled** our hopes for victory.
2. Mrs. Keet stomped her foot in **indignation** when the workman said he wasn't done.
3. The **Celestial** Café is appropriately named; its food is truly divine.

Literary Tools

1. What is an allusion? **An allusion is a reference to a work, person, or event.**
2. What is an ode? **An ode is a lofty lyric poem on a serious theme.**
3. What is the theme of Dryden's ode? **The theme is the role of harmony in the universe.**
4. Mark the stressed syllables in the following lines:

/ /
The **trum** pet's loud **clang** or
/ /
Ex **cites** us to **arms,**
/ /
With **shrill** notes of **an** ger,
/ /
And **mor** tal a **larms.**

RESPOND TO THE SELECTION

Students can use a cluster chart or other graphic organizer to explore the idea of harmony.

ANSWERS TO INVESTIGATE, INQUIRE, IMAGINE

RECALL

1a. The "universal frame" was created out of "heavenly harmony." Music began this process of creation. In stanza 2, the powers to raise and subdue passion are attributed to music.

2a. In stanza 7, an angel mistakes earth for heaven upon hearing Cecilia's organ.

3a. The trumpet shall be heard; the dead shall live; the living will die; music will untune the sky.

INTERPRET

1b. The Christian story of creation and the musical scale have the number seven in common—seven days of creation and seven notes on the musical scale. Harmony connects different aspects of the universe. The speaker implies that the created world functions harmoniously and that humans are part of that harmony.

2b. Cecilia's organ made the angel think earth was heaven.

3b. Music will signal the end of the world and the call to judgment.

ANALYZE

4a. A trumpet's sounds are loud, clear, and often staccato; the poet mirrors this with short, staccato lines. A drum's "double double double beat" and thunder are abrupt and loud, reflecting the insistent, repetitive call to action. A flute's sounds are softer and smoother; the poet's language, such as the initial *w*s in line 36, creates a soft, subdued tone. A violin's sounds range from soft and mournful to loud and furious, and the poet's description of the ups and downs of human passion echoes the violin.

SYNTHESIZE

Responses will vary. Possible responses are given.

4b. Both music and nature are governed by harmony; they are both expressions of the order of the universe. In the opening lines, the speaker says the universal frame stems from harmony, and in the poem's conclusion says that the spheres, or planets, move to their own harmonious music: "As from the power of sacred lays / The spheres began to move."

INVESTIGATE, Inquire, Imagine

Recall: GATHERING FACTS → **Interpret:** FINDING MEANING

1a. Out of what was the "universal frame" created? Who or what began this process of creation? What powers are attributed to music in stanza 2?

1b. What is the similarity between the process of creation and the notes of the musical scale? What role did harmony play in creation? What might the speaker be implying about the role of harmony in the created world in which we live?

2a. In stanza 7, who makes a mistake? What is the mistake?

2b. What role does Cecilia's invention have in this mistake? How does her creation transform the earth?

3a. According to the Grand Chorus, what shall happen to humans during the "last and dreadful hour"?

3b. How will music be involved in the end of the world?

Analyze: TAKING THINGS APART → **Synthesize:** BRINGING THINGS TOGETHER

4a. Describe the sounds the instruments praised in stanzas 3–7 make. How do the sounds of the poet's language compare to the instruments' sounds?

4b. What similarities exist between music and nature, according to the speaker? What aspects of this poem suggest that the speaker views the universe as an orderly, harmonious place, governed or regulated by rational, discoverable laws?

Evaluate: MAKING JUDGMENTS → **Extend:** CONNECTING IDEAS

5a. What non-English persons are mentioned in the poem? To what effect? What other persons or things are mentioned that might distinguish the topic or occasion as special?

5b. How does Dryden make the celebration of music extend beyond everyday experience?

Understanding Literature

ODE. Review the definition for **ode** in the Handbook of Literary Terms. An ode praises or celebrates its subject. What does Dryden praise in this ode? Identify three specific examples of this praise.

ALLUSION. Review the definition for **allusion** and the chart you made for Literary Tools in Prereading on page 578. An allusion suggests a literal, metaphorical, or symbolic parallel or contrast with another work, character, or story. An allusion may be made in a paragraph, sentence, phrase, or single word. Dryden makes several references to classical Greek and Roman literature and to the Bible. Identify two allusions. What connection exists in each allusion? What effect does the use of these allusions have?

ANSWERS TO INVESTIGATE, INQUIRE, IMAGINE (CONT.)

EVALUATE

5a. Non-English personages such as Jubal and Orpheus, both from ancient times, are mentioned in the poem to show the long-standing place of music in human society.

EXTEND

5b. *Responses will vary.* By comparing Cecilia's creation of the organ to the creation of the universe, Dryden makes the celebration of music extend to the very meaning of human experience.

Answers to Understanding Literature can be found on page 583.

WRITER'S JOURNAL

1. Write a **speech** of praise about music. You may choose to write about music in general, about a specific type of music, or about a specific musician or song.
2. Write a **song** to commemorate a special event. Your song may be a narrative that explains the details of the event, or it may be a lyric piece that tries to capture the mood of the event.
3. Write an **ode** about something that you find very moving. Remember your ode should praise or celebrate the subject you choose.

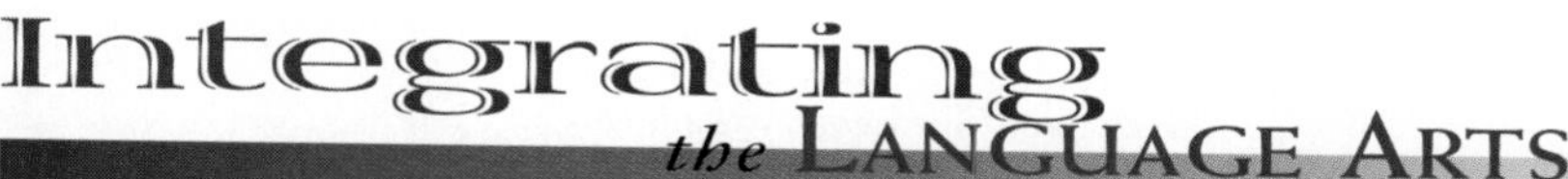

Language, Grammar, and Style

SUBJECT/VERB AGREEMENT. Read the Language Arts Survey 3.40, "Getting Subject and Verb to Agree." Then complete the following sentences by modifying the verb in parentheses to make it agree with its subject. Use the present tense.

1. In preparation for the performance, the orchestra ____________ tuning. (be)
2. The violin section ____________ two more chairs. (need)
3. Each member of the audience ____________ sitting in quiet anticipation. (be)
4. The audience ____________ to enjoy the performance immensely. (appear)
5. As the song ends, the chorus ____________ for the finale. (stand)

Study and Research & Speaking and Listening

MULTIMEDIA PRESENTATION. Dryden lists some important figures in music history. Who do you think has had a powerful impact on music history within the last fifty years? Choose one performer, composer, songwriter, or other person from the music industry. Research your subject. Then, prepare a brief multimedia presentation about this figure, and be prepared to defend your choice. You may wish to include short musical excerpts to help illustrate your point.

Applied English

PRESS RELEASE. Write a press release about the festival of St. Cecilia. Use information from the introduction and from additional research if necessary. Or, if you choose to create a festival of your own, write a press release about that event.

Collaborative Learning

CELEBRATION. Dryden's poem honors the power and glory of music. In groups of four to eight students, choose a different art form you wish to honor in a public celebration. Think about the following questions: Why is your chosen art form important? What power does it have? Where, when, and how do people experience it? What tools or materials are used to create it? How does it compare to other art forms? Work together to plan a ceremony in which to share your ideas with other people. Create samples of your art form to display or perform during your celebration.

ANSWERS TO UNDERSTANDING LITERATURE

Responses will vary. Possible responses are given.

ODE. Dryden praises music. He refers to Jubal's music as "celestial sound." He praises the organ for its ability to inspire "holy love." He says that Cecilia "raised the wonder higher" when she played the organ (giving it "vocal breath").

ALLUSION. Dryden makes an allusion to Jubal, creator of the lyre and pipe, and Orpheus, who entrances animals and trees with his music. These allusions serve to point out the harmonious power of music, suggesting that from the beginning of human history, music has triggered spiritual worship of the "celestial sound." At the same time, music also stirs human passion. Music is a balance between the natural and spiritual worlds.

ANSWERS TO INTEGRATING THE LANGUAGE ARTS

Language, Grammar, and Style

1. In preparation for the performance, the orchestra is tuning.
2. The violin section needs two more chairs.
3. Each member of the audience is sitting in quiet anticipation.
4. The audience appears to enjoy the performance immensely.
5. As the song ends, the chorus stands for the finale.

FOR MORE PRACTICE

PROBLEM. In the next morning's newspapers, the press _____ the performance. (praise)

Answer

In the next morning's newspapers, the press praises the performance.

Applied English

If students do hold a celebration, a press release can be used to inform the school and local communities.

Collaborative Learning

CELEBRATION. Students should try to demonstrate the power of the art form rather than merely explain it.

ADDITIONAL RESOURCES

Unit 7 Resource Book

- Selection Worksheet 7.3
- Selection Check Test 4.7.7
- Selection Test 4.7.8
- Language, Grammar, and Style Resource 3.39

GRAPHIC ORGANIZER

Line	Words	Repeated Sounds
1	moon, mute	*m*
3	sea, swelling, surge	*s*
4	shrinking, sublimely	*s*
6	blast, bed	*b*
8	silent, Sabbath	*s*
9	shells, seaweed, shore	*s*
10-12	whiten, wave, winds, waters, warring	*w*
13	life's long	*l*
14	gaze, gloomy	*g*

READER'S JOURNAL

Suggest that students consider whether they felt connected to or separate from nature during the event.

VOCABULARY FROM THE SELECTION

sublimely

Literary TOOLS

Anaphora. Anaphora is any word or phrase that repeats or refers to something that precedes or follows it. As you read look for examples of anaphora.

Alliteration. Alliteration is the repetition of initial consonant sounds, as in "wild wind." Make a chart to keep track of examples of alliteration you find in this sonnet.

Line	Words	Repeated Sounds
1	moon, mute	*m*

About the SELECTION

"Pressed by the Moon, Mute Arbitress of Tides" is more than a sonnet describing the activity of nature. A close reading shows that it also contains elements of inward reflection that are true to the spirit of later Romanticism (For more on Romantism, see the entry in the Handbook of Literary Terms.) In this poem, Smith evokes the powerful forces of nature and relates those forces to inner human experience, much as Byron, Shelley, and Keats would do years afterward. Its use of nature imagery, its strong emotions, and its preoccupation with death makes the poem one of the first major expressions of the Romantic spirit in English literature.

"Pressed by the

Mute Arbitress of Tides"

BY CHARLOTTE SMITH

About the AUTHOR

Charlotte (Turner) Smith (1749–1806) began her literary career relatively late in life. Married at age sixteen, she bore and reared ten children. She began writing to earn money when her husband was sent to debtor's prison. Her book of poems, *Elegiac Sonnets* (1784), was so popular that it eventually went through eleven editions. It also influenced major Romantic poets such as Samuel Taylor Coleridge and William Wordsworth, as well as the Victorian poet Elizabeth Barrett Browning. Smith's poems presage the Romantic Era both in their preoccupation with self-analysis and in their focus on nature and natural beauty, the latter reflecting Smith's attachment to the Sussex countryside of her youth.

Although Smith continued to write poetry after the success of her first book, this work did not by itself provide sufficient income for her family, so she began writing novels. Her first novel, *Emmeline, the Orphan of the Castle* (1788), was very successful. For several years she produced a book each year, and in all, published over twenty books. *The Old Manor House* (1793) is considered her finest fiction work. Many of her novels, such as *Desmond* (1792), express her sympathy with the ideals of Rousseau and the French Revolution (1789). However, critics considered her novels too political for a woman and disparaged her belief in the moral equality of the social classes. Thus, although her writing was highly regarded by major writers and was popular enough to produce an income sufficient to support a family of eleven, her work eventually fell into obscurity.

Reader's Journal

Write about a natural event that had a powerful effect on you.

GOALS/OBJECTIVES

Studying this lesson will enable students to

- interpret and appreciate natural description in a poem and relate that description to a speaker's inner emotions
- describe Charlotte Smith's literary accomplishments and explain why her work fell into obscurity
- define *alliteration* and identify and interpret its effect in a poem
- define anaphora and recognize anaphora in a poem
- use vivid verbs in writing
- use observing skills

November Moon, Wigeon with the Tide, c.1900s. Julian Novorol.

Pressed by the MOON Mute Arbitress[1] of Tides

CHARLOTTE SMITH

Written in the churchyard at Middleton in Sussex

Pressed by the moon, mute arbitress of tides,
While the loud equinox[2] its power combines,
The sea no more its swelling surge confines,
But o'er the shrinking land sublimely rides.
The wild blast, rising from the western cave,
Drives the huge billows from their heaving bed,
Tears from their grassy tombs the village dead,
And breaks the silent sabbath[3] of the grave!
With shells and seaweed mingled, on the shore
Lo! their bones whiten in the frequent wave;
But vain to them the winds and waters rave;
They hear the warring elements no more:
While I am doomed—by life's long storm oppressed,
To gaze with envy on their gloomy rest. ■

Who or what is "pressed by the moon"?

How do you feel when you imagine or observe a stormy sea?

What does the speaker compare to a storm?

1. **Arbitress.** Archaic feminine form of *arbiter,* a person selected to judge a dispute. The moon affects the changing tides of the ocean.
2. **equinox.** A storm that occurs when the sun crosses the equator, making night and day of equal length
3. **sabbath.** Rest

WORDS FOR EVERYDAY USE

sub • lime • ly (sə blīm´ lē) *adv.,* nobly; majestically. *The papal procession moved sublimely down the cathedral's velvet-carpeted aisle.*

ANSWERS TO GUIDED READING QUESTIONS

1. The sea is "pressed by the moon."
2. *Responses will vary.*
3. The speaker compares life (or the difficulties of life) to a storm.

INDIVIDUAL LEARNING STRATEGIES

MOTIVATION
This sonnet differs from many others students will have read, because its theme is not related to romantic love. However, the sonnet's reference to the moon gives it a surface similarity to other poems. Ask students to compare the use of the moon as a symbol both here and in Sidney's Sonnet 31 from *Astrophil and Stella* (page 293).

READING PROFICIENCY
Read the poem aloud to students once, pointing out the footnotes and answering comprehension questions. Have students form pairs to answer the Guided Reading and Recall questions.

ENGLISH LANGUAGE LEARNING
In addition to following the suggestions for Reading Proficiency and for Special Needs, give students the following additional vocabulary:
surge—sudden and forceful rolling or sweeping motion
billow—large wave
heaving—rising; swelling
vain to—unknown by

SPECIAL NEEDS
Follow the suggestions for Reading Proficiency. Then, to check student comprehension, encourage these students to sketch or draw their impressions of the scene described in the poem.

ENRICHMENT
Students in small groups can research folklore about the moon—its origins, effects on humans, and role in nature. Students can present their research in oral reports, works of art, recordings of folk tales, or other engaging forms.

CROSS-CURRICULAR ACTIVITIES

EARTH SCIENCE. Ask interested students to research and report to the class on the physics of the tides and of waves.

RESPOND TO THE SELECTION

Have students discuss their responses. Remind students to share ideas and listen to one another without criticizing.

ANSWERS TO INVESTIGATE, INQUIRE, IMAGINE

RECALL

1a. The "loud equinox," or storm, combines its power with the sea. The sea no longer stays in its place, but covers the land.

2a. The huge billows tear the dead from their tombs.

3a. The speaker is doomed to "gaze with envy" on the resting dead.

INTERPRET

1b. The speaker is in awe of what she sees.

2b. The action is violent, powerful, and destructive.

3b. The speaker is still alive. She must face the parts of life that are troubling her.

ANALYZE

4a. Smith refers to the moon, a powerful storm, wind, waves, the billowing ocean.

SYNTHESIZE

4b. The speaker is impressed and awed by the power of the storm. She wants the water to free her as well.

EVALUATE

5a. The speaker compares the combative nature of humans to the "warring" nature of the waves. Unlike the powerful waves that will always blast the shore, all people eventually will die and be released from their struggles. The poet seems to view people as part of nature: Like the waves, they are governed by imposing forces over which they have no control.

EXTEND

5b. *Responses will vary.* Students will probably say that women in the eighteenth century felt oppressed by their male-dominated society.

Respond *to the* SELECTION

Make a list of five feelings toward the sea that the poem arouses in you. Identify details in the poem that produced the feelings.

INVESTIGATE, Inquire, Imagine

Recall: GATHERING FACTS →

1a. What combines its power with the sea? What does the sea stop doing?

2a. What do the huge billows do?

3a. What is the speaker doomed to do?

Interpret: FINDING MEANING

1b. How does the speaker feel in relation to the natural forces she witnesses?

2b. How would you characterize this action? Explain your response.

3b. In what way does the speaker differ from the people she calls "they"?

Analyze: TAKING THINGS APART →

4a. Identify the natural elements Smith refers to in this sonnet.

Synthesize: BRINGING THINGS TOGETHER

4b. What attitude does the speaker express toward nature?

Evaluate: MAKING JUDGMENTS →

5a. Evaluate Smith's descriptions of nature. Also evaluate how she relates those descriptions to human experience.

Extend: CONNECTING IDEAS

5b. Conduct a survey to determine whether men and women react similarly to the idea that to live is to be oppressed by a long storm. Why might a woman of the eighteenth century, such as Smith, have felt like this?

Understanding Literature

ANAPHORA. Review the definition for **anaphora** in the Handbook of Literary Terms. Find the first references in the poem to the moon, the storm, the waves, and the wind. What words or phrases are used as anaphora for these things?

ALLITERATION. Review the definition for **alliteration** and the chart you made for Literary Tools in Prereading on page 584. Find instances of alliteration in Smith's sonnet. What sounds are repeated? How frequently are these sounds used elsewhere in the poem? Why do you think Smith may have chosen to use these particular sounds?

ANSWERS TO UNDERSTANDING LITERATURE

Responses will vary. Possible responses are given.

ANAPHORA. The first reference to the moon is "moon" (line 1); the first reference to the storm is "equinox" (line 2); the first reference to the waves is "swelling surge" (line 3); the first reference to the wind is "wild blast" (line 5). The phrase "mute arbitress of tides" (line 1) and "its" (line 2) are anaphora for the moon; "wild blast" (line 5) refers to the wind; "huge billows" (line 6) refers to the waves; "warring elements" (line 12) refers to the winds and the waters together.

ALLITERATION. Instances of alliteration include "moon, mute" in line 1; "swelling surge" in line 3; "silent sabbath" in line 8; "shells and seaweed mingled, on the shore" in line 9; "winds and waters" in line 11; and "life's long" in line 13. Smith frequently repeats the *s* and *w* sounds. Smith may have chosen these particular sounds because they echo the sounds of nature; the hissing *s* sounds like the waves and foam of the sea, and the breathy *w* sounds like the winds.

Writer's Journal

1. Write a **description** of a natural event you have witnessed. It can be a dramatic event, like a storm, or a more common event, such as a sunset.
2. Write a **newspaper article** about the events described by the speaker of this poem. In your article, answer the questions *who, what, when, where, why,* and *how.*
3. Write your own **sonnet** or other lyric poem about a dramatic event and how it made you feel.

Integrating *the* Language Arts

Language, Grammar, and Style

Vivid Verbs. Charlotte Smith forcefully describes the tides by carefully selecting colorful action words. Read the Language Arts Survey 3.39, "Adding Colorful Language to Sentences." Then replace the verbs or verb phrases in the following sentences with more vivid and effective words. Some sentences have more than one verb or verb phrase. Use a thesaurus or a dictionary as necessary.

1. The moon affects the tides.
2. In line 4 of the sonnet, the tide arrives on the land.
3. Line 6 tells about how a wave begins.
4. Charlotte Smith influenced the Romantic poets who followed her.
5. Smith worked hard to support her ten children.

Critical Thinking

Observing. Charlotte Smith had surely observed the sea carefully before she composed her poem. From the list below, choose two perspectives from which to observe the moon, the sea, a storm, clouds, or some other astronomical or natural object or event. From each perspective, conduct your observations for five minutes, taking careful notes. Prepare observation charts or checklists before observing, and use a separate sheet of paper for each set of observations. Try to avoid making judgments.

- a writer planning a short story about the future
- a designer planning an advertising campaign
- a painter planning a landscape or seascape
- a poet planning a poem about hope or about emptiness

Study and Research

Storms at Sea. The ocean is powerful as Smith describes it in this poem. Choose a topic to research related to storms and the sea. When you are done, compile your findings into a book about the sea. You can also include creative writing or artwork on the subject. Some possible topics include tracking hurricanes, outlining the effects of a particular hurricane, predicting tsunamis, or identifying ships lost at sea.

Applied English

Public Service Announcement. Would you know what to do in the case of a severe storm like the one Smith describes? Identify the kind of storm or other natural disaster most likely to hit your community. Research what to do in case of such a disaster. Then write a public service announcement to share what you have learned.

Answers to Integrating the Language Arts

Language, Grammar, and Style
Answers will vary. Possible answers are given.
1. The moon **toys with** the tides.
2. In line 4 of the sonnet, the tide **conquers** the land.
3. Line 6 **presents a powerful image of** how a wave begins.
4. Charlotte Smith **moved and inspired** the Romantic poets who **emulated** her.
5. Smith **toiled** to **feed and clothe** her ten children.

For More Practice
Problem. The wind along the shore is loud.
Answer
The wind screams along the shore.

Study and Research
Students should make observations from two perspectives. For each perspective, students should show careful note-taking and demonstrate the use of charts, checklists, or other planning devices.

Applied English
Students might work in teams to address different types of disasters. If equipment is available, students can record their public service announcements and share them with other classes.

Selection Check Test 4.7.7 with Answers

Checking Your Reading
1. What effect do the moon and the storm have on the sea? **They cause the sea to surge over the land.**
2. What does the storm do to the bones of the dead? **Responses could vary slightly; it tears them from their graves and tosses them on the shore.**
3. How do the dead react to the "warring elements"? **They don't; they are deaf to it.**
4. What oppresses the speaker? **She is oppressed by life (or life's long storm).**
5. What emotion does she feel toward the dead? **She is envious.**

Literary Tools
Fill in the blanks using the following terms. You may not use every term, and you may use some terms more than once.

Romantic metaphor Modern
alliteration Neoclassicist anaphora
epigraph

Selection Check Test 4.7.7 with Answers (cont.)

1. Repeated references to the moon and the storm show the poet's use of **anaphora**.
2. The line "With shells and seaweed mingled, on the shore" illustrates **alliteration**.
3. This poem is one of the earliest examples of **Romantic** elements in poetry.

ADDITIONAL RESOURCES

Unit 7 Resource Book
- Selection Worksheet 7.4
- Selection Check Test 4.7.9
- Selection Test 4.7.10
- Language, Grammar, and Style Resource 3.2

GRAPHIC ORGANIZER

Outward
saw *Romeo* and *Julett*
reports on the plague
reports on the fire of London

Inward
troubled by money spent
troubled by the effects of the plague (no more wigs)

VOCABULARY FROM THE SELECTION

ague
endeavor

READER'S JOURNAL

If students have kept journals in the past, encourage them to look back at their journals. Then have students write their impressions of the "person" who made the entries. Do the journals accurately reflect the writer? What do the entries reveal?

Literary TOOLS

Point of View. Point of view is the vantage point from which a story is told. This diary is written from Pepys' perspective.

Journal. A **journal,** like a diary, is a day-to-day record of a person's activities, experiences, thoughts, and feelings. In contrast to the word *diary,* the word *journal* connotes an outward rather than an inward focus. Make a chart and track some of the outward and inward observations Pepys makes.

Outward	Inward
saw Romeo and Juliet	

Reader's Journal

Think back over your life. During which times would it have been most interesting to have kept a journal? Why?

FROM *The Diary of Samuel Pepys*

BY SAMUEL PEPYS

About the AUTHOR

Samuel Pepys (1633–1703) wrote what many consider to be one of the most interesting accounts of daily English life in existence. Born the son of a tailor, Pepys (pronounced *peeps*) received a scholarship to Cambridge University, where he earned both bachelor's and master's degrees. Pepys was appointed to the Navy Office and rose to become Secretary of the Admiralty. During this time he studied shipbuilding and mastered navigational mathematics, trying to become a naval expert. He eventually won a seat in Parliament by convincing people of the importance of the navy and of sea power. Known as an honest, hardworking man, Pepys had along with an interest in the navy, a strong interest in theater, art, and literature. He counted among his friends such luminaries as scientist Sir Isaac Newton and writer John Dryden.

About the SELECTION

The Diary of Samuel Pepys is a clear and interesting account of the daily life of a successful, middle-class Englishman. The journal begins in the year of the Restoration—January 1, 1660—and ends on May 31, 1669. In it, Pepys writes about a variety of important and earth-shattering events, including the plague and the Great London Fire of 1666. Oddly, Pepys wrote his journal in an obscure shorthand that had to be deciphered before the book was published for the first time in 1825. In this selection, the spellings of some words differ from those now in use, and some spellings are inconsistent. However, these irregularities have been left in the text to provide something of the flavor of Pepys's work. It is a diary, written hastily, in the midst of a busy life.

GOALS/OBJECTIVES

Studying this lesson will enable students to
- identify with an Enlightenment speaker and glean relevant historical information from the speaker's account
- describe Samuel Pepys's place in history and his contribution to the literature of the seventeenth century
- define *point of view* and identify and interpret its effects on literature they read
- define *journal* and analyze journal entries that they encounter in their reading
- distinguish between formal and informal English and rewrite text in order to make it standard and formal

FROM

The Diary of Samuel Pepys

SAMUEL PEPYS

On Seeing a Play by Shakespeare

MARCH 1, 1662

This morning I paid Sir Wm. Batten 40*l*, which I have owed him this half year, having borrowed it of him.

Then to the office all the morning. So dined at home. And after dinner comes my uncle Thomas, with whom I have some high words of difference; but ended quietly, though I fear I shall do no good by fair means upon him.

Then my wife and I by coach, first to see my little picture that is a-drawing, and thence to the Opera and there saw *Romeo and Julett*, the first time it was ever acted.[1] But it is the play of itself the worst that ever I heard in my life, and the worst acted that ever I saw these people do; and I am resolved to go no more to see the first time of acting, for they were all of them out more or less. Thence home, and after supper and wrote by the post—I settled to what I have long entended, to cast up my accounts with myself; and after much pains to do it and great fear, I do find that I am 500*l* in money beforehand in the world, which I was afeared I was not. But I find that I have spent above 250*l* this last half year, which troubles me much. But by God's blessing, I am now resolved to take up, having furnished myself with all things for a great while, and tomorrow to think upon some rules and obligacions upon myself to walk by.

What trouble did Pepys write about in his first entry? What did he decide to do to deal with that trouble?

So with my mind eased of a great deal of trouble, though with no great content to find myself above 100*l* worse now then I was half a year ago, I went to bed.

The Plague of 1665

JUNE 7, 1665

This day, much against my Will, I did in Drury-lane see two or three houses marked with a red cross[2] upon the doors, and "Lord have mercy upon us" writ there—which was a sad sight to me, being the first of that kind that to my remembrance I ever saw. It put me into an ill conception of myself and my smell, so that I was forced to buy some roll-tobacco to smell to and chaw—which took away the apprehension.[3]

What did Pepys see that made him uneasy?

AUGUST 3, 1665

Up, and betimes to Deptford to Sir G. Carteret's; where not liking the horse which had been hired by Mr. Uthwayt for me, I did desire Sir G. Carteret to let me ride his new 40*l* horse; which he did and so I left my hacquenee[4] behind. And so after staying a good while in their bedchamber while they were dressing themselfs, discoursing merrily, I parted and to the Ferry, where I was forced to stay a great while before I could get my horse brought over. And then mounted and rode very finely to Dagenham's—all the way, people, Citizens, walking to and again to enquire how the plague is in the City this week by the Bill—which by chance at Greenwich I had heard was 2010 of the plague, and 3000 and odd of all diseases; but methought it was a sad question to be so often asked me. Coming to Dagenham's, I there met our company coming out of the house,

1. ***Romeo and Julett* . . . acted.** Pepys saw *Romeo and Juliet* acted for the first time since the Restoration.
2. **red cross.** A quarantine mark used during the plague
3. **roll-tobacco . . . apprehension.** Tobacco was believed to have medicinal value.
4. **hacquenee.** Horse for riding

ANSWERS TO GUIDED READING QUESTIONS

1. Pepys was troubled that he was spending too much money. He decided to think about some "rules and obligacions" to curb his spending.
2. He saw a few houses marked with a red cross, a sign of the plague.

ADDITIONAL QUESTIONS AND ACTIVITIES

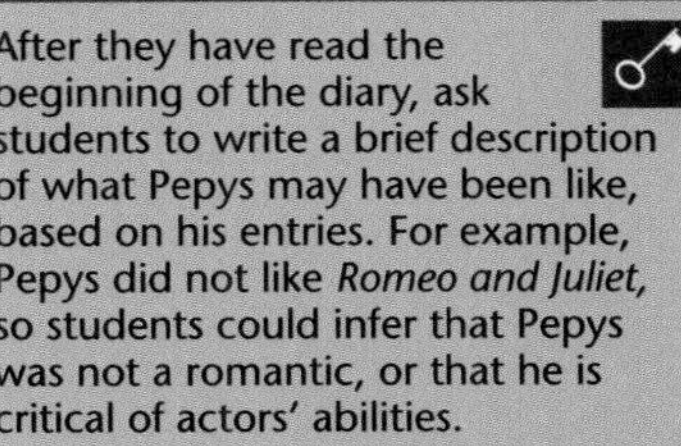

After they have read the beginning of the diary, ask students to write a brief description of what Pepys may have been like, based on his entries. For example, Pepys did not like *Romeo and Juliet*, so students could infer that Pepys was not a romantic, or that he is critical of actors' abilities.

INDIVIDUAL LEARNING STRATEGIES

MOTIVATION
Have students read the Language Arts Survey 5.5, "Generalizing." Then have them read the Pepys selection and make a list of four generalizations about life in London during Pepys's time. Have students discuss their generalizations in small groups. Each student should back up their generalizations with evidence from the selection.

READING PROFICIENCY
Make sure to tell all students that *Pepys* is pronounced like *peeps*. Explain that English spelling and capitalization were not standardized in Pepys's time. Students might want to work with another student for help with unfamiliar spellings or capitalization of words.

ENGLISH LANGUAGE LEARNING
Follow the suggestions above for Reading Proficiency. Also, share the following additional vocabulary with students:
buttery—place where supplies are available
malicious—spiteful; harmful

SPECIAL NEEDS
Ask students to make a graphic organizer listing the types of information Pepys includes in his diary. Which bits of information have to do with historical moments in London? Which are personal and

INDIVIDUAL LEARNING STRATEGIES (CONT.)

trivial? Students may illustrate one of the scenes Pepys describes in his diary entries.

ENRICHMENT
A small group of students can stage a talk-show interview with Samuel Pepys. Students should decide what topics the host will discuss with Pepys and then write questions for the host. The students who role play Pepys and the host should loosely follow the outline of these questions, but should also leave room for improvisation.

ANSWERS TO GUIDED READING QUESTIONS

1. There were so many people dying that they could not all be buried during the night.
2. Pepys didn't want to wear wigs because he feared the hair may have been cut from the heads of plague victims, and wearing such a wig would risk infection.

CROSS-CURRICULAR ACTIVITIES

MATHEMATICS AND SCIENCES. Have students do research on the plague. They should find out the causes of plague, the types of plague, and the treatments, if any, for the disease. Students can present their research in written reports and should try to include graphs, illustrations, or other visual means of representing data.

SOCIAL STUDIES. Other students might research the social effects of the plague. How were traveling, communication, and social gatherings affected? Students who have an interest in modern literature may examine Albert Camus's Existentialist novel *The Plague* in order to see how a twentieth-century society could potentially be affected by an outbreak of plague.

HISTORICAL NOTE

In the sixteenth and seventeenth centuries, people commonly believed that bathing could endanger one's health. In fact, it was believed that bathing, done either in public bathhouses or in the privacy of one's home, could spread disease. During times of plague, doctors discouraged their patients from bathing because they feared that hot vapors would open skin pores and let in contagions.

having stayed as long as they could for me. So I let them go a little before, and went and took leave of my Lady Sandwich—good woman, who seems very sensible of my service and this late business—and having her directions in some things; among others, to get Sir G. Carteret and my Lord to settle the portion and what Sir G. Carteret is to settle into land as soon as may be; she not liking that it should lie long undone, for fear of death on either side. So took leave of her, and then down to the buttery and eat a piece of cold venison-pie and drank and took some bread and cheese in my hand; and so mounted after them, Mr. Marr very kindly staying to lead me the way. By and by met my Lord Crew returning, after having accompanied them a little way. And so after them, Mr. Marr telling me by the way how a maid-servant of Mr. John Wrights (who lives thereabouts), falling sick of the plague, she was removed to an out-house, and a nurse appointed to look to her—who being once absent, the maid got out of the house at the window and run away. The nurse coming and knocking, and having no answer, believed she was dead, and went and told Mr. Wright so; who, and his lady, were in great strait what to do to get her buried. At last resolved to go to Burntwood hard by, being in that parish, and there get people to do it—but they would not; so he went home full of trouble, and in the way met the wench walking over the Common, which frighted him worse then before. And was forced to send people to take her; which he did, and they got one of the pest Coaches and put her into it to carry her to a pest-house. And passing in a narrow lane, Sir Anthony Browne, with his brother and some friends in the coach, met this coach with the Curtains drawn close. The brother being a young man, and believing there might be some lady in it that would not be seen, and the way being narrow, he thrust his head out of his own into her coach to look, and there saw somebody look very ill, and in a sick dress and stunk mightily; which the coachman also cried out upon. And presently they came up to some people that stood looking after it; and told our gallants that it was a maid of Mr. Wrights carried away sick of the plague—which put the young gentleman into a fright had almost cost him his life, but is now well again.

AUGUST 12, 1665

The people die so, that now it seems they are fain to carry the dead to be buried by daylight, the nights not sufficing to do it in. And my Lord Mayor commands people to be within at 9 at night, all (as they say) that the sick may have liberty to go abroad for ayre. There is one also dead out of one of our ships at Deptford, which troubles us mightily—the *Providence* fire-ship, which was just fitted to go to sea. But they tell me today, no more sick on board. And this day W Bodham tells me that one is dead at Woolwich, not far from the Ropeyard. I am told too, that a wife of one of the groomes at Court is dead at Salsbury, so that the King and Queene are speedily to be all gone to Milton. God preserve us.

Why might people have started carrying the dead to be buried during the day?

SEPTEMBER 3, 1665

Lords day. Up, and put on my colourd silk suit, very fine, and my new periwigg, bought a good while since, but darst not wear it because the plague was in Westminster when I bought it. And it is a wonder what will be the fashion after the plague is done as to periwigs, for nobody will dare to buy any haire for fear of the infection—that it had been cut off of the heads of people dead of the plague. . . .

Why did Pepys not want to wear his wigs?

Church being done, my Lord Brouncker, Sir J. Mennes, and I up to the Vestry at the desire of the Justices of the Peace, Sir Th Bidolph and Sir W Boreman and Alderman Hooker—in order to the doing something for the keeping of the plague from growing; but Lord, to consider the madness of people of the town, who will (because they are forbid) come in Crowds along with the dead Corps to see them buried. But we agreed on some orders for the prevention thereof.[5] Among other stories, one was very passionate methought—of a complaint brought against a man in the town for taking a child from London from an infected house. Alderman Hooker told us it was the child of a very able citizen in Gracious-street, a saddler, who had buried all the rest of his children of the plague; and himself and wife now being shut up, and in despair of escaping, did desire only to save the life of this little child; and so prevailed to have it received stark-naked into the arms of a friend, who brought it (having put it into new fresh clothes) to Grenwich; where, upon hearing the story, we did agree it should be [permitted to be] received and kept in the town. Thence with my Lord Brouncker to Captain Cockes, where we mighty merry, and supped; and very late, I by water to Woolwich, in great apprehensions of an Ague. Here was my Lord Brouncker's lady of pleasure, who I perceive goes everywhere with him, and he I find is obliged to carry her and make all the Courtship to her that can be.

The Great Fire of London
SEPTEMBER 2, 1666

Lords day. Some of our maids sitting up late last night to get things ready against our feast today, Jane called us up, about 3 in the morning, to tell us of a great fire they saw in the City.[6] So I rose, and slipped on my nightgown and went to her window, and thought it to be on the back side of Markelane at the furthest; but being unused to such fires as fallowed, I thought it far enough off, and so went to bed again and to sleep. About 7 rose again to dress myself, and there looked out at the window and saw the fire not so much as it was, and further off. So to my closet to set things to rights after yesterday's cleaning. By and by Jane comes and tells me that she hears that above 300 houses have been burned down tonight by the fire we saw, and that it was now burning down all Fishstreet by London Bridge. So I made myself ready presently, and walked to the Tower and there got up upon one of the high places, Sir J Robinsons little son going up with me; and there I did see the houses at that end of the bridge all on fire, and an infinite great fire on this and the other side the end of the bridge—which, among other people, did trouble me for poor little Michell and our Sarah on the Bridge. So down, with my heart full of trouble, to the Lieutenant of the Tower, who tells me that it begun this morning in the King's bakers house in Pudding-lane, and that it hath burned down St. Magnes Church and most part of Fishstreete already. So I down to the water-side and there got a boat and through bridge, and there saw a lamentable fire. Poor Michells house, as far as the Old Swan, already burned that way and the fire running further, that in a very little time it got as far as the Stillyard while I was there. Everybody endeavouring to remove their goods, and flinging into the River or bringing them into lighters that lay off. Poor people staying in their houses as long as till the very fire touched them, and then running into boats or clambering from one pair of stair by the water-side to another. And among other things, the poor

When and where did the fire begin?

5. **orders . . . thereof.** Laws were made forbiddng funeral processions during the plague.
6. **fire . . . City.** This was the Great Fire of London, which burned for four days and nights.

WORDS FOR EVERYDAY USE

a • gue (ā´gyo͞o) *n.*, fever and chills. *Because of his ague, the patient would push aside the bedcovers one minute and pull them up to his chin the next.*

ANSWER TO GUIDED READING QUESTION

1. The fire began on the morning of September 2, 1666, in the king's baker's house in Pudding-lane.

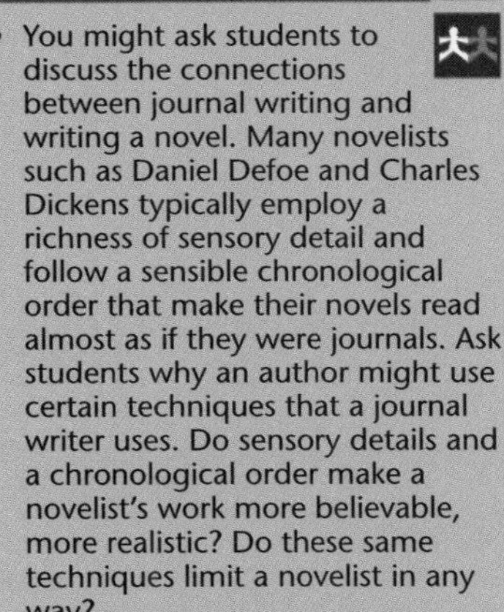

ADDITIONAL QUESTIONS AND ACTIVITIES

- You might ask students to discuss the connections between journal writing and writing a novel. Many novelists such as Daniel Defoe and Charles Dickens typically employ a richness of sensory detail and follow a sensible chronological order that make their novels read almost as if they were journals. Ask students why an author might use certain techniques that a journal writer uses. Do sensory details and a chronological order make a novelist's work more believable, more realistic? Do these same techniques limit a novelist in any way?
- Students can discuss "the madness of people in the town, who will (because they are forbid) come in Crowds along with the dead Corps to see them buried." Is the crowd's behavior exclusively a seventeenth-century phenomenon? Why, or why not?

HISTORICAL NOTE

Attracted by the hope of work in urban areas, many poor people crowded the workers' quarters of London. Fires were a common threat in seventeenth-century cities, and flimsy housing and overcrowding among the poor increased the threat. The wealthy often built their houses of brick or stone. Even so, the Great Fire of 1666 destroyed 75 percent of London, including thirteen thousand houses.

Quotables

"How great a matter a little fire kindleth."

—James 3:5

ANSWER TO GUIDED READING QUESTION

1. The high winds and a recent drought made the fire especially destructive.

ADDITIONAL QUESTIONS AND ACTIVITIES

1. Why might Pepys have suggested that the Lord Mayor "pull down houses" in order to stop the fire?

Answer

1. Pepys might have made the suggestion because the bricks, stone, and other rubble from the houses were not as combustible and might slow down the fire.

INTERNET ACTIVITIES

Students may be curious to read more of Samuel Pepys's diary and learn more about his life. The full text of an 1825 edition of his diary can be found at **Bibliomania,** at the address http://www.bibliomania.com/NonFiction/Pepys/Diary/. Selected entries and commentary can be found at http://beebo.org/journal/about.html and http://beebo.org/journal. Students might write about some of their favorite entries and what these entries revealed about Pepys and his times.

Great Fire of London, 1666. Museum of London.

pigeons I perceive were loath to leave their houses, but hovered about the windows and balconies till they were some of them burned, their wings, and fell down.

Having stayed, and in an hour's time seen the fire rage every way, and nobody to my sight endeavouring to quench it, but to remove their goods and leave all to the fire; and having seen it get as far as the Steeleyard, and the wind mighty high and driving it into the city, and everything, after so long a drougth, proving combustible, even the very stones of churches, and among other things, the poor steeple by which pretty Mrs. _____ lives, and whereof my old school-fellow Elborough is parson, taken fire in the very top and there burned till it fall down—I to Whitehall with a gentleman with me who desired to go off from the Tower to see the fire in my boat—to White-hall, and there up to the King's closet in the chapel, where people came about me and I did give them an account dismayed them all; and word was carried in to the King, so I was called for and did tell the King and Duke of York what I saw, and that unless his Majesty did command houses to be pulled down, nothing could stop the fire. They seemed much troubled, and the King commanded me to go to my

What factors contributed to making the fire especially destructive?

ArtNote

Great Fire of London, 1666. Museum of London. The Great Fire of London lasted from September 2 to September 5, 1666. It remains the worst fire in the history of London. More than thirteen thousand homes and many important civic buildings were burned. People fled from the city to the countryside and swarmed the river Thames.

WORDS FOR EVERYDAY USE

en • deav • or (en dev´ər) *vi.,* try, attempt. *Should we endeavor to cross the river in this storm?*

Lord Mayor from him and command him to spare no houses but to pull down before the fire every way. The Duke of York bid me tell him that if he would have any more soldiers, he shall; and so did my Lord Arlington afterward, as a great secret. Here meeting with Captain Cocke, I in his coach, which he lent me, and Creed with me, to Pauls; and there walked along Watling-street as well as I could, every creature coming away loaden with goods to save—and here and there sick people carried away in beds. Extraordinary good goods carried in carts and on backs. At last met my Lord Mayor in Canning Streete, like a man spent, with a hankercher about his neck. To the King's message, he cried like a fainting woman, "Lord, what can I do? I am spent. People will not obey me. I have been pull[ing] down houses. But the fire overtakes us faster then we can do it." That he needed no more soldiers; and that for himself, he must go and refresh himself, having been up all night. So he left me, and I him, and walked home—seeing people all almost distracted and no manner of means used to quench the fire. The houses too, so very thick thereabouts, and full of matter for burning, as pitch and tar, in Thames-street—and warehouses of oyle and wines and Brandy and other things. Here I saw Mr. Isaccke Houblon, that handsome man—prettily dressed and dirty at his door at Dowgate, receiving some of his brothers things whose houses were on fire; and as he says, have been removed twice already, and he doubts (as it soon proved) that they must be in a little time removed from his house also—which was a sad consideration. And to see the churches all filling with goods, by people who themselfs should have been quietly there at this time.

About what did the Lord Mayor complain?

By this time it was about 12 a-clock, and so home and there find my guests, which was Mr. Wood and his wife, Barbary Shelden, and also Mr. Moone—she mighty fine, and her husband, for aught I see, a likely man. But Mr. Moones design and mine, which was to look over my closet and please him with the sight thereof, which he hath long desired, was wholly disappointed, for we were in great trouble and disturbance at this fire, not knowing what to think of it. However, we had an extraordinary good dinner, and as merry as at this time we could be.

While at dinner, Mrs. Batelier came to enquire after Mr. Woolfe and Stanes (who it seems are related to them), whose houses in Fishstreet are all burned, and they in a sad condition. She would not stay in the fright.

As soon as dined, I and Moone away and walked through the City, the streets full of nothing but people and horses and carts loaden with goods, ready to run over one another, and removing goods from one burned house to another—they now removing out of Canning-street (which received goods in the morning) into Lumbard Streete and further; and among others, I now saw my little goldsmith Stokes receiving some friend's goods, whose house itself was burned the day after. We parted at Pauls, he home and I to Pauls-Wharf, where I had appointed a boat to attend me; and took in Mr. Carcasse and his brother, whom I met in the street, and carried them below and above bridge, to and again, to see the fire, which was now got further, both below and above, and no likelihood of stopping it. Met with the King and Duke of York in their Barge, and with them to Queen-Hith and there called Sir Rd. Browne to them. Their order was only to pull down houses apace, and so below bridge at the water-side; but little was or could be done, the fire coming upon them so fast. Good hopes there was of stopping it at the Three Cranes above, and at Buttolphs-Wharf below bridge, if care be used; but the wind carries it into the City, so as we know not by the water-side what it doth there. River full of lighter[s] and boats taking in goods, and good goods swimming in the water; and only, I

What type of activity was taking place in the city when Pepys and Mr. Moone went for a walk?

ANSWERS TO GUIDED READING QUESTIONS

1. The Lord Mayor complained that people would not obey his orders and that the fire was moving faster than he and his workers could tear down houses.
2. As Pepys and Mr. Moone walked through the city, people were frantically carting goods from one house to another to save their possessions from the fire.

CROSS-CURRICULAR ACTIVITIES

Architecture. Students can research the work of architect Christopher Wren (1632–1723), who redesigned St. Paul's Cathedral after the fire. Have students present in a written or oral report their research about Wren and his design for St. Paul's.

ANSWERS TO GUIDED READING QUESTIONS

1. People were escaping from the fire by boats and other small craft on the river.
2. Pepys finally had to begin removing goods from his own home, carrying them out into the garden or storing them in iron chests in the cellar.
3. The rumor was that the French had started the fire and that they were invading the city.

ADDITIONAL QUESTIONS AND ACTIVITIES

While Pepys does provide a detailed account of the lives of the bourgeois class in London during the Enlightenment, there exist few similar accounts from the perspective of the impoverished classes in London. One of the first writers to document the lives of impoverished London dwellers was the Victorian journalist Henry Mayhew.

Students who are interested in London life or the inequalities present in the British class structure should be encouraged to read a few brief selections from Mayhew's *London Labour and the London Poor,* 1849–1850.

How were people escaping from the fire?

observed that hardly one lighter or boat in three that had the goods of a house in, but there was a pair of virginalls[7] in it. Having seen as much as I could now, I away to White-hall by appointment, and there walked to St. James's Park, and there met my wife and Creed and Wood and his wife and walked to my boat, and there upon the water again, and to the fire up and down, it still increasing and the wind great. So near the fire as we could for smoke; and all over the Thames, with one's face in the wind you were almost burned with a shower of Firedrops—this is very true—so as houses were burned by these drops and flakes of fire, three or four, nay five or six houses, one from another. When we could endure no more upon the water, we to a little alehouse on the Bankside over against the Three Cranes, and there stayed till it was dark almost and saw the fire grow; and as it grow darker, appeared more and more, and in Corners and upon steeples and between churches and houses, as far as we courd see up the hill of the City, in a most horrid malicious bloody flame, not like the fine flame of an ordinary fire. Barbary and her husband away before us. We stayed till, it being darkish, we saw the fire as only one entire arch of fire from this to the other side the bridge, and in a bow up the hill, for an arch of above a mile long. It made me weep to see it. The churches, houses, and all on fire and flaming at once, and a horrid noise the flames made, and the cracking of houses at their ruine. So home with a sad heart, and there find everybody discoursing and lamenting the fire; and poor Tom Hater came with some few of his goods saved out of his house, which is burned upon Fish-street hill. I invited him to lie at my house, and did receive his goods: but was deceived in his lying there, the noise coming every moment of the growth of the Fire, so as we were forced to begin to pack up our own goods and prepare for their removal. And did by Moone-shine (it being brave, dry, and moonshine and warm weather) carry much of my goods into the garden, and Mr. Hater and I did remove my money and Iron-chests into my cellar—as thinking that the safest place. And got my bags of gold into my office ready to carry away, and my chief papers of accounts also there, and my tallies into a box by themselfs. So great was our fear, as Sir W. Batten had carts come out of the country to fetch away his goods this night. We did put Mr. Hater, poor man, to bed a little; but he got but very little rest, so much noise being in my house, taking down of goods.

What did Pepys finally have to do about his own home?

September 5, 1666

I lay down in the office again upon W. Hewer's quilt, being mighty weary and sore in my feet with going till I was hardly able to stand. About 2 in the morning my wife calls me up and tells of new Cryes of "Fyre!"—it being come to Barkeing Church, which is the bottom of our lane. I up; and finding it so, resolved presently to take her away; and did, and took my gold (which was about 2350*l*), W. Hewer, and Jane down by Poundy's boat to Woolwich. But Lord, what a sad sight it was by moonlight to see the whole City almost on fire—that you might see it plain at Woolwich, as if you were by it. There when I came, I find the gates[8] shut, but no guard kept at all; which troubled me, because of discourses now begun that there is plot in it and that the French had done it.[9] I got the gates open, and to Mr. Shelden's, where I locked up my gold and charged my wife and W. Hewer never to leave the room without one of them in it night nor day. So back again, by the way seeing my goods well in the lighters at Deptford

What was the rumor about how the fire had started?

7. **pair of virginalls.** Small rectangular harpsichord of the sixteenth century, usually held in the lap
8. **gates.** Dockyard gates
9. **discourses . . . it.** Rumors that the French had started the fire and were now entering the city

and watched well by people. Home, and whereas I expected to have seen our house on fire, it being now about 7 a-clock, it was not. But to the Fyre, and there find greater hopes then I expected; for my confidence of finding our office on fire was such, that I durst not ask anybody how it was with us, till I came and saw it not burned. But going to the fire, I find, by the blowing up of houses and the great help given by the workmen out of the King's yards, sent up by Sir W. Penn, there is a good stop given to it, as well at Marke-lane end as ours—it having only burned the Dyall of Barkeing Church, and part of the porch, and was there quenched. I up to the top of Barkeing steeple, and there saw the saddest sight of desolation that I ever saw. Everywhere great fires. Oyle-cellars and brimstone and other things burning. I became afeared to stay there long; and therefore down again as fast as I could, the fire being spread as far as I could see it, and to Sir W. Penn's and there eat a piece of cold meat, having eaten nothing since Sunday but the remains of Sunday's dinner.

What did Pepys see when he reached the top of Barkeing steeple?

Here I met with Mr. Young and Whistler; and having removed all my things, and received good hopes that the fire at our end is stopped, they and I walked into the town and find Fanchurch street, Gracious-street, and Lumbard-street all in dust. The Exchange a sad sight, nothing standing there of all the statues or pillars but Sir Tho. Gresham's picture in the corner.[10] Walked into Moore-fields (our feet ready to burn, walking through the town among the hot coles) and find that full of people, and poor wretches carrying their goods there, and everybody keeping his goods together by themselfs (and a great blessing it is to them that it is fair weather for them to keep abroad night and day); drank there, and paid twopence for a plain penny loaf.

Thence homeward, having passed through Cheapside and Newgate-market, all burned—and seen Anthony Joyces house in fire. And took up (which I keep by me) a piece of glass of Mercer's chapel in the street, where much more was, so melted and buckled with the heat of the fire, like parchment. I also did see a poor Catt taken out of a hole in the chimney joyning to the wall of the Exchange, with the hair all burned off the body and yet alive. So home at night, and find there good hopes of saving our office—but great endeavours of watching all night and having men ready; and so we lodged them in the office, and had drink and bread and cheese for them. And I lay down and slept a good night about midnight—though when I rose, I hear that there had been a great alarme of French and Duch being risen—which proved nothing. But it is a strange thing to see how long this time did look since Sunday, having been alway full of variety of actions, and little sleep, that it looked like a week or more. And I had forgot almost the day of the week. ■

Why had Pepys almost forgotten the day of the week?

10. **Exchange . . . corner.** The stock exchange was destroyed except for the statue of Gresham, the founder.

Respond *to the* SELECTION

What are your impressions of Pepys? Is he someone who you would have liked to have known had you lived in his day? Why, or why not?

ANSWERS TO GUIDED READING QUESTIONS

1. When he reached the top of Barkeing steeple, Pepys saw fires burning everywhere and the destruction left in the fire's wake.
2. Pepys had forgotten the day of the week because of the harried events of the fire and his lack of sleep.

SELECTION CHECK TEST 4.7.9 WITH ANSWERS

Checking Your Reading

1. In his first entry, what does Pepys resolve to do about his finances? **He resolves to be more careful and to set himself some rules to live by.**
2. What gives Anthony Browne's brother a fright "that almost cost him his life"? **He's told that the woman in the coach has the plague.**
3. Why is a 9 PM curfew imposed? **The curfew allows the sick to go out at night.**
4. What did Pepys advise the King to do to try to stop the spread of the fire? **He recommended pulling down houses in its way.**
5. What happens to Pepys' personal goods and his house? **He moves his goods into the garden and sends his wife away with their gold, but his house is spared.**

Literary Tools

1. What is the difference between a diary and a journal? **In contrast to a diary, the word *journal* connotes an outward rather than an inward focus. Students may disagree with this definition, however, since the terms are often used** interchangeably.
2. From what point of view is this selection told? **It is in first-person point of view.**
3. Describe Pepys' language and writing style. **The language is informal and straightforward.**

RESPOND TO THE SELECTION

As an alternate activity, students might create a list of questions they would like to ask Pepys if they could meet him. These questions could be about the events that Pepys witnessed or they could be about him personally.

ANSWERS TO INVESTIGATE, INQUIRE, IMAGINE

RECALL

1a. Pepys saw the play *Romeo and Juliet.* He thought that it was "the worst that I have ever seen in my life" and that it was poorly acted.

2a. The words were written on doors because the people within had the plague. Anthony Browne's brother saw a plague-ridden woman inside the coach. According to Pepys, people stopped buying wigs because they feared the wig hair had been cut from the heads of plague victims.

3a. Pepys likened the fire as seen from the alehouse to an "arch" (p. 594). He says that it was a "most horrid malicious bloody flame." He said the fire spread over a mile. After this description, Pepys describes the churches and houses that are on fire and the "horrid noise the flames made, and the cracking of houses at their ruine." Next, Pepys tells of his having to remove his possessions from his own home as the fire steadily grows.

INTERPRET

1b. *Responses will vary.* Pepys seems a very straightforward, analytical person. He might not have enjoyed the play because of its romantic theme. Another reason he did not enjoy the play was that he felt the theater was too crowded, being that it was opening night.

2b. Pepys's note on August 12, that so many people are dying they cannot be buried at night, proves that the plague was quite extensive in 1665. Pepys's description creates a mood of foreboding.

3b. Describing this specific event increases the horror of the whole because it emphasizes the destruction on a smaller, more personal scale, as the fire comes closer and closer to Pepys.

ANALYZE

4a. Pepys chose to record major public events of his time. He wrote about the plague and the great fire of London. These events had a major impact on life in England. He also writes about personal matters, such as his relationships with relatives, his finances, and entertainment he partakes in in his leisure time. He mentions many acquaintances, bringing alive the social scene of his day.

SYNTHESIZE

4b. The things Pepys chose to record seem to indicate that Pepys is a fairly objective observer. Also, if the

INVESTIGATE Inquire, Imagine

Recall: GATHERING FACTS

1a. What play did Pepys record having seen in the entry for March 1, 1662? What did he think of the play?

2a. Why were the words "Lord have mercy upon us" written on the doors of the houses in Drury Lane? What did Anthony Browne's brother see when he looked inside the coach? Why, according to Pepys, did people stop buying wigs?

3a. To what did Pepys liken the fire in the city as it appeared to him from the tavern? How large was the fire? What did Pepys describe immediately after describing the arch of fire over the city?

→ **Interpret:** FINDING MEANING

1b. What sort of person do you think Pepys was? Why might he not have enjoyed a dramatic, romantic play like the one described in the entry for March 1?

2b. How extensive was the plague in 1665? What mood is created by Pepys's description of it?

3b. How does describing a specific event increase the horror of the whole?

Analyze: TAKING THINGS APART

4a. Analyze the kinds of events Pepys chose to record.

→ **Synthesize:** BRINGING THINGS TOGETHER

4b. What can you infer about Pepys based on the subjects he chose to write about and the kinds of details he used?

Evaluate: MAKING JUDGMENTS

5a. Judge whether Pepys was a reliable record keeper. Is he an objective one?

→ **Extend:** CONNECTING IDEAS

5b. Compare Pepys' diary to the selection from *The Book of Margery Kempe* on page 211.

Understanding Literature

POINT OF VIEW. Review the definition for **point of view** in The Handbook of Literary Terms. How much does Pepys's point of view affect how you perceive the events he describes? How is a person's diary entry about a historical event different from a newspaper article of an event? How is one person's point of view about something like the plague valuable in its own way?

JOURNAL. Review the definitions for **journal** and *diary* in Literary Tools on page 588. Given these definitions, would you characterize Pepys's work as a diary or a journal? How often does Pepys give us insight into his interior world? Does he express his emotions freely, or are his writings more a documentation of the time during which he lived?

ANSWERS TO INVESTIGATE, INQUIRE, IMAGINE (CONT.)

reader believes that Pepys advised the king in the matter of the fire, the reader can conclude that Pepys was probably an important and respected man ofhis time.

EVALUATE

5a. Pepys's attitude toward himself and others seems rather objective. Because of his matter-of-fact, methodical manner of recording events and his reactions to them, Pepys seems like a reliable record-keeper.

EXTEND

5b. *Responses will vary.* Students should note that Pepys's diary focuses more on public events and Kempe's autobiography has a more personal focus.

WRITER'S JOURNAL

1. Keep a **diary** or **journal** for a week. Each day, decide what events you wish to include. They may be world, national, local, or personal events.
2. Choose a newsworthy event. Write a **personal account** in a series of journal articles from the point of view of somebody involved in the event.
3. Write a short piece of **historical fiction** based on one or more of the events Pepys includes in his diary. Consider the details Pepys uses and the mood he creates. Consider how these will affect your story.

Integrating *the* LANGUAGE ARTS

Language, Grammar, and Style

STANDARD, FORMAL ENGLISH. Because of the informal style of a diary, the language in this selection is often not standard. Choose a paragraph and rewrite it in standard, formal English. This includes using full sentences, proper punctuation, and standard syntax or word order. Refer to the Language Arts Survey 3.2, "Formal and Informal English" for more information.

Study and Research

SUMMARY. What do others have to say about the events Pepys writes about in his diary? Choose a topic, such as the plague or the Great Fire of London. Use a library catalog to find books on English history. Do some research on your topic. Then write a summary of your findings. In your summary explain how well Pepys' account matches the other information you found.

Applied English

WRITING A LETTER IN RESPONSE TO A REVIEW. Pepys did not like the performance of *Romeo and Juliet* he saw. Critics present both positive and negative comments in their reviews. Newspapers sometimes publish letters in response to reviews. Find a review of a movie or play you have seen, a book you have read, or a musical recording you have heard. A reliable online source for book, movie, and film reviews is *The New York Times* website at http://www.nytimes.com/info/contents/siteindex.html. Decide whether you agree with the review that you choose to read. Then write a letter expressing your opinion and explaining why you do or do not agree with the review.

Collaborative Learning & Media Literacy

TIME CAPSULE. A diary is one way of preserving a record of the past. A time capsule is another. As a class, create a time capsule to record the important events of your years in high school. You may wish to include newspaper articles, magazines, CDs, photographs, and other items that show important events and icons of this age. You might also include recorded interviews with classmates describing the event that most impressed them.

ANSWERS TO UNDERSTANDING LITERATURE

POINT OF VIEW. Pepys's point of view has a strong but not overwhelming effect on the reader's perception of events. Pepys's detachment from what he describes doesn't block the reader's view of happenings. However, his point of view as a middle-class male does color his account. One would imagine that the plague-ridden maid-servant would have far graver concerns than Pepys's fear of infected periwigs. A journal entry about a historical event differs from other straight, factual accounts because it reveals only one person's experience. The reader can know only what happens to and around the journal writer and must see events through the journal writer's eyes. However, a personal view of an event such as the plague is valuable because it personalizes an event that appears static in most other historical accounts.
NOTE: Students can discuss how the events of the plague or the fire might have been recorded by some of the people named in Pepys's journal, such as the maid-servant or the Lord Mayor.

JOURNAL. Pepys rarely gives insight into his interior world. Most often, he chooses to note his reactions to events rather than detail his ruminations about them. For example, he writes that seeing the houses marked for plague "put me into an ill conception of myself and my smell, so that I was forced to buy some roll-tobacco to smell and to chaw—which took away the apprehension." Pepys notes his discomfort but doesn't dwell on it; at the same time, he gives later readers an interesting bit of social history. Pepys's journal is a record of events first and a personal log second; most glimpses of his personality emerge through his documentation of events rather than through straightforward statements of feeling.
NOTE: Students should support their opinions with direct quotations from the selection.

ANSWERS TO INTEGRATING THE LANGUAGE ARTS

Language, Grammar, and Style
Responses will vary depending on the section students choose.

Study and Research
Students might choose to create visual representations of the events they write about. Illustrations or other visual aids should accompany a written description.

Applied English
Students can send their letters to the publication in which they read the original review.

ADDITIONAL RESOURCES

UNIT 7 RESOURCE BOOK
- Selection Worksheet 7.5
- Selection Check Test 4.7.11
- Selection Test 4.7.12
- Language, Grammar, and Style Resource 3.3
- Applied English Resource 6.4

INDIVIDUAL LEARNING STRATEGIES

MOTIVATION
Have students discuss aspects of modern society that they find disturbing or would like to see changed. (Examples might include pollution; cultural tensions; politics.) Ask students what elements of humor they can find in these troubling situations.

READING PROFICIENCY
Identify some of the major elements, such as the imaginary country of Lilliput, before students begin reading. The advanced vocabulary and syntax of the selection may be difficult for some students. Encourage them to stop periodically to make notes about what they have read.

ENGLISH LANGUAGE LEARNING
In addition to following the suggestions for Reading Proficiency above, share with students the following additional vocabulary:
plumb—determine depth
expedient—device used in an emergency
discompose—disarrange; disturb the order of
viceroy—person ruling a county as the deputy of a sovereign
procurement—obtaining; securing
integrity—honesty; sincerity
privy to—privately informed about

SPECIAL NEEDS
Read through the selection once with students, and then work together as a class to complete the graphic organizer in Literary Tools.

ENRICHMENT
Students may discuss troubles in modern society as suggested in Motivation. Then, they may choose a particular issue and write a satiric paragraph, mixing critique with humor. They may also choose to create a skit based on their satiric paragraph; for example, they could portray a parent scolding his or her child because the child is paying too much attention to the real world and not watching enough television.

FROM Gulliver's Travels
FROM "A Voyage to Lilliput"
FROM "A Voyage to Brobdingnag"

BY JONATHAN SWIFT

About *the* AUTHOR

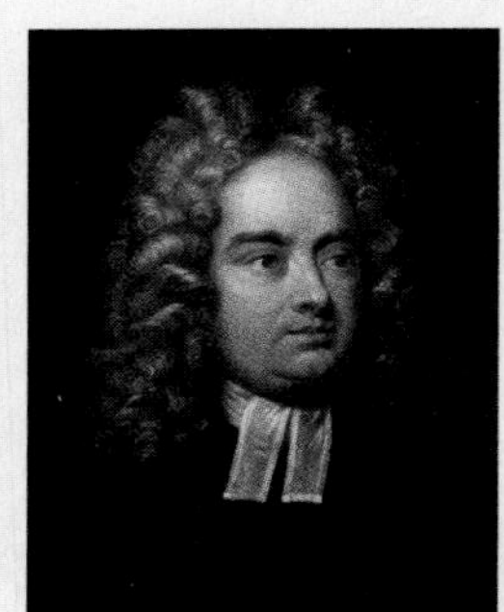

Jonathan Swift's (1667–1745) family was poor, but a generous uncle funded Jonathan's education at Kilkenny Grammar School and at Trinity College, Dublin. Undecided about what career to pursue, Swift went to live with and work for Sir William Temple in Surrey. There he met "Stella," to whom he dedicated much of his work. Swift was buried by her side, although in life their relationship was unsteady. After reading one of Swift's first publications, John Dryden told him, "Cousin Swift, you will never be a poet." Very soon after this, Swift left Temple's home for Ireland and became an Anglican priest. Two years later, though, he rededicated himself to a writing career.

Swift suffered from dizziness and nausea (probably Ménière's syndrome) for most of his life. While he said that he "liked individuals but hated humanity," he cared enough to try to mend the evils that he saw in the world. Swift wrote biting commentaries and satires for numerous periodicals and journals, and, as its official pamphleteer, wrote position papers for the Tory government, as well as his own epitaph: "Where fierce indignation no longer tears the heart." Notable satirical works by Swift include *The Battle of the Books* (1704, composed 1697), *A Tale of a Tub* (1704), *Gulliver's Travels* (1726), and "A Modest Proposal" (1729, see page 643).

About *the* SELECTIONS

While enjoyable as a fantastic travel account, ***Gulliver's Travels*** (1726) is at the same time a wicked **satire** on politics and political morals. Originally titled *"Travels into Several Remote Nations of the World," by Lemuel Gulliver,* the book tells of Gulliver's experiences in four fantastic lands.

This selection includes excerpts from Part I, "A Voyage to Lilliput," where the people are one-twelfth the size of Gulliver and are proportionally small-minded and petty; and from Part II, "A Voyage to Brobdingnag," where the people are twelve times Gulliver's size and, after hearing his tales of European social and technological achievements, come to view Europeans as "a pernicious race of little odious vermin."

In Part III Gulliver visits Laputa, a flying island inhabited by "wise" scholars with their heads in the clouds, who are completely inept in practical endeavors; and in Part IV he visits the land of the Houyhnhnms, inhabited by speaking horses whose good sense, gentleness, and gentility contrast sharply with the vigorous stupidity of the human-like Yahoos.

GOALS/OBJECTIVES

Studying this lesson will enable students to
- have positive experiences reading satire
- describe Jonathan Swift's literary accomplishments and explain the historical significance of his writings
- define *satire, irony,* and *fantasy* and recognize and interpret these techniques as they encounter them in their reading
- characterize *tone* in literature they read and rewrite to change tone
- compose a peace treaty

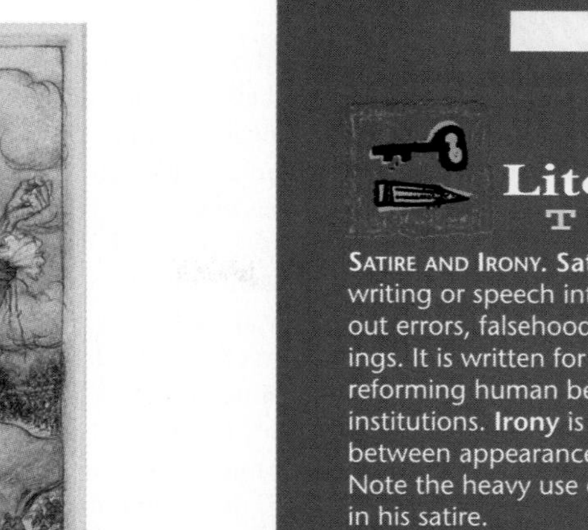

Gulliver Released from the Strings. Arthur Rackham. Wellesley College.

FROM

Gulliver's Travels

JONATHAN SWIFT

FROM

A Voyage to Lilliput

CHAPTER 5. THE AUTHOR BY AN EXTRAORDINARY STRATAGEM PREVENTS AN INVASION. A HIGH TITLE OF HONOR IS CONFERRED UPON HIM. . . .

The empire of Blefuscu is an island situated to the north north-east side of Lilliput, from whence it is parted only by a channel of eight hundred yards wide. I had not yet seen it, and upon this notice of an intended invasion, I avoided appearing on that side of the coast, for fear of being discovered by

WORDS FOR EVERYDAY USE

strat • a • gem (strat´ ə jəm) *n.*, trick or plan. *The team devised a stratagem to defeat their opponents.*

SHORT STORY

Literary TOOLS

SATIRE AND IRONY. Satire is humorous writing or speech intended to point out errors, falsehoods, foibles, or failings. It is written for the purpose of reforming human behavior or human institutions. **Irony** is a difference between appearance and reality. Note the heavy use of irony by Swift in his satire.

FANTASY. A **fantasy** is a literary work that contains highly unrealistic elements. Keep a chart of fantastic elements. Classify them as exaggerations or adaptations of reality or as completely made up.

Based in reality	Completely made up
	Blefuscu and Lilliput

Reader's Journal

If aliens landed in your community, what conclusions do you think they would come to about humans?

GRAPHIC ORGANIZER

Students may include the following in their graphic organizers:

BASED IN REALITY
the emperor's plan to become the monarch of the whole world
warring situations are similar to real ones

COMPLETELY MADE UP
Blefuscu and Lilliput
the measurement *glumgluff*
people 1/12 the size or 12 times the size of a human

READER'S JOURNAL

Suggest that students focus on one specific event or experience. For example, what would an alien think of a traffic jam on the highway? a high-school football game? a birthday party?

VOCABULARY FROM THE SELECTION

abominate	ingratiate
acute	junta
agitation	lenity
confounded	odious
contriver	panegyric
desolation	pernicious
detract	pervert
elude	procure
embargo	recapitulate
extremities	scruple
hitherto	stratagem
impotent	tribute
infallibly	veneration

ANSWER TO GUIDED READING QUESTION

1. Gulliver hooks and ties together all the enemy ships and carries them away in order to aid the Lilliputians in their war against the Blefuscudians.

HISTORICAL NOTE

In 1714, the Scriblerus Club was formed to satirize false teachings and pedantry. The group included Swift and other writers such as Alexander Pope, John Arbuthnot, John Gay, and Thomas Parnell. Although the club discontinued meetings after the first year, Swift's association with these writers and thinkers influenced his development of Part Three of *Gulliver's Travels.*

LITERARY NOTE

For another example of Swift's satire, refer students to "A Modest Proposal," which appears as a Selection for Additional Reading on page 643 of this unit.

some of the enemy's ships, who had received no intelligence of me; all intercourse between the two empires having been strictly forbidden during the war, upon pain of death; and an embargo laid by our Emperor upon all vessels whatsoever. I communicated to his Majesty a project I had formed of seizing the enemy's whole fleet; which, as our scouts assured us, lay at anchor in the harbor ready to sail with the first fair wind. I consulted the most experienced seamen upon the depth of the channel, which they had often plumbed; who told me, that in the middle at high water it was seventy *glumgluffs* deep, which is about six foot of European measure; and the rest of it fifty *glumgluffs* at most. I walked to the northeast coast over against Blefuscu; where, lying down behind a hillock, I took out my small pocket perspective glass,[1] and viewed the enemy's fleet at anchor, consisting of about fifty men of war, and a great number of transports: I then came back to my house, and gave order (for which I had a warrant) for a great quantity of the strongest cable and bars of iron. The cable was about as thick as packthread, and the bars of the length and size of a knitting-needle. I trebled the cable to make it stronger, and for the same reason I twisted three of the iron bars together, bending the extremities into a hook. Having thus fixed fifty hooks to as many cables, I went back to the northeast coast, and putting off my coat, shoes, and stockings, walked into the sea in my leathern jerkin,[2] about half an hour before high water. I waded with what haste I could, and swam in the middle about thirty yards until I felt the ground; I arrived at the fleet in less than half an hour. The enemy was so frighted when they saw me, that they leaped out of their ships, and swam to shore, where there could not be fewer than thirty thousand souls. I then took my tackling, and fastening a hook to the hole at the prow of each, I tied all the cords together at the end. While I was thus employed, the enemy discharged several thousand arrows, many of which stuck in my hands and face; and besides the excessive smart, gave me much disturbance in my work. My greatest apprehension was for my eyes, which I should have infallibly lost, if I had not suddenly thought of an expedient. I kept, among other little necessaries, a pair of spectacles in a private pocket, which, as I observed before, had escaped the Emperor's searchers. These I took out, and fastened as strongly as I could upon my nose; and thus armed went on boldly with my work in spite of the enemy's arrows; many of which struck against the glasses of my spectacles, but without any other effect, further than a little to discompose them. I had now fastened all the hooks, and taking the knot in my hand, began to pull; but not a ship would stir, for they were all too fast by their anchors, so that the boldest part of my enterprise remained. I therefore let go the cord, and leaving the hooks fixed to the ships, I resolutely cut with my knife the cables that fastened the anchors, receiving about two hundred shots in my face and hands; then I took up the knotted end of the cables to which my hooks were tied; and with great ease drew fifty of the enemy's largest men-of-war after me.

How does Gulliver aid the Lilliputians in their war against the Blefuscudians?

The Blefuscudians, who had not the least imagination of what I intended, were at first confounded with astonishment. They had seen

1. **perspective glass.** Telescope
2. **jerkin.** Vest or sleeveless jacket

WORDS FOR EVERYDAY USE

em • bar • go (em bär´gō) *n.,* government order prohibiting the entry or departure of ships. *Because of the grain embargo, many farmers could not sell their crops abroad.*

ex • trem • i • ties (ek strem´ə tēz) *n.,* outermost parts. *Frostbite first affects a person's extremities, such as the fingers and the toes.*

in • fal • li • bly (in fal´ə blē) *adv.,* unmistakedly. *Can you infallibly identify the constellations without looking through a telescope?*

con • found • ed (kən found´əd) *adj.,* confused. *The overlapping sets of animal tracks confounded the hunters.*

me cut the cables, and thought my design was only to let the ships run adrift, or fall foul on each other: but when they perceived the whole fleet moving in order, and saw me pulling at the end, they set up such a scream of grief and despair, that it is almost impossible to describe or conceive. When I had got out of danger, I stopped a while to pick out the arrows that stuck in my hands and face, and rubbed on some of the same ointment that was given me at my first arrival, as I have formerly mentioned. I then took off my spectacles, and waiting about an hour until the tide was a little fallen, I waded through the middle with my cargo, and arrived safe at the royal port of Lilliput.

The Emperor and his whole court stood on the shore, expecting the issue of this great adventure. They saw the ships move forward in a large half-moon, but could not discern me, who was up to my breast in water. When I advanced to the middle of the channel, they were yet more in pain, because I was under water to my neck. The Emperor concluded me to be drowned, and that the enemy's fleet was approaching in a hostile manner: but he was soon eased of his fears, for the channel growing shallower every step I made, I came in a short time within hearing; and holding up the end of the cable by which the fleet was fastened, I cried in a loud voice, Long live the most puissant[3] Emperor of Lilliput! This great prince received me at my landing with all possible encomiums,[4] and created me a *Nardac* upon the spot, which is the highest title of honor among them.

His Majesty desired I would take some other opportunity of bringing all the rest of his enemy's ships into his ports. And so unmeasurable is the ambition of princes, that he seemed to think of nothing less than reducing the whole empire of Blefuscu into a province, and governing it by a viceroy; of destroying the Big-Endian exiles, and compelling that people to break the smaller end of their eggs,[5] by which he would remain sole monarch of the whole world. But I endeavored to divert him from this design, by many arguments drawn from the topics of policy as well as justice: and I plainly protested, that I would never be an instrument of bringing a free and brave people into slavery. And when the matter was debated in council, the wisest part of the ministry were of my opinion.

What does Gulliver refuse to do?

This open bold declaration of mine was so opposite to the schemes and politics of his Imperial Majesty, that he could never forgive me; he mentioned it in a very artful manner at council, where I was told that some of the wisest appeared, at least by their silence, to be of my opinion; but others, who were my secret enemies, could not forbear some expressions, which by a side-wind[6] reflected on me. And from this time began an intrigue between his Majesty and a junta of ministers maliciously bent against me, which broke out in less than two months, and had like to have ended in my utter des-truction. Of so little weight are the greatest services to princes, when put into the balance with a refusal to gratify their passions.

◆ ◆ ◆

3. **puissant.** Powerful
4. **encomiums.** Expressions of high praise
5. **Big-Endian . . . eggs.** In Chapter 4, Gulliver explains that this dispute started with the Emperor's decree that all his subjects must break their eggs at the small end. This dispute is Swift's allegorical and satirical portrayal of the schism between Catholics and Protestants during his time.
6. **side-wind.** Indirect means, method, or manner

WORDS FOR EVERYDAY USE

jun • ta (hōōn´tə) *n.*, council. *According to recent news reports, the ruler has refused the advice of his junta.*

ANSWER TO GUIDED READING QUESTION

1. Gulliver refuses to aid the Lilliputians in conquering and enslaving other enemies.

ADDITIONAL QUESTIONS AND ACTIVITIES

Students can discuss Gulliver's assertion that "Of so little weight are the greatest services to princes, when put into the balance with a refusal to gratify their passions." What does Gulliver mean? How does this sentiment relate to modern politics?

ANSWERS TO GUIDED READING QUESTIONS

1. The king thinks the government of Gulliver's people is controlled by those who exhibit "ignorance, idleness, and vice."
2. Gulliver describes gunpowder to the king in order to gain his favor.

Quotables

"I have ever hated all nations, professions and communities, and all my love is towards individuals . . . But principally I hate and detest that animal called man; although I heartily love John, Peter, Thomas, and so forth."

—Jonathan Swift

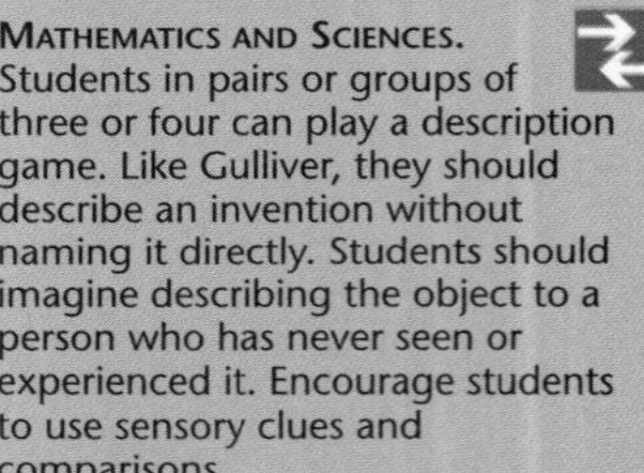

CROSS-CURRICULAR ACTIVITIES

Mathematics and Sciences. Students in pairs or groups of three or four can play a description game. Like Gulliver, they should describe an invention without naming it directly. Students should imagine describing the object to a person who has never seen or experienced it. Encourage students to use sensory clues and comparisons.

FROM A Voyage to Brobdingnag

From Chapter 6.

His Majesty in another audience was at the pains to recapitulate the sum of all I had spoken; compared the questions he made with the answers I had given; then taking me into his hands, and stroking me gently, delivered himself in these words, which I shall never forget, nor the manner he spoke them in. "My little friend Grildrig,[7] you have made a most admirable panegyric upon your country. You have clearly proved that ignorance, idleness, and vice are the proper ingredients for qualifying a legislator. That laws are best explained, interpreted, and applied by those whose interests and abilities lie in perverting, confounding, and eluding them. I observe among you some lines of an institution which in its original might have been tolerable; but these half erased, and the rest wholly blurred and blotted by corruptions. It doth not appear from all you have said how any one virtue is required towards the procurement of any one station among you; much less that men are ennobled on account of their virtue, that priests are advanced for their piety or learning, soldiers for their conduct or valor, judges for their integrity, senators for the love of their country, or counselors for their wisdom. As for yourself," continued the King, "who have spent the greatest part of your life in traveling, I am well disposed to hope you may hitherto have escaped many vices of your country. But by what I have gathered from your own relation, and the answers I have with much pains wringed and extorted from you, I cannot but conclude the bulk of your natives to be the most pernicious race of little odious vermin that nature ever suffered to crawl upon the surface of the earth."

What does the king think of European government as it has been described to him by Gulliver?

◆ ◆ ◆

From Chapter 7.

In hopes to ingratiate myself farther into his Majesty's favor, I told him of an invention discovered between three and four hundred years ago, to make a certain powder, into an heap of which the smallest spark of fire falling would kindle the whole in a moment, although it were as big as a mountain, and make it all fly up in the air together, with a noise and agitation greater than thunder. That a proper quantity of this powder rammed into an hollow tube of brass or iron, according to its bigness, would drive a ball of iron or lead with such violence and speed as

What secret does Gulliver share with the king and why?

7. **Grildrig.** King's name for Gulliver

Words for Everyday Use

re • ca • pit • u • late (rē´ kə pich´ə lāt) *vt.*, summarize. *Professor Barlow usually asks one of her students to recapitulate the readings.*

pan • e • gyr • ic (pan´ə jir´ik) *n.*, high praise. *I was grateful for the panegyric I received for my hard work.*

per • vert (pər vurt´) *v.*, distort, misinterpret. *Researchers complain that superficial news reports pervert.*

e • lude (ē lo͞od´) *vt.*, evade, escape. *How has the criminal eluded capture for so many years?*

per • ni • cious (pər nish´əs) *adj.*, wicked. *Democracies throughout the world have condemned the dictator's pernicious acts.*

o • di • ous (ō´dē əs) *adj.*, arousing disgust, offensive. *Sulfur has a strong, odious smell.*

in • gra • ti • ate (in grā´shē āt) *vt.*, bring into favor. *A simple gift will ingratiate you with the host.*

ag • i • ta • tion (aj´ə tā´shən) *n.*, violent motion. *The worried parents paced the room in agitation, waiting for news of their son.*

> The King was struck with horror at the description I had given of those terrible engines and the proposal I had made.

nothing was able to sustain its force. That the largest balls thus discharged would not only destroy whole ranks of an army at once, but batter the strongest walls to the ground; sink down ships with a thousand men in each, to the bottom of the sea; and, when linked together by a chain, would cut through masts and rigging; divide hundreds of bodies in the middle, and lay all waste before them. That we often put this powder into large hollow balls of iron, and discharged them by an engine into some city we were besieging; which would rip up the pavements, tear the houses to pieces, burst and throw splinters on every side, dashing out the brains of all who came near. That I knew the ingredients very well, which were cheap and common; I understood the manner of compounding them, and could direct his workmen how to make those tubes of a size proportionable to all other things in his Majesty's kingdom, and the largest need not be above two hundred foot long; twenty or thirty of which tubes, charged with the proper quantity of powder and balls, would batter down the walls of the strongest town in his dominions in a few hours; or destroy the whole metropolis, if ever it should pretend to dispute his absolute commands. This I humbly offered to his Majesty as a small tribute of acknowledgement in return of so many marks that I had received of his royal favor and protection.

The King was struck with horror at the description I had given of those terrible engines and the proposal I had made. He was amazed how so impotent and groveling an insect as I (these were his expressions) could entertain such inhuman ideas, and in so familiar a manner as to appear wholly unmoved at all the scenes of blood and desolation which I had painted as the common effects of those destructive machines; whereof he said some evil genius, enemy to mankind, must have been the first contriver. As for himself, he protested that although few things delighted him so much as new discoveries in art or in nature, yet he would rather lose half his kingdom than be privy to such a secret, which he commanded me, as I valued my life, never to mention any more.

How does the king react to Gulliver's proposal to share the secrets of gunpowder?

A strange effect of *narrow principles* and *short views!* that a prince possessed of every quality which procures veneration, love, and esteem; of strong parts, great wisdom, and profound learning; endued[8] with admirable talents for government, and almost adored by his subjects; should from a *nice, unnecessary scruple*, whereof in Europe we can have no conception, let slip an opportunity put into his hands that would have made him absolute master of the lives, the lib-

8. **endued.** Endowed with certain qualities

Words for Everyday Use

trib • ute (trib´yo͞ot) *n.*, homage. *In the dedication to her first novel, the writer paid tribute to her mentor.*

im • po • tent (im´pə tənt) *adj.*, powerless. *The rescue workers were impotent in the face of such strong winds.*

des • o • la • tion (des´ə lā´shən) *n.*, ruin. *In the tornado's wake, the tiny town was left in desolation.*

con • triv • er (kən triv´ər) *n.*, one who plans. *The principal demanded the name of the contriver who led the group of vandals.*

pro • cure (prō´kyo͝or´) *vt.*, obtain. *The art gallery has procured a rare painting by Vincent Van Gogh.*

ven • er • a • tion (ven´ər ā´shən) *n.*, deep respect. *Many cultures have special ceremonies to show veneration for their ancestors.*

scru • ple (scro͞o´pəl) *n.*, qualm about something one feels is wrong. *Her scruples would not allow her to lie to her parents.*

ANSWER TO GUIDED READING QUESTION

1. The king vows that he would never want to use Gulliver's knowledge of gunpowder and he commands Gulliver never to speak of it again.

HISTORICAL NOTE

As with most other male-dominated arenas of the Enlightenment era, politics and journalism largely excluded women. A few women, however, managed to contribute their political opinions and writing talents. One of them was **Mary de la Rivière Manley** (1663–1724), who published a satirical newspaper, the *Female Tatler*, in 1709. After serving a jail term for libel, Manley found a new friend and supporter in Jonathan Swift, who respected Manley as a writer and political satirist. Swift hired her to assume the editorship of his periodical, *The Examiner*, in 1711.

CROSS-CURRICULAR ACTIVITIES

Applied Arts. Have students use the Internet to research a country to which they would like to travel and create an itinerary for a one-week visit. They should give a brief description of each place, activity, or event in their itinerary. They should also write an introduction to their itinerary, including background information on the country. Ask them to record the Internet addresses of pages they used for their research.

ANSWER TO GUIDED READING QUESTION

1. Gulliver names ignorance as the reason for the king's reaction. He declares that the European mind, unlike the Brobdingnagian one, views politics as a science. The comparison is funny because the Brobdingnagians actually have a more civilized and sophisticated view of politics. Swift is critiquing European politics, in which gunpowder and the use of violence are not frowned upon.

RESPOND TO THE SELECTION

If students say they wouldn't like to live in either place, they should still provide reasons for their response.

SELECTION CHECK TEST 4.7.11 WITH ANSWERS

Checking Your Reading

1. What does Gulliver steal from the Blefuscudians? **He steals their ships.**
2. Why is the Emperor of Lilliput angry with Gulliver? **He refuses to destroy Blefuscu.**
3. What does the King of Brobdingnag think of Gulliver's countrymen? **He thinks them to be a "most pernicious race of little odious vermin."**
4. What does Gulliver think the gunpowder could do for the King of Brobdingnag? **He thinks it could help him rule absolutely.**
5. How does the king react to Gulliver's offer to share the invention of gunpowder? **The king reacts with horror.**

Vocabulary in Context

Fill each blank with the most appropriate word from the Words for Everyday Use from Gulliver's Travels. You may have to change the tense of the word.

ingratiate abominate elude
recapitulate stratagem
agitation procure

1. The right fielder dove for the ball, but it bounced on the turf and **eluded** him.
2. The party was full of agents trying to **ingratiate** themselves with the hot new author.
3. One of Elsie's duties was to **procure** materials to build sets for the stage.

erties, and the fortunes of his people. Neither do I say this with the least intention to <u>detract</u> from the many virtues of that excellent King, whose character I am sensible will on this account be very much lessened in the opinion of an English reader: but I take this defect among them to have risen from their ignorance; they not having <u>hitherto</u> reduced politics into a science, as the more <u>acute</u> wits of Europe have done. For I remember very well, in a discourse one day with the King, when I happened to say there were several thousand books among us written upon the art of government, it gave him (directly contrary to my intention) a very mean opinion of our understandings. He professed both to <u>abominate</u> and despise all *mystery, refinement,* and *intrigue,* either in a prince or a minister. He could not tell what I meant by *secrets of state,* where an enemy or some rival nation were not in the case. He confined the knowledge of governing within very *narrow bounds:* to common sense and reason, to justice and <u>lenity</u>, to the speedy determination of civil and criminal causes, with some other obvious topics which are not worth considering. And he gave it for his opinion that whoever could make two ears of corn or two blades of grass to grow upon a spot of ground where only one grew before would deserve better of mankind and do more essential service to his country than the whole race of politicians[9] put together. ■

What reason does Gulliver give for the king's reaction? What comparison does Gulliver make between Brobdingnagian and European politics? What makes this comparison funny? What message does Swift actually mean to communicate?

9. **politicians.** Political scientists

WORDS FOR EVERYDAY USE

de • tract (dē trakt) *vi.,* take or draw away. *Do you think the mural's secluded location <u>detracts</u> from its impact on the public?*
hith • er • to (hith´ər to͞o) *adv.,* until this time. *The sprinter's world record was <u>hitherto</u> unchallenged.*
a • cute (ə kyo͞ot´) *adj.,* keenly intelligent. *The <u>acute</u> child learned to played chess simply by watching others.*
a • bom • i • nate (ə bäm´ə nāt´) *vt.,* dislike very much. *I <u>abominate</u> stinginess, particularly in the wealthy.*
len • i • ty (len´ə tē) *n.,* leniency; mildness. *Activists criticize the <u>lenity</u> of the state's sentencing guidelines.*

Respond *to the* SELECTION

Would you rather live in Lilliput or Brobdingnag? Why?

SELECTION CHECK TEST 4.7.11 WITH ANSWERS (CONT.)

4. The museum docent **recapitulated** what we had seen and heard on the tour.
5. The **agitation** of the gem polisher smoothed the stones until they gleamed.

Literary Tools

1. What is satire? **Satire is humorous writing intended to point out errors, falsehoods, foibles, or failings. It is written for the purpose of reforming human behavior or human institutions.**
2. What is irony? **Irony is a difference between appearance and reality.**
3. Give an example of irony from the selection. **Responses will vary.**
4. Give an example of a fantastic, or unrealistic, element from the selection. **Responses will vary.**

Investigate, Inquire, Imagine

Recall: Gathering Facts → **Interpret:** Finding Meaning

1a. What does the emperor of Lilliput want after Gulliver's victory over the Blefuscudians? How does Gulliver respond to the emperor's request?

1b. What does this show about the emperor of Lilliput?

2a. Based on Gulliver's stories, what does the Brobdingnagian king conclude are qualifications for a legislator? What does the king believe is the proper purpose of government?

2b. Contrast the the government Gulliver knows with the Brobdingnagian government.

3a. What does Gulliver describe to the king of Brobdingnag? How does the king react?

3b. What reaction does Gulliver expect from the king? Why does he expect this reaction? What does this incident suggest about Gulliver and the English?

Analyze: Taking Things Apart → **Synthesize:** Bringing Things Together

4a. The Lilliputians are physically small. Are they small in other respects? Explain. The Brobdingnagians are physically large. Are they large in other respects? Explain.

4b. Why do you think Swift chose to play with size in these ways? What insight does Gulliver gain into the nature of the emperor in the ship episode? Compare Gulliver's opinion of the emperor to Swift's opinion of politicians generally.

Evaluate: Making Judgments → **Extend:** Connecting Ideas

5a. Judge whether Gulliver respected the people in either of the places he visited.

5b. In what way might Gulliver's travels reflect historical events of Swift's day?

Understanding Literature

Satire and Irony. Review the definitions for **satire** and **irony** in the Handbook of Literary Terms. Swift's satires make heavy use of irony. What examples of irony can you find in the selections? In each case, what appears to be true? How does appearance differ from reality? In each case, what point does Swift make by establishing this contrast?

Fantasy. Review the definition for **fantasy** and the chart you made for Literary Tools in Prereading on page 598. *Gulliver's Travels* has many imaginative elements. What unrealistic elements can you find? In what ways are they unrealistic? Which seem to be products of exaggeration? Which seem to add something imaginative to reality? Which seem to be wholly new creations?

Answers to Investigate, Inquire, Imagine

Recall

1a. The emperor wants Gulliver to bring all of his enemy's ships into port and defeat the whole empire of Blefuscu. Gulliver responds that he cannot "be an instrument" used to enslave "a brave and free people."

2a. The qualifications are "ignorance, idleness, and vice." The king believes the purpose of government is to serve citizens fairly with "common sense and reason," "justice and lenity."

3a. Gulliver describes gunpowder to the king. The king reacts with horror. He finds the idea "inhuman" and believes it must have been invented by some "evil genius," an enemy to mankind. He tells Gulliver never to speak of gunpowder again.

Interpret

1b. The emperor's desire reveals his cold ambition and quest for power.

2b. Gulliver describes a corrupt government that is not concerned with the people being governed. The Brobdingnagian government is based on service to and care for the people.

3b. Gulliver expects that the king will be excited and intrigued by the gunpowder. He expects this reaction because no king of Europe would ever reject something that "would have made him absolute master of the lives, the liberties, and the fortunes of his people." This incident shows that Gulliver and the English think the purpose of government is to conquer and to rule absolutely.

Analyze

4a. *Responses will vary.* Students may say that the Lilliputians are small in size and also small-minded, while the large Brobdingnagians are broad-minded. Although the Lilliputians are physically small, their ambition is huge; the emperor wants to become "sole monarch of the whole world." The political ambition of the Brobdingnagians, unlike their size, is very small. They only want to govern themselves peaceably.

Synthesize

4b. *Responses will vary.* Swift probably chose to play with size in these ways to surprise his readers and to play up the ironies in his piece. Gulliver has learned that the emperor is essentially selfish and self-motivated. Swift believes that politicians undertake causes that will give them absolute power, just as the emperor desires to do.

Answers to Investigate, Inquire, Imagine (cont.)

Evaluate

5a. *Responses will vary.* Some students may say that Gulliver did not respect these people because he did not understand them and thought they should adopt his ways.

Extend

5b. *Responses will vary.* Gulliver's travels came at a time when travels to other lands and encounters with other cultures was becoming quite common. There was a sense of exploration and interest in other peoples, and also, European travelers tended to feel themselves superior to the other peoples they encountered, just as Gulliver does.

Answers to Understanding Literature can be found on page 606.

ANSWERS TO UNDERSTANDING LITERATURE

Satire and Irony. It appears to the Brobdingnagian king that the English government elects the legislators most likely to mishandle their positions and that laws are interpreted by those most likely to confuse them; however, the reality is that the English attempted to elect the most qualified individual, not the least. Swift's point is that often government officials are incapable of doing their duties properly. Another example is that it appears to Gulliver that the Brobdingnagian king is ignorant because he disapproves of the use of gunpowder, abominates political intrigue, and confines governing to justice and lenity. The reality is that the Brobdingnagian king is more civilized and intelligent than the narrator in his disapproval of violence and in his ideal of a just government.

Fantasy. The Lilliputians, who are one-twelfth the size of Gulliver, and the Brobdingnagians, who are twelve times the size of Gulliver, are both unrealistic elements, as is the tale of Gulliver walking through the channel and carrying away the Blefuscudian ships. The Lilliputian measure of depth, a *glumgluff,* is an imaginative description of an actual measure. The emperor's plan to become "sole monarch of the whole world" is exaggerated, but not unlike the plans of many historical monarchs or despots. Many names of people, places, and ideas are wholly new creations; however, they are based on things or people that Swift's readers would have recognized, such as the Big-Endian exiles. NOTE: You may want to combine this discussion with a discussion about satire. Refer students to the Handbook of Literary Terms for a definition of satire.

ANSWERS TO INTEGRATING THE LANGUAGE ARTS

Language, Grammar, and Style

Responses will vary. Possible responses are given.

1. If you cross from the Lilliputian side of the narrow channel, you will reach the island empire of Blefuscu.
2. My concentration was disturbed by the thousands of tiny arrows that stung and stuck in my face and hands.
3. I tried to convince him that he was crazy to attempt such a mission.
4. I remember another time when the king tried to make sense of everything I had told him.
5. You make it sound as if anyone can get a job, no matter how unqualified the person is!

Writer's Journal

1. Write a **postcard** from from Gulliver to somebody at home. In the card write about either Lilliput or Brobdingnag. You may wish to illustrate the other side with a scene from the place you choose.
2. Gulliver and the king of Brobingnag have differing opinions on gunpowder. How do you feel about this subject? Write an **editorial** about guns and society.
3. Imagine that Gulliver arrives in another land. Write a **scene** that includes description of the land and its citizens and shows Gulliver interacting with the citizens.

Integrating the Language Arts

Language, Grammar, and Style

Tone. Read the Language Arts Survey 3.3, "Register, Tone, and Voice." Decide how you would characterize Swift's tone in *Gulliver's Travels.* Then rewrite the following sentences or phrases from *Gulliver's Travels* to give them a completely different tone. You need not use the same tone for each revised sentence.

1. The empire of Blefuscu is an island situated to the north northeast side of Lilliput, from whence it is parted only by a channel of eight hundred yards wide.
2. While I was thus employed, the enemy discharged several thousand arrows, many of which stuck in my hands and face; and besides the excessive smart, gave me much disturbance in my work.
3. But I endeavored to divert him from this design, by many arguments drawn from the topics of policy as well as justice.
4. His majesty in another audience was at the pains to recapitulate the sum of all I had spoken.
5. It doth not appear from all you have said how any one virtue is required towards the procurement of any one station among you.

Collaborative Learning & Speaking and Listening

Treaty. Lilliput and Blefuscu have agreed to end their hostilities. They now need a treaty that will make explicit the terms of the agreement. Negotiate the terms of the treaty. Form groups of four or six, and divide each group in half, with one part representing Lilliput and the other representing Blefuscu. After you have reached agreement on the terms of the treaty, prepare a written document. In your treaty, tell why you chose to negotiate, what terms each party to the treaty must abide by, what the consequences of breeching the agreement will be, and how peace will be maintained in the future.

Applied English

Writing Instruction. Gulliver offers instruction to the Brobdingnagians, but the king turns him down. Imagine that you wanted to teach the Brobdingnagians how to do something. Choose a task that you are familiar with and that might involve technology or equipment that the Brobdingnagians do not have. Write a set of instructions. Refer to the Language Arts Survey 6.4, "Writing a Step-by-Step Procedure" for help in organizing your directions.

ANSWERS TO INTEGRATING THE LANGUAGE ARTS (cont.)

Applied English

Students can share their instructions in pairs. Each partner should read the instructions for logical order and general comprehension, noting any places that are unclear or that generate questions. Each writer can then revise the instructions based on the feedback he or she received.

Collaborative Learning & Speaking and Listening

A third group of students might act as moderator and scribe as the other groups hash out their differences.

FROM

Oroonoko

BY APHRA BEHN

About the AUTHOR

Aphra Behn (1640–1689) is today honored as a great literary pioneer. The first woman in England to earn her living as a writer, she became one of the finest dramatists of her day and wrote what is arguably the first English novel. Her life, like her work, was interesting and unusual. As a child, she traveled with her foster family to the West Indies. While living in Suriname, she participated in a slave rebellion. On returning to England, she married, but her husband soon died. To earn money, she became a spy in Antwerp, Belgium, for King Charles II. When she was poorly paid for her spying, she ended up in debtor's prison. To rectify her situation, Behn began writing to earn money. This was an unusual motive for women writers in her day, for most were aristocrats who wrote for pleasure, not for pay. Over the next several years, Behn would write fourteen plays, many of which were favorably received in London. The fortunes of London theaters declined around 1680, and with them Behn's income. Still resourceful, she began writing fiction, and though she died poor, she left behind a rich legacy not just in her writings, but also in the ambitious, adventurous, and inspiring life she had lived.

About the SELECTION

Written just a year before Behn died, ***Oroonoko, or the Royal Slave,*** combines elements of autobiography, travel narrative, and fictional prose. Drawing on her own experiences in Suriname, Behn tells in this short novel the story of an African prince, Oroonoko, who is deceived by an Englishman and sold into slavery. Oroonoko falls in love with Imoinda, the daughter of one of the king's generals. Unfortunately, the king loves Imoinda as well. He chooses her as his own by bestowing upon her a royal veil. When he learns that Oroonoko has secretly visited Imoinda, he is very angry. Imoinda tells the king a lie to save her life. As a result, the king decides she is not fit for him or for Oroonoko, so he has her sold into slavery. In the meantime, Oroonoko is away at battle. This selection picks up upon Oroonoko's return from battle. Behn's book, with its noble hero, did much to turn British public opinion against the slave trade, which was outlawed in all British colonies in 1833.

Literary TOOLS

NOVEL. A **novel** is a long work of prose fiction. *Oroonoko* is considered to be one of the, if not *the*, first British novel. Novels usually have subplots in addition to their main plot. Furthermore, novels often realistically portray the interior psychological states of characters. Note the changes that Oroonoko undergoes in this selection.

CHARACTERIZATION. Characterization is the use of literary techniques to create a character. Writers use three major techniques to create characters—direct description, in which the writer through a narrator or other character comments directly on the character; portrayal of character's behavior, in which the writer presents the actions or speech of the character allowing the reader to draw his or her own conclusions; and representations of internal states, in which the writer reveals a character's private thoughts and emotions. As you read, keep a chart to show how Behn creates the character of Oroonoko.

Direct Description	Behavior	Internal States
beloved like a deity		

Reader's Journal

Write about a time when somebody deceived you. What did the deception cost you? How did you react to it?

ADDITIONAL RESOURCES

UNIT 7 RESOURCE BOOK
- Selection Worksheet 7.6
- Selection Check Test 4.7.13
- Selection Test 4.7.14
- Language, Grammar, and Style Resource 3.94

GRAPHIC ORGANIZER

Students might include the following in their graphic organizers.

DIRECT DESCRIPTION
beloved like a deity
extremely civilized
generous

BEHAVIOR
decides not to eat, to die, so he won't have to endure slavery
never violated his word in his life
believes captain will keep his word
tells captain it was worth his suffering to understand the captain and the gods by which he swears

Quotables

"All women together ought to let flowers fall upon the tomb of Aphra Behn, for it was she who earned them the right to speak their minds."

—Virginia Woolf

READER'S JOURNAL

Students might brainstorm a list of emotions that they felt before they realized the deception and a list of those they felt afterward.

GOALS/OBJECTIVES

Studying this lesson will enable students to
- empathize with a main character in a novel
- describe Aphra Behn's literary accomplishments and explain the historical significance of her writings
- define *novel* and identify the elements of a novel in literature they read
- define *characterization* and identify the major techniques of characterization as used in their reading
- edit for errors in capitalization
- evaluate a film for its portrayals of race

VOCABULARY FROM THE SELECTION

asseveration
ignominiously
repose

ANSWER TO GUIDED READING QUESTION

1. Oroonoko has a genial business relationship with the European slave traders; he sells them slaves. The Europeans consider Prince Oroonoko to be more civilized than any of his predecessors.

ART NOTE

Joseph Turner painted *Slave Ship* in 1840, almost two hundred years after Behn wrote her story. During that time, however, the activities of slave traders had changed little. Turner's painting illustrates the common practice of pitching enslaved humans overboard, which was done either because of epidemics or to avoid unrest. In this case, because of an approaching typhoon, they are throwing overboard the dead and the dying. Have students discuss their reactions to the painting. What mood does the painting evoke? What connections do students make between this scene and the scene they imagine on the English captain's ship?

INDIVIDUAL LEARNING STRATEGIES

MOTIVATION
Students can write about or discuss the opposition that Behn might have faced as a woman, as a writer, and as an outspoken opponent of slavery.

READING PROFICIENCY
Read through the selection once as a class, and then have them form partners in order to summarize each paragraph and answer the Guided Reading and Recall questions.

ENGLISH LANGUAGE LEARNING
Explain that the selection contains some uncommon contractions, such as *'em* for *them* and *'twas* for it *was*. This might be a good time to review contractions with students. Remind them that the apostrophe takes the place of dropped letters. Share with students the following additional vocabulary.

oblige—compel
indignity—affront; disgrace
circumventing—surrounding with evils
cognizance—perception; observation

Slave Ship, 1840. Joseph Mallord Turner. Museum of Fine Arts, Boston.

FROM

Oroonoko

APHRA BEHN

Oroonoko was no sooner returned from this last conquest, and received at court with all the joy and magnificence that could be expressed to a young victor, who was not only returned triumphant but beloved like a deity, when there arrived in the port an English ship.

This person had often before been in these countries and was very well known to Oroonoko, with whom he had trafficked for slaves, and had used to do the same with his predecessors.[1]

This commander was a man of a finer sort of address and conversation, better bred and more engaging than most of that sort of men are, so that he seemed rather never to have been bred out of a court than almost all his life at sea. This captain therefore was always better received at court than most of the traders to those countries were; and especially by Oroonoko, who was more civilized, according to the European mode, than any other had been, and took more delight in the white nations, and above all men of parts and wit. To this captain he sold abundance of his slaves, and for the favor and esteem he had for him, made him many presents, and obliged him to stay at court as long as possibly he could. Which the captain seemed to take as a very great honor done him, entertaining the Prince every day with globes and maps, and mathematical discourses and instruments; eating, drinking, hunting, and living with him with so much familiarity that it was not to be doubted but he had gained very greatly upon the heart of this gallant young man. And the captain, in return of all these mighty favors, besought[2] the Prince to honor his vessel with his presence, some day or other, to dinner, before he should set sail; which he condescended to accept, and appointed his day. The captain, on his part, failed not to have all things in a readiness, in the most magnificent order he could possibly. And the day being come, the captain in his boat, richly adorned with carpets and velvet cushions, rowed to the shore to receive the Prince, with another longboat where was placed all his music and trumpets, with which Oroonoko was extremely delighted; who met him on the shore attended by his French governor, Jamoan Aboan, and about a hundred of the noblest of the youths of the court. And after they had first carried the

At the beginning of the selection, what sort of relationship does Oroonoko have with the European slave traders?

1. **This . . . predecessors.** Throughout the history of Africa and the Middle East, the selling of war captives into slavery was common.
2. **besought.** Asked earnestly

INDIVIDUAL LEARNING STRATEGIES (CONT.)

SPECIAL NEEDS
Ask students to create a story map listing the main events in this excerpt. They should also note the state of mind of Oroonoko as it changes throughout the story.

ENRICHMENT
Students may wish to research the history of slavery in the British West Indies. For what purpose were slaves transported there? For how long was slavery legal in the West Indies, and how did it finally become abolished?

Prince on board, the boats fetched the rest off; where they found a very splendid treat, with all sorts of fine wines, and were as well entertained as 'twas possible in such a place to be.

The Prince, having drunk hard of punch and several sorts of wine, as did all the rest (for great care was taken they should want nothing of that part of the entertainment), was very merry, and in great admiration of the ship, for he had never been in one before; so that he was curious of beholding every place where he decently might descend. The rest, no less curious, who were not quite overcome with drinking, rambled at their pleasure fore and aft, as their fancies guided 'em. So that the captain, who had well laid his design before, gave the word, and seized on all his guests; they clapping great irons suddenly on the Prince, when he was leaped down in the hold to view that part of the vessel, and locking him fast down, secured him. The same treachery was used to all the rest; and all in one instant, in several places of the ship, were lashed fast in irons, and betrayed to slavery. That great design over, they set all hands to work to hoise[3] sail; and with as treacherous and fair a wind, they made from the shore with this innocent and glorious prize, who thought of nothing less than such an entertainment.

What does the captain do to Oroonoko and to the other "guests"?

Some have commended this act as brave in the captain; but I will spare my sense of it, and leave it to my reader to judge as he pleases.

It may be easily guessed in what manner the Prince resented this indignity, who may be best resembled to a lion taken in a toil; so he raged, so he struggled for liberty, but all in vain; and they had so wisely managed his fetters that he could not use a hand in his defense, to quit himself of a life that would by no means endure slavery, nor could he move from the place where he was tied to any solid part of the ship, against which he might have beat his head, and have finished his disgrace that way. So that being deprived of all other means, he resolved to perish for want of food. And pleased at last with that thought, and toiled and tired by rage and indignation, he laid himself down, and sullenly resolved upon dying, and refused all things that were brought him.

This did not a little vex the captain, and the more so because he found almost all of 'em of the same humor; so that the loss of so many brave slaves, so tall and goodly to behold, would have been very considerable. He therefore ordered one to go from him (for he would not be seen himself) to Oroonoko, and to assure him he was afflicted for having rashly done so unhospitable a deed, and which could not be now remedied, since they were far from shore; but since he resented it in so high a nature, he assured him he would revoke his resolution, and set both him and his friends ashore on the next land they should touch at; and of this the messenger gave him his oath, provided he would resolve to live. And Oroonoko, whose honor was such as he never had violated a word in his life himself, much less a solemn <u>asseveration</u>, believed in an instant what this man said, but replied, he expected for a confirmation of this to have his shameful fetters dismissed. This demand was carried to the captain, who returned him answer that the offense had been so great which he had put upon the

How does Oroonoko fight back? Why does this "vex," or bother, the captain? What is the deal that the captain tries to make with Oroonoko?

3. **hoise.** Hoist

WORDS FOR EVERYDAY USE

as • sev • er • a • tion (ə sev´ə rā shən) *n.,* act of stating positively; an assertion. *He punctuated his <u>asseveration</u> with affirming nods of the head.*

ANSWERS TO GUIDED READING QUESTIONS

1. The captain tricks and enslaves Oroonoko and the other Africans who were invited aboard the ship.
2. Oroonoko fights back by refusing to eat. This vexes the captain because he fears losing a valuable slave. The captain tries to make a deal with Oroonoko by telling him that he was wrong to enslave him and that he will remedy his action by letting Oroonoko and his friends off the ship when they next reach land.

ADDITIONAL QUESTIONS AND ACTIVITIES

In the eighteenth century James Thomson wrote these lyrics for a popular song:
"Rule, Britannia, rule the waves;
Britons never will be slaves."
Have students discuss to what extent *Oroonoko* can be seen as a repudiation of such imperialist attitudes. Ask students what characteristics Oroonoko possesses that make his enslavement startling. What point do they think Behn is trying to make about the nature of freedom and slavery? Is it true that Britons never will be slaves? Point out to students that in the Victorian period, Henry Mayhew, a journalist, reported in his *London Labour and the London Poor* that this song was popular among the impoverished classes; however, they rendered the lyrics, "Britons always will be slaves." What are the more subtle aspects of slavery? Do students see any of these aspects present in society today?

HISTORICAL NOTE

The slave trade was an integral part of the English economy, and the wealth generated by the slave trade helped build the British colonial empire. European slave trafficking reached its peak in the eighteenth century, the period during which six million Africans were shipped across the Atlantic. As the writer of the first novel that criticized slavery, Behn did not voice a popular view. Most Europeans did not denounce the practice of slavery until one hundred years after Behn wrote *Oroonoko,* near the end of the eighteenth century.

ANSWERS TO GUIDED READING QUESTIONS

1. The captain says he hesitates to remove Oroonoko's fetters because he fears that Oroonoko might "commit some outrage fatal to himself and the King his [the captain's] master."
2. Oroonoko responds that he doubts the principles of the captain's gods, which lead him to such distrust of another man's solemn oath.
3. The captain wants the unfettered Oroonoko to persuade the other chained men to eat and to assure them of their promised freedom.

CROSS-CURRICULAR ACTIVITIES

Social Studies. Have students research the history of the slave trade to discover the main routes used by European slave traders. Then have students make maps illustrating the routes used during the seventeenth and eighteenth centuries. Maps should indicate where the traders bought slaves and where they sold them.

CROSS-CURRICULAR ACTIVITIES

Geography. Have students research the location of Suriname, where Oroonoko lived and where Behn had actually participated in a slave rebellion. Where is it located? What is it called today?

LITERARY NOTE

Discuss with students the idea of the noble savage—the idea that primitive human beings are naturally good and that any evil they develop is a result of the corrupting force of civilization. This attitude was spawned at the end of the fifteenth century as European explorers "discovered:" new lands and peoples. The idea of the noble savage gained full flower in the Romantic era. Ask students how this idea might color Behn's writing.

Prince that he durst not trust him with liberty while he remained in the ship, for fear lest by a valor natural to him, and a revenge that would animate that valor, he might commit some outrage fatal to himself and the King his master, to whom his vessel did belong. To this Oroonoko replied, he would engage his honor to behave himself in all friendly order and manner, and obey the command of the captain, as he was lord of the King's vessel and general of those men under his command.

Why does the captain hesitate to remove Oroonoko's fetters?

This was delivered to the still doubting captain, who could not resolve to trust a heathen, he said, upon his parole, a man that had no sense or notion of the God that he worshiped. Oroonoko then replied, he was very sorry to hear that the captain pretended to the knowledge and worship of any gods who had taught him no better principles than not to credit as he would be credited; but they told him the difference of their faith occasioned that distrust. For the captain had protested to him upon the word of a Christian, and sworn in the name of a great god, which if he should violate, he would expect eternal torment in the world to come. "Is that all the obligation he has to be just to his oath?" replied Oroonoko. "Let him know I swear by my honor; which to violate, would not only render me contemptible and despised by all brave and honest men, and so give myself perpetual pain, but it would be eternally offending and diseasing all mankind, harming, betraying, circumventing and outraging all men; but punishments hereafter are suffered by one's self, and the world takes no cognizances whether this god have revenged 'em or not, 'tis done so secretly and deferred so long. While the man of no honor suffers every moment the scorn and contempt of the honester world, and dies every day ignominiously in his fame, which is more valuable than life. I speak not this to move belief, but to show you how you mistake, when you imagine that he who will violate his honor will keep his word with his gods." So turning from him with a disdainful smile, he refused to answer him, when he urged him to know what answer he should carry back to his captain; so that he departed without saying any more.

When the captain persists in doubting Oroonoko's honesty, how does Oroonoko respond?

The captain pondering and consulting what to do, it was concluded that nothing but Oroonoko's liberty would encourage any of the rest to eat, except the Frenchman, whom the captain could not pretend to keep prisoner, but only told him he was secured because he might act something in favor of the Prince, but that he should be freed as soon as they came to land. So that they concluded it wholly necessary to free the Prince from his irons, that he might show himself to the rest; that they might have an eye upon him, and that they could not fear a single man.

This being resolved, to make the obligation the greater, the captain himself went to Oroonoko; where after many compliments, and assurances of what he had already promised, he receiving from the Prince his parole and his hand for his good behavior, dismissed his irons and brought him to his own cabin; where after having treated and reposed him a while, for he had neither eat nor slept in four days before, he besought him to visit those obstinate people in

What does the captain want the unfettered Oroonoko to do?

Words For Everyday Use

ig • no • min • i • ous • ly (ig´nə min´ē əs lē) *adv.,* shamefully; disgracefully. *People will speak of you ignominiously if you continue such disgraceful behavior.*

re • pose (rē pōs) *vt.,* rest. *The hikers removed their heavy packs and reposed themselves a few minutes by the stream before continuing up the mountain.*

chains, who refused all manner of sustenance, and entreated him to oblige 'em to eat, and assure 'em of their liberty the first opportunity.

Oroonoko, who was too generous not to give credit to his words, showed himself to his people, who were transported with excess of joy at the sight of their darling prince, falling at his feet and kissing and embracing 'em, believing, as some divine oracle, all he assured 'em. But he besought 'em to bear their chains with that bravery that became those whom he had seen act so nobly in arms; and that they could not give him greater proofs of their love and friendship, since 'twas all the security the captain (his friend) could have, against the revenge, he said, they might possibly justly take for the injuries sustained by him. And they all with one accord assured him, they could not suffer enough, when it was for his repose and safety.

After this they no longer refused to eat, but took what was brought 'em, and were pleased with their captivity, since by it they hoped to redeem the Prince, who, all the rest of the voyage, was treated with all the respect due to his birth, though nothing could divert his melancholy; and he would often sigh for Imoinda, and think this a punishment due to his misfortune, in having left that noble maid behind him that fatal night, in the Otan, when he fled to the camp.

Possessed with a thousand thoughts of past joys with this fair young person, and a thousand griefs for her eternal loss, he endured a tedious voyage, and at last arrived at the mouth of the river of Surinam, a colony belonging to the King of England, and where they were to deliver some part of their slaves. There the merchants and gentlemen of the country going on board to demand those lots of slaves they had already agreed on, and, amongst those, the overseers of those plantations where I then chanced to be, the captain, who had given the word, ordered his men to bring up those noble slaves in fetters whom I have spoken of; and having put 'em some in one and some in other lots, with women and children . . . they sold 'em off as slaves to several merchants and gentlemen; not putting any two in one lot, because they would separate 'em far from each other, not daring to trust 'em together, lest rage and courage should put 'em upon contriving some great action, to the ruin of the colony.

Oroonoko was first seized on, and sold to our overseer, who had the first lot, with seventeen more of all sorts and sizes, but not one of quality with him. When he saw this, he found what they meant, for, as I said, he understood English pretty well; and being wholly unarmed and defenseless, so as it was in vain to make any resistance, he only beheld the captain with a look all fierce and disdainful, upbraiding him with eyes that forced blushes on his guilty cheeks; he only cried, in passing over the side of the ship, "Farewell, sir. 'Tis worth my suffering, to gain so true a knowledge both of you and of your gods by whom you swear." And desiring those that held him to forbear their pains, and telling 'em he would make no resistance, he cried, "Come, my fellow slaves; let us descend, and see if we can meet with more honor and honesty in the next world we shall touch upon." So he nimbly leaped into the boat, and showing no more concern, suffered himself to be rowed up the river with his seventeen companions. ■

What sort of look does Oroonoko give to the captain when he realizes what is happening? What does Oroonoko say?

Respond *to the* SELECTION

After reading this piece, how do you feel toward its main character, Oroonoko? toward the captain of the ship?

RESPOND TO THE SELECTION

Students might work in pairs to role play an meeting between the captain and Oroonoko years after this selection takes place. Each character should speak about the selling of Oroonoko into slavery.

ANSWER TO GUIDED READING QUESTION

1. When he realizes what is happening, Oroonoko looks at the captain with fierceness and disdain. He tells the captain that his suffering was worthwhile because he gained a true "knowledge both of you and of your gods by whom you swear."

ADDITIONAL QUESTIONS AND ACTIVITIES

Ask students the following questions. Students may discuss these or write about them in their journals. What contradictions does Behn point out between the professed religious beliefs of the captain and the way in which he behaves? What indictment does Behn make in this piece of the English supporters of the slave trade? How do you feel when you think of the history of slavery and of the slave trade? What do you think can be learned from study of that history?

SELECTION CHECK TEST 4.7.13 WITH ANSWERS

Checking Your Reading

1. What business transactions had Oroonoko and the Captain had? **Oroonoko has sold slaves to him.**
2. How is Oroonoko captured? **He is ambushed while at dinner on the ship.**
3. Why does Oroonoko refuse to eat? **He would rather die than be a slave.**
4. What promise of the captain's does Ooronoko believe? **He says he will be set free.**
5. As he's led away, what does Ooronoko say he's gained a "true knowledge" of? **He's gained knowledge of the English captain and of his gods.**

Literary Tools

1. What is the relationship of the narrator to Oroonoko? **Oroonoko is sold to the narrator's overseer.**
2. Describe the personal characteristics of Oroonoko. **Responses will vary, but should note that he is honorable and noble.**
3. Describe the personal characteristics of the English captain. **Responses will vary, but should note that he is deceitful and dishonorable.**

ANSWERS FOR INVESTIGATE, INQUIRE, IMAGINE

RECALL

1a. Oroonoko is described as "a young victor," who was "beloved like a deity" by his people. He has recently returned from a conquest.

2a. The captain of the ship entertains Oroonoko "with globes and maps, and mathematical discourses and instruments; eating, drinking, hunting, and living with him."

3a. Oroonoko and his fellow captives show their nobility and their spirit by their quiet determination to refuse food. The captain feels compelled to release Oroonoko from his fetters because he knows that all the slaves, following Oroonoko's refusal to eat, will die and, therefore, be of no profit to him.

INTERPRET

1b. The adoration given Oroonoko and the description "young victor" establish him as a heroic character.

2b. Oroonoko might think that the captain is a friend because the captain seems to enjoy Oroonoko's company and to treat him as an equal.

3b. Oroonoko possesses both honesty and integrity, unlike the captain who believes he needs to be honest only with people who share his beliefs. The captain lies to gain an advantage over Oroonoko; unfortunately, Oroonoko believes the captain's lies because he himself would never be so dishonest.

ANALYZE

4a. Behn presents the Africans as noble, honest, trusting people. The slave traders are portrayed as unscrupulous, conniving liars who do and say what they have to in order to capture slaves.

SYNTHESIZE

4b. Oroonoko's naiveté and trust of the captain made him easy prey. He judges the captain by his own standards of behavior.

EVALUATE

5a. *Responses will vary.* Students may say that Behn is not completely objective, but that her intent is to portray Oroonoko as a heroic figure.

EXTEND

Responses will vary. Possible responses are given.

5b. Students may say that Behn views the Africans as a primitive people, still innocent and untouched by the corruption that Behn sees in the "civilized" people of Europe.

Investigate, Inquire, Imagine

Recall: GATHERING FACTS →

1a. How is Oroonoko described in the first paragraph of the selection? From what has he recently returned?

2a. With what does the captain of the ship entertain Oroonoko in the third paragraph of the selection?

3a. What actions on the part of Oroonoko and his fellow captives show their nobility and their spirit? Why does the captain feel compelled to release Oroonoko from his fetters?

Interpret: FINDING MEANING

1b. What information given at the beginning of the selection establishes Oroonoko as a heroic character?

2b. What reason might Oroonoko have at the beginning of the selection to think that the English captain is a friend?

3b. How do the captain and Oroonoko differ with respect to their honesty and integrity? How do the negotiations over freeing Oroonoko from his fetters demonstrate this difference?

Analyze: TAKING THINGS APART →

4a. Identify the main characteristic Behn presents of the Africans and of the slave traders.

Synthesize: BRINGING THINGS TOGETHER

4b. Explain the role their differences had in Oroonoko's capture.

Evaluate: MAKING JUDGMENTS →

5a. Judge whether Behn is objective in her portrayal of the captain and of Oroonoko.

Extend: CONNECTING IDEAS

5b. Earlier in the novel, Behn writes, "And these People represented to me an absolute *Idea* of the first State of Innocence, before *Man* knew how to sin." How does Behn view the African people?

Understanding Literature

NOVEL. Review the definition for **novel** in the Handbook of Literary Terms. One characteristic that sets novels apart from earlier types of prose fiction is their realistic portrayals of the interior psychological states of characters. What does Oroonoko learn about the differences between his values and those of the captain? In what sense does Oroonoko lose a certain innocence about the world?

CHARACTERIZATION. Review the definition for **characterization** and the graphic organizer you made for Literary Tools in the Prereading for this selection. Briefly describe the character of Oroonoko, using information you learn from all three techniques of characterization.

ANSWERS TO UNDERSTANDING LITERATURE

NOVEL. In the beginning of the selection, Oroonoko naturally believes that others share his values; he accepts the English captain at face value and never suspects his intentions. By the end of the selection, Oroonoko realizes that not everyone functions within his system of honor. Whereas Oroonoko's values are unconditional and applicable to all people, the captain's values are relative. Oroonoko loses a certain sense of innocence about the world because he discovers that not all people are honorable and that his responses must now always be guarded.

NOTE: Students should examine the characters' words as well as their actions for clues about changes in their psychological states.

CHARACTERIZATION. Oroonoko is a highly respected, heroic figure. He is a popular leader. He is honest and true to his word and he expects others to be the same.

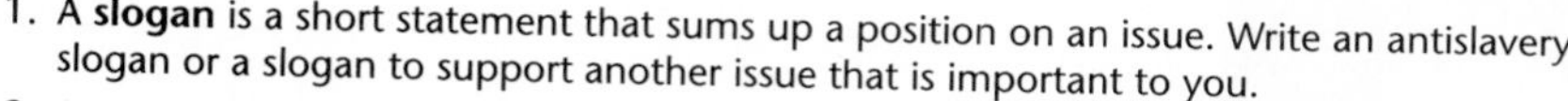

Writer's Journal

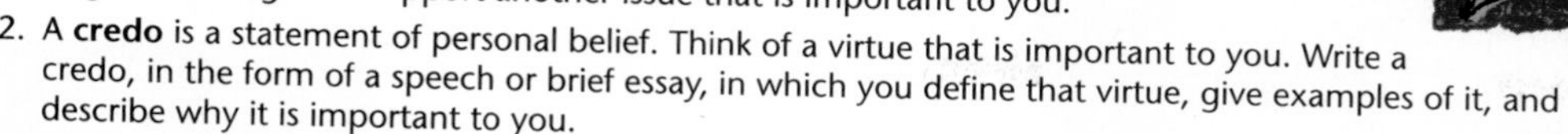

1. A **slogan** is a short statement that sums up a position on an issue. Write an antislavery slogan or a slogan to support another issue that is important to you.
2. A **credo** is a statement of personal belief. Think of a virtue that is important to you. Write a credo, in the form of a speech or brief essay, in which you define that virtue, give examples of it, and describe why it is important to you.
3. Write a dramatic **adaptation** of this selection from Oroonoko. Remember that characters will have to convey meaning by words or actions, without the help of a narrator.

Integrating *the* Language Arts

Language, Grammar, and Style

Editing for Capitalization. Read the Language Arts Survey 3.94 "Editing for Capitalization Errors." Then, rewrite the following sentences correcting any errors in capitalization.

1. Aphra Behn based this novel on her experiences in suriname.
2. She, herself, took part in a Slave Rebellion.
3. This novel tells of oroonoko, a Prince.
4. The novel is called *Oroonoko, Or the royal slave.*
5. Behn's book was outlawed in all british colonies.

Study and Research

Researching Slavery. Use library resources to find more information on the slave trade and the anti-slavery movement. What was happening at the time Behn wrote Oroonoko? Create a bibliography of sources you use to answer these questions.

Speaking and Listening

Persuasive Speech. What issue do you think is most pressing today? Prepare a short persuasive speech and deliver it to your class. In your speech, use statistics, anecdotes, or other elements that you think will be effective to convey your point.

Media Literacy & Collaborative Learning

Evaluating a Film. Look at how different races are portrayed in *Oroonoko.* Then choose a contemporary film. Examine the film for the message it sends about race. Discuss your findings in small groups.

ANSWERS TO INTEGRATING THE LANGUAGE ARTS

Language, Grammar, and Style

1. Aphra Behn based this novel on her experiences in Suriname.
2. She, herself, took part in a slave rebellion.
3. This novel tells of Oroonoko, a prince.
4. The novel is called *Oroonoko, or The Royal Slave.*
5. Behn's book was outlawed in all British colonies.

Study and Research

Students can focus on the slave-trade and anti-slavery movements in different countries.

Speaking and Listening

Students can work in pairs to practice their speeches. Partners can critique each other's speeches before the final presentation.

Evaluating Films

Students might also consider how different genders or ages are portrayed in the film they chose.

ADDITIONAL RESOURCES

UNIT 7 RESOURCE BOOK
- Selection Worksheet 7.7
- Selection Check Test 4.7.15
- Selection Test 4.7.16
- Language, Grammar, and Style Resource 3.35
- Study and Research Resource 5.53

READER'S JOURNAL

Students should consider whether the meaning of the saying is literal or whether it has come to have a different meaning than the sum of its words.

INDIVIDUAL LEARNING STRATEGIES

MOTIVATION
Have students choose one of the couplets from this selection and use a thesaurus, to find complicated synonyms for several of the words. (Refer them to the Language Arts Survey 5.22, "Using a Thesaurus" for help.) Students might then copy one their couplets on their own paper, inserting the synonyms they found, to compare the effectiveness of simple and complex language. Discuss why Pope might have used simple language to express his ideas.

READING PROFICIENCY
Syntax in some of the couplets might pose a problem for students. Have students check their comprehension by paraphrasing each couplet.

ENGLISH LANGUAGE LEARNING
Ask students if to share with the class any sayings from their own language that are similar to the sayings in this selection. Share with students the following additional vocabulary.
vast—great in extent
draught—draft; drink
joint—joined; combined
oft—often
torrent—violent flood
shun—avoid consistently

Continued on page 615

Literary TOOLS

EPIGRAM. An **epigram** is a short, often witty, saying. Pope's couplets are famous not only for their poetic excellence, but for the wit and insight they contain. In this respect, they have philosophical as well as literary value.

COUPLET. A **couplet** is a pair of rhyming lines that expresses a complete thought. The form which Pope mastered is the *heroic couplet,* the lines of which are in iambic pentameter. As you read, notice that the rhyme, like the rhythm, or sound of the words, is often very simple.

Reader's Journal

Think of a short saying or piece of folk wisdom familiar to you. Explain its meaning and give examples of a few situations to which it applies.

COUPLETS FROM
An Essay on Criticism
BY ALEXANDER POPE

About the AUTHOR

The insight and wisdom **Alexander Pope** (1688–1744) was able to capture in epigrams from his verses makes him one of the most frequently quoted authors in the English language. As a young boy, Pope was educated primarily at home by Catholic priests. An extremely bright child, he learned Greek, Latin, French, and Italian. At the age of twelve, he produced some of his first poetry, imitating the style of the poets he was already reading. By young adulthood, Pope had begun his extensive output of literary work. This output included numerous volumes of verse and ambitious projects—complete translations of Homer's *Iliad* and *Odyssey.* In his mature years, Pope lived and wrote on his country estate on the Thames outside of London and befriended many noteworthy writers, including Jonathan Swift. By the end of his life, he was immersed in a multitude of literary endeavors, though his death left some unfinished.

About the SELECTION

Pope wrote his ***Essay on Criticism*** when he was only twenty-one years old and published it a few years later, in 1711. The poem, excerpts of which appear on the following pages, wittily presents critical precepts derived from Greek and Latin authorities. It is written in Pope's favorite meter, ten-syllable **iambic pentameter.** An **iamb** is a poetic foot with one weakly stressed syllable and one strongly stressed syllable, as in the word *alone.* A **pentameter** line has five feet. Paired lines of rhymed iambic pentameter such as those used in this poem are known as **heroic couplets.**

The couplets included here demonstrate Pope's special ability to capture perceptive insights in a few words that please the ear and enlighten the mind. So appealing are these excerpts that they have gained the status of proverbs used commonly by English speakers around the globe, often by people who do not know their source.

GOALS/OBJECTIVES

Studying this lesson will enable students to
- enjoy and appreciate Alexander Pope's wit and humor
- describe Pope's literary accomplishments and explain the historical significance of his writings
- define *epigram* and interpret epigrams that they encounter in their reading
- define *couplet* and identify couplets in poems
- define *antithesis* and recognize and interpret examples of antithesis in literature that they read
- rewrite to correct wordy sentences
- document sources using correct bibliographic form

COUPLETS FROM

An Essay on Criticism

ALEXANDER POPE

'Tis with our judgments as our watches; none
Go just alike, yet each believes his own.

Can you think of situations in which people have radically different but strongly held convictions?

◆ ◆ ◆

One science only will one genius fit;
So vast is art, so narrow human wit:

Does Pope believe that a person can be a jack-of-all-trades? Why, or why not?

◆ ◆ ◆

A little learning is a dangerous thing;
Drink deep, or taste not the Pierian spring:[1]
There shallow draughts intoxicate the brain,
And drinking largely sobers us again.

Why might "A little learning" be "a dangerous thing"?

◆ ◆ ◆

In wit, as nature, what affects our hearts
Is not the exactness of peculiar parts;
'Tis not a lip, or eye, we beauty call,
But the joint force and full result of all.

Thinkers of the Enlightenment Era were enamored of generality. How does Pope's conception of beauty reflect his era's love for general principles?

◆ ◆ ◆

True wit is nature to advantage dressed,
What oft was thought, but ne'er so well expressed;

The Neoclassicists favored human artifice over untamed nature. How does Pope apply this concept to writing?

◆ ◆ ◆

Words are like leaves; and where they most abound,
Much fruit of sense beneath is rarely found;

Would Pope agree that writers should use as few words as possible? Explain.

◆ ◆ ◆

1. **Pierian spring.** The Pierian spring is said to be the birthplace of the Muses. To drink of it is to drink inspiration.

ANSWERS TO GUIDED READING QUESTIONS

1. *Responses will vary.*
2. Pope does not believe a person should be a jack-of-all-trades because a person can only have skill enough to master one.
3. A little learning might be dangerous because it could inspire false confidence untempered by deeper knowledge.
4. Pope does not love a part or a feature of beauty, but the general result of all the features combined.
5. Pope says that natural thought is not as elegant as the human artifice for expressing thought—writings.
6. Pope would agree that writers should avoid wordiness because when words are as abundant as "leaves," they produce little sense, or "fruit."

INDIVIDUAL LEARNING STRATEGIES (CONT. FROM PAGE 614)

SPECIAL NEEDS
Have students rephrase each couplet in their own words and write a brief fable in which each saying can work as a moral. They can then act out their fables as skits in front of the class.

ENRICHMENT
Students can discuss or write a comparison-contrast essay about the similarities and differences between Pope's aphorisms and those of a famous American writer, such as Benjamin Franklin. How are they similar? How are they different?

LITERARY NOTE

Tell students that Pope is the second most quoted poet in the English language, Shakespeare being first. Most people who quote him know the lines but not the source of aphorisms such as "For fools rush in where angels fear to tread." Ask students how many of the couplets presented in the passage they have heard before. Did they know the source of these quotations?

LITERARY TECHNIQUE

ANTITHESIS. Antithesis is a rhetorical technique in which words, phrases, or ideas are strongly contrasted, often by means of a repetition of grammatical structures. Ask students to identify which of these couplets use antithesis.

LITERARY NOTE

In his *Essay on Criticism* (1711), Pope set the intellectual tone for the Augustan Age. Focal words in the essay, such as *wit, Nature,* and *genius,* would be used as a measure for writers throughout the remainder of the century.

VOCABULARY FROM THE SELECTION

err

ANSWERS TO GUIDED READING QUESTIONS

1. Pope writes lines that echo their meanings by employing techniques such as the alliteration that creates the sound of soft wind in line 5: "Soft is the strain when Zephyr gently blows." Pope also uses a cæsura to make a line move slowly: "The line too labors, and the words move slow."
2. Restraint and moderation are practiced by avoiding extremes and being too little or too much pleased.
3. As people grow older they think themselves wiser than their fathers.
4. Pope's advice calls for trying to combine natural talents with sense, or wit, but mistakes are inevitable both in writing and in life.

SELECTION CHECK TEST 4.7.15 WITH ANSWERS

Checking Your Reading

1. What effect does a little learning have? **A little learning can "intoxicate the brain" or inspire false confidence, and therefore is dangerous.**
2. What are like leaves? **Words are like leaves.**
3. What is rarely found beneath these leaves? **Good sense is rarely found there.**
4. Who do we consider to be fools? **We think our fathers are fools.**
5. What must we join with "good-nature"? **We must join sense with good nature.**

Literary Tools

1. An **epigram** is ...
 a. a quotation or motto used at the beginning of a literary work to help establish the work's theme
 b. an inscription or verse written to be used on a tomb
 c. a word or phrase used to describe a characteristic of a person
 d. a short, often witty saying

2. The line, "So vast is art, so narrow human wit" illustrates **antithesis** because
 a. it assigns human qualities to nonhuman things
 b. it says one thing but implies something else
 c. it joins two contrasting ideas to make a point
 d. it directly opposes the ideas in the rest of the poem

3. Pope's lines are called **heroic couplets** because

True ease in writing comes from art, not chance,
As those move easiest who have learned to dance.
'Tis not enough no harshness gives offense,
The sound must seem an echo to the sense:
Soft is the strain when Zephyr[2] gently blows,
And the smooth stream in smoother numbers flows;
But when loud surges lash the sounding shore,
The hoarse, rough verse should like the torrent roar:
When Ajax[3] strives some rock's vast weight to throw,
The line too labors, and the words move slow;
Not so, when swift Camilla[4] scours the plain,
Flies o'er the unbending corn, and skims along the main.

In what ways do the sounds of lines in this section of the poem echo their sense?

◆ ◆ ◆

Avoid extremes; and shun the fault of such,
Who still are pleased too little or too much,

How do these lines reflect the Neoclassical idea of restraint and moderation?

◆ ◆ ◆

We think our fathers fools, so wise we grow;
Our wiser sons, no doubt, will think us so.

According to Pope, what happens as each generation grows?

◆ ◆ ◆

Good-nature and good-sense must ever join;
To err is human, to forgive, divine. ■

How might Pope's advice apply to judging someone else's writing? to other aspects of life?

2. **Zephyr.** The west wind
3. **Ajax.** A Greek hero known for his size and strength
4. **Camilla.** A female warrior killed in the Trojan War

WORDS FOR EVERYDAY USE

err (ʉr) *vi.,* be wrong. *Did I err in calling you so late at night?*

SELECTION CHECK TEST 4.7.15 WITH ANSWERS (CONT.)

 a. they deal with lofty subjects, like heroes or God
 b. they are modeled after Greek and Roman classics
 c. they are written in iambic pentameter
 d. they are written to be recited at the court of the King

Quotables

"A man should never be ashamed to own he has been in the wrong, which is but saying, in other words, that he is wiser today than he was yesterday."

—Alexander Pope, "Thoughts on Various Subjects"

Respond to the SELECTION

Choose one of these epigrams and explain why it has particular meaning for you or how it might apply to your life.

INVESTIGATE, Inquire, Imagine

Recall: GATHERING FACTS

1a. To what does Pope compare watches?

2a. To what does Pope compare words and wordiness?

3a. What, according to Pope, is "nature to advantage dressed"?

→ **Interpret:** FINDING MEANING

1b. In what sense are judgments like watches, according to Pope?

2b. What, in Pope's view, is usually true of wordy writing?

3b. In what ways might a writer "dress up" a thought?

Analyze: TAKING THINGS APART

4a. What general principles for writing and criticism can you find in these selections? State these principles in your own words.

→ **Synthesize:** BRINGING THINGS TOGETHER

4b. Does Pope follows his own advice? Explain.

Evaluate: MAKING JUDGMENTS

5a. Evaluate Pope's epigrams as a neoclassical work. What elements of neoclassicism does this writing represent?

→ **Extend:** CONNECTING IDEAS

5b. Compare this neoclassical work to the sonnet in this unit by Charlotte Smith. Smith's poem in many ways reflects Romanticism. Using Pope's and Smith's works, contrast the two movements.

Understanding Literature

EPIGRAM. Review the definition for **epigram** in the Handbook of Literary Terms. What makes an epigram valuable is that it can apply to many situations and circumstances. Choose one of Pope's epigrams and discuss situations to which it applies. How does the form itself help make an epigram effective?

COUPLET. Review the definition for **couplet** in Literary Tools in the Prereading for this selection. Why would Pope have chosen this form to express his insights? Why do think his lines are so often quoted?

RESPOND TO THE SELECTION

Students might break into groups based on which epigram they chose. They can discuss their response and ideas about the application of the epigram.

ANSWERS TO INVESTIGATE, INQUIRE, IMAGINE

RECALL

1a. Pope compares personal judgment to watches.

2a. Pope compares words, and wordiness, to a leafy tree that bears little fruit.

3a. According to Pope, "True wit is nature to advantage dressed." In other words, to take a basic, natural human thought and express it with particular eloquence is what wittiness is all about.

INTERPRET

1b. Pope says that no person's judgment is exactly like anyone else's, just as watches always run a little differently—but that every person believes his or her own judgment to be the most accurate, just as every person believes his or her watch to have the correct time.

2b. According to Pope, wordy writing often contains little sense.

3b. A writer might dress up a common thought by using literary techniques such as metaphors, similes, personification, or anaphora in order to express the thought in a new and original way.

ANALYZE

4a. Pope stresses the importance of conciseness, preciseness, and humor in writing and criticism.

SYNTHESIZE

4b. Pope writes in couplets, a short, compact form. He does not use a lot of extra words. He chooses his words carefully and generally uses simple words that say what he means.

EVALUATE

Responses will vary. Possible responses are given.

5a. Students should refer to the section "Neoclassical Literature"in the introduction to this unit. They can read there that neoclassical literature made use of classical forms and allusions; promoted ideals of harmony, tradition, and reason; and is notable for its wittiness and its emphasis on social interactions.

ANSWERS TO INVESTIGATE, INQUIRE, IMAGINE (CONT.)

Pope makes many allusions to classical Greek mythology; Pope's work is witty and philosophical. He writes about criticism, creating rules or suggestions that are based on a desire for orderliness and logic in personal comportment and social interaction. His style as well as his topic reflect neoclassical ideas.

EXTEND

5b. *Responses will vary.* Smith's poem celebrates wild disorder, while Pope's lines are aimed at creating order. Smith's poem expresses more emotion, while Pope's work is more based in logic or rational thought.

Answers to Understanding Literature can be found on page 618.

ANSWERS TO UNDERSTANDING LITERATURE

Epigram. *Responses will vary.* Students may find many applications for some of these epigrams. Because an epigram refers to a topic broadly, it can be applied in many situations. For example, Pope's couplet "One science only will one genius fit; / So vast is art, so narrow human wit" applies to the hundreds of artistic endeavors pursued by humans. An epigram is effective because its brevity makes it memorable; in the case of Pope's couplets, their rhyming quality, rhythm, and wit makes them even more memorable.
NOTE: Students might read one of Pope's couplets and brainstorm a list of stiuations to which it might apply.

Couplet. *Responses will vary.* Pope might have chosen the couplet form to express his thoughts because he found its restrictions challenging. If Pope had written a long essay on one of his themes, he might have lost his reader's interest or belabored his point. As he states in one of his own couplets, "Words are like leaves; and where they most abound, / Much fruit of sense is rarely found." By using the couplet form, he impresses his audience with a strikingly succinct and memorable idea.
NOTE: Have students write a longer, prose paraphrase of the theme of one of Pope's couplets. Then have students compare the effectiveness of each format.

ANSWERS TO INTEGRATING THE LANGUAGE ARTS

Language, Grammar, and Style
Responses will vary. A possible response is given.
Pope wrote, "The vulgar thus through imitation err; / as oft the learn'd by being singular; / So much they scorn the crowd, that if the throng / By chance go right , they purposely go wrong." This criticizes people who go their own way simply for the sake of being different. Following the crowd isn't always the best way to go, but sometimes the crowd will be right. It is important to approach each situation thoughtfully.

Study and Research
Responses will vary. Students should write an organized essay that includes a brief introduction with a clearly stated thesis, several supporting points and a conclusion. Students might use examples from their lives, from the news, from literature, or any other source to support their opinion.

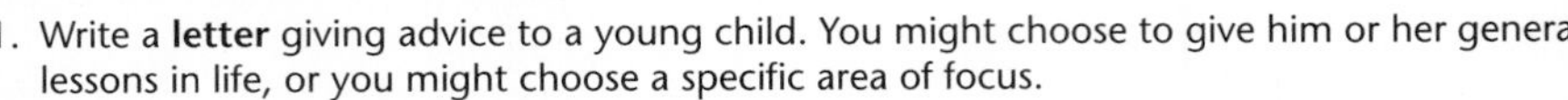

Writer's Journal

1. Write a **letter** giving advice to a young child. You might choose to give him or her general lessons in life, or you might choose a specific area of focus.
2. Think of the rules by which you live, things that you would not do, and standards or principles that you think are important. These should be general enough to apply to many relationships and circumstances. Write a short **statement** that captures the meaning of one of your rules. Revise this personal aphorism into a heroic couplet.
3. Choose one of Pope's epigrams. Write a **fable** that uses the epigram as its moral. Fables are short stories, often with animals as characters, which teach a lesson.

Integrating *the* Language Arts

Language, Grammar, and Style

Avoiding Wordiness. As Pope pointed out, wordy prose is not necessarily good, accurate, or sensible prose. Read the Language Arts Survey 3.35, "Correcting Wordy Sentences." Rewrite the following paragraph to avoid wordiness and increase clarity.

Pope wrote, "The vulgar thus through imitation err;/as oft the learn'd by being singular;/So much they scorn the crowd, that if the throng/By chance go right , they purposely go wrong." This is a scathing and searing criticism of freethinkers, or people who go their own way, but only if they do their own thing for the sole purpose of being different. Pope's statement presents an idea similar to that of the much quoted, "If your friends jumped off a bridge, would you do that too?" The latter suggests or implies that following the crowd is not the best way to go. Pope does not deny that people should think on their own or follow their own minds, but he cautions that they should make sure that they always continue to think. That is they should always evaluate a position or an action, even if it is a popular one. Sometimes the crowd will get it right.

Study and Research

Bibliography. People often quote Pope without knowing the source. In research, this is a dangerous practice known as plagiarism. Properly documenting sources is important. Find five interesting facts about Pope. Use at least three sources. Create a bibliography that shows the sources you used.

Study and Research

Essay Test. Review the Language Arts Survey 5.57, "Taking Essay Tests." Then write a response to the following: Alexander Pope wrote, "Be silent always when you doubt your sense." In an essay, support or contradict Pope's advice.

Collaborative Learning

Posters. As a class, choose epigrams from Pope that you think are most applicable to life at your school. Create a series of posters that use Pope's words as a way to convey messages to other students. Use illustrations or other words as well to convey your ideas.

CROSS-CURRICULAR ACTIVITIES

Logic. The use of logic was popular in neoclassical writing. Ask students to read the Language Arts Survey 5.7, "Deductive versus Inductive Reasoning." Then ask them to determine the reasoning Pope mimics in the following quote: "Sir, I admit your gen'ral rule / That every poet is a fool; / But you yourself may serve to show it, / That every fool is not a poet." (Alexander Pope, "Epigram from the French"). They should be able to see that the statement "Every poet is a fool" is a general statement that leads, through deductive reasoning, to the more specific implication that "Alexander Pope, the poet, is a fool." The statement "Every fool is not a poet" is a generalization that Pope makes, using inductive reasoning, from an implied specific that "You, sir, are not a poet, but you are a fool." Make sure that students know that true logic can only stem from observable facts, not subjective opinions such as "you are a fool."

FROM A Dictionary of the English Language

"A Brief to Free a Slave" BY SAMUEL JOHNSON

About the AUTHOR

Samuel Johnson's (1709–1784) influence reached far beyond his times to touch all of British literature. Johnson was exposed to literature early, for his father was a bookseller in the village of Litchfield, Staffordshire. After attempting unsuccessfully to start a school, Johnson moved to London and took up writing. His political writings brought him popular attention. He also wrote literary criticism, including a series of essays on Shakespeare. Later he compiled an edition of Shakespeare's plays (1765). In 1750 he started a periodical, *The Rambler,* which he published successfully until 1752, the year his wife died. Six years later he began a second periodical, *The Idler.* Besides writing essays for periodicals, Johnson also wrote poetry, articles, and travelogues. However, his greatest achievement is his ***Dictionary of the English Language*** (1755), which took Johnson eight years to complete. He was always known among his friends for his witty and honest conversation, some of which was recorded by his friend **James Boswell** (see page 627), whom he met in 1763. Johnson was awarded an honorary degree by Trinity College, Dublin (1765), and a lifetime pension by King George III (1762).

About the SELECTIONS

Normally we think of a dictionary as a reference guide to the standard meanings of words, and indeed Johnson's ***A Dictionary of the English Language*** is such a reference, the first great work of its kind in English. However, Johnson's *Dictionary* is also a piece of literature. Its definitions include insightful, witty commentaries on politics, mores, literature, and humanity.

"A Brief to Free a Slave" (1777) was written to aid Joseph Knight, a slave, in his legal action to obtain freedom from his Scottish master. While Scotland permitted serfdom, slavery had been abolished in England in 1772; however, the British slave trade continued until 1807, since slavery had always been integral to British colonialism.

Literary TOOLS

DENOTATION AND CONNOTATION. The **denotation** is the basic meaning or reference of an expression, excluding its emotional associations. These emotional associations or implications are called **connotations.** Pay attention to the denotations and connotations of Johnson's definitions from *A Dictionary of the English Language.*

THESIS AND ARGUMENT. A **thesis** is a main idea that is supported in a work of nonfiction prose. An **argument** presents reasons for accepting or rejecting a thesis. As you read, determine Johnson's thesis in "A Brief to Free a Slave." Use an outline to track his thesis and argument.

Thesis:
I. II. III. IV.

Reader's Journal

Choose a word that you like. In your journal define the word. Use both a standard meaning and any special meanings the word has for you.

ADDITIONAL RESOURCES

UNIT 7 RESOURCE BOOK

From *A Dictionary of the English Language*
- Selection Worksheet 7.8
- Selection Check Test 4.7.17
- Selection Test 4.7.18

"A Brief to Free a Slave"
- Selection Worksheet 7.9
- Selection Check Test 4.7.19
- Selection Test 4.7.20
- Reading Resource 1.17, 1.24
- Study and Research Resource 5.30
- Applied English Resource 6.9

GRAPHIC ORGANIZER

Responses will vary. Students might include the following thesis and supporting arguments in their graphic organizers.

THESIS: All people possess the same right to freedom and that right cannot be taken away unless a person forfeits his or her own freedom.

I. Criminal forfeits freedom, but not that of his or her children, same for conquered
II. Defendant made slave only by violence
III. Even if slavery is legal, people are often sold into it through fraud, violence, or trickery.
IV. Defendant is free by nature.

READER'S JOURNAL

Students might also write about a word that they had to explain to somebody else. For example, they might choose a slang term that they have had to explain to their parents or sports jargon they have had to explain to someone who was unfamiliar with the game.

VOCABULARY FROM THE SELECTIONS

abhorrence	insolence
avail	lament
compulsion	perpetual
disposition	redress
drudge	stipulate
entail	

GOALS/OBJECTIVES

Studying this lesson will enable students to
- appreciate a selection from an early dictionary as a piece of literature
- interpret a legal brief and infer the beliefs of the author from his writing
- describe Samuel Johnson's literary accomplishments and explain the historical significance of his writings
- define *denotation* and *connotation* and distinguish between denotations and connotations that they encounter in their reading
- define *thesis* and *argument* and identify these elements in prose works
- use a dictionary to find specific information
- write a public service announcement about the violation of human rights

ANSWERS TO GUIDED READING QUESTIONS

1. A collection of poems or stories is similar to a collection of flowers because both are pleasing, and, while pieces of the collection seem alike at first glance, each piece has its individual beauty and appeal.
2. *Responses will vary.*

INDIVIDUAL LEARNING STRATEGIES

MOTIVATION
Refer students to the Language Arts Survey 1.17, "Using a Dictionary," paying attention to the information on etymology. Then, they should examine both selections by Johnson to find words with Greek or Latin roots, making a list as they go. On their lists, they should underline the root and identify it as Greek or Latin. They can consult a dictionary as needed. Or, discuss a court case that is in the news. Students may be familiar with a local case, a case involving other students, or a particularly sensation case. Ask students to identify the arguments being made by each side. If the trial is ongoing, students might track the case as it unfolds.

READING PROFICIENCY
Explain that some of Johnson's definitions are not literal meanings of words. Have students look up the words from the selection in a dictionary and compare those definitions to Johnson's definitions. For "A Brief to Free a Slave," you might begin by discussing the end of the brief where Johnson sums up this argument. Once students understand Johnson's position, have them read the rest of the brief.

ENGLISH LANGUAGE LEARNING
Share with students the following additional vocabulary.
For *Dictionary:*
constitution—physical makeup of a person
animated—alive
compass—range, scope
countenance—give support to
wretch—despicable person

For "A Brief":
forfeit—lose; give up
inhabitant—permanent resident

SPECIAL NEEDS
Read through the selection "A Brief to Free a Slave" once with students, asking volunteers to

FROM A Dictionary of the English Language

SAMUEL JOHNSON

ANTHO´LOGY. *n.*
1. A collection of flowers.

In what ways is a collection of poems or stories similar to a collection of flowers?

GANG. *n.*
A number herding together; a troop; a company; a tribe; a herd. It is seldom used but in contempt or abhorrence.

LEXICO´GRAPHER. *n.*
A writer of dictionaries; a harmless drudge, that busies himself in tracing the original, and detailing the signification of words.

NA´TURE. *n.*

Can you make sentences using the word nature in each of these different ways?

1. An imaginary being supposed to preside over the material and animal world.

   Though, *nature*, art my goddess; to thy law
   My services are bound.—*Shakespeare*

2. The native state or properties of anything, by which it is discriminated from others.
3. The constitution of an animated body.
4. Disposition of mind; temper.
5. The regular course of things.
6. The compass of natural existence.
7. Natural affection, or reverence; native sensations.
8. The state or operation of the material world.
9. Sort; species.
10. Sentiments or images adapted to nature, or comformable to truth and reality.
11. Physics; the science which teaches the qualities of things.

   Nature and *nature's* laws lay hid in night,
   God said, Let Newton be, and all was light.—*Pope.*

WORDS FOR EVERYDAY USE

ab • hor • rence (ab hôr´ əns) *n.*, loathing. *On the playground, the elementary school boys and girls eyed each other with abhorrence.*

drudge (druj) *n.*, person who does tedious work. *The assembly-line work made her feel like a drudge.*

dis • po • si • tion (dis´ pə zish´ ən) *n.*, tendency, habit. *I hope you don't have a disposition for tardiness because this job requires promptness.*

INDIVIDUAL LEARNING STRATEGIES (CONT.)

summarize the main points of each paragraph as you go. Then, help students complete the graphic organizer in Literary Tools.

ENRICHMENT
Explain that the years between 1750 and 1798 are commonly called the Age of Johnson, in reference to Samuel Johnson. After students read the selections, have them write about or discuss what they believe are the defining characteristics of the Age of Johnson, based on the selections.

154 RELIQUES OF ANCIENT POETRY.

This mayden in a morne betime
Went forth, when May was in her prime,
To get sweete cetywall,[1]
The honey-suckle, the harlocke,[2]
The lilly and the lady-smocke,
To deck her summer hall.

Thus, as she wandred here and there,
Y-picking of the bloomed breere,
She chanced to espie
A shepheard sitting on a bancke,
Like chanteclere he crowed crancke,[3]
And pip'd full merrilie.

He lear'd[4] his sheepe as he him list,[5]
When he would whistle in his fist,
To feede about him round;
Whilst he full many a carroll sung,
Untill the fields and medowes rung,
And all the woods did sound.

In favour this same shepheards swayne
Was like the bedlam Tamburlayne,[6]
Which helde prowd kings in awe;
But meeke he was as lamb mought be;
An innocent of ill as he[7]
Whom his lewd brother slaw.

The shepheard ware a sheepe-gray cloke,
Which was of the finest loke,[8]
That could be cut with sheere:
His mitens[9] were of bauzens skinne,
His cockers[10] were of cordiwin,[11]
His hood of meniveere.[12]

His awle and lingell[13] in a thong,
His tar-boxe on his broad belt hong,
His breech of coyntrie blewe:
Full crispe and curled were his lockes,
His browes as white as Albion rocks:
So like a lover true,

DOWSABELL.

"This mayden in a morne betime
Went forth when May was in her prime."

OATS. *n.*

A grain, which in England is generally given to horses, but in Scotland supports the people.

PA´TRON. *n.*

1. One who countenances, supports, or protects. Commonly a wretch who supports with <u>insolence</u>, and is paid with flattery. ■

Based on this definition, how do you think Johnson felt about depending, for his livelihood as a writer, on the largess of patrons?

WORDS FOR EVERYDAY USE

in • so • lence (in´ sə lens) *n.,* disrespect, contempt. *The teacher reprimanded the rowdy student's <u>insolence</u>.*

Respond *to the* SELECTION

Which of Johnson's definitions seem accurate to you? most useful? most amusing? Which definition do you like the best? Why?

ANSWER TO GUIDED READING QUESTION

1. Johnson seems to have resented having to depend on the support of the wealthy, who were snobbish and treated him with disrespect, and who expected him to flatter them in his writings.

RESPOND TO THE SELECTION

Ask students to create their own definitions for each of the words in this selection.

SELECTION CHECK TEST 4.7.17 WITH ANSWERS

Checking Your Reading

1. Name one synonym given for gang. **Responses could include company, troop, tribe, or herd.**
2. How is the word gang usually used? **It is used with contempt or abhorrence.**
3. What is defined as "a harmless drudge"? **A lexicographer is a harmless drudge.**
4. What is eaten by English horses but Scottish people? **Oats are eaten thus.**
5. What is a "wretch who supports with insolence"? **This is a patron.**

Vocabulary in Context

Fill each blank with the most appropriate word of the *Words for Everyday Use* for the selection from *A Dictionary of the English Language.* You may have to change the tense of the word.

abhorrence drudge disposition insolence

1. Many people greet telemarketers with **<u>abhorrence</u>**.
2. Over the years, Martha took on a settled **<u>disposition</u>** and enjoyed her routines.
3. Although he was silent, the prisoner's **<u>insolence</u>** was obvious.

Literary Tools

1. How does Johnson's dictionary differ from common dictionaries? **His is a work of literature, that includes personal commentaries, witty statements, and insights.**
2. What is the difference between denotation and connotation?

SELECTION CHECK TEST 4.7.17 WITH ANSWERS (CONT.)

Denotation is a literal definition, and connotation is the emotional association the word carries.

3. Identify one definition in the selection from *A Dictionary of the English Language* that includes a connotation, and explain the connotation. **Students may point to the definition for gang, in which Johnson notes that the word connotes a contemptible group of people.**

ANSWERS TO INVESTIGATE, INQUIRE, IMAGINE

RECALL

1a. Johnson defines *lexicographer* as "A writer of dictionaries" and "a harmless drudge."

2a. Eleven definitions are given for *nature*. The first is "An imaginary being supposed to preside over the material and animal world."

3a. Oats are used to feed horses in England and people in Scotland.

INTERPRET

1b. "A harmless drudge…" is meant to be taken as tongue-in-cheek. "A writer of dictionaries" is meant to be taken seriously. One can determine that part of the definition is meant to be humorous because it is set off as an appositive bit of self-deprecation.

2b. Johnson equates nature to a spirit in his first definition. In his last definition, Newton's scientific discoveries account for science's "light" being shed.

3b. *Responses will vary.* Johnson doesn't think that oats are good food for people. Students may say that he finds humor in the fact that the Scots eat oats, and intends his definition as a mild barb at the Scots. Perhaps he is suggesting that the Scots are too poor to afford anything better than "animal food."

ANALYZE

4a. *Responses will vary.* Johnson offers opinions on various topics. By including a definition for *anthology* that refers back to its Greek roots as a word for flower-gathering, Johnson shows that he finds literature to be beautiful. In his definitions of *gang* and *patron,* he states a dislike for all forms of coercion. His definition of *oats* includes a poke at the people of Scotland.

SYNTHESIZE

4b. Johnson was opinionated, precise and sharp-witted. His definitions suggest that he doesn't take everything at face value. Johnson despises the snobbery of his patrons. Any future patron of Johnson cannot expect flattery or humility.

EVALUATE

5a. Johnson fits his own definition of *lexicographer* because he is a "writer of dictionaries" who traces the original meaning of words and details their "signification." However, his strong opinions and decidedly subjective definitions hardly make him "a harmless drudge."

EXTEND

5b. Johnson took on a difficult and arduous task. He is able to poke fun at himself.

INVESTIGATE, Inquire, Imagine

Recall: GATHERING FACTS

1a. How does Johnson define *lexicographer*?

2a. How many definitions of *nature* are given? What is the first definition?

3a. What are the two uses of oats? In which countries, respectively, are oats used in these ways?

→ **Interpret:** FINDING MEANING

1b. What part of Johnson's definition of *lexicographer* is meant to be taken as tongue-in-cheek? What part is meant to be taken seriously? How do you know?

2b. To what does Johnson equate nature in his first definition? In his last definition of *nature,* what accounts for science's "light" being shed?

3b. What is Johnson's opinion of how oats are used in Scotland?

Analyze: TAKING THINGS APART

4a. Identify the kinds of topics on which Johnson injects his opinions.

→ **Synthesize:** BRINGING THINGS TOGETHER

4b. What kind of person do you think Johnson was, based on these definitions?

Evaluate: MAKING JUDGMENTS

5a. Judge whether Johnson fits his definition of *lexicographer.*

→ **Extend:** CONNECTING IDEAS

5b. What does Johnson's definition of *lexicographer* tell you about him?

Understanding Literature

DENOTATION AND CONNOTATION. Review the definitions for **denotation** and **connotation** in the Handbook of Literary Terms. Which of Johnson's definitions provide denotations? What connotations does Johnson emphasize? Are these connotations widespread today?

ANSWERS TO UNDERSTANDING LITERATURE

DENOTATION AND CONNOTATION. All of these definitions provide denotations, or referents. However, these are not all straightforward: the definitions for *lexicographer, oats,* and *patron* are meant to be tongue-in-cheek. Point out to your students that the editors of this anthology have selected humorous definitions from Johnson's *Dictionary* but that most of the definitions in that dictionary are serious ones of the kind found in dictionaries today, which are, of course, the progeny of Johnson's seminal work. Johnson's definitions of *anthology, gang, oats,* and *patron* focus on connotations. With the exception of *anthology,* these definitions emphasize negative connotations. His connotation of *gang* is widespread today, but words such as *patron* and *oats* do not have the same connotations and are seldom used today in the same way.

Reader's *Journal*

Think about the freedoms you have. In your journal, write about what freedom means to you and how you value it.

A Brief to Free a Slave

SAMUEL JOHNSON

Why does the author discuss the history of slavery? What argument is Johnson refuting? What sentence shows that he subscribed to the notion that people are "created equal"?

It must be agreed that in most ages many countries have had part of their inhabitants in a state of slavery; yet it may be doubted whether slavery can ever be supposed the natural condition of man. It is impossible not to conceive that men in their original state were equal; and very difficult to imagine how one would be subjected to another but by violent compulsion. An individual may, indeed, forfeit his liberty by a crime; but he cannot by that crime forfeit the liberty of his children. What is true of a criminal seems true likewise of a captive. A man may accept life from a conquering enemy on condition of perpetual servitude; but it is very doubtful whether he can entail that servitude on his descendants; for no man can stipulate without commission for another. The condition which he himself accepts, his son or grandson perhaps would have rejected. If we should admit, what perhaps may with more reason be denied, that there are certain relations between man and man which may make slavery necessary and just, yet it can never be proved that he who is now suing for his freedom ever stood in any of those relations. He is certainly subject by no law, but that of violence, to his present master, who pretends no claim to his obedience, but that he bought him from a merchant of slaves, whose right to sell him never was examined. It is said that, according to the constitutions of Jamaica, he was legally enslaved; these constitutions are merely positive; and apparently injurious to the rights of mankind, because whoever is exposed to sale is condemned to slavery without appeal; by whatever fraud or violence he might have been originally brought into the merchant's power. In our own time princes have been sold, by wretches to whose care they were entrusted, that they might have an European education;

How would you paraphrase Johnson's statement that "no man can stipulate without commission for another"? Do you agree? Why, or why not?

WORDS FOR EVERYDAY USE

com • pul • sion (kəm pul´ shən) *n.*, coercion, driving force. *Fear of being caught, rather than a genuine sense of remorse, was the thief's main compulsion for turning himself in.*

per • pet • u • al (pər pech´ o͞o əl) *adj.*, lasting forever. *The swinging pendulum demonstrates the theory of perpetual motion.*

en • tail (en tāl) *vt.*, require. *In the job interview, the supervisor explained that the job entailed organizational skills.*

stip • u • late (stip´ yo͞o lāt) *vi.*, specify conditions of an agreement. *Does the lease stipulate when rent should be paid?*

ANSWERS TO GUIDED READING QUESTIONS

1. The author discusses the history of slavery to point out that slavery is not the natural condition of humans. "It is impossible not to conceive that men in their original state were equal" shows that Johnson believed people were "created equal."
2. Answers will vary. Johnson's statement can be paraphrased, "No man can agree to a condition concerning another individual without that individual's consent."

ADDITIONAL QUESTIONS AND ACTIVITIES

Before they read Johnson's "Brief," refer students to the Language Arts Survey 1.12, "Seeking Knowledge as an Active Reader." Then have students make five predictions about the contents of what they are about to read, indicating what information they used to make their predictions.

READER'S JOURNAL

Ask students to write about whether freedom is important to them and whether they use their freedoms wisely. Are they comfortable with the amount of freedom they have? How do they react to restrictions on their freedom? As an alternative, students might assume the role of a person who has lost his or her freedom.

HISTORICAL NOTE

Samuel Johnson's feelings about slavery were summed up in a toast he delivered at Oxford University: "Here's to the next insurrection of Negroes in the West Indies."

LITERARY NOTE

Inform students that in the practice of law, a **brief** is a formal outline that sets forth a lawyer's main contentions with suporting statements or evidence.

ANSWER TO GUIDED READING QUESTION

1. The author's argument is based on morality.

ART NOTE

The diagram on page 624 is titled "Stowage of the British Slave Ship 'Brookes' Under the Regulated Slave Trade— Act of 1788." Figure 1 is titled *"Fig I— Longitudinal Section."* The caption for figure 2 reads: "Plan of lower deck with the stowage of 202 slaves—130 of these being stowed <u>under</u> the shelves as shewn in figure 6 and figure 3." The caption for figure 3 reads: "Plan shewing the stowage of 130 additional slaves round the wings or sides of the lower deck by means of platforms or shelves (in the manner of galleries in a church) the slaves stowed <u>on</u> the shelves and <u>below</u> them have only a height of 2 feet 7 inches between the beams and far less under the beams—See fig 1." Caption for figure 4: "Cross Section of the Poop"; figure 5: "Cross section midships"; figure 6: "Lower kiss of slaves under the Poop."

SELECTION CHECK TEST 4.7.19 WITH ANSWERS

Checking Your Reading

1. What does Johnson say people are in "their original state"? **They are equal.**
2. How *can* an individual forfeit his liberty? **He or she can forfeit it by committing a crime.**
3. What do Jamaica's laws say about Knight's situation? **They give him no redress.**
4. What is considered "sufficient testimony" against Knight's bid for freedom? **His color is given as sufficient testimony.**
5. What should never give in to political convenience? **Moral right should not give in.**

Vocabulary in Context

Fill each blank with the most appropriate word from the *Words for Everyday Use* from "A Brief to Free a Slave." You may have to change the tense of the word.

avail entail stipulate compulsion redress perpetual lament

1. When she learned of his misdeeds in office, Janelle **<u>lamented</u>** voting for him.

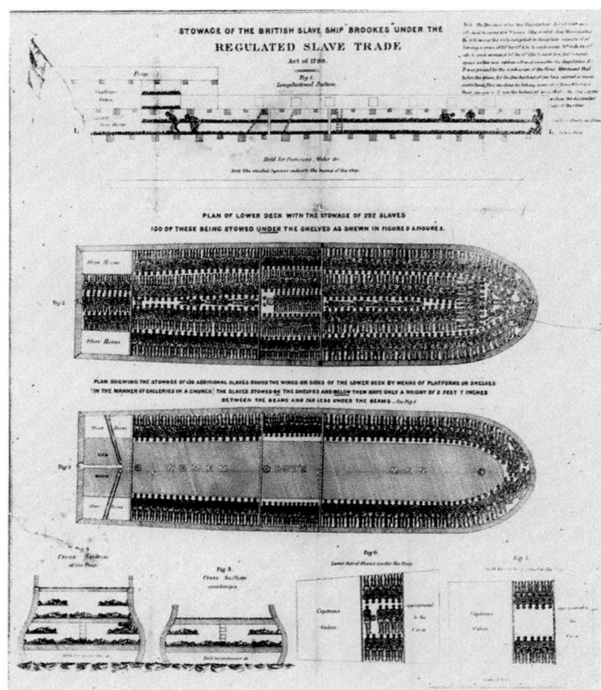

Plan for a British slave ship.

but when once they were brought to a market in the plantations, little would <u>avail</u> either their dignity or their wrongs. The laws of Jamaica afford a Negro no <u>redress</u>. His color is considered as a sufficient testimony against him. It is to be <u>lamented</u> that moral right should ever give way to political convenience. But if temptations of interest are sometimes too strong for human virtue, let us at least retain a virtue where there is no temptation to quit it. In the present case there is apparent right on one side, and no convenience on the other. Inhabitants of this island can neither gain riches nor power by taking away the liberty of any part of the human species. The sum of the argument is this:—No man is by nature the property of another: The defendant is, therefore, by nature free: The rights of nature must be some way forfeited before they can be justly taken away: That the defendant has by any act forfeited the rights of nature we require to be proved; and if no proof of such forfeiture can be given, we doubt not but the justice of the court will declare him free. ■

Is the author's argument based on law, morality, or political convenience?

WORDS FOR EVERYDAY USE

a • vail (ə vāl) *vi.,vt.*, be of use, help. *I hope the volunteer corps can <u>avail</u> the overworked hospital staff.*

re • dress (rē´ dres´) *n.*, compensation for wrong done. *As a form of <u>redress</u>, the truck driver planted a new tree to replace the one he had accidentally toppled.*

la • ment (lə ment´) *vt.*, regret. *In the confessional, many repentant churchgoers <u>lamented</u> their wrongful actions.*

SELECTION CHECK TEST 4.7.19 WITH ANSWERS (CONT.)

2. If a sales offer sounds too good to be true, make sure you know all it **<u>entails</u>**.
3. Our lease **<u>stipulates</u>** that we are responsible for the phone, electric, and water bills.
4. I can't understand your **<u>compulsion</u>** to eat fast food for every meal.
5. Sound waves are not **<u>perpetual</u>**: eventually they fade away to silence.

Literary Tools

1. What is a thesis? **A thesis is a main idea that is supported in a work of nonfiction prose.**
2. What purpose does an argument serve in nonfiction? **An argument presents reasons for accepting or rejecting a thesis.**

Respond *to the* SELECTION

Explain why you think Johnson's argument is or is not compelling or convincing.

INVESTIGATE, Inquire, Imagine

Recall: GATHERING FACTS → **Interpret:** FINDING MEANING

1a. According to the author, what is a person's "natural condition"? Under what conditions might a person forfeit, or give up the right to, his or her liberty?

1b. Why does Johnson believe that no one can forfeit the liberty of his of her children?

2a. How did Joseph Knight become a slave? On what basis does Knight's would-be master rest his claim?

2b. What flaw does Johnson see in the argument for Joseph Knight's enslavement?

3a. For what reasons might slavery seem attractive to some people, according to Johnson?

3b. Why does Johnson believe any reasons that might make slavery seem attractive are inapplicable in the case of Knight?

Analyze: TAKING THINGS APART → **Synthesize:** BRINGING THINGS TOGETHER

4a. What arguments are being made in favor of slavery?

4b. Why does Johnson bring up these arguments in his brief?

Evaluate: MAKING JUDGMENTS → **Extend:** CONNECTING IDEAS

5a. Judge whether Johnson thinks slavery is morally wrong. Explain your response.

5b. Compare Johnson's view on slavery with that presented by Aphra Behn in *Oroonoko* on page 607.

Understanding Literature

THESIS AND ARGUMENT. Review the definitions for **thesis** and **argument** in the Handbook of Literary Terms and the graphic organizer you made for Literary Tools on page 619. What is Johnson's thesis? What are the main arguments he uses to support his thesis?

RESPOND TO THE SELECTION

Ask students whether Johnson offers the best reasons against slavery, or if they find other reasons more compelling. They should discuss the arguments they would make in their own "Brief to Free a Slave."

ANSWERS TO INVESTIGATE, INQUIRE, IMAGINE

RECALL

1a. A person's "natural condition" is freedom. A person who commits a crime gives up his or her right to freedom.

2a. The brief does not state how Knight was originally enslaved. Knight's would-be master claims control because he purchased him according to the laws of Jamaica.

3a. Slavery might seem attractive because it brings some people wealth and power.

INTERPRET

1b. A person cannot forfeit someone else's freedom because that freedom belongs to that individual and only that individual can choose to forfeit it.

2b. No proof has been offered that the person from whom Knight's would-be owner bought Knight had legal ownership, or the right to sell him.

3b. Johnson believes that no one can be the property of another unless he or she consents, and that Knight has done nothing to forfeit his freedom.

ANALYZE

4a. Slavery has been a practice in many places and at many times. Slaves are often enslaved in places where it is legal to do so. Color is considered sufficient reason to keep a person enslaved. It has been considered politically convenient to keep up the practice of slavery. Some people gain riches and power through the use of slaves.

SYNTHESIZE

4b. Johnson identifies arguments for slavery in order to refute them. Rather than simply state why slavery is wrong, he presents a case that directly opposes the cases for slavery.

EVALUATE

5a. Johnson thinks slavery is morally wrong and illegal because he believes that no person is "by nature the property of another." He thinks that all people were born equal. He

ANSWERS TO INVESTIGATE, INQUIRE, IMAGINE (CONT.)

also thinks slavery is impractical because he believes that no real gain can be had by "taking away the liberty of any part of the human species."

EXTEND

5b. *Responses will vary.* Both Johnson and Behn present cases against slavery. Both authors refer to the native state of people and to slaves being tricked into slavery. Johnson presents a rational, legal case against slavery, while Behn presses a moral view through empathy for her main character.

Answers to Understanding Literature can be found on page 626.

ANSWERS TO UNDERSTANDING LITERATURE

Thesis and Argument. Johnson's thesis is that all people possess the same right to freedom and that that right cannot be taken away unless a person forfeits his or her own freedom. He states his these most explicitly near the end of the brief: "The sum of the argument is this:—No man is by nature the property of another: The defendant is, therefore, by nature free: The rights of nature must be some way forfeited before they can be justly taken away." Students may list the following supporting arguments: 1. Slavery is not the natural condition of man; 2. just as a criminal forfeits his or her freedom, but not that of his or her children, so for the captive; 3. the defendant was made a slave only by violence and through no just reason is he bound to serve his would-be master; 4. even if slavery is legal, people are often sold into it through fraud, violence, or trickery.

ANSWERS TO INTEGRATING THE LANGUAGE ARTS

Language, Grammar, and Style

Students should recognize that the words in each pair have similar denotations, but differing connotations. For example, tenacity is often applauded, while stubbornness is seen as a fault. *Traditional* suggests a sense honoring old ways, while *set-in-one's ways* suggests a negative unwillingness to change. *Economical* and *cheap* both mean low in cost, but *cheap* has connotations of shoddiness or poor value.

Study and Research

1. *ISBN* stands for *International Standard Book Number.*
2. The use of grammar dates to the fourteenth century. It came from the Middle English *gramere,* which was a form of the Middle French *gramaire. Gramaire* was a modification of the Latin *grammatica,* which developed from the Greek word *grammatikos,* meaning "of letters."
3. There are two ways to pronounce *commensurate;* the end of the second syllable can be pronounced with a ts sound or with a *ch* sound.
4. *That* can be used as a pronoun, an adjective,
a conjunction, and an adverb.
5. As a creator of a pasquinade, I would more likely be engaging in calumniation, because a pasquinade is a form of satiric writing and a calumniation is a maliciously false statement. A columniation is an arrangement of columns.

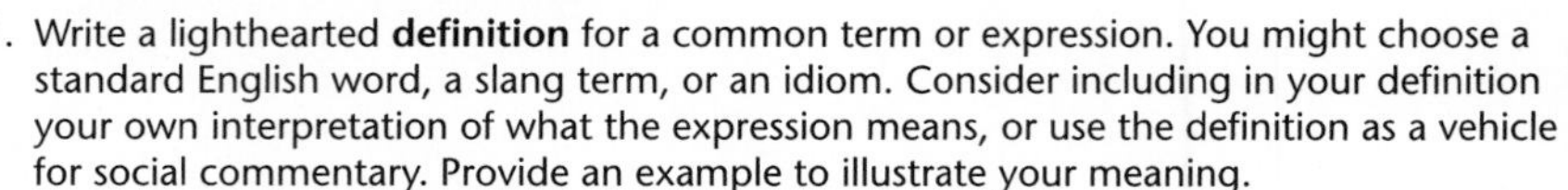

Writer's Journal

1. Write a lighthearted **definition** for a common term or expression. You might choose a standard English word, a slang term, or an idiom. Consider including in your definition your own interpretation of what the expression means, or use the definition as a vehicle for social commentary. Provide an example to illustrate your meaning.
2. Abstract concepts—such as freedom, trust, and success—are hard to define briefly because they mean different things to different people. Write a one-page "definition" in the form of a short **essay** on *freedom.* Be sure to use numerous examples to illustrate what you mean and include counterexamples to show what you do not mean.
3. Imagine that you are the presiding judge in Joseph Knight's case. Write a **judicial opinion** in which you state your decision and explain your reasons for deciding as you did. Include in your opinion a summary and evaluation of Johnson's "Brief."

Integrating the Language Arts

Vocabulary

Connotation and Denotation. Read the Language Arts Survey 1.24, "Connotation and Denotation." Look at the following pairs of words. They have similar denotations, but different connotations. Discuss the differences between the meaning of each pair.

1. tenacious — stubborn
2. traditional — set-in-one's ways
3. economical — cheap
4. inquisitive — prying
5. humorous — laughable

Study and Research

Using Dictionaries. Read the Language Arts Survey 1.17, "Using a Dictionary." Then use a dictionary to answer the following questions.

1. What does *ISBN* stand for?
2. Explain the etymology of the word *grammar.*
3. How many ways are there to pronounce the word *commensurate?* How do the ways differ?
4. As what parts of speech can *that* be used?
5. As the creator of a *pasquinade,* would you more likely be engaging in *columniation* or *calumniation*? Explain your answer.

Speaking and Listening

Interview. Choose five words that you think may have different meanings to different people. Interview several people and ask to define each word. Compile the responses. Discuss your findings with others in your class.

Applied English & Study and Research

Public Service Announcement. Slavery is a violation of human rights. Many violations of human rights go on each day. Use the Internet to research human rights violations. After evaluating each source you use, prepare a public service announcement about the area you researched. In your announcement, give listeners tips on what they can do to help. For more information refer to the Language Arts Survey 5.30, "Evaluating Information and Media Sources," and 6.9, "Delivering a Press Release."

FROM "The Life of
Samuel Johnson, LL.D."

BY JAMES BOSWELL

About the AUTHOR

James Boswell (1740–1795) was the son of a judge. His father had gained the title Lord Auchinleck, which opened the door for Boswell to enter high society in London and Edinborough. Boswell studied law and even opened a successful practice, but he had literary ambitions. Although the active social life of London attracted him, it sometimes got the better of him. Apparently one of his major goals was to befriend noted writers, and this he did persistently and remarkably well. His meeting with Samuel Johnson in 1763 proved to be the most influential. Thirty years separated the two men in age, but after a shaky beginning, they remained friends for life, even through a long tour through the sparsely populated Scottish Highlands and the Hebrides Islands. After Johnson died in 1785, Boswell spent a great deal of time completing *The Life of Samuel Johnson, LL. D.,* which stands today as his greatest literary accomplishment. Though he took great pleasure in his own reputation as a writer, in some ways he always saw himself as a failure.

Besides the *Life of Johnson,* Boswell published *An Account of Corsica* (1768) and *Journal of a Tour to the Hebrides with Dr. Johnson* (1785). He was working on a third volume of the biography of his famous friend when he died in 1795.

About the SELECTION

Soon after befriending Johnson, Boswell conceived a plan to write a new type of biography, one that told less about dates and observable events and more about the subject's thoughts and personality. ***The Life of Samuel Johnson, LL. D.*** (1791) shows Boswell's genius for drawing out Johnson and for recognizing and selecting quotations and anecdotes that depict his subject intimately. Boswell's willingness to reveal his own foibles made the work a surpassing novelty when it appeared.

Literary TOOLS

CHARACTERIZATION. **Characterization** is the use of literary techniques to create a character. Writers use three major techniques to create characters: direct description, portrayal of characters' behavior, and representations of characters' internal states. Notice how in his biography Boswell employed **characterization** to create the character of Johnson for the reader.

ANECDOTE. An **anecdote** is a brief story, usually with a specific point or moral. Boswell uses anecdotes to illuminate aspects of Johnson's character. As you read, keep a chart that identifies anecdotes and what they show about Johnson.

Anecdote	Johnson's Characteristics
Johnson's response to Adams	shows Johnson's belief in his ability and a fondness for the English over the French

Reader's Journal

If you were writing a biography about your best friend, what would you want people to know about him or her?

ADDITIONAL RESOURCES

UNIT 7 RESOURCE BOOK
- Selection Worksheet 7.10
- Selection Check Test 4.7.21
- Selection Test 4.7.22
- Language, Grammar, and Style Resource 3.85
- Applied English Resource 6.12

GRAPHIC ORGANIZER

Students might include the following in their graphic organizers.

ANECDOTE
Johnson's response to Adams
Johnson was kept was kept waiting by Lord Chesterfield
Chesterfield's attempt to curry favor and Johnson's reply

JOHNSON'S CHARACTERISTICS
shows Johnson's belief in his ability and a fondness for the English over the French
suggests Johnson had a temper, was a bit impatient, and didn't care for Cibber
uses wit and sarcasm to put Chesterfield in his place

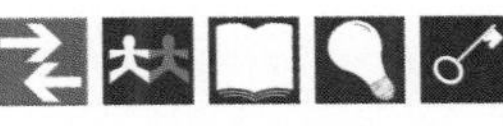

READER'S JOURNAL

As an alternate activity, students can write about what they would want somebody else to say about them. For either topic, students might think about both accomplishments and personal traits they would like to include.

VOCABULARY FROM THE SELECTION

arduous
asperity
conciliate
cynical
eminent
epoch
etymology
implicitly
insinuate
posterity
prodigious
solicit

GOALS/OBJECTIVES

Studying this lesson will enable students to
- enjoy an anecdotal style of biography
- describe Boswell's literary accomplishments and explain the historical significance of his writings
- define *characterization,* name the three major techniques writers use to create a character, and identify these techniques in their reading
- define *anecdote* and identify anecdotes as they encounter them in their reading
- write an anecdote of their own
- edit for punctuation errors

ANSWER TO GUIDED READING QUESTION

1. The enlarged, clear, and accurate views in the Plan for Johnson's dictionary shows that Johnson had thought carefully about the subject.

INDIVIDUAL LEARNING STRATEGIES

MOTIVATION
Point out that Boswell learned a lot about Johnson and others through listening carefully during conversations. Have students work in pairs to interview each other or to practice active listening during a conversation. In either case, their goal should be to learn something new about their partner. For an interview, students should develop five questions. For a discussion, students may suggest a topic. If they need help getting started, suggest they talk about a family tradition, their most frightening experiences, or their favorite hobby or activity.

READING PROFICIENCY
Many of Boswell's sentences are long and complex. Students can work in pairs to untangle each sentence. Explain that some spelling has changed since Boswell wrote his biography. Students might make note of words with unfamiliar spellings and then jot down the spelling that is standard today.

ENGLISH LANGUAGE LEARNING
Share with students the following additional vocabulary.
immense—very large; vast
contemplation—study; inspection
accumulate—heap; pile up; collect
insensibly—unconsciously
confidently—privately; secretly
artifice—trickery, craft
antechamber—small room leading into a larger room

SPECIAL NEEDS
Have students stop at each break and summarize what they have read. In each case, students should first note what Johnson did or said as well as what others did and said. For each section, ask students what they have learned about Johnson.

ENRICHMENT
Students can write about or discuss methods for writing a biography of a famous person. What methods would they employ? Would they take notes, and if so, in what manner? How close would they have to be to the subject of the biography?

Lord Chesterfield's Ante-Room in 1748, c.1800s. Edward Mathew Ward.

FROM The Life of Samuel Johnson, LL.D.

JAMES BOSWELL

But the year 1747 is distinguished as the <u>epoch</u>, when Johnson's <u>arduous</u> and important work, his *Dictionary of the English Language*, was announced to the world, by the publication of its *Plan* or *Prospectus*.

How long this immense undertaking had been the object of his contemplation, I do not know. I once asked him by what means he had attained to that astonishing knowledge of our language, by which he was enabled to realize a design of such extent, and accumulated difficulty. He told me, that "it was not the effect of particular study; but that it had grown up in his mind insensibly." I have been informed by Mr. James Dodsley, that several years before this period, when Johnson was one day sitting in his brother Robert's shop, he heard his brother suggest to him, that a Dictionary of the English Language would be a work that would be well received by the publick; that Johnson seemed at first to catch at the proposition, but, after a pause, said, in his abrupt decisive manner, "I believe I shall not undertake it." That he, however, had bestowed much thought upon the subject, before he pub-

WORDS FOR EVERYDAY USE

ep • och (ep´ ək) *n.*, period of time. *The Renaissance was an <u>epoch</u> that saw remarkable achievements in art and the sciences.*
ar • du • ous (är´ jo͞o əs) *adj.*, extremely difficult. *Few people have completed the <u>arduous</u> ascent of Mt. Everest.*

lished his *Plan*, is evident from the enlarged, clear, and accurate views which it exhibits and we find him mentioning in that tract, that many of the writers whose testimonies were to be produced as authorities, were selected by Pope; which proves that he had been furnished, probably by Mr. Robert Dodsley, with whatever hints that eminent poet had contributed towards a great literary project, that had been the subject of important consideration in a former reign.

What shows that Johnson thought carefully about his plan?

◆ ◆ ◆

Dr. Adams found him one day busy at his *Dictionary*, when the following dialogue ensued. "ADAMS. This is a great work, Sir. How are you to get all the etymologies? JOHNSON. Why, Sir, here is a shelf with Junius, and Skinner, and others; and there is a Welch gentleman who has published a collection of Welch proverbs, who will help me with the Welch. ADAMS. But, Sir, how can you do this in three years? JOHNSON. Sir, I have no doubt that I can do it in three years. ADAMS. But the French Academy, which consists of forty members, took forty years to compile their Dictionary. JOHNSON. Sir, thus it is. This is the proportion. Let me see; forty times forty is sixteen hundred. As three to sixteen hundred, so is the proportion of an Englishman to a Frenchman." With so much ease and pleasantry could he talk of that prodigious labor which he had undertaken to execute.

What do others think of Johnson's ambitions?

◆ ◆ ◆

Lord Chesterfield, to whom Johnson had paid the high compliment of addressing to his

Dr. Johnson, 1775. Joshua Reynolds.

Lordship the *Plan* of his *Dictionary*, had behaved to him in such a manner as to excite his contempt and indignation. The world has been for many years amused with a story confidently told, and as confidently repeated with additional circumstances, that a sudden disgust was taken by Johnson upon occasion of his having been one day kept long in waiting in his Lordship's antechamber, for which the reason assigned was, that he had company with him; and that at last, when the door opened, out walked Colley Cibber;[1] and that Johnson was so violently provoked when he found for whom he had been so long excluded, that he went away in a passion, and never would return. I remember

To whom did Johnson dedicate the Plan *of his dictionary?*

1. **Colley Cibber.** Minor English poet whom Pope ridiculed

WORDS FOR EVERYDAY USE

em • i • nent (em´ ə nənt) *adj.*, noteworthy. *The orchestra was honored when the eminent violinist sat in with them for the evening.*

et • y • mol • o • gy (et´ə mäl´ə je) *n.*, origin and development of a word. *The etymologies of many English words show Greek and Latin influences.*

pro • di • gious (prō dij´əs) *adj.*, amazing, huge. *The prodigious task of planning and building the skyscraper took four years.*

ANSWERS TO GUIDED READING QUESTIONS

1. Others think that Johnson's ambitions are unrealistic.
2. Johnson's *Plan* was dedicated to Lord Chesterfield.

BIOGRAPHICAL NOTE

Boswell's approach to biography was somewhat unusual. At the age of twenty-three, he attached himself to Johnson, who was the preeminent literary figure in England at that time. Boswell rarely took notes of conversations. Instead, he was a skilled observer and listener who had a highly precise memory for events, conversations, and scenes; only later would he write down what he saw and heard.

Quotables

"Johnson: Well, we had a good talk.

Boswell: Yes, Sir; you tossed and gored several persons."

—James Boswell

INTERNET ACTIVITIES

There is an impressive variety of dictionaries on the Internet. Ask students to research online dictionaries. What types of dictionaries are available? What is the most quirky dictionary they could find? For slang dictionaries, students might check out **Slanguage Links** at http://people.enternet.com.au/~goeldner/lingolnk.htm. Or, you may suggest any of the following sites:
Dictionary of Mountain Bike Slang http://world.std.com/~jimf/biking/slang.html **College Slang** Page at http://www.intranet.csupomona.edu/~jasanders/slang/index.html
Online Rhyming Dictionary for Poetry and Songwriting, at http://www.WriteExpress.com/cgi-bin/rhymer.cgi
Many sites are dedicated to Internet lingo such as emoticons and smilies. Here are two such sites:
Smilies Unlimited at http://www.parscom.cz/clients/smilies/index.html
The Unofficial Smiley Dictionary, at http://paul.merton.ox.ac.uk/ascii/smileys.html

ANSWERS TO GUIDED READING QUESTIONS

1. Johnson's attitude toward Chesterfield has become negative; he has "resolved to have no connection with him."
2. Boswell assesses Chesterfield to be opportunistic; the lord expects that Johnson will dedicate his book to him and wants to smooth over their differences.
3. Johnson thought that Chesterfield's flattery was "false and hollow."

BIOGRAPHICAL NOTE

Johnson himself wrote two biographies, *Lives of the Poets* and *The Life of Richard Savage*. Prior to Johnson's books, most English biographies either blindly praised or scandalized their subjects. Johnson felt that a biography should attempt to get as close to the "truth" of the living person as possible, so he included character defects as well as strengths of his subjects, and concrete details about their lives. He believed that this sort of biography reveals universal aspects of human nature.

LITERARY TECHNIQUE

Characterization. Characterization is the act of creating or describing a characer. As a biographer, Boswell employed characterization to create the character of Johnson for the reader. Three techniques for creating a character are direct description, portrayal of the character's behavior, and representations of the character's internal state. What technique did Boswell use in this passage about Johnson's response to Chesterfield's actions? How do you know? What does Johnson's response reveal about his character?

Answers

Boswell portrayed Johnson's behavior through descriptive words and phrases such as "despised the honeyed words" and "indignant." These highly emotional words reveal that Johnson was at times dramatic and passionate and perhaps easily angered.

having mentioned this story to George Lord Lyttelton, who told me, he was very intimate with Lord Chesterfield; and holding it as a well-known truth, defended Lord Chesterfield, by saying, that "Cibber, who had been introduced familiarly by the back-stairs, had probably not been there above ten minutes." It may seem strange even to entertain a doubt concerning a story so long and so widely current, and thus implicitly adopted, if not sanctioned, by the authority which I have mentioned; but Johnson himself assured me, that there was not the least foundation for it. He told me, that there never was any particular incident which produced a quarrel between Lord Chesterfield and him; but that his Lordship's continued neglect was the reason why he resolved to have no connection with him. When the *Dictionary* was upon the eve of publication, Lord Chesterfield, who, it is said, had flattered himself with expectations that Johnson would dedicate the work to him, attempted, in a courtly manner, to sooth, and insinuate himself with the Sage, conscious, as it should seem, of the cold indifference with which he had treated its learned author; and further attempted to conciliate him, by writing two papers in *The World*, in recommendation of the work; and it must be confessed, that they contain some studied compliments, so finely turned, that if there had been no previous offense, it is probable that Johnson would have been highly delighted. Praise, in general, was pleasing to him; but by praise from a man of rank and elegant accomplishments, he was peculiarly gratified.

What attitude has Johnson developed toward Chesterfield?

What assessment does Boswell make of Chesterfield?

◆ ◆ ◆

This courtly device failed of its effect. Johnson, who thought that "all was false and hollow," despised the honeyed words, and was even indignant that Lord Chesterfield should, for a moment, imagine that he could be the dupe of such an artifice. His expression to me concerning Lord Chesterfield, upon this occasion, was, "Sir, after making great professions, he had, for many years, taken no notice of me; but when my *Dictionary* was coming out, he fell a scribbling in *The World* about it. Upon which, I wrote him a letter expressed in civil terms, but such as might shew him that I did not mind what he said or wrote, and that I had done with him."

What did Johnson think of Chesterfield's flattery?

This is that celebrated letter of which so much has been said, and about which curiosity has been so long excited, without being gratified. I for many years solicited Johnson to favor me with a copy of it, that so excellent a composition might not be lost to posterity. He delayed from time to time to give it me; till at last in 1781, when we were on a visit at Mr. Dilly's, at Southill in Bedfordshire, he was pleased to dictate it to me from memory. He afterwards found among his papers a copy of it, which he had dictated to Mr. Baretti, with its title and corrections, in his own handwriting. This he gave to Mr. Langton; adding that if it were to come into print, he wished it to be from that copy. By Mr. Langton's kindness, I am enabled to enrich my work with a perfect transcript of what the world has so eagerly desired to see.

To The Right Honorable the Earl of Chesterfield

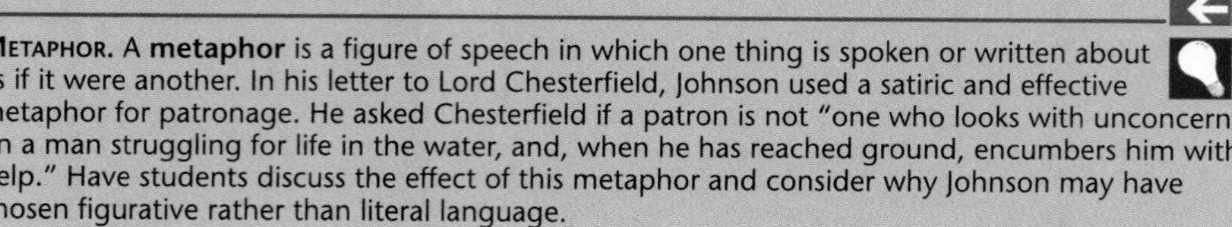

Words for Everyday Use

im • plic • it • ly (im plis ´it lē) *adv.*, doubtlessly. *The mother believed her child's side of the story implicitly.*

in • sin • u • ate (in sin´yo͞o āt´) *vt.*, work into gradually. *Lobbyists try to insinuate themselves into relationships with politicians.*

con • cil • i • ate (kən sil´ē āt´) *vt.*, win over. *With the strike in its third month, a negotiator has been brought in to conciliate the union members.*

so • lic • it (sə lis´it) *vt.*, ask or seek pleadingly. *No one is allowed to solicit money on the subway.*

pos • ter • i • ty (päs ter´ ə tē) *n.*, succeeding generations. *The advent of photography allowed people to record family histories for posterity.*

LITERARY TECHNIQUE

Metaphor. A **metaphor** is a figure of speech in which one thing is spoken or written about as if it were another. In his letter to Lord Chesterfield, Johnson used a satiric and effective metaphor for patronage. He asked Chesterfield if a patron is not "one who looks with unconcern on a man struggling for life in the water, and, when he has reached ground, encumbers him with help." Have students discuss the effect of this metaphor and consider why Johnson may have chosen figurative rather than literal language.

'My Lord, February 1755

"I have been lately informed, by the proprietor of *The World*, that two papers, in which my Dictionary is recommended to the publick, were written by your Lordship. To be so distinguished, is an honor, which, being very little accustomed to favors from the great, I know not well how to receive, or in what terms to acknowledge.

"When, upon some slight encouragement, I first visited your Lordship, I was overpowered, like the rest of mankind, by the enchantment of your address; and could not forbear to wish that I might boast myself *Le vainqueur du vainqueur de la terre*;[2]—that I might obtain that regard for which I saw the world contending; but I found my attendance so little encouraged, that neither pride nor modesty would suffer me to continue it. When I had once addressed your Lordship in publick, I had exhausted all the art of pleasing which a retired and uncourtly scholar can possess. I had done all that I could; and no man is well pleased to have his all neglected, be it ever so little.

"Seven years, my Lord, have now passed, since I waited in your outward rooms, or was repulsed from your door; during which time I have been pushing on my work through difficulties, of which it is useless to complain, and have brought it, at last, to the verge of publication, without one act of assistance, one word of encouragement, or one smile of favor. Such treatment I did not expect, for I never had a Patron before.

"The shepherd in Virgil grew at last acquainted with Love, and found him a native of the rocks.

"Is not a Patron, my Lord, one who looks with unconcern on a man struggling for life in the water, and, when he has reached ground, encumbers him with help? The notice which you have been pleased to take of my labors, had it been early, had been kind; but it has been delayed till I am indifferent, and cannot enjoy it; till I am solitary, and cannot impart it; till I am known, and do not want it. I hope it is no very cynical asperity not to confess obligations where no benefit has been received, or to be unwilling that the Publick should consider me as owing that to a Patron, which Providence has enabled me to do for myself.

"Having carried on my work thus far with so little obligation to any favorer of learning, I shall not be disappointed though I should conclude it, if less be possible, with less; for I have been long wakened from that dream of hope, in which I once boasted myself with so much exultation, my Lord, your Lordship's most humble, most obedient servant,

'Sam. Johnson.' ■

2. ***Le vainqueur . . . terre.*** "The conqueror of the conqueror of the world"

Words For Everyday Use

cyn • i • cal (sin´i kəl) *adj.*, believing that people are insincere or selfish; sarcastic or sneering. *Are you so cynical that you believe that all politicians are corrupt?*

as • per • i • ty (ə sper´ ə tē) *n.*, harshness. *The old man's asperity frightened the neighborhood children.*

Respond *to the* Selection

This selection, though about Johnson, reveals much about Boswell. What do you think of Boswell based on this selection?

SELECTION CHECK TEST 4.7.21

Checking Your Reading

1. How does Johnson respond to Dodsley's suggestion that a dictionary would be well received? **He first seems enthusiastic, then says he won't do it.**
2. How long does Johnson expect spend writing it? **He predicts three years.**
3. What does Chesterfield do as the dictionary is published? **He publicly praises it.**
4. What does Johnson say in the letter he sends Chesterfield? **He declines his help.**
5. Why does Johnson react in this way? **He feels Chesterfield had neglected him.**

Vocabulary in Context

Fill each blank with the most appropriate word from the *Words for Everyday Use* from *The Life of Samuel Johnson, LL. D.* You may have to change the tense of the word.

posterity epoch prodigious
arduous solicit implicitly asperity

1. Cross-country travel was long and **arduous** before the construction of the railroad.
2. Violet said the fossil came from Pleistocene times, but Lyn argued for a later **epoch**.
3. The audience was shocked at the **asperity** of the presenter's criticism.
4. Every season, our local public radio station **solicits** donations on the air.
5. The new legislators heard a lecture on the **prodigious** responsibility they now held.

Literary Tools

1. What is an anecdote? **An anecdote is a brief story told to make a point.**
2. What anecdote is used in this selection? **The anecdote is of Johnson being rebuffed as he waits for Lord Chesterton one day.**
3. What does Boswell say he later learned about this anecdote? **He learned that it was not true.**
4. What is characterization? What are three major techniques of characterization? **Characterization is the use of literary techniques to create a character. Writers use three major techniques: direct description, portrayal of characters' behavior, and representation of characters' internal states.**
5. Cite an example of characterization from this selection. ***Responses will vary.***

RESPOND TO THE SELECTION

Ask students what kind of character they think Boswell wants to present of himself. Students might write their response in the form of a character sketch of Boswell.

ANSWERS TO INVESTIGATE, INQUIRE, IMAGINE

Recall

1a. Johnson expected to take three years to complete his dictionary. The French Academy took forty years to complete its dictionary and it consisted of forty members.

2a. Johnson was supposedly offended that Lord Chesterfield kept him waiting a long time in his antechamber. Johnson tells Boswell that there was no one incident that offended him but that he had been offended by Chesterfield's "continued neglect."

3a. Lord Chesterfield later wrote editorials praising Johnson to win his favor. Johnson responded by writing a letter to Chesterfield. Johnson states that he did not value Chesterfield's recommendation of the Dictionary because the latter did not lend his support during its writing.

Interpret

1b. Boswell's discussion indicates that he believes the project is a huge undertaking. Boswell sees Johnson's attitude toward the task as amazingly optimistic.

2b. Many people probably believed the story about Johnson and Chesterfield because it is dramatic and gossipy.

9b. Chesterfield might have wanted to win Johnson's goodwill because he knew that Johnson's Dictionary would be successful and he wanted some credit for it. His attempt seemed insincere because of its opportunistic timing.

Analyze

4a. *Responses will vary.* Boswell reveals his admiration for Johnson's undertaking and an amusement at his wit. He admits his own curiosity to see the letter Johnson wrote to Chesterfield. He relates an anecdote in which Johnson appears childishly jealous of Colley Cibber, and notes that Johnson was "peculiarly gratified" by praise from important people.

Synthesize

4b. *Responses will vary.* Boswell's treatment of Johnson seems evenhanded because he sometimes relates unflattering details about Johnson's personality. Boswell's self-admissions, along with his details about Johnson, add to Boswell's credibility because he seems willing to include unflattering aspects of his subject and himself in order to create a more personal account.

INVESTIGATE, Inquire, Imagine

Recall: GATHERING FACTS → **Interpret:** FINDING MEANING

1a. How long did Johnson expect to take to complete his dictionary? How did this amount of time compare to the time it took the French Academy to complete its dictionary?

1b. What does Boswell's discussion indicate about Boswell's assessment of the project? What does Boswell see as Johnson's attitude toward the task he had undertaken?

2a. What incident supposedly offended Johnson in his visit to Lord Chesterfield's? What does Johnson tell Boswell about the incident?

2b. Why do you think so many people found the story about Johnson and Chesterfield plausible?

3a. What did Lord Chesterfield later do to win Johnson's favor? In his letter to Lord Chesterfield, what reason does Johnson give for not valuing his recommendation of the *Dictionary?*

3b. Why might Chesterfield have wanted to win Johnson's goodwill? Explain whether you think his attempt was sincere.

Analyze: TAKING THINGS APART → **Synthesize:** BRINGING THINGS TOGETHER

4a. Analyze the details Boswell chooses to include. What do they reveal about him? What negative aspects of Johnson does he reveal?

4b. Does Boswell's treatment of Johnson seem evenhanded? Do Boswell's self-admissions add to or detract from his credibility? Explain.

Evaluate: MAKING JUDGMENTS → **Extend:** CONNECTING IDEAS

5a. Evaluate Johnson's assessment of Chesterfield as a patron. Do you agree with Johnson that Chesterfield was insincere and self-serving? Explain.

5b. How might Lord Chesterfield's actions have related to the definition of *patron* Samuel Johnson includes in his *Dictionary of the English Language* on page 620?

Understanding Literature

Characterization. Review the definition for **characterization** in the Handbook of Literary Terms. What techniques did Boswell use in the passage about Johnson's response to Chesterfield's actions? How do you know? What does Johnson's response reveal about his character?

Anecdote. Review the definition for **anecdote** and the chart you made for Literary Tools on page 627. The story of Johnson's wait at Lord Chesterfield's is an example of an anecdote. Is Boswell's anecdote elaborate or sketchy? To support your answer, give examples of details that are or are not included. What do you think was Boswell's purpose in including or omitting these details? How might he have achieved a different effect?

ANSWERS TO INVESTIGATE, INQUIRE, IMAGINE (CONT.)

Evaluate

5a. *Responses will vary.* Students might say they agree with Johnson that Chesterfield was insincere and self-serving. He apparently ignored Johnson, neglecting to give him any support, until Johnson's book was about to be published. Chesterfield must have known that Johnson was unhappy with him and should have attempted to reconcile with him sooner. Students may say that when Chesterfield finally wrote something in support of Johnson, it was too late and was an obvious attempt to ingratiate himself in order to be acknowledged in the book's dedication. In

Continued on page 633

Writer's Journal

1. Based on what you know from this selection, write a **definition** of biographer. As you write the definition, keep in mind not only your understanding of the word but also the kind of humor Johnson used in his definitions and his feelings toward Boswell.
2. Write an **anecdote** that reveals something about your character. Before writing your anecdote, make sure you are clear on the point you are trying to make. The details you decide to include should highlight this point.
3. Write a **biographical essay** about somebody you know well. As Boswell did, focus less on events and dates and more on the personality of the individual, what makes him or her tick.

Integrating *the* Language Arts

Language, Grammar, and Style

Editing for Punctuation Errors. Review the Language Arts Survey 3.85, "Editing for Punctuation Errors." Then rewrite the following sentences, correcting any errors in punctuation.

1. James Boswell didnt' take notes very often.
2. Instead he practiced remembering what he heard until he could write it down.
3. Do you suppose that practice put his subjects at ease.
4. It seems to have worked at least in the case of his biography of Johnson.
5. Adams said this is a great work, sir.

Speaking and Listening

Delivering a Toast. Write and deliver a toast in honor of someone you know well. You might toast a teacher, coach, friend, or parent. In your toast, highlight the qualities or achievements you admire and express what the honoree has meant to you personally.

Applied English & Collaborative Learning

Team Research. Working in research groups, prepare a report on a noteworthy figure in your community, past or present. Make a list of the tasks that must be done to complete your project, such as identifying sources of information, gathering information, and producing the final product. Decide how you will divide up the tasks and in what form you will present your report to the class. Will you make a wall display? produce a video? stage a series of vignettes? For additional help, refer to the Language Arts Survey 6.12, "Working on a Team."

ANSWERS TO UNDERSTANDING LITERATURE

Responses will vary. Possible responses are given.

Characterization. Boswell portrayed Johnson's internal state through descriptive words and phrases such as "despised the honeyed words" and "indignant." These highly emotional words reveal that Johnson was at times dramatic and passionate and perhaps easily angered.

Anecdote. Boswell's anecdote is sketchy. He gives only the barest and most important details of Johnson's wait. A more complete anecdote would probably be more narrative, creating a mood of Johnson's growing indignation. It might have provided more background on the relationship between Johnson and Chesterfield and why Johnson was waiting for Lord Chesterfield that day. It might also have explicitly described Johnson's reaction, rather than simply stating "that he went away in a passion." By omitting these details, Boswell seems to confirm that the story is hearsay and was not related to him by Johnson himself. The sketchiness achieves the effect of drawing-room gossip. If Boswell had told a more detailed story, he might have implied a more intimate knowledge of the incident.

ANSWERS TO INTEGRATING THE LANGUAGE ARTS

Language, Grammar, and Style

1. James Boswell didn't take notes very often.
2. Instead, he practiced remembering what he heard until he could write it down.
3. Do you suppose that practice put his subjects at ease?
4. It seems to have worked, at least in the case of his biography of Johnson.
5. Adams said, "This is a great work, Sir."

Speaking and Listening

Students might deliver their toasts if an appropriate opportunity arises. If not, students may wish to share their ideas in a letter to the person they honor.

Applied English & Collaborative Learning

Students should consider their audience as they choose a method of presentation. Since the topic is one of local interest, students might find a community center, library, or other public area where they can present their reports.

ANSWERS TO INVESTIGATE, INQUIRE, IMAGINE (cont. from page 634)

addition, students may note that if Chesterfield truly wanted to reconcile with Johnson, he should have done so privately rather than in public. His public action seems to confirm that Chesterfield was more interested in being praised by the public than in what Johnson really thought of him.

Extend

5b. Johnson's definition includes the phrase "commonly a wretch who supports with insolence, and is paid with flattery." Johnson may have been angry with Chesterfield when he wrote that definition and included the definition as a barb aimed at Chesterfield.

ADDITIONAL RESOURCES

UNIT 7 RESOURCE BOOK
- Selection Worksheet 7.11
- Selection Check Test 4.7.23
- Selection Test 4.7.24
- Study and Research Resource 5.19, 5.26
- Applied English Resource 6.6

GRAPHIC ORGANIZER

Students may include the following in their graphic organizers.

WHAT WAS SAID

Baron is one of most powerful lords in Germany

Baronness was greatly respected

Pangloss was an "oracle" and proved "admirably" that there is no effect without a cause and that this was the best of all possible worlds

"by virtue of that gift of God which is called liberty," Candide chooses to run the gauntlet thirty-six times

The Bulgarian war called "heroic butchery"

Village burned "in accordance with international law"

WHAT WAS MEANT

Baron's power wasn't worth much because apparently all the other lords were impoverished and he merely had a door and windows on his castle!

Perhaps people feared the Baronness because of her size.

It is evident from what follows that Pangloss is actually a fool. His first insight that there is "no effect without a cause" is completely obvious. He has not proven anything "admirably"—his reasoning is completely faulty.

Candide does not make a free choice out of liberty—he is actually not free at all!

The author does not think the war was heroic at all; it was slaughter.

The burning of the village was most likely a terrible violation of international law.

READER'S JOURNAL

Ask students to discuss the meaning of the word hypocrisy and brainstorm some of the hypocrisies they have heard in political rhetoric.

MULTICULTURAL EXTENSIONS

Literary TOOLS

SATIRE. Satire is humorous writing intended to point out errors, falsehoods, foibles, or failings. It is written for the purpose of reforming human behavior or human institutions. As you read the selection, observe the behaviors and attitudes of humans Voltaire is satirizing.

IRONY. Irony is the difference between appearance and reality. Words may say one thing, but they may imply something quite different. Look for examples of irony as you read the selection. Use the graphic organizer below to help you better understand how irony is used.

What was said	What it really meant

Reader's Journal

What hypocrisies in word or deed have you observed in our society? How do you feel when you hear or witness these hypocrisies?

FROM *Candide*

BY FRANÇOIS MARIE AROUET DE VOLTAIRE

About the AUTHOR

François Marie Arouet (1694–1778) was born into a well-to-do family in Paris. He was educated at an excellent Jesuit school, where his teachers found him to be brilliant but difficult to control. His father wanted François to follow him in the profession of law, but the young man chose instead to pursue a life in literature. At the age of twenty-three, he added the words ***de Voltaire*** to his name, creating a pen name under which he became famous. In fencing, a *volt* is a step aside to avoid an opponent's thrust. The name *Voltaire* appropriately reflects the razor-sharp wit and adroit maneuvering of Voltaire's writing. As a young writer, Voltaire won acclaim for his dramatic works. However, he ran afoul of certain French nobles and was twice imprisoned in the Bastille. In his mid-thirties, he was exiled to England, where he became friends with Swift, Pope, and other leading writers and thinkers. Impressed by the relative freedom of thought in England, Voltaire wrote his *Lettres philosophiques sur les Anglais (Philosophical Letters on the English).* Upon returning to France, he published this work, a satirical attack on the French church and state, and was forced into exile once again. For most of the rest of his life, he lived outside France, making brilliant contributions to Diderot's *Encyclopédie* and writing satirical tales such as *Zadig* (1747) and *Candide* (1759). Voltaire's name has become synonymous with wit and frank good sense in opposition to all forms of intolerance, tyranny, hereditary privilege, dogma, and unexamined convention.

About the SELECTION

Candide was written after the death of Voltaire's beloved Emilie, Marquise du Chatelet. Mme du Chatelet was a believer in the "philosophical optimism" of the German philosopher Gottfried Wilhelm von Leibniz. Leibniz had argued that the world as it is, with all its problems, is the best of all possible worlds. Despairing over the death of Emilie and suffering from political and religious persecution, Voltaire wrote *Candide,* a satirical attack on philosophical optimism that has become one of the world's great classics.

GOALS/OBJECTIVES

Studying this lesson will enable students to
- interpret and appreciate humor and criticism in a work of satire
- describe Voltaire's literary accomplishments and explain the historical significance of his writings
- explain the connections between Voltaire's writing and the English literature in this unit
- define *satire* and identify satire and its effects in literature they read
- define *irony* and identify and interpret its effect as they encounter it in their reading

FROM

Candide

François Marie Arouet de Voltaire

CHAPTER I

HOW CANDIDE WAS BROUGHT UP IN A NOBLE CASTLE AND HOW HE WAS EXPELLED FROM THE SAME

In the castle of Baron Thunder ten-tronckh in Westphalia[1] there lived a youth, endowed by Nature with the most gentle character. His face was the expression of his soul. His judgment was quite honest and he was extremely simple-minded; and this was the reason, I think, that he was named Candide.[2] Old servants in the house suspected that he was the son of the Baron's sister and a decent honest gentleman of the neighborhood, whom this young lady would never marry because he could only prove seventy-one quarterings,[3] and the rest of his genealogical tree was lost, owing to the injuries of time. The Baron was one of the most powerful lords in Westphalia,[3] for his castle possessed a door and windows. His Great Hall was even decorated with a piece of tapestry. The dogs in his stable-yards formed a pack of hounds when necessary; his grooms were his huntsmen; the village curate was his Grand Almoner.[4] They all called him "My Lord," and laughed heartily at his stories. The Baroness weighed about three hundred and fifty pounds, was therefore greatly respected, and did the honors of the house with a dignity which rendered her still more respectable. Her daughter Cunegonde, aged seventeen, was rosy-cheeked, fresh, plump and tempting. The Baron's son appeared in every

What makes Candide's name fitting? Why might Voltaire have chosen such a name?

1. **Westphalia.** Region in northwestern Germany
2. **Candide.** The word *candid* means "frank" or "honest."
3. **quarterings.** Divisions of a coat of arms showing degrees of nobility
4. **Grand Almoner.** Distributor of alms or charity

ANSWER TO GUIDED READING QUESTION

1. Candide's name, which meant "frank" or "honest," was fitting because he was honest and simple-minded. Voltaire might have chosen such a character to symbolize the philosophical optimism that he wanted to satirize.

MULTICULTURAL EXTENSIONS

The Enlightenment was not limited to England. Other writers, such as Voltaire in France, celebrated the power of the intellect. Like Pope, Voltaire aimed his wit at pedantry and intellectual narrow-mindedness. Like Swift, he satirized the political events of Europe.

INDIVIDUAL LEARNING STRATEGIES

Motivation
Students can hold a debate on the idea that "this is the best of all possible worlds." Students should work in separate teams of three or four students each, and each team should develop logical arguments in agreement or disagreement with the idea. Students may also present some illogical arguments such as those expressed by Pangloss in the selection, and the other team must demonstrate why these are illogical.

Reading Proficiency
Point out that many sentences in the selection are rather long. Students should pay attention to the semicolons that signal the end of complete thoughts. Also point out to students that some of the names of places are fictional.

English Language Learning
In addition to following the suggestions for Reading Proficiency, share with students the following additional vocabulary.
genealogy—tracing a line of descent
consternation—fear or shock that makes one feel helpless
accordance—agreement; conformity
ignominious—shameful; dishonorable

Special Needs
Read over the selection with students, making sure they understand that the tone of the selection is satirical and ironic. Help them to fill out the graphic organizer in Literary Tools.

VOCABULARY FROM THE SELECTION

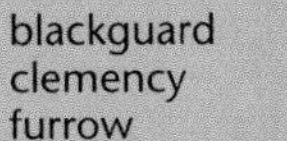

blackguard	oracle
clemency	prodigy
furrow	regiment
metaphysician	vivacity

INDIVIDUAL LEARNING STRATEGIES (CONT.)

Enrichment
Students might be interested in reading the entire story of Candide and writing an essay about the work. As an alternative, ask them to research the theories of German philosopher Gottfried Leibniz, which Voltaire satirizes in *Candide.*

ANSWER TO GUIDED READING QUESTION

1. Pangloss taught Candide the views of philosophical optimism, which holds that "this is the best of all possible worlds."

Quotables

"I disapprove of what you say, but I will defend to the death your right to say it."

—Voltaire

HISTORICAL NOTE

Point out that Pangloss taught only Candide and not the young baroness, Mademoiselle Cunegonde. Boys and girls born to aristocratic families were usually educated at home; however, a girl's education focused more on domestic tasks than on intellectual ones. While some educators advocated teaching the same subjects to girls and boys alike, most girls received an education limited to religion, the three *Rs*, and sewing skills. Still, only about 27 percent of French women were literate in 1786.

CROSS-CURRICULAR ACTIVITIES

LOGIC. Ask students to read the Language Arts Survey 5.3, "Avoiding False Arguments and Propaganda." Then, ask them whether Pangloss's arguments for why this is "the best of all possible worlds" fits into any of the categories of false arguments. Students should be able to see that Pangloss's arguments are examples of circular reasoning. When he says that this is the best of all possible worlds, he is really saying that because the world is the way it is, therefore it should be the way it is. Then he says that "since everything is made for an end, everything is necessarily for the best end" and that pigs are eaten because they are supposed to be eaten. He offers no real reasons to back up his opinion and only restates his opinion in other ways.

The Kiss, c.1800s. Francesco Hayez. Pinacoteca di Brera, Milan, Italy.

respect worthy of his father. The tutor Pangloss[5] was the oracle of the house, and little Candide followed his lessons with all the candor of his age and character. Pangloss taught metaphysico-theologo-cosmol-onigology. He proved admirably that there is no effect without a cause and that in this best of all possible worlds,[6] My Lord the Baron's castle was the best of castles and his wife the best of all possible Baronesses. "'Tis demonstrated," said he, "that things cannot be otherwise; for, since everything is made for an end, everything is necessarily for the best end. Observe that noses were made to wear spectacles; and so we have spectacles. Legs were visibly instituted to be breeched, and we have breeches. Stones were formed to be quarried and to build castles; and My Lord has a very noble castle; the greatest Baron in the province should have the best house; and as pigs were made to be eaten, we eat pork all the year round; consequently, those who have asserted that all is well talk nonsense; they ought to have said that all is for the best." Candide listened attentively and believed innocently; for he thought Mademoiselle Cunegonde extremely beautiful, although he was never bold enough to tell her so. He decided that after the happiness of being born Baron of Thunder-ten-tronckh, the second degree of happiness was to be Mademoiselle Cunegonde; the third, to see her every day; and the fourth to listen to Doctor Pangloss, the greatest philosopher

What philosophical views did Pangloss teach Candide?

5. **Pangloss.** The name means, in Greek, "all tongue."
6. **best of all possible worlds.** Voltaire is satirizing the beliefs of the German philosopher Leibniz.

WORDS FOR EVERYDAY USE

or • a • cle (ôr´ə kəl) *n.*, person in communication with the gods; person of great knowledge or wisdom. *People in ancient Greece would seek answers from the oracle.*

of the province and therefore of the whole world. . . .

◆ ◆ ◆

Next day, when they left the table after dinner, Cunegonde and Candide found themselves behind a screen; Cunegonde dropped her handkerchief, Candide picked it up; she innocently held his hand; the young man innocently kissed the young lady's hand with remarkable vivacity, tenderness and grace; their lips met, their eyes sparkled, their knees trembled, their hands wandered. Baron Thunder ten-tronckh passed near the screen, and, observing this cause and effect, expelled Candide from the castle by kicking him in the backside frequently and hard. Cunegonde swooned; when she recovered her senses, the Baroness slapped her in the face; and all was in consternation in the noblest and most agreeable of all possible castles.

CHAPTER II

WHAT HAPPENED TO CANDIDE AMONG THE BULGARIANS

Candide, expelled from the earthly paradise, wandered for a long time without knowing where he was going, turning up his eyes to Heaven, gazing back frequently at the noblest of castles which held the most beautiful of young Baronesses; he lay down to sleep supperless between two furrows in the open fields; it snowed heavily in large flakes. The next morning the shivering Candide, penniless, dying of cold and exhaustion, dragged himself towards the neighboring town, which was called Waldberghoff-trarbk-dikdorff. He halted sadly at the door of an inn. Two men dressed in blue noticed him. "Comrade," said one, "there's a well-built young man of the right height." They went up to Candide and very civilly invited him to dinner. "Gentlemen," said Candide with charming modesty, "you do me a great honor, but I have no money to pay my share." "Ah, sir," said one of the men in blue, "persons of your figure and merit never pay anything; are you not five feet five tall?" "Yes, gentlemen," said he, bowing, "that is my height." "Ah, sir, come to table; we will not only pay your expenses, we will never allow a man like you to be short of money; men were only made to help each other." "You are in the right," said Candide, "that is what Doctor Pangloss was always telling me, and I see that everything is for the best." They begged him to accept a few crowns, he took them and wished to give them an IOU; they refused to take it and all sat down to table. "Do you not love tenderly . . ." "Oh, yes," said he. "I love Mademoiselle Cunegonde tenderly." "No," said one of the gentlemen. "We were asking if you do not tenderly love the King of the Bulgarians." "Not a bit," said he, "for I have never seen him." "What! He is the most charming of Kings, and you must drink his health." "Oh, gladly, gentlemen." And he drank. "That is sufficient," he was told. "You are now the support, the aid, the defender, the hero of the Bulgarians; your fortune is made and your glory assured." They immediately put irons on his legs and took him to a regiment. He was made to turn to the right and left, to raise the ramrod[7] and return the ramrod, to take aim, to fire, to double up, and he was given thirty strokes with a stick; the next day he drilled not quite so badly, and received only twenty strokes; the day after, he only had ten and was looked on as a prodigy by his comrades. Candide was completely mystified and could not make out how

7. **ramrod.** Poker used for loading a muzzle-loaded rifle

WORDS FOR EVERYDAY USE

vi • vac • i • ty (vī vas´ə tē) *n.,* liveliness. *Exhausted from a long day of traveling, the entertainer lacked her usual vivacity.*
fur • row (fur´ō) *n.,* groove made in the earth by a plow. *The planter followed behind the plow, dropping seeds into the furrow.*
reg • i • ment (rej´ə ment) *n.,* unit of soldiers. *The regiment is housed in that barracks.*
prod • i • gy (präd´ə jē) *n.,* person with talent or genius. *The prodigy Mozart performed for royal audiences at age six.*

ANSWER TO GUIDED READING QUESTION

1. Candide is punished by the army because they think he tried to desert the army. He is allowed to exercise his "liberty" by choosing his method of punishment.

LITERARY TECHNIQUE

ALLUSION. An **allusion** is a rhetorical technique in which reference is made to a person, event, object, or work from history or literature. The story of Candide's expulsion from the castle is an allusion to the Christian story of the Garden of Eden. Candide is "expelled from the earthly paradise" because of the sin of kissing Cunegonde.

CROSS-CURRICULAR ACTIVITY

History. Students may wish to research Frederick the Great or the war between the Prussians under Frederick the Great and the French, which Voltaire satirizes in this selection. Encourage them to visit a local library to research their topic. They should prepare a short oral report to be delivered to the class and display visuals, including a portrait of Frederick the Great if they are able to find one in a book and either photocopy it or bring the book to show.

HISTORICAL NOTE

The period from 1660 to 1789 in Europe is called the Age of Absolutism. As state sovereigns gained greater legal and administrative power, they gained greater control over their subjects. However, these rulers were not despots; they realized that their power was somewhat limited by laws and the strength of neighboring rulers. The French monarchs during this period most clearly exemplified the absolutist goals of creating a state army, controlling legal matters, and generating revenue through taxation.

he was a hero. One fine spring day he thought he would take a walk, going straight ahead, in the belief that to use his legs as he pleased was a privilege of the human species as well as of animals. He had not gone two leagues when four other heroes, each six feet tall, fell upon him, bound him and dragged him back to a cell. He was asked by his judges whether he would rather be thrashed thirty-six times by the whole regiment or receive a dozen lead bullets at once in his brain. Although he protested that men's wills are free and that he wanted neither one nor the other, he had to make a choice; by virtue of that gift of God which is called *liberty,* he determined to run the gauntlet[8] thirty-six times and actually did so twice. There were two thousand men in the regiment. That made four thousand strokes which laid bare the muscles and nerves from his neck to his backside. As they were about to proceed to a third turn, Candide, utterly exhausted, begged as a favor that they would be so kind as to smash his head; he obtained this favor; they bound his eyes and he was made to kneel down. At that moment the King of the Bulgarians came by and inquired the victim's crime; and as this King was possessed of a vast genius, he perceived from what he learned about Candide that he was a young metaphysician very ignorant in worldly matters, and therefore pardoned him with a clemency which will be praised in all newspapers and all ages. An honest surgeon healed Candide in three weeks with the ointments recommended by Dioscorides. He had already regained a little skin and could walk when the King of the Bulgarians went to war with the King of the Abares.[9]

Why is Candide punished by the army? In what way is he allowed to exercise his "liberty"?

CHAPTER III

HOW CANDIDE ESCAPED FROM THE BULGARIANS AND WHAT BECAME OF HIM

Nothing could be smarter, more splendid, more brilliant, better drawn up than the two armies. Trumpets, fifes, hautboys, drums, cannons, formed a harmony such as has never been heard even in hell. The cannons first of all laid flat about six thousand men on each side; then the musketry removed from the best of worlds some nine or ten thousand blackguards who infested its surface. The bayonet also was the sufficient reason for the death of some thousands of men. The whole might amount to thirty thousand souls. Candide, who trembled like a philosopher, hid himself as well as he could during this heroic butchery. At last, while the two Kings each commanded a Te Deum[10] in his camp, Candide decided to go elsewhere to reason about effects and causes. He clambered over heaps of dead and dying men and reached a neighboring village, which was in ashes; it was an Abare village which the Bulgarians had burned in accordance with international law. . . .

◆ ◆ ◆

Candide fled to another village as fast as he could; it belonged to the Bulgarians, and Abarian heroes had treated it in the same way. Candide, stumbling over quivering limbs or across ruins, at last escaped from the theatre of war, carrying a little food in his knapsack, and

8. **to run the gauntlet.** To face an ordeal, in this case passing by soldiers, each of whom will strike him
9. **Bulgarians . . . Abares.** Voltaire's Bulgarians and Abarians represent, respectively, the Prussians under Frederick the Great and the French.
10. **Te Deum.** A hymn of thanksgiving beginning with the Latin words *Te Deum laudamus* ("We praise thee, O God")

Words for Everyday Use

met • a • phy • si • cian (met´ə fə zish´ən) *n.,* one who studies metaphysics, that branch of philosophy that deals with ultimate realities and the nature of being. *Metaphysicians from many countries participated in panel discussion on the nature of knowledge.*

clem • en • cy (klem´ən sē) *n.,* leniency, mercy. *The governor showed clemency by granting a stay of execution.*

black • guard (blag´ərd) *n.,* scoundrel, villain, low person. *In the movies of the silent era, the blackguard rarely wins.*

never forgetting Mademoiselle Cunegonde. His provisions were all gone when he reached Holland; but, having heard that everyone in that country was rich and a Christian, he had no doubt at all but that he would be as well treated as he had been in the Baron's castle before he had been expelled on account of Mademoiselle Cunegonde's pretty eyes. He asked an alms of several grave persons, who all replied that if he continued in that way he would be shut up in a house of correction to teach him how to live. He then addressed himself to a man who had been discoursing on charity in a large assembly for an hour on end. This orator, glancing at him askance, said: "What are you doing here? Are you for the good cause?" "There is no effect without a cause," said Candide modestly. "Everything is necessarily linked up and arranged for the best. It was necessary that I should be expelled from the company of Mademoiselle Cunegonde, that I ran the gauntlet, and that I beg my bread until I can earn it; all this could not have happened differently." "My friend," said the orator, "do you believe that the Pope is Anti-Christ?" "I had never heard so before," said Candide, "but whether he is or isn't, I am starving." "You don't deserve to eat," said the other. "Hence, rascal; hence, you wretch; and never come near me again." The orator's wife thrust her head out of the window and seeing a man who did not believe that the Pope was Anti-Christ, she poured on his head a full . . . O Heavens! To what excess religious zeal is carried by ladies! A man who had not been baptized, an honest Anabaptist[11] named Jacques, saw the cruel and ignominious treatment of one of his brothers, a featherless two-legged creature with a soul; he took him home, cleaned him up, gave him bread and beer, presented him with two florins,[12] and even offered to teach him to work at the manufacture of Persian stuffs which are made in Holland. Candide threw himself at the man's feet, exclaiming: "Doctor Pangloss was right in telling me that all is for the best in this world, for I am vastly more touched by your extreme generosity than by the harshness of the gentleman in the black cloak and his good lady." The next day when he walked out he met a beggar covered with sores, dull-eyed, with the end of his nose fallen away, his mouth awry, his teeth black, who talked huskily, was tormented with a violent cough and spat out a tooth at every cough.

How does the "charity" orator respond to Candide's request for alms? How do his preachings correspond to his own actions?

CHAPTER IV

HOW CANDIDE MET HIS OLD MASTER IN PHILOSOPHY, DOCTOR PANGLOSS, AND WHAT HAPPENED

Candide, moved even more by compassion than by horror, gave this horrible beggar the two florins he had received from the honest Anabaptist, Jacques. The phantom gazed fixedly at him, shed tears and threw its arms round his neck. Candide recoiled in terror. "Alas!" said the wretch to the other wretch, "don't you recognize your dear Pangloss?" ■

What state is Pangloss in when Candide meets him again? Can Pangloss's current condition be explained by his own philosophy?

11. **Anabaptist.** Member of a radical Protestant sect that opposed infant baptism
12. **florins.** Coins

ANSWERS TO GUIDED READING QUESTIONS

1. The "charity" orator responds to Candide's request for alms by demanding to know why he is attending the assembly. The orator's own actions contradict his preachings.
2. When Candide meets Pangloss again, the doctor is a sick beggar covered with sore. Pangloss's current conditions cannot logically be explained by his own philosophy.

BIOGRAPHICAL NOTE

Some of the articles that Voltaire contributed to Diderot's *Encyclopédie* generated much religious controversy. In 1758, the religious opposition was so great that Voltaire moved to Ferney, Switzerland, to escape persecution. From there, Voltaire continued to write about religious and political oppression.

RESPOND TO THE SELECTION

Students may also imagine they are a friend of Candide's. What advice would they give him?

ANSWERS TO INVESTIGATE, INQUIRE, IMAGINE

Recall

1a. Candide is tricked by the flattery of Bulgarian soldiers into enlisting with the Bulgarian army.

2a. Voltaire says that the burning of the Abare village was done "in accordance with international law."

3a. The anti-Catholic orator's actions contradict his statements because he preaches charity but condemns Candide, who requests it.

Interpret

1b. The military is satirized by details such as Candide being made "to turn to the right and left" and being "looked on as a prodigy by his comrades" for gradually receiving fewer strokes.

2b. Voltaire is trying to make the point that rulers of nations establish self-serving "laws" merely to justify their brutality.

3b. Voltaire is revealing the hypocrisy of religious people who speak of good deeds but rarely practice them.

Analyze

4a. Candide's misfortunes contradict the idea that all things are connected in a series of causes and effects to create the "best of all possible worlds." His misfortunes begin because of his attraction to Mademoiselle Cunegonde, whom Candide considers his third degree of happiness. The effect of his happiness, however, is that he is disowned, enslaved in the army, beaten close to death, and reduced to the status of a beggar.

Synthesize

4b. *Responses will vary.* Students will most likely say that if they were in Candide's place, they would no longer believe in Pangloss's philosophy on life. Candide would tell Pangloss about all the terrible things he experienced and that it couldn't possibly be the best of all possible worlds because he is miserable. Then he'd prove his point further by pointing out to Pangloss that Pangloss's own situation is wretched.

Respond to the Selection

If you were Candide, how would you have responded to all the troubles you faced since being thrown out of the castle? What things would you have done or said to yourself to find comfort in your situation?

Investigate, Inquire, Imagine

Recall: Gathering Facts → **Interpret:** Finding Meaning

1a. How does Candide come to be enlisted in the Bulgarian army?

1b. What details in the description of Candide's training as a soldier satirize the military?

2a. How does Voltaire describe the burning of the Abare village in the first paragraph of Chapter III?

2b. What point is Voltaire making about the justifications that rulers of nations make for their actions?

3a. How do the anti-Catholic orator's actions contradict his statements?

3b. What hypocrisy is Voltaire revealing in his description of the orator?

Analyze: Taking Things Apart → **Synthesize:** Bringing Things Together

4a. What evidence is offered in the selection to contradict the idea that all things are connected in a series of causes and effects to create the "best of all possible worlds"?

4b. Imagine you are Candide. The turmoil and troubles you have experienced have given you a new perspective on life. What things would you say to Pangloss upon meeting him at the end of the selection?

Evaluate: Making Judgments → **Extend:** Connecting Ideas

5a. How would you judge Pangloss's philosophy on life that "there is no effect without a cause" and that "everything is necessarily for the best end"?

5b. In what ways is Pangloss's perception of life positive? In what ways is this philosophical belief about life dangerous?

Understanding Literature

Satire. Review the definition for **satire** in the Handbook of Literary Terms. What similarities can you find in the attitudes of Voltaire, in *Candide,* and Swift, in *Gulliver's Travels,* toward governments, rulers, and warfare? What absurdities and injustices do these authors satirize?

Irony. Review the definition for **irony** and the graphic organizer you made for Literary Tools in Prereading. Verbal irony is a statement that implies its opposite. Find examples of verbal irony in the sections of *Candide* you just read. What human follies, or lack of reason, are revealed through these examples?

ANSWERS TO INVESTIGATE, INQUIRE, IMAGINE (CONT.)

Evaluate

5a. *Responses will vary.* Students should see that Pangloss is right that "there is no effect without a cause," because an effect is by definition something which was brought about by some other factor. His theory is so obvious as to be ridiculous. Students will likely say that Pangloss's argument that "this is the best of all possible worlds" is nonsensical. It makes no sense to say that simply because a situation exists, it is the best of all possible situations. Pangloss has no way of knowing whether this is the best of all possible worlds because he has no other world to compare it to—this is the only one that exists!

Continued on page 641

Answers to Understanding Literature can be found on page 641.

Writer's Journal

1. Finish the **dialogue** that you predict would take place between Candide and Pangloss.
2. Write your own **statement of belief** on the meaning of life or how our world works.
3. Outline Candide's adventures by making a **time line** of the events he experienced. Begin with his stay at the baron's castle in Westphalia.

Integrating *the* Language Arts

Applied English

Writing a Memo. Imagine you work for the government. Write a memo to the agency you work for, addressing a hypocritical situation, error, or failing in the organization. Use satire and irony as you write your memo. Remember that a satire not only points out the errors of our society and institutions, but it also subtly offers ways in which to correct our errors. Include in your memoranda how we could correct those errors. Read the Language Arts Survey 6.6, "Writing a Memo" for more information.

Study and Research

Getting to Know a Philosopher. The search to define the meaning of life or how the world works has become an endless task. Philosophers continually reflect on the foundations of various subjects to provide us with a deeper understanding of those subjects. They also try to teach us about practical daily life, about what is right and what is wrong, and how we should live our lives. Use library materials and Internet resources to help you research a philosopher and his or her philosophy about life, religion, science, ethics, and/or politics. Because there are so many philosophers who are in search of answers to the same question, you may want to decide on whether you want to study a western or eastern philosophy. From there, choose a philosopher or philosophy that most interests you. Possible philosophers are Confucius, Nietzche, Aristotle, Aquinas, Thoreau, Emerson, Simone de Beauvoir, Mary Wollstonecraft, Hypatia, Kierkegaard, Hannah Arendt. Refer to the Language Arts Survey 5.19 "How to Locate Library Materials" and 5.26 "Using the Internet" to help you with your research. After you have organized your findings, teach the rest of your class in an oral presentation about the philosophy and the philosopher you studied.

Answers to Understanding Literature

Responses will vary. Possible responses are given.

Satire. Voltaire and Swift both satirize the self-serving nature of rulers and governments. In Swift's *Gulliver's Travels,* the emperor of Lilliput seeks to become "sole monarch of the whole world," justifying this ambition with might. Through Gulliver, Swift also satirizes the "secrets of state" and political intrigue of "rival nations." Gulliver seems as surprised by the Lilliputian emperor's voracious desire for power as he is by the Brobdingnagian king's disinterest in such control. Likewise, Voltaire satirizes the self-serving actions of the Bulgarian king, whose pardon of Candide he says "will be praised in all newspapers and all ages." Voltaire also satirizes the absurdity of the Bulgarian and Abarian kings, who both give thanks for a day filled with destruction and death.

Irony. In *Candide,* Voltaire uses many statements of verbal irony to demonstrate the lack of reason behind the philosophical optimism. For example, the statement that "all was in consternation in the nobles and most agreeable of all possible castles" reveals the lack of reason behind Pangloss's assessment of Candide's world. Another example of irony can be found in the exchange between the orator and Candide. The orator, who is speaking about charity, determines that Candide does not deserve charity because he refuses to name the Pope as Anti-Christ. This example of situational irony shows the human folly of hypocrisy and religious intolerance.

Answers to Investigate, Inquire, Imagine (cont.)

Extend

5b. *Responses will vary.* Students may say that Pangloss's perception can be positive because it involves seeing the good in life and encourages one to accept what one cannot change. In some ways, then, Pangloss's view could be comforting. Yet, it could be dangerous because people who suffer extreme poverty or are in another desperate situation might accept their lot without trying to make their life better. People following Panglossian philosophy might become complacent—they might just accept whatever life throws at them without taking the initiative to make something out of the life that they have.

"TO ALL WRITING LADIES"

About the Author. Margaret Cavendish (1623–1674), duchess of Newcastle, wrote in various genres, including poetry, drama, letters, orations, and memoirs. She is best known for *The Life of William Cavendish* (1667), a biography of her husband, duke of Newcastle, and for her Sociable Letters (1664).

About the Selection. Cavendish implores her fellow women to take advantage of their moment in history and make a name for themselves. Because of her aristocratic standing, Cavendish was excused for the supposed audacity of writing about feminist issues.

ADDITIONAL QUESTIONS AND ACTIVITIES

Why does Cavendish relate instances of change in human history? What does she want "our Sex" to do? Why?

Answers

Cavendish relates instances of change in human history to demonstrate that the preferences and privileges of each age change. She wants women, or "our Sex," to pursue roles formerly accorded only to men because she believes the "spirits of the Fæminine Gender" have been at work in the past and that they are at work in her age.

"EPIGRAM ON MILTON"

About the Author. A biography of **Dryden** appears on page 578.

About the Selection. "Epigram on Milton," with its references to Homer and Virgil, reveals the influences of ancient Greek and Roman literature on Dryden.

ADDITIONAL QUESTIONS AND ACTIVITIES

According to the speaker, which two poets did Nature join? What was the result? What is the speaker implying?

Answers

Nature joined Homer and Virgil. The result was Milton. The speaker is implying that Milton's talent and poetry was a combination of the influences of Homer and Virgil.

Selections for Additional Reading: The Restoration and the Eighteenth Century

"To All Writing Ladies"
by Margaret Cavendish

It is to be observed, that there is a secret working by Nature, as to cast an influence upon the mindes of men: like as in Contagions, when as the Aire is corrupted, it produces severall Diseases; so severall distempers[1] of the minde, by the inflammations of the spirits. And as in healthfull Ages, bodies are purified, so wits are refined; yet it seemes to me as if there were severall invisible spirits, that have severall, but visible powers, to worke in severall Ages upon the mindes of men. For in many Ages men will be affected, and disaffected alike: as in some Ages so strongly, and superstitiously devout, that they make many gods: and in another Age so Atheisticall, as they beleeve in no God at all, and live to those Principles. Some Ages againe have such strong faiths, that they will not only dye in their severall Opinions, but they will Massacre, and cut one anothers throats, because their opinions are different. In some Ages all men seek absolute power, and every man would be Emperour of the World; which makes Civil Wars: for their ambition makes them restlesse, and their restlessnesse makes them seek change. Then in another Age all live peaceable, and so obedient, that the very Governours rule with obedient power. In some Ages againe, all run after Imitation, like a company of Apes, as to imitate such a Poet, to be of such a Philosophers opinion. Some Ages mixt, as Moralists, Poets, Philosophers, and the like: and in some Age agen, all affect singularity; and they are thought the wisest, that can have the most extravagant opinions. In some Ages Learning flourisheth in Arts, and Sciences, other Ages so dull, as they loose what former Ages had taught. And in some Ages it seemes as if there were a Common-wealth of those governing spirits, where most rule at one time. Some Ages, as in Aristocracy, when some part did rule; and other Ages a pure Monarchy, when but one rules; and in some Ages, it seemes as if all those spirits were at defiance, who should have most power, which makes them in confusion, and War; so confused are some Ages, and it seemes as if there were spirits of the Fæminine Gender, as also the Masculine. There will be many Heroick Women in some Ages, in others very Propheticall; in some Ages very pious, and devout: For our Sex is wonderfully addicted to the spirits. But this Age hath produced many effeminate Writers, as well as Preachers, and many effeminate Rulers, as well as Actors. And if it be an Age when the effeminate spirits rule, as most visible they doe in every Kingdome, let us take the advantage, and make the best of our time, for feare their reigne should not last long; whether it be in the Amazonian Government, or in the Politick Common-wealth, or in flourishing Monarchy, or in Schooles of Divinity, or in Lectures of Philosophy, or in witty Poetry, or any thing that may bring honour to our Sex: for they are poore, dejected spirits, that are not ambitious of Fame. And though we be inferiour to Men, let us shew our selves a degree above Beasts; and not eate, and drink, and sleep away our time as they doe; and live only to the sense, not to the reason; and so turne into forgotten dust. But let us strive to build us Tombs while we live, of Noble, Honourable, and good Actions, at least harmlesse;

That though our Bodies dye,
Our Names may live to after memory.

"Epigram on Milton"
by John Dryden

Three poets,[2] in three distant ages born,
Greece, Italy, and England did adorn.
The first in loftiness of thought surpassed,
The next in majesty, in both the last:
The force of Nature could no farther go;
To make a third, she joined the former two.

"Love Armed"[3]
by Aphra Behn

Love in fantastic triumph[4] sat
Whilst bleeding hearts around him flowed,
For whom fresh pains he did create
And strange tyrannic power he showed.

From thy bright eyes he took the fires
Which round about in sport he hurled,
But 'twas from mine he took desires
Enough t'undo the amorous world.[5]
From me he took his sighs and tears,
From thee his pride and cruelty;
From me his languishments and fears.
And every killing dart[6] from thee.

Thus thou and I the God have armed
And set him up a deity;
But my poor heart alone is harmed,
Whilst thine the victor is, and free.

1. **distempers.** Disturbances
2. **Three poets.** Refers to Homer, Virgil, and Milton
3. **"Love Armed."** Cupid, often depicted with a bow and arrow
4. **fantastic triumph.** In a grand procession
5. **Enough . . . world.** Enough to drown all lovers in suffering caused by desire
6. **dart.** Cupid's arrow

"LOVE ARMED"

About the Author. A biography of **Behn** appears on page 607.

About the Selection. "Love Armed" demonstrates both Neoclassical influences and Behn's own feminist perspective on the traditional love poem.

"THE LOVER: A BALLAD"

About the Author. Lady Mary Wortley Montagu (1689–1762) was well known in her time for her letter writing, although she also wrote some poetry and plays. She led a rather unconventional life for an eighteenth-century woman. She married her husband, Edward Wortley Montagu, for love; she followed him to Constantinople when he was appointed ambassador in 1716. Upon her return in 1718, she introduced the

from *An Essay on Man*
by Alexander Pope

From *Epistle 2. Of the Nature and State of Man With Respect to Himself, as an Individual*

1. Know then thyself, presume not God to scan;
The proper study of mankind is Man.
Placed on this isthmus of a middle state,
And being darkly wise, and rudely great:
With too much knowledge for the skeptic side,
With too much weakness for the Stoic's pride,
He hangs between; in doubt to act, or rest,
In doubt to deem himself a god, or beast;
In doubt his mind or body to prefer,
Born but to die, and reasoning but to err;
Alike in ignorance, his reason such,
Whether he thinks too little, or too much:
Chaos of through and passion, all confused;
Still by himself abused, or disabused;
Created half to rise, and half to fall;
Great lord of all things, yet a prey to all;
Sole judge of truth, in endless error hurled:
The glory, jest, and riddle of the world!

"The Lover: A Ballad"
by Lady Mary Wortley Montagu

At length, by so much importunity pressed,
Take, (Molly),[1] at once, the inside of my breast;
This stupid indifference so often you blame
Is not owing to nature, to fear, or to shame;
I am not as cold as a Virgin in lead,[2]
Nor is Sunday's sermon so strong in my head;
I know but too well how time flies along,
That we live but few years and yet fewer are young.

But I hate to be cheated, and never will buy
Long years of repentance for moments of joy.
Oh was there a man (but where shall I find
Good sense and good nature so equally joined?)
Would value his pleasure, contribute to mine,
Not meanly would boast, nor lewdly design,
Not over severe, yet not stupidly vain,
For I would have the power though not give the pain;

No pedant yet learnèd, not rakehelly gay
Or laughing because he has nothing to say,
To all my whole sex obliging and free,
Yet never be fond of any but me;
In public preserve the decorums are just,
And show in his eyes he is true to his trust,
Then rarely approach, and respectfully bow,
Yet not fulsomely pert, nor yet foppishly low.

But when the long hours of public are past
And we meet with champagne and a chicken at last,
May every fond pleasure that hour endear,
Be banished afar both discretion and fear,
Forgetting or scorning the airs of the crowd
He may cease to be formal, and I to be proud,
Till lost in the joy we confess that we live,
And he may be rude, and yet I may forgive.

And that my delight may be solidly fixed,
Let the friend and the lover be handsomely mixed,
In whose tender bosom my soul might confide,
Whose kindness can sooth me, whose counsel could guide.
From such a dear lover as here I describe
No danger should fright me, no millions should bribe;
But till this astonishing creature I know,
As I long have lived chaste, I will keep myself so.

I never will share with the wanton coquette,
Or be caught by a vain affectation of wit.
The toasters and songsters may try all their art
But never shall enter the pass of my heart.
I loathe the lewd rake, the dressed fopling despise;
Before such pursuers the nice virgin flies;
And as Ovid has sweetly in parables told
We harden like trees, and like rivers are cold.[3]

"A Modest Proposal"[4]
by Jonathan Swift

FOR PREVENTING THE CHILDREN OF POOR PEOPLE IN IRELAND FROM BEING A BURDEN TO THEIR PARENTS OR COUNTRY, AND FOR MAKING THEM BENEFICIAL TO THE PUBLIC

It is a melancholy object to those who walk through this great town or travel in the country, when they see the streets, the roads, and cabin doors, crowded with beggars of the female sex, followed by three, four, or six children, all in rags and importuning every passenger for an alms. These mothers, instead of being able to work for their honest livelihood, are forced to employ all their time in strolling to beg sustenance for their helpless infants, who, as they grow up, either turn thieves for want of work, or leave their dear native country

---

1. **Molly.** Molly Skerrett was a friend of Lady Mary and the mistress of Sir Robert Walpole.
2. **Virgin in lead.** Image of the Virgin Mary cast in lead or in a stained-glass window framed in lead.
3. **Ovid . . . cold.** In *Metamorphoses*, Ovid relates how Daphne was turned into a laurel tree to escape Apollo and how Arethusa became a fountain to escape Alpheus.
4. **"A Modest Proposal."** A satiric pamphlet by Swift that offers a supposed solution to the problem of the populous, oppressed peasants of Ireland. Swift uses irony, beginning with the use of the word *modest* in the title; parody of humanitarians who sought to solve social problems through theoretical approaches; and logic to reach his shocking conclusion.

FROM *AN ESSAY ON MAN*

ABOUT THE AUTHOR. A biography of **Pope** appears on page 614.

ABOUT THE SELECTION. ***An Essay on Man,*** like Pope's earlier work *An Essay on Criticism,* is a philosophical poem written in heroic couplets. It was published between 1732 and 1734. The essay discusses the nature of humankind and, though it is not explicitly Christian, attempts to warn human beings that, despite what they think, they are not the center of the universe and must seek salvation through God. Pope planned to write a larger work, with *Essay on Man* at its center, to put forth an entire system of ethics, but he did not live to complete this project.

ADDITIONAL QUESTIONS AND ACTIVITIES

Why does Pope say that the proper study of humankind is "Man" and not God? In what ways is humankind "on this isthmus of a middle state"—or in other words, torn between two extremes? In what way does the situation of humankind illustrate a **paradox,** or a seemingly contradictory state?

Answers

Pope implies that it would be presumptuous, or overly bold, of humans to "scan" God. Humankind is torn between the extremes of skepticism and Stoicism, acting and resting, being a god or a beast, the demands of the mind or the body, thinking too little or too much, abuse and disabuse. The situation of humankind is paradoxical in that humans are "darkly wise"—darkness implies lack of wisdom—and "rudely great"—rudeness implies commonness, the opposite of greatness. It is also paradoxical that humans were "born but to die," "Created half to rise, and half to fall," and "Great lord of things, yet a prey to all."

Turkish method of inoculation against smallpox in England. At one time friendly with Pope, she had a bitter falling out with him in 1728–1729. Her publications include *Court Poems by a Lady of Quality* (1716) and *Turkish Letters* (1763).

ABOUT THE SELECTION. "The Lover: A Ballad" expresses Montagu's belief that women have every right to think of themselves as men's equals, both in matters of the mind and of the heart.

ADDITIONAL QUESTIONS AND ACTIVITIES

According to the speaker, what is the cause of what others call her "stupid indifference"?

Answer

Her "stupid indifference" is caused by her desire to find a man who possesses the qualities she values and to whom she feels equal.

ADDITIONAL QUESTIONS AND ACTIVITIES

1. Who does Swift say would be "set up for a preserver of the nation"?
2. What solution does Swift "humbly propose"?

Answer

1. He says that the person who could devise a plan to make the children of poor Irish parents "sound, useful members of the commonwealth" would be hailed as "a preserver of the nation."
2. He proposes that infants be reared to the age of one year so that they can be killed and sold for food.

Quotables

"Satire is a sort of glass, wherein beholders do generally discover everybody's face but their own."

—Jonathan Swift

LITERARY TECHNIQUE

- **Tone.** Remind students that **tone** is the emotional attitude toward the reader or toward the subject implied by a literary work. Examples of the different tones that a work may have include familiar, ironic, playful, sarcastic, serious, and sincere. Students can discuss the **tone** Swift uses in this selection, which is that of a dispassionate economist. Have them consider how the tone contributes to the satiric effect.
- **Metaphor.** Remind students that a **metaphor** is a figure of speech in which one thing is spoken or written about as if it were another. Ask them what point Swift makes with his **metaphorical** use of the word *devour* in the following sentence: "I grant this food will be somewhat dear, and therefore very proper for landlords, who, as they have already devoured most of the parents, seem to have the best title to the children."

Answers

By using *devour* metaphorically, Swift makes the point that English landowners are draining the resources of the Irish workers.

to fight for the Pretender in Spain, or sell themselves to the Barbadoes.[1]

I think it is agreed by all parties that this prodigious number of children in the arms, or on the backs, or at the heels of their mothers, and frequently of their fathers, is in the present deplorable state of the kingdom a very great additional grievance; and therefore whoever could find out a fair, cheap, and easy method of making these children sound, useful members of the commonwealth would deserve so well of the public as to have his statue set up for a preserver of the nation.

But my intention is very far from being confined to provide only for the children of professed beggars; it is of a much greater extent, and shall take in the whole number of infants at a certain age who are born of parents in effect as little able to support them as those who demand our charity in the streets.

As to my own part, having turned my thoughts for many years upon this important subject, and maturely weighed the several schemes of other projectors, I have always found them grossly mistaken in their computation. It is true, a child just dropped from its dam may be supported by her milk for a solar year, with little other nourishment; at most not above the value of two shillings, which the mother may certainly get, or the value in scraps, by her lawful occupation of begging; and it is exactly at one year old that I propose to provide for them in such a manner as instead of being a charge upon their parents or the parish, or wanting food and raiment for the rest of their lives, they shall on the contrary contribute to the feeding, and partly to the clothing, of many thousands.

There is likewise another great advantage in my scheme, that it will prevent those voluntary abortions, and that horrid practice of women murdering their bastard children, alas, too frequent among us, sacrificing the poor innocent babes, I doubt, more to avoid the expense than the shame, which would move tears and pity in the most savage and inhuman breast.

The number of souls in this kingdom being usually reckoned one million and a half, of these I calculate there may be about two hundred thousand couples whose wives are breeders; from which number I subtract thirty thousand couples who are able to maintain their own children, although I apprehend there cannot be so many under the present distresses of the kingdom; but this being granted, there will remain an hundred and seventy thousand breeders. I again subtract fifty thousand for those women who miscarry, or whose children die by accident or disease within the year. There only remain an hundred and twenty thousand children of poor parents annually born. The question therefore is, how this number shall be reared and provided for, which, as I have already said, under the present situation of affairs, is utterly impossible by all the methods hitherto proposed. For we can neither employ them in handicraft or agriculture; we neither build houses (I mean in the country) nor cultivate land. They can very seldom pick up a livelihood by stealing till they arrive at six years old, except where they are of towardly parts;[2] although I confess they learn the rudiments much earlier, during which time they can however be looked upon only as probationers, as I have been informed by a principal gentleman in the county of Cavan, who protested to me that he never knew above one or two instances under the ages of six, even in a part of the kingdom so renowned for the quickest proficiency in that art.

I am assured by our merchants that a boy or a girl before twelve years old is no salable commodity; and even when they come to this age they will not yield above three pounds, or three pounds and half a crown at most on the Exchange; which cannot turn to account either to the parents or the kingdom, the charge of nutriment and rags having been at least four times that value.

I shall now therefore humbly propose my own thoughts, which I hope will not be liable to the least objection.

I have been assured by a very knowing American of my acquaintance in London, that a young healthy child well nursed is at a year old a most delicious, nourishing, and wholesome food, whether stewed, roasted, baked, or boiled; and I make no doubt that it will equally serve in a fricassee or a ragout.

I do therefore humbly offer it to public consideration that of the hundred and twenty thousand children, already computed, twenty thousand may be reserved for breed, whereof only one fourth part to be males, which is more than we allow to sheep, black cattle, or swine; and my reason is that these children are seldom the fruits of marriage, a circumstance not much regarded by our savages, therefore one male will be sufficient to serve four females. That the remaining hundred thousand may at a year old be offered in sale to the persons of quality and fortune through the kingdom, always advising the mother to let them suck plentifully in the last month, so as to render them plump and fat for a good table. A child will make two dishes at an entertainment for friends; and when the family dines alone, the fore or hind quarter will make a reasonable dish, and seasoned with a little pepper or salt will be very good boiled on the fourth day, especially in winter.

I have reckoned upon a medium that a child just born will weigh twelve pounds, and in a solar year if tolerably nursed increaseth to twenty-eight pounds.

I grant this food will be somewhat dear, and therefore very proper for landlords, who, as they have already devoured most of the parents, seem to have the best title to the children.

Infant's flesh will be in season throughout the year, but more plentiful in March, and a little before and after. For we are told by a grave author, an eminent French physician,[3] that fish being a prolific diet, there are more children born in Roman

1. **Pretender . . . Barbadoes.** The Pretender refers to James Francis Edward Stuart, son of James II, who had been barred from the succession. He was exiled to the Continent, and Catholic Irish loyals joined him there. Poverty caused others to leave Ireland, and many traveled to the West Indies as indentured servants.
2. **towardly parts.** Promising abilities
3. **grave . . . physician.** Refers to François Rabelais, a French satirist

"A MODEST PROPOSAL"

About the Author. After being made dean of St. Patrick's Cathedral in Dublin in 1713, **Jonathan Swift** took up residence in Ireland. In 1724, he became a spokesperson for the Irish, airing their grievances against English oppression in pamphlets and a series of letters published under a pseudonym. For more information, see the biography on page 598.

About the Selection. Swift wrote **"A Modest Proposal"** in 1729 to express his sympathy for the plight of the oppressed Irish peasants and to express his anger at the English ruling class whom he faulted for creating that plight.

Catholic countries about nine months after Lent than at any other season; therefore, reckoning a year after Lent, the markets will be more glutted than usual, because the number of popish infants is at least three to one in this kingdom; and therefore it will have one other collateral advantage, by lessening the number of Papists among us.

I have already computed the charge of nursing a beggar's child (in which list I reckon all cottagers, laborers, and four fifths of the farmers) to be about two shillings per annum, rags included; and I believe no gentleman would repine to give ten shillings for the carcass of a good fat child, which, as I have said, will make four dishes of excellent nutritive meat, when he hath only some particular friend or his own family to dine with him. Thus the squire will learn to be a good landlord, and grow popular among the tenants; the mother will have eight shillings net profit, and be fit for the work till she produces another child.

Those who are more thrifty (as I must confess the times require) may flay the carcass; the skin of which artificially dressed will make admirable gloves for ladies, and summer boots for fine gentlemen.

As to our city of Dublin, shambles[1] may be appointed for this purpose in the most convenient parts of it, and butchers we may be assured will not be wanting; although I rather recommend buying the children alive, and dressing them hot from the knife as we do roasting pigs.

A very worthy person, a true lover of his country, and whose virtues I highly esteem, was lately pleased in discoursing on this matter to offer a refinement upon my scheme. He said that many gentlemen of this kingdom, having of late destroyed their deer, he conceived that the want of venison might be well supplied by the bodies of young lads and maidens, not exceeding fourteen years of age nor under twelve, so great a number of both sexes in every county being now ready to starve for want of work and service; and these to be disposed of by their parents, if alive, or otherwise by their nearest relations. But with due deference to so excellent a friend and so deserving a patriot, I cannot be altogether in his sentiments; for as to the males, my American acquaintance assured me from frequent experience that their flesh was generally tough and lean, like that of our schoolboys, by continual exercise, and their taste disagreeable; and to fatten them would not answer the charge. Then as to the females, it would, I think with humble submission, be a loss to the public, because they soon would become breeders themselves; and besides, it is not improbable that some scrupulous people might be apt to censure such a practice (although indeed very unjustly) as a little bordering upon cruelty; which I confess, hath always been with me the strongest objection against any project, how well soever intended.

But in order to justify my friend, he confessed that this expedient was put into his head by the famous Psalmanazar,[2] a native of the island Formosa, who came from thence to London above twenty years ago, and in conversation told my friend that in his country when any young person happened to be put to death, the executioner sold the carcass to persons of quality as a prime dainty; and that in his time the body of a plump girl of fifteen, who was crucified for an attempt to poison the emperor, was sold to his Imperial Majesty's prime minister of state, and other great mandarins of the court, in joints from the gibbet, at four hundred crowns. Neither indeed can I deny that if the same use were made of several plump young girls in this town, who without one single groat to their fortunes cannot stir abroad without a chair, and appear at the playhouse and assemblies in foreign fineries which they never will pay for, the kingdom would not be the worse.

Some persons of a desponding spirit are in great concern about that vast number of poor people who are aged, diseased, or maimed, and I have been desired to employ my thoughts what course may be taken to ease the nation of so grievous an encumbrance. But I am not in the least pain upon that matter, because it is very well known that they are every day dying and rotting by cold and famine, and filth and vermin, as fast as can be reasonably expected. And as to the younger laborers, they are now in almost as hopeful a condition. They cannot get work, and consequently pine away for want of nourishment to a degree that if at any time they are accidentally hired to common labor, they have not strength to perform it; and thus the country and themselves are happily delivered from the evils to come.

I have too long digressed, and therefore shall return to my subject. I think the advantages by the proposal which I have made are obvious and many, as well as of the highest importance.

For first, as I have already observed, it would greatly lessen the number of Papists, with whom we are yearly overrun, being the principal breeders of the nation as well as our most dangerous enemies; and who stay at home on purpose to deliver the kingdom to the Pretender, hoping to take their advantage by the absence of so many good Protestants, who have chosen rather to leave their country than stay at home and pay tithes against their conscience to an Episcopal curate.

Secondly, the poorer tenants will have something valuable of their own, which by law may be made liable to distress, and help to pay their landlord's rent, their corn and cattle being already seized and money a thing unknown.

Thirdly, whereas the maintenance of an hundred thousand children, from two years old and upwards, cannot be computed at less than ten shillings a piece per annum, the nation's stock will be thereby increased fifty thousand pounds per annum, besides the profit of a new dish introduced to the tables of all gentlemen of fortune in the kingdom who have any refinement in taste. And the money will circulate among ourselves, the goods being entirely of our own growth and manufacture.

Fourthly, the constant breeders, besides the gain of eight shillings sterling per annum by the sale of their children, will be rid of the charge of maintaining them after the first year.

Fifthly, this food would likewise bring great custom to taverns, where the vintners will certainly be so prudent as to procure the best receipts for dressing it to perfection, and

1. **shambles.** Slaughterhouses

2. **Psalmanazar.** George Psalmanazar was a famous impostor. A Frenchman, he pretended to be a Formosan and wrote fictitious accounts of Formosa in which he described human sacrifices and cannibalism.

ADDITIONAL QUESTIONS AND ACTIVITIES

Inform students that "A Modest Proposal" is the longest-sustained piece of irony in the English language. It has often been attacked by critics who do not infer the ironic tone and believe that Swift is seriously recom-mending that babies be eaten. Ask students why critics might miss the irony in this piece. Is it simply because of Swift's skill as a satirist? What type of individual is most likely to misunderstand Swift's piece—the Irish Catholic, whom he is obliquely supporting, or the English Protestant noble, whom he is obliquely critiquing?

LITERARY TECHNIQUE

Verbal Irony. Remind students that **verbal irony** is a statement that implies its opposite. Ask students what reasons Swift gives for not using adolescent boys and girls for food as well. What is **ironic** about his reasoning?

Answers

He reasons that the flesh of boys would be too tough and that girls should be saved to become "breeders" and that, in any case, such a practice might be perceived as "cruelty." He suggests that he wants to avoid being cruel, which is ironic because everything he has proposed so far—killing babies for food—is horribly cruel. What Swift actually means by his statement is that killing babies *is* cruel, but so is overcharging people for rent so that they end up starving to death, or ignoring the plight of poor Irish people in England.

ADDITIONAL QUESTIONS AND ACTIVITIES

What does Swift's first argument for the proposal reveal about common attitudes toward Papists, or Catholics?

Answer

Many people were probably prejudiced against Catholics, believing them to be disloyal to Protestant England.

ADDITIONAL QUESTIONS AND ACTIVITIES

1. Refer to Swift's sixth argument for his proposal. How is Swift's statement that the proposal "would increase the care and tenderness of mothers toward their children" an example of verbal irony?
2. What purpose does Swift have in listing "other expedients"?
3. What does Swift's satiric proposal indicate about the attitude of most English toward the plight of the Irish?

Answer

1. The statement is an example of verbal irony because it implies the opposite meaning; such a proposal, if it were to be employed, would demonstrate a mother's callousness and indifference toward her children, not her affection for them.
2. These proposals are all reasonable suggestions to solving the problem. Swift juxtaposes them with his absurd, satirical proposal to make the point that there are reasonable alternatives to the problem, if the English are willing to explore them.
3. His proposal reveals that most English were indifferent to the plight of the Irish and that they believed the Irish poor were responsible for their own ills

Have students brainstorm a list of social problems faced in this country that seem to go unnoticed by the government.

LITERARY TECHNIQUE

You might ask students to find places in the proposal where Swift allows the persona he has created to slip. Where does the indignant, enraged Swift drop the mask of the cold economist?

consequently have their houses frequented by all the fine gentlemen, who justly value themselves upon their knowledge in good eating; and a skillful cook, who understands how to oblige his guests, will contrive to make it as expensive as they please.

Sixthly, this would be a great inducement to marriage, which all wise nations have either encouraged by rewards or enforced by laws and penalties. It would increase the care and tenderness of mothers toward their children, when they were sure of a settlement for life to the poor babes, provided in some sort by the public, to their annual profit instead of expense. We should see an honest emulation among the married women, which of them could bring the fattest child to the market. Men would become as fond of their wives during the time of their pregnancy as they are now of their mares in foal, their cows in calf, or sows when they are ready to farrow; nor offer to beat or kick them (as is too frequent a practice) for fear of a miscarriage.

Many other advantages might be enumerated. For instance, the addition of some thousand carcasses in our exportation of barreled beef, the propagation of swine's flesh, and improvement in the art of making good bacon, so much wanted among us by the great destruction of pigs, too frequent at our tables, which are no way comparable in taste or magnificence to a well-grown, fat, yearling child, which roasted whole will make a considerable figure at a lord mayor's feast or any other public entertainment. But this and many others I omit, being studious of brevity.

Supposing that one thousand families in this city would be constant customers for infants' flesh, besides others who might have it at merry meetings, particularly weddings and christenings, I compute that Dublin would take off annually about twenty thousand carcasses, and the rest of the kingdom (where probably they will be sold somewhat cheaper) the remaining eighty thousand.

I can think of no one objection that will probably be raised against this proposal, unless it should be urged that the number of people will be thereby much lessened in the kingdom. This I freely own, and it was indeed one principal design in offering it to the world. I desire the reader will observe, that I calculate my remedy for this one individual kingdom of Ireland and for no other that ever was, is, or I think ever can be upon earth. Therefore let no man talk to me of other expedients: of taxing our absentees at five shillings a pound: of using neither clothes nor household furniture except what is of our own growth and manufacture: of utterly rejecting the materials and instruments that promote foreign luxury: of curing the expensiveness of pride, vanity, idleness, and gaming in our women: of introducing a vein of parsimony, prudence, and temperance: of learning to love our country, in the want of which we differ even from Laplanders and the inhabitants of Topinamboo:[1] of quitting our animosities and factions, nor acting any longer like the Jews, who were murdering one another at the very moment their city was taken:[2] of being a little cautious not to sell our country and conscience for nothing: of teaching landlords to have at least one degree of mercy toward their tenants: lastly, of putting a spirit of honesty, industry, and skill into our shopkeepers; who, if a resolution could now be taken to buy only our native goods, would immediately unite to cheat and exact upon us in the price, the measure, and the goodness, nor could ever yet be brought to make one fair proposal of just dealing, though often and earnestly invited to it.[3]

Therefore I repeat, let no man talk to me of these and the like expedients, till he hath at least some glimpse of hope that there will ever be some hearty and sincere attempt to put them in practice.

But as to myself, having been wearied out for many years with offering vain, idle, visionary thoughts, and at length utterly despairing of success, I fortunately fell upon this proposal, which, as it is wholly new, so it hath something solid and real, of no expense and little trouble, full in our own power, and whereby we can incur no danger in disobliging England. For this kind of commodity will not bear exportation, the flesh being of too tender a consistence to admit a long continuance in salt, although perhaps I could name a country which would be glad to eat up our whole nation without it.

After all, I am not so violently bent upon my own opinion as to reject any offer proposed by wise men, which shall be found equally innocent, cheap, easy, and effectual. But before something of that kind shall be advanced in contradiction to my scheme, and offering a better, I desire the author or authors will be pleased maturely to consider two points. First, as things now stand, how they will be able to find food and raiment for an hundred thousand useless mouths and backs. And secondly, there being a round million of creatures in human figure throughout this kingdom, whose sole subsistence put into a common stock would leave them in debt two millions of pounds sterling, adding those who are beggars by profession to the bulk of farmers, cottagers, and laborers, with their wives and children who are beggars in effect; I desire those politicians who dislike my overture, and may perhaps be so bold to attempt an answer, that they will first ask the parents of these mortals whether they would not at this day think it a great happiness to have been sold for food at a year old in the manner I prescribe, and thereby have avoided such a perpetual sense of misfortunes as they have since gone through by the oppression of landlords, the impossibility of paying rent without money or trade, the want of common sustenance, with neither house nor clothes to cover them from the inclemencies of the weather, and the most inevitable prospect of entailing the like or greater miseries upon their breed forever.

I profess, in the sincerity of my heart, that I have not the least personal interest in endeavoring to promote this necessary work, having no other motive than the public good of my country, by advancing our trade, providing for infants, relieving the poor, and giving some pleasure to the rich. I have no children by which I can propose to get a single penny; the youngest being nine years old, and my wife past childbearing.

1. **Laplanders . . . Topinamboo.** The Anglo-Irish do not love Ireland in the way Laplanders love their frozen land or the Topinamboo love their wild jungles in Brazil.
2. **Jews . . . taken.** Fighting factions of Jews destroyed Jerusalem during the siege by the Roman emperor Titus in AD 70.
3. **being . . . to it.** These are all proposals Swift had made in various pamphlets.

from The Spectator, *No. 62, Friday, March 11, 1711*
by Joseph Addison

Mr. Locke has an admirable reflection upon the difference of wit and judgment, whereby he endeavors to show the reason why they are not always the talents of the same person. His words are as follow: "And hence, perhaps, may be given some reason of that common observation, that men who have a great deal of wit and prompt memories, have not always the clearest judgment, or deepest reason. For wit lying most in the assemblage of ideas, and putting those together with quickness and variety, wherein can be found any resemblance or congruity, thereby to make up pleasant pictures and agreeable visions in the fancy; judgment, on the contrary, lies quite on the other side, in separating carefully one from another, ideas wherein can be found the least difference, thereby to avoid being misled by similitude, and by affinity to take one thing for another. This is a way of proceeding quite contrary to metaphor and allusion; wherein, for the most part, lies that entertainment and pleasantry of wit which strikes so lively on the fancy, and is therefore so acceptable to all people."[1]

This is, I think, the best and most philosophical account that I have ever met with of wit, which generally, though not always, consists in such a resemblance and congruity of ideas as this author mentions. I shall only add to it, by way of explanation, that every resemblance of ideas is not that which we call wit, unless it be such an one that gives delight and surprise to the reader. These two properties seem essential to wit, more particularly the last of them. In order therefore that the resemblance in the ideas be wit, it is necessary that the ideas should not lie too near one another in the nature of things; for where the likeness is obvious, it gives no surprise. To compare one man's singing to that of another, or to represent the whiteness of any object by that of milk and snow, or the variety of its colors by those of the rainbow, cannot be called wit, unless, besides this obvious resemblance, there be some further congruity discovered in the two ideas that is capable of giving the reader some surprise. Thus when a poet tells us, the bosom of his mistress is as white as snow, there is no wit in the comparison; but when he adds, with a sigh, that it is as cold too, it then grows into wit. Every reader's memory may supply him with innumerable instances of the same nature. For this reason, the similitudes in heroic poets, who endeavor rather to fill the mind with great conceptions, than to divert it with such as are new and surprising, have seldom anything in them that can be called wit. Mr. Locke's account of wit, with this short explanation, comprehends most of the species of wit, as metaphors, similitudes, allegories, enigmas, mottoes, parables, fables, dreams, visions, dramatic writings, burlesque, and all the methods of allusion: as there are many other pieces of wit (how remote soever they may appear at first sight from the foregoing description) which upon examination will be found to agree with it.

As true wit generally consists in this resemblance and congruity of ideas, false wit chiefly consists in the resemblance and congruity sometimes of single letters, as in anagrams, chronograms, lipograms,[2] and acrostics; sometimes of syllables, as in echoes and doggerel rhymes; sometimes of words, as in puns and quibbles; and sometimes of whole sentences or poems, cast into the figures of eggs, axes, or altars: nay, some carry the notion of wit so far, as to ascribe it even to external mimicry; and to look upon a man as an ingenious person, that can resemble the tone, posture, or face of another.

As true wit consists in the resemblance of ideas, and false wit in the resemblance of words, according to the foregoing instances; there is another kind of wit which consists partly in the resemblance of ideas, and partly in the resemblance of words; which for distinction's sake I shall call mixed wit.

◆ ◆ ◆

Out of the innumerable branches of mixed wit, I shall choose one instance which may be met with in all the writers of this class. The passion of love in its nature has been thought to resemble fire; for which reason the words fire and flame are made use of to signify love. The witty poets therefore have taken an advantage from the doubtful meaning of the word fire, to make an infinite number of witticisms. Cowley, observing the cold regard of his mistress's eyes, and at the same time their power of producing love in him, considers them as burning-glasses made of ice; and finding himself able to live in the greatest extremities of love, concludes the torrid zone to be habitable. When his mistress has read his letter written in juice of lemon by holding it to the fire, he desires her to read it over a second time by love's flames. When she weeps, he wishes it were inward heat that distilled those drops from the limbec. When she is absent he is beyond eighty, that is, thirty degrees nearer the pole than when she is with him. His ambitious love is a fire that naturally mounts upwards; his happy love is the beams of heaven, and his unhappy love flames of hell. When it does not let him sleep, it is a flame that sends up no smoke; when it is opposed by counsel and advice, it is a fire that rages the more by the wind's blowing upon it. Upon the dying of a tree in which he had cut his loves, he observes that his written flames had burned up and withered the tree. When he resolves to give over his passion, he tells us that one burnt like him for ever dreads the fire. His heart is an Aetna, that instead of Vulcan's shop[3] encloses Cupid's forge in it. His endeavoring to drown his love in wine, is throwing oil upon the fire. He would insinuate to his mistress, that the fire of love, like that of the sun (which produces so many living creatures) should not only warm but beget. Love in another place cooks pleasure at his fire. Sometimes the poet's heart is frozen in every breast, and sometimes scorched in every eye. Sometimes he is drowned in tears, and burnt in love, like a ship set on fire in the middle of the sea.

The reader may observe in every one of these instances, that the poet mixes the qualities of fire with those of love; and in

1. **" And . . . people."** From *An Essay Concerning Human Understanding* by John Locke

2. **chronograms, lipograms.** A chronogram is a phrase in which certain letters express a date. A lipogram is a composition that omits all words that contain a certain letter.

3. **Aetna . . . shop.** Mount Etna, the workshop of Vulcan, the Roman god of fire and metalwork

FROM *THE SPECTATOR,* NO. 62, FRIDAY, MARCH 11, 1711

About the Author. Joseph Addison (1672–1719), along with friend and fellow journalist **Richard Steele** (1672–1729), is credited with the creation of the periodical essay. These essays were intended both for amusement and instruction; Addison's commentary on the morals of his time was influential in developing a middle-class code of conduct. Addison and Steele published a series of essays in The Spectator from March 1711 to December 1712 (Addison resumed briefly in 1714). Alexander Pope satirized Addison and his moralizing in his *Epistle to Dr. Arbuthnot* (1735).

About the Selection. In this essay, which appeared in *The Spectator,* Addison discusses the nature of wit.

ADDITIONAL QUESTIONS AND ACTIVITIES

1. What does Addison believe are the defining characteristics of wit?
2. According to Addison, how many types of wit are there? What are they?
3. What type of resemblance makes up "false wit"? What are some examples of false wit?
4. According to Addison, what is mixed wit?

Answer

1. He believes that wit must have "a resemblance of ideas" and "give the reader some surprise."
2. There are three types of wit: true wit, false wit, and mixed wit.
3. The resemblance of words makes up false wit. Anagrams, puns, and sentences or poems that form shapes are examples of false wit.
4. Mixed wit is a combination of true wit and false wit; it consists partly in the resemblance of ideas and partly in the resemblance of words.

"A SHORT SONG OF CONGRATULATION"

About the Author. A biography of **Johnson** appears on page 619.

About the Selection. In **"A Short Song of Congratulation,"** the speaker addresses a young man who has recently come into an inheritance and who will soon foolishly spend his money.

ADDITIONAL QUESTIONS AND ACTIVITIES

1. What event occasions the speaker's words?
2. How does the speaker predict Sir John will manage his inheritance?

Answer

1. Sir John has just turned twenty-one years of age and has inherited property.
2. He predicts that Sir John will fall prey to the temptations of "vice and folly" and lose his money to "the jockey" and "the pander."

LITERARY TECHNIQUE

After they have read the poem, have students discuss its title. Is the title to be taken at face value, or is it **ironic**? What does it imply about the speaker's attitude? Students should support their answers with specific examples from the poem.

Answers

The title of the poem is ironic because it implies that the time of congratulation will be short-lived. The speaker details how great Sir John will "Bid the slaves of thrift farewell" and eventually "hang or drown" for his debts.

the same sentence speaking of it both as a passion, and as a real fire, surprises the reader with those seeming resemblances or contradictions that make up all the wit in this kind of writing. Mixed wit therefore is a composition of pun and true wit, and is more or less perfect as the resemblance lies in the ideas or in the words. Its foundations are laid partly in falsehood and partly in truth: reason puts in her claim for one half of it, and extravagance for the other. ■

"A Short Song of Congratulation"
by Samuel Johnson

Long expected one and twenty
  Lingering year at last is flown,
Pomp and Pleasure, Pride and Plenty,
  Great Sir John,[1] are all your own.

Loosened from the minor's tether,
  Free to mortgage or to sell,
Wild as wind, and light as feather
  Bid the slaves of thrift farewell.

Call the Bettys, Kates, and Jennys
  Every name that laughs at Care,
Lavish of your grandsire's guineas,
  Show the spirit of an heir.

All that prey on vice and folly
  Joy to see their quarry fly,
Here the gamester light and jolly
  There the lender grave and sly.

Wealth, Sir John, was made to wander,
  Let it wander as it will;
See the jockey, see the pander,
  Bid them come, and take their fill.

When the bonny blade carouses,
  Pockets full, and spirits high,
What are acres? What are houses?
  Only dirt, or wet or dry.

If the guardian or the mother
  Tell the woes of willful waste,
Scorn their counsel and their pother,
  You can hang or drown at last. ■

1. **Sir John.** Sir John Lade, the nephew of one of Johnson's friends, inherited property in 1780, only to squander it all.

COMPOSING A PROSE SATIRE

A sense of humor is an elusive human attribute—teasing the "funny bone" is an idiosyncratic event, unique to each individual, a certain time, a specific place. One person will laugh at a standup comedian while another will yawn, another will groan. One way to approach humor is through satire.

Satire is humorous writing or speech intended to point out errors, falsehoods, foibles, or failings. It is written for the purpose of reforming human behavior or human institutions.

WRITING ASSIGNMENT. In this assignment you will write a prose satire aimed at changing the behavior or attitude of your audience.

"Satire is a sort of glass (i.e., mirror) wherein beholders do generally discover everybody's face but their own; which is the chief reason for the kind of reception it meets in the world, and that so very few are offended with it."

—*Jonathan Swift*

Professional Model

from "A Modest Proposal" by Jonathan Swift
page 643

It is a melancholy object to those who walk through this great town, or travel in the country, when they see the streets, the roads, and cabin doors crowded with beggars of the female sex, followed by three, four, or six children, all in rags, and importuning every passenger for an alms. These mothers, instead of being able to work for their honest livelihood, are forced to employ all their time in strolling to beg sustenance for their helpless infants—who, as they grow up, either turn thieves for want of work, or leave their dear native country in flight for the Pretender in Spain, or sell themselves to the Barbadoes.

I think it is agreed by all parties that this prodigious number of children in the arms, or on the backs, or at the heels of their mothers, and frequently of their fathers, is, in the present deplorable state of the kingdom, a very great additional grievance; and therefore whoever could find out a fair, cheap, and easy method of making these children sound and useful members of the commonwealth would deserve so well of the public as to have his statue set up for a preserver of the nation. . . .

EXAMINING THE MODEL. Swift uses several effective techniques of satirical writing.

First, he has selected a complex social problem: poverty and survival in a society of "haves" and "have-nots," Irish grievances against English oppression in the 18th century, and a religious clash between Protestant English and Catholic Irish. Satire is often used to point out political injustices, societal failings, or perversities of human nature. The subject of Swift's work covers all three.

Second, Swift speaks formally, using the tone of a concerned but realistic economist. The outrageousness of his idea to raise the children of the poor to be sold as food items is

continued on page 650

LESSON OVERVIEW

EXPRESSIVE/PERSUASIVE WRITING
Composing a Prose Satire

Language, Grammar, and Style

REGISTER AND TONE

INDIVIDUAL LEARNING STRATEGIES

MOTIVATION
Refer students to the complete selection, "A Modest Proposal" on page 643. Then have students take turns reading paragraphs, exaggerating the satirical tone of the piece.

READING PROFICIENCY
Have students summarize what they are being asked to do for each step of the assignment.

ENGLISH LANGUAGE LEARNING
See strategies for Reading Proficiency above that will also benefit students who are English language learners. It may also be helpful to have students work on vocabulary development by reviewing the Language Arts Survey 1.16, "Using Context Clues to Estimate Word Meaning."

SPECIAL NEEDS
You may want to pair students with special needs with another student or an aide who can help them complete their Graphic Organizer and develop their thesis. If students are having difficulty deciding on a topic, refer them to the table "Ways to Find a

INDIVIDUAL LEARNING STRATEGIES (CONT.)

Writing Topic" in the Language Arts Survey 2.7, "Choosing a Topic."

ENRICHMENT
Have students research other works of satire that they could use as models. One example is *The Rape of the Lock* by Alexander Pope. The poem recounts the story of a young woman, Belinda, whose lock of hair is stolen by an admirer. The event is treated like an epic tragedy, as the poem satirizes the superficial concerns of society women.

Prewriting

Finding Your Voice. Refer students to the Language Arts Survey 3.3, "Register, Tone, and Voice," for more information.

Identifying Your Audience. Remind students that satire will always poke fun at someone or something, and not everyone will like that, but that's okay. However, warn that if they are too harsh in their criticism, students may alienate some members of their audience. They should carefully evaluate their writing to make sure they are not being overly harsh or offensive. Refer students to the Language Arts Survey 2.4, "Identifying Your Audience" for a helpful chart on "Thinking About Your Audience."

Writing with a Plan. Refer students to the Language Arts Survey 2.7, "Choosing a Topic," and 2.12, "Freewriting."

GUIDED WRITING *Software*

See the Guided Writing Software for an extended version of this lesson that includes printable graphic organizers, extensive student models and student-friendly checklists, and self-, peer, and teacher evaluation features.

shocking in contrast to the seriousness of his tone.

Notice how his lofty diction, appearing to be sensitive and rational, appeals at the outset to the sadness of the street scene. It is a characteristic of satire to say nearly the opposite of what you mean.

He also exaggerates the negativity of the future for the children of the poor, doomed to a life of crime, immigration to a less "dear" country, or to become indentured servants. He is undoubtedly mocking the citizens who consider their society superior to others.

Swift maintains a mocking tone that is true to his voice. Later in the essay, he opines, "I shall now therefore humbly propose my own thoughts, which I hope will not be liable to the least objection and again, I do therefore humbly offer it to public consideration..." when it is becoming obvious that his proposal is anything but humble or unobjectionable, suggesting the English should eat Irish babies.

Prewriting

Finding Your Voice. Voice is the quality of a work that tells you that one person in particular wrote it. Your voice is inherent in everything you write. When you compose satire, choose a topic that you care about, and work to disguise that caring. The humor in the piece must be layered under your words. Your natural voice will be in the layers that hint at your concern.

Identifying Your Audience. Certainly your audience for this piece will include your peers. But, you will also want to appeal to a broader audience. Write about a topic of interest to adults as well as teens.

Writing with a Plan. As you write satire, consider first what you will satirize, and then the attitude you naturally feel toward the subject.

Much in modern life deserves to be satirized. Television programs deal with social realities and can be a starting point for your preparation. But avoid satirizing something that has been covered already. Tackle a contemporary problem area, a dilemma you have not seen satirized before. Or take a completely original approach to a persistent human shortcoming.

Sensational topics aren't appropriate. Examining violence in our culture, for example, is too agonizing to be subtly humorous, likewise human tragedy. Avoid a topic that would disparage other cultures, unless you are gently poking fun at your own.

Brainstorm ideas with your classmates. Consider current issues in the newspaper and everyday life:

- political and social institutions such as advertising, materialism and consumerism
- pervasive fast food chains
- television's place in our households
- cell phone mania
- our increasingly two class society
- a sports utility vehicle in every driveway
- ways we appreciate nature—or fail to
- music we listen to
- heroes we lionize
- styles and trends we follow

Choose two or three potential topics that interest you. Identify a problem within that topic area. Write out your opinion about that problem. Create an entirely original, outlandish solution to the problem. Think outside the box of conventional wisdom as you complete the following graphic organizer. Adam Costello plotted his satire this way:

Student Model—Graphic Organizer

TOPIC	PROBLEM	CAUSE	ORIGINAL SOLUTION
Senioritis	nonperformance in classes and/or easy	attitude: deserve a break, worked so hard classes	abolish attendance requirements senior year
TOPIC	PROBLEM	CAUSE	ORIGINAL SOLUTION

Drafting

Freewrite the first draft of the solution, keeping in mind the tone you wish to set, true to an audience of both adults and teens. Model Swift and maintain a serious tone and unemotional, formal diction. Persuade your audience of the benefits of your solution and build a convincing case for adopting your proposal, no matter how impractical it is. Do not be deterred by the arguments that people might make against your solution. Satire does not expect a counter-argument since it is meant to sound practical while being totally impractical. The layer of protest underneath the words is what the reader will internalize.

Student Model—Draft

An excerpt from Adam's rough draft

Limp Brain Eradication

Gives away too much. Too Critical!

Try to sound as though you're on the side of poor, overworked seniors from the beginning

Every high school student reaches a point where it's time to leave the high school halls. For most, it seems to be at the end of their fourth year of high school education, but in reality, the "leaving" occurs at the close of the junior year. Everyone chooses

"Words are the legs of the mind, they bear it about, carry it from point to point, bed it down at night, and keep it off the ground and out of the marsh and mists."

—Richard Edler

Self- and Peer Evaluation

Check your draft with these questions in mind.

- Where, if anywhere, have you given away too much about your solution too early in the piece?
- Is your tone considered and prudent, and the register of your voice diplomatic and professional throughout the piece?
- Where are examples of reasonableness leading up to your revelation of the "fix"?
- Where, are there examples of indignation at the cause of the problem? (These hints would allow the reader to infer true opinions.)
- Where, if anywhere, have you lapsed and come right out and stated your opinion?
- How innovative is your solution to the problem? How fresh is your overall approach?

Graphic Organizer

See the Guided Writing Resource for a blackline master of the Graphic Organizer for this lesson.

Drafting

Encourage students to use their completed Graphic Organizer modeled on page 651 to help them make sure they have gathered the essential information for their essays. For additional help, refer students to the Language Arts Survey 2.31–2.35, "Drafting."

Self- and Peer Evaluation

Have students use the checklist on this page for self- and peer evaluation.The checklist is intended to act as a student-friendly rubric that should help students identify specific evidence of writing strengths and areas needing improvement. Make sure they provide concrete suggestions for improvement or specific evidence of why the writing works. A blackline master of the checklist is available in the Guided Writing Resource.

Language, Grammar, and Style

Register and Tone

Lesson Overview

- In this lesson, students will be asked to do the following:
- Identify Register and Tone, 652
- Revise Use of Register and Tone, 654
- Use Register and Tone Effectively, 655

Introducing the Skill. Explain to students that using the right register and tone will help them in all areas of writing, not just satire.

Previewing the Skill. Refer students to the Language Arts Survey 3.3, "Register, Tone, and Voice" if you have not done so already.

Revising and Proofreading

A handout of the proofreading checklist is available in the Teacher's Resource Kit, Guided Writing Resource Book 2.45.

Language, Grammar, and Style

Register and Tone

Identifying Register and Tone. A **register** is a subset of language usage specific to a particular relationship between people. In talking to a friend, you usually speak in a register that is casual, warm, and open. In speaking to an official, you speak in a register that is polite but firm—the same register that person would use with you.

Swift's satirical essay demonstrates the use of a register that is pragmatic, that of the level-headed economist. He writes as though he is suggesting a marketing philosophy, having weighed the issue thoughtfully. Speaking within a different register would be too blatantly preposterous to be taken seriously:

> You know, it's really disgusting to walk anywhere in this city and run into these beggars with their filthy, snot-nosed, crying little brats, always begging for money. Why don't they just go out and get a job? Maybe we should just fatten up the little ones and barbecue the lot. At least they'd be useful!

Swift's **diction**, or word choice, contributes to the register of the dispassionate economist in this passage:

continued on page 653

simple classes for their final year of fun and games, or they make arrangements for release time to pursue other transitional interests, maybe a college class or two, etc. Their parents allow this lazy application of 1/18th of their child's life, 365 days of a year lost, because they know their darlings have worked very hard in those tough high school classes.

I would propose that we abolish attendance during the senior year entirely. No more waste of public education resources in teachers, buildings, athletic teams, and no more sleepy seniors, springtime disappearances, or poor role models for the underclassmen.

too negative

Sarcastic and judgmental

Too mean-spirited to be funny

can you soften?

Recast—you are negative and sarcastic, not satirical

Revising and Proofreading

As Adam examined his draft, he realized that he was too bluntly revealing his true feelings about slacking seniors. His first two paragraphs expressed negative facts about seniors and his title hinted too strongly at his solution. Adam decided that taking the position of a supporter of senioritis would allow him to exaggerate the position of the critics, and remain "in satirical character." He revised both his first paragraph and his title, which set his satire in motion.

Adam made his satire work by never alluding to the proclivity of seniors to take easy classes or slack off from school, thus wasting a year of their secondary education. This, of course, was his underlying point.

Take time now to look at your first draft. Revise your writing after considering the comments about Adam's draft and those you received during the self- and peer editing stage. Proofread your work to make sure it is free of errors in spelling, grammar, and punctuation.

Student Model—Revision

Reaching the Top
by Adam Costello

There comes a time in the affairs of high school students when they must lounge back and revel in their accomplishments. Eleven years of education is a long, hard road when you are young. It is right and appropriate that the senior year of high school be reserved for a well-deserved rest, a sabbatical from brain torque. The senior has reached the pinnacle of life and truly deserves some beach time, some sleep-in time, some late night movie time, to reflect on how far these efforts have carried him or her.

It is a known fact that as the senior year begins most students already know what they're going to do after that golden Graduation Day. Their mailboxes will have been stuffed with college literature and transcripts ready to be mailed out. True, some persnickety colleges hold applicants in limbo, waiting for senior year transcripts, but they aren't the colleges most seniors end up going to anyway. Statistics show this: very few high school graduates go to those colleges.

Parental support is critical—parents need to fend off any criticisms by overzealous teachers or counselors seemingly concerned about Johnny's reading and math abilities. With computers and our one-world marketplace, students don't really need all of those classes anyway. Maybe students from other countries could take a few of those jobs that require a stronger background in literature or math theory.

In the best interests of seniors and their ever-expanding world, I propose scaling back the senior year. This would best be accomplished by allowing seniors to check in with an attendance secretary once a week, midafternoon being most convenient for them (except in the

> …I propose to provide for them in such a manner as instead of being a charge upon their parents or the parish, or wanting food and raiment for the rest of their lives, they shall on the contrary contribute to the feeding, and partly to the clothing, of many thousands.

In this manner he uses logic to disguise the atrocity of killing babies of the poor and tanning their skins.

Tone is a writer's or speaker's attitude toward a subject. In exposition, tone reflects a writer's attitude toward the subject, but in satire that attitude is intentionally hidden. The writer maintains this tone by using **verbal irony**, in which the writer states the opposite of what he or she means in order to make a point. Verbal irony can be funny or serious. Satire, by definition, uses a tone that gives the writer's opinion authenticity in the midst of its very contrariness. Swift uses verbal irony when he knows readers will be disgusted by his suggestion and think he's gone too far in protesting the treatment of the Irish by the British:

> …and therefore whoever could find out a fair, cheap, and easy method of making these children sound and useful members of the commonwealth would deserve so well of the public as to have his statue set up for a preserver of the nation.

continued on page 654

Practicing the Skill. For additional practice revising and using the use of register and tone, have students work through the exercises in the following sections of the Language Arts Survey Resource located in the Teacher's Resource Kit: 3.3, "Register, Tone, and Voice," and 3.4, "Irony, Sarcasm, and Rudeness."

Sarcasm is another form of irony, but the difference is the speaker's intentions. People use sarcasm in order to criticize, hurt, or humiliate someone. Sarcasm differs from other forms of irony because it is mean-spirited.

Writers of satire should avoid sarcasm because it is openly unkind and reactions to it will dilute the effectiveness of your argument. Remember that the purpose of your prose satire is ultimately to persuade readers to change their behavior or at least to change the way they think about something—not to humiliate them.

Revising Use of Register and Tone. Adam's rough draft had sarcastic statements that required modification and rewriting. How would you rewrite this passage?

> Their parents allow this lazy application of 1/18th of their child's life, 365 days of a year lost, because they know their darlings have worked very hard in those tough high school classes.

To sharpen your ability to work with satire and avoid sarcasm, try this:

- Write down three sarcastic comments you have heard or said.
- Trade your statements with a classmate.
- Rewrite those three comments to show **verbal irony**, according to your understanding of the meaning.

continued on page 655

spring, as beach/sun time becomes critical), to check off a list of thoughts they've had during the week. This would keep seniors in the thinking mode and not allow them to slip backwards and forget everything they know. Everyone could earn A's and more credits by thinking.

Their critical thinking skills would be steadily reinforced, of course, by the accessibility of television, videotapes, movies, and computer games. Daytime television and talk shows would keep seniors grounded in reality and present the dilemmas and solutions to contemporary life—the life they must join all too soon. However, strategizing skills could be sharpened through computer games and the spirit of one-on-one competition. Never has there been a generation with so many resources at their very fingertips.

Practically speaking, the year would also be well spent accumulating Internet sites that could be used for upcoming college research papers. Setting up his or her files before going to college would allow the new college student to devote more time to those all important social skills.

Two additional benefits would accrue directly to the high school itself. By abolishing attendance in the senior year, there would be no further waste of public education resources in teachers, buildings, and athletic teams, freeing up monies for additional technology. Those teachers who have been around too long could be let go—who needs Brit Lit anyway? Moreover, underclassmen would enjoy smaller classes with no more sleepy seniors, and avoid the bad example of poor attendance during either the ski season or the beach season. This plan would spur on the underclassmen to stay in school and become seniors themselves, solving the dropout problem.

With a senior year devoted to rest, the first year of college would be smoother and more in line with making that transition to one last year of being young and carefree. College freshmen would be better able to cope with the targeted socializing required of their first year, and their enrichment in the social graces and circles of friendships would be enhanced. Contacts—it's all about contacts. These students would be ready to succeed.

I can see it now—rows of tanned, robust seniors on a golden Graduation Day in June, refreshed and smiling, arms around one another, with perfect handshakes and a joke for every occasion. We would not regret the respite this plan provides. Education would be put in its proper place as the incredibly hard work of eleven years of American schooling jelled in the mind of our talented youth, trained in the truly virtual life of the unburdened senior.

Publishing and Presenting

Satires deserve an audience, for they incite discussion. Approach the school newspaper about a series of editorials on topics of wide discussion or concern. Select satires appropriate for your community to submit to your local newspaper. Approach debaters in your school or world studies classes, to debate the issues that your satire addresses. Satire is supposed to prompt controversy. Stir one up!

Reflecting

Select one of the satires produced in your class and write a journal response to the position it takes. Address both sides of the issue, for there are always two sides. The ability to argue any point well is directly related to how well you understand your opponent's position.

Using Register and Tone Effectively. Look at your satire. Is the register you used the most appropriate for this piece? Are there sarcastic statements that need to be rewritten? Is your tone consistent with satire? Can you find examples where you could use verbal irony to achieve your satirical purpose(s)? Is your voice in tune with the satirical effect you wish to achieve?

For more information, see the Language Arts Survey 3.3, "Register, Tone, and Voice" and 3.4, "Irony, Sarcasm, and Rudeness."

"I have made my world and it is a much better world than I ever see outside."

—*Louise Nevelson*

Publishing and Presenting

Students may want to keep a portfolio of their writing. Refer students to the Language Arts Survey 2.48, "Maintaining a Writing Portfolio."

VOCABULARY DEVELOPMENT EXERCISES

Give students the following exercise.

Choose twenty words from the list on page 656. For each word, write a sentence that relates to something you have read in this unit. The vocabulary word need not have appeared in the selection to which you refer.

Example. Women writers like Anne Finch felt strong indignation when male writers told them writing was "unfeminine."

ADDITIONAL RESOURCES

UNIT 7 RESOURCE BOOK

- Vocabulary Worksheet
- Study Guide: Unit 7 Test
- Unit 7 Test

UNIT 7 REVIEW

The Restoration and the Eighteenth Century

Words for Everyday Use

Check your knowledge of the following vocabulary words from the selections in this unit. Write short sentences using these words in context to make the meaning clear. To review the definition or usage of a word, refer to the page number listed or the Glossary of Words for Everyday Use.

abhorrence, 620
abominate, 604
acute, 604
agitation, 602
ague, 591
arduous, 628
asperity, 631
asseveration, 609
avail, 624
blackguard, 638
celestial, 580
clemency, 638
compulsion, 623
conciliate, 630
confounded, 600
contriver, 603
cynical, 631
debarred, 575
desolation, 603
detract, 604
diffusive, 574
disdainful, 580
disposition, 620
drudge, 620
elude, 602
embargo, 600
eminent, 629
endeavor, 592
entail, 623
epoch, 628
err, 616
etymology, 629
extremities, 600
furrow, 637
hitherto, 604
ignominiously, 610
implicitly, 630
impotent, 603
indignation, 580
infallibly, 600
ingratiate, 602
insinuate, 630
insipid, 573
insolence, 621
junta, 600
lament, 624
lenity, 604
metaphysician, 638
odious, 602
oracle, 636
panegyric, 602
pernicious, 602
perpetual, 623
pervert, 602
posterity, 630
procure, 603
prodigious, 629
prodigy, 638
quell, 580
recapitulate, 602
redress, 624
regiment, 637
repose, 610
retired, 575
scruple, 603
solicit, 630
stipulate, 623
stratagem, 599
sublimely, 585
tribute, 603
veneration, 603
vivacity, 637

Literary Tools

Define the following terms, giving concrete examples of how they are used in the selections in this unit. To review a term, refer to the page number indicated or to the Handbook of Literary Terms.

alliteration, 584
allusion, 572, 578
anaphora, 584
anecdote, 627
argument, 619
assonance, 572
characterization, 607, 627
connotation, 619
consonance, 572
couplet, 614
denotation, 619
epigram, 614
fantasy, 599
irony, 599, 634
journal, 588
novel, 607
ode, 578
point of view, 588
satire, 599, 634
slant rhyme, 572
thesis, 619

Reflecting *on* Your Reading

Genre Studies

1. **Satire.** What is satire? What is being satirized in the following works in this unit: the selections from *Gulliver's Travels,* the selection from *The Life of Samuel Johnson,* "A Modest Proposal" (the Selections for Additional Reading), and the selection from *Candide* (in the Multicultural Extensions, page 635).

2. **Journals and Travelogues.** The eighteenth century was a great age for nonfiction writing. Among the most popular types of writing in that age were journals, travelogues, and biographies. Explain how each of the following works embodies this interest: *The Diary of Samuel Pepys, Gulliver's Travels, Oroonoko, The Life of Samuel Johnson,* and *Candide* (in the Multicultural Extensions, page 635).

Thematic Studies

3. **Reason.** Reread the couplets from Pope's *An Essay on Criticism.* What lines from Pope show that he highly valued reason and order? What lines show that he believed nature to be ruled by orderly laws? What arguments are set forth in "The Introduction," the selections from *Gulliver's Travels,* and "A Brief to Free a Slave"? What arguments are set forth in the following Selections for Additional Reading: "A Modest Proposal," the selection from *The Spectator,* and "A Short Song of Congratulations." How do these pieces demonstrate the importance that eighteenth-century writers placed on reason?

Historical and Biographical Studies

4. **Slavery.** Compare and contrast the selection from Aphra Behn's *Oroonoko* with Samuel Johnson's "A Brief to Free a Slave." What case does each work make against slavery?

REFLECTING ON YOUR READING

The prompts in "Reflecting on Your Reading" are suitable as topics for research papers. Refer to the Language Arts Survey, "Research Skills." (To evaluate research papers, see the evaluation forms for writing, revising, and proofreading in the Assessment Resource.)

These prompts in "Reflecting on Your Reading" can also be adapted for use as topics for oral reports or debates. Refer students to the Language Arts Survey 4, "Speaking and Listening." (To evaluate these projects, see the evaluation forms in the Assessment Resource.)

UNIT SKILLS OUTLINE

Literary Concepts
Allegory, 680, 681
Alliteration, 682, 684, 704, 708
Allusion, 694, 695
Apostrophe, 731, 734
Autobiography, 742, 747
Blank Verse, 696, 702
Byronic Hero, 724, 726
Catharsis, 742, 747
Character, 682, 684, 711, 713
Definition, 690, 693
Dialect, 672, 675
Didactic Criticism, 736, 740
Elegy, 664, 670
Free Verse, 696, 702
Haiku, 749, 751
Hymn, 672,675
Iambic Tetrameter, 720, 723
Image, 676, 677, 685, 687, 704, 708
Irony of Situation, 711, 713
Metaphor, 676, 677, 736, 740
Ode, 696, 702
Paradox, 731, 734
Parallelism, 724, 726
Pastoral, 680, 681
Personification, 714, 718
Repetition, 724, 726
Sensory Details, 749, 751
Setting, 685, 687
Simile, 720, 723
Sonnet, 694, 695, 729, 730
Speaker, 664, 670
Terza Rima, 714, 718
Theme, 690, 693, 729, 730

Writing Skills and Concepts
Travelogue, 752
Writing a Research Paper, 756

Language, Grammar, and Style
Cliché's and Euphemisms, 748
Common and Proper Nouns, 719
Compound Sentences, 678
Correcting Sentence Run-Ons, 727
Effective Documentation, 760
Identifying Direct and Indirect Objects, 752
Prepositional Phrases, 688
Split Infinitives, 741
Subject-Verb Agreement, 735
Verb Tense, 703

Painter's Honeymoon, 1864. Frederick Leighton.
Museum of Fine Arts, Boston.

GOALS/OBJECTIVES

Studying this unit will enable students to

- explore works written during the Romantic Era and ideas and themes characteristic of the Romantic Period
- enjoy and appreciate Romantic poetry and prose
- summarize Wordsworth's theory of poetry and explain its significance for English literature
- describe the status of women in England during the Romantic Era
- define Romanticism
- write a research paper
- use effective documentation

Thanks to the human heart by which we live,
Thanks to its tenderness, its joys, and fears,
To me the meanest flower that blows can give
Thoughts that do often lie too deep for tears.

—William Wordsworth
"Ode: Intimations of Immortality"

CROSS-CURRICULAR CONNECTIONS

TEACHING THE MULTIPLE INTELLIGENCES

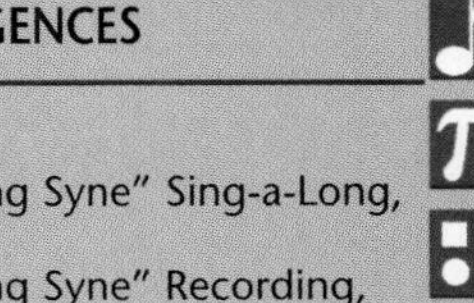

TEACHING THE MULTIPLE INTELLIGENCES (CONT.)

Continued on page 660

ADDITIONAL RESOURCES

Unit 8 Resource Book
- Selection Check Test 4.8.1
- Selection Test 4.8.2

CROSS-CURRICULAR CONNECTION

History. Several Romantic poets and writers were active supporters of the French Revolution. Robert Burns voiced his unreserved support. Mary Wollstonecraft wrote *A Vindication of the Rights of Men* as a direct response to Edmund Burke's *Reflections on the Revolution in France*, published in 1790, which attacked the French Revolution and its English supporters. To observe the revolution herself, Wollstonecraft moved to Paris at the end of 1792 and lived there until 1794. Wordsworth lived in France from November 1791 to December 1792 and became a passionate supporter of the democratic revolution, although he later became disillusioned with events in France.

CROSS-CURRICULAR ACTIVITIES

History. Students can work independently or in small groups to research trends in American literature during this time period. Have students consider the following questions: Did literary trends in England make their way to America? Were American poets affected by revolutionary ideals in the same way?

TEACHING THE MULTIPLE INTELLIGENCES (CONT. FROM PAGE 659)

Romantic Perspectives, 721
Role Play, 728
Nature Metaphor, 749

Intra/Interpersonal
Epitaph on Elizabeth, L.H., 668
Women's Rights Panel Discussion

Naturalist
Cemetary Visitation, 665
Ecology, 666
Environmental Science, 698
Aspects of Nature, 699
Nature Reflection, 710
Nature Metaphor, 749

THE ROMANTIC ERA (1785–1832)

During the **Romantic Era,** from 1785 to 1832, artists, philosophers, and writers rebelled against the rational, orderly forms of Neoclassicism, creating works that celebrated emotion over reason, nature over human artifice, ordinary people over aristocrats, and spontaneity and wildness over decorum and control. This era of dramatic change encompassed the early years of America as an independent nation, the French Revolution, and major civil and political reforms in England.

Capture of the Bastille, July 14, 1789. Claude Cholat. The Granger Collection, NY.

Political Developments in the Romantic Era

King George III, of the royal house of Hanover, was king of England from 1760 to 1820. According to some historians, his antagonistic policies toward the American colonies were directly responsible for the **American Revolution.** The American Revolution officially ended with the signing of the Treaty of Paris in 1783. The **French Revolution** began in 1789 with an attack on the Bastille prison by citizen revolutionaries. Few times in history have seen such political and social tumult. As Dickens characterized them half a century later, these were "the best of times and the worst of times"—the best because they saw a birth of freedom and equality, the worst because the cost of freedom and equality was bloodshed.

France declared war on England in 1793. **Napoleon Bonaparte** (1769–1821) and the French army were finally defeated by the Duke of Wellington at Waterloo in 1815.

When George III died in 1820, **George IV** took the throne and held it until his death in 1830. **William IV,** brother of George IV, ruled from 1830 to 1837. The weaknesses of these three kings led to strong prime ministers, which in turn led to civil reforms,

Literary Events

➤ = British Events

1712–78. French philosopher Jean-Jacques Rousseau plants seeds of Romanticism and revolution by praising nature and emotion and by championing rights of ordinary people

➤1796. Robert Burns dies

➤1798. Wordsworth and Coleridge publish *Lyrical Ballads*

1785 — 1790 — 1795 — 1800 — 1805

➤1783. Treaty of Paris ends American Revolution against British rule

1789. French Revolution begins

1799. Napoleon becomes head of French government

➤1801. Act of Union creates United Kingdom of Great Britain, annexing Ireland

1802. In Haiti, Toussaint L'Ouverture leads slave rebellion

1803. United States purchases Louisiana Territory from France

1804. Napoleon becomes emperor of France, betraying revolutionary ideals

Historical Events

including laws allowing labor unions to organize and restoring economic and religious freedoms to Roman Catholics. By 1832, parliamentary seats were redistributed in a more equitable apportionment, and the right to vote was given to men of the middle class, thereby depriving aristocrats of overwhelming majorities in Parliament.

The Meeting of Sir Walter Scott and Robert Burns. C. M. Hardie. The Granger Collection, NY.

The Pre-Romantic Poets

The late eighteenth century marked the end of the Enlightenment and the beginning of the Romantic Era. The end of the century was notable for the emergence of **Pre-Romantic poetry.** The poets of this period showed tendencies toward Romanticism in their emotional explorations and in their perceptions of nature as wild and untamed. However, they followed the Neoclassical model of imitating traditional literary forms. Among the best of these transitional poets were Thomas Gray, Robert Burns, and William Blake.

Thomas Gray (1716–1771), a lifelong scholar, was not a prolific poet, but the few poems that he wrote reflect a combination of Neoclassical and Romantic ideals. His most famous poem, **"Elegy Written in a Country Courtyard"** (page 575), is written in a style emulating the classical Greek elegy, but it is thoroughly Romantic in its praise of common people.

Robert Burns (1759–1796) won acclaim as the national poet of Scotland. Burns avoided the formal, restrained language of the Neoclassical writers and used instead his native Scottish dialect. This use of everyday speech in literature shocked some of Burns's contemporaries, but it endeared Burns to the rural and working classes of Scotland. In addition to writing poetry, Burns preserved old Scottish folk songs, which he collected and compiled.

William Blake (1757–1827) was a poet, painter, mystic, and visionary. Much of Blake's writing is an attack on the complacent rationality and orderliness of the

➤1812. Lord Byron publishes *Childe Harold's Pilgrimage*

➤1820. Keats publishes "Ode on a Grecian Urn"

➤1819. Percy Bysshe Shelley publishes "Ode to the West Wind"

➤1818. Mary Shelley publishes *Frankenstein, or the Modern Prometheus*

➤1813. Jane Austen publishes *Pride and Prejudice*

1810 | 1815 | 1820 | 1825 | 1830

1810. Simón Bolívar leads rebellions against Spanish colonial rule in South America

➤1811. King George III is declared insane and removed from throne

1815. Napoleon is defeated at Waterloo

➤1829. Catholic Emancipation Act passed

➤1832. First Reform Act extends voting rights to more males

Cross-Curricular Activities

Science. Point out that the Romantic Era began at the end of the eighteenth century, a period of great advances in the scientific world. Have students research events that happened in the world of science during the Romantic Era. Students should then discuss or write about whether the revolutionary spirit of the age affected scientific endeavors as it did political and artistic ones.

Social Studies. The Romantic Era was a period of turbulence with revolutions erupting in the United States, France, and South America. Have students consider the cost of change to the average person. Students can research a particular country and write an article about the changes that occurred.

SELECTION CHECK TEST 4.8.1 WITH ANSWERS

Political Developments in the Romantic Era

1. How might King George have contributed to the American Revolution? **Some believe that his antagonism toward the American colonies caused the Revolution.**
2. The French Revolution began when the citizens of Paris attacked what structure? **They attacked the Bastille prison.**
3. How did English aristocrats lose political power during this period? **Responses may vary; parliamentary seats were redistributed and middle-class men could vote.**
4. What did Rousseau's idea of a social contract say about government's power? **It says that governments hold power only by the consent of the governed.**
5. Why did Dickens call this period "the best of times and the worst of times"? **He suggested this because great suffering led to great social achievements.**

Neoclassic and Romantic Literature

The following elements and descriptors identify either Neoclassical or Romantic writing.

Put an (N) by any associated with Neoclassical writing and an (R) by those that are generally associated with Romantic writing.

1. traditional rhythms and elements **N**
2. lives of aristocrats **N**
3. spontaneity **R**
4. emotion **R**
5. reason **N**
6. compliance with authority **N**
7. religious freedom **R**
8. lives of ordinary people **R**
9. rebellion **R**
10. joy of nature **R**

Works of the Pre-Romantic and Romantic periods

1. considered the major literary form of the Romantic era **B**
2. contains elements of mystery, suspense, magic, and the macabre **E**
3. epitomized by the works of Jane Austen **F**
4. may be published each day, week, month, or year **A**
5. often set in haunted castles or the wild outdoors **E**
6. often contained both fictional and nonfictional characters **C**
7. epitomized by the works of Coleridge, Wordsworth, Keats, and Byron **B**

Enlightenment. Blake was unconventional not only in his poetry, but also in the way in which he published his books. He engraved designs and text onto a copper plate covered with wax; then, after applying acid to bring the design into relief, he printed a page. Each page was hand-painted with watercolors. This process limited Blake's production but made each book a work of art.

Poetry in the Romantic Era

The true beginning of the Romantic Era came with the publication in 1798 of ***Lyrical Ballads,*** a collection of poems by **William Wordsworth** (1770–1850) and **Samuel Taylor Coleridge** (1772–1834). In the preface to that book, Wordsworth explained his revolutionary theory of poetry. He stated that poetry should be about common people and events and should be written in the language of ordinary men and women. This idea of the nobility of ordinary people owed much to the American and French Revolutions and to the writings of the French philosopher **Jean-Jacques Rousseau.** Rousseau celebrated the **noble savage** and held that governments derive power only from the consent of the governed, through what he called the **social contract.**

Following in the footsteps of Wordsworth and Coleridge were the "second generation" of Romantic Era poets. These younger poets—**George Gordon, Lord Byron** (1788–1824), **Percy Bysshe Shelley** (1792–1822), and **John Keats** (1795–1821)—carried on the tradition of Wordsworth and Coleridge, celebrating emotion over reason and nature over science.

Prose in the Romantic Era

Although poetry was the major literary form during the Romantic Era, major strides were also made during this time in the development of two forms of prose—the **essay** and the **novel.** Periodicals became popular, providing outlets for essayists such as **Charles Lamb** (1775–1834), **William Hazlitt** (1778–1830), and **Thomas DeQuincey** (1785–1859), and new types of novels emerged. Three major types of Romantic Era novels are the Gothic novel, the novel of manners, and the historical romance.

Gothic novels, or **Gothic romances,** are long stories containing elements of suspense, mystery, magic, and the macabre, with exotic settings such as haunted castles and untamed wildernesses. Although the word Gothic originally implied "medieval," by the time of the Romantic Era, the word had assumed connotations of the supernatural and the macabre. ***The Castle of Otranto*** by Hugh Walpole (1717–1797) was the first Gothic novel. **Anne Radcliffe's** (1764–1823) ***The Mysteries of Udolpho,*** published in 1794, and **Mary Shelley's** (1797–1851) ***Frankenstein,*** published in 1818, are examples of other Gothic novels of the period.

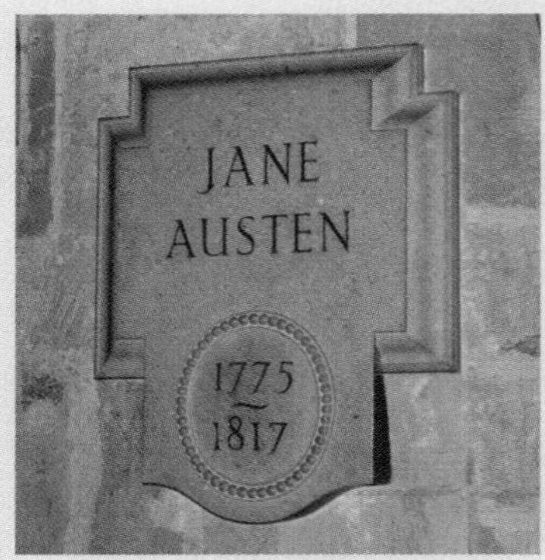

Jane Austen's plaque, Poets' Corner, Westminster Abbey. Courtesy, The Dean and Chaplaincy, Westminster Abbey.

The **novel of manners** presented a satirical look at society in book-length prose reminiscent of earlier works by Swift and others. In the Romantic Era, **Jane Austen** (1775–1817) produced what are widely considered to be the greatest works in the genre, including ***Sense and Sensibility*** (1811) and ***Pride and Prejudice*** (1813).

Historical romance novels, set in a period before the life of the author, usually depict historical events and contain both fictional and nonfictional characters. Early historical romance novels were often set in medieval days, with knights and fair damsels as main characters. **Sir Walter Scott's** (1771–1832) ***Waverly*** (1814) and ***Ivanhoe*** (1820) epitomize the genre.

SELECTION CHECK TEST 4.8.1 WITH ANSWERS (CONT.)

8. emotional and enamored with nature, but written in traditional literary forms **G**
9. exemplified by the works of Lamb, Hazlitt, and DeQuincey **D**
10. exemplified by the works of Gray, Burns, and Blake **G**

a. periodical
b. poetry
c. historic romance novel
d. essay
e. Gothic novel
f. novel of manners
g. Pre-Romantic poetry

ECHOES

THE ROMANTIC ERA

"Liberty, equality, fraternity."

—Rallying cry of the French Revolution

"The road of excess leads to the palace of wisdom."

—William Blake, *The Marriage of Heaven and Hell*

"Every thing that lives is holy."

—William Blake, "A Song of Liberty"

"Dismissing then those pretty feminine phrases, which the men condescendingly use to soften our slavish dependence, and despising that weak elegancy of mind, exquisite sensibility, and sweet docility of manners, supposed to be the sexual characteristics of the weaker vessel, I wish to shew that elegance is inferior to virtue, that the first object of laudable ambition is to obtain a character as a human being, regardless of the distinction of sex."

—Mary Wollstonecraft, *A Vindication of the Rights of Woman*

"To combine the child's sense of wonder and novelty with . . . appearances . . . familiar . . . this is the character and privilege of genius."

—Samuel Taylor Coleridge, *Biographia Literaria*

"His popular, inartificial style gets rid (at a blow) of all the trappings of verse, of all the high places of poetry . . . to return to the simplicity of truth and nature."

—William Hazlitt, writing about William Wordsworth

"Then, dearest Maiden, move along these
shades
In gentleness of heart; with gentle hand
Touch—for there is a spirit in the woods."

—William Wordsworth, "Nutting"

"Men of England, wherefore plough
For the lords who lay ye low?
Wherefore weave with toil and care
The rich robes your tyrants wear?"

—Percy Bysshe Shelley, "A Song"

Painter's Honeymoon, [Detail], 1864. Frederick Lord Leighton. Museum of Fine Arts, Boston.

ADDITIONAL QUESTIONS AND ACTIVITIES

In small groups, have students take turns reading quotations aloud. After each quotation is read, have students brainstorm to make predictions about Romantic poetry and Romantic poets. For additional instruction, refer students to the Language Arts Survey, 1.12, "Seeking Knowledge as an Active Reader."

Have students write the following four categories on a piece of paper: *Emotion versus Reason, Nature versus Human Artifice, Ordinary People versus Aristocrats, Spontaneity/ Wildness versus Control.* Then ask students to read the quotations on this page and to assign each quotation to one or more of the categories. Students can discuss reasons for their decisions in small groups or as a class.

Have students discuss how Wollstonecraft's quote could be taken as a rallying cry for a feminist revolution.

ADDITIONAL RESOURCES

UNIT 8 RESOURCE BOOK
- Selection Worksheet 8.1
- Selection Check Test 4.8.3
- Selection Test 4.8.4
- Speaking and Listening Resource 4.19

VOCABULARY FROM THE SELECTION

dirge	jocund
ignoble	obscure
ingenuous	provoke

GRAPHIC ORGANIZER

Speaker: intelligent, honest, melancholy

READER'S JOURNAL

Suggest that students think about what friends or family members might say about them.

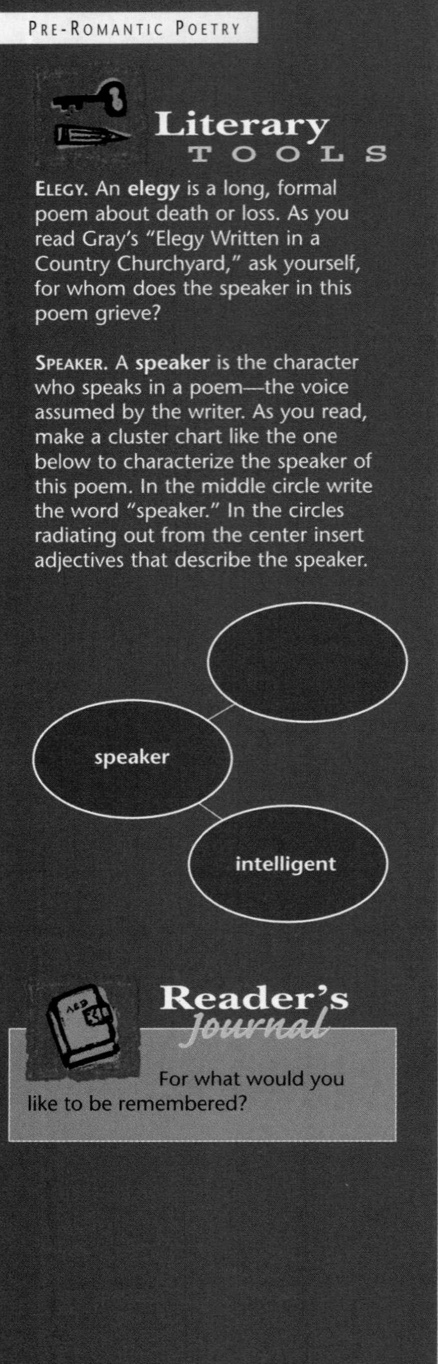

Literary TOOLS

ELEGY. An **elegy** is a long, formal poem about death or loss. As you read Gray's "Elegy Written in a Country Churchyard," ask yourself, for whom does the speaker in this poem grieve?

SPEAKER. A **speaker** is the character who speaks in a poem—the voice assumed by the writer. As you read, make a cluster chart like the one below to characterize the speaker of this poem. In the middle circle write the word "speaker." In the circles radiating out from the center insert adjectives that describe the speaker.

Reader's Journal

For what would you like to be remembered?

"ELEGY WRITTEN IN A Country Churchyard"

BY THOMAS GRAY

About the AUTHOR

Thomas Gray (1716–1771) was born in London to middle-class parents. Educated at Eton and later at Cambridge, he left the university without a degree to travel in Europe. Gray returned to Cambridge in 1742, where he began to write poetry, his first odes publishing in 1747.

Gray did not produce a great volume of verse, but he wrote carefully, bringing each poem to a level of perfection rarely achieved before or since. Characteristics that distinguish Gray's verse include a unique sensitivity to landscape and a strain of melancholy that shows him to have had a dignified, tragic view of life. Some contemporaries criticized Gray's frequent use of inverted sentences. However, Gray countered that "the language of the age is never the language of poetry." Continuing to write poetry through 1769, he lived the life of a scholar, traveling and devoting himself to the study of pre-Elizabethan poetry and Old Norse and Welsh literature.

About the SELECTION

Although Thomas Gray was a scholar and an eccentric recluse, he wrote the most well-known and beloved tribute to common people in English poetry: **"Elegy Written in a Country Churchyard."** An *elegy* is a long, formal poem about death or loss. Even Gray's harshest critics have acknowledged the importance of this poem. One critic pointed out that although the language of the poem is unique and original, readers recognize in it an echo of their own feelings and ideas. The universality of this work—its applicability to all times and places—makes it one of the masterpieces of world literature.

GOALS/OBJECTIVES

Studying this lesson will enable student to
- empathize with the speaker's feelings of loss and grief and the speaker's celebration of simple lives
- describe Gray's literary contributions and explain why some of his peers criticized his writing style
- define *elegy* and *speaker* and recognize and explain examples of each in the selection
- conduct a research on local churchyards

ELEGY WRITTEN IN A
Country Churchyard

THOMAS GRAY

A Country Churchyard, c.1797–98. Thomas Girtin. Fitzwilliam Museum, University of Cambridge, UK.

The curfew tolls the knell of parting day,
  The lowing herd wind slowly o'er the lea,[1]
The plowman homeward plods his weary way,
  And leaves the world to darkness and to me.

Now fades the glimmering landscape on the sight,
  And all the air a solemn stillness holds,
Save where the beetle wheels his droning flight,
  And drowsy tinklings lull the distant folds;

Save that from yonder ivy-mantled tower
  The moping owl does to the moon complain
Of such, as wandering near her secret bower,
  Molest her ancient solitary reign.

At what time of day does the poem take place?

1. **lea.** Meadow

ANSWER TO GUIDED READING QUESTION

1. The poem takes place at dusk.

INDIVIDUAL LEARNING STRATEGIES

MOTIVATION
If possible, allow students to visit a cemetery. What kind of things do they see? Which epitaph is most intriguing? Why?

READING PROFICIENCY
Students may benefit from reading the Prereading page before they begin reading the selection. Also suggest that students read through the vocabulary words and footnotes.

ENGLISH LANGUAGE LEARNERS
Remind students that the poem's word order often does not follow the usual patterns of spoken English.

SPECIAL NEEDS
Allow students to work together on answering the Guided Reading questions, and the Recall questions in the Investigate, Inquire, and Imagine section.

ENRICHMENT
Encourage students to discuss Gray's statement that "the language of the age is never the language of poetry." Ask them to suggest modern-day poetry or other literary forms that support or contradict Gray's belief.

ANSWERS TO GUIDED READING QUESTIONS

1. The "narrow cell" is the grave.
2. The speaker is referring to the village forefathers, who were farmers.
3. Ambition and grandeur discredit the value of simplicity and usefulness.
4. The paths of glory eventually lead to the grave, or to death.

CROSS-CURRICULAR ACTIVITIES

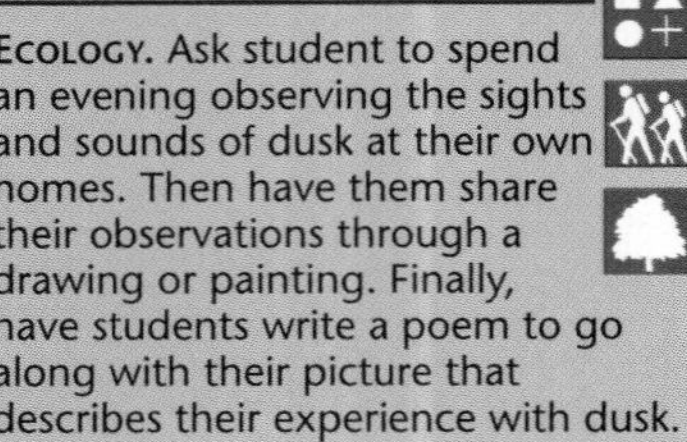

Ecology. Ask student to spend an evening observing the sights and sounds of dusk at their own homes. Then have them share their observations through a drawing or painting. Finally, have students write a poem to go along with their picture that describes their experience with dusk.

LITERARY TECHNIQUE

Elegy. The term **elegy** is sometimes applied to any poem written in elegiac meter. Elegiac meter consists of a dactylic hexameter line. This meter was thought to be appropriate for elegies and reflective or meditative poems. It was only in the seventeenth century that the term became limited to poems of death and loss. Milton's *Lycidas* (1637), which mourns the death of Edward King, a student of Milton, seems to have been of importance in this change. In the twentieth century the term has again expanded to include works of deep reflection and nostalgia.

Beneath those rugged elms, that yew tree's shade,
Where heaves the turf in many a moldering heap,
Each in his narrow cell forever laid,
The rude[2] forefathers of the hamlet[3] sleep.

Yew trees were often planted in cemeteries. What is the "narrow cell" referred to in line 15?

The breezy call of incense-breathing Morn,
The swallow twittering from the straw-built shed,
The cock's shrill clarion, or the echoing horn,
No more shall rouse them from their lowly bed.

For them no more the blazing hearth shall burn,
Or busy housewife ply her evening care;
No children run to lisp their sire's return,
Or climb his knees the envied kiss to share.

To whom is the speaker referring?

Oft did the harvest to their sickle yield,
Their furrow oft the stubborn glebe[4] has broke;
How jocund did they drive their team afield!
How bowed the woods beneath their sturdy stroke!

Let not Ambition mock their useful toil,
Their homely joys, and destiny obscure;
Nor Grandeur hear with a disdainful smile
The short and simple annals of the poor.

How does the speaker feel about ambition and grandeur?

The boast of heraldry, the pomp of power,
And all that beauty, all that wealth e'er gave,
Awaits alike the inevitable hour.
The paths of glory lead but to the grave.

What does the speaker say about the paths of glory?

Nor you, ye proud, impute[5] to these the fault,
If Memory o'er their tomb no trophies raise,
Where through the long-drawn aisle and fretted[6] vault
The pealing anthem swells the note of praise.

Can storied urn or animated bust
Back to its mansion call the fleeting breath?

2. **rude.** Ignorant
3. **hamlet.** Small village
4. **glebe.** Soil
5. **impute.** To attribute
6. **fretted.** Decorated with a raised design of intersecting lines

Words for Everyday Use

jo • cund (jäk´ ənd) *adj.*, cheerful, pleasant (used in poem as an adverb). *The jocund host set the tone for the lively party.*

ob • scure (əb skyo͞or´) *adj.*, faint, undefined. *The point of the lecturer's speech was so obscure that most people left the auditorium confused.*

Can Honor's voice provoke the silent dust,
Or Flattery soothe the dull cold ear of Death?

Perhaps in this neglected spot is laid
Some heart once pregnant with celestial fire;
Hands that the rod of empire might have swayed,
Or waked to ecstasy the living lyre.

But Knowledge to their eyes her ample page
Rich with the spoils of time did ne'er unroll;
Chill Penury[7] repressed their noble rage,
And froze the genial current of the soul.

Full many a gem of purest ray serene,
The dark unfathomed caves of ocean bear:
Full many a flower is born to blush unseen,
And waste its sweetness on the desert air.

To what or whom does the speaker compare a flower in the desert?

Some village Hampden,[8] that with dauntless breast
The little tyrant of his fields withstood;
Some mute inglorious Milton[9] here may rest,
Some Cromwell[10] guiltless of his country's blood.

The applause of listening senates to command,
The threats of pain and ruin to despise,
To scatter plenty o'er a smiling land,
And read their history in a nation's eyes,

Their lot forbade: nor circumscribed alone
Their growing virtues, but their crimes confined;
Forbade to wade through slaughter to a throne,
And shut the gates of mercy on mankind,

What positive side of living a simple life is pointed out in this stanza?

The struggling pangs of conscious truth to hide,
To quench the blushes of ingenuous shame,

7. **Penury.** Poverty
8. **Hampden.** John Hampden was a member of Parliament who defended the rights of the people.
9. **Milton.** English poet, author of *Paradise Lost*
10. **Cromwell.** Oliver Cromwell, ruler of England during the Commonwealth Period, or Puritan Interregnum

WORDS FOR EVERYDAY USE

pro • voke (prō vōk´) *vt.*, stir up action or feeling. *Such angry threats are sure to provoke a fight.*

in • gen • u • ous (in jen´ yo͞o əs) *adj.*, artless, naive. *The child's ingenuous answers charmed the reporters.*

ANSWERS TO GUIDED READING QUESTIONS

1. The speaker compares a flower in the desert to the life of a poor villager whose potential is never realized.
2. Simple life shuns following an evil path to grandeur and upholds mercy toward others.

ADDITIONAL QUESTIONS AND ACTIVITIES

Why is Hampden an appropriate figure for the speaker to invoke? How is Hampden related to the poem's theme?

Answers

Hampden defended the rights of the people. During his life, he spoke for the poor, unrecognized people, just as the speaker does in the poem.

ANSWERS TO GUIDED READING QUESTIONS

1. The sight of the "frail memorial"—the gravestone—causes the speaker to sigh.
2. Religious inscriptions appear on many gravestones. The purpose of these "holy texts" is to teach and speak to death.
3. The lines recall pleasures such as sunrise, morning dew, and a babbling brook. The lines recall human woes such as "hopeless love."

LITERARY TECHNIQUE

Neoclassical Elements. Gray's poetry bridges the Neoclassical and Romantic movements. Neoclassical elements, such as elegiac form and reference to the Muse, are combined with the Romantic subject of the common person.

Or heap the shrine of Luxury and Pride
With incense kindled at the Muse's flame.

Far from the madding crowd's ignoble strife,
Their sober wishes never learned to stray;
Along the cool sequestered vale of life
They kept the noiseless tenor of their way.

Yet even these bones from insult to protect
Some frail memorial still erected nigh,
With uncouth rhymes and shapeless sculpture decked,
Implores the passing tribute of a sigh.

What causes the speaker to sigh?

Their name, their years, spelt by the unlettered Muse,
The place of fame and elegy supply:
And many a holy text around she strews,
That teach the rustic moralist to die.

What is written on the gravestones? What purpose is served by these "holy texts"?

For who to dumb Forgetfulness a prey,
This pleasing anxious being e'er resigned,
Left the warm precincts of the cheerful day,
Nor cast one longing lingering look behind?

On some fond breast the parting soul relies,
Some pious drops the closing eye requires;
Even from the tomb the voice of Nature cries,
Even in our ashes live their wonted fires.

For thee, who mindful of the unhonored dead
Dost in these lines their artless tale relate;
If chance, by lonely contemplation led,
Some kindred spirit shall inquire thy fate,

Haply some hoary-headed swain may say,
"Oft have we seen him at the peep of dawn
Brushing with hasty steps the dews away
To meet the sun upon the upland lawn.

What simple pleasures of the rustic life are recalled in these lines? What human woes are also recalled?

"There at the foot of yonder nodding beech
That wreathes its old fantastic roots so high,

Words for Everyday Use

ig • no • ble (ig nō´ bəl) *adj.*, dishonorable, mean. *The politician's cruel lies about his opponent confirm the reports of his ignoble behavior.*

His listless length at noontide would he stretch,
And pore upon the brook that babbles by.

"Hard by yon wood, now smiling as in scorn,
Muttering his wayward fancies he would rove,
Now drooping, woeful wan, like one forlorn,
Or crazed with care, or crossed in hopeless love.

"One morn I missed him on the customed hill,
Along the heath and near his favorite tree;
Another came; nor yet beside the rill,
Nor up the lawn, nor at the wood was he;

What line in the poem shows that death comes unexpectedly, in the middle of life's pleasures and woes?

"The next with <u>dirges</u> due in sad array
Slow through the churchway path we saw him borne.
Approach and read (for thou canst read) the lay,
Graved on the stone beneath yon aged thorn."

The Epitaph

Here rests his head upon the lap of Earth
A youth to Fortune and to Fame unknown.
Fair Science[11] *frowned not on his humble birth,*
And Melancholy marked him for her own.

Large was his bounty, and his soul sincere,
Heaven did a recompense as largely send:
He gave to Misery all he had, a tear,
He gained from Heaven ('twas all he wished) a friend.

What did the simple person give during his life? What did he receive?

No farther seek his merits to disclose,
Or draw his frailties from their dread abode
(There they alike in trembling hope repose),
The bosom of his Father and his God. ■

11. **Science.** Learning

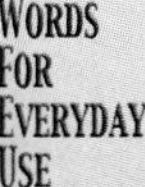

dirge (durj) *n.*, funeral song. *As the mourners entered the cathedral, the organist began to play a <u>dirge</u>.*

ANSWERS TO GUIDED READING QUESTIONS

1. "One morn I missed him on the customed hill" (line 109) speaks of sudden loss.
2. The simple person gave "to Misery all he had, a tear,/He gained from Heaven . . . a friend."

SELECTION CHECK TEST 4.8.3 WITH ANSWERS

Checking Your Reading

1. At dusk, what is left "to darkness and to me"? **The world is left.**
2. Where do paths of glory lead? **They lead to the grave.**
3. What might the villagers have done if they weren't born as poor villagers? **They might have achieved greatness.**
4. What does the "hoary-headed swain" say happened to the younger man? **He died.**
5. What are the last three stanzas about? **They are an epitaph for the young man.**

Vocabulary in Context

Fill each blank with the most appropriate word from the Words for Everyday Use. You may have to change the tense of the word.

jocund obscure provoke
ingenuous ignoble dirge

1. Della realized that purchasing the car had been a(n) **<u>ingenuous</u>** mistake.
2. The rainwater made the route marked on the map **<u>obscure</u>**, so we soon got lost.
3. In his will, my uncle requested that no **<u>dirges</u>** be played at his funeral.
4. The **<u>jocund</u>** sales associate put us in such good humor that we bought many things.
5. We couldn't help but be **<u>provoked</u>** by the speaker's moving account of the tragedy.

Literary Tools

1. What is an elegy? **An elegy is a long, formal poem about death or loss.**
2. What is an epitaph? **An epitaph is an inscription or verse on a tomb.**

SELECTION CHECK TEST 4.8.3 WITH ANSWERS (CONT.)

3. What is the rhyme scheme of the following stanza? **The rhyme scheme is abab.**

The breezy call of incense-breathing Morn,
The swallow twittering from the straw-built shed,
The cock's shrill clarion, or the echoing horn,
No more shall rouse them from their lowly bed.

RESPOND TO THE SELECTION

Suggest that students start their search for examples by examining the epitaph, in which the speaker mentions fame.

ANSWERS TO INVESTIGATE, INQUIRE, AND IMAGINE

RECALL

1a. They lament the deaths of the village forefathers, who were poor farmers.

2a. The speaker warns that those in power should not believe themselves beyond the reach of death or believe themselves to be innately superior to the poor.

3a. Someone not born to wealth and privilege might have many talents that will never be recognized.

INTERPRET

1b. The farmers' closeness to nature, their loving families, and their hard work appeals to the speaker.

2b. In the late eighteenth century in England, the rich believed themselves superior to the poor.

3b. The common people might have developed their talents if they had been given the opportunities of the privileged classes such as education.

ANALYZE

4a. Gray uses images of animals returning to the barns from the fields: lowing herds, droning beetles, moping owls. There are also images of fading light, stillness and "drowsy" bells tinkling. These images create a mood of quietude and peace, and encourage contemplation and stillness. They also are traditionally images that call to mind death—sleeping, fading light, and the end of the day.

SYNTHESIZE

4b. The lives of the farmers are simple, linked to nature, and unclouded by the frantic rush for power and wealth that drives the lives of so many. It is the very simplicity, honesty, and peace of the rural life that appeals to Gray and which he honors in this poem. A mood of stillness, contemplation and peace in the context of the natural world is, therefore an appropriate mood to open this poem.

Respond *to the* SELECTION

Do you agree with Gray that a simple life of honest hard work is as desirable as a life of fame and fortune? Why or why not?

INVESTIGATE, Inquire, *Imagine*

Recall: GATHERING FACTS

1a. What do lines 13 through 28 lament?

2a. Of what does the speaker warn in lines 29 through 44?

3a. Paraphrase the speaker's message in lines 45 through 80?

Interpret: FINDING MEANING

1b. What about the farmers' lives does the speaker find appealing?

2b. Why does the speaker assume that the powerful will criticize the poor?

3b. What might give these common people an opportunity to express their talents in the world at large?

Analyze: TAKING THINGS APART

4a. What images are used in the opening four stanzas of the poem? What mood or feeling is created by these images?

Synthesize: BRINGING THINGS TOGETHER

4b. How does this mood relate to the theme of the poem? What is it about the rustic lives of the farmers buried in the churchyard that makes this mood an appropriate opening for this poem?

Evaluate: MAKING JUDGMENTS

5a. How does Gray attempt to portray the simple, rustic life as attractive and desirable? How effectively does the poem do this?

Extend: CONNECTING IDEAS

5b. In what way are the poor equal to the rich? Do you think modern attitudes toward the poor and uneducated would have pleased Gray? Do those with power and wealth view the poor as potential Miltons and Cromwells but for the lack of education, as he hopes in lines 59-60, or would they see the poor with mocking and disdain, as he fears in lines 29-32? Do you agree with Gray's attitude toward a simple, uneducated life? Why, or why not?

Understanding *Literature*

ELEGY. Review the definition for **elegy** in the Handbook of Literary Terms. For whom does the speaker in this poem grieve? Given that elegies are usually written about famous people, what makes this elegy unique? Explain.

SPEAKER. Review the definition for **speaker** and the cluster chart you made for Literary Tools in the Prereading for this selection. What can you infer about the speaker of this poem? What sort of person is he?

ANSWERS TO INVESTIGATE, INQUIRE, AND IMAGINE (CONT.)

EVALUATE

5a. Gray points out that riches, fame and power are no guarantee against death. The rich and poor alike must face the end of life. He also points out that while the rich may be tempted to act in evil, greedy or cruel ways in order to gain and keep wealth and power, the simple, uneducated poor are not so tempted. Finally, he points out the simple pleasures of the rustic life: hard work, the beauties of nature, a "blazing hearth" and children to "climb his knees the envied kiss to share." Responses will vary as to how effectively this makes such a life seem attractive.

(Continued on page 671)

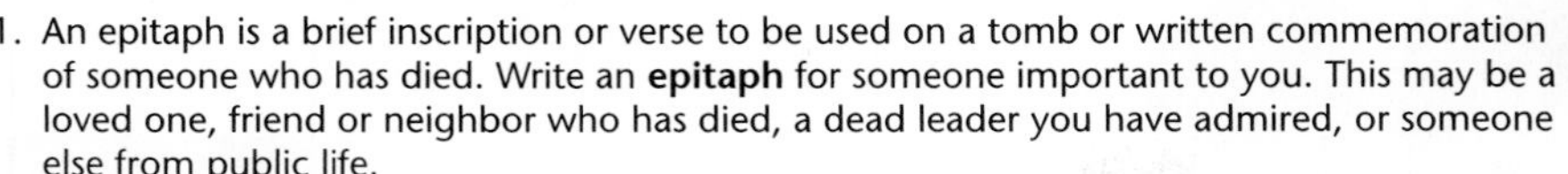

Writer's Journal

1. An epitaph is a brief inscription or verse to be used on a tomb or written commemoration of someone who has died. Write an **epitaph** for someone important to you. This may be a loved one, friend or neighbor who has died, a dead leader you have admired, or someone else from public life.
2. A paraphrase is a rewriting of a passage in different words. Review the epitaph of this poem and write a **paraphrase** that would help someone with limited education or ability to speak English understand. Do your best to preserve the meaning as well as the feeling expressed in these words.
3. Graveyards and churches provoke strong feelings in many of us. What feelings do they cause you to have? Contemplate a church or graveyard that you have visited or seen in passing. You may wish to visit it again for the purposes of this exercise. What sounds do you hear? What is the quality of the light? What colors and shapes and images do you see? Write a brief (two to four stanza) **poem** about this experience. You may write in rhymed or free verse, as you choose.

Integrating *the* Language Arts

Critical Thinking

Remembering and Visualizing. Often you will want to visualize a person, scene, or object so you can write about it and describe it accurately and vividly. When trying to remember and visualize, you may find it helpful to use clues to remind yourself of details. For instance, if you try to visualize a friend, you may think about articles of clothing that he or she typically wears, places where the two of you have gone together, activities you have shared, or characteristic facial or verbal expressions that he or she uses. Use your remembering and visualizing skills to answer the following questions.

1. What is the quality of light in the graveyard at the beginning of the poem?
2. What do you visualize around the hearth after reading stanza 6?
3. How do you visualize the deceased after reading stanza 14?
4. How do you visualize the lives of the deceased after reading stanza 19?
5. What do you imagine as you read stanza 25?

Speaking and Listening

Oral Interpretation of Poetry. It is often said that poetry is meant to be read aloud rather than silently. The music of poetry—its rhythms and rhymes—as much as the meaning of the words themselves contributes to the total experience. Review Language Arts Survey 4.19, "Oral Interpretation." Then practice reading aloud the first four stanzas of this poem. Think carefully about the mood these stanzas set and about how to best contribute to that mood via the tone, pacing and inflection you choose. Deliver your reading to the class.

Study and Research & Collaborative Learning

Researching Your Local Churchyard. Using the resources available in your school and public libraries as well as the recollections of people in the community, research the history of a church graveyard in your community. Working in small groups, select a church graveyard near your school and develop a list of questions about the history of the graveyard and the kinds of people buried there. Interview the minister, rabbi, priest or other official of the church if possible. If a member of your group has a camera, take photographs. Prepare a presentation for your class designed to help them share the experience of being in this particular churchyard.

Answers to Investigate, Inquire, and Imagine
(cont. from page 670)

Extend

5b. The poor and the rich are equal in that we must all die someday. Responses will vary as to the rest of the question. One might ask, however, whether disdain or acceptance are the only options for viewing a simple, uneducated life. Might it be possible to value the sincerity and honor of such people and still desire to provide them with an education that would give them a wider range of choices in life?

Answers to Understanding Literature

Elegy. The speaker grieves the loss of people whose lives were not celebrated when they were alive; the loss expressed is the waste of those people's (and perhaps his own) energy and talents. This elegy is unique because it mourns the loss of unnamed commoners, rather than well-known aristocrats or nobles.

Speaker. At the beginning of the poem, the speaker stands in the churchyard sharing his thoughts about the dead. At the end, the speaker reveals that he himself is buried in the churchyard. He characterizes himself as intelligent, honest, and melancholy.

Answers to Integrating the Language Arts

Critical Thinking
For students who are artistically inclined, ask them to draw a picture or painting of the image that is created in their mind as they undergo this visualizing activity.

Speaking and Listening
Encourage students to use the suggestions for listening to their classmates deliver their poem in the Language Arts Survey 4.6, "Adapting Listening Skills to Specific Task."

Study and Research
Students may find it helpful to read the Language Arts Survey 6.11, "Displaying Effective Visual Information" as they organize their photographs to present to the class.

ADDITIONAL RESOURCES

Unit 8 Resource Book
"Auld Lang Syne"
- Selection Worksheet 8.2
- Selection Check Test 4.8.5
- Selection Test 4.8.6

"John Anderson, My Jo"
- Selection Worksheet 8.3
- Selection Check Test 4.8.7
- Selection Test 4.8.8
- Language, Grammar, and Style Resource 3.28
- Speaking and Listening Resource 4.19
- Study and Research Resource 5.47

GRAPHIC ORGANIZER

Dialect: But we've wandered mony a weary foot, Sin' auld lange syne.
Standard English: But we have wondered many miles since long ago.

Dialect: But seas between us braid hae roared, Sin' auld lange syne.
Standard English: But broad seas between us have roared since long ago.

READER'S JOURNAL

Students might begin by listing adjectives associated with the experience, such as *happy, touching,* or *life changing.*

Literary Tools

Hymn. A **hymn** is a song or verse of praise. As you read this familiar song, consider it as a song of praise—what or who is being praised?

Dialect. **Dialect** is a version of a language spoken by the people of a particular place, time or social group. This poem, like most of Burns's work, is written in Scots, a northern dialect of the English language spoken by Scottish peasants. You may find it helpful to read the song through once, using the footnotes, and then again for fluidity. Make a chart listing examples of dialect you find in this selection. In the left column write the example of dialect and in the right column explain the meaning in Standard English. One example has been done for you.

Dialect	Standard English
We twa hae run about the braes	We two have run about the slopes

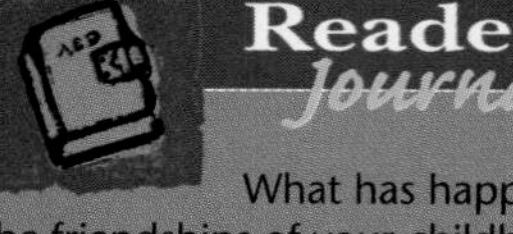

Reader's Journal

What has happened to the friendships of your childhood, and how do you feel about that?

"Auld Lang Syne"
"John Anderson, My Jo"

by Robert Burns

About the Author

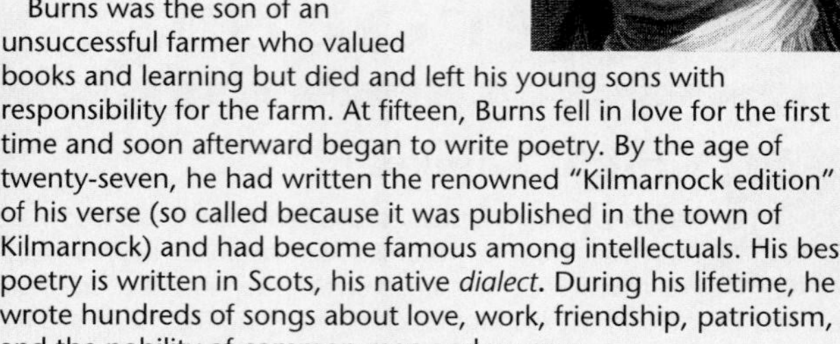

Robert Burns (1759–1796), the national poet of Scotland, had a natural gift for poetry and was largely self-educated. He chose his style deliberately from the Scottish folkloric and literary traditions.

Burns was the son of an unsuccessful farmer who valued books and learning but died and left his young sons with responsibility for the farm. At fifteen, Burns fell in love for the first time and soon afterward began to write poetry. By the age of twenty-seven, he had written the renowned "Kilmarnock edition" of his verse (so called because it was published in the town of Kilmarnock) and had become famous among intellectuals. His best poetry is written in Scots, his native *dialect.* During his lifetime, he wrote hundreds of songs about love, work, friendship, patriotism, and the nobility of common men and women.

A social rebel, Burns had great sympathy for the revolutions in America and France, which took place during his lifetime. Strongly opposed to Calvinism, the religion in which he had been raised, he was considered to be a social radical, one whose lifestyle left him open to criticism.

In his late twenties, Burns settled down, married Jean Armour, and began working as a tax inspector in Dumfries. Extremely patriotic and passionate about Scotland, during his last years he worked feverishly to preserve his country's music in published form. Although often in need of money, he would take no financial compensation for his work on volumes of Scottish lyrics. He continued to work on the Scottish anthologies until he died of heart disease at thirty-seven.

About the Selections

The poem **"Auld Lang Syne"** is perhaps the best known of all Scottish songs. Its first verse and chorus are sung traditionally at midnight on New Year's Eve. The poem expresses the tenderness of friendship, the joy of celebration, and the value of memories. In **"John Anderson, My Jo,"** Burns celebrates lifelong friendship, honoring a couple who have shared the joys and hard work of youth and now share their later years.

GOALS/OBJECTIVES

Studying this lesson will enable student to
- enjoy Burns's lighthearted musical verse and celebration of friendship and memories
- explain the importance of the Scots dialect in Burns's writing
- define *hymn, dialect, metaphor,* and *image* and recognize and explain examples of each that they encounter in their reading
- demonstrate the ability to work with compound sentences
- answer true/false test questions

Auld Lang Syne

ROBERT BURNS

Should auld acquaintance be forgot,
And never brought to min'?
Should auld acquaintance be forgot,
And days o' lang syne?

Chorus
For auld lang syne, my dear,
For auld lang syne,
We'll tak a cup o' kindness yet,
For auld lang syne.

We twa hae run about the braes,[2]
And pu'd the gowans[3] fine,
But we've wandered mony a weary foot,
Sin' auld lang syne.
(Chorus)

We twa hae paidled i' the burn,[4]
From morning sun till dine,[5]
But seas between us braid[6] hae roared,
Sin' auld lang syne.
(Chorus)

What questions are posed in the opening stanza?

What three things does the speaker remember doing with his friend?

1. **Lang Syne.** Long ago
2. **braes.** Slopes
3. **gowans.** Daisies
4. **twa . . . burn.** Two have paddled in the stream
5. **dine.** Dinner
6. **braid.** Broad

ANSWERS TO GUIDED READING QUESTIONS

1. The opening stanza asks if old friends and experiences should be forgotten.
2. The speaker remembers running about the slopes, picking daisies, and paddling in the stream.

INDIVIDUAL LEARNING STRATEGIES

MOTIVATION
Bring in a tape or CD with the song "Auld Lang Syne" to play for the class. You may even suggest that students sing along while you play it.

READING PROFICIENCY
Have students read through the Prereading page and the About the Author page before they read the poems to have a better understanding of their background and history.

ENGLISH LANGUAGE LEARNING
Most students will have extreme difficulty with the dialect in Burns's poems. Play the reading of "Auld Lang Syne" on the audiocassette and ask students to follow along.

SPECIAL NEEDS
You might want to translate the Scots dialect used in the following poems into standard English to help students better understand each poem.

ENRICHMENT
Have students who play musical instruments and/or sing perform the song for the class.

LITERARY NOTE 

"Auld Lang Syne" had long existed in Scottish oral tradition before Burns wrote his version of it. The poet wrote down the words while listening to an old man's song.

SELECTION CHECK TEST 4.8.5 WITH ANSWERS

Checking Your Reading

1. What does "lang syne" mean? **It means "long ago."**
2. What will the speaker take a cup of? **He will take a cup of kindness.**
3. What had the two friends once done, from morning until dinner (evening)? **They rowed in the stream.**
4. What does the speaker offer his friend? **He offers a hand.**
5. What will each person pay for? **Each will pay for his own drink.**

Literary Tools

1. What is being praised in this song? **A lifelong friendship is being praised.**
2. What might a theme for this song be? **Responses will vary, but could include friendship, continuity, the importance of celebrations, or the value of memories.**
3. Why do you think this song is traditionally sung on New Year's Eve? **Responses will vary, but it toasts maintaining relationships over the years.**

RESPOND TO THE SELECTION

Why do you think Americans sing "Auld Lang Syne" at the stroke of midnight on New Year's Day?

The Village Holiday or Dance of the Peasants, c.1650. David Teniers, The Younger. Virginia Museum of Fine Arts, Richmond, VA.

And there's a hand, my trusty fiere,[7]
   And gie's a hand o' thine;
And we'll tak a right gude-willie waught,[8]
   For auld lang syne.
         (Chorus)

And surely ye'll be your pint-stowp,[9]
   And surely I'll be mine;
And we'll tak a cup o' kindness yet,
   For auld lang syne.
         (Chorus) ■

7. **fiere.** Friend
8. **gude-willie waught.** A big swig
9. **be your pint-stowp.** Pay for your pint-cup

Respond *to the* SELECTION

What experiences have you had that are similar to the bonding experiences described in Burns's poem?

Investigate, Inquire, Imagine

Recall: Gathering Facts

1a. What is the question asked in lines 1–4?

2a. In lines 9 and 10, what does the speaker remember doing with his friend?

3a. What is the speaker offering his friend in lines 17 and 18?

Interpret: Finding Meaning

1b. Is this a real question—does the speaker want to know the opinion of someone else? Or is it a rhetorical question, and if so, what point is he making?

2b. What stage of life is the speaker recalling?

3b. What are the friends sharing besides a drink?

Analyze: Taking Things Apart

4a. What values are being expressed in this song? Cite evidence that it expresses the voices of hard-working people who have little material wealth?

Synthesize: Bringing Things Together

4b. How would you characterize the tone of this song—as intellectual and rational, or as spontaneous and emotional? How does it reflect the Romantic tradition?

Evaluate: Making Judgments

5a. Evaluate the enduring appeal of this song.

Extend: Connecting Ideas

5b. Burns, an ardent supporter of the French Revolution, wrote "Auld Lang Syne" a year before that fighting broke out. Does this song supports the ideals of the French Revolution: Liberty, Equality and Fraternity?

Understanding Literature

Hymn. Review the definition for **hymn** in the Handbook of Literary Terms. What is Burns praising in this song? What particular characteristics make this piece sound like a hymn? Why do you think this song has continued to be so popular over the years?

Dialect. Review the definition for **dialect** and the chart you made for Literary Tools in Prereading. How does the use of the Scots dialect affect the song? How would the song be different if written in a more formal version of English?

ANSWERS TO INVESTIGATE, INQUIRE, AND IMAGINE

Recall

1a. The question asked is, "Should we forget friends from long ago?"

2a. The speaker remembers running on hills and picking daisies.

3a. In lines 17 and 18, the speaker is offering to shake hands with his friend.

Interpret

1b. This is a rhetorical question. The speaker is saying that we should certainly not forget old acquaintances.

2b. The speaker is recalling his childhood.

3b. Besides a beverage, the friends are sharing their memories and affection for one another.

Analyze

4a. The values being expressed here are an appreciation for loyalty and friendship. Hard-working people make strong friendships through sharing difficulties and growing to trust and rely on one another for help in a difficult world.

Synthesize

4b. The tone of the song is spontaneous and emotional, full of nostalgia, hearty fellowship and backslapping camaraderie. It fits the Romantic tradition as it is told in the words of common people, about common people; and it reflects the spontaneous overflow of emotion, rather than dry rationality.

Evaluate

5a. *Responses will vary.*

Extend

5b. Certainly; fraternity, or brotherhood, is a central theme of this song. It deals with long-term friendships. It might also be said to support the ideal of equality in that it celebrates the lives and loyalties of common people, rather than those of the wealthy or powerful. The French Revolution was a revolt by the same sort of common laborers as those in this song.

ANSWERS TO UNDERSTANDING LITERATURE

Hymn. Burns is praising loyalty to friends over time. The chorus, with its repetition of the phrase "For auld lang syne," makes the piece sound like a hymn. The form is popular among everyday people because of its short lines and repeated chorus that celebrate the common theme of friendship.

Dialect. If the song were written in standard, more formal English, it would seem less authentic.

ANSWER TO GUIDED READING QUESTION

1. John Anderson's hair is "like the snow," and he is also balding.

READER'S JOURNAL

Students might want to refer to photographs to help them with their descriptions.

SELECTION CHECK TEST 4.8.7 WITH ANSWERS

Checking Your Reading

1. What is a "jo"? **A jo is a sweetheart.**
2. What was like the raven? **John's hair was like the raven.**
3. How has John's brow changed since the speaker met him? **It is now bald.**
4. What does the speaker recall spending together? **She recalls happy days.**
5. Where will the two share together now? **They will share a grave.**

Literary Tools

1. What is the relationship between the speaker and the person she is addressing? **They are a couple, most likely married.**
2. What suggests that the two have known each other a long time? **The physical changes in John—his hair is white and his brow bald.**
3. What might the hill in the poem symbolize? **Responses will vary, but it probably symbolizes life, with its ups and downs.**

Literary TOOLS

METAPHOR. A **metaphor** is a figure of speech in which one thing is spoken or written about as if it were another. In the second stanza, the speaker mentions a hill. Consider the hill as a metaphor—what does this metaphor describe?

IMAGE. An **image** is a word or phrase that names something that can be seen, heard, touched, tasted or smelled. As you read, note the images used in this poem.

Reader's Journal

How has the appearance of someone close to you changed over the years?

Portrait of Newlyweds, c.1800s. American Artist. American Museum, Bath, UK.

John Anderson, My Jo

ROBERT BURNS

John Anderson, my jo,[1] John,
  When we were first acquent,
Your locks were like the raven,
  Your bonnie brow was brent;[2]
But now your brow is beld,[3] John,
  Your locks are like the snow,
But blessings on your frosty pow,[4]
  John Anderson, my jo!

John Anderson, my jo, John,
  We clamb the hill thegither,
And monie a cantie[5] day, John,
  We've had wi' ane anither;
Now we maun[6] totter down, John,
  And hand in hand we'll go,
And sleep thegither at the foot,
  John Anderson, my jo! ■

How has John Anderson's appearance changed over the years?

1. **jo.** Sweetheart
2. **brent.** Smooth
3. **beld.** Bald
4. **pow.** Head
5. **cantie.** Happy
6. **maun.** Must

Respond *to the* SELECTION

How does the speaker feel toward John Anderson, and how do you feel toward him after reading this poem?

INVESTIGATE, Inquire, Imagine

Recall: Gathering Facts → **Interpret:** Finding Meaning

1a. What did John Anderson look like when the speaker first knew him?

1b. What are the speaker's feelings on remembering John's appearance as a young man?

2a. What does John Anderson look like now?

2b. How does the speaker feel about John Anderson's appearance now?

3a. What does the speaker remember doing with John Anderson, and what does she anticipate doing now?

3b. What might the hill represent and what are the speaker's feelings about the future with John?

Analyze: Taking Things Apart → **Synthesize:** Bringing Things Together

4a. What have the speaker and John done together in the past, and what will they do together in the future? What might these actions symbolize?

4b. What might you say about the relationship between the two people in this poem?

Evaluate: Making Judgments → **Extend:** Connecting Ideas

5a. What attitude is expressed toward loyalty and commitment in this poem? What evidence do you find in the poem for your opinion?

5b. In what way are the themes of this poem and of "Auld Lang Syne" similar?

Understanding Literature

Metaphor. Review the definition of **metaphor** in the Handbook of Literary Terms. Analyze the metaphor of the hill that the speaker and John have climbed and will now "totter" down. What does it represent? Why is a hill an appropriate metaphor for this?

Image. Review the definition of **image** in the Handbook of Literary Terms, and complete the following sensory details chart with images in this poem. What attitudes do these images express?

Sight	Sound	Touch	Taste	Smell
raven locks		climbing hill		

ANSWERS TO UNDERSTANDING LITERATURE

Metaphor. The poem uses the metaphor of climbing and descending a hill for the journey of life. The hill is appropriate to describe the way the two have climbed or surmounted life's challenges going up and now begin the descent of the end of their lives together. They will sleep together at the foot, symbolizing death. They are older but still together and still happy.

Image.

Sight	Sound	Touch	Taste	Smell
Raven locks		climbing hill		
Smooth brow		hand in hand		
Bald head		sleeping on grass		
Snowy locks		Tottering		

These images express an attitude of delight in and connection with the natural world.

RESPOND TO THE SELECTION

With a partner, have students create a dialogue between the speaker and John Anderson.

ANSWERS TO INVESTIGATE, INQUIRE, AND IMAGINE

Recall

1a. He had black hair and a smooth forehead.

2a. He has white hair and is balding.

3a. The speaker remembers climbing the hill with John and spending many a happy day. Now, the speaker expects to "totter" down the hill with John.

Interpret

1b. The speaker remembers him with affection and love.

2b. The speaker has as much love for John and his appearance now as before.

3b. The hill may represent life's difficulties and the speaker is happy to contemplate growing old with John.

Analyze

4a. They have climbed the hill together and will now totter down that hill and sleep together at the bottom. These actions may symbolize life and death, with sleep at the foot of the hill symbolizing death at the end of the journey.

Synthesize

4b. You might conclude that the two people in this poem are long-term friends or are married. The fact that the speaker calls John "jo" meaning sweetheart, would indicate that they share a strong love for one another.

Evaluate

5a. This poem honors loyalty and commitment to another in a long-term friendship or marriage. The speaker loves John as much as she did in her youth and finds him as beautiful in old age as when he as a young man

Extend

5b. Both "Auld Lang Syne" and "John Anderson, My Jo" honor long-term friendship, loyalty and love over the years.

ANSWERS TO INTEGRATING THE LANGUAGE ARTS

Language, Grammar, and Style

1. Your hair was like the raven, and your bonny brow was smooth.
2. Your hair is like the snow, so blessing on your frosty head!
3. We climbed the hill together and had many a happy day.
4. We have to trudge down while we go hand in hand.
5. We'll sleep together at the foot and we'll always be friends.

Study and Research

Test-Taking Skills.

1. F
2. F
3. T
4. T
5. T

1. Write a **personal letter** to a childhood friend recounting a special memory you have of a time the two of you shared.
2. Write brief **character sketches** of the two people featured in this poem. Base your sketches on information provided in the poem; however, use your imagination and fill in the blanks when necessary.
3. Write a **monologue** by the speaker of the poem. You might have the person comment about marriage, life on a farm, or poetry.

Integrating *the* LANGUAGE ARTS

Language, Grammar, and Style

COMPOUND SENTENCES. Read the Language Arts Survey 3.28, " Working with Compound Sentences, Subjects, and Verbs." Then rewrite the sentences below to make them compound sentences.

1. Your hair was like the raven. Your bonny brow was smooth.
2. Your hair is like the snow. Blessings on your frosty head!
3. We climbed the hill together. We had many a happy day.
4. We have to trudge down. Hand in hand we'll go.
5. We'll sleep together at the foot. We'll always be friends.

Speaking and Listening

READING DIALECT ALOUD. The dialect of Robert Burns' work is difficult for many readers. This difficulty is often an unfortunate barrier which prevents the reader from appreciating the musical quality of his poetry. Try reading either of the two selections by Burns aloud several times. To familiarize yourself with pronunciation and rhythm you may find it helpful to listen to the recording of "Auld Lang Syne" on the audiocassette in your teacher's materials. Practice reading one of the poems aloud a sufficient number of times to be able to do it fluidly. Then deliver your reading before the class. Language Arts Survey 4.19, "Oral Interpretation," may also be helpful to you.

Study and Research

RESEARCHING CALVINISM. In the About the Author section, we learned that Burns rejected the Calvinism of his youth. Using the library and perhaps your own church resources, research Calvinism. What are the central tenets of this movement within the Christian church? Why might a Romantic reject Calvinism? Prepare a report for your teacher.

Study and Research

TEST-TAKING SKILLS. Read the Language Arts Survey 5.47, "Taking Objective Tests." Then answer the following questions on your own paper by writing T if a sentence is true and F if a sentence is false.

1. As a young boy, John Anderson had red hair.
2. The two friends met recently.
3. John and the speaker had many happy days together.
4. John and the speaker are no longer young.
5. John Anderson is probably the speaker's husband.

"The Lamb" "The Tyger" "London"

BY WILLIAM BLAKE

About the AUTHOR

Born to a middle-class family in London, **William Blake** (1757–1827) received his formal education in art, studying at the Royal Academy of Arts. When he was fourteen, he was apprenticed to James Basire, a well-known engraver. During his free time, Blake wrote poetry and read.

As a child, Blake had a number of "visions." The earliest one was of God looking through his bedroom window, a vision which left him screaming in fear. When he was eight or nine, he told his father he had seen a tree filled with bright, shining angels. He grew accustomed to his visions and later reported talking with spirits and angels. Thus, Blake's experience of the world was intensely visual and was reflected in both the imagery of his poetry and in his other love, painting and drawing. He told the people around him that his poetry and his drawings were "copied" from the visions he saw.

Blake earned a living giving drawing lessons, illustrating books, and engraving. Later, when work was not plentiful, he and his wife moved to the Sussex seacoast. A wealthy patron of the arts supported the Blakes and tried to convince William to work with a more conventional style. Blake, however, rebelled, insisting that his poems reflected a passionate, spiritual world and that this world must be kept separate from the "corporeal," or physical, world. Consequently, he kept his own style and lived for a time in poverty and isolation because his work was so contrary to the tastes and conventions of his time.

In his sixties, Blake left his poetry behind, attracted a small group of painters, and began to concentrate on his visual work. He died at the age of seventy.

About the SELECTIONS

Both **"The Lamb"** and **"The Tyger"** are included in Blake's *Songs of Innocence and of Experience.* The two poems are almost mirror images of one another in structure. Each of the poems makes use of a regular rhyme scheme and frequent repetition. One uses a symbol for innocence the other uses a symbol for experience. Blake considered these poems representative of "two contrary states of the human soul." The poem **"London,"** like "The Tyger," is also a song of experience. In this poem, Blake writes poignantly about some of the evils of urban life.

In the *Songs of Innocence,* Blake presents a vision of the "fallen world"—the world after the expulsion of man from the Garden of Eden—through the naïve eyes of innocence. In *The Songs of Experience,* he presents this same world in all the truth of its ugliness and fearsomeness. He thought that one must pass through the stage of childlike innocence, to see the world as it is and then to assimilate both visions. In other words, both are true—the world is beautiful and bountiful, and ugly and painful. One might then reach a mature vision of the world and of life which incorporates both, a state he called "organized innocence."

ADDITIONAL RESOURCES

UNIT 8 RESOURCE BOOK

"The Lamb"
- Selection Worksheet 8.4
- Selection Check Test 4.8.9
- Selection Test 4.8.10

"The Tyger"
- Selection Worksheet 8.5
- Selection Check Test 4.8.11
- Selection Test 4.8.12

"London"
- Selection Worksheet 8.6
- Selection Check Test 4.8.13
- Selection Test 4.8.14
- Language, Grammar, and Style Resource 3.30

INDIVIDUAL LEARNING STRATEGIES

MOTIVATION
These three poems by Blake center around symbols to represent something about humanity and life. Ask students to choose a symbol to represent a certain aspect of life such as love, joy, sadness, etc. Then have them explain why they chose that symbol.

READING PROFICIENCY
Encourage students to read through the vocabulary words and footnotes before they begin reading these poems.

ENGLISH LANGUAGE LEARNING
Point out that in the poem, "London," the word *mark* has two meanings—as a verb it means "to notice" and as a noun it means "a sign." Explain that knowing the various meanings of certain words can help students gain a deeper understanding and appreciation for poetic language and conventions.

SPECIAL NEEDS
Students might enjoy the selection read aloud to hear the childlike rhymes of the poems. Also have students focus on answering the Guided Reading Questions as they read.

ENRICHMENT
Blake was an important influence on the artist Samuel Palmer, whose *A Shoreham Garden* appears on page 28. Have students compare Palmer's painting with that of Blake.

GOALS/OBJECTIVES

Studying this lesson will enable student to
- interpret and appreciate the poet's ideas about innocence, experience, and the human soul
- describe Blake's literary accomplishment and explain the historical significance of his work
- define *pastoral, allegory, alliteration, character, setting,* and *image* and recognize and explain example each in the selection
- demonstrate ability to identify prepositional phrases
- conduct a research on London, England

ANSWER TO GUIDED READING QUESTION

1. Both the lamb and its maker, the Lamb of God, have the same name.

GRAPHIC ORGANIZER

The lamb represents Jesus Christ; childhood; innocence; giver of life and food; giver of clothing; giver of a tender voice; humanity.

SELECTION CHECK TEST 4.8.9 WITH ANSWERS

Checking Your Reading

1. With what question does the poem open? **The poem asks the lamb who made it.**
2. What is the lamb's clothing? **Soft wool is its clothing.**
3. What makes "all the vales rejoice"? **The lamb's voice makes the vales rejoice.**
4. Who became a little child? **The lamb's maker, or Jesus, became a child.**
5. With what blessing does the poem end? **It ends with, "God bless thee."**

Literary Tools

Fill in the blanks using the following terms. You may not use every term, and you may use some terms more than once.

symbol   Romantic poem   allegory
pastoral poem   mood   repetition

1. **Pastoral poems** present idealized renditions of rural life.
2. The emotion a poem creates in the reader is the work's **mood**.
3. **Allegories** are works in which each various element symbolizes something else.

READER'S JOURNAL

Students might begin their freewriting by focusing on a topic such as childhood games.

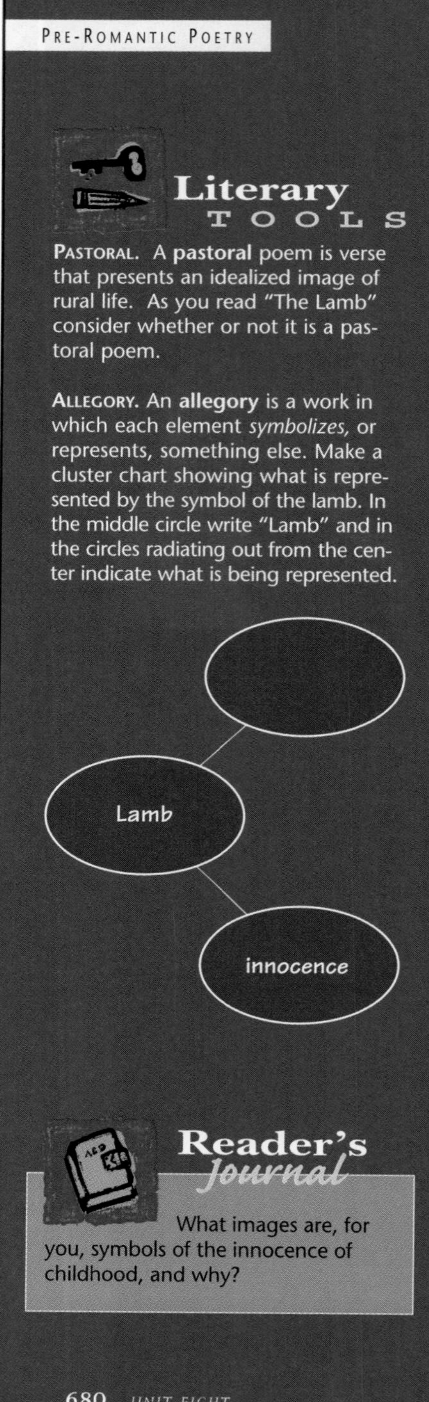

Literary TOOLS

PASTORAL. A **pastoral** poem is verse that presents an idealized image of rural life. As you read "The Lamb" consider whether or not it is a pastoral poem.

ALLEGORY. An **allegory** is a work in which each element *symbolizes*, or represents, something else. Make a cluster chart showing what is represented by the symbol of the lamb. In the middle circle write "Lamb" and in the circles radiating out from the center indicate what is being represented.

Reader's Journal

What images are, for you, symbols of the innocence of childhood, and why?

The Lamb

WILLIAM BLAKE

Little Lamb, who made thee?
Dost thou know who made thee?
Gave thee life & bid thee feed,
By the stream & o'er the mead;[1]
Gave thee clothing of delight,
Softest clothing wooly bright;
Gave thee such a tender voice,
Making all the vales[2] rejoice!
Little Lamb who made thee?
Dost thou know who made thee?

Little Lamb I'll tell thee,
Little Lamb I'll tell thee!
He is callèd[3] by thy name,
For he calls himself a Lamb;[4]
He is meek & he is mild,
He became a little child;
I a child & thou a lamb,
We are callèd by his name.
Little Lamb God bless thee.
Little Lamb God bless thee. ■

In what way is the lamb similar to its maker?

1. **mead.** Meadow
2. **Vales.** Valleys.
3. **callèd.** (with accent over the 'e') The accent over the 'e' indicates that the \ed\ is a stressed syllable, making this a two-syllable word, in order to fit the meter of the poem.
4. **Lamb.** Jesus is often referred to as "the Lamb of God."

Respond *to the* Selection

Do you agree that childhood is a time of innocence? Why or why not?

Investigate, Inquire, *Imagine*

Recall: Gathering Facts → **Interpret:** Finding Meaning

1a. What questions are asked in stanza 1?

1b. What is the attitude of the speaker as he questions the lamb?

2a. What answer does the speaker give to the lamb?

2b. In stanza 2 how does the speaker compare the lamb to the one who became a lamb?

3a. To whom does the speaker compare the lamb?

3b. How does the speaker explain humanity's relationship to the lamb?

Analyze: Taking Things Apart → **Synthesize:** Bringing Things Together

4a. How is this poem like a prayer? What elements give this impression?

4b. What sort of speaker might offer this kind of prayer? What conclusions can you draw, then, about the speaker we hear in this poem? Why?

Evaluate: Making Judgments → **Extend:** Connecting Ideas

5a. Evaluate the mood of the poem. What elements help to create that mood?

5b. What other animals might the poet have used to symbolize innocence? What characteristics and traditional associations make the lamb an appropriate symbol for innocence?

Understanding *Literature*

Pastoral Poem. Review the definition of a **pastoral** poem in the Handbook of Literary Terms. Does "The Lamb" fit this definition of a pastoral poem? Explain.

Allegory. Review the definition of **allegory** in the Handbook of Literary Terms and the chart you made for Literary Tools in Prereading. In one sense all literature can be viewed as allegorical in that individual characters, objects, places, and actions are types representing others of their kind. In *naïve allegory,* characters, objects, places, and actions are personifications of abstractions such as Good Deeds, Beauty, and Vanity. In more sophisticated allegories, the elements of the work make up an *extended metaphor* in which the literal elements are described, but their part-by-part interpretation is left up to the reader. Explain whether "The Lamb" is an example of naïve allegory or an extended metaphor.

Answers to Understanding Literature

Pastoral Poem. The poem idealizes the lamb, a country animal. It also idealizes the lamb's home near the stream, the mead, and the vale.

Allegory. "The Lamb" is an example of naïve allegory because the lamb not only represents Jesus Christ, but also the abstract qualities of innocence, childhood, and humanity.

Respond to the Selection

What other animals besides the lamb might the speaker have chosen as subjects for this poem? What characteristics make the lamb an appropriate symbol of innocence?

Answer to Investigate, Inquire, and Imagine

Recall

1a. Stanza 1 asks who made the lamb; who gave it life, food, wool, and a tender voice; and if the lamb knows who made it.

2a. The speaker tells the lamb that its maker is also called a Lamb.

3a. The speaker compares the lamb to Jesus, or the Lamb of God.

Interpret

1b. The speaker's attitude is gentle and loving.

2b. Both are meek, mild, and childlike.

3b. Like the lamb, people are called by Jesus' name.

Analyze

4a. Like a prayer, the poem praises God and has a chanting, rhythmic quality. The last two lines are like a benediction.

Synthesize

4b. The lilting, nursery rhyme-like rhythm noted in 4a as well as the gentle, loving feeling expressed toward the lamb, may lead the reader to see a child as the speaker. The rhythm and rhyme scheme of the poem in lines 3-8 and lines 13-18 are the same as the traditional children's prayer:
Now I lay me down to sleep
I pray the Lord my soul to keep.
If I should die before I wake,
I pray the Lord my soul to take.
Others may see a nurturing, parental quality in the speaker.

Evaluate

5a. The mood of the poem is light and joyful. The rhythm is lilting and singsong, like a child's nursery rhyme. The speaker expresses affection towards the lamb, comparing it to Jesus as the "Lamb of God." There is no hint of anything negative.

Extend

5b. *Responses will vary.* The lamb's characteristics are gentleness, meekness and softness, which are associated with innocence. Traditional associations, other than that with Jesus, include the "Mary Had a Little Lamb," "Baa Baa Black Sheep" and "Little Bo Peep" nursery rhymes.

ANSWERS TO GUIDED READING QUESTIONS

1. The speaker asks the tiger what "immortal hand or eye" made him.
2. The stars throw down their spears.

GRAPHIC ORGANIZER

Descriptive words that describe the Tiger: bright, fearful symmetry, fire of thine eyes, deadly terrors

READER'S JOURNAL

Why might ferocious animals like a tiger be intimidating to people? What qualities do they have that make people fearful of them?

VOCABULARY FROM THE SELECTION

aspire
sinew

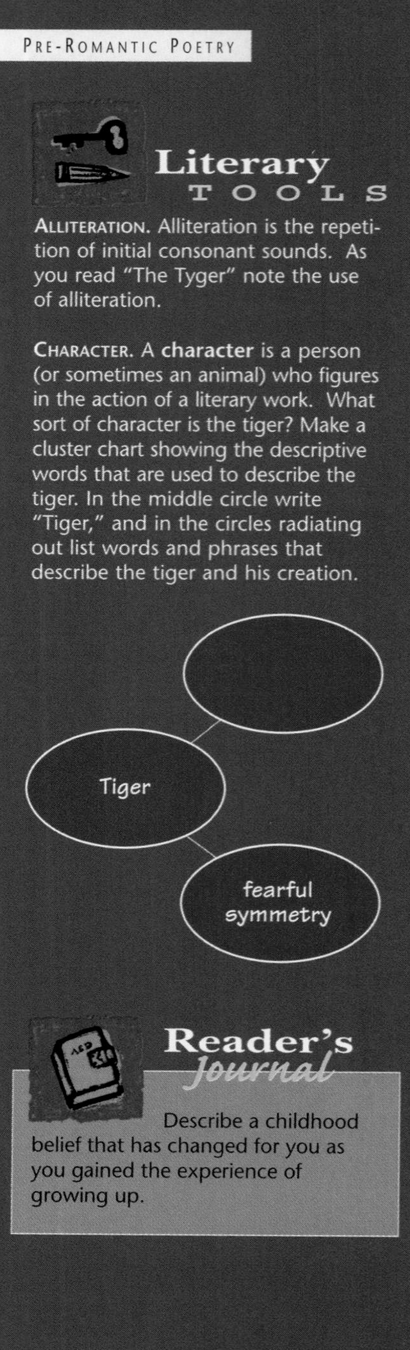

Literary TOOLS

ALLITERATION. Alliteration is the repetition of initial consonant sounds. As you read "The Tyger" note the use of alliteration.

CHARACTER. A **character** is a person (or sometimes an animal) who figures in the action of a literary work. What sort of character is the tiger? Make a cluster chart showing the descriptive words that are used to describe the tiger. In the middle circle write "Tiger," and in the circles radiating out list words and phrases that describe the tiger and his creation.

Reader's Journal

Describe a childhood belief that has changed for you as you gained the experience of growing up.

The Tyger

WILLIAM BLAKE

Tyger! Tyger! burning bright
In the forests of the night,
What immortal hand or eye
Could frame thy fearful symmetry?

What question does the speaker ask of the tiger?

In what distant deeps or skies
Burnt the fire of thine eyes?
On what wings dare he aspire?
What the hand dare seize the fire?

And what shoulder, & what art,
Could twist the sinews of thy heart?
And when thy heart began to beat,
What dread hand? & what dread feet?

What the hammer? what the chain?
In what furnace was thy brain?
What the anvil? what dread grasp
Dare its deadly terrors clasp?
When the stars threw down[1] their spears
And water'd heaven with their tears,
Did he smile his work to see?
Did he who made the Lamb make thee?

How do the stars react to the creation of the tiger?

1. **threw down.** Surrendered or hurled down

WORDS FOR EVERYDAY USE

as • pire (ə spīr´) *vi.,* seek to achieve lofty goals. *Many of this year's college graduates aspire to professional careers as lawyers and doctors.*

si • new (sin´ yü) *n.* tendon or nerve. *The strenuous exercises stretched the sinews of Tara's leg muscles.*

The Tyger. William Blake, 1789. Yale Center for British Art, Paul Mellon Collection.

ArtNote

Blake's first book of poems, *Poetical Sketches,* was printed when he was twenty-six. Later, he began illustrating his poetry with a technique called *illuminated printing.* He would work with pens and brushes in an acid-resistant medium on a copper plate. He wrote in mirror images, so that the plate would print the characters correctly. Then he etched the plate with acid to make the image stand out. He colored the printed pages with watercolors and stitched them together. His well-known *Songs of Innocence and of Experience* was printed this way.

Tyger! Tyger! burning bright
In the forests of the night,
What immortal hand or eye
Dare frame thy fearful symmetry? ■

Respond *to the* SELECTION

What other animals or things might symbolize experience for you?

SELECTION CHECK TEST 4.8.11 WITH ANSWERS

Checking Your Reading

1. Where is the tiger? **It is in the forests of the night.**
2. Where does fire burn? **It burns in the tiger's eyes.**
3. Who threw down their spears? **The stars threw down their spears.**
4. With what were the heavens watered? **They were watered with the stars' tears.**
5. What does the speaker wonder about the lamb? **He wonders "Did he who made the Lamb make thee"?**

Literary Tools

1. Mark the stressed syllables in the following lines:

   / / / /
   And what shoulder, & what art,
   / / /
   Could twist the sinews of thy heart?
   / / / /
   And when thy heart began to beat,
   / / / /
   What dread hand? & what dread feet?

2. What is the rhyme scheme of the above lines? **The rhyme scheme is *aabb*.**
3. How is repetition used in this poem? **Responses may vary, but the word "Tyger" is repeated, and the first stanza is repeated.**
4. What is alliteration? **Alliteration is the repetition of initial consonant sounds.**
5. What might the tiger symbolize? **Responses will vary, but could include experience or evil.**

RESPONDING TO THE SELECTION

Why do you think Blake chose a tiger to symbolize experience? What makes a tiger "experienced" and not innocent?

ANSWERS TO INVESTIGATE, INQUIRE, AND IMAGINE

RECALL

1a. The tiger is described as having fiery eyes and a sinewy heart.
2a. The speaker describes the process of something being created in a furnace.
3a. The speaker asks if the creator smiled at the tiger and if the lamb's creator also made the tiger.

INTERPRET

1b. The speaker characterizes the tiger as fierce and terrifying.
2b. The image of the furnace might draw a parallel to hell.
3b. In wondering whether God could be pleased with a creation that kills, the speaker questions the nature of God.

ANALYZE

4a. "The Tyger" uses words and phrases like "fearful," "dread" (three times), "deadly terrors," and the images of fires burning and night. These are all images of power and fear. In contrast, the images and words and phrases in "The Lamb" are all gentle and peaceful, like "tender," "softest clothing wooly bright," and "meek and mild." In "The Lamb," each question is asked and answered by a benevolent speaker. In "The Tyger," however, every sentence is a question, many of which have an urgent quality due to the fact that they are shortened to sentence fragments, such as "What dread hand? & what dread feet?" No answers are given.

SYNTHESIZE

4b. Experience is not necessarily peaceful or gentle, but rather sometimes violent and fearsome. In innocence we believe our questions are answered but experience involves fewer answers and continuing mystery.

EVALUATE

5a. Blake seems to say that experience is difficult and frightening, and fraught with mystery. But he also presents it as having both destructive and creative elements. The tiger is a predator that is portrayed as powerful and fearsome but the image of the blacksmith's fires introduces a creative element—out of the fires of experience comes a new creation.

EXTEND

5b. The poem reflects a fear of the primitive because the tiger dwells in the threatening, mysterious "forests of the night," not in the peaceful, familiar meadows of England. So-called civilized people fear the primitive because it represents the unknown.

INVESTIGATE, Inquire, Imagine

Recall: GATHERING FACTS →

1a. What characteristics of the tiger are described in stanzas 2 and 3?
2a. What process does the speaker describe in stanza 4?
3a. What question does the speaker ask in stanza 5?

Interpret: FINDING MEANING

1b. How does the speaker characterize the tiger through this physical description?
2b. To what process involving furnaces and anvils does the speaker compare the creation of the tiger?
3b. Why does the speaker wonder whether God was happy with the creation of the tiger?

Analyze: TAKING THINGS APART →

4a. Analyze the descriptive words and phrases used to describe the tiger. Compare them to the descriptive words and phrases used in "The Lamb." Compare also the use of questions in each poem.

Synthesize: BRINGING THINGS TOGETHER

4b. If the tiger symbolizes experience and the lamb symbolizes innocence, how does experience differ from innocence?

Evaluate: MAKING JUDGMENTS →

5a. What judgment on experience does Blake suggest? Is it a positive or a negative thing? Or is it some combination? What elements of the poem lead you to this conclusion? Do you agree or disagree with Blake?

Extend: CONNECTING IDEAS

5b. How does this poem reflect a fear of the primitive? Why do "civilized people" have this fear?

Understanding Literature

ALLITERATION. Review the definition for **alliteration** in the Handbook of Literary Terms. List examples of alliteration in "The Tyger." Then review "The Lamb" and compare the uses of alliteration in the two poems.

CHARACTER. Review the definition for **character** and the cluster chart you made for Literary Tools in Prereading. Compare the characters in "The Lamb" and "The Tyger." What characteristics make one character clearly a symbol of innocence and the other clearly a symbol of experience?

ANSWERS TO UNDERSTANDING LITERATURE

ALLITERATION. Examples of alliteration in "The Tyger" include "Tyger! Tyger!," "burning bright," and "distant deeps." The words "Little Lamb" and "meek and mild" are examples of alliteration in "The Lamb." Both poems use alliteration to emphasize their subject. Alliteration in "The Tyger" underscores the tiger's terrifying or mysterious aspects, whereas alliteration in "The Lamb" emphasizes the innocence and gentleness of the lamb.

CHARACTER. The lamb is a clear symbol of innocence because of its gentleness and its symbolic connection to Jesus Christ, believed to be without sin. In contrast, the tiger symbolizes experience because of its ferocity and connotation of violence. In the natural world, the tiger is a predator and a threat to the defenseless lamb. The lamb is also representative of natural, pastoral beauty while the tiger represents a tough, ugly urban world.

London

WILLIAM BLAKE

I wander thro' each charter'd[1] street,
Near where the charter'd Thames does flow,
And mark in every face I meet
Marks of weakness, marks of woe.

In every cry of every Man,
In every Infant's cry of fear,
In every voice, in every ban,[2]
The mind-forg'd manacles I hear:

What does the speaker hear in every voice?

How the Chimney-sweeper's cry
Every blackning Church appalls,
And the hapless Soldier's sigh
Runs in blood down Palace walls.

What social institutions are mentioned here? Who is wronged by them?

1. **Charter'd.** Established or created as a free entity, as in "given a charter" but also bound, or rented out to someone by its owner, as in to charter a hall or a carriage.
2. **ban.** A proclamation, a prohibition, or an announcement of marriage

WORDS FOR EVERYDAY USE

man • a • cle (man´ ə kəl) *n.,* handcuff, shackle. *Rusted manacles hung from hooks on the old prison's walls.*
hap • less (ha' pləs) *adj.* having no luck. *One accident after another had befallen the hapless student.*

Literary TOOLS

SETTING. The **setting** of a literary work is the time and place in which it occurs, together with the details used to create a sense of a particular time and place. As you read, note the details that create the setting of "London."

IMAGE. An **image** is a word or phrase that names something that can be seen, heard, touched tasted or smelled. As you read, jot down the sensory details in "London" in a sensory details chart like the one below.

SIGHT	SOUND	TOUCH	TASTE	SMELL
	every cry of every man			

Reader's Journal

Which do you prefer, city life or rural life, and why?

ANSWERS TO GUIDED READING QUESTIONS

1. The speaker hears "ming-forg'd manacles."
2. The church is mentioned, with the chimney-sweeper's cry attributed to it. The palace is mentioned and the soldier's sigh is attributed to it.

VOCABULARY FROM THE SELECTION

blight
manacle

GRAPHIC ORGANIZER

SIGHT: every face I meet; marks of weakness; marks of woe
SOUND: every cry of every Man; every infant's cry of fear; every voice; sound of mind-forged manacles; the chimney sweeper's cry; the hapless soldier's sigh; the youthful Harlot's curse

READER'S JOURNAL

What images are created in your mind when you think about the city? What do you believe are the postive aspects of urban life? What are the negative aspects?

ANSWER TO GUIDED READING QUESTION

1. The two tragedies are a newborn's blindness and a newlywed's death. Both are caused by a disease.

SELECTION CHECK TEST 4.8.13 WITH ANSWERS

Checking Your Reading

1. In what are seen marks of weakness and woe? **They are in people's faces.**
2. Who cries in fear? **The infant cries in fear.**
3. What "runs in blood down palace walls"? **The soldier's sigh does.**
4. Who is inflicted with a "curse"? **The harlot has a curse.**
5. What becomes a hearse? **The wedding carriage becomes a hearse.**

Literary Tools

1. What is setting? **Setting is the time and place in which a work takes place.**
2. What is the setting of this poem? **The setting is 18th-century London.**
3. What image of this setting does Blake create? **Responses will vary, but should indicate that it is dark, frightening, sorrowful.**

The Heart of the Empire, c.1800s. Niels Moiler Lund. Guildhall Art Gallery, London.

But most thro' midnight streets I hear
How the youthful Harlot's curse
Blasts the new-born Infant's tear,[3]
And blights with plagues the Marriage hearse.[4] ■

What two tragedies are mentioned here? What caused them?

3. **Harlot's curse . . . Infants' tear.** The infant may have been born blind due to a disease.
4. **Marriage hearse.** The wedding carriage transformed into a funeral hearse

WORDS FOR EVERYDAY USE

blight (blīt) *vt.*, destroy, prevent growth. *Farmers worry that the locusts will blight their crops.*

Respond *to the* SELECTION

If you could give advice to a newcomer to London, what would it be?

INVESTIGATE

Inquire, *Imagine*

Recall: Gathering Facts →

1a. In stanza 2, what does the speaker hear in every voice?

2a. What two people are mentioned in stanza 3? what two social institutions?

3a. What harm is done by the "curse" mentioned in stanza 4?

Interpret: Finding Meaning

1b. In what ways are the people of the city "manacled"?

2b. What wrongs are referred to in stanza 3? What implied criticism is made of the two institutions mentioned in stanza 3?

3b. What double meaning can we draw from the word "curse" here? What is the significance of the "marriage hearse?"

Analyze: Taking Things Apart →

4a. Analyze the people who are wronged in this poem. What sort of people are they? Who or what seems to be the wrongdoer in the poem?

Synthesize: Bringing Things Together

4b. How does the poet seem to feel about the common people of London? What leads you to this conclusion? How is this consistent or not consistent with Romantic ideals?

Evaluate: Making Judgments →

5a. What judgment is Blake making about urban life?

Extend: Connecting Ideas

5b. Given what you know about the Romantics from the introduction to this unit, what sort of life do you think Blake would prefer to live in urban London? Why?

Understanding *Literature*

Setting. Review the definition for **setting** in the Handbook of Literary Terms. Describe this poem's setting. Why is its setting particularly important?

Image. Review the definition for **image** and the sensory details you listed as you read "London." What senses are employed? What sort of mood do these sensory details help to create?

RESPOND TO THE SELECTION

Write about an incident where you moved to or visited an unfamiliar place. How did you feel? What questions or fears did you have?

ANSWERS TO INVESTIGATE, INQUIRE, AND IMAGINE

Recall

1a. He hears "mind-forg'd manacles."

2a. The chimney-sweeper and the soldier are mentioned and connected with the institutions of church and palace, respectively.

3a. The curse results in the baby being blinded and the marriage coach being turned into a funeral hearse.

Interpret

1b. The "mind-forg'd manacles" represent the way we create our own imprisonment in our minds—by limiting ourselves with things like self doubt, fear and closed-mindedness.

2b. The chimney sweeper's cry shows on the church as a black stain, implying that the church is impure—so much so that the sweeper cannot clean it, or that the church does not care for the poor like the sweeper. The soldier's blood in the palace implies that soldiers die to protect the interests of the nobility.

3b. The word, "curse" can mean that the harlot swears an epithet, in anger or despair. It might also mean that she has contracted a disease, and that this disease affects her and her child. This double meaning implies that she is a victim herself as well as one who victimizes the infant. The significance of the "marriage hearse" is that the life-affirming nature of new love and marriage is perverted to become death.

Analyze

4a. The people who seem to be wronged are the chimney-sweeper, the soldier, the infant and even the young harlot. Indeed, "every Man" is full of woe. The finger of blame is pointed at institutions, like the church and the palace.

Synthesize

4b. The poet seems to feel that the common people are victimized by the big institutions of the city and by the nobility. The artificial construction of the city has deadened the spirits of the common people and led to their despair. The Romantics celebrated the ordinary

ANSWERS TO INVESTIGATE, INQUIRE, AND IMAGINE (cont.)

people over the aristocracy and trusted human emotion and sympathy, and nature over the creations of the orderly, rational/logical mind.

Evaluate

5a. Blake judges urban life to be full of despair, pain and woe. It breaks the spirit and leads to the isolation of people from one another.

Extend

5b. Given the Romantic celebration of "nature over human artifice" and "emotion over reason, we can assume that Blake would value rural life, in the wilds of nature, over this city created by man's rational mind, which deadens his heart and emotions.

Answers to Understanding Literature can be found on page 688.

ANSWERS TO UNDERSTANDING LITERATURE

Setting. The poem is set in nineteenth-century London at night. The chimney-sweeper and marriage hearse establish the historical setting, and "midnight streets" establishes the time. Because he hears a harlot, the speaker is probably in a disreputable part of the city.

Image. The sound images (every man's and infant's cries, soldier's sigh, and harlot's curse) create a woeful mood. The sight images (blood running "down Palace walls" and the infant's tear) reinforce the loss of hope in a city devoid of natural elements. Note that there are no images of any form of nature other than the people, who are in a state of despair. There are no trees, plants, clouds, stars, birds or animals. The only natural thing, the Thames River, is ironically described as "chartered" with the double meaning of free and bound.

ANSWERS TO INTEGRATING THE LANGUAGE ARTS

Language, Grammar, and Style

Responses may vary.

1. By hearing the said voices of people, I knew they were in pain.
2. I could see the weakness and pain in the people's faces.
3. People in mind-forged manacles are imprisoned.
4. By the cry I heard, I knew it was an infant's cry.
5. In the act of crying, the chimney-sweeper appalled the church.

Collaborative Learning

Refer students to the Language Arts Survey 4.8, "Communicating in a Small Group" to help them communicate effectively in their groups.

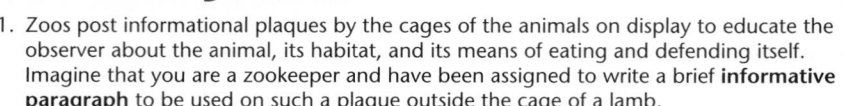

Writer's Journal

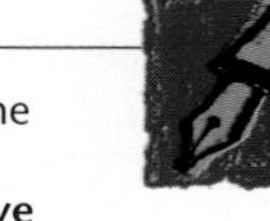

1. Zoos post informational plaques by the cages of the animals on display to educate the observer about the animal, its habitat, and its means of eating and defending itself. Imagine that you are a zookeeper and have been assigned to write a brief **informative paragraph** to be used on such a plaque outside the cage of a lamb.
2. Write an allegorical **poem** about an animal, perhaps a pet or an animal you have seen in a zoo or in the wild. Using your imagination, ask yourself what that animal might symbolize for you. Then, use descriptive detail that will appeal to your reader's senses of touch, taste, sight, smell and hearing to describe the animal and develop the symbolic association you have in mind.
3. Imagine yourself to be a nineteenth century social reformer who has observed the conditions portrayed by Blake in "London." Write an **expose** (a formal statement of facts) to be published in the newspaper pointing out these conditions and offering a proposal for correcting them.

Integrating *the* Language Arts

Language, Grammar, and Style

Prepositional Phrases. Read the Language Arts Survey 2.47, "Identifying Prepositional Phrases." Then combine each of the pairs of sentences using prepositional phrases beginning with *in, on, of,* or *by.*

1. I hear the sad voices of people. The people are in pain.
2. I see weakness and pain. The weakness and pain show on people's faces.
3. People are imprisoned. Mind-forged manacles imprison them.
4. I hear a cry. It is an infant's cry.
5. The chimney-sweeper cries. His cries appall the church.

Study and Research

Researching London. Research the actual living conditions in London for the common person in the early nineteenth century. What was an average day like for a chimney sweep or a soldier? How realistic is Blake's setting and mood in "London"? Prepare a report for your teacher.

Collaborative Learning

Art Creations. In small groups, think about how you might illustrate Blake's poems. Keep in mind that Blake was not afraid to express his creative ideas in unconventional ways. What are the different tools, colors, and objects with which you might illustrate the poems?

FROM Preface to *Lyrical Ballads*
"The World Is Too Much with Us"
"Lines Composed a Few Miles above Tintern Abbey"

BY WILLIAM WORDSWORTH

About the AUTHOR

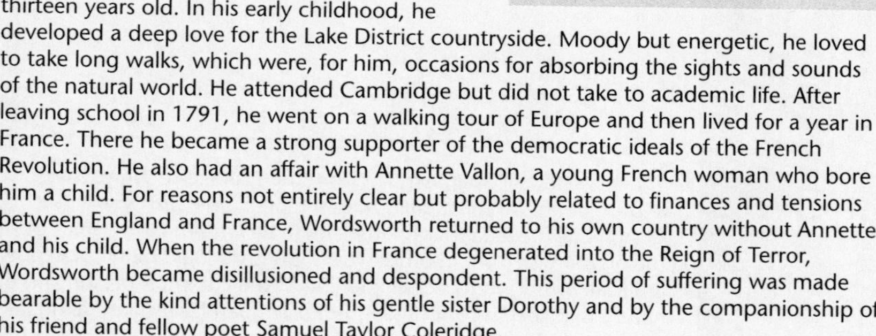

William Wordsworth (1770–1850), the father of the Romantic Movement in England, had more influence on English poetry than any other writer since Shakespeare. Before Wordsworth, people for the most part viewed nature as something to be tamed, controlled, and turned to human uses. A tree was something to be chopped down and turned into a house or a boat or a bridge. Wordsworth taught people to look at the tree itself, to see it as a thing of beauty that could inspire elevated emotions.

Wordsworth was born in the English Lake District to parents who both died before he was thirteen years old. In his early childhood, he developed a deep love for the Lake District countryside. Moody but energetic, he loved to take long walks, which were, for him, occasions for absorbing the sights and sounds of the natural world. He attended Cambridge but did not take to academic life. After leaving school in 1791, he went on a walking tour of Europe and then lived for a year in France. There he became a strong supporter of the democratic ideals of the French Revolution. He also had an affair with Annette Vallon, a young French woman who bore him a child. For reasons not entirely clear but probably related to finances and tensions between England and France, Wordsworth returned to his own country without Annette and his child. When the revolution in France degenerated into the Reign of Terror, Wordsworth became disillusioned and despondent. This period of suffering was made bearable by the kind attentions of his gentle sister Dorothy and by the companionship of his friend and fellow poet Samuel Taylor Coleridge.

Wordsworth met Coleridge in 1795. Each was extremely impressed with the talents of the other. Living in a cottage in Dorsetshire with Dorothy, Wordsworth visited almost daily with Coleridge, who called his friend "the best poet of the age." Together they walked through the countryside, spoke of poetry and philosophy, and conceived radical new ideas about verse. These ideas would find fruit in *Lyrical Ballads* (1798), a collection of poems that they co-authored. Later editions of this volume contained various versions of Wordsworth's magnificent, controversial **Preface,** which argues, in keeping with the poet's revolutionary, democratic principles, that poetry should be written not in stilted,

ADDITIONAL RESOURCES

UNIT 8 RESOURCE BOOK

From Preface to *Lyrical Ballads*
- Selection Worksheet 8.7
- Selection Check Test 4.8.15
- Selection Test 4.8.16

"The World Is Too Much with Us"
- Selection Worksheet 8.8
- Selection Check Test 4.8.17
- Selection Test 4.8.18

"Lines Composed a Few Miles above Tintern Abbey"
- Selection Worksheet 8.9
- Selection Check Test 4.8.19
- Selection Test 4.8.20
- Language, Grammar, and Style Resource 3.62
- Speaking and Listening Resource 4.15

INDIVIDUAL LEARNING STRATEGIES

MOTIVATION
Have students find poems or sayings about poetry that reflect their definition of poetry. They may need to search the Internet or browse through books about poetry. Then have the share their poem or saying.

READING PROFICIENCY
Have students read through the Prereading page and the About the Author page before they read the poems to have a better understanding of how Wordsworth's theory about poetry developed and from where his ideas came.

ENGLISH LANGUAGE LEARNING
Help students identify the mode, purpose or aim, and audience of these works. They can get important information from the title.

SPECIAL NEEDS
Students may benefit from hearing the selection read aloud. Also have students focus on the Guided Reading questions and the Recall questions in the Investigate, Inquire, and Imagine section.

ENRICHMENT
After reading the poem, "Lines Composed a Few Miles above Tintern Abbey," have students assume the role of a travel writer and organize the information for a travel brochure. Students may want to access a computerized atlas.

GOALS/OBJECTIVES

Studying this lesson will enable students to
- interpret and appreciate Wordsworth's ideas and feelings about poetry
- describe Wordsworth's theory of poetry and its connection to the ordinary person
- define *definition, theme, allusion, sonnet, free verse,* and *ode* and explain and identify examples of each that they encounter in their reading
- demonstrate the ability to use proper verb forms and tense
- conduct a research on the French Revolution

VOCABULARY FROM THE SELECTION

contemplate
emphatic
endeavor
erroneous
kindred
organic
ostentatiously
principal

GRAPHIC ORGANIZER

Themes: Poetry should reflect the language spoken by ordinary people—to "adopt the language of men"; poems should be about situations and incidents from common, everyday life; emotions should be recollected in tranquility and contemplated until a poem develops

READER'S JOURNAL

How would you define poetry? Why do you think people write poetry?

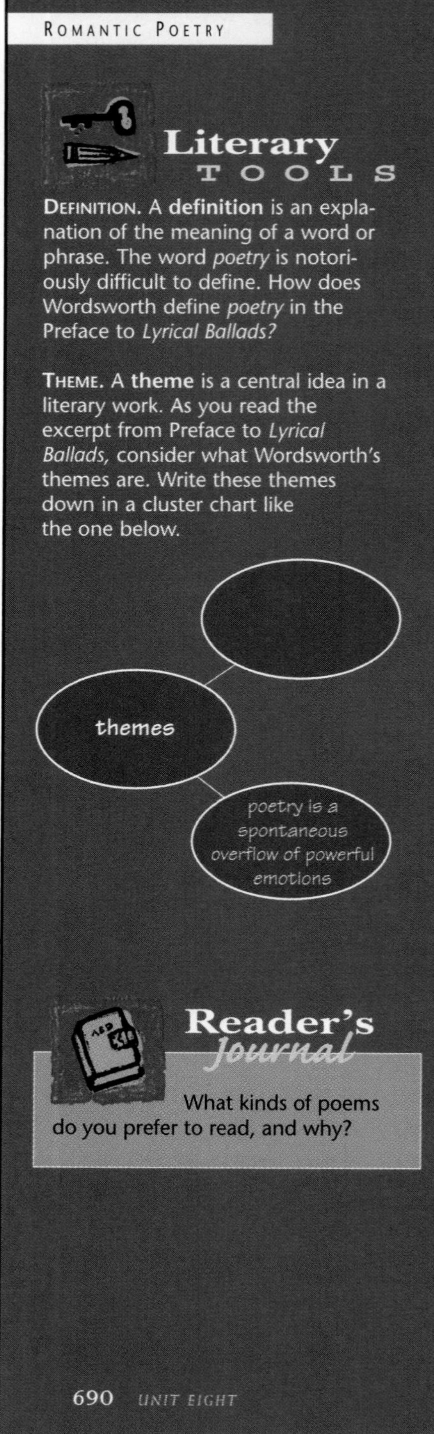

Literary TOOLS

DEFINITION. A **definition** is an explanation of the meaning of a word or phrase. The word *poetry* is notoriously difficult to define. How does Wordsworth define *poetry* in the Preface to *Lyrical Ballads?*

THEME. A **theme** is a central idea in a literary work. As you read the excerpt from Preface to *Lyrical Ballads,* consider what Wordsworth's themes are. Write these themes down in a cluster chart like the one below.

Reader's Journal

What kinds of poems do you prefer to read, and why?

flowery, formal language but rather in the voice of the common person. The verse in *Lyrical Ballads* contains portraits of nature and of ordinary but noble people; it eschews artificial, mechanical devices of style in favor of "a selection of the language actually used by men"; and it records remembered moments of spontaneous emotional transport over which had been thrown "a certain coloring of the imagination."

In 1802, Wordsworth married Mary Hutchinson, with whom he was to have five children. In 1805 he completed his long masterwork, *The Prelude,* an autobiographical portrait of the development of a poet from childhood through maturity. This poem was meant to be the introduction to a longer work that was never completed.

The period from 1797 to 1807 saw the creation of Wordsworth's finest poems, most of which dealt with the elevation of the soul through communion with nature. Thereafter, Wordsworth's poetic powers declined as his conservatism, derived from bitterness over the failures of the French Revolution, increased. This conservatism earned him the scorn of younger, more radical poets, including Shelley, Byron, Keats, and Robert Browning, a scorn most famously expressed in Browning's poem "The Lost Leader."

In 1843 Wordsworth accepted the position of poet laureate of England under the condition that he not be required to write occasional or official verse. In his later years, he cared patiently and devotedly for his beloved sister Dorothy, who suffered from senile dementia. When Wordsworth himself died, he was buried in Grasmere Churchyard in the Lake District that he had immortalized in his work.

About the SELECTIONS

The first selection is an excerpt from the **Preface** to Wordsworth and Coleridge's ***Lyrical Ballads.*** In the preface, Wordsworth champions the idea that poetry should be written in the voice of the ordinary person. In other words, poetry should be natural, not artificial. Wordsworth's championing of the common person and of nature is in keeping with his youthful sympathies for natural rights as embodied in the rhetoric of the French Revolution. **"The World Is Too Much with Us"** a sonnet reminiscent of Blake's poem "London," bemoans humanity's separation from nature. **"Lines Composed a Few Miles above Tintern Abbey"** is a poem inspired by a four- or five-day walk that Wordsworth took from Tintern to Bristol with his sister.

FROM Preface to *Lyrical Ballads*

WILLIAM WORDSWORTH

The principal object, then, which I myself proposed in these poems was to choose incidents and situations from common life, and to relate or describe them, throughout, as far as was possible in a selection of language really used by men; and, at the same time to throw over them a certain coloring of imagination, whereby ordinary things should be presented to the mind in an unusual way; and, further, and above all, to make these incidents and situations interesting by tracing in them, truly though not ostentatiously, the primary laws of our nature: chiefly, as far as regards the manner in which we associate ideas in a state of excitement. Humble and rustic life was generally chosen, because in that condition, the essential passions of the heart find a better soil in which they can attain their maturity, are less under restraint, and speak a plainer and more emphatic language; because in that condition of life our elementary feelings coexist in a state of greater simplicity, and, consequently, may be more accurately contemplated, and more forcibly communicated . . .

What sorts of incidents did Wordsworth propose to write about? What sort of language did he propose to use? In what ways did he wish to present these incidents and for what purpose?

◆ ◆ ◆

Not that I . . . always began to write with a distinct purpose formally conceived; but I believe that habits of meditation have so formed my feelings that my descriptions of such objects as strongly excite those feelings will be found to carry along with them a *purpose*. If this opinion be erroneous, I can have little right to the name of a poet. For all good poetry is the spontaneous overflow of powerful feelings: but though this be true, poems to which any value can be attached were never produced on any variety of subjects but by a man who, being possessed of more than usual organic sensibility had also thought long and deeply.

What two things are necessary for a poem to be of value?

◆ ◆ ◆

The reader will find that personifications of abstract ideas rarely occur in these volumes; and are utterly rejected, as an ordinary device, to elevate the style and raise it above prose. My purpose was to imitate, and, as far as possible, to adopt the very language of men; and

WORDS FOR EVERYDAY USE

prin • ci • pal (prin´ sə pəl) *adj.*, main or chief. *The principal damage from the fire was caused by smoke.*

os • ten • ta • tious • ly (äs´ tən tā´ shəs lē) *adv.*, in a showy display. *Expensive homes are featured ostentatiously in the architectural magazine.*

em • phat • ic (em fat´ ik) *adj.*, forceful, definite. *The soldiers' emphatic replies satisfied the officers.*

con • tem • plate (kän´ təm plāt) *vt.*, think about carefully. *You should contemplate the consequences of your actions.*

er • ro • ne • ous (ər rōn´ nē əs) *adj.*, based on error, wrong. *When they discovered a miscalculation, the scientists declared that the lab results were erroneous.*

or • gan • ic (ôr gan´ ik) *adj.*, inherent, inborn. *The judge possesses an organic sense of fairness.*

ANSWERS TO GUIDED READING QUESTIONS

1. Wordsworth proposed to write about situations from common life. These situations should be described imaginatively but simply, with language used by ordinary people. They should also be presented to the mind in an unusual way, and in them, readers should be able to trace the primary laws of nature.
2. "All good poetry is the spontaneous overflow of powerful feelings; but...poems to which any value can be attached..." are created by poets who have also "thought long and deeply."

LITERARY NOTE

The first edition of *Lyrical Ballads,* published in 1798, did not contain a preface. Wordsworth added the preface to the second edition, which was published in 1800, and revised it two years later for the third edition.

ANSWER TO GUIDED READING QUESTION

1. The origin of poetry is "emotion recollected in tranquility."

SELECTION CHECK TEST 4.8.15 WITH ANSWERS

Checking Your Reading

1. What does the "humble and rustic life" allow us to experience fully? **Responses will vary, but could include passions, feelings, or emotions.**
2. In what language does Wordsworth strive to write? **He writes in ordinary language.**
3. When will Wordsworth use personification? **He uses it when incited by passion.**
4. From where does poetry take its origin? **It takes its origin in emotion.**
5. How does the poet access this origin? **He thinks long and deeply; in tranquillity.**

Vocabulary in Context

Fill each blank with the most appropriate word from the Words for Everyday Use. You may have to change the tense of the word.

principal ostentatious emphatic contemplate erroneous organic endeavor

1. Before Duncan's on-the-buzzer basket, we heard the **erroneous** announcement that the Raptors had lost.
2. Jackie used the long train ride to **contemplate** what life in New York would be like.
3. The protestors painted **emphatic** slogans on cardboard and marched to the site.
4. Raquel's **ostentatious** outfit stood out among the classic gowns of the other women.
5. The Hippocratic Oath's **principal** instruction is to do no harm.

Literary Tools

Choose the sentence ending that best fits each sentence beginning. You may not use any choice more than once.

1. Wordsworth rejects… **C**
2. Poets take ordinary experiences and throw over them… **F**
3. A definition is… **G**
4. This selection can be read as… **B**
5. Lyrical Ballads was… **D**

Sunset with Fishing Boats on Loch Fyne, c.1807. Joshua Cristall. Ashmolean Museum, Oxford.

assuredly such personifications do not make any natural or regular part of that language. They are, indeed, a figure of speech occasionally prompted by passion, and I have made use of them as such; but have endeavored utterly to reject them as a mechanical device of style, or as a family language which writers in meter seem to lay claim to by prescription. I have wished to keep the reader in the company of flesh and blood, persuaded that by so doing I shall interest him.

◆ ◆ ◆

I have said that poetry is the spontaneous overflow of powerful feelings: it takes its origin from emotion recollected in tranquillity; the emotion is contemplated till, by a species of reaction, the tranquillity gradually disappears, and an emotion, kindred to that which was before the subject of contemplation, is gradually produced, and does itself actually exist in the mind. ■

What is the origin of poetry?

WORDS FOR EVERYDAY USE

en • deav • or (en dev´ ər) *vt.*, attempt, try. *The swimmer will endeavor to set a new record for crossing the English Channel.*
kin • dred (kin´ drid) *adj.*, related, similar. *Are the ideas expressed in this philosophy kindred to your own?*

Respond *to the* **SELECTION**

Have you ever tried to write poetry? If so, what was the experience like for you? If not, why not?

SELECTION CHECK TEST 4.8.15 WITH ANSWERS (CONT.)

a. a criticism of the major poets of the age.
b. an argument for Wordsworth's idea of poetry.
c. stylistic devices and flourishes.
d. co-written with Samuel Coleridge.
e. the power of nature.
f. a "certain coloring of imagination."
g. an explanation of the meaning of a word or phrase.

RESPOND TO THE SELECTION

Do you agree with Wordsworth that "poetry is a spontaneous overflow of powerful feelings"? Why, or why not?

Investigate, Inquire, Imagine

Recall: GATHERING FACTS →

1a. What kind of situations and language does Wordsworth propose to use in the poems in *Lyrical Ballads*?

2a. What, according to Wordsworth, is poetry?

3a. What does Wordsworth try to imitate in his poetry? What device does he reject?

Interpret: FINDING MEANING

1b. Why does Wordsworth feel strongly about the type of situation and language used in poetry? How does he feel about other kinds of topics and language used in poetry?

2b. Based on his notions of poetry, what can you infer about Wordsworth as a poet?

3b. Why would natural speech be the best way to express oneself in poetic form?

Analyze: TAKING THINGS APART →

4a. Identify the process Wordsworth describes for the writing of good poetry and the qualities of a good poem.

Synthesize: BRINGING THINGS TOGETHER

4b. What case does the speaker make for taking steps to remedy the social problem that brings about the curse mentioned in stanza 4?

Evaluate: MAKING JUDGMENTS →

5a. The French Revolution began in 1789 when common folk stormed the Bastille Prison to protest their treatment by the monarchy and demand equality. Having read The Preface to *Lyrical Ballads,* what would you judge the impact of the French Revolution to have been on Wordsworth's ideals and his conception of poetry?

Extend: CONNECTING IDEAS

5b. What might Wordsworth consider to be essential and universal elements of human nature?

Understanding Literature

DEFINITION. Review **definition** in the Handbook of Literary Terms. The word *poetry* is notoriously difficult to define. Wordsworth defines poetry as "a spontaneous overflow of powerful feelings." Do you consider this a complete or accurate definition? Why, or why not? Work with a group of students to arrive at your own definition of poetry. Begin by having each student write a definition. Then discuss each definition's merits and limitations. See if you can combine your definitions to come up with one that you consider accurate and useful.

THEME. Review the definition for **theme** and the cluster chart you completed for Literary Tools in Prereading. What are some important themes in Wordsworth's Preface? What kinds of poems would not fit the criteria for poetry set forth by Wordsworth?

ANSWERS TO INVESTIGATE, INQUIRE, AND IMAGINE

RECALL

1a. He proposes to use situations and language from common life.

2a. Wordsworth says that poetry is the "spontaneous overflow of powerful feelings."

3a. Wordsworth tries to imitate the way people really speak. He rejects personification.

INTERPRET

1b. Wordsworth believes that such situations and language allow true, simple passions greater room for expression. He feels that other topics and language constrict natural expression and lead away from truth.

2b. He probably wrote his poetry when he felt powerful emotions.

3b. Poetry should be "spontaneous" and filled with emotion. Even though it is later refined, poetry should reflect the natural conversational language of the poet.

ANALYZE

4a. The source of inspiration is powerful emotions, which we recall at some point after we experience them. Through deep contemplation, we can bring ourselves back to the experience of the original emotion and create a poem. The qualities of good poetry include the use of the "language of men" and the description of simple, "humble and rustic life."

SYNTHESIZE

4b. Wordsworth valued emotion over intellectualization, though he did acknowledge the need to use contemplation and thought along with the recollection of emotion. He believed in the simple, rustic life and that simple, common language allowed for more compelling communication. He valued simplicity, honesty and had an aversion to artifice and formality.

EVALUATE

5a. The French Revolution was fought for equality among the classes. Wordsworth echoes this idea in his belief that common people and their language are suitable subjects—in fact the most suitable subjects—for poetry.

EXTEND

5b. He might consider love of beauty, friendship, and compassion to be some of the essential and universal elements of human nature.

ANSWERS TO UNDERSTANDING LITERATURE

DEFINITION. Answers should respond to Wordsworth's definition and present reasonable arguments for or against it. Students may comment that the common language of nineteenth-century England does not necessarily translate to the present.

THEME. Some important themes in Wordsworth's Preface are that poetry should mirror the experience and language of common people and that poetry is a "spontaneous overflow of powerful emotion." Poems, which would not fit his definition, could include some famous epics about great heroes like the Odyssey and the Iliad of Homer as well as any poetry using very formal language. He would also have disapproved of poetry which included the personification of abstract ideals.

VOCABULARY FROM THE SELECTION

sordid

READER'S JOURNAL

Make a list of ways in which humankind has turned away from nature. What attitudes have people held in the past about the natural world?

SELECTION CHECK TEST 4.8.17 WITH ANSWERS

Checking Your Reading

1. What do we lay waste as we are "getting and spending"? **We lay waste our powers.**
2. What have we given away? **We have given our hearts away.**
3. What will be howling at all hours? **The winds will be howling at all hours.**
4. What would the speaker rather be? **He would rather be a Pagan.**
5. How would the speaker like to feel? **The speaker would like to feel less forlorn.**

Literary Tools

1. A reference to an event, person, object, or work from history or literature is:
   a. a metaphor b. an apostrophe
   c. an allusion d. an ode
2. When something nonhuman is given human characteristics, the poet is using
   a. blank verse b. allusion
   c. personification d. synecdoche
3. A contradictory statement, idea, or event is
   a. paradox b. simile
   c. alliteration d. hyperbole

ART NOTE

Nocturne in Grey and Gold: Chelsea Snow, 1876. James McNeill Whistler. American-born artist James McNeill Whistler (1834–1903) spent most of his life in England. In 1877, he exhibited a number of paintings which he called "nocturnes." The paintings outraged conservative art opinion, which did not understand his avoidance of narrative detail, his layers of atmospheric color, and his belief in art for art's sake. The art critic John Ruskin wrote a caustically critical article, and Whistler, charging slander, sued Ruskin for damages. Whistler won the case, but the expense of the trial forced him into bankruptcy.

Literary TOOLS

Allusion. An **allusion** is a figure of speech in which a reference is made to a person, event, object or work from history or literature. Note the allusions used by Wordsworth in this poem.

Sonnet. A **sonnet** is a fourteen-line poem that follows one of a number of different rhyme schemes. "The World Is Too Much with Us" is a sonnet. As you read, pay attention to the rhyme scheme of the poem.

Reader's Journal

Write about a time when you experienced nature, without any of the distractions of the modern, technological world, and what the experience meant to you.

Nocturne in Grey and Gold: Chelsea Snow, 1876. James McNeill Whistler. The Fogg Art Museum, Harvard University.

The World Is Too Much with Us

WILLIAM WORDSWORTH

The world is too much with us; late and soon,
Getting and spending, we lay waste our powers:
Little we see in Nature that is ours;
We have given our hearts away, a sordid boon![1]
This Sea that bares her bosom to the moon;
The winds that will be howling at all hours,
And are up-gathered now like sleeping flowers;
For this, for every thing, we are out of tune;
It moves us not.—Great God! I'd rather be
A Pagan suckled in a creed outworn;
So might I, standing on this pleasant lea,[2]
Have glimpses that would make me less forlorn;
Have sight of Proteus[3] rising from the sea;
Or hear old Triton[4] blow his wreathèd horn. ■

According to the speaker, what happens when people focus too much on "getting and spending"?

What, according to the speaker, could the ancients see that we cannot see because we are too civilized?

1. **boon.** Gift
2. **lea.** Meadow
3. **Proteus.** In the *Odyssey,* Proteus was an old man of the sea who could change his shape at will.
4. **Triton.** A sea god

WORDS FOR EVERYDAY USE

sor • did (sôr´ did) *adj.,* ignoble, squalid. *The polite, well-dressed young man seemed out of place in his sordid surroundings.*

ANSWERS TO INVESTIGATE, INQUIRE, AND IMAGINE

Recall

1a. We waste our powers "getting and spending."
2a. We have "given our hearts away."
3a. These myths are of the Greek Proteus and the Roman Triton—the gods of the sea.

Interpret

1b. When we concentrate on material concerns, we become numb to the spiritual aspects of our environment.
2b. We have given away our hearts to the material world of possession. In doing so, we have lost our spirituality.
3b. These myths are important because they honor the elemental force of the sea, which the speaker believes is therapeutic. The speaker feels that nature is dead to modern people and needs to be resurrected.

(Continued on page 695)

Respond to the SELECTION

What aspects of modern life keep you isolated from nature? How do you feel about that?

INVESTIGATE, Inquire, Imagine

Recall: Gathering Facts →

1a. According to the speaker, how do we "lay waste our powers"?

2a. According to the speaker, what have we "given . . . away"?

3a. What are the myths from "a creed outworn" to which the speaker refers?

Interpret: Finding Meaning

1b. What might be wrong with focusing too much on "getting and spending"?

2b. Why does this action represent "a sordid boon"?

3b. What might have been felt or experienced by believers of these myths that is not felt or experienced by us today?

Analyze: Taking Things Apart →

4a. Review the selection from Preface to *Lyrical Ballads* on page 601. In it, Wordsworth rejects a kind of personification. And yet, in "The World Is Too Much with Us" he uses personification. What sort of personification does Wordsworth reject? What sort of personification does he apparently accept?

Synthesize: Bringing Things Together

4b. What Romantic view of the proper relationship between humans and nature is expressed in this poem? In other words, what makes this poem Romantic? How is the poem's use of personification consistent with the Romantic view?

Evaluate: Making Judgments →

5a. Evaluate the emotion expressed in this poem. How does the poet feel about man's relationship to nature? Do you agree? Why, or why not?

Extend: Connecting Ideas

5b. To what time and place in history might this speaker like to return? Why might he want to do this ?

Understanding Literature

Allusion. Review the definition for **allusion** in the Handbook of Literary Terms. What are the allusions in this poem?

Sonnet. Review the definition for **sonnet** in Literary Tools in Prereading. What rhyme scheme does this sonnet follow? Rewrite the last word of each line and mark the rhyme scheme as shown below.

soon *a*
powers *b*

How is this sonnet unlike the typical Petrarchan sonnet described in Unit 4 of this text?

RESPOND TO THE SELECTION

What specific environmental problems have occurred as a result of modern life and technological advances?

ANSWERS TO INVESTIGATE, INQUIRE, AND IMAGINE (CONT. FROM PAGE 694)

Analyze

4a. In the Preface to *Lyrical Ballads,* Wordsworth rejects the personification of abstract ideas, saying that it is an attempt to "elevate the style and raise it above prose." He seems to find this artificial and elitist. He attempts to maintain a style that is consistent with the way real people speak. He does, however, personify elements of nature in "The World is Too Much With Us." In it, "This sea bares her bosom to the moon," the winds howl, and flowers sleep.

Synthesize

4b. The poem is Romantic because it expresses the inherent value of human passions, the natural world, and spirituality. By personifying nature, Wordsworth portrays the kinship between nature and man that is inherent in the Romantic view. Both nature and man are infused with the same creative spirit or life force.

Evaluate:

5a. The emotions expressed in this poem are regret, despair and longing for a closer relationship to nature. Responses will vary as to agreement.

Extend

5b. He might like to return to ancient Greece or Rome because of the power of myth and strength of spirituality during these times. He might also like to return to ancient Greece or Rome because of the power of myth and strength of spirituality of that time, particularly the spiritual relationship with nature.

ANSWERS TO UNDERSTANDING LITERATURE

Allusion. The allusions are to Proteus and to Triton.

Sonnet. This Petrarchan sonnet has two parts: an octave that rhymes *abbaabba* and a sestet that rhymes *cdcdcd.* The typical Petrarchan sonnet would be addressed to a cold and distant but beautiful woman, the object of the speaker's unrequited love. Instead, this sonnet focuses on the speaker's contemplation of his spiritual alienation from the natural world.

VOCABULARY FROM THE SELECTION

beauteous
copse
corporeal
exhortation
prevail
recompense
repose
secluded
sublime
tranquil
vagrant
vain
zeal

GRAPHIC ORGANIZER

Lines1-22: description of the scene itself
Lines 22-57: description of times past, drawing comfort from memories of this scene while elsewhere
Lines 58-83: Description of his youthful experience of this scene
Lines 83-111: Description of his present feelings about nature and this scene
Lines 112-159: Description of feelings about his sister and hopes for her experience of nature in the future.

READER'S JOURNAL

Students might want to accompany their writing with photographs or pictures.

Literary TOOLS

Free Verse and Blank Verse. Free verse, or ***vers libre***, is poetry that avoids use of regular rhyme, rhythm, meter, or division into stanzas. **Blank verse** is unrhymed poetry written in iambic pentameter. As you read, try to determine whether this poem is written in blank verse or free verse.

Ode. An **ode** is a lofty lyric poem on a serious theme. Wordsworth's poetry is often described as meditative or introspective. "Lines Composed a Few Miles above Tintern Abbey" is a good example of such a poem. To track the speaker's developing feelings and changing thoughts, complete the following graphic organizer listing the time periods he describes in the lines below. An example has been done for you.

Lines 1–22:	description of the scene itself
Lines 22–57:	
Lines 58–83:	
Lines 83–111:	
Lines 112–159:	

Reader's Journal

Recall a place in nature which you visited in early childhood. Describe the way this place looked and how it made you feel then, and imagine how you might react to it now.

Lines Composed a Few Miles Above Tintern Abbey

WILLIAM WORDSWORTH

Five years have past; five summers, with the length
Of five long winters! and again I hear
These waters, rolling from their mountain-springs
With a soft inland murmur.—Once again
Do I behold these steep and lofty cliffs,
That on a wild secluded scene impress
Thoughts of more deep seclusion; and connect
The landscape with the quiet of the sky.
The day is come when I again repose
Here, under this dark sycamore, and view
These plots of cottage-ground, these orchard-tufts,
Which at this season, with their unripe fruits,
Are clad in one green hue, and lose themselves
'Mid groves and copses. Once again I see
These hedge-rows, hardly hedge-rows, little lines
Of sportive wood run wild: these pastoral farms,
Green to the very door; and wreaths of smoke
Sent up, in silence, from among the trees!
With some uncertain notice, as might seem
Of vagrant dwellers in the houseless woods,
Or of some Hermit's cave, where by his fire
The Hermit sits alone.

These beauteous forms,
Through a long absence, have not been to me
As is a landscape to a blind man's eye:
But oft, in lonely rooms, and 'mid the din
Of towns and cities, I have owed to them

WORDS FOR EVERYDAY USE

se• clud • ed (si klo͞od´ id) *adj.*, hidden from public view. *We couldn't see the secluded campsite from the highway.*

re • pose (ri pōz´) *vt.*, lie quietly, rest. *The artist's model reposes on a velvet sofa.*

copse (käps) *n.*, thicket of small trees or bushes. *That copse marks the southern border of the property.*

va • grant (vāg´ rənt) *adj.*, nomadic, wandering. *When she tired of her vagrant lifestyle, she settled down in the small town.*

beau • te • ous (byo͞o´ tē əs) *adj.*, beautiful. *Nothing matches the beauteous glow of the aurora borealis.*

Tintern Abbey on the River Wye, 1805. Philip James de Loutherbourg. Fitzwilliam Museum, Cambridge.

In hours of weariness, sensations sweet,
Felt in the blood, and felt along the heart;
And passing even into my purer mind,
With tranquil restoration:—feelings too
Of unremembered pleasure: such, perhaps,
As have no slight or trivial influence
On that best portion of a good man's life,
His little, nameless, unremembered, acts
Of kindness and of love. Nor less, I trust,
To them I may have owed another gift,
Of aspect more sublime; that blessed mood,
In which the burthen of the mystery,
In which the heavy and the weary weight
Of all this unintelligible world,
Is lightened:—that serene and blessed mood,

What effects has remembering this scene had on the speaker?

WORDS FOR EVERYDAY USE

tran • quil (tran´ kwil) *adj.,* peaceful, calm. *The siren pierced the tranquil, evening air.*
sub • lime (sə blīm´) *adj.,* noble, majestic. *The painter captured perfectly the sublime expression on the emperor's face.*

ANSWER TO GUIDED READING QUESTION

1. Remembering this scene has had a calming, sublime effect on the speaker.

LITERARY NOTE

Unlike the dramatic "I" used by most eighteenth-century poets, Wordsworth used a personal "I." In fact, the poem was originally printed with a journal-like notation that told the place and date it was written. "Tintern Abbey" and other poems in *Lyrical Ballads* set the tone for a new era of more personal and reflective poetry. Refer to the Handbook of Literary Terms for more information about the role of the speaker in poetry.

ANSWERS TO GUIDED READING QUESTIONS

1. The speaker was energetic and connected to nature in an unreflective way.
2. In his youth, the speaker experienced nature as an "appetite" which needed no deeper meaning to hold his interest that its own visual beauty.

LITERARY TECHNIQUE

Apostrophe. An **apostrophe** is a figure of speech in which an object or person is directly addressed. What is the apostrophe in stanza 3? (Refer to the Handbook of Literary Terms for more information.)

Answer

The speaker addresses the Wye.

CROSS-CURRICULAR ACTIVITIES

Environmental Science. Have students observe Nature. Tell them to go to their favorite place outside where they can experience Nature. If students don't have a place in mind, suggest they go to a park, a wooded area, or go by a lake. As students take in the wonders around them, have them jot down sensory details. Then have students use their notes to make a sensory detail chart of their experience. Refer them to the Language Arts Survey 2.18, "Sensory Detail Charts." You may also want students to use their chart to help them write a brief essay about their experience.

In which the affections gently lead us on,—
Until, the breath of this corporeal frame
And even the motion of our human blood
Almost suspended, we are laid asleep
In body, and become a living soul:
While with an eye made quiet by the power
Of harmony, and the deep power of joy,
We see into the life of things.

If this
Be but a vain belief, yet, oh! how oft—
In darkness and amid the many shapes
Of joyless daylight; when the fretful stir
Unprofitable, and the fever of the world
Have hung upon the beatings of my heart—
How oft, in spirit, have I turned to thee,
O sylvan Wye![1] thou wanderer thro' the woods,
How often has my spirit turned to thee!

And now, with gleams of half-extinguished thought,
With many recognitions dim and faint,
And somewhat of a sad perplexity,
The picture of the mind revives again:
While here I stand, not only with the sense
Of present pleasure, but with pleasing thoughts
That in this moment there is life and food
For future years. And so I dare to hope,
Though changed, no doubt, from what I was when first
I came among these hills; when like a roe[2]
I bounded o'er the mountains, by the sides
Of the deep rivers, and the lonely streams,
Wherever nature led: more like a man
Flying from something that he dreads, than one
Who sought the thing he loved. For nature then
(The coarser pleasures of my boyish days,
And their glad animal movements all gone by)
To me was all in all.—I cannot paint
What then I was. The sounding cataract

What was the speaker like in his younger years?

What was the appeal of nature to the speaker in his youth?

1. **Wye.** A river in England
2. **roe.** A type of deer

Words for Everyday Use

cor • po • re • al (kôr pôr´ ē əl) *adj.*, of a bodily or physical nature. *According to legend, the strange female figure that appears outside the cemetery is not a corporeal being, but a spirit or phantom.*

vain (vān) *adj.*, empty, worthless. *Do you expect me to believe such vain promises?*

Haunted me like a passion: the tall rock,
The mountain, and the deep and gloomy wood,
Their colors and their forms, were then to me
An appetite; a feeling and a love,
That had no need of a remoter charm,
By thought supplied, nor any interest
Unborrowed from the eye.—That time is past,
And all its aching joys are now no more,
And all its dizzy raptures. Not for this
Faint[3] I, nor mourn nor murmur; other gifts
Have followed; for such loss, I would believe,
Abundant recompense. For I have learned
To look on nature, not as in the hour
Of thoughtless youth; but hearing oftentimes
The still, sad music of humanity,
Nor harsh nor grating, though of ample power
To chasten and subdue. And I have felt
A presence that disturbs me with the joy
Of elevated thoughts; a sense sublime
Of something far more deeply interfused,
Whose dwelling is the light of setting suns,
And the round ocean and the living air,
And the blue sky, and in the mind of man:
A motion and a spirit, that impels
All thinking things, all objects of all thought,
And rolls through all things. Therefore am I still
A lover of the meadows and the woods,
And mountains; and of all that we behold
From this green earth; of all the mighty world
Of eye, and ear,—both what they half create,
And what perceive; well pleased to recognize
In nature and the language of the sense,
The anchor of my purest thoughts, the nurse,
The guide, the guardian of my heart, and soul
Of all my moral being.

Nor perchance,
If I were not thus taught, should I the more

How does the speaker regard nature now? What does the speaker sense in the natural world around him?

3. **Faint.** Lose heart

WORDS FOR EVERYDAY USE

rec • om • pense (rek´ əm pens) *n.*, repayment, reward. *The grateful parents gave recompense to the man who found their missing daughter.*

ANSWER TO GUIDED READING QUESTION

1. Now the speaker regards nature with his intellect rather than simply with his senses. He realizes that the natural world holds deep inner truths that pertain to the essence of all living things.

ADDITIONAL QUESTIONS AND ACTIVITIES

Point out to students that a plant on a windowsill, a squirrel or tree in the middle of a city, and the weather are all aspects of nature. Ask students the following questions:

1. Do you feel connected with Nature? Why, or why not?
2. Do you think modernization has enhanced or destroyed Nature? Explain.
3. Do you think people's appreciation for Nature has changed since Wordsworth's time, or has it stayed the same? Explain.

ANSWER TO GUIDED READING QUESTION

1. The speaker's sister now experiences nature as he did in his own youth, and he is reminded of his youth watching her.

BIOGRAPHICAL NOTE

- Dorothy Wordsworth was almost two years younger than her brother William. After her mother's death, the seven-year-old Dorothy lived with several relatives and spent time with William and her other brothers only during the summers. William and Dorothy were finally reunited in 1795, when William came into some money and Dorothy moved into his house to care for him.
- A selection from Dorothy Wordsworth's *The Grasmere Journals* appears on page 674.

SELECTION CHECK TEST 4.8.19 WITH ANSWERS

Checking Your Reading

1. How long has it been since the speaker visited this place? **It has been five years.**
2. What thoughts have comforted the speaker in times of stress? **He has been comforted by thoughts of this place along the Wye River.**
3. What did the speaker think of nature when he was younger? **He enjoyed it, but did not appreciate it as he does now.**
4. How does the speaker feel about having grown older? **He is glad for the lessons he's learned.**
5. What person does the speaker address in this poem? **He addresses his sister.**

Vocabulary in Context

Fill each blank with the most appropriate word from the Words for Everyday Use. You may have to change the tense of the word.

recompense repose secluded tranquil vagrant vain zeal

1. The chess player made several **vain** moves before conceding that he had lost.
2. Japanese gardens are designed to be **tranquil** escapes from a busy life.
3. Each afternoon, my mother tries to have an hour of **repose** before we all get home.

Suffer my genial spirits[4] to decay:
For thou art with me here upon the banks
Of this fair river; thou my dearest Friend,[5]
My dear, dear Friend; and in thy voice I catch
The language of my former heart, and read
My former pleasures in the shooting lights
Of thy wild eyes. Oh! yet a little while
May I behold in thee what I was once,
My dear, dear Sister! and this prayer I make,
Knowing that Nature never did betray
The heart that loved her; 'tis her privilege,
Through all the years of this our life, to lead
From joy to joy: for she can so inform
The mind that is within us, so impress
With quietness and beauty, and so feed
With lofty thoughts, that neither evil tongues,
Rash judgments, nor the sneers of selfish men,
Nor greetings where no kindness is, nor all
The dreary intercourse of daily life,
Shall e'er prevail against us, or disturb
Our cheerful faith, that all which we behold
Is full of blessings. Therefore let the moon
Shine on thee in thy solitary walk;
And let the misty mountain-winds be free
To blow against thee: and, in after years,
When these wild ecstasies shall be matured
Into a sober pleasure; when thy mind
Shall be a mansion for all lovely forms,
Thy memory be as a dwelling-place
For all sweet sounds and harmonies; oh! then,
If solitude, or fear, or pain, or grief,
Should be thy portion, with what healing thoughts
Of tender joy wilt thou remember me,
And these my exhortations! Nor, perchance—
If I should be where I no more can hear
Thy voice, nor catch from thy wild eyes these gleams
Of past existence—wilt thou then forget

Whose reaction now, to this scene, reminds the speaker of his own, youthful reaction?

4. **genial spirits.** Creative spirit, from the noun *genius*
5. **dearest Friend.** Dorothy, his sister

WORDS FOR EVERYDAY USE

pre • vail (prē vāl´) *vi.*, be victorious. *Did the school board prevail in its fight against the budget cuts?*

ex • hor • ta • tion (eg´ zôr tā´ shən) *n.*, strong urging. *The speaker's exhortations convinced me to join the cause.*

SELECTION CHECK TEST 4.8.19 WITH ANSWERS (CONT.)

4. At fifty, it seems unlikely that Joe will give up his **vagrant** lifestyle.
5. The protestors argued for appropriate **recompense** for the factory's workers.

Literary Tools

1. The lines "I came among these hills; when like a roe/ I bounded o'er the mountains..." illustrate
   a. allegory
   b. hyperbole
   c. free verse
   d. metaphor
2. The line "Of the deep rivers, and the lonely streams," illustrates

Continued on page 701

That on the banks of this delightful stream
We stood together; and that I, so long
A worshiper of Nature, hither came
Unwearied in that service; rather say
With warmer love—oh! with far deeper zeal
Of holier love. Nor wilt thou then forget,
That after many wanderings, many years
Of absence, these steep woods and lofty cliffs,
And this green pastoral landscape, were to me
More dear, both for themselves and for thy sake! ■

Why is this place special to the speaker, beyond the fact that he is "A worshiper of Nature"?

WORDS FOR EVERYDAY USE

zeal (zēl) *n.*, passion, fervor. *The conductor's creative zeal spread through the entire orchestra.*

Respond *to the* Selection

What special place gives you a feeling of comfort and peace? How would you describe it to someone you love?

ANSWER TO GUIDED READING QUESTION

1. This place is special because it reminds him of his sister and the time they shared there.

RESPOND TO THE SELECTION

If students have difficulty imagining Dorothy's responses, read them the biographical information about her on page 674.

SELECTION CHECK TEST 4.8.19 WITH ANSWERS (CONT. FROM PAGE 700)

a. simile
b. personification
c. hyperbole
d. credo

3. A poem that does not rhyme and is written in iambic pentameter is
   a. a pastoral poem
   b. blank verse
   c. free verse
   d. an ode

ANSWERS TO INVESTIGATE, INQUIRE, AND IMAGINE

RECALL

1a. The speaker describes his youth, when he first experienced this place.

2a. The speaker says he does not "mourn nor murmur." He is not sad because he has found something else that offers recompense.

3a. He values her youthful passion for nature and sees his youthful joy in nature in her reactions.

INTERPRET

1b. He uses the metaphor of a roe—or a young deer bounding over the hills. This implies that his relationship to nature was a simple one of exuberant joy at the sensual experience of nature. He responded to it as if it were an urge or an appetite [see lines79-83] rather than something to contemplate or understand.

2a. The speaker has learned to hear the "still, sad music of humanity" in nature and to feel the presence of something "sublime / Of something far more deeply interfused..." [lines 94-96] He has learned to relate to nature with his mind as well as his emotions and to sense in nature a moral anchor he describes in lines 109-111: "The anchor of my purest thoughts, the nurse, / The guide, the guardian of my heart, and soul / Of all my moral being."

3b. He believes that the "quietness and beauty" (line 127) of nature can protect people from the "dreary intercourse of daily life" (line 131).

ANALYZE

4a. In his youth, the speaker reacted to nature with the joy of a deer bounding over the hills. His relationship to nature depended only on its visual appeal, not on any intellectual appreciation. He says in lines 81-83 that he "had no need of a remoter charm, / By thought supplied, nor any interest / Unborrowed from the eye." As a man, however, he has lost those "dizzy raptures" and developed an appreciation for nature that includes a sense of a healing presence that runs throughout all of nature. He appreciates nature now with his sight and his emotions as well as with his mind and his intellect.

SYNTHESIZE

4b. The speaker is not sad or mournful about this change. He describes a deeper, more satisfying relationship to nature that is, for him, a healing and guiding presence. This presence might be described as divine. Indeed, throughout Wordsworth's poetry, he uses the word "presence" often to describe the idea that there

INVESTIGATE, Inquire, Imagine

Recall: GATHERING FACTS → **Interpret:** FINDING MEANING

1a. What period of the speaker's life is described in lines 66–83?

1b. What metaphor from nature does he use to describe himself in his earliest visit to Tintern Abbey? What does this imply about his relationship to nature at that time?

2a. What feelings does the speaker describe having over the loss of this youthful relationship to nature?

2b. What things offer recompense to the speaker for having lost the "aching joys" of his youthful relationship with nature?

3a. What does the speaker value most in his sister?

3b. Why does the speaker view nature as a protector of the human spirit?

Analyze: TAKING THINGS APART → **Synthesize:** BRINGING THINGS TOGETHER

4a. In lines 66–83, the speaker describes his relationship to nature in his youth. In lines 88-111, he describes his relationship to nature as a man, in the present. Compare the two different descriptions and analyze the change in his relationship to nature.

4b. How does the speaker feel about this change? How do you interpret this "presence" in nature that the speaker describes?

Evaluate: MAKING JUDGMENTS → **Extend:** CONNECTING IDEAS

5a. Consider the speaker's feeling that a more contemplative relationship to nature, one that involves both emotion and reason, is preferable to the relationship of his youth, in which he reacted to nature as if to an instinct, with the passion and joyous abandon of a deer. Why do you think he feels this way? Do you share those feelings? Explain.

5b. The speaker compares his young sister and her relationship to nature to his own relationship when he was young. What does this comparison tell you about his feelings toward his sister and his hopes for her as she lives out her life?

Understanding Literature

FREE VERSE AND BLANK VERSE. Review the definitions for **free verse** and **blank verse** in the Handbook of Literary Terms. To which category does this selection belong? Explain your answer. Refer to specific aspects of the poem.

ODE. Review the definition for ode in Literary Tools in Prereading. Odes are often addressed to someone or something. To whom is this ode addressed and how are they related?

ANSWERS TO INVESTIGATE, INQUIRE, AND IMAGINE (CONT.)

is a common life force that runs throughout all of existence—all living and all inanimate things in nature.

EVALUATE

5a. *Responses will vary.* The speaker feels that he has a deeper appreciation of nature and that he finds a moral anchor and guide therein. He seems to take a great deal of comfort in his sense that there is a larger presence in all of nature, guiding and guarding him.

EXTEND

5b. The speaker describes a warm, loving and protective relationship towards his sister, whom he hopes will come to find the same sort of comfort, and sense of protection and guidance that he has found in nature.

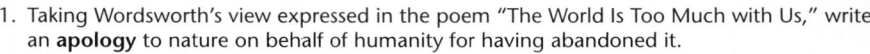

Writer's Journal

1. Taking Wordsworth's view expressed in the poem "The World Is Too Much with Us," write an **apology** to nature on behalf of humanity for having abandoned it.
2. Take an imaginary journey to a world in which people are completely in touch with nature. Write a few entries in a **travel journal** about this new land. Describe the place and your impressions of it. How do the people live? What is important to them? You may wish to make comparisons to your own homeland as well.
3. Write a **free verse poem** of at least two stanzas on a childhood memory and what it now means to you. You may choose a place you recall, a family event, a person or a special possession. What did it mean to you at the time and what is its significance to you now? If its significance has changed, why do you think this is so?

Integrating *the* Language Arts

Language, Grammar, and Style

Verb Tense. Read the Language Arts Survey 3.62, "Properties of Verbs: Tense." Then complete each sentence below by writing the verb form described in parentheses.

1. Since I was here last, five years _____. (present perfect of *pass*)
2. Those landscapes _____ me many moments of tranquil recollection over the years. (past perfect of *give*)
3. When we are quiet and thoughtful, we _____ into the life of things. (present of *see*)
4. As you mature, you _____ more fully the value of quiet time and of friends. (future of *appreciate*)
5. The memory of that landscape is more powerful to me because you ____ it and _____ it with me. (past of *see* and *share*)

Media Literacy & Speaking and Listening

Effects of Mass Media. Wordsworth believed that imaginative literature is important because it keeps people emotionally alive and morally aware. He also believed that, in contrast, mass culture has the effect of reducing the mind to a "savage torpor," that is, to dullness brought on by being deluged by trivia and sensationalism. Think about the meaning of this phrase in terms of your own life. What are the effects of the avalanche of trivia that we are exposed to daily in the mass media? Do the trivial, unimaginative, sensationalistic products of mass culture dull the mind? Review Language Arts Survey 4.15, "Giving a Speech." Then prepare a speech outlining your thoughts on these questions, and deliver it to your class.

Study and Research

Researching the French Revolution. Using the library and world history texts, research the French Revolution in order to better understand the revolutionary ideas that so inspired the Romantics. What events led to the revolt? Who were the leaders, and what were their ideals? How did the rest of the world react? What was the ultimate outcome of the revolution? Prepare a report and share your findings with your class. You may wish to lead a classroom discussion on how the ideals of the French Revolution are represented in the poetry of the Romantics.

ANSWERS TO INTEGRATING THE LANGUAGE ARTS

Language, Grammar, and Style

1. have passed
2. had given
3. see
4. will appreciate
5. saw, shared

Media Literacy & Speaking and Listening

To prompt students' thinking, you might suggest that they look over magazines, TV commercials, and other aspects of mass media. Before they critique and analyze the trivia and sensationalism of mass media, have them read the Language Arts Survey 5.29, "Evaluating Information and Media Sources."

ANSWERS TO UNDERSTANDING LITERATURE

Free Verse and **Blank Verse.** This poem is written in blank verse. It is divided into five stanzas. Although there are a few exceptions of irregularly stressed feet, it is written in unrhyming iambic pentameter: "I came among these hills; when like a roe/I bounded o'er the mountains, by the sides/Of the deep rivers, and the lonely streams" (lines 67–69).

Ode. The ode is addressed to both Nature and the speaker's sister Nature and the speaker's sister are related in that they both bring the speaker joy.

ADDITIONAL RESOURCES

Unit 8 Resource Book
- Selection Worksheet 8.10
- Selection Check Test 4.8.21
- Selection Test 4.8.22
- Speaking and Listening Resource 4.19
- Study and Research Resource 5.26

VOCABULARY FROM THE SELECTION

cavern
chasm
meander
tumult

READER'S JOURNAL

Suggest that students write the word *paradise* in their journals and create a cluster diagram for the word, writing whatever words and phrases come to mind. Students might then share their ideas and discuss the difference in people's views of paradise.

Alliteration. **Alliteration** is the repetition of initial consonant sounds. The title itself, "Kubla Kahn," is an example of alliteration. As you read, note the instances of alliteration you find in this poem.

dome decree
river, ran

Image. An **image** is a word picture—a word or phrase that names something that can be seen, heard, touched, tasted, or smelled. In "Kubla Kahn," Coleridge uses several images of opposites.

About the SELECTION

In a preface to **"Kubla Khan,"** Coleridge writes that he awoke from a dream with the poem fully formed in his mind. In ill health and taking medication, he had fallen asleep while reading *Purchase his Pilgrimage* by Samuel Purchase, which contains the line "In Xanadu did Cublai Can build a stately Palace." Kubla Khan founded the Chinese Mongol Dynasty in the thirteenth century. Coleridge's poem is a classic rendering of an instance of poetic reverie and inspiration.

Reader's Journal

If you could imagine a paradise for yourself and include any real or imaginary mystical elements you would choose, how would you describe such a place?

"Kubla Khan"

BY SAMUEL TAYLOR COLERIDGE

About the AUTHOR

Samuel Taylor Coleridge (1772–1834), born in rural Devonshire, attended school in London and later in Cambridge. A sensitive, intelligent, but often rather lonely student, he left school in debt, dissolution, and disgrace to enlist in the Light Dragoons. Not suited to the military life, he was soon rescued by friends and returned to the university, although he never graduated.

In 1795, Coleridge met William Wordsworth, the friend and fellow poet with whom he would collaborate on the influential *Lyrical Ballads,* which championed poetry written in the language of common people. Coleridge suffered from rheumatism and took laudanum (an opium derivative), following the standard medical procedures of the day. He became addicted to the drug around 1800, soon after becoming estranged from his wife. In 1810, at his lowest point, he had a terrible argument with his friend Wordsworth. Despite his agonies, Coleridge continued to write, lecture, and publish. After finding a caring physician who reduced the strength of his addiction, Coleridge regained his tranquility, reconciled with Wordsworth, and made peace with his former wife.

Perhaps because of his tragic addiction, many of Coleridge's most intense work efforts, including "Kubla Khan," remain unfinished and exist only in the form of scrawled notes. Nonetheless, Coleridge is considered today one of the great poets of his era and an influential literary theorist. In his *Biographia Literaria,* Coleridge introduced the idea of the "willing suspension of disbelief" central to the reading of literature. He also drew an interesting distinction between fancy, which he thought of as "memory emancipated from the order of time and space," and the higher faculty of imagination, which transcends the senses and brings knowledge of ultimate realities.

GOALS/OBJECTIVES

Studying this lesson will enable students to
- enjoy Coleridge's colorful imagery as he describes the pleasure dome
- describe Coleridge's contributions to Romantic literature and to literary theory
- define *alliteration* and *image* and recognize and explain examples of each that they encounter in their reading
- research information using a computer
- conduct research on creation myths

SAMUEL TAYLOR COLERIDGE

In Xanadu did Kubla Khan
A stately pleasure dome decree:
Where Alph,[1] the sacred river, ran
Through caverns measureless to man
   Down to a sunless sea.
So twice five miles of fertile ground
With walls and towers were girdled round:
And there were gardens bright with sinuous rills,[2]
Where blossomed many an incense-bearing tree;
And here were forests ancient as the hills,
Enfolding sunny spots of greenery.

But oh! that deep romantic chasm which slanted
Down the green hill athwart a cedarn cover![3]
A savage place! as holy and enchanted
As e'er beneath a waning moon was haunted
By woman wailing for her demon lover!
And from this chasm, with ceaseless turmoil seething,
As if this earth in fast thick pants were breathing,
A mighty fountain momently was forced:[4]
Amid whose swift half-intermitted burst
Huge fragments vaulted like rebounding hail,
Or chaffy grain beneath the thresher's flail:
And 'mid these dancing rocks at once and ever
It flung up momently the sacred river.
Five miles meandering with a mazy motion

Where is the dome to be created?

What is forced out of the chasm?

1. **Alph.** Probably the Alpheus river in Greece
2. **sinuous rills.** Winding streams
3. **athwart a cedarn cover.** The chasm cut across the cedar-covered hill on a downward slant.
4. **A . . . forced.** Waters springing from under the ground have long been a symbol for poetic inspiration.

WORDS FOR EVERYDAY USE

cav • ern (kav´ ərn) *n.*, cave. *Mammoth Cave, an underground cavern in Kentucky, has over three hundred miles of passageways.*

chasm (ka' zəm) *n.*, deep cleft in the earth. *A bridge went over the chasm that dropped 1000 feet.*

me • an • der (mē an´ dər) *vi.*, follow a winding course. *We meandered up the steep, hillside path.*

ANSWERS TO GUIDED READING QUESTIONS

1. The dome is to be where "Alph, the sacred river" runs through "caverns measureless to man / Down to a sunless sea.
2. A fountain is forced up out of the chasm.

INDIVIDUAL LEARNING STRATEGIES

MOTIVATION
Explain to students that it is not uncommon for poets to dedicate poems to great leaders or figures. Have them find a poem that is a tribute to a great leader (past or present) and also to read aloud their poem to the class.

READING PROFICIENCY
Students might find it beneficial to hear the story read aloud as they will better understand the action and the mood if it is read expressively.

ENGLISH LANGUAGE LEARNING
Explain to students that Coleridge achieves a lofty tone in the poem by using archaic language and by inverting normal word order.

SPECIAL NEEDS
Have students work together in small groups to answer the Guided Reading questions and the Recall questions in the Investigate, Inquire, and Imagine section. Then check their understanding with the selection check test.

ENRICHMENT
Students can write about or discuss what they know about Coleridge's idea of the "willing suspension of disbelief." What does it mean? Is it right for a writer to expect this from a reader? In what other mediums is suspension of disbelief required of an audience?

CROSS-CURRICULAR ACTIVITIES

SCIENCE AND MEDICINE. Research the effects of opium on the mind, both the short term and long term effects. What is opium used for in the medical field? Where does it come from? Why is it so addictive? Ask students to also research the affect it had on Coleridge.

LITERARY NOTE

Coleridge reported that he was reading the following sentence just before he fell asleep: "Here the Kubla Khan commanded a palace to be built, and a stately garden thereunto. And thus ten miles of fertile ground were inclosed [sic] with a wall."

CROSS-CURRICULAR ACTIVITY

Psychology. Coleridge said he had just read a sentence that read, "Here the Kubla Kahn commanded a palace to be...." Psychologists, looking into how we learn and how our minds work, have researched the possibility of "programming" ourselves to dream about certain issues through the use of suggestions given immediately before sleep. Research this and share with the class.

Princess Badoura, a Tale from the Arabian Nights, c.1800s. Edmund Dulac.

Through wood and dale the sacred river ran,
Then reached the caverns measureless to man,
And sank in tumult to a lifeless ocean:
And 'mid this tumult Kubla heard from far
Ancestral voices prophesying war!
   The shadow of the dome of pleasure
   Floated midway on the waves;
   Where was heard the mingled measure
   From the fountain and the caves.

Words for Everyday Use

tu • mult (to͞o´mult) *n.,* a loud commotion. *The tumult signaled the volcano's violent eruption.*

It was a miracle of rare device,
A sunny pleasure dome with caves of ice!

A damsel with a dulcimer
In a vision once I saw:
It was an Abyssinian maid,
And on her dulcimer she played,
Singing of Mount Abora.[5]
Could I revive within me
Her symphony and song,
To such a deep delight 'twould win me,
That with music loud and long,
I would build that dome in air,
That sunny dome! those caves of ice!
And all who heard should see them there,
And all should cry, Beware! Beware!
His flashing eyes, his floating hair!
Weave a circle round him thrice,[6]
And close your eyes with holy dread,
For he on honeydew hath fed,
And drunk the milk of Paradise. ■

What other vision does the speaker recall? What does the speaker want to revive within himself?

What would observers say about the poet if he were able to build that pleasure dome?

---

5. **Mount Abora.** Apparently a reference to Milton's *Paradise Lost*, Book IV, Lines 280-282, in which he refers to "Mount Amara" where Abyssinian kings were believed to have built a palatial paradise.
6. **Weave . . . thrice.** A magical ritual

Respond *to the* Selection

Does Kubla Kahn's pleasure dome sound to you like paradise? Why or why not?

ANSWERS TO GUIDED READING QUESTIONS

1. The speaker recalls a vision of a young woman playing a dulcimer and singing. The speaker wants to revive the song within himself and reexpe-rience his feelings upon hearing the song so that he would be inspired to rebuild the pleasure dome.
2. All who saw him would cry, "Beware! Beware! / His flashing eyes, his floating hair!"

SELECTION CHECK TEST 4.8.21 WITH ANSWERS

Checking Your Reading

1. What kind of trees blossom in the pleasure dome? **Incense-bearing trees blossom.**
2. What disrupts the quiet of the dome? **The chasm erupts.**
3. What does the sacred river sink into? **It sinks into the lifeless ocean.**
4. What does Kubla hear from far? **He hears voices prophesying war.**
5. What is the damsel in the vision doing? **She is playing the dulcimer and singing.**

Literary Tools

1. The line, "Huge fragments vaulted like rebounding hail" illustrates
   a. allegory
   b. consonance
   c. metaphor
   d. assonance

2. The line, "Where was heard the mingled measure" illustrates
   a. alliteration
   b. personification
   c. metaphor
   d. assonance

3. Coleridge claimed that the idea for this poem came from
   a. a course he took in college
   b. a Greek poem
   c. a dream
   d. his friend William Wordsworth

RESPOND TO THE SELECTION

Do you think Kubla Khans' "stately pleasure dome" will last? How does it compare to your own paradise?

ANSWERS TO INVESTIGATE, INQUIRE, AND IMAGINE

Recall

1a. It is in Xanadu, and it covers ten miles of land.

2a. It is "deep" and "romantic" and "holy and enchanted." The sacred river erupts from the chasm in the form of a fountain.

3a. The speaker once saw a "damsel with a dulcimer...[s]inging of Mount Abora."

Interpret

1b. The mood in the first stanza is idyllic and peaceful.

2b. In the second stanza the chasm erupts in tumult and disrupts the orderliness of the garden. Compared to the stateliness of the first stanza, the second stanza is wild and chaotic.

3b. If he were able to recreate the damsel's song, he would be overtaken with deep delight and would create the pleasure dome of sunny caves of ice and would be seen as wild and dangerous by those who saw him.

Analyze

4a. The river, as noted, symbolizes the source of inspiration or creative life force. The images of the first stanza recall the Garden of Eden, the scene of God's original creation in Judeo-Christian terms, with reference to "fertile ground," "incense-bearing tree," and "gardens." The forcing of the fountain out of the chasm, after breathing in "thick pants" calls to mind a birth—also a traditional symbol of artistic creation. The damsel's song is an artistic creation. And finally, in the final lines, the poet says others would warn that he "on honeydew hath fed, / And drunk the milk of Paradise," another reference to Eden. Thus, not only do several images symbolize creations, there are some very clear references to the original act of creation in religious terms.

Synthesize

4b. The poet writes that, if he could "revive within me / Her symphony and song"—i.e. achieve that inspiration, it would lead him to such "deep delight" that he could build the pleasure dome. The emotions this would arouse in him are joy and exhilaration. He says that those who saw this would say, "Beware! Beware! / His flashing eyes, his floating hair! / Weave a circle around him thrice, / And close your eyes with holy dread..." The poet seems to be saying that others who observe this act of creation would be both frightened and struck with awe. He would seem a crazy man,

INVESTIGATE, Inquire, Imagine

Recall: GATHERING FACTS → **Interpret:** FINDING MEANING

1a. Where is Kubla Khan's pleasure dome? How large an area of land does it cover? → 1b. What is the mood created in the first stanza by the description of the garden?

2a. How is the "chasm" described in the second stanza? What issues out of the chasm? → 2b. What is happening in the second stanza? How does that scene compare to the scene of the first stanza?

3a. Whom did the speaker once see in a vision? What was she doing? → 3b. What would happen, according to the speaker, if he were able to revive within himself the maid's song?

Analyze: TAKING THINGS APART → **Synthesize:** BRINGING THINGS TOGETHER

4a. "Kubla Kahn" is frequently interpreted as a poem about the act of poetic or artistic creation. The central image of the first stanza is a river, a traditional symbol for the source of life or the source of creative inspiration. Analyze the images used in the poem, and identify those which support this interpretation. → 4b. If "Kubla Kahn" is about artistic creation, how does Coleridge seem to feel about the creative process? What indications do we have, in this poem, of the emotions it arouses in him and in those who might observe him?

Evaluate: MAKING JUDGMENTS → **Extend:** CONNECTING IDEAS

5a. Coleridge calls this poem "a vision in a dream." Does it seem like a dream to you? Which images are most dreamlike? How does the progression of the poem compare to that of a dream? → 5b. Throughout history, many artists have also spoken of having visions or dreams, or being caught up in trances in which their creative imaginations were freed of inhibitions and their best creative work was possible. Many of us find our dreams to be sources of vivid imagery and creative insights. How does this identification of the dream state as a creative source fit the Romantic ideals you read about in the introduction to this unit?

Understanding Literature

ALLITERATION. Review the definition for **alliteration** in Literary Tools in Prereading. What other examples of alliteration can you find in "Kubla Khan"? How does the alliteration contribute to the mood of the poem?

IMAGE. Review the definition for **image** in the Handbook of Literary Terms. Reread "Kubla Kahn" and complete the following graphic organizer noting the images of opposites. One is completed for you. In his important work of literary criticism, *Biographia Literaria* (Chapter XIV), Coleridge said that imagination "reveals itself in the balance or reconciliation of opposite or discordant qualities." What do you think his use of images of opposites indicates about the theme of this poem?

Images of Opposites		
A savage place, demon lover	holy	lines 14-16

ANSWERS TO INVESTIGATE, INQUIRE, AND IMAGINE (CONT.)

consumed by the powerful act of creation.

Evaluate

5a. The images of the woman wailing for her demon-lover, and the ancestral voices prophesying war seem dreamlike and somewhat supernatural. The recurrence of the river and the caves and the dome recall the way images pop up over and over, often without direct connection, in a dream. And finally, the poem starts with a relatively straightforward narrative about Kubla Kahn's decree in the first stanza and becomes increasingly turbulent and chaotic as it progresses, much as dreams often begin with a coherent series of images that become more and more fragmented as the dream progresses.

Answers to Understanding Literature can be found on page 709.

Writer's Journal

1. If the pleasure dome were a real place, it would be a wonder to see. Write a **travel brochure** designed to entice tourists to visit Kubla Kahn's paradise.
2. Recall a particularly vivid dream you have had and write a **dream report.** What happened in your dream? Describe the images you experienced and the sometimes inexplicable path of your dream. Did it have a definite ending, or did it simply break off? What did it mean to you?
3. Coleridge wrote that "Kubla Khan" was only a fragment and that he was unable to finish the poem because he was interrupted in the middle of transcribing it after his dream. Although you cannot know what Coleridge would have written if he had continued, you can use your imagination to come up with an extension of the poem. Write your **continuation** in verse or in prose.

Media Literacy & Study and Research

Computer-Assisted Research. Read the Language Arts Survey, 5.26, "Using the Internet." Then do some research on Kubla Khan and answer the following questions.

1. When did Kubla Khan live?
2. Where was Kubla Khan's empire?
3. How large was Kubla Khan's empire?
4. Who were the people ruled by Kubla Khan?
5. What other nations or people did Kubla Khan conquer during his reign?

Speaking and Listening

Oral Interpretation. Review Language Arts Survey 4.19, "Oral Interpretation." Then prepare an oral interpretation of "Kubla Kahn." Before reading, consider the mood and tone as well as the theme of the poem. What sort of pacing will be appropriate? What inflection and tone will you use? Will gestures and body language add to the effect you are attempting to create? It is often best to rehearse your oral interpretation aloud before a mirror and to try several different approaches to select the effect you wish to deliver. Give your oral interpretation before your class.

Study and Research

Creation Myths. In "Kubla Kahn," Coleridge uses images that bring to mind the story of the Garden of Eden and the creation story of the Judeo-Christian tradition. Many scholars have noted that most major world religions have a creation story that is similar in some significant ways. Using library resources as well as local religious institutions, research the creation stories of two or more religions and compare them. How are they similar and how different? Share your findings with your class.

ANSWERS TO INVESTIGATE, INQUIRE, AND IMAGINE (CONT. FROM PAGE 708)

Extend

5b. *Responses will vary.* Our dreams are not subject to the control or censorship of our rational/logical mind and therefore are unrestrained and represent our feelings in their "natural" state.

ANSWERS TO UNDERSTANDING LITERATURE

Alliteration. Other examples of alliteration include the "woman wailing," "miles meandering with a mazy motion," and "mingled measure."

Image. Responses will vary, but it seems that images of opposites together is a portrayal of the working of imagination, according to Coleridge's words above. This supports the interpretation that the poem is about artistic creation.

Images of Opposites

A savage place, demon lover	holy	line14–16
thick	pants	line 18
cave (concave)	dome (convex)	line 36
sunny dome	caves of ice	line 36

ANSWERS TO INTEGRATING THE LANGUAGE ARTS

Medial Literacy & Study and Research

1. Kubla Khan lived from AD 1215 to 1294
2. It encompassed present-day China, southern Russia, and Iran
3. His empire was large; he conquered China and became the overlord of all Mongol dominions.
4. He ruled the Mongols, his own nomad race, and the other peoples of China (which was unified during his reign.)
5. He also ruled the Mongols of southern Russia and present-day Iran.

Speaking and Listening

Remind students to be respectful audience members by having them read the Language Arts Survey 4.6, "Adapting Listening Skills to Specific Tasks."

Study and Research

To help students in their comparing and contrasting of creation myths, refer them to the Language Arts Survey 5.9, "Comparing and Contrasting."

"Ozymandias"

"Ode to the West Wind"

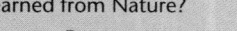

BY PERCY BYSSHE SHELLEY

About the AUTHOR

Percy Bysshe Shelley (1792–1822) was born to a wealthy family of Sussex aristocrats, merchants, and politicians. He was sent to Eton and Oxford, where he endured teasing because of his slight build and eccentric manner. Perhaps as a consequence of being belittled, he developed a passionate will to defeat injustice by being "meek and bold."

His closest friend at Oxford was Thomas Jefferson Hogg. They both loved philosophy and were opposed to conventional ideas. Shelley's passion for justice and intellectual freedom, combined with his determination to live consistently with his ideals, led him into a number of difficult spots. After only six months at Oxford, he was expelled for having circulated a pamphlet titled "The Necessity of Atheism," behavior which did not sit well with Oxford officials. Soon afterward, he moved to Ireland, determined to reform the world, beginning with organizing the Irish into what he called a "society of peace and love." After the failure of this venture, he moved to Wales at the age of nineteen and wrote a pamphlet called "Declaration of Rights," which he published by putting copies in green bottles he threw in the ocean and in balloons he released into the air. He was an idealistic young man who was unafraid to proclaim and live his ideals. Shelley traveled to London and eloped to Edinburgh with the daughter of a London tavern keeper. Shelley and his wife then went to Ireland, where he delivered his *Address to the Irish People,* which favored Catholic emancipation and social justice for Ireland.

In 1813, Shelley printed his first serious piece, *Queen Mab,* a poem that prophesied a future of happiness, equality, and a return to nature for humankind. Soon afterward, Shelley fell in love with Mary Wollstonecraft Godwin, the daughter of Mary Wollstonecraft and William Godwin. Shelley left his wife, Harriet, and fled to France with Mary, though he later invited Harriet to come live in a "sisterly" relationship with him. Mary's father, despite being a social radical himself, was furious with Shelley for compromising his daughter. When Shelley returned to London, he found that he had created something of a scandal.

The Shelleys later moved to Pisa, Italy. On July 8, 1822, Shelley and a friend were sailing in an open boat, the *Don Juan,* when a storm capsized their vessel. Neither survived. At the age of twenty-nine, Shelley was buried in Rome near his fellow poet John Keats.

ADDITIONAL RESOURCES

UNIT 8 RESOURCE BOOK

"Ozymandias"
- Selection Worksheet 8.11
- Selection Check Test 4.8.23
- Selection Test 4.8.24

"Ode to the West Wind"
- Selection Worksheet 8.12
- Selection Check Test 4.8.25
- Selection Test 4.8.26
- Language, Grammar, and Style Resource 3.51
- Speaking and Listening Resource 4.19, 5.51

INDIVIDUAL LEARNING STRATEGIES

MOTIVATION
Ask students to spend time outdoors completely surrounded by Nature. Have them reflect on the following questions in their journals: Does Nature inspire you? Why, or why not? What things have you learned from Nature?

READING PROFICIENCY
To help students better understand the writer's aim of the selection, students might benefit from hearing the selection read aloud. Also ask students to read the Prereading page before they begin reading the selection on their own.

ENGLISH LANGUAGE LEARNING
Some formal language, such as "thou," "thy," and "didst," may be difficult for student to understand. Have them make translation flash cards for these words. For example, students write *thou* on the front of the card and *you* on the back. Encourage student to use this technique for unfamiliar vocabulary words.

SPECIAL NEEDS
Have students work in pairs to answer the Guided Reading questions and the Recall questions in the Investigate, Inquire, and Imagine section.

ENRICHMENT
Have students research political events in Great Britain and Ireland during Shelley's lifetime that related to Catholic Emancipation. Then ask them to report their findings to the class.

GOALS/OBJECTIVES

Studying this lesson will enable students to
- empathize with feelings of desolation and ruin and exalt in the power of nature
- describe the historical significance of Shelley's work
- define *character, irony of situation, terza rima,* and *personification* and identify and explain examples of each that they encounter in their reading
- identify and correct common and proper nouns
- demonstrate the ability to answer sentence-completion questions

About the SELECTIONS

The first selection, **"Ozymandias,"** deals with an ancient king of Egypt and is a classic statement of the fleeting nature of worldly pomp and glory. Ozymandias is the Greek name for Ramses II, who reigned in the thirteenth century BC. During his sixty-seven-year reign, Egypt acquired unprecedented splendor. On his statue, which prompts the sonnet, is inscribed, "Look on my Works, ye Mighty, and despair!" Published in 1818, the sonnet is ironic in tone.

"Ode to the West Wind" was written in a single sitting near Florence, Italy on a mild, windy day in early fall—October 25, 1819. In keeping with Romantic ideals, the poem calls upon a force of nature to inspire the poet's creative endeavors. Considered a prime example of the poet's passionate language and symbolic imagery, the ode invokes the spirit of the West Wind, "Destroyer and Preserver." This ode is important because it introduced a new stanzaic form composed of five sonnets, each of which has four tercets (units of three lines each). The rhyme scheme is based on Italian terza rima, rhyming *aba, bcb, cdc,* and *ded* followed by a rhyming ee couplet.

ArtNote

The Evacuation of the Great Temple of Ramsses II, Abu Simel, c.1800s. Louis Linant de Bellefonds.

Louis Linant de Bellefonds (1799-1883) was an archeologist and artist who explored the Nile in the 19th century. The watercolor painting on page 712 shows the uncovering of Abu Simbel near the present day border of Sudan. Ramses II, the most prolific monument builder of Ancient Egypt, raised the temple about 1250 BC. to honor the gods and himself, and to demonstrate his power to a foreign land. Four enormous statues of Ramses II surround the entrance. Twice a year, on February 21, Ramses II's birthday, and October 22, the date of his coronation, the sun penetrates the entrance of the temple and illuminates the statues of Amon, Hamarkhis, and Ramses II. In the 1960s the temple was dismantled and reconstructed on higher ground to save it from flooding caused by the Aswan Dam.

Literary TOOLS

CHARACTER. A **character** is a person who figures in the action of a literary work. As you read "Ozymandias," note the details Shelley uses to develop his character.

IRONY OF SITUATION. Irony of situation is when an event occurs that violates the expectations of a character, the reader or the audience. Observe the use of irony in "Ozymandias."

Reader's Journal

In what ways does power change people?

VOCABULARY FROM THE SELECTION

visage

READER'S JOURNAL

Do you think gain in power ultimately leads to corruption? Why, or why not? What rulers or famous figures can think of who have become corrupted by power?

ANSWER TO GUIDED READING QUESTION

1. Nothing is to be seen—only the bare sands surround the remains of the statue.

SELECTION CHECK TEST 4.8.23 WITH ANSWERS

Checking Your Reading

1. Where was the traveler from? **He was from an antique land.**
2. What expression is on the statue's face? **The statue is frowning or sneering.**
3. Who was Ozymandias? **Ozymandias was a king, Ramses II of Egypt.**
4. What does the inscription tell "ye Mighty" to do? **Look on his Works and despair.**
5. Describe where the statue lies. What surrounds it? **Bare desert surrounds it.**

Literary Tools

1. What is irony of situation? **Irony of situation is when an event occurs that contradicts the expectations of the characters or audience.**
2. Who is the speaker in this poem? **The speaker is someone who met a traveler.**
3. Describe the character of Ozymandias. **He was powerful, commanding, cold.**

RESPOND TO THE SELECTION

Imagine you have the opportunity to interwiew Ozymandias. What type of questions would you ask him? Begin your questions with the words who, what, when, why, and how.

The Excavation of the Great Temple of Ramses II, Abu Simel, c.1800s. Louis Linant de Bellefonds. Private Collection.

Ozymandias

PERCY BYSSHE SHELLEY

I met a traveller from an antique land,
Who said—"Two vast and trunkless legs of stone
Stand in the desert. . . . Near them, on the sand,
Half sunk a shattered visage lies, whose frown,
And wrinkled lip, and sneer of cold command,
Tell that its sculptor well those passions read
Which yet survive, stamped on these lifeless things,
The hand that mocked them, and the heart that fed;
And on the pedestal, these words appear:
My name is Ozymandias, King of Kings,
Look on my Works, ye Mighty, and despair!
Nothing beside remains. Round the decay
Of that colossal Wreck, boundless and bare
The lone and level sands stretch far away." ■

What "works" of Ozymandias are to be seen?

WORDS FOR EVERYDAY USE

vis • age (viz´ ij) *n.*, a face. *The monarch's visage appears on British currency.*

Respond *to the* SELECTION

What might be the moral of this poem?

Inquire, *Imagine*

Recall: GATHERING FACTS

1a. What does the traveler describe to the speaker?

2a. What does the inscription on the pedestal say?

3a. What remains in the environment around the statue?

Interpret: FINDING MEANING

1b. Why does the statue interest the traveler and the speaker?

2b. Of what flaw was the king apparently guilty?

3b. What is the significance of the description in the last three lines of the poem? What kingdom has the powerful king inherited?

Analyze: TAKING THINGS APART

4a. Look at lines 11 and 12 closely. What does this poem say about earthly power and greed?

Synthesize: BRINGING THINGS TOGETHER

4b. What attitude does this poem express towards its subject? Explain your answer.

Evaluate: MAKING JUDGMENTS

5a. In this poem, Shelley expresses his feelings about worldly power and glory. What are those feelings? How effectively are they expressed in this poem? Is this poem either more or less effective than stating these feelings more directly? Why?

Extend: CONNECTING IDEAS

5b. What message might Shelley give to today's leaders?

Understanding *Literature*

CHARACTER. Review the definition for **character** in Literary Tools in Prereading. What description does the speaker give of Ozymandias? What do the details of this description reveal about the ancient kings?

IRONY OF SITUATION. Review the definition of **irony of situation** in the Handbook of Literary Terms. What is the irony of the last few lines of this poem? Whose expectations are violated and in what way?

ANSWERS TO INVESTIGATE, INQUIRE AND IMAGINE

RECALL

1a. He describes a gigantic, fallen statue of a king in the desert.

2a. The inscription says, "My name is Ozymandias, King of Kings,/Look on my Works, ye Mighty, and despair!"

3a. Nothing remains but the empty desert.

INTERPRET

1b. The statue interests them because it is all that remains of a man who boasted of ultimate power.

2b. He was apparently guilty of pride.

3b. The last three lines describe all that remains of the once powerful king's empire. He has inherited a kingdom of ruins and sand.

ANALYZE

4a. It says that greed is not rewarded and earthly power lasts only for the brief period of a person's life; everything decays.

SYNTHESIZE

4b. It expresses disdain for its subject. Although Ozymandias is the subject of the poem, he is described as a ruin rather than as a great and powerful ruler, as he wished to be remembered.

EVALUATE

5a. Shelley expresses the feeling that worldly power and glory are transitory and, because they do not last, they only feed our vanity and greed. Opinions will vary as to the effectiveness of this poem. Shelley paints a picture of the way time has dealt with the power and glory of one man. This has the effect of portraying a fact, from which the reader may draw his or her own opinion. Were he to state his opinion directly, the poem might have less power.

EXTEND

5b. *Responses will vary.*

ANSWERS TO UNDERSTANDING LITERATURE

CHARACTER. He describes Ozymandias as wearing a frowning and sneering look of command. The ancient kings were probably accustomed to absolute power and, as a result, were vain and cold.

IRONY OF SITUATION. The irony is that Ozymandias believed that his power and glory would live on but all that is left of him is the wreck of this statue. He says, "Look on my works, ye Mighty and despair!" Yet the despair of the onlooker would not be due to envy or fear of Ozymandias's power. Rather, Ozymandias and others like him who value earthly power and glory would despair because such power and glory is so temporary.

ANSWER TO GUIDED READING QUESTION

1. The West Wind is wild and fast. Unlike the life-giving wind of spring, the West Wind brings all things to their death.

GRAPHIC ORGANIZER

The following are additional circles to be included:
Seeds go to their graves
Spring wind is west wind's sister
Angels of rain and lightening
Wind awakens the sea
Mediterranean sea dreams
Wind has a voice
Sea blooms tremble with fear
Wind wanders
Wind is destroyer and preserver

READER'S JOURNAL

Suggest that students think about how they feel when seasons change or when they feel like they failed at something in which they knew they could succeed.

VOCABULARY FROM THE SELECTION

chasm	sepulcher
dirge	tumult
impetuous	zenith
pestilence	

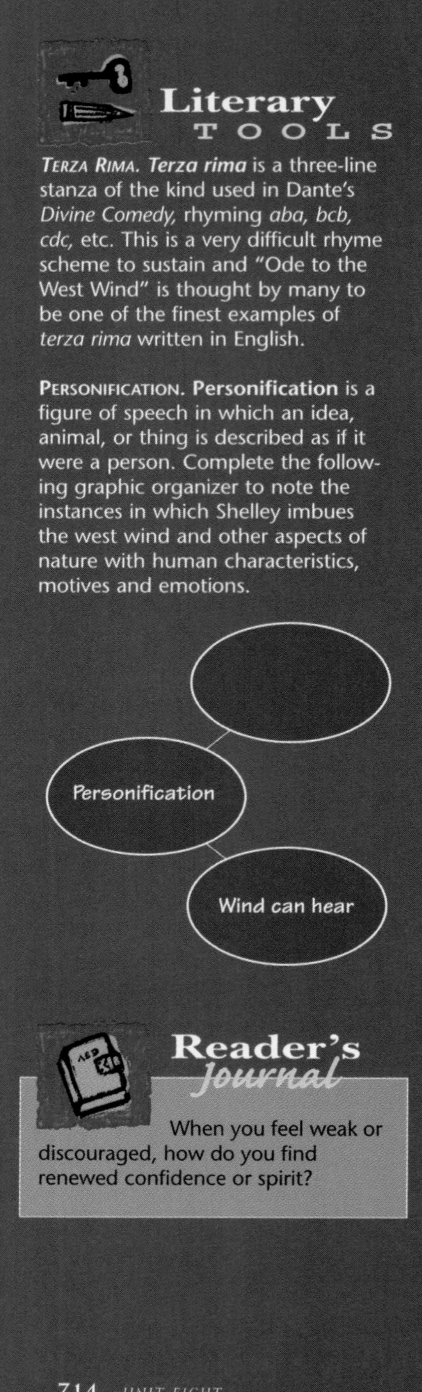

Literary TOOLS

TERZA RIMA. ***Terza rima*** is a three-line stanza of the kind used in Dante's *Divine Comedy,* rhyming *aba, bcb, cdc,* etc. This is a very difficult rhyme scheme to sustain and "Ode to the West Wind" is thought by many to be one of the finest examples of *terza rima* written in English.

PERSONIFICATION. **Personification** is a figure of speech in which an idea, animal, or thing is described as if it were a person. Complete the following graphic organizer to note the instances in which Shelley imbues the west wind and other aspects of nature with human characteristics, motives and emotions.

Reader's Journal

When you feel weak or discouraged, how do you find renewed confidence or spirit?

Ode to the West Wind

PERCY BYSSHE SHELLEY

1

O wild West Wind, thou breath of Autumn's being,
Thou, from whose unseen presence the leaves dead
Are driven, like ghosts from an enchanter fleeing,

Yellow, and black, and pale, and hectic[1] red,
Pestilence-stricken multitudes: O Thou,
Who chariotest to their dark wintry bed

The winged seeds, where they lie cold and low,
Each like a corpse within its grave, until
Thine azure sister of the Spring[2] shall blow

Her clarion[3] o'er the dreaming earth, and fill
(Driving sweet buds like flocks to feed in air)
With living hues and odors plain and hill:

Wild Spirit, which art moving everywhere;
Destroyer and Preserver;[4] hear, O hear!

How does the speaker describe the West Wind? How does it compare to the Wind of Spring?

2

Thou on whose stream, 'mid the steep sky's commotion,
Loose clouds like Earth's decaying leaves are shed,
Shook from the tangled boughs of Heaven and Ocean,

1. **hectic.** Characteristic of the fever of tuberculosis
2. **Thine . . . Spring.** The west wind of the spring
3. **clarion.** A high-pitched trumpet
4. **Destroyer and Preserver.** Shelley is perhaps likening the wind to those Hindu gods, Vishnu and Shiva, who respectively preserve and destroy the numerous worlds that come into existence, one after the other, of which ours is but the latest.

WORDS FOR EVERYDAY USE

pes • ti • lence (pes´tə ləns) *n.,* virulent or infectious disease of epidemic proportions. *In the Middle Ages, the Black Plague and other pestilences ravaged Europe.*

A Whole Gale of Wind, c.1900s. William Lionel Wyllie. Bonhams, London.

Angels of rain and lightning: there are spread
On the blue surface of thine aery surge,
Like the bright hair uplifted from the head

Of some fierce Mænad,[5] even from the dim verge
Of the horizon to the zenith's height
The locks of the approaching storm. Thou Dirge

Of the dying year, to which this closing night
Will be the dome of a vast sepulchre,
Vaulted with all thy congregated might

Of vapors,[6] from whose solid atmosphere
Black rain and fire and hail will burst: O hear!

To what are the clouds compared?

5. **Mænad.** A female follower who danced in worship of Dionysius, Greek god of wine and vegetation
6. **vapors.** Clouds

WORDS FOR EVERYDAY USE

ze • nith (zē´nith) *n.,* the highest point in the sky. *At twelve noon the sun will be at its zenith.*

dirge (durj) *n.,* funeral song. *Bagpipes spread the mournful dirge across the cemetery.*

sep • ul • chre or **sep • ul • cher** (sep´əl kər) *n.,* burial vault or tomb. *Mourners laid flowers at the sepulcher's entrance.*

ANSWER TO GUIDED READING QUESTION

1. The clouds are compared to decaying leaves and the hair of a woman who worships Dionysius.

LITERARY TECHNIQUE 

ANAPHORA. An **anaphora** is any word or phrase the repeats or refers to something that precedes or follows it. In the first line, "thou" and "breath of Autumn's being" both refer back to the West Wind. Ask students to look for other examples of anaphora as they read.

ANSWERS TO GUIDED READING QUESTIONS

1. The speaker wishes to be a dead leaf, a cloud, and a wave. These are the subjects of the first three stanzas.
2. Like the West Wind, the speaker was strong, capable, and at one with nature. Now, he doubts himself and must ask for help.

3

Thou who didst waken from his summer dreams
The blue Mediterranean, where he lay,
Lulled by the coil of his chrystalline streams,[7]

Beside a pumice isle in Baiæ's bay,[8]
And saw in sleep old palaces and towers
Quivering within the wave's intenser day,[9]

All overgrown with azure moss and flowers
So sweet, the sense faints picturing them! Thou
For whose path the Atlantic's level powers

Cleave themselves into chasms, while far below
The sea-blooms and the oozy woods which wear
The sapless foliage of the ocean, know

Thy voice, and suddenly grow grey with fear,
And tremble and despoil themselves: O hear!

4

If I were a dead leaf thou mightest bear;
If I were a swift cloud to fly with thee;
A wave to pant beneath thy power, and share

The impulse of thy strength, only less free
Than thou, O Uncontrollable! If even
I were as in my boyhood, and could be

The comrade of thy wanderings over Heaven,
As then, when to outstrip thy skiey speed
Scarce seemed a vision; I would ne'er have striven

As thus with thee in prayer in my sore need.
Oh! lift me as a wave, a leaf, a cloud!

What three objects does the speaker wish to be? How do these objects relate to the preceding stanzas?

In what way was the speaker, as a child, like the West Wind? How has he changed? Why?

7. **coil of his chrystalline streams.** Currents of the Mediterranean Sea often have differences in color.
8. **Baiæ's bay.** Located west of Naples, Italy, it is the site of many villas built by Roman emperors.
9. **wave's intenser day.** Shelley thought that colors reflected in water were more vivid yet more blended.

WORDS FOR EVERYDAY USE

chasm (kaz´əm) *n.*, a crack in the surface of the earth. *Chasms spread like veins across the canyon's parched floor.*

I fall upon the thorns of life! I bleed!
A heavy weight of hours has chained and bowed
One too like thee: tameless, and swift, and proud.

5

Make me thy lyre,[10] even as the forest is:
What if my leaves are falling like its own!
The tumult of thy mighty harmonies

Will take from both a deep, autumnal tone,
Sweet though in sadness. Be thou, Spirit fierce,
My spirit! Be thou me, impetuous one!

Drive my dead thoughts over the universe
Like withered leaves to quicken a new birth!
And, by the incantation of this verse,

Scatter, as from an unextinguished hearth
Ashes and sparks, my words among mankind!
Be through my lips to unawakened Earth

The trumpet of a prophecy! O Wind,
If Winter comes, can Spring be far behind? ■

What does the speaker ask of the wind? What does the speaker want to do with his verse?

10. **lyre.** A harp-like stringed instrument, here played by the wind

WORDS FOR EVERYDAY USE

tu • mult (tü´mult) *n.*, loud commotion. *We awakened to a tumult of breaking glass as the earthquake hit.*

im • pet • u • ous (im pech´o͞o əs) *adj.*, acting on impulse. *Although I prefer not to plan things, my impetuous actions sometimes get me into trouble.*

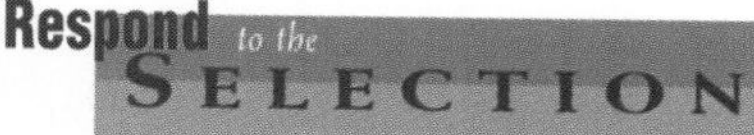

How would you answer the question asked in the last line of the poem?

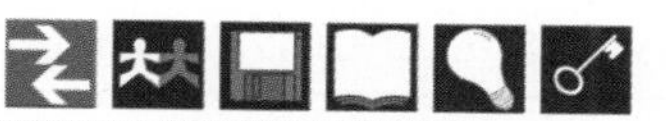

RESPOND TO THE SELECTION

If you were a poet, what aspect of a nature would you praise? Complete the following title and describe the details you would include in your poem: "Ode to the _________."

ANSWER TO GUIDED READING QUESTION

1. The speaker asks the wind to revive his thoughts. He wants the wind to scatter his verse over the earth and make him a "trumpet of prophecy."

SELECTION CHECK TEST 4.8.25 WITH ANSWERS

Checking Your Reading

1. What lies "like a corpse within its grave" until spring? **Seeds lie and wait for spring.**
2. What will arrive in spring to waken the earth? **The west wind of spring will arrive.**
3. What are "shook from the tangled boughs of Heaven."? **Clouds are shook free.**
4. Who used to be like the west wind? **The speaker used to be like the west wind.**
5. The speaker asks the wind to do what with his words? **He wants them scattered among mankind.**

Vocabulary in Context

Fill each blank with the most appropriate word from the Words for Everyday Use. You may have to change the tense of the word.

tumult impetuous chasm zenith
dirge sepulcher pestilence

1. Our company dislikes **impetuous** decisions; everything is discussed in committees.
2. My class watched as the rocket we made reached its **zenith** and fell toward earth.
3. The helicopter hovered over the **chasm** so scientists could lower equipment into it.
4. The **tumult** of lunchtime gave way to quiet as the kindergartners lay down for naps.
5. Marcie liked band, but she hated playing **dirges**.

Literary Tools

Fill in the blanks using the following terms. You may not use every term, and you may use some terms more than once.

sonnet terza rima anaphora
personification simile

1. The line "…the leaves dead/Are driven, like ghosts from an enchanter fleeing" contains a(n) **simile**.
2. Addressing something that is not human as if it were human is **personification**.
3. This poem is written in **terza rima**, three-lined stanzas that rhyme aba, cdc, efe, etc.

ANSWERS TO INVESTIGATE, INQUIRE AND IMAGINE

RECALL

1a. The speaker describes an autumn scene in which brightly colored leaves and seeds are blown around and to the ground.
2a. Three effects of the wind are clouds, rain, and waves.
3a. He asks the wind to instill him with its power and spirit.

INTERPRET

1b. His attitude is worshipful and somewhat awestruck.
2b. The language compares the clouds to leaves being shed and shaken from the branches of heaven.
3b. The exclamations that make up the final stanza show that the intensity of his request increases.

ANALYZE

4a. In stanza 1, Shelley describes the wind as driving leaves before it "like ghosts." In stanza 2, "clouds like Earth's decaying leaves are shed." In stanza 3, below the surface of the ocean, "sea-blooms…wear / The sapless foliage of the ocean." In all three stanzas, the imagery used is of dead and dying leaves being blown before the power of the west wind as it blows trees on land, clouds in the air and waves in the sea. The west wind ushers in death and endings.

SYNTHESIZE

4b. The wind blows the dead and dying away in order that the winds of Spring can bring new life. The speaker is despondent in stanza 4, saying in lines 55-56, "A heavy weight of hours has chained and bowed / One too like thee: tameless, and swift and proud." He hopes for renewal like that which takes place in nature, a rebirth after the death.

EVALUATE

5a. *Responses will vary.* The last lines of the poem seem to indicate hope—the rebirth of spring after the death of winter. The speaker is despondent and says he is "chained and bowed" by the burdens of his life. He finds hope in the renewal of nature he sees enacted by the west wind.

EXTEND.

5b. *Responses will vary.* The movies mentioned deal with the theme of returning to live a certain time period over again. The idea of getting a second chance, the ability to start over with renewed energy, purpose, power, strength, etc is very powerful to anyone who has ever experienced regret.

INVESTIGATE, Inquire, Imagine

Recall: GATHERING FACTS →

1a. What scene is described by the speaker in section 1?
2a. What are three effects of the wind described in sections 2 and 3?
3a. In section 5, what is the speaker asking the wind to do?

Interpret: FINDING MEANING

1b. With what attitude is the speaker addressing the wind in section 1?
2b. How does the figurative language in section 2 connect the images of the clouds to the previous images of the trees?
3b. What happens to the intensity of the speaker's request in section 5? How do you know?

Analyze: TAKING THINGS APART →

4a. In stanzas 1,2 and 3, Shelley uses leaf imagery to describe the wind's effect on land, air and sea. Analyze the leaf imagery used. What is Shelley saying about the effect the west wind has on these aspects of nature?

Synthesize: BRINGING THINGS TOGETHER

4b. What is the promise of the west wind's act of blowing away the dead and dying leaves? Why do you think the speaker wants the wind to work its powers on him as it does on the leaves, the clouds and the waves?

Evaluate: MAKING JUDGMENTS →

5a. Evaluate the tone of this poem. To what degree is it despairing? To what degree is it hopeful? What leads you to this conclusion?

Extend: CONNECTING IDEAS

5b. The theme of rebirth is one that strikes a chord with many people. We see it in popular movies like *Groundhog Day* and *Big* as well as in the religious beliefs of many who believe in reincarnation, resurrection or being "born again" spiritually. Why do you think this idea is so powerful for so many people? What great longing in human nature does it address?

Understanding Literature

TERZA RIMA. Review the definition for ***terza rima*** in Literary Tools in Prereading. In this poem the last two lines of each stanza are a couplet. How does the rhyme scheme of the couplet relate to the rest of the stanza? Mark the complete rhyme scheme of a full stanza.

PERSONIFICATION. Review the definition for **personification** and the graphic organizer you completed for Literary Tools in Prereading. In this poem, how does personification work to establish a relationship between the speaker and the personified thing? How would the poem be different if Shelley had referred to the wind impersonally?

ANSWERS TO UNDERSTANDING LITERATURE

TERZA RIMA. The couplets rhyme with the middle line of the preceding tercet. The rhyme scheme of each stanza is: *aba, bcb, cdc, ded, ee.*

PERSONIFICATION. Personification helps establish a relationship between the speaker and the personified object by assigning recognizable, human qualities to the object. The speaker reveals his values and feelings through what he says about the personified object. If Shelley had referred to the wind impersonally, the poem might have had a stilted feeling and seemed more like a descriptive exercise than a revelation of profound feeling.

Writer's Journal

1. Ozymandias inscribed his own epitaph on the base of the statue in the poem "Ozymandias." In reading the poem, however, we see the irony of the words he chose. Having read the poem, what words would you choose? Write an **epitaph** for Ozymandias.
2. The speaker in "Ode to the West Wind" recalls his childhood as a time in which his own spirit paralleled or equalled that of the West Wind. He then describes how that spirit has been beaten down by life. Write a **memoir** that compares your childhood with your present life. Have things changed for you? In what ways?
3. A myth is a story that explains objects or events in the natural world as resulting from the action of some supernatural force or entity. In this poem, the speaker calls upon the wind to inspire him and to renew his spirit, so that he can be a powerful voice prophesying change. Use Shelley's technique to create a prose **myth** of your own in which you evoke the aid of a force of nature to help you to achieve some end.

Integrating *the* Language Arts

Language, Grammar, and Style

Common and Proper Nouns. Read the Language Arts Survey 2.3, "Common and Proper Nouns." Then list each of the nouns from the following sentences and correct any errors in capitalization. (Note: These nouns come from the selections. Remember that poets do not always follow rules of capitalization, but you should attempt to follow them in this exercise.)

1. I am Ozymandias, and I am King of kings.
2. The real ozymandias was ramses II of egypt, who lived around 1300 BC.
3. The West Wind is the breath of Autumn's being.
4. The blue mediterranean sea was awakened in the Fall.
5. "Ode to the West Wind" was written near florence, Italy.

Study and Research

Test Taking Skills. Read the Language Arts Survey 4.41, "Sentence-Completion Questions." Then add words and punctuation to the following sentence fragments to make them complete sentences.

1. The real Ozymandias was a ______________ .
2. To the speaker of the poem, the West Wind represents ______________ .
3. The Romantics valued nature and wildness above ______________ .
4. The speaker asks the wind to ______________ .
5. At the end of "Ode to the West Wind," the reader feels ______________ .

Speaking and Listening

Oral Interpretation of Poetry. Review Language Arts Survey 4.19, "Oral Interpretation of Poetry," and prepare an oral interpretation of "Ozymandias." You should rehearse this several times, experimenting with different volume, inflection, tempo, and tone. Deliver your interpretation before your class.

Answers to Integrating the Language Arts

Language, Grammar, and Style

1. Ozymanidas, king of kings
2. Ozymanidas, Ramses II, Egypt
3. wind, autumn's being
4. Mediterranean Sea, fall
5. Florence, Italy

Study and Research

1. king of Egypt.
2. inspiration
3. human works
4. become him
5. hopeful

ADDITIONAL RESOURCES

UNIT 8 RESOURCE BOOK
"She Walks in Beauty"
Selection Worksheet 8.13
Selection Check Test 4.8.27
Selection Test 4.8.28

From *Childe Harold's Pilgrimage*
- Selection Worksheet 8.14
- Selection Check Test 4.8.29
- Selection Test 4.8.30
- Language, Grammar, and Style Resource 3.34
- Speaking and Listening Resource 4.15

VOCABULARY FROM THE SELECTION

serenely

CROSS-CURRICULAR ACTIVITIES

ARTS AND HUMANITIES. Have students draw or paint a picture of the woman whom the speaker describes. Encourage them to use both their imagination and details from the poem. For students who are not comfortable with illustration, suggest that they find a picture that represents their image of the woman. They can explain why they chose the picture and what, if any, discrepancies there are between the picture and the image.

READER'S JOURNAL

What qualities make a person beautiful? Who do you consider beautiful? Describe him or her using figurative language such as similes and metaphors.

Literary TOOLS

IAMBIC TETRAMETER. An **iamb** is a poetic foot consisting of one weakly stressed syllable followed by one strongly stressed syllable. A line of poetry made up of four iambs is called iambic tetrameter. "She Walks in Beauty" is generally iambic tetrameter, though there are two lines which do not follow this pattern. Note the rhythm of "She Walks in Beauty" and note the lines which are not iambic tetrameter.

SIMILE. A **simile** is a comparison using like or as. As you read, identify the simile in "She Walks in Beauty."

About the SELECTIONS

Byron wrote the first selection, **"She Walks in Beauty,"** after seeing Lady Wilmot Horton, his cousin by marriage, at an evening party where she was wearing a black mourning gown with glittering spangles. The next two selections, stanzas from ***Childe Harold's Pilgrimage,*** are among the clearest and loftiest expressions of the Romantic view of nature as a source of spiritual renewal and inspiration.

Reader's Journal

How do you think a person's personality affects his or her appearance to others?

"She Walks in Beauty"

FROM *Childe Harold's Pilgrimage*

BY GEORGE GORDON, LORD BYRON

About the AUTHOR

George Gordon, Lord Byron (1788–1824) came from an aristocratic family but was raised in poverty. When his great-uncle died, he became the sixth Lord Byron. Born with a clubfoot, he nonetheless became a capable athlete. At Cambridge his extravagance led to indebtedness, but he formed close friendships there and began to write lyric verse. After completing his studies, Byron toured the Mediterranean, gathering ideas and experiences for his most important poems, such as *Childe Harold's Pilgrimage* and *Don Juan.* His romantic image, his good looks, his title, and his deeply emotional, sometimes sensational work combined to make him the most popular author of his day. Despite financial difficulties, he took no income from his publications because of his aristocratic status. He occupied his family's seat in the House of Lords and spoke as a liberal in support of laborers and Catholic Emancipation.

Lord Byron found himself entangled in a number of difficult romantic situations throughout his life. Like Percy Shelley, Byron was forced to leave England because of his eccentric behavior. He lived first in Switzerland and then in Italy, where he became involved in political intrigues. In his thirties, Byron settled into a relationship with an Italian countess and lived near Shelley in Pisa. He continued working on *Childe Harold* and completed *Don Juan,* a book-length, best-selling poem that scandalized Europe.

In the 1820s, Byron's writings stirred popular support for Greek independence from the Turks. Byron left his literary work and organized an expedition to aid in the Greek war. However, he was not a gifted soldier. He succumbed to a fever and died just before turning thirty-six. When news of his death reached England, a fifteen-year-old boy went into the forest and wrote on a rock, "Byron is dead." The boy would grow to become another of England's greatest poets, Alfred Tennyson, who later said "On that day, the whole world seemed to be darkened for me." The Greek people today still honor Byron as a national hero.

GOALS/OBJECTIVES

Studying this lesson will enable students to
- experience the speaker's awe at the wonder of nature
- describe the characteristics of the Byronic hero and relate them to the ideals of the Romantic Era
- define *iambic tetrameter, simile, repetition, parallelism,* and *Byronic hero* and identify and explain examples of each that they encounter in their reading
- identify and correct sentence run-ons
- conducting a research on Greek wars

She Walks in Beauty

GEORGE GORDON, LORD BYRON

Portrait of Lady Caroline Lamb, 1809. Sir Thomas Lawrence.
Bristol City Museum and Art Gallery, UK.

She walks in beauty, like the night
Of cloudless climes and starry skies;
And all that's best of dark and bright
Meet in her aspect[1] and her eyes:
Thus mellow'd to that tender light
Which heaven to gaudy day denies.

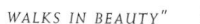

To what does the speaker compare the woman's beauty?

1. **aspect.** Appearance

ANSWER TO GUIDED READING QUESTION

1. The speaker compares the woman's beauty to the night, cloudless climes, and starry skies.

INDIVIDUAL LEARNING STRATEGIES

MOTIVATION
Have students discuss the statement, "Art imitates life." Do they agree with this saying? Do they think it applies to Byron and his work? Why, or why not? Students might present their opinions as a debate for the class.

READING PROFICIENCY
Encourage students to read through the vocabulary words and the Prereading page before they begin reading. Students might also benefit from hearing the poems read aloud.

ENGLISH LANGUAGE LEARNING
Students may have difficulty with the inverted word order in the poems. Have students use colored markers or pencils to identify nouns, verbs, adjectives, adverbs, and other parts of speech in the poems.

SPECIAL NEEDS
Once students have answered the Guided Reading questions and the Recall questions from the Investigate, Inquire, and Imagine section, ask them to get together in small groups to discuss their answers.

ENRICHMENT
Students should have a firm grasp on what the Romantic Era was about and what defines Romantic poems or prose. Have students present a lecture to the class, teaching them about the Romantic Era and its views toward Nature, poetry, and humanity.

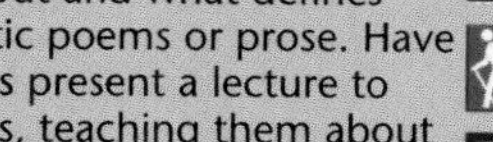

ANSWER TO GUIDED READING QUESTION

1. One can tell that the woman has spent happy days and that she is at peace with herself.

SELECTION CHECK TEST 4.8.27 WITH ANSWERS

Checking Your Reading

1. Where do "all that's best of dark and bright" meet? **They meet in her face and eyes.**
2. What color is her hair? **Her hair is raven colored, or black.**
3. What expression is on the woman's face? **She has a sweet, gentle expression.**
4. How does the woman spend her days? **She spends her days in goodness.**
5. How is the woman's love described? **Her love is innocent.**

Literary Tools

1. What figure of speech is in the first line, "She walks in beauty, like the night"? **This line contains a simile.**
2. What is an iamb? **It is a poetic foot with one weak and one strong syllable.**
3. What is iambic tetrameter? **A line of poetry with four iambs is iambic tetrameter.**

RESPOND TO THE SELECTION

What do you admire in people? How do your qualities compare to Byron's?

One shade the more, one ray the less,
   Had half impair'd the nameless grace
Which waves in every raven tress,
   Or softly lightens o'er her face;
Where thoughts serenely sweet express
   How pure, how dear their dwelling place.

And on that cheek, and o'er that brow,
   So soft, so calm, yet eloquent,
The smiles that win, the tints that glow,
   But tell of days in goodness spent,
A mind at peace with all below,
   A heart whose love is innocent! ■

What can one tell about this woman from her appearance?

WORDS FOR EVERYDAY USE

se • rene • ly (sə rēn´lē) *adv.*, peacefully. *The rowers glided serenely across the quiet lake.*

Respond to the SELECTION

What do you think the speaker admires in this woman?

Investigate, Inquire, Imagine

Recall: Gathering Facts →

1a. Where, according to the poem, does "all that's best of dark and bright" meet?

2a. What personality trait does the speaker feel is reflected in the woman's raven tresses and in her face?

3a. What, according to the speaker, can one tell from the woman's smiles?

Interpret: Finding Meaning

1b. What characteristics of the woman are suggested by the comparison in lines 1 and 2?

2b. What does the speaker have to say about the "dwelling place" of her thoughts?

3b. What does it mean to say that a mind is "at peace with all below" it? How would someone who is at peace with his or her physical being differ from someone who is not?

Analyze: Taking Things Apart →

4a. What modifiers (adverbs and adjectives) are used in the poem to describe the woman? Are these modifiers consistent with the speaker's description of the woman as mellower than "gaudy day"? Explain.

Synthesize: Bringing Things Together

4b. What words and phrases in the poem suggest moderation and temperance? How might these qualities bring one peace?

Evaluate: Making Judgments →

5a. A more traditional metaphor or simile for beauty and purity has been sunlight and morning. How effective do you find the simile of night for beauty in this poem? Why do you suppose Byron chose night, and how is the effect different than it would have been if he had chosen day?

Extend: Connecting Ideas

5b. William Blake's poem "The Lamb" is a rather different poetic description of innocence than "She Walks in Beauty." Compare the two. In what ways are they similar, and how do they differ?

Understanding Literature

Iambic Tetrameter. Review the definition for **iambic tetrameter** in Literary Tools in Prereading. A line of poetry made up of four iambs is called iambic tetrameter. Find the first line in the poem that is not in strict iambic tetrameter. Write that line down and mark its rhythmical pattern. Divide the line into feet and mark its weak and strong stresses.

Simile. Review the definition for **simile** in the Handbook of Literary Terms. With what simile does this poem begin? How is that simile extended, or elaborated, in the rest of the poem?

ANSWERS TO UNDERSTANDING LITERATURE

Iambic Tetrameter. Line 4 is the first line that is not in strict iambic tetrameter. It uses one trochee followed by three iambs.

Simile. The poem begins with the simile "She walks in beauty, like the night." The simile is extended as the speaker compares the lady's eyes, face, hair, and personality to the night as well.

ANSWERS TO INVESTIGATE, INQUIRE AND IMAGINE

Recall

1a. They meet in her aspect, or face, and her eyes.

2a. These characteristics reflect her grace and gentleness.

3a. The smiles tell that she is at peace with herself.

Interpret

1b. The comparison suggests that she is dark-haired or that she wears dark clothing. It also suggests that she moves smoothly and flawlessly.

2b. The speaker says that her head is "pure and dear", or innocent.

3b. It means that one is self-assured. A person at peace with his or her physical being appears confident, whereas one who isn't at peace might betray signs of physical self-consciousness such as fidgeting or slouching.

Analyze

4a. Modifiers such as "soft," "calm," "eloquent," and "innocent" describe the woman. They are consistent with the speaker's description because they all imply something opposite of the harsh, obvious light of "gaudy day." They imply subtlety and smoothness.

Synthesize.

4b. Words and phrases such as "mellow'd," "nameless grace," "serenely," "pure," and "days in goodness spent" all suggest moderation and temperance. These qualities might bring one peace because they involve thought and reflection rather than impetuousness, which often leads to turmoil.

Evaluate.

5a. *Responses will vary.* One might guess that night, when man is less likely to be about, seems a bit closer to nature unadulterated by the influence of man, a value that would have appealed to the Romantics. Night is also more still and quiet than day—a fitting simile for a woman at peace with herself.

Extend

5b. *Responses will vary.* The similarities lie in the common theme of innocence. Blake uses a creature of nature and Byron compares the woman to an aspect of nature. Byron portrays her beauty as evidence of her innocence—i.e. innocence, purity and a lack of artifice is beautiful. Because nature is also innocent, pure and without artifice, it is the metaphor. Blake also sees nature, as a creation of God without intervention of man, as beautiful. "She Walks in Beauty," however, is also a love poem, an aspect it does not share with Blake's poem.

ANSWERS TO GUIDED READING QUESTIONS

1. The ancient Persians worshiped atop the mountains.
2. The speaker loves nature more than humankind.

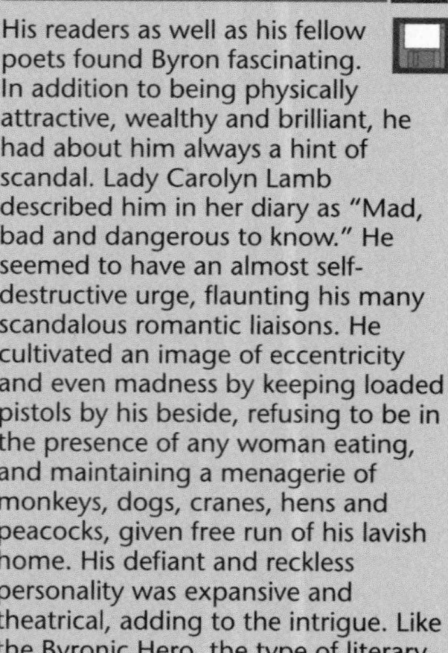

BIOGRAPHICAL NOTE

His readers as well as his fellow poets found Byron fascinating. In addition to being physically attractive, wealthy and brilliant, he had about him always a hint of scandal. Lady Carolyn Lamb described him in her diary as "Mad, bad and dangerous to know." He seemed to have an almost self-destructive urge, flaunting his many scandalous romantic liaisons. He cultivated an image of eccentricity and even madness by keeping loaded pistols by his beside, refusing to be in the presence of any woman eating, and maintaining a menagerie of monkeys, dogs, cranes, hens and peacocks, given free run of his lavish home. His defiant and reckless personality was expansive and theatrical, adding to the intrigue. Like the Byronic Hero, the type of literary character which is his namesake, he was given to extremes of profound emotion—towering rage, soaring joy, and tormenting guilt.

READER'S JOURNAL

Encourage students to write about the feelings created by being in that place, not just what they find intriguing about its physicality.

VOCABULARY FROM THE SELECTION

circumscribe
vainly

Literary TOOLS

REPETITION AND PARALLELISM. **Repetition** is the author's reuse of a sound, word, phrase, sentence, or other element. **Parallelism** is a literary technique in which a writer emphasizes the equal value or weight of two or more ideas by expressing them in the same grammatical form. As you read, note Byron's use of repetition and parallelism.

BYRONIC HERO. The **Byronic hero** is a leading figure in a literary work who, like a hero in Byron's works, is moody, passionate, proud, gloomy, adventurous, great-spirited, introverted, a bit disreputable by conventional standards, and a loner. As you read these selections from *Childe Harold's Pilgrimage,* consider whether or not the speaker can be characterized as a "Byronic hero."

Reader's Journal

If you could visit any natural wonder in the world, which would you choose: the Swiss Alps, the Grand Canyon, the fjords of Norway, or some place else? Why?

FROM

Childe Harold's Pilgrimage

GEORGE GORDON, LORD BYRON

FROM CANTO 3

91

Where did the ancient Persians worship?

Not vainly did the early Persian make
His altar the high places and the peak
Of earth-o'ergazing mountains, and thus take
A fit and unwall'd temple, there to seek
The Spirit, in whose honor shrines are weak,
Uprear'd of human hands. Come, and compare
Columns and idol-dwellings, Goth or Greek,
With Nature's realms of worship, earth and air,
Nor fix on fond abodes to circumscribe thy prayer!

FROM CANTO 4

178

There is a pleasure in the pathless woods,
There is a rapture on the lonely shore,
There is society, where none intrudes,
By the deep Sea, and music in its roar:
I love not Man the less, but Nature more,
From these our interviews, in which I steal
From all I may be, or have been before,
To mingle with the Universe, and feel
What I can ne'er express, yet can not all conceal. ■

What does the speaker love more than humankind?

WORDS FOR EVERYDAY USE

vain • ly (vān ´lē) *adv.*, uselessly. *The knight vainly courted the indeifferent lady.*

cir • cum • scribe (sər ´kəm scrīb) *vt.*, constrict, enclose. *A rustic stone fence circumscribes the farmer's land.*

Landscape with Lake and Mountains, c.1800s. John Knox. The Fine Art Society, London.

Respond *to the* SELECTION

Do you agree with the speaker's opinion about nature versus man-made shrines as places of worship and inspiration? Why, or why not?

LITERARY NOTE

Childe Harold's Pilgrimage was published in four cantos: Cantos 1 and 2 in 1812, Canto 3 in 1816, and Canto 4 in 1818. Byron traveled through Europe during these years and incorporated contemporary events, such as the Napoleonic Wars, into his poetic travelogue.

SELECTION CHECK TEST 4.8.29 WITH ANSWERS

Checking Your Reading

CANTO 3

1. What did early Persians use for altars? **They used mountaintops for altars.**
2. What is the reader asked to compare? **He is asked to compare mountaintops to manmade temples.**

CANTO 4

3. Where does the speaker find rapture? **He finds rapture on the lonely shore.**
4. With what does the speaker mingle? **He mingles with the Universe.**
5. What can the speaker never express? **He can never express his feelings.**

Literary Tools

1. How is repetition used in Canto 4? **The phrase "There is" is repeated.**
2. What is a Byronic hero? **A Byronic hero is moody, passionate, proud, gloomy, adventurous, great-spirited, introverted, and a bit disreputable.**
3. Identify two traits that suggest the speaker is a Byronic hero. ***Responses will vary.***

RESPOND TO THE SELECTION

Consider the feelings that the speaker in stanza 178 has about nature and solitude. Do you share these feelings? Why, or why not?

ANSWERS TO INVESTIGATE, INQUIRE AND IMAGINE

Recall

1a. It suggests that the reader not limit himself or herself to praying in artificial shrines.

2a. He finds pleasure, rapture, and society.

3a. He uses the metaphor of an interview.

Interpret

1b. They sometimes circumscribe their prayer by doing it only in human-made places. The speaker would rather that people prayed and worshiped at nature's shrine.

2b. He doesn't despise human company, but he simply loves nature more. He says "I love not man the less, but Nature more."

3b. He experiences some sort of communion, or two-way interaction with nature, evidenced by the use of the words, "society" and "interview."

Analyze

4a. The speaker is independent, passionate, and contemplative. He finds pleasure in "the lonely shore" and prefers nature when he is alone, when "none intrude(s)." He feels what he "can ne'er express"—feelings too large and complex for words. He prefers to worship in the limitless outdoors than in the circumscribing confines of buildings.

Synthesize

4b. *Responses will vary.* Many will find it attractive as this personality seems to enjoy life to the fullest, without inhibition. Some may feel this type of personality may not be successful in society.

Evaluate

5a. In stanza 91, the speaker urges readers to consider nature a more fitting place of worship than a temple. In stanza 178, the speaker reveals that he finds greater pleasure in nature's company than in human company.

Extend

5b. *Responses will vary.*

Investigate, Inquire, Imagine

Recall: Gathering Facts → **Interpret:** Finding Meaning

1a. What does the last line in stanza 91 suggest that the reader not do?

1b. In what way, according to the speaker, do people sometimes "circumscribe [their] prayer"? What would the speaker rather have people do?

2a. In stanza 178, what does the speaker find in the woods, the shore, and the sea?

2b. Does the speaker despise people and human company? How do you know?

3a. What metaphor does the speaker use in stanza 178 to describe encounters with nature?

3b. What relationship toward the universe does the speaker feel when spending time in nature?

Analyze: Taking Things Apart → **Synthesize:** Bringing Things Together

4a. How would you characterize the personality of the speaker of these two stanzas? Does this person favor rationality or emotion? human company or solitude? limits and constraints or boundlessness and freedom? How do you know?

4b. Based on these two stanzas, do you find the personality of the speaker attractive? Why or why not?

Evaluate: Making Judgments → **Extend:** Connecting Ideas

5a. The Romantic poets believed that the natural world was more important than the world made by human hands. In what different ways is this sentiment expressed in these two poems? How effectively is this sentiment expressed?

5b. What kinds of places seem holy or sacred to you? Why?

Understanding Literature

Repetition and Parallelism. Review the definitions for **repetition** and **parallelism** in the Handbook of Literary Terms. What examples of repetition and parallelism can you find in stanza 178?

Byronic Hero. Review the definition for **Byronic hero** in Literary Tools in Prereading. Complete the following cluster chart of aspects of the speaker's personality that fit the "Byronic hero" mold. All in all, do you think the speaker is a "Byronic hero?" Why or why not?

ANSWERS TO UNDERSTANDING LITERATURE

Repetition and Parallelism. The first three lines of stanza 178 exhibit both repetition and parallelism. Each begins with the phrase "There is" and ends with a parallel phrase: "a pleasure in the pathless woods," "a rapture on the lonely shore," "society, where none intrudes/By the deep Sea."

Byronic hero. Responses will vary as to whether or not he fits the "Byronic hero" mold. Certainly, he fits several of the characteristics.
Others characteristics of a Byronic hero:
Adventurous traveler
Loner—prefers solitude
Lofty ideals—mingles with Universe
Dislikes limits—wants freedom

WRITER'S JOURNAL

1. Pretend that you are the speaker of *Childe Harold's Pilgrimage* and that you are honoring a person by erecting a statue or fountain. Write a short **inscription** for this memorial. Who was this person, and why are you honoring him or her?
2. Write a brief **essay** describing a moment of deep connection to the universe that you have experienced or imagined. The moment could have taken place during a walk by the ocean, after winning a soccer game, or while playing with a small child.
3. Byron admires the woman in "She Walks in Beauty" for her serenity. She seems to be at peace with herself, and this adds to her beauty. Write a peace treaty with yourself. Identify what makes you feel angry, annoyed, worried, etc. Then think about what you can do to avert the feelings, such as avoiding something stressful, practicing relaxation techniques, or exercising. Write a **plan** to follow to rid yourself of negative energy.

Integrating *the* Language Arts

Language, Grammar, and Style

Correcting Sentence Run-ons. Read the Language Arts Survey 2.62, "Correcting Run-ons." Revise the following items, correcting the run-ons.

1. She walks in beauty, all that's best of dark and bright meet in her eyes.
2. One shade deeper would be too deep, one shade brighter would be too bright.
3. I love human beings, however, I love nature more.
4. The woods hold magic, the sea holds rapture they make me feel as if I mingle with the universe.
5. I give myself to nature, and I mingle with the universe and I can never express what I feel.

Collaborative Learning & Speaking and Listening

Speech Writing. Imagine that Byron could return to life and that he observed our modern urban sprawl, our clearing of forests for new highways and subdivisions, and our time spent in front of televisions. What do you think he would say to us? Working in small groups, prepare a speech that Byron might make to a high school graduating class. What would he say to the students? What language might he use? What rationale would he offer for his ideas? Consider the tone, volume, inflection, and rate he would use. One member of your group should rehearse delivery of the speech with the rest of the group offering coaching. Then deliver the speech to the whole class. You may find it helpful to refer to Language Arts Survey 4.15, "Giving a Speech," in your preparation.

Study and Research

Researching Greek History. Using library resources, research the Greek war for independence from the Turks. Prepare a report for your class on the factors that precipitated the war. Why do you think this cause inspired Byron to travel there with money and medical supplies to aid the Greeks? How do the Greeks see Byron today?

ANSWERS TO INTEGRATING THE LANGUAGE ARTS

Language, Grammar, and Style

Responses will vary.

1. She walks in beauty, and all that's best of dark and bright meet in her eyes.
2. One shade deeper would be too deep, but one shade brighter would be too bright.
3. I love human beings; however, I love nature more.
4. The woods hold magic; the sea holds rapture. They make me feel as if I mingle with the universe.
5. I give myself to nature; I mingle with the universe, and I can never express what I feel.

Study and Research

Students may also want to search the Internet under "Greek wars" to help them find information about the war for independence from the Turks. Refer students to the Language Arts Survey 5.26, "Browsing versus Searching on the Internet."

ADDITIONAL RESOURCES

UNIT 8 RESOURCE BOOK
"When I Have Fears"
- Selection Worksheet 8.15
- Selection Check Test 4.8.31
- Selection Test 4.8.32

"Ode on a Grecian Urn"
- Selection Worksheet 8.16
- Selection Check Test 4.8.33
- Selection Test 4.8.34
- Language, Grammar, and Style Resource 3.40

INDIVIDUAL LEARNING STRATEGIES

MOTIVATION
Ask students to discuss the saying "Live every day as it if were your last." What does this mean? Why do you think this saying is so popular? What is the motivation behind this saying?

READING PROFICIENCY
Read the poem, "Ode on a Grecian Urn," aloud to students before they read it on their own. Ask them to listen to the questions the speaker asks. Do these questions get answered or are they rhetorical questions? Why do they think the speaker asks so many questions?

ENGLISH LANGUAGE LEARNING
After students read "Ode on a Grecian Urn," have students role play the scenes described on the urn. Students may also describe the scenes in writing or draw pictures of the scenes.

SPECIAL NEEDS
Have students work with a partner to answer the questions in the Literary Tools section and to fill out the Graphic Organizer on page 731.Test their comprehension with the selection check test.

ENRICHMENT
Ask students to read the Language Arts Survey 4.18, "Guidelines for Giving a Speech." Then have them choose a song, a story, a poem, or a work of art that inspires them. Finally, have them write a brief speech that expresses their feelings about the work they chose. Make sure students quote from or describe the work.

"When I Have FEARS" "Ode on a Grecian Urn"

BY JOHN KEATS

About the AUTHOR

John Keats (1795–1821) came from the least privileged background of all the major British poets. His father was head stableman at a London livery stable. The eldest of five children, Keats was an energetic, boisterous child. One of his teachers encouraged him to write and read poetry, including the work of Edmund Spenser.

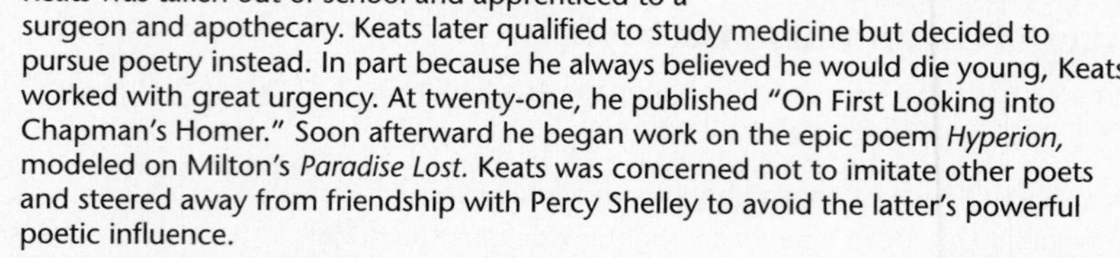

At the age of fifteen, after the death of his parents, Keats was taken out of school and apprenticed to a surgeon and apothecary. Keats later qualified to study medicine but decided to pursue poetry instead. In part because he always believed he would die young, Keats worked with great urgency. At twenty-one, he published "On First Looking into Chapman's Homer." Soon afterward he began work on the epic poem *Hyperion,* modeled on Milton's *Paradise Lost.* Keats was concerned not to imitate other poets and steered away from friendship with Percy Shelley to avoid the latter's powerful poetic influence.

In 1818, Keats became mortally ill with tuberculosis; some people attributed his sickness to the criticism that he received in the literary press after publishing *Hyperion.* Despite his illness, Keats was extremely creative and prolific during the year that followed. He published a series of masterpieces, including his great odes and sonnets. Critics have compared his language to that of William Shakespeare because of its richness of detail and its celebration of existence.

Keats's respiratory illness intensified in 1820. A year later, he died in Rome at age twenty-five. His early death was a great tragedy, for we shall never know what his genius might have produced had he lived.

About the SELECTIONS

Keats's sonnet **"When I Have Fears"** is a moving meditation on death written by a young poet who knew that his own life would be cut short. **"Ode on a Grecian Urn"** is an exploration of the value and purpose of art. The skilled potters of ancient Greece made urns for various purposes, including storage of wine and a variety of foods. These urns were often decorated with figures. In Keats's poem, the speaker addresses a Grecian urn and the various figures that appear on it: a bride, men or gods, maidens, a pipe-playing youth, a lover, and a priest leading a cow to sacrifice.

GOALS/OBJECTIVES

Studying the lessons will enable students to
- experience the speaker's feeling about love, death, and beauty
- describe Keat's poetry and it literary significance
- define *sonnet, theme, apostrophe*, and *paradox* and recognize and explain examples of each that they encounter in their reading
- demonstrate the ability to achieve subject-verb agreement
- conduct a research on Greek classical art

Branch Hill Pond, Hampstead, c.1800s. John Constable. Victoria and Albert Museum, London.

When I Have FEARS

JOHN KEATS

When I have fears that I may cease to be
Before my pen has glean'd[1] my teeming brain,
Before high piled books, in charactry,[2]
Hold like rich garners[3] the full ripen'd grain;
When I behold, upon the night's starr'd face,
Huge cloudy symbols of a high romance,
And think that I may never live to trace
Their shadows, with the magic hand of chance;
And when I feel, fair creature of an hour,
That I shall never look upon thee more,
Never have relish in the fairy power
Of unreflecting love;—then on the shore
Of the wide world I stand alone, and think
Till love and fame to nothingness do sink. ■

1. **glean'd.** Gathered the last remains
2. **charactry.** Printed letters of the alphabet
3. **garner.** Granary, place to store grain

WORDS FOR EVERYDAY USE

teem • ing. (tem iŋ) *part.,* overflowing. *The meadow was teeming with wild flowers.*

Literary TOOLS

SONNET. A **sonnet** is a fourteen-line poem that follows one of a number of different rhyme schemes. "When I Have Fears" follows the rhyme scheme of the Elizabethan or Shakespearean sonnet. Notice that it is divided into four parts: three quatrains, or four line sections, and a final couplet, or two-line section.

THEME. A **theme** is a central idea in a literary work. As you read, consider what the overall theme of this poem might be.

Reader's Journal

What would you most like to accomplish before you die?

What does the speaker fear will prevent him from doing all that he wants to do?

ANSWER TO GUIDED READING QUESTION

1. The speaker fears that death will prevent him from doing and experiencing all that he wants.

VOCABULARY FROM THE SELECTIONS

teeming

READER'S JOURNAL

To prompt students' thinking, ask them to reflect on these questions: "What are the five things that are most important in your life? What would you do if you had only a few months to live?

SELECTION CHECK TEST 4.8.31 WITH ANSWERS

Checking Your Reading

1. The speaker fears what will happen before he becomes a great poet? **He will die.**
2. Who does the speaker address in this poem? **He addresses a "fair creature."**
3. What is he afraid will happen with this person? **He won't see her again.**
4. On what shore does he stand? **He stands on the shore of the wide world.**
5. What happens to love and fame? **Love and fame sink to nothingness.**

Literary Tools

Fill in the blanks using the following terms. You may not use every term, and you may use some terms more than once.

sonnet metaphor quatrain
couplet theme

1. The line "Hold like rich garners the full ripen'd grain" illustrates **metaphor**.
2. **Sonnets** may have various rhyme schemes but always have fourteen lines.
3. Elizabethan sonnets generally contain three **quatrains**.

RESPOND TO THE SELECTION

What fears do you have? What do you do "when [you] have fears"? How do you react to fear?

ANSWERS TO INVESTIGATE, INQUIRE AND IMAGINE

Recall

1a. He is afraid he will not have the opportunity to gather and write about as much as he could in a normal lifetime.
2a. He sees clouds in the night sky.
3a. He fears to lose the ability to fall in love completely.

Interpret

1b. "Gleaning" is gathering grain. "Teeming" means overflowing. Gleaning a teeming brain might mean harvesting, or making use of, an abundance of thought and creativity.
2b. He fears he will not be able to experience the fullness of nature.
3b. Something that is "fairy-like" would be magical and entrancing but somewhat unreal. Unreflecting love is unconditional love, free of everyday concerns and criticisms. He reveals that he would like to believe the magical idea that love can exist in a sphere separate from everyday problems and concerns.

Analyze

4a. The speaker fears he will die before he is able to write all of the poetry in his mind, experience the fullness and glory of nature and experience the heady, magical feeling of love untamed by rational thought.

Synthesize

4b. Reflecting on death subdues the speaker's desire for fame and approval as he considers that everything of this world is temporary.

Evaluate

5a. The speaker concludes that love and fame sink to nothingness, because this life is short and death might take him before he is able to do the things that really matter to him.

Extend

5b. The speaker of "Ozymandias" says that earthly fame and glory are only temporary and, like the lost glories of Ozymandias's reign, fall to the relentless march of time. He seems to say that vanity and arrogance lead one to value fame and glory. The speaker of "When I Have Fears" seems to say that earthly fame and glory are insignificant in the face of the really important things—love, art, nature, and that our lives are too short to waste time on fame. The speaker of "When I Have Fears" is somewhat sad and mourns that he may not have enough time for those things he feels are most important.

Respond *to the* SELECTION

Why do you think the speaker feels alone?

INVESTIGATE, Inquire, *Imagine*

Recall: GATHERING FACTS → **Interpret:** FINDING MEANING

1a. In lines 1–4, what is the speaker afraid will not happen before he dies?

1b. What is "gleaning"? What does "teeming" mean? What might it mean to glean a teeming brain?

2a. In lines 5–8, what does the speaker see in the sky?

2b. In lines 5–8, what does the speaker fear he will not be able to do?

3a. In lines 9–12, what is the speaker fearing to lose?

3b. What qualities would something that is "fairy-like" have? How might "unreflecting love" differ from feelings based on a critical examination of someone else? What is the speaker saying about his feelings when he refers to "the fairy power/Of unreflecting love"?

Analyze: TAKING THINGS APART → **Synthesize:** BRINGING THINGS TOGETHER

4a. What three things does the speaker fear he will not be able to do before he dies?

4b. How does reflecting on death change the speaker's desires for fame as a writer and for continuation of his "unreflecting love"?

Evaluate: MAKING JUDGMENTS → **Extend:** CONNECTING IDEAS

5a. Evaluate the speaker's reasons for concluding that fame and love sink to "nothingness." It has been suggested by some critics that the love he refers to in line 14 is to be interpreted as approval or popularity—different from the "unreflecting love" of line 12, which is to be interpreted as romantic love. Do you agree with his thoughts on fame and approval? Why, or why not?

5b. Consider the way in which both "When I Have Fears" by Keats and "Ozymandias" by Shelley deal with the nature of fame and earthly glory. What is the speaker of each poem saying about this subject?

Understanding *Literature*

SONNET. Review the definition of **sonnet** in the Literary Tools in Prereading. What is the subject of each of the three quatrains and of the final couplet?

THEME. Review the definition for **theme** in the Handbook of Literary Terms. Why does the speaker call the person to whom this poem is addressed the "fair creature of an hour"? What is the speaker saying about love and life? How does this statement fit with the theme of the poem as a whole?

ANSWERS TO INVESTIGATE, INQUIRE AND IMAGINE (CONT.)

Answers to Understanding Literature can be found on page 731.

Ode on a Grecian Urn

JOHN KEATS

Grecian water jug. c.510 BC. Museum of Fine Arts, Boston.

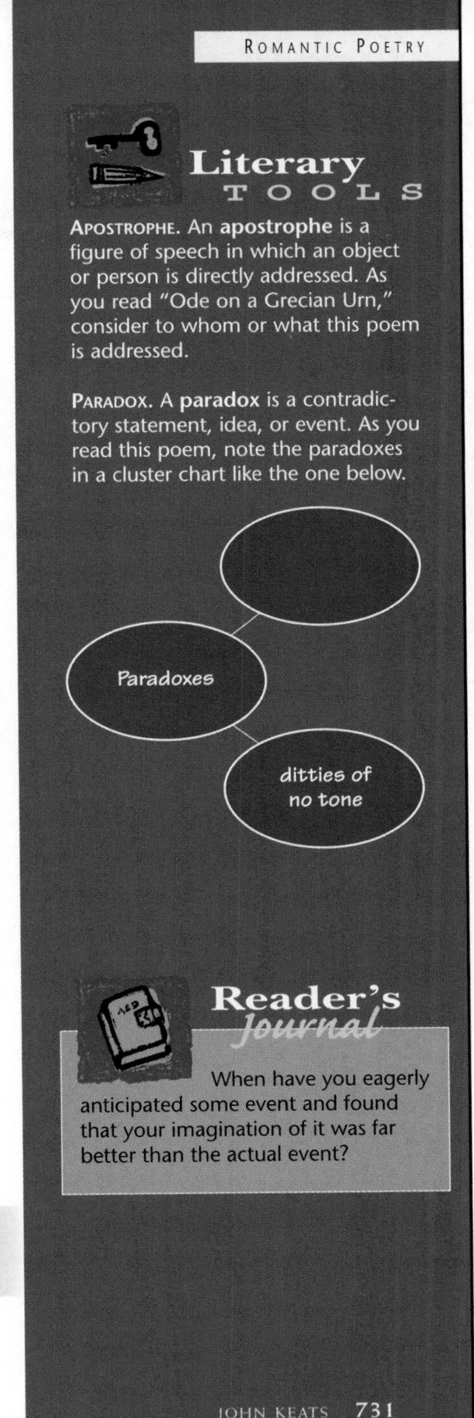

Literary TOOLS

APOSTROPHE. An **apostrophe** is a figure of speech in which an object or person is directly addressed. As you read "Ode on a Grecian Urn," consider to whom or what this poem is addressed.

PARADOX. A **paradox** is a contradictory statement, idea, or event. As you read this poem, note the paradoxes in a cluster chart like the one below.

Reader's Journal

When have you eagerly anticipated some event and found that your imagination of it was far better than the actual event?

1

Thou still unravish'd bride of quietness,
Thou foster-child of silence and slow time,
Sylvan[1] historian, who canst thus express
A flowery tale more sweetly than our rhyme:

What is pictured on the urn?

1. **Sylvan.** Rustic

ANSWER TO GUIDED READING QUESTION

1. A bride, men or gods, and maidens are pictured on the urn.

GRAPHIC ORGANIZER

In the poem, the following paradoxes occur: the unheard melody is sweeter than the one heard, "ditties of no tone," the lover can never kiss his beloved yet he will always love her and she will always be fair, the piper forever pipes songs that remain forever new, a love that is warm—i.e. felt hotly—and is yet still to be felt. There are several instances of things that exist and yet are not yet experienced.

READER'S JOURNAL

Look through your textbook to find a picture of people gathering together. What is the significance of the gathering? Is it for celebration, mourning, religious worship, or some other purpose? How can you tell?

VOCABULARY FROM THE SELECTIONS

adieu
citadel
cloy'd
deity

ANSWERS TO UNDERSTANDING LITERATURE

SONNET. The speaker's fear of not becoming a great poet is the subject of the first quatrain. His fear of not experiencing the fullness of nature is the subject of the second quatrain. His fear of not experiencing a great love is the subject of the third quatrain, and his contemplation of an early death is the subject of the final couplet. The paraphrased poem might read: "When I fear that I might die before I've written and read everything that I possibly can, seen everything in nature, and experienced an all-consuming, passionate love, then I forget all about love and fame and become lost in thoughts about dying young."

THEME. He calls her "fair creature of an hour" because he realizes both the inevitability of his own death and the possibility that she is but a fleeting love. The speaker is saying that love and life are transitory and that there is no knowing when they might be lost. The statement fits with the theme of the poem as a whole because it acknowledges the fragile nature of life and love.

SELECTION CHECK TEST 4.8.33 WITH ANSWERS

Checking Your Reading

1. What does Stanza 1 describe? **It describes the scene on the urn (bride, men or gods, maidens).**
2. What is said about heard and unheard melodies? **Unheard melodies are sweeter.**
3. What can the bold lover never, never do? **He can never kiss his love.**
4. What will happen to people, but not to the urn? **People die, but the urn remains.**
5. What does the urn "say" to man? **It says, "Beauty is truth, truth beauty."**

Literary Tools

Fill in the blanks using the following terms. You may not use every term, and you may use some terms more than once.

paradox ode theme
aphorism apostrophe

1. A poem demonstrates **apostrophe** when it directly addresses a person or object.
2. The fragility of human existence is a central **theme** in this poem.
3. A contradictory statement, idea, or event is a(n) **paradox**.

What leaf-fring'd legend haunts about thy shape
Of deities or mortals, or of both,
In Tempe or the dales of Arcady?[2]
What men or gods are these? What maidens loth?
What mad pursuit? What struggle to escape?
What pipes and timbrels?[3] What wild ecstasy?

2

Heard melodies are sweet, but those unheard
Are sweeter; therefore, ye soft pipes, play on;
Not to the sensual ear,[4] but, more endear'd,
Pipe to the spirit ditties of no tone:
Fair youth, beneath the trees, thou canst not leave
Thy song, nor ever can those trees be bare;
Bold lover, never, never canst thou kiss,
Though winning near the goal—yet, do not grieve;
She cannot fade, though thou hast not thy bliss,
For ever wilt thou love, and she be fair!

3

Ah, happy, happy boughs! that cannot shed
Your leaves, nor ever bid the spring adieu;
And, happy melodist, unwearied,
For ever piping songs for ever new;
More happy love! more happy, happy love!
For ever warm and still to be enjoy'd,
For ever panting, and for ever young;
All breathing human passion far above,
That leaves a heart high-sorrowful and cloy'd,
A burning forehead, and a parching tongue.

2. **Tempe . . . Arcady.** Tempe and Arcadia are both places in Greece that have become symbols for ideal rural beauty.
3. **timbrels.** Ancient tambourines
4. **sensual ear.** The ear that actually hears, not that of imagination

WORDS FOR EVERYDAY USE

de • i • ty (dē´ ə tē) *n.,* a god. *Vishnu is an Indian deity.*
a • dieu (ə dyo͞o´) *interj.,* goodbye. *As the train pulled out of the station, travelers leaned out the windows shouting "Adieu!"*
cloy'd (klȯid) *adj.,* to have had too much; surfeited. *Cloyed from eating too much cake and candy, the boy spent the rest of his birthday in bed.*

4

Who are these coming to the sacrifice?
To what green altar, O mysterious priest,
Lead'st thou that heifer lowing at the skies,
And all her silken flanks with garlands drest?
What little town by river or sea shore,
Or mountain-built with peaceful citadel,
Is emptied of this folk, this pious morn?
And, little town, thy streets for evermore
Will silent be; and not a soul to tell
Why thou art desolate, can e'er return.

What can the lover never do? What will his beloved never do?

5

O Attic[5] shape! Fair attitude! with brede[6]
Of marble men and maidens overwrought,
With forest branches and the trodden weed;
Thou, silent form, dost tease us out of thought
As doth eternity: Cold Pastoral!
When old age shall this generation waste,
Thou shalt remain, in midst of other woe
Than ours, a friend to man, to whom thou say'st,
"Beauty is truth, truth beauty,"—that is all
Ye know on earth, and all ye need to know. ■

What will remain when this generation is old and gone?

5. **Attic.** Characteristic of Attica, a region of Greece where Athens is located

6. **Brede.** An archaic word meaning an embroidered or braided edge.

WORDS FOR EVERYDAY USE

cit • a • del (sit′ə del) *n.*, fortress, safe place. *At dawn, soldiers advanced on the citadel.*

Respond to the SELECTION

What does "beauty" mean to the speaker?

ANSWERS TO GUIDED READING QUESTIONS

1. The lover can never kiss his beloved, yet she will always be fair and he will always love her.
2. The urn will remain when this generation is old and gone.

ADDITIONAL QUESTIONS AND ACTIVITIES

In "Endymion," Keats gives us another aphorism about beauty: "A thing of beauty is a joy forever." Compare this to line 49 of "Ode on a Grecian Urn." Ask students what they believe the poet is saying in each case.

Answer

Responses will vary. The line from "Endymion" certainly expresses the sentiment that beauty is lasting and timeless, as does the common interpretation of the line from "Ode on a Grecian Urn."

RESPOND TO THE SELECTION

How would you define beauty and truth? How does your definition compare to the speaker's definition of these terms?

ANSWERS TO INVESTIGATE, INQUIRE AND IMAGINE

RECALL

1a. The imagined melody is sweeter.
2a. They never lose their leaves.
3a. He asks which town it is.

INTERPRET

1b. An imagined melody might be sweeter because its possibilities are unlimited.
2b. They are frozen in time; they will never change or die.
3b. He speculates that the town is on a river, sea shore, or mountain. Its people might have left to attend a sacrifice (line 3). The town will be silent forever more because it is not pictured on the urn, and no one will ever know about it.

ANALYZE

4a. When "this generation" is old, the urn will remain unchanged, a "friend to man." All the things pictured on the urn are special because they preserve the youth and beauty of humans.

SYNTHESIZE

4b. The urn depicts the joy of love and the pain of being unable to attain the object of that love. It shows music being played which cannot be heard. And the images portray a moment in time—brief and fleeting—that is nonetheless frozen and made permanent. The poem is an artistic rendering of the very state Keats describes—"being in uncertainties, Mysteries" with no resolution offered.

EVALUATE

5a. *Responses will vary.*

EXTEND

5b. Common themes of these poems are that human experience is short and fleeting and that peace and beauty can be found in things external. The speaker in "When I Have Fears" speaks of the "fair creature of an hour" who might never be seen again. The speaker in "Ode on a Grecian Urn" urges a youth to be happy because his lover "cannot fade."

INVESTIGATE, Inquire, Imagine

Recall: GATHERING FACTS →

1a. Which, according to the speaker, is "sweeter," an actual melody or an imagined one?
2a. What is true of the boughs from the first line of stanza 3 that is not true of boughs in the real world?
3a. What question does the speaker ask about the town in stanza 4?

Interpret: FINDING MEANING

1b. Why might this be so?
2b. What similarity do the boughs, the melody, and the love that are described in stanza 3 have?
3b. What speculations does the speaker make about the town in stanza 4? Why might the people have left the town? Why will it be silent forever more?

Analyze: TAKING THINGS APART →

4a. Consider lines 45-47. What will be true when "this generation" is old? What is special about the people, trees, melodies, and other things pictured on the urn?

Synthesize: BRINGING THINGS TOGETHER

4b. Keats presents life as an enigma of unresolved opposites: joy and pain, permanence and transience, detachment and wild passion. He once said in a letter that the ideal state is "being in uncertainties, Mysteries and doubts without any irritable reaching after fact and reason." How is "Ode on a Grecian Urn" a reflection of this sentiment?

Evaluate: MAKING JUDGMENTS →

5a. In what sense might beauty be truth and truth beauty? Do you agree? Is this aphorism consistent with or contradictory of another familiar one, "beauty is only skin deep?"

Extend: CONNECTING IDEAS

5b. Compare Keats's "Ode on a Grecian Urn" with "When I Have Fears." Is there a common theme in these selections? Explain.

Understanding Literature

APOSTROPHE. Review the definition of **apostrophe** in the Handbook of Literary Terms. What objects or figures are addressed by the speaker in this poem? Discuss with your classmates how Keats uses the technique of apostrophe to express his thoughts about the urn and about art.

Paradox. Review the definition of **paradox** and the cluster chart you made for Literary Tools in Prereading. The well-known critic Harold Bloom has said that "Fulfillment, for Keats, is a betrayal of potential. The ideal for Keats is to be poised before experience." How do you interpret this comment in light of the paradoxes in "Ode on a Grecian Urn?"

ANSWERS TO UNDERSTANDING LITERATURE

APOSTROPHE. The speaker addresses the urn and some of the figures and objects that are depicted on it: in stanza 1, the speaker may be addressing a bride and a historian, or perhaps the urn itself; in stanza 2, pipes and the pipe-playing youth; in stanza 3, boughs and another piper; in stanza 4, the urn, a priest, and a town; in stanza 5, the urn.

PARADOX. Each of the paradoxes in the poem centers on a frozen moment in time, in which we can feel the anticipation of some event but never experience the realization. The urn is a depiction of being poised on the verge of experience, and in this sense, it represents perfection.

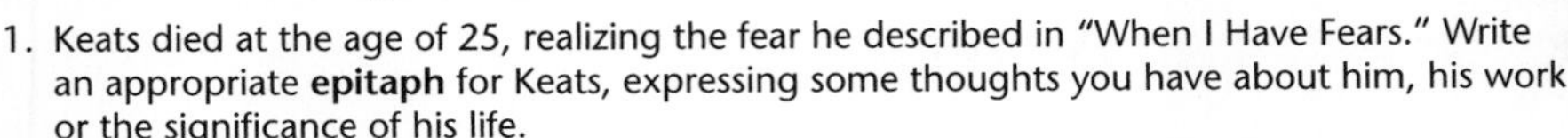

Writer's Journal

1. Keats died at the age of 25, realizing the fear he described in "When I Have Fears." Write an appropriate **epitaph** for Keats, expressing some thoughts you have about him, his work or the significance of his life.
2. Metaphors are important literary tools that give a simple description a color, taste, smell or feeling that the reader recognizes. They bring the reader into the experience of the poem or story. What metaphors would you use to describe death, mortality or immortality? Write several **metaphors** on this theme. First, write the tenor, the actual subject; then write the vehicle, the thing to which the subject will be likened. For example, if the tenor were "death," the vehicle could be "sleep" or "darkness."
3. A myth is a story that explains objects or events in the natural world as resulting from the action of some supernatural force or entity, most often a god. Write your own **myth** about the origins of art. In your myth, tell why some art form, such as music, painting, pottery-making, poetry, drama, or storytelling, was given to human beings. In other words, explain the importance of that art form to people. Tell what function or functions it serves. To prepare for writing your myth, you might want to read a few Greek or Native American myths in books from your school or community library.

Integrating *the* Language Arts

Language, Grammar, and Style.

Subject-verb Agreement. Review the Language Arts Survey 3.40, "Getting Subject and Verb to Agree". Correct the following sentences to make subjects and verbs agree.

1. Each of the figures on the urn have a story to tell.
2. The maiden and her lover stands forever still.
3. Neither the melodies of the piper nor the song of the lover are heard.
4. One of the maidens are playing a harp.
5. Neither the poet nor his contemporaries was in favor of using reason to overrule emotion.

Study and Research

Researching Art. Research the vase art of classical Greece. Using, if possible, the library and art history texts as well as museums in your area determine the various forms and uses of vases and urns in classical Greece. What sorts of scenes were typically depicted on them? How were they made? Can you find a vase or urn with scenes similar to those described in "Ode on a Grecian Urn?" Share your findings with your class.

Collaborative Learning

Time Capsule. Keats was concerned about his legacy to future generations. With other students, plan a time capsule—a box to be opened by people two hundred years from now. What items would you put in the box to tell future generations about you, your lives, your time, and your place?

ANSWERS TO INTEGRATING THE LANGUAGE ARTS

Language, Grammar, and Style

1. Each of the figures on the urn has a story to tell.
2. The maiden and her lover stand forever still.
3. Neither the melodies of the piper nor the song of the lover is heard.
4. One of the maidens is playing a harp.
5. Neither the poet nor his contemporaries were in favor of using reason to overrule emotion.

Collaborative Learning

Tell students that items they choose to be in the time capsule should symbolize the major events and ideology of their generation. For example, they may choose the American flag to symbolize freedom or a CD of a popular rap group to symbolize hip-hop culture.

ADDITIONAL RESOURCES

UNIT 8 RESOURCE BOOK
- Selection Worksheet 8.17
- Selection Check Test 4.8.35
- Selection Test 4.8.36
- Language, Grammar, and Style Resource 3.42

VOCABULARY FROM THE SELECTION

caprice
epithet
ignoble
ingenious
insinuate
puerile
satirize
scrupulous
specious

GRAPHIC ORGANIZER

Tenor: emotions and behavior of women	**Vehicle:** current
Tenor: limiting education to women	**Vehicle:** barriers
Tenor: education	**Vehicle:** fountain of light
Tenor: man	**Vehicle:** satellite

READER'S JOURNAL

Do you think education is important? Why, or why not?

DIDACTIC CRITICISM. Didactic criticism evaluates works of art in terms of the moral, ethical, or political message that they convey. Note the use of didactic criticism in this selection as Mary Wollstonecraft refers to Milton's work.

METAPHOR. A metaphor is a figure of speech in which one thing is spoken or written about as if it were another. This figure of speech invites the reader to make a comparison between the two things. The tenor of the metaphor is the actual subject, and the vehicle is the thing to which the subject is being compared. As you read, make a chart listing the tenor and vehicle of the metaphors Wollstonecraft uses to make her point in this except from "A Vindication of the Rights of Woman."

TENOR	VEHICLE
behavior of women	*current*

What do you think happens to people when they are denied the right to education, ownership of property, or participation in government or the work force?

FROM
A Vindication of the Rights of Woman
BY MARY WOLLSTONECRAFT

About the AUTHOR

Mary Wollstonecraft (1759–1797) is widely recognized as one of the first great feminist writers and thinkers. At the age of nineteen, she took a position as a governess but had to give it up to care for her mother during a protracted, terminal illness. In 1784, she helped her sister escape from a cruel husband. The two sisters, along with a friend, fled to London, where they started a school. Although initially a success, the school ran into financial difficulties and closed. Wollstonecraft wrote her first book, *Thoughts on the Education of Daughters,* in 1786. This work was followed in 1788 by a novel, *Mary, a Fiction;* in 1790 by a book on the French Revolution, *A Vindication of the Rights of Men;* and in 1792 by Wollstonecraft's masterpiece, *A Vindication of the Rights of Woman.* During the years 1793–94, she went to France to observe the French Revolution firsthand. After adventures and misadventures, she returned to London and married the radical social philosopher William Godwin. The couple's child, Mary Wollstonecraft Godwin, grew up to write that astonishing Romantic novel *Frankenstein.* However, Wollstonecraft was not to know her daughter, for she died as a result of childbirth. A memoir written by Godwin after Wollstonecraft's death scandalized the public and led to a suppression of her work. However, twentieth-century women's rights advocates have come to view *A Vindication of the Rights of Woman* as a pioneering work on the necessity of equal education and opportunity for women.

About the SELECTION

Mary Wollstonecraft lived in a time when women had few rights under the law. They could neither vote nor sue in court. They had limited educational opportunities and were not allowed to attend universities. When they married, their husbands inherited all of their property. They had very few opportunities for work except as servants, nurses, or governesses (who performed tutoring and child-care duties). In ***A Vindication of the Rights of Woman,*** Wollstonecraft argued that such inequities reduced women to the dependent state of children; robbed them of self-sufficiency; made them weak, docile, and overly emotional; and kept them from becoming fully human. In contemporary terms, one might put Wollstonecraft's argument as follows: lack of opportunity and education made it impossible for women in Wollstonecraft's day to achieve their full potential.

GOALS/OBJECTIVES

Studying this lesson will enable students to
- understand and empathize with women of the Romantic Era who did not have the educational opportunities available today
- describe Wollstonecraft's contributions to the women's rights movement
- define *didactic criticism* and *metaphor* and recognize and explain examples of each that they encounter in their reading
- identify and correct split infinitives
- conduct a survey of works about Women's Rights

FROM

A Vindication of the Rights of Woman

MARY WOLLSTONECRAFT

To account for, and excuse the tyranny of man, many ingenious arguments have been brought forward to prove, that the two sexes, in the acquirement of virtue, ought to aim at attaining a very different character: or, to speak explicitly, women are not allowed to have sufficient strength of mind to acquire what really deserves the name of virtue. Yet it should seem, allowing them to have souls, that there is but one way appointed by Providence to lead *mankind* to either virtue or happiness.

If then women are not a swarm of ephemeron[1] triflers, why should they be kept in ignorance under the specious name of innocence? Men complain, and with reason, of the follies and caprices of our sex, when they do not keenly satirize our headstrong passions and groveling vices.—Behold, I should answer, the natural effect of ignorance! The mind will ever be unstable that has only prejudices to rest on, and the current will run with destructive fury when there are no barriers to break its force. Women are told from their infancy, and taught by the example of their mothers, that a little knowledge of human weakness, justly termed cunning, softness of temper, *outward* obedience, and a scrupulous attention to a puerile kind of propriety, will obtain for them the protection of man; and should they be beautiful, every thing else is needless, for, at least, twenty years of their lives.

What do men complain about in women, and what does Mary Wollstonecraft say causes this behavior?

Thus Milton describes our first frail mother; though when he tells us that women are formed for softness and sweet attractive grace,[2] I cannot comprehend his meaning, unless, in the true Mahometan strain, he meant to deprive us of souls, and insinuate that we were beings only designed by sweet attractive grace, and docile blind obedience, to gratify the senses of man when he can no longer soar on the wing of contemplation.

How grossly do they insult us who thus advise us only to render ourselves gentle, domestic brutes! For instance, the winning softness so warmly, and frequently, recommended, that governs by obeying. What childish expressions, and how insignificant is the being—can it be an immortal one? who will condescend to govern by such sinister methods! "Certainly," says Lord Bacon, "man is of kin to the beasts by his body; and if he be not of kin to God by his

1. **ephemeron.** An insect that lives only one day
2. **Milton . . . grace.** In *Paradise Lost* (IV. 297–99), Milton wrote that men were formed for "contemplation" and "valor," while women were made for "softness" and "sweet attractive grace."

WORDS FOR EVERYDAY USE

spe • cious (spē shəs) *adj.*, seeming sound or logical while not really being so. *The detectives weren't deceived by the thief's specious alibi.*

ca • price (kə prēs´) *n.*, whim. *What caprice led you to spend your money so foolishly?*

sat • i • rize (sat´ə rīz) *vt.*, attack or ridicule with satire. *The witty comedy team satirizes political events.*

scru • pu • lous (skrōō´ pyə ləs) *adj.*, extremely careful. *Make a scrupulous review of the material, because it has to be perfect for publication.*

pu • er • ile (pyōō´ər il) *adj.*, childish; immature. *Why would a mature adult still engage in such puerile activities?*

in • sin • u • ate (in sin´yōō āt´) *vt.*, suggest, imply. *Your critical tone insinuates that you don't agree with me.*

ANSWER TO GUIDED READING QUESTION

1. Men complain that women are given to folly and whim and are ruled by their passions and vices. This silly and emotional behavior is due to the fact that women are kept in ignorance, according to Wollstonecraft.

INDIVIDUAL LEARNING STRATEGIES

MOTIVATION
Ask students to discuss the following questions: What stereotypes are there about men and women? Do you think men and women have equal rights at this time? Why, or why not? If not, what rights do men have that women still do not have?

READING PROFICIENCY
Suggest that students stop at the end of each paragraph and ask themselves if they understand what they have read. If they do not, have them ask a more advanced reader to help them understand.

ENGLISH LANGUAGE LEARNING
Share with students the additional vocabulary words from this selection. Ask them to look up the definition of each word and to write a contextual sentence:

tyranny	contemplation
cunning	indefeasible
propriety	expostulate

SPECIAL NEEDS
You may want to help students complete the graphic organizer in the Literary Tools section, or allow them to work with a partner.

ENRICHMENT
Have students hold a panel discussion on women's rights. Have them compare the rights of modern women to the rights of women in Wollstonecraft's era. Do students feel there has been progress made in the area of women's rights? Why, or why not? (Research may be required in order to participate in this discussion.)

LITERARY NOTE

Although he was a Humanist, John Milton did not extend his belief in the possibilities of human nature to many of the women in his life. He had a difficult relationship with his first wife and showed little consideration for his three daughters.

ADDITIONAL QUESTIONS AND ACTIVITIES

Ask students the following questions:

1. According to Wollstonecraft, what effect does Rousseau believe education has on men? on women?
2. What does Wollstonecraft mean when she says women should not be "forced to shape their course by the twinkling of a mere satellite" (paragraph 5)? What figure of speech is this phrase?
3. What advantages do men gain when women are also free?

Answers

1. She says that Rousseau believes education corrupts men and that women educated by men would become corrupt as well.
2. She means that women should be given equal access to education, or "the fountain of light," rather than settling for second-rate education. This figure of speech is a metaphor.
3. Women's freedom would enable both women and men to enjoy true fellowship, which, according to both Wollstonecraft and Milton, is possible only between equals. As well, men could choose their own professions, too, including those traditionally reserved for women.

ART NOTE

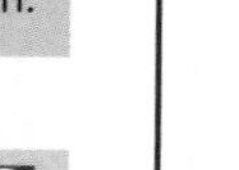

Day Dream, 1880. Dante Gabriel Rossetti. The book in her lap tells us that she is educated. Her expression is thoughtful. She appears to be someone of strong character.

Day Dream, 1880. Dante Gabriel Rossetti. Victoria and Albert Museum, London.

ArtNote

Dante Gabriel Rossetti (1828-1882) was a founding member of the Pre-Raphaelite Brotherhood (see page 302). His most common subject was portraits of women, during a period when women's role in society was rapidly changing. This is a painting of Jane Morris, who modeled for him many times throughout his career. Judging from this portrait, how would you describe Jane Morris's character in relation to Wollstonecraft's discussion of the nature of women?

spirit, he is a base and ignoble creature!" Men, indeed, appear to me to act in a very unphilosophical manner when they try to secure the good conduct of women by attempting to keep them always in a state of childhood. Rousseau was more consistent when he wished to stop the progress of reason in both sexes, for if men eat of the tree of knowledge, women will come in for a taste; but, from the imperfect cultivation which their understandings now receive, they only attain a knowledge of evil.

How do men try to insure that women will behave well?

Children, I grant, should be innocent; but when the epithet is applied to men, or women, it is but a civil term for weakness. For if it be allowed that women were destined by Providence to acquire human virtues, and by the exercise of their understandings, that stability of character which is the firmest ground to rest our future hopes upon, they must be permitted to turn to the fountain of light, and not forced to shape their course by the twinkling of a mere satellite.[3] Milton, I grant, was of a very different opinion; for he only bends to the indefeasible right of beauty, though it would be difficult to render two passages which I now mean to contrast, consistent. But into similar inconsistencies are great men often led by their senses.

When women are called "innocent" what does the term really mean?

To whom thus Eve with *perfect beauty* adorned.
My Author and Disposer, what thou bidst
Unargued I obey; So God ordains;
God is thy *law, thou mine:*—to know no more
Is Woman's *happiest* knowledge and her *praise.*[4]

These are exactly the arguments that I have used to children; but I have added, your reason is now gaining strength, and, till it arrives at some degree of maturity, you must look up to me for advice—then you ought to *think*, and only rely on God.

Yet in the following lines Milton seems to coincide with me; when he makes Adam thus expostulate with his Maker.

Hast thou not made me here thy substitute,
And these inferior far beneath me set?
Among *unequals* what society
Can sort, what harmony or
true delight?
Which must be mutual, in
proportion due
Giv'n and *received;* but in
disparity
The one intense, the other still remiss
Cannot well suit with either, but soon prove
Tedious alike: of *fellowship* I speak
Such as I seek, fit to participate
All rational delight—[5]

According to Milton, in this passage, what cannot be achieved between unequals?

In treating, therefore, of the manners of women, let us, disregarding sensual arguments, trace what we should endeavor to make them in order to cooperate, if the expression be not too bold, with the supreme Being. ■

3. **satellite.** Body that orbits a larger body
4. **To whom . . . praise.** *Paradise Lost* IV. 634–38; Wollstonecraft has added italics to emphasize her point
5. **Hast . . . delight.** *Paradise Lost* VII. 381–92; Wollstonecraft has added italics to show the inconsistency between this and the previous passage

WORDS FOR EVERYDAY USE

ep • i • thet (ep´ə thet´) *n.*, word or phrase used to characterize a person or thing. *When asked to describe the spy, the general could only mutter the epithet "traitor."*

Respond *to the* SELECTION

How do you feel about Milton's portrayal of Eve in the passage from *Paradise Lost*?

RESPOND TO THE SELECTION

Imagine you are Eve. What would you say to Milton? to Wollstonecraft?

ANSWERS TO GUIDED READING QUESTIONS

1. Men try to insure women's good behavior by keeping them childlike.
2. Innocence is a "civil term for weakness."
3. Between unequals, society, harmony and "true delight" cannot be realized.

SELECTION CHECK TEST 4.8.35 WITH ANSWERS

Checking Your Reading

1. What is blamed for women's "follies and caprices"? **Ignorance is blamed.**
2. Who does Milton describe? **He describes "our first frail mother," or Eve.**
3. In what state do men keep women, in order to secure their obedience? **Men keep women in a state of childhood.**
4. Who does she tell to look up to her for advice? **She tells children to look up to her.**
5. True fellowship is possible only among whom? **It is possible only among equals.**

Vocabulary in Context

Fill each blank with the most appropriate word from the Words for Everyday Use. You may have to change the tense of the word.

satirize scrupulous caprice
ingenious puerile insinuate
epithet

1. The scrub nurse was always **scrupulous** in preparing the operating room.
2. Max had little regard for the speaker, and disrupted her talk with **puerile** comments.
3. The captain's tone **insinuated** that he was angry that we skipped the lifeboat drill.
4. The comedy writers passed the time creating **epithets** for one other.
5. It's difficult to separate Casey's **caprices** from her serious ideas.

Literary Tools

1. What is an allusion? **An allusion is a reference to a person, event, object or work from history or literature.**
2. How is allusion used in this selection? ***Responses will vary.* The selection alludes to Milton, Rousseau and Lord Bacon.**
3. What is didactic criticism? **Didactic criticism evaluates works of art in terms of the moral, ethical, or political message that they convey.**

ANSWERS TO INVESTIGATE, INQUIRE AND IMAGINE

RECALL

1a. Her contemporaries reasoned that women didn't have "sufficient strength of mind."

2a. Women were kept in an ignorant state. The reason was that women were capricious and passionate rather than given to reason.

3a. Women were kept in a state of childhood.

INTERPRET

1b. Wollstonecraft strongly disagrees with the contention. She expresses her opinion by using words such as *tyranny* and *ingenious* to describe the common belief.

2b. Women exhibited this behavior because they were trained to do so and praised for complying.

3b. Women must be allowed to be educated and attain knowledge in order to become virtuous.

ANALYZE

4a. In the first passage, Eve says that she answers to Adam as her law and that she does as he bids, without argument. To know him as her law is her "happiest knowledge." In the second, however, Adam pleads the case with God that there can be no true society—no real relationship—between unequal parties. The contradiction is that he seems to say women should be subservient in one passage and, in the other, to say that women must be equal to men in order to fulfill God's desire that man and woman shall live in harmonious relationship.

SYNTHESIZE

4b. Wollstonecraft would agree with the second argument, that women must be equal to men in order to fulfill God's plan. She thinks that others hold the opposite belief because they want to keep women childlike in order to be sure their behavior is docile and obedient.

EVALUATE

5a. Wollstonecraft wants women to have equal access to education, arguing that the ignorance imposed upon them is the cause of women's irrational and unstable behavior. She argues that treating men and women as equals will change the weak and emotional behavior to which women have been trained, and will allow women to develop strength of character. Only then can women and men enjoy the true fellowship which is God's plan. Responses will vary as the effectiveness of this argument.

Investigate, Inquire, Imagine

Recall: GATHERING FACTS → Interpret: FINDING MEANING

1a. According to the first paragraph, what reason was given by Wollstonecraft's contemporaries to support the belief that women cannot acquire virtue?

1b. How does Wollstonecraft feel about the contention that women are incapable of attaining virtue? How do you know?

2a. According to the beginning of paragraph 2, in what state were women in Wollstonecraft's time generally kept? What reason was given for keeping them in that state?

2b. According to paragraph 2, why did women in Wollstonecraft's day often exhibit follies, caprices, headstrong passions, and groveling vices?

3a. According to paragraph 4, in what state were women kept?

3b. According to Wollstonecraft, what must women be allowed if they are indeed to be virtuous?

Analyze: TAKING THINGS APART → Synthesize: BRINGING THINGS TOGETHER

4a. Analyze the two passages from Milton to which Wollstonecraft refers. What contradictions are there between the two?

4b. With which argument does Wollstonecraft agree? Why would some agree with the other argument, according to Wollstonecraft?

Evaluate: MAKING JUDGMENTS → Extend: CONNECTING IDEAS

5a. Evaluate Mary Wollstonecraft's argument. What does she want for women? What reasons does she give? Is her argument effective? Why or why not?

5b. Think back over what you have learned about the treatment of slaves, servants, and oppressed people by those in control through history. What similarities do you note about the arguments against educating women and the arguments against educating African slaves, Native Americans and others? Why do you think these arguments were used?

Understanding Literature

DIDACTIC CRITICISM. Review the definition of **didactic criticism** in the Handbook of Literary Terms. What criticism does Wollstonecraft level at Milton in this piece? What does she dislike about Milton's portrayal of Eve? What contradiction does she point out in Milton's thought? Do you agree with Wollstonecraft? Why, or why not?

METAPHOR. Review the definition of **metaphor** and the chart you made for Literary Tools in Prereading. In this selection, Wollstonecraft uses two vivid metaphors. Identify the tenor and vehicle of each and analyze the point the author is making with each metaphor.

ANSWERS TO INVESTIGATE, INQUIRE AND IMAGINE (CONT.)

EXTEND

5b. Students will note that slaveholders resisted education for African slaves on the assertion that the slaves were not fully human and not capable of intellectual achievement, as well as the assertion that education would confuse them and upset their "natural" docile behavior. Native Americans were called "savages" and were thought to be incapable of learning as well. In many cases the root of this may have been a desire to do exactly what Wollstonecraft accuses: to keep them ignorant and their behavior childlike in order to more easily control them.

Answers to Understanding Literature can be found on page 741.

Writer's Journal

1. If Mary Wollstonecraft published her treatise today, some enterprising person would probably have printed bumper stickers to sell to her fans. Write a **bumper sticker** that might appeal to those who agree with Mary Wollstonecraft.
2. Imagine that a debate were held between Wollstonecraft and Milton. The proposition to be debated is: Women should be granted full and equal rights to own property, obtain an education and to vote, and participate in the government of the land. Create a **poster** advertising this event, designed to attract as large an audience as possible.
3. Suppose you could travel back in time to Wollstonecraft's day and draft a Bill of Women's Rights to protect women against the abuses that they suffered then. What rights would you grant to women? Write a **bill of rights** for women to be included in a constitution for England in the late 1700s.

Integrating *the* Language Arts

Language, Grammar, and Style

Split Infinitives. Read the Language Arts Survey 3.42, "Avoiding Split Infinitives." Then rewrite the sentences below, correcting the split infinitives that you find.

1. Mary Wollstonecraft was moved to eloquently and persuasively write about the importance of equal access to education.
2. She considered education to obviously be key to improving the status of women because only by that means could they rise above the artificial "state of childhood" in which they were kept.
3. It is too facile to today anachronistically conclude that Wollstonecraft was too hard on other women of her time.
4. She often pauses to passionately rail against the silliness, coquetishness, follies, caprices, and overriding passions of many of her female contemporaries.
5. Reading her book, it is important for us to always remember that she is speaking about a time in which women were expected to behave in these ways.

Study and Research

Survey of the History of Writing about Women's Rights. Divide into groups of four to six students each. Assign each group one of the following major works on women's rights: Mary Wollstonecraft's *A Vindication of the Rights of Woman,* John Stuart Mill's *On the Subjugation of Women,* Simon de Beauvoir's *The Second Sex,* Betty Friedan's *The Feminine Mystique,* and Susan Faludi's *Backlash.* Have each group study the work assigned to it and report to the class about the social conditions of the time in which the work was produced, as well as about the work's major ideas.

Speaking and Listening

Panel Discussion. Do social norms, including attitudes and behaviors, still favor the development of men's abilities over those of women? Do men still have more opportunities than women to develop their physical and mental skills and to apply those skills in the world? Hold a panel discussion in class to consider these issues. Choose an equal number of men and women from among your classmates to sit on the panel (three of each would be a reasonable number). Elect a moderator to pose questions to the panel.

ANSWERS TO UNDERSTANDING LITERATURE

Didactic Criticism. She argues that Milton contradicts himself in applying different standards of virtue to men and women, both of whom are God's creations. She dislikes Milton's portrayal of Eve as merely a beautiful subject of God's law and man's control. She points out that Milton contradicts himself by saying there can be no har-mony in a society of unequals.

Metaphor. Metaphor: "the current will run with destructive fury when there are no barriers to break its force."
Tenor: emotions and behavior of women
Vehicle: current
The current is the emotions and behavior of women, which will run amok without the balancing and normalizing effects of education. Education is the barrier to this dangerous course.

Metaphor: "they [women] must be permitted to turn to the fountain of light, and not forced to shape their course by the twinkling of a mere satellite."
Tenor: education
Vehicle: fountain of light
The fountain of light is education, which can allow women to set a true course for their lives. If denied education, woman's only option is to set her course by the reflection of the fountain's light in a satellite—man. The metaphor makes the point that if women may only do what they are told by men, it is like relying on the light of the moon—the reflection of the sun—rather than using the full light of the sun.

ANSWERS TO INTEGRATING THE LANGUAGE ARTS

Language, Grammar, and Style

1. Mary Wollstonecraft was moved to write eloquently and persuasively about the importance of equal access to education.
2. She considered education to be obviously key to improving the status of women because only by that means could they rise above the artificial "state of childhood" in which they were kept.

ANSWERS TO INTEGRATING THE LANGUAGE ARTS (cont.)

3. It is too facile, today, to conclude anachronistically that Wollstonecraft was too hard on other women of her time.
4. She often pauses to rail passionately against the silliness, coquetishness, follies, caprices, and overriding passions of many of her female contemporaries.
5. Reading her book, it is important for us always to remember that she is speaking about a time in which women were expected to behave in these ways.

Speaking and Listening
Refer students to the Language Arts Survey 4.4, "Listening in Conversations" and 4.10, "Asking and Answer Questions" for this activity.

ADDITIONAL RESOURCES

UNIT 8 RESOURCE BOOK
- Selection Worksheet 8.18
- Selection Check Test 4.8.37
- Selection Test 4.8.38
- Language, Grammar, and Style Resource 3.22
- Applied English Resource 6.1

VOCABULARY FROM THE SELECTION

platitude
progeny
reverie
ungenial

ADDITIONAL QUESTIONS AND ACTIVITIES

Consider the most important people in Mary Shelley's life. Her father was a famous radical philosopher and social reformer. Her mother was a famous writer and advocate for women's rights. Her husband, the poet Shelley, was also a revolutionary poet and social activist. All three were idealistic reformers advocating change to improve society. Each seemed to believe that mankind could create a better world. How might this environment have influenced her choice of subject?

READER'S JOURNAL

Do you think it is moral for scientists to create new species through genetic engineering? What are the positive and negative effects that might result from such experiments?

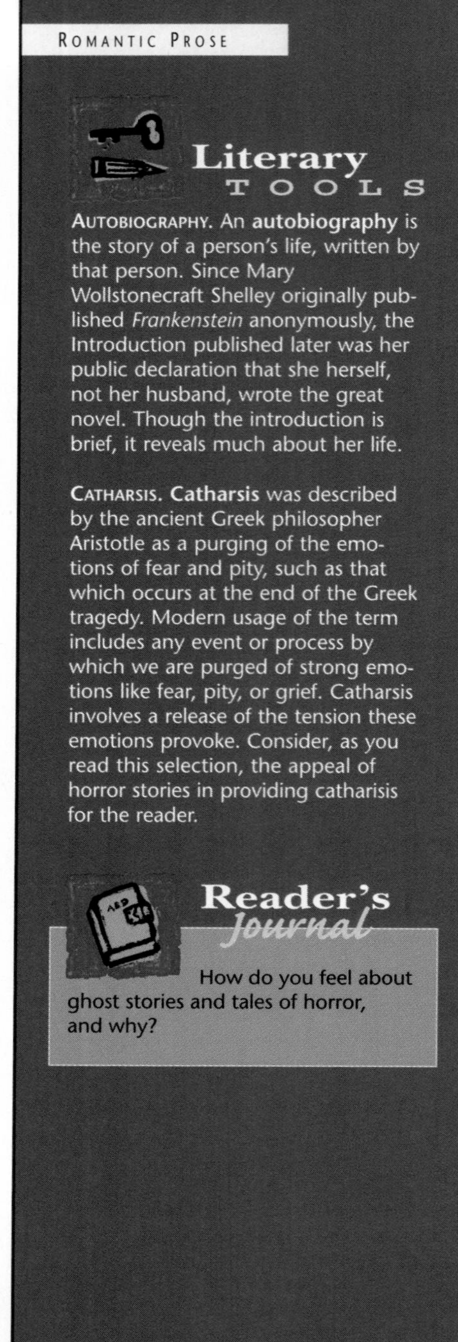

Literary TOOLS

AUTOBIOGRAPHY. An **autobiography** is the story of a person's life, written by that person. Since Mary Wollstonecraft Shelley originally published *Frankenstein* anonymously, the Introduction published later was her public declaration that she herself, not her husband, wrote the great novel. Though the introduction is brief, it reveals much about her life.

CATHARSIS. **Catharsis** was described by the ancient Greek philosopher Aristotle as a purging of the emotions of fear and pity, such as that which occurs at the end of the Greek tragedy. Modern usage of the term includes any event or process by which we are purged of strong emotions like fear, pity, or grief. Catharsis involves a release of the tension these emotions provoke. Consider, as you read this selection, the appeal of horror stories in providing catharisis for the reader.

Reader's Journal

How do you feel about ghost stories and tales of horror, and why?

FROM *the Introduction to* Frankenstein

BY MARY WOLLSTONECRAFT SHELLEY

About the AUTHOR

Mary Wollstonecraft Shelley (1797–1851) was the daughter of William Godwin, a leading radical thinker of his time, and Mary Wollstonecraft, the famous women's rights activist who wrote *A Vindication of the Rights of Woman* (page 647). After Mary's mother died in childbirth, the little girl and her four siblings were raised by a stepmother. When she was fourteen, Mary was sent to Dundee, Scotland, to live with the family of one of her father's admirers. She lived there happily for two years and returned to London at age sixteen.

In London she met Percy Bysshe Shelley and soon eloped with him to Europe, despite her father's protests. The young couple faced many challenges, both financial and personal. Their first three children died before Mary was twenty-one, and several of the couple's close relatives died untimely deaths during this period as well.

In this time of personal upheaval, Mary was inspired to write. She spent long hours discussing ideas with Lord Byron and Percy, and during this period wrote *Frankenstein, or the Modern Prometheus,* which was eventually published in 1818.

The multiple tragedies in their lives, including the deaths of their children and several close friends, caused Mary to emotionally retreat from Percy during his last years. As a result of this estrangement, Mary felt deep guilt when her dear husband and co-worker died suddenly in 1822 in a boating accident. She is largely responsible for preserving Percy's work by annotating and publishing several editions after his death.

During the remaining twenty-five years of her life, Mary wrote five more novels, twenty-five short tales, and several volumes of literary criticism.

About the SELECTION

In Switzerland, during the rainy summer of 1816, Mary Shelley wrote *Frankenstein,* probably the greatest Gothic novel and science fiction fantasy ever written. The well-known story of the creation of a monster from human parts has been presented in several movies. More than a horror story, *Frankenstein* explores themes of creation and responsibility, remaining fascinating today as we ponder whether science has gone too far in some of the strides it has made. The **Introduction** was written for the third edition of *Frankenstein,* fifteen years after the book was first published.

GOALS/OBJECTIVES

Studying this lesson will enable students to
- experience the speaker's excitement about the creative process
- describe Mary Shelley's connections and contributions to the Romantic Era
- define *autobiography* and *catharsis* and identify and explain examples of each in the selection
- identify and eliminate cliches and euphemisms
- participate in a discussion about various film versions of Frankenstein

FROM *the Introduction to*

Frankenstein

MARY WOLLSTONECRAFT SHELLEY

In the summer of 1816, we[1] visited Switzerland and became the neighbors of Lord Byron. At first we spent our pleasant hours on the lake or wandering on its shores; and Lord Byron, who was writing the third canto of *Childe Harold,* was the only one among us who put his thoughts upon paper. These, as he brought them successively to us, clothed in all the light and harmony of poetry, seemed to stamp as divine the glories of heaven and earth, whose influences we partook with him.

But it proved a wet, ungenial summer, and incessant rain often confined us for days to the house. Some volumes of ghost stories, translated from the German into French, fell into our hands. There was the *History of the Inconstant Lover,* who, when he thought to clasp the bride to whom he had pledged his vows, found himself in the arms of the pale ghost of her whom he had deserted. There was the tale of the sinful founder of his race whose miserable doom it was to bestow the kiss of death on all the younger sons of his fated house, just when they reached the age of promise. His gigantic, shadowy form, clothed like the ghost in *Hamlet,* in complete armor but with the beaver[2] up, was seen at midnight, by the moon's fitful beams, to advance slowly along the gloomy avenue. The shape was lost beneath the shadow of the castle walls; but soon a gate swung back, a step was heard, the door of the chamber opened, and he advanced to the couch of the blooming youths, cradled in healthy sleep. Eternal sorrow sat upon his face as he bent down and kissed the forehead of the boys, who from that hour withered like flowers snapped upon the stalk. I have not seen these stories since then, but their incidents are as fresh in my mind as if I had read them yesterday.

How did the group of friends entertain themselves that rainy summer?

"We will each write a ghost story," said Lord Byron, and his proposition was acceded to. There were four of us.[3] The noble author began a tale, a fragment of which he printed at the end of his poem of Mazeppa. Shelley, more apt to embody ideas and sentiments in the radiance of brilliant imagery and in the music of the most melodious verse that adorns our language than to invent the machinery of a story, commenced one founded on the experiences of his early life. Poor Polidori had some terrible idea about a skull-headed lady who was so punished for peeping through a keyhole—what to see I forget: something very shocking and wrong of course; but when she was reduced to a worse condition than the renowned Tom of Coventry,[4] he did not know what to do with her, and was obliged to dispatch her to the

What proposition did Lord Byron make to the group?

1. **we.** Mary Shelley, Percy Bysshe Shelley, and their children
2. **beaver.** Piece of armor that covers the face
3. **four of us.** Byron, Mary and Percy Bysshe Shelley, and John William Polidori
4. **Tom of Coventry.** Tom of Coventry, or Peeping Tom, was, according to legend, struck blind for looking at the naked Lady Godiva.

WORDS FOR EVERYDAY USE

un • gen • i • al (un jēn´yəl) *adj.,* unpleasant. *The rude man's ungenial remarks made everyone feel uncomfortable.*

ac • ced • ed (ak sēd´ əd) *vi.,* agreed. *The judge acceded to the defending council's request for a continuance.*

ANSWERS TO GUIDED READING QUESTIONS

1. When rains prevented them from boating and walking, they read ghost stories.
2. Byron proposed that they each write a ghost story.

INDIVIDUAL LEARNING STRATEGIES

MOTIVATION
Ask students, "What do you think of when you hear the word *Frankenstein?"* Then have them predict how the story was created. After they have read the selection, have students check to see if their predictions were correct or incorrect.

READING PROFICIENCY
Have students pause after reading each paragraph of the selection to write the main idea.

ENGLISH LANGUAGE LEARNING
Explain to students that they will be reading a piece of nonfiction—the introduction to Shelley's fictional work. Encourage students to create a time line of events that led up to Shelley's writing of Frankenstein, adding key events as they read.

SPECIAL NEEDS
Consider reading the selection aloud to students, paraphrasing each paragraph for them.

ENRICHMENT
Frankenstein's monster is a human creation. Students can discuss or write about the idea that all people are human creations. How much of what people are like is due to nature and how much is a product of society? Have them consider social functions such as education, morals, laws, and language.

ANSWERS TO GUIDED READING QUESTIONS

1. Chaos must exist before invention can take place.
2. She got the idea about using electricity to animate a corpse.
3. Her dream was frightful because the human creator had made something that defied the natural order of God's creation and that was beyond his control.

LITERARY NOTE

Erasmus Darwin (1731–1802) was an English doctor who also studied botany and wrote poetry. His book *Zoönomia* (1794–1796) set forth theories on evolutionary development. His grandson, Charles Darwin, established the theory of evolution as it is known today.

tomb of the Capulets, the only place for which she was fitted. The illustrious poets also, annoyed by the platitude of prose, speedily relinquished their uncongenial task.

I busied myself *to think of a story*—a story to rival those which had excited us to this task. One which would speak to the mysterious fears of our nature and awaken thrilling horror—one to make the reader dread to look round, to curdle the blood, and quicken the beatings of the heart. If I did not accomplish these things, my ghost story would be unworthy of its name. I thought and pondered—vainly. I felt that blank incapability of invention which is the greatest misery of authorship, when dull Nothing replies to our anxious invocations. "Have you thought of a story?" I was asked each morning, and each morning I was forced to reply with a mortifying negative.

Everything must have a beginning, to speak in Sanchean phrase; and that beginning must be linked to something that went before. The Hindus give the world an elephant to support it, but they make the elephant stand upon a tortoise. Invention, it must be humbly admitted, does not consist in creating out of void, but out of chaos; the materials must, in the first place, be afforded: it can give form to dark, shapeless substances but cannot bring into being the substance itself. In all matters of discovery and invention, even of those that appertain to the imagination, we are continually reminded of the story of Columbus and his egg. Invention consists in the capacity of seizing on the capabilities of a subject and in the power of molding and fashioning ideas suggested by it.

What must exist as a prerequisite to invention?

Many and long were the conversations between Lord Byron and Shelley to which I was a devout, but nearly silent, listener. During one of these, various philosophical doctrines were discussed, and among others the nature of the principle of life and whether there was any probability of its ever being discovered and communicated. They talked of the experiments of Dr. Darwin[5] (I speak not of what the doctor really did or said that he did, but, as more to my purpose, of what was then spoken of as having been done by him), who preserved a piece of vermicelli in a glass case till by some extraordinary means it began to move with voluntary motion. Not thus, after all, would life be given. Perhaps a corpse would be reanimated; galvanism[6] had given token of such things: perhaps the component parts of a creature might be manufactured, brought together, and endued with vital warmth.

What idea did Mary get from the conversation between Percy and Lord Byron?

Night waned upon this talk, and even the witching hour had gone by before we retired to rest. When I placed my head on my pillow, I did not sleep, nor could I be said to think. My imagination, unbidden, possessed and guided me, gifting the successive images that arose in my mind with a vividness far beyond the usual bounds of reverie. I saw—with shut eyes, but acute mental vision—I saw the pale student of unhallowed arts kneeling beside the thing he had put together. I saw the hideous phantasm of a man stretched out, and then, on the working of some powerful engine, show signs of life, and stir with an uneasy, half-vital motion. Frightful must it be, for supremely frightful would be the effect of any human

Why was Mary's dream so frightful?

5. **Dr. Darwin.** Erasmus Darwin was a scientist and a poet.
6. **galvanism.** Galvanism uses electric currents to cause movement in dead muscles.

WORDS FOR EVERYDAY USE

plat • i • tude (plat´ ə to͞od´) *n.*, commonplace saying. *I found her ideas a delightful change from the platitudes voiced by the other speakers.*

rev • er • ie (rev´ər ē) *n.*, dreaming. *I was startled out of my reverie by a telephone's abrupt ringing.*

Illustration from *"**Frankenstein,**"* c. 1800s. English Artist. Private Collection.

ADDITIONAL QUESTIONS AND ACTIVITIES

Point out Mary Shelley's discussion about the nature of the creative process. Have students discuss her idea that "invention . . . does not consist in creating out of void, but out of chaos." Do they agree? What experiences have they had with the creative process, either in their writing or in other creative endeavors? What else have they read that discusses the creative process? Do other authors agree? How is brainstorming or story mapping beneficial to the creative process?

ANSWER TO GUIDED READING QUESTION

1. She has special affection for her creation because it reminds her of a happy time in her life, before her husband and children died. As she writes this, she is feeling sad and alone.

SELECTION CHECK TEST 4.8.37 WITH ANSWERS

Checking Your Reading

1. What does Byron tell each adult to do? **He tells everyone to write a ghost story.**
2. What does invention require? **It requires raw materials, or "chaos."**
3. What did Percy Shelley and Byron debate about the nature of life? **They debated whether or not it could be created.**
4. What did Mary Shelley see in her dream? **She saw a creature brought to life.**
5. For what does Mary credit her husband? **He encouraged her to develop the story.**

Literary Tools

1. What is a catharsis? **A catharsis is a purging of feelings of fear or pity.**
2. How might a ghost story cause a catharsis in a reader? **It elicits fear in a safe way.**
3. What is a Gothic tale? **A story with horror, suspense, magic, and mystery.**

RESPOND TO THE SELECTION

Ask students to recall a nightmare they had from the past. What was it about? How did it compare to Shelley's dream?

endeavor to mock the stupendous mechanism of the Creator of the world. His success would terrify the artist; he would rush away from his odious handiwork, horror-stricken. He would hope that, left to itself, the slight spark of life which he had communicated would fade, that this thing which had received such imperfect animation would subside into dead matter, and he might sleep in the belief that the silence of the grave would quench forever the transient existence of the hideous corpse which he had looked upon as the cradle of life. He sleeps; but he is awakened; he opens his eyes; behold, the horrid thing stands at his bedside, opening his curtains, and looking on him with yellow, watery, but speculative eyes.

I opened mine in terror. The idea so possessed my mind that a thrill of fear ran through me, and I wished to exchange the ghastly image of my fancy for the realities around. I see them still: the very room, the dark parquet, the closed shutters with the moonlight struggling through, and the sense I had that the glassy lake and white high Alps were beyond. I could not so easily get rid of my hideous phantom; still it haunted me. I must try to think of something else. I recurred to my ghost story—my tiresome unlucky ghost story! O! if I could only contrive one which would frighten my reader as I myself had been frightened that night!

Swift as light and as cheering was the idea that broke in upon me. "I have found it! What terrified me will terrify others; and I need only describe the specter which had haunted my midnight pillow." On the morrow I announced that I had *thought of a story*. I began that day with the words "It was on a dreary night of November," making only a transcript of the grim terrors of my waking dream.

At first I thought but of a few pages, of a short tale, but Shelley urged me to develop the idea at greater length. I certainly did not owe the suggestion of one incident, nor scarcely of one train of feeling, to my husband, and yet but for his incitement, it would never have taken the form in which it was presented to the world. From this declaration I must except the preface. As far as I can recollect, it was entirely written by him.

And now, once again, I bid my hideous progeny go forth and prosper. I have an affection for it, for it was the offspring of happy days, when death and grief were but words which found no true echo in my heart. Its several pages speak of many a walk, many a drive, and many a conversation, when I was not alone; and my companion was one who, in this world, I shall never see more. But this is for myself: my readers have nothing to do with these associations. ■

Why does Mary have special affection for her creation? How is she feeling as she writes this?

Words For Everyday Use

prog • e • ny (präj´ə nē) *n.*, offspring. *The king's first-born son succeeded him on the throne, and his other progeny became rulers of principalities.*

Respond *to the* Selection

How do you think Mary Wollstonecraft, Mary Shelley's mother, would have felt about her daughter, had she lived to see her grow and achieve what she did as a woman?

Investigate, Inquire, Imagine

Recall: Gathering Facts →

1a. What was Lord Byron's idea for the group?

2a. What was the nature of the discussion between Byron and Percy Shelley that led to Mary's idea for her story?

3a. What is the reason for Mary Shelley's affection for the monster, according to the last paragraph of the selection?

Interpret: Finding Meaning

1b. Why might Mary Shelley have felt fearful about presenting her writing to this gathering?

2b. What does Shelley mean by "mock the stupendous mechanism of the Creator of the world" in paragraph 7 of the selection?

3b. What does Shelley mean by "I bid my hideous progeny go forth and prosper" in the last paragraph of the selection?

Analyze: Taking Things Apart →

4a. Reread Mary Shelley's biography on page 652. What special significance might the idea of creating life have for her, in terms of motherhood and personal grief?

Synthesize: Bringing Things Together

4b. Do you see the Frankenstein monster as a commentary on the idea that mankind can create an ideal world? Why, or why not?

Evaluate: Making Judgments →

5a. Shelley says, in this selection, "invention…does not consist in creating out of void, but out of chaos." Do you agree? What raw material—experiences, ideas, emotions—do you think she used to create her novel? What creative experiences have you had? Did your creations arise out of nothing, or out of some "materials" in your life? Explain.

Extend: Connecting Ideas

5b. Mary Shelley might have thought truth stranger than fiction had she lived to see the things which modern science can now do, such as genetic engineering. How far do you think science should go in exploring ways to change the outcomes of nature? Is there a limit to what scientists should attempt?

Understanding Literature

Autobiography. Review the definition for **autobiography** in Literary Tools in Prereading. Although this introduction tells only part of Mary Shelley's life, it is very revealing. What do you learn about Shelley's life from this selection? Why do you think she felt compelled to include this autobiographical information in the introduction to her book?

Catharsis. Review the definition for **catharsis** in Literary Tools. Discuss the role of catharsis in the telling of ghost stories and its role in Mary Shelley's idea for the novel *Frankenstein.*

ANSWERS TO UNDERSTANDING LITERATURE

Autobiography. Shelley reveals herself as imaginative, driven to think of a story yet uncertain of her abilities. She may have included this information as an explanation since many people felt it improbable that a young woman could have written this story.

Catharsis. At first the Shelleys told ghost stories to entertain themselves when the weather kept them indoors. For Byron, Polidori, and Percy Shelley, telling ghost stories was not especially cathartic; Mary Shelley does not mention the effect of their stories. However, she decided to write her story both to rid herself of the terrifying images of her dream and to incite the same fear in her readers.

ANSWERS TO INVESTIGATE, INQUIRE AND IMAGINE

Recall

1a. Byron proposed that each person write a ghost story.

2a. Byron and Shelley discussed whether it was possible for humans to discover the mechanisms for creating life, specifically the use of electricity to bring a corpse to life.

3a. She has affection for the monster because she created the idea of the monster during a happy time in her life.

Interpret

1b. She may have felt intimidated by Byron and Shelley, who were writers by trade. She might also have felt additional pressure because she was the only woman.

2b. She means that the human creator has crossed the natural boundary between humans and God; the complex nature of creation is not something to be undertaken by humans.

3b. She wishes for the book to be successful.

Analyze

4a. Mary Shelley lost three of her young children shortly before beginning her story. The experience of helping to create her children's lives and then losing them adds special significance to the idea of creating life in her work.

Synthesize

4b. Mary Shelley chose to write about a man who tried to create new life. It is possible to see the novel as a commentary on the notion that mankind can create an ideal world and eliminate all of the negative aspects of human nature. Frankenstein's creature is a monster—not at all what he had hoped for. It brings out the worst in those around it and Frankenstein himself is terrified by his creation. Ultimately, he is driven to his death by it. It is an aberration and not at all an improvement on nature.

Evaluate

5a. Shelley's materials may have included her own feelings about giving birth to life in her children and then losing them to death. She may also have used the emotions she felt in observing her husband and his friends create art and her own desire to create. She certainly used the experience of discussing scientific advances in using Galvanism and electricity as fodder for her story.

Extend

5b. *Responses will vary.*

ANSWERS TO INTEGRATING THE LANGUAGE ARTS

Language, Grammar, and Style
Pick up from page 660 under "Answers for Language Lab" excluding Additional practice note

Study and Research
This activity will require students to use critical thinking skills such as analyzing and synthesizing, and comparing and contrasting. Refer students to the Language Arts Survey 5.8 and 5.9 as they begin outlining their essays.

Writer's Journal

1. A *gothic tale* is a story containing elements of horror, suspense, mystery, and magic. Write a **one-paragraph description** of a haunted house. Before you begin drafting your paragraph, think about how haunted houses have been depicted in books and movies. Then freewrite your own details about a Gothic haunted house.
2. Write a **letter to the editor**, expressing your feelings on the morality of genetic engineering and the advances of modern science.
3. Imagine that you are a talk-show host given the opportunity to interview Mary Shelley about her famous novel. What would you like to ask her? Perhaps you are curious about her personal life with Shelley or about the influence of her parents. You may wish to know her reaction to the enduring popularity of her story or her reaction to the many ways in which modern versions have treated it. Prepare a set of **interview questions** for Mary Shelley.

Integrating *the* Language Arts

Language, Grammar, and Style

Clichés and Euphemisms. Read the Language Arts Survey 1.23, "Clichés and Euphemisms." Then rewrite the underlined phrase in each sentence to eliminate either the cliché or the euphemism.

1. When she was a child, Mary Shelley worshiped the ground her father walked on.
2. Mary Shelley appears to have been fascinated with the end of life as we know it.
3. The young authoress was white as a sheet after she awakened from her nightmare.
4. The unusual being created by Dr. Frankenstein was lonely and felt abandoned by his creator.
5. The Romantic writers cherished their individuality and their emotions, though their feelings sometimes caused them to tear their hair and gnash their teeth.

Media Literacy & Speaking and Listening

Film Discussion Group. Mary Shelley's *Frankenstein* has become a cultural icon—a figure that nearly every child or adult recognizes. Select one of the film versions of the novel and watch it together. Then, in small groups of four or five, conduct a discussion of the film. In what ways did it illustrate Mary Shelley's statement, "supremely frightful would be the effect of any human endeavor to mock the stupendous mechanism of the Creator of the world." Is the monster a sympathetic character or not? Is Dr. Frankenstein sympathetic? What commentary do you think Shelley and the filmmaker are making on creativity and human nature? You may find it helpful to review Language Arts Survey 4.8, "Communicating in Small Groups" before you begin your discussion.

Study and Research

Researching Prometheus. In your school or local library, research the Prometheus myth. Why did Mary Shelley subtitle her novel, *The Modern Prometheus?* Write an essay outlining the parallels of the Prometheus story with Frankenstein and providing your answer to this question for your teacher.

POEMS FROM

The Narrow Road to the Deep North and Other Travel Sketches

MATSUO BASHŌ, TRANSLATED BY NOBUYUKI YUASA

About the Author

Matsuo Bashō (1644–1694) was the pen name of Matsuo Munefusa, the greatest of the Japanese haiku poets. Born near the holy city of Kyoto, he became interested in poetry while still a youth. However, until 1666, he put his literary interests aside while serving a local lord. Munefusa was a member of the samurai, or warrior, class, but after the death of his lord, he gave up that status to pursue a literary career. He moved to Edo (modern-day Tokyo) and worked as a poet and critic. Later, influenced by his study of Zen philosophy, he was drawn to a simple, reclusive life. He moved to the country and adopted the name *Bashō,* from *Bashō-an,* the word for the simple hut in which he lived. Bashō's poetry, like Zen philosophy, finds beauty and meaning in the simplest of natural phenomena. Bashō views blossoms on a mountainside, an ear of wheat, or the antlers of a deer and sees in each of them an eternal truth. The natural object becomes a symbol of the affinity or interconnectedness of all things.

About the Selections

In 1694, Bashō wrote ***The Narrow Road to the Deep North,*** a book describing one of the many journeys that he took during his lifetime. During these journeys, he stayed with other poets or at Buddhist temples. The book has become one of the great classics of the world's literature, not only for the beauty of its prose descriptions, but also for the incidental poetry that it contains. The selections that follow are examples of haiku from *The Narrow Road to the Deep North.*

MULTICULTURAL EXTENSIONS

Literary Tools

HAIKU. Haiku is a short, unrhymed poem of seventeen syllables divided into three lines of five syllables, seven syllables, and five again (although in translation, this scheme is often varied). Haiku presents one or more images—words that describe things that can be seen, touched, tasted, heard, or smelled—in an attempt to capture a passing moment of reflection. As you read the poem, identify the images presented in the poem.

SENSORY DETAILS. Sensory details are words and phrases that describe how things look, sound, smell, taste, or feel. Because haiku is centered on images, sensory details are prevalent in this form of poetry. Use the graphic organizer below to help you thoroughly describe the images presented in the poems.

Sight	Sound	Touch	Taste	Smell
show me your face				

Reader's Journal

Spend some time observing nature. If you can, go outside; otherwise observe nature from a window. What things do you see? What catches your eye the most? In what ways can Nature reflect truths about us and about humanity?

GRAPHIC ORGANIZER

Sight: show me your face; dawning blossoms; stags antlers split into tines; seedling; pine
Touch: sharing a grass pillow
Taste: let us eat ears of wheat

READER'S JOURNAL

What is your favorite aspect of nature? Stars, moon, trees, flowers? Explain.

INDIVIDUAL LEARNING STRATEGIES

MOTIVATION
Explain to students that the haiku they will be reading uses metaphors from nature to describe life. Have students observe nature in order to find a metaphor that describes at least one aspect of life.

READING PROFICIENCY
This selection used simplistic language, but students may still have difficulty understanding the haiku. Ask students to summarize each poem. Then have them compare their summaries with advanced students.

ENGLISH LANGUAGE LEARNING
Students whose first language is Japanese might be able to locate these haiku or others written by Basho in Japanese. Have these students work with students who have difficulty appreciating or understanding the haiku.

SPECIAL NEEDS
Despite the simple words and word order of this selection, students may have difficulty understanding the poems. You may wish to paraphrase each stanza for students.

ENRICHMENT
Ask students to write about the similarities and differences between Basho's life and the life of Wordsworth, Percy Shelley, Byron, or another of the English Romantic poets. They will need to do biographical research on Basho and an English Romantic poet in order to do this activity.

GOALS/OBJECTIVES

Studying this lesson will enable students to
- interpret and appreciate haiku poems
- describe how Matsuo Basho's poetry relates to poetry of the Romantic Era in England
- define *haiku* and *sensory details* and identify and explain examples of each that they encounter in their reading
- identify direct and indirect objects
- explore the opportunity to adopt an acre of rainforest land

SELECTION CHECK TEST 4.8.39 WITH ANSWERS

Checking Your Reading

1. Of what does the speaker of the first poem ask a question? **The speaker asks a question of the "God of this mountain."**
2. How are the blossoms in the first poem described? **The blossoms are described as "dawning."**
3. In the second poem, what do the two friends do together? **Together the friends eat ears of wheat and share a grass pillow.**
4. To what are a stag's antlers compared in the third poem? **A stag's antlers are compared to a friendship.**
5. When was the pine tree in the fourth poem a "mere seedling"? **The pine tree was a seedling in the days of the ancient gods.**

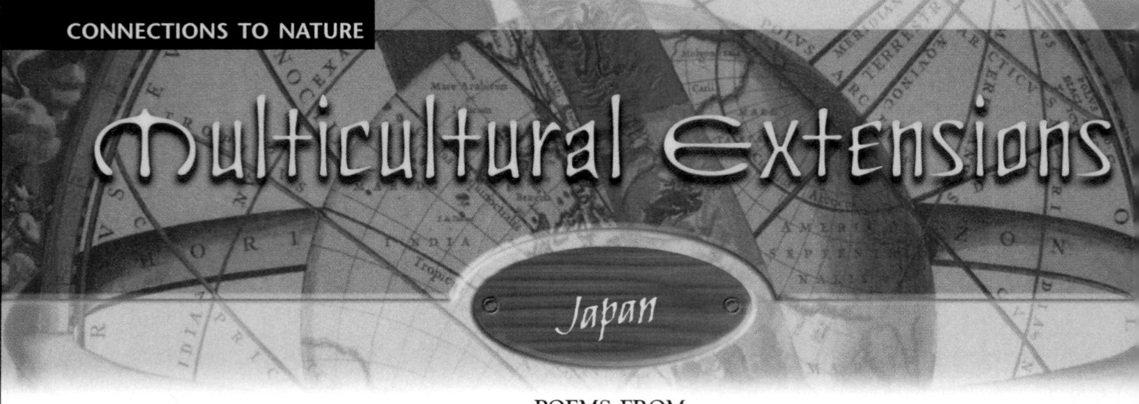

POEMS FROM

The Narrow Road to the Deep North and Other Travel Sketches

MATSUO BASHŌ, TRANSLATED BY NOBUYUKI YUASA

1

God of this mountain,
May you be kind enough
To show me your face
Among the dawning blossoms?

2

Together let us eat
Ears of wheat,
Sharing at night
A grass pillow.

3

Just as a stag's antlers
Are split into tines,
So I must go willy-nilly
Separated from my friend.

4

In the days
Of the ancient gods,
A mere seedling
This pine must have been.

Fuji from the Mountains of Isu**,** 1858. Ando Hiroshige. Fitzwilliam Museum, University of Cambridge, UK.

Respond *to the* SELECTION

With which haiku could you most identify? What image is most meaningful to you? Explain.

INVESTIGATE, Inquire, *Imagine*

Recall: GATHERING FACTS

1a. What does the speaker ask of the "God of this mountain"?

2a. What simple actions in the second haiku show a deep connection between two people?

3a. What thought does the speaker have on viewing a pine tree?

Interpret: FINDING MEANING

1b. In what sense might blossoms be described as "dawning"?

2b. What similarity exists between the speaker and his friend and the antlers of a stag?

3b. What does the speaker's reflection on the pine tree say about the type of person he is?

Analyze: TAKING THINGS APART →

4a. What is the sentiment Bashō is expressing in the first haiku?

Synthesize: BRINGING THINGS TOGETHER

4b. Reread the selections from Byron's *Childe Harold's Pilgrimage* on p. 634. Given what Byron has to say in those selections, would he understand the sentiment expressed in the first haiku by Bashō? Explain.

Evaluate: MAKING JUDGMENTS →

5a. In the poems that Basho wrote, he tried to express the theme of harmony that can be achieved between humans and Nature. Do you think Basho achieves this?

Extend: CONNECTING IDEAS

5b. Have you ever felt in harmony with Nature? How have your experiences with Nature been similar to or different from Basho's experiences?

Understanding *Literature*

HAIKU. Review the definition for **haiku** in the Handbook of Literary Terms. In the greatest of haiku, like those of Bashō, observation of some simple phenomenon in nature suggests a deeper meaning. The overall effect is of sudden revelation, or a deep truth emerging from a fleeting experience and compressed into a few words. What sudden revelations or truths emerge from the haiku of Bashō?

SENSORY DETAILS. Review the definition for **sensory details** and the chart you made for Literary Tools in Prereading. Because haiku is centered on images, sensory details are prevalent in this type of poetry. What images presented in these selections bring both humans and Nature together?

RESPOND TO THE SELECTION

Imagine you are the poet. What images would you include in your haiku? Explain.

ANSWERS TO INVESTIGATE, INQUIRE, AND IMAGINE

RECALL

1a. He asks the god to "show me your face."

2a. Eating together and sleeping together show a deep connection between two people.

3a. The speaker wonders at how old the pine is and how long ago it was a seedling.

INTERPRET

1b. Blossoms might be described as "dawning" when they first begin opening.

2b. Like the antlers of a stag, the two friends share a closeness that comes from the same source.

3b. The speaker is deeply reflective by thinking about the past and the changes that Nature has undergone since ancient times.

ANALYZE

4a. The sentiment he is expressing is that spirituality and spiritual things reside in Nature. Nature reflects god-like qualities such as power, mercy, and the ability to create.

SYNTHESIZE

4b. Byron would probably agree with the sentiment expressed in the first haiku. Like Byron, Basho sees an inherent spirituality in nature. Stanza 91 of Childe Harold's Pilgrimage and Basho's first haiku both speak of mountains as spiritual places, where humans strive to be close to the spiritual aspect of nature. The speakers of stanza 178 of Childe Harold's Pilgrimage and of the first haiku both address nature directly, indicating that they have or desire an intimate relationship.

EVALUATE

5a. *Responses will vary.*

EXTEND:

5b. *Responses will vary.*

ANSWERS TO UNDERSTANDING LITERATURE

HAIKU. *Responses will vary.* In the first haiku, Basho realizes that there is a deep spiritual aspect in Nature. In the second and third haiku, Basho expresses the truth that an intimate friendship can be established between humans and Nature. And in the fourth haiku, Basho realizes that Nature is more permanent than humans; it outlives humans.

SENSORY DETAILS. The image of the mountain and the flower blossoms brings humans closer to Nature by observing and experiencing its beauty. The images of a stag's antlers, eating ears of wheat, and sharing a pillow made of grass bring Nature and humans into an intimate relationship one would have with a close friend.

ANSWERS TO INTEGRATING THE LANGUAGE ARTS

Language, Grammar, and Style

1. DO
2. IO
3. DO
4. DO
5. IO

WRITER'S JOURNAL

1. Write a **haiku** about nature and its relationship with humans.
2. Write a **journal entry** about a time you communed with nature or encountered nature in an extraordinary way. What happened? What did you learn about nature during that experience? What did you learn about yourself?
3. Create a **title** for each haiku on page **660** based on the content of the poem.

Integrating *the* LANGUAGE ARTS

Language, Grammar, and Style

IDENTIFYING DIRECT AND INDIRECT OBJECTS. Read the Language Arts Survey 3.22, "Sentence Completers for Action Verbs: Direct and Indirect Objects." Then identify the underlined nouns as direct or indirect objects.

1. Matsuo Basho took a pen name.
2. He gave his lord his loyalty until his lord died.
3. Basho wrote haiku and renga poems.
4. In 1666 Basho abandoned his samurai status to devote himself to poetry.
5. He tried to show his readers the interdependence of all things.

Collaborative Learning & Applied English

ADOPT AN ACRE. The poets in this unit express the importance nature plays in our lives. They believe that nature reveals truths about humanity and spirituality; it also is a source of imagination and creativity. In recent years, rainforests have been the subject of many literary works and artistic expressions. The problem of rainforest destruction is complex and enormous. However, the Adopt an Acre program proposes a simple, yet highly effective solution—to provide funds to purchase and actively protect threatened rainforest. For only $35, your class can adopt one acre of rainforest land. As a class, log onto The Nature Conservancy webpage at http://www.tnc.org/frames/index.html?/html/list.html. Print out the Adoption Information form. Fill in the boxes that are applicable to your class. Read the Language Arts Survey 6.1, "Filling Out Forms" to help you correctly fill out the form.

Applied English

TRAVELOGUE. Bashō's *The Narrow Road to the Deep North and Other Travel Sketches* was written as the poet traveled and communed with nature. Write a travelogue chronicling a trip you have taken or a trip you would like to take to a nature area. Make sure to include sensory details that you experience along the way.

"She Dwelt among the Untrodden Ways" by William Wordsworth

She dwelt among the untrodden ways
Beside the springs of Dove,[1]
A Maid whom there were none to praise
And very few to love:

A violet by a mossy stone
Half hidden from the eye!
—Fair as a star, when only one
Is shining in the sky.

She lived unknown, and few could know
When Lucy ceased to be;
But she is in her grave, and, oh,
The difference to me!

"Dirce" by Walter Savage Landor

Stand close around, ye Stygian set,[2]
With Dirce in one boat conveyed!
Or Charon, seeing, may forget
That he is old and she a shade.

"The Harp That Once through Tara's[3] Halls" by Thomas Moore

The harp that once through Tara's halls
The soul of music shed,
Now hangs as mute on Tara's walls
As if that soul were fled.—
So sleeps the pride of former days,
So glory's thrill is o'er.
And hearts that once beat high for praise
Now feel that pulse no more.

No more to chiefs and ladies bright
The harp of Tara swells;
The chord alone that breaks at night
Its tale of ruin tells.
Thus Freedom now so seldom wakes,
The only throb she gives,
Is when some heart indignant breaks,
To show that still she lives.

1. **Dove.** A river in England
2. **Stygian set.** Ghosts of the dead who were ferried by Charon across the Styx river to Hades
3. **Tara.** In the Middle Ages, the capital of Ireland, which was a center of learning

"Casabianca"[4] by Felicia Dorothea Hemans

The boy stood on the burning deck
Whence all but he had fled;
The flame that lit the battle's wreck
Shone round him o'er the dead.

Yet beautiful and bright he stood,
As born to rule the storm;
A creature of heroic blood,
A proud, though childlike form.

The flames roll'd on—he would not go
Without his father's word;
That father, faint in death below,
His voice no longer heard.

He call'd aloud:—"Say, Father, say
If yet my task is done?"
He knew not that the chieftain lay
Unconscious of his son.

"Speak, Father!" once again he cried,
"If I may yet be gone!"
And but the booming shots replied,
And fast the flames roll'd on.

Upon his brow he felt their breath,
And in his waving hair,
And look'd from that lone post of death
In still, yet brave despair.

And shouted but once more aloud,
"My Father! must I stay?"
While o'er him fast, through sail and shroud,
The wreathing fires made way.

They wrapt the ship in splendor wild,
They caught the flag on high,
And stream'd above the gallant child,
Like banners in the sky.

4. **Casabianca.** A thirteen-year-old boy who remained at his post on the Orient after it had been abandoned during the Battle of the Nile, August 1, 1798

"She Dwelt among the Untrodden Ways"
About the Author. A biography of **William Wordsworth** appears on page 689.
About the Selection. **"She Dwelt among the Untrodden Ways,"** which appeared in *Lyrical Ballads,* exemplifies one of the "situations from common life" that Wordsworth believed were the essence of poetry.

"Dirce"
About the Author. Walter Savage Landor (1775–1864) lived and wrote in both the Romantic Era and the Victorian Age. Although his poetry was never popular in his lifetime, Landor is best known today for his short, elegant lyrics. He modeled many of these poems after Greek and Latin lyrics.
About the Selection. "Dirce" approximates the terse style and mythological subject of Greek lyrics.

"The Harp That Once through Tara's Halls"
About the Author. Thomas Moore (1779–1852) was an Irish poet, best known for the lyrics and folk songs of his *Irish Melodies.* He was a close friend of Byron and wrote a biography of the poet, *Life of Byron,* in 1830. Although Moore's writing was very popular during the Romantic Era, much of his work was deemed sentimental by later readers and critics.
About the Selection. Like many of the songs in *Irish Melodies,* **"The Harp That Once through Tara's Halls"** was set to a traditional Irish tune.

"Casabianca"
About the Author. Felicia Dorothea Hemans (1793–1835) was best known for her Romantic lyric poetry. She was much admired as a poet by William Wordsworth and Sir Walter Scott. She wrote her *Poems,* published in 1808, between the ages of eight and thirteen. After separating from her husband, she was able to support five children by selling her poems.
About the Selection. The lyric poem **"Casabianca"** also has the elements of a ballad, telling the story of a young, doomed soldier. This poem has been committed to memory by countless students over the years.

FROM *MACBETH*
About the Author. A biography on **William Shakespeare** appears on page 374.
About the Selection. Background information about the selection appears on page 375.

There came a burst of thunder sound—
The boy—oh! where was he?
Ask of the winds that far around
With fragments strew'd the sea!—

With mast, and helm, and pennon fair,
That well had borne their part,
But the noblest thing which perish'd there
Was that young faithful heart!

from "Macbeth" by William Hazlitt

"The poet's eye in a fine
frenzy rolling
Doth glance from heaven to
earth, from earth to heaven;
And as imagination bodies forth
The forms of things
unknown, the poet's pen
Turns them to shape, and
gives to airy nothing
A local habitation and a name."[1]

Macbeth and *Lear*, *Othello* and *Hamlet*, are usually reckoned Shakespeare's four principal tragedies. *Lear* stands first for the profound intensity of the passion; *Macbeth* for the wildness of the imagination and the rapidity of the action; *Othello* for the progressive interest and powerful alternations of feeling; *Hamlet* for the refined development of thought and sentiment. If the force of genius shown in each of these works is astonishing, their variety is not less so. They are like different creations of the same mind, not one of which has the slightest reference to the rest. This distinctness and originality is indeed the necessary consequence of truth and nature. Shakespeare's genius alone appeared to possess the resources of nature. He is "your only *tragedy maker*." His plays have the force of things upon the mind. What he represents is brought home to the bosom as a part of our experience, implanted in the memory as if we had known the places, persons, and things of which he treats. *Macbeth* is like a record of a preternatural and tragical event. It has the rugged severity of an old chronicle with all that the imagination of the poet can engraft upon traditional belief. The castle of Macbeth, round which "the air smells wooingly," and where "the temple-haunting martlet builds," has a real subsistence in the mind; the Weird Sisters meet us in person on "the blasted heath"; the "air-drawn dagger" moves slowly before our eyes; the "gracious Duncan," the "blood-boltered Banquo" stand before us; all that passed through the mind of Macbeth passes, without the loss of a tittle, through ours. All that could actually take place, and all that is only possible to be conceived, what was said and what was done, the workings of passion, the spells of magic, are brought before us with the same absolute truth and vividness.

Shakespeare excelled in the openings of his plays: that of *Macbeth* is the most striking of any. The wildness of the scenery, the sudden shifting of the situations and characters, the bustle, the expectations excited, are equally extraordinary. From the first entrance of the Witches and the description of them when they meet Macbeth:

What are these
So wither'd and so wild
in their attire,
That look not like the
inhabitants of th' earth
And yet are on't?

the mind is prepared for all that follows.

This tragedy is alike distinguished for the lofty imagination it displays, and for the tumultuous vehemence of the action; and the one is made the moving principle of the other. The overwhelming pressure of preternatural agency urges on the tide of human passion with redoubled force. Macbeth himself appears driven along by the violence of his fate like a vessel drifting before a storm: he reels to and fro like a drunken man; he staggers under the weight of his own purposes and the suggestions of others; he stands at bay with his situation; and from the superstitious awe and breathless suspense into which the communications of the Weird Sisters throw him is hurried on with daring impatience to verify their predictions, and with impious and bloody hand to tear aside the veil which hides the uncertainty of the future. He is not equal to the struggle with fate and conscience. He now "bends up each corporal instrument to the terrible feat"; at other times his heart misgives him, and he is cowed and abashed by his success. "The deed, no less than the attempt, confounds him." His mind is assailed by the stings of remorse, and full of "preternatural solicitings." His speeches and soliloquies are dark riddles on human life, baffling solution, and entangling him in their labyrinths. In thought he is absent and perplexed, sudden and desperate in act, from a distrust of his own resolution. His energy springs from the anxiety and agitation of his mind. His blindly rushing forward on the objects of his ambition and revenge, or his recoiling from them, equally betrays the harassed state of his feelings. This part of his character is admirably set off by being brought in connection with that of Lady Macbeth, whose obdurate strength of will and masculine firmness give her the ascendancy over her husband's faltering virtue. She at once seizes on the opportunity that offers for the accom-

1. **"The poet's . . . name."** From Shakespeare's *A Midsummer Night's Dream*, Act V. scene i.

plishment of all their wished-for greatness, and never flinches from her object till all is over. The magnitude of her resolution almost covers the magnitude of her guilt. She is a great bad woman, whom we hate, but whom we fear more than we hate. She does not excite our loathing and abhorrence like Regan and Goneril.[2] She is only wicked to gain a great end and is perhaps more distinguished by her commanding presence of mind and inexorable self-will, which do not suffer her to be diverted from a bad purpose, when once formed, by weak and womanly regrets, than by the hardness of her heart or want of natural affections. The impression which her lofty determination of character makes on the mind of Macbeth is well described where he exclaims:

Bring forth men children only;
For thy undaunted mettle should compose
Nothing but males!

Nor do the pains she is at to "screw his courage to the sticking-place," the reproach to him, not to be "lost so poorly in himself," the assurance that "a little water clears them of this deed," show anything but her greater consistency in depravity. Her strong-nerved ambition furnishes ribs of steel to "the sides of his intent"; and she is herself wound up to the execution of her baneful project with the same unshrinking fortitude in crime, that in other circumstances she would probably have shown patience in suffering. The deliberate sacrifice of all other considerations to the gaining "for their future days and nights sole sovereign sway and masterdom," by the murder of Duncan, is gorgeously expressed in her invocation on hearing of "his fatal entrance under her battlements":

Come all you spirits
That tend on mortal thoughts, unsex me here:
And fill me, from the crown to th' toe, top-full
Of direst cruelty; make thick my blood,
Stop up the access and passage to remorse,
That no compunctious visitings of nature
Shake my fell purpose, nor keep peace between
The effect and it. Come to my woman's breasts,
And take my milk for gall, you murthering ministers,
Wherever in your sightless substances
You wait on nature's mischief. Come, thick night!
And pall thee in the dunnest smoke of hell,
That my keen knife see not the wound it makes,
Nor heav'n peep through the blanket of the dark,
To cry, hold, hold!

When she first hears that "Duncan comes there to sleep" she is so overcome by the news, which is beyond her utmost expectations, that she answers the messenger, "Thou 'rt mad to say it"; and on receiving her husband's account of the predictions of the Witches, conscious of his instability of purpose, and that her presence is necessary to goad him on to the consummation of his promised greatness, she exclaims:

Hie thee hither,
That I may pour my spirits in thine ear,
And chastise with the valor of my tongue
All that impedes thee from the golden round,
Which fate and metaphysical aid doth seem
To have thee crowned withal.

This swelling exultation and keen spirit of triumph, this uncontrollable eagerness of anticipation, which seems to dilate her form and take possession of all her faculties, this solid, substantial flesh and blood display of passion, exhibit a striking contrast to the cold, abstracted, gratuitous, servile malignity of the Witches, who are equally instrumental in urging Macbeth to his fate for the mere love of mischief, and from a disinterested delight in deformity and cruelty. They are hags of mischief, obscene panders to iniquity, malicious from their impotence of enjoyment, enamored of destruction, because they are themselves unreal, abortive, half-existences, who become sublime from their exemption from all human sympathies and contempt for all human affairs, as Lady Macbeth does by the force of passion! Her fault seems to have been an excess of that strong principle of self-interest and family aggrandizement, not amenable to the common feelings of compassion and justice, which is so marked a feature in barbarous nations and times. A passing reflection of this kind, on the resemblance of the sleeping king to her father, alone prevents her from slaying Duncan with her own hand. . . .

Macbeth (generally speaking) is done upon a stronger and more systematic principle of contrast than any other of Shakespeare's plays. It moves upon the verge of an abyss and is a constant struggle between life and death. The action is desperate and the reaction is dreadful. It is a huddling together of fierce extremes, a war of opposite natures, which of them shall destroy the other. There is nothing but what has a violent end or violent beginnings. The lights and shades are laid on with a determined hand; the transitions from triumph to despair, from the height of terror to the repose of death, are sudden and startling; every passion brings in its fellow-contrary, and the thoughts pitch and jostle against each other as in the dark. The whole play is an unruly chaos of strange and forbidden things, where the ground rocks under our feet. Shakespeare's genius here took its full swing, and trod upon the farthest bounds of nature and passion.

1. **Regan and Goneril.** The two evil daughters in Shakespeare's *King Lear*

ADDITIONAL QUESTIONS AND ACTIVITIES

William Hazlitt gives critical commentary and insight on Shakespeare's *The Tragedy of Macbeth*. What do you think about his statement: "Macbeth (generally speaking) is done upon a stronger and more systematic principle of contrast than any other of Shakespeare's plays. It moves upon the verge of an abyss and is a constant struggle between life and death." After reading the play in Unit 5, do you agree or disagree with this statement? Why, or why not? Give specific examples from the text to back up your opinion.

LESSON OVERVIEW

GUIDED WRITING *Software*

See the Guided Writing Software for an extended version of this lesson that includes printable graphic organizers, extensive student models and student-friendly checklists, and self-, peer, and teacher evaluation features.

INDIVIDUAL LEARNING STRATEGIES

MOTIVATION
Make students aware that being able to write a research paper is a required skill for post-secondary education.
Encourage students to share past experiences they have had in writing research papers.

READING PROFICIENCY
As students are now familiar with the Guided Writing lessons, have them tell you what sections they anticipate seeing in this lesson before they begin reading.

ENGLISH LANGUAGE LEARNING
Point out to students who feel overwhelmed by the assignments of writing a research paper that it is a process and they will learn to do it one step at a time.

Pure logic is the ruin of the spirit.
—*Antoine de Saint-Exupery*

WRITING A RESEARCH PAPER

We live in an era that emphasizes fact and technology. However, not all scholars, philosophers, educators, or scientists are in total agreement on their importance. The Romantic period (1785–1832) was a similar time: while some people accepted things as they were, others questioned, and still others literally rebelled against the rational. For some Romantics, emotion was celebrated over reason, nature played a larger role than man's accomplishments, and spontaneity and wildness were considered more important than control and propriety.

WRITING ASSIGNMENT. In this assignment you will write a research paper about developments in literature, science, or society during the Romantic Period (1785–1832).

EXAMINING THE MODEL. Mary Shelley's Introduction to *Frankenstein*, triggered Marin's memory: she remembered a science fiction unit back in middle school when her class had read a play based on the novel. Marin wanted to explore the background of that pre-science fiction novel and discover, if she could, what might have compelled a young woman, still in her teens, to write such a forceful tale with all the right ingredients: obsession, suspense, love, and horror. Mary Shelley's creation intrigued her from the start.

Marin begins her research paper by suggesting possible sources for Mary Shelley's

Student Model

from "It Came Alive: The Birth of Mary Shelley's *Frankenstein*" by Marin Lix

Among the many essential elements required when composing a novel, authors often employ imagination and inspiration, whether positive or negative, drawn from the experiences of their lives, or strictly fictitious circumstances. Perhaps Mary Wollstonecraft Shelley applied and combined both the tools of creativity and passion to compose her novel, *Frankenstein*. Many people believe tragedies in her life spawned the plot of the horrifying story, while others contend that a dream provoked her to produce the frightening myth. Possibly a combination of factors motivated Mary Shelley to write a story predicated on the power of futuristic science to form and give life to an imaginary human monster.

Mary Wollstonecraft Shelley, destined to become a "prominent, though often overlooked, literary figure during the Romantic Era of English Literature" (Life) entered the world on August 30, 1797. Her birth preceded her mother's death by only several days. Many people believe the loss of her mother during Mary's infancy

INDIVIDUAL LEARNING STRATEGIES

SPECIAL NEEDS
You might want to give students a list of easier topics to write about or have them choose a topic of their own. For students who are incapable of completing this assignment, ask them to write a short summary of the process of writing a research paper.

ENRICHMENT
Suggest that students make a multimedia presentation of their research paper topic once they have completed the paper. Refer students to the Language Arts Survey 4.22, "Preparing a Multimedia Presentation."

influenced her to write *Frankenstein*, but an equally prominent factor may have been her upbringing.

Her father reared and educated Mary and her four other siblings. Little distinction existed between genders in her family, allowing Mary to obtain an education of considerable breadth. Mary Wollstonecraft's father exposed his children to scientists such as Humphrey Davy and William Nicholson, both of whom conducted experiments in the emerging field of galvanic electrical science. Perhaps Mary employed a portion of her scientific background when she composed Frankenstein.

At the age of 16, Mary "ran away to live with" (Life) poet Percy Bysshe Shelley, a twenty-one-year-old married man. She was smitten with Shelley, writing to a friend how she loved "him so tenderly and entirely whose life hangs on the beam of his eye and whose whole soul is entirely wrapt up in him" (Bennett). Because of Mary Wollstonecraft's controversial and scandalous relationship with Percy Shelley, many friends and family, including her own father, shunned her. Existing as an outcast of polite society was merely one of many traumatic events in Mary Shelley's life.

inspiration to create *Frankenstein*. The reader knows where the paper is going to go because Marin provides a clear thesis statement early on. Marin provides adequate parenthetical documentation to show from where the information is derived. The writing is lively and engaging. The reader is drawn to the energy of Marin's ideas and words.

Prewriting

Writing with a Plan. Finding a suitable topic is critical. Take some time exploring the literature as well as looking at the possible cultural or scientific issues that arose during the Romantic Period and discuss how they might interest you and your audience. Remember to use your curiosity: *what do you want to know more about?*

Once you have found a general topic, you will need to find out what information is available. Gather information from the library and your electronic sources and start reading. When you have some background information, you should be ready to narrow your topic by developing a focus for presenting information about the issue.

As you read about your narrowed topic, take notes and document the sources. You will need this information later. For more information on taking notes and documenting sources, see the Language Arts Survey section in your textbook, in particular 5.36–5.45.

Next, write a thesis statement that states your topic and your focus on that topic. Your thesis statement will serve as a guide to identify and develop the main points of support needed for your research paper. Thesis statements may change, of course, as you find more information that may not support your original intent. See the Language Arts Survey 2.25, "Writing a Thesis Statement."

Finding Your Voice. The research paper is the most formal piece of writing you will do. Therefore, avoid contractions, slang, and colloquialisms. Still, don't be reluctant to let your own voice come through in this paper. If you are truly amazed at an insight your research uncovers, let that amazement show in your choice of words and sentence structure. Convey your excitement for your newfound knowledge.

Identifying Your Audience. As your primary audience for your research paper, your teacher probably has a keen interest in the product you and your classmates produce. Keep your teacher in mind as you write as well as your peers. What will interest them? You can assume this audience has more than a basic understanding about your topic. Write to inform and enlighten this group of readers.

Prewriting

Writing with a Plan
Encourage students to choose a method of organization after reading the Language Arts Survey 2.27, "Choosing a Method of Organization."

Finding Your Voice
Provide a worksheet with slang, contractions, and colloquialisms and ask students to change them to formal English before they begin writing their research paper. Tell students the more reading they do on their topic, the more authoritative they will become.

Identify Your Audience
Establish the audience beforehand. Will students be writing for you or another student?

STUDENT MODEL—GRAPHIC ORGANIZER

See the Guided Writing Resource 12.8 for a blackline master of the Graphic Organizer for this lesson.

Drafting

Encourage students to use their completed Graphic Organizer modeled on page 758 to help them make sure they have organized the main points of their paper carefully. Students might also benefit from reading the Language Arts Survey 2.32–2.35, "Drafting."

Choosing a Topic

You may use the following topics, or use them for seed to come up with your own.

Consider the literary or cultural angle:

- In what ways did literary trends in England make their way to America?
- Were American poets affected by revolutionary ideals in the same ways Romantic English poets were?
- What people, events, or experiences influenced Romantic writers?
- Examine the life of a great Romantic artist or musician.

Consider the science angle:

- What events occurred in the world of science during the Romantic Era?
- Did the revolutionary spirit of the age affect scientific endeavors as it did political and artistic ones? How?
- What advances in science can one trace to the 21st century?

Consider the sociological angle:

- Research a particular country and write about specific changes that happened.
- Examine the life of an ordinary person who lived during the Romantic period in France, England, or America.
- Compare the rights of women during this time to that of men or compare the rights of women in one part of the world to that of another.

After you have gathered information, organize it around the main points that support your thesis. Writers frequently organize their research in an outline to give their paper structure and order. Many students, however, don't like to create an outline because they think an outline is limiting. Consider, then, creating a graphic organizer instead, especially if you favor a structure that is more visual or spatial. If your teacher requires an outline, the graphic organizer can easily be converted to one. If it is difficult to put together either an outline or a graphic organizer, you may have some serious problems with the thesis, main points of support, research information, and structure of the paper. If you have trouble conceptualizing these elements, you might need to rethink your approach to the topic.

Details for some parts of the outline, such as the introduction and conclusion, may best be filled in as you develop your draft for the paper.

As she took notes from her research materials and began to formulate her narrowed topic and thesis, Marin used a cluster chart for her paper on Mary Shelley.

Student Model—Graphic Organizer

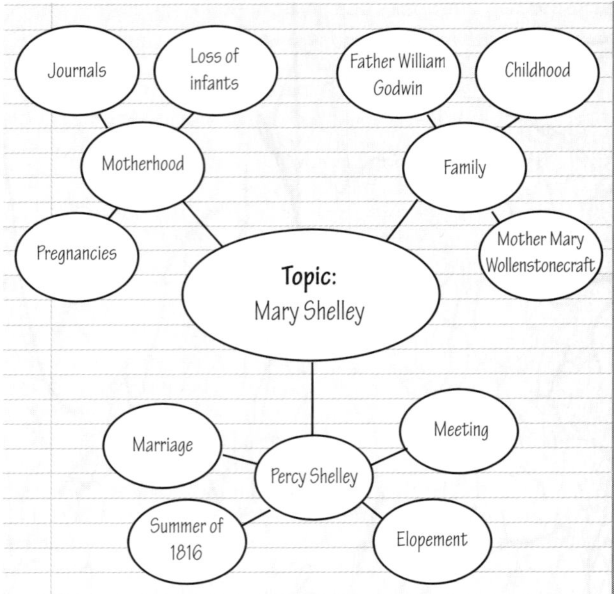

Drafting

It is easier to write a good introduction for your paper if you wait until the body of the paper is written; then you know what your paper says, and what you need to finalize it. Begin instead with your thesis statement: What do you want to say about your topic? What are you trying to show to your audience? Starting with a thesis will give your paper some direction.

From the thesis write about the main points that will support it. Write about only one point at a time. Insert the necessary parenthetical documentation as you quote or paraphrase specific information from your sources. After you finish a point, take a break before you go on to the next. Keeping a fresh mind is important while you are writing, for you may forget to include key information. Documenting sources as you go along will ultimately save you time later.

After you have finished developing all of the main points and their supporting information, read through your draft to see if the points are coherent and work together. Then draft an introduction that uses an appropriate technique to develop interest in your topic. Include your thesis in the introduction. Finally, draft a conclusion that summarizes the essence of your paper.

Self- and Peer Evaluation

After you finish your first draft, complete a self-evaluation of your research paper. Try to read your draft as though you were uninformed about the topic. Identify background information or support that may be missing. As time allows, obtain one or more peer evaluations. As you evaluate your draft or that of classmate, respond to the following questions:

- How does this topic relate to the Romantic Period?
- What additional information is needed for the reader to have a more thorough understanding?
- What would make the introduction more interesting or more focused?
- How clearly does the thesis statement present the issue?
- What main point is developed in each of the body paragraphs?
- How does each body paragraph relate to the thesis?
- How logically do the main points support the thesis? What points might be missing? Which points might be extraneous to the issue?
- What do direct quotations add? What additional quotations would add meaningful support? Which quotations seem unnecessary?
- How effective is the conclusion?
- Where, if anywhere, does the documentation fail to follow correct MLA form?

Student Model—Revised

A continuation of Marin Lix's paper on Mary Shelley appears on the next page. Note her strong body paragraphs and effective documentation. Also note the way her voice reflects her interest in her topic as she concludes her paper.

Writing Plan Checklist:

- –Fascinating topic
- –Explore areas to develop (complete a graphic organizer)
- –Narrow topic
- –Locate sources (5–8 total, including at least one on-line source)
- –Take notes and document sources
- –Write Introduction
- –Write thesis statement
- –Determine main points
- –Organize information
- –Write strong body paragraphs
- –Write conclusion effective

Revising and Proofreading

Review your self- and peer evaluations. Revise your writing after considering these comments. Check that each paragraph has a topic sentence that relates to your thesis statement. Proofread your revised draft for spelling, mechanical, and usage errors. Invite one or two friends to proofread, also. See the language Arts Survey 2.45 for a proofreading checklist.

Be sure that each source is referenced correctly in the paper and that the Works Cited page is also done correctly. Remember that each source listed at the end of the paper must be cited internally at least once. Finish the paper by including a title page. Follow the Modern Language Association format for the title page as well as for the works cited.

Self- and Peer Evaluation

Have students review the Language Arts Survey 2.37, "Self- and Peer Evaluation." Then have students use the checklist on page 759 for self- and peer evaluation. The checklist is intended to act as a student-friendly rubric that should help students identify specific evidence of writing strengths and areas needing improvement. Make sure they provide concrete suggestions for improvement or specific evidence of why the writing works.

Revising and Proofreading

A handout of the proofreading checklist in the Language Arts Survey is available in the Teacher's Resource Kit, Guided Writing Resource Book 2.45. Students critiquing their classmates' work might be interested in using common proofreader's symbols, which are found in the Language Arts Survey 2.44, "Using Proofreader's Marks."

Language, Grammar, and Style

EFFECTIVE DOCUMENTATION
Lesson Overview
In this lesson, students will be asked to do the following:

- Identify Effective Documentation
- Fix Effective Documentation
- Use Effective Documentation

INTRODUCING THE SKILL
Explain to students that they can use documentation in many of their classes. If they are going on to college, explain that it is expected that they know this skill.

Language, Grammar, and Style

Effective Documentation

IDENTIFYING EFFECTIVE DOCUMENTATION. You need to credit authors and sources for the information that you use in your research. Citing your sources allows your readers to verify your research and protects you against plagiarism. Documentation that is effective for both these purposes is accurate and presented according to accepted style.

To quote an author's exact words, put the exact words in quotation marks and reference the last name and the page where you found those words.

DIRECT QUOTATION

Frankenstein "is a birth myth, and one that was lodged in the novelist's imagination by the fact that she was herself a mother" (Moers).

At times, instead of using a direct quotation, you may paraphrase an author's idea in your essay. Even though you are paraphrasing, you must still credit the author by referencing the last name and page where you found the idea. If no author's name is available, use a shortened form of the title.

PARAPHRASED STATEMENT

Emotionally devastated by the loss of her daughter, Mary received no support from her negligent partner, Percy, who considered socializing with his controversial friends of

continued on page 761

It Came Alive: The Birth of Mary Shelley's *Frankenstein*
by Marin Lix

Before Mary Wollstonecraft and Percy Shelley married, they lost the first of her [four] children (Birth). Clara, her first child, born prematurely on February 22, 1815, died on March 6, when she was only 13 days old. Emotionally devastated by the loss of her daughter, Mary received no support from her negligent partner, Percy, who considered socializing with his controversial friends more important than comforting and consoling Mary (Birth). On March 19, she wrote in her journal: "Dream that my little baby came to life again, that it had been only cold, and that we rubbed it before the fire, and it lived. Awake and find no baby. I think about the little thing all day. Not in good spirits" (Walling 17). Shelley's Victor Frankenstein, too, desperately wants to bring his creation to life. According to Ellen Moers, author of *Literary Women, Frankenstein* "is a birth myth, and one that was lodged in the novelist's imagination by the fact that she was herself a mother" (Moers).

During the course of their relationship, Mary Wollstonecraft and Percy Shelley often traveled together. Perhaps one such journey in June, 1816, spawned the novel, *Frankenstein*. The couple visited one of Percy's friends, Lord Byron, at his home, Villa Diodati, in Geneva, Switzerland. Both *Gothic* and *Haunted Summer*, movie versions of the gathering of this creative group, embellish the events which allegedly took place that summer. The stormy night of June 16 inspired the group of adults to "read aloud a collection of German ghost stories, *Fantasmagoriana*" (Harris 9). Their host then challenged each of his guests to develop his or her own ghost story.

The following evening, the group resumed their exchange of ghost stories. At the stroke of midnight, Byron recited "Christabel" by Coleridge. Percy Shelley, upon hearing Coleridge's poem, became convinced the villainess of the poem was his partner, Mary, and created a terrible scene while running out of the room where the group had gathered. Quite naturally being affected and embarrassed by his outburst, perhaps her "feelings of guilt. . . contributed to the story ideas she later developed" (Summer). In the interim, Mary failed in her efforts to compose her own ghost story to share with Lord Byron's other guests.

Over several days at Byron's villa, those present continued to regale one another with their ghost stories. Impatience and persistence stifled Mary's creativity, stymieing all her efforts and desire to compose a horrifying tale to match those of her male cohorts. Shortly thereafter, however, on June 22, Mary had a "waking" nightmare. After awakening, Mary began writing her story, beginning with the opening lines of Chapter IV of Frankenstein. In 1817, Mary completed her novel. Of all the guests who attended Lord Byron's party and wrote their ghost stories, only Mary Wollstonecraft Shelley's reached publication.

What provoked Mary Wollstonecraft Shelley to create a story about the possible horrors of futuristic science? Mary never received a chance to acquaint herself with her mother. Was it a combination of Mary's "pregnancy and childbirth [that were] . . . "an integral part of Mary Shelley's young adult life" (Birth) and the loneliness of a motherless childhood?

Loneliness and a profound sense of loss due to her daughter's death may have consumed Mary's waking and sleeping thoughts. Creation of an

more importance than comforting and consoling Mary (Birth).

If you use two or more articles or books with the same author, include the author, title of article or book, and page number in the parenthetical reference. You also need to include this source in your works cited page at the end of your paper.

- Avoid quotations that stand alone in your paper: sentences that begin and end with quotation marks. Rather, work to blend them into your writing.
- Anything that you change or add to a quotation needs to be bracketed.
- You need not directly quote information that is common knowledge or that is found in several sources. Directly quote when passages are precise, eloquent, or unique to a source.

Fixing Documentation. You need to document sources correctly. Explain how you would fix the documentation in each example below.

(Harris, 9)
(p. 17 Walling)
(Ellen Moers)

Read the quotations below. Then add your own words, both before and after the quotation, so that the quotations are not isolated from the rest of the text.

"In truth, even *Frankenstein*, the novel by which Mary Shelley's name most surely

continued on page 762

Previewing the Skill

Refer students to the Language Arts Survey 5.43, "Paraphrasing, Summarizing, and Quoting." This is intended to reinforce the integrated Language, Grammar, and Style lesson in Unit 8.

Practicing the Skill
For additional practice, have students work through the exercise in the following section of the Language, Grammar, and Style Resource located in the Teacher's Resource Kit: 5.43, "Paraphrasing, Summarizing, and Quoting."

survives, would never have been begun without the stimulus of Shelley and his friends" (Walling 15).

"By the time [Percy] Shelley's hallucination was over, the storm had ended and the first clear light of morning was beginning to seep through the shutters, across the polished parquet floor" (Harris 10).

Using Effective Documentation. Read through your paper again. Where have you handled quotations correctly? Where do you need to strengthen your use of quotations? Check carefully for paraphrased ideas. Are there any places where you paraphrased material that you need to reference? Is your works cited page done correctly? For more information, see the Language Arts Survey 5.36–5.45, "Documenting Sources."

imaginary monster may have been Mary's only means of coping with the deaths of significant people in her life.

Subconsciously and consciously considering the tragedies of her life, Percy Shelley's negligence, and the prevalent isolation of her personal life, Mary Wollstonecraft Shelley perhaps entertained thoughts about restoring life to Clara. In her novel, the monster comes to life with the help of a scientist, Victor Frankenstein. In Mary's unwritten thoughts, Victor may have suffered from isolation and loneliness, uniting him with his creator, Mary Wollstonecraft Shelley.

Suppose, however, that loneliness, tragedies, and depression were not motivating factors for Mary Shelley's writing of *Frankenstein*? What if Mary merely desired to meet Lord Byron's challenge and to elevate her status among Percy Shelley's friends? Feeling out of her element, did Mary decide to accept the challenge and prove she was just as capable of writing horrifying tales as her male counterparts? The impetus for the monster's creation might well have been an outgrowth of Mary Wollstonecraft Shelley's unusual wealth of scientific knowledge, brought to the forefront by Lord Byron's other guests' successes in their timely responses to Byron's challenge.

Could *Frankenstein* be a rearrangement of these various elements in different combinations or even simply a matter of writing only for entertainment purposes or for her own personal pleasure? Because Mary Wollstonecraft Shelley died in 1851, we can only analyze possible catalysts, reach individual conclusions for ourselves, and graciously and gratefully accept the fact that she immortalized herself through the creation of *Frankenstein*.

Works Cited

"The 'Birth' of a Monster." 24 Feb. 2000 <http://www.desert-fairy.com/birth.shtml>.

Bennett, Betty T., ed. The Letters of Mary Wollstonecraft Shelley. Baltimore, 1980. 9 March 2000 <http://virtual.park.uga.edu/~232/>.

Gothic. Dir. Ken Russell. With Gabriel Byrne and Natasha Richardson. Writ. Stephen Volk. 87 min., 1987.

Harris, Janet. *The Woman Who Created Frankenstein*. New York: Harper & Row, 1979.

Haunted Summer. Dir. Ivan Passer. With Laura Dern and Eric Stoltz. Writ. Lewis John Carlino. Based on the novel of the same title by Anne Edwards. 106 min., 1988.

"The Life of Mary Shelley." 24 Feb. 2000 <http://www.desert-fairy.com/life.shtml>. 24 Feb. 2000.

"Mary Shelley and Knowledge." 24 Feb. 2000 <http://www.desert-fairy.com/knowledge.shtml>. 24 Feb. 2000.

Moers, Ellen. *Literary Women*. New York: Anchor Press, 1977. 6 March 2000 <http://www.engl.virginia.edu/!enec981/Group/ami.frank.html#shelley>.

"The Summer of 1816." 24 Feb. 2000 <http://www.desert-fairy.com/summer.shtml>.

Walling, William. *Mary Shelley*. New York: Twayne Publishers, Inc.: 1972.

Publishing and Presenting

Your final product should be a paper that you are proud to present. When you have done your best, share your work. You may wish to publish the papers as an anthology. Your high school library might wish to shelve a copy—or you might post it on your school's website.

Reflecting

Writing a good research paper is one of the more difficult tasks asked of students. What was the most challenging part of the project for you? What do you wish you would have done differently? What did you learn about your research and organizational skills? The subject matter? What future reading or research might you be compelled to do?

> Gie me ae spark o' Nature's fire, / That's a' the learning I desire.
>
> —*Robert Burns*

Publishing and Presenting

You might consider holding a conference called "Literary, Social, and Cultural Issues of the Romantic Period" with another English or Social Studies class and invite students from your class to present their papers. Have students in the host class ask questions of the presenters once the papers have been read. Students interested in sharing their papers might be interested in posting their papers online. Another suggestion would be to have students place their papers in a writing portfolio; have them read the Language Arts Survey 2.48, "Maintaining a Writing Portfolio."

Reflecting

Encourage students to write a journal entry reflecting on how they would do the assignment differently next time. How do they see the process of writing a research paper more clearly now?

ADDITIONAL RESOURCES

UNIT 8 RESOURCE BOOK
- Vocabulary Worksheet
- Study Guide: Unit 8 Test
- Unit 8 Test

VOCABULARY DEVELOPMENT

Give students the following exercise: Choose twenty words from the list on page 764. For each word, write a sentence that relates to something you have read in this unit. The vocabulary word need not have appeared in the selection to which you refer.

UNIT 8 REVIEW
The Romantic Era

Words for Everyday Use

Check your knowledge of the following vocabulary words from the selections in this unit. Write short sentences using these words in context to make the meaning clear. To review the definition or usage of a word, refer to the page number listed or the Glossary of Words for Everyday Use.

acceded, 743
adieu, 732
aspire, 682
beauteous, 696
blight, 686
caprice, 737
cavern, 705
chasm, 705, 716
circumscribe, 724
citadel, 733
cloy'd, 732
contemplate, 691
copse, 696
corporeal, 698
deity, 732
dirge, 669, 715
emphatic, 691
endeavor, 692
epithet, 739
erroneous, 691
exhortation, 700
hapless, 685
ignoble, 668
impetuous, 717
ingenuous, 667
insinuate, 737
jocund, 666
kindred, 692
manacle, 685
meander, 705
obscure, 666
organic, 691
ostentatiously, 691
pestilence, 714
platitude, 744
prevail, 700
principal, 691
progeny, 746
provoke, 667
puerile, 737
recompense, 699
repose, 696
reverie, 744
satirize, 737
scrupulous, 737
secluded, 696
sepulchre or sepulcher, 715
serenely, 722
sinew, 682
sordid, 694
specious, 737
sublime, 696
teeming, 729
tranquil, 696
tumult, 706, 717
ungenial, 743
vagrant, 696
vain, 698
vainly, 724
visage, 712
zeal, 701
zenith, 715

Literary Tools

Define the following terms, giving concrete examples of how they are used in the selections in this unit. To review a term, refer to the page number indicated or to the Handbook of Literary Terms.

allegory, 680
alliteration, 682, 704
allusion, 694
apostrophe, 731
autobiography, 742
blank verse, 696
Byronic hero, 724
catharsis, 742
character, 682, 711
definition, 690
dialect, 672
didactic criticism, 736
elegy, 664
free verse, 696
haiku, 749
hymn, 672
iambic tetrameter, 720
image, 676, 685, 704
irony of situation, 711
metaphor, 676, 736
ode, 696
paradox, 731
parallelism, 724
pastoral, 680
personification, 714
repetition, 724
sensory details, 749
setting, 685
simile, 720
sonnet, 694, 729
speaker, 664
terza rima, 714
theme, 690, 729

Reflecting on Your Reading

Genre Studies

1. **Lyric Poetry.** Lyric poems of the Romantic Era tended to express strong personal feelings. Compare and contrast the feelings expressed in the following poems: "John Anderson, My Jo," "She Dwelt among the Untrodden Ways," and "She Walks in Beauty." In each case, describe the speaker and what he or she is feeling. Also explain who the speaker is addressing in each case and what the speaker has to say about this person.

Thematic Studies

2. **Coping with Death.** The poets of the Romantic Era wrote often about subjects that evoke strong feelings. One such subject is death. Explore the theme of coping with death in the following poems: "Elegy Written in a Country Churchyard," "Lines Composed a Few Miles above Tintern Abbey," and "When I Have Fears." In each case, explain the feelings about death that are expressed by the speaker and what comfort, if any, the speaker offers.

3. **Nature in Romantic Poetry.** Many Romantic Era poets exalted nature over the works of human beings. Describe the view of nature and of human works expressed in the following poems: "The World Is Too Much with Us," "Ozymandias," "Ode to the West Wind," and the selection from *Childe Harold's Pilgrimage.*

Historical and Biographical Studies

4. **Human Rights.** The major events influencing the development of the spirit of the Romantic Era were the American and French Revolutions. These revolutions attempted to redress social evils, such as the inequities that existed between common people and wealthy members of the nobility. Explain the political significance of the following pieces from the unit: "Elegy Written in a Country Churchyard," "London," the selection from the Preface to *Lyrical Ballads,* "Ozymandias," the selection from *A Vindication of the Rights of Woman.*

REFLECTING ON YOUR READING

The prompts in "Reflecting on your Reading" are suitable as topics for research papers. Refer to the Language Arts Survey 5.18-5.45, "Research Skills." (To evaluate research papers, see the evaluation forms for writing, revising and proofreading in the Assessment Resource.)

These prompts can also be used as topics for oral reports. Refer students to the Language Arts Survey 4, "Speaking and Listening." (To evaluate these projects, see the evaluation forms in the Assessment Resource.)

UNIT SKILLS OUTLINE

Fair, Quiet and Sweet Rest, [detail] c. 1900s. Luke Fildes
Warrington Museum & Art Gallery, Lancs.

GOALS/OBJECTIVES

Studying this unit will enable students to

- gain an appreciation for the poetry and prose of the Victorian Age
- describe the reaction of writers and intellectuals to the scientific revolution, the Industrial Revolution, and their consequences
- describe Victorian England's ideas of the role of art and artists
- explain the concept of Realism in literature
- understand the concepts of dramatic monologue, metaphor, and symbol
- write an essay to analyze a work of art
- identify and use effective transitions

Unit 9 The Victorian Age (1832–1900)

Ah, love, let us be true
To one another! for the world, which seems
To lie before us like a land of dreams,
So various, so beautiful, so new,
Hath really neither joy, nor love, nor light,
Nor certitude, nor peace, nor help for pain. . .

—Matthew Arnold, "Dover Beach"

Cross-Curricular Connections

Teaching the Multiple Intelligences

Teaching the Multiple Intelligences (cont.)

ADDITIONAL RESOURCES

UNIT 9 RESOURCE BOOK
- Selection Check Test 4.9.1
- Selection Test 4.9.2

CROSS-CULTURAL CONNECTIONS

HISTORY. During the reign of Queen Victoria the role of the monarch in England changed drastically. Initially very intrigued by and protective of her political power, Victoria gave increasing control to Albert after their marriage. After Albert died in 1861, Victoria, deeply depressed, retreated into mourning and retirement, surrounding herself with momentos and photographs of her lost husband. Victoria remained absent from both politics and public life until the fiftieth anniversary of her coronation, the Jubilee of 1887. Originally planned as a procession through the London streets to display the restored grandeur of the monarchy and to renew the people's confidence, the Jubilee quickly became something else: an example of the Victorian love of spectacle, a consumer frenzy, and a manufacturer's dream. While the monarchy never regained the political power it held in preceding centuries, it did gain a certain appeal and mystique. Victoria, her image stamped on everything from Jubilee banners to Jubilee commemorative thimbles, became something unique to British history: a living symbol of burgeoning consumer culture. Interested students may read selections of George Grissing's novel about gender roles at that time, *In the Year of Jubilee.*

ArtNote

Fair, Quiet and Sweet Rest, [detail] c.1900s. Luke Fields, page 766.

Sir Luke Fildes, born October 18, 1843, died February 27, 1927, was a fashionable British painter of social scenes and portraits in Victorian England. He began his career in 1863 as a magazine illustrator in London, and illustrated Dickens's last novel, *Edwin Drood.* In the 1870s, he began painting. His most famous works were realistic depictions of social issues. His *Applicants for Admission to a Casual Ward* (1874; Royal Holloway College, London) and *The Doctor* (1891; Tate Gallery, London) were his two most popular works. In 1906, Fildes received a knighthood.

THE VICTORIAN AGE (1832–1900)

THE VICTORIAN LEGACY

To understand the world in which we live today, one must go back to the **Victorian Age** (1832–1900), for the titanic forces that have shaped our century emerged during that time. In those years, enormous changes occurred in political and social life in England and in the rest of the world—the scientific and technical innovations of the Industrial Revolution, the emergence of modern nationalism, and the European colonization of much of Africa, the Middle East, and the Far East. The period produced far-reaching new ideas and one of the richest outpourings of literature the world has ever seen.

VICTORIA AND ALBERT

The period takes its name from **Queen Victoria** (1819–1901), who ruled England from 1837 to 1901. Her sixty-four-year reign was the longest in British history. When Victoria became queen at the age of eighteen, she was a graceful, self-assured young woman. Throughout her reign, she maintained a sense of dignity and decorum that restored the average person's high opinion of the monarchy after a series of dissolute, ineffectual leaders. (Today, the term *Victorian* is often associated with extreme or hypocritical prudery. However, that fact probably has more to do with middle-class attitudes in Victorian England than with the character of Victoria herself.) In 1840, Victoria married a German prince, Albert of Saxe-Coburg-Gotha, who became not king, but prince consort. Together, Victoria and Albert set a standard of national pride and optimism that influenced their subjects to bring about enormous changes in the world. However, England's political leadership lay not with them but with the prime ministers and the elected members of the two bodies of Parliament, the House of Commons and the House of Lords.

THE GROWTH OF THE BRITISH EMPIRE

During the Victorian Era, England grew to become the most powerful nation on earth, ruler of a vast empire on which, in the words of Prime Minister Benjamin Disraeli, the

LITERARY EVENTS

➤ = British Events

➤1843. William Wordsworth becomes poet laureate

➤1847. Charlotte Brontë publishes *Jane Eyre;* Emil Brontë publishes *Wuthering Heights*

1848. Marx and Engels publish *The Communist Manifesto*

➤ 1850. Alfred Tennyson publishes *In Memoriam* becomes poet laureate

1830 | 1835 | 1840 | 1845 | 1850

HISTORICAL EVENTS

➤1832. First Reform Act extends suffrage to more men

➤1833. Abolitionists earn victory; Britain abolishes slavery within empire

➤1834. Poor-Law-Amendment Act extends use of workhouses

➤1837. Chartist Movement begins

➤1837. Victoria ascends throne; reigns until 1901

➤1840. Victoria marries Prince Albert

➤1842–45. Corn Laws are repealed

➤1844. YMCA is founded

➤1845. Beginning of Great Potato Famine in Ireland

➤ 1848. Dante Gabrielle Rossetti and friends found Pre-Raphaelite Brotherhood

➤ 1848. Public Health Act improves sanitation, drinking water

➤1850. Public Librarie Act establishes librari

➤1851. Great Exhibition is held

sun never set. Its dominions included the relatively independent and self-governing countries of Canada, Australia, and New Zealand, as well as imperial colonies in Hong Kong, Singapore, South Africa, Rhodesia (modern Zimbabwe), Kenya, Cyprus, British Guyana, Ceylon, and, the "jewel in the British crown," India (modern India, Pakistan, and Bangladesh).

The origins of **British Imperialism** lay in the defeat, during the Elizabethan Era, of the Spanish Armada, a defeat which made England the undisputed master of the seas. During the centuries that followed, England built a large navy and merchant fleet for purposes of trade and colonization. England imported raw materials from overseas, such as cotton from the Americas and silk from China, and exported finished goods made in British factories. By the middle of the eighteenth century, England was the largest exporter and importer, the primary manufacturer, and the wealthiest country in the world.

British dominion over much of the globe led to what most modern people would consider an overweening optimism, smugness, and arrogance among well-to-do English men and women. Many came to believe that it was their country's destiny and duty to bring English values, laws, customs, and religion to poor, benighted "savage races." The British poet **Rudyard Kipling** voiced the prejudices and the uneasiness of many of his countrymen about the costs of the Empire when he wrote,

Take up the White Man's burden—
Send forth the best ye breed—
Go bind your sons to exile
To serve your captives' need;
To wait in heavy harness,
On fluttered folk and wild—
Your new-caught, sullen peoples,
Half devil and half child.

Queen Victoria of England. *Sir George Hayter, 1838. The Granger Collection, NY.*

▶1865. Lewis Carroll publishes *Alice in Wonderland*
▶1864. Robert Browning publishes *The Ring and the Book*
▶1862. Christina Rossetti publishes *Goblin Market and Other Poems*
▶1861. Charles Dickens publishes *Great Expectations*
▶1860. George Eliot publishes *The Mill on the Floss* and *Silas Marner*
▶1857. Matthew Arnold becomes professor of poetry at Oxford
▶1869. John Stuart Mill publishes *On the Subjection of Women*

1855 1860 1865 1870 1875

▶1854–55. Britain fights against Russia in Crimean War
▶1857. British put down rebellion in India
▶1859. Darwin publishes *The Origin of Species*
▶1860. Florence Nightingale founds nursing school
1861. U.S. Civil War begins
▶1867. Suffrage is extended to more men
▶1869. Debtor's prisons are abolished
▶1871. Trade Union Act legalizes union organizing

CROSS-CURRICULAR ACTIVITIES

Social Studies. Have students research the concept of *colonialism.* Students may wish to choose one country that has been colonized by England. How did the British profit from colonization? What were the consequences for the colonized country? They should report on how, when, and why the country threw off British rule, if it did do so, and the contemporary situation in the country.

BIOGRAPHICAL NOTE

Sir Henry Morton Stanley (1841–1904) is famed as an explorer, the rescuer of David Livingstone and Elmin Pasha, and a personification of British Imperialism. It has been suggested that British Imperialism was most effective not in spreading the British political system, religion, and morals, but in spreading its consumer culture; both Stanley's work *In Darkest Africa* and his role as one of the first product endorsers lend this theory some credence. You might ask students to read selections from *In Darkest Africa.* Tell them to note Stanley's treatment of fellow human beings and the numerous product references. Ask them, "To what extent was the rescue of Elmin Pasha a media event?" (You might want to inform them that when Elmin Pasha was "rescued," he was content, was better supplied than Stanley, and seemed surprised to find that he was in need of rescue.)

Quotables

"Dr. Livingston, I presume?"
—Sir Henry Morton Stanley

CROSS-CURRICULAR ACTIVITIES

MIGRATION. Have students conduct a study of urban migration in Victorian England. They should determine percentages of population affected and show the shift on a graph. Interested students can prepare maps showing patterns of migration.

CROSS-CULTURAL CONNECTIONS

HISTORY. Throughout much of the Victorian Period, two categories of courts existed in England. The first, Courts of Common Law, dealt with criminal suits, such as murder, theft, or robbery. The second, Courts of Chancery, decided suits based on Equity rather than the Common Law. Such suits included legacy, trust, and mortgage disputes. Until the court was reformed in the second half of the nineteenth century, obtaining a decision through the Court of Chancery was an unwieldy, time-consuming, and expensive process. (Some cases lasted well over fifty years.) Dickens became involved in Chancery when he sued publishers for breach of copyright. The suit was more financially draining than it was rewarding. Dickens's *Bleak House*, with its famed *Jarndyce and Jarndyce* suit caught in Chancery, was based on Dickens's own experience with this legal institution.

Much of the history of the twentieth century has been one of undoing the ugly legacy of European colonialism in the nineteenth century.

THE INDUSTRIAL REVOLUTION AND ITS CONSEQUENCES

The **Industrial Revolution** that gave rise to the modern era began in the late 1700s with the invention of machines for weaving, including the spinning jenny and the power loom. Gradually, a **factory system** emerged in England that supplied much of the rest of the world with finished goods. English textile factories had to be supplied with coal and iron, so mining increased, and the canal and railway systems were developed. The coming of factories meant a dramatic shift in the English economy away from agriculture and toward the production of manufactured goods. Millions of people left the land and crowded into factory towns and mill towns. The old landed gentry, the aristocracy of former days, lost power, which shifted almost completely into the hands of factory owners and merchants. England made great progress during this period in developing the tools and techniques of mass production, which were brilliantly displayed in the **Great Exhibition of 1851.** The exhibition was organized by Prince Albert and housed in a marvel of modern architecture, a **Crystal Palace** of glass and iron. Visitors to the exhibition had a chance to see, firsthand, the machines that were making over the modern world, such as hydraulic presses, locomotives, power looms, reapers, and steamboats.

Industrialization in England, perhaps because it occurred there first, was attended by great social evils. While vast wealth was concentrated in a few hands, most laboring people lived in poverty. Children as young as five years old worked sixteen-hour days in factories and mines. Cities grew beyond their means, and sprawling, vermin-ridden slums appeared. Clean drinking water often could not be found, epidemics of cholera killed hundreds of thousands of people, and hunger was more common than uncommon. Such conditions bred crime and moral license. They also bred reform.

SOCIAL AND POLITICAL REFORM

The terrible conditions among the working poor in England during the Victorian Age might well have brought about bloody revolution, as they did in France at the end of the preceding century, if not for a long series of social and political reforms aimed at improving those conditions. In 1832, the **First Reform Act** was passed, extending the

LITERARY EVENTS

➤ = British Events

1880. Russian Feodor Dostoevsky publishes *The Brothers Karamazov*

➤1891. Thomas Hardy publishes *Tess of the D'Urbervilles*

➤1896. A. E. Housman publishes *A Shropshire Lad*

1880 — 1885 — 1890 — 1895 — 1900

➤1878. Salvation Army is founded

➤1879. Zulus war against British in South Africa

➤1882. Married Woman's Property Act allows women in England to possess property of their own

➤1884. William Morris founds The Socialist League

➤1888. Notorious murders by Jack the Ripper occur

➤1901. Queen Victoria dies

HISTORICAL EVENTS

vote to most middle-class men. In 1833, Britain abolished slavery in all of its colonies and passed a **Factory Act** regulating child labor. In 1834, the **Poor-Law-Amendment Act** applied to all of England a system of workhouses for indigent people, but conditions in the workhouses tended to be miserable, and poverty continued to be a major social problem. In 1842, 1845, and 1846, conservative Prime Minister **Robert Peel**, reacting to the hunger and social unrest at home and to Ireland's **Great Famine** of 1845, pushed through legislation repealing the so-called **Corn Laws** that placed high tariffs on imported grain and kept the price of bread artificially high. Other **Reform Bills** passed in 1867 and 1884–85 extended the vote to almost all English men. In 1869, debtors' prisons were abolished, and nearly universal primary education was instituted. In 1871, the **Trade Union Act** made it legal for laborers to organize to protect their rights. Throughout the Victorian Era, various laws were passed regulating food, drugs, and sanitation. One important force for social change was the **Chartist Movement**, begun in 1837. The Chartists took their name from a document called the **People's Charter**, which called for widespread political reforms, including universal male suffrage and vote by ballot.

Religious Movements in Victorian England

Much of the character of the Victorian Age can be attributed to the **Evangelical Movement**, which emphasized a Protestant faith in personal salvation through Christ. The Evangelical Movement swept through England, winning much of the population to its vision of a life lived according to a strict moral code. The movement led to an enormous outpouring of philanthropic and charitable work and to the foundation of both the **Salvation Army** and the **Young Men's Christian Association**, or **YMCA.**

In contrast to the strict Protestantism of the Evangelicals, the members of the **Oxford Movement**, or **Tractarians**, sought to bring the official English Anglican Church closer in rituals and beliefs to Roman Catholicism. The primary spokesperson for this movement, **John Henry Newman** (1801–1890), later converted to Catholicism, took holy orders, and was elevated to the position of cardinal.

Another religious thinker influential during the Victorian Era was **William Paley**, who lived in the preceding era but whose works struck a chord with Victorians. In his ***Natural Theology*** (1802), Paley presented the so-called **argument from design**. According to Paley, a person picking up a watch on the street can tell by the complexity and intricacy of its design that it must have had a maker. Similarly, one who observes the complexity and intricacy of nature may conclude that it, as well, had a maker—God.

Other Currents of Victorian Thought

The Victorian Age was a time of vigorous, intense intellectual activity in England. Leading thinkers of the period included the following:

John Stuart Mill (1806–1873), philosopher and social critic, popularized the **Utilitarianism** of the philosopher **Jeremy Bentham**, arguing that the object of moral action was to bring about "the greatest good for the greatest number" of people. Mill also championed **Liberalism**, arguing that governments had the right to restrict the actions of individuals only when those actions harmed others and that society should use its collective resources to provide for the basic welfare of its members. In ***The Subjection of Women***, Mill argues that women should be treated as equals under the law and provided with opportunities for education.

CROSS-CULTURAL CONNECTIONS

Social Studies. In 1867, working men in England began to receive the attention of the British ruling class. This is the year that Benjamin Disraeli, the leader of Parliament's Conservative party (formerly Tory party), introduced a new and radical bill that allowed urban workmen the right to vote on government issues. Disraeli believed that this would encourage support for the Conservative party. He reasoned that the workers would want to vote against the party to which most of their employers belonged—the Liberal party. He also reasoned that they would vote for the Conservative party out of appreciation for being given the right to vote. A few years later the leader of the Liberal party, William Ewart Gladstone, extended the same right to agricultural laborers. Gladstone expected that these people would naturally want to vote against the Conservative party because most of their landlord employers belonged to this party. Although instigated as part of competition between political parties, a workingman's right to vote was established in England.

CROSS-CURRICULAR ACTIVITIES

DARWINISM. Darwin's theory of the evolution of species did not appear out of a vacuum. The idea was on par with much of contemporary Victorian thought. The favored theory of governmental *laissez faire* espoused that the strong would survive and that a vital economy was one in which competition was unchecked, a "survival of the fittest," in a sense. Invite students to compare Darwin's theory of natural selection, as described in *The Origin of Species* (1859), and Adam Smith's theory of the invisible hand, as described in *The Wealth of Nations* (1776), with Victorian ideas about *laissez faire* capitalism.

Charles Darwin. *The Granger Collection, NY.*

Charles Lyell (1797–1875) wrote an influential work, ***Principles of Geology***, that showed that geological features on Earth had developed continuously and slowly over immense periods of time. Lyell's **Gradualism** provided an alternative to the **Catastrophism** of such nineteenth-century scientists as the French naturalist **George Cuvier**.

Charles Darwin (1809–1882) advanced in his book ***The Origin of Species*** the not-entirely-new idea that the earth's many species of animals and plants had evolved, over time, from common ancestors. The idea had been advanced by Darwin's grandfather, Erasmus, and was separately arrived at by the biologist Alfred Wallace. Darwin's chief contribution to **evolutionary theory** was the mechanism that he provided to explain it. Darwin found his explanation in the writings of **Thomas Malthus** (1766–1834), who argued in his ***Essay on the Principle of Population*** that populations naturally increase geometrically, while available resources increase only arithmetically. This leads to fierce competition for resources and inevitably to famine, disease, and war. According to Darwin, species changed, or evolved, as a result of such competition. In every generation of individuals, there were random variations. Fierce competition for limited resources led to the selective **survival of the fittest**—those creatures best suited to taking advantage of the available resources.

Herbert Spencer (1820–1903) attempted to apply the ideas of Darwin to many areas of human endeavor and thought. Proponents of Spencer's **Social Darwinism** held that in human society, as in nature, survival properly belonged to the fittest—those most able to survive. Social Darwinism was used by many Victorians to justify inequalities based on race, social or economic class, and gender.

The Social Darwinists championed not only the ideas of Spencer, but also those of the eighteenth-century economist Adam Smith. Smith held that the best government economic policy was to leave the market alone, to follow a ***laissez-faire*** or "let it be" policy of little or no government intervention. Followers of Mill and other Liberals argued that government did have a proper role in protecting the weak against the strong, the poor against the wealthy. Still more radical thinkers, the Socialists, believed in far-reaching government control and in the abolition of private property in favor of publicly or communally owned lands and businesses. These debates about the proper role of government in public affairs continue into our own time.

Another Victorian-Era debate that has continued into our own time is the one generated by the theory of evolution. In Victorian times, this theory presented for many people a crisis of faith, for it contradicted widely held beliefs, such as the idea expressed by Archbishop Ussher that the world had been created in 4004 BC. Then, as now, many people followed the line of the poet Alfred, Lord Tennyson, who struggled toward a middle path, one that would reconcile his faith with the discoveries of science.

CURRENTS IN VICTORIAN LITERATURE: REALISM AND NATURALISM

In response to the difficult conditions in many of England's cities during the Victorian Era, a new style of literary expression was born: **Realism**. Realism is the attempt to render in art or literature an accurate portrayal of reality. Although the development of the novel in the eighteenth century, with its detailed descriptions of characters and settings, could be considered Realist, literary historians usually apply the term to works of the late nineteenth century that deal with the harsher details of ordinary lives.

As literacy became more common among the middle class, the popularity of the novel increased dramatically. Realistic, detailed descriptions of everyday life, and especially of its darker aspects, appealed to many readers, disillusioned by the "progress"

The Heart of the Empire. Niels Moiler Lund. Guildhall Art Gallery, London.

going on around them. Topics in Realist writing included families, religion, and social reform.

Another literary movement founded in the Victorian Age was **Naturalism**. Naturalism is based on the philosophical theory that actions and events are determined, not by human intentions, but by largely uncontrollable external forces. Naturalist writers, like Realists, chose subjects and themes common to the lower and middle classes. They were also attentive to details, striving for accuracy and authenticity in their descriptions. Naturalism had its greatest influence in France and in the United States. However, there are Naturalist elements in the works of the English poet and novelist **Thomas Hardy**, whose characters are typically hapless victims of fate.

The Novel in Victorian England

In the early part of the Victorian Age, there was still a flavor of Romanticism in the novels being written. Works such as **Emily Brontë's *Wuthering Heights*** (1847) and **Charlotte Brontë's *Jane Eyre*** (1847) contained many elements of the passionate and the mysterious and made use of Gothic settings.

Charles Dickens (1812–1870), perhaps the most famous of the Victorian novelists, was wildly popular in his day. Many of his novels were published in serial form in monthly magazine installments or in magazines. This form of publication, and his comic and sentimental descriptions of the lives of people of diverse occupations and social classes, gave Dickens an exceptionally large and varied audience. Novels such as ***A Christmas Carol*** (1843), ***David Copperfield*** (1850), and ***Great Expectations*** (1861) are typical of Dickens's fiction in their attacks on social indifference to poverty and injustice, their comic invention, and their call on charity and love to resolve, or at least to alleviate, the troubles of the Victorian Age.

SELECTION CHECK TEST 4.9.1 WITH ANSWERS

Checking Your Reading

Political Developments in the Romantic Era

1. Identify three countries/imperial colonies ruled by Britain during the Victorian Age. **Responses will vary but could include Canada, Australia, New Zealand, Hong Kong, Singapore, South Africa, Rhodesia/Zimbabwe, Kenya, Cyprus, British Guyana, Ceylon, or India/Pakistan/Bangladesh.**
2. How did Queen Victoria restore the average person's high regard for the monarchy? **Responses may vary but could note that she was an effective ruler who followed a series of ineffective rulers, or that she behaved with dignity and decorum.**
3. How did industrialization shift power away from the aristocracy? **Agriculture waned and people left the land to work in cities, shifting power to factory owners.**
4. What was displayed in the Crystal Palace at the Great Exhibition of 1851? **The great machines "that were taking over the world" were displayed.**
5. What is Social Darwinism? **This is the belief that the law of "survival of the fittest" applies to human society as well as to nature.**

Social Movements during the Victorian Age

Fill in the blanks using the following terms. You will not use every term, and you may use some terms more than once.

Catastrophism Gradualism
Liberalism Chartist Movement
Evangelical Movement Utilitarianism
Industrialization

1. The **Evangelical Movement** led to an increase in charitable work, including the establishment of the Salvation Army and the YMCA.
2. **Gradualism** argued that geological features on Earth developed continuously over immense periods of time.
3. The **Chartist Movement** called for widespread political reforms.
4. Mill popularized **Utilitarianism**, arguing that moral action was that which brought about "the greatest good for the greatest number of people."
5. Much of the spirit of the Victorian Age arose from the **Evangelical Movement**, which emphasized faith in personal salvation through Christ.

SELECTION CHECK TEST 4.9.1 WITH ANSWERS (cont.)

Naturalism and Realism in Literature

The following elements and descriptors identify either Naturalistic or Realistic writing.
Put an (N) by those that are generally associated with Naturalism, an (R) by those that are generally associated with Realism, or (B) by any that apply to both.

__B__ 1. addressed themes that appealed to the lower and middle classes

__N__ 2. argued that humans had little control over the forces that shaped their lives

__N__ 3. had greater influence in France and the United States than in England

__B__ 4. known for attention to detail and authentic descriptions

__R__ 5. influenced poets such as the Brownings and Arnold, and the writer George Eliot

Quotables

"At length a caged goldfinch met his eye. The cage was a plain and small one, the shop humble, and on inquiry he concluded he could afford the modest sum asked. A sheet of newspaper was tied around the little creature's wire prison, and with the wrapped up cage in his hand Henchard sought a lodging for the night."

—Thomas Hardy

LITERARY NOTE

Many of Thomas Hardy's novels reveal his admiration for Shakespeare. Hardy shares Shakespeare's keen eye for life's tragic elements and his talent for emphasizing the grandeur of passion a character can reach when caught in the web of fate. There are many parallels in the two artists' work, and an excellent, if ambitious, project for a student would be to compare a work of Hardy to a work of Shakespeare. Hardy's *The Mayor of Casterbridge* is similar in characterization, theme, and tragic intensity to Shakespeare's *The Tragedy of King Lear.*

CROSS-CURRICULAR ACTIVITIES

Marketing. The Victorian Period was the age in which advertising as we know it first became an important industry. Many ideals that were important to Victorians can be seen in their advertising. The importance of family, British Imperialism, and Social Darwinism are revealed in period advertisements for products such as Pear's Soap, Eno's Fruit Salts, and even beef bullion. H. G. Wells's novel, *Tono-Bungay,* is an excellent satire of both the Victorian advertising industry and the unregulated "quack medicines" that produced much of this advertising. You might show students examples of Victorian advertisements, and read them some of the satirical advertisements Wells creates. Encourage a discussion on advertising in the Victorian Period and today. What elements of modern advertising stem from the Victorian Period? How has advertising changed? To what extent have our methods of representing the commercial object stayed the same?

The greatest novels in the Realist tradition produced during the period were those of **George Eliot** (1819–1880), author of ***Middlemarch*** and ***The Mill on the Floss***, and **Thomas Hardy**, author of ***Far from the Madding Crowd***, ***Tess of the D'Urbervilles***, and ***Jude the Obscure.*** Other famous novelists of the Victorian Era include William Makepeace Thackeray, Anthony Trollope, and Samuel Butler.

Caricature of Charles Dickens. *Alfred Bryan. The Pierpont Morgan Library, NY.*

Victorian Poetry

Even though the Victorian Age could well be called the "Age of the Novel," poetry was not a forgotten literary form. **Alfred, Lord Tennyson** (1809–1892) was the most popular poet of his time. Writing in the style of the Romantics, Tennyson produced long narrative poems, often on themes taken from classical myth or from medieval romance and legend. Gradually, the philosophies of Realism and Naturalism, propelled by reactions to the Industrial Revolution, insinuated their way into the poetry of the day.

The poets influenced by Realism include **Robert Browning** (1812–1889), **Elizabeth Barrett Browning** (1806–1861), and **Matthew Arnold** (1822–1888). In poems such as **"My Last Duchess"** and **"Andrea del Sarto,"** Robert Browning raised the **dramatic monologue** to great heights, making it a superb vehicle for deep psychological probing and character study. Elizabeth Barrett, the other half of one of literature's greatest love affairs, was the more prominent poet at the time of her elopement with Robert Browning in 1846. Her most well-known work is ***Sonnets from the Portuguese,*** a collection of love sonnets valued for their lyrical beauty, but she also wrote poetry on serious political themes, including **"Runaway Slave."** Arnold's **"Dover Beach"** (1867), partly written during his honeymoon, foreshadowed much of twentieth-century poetry with its ironic pathos, its concern with love as the only remedy for alienation, its use of literary allusion, and its compact, precise, plain language.

The Victorian Age closed with the dawn of the twentieth century. The Realism of the great literature of that time infuses the modern reader with a sense of what one's everyday life would be like in a time that seems so far away, yet in a sense is very near, for the issues that we continue to grapple with were born in that era.

ECHOES

VICTORIAN ENGLAND

The general average of mankind . . . have no tastes or wishes strong enough to incline them to do anything unusual, and they consequently do not understand those who have, and class all such with the wild and intemperate whom they are accustomed to look down upon. Now, in addition to this fact which is general, we have only to suppose that a strong movement has set in towards the improvement of morals, and it is evident what we have to expect. . . . much has actually been effected in the way of increased regularity of conduct, and discouragement of excesses; . . . . These tendencies of the times cause the public to be more disposed than at most former periods to prescribe general rules of conduct, and endeavor to make everyone conform to the approved standard. . . . Its ideal of character is to be without any marked character, to maim by compression, like a Chinese lady's foot, every part of human nature which stands out prominently.

—John Stuart Mill, *On Liberty*

Fair, Quiet and Sweet Rest, [detail] c. 1900s. Luke Fildes. Warrington Museum & Art Gallery, Lancs.

When I was young, it was not thought proper for young ladies to study very conspicuously; and especially with pen in hand. Young ladies (at least in provincial towns) were expected to sit down in the parlor to sew,—during which reading aloud was permitted,—or to practice their music. . . . Jane Austen herself, the Queen of novelists . . . was compelled by the feelings of her family to cover up her manuscripts with a large piece of muslin work.

—Harriet Martineau, *Autobiography*

ADDITIONAL QUESTIONS AND ACTIVITIES

Have students read the quotations carefully. Then, ask them to think about how social pressures restrict people's freedom. Does it seem to them that these pressures were greater in Victorian England than they are today? Ask them what restrictions are placed on their liberty. Which of these restrictions are in place because of age, because of gender, or for other reasons?

PREREADING

"The Lady of Shalott"
"Ulysses"
FROM In Memoriam

BY ALFRED, LORD TENNYSON

About the AUTHOR

Alfred, Lord Tennyson (1809–1892) was born into a family of twelve children. While still in his teens, he collaborated with two of his brothers on a book of verse that was published in 1827. He attended Cambridge University, where he won a Chancellor's medal for poetry and joined a group of talented undergraduates who called themselves the Apostles. One member of this group, Arthur Hallam, became Tennyson's best friend. In 1833, Hallam died suddenly, sending Tennyson into a deep depression. In the decade that followed, Tennyson fell in love with Emily Sellwood but was unable to marry because of poverty. In 1850 his fortunes changed. In that year, England's poet laureate, William Wordsworth, died, and Tennyson was named to replace him. Tennyson married Emily, and his fame as a poet grew steadily. In 1884 he was made a peer. His work, which often dealt with patriotic themes and subjects from medieval romance, was enormously popular. When the much-loved, legendary poet died, he was buried in Westminster Abbey.

About the SELECTIONS

"The Lady of Shalott" tells a story set in the legendary days of King Arthur and his Knights of the Round Table. The city of Camelot, mentioned repeatedly in the poem, was the capital of Arthur's kingdom. Sir Lancelot, also mentioned, was one of Arthur's most capable knights.

Ulysses was the Roman name of Odysseus, a hero from those ancient Greek epic poems attributed to Homer, the *Iliad* and the *Odyssey*. Ulysses fought in the Trojan War and returned to his kingdom, Ithaca. On the decade-long return journey, he saw many strange lands and had many marvelous, heroic adventures. In Tennyson's poem **"Ulysses,"** the aged king Ulysses longs for one last adventure to culminate his career.

In Memoriam is an elegy written by Tennyson over the course of seventeen years, in response to the death of his friend Arthur Hallam. The poem is a moving record of Tennyson's struggle through loss, grief, and doubt toward spiritual renewal.

ADDITIONAL RESOURCES

UNIT 9 RESOURCE BOOK

"The Lady of Shalott"
- Selection Worksheet 9.1
- Selection Check Test 4.9.3
- Selection Test 4.9.4

"Ulysses"
- Selection Worksheet 9.2
- Selection Check Test 4.9.5
- Selection Test 4.9.6

From In Memoriam
- Selection Worksheet 9.3
- Selection Check Test 4.9.7
- Selection Test 4.9.8
- Language, Grammar, and Style Resource 1.23
- Speaking and Listening Resource 5.39

INDIVIDUAL LEARNING STRATEGIES

MOTIVATION
"The Lady of Shalott" is an excellent poem for reading aloud. Have a different person read each line of each stanza, except for the fifth and ninth lines, which are refrains. When you come to these refrain lines, read them together. You may wish to have students do this activity in small groups.

READING PROFICIENCY
Explain that some writers retain the now obsolete practice of ending some verbs with –th rather than –s. Examples in the poem include hath rather than has and weaveth rather than weaves. The old-fashioned verbs are appropriate for the medieval setting of the poem.

ENGLISH LANGUAGE LEARNING
In addition to following the suggestions for Reading Proficiency, share with students the following additional vocabulary.
casement—window frame
reaper—fieldworker
damsels—young ladies
bowshot—distance an arrow could fly
bower—lady's room or apartment within a house

SPECIAL NEEDS
Work with students to help them fill out the graphic organizer in Literary Tools.

ENRICHMENT

Have students debate in class the proper relationship of the artist to the rest of the world. Pose the following questions:
1. Should artists devote themselves entirely to art

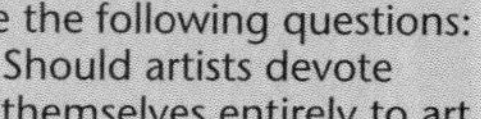

INDIVIDUAL LEARNING STRATEGIES (CONT.)

and remain aloof from the world, or should they have ordinary careers and do their artwork on the side?
2. Which is a better story, one written primarily to teach a lesson or one written primarily to entertain? Which is a better painting, one created to communicate a message or one created simply to be beautiful?
3. Do governments or communities have the right to censor art that does not present ideas or attitudes that most people consider acceptable?

The Lady of Shalott

ALFRED, LORD TENNYSON

Part 1

On either side the river lie
Long fields of barley and of rye,
That clothe the wold[1] and meet the sky;
And through the field the road runs by
To many-towered Camelot;
And up and down the people go,
Gazing where the lilies blow
Round an island there below,
The island of Shalott.

What grows on either side of the river? What runs through the field?

What city lies in the distance? What is the name of the island in the river?

Willows whiten, aspens quiver,
Little breezes dusk and shiver
Through the wave that runs forever
By the island in the river
Flowing down to Camelot.
Four gray walls, and four gray towers,
Overlook a space of flowers,
And the silent isle imbowers[2]
The Lady of Shalott.

Who is in the castle?

By the margin, willow-veiled,
Slide the heavy barges trailed
By slow horses; and unhailed
The shallop[3] flitteth silken-sailed
Skimming down to Camelot:
But who hath seen her wave her hand?
Or at the casement seen her stand?
Or is she known in all the land,

1. **wold.** Plains
2. **imbowers.** Encloses or shelters
3. **shallop.** Open boat

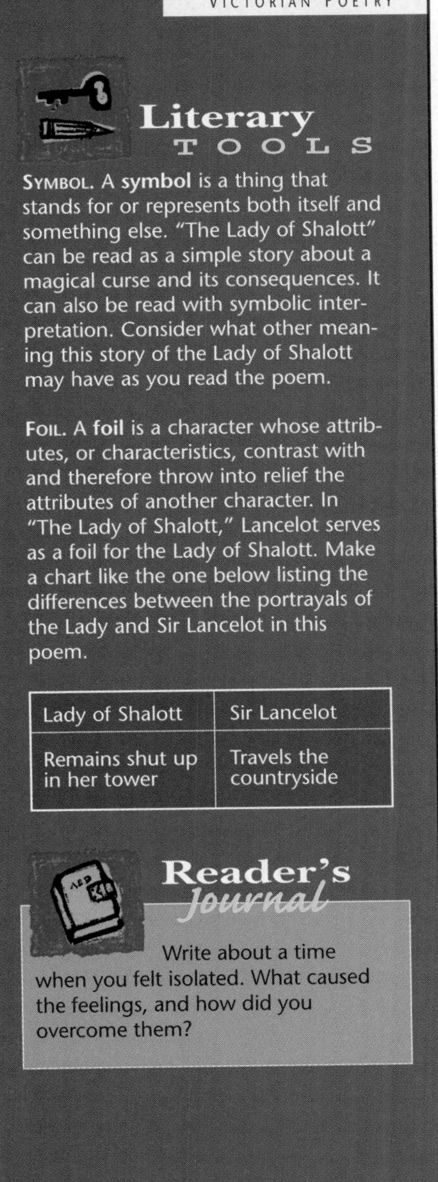

Literary TOOLS

SYMBOL. A **symbol** is a thing that stands for or represents both itself and something else. "The Lady of Shalott" can be read as a simple story about a magical curse and its consequences. It can also be read with symbolic interpretation. Consider what other meaning this story of the Lady of Shalott may have as you read the poem.

FOIL. A **foil** is a character whose attributes, or characteristics, contrast with and therefore throw into relief the attributes of another character. In "The Lady of Shalott," Lancelot serves as a foil for the Lady of Shalott. Make a chart like the one below listing the differences between the portrayals of the Lady and Sir Lancelot in this poem.

Lady of Shalott	Sir Lancelot
Remains shut up in her tower	Travels the countryside

Reader's Journal

Write about a time when you felt isolated. What caused the feelings, and how did you overcome them?

ANSWERS TO GUIDED READING QUESTIONS

1. Fields of barley and rye grow on either side of the river. The road to Camelot runs through the field.
2. The city of Camelot lies in the distance. The name of the island is Shalott.
3. The Lady of Shalott lives in the castle.

GRAPHIC ORGANIZER ANSWERS

LADY OF SHALOTT
Is seen by no one
Lives among shadows
Lives in fear of a curse
Has no loyal knight
Sings a "mournful, holy" carol, which is her last song

SIR LANCELOT
Is bright and shining like a "burning flame"—probably calling much attention and admiration
Lives in the dazzling sun and glowing sunlight
Is "bold" and his bridle bells ring "merrily"—he has no fears and seems blessed by the world
His shield shows a knight "forever" kneeling before a lady, suggesting that Sir Lancelot serves many noble ladies
Sings gaily, "Tirra lirra"

READER'S JOURNAL

Ask students if they know what it is like to feel cut off from the rest of the world or to feel as though life were passing them by. They can freewrite about these feelings in their journal, but need not share their writing with anyone else in the class.

GOALS/OBJECTIVES

Studying this lesson will enable students to
- enjoy lyric poetry and empathize with the isolation of the artist in society
- describe Alfred, Lord Tennyson's literary accomplishments and explain the historical significance of his writings
- define *symbol* and recognize and interpret symbols in a poem
- define *foil* and recognize foils in their reading

ANSWERS TO GUIDED READING QUESTIONS

1. The presence of a "fairy Lady" suggests that the story is about supernatural or magical occurrences.
2. Night and day, the Lady weaves a magic web. She is under a curse that forbids her to look out the window toward Camelot. She doesn't know the exact nature of the curse (i.e., she doesn't know what will happen if she does look toward Camelot).
3. The Lady sees the world indirectly, viewing its reflection in a mirror. She doesn't look out the window and view the world directly because the curse forbids her to do so.

VOCABULARY FROM THE SELECTION

ambling
countenance
wane

LITERARY NOTE

Biographical Criticism. "The Lady of Shalott" can be read as an allegory about an important issue in Tennyson's own life. After he became poet laureate in 1850, Tennyson was expected to write works that treated social and political themes, and he had responsibilities that necessarily involved him in the affairs of the country. Tennyson's later works, such as "The Charge of the Light Brigade," tended toward **didacticism**—the teaching of moral lessons related to human affairs such as soldierly duty. "The Lady of Shalott" shows that Tennyson had reservations about such engagement in worldly matters. In the poem, when the artist enters the world her art is destroyed and she dies. On the other hand, the poem shows the life of the unengaged, isolated artist to be unsatisfying, one of shadows and reflections rather than reality. In his own life, Tennyson opted for engaging in the world and for producing art that served the public good, but some critics would argue that he did so at a price, that his later didactic works do not reach the same high artistic level of his ear-lier, less worldly poetry, of which "The Lady of Shalott" is an example. Refer to *didacticism* in the Handbook of Literary Terms.

The Lady of Shalott?
Only reapers, reaping early
In among the bearded barley,
Hear a song that echoes cheerly
From the river winding clearly,
Down to towered Camelot;
And by the moon the reaper weary,
Piling sheaves in uplands airy,
Listening, whispers " 'Tis the fairy
Lady of Shalott."

What tells you that you are reading a story about magical occurrences?

Part 2

There she weaves by night and day
A magic web with colors gay.
She has heard a whisper say,
A curse is on her if she stay
To look down to Camelot.
She knows not what the curse may be,
And so she weaveth steadily,
And little other care hath she,
The Lady of Shalott.

What does the Lady do night and day? What curse is on her?

And moving through a mirror clear[4]
That hangs before her all the year,
Shadows of the world appear.
There she sees the highway near
Winding down to Camelot;
There the river eddy whirls,
And there the surly village churls,[5]
And the red cloaks of market girls,
Pass onward from Shalott.

By what means does the Lady see what is happening in the world? Why doesn't she just look out the window and view the world directly?

Sometimes a troop of damsels glad,
An abbot on an ambling pad,[6]
Sometimes a curly shepherd lad,

4. **mirror clear.** Weavers often use mirrors to see the progress of their work.
5. **churls.** Peasants
6. **pad.** Horse with an easy pace

Words for Everyday Use

am • bling (am′ bliŋ) *part.*, moving with a smooth, easy gait. *The ambling hitchhiker stopped to put out his thumb when he heard a car approaching.*

CROSS-CURRICULAR CONNECTION

Art. Explain to students that in the late nineteenth century, a great debate raged over the role of art in human life. The literary critic Matthew Arnold argued that art presents a "criticism of life" and thus serves a moral and social purpose. In contrast, the art critic Walter Pater argued that art exists for its own sake, that its value lies not in moral or social lessons but rather in its beauty or aesthetic value.

During the early twentieth century, many artists accepted the "art for art's sake" position. They believed that artists should live apart from the ordinary world and devote themselves entirely to art. In France, especially, artists adopted "bohemian" lifestyles. They shunned middle-class occupations, habits, and dress. They kept company with other artists in cafés and salons and created the modern conception of artists as a breed apart, concerned only with beauty and not with moral, social, or political affairs.

Or long-haired page in crimson clad,
Goes by to towered Camelot;
And sometimes through the mirror blue
The knights come riding two and two:
She hath no loyal knight and true,
The Lady of Shalott.

But in her web she still delights
To weave the mirror's magic sights,
For often through the silent nights
A funeral, with plumes and lights
And music, went to Camelot;
Or when the moon was overhead,
Came two young lovers lately wed:
"I am half sick of shadows," said
The Lady of Shalott.

Is there a mate in the Lady's life? How do you know?

What causes the Lady to say that she is "half sick of shadows"? What does she see that fills her with yearning?

Part 3

A bowshot from her bower eaves,
He rode between the barley sheaves,
The sun came dazzling through the leaves,
And flamed upon the brazen greaves[7]
Of bold Sir Lancelot.
A red-cross knight forever kneeled
To a lady in his shield,
That sparkled on the yellow field,
Beside remote Shalott.

How is Sir Lancelot described? What about him would be attractive to the Lady?

The gemmy bridle glittered free,
Like to some branch of stars we see
Hung in the golden Galaxy.
The bridle bells rang merrily
As he rode down to Camelot;
And from his blazoned baldric[8] slung
A mighty silver bugle hung,
And as he rode his armor rung,
Beside remote Shalott.

All in the blue unclouded weather
Thick-jeweled shone the saddle leather,
The helmet and the helmet-feather

7. **greaves.** Pieces of armor that protect the lower leg
8. **baldric.** An ornamented belt used to support a sword or bugle

ANSWERS TO GUIDED READING QUESTIONS

1. No, the poem says she has no loyal and true knight.
2. In her mirror, the Lady sees the reflection, or the "shadow," of two newlyweds. Seeing them fills her with yearning. She seems to wish that she, too, could have a mate and be wed.
3. He is described as bold and chivalrous. His shield shows a knight kneeling before a lady.

LITERARY NOTE

Lancelot is the hero of many medieval romances. For example, he figures prominently in Sir Thomas Malory's Le Morte d'Arthur. (See page 199.) The Lady in "The Lady of Shalott" is based on Elaine of Astolat. According to Arthurian legend, Elaine of Astolat fell in love with Lancelot, but her love was not returned. She died of unrequited love and, as she had requested, she was placed in a boat in the Thames and was steered down that river to Camelot.

In the romances, Lancelot is a nearly perfect knight, handsome, brave, strong, courteous, persevering, and devout. However, he has some failings that keep him from being pure enough to achieve the Holy Grail. That feat is accomplished by Galahad, the most perfect of all the knights of medieval legend.

ANSWERS TO GUIDED READING QUESTIONS

1. The Lady of Shalott looks out because she hears Lancelot singing and wants to see him. She probably takes the risk because she is "sick of shadows."
2. Her web flies out and floats wide. Perhaps it flies through the window. Her mirror breaks.
3. The Lady finds a boat and writes on the prow: *The Lady of Shalott.*

CROSS-CURRICULAR ACTIVITIES

Social Studies. Suggest that students work in a small group to research historical aspects of medieval England. Of special interest might be the role of women. Excellent sources of information on medieval women include the following:

Thiébaux, Marcelle. *The Writings of Medieval Women.* 1994.

Klapisch-Zuber, Christiane, ed. *Silences of the Middle Ages.* Vol. 2. *A History of Women.* Ed. Georges Duby and Michelle Perrot. 1992.

Power, Eileen. *Medieval People.* 1965.

LITERARY TECHNIQUE

Refrain. A **refrain** is a line or group of lines repeated in a poem or song. What refrains appear in "The Lady of Shalott"? How are these refrains varied throughout the poem? What effect does this use of refrains have on the sound of the poem? What other techniques does Tennyson use in this poem to give it a musical quality?

Answers

The refrains in "The Lady of Shalott" include "To many-towered Camelot," "The island of Shalott," "Flowing down to Camelot," "The Lady of Shalott," "Skimming down to Camelot," "Down to towered Camelot," "To look down to Camelot," "Winding down to Camelot," "Pass onward from Shalott," "Goes by to towered Camelot," "And music, went to Camelot," "Of bold Sir Lance-lot," "Beside remote Shalott," "As he rode down to Camelot," "Moves over still Shalott," "Sang Sir Lancelot," "She looked down to Camelot," "Over towered Camelot," "Did she look to Camelot," "She floated down to Camelot," "Turned to towered Camelot," "Silent into Camelot," and

Burned like one burning flame together,
 As he rode down to Camelot;
As often through the purple night,
Below the starry clusters bright,
Some bearded meteor, trailing light,
 Moves over still Shalott.

His broad clear brow in sunlight glowed;
On burnished hooves his war horse trode;
From underneath his helmet flowed
His coal-black curls as on he rode,
 As he rode down to Camelot.
From the bank and from the river
He flashed into the crystal mirror,
"Tirra lirra," by the river
 Sang Sir Lancelot.

Why does the Lady look out? Why does she take this risk?

She left the web, she left the loom,
She made three paces through the room,
She saw the water lily bloom,
She saw the helmet and the plume,
 She looked down to Camelot.
Out flew the web and floated wide;
The mirror cracked from side to side;
"The curse is come upon me," cried
 The Lady of Shalott.

What happens when the Lady turns her attention to the world?

Part 4

In the stormy east wind straining,
The pale yellow woods were waning,
The broad stream in his banks complaining,
Heavily the low sky raining
 Over towered Camelot;
Down she came and found a boat
Beneath a willow left afloat,
And round about the prow she wrote
 The Lady of Shalott.

What does the Lady do when she leaves the tower?

And down the river's dim expanse

Words for Everyday Use

wane (wān) *vi.,* lose strength. *The moon has passed full and is now in the waning phase.*

LITERARY TECHNIQUE (CONT.)

"All the knights at Camelot." The vast majority of the refrains are some variation of going down to Camelot and the Lady of Shalott. The refrains make the poem sound like a song and give a sense of inevitability to the end of the poem. Tennyson uses end rhyme to give this poem a musical quality.

The Lady of Shalott. John William Waterhouse. Tate Gallery, London.

Like some bold seër[9] in a trance,
Seeing all his own mischance—
With a glassy <u>countenance</u>
Did she look to Camelot.
And at the closing of the day
She loosed the chain, and down she lay;
The broad steam bore her far away,
The Lady of Shalott.

Lying, robed in snowy white
That loosely flew to left and right—
The leaves upon her falling light—
Through the noises of the night

9. **seër.** Prophet

WORDS FOR EVERYDAY USE

coun • te • nance (koun' tə nəns) *n.*, facial expression. *I could tell that he was furious with me when his <u>countenance</u> changed from a smile to a grimace.*

ART NOTE

Because of its vivid imagery, Tennyson's "The Lady of Shalott" inspired many illustrative paintings. One of the most famous is this work by **John William Waterhouse** (1849–1917). Waterhouse began his career painting in the Classical mode but developed a Romantic style in his mature years. His works were influenced by those of Dante Gabriel Rossetti and other members of the Pre-Raphaelite Brotherhood. The Pre-Raphaelites attempted to restore painting to an imagined purity that existed in the late Middle Ages and early Renaissance. They often treated medieval subjects in a highly Romantic manner tinged with mysticism. Ask students to identify Romantic elements in this painting, such as the three candles blowing in the wind and the wild disarray of the reeds, the trees, and the Lady's hair. Students might notice that two of the three candles are burned out, and the other is flickering. These candles may symbolize the Lady's life force, which is also flickering out. Students might also notice that the right-most scene on the tapestry draped over the boat is the picture of Lancelot as seen in the Lady's mirror.

CROSS-CURRICULAR ACTIVITIES

ART. Have students find other works of art that illustrate "The Lady of Shalott." Ask students to compare the imagery, mood, and other aspects of the painting with those of the poem. Students can also compare the works of art they find with the painting by Waterhouse on this page.

CROSS-CURRICULAR ACTIVITIES

APPLIED ARTS.

- Suggest that students conduct research into weaving. How does a loom work? How does one weave cloth? How much of the work is done by machines?
- Students may wish to invite a local weaver to demonstrate the process of weaving.

ANSWERS TO GUIDED READING QUESTIONS

1. The Lady sings her last song while floating down to Camelot. Her blood is slowly frozen and she dies.
2. The crowd is afraid of the Lady. Sir Lancelot says she is lovely and that God should bless her.

SELECTION CHECK TEST 4.9.3 WITH ANSWERS

Checking Your Reading

1. What do the reapers hear each morning? **They hear the Lady of Shalott singing.**
2. What does the Lady see in her mirror? **She sees shadows of the world.**
3. What does the Lady weave? **She weaves a web of the images she sees.**
4. How does the Lady cause the curse to fall on her? **She looks out a window.**
5. How does the Lady reach Camelot? **She lies down in a boat that drifts down the river.**

Literary Tools

1. A **symbol** represents
   a. an emotion
   b. the author's message
   c. the theme of a work
   d. itself and something else

2. A **foil** is a character who
   a. communicates the author's message
   b. solves the main conflict in the work
   c. creates problems for the protagonist
   d. contrasts with another character

3. In this poem, Lancelot
   a. is a foil
   b. narrates the story
   c. is the protagonist
   d. symbolizes evil

She floated down to Camelot;
And as the boat-head wound along
The willowy hills and fields among,
They heard her singing her last song,
The Lady of Shalott.

What does the Lady do in the boat? What happens to her?

Heard a carol, mournful, holy,
Chanted loudly, chanted lowly,
Till her blood was frozen slowly,
And her eyes were darkened wholly,
Turned to towered Camelot.
For ere she reached upon the tide
The first house by the waterside,
Singing in her song she died,
The Lady of Shalott.

Under tower and balcony,
By garden wall and gallery,
A gleaming shape she floated by,
Dead-pale between the houses high,
Silent into Camelot.
Out upon the wharfs they came,
Knight and burgher, lord and dame,
And round the prow they read her name,
The Lady of Shalott.

Who is this? and what is here?
And in the lighted palace near
Died the sound of royal cheer;
And they crossed themselves for fear,
All the knights at Camelot:
But Lancelot mused a little space;
He said, "She has a lovely face;
God in his mercy lend her grace,
The Lady of Shalott." ■

How does the crowd react on seeing the Lady? How does Sir Lancelot react?

Respond *to the* SELECTION

What are your feelings toward the Lady of Shalott? What might you say if you were one of the people who found her in her boat?

INVESTIGATE, Inquire, *Imagine*

Recall: GATHERING FACTS → **Interpret:** FINDING MEANING

1a. How does the Lady of Shalott see what is going on in the outside world? What art does the Lady practice? What does she portray in her art?

1b. How do the arts the Lady practices show her distance from the world?

2a. Whom does the Lady see just before going to the window and "looking down to Camelot"?

2b. What might have motivated the Lady to look toward Camelot despite the curse that is upon her?

3a. What happens to the Lady when she leaves the tower?

3b. How do the people respond when they see her in the boat?

Analyze: TAKING THINGS APART → **Synthesize:** BRINGING THINGS TOGETHER

4a. Compare and contrast the worlds of the Lady of Shalott and of the people outside her window.

4b. Do you think the Lady of Shalott was really cursed? Explain.

Evaluate: MAKING JUDGMENTS → **Extend:** CONNECTING IDEAS

5a. Judge whether the Lady of Shalott was ever content with her life.

5b. Why is isolation hard to bear? Why is human interaction important?

Understanding *Literature*

SYMBOL. Review the definition of **symbol** in the Handbook of Literary Terms. One interpretation of this poem views the Lady as representative of the artist who is removed from the world, viewing it in the mirror of his or her imagination. Following this interpretation, what might the Lady's web symbolize? What might the poem be saying about the world of imagination versus the world of reality?

FOIL. Review the definition of **foil** and the chart you made for Literary Tools in Prereading. Explain why the Lady and Sir Lancelot are foils for one another. What does Tennyson suggest about the differences between artists and "public people"?

RESPOND TO THE SELECTION

Students might also consider what questions they would have about this woman and her death.

ANSWERS TO INVESTIGATE, INQUIRE, IMAGINE

RECALL

1a. She sees the reflection of life in the mirror on her loom. She practices weaving, and portrays in her weaving "the mirror's magic sights," such as funerals or young lovers.

2a. She sees Sir Lancelot.

3a. When she leaves the tower, the Lady lies down in a boat and floats downriver to Camelot. Her blood freezes and she dies.

INTERPRET

Responses will vary.

1b. Her art is a reflection of a reflection, which shows how far removed from the world she is.

2b. The Lady may have fallen in love with Lancelot.

3b. The people are afraid of her and make the sign of the cross.

ANALYZE

4a. The people outside the tower live in an interactive social world, while the Lady of Shalott lives in a private, imaginative world.

SYNTHESIZE

4b. *Responses will vary.* Students may say that the Lady of Shalott's isolation was a kind of a curse. Others may suggest that the Lady made what was only a supposed curse come true.

EVALUATE

5a. *Responses will vary.* Students may suggest that the Lady of Shalott was never content because she always felt trapped by the curse. Others may suggest that for some time she was content, but became lonely upon seeing Lancelot and happy couples.

EXTEND

5b. *Responses will vary.* People are social beings. We need interaction with others. Even babies need human touch to grow healthy and happy. You may wish to ask students to distinguish between feeling lonely and being alone.

ANSWERS TO UNDERSTANDING LITERATURE

SYMBOL. The web is the Lady's interpretation of reality. The poem presents a paradox. On one hand, the Lady's art represents reality, but the only reality she experiences is that which she sees in a mirror. As in any reflection in a mirror, she views reality in reverse. On the other hand, when she leaves the tower and her world of imagination for the outside world, she dies.

FOIL. The Lady remains shut up in her tower, doing the same thing day after day, and only observes life in the reflection of a mirror. Lancelot travels the countryside having adventures.

The Lady and Lancelot seem to be exact opposites of one another. Stereotypically, artists are thought of as mysterious people who sit alone in a room with their imaginations so that they can create great works of art.

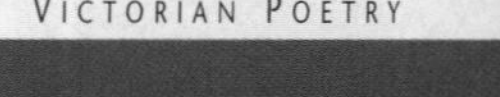

ANSWERS TO GUIDED READING QUESTIONS

1. Ulysses and his wife are getting older, he is dissatisfied with his isolated life as ruler of his people, and his life has none of the danger or adventure he encountered in his travels.
2. Ulysses became famous for his great journeys.

READER'S JOURNAL

Suggest that students consider what Ulysses has already done with his life. What other feats might he accomplish before he dies?

VOCABULARY FROM THE SELECTION

discerning
yearn

INDIVIDUAL LEARNING STRATEGIES

MOTIVATION

Have students discuss what they know of Ulysses, or Odysseus, from the *Iliad* and the *Odyssey*. What were their opinions of Ulysses upon reading these works? For example, did they feel sorry for the exiled Ulysses, or did they blame him for delaying his own return to Ithaca? Was he guilty of *hubris?*

READING PROFICIENCY

Have students read the Language Arts Survey, 3.65, "Modifiers—Adverbs and Adjectives." Point out that Tennyson uses vivid modifiers throughout "Ulysses." Have students keep a list of modifiers as they read. Students can use a thesaurus to find other words with similar meanings.

ENGLISH LANGUAGE LEARNING

A common colloquialism in English is the use of the phrase "to make a name for oneself" to mean "become famous." Tennyson uses a form of this colloquialism in line 11. Share with students the following additional vocabulary.

vexed—angered, upset

Continued on page 785

Literary TOOLS

DRAMATIC MONOLOGUE. A **dramatic monologue** is a poem that presents the speech of a single character in a dramatic situation. The technique is often used to explore the psychological state—the thoughts, sensations, and feelings—of characters in times of crises.

CHARACTER AND MOTIVATION. A **character** is a person who figures in the action of a literary work. A **motivation** is a force that moves a character to think, feel, or behave in a certain way. The sociologist and psychologist Erik Erikson wrote that in advanced age, people struggle between acceptance and defeat. Keep this in mind as you read "Ulysses" and consider his motivation.

Reader's Journal

Suppose that you had very little time in which to live. What would you want to accomplish before you died?

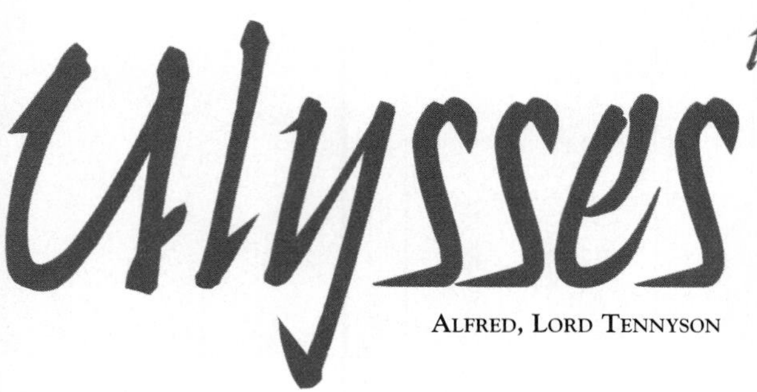

Ulysses[1]

ALFRED, LORD TENNYSON

What elements in Ulysses's present life are unsatisfying?

It little profits that an idle king,
By this still hearth, among these barren crags,
Matched with an aged wife, I mete and dole
Unequal laws[2] unto a savage race,
That hoard, and sleep, and feed, and know not me.
I cannot rest from travel; I will drink
Life to the lees.[3] All times I have enjoyed
Greatly, have suffered greatly, both with those
That loved me, and alone; on shore, and when
Through scudding drifts the rainy Hyades[4]
Vexed the dim sea. I am become a name;
For always roaming with a hungry heart
Much have I seen and known—cities of men
And manners, climates, councils, governments,
Myself not least, but honored of them all—
And drunk delight of battle with my peers,
Far on the ringing plains of windy Troy,
I am a part of all that I have met;
Yet all experience is an arch wherethrough
Gleams that untraveled world whose margin fades
Forever and forever when I move.
How dull it is to pause, to make an end,
To rust unburnished, not to shine in use!
As though to breathe were life! Life piled on life

For what did Ulysses become famous? In other words, what made him "become a name"?

1. **Ulysses.** Ulysses was a king of Ithaca who fought in the Trojan War. The story of Ulysses is told in Homer's epic poems, the *Iliad* and the *Odyssey*.
2. **mete . . . laws.** Give out rewards and punishments
3. **lees.** Dregs
4. **Through . . . Hyades.** Through driving rain showers which were said to follow the rising of the group of stars known as the Hyades

GOALS/OBJECTIVES

Studying this lesson will enable students to

- empathize with the main character's view of life
- define dramatic *monologue* and *blank verse* and identify these forms in their reading
- describe Alfred, Lord Tennyson's literary accomplishments and explain the historical significance of his writings
- define *character* and *motivation* and recognize and interpret the motivation of characters they encounter in their reading
- write a thematic comparison essay

The Return of Ulysses. 1976. Romare Bearden. National Museum of American Art.

Were all too little, and of one to me
Little remains; but every hour is saved
From that eternal silence, something more,
A bringer of new things; and vile it were
For some three suns to store and hoard myself,
And this gray spirit yearning in desire
To follow knowledge like a sinking star,
Beyond the utmost bound of human thought.

This is my son, mine own Telemachus,
To whom I leave the scepter and the isle—
Well-loved of me, discerning to fulfill

What kind of life does Ulysses find dull? For what does he yearn?

Words for Everyday Use

yearn (yərn′) *vi.,* filled with longing. *My sister has been yearning to see the Grand Canyon before she moves to Tokyo.*

dis • cern • ing (di zərn′ iŋ) *part.,* showing good judgment. *The jury was discerning in their refusal to be persuaded by the flimsy evidence presented by the prosecution.*

ANSWER TO GUIDED READING QUESTION

1. Ulysses thinks that a life of inaction is dull. He yearns to pursue knowledge—to go beyond the boundaries of human thought.

INDIVIDUAL LEARNING STRATEGIES (CONT. FROM PAGE 784)

scepter—staff or baton carried by a king as symbol of royal authority
prudence—careful wisdom

Special Needs
Ask students to talk about how it must feel to be getting older and being unable to do the same things you did when you were younger. Have students read through the poem with a partner, noting what feelings Ulysses expresses.

Enrichment
Suggest that students analyze how United States culture as a whole responds to aging and to older people. Students should contrast another culture's treatment of aging with that of the United States.

LITERARY TECHNIQUE

Blank Verse. Blank verse is unrhymed poetry written in iambic pentameter. Many of the great tragic and heroic works in the English language are written in blank verse, including much of Shakespeare's *Macbeth* and all of Milton's *Paradise Lost.* Because blank verse is unrhymed, it sounds more like ordinary speech than poetry often does. However, because of its regular metrical pattern, it sounds more formal, elevated, or lofty than ordinary speech. In other words, writing in blank verse enables a poet to render realistic characters elevated to a lofty plane. Ask students what is realistic about the character Ulysses in this poem. What about him is lofty or heroic? Then ask them to compare the sound of "Ulysses" to that of "The Lady of Shalott." What makes these poems sound different?

Answers
Ulysses's frustration and anger with getting older are realistic. His refusal to succumb to the inevitable and his determination to go on another journey are heroic. "The Lady of Shalott" is very musical while "Ulysses" reads more like a dramatic speech. "The Lady of Shalott" has end rhymes and refrains. "Ulysses" has blank verse and elevated language.

ANSWERS TO GUIDED READING QUESTIONS

1. Telemachus is discerning, prudent, honest, caring, and reverent. Ulysses does not have the patience to rule and is much less family-centered than his son.
2. Ulysses is very fond of his fellow mariners. Though they have all grown old, Ulysses believes that because they once accomplished great things, they may do so again. Ulysses admits that they do not have the strength of their youth, but they have heroic hearts and strong wills.

ADDITIONAL QUESTIONS AND ACTIVITIES

Discuss the following questions with students. What is a hero or a heroic pursuit? Is the modern-day definition of a hero different from that of Ulysses's time, or even Tennyson's time? Rewrite the story told in the poem so that Ulysses embodies modern-day heroic qualities.

SELECTION CHECK TEST 4.9.5 WITH ANSWERS

Checking Your Reading

1. What is Ulysses's position in his society? **He is the king.**
2. For what did Ulysses become famous? **He became famous for bravery in battle.**
3. What will Ulysses leave his son, Telemachus? **His son will rule the kingdom.**
4. What effect does Ulysses expect his son to have on people? **He expects him to soften them, to make them "useful and good."**
5. What does Ulysses want to do now? **He wants to sail on an adventure, to do "Some work of noble note."**

Literary Tools

Fill in the blanks using the following terms. You will not use every term, and you may use some terms more than once.

symbol dramatic monologue
character psychological state
motivation

1. Characters' inner feelings and thoughts are shared through **dramatic monologue**.
2. A force that drives a character to think or act a certain way is **motivation**.
3. A speech from a single character is a **dramatic monologue**.

This labor, by slow prudence to make mild
A rugged people, and through soft degrees
Subdue them to the useful and the good.
Most blameless is he, centered in the sphere
Of common duties, decent not to fail
In offices of tenderness, and pay
Meet adoration to my household gods,
When I am gone. He works his work, I mine.

What fine qualities does Telemachus have? Does Ulysses have these same qualities?

There lies the port, the vessel puffs her sail;
There gloom the dark, broad seas. My mariners,
Souls that have toiled, and wrought, and thought with me—
That ever with a frolic welcome took
The thunder and the sunshine, and opposed
Free hearts, free foreheads—you and I are old;
Old age hath yet his honor and his toil.
Death closes all; but something ere the end,
Some work of noble note, may yet be done,
Not unbecoming men that strove with Gods.
The lights begin to twinkle from the rocks;
The long day wanes; the slow moon climbs; the deep
Moans round with many voices. Come, my friends,
'Tis not too late to seek a newer world.
Push off, and sitting well in order smite
The sounding furrows; for my purpose holds
To sail beyond the sunset, and the baths
Of all the western stars, until I die.
It may be that the gulfs will wash us down;
It may be we shall touch the Happy Isles,[5]
And see the great Achilles,[6] whom we knew.
Though much is taken, much abides; and though
We are not now that strength which in old days
Moved earth and heaven, that which we are, we are—
One equal temper of heroic hearts,
Made weak by time and fate, but strong in will
To strive, to seek, to find, and not to yield. ■

How does Ulysses feel toward his fellow mariners, now grown old? Why does he still believe that he and they can do great things?

5. **Happy Isles.** Paradise islands of perpetual summer located in the western ocean according to Greek myth
6. **Achilles.** A Greek warrior in the Trojan War whose only vulnerable spot was his heel.

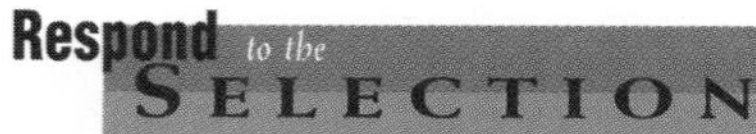

Review lines 33-43. Do you think you are more like Ulysses or his son Telemachus? Why?

RESPOND TO THE SELECTION

Students should identify the characteristics they see in themselves and the character they choose. They might also point out specific characteristics that make them different from one of the characters.

INVESTIGATE, Inquire, Imagine

Recall: GATHERING FACTS →

1a. With what specific aspects of his life does Ulysses express displeasure in lines 1–5?

2a. For what has Ulysses become famous?

3a. What does Ulysses think of his fellow mariners in their old age?

Interpret: FINDING MEANING

1b. What does this dissatisfaction suggest about his earlier life?

2b. Why isn't Ulysses satisfied with his adventures?

3b. What might prompt Ulysses to be so sure in these beliefs?

Analyze: TAKING THINGS APART →

4a. Analyze the character of Ulysses's son Telemachus.

Synthesize: BRINGING THINGS TOGETHER

4b. Based on your analysis, explain whether Telemachus will make a good king.

Evaluate: MAKING JUDGMENTS →

5a. Judge whether Ulysses is still a hero or just an old man reluctant to give up the pleasures of his youth.

Extend: CONNECTING IDEAS

5b. How do you define heroism?

Understanding Literature

DRAMATIC MONOLOGUE. Review the definition of **dramatic monologue** in the Handbook of Literary Terms. What crisis is Ulysses facing in this poem? What has he resolved to do?

CHARACTER AND MOTIVATION. Review the definitions of **character** and **motivation** in the Handbook of Literary Terms. Why might Ulysses see staying in Ithaca as a defeat? What does he refuse to accept?

ArtNote

The Return of Ulysses. 1976. Romare Bearden.

The archetypal story of Ulysses has been a subject for many artists through the centuries. Romare Bearden (1914-1988), an African American collage and print artist, created the scene on page 785 of Ulysses returning to his home and family. What symbols did Bearden use to represent travel and domesticity?

ANSWERS TO INVESTIGATE, INQUIRE, IMAGINE

RECALL

1a. Ulysses is displeased because he feels that the people he rules are "savage" and do not know or respect their own king. His wife is aged and he is bored by the lack of activity.

2a. Ulysses became famous for "roaming with a hungry heart." He has known places and been known all over the world.

3a. Ulysses believes there is life in his old mariners yet and that they yearn for new accomplishments as he does. He says that though they are no longer as strong as they were in the old days, but they have heroic hearts and strong wills.

INTERPRET

1b. This dissatisfaction suggests that Ulysses led an exciting life away from the people he now rules.

2b. Ulysses wants to continue to adventure. He feels that life is more than just breathing. He still wants new challenges.

3b. Ulysses knows these men very well having been through all kinds of toils and trials with them. He may also be projecting some of his own feelings on to them.

ANALYZE

4a. Telemachus is discerning, prudent, honest, caring, and reverent. Ulysses respects his son for having strengths that he does not have himself.

SYNTHESIZE

4b. *Responses will vary.* Telemachus seems to have many qualities that would make him a fair and able leader.

EVALUATE

5a. *Responses will vary.* Responses may in part be based on students' definitions of heroism. Ulysses's goals seem to be very self-centered—a desire for adventure and greatness. If serving others is part of being a hero, this does not apply to Ulysses. Some might find his willingness to continue to take risks and seek new challenges despite obstacles, such as age and physical weakening, to be heroic. In this regard Ulysses would be a hero.

EXTEND

5b. *Responses will vary.* Suggest that students identify characteristics of a hero and give examples of contemporary heroes.

ANSWERS TO UNDERSTANDING LITERATURE

DRAMATIC MONOLOGUE. Ulysses is facing the end of his life. He has decided that he would rather die at sea in the middle of an adventure than waste away at home.

CHARACTER AND MOTIVATION. Ulysses does not want to die quietly in his home. He refuses to accept that his days of exploring and conquest are over.

ART NOTE

The Return of Ulysses, 1976. Romare Bearden. Students may point out that the loom represents domesticity as does the cat. The ships in the background represent Ulysses' travels.

ANSWERS TO GUIDED READING QUESTIONS

1. A helmless life would be one without an aim (a helm is a steering wheel on a boat); the person would have no control over events.
2. At night the speaker is despondent. In the morning, the speaker's will once again comes under control.
3. Words are not sufficient to epxress the extent of his grief.
4. Working to put his feelings into words seems to numb his pain.

READER'S JOURNAL

Some students may not have experienced the death of someone close to them. Suggest other types of loss such as losing one's home in a fire, experiencing the death of a favorite pet, or moving to another country.

VOCABULARY FROM THE SELECTION

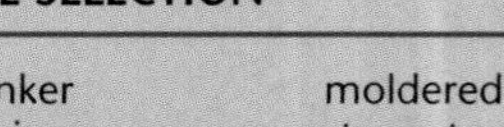

canker
derive
diffusive
fickle
moldered
stagnate
tumult

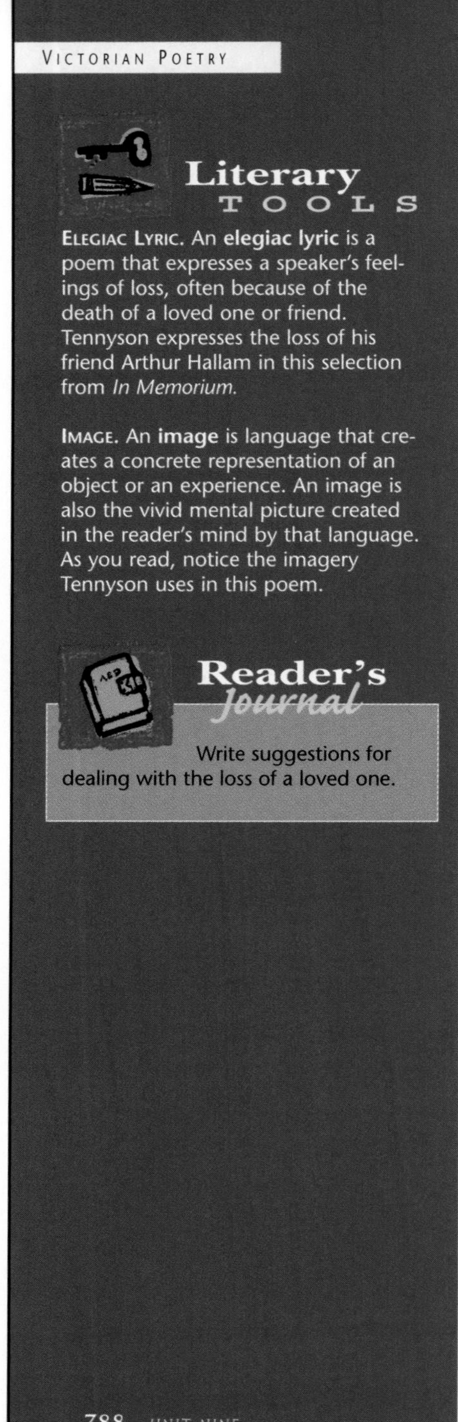

Literary TOOLS

ELEGIAC LYRIC. An **elegiac lyric** is a poem that expresses a speaker's feelings of loss, often because of the death of a loved one or friend. Tennyson expresses the loss of his friend Arthur Hallam in this selection from *In Memorium.*

IMAGE. An **image** is language that creates a concrete representation of an object or an experience. An image is also the vivid mental picture created in the reader's mind by that language. As you read, notice the imagery Tennyson uses in this poem.

Reader's Journal

Write suggestions for dealing with the loss of a loved one.

FROM

In Memoriam

ALFRED, LORD TENNYSON

4

To Sleep I give my powers away;
My will is bondsman to the dark;
I sit within a helmless bark,[1]
And with my heart I muse and say:

What would a helmless life be like?

O heart, how fares it with thee now,
That thou should fail from thy desire,
Who scarcely darest to inquire,
"What is it makes me beat so low?"

Something it is which thou hast lost,
Some pleasure from thine early years.
Break thou deep vase of chilling tears,
That grief hath shaken into frost!

Such clouds of nameless trouble cross
All night below the darkened eyes;
With morning wakes the will, and cries,
"Thou shalt not be the fool of loss."

How do the speaker's nights differ from his mornings?

5

I sometimes hold it half a sin
To put in words the grief I feel;
For words, like Nature, half reveal
And half conceal the Soul within.

Why does the speaker sometimes think it "half a sin" to try to express his feelings in words?

But, for the unquiet heart and brain,
A use in measured language lies;
The sad mechanic exercise,
Like dull narcotics, numbing pain.

What comfort does writing give him?

In words, like weeds,[2] I'll wrap me o'er,
Like coarsest clothes against the cold;
But that large grief which these enfold
Is given in outline and no more.

1. **helmless bark.** Unsteered boat
2. **weeds.** Clothes

GOALS/OBJECTIVES

Studying this lesson will enable students to

- experience and interpret an elegiac lyric and appreciate a speaker's sense of loss
- describe Alfred, Lord Tennyson's literary accomplishments and explain the historical significance of his writings
- define *elegiac lyric* and identify elegiac lyrics they encounter in future reading
- define *image* and identify imagery in poems that they read
- recognize and correct clichés and euphemisms

The Pine Tree at St. Tropez, 1909. Paul Signac. Pushkin Museum, Moscow.

◆ ◆ ◆

26

Still onward winds the dreary way;
  I with it, for I long to prove
  No lapse of moons can canker Love,
Whatever fickle tongues may say.

And if that eye which watches guilt
  And goodness, and hath power to see
  Within the green the mouldered tree,
And towers fallen as soon as built—

What does the speaker long to prove? What claim made by "fickle tongues" does the speaker remark?

Words for Everyday Use

can • ker (kaŋ′ kər) *vt.,* infect with corruption. *Just one bad apple in a basket can canker the rest of the bushel.*

fick • le (fik′ əl) *adj.,* unstable in affection, loyalty, interest, etc. *My fickle dog scurries from one person to the next, hoping for a discarded morsel.*

mould • ered or **mold • ered** (mōl′ derd) *adj.,* decayed. *We had to throw away the moldered quilt we had found in the trunk in the damp basement.*

ANSWER TO GUIDED READING QUESTION

1. The speaker longs to prove that a lapse of time will not corrupt love. He detests the idea that his feelings of loss will lessen with time.

INDIVIDUAL LEARNING SKILLS

Motivation
Ask students to read the Language Arts Survey 5.9, "Analyzing and Synthesizing." As they read, have them analyze the stages of grief the speaker goes through. They might map out the poem on a separate piece of paper. As they encounter a form of grief, they can write the line in which the reference occurs and a description of the grief next to it.

Reading Proficiency
Point out to students that in this poem, Tennyson uses archaic word forms that are rarely used in modern speech. For example, *thou* (you), *hast* (have), and *shalt* (shall or will).

English Language Learning
Share with students the information in Reading Proficiency, as well as the additional vocabulary below:
coarsest—roughest
envy—want, be jealous of
unfettered—unbound, free
sloth—laziness
cloven—split
aptest—most fitting

Special Needs
Read the poem with students and help them to interpret each stanza. Then, work with them through the Motivation activity.

Enrichment Activities
Suggest that students write a poem in memory of someone or something they have lost. As an alternate activity students might write a prose obituary. Students should include their own feelings as well as details about their subject in their writing.

ANSWERS TO GUIDED READING QUESTIONS

1. The speaker says that the difference between people and animals is that animals don't have a conscience or feel outrage in the same way the people do.
2. The speaker feels that is "better to have loved and lost / Than never to have loved at all." He feels that loving is an important part of life and that one should not avoid loving people simply in order to avoid the pain of losing them.

LITERARY TECHNIQUE

Punctuation. Ask students to look for words that are capitalized in the poem, other than those at the beginning of lines. Why might Tennyson have chosen to capitalize those words? Do their meanings differ when they are capitalized? If so, how?

ADDITIONAL QUESTIONS AND ACTIVITIES

Discuss with students the often quoted lines, "'Tis better to have loved and lost/Than never to have loved at all." Why might these lines resonate with some readers more than other lines? Find lines in the poem that seem to speak to you, that resonate with you. Discuss with the class why you chose these lines.

O, if indeed that eye foresee
Or see—in Him is no before—
In more of life true life no more
And Love the indifference to be,

Then might I find, ere yet the morn
Breaks hither over Indian seas,
That Shadow waiting with the keys,
To shroud me from my proper scorn.[3]

27

I envy not in any moods
The captive void of noble rage,
The linnet[4] born within the cage,
That never knew the summer woods;

I envy not the beast that takes
His license in the field of time,
Unfettered by the sense of crime,
To whom a conscience never wakes;

What is the speaker saying about the difference between people and animals?

Nor, what may count itself as blest,
The heart that never plighted troth
But stagnates in the weeds of sloth;
Nor any want-begotten rest.[5]

I hold it true, whate'er befall;
I feel it, when I sorrow most;
'Tis better to have loved and lost
Than never to have loved at all.

What are the speaker's feelings about love and loss?

28

The time draws near the birth of Christ.[6]
The moon is hid, the night is still;
The Christmas bells from hill to hill
Answer each other in the mist.

3. **eye . . . scorn.** If God, who sees everything, sees that the rest of my life will be as it is now, then let me die tonight so that I won't live to scorn myself as one who could not prove that love can outlast change.
4. **linnet.** A type of bird
5. **But . . . rest.** A need or desire has led to complacency.
6. **birth of Christ.** This was the first Christmas after Tennyson's friend Hallam had died.

Words For Everyday Use

stag • nate (stag′ nāt′) *vi.,* become sluggish. *Once the dam was built, the formerly swift-moving river stagnated.*

Four voices of four hamlets round,
From far and near, on mead and moor,
Swell out and fail, as if a door
Were shut between me and the sound;

Each voice four changes on the wind,
That now dilate, and now decrease,
Peace and goodwill, goodwill and peace,
Peace and goodwill, to all mankind.

This year I slept and woke with pain,
I almost wished no more to wake,
And that my hold on life would break
Before I heard those bells again;

But they my troubled spirit rule,
For they controlled me when a boy;
They bring me sorrow touched with joy,
The merry, merry bells of Yule.

◆ ◆ ◆

48

If these brief lays, of Sorrow born,
Were taken to be such as closed
Grave doubts and answers here proposed,
Then these were such as men might scorn.

Her[7] care is not to part and prove;
She takes, when harsher moods remit,
What slender shade of doubt may flit,
And makes it vassal unto love;

And hence, indeed, she sports with words,
But better serves a wholesome law,
And holds it sin and shame to draw
The deepest measure from the chords;

Nor dare she trust a larger lay,
But rather loosens from the lip
Short swallow-flights of song, that dip
Their wings in tears, and skim away.

How does the speaker respond to the Christmas caroling? Why?

What conflicting emotions is the speaker feeling? What is the source of his sorrow? of his joy?

What kinds of poetry does the poet reject in the first stanza of section 48?

What kind of poetry does his sorrow allow him to write?

7. **Her.** Sorrow's

ANSWERS TO GUIDED READING QUESTIONS

1. The speaker hears the caroling but is unaffected. He still mourns the death of his friend.
2. The speaker feels both sorrow and joy. The source of the speaker's sorrow is the death of his friend and possibly the loss of his boyhood innocence. The speaker's joy comes from hearing the bells, which remind him of his happy boyhood.
3. The poet rejects poems that provide easy answers.
4. The poet's sorrow allows him to write poems that only touch the surface of his feelings, and do not express his deepest sense of loss.

Quotables

"[William] Wordsworth, Tennyson and [Robert] Browning; or, Pure, Ornate, and Grotesque Art in English Poetry."

—Walter Bagehot

ANSWERS TO GUIDED READING QUESTIONS

1. People trust that good will somehow come out of bad events.
2. An example of good coming out of ill is spring coming out of winter.
3. The speaker likens himself to a crying infant. He has not accepted the idea that everything happens for a reason or that good will come of ill—it is still a "dream" for him.
4. People hope that life will continue "beyond the grave."
5. The speaker finds it ironic that life is so precious while nature is "careless of the single life," that is, while nature has no concern for the individual soul.

◆ ◆ ◆

54

O, yet we trust that somehow good
Will be the final goal of ill,
To pangs of nature, sins of will,
Defects of doubt, and taints of blood;
That nothing walks with aimless feet;
That not one life shall be destroyed,
Or cast as rubbish to the void,
When God hath made the pile complete;

That not a worm is cloven in vain;
That not a moth with vain desire
Is shriveled in a fruitless fire,
Or but subserves another's gain.

Behold, we know not anything;
I can but trust that good shall fall
At last—far off—at last, to all,
And every winter change to spring.

So runs my dream; but what am I?
An infant crying in the night;
An infant crying for the light,
And with no language but a cry.

55

The wish, that of the living whole
No life may fail beyond the grave,
Derives it not from what we have
The likest God within the soul?

Are God and Nature then at strife,
That Nature lends such evil dreams?
So careful of the type she seems,
So careless of the single life,

That I, considering everywhere
Her secret meaning in her deeds,

What trust do people have, according to the speaker?

What event in nature symbolizes, for the speaker, the idea that good can come of ill?

To what does the speaker liken himself? Has he truly accepted the idea that everything happens for a reason and that good will come of ill?

What hope do people have about life?

What in the way that nature treats life seems ironic to the speaker?

WORDS FOR EVERYDAY USE

de • rive (di rīv′) *vt.*, get from a source. *I derive satisfaction from a job well done.*

And finding that of fifty seeds
She often brings but one to bear,

I falter where I firmly trod,
And falling with my weight of cares
Upon the great world's altar-stairs
That slope through darkness up to God,

I stretch lame hands of faith, and grope,
And gather dust and chaff, and call
To what I feel is Lord of all,
And faintly trust the larger hope.

What faith is the speaker groping toward? What is he learning to trust?

◆ ◆ ◆

59

O Sorrow, wilt thou live with me
No casual mistress, but a wife,
My bosom friend and half of life;
As I confess it needs must be?

To what is the speaker proposing to wed himself?

O Sorrow, wilt thou rule my blood,
Be sometimes lovely like a bride,
And put thy harsher moods aside,
If thou wilt have me wise and good?

What good might come of the speaker's sorrow? What changes might sorrow bring about in him?

My centered passion cannot move,
Nor will it lessen from today;
But I'll have leave at times to play
As with the creature of my love;

And set thee forth, for thou art mine,
With so much hope for years to come,
That, howsoe'er I know thee, some
Could hardly tell what name were thine.

◆ ◆ ◆

75

I leave thy praises unexpressed
In verse that brings myself relief,
And by the measure of my grief
I leave thy greatness to be guessed.

Why doesn't the speaker write verse to praise the qualities of his lost friend?

ANSWERS TO GUIDED READING QUESTIONS

1. The speaker is groping toward faith in the Lord of all. He is learning to trust the larger hope.
2. The speaker is proposing to wed himself to sorrow.
3. Sorrow may put her "harsher moods aside," his grief may not be so painful. The speaker may become wise and good.
4. The speaker is unable to express in words the fine qualities of his friend.

ANSWERS TO GUIDED READING QUESTIONS

1. The world praises a person's actions; the world is cold to a person's unrealized potential.
2. The place "somewhere, out of human view" is the afterworld. There the talents of the speaker's dead friend will be known.
3. The speaker enjoyed many of the Christmas foods and events that he used to enjoy before the death of his friend, such as the Yule log, dances, games, and songs.

ADDITIONAL QUESTIONS AND ACTIVITIES

Ask the students the following questions: What stages does his grief go through? What conclusions does Tennysong come to about the role played by sorrow in people's lives, about life after death, and about the spiritual bonds of connectedness between people? Explain your answers based on evidence from the poem.

Answer

Initially, the speaker is despondent and feels powerless; he then vows always to suffer the pain of his loss; with time he is less angry and becomes very sad; after a few years, his grief is still very strong, but quieter; and finally, he comes to a higher understanding of death and realizes that his friend is an inextricable part of his memory and of nature. He concludes that sorrow makes people wiser and better (poem 59, line 8). In poem 131, lines 1–8, Tennyson supports the Christian concept of Judgment Day and life after death. All of poem 130 describes Tennyson's feelings of spiritual connection with his dead friend.

What practice howsoe'er expert
In fitting aptest words to things,
Or voice the richest-toned that sings,
Hath power to give thee as thou wert?

I care not in these fading days
To raise a cry that lasts not long,
And round thee with the breeze of song
To stir a little dust of praise.

Thy leaf has perished in the green,
And, while we breathe beneath the sun,
The world which credits what is done
Is cold to all that might have been.

What does the world praise? To what is the world cold?

So here shall silence guard thy fame;
But somewhere, out of human view,
Whate'er thy hands are set to do
Is wrought with <u>tumult</u> of acclaim.

What is the place "somewhere, out of human view"? What will be known there that is not known now?

◆ ◆ ◆

78

Again at Christmas did we weave
The holly round the Christmas hearth;
The silent snow possessed the earth,
And calmly fell our Christmas eve.

The yule clog[8] sparkled keen with frost,
No wing of wind the region swept,
But over all things brooding slept
The quiet sense of something lost.

As in the winters left behind,
Again our ancient games had place,
The mimic picture's[9] breathing grace,
And dance and song and hoodman-blind.[10]

What joys did the speaker experience at this Christmastime?

---

8. **clog.** Log
9. **mimic picture.** A game in which players pose as a famous statue or painting while others try to guess the source
10. **hoodman-blind.** The blindfolded person in a game of blindman's bluff

WORDS FOR EVERYDAY USE

tu • mult (tōō´ mult) *n.*, commotion; agitation. *The <u>tumult</u> from the New Year's Eve party next door was more than I could stand or sleep through.*

Who showed a token of distress?
No single tear, no mark of pain—
O sorrow, then can sorrow wane?
O grief, can grief be changed to less?

O last regret, regret can die!
No—mixed with all this mystic frame,
Her deep relations are the same,
But with long use her tears are dry.

Does the speaker really believe that regret can die? What conclusion does he come to on that subject?

◆ ◆ ◆

130

Thy voice is on the rolling air
I hear thee where the waters run;
Thou standest in the rising sun,
And in the setting thou art fair.

In what does the speaker hear and see his departed friend?

What art thou then? I cannot guess;
But though I seem in star and flower
To feel thee some diffusive power,
I do not therefore love thee less.

My love involves the love before;
My love is vaster passion now;
Tho' mix'd with God and Nature thou,
I seem to love thee more and more.

Far off thou art, but ever nigh;
I have thee still, and I rejoice;
I prosper, circled with thy voice;
I shall not lose thee tho' I die.

In what sense does the speaker still have his friend? How could he not lose his friend even if he lost his own life?

131

O living will[11] that shalt endure
When all that seems shall suffer shock,
Rise in the spiritual rock,[12]
Flow through our deeds and make them pure,

11. **living will.** Humankind's moral will
12. **spiritual rock.** Christ

Words for Everyday Use

dif • fu • sive (di fyo͞o siv) *adj.*, tending to disperse. *The snake oil salesman's crowd was diffusive, no matter what wondrous cures he effected.*

ANSWERS TO GUIDED READING QUESTIONS

1. No. His regret remains deep, but with time the outward display of loss ceases, or runs dry.
2. The speaker hears his departed friend's voice in the wind and in rivers, and sees him in the rising and setting of the sun.
3. The speaker feels that the spirit of his friend is evident in all of nature. The speaker feels that he would always be surrounded by his friend's voice, even if he were to die.

ADDITIONAL QUESTIONS AND ACTIVITIES

Discuss with students why Tennyson might have chosen Christmas as a way to mark the passing of time. What ideas was he trying to communicate by referring to that holiday?

Answer

Christmas marks the end of one year and the beginning of the next. Christians also consider the first Christmas as the beginning of a new era on Earth, so the holiday signifies renewal.

ANSWER TO GUIDED READING QUESTION

1. He might be referring to truths having to do with the meaning of life and death. To close with all you have loved and with all that you flow from means to attain unity in the afterlife, presumably in heaven.

RESPOND TO THE SELECTION

Students may also consider at which points they were most moved by the speaker's feelings.

SELECTION CHECK TEST 4.9.7 WITH ANSWERS

Checking Your Reading

1. What holiday is referenced in the poem? **Christmas is referenced in the poem.**
2. What is better than never having loved? **It is better to lose a loved one than to never love.**
3. What do the four voices wish to all mankind? **They wish "peace and goodwill."**
4. What force seems at odds with God and careless toward man? **Nature does.**
5. As the poem concludes, what has happened to the speaker's love for his friend? **His love has grown; he claims to "love thee more and more."**

Vocabulary in Context

Fill each blank with the most appropriate word from the Words for Everyday Use. You may have to change the tense of the word.

moldered tumult diffusive
canker stagnate derive fickle

1. In the forties, some feared that television would **canker** society if it became popular.
2. The arrival of the principal was enough to quiet the **tumult** in the lunchroom.
3. Josette is a **fickle** employee who changes jobs often.
4. The actor's career **stagnated** after his television show was cancelled.
5. The old documents were **moldered** and barely legible.

Literary Tools

1. An elegiac lyric is
   a. a poem that tells a story
   b. a poem that expresses feelings of grief or loss
   c. a poem that originally was a song
   d. a love song

That we may lift from out of dust
  A voice as unto him that hears,
  A cry above the conquered years
To one that with us works, and trust,

With faith that comes of self-control,
  The truths that never can be proved
  Until we close with all we loved,
And all we flow from, soul in soul. ■

What does it mean to close with all that you have loved and with all that you flow from?

Respond *to the* SELECTION

Which of the speaker's feelings about love, death, the spirit, and immortality do you agree with? With which do you disagree?

SELECTION CHECK TEST 4.9.7 WITH ANSWERS (CONT.)

2. An example of **imagery** from *In Memoriam* can be found in the lines:
   a. "Something it is which thou hast lost / Some pleasure from thine early years."
   b. "Break thou deep vase of chilling tears / That grief hath shaken into frost!"
   c. "'Tis better to have loved and lost / Than never to have loved at all."
   d. "I leave thy praises unexpressed / In verse that brings myself relief…"

3. The primary rhyme scheme of this poem is:
   a. *aabb ccdd ee*
   b. *abba cddc effe ghhg*
   c. abba abba cdecde
   d. none; it is unrhymed

Investigate, Inquire, Imagine

Recall: Gathering Facts →

1a. In canto 4, how does the speaker feel at night and in the morning?

2a. According to canto 26, what do "fickle tongues" say about love?

3a. Contrast the speaker's feelings at Christmas in canto 28 with those in canto 78.

Interpret: Finding Meaning

1b. Based on the poem as a whole, explain whether the speaker became "the fool of loss."

2b. Based on the speaker's experience, are "fickle tongues" right?

3b. Why have the speaker's feelings changed?

Analyze: Taking Things Apart →

4a. Summarize the development of the speaker's feelings throughout the excerpts.

Synthesize: Bringing Things Together

4b. How do you think the speaker would react if he lost another very close friend?

Evaluate: Making Judgments →

5a. Evaluate the speaker's claim that "it is better to have loved and lost than never to have loved at all."

Extend: Connecting Ideas

5b. Do you think the Lady of Shalott would agree with this statement? Would Ulysses? Why, or why not?

Understanding Literature

Elegiac Lyric. Review the definition of **elegiac lyric** in the Handbook of Literary Terms. Based on the poem, what kind of person do you think Arthur Hallam was? Why is it particularly tragic for someone to die so young?

Imagery. Review the definition of **imagery** in the Literary Tools in Prereading. What images are evoked in lines 9-12 of canto 75? How has the poet's imagery been affected by death? What does a still, dusty place bring to mind? Because the poet is grieving, is he in any sense eternally in a vault or mausoleum of his own creation?

ANSWERS TO INVESTIGATE, INQUIRE, IMAGINE

Recall

1a. At night the speaker feels despair, as if his life is without aim. In the morning his spirit rallies and he resolves not to have his life destroyed by grief.

2a. "Fickle tongues" say that love will become less intense over time. In other words, the speaker will recover from the death of his friend with time.

3a. The speaker felt great pain and isolation and wanted to die in poem 28. The speaker was able to join in the festivities during the second Christmas. During the first Christmas, the speaker almost wanted to die, but by the second Christmas he was able to experience some pleasure.

Interpret

1b. Students may notice that the speaker used the term "fool of loss" when he was still very angry and full of despair. Later on, he was better able to deal with his loss.

2b. No. His love and grief did not die, but they changed. The speaker realized that he hadn't completely lost his friend; he could still feel his spirit in nature.

3b. The speaker still feels loss, but the outward show of his grief has dried out with long use.

Analyze

4a. The speaker's spiritual ideas evolve from anger and despair into a more complex concept of the inseparability of nature and the human spirit. One of the speaker's conclusions is that some questions cannot be answered until after death.

Synthesize

4b. *Responses will vary.* He might go through a similar grieving process. The depth of his grief may vary based on the importance of the person in his life.

Evaluate

5a. *Responses will vary.* Students may say that the pain of losing is not worth loving. Others may agree that all kinds of love are so important in our lives that we should not forgo it for fear of loss.

Extend

5b. *Responses will vary.* The Lady of Shalott would probably agree. She was cursed by isolation and would probably have cherished a chance to love even if it ended in grief. Ulysses would probably agree as well. He seems to want to take everything possible from life, so avoiding love simply to avoid pain seems out of character.

ANSWERS TO UNDERSTANDING LITERATURE

Responses will vary.

Elegaic Lyric. It seems clear that Arthur Hallam was a very good friend, and he was probably quite talented in some way. Hallam died at a young age, before he had "ripened" or matured. It is tragic when a young person dies, because there are so many things he or she was not able to experience, and the death is unexpected and therefore shocking.

Imagery. Students may say that the images in these lines remind them of death. The speaker mentions fading (dying) days, a cry that lasts not long (but soon dies), and dust (as in "to dust you shall return"). A still, dusty place recalls a tomb. Students may say that while the poet grieves on the death of his friend, he mentally places himself in a mausoleum as well, perhaps contemplating his own inevitable end.

ANSWERS TO INTEGRATING THE LANGUAGE ARTS

Language, Grammar, and Style
Responses may vary.

1. Arthur Hallam was a talented artist and an excellent friend.
2. Tennyson was despondent when Hallam died.
3. Tennyson spent seventeen years composing a poem eulogizing his dead friend.
4. Writing *In Memoriam* helped Tennyson to analyze and understand his grief.
5. Through dealing with his friend's death, Tennyson gained a more complex understanding of love and death, of his relationship to nature, and of his own spirituality.

Collaborative Learning & Study and Research
Make sure that the two memorial rituals that students compare are contemporaneous.

Media Literacy
Responses will vary.

- Grief might be signified by crying or covering one's face with one's hands. A person's shoulders would probably be slumped and his or her facial expression might be very sad or vacant.
- Joy might be shown by a smile, laughter, wide eyes, and a desire for eye contact in order to share the emotion with others. People sometimes clap, shout, or jump up and down when joyful.
- When people are in awe, their eyes and mouth are usually open and they don't say anything, or they speak only gibberish. Oftentimes people may act awkwardly when they are in awe.
- Fear often makes people jump back from the object they are afraid of. A person will often have wide eyes and may scream. Sometimes people will fidget and become excitable when fearful.

Writer's Journal

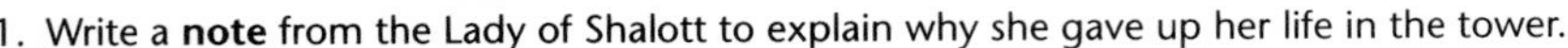
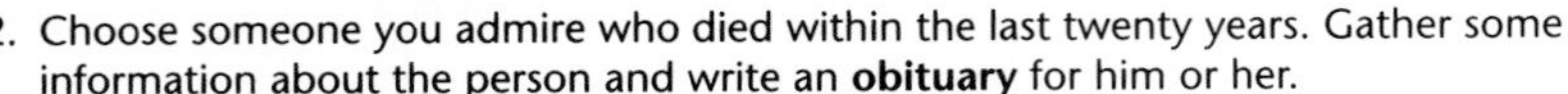

1. Write a **note** from the Lady of Shalott to explain why she gave up her life in the tower.
2. Choose someone you admire who died within the last twenty years. Gather some information about the person and write an **obituary** for him or her.
3. Imagine Ulysses has one last adventure. Write an **adventure story** about his last exploits.

Integrating *the* Language Arts

Language, Grammar, and Style

Clichés and Euphemisms. Read the Language Arts Survey 1.23, "Clichés and Euphemisms." Then rewrite the following sentences, replacing the clichés and euphemisms that you find in them.

1. Arthur Hallam must have been a fine young man.
2. When Hallam passed away, it broke Tennyson's heart.
3. Tennyson spent seventeen years composing a poem eulogizing the dearly departed.
4. Writing *In Memoriam* helped Tennyson to look on the sunny side of things.
5. Tennyson came to recognize that every cloud has a silver lining and that the passing on of the young Arthur Hallam had deepened his own life, making it more meaningful.

Speaking and Listening

Oral History. As Tennyson's "Ulysses" vividly demonstrates, advanced age does not mean that a person no longer has a great deal to offer. Quite the contrary, elderly people have a lifetime of acquired knowledge and experience, and one can learn much from them. Visit someone at a home for elderly people or seek out an elderly person in your own family, and interview that person to prepare an oral history of his or her life at some specific period in the past. If possible, tape record and transcribe the stories that the person tells you. If you do not have access to a tape recorder, take detailed notes and then write them up in the form of a brief report. (See the Language Arts Survey 5.39, "Formal and Informal Note-Taking.")

Collaborative Learning & Study and Research

Research Report. Tennyson memorialized his friend Arthur Hallam by writing *In Memoriam.* With two or three other classmates, prepare a research report on ways in which people around the world memorialize others who have died. You may wish to choose two cultures, such as yours and that of one foreign country, and concentrate on comparing and contrasting memorial rituals in those countries. For example, you might compare and contrast what people do after someone dies in Japan and in the United States.

Media Literacy

Media Death Watch. Some people think that death is so commonplace on television, in movies, and in the news that people have become desensitized to it. For one week, monitor what you see. Take notes on how often death is shown, whether it is shown realistically, and what you see after the death has taken place. Do you agree that death has become commonplace and that people just don't care much any more? Use your findings to support your response.

"My Last Duchess"
"Andrea del Sarto"

BY ROBERT BROWNING

About the AUTHOR

Robert Browning (1812–1889) grew up in a remarkable household with parents who loved literature and music. Tutored at home, he became one of the most learned men in Europe. While still quite young, he published two volumes of poetry, but neither met with success. He also failed in his first attempt at writing for the stage. His play *Strafford*, produced in 1837, closed after running for only five nights. In subsequent years, he gained some reputation as a writer of verse in which characters speak in their own voices without narrative commentary. In 1846, Robert married Elizabeth Barrett, a poet six years older than he with a far greater reputation than his own. Elizabeth and Robert moved to Italy, partially because of Elizabeth's poor health, but primarily to escape her domineering father. Theirs was one of the great love stories of all time. They had an exceedingly happy marriage and lived in Italy for thirteen years, until Elizabeth's death. Robert then returned to England to teach and write. In his own day, many people considered Browning's poetry to be too unpoetic and obscure. However, in the twentieth century, Browning's reputation has grown enormously. His poetry is modern in its use of realistic speech and its portrayal of the psychological states of characters.

About the SELECTIONS

Browning had a lifelong obsession with Italy and with the Italian Renaissance. In **"My Last Duchess,"** the speaker prattles on, seemingly unaware that he is revealing something horrible about himself. The poem shows Browning's gift for allowing characters to speak in their own voices, inadvertently exposing their innermost conflicts and desires.

The speaker in **"Andrea del Sarto"** is Andrea d'Angelo di Francesca, an Italian Renaissance painter who was called "del Sarto" because his father was a *sarto*, or tailor. Del Sarto gained a reputation for painting flawless works. In the poem, del Sarto addresses his wife, Lucrezia del Fede, whose influence was disastrous for his art.

Literary TOOLS

DRAMATIC MONOLOGUE. A **dramatic monologue** is a poem that presents the speech of a single character in a dramatic situation. The speech is one side of an imagined conversation. Robert Browning's reputation rests primarily on his dramatic monologues. As you read, identify the speaker in "My Last Duchess."

DICTION. **Diction**, when applied to writing, refers to word choice. Much of a writer's style is determined by his or her diction, the types of words that he or she chooses. Browning was known for writing poetry that sounded just like ordinary speech. He avoided lofty, sentimental, flowery, "poetic" diction in favor of words and phrases that might be spoken. Chart the examples you can find in the poem of the following elements from ordinary speech:

contractions	that's
exclamations	
interrupted statements	
words of direct address	
rhetorical questions	

Reader's Journal

What would you do if you suspected someone of having committed a horrible crime?

ADDITIONAL RESOURCES

UNIT 9 RESOURCE BOOK
"My Last Duchess"
- Selection Worksheet 9.4
- Selection Check Test 4.9.9
- Selection Test 4.9.10

"Andrea del Sarto"
- Selection Worksheet 9.5
- Selection Check Test 4.9.11
- Selection Test 4.9.12
- Language, Grammar, and Style Resource 3.36
- Applied English Resource 6.10

VOCABULARY FROM THE SELECTION

countenance
munificence
officious

GRAPHIC ORGANIZER

DICTION. Students may include the following in their graphic organizers. Examples of contractions include *Will't, 'twas,* and *who'd.* Examples of exclamations include: "Sir, 'twas all one!" and "good!" Examples of interrupted statements include: "A heart—how shall I say?—too soon made glad" and "but thanked / Somehow—I know not how—as if she ranked / My gift..." Examples of words of direct address include: "Will't please you sit and look at her?" and "Will't please you rise?" Examples of rhetorical questions include "how shall I say?" and "Who'd stoop to blame / This sort of trifling?"

READER'S JOURNAL

Ask students to determine if there is enough evidence in this poem to report the Duke to the police.

GOALS/OBJECTIVES

Studying this lesson will enable students to
- have positive experiences reading dramatic monologues
- describe Browning's literary accomplishments and explain the historical significance of his writings
- define *dramatic monologue* and identify poems that are written as dramatic monologues
- define *theme* and identify themes of a poem
- define *diction* and *paradox* and recognize and interpret these techniques as used in a poem
- write a dramatic monologue and dramatic skit
- revise sentences to vary length and structure

ANSWER TO GUIDED READING QUESTION

1. The Duke is showing his visitor a portrait of the late Duchess. People question the Duchess's lifelike look of passion and joy.

INDIVIDUAL LEARNING STRATEGIES

Motivation
Have students role play an interview between the police and the Duke using the information about the Duke and the late Duchess found in the poem.

Reading Proficiency
Ask students to determine who is speaking the monologue and whom this person is addressing. Discuss with students what different punctuation marks signify in the dramatic monologue. Quotation marks mean that the speaker is using words as words or that he is quoting someone else. Parentheses indicate an aside.

Additional Vocabulary
In addition to following the suggestions in Reading Proficiency above, share with students the following additional vocabulary.
mantle—shawl
pretense—claim
avow—promise

Special Needs
Read the poem aloud to students and ask them what they think of the speaker. What is revealed about him?

Enrichment
Encourage students to prepare a brief (one to two pages) speech that reveals an aspect of their personalities or tells about their lives. Students who are comfortable doing so can read their speeches out loud in class. Have other students critique their speeches, noting what the speakers might have unwittingly revealed. As an alternative, students may wish to invent a persona and write a dramatic monologue from that character's perspective.

My Last Duchess[1]

Robert Browning

Portrait of a Woman, 1500s. Titian. Palazzo Pitti, Florence, Italy

That's my last Duchess painted on the wall,
Looking as if she were alive. I call
That piece a wonder, now: Frà Pandolf's[2] hands
Worked busily a day, and there she stands.
Will 't please you sit and look at her? I said
"Frà Pandolf" by design, for never read
Strangers like you that pictured <u>countenance</u>,
The depth and passion of its earnest glance,
But to myself they turned (since none puts by
The curtain I have drawn for you, but I)
And seemed as they would ask me, if they durst,
How such a glance came there; so, not the first
Are you to turn and ask thus. Sir, 'twas not
Her husband's presence only, called that spot
Of joy into the Duchess' cheek: perhaps
Frà Pandolf chanced to say "Her mantle laps
Over my lady's wrist too much," or "Paint
Must never hope to reproduce the faint

Whose portrait is the Duke showing to his visitor? What about the portrait causes people to ask questions about it?

1. **My Last Duchess.** The speaker is Alfonso II, duke of Ferrara, Italy. His wife Lucrezia has died. In the poem he is addressing an agent who is negotiating his next marriage.
2. **Frà Pandolf.** An imaginary painter. *Frà* is short for *Fratello,* Italian for "brother." The painter was a monk.

Words For Everyday Use

coun • te • nance (koun′ tə nəns) *n.,* look on a person's face. *The condemned man had a stoic <u>countenance</u>.*

LITERARY NOTE

Irony. Remind students that **irony** is a difference between appearance and reality. Ask them what is ironic in the Duke's attempt to present an ugly characterization of his Duchess.

Answer
In trying to present an ugly characterization of his wife, the Duke ironically reveals his own hideous character.

Half-flush that dies along her throat": such stuff
Was courtesy, she thought, and cause enough
For calling up that spot of joy. She had
A heart—how shall I say?—too soon made glad,
Too easily impressed, she liked whate'er
She looked on, and her looks went everywhere.
Sir, 'twas all one! My favor at her breast,
The dropping of the daylight in the West,
The bough of cherries some officious fool
Broke in the orchard for her, the white mule
She rode with round the terrace—all and each
Would draw from her alike the approving speech,
Or blush, at least. She thanked men—good! but thanked
Somehow—I know not how—as if she ranked
My gift of a nine-hundred-years-old name
With anybody's gift. Who'd stoop to blame
This sort of trifling? Even had you skill
In speech—(which I have not)—to make your will
Quite clear to such an one, and say, "Just this
Or that in you disgusts me; here you miss,
Or there exceed the mark"—and if she let
Herself be lessoned so, nor plainly set
Her wits to yours, forsooth, and made excuse
—E'en then would be some stooping, and I choose
Never to stoop. Oh sir, she smiled, no doubt,
Whene'er I passed her; but who passed without
Much the same smile? This grew; I gave commands;
Then all smiles stopped together. There she stands
As if alive. Will 't please you rise? We'll meet
The company below, then. I repeat,
The Count your master's known munificence
Is ample warrant that no just pretense
Of mine for dowry will be disallowed;
Though his fair daughter's self, as I avowed
At starting, is my object. Nay, we'll go
Together down, sir. Notice Neptune, though,
Taming a sea horse, thought a rarity,
Which Claus of Innsbruck[3] cast in bronze for me! ■

To what does the Duke attribute the look on the Duchess's face in the portrait?

What is the implication of the Duke's statement that "her looks went everywhere"?

Why did the Duke not tell the Duchess what displeased him about her conduct?

What had happened to the Duke's relationship with his wife before she died? What makes this fact ominous?

What is ominous about the Duke's choice of words in lines 50–53?

3. **Claus of Innsbruck.** An imaginary sculptor

Words for Everyday Use

of • fi • cious (ə fish′ əs) *adj.*, meddlesome. *Todd became officious when the president of the company walked into the room.*

mu • nif • i • cence (myo͞o nif′ ə səns) *n.*, generosity. *Todd slithered up to Ms. Brahm and said, "The munificence with which you replied to my report was awe-inspiring."*

ANSWERS TO GUIDED READING QUESTIONS

1. The Duke attributes the look to either his own presence or an offhand courteous remark by the artist.
2. The implication is that the Duchess was a flirt—or worse.
3. The Duke felt he would be lowering himself if he revealed that her behavior upset him.
4. The Duke became increasingly jealous because the Duchess gave others the same smile she gave him. That is ominous because he then commanded the cessation of her smiles (and possibly commended her death).
5. The Duke's choice of words is ominous because they suggest he is already planning on finding another bride, and perhaps, another work of "art."

LITERARY NOTE

- Browning based this poem on historical events that took place in Renaissance Italy. Alfonso II d'Este, Duke of Ferrara (1533–1597), married the daughter of Cosimo I de'Medici, the Duke of Florence, in 1558, when she was fourteen. The young duchess died April 21, 1561, under suspicious circumstances. Soon afterwards, the Duke began negotiating for the hand of the niece of the Count of Tyrol, whose court was seated in Innsbruck, Austria.
- Neptune is the Roman name for the god of the sea, Poseidon. He was considered a violent and powerful god, and was renowned for his many love affairs.

SELECTION CHECK TEST 4.9.9 WITH ANSWERS

Checking Your Reading

1. What hangs on the wall? **A portrait of the late duchess hangs on the wall.**
2. How did the Duchess feel about "whate'er she looked on"? **She liked everything.**
3. What does the speaker say he chooses never to do? **He never stoops.**
4. What happened after the speaker "gave commands"? **All smiles stopped.**
5. What does the speaker want from the Count? **He wants to marry the Count's daughter.**

SELECTION CHECK TEST 4.9.9 WITH ANSWERS (CONT.)

Literary Tools

1. What is a dramatic monologue? A dramatic monologue presents the speech of a single character in a dramatic situation.
2. In writing, to what does diction refer? In writing, diction refers to word choice.
3. For what sort of diction is Browning known? He used everyday, common diction.

RESPOND TO THE SELECTION

Ask students to consider what they would do if somebody said something that made them think a crime had been committed or if they thought somebody was in danger.

ANSWERS TO INVESTIGATE, INQUIRE, IMAGINE

Recall

1a. The Duke refers to the person in the painting as "my last Duchess."

2a. He attributes her look to either his own presence or to a courteous remark made by the artist.

3a. The Duke considered his marrying her to be a greater gift than anyone else could hope to give her.

Interpret

1b. The Duke despised her and thought of her as a possession.

2b. The late Duchess was a very kindhearted, joyful person. The Duchess found joy in everything. The Duke wanted to be the only thing that made her smile. The Duke was arrogant in feeling that way.

3b. The Duke is snobby and self-obsessed. He is a shallow person.

Analyze

4a. *Responses will vary.* Possible responses are given. The late Duchess was a very kindhearted, joyful person, who found joy in everything around her. Some might view her behavior as innocently flirtatious, but others may say she simply showed gratitude to those who did kind and courteous things for her.

Synthesize

4b. *Responses will vary.* Students may say that the Duchess would say that the Duke was very controlling and jealous. Others may say that the Duchess seems to have a positive view of the world and might have nice things to say about the Duke.

Evaluate

5a. The Duke seems to have intended to justify his feelings for the late Duchess and to encourage the emissary to view the Duchess through his own eyes. Instead, he painted a charming picture of the Duchess and cast himself as a despicable, jealous man who had her killed.

Extend

5b. *Responses will vary.*

Respond to the SELECTION

If you were the visitor, how would you respond to the Duke?

INVESTIGATE, Inquire, Imagine

Recall: Gathering Facts

1a. In line 1, how does the Duke refer to the person in the portrait?

2a. To what causes does the Duke attribute the Duchess's smile in the painting?

3a. What did the Duke give his Duchess that he thought was greater than all other gifts?

Interpret: Finding Meaning

1b. What can you infer about the Duke from this comment?

2b. Why does the Duke dislike the Duchess's smile?

3b. What does the Duke think of himself?

Analyze: Taking Things Apart →

4a. Identify the main characteristics of the Duchess.

Synthesize: Bringing Things Together

4b. If the portrait could talk, what do you think the Duchess would say about the Duke?

Evaluate: Making Judgments →

5a. Evaluate the Duke's comments. Consider both their intent and their effect.

Extend: Connecting Ideas

5b. What would you do if you heard somebody talk like this?

Understanding Literature

Dramatic Monologue. Review the definition of **dramatic monologue** in the Handbook of Literary Terms. Explain the situation behind this dramatic monologue. What does the speaker reveal about himself through his speech?

Diction. Review the definition of **diction** and the chart you made in Literary Tools on page 799. What is the significance of the Duke's choice of the word *object* to refer to the woman whom he wants to marry? What other objects does the Duke collect? What might be the reaction of the Duke's visitor?

ANSWERS TO UNDERSTANDING LITERATURE

Dramatic Monologue. The speaker in the poem is the Duke. The Duke is speaking with an agent who is negotiating his next marriage. The Duke shows his visitor the portrait of his late wife. The Duke imagines that the agent wonders why the Duchess has that look on her face. He replies that the look is a result of his presence or of a remark made by the artist. The monologue reveals that the Duke is a self-obsessed, cruel, shallow man.

Diction. By using the word *object,* the Duke makes it clear that he never considers his wives as equals, or even as human beings. The Duke also collects art. The visitor may realize that the Duke's attitude might have led to the Duchess's death. The visitor may now hesitate to help negotiate this new match for the Duke, worrying that the same thing will happen with a new wife.

"Andrea del Sarto"[1]

ROBERT BROWNING

But do not let us quarrel any more,
No, my Lucrezia; bear with me for once:
Sit down and all shall happen as you wish.
You turn your face, but does it bring your heart?
I'll work then for your friend's friend, never fear,
Treat his own subject after his own way,
Fix his own time, accept too his own price,
And shut the money into this small hand
When next it takes mine. Will it? tenderly?
Oh, I'll content him—but tomorrow, Love!
I often am much wearier than you think,
This evening more than usual, and it seems
As if—forgive now—should you let me sit
Here by the window with your hand in mine
And look a half-hour forth on Fiesole,[2]
Both of one mind, as married people use,
Quietly, quietly the evening through,
I might get up tomorrow to my work
Cheerful and fresh as ever. Let us try.
Tomorrow, how you shall be glad for this!
Your soft hand is a woman of itself,
And mine the man's bared breast she curls inside.
Don't count the time lost, neither; you must serve
For each of the five pictures we require:

What is the painter agreeing to do? What will he do with the money that he earns? What does he hope for in return?

What does the painter want to do this evening?

1. **Andrea del Sarto.** Andrea del Sarto was a Florentine painter. Browning draws his information from a biography in Vasari's *The Lives of the Painters.* Del Sarto never fulfilled early signs of promise in his career. Lucrezia, his wife, had great influence on him, and his infatuation with her led to some neglect of his art.
2. **Fiesole.** A hill town overlooking Florence

Literary TOOLS

PARADOX. A **paradox** is a seemingly contradictory statement, idea, or event. As you read "Andrea del Sarto," try to figure out what is meant by the paradox, "Less is more."

THEME. A **theme** is a central idea in a literary work. As you read, try to identify one theme of "Andrea del Sarto."

Reader's Journal

Which do you prefer in art: technical perfection or inspired passion? Explain.

ANSWERS TO GUIDED READING QUESTIONS

1. The painter will paint a portrait for a friend of Lucrezia's friend. He will give the money to Lucrezia. The painter hopes that Lucrezia will tenderly hold his hand.
2. The painter wants to sit for one half hour and look out the window with Lucrezia.

READER'S JOURNAL

You may wish to show students a selection of works by artists with varying styles. Or, have students find examples of art of a style they like from the works shown in this book.

VOCABULARY FROM THE SELECTION

demur
profusely

INDIVIDUAL LEARNING STRATEGIES

MOTIVATION
Students should work together to role play the scene depicted in this poem. They might give some poetic lines to del Sarto's wife and to her "Cousin" to create dialogue instead of a monologue.

READING PROFICIENCY
Remind students that making predictions is one way of reading actively. Ask them to make some predictions about the outcome of the request that the speaker makes at the beginning of "Andrea del Sarto."

ENGLISH LANGUAGE LEARNING
Explain that del Sarto refers to Lucrezia's love as her "cousin," but he is probably not really her cousin.

ADDITIONAL VOCABULARY
quarrel—argue
serpentining—winding
convent—monastery
fetter—bond
strive—try hard
replenish—refill; replace
avail—be effective
illumined—lit
suffice—be enough

INDIVIDUAL LEARNING STRATEGIES (CONT.)

SPECIAL NEEDS
Read the selection aloud to students, or have them listen to a recording of the poem. Ask them to discuss the conflict that del Sarto is experiencing. What would they do in his situation—spend less energy on Lucrezia and strive for a more inspired art? Or be happy with the perfection of artistic technique?

ENRICHMENT

Have students find examples of the works of Andrea del Sarto. Students can choose one or more works to analyze. Students might also compare del Sarto's work to that of Michelangelo.

ANSWER TO GUIDED READING QUESTION

1. The painter is obsessed by his wife's beauty. She does not love him anymore. The line "which everybody looks on and calls his" points to her promiscuous lifestyle.

ART NOTE

Andrea del Sarto (1486–1530) was the most gifted of the Florentine painters of his generation. *Holy Family* is one of his last and greatest works, a developed, somewhat complex High Renaissance painting. Its color is the most outstanding thing about the painting, and the color seems to be not naturalistic but expressive. The globe with the cross refers to Christianity's expansion around the world. John the Baptist, the traditional patron saint of Florence, seems to be handing the globe to Christ. Lucrezia del Fede is the model for the Virgin Mary in this painting, as she was for many of his works. Refer students to lines 24–34 and 175–179 of the poem, in which the speaker refers to this practice of using his wife as a model.

CROSS-CURRICULAR CONNECTIONS

History. Robert Browning was devoted to his wife, Elizabeth Barrett Browning. Theirs, however, was a more fortunate relationship than that of del Sarto and his wife. After the death of Elizabeth Barrett Browning, Robert Browning responded to criticism of her with the following words.

"How to return your thanks would pass my wits.
Kicking you seems the common lot of ours—
While more appropriate greeting lends you grace!
Spitting from lips once sacrificed by Hers."

That Browning's rejoinder was indignant is understandable, that it was also poetic is remarkable.

The Holy Family with the Infant Saint John, c.1530. Andrea del Sarto. The Metropolitan Museum of Art.

It saves a model. So! keep looking so—
My serpentining beauty, rounds on rounds![3]
—How could you ever prick those perfect ears,
Even to put the pearl there! oh, so sweet—
My face, my moon, my everybody's moon,
Which everybody looks on and calls his,
And, I suppose, is looked on by in turn,
While she looks—no one's: very dear, no less.
You smile? why, there's my picture ready made,

How does the painter feel toward his wife? How does she act toward him? How do you know?

3. **My . . . rounds.** Hair coiled like a serpent

There's what we painters call our harmony!
A common grayness silvers[4] everything—
All in a twilight, you and I alike
—You, at the point of your first pride in me
(That's gone you know)—but I, at every point;
My youth, my hope, my art, being all toned down
To yonder sober pleasant Fiesole.
There's the bell clinking from the chapel top;
That length of convent wall across the way
Holds the trees safer, huddled more inside;
The last monk leaves the garden; days decrease,
And autumn grows, autumn in everything.
Eh? the whole seems to fall into a shape
As if I saw alike my work and self
And all that I was born to be and do,
A twilight-piece. Love, we are in God's hand.
How strange now, looks the life he makes us lead;
So free we seem, so fettered fast we are!
I feel he laid the fetter: let it lie!
This chamber for example—turn your head—
All that's behind us! You don't understand
Nor care to understand about my art,
But you can hear at least when people speak:
And that cartoon,[5] the second from the door
—It is the thing, Love! so such things should be—
Behold Madonna!—I am bold to say.
I can do with my pencil what I know,
What I see, what at bottom of my heart
I wish for, if I ever wish so deep—
Do easily, too—when I say, perfectly,
I do not boast, perhaps: yourself are judge,
Who listened to the Legate's[6] talk last week,
And just as much they used to say in France.
At any rate 'tis easy, all of it!
No sketches first, no studies, that's long past:
I do what many dream of, all their lives,
—Dream? strive to do, and agonize to do,
And fail in doing. I could count twenty such
On twice your fingers, and not leave this town,
Who strive—you don't know how the others strive
To paint a little thing like that you smeared

How does the painter characterize his present life? To what does he compare it?

What is the painter capable of doing?

4. **grayness silvers.** Silver gray was a predominant color in del Sarto's paintings.
5. **cartoon.** Drawing
6. **Legate.** One of the pope's deputies

ANSWERS TO GUIDED READING QUESTIONS

1. The painter sees his life as a lesser verision of what it might have been had he not moved to Fiesole. He compares his life to a twilight-piece, or something that is at the point just before being extinguished.
2. The artist is capable of drawing perfectly anything that he wishes.

LITERARY TECHNIQUE

Image. An **image** is a word picture—a word or phrase that names something that can be seen, heard, touched, tasted, or smelled. Ask students to list the predominant images in lines 35–49. What do images such as "grayness," twilight," the clinking of the chapel bell, autumn, and a "twilight-piece" seem to suggest? Ask students to think of all the words or ideas that they associate with the color gray. Ask students, "What is coming to an end for del Sarto—his art, his love, his life, his hopes?"

Metaphor. A **metaphor** is a figure of speech in which one thing is spoken or written about as if it were another. This figure of speech invites the reader to make a comparison between the two things. The image in lines 35–49, in which del Sarto describes his "work and self," all that he was "born to be and do" as "a twilight" piece, can also be considered a metaphor. His life and his work are both like a painting of a twilight scene, in which "A common grayness silvers everything." Ask students what things are being compared in this metaphor. What is del Sarto saying about his life and his work? What makes his house and his life seem gray? In what sense is his work also like the twilight, like grayness, and not like daytime and brightness?

Answers

This metaphor compares the waning of the day to the waning of del Sarto's life and talent. His house and his life are gray because he is not living his life as he should. His work is only a shadow of what it should be.

ANSWER TO GUIDED READING QUESTION

1. The artist feels that in other artists' paintings burns a truer light of God, or divine inspiration.

ADDITIONAL QUESTIONS AND ACTIVITIES

One theme of "Andrea del Sarto" is stated in the lines "Ah, but a man's reach should exceed his grasp, / Or what's a heaven for?" Ask students what they think is meant by these lines.

Answer

These lines mean that a person shouldn't settle for accomplishing those things that are easy or even possible. Instead, a person should reach for heaven—for the divine ideal—even if she or he believes it would be impossible to grasp.

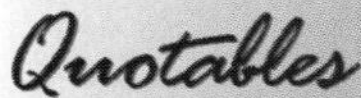

"I find earth not grey but rosy,
Heaven not grim but fair of hue.
Do I stoop? I pluck a posy.
Do I stand and stare? All's blue."

—Robert Browning

Carelessly passing with your robes afloat—
Yet do much less, so much less, Someone[7] says
(I know his name, no matter)—so much less!
Well, less is more, Lucrezia: I am judged.
There burns a truer light of God in them,
In their vexed beating stuffed and stopped-up brain,
Heart, or whate'er else, than goes on to prompt
This low-pulsed forthright craftsman's hand of mine.
Their works drop groundward, but themselves, I know,
Reach many a time a heaven that's shut to me,
Enter and take their place there sure enough,
Though they come back and cannot tell the world.
My works are nearer heaven, but I sit here.
The sudden blood of these men! at a word—
Praise them, it boils, or blame them, it boils too.
I, painting from myself and to myself,
Know what I do, am unmoved by men's blame
Or their praise either. Somebody remarks
Morello's[8] outline there is wrongly traced,
His hue mistaken; what of that? or else,
Rightly traced and well ordered; what of that?
Speak as they please, what does the mountain care?
Ah, but a man's reach should exceed his grasp,
Or what's a heaven for? All is silver-gray
Placid and perfect with my art: the worse!
I know both what I want and what might gain,
And yet how profitless to know, to sigh
"Had I been two, another and myself,
Our head would have o'erlooked the world!"[9] No doubt.
Yonder's a work now, of that famous youth
The Urbinate[10] who died five years ago.
('Tis copied, George Vasari sent it me.)
Well, I can fancy how he did it all,
Pouring his soul, with kings and popes to see,
Reaching, that heaven might so replenish him,
Above and through his art—for it gives way;
That arm is wrongly put—and there again—
A fault to pardon in the drawing's lines,
Its body, so to speak: its soul is right,
He means right—that, a child may understand.

Del Sarto paints flawlessly, but he feels that there is something lacking in his work. What is lacking that he finds in other painters?

7. **Someone.** Probably Michelangelo
8. **Morello.** A mountain outside Florence
9. **Had . . . world.** Andrea acknowledges the need for aspiration and dedication combined with the skill he possessed to make a truly great artist.
10. **Urbinate.** Raphael, who was born in Urbino

Still, what an arm! and I could alter it:
But all the play, the insight and the stretch—
Out of me, out of me! And wherefore out?
Had you enjoined them on me, given me soul,
We might have risen to Rafael, I and you!
Nay, Love, you did give all I asked, I think—
More than I merit, yes, by many times.
But had you—oh, with the same perfect brow,
And perfect eyes, and more than perfect mouth,
And the low voice my soul hears, as a bird
The fowler's pipe,[11] and follows to the snare—
Had you, with these the same, but brought a mind!
Some women do so. Had the mouth there urged
"God and the glory! never care for gain.
The present by the future, what is that?
Live for fame, side by side with Agnolo![12]
Rafael is waiting: up to God, all three!"
I might have done it for you. So it seems:
Perhaps not. All is as God overrules.
Beside, incentives come from the soul's self;
The rest avail not. Why do I need you?
What wife had Rafael, or has Agnolo?
In this world, who can do a thing, will not;
And who would do it, cannot, I perceive:
Yet the will's somewhat—somewhat, too, the power—
And thus we half-men struggle. At the end,
God, I conclude, compensates, punishes.
'Tis safer for me, if the award be strict,
That I am something underrated here.
Poor this long while, despised, to speak the truth.
I dared not, do you know, leave home all day,
For fear of chancing on the Paris lords.
The best is when they pass and look aside;
But they speak sometimes; I must bear it all.
Well may they speak! That Francis,[13] that first time,
And that long festal year at Fontainebleau!
I surely then could sometimes leave the ground,
Put on the glory, Rafael's daily wear,
In that humane great monarch's golden look—
One finger in his beard or twisted curl
Over his mouth's good mark that made the smile,

What does del Sarto mean when he says of Raphael's painting that its body is wrong but its soul is right? In what sense is del Sarto the better painter? In what sense is Raphael the better painter?

What does del Sarto wish his wife had given him?

Does del Sarto blame his wife or himself for his failure to create great work? How do you know?

---

11. **fowler's pipe.** Hunter's call
12. **Agnolo.** Michelangelo
13. **Francis.** Andrea was encouraged by King Francis I of France whose court was at Fontainebleau. Andrea supposedly stole funds from Francis which he used to build a house.

ANSWERS TO GUIDED READING QUESTIONS

1. The body of the subject in the painting is depicted imperfectly: the arm is bent or shaped unnaturally. However, the soul of the person is depicted correctly. The viewer can see a personality there. Del Sarto can draw great arms, while Raphael represents great ideas.
2. Del Sarto wishes that his wife had a mind to match her beautiful body.
3. Del Sarto blames himself. He says that incentives to create art come from the soul's self. He adds that other great painters didn't have wives to urge them on to creating great works.

ADDITIONAL QUESTIONS AND ACTIVITIES

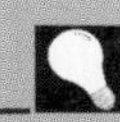

Discuss with students what they feel is del Sarto's biggest obstacle to artistic success. Why?

Answer

Possible responses include his self-obsession, his interest in his wife, his lack of encouragement from his wife, his laziness or his lack of will, and his overly high expectations.

CROSS-CURRICULAR CONNECTIONS

ART. Giorgio Vasari's *The Lives of the Most Eminent Italian Architects, Painters, and Sculptors* (1550) is one of the most influential sources on Renaissance art. Vasari himself was a painter of some notoriety, and as an architect he designed the Uffizi gallery in Florence, which houses one of the great collections of Italian Renaissance painting, but he is known today for his book. Browning refers to Vasari (line 106) and repeats Vasari's low opinion of Andrea del Sarto. It is not obvious to the modern observer that del Sarto's lack of ambition for money or fame, for which Vasari criticized him, implies a lack of artistic ambition.

ANSWERS TO GUIDED READING QUESTIONS

1. Del Sarto doesn't want to blame his wife for his lack of success.
2. If del Sarto worked under the same system as did Raphael, del Sarto would offer stiff competition. Del Sarto believes that Michelangelo was right because he knows that Raphael's technical skills are wanting.

LITERARY NOTE

Michel Agnolo is now called Michelangelo.

Quotables

"The making of a poem is like that of a painting."

—Horace

ADDITIONAL QUESTIONS AND ACTIVITIES

Have students discuss the above quotation. How do painting and poetry interact in this selection? What are the tools with which a poet "paints"? Does Browning successfully describe painting?

One arm about my shoulder, round my neck,
The jingle of his gold chain in my ear,
I painting proudly with his breath on me,
All his court round him, seeing with his eyes,
Such frank French eyes, and such a fire of souls
Profuse, my hand kept plying by those hearts—
And, best of all, this, this, this face beyond,
This in the background, waiting on my work,
To crown the issue with a last reward!
A good time, was it not, my kingly days?
And had you not grown restless . . . but I know—
'Tis done and past; 'twas right, my instinct said;
Too live the life grew, golden and not gray,
And I'm the weak-eyed bat no sun should tempt
Out of the grange whose four walls make his world.
How could it end in any other way?
You called me, and I came home to your heart.
The triumph was—to reach and stay there; since
I reached it ere the triumph, what is lost?
Let my hands frame your face in your hair's gold,
You beautiful Lucrezia that are mine!
"Rafael did this, Andrea painted that;
The Roman's is the better when you pray,
But still the other's Virgin was his wife—"
Men will excuse me. I am glad to judge
Both pictures in your presence; clearer grows
My better fortune, I resolve to think.
For, do you know, Lucrezia, as God lives,
Said one day Agnolo, his very self,
To Rafael . . . I have known it all these years . . .
(When the young man was flaming out his thoughts
Upon a palace wall for Rome to see,
Too lifted up in heart because of it)
"Friend, there's a certain sorry little scrub
Goes up and down our Florence, none cares how,
Who, were he set to plan and execute
As you are, pricked on by your popes and kings,
Would bring the sweat into that brow of yours!"
To Rafael's—And indeed the arm is wrong.
I hardly dare . . . yet, only you to see,
Give the chalk here—quick, thus the line should go!
Aye, but the soul! he's Rafael! rub it out!
Still, all I care for, if he spoke the truth,
(What he? why, who but Michel Agnolo?
Do you forget already words like those?)

Why doesn't del Sarto finish the statement that begins, "had you not grown restless"? What is he thinking about here?

What did the great Michelangelo tell Raphael about del Sarto? Does del Sarto believe that Michelangelo was right?

If really there was such a chance, so lost—
Is, whether you're—not grateful—but more pleased.
Well, let me think so. And you smile indeed!
This hour has been an hour! Another smile?
If you would sit thus by me every night
I should work better, do you comprehend?
I mean that I should earn more, give you more.
See, it is settled dusk now; there's a star;
Morello's gone, the watch-lights show the wall,
The cue-owls[14] speak the name we call them by.
Come from the window, love—come in, at last,
Inside the melancholy little house
We built to be so gay with. God is just.
King Francis may forgive me: oft at nights
When I look up from painting, eyes tired out,
The walls become illumined, brick from brick
Distinct, instead of mortar, fierce bright gold,
That gold of his I did cement them with!
Let us but love each other. Must you go?
That Cousin here again? he waits outside?
Must see you—you—and not with me? Those loans?
More gaming debts to pay?[15] you smiled for that?
Well, let smiles buy me! have you more to spend?
While hand and eye and something of a heart
Are left me, work's my ware, and what's it worth?
I'll pay my fancy. Only let me sit
The gray remainder of the evening out,
Idle, you call it, and muse perfectly
How I could paint, were I but back in France,
One picture, just one more—the Virgin's face,
Not yours this time! I want you at my side
To hear them—that is, Michel Agnolo—
Judge all I do and tell you of its worth.
Will you? Tomorrow, satisfy your friend.
I take the subjects for his corridor,
Finish the portrait out of hand—there, there,
And throw him in another thing or two
If he demurs; the whole should prove enough

What does del Sarto implore his wife to do? How might this affect his work? Why?

Who has come to see del Sarto's wife? Why is he there? Why does she want him to do the painting mentioned at the beginning of the poem?

14. **cue-owls.** Owls that make a noise like the Italian word *ciu*
15. **Cousin . . . pay.** Lucrezia's lover had gambling debts that Andrea agreed to cover by painting some pictures.

WORDS FOR EVERYDAY USE

de • mur (dē mur′) *vi.,* hesitate, object. *Do not demur upon my proposal of marriage.*

ANSWERS TO GUIDED READING QUESTIONS

1. Del Sarto wants his wife to sit by him every night while he works. Del Sarto might be able to work better knowing that his wife cared about him and was near him.
2. A lover has come to see del Sarto's wife. The lover is there to borrow money. Lucrezia wants del Sarto to do the painting to raise money to pay off her lover's gambling debts.

BIBLIOGRAPHICAL NOTE

George Meredith (1828–1909) was known as the author of *The Ordeal of Richard Feverel* (1859) and The Egoist (1879). Meredith, however, preferred writing poetry. Meredith's sonnet sequence "Modern Love" shares a common theme with "Andrea del Sarto"—a difficult marriage that causes suffering. Indeed, like Meredith's narrator, Browning's Andrea del Sarto too might have said, "But, oh, the bitter taste her beauty had!"

Quotables

"'Will you very kindly tell me, Mr. Wilde, in your own words, your viewpoint of George Meredith?'
'George Meredith is a prose Browning, and so is Browning.'
'Thank you. His style?'
'Chaos, illumined by flashes of lightning.'"

—Oscar Wilde

ANSWERS TO GUIDED READING QUESTIONS

1. Del Sarto is attempting to justify spending all of his money on Lucrezia while his parents were living in poverty.
2. The other artists would outpaint del Sarto because he would still be with Lucrezia. Del Sarto would still be worrying too much about his wife to paint well. Ultimately, del Sarto blames himself for not doing great work.

SELECTION CHECK TEST 4.9.11 WITH ANSWERS

Checking Your Reading

1. What does Lucrezia not understand? **She does not understand her husband's art.**
2. What two great artists inspired del Sarto? **Rafael and Michelangelo inspired him.**
3. Why did del Sarto leave Fountainebleau? **His wife called him home.**
4. What does del Sarto do with the money he steals from Francis? **He builds a house.**
5. Who whistles for Lucrezia? **Her "cousin"—her lover.**

Literary Tools

Fill in the blanks using the following terms. You will not use every term, and you may use some terms more than once.

character theme metaphor
hyperbole paradox

1. A central idea in a literary work is called a **theme**.
2. The line, "Your soft hand is a woman of itself" contains a **metaphor**.
3. A contradictory statement, idea, or event is a **paradox**.

RESPOND TO THE SELECTION

Students may want to consider how this poem might have affected them if the gender of the characters were reversed.

To pay for this same Cousin's freak. Beside,
What's better and what's all I care about,
Get you the thirteen scudi[16] for the ruff!
Love, does that please you? Ah, but what does he,
The Cousin! What does he to please you more?

I am grown peaceful as old age tonight.
I regret little, I would change still less.
Since there my past life lies, why alter it?
The very wrong to Francis!—it is true
I took his coin, was tempted and complied,
And built this house and sinned, and all is said.
My father and my mother died of want.[17]
Well, had I riches of my own? you see
How one gets rich! Let each one bear his lot.
They were born poor, lived poor, and poor they died:
And I have labored somewhat in my time
And not been paid profusely. Some good son
Paint my two hundred pictures—let him try!
No doubt, there's something strikes a balance. Yes,
You loved me quite enough, it seems tonight.
This must suffice me here. What would one have?
In heaven, perhaps, new chances, one more chance—
Four great walls in the New Jerusalem,
Meted on each side by the angel's reed,
For Leonard,[18] Rafael, Agnolo and me
To cover—the three first without a wife,
While I have mine! So—still they overcome
Because there's still Lucrezia—as I choose.

Again the Cousin's whistle! Go my Love. ■

What is del Sarto attempting to justify here?

Even in heaven, if given one last chance to paint greatly, del Sarto believes that he would be outdone by Leonardo, Raphael, and Michelangelo. Why? What would keep him from having spirit enough to do great work? On whom does the blame ultimately rest for his not doing great work?

16. **scudi.** Italian coins
17. **My . . . want.** Vasari claims Andrea stopped supporting his poor parents because of his infatuation for Lucrezia.
18. **Leonard.** Leonardo da Vinci

Words For Everyday Use

pro • fuse • ly (prō fyo͞os′ lē) *adv.*, generously; freely. *I bled profusely when I cut my finger.*

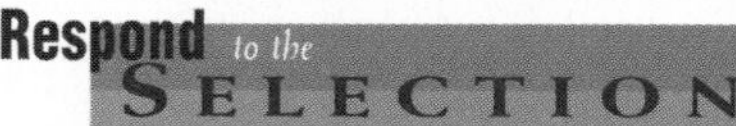

Respond to the Selection

What compromise has del Sarto made? Do you respect him for this decision? Why, or why not?

INVESTIGATE, Inquire, Imagine

Recall: GATHERING FACTS →

1a. What has del Sarto's wife asked him to do at the beginning of the poem? What does del Sarto ask his wife to do this evening?

2a. What is del Sarto's skill as a painter? What does his painting lack?

3a. Why did del Sarto leave his "kingly days" behind?

Interpret: FINDING MEANING

1b. How does del Sarto feel toward his wife? How do you know?

2b. Which quality does del Sarto think is more important? How do you know?

3b. What effect has Lucrezia had on del Sarto's work?

Analyze: TAKING THINGS APART →

4a. Analyze del Sarto's lack of success. What aspects of his life led him toward success? Which stood in his way?

Synthesize: BRINGING THINGS TOGETHER

4b. What do you think would have happened if del Sarto left Lucrezia?

Evaluate: MAKING JUDGMENTS →

5a. Near the beginning of the poem, del Sarto says that he regrets little and "would change still less." Judge whether he is being honest.

Extend: CONNECTING IDEAS

5b. Is it possible to regret something, but not want to change it? Explain.

Understanding Literature

PARADOX. Review the definition for **paradox** in the Handbook of Literary Terms. In the poem, del Sarto says of other painters in Florence that they are not as skilled as he, that they are able to do less than he can. Then he states a paradox, that "Less is more." What does he mean by that paradox? In what sense is their work greater than his, even though it is less technically perfect?

THEME. Review the definition for **theme** in the Handbook of Literary Terms. One central idea, perhaps the central idea, of this poem is stated in the lines "Ah, but a man's reach should exceed his grasp, / Or what's a heaven for?" What does it mean to have a reach that exceeds your grasp? What is within del Sarto's grasp? For what should he be reaching? What keeps him from doing so? How might reaching beyond one's grasp account for the great works done by human beings? What is Browning saying about the human spirit and its role in creating great art and wonderful lives?

ANSWERS TO INVESTIGATE, INQUIRE, IMAGINE

RECALL

1a. Lucrezia wants him to paint for a friend of a friend of hers. Del Sarto asks his wife to stay with him that evening.

2a. Del Sarto is very technically accurate as a painter, but his art lacks passion.

3a. Lucrezia grew restless.

INTERPRET

1b. He loves her, but he also knows that his feelings for her are his downfall. He mentions a number of times that if he were to apply himself, his skills could make him famous, but he is too involved in his feelings for Lucrezia.

2b. Which quality does del Sarto think is more important? How do you know?

3b. She has encouraged him to work for money and to give up opportunities to be with her.

ANALYZE

4a. Del Sarto has great talent and technical skill. He believes that he is unable to achieve his goal because of the relationship he has with his wife. He is devoted to a wife who only wants the money he is able to earn from his paintings.

SYNTHESIZE

4b. *Responses will vary.* Students may say del Sarto might finally achieve his potential. Others may say that he does not want to leave Lucrezia, and so might not benefit from being free of her.

EVALUATE

5a. The fact that del Sarto does not change indicates that he would not exchange his wife for greater talent. He does, however, realize that he has settled for being married to a woman who doesn't love him and for painting second-rate pictures for people who don't know real art. Doing this has cost him fame, respect, and a decent life.

EXTEND

5b. *Responses will vary.*

ANSWERS TO UNDERSTANDING LITERATURE

PARADOX. This is the great paradox of del Sarto's life: he has the ability to be great, but not the passion, and so the work of other, less technically talented artists surpasses his. The work of the other artists is inspired by great ideas and displays their passion for their work. All of del Sarto's passion is wrapped up in his unfaithful wife.

THEME. People should strive to accomplish more than those things easily in reach. Those things in del Sarto's grasp include producing technically perfect, but emotionally bankrupt, art and being an emotional slave to his wife. Del Sarto should be reaching for subjects that would inspire him and fill his art with passion. He is prevented from reaching beyond his grasp because of both his devotion to a bad marriage and his tendency to make excuses for his lack of inspiration. When an artist reaches beyond his or her grasp to create, that effort is reflected in the work.Great art and a wonderful life can only be accomplished by those who attempt to reach beyond their limitations.

ANSWERS TO INTEGRATING THE LANGUAGE ARTS

Language, Grammar, and Style
Responses will vary.
Robert Browning wrote the famous poem, "The Pied Piper of Hamlin." It is a marvelous story about a city plagued by rats often retold in children's books. A piper offers to rid the town of rats and the worried city fathers agree to pay him. The piper plays. Even though the rats follow him out of town, the town refuses to pay the piper. The piper therefore takes his revenge. He plays his pipe. The city's children hear the music, follow him out of town, and are not seen or heard of again.

Study and Research
Review with students where they might find information on the various artists, including which libraries they might visit.

Speaking and Listening & Collaborative Learning
Student groups may want to choose different events in the lives of the Duke and Duchess so that the skits won't be repetitive.

Applied English
Students might work in groups to create a series of announcements with a similar theme or focus.

Writer's Journal

1. Write a **thank you note** to somebody who has supported you in some endeavor or helped you to succeed in some way.
2. Write a **personal essay** about a dream you are trying to achieve, your own attempt to reach beyond your grasp.
3. Imagine that you are the Duke's visitor or Lucrezia, Andrea del Sarto's wife. Write a **dramatic monologue** in response to one of these poems.

Integrating *the* Language Arts

Language, Grammar, and Style

Writing Varied Sentences. Read the Language Arts Survey 3.36, "Combining and Expanding Sentences." Then rewrite the following paragraph to vary the length and structure of its sentences.

Robert Browning wrote "The Pied Piper of Hamlin." It is a famous poem. It tells a marvelous story. The story is often retold in children's books. The story goes like this: A city is plagued with rats. The city fathers are worried. A piper offers to rid the town of rats. The city agrees to pay him. The piper plays. The rats follow him out of the town. The city then refuses to pay the piper. The piper therefore takes revenge. He plays his pipe. The city's children hear the music. They follow him out of town and are not seen or heard of again.

Study and Research

Art History. As a class, do research on some or all of the following Italian Renaissance painters: Andrea del Sarto, Giotto di Bondone, Michelangelo Buonarroti, Leonardo da Vinci, Raphael (Raffaello Santi), Titian (Tiziano Vecellio), Tintoretto (Jacopo Robusti), and Michelangelo da Caravaggio. Divide into groups. Assign one painter to each group. Research the life and works of these painters. Then present the results of your research in class, combining oral reporting with slides, prints, or pictures from books.

Speaking and Listening & Collaborative Learning

Dramatic Skit. Collaborate with one or two other students to write a dramatic scene that presents a confrontation between the Duke in Browning's "My Last Duchess" and his former wife. (This scene will, of course, take place before the time of Browning's poem.) In your scene, portray the characters as they are portrayed in the poem. Write parts for each student in your group, including, if your group has three students, a third character such as the "officious fool" mentioned in line 27 of the poem. Rehearse your skit and present it to the rest of the class.

Applied English

Public Service Announcement. Write a public service announcement about domestic abuse or dating violence. You may need to research the subject to get statistics or other facts. This is a broad topic, so you will need to decide on a concise message you wish to convey. For additional help, read the Language Arts Survey 6.10, "Writing a Public Service Announcement."

"Dover Beach"

BY MATTHEW ARNOLD

About the AUTHOR

Matthew Arnold (1822–1888) was a multitalented man, a great classics scholar, a distinguished poet and literary critic, and a commentator on education, religion, and culture. The son of the headmaster of Rugby school, he attended Rugby and Oxford. While at Oxford, he received the Newdigate prize for a poem about Oliver Cromwell, leader of England during the Puritan Interregnum. After graduating, Arnold took a government post as inspector of schools, a position that he held for the rest of his working life. In 1853, he published a book entitled *Poems,* which established his reputation as a writer of verse. In 1857, he was appointed to the poetry chair at Oxford, a position that he held for ten years. In 1859, he was appointed foreign assistant commissioner on education and traveled to the continent to observe school systems there. His *New Poems,* containing "Dover Beach," appeared in 1867, but by that time he was devoting his writing primarily to critical essays. He admired the calmness, clarity, and restraint of the great writers of classical Greece and Rome and believed that culture—"the best that has been thought and said in the world"—was the proper antidote for the worries, materialism, and decay of his times. In 1883 he made a lecture tour in the United States, published as *Discourses in America.*

About the SELECTION

No work more typifies the struggle between faith and doubt faced by thinking men and women of the Victorian Age than Matthew Arnold's **"Dover Beach."** Arnold lived in a time when religion was coming under attack from science and many people were questioning their faith. He felt the loss of his own faith keenly and wrote about it in this famous poem. The poem fully meets Arnold's own criteria for poetry, that it have a "high seriousness" and that it provide a "criticism of life." Many critics have called Arnold's poetry severe and melancholic, and indeed "Dover Beach" is one of the most melancholic poems ever written. However, a close reading of the selection will reveal that Arnold did have some Victorian optimism in him, for the poem offers as a stay against the anarchy and confusion of life the possibility that people can be "true / To one another."

Literary TOOLS

ALLUSION. An **allusion** is a rhetorical technique in which a reference is made to a person, event, object, or work from history or literature. Note the allusion that Arnold makes in "Dover Beach."

SYMBOL. A **symbol** is a thing that stands for or represents both itself and something else. Make a cluster chart like the one below to indicate what the sea represents in this poem.

Reader's Journal

What sights or sounds make you feel melancholy, or blue?

ADDITIONAL RESOURCES

UNIT 9 RESOURCE BOOK
- Selection Worksheet 9.6
- Selection Check Test 4.9.13
- Selection Test 4.9.14
- Writing Resource 2.24

VOCABULARY FROM THE SELECTON

certitude
shingle
strand
tremulous
turbid

GRAPHIC ORGANIZER

Students may include the following in their cluster charts:
ebb and flow of human misery (to Sophocles); Sea of Faith; religion; retreating tide represents the diminishing of human faith.

READER'S JOURNAL

Students may wish to consider weather, times of day, times of year, or other aspects that contribute to their mood. Students may also discuss sights and sounds that draw them out of gloomy moods.

GOALS/OBJECTIVES

Studying this lesson will enable students to
- interpret and appreciate a lyric poem
- describe Matthew Arnold's literary accomplishments and explain the historical significance of his writings
- define *allusion* and *symbol* and identify examples of each that they encounter in their reading
- write topic sentences

ANSWERS TO GUIDED READING QUESTIONS

1. The speaker hears the "grating roar" of pebbles drawn back and flung up by the waves over and over. The speaker feels an "eternal note of sadness" communicated by the slow rhythm of the waves.
2. Sophocles thought of human misery when he heard the sound of the Aegean Sea.
3. The "Sea of Faith" is shrinking, retreating from its banks.

INDIVIDUAL LEARNING STRATEGIES

Motivation
Explain that "straits" (line 3) refers to the Straits of Dover in the English Channel. Have students find Dover and the Aegean on a map of Europe and discuss the similarities.

Reading Proficiency
Suggest that students work with a reading partner. The partners can work together to determine the meaning of unfamiliar words or phrases.

English Language Learning
In addition to following the suggestions for Reading Proficiency above, share with students the following additional vocabulary.
glimmering—flickering faintly
tranquil—peaceful and calm
blanched—whitened
darkling—dim; obscure

Special Needs
Have students read the Language Arts Survey 5.4, "Classifying." Then, have them look up sanguine and melancholic in a dictionary. As they read the poem, they should decide which classification, sanguine or melancholic, fits the speaker of Arnold's poem.

Enrichment
In Victorian times, religion was a very important part of political life. Members of the government were overwhelmingly Anglican. In 1851, Great Britain conducted the only census to ever attempt to determine religious affiliation. Have students research the results of that census and analyze how those results affected British politics.

Dover Beach

Matthew Arnold

The sea is calm tonight.
The tide is full, the moon lies fair
Upon the straits—on the French coast the light
Gleams and is gone; the cliffs of England stand,
Glimmering and vast, out in the tranquil bay.
Come to the window, sweet is the night air!
Only, from the long line of spray
Where the sea meets the moon-blanched land,
Listen! you hear the grating roar
Of pebbles which the waves draw back, and fling,
At their return, up the high strand,
Begin, and cease, and then again begin,
With tremulous cadence slow, and bring
The eternal note of sadness in.

What does the speaker hear? How does this sound make the speaker feel?

Sophocles[1] long ago
Heard it on the Aegean, and it brought
Into his mind the turbid ebb and flow
Of human misery; we
Find also in the sound a thought,
Hearing it by this distant northern sea.

What did Sophocles think of when he heard the sound of the waves on the Aegean Sea centuries before?

The Sea of Faith
Was once, too, at the full, and round earth's shore
Lay like the folds of a bright girdle furled.[2]
But now I only hear
Its melancholy, long, withdrawing roar,
Retreating, to the breath
Of the night wind, down the vast edges drear
And naked shingles[3] of the world.

What, according to the speaker, has happened to the "Sea of Faith"?

1. **Sophocles.** Greek playwright (496–406 BC)
2. **Lay . . . furled.** At high tide, the sea tightly envelopes the land like a girdle.
3. **shingle.** Rocky beach

Words for Everyday Use

strand (strand) *n.*, shore. *My brother and I sat upon the strand and watched the waves roll in.*
trem • u • lous (trem´yo͞o ləs) *adj.*, trembling. *The leaves in the willow tree were tremulous in the light breeze.*
tur • bid (tur´bid) *adj.*, muddled. *Never drink from a turbid stream.*

White Cliffs of Dover, c.1900s. Noel Coward. Roy Miles Gallery, London.

Ah, love, let us be true
To one another! for the world, which seems
To lie before us like a land of dreams,
So various, so beautiful, so new,
Hath really neither joy, nor love, nor light,
Nor certitude, nor peace, nor help for pain;
And we are here as on a darkling plain
Swept with confused alarms of struggle and flight,
Where ignorant armies clash by night. ■

What does the speaker ask of his love? Why, according to the speaker, is this necessary?

WORDS FOR EVERYDAY USE

cer • ti • tude (surt´ ə to͞od´) *n.,* absolute sureness. *With certitude I raised my hand and strode to the chalkboard to work the arithmetic problem.*

ANSWER TO GUIDED READING QUESTION

1. The speaker asks that he and his love be true to one another, that they love each other. Doing so is necessary because the rest of the world has no joy, love, light, certitude, peace, or help for pain. Their relationship is the only place where they will experience such feelings.

ADDITIONAL QUESTIONS AND ACTIVITIES

If students have not read the poems by Tennyson (pages 777, 784, 789) and Robert Browning (pages 800 and 803), suggest that they do so. Ask students to compare the roles that women play in these poems and in "Dover Beach." How do the roles of the women differ from those of the men? Why might this be so?

SELECTION CHECK TEST 4.9.13 WITH ANSWERS

Checking Your Reading

1. What causes the "grating roar"? **This is the sound of pebbles thrown by waves.**
2. What "sea" was "once, too, at the full"? **The Sea of Faith was once full.**
3. What does the speaker ask his love? **He asks her to be true.**
4. What does the world seem to be? **It seems to be full of dreams.**
5. What is the world really like? **It is joyless, frightening, confusing, and troubled.**

Literary Tools

1. What is an allusion? **An allusion is a reference to a person, event, or work from history or literature.**
2. What allusion is used in this poem? **A reference is made to Sophocles, specifically, to lines from his play *Antigone*.**
3. What might the sea symbolize in this poem? **Responses will vary.**

RESPOND TO THE SELECTION

Students should cite examples of the things that are happening today that support their response.

ANSWERS TO INVESTIGATE, INQUIRE, IMAGINE

Recall

1a. The sea is calm, the tide is full, the moon gently shines on the land, the cliffs stand glimmering and vast, the bay is tranquil, and the night air is sweet.

2a. Sophocles thought about the cycle of human misery when he heard the sea.

3a. The speaker asks that he and his love be true to one another, that they love each other.

Interpret

1b. At the beginning of the poem, the mood is calm and tranquil. The mood of tranquillity soon changes to one of melancholy.

2b. The speaker connects Sophocles's thought with his sense that human faith is shrinking or ebbing like the tide. He sees a great deal of misery and confusion in the world.

3b. The speaker knows that only in their relationship can they feel joy, love, certitude, and peace.

Analyze

4a. *Responses will vary.* People expect life to be like a land of dreams, various, beautiful, and new. They actually find that life is full of ignorance and strife.

Synthesize

4b. *Responses will vary.* The speaker might feel better if he saw a greater show of faith or of caring and humanity in the world.

Evaluate

5a. *Responses will vary.* Students might bring in a newspaper and find events that support their position.

Extend

5b. *Responses will vary.* When creating metaphors, students should consider not only whether they feel that the general state of the world is positive or negative now, but also whether there is hope for the future.

Respond *to the* Selection

Explain why you agree or disagree with the speaker's assessment of the world in stanza 3.

Investigate, Inquire, Imagine

Recall: Gathering Facts

1a. How does the speaker describe the sea, the tide, the moon, the cliffs, the bay, and the night air in the first few lines of the poem?

2a. What thought did Sophocles have when listening to the sea?

3a. What does the speaker ask of his love in the last stanza?

Interpret: Finding Meaning

1b. What mood is created by the description of the environment at the beginning of the poem? How does this mood change?

2b. What connection does the speaker make to Sophocles's thought?

3b. In the last stanza, why does the speaker make the request that he makes of his love?

Analyze: Taking Things Apart →

4a. Compare and contrast the world as it seems to be and the way it really is according to the speaker.

Synthesize: Bringing Things Together

4b. What do you think would make the speaker have a more positive view of the world?

Evaluate: Making Judgments →

5a. Judge whether the events in the daily news provide evidence for or against Arnold's idea that life is a "darkling plain."

Extend: Connecting Ideas

5b. What metaphor or comparison might you use today to describe the state of the world?

Understanding Literature

Allusion. Review the definition for **allusion** in Literary Tools in Prereading. What allusion does the speaker make in the second stanza of this poem? What is the purpose of this allusion? What idea does the allusion introduce?

Symbol. Review the definition for **symbol** and the cluster chart you completed for Literary Tools in Prereading. Of what is the ebb and flow of the sea a symbol in this poem? What did Sophocles hear in this ebb and flow? What other symbolic significance does the sea have for the speaker? With what does the speaker associate the sea in the third stanza? What has happened to that sea?

ANSWERS FOR UNDERSTANDING LITERATURE

Allusion. The speaker alludes to Sophocles. The purpose of the allusion is to stress that though centuries have passed, the human condition is much the same. (This point is made by Sophocles as well.) The idea of human misery is introduced.

Symbol. The ebb and flow of the sea represent the cycle of life and death. Sophocles heard the ebb and flow of human misery. The speaker also links the retreat of the sea to the diminishing of human faith. The speaker associates the sea with religion, the Sea of Faith, which is retreating.

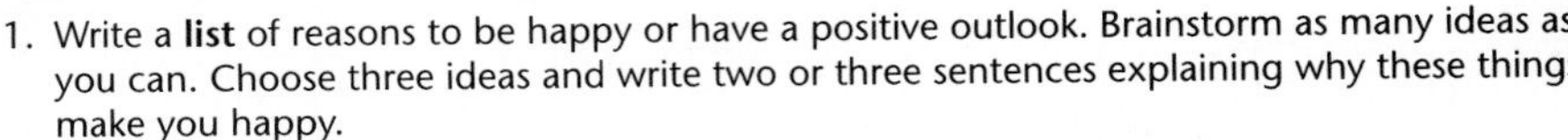

Writer's Journal

1. Write a **list** of reasons to be happy or have a positive outlook. Brainstorm as many ideas as you can. Choose three ideas and write two or three sentences explaining why these things make you happy.
2. Write an **editorial** that expresses your opinion about the state of the world. Whether you choose a positive or negative outlook, support your response with examples and offer reasons for your perception of the state of the world.
3. Choose a sound that you hear often. Make a connection between this sound and a feeling or idea. For example, a dripping faucet might keep you up at night like a nagging worry. Write a **personal essay** in which you explore such a connection.

Integrating *the* Language Arts

Language, Grammar, and Style

Writing Topic Sentences. Review the Language Arts Survey 2.24, "Paragraphs with Topic Sentences." Imagine each stanza of this poem is a paragraph. Write an appropriate topic sentence for each stanza.

Study and Research

Researching Dover. Dover, England is known for its white cliffs. Using guidebooks, travel magazines, and the Internet, research Dover. Then, write a brief description of the city and identify anything you would want to see or do if you visited Dover.

Media Literacy

Evaluating Media. What kinds of stories dominate the news? For several days in a row, watch the news on television, or read the news sections of the paper. How many stories are about negative events? positive events? How many "negative" stories have positive elements or slants, such as people reaching out to help flood victims? Do you think these news stories create an accurate portrait of what the world is like today?

ANSWERS TO INTEGRATING THE LANGUAGE ARTS

Language, Grammar, and Style
Responses will vary.
The repetitive sound of the sea is filled with sadness.
This timeless sound is a sign of human misery and diminishing faith.
The world seems fine on the surface, but that is just an illusion.

Study and Research
Students might use their findings to create a travel brochure for Dover and the surrounding area.

ADDITIONAL RESOURCES

UNIT 9 RESOURCE BOOK

"The Man He Killed"
- Selection Worksheet 9.7
- Selection Check Test 4.9.15
- Selection Test 4.9.16

"Channel Firing"
- Selection Worksheet 9.8
- Selection Check Test 4.9.17
- Selection Test 4.9.18

"The Darkling Thrush"
- Selection Worksheet 9.9
- Selection Check Test 4.9.19
- Selection Test 4.9.20
- Language, Grammar, and Style Resource 3.5
- Speaking and Listening Resource 4.21

INDIVIDUAL LEARNING STRATEGIES

MOTIVATION
Have students read the Language Arts Survey, 5.3, "Avoiding False Arguments and Propaganda." As students read the poem, they should look for the faulty reason the speaker gives for killing a man.

READING PROFICIENCY
Point out the Hardy uses non-standard dialect. Students might with work with another student to put the dialect into standard dialect, or into a dialect more familiar to them.

ENGLISH LANGUAGE LEARNING
Share with students the following additional vocabulary and help them to understand the dialect used in the poem.
ranged—arranged
quaint—unusual, odd

SPECIAL NEEDS
Read the poem aloud to the class. Ask students to discuss the tone of the poem. Is it one of sadness, or wonder, or of horror? Or does it have elements of all three?

ENRICHMENT
Just before the Victorian Age began, many people believed that state education was the best way to convert the masses to the Church of England and prevent a working class revolution. In his book *Culture and Anarchy* (1896), Matthew Arnold described those people living in the east end of London as "those vast, miserable, unmanageable masses of paupers." Conduct research into the plight of the working class in Victorian England. Write a short report on what it might have been like to be part of that working class. Stage a debate on the role of state education and what students should be taught.

PREREADING

"The Man He Killed," "Channel Firing," "The Darkling Thrush"

BY THOMAS HARDY

About the AUTHOR

Thomas Hardy (1840–1928) is perhaps best known for his memorable novels, such as *The Return of the Native, The Mayor of Casterbridge, Tess of the D'Urbervilles,* and *Jude the Obscure.* However, Hardy's first love was poetry, and today he is recognized as one of the great forerunners of modern Realism in verse. Hardy was born in the English west country, the "Wessex" of his novels. Under the influence of his father, a building constructor, he became as a young man apprenticed to a local church architect. Though he showed great talent for architecture, he gave his free time to writing. In 1871, he published his first novel, *Desperate Remedies,* and in 1874, *Far from the Madding Crowd,* which won him much acclaim. Over the years, Hardy reached a wide reading public with his novels about characters buffeted by terrible fates. However, he also faced criticism and censorship because of his sympathetic treatment of characters who were driven by circumstances to commit terrible deeds. Financially secure and disgusted with the censorship leveled at his novels, he turned in the later part of his career to his original love, writing poetry. Both Hardy's novels and his poems present a pessimistic view of life, but Hardy himself argued that he was a "meliorist," someone who thinks that the human condition can be improved. His writing about tragic circumstances and lives was intended to arouse human sympathy and compassion by showing readers how people come to be as they are. Hardy is buried in the Poet's Corner of Westminster Abbey. His heart, however, is buried in the churchyard at Stinsford in the west country, near Dorchester.

About the SELECTIONS

"The Man He Killed" is perhaps the most famous of Hardy's antiwar poems. The poem places an eloquent argument against the inhumanity of war in the mouth of an uneducated speaker.

"Channel Firing" again addresses the subject of war. The poem is remarkable for its combination of humor with high seriousness. It is also remarkable for its visual clarity, which rises to a cinemagraphic climax.

"The Darkling Thrush" demonstrates Hardy's ability to create a somber mood through a few deft strokes of his poetic brush. The poem reflects Hardy's disillusionment with the age in which he lived and contrasts this disillusionment with a message of hope from a source in nature.

GOALS/OBJECTIVES

Studying this lesson will enable students to
- experience a speaker's feelings toward war death, hope, and nature
- describe the literary significance of Thomas Hardy's writings
- recognize and analyze themes that they encounter in their reading
- explain the concepts of *irony, understatement, satire, dialect, metaphor,* and *simile,* and identify and interpret these in poetry
- complete reading comprehension test questions

The Man He Killed

THOMAS HARDY

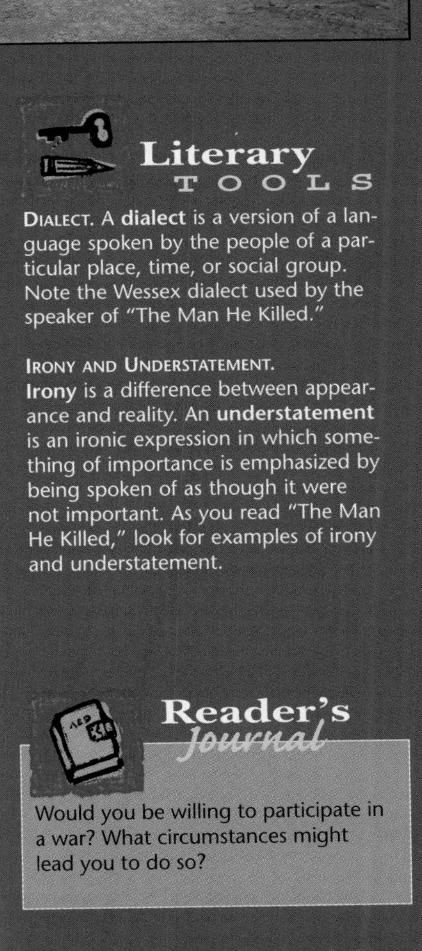

The Queen, God Bless Her, c. 1800s. John Evan Hodgson. Forbes Magazine Collection, New York.

"Had he and I but met
By some old ancient inn,
We should have sat us down to wet
Right many a nipperkin![1]

"But ranged as infantry,
And staring face to face,
I shot at him as he at me,
And killed him in his place.

"I shot him dead because—
Because he was my foe,
Just so—my foe of course he was;
That's clear enough; although

"He thought he'd 'list,[2] perhaps,
Off-hand like—just as I—
Was out of work—had sold his traps—[3]
No other reason why.

"Yes; quaint and curious war is!
You shoot a fellow down
You'd treat if met where any bar is,
Or help to half-a-crown."[4] ■

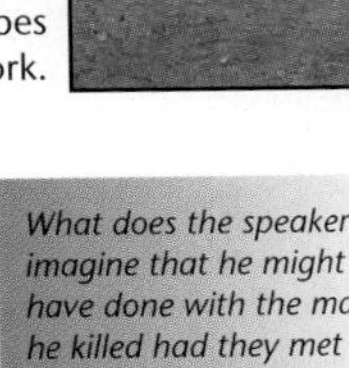

What does the speaker imagine that he might have done with the man he killed had they met in other circumstances?

Why does shooting the enemy soldier seem curious to the speaker?

1. **nipperkin.** Half pint of ale
2. **'list.** Enlist
3. **traps.** Traps for hunting
4. **half-a-crown.** English coin

Literary TOOLS

DIALECT. A **dialect** is a version of a language spoken by the people of a particular place, time, or social group. Note the Wessex dialect used by the speaker of "The Man He Killed."

IRONY AND UNDERSTATEMENT. **Irony** is a difference between appearance and reality. An **understatement** is an ironic expression in which something of importance is emphasized by being spoken of as though it were not important. As you read "The Man He Killed," look for examples of irony and understatement.

Reader's Journal

Would you be willing to participate in a war? What circumstances might lead you to do so?

ANSWERS TO GUIDED READING QUESTIONS

1. Had the speaker met the man under different circumstances, they probably would have sat and drunk ale together.
2. Shooting a soldier seems curious to the speaker because in any other situation, he would buy him a drink or loan him money.

READER'S JOURNAL

Students might consider the following questions: Do they think war is ever justified? Would they be willing to participate in a war? Students may wish to consider a specific war as they write about this question.

SELECTION CHECK TEST 4.9.15 WITH ANSWERS

Checking Your Reading

1. What would the men have done if they'd met at an inn? **They'd have shared drinks.**
2. What had the two men done to each other? **They'd shot at each other.**
3. Why did the speaker kill the man? **He killed him because he "was my foe."**
4. What had the speaker done when he was out of work? **He had enlisted in the army.**
5. What is "quaint and curious"? **War is quaint and curious.**

Literary Tools

1. How is dialect used in this poem? **Dialect is used to evoke the speech of a common man.**
2. What is irony? **Irony is the difference between appearance and reality.**
3. What is the central irony of this poem? **Responses will vary, but should suggest that war forces men to kill people they might otherwise befriend.**

RESPOND TO THE SELECTION

Students might also consider how the man feels about what he has done and whether he is responsible for his actions or is merely a pawn.

ANSWERS TO INVESTIGATE, INQUIRE, IMAGINE

RECALL

1a. He probably would have stopped for a drink with the man under other circumstances.

2a. He killed the other man because he was his foe.

3a. The speaker says war is "quaint" and "curious."

INTERPRET

1b. The speaker is probably a friendly, outgoing man who likes to socialize.

2b. The speaker can thnk of no good reason for killing the man. Even when he says he did it because the man was his foe, he was not convinced because he saw the man as very similar to himself.

3b. The speaker is understating the gravity of his situation. He is struggling to make sense of a situation that makes no sense.

ANALYZE

4a. The speaker says that under other circumstances he probably would have had a few drinks with the man. He considers that the man probably enlisted without much thought as he, himself, did because he was out of work.

SYNTHESIZE

4b. The speaker already identifies with the man. Having known him and perhaps having related to him even more, the speaker might have had a difficult time seeing the man as a foe. If he shot the man, he probably would have an even more difficult time explaining to himself why he did it.

EVALUATE

5a. The speaker is disturbed by what he has done. He finds it strange and inexplicable to kill somebody who normally you would see as a friend.

EXTEND

5b. It may be easier to kill a stranger or someone who is dehumanized because you don't associate yourself with the life you are killing.

Respond *to the* SELECTION

How do you feel toward the speaker? toward his actions?

INVESTIGATE, Inquire, *Imagine*

Recall: GATHERING FACTS → **Interpret:** FINDING MEANING

1a. What does the speaker say he might have done if he had met the man under other circumstances? → 1b. What kind of person do these actions suggest the speaker is?

2a. Why did the speaker kill the other man? → 2b. Why do you think the speaker hesitates in line 10?

3a. What words does the speaker use to describe war? → 3b. These are not the kinds of words people usually use to describe war. Why do you think the speaker uses these words?

Analyze: TAKING THINGS APART → **Synthesize:** BRINGING THINGS TOGETHER

4a. Identify elements that show the speaker identifies with the man he killed. → 4b. If the speaker had met the man first in a bar and then on the battlefield as an enemy, how do you think the speaker would have reacted to seeing him on the battlefield?

Evaluate: MAKING JUDGMENTS → **Extend:** CONNECTING IDEAS

5a. Evaluate the speaker's feelings toward what he has done. → 5b. Why is it important to dehumanize the enemy in a war?

Understanding *Literature*

DIALECT. What nonstandard, dialectical expressions are used in this poem? What does the use of dialect reveal about the speaker? How does the use of dialect help to relate the speaker to the man he killed?

IRONY AND UNDERSTATEMENT. What was the apparent situation between the two men when they met face to face? What was the common reality that they shared? What makes the killing of the other man ironic? Why is the speaker's description of war as "quaint and curious" ironic?

ANSWERS TO UNDERSTANDING LITERATURE

DIALECT. The speaker uses the phrases "sat us down to wet/Right many a nipperkin," "He thought he'd 'list, perhaps,/Off-hand like—just as I," and "You'd treat if met where any bar is,/Or help to half-a-crown." Hardy may have used dialect to place the speaker in the working class. Hardy may have used dialect to suggest that the speaker and the man he killed were both common people.

IRONY. The two men appeared to be enemies, yet they had no quarrel. They were both common men who had enlisted because they were out of work. Neither was fighting for a great cause; they both just needed work. Referring to killing a person as unusual and odd rather than tragic or horrifying is an understatement. It is nonetheless unusual and strange to be encouraged to kill other people.

Channel Firing[1]

BY THOMAS HARDY

That night your great guns, unawares,
Shook all our coffins as we lay,
And broke the chancel[2] window-squares,
We thought it was the Judgment-day

And sat upright. While drearisome
Arose the howl of wakened hounds:
The mouse let fall the altar-crumb,
The worms drew back into the mounds,

The glebe[3] cow drooled. Till God called, "No;
It's gunnery practice out at sea
Just as before you went below;
The world is as it used to be:

"All nations striving strong to make
Red war yet redder. Mad as hatters
They do no more for Christès[4] sake
Than you who are helpless in such matters.

Who is speaking at the beginning of the poem? What has awakened this person?

What did the speaker think was happening? What is actually happening?

1. **Channel Firing.** In the months preceding World War I, gunnery practice was done in the English Channel.
2. **chancel.** Part of a church near the altar
3. **glebe.** A small field belonging to a church
4. **Christès.** The archaic spelling of Christ is meant to suggest a sense of doom, as was common in ballads.

WORDS FOR EVERYDAY USE

drear • i • some (drir′ ē sum) *adj.*, sad. *The brown stubble and frozen mud of the garden in winter is a* drearisome *sight.*

Literary TOOLS

SATIRE. Satire is humorous writing or speech intended to point out errors, falshoods, foibles, or failings. Satire is written with the purpose of reforming human behavior or institutions. Note Hardy's use of satire in "Channel Crossing," a poem about war.

CONCRETE UNIVERSAL. A **concrete universal** is a particular object, person, action, or event that provides an instance or example of a general type. What concrete universal does Hardy present in this poem?

Reader's Journal

Imagine how somebody who has died might view the events of the world today.

ANSWERS TO GUIDED READING QUESTIONS

1. A corpse resting in the churchyard is the speaker in the beginning of the poem. The explosions of large guns have awakened the dead person.
2. The speaker thought it was Judgment Day. It is really only shooting practice for the gunners.

READER'S JOURNAL

Remind people of other examples in which dead people observe the living, such as Charles Dickens's *A Christmas Carol* and Thorton Wilder's *Our Town*. Ask students to think of other examples of the dead observing the living from books or movies.

VOCABULARY FROM THE SELECTION

avenge
drearisome

CROSS-CURRICULAR ACTIVITIES

BIOLOGY. Give background on the phrase "mad as hatters." This phrase described an actual occupational disease encountered by people who made hats in the nineteenth century. Mercury was used in the preparation of felt. Many "hatters" suffered from nerve damage caused by exposure to mercury. You may have some students who could research the mechanisms of mercury poisoning and report to the class. Give them time to prepare so they can report as you begin the lesson.

ANSWERS TO GUIDED READING QUESTIONS

1. If it were Judgment Day, the gunners would be in hell.
2. The parson wishes he had stuck to drinking and smoking rather than preaching for forty years, because after preaching that one should love thy neighbor, people still prepare for war.

SELECTION CHECK TEST 4.9.17 WITH ANSWERS

Checking Your Reading

1. What causes the speaker to sit upright? **He hears cannon-fire.**
2. What day does the speaker think it is? **He thinks it is Judgment Day.**
3. What actually caused the disturbance? Gunnery practice caused the noise.
4. What does Parson Thirdly wish he'd done? **He wishes he'd had more fun.**
5. What is the speaker? **The speaker is a skeleton, or a corpse in a coffin.**

Literary Tools

1. Satire points out lies, errors, or failings through the use of what? **It uses humor.**
2. Writers use satire for what purpose? **Writers use satire to reform human behavior.**
3. What is a concrete universal? **It is an object, person, action, or event that provides an example of a general type.**

RESPOND TO THE SELECTION

As an alternate activity, have students discuss the opinons of humanity expressed by the dead and by God.

"That this is not the judgment-hour
For some of them's a blessed thing,
For if it were they'd have to scour
Hell's floor for so much threatening. . . .

"Ha, ha. It will be warmer when
I blow the trumpet (if indeed
I ever do; for you are men,
And rest eternal sorely need)."

So down we lay again. "I wonder,
Will the world ever saner be,"
Said one, "than when He sent us under
In our indifferent century!"

And many a skeleton shook his head.
"Instead of preaching forty year,"
My neighbor Parson Thirdly said,
"I wish I had stuck to pipes and beer."

Again the guns disturbed the hour,
Roaring their readiness to avenge,
As far inland as Stourton Tower,
And Camelot, and starlit Stonehenge.[5] ■

What does God suggest might happen to the gunners if this were indeed Judgment Day?

What does the parson's comment tell you about how successful he considers his work to have been? Why might the parson feel that he failed?

5. **Stourton . . . Stonehenge.** The sound of the guns reached Stourton Tower, where King Alfred defeated the Danes in 879; Arthur's court at Camelot; and the prehistoric circle of stones at Stonehenge. The view encompasses much of England both geographically and throughout time.

Words For Everyday Use

a • venge (ə venj') *vt.*, get revenge for. *I will avenge my brother's death by bringing his enemy to justice!*

Respond *to the* Selection

If you were one of the gunners how would you defend your position?

INVESTIGATE, Inquire, Imagine

Recall: GATHERING FACTS → **Interpret:** FINDING MEANING

1a. What awakens the dead at the beginning of the poem?

1b. How do you know the speakers are dead?

2a. Of what does God assure the dead? What would happen if it were Judgment Day?

2b. How does God feel about people? How do you know?

3a. What does Parson Thirdly wish he had done?

3b. What does the parson's attitude suggest about the state of humankind?

Analyze: TAKING THINGS APART → **Synthesize:** BRINGING THINGS TOGETHER

4a. Identify the events in English history that are alluded to in the last stanza.

4b. Why might Hardy have chosen to make there allusions? What do they suggest about England as a whole?

Evaluate: MAKING JUDGMENTS → **Extend:** CONNECTING IDEAS

5a. Do you think the attitude toward war expressed in this poem is justified? Why or why not?

5b. Compare and contrast Hardy's attitude toward war with that expressed by Arnold in "Dover Beach."

Understanding Literature

SATIRE. Review the definition for **satire** in the Literary Tools in Prereading. Psychologists have often pointed out that there is a dark undercurrent to what people consider humorous. What elements of this poem are darkly humorous? What failings do you think this satiric approach aims to reform?

CONCRETE UNIVERSAL. Review the definition of **concrete universal** in the Handbook of Literary Terms. What concrete example does the author give in this poem of people's absurd preoccupation with war? How does the ending of the poem serve to universalize the comments made about that example?

ANSWERS TO INVESTIGATE, INQUIRE, IMAGINE

RECALL

1a. The shaking and sounds from the gunnery practice wake the dead.

2a. God assures the dead that it is not Judgment Day; the world is the same as when they died. If it were Judgment Day, many people would go to hell.

3a. Parson Thirdly wishes he had stuck to pipes and beer instead of preaching.

INTERPRET

1b. Line 2 refers to the coffins that were shook. Lines 11-12 refer to the time before these people "went below." These are signs that the people are dead.

2b. God is frustrated that people don't live better lives. He says that men are "mad as hatters"; they don't live a Christian life and would surely go to hell if it were Judgment Day. God shows that He is understanding by saying that people sorely need eternal rest.

3b. His attitude suggests that people do not follow the teachings of the church. It also suggests that he, like others, would rather have a good time than live a responsible life.

ANALYZE

4a. Hardy alludes to King Alfred's defeat of the Danes in 879, King Arthur's court at Camelot, and Stonehenge.

SYNTHESIZE

4b. Hardy wants to stress that England has a violent history. He suggests that, while nations may advance in some respects, with regard to war they remain as primitive as ever.

EVALUATE

5a. War is depicted as yet another failing of humanity. It disturbs the dead and suggests that the end or Judgement Day is near at hand.

EXTEND

5b. Both poems express a disappointment or despair at the state of humanity. However, Hardy uses more humor in his poem than Arnold does.

ANSWERS TO UNDERSTANDING LITERATURE

SATIRE. It is humorous that dead people have been wakened because they mistook gunfire for Judgment Day. God says that humanity is lucky that He hasn't blown his horn, because we are destined for hell, and what people really need is eternal rest. The parson says that he wishes he had stayed with drinking and smoking rather than trying to preach for the last forty years. Underlying all of this humor is the sad state of humanity.

CONCRETE UNIVERSAL. The author uses the example of gunnery practice at sea. By listing places that cover much of England geographically as well as chronologically, the author universalizes his comments.

ANSWER TO GUIDED READING QUESTION

1. The land symbolizes the body of the dead century laid out on the ground.

READER'S JOURNAL

Students should keep this experience in mind as they read "The Darkling Thrush." As they read they can determine how the speaker's mood changes.

INDIVIDUAL LEARNING STRATEGIES

Motivation
Have students research the events occurring in the world at the time that Hardy wrote "The Darkling Thrush." Why might Hardy feel so depressed?

Reading Proficiency
The punch line of the poem, the last stanza, may be difficult for some students to comprehend, as it is one very long sentence. Have students work with a partner to decipher the stanza.

English Language Learning
Share with students the following additional vocabulary.
dregs—residue; scum
score—scratch lines in
crypt—grave; tomb
canopy—awning (sky)
plume—feathers

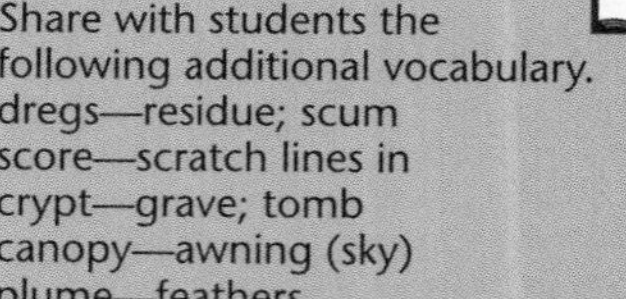

Special Needs
As they read, students can keep a sensory detail chart. Ask students to identify the speaker's mood as it is revealed through these details.

Enrichment
Discuss with students the term *fin de siècle,* French for "end of the century." *Fin de siècle* refers to a decadent ideal, a "get it all in before the party is over" mentality, such as might be found in the writings of Oscar Wilde or the illustrations of Aubrey Beardsley. *Fin de siècle* thought also manifests itself in an apocalyptic, sometimes self-indulgently hopeless worldview. Discuss how this and other poems that students have read might express a *fin de siècle* mentality.

Literary TOOLS

Stanza and Slant Rhyme. A **stanza** is a group of lines in a poem. A **slant rhyme** is the substitution of assonance or consonance for true rhyme. "The Darkling Thrush" uses an eight-line stanza known as an octave or octet. As you read this poem, note the rhyme scheme of each stanza.

Simile and Metaphor. A **simile** is a comparison using *like* or *as*. A **metaphor** is a figure of speech in which one thing is spoken or written about as if it were another. In metaphors and similes, the writer either makes a comparison or invites the reader to make a comparison between the two things. The speaker's actual subject is the tenor of the simile or metaphor. The thing to which the subject is compared is the *vehicle*. As you read, observe Hardy's use of simile and metaphor in "The Darkling Thrush."

Reader's Journal

Write in your journal about an event that caused in you a sudden change in mood. Describe your initial mood, the event, and the mood that resulted.

The Darkling[1] Thrush

Thomas Hardy

I leant upon a coppice gate[2]
When Frost was spectre-gray,
And Winter's dregs made desolate
The weakening eye of day.
The tangled bine-stems[3] scored the sky
Like strings of broken lyres,[4]
And all mankind that haunted nigh
Had sought their household fires.

The land's sharp features seemed to be
The Century's corpse outleant,[5]
His crypt the cloudy canopy,
The wind his death-lament.
The ancient pulse of germ and birth
Was shrunken hard and dry,
And every spirit upon earth
Seemed fervourless[6] as I.

What does the sharp-featured land symbolize for the speaker?

1. **Darkling.** In the dark
2. **coppice gate.** Gate leading into a wooded area
3. **tangled bine-stems.** Intertwined stems of shrubs
4. **lyres.** Small stringed instruments like harps
5. **Century's corpse outleant.** The poem was written on Dec. 31, 1900, so the nineteenth century was dead.
6. **fervourless.** Without passion

At once a voice arose among
   The bleak twigs overhead
In a full-hearted evensong
   Of joy illimited;
An aged thrush, frail, gaunt, and small,
   In blast-beruffled plume,
Had chosen thus to fling his soul
   Upon the growing gloom.

So little cause for carolings
   Of such ecstatic sound
Was written on terrestrial things
   Afar or nigh around,
That I could think there trembled through
   His happy good-night air
Some blessed Hope, whereof he knew
   And I was unaware. ■

What does the speaker hear? How does this sound contrast with the speaker's environment?

What possibility does the speaker entertain as a result of hearing the thrush's song?

WORDS FOR EVERYDAY USE

gaunt (gônt) *adj.*, haggard; emaciated. *The stray dog looked gaunt and scruffy.*

Respond *to the* Selection

What makes the thrush's song particularly surprising?

ANSWERS TO GUIDED READING QUESTIONS

1. The speaker hears a thrush. The joyous song of the thrush contrasts with the bleak landscape.
2. The speaker feels the thrush knows of some hope for the future of which he himself isn't aware.

SELECTION CHECK TEST 4.9.19 WITH ANSWERS

Checking Your Reading

1. At what time of day does this poem take place? It is early evening.
2. What has all mankind sought? They'd sought their household fires.
3. The wind is a "death-lament" for what? It is a lament for the previous century.
4. How does the speaker describe the bird's song? It is joyous and ecstatic.
5. What does the bird know that the speaker does not? The bird knows Hope.

Literary Tools

Fill in the blanks using the following terms. You will not use every term, and you may use some terms more than once.

slant rhyme   octave   consonance
metaphor   tenor   vehicle

1. In a comparison, the **tenor** is the actual subject of the comparison.
2. The stanzas of this poem are arranged into **octaves**.
3. In **metaphor**, one thing is spoken of as if it were something else.
4. **Slant rhyme** is the substitution of assonance or **consonance** for true rhyme.

RESPOND TO THE SELECTION

Students should look to lines 21–24 for the physical description of the thrush. They should discuss the context of the bleak setting in considering the surprise of the thrush's ecstatic song.

ANSWERS TO INVESTIGATE, INQUIRE, IMAGINE

Recall

1a. The speaker describes frost, the waning daylight, and shrubs.

2a. The speaker compares the land to the corpse of the dead century.

3a. The song of the thrush surprises the speaker.

Interpret

1b. The poem is set at dusk in winter.

2b. The speaker feels depressed and hopeless about his time, because the century has ended and he is not optimistic about the path that events are taking.

3b. The speaker thinks the thrush must know of something hopeful to make a joyful sound on such a gloomy night.

Analyze

4a. Gloomy or grim elements include: the spectre-gray frost, the dregs of winter weakening the sun, the wind sounded like a death lament, everyone seemed passionless, the twigs were bleak. The thrush itself was frail, gaunt and small.

Synthesize

4b. *Responses will vary.* The speaker might have been in a cheerier mood, so the song of the thrush might not have seemed as joyful in contrast. The bird might have even seemed slightly pathetic in its state of disarray.

Evaluate

5a. The speaker learns that there may be some cause for hope. The thrush is small and weak, yet persists in singing joyfully despite the gloomy setting. Yes, there seems to be so little cause for celebration that the thrush must know something the speaker does not.

Extend

5b. *Responses will vary.*

INVESTIGATE, Inquire, Imagine

Recall: GATHERING FACTS

1a. What details of the environment does the speaker describe in stanza 1?

2a. To what does the speaker compare the land?

3a. What surprises the speaker?

Interpret: FINDING MEANING

1b. At what time of day and in what season of the year is this poem set?

2b. How does the speaker feel toward his own time? Why might he feel this way?

3b. Why does this give the speaker hope?

Analyze: TAKING THINGS APART →

4a. Identify elements that create a gloomy or grim mood through most of the poem.

Synthesize: BRINGING THINGS TOGETHER

4b. What if the speaker had heard the thrush on a sunny day? Do you think it would have the same effect? Why, or why not?

Evaluate: MAKING JUDGMENTS →

5a. Evaluate whether the end of the poem is optimistic.

Extend: CONNECTING IDEAS

5b. What has given you hope at a time when you were feeling down?

Understanding Literature

SIMILE AND METAPHOR. Review the definitions for **simile** and **metaphor** in the Handbook of Literary Tools. Identify each of the following as a metaphor or a simile. Then identify the tenor and vehicle of each.

a. Winter's dregs
b. tangled bine-stems . . . / Like strings of broken lyres
c. The weakening eye of day
d. The land's sharp features seemed to be / The Century's corpse
e. His crypt the cloudy canopy
f. The wind his death-lament
g. to fling his soul
h. there trembled through / His happy good-night air / Some blessed Hope

STANZA AND SLANT RHYME. Review the definitions for **stanza** and **rhyme scheme** in Literary Tools in Prereading. What is the rhyme scheme of each stanza? Chart the rhyme scheme of the poem, identifying any slant rhymes.

Last word in line	Rhyme	Rhyme or Slant
gate	a	slant
gray	b	
desolate	a	slant

ANSWERS TO UNDERSTANDING LITERATURE

SIMILE AND METAPHOR.

a. metaphor; tenor = winter; vehicle = a glass of liquid
b. simile; tenor = bine-stems; vehicle = the strings of a broken lyre
c. metaphor; tenor = dusk; vehicle = an eye that is losing its sight
d. metaphor; tenor = the land; vehicle = a corpse
e. metaphor; tenor = a crypt; vehicle = cloudy sky
f. metaphor; tenor = the wind; vehicle = his death-lament
g. metaphor; tenor = his soul; vehicle = an object that might be flung
h. metaphor; tenor = hope; vehicle = something that might tremble through a song

Continued on page 826

WRITER'S JOURNAL

1. Write a **note of encouragement** to somebody you know who is struggling. He or she may be trying to accomplish something, facing a loss or difficult decision, or confronting some other personal struggle.
2. Imagine that the speaker of "The Man He Killed" had met his enemy under different circumstances. Write a **dialogue** between the two of them.
3. In "Channel Firing" the speakers are dead. Write a **ghost story** based on the thoughts and actions of these or other dead people.

Integrating *the* LANGUAGE ARTS

Language, Grammar, and Style

TRANSLATING DIALECT. Dialect is a version of a language used in a particular time or place. Rewrite the dialectical language in "The Man He Killed" in standard English. Then rewrite it in dialect or slang that is particular to your current time and place. Refer to the Language Arts Survey 3.5, "Dialects of English" for additional help.

Critical Thinking & Collaborative Learning

POETRY DISCUSSION GROUP. A *theme* is a central idea in a literary work. In small groups discuss the following questions about the theme of "The Darkling Thrush."

- What does the speaker of this poem make of "terrestrial things" both "Afar"and "nigh around"?
- What two possible references might the word *His* in line 30 have?
- Whose air might this be?
- What words in the stanza have connotations of religion?
- What hope might the speaker be intimating by these references?

Study and Research

RESEARCHING WORLD EVENTS. Research the events occurring in the world at the time that Hardy wrote "The Darkling Thrush." Why might Hardy feel so depressed? Write a report about your findings.

Collaborative Learning

DEBATE. Consider Tennyson's and Arnold's opinions about the role of the artist. Does Hardy share their opinion? Hold a class debate between Hardyites and Tennysonians or Arnoldites about their views on the role of the artist. To prepare, review the Language Arts Survey 4.21, "Participating in a Debate."

ANSWERS TO INTEGRATING THE LANGUAGE ARTS

Language, Grammar, and Style
Responses will vary.

ANSWERS TO UNDERSTANDING LITERATURE (CONT. FROM PAGE 826)

STANZA AND SLANT RHYME. The rhyme scheme for each stanza is *ababcdcd.* The following should be included in students' charts:
for stanza 1: gate (a, slant); gray (b); desolate (a, slant); day (b); sky (c); lyres (d); nigh (c); fires (d)

stanza 2: be (a); outleant (b, slant); canopy (a); death-lament (b, slant); birth (c); dry (d); earth (c); I (d)
stanza 3: among (a, slant); overhead (b, slant), evensong (b, slant); illimited (b, slant); small (c, slant); plume (d); soul (c, slant); gloom (d)

stanza 4: carolings (a); sound (b); things (a); around (b); through (c); air (d); knew (c); unaware (d)

ADDITIONAL RESOURCES

UNIT 9 RESOURCE BOOK
- Selection Worksheet 9.10
- Selection Check Test 4.9.21
- Selection Test 4.9.22
- Writing Resource 2.27

INDIVIDUAL LEARNING STRATEGIES

MOTIVATION
Suggest that students read other poems from *Sonnets from the Portuguese.* Have them choose two poems and compare the roles of the speaker and the type of love described. Students can compare their findings in small groups or in expository essays.

READING PROFICIENCY
Line breaks in the middle of sentences may make the poem difficult for students to parse out. Read the poem aloud for students.

ENGLISH LANGUAGE LEARNING
Point out that Browning uses the old pronoun *thee* instead of *you.* Also discuss with students the use of capitalization to signify a divine or otherworldly quality.

SPECIAL NEEDS
Have students make a graphic organizer showing each of the eight ways the speaker loves her subject. Students should then write about the image they get when they think of each of those eight ways. For example, they might picture a soul reaching out in the dark.

ENRICHMENT
Ask students to read the Language Arts Survey 5.6, "Making Inferences, Predictions, and Hypotheses." Then they should think about Robert and Elizabeth Barrett Browning. Based on the information in this book and in one other source, they should form a hypothesis about spouses or siblings who simultaneously pursue literary careers. Then they should read about the following people: Mary and Percy Shelley, Dorothy and William Wordsworth, and Dante Gabriel and Christina Rossetti. Do their hypotheses hold true in these situations? Why, or why not?

Sonnet 43 ("How do I love thee . . .")

from Sonnets from the Portuguese

BY ELIZABETH BARRETT BROWNING

About the AUTHOR

In her own era, **Elizabeth Barrett Browning** (1806–1861) was one of England's most well-known female poets. She is most often associated with the love poetry she wrote for her husband, Robert Browning. However, at the time during which she wrote, she was respected as a scholarly poet, and her large body of work raised many moral and political issues. During her early years, Browning received a thorough education in Latin and Greek, philosophy, and literature. As a young child she began to write poetry, and at the age of fourteen she composed an epic poem that her father privately printed. Elizabeth's father, although supportive of his daughter's obvious talent, was overprotective and kept careful watch over the poet. His overprotection was especially true when Elizabeth's health began to fail, and she was later confined to her home. She was an invalid living in the family home in London when her literary career began to thrive. At the age of thirty-nine, Elizabeth received her first letter from Robert Browning, an unknown poet who admired her work. She wrote back, and the two began their famous romance and eventually married. Although Elizabeth and Robert were supportive of one another in their individual literary careers, at the time of Elizabeth's death in 1861, her work was much more popular than his. Today, her most recognizable pieces come from the book *Sonnets from the Portuguese.* Other important pieces include the lengthy poem "Aurora Leigh" and the ambitious piece "Runaway Slave at Pilgrim's Point."

About the SELECTION

Sonnet 43 ("How do I love thee . . .") comes from Browning's book, *Sonnets from the Portuguese,* which is a sequence of forty-five sonnets that Browning wrote to chronicle the stages of her love for her husband Robert. "The Portuguese" was one of Robert's pet names for Elizabeth. Because of the deeply personal nature of the poems, Elizabeth didn't intend for them to be published and read by the general public. However, she finally decided to publish the pieces under the title ***Sonnets from the Portuguese.*** This title was meant to imply that the poems were translations of pieces written in Portuguese, not her original work. The best-known sonnet sequences had been written by men, and it was unusual to use the form to tell a love story from the point of view of a woman. Sonnet 43 is by far the most recognizable of any of the poems in the sequence.

GOALS/OBJECTIVES

Studying this lesson will enable students to
- enjoy reading a love sonnet
- describe Elizabeth Barrett Browning's literary accomplishments and explain the historical significance of her writings
- define *repetition* and identify and analyze how it is used in a poem
- define *sonnet* and identify sonnets that they encounter in their reading
- write a question poem and a comparison essay

Sonnet 43
How do I love thee . . .

Elizabeth Barrett Browning

The Anniversary, 1909. Albert Chevallier Tayler. Harris Museum and Art Gallery, Preston, UK.

How do I love thee? Let me count the ways.
I love thee to the depth and breadth and height
My soul can reach, when feeling out of sight
For the ends of Being and ideal Grace.
I love thee to the level of everyday's
Most quiet need, by sun and candle-light.
I love thee freely, as men strive for Right;
I love thee purely, as they turn from Praise.
I love thee with the passion put to use
In my old griefs, and with my childhood's faith.
I love thee with a love I seemed to lose
With my lost saints,—I love thee with the breath,
Smiles, tears, of all my life!—and, if God choose,
I shall but love thee better after death. ■

What is the speaker counting?

How strong is the love this speaker feels? How long will it last?

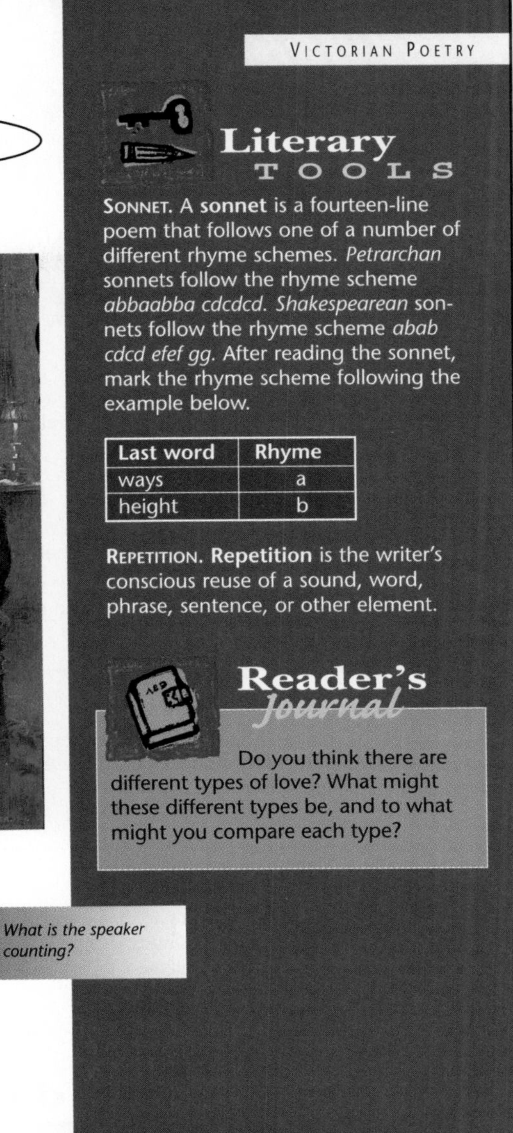

Literary Tools

Sonnet. A **sonnet** is a fourteen-line poem that follows one of a number of different rhyme schemes. *Petrarchan* sonnets follow the rhyme scheme *abbaabba cdcdcd. Shakespearean* sonnets follow the rhyme scheme *abab cdcd efef gg.* After reading the sonnet, mark the rhyme scheme following the example below.

Last word	Rhyme
ways	a
height	b

Repetition. **Repetition** is the writer's conscious reuse of a sound, word, phrase, sentence, or other element.

Reader's Journal

Do you think there are different types of love? What might these different types be, and to what might you compare each type?

ANSWERS TO GUIDED READING QUESTIONS

1. The speaker is counting the number of ways in which she loves the subject of the poem.
2. The speaker's love is very strong and will last even after she dies.

GRAPHIC ORGANIZER

After filling out their graphic organizers, students should note that the rhyme scheme of the poem is *abbaabba cdcdcd.*

READER'S JOURNAL

Students may want to think about specific people in their lives and how their feelings for each person differ.

ADDITIONAL QUESTIONS AND ACTIVITIES

Ask students how many references to religion they can find in the poem. Why might the speaker be making these references? What is the speaker's attitude toward religion?

Answer

The poem includes four references to religion, in lines 3–4 ("soul...Grace"), 10 ("faith"), 12 ("saints"), and 13 ("God"). The poet likens her religious faith to her faith in her beloved. Love and religious faith and grace seem to be the highest forms of human experience for her.

SELECTION CHECK TEST 4.9.21 WITH ANSWERS

Checking Your Reading

1. For what do some men strive? **Some men strive for right.**
2. From what do some men turn away? **Some men turn away from praise.**
3. What does the speaker recall from childhood? **She recalls her faith.**
4. On what has the speaker used her passion in the past? **She has used it in grieving.**
5. When will the speaker love the listener better, if God choose? **She will love him better after death.**

SELECTION CHECK TEST 4.9.21 WITH ANSWERS (CONT.)

Literary Tools

1. How is repetition used in this poem? ***Responses will vary.***
2. What is the rhyme scheme of the following lines? **The scheme is *abba.***

How do I love thee? Let me count the ways.
I love thee to the depth and breadth and height
My soul can reach, when feeling out of sight
For the ends of Being and ideal Grace.

3. What type of sonnet is this? **This is a Petrarchan sonnet.**

RESPOND TO THE SELECTION

Students may want to consider how they would feel if they received a poem like this.

ANSWERS TO INVESTIGATE, INQUIRE, IMAGINE

RECALL

1a. The speaker refers to night and day by the way that each time is illuminated, by sun and by candlelight.

2a. The speaker loves with the same intensity that she grieved in the past. It seems that she had a previous love who died or who broke off their relationship.

3a. The speaker says that she will love the subject of the poem even after she dies.

INTERPRET

1b. The speaker means that her love can be humble and quiet as well as passionate and grand. The speaker's love encompasses many levels and types of feeling. It is not a feeling that will easily dissipate.

2b. Both "childhood's faith" and "old griefs" are very powerful and pure emotions. These comparisons reflect the intensity and purity of her love.

3b. The speaker's love is so strong that she will be able to love even after she dies. The speaker's love will survive forever, no matter what happens, even death.

ANALYZE

4a. The speaker says she loves "to the depth and breadth and height [her] soul can reach; "to the level of everyday's most quiet need by sun and candle-light"; "freely, as men strive for Right"; "purely, as they turn from Praise"; "with the passion put to use in [her] old griefs, and with [her] childhood's faith"; with a love [she] seemed to lose with [her] lost saints"; "with the breath, smiles tears of [her] life"; and she shall love better after death. All of these things show a great depth and intensity of feeling.

SYNTHESIZE

4b. *Responses will vary.* Students may say that Browning chooses examples that show the depth and breadth of her love. Others may say that if she is going to count the ways, she should include more.

EVALUATE

5a. *Responses will vary.* Each example demonstrates a different "way" the speaker loves. She intends to show that she loves her subject in all possible ways. Students may say that the poem has a cumulative effect.

EXTEND

5b. *Responses will vary.*

Respond *to the* SELECTION

Explain whether the feelings Browning describes are similar to your own feelings about love.

Investigate, Inquire, Imagine

Recall: GATHERING FACTS → **Interpret:** FINDING MEANING

1a. In line 6, how does the speaker refer to night and day?

1b. What does the speaker mean by saying that she loves "to the level of everyday's/Most quiet need"? What does this say about the speaker's love and its importance?

2a. How does the speaker love with a "passion put to use/In my old griefs"? Where has she loved before?

2b. Why does the speaker refer to "childhood's faith" and "old griefs"? Explain your answer.

3a. What does the speaker say about death in the last line of the poem?

3b. What does this answer suggest about the speaker's love?

Analyze: TAKING THINGS APART → **Synthesize:** BRINGING THINGS TOGETHER

4a. Identify the eight answers the speaker gives to her initial question. What do these things have in common?

4b. Do you think this sonnet expresses the depth of the speaker's love? Would the response have been stronger if Browning had written a longer poem?

Evaluate: MAKING JUDGMENTS → **Extend:** CONNECTING IDEAS

5a. Evaluate one way in which the speaker professes her love. Does the item stand on its own, or is it a cumulative effect?

5b. At her death, Elizabeth Barrett Browning was a more popular poet than her husband, Robert. Based on the works you have read by each, which do you prefer? Why?

Understanding *Literature*

SONNET. Review the definition for **sonnet** in the Handbook of Literary Terms. Based on the rhyme scheme, which type of sonnet is this? Explain whether this poem has the traditional breaks of such a sonnet.

REPETITION. Review the definition for **repetition** in the Handbook of Literary Terms. Identify examples of repetition in this poem. How does the repetition emphasize the poem's theme?

ANSWERS TO UNDERSTANDING LITERATURE

SONNET. This poem has the rhyme scheme of a Petrachan sonnet. However, it does not have the thematic break that Petrarchan sonnets often have between the octave and the sestet.

REPETITION. The phrase "I love thee" is used repeatedly and stresses the breadth of the speaker's love for the subject of the poem. The speaker links the phrase to different kinds of love in order to lend a number of levels of meaning to the phrase.

WRITER'S JOURNAL

1. Imagine somebody has just written this poem for you. Write a **journal entry** about your feelings.
2. Write your own **love poem**. Begin with the question, "How do I love thee? Let me count the ways." You may address your poem to anyone you love.
3. Create an **advice column** about love. First write a letter with a question or problem that somebody might have. Then create a response.

Integrating *the* LANGUAGE ARTS

Language, Grammar, and Style

SENTENCE VARIETY. In some cases, repetition is intentional and has a purpose. Other times, you will want to vary your sentence structures and wording. Rewrite the following passage to improve sentence style and avoid repetition.

Elizabeth Browning was a poet. Robert Browning was also a poet. Elizabeth Browning was a more popular poet during her lifetime. She is best known for her love poems written to her husband. She also wrote about many moral and political issues. She wrote "The Runaway Slave at Pilgrim's Point" in 1850. That was just seventeen years after slavery was outlawed in Great Britain and its colonies.

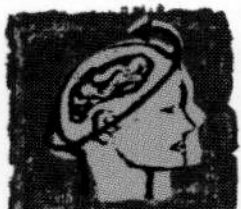

Critical Thinking

COMPARING AND CONTRASTING. Read in the Language Arts Survey 2.27, "Choosing a Method of Organization." Then compare and contrast this poem with any other love poem in this book. Identify which poem you think more strongly expresses genuine feelings of love. Use examples from both poems to support your thesis.

Media Literacy & Collaborative Learning

MEDIA COLLAGE. Create a collage that uses words and pictures to relay images of love in the popular media, including movies, television, and music. Then discuss the images you find. Which of them are unique? Which are cliched? Do any express your own ideas about love? If so, which? If not, what images or words would express your ideas?

ANSWERS TO INTEGRATING THE LANGUAGE ARTS

Language, Grammar, and Style
Responses will vary.
Elizabeth Browning and Robert Browning were both poets. During her lifetime, Elizabeth Browning was a more popular poet. She is best known for her love poems written to her husband, but she also wrote about many moral and political issues. In 1850, just seventeen years after slavery was outlawed in Great Britain and its colonies, she wrote "The Runaway Slave at Pilgrim's Point."

Critical Thinking
Suggest that students use a Venn diagram to make notes about each poem.

"Pied Beauty," "God's Grandeur," "Spring and Fall: To a Young Child"

BY GERARD MANLEY HOPKINS

About the Author

Gerard Manley Hopkins (1844–1889) grew up in a political and poetical family. His father was a poet who had served as the British consul general in Hawaii. Hopkins attended Oxford University and was attracted to the ideas of the Oxford Movement, which, in response to the increased skepticism of the age, attempted to connect the Anglican Church to the tenets and rituals of the early Christian church. Like John Henry Newman, one of the founders of the Oxford Movement, Hopkins found himself unable to resist the conclusion that the Roman Catholic Church was the true heir of early Christianity, and he converted to Catholicism. In 1868 he joined the Society of Jesus, or Jesuits, and in 1877 he was ordained a priest, after which he burned the poetry he had written as a youth, considering it unworthy of his high vocation. Although some of his superiors encouraged him to resume writing poetry, one of his most ambitious poems, "The Wreck of the Deutschland," about a shipwreck in which five nuns were drowned, was not accepted for publication by the Jesuit periodical to which he submitted it. Few of Hopkins's poems were published during his lifetime because most readers could not understand their unusual words, highly compressed images, and odd rhythms. This poetry is among the most beautiful but also among the oddest in the English language. Its conciseness of expression and unconventional rhythm have strongly influenced a number of twentieth-century poets.

About the Selections

"Pied Beauty" is a celebration of the variety and abundance of nature and of the ultimate source of that variety and abundance. **"God's Grandeur"** is an example of what an extremely original poet can do with a conventional form, such as a sonnet. **"Spring and Fall: To a Young Child"** is one of Hopkins' best-known poems. It uses the unusual rhythm common to his poems.

ADDITIONAL RESOURCES

UNIT 9 RESOURCE BOOK

"Pied Beauty"
- Selection Worksheet 9.11
- Selection Check Test 4.9.23
- Selection Test 4.9.24

"God's Grandeur"
- Selection Worksheet 9.12
- Selection Check Test 4.9.25
- Selection Test 4.9.26

"Spring and Fall: To a Young Child"
- Selection Worksheet 9.13
- Selection Check Test 4.9.27
- Selection Test 4.9.28
- Language, Grammar, and Style Resource 3.6–3.7
- Speaking and Listening Resource 4.21

INDIVIDUAL LEARNING STRATEGIES

MOTIVATION
Have students look up the word *pied* (or *piebald*) or *beauty* in a thesaurus and list the synonyms and antonyms in their journals. They should think about the specific connotations each word has.

READING PROFICIENCY
Students might work with a partner on these poems. Suggest to students that the beauty of Hopkins's poems lies as much in how the words sound when read as in what they mean.

ENGLISH LANGUAGE LEARNING
Point out to students the sets of antonyms, or opposites, in line 9 of "Pied Beauty." Students can try to name other pairs of opposites. Students should pay special attention to the first line of each stanza in "God's Grandeur." These two lines identify Hopkins's main points. The other lines tend to support these ideas.

SPECIAL NEEDS
Students should map out the rhyme scheme of these poems. Also, have them discuss the imagery in the poems. What images does each poem bring to mind? Students might want to draw something in response to one of the poems.

ENRICHMENT ACTIVITIES
Suggest that students read other poems by Hopkins in order to become more familiar with the concept of sprung rhythm. Have students write a few lines that celebrate nature, using sprung rhythm.

GOALS/OBJECTIVES

Studying this lesson will enable students to
- experience the speaker's feelings of joy in the variety of wonders in the world
- describe the significance of Gerard Manley Hopkins's writings
- define *sprung rhythm* and identify it in a poem
- define *sonnet* and identify an Italian, or Petrarchan, sonnet
- define *alliteration, metaphor, repetition,* and *theme* and recognize and analyze them in a poem
- identify the parts of speech
- create a nature guide
- participate in a debate

Pied[1] *Beauty*

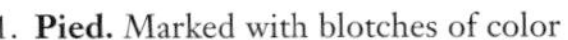

GERARD MANLEY HOPKINS

Glory be to God for dappled things—
For skies of couple-colour as a brinded[2] cow;
For rose-moles all in stipple upon trout that swim;
Fresh-firecoal chestnut-falls,[3] finches' wings;
Landscape plotted and pieced—fold, fallow, and plough;[4]
And áll trádes, their gear and tackle and trim.

All things counter, original, spare,[5] strange;
Whatever is fickle, freckled (who knows how?)
With swift, slow; sweet, sour; adazzle, dim;
He fathers-forth whose beauty is past change:
Praise him. ■

What is the main idea of this poem, expressed in the first line?

According to the speaker, how does God differ from the world, which is so varied and changeable?

1. **Pied.** Marked with blotches of color
2. **brinded.** Brownish orange streaked with gray
3. **Fresh-firecoal chestnut-falls.** Freshly fallen chestnuts, red as coals
4. **fold . . . plough.** The land is colored in patches from the pastures or folds, fallow, unplowed fields, and plowed land.
5. **spare.** Rare

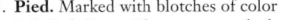

WORDS FOR EVERYDAY USE

dap • pled (dap´ əld) *adj.,* marked with spots. *The Dalmatian was white dappled with black.*

stip • ple (stip´ əl) *adj.,* flecked. *You can create a stippled look by shaking a paintbrush over your canvas.*

Literary TOOLS

SPRUNG RHYTHM. **Sprung rhythm** is the term coined by Gerard Manley Hopkins to describe the unique metrical forms of his verse. Sprung rhythm is a system in which each line has the same number of stressed syllables but a variable number of unstressed syllables. The lines, therefore, can be of unequal lengths, and the stresses do not fall in a regular pattern; several strong stresses can be placed next to one another.

ALLITERATION. **Alliteration** is the repetition of initial consonant sounds. Hopkins used this technique frequently in his poetry. Note the alliteration in "Pied Beauty."

Reader's Journal

What things in the natural world do you find most intriguing to look at?

ANSWERS TO GUIDED READING QUESTIONS

1. The main idea of the poem is to praise God for natural beauty.
2. God does not change.

READER'S JOURNAL

Students might consider both things they have actually seen in the wild, such as a fiery red maple tree in the fall or a lightning storm, and things they have seen in zoos, sanctuaries, pictures, or documentaries.

SELECTION CHECK TEST 4.9.23 WITH ANSWERS

Checking Your Reading

1. With what animal is the color of the sky compared? **It is compared to a cow.**
2. What fish is stippled with "rose moles"? **The trout is stippled with rose moles.**
3. What is "plotted and pieced"? **The landscape is plotted and pieced.**
4. Whose beauty is "past change"? **God's beauty is past change.**
5. What command concludes the poem? **It ends with the command to "praise him."**

Literary Tools

1. A poem written in sprung rhythm:
   a. substitutes assonance and consonance for true rhyme
   b. has the same number of lines as a sonnet but does not rhyme
   c. has the same number of stressed syllables in each line
   d. uses iambic pentameter but does not rhyme

2. The repetition of initial consonant sounds in words is
   a. alliteration
   b. assonance
   c. consonance
   d. meter

3. Sprung rhythm
   a. was a tradition begun by Shakespeare
   b. was popular among Victorian-Age poets
   c. was first used by Hopkins
   d. is frowned upon by critics

RESPOND TO THE SELECTION

Students may say that Hopkins meant that God's beauty, being divine, cannot be touched by time and change—it is are everlasting and constant.

ANSWERS TO INVESTIGATE, INQUIRE, IMAGINE

RECALL

1a. The speaker says "Glory be to God for dappled things." The speaker then gives examples of dappled things.

2a. The patterns in the field were created by humans, who planted the fields.

3a. The poem ends with the request that we praise God.

INTERPRET

1b. All of these things are beautiful, multicolored, unique, and created by God.

2b. God created the earth and the plants that created these patterns and gave life to the humans who tend to the fields.

3b. The speaker wants the reader to praise the fact that God can create beautiful things in infinite variety, yet be unchanging.

ANALYZE

4a. Lines 1–5 mention skies, trout, chestnut–falls, finches' wings, and a plotted and pieced landscape. All of these things are either dappled themselves or create a dappled appearance, such as chestnuts on the ground.

SYNTHESIZE

4b. *Responses will vary.* Some items might include the hide of a dalmatian, the waves in the sea with many shades of blue and green, the patterns of different colors of greenery covering a mountain, the feathers of a parrot.

EVALUATE

5a. In lines 7–9, the speaker discusses the uniqueness and curiosity of God's creations. In lines 1–5, the speaker lists specific ordinary things that are unique and curious because they are dappled, or variegated. These provide examples of the beautiful variety in the world.

EXTEND

5b. *Responses will vary.*

Respond *to the* SELECTION

How is beauty "past change"?

INVESTIGATE, Inquire, *Imagine*

Recall: GATHERING FACTS →

1a. For what does the speaker say glory be to God?

2a. In what way do the fields mentioned in line 5 differ from the things mentioned in lines 1–4?

3a. With what request does the poem end?

Interpret: FINDING MEANING

1b. Why are these things so impressive?

2b. Explain how God is still responsible for these things.

3b. What aspect of God does the speaker want the reader to see as worthy of praise?

Analyze: TAKING THINGS APART →

4a. Identify the things from nature that are mentioned in lines 1–5. What do these things have in common?

Synthesize: BRINGING THINGS TOGETHER

4b. What else could you include in this list?

Evaluate: MAKING JUDGMENTS →

5a. Consider the connection between lines 7–9 and 1–6. How do lines 1-6 support the ideas in lines 7–9?

Extend: CONNECTING IDEAS

5b. What do you think of when you see the beauty and variety in nature?

Understanding *Literature*

SPRUNG RHYTHM. Review the definition of **sprung rhythm** in the Handbook of Literary Terms. Scan the poem. Write each line and mark the stressed syllables. At what point do several strongly stressed syllables appear in a row?

ALLITERATION. Review the definition of **alliteration** in Literary Tools in Prereading. What examples of alliteration can you find in this poem? What other repeated sounds can you find?

ANSWERS TO UNDERSTANDING LITERATURE

SPRUNG RHYTHM. Line 5 has two strong stresses in a row at its beginning, on the words *fresh* and *fire,* and two more on *fold* and *fallow.* Line 6 has several strongly stressed syllables in a row: *all* and *trades.*

ALLITERATION. Examples of alliteration in this poem include: "Glory be to God," "couple-color," "Fresh-firecoal chestnut-falls, finches' wings," "plotted and pieced—fold, fallow, and plough," "fickle, freckled," "swift, slow; sweet, sour," and "fathers-forth." Another repeated sound occurs in "fickle, freckled."

GOD'S *Grandeur*

GERARD MANLEY HOPKINS

The world is charged with the grandeur of God.
　It will flame out, like shining from shook foil;[1]
　It gathers to a greatness, like the ooze of oil
Crushed.[2] Why do men then now not reck[3] his rod?
Generations have trod, have trod, have trod;
　And all is seared with trade; bleared, smeared with toil;
　And wears man's smudge and shares man's smell: the
　soil
Is bare now, nor can foot feel, being shod.

And for all this, nature is never spent;
　There lives the dearest freshness deep down things;
And though the last lights off the black West went
　Oh, morning, at the brown brink eastward,
　springs—
Because the Holy Ghost over the bent
　World broods with warm breast and with ah! bright
　wings. ■

1. **foil.** Gold foil which glares in the light
2. **ooze . . . Crushed.** Droplets of oil scattered by crushing, gathered back together again. The idea here is that the greatness of God, however diffused in the world, cannot be diminished.
3. **reck.** Reckon with; heed

Literary TOOLS

SONNET. A **sonnet** is a fourteen-line poem that follows one of a number of different rhyme schemes. The *Italian* or *Petrarchan* sonnet is divided into two parts: an octave, or eight-line stanza, followed by a sestet, or six-line stanza. See how Hopkins uses this very traditional form.

REPETITION. **Repetition** is a writer's conscious reuse of a word, phrase, sentence, or other element. As you read in "God's Grandeur," look for repeated elements.

Reader's *Journal*

What impact have humans had on the natural environment?

Despite the great age of the world and the many generations that have come and gone, what remains true of nature, according to the speaker?

ANSWER TO GUIDED READING QUESTION

1. Nature never runs out.

READER'S JOURNAL

Ask students to consider what has happened to the environment as a result of human industry. How resilient is nature? How capable is nature of absorbing the shocks of human actions such as building factories and roads?

ADDITIONAL QUESTIONS AND ACTIVITIES

Students should think about how recent discoveries about ecology and the environment affect the message of Hopkins's poem.

- Students should decide whether the passage of almost one hundred years should have any effect on the interpretation of this poem.
- If students were reading this poem one hundred years ago, might they agree with Hopkins's argument?
- Might Hopkins be so optimistic about nature if he were writing the poem today?

SELECTION CHECK TEST 4.9.25 WITH ANSWERS

Checking Your Reading

1. What is charged with the grandeur of God? **The world is charged.**
2. Who "have trod, have trod, have trod"? **Generations have trod.**
3. Why can't the foot feel the soil? **It can't feel the soil because it is shod.**
4. What is never spent, despite all this? **Nature is never spent.**
5. Who broods over the "bent world"? **The Holy Ghost broods over the world.**

Literary Tools

1. This poem can be considered a version of
   a. **a Petrarchan sonnet**
   b. a Shakespearean sonnet
   c. an unrhymed sonnet
   d. a sonnet sequence

SELECTION CHECK TEST 4.9.25 WITH ANSWERS (CONT.)

2. This poem contains
   a. three quatrains and a couplet
   b. an octave and a sestet
   c. two quatrains and a series of unrhymed lines
   d. no rhyming lines
3. The line "And wears man's smudge and shares man's smell: the soil" contains
   a. assonance
   b. hyperbole
   c. alliteration
   d. slant rhyme

RESPOND TO THE SELECTION

Students should give reasons to support their responses. If students disagree, they might also give reasons that refute the reasons Hopkins gives.

ANSWERS TO INVESTIGATE, INQUIRE, IMAGINE

RECALL

1a. The world is charged with the greatness of God.
2a. Generations "have trod, have trod, have trod." They have seared the world with trade and bleared and smeared it with toil. The soil is bare and the foot cannot feel it.
3a. Nature is never spent because a freshness continues and the Holy Ghost broods with a warm breast and bright wings.

INTERPRET

1b. The word *charge* is usually associated with electricity. Here it means that God is the motivating force—the energy—in the world.
2b. Humans have ruined parts of the world. They have dirtied or destroyed some natural things with industry, but they have not killed or completely destroyed nature.
3b. Hopkins has an optimistic belief in nature's ability to regenerate because of God's greatness. Analyze
4a. People have overtrod the land. We have burned and dirtied it with work and industry. We have stripped it bare.

SYNTHESIZE

4b. *Responses will vary.* Recent abuses have in some cases increased those Hopkins identified. For example, destruction of the rain forests, oil spills, air and water pollution, and development of previously open places.

EVALUATE

5a. *Responses will vary.* Students may suggest that some aspects of nature are not renewable. For example water supplies that become contaminated or species that become extinct. Others may suggest that nature continues to adapt even if certain things are lost.

EXTEND

5b. *Responses will vary.* Hopkins might remain optimistic in the power of God and nature to continue.

Respond *to the* SELECTION

Do you share Hopkins' attitude toward the state of the world?

INVESTIGATE, Inquire, *Imagine*

Recall: GATHERING FACTS →

1a. What according to line 1, is the world charged with?
2a. What, according to lines 5–8, have generations done to the world?
3a. Why is nature never spent?

Interpret: FINDING MEANING

1b. With what force is the word *charge* ordinarily associated? What is Hopkins saying about the relationship of God to the world?
2b. What overall effect have humans had on the natural world?
3b. What attitude does Hopkins have toward the natural world?

Analyze: TAKING THINGS APART →

4a. What abuses of nature are mentioned in this poem?

Synthesize: BRINGING THINGS TOGETHER

4b. What more recent abuses might you add to this list?

Evaluate: MAKING JUDGMENTS →

5a. Do you agree with Hopkins that "There lives the dearest freshness deep down things"?

Extend: CONNECTING IDEAS

5b. Do you think Hopkins would change his mind if he saw the world today?

Understanding *Literature*

SONNET. Review the definition of **sonnet** in the Handbook of Literary Terms. What description is presented in the first four lines of the octave? What description is presented in the second four lines of the octave? What point is made about nature in the opening of the sestet? To what does the speaker attribute nature's characteristics in the rest of the sestet?

REPETITION. Review the definition of **repetition** in Literary Tools on page 835. In this poem, Hopkins uses repetition to tie together key ideas. What example of repetition appears in line 5? How does this repetition mirror the sense of the line?

ANSWERS TO UNDERSTANDING LITERATURE

SONNET. The first four lines discuss the grandeur of God. The second four lines describe how the earth has been worn by humanity. The sestet insists that nature is never worn out. Nature will never wear out because God is watching over us.
Teaching Note: Discuss with students the types of rhyme Hopkins uses in this poem, specifically end, slant, and exact. Point out the internal rhymes in lines 6 and 7, which highlight the idea that the earth has been dirtied by humanity.

REPETITION. The repetition in line 5 is "have trod, have trod, have trod." This repetition mirrors the countless numbers of feet that have trod over the earth.
Teaching Note: Ask students to find examples of alliteration in the poem.

Child in a White Dress, c.1880. Kate Greenaway.

SPRING AND FALL: TO A YOUNG CHILD

GERARD MANLEY HOPKINS

Márgarét, áre you gríeving
Over Goldengrove unleaving?
Leáves, líke the things of man, you
With your fresh thoughts care for, can you?
Áh! ás the heart grows older
It will come to such sights colder
By and by, nor spare a sigh
Though worlds of wanwood leafmeal[1] lie;
And yet you *will* weep and know why.
Now no matter, child, the name:
Sórrow's spríngs áre the same.
Nor mouth had, no nor mind, expressed
What heart heard of, ghost guessed:
It ís the blight man was born for,
It is Margaret you mourn for. ■

What happens as people grow older?

According to the speaker what does Margaret mourn for?

1. **wanwood leafmeal.** Leaves that have fallen and begun to decay

Literary TOOLS

METAPHOR. A **metaphor** is a figure of speech in which one thing is written about as if it were another. Metaphors invite the reader to make a comparison between two things. Look for metaphors as you read "Spring and Fall: To a Young Child."

THEME. A **theme** is a main idea in a literary work. As you read this poem, identify the theme.

Reader's Journal

How does the fall season make you feel?

ANSWERS TO GUIDED READING QUESTIONS

1. People find colder sights as they grow older.
2. She is grieving for Margaret—for herself.

READER'S JOURNAL

Students might also write about their feelings during the other seasons. Students should think more about their mood during certain seasons rather than whether they like certain seasons. For example, do they think of spring as a time of hope and rebirth or one of mud and dreariness?

SELECTION CHECK TEST 4.9.27 WITH ANSWERS

Checking Your Reading

1. What is Goldengrove doing? **It is unleaving, or losing its leaves.**
2. What does the child care about? **She cares about the leaves.**
3. How will the heart approach such sights as it gets older? **It will be colder.**
4. In time, the child will know why she does what? **She will know why she weeps.**
5. What does the speaker think the child really mourns for? **She mourns for herself.**

Literary Tools

1. Identify one metaphor from this poem. **Responses will vary, but could include the comparison of fall and spring to stages of life.**
2. What might be a theme for this poem? ***Responses will vary.***
3. Who does the speaker address in this poem? **He addresses Margaret.**

RESPOND TO THE SELECTION

You might have students make predictions before they read the poem. Then they can look back on their predictions after they have read it.

ANSWERS TO INVESTIGATE, INQUIRE, IMAGINE

Recall

1a. The speaker asks Margaret if she is grieving over Goldengrove "unleaving"—over the fact that the grove of trees is losing its leaves.
2a. Colder sights will come.
3a. Margaret mourns for herself.

Interpret

1b. The falling leaves may seem to be the only change. It may seem like a great loss to a child, who does not know why this happens.
2b. The speaker seems to have a negative or pessimistic attitude toward life.
3b. A child might react to a simple change in the environment. It is an adult who looks at the child and knows what she has to lose who suspects such a mourning.

Analyze

4a. The speaker begins by asking whether the child mourns the falling leaves. Then, he or she points out that the child, who has had little experience in life, can care about something so simple. He or she explains that life gets harder as you get older and every season becomes sorrowful. In the end it is a sense of your own mortality that causes you to weep.

Synthesize

54b. *Responses will vary.* Margaret might have said that she was sad because all the leaves were falling. She may feel bad for the trees. Perhaps she will miss a summer friend or activity. She may sense a change and not be sure that she likes it. It is unlikely that she would come to a sophisticated conclusion such as the speaker's.

Evaluate

5a. *Responses will vary.* The speaker has a negative attitude toward aging. He or she expresses a sense that life gets harder and more full of sorrow as we age. The sense that we must age and die can affect us at any age.

Respond *to the* Selection

Does this poem meet the expectations you had based on the title, "Spring and Fall: To a Young Child"? Why, or why not?

Investigate, Inquire, *Imagine*

Recall: Gathering Facts

1a. What question does the speaker ask in lines 1–2?
2a. What will come as "the heart grows older"?
3a. According to line 15, what is it Margaret mourns for?

Interpret: Finding Meaning

1b. Why might the speaker think this is the reason for Margaret's grieving?
2b. What does this prophecy suggest about the speaker's attitude toward life?
3b. Why would a child mourn this way?

Analyze: Taking Things Apart

4a. Outline the speaker's argument.

Synthesize: Bringing Things Together

4b. What if Margaret had answered the speaker's first question? What might she have said?

Evaluate: Making Judgments

5a. Evaluate the speaker's feelings about aging.

Extend: Connecting Ideas

5b. Compare and contrast the attitude toward life expressed in this poem with that expressed in "Pied Beauty" and "God's Grandeur."

Understanding *Literature*

Metaphor. Metaphor. Review the definition of **metaphor** in Literary Tools in Prereading. The seasons fall and spring are often used metaphorically. To what are they compared in this poem?

Theme. Review the definition of **theme** in the Handbook of Literary Terms. What theme does the metaphor of the seasons express in "Spring and Fall: To a Young Child"?

ANSWERS TO INVESTIGATE, INQUIRE, IMAGINE (cont.)

Extend

5b. *Responses will vary.* Both "Pied Beauty" and "God's Grandeur" are more optimistic. They both profess the greatness of God and the wonders of the world he created. In a similar vein, this poem might have praised the glory of the falling leaves and pointed to the regeneration that would come with spring. Instead, this poem points to the inevitable mortality of humans.

Answers to Understanding Literature can be found on page 839.

WRITER'S JOURNAL

1. Write a **cheer** for something unusual that you find beautiful. In the cheer identify some important characteristics of this thing.
2. Write an **editorial** about humans' effects on the natural world.
3. Write a **short story** about a young person realizing his or her mortality.

Integrating *the* LANGUAGE ARTS

Language, Grammar, and Style

IDENTIFYING PARTS OF SPEECH. The word *leaves* is both a verb and a noun. The following words can be assigned different parts of speech as well. Using a dictionary, determine the definition for each part of speech for each word. You may also want to refer to the Language Arts Survey 3.6–3.7, "Identifying the Parts of Speech."

1. fold
2. spring
3. spare
4. fall
5. lie

Study and Research

PIED BEAUTY NATURE GUIDE. Make a nature guide celebrating pied beauty. Choose animals that show distinctive coloring or markings. Use encyclopedias, field guides, and other resources to learn more about your subject. Write a brief description of the animal, its habitat, habits, and other key points. Include an illustration to show the pied beauty of the beast you chose.

Speaking and Listening & Collaborative Learning

DEBATE. Hopkins argues that "nature is never spent." His statement was made at the beginning of the Industrial Revolution. Look at the natural world today. Does Hopkins claim remain true? Split into two teams to debate this issue. Refer to the Language Arts Survey 4.21, "Participating in a Debate" for guidelines on setting up the debate.

ANSWERS TO UNDERSTANDING LITERATURE

METAPHOR. Spring and fall are often related to stages in the life of a person. Spring is a time of youth and birth. Fall is an aging period of decline and time of sorrow. Spring, usually a time of joy and regeneration, is also connected to sorrow in this poem. The metaphor suggests that life passes through different periods.

THEME. The metaphor suggests that life leads each person to his or her own fall.

ANSWERS TO INTEGRATING THE LANGUAGE ARTS

Language, Grammar, and Style
Responses will vary.

1. Fold is a verb meaning to bend. In cooking it means to mix in gently. In card games it means to remove oneself from a hand. It is also a noun meaning an area that is fenced in for animals.
2. Spring is a verb meaning to jump suddenly or to arise from a source. It is also a noun meaning the season between winter and summer. It also means a small brook or stream.
3. Spare is a verb meaning to treat mercifully or to save. It can also mean to give out one's resources. As an adjective it can mean extra or replacement.
4. Fall is a verb meaning to tumble from or plummet. It is also a noun meaning the season also known as autumn.
5. Lie is a verb meaning assume a horizontal position. It can also mean to deceive or make an untrue statement. It is also a noun meaning an untrue or inaccurate statement.

ADDITIONAL RESOURCES

UNIT 9 RESOURCE BOOK
"Promises Like Pie-Crust"
- Selection Worksheet 9.14
- Selection Check Test 4.9.29
- Selection Test 4.9.30

"A Birthday"
- Selection Worksheet 9.15
- Selection Check Test 4.9.31
- Selection Test 4.9.32
- Language, Grammar, and Style Resource 3.80
- Speaking and Listening Resource 4.22

INDIVIDUAL LEARNING STRATEGIES

MOTIVATION
Ask them the following questions for "Promises…": Why has the speaker decided not to enter into a lifelong union with the person whom she is addressing? Do you consider the reasons that she offers to be sound? Why, or why not? Ask students the following questions about "A Birthday": As you read the first stanza of the poem, ask yourself what similarities there are between the speaker's heart and the things to which the heart is compared.

ENGLISH LANGUAGE LEARNING
In "Promises…," Rossetti uses two phrases to refer to fortune telling or the role of fate. The first is "Let us hold the die uncast." A die or dice are used in gambling. The cast die can also refer to the role of fate. The second is "Fades the image from the glass / And the fortune is not told." The glass refers to a gazing crystal used to tell fortunes or foresee the future.

SPECIAL NEEDS
Have students work with a partner to complete the Guided Reading and Recall questions.

ENRICHMENT ACTIVITIES
Rossetti wrote poetry that dealt with contemporary issues of sexual politics, of which "Promises Like Pie-Crust" is an example. Have students research other politically conscious poetry by Rossetti and present their findings to the class.

PREREADING

"PROMISES LIKE PIE-CRUST," "A BIRTHDAY"

BY CHRISTINA ROSSETTI

About the AUTHOR

Christina Rossetti (1830–1894) grew up in a stimulating Anglo-Italian family, the daughter of an exiled Italian poet and politician. In her household, Italian exiles gathered and talked of politics, art, and literature. She and her brothers, Dante and William, wrote poetry and did artwork from childhood on. A deeply religious person, Rossetti became involved in a contemporary movement to restore elements of Catholicism to Anglican religious services. However, her commitment to the Anglican Church was strong enough that she broke off an engagement with one suitor because of his conversion to Catholicism. She later broke off a second relationship because her suitor was insufficiently interested in religion.

Rossetti lived a quiet, thoughtful life, often doing charitable works such as volunteering at a home that we would today call a "women's shelter." Rossetti's first book of poetry, *Goblin Market and Other Poems,* published in 1862, was an immediate success. On the surface, the title poem seems to tell a simple children's story, but beneath the simplicity lies a depth of religious symbolism.

Rossetti's brother Dante helped to found a group of writers, artists, and critics known as the Pre-Raphaelite Brotherhood whose purpose was to promote simplicity, naturalness, and expressiveness in art and literature, on the model of artwork done in Italy before the Renaissance. Christina Rossetti's exquisite poetry is often described as Pre-Raphaelite because of its surface simplicity and gracefulness achieved through a rarely paralleled technical mastery. However, the simplicity of surface in Rossetti's poetry masks a complexity of thought and feeling. Her poems bear reading again and again.

For years, readers and critics tended to dismiss Rossetti because of the sheer variety and magnitude of work by her more famous male contemporaries Tennyson and Browning. However, in recent years her reputation has grown as readers have rediscovered the fine artistry of her work. More than any other poet of her age, she exemplifies the common critical observation that a writer must work hard to make a piece seem simple and easy.

About the SELECTIONS

In both **"Promises Like Pie-Crust"** and **"A Birthday,"** Rossetti deals with the subject of love. The poems deal with different themes and tones, however. Both are excellent examples of Rossetti's apparently simple, yet actually quite complex, style.

GOALS/OBJECTIVES

Studying this lesson will enable students to
- enjoy the simple beauty of Rossetti's lyric poetry
- describe Rossetti's literary accomplishments and explain the historical significance of her writings
- define *parallelism, alliteration,* and *chiasmus* and recognize and analyze them in a poem
- define *metaphor, connotation,* and *symbol,* and recognize and interpret them in a poem
- identify participles, gerunds, and infinitives
- write nursery rhymes, art criticism, and comparison and contrast essays

PROMISES Like Pie-Crust

CHRISTINA ROSSETTI

Promise me no promises,
So will I not promise you:
Keep we both our liberties,
Never false and never true:
Let us hold the die uncast,
Free to come as free to go:
For I cannot know your past,
And of mine what can you know?

You, so warm, may once have been
Warmer towards another one:
I, so cold, may once have seen
Sunlight, once have felt the sun:
Who shall show us if it was
Thus indeed in time of old?
Fades the image from the glass,
And the fortune is not told.

If you promised, you might grieve
For lost liberty again:
If I promised, I believe
I should fret to break the chain.
Let us be the friends we were,
Nothing more but nothing less:
Many thrive on frugal fare
Who would perish of excess. ■

What does the speaker want the person addressed not to do?

What sort of relationship does the speaker want to have?

Literary TOOLS

METAPHOR AND SIMILE. A **metaphor** is a figure of speech in which one thing is spoken or written about as if it were another. This figure of speech asks the reader to make a comparison between the two things. A **simile**, a comparison using *like* or *as*, is a kind of metaphor. The title "Promises Like Pie-Crust" is a simile. As you read, note the metaphors Rossetti uses in this poem.

PARALLELISM. **Parallelism** is a rhetorical technique in which a writer emphasizes the equal value or weight of two or more ideas by expressing them in the same grammatical form. Look for parallelism in "A Birthday."

ALLITERATION. **Alliteration** is the repetition of initial consonant sounds. Rossetti uses alliteration to create a musical effect in "A Birthday."

Reader's *Journal*

Have you ever had to deny someone something that he or she wanted of you? How did you handle the situation?

ANSWERS TO GUIDED READING QUESTIONS

1. She asks the person not to make any promises.
2. The speaker wants to remain friends—"nothing more, nothing less."

READER'S JOURNAL

Ask students to consider the saying, "Promises are made to be broken." Ask them if they agree or disagree with this idea.

SELECTION CHECK TEST 4.9.29 WITH ANSWERS

Checking Your Reading

1. What does the speaker ask the listener not to do? **She asks the listener not to make promises.**
2. What can the two people not really know about each other? **They cannot truly know each other's pasts.**
3. What may the speaker, "so cold," once have felt? **She once may have felt the sun.**
4. What might the listener grieve for if it were lost? **He might grieve for lost liberty.**
5. What do many thrive on? **Many thrive on "frugal fare."**

Literary Tools

1. Writers use parallelism to:
   a. achieve even rhythm
   b. give two or more ideas equal value
   c. indicate the importance of a central idea
   d. help the reader remember an element of the poem
2. What metaphor does Rossetti use for commitment?
   a. a rope
   b. a chain
   c. a cell
   d. a lock without a key
3. The speaker of this poem is most likely addressing
   a. her husband
   b. her child
   c. her mother
   d. her friend

RESPOND TO THE SELECTION
Students might consider how they would feel right away and also how they might feel after some time had passed.

ANSWERS TO INVESTIGATE, INQUIRE, IMAGINE

RECALL

1a. The speaker asks her suitor not make any promises. She also says, "Let us hold the die uncast."

2a. The suitor is warm and the speaker is cold.

3a. They might grieve for their lost liberty or try to break the chains.

INTERPRET

1b. The speaker is afraid that any promises they make might be broken. She is happy with the kind of relationship they have and does not want to make changes that might make her unhappy.

2b. These words suggest that the suitor cares more for the speaker than the speaker does for her suitor.

3b. *Responses will vary.* Because of the suitor's strong feelings, it seems unlikely that they will be able to maintain their friendship.

ANALYZE

4a. The speaker does not want to pursue the relationship because she fears the commitment. She is afraid that both she and her suitor will miss their freedom. She mentions that she is "cold" to her suitor, showing that she does not have strong feelings for him. In the second stanza, the speaker alludes to the possibility of other, warmer loves, loves they might miss if they were together.

SYNTHESIZE

4b. *Responses will vary.* It is likely that the speaker would be unhappy in the relationship. She might break her promises and break off the relationship or seek happiness elsewhere. The suitor might be unhappy with the relationship if the speaker does not have the feeling he would like her to have.

EVALUATE

5a. The speaker wants a friendship. She wants a relationship between equals. She values her liberty or freedom.

EXTEND

5b. *Responses will vary.* Students should note that a good relationship should not diminish either individual.

Respond to the SELECTION

How would you feel if somebody you loved said, "Let us be the friends we were,/Nothing more but nothing less"?

INVESTIGATE, Inquire, Imagine

Recall: GATHERING FACTS → **Interpret:** FINDING MEANING

1a. What requests does the speaker make in stanza 1?

1b. Why does the speaker want to act this way?

2a. What words describe the speaker and her suitor in lines 9–11?

2b. What do these words suggest about their relationship?

3a. What might happen if the speaker and her suitor made promises?

3b. Do you think the speaker and her suitor can "be the friends [they] were? Explain.

Analyze: TAKING THINGS APART → **Synthesize:** BRINGING THINGS TOGETHER

4a. Analyze the speaker's reasons for not pursuing this relationship.

4b. Imagine what might happen if the speaker gave in and made promises with her suitor.

Evaluate: MAKING JUDGMENTS → **Extend:** CONNECTING IDEAS

5a. What kind of relationship does the speaker want? What else does she seem to value in her life?

5b. Explain how individuality or independence can coexist with a close relationship.

Understanding Literature

METAPHOR AND SIMILE. Review the definitions for **metaphor** and **simile** in the Handbook of Literary Terms. In what way are promises like pie crust? What does the speaker mean by, "Let us hold the die uncast"? by "Many thrive on frugal fare / Who would perish of excess"?

ANSWERS TO UNDERSTANDING LITERATURE

METAPHOR AND SIMILE. *Responses will vary.* Promises are like pie crust in that they can be difficult to make and easy to break. The die uncast shows that the speaker feels that love is a gamble. Frugal fare is their friendship as opposed to the excess of a love affair.

Apple Trees in Flower, c. 1900s. Ernest Quost. Private Collection.

A BIRTHDAY

CHRISTINA ROSSETTI

My heart is like a singing bird
  Whose nest is in a watered shoot;
My heart is like an apple tree
  Whose boughs are bent with thickset fruit;
My heart is like a rainbow shell
  That paddles in a halcyon sea;
My heart is gladder than all these
  Because my love is come to me.

Raise me a dais of silk and down;
  Hang it with vair[1] and purple dyes;[2]
Carve it in doves[3] and pomegranates,[4]
  And peacocks[5] with a hundred eyes;
Work in it gold and silver grapes,
  In leaves and silver fleurs-de-lys;[6]
Because the birthday of my life
  Is come, my love is come to me. ■

To what does the speaker compare her heart?

In what sense has the speaker had a second birthday? How important is the speaker's love to her?

1. **vair.** Gray and white fur used to trim fancy garments
2. **purple dyes.** In former days only royals were allowed to wear cloth dyed purple.
3. **doves.** Traditional symbols of peace
4. **pomegranates.** Type of fruit
5. **peacocks.** Splendid birds often kept in royal gardens
6. **fleurs-de-lys.** Flowers of the lily, found on coat of arms of the former French royal family

WORDS FOR EVERYDAY USE

hal • cy • on (hal´sē ən) *adj.,* tranquil; happy. *The halcyon days of my childhood were those days I spent playing chess by the lake.*

da • is (dā´is *or* dī´is) *n.,* raised platform, as for a seat of honor. *The speakers were seated at the front of the auditorium on the dais.*

ANSWERS TO GUIDED READING QUESTIONS

1. The speaker compares her heart to a singing bird, an apple tree, and a rainbow shell.
2. The first birthday is when the speaker was born. The second birthday is when the speaker found love. The speaker's love is important enough to seem like a rebirth.

VOCABULARY FROM THE SELECTION

dais
halcyon

SELECTION CHECK TEST 4.9.31 WITH ANSWERS

Checking Your Reading

1. What paddles in the sea? **The rainbow shell paddles in the sea.**
2. What is "gladder than all these"? **Her heart is gladder than all these.**
3. What does the speaker ask to be raised for her? **She wants a dais.**
4. What has "a hundred eyes"? **The peacock has a hundred eyes.**
5. Who has joined the speaker? **Her love has joined her.**

Literary Tools

1. How is parallelism used in this poem? **The phrase "My heart is like…" is repeated.**
2. How is "birthday" used as a metaphor in this poem? **The speaker talks of the day her love joined her as the first day of her life.**
3. Identify a simile from the poem. ***Responses will vary.***

RESPOND TO THE SELECTION

Students may wish to create a sketch along with a written description of their celebration.

ANSWERS TO INVESTIGATE, INQUIRE, IMAGINE

RECALL

1a. The speaker compares her heart to a singing bird, an apple tree, and a rainbow shell.

2a. The speaker's love has come to her.

3a. The speaker has the birthday of her life because her love has come to her.

INTERPRET

1b. The speaker's heart may be said to be singing or flying. The speaker's heart may be said to be luxuriant or rich, or the love could be considered successful.

2b. The speaker's gladness is beyond words because even the three comparisons she made were inadequate to express her feelings.

3b. The speaker's life has completely changed, so much so that she feels reborn. Perhaps the emotions or qualities associated with childhood birthdays, such as joy and innocence, have returned to the speaker. The speaker's new love makes the speaker feel reborn.

ANALYZE

4a. The speaker mentions a dais of silk and down, vair and purple dyes, doves, pomegranates and peacocks. She also mentions gold and silver grapes and fleurs-de-lys. These things all signify luxury or royalty.

SYNTHESIZE

4b. The images in stanza 1 are similes drawn from nature. They are in stark contrast to the opulence expressed in the second stanza. This contrast shows depth or breadth to the speaker's feelings. The feelings are both natural and abundant. They include the wonder at the simple things in life and the overwhelming wonder of the most and best of everything.

EVALUATE

5a. *Responses will vary.* Students may say that it is difficult to express fully the deepness of a true love. The variety of ways in which the speaker expresses help demonstrate this love. Also, the sense that this love is like a rebirth is very telling.

Respond *to the* SELECTION

If you were going to create a celebration of a great moment of happiness, what would it be like?

INVESTIGATE, Inquire, *Imagine*

Recall: GATHERING FACTS →

1a. To what three things does the speaker compare her heart?

2a. What has come to the speaker?

3a. What "birthday" does the speaker have?

Interpret: FINDING MEANING

1b. What do these comparisons suggest about the speaker's feelings?

2b. How does this make the speaker feel?

3b. In what way has the speaker been reborn?

Analyze: TAKING THINGS APART →

4a. Analyze the images the speaker uses in lines 9–14. What do these things have in common?

Synthesize: BRINGING THINGS TOGETHER

4b. How do the images used in stanza 2 contrast with those in stanza 1? Why do you think Rosetti used this contrast?

Evaluate: MAKING JUDGMENTS →

5a. Judge whether the speaker is able to express her feelings adequately.

Extend: CONNECTING IDEAS

5b. Contrast these feelings to the feelings expressed in "Promises Like Pie-Crust."

Understanding *Literature*

PARALLELISM. Review the definition of **parallelism** in the Handbook of Literary Terms. What examples of parallelism can you find in stanza 1?

ALLITERATION. Review the definition of **alliteration** in Literary Tools on page 841. Identify six examples of alliteration in this poem.

ANSWERS TO INVESTIGATE, INQUIRE, IMAGINE (CONT.)

EXTEND

5b. *Responses will vary.* The speaker in this poem could hardly be more in love. The speaker in "Promises Like Pie-Crust" is not in love with her suitor and reacts quite coolly.

Answers to Understanding Literature can be found on page 845

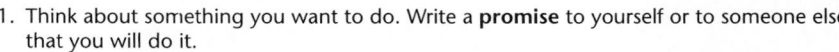

Writer's Journal

1. Think about something you want to do. Write a **promise** to yourself or to someone else that you will do it.
2. Choose a time when you had very strong emotions. Write a **poem** about this time. Use similes to express your feelings.
3. Write a **comparison and contrast essay** about the themes of Rossetti's "A Birthday" and Browning's Sonnet 43 on page 829.

Integrating *the* Language Arts

Language, Grammar, and Style

Verbals. Read the Language Arts Survey 3.80, "Verbals: Participles, Gerunds, and Infinitives." Then find the participles, gerunds, and infinitives in the following lines from Rossetti's poems.

1. The wind has such a rainy sound
   Moaning through the town,
2. But when the leaves hang trembling
   The wind is passing through.
3. Not wan with waiting, not with sorrow dim;
4. Let us hold the die uncast,
   Free to come as free to go:
5. If I promised, I believe
   I should fret to break the chain.

Speaking and Listening

Multimedia Presentation. Choose an upcoming event such as a birthday, graduation, or anniversary. Create a multimedia presentation to be part of the celebration of this event. You might use photographs, video clips, interviews with those who know the person being honored, or any other audio or visual elements that will enhance your message. Refer to the Language Arts Survey 4.22, "Preparing a Multimedia Presentation" to find guidelines for creating a multimedia presentation.

Collaborative Learning

Chapbook. A **chapbook** is a collection of works from different sources prepared for one's own pleasure or use. Christina Rossetti wrote some of the finest poems in our language on the subject of romantic love. Do some research to identify poems on other kinds of love—love for family members, friends, teachers, mentors; love for one's community, land, or country; love of learning or of art; and so on. Working with other members of your class, design and illustrate an anthology of poems on other kinds of love. You may wish to add works by classmates to the collection.

ANSWERS TO UNDERSTANDING LITERATURE

Parallelism. Examples of parallelism in the first stanza are a singing bird, an apple tree, and a rainbow shell.

Alliteration. Examples include "boughs are bent"; "dais of silk and down"; purple, pomegranates, and peacocks; "gold and silver grapes"; "leaves and silver fleurs-de-lys"; and "Because the birthday."

ANSWERS TO INTEGRATING THE LANGUAGE ARTS

Language, Grammar, and Style

1. participle—moaning
2. participles—trembling, passing
3. gerund—waiting
4. infinitives—to come, to go
5. participles—promised, fret;
   infinitive—to break

Collaborative Learning

Students may wish to produce their chapbook on a computer, inserting ClipArt images, scanning their own images, or using images from CD/ROM, if available.

ADDITIONAL RESOURCES

Unit 9 Resource Book
- Selection Worksheet 9.16
- Selection Check Test 4.9.33
- Selection Test 4.9.34
- Speaking and Listening Resource 4.21
- Applied English Resource 6.9

GRAPHIC ORGANIZER

Students may list some of the words that illustrate the solemn tone of the poem: laurel; shady night; echoes fade; low lintel; strengthless dead; garland briefer than a girl's.

READER'S JOURNAL

Students should also consider these questions: Why do people value athletes? What causes athletes' fame to fade? Is the public always fair in the way it hands out and takes away fame and adoration?

Quotables

In the future, everyone will be world-famous for fifteen minutes.

—Andy Warhol

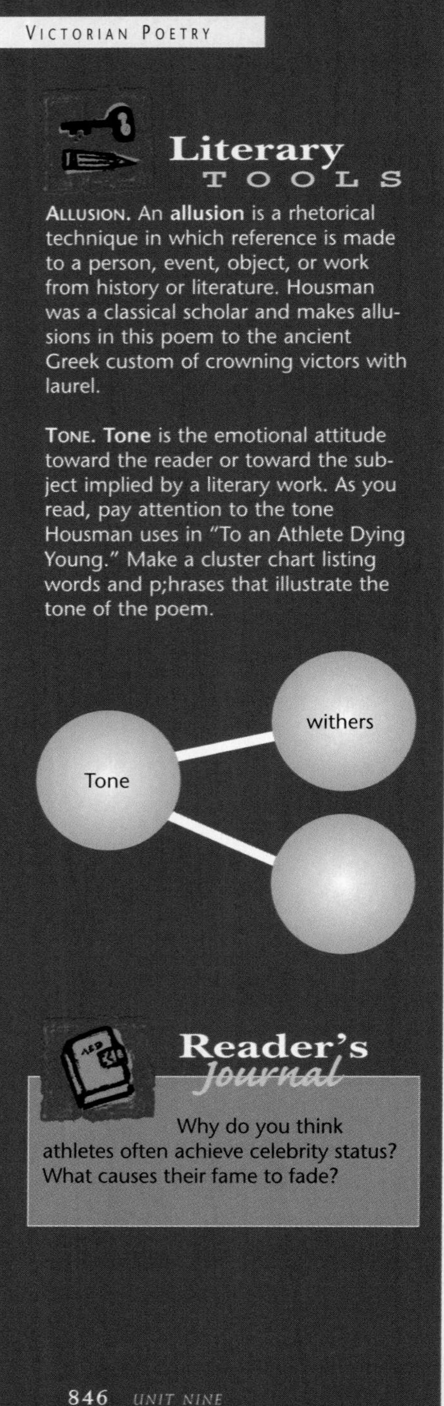

Literary Tools

Allusion. An **allusion** is a rhetorical technique in which reference is made to a person, event, object, or work from history or literature. Housman was a classical scholar and makes allusions in this poem to the ancient Greek custom of crowning victors with laurel.

Tone. **Tone** is the emotional attitude toward the reader or toward the subject implied by a literary work. As you read, pay attention to the tone Housman uses in "To an Athlete Dying Young." Make a cluster chart listing words and p;hrases that illustrate the tone of the poem.

Reader's Journal

Why do you think athletes often achieve celebrity status? What causes their fame to fade?

"To an Athlete Dying Young"

By A. E. Housman

About the Author

Alfred Edward Housman (1859–1936) was a classical scholar and distinguished poet. Although Housman did not produce a large body of work, his polished, simple style has influenced a great many other poets.

Housman was born in Worcestershire, near the Shropshire countryside which often appears in his poetry. He attended Oxford University, and although a brilliant student, he failed his final examination because of personal problems. Housman then went to work as a clerk in the Patent Office, where he spent ten years. During this time, he spent evenings at the British Museum reading room studying Latin texts. When he wrote articles about his studies and sent them to scholarly journals, fellow scholars eventually took notice of his work, and in 1892 he was appointed professor of Latin at University College, London. Housman's major scholarly work was an annotated edition of the writings of Manilius. His volumes of poetry are *A Shropshire Lad,* which appeared in 1896, and *Last Poems,* which appeared nearly twenty-five years later. After Housman passed away, his brother published another volume called *More Poems.*

About the Selection

"To an Athlete Dying Young" appears in Housman's first book, *A Shropshire Lad* (1896). The poem, like his others, is written in a simple style, one which expresses Housman's common theme of the transience of youth, beauty, and friendship. The poem harkens back to classical elegies of Greece and Rome, which often dealt with the death of a young athlete or hero.

GOALS/OBJECTIVES

Studying this lesson will enable students to
- experience the speaker's feelings toward youth, glory, and death
- define *allusion* and recognize and interpret allusions in a poem
- define *aim* and *tone* and analyze examples of each in the poems they read
- write a eulogy, a newspaper article, and images of change and victory

The Race, 1930. Museo d'Arte Moderno di Ca Pesaro, Venice.

To An Athlete Dying Young

A. E. Housman

The time you won your town the race
We chaired[1] you through the
market-place;
Man and boy stood cheering by,
And home we brought you
shoulder-high.

Today, the road all runners come,
Shoulder-high we bring you home,
And set you at your threshold down,
Townsman of a
stiller town.

What takes place in the first stanza? What takes place in the second stanza?

Smart lad, to slip
betimes away
From fields where glory does not stay
And early though
the laurel[2] grows
It withers quicker
than the rose.

According to the speaker, what happens to an athlete's "glory"?

Eyes the shady night has shut
Cannot see the record cut,[3]
And silence sounds no worse than cheers
After earth has stopped the ears:

Now you will not swell the rout
Of lads that wore their honors out,
Runners whom renown outran
And the name died before the man.

So set, before its echoes fade
The fleet foot on the sill of shade,
And hold to the low lintel up
The still-defended challenge-cup.

And round that early laurelled head
Will flock to gaze the strengthless dead
And find unwithered on its curls
The garland briefer than a girl's. ■

1. **chaired.** Carried you home in victory
2. **laurel.** Laurel wreaths are traditional signs of victory.
3. **cut.** Broken

ANSWERS TO GUIDED READING QUESTIONS

1. In the first stanza the speaker refers to a time when the athlete won a race. The dead athlete is brought home in the second stanza.
2. An athlete's "glory" slips away very quickly—it "withers quicker than a rose."

INDIVIDUAL LEARNING STRATEGIES

MOTIVATION
Have students use an almanac or yearbook to find a list of athletes who died last year. Students should note the age of the youngest athlete. Then ask students to find information about the athlete's accomplishments.

READING PROFICIENCY
Point out to students that again in this poem, syntax is reordered so that the subject sometimes comes after a verb. One example of the former is in line 27: the subject, *the dead,* comes after the verb, *flock.* Ask them what is meant by the phrase in line 19: "Runners whom renown outran / And the name died before the man."

ENGLISH LANGUAGE LEARNING
Housman uses "name" to mean fame. This is similar to the way Tennyson used the term "make a name" in "Ulysses." Students can work in small groups to list other terms for becoming successful or famous.

SPECIAL NEEDS
Have students work together to answer the Guided Reading and Recall questions.

ENRICHMENT ACTIVITIES
English composer John Nicholson Ireland (1879–1962) wrote a number of short pieces set to poems by Thomas Hardy and A. E. Housman. (Some of these are recorded on the CD *John Ireland: English Songs*, by Rachel Ann Morgan and Tan Crone. EtCetera Records. KTC 1128.) Play a selection for students. Students should research other poems set to music and share their findings and the music with the class.

SELECTION CHECK TEST 4.9.33 WITH ANSWERS

Checking Your Reading

1. Why had the athlete once been "chaired" through town? **He won a race.**
2. Of what is he now a "townsman"? **He is townsman of a stiller town—the graveyard.**
3. What withers quicker than the rose? **Laurel withers quicker than the rose.**
4. What can eyes that "night has shut" not see? **They cannot see the record broken.**
5. For an aging athlete, what often "dies" before he does? **His name dies before him.**

Literary Tools

1. What is an elegy? **An elegy is a poem that expresses grief or loss.**
2. What is an allusion? **An allusion is a reference to a person, event, object, or work from history or literature.**
3. What is a poem's tone? **Tone is the emotional attitude toward the reader or subject that is implied by a literary work.**

RESPOND TO THE SELECTION

If students know somebody who has died young, they might express their feelings about this event.

ANSWERS TO INVESTIGATE, INQUIRE, IMAGINE

Recall

1a. The crowd carries him home in victory.

2a. The boy slipped away from life where glory does not stay. He died before his fame could.

3a. The athlete sets his fleet foot on the "sill of shade." He holds his cup to the low lintel. Both of these refer to the grave.

Interpret

1b. This probably makes the boy feel proud, praised, and popular. It is probably very exciting.

2b. The boy has given up his life. The speaker thinks the boy has gained immortality. He dies before his fame withers or fades to the glory of some one else.

3b. The speaker refers to the fact that the athlete can never be defeated.

Analyze

4a. The crowd was cheering and proud of the boy when he won the race. They still honor and carry him, but the mood is somber when they carry him to his grave.

Synthesize

4b. *Responses will vary.* The crowd might have continued to love and be proud of the athlete if he had continued to live and win. He might have been eclipsed by other athletes. Actions unrelated to his athletic endeavors might have turned the crowd against him. He might have been sidelined by injuries and forgotten.

Evaluate

5a. The speaker seems to think that public adoration and fame is fickle. One cannot count on it to last. He seems to see death as a way to escape a loss of public adoration.

Extend

5b. *Responses will vary.*

Respond *to the* Selection

Do you think the speaker is cynical or realistic? Explain your response.

Investigate, Inquire, Imagine

Recall: Gathering Facts →

1a. What does the crowd do when the boy wins the race?

2a. Why, according to the speaker, is the boy smart?

3a. Where is the athlete to set his "fleet foot" and hold up his trophy?

Interpret: Finding Meaning

1b. How do you think this makes the boy feel?

2b. What has the boy given up? What does the speaker think he has gained?

3b. Why does the speaker refer to the "still-defended challenge-cup"?

Analyze: Taking Things Apart →

4a. Compare and contrast the crowd's actions in the situations described in stanza 1 and stanza 2.

Synthesize: Bringing Things Together

4b. How might the crowd have reacted to the death of the athlete if he had lived to be an old man?

Evaluate: Making Judgments →

5a. Evaluate the speaker's attitudes toward pubic adoration and toward death.

Extend: Connecting Ideas

5b. How do you react when somebody (either famous or well-known to you) dies young?

Understanding Literature

Allusion. Review the definition for **allusion** in the Handbook of Literary Terms. Why do you think Housman alludes to the Greek tradition of crowning victors with laurel?

Tone. Review the definition for **tone** in Literary Tools in Prereading. What is the prevailing tone of the poem? Identify words and phrases that contribute to this tone.

ANSWERS FOR UNDERSTANDING LITERATURE

Allusion. The allusions to crowns of laurel represent a celebration of greatness and a bestowing of fame. The allusions elevate the subject of the poem to legendary status, rather than chronicling the untimely death of a local boy who won a town footrace.

Tone. *Responses will vary.* Some students may say the tone is disturbingly unemotional for such an emotional topic, so much so that it is debatable whether Housman is being serious or ironic. Others may say that the tone is solemn; some might call it bitter and cynical. Words such as home, town, and lad imply the commonplace, whereas the poem's subject—the death of a young hero—is highly uncommon and even shocking.

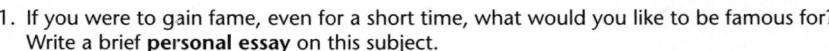

WRITER'S JOURNAL

1. If you were to gain fame, even for a short time, what would you like to be famous for? Write a brief **personal essay** on this subject.
2. Choose a local athlete and write a **profile** of him or her. You may choose to focus solely on the individual's athletic skills, or you may wish to include additional details about this person.
3. Write a **eulogy** for the funeral of an athlete. Consider the effect this person had on his community and what you know about his accomplishments. Fill in the gaps with your imagination.

Integrating *the* LANGUAGE ARTS

Study and Research

NEWSPAPER ARTICLE. Choose an athlete that inspires or intrigues you. Do some research to answer these questions: When did this person first gain public attention? How fast did his or her career flourish from that point? What, if any, incidents caused the athlete to lose public favor? What was the pinnacle of the person's career? When did fame begin to fade? Why? You may also wish to explore other aspects of the athlete's life or career. Then write a series of short newspaper or magazine article on this athlete.

Speaking and Listening & Collaborative Learning

DEBATE. Consider that many athletes become celebrities and achieve hero status. Some people think that with this status comes a responsibility to be a good role model. Others disagree. Divide into two teams to debate this idea: Athletes, because of their status, should be role models for young people. You may find it helpful to refer to the Language Arts Survey 4.21, "Participating in a Debate."

Applied English & Collaborative Learning

WRITING PRESS RELEASES. With your classmates, create a list of school events. Divide up the events by theme; for example; sports, performing and visual arts, class events, fundraisers, etc. Working in small groups, write a series of press releases about these events. Consider submitting these releases to local media to inform your community and encourage citizens' participation. Refer to the Language Arts Survey 6.9, "Delivering a Press Release," to find guidelines for writing a press release.

ANSWERS TO INTEGRATING THE LANGUAGE ARTS

Study and Research
Students might choose to give an oral presentation or create a display to share what they have learned. Students should include proper documentation for any sources they use.

Speaking and Listening & Collaborative Learning
Students may also wish to consider the whether other famous people are considered or should be role models. For example, are actors, musicians, or political figures held accountable for their actions and how they are viewed by young people?

ADDITIONAL RESOURCES

UNIT 9 RESOURCE BOOK
- Selection Worksheet 9.17
- Selection Check Test 4.9.35
- Selection Test 4.9.36
- Language, Grammar, and Style Resource 3.36
- Speaking and Listening Resource 4.20
- Study and Research Resource 5.19

GRAPHIC ORGANIZER

Students may include the following in their cluster charts: deep trench; solitary and dismal place; dripping-wet wall of jagged stone; great dungeon terminating in a gloomy red light; massive architecture; barbarous, depressing, and forbidding air; struck chill...as if I had left the natural world.

READER'S JOURNAL

If students do not find ghost stories frightening, they might write about other kinds of stories they find frightening. Students should consider the elements that make these stories scary—is it fear of the unknown? fear that it could really happen? simply an active imagination? Students might write about one of the scariest stories they know.

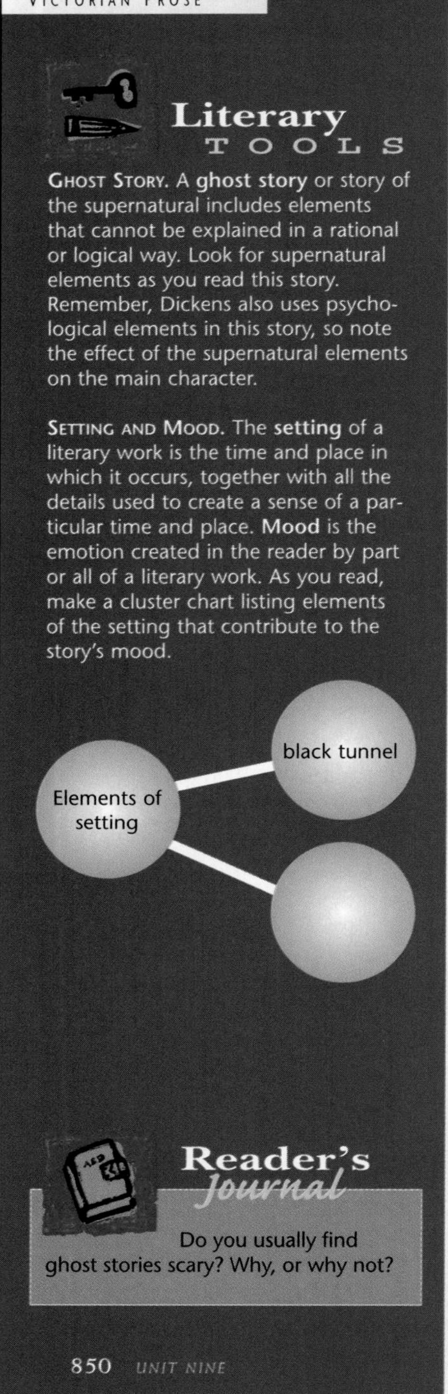

Literary TOOLS

GHOST STORY. A **ghost story** or story of the supernatural includes elements that cannot be explained in a rational or logical way. Look for supernatural elements as you read this story. Remember, Dickens also uses psychological elements in this story, so note the effect of the supernatural elements on the main character.

SETTING AND MOOD. The **setting** of a literary work is the time and place in which it occurs, together with all the details used to create a sense of a particular time and place. **Mood** is the emotion created in the reader by part or all of a literary work. As you read, make a cluster chart listing elements of the setting that contribute to the story's mood.

Reader's Journal

Do you usually find ghost stories scary? Why, or why not?

"THE SIGNALMAN"

BY CHARLES DICKENS

About the AUTHOR

Much of the life of **Charles Dickens** (1812–1870) appeared in fictional form in his literary work. His childhood began happily, but it dramatically changed in his eleventh year when the family moved from Chatham, a port town, to the city of London. Soon after the move, his father was sent to prison for unpaid debts. Young Charles was taken out of school and eventually put to work in a warehouse. The mark that these two experiences left on him was profound. Later in life he became an ardent social critic on behalf of the poor and downtrodden who filled London's streets in the mid-nineteenth century.

Eventually Charles returned to school, but he left again at the age of fifteen to work as a legal clerk and legal reporter. When he was twenty-one, he began contributing stories, many of them humorous, to various newspapers and magazines. His unique writing style and social awareness won him wide popularity. Having found a market and an audience, Dickens began to publish his longer works in serial form, or installments. His first novel, *Pickwick Papers,* was published in serial form from 1836 to 1837 and gained him substantial fame. Dickens soon became one of the most popular and renowned writers of his day, both in England and the United States. Despite his commercial success, the pain of his childhood haunted him, and many of his novels sympathetically describe the poverty and insecurity of children, clerks, and small merchants struggling on their own in the city.

A Christmas Carol (1843), featuring the character Ebenezer Scrooge, is perhaps Dickens's most well-known work. *A Tale of Two Cities* (1859), a historical novel set in France and England during the French Revolution, is extremely well regarded. Other major works include *Oliver Twist* (1838), *Nicholas Nickleby* (1839), *Bleak House* (1853), and *Hard Times* (1854).

About the SELECTION

In *A Christmas Carol,* Dickens introduces several now famous spirits, including the ghost of Marley and three Christmas spirits. Dickens also included supernatural beings in short stories, such as "The Haunted House" and "The Lawyer and the Ghost." **"The Signalman"** is also a tale of the supernatural. In "The Signalman," Dickens mixes psychological elements with the supernatural.

GOALS/OBJECTIVES

Studying this lesson will enable students to
- appreciate a story with supernatural and psychological elements
- describe Dickens's literary accomplishments and explain the historical significance of his writings
- define *setting* and *mood* and identify these elements in their reading
- explain the connection between setting and mood
- recognize both supernatural and psychological elements in a story

Liverpool to Manchester Railway.

The SIGNALMAN

Charles Dickens

"Halloa! Below there!"

When he heard a voice thus calling to him, he was standing at the door of his box, with a flag in his hand, furled round its short pole. One would have thought, considering the nature of the ground, that he could not have doubted from what quarter the voice came; but instead of looking up to where I stood on the top of the steep cutting nearly over his head, he turned himself about, and looked down the Line. There was something remarkable in his manner of doing so, though I could not have said for my life what. But I

What greeting does the narrator shout to the signalman?

Where does the signalman look when he hears this noise?

Words For Everyday Use

steep (stēp) *adj.*, mounting or falling precipitously. *It took Grandma ten minutes to climb the steep steps.*

ANSWERS TO GUIDED READING QUESTIONS

1. The narrator shouts "Halloa! Below there!"
2. The signalman looks down the Line.

INDIVIDUAL LEARNING STRATEGIES

Motivation
Ask students to share ghost stories they have heard, as suggested in the Speaking and Listening activity on page 862. What makes some stories scary and others silly?

Reading Proficiency
This story includes both supernatural and psychological elements. Make sure that students understand both terms. The supernatural elements are those that are beyond natural explanation. The psychological elements are ones that play with the mind and effect the thinking of the characters.

English Language Learning
Share with students the following additional vocabulary.
dint—effort
saturnine—gloomy
singular—peculiar, strange
vehemence—violent or passionate expression of conviction
painstaking—taking care to do things correctly or properly
oppressed—weighed heavily upon, depressed the spirits

Special Needs
Have students work in pairs on the cluster charts in Literary Tools. As an alternative, they can keep a sensory detail chart about the setting of the story.

Enrichment Activities
Dickens was well known for encouraging many social reforms. One outlet for his ideas was the periodical he created, *Household Words.* Suggest that students create their own magazine to deal with social issues. What issues would they address? How would they attract an audience?

ANSWERS TO GUIDED READING QUESTIONS

1. The signalman seemed reluctant to point out the path.
2. The signalman works in a gloomy, dark place that smells earthy and deadly. It makes the speaker feel as if he has left the natural world.

VOCABULARY FROM THE SELECTION

apprise	inexplicable
asunder	peruse
avert	prominent
calamity	redoubled
compose	rejoin
compulsion	ruminating
daunt	steep
derive	treacherous
idle	vehemence
incongruity	vigilant

know it was remarkable enough to attract my notice, even though his figure was foreshortened and shadowed, down in the deep trench, and mine was high above him, so steeped in the glow of an angry sunset, that I had shaded my eyes with my hand before I saw him at all.

"Halloa! Below!"

From looking down the Line, he turned himself about again, and, raising his eyes, saw my figure high above him.

"Is there any path by which I can come down and speak to you?"

He looked up at me without replying, and I looked down at him without pressing him too soon with a repetition of my idle question. Just then there came a vague vibration in the earth and air, quickly changing into a violent pulsation, and an oncoming rush that caused me to start back, as though it had force to draw me down. When such vapor as rose to my height from this rapid train had passed me and was skimming away over the landscape, I looked down again, and saw him refurling the flag he had shown while the train went by.

I repeated my inquiry. After a pause, during which he seemed to regard me with fixed attention, he motioned with his rolled-up flag towards a point on my level, some two or three hundred yards distant. I called down to him, "All right!" and made for that point. There, by dint of looking closely about me, I found a rough zigzag descending path notched out, which I followed.

HIS POST WAS IN AS SOLITARY AND DISMAL A PLACE AS EVER I SAW.

The cutting was extremely deep, and unusually precipitate.[1] It was made through a clammy stone, that become oozier and wetter as I went down. For these reasons, I found the way long enough to give me time to recall a singular air of reluctance or compulsion with which he had pointed out the path.

What kind of reaction did the signalman have to pointing out the path?

When I came down low enough upon the zigzag descent to see him again, I saw that he was standing between the rails on the way by which the train had lately passed, in an attitude as if he were waiting for me to appear. He had his left hand at his chin, and that left elbow rested on his right hand, crossed over his breast. His attitude was one of such expectation and watchfulness, that I stopped a moment, wondering at it.

I resumed my downward way, and stepping out upon the level of the railroad, and drawing nearer to him, saw that he was a dark sallow man, with a dark beard and rather heavy eyebrows. His post was in as solitary and dismal a place as ever I saw. On either side, a dripping-wet wall of jagged stone, excluding all view but a strip of sky; the perspective one way only a crooked prolongation of this great dungeon; the shorter perspective in the other direction terminating in a gloomy red light, and the gloomier entrance to a black tunnel, in whose massive architecture there was a barbarous,

Describe the place where the signalman works. How does it make the narrator feel?

1. **precipitate.** Steep

WORDS FOR EVERYDAY USE

i • dle (ī′ dəl) *adj.*, useless; having no value. *Marc never followed through on his idle curiosity.*

com • pul • sion (kəm pəl′ shən) *n.*, irresistible, irrational impulse. *Gaisha fought the compulsion to run every time she passed a cemetery.*

depressing, and forbidding air. So little sunlight ever found its way to this spot, that it had an earthy, deadly smell; and so much cold wind rushed through it, that it struck chill to me, as if I had left the natural world.

Before he stirred, I was near enough to him to have touched him. Not even then removing his eyes from mine, he stepped back one step, and lifted his hand.

This was a lonesome post to occupy (I said), and it had riveted my attention when I looked down from up yonder. A visitor was a rarity, I should suppose; not an unwelcome rarity, I hoped? In me, he merely saw a man who had been shut up within narrow limits all his life, and who, being at last set free, had a newly awakened interest in these great works. To such purpose I spoke to him; but I am far from sure of the terms I used; for, besides that I am not happy in opening any conversation, there was something in the man that daunted me.

What does the narrator notice the signalman doing?

He directed a most curious look towards the red light near the tunnel's mouth, and looked all about it, as if something were missing from it, and then looked at me.

That light was part of his charge? Was it not?

He answered in a low voice, "Don't you know it is?"

The monstrous thought came into my mind, as I perused the fixed eyes and the saturnine face, that this was a spirit, not a man. I have speculated since, whether there may have been infection in his mind.

What did the narrator later think about the man's face?

In my turn, I stepped back. But in making the action, I detected in his eyes some latent fear of me. This put the monstrous thought to flight.

"You look at me," I said, forcing a smile, "as if you had a dread of me."

"I was doubtful," he returned, "whether I had seen you before."

"Where?"

He pointed to the red light he had looked at.

"There?" I said.

Intently watchful of me, he replied (but without sound), "Yes."

"My good fellow, what should I do there? However, be that as it may, I never was there, you may swear."

"I think I may," he rejoined. "Yes, I am sure I may."

His manner cleared, like my own. He replied to my remarks with readiness, and in well-chosen words. Had he much to do there? Yes; that was to say, he had enough responsibility to bear; but exactness and watchfulness were what was required of him, and of actual work—manual labor—he had next to none. To change that signal, to trim those lights, and to turn this iron handle now and then, was all he had to do under that head. Regarding those many long and lonely hours of which I seemed to make so much, he could only say that the routine of his life had shaped itself into that form, and he had grown used to it. He had taught himself a language down here—if only to know it by sight, and to have formed his own crude ideas of its pronunciation, could be called learning it. He had also worked at fractions and decimals, and tried a little algebra; but he was, and had been as a boy, a poor hand at figures. Was it necessary for him when on duty always to remain in that channel of damp air, and could he never rise into the sunshine from between those high stone walls? Why, that depended upon times and circumstances. Under

What has the signalman done with his free time?

WORDS FOR EVERYDAY USE

daunt (dônt) *vt.*, make afraid or discouraged. *The rugged terrain daunted the faint-hearted hikers.*

pe • ruse (pə rüz′) *vt.*, examine carefully. *Edgar perused the map before choosing his route.*

ANSWERS TO GUIDED READING QUESTIONS

1. He sees the signalman giving a curious look towards the red light near the tunnel's mouth.
2. The narrator later thought the man was a spirit, and not a man. Later, he thought there might have been an infection in the man's mind.
3. The signalman has spent his time learning or educating himself.

LITERARY NOTE

Although dedicated to social reform, Dickens was not above satirizing fellow reformers. One of Dickens's most memorable character sketches is that of Mrs. Jellyby, a professional philanthropist. Perhaps what Dickens found objectionable in many philanthropists was their focus on foreign charity. This sentiment is evident in his characterization of Mrs. Jellyby who sacrifices her family's well-being for "Educating the natives of Borrioboola-Gha, on the left bank of the Niger" (*Bleak House,* chapter 4).

Quotables

"It was the best of times, it was the worst of times, it was the age of wisdom, it was the age of foolishness, it was the epoch of belief, it was the epoch of incredulity, it was the season of Light, it was the season of Darkness, it was the spring of hope, it was the winter of despair, we had everything before us, we had nothing before us, we were all going direct to Heaven, we were all going direct the other way."

—Charles Dickens

ANSWERS TO GUIDED READING QUESTIONS

1. The narrator observes the signalman to be remarkably exact and vigilant.
2. The narrator found it odd when the signalman looks at the bell when it does not ring and goes to the door and stares at the tunnel.

CROSS-CURRICULAR ACTIVITIES

Science. Students can research the telegraph and its importance to the railroad. When was the telegraph invented, by whom, and how did that person discover the technology? What procedures were replaced by the telegraph? If you have a railroad museum in your community, students may visit it to learn about and try using the telegraph, as well as seeing other train procedures demonstrated.

some conditions there would be less upon the Line than under others, and the same held good as to certain hours of the day and night. In bright weather, he did choose occasions for getting a little above these lower shadows; but, being at all times liable to be called by his electric bell, and at such times listening for it with redoubled anxiety, the relief was less than I would suppose.

He took me into his box, where there was a fire, a desk for an official book in which he had to make certain entries, a telegraphic instrument[2] with its dial, face, and needles, and the little bell of which he had spoken. On my trusting that he would excuse the remark that he had been well educated, and (I hoped I might say without offense) perhaps educated above that station, he observed that instances of slight incongruity in such wise would rarely be found wanting among large bodies of men; that he had heard it was so in workhouses, in the police force, even in that last desperate resource, the army; and that he knew it was so, more or less, in any great railway staff. He had been, when young (if I could believe it, sitting in that hut—he scarcely could), a student of natural philosophy, and had attended lectures; but he had run wild, misused his opportunities, gone down, and never risen again. He had no complaint to offer about that. He had made his bed, and he lay upon it. It was far too late to make another.

All that I have here condensed, he said in a quiet manner, with his grave dark regards divided between me and the fire. He threw in the word, "Sir," from time to time, and especially when he referred to his youth, as though to request me to understand that he claimed to be nothing but what I found him. He was several times interrupted by the little bell, and had to read off messages, and send replies. Once he had to stand without the door, and display a flag as a train passed, and make some verbal communication to the driver. In the discharge of his duties, I observed him to be remarkably exact and vigilant, breaking off his discourse at a syllable, and remaining silent until what he had to do was done.

What kind of worker does the narrator observe the signalman to be?

In a word, I should have set this man down as one of the safest of men to be employed in that capacity, but for the circumstance that while he was speaking to me he twice broke off with a fallen color, turned his face towards the little bell when it did NOT ring, opened the door of the hut (which was kept shut to exclude the unhealthy damp), and looked out towards the red light near the mouth of the tunnel. On both of those occasions, he came back to the fire with the inexplicable air upon him which I had remarked, without being able to define, when we were so far asunder.

What actions does the narrator find surprising?

Said I, when I rose to leave him, "You almost make me think that I have met with a contented man."

(I am afraid I must acknowledge that I said it to lead him on.)

"I believe I used to be so," he rejoined, in the low voice in which he had first spoken; "but I am troubled, sir, I am troubled."

He would have recalled the words if he could. He had said them, however, and I took them up quickly.

"With what? What is your trouble?"

2. **telegraphic instrument.** Equipment, now obsolete, for sending messages

Words for Everyday Use

re • dou • bled (rē də′ bəld) *adj.,* twice intensified. *The team redoubled its efforts in the second half and won the game.*

in • con • gru • i • ty (in kən grü′ ə tē) *n.,* lack of appropriateness or fitness. *I was struck by the incongruity of the band practicing in the library.*

vig • i • lant (vi′ jə lənt) *adj.,* warchful and alert. *Our vigilant dog barks when anyone approaches the house.*

in • ex • pli • ca • ble (i nik spli′ kə bəl) *adj.,* that cannot be explained or understood. *There was an inexplicable chill as we entered the room.*

a • sun • der (ə sən′ dər) *adv.,* apart or separate. *The torn pages were scattered asunder.*

"It is very difficult to impart, sir. It is very, very difficult to speak of. If ever you make me another visit, I will try to tell you."

"But I expressly intend to make you another visit. Say, when shall it be?"

"I go off early in the morning, and I shall be on again at ten tomorrow night, sir."

"I will come at eleven."

He thanked me, and went out at the door with me. "I'll show my white light, sir," he said, in his peculiar low voice, "till you have found the way up. When you have found it, don't call out! And when you are at the top, don't call out!"

His manner seemed to make the place strike colder to me, but I said no more than, "Very well."

"And when you come down tomorrow night, don't call out! Let me ask you a parting question. What made you cry, 'Halloa! Below there!' tonight?"

What request does the signalman make? How does it make the narrator feel?

"Heaven knows," said I. "I cried something to that effect—"

"Not to that effect, sir. Those were the very words. I know them well."

"Admit those were the very words, I said them, no doubt, because I saw you below."

"For no other reason?"

"What other reason could I possibly have?"

"You had no feeling that they were conveyed to you in any supernatural way?"

What questions does the signalman ask?

"No."

He wished me good night, and held up his light. I walked by the side of the down Line of rails (with a very disagreeable sensation of a train coming behind me) until I found the path. It was easier to mount than to descend, and I got back to my inn without any adventure.

Punctual to my appointment, I placed my foot on the first notch of the zigzag next night, as the distant clocks were striking eleven. He was waiting for me at the bottom, with his white light on. "I have not called out," I said, when we came close together; "may I speak now?" "By all means, sir." "Good night, then, and here's my hand." "Good night, sir, and here's mine." With that we walked side by side to his box, entered it, closed the door, and sat down by the fire.

"I have made up my mind, sir," he began, bending forward as soon as we were seated, and speaking in a tone but a little above a whisper, "that you shall not have to ask me twice what troubles me. I took you for someone else yesterday evening. That troubles me."

"That mistake?"

"No. That someone else."

"Who is it?"

"I don't know."

"Like me?"

What troubles the signalman?

"I don't know. I never saw the face. The left arm is across the face, and the right arm is waved—violently waved. This way."

I followed his action with my eyes, and it was the action of an arm gesticulating, with the utmost passion and vehemence, "For God's sake, clear the way!"

"One moonlight night," said the man, "I was sitting here, when I heard a voice cry, 'Halloa! Below there!' I started up, looked from that door, and saw this Someone else standing by the red light near the tunnel, waving as I just now showed you. The voice seemed hoarse with shouting, and it cried, 'Look out! Look out!' and then again, 'Halloa! Below there! Look out!' I caught up my lamp, turned it on red, and ran towards the figure, calling, 'What's wrong? What has happened? Where?' It stood

WORDS FOR EVERYDAY USE

ve • he • mence (vē' ə mənts) *n.*, great force and strong feeling. *Refusing to give in, Toby protested with vehemence.*

ANSWERS TO GUIDED READING QUESTIONS

1. The signalman asks the narrator not to call out. It makes the narrator feel that the place has become colder.
2. The signalman asks why the narrator called out as he did and why he chose those specific words.
3. The signalman is troubled by a figure holding a hand in front of its face and waving its other arm as if to say, "For God's sake, clear the way!"

LITERARY NOTE 

Point out to students that the title, "The Signalman," has a double meaning when one considers that the man not only gives and receives signals to passing trains, but actually receives signals from some supernatural source.

ANSWERS TO GUIDED READING QUESTIONS

1. The narrator feels a cold finger trace his spine. He then tries to give explanations for all the things the signalman has told him of.
2. The accident that happened after the first sighting made the story even more telling.
3. The narrator does not think much of coincidences.

LITERARY NOTE 

One of Dickens's best-known works, *A Christmas Carol,* also features ghosts. The subject matter of Dickens's *A Christmas Carol,* one of the most famed yuletide tales, was not so much a unique creation but part of a Victorian tradition. Like many novelists, Dickens produced a number of Christmas stories that were sold in special editions before the holiday. Many of Dickens's Christmas stories are collected in *The Christmas Books*. For the most part, these works reach the height of Victorian sentimentality and lack the richness of Dickens's other works. They are, however, interesting documents of how Christmas was rapidly changing in Victorian England from a religious and spiritual holiday to a commercial and sentimental one. In *The Christmas Books* religious overtones are scarce, but gifts, turkeys, and money (and the equation of moral worth with consumerism) abound.

just outside the blackness of the tunnel. I advanced so close upon it that I wondered at its keeping the sleeve across its eyes. I ran right up at it, and had my hand stretched out to pull the sleeve away, when it was gone."

"Into the tunnel," said I.

"No. I ran on into the tunnel, five hundred yards. I stopped, and held my lamp above my head, and saw the figures of the measured distance, and saw the wet stains stealing down the walls and trickling through the arch. I ran out again faster than I had run in (for I had a mortal abhorrence[3] of the place upon me), and I looked all round the red light with my own red light, and I went up the iron ladder to the gallery top of it, and I came down again, and ran back here. I telegraphed both ways, 'An alarm has been given. Is anything wrong?' The answer came back, both ways, 'All well.' "

How does the narrator react to the signalman's story?

Resisting the slow touch of a frozen finger tracing out my spine, I showed him how that this figure must be a deception of his sense of sight; and how that figures, originating in disease of the delicate nerves that minister to the functions of the eye, were known to have often troubled patients, some of whom had become conscious of the nature of their affliction, and had even proved it my experiments upon themselves. "As to an imaginary cry," said I, "do but listen for a moment to the wind in this unnatural valley while we speak so low, and to the wild harp it makes of the telegraph wires!"

That was all very well, he returned, after we had sat listening for a while, and he ought to know something of the wind and the wires—he who so often passed long winter nights there, alone and watching. But he would beg to remark that he had not finished.

I asked his pardon, and he slowly added these words, touching my arm:

"Within six hours after the Appearance, the memorable accident on this Line happened, and within ten hours the dead and wounded were brought along through the tunnel over the spot where the figure had stood."

What event made the signalman's story even more chilling?

A disagreeable shudder crept over me, but I did my best against it. It was not to be denied, I rejoined, that this was a remarkable coincidence, calculated deeply to impress his mind. But it was unquestionable that remarkable coincidences did continually occur, and they must be taken into account in dealing with such a subject. Though to be sure I must admit, I added (for I thought I saw that he was going to bring the objection to bear upon me), men of common sense did not allow much for coincidences in making the ordinary calculations of life.

What does the narrator think of coincidences?

He again begged to remark that he had not finished.

I again begged his pardon for being betrayed into interruptions.

"This," he said, again laying his hand upon my arm, and glancing over his shoulder with hollow eyes, "was just a year ago. Six or seven months passed, and I had recovered from the surprise and shock, when one morning, as the day was breaking, I, standing at the door, looked towards the red light, and saw the specter[4] again." He stopped, with a fixed look at me.

"Did it cry out?"

"No. It was silent."

3. **mortal abhorrence.** Fear and loathing
4. **specter.** Spirit or ghost

WORDS FOR EVERYDAY USE

re join (ri jôin') *vi.,* answer. *"Count me out," I rejoined.*

Metropolitan Railway, 1860.

"Did it wave its arm?"

"No. It leaned against the shaft of the light, with both hands before the face. Like this."

Once more I followed his action with my eyes. It was an action of mourning. I have seen such an attitude in stone figures on tombs.

"Did you go up to it?"

"I came in and sat down, partly to collect my thoughts, partly because it had turned me faint. When I went to the door again, daylight was above me, and the ghost was gone."

"But nothing followed? Nothing came of this?"

He touched me on the arm with his forefinger twice or thrice, giving a ghastly nod each time:

"That very day, as a train came out of the tunnel, I noticed, at a carriage window on my side, what looked like a confusion of hands and heads, and something waved. I saw it just in time to signal the driver. Stop! He shut off, and put his brake on, but the train drifted past here a hundred and fifty yards or more. I ran after it, and, as I went along, heard terrible screams and cries. A beautiful young lady had died instantaneously in one of the compartments, and was brought in here, and laid on this floor between us."

What happens after the signalman sees the mysterious figure again?

Involuntarily I pushed my chair back, as I looked from the boards at which he pointed to himself.

"True, sir. True. Precisely as it happened, so I tell it you."

I could think of nothing to say, to any purpose, and my mouth was very dry. The wind and the wires took up the story with a long lamenting wail.

He resumed. "Now, sir, mark this, and judge how my mind is troubled. The

Why is the signalman troubled?

ANSWERS TO GUIDED READING QUESTIONS

1. He flags the train to stop and finds that a woman has died suddenly on the train.
2. He is troubled because the specter is back.

ANSWERS TO GUIDED READING QUESTIONS

1. The narrator thinks the story cannot be true because he himself did not hear the bell the several times he noticed the signalman looking at it.
2. The signalman is troubled because he does not know what the specter means.

specter came back a week ago. Ever since, it has been there, now and again, by fits and starts."

"At the light?"

"At the Danger light."

"What does it seem to do?"

He repeated, if possible with increased passion and vehemence, that former gesticulation of, "For God's sake, clear the way!'

Then he went on. "I have no peace or rest for it. It calls to me, for many minutes together, in an agonized manner, 'Below there! Look out! Look out!' It stands waving to me. It rings my little bell—"

I caught at that. "Did it ring your bell yesterday evening when I was here, and you went to the door?"

"Twice."

"Why, see," said I, "how your imagination misleads you. My eyes were on the bell, and my ears were open to the bell, and if I am a living man, it did NOT ring at those times. No, nor at any other time, except when it was rung in the natural course of physical things by the station communicating with you."

What makes the narrator think the story cannot be true?

He shook his head. "I have never made a mistake as to that yet, sir. I have never confused the specter's ring with the man's. The ghost's ring is a strange vibration in the bell that it <u>derives</u> from nothing else, and I have not asserted that the bell stirs to the eye. I don't wonder that you failed to hear it. But I heard it."

"And did the specter seem to be there, when you looked out?"

"It WAS there."

"Both times?"

He repeated firmly: "Both times."

"Will you come to the door with me, and look for it now?"

He bit his under lip as though he were somewhat unwilling, but arose. I opened the door, and stood on the step, while he stood in the doorway. There was the Danger light. There was the dismal mouth of the tunnel. There were the high, wet stone walls of the cutting. There were the stars above them.

"Do you see it?" I asked him, taking particular note of his face. His eyes were <u>prominent</u> and strained, but not very much more so, perhaps, than my own had been when I had directed them earnestly towards the same spot.

THERE IS DANGER OVERHANGING SOMEWHERE ON THE LINE.

"No," he answered. "It is not there."

"Agreed," said I.

We went in again, shut the door, and resumed our seats. I was thinking how best to improve this advantage, if it might be called one, when he took up the conversation in such a matter-of-course way, so assuming that there could be no serious question of fact between us, that I felt myself placed in the weakest of positions.

"By this time you will fully understand, sir," he said, "that what troubles me so dreadfully is the question, What does the specter mean?"

I was not sure, I told him, that I did fully understand.

What question troubles the signalman?

"What is its warning against?" he said, <u>ruminating</u>, with his eyes on the fire, and only by times turning them on me. "What is the danger? Where is the danger? There is danger overhanging somewhere on the Line. Some dreadful <u>calamity</u> will

WORDS FOR EVERYDAY USE

de • rive (di rīv′) *vi.*, come from. *The rustling <u>derives</u> from the wind in the trees.*

prom • i • nent (prä′ mə nənt) *adj.*, noticeable; obvious. *Lucia's red hair is her most <u>prominent</u> feature.*

ru • mi • nat • ing (rü′ mə nāt iŋ) *part.*, turn something over in the mind. *I waited patiently while Lars continued <u>ruminating</u> about his old pal.*

ca • la • mi • ty (kə la′ mə tē) *n.*, disaster. *Rushville was hit by one <u>calamity</u> after another—flood, mudslides, and wild fire.*

happen. It is not to be doubted this third time, after what has gone before. But surely this is a cruel haunting of me. What can I do?"

He pulled out his handkerchief, and wiped the drops from his heated forehead.

"If I telegraph Danger, on either side of me, or on both, I can give no reason for it," he went on, wiping the palms of his hands. "I should get into trouble, and do no good. They would think I was mad. This is the way it would work: Message: "Danger! Take care!" Answer: "What Danger? Where?" Message: "Don't know. But for God's sake, take care!" They would displace me. What else could they do?"

His pain of mind was most pitiable to see. It was the mental torture of a conscientious man, oppressed beyond endurance by an unintelligible responsibility involving life.

What tortures the signalman?

"When it first stood under the Danger light," he went on, putting his dark hair back from his head, and drawing his hands outward across and across his temples in an extremity of feverish distress, "why not tell me where that accident was to happen—if it must happen? Why not tell me how it could be averted—if it could have been averted? When on its second coming it hid its face, why not tell me, instead, "She is going to die. Let them keep her at home"? If it came, on those two occasions, only to show me that its warnings were true, and so to prepare me for the third, why not warn me plainly now? And I, Lord help me! A mere poor signalman on this solitary station! Why not go to somebody with credit to be believed, and power to act?"

When I saw him in this state, I saw that for the poor man's sake, as well as for the public safety, what I had to do for the time was to compose his mind. Therefore, setting aside all question of reality or unreality between us, I represented to him that whoever thoroughly discharged his duty must do well, and that at least it was his comfort that he understood his duty, though he did not understand these confounding Appearances. In this effort I succeeded far better than in the attempt to reason him out of his conviction. He became calm; the occupations incidental to his post as the night advanced began to make larger demands on his attention: and I left him at two in the morning. I had offered to stay through the night, but he would not hear of it.

What course of action does the narrator decide upon?

That I more than once looked back at the red light as I ascended the pathway, that I did not like the red light, and that I should have slept but poorly if my bed had been under it, I see no reason to conceal. Nor did I like the two sequences of the accident and the dead girl. I see no reason to conceal that either.

But what ran most in my thoughts was the consideration how ought I to act, having become the recipient of this disclosure? I had proved the man to be intelligent, vigilant, painstaking, and exact; but how long might he remain so, in his state of mind? Though in a subordinate position, still he held a most important trust, and would I (for instance) like to stake my own life on the chances of his continuing to execute it with precision?

Unable to overcome a feeling that there would be something treacherous in my communicating what he had told me to his superiors in the Company, without first being plain with himself and proposing a middle course to him, I ultimately resolved to offer to accompany him (otherwise keeping his secret for the present) to the wisest medical practitioner we could hear of in those parts, and to take his opinion. A change in his time of duty would come round next night, he had apprised me, and he would

WORDS FOR EVERYDAY USE

a • vert (ə vərt') *vt.*, avoid, keep from happening. *The pilot handled the tricky landing and averted disaster.*
com • pose (kəm pōz) *vt.*, calm; put in order. *Deshawn took a deep breath to compose himself before his speech.*
treach • er • ous (tre' chə rəs) *adj.*, untrustworthy, with a false sense of safety. *Many ships are stranded on the treacherous rocky shore.*
ap • prise (ə prīz') *vt.*, inform; notify. *Ms. DeLucca apprised us of the deadline for the poetry contest.*

ANSWERS TO GUIDED READING QUESTIONS

1. He is a conscientious man, and is tortured by the feeling that he will be responsible for deaths if he cannot prevent some mysterious future tragedy.
2. The narrator decides that for the time being, he will try to calm the man down and compose his mind. Later, he will convince the man to go with him to see a doctor.

SELECTION CHECK TEST 4.9.35 WITH ANSWERS

Checking Your Reading

1. How does the signalman react when the narrator first calls out to him? **The signalman first looks down the tracks, instead of up to where the voice is calling from.**
2. Describe the signalman's workplace and his job responsibilities. **The signalman works in a trench down near the tracks. There are high rocky walls on either side of him, and it is cold, damp, and gloomy there. He is responsible for relaying messages to and from the trains that pass.**
3. What is troubling the signalman? **He has been troubled by a ghost who twice warned him of tragedies that were about to occur.**
4. What does the narrator think about the signalman's story? **He doesn't believe him and worries that the man might be insane.**
5. What happens to the signalman at the end of the story? **What makes this event particularly eerie or coincidental? The signalman is hit and killed by a train. This event is particularly eerie or coincidental because the man had been tormented by a ghost who shouted, "For God's sake, clear the way!" and waved his arm, while holding the left arm over his face. These were the exact words and actions of the train engineer at the moment the train hit the signalman.**

Continued on page 860

ANSWERS TO GUIDED READING QUESTIONS

1. The narrator sees a man with a hand over his face and his other arm waving in warning, just like the actions of the specter that the signalman had shown him.
2. Tom called out, "Below there! Look out! Look out! For God's sake, clear the way!"

SELECTION CHECK TEST 4.9.35 WITH ANSWERS

(CONT. FROM PAGE 859)

Vocabulary in Context
Fill in each blank below with the most appropriate word from the following Words for Everyday Use from "The Signalman." You may have to change the tense of certain verbs.

peruse daunt vigilant
avert vehemence rejoin
asunder prominent

1. I **perused** the anonymous note, hoping to find clues as to who had sent it.
2. The watchdog being less than **vigilant**, the thieves were able to break into the house.
3. Emily prepared for the debate carefully, but was **daunted** by the sight of the full auditorium.
4. "This problem could have been **averted** if you had asked for proper instructions," Dad scolded me.
5. "That's a great idea!" Mark **rejoined** when he heard my suggestion.

Literary Tools
Select the letter of the best answer for each question below.

1. What is another name for a ghost story? **Another name is "story of the supernatural."**
2. What cannot be explained in a logical or rational way? **Supernatural elements cannot be explained in a logical or rational way.**
3. What is the setting of a literary work? **The setting is the time and place in which the story occurs, along with all the details used to create a sense of a particular time and place.**
4. How might you describe the mood of "The Signalman"? **Students may say the mood is eerie.**
5. What are some elements that contribute to this mood? **Details such as the black tunnel, the high, jagged rock walls, the icy chill that makes the narrator think the place is outside of the earthly world, all contribute to this mood.**

be off an hour or two after sunrise, and on again soon after sunset, I had appointed to return accordingly.

Next evening was a lovely evening, and I walked out early to enjoy it. The sun was not yet quite down when I traversed the fieldpath near the top of the deep cutting. I would extend my walk for an hour, I said to myself, half an hour on and half an hour back, and it would then be time to go to my signalman's box.

Before pursuing my stroll, I stepped to the brink, and mechanically looked down, from the point from which I had first seen him. I cannot describe the thrill that seized upon me, when, close at the mouth of the tunnel, I saw the appearance of a man, with his left sleeve across his eyes, passionately waving his right arm.

The nameless horror that oppressed me passed in a moment, for in a moment I saw that this appearance of a man was a man indeed, and that there was a little group of other men, standing at a short distance, to whom he seemed to be rehearsing the gesture he made. The Danger light was not yet lighted. Against its shaft, a little low hut, entirely new to me, had been made of some wooden supports and tarpaulin. It looked no bigger than a bed.

What does the narrator see by the tunnel?

With an irresistible sense that something was wrong—with a flashing self-reproachful fear that fatal mischief had come of my leaving the man there, and causing no one to be sent to overlook or correct what he did—I descended the notched path with all the speed I could make.

"What is the matter?" I asked the men.

"Signalman killed this morning, sir."

"Not the man belonging to that box?"

"Yes, sir."

"Not the man I know?"

"You will recognize him, sir, if you knew him," said the man who spoke for the others, solemnly uncovering his own head, and raising an end of the tarpaulin, "for his face is quite composed."

How did the narrator react when he saw the signalman on the path?

"O, how did this happen, how did this happen?" I asked, turning from one to another as the hut closed in again.

"He was cut down by an engine, sir. No man in England knew his work better. But somehow he was not clear of the outer rail. It was just at broad day. He had struck the light, and had the lamp in his hand. As the engine came out of the tunnel, his back was toward her, and she cut him down. That man drove her, and was showing how it happened. Show the gentleman, Tom."

The man, who wore a rough dark dress, stepped back to his former place at the mouth of the tunnel.

"Coming round the curve in the tunnel, sir," he said, "I saw him at the end, like as if I saw him down a perspective-glass. There was no time to check speed, and I knew him to be very careful. As he didn't seem to take heed of the whistle, I shut it off when we were running down upon him, and called to him as loud as I could call."

"What did you say?"

"I said, 'Below there! Look out! Look out! For God's sake, clear the way!' "

I started.

"Ah! it was a dreadful time, sir. I never left off calling to him. I put this arm before my eyes not to see, and I waved this arm to the last; but it was no use."

Without prolonging the narrative to dwell on any time to dwell on any one of its curious circumstances more than on any other, I may, in closing it, point out the coincidence that the warning of the Engine Driver included, not only the words which the unfortunate Signalman had repeated to me as haunting him, but also the words which I myself—not he—had attached and that only in my own mind, to the gesticulation he had imitated.

Respond to the SELECTION

Do you find the ending to this story satisfying? Why, or why not?

INVESTIGATE

Inquire, Imagine

Recall: GATHERING FACTS → **Interpret:** FINDING MEANING

1a. What does the narrator shout when he first sees the signalman? What is the signalman's reaction?

1b. Why is the signalman's action surprising?

2a. What observations does the narrator make about the signalman's abilities the first night he visits?

2b. Why are these details important?

3a. What sight and sound troubles the signalman?

3b. Does the ending explain what the signalman heard and saw? Explain.

Analyze: TAKING THINGS APART → **Synthesize:** BRINGING THINGS TOGETHER

4a. Analyze the narrator's connection to the signalman's experience.

4b. Could this tragedy have been averted? Explain.

Evaluate: MAKING JUDGMENTS → **Extend:** CONNECTING IDEAS

5a. Judge whether the narrator believes the signalman. Use examples from his reactions to the signalman throughout the story to support your response.

5b. Why does the narrator want to find a rational explanation for the story?

Understanding Literature

GHOST STORY. Review the definition for **ghost story** in Literary Tools in Prereading. Identify supernatural elements in this story. What effect do these elements have on the signalman psychologically? Does the end of the story explain the supernatural elements?

SETTING AND MOOD. Review the definitions for **setting** and **mood** in the Handbook of Literary Terms and the cluster chart you made for Literary Tools on page 850. Where is this story set? How does the narrator describe this place when he first visits? What aspects of this setting create an appropriate mood for a ghost story?

RESPOND TO THE SELECTION

If students do not find the ending satisfying, they should explain how they would rewrite the ending.

ANSWERS TO INVESTIGATE, INQUIRE, IMAGINE

RECALL

1a. The narrator shouts, "Halloa! Below there!" The signalman looks down the line instead of up at the narrator.

2a. The narrator notices that the signalman is very exact and vigilant in attending to his duties.

3a. The signalman hears a certain bell that he knows is being rung by a specter. The specter he sees holds one arm in front of its face and waves the other arm in warning.

INTERPRET

1b. The signalman should be able to tell where the voice is coming from. It is surprising that he looks someplace else.

2b. These details suggest that the signal man is clear-headed, thinks things through, and is generally steady and dependable.

3b. *Responses will vary.* What the signalman saw and heard seemed to be a premonition of what was to happen to him. Why he saw these things is not explained.

ANALYZE

4a. The narrator is the only one who knows about what the signalman heard and saw. If he had not learned of these visions, nobody would understand the significance of how the signalman had died and the uncanny coincidence would not be exposed.

SYNTHESIZE

4b. *Responses will vary.* If the narrator had been with the signalman, perhaps he would have kept him off the tracks. Perhaps the narrator could have gotten help for the signalman if it were a psychological problem.

EVALUATE

5a. *Responses will vary.* The narrator seems to discount the signalman's story. He tries repeatedly to explain in a rational way the odd happenings the signalman describes. He is touched by a bit of fear, as shown by the cold chill that goes down his spine. He does think some of the coincidences are

ANSWERS TO INVESTIGATE, INQUIRE, IMAGINE (CONT.)

disturbing, but he doesn't pay much attention to them. He finds the signalman's work area disconcerting, however, and thinks there is an otherworldly mood to it.

EXTEND

5b. The narrator is disturbed by the coincidences. He finds this last one the most difficult to explain. He is disturbed because he knew the man and perhaps could have helped save him.

Answers to Understanding Literature can be found on page 862.

ANSWERS TO UNDERSTANDING LITERATURE

Ghost Story. The specter and the the unnatural ringing of the bell are supernatual elements. The fact that the appearance of the specter may actually have been a premonition is also a supernatural element. These elements disturb the signalman. He is worried by what he perceives as a responsibility to save human lives. The supernatural elements are not explained at the end of the story. The reader is left to wonder whether the signalman was psychologically disturbed and that the manner of his death was a horrible coincidence, or whether the supernatural did play a role.

Setting and Mood. The story is set in the signalman's work area, in a trench surrounded by tall, jagged stone walls and a train tunnel. It is dark, cold, and damp and has "an earthy, deadly smell" and an otherworldly feel. All of these elements contribute to the mood of a ghost story.

ANSWERS TO INTEGRATING THE LANGUAGE ARTS

Language, Grammar, and Style

1. Dickens faced a hard childhood, and he struggled to rise above his family's poverty.
2. As Pip walked through Miss Havisham's ruined estate, he noticed how it had changed since the days of his youth.
3. At middle age, Dickens had acquired a wide following of readers of his novels, which were circulated in magazines and periodicals of the time.
4. Victorian-era London was populated with the rich and the destitute, both of whom filled the city's narrow, dirty streets.
5. Estella saw Pip through the evening mist, and she called out his name.

Writer's Journal

1. Write an **obituary** for the signalman. Use information from the story to help you illuminate this character.
2. Write a one-paragraph **review** of this story. Describe your reaction to the story and why you think others would or would not like it.
3. Write your own **ghost story**. You might begin by choosing a setting and writing a description that creates an eerie mood.

Integrating *the* Language Arts

Language, Grammar, and Style

Combining Sentences. Read the Language Arts Survey 2.53, "Combining Sentences Using Clauses." Then combine each pair of sentences below into a single sentence by changing one of the pair into a clause.

1. Dickens faced a hard childhood. He struggled to rise above his family's poverty.
2. Pip walked through Miss Havisham's ruined estate. He noticed how it had changed since the days of his youth.
3. At middle age, Dickens had acquired a wide following of readers of his novels. His novels were circulated in magazines and periodicals of the time.
4. Victorian-era London was populated with the rich and the destitute. Both the rich and the destitute filled the city's narrow, dirty streets.
5. Estella saw Pip through the evening mist. She called out his name.

Speaking and Listening

Telling Ghost Stories. Ghost stories are perhaps most effective when they are told orally. This is because the teller can add drama by the use of tone, pacing, and different voices. Think about a ghost story you have heard or an original one you have written. Practice telling this story. Then tell it to your classmates. Refer to the Language Arts 4.20, "Telling a Story" for advice on using elements of verbal communication to make your telling more effective.

Study and Research

Research Skills. Using your library, find the following:

- Two other short stories by Charles Dickens
- An analysis of one or more of Dickens' works
- A collection of ghost stories
- A biography of Dickens
- A book about psychological disorders.

You may want to refer to the Language Arts Survey 5.19, "How to Locate Library Materials" for assistance in your research.

FROM *Through the Looking Glass*

BY LEWIS CARROLL

About *the* AUTHOR

Lewis Carroll was the pen name of Charles Lutwidge Dodgson (1832–1898), the son of an Anglican minister. Like his father, Carroll went to Oxford and was ordained as an Anglican priest. He remained at Christ Church, Oxford, as a mathematics tutor, and he also became a skilled photographer. He is best known today, however, as an author of children's books. His popularity as a children's writer is based on his inventive tales *Alice's Adventures in Wonderland* (1865) and *Through the Looking Glass and What Alice Found There* (1871).

The first book, *Alice's Adventures in Wonderland*, grew out of tales that Carroll told to a group of children on a boat trip up the Thames River. Alice Liddell, the young daughter of the dean of Carroll's school, pleaded with Carroll to write a story featuring her as the heroine. She wanted him to call these tales "Alice's adventures." He soon created a hand-printed storybook called *Alice's Adventures Underground.* Carroll became convinced the story was publishable, and *Alice's Adventures* soon became one of the most popular works of children's literature in the world. After its publication, Carroll wrote several more books for children as well as some books on mathematics.

About *the* SELECTION

Through the Looking Glass, the sequel to *Alice in Wonderland*, was written in 1871. It continues the adventures of Alice through the make-believe world that Carroll had created, populated with live chessmen, talking insects, and the famous character of Humpty Dumpty (who Alice meets in this selection). This story, like the first *Alice* book, displays Carroll's creative genius and love of puzzles and riddles. Some of the songs and poems are parodies of society, while some are comical bits of nonsense verse. The tales are amazingly intricate and complex, but they are also celebrations of the world of fantasy from which adults, unlike children, are too often separated.

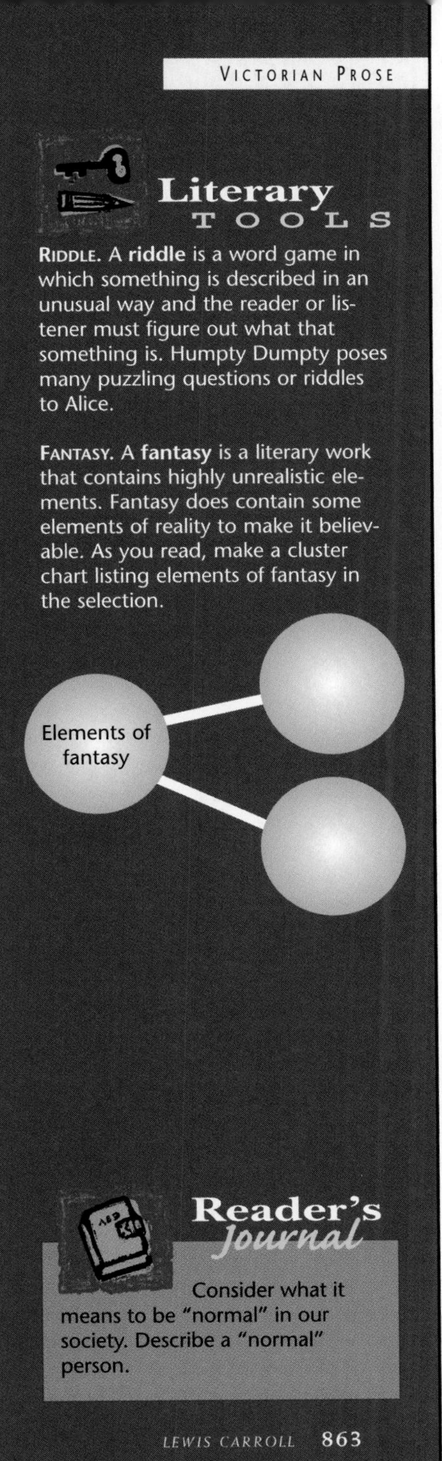

Literary TOOLS
RIDDLE. A **riddle** is a word game in which something is described in an unusual way and the reader or listener must figure out what that something is. Humpty Dumpty poses many puzzling questions or riddles to Alice.
FANTASY. A **fantasy** is a literary work that contains highly unrealistic elements. Fantasy does contain some elements of reality to make it believable. As you read, make a cluster chart listing elements of fantasy in the selection.
Elements of fantasy
Reader's Journal
Consider what it means to be "normal" in our society. Describe a "normal" person.

ADDITIONAL RESOURCES

UNIT 9 RESOURCE BOOK
- Selection Worksheet 9.18
- Selection Check Test 4.9.37
- Selection Test 4.9.38
- Reading Resource 1.21
- Speaking and Listening Resource 4.7–4.10

GRAPHIC ORGANIZER

Students may include the following in their cluster charts: Humpty Dumpty is a character from children's verse but doesn't know it; Humpty Dumpty is a giant talking egg; the White King and Queen are not real; words have tempers, especially verbs; Humpty Dumpty pays words to do what he asks; toves, borogoves, and raths are fantasy animals; the fishes in Humpty Dumpty's song can talk and sleep in a bed.

VOCABULARY FROM THE SELECTION

contemptuously

READER'S JOURNAL

What are the challenges inherent in being perceived as unconventional? Students should consider this question as they read the selection.

GOALS/OBJECTIVES

Studying this lesson will enable students to
- enjoy a work of fantasy filled with wordplay
- describe Lewis Carroll's literary accomplishments and explain the historical significance of his writings
- define *riddle* and *fantasy* and identify and analyze examples of each that they encounter in their reading
- use the *Oxford English Dictionary* to research word histories
- critique conversation techniques
- analyze a children's show

INDIVIDUAL LEARNING STRATEGIES

MOTIVATION
Ask students to read the Language Arts Survey 5.4, "Classifying." Then, have them devise a system for classifying the items with strange names that Humpty Dumpty describes to Alice. They should avoid obvious categories like "animals," and use their imaginations to create categories of their own. Some of the words that Humpty Dumpty explains are combinations of conventional words; others are descriptive of what they stand for. Have students think of real-life examples of these kinds of combination and onomatopoeic words.

READING PROFICIENCY
Stress that much of this selection contains words used to stand for ideas completely different from their customary associations. Also explain to them that Carroll's spelling of the word can't (he spells it "ca'n't") is unconventional today.

ENGLISH LANGUAGE LEARNING
Explain to students that Humpty Dumpty is a character from children's verse. Share with students the following additional vocabulary:
provoking—annoying
queer—odd
indignantly—with anger at injustice or ingratitude
impenetrable—not solvable; not comprehensible
gimlet—small tool for boring
ingenuity—clever inventiveness
hastily—in a hurry
civil—friendly and polite

SPECIAL NEEDS
Have students work in pairs to answer the Guided Reading and Recall questions.

ENRICHMENT
One of the contributions Lewis Carroll made to the English language is the word *chortle,* a combination of *snort* and *chuckle.* Students should try to discover a number of words in the English language that are combination, or portmanteau, words. Then in a game-show format, one group can challenge another group to figure out the two words from which their portmanteau originally came.

FROM THROUGH the Looking Glass

LEWIS CARROLL

Humpty Dumpty. From Lewis Carroll's *Through the Looking Glass.*

Humpty Dumpty

HOWEVER, the egg only got larger and larger, and more and more human: when she had come within a few yards of it, she saw that it had eyes and a nose and mouth; and, when she had come close to it, she saw clearly that it was HUMPTY DUMPTY himself. "It ca'n't be anybody else!" she said to herself. "I'm as certain of it, as if his name were written all over his face!"

It might have been written a hundred times, easily, on that enormous face. Humpty Dumpty was sitting, with his legs crossed like a Turk, on the top of a high wall—such a narrow one that Alice quite wondered how he could keep his balance—and, as his eyes were steadily fixed in the opposite direction, and he didn't take the least notice of her, she thought he must be a stuffed figure, after all.

"And how exactly like an egg he is !" she said aloud, standing with her hands ready to catch him, for she was every moment expecting him to fall.

What does Alice say aloud? How does the egg respond?

"It's *very* provoking," Humpty Dumpty said after a long silence, looking away from Alice as he spoke, "to be called an egg—*very*!"

"I said you *looked* like an egg, Sir," Alice gently explained. "And some eggs are very pretty, you know," she added, hoping to turn her remark into a sort of compliment.

"Some people," said Humpty Dumpty, looking away from her as usual, "have no more sense than a baby!"

What was strange about Alice's conversation with Humpty Dumpty?

Alice didn't know what to say to this: it wasn't at all like conversation, she thought, as he never said anything to *her*: in fact, his last remark was evidently addressed to a tree—so she stood and softly repeated to herself:—

Humpty Dumpty sat on a wall:
Humpty Dumpty had a great fall.
All the King's horses and all the King's men
Couldn't put Humpty Dumpty in his place again.

"That last line is much too long for the poetry," she added, almost out loud, forgetting that Humpty Dumpty would hear her.

"Don't stand chattering to yourself like that," Humpty Dumpty said, looking at her for the first time, "but tell me your name and your business."

"My name is Alice, but—"

"It's a stupid name enough!" Humpty Dumpty interrupted impatiently. "What does it mean?"

"*Must* a name mean something?" Alice asked doubtfully.

"Of course it must," Humpty Dumpty said with a short laugh: *my* name means the shape I am—and a good handsome shape it is, too. With a name like yours, you might be any shape, almost."

"Why do you sit out here all alone?" said Alice, not wishing to begin an argument.

"Why, because there's nobody with me!" cried Humpty Dumpty. Did you think I didn't know the answer to *that*? Ask another."

"Don't you think you'd be safer down on the ground?" Alice went on, not with any idea of making another riddle, but simply in her good-natured anxiety for the queer creature. "That wall is so *very* narrow!"

What is Humpty Dumpty's attitude toward Alice? How does he speak to her?

"What tremendously easy riddles you ask!" Humpty Dumpty growled out. "Of course I don't think so! Why, if ever I *did* fall off—which there's no chance of—but *if* I did—" Here he pursed up his lips, and looked so solemn and grand that Alice could hardly help laughing. "*If* I *did* fall," he went on, "*the King has promised me*—ah, you may turn pale, if you like! You didn't think I was going to say that, did you? *The King has promised me—with his very own mouth*—to—to—"

How does Alice respond when Humpty Dumpty tells her about what they king has promised? How does he respond to her?

"To send all his horses and all his men," Alice interrupted, rather unwisely.

"Now I declare that's too bad!" Humpty Dumpty cried, breaking into a sudden passion. "You've been listening at doors—and behind trees—and down chimneys—or you couldn't have known it!"

"I haven't, indeed!" Alice said very gently. "It's in a book."

"Ah, well! They may write such things in a *book*," Humpty Dumpty said in a calmer tone. "That's what you call a History of England, that is. Now, take a good look at me! I'm one that has

ANSWERS TO GUIDED READING QUESTIONS

1. Alice says, "And how exactly like an egg he is!" Humpty responds, "It's very provoking to be called an egg."
2. Humpty never said anything to her; his remarks seem to be addressed to trees.
3. Alice finishes Humpty's sentence for him by saying, "To send all his horses and all his men." Humpty accuses Alice of eavesdropping.
4. Humpty is rude to Alice and insults her. He speaks very condescendingly to her.

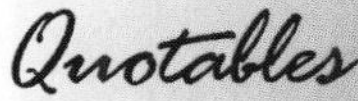

"'What is the use of a book,' thought Alice, 'without pictures or conversations?'"

—Lewis Carroll

ANSWERS TO GUIDED READING QUESTIONS

1. The question Humpty asked was, "How old did you say you were?" even though the subject had not yet come up. Alice interpreted his question as a request to know how old she was rather than as a request to repeat herself.
2. Humpty received his cravat from the White King and Queen for his un-birthday.

LITERARY TECHNIQUE

Satire. A **satire** is humorous writing or speech intended to point out errors, falsehoods, foibles, or failings. Carroll included both satiric and absurd elements in his writing. Students should identify what in this selection is satiric and what is being satirized.

ADDITIONAL QUESTIONS AND ACTIVITIES

Ask students if Carroll has succeeded in believably writing from the point of view of a child. To what extent is Humpty's behavior characteristic of some adults' behavior to very young children?

spoken to a King, *I* am: mayhap you'll never see such another: and, to show you I'm not proud, you may shake hands with me!" And he grinned almost from ear to ear, as he leant forwards (and as nearly as possible fell off the wall in doing so) and offered Alice his hand. She watched him a little anxiously as she took it. "If he smiled much more the ends of his mouth might meet behind," she thought: "And then I don't know *what* would happen to his head! I'm afraid it would come off!"

"Yes, all his horses and all his men," Humpty Dumpty went on. "They'd pick me up again in a minute, *they* would! However, this conversation is going on a little too fast: let's go back to the last remark but one."

"I'm afraid I ca'n't quite remember it," Alice said, very politely.

"In that case we start afresh," said Humpty Dumpty, "and it's my turn to choose a subject—" ("He talks about it just as if it was a game!" thought Alice.) "So here's a question for you. How old did you say you were?"

Alice made a short calculation, and said "Seven years and six months."

"Wrong!" Humpty Dumpty exclaimed triumphantly. "You never said a word like it!"

How does Humpty Dumpty turn a simple question about Alice's age into a trick question?

"I thought you meant 'How old *are* you?' " Alice explained.

"If I'd meant that, I'd have said it," said Humpty Dumpty.

Alice didn't want to begin another argument, so she said nothing.

"Seven years and six months!" Humpty Dumpty repeated thoughtfully. "An uncomfortable sort of age. Now if you'd asked *my* advice, I'd have said 'Leave off at seven'—but it's too late now."

"I never ask advice about growing," Alice said indignantly.

"Too proud?" the other enquired.

Alice felt even more indignant at this suggestion. "I mean," she said, "that one ca'n't help growing older."

"*One* ca'n't, perhaps," said Humpty Dumpty; "but *two* can. With proper assistance, you might have left off at seven."

"What a beautiful belt you've got on!" Alice suddenly remarked. (They had had quite enough of the subject of age, she thought: and, if they really were to take turns in choosing subjects, it was *her* turn now.) "At least," she corrected herself on second thoughts, "a beautiful cravat,[1] I should have said—no, a belt, I mean—I beg your pardon!" she added in dismay, for Humpty Dumpty looked thoroughly offended, and she began to wish she hadn't chosen that subject. "If only I knew," she thought to herself, "which was neck and which was waist!"

Evidently Humpty Dumpty was very angry, though he said nothing for a minute or two. When he *did* speak again, it was in a deep growl.

"It is a—*most*—*provoking*—thing," he said at last, "when a person doesn't know a cravat from a belt!"

"I know it's very ignorant of me," Alice said, in so humble a tone that Humpty Dumpty relented.

"It's a cravat, child, and a beautiful one, as you say. It's a present from the White King and Queen. There now!"

"Is it really?" said Alice, quite pleased to find that she *had* chosen a good subject after all.

"They gave it me," Humpty Dumpty continued thoughtfully as he crossed one knee over the other and clasped his hands round it, "they gave it me—for an un-birthday present."

On what occasion did Humpty Dumpty receive his cravat? from whom?

"I beg your pardon?" Alice said with a puzzled air.

"I'm not offended," said Humpty Dumpty.

"I mean, what *is* an un-birthday present?"

"A present given when it isn't your birthday, of course."

1. **cravat.** Scarf, necktie, or any article of clothing worn around the neck

Alice considered a little. "I like birthday presents best," she said at last.

"You don't know what you're talking about!" cried Humpty Dumpty. "How many days are there in a year?"

"Three hundred and sixty-five," said Alice.

"And how many birthdays have you?"

"One."

"And if you take one from three hundred and sixty-five what remains?"

"Three hundred and sixty-four, of course."

Humpty Dumpty looked doubtful. "I'd rather see that done on paper," he said.

Alice couldn't help smiling as she took out her memorandum-book, and worked the sum for him:

$$\begin{array}{r} 365 \\ \underline{1} \\ 364 \end{array}$$

Humpty Dumpty took the book and looked at it carefully. "That seems to be done right—" he began.

"You're holding it upside down!" Alice interrupted.

"To be sure I was!" Humpty Dumpty said gaily as she turned it round for him. "I thought it looked a little queer. As I was saying, that *seems* to be done right—though I haven't time to look it over thoroughly just now—and that shows that there are three hundred and sixty-four days when you might get un-birthday presents—"

"Certainly," said Alice.

"And only *one* for birthday presents, you know. There's glory for you!"

"I don't know what you mean by 'glory,' " Alice said.

Humpty Dumpty smiled contemptuously. "Of course you don't—till I tell you. I meant 'there's a nice knock-down argument for you!' "

"But 'glory' doesn't mean 'a nice knock-down argument,' " Alice objected.

"When *I* use a word," Humpty Dumpty said, in rather a scornful tone, "it means just what I choose it to mean—neither more nor less."

What does Humpty Dumpty say about the meanings of words? What does this say about his character? What does this say about the society in which he lives?

"The question is," said Alice, "whether you *can* make words mean so many different things."

"The question is," said Humpty Dumpty, "which is to be master—that's all."

Alice was too much puzzled to say anything; so after a minute Humpty Dumpty began again. "They've a temper, some of them—particularly verbs: they're the proudest—adjectives you can do anything with, but not verbs—however, *I* can manage the whole lot of them! Impenetrability! That's what *I* say!"

"Would you tell me please," said Alice, "what that means?"

"Now you talk like a reasonable child," said Humpty Dumpty, looking very much pleased. "I meant by 'impenetrability' that we've had

"HOW OLD did you say you were?"

WORDS FOR EVERYDAY USE

con • temp • tu • ous • ly (kən temp´cho͞o əs lē) *adv.*, scornfully. *He spat out contemptuously, "I am not a waiter, I am the maitre d'!"*

ANSWER TO GUIDED READING QUESTION

1. Humpty says that the words he uses mean whatever he wants them to mean. His character is bizarre and difficult to communicate with. The society is probably confusing and somewhat anarchic.

ADDITIONAL QUESTIONS AND ACTIVITIES

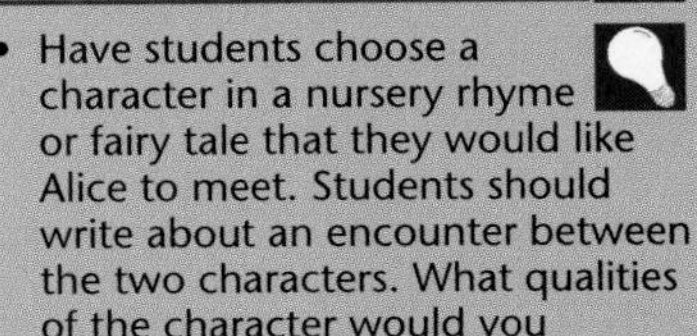

- Have students choose a character in a nursery rhyme or fairy tale that they would like Alice to meet. Students should write about an encounter between the two characters. What qualities of the character would you emphasize? How might you use that character in a satirical way?
- Ask students if Humpty Dumpty has anything in common with writers and, in particular, the author of this novel. Point out that Carroll poses riddles to the reader, much like Humpty does to Alice. Humpty shares the writer's freedom to use words as he wills. Also, Carroll and Humpty are both perched precariously on a wall—both are in danger of having their wordplay and riddling alienate a reader or listener. Should the reader be as annoyed with Carroll as Alice is with Humpty? Should the reader admire both Carroll and Humpty's wordplay?

ANSWER TO GUIDED READING QUESTION

1. Alice asks Humpty to explain the poem "Jabberwocky." Because the poem is nonsensical and Humpty makes up his own meanings for words, he is the perfect person to interpret the poem.

ADDITIONAL QUESTIONS AND ACTIVITIES

Have students think of other objects or pieces of furniture that might be used to represent certain kinds of words. For example, a sleeper-sofa word might be a word with a hidden meaning. Share these categories and examples of words with the class.

Quotables

"'Where shall I begin, please your Majesty?' he asked. 'Begin at the beginning,' the King said, gravely, 'and go on till you come to the end: then stop.'"

—Lewis Carroll

enough of that subject, and it would be just as well if you'd mention what you mean to do next, as I suppose you don't mean to stop here all the rest of your life."

"That's a great deal to make one word mean," Alice said in a thoughtful tone.

"When I make a word do a lot of work like that," said Humpty Dumpty, "I always pay it extra."

"Oh!" said Alice. She was too much puzzled to make any other remark.

"Ah, you should see 'em come round me of a Saturday night," Humpty Dumpty went on, wagging his head gravely from side to side, "for to get their wages, you know."

(Alice didn't venture to ask what he paid them with; and so you see I ca'n't tell *you*.)

"You seem very clever at explaining words, Sir," said Alice. "Would you kindly tell me the meaning of the poem called 'Jabberwocky'?"

What does Alice ask Humpty Dumpty to explain to her? Why does she ask him to do this?

"Let's hear it," said Humpty Dumpty. "I can explain all the poems that ever were invented—and a good many that haven't been invented just yet."

This sounded very hopeful, so Alice repeated the first verse:—

" *'Twas brillig, and the slithy toves*
Did gyre and gimble in the wabe:
All mimsy were the borogoves,
And the mome raths outgrabe."

"That's enough to begin with," Humpty Dumpty interrupted: "there are plenty of hard words there. '*Brillig*' means four o'clock in the afternoon—the time when you begin *broiling* things for dinner."

"That'll do very well," said Alice: "and '*slithy*'?"

"Well, '*slithy*' means 'lithe and slimy.' 'Lithe' is the same as 'active.' You see it's like a portmanteau[2]— there are two meanings packed up into one word."

"I see it now," Alice remarked thoughtfully: "and what are '*toves*'?"

"Well, '*toves*' are something like badgers—they're something like lizards—and they're something like corkscrews."

"They must be very curious-looking creatures."

"They are that," said Humpty Dumpty: "also they make their nests under sun-dials—also they live on cheese."

"And what's to '*gyre*' and to '*gimble*'?"

"To '*gyre*' is to go round and round like a gyroscope. To '*gimble*' is to make holes like a gimlet."

"And '*the wabe*' is the grass-plot round a sun-dial, I suppose?" said Alice, surprised at her own ingenuity.

"Of course it is. It's called '*wabe*' you know, because it goes a long way before it, and a long way behind it—"

"And a long way beyond it on each side," Alice added.

"Exactly so. Well then, '*mimsy*' is 'flimsy and miserable' (there's another portmanteau for you). And a '*borogove*' is a thin shabby-looking bird with its feathers sticking out all round—something like a live mop."

"And then '*mome raths*'?" said Alice. "I'm afraid I'm giving you a great deal of trouble."

"Well, a '*rath*' is a sort of green pig: but '*mome*' I'm not certain about. I think it's short for 'from home'— meaning that they'd lost their way, you know."

"And what does '*outgrabe*' mean?"

"Well, '*outgribing*' is something between bellowing and whistling, with a kind of sneeze in the middle: however, you'll hear it done, maybe—down in the wood yonder—and, when you've once heard it, you'll be *quite* content. Who's been repeating all that hard stuff to you?"

"I read it in a book" said Alice. "But I had some poetry repeated to me much easier than

2. **portmanteau.** Traveling case that opens into two compartments

that, by— 'Tweedledee, I think it was."

Where has Alice heard these difficult words?

"As to poetry, you know," said Humpty Dumpty, stretching out one of his great hands, "*I* can repeat poetry as well as other folk, if it comes to that—"

"Oh, it needn't come to that!" Alice hastily said, hoping to keep him from beginning.

"The piece I'm going to repeat," he went on without noticing her remark, "was written entirely for your amusement."

Why does Alice feel she has to listen to Humpty Dumpty's poem?

Alice felt that in that case she really *ought* to listen to it; so she sat down, and said "Thank you" rather sadly.

"In winter, when the fields are white,
I sing this song for your delight—

only I don't sing it," he added, as an explanation.

"I see you don't," said Alice.

"If you can *see* whether I'm singing or not, you've sharper eyes than most," Humpty Dumpty remarked severely. Alice was silent.

"In spring, when woods are getting green,
I'll try and tell you what I mean:"

"Thank you very much," said Alice.

"In summer, when the days are long,
Perhaps you'll understand the song:

In autumn, when the leaves are brown,
Take pen and ink, and write it down."

"I will, if I can remember it so long," said Alice.

"You needn't go on making remarks like that," Humpty Dumpty said: "they're not sensible, and they put me out."

What does Humpty Dumpty say about Alice's remarks after his verses?

"I sent a message to the fish:
I told them 'This is what I wish.'

The little fishes of the sea
They sent an answer back to me.

The little fishes' answer was
'We cannot do it, Sir, because —'"

"I'm afraid I don't quite understand," said Alice.

"It gets easier further on," Humpty Dumpty replied.

"I sent to them again to say
'It will be better to obey.'

The fishes answered, with a grin,
'Why, what a temper you are in!'

I told them once, I told them twice:
They would not listen to advice.

I took a kettle large and new,
Fit for the deed I had to do.

My heart went hop, my heart went thump:
I filled the kettle at the pump.

Then some one came to me and said
'The little fishes are in bed.'

"In WINTER when the fields are white"

ANSWERS TO GUIDED READING QUESTIONS

1. Alice found these difficult words in a book.
2. Alice feels she must listen to the poem because Humpty said he created it entirely for her amusement.
3. Humpty says that Alice's remarks aren't sensible and that they "put [him] out," or put him in a bad mood.

ADDITIONAL QUESTIONS AND ACTIVITIES

Have students read the poem "Jabberwocky" and, using Humpty Dumpty's interpretation as a model, translate the rest of the poem.

ADDITIONAL QUESTIONS AND ACTIVITIES

Have students briefly review what they learned about the medieval romance. Then have them identify the elements of "Jabberwocky" that seem to come from medieval romance, or works of chivalry.

ANSWERS TO GUIDED READING QUESTIONS

1. Humpty Dumpty tells Alice "Goodbye."
2. Humpty says that Alice has a face just like everyone else. Her face has two eyes, one nose, and one mouth arranged in the customary way.
3. Alice doesn't like Humpty Dumpty. He is rude, self-centered, and confusing. The great crash is Humpty Dumpty falling off the wall.

RESPOND TO THE SELECTION

Students might work in pairs to act out their responses. Students may wish to write their responses first.

SELECTION CHECK TEST 4.9.37 WITH ANSWERS

Checking Your Reading

1. Humpty says that it is very provoking to be called what? **He says that it is very provoking to be called an egg.**
2. Why does Humpty think that Alice's name is "stupid"? **He thinks that because the name doesn't have a meaning.**
3. What has the king promised Humpty should he fall? **The king has promised to send all his horses and all his men.**
4. For what does Alice mistake Humpty Dumpty's cravat? **She mistakes it for a belt.**
5. What is the title of the poem that Humpty explains to Alice? **The title is "Jabberwocky."**

I said to him, I said it plain,
'Then you must wake them up again.'

I said it very loud and clear:
I went and shouted in his ear."

Humpty Dumpty raised his voice almost to a scream as he repeated this verse, and Alice thought, with a shudder, "I wouldn't have been the messenger for *anything*!"

"But he was very stiff and proud:
He said, 'You needn't shout so loud!'

And he was very proud and stiff:
He said 'I'd go and wake them, if—'

I took a corkscrew from the shelf:
I went to wake them up myself.

And when I found the door was locked,
I pulled and pushed and kicked and knocked.

And when I found the door was shut,
I tried to turn the handle, but—"

There was a long pause.

"Is that all?" Alice timidly asked.

"That's all," said Humpty Dumpty. "Good-bye."

How does Humpty Dumpty let Alice know that she should leave?

This was rather sudden, Alice thought: but, after such a *very* strong hint that she ought to be going, she felt that it would hardly be civil to stay. So she got up, and held out her hand. "Good-bye, till we meet again!" she said as cheerfully as she could.

"I shouldn't know you again if we *did* meet," Humpty Dumpty replied in a discontented tone, giving her one of his fingers to shake: "you're so exactly like other people."

"The face is what one goes by, generally," Alice remarked in a thoughtful tone.

"That's just what I complain of," said Humpty Dumpty. "Your face is the same as everybody has—the two eyes, so—" (marking their places in the air with his thumb) "nose in the middle, mouth under. It's always the same. Now if you had the two eyes on the same side of the nose, for instance—or the mouth at the top—that would be *some* help."

What does Humpty Dumpty say about Alice? What does he mean?

"It wouldn't look nice," Alice objected. But Humpty Dumpty only shut his eyes, and said "Wait till you've tried."

Alice waited a minute to see if he would speak again, but, as he never opened his eyes or took any further notice of her, she said "Good-bye!" once more, and, getting no answer to this, she quietly walked way: but she couldn't help saying to herself, as she went, "of all the unsatisfactory—" (she repeated this aloud, as it was a great comfort to have such a long word to say) "of all the unsatisfactory people I *ever* met—" She never finished the sentence, for at this moment a heavy crash shook the forest from end to end. ■

How does Alice feel about Humpty Dumpty? Why does she feel this way? What is the great crash? What has happened to Humpty Dumpty?

Respond to the SELECTION

If you were Alice, how would you react to meeting Humpty Dumpty?

Investigate, Inquire, Imagine

Recall: GATHERING FACTS

1a. What does Alice say that upsets Humpty Dumpty when they first meet?

2a. What comment does Alice make to turn the conversation from her age?

3a. What does Humpty Dumpty say about words and their meaning?

Interpret: FINDING MEANING

1b. Why does Alice have trouble communicating with Humpty Dumpty?

2b. How does Humpty Dumpty react to Alice's confusion? Why does he change his attitude?

3b. What do his ideas about language suggest about his character and his attitude toward rules?

Analyze: TAKING THINGS APART →

4a. Analyze the different ways Humpty Dumpty challenges and confuses Alice.

Synthesize: BRINGING THINGS TOGETHER

4b. What would happen if everyone treated words as Humpty Dumpty does?

Evaluate: MAKING JUDGMENTS →

5a. Evaluate Humpty Dumpty's conversation skills. Compare them to Alice's.

Extend: CONNECTING IDEAS

5b. With whom would you rather have a conversation—Alice or Humpty Dumpty? Why?

Understanding Literature

RIDDLE. Review the definition for **riddle** in Literary Tools in Prereading on page 863. In what way is Humpty Dumpty's use of language riddle-like? Why do you think Carroll created this encounter?

FANTASY. Review the definition for **fantasy** in the Handbook of Literary Terms. Identify elements of fantasy in this selection.

ANSWERS TO INVESTIGATE, INQUIRE, IMAGINE

RECALL

1a. Alice says he is like an egg.

2a. She says, "What a beautiful belt you've got on!" She then corrects herself since she is not sure if it is a belt or a cravat.

3a. He says they mean what he wants them to mean.

INTERPRET

1b. Humpty Dumpty sometimes means exactly what he says. For example, he says "How old did you say you were?" Alice wrongly assumes he means, "How old are you?" Other times, Humpty Dumpty simply makes up words or uses them in very unconventional ways, making it difficult for anyone to communicate effectively with him.

2b. He gets very angry. When she apologizes humbly for being ignorant, his whole tone changes.

3b. Humpty's distortions of language point to his arrogance and distaste for rules he sees as intended for the small-minded.

ANALYZE

4a. Humpty Dumpty begins by speaking in an antagonistic tone without looking at Alice. He criticizes her name and asks what it means. He reacts to her questions as if they were riddles or tricks and accuses her of eavesdropping. He asks her how old she said she was, a trick question. He then begins to make up meanings for words. He gets angry with her because she makes a simple mistake.

SYNTHESIZE

4b. Communication would be difficult or impossible. However, you may point out that slang often involves taking a word and giving it a new or modified meaning. Have students consider words they have given new meanings to.

EVALUATE

5a. Humpty bewildered Alice, insulted her, and annoyed her. His conversation skills do not enable him to communicate with other persons. Alice's conversation methods show an awareness of the other person's intentions and feelings. She attempts to be polite, and avoids conflicts and arguments.

EXTEND

5b. *Responses will vary.*

Answers to Understanding Literature can be found on page 872.

ANSWERS TO UNDERSTANDING LITERATURE

FANTASY. The most obvious element of fantasy is that Humpty Dumpty is a giant talking eff. His personality is also fantastically absurd. It might be said that the conversation they have, while surreal in parts, is realistic in that it is awkward and unsatisfying.

Teaching Note: Discuss with students why it is important that all fantasies have realistic elements in them.

RIDDLE. Humpty Dumpty's language has to be "solved" like a riddle. He uses words that do not always say what they mean. Humpty Dumpty wants to confuse Alice, and, in doing so, make himself appear superior. Humpty Dumpty's arrogance is an exaggerated version of how many adults treat children. Carroll also emphasizes Alice's good manners and polite behavior in contrast to Humpty Dumpty's rudeness.

Teaching Note: Riddles have been a part of literature for thousands of years. Ask students a famous riddle, from Sophocles's play Oedipus Rex: "What goes on four feet in the morning, two at noon, and in the evening on three?" Answer. A person in three stages of life—infancy, maturity, and infirm old age.

ANSWERS TO INTEGRATING THE LANGUAGE ARTS

Language, Grammar, and Style
Responses will vary. Student responses should address each of the five elements of the activity and be clearly written. Praise responses that provide extensive histories, multiple definitions, or multiple related words.

Speaking and Listening
Responses will vary. Students should note the language difficulties between Alice and Humpty Dumpty. They should also notice poor communication skills, such as Humpty refusing to look at Alice when he first speaks to her, Humpty's scornful tone, and superior attitude.

WRITER'S JOURNAL

1. Choose five words. Write **definitions** for each word. Include a short explanation of each definition as Humpty Dumpty does as he explains the first few lines of *Jaberwocky* to Alice.
2. Write a **rhyming poem** that tells a simple story. Use the poem Humpty Dumpty recites to Alice as a model.
3. Choose an inanimate object and give it human characteristics. Create a **comic strip** about this object.

Integrating *the* LANGUAGE ARTS

Language, Grammar, and Style

WORD ORIGINS. Read the Language Arts Survey 1.21, "Exploring Word Origins and Word Families." Then, using the *Oxford English Dictionary* in your library, look up a word that has a particularly long entry and prepare a short report describing the word's:

1. history—the original form of the word
2. spelling and pronunciation—how it may have changed through time
3. archaic forms—forms which are no longer in use
4. various definitions—if it can be used in more than one way
5. "relatives"—other words or uses that are related to it

Speaking and Listening

COMMUNICATION CRITIQUE. Review the Language Arts Survey 4.7–4.9 "Communicating with Others." Examine the exchange between Alice and Humpty Dumpty. Write a critique of their conversation. Why aren't they communicating well?

Media Literacy

ANALYZING MEDIA. Carroll's books about Alice are often considered children's stories. But, if you look at them closely, they include parodies, commentary, and word play that appeal to adults. Choose and watch a current movie or television show that is for children. Analyze the movie or show. Is it really appropriate for children? Does it appeal to children on one level and adults on another? Present your findings to your class.

FROM *Madame Bovary*

BY GUSTAVE FLAUBERT

About the AUTHOR

Gustave Flaubert (1821–1880) was born December 12, 1821, in Rouen, France. Flaubert showed an interest in literature, particularly the work of Romantic novelists, at an early age. To satisfy his father's wishes, Flaubert went to Paris to study law in 1841. He later left to devote his life to literature. He received a large inheritance that allowed him to retire to his family's estate and write. In 1875 he lost his fortune trying to help his niece and her husband financially. Flaubert was a meticulous writer who would sometimes spend days trying to find the precise word or formulating a flawless sentence. He spent five years writing his best-known work, *Madame Bovary.* His other works include *L'Education Sentimentale* and *La Tentation de St. Antoine.*

About the SELECTION

Madame Bovary, Flaubert's masterpiece, is a novel about a young married woman who, stirred by romantic ideals and dissatisfaction with her marriage, rebels against her middle-class lifestyle by having love affairs and trying to live an extravagant lifestyle.

When *Madame Bovary* was first published as a magazine serial in 1856, the public was shocked by its subject matter. In fact, Flaubert was bought to trial for publishing a work that was morally offensive. He defended himself against a conservative and judgmental public by saying that, far from making adultery look attractive, the tragic results of Emma Bovary's extravagance and romantic encounters serve as a lesson in using good moral judgment. Flaubert was acquitted in 1857, and the story came out in book form that same year.

The selection you are about to read is chapter 8 of *Madame Bovary.* Emma Bovary, the title character, and her husband Charles have just arrived at Vaubyessard, a chateau owned by the Marquis d'Andervilliers. They have received an invitation to an elegant ball at the chateau, and Emma, who feels trapped in her marriage and in her middle-class life, is looking forward to escaping for the evening into a world she sees as romantic and exciting.

MULTICULTURAL EXTENSIONS

Literary TOOLS

FLASHBACK. A **flashback** is a section of a literary work that presents an event or series of events that occurred earlier than the current time in the work. As you read, look for instances of flashback.

DESCRIPTION. **Description** is a type of writing that portrays a character, an object, or a scene. Descriptions make use of sensory details—words and phrases that describe how things look, sound, smell, taste, or feel. Effective descriptions contain precise nouns, verbs, adverbs, and adjectives. Create a sensory details chart like the one below to help you identify some of the many examples of sensory detail Flaubert creates.

Sight	Sound	Touch	Taste	Smell
	sound of foot-steps			

Reader's Journal

Have you ever wished you lived a life different from the one you have now? Describe it. How has this wish kept you from appreciating the life you currently live?

ADDITIONAL RESOURCES

UNIT 9 RESOURCE BOOK
- Selection Worksheet 9.19
- Selection Check Test 4.9.39
- Selection Test 4.9.40
- Reading Resource 1.15
- Language, Grammar, and Style Resource 3.34
- Study and Research Resource 5.26

GRAPHIC ORGANIZER

This selection contains a wealth of descriptive sensory detail. Students may include details such as the following in their sensory detail charts: Sight: Italian-style château with an immense green yard; light of lamps over green cloth; silver dish covers reflecting the lighted wax candles; hair of men glossy with pomades. Sound: reechoing voices as in a church; clicking of billiards; flourish of a violin; music murmuring in her ears. Touch: wrapped around by warm air; shivering because of iced champagne. Taste: pomegranates and pineapples. Smell: perfume of flowers and of fine linen, fumes of the viands, odor of truffles.

READER'S JOURNAL

Students might write about the materialism in teen culture. How does it feel to not be able to afford certain clothes and certain possessions?

VOCABULARY FROM THE SELECTION

amicably
cotillion
effaced
fain
satiated
torpor
undulating

GOALS/OBJECTIVES

Studying this lesson will enable students to
- appreciate Gustave Flaubert's skill as a novelist
- describe Flaubert's literary accomplishments and explain the historical significance of his writings
- explain the connection between Flaubert's writing and the English literature in this unit
- define *flashback* and *description* and identify examples of each in their reading

ANSWER TO GUIDED READING QUESTION

1. Life at Vaubyessard is luxurious and elegant.

INDIVIDUAL LEARNING STRATEGIES

MOTIVATION
Madame Bovary is one of the most famous characters in literature. For Flaubert, she was a symbol of the bourgeois, or middle-class, mentality of French people in his time: she was small-minded, easily impressed by wealth and very materialistic. Her name, Bovary, is meant to suggest that she is like a cow (bovine means "cowlike" in both French and English), or someone who cannot think for herself. Students can discuss their opinions of Madame Bovary after reading the selection.

READING PROFICIENCY
This selection may be difficult for students because there are many French names that may be hard to pronounce and many particular words for plants, foods, ornaments, and clothing that may be unfamiliar to them. Encourage them to read through the selection once to get the general idea, and not to worry about the meanings of words unless they obstruct the meaning or unless they are curious to learn them. You may wish to read the selection aloud for students.

ENGLISH LANGUAGE LEARNING
Follow the suggestions in Reading Proficiency above. You may wish to share with students the following additional vocabulary:
château—French house
greensward—lawn
billiards—game of pool
Marquis, Marchioness, Viscount—titles of minor nobility
peasants—poor farmers

SPECIAL NEEDS
Students may work in pairs to complete the sensory detail chart in Literary Tools. Ask them what effect the details have in conveying what Madame Bovary feels at the ball.

ENRICHMENT
Students may wish to read the entire book *Madame Bovary* and write a review of the book.

FROM MADAME BOVARY

GUSTAVE FLAUBERT

The château, a modern building in Italian style, with two projecting wings and three flights of steps, lay at the foot of an immense greensward, on which some cows were grazing among groups of large trees set out at regular intervals, while large beds of arbutus, rhododendron, syringas, and guelder roses bulged out their irregular clusters of green along the curve of the gravel path. A river flowed under a bridge; through the mist one could distinguish buildings with thatched roofs scattered over the field bordered by two gently sloping well-timbered hillocks, and in the background amid the trees rose in two parallel lines the coach houses and stables, all that was left of the ruined old château.

What is life like at Vaubyessard, the place where Emma and Charles visit?

Charles's dogcart pulled up before the middle flight of steps; servants appeared; the Marquis came forward, and offering his arm to the doctor's wife, conducted her to the vestibule.

It was paved with marble slabs, was very lofty, and the sound of footsteps and that of voices reechoed through it as in a church. Opposite rose a straight staircase, and on the left a gallery overlooking the garden led to the billiard room, through whose door one could hear the click of the ivory balls. As she crossed it to go to the drawing room, Emma saw standing around the table men with grave faces, their chins resting on high cravats.[1] They all wore orders, and smiled silently as they made their strokes. On the dark wainscoting of the walls large gold frames bore at the bottom names written in black letters. She read: "Jean-Antoine d'Andervilliers d'Yverbonville, Count de la Vaubyessard and Baron de la Fresnaye, killed at the battle of Coutras on the 20th of October 1587." And on another: "Jean-Antoine-Henri-Guy d'Andervilliers de la Vaubyessard, Admiral of France and Chevalier of the Order of St. Michael, wounded at the battle of the Hougue-Saint-Vaast on the 29th of May 1692; died at Vaubyessard on the 23rd of January 1693." One could hardly make out those that followed, for the light of the lamps lowered over the green cloth threw a dim shadow around the room. Burnishing the horizontal pictures, it broke up against these in delicate lines where there were cracks in the varnish and from all these great black squares framed in with gold stood out here and there some lighter portion of the painting—a pale brow, two eyes that looked at you, perukes[2] flowing over and powdering red-coated shoulders, or the buckle of a garter above a well-rounded calf.

1. **cravats.** Neckerchiefs or scarves; neckties
2. **perukes.** Powdered wigs worn by men in the seventeenth and eighteenth centuries

The Marquis opened the drawing-room door; one of the ladies, the Marchioness herself, came to meet Emma. She made her sit down by her on an ottoman, and began talking to her as amicably as if she had known her a long time. She was a woman of about forty, with fine shoulders, a hook nose, a drawling voice, and on this evening she wore over her brown hair a simple guipure fichu[3] that fell in a point at the back. A fair young woman was by her side in a high-backed chair, and gentlemen with flowers in their buttonholes were talking to ladies around the fire.

At seven dinner was served. The men, who were in the majority, sat down at the first table in the vestibule; the ladies at the second in the dining room with the Marquis and Marchioness.

Emma, on entering, felt herself wrapped around by the warm air, a blending of the perfume of flowers and of the fine linen, of the fumes of the viands, and the odor of the truffles. The silver dish covers reflected the lighted wax candles in the candelabra, the cut crystal covered with light steam reflected from one to the other pale rays; bouquets were placed in a row the whole length of the table; and in the large bordered plates each napkin, arranged after the fashion of a bishop's miter,[4] held between its two gaping folds a small oval-shaped roll. The red claws of lobsters hung over the dishes; rich fruit in open baskets was piled up on moss; there were quails in their plumage; smoke was rising; and in silk stockings, knee breeches, white cravat, and frilled shirt, the steward, grave as a judge, offering ready carved dishes between the shoulders of the guests, with a touch of the spoon gave you the piece chosen. On the large stove of porcelain inlaid with copper baguettes the statue of a woman, draped to the chin, gazed motionless on the room full of life.

How does Emma feel about visiting Vaubyessard and attending the ball?

Madame Bovary noticed that many ladies had not put their gloves in their glasses.

But at the upper end of the table, alone among all these women, bent over his full plate, and his napkin tied around his neck like a child, an old man sat eating, letting drops of gravy drip from his mouth. His eyes were bloodshot, and he wore a little queue[5] tied with a black ribbon. He was the Marquis's father-in-law, the old Duke de Laverdière, once on a time favorite of the Count d'Artois, in the days of the Vaudreuil hunting parties at the Marquis de Conflans', and had been, it was said, the lover of Queen Marie Antoinette, between Monsieur de Coigny and Monsieur de Lauzun. He had lived a life of noisy debauch, full of duels, bets, elopements; he had squandered his fortune and frightened all his family. A servant behind his chair named aloud to him in his ear the dishes that he pointed to stammering, and constantly Emma's eyes turned involuntarily to this old man with hanging lips, as to something extraordinary. He had lived at court and slept in the bed of queens!

What new sights and tastes does Emma experience during her time at Vaubyessard?

Iced champagne was poured out. Emma shivered all over as she felt it cold in her mouth. She had never seen pomegranates nor tasted pineapples. The powdered sugar even seemed to her whiter and finer than elsewhere.

The ladies afterwards went to their rooms to prepare for the ball.

Emma made her toilet with the fastidious care of an actress on her début. She did her hair according to the directions of the hairdresser, and

3. **guipure fichu.** Lace cape worn with the ends crossed or fastened in front
4. **miter.** Headdress; tall ornamental cap with peaks in front and back
5. **queue.** Braid of hair at the back of the head

Words for Everyday Use

am • i • ca • bly (a' mi kə blē) *adv.*, in a friendly manner. *Mr. and Mrs. Nguyen greeted us amicably, shaking our hands and asking how we were.*

ANSWERS TO GUIDED READING QUESTIONS

1. Emma is thrilled to visit Vaubyessard and attend the ball.
2. She sees beautiful bouquets of flowers, elegant china, and pomegranates. She tastes pineapple and several gourmet dishes for the first time.

CROSS-CURRICULAR ACTIVITIES

Botany. Students can research the flowers mentioned in the first paragraph of the selection. They may find photographs or drawings of the plants, describe their characteristics and what conditions are needed to grow them.

ANSWER TO GUIDED READING QUESTION

1. Her heart begins to beat faster as she takes her partner's hand, but she soon forgets her anxiousness when the music starts.

put on the barège dress spread out upon the bed. Charles's trousers were tight across the belly.

"My trouser-straps will be rather awkward for dancing," he said.

"Dancing?" repeated Emma.

"Yes!"

"Why, you must be mad! They would make fun of you; keep your place. Besides, it is more becoming for a doctor," she added.

Charles was silent. He walked up and down waiting for Emma to finish dressing.

He saw her from behind in the glass between two lights. Her black eyes seemed blacker than ever. Her hair, undulating towards the ears, shone with a blue luster; a rose in her chignon[6] trembled on its mobile stalk, with artificial dew-drops on the tip of the leaves. She wore a gown of pale saffron trimmed with three bouquets of pompon roses mixed with green.

Charles came and kissed her on her shoulder.

"Let me alone!" she said; "you are tumbling me."

One could hear the flourish of the violin and the notes of a horn. She went downstairs restraining herself from running.

Dancing had begun. Guests were arriving. There was some crushing. She sat down on a form near the door.

The quadrille[7] over, the floor was occupied by groups of men standing up and talking and servants in livery bearing large trays. Along the line of seated women painted fans were fluttering, bouquets half hid smiling faces, and gold stoppered scent bottles were turned in partly closed hands, whose white gloves outlined the nails and tightened on the flesh at the wrists. Lace trimmings, diamond brooches, medallion bracelets trembled on bodices, gleamed on breasts, clinked on bare arms. The hair, well smoothed over the temples and knotted at the nape, bore crowns, or bunches, or sprays of myosotis, jasmine, pomegranate blossoms, ears of corn, and cornflowers. Calmly seated in their places, mothers with forbidding countenances were wearing red turbans.

Emma's heart beat rather faster when, her partner holding her by the tips of the fingers, she took her place in a line with the dancers, and waited for the first note to start. But her emotion soon vanished, and, swaying to the rhythm of the orchestra. she glided forward with slight movements of the neck. A smile rose to her lips at certain delicate phrases of the violin, that sometimes played alone while the other instruments were silent; one could hear the clear clink of the louis d'or that were being thrown down upon the card tables in the next room; then all struck in again, the cornet-a-piston uttered its sonorous note, feet marked time, skirts swelled and rustled, hands touched and parted; the same eyes falling before you met yours again.

What happens to Emma as she dances her first dance of the evening?

A few men (some fifteen or so) of twenty-five to forty, scattered here and there among the dancers or talking at the doorways, distinguished themselves from the crowd by a certain air of breeding, whatever their differences in age, dress or face.

Their clothes, better made, seemed of finer cloth, and their hair, brought forward in curls towards the temples, glossy with more delicate pomades.[8] They had the complexion of wealth—that clear complexion that is heightened by the pallor of porcelain, the shimmer of satin, the veneer of old furniture, and that an ordered regimen of exquisite nurture maintains at its best. Their necks

6. **chignon.** Knot or coil of hair worn at the back of the neck
7. **quadrille.** Dance performed by four couples
8. **pomades.** Perfumed ointments for the hair

WORDS FOR EVERYDAY USE

un • du • lat • ing (ən′ jə lāt iŋ) *part.*, moving in a wavy or flowing manner. *The undulating flag of the ship was visible on shore.*

moved easily in their low cravats, their long whiskers fell over their turned-down collars, they wiped their lips upon handkerchiefs with embroidered initials that gave forth a subtle perfume. Those who were beginning to grow old had an air of youth, while there was something mature in the faces of the young. In their unconcerned looks was the calm of passions daily satiated, and through all their gentleness of manner pierced that peculiar brutality, the result of a command of half easy things, in which force is exercised and vanity amused—the management of thoroughbred horses and the society of loose women.

A few steps from Emma a gentleman in a blue coat was talking of Italy with a pale young woman wearing a parure of pearls.

They were praising the breadth of the columns of St. Peter's, Tivoli, Vesuvius, Castellamare, and Cassines, the roses of Genoa, the Coliseum by moonlight. With her other ear Emma was listening to a conversation full of words she did not understand. A circle gathered round a very young man who the week before had beaten "Miss Arabella" and "Romolus," and won two thousand louis jumping a ditch in England. One complained that his race horses were growing fat; another of the printers' errors that had disfigured the name of his horse.

The atmosphere of the ball was heavy; the lamps were growing dim. Guests were flocking to the billiard room. A servant got upon a chair and broke the window panes. At the crash of the glass Madame Bovary turned her head and saw in the garden the faces of peasants pressed against the window looking in at them. Then the memory of the Bertaux came back to her. She saw the farm again, the muddy pond, her father in a blouse under the apple trees, and she saw herself again as formerly, skimming with her finger the cream off the milk pans in the dairy. But in the refulgence of the present hour her past life, so distinct until then, faded away completely, and she almost doubted having lived it. She was there; beyond the ball was only shadow overspreading all the rest. . . .

What caused the crash of glass?

After supper, where were plenty of Spanish and Rhine wines, soups *à la bisque* and *au lait d'amandes*, puddings *à la Trafalgar*, and all sorts of cold meats with jellies that trembled in the dishes, the carriages one after the other began to drive off. Raising the corners of the muslin[9] curtain, one could see the light of their lanterns glimmering through the darkness. The seats began to empty, some card players were still left; the musicians were cooling the tips of their fingers on their tongues. Charles was half asleep, his back propped against a door.

At three o'clock the cotillion began. Emma did not know how to waltz. Everyone was waltzing, Mademoiselle d'Andervilliers herself and the Marquis; only the guests staying at the castle were still there, about a dozen persons.

One of the waltzers, however, who was familiarly called Viscount, and whose low cut waistcoat seemed molded to his chest, came a second time to ask Madame Bovary to dance, assuring her that he would guide her, and that she would get through it very well.

They began slowly, then went more rapidly. They turned; all around them was turning—the lamps, the furniture, the wainscoting, the floor, like a disc on a pivot. On passing near the doors the bottom of Emma's dress caught against his trousers. Their legs commingled; he looked down at her; she raised her eyes to his. A torpor seized her; she stopped. They started again, and with a more rapid movement; the Viscount, dragging

9. **muslin.** Strong and sheer cotton cloth of plain weave

Words For Everyday Use

sa • ti • at • ed (sā′ shē āt′ əd) *part.*, to satisfy fully or to excess. *I was fully satiated after eating a three-course meal.*

co • til • lion (kō til′ yən) *n.*, a formal ball. *Gena was invited to a cotillion during the holidays.*

tor • por (tōr′ pər) *n.*, extreme sluggishness; lethargy. *After the 5K race, the runners experienced torpor.*

ANSWER TO GUIDED READING QUESTION

1. A servant got up on a chair, perhaps to see better, and broke the window panes. He or she may have fallen.

ANSWER TO GUIDED READING QUESTION

1. The grace and poise of the two dancers spellbind them. They are also impressed with their amount of endurance.

her along, disappeared with her to the end of the gallery, where, panting, she almost fell, and for a moment rested her head upon his breast. And then, still turning, but more slowly, he guided her back to her seat. She leaned back against the wall and covered her eyes with her hands.

When she opened them again, in the middle of the drawing-room three waltzers were kneeling before a lady sitting on a stool. She chose the Viscount, and the violin struck up once more.

Everyone looked at them. They passed and repassed, she with rigid body, her chin bent downward, and he always in the same pose, his figure curved, his elbow rounded, his chin thrown forward. That woman knew how to waltz! They kept up a long time, and tired out all the others.

Describe the reactions of people as they watch Emma waltz with the Viscount.

Then they talked a few moments longer, and after the good nights, or rather good mornings, the guests of the château retired to bed.

Charles dragged himself up by the balusters. His "knees were going up into his body." He had spent five consecutive hours standing bolt upright at the card tables, watching them play whist, without understanding anything about it, and it was with a deep sigh of relief that he pulled off his boots.

Emma threw a shawl over her shoulders, opened the window, and leaned out.

The night was dark; some drops of rain were falling. She breathed in the damp wind that refreshed her eyelids. The music of the ball was still murmuring in her ears, and she tried to keep herself awake in order to prolong the illusion of this luxurious life that she would soon have to give up.

Day began to break. She looked long at the windows of the château, trying to guess which were the rooms of all those she had noticed the evening before. She would fain have known their lives, have penetrated, blended with them. But she was shivering with cold. She undressed, and cowered down between the sheets against Charles, who was asleep.

There were a great many people to luncheon. The repast lasted ten minutes; no liquors were served, which astonished the doctor. Next, Mademoiselle d'Andervilliers collected some pieces of roll in a small basket to take them to the swans on the ornamental waters, and they went to walk in the hot houses, where strange plants, bristling with hairs, rose in pyramids under hanging vases, where, as from overfilled nests of serpents, fell long green cords interlacing. The orangery, which was at the other end, led by a covered way to the outhouses of the château. The Marquis, to amuse the young woman, took her to see the stables. Above the basketshaped racks porcelain slabs bore the names of the horses in black letters. Each animal in its stall whisked its tail when anyone went near and said "Tchk! tchk!" The boards of the harness room shone like the flooring of a drawing-room. . . .

Charles, meanwhile, went to ask a groom to put his horse to. The dogcart was brought to the foot of the steps, and all the parcels being crammed in, the Bovarys paid their respects to the Marquis and Marchioness and set out again for Tostes.

Emma watched the turning wheels in silence. Charles, on the extreme edge of the seat, held the reins with his two arms wide apart, and the little horse ambled along in the shafts that were too big for him. The loose reins hanging over his crupper[10] were wet with foam, and the box fastened on behind the chaise gave great regular bumps against it.

10. **crupper.** Part of a padded leather saddle-strap passed around the base of a horse's tail to keep the saddle from moving forward

WORDS FOR EVERYDAY USE

fain (fān) *adv.*, with pleasure; gladly. *My grandmother would fain make me chocolate chip cookies for our school bake sale.*

They were on the heights of Thibourville when suddenly some horsemen with cigars between their lips passed laughing. Emma thought she recognized the Viscount, turned back, and caught on the horizon only the movement of the heads rising or falling with the unequal cadence of the trot or gallop.

A mile farther on they had to stop to mend with some string the traces that had broken.

But Charles, giving a last look to the harness, saw something on the ground between his horse's legs, and he picked up a cigar case with a green silk border and emblazoned in the center like the door of a carriage.

What does Charles find on the ground as he and Emma leave Vaubyessard?

"There are even two cigars in it," said he; "they'll do for this evening after dinner."

"Why, do you smoke?" she asked.

"Sometimes, when I get a chance."

He put his find in his pocket and whipped up the nag.

When they reached home the dinner was not ready. Madame lost her temper. Natasie answered rudely.

"Leave the room!" said Emma. "You are forgetting yourself. I give you warning."

For dinner there was onion soup and a piece of veal with sorrel. Charles, seated opposite Emma, rubbed his hands gleefully.

"How good it is to be at home again!"

Natasie could be heard crying. He was rather fond of the poor girl. She had formerly, during the wearisome time of his widowhood, kept him company many an evening. She had been his first patient, his oldest acquaintance in the place.

"Have you given her warning for good?" he asked at last.

"Yes. Who is to prevent me?" she replied.

Then they warmed themselves in the kitchen while their room was being made ready. Charles began to smoke. He smoked with lips protruding, spitting every moment, recoiling at every puff.

"You'll make yourself ill," she said scornfully.

He put down his cigar and ran to swallow a glass of cold water at the pump. Emma seizing hold of the cigar case threw it quickly to the back of the cupboard.

The next day was a long one. She walked about her little garden, up and down the same walks, stopping before the beds, before the espalier,[11] before the plaster curate, looking with amazement at all these things of once-on-a-time that she knew so well. How far off the ball seemed already! What was it that thus set so far asunder the morning of the day before yesterday and the evening of today? Her journey to Vaubyessard had made a hole in her life, like one of those great crevasses that a storm will sometimes make in one night in mountains. Still she was resigned. She devoutly put away in her drawers her beautiful dress, down to the satin shoes whose soles were yellowed with the slippery wax of the dancing floor. Her heart was like these. In its friction against wealth something had come over it that could not be <u>effaced</u>.

The memory of this ball, then, became an occupation for Emma. Whenever the Wednesday came round she said to herself as she awoke, "Ah! I was there a week—a fortnight—three weeks ago." And little by little the faces grew confused in her remembrance. She forgot the tune of the quadrilles; she no longer saw the liveries and appointments so distinctly; some details escaped her, but the regret remained with her. ■

How has the ball affected Emma?

11. **espalier.** Lattice or trellis on which shrubs are trained to grow flat

Words for Everyday Use

ef • faced (e fāsd′) *vt.,* to eliminate; to vanish. *The rising of the sun <u>effaced</u> the stars.*

ANSWERS TO GUIDED READING QUESTIONS

1. Charles finds a cigar case encasing two cigars on the ground.
2. She is preoccupied by the memory of the ball. She feels that her life is ordinary compared with the grandeur she witnessed there, and feels intense regret that she herself is not wealthy.

RESPOND TO THE SELECTION

Students may imagine that Madame Bovary is a friend. What would they advise her to do about her frustrations?

ANSWERS TO INVESTIGATE, INQUIRE, AND IMAGINE

RECALL

1a. The Marquis's father-in-law is described as having a napkin tied around his neck like a child, drops of gravy falling from his mouth, and bloodshot eyes. He has lived a wild life, frightening his family and squandering his money.

2a. Emma responds to Charles's questions and his kiss on her shoulder with disdain.

3a. Emma gets mad at Natasie because dinner is late, Natasie answers rudely, and Emma fires her.

INTERPRET

1b. Emma thinks only about the fact that he has lived in court and mingled with queens. Emma is so impressed with the man's social status that she cannot see his true nature.

2b. Emma is annoyed with her life with Charles and the fact that he is not part of this elegant world.

3b. Emma is hostile because she does not live in the luxurious world that she just left and feels powerless to get out of her won world, in which she is bored and unhappy.

ANALYZE

4a. Charles is sleeping, standing up, by the card tables. When Charles returns to the room, he takes his boots off and prepares for sleep. When Emma returns to the room, she leans out of the window and breathes in the night air, not wanting the elegant night to end.

SYNTHESIZE

4b. They are both satisfied with different things—Charles is happy being a middle-class doctor and living an average life. Emma wants to be part of the elegant world of Vaubyessard. They do not agree on this major point, and they do not seem to communicate well or understand each other.

Respond *to the* SELECTION

How would you feel if you were in Emma Bovary's situation? What would you do about your unhappiness or discontentment?

INVESTIGATE, Inquire, *Imagine*

Recall: GATHERING FACTS → **Interpret:** FINDING MEANING

1a. What details are used to describe the Marquis's father-in-law? → 1b. What is Emma's perception of the Marquis's father-in-law and why is it so different from the actual description of him?

2a. As they dress for the ball, how does Emma respond to Charles's questions and his kiss on her shoulder? → 2b. What does Emma's treatment of Charles say about her feeling for him?

3a. What happens between Emma and the maid, Natasie, when Charles and Emma arrive home? → 3b. What might be the reason behind Emma's hostility?

Analyze: TAKING THINGS APART → **Synthesize:** BRINGING THINGS TOGETHER

4a. What is Charles doing just before the ball ends? What is the first thing Charles and Emma do when they return to the room? → 4b. What do the reactions of Charles and Emma at the end of the dance reveal about their individual perspectives on their lives and their relationship?

Perspective: LOOKING AT OTHER VIEWS → **Empathy:** SEEING FROM INSIDE

5a. Why do you think Emma Bovary was greatly affected by her visit to Vaubyessard? → 5b. Can you identify with Emma Bovary? Are you able to understand the feelings she has toward her life? Why, or why not? If you were her friend, what would you say to her about her life and about her behavior?

Understanding *Literature*

FLASHBACK. Review the definition for **flashback** in Literary Tools in Prereading on page 873. In what way did the use of flashback help you to know that the scene at the ball was rather foreign to Emma?

DESCRIPTION. Review the definition of **description** and the sensory details chart you completed for Literary Tools in Prereading. How do Flaubert's descriptions add to the luxurious setting of the ball? What is your favorite description? Why?

ANSWERS TO INVESTIGATE, INQUIRE, AND IMAGINE (CONT.)

PERSPECTIVE

5a. Responses may vary. Emma saw, tasted, and experienced things she never experienced before living as a middle-class citizen and raised on a farm. Her visit to Vaubyessard opened her eyes to a new kind of life that was attractive to her since she was already unhappy and bored with her current lifestyle.

EMPATHY

5b. *Responses will vary.*

Answers to Understanding Literature can be found on page 881.

Writer's Journal

1. Pretend you are the hosts of the ball. Write a **party invitation** that Charles and Emma Bovary might have received to the cotillion.
2. Imagine you are Madame Bovary. Upon returning to your bedroom after the ball ended, a flood of emotions rise up in you. Write a **journal entry** that describes your experience at the ball to help you sort through your emotions.
3. Imagine you are Natasie, the maid. Write a **letter of apology** that expresses your repentance for answering rudely and that pleads for getting back your job.

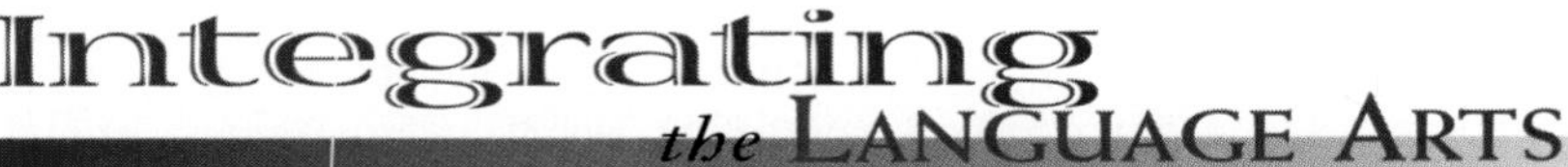

Language, Grammar, and Style

Correcting Run-Ons. Read the Language Arts Survey 3.34, "Correcting Sentence Run-Ons." Then rewrite the following run-ons. Correct each one either by making it into two separate sentences or by adding a comma and a coordinating conjunction.

1. Bouquets of flowers filled the foyer of the ballroom its scent was like a beautiful blend of perfumes.
2. Lobster, champagne, and exotic fruits were served for dinner Emma could not eat because of her excitement.
3. The guests gazed upon the couple in amazement the couple waltzed the entire night together.
4. Charles fell asleep to the dance music he was bored.
5. Emma dreaded going back home she would miss the excitement and newness that the world of Vaubyessard offered.

Collaborative Learning

Travel Guide. Working in groups of three or four, find the places that are mentioned in the selection using a map. Create a travel guide that includes the location of each town, one distinguishing fact about the town, and a list of things that tourists might enjoy seeing or doing. Refer to Language Arts Survey 1.15, "Using Graphic Aids" and 5.26, "Using the Internet" to help complete this project.

Media Literacy & Speaking and Listening

Morality Debate. View the 2000 BBC production of the film, *Madame Bovary*, which stars Frances O'Connor. Do you agree with Flaubert's comment that "far from making adultery look attractive, the tragic results of Emma Bovary's extravagance and romantic encounters serve as a lesson in using good moral judgment"? Or do you agree with the public who deemed his book morally offensive in 1856? Debate these questions in small groups. After the debate, discuss the societal attitudes that have changed throughout the years in regards to what is morally offensive and what is not.

Answers to Understanding Literature

Flashback. The flashback on page 877 informs the reader about Emma's childhood on her parents' farm—a life far different from the upper-class life of the Marquis and Marchioness. The flashback clearly shows why Madame Bovary feels overwhelmed by the elegance at Vaubyessard. She is looking in at this particular social world from its outskirts.

Description. *Responses will vary.* Flaubert's descriptions add to the elegant setting of the ball by making use of sensory details that describe rich and expensive things. For example, the description of hair ("and on this evening she wore over her brown hair a simple guipure fichu that fell in a point at the back"), attire ("gentleman with flowers in their buttonholes"), food ("The red claws of lobsters hung over the dishes: rich fruit in open baskets was piled up on moss"), and décor ("The silver dish covers reflected the lighted wax candles in the candelabra, the cut crystal covered with light steam reflected from one to the other pale rays"), all described in a way that makes the reader think of high society and their expensive lifestyle.

Answers to Integrating the Language Arts

Language, Grammar, and Style

1. Bouquets of flowers filled the foyer of the ballroom; its scent was like a beautiful blend of perfumes.
2. Although lobster, champagne, and exotic fruits were served for dinner, Emma could not eat because of her excitement.
3. The guests gazed upon the couple in amazement; the couple waltzed the entire night together.
4. Charles fell asleep to the dance music because he was bored.
5. Emma dreaded going back home because she would miss the excitement and newness that the world of Vaubyessard offered.

"FLOWER IN THE CRANNIED WALL"

About the Author. A biography of **Alfred, Lord Tennyson** appears on page 776.

About the Selection. This poem is reminiscent of "In Memoriam" inasmuch as the poet thinks of nature as being inextricably joined with God.

"WHEN I WAS ONE-AND-TWENTY" "LOVELIEST OF TREES"

About the Author. A biography of **A. E. Housman** appears on page 846.

About the Selections. Both selections can be linked with "To an Athlete Dying Young" in that they deal with the futility of achievement and the inevitability of death.

"THE NIGHT IS DARKENING"

About the Author. Emily Brontë (1818–1848) was born and raised in the Yorkshire district of northern England—on the same Yorkshire moors that serve as the setting for *Wuthering Heights*. Brontë was a passionate and talented person, although she was also quiet and reserved and left few records of her personal life. Brontë's father, a rector, moved the family to Haworth, Yorkshire, in 1820. After the death of her mother in 1821, Emily and her siblings were left almost entirely on their own in the moorland rectory. The children were educated at home and spent a great deal of time reading and writing. In 1841, Emily and her sister Charlotte traveled to Brussels, Belgium, to study languages and school management. They were hoping to establish a school for girls in England. After the death of one of their aunts, however, the sisters returned home. Emily never went back to the Belgian school, and in fact never left the moorlands again. In 1845, Emily, Charlotte, and another sister, Anne, published a book of their poetry. The book, which was published under the pseudonyms Currer Bell, Ellis Bell, and Acton Bell, was unsuccessful at the time; however, the work is now being looked at with new respect, mainly because of Emily's poetry. Her only novel and greatest artistic achievement, *Wuthering Heights,* appeared two years later along with Charlotte's classic work, *Jane Eyre.* Although Charlotte's work had a much stronger reputation at first, Emily is now considered by many to be the family genius.

About the Selection. Many of Emily Brontë's poems dealt with the relationship between the speaker and nature.

Selections for Additional Reading: The Victorian Age

"Flower in the Crannied Wall"
by Alfred, Lord Tennyson

Flower in the crannied wall,
I pluck you out of the crannies,
I hold you here, root and all, in my hand,
Little flower—but if I could understand
What you are, root and all, and all in all,
I should know what God and man is.

"When I Was One-and-Twenty"
by A. E. Housman

When I was one-and-twenty
I heard a wise man say,
"Give crowns and pounds and guineas[1]
But not your heart away;
Give pearls away and rubies
But keep your fancy free."
But I was one-and-twenty,
No use to talk to me.

When I was one-and-twenty
I heard him say again,
"The heart out of the bosom
Was never given in vain;
'Tis paid with sighs a plenty
And sold for endless rue."
And I am two-and-twenty,
And oh, 'tis true, 'tis true.

"Loveliest of Trees" by A. E. Housman

Loveliest of trees, the cherry now
Is hung with bloom along the bough,
And stands about the woodland ride
Wearing white for Eastertide.

Now, of my threescore years and ten,
Twenty will not come again,
And take from seventy springs a score,
It only leaves me fifty more.

And since to look at things in bloom
Fifty springs are little room,
About the woodlands I will go
To see the cherry hung with snow.

"The Night is Darkening"
by Emily Brontë

The night is darkening round me,
The wild winds coldly blow;
But a tyrant spell has bound me,
And I cannot, cannot go.

The giant trees are bending
Their bare boughs weighed with snow;
The storm is fast descending,
And yet I cannot go.

Clouds beyond clouds above me,
Wastes beyond wastes below;
But nothing drear can move me:
I will not, cannot go.

from *The Subjection of Women*
by John Stuart Mill

The social subordination of women thus stands out an isolated fact in modern social institutions; a solitary breach of what has become their fundamental law; a single relic of an old world of thought and practice exploded in everything else, but retained in the one thing of most universal interest; as if a gigantic dolmen,[2] or a vast temple of Jupiter Olympius, occupied the site of St. Paul's and received daily worship, while the surrounding Christian churches were only resorted to on fasts and festivals. This entire discrepancy between one social fact and all those which accompany it, and the radical opposition between its nature and the progressive movement which is the boast of the modern world, and which has successively swept away everything else of an analogous character, surely affords, to a conscientious observer of human tendencies, serious matter for reflection. It raises a *primâ facie*[3] presumption on the unfavorable side, far outweighing any which custom and usage could in such circumstances create on the favorable; and should at least suffice to make this, like the choice between republicanism and royalty, a balanced question.

1. **crowns . . . guineas.** Different units of money
2. **dolmen.** A neolithic stone monument associated with pagan rites
3. ***primâ facie.*** First view before further examination

"The Slave Ship,"[1] from *Modern Painters*
by John Ruskin
(see painting on page 608)

But I think the noblest sea that Turner has ever painted, and, if so, the noblest certainly ever painted by man, is that of "The Slave Ship," the chief Academy picture of the exhibition of 1840. It is a sunset on the Atlantic after prolonged storm; but the storm is partially lulled, and the torn and streaming rain clouds are moving in scarlet lines to lose themselves in the hollow of the night. The whole surface of sea included in the picture is divided into two ridges of enormous swell, not high, nor local, but a low, broad heaving of the whole ocean, like the lifting of its bosom by deep-drawn breath after the torture of the storm. Between these two ridges the fire of the sunset falls along the trough of the sea, dyeing it with an awful but glorious light, the intense and lurid splendor which burns like gold and bathes like blood. Along this fiery path and valley the tossing waves by which the swell of the sea is restlessly divided lift themselves in dark, indefinite, fantastic forms, each casting a faint and ghastly shadow behind it along the illumined foam. They do not rise everywhere, but three or four together in wild groups, fitfully and furiously, as the under-strength of the swell compels or permits them; leaving between them treacherous spaces of level and whirling water, now lighted with green and lamplike fire, now flashing back the gold of the declining sun, now fearfully shed from above with the indistinguishable images of the burning clouds, which fall upon them in flakes of crimson and scarlet and give to the reckless waves the added motion of their own fiery being. Purple and blue, the lurid shadows of the hollow breakers are cast upon the mist of night, which gathers cold and low, advancing like the shadow of death upon the guilty ship as it labors amidst the lightning of the sea, its thin masts written upon the sky in lines of blood, girded with condemnation in that fearful hue which signs the sky with horror, and mixes its flaming flood with the sunlight, and, cast far along the desolate heave of the sepulchral waves, incarnadines the multitudinous sea.

I believe, if I were reduced to rest Turner's immortality upon any single work, I should choose this. Its daring conception—ideal in the highest sense of the word—is based on the purest truth, and wrought out with the concentrated knowledge of a life; its color is absolutely perfect, not one false or morbid hue in any part or line, and so modulated that every square inch of canvas is a perfect composition; its drawing as accurate as fearless; the ship buoyant, bending, and full of motion; its tones as true as they are wonderful; and the whole picture dedicated to the most sublime of subjects and impressions—completing thus the perfect system of all truth which we have shown to be formed by Turner's works—the power, majesty, and deathfulness of the open, deep, illimitable Sea.

1. **"The Slave Ship."** A painting by Turner, picturing a slave ship at sunset with dead slaves being thrown overboard

FROM *THE SUBJECTION OF WOMEN*

About the Author. John Stuart Mill (1806–1873) was perhaps the most influential thinker of his time. An extremely precocious child, he read Greek at the age of three and received a strict and extensive education under the tutelage of his father.

Primarily an economist and philosopher, John Stuart Mill was elected to Parliament where he introduced the first proposal ever offered to a legislative body regarding the rights of women. A few years later, in 1868, he published his last work, *The Subjection of Women.*

Among Mill's major works are his essays *On Liberty* and *Considerations on Representative Government.*

About the Selection. The public response to ***The Subjection of Women*** was extremely harsh. Women did not receive equal voting rights in England until 1928.

LITERARY NOTE

Some people believe that Mill's longtime friend Harriet Taylor was responsible for the bulk of the ideas expressed in the essay, and even for much of the writing. Students may be interested in researching this theory, as well as Harriet Taylor's life and her relationship with Mill.

"THE SLAVE SHIP"

About the Author. John Ruskin (1819–1900) was an important art critic and social reformer in Victorian England. As a boy, he developed an interest in art and architecture. Later at Oxford, he studied art seriously, which led him to write the five-volume work *Modern Painters.*

About the Selection. Ruskin believed that art reflects the morality of society and wrote numerous essays on the subject. He lectured extensively on social change.

He was a brilliant writer whose work dictated how Victorians would think about art. Ruskin believed that the art that one gravitated toward reflected one's intellect and spirituality.

LESSON OVERVIEW

Informative Writing

ANALYZING ART

Language, Grammar, and Style

SENTENCE VARIETY

GUIDED WRITING *Software*

See the Guided Writing Software for an extended version of this lesson that includes printable graphic organizers, extensive student models and student-friendly checklists, and self-, peer, and teacher evaluation features.

Examining the Model

Read aloud the Professional Model to students and have them listen for the description Ruskin provides. Tell them that their own writing should strive for the same evocative detail.

"All great art is the work of the whole living creature, body and soul, and chiefly of the soul."

—*John Ruskin*

Guided Writing

ANALYZING ART

Something strange happens when you begin to look closely at a work of art: you discover hidden parts and pieces. And the minute you begin to ask yourself how all these pieces fit together and why they work as they do, you enter analysis, one of the finest vehicles for stretching your intellect.

WRITING ASSIGMENT. In this lesson, you will choose a British painting from the Victorian era, look closely, and write an analysis that springs from your own careful observation. You will think about how this painting connects with the literature of the time and see where your analysis takes you.

EXAMINING THE MODEL. The opening of this critical analysis introduces the reader to the painting with a description of the piece, the painter's name, and the date of his work. A critical analysis typically starts out with an intriguing fact, description, or story and then moves on to express a strong statement or viewpoint that explains or evaluates.

The writer takes a stand and then proves or shows the reader why he or she holds that stand. Which sentences in the opening paragraph would you say are the thesis or main idea of this analysis?

What are several points that the author makes in the body of the essay to show that the painting is "the noblest sea ever painted by man"? Are the examples convincing?

Professional Model

"The Slave Ship," from *Modern Painters*
by John Ruskin, page 883 (see painting on page 608)

But I think the noblest sea that Turner has ever painted, and, if so, the noblest certainly ever painted by man, is that of "The Slave Ship," the chief Academy picture of the exhibition of 1840. It is a sunset on the Atlantic after prolonged storm; but the storm is partially lulled, and the torn and streaming rain clouds are moving in scarlet lines to lose themselves in the hollow of the night. The whole surface of sea included in the picture is divided into two ridges of enormous swell, not high, nor local, but a low, broad heaving of the whole ocean, like the lifting of its bosom by deep-drawn breath after the torture of the storm. Between these two ridges the fire of the sunset falls along the trough of the sea, dyeing it with an awful but glorious light, the intense and lurid splendor which burns like gold and bathes like blood. Along this fiery path and valley the tossing waves by which the swell of the sea is restlessly divided lift themselves in dark, indefinite, fantastic forms, each casting a faint and ghastly shadow behind it along the illumined foam. They do not rise everywhere, but three or four together in wild groups, fitfully and furiously, as the under-strength of the swell compels or permits them; leaving between them treacherous spaces of level and whirling water, now lighted with green and lamplike fire, now flashing back the gold of the declining sun, now fearfully shed from above with the indistinguishable images of the burning clouds, which fall upon them in flakes of crimson and scarlet and give to the reckless waves the added motion of their own fiery being. Purple and blue, the lurid shadows of the hollow breakers are cast upon the mist of night, which gathers cold and low, advancing like the shadow of death upon the guilty ship as it labors amidst the lightning of the sea, its thin masts written upon the sky in lines of blood, girded with condemnation in that fearful hue which signs the sky with horror, and mixes its flaming flood with the sunlight, and, cast far along the desolate heave of the sepulchral waves, incarnadines the multitudinous sea.

I believe, if I were reduced to rest Turner's immortality upon any single work, I should choose this. Its daring conception—ideal in the highest sense of the word—is based on the purest truth, and wrought out with the concentrated knowledge of a life; its color is absolutely perfect, not one false or morbid hue in any part or line, and so modulated that every square inch of canvas is a perfect composition; its drawing as accurate as fearless; the ship buoyant, bending, and full of motion; its tones as true as they are wonderful; and the whole picture dedicated to the most sublime of subjects and impressions—completing thus the perfect system of all truth which we have shown to be formed by Turner's works—the power, majesty, and deathfulness of the open, deep, illimitable Sea.

Prewriting

Writing with a Plan. A critical analysis is more than a description of a work of art. Analysis makes sense of a subject by asking **what**, **how**, and **why** questions. What are you seeing in the painting in terms of composition and color? How do these parts add to the whole? What is the context of the painting? That is, when was it painted and what were the historical circumstances? Does the painting tell a story? How does the painting relate to the literature and thought of its time period? How does the painting hold up to our modern sensibilities?

For this assignment, choose a British painting from the Victorian era, 1832–1900, one that you have some feelings about. If you can, try to see paintings firsthand in a museum. Many local university and city museums have paintings from the Victorian era in their collections. Libraries also have many art

A Few Terms For Art Analysis

Color
intensity — degree of purity of color value — degree of lightness or darkness
temperature — warm or cool

Composition
combination of parts; ordering or arrangement of elements to make a whole

Focal Point
the center of concentration, attraction, or attention

Narrative
the story the painting tells

Unity
the wholeness of the design

INDIVIDUAL LEARNING STRATEGIES

Motivation
Focus on the points made in the lesson in Analyzing Art. In this introduction, students are asked to write a close analysis of a painting and consider how the painting connects with Victorian literature. Ask them to discuss how a painting differs from a piece of literature in the way it conveys meaning and information. Encourage students to discuss the elements of painting as outlined on page 885.

Reading Proficiency
Encourage students to read the Guided Writing lesson one section at a time, summarizing each section as they work through the lesson.

English Language Learning
Go over the terms for art analysis on this page. Be sure students understand the goal of the essay they will write. They should not just describe the features of the painting but write about its message and how that message relates to the literature of Victorian-era England.

Special Needs
Ask students to discuss what a person can learn from a painting. What kinds of paintings do they like? What kinds of paintings do they think are not particularly nice to look at, but which convey important messages?

Enrichment
Students may wish to research the artistic movements of the 19th century. Who were the major painters of the time? In what ways had the style changed from previous centuries? Students may write a brief report to be delivered to the class before the rest of the class begins their research.

Prewriting

WRITING WITH A PLAN
Students should select a painting that has a theme similar to one of the works of literature in this unit. Refer students to the Language Arts Survey 2.1, "The Writing Process," and 2.2, "Prewriting" to give them a review of the writing process.

Prewriting

FINDING YOUR VOICE
This section introduces the idea of voice. Refer students to the Language Arts Survey 2.5, "Finding Your Voice." Tell students that, while they might make conscious decisions in shaping their voice, their writing will reveal voice as they proceed.

IDENTIFYING YOUR AUDIENCE
Suggest that students write their essay for a high school student. Have students discuss the different ways they would approach this essay with such a student, as opposed to someone older than themselves. Refer students to the Language Arts Survey 2.4, "Identifying Your Audience."

Graphic Organizer

See the Guided Writing Resource for a blackline master of the Graphic Organizer for this lesson.

Finding Your Voice. Art criticism should reflect a genuine, thoughtful voice. Whether you are questioning or full of conviction, you will want to use your natural voice, avoiding fancy or abstract words.

Identifying Your Audience. Write your critical analysis for your peers and others who enjoy art. Assume that your reader is an intelligent person who has not seen the painting you are analyzing and will want to know what makes the piece worth looking at.

books with excellent reproductions. You could also check the Internet for art museum websites.

Be aware that models in this lesson discuss very early Victorian work. You may want to look at the later painters and compare their art to Realism and Naturalism, the literary movements that followed Romanticism.

Once you have chosen a painting, ask and answer questions that will help you generate ideas. Copy the following graphic organizer onto your own paper and write as many responses as you can.

Fred Harnett began his graphic organizer as follows:

Student Model—Graphic Organizer

Painting:
The Cornfield, by John Constable, 1826

What are the most surprising, remarkable or memorable qualities of this painting? Write your first and strongest impressions.

- moody clouds
- spots of sunlight
- dark trees
- golden field
- peaceful
- lush
- grand
- old fashioned

Select the three strongest art elements in the painting and explain why they are notable.

- color: rich greens and browns, complex blues, not intense but mixed with other colors — you can almost smell the earth and trees and wind
- composition: the trees on either side of the painting create a passage where your eye goes to see the fields and the hills beyond
- unity: the green in the trees matches the green on the grass. The light on the trees matches the light on the ground, the sheep and the golden field.

List three or more connections between this painting and the literature of the Victorian era.

early Victorian (actually Constable painted this before Victoria took the throne)
Romanticism/Romantic characteristics in *The Cornfield*:

- Nature
- dramatic emotional sky
- panorama
- pastoral — the beauty of the country
- children and animals — represent innocence, simplicity
- nostalgia — shows a time when things were better

Write two or three possible thesis statements for your analysis. These should clearly state your explanation of the painting and possibly include reasons for your opinion.
- The painting expresses an old fashioned vision of the countryside.
- This painting shows the Romantics' longing for the past.
- This is a sentimental piece about innocence.

Circle the thesis statement you think has the most promise.

Now list below at least three ideas, examples, or reasons that support your thesis.

—everything is perfect, in harmony, the trees are balanced, the colors are balanced and repeating

—the subjects are about old fashioned things: farming, drinking fresh water from a stream, clean air

—the sky is panoramic and the trees are huge — nature rules in this painting

Drafting

Use your prewriting notes to write a quick first draft. Try to begin your analysis with a sentence that makes your reader want to know more. You may include bits of biographical information about the painter, compelling elements in the painting, or historical notes.

State your opinion in the thesis which is usually placed toward the end of the introductory paragraph. In the body of the analysis, support your opinion with examples of the painting's elements and literary comparisons. If you quote directly from a book, remember to use quotation marks.

Conclude your review with a strong statement of your opinion. Try to end with an intriguing sentence.

Self- and Peer Evaluation

After you write your rough draft, complete a self-evaluation of your piece. If time allows, have one or two other students give you peer evaluations.

- Does the opening paragraph contain a thesis statement that expresses a viewpoint about the painting? Is the thesis clear?
- How does each paragraph in the body of the paper support the writer's analysis of the painting? Do the supporting paragraphs include examples from both the painting and the literature of the times? If not, what kind of examples are needed and where?

Language, Grammar, and Style

Effective Transitions

Identifying Transitions. Here is one tip you can use to improve coherence in your writing.

Repetition/Paraphrase = Echo Transition

One professional writer, Max Gunther, calls this technique an echo transition because you connect ideas by repeating or echoing phrases or words. To create a connection between paragraphs, find words or phrases from the last sentence of a paragraph to use in the first sentence of the next paragraph.

EXAMPLE:

See how Fred used the echo transition to strengthen the connection between these two paragraphs:

"The repetition of colors give the painting a calm feeling. The green in the trees matches the green on the grass. The light on the trees echoes the light on the ground, the sheep and the golden field. These repeating elements give the painting a sense of unity and peace.

The composition of the painting adds to the sense of peace as well. The trees on either side of the painting create a passage where your eye goes to see the fields and the hills beyond. They frame the beautiful pastoral scene."

continued on page 888

Drafting

Encourage students to work through the Graphic Organizer on pages 886–887 to help identify their thesis, build their introductory paragraph, and write their body and concluding paragraphs.

Self- and Peer Evaluation

Have students use the checklist on page 887–888 for self- and peer evaluation. The checklist is intended to act as a student-friendly rubric that should help students identify specific evidence of writing strengths and areas needing improvement. Make sure they provide concrete suggestions for improvement or specific evidence of why the writing works. A blackline master of the checklist is available in the Guided Writing Resource.

Language, Grammar, and Style

Effective Transitions

LESSON OVERVIEW

In this lesson, students will be asked to do the following:
- Identify Transitions, 887
- Fix Transitions, 888
- Use Transitions, 888

INTRODUCING THE SKILL

Explain to students that learning to use effective transitions will help them improve all of their writing, not just informative essays. Using effective transitions helps guide the reader and keeps the writing cohesive and orderly.

PREVIEWING THE SKILL
Refer students to the Language Arts Survey 2.35, "Using Transitions Effectively." This is the basis for the Language, Grammar, and Style lesson.

PRACTICING THE SKILL
For additional practice, have students work through the exercises in the Language, Grammar, and Style Resource Book 2.35, "Using Transitions Effectively," located in the Teacher's Resource Book.

Revising and Proofreading

A handout of the proofreading checklist found in the Language Arts Survey 2.45 is available in the Teacher's Resource Kit, Guided Writing Resource Book 2.45. Students critiquing their classmates' work may be interested in using common proofreader's symbols, which are found in the Language Arts Survey 2.44, "Using Proofreader's Marks."

By repeating the word peace, the second paragraph shows a clear connection to the first. The reader is told that new information will now be added to the concept of calm or peaceful feelings.

The echo transition guides your reader from one point to another, and your reader will call it good writing when he or she can follow you perfectly.

Fixing transitions. Now try your hand at connecting the following paragraphs by using an echo transition. Paraphrase or repeat words from the end of one paragraph in the beginning of the next:

The romantics presented a heroic and picturesque world: they portrayed life as we would wish it to be. The realists sought to accurately reflect life as if seems to the ordinary reader.

Naturalism presented subjects with a scientific and objective attitude. Writers spoke of bodily functions and characters driven by grim desires, such as greed and lust, characters who seemed to be pushed about by circumstances.

Using transitions. Find and underline places in your writing where you move from one idea to the next. Do you have a transition there? How could you improve the flow by using either transition words or an echo transition between paragraphs? Add them in as needed and read your piece aloud to see how it sounds.

- Would this art analysis benefit from the addition of biographical or historical information? If so, where would it be appropriate?
- Does the essay contain excessive description? How and where could this be more concise?
- Does each paragraph connect to the paragraphs around it? Where are transitions needed?
- Are the titles of paintings and historical events capitalized? Are titles of paintings italized or, if the paper is handwritten, are the titles underlined ?

Revising and Proofreading

Review your self- and peer evaluations and revise your writing according to these comments. Is your viewpoint about the painting clearly stated in your opening paragraph? Have you kept the descriptions and historical summaries to a minimum and used your skills of critical analysis to explain the painting?

When you are satisfied with your draft, revise it for errors in spelling, grammar, punctuation, capitalization and other details.

Student Model—Revised

The Cornfield by John Constable, 1826
Analysis by Fred Harnett

John Constable's *The Cornfield* is like a Romantic poem come to life. You have a young shepherd drinking from a stream, sheep ambling down a path, fluffy clouds, huge trees, and a golden field of corn in the distance. Everything about this painting speaks to the Romantics' longing for the peaceful, pastoral life of old.

The Romantic poets like Wordsworth and Shelley focused on a return to nature in their work. They valued solitude, panorama, and moods. In Constable's painting we see these elements in the woods and sky. The rich, intense greens and browns of the trees and earth give the painting the feeling of nature's lushness and the muted blues of the sky create a summer mood you can almost smell.

The repetition of colors give the painting a calm feeling. The green in the trees matches the green on the grass. The light on the trees echoes the light on the ground, the sheep and the golden field. These repeating elements give the painting a sense of unity and peace.

The composition of the painting adds to the sense of peace as well. The trees on either side of the painting create a passage where your eye goes to see the fields and the hills beyond. They frame the beautiful pastoral scene.

The Cornfield is an old fashioned picture with a feeling of innocence. The child, the sheep, the panoramic sky suggest a better time, when people were free from society to live as part of nature, or in Wordsworth's words: "A blended holiness of earth and sky."

Publishing and Presenting

Consider creating a classroom or hall bulletin board of students' critical analyses. Attach the typed essays along with black and white or color copies of the paintings you have analyzed.

Reflecting

What new insights have you gained about the painting, about the historical time period, or about your own artistic tastes from your critical analysis?

There was a time when a painting could only be viewed by standing in front of it. Now that film and video dominate our lives, we are frequently removed from artwork as objects. That is, we see artwork secondhand on a screen or page and lose some of the ability for a piece to affect us physically. When you see a painting on the page of a book, or on a computer screen, you don't know whether it is the size of a postage stamp or a wall. What other elements of a work of art are lost when you view a reproduction instead of the real object?

Tips For Capitalizing

EXAMPLES

Mona Lisa, The Banjo Lesson, The Persistence of Memory

Capitalize the names of historical events or times.

EXAMPLES

French Revolution, Victorian era

For cultural movements, capitalize names that come from proper nouns. Otherwise, use lowercase unless you need the capitals to distinguish the word from its general meaning.

EXAMPLES

naturalism, neoclassicism, Aristotelian, Romanesque, romantic (or *Romantic* if you need to show that you are talking about a movement and not a feeling)

"There is a logic of colors, and it is with this alone, and not with the logic of the brain, that the painter should conform."

—*Paul Cézanne*

Publishing and Presenting

Students might also like to present their writing as oral reports to a larger group of art history students (if your school offers such a course), literature students, and perhaps even history students.

Reflecting

You may want to have students write about the questions presented in Reflecting and submit them when they turn in their papers to you for evaluation.

ADDITIONAL RESOURCES

UNIT 9 RESOURCE BOOK
- Vocabulary Worksheet: Unit 9
- Study Guide: Unit 9 Test
- Unit 9 Test

VOCABULARY DEVELOPMENT

Give students the following exercise: Write a dialogue for two people that incorporates fifteen words from the list on page 890. Then, with a partner, practice both dialogues aloud, paying attention to the correct pronunciation of the new vocabulary words.

UNIT 9 REVIEW
The Victorian Age

Words for Everyday Use

Check your knowledge of the following vocabulary words from the selections in this unit. Write short sentences using these words in context to make the meaning clear. To review the definition or usage of a word, refer to the page number listed or the Glossary of Words for Everyday Use.

ambling, 778
amicably, 875
apprise, 859
asunder, 854
avenge, 822
avert, 859
calamity, 858
canker, 789
certitude, 815
compose, 859
compulsion, 852
contemptuously, 867
cotillion, 877
countenance, 781, 800
dais, 843
dappled, 833
daunt, 853
demur, 809
derive, 792, 858
diffusive, 795
discerning, 785
drearisome, 821
effaced, 879
fain, 878
fickle, 789
gaunt, 825
halcyon, 843
idle, 852
incongruity, 854
inexplicable, 854
mouldered, 789
munificence, 801
officious, 801
peruse, 853
profusely, 810
prominent, 858
redoubled, 854
rejoin, 856
ruminating, 858
satiated, 877
stagnate, 790
steep, 851
stipple, 833
strand, 814
tremulous, 814
torpor, 877
treacherous, 859
tumult, 794
turbid, 814
undulating, 876
vehemence, 855
vigilant, 854
wane, 780
yearn, 785

Literary Tools

Define the following terms, giving concrete examples of how they are used in the selections in this unit. To review a term, refer to the page number indicated or to the Handbook of Literary Terms.

alliteration, 833, 841, 846
allusion, 813
character, 784
concrete universal, 821
description, 873
dialect, 819
diction, 799
dramatic monologue, 784, 799
elegiac lyric, 788
fantasy, 863
flashback, 873
foil, 777
ghost story, 850
image, 788
irony, 819
metaphor, 824, 837, 841
mood, 850
motivation, 784
paradox, 803
parallelism, 841
repetition, 829, 835
riddle, 863
satire, 821
setting, 850
simile, 824, 841
slant rhyme, 824
sonnet, 829
sprung rhythm, 833
stanza, 824
symbol, 777, 813
theme, 803, 837
tone, 846
understatement, 819

Reflecting on Your Reading

Genre Studies

1. **The Dramatic Monologue.** Compare the following dramatic monologues from the unit: "Ulysses," "My Last Duchess," and "Andrea del Sarto." What moment of crisis is presented in each poem? Who is the speaker in each poem? Who is being addressed? What does the speaker reveal about himself through his speech?

2. **Lyric Poetry.** Contrast the styles of Christina Rossetti and Gerard Manley Hopkins. What differences can you find in the rhythms of their poems; in their diction, or word choice; and in their use of figurative language?

Thematic Studies

3. **Challenges to Conventional Thinking.** The Victorian Age has become synonymous with smug, complacent, conventional thinking. However, many writers of that period challenged accepted ideas. What conventional ideas are challenged in the following selections: "The Man He Killed," "Channel Firing," and the selection from *The Subjection of Women*?

4. **Aging and Mortality.** Examine the following selections: "Ulysses," "To an Athlete Dying Young," and "Spring and Fall: To a Young Child." Compare and contrast the ideas about aging and dying expressed in these poems.

Historical and Biographical Studies

5. **Biographical Criticism.** Do some research on the lives of George Eliot, Emily Brontë, Charlotte Brontë, and Lewis Carroll. Explain what elements in the selections in this unit can be traced to experiences in the lives of the authors.

REFLECTING ON YOUR READING

The prompts in "Reflecting on Your Reading" are suitable as topics for research papers. Refer to the Language Arts Survey 5.18–5.45, "Research Skills." (To evaluate research papers, see the evaluation forms for writing, revising, and proofreading in the Assessment Resource.)

The prompts in "Reflecting on Your Reading can also be adapted for use as topics for oral reports or debates. Refer students to the Language Arts Survey 4, Speaking and Listening. (To evaluate these projects, see the evaluation forms in the Assessment Resource.)

UNIT SKILLS OUTLINE

Literary Skills and Concepts
Alliteration, 932
Allusion, 907, 948, 963, 976
Caesura, 956
Diction, 937
Figurative Language, 952
Free Verse, 976
Image, 907
Image, 916, 932, 956
Irony, 945
Irony, 952, 960
Objective Correlative, 916
Oxymoron, 956
Point of View, 966
Prose Poem, 966
Pun, 941
Rhyme Scheme, 907, 928, 941, 971
Sight Rhyme, 971
Simile, 937
Simile, 960
Sonnet, 928
Sonnet, 945
Speaker, 916
Stanza, 971
Symbol, 907, 921, 941
Theme, 921, 928, 948
Tone, 916
Tone, 966
Verbal Irony, 932
Villanelle, 941

Writing Skills and Concepts
Letter-Writing Campaign, 970
Public Service Announcement, 927, 940, 955
Writing a Dialogue, 936
Writing a Film Introduction, 965
Writing a Poetry Explication, 980
Writing a Resume, 915
Writing a Summary, 975
Writing an Introduction, 979
Writing and Performing a Play, 970

Language, Grammar, and Style
Adjectives and Participles, 915
Avoiding Split Infinitives, 965
Classifying Pronouns, 970
Combining Sentences, 959
Effective Titles, 985
Functions of Sentences, 951
Hyphens, Dashes, and Capital Letters, 979
Imperative Sentences, 944
Inverted Sentences, 931
Proofreading, 955
Sentence Fragments, 940
Sentence Run-Ons, 920
The Subjunctive Mood, 975
Verbals: Participles and Gerunds, 936

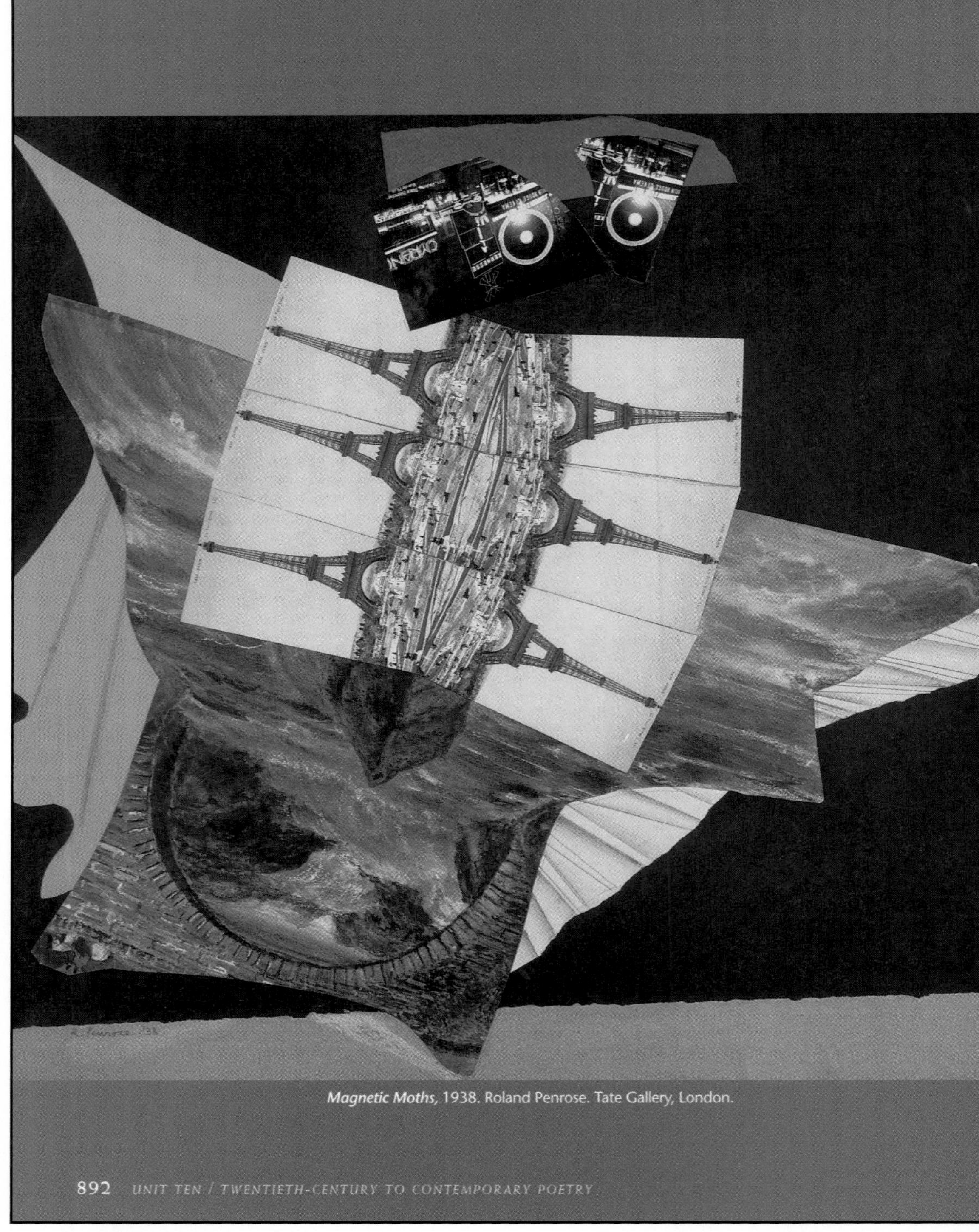

Magnetic Moths, 1938. Roland Penrose. Tate Gallery, London.

GOALS/OBJECTIVES

Studying this unit will enable students to

- interpret and appreciate twentieth-century British poetry
- describe how English-speaking writers responded to the social and economic upheaval of the twentieth century
- name and describe the literary accomplishments of some of the main figures of twentieth-century poetry
- define *rhyme scheme, image, allusion, symbol, speaker, tone, objective correlative, theme, sonnet, diction, simile, pun, villanelle, verbal irony, alliteration, irony, figurative language, oxymoron, caesura, tone, point of view, prose poem, stanza, sight rhyme*, and *free verse* and recognize the use of these techniques in the selections
- write a poetry explication
- create a good title

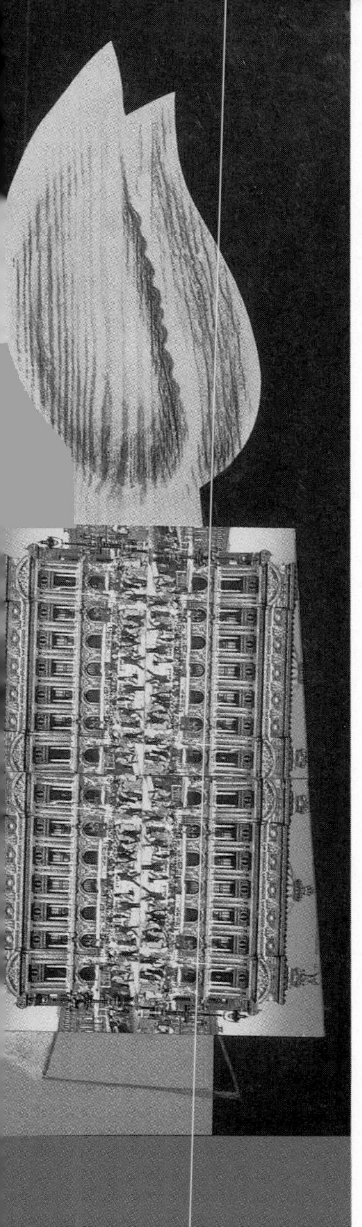

And now for something completely different.

—Monty Python's Flying Circus

CROSS-CURRICULAR CONNECTIONS

Arts and Humanities
Horoscopes, 912
Apocalypse Poetry, 913
Gorillas in the Mist, 922
Millennium: Tribal Wisdom and the Modern World, 922
Ryan's Daughter, 933
How Many Miles to Babylon?, 933
Poems by Stephen Spender, 938
Dangerous Minds, 941
W.H. Auden Biography, 946
Pieter Bruegel's Art, 948
16th-Century Dutch and Flemish Paintings, 948
Performance of the play, *Stevie*, 952
Greek Mythology, 957
Odysseus Reference Poems, 976

Mathematics and Sciences
Freudian Criticism, 923
World Hunger Organizations, 967

Social Studies
Judith Wright in Australia, 972

Applied Arts
Performance of the play, Stevie, 952
Bread-Baking, 967

TEACHING THE MULTIPLE INTELLIGENCES

Musical
British National Anthem, 928
Dylan Thomas Recordings, 942

Spatial
Sensory Details Chart, 917
Gorillas in the Mist, 922
Millennium: Tribal Wisdom and the Modern World, 922
Ryan's Daughter, 933
How Many Miles to Babylon?, 933
Dangerous Minds, 941
Pieter Bruegel's Art, 948
16th-Century Dutch and Flemish Paintings, 948
Performance of the play, *Stevie*, 952

Kinesthetic
Performance of the play, *Stevie*, 952
Bread-Baking, 967

ADDITIONAL RESOURCES

Unit 10 Resource Book
- Selection Check Test 4.10.1
- Selection Test 4.10.2

ADDITIONAL QUESTIONS AND ACTIVITIES

Ask students if they think Yeats's apocalyptic lines are applicable today. Do they feel "things" are falling apart, coming together, or staying about the same? Are innocent things in jeopardy? Ask them to compare and contrast the events of the twentieth century with their own expectations of the century to come as they read this unit introduction. When they have finished reading the introduction, they can write a comparative essay explaining their thoughts on how the next hundred years will differ from the last hundred years.

Quotables

"I have many times asked myself whether there can be more potent advocates of peace upon earth through the years to come than this massed multitude of silent witnesses to the desolation of war."

—King George V
(on the battlefield cemeteries in Flanders)

TWENTIETH-CENTURY TO CONTEMPORARY BRITISH LITERATURE (1900–PRESENT)

The Twentieth Century

At the beginning of the twentieth century, Britain controlled a vast empire and was arguably the wealthiest, most powerful country in the world. During the following decades, Britain lost most of its colonial possessions, fought in two bloody and prolonged world wars, and experienced repeated economic depressions. At times, **William Butler Yeats's** (1865–1939) lines, written in "The Second Coming" (1919), seemed like a prophecy come true:

Things fall apart; the center cannot hold;
Mere anarchy is loosed upon the world,
The blood-dimmed tide is loosed, and everywhere
The ceremony of innocence is drowned.

The Edwardian and Georgian Eras

Like many Irish writers of the early part of the century, Yeats felt a deep conflict between his nationalism and his loathing for the ambitions of the emerging Irish middle class. During his middle years, Yeats spent considerable time in the homes of the privileged, most notably at the country estate of his friend and fellow author of the **Celtic Twilight**, or **Irish Renaissance**, **Lady Augusta Gregory** (1852–1932). In these homes he conceived the idea of "the ceremony of innocence," for he admired the cultivation possible among the upper classes, who had leisure to enjoy the arts, literature, and philosophy. Such attitudes came easily in the early years of the twentieth century. When Queen Victoria died in 1901, her son became King Edward VII. The **Edwardian Age**, from 1901 to 1910, was characterized by extravagance among the wealthy and relative ease among the middle and lower classes, who were enjoying near full employment and such amenities as universal education, public libraries, and male suffrage, introduced during the Victorian Age. The **Georgian Age**, named for George V, king from 1910 to 1936, proved to be the last golden moment before the mid-century darkness. Even in that time, many writers were disturbed by inequities between the social classes. Georgian literature dealing with such inequities includes **George**

Literary Events

➤ = British Events

➤1905. E. M. Forster (1879–1970) publishes *Where Angels Fear to Tread*

➤1906. Siegfied Sassoon publishes *Poems*

➤1912. Joseph Conrad publishes *Twixt Land and Sea*, a collection of stories

➤1913. D. H. Lawrence publishes *Sons and Lovers*

➤1914. James Joyce publishes *Dubliners* and *A Portrait of the Artist as a Young Man*

➤1914. *Pygmalion* by George Bernard Shaw is performed at His Majesty's Theater, London

1900 — 1905 — 1910

Historical Events

➤1901. Queen Victoria dies; Edward VII becomes king

➤1910. Edward VII dies; reign of George V begins

➤1910. South Africa is established as a dominion within the British Empire

➤1914. World War I begins following the assassination of Franz Ferdinand, Archduke of Austria

Bernard Shaw's (1856–1950) play *Pygmalion* and **Katherine Mansfield's** (1888–1923) story **"The Garden-Party."**

World War I

In the early years of the century, England was allied with France and Russia, and Austria-Hungary was allied with Germany. In 1914, a Serbian nationalist murdered Archduke Franz Ferdinand, heir to the throne of Austria-Hungary. Austria declared war on Serbia, and Russia entered the war to protect Serbia, another Slavic state. Soon France and Germany entered the conflict, and Germany invaded Belgium, a neutral country that lay in its path toward France. This violation of Belgian neutrality led England into one of the costliest wars in its history.

Battle of the Somme, August 1916.

None of the participants in **The Great War,** later called **World War I,** knew at first what lay ahead. In the past, war had been by modern sights relatively benign, even, some thought, glorious. However, modern technology made possible a new kind of warfare. Submarines, battleships, barbed wire, exploding bullets, machine guns, hand grenades, poison gas, and tanks led to carnage on an enormous scale. By the end of the war in 1918, nearly nine million people had died, including almost eight hundred thousand from Britain alone. Many of these casualties resulted from trench warfare, in which both sides dug into foxholes along the Western Front between France and Switzerland. For three years soldiers fought in rain-filled, rat-infested trenches, bombarded by heavy artillery and by poison gas. To many who experienced this hell, old slogans about the glories of war seemed not just foolish but demented.

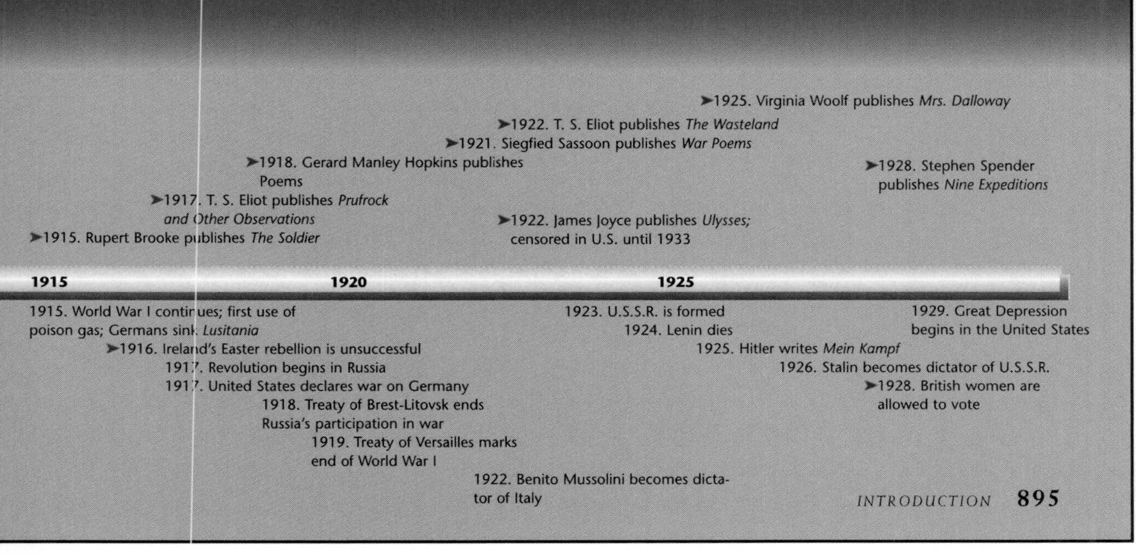

➤1925. Virginia Woolf publishes *Mrs. Dalloway*
➤1922. T. S. Eliot publishes *The Wasteland*
➤1921. Siegfied Sassoon publishes *War Poems*
➤1918. Gerard Manley Hopkins publishes Poems
➤1928. Stephen Spender publishes *Nine Expeditions*
➤1917. T. S. Eliot publishes *Prufrock and Other Observations*
➤1922. James Joyce publishes *Ulysses;* censored in U.S. until 1933
➤1915. Rupert Brooke publishes *The Soldier*
1915
1920
1925
1915. World War I continues; first use of poison gas; Germans sink *Lusitania*
➤1916. Ireland's Easter rebellion is unsuccessful
1917. Revolution begins in Russia
1917. United States declares war on Germany
1918. Treaty of Brest-Litovsk ends Russia's participation in war
1919. Treaty of Versailles marks end of World War I
1922. Benito Mussolini becomes dictator of Italy
1923. U.S.S.R. is formed
1924. Lenin dies
1925. Hitler writes *Mein Kampf*
1926. Stalin becomes dictator of U.S.S.R.
1929. Great Depression begins in the United States
➤1928. British women are allowed to vote

CROSS-CURRICULAR CONNECTIONS

History. As an example of the scale of destruction of The Great War, in the First Battle of the Somme (July–October 1916), the British sustained four hundred twenty thousand casualties, the French one hundred ninety-four thousand, and the Germans four hundred forty thousand—over a million dead and wounded in all. In 1916 alone, the Italians sustained five hundred thousand casualties. Although the new technology of warfare left many of the younger generation of Europeans maimed or blind, still more extensive than the physical damage were the social consequences: poor, middle class, and rich alike in country after country were broken and embittered. The failure to heal the social wounds of The Great War led to its continuation in 1939.

ADDITIONAL QUESTIONS AND ACTIVITIES

Mustard gas, which was used in World War I, was later outlawed. Students can research the effects of mustard gas and other gases and then write an editorial urging continued vigilance in the ban on chemical warfare.

ADDITIONAL QUESTIONS AND ACTIVITIES

Students can do additional reading to understand the central importance of the Russian Revolution in twentieth-century history. Students might also research the career of Josef Stalin or examine why the Russian Communist experiment had failed by the late twentieth century.

BIOGRAPHICAL NOTE

George Orwell was the son of a minor British civil servant in India. Though he attended the British preparatory school Eton and could have gone on to a university, he opted to enter the civil service. As a police official in Burma he came face to face with the contradictions of British imperialism, an experience that proved radicalizing. He resigned his job and then deliberately sought out the companionship of the poor of London and Paris. Though he fought against Fascism in Spain during its civil war, by the end of that conflict he also found himself battling Com-munists who had turned on their political opponents. From this turnabout he learned the frightening lesson that Communism and Fascism have common totalitarian elements. His brilliant allegorical exposé of Soviet Communism, *Animal Farm,* appeared in 1945; his last work, *Nineteen Eighty-four,* the anti-utopian depiction of totalitarianism taken to its logical extreme, was published a year before his death in 1950.

THE WAR POETS

Rupert Brooke (1887–1915), who died of blood poisoning during the war, typified for the English a whole generation of patriotic young men who sacrificed all for their country. His poetry, Georgian in its optimism and nationalistic pride, helped to sustain English spirits during this time when the country lost many of its young people. **Wilfred Owen** (1893–1918) and **Siegfried Sassoon** (1886–1967) depicted in their poetry the other side of war, the massive slaughter and waste that resulted from mechanized killing.

THE RUSSIAN REVOLUTION

Unable to sustain the costs of war, the Russian monarchy toppled in 1917. Czar Nicholas II and his family were executed, and a short-lived democratic government was established. Soon afterward, the **October Revolution** brought **Lenin** (born Vladimir Ilyich Ulanov, 1870–1924) to the head of the first Communist state. This state was founded on the ideas of German economist **Karl Marx** (1818–1883), who did much of his writing while in exile in Britain. Marx theorized that capitalist excesses would lead inevitably to worldwide revolution and to the establishment of worker-run states. These states would eventually evolve into perfect democracies operating for the common good, taking from each "according to his means" and giving to "each according to his needs." In Britain, many idealistic young men and women, such as poets **Stephen Spender** (1909–1995) and **W. H. Auden** (1907–1973), flirted with Communism and Socialism but later became disillusioned when they saw the results of the Russian Revolution. Russia under Lenin and his successor **Joseph Stalin** (1879–1953) turned out to be not a worker's paradise but a ruthless dictatorship that suppressed free speech and massacred or imprisoned citizens who voiced opposition to government policies. The English novelist **George Orwell** (1903–1950) at first supported the Russian Revolution and its ideals. However, seeing what became of those ideals, Orwell bitterly critiqued the revolution, writing notable attacks on totalitarian dictatorship, including ***Animal Farm*** and ***Nineteen Eighty-four.***

BRITAIN AFTER WORLD WAR I

Socialist Politics and the Labour Party. With most of an entire generation of its young men dead, and deeply in debt because of wartime expenditures, postwar

LITERARY EVENTS

➤ = British Events

➤1930. W. H. Auden publishes *Poems*

➤1930. Virginia Woolf publishes *A Room of One's Own*; T. S. Eliot publishes "Ash Wednesday"

➤1936. Dylan Thomas publishes *Twenty-five Poems*

➤1938. Elizabeth Bowen publishes *The Death of the Heart*

1930 — 1935 — 1940

HISTORICAL EVENTS

1933. Nazi party gains control of Reichstag; Adolf Hitler becomes dictator

1936. Edward VIII becomes king and then abdicates

➤1938. British Prime Minister Neville Chamberlain accedes to Hitler's demands of Czechoslovakia

1939. Germany invades Poland, beginning World War II

1941. Germans invade Soviet Union; Japanese bomb Pearl Harbor

1944. D-day—Allied forces invade Normandy

Britain reeled. The period saw economic depression and radical demand for change. Socialism gained ground, supported by labor unions, by working people who felt they deserved more in return for their contributions to the war effort, and by radical members of the intelligentsia. The socialists believed in strong, centralized government as a means for achieving equality among the social classes. In the elections of 1922, the once-weak Labour Party came in second to the Conservatives. In 1924, Labour won, installing the first Socialist prime minister. During the rest of the twentieth century, the Conservative and Labour parties vied for power, but for most of the century, socialist ideas held sway. Major businesses were nationalized, and government-run national health care was established.

Demonstration of the unemployed, Tower Hill, 1930.

The Women's Movement. During this time, women in Britain gained enormous ground. In 1918, after years of protest, including pamphleteering and marching in the streets, women of age thirty and over won the right to vote. In 1928, this right was extended to women who had reached the age of twenty-one, putting British women for the first time on a par with British men. However, the right to vote was but the beginning of a continuing struggle for equal opportunity. Nowhere, perhaps, have the motivating forces for this struggle been more eloquently expressed than in **Virginia Woolf's** (1882–1941) ***A Room of One's Own*** (1929). In this classic document of the women's movement, Woolf describes the tragic loss that occurs when women are barred from achieving their full potential.

Irish Rebellion. At home, the British faced protest against traditional ideas. In Ireland, they faced armed conflict. Clamor for Irish independence among Catholics had reached a fever pitch at the turn of the century, but famine and migration had

➤1954. Stephen Spender's collected poems are published

➤1953. Samuel Becket introduces the theater of the absurd with *Waiting for Godot*

➤1952. Dylan Thomas writes "Do Not Go Gentle Into That Good Night"

➤1949. George Orwell publishes *Nineteen Eighty-four*

➤1947. Judith Wright publishes first book of poetry

➤1946. Denise Levertov publishes *The Double Image*

➤1945. George Orwell publishes *Animal Farm*

➤1954. Iris Murdoch publishes *Under the Net*

1945 **1950** **1955**

1945. May 8, war in Europe ends; U.S. drops two atomic bombs on Japan; August 10, war in Japan ends

1946. United Nations begins its first session

1948. State of Israel is established

1949. NATO is formed

1950. First protest occurs against apartheid in South Africa

➤1952. Elizabeth II ascends throne

1956. Sputnik I is launched by U.S.S.R.

1957. Treaty of Rome establishes the European Common Market

CROSS-CURRICULAR CONNECTIONS 

History. Three great leaders of the fight for women's suffrage in Great Britain were Emmeline Goulden Pankhurst (1858–1928), her daughter Christabel Harriette Pankhurst (1880–1985), and Millicent Garrett Fawcett (1847–1929). The Pankhursts believed in brash confrontation with the establishment; they were jailed repeatedly for such then daring acts as unfurling a suffrage banner at a political rally. (Not all their demonstrations were so benign, however; their organization and the Women's Social and Political Union advocated bombing and arson to effect its goals.) Fawcett, the daughter of one of the first women physicians, frowned on illegal confrontation as a means to achieving suffrage in her role as the president of the National Union of Women's Suffrage Societies. The combined efforts of thousands of women like the Pankhursts and Fawcett resulted in limited suffrage for women in 1918 and full political equality in 1928.

Students can research and compare the movement for women's suffrage in Great Britain to the women's suffrage movement in the United States.

Quotables

"And Britannia's sons with their long-range guns sailed into the Foggy Dew."

—"The Foggy Dew," a song about the Easter 1916 uprising in Dublin

CROSS-CURRICULAR ACTIVITIES

Social Studies. By the mid-1990s, the two sides in the centuries-old feud between Britain and Ireland seemed to have achieved a truce. Students can divide into three groups to research the current status of the conflict among (1) Britain, (2) the nationalists in Ireland who want to see the entire island united, and (3) Unionists in Northern Ireland who want to perpetuate their political connection with Great Britain. Each group should focus on the point of view of one of the parties involved. Group reports should include recommendations for resolving any remaining sources of conflict among the three parties.

CROSS-CURRICULAR CONNECTIONS

History. The Great Depression in the United States has achieved mythic status in the American consciousness, but few Americans know of its effect on Britain. One index puts the rate of unemployment in that country at 23 percent in 1931, with a smaller overall decrease in production. Britain recovered from the great crash of 1929 much sooner than did the United States. By as early as 1933, production had begun to rise again, and by 1937, it exceeded 1929 levels by 34 percent; unemployment was significantly reduced. By most measures, life for the British working classes was better during the decade of the 1930s than it had been in the 1920s. Overall, however, British exports continued the decline begun earlier in the century.

kept rebellion in check. After the turn of the century, resentments against English rule blossomed into insurrection. In 1916, members of the Irish Republican Brotherhood (later the Irish Republican Army) seized the Dublin Post Office. The Irish rebels knew that they would not be able to resist the British forces that would be mobilized against them, but they were willing to be martyred for their cause. The insurrection was ruthlessly put down, and its leaders were exiled or publicly hanged. Britain's reaction increased Irish nationalism. Much of the literature produced in Ireland during the period, including Lady Augusta Gregory's play ***The Rising of the Moon*** (see page 48), reflects this national feeling. William Butler Yeats, in his famous poem about the uprising, **"Easter, 1916,"** observed that, "All changed, changed utterly: A terrible beauty is born." In 1922, the British Parliament partitioned Ireland into a northern Protestant section under British control and a southern Irish Free State, of which Yeats became a senator. Fighting between Protestants and Catholics in the north continued throughout much of the century, punctuated by sporadic outbreaks of terrorist violence on both sides.

Children sheltering from the Blitz.

The British Commonwealth. During the years leading up to World War II, British colonies around the world began clamoring for self-rule. Canada, South Africa, Australia, and New Zealand were already relatively independent, self-governing parts of the empire. In 1926, Parliament officially recognized the autonomy of these countries by passing a resolution naming them as free, equal partners with England in the British Commonwealth of Nations.

Economic Depression. In 1929, a crash at the New York Stock Exchange began a worldwide economic depression already felt keenly in Britain, which was suffering from the costs of World War I, the loss of colonial revenues, and increased global competition for trade. Unemployment soared, fueling Socialist idealism and conservative reaction.

World War II

The Great Depression of the 1930s had dramatic consequences for all of Europe. Desperate to improve their economic conditions, Europeans turned to political extremes. In Italy and in Germany, ultranationalist, fascist dictatorships emerged under **Benito Mussolini** (1883–1945) and **Adolf Hitler**

Literary Events

➤ = British Events

➤1962. Doris Lessing publishes *The Golden Notebook*

➤1965. Wole Soyinka publishes *The Interlopers*

➤1965. T. S. Eliot dies

➤1966. Margaret Atwood publishes *The Circle Game*

1960 — 1965 — 1970

1961. Berlin Wall is built

1962–1965. Second Vatican Council convenes

1964. U.S. escalates undeclared war in Viet Nam

1968. Russia invades Czechoslovakia, ending Prague Spring

➤1972. Britain imposes direct rule over Northern Ireland

Historical Events

(1889–1945). In 1938, Hitler invaded Czechoslovakia. Then, in 1939, he entered Poland. This move ignited World War II, pitting Germany and Italy—the Axis powers—against France, England, Russia, and the United States—the Allies. Japan joined the fray by attacking the United States fleet at Pearl Harbor in 1941. For most of the war, Germany occupied France and conducted aerial bombardments of Britain known as the Blitz. In London especially, the British huddled in shelters and subway tunnels under a rain of German V-2 rockets. During this dark time, Prime Minister **Winston Churchill** (1874–1965) kept spirits alive with his famous radio addresses:

Wrens fitting smoke floats on to a plane.

> You ask, What is our policy? I will say: "It is to wage war, by sea, land and air, with all our might and with all the strength that God can give us: to wage war against a monstrous tyranny, never surpassed in the dark, lamentable catalog of human crime."

Only at war's end was the nature of that "monstrous tyranny" fully known. Before the war, Hitler's National Socialist Party, the Nazis, built nationalist fervor by making scapegoats of subgroups within the European population, particularly Jews, gypsies, homosexuals, and mentally retarded persons. During the war, the Nazis implemented what they called the "final solution" to the "Jewish problem." Millions of Jews and others considered undesirable by the Nazis were put to death in extermination camps.

World War II ended in 1945 when Allied forces invaded Germany, and the United States dropped atomic bombs on the Japanese cities of Hiroshima and Nagasaki. Estimates of wartime casualties differ, but about forty million people died in all, including almost nine million in German concentration and extermination camps. For the rest of the century, the world would live in the shadow of nuclear weapons.

1974. Alexander Solzhenitsyn publishes *Gulag Archipelago*

➤1986. Margaret Atwood publishes *A Handmaiden's Tale*

➤1984. Ted Hughes becomes poet laureate of Great Britain

1981. Nadine Gordimer publishes *July's People*

1975 **1980** **1985**

➤1973. Great Britain joins European Economic Community

1974. Sears Tower is built in Chicago, the world's tallest building (110 stories)

➤1979. Margaret Thatcher becomes Prime Minister

1979. Accident at Three-Mile Island nuclear power plant occurs

➤1982. Argentina invades Britain's Falkland Islands

1989. Berlin Wall is torn down

ADDITIONAL QUESTIONS AND ACTIVITIES

Winston Churchill's speeches are available on audio recordings. Students can obtain these from area libraries and listen to them in class. To provide the correct ambience for the speeches, darken the room and suggest that students imagine that they are in wartime London, listening to Churchill on the radio at night during an air raid.

Students can freewrite in their journals about how American soldiers might have felt when they first reached the sites of the Nazi extermination camps and found thousands of prisoners who had been waiting to die.

Quotables

"Victory at all costs, victory in spite of all terror, victory however long and hard the road may be; for without victory there is no survival."

—Winston Churchill

CROSS-CURRICULAR CONNECTIONS

SOCIAL STUDIES. Mohandas K. Gandhi was a brilliant social philosopher as well as a political leader. Discuss with the class the following excerpt from Gandhi, titled "The Seven Roots of Violence":

Wealth without work.

Pleasure without conscience.

Knowledge without character.

Commerce without morality.

Science without humanity.

Worship without sacrifice.

Politics without principles.

ADDITIONAL QUESTIONS AND ACTIVITIES

Students can write a position paper in which they defend the royal family of Britain or call for an end to its officially recognized status.

Quotables

"Let us not be deceived—we are today in the midst of a cold war."

—Bernard Baruch, 1947

Queen Elizabeth II making her first Christmas broadcast, 1952.

POST-WAR BRITAIN

In the years immediately following World War II, Britain's Labour government increased its control over industry and the economy, nationalizing more industries, rationing essential goods, controlling prices, and instituting the sorts of social programs associated with modern "welfare states." Meanwhile, the British economy continued to decline.

On the international scene, Britain lost its empire. India was granted independence in 1947, following successful nonviolent protests led by **Mohandas Gandhi** (1869–1948). Many other former colonies and territories became independent, including Burma, Ceylon (now Sri Lanka), Ghana, Kenya, Nigeria, Rhodesia (now Zimbabwe), Sudan, Trinidad and Tobago, and Uganda.

Immediately following the war, Russia extended its Communist dictatorship over much of Eastern Europe and the Balkan states. Speaking in the United States in 1946, Winston Churchill declared that an **"Iron Curtain"** had fallen across the continent, dividing East and West. Symbolic of the division of Europe was the **Berlin Wall,** which the Communists erected in 1961 to divide Russian-controlled East Berlin from West Berlin. For the next several decades, world politics was dominated by struggles between the Communist states, especially the Soviet Union, and democratic states of Western Europe and North America. Western Europe and the United States formed the **North Atlantic Treaty Organization,** or NATO, in defense against the Communists. England also joined the **Common Market,** or **European Economic Community (EEC),** an organization of Western European states formed to oversee trade between member countries.

In 1953, **Queen Elizabeth II** (1926–) was crowned. The once-powerful English monarchy had been reduced to a largely ceremonial position, but most English men and women continued to support it for the sake of tradition.

The 1960s and 1970s saw a radical revolt among the youth of England, who challenged the values and traditions of their elders. In the early sixties, English rock-and-roll groups such as the Beatles and the Rolling Stones became extremely popular, and teenagers around the globe imitated these groups' hairstyles and modes of dress.

LITERARY EVENTS

➤ = British Events

➤1990. Derek Walcott publishes *Omeros*

➤1991. Novelist Graham Greene dies

1991. Nadine Gordimer wins the Nobel Prize for literature

1992. Michael Ondaatje's *The English Patient* wins the Booker Prize

1992. Derek Walcott wins the Nobel Prize for literature

1993. Toni Morrison wins the Nobel Prize for literature

1993. Margaret Atwood publishes *The Robber Bride*

1994. Alice Munro publishes *Open Secrets* and *A Wilderness Station*

1995. Seamus Heaney wins the Nobel Prize for literature

1996. Frank McCourt publishes *Angela's Ashes*

1997. Frank McCourt wins Pulitzer Prize

➤1998. Poet Ted Hughes dies

1999. J. M. Coetzee wins the Brooker Prize for *Disgrace*

1999. Frank McCourt publishes *'Tis*

1990 — 1995

HISTORICAL EVENTS

➤1990. John Major becomes Prime Minister

1990. East and West Germany are reunified.

1991. U. S. and allies wage war against Iraq and liberate Kuwait

1991. Maastricht Treaty signed by members of the European Union

1991.The USSR is dissolved

1991.Civil war breaks out in Yugoslavia

1994. Nelson Mandela is elected the first black president of South Africa

➤1994. Cease fire is proclaimed in Northern Ireland

➤1997. Tony Blair is elected Prime Minister

Throughout the world, the sixties and the seventies were an era of radical experimentation in all the arts, partially fueled by the youth movement.

During the postwar period, modern forms of technologically based entertainment, notably radio, television, and the cinema, came into their own, further increasing the division between lowbrow and highbrow culture that characterized much of the twentieth century.

In 1979, Britain elected its first female prime minister, **Margaret Thatcher** (1925–), a conservative who privatized some British industries and radically cut back social programs. She became Britian's longest-serving prime minister in history. In 1982, under Thatcher, Britain fought a short war with Argentina over control of the Falkland Islands, one of Britain's few remaining colonial possessions. The British lease on Hong Kong expired in 1999. In 1989, the Soviet Union collapsed, and the Berlin Wall came down, signaling the possibility of a future not dominated by East-West tensions. Britain moved toward reducing its isolation by joining with France to build the so-called **Chunnel,** a tunnel beneath the English Channel. In 1993, the last of the European states joined in ratifying the **Maastricht Treaty,** creating a new continent-wide economic entity, the **European Union,** or **EU.** Today, England remains a shadow of its former economic self. However, because of immigration, its population has become more diverse, and with diversity come new possibilities for the future.

Margaret Thatcher, Britain's longest-serving prime minister.

Realism

During the late Victorian Era the pressures of modern urban life helped to create a kind of writing known as **Realism** for its realistic portrayal of life in all its gritty, often disturbing detail. Important late Victorian Realist writers include English novelists **George Eliot,** born Mary Ann Evans (1819–1880), and **Thomas Hardy** (1840–1928) and French novelists **Honoré de Balzac** (1799–1850) and **Émile Zola** (1840–1902). Their writings inspired fine works in the Realist tradition in the early part of the twentieth century. Polish-born **Joseph Conrad** (1857–1924) wrote Realist stories and novels full of psychological probing and dark symbolic undercurrents, including ***Lord Jim*** (1900) and ***Heart of Darkness*** (1902). An example of Conrad's fiction, **"The Lagoon,"** can be found on page 967. The early stories of the Irish writer **James Joyce** (1882–1941) were likewise Realist. Other English writers of the early twentieth century who worked in the Realist tradition include **H. G. Wells** (1866–1946), **John Galsworthy** (1867–1933), **Katherine Mansfield** (1888–1923), **E. M. Forster** (1879–1970), and **George Orwell** (1903–1950). The early twentieth century was also the heyday of Realism on the stage. Lady Gregory's ***The Rising of the Moon,*** Unit 1, and George Bernard Shaw's ***Pygmalion,*** Unit 12, are examples.

Modernism

Perhaps ironically, Realism contributed to growing discontent with traditional ways of thinking, which in turn helped to create a number of anti-Realist literary and artistic movements collectively referred to as **Modernism.** Modernist art and literature are characterized by several related trends: technicality, primitivism, impersonalism, imagism, aestheticism, and intellectualism.

Technicality. Modernist art often emphasizes technique and materials over representational content. This trend found perhaps its clearest expression in painting and music. The **Cubist** paintings of **Pablo Picasso** (1881–1973) and **Georges Braque** (1882–1963) represented people, buildings, and everyday objects as abstract arrangements of geometric shapes. Other forms of abstract art, such as **Abstract Expressionism** and **Minimalism,** moved still further away from representation. **Surrealism** explored the subconscious mind, sometimes through abstraction, as in

CROSS-CURRICULAR CONNECTIONS

History. The poets of The Movement included Roy Fuller, Philip Larkin, John Wain, Kingsley Amis, and D. J. Enright. The manifesto, so to speak, of The Movement was an anthology edited by Robert Conquest titled *New Lines* (1956). Movement poetry has been characterized as wry but slightly flat. Ted Hughes, in a spin-off of The Movement (which was short-lived), brought an infusion of power to the simplicity of The Movement's style; this vigor swept him into his seat as poet laureate of Britain.

ADDITIONAL QUESTIONS AND ACTIVITIES

For excellent distinctions between Romanticism, Classicism, Realism, and Symbolist (Modernist) writing, refer advanced students to the opening essay of Edmund Wilson's *Axel's Castle.*

CROSS-CURRICULAR ACTIVITIES

Arts and Humanities. Play a recording by Schönberg, Webern, or Stravinsky to demonstrate the effect of Modernism on music. An excellent choice would be the famous opening of Stravinsky's *Le Sacre du Printemps*. For a contrast, play a short piece of classical music by Mozart, Beethoven, or Brahms before playing the Modernist piece. One possibility would be the opening of the first movement of Beethoven's Symphony No. 1 in C major. While the Modernist music is playing, students can then freewrite in their journals to describe the differences between the two types of music.

Arts and Humanities. Although great art is always difficult to achieve, the very simplicity of Primitivism encourages people who are not artists to give it a try. Arrange to have art books put on reserve at your school or local library so that students can study examples of Primitivism in art. They can then attempt a Primitivist work of art of their own, using any medium they like—tempera, felt-tip pens, collage, watercolor, sculpture, etc. When their works are completed, display them in the classroom or elsewhere in the school. Each student should have a chance to explain to the class why he or she believes his or her art is Primitivist.

Three Musicians, 1921. Pablo Picasso.The Museum of Modern Art, NY.

the work of **Joan Miró**, and sometimes through a hallucinatory realism, like the paintings of **Salvador Dali. Pop Art**, which both celebrated and parodied consumerism through mass media imagery, had its beginnings in London in the late 1950s and was soon joined by American artists, most notably, **Andy Warhol.** Architects such as **Walter Gropius** (Germany, 1883–1969), **Le Corbusier** (Switzerland, 1887–1965), and **Ludwig Mies Van der Rohe** (Germany, 1886–1969) introduced severely functional buildings viewed as abstract, nondecorated forms, from which evolved the modern skyscraper.

Two Austrian-born musicians, **Arnold Schönberg** (1874–1951) and **Anton Webern** (1883–1945), moved away from traditional tonal music, creating **twelve-tone, atonal** compositions written in no particular key and making extensive use of discordances. **Igor Stravinsky** of Russia (1882–1971) and **Béla Bartók** of Hungary (1881–1945) experimented with alternatives to traditional tonal music, often drawing inspiration from primitive folk sources.

Primitivism. Modernists were attracted to the primitive for two major reasons. First, primitive art and music tended toward abstraction and stylization. Second, Modernists sought in primitive sources a deeper connection to the dark, hidden elements of the human spirit suppressed by Western "civilized" culture. This attraction to the primitive for inspiration owed a debt to the Austrian founder of **psychoanalysis, Sigmund Freud** (1856–1939). Freud proposed that people, in the course of growing up, learn to suppress their primitive, basic impulses, which then find expression in jokes; slips of the tongue; fantasies; wish-fulfilling, symbolic dreams; and works of art (music, dance, theater, painting, sculpture, and literature).

Impersonalism. Modernist literature often deals with subjective feelings in an impersonal, intellectualized style. This contrast between personal subject matter and an impersonal style reflects the alienation of many modern writers—their sense that, more than ever before, people are isolated from one another, crowded together in cities but lacking the interpersonal connections that bound together peasant communities of the past. In Britain, Modernism found expression in different ways in the writings of **James Joyce, Virginia Woolf, D. H. Lawrence** (1885–1930), U.S.-born **T. S. Eliot** (1888–1965), and **Dylan Thomas** (1914–1953).

Major English poets of the period included Ted Hughes (1930–1998) and **Philip Larkin** (1922–1985), members of **The Movement,** a group of poets dedicated to clear, precise, non-Romantic verse in ordinary speech.

Joyce and Woolf experimented with a new kind of fiction writing that used a **stream-of-consciousness** style that attempted to render in prose the subjective flow of thoughts and emotions in a character's mind. Novels such as Virginia Woolf's ***Mrs. Dalloway*** (1925) and ***To the Lighthouse*** (1927) and James Joyce's ***A Portrait of the Artist as a Young Man*** (1914–1915) and ***Ulysses*** (1922) violated standard fictional conventions by placing the reader inside characters' minds in all their jumbled confusion. Such literature placed high demands on readers and further accentuated the rift between highbrow and lowbrow culture. An example of stream-of-consciousness technique is the excerpt from Joyce's ***A Portrait of the Artist*** on page 921.

Imagism. American-born **Ezra Pound** (1885–1972) was, perhaps, the primary spokesperson for Modernism in poetry. Pound was initially attracted to **Imagism**, an attempt to free poetry of the speaker's or author's comment about feeling or meaning. A typical Imagist poem presents a single, clear snapshot of a moment of perception. It does not tell the reader how to feel about the picture that is presented. Instead, it presents the picture, or image, and lets it evoke the emotion in the reader. The author or speaker assumes an "impersonal" stance, not sharing his or her emotions directly, but presenting emotion-creating images. Such impersonality is a hallmark of much Modernist writing. To this day, a major distinction between highbrow literature and lowbrow literature (such as popular romances and mystery stories) is that the latter tends to state feelings directly, while the former tends to present surface details and to let the reader infer what is to be felt about these details. T. S. Eliot, who was born in America but later became an English citizen, coined a term, the ***objective correlative,*** to describe a group of images that produce a particular emotion in the reader.

Aestheticism. The alienation between high culture and popular culture reflected in Modernism began with the **Aesthetic Movement** at the close of the nineteenth century, the motto of which was "Art for art's sake." **Oscar Wilde's** (1854–1900) preface to *The Picture of Dorian Gray* (1891) expresses this idea in a bold and absolute distinction between the artistic and the useful. The German Nobel Prize winner **Thomas Mann** (1875–1955), in such works as *Buddenbrooks* (1900), *Death in Venice* (1912), and *The Magic Mountain* (1924), wrote about the incompatibility of artistic and utilitarian values and lifestyles. In James Joyce's ***A Portrait of the Artist as a Young Man*** (1916), the main character, Stephen Dedalus, experiences deep conflicts between his inner artistic nature and the pressures of the practical exterior world.

Intellectualism and Alienation from Popular Culture. The emphasis on technique over representation, on impersonality, and on aestheticism in Modernist art and literature reflects the intellectual revolution of the late nineteenth century. The work of Freud, Marx, **Charles Darwin** (1809–1882), and **Albert Einstein** (1879–1955) forced scholars in every field to rethink the foundations of their disciplines and led to a primary concern with theory per se. Art, music, and literature were seen by many as little more than vehicles through which to express ideas about art, music, and literature. Art appreciation became an intellectual task requiring years of training in history and theory. Such ideas fueled a growing separation between artists and the public. Artistic alienation is expressed powerfully in the writings of Czech **Franz Kafka** (1883–1924) and in the famous painting *The Scream* by Norwegian **Edvard Munch** (1863–1944).

Representative Modern Writers

Eliot's poetry is the prime example of Modernism in literature. The work is detached and impersonal in style but deals with personal, subjective feelings. It tends to be highly intellectual, alluding to other literature and to historical events. Often the symbols used are peculiar to the individual. Instead of using traditional symbols, such as a rose for love or the moon for inconstancy, a Modernist poet is likely to present symbols that have personal meaning or associations that must be inferred by the reader. Such use of symbolism was strongly influenced by the **French Symbolist** poets of the nineteenth century, including **Stéphane Mallarmé** (1842–1898), **Arthur Rimbaud**

CROSS-CURRICULAR CONNECTIONS

History. Besides Pound, poets openly espousing Imagism or influenced by it included Conrad Aiken, Richard Aldington, Hilda Doolittle (H. D.), T. S. Eliot, John Gould Fletcher, F. S. Flint, Amy Lowell, Harriet Monroe, Marianne Moore, and Wallace Stevens. The most important Imagist work appeared between 1914 and 1917 in the anthologies *Des Imagistes* and *Some Imagists*, the latter appearing in three separate volumes.

Quotables

"The only way of expressing emotion in the form of art is by finding an 'objective correlative,' in other words, a set of objects, a situation, a chain of events which shall be the formula of that *particular* emotion; such that when the external facts, which must terminate in sensory experiences, are given, the emotion is immediately evoked."

—T. S. Eliot

SELECTION CHECK TEST 12.10.1 WITH ANSWERS

Checking Your Reading

1. What happened to many British colonies after World War II? **They became independent.**
2. What was the European Economic Community? **It was an organization of Western European states formed to oversee trade between member countries.**
3. What did Sigmund Freud believe people suppress? **He believed that people suppress their primitive, basic impulses.**
4. What was the motto of the Aesthetic Movement? **It was "Art for art's sake."**
5. During the 1950s what was the goal of members of "the Movement"? **They sought to revivify inherited artistic forms and the humanist tradition of Western cultural values.**

Terms and People

Match each definition below with the letter of the most appropriate term or person discussed in the Unit Ten Introduction.

TERMS

a. NATO
b. stream-of-consciousness
c. Modernism
d. free verse
e. Imagism

1. Movement characterized by technicality, primitivism, impersonalism, imagism, aestheticism, and intellectualism. **C**
2. Organization formed by Western Europe and the United States for self-defense. **A**
3. Movement that sought to present a single, clear snapshot of a moment of perception in poetry. **E**
4. Literary work that attempts to render the flow of feelings, thoughts, and impressions within the minds of characters. **F**
5. Poetry that avoids use of regular rhyme, meter, or division into stanzas. **D**

PEOPLE

a. Georges Braque
b. Harold Pinter
c. Mohandas Gandhi
d. D. H. Lawrence
e. Margaret Thatcher

1. led successful nonviolent protests to gain independence for India **C**
2. wrote plays during the 1950s and 1960s characterized by a surface realism of violence and vulgarity

(1854–1891), and **Charles Baudelaire** (1821–1867). Modernist intellectualism, allusiveness, and use of nontraditionally poetic speech owed debts to the Metaphysical poetry of **John Donne** (1572–1631) and to the poetry of **Gerard Manley Hopkins** (1844–1889) published in 1918. In meter as in other areas, Modernist poets were innovators. Conventions of rhythm, rhyme, and stanza form were thrown off in favor of ***vers libre,*** or **free verse,** that conformed more readily to the stream of the speaker's thought, or, in Pound's famous statement, "to the musical phrase, not to the metronome."

Dylan Thomas and **D. H. Lawrence** represent a different trend in Modernism. Each wrote often in conventional forms but adapted those forms to Modernist purposes. Both writers, influenced by Freud, dealt with basic human impulses, often ones repressed by society. Both made use of personal rather than conventional symbols. Thomas's poetry, in particular, makes great demands on readers because of his often startling and unique symbolism. Despite its difficulty, the Welsh poet's work was and still is extremely popular. Thomas had a beautiful speaking voice and popularized his poetry through public readings. Many people are attracted to his work for its sheer lyrical beauty, aside from any interpretations that they might give to it. Lawrence is known primarily for his novels, notably ***Sons and Lovers*** (1913), ***The Rainbow*** (1915), ***Women in Love*** (1916, published 1920), and ***Lady Chatterley's Lover*** (1928). These novels challenged the moral sensibilities of many people of the time and were subject to censorship, though by today's standards they are generally considered quite tame. In addition to his novels, Lawrence wrote fine short fiction and poetry, examples of which can be found on pages 33 and 922 of this text.

ANTI-CULTURE AND THE NEW TRADITIONALISM

In the early twentieth century British literature was influenced by expressionist, surrealist, symbolist, and existentialist movements on the continent. Literature in the latter half of the twentieth century was marked by themes of alienation, negation, and emptiness resulting from wars, depressions, population increases, a pervasive sense that technology was out of control, and a cynicism about culture itself. Novels such as **Kingsley Amis's *Lucky Jim*** (1954) expressed protest against an Establishment which seemed to retain its power over characters' minds even as its outer forms were melting away. On the stage **Harold Pinter's** plays (***The Birthday Party,*** 1959; ***The Caretaker,*** 1960; ***The Homecoming,*** 1965) were characterized by a surface realism of violence and vulgarity playing against symbolic suggestions and a multiplicity of motivations that were deliberately left obscure. During the 1950s members of "the Movement" sought to revivify inherited artistic forms and the humanist tradition of Western cultural values. Two poets of the period generally considered in England to be the best of their generation were **Thom Gunn** and **Ted Hughes.** Hughes was named poet laureate of Great Britain in 1984.

Contemporary Irish writers have been prominent recently with **Seamus Heaney** winning the Nobel Prize for Literature in 1995 and **Frank McCourt** winning a Pulizer Prize for his memoir ***Angela's Ashes*** in 1997. Other important twentieth-century and contemporary British writers include **Virginia Woolf, Katherine Mansfield, W. H. Auden, Joseph Conrad, Wilfred Owen, Stevie Smith, Alice Munro, Doris Lessing, Iris Murdoch,** and **Graham Greene.**

SELECTION CHECK TEST 12.10.1 WITH ANSWERS (CONT.)

playing against symbolic suggestions and a multiplicity of motivations deliberately left obscure **B**

3. served Britain as a conservative prime minister who privatized some British industries and radically cut back social programs **E**
4. painted people, buildings, and everyday objects as abstract arrangements of geometric shapes **A**
5. wrote Sons and Lovers and Lady Chatterly's Lover **D**

ECHOES

TWENTIETH-CENTURY TO CONTEMPORARY POETRY

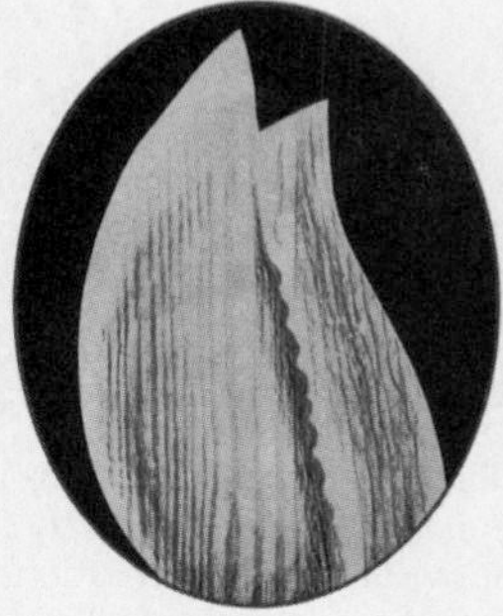

We are created from and with the world
To suffer with and from it day by day:
Whether we meet in a majestic world
Of solid measurements or a dream world
Of swans and gold, we are required to love
All homeless objects that require a world.
Our claim to own our bodies and our world
Is our catastrophe. What can we know
But panic and caprice until we know
Our dreadful appetite demands a world
Whose order, origin, and purpose will
Be fluent satisfaction of our will?

—W. H. Auden, "Canzone"

It's certain there's no fine thing
Since Adam's fall but needs much laboring.

—William Butler Yeats, "Adam's Curse"

I am moved by fancies that are curled
Around these images, and cling:
The notion of some infinitely gentle
Infinitely suffering thing.

—T. S. Eliot, "Preludes"

If in some smothering dreams you too could pace
Behind the wagon that we flung him in . . .
My friend, you would not tell with such high zest
To children ardent for some desperate glory,
The old lie: Dulce et decorum est
Pro patria mori.

—Wilfred Owen, "Dulce et Decorum Est"

The impact of poetry is so hard and direct that for the moment there is no other sensation except that of the poem itself. What profound depths we visit then—how sudden and complete is our immersion.

—Virginia Woolf

Things fall apart; the center cannot hold;
Mere anarchy is loosed upon the world.

—William Butler Yeats, "The Second Coming"

And so, I missed my chance with one of the
lords of life.
And I have something to expiate:
A pettiness.

—D. H. Lawrence, "Snake"

Imagine a famine. Now imagine a piece of bread. Both things are real but you happen to be in the same room with only one of them.

—Margaret Atwood, "Bread"

ADDITIONAL QUESTIONS AND ACTIVITIES

- Unlike other units, all but two of the quotes (Auden, Woolf) on this page come from selections in this unit. Ask students to hypothesize what these poems are about based on the quotes. When they read these poems, it will be interesting for them to reread what they wrote. Students will appreciate that a poem needs to be examined in its entirety.
- Ask students to make a list of topics twentieth-century writers are interested in. Then have students compare and contrast these concerns with the topics the poets in Unit 6 wrote about. In these quotations students should be able to recognize these topics: the nature of humankind, suffering, war, apocalyptic visions of the future, psychology, and social consciousness.

BIOGRAPHICAL NOTES

For information about the poets on this page, see About the Author on the following pages.
W. H. Auden, page 945
William Butler Yeats, page 906
T. S. Eliot, page 916
Wilfred Owen, page 932
D. H. Lawrence, page 921
Margaret Atwood, page 966

ADDITIONAL RESOURCES

UNIT 10 RESOURCE BOOK
"THE LAKE ISLE OF INNISFREE"
- Selection Worksheet 10.1
- Selection Check Test 4.10.3
- Selection Test 4.10.4

"ADAM'S CURSE"
- Selection Worksheet 10.2
- Selection Check Test 4.10.5
- Selection Test 4.10.6

"THE SECOND COMING"
- Selection Worksheet 10.3
- Selection Check Test 4.10.7
- Selection Test 4.10.8

- Language, Grammar, and Style Resource 3.66, 3.80
- Applied English Resource 6.8

INDIVIDUAL LEARNING STRATEGIES

MOTIVATION
In small groups, have students describe a positive experience they have had in nature.

READING PROFICIENCY
Ask students what sounds in lines 3 and 4 suggest the buzzing and humming of bees.

ENGLISH LANGUAGE LEARNING
Read aloud stanza 2. Students should get a sense for the peacefulness from the sound and rhythm of this section. Point out the descriptive language Yeats uses in stanza 2 to refer to different parts of the day. Make sure students understand what times of day Yeats refers to with these sensory details.

SPECIAL NEEDS
Make sure students understand the Guided Reading Questions and the Recall questions in Investigate, Inquire, and Imagine.

ENRICHMENT
Have students read "Economy," the first chapter of Henry David Thoreau's *Walden*. Point out that "The Lake Isle of Innisfree" was influenced by the first chapter of Walden. Have students write a critical essay supporting this relationship. You might also ask students to give Donne's viewpoint on living alone after having students review his "No man is an island" analogy from "Meditation 17."

"The Lake Isle of Innisfree"
"ADAM'S CURSE"
"THE SECOND COMING"

BY WILLIAM BUTLER YEATS

About the AUTHOR

William Butler Yeats (1865–1939) was born near Dublin and grew up there, in London, and in the County Sligo countryside. In Sligo, under the shadow of Ben Bulben Mountain, said by locals to be home to the fairy people known as the Sidhe (She), Yeats imbibed Irish folk tales and legends. He studied painting in Dublin but left school to pursue a literary career. His early poetry drew heavily on traditional legends and myths. As a young man, he fell deeply in love with an actress and Irish revolutionary named Maude Gonne. However, Gonne did not return his affections. His unrequited love for her led to the creation of many of his finest poems. In the late 1890s, Yeats and Lady Augusta Gregory founded the Irish National Theatre, later the Abbey Theatre, and Yeats became its director. For that theater he wrote plays based on Irish themes, some of which used innovative costuming and movement derived from Japanese Nō drama. In 1917, he married Georgie Hyde-Lees and moved into a restored Norman tower called Thoor Ballylee. Yeats had always had a keen interest in spiritualism, and much of the symbolism of his later poetry derives from the "spirit writing" that his wife Georgie did in trancelike states. In 1922, Yeats was named a senator of the new Irish Free State (Eire). When he died in January 1939, he left behind a varied, fascinating body of work that reveals him as one of the great poets of the twentieth century.

About the SELECTIONS

"The Lake Isle of Innisfree" is one of Yeats's most well-known and well-loved poems. Technically a pastoral verse, it deals with a modern speaker's desire to escape from city life to a life of peace in the countryside.

"Adam's Curse" is an autobiographical poem telling of one small event in the history of Yeats's relationship with Maude Gonne. The poem reveals Yeats's belief that nothing wonderful—poetry, beauty, or love—comes without hard work and sacrifice.

"The Second Coming," published in 1921, shows his mastery of visionary symbolism and of a terse, strong, modern style quite different from that of his dreamy early verse. Written shortly after World War I and the Russian Revolution, the poem prophesies the beginning of a new and frightening cycle of history.

GOALS/OBJECTIVES

Studying this lesson will enable students to
- interpret and appreciate the poetry of William Butler Yeats
- describe Yeats's literary accomplishments and explain the historical significance of his writings
- define *rhyme scheme, image, allusion,* and *symbol* and recognize the use of these techniques in the selections
- identify adjectives and participles
- select titles from phrases in Yeats's poetry
- write a résumé
- plan and participate in a Nobel Prize Winners festival

Sligo, c.1900s. Eveleen Buckton. Victoria and Albert Museum, London.

The Lake Isle of Innisfree[1]

WILLIAM BUTLER YEATS

I will arise and go now, and go to Innisfree,
And a small cabin build there, of clay and wattles[2] made;
Nine bean-rows will I have there, a hive for the honey-bee,
And live alone in the bee-loud glade.

And I shall have some peace there, for peace
comes dropping slow,
Dropping from the veils of the morning to
where the cricket sings;
There midnight's all a glimmer, and noon a purple glow,
And evening full of the linnet's[3] wings.

I will arise and go now, for always night and day
I hear lake water lapping with low sounds by the shore;
While I stand on the roadway, or on the pavements gray,
I hear it in the deep heart's core. ■

What details in the first two stanzas suggest a simple, peaceful, rustic existence?

1. **Lake Isle of Innisfree.** Island in County Sligo, Ireland
2. **wattles.** Woven twigs and branches
3. **linnet.** Finch

WORDS FOR EVERYDAY USE

glade (glād) *n.*, open space in a forest. *Ayesha followed the forest stream through the trees until she came out into a sunny glade.*

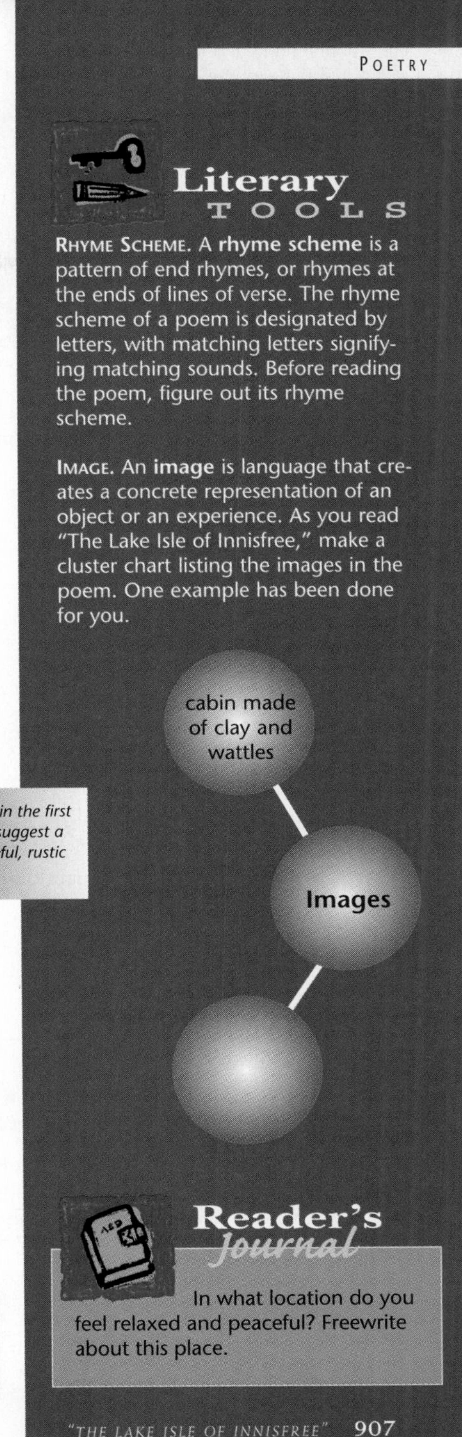

POETRY
Literary TOOLS
RHYME SCHEME. A **rhyme scheme** is a pattern of end rhymes, or rhymes at the ends of lines of verse. The rhyme scheme of a poem is designated by letters, with matching letters signifying matching sounds. Before reading the poem, figure out its rhyme scheme.
IMAGE. An **image** is language that creates a concrete representation of an object or an experience. As you read "The Lake Isle of Innisfree," make a cluster chart listing the images in the poem. One example has been done for you.
cabin made of clay and wattles
Images
Reader's Journal
In what location do you feel relaxed and peaceful? Freewrite about this place.

GRAPHIC ORGANIZER

Students should include the following images in their cluster charts:
bee-loud glade, singing cricket, flutter of the linnet's wings, sounds of lake water lapping.

READER'S JOURNAL

Students should focus on any of the five senses that are relevant to their associations with the place.

SELECTION CHECK TEST 12.10.3 WITH ANSWERS

Checking Your Reading

1. What will the speaker have on Innisfree? **The speaker will have a small cabin made of clay and wattles, nine bean-rows, and a beehive.**
2. Will the speaker live with anyone else? **No, the speaker will live alone.**
3. What adjective best describes the speaker's life on Innisfree? **Peaceful best describes the speaker's life on Innisfree.**
4. What does the speaker hear day and night? **The speaker hears "lake water lapping."**
5. Where does the speaker currently live, in the city or in the country? **The speaker now lives in the city.**

Literary Tools

Fill in the blanks with an appropriate literary tool from the list below.

rhyme scheme objective correlative image speaker point of view

1. The **speaker** wants to go to Innisfree to live.
2. The cabin made of clay and wattles is an example of a(n) **image** used by Yeats to create a concrete representation of an experience he longs to have.
3. The **rhyme scheme** of a poem is designated by letters, with matching letters signifying matching sounds.

RESPOND TO THE SELECTION

Point out that in describing an ideal place to live, students are making a statement about their needs, desires, and their attitude toward humanity. For this reason students may wish to describe more than one spot.

ANSWERS TO INVESTIGATE, INQUIRE, AND IMAGINE

RECALL

1a. The speaker plans to rise, go to Innisfree, build a cabin, have a garden and beehive, and live alone.

2a. The speaker remembers the sound of lake water lapping on the shore.

3a. The speaker evidently lives in an urban environment because he mentions a roadway and gray pavements.

INTERPRET

1b. The speaker wants to find a peaceful life alone with only the company of nature.

2b. An island is effectively cut off from neighbors.

3b. The last stanza implies a contrast between road sounds and lake water lapping on a shore and between the gray pavement of the city and the vivid colors of the island.

ANALYZE

4a. Morning is veiled; crickets sing and linnets flap their wings in the evening; midnight glimmers; noon glows purple.

SYNTHESIZE

4b. The sounds make the speaker feel peaceful.

EVALUATE

5a. People still want to get away from it all, so the poem is still relevant. Ironically, many people bring the trappings of civilization (cell phones, pagers, laptop computers) with them when they try to escape. Because of modern technology, an island is not necessarily the isolated escape it once was.

EXTEND

5b. Yeats and Thoreau both want to learn from nature and to live a solitary life.

Respond *to the* SELECTION

Compare your ideal life with the vision of an ideal life described by Yeats.

INVESTIGATE, Inquire, Imagine

Recall: GATHERING FACTS → **Interpret:** FINDING MEANING

1a. In the first stanza, what specific plans does the speaker relate?

1b. What kind of lifestyle does the speaker want to find on Innisfree?

2a. In the third stanza, what memory of Innisfree is strongest when the speaker is not there?

2b. Why might it be important for the speaker's retreat to be an island?

3a. Where does the speaker live now? How do you know?

3b. What contrasts in sights and sounds are described or implied by the last stanza?

Analyze: TAKING THINGS APART → **Synthesize:** BRINGING THINGS TOGETHER

4a. Describe the different times of day at the Isle of Innisfree.

4b. The speaker says "night and day / I hear lake water lapping with low sounds by the shore." How does this sound make the speaker feel?

Evaluate: MAKING JUDGMENTS → **Extend:** CONNECTING IDEAS

5a. Yeats wrote "The Lake Isle of Innisfree" more than 100 years ago. Evaluate the relevance of this poem to life today.

5b. In *Walden,* Henry David Thoreau said, "I went to the woods because I wished to live deliberately, to front only the essential facts of life, and see if I could not learn what it had to teach, and not, when I came to die, discover that I had not lived." What common vision do Yeats and Thoreau share?

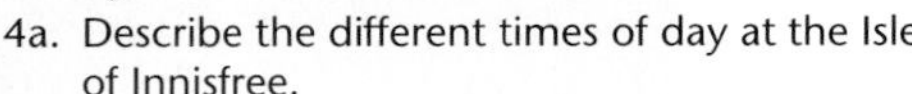

Understanding Literature

RHYME SCHEME. Review the definition for **rhyme scheme** in Literary Tools on page 907. What is the rhyme scheme of "The Lake Isle of Innisfree"?

IMAGE. Review the definition for **image** in the Handbook of Literary Terms and the cluster chart you made for Literary Tools on page 907. What images in the poem appeal to the sense of hearing?

ANSWERS TO UNDERSTANDING LITERATURE

RHYME SCHEME. The rhyme scheme of the poem is *abab cdcd efef.*

IMAGE. In the first stanza, the image of the "bee-loud glade" appeals to the sense of hearing. Other auditory images are the singing cricket, the flutter of the linnet's wings, and the sounds of "lake water lapping with low sounds by the shore."

ADAM'S CURSE[1]

WILLIAM BUTLER YEATS

We sat together at one summer's end,
That beautiful mild woman, your close friend,
And you[2] and I, and talked of poetry.
I said: "A line will take us hours maybe;
Yet if it does not seem a moment's thought,
Our stitching and unstitching has been naught.
Better go down upon your marrow-bones
And scrub a kitchen pavement, or break stones
Like an old pauper, in all kinds of weather;
For to articulate sweet sounds together
Is to work harder than all these, and yet
Be thought an idler by the noisy set
Of bankers, schoolmasters, and clergymen
The martyrs call the world."

And thereupon
That beautiful mild woman for whose sake
There's many a one shall find out all heartache
On finding that her voice is sweet and low
Replied: "To be born woman is to know—
Although they do not talk of it at school—
That we must labor to be beautiful."

According to the speaker, what paradox does writing poetry involve?

1. **Adam's Curse.** In Genesis, Adam is cursed after the Fall with having to die and with having to live by the sweat of his brow, to work.
2. **you.** This autobiographical poem is addressed to Maude Gonne, the beautiful actress and revolutionary for whom Yeats felt unrequited love during most of his adult life.

WORDS FOR EVERYDAY USE

ar • ti • cu • late (är tik´ yo̅o̅ lāt´) *vt.,* express clearly; join or connect. *Though Paolo loved Francesca, he was unable to articulate his feelings for her.*

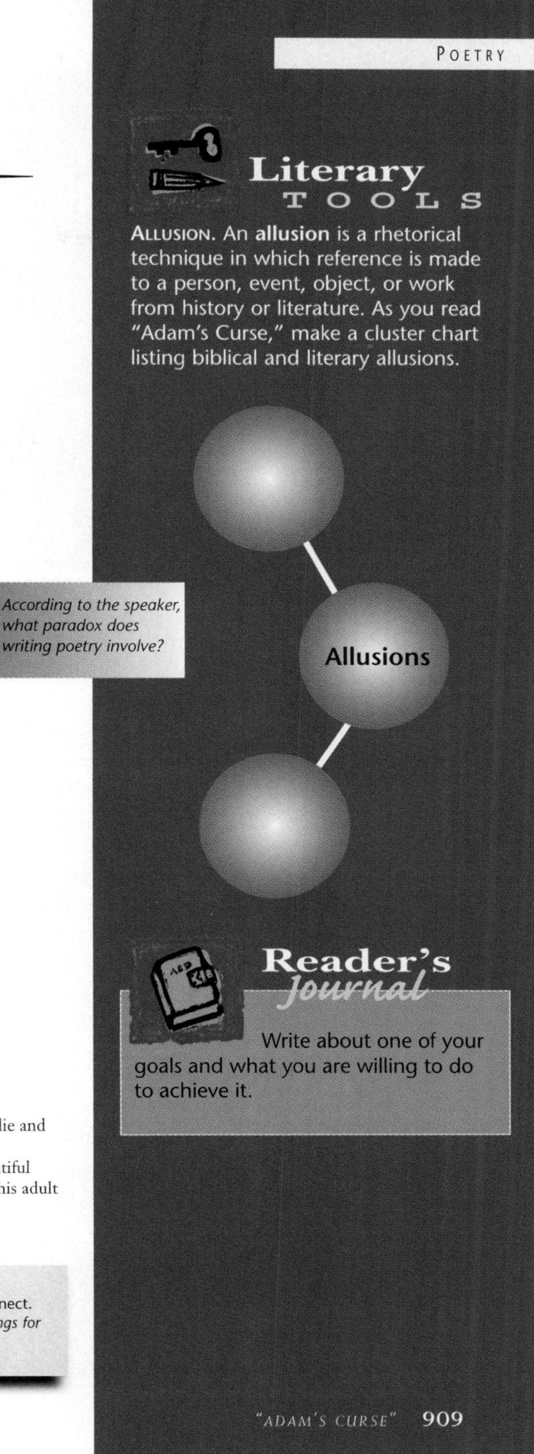

Literary TOOLS
ALLUSION. An **allusion** is a rhetorical technique in which reference is made to a person, event, object, or work from history or literature. As you read "Adam's Curse," make a cluster chart listing biblical and literary allusions.
Allusions
Reader's Journal
Write about one of your goals and what you are willing to do to achieve it.

GRAPHIC ORGANIZER

The speaker alludes to romance literature in line 27 and the story of Adam and Eve in line 23.

READER'S JOURNAL

Observe to students that the goals they discuss may be entirely personal or may focus on changes they wish to see in society at large. What satisfaction might achieving such a goal bring? What disadvantages would pursuing such a goal involve? Have students review the sections on problem solving in the Language Arts Survey and then identify some strategies for achieving their goal.

INDIVIDUAL LEARNING STRATEGIES

MOTIVATION
Discuss with students whether love or any other goal means more if it is come by with difficulty.

READING PROFICIENCY
Remind students that this poem expresses Yeats's belief that one must work for all wonderful things. Point out that each stanza addresses something that one must work for: stanza 1 addresses poetry, stanza 2 addresses beauty, stanza 3 addresses love. The last two stanzas are also devoted to the idea of love.
Provide students with the following additional vocabulary words:
naught—nothing
pauper—extremely poor person
idler—lazy person
compound—create through the combining of elements
precedent—example
strove—tried hard; endeavored

ENGLISH LANGUAGE LEARNING
See above strategies under Reading Proficiency. Also point out the following additional vocabulary words:
stitching and unstitching—writing and rewriting
noisy set—people who are not writers or do not respect poetry
idle trade—easy work

INDIVIDUAL LEARNING STRATEGIES (CONT.)

SPECIAL NEEDS
Explain the organization of the poem as outlined in Reading Proficiency. Review the phrases defined in the same section. Make sure students can answer the Guided Reading Questions and the Recall questions in Investigate, Inquire, and Imagine.

ENRICHMENT
Have students review the biography of Yeats and do additional research about him. Then they can write a critical essay of biographical criticism, examining "Adam's Curse" as it relates to Yeats's life.

ANSWER TO GUIDED READING QUESTION

1. Labor and hard work is required to create any "fine thing."

SELECTION CHECK TEST 12.10.5 WITH ANSWERS

Checking Your Reading

1. What subject of discussion does the speaker recall at the beginning of the poem? **The speaker recalls a discussion about poetry.**
2. What curse was placed on Adam? **He was required to work.**
3. What examples does the poem give of things that require work? **The examples are a poet writing poetry, a woman beautifying herself, and a lover wooing.**
4. What do lovers quote? **Lovers quote "beautiful old books."**
5. The speaker and the person to whom the poem is addressed have grown as "weary-hearted" as what? **They have grown as "weary-hearted as that hollow moon."**

Literary Tools

Fill in the blank with the appropriate literary tool from the following list.

courtly love   allusion   stanza

1. The poem is divided into five __stanzas__.
2. Yeats makes __allusions__ to the story of Adam and Eve and courtly love.
3. __Courtly love__ is a code of romantic love celebrated in songs and romances of the Medieval Period in France and England.

RESPOND TO THE SELECTION

Ask students to explain why some things might be worth working for, while others are not. If students are comfortable doing so, they can cite examples of things they have worked hard for, whether or not they succeeded.

Adam and Eve, 1908. Edvard Munch. Munch Museet, Olso, Norway.

I said: "It's certain there is no fine thing
Since Adam's fall but needs much laboring.
There have been lovers who thought love should be
So much compounded of high courtesy
That they would sigh and quote with learned looks
Precedents out of beautiful old books;
Yet now it seems an idle trade enough."

We sat grown quiet at the name of love;
We saw the last embers of daylight die,
And in the trembling blue-green of the sky
A moon, worn as if it had been a shell
Washed by time's waters as they rose and fell
About the stars and broke in days and years.

I had a thought for no one's but your ears:
That you were beautiful, and that I strove
To love you in the old high way of love;
That it had all seemed happy, and yet we'd grown
As weary-hearted as that hollow moon. ■

What, according to the speaker, is required in order to create any "fine thing"?

Respond *to the* SELECTION

Do you agree with the speaker's ideas about what requires hard work? Why, or why not?

Inquire, Imagine

Recall: GATHERING FACTS →

1a. According to the speaker, what is harder than scrubbing a floor or breaking stones?

2a. What comment does the "beautiful woman" make in stanza 2?

3a. What third subject is introduced by the speaker in stanza 3?

Interpret: FINDING MEANING

1b. What do many people think about this activity? Why?

2b. How is this comment related to the speaker's initial comments?

3b. What hard work is related to this subject?

Analyze: TAKING THINGS APART →

4a. Which person in the poem has labored to be beautiful? Which has labored to love in the old way, "compounded of high courtesy"?

Synthesize: BRINGING THINGS TOGETHER

4b. How does the conversation in this poem relate to Yeats' life and love for Maude Gonne?

Evaluate: MAKING JUDGMENTS →

5a. Evaluate the speaker's success at the things he has worked for.

Extend: CONNECTING IDEAS

5b. What makes it worthwhile to work at something hard, even when there is a chance of failure?

Understanding Literature

ALLUSION. Review the definition for **allusion** in the Handbook of Literary Terms and the cluster chart you made for Literary Tools on page 909. What allusions does Yeats make in the poem? What do they reveal about the speaker?

ANSWERS TO INVESTIGATE, INQUIRE, AND IMAGINE

RECALL

1a. Writing poetry is harder than these things.

2a. The beautiful woman says women must work hard at being beautiful.

3a. Love is introduced in stanza

INTERPRET

1b. Many people think writing poetry is easy or a lazy person's task. This may be because it does not involve physical labor, because people have not tried to write poetry, or they do not respect poetry and thus the work of poets.

2b. The woman draws a parallel between creating a beautiful poem and creating an image of physical beauty. Both require labor but must look effortless.

3b. In former times, people worked at love by maintaining a high level of courtesy and doing romantic things such as sighing and quoting from beautiful books.

ANALYZE

4a. The beautiful woman has worked hard to look the way she does. The speaker has labored hard to love in the old way.

SYNTHESIZE

4b. Yeats may have felt that his hard work went unrewarded because his love for Maude Gonne was unrequited.

EVALUATE

5a. The speaker has been successful as a poet, but unsuccessful in love.

EXTEND

5b. *Responses will vary.* Students may mention the satisfaction of reaching a goal or that life is dull without taking the risk of working for something.

UNDERSTANDING LITERATURE

ALLUSION. In the title and line 23, the speaker alludes to Adam's curse from Genesis 3:17-19, which tells of the curse laid on Adam requiring him to work after sinning against God in the Garden of Eden. This allusion relates to the speaker's hard work of writing poetry and his unsuccessful efforts at wooing the woman he loves. The reference to "high courtesy" in line 25 alludes to chivalry, courtly love, and romance. This allusion reveals that the speaker has been trying to win the woman's love using old-fashioned methods which have not worked.

ANSWER TO GUIDED READING QUESTION

1. The speaker characterizes the times in which he lives as chaotic, violent, and in the hands of the worst elements.

GRAPHIC ORGANIZER

Students should include the following information in their charts.

Symbols	Meaning
sphinx	imminent birth of a new, even more difficult age
slouching beast	guiding spirit of the new age

READER'S JOURNAL

Before students write, discuss with them what the world was like in past times and what it may be like in the future.

INDIVIDUAL LEARNING STRATEGIES

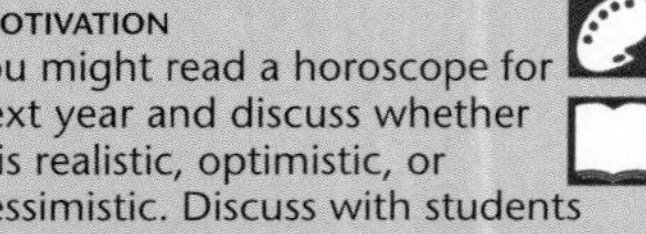

Motivation
You might read a horoscope for next year and discuss whether it is realistic, optimistic, or pessimistic. Discuss with students signs that indicate what this century might be like.

Reading Proficiency
Students might find the lines "twenty centuries of stony sleep / Were vexed to nightmare by a rocking cradle" difficult. Explain that it might mean the birth of Jesus was, for the old order, a "nightmare" because that order was thrown into upheaval.

English Language Learning
The first stanza is one long sentence. Have students stop at each semicolon and evaluate the meaning of what they have read. Each segment builds on the sense of dread, the idea that the something terrible is afoot in the world. If students have trouble with lines 19–20, provide the explanation given in Reading Proficiency.

Special Needs
Help students understand answers to the Guided Reading Questions and the Recall questions in Investigate, Inquire, and Imagine. Students will also benefit from doing

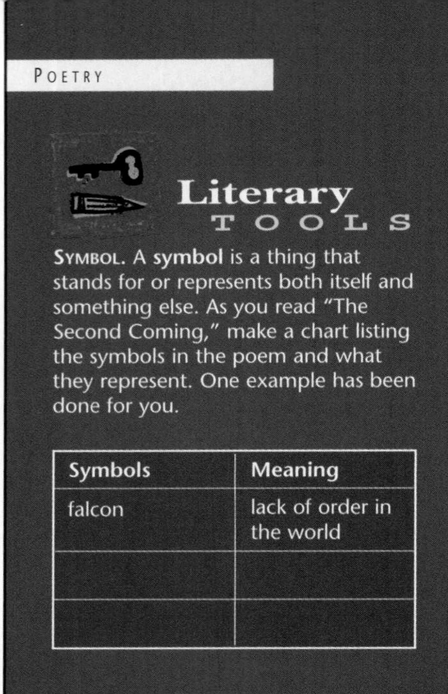

Literary TOOLS

Symbol. A **symbol** is a thing that stands for or represents both itself and something else. As you read "The Second Coming," make a chart listing the symbols in the poem and what they represent. One example has been done for you.

Symbols	Meaning
falcon	lack of order in the world

Reader's Journal

Explain why you think life is better or worse now than in former times. Are you hopeful or pessimistic about the future?

THE SECOND COMING

WILLIAM BUTLER YEATS

Turning and turning in the widening gyre[1]
The falcon cannot hear the falconer;[2]
Things fall apart; the center cannot hold;
Mere anarchy is loosed upon the world,
The blood-dimmed tide is loosed, and everywhere
The ceremony of innocence is drowned;
The best lack all conviction, while
the worst
Are full of passionate intensity.

How does the speaker characterize the times in which he lives?

Surely some revelation is at hand;
Surely the Second Coming[3] is at hand.
The Second Coming! Hardly are those words out
When a vast image out of *Spiritus Mundi*[4]
Troubles my sight: somewhere in sands of the desert
A shape with lion body and the head of a man,[5]

---

1. **gyre.** Circle or cycle. Yeats believed that history occurred in cycles punctuated by revolutionary events in which the spirit world intersected this world. He called these cycles of history *gyres,* which he pronounced with a hard *g.*
2. **falcon . . . falconer.** The reference is to the sport of falconry, in which a trained falcon is used for hunting. The image suggests violence that is uncontrolled by any authority.
3. **Second Coming.** Many Christian sects believe Jesus will come again to earth at the end of time as we know it. This event is known as the Second Coming.
4. ***Spiritus Mundi.*** Latin for "the world spirit," Yeats used it as the name for the collective, inherited body of symbols common to all people. The concept is similar to Carl Jung's archetypes of the collective unconscious. See the entries on *Jungian Criticism* and *archetype* in the Handbook of Literary Terms.
5. **lion . . . man.** The Egyptian sphinx

INDIVIDUAL LEARNING STRATEGIES (CONT.)

the activities in Reading Proficiency and English Language Learning.

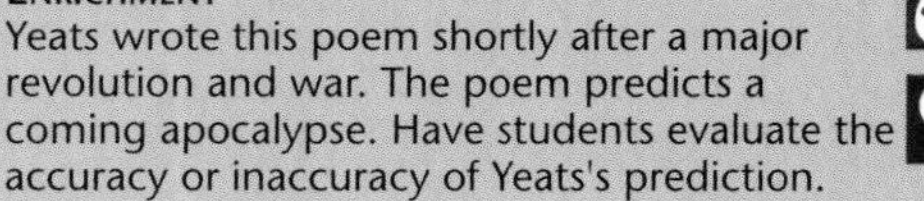

Enrichment
Yeats wrote this poem shortly after a major revolution and war. The poem predicts a coming apocalypse. Have students evaluate the accuracy or inaccuracy of Yeats's prediction.

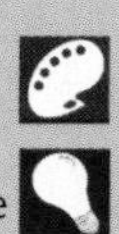

They should consider the apocalyptic events that did occur in the twentieth century. Students might also consider whether there is reason to feel more optimistic about the future than Yeats did. For another poem on this theme, refer students to Eliot's "The Journey of the Magi." Have students compare and contrast these two poems.

Rest on the Flight into Egypt, 1874. Luc Olivier Merson. Museum of Fine Arts, Boston.

A gaze blank and pitiless as the sun,
Is moving its slow thighs, while all about it
Reel shadows of the indignant desert birds.[6]
The darkness drops again; but now I know
That twenty centuries[7] of stony
sleep
Were vexed to nightmare by a
rocking cradle,[8]
And what rough beast, its hour
come round at last,
Slouches towards Bethlehem[9] to be born? ■

What prophesy is implied by the speaker's closing question?

6. **Reel . . . birds.** Birds are traditionally associated with omens or predictions. Unscientific peoples often observe their behavior to predict the future. The reeling suggests Yeats's gyres.
7. **twenty centuries.** The two-thousand-year period before the birth of Jesus, thought of by Yeats as the Heroic Age
8. **rocking cradle.** The birth of Jesus
9. **Bethlehem.** The birthplace of Jesus

Respond *to the* SELECTION

"The Second Coming" is one of the most famous and most-quoted poems of the twentieth century. Why do you think this is so?

ANSWER TO GUIDED READING QUESTION

1. The closing question implies a prophecy of the birth of some horrible beast (instead of Jesus) whose rule will change the world.

SELECTION CHECK TEST 12.10.7 WITH ANSWERS

Checking Your Reading

1. According to the speaker, what has been drowned? **The ceremony of innocence has been drowned.**
2. What does the speaker say the worst people are full of? **They are "full of passionate intensity."**
3. What astonishing event is at hand? **The Second Coming is at hand.**
4. What does the speaker envision in the sands of the desert? **The speaker envisions a shape with a lion's body and a man's head.**
5. At the end of the poem, what does the speaker say is slouching "towards Bethlehem to be born"? **A "rough beast" is slouching "towards Bethlehem to be born."**

Literary Tools

Fill in the blank with the appropriate literary tool from the following list.

symbol allusion metaphor image

1. The "shape with lion body and the head of a man" is a(n) **allusion** to the Egyptian sphinx.
2. The falcon may be a(n) **symbol** for the lack of order in the modern world.
3. The "rocking cradle" is an **allusion** to Jesus's birth in Bethlehem.

RESPOND TO THE SELECTION

Do you believe that we are approaching the apocalypse, or the "end times"? Why, or why not?

ANSWERS TO INVESTIGATE, INQUIRE, AND IMAGINE

Recall

1a. The speaker draws a picture of a world in which everything is falling apart, violence is rampant, innocence is lost, the best people lack convictions, and the worst are full of passion.

2a. The opening of stanza 2 refers to the Second Coming (i.e., the return of Jesus to the earth), described in the Bible as occurring after a time of trouble and tribulation. The speaker sees a creature that looks like a lion's body with the head of a man.

3a. "Twenty centuries" refers to a period of time before the birth of Jesus and a period of time after the birth of Jesus, a cycle coming around again; "a rocking cradle" and "Bethlehem" refer to the birth of Jesus and therefore possibly indicate that some other similarly major event is going to occur now.

INTERPRET

1b. The failure of order, the tide of violence, the end of the "ceremony of innocence," the apathy of the best people, and the enthusiasm of the worst are all changes that trouble the speaker.

2b. The speaker predicts the coming of Jesus, but instead sees an unfeeling beast.

3b. The speaker seems to suggest that an age guided or ruled by some rough beast (a totalitarian government?) will succeed the present age.

ANALYZE

4a. The first cycle is the twenty centuries before the birth of Jesus, the second cycle the period between the birth of Jesus and the present, and the third cycle the time after the Second Coming, whatever form that event takes. The speaker feels dread or foreboding.

SYNTHESIZE

4b. There was a great deal of upheaval during Yeats's life, including the Irish Rebellion, worldwide depression, and world war.

EVALUATE

5a. *Responses will vary.*

EXTEND

5b. Yeats's "Leda and the Swan" and "The Magi" are two poems in which he expresses his views on the cycles of history. Students should summarize Yeats's views about the cycles of history in one of these poems.

Investigate, Inquire, Imagine

Recall: GATHERING FACTS

1a. What picture of the state of the world does the speaker draw in stanza 1?

2a. What does the opening of stanza 2 predict? What shape does the speaker see in a vision?

3a. In the last four lines, what is the meaning of the references to "twenty centuries," "a rocking cradle," and "Bethlehem"?

→ **Interpret:** FINDING MEANING

1b. How does the speaker feel about these changes?

2b. How does the speaker's vision differ from the opening prediction of stanza 2?

3b. In the final lines, what does the speaker seem to suggest will be the successor to the age begun, two thousand years ago, by the birth of Jesus?

Analyze: TAKING THINGS APART

4a. Yeats used the term *gyre*, which he pronounced with a hard *g*, to refer to the cycles of history. What three cycles of history are referred to in the poem? How does the speaker feel about the second and third periods?

→ **Synthesize:** BRINGING THINGS TOGETHER

4b. What events might have led to Yeats's feelings?

Evaluate: MAKING JUDGMENTS

5a. Evaluate whether the speaker is realistic, optimistic, or pessimistic about the future.

→ **Extend:** CONNECTING IDEAS

5b. Yeats expressed his views on the cycles of history in other poems he wrote. Find one of these poems and summarize the poet's views.

Understanding Literature

SYMBOL. Review the definition for **symbol** in the Handbook of Literary Terms and the chart you made for Literary Tools on page 912. What symbols did you find in the poem? What do they represent?

ANSWERS TO UNDERSTANDING LITERATURE

SYMBOL. The falcon symbolizes the lack of order in the world. The sphinx might symbolize the imminent birth of a new, even more difficult age. The slouching beast might symbolize the guiding spirit of the world in the next age.

WRITER'S JOURNAL

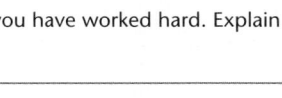

1. "The Second Coming" makes a prediction about what is to come in the world. Write your own **prediction** about the fate of the twenty-first century.
2. Create a **travel brochure** for a place that, like Innisfree, is wild and beautiful. In your brochure, use description of the place to create a mood and explain how people will benefit from visiting.
3. Write a **paragraph** or two about something for which you have worked hard. Explain what you did and why your efforts were important to you.

Integrating *the* LANGUAGE ARTS

Language, Grammar, and Style

ADJECTIVES AND PARTICIPLES. Read the Language Arts Survey 3.66, "Adjectives" and 3.80, "Verbals: Participles, Gerunds, and Infinitives." Then identify the adjectives and participles in the following lines from Yeats's poem "The Stolen Child."

1. Where dips the rocky highland
2. There lies a leafy island
3. Where flapping herons wake
4. The drowsy water-rats
5. And of reddest stolen cherries
6. The dim gray sands with light
7. Weaving olden dances
8. And chase the frothy bubbles
9. Where the wandering water gushes
10. We seek for slumbering trout

Speaking and Listening

TITLES. *The Widening Gyre* and *Things Fall Apart* are twentieth-century books whose titles are quotations from Yeats's "The Second Coming." Look back at the Yeats poems in this unit and choose a phrase that you might use as a title. Then give a brief verbal explanation to your class about what your book is about and why the title is appropriate.

Applied English & Study and Research

WRITING A RÉSUMÉ. Read the Language Arts Survey 6.8, "Writing a Résumé." Then reread the information about Yeats on page 840. Consult several reference works to learn more about Yeats's life. Based on the information that you gather, write a résumé for W. B. Yeats. Imagine that the year is 1930 and that Yeats is applying for a position as the director of a new theater department at Dublin University.

Collaborative Learning & Study and Research

NOBEL PRIZE WINNERS. As a class, organize a festival honoring men and women who, like Yeats, won the Nobel Prize for literature. A list of Nobel Prize winners can be found in a standard reference work such as an encyclopedia. Choose representative works by ten of these prize winners. Invite parents, teachers, and other students to hear your oral interpretations. You might include exhibits of pictures of the authors, copies of their works, and posters showing major events and accomplishments in their lives.

ANSWERS TO INTEGRATING THE LANGUAGE ARTS

Language, Grammar, and Style

1. Adjective: rocky
2. Adjective: leafy
3. Participle: flapping
4. Adjective: drowsy
5. Adjective: reddest; participle: stolen
6. Adjectives: dim, gray
7. Participle: weaving; adjective: olden
8. Adjective: frothy
9. Participle: wandering
10. Participle: slumbering

Applied English & Study and Research

Students should follow the résumé form set out in the Language Arts Survey 6.8, "Writing a Résumé." Résumés should accurately cite important credentials from Yeats's career.

Collaborative Learning & Study and Research

Students may also perform a play at the festival. Several Nobel Prize winners wrote plays. (Yeats is an example.)

Encourage students to contribute in ways that most interest them or best suit their skills. Some may find preparing posters or decorating the festival location more exciting than actually performing, while others may thrive on performance.

Students should strive to make their mix of readings broad enough to include something of interest to everyone who will attend.

ADDITIONAL RESOURCES

Unit 10 Resource Book
- Selection Worksheet 10.4
- Selection Check Test 4.10.9
- Selection Test 4.10.10
- Language, Grammar, and Style Resource 3.34
- Study and Research Resource 5.19

GRAPHIC ORGANIZER

Image and Objective Correlative. Students should note the following images in their sensory details chart:
Sight: "the burnt-out ends of smoky days"; "a gusty shower wraps / The grimy scraps / Of withered leaves about your feet / And newspapers from vacant lots"; "A lonely cab-horse steams and stamps"; "the lighting of the lamps"; "sawdust-trampled street / With all its muddy feet"; "all the hands / That are raising dingy shades / In a thousand furnished rooms"; "the thousand sordid images"; "light crept up between the shutters"; "short square fingers stuffing pipes"; "evening newspapers"; "ancient women / Gathering fuel in vacant lots"
Sound: "The showers beat / On broken blinds and chimney-pots"; "you heard the sparrows in the gutters"
Touch: "You curled the papers from your hair, / Or clasped the yellow soles of feet"
Smell: steak, "faint stale smells of beer"

READER'S JOURNAL

Encourage students to notice the sights, sounds, smells, tastes, and touching associated with that time of day.

Literary Tools

Speaker and Tone. The **speaker** is the character who speaks in, or narrates, a poem—the voice assumed by the writer. **Tone** is the emotional attitude toward the reader or toward the subject implied by a literary work. As you read, notice where the tone of the poem shifts and determine the attitude toward the subject that the speaker reveals in these places.

Image and Objective Correlative. An **image** is language that creates a concrete representation of an object or an experience. An **objective correlative** is a group of images that together create a particular emotion in the reader. This term was coined by T. S. Eliot. As you read, make a sensory details chart that lists the images in the poem. One example has been done for you.

Sight	Sound	Touch	Taste	Smell
				steaks

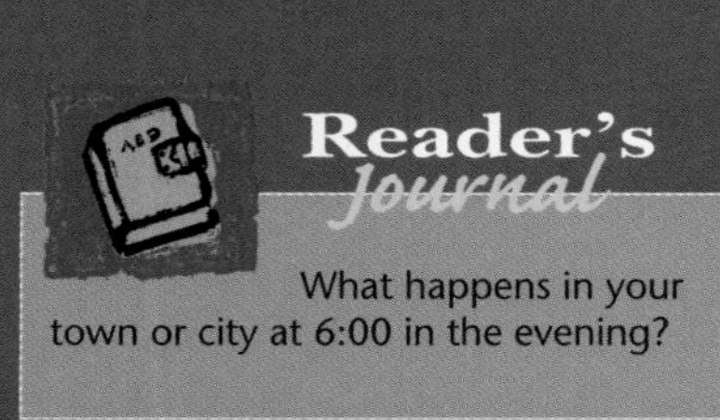

Reader's Journal

What happens in your town or city at 6:00 in the evening?

"Preludes"

by T. S. Eliot

About the Author

Thomas Stearns Eliot (1888–1965) was born and raised in St. Louis, Missouri but lived much of his adult life in England where he eventually became a citizen. Educated at Harvard, the Sorbonne, and Oxford, Eliot steeped himself in philosophy and linguistics. He wrote his first major poems, including "The Love Song of J. Alfred Prufrock" (1910–11), while he was a student in Paris. Eliot's early poems established the major themes of his body of work: the problem of isolation from other people and from God in modern urban life and the search for purpose and meaning. Eliot returned to these themes again and again in poems such as *The Waste Land* (1922), a long narrative poem published as a book; "The Hollow Men" (1927); and "Ash Wednesday" (1930).

Eliot's influence on twentieth-century poetry was tremendous, particularly in the years between the world wars. His poems departed radically from nineteenth-century poetry, not only in theme but in form. Considered one of the inventors of modern poetry, Eliot wrote in **free verse**. Free verse is a flexible form of poetry without regular patterns of rhyme, rhythm, or division into stanzas. It usually has irregular line lengths and, like prose, suits the rhythm and length of the lines to what is being said. In addition to being one of the century's leading poets, Eliot was a distinguished literary critic, editor, and dramatist. In 1948, he was awarded the Nobel Prize in literature.

About the Selection

"Preludes" (1915) is one of Eliot's early poems. Its drab and seedy images of city life are typical of the view of modern life he expressed in his work. Eliot once explained, "My urban imagery was that of St. Louis, upon which that of Paris and London had been superimposed." The poem is remarkable for finding hope amid the futility and dreariness of modern life.

GOALS/OBJECTIVES

Studying this lesson will enable students to
- appreciate the poetry of T. S. Eliot
- understand the associations connected with a description of an urban setting
- describe T. S. Eliot's literary accomplishments and explain the historical significance of his writings
- define *speaker, tone, image,* and *objective correlative* and recognize the use of these techniques in the selection
- correct sentence fragments
- tell a story
- compile a bibliography

Preludes

T. S. Eliot

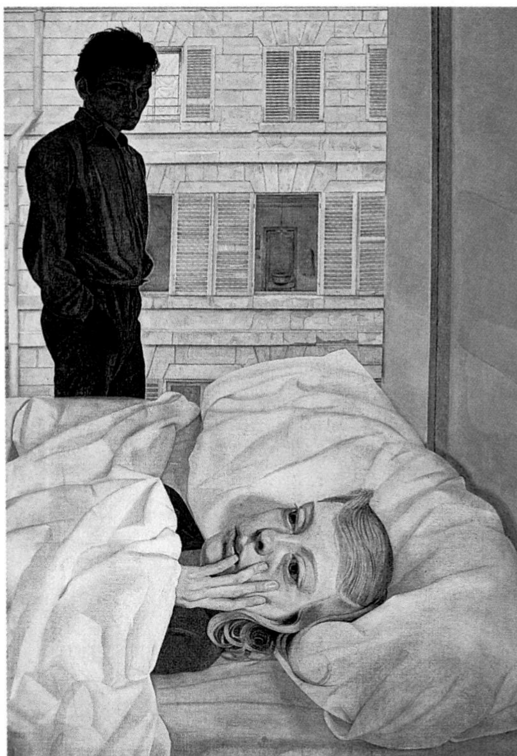

Hotel Bedroom, c.1900s. Lucian Freud. Beaverbrook Art Gallery, Frederickton, New Brunswick, Canada.

I

The winter evening settles down
With smell of steaks in passageways.
Six o'clock.
The burnt-out ends of smoky days.
And now a gusty shower wraps
The grimy scraps
Of withered leaves about your feet
And newspapers from vacant lots;
The showers beat
On broken blinds and chimney-pots,
And at the corner of the street
A lonely cab-horse steams and stamps.

And then the lighting of the lamps.

How does line 13 affect the mood of the first stanza?

II

The morning comes to consciousness
Of faint stale smells of beer
From the sawdust-trampled street
With all its muddy feet that press
To early coffee-stands.

With the other masquerades
That time resumes,
One thinks of all the hands
That are raising dingy shades
In a thousand furnished rooms.

Words for Everyday Use

mas • quer • ade (mas´kər ād´) *n.,* ball or party at which masks and fancy costumes or disguises are worn. *As the prom was a masquerade, I was not aware that I was dancing with my sworn enemy.*

Answer to Guided Reading Question

1. A mood of dreariness, futility, loneliness, and depression is created in the first stanza. Line 12 increases the loneliness of the stanza; line 13 may be seen as one more futile act that sheds light on the grit and grime of the city or as an illumination that softens and improves it. Point out to students that each stanza of the poem moves from some sordid or desperate image to some actual or metaphorical illumination (the lighting of lamps, the raising of window shades, the vision of the street, and the notion of "some infinitely gentle/Infinitely suffering thing").

Individual Learning Strategies

Motivation
Have students make a sensory details charts listing images of the city in which they live.

Reading Proficiency
Explain that Eliot sometimes uses phrases as sentences that do not have verbs and so are not really complete sentences. Point out that while this type of sentence is frequent in modern poetry, it is not a proper form of sentence to use in schoolwork or in prose in general; it may be confusing to the reader, who will think something is missing.

English Language Learning
Point out that "Preludes" presents urban scenes from shortly after the turn of the century. Ask students to look for references to this time period, such as the "lonely cab-horse" and the "lighting of lamps" in section 1. Give students definitions for the following additional vocabulary from the selection:
insistent—persistent in demands or assertions
resume—begin again

Special Needs
Make sure students can answer the Guided Reading Questions and the Recall questions from Investigate, Inquire, and Imagine. Students will also benefit from doing the activities in Reading Proficiency and English Language Learning.

Enrichment
Have students compare and contrast Eliot's urban imagery with the rustic imagery of Yeats's poem "The Lake Isle of Innisfree" in this unit.

Vocabulary from the Selection

constitute
masquerade
sordid

ANSWERS TO GUIDED READING QUESTIONS

1. At night the person described in the poem lies upon her back and waits, she dozes, and she watches the night revealing the nightmare or subconscious images of her life in a kind of flickering show on the ceiling.
2. "His" soul has been stretched across the skies or trampled by feet. This has happened because he has internal-lized or become a part of the city environment and so suffers physically with every sight he sees and sound he hears.

SELECTION CHECK TEST 12.10.9 WITH ANSWERS

Checking Your Reading

1. What season and time of day does Eliot describe in stanza 1? **He describes a wintry night.**
2. What images in stanza 1 fix the time period? **The "lonely cab-horse" and the lighting of the lamps fix the time period.**
3. What is being raised by hands "In a thousand furnished rooms"? **Dingy shades are being raised by hands "In a thousand furnished rooms.**
4. The speaker of the poem is moved by the notion of what? **The speaker is moved by the notion of "some infinitely gentle / Infinitely suffering thing."**
5. The worlds revolve like what? **They "revolve like ancient women / Gathering fuel in vacant lots."**

Vocabulary in Context

Fill in each blank below with the most appropriate word from the following Words for Everyday Use. You may have to change the tense of certain verbs.

constitute masquerade sordid

1. From the period costumes, the reporter could see that the ball was a **masquerade**.
2. Two hundred Burger Barn restaurants **constitute** the national franchise.
3. In the **sordid** tavern Meridel saw peanut shells and spilled beer on the floor.

Literary Tools

Fill in the blank with the appropriate literary tool from the following list.

image speaker objective correlative tone

1. Images are needed to make an **objective correlative**.
2. The **speaker** describes a mood of dreariness, futility, loneliness, and depression in the first stanza.
3. The **tone** of the poem changes from one of weary cynicism in section 1 to one of sensitivity and compassion in section 2.

III

You tossed a blanket from the bed,
You lay upon your back, and waited;
You dozed, and watched the night revealing
The thousand sordid images
Of which your soul was constituted;
They flickered against the ceiling.
And when all the world came back
And the light crept up between the shutters
And you heard the sparrows in the gutters,
You had such a vision of the street
As the street hardly understands;
Sitting along the bed's edge, where
You curled the papers from your hair,
Or clasped the yellow soles of feet
In the palms of both soiled hands.

What happens at night?

IV

His soul stretched tight across the skies
That fade behind a city block,
Or trampled by insistent feet
At four and five and six o'clock;
And short square fingers stuffing pipes,
And evening newspapers, and eyes
Assured of certain certainties,
The conscience of a blackened street
Impatient to assume the world.

What has happened to "His" soul? Why has this happened?

I am moved by fancies that are curled
Around these images, and cling:
The notion of some infinitely gentle
Infinitely suffering thing.

Wipe your hand across your mouth, and laugh;
The worlds revolve like ancient women
Gathering fuel in vacant lots. ■

WORDS FOR EVERYDAY USE

sor • did (sôr´did) *adj.*, dirty; filthy. *The problem with writing about sordid scenes is that one's own writing quickly becomes depressing and grim.*

con • sti • tute (kän´stə to͞ot´) *vt.*, make up; be the components or elements of; form; compose. *The fifty states together constitute the United States.*

Respond *to the* **SELECTION**

Jot down a few words that describe your mood after reading "Preludes." What in this poem creates such a mood?

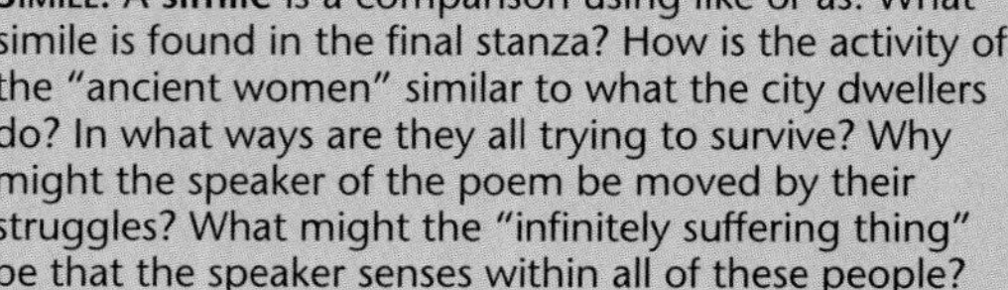

LITERARY TECHNIQUE

SIMILE. A **simile** is a comparison using like or as. What simile is found in the final stanza? How is the activity of the "ancient women" similar to what the city dwellers do? In what ways are they all trying to survive? Why might the speaker of the poem be moved by their struggles? What might the "infinitely suffering thing" be that the speaker senses within all of these people?

Answer

The last stanza contains a simile that compares revolving worlds to ancient women gathering fuel in vacant lots. The ancient women, like the other city dwellers, are going about their business gathering the necessities of life. The activity of the city is determined by the occupations of its dwellers. The speaker might be moved by their lives because he sees them as typical of humans everywhere, including himself. The "infinitely suffering thing" may be their essential humanity, their souls, or their need to struggle to survive though their environment offers them little beauty or peace to compensate them.

INVESTIGATE

Inquire, Imagine

Recall: GATHERING FACTS

1a. What setting does the speaker describe in stanza 1?

2a. What resumes in the morning?

3a. What moves the speaker at the end of the poem?

→ **Interpret:** FINDING MEANING

1b. What mood is evoked in stanza 1? What images are used to create this mood?

2b. How are the images of the night compared with the human soul?

3b. The speaker has a notion of some "Infinitely suffering thing." To what in the poem might this phrase refer? To what might it refer beyond the poem?

Analyze: TAKING THINGS APART

4a. Identify the impact of the urban environment on the woman in stanza 3.

→ **Synthesize:** BRINGING THINGS TOGETHER

4b. The woman in stanza 3 has a "vision of the street / As the street hardly understands." What characterizes this vision? What does this vision have in common with the "lighting of the lamps" in stanza 1 and the raising of the window shades in stanza 2?

Evaluate: MAKING JUDGMENTS

5a. Do you think the portrait of the world as portrayed in "Preludes" is an accurate representation of the world today? Is the mood evoked in the poem a prevalent one? Are there times when this is more so than others?

→ **Extend:** CONNECTING IDEAS

5b. What similarities do you find between this poem and Yeats's "The Lake Isle of Innisfree" and "The Second Coming"?

Understanding Literature

SPEAKER AND TONE. Review the definitions of **speaker** and **tone** in the Handbook of Literary Terms. Where does the tone of the poem shift? What is the attitude toward the subject that the speaker reveals in these places?

IMAGE AND OBJECTIVE CORRELATIVE. Review the definitions of **image** and **objective correlative** in the Handbook of Literary Terms and the graphic organizer you made for Literary Tools on page 916. What images are used in stanza 1 to describe the scene observed by the speaker? What emotions are created by these images?

RESPOND TO THE SELECTION

Students might suggest a depressed or lonely mood after reading the poem. Sordid images create the mood.

ANSWERS TO INVESTIGATE, INQUIRE, AND IMAGINE

RECALL

1a. The speaker describes an urban setting on a rainy evening in winter.

2a. Masquerades, such as the raising of shades, resume in the morning.

3a. The speaker is moved by fancies associated with "these images" of dismal city life. These fancies involve "some infinitely gentle / Infinitely suffering thing," perhaps the human soul rising above its circumstances.

INTERPRET

1b. A mood of dreariness, futility, loneliness, and depression is evoked in the first stanza. This mood is created by images such as the winter evening settling down, day described as being "smoky" and having a burnt-out end like a dead cigarette, and the grimy scraps of withered leaves wrapping around one's feet.

2b. The thousand sordid images revealed by the night are compared to the constitution of the human soul.

3b. The "infinitely suffering thing" may refer to humanity as represented by the humans in the poem, or it may represent the soul stretched tight across the skies. Beyond the poem, the phrase may perhaps refer to the willingness to live; to God (who may be the soul stretched across the sky), to life in general, or to the universe.

ANALYZE

4a. The sordid environment has a direct connection to the sordid images that play in the woman's mind. They constitute her soul, as if years of living in a sordid urban environment have transformed her internally.

SYNTHESIZE

4b. The woman's vision opposes the sordid street scene and appears to be elevated in comparison, perhaps optimistic or romantic. The sordidness of city life is transmuted by images of actual or metaphorical illumination throughout the poem, such as the "lighting of the lamps" in stanza 1 and the raising of the window shades in stanza 2.

EVALUATE

Responses will vary.

5a. The urban world as portrayed in "Preludes" has not significantly

INVESTIGATE, INQUIRE, AND IMAGINE (CONT.)

changed since Eliot wrote this poem. The mood of awareness of this sordidness is probably not prevalent,, although arguably the sordidness is. Times of economic depression may make the sordidness more intrusive.

EXTEND

5b. Eliot's view of urban life recalls Yeats's description of the city in "The Lake Isle of Innisfree." Lines 27-28 of "Preludes" recalls the vision of the speaker in "The Second Coming." Lines 50-51 refer to an "infinitely suffering thing" that may be compared to the beast slouching to Bethlehem in "The Second Coming." The revolving words mentioned in line 53 suggest Yeats's cycles of history in "The Second Coming."

Answers to Understanding Literature can be found on page 920.

ANSWERS TO UNDERSTANDING LITERATURE

Speaker and Tone. The tone of weary cynicism in lines 1-47 of the poem is fairly consistent. It changes in lines 48-51 to a tone of sensitivity and compassion and shifts again in lines 52-54 to a tone of ironic awareness of the inextricable connection in this world of the positive (gathering fuel) and the negative (being ancient and working to gather fuel as the desperately poor do, in vacant lots).

Image and Objective Correlative. The speaker mentions the winter evening settling down; the smell of meat; the "smoky" day with a burnt-out end like a dead cigarette; a gusty shower; the grimy scraps of withered leaves wrapping around one's feet, along with newspapers from vacant lots; showers beating on broken blinds; and a lonely cab-horse. Emotions of loneliness and depression are evoked by these images.

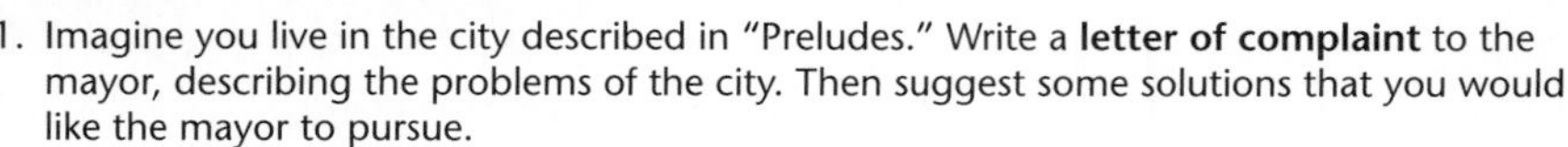

Writer's Journal

1. Imagine you live in the city described in "Preludes." Write a **letter of complaint** to the mayor, describing the problems of the city. Then suggest some solutions that you would like the mayor to pursue.
2. Write a **paragraph** paraphrasing one of the stanzas of the poem. In your paraphrase, restate the ideas that seem essential.
3. Write a **poem** describing a city that you know, using vivid images.

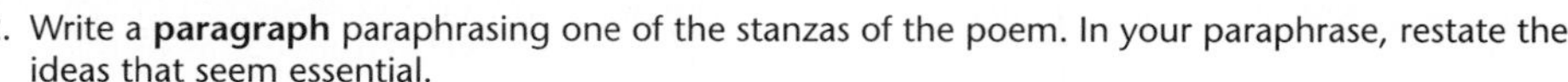

Integrating the Language Arts

Language, Grammar, and Style

Sentence Run-ons. Read the Language Arts Survey 3.34, "Correcting Sentence Run-ons." Then rewrite the following sentences, correcting the sentence run-ons. If a sentence is correct, write OK.

1. Thomas Stearns Eliot was a poet and playwright he lived in the United States and England.
2. His early poems express the anguish and barrenness of modern life in many poems he focuses on the isolation of the individual.
3. Born in the United States, Eliot became a British subject in 1927.
4. The *Sacred Wood, Essays Ancient and Modern* and *Notes Towards a Definition of Culture* are Eliot's works of literary criticism.
5. In 1948 he was awarded the Nobel Prize for Literature he was 60 years old.

Speaking and Listening & Collaborative Learning

Telling a Story. With a partner, take turns telling a story about a character who lives in the city described in "Preludes." Try to evoke a mood similar to the one expressed in "Preludes."

Study and Research

Catalog Search. Read about using computerized and card catalogs in the Language Arts Survey 5.19, "How to Locate Library Materials." Depending on the cataloging system used in your library, use the card catalog or database to look up works available by T. S. Eliot. Compile a selective bibliography that includes a sampling of Eliot's poetry, plays, and critical essays from all stages of his career.

INTEGRATING THE LANGUAGE ARTS

Language, Grammar, and Style

1. Thomas Stearns Eliot was a poet and playwright who lived in the United States and England.
2. His early poems express the anguish and barrenness of modern life; in many poem he focuses on the isolation of the individual.
3. OK
4. OK
5. In 1948, when he was 60 years old, Eliot was awarded the Nobel Prize for Literature.

"Snake"

By D. H. Lawrence

About the Author

David Herbert Lawrence (1885–1930) led a restless, colorful, controversial life. Born in Nottinghamshire, he was the son of a rough coal miner and a genteel mother. Lawrence's mother longed to have her children rise above their working-class origins, and the young boy identified strongly with her. However, as an adult, Lawrence came to appreciate the primitive, natural integrity of his father and others of his class as opposed to the smothering conventional aspirations of his mother and other members of the higher social classes. In 1909, Lawrence published his first poems, and in the following year a novel. He taught school for a while but gave this up after meeting Frieda von Richthofen, a German woman whom he married. Lawrence's first major novel, the autobiographical *Sons and Lovers,* was finished shortly thereafter. The novel deals with a boy's attempt to break away from a domineering mother and to establish his own identity. This novel was followed by *The Rainbow,* the first of several of Lawrence's works to be banned in England because of their controversial treatment of human sexuality.

Lawrence traveled widely and lived, at different times, in Germany, Italy, Mexico, Australia, and New Mexico. He and his wife Frieda were at the center of the artists' colony in Taos, New Mexico. In addition to his novels, Lawrence wrote poetry, criticism, short stories, and colorful travel sketches. He was also a gifted painter. Lawrence's novel *Lady Chatterley's Lover* became the focus of a legal battle in the United States, ending in a famous victory over censorship. In his mature work, Lawrence championed the primitive, basic instincts of men and women over what he believed to be the artificial, mechanical impositions of contemporary civilized society.

About the Selection

D. H. Lawrence explored the psychology and subconscious minds of his characters, using intense imagery and symbolism. He wanted his work to be free of conventional rhythms and phrases and to capture the feeling of the immediate moment. **"Snake"** was published in the 1923 collection *Birds, Beasts and Flowers,* which contains poems set in many different places around the world. This poem, set in Sicily, shows the speaker's desire to be connected with primitive forces in nature and his opposition to the voices of his "accursed human education."

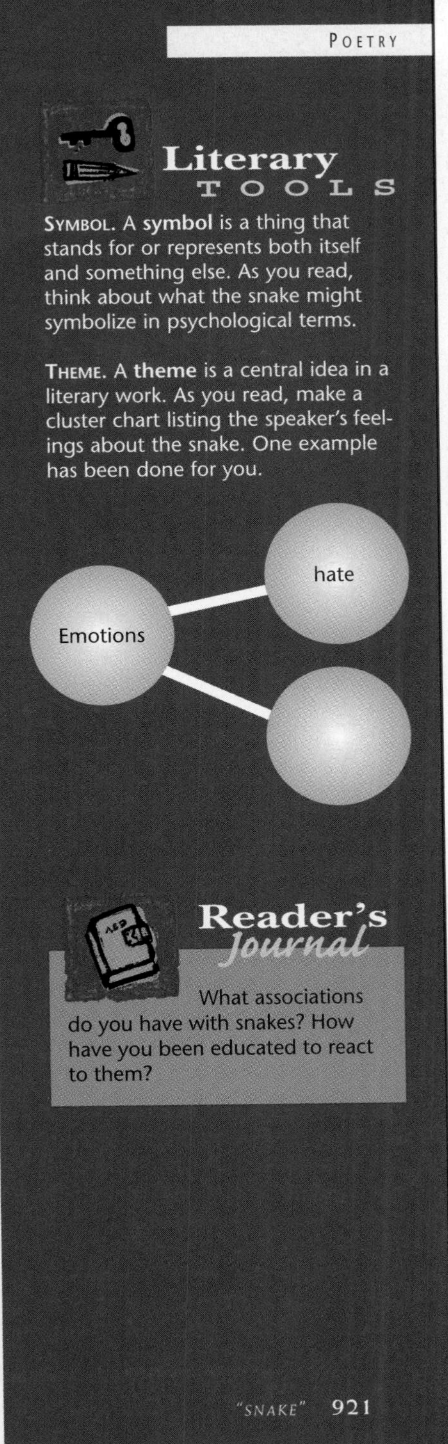

Literary Tools

Symbol. A **symbol** is a thing that stands for or represents both itself and something else. As you read, think about what the snake might symbolize in psychological terms.

Theme. A **theme** is a central idea in a literary work. As you read, make a cluster chart listing the speaker's feelings about the snake. One example has been done for you.

Reader's Journal

What associations do you have with snakes? How have you been educated to react to them?

ADDITIONAL RESOURCES

Unit 10 Resource Book

- Selection Worksheet 10.5
- Selection Check Test 4.10.11
- Selection Test 4.10.12
- Speaking and Listening Resource 4.21
- Applied English Resource 6.4

GRAPHIC ORGANIZER

Students should include the following emotions in their charts: fear, revulsion, honor.

VOCABULARY FROM THE SELECTION

carob
convulse
fissure
humility
muse
paltry
perversity

READER'S JOURNAL

You might discuss that, in the Judeo-Christian tradition, the snake was the original tempter of the human race and has always represented evil. Students may or may not be aware of this association with the snake.

GOALS/OBJECTIVES

Studying this lesson will enable students to

- appreciate the speaker's desire to become connected with primitive, vital natural forces often buried by such "civilizing" forces as education
- describe D.H. Lawrences' literary accomplishments and explain the historical significance of his writings
- define *allusion, symbol,* and *theme* and recognize the use of these techniques in the selection
- research the culture of snakes
- participate in a debate
- write a public service announcement

INDIVIDUAL LEARNING STRATEGIES

MOTIVATION
Play the segment from the movie *Gorillas in the Mist* when the protagonist first sees gorillas in the wild. Tell students to analyze her emotions. Then have students share their experiences of encountering a wild animal in its natural habitat.

READING PROFICIENCY
Explain to students how writers sometimes use italics to indicate the thoughts of characters. Point out line 36 as an example of italics showing internal "voices" of the speaker.

ENGLISH LANGUAGE LEARNING
Review the following additional vocabulary with students:
trough—long shallow receptacle holding drinking water
slackness—lacking in firmness
venomous—poisonous
thrice—three times
writhe—twist into coils
exile—forced absence from one's country

SPECIAL NEEDS
Review with students the answers to the Guided Reading Questions and the answers to the Recall questions in Investigate, Inquire, and Imagine. Students will also benefit from doing the activities in Reading Proficiency and English Language Learning.

ENRICHMENT
Students usually find Lawrence's work interesting because it explores many of the challenging issues of relationship to authority, reaction to tradition, and the embracing of vital instincts with which teenagers are often concerned. Lawrence viewed modern "civilized" society with some skepticism. Pose the following questions to students: What are the forces in society that work to uncivilize people? What feelings or experiences, now generally lost, might have been common among our uncivilized ancestors long ago? For a fascinating exploration of what might be learned from so-called "primitive" peoples, refer students to Maybury-Lewis, David. *Millennium: Tribal Wisdom and the Modern World.* 1992. This book is based on a PBS series hosted by Maybury-Lewis, which may be viewed on videotape.

Snake

D. H. LAWRENCE

A snake came to my water trough
On a hot, hot day, and I in pajamas for the heat,
To drink there.

In the deep, strange-scented shade of the great dark carob tree
I came down the steps with my pitcher
And must wait, must stand and wait, for there he was at the trough before me.

He reached down from a fissure in the earth-wall in the gloom
And trailed his yellow-brown slackness soft-bellied down, over the edge of the stone trough
And rested his throat upon the stone bottom,
And where the water had dripped from the tap, in a small clearness,
He sipped with his straight mouth,
Softly drank through his straight gums, into his slack long body,
Silently.

Someone was before me at my water trough,
And I, like a second-comer, waiting.

He lifted his head from his drinking, as cattle do,
And looked at me vaguely, as drinking cattle do,
And flickered his two-forked tongue from his lips, and mused a moment,
And stooped and drank a little more,

WORDS FOR EVERYDAY USE

car • ob (kar´ əb) *n.*, leguminous tree of the eastern Mediterranean, bearing long, flat, leathery, brown pods with a sweet pulp. *The fruit of the carob tree, when dried and made into a powder, serves as a substitute for chocolate.*

fis • sure (fish´ ər) *n.*, long, narrow, deep cleft or crack. *In a fairy tale, a young man makes his fortune with a magic stick he finds in a fissure that has opened in the ground during an earthquake.*

muse (myo͞oz) *vi.*, think deeply and at length; meditate. *While he mused on the stars, the philosopher fell into a well.*

Serpent, c.1900s. Raoul Dufy. Sheldon Memorial Art Gallery, Lincoln, Nebraska.

Being earth-brown, earth-golden from the burning bowels of the earth
On the day of Sicilian July, with Etna smoking.[1]

The voice of my education said to me
He must be killed,
For in Sicily the black black snakes are innocent, the gold are venomous.

And voices in me said, If you were a man
You would take a stick and break him now, and finish him off.

What tells the speaker that he should kill the snake?

1. **Etna smoking.** Etna is a volcanic mountain in eastern Sicily.

ANSWERS TO GUIDED READING QUESTIONS

1. The voice of the speaker's education tells him that he should kill the snake. The voice says that if he were a man, he would kill the snake with a stick.

LITERARY TECHNIQUE

Freudian Criticism. Freudian criticism draws upon the works of the founder of psychoanalysis, Sigmund Freud, and generally views literary works or the parts thereof as expressions of unconscious desires, as wish fulfillments, or as neurotic sublimations of unresolved conflicts from childhood. Freud believed that children are born with basic, primitive instinctual desires that he called the *id.* As they grow up, according to Freud, children encounter limitations on these desires in the form of rules and codes of behavior enforced by their parents and others. These rules, internalized, become another part of the personality which Freud called the *superego*—what in ordinary speech is called the *conscience.* The desires of the id are suppressed but come out in dreams, fantasies, slips of the tongue, and neurotic behaviors. How do Freud's ideas help to explain Lawrence's poem? With what would he associate Lawrence's "voices of my accursed human education"? The speaker's impulse to destroy the snake can be identified with the limitations imposed on the id by external rules. Freud would probably identify the snake with the id. He would associate the voices Lawrence hears with the limitations imposed on the id. (Other interpretations are possible: The remorse felt by the speaker could be interpreted as the voice of the superego chastising him for his unnecessary actions.)

ANSWERS TO GUIDED READING QUESTIONS

1. The speaker experiences feelings of cowardice because he does not kill the snake, eccentricity because he wants to talk to the snake, and humility because he feels honored at the snake's presence.
2. The speaker decides to act because he feels horror at the idea that the snake is going into a hole. This may make the reader feel sympathy with the speaker because he did not want the snake to have to go into the hole, or irritation with the speaker because he should have restrained his impulse and let the snake go into the hole without interruption.

SELECTION CHECK TEST 12.10.11 WITH ANSWERS

Checking Your Answers

1. Why do the speaker and the snake go to the trough? **They want some water.**
2. Why does the speaker think that the snake must be killed? **It is a gold snake, which is venomous.**
3. Why does the speaker throw the log at the snake? **The speaker throws the log to prove to himself that he is not cowardly.**
4. Why does the speaker think of the albatross? **The speaker thinks of the albatross because, like the mariner, he hurt a noble creature.**
5. How does the speaker describe his behavior toward the snake? **The speaker thinks of his behavior as a "pettiness" that he must expiate.**

Vocabulary in Context

Fill in each blank with the most appropriate word from the following Words for Everyday Use from "Snake."

muse perversity fissure humility

1. Mr. Takimoto showed his **humility** each time he bowed to his employer.
2. When Danielle **muses**, she gets a faraway look in her eyes and sometimes inspiration for a song.
3. Jack showed his **perversity** when he double-parked next to a car in which the driver was trying to get out.

Literary Tools

Fill in the blanks with the appropriate literary tool from the following list.

symbol theme allusion image

1. Lawrence makes a(n) **allusion** to "The Rime of the Ancient Mariner" when he mentions the albatross.
2. The snake is a(n) **symbol** for the hidden, primitive forces of life that dwell in the dark of the subconscious.
3. The **theme** of the poem may be the inability of modern humans to connect with the divine in nature, as represented by the snake.

But must I confess how I liked him,
How glad I was he had come like a guest in quiet, to drink at my water trough
And depart peaceful, pacified, and thankless
Into the burning bowels of this earth?

Was it cowardice, that I dared not kill him?
Was it perversity, that I longed to talk to him?
Was it humility, to feel so honored?
I felt so honored.

What contradictory feelings does the speaker have about the snake?

And yet those voices:
If you were not afraid, you would kill him!

And truly I was afraid, I was most afraid,
But even so, honored still more
That he should seek my hospitality
From out the dark door of the secret earth.

He drank enough
And lifted his head, dreamily, as one who has drunken,
And flickered his tongue like a forked night on the air, so black,
Seeming to lick his lips,
And looked around like a god, unseeing, into the air,
And slowly turned his head,
And slowly, very slowly, as if thrice adream

Proceeded to draw his slow length curving round
And climb the broken bank of my wall-face.

And as he put his head into that dreadful hole,
And as he slowly drew up, snake-easing his shoulders, and entered further,
A sort of horror, a sort of protest against his withdrawing into that horrid
black hole,
Deliberately going into the blackness, and slowly drawing himself after,
Overcame me now his back was turned.

Why does the speaker decide to act at this point? How does this make you feel toward the speaker?

I looked round, I put down my pitcher,
I picked up a clumsy log
And threw it at the water trough with a clatter.

WORDS FOR EVERYDAY USE

per • ver • si • ty (pər vʉr´ sə tē) *n.*, quality or condition of deviating from what is considered right or good. *They thought they were ready to depart when they had packed the car, but out of sheer perversity the engine would not start.*

hu • mil • i • ty (hyo͞o mil´ ə tē) *n.*, absence of pride or self-assertion. *Said the old man of the hills, "Humility is a basic requirement for perfection."*

I think it did not hit him;
But suddenly that part of him that was left behind convulsed in undignified haste,
Writhed like lightning, and was gone
Into the black hole, the earth-lipped fissure in the wall-front
At which, in the intense still noon, I stared with fascination.

And immediately I regretted it.
I thought how paltry, how vulgar, what a mean act!
I despised myself and the voices of my accursed human education.

And I thought of the albatross,[2]
And I wished he would come back, my snake.

For he seemed to me again like a king,
Like a king in exile, uncrowned in the underworld,
Now due to be crowned again.

And so, I missed my chance with one of the lords
Of life.
And I have something to expiate:[3]
A pettiness.

How does the speaker feel about himself at the end of the poem?

■

2. **albatross.** In Coleridge's "The Rime of the Ancient Mariner," the mariner kills a friendly sea bird, the albatross, and so brings ghoulish misfortune on himself and on his shipmates.
3. **expiate.** Get rid of (in myself)

WORDS FOR EVERYDAY USE

con • vulse (kən vuls´) *vt.*, shake or disturb violently; agitate. *The film was so funny that the audience was convulsed with laughter.*

pal • try (pôl´ trē) *adj.*, practically worthless; trifling; insignificant; contemptible; petty. *In some countries, workers earn the paltry sum of a dollar a week.*

Respond to the SELECTION

What first, unexamined reaction does the speaker have to the snake?

ANSWER TO GUIDED READING QUESTION

1. The speaker regrets his actions and feels ashamed of his own pettiness.

RESPOND TO THE SELECTION

The speaker's first reaction is to think the snake should be killed. Students may recognize that this impulse is part of an unthinking desire to act in an outward way to exert control over an unnerving situation; the real necessity is to exert inward control, remain calm, and assess the circumstances.

ANSWERS TO INVESTIGATE, INQUIRE, AND IMAGINE

Recall

1a. The snake and the speaker have come for water.

2a. The voice of his education tells the speaker that if he were a man, he would kill the snake with a stick.

3a. The speaker wonders if he is a coward because he does not kill the snake, or eccentric because he wants to talk to the snake, or merely humble because he feels honored at the snake's presence.

Interpret

1b. The speaker acknowledges that the heat affects the snake just as it affects him. They share a need for water.

2b. Conventional wisdom tells the speaker that the snake is venomous. He is also very afraid of the snake.

3b. The speaker reacts when the snake returns to a hole in the wall; he feels a horror at the idea that the snake is going into a hole. He does not like the idea that the snake is "deliberately going into the blackness."

Analyze

4a. The speaker is happy and honored that the snake has come for water. The speaker fears the snake and is nagged by the voice of education or civilization that tells him that he should kill the snake.

Synthesize

4b. The positive feelings seem stronger, though the negative feelings are more persistent. The speaker's action suggest that the "educated, " negative feelings toward the snake have won, but his reaction to his action suggest that his positive feelings toward the snake have won out.

Evaluate

5a. *Responses will vary.*

Extend

Responses will vary.

5b. The serpent in "Paradise Lost" is the devil and incarnates evil. He is sly, manipulative, and intelligent. In his Christian education Lawrence would have been aware of these associations with snakes.

Investigate, Inquire, Imagine

Recall: Gathering Facts

1a. For what purpose have both the snake and the speaker come out on this hot, hot day?

2a. What does the voice of the speaker's education tell him?

3a. What contradictory feelings does the speaker find himself having about the snake?

Interpret: Finding Meaning

1b. How does the speaker establish, from the very beginning of the poem, an animal bond between himself and the snake? What need to they both share?

2b. What practical reason does the speaker have for thinking he must do something to the snake? What emotional reason also leads him to this thought?

3b. What finally causes the speaker to react physically to the snake? How is he feeling at that moment? Why?

Analyze: Taking Things Apart →

4a. Identify positive thoughts the speaker has toward the snake. Identify reasons the speaker feels he should harm the snake.

Synthesize: Bringing Things Together

4b. Which feelings toward the snake seem stronger? What do the speaker's final actions suggest?

Evaluate: Making Judgments →

5a. Judge whether the speaker is benig too hard on himself at the end of the poem.

Extend: Connecting Ideas

5b. What are the characteristics of the serpent in Milton's "Paradise Lost"? How might Milton's snake have informed Lawrence and been a part of his education regarding snakes?

Understanding Literature

Symbol. Review the definition for **symbol** in Literary Tools on page 921. What do you think the snake in this poem symbolizes? Why might the speaker be frightened of his own more primitive nature, his basic animal instincts, and the dark, subterranean recesses of his own spirit? Why might the voices of his human education tell him that these parts of himself should be suppressed?

Theme. Review the definition for **theme** in the Handbook of Literary Terms and the cluster chart you made for Literary Tools on page 921. What does the speaker in this poem think has happened to people as a result of civilizing influences like education? Why does the speaker think that his action was paltry, vulgar, mean, and petty? Read or reread William Wordsworth's "The World Is Too Much with Us" on page 611. What similarity in theme can you find in the two poems?

ANSWERS TO UNDERSTANDING LITERATURE

Symbol. The snake seems to symbolize the hidden, primitive forces of life that dwell in the dark of the subconscious. The speaker is an educated man who has been taught to distrust the primitive within him. The voices of his human education recognize that his primitive impulses are not always comprehensible or controllable.

Theme. The speaker believes that people have become prone to paltry, petty acts in rejecting animal powers such as are represented by the snake. The speaker despises his own action because it was unnecessary and ineffectual. Wordsworth spells out his theme by saying, "Little we see in Nature that is ours"; the speaker in Lawrence's poem sees a similar failure of connection between himself and nature as represented by the snake.

WRITER'S JOURNAL

1. Write a **note** in which the speaker apologizes to the snake for throwing the log.
2. Write a **dialogue** between the speaker and his wife in which the speaker explains the reactions he had to the snake and his wife gives her opinions about snakes and what the speaker should have done.
3. Choose an animal with which you have strong emotional associations. Do some reading about the habits of your chosen animal. Then write a **story** about a character who encounters that animal in the wild and learns a lesson from it.

Integrating *the* LANGUAGE ARTS

Speaking and Listening & Collaborative Learning

PARTICIPATING IN A DEBATE. The wolf, like the snake, is seen by many as a dangerous predator. Research facts about the wolf. Do they ever harm humans? How often do they kill livestock? Why are they on the endangered species list? Debate whether wolves should be hunted. Half the students in your group should provide arguments in favor of this proposition, and half should provide arguments against it. No matter which side you are on, prepare both constructive speeches and rebuttal speeches. Before holding your debate, you may want to review the Language Arts Survey 4.21, "Participating in a Debate."

Applied English & Study and Research

PUBLIC SERVICE ANNOUNCEMENT. Write a public service announcement about what steps to take after being bitten by a poisonous snake. First research the topic. Then write step-by-step directions. You may find it useful to review the Language Arts Survey 6.4, "Writing a Step-by-Step Procedure."

Study and Research

RESEARCHING THE CULTURE OF SNAKES. Research associations, ceremonies, and myths relevant to the snake in Indian, Native American, African, Cretan, Aztec, or another culture. Share your findings with a small group of your classmates.

ANSWERS TO INTEGRATING THE LANGUAGE ARTS

Applied English
Assign a score from 1 to 25 for each grading criterion below. (For more detailed evaluation, see the evaluation forms for writing, revising, and proofreading, Assessment Resource, 7.1–7.10.)

Public Service Announcement

- Content/Unity. The public service announcement gives steps for dealing with a poisonous snake bite.
- Organization/Coherence. The steps included in the public service announcement are in the order in which they should be performed.
- Language/Style. The English in the public service announcement is clear and concise.
- Conventions. The public service announcement avoids errors in spelling, grammar, usage, and manuscript form.

ADDITIONAL RESOURCES

Unit 10 Resource Book
- Selection Worksheet 10.6
- Selection Check Test 4.10.13
- Selection Test 4.10.14
- Language, Grammar, and Style Resource 3.26
- Study and Research Resource 5.21

GRAPHIC ORGANIZER

Theme. Students should list the following themes in their Graphic Organizers: purification, love for and duty toward one's country, gratitude, eternal life, and the meaning imparted to life by one's environs and by friends.

READER'S JOURNAL

Ask students if it is possible to be proud of one's country and still find faults with it. Ask them how they would react if someone from another country criticized this country.

INDIVIDUAL LEARNING STRATEGIES

Motivation
Play the British national anthem and ask students what feelings it evokes in them.

Reading Proficiency
Have students review the Language Arts Survey 3.87, "Commas." Brooke uses seventeen commas in the fourteen lines of poetry in this selection. Students may have difficulty tracking the sense through these commas. After students have read the poem themselves, develop a paraphrase of it with them to elucidate the purpose of the various clauses and phrases set off by commas.

English Language Learning
Point out the following vocabulary words.
roam—travel; wander
shed—discard

Special Needs
Make sure students can answer the Guided Reading Questions and the Recall questions in Investigate, Inquire, and Imagine. Students will also benefit from doing the activities described in Reading Proficiency and English Language Learning.

(Continued on page 929)

Sonnet and Rhyme Scheme. A **sonnet** is a fourteen-line poem that follows one of a number of different rhyme schemes. Read more about sonnets in the Handbook of Literary Terms. A **rhyme scheme** is a pattern of end rhymes, or rhymes at the ends of lines of verse. The rhyme scheme of a poem is designated by letters, with matching letters signifying matching sounds.

Theme. A **theme** is a central idea in a literary work. "The Soldier" is thematically very rich for such a short piece. As you read, make a cluster chart listing the themes of the poem.

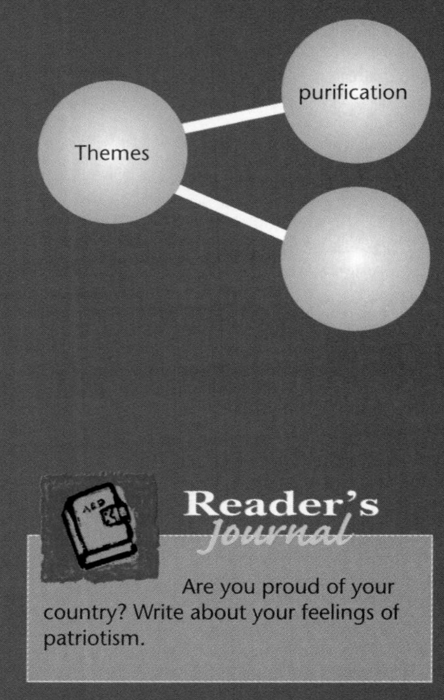

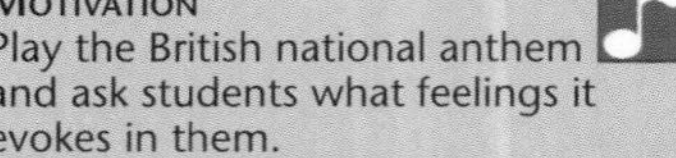

Reader's Journal

Are you proud of your country? Write about your feelings of patriotism.

"The Soldier"

by Rupert Brooke

About the Author

Of all the young Englishmen who died in World War I, perhaps the most romanticized as a hero was **Rupert Brooke** (1887–1915). Brooke seemed in many respects an ideal young man. Intelligent and athletic, he performed well in his classes and on the cricket and "football" fields at the Rugby School. He entered King's College, Cambridge, in 1906; made many friends; and was active in university life. He then studied in Europe and traveled to Canada and the South Seas, writing travel articles and publishing a book, *Poems,* in 1911. When war began, Brooke joined the Royal Navy. The sequence of patriotic, idealistic sonnets called *1914* made him famous. On the way to fight in the Gallipoli campaign after a disastrous battle in the North Sea, Brooke contracted blood poisoning and died. He was buried on the Greek island of Skyros. After his death, Winston Churchill wrote an obituary describing Brooke as "all that one would wish England's noblest sons to be."

About the Selection

World War I—the first "total war"—was so brutal and destructive that it shattered some earlier ideas of war as a heroic occupation for "gentlemen." **"The Soldier,"** like much of Brooke's poetry, written early in the war, presents an idealized view of the war and a stirring heroism. Speaking after the poet's death, Winston Churchill said that the thoughts in Brooke's sonnets "will be shared by many thousands of young men moving resolutely and blithely forward into this, the hardest, the cruelest, and the least rewarded of all the wars that men have fought." Brooke's early death made him a tragic symbol for the English public, even though much of his poetry is joyful. Over the next decade, two volumes of poetry—*1914 and Other Poems* and *Collected Poems*—sold over three hundred thousand copies.

GOALS/OBJECTIVES

Studying this lesson will enable students to
- experience the speaker's feelings of love for his country
- describe Rupert Brooke's literary accomplishments and explain the historical significance of his writings
- define *sonnet, rhyme scheme,* and *theme* and recognize the use of these techniques in the selection
- rewrite inverted sentences
- practice using the dictionary
- create a poetry booklet about war

Column on the March, c. 1914. Christopher Nevinson. Birmingham Museums and Art Gallery, UK.

The Soldier

RUPERT BROOKE

If I should die, think only this of me:
That there's some corner of a foreign field
That is forever England. There shall be
In that rich earth a richer dust concealed;
A dust whom England bore, shaped, made aware,
Gave, once, her flowers to love, her ways to roam,
A body of England's, breathing English air,
Washed by the rivers, blest by suns of home.

And think, this heart, all evil shed away,
A pulse in the Eternal mind, no less
Gives somewhere back the thoughts by England given,
Her sights and sounds; dreams happy as her day;
And laughter, learnt of friends; and gentleness,
In hearts at peace, under an English heaven. ■

What has England done for this speaker?

What will happen to the happy thoughts given to the speaker by England?

ANSWERS TO GUIDED READING QUESTIONS

1. England has borne, shaped, and made the speaker aware; given him flowers to love and places to roam; and provided him with an active body.
2. The speaker believes that his thoughts will become a part of the "Eternal mind," and so will be given back to people someday.

INDIVIDUAL LEARNING STRATEGIES (CONT. FROM PAGE 928)

ENRICHMENT
Siegfried Sassoon was a British World War I soldier known for his anti–war poetry. Have students read a Sassoon poem and compare its content to that of "The Soldier."

SELECTION CHECK TEST 12.10.13 WITH ANSWERS

Checking Your Reading

1. What does the speaker contemplate in the first line? **The speaker contemplates the possibility of his death.**
2. If the speaker dies, what will be true of "some corner of a foreign field"? **The "corner of a foreign field" will be "forever England."**
3. What will be concealed in the rich earth of that place? **A "richer dust" will be concealed there (i.e., the speaker's body).**
4. What bore that dust, shaped it, and made it aware? **England did.**
5. What does the speaker imagine being shed away after death? **The speaker imagines all evil in his heart being shed away.**

Literary Tools
Fill in the blank with the appropriate literary tool from the following list.

image theme
rhyme scheme sonnet

1. This **sonnet** is divided into an octet and a sestet.
2. The **rhyme scheme** of the octet is ababcdcd.
3. The main **theme** of the poem is love for and duty toward one's country.

RESPOND TO THE SELECTION

Students can consider how they might feel in the speaker's situation. They may also wish to discuss how they feel about the speaker's attitude based on their own feelings about war.

ANSWERS TO INVESTIGATE, INQUIRE, AND IMAGINE

RECALL

1a. The speaker would like the reader to think that there is a corner of a foreign field that is forever England.

2a. England bore, shaped, and made aware the speaker.

3a. The speaker will return the happy thoughts under an English heaven.

INTERPRET

1b. The richer dust is the speaker's corpse. The speaker claims it is "richer" perhaps because it is English, or perhaps because literally it is organically richer.

2b. The speaker loves England and is proud to represent his country in war.

3b. The speaker will give himself, give his life for England.

ANALYZE

4a. The speaker is connected to England because he was born and raised there. He is connected to England spiritually because of his great love for the country.

SYNTHESIZE

4b. Brooke might have been moved by England's efforts in the war. He may have felt great patriotism that he was taking part in what he might have considered a worthy cause. He may have wanted to rally support.

EVALUATE

5a. The final mood is upbeat. Words and phrases such as "dreams happy as her day," "laughter, learnt of friends," "gentleness," and "hearts at peace" create this mood.

EXTEND

Responses will vary.

5b. Brooke's would probably have agreed with Shakespeare's patriotic words.

Respond to the SELECTION

What is the speaker's general attitude toward his situation? Why does he have this attitude?

INVESTIGATE, Inquire, Imagine

Recall: GATHERING FACTS → **Interpret:** FINDING MEANING

1a. What would the speaker like the reader to think if he dies? → 1b. What is the "richer dust" buried in the foreign earth?

2a. What has England done for the speaker? → 2b. How does the speaker feel about England?

3a. What will become of the happy thoughts given to the speaker by England? → 3b. What will the speaker give back to England?

Analyze: TAKING THINGS APART → **Synthesize:** BRINGING THINGS TOGETHER

4a. How is the speaker connected to England? → 4b. Why might Brooke have written such a patriotic poem?

Evaluate: MAKING JUDGMENTS → **Extend:** CONNECTING IDEAS

5a. Evaluate the mood at the end of this poem. What phrases help to create this mood? → 5b. Would Brooke agree or disagree with the attitude expressed in the following lines from *Richard II*? Explain.

"This happy breed of men, this little world,
This precious stone set in the silver sea,
Which serves it in the office of a wall,
Or as a moat defensive to a house,
Against the envy of less happier lands,
This blessed plot, this earth, this realm, this England. . . ."

Understanding Literature

SONNET AND RHYME SCHEME. Review the definitions for **sonnet** and **rhyme scheme** in Literary Tools on page 928. How is this sonnet divided? What is its rhyme scheme?

THEME. Review the definition for **theme** in the Handbook of Literary Terms and the cluster chart you made for Literary Tools on page 928. What are the themes of this poem?

ANSWERS TO UNDERSTANDING LITERATURE

SONNET AND RHYME SCHEME. The sonnet is divided into an octave and a sestet. The rhyme scheme of the sonnet is ababcdcd efgefg.

THEME. The main theme of the poem is love for and duty toward one's country. Other themes may include gratitude, eternal life, and the meaning imparted to life by one's environs and friends.

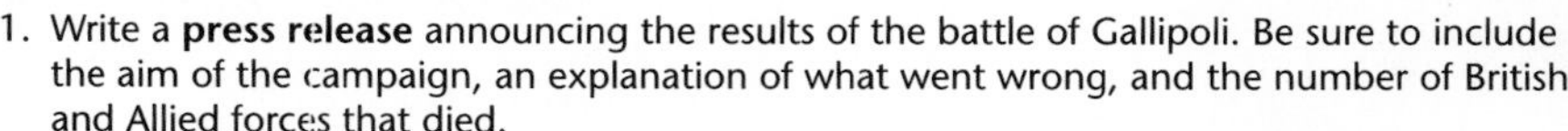

Writer's Journal

1. Write a **press release** announcing the results of the battle of Gallipoli. Be sure to include the aim of the campaign, an explanation of what went wrong, and the number of British and Allied forces that died.
2. Brooke's poem mentions a number of things that made England a special place for him—both physical things such as air and rivers and abstract things such as friendship. Write a short **editorial** describing some of the things that make your school, community, or country special to you.
3. This poem was written early in the war and expresses an idealized view of war. Write a **poem or essay** that expresses a more realistic or pessimistic portrait of war.

Integrating the Language Arts

Language, Grammar, and Style

Inverted Sentences. Read the Language Arts Survey 3.26, "Working with Inverted Sentences." Poets frequently use inverted word order for poetic effect, but such syntax sometimes makes poetry harder to understand. In each sentence below, underline the word or phrase that is the subject of the sentence. Then rewrite each sentence in normal word order. Drop or add words if you need to do so. (The examples are adapted from Brooke's poetry.)

1. There shall be in that rich earth a richer dust concealed.
2. Forever shall some corner of a foreign field be England.
3. Proud we were.
4. Washed by England's rivers was this body.
5. This heart the thoughts gives back.

Vocabulary

Finding Alternative Meanings. Read the Language Arts Survey 5.21, "Using a Dictionary." Then look in a dictionary to discover alternative meanings of the italicized words in these phrases from "The Soldier." For each word, first list the meaning used in the poem. Then, in your own words, give at least two other dictionary meanings for the word.

1. *rich* earth
2. whom England *bore*
3. breathing English *air*
4. all evil *shed*
5. a *pulse* in the eternal mind

Collaborative Learning & Media Literacy

Poetry Booklet. With the help of several classmates, select poems for a poetry booklet dedicated to war. You may choose to organize it chronologically or thematically. Write a short biography of each poet and an introduction before each poem. Use a computer to print your poetry booklet.

ANSWERS TO INTEGRATING THE LANGUAGE ARTS

Language, Grammar, and Style

1. a richer dust; A richer dust shall be concealed in that rich earth.
2. some corner; Some corner of a foreign field shall be England forever.
3. we; We were proud.
4. this body; This body was washed by England's rivers.
5. heart; This heart gives back the thoughts.

Vocabulary

Responses will vary.

1. *rich:* abundantly supplied with plant nutrients; of high quality; magnificent or impressive
2. *bore:* gave birth to; carried; supported
3. *air:* mixture of invisible gases that sustain life; atmosphere; demeanor
4. *shed:* cast off; repel; spill
5. *pulse:* sign of life; rhythmic beat; contraction

ADDITIONAL RESOURCE

UNIT 10 RESOURCE BOOK
- Selection Worksheet 10.7
- Selection Check Test 4.10.15
- Selection Test 4.10.16
- Language, Grammar, and Style Resource 3.80

GRAPHIC ORGANIZER

Students should include the following images in their cluster charts: white eyes writhing, hanging face, the sound of blood gargling from froth-corrupted lungs.

VOCABULARY FROM THE SELECTION

ardent
gutter

READER'S JOURNAL

Ask students to share stories about war they have heard from veterans who are family members or friends.

POETRY

VERBAL IRONY. Verbal irony occurs when a writer or speaker makes a statement that implies its opposite. As you read, consider what is ironic about the title "Dulce et Decorum Est."

ALLITERATION. Alliteration is the repetition of initial consonant sounds. As you read, look for examples of alliteration.

IMAGE. An **image** is language that creates a concrete representation of an object or an experience. In the poem, Owen paints a picture of a gassed soldier. As you read, make a cluster chart of the images used in this description. One example has been done for you.

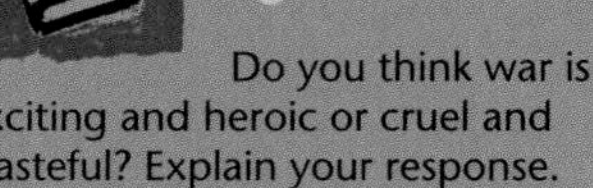

Do you think war is exciting and heroic or cruel and wasteful? Explain your response.

"Dulce et Decorum Est"

BY WILFRED OWEN

About the AUTHOR

World War I shaped the lives of several young British soldier-poets. One was **Wilfred Owen** (1893–1918), who was killed in action in France just a week before the Armistice that ended the war (November 11, 1918). Born in Shropshire, he enrolled in the University of London but dropped out because of illness in 1913 and then went to live in France. Working as a tutor, he began to write lyric poetry that was influenced by Keats and Shelley (see Unit 8). In 1915, Owen enlisted in the army and soon was writing angrily about the war and its horrors. In June 1917, suffering from shell shock, he was sent to a hospital in Scotland, where he met the poet Siegfried Sassoon. Both were strongly antiwar, and Sassoon's ideas about poetry also influenced Owen. Though friends tried to find him a staff job behind the lines, Owen went back to France as a platoon commander in August 1918. He won the Military Cross in October and was killed soon afterward.

About the SELECTION

Owen's poems, including the selection **"Dulce et Decorum Est,"** were published after his death by Siegfried Sassoon. His works contain become some of the most quoted lines about the cruelty and wastefulness of war. Owen's preface to the volume reads: "Above all, this book is not concerned with/ Poetry, The subject of it is War, and the pity of/ War. The Poetry is in the pity. All a poet can do is warn." *Dulce et decorum est pro patria mori* is a line from the *Odes* of the Roman poet Horace. It means: "It is sweet and proper to die for your country."

GOALS/OBJECTIVES

Studying this lesson will enable students to
- experience the speaker's disgust and horror at the cruelty of war
- describe Wilfred Owen's literary accomplishments and explain the historical significance of his writings
- define *verbal irony, alliteration,* and *image* and recognize the use of these techniques in the selection
- identify participles and gerunds
- research wartime technology during World War I
- write a dialogue between Wilfred Owen and Siegfried Sassoon

Paths of Glory, 1917. Christopher Nevinson. Imperial War Museum, London.

Dulce et Decorum Est

Wilfred Owen

Bent double, like old beggars under sacks,
Knock-kneed, coughing like hags, we cursed through sludge,
Till on the haunting flares we turned our backs
And towards our distant rest began to trudge.
Men marched asleep. Many had lost their boots
But limped on, blood-shod. All went lame; all blind;
Drunk with fatigue; deaf even to the hoots
Of tired, outstripped Five-Nines[1] that dropped behind.

1. **Five-Nines.** Common artillery shells

INDIVIDUAL LEARNING STRATEGIES

Motivation
Many veterans of World War I experienced shell shock after the war. You might introduce students to the after affects of combat by showing the segment from the film *Ryan's Daughter* in which the soldier displays signs of shell shock.

Reading Proficiency
Point out the similes in lines 23–24 that describe the gassed soldier's blood.

English Language Learning
Explain the Latin phrase from which the title and the last line of the poem are taken. Point out English words derived from the same roots as the Latin words: *dulcet, decorous, pro* (as in "pro and con"), *patriot,* and *mortal.* Have students look up these English words and their etymologies.

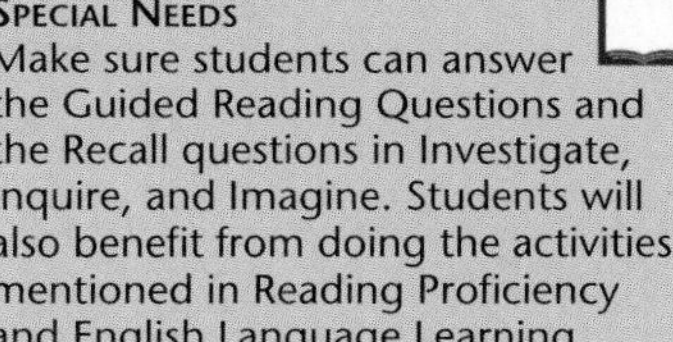

Special Needs
Make sure students can answer the Guided Reading Questions and the Recall questions in Investigate, Inquire, and Imagine. Students will also benefit from doing the activities mentioned in Reading Proficiency and English Language Learning.

Enrichment
World War I was fought in the trenches. To illustrate this aspect of the war, show the film *How Many Miles to Babylon?* Have students compare the experiences of the soldiers in the film to the soldiers in the poem.

ANSWERS TO GUIDED READING QUESTIONS

1. The soldiers are forced to slog through sludge and to march long hours beyond the point of exhaustion in order to keep ahead of the shelling; some lose their boots but must continue walking. Poison gas descends upon the soldiers.
2. "The old Lie" is that it is sweet and proper to die for one's country. No one who has experienced directly the suffering of soldiers in war could repeat this lie with zest.

ADDITIONAL QUESTIONS AND ACTIVITIES

You might have students read the Language Arts Survey 3.39, "Adding Colorful Language to Sentences." Then have students identify vivid verbs that make the poem come alive. Answers: Some of the vivid verbs used include "coughing," "cursed" (line 2); "stumbling" (line 11); "flound'ring" (line 12); "plunges," "guttering" (line 16); and 'writhing" (line 19).

SELECTION CHECK TEST 12.10.19 WITH ANSWERS

Checking Your Reading

1. Who were like "old beggars under sacks"? **The speaker and the other soldiers were like "old beggars under sacks."**
2. With what are the soldiers "drunk"? **They are "drunk" with fatigue.**
3. What caused the man to become so sick that he had to be flung into a wagon? **He was gassed.**
4. What do people sometimes tell to children "with such high zest"? **They sometimes tell children "The old Lie."**
5. What does the Latin sentence "Dulce et decorum est / Pro patria mori" mean? **The sentence means "It is sweet and proper to die for one's country.**

Literary Tools

Fill in the blank with the appropriate literary tool from the following list.

alliteration verbal irony
consonance image

1. To describe the horrors of war, Owen creates **images** of the gassed soldier.
2. "White eyes writhing" and "fumbling, Fitting" are examples of **alliteration**.
3. **Verbal irony** is evident in the title of the poem since the scenes Owen is describing are not "sweet and proper."

Gas! Gas! Quick, boys!—An ecstasy of fumbling,
Fitting the clumsy helmets just in time;
But someone still was yelling out and stumbling,
And flound'ring like a man in fire or lime . . .
Dim, through the misty panes and thick green light,
As under a green sea, I saw him drowning.

In all my dreams, before my helpless sight,
He plunges at me, guttering, choking, drowning.
If in some smothering dreams you too could pace
Behind the wagon that we flung him in,
And watch the white eyes writhing in his face,
His hanging face, like a devil's sick of sin;
If you could hear, at every jolt, the blood
Come gargling from the froth-corrupted lungs,
Obscene as cancer, bitter as the cud
Of vile, incurable sores on innocent tongues,—
My friend, you would not tell with such high zest
To children ardent for some desperate glory,
The old Lie: Dulce et decorum est
Pro patria mori.[2] ■

What do soldiers endure? What descends upon the soldiers?

What is "The old Lie"? What would cause someone not to tell this lie with "such high zest"?

2. **Dulce . . . mori.** Latin phrase from Horace meaning "It is sweet and proper to die for your country."

WORDS FOR EVERYDAY USE

gut • ter (gut´ər) *vi.,* gurgle and sputter. *The last thing I saw before all grew black was a face lit by a guttering candle.*

ar • dent (ärd´'nt) *adj.,* intensely enthusiastic or devoted; zealous. *Only the most ardent fans braved the rain to watch the soccer match.*

ArtNote

Paths of Glory, 1917. Christopher Nevinson.

Christopher Nevinson (1889-1946) was a painter for the British government's official war art program during World War I. Early in the war he produced patriotic images such as *Column on the March* (page 929). Later in the war his paintings recorded the horrors he had witnessed, such as the scene of dead British soldiers (page 933) which takes its ironic title from Thomas Gray's "Elegy Written in a Country Churchyard" (unit 8). The government banned its exhibition, fearing that it would undermine morale. Why did Nevinson choose the title *Paths of Glory*?

Respond *to the* SELECTION

What would you say to either promote or refute "the old Lie"?

INVESTIGATE, Inquire, *Imagine*

Recall: GATHERING FACTS → **Interpret:** FINDING MEANING

1a. What physical hardships do the soldiers face as they march?

1b. What is the mood of the soldiers?

2a. What does the speaker see when one soldier does not get his gas mask on?

2b. Why does this sight live on in the speaker's dreams?

3a. What is "the old Lie"?

3b. Who do you think perpetrates the lie?

Analyze: TAKING THINGS APART → **Synthesize:** BRINGING THINGS TOGETHER

4a. What emotions does the speaker feel after seeing the gassed soldier?

4b. What ideal does the speaker oppose?

Evaluate: MAKING JUDGMENTS → **Extend:** CONNECTING IDEAS

5a. Why might people have told "the old Lie"? Evaluate reasons for perpetuating the notion that it is glorious to die for your country.

5b. Compare and contrast Owen's view of war with that of Brooke in "The Soldier."

Understanding *Literature*

VERBAL IRONY. Review the definition for **verbal irony** in the Handbook of Literary Terms. How is the title of the poem ironic?

ALLITERATION. Review the definition for **alliteration** in Literary Tools on page 932. What consonant sounds are repeated in lines 5–7? Where else does Owen use alliteration?

IMAGE. Review the definition for image in the Handbook of Literary Terms and the cluster chart you made for Literary Tools on page 932. How do the images of the gassed soldier contribute to Owen's purpose?

RESPOND TO THE SELECTION

Ask students to discuss different motives for either stance. Why might some people want to believe "the old Lie"? Why might others want to dispel it?

ANSWERS TO INVESTIGATE, INQUIRE, AND IMAGINE

RECALL

1a. The soldiers have to carry heavy loads; they are sick; they have to march through mud; they are weary nearly to sleep; many have lost their boots; they are virtually lame, blind, and deaf; they are assaulted by poison gas.

INTERPRET

1b. The mood of the soldiers is exhausted and defeated.

2b. The sight lives on because it was so horrifying. The speaker saw somebody die an agonizing death, stripped of dignity.

3b. Teachers, veterans, and politicians may be responsible for perpetuating "the old Lie."

ANALYZE

4a. The speaker feels haunted, helpless, and smothered.

SYNTHESIZE

4b. The speaker opposes the ideal that fighting for one's country is glorious and the epitome of patriotism.

EVALUATE

5a. People might have told the lie because it was traditional. They may not have experienced war so they have unrealistic ideas about it. They may have heard the heroic stories that soldiers wanted to tell rather than the stories or carnage, injury, and death. They may have been trying to garner support for the war or to build pride in their country. Some may feel that the reasons for fighting such as nationalism, colonialism, and economic expansion justify war.

EXTEND

Responses will vary.

5b. In "The Soldier" Brooke expresses an idealism in the face of death. Owen portrays wars horrifying realism. The two poets had opposing viewpoints about World War I.

ANSWERS TO UNDERSTANDING LITERATURE

VERBAL IRONY. The title of the poem is ironic because Owen is deliber-ately describing a situation that is not "sweet and becoming." The imagery is so direct and realistic that it does not allow for much irony. It is only when the entire description of war is contrasted with the glorious image of war in the last lines that the horror becomes ironic.

ALLITERATION. The consonant sounds of *b, l, m,* and *d* are the most prominent in these lines. Another example of alliteration can be found in lines 18 and 19: "Behind the *wagon* that *we* flung him in,/And *watch* the *white* eyes *writhing* in his face."

IMAGE. Owen's aim is to present a realistic portrait of war that is not glorious. He does this by depicting the death of a gassed soldier. The images present the horror of his death.

ANSWERS TO INTEGRATING THE LANGUAGE ARTS

Language, Grammar, and Style

1. "Bent" (past participle modifying "we"), "coughing" (present participle modifying "we")
2. "Haunting" (present participle modifying "flares")
3. "Fumbling" (G), "fitting" (G)
4. "Drowning" (present participle modifying "him")
5. "Smothering" (present participle modifying "dreams")

Study and Research

In addition to books, there exist abundant video materials on World War I that can supply information on the technology of the war.

Mention to students that, considering the nature of Owen's poem, it would be inappropriate for their presentation to glamorize or glorify the technology used during World War I.

Writer's Journal

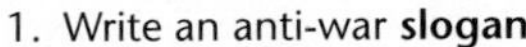

1. Write an anti-war **slogan**.

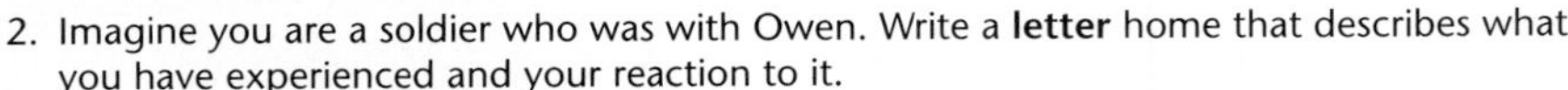

2. Imagine you are a soldier who was with Owen. Write a **letter** home that describes what you have experienced and your reaction to it.

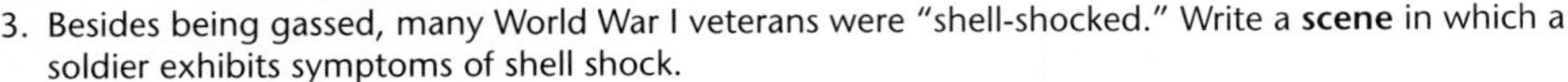

3. Besides being gassed, many World War I veterans were "shell-shocked." Write a **scene** in which a soldier exhibits symptoms of shell shock.

Integrating the Language Arts

Language, Grammar, and Style

Verbals: Participles and Gerunds. Read the Language Arts Survey 3.80, "Verbals: Participles, Gerunds, and Infinitives." Much of the strength of Owen's writing lies in his use of strong verbs and verbals. In each of the excerpts below, identify the verbals. If a participle is used as an adjective, identify the noun that it modifies. (Look for both past participles and present participles.) Write *G* after a gerund and *P* after a participle.

1. Bent double, like old beggars under sacks, / Knock-kneed, coughing like hags, we cursed through sludge.
2. Till on the haunting flares we turned our backs.
3. An ecstasy of fumbling, / Fitting the clumsy helmets just in time . . .
4. As under a green sea, I saw him drowning . . .
5. If in some smothering dreams you too could pace / Behind the wagon that we flung him in . . .

Study and Research

Wartime Technology. One reason for the horrors and huge casualties of World War I was the introduction of new kinds of weapons and equipment, including machine guns, tanks, modern submarines, and poison gas (as Owen described in his poem). During World War I, airplanes were also used in battle for the first time. With a group of other students, research World War I technology, finding photographs or drawings that illustrate your research. Prepare a presentation on this technology for your class.

Speaking and Listening & Collaborative Learning

Writing a Dialogue. Confined for a time in a sanatorium during World War I, Wilfred Owen met poet Siegfried Sassoon, who shared his anti-war views. Write a dialogue that might have taken place between Owen and Sassoon in which they discuss their views and the work of Rupert Brooke. Then read your dialogue for the class. In preparation, you might consider reading part of Jon Stallworthy's *Wilfred Owen: a Biography* (Oxford University Press and Chatto and Windus, 1974), which discusses Sassoon's influence on Owen.

"Rough"

BY STEPHEN SPENDER

About the AUTHOR

Stephen Spender (1909–1995) was a leading member of a group of socially conscious British writers of the 1930s. This group took part in "new left" politics and worked for social reform. Born in London, Spender attended University College, Oxford, where he became friends with other writers, including W. H. Auden. While his contemporaries focused on society and its problems, Spender wrote poetry with a more personal and individual voice. Because he was a pacifist, he did not fight in either the Spanish Civil War, as many liberal writers did, or World War II. He was a firefighter in London during the Blitz. By the 1950s, he wrote less poetry and became better known as a critic and lecturer, both in Britain and in the United States. He edited the literary review *Encounter* from 1953 to 1967. *The Creative Element* (1953) is one of Spender's well-known critical works. His autobiography, *World Within World,* was published in 1951 and reissued in 1994.

About the SELECTION

Spender is part of the generation of British writers who grew up between the two world wars, during the political upheavals of the 1930s in Europe. His "new poetry" was a bridge between the work of earlier modern poets such as Eliot and that of poets who began to write after World War II. Rapid changes in technology and politics made the interwar years an edgy, uneasy period, as did the worldwide economic depression. Many writers of this period turned to private, personal subjects. **"Rough"** is a highly personal poem in which the speaker deals from an adult perspective with an issue that confronted him in childhood. The poem appears in Spender's *Selected Poems.*

Literary TOOLS

DICTION. Diction, when applied to writing, refers to word choice. As you read, make a list of the verbs and adjectives associated with the rough children and one of the verbs and adjectives associated with the speaker.

SIMILE. A **simile** is a comparison using *like* or *as*. This figure of speech invites the reader to make a comparison between the two things. The two "things" involved are the writer's actual subject, the *tenor* of the simile, and another thing to which the subject is likened, the *vehicle* of the simile. As you read, make a chart listing the tenor and vehicle for each simile in the poem. One example has been done for you.

Tenor	Vehicle
words	stones

Reader's Journal

Write about a time when you were bullied.

ADDITIONAL RESOURCES

UNIT 10 RESOURCE BOOK
- Selection Worksheet 10.8
- Selection Check Test 4.10.17
- Selection Test 4.10.18
- Language, Grammar, and Style Resource 3.33
- Study and Research Resource 5.19

GRAPHIC ORGANIZER

Students should fill in their Graphic Organizer as follows:

Tenor	Vehicle
words	stones
muscles	iron
rough children	dogs

READER'S JOURNAL

Before students begin writing you may wish to discuss with them the classic psychological profile of the bully, which suggests that he or she is someone who attempts to compensate for his or her insecurities by acting out physically against others; his or her victims are generally those who are psychologically stronger and thus threatening to him or her. Signs of physical weakness or of any emotional susceptibility to harsh treatment attract the attention of bullies. You may also wish to discuss whether physically weak people who are bullied as children may compensate for that feeling of powerlessness by bullying others as they grow and gain power in other fields of endeavor besides the physical.

GOALS/OBJECTIVES

Studying this lesson will enable students to
- empathize with the physical and emotional pain the speaker suffered as a child
- describe Stephen Spender's literary accomplishments and explain the historical significance of his writings
- define *diction* and *simile* and recognize the use of these techniques in the selection
- correct sentence fragments
- compile a bibliography of Spender's works
- participate in a panel discussion
- write a public service announcement

INDIVIDUAL LEARNING STRATEGIES

Motivation
Hold a class discussion about how children who are different are treated by their peers. What makes some children act cruelly to other children?

Reading Proficiency
Have students review the section on active reading in the Language Arts Survey. Then, ask them to read the first line of the poem and predict what it will be about. Students can suggest what they would include in a poem with such a beginning.

English Language Learning
Several of the phrases in the poem are elliptical and may be difficult for students to understand. "Stripped," for instance, means "took off their clothes to go swimming"; "salt coarse pointing" suggests that the speaker feels the effect of the boys' pointing at him as if it were coarse salt rubbed into a wound or forced into his mouth. Encourage students from other cultures to share how children interact in their country. Do they find Americans more or less aggressive than people from their own culture?
Point out the following additional vocabulary words:
salt—that which lends a tang or sharpness
coarse—rough; harsh
lithe—bending easily; flexible; supple

Special Needs
Have students make a list of the activities of the rough children that are described in the poem. Make sure students can answer the Guided Reading Questions and the Recall questions in Investigate, Inquire, and Imagine.

Enrichment
Have students look for poems by other poets in this unit that reveal an aspect of their childhoods. Ask students to hypothesize how these described experiences might have influenced the poets. For a fuller perspective on Spender, students can read his autobiography (cited in "About the Author"), or read his work, *Selected Poems*. Students can then compose a letter to Spender in which they describe their response to his life and accomplishments.

STEPHEN SPENDER

My parents kept me from children who were rough
Who threw words like stones and who wore torn clothes.
Their thighs showed through rags. They ran in the street
And climbed cliffs and stripped by the country streams.

From whom was the speaker kept?

I feared more than tigers their muscles like iron
Their jerking hands and their knees tight on my arms.
I feared the salt coarse pointing of those boys
Who copied my lisp behind me on the road.

They were lithe, they sprang out behind hedges
Like dogs to bark at my world. They threw mud
While I looked the other way, pretending to smile.
I longed to forgive them, but they never smiled. ■

What did the speaker long to do? Was he given the opportunity to do so?

Respond to the Selection

Imagine you are one of the "rough" children. How would you describe the speaker?

RESPOND TO THE SELECTION

In their descriptions, suggest students explain how they feel about the speaker and perhaps why they treat him as they do.

INVESTIGATE, Inquire, Imagine

Recall: GATHERING FACTS → **Interpret:** FINDING MEANING

1a. In stanza 1, in what activities does the speaker recall the rough children engaging?

1b. What does it tell you about the speaker's situation that he was not allowed to engage in such activities?

2a. In stanza 2, what does the speaker recall having feared?

2b. In what circumstances would knees be "tight on my arms"? What evidently happened to the speaker during his childhood?

3a. What does the speaker do while the children are throwing mud? What did he long to do?

3b. Why do you think the speaker pretended to smile? Why did he long to forgive the rough children?

Analyze: TAKING THINGS APART → **Synthesize:** BRINGING THINGS TOGETHER

4a. What images in the poem show that the speaker now has some admiration for those rough children? What recalled images and events show that, despite this admiration, the speaker has not forgotten the pain that he felt as a child?

4b. How do you think the speaker would react if he met one of the rough children as an adult?

Evaluate: MAKING JUDGMENTS → **Extend:** CONNECTING IDEAS

5a. Decide whether the speaker has forgiven the rough children. Explain your response.

5b. Is it possible to forgive and still not forget? Give an example that supports your response.

Understanding Literature

DICTION. Review the definition for **diction** in Literary Tools on page 937. Based on these descriptions, summarize what you know about the rough children and about the narrator. What verbs and adjectives describe the rough children and the speaker? What do these words reveal about the rough children and the speaker?

SIMILE. Review the definition for **simile** in the Handbook of Literary Terms and the chart you made for Literary Tools on page 937. What do the similes reveal about the rough children?

SELECTION CHECK TEST 12.10.15 WITH ANSWERS

Checking Your Reading

1. The speaker's parents kept him away from whom? **They kept him away from children who were rough.**
2. What were the other children's words like? **The other children's words were like stones.**
3. How did the rough children hold the speaker? **They put their knees on his arms.**
4. What did the rough children copy? **They copied the speaker's lisp.**
5. What prevented the speaker from forgiving the rough children? **They never smiled.**

Literary Tools

Fill in the blank with an appropriate literary tool from the following list.

diction speaker metaphor simile

1. The **speaker** feared the muscles of the rough children "more than tigers."
2. "Rough," "threw, "torn," "sprang," words that describe the rough children, are examples of Spender's **diction**.
3. When Spender says the rough children "threw words like stones," he is using a **simile**.

ANSWERS TO INVESTIGATE, INQUIRE, AND IMAGINE

RECALL

1a. He recalls them taunting him, wearing torn clothes, running in the street, climbing cliffs, and swimming in streams.

2a. The speaker recalls having feared the boys' muscles, their hands, their knees, and their pointing.

3a. He looks the other way, pretending to smile. He longed to forgive them.

INTERPRET

1b. The speaker apparently could not play if it involved any danger or physical exertion.

2b. Evidently the speaker was once pinned down by bullies who put their knees on his arms.

3b. The speaker pretended to smile, trying to ingratiate himself with the rough children or to feign nonchalance. He wanted to forgive them because he preferred to be friends with them than to continue to be a victim of their abuse.

ANALYZE

4a. The images of the children as tigers and as being lithe and like dogs suggest the speaker admires their animal vitality and strength. The speaker has not forgotten the pain they caused—he speaks in terms of his remembered fear, and mentions "words like stones," "jerking hands," and their knees on his arms.

ANSWERS TO INVESTIGATE, INQUIRE, AND IMAGINE (CONT.)

SYNTHESIZE

4b. The speaker might have envied the rough children their freedom and physical vitality. He clearly did not want to be callous and cruel as the rough children were.

EVALUATE

5a. The speaker seems to have forgiven the rough children although he can still sometimes feel the sting of how they treated him. He is, however, still traumatized by his childhood experiences.

EXTEND

5b. *Responses will vary.*

Answers to Understanding Literature can be found on page 940.

ANSWERS TO UNDERSTANDING LITERATURE

DICTION. Significant verbs and adjectives associated with the rough children are "rough" (line 1); "threw," "torn" (line 2); "ran" (line 3); "climbed," "stripped" (line 4); "copied" (line 8); "lithe," "sprang" (line 9); "bark," "threw" (line 10); and "[never] smiled" (line 12). These verbs and adjectives indicate wildness, activity, and hostility. Verbs and verbals associated with the speaker are "feared" (lines 5 and 7); "looked," "pretending" (line 11); and "longed" (line 12). These indicate mildness and passivity.

SIMILE. The similes suggest that the rough children are fierce.

ANSWERS TO INTEGRATING THE LANGUAGE ARTS

Language, Grammar, and Style
Responses will vary.

1. In the 1930s, Spender's writing dealt with modern technology, such as airfields and express trains.
2. The young poet became an immediate popular success in a few years.
3. As an older man in the 1960s, Spender wrote sympathetically about student rebellions in Europe and the United States.
4. OK
5. Spender later wrote books of memoirs, travel articles, and history.

Speaking and Listening & Collaborative Learning
Some authorities con-sider television to be a major cause of violence among the young. Students can investigate some of the literature available on this subject in popular magazines by checking the *Reader's Guide to Periodical Literature.*

Ask students on the panel to plan to offer concrete proposals for eliminating the root causes of violence they discuss.

Applied English
You might have students videotape their public service announcements and then have the class watch them.

Assign a score from 1 to 25 for each grading criterion below. (For more detailed evaluation, see the evaluation forms for writing, revising, and proofreading, Assessment Portfolio, 7.1–7.10.)

Public Service Announcement
Content/Unity. The public service announcement gives tips on how to change negative behavior.

WRITER'S JOURNAL

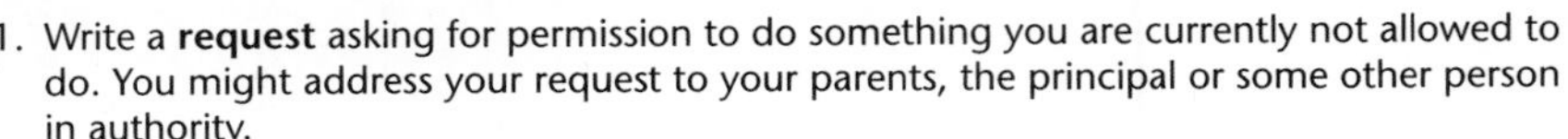

1. Write a **request** asking for permission to do something you are currently not allowed to do. You might address your request to your parents, the principal or some other person in authority.
2. Write a **description** of the speaker from the point of view of one of the rough children.
3. Assuming that the speaker is the poet Spender, write a **critical analysis** of what his childhood must have been like and how it may have affected the later course of his life. For example, in line 8, Spender talks about having a lisp. How might this have influenced him to become a writer?

Integrating *the* LANGUAGE ARTS

Language, Grammar, and Style

SENTENCE FRAGMENTS. Read the Language Arts Survey 3.33, "Correcting Sentence Fragments." Sentence fragments are common in poetry but should generally be avoided in most other kinds of writing. Some of the examples below are fragments; some are not. Rewrite the fragments as complete sentences, adding words as needed. If a sentence is not a fragment, write OK by its number.

1. In the 1930s Spender's writing about modern technology, such as airfields and express trains.
2. The young poet an immediate popular success in a few years.
3. As an older man in the 1960s, wrote sympathetically about student rebellions in Europe and the United States.
4. Spender's autobiography, *World Within World,* portrays many other famous writers.
5. Later books of memoirs, travel articles, and history.

Study and Research

COMPILING A BIBLIOGRAPHY. Read about computerized and card catalogs in the Language Arts Survey 5.19, "How to Locate Library Materials." Depending on the cataloging system used in your library, use the card catalog or database to look up works available by Stephen Spender. Compile a selective bibliography that includes a sampling of Spender's poetry, travel writing, and memoirs from all stages of his career.

Speaking and Listening & Collaborative Learning

PANEL DISCUSSION. In class, hold a panel discussion about violence among young people. Consider these questions: What are the causes of violence among the young? What can be done to protect young people from violence? What can be done to eliminate or change its root causes?

Applied English

PUBLIC SERVICE ANNOUNCEMENT. On TV you have probably seen public service announcements about the dangers of telling racial jokes, using drugs, and perpetuating stereotypes. Write a public service announcement about one of these topics:

- accepting rather than ridiculing differences
- how cliques divide a community
- the harmful effects of aggression

ANSWERS TO INTEGRATING THE LANGUAGE ARTS (CONT.)

Organization/Coherence. The public service announcement is logically organized.
Language/Style. The public service announcement avoids slang and colloquial English.
Conventions. The public service announcement avoids errors in spelling, grammar, usage, mechanics, and manuscript form.

"Do Not Go Gentle into That Good Night"

BY DYLAN THOMAS

About the AUTHOR

During his lifetime, **Dylan Thomas** (1914–1953) was almost as famous a colorful personality as he was a poet. He grew up in the industrial city of Swansea, Wales, the son of a schoolteacher. Journals that he kept show him to have had a considerable poetic gift from an early age. He worked briefly as a news reporter, published his first book of poems when he was twenty years old, and then moved to London. Besides writing poetry, Thomas worked for the BBC (British Broadcasting Corporation) and wrote stories and plays, including the play for voices *Under Milk Wood* (1954). His prose memoir *A Child's Christmas in Wales* is a popular classic. Thomas gave many public readings in a rich, Welsh-accented voice that captivated audiences. These readings made him quite popular, even among people who ordinarily did not appreciate poetry. Although Thomas's verse often makes great demands on the reader or listener, most people respond to its passion and to its vivid, charged language, reminiscent of the King James Bible and of Welsh preaching. In person, Thomas was often talkative and witty. However, his alcoholism made a ruin of much of his life, including his marriage to Caitlin Macnamara. Heavy drinking, especially on reading tours, interfered with his writing; his total output of poetry was rather small, and he died of acute alcoholism before reaching his fortieth birthday.

About the SELECTION

Dylan Thomas's poems are rich with imagery and music. Reading his first works, critics thought of him as a wild Romantic. However, it soon became clear that Thomas was a serious craftsman. **"Do Not Go Gentle into That Good Night"** shows Thomas's technical mastery. This poem, written about the approaching death of his father, is an example of the complex French verse form known as the *villanelle*. It may well be the finest example of the form ever produced. It is certainly the most famous.

Literary TOOLS

PUN. A **pun** is a play on words, one that wittily exploits a double meaning. As you read "Do Not Go Gentle into That Good Night," look for the pun in stanza 5.

SYMBOL. A **symbol** is a thing that stands for or represents both itself and something else. As you read, decide what *night* and *light* symbolize.

VILLANELLE AND RHYME SCHEME. A **villanelle** is a complex and intricate nineteen-line French verse form. The rhyme scheme is *aba aba aba aba abaa*. The first fifteen lines are organized into three-line stanzas, or tercets. The first and last lines of the opening stanza are repeated, alternately as the last lines of stanzas 2–5 and the concluding couplet of the last stanza, which is a four-line quatrain. A **rhyme scheme** is a pattern of end rhymes, or rhymes at the ends of lines of verse. The rhyme scheme of a poem is designated by letters, with matching letters signifying matching sounds. Write out the words that correspond with the *a* and *b* rhymes in the poem. The first stanza has been done for you.

Rhyming Words	Corresponding Letters
night / light	*a*
day	*b*

Reader's Journal

Are you afraid of death? Explain.

ADDITIONAL RESOURCES

UNIT 10 RESOURCE BOOK
- Selection Worksheet 10.9
- Selection Check Test 4.10.19
- Selection Test 4.10.20
- Speaking and Listening Resource 4.21

GRAPHIC ORGANIZER

VILLANELLE AND RHYME SCHEME. Students should complete their charts as follows:

Rhyming Words	Corresponding Letters
night-light	a
day	b
right-night	a
they	b
bright-light	a
bay	b
flight-night	a
way	b
sight-light	a
gay	b
height-night-light	a
pray	b

READER'S JOURNAL

Due to the personal nature of the question, students may not want to share their Reader's Journal entries.

INDIVIDUAL LEARNING STRATEGIES

MOTIVATION
Show the segment from the movie *Dangerous Minds* in which students participate in the Dylan-Dylan (Bob Dylan and Dylan Thomas) contest. Then discuss what the Bob Dylan song and the Dylan Thomas poem have in common.

READING PROFICIENCY
Pointing out the structure of the poem may help students to understand it better. The opening stanza serves as an introduction to the theme, and the closing stanza serves as a conclusion and summation. The four stanzas in the center of the poem each give an example of a type of person and then explain why that type does not face death with resignation.

(Continued on page 942)

GOALS/OBJECTIVES

Studying this lesson will enable students to
- empathize with the speaker's feelings about death
- describe Dylan Thomas's literary accomplishments and explain the historical significance of his writings
- define *pun, symbol*, and *villanelle* and recognize the use of these techniques in the selection
- write imperative sentences
- participate in a debate
- participate in a panel discussion

ANSWERS TO GUIDED READING QUESTIONS

1. Old age should "burn & rave at close of day."
2. Even "wise men" do not go gentle into death because "their words had forked no lightning," by which Thomas may mean that their wisdom has not yet produced the effect on others that they intended.

INDIVIDUAL LEARNING STRATEGIES (CONT. FROM PAGE 941)

English Language Learning
Make sure that students understand that Thomas is referring to death when he says "that good night." The phrases "close of day" and "the sad height" refer to a period of life when a person is close to death.

Special Needs
Make sure students can answer the Guided Reading Questions and the Recall questions in Investigate, Inquire, and Imagine. Students will also benefit from doing the Reading Proficiency and English Language Learning activities with students.

Enrichment
Excellent recordings of Dylan Thomas reading his works are available on audiocassette. Assign several students to find a library in the area that has one of Thomas's recordings and borrow it to play during class.

SELECTION CHECK TEST 12.10.17 WITH ANSWERS

Checking Your Reading

1. According to the speaker, what should old age do "at close of day"? **It should "burn and rave."**
2. What does the speaker say people near death should rage against? **They should rage against the "dying of the light."**
3. What do good men cry? **They cry "how bright / Their frail deeds might have danced in a green bay."**
4. Who "caught and sang the sun in flight"? **Wild men "caught and sang the sun in flight."**
5. Whom does the speaker address? **The speaker addresses his dying father.**

Do Not Go Gentle into That Good Night

DYLAN THOMAS

Do not go gentle into that good night,
Old age should burn and rave at close of day;
Rage, rage against the dying of the light.

Though wise men at their end know dark is right,
Because their words had forked no lightning they
Do not go gentle into that good night.

Good men, the last wave by, crying how bright
Their frail deeds might have danced in a green bay,
Rage, rage against the dying of the light.

Wild men who caught and sang the sun in flight,
And learn, too late, they grieved it on its way,
Do not go gentle into that good night.

Grave men, near death, who see with blinding sight
Blind eyes could blaze like meteors and be gay,
Rage, rage against the dying of the light.

And you, my father, there on the sad height,
Curse, bless, me now with your fierce tears, I pray.
Do not go gentle into that good night.
Rage, rage against the dying of the light. ■

What should old age do at "close of day"?

Why do even "wise men" not go gentle into that good night?

Respond *to the* **SELECTION**

Do you agree with the speaker about how someone should confront death? Explain.

SELECTION CHECK TEST 12.10.17 WITH ANSWERS (CONT.)

Literary Tools
Fill in the blank with the appropriate literary tool from the following list.

mood villanelle symbol pun

1. "Do Not Go Gentle into That Good Night," which has a rhyme scheme of aba aba aba aba aba abaa, is an example of a **villanelle**.
2. Calling dying men "grave" is an example of a **pun** because it refers both to the men's seriousness and a hole in the earth where they will be buried.
3. In the poem, night is a **symbol** of death.

INVESTIGATE, Inquire, Imagine

Recall: GATHERING FACTS → **Interpret:** FINDING MEANING

1a. What terms are used to describe death in stanza 1? What does the speaker urge the dying person to do?
→ 1b. What attitude does the speaker believe that people should adopt when near death?

2a. What do wise men know when they are close to death?
→ 2b. How is the knowledge of wise men related to the speaker's reference to death as "that good night"?

3a. Where, according to stanza 6, is the speaker's father?
→ 3b. What might this phrase refer to?

Analyze: TAKING THINGS APART → **Synthesize:** BRINGING THINGS TOGETHER

4a. Identify the reactions of different types of men as they approach death.
→ 4b. Summarize the reaction to death that the speaker describes.

Evaluate: MAKING JUDGMENTS → **Extend:** CONNECTING IDEAS

5a. The speaker asks his father to curse or bless him. Evaluate the speaker's reasons for wanting such a reaction.
→ 5b. What would you say to someone you knew who was close to death?

Understanding Literature

PUN. Review the definition for **pun** in the Handbook of Literary Terms. What pun appears in line 13 of this poem? What two meanings does this pun play upon?

SYMBOL. Review the definition for **symbol** in Literary Terms on page 941. What do night and light symbolize in stanza 1?

VILLANELLE AND RHYME SCHEME. Review the definitions for **villanelle** and **rhyme scheme** in the Handbook of Literary Terms and the chart you made for Literary Tools on page 941. What two lines are repeated throughout this poem? Does the poem meet the requirements of the villanelle form? What is the poem's rhyme scheme?

ANSWERS TO UNDERSTANDING LITERATURE

PUN. The pun in line 13 is grave. It can be an adjective meaning "sad" or "somber" and a noun referring to a hole in the earth where the dead are buried.

SYMBOL. Night symbolizes death and light symbolizes life.

VILLANELLE AND RHYME SCHEME. The two repeated lines in Thomas's poem are "Do not go gentle into that good night," and "Rage, rage against the dying of the light." The poem meets the villanelle requirements. The rhyme scheme is *aba aba aba aba aba abaa.*

RESPOND TO THE SELECTION

Ask students to consider the role age, health, or other criteria play in a person's attitude toward death. Students should also consider what they think death means: is it the end of everything or a transitional experience?

ANSWERS TO INVESTIGATE, INQUIRE, AND IMAGINE

RECALL

1a. "That good night" and "dying of the light" refer to death. The speaker urges the dying person to "burn and rave" and "rage" against death.
2a. Wise men know that dark is right.
3a. The speaker's father is on the "sad height."

INTERPRET

1b. The speaker thinks people should adopt an attitude of anger or determination to continue to live.
2b. Wise men know that "dark is right" or that death is in some way good.
3b. It might refer to the end of life, a period when one is close to death.

ANALYZE

4a. Wise men "know dark is right" and they do not go gently. Good men cry about their frail deeds and rage against death. Wild men learn too late and do not go gently. Grave men see with blinding sight and rage against death.

SYNTHESIZE

4b. In stanzas 2-5 the speaker describes men who rage against death.

EVALUATE

5a. Although a curse or a blessing seem very different actions, they both connect the father to the speaker and make him react in some way. If his father cursed the speaker, the father would be expressing the rage the speaker wants to see; it would mean he was still engaged in life. If his father blessed the speaker, the father would be expressing the love that the speaker wants to know is still there.

EXTEND

5b. *Responses will vary.*

ANSWERS TO INTEGRATING THE LANGUAGE ARTS

Language, Grammar, and Style

1. Do not go gentle into that good night!
2. When death draws near, rage against it!
3. Show respect for people who have died!
4. Father, live!
5. Say goodbye!

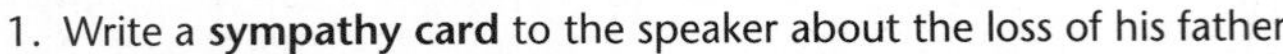
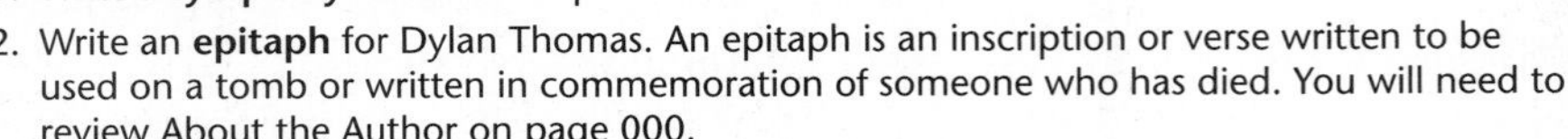

Writer's Journal

1. Write a **sympathy card** to the speaker about the loss of his father.
2. Write an **epitaph** for Dylan Thomas. An epitaph is an inscription or verse written to be used on a tomb or written in commemoration of someone who has died. You will need to review About the Author on page 000.
3. In this poem, Thomas tells his father how to approach death. Write a **personal statement** about how you think people should approach life.

Integrating *the* Language Arts

Language, Grammar, and Style

Imperative sentences give orders or make requests. "Write your answer on a separate sheet of paper" is an imperative sentence. Rewrite each of the sentences below as an imperative sentence.

1. You should not go gentle into that good night.
2. When death draws near, people should rage against it.
3. You should show respect for people who have died.
4. Father, I want you to live.
5. Shall we say goodbye?

Speaking and Listening & Collaborative Learning

Participating in a Debate. With a small group of classmates, debate whether laws protecting euthanasia should be enacted. Choose whether to support or refute the proposition. Write both constructive and rebuttal speeches. You may find it useful to review the Language Arts Survey 4.21, "Participating in a Debate."

Collaborative Learning & Speaking and Listening

Panel Discussion. Is it normal for dying people to "rage against the dying of the light"? Read *On Death and Dying* by Elizabeth Kübler-Ross. Then hold a panel discussion about the five stages of dying, and decide which stage is described in Thomas's poem.

"Who's Who"

"Musée des Beaux Arts"

By W. H. Auden

About the Author

Wystan Hugh Auden (1907-1973) was considered the leader of the young, politically conscious British poets of the 1930s. As fascism gained ground in Germany and Italy, this group of poets supported left-wing ideas and tried to bring change to British society. At Oxford University, Auden became friends with other writers who achieved fame, including the playwright Christopher Isherwood and the poet Stephen Spender. After spending a year in Germany, Auden returned to England and began teaching. His early poetry soon made him famous. During the 1930s, Auden also wrote dramas, light verse, and political observations, sometimes working with other writers. In 1939, he moved to the United States, where he spent more than thirty years and won the Pulitzer Prize for poetry. He returned to Oxford in 1972. Over time, Auden's style, outlook, and religious beliefs changed, but his social awareness never failed. In the tense Cold War era, he coined the term "Age of Anxiety."

About the Selections

Most of the important themes of Auden's times are represented in his poems. The sonnet **"Who's Who"** reflects his interest in different verse forms as well as his ironic view of worldly fame. Visual arts and music have often inspired modern poets. **"Musée des Beaux Arts"** is a reflection on the sixteenth-century Flemish painting "The Fall of Icarus," by Pieter Brueghel, which is in the collection of the Museum of Fine Arts in Brussels, Belgium. In Greek mythology, Icarus and his father, the architect Daedalus, tried to escape from prison by flying with wings made of wax and feathers. Ignoring his father's warning, Icarus flew too near the sun, which melted his wings, sending him plunging into the sea. Auden uses the poem to comment on suffering and its place in human life.

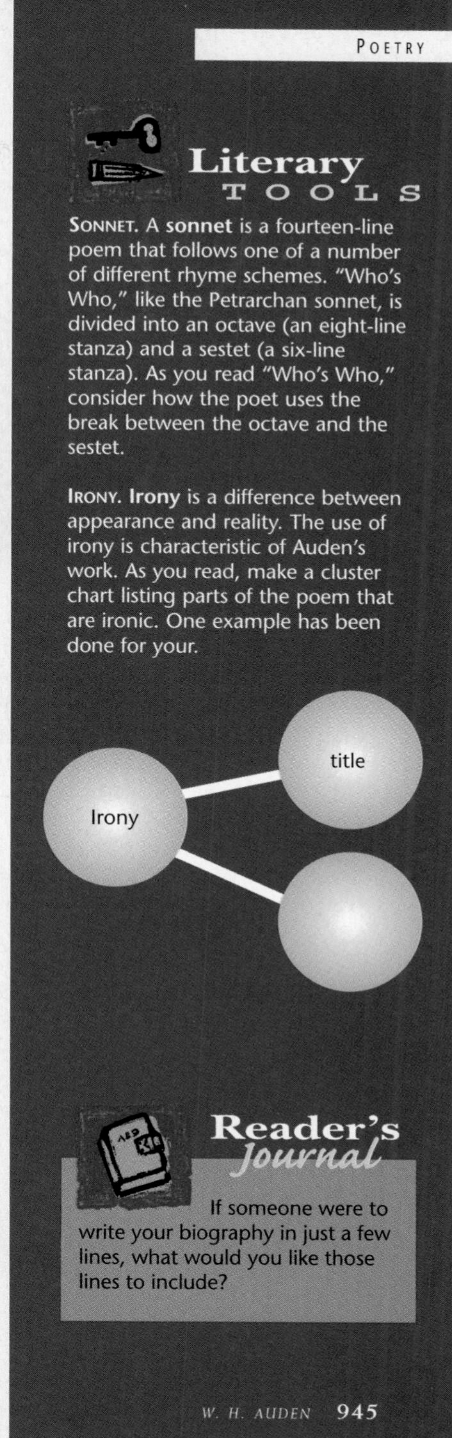

Literary Tools

Sonnet. A **sonnet** is a fourteen-line poem that follows one of a number of different rhyme schemes. "Who's Who," like the Petrarchan sonnet, is divided into an octave (an eight-line stanza) and a sestet (a six-line stanza). As you read "Who's Who," consider how the poet uses the break between the octave and the sestet.

Irony. **Irony** is a difference between appearance and reality. The use of irony is characteristic of Auden's work. As you read, make a cluster chart listing parts of the poem that are ironic. One example has been done for your.

Reader's Journal

If someone were to write your biography in just a few lines, what would you like those lines to include?

GOALS/OBJECTIVES

Studying this lesson will enable students to

- empathize with the speaker's attitudes toward fame and suffering
- describe W. H. Auden's literary accomplishments and explain the historical significance of his writings
- define *sonnet, irony, theme*, and *allusion* and recognize the use of these techniques in the selections
- identify the functions of sentences
- identify synonyms
- present an oral history

ADDITIONAL RESOURCES

Unit 10 Resource Book
"WHO'S WHO"
- Selection Worksheet 10.10
- Selection Check Test 4.10.21
- Selection Test 4.10.22

"MUSÉE DES BEAUX ARTS"
- Selection Worksheet 10.11
- Selection Check Test 4.10.23
- Selection Test 4.10.24

- Language, Grammar, and Style Resource 3.17
- Study and Research Resource 5.50

GRAPHIC ORGANIZER

Irony. Students should list the following examples of irony in their charts: the "shilling life" and the "marvelous" letters.

READER'S JOURNAL

Students might consider one incident, one relationship or one small details that could give the world a picture of their life. Students might write a one paragraph biography based on these ideas.

INDIVIDUAL LEARNING STRATEGIES

Motivation
Examine an entry from "Who's Who" with students and have them make a list of character traits the person probably possesses in order to have accomplished what he or she did.

Reading Proficiency
Point out that a different character is examined in the octet and the sestet. Have students review the Language Arts Survey 3.89, "Colons." Discuss with students the use of colons in lines 1, 4, and 6.

English Language Learning
Point out the additional vocabulary words below.
figure—person, especially one thought of in a specified way
giddy—feeling dizzy or unsteady
potter—busy oneself in a trifling or aimless way

Special Needs
Point out that there is a relationship between the person

(Continued on page 946)

ANSWERS TO GUIDED READING QUESTIONS

1. The subject of the poem has led a life of great activity, struggle, and exploration that has brought him fame.
2. He "sighs for" someone who is a homebody.

INDIVIDUAL LEARNING STRATEGIES (CONT. FROM PAGE 945)

described in stanza 1 and the person described in stanza 2. Ask students how they communicate. Make sure students can answer the Guided Reading Questions and the Recall questions from Investigate, Inquire, and Imagine.

ENRICHMENT

"Poetry makes nothing happen," says Auden, commenting on how little literature affects life. Life, however, has a great influence on literature; and a poet's character and times appear in his verse as in a dark mirror. Students can write a speculative paragraph on what they think Auden and his life were like, based on the Prereading information and on the selections. They can then do research and compare the facts of Auden's personality and biography with their conjectures.

SELECTION CHECK TEST 12.10.21 WITH ANSWERS

Checking Your Reading

1. What will a "shilling life" reveal? **It will reveal "all the facts" about the explorer's life.**
2. What did the subject of the poem name? **He named a sea.**
3. Why did the explorer "weep his pints like you and me"? **His love was unrequited.**
4. How did the explorer's love interest live? **He or she lived a quiet, very ordinary life at home, doing "little jobs about the house with skill."**
5. What did the ordinary person do with the letters from the explorer? **He or she answered some of them but kept none.**

Literary Tools

Fill in the blank with the appropriate literary tool from the following list.

irony   rhyme scheme   sonnet   dramatic irony

Who's Who

W. H. AUDEN

A shilling life[1] will give you all the facts:
How Father beat him, how he ran away,
What were the struggles of his youth, what acts
Made him the greatest figure of his day:
Of how he fought, fished, hunted, worked all night,
Though giddy, climbed new mountains; named a sea:
Some of the last researchers even write
Love made him weep his pints like you and me.

With all his honors on, he sighed for one
Who, say astonished critics, lived at home;
Did little jobs about the house with skill
And nothing else; could whistle; would sit still
Or potter round the garden; answered some
Of his long marvellous letters but kept none. ■

What sort of life has this person led?

Despite fame, for whom does this person "sigh"?

1. **shilling life.** A short biography sold in England in Auden's day for a shilling; a shilling was approximately equal in value to a dime.

Respond *to the* **SELECTION**

Imagining you are the recipient of the letters, explain why you did not keep them.

SELECTION CHECK TEST 12.10.21 WITH ANSWERS (CONT.)

1. "Who's Who" is a **sonnet**, divided into an octave and a sestet.
2. The **rhyme scheme** of the poem is ababcdcd efggfe.
3. **Irony** occurs when the "marvelous" letters are not considered worth keeping by the ordinary person described in the sestet.

RESPOND TO THE SELECTION

Students may discuss their responses or they might write a letter to the man in stanza 1 that gives their explanation.

INVESTIGATE, **Inquire,** *Imagine*

Recall: GATHERING FACTS → **Interpret:** FINDING MEANING

1a. What facts will a "shilling life" give you?
1b. How do you think most people react to such facts?

2a. What do you know about the person described in stanza 2?
2b. Why are critics astonished that the subject loves this person?

3a. What does the recipient of the letters do with them?
3b. What does this action suggest about the feelings of the recipient for the writer of the letters?

Analyze: TAKING THINGS APART → **Synthesize:** BRINGING THINGS TOGETHER

4a. Compare and contrast the two people described in this poem.
4b. Does the recipient of the letters seem impressed by the explorer?

Evaluate: MAKING JUDGMENTS → **Extend:** CONNECTING IDEAS

5a. Evaluate the life of the person described in stanza 1. Is it a happy life? a successful one? How else can you characterize it?
5b. Some say that letter writing is a lost art. Explain whether you agree with this position.

Understanding *Literature*

SONNET. Review the definition of **sonnet** in the Handbook of Literary Terms. What does Auden use the stanza break for? How might you summarize the octet? the sestet? How does the rhyme scheme change between the octave and the sestet?

IRONY. Review the definition of **irony** in the Handbook of Literary Terms and the cluster chart you made for Literary Tools on page 945. *Who's Who* is the title of a book that gives short biographies of famous or accomplished people. How is the title of Auden's poem ironic? What other examples of irony did you find in the poem?

ANSWERS TO INVESTIGATE, INQUIRE, AND IMAGINE

RECALL

1a. Such a biography would tell you that the subject of the poem was beaten by his father, ran away, struggled as a youth, became a great figure, fought, fished, hunted, worked, climbed new mountains, and named a sea.

2a. The person lived at home, did jobs about the house, could whistle, would sit still or putter about the garden, answered some of the letters from the explorer, but kept none of them.

3a. The recipient answers some of them, but does not keep any.

INTERPRET

1b. Most people probably think the explorer, despite a difficult childhood, has made quite a life for himself and must not want for anything.

2b. The critics cannot understand how such an accomplished and worldly man could love someone who stayed at home and was content with doing very little.

3b. The recipient of the letters respects the sender enough to answer him, but not enough to treasure his letters.

ANALYZE

4a. The explorer in stanza 1 is famous and applauded for his impressive, exciting actions, but he is not content. The person he loves is unknown and lives a mundane life. Unlike the speaker, this person seems to be content with his or her life.

SYNTHESIZE

4b. No, the recipient of the letters does not seem unduly impressed by the explorer. If the recipient of the letters were really impressed, he or should would have kept the letters.

EVALUATE

5a. *Responses will vary.* The explorer's life does not seem to be happy. He had a difficult childhood, and despite the exciting things he has done, he does not seem happy. Also, his love is unrequited. Whether the explorer's life is successful depends on an individual's definition of success. He is certainly not as content as the person described in stanza 2.

EXTEND

5b. *Responses will vary.*

ANSWERS TO UNDERSTANDING LITERATURE

SONNET. Auden uses the break between stanzas to switch from recounting the successes of the subject of the poem to describing his failed love for the second person. The octave outlines the success of the first person; the sestet describes the second person in terms that contrast with the first person. The rhyme scheme changes from *ababcdcd* to *efggfe.*

IRONY. The title of the poem is ironic because it refers to a book with collections of supposedly notable people, and yet also poses the question "Who's who?" That is, who's better off—the famous person or the person who is not famous? In the eyes of the world, the former is the important one; in the eyes of the explorer, the latter is the person of true importance. Other examples of irony are the notion that a cheap biography can sum up all the facts about the explorer that are worth knowing, and that although the letters were "marvelous," the recipient did not feel compelled to keep any of them.

ANSWER TO GUIDED READING QUESTION

1. They understood that suffering takes place while someone else is engaged in some mundane activity.

GRAPHIC ORGANIZER

ALLUSION. Students should fill in their charts as follows.

Allusions	Type
Brueghel's Icarus	artistic
the myth of Daedalus and Icarus	literary
the Old Masters	historical

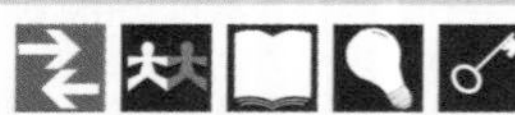

READER'S JOURNAL

Due to the personal nature of the question, students may not want to share their Reader's Journal entries.

INDIVIDUAL LEARNING STRATEGIES

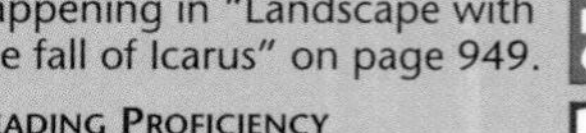

MOTIVATION
Ask students to describe what is happening in "Landscape with the fall of Icarus" on page 949.

READING PROFICIENCY
Have students read About the Selection on page 945, which describes Brueghel's painting. Students need to know the inspiration for this poem came from a painting.

ENGLISH LANGUAGE LEARNING
Point out the British spelling *ploughman* for *plowman.* Introduce the following additional vocabulary words:

leisurely—without haste; deliberately; slowly
forsaken—abandoned; forlorn; desperate

SPECIAL NEEDS
Explain the use of the colon in line 2. Make sure students can answer the Guided Reading Questions and the Recall questions in Investigate, Inquire, and Imagine.

ENRICHMENT
Have students review how to search for library materials. Then, they should use the library to find one or more art books about sixteenth-century Dutch and Flemish painting. Using the source or sources they find, they should make a note of biographical information about Brueghel and the names of at least two of Brueghel's paintings besides "Landscape with the fall of Icarus."

Literary TOOLS

THEME. A **theme** is a central idea in a literary work. As you read the poem, try to figure out its theme.

ALLUSION. An **allusion** is a rhetorical technique in which reference is made to a person, event, object, or work from history or literature. As you read "Musée des Beaux Arts," make a chart listing the allusions and identify them as historic, artistic, or literary.

Allusions	Type

Reader's Journal

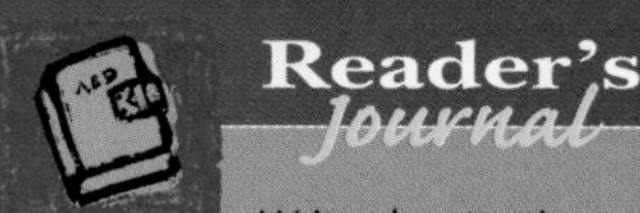

Write about a time when you suffered. Were others aware of your pain?

Musée des Beaux Arts

W. H. AUDEN

About suffering they were never wrong,
The Old Masters:[1] how well they understood
Its human position; how it takes place
While someone else is eating or
opening a window or
just walking dully along;
How, when the aged are
reverently, passionately waiting
For the miraculous birth, there always must be
Children who did not specially want it to happen,
skating
On a pond at the edge of the wood:
They never forgot
That even the dreadful martyrdom must run its course
Anyhow in a corner, some untidy spot
Where the dogs go on with their doggy life and the
torturers horse
Scratches its innocent behind on a tree.
In Brueghel's *Icarus*,[2] for instance: how everything turns
away
Quite leisurely from the disaster; the ploughman may
Have heard the splash, the forsaken cry,
But for him it was not an important failure; the sun
shone
As it had to on the white legs disappearing into the
green

What did the Old Masters understand about suffering?

1. **Old Masters.** Collective name for great European artists before the eighteenth century
2. **Brueghel's *Icarus*.** Brueghel was a Flemish painter. One of his paintings is of the legend of Icarus, who flew too close to the sun with wings made of wax and fell back to earth and died.

VOCABULARY FROM THE SELECTION

martyrdom
reverently

Landscape with the fall of Icarus, c.1558. Pieter Bruegel. Musées Royaux des Beaux-Arts, Brussels.

Water; and the expensive delicate ship that must have
seen
Something amazing, a boy falling out of the sky,
Had somewhere to get to and
sailed calmly on. ■

What was happening as Icarus fell from the sky?

WORDS FOR EVERYDAY USE

rev • er • ent • ly (rev´ər ənt lē) *adv.,* with respect or awe. *The king of Lunonia insisted upon being treated reverently by his subjects.*

mar• tyr • dom (mär' tər dəm) *n.,* death or suffering for a cause. *Many who make bad choices in life feel compelled to endure their martyrdom rather than act to make changes.*

ANSWER TO GUIDED READING QUESTION

1. A plowman was plowing and a ship was sailing by.

SELECTION CHECK TEST 12.10.23 WITH ANSWERS

Checking Your Reading

1. About what were the Old Masters never wrong? **They were never wrong about suffering.**
2. When does suffering take place? **It takes place "While someone else is eating or opening a window or just walking dully along."**
3. What famous painting is mentioned in the poem? **Brueghel's Icarus is mentioned in the poem.**
4. What happened to Icarus? **He fell into the sea.**
5. Why didn't the "delicate ship" stop when it saw a boy fall out of the sky? **It "Had somewhere to get to and sailed calmly on."**

Literary Tools

Fill in the blank with the appropriate literary tool from the following list.

free verse allusion
theme denotation

1. Auden makes a(n) **allusion** to Brueghel's painting Landscape with the fall of Icarus.
2. The **theme** of the poem is that human suffering goes largely unnoticed by others.
3. "Musée des Beaux Arts" is written in **free verse**, not having regular rhyme, rhythm, meter, or division into stanzas.

RESPOND TO THE SELECTION

Remind students about the point of the poem: those present during these great moments have other thoughts and concerns and pay very little attention to the high drama or tragedy taking place.

ANSWERS TO INVESTIGATE, INQUIRE, AND IMAGINE

Recall

1a. Human suffering occurs when mundane things, such as eating, opening a window, or walking dully along, are happening.

2a. The aged are "reverently, passionately waiting." The children did not really want it to happen.

3a. Brueghel shows everyone turning away or ignoring the event.

Interpret

1b. They understood that human suffering does not take center stage, that it is just one more thing happening at any moment. Sometimes it seems that a tragic event should make the world stop for a while, but it doesn't.

2b. Children may be less aware of an event. They may be more self-centered and think about how it will affect them.

3b. They suggest that human suffering may go unnoticed. Brueghel suggests that people are too busy to care about the suffering of others.

Analyze

4a. Mundane, ordinary actions occur.

Synthesize

4b. Auden is saying that we are alone in our suffering.

Evaluate

Responses will vary.

5a. Students who disagree with Auden might mention that people do not suffer alone in circumstances like fires and car accidents when fire fighters and police officers come to help. There are also many agencies and organizations like the Red Cross and the International Monetary Fund that try to stem human suffering.

Extend

5b. Both poems contrast extraordinary events with mundane ones. In "Who's Who," the spectacular is noticed, unlike in "Musée des Beaux Arts." But in "Who's Who" it is the extraordinary things that do not matter. In "Musée des Beaux Arts," Auden suggests, not that the tragedy doesn't matter, but that it goes unnoticed.

Respond *to the* SELECTION

Pick one of the characters in the painting and describe what he or she was thinking about when Icarus fell.

INVESTIGATE, Inquire, *Imagine*

Recall: GATHERING FACTS →

1a. According to line 1, when does human suffering occur?

2a. What different reactions to a miraculous birth are described in lines 5–8?

3a. What reaction to Icarus's fall does Brueghel show?

Interpret: FINDING MEANING

1b. Why were the Old Masters adept at depicting suffering?

2b. Why might young and old people react differently to the same event?

3b. What do these reactions suggest about human suffering or human compassion?

Analyze: TAKING THINGS APART →

4a. What kinds of things happen when tragedies or other amazing events occur?

Synthesize: BRINGING THINGS TOGETHER

4b. Is Auden saying that other people suffer with us or that we generally suffer alone?

Evaluate: MAKING JUDGMENTS →

5a. Evaluate Auden's idea that suffering often goes unnoticed because other things are happening. Does this idea reflect reality?

Extend: CONNECTING IDEAS

5b. Compare and contrast the theme of "Musée des Beaux Arts" with that of "Who's Who."

Understanding *Literature*

THEME. Review the definition for **theme** in Literary Tools on page 948. What is the theme of this poem?

ALLUSION. Review the definition for **allusion** in the Handbook of Literary Terms and the chart you made for Literary Tools on page 948. How do the allusions reinforce the theme of the poem?

Answers to Understanding Literature can be found on page 951.

Writer's Journal

1. Write a **letter** to Auden telling him how you reacted to "Who's Who" or "Musée des Beaux Arts."
2. Auden tells the reader only a few facts about the second person in "Who's Who." Write a **character sketch** that provides details about this person's age, appearance, voice, background, personality, and daily life.
3. In "Musée des Beaux Arts," Auden draws on his reactions to a painting to express his emotions and thoughts about human suffering. Choose a photograph or painting that speaks to you. Write a **poem** or short **essay** in which you use the photo or painting as a springboard for your feelings or thoughts.

Integrating *the* Language Arts

Language, Grammar, and Style

Functions of Sentences. Read the Language Arts Survey 3.17, "Functions of Sentences." Write whether each sentence below is declarative, exclamatory, interrogative, or imperative.

1. About suffering they were never wrong.
2. Were the Old Masters ever wrong about suffering?
3. Consider, for example, Pieter Brueghel's painting of Icarus.
4. Isn't it odd that the ship just sails blithely on?
5. The sailors on that ship must have seen something amazing!

Study and Research

Identifying Synonyms. Read the Language Arts Survey 5.56, "Answering Synonym and Antonym Questions." Then read the underlined words listed below. From the choices listed after each one, choose the one most similar in meaning to the underlined word.

1. reverently—hopefully, passionately, worshipfully, timidly
2. martyr—prophet, follower, sufferer, rebel
3. innocent—calculating, blameless, experienced, unknowing
4. giddy—friendly, forceful, sick, dizzy
5. astonished—amazed, fearful, wondering, supportive

Collaborative Learning & Speaking and Listening

Oral History. Auden's "Who's Who" raises interesting issues about the importance (or lack thereof) of fame. It asks us to consider, among other things, whether a simple, quiet life might be more engaging than one of high adventure. Histories are usually written about famous people. However, quite interesting historical writing can be done about people who are not famous, for everyone has interesting stories to tell. Choose an older person whom you know who is not famous and interview that person about his or her early life. Based on your interview, share your findings with a small group of your classmates.

ANSWERS TO UNDERSTANDING LITERATURE

Theme. The opening lines say that human suffering goes unnoticed by the world around it. As examples, the poem tells of a martyr being tortured and Icarus falling into the sea. The theme of the poem is that human suffering occurs in a context of general indifference; thus we are essentially alone in our suffering. The theme is elaborated by referring to the Old Masters, who made everyday objects and events the focus of their paintings, while the notable or unusual event occurred in a limited portion of the canvas.

Allusion. The reference to the myth of Daedalus and Icarus and to Brueghel's painting underlines the poem's theme of isolation in suffering; if even the suffering of mythological characters is ignored by the world, Auden seems to be saying it is logical to assume that a broken heart or a lost job goes largely unnoticed. The theme is further elaborated by referring to the Old Masters, who made everyday objects and events the focus of their paintings, while the notable or unusual event occurred in a limited portion of the canvas.

ANSWERS TO INTEGRATING THE LANGUAGE ARTS

Language, Grammar, and Style

1. declarative
2. interrogative
3. imperative
4. interrogative
5. declarative

Study and Research

1. worshipfully
2. sufferer
3. blameless
4. dizzy
5. amazed

Speaking and Listening & Collaborative Learning

Students should prepare interview questions ahead of time, but they should feel free to explore other topics of interest that arise during the interview. Students may find it useful to read the Language Arts Survey 4.14, "Conducting an Interview." After conducting their interviews, students might write up the oral histories and make a group booklet.

ADDITIONAL RESOURCES

Unit 10 Resource Book
- Selection Worksheet 10.12
- Selection Check Test 4.10.25
- Selection Test 4.10.26
- Language, Grammar, and Style Resource 3.91, 3.92

READER'S JOURNAL

If students feel comfortable doing so, they should express the emotions they felt when they were misunderstood. In any case, they should analyze the misunderstanding and state the reasons why they think it occurred.

INDIVIDUAL LEARNING STRATEGIES

Motivation
Discuss with students times when people mask their true feelings.

Reading Proficiency
Point out that the dead man is talking in lines 3-4, 9, and 11-12. The speaker's voice is also heard, and "they" speak as well.

English Language Learning
Explain to students that slant rhyme is rhyme that contrasts word endings that are not quite the same. Point out "moaning" and "drowning" as examples of slant rhyme from Stevie Smith's poem. Many great poets (Yeats is a good example) have exploited slant rhyme in an attempt to move away from strictly rhymed line endings.

Special Needs
Make sure students can answer the Guided Reading Questions and Recall questions in Investigate, Inquire, and Imagine. Students will also benefit from doing the activities in Reading Proficiency and English Language Learning.

Enrichment
Students can read or perform the play *Stevie*, by Hugh Whitemore (published 1977). (Students may want to stage contrasting scenes from *The Belle of Amherst*, a play about Dickinson.)

Whitemore also wrote the screenplay for the film *Stevie* (1978), starring Glenda Jackson. Students may be interested in obtaining this film from a library or video rental company.

POETRY

Literary Tools

Figurative Language. Figurative language is writing or speech meant to be understood imaginatively instead of literally. As you read the poem, decide what the poet wants you to interpret figuratively as well as literally.

Irony. Irony is a difference between appearance and reality. Irony may be presented as a contradiction of expectation. As you read, look for examples of irony in the poem.

Reader's Journal

Write about a time you felt misunderstood.

"Not Waving but Drowning"

by Stevie Smith

About the Author

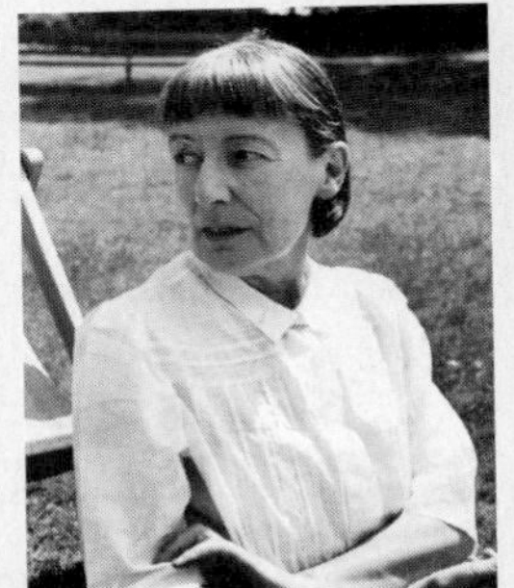

Recognition as a poet came late for **Stevie Smith** (1902–1971), whose real name was Florence Margaret Smith. Born in Yorkshire, she lived nearly all her life with an elderly aunt in a London suburb. She led a quiet life, and her wit appeared mainly in her poems and drawings. In 1923 she took a job as a secretary in a publishing firm and kept the same job for thirty years. However, for two brief periods, Stevie Smith was famous. In the 1930s, she became well known for her *Novel on Yellow Paper* (1936) and for some published poems. Then in the 1960s, after the publication of her collection of poems *Not Waving but Drowning,* Smith became a popular British radio personality and gained new recognition as a contemporary poet. Originality and a strong feminist outlook made her a popular figure in London, where she read and chanted her poems on stage. Smith was given the Gold Medal for Poetry in 1969 by Queen Elizabeth II. After her death, a play and a movie were produced about her career.

About the Selection

Stevie Smith writes in a conversational style, looking at everyday unhappiness in a wry, unsentimental way. Unlike most of her contemporaries, she did not go to university or become part of any literary group but instead developed her voice on her own. One critic says that she wrote in three voices: little girl, lonely and cynical woman, and skeptical philosopher. The mood changes quickly from solemnity to humor. Stevie Smith's most famous poem, **"Not Waving but Drowning,"** is the title of a collection of poems and drawings published in 1957. The poem itself was written in 1953, and its black humor reflects the poet's deep depression at the time.

GOALS/OBJECTIVES

Studying this lesson will enable students to
- empathize with the drowning man's isolation and helplessness
- describe Stevie Smith's literary accomplishments and explain the historical significance of her writings
- define *figurative language* and *irony* and recognize the use of these techniques in the selection
- insert italics and quotation marks as necessary
- make a study plan
- write a monologue or a dialogue
- write a public service announcement

Swimmer, 1919. Erich Heckel. Stadtisches Museum, Mulheim, Germany.

Not Waving but Drowning

STEVIE SMITH

Nobody heard him, the dead man,
But still he lay moaning:
I was much further out than you thought
And not waving but drowning.

Poor chap, he always loved larking[1]
And now he's dead
It must have been too cold for him his heart gave way,
They said.

What do people say happened to the man?

Oh, no no no, it was too cold always
(Still the dead one lay moaning)
I was much too far out all my life
And not waving but drowning. ■

How does the man respond?

1. **larking.** Kidding around, having fun

ANSWERS TO GUIDED READING QUESTIONS

1. People say that his heart gave way due to the cold while he was having a good time fooling around.
2. The man responds that they are wrong, that the coldness was nothing new to him, and that he was always too far out or isolated in his life.

SELECTION CHECK TEST 12.10.25 WITH ANSWERS

Checking Your Reading

1. What did the people think that the man was doing? **They thought that he was waving.**
2. What was really happening? **The man was drowning.**
3. Who says "he always loved larking"? **"They," the spectators, say it.**
4. On what did the bystanders blame the man's death? **They thought the water must have been too cold for him.**
5. Who says "I was much too far out all my life"? **The drowning man says it.**

Literary Tools

Fill in the blank with the appropriate literary tool from the following list.

figurative language   point of view
irony   personification

1. **Figurative language** is evident in "Not Waving but Drowning" when Smith mentions the coldness the man lived with during his whole life.
2. **Irony** occurs when the bystanders think the drowning man is larking in the water.
3. Smith gives the **point of view** of the drowning man and the spectators.

ADDITIONAL QUESTIONS AND ACTIVITIES

Ask students to make some generalizations as they read the poem. They should consider these questions: What generalizations can you make about the man who is the subject of the poem? On what evidence are these generalizations based?

Answers

Students should be able to generalize that the man in the poem was not happy in life, though he appeared to others to be so; the evidence for this consists of his statement that "it was too cold always/. . . I was much too far out all my life," and that the other speakers in the poem claim "he always loved larking." Point out that the man is, as a symbol, a generalization for the human experience.

RESPOND TO THE SELECTION

Insofar as students don't know whether the man felt "too far out" in his personal or professional life, comments should be general.

ANSWERS TO INVESTIGATE, INQUIRE, AND IMAGINE

Recall
1a. People thought the drowning man was waving.
2a. They say that the man's heart gave way because of the cold.
3a. The drowning man says it was always too cold, that he was always out too far, and that he was always drowning, not waving.

Interpret
1b. The man liked to fool around.
2b. People do not seem very moved by his death.
3b. The man felt overwhelm and unhappy all his life.

Analyze
4a. The man felt that his life was cold and that he was in over his head all the time. Others thought he was having a great time most of his life, playing jokes and having fun.

Synthesize
4b. The man might have stopped feeling like he was drowning. Other people might have understood him better.

Evaluate
5a. The people seem to think it is a shame, but they do not seem very sad. Perhaps this is because they thought the man was kidding around when he died. Or perhaps they do not feel deep emotion because they did not really know him well.

Extend
5b. In both cases a tragedy occurs without receiving the proper recognition. In Auden's poem, people seem too busy to notice what is happening around them. In Smith's poem, people notice but misinterpret what is happening. In both cases, the tragedies seem to be taken lightly.

Respond *to the* Selection

How might someone have made a difference to the chap who was "too far out" all his life?

Investigate, Inquire, Imagine

Recall: Gathering Facts
1a. What did people think the drowning man was doing?
2a. What do people say caused the man's death?
3a. What does the dying man say about his life?

Interpret: Finding Meaning
1b. Why did people make this assumption?
2b. How do people feel about his death?
3b. How did the dying man feel throughout his life?

Analyze: Taking Things Apart
4a. Compare and contrast the way the man saw himself and how others saw him.

Synthesize: Bringing Things Together
4b. What if the man had been able to ask for help? What difference might this have made?

Evaluate: Making Judgments
5a. Assess the attitude of the people who knew the drowning man toward his death.

Extend: Connecting Ideas
5b. Compare the attitude toward tragedy in this poem with that in Auden's "Musée des Beaux Arts."

Understanding Literature

Figurative Language. Review the definition for **figurative language** in Literary Tools on page 952. In what way can people drown figuratively? How might one's surroundings be figuratively cold?

Irony. Review the definition for **irony** in the Handbook of Literary Terms. What is ironic about the attitude of "they" in stanza 2?

ANSWERS TO UNDERSTANDING LITERATURE

Figurative Language. A person may suffer from depression or isolation after experiencing a loss, for instance, and conceal his or her problem from others until the problem reaches a point where it seems insoluble. A person also might act cheerful out of a desire not to burden others, and so never indicate his or her pain. Others may be too busy or preoccupied to notice, or may underestimate the magnitude of the problems involved. One's surroundings may be "cold" if one feels one does not receive attention, interest, or response from others.

Irony. The attitude of the observers referred to as "they" is ironic because they believe the dead man was having fun up to the instant he died; the dead man points out that he was never having fun. The title is ironic; it reflects the drowning man's insistence that he was never happy, though he was believed to be so, a contrast between appearance and reality.

Writer's Journal

1. Write a **journal entry** from the point of view of the drowned man before he died.
2. Imagine you are a reporter. Write a **newspaper article** about the drowning. Include an interview with someone who observed the man's behavior in the water.
3. Write a **poem** about someone drowning figuratively. You may or may not want to use images of literal drowning.

Integrating *the* Language Arts

Language, Grammar, and Style

Proofreading. Read the Language Arts Survey 3.91, "Underlining and Italics" and 3.92, "Quotation Marks." Revise the sentences below as needed to correct errors in those forms of punctuation. If the punctuation is correct, write OK.

1. The heroine of Stevie Smith's first novels, *Novel on Yellow Paper* and "Over the Frontier", is much like the writer herself.
2. Her first book of poetry was called A Good Time Was Had by All.
3. After World War II ended, Stevie began to give public readings of her "poems," sometimes chanting them to the tunes of hymns or "folk songs."
4. Stevie's poem "Thoughts about the Person from Porlock refers to the person who interrupted the poet Coleridge as he was writing his famous poem *Kubla Khan.*
5. The Frog Prince is the best-known poem in Smith's popular 1966 collection of verse.

Study and Research

Making a Study Plan. Keeping track of your responsibilities and planning how to get done what you have to do can help keep you from feeling that you are drowning. Make a study plan for the next two weeks. Include any items that are due over the next two weeks and any work you plan to do on long-term projects.

Speaking and Listening

Monologue/Dialogue. Pieces like "Not Waving but Drowning," which feature only one or two characters and a single incident, can be surprisingly complex and powerful. Many contemporary plays are written as monologues or dialogues. Think of a crisis situation involving one or two actors (for instance, one person on the telephone or two people at a fast-food restaurant). Write and deliver a short monologue or dialogue based on the situation and characters you have chosen. Then share your monologue or dialogue with the class.

Applied English & Study and Research

Public Service Announcement. Research CPR procedures. Then write step-by-step directions for how to give CPR to a person who has almost drowned.

ANSWERS TO INTEGRATING THE LANGUAGE ARTS

Language, Grammar, and Style

1. The heroine of Stevie Smith's first novels, *Novel on Yellow Paper* and *Over the Frontier,* is much like the writer herself.
2. Her first book of poetry was called *A Good Time Was Had by All.*
3. After World War II ended, Smith began to give public readings of her poems, sometimes chanting them to the tunes of hymns or folk songs.
4. Stevie's poem "Thoughts about the Person from Porlock" refers to the person who interrupted the poet Coleridge as he was writing his famous poem "Kubla Kahn."
5. "The Frog Prince" is the best-known poem in Smith's popular 1966 collection of verse.

Speaking and Listening
Students should go through the process of writing, beginning with free writing or another kind of prewriting to gather ideas. If students choose to write dialogues, they might work in pairs to both write and present the dialogue.

Applied English
Assign a score from 1 to 25 for each grading criterion below. (For more detailed evaluation see the evaluation forms for writing, revising, and proofreading, Assessment Resource.)

Public Service Announcement
Content/Unity. The public service announcement gives CPR instructions that could be administrated to a person who was saved from drowning.
Organization/Coherence. The public service announcement gives the steps in chronological order.
Language/Style. The public service announcement uses clear and precise language.
Conventions. The public service announcement avoids errors in spelling, grammar, usage, mechanics, and manuscript form.

ADDITIONAL RESOURCES

Unit 10 Resource Book
- Selection Worksheet 10.13
- Selection Check Test 4.10.27
- Selection Test 4.10.28
- Language, Grammar, and Style Resource 3.36
- Speaking and Listening Resource 4.19

GRAPHIC ORGANIZER

Students should include the following images in their cluster charts: fistfuls of splintered weapons, a flower as a plume of blood, thistles going to seed and turning white.

READER'S JOURNAL

Students should be aware that humans project human attitudes, such as hostility, on nature.

INDIVIDUAL LEARNING STRATEGIES

Motivation
Have students write a poem in which an element of nature demonstrates a human characteristic.

Reading Proficiency
Explain to students that for centuries in the Middle Ages the British Isles underwent constant invasion by Vikings, a warlike people who lived in northern Europe and in Iceland. The Vikings were known for their pale, or blond, hair; their Germanic speech is commonly viewed as guttural, that is, as including many sounds produced deep in the throat. In the poem, Hughes imagines that thistles rise up from the bodies of Vikings buried under the ground. This information will allow students to understand many of the references in the poem.

English Language Learning
Explain that thistles are a weed. They are beautiful, but they are difficult to kill. Tell students that this poem describes the life cycle of the thistle in figurative language.

Special Needs
Review Guided Reading Questions and Recall questions from Investigate, Inquire, and Imagine with students.

Enrichment
In Greek mythology, Jason sowed dragon's teeth and warriors sprang up from the teeth as if they were seeds. Have students read a version of this myth.

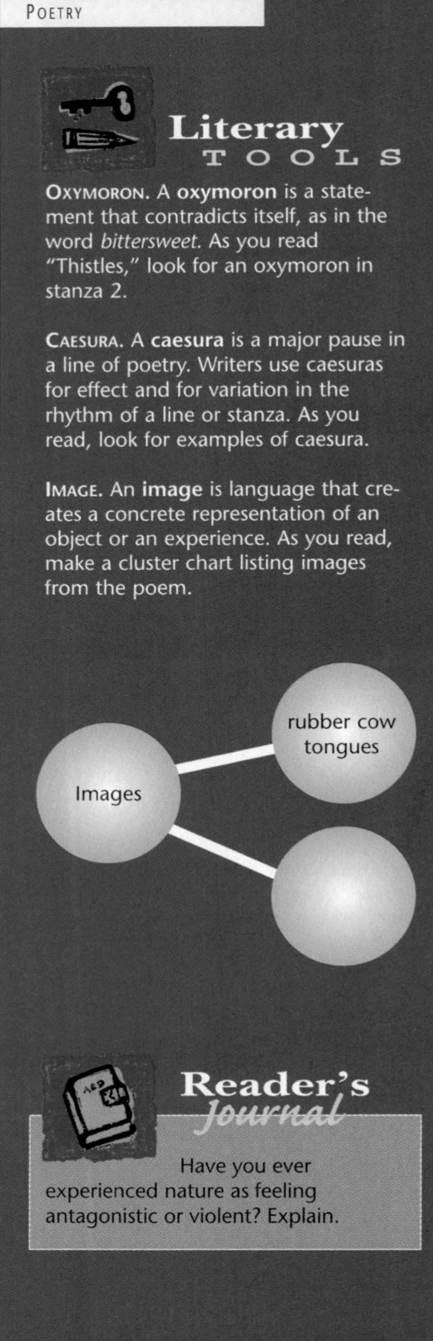

POETRY

Literary TOOLS

Oxymoron. A **oxymoron** is a statement that contradicts itself, as in the word *bittersweet.* As you read "Thistles," look for an oxymoron in stanza 2.

Caesura. A **caesura** is a major pause in a line of poetry. Writers use caesuras for effect and for variation in the rhythm of a line or stanza. As you read, look for examples of caesura.

Image. An **image** is language that creates a concrete representation of an object or an experience. As you read, make a cluster chart listing images from the poem.

Reader's Journal

Have you ever experienced nature as feeling antagonistic or violent? Explain.

956 UNIT TEN

PREREADING

"Thistles"

by Ted Hughes

About the Author

Ted Hughes (1930–1998) was born in Mytholmroyd, a milltown in Yorkshire. The experience of growing up in a milltown shaped the unsentimental and often violent view of life that Hughes expresses in his poetry; his dialect, native to the West Riding area of Yorkshire, establishes the vocabulary and tone in his poetry. Another vital influence on Hughes's verse was his early introduction to the poetry of D. H. Lawrence. In 1954, Hughes earned a bachelor's degree at Cambridge, where he studied anthropology, mythology, and folklore. While at Cambridge, he met the American poet Sylvia Plath, whom he married in 1956. In 1957, Hughes published his first volume of poetry, *The Hawk in the Rain,* which won immediate critical acclaim. The volume introduced readers to many of the themes characteristic of his work, primarily the violence found in nature and in legend. His second volume, *Lupercal,* was published in 1960. Subsequent volumes include *Wodwo,* a collection of stories, verse, and prose poems; *Crow; Selected Poems: 1957–1967; Season Songs; Cave Birds; Moortown; Under the North Star* (poems for children); *What Is the Truth?;* and *Birthday Letters.* Hughes also published stories and plays. Considered one of the most individual poetic voices in England since Dylan Thomas, Hughes was appointed poet laureate in 1984.

About the Selection

"Thistles" is from the volume *New Selected Poems,* published in 1982. The selection shows many of the elements characteristic of Hughes's work—violence of feeling, vivid and concrete images of nature and animals, direct vocabulary, and surprising meter and rhyme. Also characteristic is the pessimistic, yet vital, point of view toward the human condition.

GOALS/OBJECTIVES

Studying this lesson will enable students to
- appreciate the fierce tenacity projected by the speaker onto his subject
- describe Ted Hughes's literary contributions and explain the historical significance of his writings
- define *oxymoron, caesura,* and *image* and recognize the use of these techniques in the selection
- combine sentences
- orally interpret a poem
- participate in a panel discussion

Fleet of Viking Ships in a Rough Sea, c.1900s.
Edward Moran. Private Collection.

Thistles

TED HUGHES

Against the rubber tongues of cows and the hoeing hands of men
Thistles spike the summer air
Or crackle open under a blue-black pressure.

Every one a revengeful burst
Of resurrection, a grasped fistful
Of splintered weapons and Icelandic frost thrust up

From the underground stain of a decayed Viking.
They are like pale hair and the gutturals of dialects.
Every one manages a plume of blood.

Then they grow gray, like men.
Mown down, it is a feud. Their sons appear,
Stiff with weapons, fighting back over the same ground. ■

According to the poem, what is each thistle?

What happens to the thistles? What appears in their place? What sort of "battle" is taking place?

ANSWERS TO GUIDED READING QUESTIONS

1. Each thistle is like the resurrection of a Viking.
2. The thistles are mown down, but other thistle plants ("their sons") appear in their place. A battle between the thistles and the farmers, of nature against humankind, is taking place.

SELECTION CHECK TEST 12.10.27 WITH ANSWERS

Checking Your Reading

1. What two forces work to destroy the thistles? **The "rubber tongues of cows and the hoeing hands of men" work to destroy the thistles.**
2. What do thistles spike? **They spike the "summer air."**
3. What does the speaker imagine feeds the thistles? **The speaker imagines that decayed Vikings feed the thistles.**
4. In what ways are the thistles like men? **They have pale hair, speak in a guttural dialect, and grow gray in their old age.**
5. What do the sons of the thistles do? **They fight back over the same ground.**

Literary Tools
Fill in the blank with the appropriate literary tool from the following list.

caesura oxymoron
image palindrome

1. Bittersweet is a(n) **oxymoron** because bitter and sweet contradict each other.
2. In "Thistles" commas create **caesuras**.
3. "Plume of blood" is an ***image*** that contributes to the violent tone of the poem.

ADDITIONAL QUESTIONS AND ACTIVITIES

As students read, have them make lists of precise nouns and vivid verbs from the selection.

Vivid nouns include "pressure," "burst," "fistful," "frost," "stain," "gutturals," "plume," and "feud." Two especially vivid verbs are "spike" and "crackle."

Students can rephrase the following clauses to replace the colorless verbs used by Hughes: "They are like pale hair"; "it is a feud." Ask why the poet might have chosen to use less vivid and specific words.

RESPOND TO THE SELECTION

Students might consider how they feel about weeds in general.

ANSWERS TO INVESTIGATE, INQUIRE, AND IMAGINE

Recall

1a. The thistles are fighting against "the rubber tongues of cows and the hoeing hands of men."
2a. They reappear like revengeful Vikings with fistfuls of weapons.
3a. They "grow gray" like old men.

Interpret

1b. The thistles' opponents are both susceptible to the thistles' prickles.
2b. The image suggests that nature resurrects itself to fight again even when "slain."
3b. The sons of the thistles appear to fight back.

Analyze

4a. Hughes shows the thistles as vengeful, powerful, steeped in history, recurring, and victorious in the battle to survive.

Synthesize

4b. Nature has powerful renewing energies, which usually ensure that plants reproduce despite the actions of humans.

Evaluate

5a. Neither side really wins in the poem; the battle simply continues. The reader can conclude that the battle will be perpetual.

Extend

5b. In Yeats's poem "The Lake Isle of Innisfree," the speaker feels at one with nature, which is perceived as benevolent. The speaker enjoys the peacefulness of Innisfree where crickets sing linnets fly. "There midnight's all a glimmer, and noon a purple glow." In Hughes's "Thistles" the speaker perceives nature as antagonistic to humans. The thistles sprout up like Viking warriors, each one managing "a plume of blood."

Respond *to the* Selection

How does this poem make you feel about thistles?

Investigate, Inquire, Imagine

Recall: Gathering Facts

1a. What are the thistles fighting against?

2a. How do thistles reappear in stanza 2?

3a. Like what do the thistles "grow gray"?

→ **Interpret:** Finding Meaning

1b. What do the thistles' "opponents" have in common?

2b. What does this image suggest about the ability of human beings to battle nature?

3b. What evidence at the end of the poem suggests the thistles' renewal?

Analyze: Taking Things Apart

4a. What characteristics does Hughes identify in the thistles?

→ **Synthesize:** Bringing Things Together

4b. What power do thistles have that human beings cannot completely conquer?

Evaluate: Making Judgments

5a. Assess which side wins the battle in the poem.

→ **Extend:** Connecting Ideas

5b. Compare the attitude toward nature expressed in Yeats's poem "The Lake Isle of Innisfree" on page 907 and Hughes's "Thistles."

Understanding *Literature*

Oxymoron. Review the definition for **oxymoron** in the Handbook of Literary Terms. Identify an oxymoron in stanza 2. Explain how this oxymoron reflects the tone of the poem.

Caesura. Review the definition for **caesura** in Literary Tools on page 956. Lines 4–7 contain three caesuras. What effect do they create? What effect do they have on the rhythm of the stanza?

Image. Review the definition for **image** in the Handbook of Literary Terms and the cluster chart you made for Literary Tools on page 956. What type of relationship between nature and humans does Hughes portray?

ANSWERS TO UNDERSTANDING LITERATURE

Oxymoron. "A revengeful burst / Of resurrection" in lines 4-5 is an oxymoron. The phrase suggests that new life is born out of an impulse to "get back at" those who have killed the previous generation. The phrase reflects the violent tone of the poem.

Cæsura. The cæsuras occur after "resurrection," "weapons," and "stain." They make the rhythm mimic the breaking action described in the poem. They slow the rhythm of the stanza.

Image. Many of the images are violent and reflect a warlike relationship between nature and humans.

WRITER'S JOURNAL

1. Write **catalog copy** about thistles for a seed catalog. Include vivid images in your copy.
2. Write a **magazine article** for an outdoors publication. Choose one aspect of nature that appeals to you. Write in unsentimental language about your subject.
3. Write a **poem** about the cycle of life. You may wish to try writing in free verse.

Integrating *the* LANGUAGE ARTS

Language, Grammar, and Style

COMBINING SENTENCES. Read the Language Arts Survey 3.36, "Combining and Expanding Sentences." Then combine the following pairs of sentences using single words, phrases, or clauses.

1. Hughes's most characteristic work is without sentimentality. He emphasizes the cunning and savagery of animal life in harsh, sometimes disjunctive lines.
2. The dialect of Hughes's native region set the tone of his verse. He came from the West Riding area of Yorkshire.
3. In his twenties Hughes married the American poet Sylvia Plath. He published his first volume of verse at 27.
4. Hughes published prolifically. He liked to collaborate with photographers and illustrators.
5. Hughes wrote many volumes for children. *Under the North Star* and *A Farmyard Fable for the Young* were children's books.

Speaking and Listening

ORAL INTERPRETATION. With several classmates, have a poetry reading of poems by Ted Hughes. Each person should choose a different poem by Hughes. Review the Language Arts Survey 4.19, "Oral Interpretation of Poetry." Spend some time preparing and practicing your interpretation before presenting it to your group.

Study and Research & Collaborative Learning

PANEL DISCUSSION. Research biologically engineered crops to look at one way humans try to control nature. What are the advantages of these crops? What are the disadvantages? How wide-spread is the use of biologically engineered crops? What happens when the seeds from these crops come in contact with crops that are not biologi-cally engineered? What arguments do opponents of biologically engineered crops present? What are the arguments of the proponents? Discuss these and other questions with your panel.

ANSWERS TO INTEGRATING THE LANGUAGE ARTS

Language, Grammar, and Style

1. Hughes's most characteristic work is without sentimentality, emphasizing the cunning and savagery of animal life in harsh, sometimes disjunctive lines.
2. The dialect of Hughes's native West Riding area of Yorkshire set the tone of his verse.
3. In his twenties Hughes married the American poet Sylvia Plath and published his first volume of verse.
4. Hughes published prolifically, often collaborating with photographers and illustrators.
5. Hughes wrote many volumes for children, including Under the North Star and A Farmyard Fable for the Young.

ADDITIONAL RESOURCES

UNIT 10 RESOURCE BOOK
"FOLLOWER"
- Selection Worksheet 10.14
- Selection Check Test 4.10.29
- Selection Test 4.10.30

"A CALL"
- Selection Worksheet 10.15
- Selection Check Test 4.10.31
- Selection Test 4.10.32
- Language, Grammar, and Style Resource 3.42

GRAPHIC ORGANIZER

Irony. Students should complete their charts as follows.

Beginning	Conclusion
The son follows the father.	The father follows the son.

READER'S JOURNAL

Students might choose to write about a celebrity or a person actually present in their lives when they were growing up.

INDIVIDUAL LEARNING STRATEGIES

MOTIVATION
Ask students to brainstorm a list of five characteristics of a good father.

READING PROFICIENCY
Ask students which stanza does not contain a complete thought and continues in the next stanza.

ENGLISH LANGUAGE LEARNING
Point out that *plough* is the British spelling of *plow*. Have students identify words that have to do with plowing. Point out the definition for the additional vocabulary word below.
furrow—line where the ground is broken by a plow

SPECIAL NEEDS
Review with students the answers to the Guided Reading Questions and the Recall questions in Investigate, Inquire, and Imagine. Students will also benefit from doing the activities mentioned in Reading Proficiency and English Language Learning.

ENRICHMENT
Have students find other poems in which Heaney discusses his relationship with his father. Then have students write an essay exploring Heaney's relationship with his father.

Literary TOOLS

SIMILE. A **simile** is a comparison using *like* or *as*. As you read "Follower," look for a simile in stanza 1.

IRONY. **Irony** is a difference between appearance and reality. In **irony of situation** an event occurs that violates the expectations of the characters, the reader, or the audience. As you read, make a chart describing the relationship of the father and son at the beginning and at the end of the poem.

Beginning	Conclusion

Reader's Journal

Who did you want to grow up to be like?

"Follower"
"A CALL"

BY SEAMUS HEANEY

About the AUTHOR

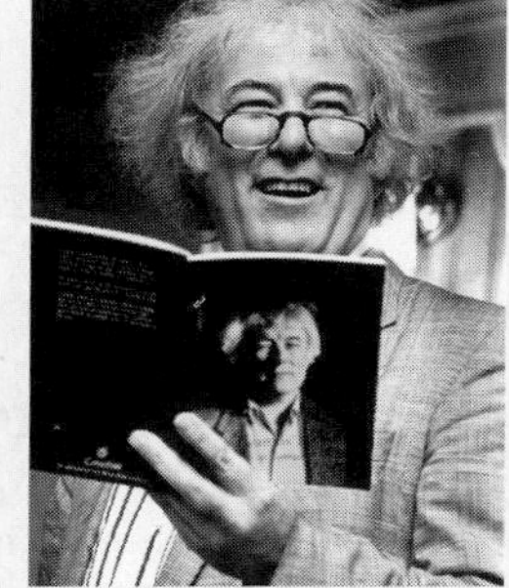

Seamus Heaney (1939–) was born in Northern Ireland, the oldest of nine children. He grew up on a farm in County Derry near the border of the Irish Republic. After graduating from Queen's University, Belfast, Heaney taught secondary school and lectured in colleges and universities in Belfast and Dublin. He has taught at Harvard University and at the University of Oxford.

Heaney has published may volumes of verse, including *Death of a Naturalist* (1966), *Door into the Dark* (1969), *Wintering Out* (1972), *North* (1975), *Field Work* (1979), *Station Island* (1984), *The Haw Lantern* (1987), and *Seeing Things* (1991). His translation of *Beowulf* appeared in 2000. Often called the greatest Irish poet since W. B. Yeats, he received the Nobel Prize for literature in 1995. Heaney's poems evoke Irish history and draw on myth and unique aspects of the Irish experience. Simplicity and clarity distinguish his style.

About the SELECTIONS

Heaney digs into memory and the past, using his father and grandfather as subjects of many of his poems. The Irish countryside often figures in his poetry as well. Heaney treats both subjects in "Follower" and "A Call." *"Follower"* is from his first collection, *Death of a Naturalist* (1966). It is written in six stanzas of four lines each. *"A Call"* is from his collection *The Spirit Level.* It is written in free verse without a regular rhyme scheme or stanza pattern.

GOALS/OBJECTIVES

Studying this lesson will enable students to:
- understand the speaker's relationship with his father
- describe Seamus Heaney's literary accomplishments and explain the historical significance of his writings
- define *allusion, simile,* and *irony* and recognize the use of these techniques in the selections
- correct split infinitives
- write an introduction to an Irish film about the Troubles
- conduct an informational interview

Ploughing, c.1900s. Cecil Aldin. Private Collection.

Follower

SEAMUS HEANEY

My father worked with a horse plough,
His shoulders globed like a full sail strung
Between the shafts[1] and the furrow.
The horses strained at his clicking tongue.

What kind of work did the speaker's father do?

An expert. He would set the wing
And fit the bright steel-pointed sock.
The sod rolled over without breaking.
At the headrig, with a single pluck

Of reins, the sweating team turned round
And back into the land. His eye
Narrowed and angled at the ground,
Mapping the furrow exactly.

I stumbled in his hobnailed wake,
Fell sometimes on the polished sod;
Sometimes he rode me on his back
Dipping and rising to his plod.

I wanted to grow up and plough,
To close one eye, stiffen my arm.
All I ever did was follow
In his broad shadow round the farm.

What did the speaker do while his father plowed?

I was a nuisance, tripping, falling,
Yapping always. But today
It is my father who keeps stumbling
Behind me, and will not go away. ■

What has happened today?

1. **shafts.** Parts of a plow

ANSWERS TO GUIDED READING QUESTIONS

1. The speaker's father was a farmer who worked the land with a horse and a plow.
2. The speaker stumbled behind his father and sometimes rode on his back.
3. Today the speaker's father is stumbling behind him and will not go away.

SELECTION CHECK TEST 12.10.29 WITH ANSWERS

Checking Your Reading

1. What was the profession of the speaker's father? **He was a farmer.**
2. What could the father map exactly? **He could map the furrows exactly.**
3. What happened to the speaker when, as a child, he tried to follow his father while he plowed? **The speaker stumbled.**
4. Why did the speaker want to be a farmer when he grew up? **He wanted to be just like his father.**
5. How has the relationship between the father and the speaker changed? **It is now the father who stumbles, following after his son.**

Literary Tools

Fill in the blank with the appropriate literary tool from the following list.

metaphor simile stanza irony

1. When Heaney says his father's shoulders globed "like a full sail," he is using a **simile**.
2. **Irony** occurs when the father stumbles after his son because the son used to stumble after the father.
3. Each **stanza** in the poem contains four lines.

RESPOND TO THE SELECTION

Students should realize that much time has passed since the speaker was a boy and his father has grown old.

ANSWERS TO INVESTIGATE, INQUIRE, AND IMAGINE

Recall
1a. The speaker's father was an expert at plowing.
2a. The speaker wanted to plow when he grew up.
3a. The father sometimes carried the speaker on his back.

Interpret
1b. The speaker's father took pride in his work.
2b. The speaker felt proud of his father and respected him.
3b. He was kind to his son. He did not yell at him when he fell or chattered. He seemed to enjoy his company.

Analyze
4a. In stanzas 1-5, the father is depicted as sure and confident in his actions, exact and expert at what he does. He is kind and patient with the speaker. In the last stanza, the father stumbles.

Synthesize
4b. The speaker still wants his father to be strong and someone he can look up to.

Evaluate
5a. The speaker is annoyed and impatient with his father, unlike his father was with him.

Extend
5a. *Responses will vary.*

ANSWERS TO UNDERSTANDING LITERATURE

Simile. The poet compares his father's stance at the plow to a "full sail." The father's purposefulness is expressed with this simile.

Irony. In lines 23-24 the father now follows the speaker, which is a reversal of the speaker following his father in his childhood, which is described in lines 1–22.

Respond *to the* Selection

If you were the speaker, what would you say to your father?

Investigate, Inquire, *Imagine*

Recall: Gathering Facts →
1a. At what was the speaker's father an expert?
2a. What did the speaker want to do when he grew up?
3a. In stanza 4, how did the father include the speaker?

Interpret: Finding Meaning
1b. How did the speaker's father feel about his work?
2b. How did the speaker feel about his father?
3b. How did the father treat his son?

Analyze: Taking Things Apart →
4a. Compare and contrast the father as he is pictured in stanzas 1-5 and in stanza 6.

Synthesize: Bringing Things Together
4b. What does the speaker want from his father today?

Evaluate: Making Judgments →
5a. Evaluate the speaker's present attitude toward his father.

Extend: Connecting Ideas
5b. What things annoy children about their parents? What things do children respect about their parents?

Understanding *Literature*

Simile. Review the definition for **simile** in Literary Tools on page 960. What simile did you find in stanza 1? What characteristic of the father is expressed with this simile?

Irony. Review the definition for **irony** in the Handbook of Literary Terms and the chart you made for Literary Tools on page 960. What is ironic about the roles of the father and the speaker at the end of the poem?

A CALL

SEAMUS HEANEY

"Hold on," she said, "I'll just run out and get him.
The weather here's so good, he took the chance
To do a bit of weeding."
                                        So I saw him
Down on his hands and knees beside the leek rig,[1]
Touching, inspecting, separating one
Stalk from the other, gently pulling up
Everything not tapered, frail and leafless,
Pleased to feel each little weed-root break,
But rueful also . . .
                                        Then found myself listening to
The amplified grave ticking of hall clocks
Where the phone lay unattended in a calm
Of mirror glass and sunstruck pendulums . . .

And found myself then thinking: if it were nowadays,
This is how Death would summon Everyman.[2]

Next thing he spoke and I nearly said I loved him. ■

1. **leek rig.** Place where leeks, a type of onion, are grown
2. **Death would summon Everyman.** Refers to a medieval morality play in which Death comes and Everyman must face the end of his life

What does the speaker think about while he waits to talk to his father on the phone?

WORDS FOR EVERYDAY USE

rue • ful (rü' fəl) *adj.,* exciting pity or sympathy; mournful. *The rueful plight of David Copperfield touched his aunt, and she decided to adopt him.*

am • pli • fy (am' plə fī) *vt.,* make stronger; increase. *The megaphone amplified Henry's voice.*

Literary TOOLS

ALLUSION. An **allusion** is a rhetorical technique in which reference is made to a person, event, object, or work from history or literature. Allusions allow the reader to make connections between the subject of their reading and something else. This comparison illuminates some aspect of the subject of the work. As you read "A Call," look for an allusion the poet makes.

Reader's Journal

Why do you think people do not always express how they really feel?

ANSWER TO GUIDED READING QUESTIONS

1. The speaker thinks that, these days, Death would summon Everyman with a phone call.

READER'S JOURNAL

Ask students to recall a time when they kept their true feelings to themselves.

INDIVIDUAL LEARNING STRATEGIES

MOTIVATION
Ask students to describe an activity they associate with one of their parents.

READING PROFICIENCY
Point out that the activities the speaker's father does in the "leek rig" are seen through the speaker's memory. Ask students which expression in line 1 gives the clue that this poem is about a phone call rather than a physical visit.

ENGLISH LANGUAGE LEARNING
Heaney uses several verbs to identify weeding (touching, inspecting, separating, pulling). Have students create a list of verbs associated with some other activity, such as cooking (stirring, measuring, chopping).

SPECIAL NEEDS
Make sure students know the answers to the Guided Reading Questions and the Recall questions in Investigate, Inquire, and Imagine. Students will also benefit from doing the activities mentioned in Reading Proficiency and English Language Learning.

ENRICHMENT
Another poet who writes frequently about his relationship with his father is Robert Bly. Have students select a relevant Bly poem and compare and contrast Bly's relationship with his father with those described in the Heaney poems. What common themes do the two poets develop in their poems about their fathers?

VOCABULARY FROM THE SELECTION

amplify
rueful

RESPOND TO THE SELECTION

Students should consider whether the speaker is impatient or anxious, and whether there is any evidence in the poem to support their assessment.

SELECTION CHECK TEST 12.10.31 WITH ANSWERS

Checking Your Reading

1. With whom does the speaker want to speak? The speaker wants to speak to the man who is weeding the leek rig.
2. How does the man approach the task of weeding? **He is methodical and rueful.**
3. Whose house has a ticking clock? **The man who is weeding has a house with a ticking clock; the speaker hears the clock over the "unattended" phone.**
4. According to the speaker, how would Death summon Everyman in contemporary society? **Death would make a phone call to Everyman.**
5. What does the speaker almost tell the man? **The speaker almost tells the man he loves him.**

Literary Tools

Fill in the blank with the appropriate literary tool from the following list.

speaker characterization
character allusion

1. In "A Call" Heaney makes an **allusion** to a medieval morality play called Everyman.
2. The **speaker** is probably the weeding man's son.
3. Presenting the actions of the man weeding is an example of **characterization**.

ANSWERS TO UNDERSTANDING LITERATURE

Allusion. The poet makes an allusion to the medieval play "Everyman" in which Death comes to claim Everyman. This allusion illuminates the fact that the speaker is thinking about his father's mortality and wondering when he will die because he is old.

Respond *to the* Selection

How do you think the speaker feels while he is waiting for his father to come to the phone?

Investigate, Inquire, *Imagine*

Recall: Gathering Facts → **Interpret:** Finding Meaning

1a. What is the father doing when the speaker calls?
1b. With what type of concentration does the speaker's father do his task?

2a. What does the speaker notice as he waits?
2b. Why might this situation make the speaker think of death?

3a. What does the speaker nearly say?
3b. What evokes feelings of love in the speaker?

Analyze: Taking Things Apart → **Synthesize:** Bringing Things Together

4a. Identify the actions that the speaker, in his mind, observes his father doing.
4b. Why is it so easy for the speaker to see how his father is weeding? What do you learn about the speaker's father from these actions?

Evaluate: Making Judgments → **Extend:** Connecting Ideas

5a. Evaluate the relationship between the speaker and his father.
5b. What similarity exists between the speaker of "Do Not Go Gentle into That Good Night" by Dylan Thomas and the speaker in "A Call"?

Understanding *Literature*

Allusion. Review the definition for **allusion** in the Handbook of Literary Terms. What allusion does Heaney make in this poem? What thought on the part of the speaker does this allusion illuminate?

Writer's Journal

1. Imagine you are the speaker in "Follower." Write a **father's day card** to your father describing the times you feel closest to him and what that means to you.
2. Imagine you are the speaker in "Follower." Write a **toast** to celebrate your father's seventy-fifth birthday.
3. Write a **dialogue** between the father and son in "A Call."

Integrating *the* Language Arts

Language, Grammar, and Style

Avoiding Split Infinitives. Read the Language Arts Survey 3.42, "Avoiding Split Infinitives." Then rewrite the sentences below correcting any split infinitives.

1. To cleverly disguise himself, Heaney wrote under the pseudonym Incertus in college.
2. Heaney stopped teaching to solely focus on his writing.
3. Later he began to again teach.
4. His poems are known for their ability to firmly draw the reader into the actions they describe.
5. Heaney likes to clearly and simply write.

Speaking and Listening

Conducting an Informational Interview. The speaker in "Follower" decided he wanted to plow when he grew up because he saw his father do it. But selecting a career for the twenty-first century sometimes requires real investigating. Think about a profession that interests you. Then write several questions to ask someone in that profession. If you do not personally know someone in that profession, contact the Human Resources Department of an appropriate company or firm, explain your goal, and ask for a contact person in that company or firm. After conducting your interview, hold a panel discussion with several classmates to share what you have learned about the education required for the profession you investigated and about the tasks required on the job.

Media Literacy & Study and Research

Writing a Film Introduction. Seamus Heaney grew up in Northern Ireland, an area filled with violent conflict since the 1970s. Watch the film *Some Mother's Son.* Then research the Troubles in Northern Ireland. Write an introduction to the Jim Sheridan film that will give background information for Americans about what was happening in Northern Ireland that led to the hunger strikes depicted in the film.

Answers to Investigate, Inquire, and Imagine

Recall

1a. The speaker's father is weeding the leek rig.

2a. The speaker notices the "amplified grave ticking" of hall clocks, the unattended phone, the mirror, and the sun striking the pendulums.

3a. The speaker nearly says he loves his father.

Interpret

1b. The speaker's father is engrossed in his task.

2b. The act of summoning his father makes him think how Death was perceived to summon Everyman in the past.

3b. The memory of how his father weeds the leek rig and the sound of his father's voice on the phone evoke feelings of love in the speaker.

Analyze

4a. The speaker sees his father "Touching, inspecting, separating one / Stalk from the other, gently pulling up / Everything not tapered, frail and leafless."

Synthesize

4b. The speaker probably saw his father weeding when he was a child. The speaker's father is hardworking and meticulous.

Evaluate

5a. The speaker and his father keep in touch by telephone. The speaker knows the details of his father's life from memory. It is not easy for father and son to express their feelings for each other.

Extend

5b. Both poems deal with relationships between a father and a son and the son's need to come to terms with his father's approaching death.

Answers to Integrating the Language Arts

Language, Grammar, and Style

1. To disguise himself cleverly, Heaney wrote under the pseudonym Incertus in college.
2. Heaney stopped teaching to focus solely on his writing.
3. Later he began to teach again.
4. His poems are known for their ability to draw the reader firmly into the actions they describe.
5. Heaney likes to write clearly and simply.

ADDITIONAL RESOURCES

Unit 10 Resource Book
- Selection Worksheet 10.16
- Selection Check Test 4.10.33
- Selection Test 4.10.34
- Language, Grammar, and Style Resource 3.55, 3.58
- Applied English Resource 6.5

GRAPHIC ORGANIZER

Students should list the following images in their cluster charts: the honey running onto your fingers, the brownness of the bread, the moldy heel of rye in the refrigerator.

VOCABULARY FROM THE SELECTION

conjure
dupe
infest
subversive
treacherous

READER'S JOURNAL

Students might think of social, religious, and cultural associations they have with bread.

Literary TOOLS

Tone. Tone is the emotional attitude toward the reader or toward the subject implied by a literary work. The speaker uses a manipulative tone throughout "Bread." As you read, look for examples of this tone.

Point of View. Point of view is the vantage point from which a story is told. Stories are typically written from a *first-person point of view,* in which the narrator uses words such as *I* and *we;* from a *second-person point of view,* in which the narrator uses *you;* or from a *third-person point of view,* in which the narrator uses words such as *he, she, it* and *they.* As you read, determine the point of view of "Bread."

Prose Poem. A **prose poem** is a work of prose, usually a short work, that make such extensive use of poetic language, such as figures of speech and words that echo their sense, that the line between prose and poetry, which is never clear, becomes blurred. Unlike conventional poetry, prose poems are usually written in paragraph form, with no formal rhyme or meter. They still have other characteristics that set them apart from ordinary prose, including the use of rich imagery, metaphor, repetition, and indirect or implied meaning. As you read "Bread," make a cluster chart of the sensory images in the first paragraph.

Reader's Journal

Freewrite about associations you have with bread.

"Bread"

BY MARGARET ATWOOD

About the AUTHOR

Although she first became famous as a poet, Canadian writer **Margaret Atwood** (1939–) is also well known for her intense, ironic, and sometimes disturbing novels and stories, such as *Surfacing* (1972), *The Handmaid's Tale* (1986), *Cat's Eye* (1988), and *The Robber Bride* (1993). She grew up in Ottawa and Toronto, Ontario, but came to know the Canadian wilderness during summers spent in northern Quebec. She graduated from the University of Toronto and received a master's degree at Radcliffe (Cambridge, MA) in 1962.

Her first book of poetry, *The Circle Game,* won a Governor General's Award in 1966, and she has won many other awards since. Atwood's writing probes varied subjects, including male-female relationships, the Canadian pioneer spirit, the influence of myth, and international human rights. Atwood is also an editor and critic; in a critical study of Canadian literature, she suggested that survival has been the dominant theme in Canadian writing.

About the SELECTION

Atwood's poetry is often short, terse, written in everyday language, and filled with sharp or witty observations. Her longer, interconnected poems, like her novels, are rich with symbolism and irony. **"Bread"** is a prose poem taken from *Murder in the Dark,* a 1984 collection of short experimental pieces. Like several other works, including the novel *Bodily Harm* (1981) and the poem "Notes Towards a Poem That Can Never Be Written," this poem reflects her personal concern with human rights abuses and repression everywhere.

GOALS/OBJECTIVES

Studying this lesson will enable students to
- understand the speaker's intense feelings of social concern as expressed in the prose poem
- describe Margaret Atwood's literary accomplishments and explain the historical significance of her writings
- define *tone, point of view,* and *prose poem* and recognize the use of these techniques in the poem
- classify pronouns
- write and perform a play
- participate in a human rights letter-writing campaign

Breadstuffs, 1912. Ilya Maskov. State Russian Museum, St. Petersburg, Russia.

Bread

Margaret Atwood

◆ ◆ ◆

Imagine a piece of bread. You don't have to imagine it, it's right here in the kitchen, on the bread board, in its plastic bag, lying beside the bread knife. The bread knife is an old one you picked up at an auction; it has the word BREAD carved into the wooden handle. You open the bag, pull back the wrapper, cut yourself a slice. You put butter on it, then peanut butter, then honey, and you fold it over. Some of the honey runs out onto your fingers and you lick it off. It takes you about a minute to eat the bread. This bread happens to be brown, but there is also white bread, in the refrigerator, and a heel of rye you got last week, round as a full stomach then, now going mouldy. Occasionally you make bread. You think of it as something relaxing to do with your hands.

Imagine a famine. Now imagine a piece of bread. Both of these things are real but you happen to be in the same room with only one of them. Put yourself into a different room, that's what the mind is for. You are now lying on a thin mattress in a hot room. The walls are made of dried earth and your sister, who is younger than you are, is in the room with you. She is starving, her belly is bloated, flies land on her eyes; you brush them off with your hand. You have a cloth too, filthy but damp, and you press it to her lips and forehead. The piece of bread is the bread you've been

What does bread mean to the person in the first paragraph? What does bread mean to the person in the second paragraph?

ANSWER TO GUIDED READING QUESTION

1. Bread is something pleasant that is taken for granted by the person in the first paragraph. For the person in the second paragraph, bread is both a link with life and the cause of a terrible moral dilemma.

INDIVIDUAL LEARNING STRATEGIES

MOTIVATION
Have students make a list of issues a socially conscious person would deem important.

READING PROFICIENCY
Point out that in this selection, each break in the text indicates a shift to another manner of considering the subject, bread. Alert students to the loose connection between the sections of the poem so that they will not be looking for a continuation of thought that is not there. Suggest that students look upon the piece as a connected essay about bread that offers three examples of new ways to look at the subject.

ENGLISH LANGUAGE LEARNING
Explain that the writer is trying to make the readers put themselves in the situations described. English Language Learners might share what bread is like in their cultures. Point out the following additional vocabulary words.
bloated—swollen
scavenger—one who gathers or collects waste

SPECIAL NEEDS
Make sure students can answer the Guided Reading Questions and the Recall questions in Investigate, Inquire, and Imagine. Students will also benefit from doing the activities described in Reading Proficiency and English Language Learning.

ENRICHMENT
Students can arrange for a visit from a representative of a local organization (such as a branch of Oxfam America) that is working to end world hunger.

Students can bake a loaf of bread and serve it before giving a reading of the poem.

ANSWERS TO GUIDED READING QUESTIONS

1. The yellow bowl held apples and pears. It was in the home. It means food, home, and all the good things the person in prison does not have.
2. When the sister's husband cut himself a slice of bread, blood flowed from the cut.
3. The bread has more meaning for the reader by the last paragraph. The writer claims that the reader will no longer be interested in eating the bread.

SELECTION CHECK TEST 12.10.33 WITH ANSWERS

Checking Your Reading

1. What is the setting for the bread in the first section? **The bread is in a Western kitchen.**
2. What decision does the famine victim have to make? **The famine victim has to decide whether to give the bread to his or her sister or eat it himself or herself.**
3. What memory does the bread bring back to the prisoner? **It brings back the memory of a yellow bowl.**
4. In the fairy-tale, what happened when the husband of the rich sister cut the bread? **Blood flowed out.**
5. Where is the bread in the last section? **It is floating above the kitchen table.**

Vocabulary in Context
Fill in each blank with the most appropriate word from the following Words for Everyday Use. You may have to change the tense of certain verbs.

infest subversive
conjure treacherous

1. The magician **conjured** a rabbit out of his hat.
2. Rats **infested** the sewers.
3. The book alleged that **subversive** CIA agents masterminded the South American rebellion.

Literary Tools
Fill in the blank with the appropriate literary tool from the following list.

villanelle tone
point of view mood

1. "Bread" is a **prose poem** because it merges elements of poetry and prose.
2. Because Atwood wants the reader to feel part of each situation described, she uses the second-person **point of view**.
3. The **tone** of the poem can be described as manipulative.

saving, for days it seems. You are as hungry as she is, but not yet as weak. How long does this take? When will someone come with more bread? You think of going out to see if you might find something that could be eaten, but outside the streets are infested with scavengers and the stink of corpses is everywhere.

Should you share the bread or give the whole piece to your sister? Should you eat the piece of bread yourself? After all, you have a better chance of living, you're stronger. How long does it take to decide?

◆ ◆ ◆

Imagine a prison. There is something you know that you have not yet told. Those in control of the prison know that you know. So do those not in control. If you tell, thirty or forty or a hundred of your friends, your comrades, will be caught and will die. If you refuse to tell, tonight will be like last night. They always choose the night. You don't think about the night however, but about the piece of bread they offered you. How long does it take? The piece of bread was brown and fresh and reminded you of sunlight falling across a wooden floor. It reminded you of a bowl, a yellow bowl that was once in your home. It held apples and pears; it stood on a table you can also remember. It's not the hunger or the pain that is killing you but the absence of the yellow bowl. If you could only hold the bowl in your hands, right here, you could withstand anything, you tell yourself. The bread they offered you is subversive, it's treacherous, it does not mean life.

What did the yellow bowl hold? Where was the yellow bowl? What does it mean to the person in prison?

◆ ◆ ◆

There were once two sisters. One was rich and had no children, the other had five children and was a widow, so poor that she no longer had any food left. She went to her sister and asked her for a mouthful of bread. "My children are dying," she said. The rich sister said, "I do not have enough for myself," and drove her away from the door. Then the husband of the rich sister came home and wanted to cut himself a piece of bread; but when he made the first cut, out flowed red blood.

What happened as a result of the sister's selfishness?

Everyone knew what that meant.

This is a traditional German fairy-tale.

◆ ◆ ◆

The loaf of bread I have conjured for you floats about a foot above your kitchen table. The table is normal, there are no trap doors in it. A blue tea towel floats beneath the bread, and there are no strings attaching the cloth to the bread or the bread to the ceiling or the table to the cloth, you've proved it by passing your hand above and below. You didn't touch the bread though. What stopped you? You don't want to know whether the bread is real or whether it's just a hallucination I've somehow duped you into seeing. There's no doubt that you can see the bread, you can even smell it, it smells like yeast, and it looks solid enough, solid as your own arm. But can you trust it? Can you eat it? You don't want to know, imagine that. ■

By the last paragraph, does a loaf of bread hold more meaning for the reader? How does the author show this?

WORDS FOR EVERYDAY USE

in • fest (in fest´) *vt.,* overrun in large numbers. *After the math exam, Gilbert dreamed that his bed was infested with real numbers.*

sub • ver • sive (səb vʉr´ siv) *adj.,* with a goal to undermine or corrupt. *The king of Lunonia cracked down harshly on people who insulted his mustache, as well as other elements of the population that he considered dangerous and subversive.*

treach • er • ous (trech´ ər əs) *adj.,* traitorous, disloyal. *The treacherous goalie let the soccer ball into the goal without attempting to stop it, and his team lost the championship.*

con • jure (kôn´ jər) *vt.,* make appear as by magic. *A truly great poet can conjure a golden world out of a hatful of ordinary words.*

dupe (do͞op) *vt.,* deceive by trickery. *When threatened by the evil genie, the girl duped him into returning to his bottle.*

Respond *to the* SELECTION

Have your feelings or thoughts about bread changed since you read the poem?

INVESTIGATE, Inquire, *Imagine*

Recall: GATHERING FACTS

1a. What are the setting and events of paragraph 1?

2a. How does the scene change in paragraph 2? What happens there?

3a. What is the setting of paragraph 3? What is happening there?

Interpret: FINDING MEANING

1b. What mood is Atwood trying to create in paragraph 1? What words and phrases create this mood?

2b. How does this scene contrast with the previous scene?

3b. What is the significance of the yellow bowl in paragraph 3?

Analyze: TAKING THINGS APART

4a. Analyze the meaning of the bread in each scene described by the speaker.

Synthesize: BRINGING THINGS TOGETHER

4b. What has happened to the bread at the end of the selection?

Evaluate: MAKING JUDGMENTS

5a. Assess which scene is the most provocative.

Extend: CONNECTING IDEAS

5b. Is it possible to know how you would react without being in those situations? What does this suggest about judging the actions of others?

Understanding *Literature*

TONE. Review the definition for **tone** in the Handbook of Literary Terms. How is the speaker manipulative?

POINT OF VIEW. Review the definition for **point of view** in Literary Tools on page 966. What is the point of view used in this selection? Why did Atwood select this point of view?

PROSE POEM. Review the definition for **prose poem** in the Handbook of Literary Terms. Give three examples of poetic techniques you find in "Bread." How might the selection be different if it were written as "pure prose" or "pure poetry"?

Answers to Understanding Literature can be found on page 970.

RESPOND TO THE SELECTION

Students might discuss what Atwood wants the reader to do after reading the poem.

ANSWERS TO INVESTIGATE, INQUIRE, AND IMAGINE

RECALL

1a. The setting is your own home. The events are those that take place when you eat bread.

2a. The scene shifts to a room where two people are starving. There you are faced with the question of whether to feed a piece of bread to your sister or eat it yourself.

3a. The setting of paragraph 3 is a prison. There bread is being used to torture you into revealing information about your friends and comrades.

INTERPRET

1b. Atwood is trying to create a mood of ease and abundance. The description of the spreading of butter, peanut butter, and honey on the bread; the description of the running of the honey, of licking the honey; and the list of the bread available all contribute to the picture of abundance Atwood is sketching.

2b. The abundance in the first scene contrasts sharply with the deprivation in the second scene.

3b. The bowl means food and home and all the good things you do not have at this time.

ANALYZE

4a. In the first scene the bread is an item that goes almost unnoticed in a place of abundance. In the second scene, bread is a precious commodity that is needed to sustain life. It forces a moral dilemma: Who will get the bread? In the third scenario, the bread is subversive because it is used as a bribe In the fourth scene, mythic connections with bread are revealed. In the last scene, the meaning of bread is questioned.

SYNTHESIZE

4b. The loaf of bread has become untouchable through its association with guilt. It supposedly has changed from a commodity casually taken for granted to one that cannot be eaten because it is charged with so much guilt.

EVALUATE

5a. *Responses will vary.*

EXTEND

5b. *Responses will vary.*

ANSWERS TO UNDERSTANDING LITERATURE

Tone. The speaker is manipulative when asking direct questions: "How long does this take? When will someone come with more bread? . . . Should you share the bread or give the whole piece to your sister? Should you eat the bread yourself? How long does it take to decide?" The reader is asked to answer these questions for himself or herself.

Point of View. This selection uses the second-person point of view in order to make the reader feel that he or she is present in each situation, making life or death decisions.

Prose Poem. Atwood uses very vivid images such as the bloated belly and flies landing on the eyes of the starving sister. She uses parallelism when she begins each section with "Imagine . . . " Atwood also uses repetition when she states "Imagine . . ." and asks "How long does it take?" If "Bread" were written as "pure prose," it would probably develop characterization more. If it were written as "pure poetry," it would probably be more lyrical.

ANSWERS TO INTEGRATING THE LANGUAGE ARTS

Language, Grammar, and Style

1. You [P]; it [P]; you [P]; it [P]
2. these [D]; you [P]; them [P] (Note that the word *one* is used as a noun.)
3. this [D]; someone [I]
4. you [P]; yourself [R]
5. it [P]

Critical Thinking

You were then lying on a thin mattress in a hot room. The walls were made of dried earth and your sister, who was younger than you were, was in the room with you. She was starving, her belly was bloated, flies landed on her eyes; you brushed them off with your hand. You had a cloth too, filthy but damp, and you pressed it to her lips and forehead. The piece of bread was the bread you had been saving, for days it seems. You were as hungry as she was, but not yet as weak.

WRITER'S JOURNAL

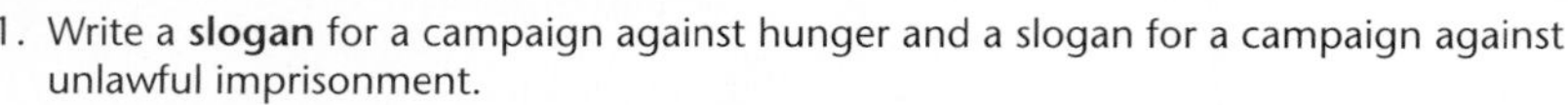

1. Write a **slogan** for a campaign against hunger and a slogan for a campaign against unlawful imprisonment.
2. Write a **personal essay** about a simple object that has special or symbolic meaning to you.
3. Write an additional **scene** for "Bread." For example, the scene could take place in a church.

Integrating *the* Language Arts

Language, Grammar, and Style

Classifying Pronouns. Read the Language Arts Survey 3.55, "Personal Pronouns," 3.58, "Reflexive Pronouns, and 3.56, "Demonstrative and Indefinite Pronouns." Then identify all the pronouns in the following sentences taken from "Bread." After each pronoun, write P (Personal), R (Reflexive), D (Demonstrative), or I (Indefinite).

1. You put butter on it, then peanut butter, then honey, and you fold it over.
2. Both of these things are real but you happen to be in the same room with only one of them.
3. How long does this take? When will someone come with more bread?
4. Should you eat the piece of bread yourself?
5. How long does it take to decide?

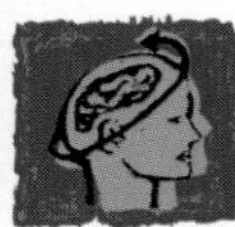

Critical Thinking

Point of View. "Bread" uses a second-person point of view and the present tense. Rewrite the second section beginning with "You are now lying. . ." and ending with "but not yet as weak" using a third-person point of view and the past tense to see how these changes alter the meaning of the poem.

Speaking and Listening & Collaborative Learning

Writing and Performing a Play. Read the separate sections of "Bread" as five different scenes in a play. Use Atwood's ideas and words to create a script for this play, describing the setting and characters, and creating dialogue. Then select a narrator and characters to read the play for the class.

Applied English & Media Literacy

Letter-Writing Campaign. Write a letter to get someone out of prison who is falsely incarcerated. For a list of names and addresses to write to, access Amnesty International's Freedom Writers site at http://www.amnestyusa.org/group/aicasework/fw.html. For a model of how to write a business letter, review the Language Arts Survey 6.5, "Writing a Business Letter."

"Naked Girl and Mirror"

BY JUDITH WRIGHT

About the AUTHOR

Judith Wright (1915–) was born in Armidale, Australia. After graduating from the University of Sydney, Wright worked in an advertising agency. Later she was employed as a secretary for the University of Sydney, as a clerk in Brisbane, and as a statistician. In 1946, Wright published her first volume of poetry, *The Moving Image.* Three years later, she began lecturing part-time at various universities in Australia and published her second volume of poetry, *Woman to Man.* Her first two volumes of poetry were followed by *The Gateway; The Two Fires; City Sunrise; The Nature of Love, a collection of short stories; Collected Poems 1942–1970;* and *The Double Tree,* an updated selection of Wright's poetry. In addition to poetry, Wright has written literary criticism, children's books, a biography of the Australian poet Charles Harpur, a book on the Australian short story writer Charles Lawson, and a book on her pioneering grandparents' settlement in Australia, a former British colony.

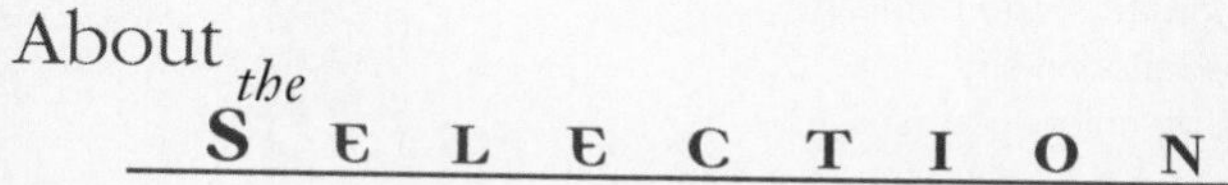

About the SELECTION

"Naked Girl and Mirror" shows Wright's exploration of the dynamics of human and biological relationships. Characteristic of Wright's work, the exploration into the mysteries of those relationships is progressive and thoroughly modern in idiom. The selection also shows Wright's skill in poetic techniques, such as rhyme and meter, for which she is noted.

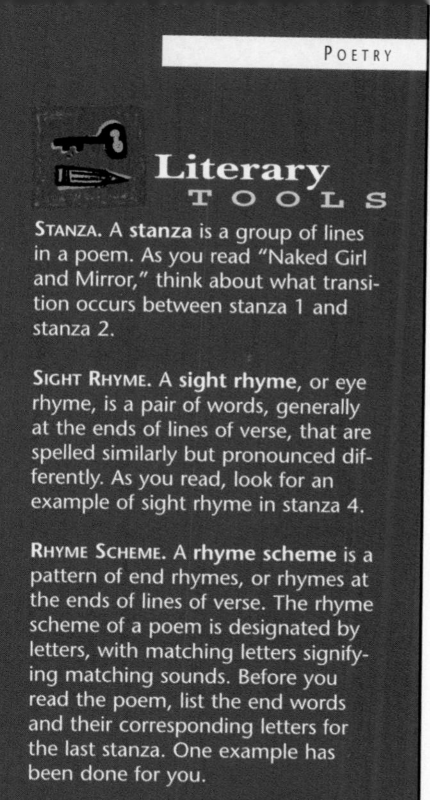

Literary TOOLS

STANZA. A **stanza** is a group of lines in a poem. As you read "Naked Girl and Mirror," think about what transition occurs between stanza 1 and stanza 2.

SIGHT RHYME. A **sight rhyme**, or eye rhyme, is a pair of words, generally at the ends of lines of verse, that are spelled similarly but pronounced differently. As you read, look for an example of sight rhyme in stanza 4.

RHYME SCHEME. A **rhyme scheme** is a pattern of end rhymes, or rhymes at the ends of lines of verse. The rhyme scheme of a poem is designated by letters, with matching letters signifying matching sounds. Before you read the poem, list the end words and their corresponding letters for the last stanza. One example has been done for you.

Rhyming Words	Corresponding Letters
tears / years	*a*

Reader's Journal

What do you see when you look in a mirror?

ADDITIONAL RESOURCES

UNIT 10 RESOURCE BOOK
- Selection Worksheet 10.17
- Selection Check Test 4.10.35
- Selection Test 4.10.36
- Language, Grammar, and Style Resource 3.64
- Study and Research Resource 5.53

GRAPHIC ORGANIZER

Rhyme Scheme. Students should complete their charts as follows:

Rhyming Words	Corresponding Letters
tears-years	*a*
obey-day	*b*
too-you	*c*

VOCABULARY FROM THE SELECTION

hermaphrodite
immoderate
quicksilver
tentatively

READER'S JOURNAL

You might ask students to describe their reflection using the third person.

GOALS/OBJECTIVES

Studying this lesson will enable students to
- experience the speaker's feelings of ambivalence about her transition into adulthood
- describe Judith Wright's literary accomplishments and explain the historical significance of her writings
- define *stanza, sight rhyme,* and *rhyme scheme* and recognize the use of these techniques in the selection
- identify verbs in the subjunctive mood
- write the answer to an essay test question
- write a summary

ANSWERS TO GUIDED READING QUESTIONS

1. The speaker was free and uninhibited during her childhood. She now realizes that she has a body in which she feels trapped.
2. She is fearful of her new body. It pleads with her to recognize "that you were always here; know me—be me."
3. The person may be betrayed.

INDIVIDUAL LEARNING STRATEGIES

Motivation
Have students brainstorm a list of the five top concerns of adolescents.

Reading Proficiency
Ask students to identify which stanza is not complete and which stanzas can stand by themselves as a complete thought. Students might also count how many sentences there are in the poem.

English Language Learning
Point out the dashes used in the poem and explain that dashes are used to show a sudden break or change in thought. Students might benefit from reading the Language Arts Survey 3.93, "Hyphens and Dashes."

Special Needs
Make sure students can answer the Guided Reading Questions and the Recall questions in Investigate, Inquire, and Imagine. Students will also benefit from doing the activities mentioned in Reading Proficiency and English Language Learning.

Enrichment
Using the Internet, have students research other subjects and themes that Judith Wright writes about. Students may also be interested to research the work she has done on behalf the Aborigines in Australia.

Naked Girl and Mirror

JUDITH WRIGHT

This is not I. I had no body once—
only what served my need to laugh and run
and stare at stars and tentatively dance
on the fringe of foam and wave and sand and sun.
Eyes loved, hands reached for me, but I was gone
on my own currents, quicksilver, thistledown.
Can I be trapped at last in that soft face?

What was the speaker like in her childhood? How has she changed?

I stare at you in fear, dark brimming eyes.
Why do you watch me with that immoderate plea—
"Look under these curled lashes, recognize
that you were always here; know me—be me."
Smooth once-hermaphrodite shoulders, too tenderly
your long slope runs, above those sudden shy
curves furred with light that spring below your space.

How does the speaker feel about her new body? What does her new body plead with her to do?

No, I have been betrayed. If I had known
that this girl waited between a year and a year,
I'd not have chosen her bough to dance upon.
Betrayed, by that little darkness here, and here
this swelling softness and that frightened stare
from eyes I will not answer; shut out here
from my own self, by its new body's grace—

What might happen to a person who danced on a bough?

for I am betrayed by someone lovely. Yes,
I see you are lovely, hateful naked girl.

Words for Everyday Use

ten • ta • tive • ly (ten' tə tiv lē) *adv.*, hesitantly; uncertainly. *Marlee raised her hand tentatively because she was not completely sure of the answer.*

quick • sil • ver (kwik' sil vər) *adj.*, resembling mercury or its properties. *The quicksilver dancer moved quickly across the stage.*

im • mod • er • ate (im mä' də rət) *adj.*, exceeding just, usual, or suitable bounds. *Because of her husband's immoderate appetite, Mrs. Duncan baked an extra pie.*

her • maph • ro • dite (hər maf´ro dīt´) *adj.*, with both male and female characteristics. *Some hermaphrodite gods are represented as having characteristics of both sexes.*

The Mirror. Thomas Wilmer Dewing, c.1907. Freer Gallery of Art, Smithsonian Institution, Washington, DC.

Your lips in the mirror tremble as I refuse
to know or claim you. Let me go—let me be gone.
You are half of some other who may never come.
Why should I tend you? You are not my own;
you seek that other—he will be your home.

Yet I pity your eyes in the mirror, misted with tears;
I lean to your kiss. I must serve you; I will obey.
Some day we may love. I may miss your going, some day,
though I shall always resent your dumb and fruitful years.
Your lovers shall learn better, and bitterly too,
if their arrogance dares to think I am part of you. ■

How does the speaker view her "self" in relation to her body?

Respond *to the* SELECTION

If you were the speaker, what would help you to accept your new body?

RESPOND TO THE SELECTION

Students might mention the approval or admiration of others.

ANSWER TO GUIDED READING QUESTION

1. She sees herself as arrogant in relation to her body.

SELECTION CHECK TEST 12.10.35 WITH ANSWERS

Checking Your Reading

1. When did the speaker "stare at stars and tentatively dance"? **The speaker stared at stars and tentatively danced as a child.**
2. With what emotion does the speaker look at her reflection in the mirror? **The speaker looks at herself with fear.**
3. What changes in her body does the speaker notice? **She notices "that little darkness here" and "this swelling softness."**
4. What does the speaker "refuse / to know or claim"? **She refuses to know or claim the maturing self she sees reflected.**
5. What must the speaker's future lovers learn? **They must learn that underneath the speaker's new appearance lies her true self.**

Vocabulary in Context

Fill in each blank with the most appropriate word from the following Words for Everyday Use.

quicksilver immoderate
hermaphrodite tentatively

1. I **tentatively** agreed to go on the picnic; I told my friends I would make up my mind for sure in a couple days.
2. The **quicksilver** dragonfly darted across the pond.
3. Chad frustrated his teacher because he had an **immoderate** need for continual attention.

Literary Tools

Fill in the blank with the appropriate literary tool from the following list.

slant rhyme sight rhyme
stanza rhyme scheme

1. Each **stanza** of "Naked Girl and Mirror" has six or seven lines.
2. The poem has an inconsistent **rhyme scheme** since the pattern of end rhymes changes from stanza to stanza.
3. Since come and home do not rhyme conventionally, they comprise a **sight rhyme**.

ANSWERS TO INVESTIGATE, INQUIRE, AND IMAGINE

RECALL

1a. The speaker is looking at her body in the mirror.

2a. The speaker feels betrayed by her body.

3a. Her body will seek "that other," a man.

INTERPRET

1b. The speaker fears her body has grown up.

2b. Her "dark brimming eyes" tell her to recognize the body in the mirror as her own.

3b. The speaker feels pity for her body.

ANALYZE

4a. The speaker cites "that little darkness here" (line 18), "this swelling softness" (line 19), "that frightened stare" (line 19), and her new loveliness (lines 22-23).

SYNTHESIZE

4b. The speaker decides to accept her new body and says that "someday we may love" and that "I may miss your going, someday."

EVALUATE

5a. The speaker wants a mate who will realize her body is not her true self. She wants to be appreciated for her inner qualities that she sees as being constant since childhood. The speaker is probably an adolescent changing from girlhood to womanhood.

EXTEND

5b. In Wright's poem, the speaker confronts her emerging woman's body, reluctant to let go of her girl's body, which she identifies with her essential self. In Lawrence's poem, the speaker confronts a pettiness in himself that fears the primitive, instinctive natural forces. In the former poem, the speaker learns that her essential self and her body are different things. In the latter poem, the speaker learns that he wishes to get rid of, or expiate, his pettiness.

INVESTIGATE, Inquire, *Imagine*

Recall: GATHERING FACTS

1a. What is the speaker looking at in the mirror?

2a. How does the speaker feel about her body?

3a. What will her body seek?

Interpret: FINDING MEANING

1b. What does the speaker fear her body has done?

2b. What do her "dark brimming eyes" tell her?

3b. What feeling does the speaker have for her body in the last stanza?

Analyze: TAKING THINGS APART →

4a. What physical evidence does the speaker give to support her feelings of betrayal? In other words, what changes has she undergone?

Synthesize: BRINGING THINGS TOGETHER

4b. What response does the speaker decide to take toward her new body?

Evaluate: MAKING JUDGMENTS →

5a. Assess what the speaker is looking for in a mate. Then evaluate the age of the speaker.

Extend: CONNECTING IDEAS

5b. Much contemporary poetry, like Judith Wright's "Naked Girl and Mirror," deals with moments of self-revelation or insight, often ones that are psychologically challenging or wrenching. Consider Wright's poem in relation to D. H. Lawrence's "Snake." In each poem, what issue does the speaker confront? What does each speaker learn about himself or herself?

Understanding *Literature*

STANZA. Review the definition for **stanza** in the Handbook of Literary Terms. What transition occurs between stanza 1 and stanza 2?

SIGHT RHYME. Review the definition for **sight rhyme** in Literary Tools on page 971. What example of sight rhyme did you find in stanza 4?

RHYME SCHEME. Review the definition for **rhyme scheme** in the Handbook of Literary Terms and the chart you made for Literary Tools on page 971. What is the rhyme scheme of the final stanza? Is this rhyme scheme repeated throughout the poem?

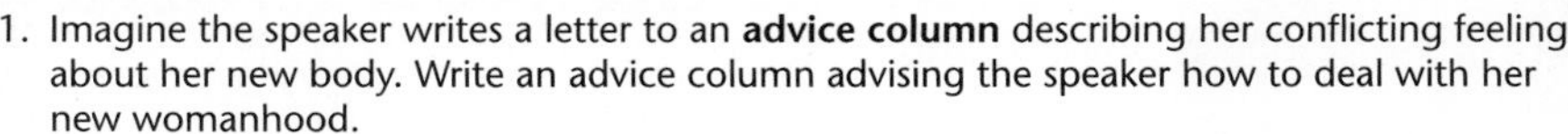

Writer's Journal

1. Imagine the speaker writes a letter to an **advice column** describing her conflicting feelings about her new body. Write an advice column advising the speaker how to deal with her new womanhood.
2. Imagine you are the speaker and you have met a man you love. Write him a **letter** telling him your expectations of him. What do you want him to see in you?
3. Imagine you are the speaker and you are now an old woman. Write a **poem** describing what you see in the mirror and how that makes you feel. Which body seems like your real body now?

Integrating *the* Language Arts

Language, Grammar, and Style

The Subjunctive Mood. Read the Language Arts Survey 3.64, "Properties of Verbs: Mood," on the present and past subjunctive mood. Then list each verb that is used in the subjunctive mood.

1. If the speaker were still a child, she would stare at stars.
2. To understand the speaker's dilemma, it is necessary that the reader remember she felt unconnected to her body in childhood.
3. Society required that she accept her new womanhood.
4. Can you imagine the speaker's surprise if she were to learn that other young women felt as she did?
5. It is important that the speaker be appreciated for her inner qualities.

Study and Research & Critical Thinkings

Taking an Essay Test. Read the Language Arts Survey 5.53, "Taking Essay Tests." Then answer the test question below.

Modern so-called confessional poetry often deals with the private experiences had by people as they were growing up. What other poem in this unit deals directly with intense experiences from childhood? What personal experiences from childhood are described in each poem?

Media Literacy

Writing a Summary. Judith Wright's many nonfiction works include a biography of the nineteenth-century Australian poet Charles Harpur. Write a summary of Harpur's contributions to Australian poetry. You may find it useful to access Bartleby.com The Literature of Australia and New Zealand at http://www.bartleby.com/224/1201.html.

Answers to Understanding Literature

Stanza. The speaker switches from remembering her childhood to contemplating her new womanhood.

Sight Rhyme. The two words that are spelled similarly but pronounced differently are come/home at the end of lines 26 and 28.

Rhyme Scheme. The rhyme scheme of the final stanza is abbacc. This rhyme scheme is not repeated throughout the poem; each stanza has a different rhyme scheme.

Answers to Integrating the Language Arts

Language, Grammar, and Style

1. were
2. remember
3. accept
4. were
5. be

Study and Research & Critical Thinking

The other poem in the unit that deals directly with intense feelings from childhood is Stephen Spender's "Rough." In "Rough," the speaker describes being teased by rough children during his childhood and longing to be accepted by them. In "Naked Girl and Mirror," the speaker describes carefree times from childhood when she was not at all conscious of even having a body, times when she would "laugh and run / and stare at stars and tentatively dance / on the fringe of foam and wave and sand and sun."

Media Literacy

Assign a score from 1 to 25 for each grading criterion below.

Summary

Content/Unity. The summary details Australian poet Charles Harpur's main contributions to Australian poetry.
Organization/Coherence. The summary is logically organized.
Language/Style. The summary uses vivid and precise nouns, verbs, and modifiers. It is written in formal English.
Conventions. The summary avoids errors in spelling, grammar, usage, and manuscript form.

ADDITIONAL RESOURCES

Unit 10 Resource Book

- Selection Worksheet 10.18
- Selection Check Test 4.10.37
- Selection Test 4.10.38
- Language, Grammar, and Style Resource 3.93

GRAPHIC ORGANIZER

Students should complete the chart as follows: the ruins of Troy (event), Helen (person), Homer (person), the Odyssey (literary work).

READER'S JOURNAL

Some students might say they use a quotation to shape their writing. Others might prefer anecdotes.

INDIVIDUAL LEARNING STRATEGIES

Motivation
Discuss with students how they begin a writing assignment.

Reading Proficiency
Point out the metaphor of the harp in the last stanza that is used to express the beginning of the writing process.

English Language Learning
Introduce students to Odysseus and the Trojan War.

Special Needs
Make sure students can answer the Guided Reading Questions and the Recall questions in Investigate, Inquire, and Imagine. Students will also benefit from doing the activities mentioned in Reading Proficiency and English Language Learning.

Enrichment
Odysseus is one of the most frequently mentioned characters in Western literature. Working in small groups, have students compile a list of poem titles with references to Odysseus.

"Map of the New World"

by Derek Walcott

Literary Tools

Free Verse. **Free verse** is poetry that avoids use of regular rhymes, meter, or division into stanzas. As you read the selection, think about why the author chose to write in free verse instead of a more strict poetic form.

Allusion. An **allusion** is a rhetorical technique in which reference is made to a person, event, object, or work from history or literature. What things does the speaker of the poem allude to in "Map of the World"? Use the graphic organizer below to classify each allusion made in the poem. Is it a person, event, object, or literary/historical work? One example has been done for you.

Person	Event	Object	Literary/ Historical Work
Homer			

Reader's Journal

What techniques do you use to shape your writing?

About the Author

The 1992 Nobel Prize for literature went to West Indian poet and playwright **Derek Walcott** (1930–). Born on the island of St. Lucia in the Caribbean, he attended the University of the West Indies in Jamaica, and then moved to Trinidad. Walcott began as a painter, then became a writer and teacher. His first book of poems was published in 1948. His work combines the English tradition of lyric poetry with the scenery, attitudes, and sounds of the Caribbean and urban America. Since the 1950s he has lived and taught at universities in Boston and New York but spends part of each year in the West Indies. Walcott has written several book-length poems and numerous plays. *Another Life* (1973) is a saga of a poet's development, written in episodes like scenes in a play. Another of his major works is *Omeros* (1990), an epic poem that takes a new, imaginative look at the epics of the Greek poet Homer.

About the Selection

Walcott's work dwells on the division between "Englishness" and the black Afro-Caribbean heritage of colonialism. Images and ideas from Homer's *Iliad* and *Odyssey* have long influenced Walcott. They are the background for **"Map of the New World,"** which is an example of a self-referencing poem. It is a poem about the writing of Homer's *Odyssey* that begins by describing its own writing. The subject is the creation by a poet of a world of the imagination.

GOALS/OBJECTIVES

Studying this lesson will enable students to

- appreciate the poet's description of the creative process
- describe Derek Walcott's literary accomplishments and explain the historical significance of his writings
- define *free verse* and *allusion* and recognize the use of these techniques in the selection
- use hyphens, dashes, and capital letters correctly
- organize an art exhibit
- write an introduction

MAP OF THE NEW WORLD

DEREK WALCOTT

I *Archipelagoes*[1]

At the end of this sentence, rain will begin.
At the rain's edge, a sail.

Slowly the sail will lose sight of islands;
into a mist will go the belief in harbours
of an entire race.

The ten-years war is finished.
Helen's hair, a grey cloud.
Troy, a white ashpit
by the drizzling sea.

The drizzle tightens like the strings of a harp.
A man with clouded eyes picks up the rain
and plucks the first line of the *Odyssey*.[2] ■

In what way does the opening sentence actually carry out, or perform, what it describes?

What feelings are created in you by this description of the ruin of Helen and of Troy?

Who is the man with clouded eyes? What is he doing?

1. ***Archipelagoes.*** Seas with many islands in them
2. ***Odyssey.*** References to Homer's *Odyssey*, an ancient Greek epic poem about the wanderings of Odysseus after the fall of Troy in the Trojan War

ANSWERS TO GUIDED READING QUESTIONS

1. The sentence in a sense performs the very act that it describes being performed. The words "rain will begin" both predict what will happen at the end of the sentence and are what happens, in the reader's imagination, at the end of the sentence.
2. *Responses may vary.* Most readers will sense desolation and sadness in these lines.
3. The man with clouded eyes is the poet Homer. He is beginning to compose the *Odyssey*.

SELECTION CHECK TEST 12.10.37 WITH ANSWERS

Checking Your Reading

1. What will begin at the end of the first sentence? **Rain will begin.**
2. What will go "into a mist"? **"The belief in harbours / of an entire race" will go "into a mist."**
3. What war is finished? **The Trojan War is finished.**
4. Who is the man "with clouded eyes"? **Homer is the man "with clouded eyes."**
5. What does the man pluck? **The man "plucks the first line of the Odyssey."**

Literary Tools

Fill in the blank with the appropriate literary tool from the following list.

metaphor free verse
simile allusion

1. "Map of the New World" is written in **free verse**, without regular rhyme, rhythm, meter, or division into stanzas.
2. In the poem Walcott makes several **allusions** to the Odyssey.
3. When the poet says that tightening drizzle is "like the strings of a harp," he is using a(n) **simile**.

RESPOND TO THE SELECTION

Students should realize that Walcott uses allusions to shape his poem.

ANSWERS TO INVESTIGATE, INQUIRE, AND IMAGINE

RECALL

1a. Rain begins at the end of the first sentence.
2a. The scene being left by the sailors is the desolation of Troy after the city was destroyed by the Greeks.
3a. Homer begins to create the *Odyssey* with tragic wisdom.

INTERPRET

1b. A writer has the power to bring images into existence in the imagination of readers (or listeners). Walcott demonstrates this power by simultaneously describing the act of creating images and actually creating them.
2b. As a result of the war, the *Odyssey* was composed.
3b. The last stanza seems sad and tragic.

ANALYZE

4a. Images used by Walcott include rain, "grey cloud," "white ashpit," "drizzling sea," and "clouded eyes."

SYNTHESIZE

4b. These images convey a melancholy and solemn mood.

EVALUATE

5a. *Responses will vary.* Walcott is trying to create a sense of sadness, desolation, and melancholy through the allusions of the Trojan War and the epic poem the *Odyssey* in which Odysseus is separated from his family for many years and endures hardships. Walcott accomplishes this effect by having a sad Homer pluck "the first line of the *Odyssey*."

EXTEND

5b. Students may say that the poem would be less powerful without the illusions Walcott uses.

Respond to the SELECTION

What techniques does Walcott use to shape his writing?

INVESTIGATE, Inquire, Imagine

Recall: GATHERING FACTS →

1a. What begins at the end of the first sentence?

2a. What scene described in stanza 3 is being left behind by the sailors?

3a. In what mood does Homer begin to create the *Odyssey*?

Interpret: FINDING MEANING

1b. What power does a writer have that is illustrated by the first two lines of the poem? How does Walcott illustrate the act of poetic creation?

2b. What creative act happened as a result of this war?

3b. With what kind of wisdom does Homer begin to create the *Odyssey*?

Analyze: TAKING THINGS APART →

4a. What images does Walcott use?

Synthesize: BRINGING THINGS TOGETHER

4b. What mood do these images convey?

Evaluate: MAKING JUDGMENTS →

5a. What effect is Walcott trying to create by the use of allusions? Do you think he accomplishes this effect?

Extend: CONNECTING IDEAS

5b. How do you think this poem would be different without the use of allusions?

Understanding Literature

FREE VERSE. Review the definition for **free verse** in Literary Tools on page 976. Which poems in this unit are written in free verse? Why do many poets choose free verse?

ALLUSION. Review the definition for **allusion** in the Handbook of Literary Terms and the chart you made for Literary Tools on page 976. To what does Walcott allude in his poem? What does Walcott demonstrate with his allusions?

ANSWERS TO UNDERSTANDING LITERATURE

FREE VERSE. Poems in this unit that are written in free verse are "The Second Coming," "Preludes," "Snake," "Rough," "Not Waving but Drowning," "Thistles," and "Map of the World." Many poets prefer writing in free verse because it gives them the freedom to choose precisely the right word, as opposed to a word that merely fits the rhyme scheme or metrical pattern.

ALLUSION. Walcott alludes to the Greeks sailing away from the ruins of Troy, to Helen, to Troy itself, to Homer, and to the Odyssey. Walcott uses his allusions to demonstrate how, out of events and feeling, a poet shapes his or her work.

Writer's Journal

1. Write a **footnote** describing one of the following allusions made in "Map of the New World": the Trojan War, the fall of Troy, or Helen.
2. Homer greatly influenced Walcott's work. Pretend you are Walcott. Write a **eulogy** that praises Homer.
3. Imagine you are a literary critic. Write a **poetry review** of "Map of the New World."

Integrating *the* Language Arts

Language, Grammar, and Style

Hyphens, Dashes, and Capital Letters. Hyphens are used to make a compound word. Dashes are used to show a sudden break or change in thought. Correctly punctuate the sentences below by inserting hyphens or dashes in each sentence. In addition, correct errors in capitalization. Refer to Language Arts 3.83, "Hyphens and Dashes" and 3.94, "Editing for Capitalization Errors" for more information.

1. odysseus the hero of the *Odyssey* is one of the most frequently portrayed figures in Western literature.
2. Odysseus has many adventures after the end of the trojan war.
3. In the land of the Lotus-Eaters, Odysseus struggles with lotus induced lethargy.
4. Guiltridden, Odysseus returns home to ithaca, only to find that many suitors are courting his wife penelope.
5. What twentieth century poem are you familiar with that alludes to homer's *Odyssey*?

Study and Research & Speaking and Listening

Art Exhibit. In the library find a copy of a painting that illustrates an episode from the *Odyssey*. Display the painting and describe to the class what is happening in the painting. Along with your classmates, display the paintings in the classroom in order to create an art exhibit on the *Odyssey.*

Applied English

Writing an Introduction. Imagine your job is to write introductions to books of poetry. Write an introduction to Walcott's poem *Omeros.* Be sure to define his purpose and influence.

ANSWERS TO INTEGRATING THE LANGUAGE ARTS

Language, Grammar, and Style

1. Odysseus—the hero of the Odyssey—is one of the most frequently portrayed figures in Western literature.
2. Odysseus has many adventures after the end of the Trojan War.
3. In the land of the Lotus-Eaters, Odysseus struggles with lotus-induced lethargy.
4. Guilt-ridden, Odysseus returns home to Ithaca, only to find that many suitors are courting his wife Penelope.
5. What twentieth-century poem are you familiar with that alludes to Homer's Odyssey?

Applied English

Walcott's purpose in writing Omeros is to link the world of the Caribbean with that of Homer by recalling the dramas of Homer's *Iliad* and *Odyssey* in a Caribbean setting. Through writing *Omeros*, Walcott was able to fuse his Caribbean and African roots with his British upbringing. In doing so, his quest for self-identification was accomplished. Walcott's influence is Homer, specifically, the *Iliad* and the *Odyssey*.

Assign a score from 1 to 25 for each grading criterion below.

Poetry Introduction

Content/Unity. The poetry introduction establishes Walcott's purpose and influences in writing Omeros.
Organization/Coherence. The introduction is logically organized.
Language/Style. The introduction uses formal English.
Conventions. The introduction avoids errors in spelling, grammar, usage, and manuscript form.

LESSON OVERVIEW

INDIVIDUAL LEARNING STRATEGIES

Motivation
Ask students to write down five questions they have about poems in this unit. For example, students might wonder if Seamus Heaney writes other poems about his relationship with his father or if Yeats's view of the future is always as bleak as in "The Second Coming." Students might use this list to come up with an idea for a poetry explication.

Reading Proficiency
As students are now familiar with the Guided Writing lessons, ask them to tell you what sections they anticipate seeing in this lesson before they being reading.

English Language Learning
Review with students transitional phrases that will help them in their writing. Have students review the Language Arts Survey 2.35, "Using Transitions Effectively."

Special Needs
You might give special needs students a list of easier topics to write about rather than having them come up with a topic of their own. For students incapable of completing this assignment, have them summarize an explication done by another student in the class.

Enrichment
Students with a bent for literary criticism might want to research T. S. Eliot's definitions for poetry and great poetry. Eliot proposed the view that whether a work is poetry must be decided by literary standards; whether it is great poetry must be decided by standards higher

"The great poet, in writing himself, writes his time."
—*T. S. Eliot*

WRITING A POETRY EXPLICATION

Great poetry spins and vibrates in many directions at once, at many levels and speeds, as you experience one person's unique vision of the world. But how does that meaning happen? How *do* poets do it? An **explication** analyzes the meanings and relationships of the words, images, and literary techniques used to make a literary work.

Writing Assignment. Your assignment is to write a poetry explication that describes aspects that typify the work of a poet in this unit using two or three poems as source materials. You may also include information about the poet's life as it pertains to the poems you study.

Throughout this exercise, you will find yourself expanding and shifting your own notions about the poems and the issues that they raise.

Examining the Model. In his essay, Isaiah Washington picked three main characteristics of the three poems – their themes, their sounds and their irony – and demonstrated how they come together to make a larger point: Auden's pragmatism in the face of a deeply troubled world. Isaiah succinctly states this main point and its supporting ideas in a thesis statement at the end of the first paragraph:

> In "Musee des Beaux Arts," the reader finds Auden's most succinct statement of this philosophy that none of it really matters in the long view.

continued on page 981

Student Model

from "Auden's Pragmatism: What Matters?"
by Isaiah Washington

The time between World War I and World War II was a time for intense and worldwide self-examination. The world had just experienced the bloodiest war in its history and was, it seemed, inexorably heading towards another conflict. The poetry of the time took on a generally gloomy tone, as we see in T. S. Eliot's "The Wasteland" and W. B. Yeats' "The Second Coming." However, not all poets assumed this rather pessimistic mood. W. H. Auden found the time invigorating, both politically and artistically. He wasn't optimistic, though. Instead, he took an extremely realistic, or pragmatic, approach towards the events of the day. In "As I Walked Out One Evening," and "Who's Who?" W. H. Auden uses themes, word sounds, and a thinly veiled cynicism to demonstrate this pragmatic view of his world and the building holocaust. In "Musee des Beaux Arts," the reader finds Auden's most succinct statement of this philosophy that none of it really matters in the long view.

INDIVIDUAL LEARNING STRATEGIES (CONT.)

than the literary. Have students write an essay in which they agree or disagree with Eliot's position and use examples from this unit to prove their point.

Prewriting

Finding Your Voice. Explicating poetry is just like any other writing in that clear, effective writing in your own confident voice is the best way to get the job done. When writing this piece, be sure to avoid "puffery" in your word choice and sentence construction.

One common example of puffery in a poetry paper is redundancy. Another example is convoluted sentence constructions, especially those with meandering, intrusive, subordinating clauses. Also, avoid meaningless, academic-sounding phrases like "In the opinion of many authorities..." In the excerpt below, see if you can spot the puffery.

> A crucial and essential thematic device in Yeats's "Sailing to Byzantium" is aging and the fact that he was, while yet vital and lively at age 62, in the midst of that stage of human life. This is a thought that completely permeates the first line of the poem: "That is no country for old men."
>
> It is generally accepted among scholars that "that...country" is a reference to the country of Ireland, which makes it a powerful and resonant line in that Yeats loved Ireland above all other countries and that line, in effect, banishes his person from that country simply for the perceived sin of old age.

How would you rewrite this passage to make it clearer and livelier?

Identifying Your Audience. Your audience will include other students like you, but who don't know as much about the poems or poet as you do. You should not assume that your audience knows much of anything about the poet or the poems. Did you find out something about the poet that made his or her poems make more sense to you? Would your audience be aware of that insight? If not, you'll want to be sure to include it in your paper.

The identification of your audience should also take into account how you will be publishing this paper. For instance, if you plan to post this work to a student web page, you should include more explanatory detail. The wider you make the audience, the more you must assume that they won't know much about the poet or his/her work.

Writing with a Plan. Remember, poetry is wild and unpredictable—and open to many differing explications. It's going to be fun to dive into your poems, but you'll need to structure your exploration to avoid overwhelming yourself.

Read the Poems Out Loud. Begin by reading the poems—and not just once or twice—out loud to yourself. Read them until you know them well—even to the point of memorizing certain phrases or lines. Remember, poetry's oldest roots are oral. A poem barely breathes on the printed page. It's up to you to

The rest of the essay (continued on page 984) does not stray from these three points, but not because Auden's poems don't offer any other ideas. Rather, they offer too many ideas to deal with them effectively in a short essay like this one. Accordingly, Isaiah strictly limits himself to supporting only his thesis throughout in the composition. He follows the plan suggested by his thesis statement and supports his ideas with specific but short quotes from the poems.

Learning from Professional Models

Besides examining the student model by Isaiah Washington in this lesson, you might find it helpful to read poetry explications by literary scholars. Public and university libraries carry a number of periodicals that contain such essays. *PMLA*, the journal of the Modern Language Association of America, is an excellent place to start. You can find similar essays in the *New York Times*, *New York Review of Books*, and many literary magazines and scholarly reviews.

Prewriting

Finding Your Voice
It might be useful for students to review the Language Arts Survey 2.5, "Finding Your Voice."

Identifying Your Audience
Establish the audience before students begin writing. Will students be writing for you, another student, or a school publication?

Writing with a Plan
Encourage students to choose a method of organization after reading the Language Arts Survey 2.27, "Choosing a Method of Organization." Ask students to determine which method of organization Isaiah Washington used in his student model. It might be easier for students to figure out Isaiah's method of organization by looking at his graphic organizer on page 983.

Strengthening Your Explication

As you follow each step in the prewriting process, pay attention to the words, phrases, and lines of poetry that especially give you trouble. Instead of ignoring such problem areas, welcome them—they can often lead to insights that can truly anchor your paper. Think through the issues these problem spots present. Write questions that point to what you don't understand. You may find the insights of other students helpful during the discussion stage, or you may come up with a breakthrough in understanding on your own.

In engaging in this type of literary exploration, you are doing the same sort of scholarly work people in academia pursue on a regular basis. The word *explicate* is derived from the Latin and means, literally, "to unfold." The further you unfold the layers of meaning in a poem, the more you will expand your ability to think analytically, intuitively, and expansively.

"We shall not cease
from exploration
And the end of all our
exploring
Will be to arrive where
we started
And know the place
for the first time."

—T. S. Eliot, *"Little Gidding," The Four Quartets*

release it. If you can find it, a recording of the author reading the poems may help.

Map your impressions. As you read the poems, keep track of the impressions you have *at each stage*. A good way to do this is to place each poem in the center of a page, and then write around it "1st thoughts," "2nd thoughts on re-reading," "3rd thoughts," "4th thoughts on troublesome lines," "5th thoughts" and then "6th thoughts." Follow through to the end—it will really help enrich your understanding of the poems.

Discuss your poems with a small group of your classmates. At this point, you don't need to explain what the poems mean, just what they are saying on a literal level, and how they make you respond. When you're done with group discussion, take notes on what you've discovered. Express what you think. What are the poems about? How do they say that? What feelings or emotions do they leave you with?

Summarize the main characteristics of the three poems. Using a graphic organizer like the one on page 983 can help.

Find out more about the poet. Pay particular attention to the periods immediately preceding the composition of the poems. Remember, the date a poem was published does not necessarily reflect the date it was composed. A writer may work on a poem for months, even years. You may find it helpful to compare earlier drafts of a poet's work if they are available. Seeing what revisions the poet made in the drafting process can give you invaluable insights as you write your paper.

Explore the influence of the poet's life and surroundings. Ask yourself how the political and social concerns and/or the circumstances of the time period or poet's life might have affected the composition of the poems.

Make connections. Once you have contemplated the poems individually, find the connections between them. Do they have similar themes? Do they use language in the same way? If they are very different, consider why that might be. Did something happen in the poet's life between the poems? How did the change in the poet manifest itself in the poem? The answers to these questions will lead you to a thesis statement. Your thesis statement should outline the three or so similarities you've found that illustrate one key characteristic of the poet and his work, and will anchor your paper.

Once you have read the poems and studied the poet, organize the information you've generated, using a copy of the graphic organizer on page 983. Isaiah Washington, the writer of "Auden's Pragmatism: What Matters?", organized his information this way:

Student Model—Graphic Organizer

Poem	Theme	Stylistic Device(s)
"Who's Who?"	Sometimes we assume famous people are happy, but fame is less important than love	• customized sonnet • irony • tight vs. loose language (creates irony)
"Musee des Beaux Arts"	Old artists were right to always include people uninterested in the main action of a painting since nothing is important enough to interest everyone.	• ironic language • allusions to famous paintings • sounds
"As I Walked Out One Evening"	Lovers who swoon and swear undying love are ignorant about the practical nature of life.	• contrasting sounds between the two speakers (love and time) • irony

With his thoughts externalized, Isaiah was able to spot the similarity that until then had been lurking in his mind: all three poems concern themselves with arguing against what is generally held as "important." His next step was to compare this developing thesis with what he had learned about Auden's life.

Life Event	Auden's reaction	What is shows about him
World War II	Fled England and moved to California	• He was either cowardly (as his countrymen thought) or being smart and practical (I'd get out of the way too!)
The Spanish Civil War	He supported the Leftists	• I'm not sure, except that he didn't stay committed to the cause for very long, so I guess it shows he shifted as the climate suited him.

Quoting Lines of Poetry
When quoting lines of poetry, make sure that you use standard poetry conventions. Enclose exact quotes from a poem in **quotation marks** and include **line references** in parentheses.

EXAMPLE

"Who's Who" presents a great man, a man who "named the sea" (6).

If you paraphrase a passage from a poem, you must still include any relevant line references.

EXAMPLE

In "As I Walked...," the city clocks begin to chime (25-26), suggesting that love (and life) are not permanent.

Use a **slash mark** (/) to indicate a line break in the poem and keep punctuation and capitalization exactly as it appears in the poem:

EXAMPLE

The object of the man's love in "Who's Who" "Did little jobs about the house with skill / And nothing else."

Use **ellipses** (...) as needed to show that you have omitted words. Note that ellipses with three periods (...) can be used except when you wish to show that a period ends the sentence. In that case, use four periods (....).

EXAMPLES

"Let me not...admit impediments" is one of the many themes about love that Shakespeare explores in his sonnets.

continued on page 984

Student Model—Graphic Organizer

See the Guided Writing Resource for a blackline master of the Graphic Organizer for this lesson.

Drafting

Encourage students to use their completed graphic organizer modeled on this page to help them make sure they have organized the main points of their explication carefully. Students might also benefit from reviewing the Language Arts Survey 2.32, "Drafting an Introduction," 2.33, "Drafting Body Paragraphs," and 2.34, "Drafting a Conclusion."

Revising and Proofreading

A handout of the proofreading checklist found in the Language Arts Survey 2.45 is available in the Teacher's Resource Kit, Guided Writing Resource Book 2.45. Students critiquing a classmate's work may be interested in using proofreader's marks; have them refer to the Language Arts Survey 2.44, "Using Proofreader's Marks."

Self- and Peer Evaluation

Have students use the checklist on page 984 for self- and peer evaluation. The checklist is intended to act as a student-friendly rubric that should help students identify specific evidence of writing strengths and areas needing improvement. Make sure they provide concrete suggestions for improvement of specific evidence of why the writing works. A blackline master of the checklist is available in the Guided Writing Resource 12.10. For students doing peer editing, have them read the Language Arts Survey 2.37, "Self- and Peer Evaluation," "2.38, "How to Evaluate a Piece of Writing," 2.39, "How to Deliver Helpful Criticism," and 2.40, "How to Benefit from Helpful Criticism."

"Go said the bird, for the leaves were full of children, / Hidden excitedly, containing laughter..../ human kind / Cannot bear very much reality." (42–45).

Finally, if you are quoting more than three lines of poetry, start the passage on a new line and indent the passage, showing the line breaks as they actually appear in the poem itself. Do not add any quotation marks that do not appear in the original. End the indented passage with the line reference.

EXAMPLE

In the opening lines to T. S. Eliot's "Ash-Wednesday," the attitude of the speaker is marked by weariness and frustration:

Because I do not hope to
turn again
Because I do not hope
Because I do not hope to
turn
Desiring this man's gift and
that man's scope
I no longer strive to strive
towards such things...
(1-5)

For more information on citing poetry, see the current edition of the *MLA Handbook for Writers of Research Papers.*

Self- and Peer Evaluation

Read through your draft with your thesis statement in mind. If time allows, get one or two peer evaluations. As you evaluate your explication, ask yourself the following questions. Take notes to help you in the revision process.

continued on page 985

Drafting

Begin writing this paper as you would any other, with a mind toward just getting something down on paper that you can play with later. At this point you'll be giving first expression to the thoughts you generated in the prewriting exercises, so don't be discouraged if it comes out a little jumbled at first. Also keep in mind:

- Your audience—do they know what you do about the poet and his times? How much do you need to help them?
- Your thesis statement—how well is it worked in the introduction of your paper? This single sentence should encapsulate what you will flesh out in the rest of the paper, and give a general idea of the order in which you'll discuss those topics. For more information, see the Language Arts Survey 2.25, "Writing a Thesis Statement."
- Your honest voice—avoid fluffy or "academic" language.

Revising and Proofreading

Review your self- and peer evaluations. Revise your writing after considering these comments. Proofread your final draft for spelling, grammatical, and mechanical errors. See the Language Arts Survey 2.45 for a proofreading checklist.

As a final step in revising, now that you're getting in tune with your essay, begin to think of possible titles for your explication.

Student Model—Revision

Following his introduction given on page 980, Isaiah Washington continued his paper as follows. Note the strong body paragraphs and satisfying conclusion. The writing voice is formal but engaging, revealing that Isaiah put considerable effort into this explication.

Auden's Pragmatism: What Matters?
by Isaiah Washington
[continued]

All three poems are concerned with great or seemingly tragic events and the poet's reaction to them. In "As I Walked...," the event is love—that greatest of events. Beginning in the third stanza, Auden has a "lover sing" of the permanence of love. Truly, it is a very well-written ode to love, complete with hyperbole and images of staying power like "Till China and Africa meet, / And the river jumps over the mountain" (10-11). "Who's Who" presents a great man, a man who "named a sea" (6). Both poems, however, take a turn about halfway through, and counter whatever was suggested as great or important in the first half. In "As I Walked…," "the clocks in the city / Began to whirr and chime" (25-26), suggesting that love (and life) are not permanent, all the romanticism in the world notwithstanding. "Who's Who" suggests that the great adventurer was unsatisfied due to a lost love. In one poem love makes all else insignificant, while in the other, time makes love insignificant. This lends the idea that no matter how important something seems, it's not. In "Musee des Beaux Arts", Auden states this plainly. He says the ploughman in Breughel's painting, "The Fall of Icarus" probably saw the fall, "But for him it was not an important failure" (17). It's almost funny, Auden's differentiation between levels of failure, but it serves to demonstrate his serious, pragmatic point.

Another way Auden shows his regard for the things we consider important is through his use of sound. In "As I Walked…," the lover speaks in a singsong voice, with many "s" sounds like "the seven stars go squawking / Like geese about the sky" (15-16). It sounds nice, but when Time steps in to correct, heavier sounds drown out the silliness of the lover: "Time breaks the threaded dances" (35). The same thing happens in "Who's Who," except backwards. This poem is a sonnet with a Petrarchan form (an octave answered by a sestet). Sonnets are, of course, usually used for love poems, and that reinforces the idea that love conquers the great deeds listed in the octave. However, a close look shows that Auden uses softer language in the sestet, which paradoxically carries more thematic weight. The octave uses direct,

- What is the thesis statement of the explication?
- Where are the actual words from the poem used to give proof to the writer's point?
- What information about the poet's life does the writer use to inform the audience of his/her opinion?
- Where does the writer take into consideration what the audience needs to know?
- Does each paragraph point back to the thesis statement?
- Where can you find examples of the writer's honest voice?
- Where, if anywhere, can you find examples of inflated language?
- Evaluate the title of the explication. How effect is it in conveying what the paper is about?

Language, Grammar, and Style

Effective Titles

Identifying a Good Title. A good title should intrigue the reader and give a strong hint about what your essay will address—it's a sort of "sound byte." In the model, the title "Auden's Pragmatism" tells us the general subject of the paper, but then adds a surprise: "What Matters?" The first part prepares and recruits the reader. It, in effect, says, "If you're looking for Yeats, you're

continued on page 986

Language, Grammar, and Style

Effective Titles

Lesson Overview

In this lesson, students will be asked to do the following:

- identify a good title
- fix weak titles
- select an effective title

Introducing the Skill

Have students share the process they have used in the past to come up with titles for their homework. Students might mention using quotations, puns, or anecdotes, or rewording the thesis statement.

Previewing the Skill
Pass out copies of an explication by a student that was written the last time you taught this class and omit the title. Have students read the explication. Then have the class brainstorm a list of possible titles for the explication. Students can vote on the title they find the most appropriate.

Practicing the Skill
Have students think of alternate titles for some of the poems in this unit. For example, "A Call" could be retitled "I Almost Said I Love You."

in the wrong place, but if you're interested in W. H. Auden and how he looked at the world, come on in." The second part interests and engages the reader, but also fleshes out the idea presented in the first part. It is designed to provoke questions in the readers' heads, questions that can only be answered by reading the essay.

In general, titles can come from many sources besides the work itself. They might allude to other works of literature, song lyrics, art, or other places. For instance, "Musee des Beaux Arts" refers to the museum where the painting referenced in the poem hangs. In light of the meaning of the poem, what does Auden add to the title by leaving it in French instead of translating it to his native language?

Many times a catchy and funny title can help the readability of a paper, but only if it suits your essay. It is better to have a mundane title that fits than something exciting that misleads the reader.

Capitalize only the important words in your title. Do not capitalize an article or preposition unless it is the first or last word in the title. Center the title on a title page or above the main body of the text, immediately before the first paragraph. Do not underline or put the title in quotation marks. Do not put a period after it.

Fixing Weak Titles. The following is a list of other titles Isaiah considered, but rejected for his essay.

continued on page 987

punchy "d" and "t" sound-dominated phrases like "he fought, fished, hunted, worked" (5), while the sestet says "could whistle; would sit still / Or potter round the garden; answered some…" (12-13). The language relies heavily on 'l' and 's' sounds, but still they outweigh the supposed more important words and people. Again, "Musee des Beaux Arts" balances these two ideas, and uses similarly languid language for seemingly important events. Icarus falling was "amazing," but the ship that ignored the falling boy and "sailed calmly on" was "expensive" and "delicate." Auden does not differentiate or judge. The two are equal in his practical eye.

The three poems are similar in their use of irony when regarding supposed greatness or permanence. As a rule, he does not directly denounce their pretensions. Instead, he uses ironic understatements. As mentioned above, Icarus is "not an important failure" to the plowman; the object of the great man's love in "Who's Who" "Did little jobs about the house with skill / And nothing else." In "As I Walked…," the irony is revealed only when the lover's words are exposed as the simplistic platitudes they are. When Time speaks it becomes apparent that Auden is mocking the conventional love poem in the first half of the poem. It is important to note that Auden's sarcasm is light, almost chiding. He doesn't harangue, but gently points out that all things must pass, and there's not much point in getting excited about much of anything.

Auden's pragmatism hurt his reputation. When World War II became imminent, he left England for sunny California. This was pragmatic, but also cowardly in the eyes of his fellow countrymen who stayed behind to endure the Nazi bombardment. Many blamed his political views, but if they had read

```
his poems a little more closely they
might have realized that it wasn't
cowardice or politics that led him to
avoid potential death; it was just the
practical thing to do. Love passes,
fame passes, even death passes - why should
a little thing like war be any different?
```

Publishing and Presenting

Now that you've written a poetry explication, others deserve to see it. How will you get it to your audience? One easy way would be to have your class present their papers to each other at a "read-around" and discuss them at a local coffee shop or in a student lounge.

You and your classmates might also put together an anthology, complete with a table of contents, short explanations of why and how you chose your poems, and how you arrived at your paper's title. It might be fun to add short biographies of the poets, as well.

If you're more ambitious, you could make a wall display with strings or arrows pointing from verbal images in the poems to your artistic renditions of them. The display could include a picture of the poet, or a paragraph of where he or she wrote the poem. What else in your poems could be reinterpreted in visual form to aid understanding? This same idea could be expanded on a web page or hypertext stack that would use links instead of strings.

Reflecting

When you study and explicate great poetry, you do much more than simply describe what happens in a work of art—you describe how you see yourself in relationship to art, and how a poem makes you think. What new perspectives did you discover as you explored this poet and these poems? Try writing a poem, one that begins, "When I read [your author], my brain…" Then write a poem pretending you are your poet that begins "When I read [your name], my brain…"

Pragmatism as Demonstrated in Three of W. H. Auden's Poems

Who Cares? Auden's Long View and the Coming War

Looking Out for Numero Uno

Auden's Philosophy: Take It Easy

Not an Important Problem

Why do you think Isaiah rejected these? Is the current title better? Why, or why not?

Using an Effective Title. Take another look at the title of your essay. How does it inform and invite the reader to continue reading? How does it reflect the subject of your essay? What about it makes the essay intriguing?

Read your title to three people and ask them to tell you what they would expect from an essay with that title. They might not get it exactly, but they should be in the ballpark if you have a strong title.

"A poem must be felt to be understood, and before it can be felt it must be heard."
—*Stanley Kunitz*

Publishing and Presenting

You might consider convening a conference that students and teachers from other classes could attend. After selected students have presented their explications, invite questions from the audience about the topic, the poet, and the writing process.

Reflecting

Encourage students to write a journal entry reflecting on how they would do the assignment differently next time. How do they see the process of writing an explication more clearly now?

ADDITIONAL RESOURCES

Unit 10 Resource Book
- Vocabulary Worksheet: Unit 10
- Study Guide: Unit 10
- Unit 10 Test

VOCABULARY DEVELOPMENT

Ask students to number their papers from one to ten. Have students complete each sentence with a word from the Words for Everyday Use list on this page.

1. The cheerleader used a megaphone to __________ his voice so it could be heard in the last row of the bleachers.
2. In church Mrs. Del Fuente knelt down __________ before saying her prayers.
3. We had our picnic in the _______ under the shade of a sycamore tree.
4. When I speak it's easier for me to __________ my thoughts and feelings so that others can understand them.
5. High school dropouts _________ half the employees at Burger Barn.
6. Sometimes when I _______ I get a good idea for a song.
7. The Collins's thought it was pure ____________ that made their youngest son prefer reading to the sports they loved so much.
8. In many African nations, laborers earn a __________ salary of one dollar a day.
9. Jamie wrote an ______ love letter to express his feelings to Christa.
10. After being killed by the Romans, many early Christians were raised to ______________.

Answers

1. amplify
2. reverently
3. glade
4. articulate
5. constitute
6. muse
7. perversity
8. paltry
9. ardent
10. martyrdom

UNIT 10 REVIEW

Twentieth-Century to Contemporary Poetry

Words for Everyday Use

Check your knowledge of the following vocabulary words from the selections in this unit. Write short sentences using these words in context to make the meaning clear. To review the definition or usage of a word, refer to the page number listed or the Glossary of Words for Everyday Use.

amplify, 963
ardent, 934
articulate, 909
carob, 922
conjure, 968
constitute, 918
convulse, 925
dupe, 968
fissure, 922
glade, 907
gutter, 934
hermaphrodite, 972
humility, 924
immoderate, 972
infest, 968
martyrdom, 949
masquerade, 917
muse, 922
paltry, 925
perversity, 924
quicksilver, 972
reverently, 949
rueful, 963
sordid, 918
subversive, 968
tentatively, 972
treacherous, 968

Literary Tools

Define the following terms, giving concrete examples of how they are used in the selections in this unit. To review a term, refer to the page number indicated or to the Handbook of Literary Terms.

alliteration, 932
allusion, 909, 921, 948, 963, 976
cæsura, 956
diction, 937
figurative language, 952
free verse, 976
image, 907, 916, 932, 956
irony, 945, 952, 960
objective correlative, 916
oxymoron, 956
point of view, 966
prose poem, 966
pun, 941
rhyme scheme, 907, 928, 941, 971
sight rhyme, 971
simile, 937, 960
sonnet, 928, 945
speaker, 916
stanza, 971
symbol, 912, 921, 941
theme, 921, 928, 948
tone, 916, 966
verbal irony, 932
villanelle, 941

Reflecting on Your Reading

Genre Studies

1. **Free Verse.** Much of the poetry written in the twentieth century has been in free verse. Define free verse and find examples in the unit. Explain what techniques are used in each free verse poem to make the poem poetic even though it does not use traditional meters, rhythms, or rhyme schemes.

2. **Confessional Poetry.** A confessional poem is one that expresses extremely personal experiences and feelings. In a confessional poem, the speaker generally performs a self-examination or relates private experiences. Much confessional poetry is autobiographical. Which poems in this unit best fit this definition of confessional poetry and why?

Thematic Studies

3. **Irony in Modern Poetry.** The Modern Era has been called the Age of Irony, for many works produced in this century present ironic undercuttings of traditional ideas. What ironies are explored in the following works from the unit?

   "Adam's Curse"
   "Snake"
   "Dulce et Decorum Est"
   "Rough"
   "Who's Who"
   "Not Waving but Drowning"

Historical and Biographical Studies

4. **Social Consciousness.** What are Wilfred Owen and Margaret Atwood incensed about in "Dulce et Decorum Est" and "Bread"? What are their reactions to these injustices? What changes do they want to see?

5. **Attitudes Towards Death.** What attitudes towards death are expressed by Dylan Thomas and Seamus Heaney in "Do Not Go Gentle into That Good Night" and "A Call"? Whose imminent death are the poets anticipating? How do the speakers feel about these people?

6. **The War Poets.** Contrast the depictions of war in the poems of Wilfred Owen and Rupert Brooke. Refer to the works in this unit and to other works by the two poets.

REFLECTING ON YOUR READING

The prompts in "Reflecting on Your Reading" are suitable as topics for research papers. Refer to the Language Arts Survey 5.18-5.45, "Research Skills." (To evaluate research papers, see the evaluation forms for writing, revising, and proofreading in the Assessment Resource.)

The prompts in "Reflecting on Your Reading" can also be adapted for use as topics for oral reports or debates. Refer students to the Language Arts Survey 4, Speaking and Listening. (To evaluate these projects, see the evaluation forms in the Assessment Resource.)

UNIT SKILLS OUTLINE

Literary Skills and Concepts
Essay, 993, 998
Aim, 993, 998
Image, 1000,1008, 1019, 1031, 1033, 1044
Objective Correlative, 1000, 1008, 1019, 1031
Stream-of-Consciousness, 1000, 1008
Thesis, 1010, 1017
Irony, 1010, 1017
Symbol, 1019, 1031
Character, 1033, 1044
Narrator, 1046, 1049, 1082, 1087
Point of View, 1046, 1049
Naturalism, 1051, 1059
Plot, 1051, 1059, 1061, 1071
Characterization, 1061, 1071
Conflict, 1061, 1071
Memoir, 1073, 1080
Theme, 1073, 1080?
Simile, 1082, 1087

Writing Skills and Concepts
Advertisement Analysis, 1089

Language, Grammar, and Style
Achieving Parallelism, 999
Correcting Run-Ons, 1009
Reducing Wordiness, 1018
Base Words and Suffixes, 1032
Parts of Speech in Writing, 1045
Editing for Punctuation Errors, 1050
Direct and Indirect Objects and Complements, 1060
Making Passive Sentences Active, 1081
Using Quotation Marks, 1081
Dangling and Misplaced Modifiers, 1088
Using Correct Punctuation and Paragraph Formatting in Dialogue, 1091

London Bridge, 1906. Andre Derain. Museum of Modern Art, New York.

GOALS/OBJECTIVES

Studying this unit will enable students to
- interpret and appreciate modern prose
- understand the major literary movements of the twentieth century and the English writers who exemplify them
- define the stream-of-consciousness technique of writing and recognize its major practitioners
- write an analysis on a media advertisement
- demonstrate the ability to use correct punctuation and paragraph formatting in dialogue

UNIT 11 TWENTIETH-CENTURY TO CONTEMPORARY PROSE (1900–PRESENT)

"The king died and then the queen died" is a story.

"The king died, and then the queen died of grief"

is a plot.

—E. M. Forster

991

CROSS-CURRICULAR CONNECTIONS

ARTS AND HUMANITIES

MATHEMATICS AND SCIENCES

SOCIAL STUDIES

APPLIED ARTS

TEACHING THE MULTIPLE INTELLIGENCES

LOGICAL-MATHEMATICAL

SPATIAL

TEACHING THE MULTIPLE INTELLIGENCES (CONT.)

Continued on page 992

TEACHING THE MULTIPLE INTELLIGENCES
(CONT. FROM PAGE 991)

The River Shannon, 1076
Monsoon Locations, 1084

KINESTHETIC
Garden Party, 1021
Picture/Word Association, 1020
Set and Costume Designs, 1027
1940-1950s Dress, 1062
Self-Identity Project, 1062

INTERPERSONAL
Storytelling Event, 1052
Irish Immigrants, 1075
Effects of Natural Disasters, 1084

NATURALIST
Garden Party, 1021

ADDITIONAL QUESTIONS AND ACTIVITIES

Ask students to surmise who the audience is for four quotes on this page. Then hold a class discussion to compare students' assessments.

Have students choose one of the quotations on this page. In a personal essay, each student should reflect on the meaning of the quotation and its application to their personal experiences or philosophies.

ECHOES

TWENTIETH-CENTURY TO CONTEMPORARY PROSE

The whole is greater than the part. And therefore, I, who am man alive, am greater than my soul, or spirit, or body, or mind, or consciousness, or anything else that is merely a part of me. I am a man, and alive. I am man alive, and as long as I can, I intend to go on being man alive.

—D. H. Lawrence, *Why the Novel Matters*

Fiction—if it at all aspires to be art—appeals to temperament. And in truth it must be, like painting, like music, like all art, the appeal of one temperament to all the other innumerable temperaments whose subtle and resistless power endows passing events with their true meaning, and creates the moral, the emotional atmosphere of the place and time.

—Joseph Conrad

In the classic it is always the light of ordinary day, never the light that never was on land or sea. It is always perfectly human and never exaggerated: man is always man and never a god. But the awful result of romanticism is that, accustomed to this strange light, you can never live without it. Its effect on you is that of a drug.

—T. E. Hulme, "Romanticism and Classicism"

"Why should life be made endurable? I know that nothing consoles and nothing justifies except a story—but that doesn't stop all stories from being lies. Only the greatest men can speak and still be truthful. Any artist knows this obscurely; he knows that a theory is death, and that all expression is weighted with theory. Only the strongest can rise against that weight. For most of us, for almost all of us, truth can be attained, if at all, only in silence."

—Iris Murdoch, *Under the Net*

That the one and only goal of all critical endeavors, of all interpretation, appreciation, exhortation, praise, or abuse, is improvement in communication may seem an exaggeration. But in practice it is so.

—I. A. Richards, *The Critical Revolt*

"You and I are the boulder pushers. All our lives, you and I, we'll put all our energies, all our talents, into pushing a great boulder up a mountain. The boulder is the truth that the great men know by instinct, and the mountain is the stupidity of mankind. We push the boulder."

—Doris Lessing, *The Golden Notebook*

London Bridge [Detail], 1906. Andre Derain.

FROM *A Room of One's Own*

BY VIRGINIA WOOLF

About the Author

Virginia Woolf (1882–1941) was born in London, England, and educated at home by her father, Sir Leslie Stephen. There, young Virginia Stephen made good use of her father's extensive library and met many of the outstanding literary and intellectual figures of the time. After her father's death, Virginia and her sister Vanessa continued to live in Gordon Square, in the Bloomsbury section of London. They hosted gatherings of writers and artists, a circle of Cambridge-educated friends that came to be known as the Bloomsbury Group. In 1912, Virginia married one of these friends, Leonard Woolf, a writer on politics and economics. Five years later, Virginia and Leonard Woolf started Hogarth Press, which became a successful publishing house, printing works by Katherine Mansfield, E. M. Forster, T. S. Eliot, and Virginia Woolf. After Woolf's first two novels, *The Voyage Out* and *Night and Day,* she began to experiment with various elements of fiction, particularly with interior monologues and stream-of-consciousness technique. Her novels include *Jacob's Room, Mrs. Dalloway, To the Lighthouse, Orlando, The Waves,* and *Between the Acts.* Her short stories were published in the collections *Monday or Tuesday* and *A Haunted House.* One of the most distinguished critics of her time, Woolf published numerous essays and works of literary criticism, including *Mr. Bennett and Mrs. Brown, The Common Reader, A Room of One's Own, Flush, Three Guineas, Roger Fry,* and *The Death of the Moth.* In 1953, Leonard Woolf edited and published *A Writer's Diary,* extracts from the diary that Woolf had kept about her work.

About the Selection

An eloquent and ardent feminist, Virginia Woolf published ***A Room of One's Own*** (1929), a long essay on the status of women and the difficulties of being a woman artist. Woolf's essay was based on two lectures given at Cambridge University. In the essay, Woolf discussed the Elizabethan Age, the period when Queen Elizabeth I reigned in England (1558–1603). This was a time of extraordinary energy, splendor, and creativity, the age of Marlowe, Jonson, and Shakespeare. In the selection that follows, Woolf considers a dark aspect of the Elizabethan and later periods of English history—the social forces that kept women from exercising their talents. Woolf asks and answers the question, "What if Shakespeare had had an equally talented sister?"

Literary Tools

ESSAY. An **essay** is a brief work of prose nonfiction. Typically, a good essay develops a single idea and is characterized by *unity* and *coherence.* As you read, identify the single idea this essay presents.

AIM. A writer's **aim** is his or her purpose, or goal. People may write to inform, to entertain, to make a point, to reflect, or to persuade. What is Woolf's main aim in writing this essay?

Reader's Journal

Describe your feelings about a talent you have that you have been encouraged or discouraged to develop.

ADDITIONAL RESOURCES

UNIT 11 RESOURCE BOOK
- Selection Worksheet 11.1
- Selection Check Test 4.11.1
- Selection Test 4.11.2
- Language, Grammar, and Style Resource 3.38
- Study and Research Resource 5.20

READER'S JOURNAL

How have societal stereotypes about gender influenced the advice you have received about pursing your talents? How have gender stereotypes influenced your goals and dreams?

VOCABULARY FROM THE SELECTION

agog	guffaw
betrothed	omnibus
escapade	poach

GOALS/OBJECTIVES

Studying this lesson will enable students to
- empathize with the torment of a creative mind bound by society
- describe Virginia Woolf's contributions to twentieth-century literature
- define *essay* and *aim* and explain how these terms apply to this selection
- demonstrate the ability to make sentences parallel
- work collaboratively on a role-play activity

ANSWER TO GUIDED READING QUESTION

They would have discouraged her from reading or educating herself. They would have encouraged her to perform household tasks.

INDIVIDUAL LEARNING STRATEGIES

MOTIVATION
Ask students to predict what the selection will be about based on the title and what they know about Virginia Wolf and her work. Then have them check their predictions after they have read the selection.

READING PROFICIENCY
Students may need help with the conditional verb phrases, formed with *would,* in some of the Guided Reading questions. Explain that this verb construction indicates a situation that is contrary to fact. Make sure students understand that the whole essay discusses a fictional character.

ENGLISH LANGUAGE LEARNING
Give students the following idioms and words as additional vocabulary:
Idioms
on the sly—secretly
apple of one's eye—one's favorite
Additional Vocabulary
moon—behave idly
fancy—imagination
servile—submissive
asunder—into separate parts

SPECIAL NEEDS
Have advanced students help students with special needs with the Guided Reading Questions and the Graphic Organizer on page 998.

ENRICHMENT
Have students choose a woman writer or artist during Woolf's time. Ask them to research the obstacles that she faced during the early twentieth century. How do their struggles compare to the struggles women face today? They should present their information in a written report.

FROM A Room of One's Own

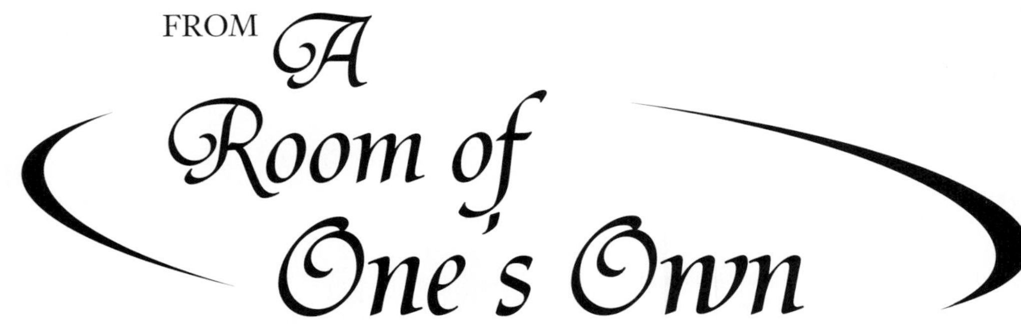

Virginia Woolf

Let me imagine, since facts are so hard to come by, what would have happened had Shakespeare had a wonderfully gifted sister, called Judith, let us say. Shakespeare himself went, very probably—his mother was an heiress—to the grammar school, where he may have learnt Latin—Ovid, Virgil and Horace—and the elements of grammar and logic. He was, it is well known, a wild boy who poached rabbits, perhaps shot a deer, and had, rather sooner than he should have done, to marry a woman in the neighborhood, who bore him a child rather quicker than was right. That escapade sent him to seek his fortune in London. He had, it seemed, a taste for the theatre; he began by holding horses at the stage door. Very soon he got work in the theatre, became a successful actor, and lived at the hub of the universe, meeting everybody, knowing everybody, practicing his art on the boards, exercising his wits in the streets, and even getting access to the palace of the queen. Meanwhile his extraordinarily gifted sister, let us suppose, remained at home. She was as adventurous, as imaginative, as agog to see the world as he was. But she was not sent to school. She had no chance of learning grammar and logic, let alone of reading Horace and Virgil. She picked up a book now and then, one of her brother's perhaps, and read a few pages. But then her parents came in and told her to mend the stockings or mind the stew and not moon about with books and papers. They would have spoken sharply but kindly, for they were substantial people who knew the conditions of life for a woman and loved their daughter—indeed, more likely than not she was the apple of her father's eye. Perhaps she scribbled some pages up in an apple loft on the sly, but was careful to hide them or set fire to them. Soon, however, before she was out of her teens, she was to be betrothed to the son of a neighboring wool-stapler. She cried out that marriage was hateful to her, and for that she was severely beaten by her father. Then he ceased to scold her. He begged

What would Judith's parents have discouraged her from doing? What would Judith have been encouraged to do with her time?

WORDS FOR EVERYDAY USE

poach (pōch) *vt.,* hunt illegally. *Any hunters who poach deer on this land will be arrested.*

es • ca • pade (es´kə pād´) *n.,* reckless adventure. *The starlet detailed her many wild escapades in her memoirs.*

a • gog (ə gäg´) *adj.,* eagerly excited. *The children were so agog to visit the amusement park that they got dressed before anyone else was awake.*

be • trothed (bē trôtht´) *adj.,* engaged to be married. *Did you hear that the bachelor was recently betrothed to an heiress?*

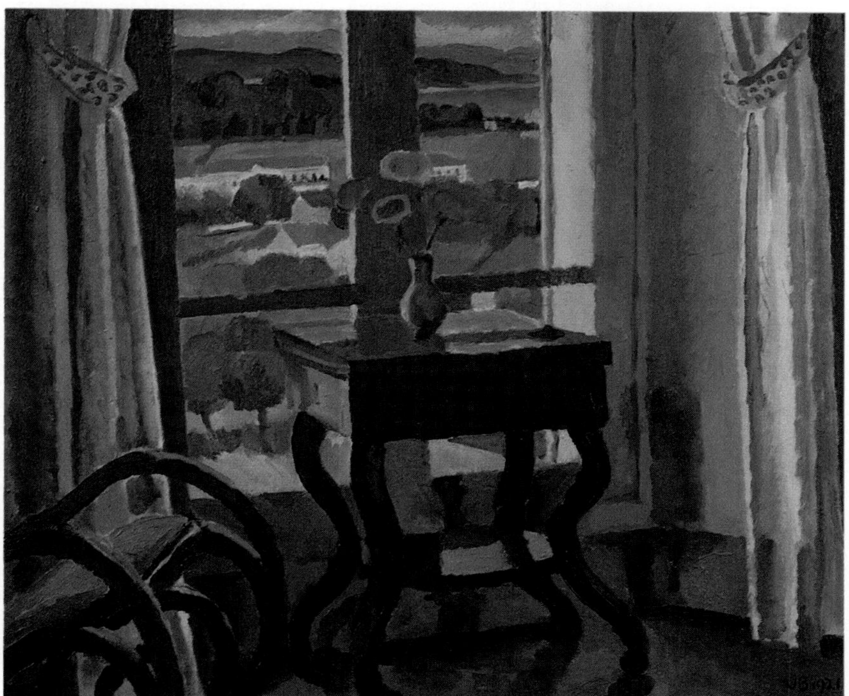

Interior with a Table, 1921. Vanessa Bell. Tate Gallery, London.

her instead not to hurt him, not to shame him in this matter of her marriage. He would give her a chain of beads or a fine petticoat, he said; and there were tears in his eyes. How could she disobey him? How could she break his heart? The force of her own gift alone drove her to it. She made up a small parcel of her belongings, let herself down by a rope one summer's night and took the road to London. She was not seventeen. The birds that sang in the hedge were not more musical than she was. She had the quickest fancy, a gift like her brother's, for the tune of words. Like him, she had a taste for the theatre. She stood at the stage door; she wanted to act, she said. Men laughed in her face. The manager—a fat, loose-lipped man—guffawed. He bellowed something about poodles dancing and women acting—no woman, he said, could

What conflict would have arisen between Judith and her father?

WORDS FOR EVERYDAY USE

guf • faw (gu fô´) *vi.*, let out a short burst of laughter. *An inappropriate guffaw erupted from the back row of the funeral parlor.*

ANSWER TO GUIDED READING QUESTION

1. Judith and her father would have fought over whether or not she would marry the son of wool-stapler.

CROSS-CURRICULAR CONNECTIONS

HISTORY. "On page 996," Woolf refers to Professor Trevelyan, author of *The History of England* (1926). As she explored Trevelyan's text, Woolf searched in vain for any mention of women in the arts during the sixteenth century. The only entries about women discussed the accepted practice of wife beating and the custom of arranged marriages.

ANSWERS TO GUIDED READING QUESTIONS

1. At the theater Judith would have been turned away. People would have laughed at her and demeaned her for thinking she could be an actor.
2. Judith kills herself after finding that she is pregnant, a "poet's heart…caught and tangled in a woman's body."

LITERARY TECHNIQUE

ALLUSION. Woolf uses an **allusion** to emphasize her point. She speaks of a "mute and inglorious Jane Austen," which recalls "Some mute inglorious Milton" (line 59) from Thomas Gray's "Elegy Written in a Country Churchyard" (page 574). In making such an allusion, Woolf underscores how women have been neglected throughout history; Gray's poem praises the common, unknown *man* but makes no mention of the common, nameless women who lie in the same graveyard.

What would have happened to Judith at the theater? How would people have reacted to her?

possibly be an actress. He hinted—you can imagine what. She could get no training in her craft. Could she even seek her dinner in a tavern or roam the streets at midnight? Yet her genius was for fiction and lusted to feed abundantly upon the lives of men and women and the study of their ways. At last—for she was very young, oddly like Shakespeare the poet in her face, with the same grey eyes and rounded brows—at last Nick Greene the actor-manager took pity on her; she found herself with child by that gentleman and so—who shall measure the heat and violence of the poet's heart when caught and tangled in a woman's body?—killed herself one winter's night and lies buried at some cross-roads where the <u>omnibuses</u> now stop outside the Elephant and Castle.

What does Judith do, and why?

For genius like Shakespeare's is not born among laboring, uneducated, servile people.

That, more or less, is how the story would run, I think, if a woman in Shakespeare's day had had Shakespeare's genius. But for my part, I agree with the deceased bishop, if such he was—it is unthinkable that any woman in Shakespeare's day should have had Shakespeare's genius. For genius like Shakespeare's is not born among laboring, uneducated, servile people. It was not born in England among the Saxons and the Brittons. It is not born today among the working classes. How, then, could it have been born among women whose work began, according to Professor Trevelyan, almost before they were out of the nursery, who were forced to it by their parents and held to it by all the power of law and custom? Yet genius of a sort must have existed among women as it must have existed among the working classes. Now and again an Emily Brontë or a Robert Burns blazes out and proves its presence. But certainly it never got itself on to paper. When, however, one reads of a witch being ducked, of a woman possessed by devils, of a wise woman selling herbs, or even of a very remarkable man who had a mother, then I think we are on the track of a lost novelist, a suppressed poet, of some mute and inglorious Jane Austen, some Emily Brontë who dashed her brains out on the moor or mopped and mowed about the highways crazed with the torture that her gift had put her to. Indeed, I would venture to guess that Anon, who wrote so many poems without signing them, was often a woman. It was a woman Edward FitzGerald, I think, suggested who made the ballads and the folk-songs, crooning them to her children, beguiling her spinning with them, or the length of the winter's night.

This may be true or it may be false—who can say?—but what is true in it, so it seemed to me, reviewing the story of Shakespeare's sister as I had made it, is that any woman born with a great gift in the sixteenth century would certainly have gone crazed, shot herself, or ended her days in some lonely cottage outside the vil-

WORDS FOR EVERYDAY USE

om • ni • bus (äm´ni bəs) *n.,* bus. *Because of her fear of flying, the singer toured the country by <u>omnibus</u>.*

lage, half witch, half wizard, feared and mocked at. For it needs little skill in psychology to be sure that a highly gifted girl who had tried to use her gift for poetry would have been so thwarted and hindered by other people, so tortured and pulled asunder by her own contrary instincts, that she must have lost her health and sanity to a certainty. No girl could have walked to London and stood at a stage door and forced her way into the presence of actor-managers without doing herself a violence and suffering an anguish which may have been irrational—for chastity may be a fetish invented by certain societies for unknown reasons—but were none the less inevitable. Chastity had then, it has even now, a religious importance in a woman's life, and has so wrapped itself round with nerves and instincts that to cut it free and bring it to the light of day demands courage of the rarest. To have lived a free life in London in the sixteenth century would have meant for a woman who was poet and playwright a nervous stress and dilemma which might well have killed her. Had she survived, whatever she had written would have been twisted and deformed, issuing from a strained and morbid imagination. And undoubtedly, I thought, looking at the shelf where there are no plays by women, her work would have gone unsigned. ■

What does Woolf suggest about poems signed "anonymous"?

Respond *to the* Selection

What does the idea of a room of your own mean to you? Do you think this is an apt title for this essay? Why, or why not?

ANSWER TO GUIDED READING QUESTION

1. Woolf suggests that poems signed "anonymous" were probably written by women.

RESPOND TO THE SELECTION

Imagine you are the sister of Shakespeare. How would you feel to have a talented brother who was given every opportunity to develop his craft and not to have such opportunities yourself? Write a letter to your parent explaining your frustrations and need to develop your own talents.

SELECTION CHECK TEST 4.11.1 WITH ANSWERS

Checking Your Reading

1. What education is Judith given? **She is only taught homemaking skills.**
2. Why does Judith run away from home? **She has been betrothed against her will.**
3. What does the bishop say is unthinkable about women in Shakespeare's day? **It is unthinkable that any women of the day had Shakespeare's genius.**
4. What do Emily Bronte and Robert Burns prove? **They prove that women and working-class people can be geniuses.**
5. What would have been the likely fate for any gifted woman born in Judith's time? **She would have gone insane.**

Vocabulary in Context

Fill each blank with the most appropriate word from the Words for Everyday Use. You may have to change the tense of the word.

betrothed omnibus escapade
guffaw poach agog

1. We gathered on the rooftop, **agog** at the sight of the comet.
2. The candidate's **escapades** as a young woman came to light during her campaign.
3. Much of the fees collected by the wild game park support the fight against **poaching**.
4. The red **omnibus** trundled out of the fog and stopped in front of us.
5. Josh could hardly wait to tell his friends that he was **betrothed**.

SELECTION CHECK TEST 4.11.1 WITH ANSWERS (CONT.)

Literary Tools

Match the descriptions with the following terms. You will not use every term, and you may use some terms more than once.

a. informative/expository b. narrative
c. imaginative d. personal/expressive
e. persuasive/argumentative f. character
g. essay h. theme

__E__ 1. influences an audience to think, feel, agree, or behave in a certain way
__G__ 2. develops a single idea with unity and coherence
__A__ 3. includes newspaper articles, journal articles, pamphlets and websites
__H__ 4. the central idea developed in a literary work
__E__ 5. includes advertisements, editorials, letters to the editor, and political speeches

ANSWERS TO INVESTIGATE, INQUIRE, AND IMAGINE

RECALL

1a. She asks them to let her imagine that Shakespeare had "a wonderfully gifted sister."

2a. He learns Latin, grammar, and logic.

3a. Shakespeare begins by holding horses at the stage door; then he works in the theatre and becomes an actor.

INTERPRET

1b. Judith is imaginative, adventurous and eager to have a career and see the world. She is not content to stay home and assume the traditional role of wife and mother.

2b. Her education consists of learning to do the things women were supposed to do during that time: mending, cooking, being a proper wife and any writing or reading (from her brother's books) that she manages to sneak in during the day.

3b. Historical evidence of witches, possessed women, herbal healers, anonymous poems, and the mothers of remarkable men put Woolf on the track of women's hidden genius during that time.

ANALYZE

4a. The reasons Judith never achieved fame include the fact that she was not educated as men were and that she was financially dependant on men, as were all women of her day. The norms of society prevented women from pursuing intellectual pursuits or independence and took a very limited view of women's potential. She had the talent and desire but was held back by society's expectations of her.

SYNTHESIZE

4b. The author is suggesting that the heart of a creative artist would be consumed by its own creative fire and destroyed if not allowed to vent that creative fire by pursuing her art. She is saying that Judith is destroyed by the conventions that limit and constrain her from doing what her creative genius must do.

EVALUATE

5a. Through Shakespeare's imaginary sister, Woolf illustrates the grim obstacles faced by a talented woman in the sixteenth century. Woolf's choice of Shakespeare is particularly persuasive, and perhaps lurking underneath the scenario of Shakespeare's sister is the question: "What if Shakespeare had been a woman?" The challenges Judith faces help to confirm Woolf's point. Details such as the back and forth of her argument with her father, her escape by rope from an upstairs window and the name of the actor

INVESTIGATE, Inquire, Imagine

Recall: GATHERING FACTS

1a. What does the author ask her audience to let her imagine?

2a. What does William Shakespeare learn in grammar school?

3a. What series of jobs gives Shakespeare the opportunity to work his way into theater?

Interpret: FINDING MEANING

1b. What sort of person does the author imagine Judith to be?

2b. What elements comprise the education of Judith Shakespeare?

3b. What evidence supports Woolf's imaginary depiction of Judith's fate?

Analyze: TAKING THINGS APART

4a. What reasons are given for Judith's obscurity? Why did she not achieve fame?

Synthesize: BRINGING THINGS TOGETHER

4b. Explain the phrase, "Who shall measure the heat and violence of the poet's heart when caught and tangled in a woman's body?"

Evaluate: MAKING JUDGMENTS

5a. What purpose does the imaginary sister of Shakespeare serve in the essay? What details make her a compelling character? How effectively does the imaginary sister serve the author's purpose?

Extend: CONNECTING IDEAS

5b. How would a modern-day Judith's fate unfold? What aspects of her life would be the same, and which would be different?

Understanding Literature

ESSAY. Review the definition for **essay** in Literary Tools in Prereading for this selection. What single idea does this essay present? What examples support and develop this idea? Use the following graphic organizer to record your thoughts, listing the main idea in the center circle, and the supporting examples in the radiating circles.

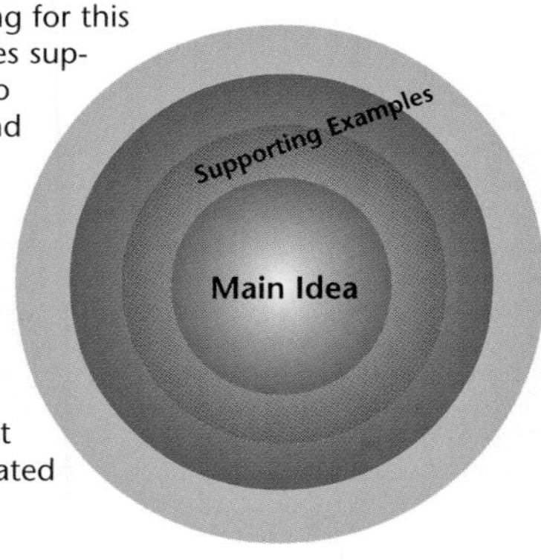

AIM. Review the definition for **aim** in the Handbook of Literary Terms. One aim of *A Room of One's Own* is to illustrate the obstacles faced by women writers in the sixteenth century. From reading the selection, can you tell whether Woolf believed that those obstacles still existed in 1928, the year in which she wrote the essay? Of what significance is the fact that the essay is based on two lectures that Woolf gave at Cambridge University? How might the aim of the essay be different if Woolf were a Cambridge-educated man?

ANSWERS TO INVESTIGATE, INQUIRE, AND IMAGINE (CONT.)

who took advantage of her, all make her seem quite real and make Judith a very effective means to make the author's point.

EXTEND

5b. *Responses will vary.* A modern-day Judith would have access to greater educational opportunity and would find that society's view of appropriate roles for women is much broader. She might create a life for herself that would not entail financial dependence on a man. However, to some extent, society still views some work as "women's work" and many women are still more likely to be financially dependent and more likely to work in traditionally female occupations. Students should be encouraged to base their idea of a modern-day Judith on the character traits that Woolf creates for her. Most likely, a modern-day Judith wouldn't let anything stop her from achieving her goals.

Writer's Journal

1. Imagine that you are Shakespeare. Write an **epitaph** for your sister, Judith.
2. Write the **letter** that Judith might have left for her parents the night she left for London.
3. Write a **character sketch** that describes one of the sixteenth-century women who published work anonomously.

Integrating the Language Arts

Language, Grammar, and Style

Achieving Parallelism. Read the Language Arts Survey 3.38, "Achieving Parallelism." Rewrite each of the following sentences to make their parts parallel.

1. Virginia Woolf and her sister Vanessa often met with their Bloomsbury friends, many of whom enjoyed discussing political issues and to write essays.
2. To educate women is as important as educating men.
3. Woolf experimented with the form of the novel more than experimentation with the form of the essay.
4. Having a profession guarantees a woman economic independence and to be free intellectually.
5. Having a room of her own and to earn a reasonable income are two necessities for a woman artist, according to Woolf.

Speaking and Listening & Collaborative Learning

Role-Play. Working in pairs, role-play a debate between Judith and her father over her course in life. One of you should play the father, a man who loves his daughter and wants her to be happy, but who also knows how harsh society can be on renegades and nonconformists. The other should play Judith, who, like her brother, longs to be able to pursue her dreams of a life in the theater. Before you begin, spend some time thinking carefully about the way your character might feel, what concerns and doubts, hopes and fears he or she might be having. What arguments will you make to convince the other? Conduct your role-play before your class.

Study and Research

Research Report. Read the Language Arts Survey 5.20, "Using Reference Works." Then use several reference works to find information about the Bloomsbury Group. Identify the members of the group, and research their views about literature, art, and politics. Organize your research information into a short report to share with your class.

ANSWERS TO UNDERSTANDING LITERATURE

Essay.
Center circle: Talented women faced huge obstacles in 16th century.
Radiating circles:
- Lack of education
- Pushed into women's work
- Arranged marriages
- Few opportunities
- Financial dependence
- Pregnancy limited opportunity
- Suicide rather than life without chance to practice art

Aim. In her essay, Woolf states that genius "is not born today among the working classes." The implication is that women born among the working classes in 1928 still did not have the advantages of education of financial independence. It is ironic that Woolf was speaking to a highly educated audience about the obstacles, including the lack of education, that faced sixteenth-century women. If Woolf had been a man, perhaps her purpose would have been to celebrate the literary feats of sixteenth-century men such as Shakespeare and Marlowe.

ANSWERS TO INTEGRATING THE LANGUAGE ARTS

Language, Grammar, and Style

1. Virginia Woolf and her sister Vanessa often met with their Bloomsbury friends, many of whom enjoyed discussing political issues and **writing** essays.
2. **Educating** women is as important as educating men.
3. Woolf experimented with the form of the novel more than **she experimented** with the form of the essay.
4. Having a profession guarantees a woman economic independence and **intellectual freedom.**
5. Having a room of her own and **earning** a reasonable income are two necessities for a woman artist, according to Woolf.

Speaking and Listening & Collaborative Learning
You might want to refer students to the Language Arts Survey 4.21, "Participating in a Debate" to help them with this activity.

ADDITIONAL RESOURCES

UNIT 11 RESOURCE BOOK
- Selection Worksheet 11.2
- Selection Check Test 4.11.3
- Selection Test 4.11.4
- Language, Grammar, and Style Resource 3.34

GRAPHIC ORGANIZER

Note that there are many other examples of stream-of consciousness writing in the excerpt and that students should be encouraged to find as many as possible. Possible answers for graphic organizer.

1. Students should complete flow chart example by following Stephen's thoughts from reading Fleming's verse and his own flynotes through to his thought that "God's real name is God." (page 1007)
2. Students should chart Stephen's thoughts from not being able to get the answer for the sum to wondering if somewhere in the world you could have a green rose. (page 1005)
3. Students should follow Stephen's thought about what the right answer to Wells' question—"...do you kiss your mother before you go to bed?"—is through to his wondering about kissing, "Why did people do that with their two faces?" (page 1006)

READER'S JOURNAL

If students can't remember their childhood vocabulary, suggest that they invent childlike names for everyday objects and explain why they chose the words they did.

Literary TOOLS

IMAGE AND OBJECTIVE CORRELATIVE. An **image** is language that creates a concrete representation of an object or an experience. An image is also the vivid mental picture created in the reader's mind by that language. An **objective correlative** is a group of images that together create a particular emotion in the reader. Note the imagery in this selection and how it affects the reader.

STREAM-OF-CONSCIOUSNESS WRITING. Stream-of-consciousness writing is a literary technique that attempts to render the flow of feelings, thoughts, and impressions within the minds of characters. As you read, note some examples of how the author accomplishes this in the excerpt from *A Portrait of the Artist as a Young Man.*

Use the diagram below as a model for tracking the stream-of-consciousness flow of Stephen's thoughts through these passages. Create a diagram for each passage you identify.

Reads Fleming's verse backwards, notes in flyleaf bottom to top, top to bottom	→	What is beyond the universe? Nothing.

Reader's Journal

Write about a time when you felt homesick, alone, or as if you did not belong.

FROM A Portrait of the Artist as a Young Man

BY JAMES JOYCE

About the AUTHOR

James Joyce (1882–1941) was born in Dublin, Ireland, and educated at Jesuit schools and at University College, Dublin. In 1902, having rebelled against Catholicism, Irish nationalism, and his family, Joyce left Dublin. He spent the rest of his life in a self-imposed exile, living in Paris, Trieste, Rome, and Zurich, returning to Ireland only for a brief visit. Accompanying him to Trieste in 1904 was Nora Barnacle, an uneducated Dublin chambermaid, whom he eventually married. Supported by Joyce's meager earnings as a clerk and as a teacher of languages, the couple wandered about Europe and had two children. In 1914, Joyce published *Dubliners,* a collection of short stories. The collection was greatly admired by the American poet and critic Ezra Pound, who assisted Joyce throughout the following years. Because of his deteriorating eyesight, Joyce relied on his memory and on the secretarial help of friends in order to work. A perfectionist, Joyce wrote and repeatedly revised his novel *Ulysses* for seven years, from 1914 to 1921. A second large, experimental novel, *Finnegan's Wake,* took seventeen years to complete. Both novels incited controversy. *Ulysses* was banned in the United States and Britain on the basis of obscenity from 1922 until a landmark ruling in 1933 in United States District court lifted the ban and permitted broad distribution of what would come to be seen as Joyce's masterwork. Readers found both *Ulysses* and *Finnegan's Wake* obscure and even nonsensical until critics explained Joyce's innovative methods and other writers began to imitate his experimental techniques. Joyce is now regarded as one of the twentieth century's greatest writers, known for his revolutionary innovations in prose style, which included the use of stream-of-consciousness technique, frequent allusions, and extensive word play.

About the SELECTION

Published in 1916, Joyce's novel ***A Portrait of the Artist as a Young Man*** is largely autobiographical. The selection portrays the childhood and school days of Stephen Dedalus, an Irish Catholic boy attending a Jesuit school; the novel continues with Dedalus's adolescence and early manhood. Stephen Dedalus later becomes one of the leading characters in Ulysses. Throughout *A Portrait of the Artist as a Young Man,* Dedalus's self-awareness as an artist grows, forcing him to reject the world in which he was raised. The novel does not follow a chronological progression but focuses instead on certain experiences that are critical to Dedalus's development as an artist.

GOALS/OBJECTIVES

Studying this lesson will enable students to
- empathize with the sensitive nature of the protagonist in a rough, unkind world
- describe James Joyce's contributions to twentieth-century literature
- define *image, objective correlative,* and *stream-of-consciousness writing* and identify examples of each that they encounter in their reading
- demonstrate the ability to correct run-on sentences
- conduct a research on Greek mythology

A Football Match, 1932. Lawrence Stephen Lowry. Private Collection.

FROM

A Portrait of the Artist as a Young Man

James Joyce

INDIVIDUAL LEARNING STRATEGIES

Motivation
Ask students to freewrite about anything that comes to their mind for ten minutes. When they are finished, explain to students that stream-of-consciousness writing is similar to the freewriting process because words and emotions flow naturally in both instances.

Reading Proficiency
Explain that the selection does not obviously exhibit the fictional elements of character, setting, and plot. To help students understand this difficult selection, establish the main character, setting, and plot for students before they begin reading. Then pair students with English-proficient students who can help answer questions as they read.

English Language Learning
See the suggestion above for Reading Proficiency. Also give students the following vocabulary words. Ask them to find a synonym and an antonym for each word.

Additional Vocabulary
throng—great number of people gathered together
scrimmage—practice football or rugby game
well-read—having read much
rhetoric—the art of using words effectively

Special Needs
Direct students' attention to About the Author and About the Selection sections to prepare them for the innovative and nonsensical writing style they will encounter in the selection.

Enrichment
Ask students to write a short story using the stream-of-consciousness technique. Encourage students to let emotions, feelings, and dialogue to flow naturally in the characters they develop.

ANSWERS TO GUIDED READING QUESTIONS

1. The point of view is third person. The observations are those of a young child.
2. Stephen notices a rhyme in what he hears and creates a poem around it.

ADDITIONAL QUESTIONS AND ACTIVITIES

Have students trace Stephen's train of thought from the scene on the playground, which begins on the preceding page, to the moment when Stephen is "caught in the whirl of a scrimmage." Suggest that students use arrows to indicate the flow of Stephen's thoughts.

What is the point of view of the opening of the novel? Through whose eyes and ears are these events observed?

Once upon a time and a very good time it was there was a moocow coming down along the road and this moocow that was coming down along the road met a nicens little boy named baby tuckoo. . . .

His father told him that story: his father looked at him through a glass: he had a hairy face.

He was baby tuckoo. The moocow came down the road where Betty Byrne lived: she sold lemon platt.

O, the wild rose blossoms
On the little green place.

He sang that song. That was his song.

O, the green wothe botheth.

When you wet the bed first it is warm then it gets cold. His mother put on the oilsheet. That had the queer smell.

His mother had a nicer smell than his father. She played on the piano the sailor's hornpipe for him to dance. He danced:

Tralala lala
Tralala tralaladdy
Tralala lala
Tralala lala.

Uncle Charles and Dante clapped. They were older than his father and mother but uncle Charles was older than Dante.

Dante had two brushes in her press. The brush with the maroon velvet back was for Michael Davitt[1] and the brush with the green velvet back was for Parnell.[2] Dante gave him a cachou[3] every time he brought her a piece of tissue paper.

The Vances lived in number seven. They had a different father and mother. They were Eileen's father and mother. When they were grown up he was going to marry Eileen. He hid under the table. His mother said:

—O, Stephen will apologise.

Dante said:

—O, if not, the eagles will come and pull out his eyes.

How does this passage illustrate that even at an early age Stephen is drawn to word play?

Pull out his eyes,
Apologise,
Apologise,
Pull out his eyes.

Apologise,
Pull out his eyes,
Pull out his eyes,
Apologise.

◆ ◆ ◆

The wide playgrounds were swarming with boys. All were shouting and the prefects[4] urged them on with strong cries. The evening air was pale and chilly and after every charge and thud of the footballers[5] the greasy leather orb[6] flew like a heavy bird through the grey light. He kept on the fringe of his line, out of sight of his prefect, out of the reach of the rude feet, feigning to run now and then. He felt his body small and weak amid the throng of players and his eyes were weak and watery. Rody Kickham was not like that: he would be captain of the third line all the fellows said.

Rody Kickham was a decent fellow but Nasty Roche was a stink. Rody Kickham had greaves[7] in his number and a hamper in the refectory.[8] Nasty Roche had big hands. He called the

1. **Michael Davitt.** Irish nationalist leader (1846–1906)
2. **Charles Stewart Parnell.** Irish nationalist leader (1846–1891)
3. **cachou.** Lozenge, or perhaps, an onomatopoetic rendering of a sneeze
4. **prefects.** Older students in position of authority
5. **footballers.** Soccer players
6. **orb.** Soccer ball
7. **greaves.** Leg armor worn below the knee to protect the shin; used here to describe soccer shin guards
8. **refectory.** Dining hall

Friday pudding dog-in-the-blanket. And one day he had asked:

—What is your name?

Stephen had answered:

—Stephen Dedalus.

Then Nasty Roche had said:

—What kind of a name is that?

And when Stephen had not been able to answer Nasty Roche had asked:

—What is your father?

Stephen had answered:

—A gentleman.

Then Nasty Roche had asked:

—Is he a magistrate?[9]

He crept about from point to point on the fringe of his line, making little runs now and then. But his hands were bluish with cold. He kept his hands in the sidepockets of his belted grey suit. That was a belt round his pocket. And belt was also to give a fellow a belt. One day a fellow had said to Cantwell:

—I'd give you such a belt in a second.

Cantwell had answered:

—Go and fight your match. Give Cecil Thunder a belt. I'd like to see you. He'd give you a toe in the rump for yourself.

That was not a nice expression. His mother had told him not to speak with the rough boys in the college. Nice mother! The first day in the hall of the castle when she had said goodbye she had put up her veil double to her nose to kiss him: and her nose and eyes were red. But he had pretended not to see that she was going to cry. She was a nice mother but she was not so nice when she cried. And his father had given him two fiveshilling pieces for pocket money. And his father had told him if he wanted anything to write home to him and, whatever he did, never to peach[10] on a fellow. Then at the door of the castle the rector had shaken hands with his father and mother, his soutane[11] fluttering in the breeze, and the car had driven off with his father and mother on it. They had cried to him from the car, waving their hands:

What does Stephen pretend not to see? What advice does his father give him?

—Goodbye, Stephen, goodbye!

—Goodbye, Stephen, goodbye!

He was caught in the whirl of a scrimmage and, fearful of the flashing eyes and muddy boots, bent down to look through the legs. The fellows were struggling and groaning and their legs were rubbing and kicking and stamping. Then Jack Lawton's yellow boots dodged out the ball and all the other boots and legs ran after. He ran after them a little way and then stopped. It was useless to run on. Soon they would be going home for the holidays. After supper in the studyhall he would change the number pasted up inside his desk from seventyseven to seventysix.

Why does Stephen change the number each day? How does he feel about school? about home?

It would be better to be in the studyhall than out there in the cold. The sky was pale and cold but there were lights in the castle. He wondered from which window Hamilton Rowan had thrown his hat on the haha[12] and had there been flowerbeds at that time under the windows. One day when he had been called to the castle the butler had shown him the marks of the soldiers' slugs in the wood of the door and had given him a piece of shortbread that the community ate. It was nice and warm to see the lights in the castle. It was like something in a book. Perhaps Leicester Abbey was like that. And there were nice sentences in Doctor Cornwell's Spelling Book. They were like poetry but they were only sentences to learn the spelling from.

Wolsey died in Leicester Abbey
Where the abbots buried him.
Canker is a disease of plants,
Cancer one of animals.

9. **magistrate.** Civil officer
10. **peach.** Give evidence against
11. **soutane.** Long, loose-fitting vestment, generally black, worn by clergymen
12. **haha.** Fence around a garden

ANSWERS TO GUIDED READING QUESTIONS

1. Stephen pretends not to see that his mother is ready to cry. His father tells him to write home for anything he needs and no matter what, never to snitch on anyone.
2. Stephen is counting the number of days until he can go home. He seems terrified of school. He wants to go home where he knows what to expect.

LITERARY TECHNIQUE

Dialogue. Dialogue is conversation involving two or more people or characters. One of the characteristics of stream-of-consciousness writing is that dialogue is not presented in conventional terms. When Joyce uses dialogue, he forgoes the quotation marks and tag lines that usually identify the speakers and their words. Have students discuss why Joyce might have used this dialogue format.

ANSWER TO GUIDED READING QUESTION

1. Stephen is sensitive to the sounds of words. He is also sensitive to the embarrassment and pain of others.

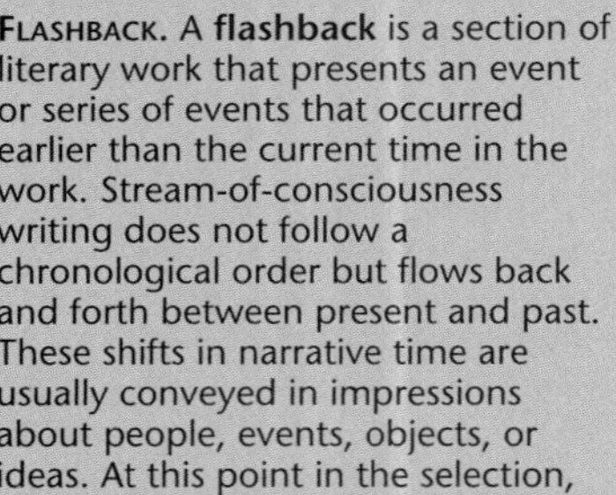

LITERARY TECHNIQUE

FLASHBACK. A **flashback** is a section of literary work that presents an event or series of events that occurred earlier than the current time in the work. Stream-of-consciousness writing does not follow a chronological order but flows back and forth between present and past. These shifts in narrative time are usually conveyed in impressions about people, events, objects, or ideas. At this point in the selection, Stephen returns to the present time of the football game after a flashback in which he reminisces about the day his parents left him at school.

CROSS-CURRICULAR CONNECTIONS

HISTORY. York and Lancaster were the opposing parties in the War of the Roses (1455–1485). Members of these two English houses, who fought over the English throne, wore roses to identify their affiliation—white for the House of York and red for the House of Lancaster. At the Battle of Bosworth in 1485, the Lancastrian Henry Tudor defeated the Yorkist Richard III. Henry was proclaimed King Henry IV, and through his marriage to Elizabeth of York, the opposing parties were united.

It would be nice to lie on the hearthrug before the fire, leaning his head upon his hands, and think on those sentences. He shivered as if he had cold slimy water next his skin. That was mean of Wells to shoulder him into the square ditch because he would not swop his little snuffbox for Wells's seasoned hacking chestnut, the conqueror of forty. How cold and slimy the water had been! A fellow had once seen a big rat jump into the scum. Mother was sitting at the fire with Dante waiting for Brigid to bring in the tea. She had her feet on the fender and her jewelly slippers were so hot and they had such a lovely warm smell! Dante knew a lot of things. She had taught him where the Mozambique Channel was and what was the longest river in America and what was the name of the highest mountain in the moon. Father Arnall knew more than Dante because he was a priest but both his father and uncle Charles said that Dante was a clever woman and a wellread woman. And when Dante made that noise after dinner and then put up her hand to her mouth: that was heartburn.

A voice cried far out on the playground:

—All in!

Then other voices cried from the lower and third lines:

—All in! All in!

The players closed around, flushed and muddy, and he went among them, glad to go in. Rody Kickham held the ball by its greasy lace. A fellow asked him to give it one last: but he walked on without even answering the fellow. Simon Moonan told him not to because the prefect was looking. The fellow turned to Simon Moonan and said:

—We all know why you speak. You are McGlade's suck.

Suck was a queer word. The fellow called Simon Moonan that name because Simon Moonan used to tie the prefect's false sleeves behind his back and the prefect used to let on to be angry. But the sound was ugly. Once he had washed his hands in the lavatory of the Wicklow Hotel and his father pulled the stopper up by the chain after and the dirty water went down through the hole in the basin. And when it had all gone down slowly the hole in the basin had made a sound like that: suck. Only louder.

What aspect of this passage reveals Stephen to be a sensitive boy?

To remember that and the white look of the lavatory made him feel cold and then hot. There were two cocks that you turned and water came out: cold and hot. He felt cold and then a little hot: and he could see the names printed on the cocks. That was a very queer thing.

And the air in the corridor chilled him too. It was queer and wettish. But soon the gas would be lit and in burning it made a light noise like a little song. Always the same: and when the fellows stopped talking in the playroom you could hear it.

It was the hour for sums. Father Arnall wrote a hard sum on the board and then said:

—Now then, who will win? Go ahead, York! Go ahead, Lancaster!

Stephen tried his best but the sum was too hard and he felt confused. The little silk badge with the white rose on it that was pinned on the breast of his jacket began to flutter. He was no good at sums but he tried his best so that York might not lose. Father Arnall's face looked very black but he was not in a wax: he was laughing. Then Jack Lawton cracked his fingers and Father Arnall looked at his copybook and said:

—Right. Bravo Lancaster! The red rose wins. Come on now, York! Forge ahead!

Jack Lawton looked over from his side. The little silk badge with the red rose on it looked very rich because he had a blue sailor top on. Stephen felt his own face red too, thinking of all the bets about who would get first place in elements, Jack Lawton or he. Some weeks Jack Lawton got the card for first and some weeks he got the card for first. His white silk badge fluttered and fluttered as he worked at the next sum and heard Father Arnall's voice. Then all his eagerness passed away and he felt his face quite cool. He thought his face must be white because it felt so cool. He could not get out the answer for the sum but it did not matter. White roses and red roses: those were beautiful colours to think of. And the cards for first place and second place and third place were beautiful colours too: pink and cream and lavender. Lavender and cream and pink roses were beautiful to think of. Perhaps a wild rose might be like those colours and he remembered the song about the wild rose blossoms on the little green place. But you could not have a green rose. But perhaps somewhere in the world you could.

Why can't Stephen concentrate on the sums? What types of things capture his attention while the others focus on calculating sums?

The bell rang and then the classes began to file out of the rooms and along the corridors towards the refectory. He sat looking at the two prints of butter on his plate but could not eat the damp bread. The tablecloth was damp and limp. But he drank off the hot weak tea which the clumsy scullion,[13] girt with a white apron, poured into his cup. He wondered whether the scullion's apron was damp too or whether all white things were cold and damp. Nasty Roche and Saurin drank cocoa that their people sent them in tins. They said they could not drink the tea; that it was hogwash. Their fathers were magistrates, the fellows said.

All the boys seemed to him very strange. They had all fathers and mothers and different clothes and voices. He longed to be at home and lay his head on his mother's lap. But he could not: and so he longed for the play and study and prayers to be over and to be in bed.

For what things does Stephen long?

He drank another cup of hot tea and Fleming said:

—What's up? Have you a pain or what's up with you?

—I don't know, Stephen said.

—Sick in your breadbasket, Fleming said, because your face looks white. It will go away.

—O yes, Stephen said.

But he was not sick there. He thought that he was sick in his heart if you could be sick in that place. Fleming was very decent to ask him. He wanted to cry. He leaned his elbows on the table and shut and opened the flaps of his ears. Then he heard the noise of the refectory every time he opened the flaps of his ears. It made a roar like a train at night. And when he closed the flaps the roar was shut off like a train going into a tunnel. That night at Dalkey the train had roared like that and then, when it went into the tunnel, the roar stopped. He closed his eyes and the train went on, roaring and then stopping; roaring again, stopping. It was nice to hear it roar and stop and then roar out of the tunnel again and then stop.

Why is Stephen "sick in his heart"?

Then the higher line fellows began to come down along the matting in the middle of the refectory, Paddy Rath and Jimmy Magee and the Spaniard who was allowed to smoke cigars and the little Portuguese who wore the woolly cap. And then the lower line tables and the tables of the third line. And every single fellow had a different way of walking.

He sat in a corner of the playroom pretending to watch a game of dominos and once or twice he was able to hear for an instant the little song of the gas. The prefect was at the door with some boys and Simon Moonan was knotting his false sleeves. He was telling them something about Tullabeg.

Then he went away from the door and Wells came over to Stephen and said:

—Tell us, Dedalus, do you kiss your mother before you go to bed?

Stephen answered:

—I do.

13. **scullion.** Kitchen servant

ANSWERS TO GUIDED READING QUESTIONS

1. Stephen can't concentrate on calculating sums because they are too hard and he gets confused. Also, he simply isn't interested in calculating sums. He is distracted by the silk badges and the colors of the roses his classmates wear on their jackets, the colors of the cards denoting first-, second-, and third-place in the math contest, and he wonders whether there might be wild roses the color of those cards, remembers a song he knows about wild roses, and wonders whether anywhere in the world there exists a green rose.
2. Stephen longs first to be at home with his head on his mother's lap. He knows that cannot be, and so he longs for the play and study and prayers to be over so he can go to bed.
3. Stephen is sick in his heart because he feels out of place and homesick.

ADDITIONAL QUESTIONS AND ACTIVITIES

How does the contest of sums mirror the historical contest between York and Lancaster? What mood does this create in the selection?

Answers

Like in the historical contest, Lancaster emerges victorious. It creates a mood of resignation, as if Stephen's failure at sums is already an historical fact. Also, Stephen wears a white rose, one of the images that creates the objective correlative and creates a mood of loneliness and isolation.

ANSWERS TO GUIDED READING QUESTIONS

1. Stephen doesn't know how to react to Well's teasing. He answers him honestly, and when all the boys laugh, he contradicts his answer, and they laugh again. He doesn't realize they are making fun of him, and he wonders what the right answer to the question is. Stephen won't look at Wells; he doesn't like his face, and he thinks Wells mean for pushing him in to a ditch full of slimy water the day before.
2. Stephen can't learn the names of the places in America. He takes a more conceptual view of geography: there are different places in America with different names, different countries on different continents that make up the world, and the world, which resides in the universe.

CROSS-CURRICULAR ACTIVITIES

GEOGRAPHY. Students can use an atlas to find Stephen's location. Then they can make their own lists of where they are. They should try to make their lists as detailed as possible.

Wells turned to the other fellows and said:

—O, I say, here's a fellow says he kisses his mother every night before he goes to bed.

The other fellows stopped their game and turned round, laughing. Stephen blushed under their eyes and said:

—I do not.

Wells said:

—O, I say, here's a fellow says he doesn't kiss his mother before he goes to bed.

They all laughed again. Stephen tried to laugh with them. He felt his whole body hot and confused in a moment. What was the right answer to the question? He had given two and still Wells laughed. But Wells must know the right answer for he was in third of grammar. He tried to think of Wells's mother but he did not dare to raise his eyes to Wells's face. He did not like Wells's face. It was Wells who had shouldered him into the square ditch the day before because he would not swop his little snuffbox for Wells's seasoned hacking chestnut, the conqueror of forty. It was a mean thing to do; all the fellows said it was. And how cold and slimy the water had been! And a fellow had once seen a big rat jump plop into the scum.

How does Stephen react to Wells' teasing? How does Stephen feel about Wells?

The cold slime of the ditch covered his whole body; and, when the bell rang for study and the lines filed out of the playrooms, he felt the cold air of the corridor and staircase inside his clothes. He still tried to think what was the right answer. Was it right to kiss his mother or wrong to kiss his mother? What did that mean, to kiss? You put your face up like that to say goodnight and then his mother put her face down. That was to kiss. His mother put her lips on his cheek; her lips were soft and they wetted his cheek; and they made a tiny little noise: kiss. Why did people do that with their two faces?

Sitting in the studyhall he opened the lid of his desk and changed the number pasted up inside from seventyseven to seventysix. But the Christmas vacation was very far away: but one time it would come because the earth moved round always.

There was a picture of the earth on the first page of his geography: a big ball in the middle of clouds. Fleming had a box of crayons and one night during free study he had coloured the earth green and the clouds maroon. That was like the two brushes in Dante's press, the brush with the green velvet back for Parnell and the brush with the maroon velvet back for Michael Davitt. But he had not told Fleming to colour them those colours. Fleming had done it himself.

He opened the geography to study the lesson; but he could not learn the names of places in America. Still they were all different places that had those different names. They were all in different countries and the countries were in continents and the continents were in the world and the world was in the universe.

What can't Stephen learn? How does he think about geography?

He turned to the flyleaf[14] of the geography and read what he had written there: himself, his name and where he was.

Stephen Dedalus
Class of Elements
Clongowes Wood College
Sallins
County Kildare
Ireland
Europe
The World
The Universe

That was in his writing: and Fleming one night for a cod had written on the opposite page:

14. **flyleaf.** A blank page at the beginning or end of a book

Stephen Dedalus is my name,
Ireland is my nation.
Clongowes is my dwellingplace
And heaven my expectation.

He read the verses backwards but then they were not poetry. Then he read the flyleaf from the bottom to the top till he came to his own name. That was he: and he read down the page again. What was after the universe? Nothing. But was there anything round the universe to show where it stopped before the nothing place began? It could not be a wall but there could be a thin thin line there all round everything. It was very big to think about everything and everywhere. Only God could do that. He tried to think what a big thought that must be but he could think only of God. God was God's name just as his name was Stephen. *Dieu* was the French for God and that was God's name too; and when anyone prayed to God and said *Dieu* then God knew at once that it was a French person that was praying. But though there were different names for God in all the different languages in the world and God understood what all the people who prayed said in their different languages still God remained always the same God and God's real name was God.

What types of things does Stephen think about when he thinks "that way"?

It made him very tired to think that way. It made him feel his head very big. He turned over the flyleaf and looked wearily at the green round earth in the middle of the maroon clouds. He wondered which was right, to be for the green or for the maroon, because Dante had ripped the green velvet back off the brush that was for Parnell one day with her scissors and had told him that Parnell was a bad man.[15] He wondered if they were arguing at home about that. That was called politics. There were two sides in it: Dante was on one side and his father and Mr. Casey were on the other side but his mother and uncle Charles were on no side. Every day there was something in the paper about it.

What things does Stephen want to understand? Why?

It pained him that he did not know well what politics meant and that he did not know where the universe ended. He felt small and weak. When would he be like the fellows in poetry and rhetoric?[16] They had big voices and big boots and they studied trigonometry. That was very far away. First came the vacation and then the next term and then vacation again and then again another term and then again the vacation. It was like a train going in and out of tunnels and that was like the noise of the boys eating in the refectory when you opened and closed the flaps of the ears. Term, vacation; tunnel, out; noise, stop. How far away it was! It was better to go to bed to sleep. Only prayers in the chapel and then bed. He shivered and yawned. It would be lovely in bed after the sheets got a bit hot. First they were so cold to get into. He shivered to think how cold they were first. But then they got hot and then he could sleep. It was lovely to be tired. He yawned again. Night prayers and then bed: he shivered and wanted to yawn. It would be lovely in a few minutes. He felt a warm glow creeping up from the cold shivering sheets, warmer and warmer till he felt warm all over, ever so warm; ever so warm and yet he shivered a little and still wanted to yawn. ■

15. **bad man.** Parnell, the Irish nationalist leader and supporter of home rule for Ireland, was involved in a scandal that ended his career.

16. **rhetoric.** Class on the art of speaking or writing effectively

Respond to the Selection

Make a list of ten words to describe Stephen Dedalus.

ANSWERS TO GUIDED READING QUESTIONS

1. Stephen's thoughts move from the verse Fleming has written to what is beyond the universe to how to define the boundaries of the universe to God and how God's name is different in different languages around the world, but how God hears the prayers of people all around the world and understands all the languages of the world to how everyone's God is really the same God and that his real name is God.
2. Stephen wants to understand politics and the universe (science), poetry and rhetoric. Not understanding these things makes him feel small and weak.

SELECTION CHECK TEST 4.11.3 WITH ANSWERS

Checking Your Reading

1. About what age is Dedalus as the selection opens? He is probably a toddler.
2. What does Dedalus play with Rody Kickham and Nasty Roche? He plays soccer.
3. To what question from Wells does Dedalus give two answers? "Do you kiss your mother before you go to bed?"
4. What does Dante argue about with Dedalus' father? They argue over politics.
5. What do the numbers Dedalus changes in his desk (from 77 to 76) stand for? The numbers indicate how many days there are until Christmas vacation.

Literary Tools

Choose the sentence ending that best fits each sentence beginning. You may not use any choice more than once.

_C_ 1. Stream-of-consciousness writing seeks to capture…
_A_ 2. Typical narrative writing presents…
_F_ 3. Images are…
_G_4. Stream-of-consciousness usually does not offer…
_B_ 5. An objective correlative is…

a. events in a logical sequence, generally arranging them in a chronological order.
b. a group of images that together create a particular emotion in the reader.

SELECTION CHECK TEST 4.11.3 WITH ANSWERS (CONT.)

c. the flow of feelings, thoughts, and impressions in the mind of a character.
d. writing that is not disrupted by dialogue.
e. the main idea, or theme, or a piece of literary writing.
f. words or phrases that name things that can be captured with one of the five senses.
g. multiple perspectives on a single event.

RESPOND TO THE SELECTION

Suggest that students expand on the images and incidents in the selection rather than limiting themselves to recalling them.

ANSWERS TO INVESTIGATE, INQUIRE, IMAGINE

RECALL

1a. His body feels "small and weak."

2a. Father Arnall knows more because he is a priest.

3a. He wrote his name followed by a series of places "where he was" and ending with "The Universe." Stephen wonders what lies beyond the universe and what separates the universe from whatever lies beyond it.

INTERPRET

1b. Stephen is not interested in football: he feels that running after the ball would be "useless." He is afraid of the other boys: he feels his body is weak, and "all the boys seemed to him very strange." He does not feel comfortable at school: he counts the days until he can leave and thinks frequently of his family.

2b. Stephen respects Dante because she knows a lot and has taught him many things.

3b. The notes about the places "where he was" and the questions about the universe indicate that he wants to understand how the world around him is constructed and is concerned about his place in that world and how he fits in.

ANALYZE

4a. *Responses will vary.* Stephen's realities include bullies like Wells, athletes like Rody Kickham, teacher's pets like the prefect's Simon Moonan, and humiliating moments such as being kicked into the ditch.

SYNTHESIZE

4b. Stephen's artistic sensibilities are revealed at an early age when he recognizes the rhymes in "Pull out his eyes" and "apologize" and forms a poem. Later they are revealed in his enjoyment of words in the sentences of his spelling book, his attention to sounds, and his pleasure in the color of cards and roses.

EVALUATE

5a. The speaker's thoughts jump from one thing to another without a linear, logical process. For example, the passage on p.1004, describes Wells pushing him into the ditch, followed by a memory of his mother with her feet up before the fire, followed by how much Dante knows and finally that Dante has heartburn and burps after dinner. The speaker often wonders about fanciful things, like "But you could not have a green rose. But perhaps somewhere in the world you could." All of these things suggest the workings of a child's mind.

INVESTIGATE, Inquire, *Imagine*

Recall: GATHERING FACTS → **Interpret:** FINDING MEANING

1a. What does the schoolboy Stephen feel his body is like "amid the throng of players"?

1b. How does Stephen feel toward football (soccer)? toward the other boys? toward school? How do you know?

2a. What reason is given for Father Arnall knowing more than Dante?

2b. How does Stephen feel about Dante? Support your response with examples from the selection.

3a. What did Stephen write on the flyleaf of his geography book? What questions does Stephen have about the universe?

3b. What do these things reveal about him?

Analyze: TAKING THINGS APART → **Synthesize:** BRINGING THINGS TOGETHER

4a. What realities are part of Stephen's everyday life at school?

4b. What aspects of this selection reveal the young Stephen to have artistic sensibilities?

Evaluate: MAKING JUDGMENTS → **Extend:** CONNECTING IDEAS

5a. How effectively does this passage recreate the workings of a child's mind? Use examples from the text to support your answer.

5b. Joyce thought that an artist had to be removed from the subject of his or her art to treat that subject objectively. He wrote about Ireland all of his career, but spent nearly all his adult life in self-imposed exile in Europe. In *A Portrait of the Artist as a Young Man,* Joyce depicts his coming of age and the beginning realization of his own alienation from the world around him. What evidence in the selection indicates that Joyce treated his own childhood objectively? Do you agree with his philosophy on maintaining a distance from the subject of one's art? Why, or why not?

Understanding *Literature*

IMAGE AND OBJECTIVE CORRELATIVE. Review the definitions for **image** and **objective correlative** in Literary Tools in Prereading for this selection. What images are used in the selection to describe dampness? What is the effect of this group of images on the reader? What images are used to describe warmth and comfort? How are these opposing images used, and what do they convey about Stephen's experience?

STREAM-OF-CONSCIOUSNESS WRITING. Review the definition for **stream-of-consciousness writing** and the diagram you completed in Literary Tools in Prereading. One characteristic of stream-of-consciousness writing that sets it apart from ordinary narratives is that ideas are presented in the order in which they occur in the mind of the protagonist, not necessarily in a logical order. How do the passages that you've charted demonstrate this characteristic? How does this type of writing provide insight into the character of Stephen Dedalus? What insights does it provide?

ANSWERS TO INVESTIGATE, INQUIRE, IMAGINE (CONT.)

EXTEND

5b. The argument to be made for distance and exile is that it allows one to observe without emotional attachment which might color one's observations. The argument for immersing oneself in the subject of one's art is that it allows the artist to absorb every aspect of the subject in order to understand and then share the experience with the viewer of the art.

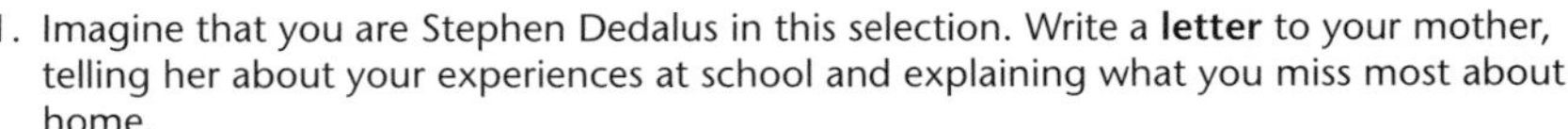

Writer's Journal

1. Imagine that you are Stephen Dedalus in this selection. Write a **letter** to your mother, telling her about your experiences at school and explaining what you miss most about home.
2. Imagine that you are the headmaster of the school that Stephen Dedalus attended. At the end of the first term, you must summarize the student's progress and behavior for his record. Write an imaginary **progress report** on Stephen Dedalus.
3. Close your eyes and think back to when you were a young child. Visualize a person, place, or object that was very important to you. Keeping that image in mind, write a **stream-of-consciousness paragraph,** freely associating words, impressions, and reactions to that image as they come to you. Write either from the point of view of yourself now, looking back on the image, or from the point of view of yourself then, actually experiencing the image.

Integrating *the* Language Arts

Language, Grammar, and Style

Correcting run-ons. Review the Language Arts Survey 3.34, "Correcting Sentence Run-ons." Revise the sentences below by changing punctuation and capitalization and adding words as necessary.

1. Joyce admired the work of Henrik Ibsen, a Norwegian poet and playwright, Joyce's first publication was an essay, "Ibsen's New Drama."
2. Joyce's *Dubliners* is a brilliant collection of short stories some of these stories are autobiographical.
3. Joyce's books were banned by censors and pirated by publishers these are just two of the reasons why Joyce earned almost nothing from his writing until his last few years.
4. Joyce's hero Stephen Dedalus says, "I will not serve that in which I no longer believe," this statement appears in the novel *A Portrait of the Artist as a Young Man.*
5. Stephen Dedalus appears again later, much older, in another novel by James Joyce, that novel is *Ulysses.*

Study and Research

Researching a Myth. Joyce often uses allusions to political and historical events and to other literary works. In this book, the main character's name is an allusion to the first Christian martyr Saint Stephen, and to Daedalus from Greek mythology. Using library and Internet resources, research the Daedalus myth. Keep in mind that Stephen Dedalus is both the son of a man named Dedalus and is named Dedalus himself. Why do you think Joyce chose this name for Stephen? Prepare a report for your teacher on the Daedalus myth and the apparent significance of Stephen Dedalus's name.

ANSWERS TO UNDERSTANDING LITERATURE

Image and Objective Correlative. Images of dampness: wet bed is warm first, then cold; cold, slimy water in ditch; damp bread in dining hall; damp tablecloth; damp apron. The images of cold and damp are most often used to describe the college and his experience there. Images of warmth: mother with feet up by fire; mother's "lovely warm smell"; bed sheets feel cold first, then warm. Images of warmth and comfort are associated with bed and sleep and home. These images create in the reader an experience of Stephen's lonely and homesick yearning to leave the school and find comfort.

Stream-of-Consciousness Writing. The passages charted directly demonstrate this characteristic by revealing the disorderly, abstract flow of Stephen's thoughts. This type of writing reveals Stephen to be an abstract thinker, a person heavily influenced by and sensitive to what he sees, hears, and feels. He is easily distracted, unable to focus on the practical or mundane, and a social misfit.

ANSWERS TO INTEGRATING THE LANGUAGE ARTS

Language, Grammar, and Style
Responses will vary.

1. Joyce admired the work of Henrik Ibsen, a Norwegian poet and playwright. Joyce's first publication was an essay, "Ibsen's New Drama."
2. Joyce's *Dubliners* is a brilliant collection of short stories; some of these stories are autobiographical.
3. Joyce's books were banned by censors and pirated by publishers. These are just two of the reasons why Joyce earned almost nothing from his writing until his last few years.
4. Joyce's hero Stephen Dedalus says, "I will not serve that in which I no longer believe"; this statement appears in the novel *A Portrait of the Artist as a Young Man.*
5. Stephen Dedalus appears again later, much older, in another novel by James Joyce. That novel is Ulysses.

Study and Research Activity
Daedalus meant "cunning craftsman." The mythological Daedalus was the architect of the labyrinth ordered by King Minos to keep the minotaur. King Minos, however, imprisoned Daedalus on an island to preserve the secret of the labyrinth. Daedalus and his son,

ANSWERS TO INTEGRATING THE LANGUAGE ARTS (CONT.)

Icarus, made wings of bird feathers and wax in order to escape the island prison but Icarus flew too close to the sun, melted the wax and fell to his death. The significance of this name for Stephen may include the idea that he is a "cunning craftsman"—an artist. It may also signify that he will be so swept up in his art that he will be consumed by it, as Icarus was destroyed when he lost himself in the glory of flight. It may also include the idea that the artist must escape—as Joyce "escaped" Ireland and went into exile.

ADDITIONAL RESOURCES

UNIT 11 RESOURCE BOOK

- Selection Worksheet 11.3
- election Check Test 4.11.5
- Selection Test 4.11.6
- Speaking and Listening Resource 4.21
- Study and Research Resource 5.1

READER'S JOURNAL

Recall a time when you felt peer pressure. Describe the situation. Did you give in or resist to the pressure? After you made your choice, did you feel feelings of regret or satisfaction?

VOCABULARY FROM THE SELECTION

despotic	prostrate
labyrinth	scored
pretext	senility

Literary TOOLS

THESIS. A **thesis** is a main idea that is supported in a work of nonfiction prose. As you read "Shooting An Elephant," make notes on the ideas Orwell explores. What do you think the main thesis of the selection is?

IRONY. **Irony** is a difference between appearance and reality. As you read this essay, consider what is ironic about the situation Orwell describes. Note examples of the divergence of appearance and reality.

Reader's Journal

When have you felt pressured by the expectations of other people to do something you did not want to do?

"Shooting an Elephant"

BY GEORGE ORWELL

About the AUTHOR

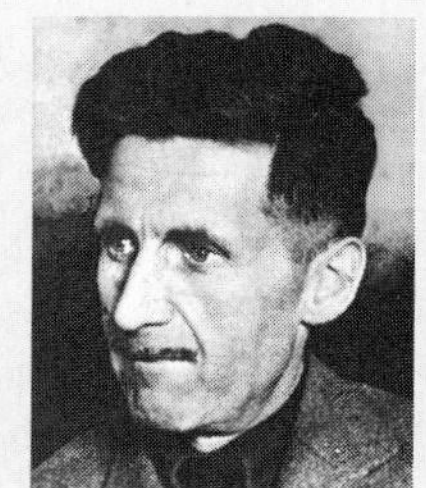

George Orwell (1903–1950) was the pseudonym of Eric Arthur Blair. Orwell was born in India, where his father served in the civil service. Orwell won a scholarship to Eton but was financially unable to continue his education at Oxford or Cambridge. From 1922 to 1927, he worked for the Imperial Police in Burma; the experience provided much of the material for his early work, including the novel *Burmese Days* (1934) and the title work in the essay collection *Shooting an Elephant* (1950). For years Orwell worked at ill-paid jobs. He described his experiences with poverty in *Down and Out in Paris and London* (1933). His experiences in the Spanish Civil War, in which he fought on the Republican side and was wounded, are recounted in *Homage to Catalonia* (1939). An early convert to Socialism, Orwell was angered by the ruthless, authoritarian policies of the Soviet Union under Lenin and Stalin. His two best-known novels, *Animal Farm* (1945) and *Nineteen Eighty-Four* (1949), are attacks on Soviet-style totalitarianism. Orwell's other works include *Keep the Aspidistra Flying* (1936), *Coming Up for Air* (1939), and the posthumously published *Collected Essays, Journalism and Letters* (1968).

About the SELECTION

"Shooting an Elephant" is an essay in which Orwell recalls an incident that took place in Burma during his years as a police officer of the Imperial British government. An elephant has run mad and trampled a man to death. Orwell is called upon to respond and finds himself having to choose between doing what he feels is right, and doing what he believes the natives expected of him as a representative of the power of the British crown.

GOALS/OBJECTIVES

Studying this lesson will enable students to

- empathize with the speaker's feeling of peer pressure
- describe George Orwell's experience as a police officer in Burma
- define *thesis* and *irony* and recognize and explain examples of each in the selection
- demonstrate the ability to reduce wordiness in sentences
- conduct a research of the history of Burma

SHOOTING AN Elephant

George Orwell

In Moulmein, in Lower Burma, I was hated by large numbers of people—the only time in my life that I have been important enough for this to happen to me. I was sub-divisional police officer of the town, and in an aimless, petty kind of way anti-European feeling was very bitter. No one had the guts to raise a riot, but if a European woman went through the bazaars alone somebody would probably spit betel juice[1] over her dress. As a police officer I was an obvious target and was baited whenever it seemed safe to do so. When a nimble Burman tripped me up on the football field and the referee (another Burman) looked the other way, the crowd yelled with hideous laughter. This happened more than once. In the end the sneering yellow faces of young men that met me everywhere, the insults hooted after me when I was at a safe distance, got badly on my nerves. The young Buddhist priests were the worst of all. There were several thousands of them in the town and none of them seemed to have anything to do except stand on street corners and jeer at Europeans.

Why was the narrator a target of hatred?

All this was perplexing and upsetting. For at that time I had already made up my mind that

1. **betel juice.** Juice of the nuts and leaves of the betel palm, a tree in Asia

ANSWER TO GUIDED READING QUESTION

1. Orwell was a target for the hatred of the natives because he was an officer in the British police.

INDIVIDUAL LEARNING STRATEGIES

Motivation
Ask students to discuss the following questions in small groups: How do you feel about hunting or killing animals? What is the moral dilemma about killing animals? Then after students have read the selection, ask them, "What was the moral conflict Orwell faced? Do you think Orwell did the right thing? Why, or why not?"

Reading Proficiency
To help students follow the events that take place in the selection, ask them to make a time line of events as they read. Have them begin their timeline with the phone call the protagonist receives about an elephant on the loose.

English Language Learning
Have students share their cultural practices in the area of killing animals. What animals in their culture are considered sacred? How would people in their culture handle the situation Orwell faced?

Special Needs
Before students read the selection, have them read the About the Selection section. Then point out the main idea of the story.

Enrichment
Ask students to conduct a research on the British rule of Burma during Orwell's time living there and the state of Burma's government today. What impact did British rule have on Burmans? Does an anti-European attitude currently exist among Burmans? Have them present their findings in an oral report.

ANSWERS TO GUIDED READING QUESTIONS

1. He hated his job and the empire, and the Burmese people, who made his job so difficult, as well.
2. He was called to do something about a rampaging elephant destroying the bazaar.

ADDITIONAL QUESTIONS AND ACTIVITIES

Orwell says, "I had already made up my mind that imperialism was an evil thing…" Why do you think he decided to work for the British Raj if he felt this way about their governmental tactics? Have you ever taken part in an activity that you believed was wrong? Why did you choose to participate in something in which you did not believe?

CROSS-CURRICULAR CONNECTIONS

History. Webster's Dictionary defines imperialism as "the policy or practice of extending the power and dominion over a nation by direct territorial acquisitions or by gaining indirect control over the political or economic life of other areas." For Britain, the word *imperialism* was the key word of the 1890s for it was during these years that the British Raj gained power and territories. The cause of the empire was not only the result of businessmen looking for materials and markets internationally, but they were also interested in keeping the traditional lustre of the crown. Despite the fact that materials and markets were most effectively acquired through trade, the British Empire continued to acquire colonies by force. Most of the acquisitions, like Burma, were located in tropical areas of the world and peopled mainly by non-Europeans.

imperialism was an evil thing and the sooner I chucked up my job and got out of it the better. Theoretically—and secretly, of course—I was all for the Burmese and all against their oppressors, the British. As for the job I was doing, I hated it more bitterly than I can perhaps make clear. In a job like that you see the dirty work of Empire at close quarters. The wretched prisoners huddling in the stinking cages of the lock-ups, the grey, cowed faces of the long-term convicts, the scarred buttocks of the men who had been flogged with bamboos—all these oppressed me with an intolerable sense of guilt. But I could get nothing into perspective. I was young and ill-educated and I had had to think out my problems in the utter silence that is imposed on every Englishman in the East. I did not even know that the British Empire is dying, still less did I know that it is a great deal better than the younger empires that are going to supplant it. All I knew was that I was stuck between my hatred of the empire I served and my rage against the evil-spirited little beasts who tried to make my job impossible. With one part of my mind I thought of the British Raj[2] as an unbreakable tyranny, as something clamped down, in saecula saeculorum,[3] upon the will of prostrate peoples; with another part I thought that the greatest joy in the world would be to drive a bayonet into a Buddhist priest's guts. Feelings like these are the normal by-products of imperialism; ask any Anglo-Indian official, if you can catch him off duty.

How did the narrator feel about his job and about the Burmese people?

One day something happened which in a roundabout way was enlightening. It was a tiny incident in itself, but it gave me a better glimpse than I had had before of the real nature of imperialism—the real motives for which despotic governments act. Early one morning the sub-inspector at a police station at the other end of the town rang me up on the 'phone and said that an elephant was ravaging the bazaar. Would I please come and do something about it? I did not know what I could do, but I wanted to see what was happening and I got on to a pony and started out. I took my rifle, an old .44 Winchester and much too small to kill an elephant, but I thought the noise might be useful in *terrorem*.[4] Various Burmans stopped me on the way and told me about the elephant's doings. It was not, of course, a wild elephant, but a tame one which had gone "must."[5] It had been chained up, as tame elephants always are when their attack of "must" is due, but on the previous night it had broken its chain and escaped. Its mahout,[6] the only person who could manage it when it was in that state, had set out in pursuit, but had taken the wrong direction and was now twelve hours' journey away, and in the morning the elephant had suddenly reappeared in the town. The Burmese population had no weapons and were quite helpless against it. It had already destroyed somebody's bamboo hut, killed a cow and raided some fruit-stalls and devoured the stock; also it had met the municipal rubbish van and, when the driver jumped out and took to his heels, had turned the van over and inflicted violences upon it.

What problem calls the narrator away from the police station?

The Burmese sub-inspector and some Indian constables were waiting for me in the quarter where the elephant had been seen. It was a very

2. **Raj.** Rule
3. **in saecula saeculorum.** Forever and ever
4. **in terrorem** for terror
5. **must.** The mating period for male elephants, characterized by dangerous frenzies
6. **mahout.** An elephant trainer or keeper

Words for Everyday Use

pros • trate (prä′ strāte) *adj.*, completely overcome and lacking the will or power to rise. *The twice-defeated boxer appeared prostrate and depressed in the interview afterward.*

des • pot • ic (des pä′ tik) *adj.*, of, relating to, or characteristic of a tyrant. *The coach's despotic behavior had a negative effect on the players.*

poor quarter, a labyrinth of squalid bamboo huts, thatched with palm-leaf, winding all over a steep hillside. I remember that it was a cloudy, stuffy morning at the beginning of the rains. We began questioning the people as to where the elephant had gone and, as usual, failed to get any definite information. That is invariably the case in the East; a story always sounds clear enough at a distance, but the nearer you get to the scene of the events the vaguer it becomes. Some of the people said that the elephant had gone in one direction, some said that he had gone in another, some professed not even to have heard of any elephant. I had almost made up my mind that the whole story was a pack of lies, when we heard yells a little distance away. There was a loud, scandalized cry of "Go away, child! Go away this instant!" and an old woman with a switch in her hand come round the corner of a hut, violently shooing away a crowd of naked children. Some more women followed, clicking their tongues and exclaiming; evidently there was something that the children ought not to have seen. I rounded the hut and saw a man's dead body sprawling in the mud. He was an Indian, a black Dravidian[7] coolie,[8] almost naked, and he could not have been dead many minutes. The people said that the elephant had come suddenly upon him round the corner of the hut, caught him with its trunk, put its foot on his back and ground him into the earth. This was the rainy season and the ground was soft, and his face had scored a trench a foot deep and a couple of yards long. He was lying on his belly with arms crucified and head sharply twisted to one side. His face was coated with mud, the eyes wide open, the teeth bared and grinning with an expression of unendurable agony. (Never tell me, by the way, that the dead look peaceful. Most of the corpses I have seen looked devilish.) The friction of the great beast's foot had stripped the skin from his back as neatly as one skins a rabbit. As soon as I saw the dead man I sent an orderly to a friend's house nearby to borrow an elephant rifle. I had already sent back the pony, not wanting it to go mad with fright and throw me if it smelt the elephant.

What disturbing sight greeted the narrator when he got to the area where the elephant was loose?

The orderly came back in a few minutes with a rifle and five cartridges, and meanwhile some Burmans had arrived and told us that the elephant was in the paddy fields[9] below, only a few hundred yards away. As I started forward practically the whole population of the quarter flocked out of the houses and followed me. They had seen the rifle and were all shouting excitedly that I was going to shoot the elephant. They had not shown much interest in the elephant when he was merely ravaging their homes, but it was different now that he was going to be shot. It was a bit of fun to them, as it would be to an English crowd; besides they wanted the meat. It made me vaguely uneasy. I had no intention of shooting the elephant—I merely sent for the rifle to defend myself if necessary—and it is always unnerving to have a crowd following you. I marched down the hill, looking and feeling a fool, with the rifle over my shoulder and an ever-growing army of people jostling at my heels. At the bottom, when you got away from the huts, there was a metalled road[10] and beyond that a miry waste of paddy fields a thousand yards across, not yet ploughed but soggy from the first rains and

7. **Dravidian.** One of a race of people living in southern India
8. **coolie.** Worker or laborer
9. **paddy fields.** Rice fields
10. **metaled road.** Road which is reinforced with metal strips

WORDS FOR EVERYDAY USE

lab • y • rinth (la' bə rinth) *n.*, a place full of intricate pathways and blind alleys. *The new city seemed to her a labyrinth of dead ends and one-way streets.*

scored (skōrd') *vt.*, to mark with lines, grooves, scratches, or notches. *He used a screwdriver to score his initials into the wooden bench.*

ANSWER TO GUIDED READING QUESTION

1. The sight of a dead coolie, apparently killed by the elephant, greeted him.

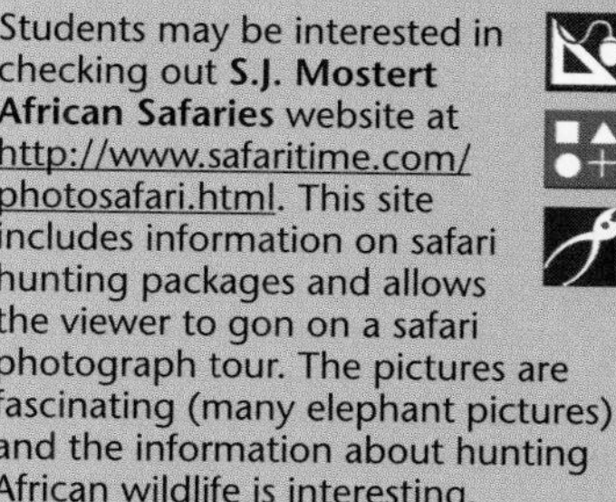

INTERNET RESOURCES

Students may be interested in checking out **S.J. Mostert African Safaries** website at http://www.safaritime.com/photosafari.html. This site includes information on safari hunting packages and allows the viewer to gon on a safari photograph tour. The pictures are fascinating (many elephant pictures) and the information about hunting African wildlife is interesting.

ANSWERS TO GUIDED READING QUESTIONS

1. The elephant's rampage was over, and it was peacefully eating grass.
2. He felt he must shoot the elephant because the crowd expected it of him.

CROSS-CURRICULAR CONNECTIONS

Science and Social Studies. Between 1979 and 1989, the worldwide demand for ivory caused elephant populations to decline to dangerously low levels. In 1997, 1.3 million elephants lived in Africa; by 1997, only 600,000 remained. Although it is illegal to kill an elephant in Africa, people continue to kill them for reasons of poaching or revenge. To a farmer, an elephant can be a five-ton garden pest, destroying the season's crop. If this happens, the culprit (elephant) may be hunted down and force to pay the price of damage with its life. Currently, scientists are working on developing a pepper-spray bomb to ward off elephants from gardens and fields by attacking their eyes with airborne pepper molecules. The elephant recovers soon after, having learned to stay clear of the crops.

dotted with coarse grass. The elephant was standing eight yards from the road, his left side towards us. He took not the slightest notice of the crowd's approach. He was tearing up bunches of grass, beating them against his knees to clean them and stuffing them into his mouth.

I had halted on the road. As soon as I saw the elephant I knew with perfect certainty that I ought not to shoot him. It is a serious matter to shoot a working elephant—it is comparable to destroying a huge and costly piece of machinery—and obviously one ought not to do it if it can possibly be avoided. And at that distance, peacefully eating, the elephant looked no more dangerous than a cow. I thought then and I think now that his attack of "must" was already passing off; in which case he would merely wander harmlessly about until the mahout came back and caught him. Moreover, I did not in the least want to shoot him. I decided that I would watch him for a little while to make sure that he did not turn savage again, and then go home.

How was the elephant behaving when the narrator approached it?

But at that moment I glanced round at the crowd that had followed me. It was an immense crowd, two thousand at the least and growing every minute. It blocked the road for a long distance on either side. I looked at the sea of yellow faces above the garish clothes—faces all happy and excited over this bit of fun, all certain that the elephant was going to be shot. They were watching me as they would watch a conjurer about to perform a trick. They did not like me, but with the magical rifle in my hands I was momentarily worth watching. And suddenly I realized that I should have to shoot the elephant after all. The people expected it of me and I had got to do it; I could feel their two thousand wills pressing me forward, irresistibly. And it was at this moment, as I stood there with the rifle in my hands, that I first grasped the hollowness, the futility of the white man's dominion in the East. Here was I, the white man with his gun, standing in front of the unarmed native crowd—seemingly the leading actor of the piece; but in reality I was only an absurd puppet pushed to and fro by the will of those yellow faces behind. I perceived in this moment that when the white man turns tyrant it is his own freedom that he destroys. He becomes a sort of hollow, posing dummy, the conventionalized figure of a sahib.[11] For it is the condition of his rule that he shall spend his life in trying to impress the "natives," and so in every crisis he has got to do what the "natives" expect of him. He wears a mask, and his face grows to fit it. I had got to shoot the elephant. I had committed myself to doing it when I sent for the rifle. A sahib has got to act like a sahib; he has got to appear resolute, to know his own mind and do definite things. To come all that way, rifle in hand, with two thousand people marching at my heels, and then to rail feebly away, having done nothing—no, that was impossible. The crowd would laugh at me. And my whole life, every white man's life in the East, was one long struggle not to be laughed at.

Why did the narrator feel he must shoot the elephant?

But I did not want to shoot the elephant. I watched him beating his bunch of grass against his knees, with that preoccupied grandmotherly air that elephants have. It seemed to me that it would be murder to shoot him. At that age I was not squeamish about killing animals, but I had never shot an elephant and never wanted

11. **sahib.** Indian word for gentleman

THE Elephant LOOKED
NO MORE DANGEROUS THAN A COW

to. (Somehow it always seems worse to kill a large animal.) Besides, there was the beast's owner to be considered. Alive, the elephant was worth at least a hundred pounds; dead, he would have only be worth the value of his tusks, five pounds, possibly. But I had got to act quickly. I turned to some experienced-looking Burmans who had been there when we arrived, and asked them how the elephant had been behaving. They all said the same thing: he took no notice of you if you left him alone, but he might charge if you went too close to him.

What would shooting the elephant be like, according to the narrator?

It was perfectly clear to me what I ought to do. I ought to walk up to within, say, twenty-five yards of the elephant and test his behavior. If he charged, I could shoot; if he took no notice of me, it would be safe to leave him until the mahout came back. But also I know that I was going to do no such thing. I was a poor shot with a rifle and the ground was soft mud into which one would sink at every step. If the elephant charged and I missed him, I should have about as much chance as a toad under a steam-roller. But even then I was not thinking particularly of my own skin, only the watchful yellow faces behind. For at that moment, with the crowd watching me, I was not afraid in the ordinary sense, as I would have been if I had been alone. A white man mustn't be frightened in front of "natives"; and so, in general, he isn't frightened. The sole thought in my mind was that if anything went wrong those two thousand Burmans would see me pursued, caught, trampled on and reduced to a grinning corpse like that Indian up the hill. And if that happened it was quite probable that some of them would laugh. That would never do. There was only one alternative. I shoved the cartridges into the magazine and lay down on the road to get a better aim.

What would be, ultimately, the worst outcome if the narrator did not shoot the elephant and something went wrong?

The crowd grew very still, and a deep, low, happy sigh, as of people who see the theatre curtain go up at last, breathed from innumerable throats. They were going to have their bit of fun after all. The rifle was a beautiful German thing with cross-hair sights. I did not then know that in shooting an elephant one would shoot to cut an imaginary bar running from ear-hole to ear-hole. I ought, therefore, as the elephant was sideways on, to have aimed straight at his ear-hole; actually I aimed several inches in front of this, thinking the brain would be further forward.

When I pulled the trigger I did not hear the bang or feel the kick—one never does when a shot goes home—but I heard the devilish roar of glee that went up from the crowd. In that instant, in too short a time, one would have thought, even for the bullet to get there, a mysterious, terrible change had come over the elephant. He neither stirred nor fell, but every line of his body had altered. He looked suddenly stricken, shrunken, immensely old, as though the frightful impact of the bullet had paralyzed him without knocking him down. At last, after what seemed a long time—it might have been five seconds, I dare say—he sagged flabbily to his knees. His mouth slobbered. An enormous <u>senility</u> seemed to have settled upon him. One could have imagined him thousands of years old. I fired again into the same spot. At the second shot he did not collapse but climbed with desperate slowness to his feet and stood weakly upright, with legs sagging and head drooping. I fired a third time. That was the shot that did for him. You could see the agony of it jolt his

WORDS FOR EVERYDAY USE

se • nil • ity (si ni′ lə tē) *n.*, the physical and mental infirmity of old age. *Ruth firmly believes a healthy diet, exercise, and lots of reading are the keys to fighting <u>senility</u>.*

ANSWERS TO GUIDED READING QUESTIONS

1. It seemed to Orwell that shooting the elephant would be murder.
2. Orwell says, "it was quite probable that some of them would laugh. That would never do."

CROSS-CURRICULAR CONNECTION

Zoology. Orwell has a difficult time killing the elephant due to its enormous size. An elephant calf is born at around 250 pounds. At the age of five, the elephant weighs nearly a ton; and as a full grown adult, an elephant can weigh up to several tons. In order to maintain their size, elephants need to eat 300 pounds of food a day! They do this with the use of their trunk, which has over 40,000 muscles.

ANSWERS TO GUIDED READING QUESTIONS

1. The elephant died slowly and in agony, taking over a half hour.
2. Orwell was glad the coolie had been killed because it gave him a legal justification for what he had done, in shooting the elephant.

SELECTION CHECK TEST 4.11.5 WITH ANSWERS

Checking Your Reading

1. How does Orwell feel about his job? **He hates it.**
2. Who has been killed by the elephant? **The elephant killed an Indian coolie.**
3. What does Orwell know "with perfect certainty" as soon as he sees the elephant? **He knows he shouldn't kill it.**
4. What does a man destroy when he "turns tyrant"? **He destroys his own freedom.**
5. Orwell wonders if anyone grasps the sole reason he shot the elephant. What is it? **He did it to avoid looking a fool.**

Vocabulary in Context

Fill each blank with the most appropriate word from the Words for Everyday Use. You may have to change the tense of the word.

prostrate despotic labyrinth
scored senility pretext

1. The farmer charged admission into the elaborate **labyrinth** he'd built in the cornfield.
2. The baker **scored** the tops of the cookies before he baked them.
3. Our new boss maintains his authority without **despotic** actions.
4. After struggling to finish the marathon, Zander lay **prostrate** on the ground.
5. We all agreed that Ralph's **pretext** for calling us together was flimsy.

Literary Tools

1. "Shooting an Elephant" is a(n)
a. novel
b. biography
c. hort story
d. essay

2. The *thesis* gives
a. the main idea
b. the topic
c. support for an argument
d. the author's reasons

3. What does Orwell find to be ironic?
a. the way the Indians live

whole body and knock the last remnant of strength from his legs. But in falling he seemed from a moment to rise, for as his hind legs collapsed beneath him he seemed to tower upward like a huge rock toppling, his trunk reaching skywards like a tree. He trumpeted, for the first and only time. And then down he came, his belly towards me, with a crash that seemed to shake the ground even where I lay.

I got up. The Burmans were already racing past me across the mud. It was obvious that the elephant would never rise again, but he was not dead. He was breathing very rhythmically with long rattling gasps, his great mound of a side painfully rising and falling. His mouth was wide open—I could see far down into caverns of pale pink throat. I waited a long time for him to die, but his breathing did not weaken. Finally I fired my two remaining shots into the spot where I thought his heart must be. The thick blood welled out of him like red velvet, but still he did not die. His body did not even jerk when the shots hit him, the tortured breathing continued without a pause. He was dying, very slowly and in great agony, but in some world remote from me where not even a bullet could damage him further. I felt that I had got to put an end to that dreadful noise. It seemed dreadful to see the great beast lying there, powerless to move and yet powerless to die, and not even to be able to finish him. I sent back for my small rifle and poured shot after shot into his heart and down his throat. They seemed to make no impression. The tortured gasps continued as steadily as the ticking of a clock.

In the end I could not stand it any longer and went away. I heard later that it took him half an hour to die. Burmans were bringing dahs[12] and baskets even before I left, and I was told they had stripped his body almost to the bones by the afternoon.

How did the elephant die?

Afterwards, of course, there were endless discussions about the shooting of the elephant. The owner was furious, but he was only an Indian and could do nothing. Besides, legally I had done the right thing, for a mad elephant has to be killed, like a mad dog, if its owner fails to control it. Among the Europeans opinion was divided. The older men said I was right, the younger men said it was a damn shame to shoot an elephant for killing a coolie, because an elephant was worth more than any damn Coringhee coolie. And afterwards I was very glad that the coolie had been killed; it put me legally in the right and it gave me a sufficient <u>pretext</u> for shooting the elephant. I often wondered whether any of the other grasped that I had done it solely to avoid looking a fool. ■

Why was the narrator glad the coolie had been killed?

12. **dahs.** Butcher knives

WORDS FOR EVERYDAY USE

pre • text (prē tekst) *n.*, an appearance assumed in order to disguise the truth. *Lily went into the store under the <u>pretext</u> of buying some gum, but she really just wanted to talk to James.*

Respond *to the* **SELECTION**

How would you act if you were placed in the same situation as the narrator in the story?

SELECTION CHECK TEST 4.11.5 WITH ANSWERS (CONT.)

b. the Indians' opinion of his role in the Empire
c. the size of the elephant
d. the order to shoot the elephant

4. From what point of view is this selection written?
a. first-person
b. second-person
c. third-person omniscient
d. third-person limited

5. Which of the following is described with the most detail?
a. the palace in which the Raj lived
b. the bazaar through which the elephant has trampled
c. Orwell's selection of the perfect weapon
d. the elephant's death

INVESTIGATE,

Inquire, Imagine

Recall: Gathering Facts →

1a. What step did the narrator take as soon as he saw the dead man?

2a. Why did the crowd follow the narrator as he searched for the elephant? How did this make him feel?

3a. What did the narrator know as soon as he saw the elephant?

Interpret: Finding Meaning

1b. How did this action set in motion a chain of events that led to the shooting of the elephant?

2b. Why did he feel this way?

3b. Why did he come to this conclusion?

Analyze: Taking Things Apart →

4a. Analyze the narrator's attitude toward imperialism and toward his role in the Empire. What is the narrator's judgement of imperialism? What conflicting feelings does he have toward the Burmese people as a result of the situation they are in?

Synthesize: Bringing Things Together

4b. What is it about the nature of imperialism that leads him to this conclusion? How does this form of government differ from our democracy?

Evaluate: Making Judgments →

5a. Evaluate the narrator's decision to shoot the elephant. Did he do the right thing? Why, or why not? Support your answer.

Extend: Connecting Ideas

5b. How would the story have been different if the narrator had lain down his rifle and quit his job rather than shoot the elephant? What does the narrator mean when he says he "grasped the hollowness, the futility of the white man's dominion in the East"?

Understanding Literature

Thesis. Review the definition for **thesis** in the Handbook of Literary Terms. What do you think is the main thesis of "Shooting An Elephant?" Do you think this story is an effective way to explore this thesis?

Irony. Review the definition of **irony** in the Handbook of Literary Terms. In what situations in this essay does appearance differ from reality? How does this use of irony contribute to the development of the main thesis or other statements expressed in the essay? Use the graphic organizer below as a guide for organizing your thoughts about the questions above.

appearance	reality	contributes to thesis
Narrator is a police officer for the Imperial Crown, a symbol of the British Empire	"As for the job I was doing, I hated it more bitterly than I can perhaps make clear. In a job like that you see the dirty work of the Empire at close quarters."	one's actions don't always correspond with one's beliefs/what is touted a being in the best interest of "the people" isn't always in the interest of *all* the people.

RESPOND TO THE SELECTION

Imagine you are a member of the crowd. Would you have tried to stop Orwell from shooting the elephant or would you have become caught up in its excitement?

ANSWERS TO INVESTIGATE, INQUIRE, AND IMAGINE

Recall

1a. As soon as he saw the dead man, the narrator sent an orderly to get him an elephant rifle.

2a. The crowd followed the narrator because he had ordered a gun, and they were excited, anticipating the entertainment of a shooting. This made the narrator "uneasy."

3a. As soon as he saw the elephant, the narrator knew that he should not shoot it.

Interpret

1b. This action created the expectation of a shooting in the minds of townspeople; their expectations made the narrator feel as though he had to shoot the elephant so as not to disappoint them, appear weak or afraid.

2b. The narrator felt uneasy because he originally had no intention of shooting the elephant, but felt the crowd willing him to do it.

3b. The narrator didn't want to shoot the elephant; he saw that the elephant had calmed down and no longer posed a threat to property or human life, and he knew the owner of the elephant would be angry with him for shooting it.

Analyze

4a. Orwell feels that imperialism is an unjust system that oppresses the colonized and the colonizer. He says, "when the white man turns tyrant it is his own freedom that he destroys" sympathy for the Burmese as victims of an unjust system, yet at the same time he feels hatred for them because they bait and jeer at him and other Europeans.

Synthesize

4b. In imperialism, a ruling country must hold power over its colony. The colonials are not allowed participation in the way they are governed, as we are in our own democratic form of government. Therefore, they are ruled without their consent and some form of power must be exercised over them—either physical force, economic force, or the force of intimidation.

Evaluate

5a. *Responses will vary.* Some students will think he made the wrong decision because he acted in opposition to his own conscience. Others may judge that Orwell had no choice but to act as he did to avoid chaos and to keep his job.

(Continued on page 1018)

ANSWERS TO INVESTIGATE, INQUIRE, AND IMAGINE
(CONT. FROM PAGE 1017)

EXTEND

5b. *Responses will vary.* The "hollowness, the futility of the white man's dominion in the East" refers to the fact that the white man's "power" is only an illusion. In fact, the situation in which both the British and the Burmese found themselves enslaved them both.

ANSWERS TO UNDERSTANDING LITERATURE

THESIS. The main idea of this essay is that the exercise of unjust power by one group of people over another group actually imprisons both groups of people.

IRONY. In this essay, Orwell appears to be in power, as he is a police officer in uniform with a gun, seemingly controlling the situation. In fact, the crowd is in control of him, as he notes when he says he was "seemingly the leading actor of the piece; but in reality I was only an absurd puppet pushed to and fro by the will of those yellow faces behind." In another instance, the elephant is supposedly a terrifying threat to life and property and yet it is described as having a "grandmotherly air" and being "shrunken, immensely old" and therefore is not threat at all.

ANSWERS TO INTEGRATING THE LANGUAGE ARTS

Language, Grammar, and Style

Responses will vary.

1. Having already picked up a gun, Orwell had to proceed to shoot the elephant.
2. The elephant slumped to the ground in slow motion.
3. Many European police officers were hated by the Burmese.
4. Shot but not killed, the elephant began to roar.
5. In a clamoring mob, the villagers gathered around Orwell.

Study and Research

To help students successfully conduct their research, refer them to the Language Arts Survey 5.19, "How to Locate Library Materials" and 5.26, "Using the Internet."

WRITER'S JOURNAL

1. Write for a British newspaper, the **newspaper headline** that might accompany the article the following day about the shooting of the elephant. Write the headline that might appear in a newspaper written and controlled by the Burmese.
2. Imagine that you are Orwell. Write up an official **police report** of the elephant shooting incident for your superiors in the Imperial Police.
3. Write the **opening paragraph of a personal essay** expressing your opinion on the issue of imperialism.

Integrating *the* LANGUAGE ARTS

Language, Grammar, and Style

REDUCING WORDINESS. Wordy sentences are cluttered and unclear. Orwell writes in a very simple and direct style, which gives his writing power and energy. Rewrite the following sentences. Eliminate the unnecessary words that clutter each sentence, but be sure to maintain the original meaning.

1. Having already picked up a gun, Orwell feared he had no choice but to proceed with his original intention to shoot the elephant.
2. The old, flabby, elderly elephant gradually slumped to the ground, in slow motion.
3. Many Europeans were hated by the Burmese because they were police officers.
4. Having been shot but not killed, the elephant began to roar.
5. The people of the village gathered around Orwell in a loud, clamoring mob.

Study and Research

A BRIEF HISTORY OF BURMA. Using library and/or Internet resources, research the history of British involvement in Burma. How and when did Great Britain first become involved in Burma, and what conflicts arose during Britain's rule there? How did British rule come to an end? What roles did religious and cultural differences play in this conflict? How is Burma (Myanmar) ruled today? Prepare a report for your class.

Speaking and Listening

CONDUCTING A DEBATE. Conduct a debate in class on the following statement: Imperialism has been a force for economic growth and positive change in the world. In preparation for this debate, you may find it helpful to review Language Arts Survey 4.21, Participating in a Debate, and the Pros and Cons chart in Language Arts Survey 5.1, "Making Decisions and Solving Problems." You will need to form two teams: one will argue the "pro" or supporting case, and one will argue the "con" or refuting case.

"The Garden-Party"

BY KATHERINE MANSFIELD

About the AUTHOR

Katherine Mansfield (1888–1923) was born in Wellington, New Zealand. In 1903, she moved to London with her family and stayed to study music at Queen's College. There she met and became friends with D. H. Lawrence and Aldous Huxley, who encouraged her to write. Mansfield returned to New Zealand in 1906, having written numerous poems, sketches, and short stories. Rebellious and ambitious by nature, Mansfield went back to London in 1908 and never returned to New Zealand. Mansfield's first volume of short stories, *In a German Pension*, was published in 1911. One year later, she met the editor and critic John Middleton Murry, whom she married in 1918. Throughout this time, Mansfield experimented with technique, refining her work to achieve a short story that would evoke insights into particular experiences through patterns of precise imagery and style. She was an ardent admirer of the stories of the Russian writer Anton Chekhov. Her grief over the death of her brother in 1915 seemed to infuse her writing with freshness and greater subtlety. During this time she produced her best stories: "Prelude," "Daughters of the Late Colonel," "At the Bay," and "The Garden-Party." Her collection *Prelude*, published in 1918, was followed two years later by *Bliss and Other Stories*. By the time of the 1922 publication of *The Garden-Party and Other Stories*, which assured Mansfield's place as a master of the short story, she was already gravely ill with tuberculosis. She died in France in 1923.

About the SELECTION

Considered to be one of her best stories, **"The Garden-Party"** was written at a time when Mansfield was looking back at her childhood experiences in New Zealand. One of the events on which Mansfield focused was a garden party given by her mother in the spring of 1907. The basis of her story was a fatal street accident that occurred to a neighbor in the midst of the festivities. The selection shows Mansfield's ability to combine incident, image, symbol, and structure to clarify her protagonist, Laura, and to capture the essential poignance of the story.

Literary TOOLS

IMAGE AND OBJECTIVE CORRELATIVE. An **image** is language that creates a concrete representation of an object or an experience. An image is also the vivid mental picture created in the reader's mind by that language. An **objective correlative** is a group of images that together create a particular emotion in the reader. As you read, pay close attention to the images used to describe the party preparations in this story.

SYMBOL. A **symbol** is a thing that stands for or represents both itself and something else. As you read, pay attention to how the hat Laura's mother gives her functions as a symbol in the story.

Reader's Journal

Recall an experience that you or someone close to you has had that caused you to look at your life in a new way. In your journal, write about the experience and how it altered your perspective.

ADDITIONAL RESOURCES

UNIT 11 RESOURCE BOOK
- Selection Worksheet 11.4
- Selection Check Test 4.11.7
- Selection Test 4.11.8
- Reading Resource 1.19

VOCABULARY FROM THE SELECTION

baize	rapturous
enigmatically	sordid
haggard	stave
marquee	veranda

READER'S JOURNAL

Suggest that students list adjectives and adverbs that reflect how they felt before and after their life-changing experience.

GOALS/OBJECTIVES

Studying this lesson will enable students to
- empathize with Laura's distress, concern, and discomfort
- describe Katherine Mansfield's contribution to twentieth-century literature and how her writing reflects the social atmosphere of the time
- define *image, objective correlative*, and *symbol* and recognize and explain examples of each that they encounter in their reading
- identify base words and suffixes

ANSWER TO GUIDED READING QUESTION

1. The weather and the roses that had opened overnight were "ideal." The gardener was mowing and sweeping the lawns to prepare for the party.

INDIVIDUAL LEARNING STRATEGIES

MOTIVATION
Plan a garden party with your students. If you cannot go outdoors, use your school gym. Who will be invited? What will the invitations say? What kind of refreshments will you have? How will you decorate the gym/outside area? What will there be for entertainment? The plans for this garden party could be used as an end of the school year party or end of the semester party.

READING PROFICIENCY
Students who are not a comfortable and familiar with the language might not realize the slightly satirical tone of the portrayal of the middle class. Have students look up satire in the Handbook of Literary terms. Then discuss this aspect of the story with them.

ENGLISH LANGUAGE LEARNING
With the additional vocabulary words listed below, ask students to draw pictures that reflect the definition of each word. This activity will especially be helpful for visual and kinesthetic learners.

Additional Vocabulary
kimono—a woman's loose dressing gown
lanky—tall and lean
affected—artificial to impress people
exquisite—very beautiful
alight—come down after flight
frock—a girl's or woman's dress

SPECIAL NEEDS
Have students focus on the Guided Reading Questions. Then with a partner, discuss what they read.

ENRICHMENT
Refer students to the historical information about the Georgian Age on page 894. Then have student research the social conditions in England during this period.

The Garden-Party

KATHERINE MANSFIELD

And after all the weather was ideal. They could not have had a more perfect day for a garden-party if they had ordered it. Windless, warm, the sky without a cloud. Only the blue was veiled with a haze of light gold, as it is sometimes in early summer. The gardener had been up since dawn, mowing the lawns and sweeping them, until the grass and the dark flat rosettes where the daisy plants had been seemed to shine. As for the roses, you could not help feeling they understood that roses are the only flowers that impress people at garden-parties; the only flowers that everybody is certain of knowing. Hundreds, yes, literally hundreds, had come out in a single night; the green bushes bowed down as though they had been visited by archangels.

In what way was the day "ideal"? What was the gardener doing to prepare for the party?

Breakfast was not yet over before the men came to put up the marquee.

"Where do you want the marquee put, mother?"

"My dear child, it's no use asking me. I'm determined to leave everything to you children this year. Forget I am your mother. Treat me as an honored guest."

But Meg could not possibly go and supervise the men. She had washed her hair before breakfast, and she sat drinking her coffee in a green turban, with a dark wet curl stamped on each cheek. Jose, the butterfly, always came down in a silk petticoat and a kimono jacket.

"You'll have to go, Laura; you're the artistic one."

Away Laura flew, still holding her piece of bread-and-butter. It's so delicious to have an excuse for eating out of doors, and besides, she loved having to arrange things; she always felt she could do it so much better than anybody else.

WORDS FOR EVERYDAY USE
mar • quee (mär kē´) *n.*, tent with open sides. *When the rain began falling, the garden-party guests took shelter under the marquee.*

Four men in their shirt-sleeves stood grouped together on the garden path. They carried staves covered with rolls of canvas, and they had big tool-bags slung on their backs. They looked impressive. Laura wished now that she had not got the bread-and-butter, but there was nowhere to put it, and she couldn't possibly throw it away. She blushed and tried to look severe and even a little bit short-sighted as she came up to them.

"Good morning," she said, copying her mother's voice. But that sounded so fearfully affected that she was ashamed, and stammered like a little girl, "Oh—er—have you come—is it about the marquee?"

Whose voice does Laura imitate when she speaks to the workers? Why does she feel ashamed?

"That's right, miss," said the tallest of the men, a lanky, freckled fellow, and he shifted his tool-bag, knocked back his straw hat and smiled down at her. "That's about it."

His smile was so easy, so friendly that Laura recovered. What nice eyes he had, small, but such a dark blue! And now she looked at the others, they were smiling too. "Cheer up, we won't bite," their smile seemed to say. How very nice workmen were! And what a beautiful morning! she mustn't mention the morning; she must be businesslike. The marquee.

"Well, what about the lily-lawn? Would that do?"

And she pointed to the lily-lawn with the hand that didn't hold the bread-and-butter. They turned, they stared in the direction. A little fat chap thrust out his under-lip, and the tall fellow frowned.

"I don't fancy it," said he. "Not conspicuous enough. You see, with a thing like a marquee," and he turned to Laura in his easy way, "you want to put it somewhere where it'll give you a bang slap in the eye, if you follow me."

Laura's upbringing made her wonder for a moment whether it was quite respectful of a workman to talk to her of bangs slap in the eye. But she did quite follow him.

What does Laura wonder?

"A corner of the tennis-court," she suggested. "But the band's going to be in one corner."

"H'm, going to have a band, are you?" said another of the workmen. He was pale. He had a haggard look as his dark eyes scanned the tennis-court. What was he thinking?

"Only a very small band," said Laura gently. Perhaps he wouldn't mind so much if the band was quite small. But the tall fellow interrupted.

"Look here, miss, that's the place. Against those trees. Over there. That'll do fine."

Against the karakas. Then the karaka-trees would be hidden. And they were so lovely, with their broad, gleaming leaves, and their clusters of yellow fruit. They were like trees you imagined growing on a desert island, proud, solitary, lifting their leaves and fruits to the sun in a kind of silent splendor. Must they be hidden by a marquee?

They must. Already the men had shouldered their staves and were making for the place. Only the tall fellow was left. He bent down, pinched a sprig of lavender, put his thumb and forefinger to his nose and snuffed up the smell. When Laura saw that gesture she forgot all about the karakas in her wonder at him caring for things like that—caring for the smell of lavender. How many men that she knew would have done such a thing? Oh, how extraordinarily nice workmen were, she thought. Why couldn't she have workmen for friends rather than the silly boys she danced with and who came to Sunday night supper? She would get on much better with men like these.

What surprises Laura about the workman?

WORDS FOR EVERYDAY USE

stave (stāv) *n.*, pole. *After the heavy rain, the staves that supported the tent were stuck in the mud.*

hag • gard (hag´ərd) *adj.*, worn, gaunt. *The haggard student had stayed up all night cramming for the exam.*

ANSWERS TO GUIDED READING QUESTIONS

1. Laura imitates her mother's voice. She feels ashamed because her imitation sounds pretentious.
2. Laura wonders if it is respectable for a workman to use slang when speaking to her.
3. Laura is surprised that the workman stops to smell the lavender.

ADDITIONAL QUESTIONS AND ACTIVITIES

What has Laura's upbringing taught her about working people, how they behave, and what her relationship to them should be?

Answer

Laura's upbringing emphasized class differences. She is concerned that she "must be businesslike" and wonders "for a moment whether it was quite respectful of a workman to talk to her of bangs slap in the eye." She is concerned about the propriety of eating in front of them. She might have learned that working-class people are unrefined or that they expect, or need, to receive orders from people of her social class.

ANSWERS TO GUIDED READING QUESTIONS

1. Laura takes a big bite of her bread and butter to prove how comfortable she feels with the workmen and how much she despises the "stupid conventions" of her social class.
2. Laura discusses lunch plans and clothing with her friend.

LITERARY TECHNIQUE

Dramatic Irony. The difference between appearance and reality is called irony, and **dramatic irony** is when something is known by the reader but unknown to the characters. Laura took a bite of the bread-and-butter "just to show the tall fellow how at home she felt" and "felt just like a work-girl" after doing so. Have students discuss how Laura's action and thoughts are an example of dramatic irony.

Answer

Her action and thoughts are ironic because she is not a work-girl; she is watching the workmen work. Although Laura claims she feels free of the "absurd class distinctions," the tall fellow, busily drawing the design for the marquee, is probably unaware of her actions.

It's all the fault, she decided, as the tall fellow drew something on the back of an envelope, something that was to be looped up or left to hang, of these absurd class distinctions. Well, for her part, she didn't feel them. Not a bit, not an atom. . . . And now there came the chock-chock of wooden hammers. Some one whistled, some one sang out, "Are you right there, matey?" "Matey!" The friendliness of it, the—the—Just to prove how happy she was, just to show the tall fellow how at home she felt, and how she despised stupid conventions, Laura took a big bite of her bread-and-butter as she stared at the little drawing. She felt just like a work-girl.

Why does Laura take a big bite of her bread-and-butter?

"Laura, Laura, where are you? Telephone, Laura!" a voice cried from the house.

"Coming!" Away she skimmed, over the lawn, up the path, up the steps, across the <u>veranda</u>, and into the porch. In the hall her father and Laurie were brushing their hats ready to go to the office.

"I say, Laura," said Laurie very fast, "you might just give a squiz at my coat before this afternoon. See if it wants pressing."

"I will," said she. Suddenly she couldn't stop herself. She ran at Laurie and gave him a small, quick squeeze. "Oh, I do love parties, don't you?" gasped Laura.

"Ra-ther," said Laurie's warm, boyish voice, and he squeezed his sister too, and gave her a gentle push. "Dash off to the telephone, old girl."

The telephone. "Yes, yes; oh yes. Kitty? Good morning, dear. Come to lunch? Do, dear. Delighted of course. It will only be a very scratch meal—just the sandwich crusts and broken meringue-shells and what's left over. Yes, isn't it a perfect morning? Your white? Oh, I certainly should. One moment—hold the line. Mother's calling." And Laura sat back. "What, mother? Can't hear."

What does Laura discuss with her friend over the phone?

Mrs. Sheridan's voice floated down the stairs. "Tell her to wear that sweet hat she had on last Sunday."

"Mother says you're to wear that *sweet* hat you had on last Sunday. Good. One o'clock. Bye-bye."

Laura put back the receiver, flung her arms over her head, took a deep breath, stretched and let them fall. "Huh," she sighed, and the moment after the sigh she sat up quickly. She was still, listening. All the doors in the house seemed to be open. The house was alive with soft, quick steps and running voices. The green <u>baize</u> door that led to the kitchen regions swung open and shut with a muffled thud. And now there came a long, chuckling absurd sound. It was the heavy piano being moved on its stiff castors. But the air! If you stopped to notice, was the air always like this? Little faint winds were playing chase, in at the tops of the windows, out at the doors. And there were two tiny spots of sun, one on the inkpot, one on a silver photograph frame, playing too. Darling little spots. Especially the one on the inkpot lid.

"Oh, I do love parties, don't you?"

Words for Everyday Use

ve • ran • da (və ran´də) *n.*, open porch. *Standing on the <u>veranda</u>, one can see across the vast lawn.*

baize (bāz) *n.*, woolen or cotton fabric made to resemble felt. *The <u>baize</u> covering on the card table prevents cards from slipping.*

It was quite warm. A warm little silver star. She could have kissed it.

The front door bell pealed, and there sounded the rustle of Sadie's print skirt on the stairs. A man's voice murmured; Sadie answered, careless, "I'm sure I don't know. Wait. I'll ask Mrs. Sheridan."

"What is it, Sadie?" Laura came into the hall.

"It's the florist, Miss Laura."

It was, indeed. There, just inside the door, stood a wide, shallow tray full of pots of pink lilies. No other kind. Nothing but lilies—canna lilies, big pink flowers, wide open, radiant, almost frighteningly alive on bright crimson stems.

"O-oh, Sadie!" said Laura, and the sound was like a little moan. She crouched down as if to warm herself at that blaze of lilies; she felt they were in her fingers, on her lips, growing in her breast.

"It's some mistake," she said faintly. "Nobody ever ordered so many. Sadie, go and find mother."

But at that moment Mrs. Sheridan joined them.

"It's quite right," she said calmly. "Yes, I ordered them. Aren't they lovely?" She pressed Laura's arm. "I was passing the shop yesterday, and I saw them in the window. And I suddenly thought for once in my life I shall have enough canna lilies. The garden-party will be a good excuse."

What mistake does Laura think has been made? How does Mother respond?

"But I thought you said you didn't mean to interfere," said Laura. Sadie had gone. The florist's man was still outside at his van. She put her arm round her mother's neck and gently, very gently, she bit her mother's ear.

"My darling child, you wouldn't like a logical mother, would you? Don't do that. Here's the man."

He carried more lilies still, another whole tray.

"Bank them up, just inside the door, on both sides of the porch, please," said Mrs. Sheridan. "Don't you agree, Laura?"

"Oh, I *do* mother."

In the drawing-room Meg, Jose and good little Hans had at last succeeded in moving the piano.

"Now, if we put this chesterfield against the wall and move everything out of the room except the chairs, don't you think?"

"Quite."

"Hans, move these tables into the smoking-room, and bring a sweeper to take these marks off the carpet and—one moment, Hans—" Jose loved giving orders to the servants, and they loved obeying her. She always made them feel they were taking part in some drama. "Tell mother and Miss Laura to come here at once."

Why does the narrator say the servants liked taking orders from Jose?

"Very good, Miss Jose."

She turned to Meg. "I want to hear what the piano sounds like, just in case I'm asked to sing this afternoon. Let's try over 'This life is Weary.'"

Pom! Ta-ta-ta *Tee*-ta! The piano burst out so passionately that Jose's face changed. She clasped her hands. She looked mournfully and enigmatically at her mother and Laura as they came in.

This Life is *Wee*-ary,
A Tear—a Sigh.
A Love that *Chan*-ges,
This Life is *Wee*-ary,
A Tear—a Sigh.
A Love that *Chan*-ges,
And then . . . Good-bye!

WORDS FOR EVERYDAY USE

en • ig • mat • i • cal • ly (en´ig mat´ik lē) *adv.*, in a perplexed manner. *Do you ever wonder why the Mona Lisa smiles so enigmatically?*

ANSWERS TO GUIDED READING QUESTIONS

1. Laura thinks the men have delivered far too many flowers, but Mother tells her she decided to have, for once, "enough" canna lilies.
2. The narrator says the servants liked taking orders from Jose because she always made them feel like they were participating in something dramatic.

LITERARY TECHNIQUE

CHARACTERIZATION. Characterization is the use of literary techniques to create a character. One way of creating a character is through the portrayal of a character's behavior, using the actions and speech of the character. Students can discuss what Mrs. Sheridan's actions and speech in the scene about the canna lilies reveal about her character.

ANSWERS TO GUIDED READING QUESTIONS

1. Jose breaks into a huge smile at the end of her song.
2. Fifteen kinds of sandwiches are made for the party.

ADDITIONAL QUESTIONS AND ACTIVITIES

Mrs. Sheridan's plans for the garden-party are whimsical and unorganized. Ask students to consider why she is able to plan this way. Then have students continue to work on the plans for the garden party as suggested under Motivation in the Individual Learning Strategies. They should set aside a budget and determine who will do what in order to prepare for the party.

What does Jose do at the end of the song?

But at the word "Good-bye," and although the piano sounded more desperate than ever, her face broke into a brilliant, dreadfully unsympathetic smile.

"Aren't I in good voice, mummy?" she beamed.

> This Life is *Wee*-ary,
> Hope comes to Die.
> A Dream—a *Wa*-kening.

But now Sadie interrupted them. "What is it, Sadie?"

"If you please, m'm, cook says have you got the flags for the sandwiches?"

"The flags for the sandwiches, Sadie?" echoed Mrs. Sheridan dreamily. And the children knew by her face that she hadn't got them. "Let me see." And she said to Sadie firmly, "Tell cook I'll let her have them in ten minutes."

Sadie went.

"Now, Laura," said her mother quickly. "Come with me into the smoking-room. I've got the names somewhere on the back of an envelope. You'll have to write them out for me. Meg, go upstairs this minute and take that wet thing off your head. Jose, run and finish dressing this instant. Do you hear me, children, or shall I have to tell your father when he comes home to-night? And—and, Jose, pacify cook if you do go into the kitchen, will you? I'm terrified of her this morning."

The envelope was found at last behind the dining-room clock, though how it had got there Mrs. Sheridan could not imagine.

"One of you children must have stolen it out of my bag, because I remember vividly—cream cheese and lemon-curd. Have you done that?"

"Yes."

"Egg and—" Mrs. Sheridan held the envelope away from her. "It looks like mice. It can't be mice, can it?"

"Olive, pet," said Laura, looking over her shoulder.

"Yes, of course, olive. What a horrible combination it sounds. Egg and olive."

They were finished at last, and Laura took them off to the kitchen. She found Jose there pacifying the cook, who did not look at all terrifying.

"I have never seen such exquisite sandwiches," said Jose's rapturous voice. "How many kinds did you say there were, cook? Fifteen?"

How many different kinds of sandwiches have been made for the party?

"Fifteen, Miss Jose."

"Well, cook, I congratulate you."

Cook swept up crusts with the long sandwich knife, and smiled broadly.

"Godber's has come," announced Sadie, issuing out of the pantry. She had seen the man pass the window.

That meant the cream puffs had come. Godber's were famous for their cream puffs. Nobody ever thought of making them at home.

"Bring them in and put them on the table, my girl," ordered cook.

Sadie brought them in and went back to the door. Of course Laura and Jose were far too grown-up to really care about such things. All the same, they couldn't help agreeing that the puffs looked very attractive. Very. Cook began arranging them, shaking off the extra icing sugar.

"Don't they carry one back to all one's parties?" said Laura.

WORDS FOR EVERYDAY USE

rap • tur • ous (rap´chər əs) *adj.,* full of pleasure. *The rapturous sounds of the Mozart concerto filled the symphony hall.*

The Idlers, c.1916–18. Maurice Prendergast. Maier Museum of Art, Randolph-Macon Woman's College, Lynchburg, VA.

"I suppose they do," said practical Jose, who never liked to be carried back. "They look beautifully light and feathery, I must say."

"Have one each, my dears," said cook in her comfortable voice. "Yer ma won't know."

Oh, impossible. Fancy cream puffs so soon after breakfast. The very idea made one shudder. All the same, two minutes later Jose and Laura were licking their fingers with that absorbed inward look that only comes from whipped cream.

"Let's go into the garden, out by the back way," suggested Laura. "I want to see how the men are getting on with the marquee. They're such awfully nice men."

But the back door was blocked by cook, Sadie, Godber's man and Hans.

Something had happened.

"Tuk-tuk-tuk," clucked cook like an agitated hen. Sadie had her hand clapped to her cheek as though she had toothache. Hans's face was screwed up in the effort to understand. Only Godber's man seemed to be enjoying himself; it was his story.

"What's the matter? What's happened?"

"There's been a horrible accident," said Cook. "A man killed."

"A man killed! Where? How? When?"

But Godber's man wasn't going to have his story snatched from under his very nose.

"Know those little cottages just below here, miss?" Know them? Of course, she knew them. "Well, there's a young chap living there, name of Scott, a carter. His horse shied at a traction-engine, corner of Hawke Street this morning, and he was thrown out on the back of his head. Killed."

What happened to the man? Why is this incident especially tragic?

"Dead!" Laura stared at Godber's man.

ANSWER TO GUIDED READING QUESTION

1. The man was thrown from his horse and killed instantly. The incident is especially tragic because the man left behind a wife and five children.

ART NOTE

Maurice Prendergast (1859–1924) was born in Newfoundland. He studied in Paris and was influenced by the French Imperialists. Although Prendergast is widely known as a watercolorist, in his later life he worked mainly with oils, as in the painting The Idlers. Ask students to compare the attitudes and lifestyles of the people in the painting to those of the people in the story.

ANSWERS TO GUIDED READING QUESTIONS

1. Laura and Laurie sometimes walk by the cottages because "one must go everywhere; one must see everything."
2. Jose assumes that he was drunk.

ADDITIONAL QUESTIONS AND ACTIVITIES

Have students use a comparison and contrast chart to compare and contrast the description of the cottages in the lane to the Sheridan property. Refer them to the Language Arts Survey, 4.8, "Comparing and Contrasting."

What do Jose's comments about the cause of the workman's death reveal about her beliefs about the working class?

Answer

Jose's assumption that the workman was drunk reveals that she believes the working class is generally unruly.

"Dead when they picked him up," said Godber's man with relish. "They were taking the body home as I come up here." And he said to the cook, "He's left a wife and five little ones."

"Jose, come here." Laura caught hold of her sister's sleeve and dragged her through the kitchen to the other side of the green baize door. There she paused and leaned against it. "Jose!" she said, horrified, "however are we going to stop everything?"

"Stop everything, Laura!" cried Jose in astonishment. "What do you mean?"

"Stop the garden-party, of course." Why did Jose pretend?

But Jose was still more amazed. "Stop the garden-party? My dear Laura, don't be so absurd. Of course we can't do anything of the kind. Nobody expects us to. Don't be so extravagant."

"But we can't possibly have a garden-party with a man dead just outside the front gate."

That really was extravagant, for the little cottages were in a lane to themselves at the very bottom of a steep rise that led up to the house. A broad road ran between. True, they were far too near. They were the greatest possible eyesore, and they had no right to be in that neighborhood at all. They were little mean dwellings painted a chocolate brown. In the garden patches there was nothing but cabbage stalks, sick hens and tomato cans. The very smoke coming out of their chimneys was poverty-stricken. Little rags and shreds of smoke, so unlike the great silvery plumes that uncurled from the Sheridans' chimneys. Washerwomen lived in the lane and sweeps and a cobbler, and a man whose house-front was studded all over with minute bird-cages. Children swarmed. When the Sheridans were little they were forbidden to set foot there because of the revolting language and of what they might catch. But since they were grown up, Laura and Laurie on their prowls sometimes walked through. It was disgusting and sordid. They came out with a shudder. But still one must go everywhere; one must see everything. So through they went.

Why do Laura and Laurie sometimes walk by the cottages?

"And just think of what the band would sound like to that poor woman," said Laura.

"Oh, Laura!" Jose began to be seriously annoyed. "If you're going to stop a band playing every time some one has an accident, you'll lead a very strenuous life. I'm every bit as sorry about it as you. I feel just as sympathetic." Her eyes hardened. She looked at her sister just as she used to when they were little and fighting together. "You won't bring a drunken workman back to life by being sentimental," she said softly.

What does Jose assume about the workman who was killed?

"Drunk! Who said he was drunk?" Laura turned furiously on Jose. She said, just as they had used to say on those occasions, "I'm going straight up to tell mother."

"Do, dear," cooed Jose.

"Mother, can I come into your room?" Laura turned the big glass doorknob.

"Of course, child. Why, what's the matter? What's given you such a color?" And Mrs. Sheridan turned round from her dressing-table. She was trying on a new hat.

"Mother, a man's been killed," began Laura.

"*Not* in the garden?" interrupted her mother.

"No, no!"

"Oh, what a fright you gave me!" Mrs. Sheridan sighed with relief, and took off the big hat and held it on her knees.

WORDS FOR EVERYDAY USE

sor • did (sôr´did) *adj.*, dirty, wretched. *The mayor condemned slum landlords for the sordid living conditions in parts of the city.*

"But listen, mother," said Laura. Breathless, half-choking, she told the dreadful story. "Of course, we can't have our party, can we?" she pleaded. "The band and everybody arriving. They'd hear us, mother; they're nearly neighbors!"

How does Laura's mother first react to the news of the man's death?

To Laura's astonishment her mother behaved just like Jose, it was harder to bear because she seemed amused. She refused to take Laura seriously.

"But, my dear child, use your common sense. It's only by accident we've heard of it. If some one had died there normally— and I can't understand how they keep alive in those poky little holes—we should still be having our party, shouldn't we?"

Laura had to say "yes" to that, but she felt it was all wrong. She sat down on her mother's sofa and pinched the cushion frill.

"Mother, isn't it really terribly heartless of us?" she asked.

"Darling!" Mrs. Sheridan got up and came over to her, carrying the hat. Before Laura could stop her she had popped it on. "My child!" said her mother, "the hat is yours. It's made for you. It's much too young for me. I have never seen you look such a picture. Look at yourself!" And she held up her hand-mirror.

"But, mother," Laura began again. She couldn't look at herself; she turned aside.

This time Mrs. Sheridan lost patience just as Jose had done.

"You are being very absurd, Laura," she said coldly. "People like that don't expect sacrifices from us. And it's not very sympathetic to spoil everybody's enjoyment as you're doing now."

What does Laura's mother accuse her of doing?

"I don't understand," said Laura, and she walked quickly out of the room into her own bedroom. There, quite by chance, the first thing she saw was this charming girl in the mirror, in her black hat trimmed with gold daisies, and a long black velvet ribbon. Never had she imagined she could look like that. Is mother right? she thought. And now she hoped her mother was right. Am I being extravagant? Perhaps it was extravagant. Just for a moment she had another glimpse of that poor woman and those little children, and the body being carried into the house. But it all seemed blurred, unreal, like a picture in the newspaper. I'll remember it again after the party's over, she decided. And somehow that seemed quite the best plan. . . .

What struggle is taking place in Laura's mind? What does she finally decide is the best plan?

Lunch was over by half-past one. By half-past two they were all ready for the fray. The green-coated band had arrived and was established in a corner of the tennis-court.

"My dear!" trilled Kitty Maitland, "aren't they too like frogs for words? You ought to have arranged them round the pond with the conductor in the middle on a leaf."

Laurie arrived and hailed them on his way to dress. At the sight of him Laura remembered the accident again. She wanted to tell him. If Laurie agreed with the others, then it was bound to be all right. And she followed him into the hall.

"Laurie!"

"Hallo!" He was half-way upstairs, but when he turned round and saw Laura he suddenly puffed out his cheeks and goggled his eyes at her. "My word, Laura; you do look stunning," said Laurie. "What an absolutely topping hat!"

Laura said faintly "Is it?" and smiled up at Laurie, and didn't tell him after all.

Soon after that people began coming in streams. The band struck up; the hired waiters ran from the house to the marquee. Wherever you looked there were couples strolling, bending to the flowers, greeting, moving on over the lawn.

ANSWERS TO GUIDED READING QUESTIONS

1. At first, Laura's mother is worried that the man has died in their garden.
2. She tells Laura that the party must go on despite their news of hearing someone died
3. Mother accuses Laura of spoiling everyone's enjoyment by her expression of concern for their neighbors in the cottages.
4. Laura struggles with the difference between her reaction to the tragedy and her mother's assessment of her behavior. She finally decides that the best plan is to forget about it until after the party.

CROSS-CURRICULAR ACTIVITIES

Location and dress are very important in this story. Students can prepare set or costume designs as though the story were to be presented as a play.

ANSWER TO GUIDED READING QUESTION

1. Mother suggests sending lilies because she says "people of that class are so impressed by lilies. Laura decides not to bring the lilies because Jose points out that the stems might ruin Laura's dress.

ADDITIONAL QUESTIONS AND ACTIVITIES

"Again, how curious, she seemed to be different from them all." How do Laura's ideas on the situation at hand differ from the ideas of the rest of her family? What other examples of Laura's difference appear throughout the story? Why do you think Laura is different?

Answers

Laura, unlike the rest of her family, does not think it a good idea to bring leftover party food to the grieving family. Laura also differs from her family in her treatment of workers, her attitudes toward the poor in general, and mainly in her reaction to the tragic accident. Laura's reaction may be different because she is especially sensitive, or because she has not yet learned all of the expectations and rules of her class.

They were like bright birds that had alighted in the Sheridans' garden for this one afternoon, on their way to—where? Ah, what happiness it is to be with people who all are happy, to press hands, press cheeks, smile into eyes.

"Darling Laura, how well you look!"

"What a becoming hat, child!"

"Laura, you look quite Spanish. I've never seen you look so striking."

And Laura, glowing, answered softly, "Have you had tea? Won't you have an ice? The passion-fruit ices really are rather special." She ran to her father and begged him. "Daddy darling, can't the band have something to drink?"

And the perfect afternoon slowly ripened, slowly faded, slowly its petals closed.

"Never a more delightful garden party . . ." "The greatest success . . ." "Quite the most . . ."

"What a becoming hat, child!"

Laura helped her mother with the good-byes. They stood side by side in the porch till it was all over.

"All over, all over, thank heaven," said Mrs. Sheridan. "Round up the others, Laura. Let's go and have some fresh coffee. I'm exhausted. Yes, it's been very successful. But oh, these parties, these parties! Why will you children insist on giving parties!" And they all of them sat down in the deserted marquee.

"Have a sandwich, daddy dear. I wrote the flag."

"Thanks." Mr. Sheridan took a bite and the sandwich was gone. He took another. "I suppose you didn't hear of a beastly accident that happened today?" he said.

"My dear," said Mrs. Sheridan, holding up her hand, "we did. It nearly ruined the party. Laura insisted we should put it off."

"Oh, mother!" Laura didn't want to be teased about it.

"It was a horrible affair all the same," said Mr. Sheridan. "The chap was married too. Lived just below in the lane, and leaves a wife and half a dozen kiddies, so they say."

An awkward little silence fell. Mrs. Sheridan fidgeted with her cup. Really, it was very tactless of father . . .

Suddenly she looked up. There on the table were all those sandwiches, cakes, puffs, all uneaten, all going to be wasted. She had one of her brilliant ideas.

"I know," she said. "Let's make up a basket. Let's send that poor creature some of this perfectly good food. At any rate, it will be the greatest treat for the children. Don't you agree? And she's sure to have neighbors calling in and so on. What a point to have it all ready prepared. Laura!" She jumped up. "Get me the big basket out of the stairs cupboard."

"But, mother, do you really think it's a good idea?" said Laura.

Again, how curious, she seemed to be different from them all. To take scraps from their party. Would the poor woman really like that?

"Of course! What's the matter with you to-day? An hour or two ago you were insisting on us being sympathetic, and now—"

Oh, well! Laura ran for the basket. It was filled, it was heaped by her mother.

"Take it yourself, darling," said she. "Run down just as you are. No, wait, take the arum lilies too. People of that class are so impressed by arum lilies."

"The stems will ruin her lace frock," said practical Jose.

Why does Mother suggest sending lilies to the widow in the lane? Why does Lara decide not to take the lilies?

So they would. Just in time. "Only the basket, then. And, Laura!"—her mother followed her out of the marquee—"don't on any account—"

"What, mother?"

No, better not put such ideas into the child's head! "Nothing! Run along."

It was just growing dusky as Laura shut their garden gates. A big dog ran by like a shadow. The road gleamed white, and down below in the hollow the little cottages were in deep shade. How quiet it seemed after the afternoon. Here she was going down the hill to somewhere where a man lay dead, and she couldn't realize it. Why couldn't she? She stopped a minute. And it seemed to her that kisses, voices, tinkling spoons, laughter, the smell of crushed grass were somehow inside her. She had no room for anything else. How strange! She looked up at the pale sky, and all she thought was, "Yes, it was the most successful party."

Now the broad road was crossed. The lane began, smoky and dark. Women in shawls and men's tweed caps hurried by. Men hung over the palings; the children played in the doorways. A low hum came from the mean little cottages. In some of them there was a flicker of light, and a shadow, crab-like, moved across the window. Laura bent her head and hurried on. She wished now she had put on a coat. How her frock shone! And the big hat with the velvet streamer—if only it was another hat! Were the people looking at her? They must be. It was a mistake to have come; she knew all along it was a mistake. Should she go back even now?

About what does Laura become self-conscious as she walks through the street?

No, too late. This was the house. It must be. A dark knot of people stood outside. Beside the gate an old, old woman with a crutch sat in a chair, watching. She had her feet on a newspaper. The voices stopped as Laura drew near. The group parted. It was as though she was expected, as though they had known she was coming here.

Laura was terribly nervous. Tossing the velvet ribbon over her shoulder, she said to a woman standing by, "Is this Mrs. Scott's house?" and the woman, smiling queerly, said, "It is, my lass."

Oh, to be away from this! She actually said, "Help me, God," as she walked up the tiny path and knocked. To be away from those staring eyes, or to be covered up in anything, one of those women's shawls even. I'll just leave the basket and go, she decided. I shan't even wait for it to be emptied.

Then the door opened. A little woman in black showed in the gloom.

Laura said, "Are you Mrs. Scott?" But to her horror the woman answered, "Walk in please, miss," and she was shut in the passage.

"No," said Laura, "I don't want to come in. I only want to leave this basket. Mother sent—"

The little woman in the gloomy passage seemed not to have heard her. "Step this way, please, miss," she said in an oily voice, and Laura followed her.

She found herself in a wretched little low kitchen, lighted by a smoky lamp. There was a woman sitting before the fire.

"Em," said the little creature who had let her in. "Em! It's a young lady." She turned to Laura. She said meaningly, "I'm 'er sister, Miss. You'll excuse 'er, won't you?"

"Oh, but of course!" said Laura. "Please, please don't disturb her. I—I only want to leave—"

But at that moment the woman at the fire turned round. Her face, puffed up, red, with swollen eyes and swollen lips, looked terrible. She seemed as though she couldn't understand why Laura was there. What did it mean? Why was this stranger standing in the kitchen with a basket? What was it all about? And the poor face puckered up again.

ANSWERS TO GUIDED READING QUESTIONS

1. Laura becomes self-conscious about her bright dress and fancy hat.
2. She feels confused and uncomfortable.

ADDITIONAL QUESTIONS AND ACTIVITIES

What do you think Mrs. Sheridan was going to say when she began to say "don't on any account"?

Answer

Students might reason that she was going to caution Laura against inviting the family to their house or suggesting that she would bring more food.

“All right, my dear,” said the other. “I’ll thank the young lady.”

And again she began, “You’ll excuse her, miss, I’m sure,” and her face, swollen too, tried an oily smile.

Laura only wanted to get out, to get away. She was back in the passage. The door opened. She walked straight through into the bedroom, where the dead man was lying.

“You’d like a look at ’im, wouldn’t you?” said Em’s sister, and she brushed past Laura over to the bed. “Don’t be afraid, my lass—” and now her voice sounded fond and sly, and fondly she drew down the sheet—“ ’e looks a picture. There’s nothing to show. Come along, my dear.”

Laura came.

There lay a young man, fast asleep—sleeping so soundly, so deeply, that he was far, far away from them both. Oh, so remote, so peaceful. He was dreaming. Never wake him up again. His head was sunk in the pillow, his eyes were closed; they were blind under the closed eyelids. He was given up to his dream. What did garden-parties and baskets and lace frocks matter to him? He was far from all those things. He was wonderful, beautiful. While they were laughing and while the band was playing, this marvel had come to the lane. Happy . . . happy. . . . All is well, said that sleeping face. This is just as it should be. I am content.

But all the same you had to cry, and she couldn’t go out of the room without saying something to him. Laura gave a loud childish sob.

“Forgive my hat,” she said.

What is Laura thinking as she looks at the dead man? What does she say to him?

And this time she didn’t wait for Em’s sister. She found her way out of the door, down the path, past all those dark people. At the corner of the lane she met Laurie.

He stepped out of the shadow. “Is that you, Laura?”

“Yes.”

“Mother was getting anxious. Was it all right?”

“Yes, quite. Oh, Laurie!” She took his arm, she pressed up against him.

“I say, you’re not crying, are you?” asked her brother.

Laura shook her head. She was.

Laurie put his arm round her shoulder. “Don’t cry,” he said in his warm, loving voice. “Was it awful?”

“No,” sobbed Laura. “It was simply marvelous. But, Laurie—” She stopped, she looked at her brother. “Isn’t life,” she stammered, “isn’t life—” But what life was she couldn’t explain. No matter. He quite understood.

“*Isn’t* it, darling?” said Laurie. ■

Respond *to the* Selection

How would you finish Laura’s sentence, “Isn’t life—?” Do you think this is how Laura meant to finish the sentence? Do you think Laurie understood what she meant? Why, or why not?

ANSWER TO GUIDED READING QUESTION

1. As she looks at the dead man, Laura is thinking that he appears merely to be sleeping and this his face is a beautiful sign that “All is well.” She says “Forgive my hat” as leaves the room.

SELECTION CHECK TEST 4.11.7 WITH ANSWERS

Checking Your Reading

1. What job does Laura supervise? **She supervises the assembly of the marquee.**
2. What does the tall workman do that surprises her? **He sniffs lavender.**
3. Why does Laura claim they must cancel the party? **A local man has been killed.**
4. How does her mother react to her saying this? **She tells her she’s being ridiculous.**
5. What does Laura ask the people to forgive? **She asks them to forgive her hat.**

Vocabulary in Context

Fill each blank with the most appropriate word from the Words for Everyday Use. You may have to change the tense of the word.

stave enigmatically marquee
rapturous haggard baize sordid

1. Wanda struck at the billiard ball with such force that her cue ripped the **baize**.
2. “You’re looking **haggard**,” Mrs. Simpson said. “A good meal will fix you up.”
3. Our manager would only smile **enigmatically** when we asked about our bonus.
4. When we saw the rain clouds gathering, we were glad we had rented a **marquee**.
5. The children were **rapturous** as the clowns tumbled onto the ground at their feet.

Literary Tools

1. In what two settings does this story take place? **It takes place at the Sheridans’ grand house and the laborer’s poor cottage.**
2. How do these two settings contrast with each other? **Responses will vary, but should suggest that the Sheridans’ house is impressive and extravagantly decorated for a party, while the cottage is squalid and darkened in mourning.**
3. Describe Mrs. Sheridan. **She is vain, self-indulgent, elitist, and shallow.**

SELECTION CHECK TEST 4.11.7 WITH ANSWERS (CONT.)

4. What is an objective correlative? **An objective correlative is a group of images that together create a particular emotion in a reader.**
5. What is irony? **Irony is the difference between appearance and reality.**

RESPOND TO THE SELECTION

Pose the same question, but instead of Laura, ask students to imagine how Mrs. Sheridan might finish this sentence.

Investigate, Inquire, Imagine

Recall: Gathering Facts →

1a. What is Mother's brilliant idea about the leftover food from the party?

2a. Upon hearing about the accident, what does Laura try to convince her family to do? What does Mother do when Laura tries to convince her to do this?

3a. What does Laura say to the dead man?

Interpret: Finding Meaning

1b. What does this reveal about Mother's character?

2b. Why do you think Mother does this?

3b. Why do you think she says this?

Analyze: Taking Things Apart →

4a. Compare and contrast the comments and attitudes of Laura and Jose toward the workers and servants. How does the view of each girl compare to reality?

Synthesize: Bringing Things Together

4b. Why is Laura so uncomfortable when she is in the dead worker's house? What commentary might the author be making about class differences?

Perspective: Looking at Other Views →

5a. What is Mother's attitude toward the poor? What evidence do you find in the story to support your conclusion?

Empathy: Seeing from Inside

5b. If you were the widow of the dead worker, how might you feel toward the Sheridans? How would you feel toward Laura, as she enters the cottage bearing a basket of leftover party food? Why?

Understanding Literature

Image and Objective Correlative. Review the definitions for **image** and **objective correlative** in Literary Tools in Prereading for this selection. What images are used to describe the preparations—the food, clothing, music—for the garden party? What reaction do you think the author hopes to evoke in the reader by these images? Why? Complete the cluster chart to the right, noting the many images used to create the scene for the garden party. Once you've completed the cluster chart, go back to page 1026 of "The Garden-Party," and reread the description of the cottages across the lane. In your own words, explain the impact the author's use of strong imagery has on this story.

Party preparations

Fifteen kinds of sandwiches

Symbol. Review the definition for **symbol** in the Literary Tools in Prereading for this selection. Consider the significance of the hat Laura wears in the story. What does the hat mean to Laura's mother? What does the hat mean at first to Laura? How does its meaning change for her?

Answers to Investigate, Inquire, and Imagine

Recall

1a. Mother's brilliant idea is to send the leftovers in a basket to the family of the man killed in the lane.

2a. Laura tries to convince her family to cancel the party.

3a. Laura says, "Forgive my hat."

Interpret

1b. This reveals that Mother is concerned only about appearances. Her idea makes her appear generous but actually requires no sacrifice on her part—the food is all leftovers that would be thrown out anyway. She shows herself to be quite unsympathetic to the plight of the man's family earlier in the day.

Analyze

4a. Laura finds the workers very attractive and wishes she could be one of them. She notices their smiles and friendly eyes and is surprised and pleased to see one of them crush a sprig of lavender to smell it. However, she seems naïve to the reader, thinking that just by eating bread and butter outside she has put herself in the workers' place. She appreciates their honesty and hard work but has no real idea how their lives differ from her own or what their struggles are, until she goes down to the lane. Jose, on the other hand, loves "giving orders to the servants" and believes they like being ordered by her. We later hear Jose patronizing the cook, marveling over her fifteen kinds of sandwiches in a "rapturous" voice. She assumes the dead worker was drunk. Jose has no second thoughts and has convinced herself that her superior status in life is the right and natural order of things. By the end of the story, Laura has a more realistic view of the workers' lives but Jose's illusions have not changed.

Synthesize

4b. Laura is self-conscious and feels guilty about her wealth and privilege in the face of the poverty of the man's family. The author may be saying that the class system at the turn of the century was unjust and that the wealthy classes deluded themselves into believing that the lower class liked the system as much as the wealthy did, thereby absolving themselves of any feelings of guilt.

Evaluate

5a. Mother's attitudes toward the poor are somewhat complex. She clearly feels superior, as evidenced in her saying things like, "People of that class are so impressed by arum lilies," and "People like that don't

Answers to Investigate, Inquire, and Imagine (cont.)

expect sacrifices from us." Her remarks indicate a desire to distance herself from those of the lower class, to remind herself and those around her that she is different from them. She says, early on, that she is "terrified of cook." In what sense would she be afraid of her servant? She avoids contact with the lower class and has forbidden her children from going to the lane as though she fears she may be somehow contaminated and become one of them! Mother is also completely unsympathetic, as evidenced in her comment to Father that the death of the worker "nearly ruined the party."

Extend

5b. *Responses will vary.*

Answers to Understanding Literature can be found on page 1032.

ANSWERS TO UNDERSTANDING LITERATURE

Image and Objective Correlative. Note: Go back to story and check to make sure list is complete.
Fifteen kinds of sandwiches
"Enough" canna lilies—hundreds
the "sweet" hat Laura's friend wears
roses the 'only flowers that impress people"
band on the tennis court
tent in front of the karakas trees
the lily lawn

The images create an emotion of distaste due to the extravagance and decadent indulgence.

Symbol. The significance of the hat is that Laura's mother gave her the hat to pacify her and to divert her attention from the accident to herself and the party. To Laura's mother, the hat symbolizes youth and beauty and parties, the refined world of privilege. To Laura, at first the hat symbolizes everything to her that it does to her mother. Later, it becomes a symbol of her insensitivity to the plight of her grieving, less-fortunate neighbors.

ANSWERS TO INTEGRATING THE LANGUAGE ARTS

Language, Grammar, and Style
Responses will vary.

1. enigmatically; grammatically, systematically
2. comfortable; reliable, predictable
3. sympathetic; magnetic, angelic
4. extravagant; occupant, defendant
5. tactless; heartless, breathless

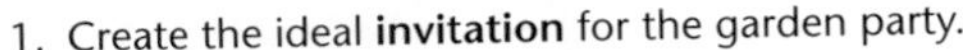

Writer's Journal

1. Create the ideal **invitation** for the garden party.
2. Imagine that you are the society editor for the local newspaper. Write a **short column** for the society section about the Sheridan's party.
3. Katherine Mansfield based this story on an actual experience from her childhood. Think about the experience you wrote about in your Reader's Journal. Choose an image, character, or line of dialogue from that experience to use as the beginning of a short story in which the protagonist gains a newfound perspective about some aspect of his or her life. Write the **opening paragraph** of this story.

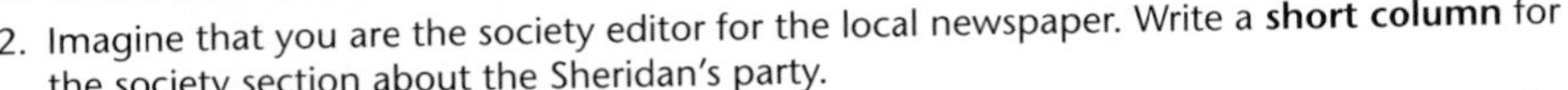

Integrating *the* Language Arts

Language, Grammar, and Style

Base Words and Suffixes. Read the Language Arts Survey 1.19, "Learning Base Words, Prefixes, and Suffixes." Underline the base word once and the suffix twice in each of the words below. Next, look up each suffix in a dictionary, and write two additional words that end with the same suffix.

1. enigmatically
2. comfortable
3. sympathetic
4. extravagant
5. tactless

Collaborative Learning

Recreating Imagery from "The Garden-Party." Form groups of three of four, and consider the two contrasting scenes in "The Garden-Party"—the Sheridan's house and yard before and during the party, and the cottages across the lane after the accident. Discuss how, as a group, you might best recreate, as a whole or in part, the stark contrast of the imagery in these scenes. You may want to write a newspaper article that details the event at the Sheridan's and the terrible accident that happened nearby. You may want to split into two groups and have each group act out part of the events that take place at the Sheridan's and part of the events that take place across the lane. You may want to draw or paint part or all of each scene side by side. Once you've completed your recreation, present it to your class.

Speaking and Listening

Dramatic Skit. Collaborate with one or two other students to write a dramatic scene to follow the closing of the story and provide completion to Laura's utterance "Isn't life...." You may choose to write the scene for Laura and her brother Laurie, or you may choose to have the scene take place between Laura and Jose, Laura and her father or Laura and her mother. Make sure to portray the characters as they are in the story.

"The Lagoon"

By Joseph Conrad

About the Author

Joseph Conrad (1857–1924) was born Jozef Teodor Konrad Korzeniowski in Berdichev, in the Ukraine. Berdichev had once been part of Poland, but in 1857 was under Russian rule, and Conrad grew up under Tsarist autocracy. In 1861, his parents, passionate Polish patriots, were exiled to northern Russia as a result of their involvement in anti-Russian politics. By the age of 12, Conrad had lost his mother and father to tuberculosis and was sent to live with his uncle in Switzerland. In the mid-1870s, he acted on his passion for the sea by joining the French Merchant Marine. In 1878, he joined the British merchant navy, staying for 16 years, and working his way up from common seaman to commanding his own ship. In 1886, he obtained British citizenship and officially changed his name to Joseph Conrad. It was during his time at sea that Conrad learned English—his third language. Conrad eventually took to life on land, marrying in 1896, and devoting himself to sharing the stories of his adventures at sea through his writing. Now considered one of the great writers of fiction, he is best known for his novella, *Heart of Darkness,* based in part on his travels on the Congo River and for his novels *Lord Jim, Typhoon,* and *The Secret Agent.*

About the Selection

"The Lagoon" includes many of the elements and themes characteristic of Conrad's work: passages rich in description and analysis; tests of human character; and concern with moral questions, isolation, and human psychology.

Literary Tools

Image. An **image** is language that creates a concrete representation of an object or an experience. An image is also the vivid mental picture created in the reader's mind by that language. The images in a literary work are referred to, collectively, as the work's *imagery.* As you read, note the rich description of setting in this story, especially the images of light and darkness and the images of stillness and immobility.

Character. **A character** is a person who figures in the action of a literary work. A *protagonist, or main character,* is the central figure in a literary work. *Minor characters* are ones who play lesser roles. As you read "The Lagoon," pay attention to what the author reveals about Arsat, the main character, and what the reader comes to know about the lesser character of Tuan.

Reader's Journal

Where do you turn when you are troubled, unhappy, or find yourself with a heavy burden to bear?

ADDITIONAL RESOURCES

Unit 11 Resource Book

- Selection Worksheet 11.5
- Selection Check Test 4.11.9
- Selection Test 4.11.10
- Language, Grammar, and Style Resource 3.39

VOCABULARY FROM THE SELECTION

audacious	ignoble
august	lagoon
conflagration	portal
discordant	propitiate
eddies	wayfarer
festoon	

READER'S JOURNAL

In times of hardship, what kind of things comfort you? What do you like to hear from a friend or family member to calm your fears?

GOALS/OBJECTIVES

Studying this lesson will enable students to

- empathize with the speaker's struggle to be loyal to both friend and family
- explain the elements and themes characteristic of Joseph Conrad
- define *image* and *character* and recognize and explain examples of each that they encounter in their reading
- demonstrate the ability to make sentences more colorful and vivid
- conduct a research on the history of Malaysia

ANSWERS TO GUIDED READING QUESTIONS

1. They will pass the night at Arsat's clearing.
2. The memory of motion seems to have departed from the land.

INDIVIDUAL LEARNING STRATEGIES

MOTIVATION
The protagonist in the selection spends a lot of time traveling on a boat to get to the lagoon. Ask students to share experiences they have had with boat, rivers, oceans, and/or lagoons. Then as they read, encourage them to compare their experience with the experience of the protagonist.

READING PROFICIENCY
Suggest that students read the story aloud with a partner, reading every other paragraph. As they read, encourage them to anticipate the answers to the Guided Reading questions.

ENGLISH LANGUAGE LEARNING
Ask students to prepare a quiz (multiple choice, matching, or fill in the blank) with the Words for Everyday Use. Have them exchange their quiz with two other students. Give students time to complete their quizzes in class.

SPECIAL NEEDS
Help students to focus on the Guided Reading questions. In addition, bring in pictures of lagoons from around the world to give students a sense of the scene and setting of the selection.

ENRICHMENT
Ask students to write a more complete and detailed About the Author by researching biographical information on Joseph Conrad. What motivated him to be a writer? What experiences led him to write stories about isolation, morality, and tests of human character and psychology? Have students present their information similar to the About the Author sections in this textbook.

JOSEPH CONRAD

The white man, leaning with both arms over the roof of the little house in the stern[1] of the boat, said to the steersman: "We will pass the night in Arsat's clearing. It is late."

Where will the white man and crew pass the night?

The Malay[2] only grunted, and went on looking fixedly at the river. The white man rested his chin on his crossed arms and gazed at the wake of the boat. At the end of the straight avenue of forests cut by the intense glitter of the river, the sun appeared unclouded and dazzling, poised low over the water that shone smoothly like a band of metal. The forests, somber and dull, stood motionless and silent on each side of the broad stream. At the foot of big, towering trees, trunkless nipa palms rose from the mud of the bank, in bunches of leaves enormous and heavy, that hung unstirring over the brown swirl of eddies. In the stillness of the air every tree, every leaf, every bough, every tendril of creeper and every petal of minute blossoms seemed to have been bewitched into an immobility perfect and final. Nothing moved on the river but the eight paddles that rose flashing regularly, dipped together with a single splash; while the steersman swept right and left with a periodic and sudden flourish of his blade describing a glinting semicircle above his head. The churned-up water frothed alongside with a confused murmur. And the white man's canoe, advancing upstream in the short-lived disturbance of its own making, seemed to enter the portals of a land from which the very memory of motion had forever departed.

What seems to have departed from the land?

The white man, turning his back upon the setting sun, looked along the empty and broad expanse of the sea-reach. For the last three miles of its course the wandering, hesitating river, as if enticed irresistibly by the freedom of an open horizon, flows straight into the sea, flows straight to the east—to the east that harbors both light and darkness. Astern[3] of the boat the repeated call of some bird, a cry discordant and feeble, skipped along over the smooth water and lost itself, before it could reach the other shore, in the breathless silence of the world.

The steersman dug his paddle into the stream, and held hard with stiffened arms, his body thrown forward. The water gurgled aloud; and suddenly the long straight reach seemed to pivot on its center, the forests swung in a semicircle, and the slanting beams of sunset touched the broadside[4] of the canoe with a fiery glow,

1. **stern.** The rear end of a boat
2. **Malay.** A member of a people of the Malay peninsula, eastern Sumatra, parts of Borneo, and some adjacent islands
3. **Astern.** Behind a boat or ship
4. **broadside.** A broad or unbroken surface

WORDS FOR EVERYDAY USE

ed • dies (e′ dēz) *n., pl,* currents of water or air running contrary to the main current; whirlpools. *Tiny minnows darted among the weeds and eddies along the shore of the river.*

por • tal (pōr′ təl) *n.,* door, entrance. *The portals of the old theatre were made of stone.*

dis • cor • dant (dis kôr′ dənt) *adj.,* quarrelsome; unmelodious. *The beginning music students collaborated and produced a decidedly discordant sound.*

throwing the slender and distorted shadows of its crew upon the streaked glitter of the river. The white man turned to look ahead. The course of the boat had been altered at right angles to the stream, and the carved dragon head of its prow was pointing now at a gap in the fringing bushes of the bank. It glided through, brushing the overhanging twigs, and disappeared from the river like some slim and amphibious creature leaving the water for its lair in the forests.

The narrow creek was like a ditch: tortuous, fabulously deep; filled with gloom under the thin strip of pure and shining blue of the heaven. Immense trees soared up, invisible behind the festooned draperies of creepers. Here and there, near the glistening blackness of the water, a twisted root of some tall tree showed amongst the tracery of small ferns, black and dull, writhing and motionless, like an arrested snake. The short words of the paddlers reverberated loudly between the thick and somber walls of vegetation. Darkness oozed out from between the trees, through the tangled maze of the creepers, from behind the great fantastic and unstirring leaves, the darkness, mysterious and invincible; the darkness scented and poisonous of impenetrable forests.

The men poled in the shoaling[5] water. The creek broadened, opening out into a wide sweep of a stagnant lagoon. The forests receded from the marshy bank, leaving a level strip of bright green, reedy grass to frame the reflected blueness of the sky. A fleecy pink cloud drifted high above, trailing the delicate coloring of its image under the floating leaves and the silvery blossoms of the lotus. A little house, perched on high piles, appeared black in the distance. Near it, two tall nibong palms, that seemed to have come out of the forests in the background, leaned slightly over the ragged roof, with a suggestion of sad tenderness and care in the droop of their leafy and soaring heads.

The steersman, pointing with his paddle, said, "Arsat is there. I see his canoe fast between the piles."

The polers ran along the sides of the boat glancing over their shoulders at the end of the day's journey. They would have preferred to spend the night somewhere else than on this lagoon of weird aspect and ghostly reputation. Moreover, they disliked Arsat, first as a stranger, and also because he who repairs a ruined house, and dwells in it, proclaims that he is not afraid to live amongst the spirits that haunt the places abandoned by mankind. Such a man can disturb the course of fate by glances or words; while his familiar ghosts are not easy to propitiate by casual wayfarers upon whom they long to wreak the malice of their human master. White men care not for such things, being unbelievers and in league with the Father of Evil, who leads them unharmed through the invisible dangers of this world. To the warnings of the righteous they oppose an offensive pretense of disbelief. What is there to be done?

Why would the men prefer to pass the night elsewhere?

So they thought, throwing their weight on the end of their long poles. The big canoe glided on swiftly, noiselessly, and smoothly, toward Arsat's clearing, till, in a great rattling of poles thrown down, and the loud murmurs of "Allah[6] be praised!" it came with a gentle knock against the crooked piles below the house.

5. **shoal.** To become shallow
6. **Allah.** Muslim God

Words for Everyday Use

fes • toon (fes tün') *vt.,* decorate. *Joy will wrap the presents and festoon them with ribbons and bows.*

la • goon (lə gün') *n.,* a shallow sound, channel, or pond near a larger body of water. *Carefully, we eased our canoe through the lily pads and tall grass of the lagoon.*

pro • pi • ti • ate (prō pi' shē āt) *vt.,* to regain the favor of; to pacify. *Bad guys in movies often use raw meat to propitiate ferocious guard dogs.*

way • far • er (wā' far ər) *n.,* a traveler, especially one who travels on foot. *The small group of wayfarers moved from town to town, living modestly on what they could beg or earn.*

ANSWER TO GUIDED READING QUESTION

1. The men would prefer to pass the night elsewhere because the lagoon is "weird" and has a "ghostly reputation." They don't like Arsat because he lives in a ruined house, and this, they fear, means he can "disturb the course of fate."

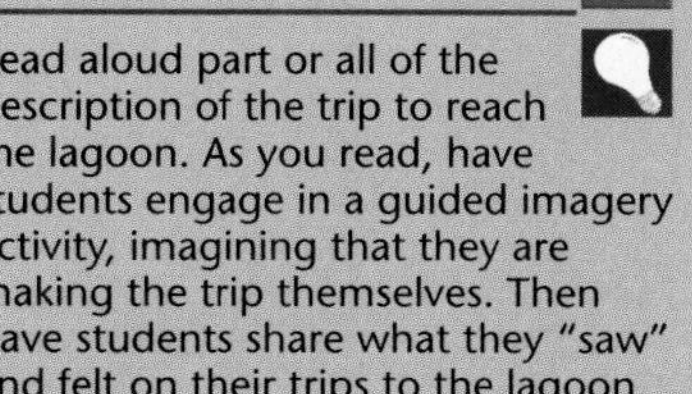

ADDITIONAL QUESTIONS AND ACTIVITIES

Read aloud part or all of the description of the trip to reach the lagoon. As you read, have students engage in a guided imagery activity, imagining that they are making the trip themselves. Then have students share what they "saw" and felt on their trips to the lagoon.

ANSWER TO GUIDED READING QUESTION

1. The woman is gravely ill. She has a high fever and is unconscious.

ADDITIONAL QUESTIONS AND ACTIVITIES

1. What description does the narrator give of Arsat?
2. Why do the polers dislike Arsat?
3. What details reveal the seriousness of the woman's illness?

Answers

1. The narrator describes Arsat as "young, powerful, with broad chest and muscular arms." He is dressed only in a sarong and has "big, soft eyes… but his voice and demeanor were composed…"
2. They dislike him because he is "a stranger" and because he has repaired a "ruined house" and lives in it "amongst the spirits that haunt the places abandoned by mankind." The polers are superstitious of such actions and believe that "such a man can disturb the course of fate."
3. Details such as "her big eyes, wide open, glittered in the gloom"; her high fever; sunken cheeks; and fixed expression reveal the seriousness of her illness.

Students in small groups can make or find recordings of environmental sounds that they imagine one would hear at the lagoon.

The boatmen with uplifted faces shouted discordantly, "Arsat! O Arsat!" Nobody came. The white man began to climb the rude ladder giving access to the bamboo platform before the house. The juragan of the boat said sulkily, "We will cook in the sampan,[7] and sleep on the water."

"Pass my blankets and the basket," said the white man, curtly.

He knelt on the edge of the platform to receive the bundle. Then the boat shoved off, and the white man, standing up, confronted Arsat, who had come out through the low door of his hut. He was a man young, powerful, with broad chest and muscular arms. He had nothing on but his sarong. His head was bare. His big, soft eyes stared eagerly at the white man, but his voice and demeanor were composed as he asked, without any words of greeting:

"Have you medicine, Tuan?"

"No," said the visitor in a startled tone. "No. Why? Is there sickness in the house?"

"Enter and see," replied Arsat, in the same calm manner, and turning short round, passed again through the small doorway. The white man, dropping his bundles, followed.

In the dim light of the dwelling he made out on a couch of bamboos a woman stretched on her back under a broad sheet of red cotton cloth. She lay still, as if dead; but her big eyes, wide open, glittered in the gloom, staring upwards at the slender rafters, motionless and unseeing. She was in a high fever, and evidently unconscious. Her cheeks were sunk slightly, her lips were partly open, and on the young face there was the ominous and fixed expression—the absorbed, contemplating expression of the unconscious who are going to die. The two men stood looking down at her in silence.

What is the woman's condition?

"Has she been long ill?" asked the traveler.

"I have not slept for five nights," answered the Malay, in a deliberate tone. "At first she heard voices calling her from the water and struggled against me who held her. But since the sun of today rose she hears nothing—she hears not me. She sees nothing. She sees not me—me!"

He remained silent for a minute, then asked softly:

"She sees nothing. She sees not me–me!"

"Tuan, will she die?"

"I fear so," said the white man, sorrowfully. He had known Arsat years ago, in a far country in times of trouble and danger, when no friendship is to be despised. And since his Malay friend had come unexpectedly to dwell in the hut on the lagoon with a strange woman, he had slept many times there, in his journeys up and down the river. He liked the man who knew how to keep faith in council and how to fight without fear by the side of his white friend. He liked him—not so much perhaps as a man likes his favorite dog—but still he liked him well enough to help and ask no questions, to think sometimes vaguely and hazily in the midst of his own pursuits, about the lonely man and the longhaired woman with audacious face and triumphant eyes, who lived together hidden

7. **sampan.** A flat-bottomed boat Chinese boat usually propelled by two short oars

WORDS FOR EVERYDAY USE

au • da • cious (ô dā′ shəs) *adj.*, bold; brave; spirited. *The officer was honored for her audacious behavior in the line of duty.*

by the forests—alone and feared.

How does Tuan feel about Arsat?

The white man came out of the hut in time to see the enormous <u>conflagration</u> of sunset put out by the swift and stealthy shadows that, rising like a black and impalpable vapor above the treetops, spread over the heaven, extinguishing the crimson glow of floating clouds and the red brilliance of departing daylight. In a few moments all the stars came out above the intense blackness of the earth and the great lagoon gleaming suddenly with reflected lights resembled an oval patch of night sky flung down into the hopeless and abysmal night of the wilderness. The white man had some supper out of the basket, then collecting a few sticks that lay about the platform, made up a small fire, not for warmth, but for the sake of the smoke, which would keep off the mosquitoes. He wrapped himself in the blankets and sat with his back against the reed wall of the house, smoking thoughtfully.

Arsat came through the doorway with noiseless steps and squatted down by the fire. The white man moved his outstretched legs a little.

"She breathes," said Arsat in a low voice, anticipating the expected question. "She breathes and burns as if with a great fire. She speaks not; she hears not—and burns!"

He paused for a moment, then asked in a quiet, incurious tone:

What does Arsat ask Tuan? How does Tuan answer?

"Tuan . . . will she die?"

The white man moved his shoulders uneasily and muttered in a hesitating manner:

"If such is her fate."

"No, Tuan," said Arsat, calmly. "If such is my fate. I hear, I see, I wait. I remember. . . . Tuan, do you remember the old days? Do you remember my brother?"

"Yes," said the white man. The Malay rose suddenly and went in. The other, sitting still outside, could hear the voice in the hut. Arsat said: "Hear me! Speak!" His words were succeeded by a complete silence. "O Diamelen!" he cried, suddenly. After that cry there was a deep sigh. Arsat came out and sank down again in his old place.

They sat in silence before the fire. There was no sound within the house, there was no sound near them; but far away on the lagoon they could hear the voices of the boatmen ringing fitful and distinct on the calm water. The fire in the bows of the sampan shone faintly in the distance with a hazy red glow. Then it died out. The voices ceased. The land and the water slept invisible, unstirring and mute. It was as though there had been nothing left in the world but the glitter of stars streaming, ceaseless and vain, through the black stillness of the night.

The white man gazed straight before him into the darkness with wide-open eyes. The fear and fascination, the inspiration and the wonder of death—of death near, unavoidable, and unseen, soothed the unrest of his race and stirred the most indistinct, the most intimate of his thoughts. The ever-ready suspicion of evil, the gnawing suspicion that lurks in our hearts, flowed out into the stillness round him—into the stillness profound and dumb, and made it appear untrustworthy and infamous, like the placid and impenetrable mask of an unjustifiable violence. In that fleeting and powerful disturbance of his being the earth enfolded in the starlight peace became a shadowy country of inhuman strife, a battlefield of phantoms terrible and charming, <u>august</u> or <u>ignoble</u>, struggling ardently for the possession of our helpless hearts. An

What stirs Tuan's thoughts? What changes the way he looks at the stillness around him? How does it change?

WORDS FOR EVERYDAY USE

con • fla • gra • tion (kän flə grā′ shən) *n.*, fire. *Firefighters are struggling to contain the <u>conflagration</u> that has taken two lives and already destroyed thousands of acres of forest.*

au • gust (ö gəst′) *adj.*, magnificent; admirable. *The plaque was an appropriate tribute to the <u>august</u> efforts of the group of volunteers.*

ig • no • ble (ig nō′ bəl) *adj.*, dishonorable; detestable. *His actions may seem sincere, but his motives are <u>ignoble.</u>*

ANSWERS TO GUIDED READING QUESTIONS

1. He likes and respects him well enough to help him.
2. He asks Arsat if the woman will die or not. Tuan answers by saying that she will die if it is her fate.
3. The fear, fascination, and wonder of death stirs Tuan's thoughts. The suspicion of evil changes the way he looks at the stillness around him by making it seem untrustworthy and infamous.

ADDITIONAL QUESTIONS AND ACTIVITIES

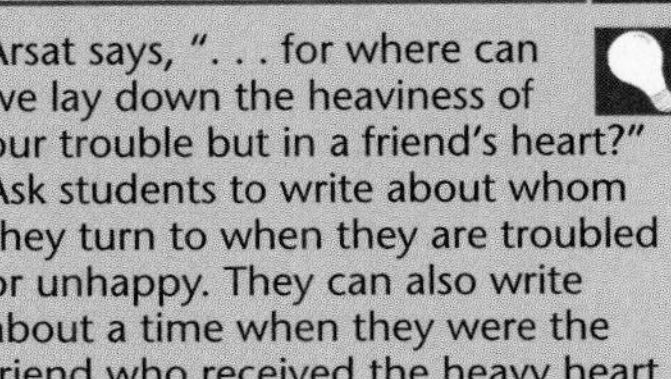

Arsat says, ". . . for where can we lay down the heaviness of our trouble but in a friend's heart?" Ask students to write about whom they turn to when they are troubled or unhappy. They can also write about a time when they were the friend who received the heavy heart.

ANSWER TO GUIDED READING QUESTION

1. Arsat could no longer see anything in his past once he had looked upon the woman.

LITERARY TECHNIQUE 

Personification. Explain that **personification** is a writing technique in which an idea, animal, or thing is described as if it were a person. Point out the personification of the woods in the following passage: "A plaintive murmur rose in the night; a murmur saddening and startling, as if the great solitudes of surrounding woods had tried to whisper into his ear the wisdom of their immense and lofty indifference." Have students identify other examples of personification in the selection.

unquiet and mysterious country of inextinguishable desires and fears.

A plaintive murmur rose in the night; a murmur saddening and startling, as if the great solitudes of surrounding woods had tried to whisper into his ear the wisdom of their immense and lofty indifference. Sounds hesitating and vague floated in the air round him, shaped themselves slowly into words; and at last flowed on gently in a murmuring stream of soft and monotonous sentences. He stirred like a man waking up and changed his position slightly. Arsat, motionless and shadowy, sitting with bowed head under the stars, was speaking in a low and dreamy tone:

". . . for where can we lay down the heaviness of our trouble but in a friend's heart? A man must speak of war and of love. You, Tuan, know what war is, and you have seen me in time of danger seek death as other men seek life! A writing may be lost; a lie may be written; but what the eye has seen is truth and remains in the mind!"

"I remember," said the white man, quietly. Arsat went on with mournful composure:

"Therefore I shall speak to you of love. Speak in the night. Speak before both night and love are gone—and the eye of day looks upon my sorrow and my shame; upon my blackened face; upon my burnt-up heart."

A sigh, short and faint, marked an almost imperceptible pause, and then his words flowed on, without a stir, without a gesture.

"After the time of trouble and war was over and you went away from my country in the pursuit of your desires, which we, men of the islands, cannot understand, I and my brother became again, as we had been before, the sword bearers of the Ruler. You know we were men of family, belonging to a ruling race, and more fit than any to carry on our right shoulder the emblem of power. And in the time of prosperity Si Dendring showed us favor, as we, in time of sorrow, had showed to him the faithfulness of our courage. It was a time of peace. A time of deer hunts and cock fights; of idle talks and foolish squabbles between men whose bellies are full and weapons are rusty. But the sower watched the young rice shoots grow up without fear, and the traders came and went, departed lean and returned fat into the river of peace. They brought news, too. Brought lies and truth mixed together, so that no man knew when to rejoice and when to be sorry. We heard from them about you also. They had seen you here and had seen you there. And I was glad to hear, for I remembered the stirring times, and I always remembered you, Tuan, till the time came when my eyes could see nothing in the past, because they had looked upon the one who is dying there—in the house."

What could Arsat no longer see, once he had laid eyes on the woman?

He stopped to exclaim in an intense whisper, "O Mara bahia! O Calamity!" then went on speaking a little louder:

"There's no worse enemy and no better friend than a brother, Tuan, for one brother knows another, and in perfect knowledge is strength for good or evil. I loved my brother. I went to him and told him that I could see nothing but one face, hear nothing but one voice. He told me: 'Open your heart so that she can see what is in it—and wait. Patience is wisdom. Inchi Midah may die or our Ruler may throw off his fear of a woman!' . . . I waited! . . . You remember the lady with the veiled face, Tuan, and the fear of our Ruler before her cunning and temper. And if she wanted her servant, what could I do? But I fed the hunger of my heart on short glances and stealthy words. I loitered on the path to the bathhouses in the daytime, and when the sun had fallen behind the forest I crept along the jasmine hedges of the women's courtyard. Unseeing, we spoke to one another through the scent of flowers, through the veil of leaves, through the blades of long grass that stood still before our lips; so great was our prudence, so faint was the murmur of our great longing. The time passed swiftly . . .

and there were whispers amongst women—and our enemies watched—my brother was gloomy, and I began to think of killing and of a fierce death. . . . We are of a people who take what they want—like you whites. There is a time when a man should forget loyalty and respect. Might and authority are given to rulers, but to all men is given love and strength and courage. My brother said, 'You shall take her from their midst. We are two who are like one.' And I answered, 'Let it be soon, for I find no warmth in sunlight that does not shine upon her.' Our time came when the Ruler and all the great people went to the mouth of the river to fish by torchlight. There were hundreds of boats, and on the white sand, between the water and the forests, dwellings of leaves were built for the households of the Rajahs.[8] The smoke of cooking fires was like a blue mist of the evening, and many voices rang in it joyfully. While they were making the boats ready to beat up the fish, my brother came to me and said, 'Tonight!' I looked to my weapons, and when the time came our canoe took its place in the circle of boats carrying the torches. The lights blazed on the water, but behind the boats there was darkness. When the shouting began and the excitement made them like mad we dropped out. The water swallowed our fire, and we floated back to the shore that was dark with only here and there the glimmer of embers. We could hear the talk of slave girls amongst the sheds. Then we found a place deserted and silent. We waited there. She came. She came running along the shore, rapid and leaving no trace, like a leaf driven by the wind into the sea. My brother said gloomily, 'Go and take her; carry her into our boat.' I lifted her in my arms. She panted. Her heart was beating against my breast. I said, 'I take you from those people. You came to the cry of my heart, but my arms take you into my boat against the will of the great!' 'It is right,' said my brother. 'We are men who take what we want and can hold it against many. We should have taken her in daylight.' I said, 'Let us be off'; for since she was in my boat I began

What did the brothers resolve to do?

Martinique, 1887. Paul Gauguin.

8. **Rajah.** An Indian or Malay prince or chief

ANSWER TO GUIDED READING QUESTION

1. The brothers resolve to take the woman from the Ruler.

ADDITIONAL QUESTIONS AND ACTIVITIES

1. Of whom is Arsat speaking when he says, "I find no warmth in sunlight that does not shine upon her"?
2. While the Ruler and other villagers are fishing at night, what do Arsat and his brother do?

Answers

1. Arsat is speaking about "the lady with the veiled face" with whom he has fallen in love.
2. They steal the woman away from the Ruler.

ANSWERS TO GUIDED READING QUESTIONS

1. Arsat begged his brother to be silent, though his brother wanted to shout a cry of defiant challenge, to let the rulers know that they were unafraid.
2. His brother was still brave and strong—"He knew not fear and no fatigue."

BIBLIOGRAPHIC NOTE

Students who are interested in reading more works by Conrad will find a number of critical editions available. Good sources include:

Heart of Darkness. Ed. Robert Kimbrough. Third ed. 1987.

Lord Jim. Ed. Thomas C. Moser. 1968.

Students also interested in Conrad's life might enjoy the following:

Najder, Zdzislaw. *Joseph Conrad: A Chronicle*. 1983.

to think of our Ruler's many men. 'Yes. Let us be off,' said my brother. 'We are cast out and this boat is our country now—and the sea is our refuge.' He lingered with his foot on the shore, and I entreated him to hasten, for I remembered the strokes of her heart against my breast and thought that two men cannot withstand a hundred. We left, paddling downstream close to the bank; and as we passed by the creek where they were fishing, the great shouting had ceased, but the murmur of voices was loud like the humming of insects flying at noonday. The boats floated, clustered together, in the red light of torches, under a black roof of smoke; and men talked of their sport. Men that boasted, and praised, and jeered—men that would have been our friends in the morning, but on that night were already our enemies. We paddled swiftly past. We had no more friends in the country of our birth. She sat in the middle of the canoe with covered face; silent as she is now; unseeing as she is now—and I had no regret at what I was leaving because I could hear her breathing close to me—as I can hear her now."

He paused, listened with his ear turned to the doorway, then shook his head and went on:

"My brother wanted to shout the cry of challenge—one cry only—to let the people know we were freeborn robbers who trusted our arms and the great sea. And again I begged him in the name of our love to be silent.

> *What did his brother want to do as they paddled away with the woman? What did Arsat beg of him?*

Could I not hear her breathing close to me? I knew the pursuit would come quick enough. My brother loved me. He dipped his paddle without a splash. He only said, 'There is half a man in you now—the other half is in that woman. I can wait. When you are a whole man again, you will come back with me here to shout defiance. We are sons of the same mother.' I made no answer. All my strength and all my spirit were in my hands that held the paddle—for I longed to be with her in a safe place beyond the reach of men's anger and of women's spite. My love was so great, that I thought it could guide me to a country where death was unknown, if I could only escape from Inchi Midah's fury and from our Ruler's sword. We paddled with haste, breathing through our teeth. The blades bit deep into the smooth water. We passed out of the river; we flew in clear channels amongst the shallows. We skirted the black coast; we skirted the sand beaches where the sea speaks in whispers to the land; and the gleam of white sand flashed back past our boat, so swiftly she ran upon the water. We spoke not. Only once I said, 'Sleep, Diamelen, for soon you may want all your strength.' I heard the sweetness of her voice, but I never turned my head. The sun rose and still we went on. Water fell from my face like rain from a cloud. We flew in the light and heat. I never looked back, but I knew that my brother's eyes, behind me, were looking steadily ahead, for the boat went as straight as a bushman's dart, when it leaves the end of the sumpitan. There was no better paddler, no better steersman than my brother. Many times, together, we had won races in that canoe. But we never had put out our strength as we did then—then, when for the last time we paddled together! There was no braver or stronger man in our country than my brother. I could not spare the strength to turn my head and look at him, but every moment I heard the hiss of his breath getting louder behind me. Still he did not speak. The sun was high. The heat clung to my back like a flame of fire. My ribs were ready to burst, but I could no longer get enough air into my chest. And then I felt I must cry out with my last breath, 'Let us rest!' . . . 'Good!' he answered; and his voice was firm. He was strong. He was brave. He knew not fear and no fatigue . . . My brother!"

> *As Arsat felt he could breathe and paddle no longer, what was his brother's condition?*

A murmur powerful and gentle, a murmur vast and

faint; the murmur of trembling leaves, of stirring boughs, ran through the tangled depths of the forests, ran over the starry smoothness of the lagoon, and the water between the piles lapped the slimy timber once with a sudden splash. A breath of warm air touched the two men's faces and passed on with a mournful sound—a breath loud and short like an uneasy sigh of the dreaming earth.

Arsat went on in an even, low voice.

"We ran our canoe on the white beach of a little bay close to a long tongue of land that seemed to bar our road; a long wooded cape going far into the sea. My brother knew that place. Beyond the cape a river has its entrance, and through the jungle of that land there is a narrow path. We made a fire and cooked rice. Then we lay down to sleep on the soft sand in the shade of our canoe, while she watched. No sooner had I closed my eyes than I heard her cry of alarm. We leaped up. The sun was halfway down the sky already, and coming in sight in the opening of the bay we saw a prau[9] manned by many paddlers. We knew it at once; it was one of our Rajah's praus. They were watching the shore, and saw us. They beat the gong, and turned the head of the prau into the bay. I felt my heart become weak within my breast. Diamelen sat on the sand and covered her face. There was no escape by sea. My brother laughed. He had the gun you had given him, Tuan, before you went away, but there was only a handful of powder. He spoke to me quickly: 'Run with her along the path. I shall keep them back, for they have no firearms, and landing in the face of a man with a gun is certain death for some. Run with her. On the other side of that wood there is a fisherman's house—and a canoe. When I have fired all the shots I will follow. I am a great runner, and before they can come up we shall be gone. I will hold out as long as I can, for she is but a woman—that can neither run nor fight, but she has your heart in her weak hands.' He dropped behind the canoe. The prau was coming. She and I ran, and as we rushed along the path I heard shots. My brother fired—once—twice—and the booming of the gong ceased. There was silence behind us. That neck of land is narrow. Before I heard my brother fire the third shot I saw the shelving shore, and I saw the water again; the mouth of a broad river. We crossed a grassy glade. We ran down to the water. I saw a low hut above the black mud, and a small canoe hauled up. I heard another shot behind me. I thought, 'That is his last charge.' We rushed down to the canoe; a man came running from the hut, but I leaped on him, and we rolled together in the mud. Then I got up, and he lay still at my feet. I don't know whether I had killed him or not. I and Diamelen pushed the canoe afloat. I heard yells behind me, and I saw my brother run across the glade. Many men were bounding after him. I took her in my arms and threw her into the boat, then leaped in myself. When I looked back I saw that my brother had fallen. He fell and was up again, but the men were closing round him. He shouted, 'I am coming!' The men were close to him. I looked. Many men. Then I looked at her. Tuan, I pushed the canoe! I pushed it into deep water. She was kneeling forward looking at me, and I said, 'Take your paddle,' while I struck the water with mine. Tuan, I heard him cry. I heard him cry my name twice; and I heard voices shouting, 'Kill! Strike!' I never turned back. I heard him calling my name again with a great shriek, as when life is going out together with the voice—and I never turned my head. My own name! . . . My brother! Three times he called—but I was not afraid of life. Was she not there in that canoe? And could I not with her find a country where death is forgotten—where death is unknown!"

How did Arsat react to the sight of the ruler's men? How did his brother react?

What did Arsat do when he saw the ruler's men close around his brother?

9 **prau.** An Indonesian boat, usually without a deck, propelled by sails or paddles

ANSWERS TO GUIDED READING QUESTIONS

1. Arsat felt his heart go weak when he saw the ruler's men but his brother laughed.
2. Arsat pushed the canoe into the water and began to paddle away when he saw his brother surrounded by the ruler's men. He never looked back.

ADDITIONAL QUESTIONS AND ACTIVITIES

1. Why does Diamelen make a "cry of alarm"? How does Arsat's brother respond?
2. What moral dilemma is described in "The Lagoon"? What consequences were suffered because of that dilemma?
3. What choice did Arsat make? What desire influenced his choice?

Answers

1. She sees a "prau manned by many paddlers" approaching the shore where she, Arsat, and Arsat's brother are sleeping. Arsat's brother tells him to take Diamelen and run for the fisherman's house and canoe; he plans to fend off the men with his gun and then run back to Arsat in the canoe.
2. The moral dilemma is the choice that Arsat must make between his brother and Diamelen. If he chooses to help his brother, chances are that both men will die and Diamelen will probably be killed. If Arsat chooses Diamelen, then his brother will die, but Arsat and Diamelen will escape. One of the consequences suffered is the guilt Arsat has lived with and now faces upon remembering his brother's cries for help and his death.
3. Arsat chose Diamelen over his brother. He desired the love of a woman and "peace in my own heart."

ANSWER TO GUIDED READING QUESTION

1. The woman has died.

ADDITIONAL QUESTIONS AND ACTIVITIES

1. What is ironic about Arsat's reasoning?
2. What response does Tuan give when Arsat says, "Tuan, I loved my brother"?

Answers

1. Arsat chose Diamelen because he desired peace but he has been wracked with guilt since making that decision.
2. Tuan replies, "We all love our brothers."

The white man sat up. Arsat rose and stood, an indistinct and silent figure above the dying embers of the fire. Over the lagoon a mist drifting and low had crept, erasing slowly the glittering images of the stars. And now a great expanse of white vapor covered the land: it flowed cold and gray in the darkness, eddied in noiseless whirls round the tree trunks and about the platform of the house, which seemed to float upon a restless and impalpable illusion of a sea. Only far away the tops of the trees stood outlined on the twinkle of heaven, like a somber and forbidding shore—a coast deceptive, pitiless and black.

Arsat's voice vibrated loudly in the profound peace.

"I had her there! I had her! To get her I would have faced all mankind. But I had her—and—"

"To get her I would have faced all mankind."

His words went out ringing into the empty distances. He paused, and seemed to listen to them dying away very far—beyond help and beyond recall. Then he said quietly:

"Tuan, I loved my brother."

A breath of wind made him shiver. High above his head, high above the silent sea of mist the drooping leaves of the palms rattled together with a mournful and expiring sound. The white man stretched his legs. His chin rested on his chest, and he murmured sadly without lifting his head:

"We all love our brothers."

Arsat burst out with an intense whispering violence:

"What did I care who died? I wanted peace in my own heart."

He seemed to hear a stir in the house—listened— then stepped in noiselessly. The white man stood up. A breeze was coming in fitful puffs. The stars shone paler as if they had retreated into the frozen depths of immense space. After a chill gust of wind there were a few seconds of perfect calm and absolute silence. Then from behind the black and wavy line of the forests a column of golden light shot up into the heavens and spread over the semicircle of the eastern horizon. The sun had risen. The mist lifted, broke into drifting patches, vanished into thin flying wreaths; and the unveiled lagoon lay, polished and black, in the heavy shadows at the foot of the wall of trees. A white eagle rose over it with a slanting and ponderous flight, reached the clear sunshine and appeared dazzlingly brilliant for a moment, then soaring higher, became a dark and motionless speck before it vanished into the blue as if it had left the earth forever. The white man, standing gazing upwards before the doorway, heard in the hut a confused and broken murmur of distracted words ending with a loud groan. Suddenly Arsat stumbled out with outstretched hands, shivered, and stood still for some time with fixed eyes. Then he said:

"She burns no more."

What has happened to the woman by morning?

Before his face the sun showed its edge above the treetops rising steadily. The breeze freshened; a great brilliance burst upon the lagoon, sparkled on the rippling water. The forests came out of the clear shadows of the morning, became distinct, as if they had rushed nearer—to stop short in a great stir of leaves, of nodding boughs, of swaying branches. In the merciless sunshine the whisper of unconscious life grew louder, speaking in an incomprehensible voice round the dumb darkness of that human sorrow. Arsat's eyes wandered slowly, then stared at the rising sun.

"I can see nothing," he said half aloud to himself.

"There is nothing," said the white man, moving to the edge of the platform and waving his hand to his boat. A shout came faintly over the lagoon and the sampan began to glide towards the abode of the friend of ghosts.

"If you want to come with me, I will wait all the morning," said the white man, looking away upon the water.

"No, Tuan," said Arsat, softly. "I shall not eat or sleep in this house, but I must first see my road. Now I can see nothing—see nothing! There is no light and no peace in the world; but there is death—death for many. We are sons of the same mother—and I left him in the midst of enemies; but I am going back now."

What guilt continues to haunt Arsat?

He drew a long breath and went on in a dreamy tone:

"In a little while I shall see clear enough to strike—to strike. But she has died, and . . . now . . . darkness."

He flung his arms wide open, let them fall along his body, then stood still with unmoved face and stony eyes, staring at the sun. The white man got down into his canoe. The polers ran smartly along the sides of the boat, looking over their shoulders at the beginning of a weary journey. High in the stern, his head muffled up in white rags, the juragan sat moody, letting his paddle trail in the water. The white man, leaning with both arms over the grass roof of the little cabin, looked back at the shining ripple of the boat's wake. Before the sampan passed out of the lagoon into the creek he lifted his eyes. Arsat had not moved. He stood lonely in the searching sunshine; and he looked beyond the great light of a cloudless day into the darkness of a world of illusions. ■

Respond *to the* SELECTION

What do you think Arsat will do now? Why?

ANSWER TO GUIDED READING QUESTION

1. The guilt of leaving his brother in the midst of enemies continues to haunt Arsat.

RESPOND TO THE SELECTION

What choice would you have made if you were Arsat? Who would have chosen to help your brother or your friend?

SELECTION CHECK TEST 4.11.9 WITH ANSWERS

Checking Your Reading

1. What is the polers' opinion of Arsat? **They dislike and distrust him.**
2. What is wrong with Diamelen? **She is dying of a fever.**
3. Why had Arsat fled his village? **His was not allowed to marry Diamelen.**
4. What happened to Arsat's brother? **He was killed by the villagers.**
5. Why won't Arsat go with Tuan now? **He plans to return to his village.**

Vocabulary in Context

Fill each blank with the most appropriate word from the Words for Everyday Use. You may have to change the tense of the word.

portal discordant festoon
wayfarer conflagration august
ignoble

1. I enjoy the **discordant** style of the modern piece, but Jo prefers the classic melody.
2. After a year backpacking through Europe, the young **wayfarer** returned to school.
3. We were criticized for behaving **ignobly** during what was otherwise a peaceful rally.
4. Although he is humble, Dr. Mason's accomplishments are **august**.
5. In the hot dry weather, the brush fire quickly became a fierce **conflagration**.

Literary Tools

1. What two meanings does "image" have in the context of a literary work? **An image is both the language that creates a concrete representation of an object or experience and the vivid mental picture created in the mind by that language.**

SELECTION CHECK TEST 4.11.9 WITH ANSWERS (CONT.)

2. What term is used for the collection of all images in a literary work? **This is imagery.**
3. Identify one element or theme common in Conrad's work. **Responses could include rich description, tests of character, moral questions, isolation, or psychology.**
4. What do you learn about Tuan in this story? **Responses will vary; he served with Arsat in a war; he's traveled extensively; he likes Arsat; he is white.**
5. What is the central conflict of this story? **Arsat's anguish over his role in his brother's death is the main conflict. Students may also note a hint of supernatural interference in the polers' superstition about Arsat's disregard for the spirits.**

ANSWERS TO INVESTIGATE, INQUIRE AND IMAGINE

RECALL

1a. The men have great respect for Arsat. The men are fearful of the spirits in Arsat's ruined house and refuse to stay there.

2a. Arsat tells Tuan twice that he hoped to find a "country where death is unknown."

3a. He tells Tuan that there is "no worse enemy and no better friend than a brother."

INTERPRET

1b. Given the tormented nature of Arsat's soul and the death of his love, one may interpret the men's fears as having been justified.

2b. He found a life tormented by guilt and death.

3b. Arsat feels a great deal of guilt about abandoning his brother because he saw him as a friend. But he also became an enemy because he would have threatened Arsat's life if he would have waited from him.

ANALYZE

4a. Arsat's dilemma was the choice he had to make between waiting for his brother and risking his own and the woman's death, or abandoning his brother to save himself and the woman. The latter choice guaranteed the death of his brother. He chose to abandon his brother to the ruler's men and death, in order to save himself and the woman.

SYNTHESIZE

4b. Arsat tells Tuan that he chose to save himself and the woman because he "wanted peace in my own heart." This is ironic because his choice ended all peace in his heart. The story implies that Arsat has set his fate by choosing to allow the death of his brother, and brought on the life of death he now knows.

EVALUATE

5a. *Responses will vary.* Some students will find him guilty of the crime of stealing the woman away from the ruler. Because of that first crime, he finds himself in a dilemma involving choices that all involve death. Others will feel he acted in love by taking the woman, and that he is a victim of capricious and arbitrary fate. Some students may feel he should have defended his brother who unselfishly defended him. This story permits several interpretations, with no simple conclusion about clear-cut guilt or innocence. Conrad's fiction is full of complex and irresolvable moral dilemmas where the emotions of the human heart are concerned.

INVESTIGATE, Inquire, Imagine

Recall: GATHERING FACTS →

1a. How do the men feel about Arsat? What do they fear about staying in the lagoon near his house?

2a. By escaping with the woman, what did Arsat hope to find?

3a. How does Arsat describe to Tuan having a brother?

Interpret: FINDING MEANING

1b. After reading the story, do you think their fears were unfounded? Why, or why not?

2b. What did Arsat find?

3b. How is this description relevant to what happens between Arsat and his brother?

Analyze: TAKING THINGS APART →

4a. What moral dilemmas did Arsat face in "The Lagoon"? What choices did Arsat make, and what consequences did he face for each choice? How did he resolve each dilemma?

Synthesize: BRINGING THINGS TOGETHER

4b. What is ironic about the choices Arsat made?

Evaluate: MAKING JUDGMENTS →

5a. Tuan tells Arsat that the woman will die "if such is her fate." Arsat replies, "No, Tuan...If such is my fate." How do you judge Arsat's guilt or innocence in this story? If you find him guilty, what is his crime? How does fate play out his sentence? Do you feel any sympathy for him? Why, or why not?

Extend: CONNECTING IDEAS

5b. Why do you think Arsat tells his story to Tuan? What does he want from Tuan? Does he get it?

Understanding Literature

IMAGE. Review the definition for **image** in Literary Tools in Prereading for this selection. As you read, you paid attention to the description of setting in the story. Complete the following chart, recording images from it that convey darkness and stillness. Two have been completed for you. Having analyzed these images, what mood do you think they create them? What is the significance of the use of light imagery at the end of the story after the death of the woman?

Darkness and Stillness
Forests stood motionless
Stagnant lagoon

CHARACTER. Review the definition for **character** in Literary Tools in Prereading for this selection. What does the reader come to know about Arsat? How does the author present information about Arsat to the reader? What does the reader come to know of Tuan? How does the reader learn about Tuan? What purpose does Tuan serve in the story?

ANSWERS TO INVESTIGATE, INQUIRE AND IMAGINE (CONT.)

EXTEND

5b. *Responses will vary.* One interpretation is that Arsat hopes that Tuan can help him understand and find absolution for his torment. However, Tuan offers no insight. Ultimately, he is alone with his guilt.

Writer's Journal

1. Write the **letter** you think Arsat might write to his dead brother, explaining why he acted the way he did and how he feels about it now.
2. Captains of ships keep logs that record the events of their voyages, facts about the weather and sea conditions, and often diary-like comments on the events of the day. Imagine that you are Tuan, and write a **captain's log entry** for the evening spent in Arsat's clearing, including not only the events but also your reaction to them.
3. Superstitions arise to explain the seemingly unexplainable. The Malay men who staff Tuan's boat are superstitious about Arsat and his clearing. Imagine you are one of the boatmen. Develop a brief **explanation** based on superstition to account for the death of the woman in Arsat's hut.

Integrating *the* Language Arts

Language, Grammar, and Style

Review the Language Arts Survey 3.39, "Adding Colorful Language to Sentences." Revise the following sentences to make them as vivid as you can by using more precise nouns, action verbs, and colorful modifiers. You may find the Speaking and Listening exercise below on guided visualization helps you to "see" and therefore describe a more vivid picture.

1. The boat floated into the dark cove.
2. The jungle was thick with vines.
3. The woman was hot with fever.
4. A small house was sitting on the edge of the lagoon.
5. Arsat was sad about the death of the woman.

Study and Research

Researching Malaysia's History. Locate Malaysia on a map and, using library and Internet resources, research the socio-political setting of this story. What was the nature of British involvement in Malaya in the late 1800s? (Malaya's name was changed to the name we know today, Malaysia, in 1963. You may want to try Internet searches on both names.) What sort of society existed in Malaya? How might white men like Tuan have viewed the Malayan natives, and how did the Malayans view the British? Prepare a brief report for your teacher on your findings.

Speaking and Listening

Recreating Imagery from "The Lagoon." Working in small groups, engage in a guided imagery exercise to envision the jungle in which this story takes place. Have one member of the group, or perhaps your teacher, read aloud the opening passages of the story, describing the jungle as the boat approaches Arsat's house. As this person reads, the other members of the group should close their eyes and listen carefully, imagining the sights, sounds, and smells of the jungle as if they were actually there. Afterward, share with each other what you "saw" and "heard" and "smelled." Working together, create illustrations for the opening of the story. You may also wish to locate or create recordings of the sort of sounds you might hear in the jungle. Experiment with creating a multi-sensory experience of "The Lagoon."

Answers to Understanding Literature

Image. Other images of darkness and stillness:

- Forests stood motionless
- Blossoms bewitched into an immobility perfect and final
- Nothing moved on the river
- Land from which the very memory of motion had forever departed
- Narrow creek...filled with gloom
- Glistening blackness of the water
- Small ferns, black and dull
- Darkness oozed out from between the trees
- Darkness mysterious and invincible; the darkness scented and poisonous of impenetrable forests
- Stagnant lagoon

The effect of these images is to create a mood of gloom and sadness. The images of darkness and immobility support the idea that there can be no solving of this situation The overall effect is an oppressive atmosphere of despair. Darkness is a common symbol of lack of enlightenment or understanding. At the end of the story, as the woman dies and Arsat endures his full fate, we see light break out and Tuan says, "There is nothing." This is, ultimately, the only understanding offered to Arsat---that there is no resolution, and that he is alone in his guilt.

Character. We learn that Arsat loved the woman obsessively and could think of nothing else but her. When his brother was captured, Arsat was apparently able to forget his loyalty to his brother and convince himself that his future with the woman would outweigh his loss. Now, he is racked with guilt. Many readers will sympathize with him, seeing in him their own ability to rationalize and give into their own, selfish desires. We learn very little about Tuan. He seems to exist in the story only to hear Arsat and to offer only "There is nothing" in response to Arsat's tale. The purpose served by Tuan is to point out that Arsat is alone. Tuan cannot take him out of the jungle and "undo" his guilt.

Answers to Integrating the Language Arts

Langauge, Grammar and Style.
Responses may vary.

1. The tiny craft slipped into the darkened void of the cove, disappearing from sight.
2. The jungle hung thick with a tangle of vines, blocking the sunlight like an emerald curtain.
3. She lay feverish, glistening and motionless in a bed sodden with her sweat.

Answers to Integrating the Language Arts (cont.)

4. A thatched hut, squeezed into the trees that crowded the shoreline, cast a small shadow on the water of the lagoon.
5. Arsat collapsed against the door and slid to the ground, his face blank with despair.

Study and Research
Refer students to the Language Arts Survey 1.15, "Using Graphic Aids," 5.19, "How to Locate Library Materials," and 5.26, "Using the Internet"

Speaking and Listening & Collaborative Learning
Refer students to the Language Arts Survey 2.18, "Sensory Detail Charts." Using a sensory detail chart for this activity will help students to organize their images.

ADDITIONAL RESOURCES

UNIT 11 RESOURCE BOOK
- Selection Worksheet 11.6
- Selection Check Test 4.11.11
- Selection Test 4.11.12
- Language, Grammar, and Style Resource 3.85–3.88
- Speaking and Listening Resource 4.2, 4.14

READER'S JOURNAL

Do you have mostly happy or sad memories from your childhood? Explain.

Literary TOOLS

NARRATOR AND POINT OF VIEW. A **narrator** is one who tells a story. Writers achieve a wide variety of ends by varying the characteristics of the narrator chosen for a particular work. Of primary importance is the narrator's **point of view.** Will the narrator be omniscient, knowing all things including the internal workings of the minds of the characters in the story, or will the narrator be limited in his or her knowledge? Will the narrator participate in the action of the story or stand outside that action and comment on it? Will the narrator be reliable or unreliable? That is, will the reader be able to trust the narrator's statements? These are all questions that a writer must consider when creating a narrator. As you read, contemplate the characteristics of the narrator Rhys has created to tell this story.

Reader's Journal

What are one or two of your most vivid memories from childhood?

"HEAT"

BY JEAN RHYS

About the AUTHOR

Jean Rhys (1894–1979) was born in Dominica, in the Windward Islands of the West Indies. The daughter of a Creole mother and a Welsh doctor, Rhys lived and went to school in Dominica until the age of sixteen, when she was sent to England to study. Unfortunately, her father died shortly after her arrival in England, and she was left penniless. To support herself, Rhys worked at various jobs, including acting. After her marriage to a Dutch journalist, Rhys moved to Paris, where she met the English novelist Ford Madox Ford. Ford encouraged Rhys in her writing, and in 1927, she published her first book, *The Left Bank and Other Stories.* Her novel *Postures,* published in 1928, was followed by the novels *After Leaving Mr. Mackenzie* and *Voyage in the Dark.* In 1939, she published *Good Morning, Midnight,* and then nearly thirty years passed before she published her enormously successful novel *Wide Sargasso Sea,* a fictional account of the character Berthe Rochester, Mr. Rochester's mad wife from Charlotte Brontë's *Jane Eyre.* Following such a success, her books were reissued, and two new collections of stories were published, *Tigers Are Better Looking* and *Sleep It Off, Lady.* Rhys's unfinished autobiography, *Smile Please,* was published posthumously.

About the SELECTION

"Heat" is written in the spare and direct style characteristic of Rhys's writing. While much of her writing revolves around the theme of the lonely woman seeking solace in a compassionless, male-dominated world, "Heat" gives a remembered first-person account of Mount Pelée's eruption in 1902. Mount Pelée, located near the city of Saint-Pierre on the island of Martinique, had last erupted in 1856; when it showed signs of erupting again, the signs were not taken seriously by officials. The ensuing volcanic explosion set fire to the island, killing nearly the entire population of Saint-Pierre. A deadly gas, emitted by the volcano, suffocated many of the people.

GOALS/OBJECTIVES

Studying this lesson will enable students to
- empathize with the people who were killed by Mount Pelee's volcanic eruption
- summarize Jean Rhys's literary accomplishments and her style of writing
- define *narrator* and *point of view* and explain and recognize examples in the selection
- demonstrate the ability to edit punctuation errors
- conduct a research on West Indian volcanoes

HEAT

Jean Rhys

Ash had fallen. Perhaps it had fallen the night before or perhaps it was still falling. I can only remember in patches. I was looking at it two feet deep on the flat roof outside my bedroom. The ash and the silence. Nobody talked in the street, nobody talked while we ate, or hardly at all. I know now that they were all frightened. They thought our volcano was going up.

Why was everyone frightened?

Our volcano was called the boiling lake. That's what it was, a sheet of water that always boiled. From what fires? I thought of it as a mysterious place that few people had ever seen. In the churchyard where we often went—for death was not then a taboo subject—quite near the grave of my little sister, was a large marble headstone. 'Sacred to the memory of Clive—, who lost his life at the boiling lake in Dominica in a heroic attempt to save his guide'. Aged twenty-seven. I remember that too.

He was a young Englishman, a visitor, who had gone exploring with two guides to the boiling lake. As they were standing looking at it one of the guides, who was a long way ahead, staggered and fell. The other seized hold of the Englishman's hand and said 'Run!' There must have been some local tradition that poisonous gases sometimes came out of the lake. After a few steps the Englishman pulled his hand away and went back and lifted up the man who had fallen. Then he too staggered and they both fell. The surviving guide ran and told what had happened.

In the afternoon two little friends were coming to see us and to my surprise they both arrived carrying large glass bottles. Both the bottles had carefully written labels pasted on: 'Ash collected from the streets of Roseau on May 8th, 1902.' The little boy asked me if I'd like to have his jar, but I refused. I didn't want to touch the ash. I don't remember the rest of the day. I must have gone to bed, for that night my mother woke me and without saying anything, led me to the window. There was a huge black cloud over Martinique. I couldn't ever describe that cloud, so huge and black it was, but I have never forgotten it. There was no moon, no stars, but the edges of the cloud were flame-coloured and in the middle what looked to me like lightning flickered, never stopping. My mother said: 'You will never see anything like this in your life again.' That was all. I must have gone to sleep at the window and been carried to bed.

What did she see when her mother wakened her?

Next morning we heard what had happened. Was it a blue or a grey day? I only know ash wasn't falling any longer. The Roseau fishermen went out very early, as they did in those days. They met the fishermen from Port de France, who knew. That was how we heard before the cablegrams, the papers and all the rest came flooding in. That was how we heard

ANSWERS TO GUIDED READING QUESTIONS

1. Everyone was frightened because they thought the falling ash meant their volcano would erupt.
2. She saw a huge cloud and flickering light over Martinique.

INDIVIDUAL LEARNING STRATEGIES

Motivation
Bring pictures of various volcanic eruptions that have taken place around the world. Also pose the following question to students: Why do you think people live in areas that have active volcanoes nearby—such as the people who live on the Hawaiian Islands—when they know it could possibly erupt?

Reading Proficiency
Have students work with a partner reading the selection and summarizing each paragraph in one or two sentences.

English Language Learning
As students read the selection, ask them to flag or write down phrases or words they do not understand. Then have them find the meaning based on the context of the word or phrase. If this fails, encourage them to ask a native English speaker for help.

Special Needs
Students should focus on the Recall questions. Also have students construct a time line of the important events that take place in the selection.

Enrichment
Ask students to research a volcano eruption that took place within the past century. Have them provide information about the date it took place, the number of fatalities, and the environmental effects of the eruption. Also have them find pictures of the eruption they research. Finally, ask them to present their information in an oral report.

ANSWERS TO GUIDED READING QUESTIONS

1. Mount Pelee, a volcano, had erupted and killed 40,000.
2. A convict being held in an underground cell survived the eruption.

SELECTION CHECK TEST 4.11.11 WITH ANSWERS

Checking Your Reading

1. What covers the flat roof? **Ash covers the flat roof.**
2. What is the "boiling lake"? **This is what the volcano is called.**
3. What happens to Clive? **He dies trying to save his guide at the volcano.**
4. What do the gossips say about St. Pierre? **They say it is a "wicked" city.**
5. What happens to the sole survivor? **He is exhibited around the world.**

Literary Tools

1. Who is the narrator of this selection? **Rhys narrates the selection.**
2. From what point of view is the selection given? **It is in first-person point of view.**
3. Is the narrator reliable or unreliable? Why? **Reliable; she is part of the action.**

RESPOND TO THE SELECTION

What is ironic about the criminal surviving the eruption?

What was the cause of the cloud?

of Mont Pelée's eruption and the deaths of 40,000 people, and that there was nothing left of St Pierre.

As soon as ships were sailing again between Dominica and Martinique my father went to see the desolation that was left. He brought back a pair of candlesticks, tall heavy brass candlesticks which must have been in a church. The heat had twisted them into an extraordinary shape. He hung them on the wall of the dining-room and I stared at them all through meals, trying to make sense of the shape.

It was after this that the gossip started. That went on for years so I can remember it well. St Pierre, they said, was a very wicked city. It had not only a theatre, but an opera house, which was probably wickeder still. Companies from Paris performed there. But worse than this was the behaviour of the women who were the prettiest in the West Indies. They tied their turbans in a particular way, a sort of language of love that all St Pierre people understood. Tied in one way it meant 'I am in love, I am not free'; tied another way it meant 'You are welcome, I am free'. Even the women who were married, or as good as, tied their kerchiefs in the 'I am free' way. And that wasn't all. The last bishop who had visited the city had taken off his shoes and solemnly shaken them over it. After that, of course, you couldn't wonder.

As I grew older I heard of a book by a man called Lafcadio Hearn who had written about St Pierre as it used to be, about Ti Marie and all the others, but I never found the book and stopped looking for it. However, one day I did discover a pile of old newspapers and magazines, some illustrated: the English version of

Mount Pelée August 30, 1902

the eruption. They said nothing about the opera house or the theatre which must have seemed to the English the height of frivolity in a Caribbean island, and very little about the city and its inhabitants. It was nearly all about the one man who had survived. He was a convict imprisoned in an underground cell, so he escaped—the only one out of 40,000. He was now travelling round the music-halls of the world being exhibited. They had taught him a little speech. He must be quite a rich man —what did he do with his money? Would he marry again? His wife and children had been killed in the eruption. . . . I read all this, then I thought but it wasn't like that, it wasn't like that at all. ■

Who survived?

Respond *to the* Selection

Respond to the narrator's comment, "...I read all this, then I thought but it wasn't like that, it wasn't like that at all." What might the narrator mean when she says this? Can you relate the narrator's response in this situation to an experience from your own life? Why, or why not?

Investigate, Inquire, Imagine

Recall: GATHERING FACTS

1a. What does the narrator's friend offer to the narrator? How does the narrator respond?

2a. What was the gossip about St. Pierre, Martinique?

3a. What do the old newspapers say about the sole survivor of the eruption?

→ **Interpret:** FINDING MEANING

1b. Why might the narrator respond this way?

2b. What do you think was the significance of St. Pierre's wicked ways, in the minds of the gossipers?

3b. Why do you think the narrator rejects newspapers' versions of the story?

Analyze: TAKING THINGS APART

4a. What sources of information on the eruption are available to the narrator? Which seem most reliable to her? Which seem most reliable to you?

→ **Synthesize:** BRINGING THINGS TOGETHER

4b. Why do you think she finds this account most reliable? What is the significance of the fact that she was a child at the time?

Evaluate: MAKING JUDGMENTS

5a. How reliable do you think the gossip about St. Pierre was? Why do you think such gossip would arise?

→ **Extend:** CONNECTING IDEAS

5b. Compare this story to Joseph Conrad's "Lagoon." How is the notion of guilt and punishment presented in each?

Understanding Literature

NARRATOR. Review the definitions for **narrator** and **point of view** in the Handbook of Literary Terms. What sort of narrator has Rhys chosen to use? Does the narrator take part in the action of the story or stand outside the events taking place? Is the narrator omniscient, or is the narrator's knowledge of the events limited? Does the narrator seem reliable to you? Do her observations seem to be accurate? How would changing the point of view from which the story is told change the story?

ANSWERS TO INVESTIGATE, INQUIRE, AND IMAGINE

RECALL

1a. He offered her a bottle with "'ash collected from the streets of Roseau on May 8th, 1902.'" The narrator refused the offer.

2a. The gossip about St. Pierre was that it was a wicked city with a theatre, an opera house and women of loose morals.

3a. The newspapers say that the only survivor was a convict, who subsequently became a celebrity.

INTERPRET

1b. The narrator does not want to remember what happened on May 8, 1902 because it was a tragic day.

2b. The gossipers appear to have felt that St. Pierre was punished for its wicked ways.)

3b. The narrator may reject this because it is inconsistent with a view that the city was punished for its wicked ways by the eruption. A convict would not be allowed to survive if this were the case.)

ANALYZE

4a. The narrator has her own recollection, the gossip she heard, the newspaper accounts, cablegrams, and reports of witnesses. She seems to find her own recollection most reliable and she rejects the newspaper accounts. Because the narrator admits that she remembers "in patches," her memory is probably not the most reliable.

SYNTHESIZE

4b. The narrator finds her memory most reliable because it is human nature to trust our own memory. Because she was a child at the time, this memory has been the version she has known for a long time and the newspaper accounts, which contradict it, are relatively new to her. This may make her less likely to trust them. It also means that her memory is likely to be less than objective and may have been colored by a child's interpretation of the events she saw.

EVALUATE

5a. *Responses will vary.* Some students will believe that God punishes the wicked as the gossip appears to imply. Others will believe that the gossip may have arisen because people want to believe that disasters are not random, and will try to blame the disaster on the behavior of the victim. Others will say that

ANSWERS TO INVESTIGATE, INQUIRE, AND IMAGINE (CONT.)

the people of Dominica poorly understood the science of volcanoes and so they created a cause they could understand.

EXTEND

5b. In Joseph Conrad's "Lagoon," Arsat feels that the death of his wife is his fate, or punishment, for his betrayal of his brother. Conrad does not present a judgment on Arsat's belief but seems to say that Arsat's agonizing guilt is his punishment. In "Heat,' Jean Rhys presents the idea of guilt and punishment as "gossip" which implies that it is not credible.

Answers to Understanding Literature can be found on page 1050.

ANSWERS TO UNDERSTANDING LITERATURE

Narrator. The narrator is a limited narrator who participates in the action of the story. She is limited in that she can only report what she remembers and her own thoughts, rather than the thoughts of all the characters. Indeed, she cannot even explain her own thoughts fully, and does not tell us why she thinks the newspaper accounts were wrong. We have the sense that she herself does not know. If she were omniscient, she would be able to tell the reader this as well as why her father hung the candlesticks on the wall and what the survivor's thoughts and plans were. The narrator is not very reliable because she admits that she remembers some things and not others. She was a child at the time so her memory is likely to be flawed and incomplete. Had Rhys used a reliable, omniscient narrator, she could not have created as effective a portrait of how the human memory interprets and changes events in order to explain reality.

ANSWERS TO INTEGRATING THE LANGUAGE ARTS

Language, Grammar, and Style

1. Having seen the young Englishman drop dead by the boiling lake, I decided never to go near it.
2. I remember a lot of talk about how wicked St. Pierre was; however, there was no mention of it in the newspaper accounts.
3. The air was full of ash and the clouds, thick and black, obscured the moon and stars.
4. There was silence in the streets, silence in the schools, and silence in our home.
5. The day the volcano erupted was the day I remember most from my childhood; it was the day I realized that we would all die someday.

Study and Research

Refer students to the Language Arts Survey 5.19, "How to Locate Library Materials" and 5.26, "Using the Internet."

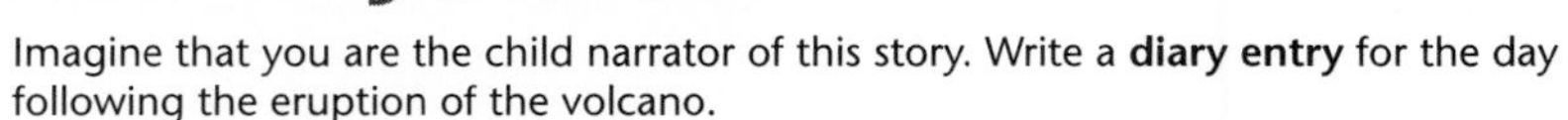

Writer's Journal

1. Imagine that you are the child narrator of this story. Write a **diary entry** for the day following the eruption of the volcano.
2. Write the **poster copy** that might have been used to advertise a lecture by the convict who survived the eruption.
3. **Myths** often arise in order to explain the mysterious forces of nature. Write a myth to explain the boiling lake, its poisonous gases, and the lives it has taken.

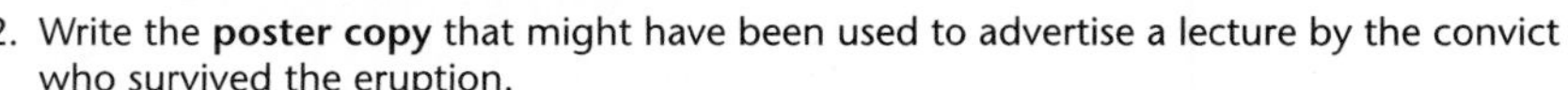

Integrating *the* Language Arts

Language, Grammar, and Style

Editing for Punctuation Errors. Review the Language Arts Survey 3.85–3.88, "Editing for Punctuation Errors: End Marks, Commas, and Semicolons." Then, edit the following sentences for proper punctuation.

1. Having seen the young Englishman drop dead by the boiling lake I decided never to go near it.
2. I remember a lot of talk about how wicked St. Pierre was however there was no mention of it in the newspaper accounts
3. The air was full of ash and the clouds thick and black obscured the moon and stars.
4. There was silence in the streets silence in the schools and silence in our home.
5. The day the volcano erupted the day I remember most from my childhood was the day I realized that we would all die someday.

Study and Research

Researching Volcanos. Using library and Internet resources, research the West Indies islands of Dominica and Martinique. What active and inactive volcanoes exist on these islands? What is the history of volcanic activity on these islands? What are the causes of volcanoes and volcanic eruptions? Are these islands high-risk areas for volcanic eruptions?

Speaking and Listening

Comparing Recollections. When several people experience the same event, they often have very different recollections and interpretations of the event afterward. Select an event that several of your schoolmates, friends, or family members have experienced. Interview them about what happened and why. You may wish to tape record your interviews. Afterward, compare the versions you heard. How are they similar? How are they different? What explanation do you have for the differences? Before you begin, you may wish to review the Language Arts Survey 4.2, "Active versus Passive Listening," and 4.14, "Conducting an Interview."

"A Sunrise on the Veld"

BY DORIS LESSING

About the AUTHOR

Doris Lessing (1919–) was born in Kermanshah, Persia (now Iran), and lived for many years in the African country of southern Rhodesia (now Zimbabwe), where she was educated. She moved to London in 1949 and one year later published her first novel, *The Grass Is Singing,* which is set in Africa. Throughout her work, Lessing's primary interest has been in the subtle and sometimes destructive interactions between women and men. Lessing's experimental novel *The Golden Notebook* (1962) has become a classic of feminist literature. The author of more than thirty books of fiction, nonfiction, poems, and plays, Lessing has published numerous short story collections including *Nine African Stories,* from which this selection is taken, *The Stories of Doris Lessing,* and *The Habit of Loving.* Her most recent work is the novel *Mara and Dann,* an adventure story.

About the SELECTION

Growing up on a farm in Africa, Lessing spent her youth exploring the bordering *veld,* a vast grassy land with sparse bushes and almost no trees. Allowed to go into the veld alone, which was uncommon for a female of her generation, she often carried a rifle to shoot game for the family's food. Lessing has claimed that her real education came from observing nature on the veld, which became the setting for many of her stories. In **"A Sunrise on the Veld"** a boy discovers his own limitations by observing the ways of nature.

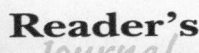

Reader's Journal

Write about a time when you learned a lesson about life that startled you or forever changed your view of the world.

Literary TOOLS

NATURALISM. Naturalism was a literary movement of the late nineteenth and early twentieth centuries that saw actions and events as resulting inevitably from biological, environmental, or natural forces. Often these forces were beyond the comprehension or control of the characters subjected to them. Taken to its extreme, Naturalism views all events as mechanically determined by external forces, including the decisions made by people. As you read, think about what naturalistic themes are present in this short story.

PLOT. A **plot** is a series of events related to a central conflict, or struggle. A typical plot involves the introduction of a conflict, its development, and its eventual resolution. Terms used to describe elements of a plot include the following:

- **exposition**, or **introduction**
- **inciting incident**
- **rising action**, or **complication**
- **climax**
- **crisis**, or **turning point**
- **falling action**
- **resolution**
- **dénouement**

Refer to **plot** in the Handbook of Literary Terms for complete definitions of each element of plot. Then, write each of the boldface terms down the side of a sheet of paper. As you read, jot down your ideas about what events in the story correspond to these terms. You may find that your ideas about what the various parts of the plot are change as you read further into the story.

ADDITIONAL RESOURCES

UNIT 11 RESOURCE BOOK
- Selection Worksheet 11.7
- Selection Check Test 4.11.13
- Selection Test 4.11.14
- Language, Grammar, and Style Resource 3.22, 3.23
- Speaking and Listening Resource 4.21

VOCABULARY FROM THE SELECTION

crook	myriad
exultation	stoicism
fastidious	sultry
fatality	superfluity
frond	tumult
incredulously	veld
lope	vigilant

READER'S JOURNAL

Have you felt regret after doing a particular thing? What did you do? Why did you feel regret?

GOALS/OBJECTIVES

Studying this lesson will enable students to
- enjoy a brief work of a naturalistic short story
- describe Doris Lessing's literary accomplishments and explain her influence on twentieth-century prose
- define *Naturalism* and *plot* and identify and explain examples of each in the selection
- identify direct and indirect objects and complements in sentences
- participate in a class debate on hunting

ANSWERS TO GUIDED READING QUESTIONS

1. The character says aloud, "Half past four!" to himself each night before he falls asleep, and then he wakes up at half past four each morning before his alarm goes off.
2. His attitude toward his own body is that his limbs and fingers are like soldiers awaiting his command. He feels that sleep is also something that he can command and refuse.

INDIVIDUAL LEARNING STRATEGIES

MOTIVATION
Have students share their thoughts about hunting wild animals such as deer. Do they think it's right or wrong? For those who hunt animals, have them share why they like to hunt and why they think it is morally acceptable to kill animals for sport.

READING PROFICIENCY
This selection will be captivating to most readers. To make it even more enjoyable, have someone from the class or from another class who competes in Storytelling within the Forensics department read this story to the class.

ENGLISH LANGUAGE LEARNING
Ask students to select five words of particular difficulty from the selection. Then have them make a flash card for each word that contains a synonym, an antonym, and a contextual sentence. Finally, ask students to use each word at least once in their conversations throughout the day.

SPECIAL NEEDS
Have students focus on the Recall questions in particular. You may also want to spend some time helping students understand the overall message of the selection.

ENRICHMENT
Ask students to do a comparison-contrast essay between this selection and "Shooting an Elephant." How are the experience and feelings of both protagonists similar or different? In what ways are the lessons they learn similar? different?

A SUNRISE ON THE VELD

DORIS LESSING

Every night that winter he said aloud into the dark of the pillow, "Half past four! Half past four!" till he felt his brain had gripped the words and held them fast. Then he fell asleep at once, as if a shutter had fallen, and lay with his face turned to the clock so that he could see it first thing when he woke.

It was half past four to the minute, every morning. Triumphantly pressing down the alarm knob of the clock, which the dark half of his mind had outwitted, remaining vigilant all night and counting the hours as he lay relaxed in sleep, he huddled down for a last warm moment under the clothes, playing with the idea of lying abed for this once only. But he played with it for the fun of knowing that it was a weakness he could defeat without effort, just as he set the alarm each night for the delight of the moment when he woke and stretched his limbs, feeling the muscles tighten, and thought: Even my brain—even that! I can control every part of myself.

What does this boy do every night? What is he able to do every morning?

Luxury of warm, rested body, with the arms and legs and fingers waiting like soldiers for a word of command! Joy of knowing that the precious hours were given to sleep voluntarily!—for he had once stayed awake three nights running, to prove that he could, and then worked all day, refusing even to admit

What is his attitude toward his own body? What is his attitude toward sleep?

WORDS FOR EVERYDAY USE

vig • i • lant (vij′ ə lənt) *adj.*, staying watchful and alert to danger or trouble. *At night, the guard dog kept a vigilant watch over its owner's home.*

that he was tired; and now sleep seemed to him a servant to be commanded and refused.

The boy stretched his frame full length, touching the wall at his head with his hands, and the bed foot with his toes; then he sprung out, like a fish leaping from water. And it was cold, cold.

He always dressed rapidly, so as to try and conserve his night warmth till the sun rose two hours later; but by the time he had on his clothes, his hands were numbed and he could scarcely hold his shoes. These he could not put on for fear of waking his parents, who never came to know how early he rose.

As soon as he stepped over the lintel,[1] the flesh of his soles contracted on the chilled earth, and his legs began to ache with cold. It was night: the stars were glittering, the trees standing black and still. He looked for signs of day, for the graying of the edge of a stone, or a lightening in the sky where the sun would rise, but there was nothing yet. Alert as an animal, he crept past the dangerous window, standing poised with his hand on the sill for one proudly fastidious moment, looking in at the stuffy blackness of the room where his parents lay.

Where does the boy go when he wakes? What does he carefully creep by?

Feeling for the grass edge of the path with his toes, he reached inside another window further along the wall, where his gun had been set in readiness the night before. The steel was icy, and numbed fingers slipped along it, so that he had to hold it in the crook of his arm for safety. Then he tiptoed to the room where the dogs slept and was fearful that they might have been tempted to go before him; but they were waiting, their haunches[2] crouched in reluctance at the cold, but ears and swinging tails greeting the gun ecstatically. His warning undertone kept them secret and silent till the house was a hundred yards back; then they bolted off into the bush, yelping excitedly. The boy imagined his parents turning in their beds and muttering, "Those dogs again!" before they were dragged back in sleep; and he smiled scornfully. He always looked back over his shoulder at the house before he passed a wall of trees that shut it from sight. It looked so low and small, crouching there under a tall and brilliant sky. Then he turned his back on it, and on the frowsting[3] sleepers, and forgot them.

He would have to hurry. Before the light grew strong, he must be four miles away; and already a tint of green stood in the hollow of a leaf, and the air smelled of morning, and the stars were dimming.

He slung the shoes over his shoulder, veld skoen[4] that were crinkled and hard with the dews of a hundred mornings. They would be necessary when the ground became too hot to bear. Now he felt the chilled dust push up between his toes, and he let the muscles of his feet spread and settle into the shapes of the earth; and he thought: I could walk a hundred miles on feet like these! I could walk all day and never tire!

What does the boy bring with him as he sets out?

He was walking swiftly through the dark tunnel of foliage that in daytime was a road. The dogs were invisibly ranging the lower travel-ways of the bush, and he heard them panting. Sometimes he felt a cold muzzle on his leg before they were off again, scouting for

1. **lintel.** Horizontal crosspiece over an opening, such as in a door or window
2. **haunches.** Part of the body including the hips and thighs
3. **frowsting.** Lounging about in a hot, stuffy room (British colloquialism)
4. **skoen.** Homemade leather shoes

WORDS FOR EVERYDAY USE

fas • tid • i • ous (fas tid′ ē əs) *adj.*, not easy to please; very critical. *Our uncle turned up his nose in a fastidious manner at the sight of the meal, but the rest of us began eating the unusual dish with delight.*

crook (krŏŏk) *n.*, hooked, bent, or curved thing or part. *The birds built their nest in a crook in the branch of the old oak tree.*

veld (velt) *n.*, in South Africa, open grassy country, with few bushes and almost no trees; grassland. *Zebras and antelopes grazed on the veld as predators like lions and cheetahs lay in wait, ready to spring.*

ANSWERS TO GUIDED READING QUESTIONS

1. The boy goes outside even though it is not yet dawn. He creeps carefully by his parents bedroom window because they lie sleeping in that room.
2. He brings his gun and his dogs.

CROSS-CURRICULAR CONNECTIONS

Biology. The Zimbabwe African veld is also known as the South African Highveld. The highveld is dominated by species of red grass and tends to be sweeter than elsewhere. It also consists of fire-resistant tress and tall perennial grasses and flowering herbs, which readily catch fire during the dry season.

Meteorology. Many students will be surprised to read about how cold the boy is since he lives in Africa. Explain to students that temperatures can range from a cool 40 degrees F to a blazing 80 degrees F over a 24-hour period. And in the desert, it can range from 35 degrees F to 110 degrees F.

ANSWERS TO GUIDED READING QUESTIONS

1. The boy learned how to maintain a steady, loping run from watching the natives. The boy feels proud and triumphant as the blood rushes through him and he maintains his steady pace.
2. The boy had gone out on the veld to hunt guinea hens. It is now too late to hunt he birds, which are no longer roosting.
3. The boy suddenly begins running wildly and yelling, filled with the joy of living because it is his fifteenth birthday.

BIBLIOGRAPHIC NOTE

Lessing's other novels include *The Good Terrorist* (1985) and *The Fifth Child* (1988); she also published two novels under the pseudonym Jane Somers (*The Diary of a Good Neighbour*, 1983 and *If the Old Could...*, 1984). In addition, she has written several nonfiction works, including books about cats, a love since childhood. *Under My Skin: Volume One of My Autobiography, to 1949* appeared in 1995 and received the James Tait Black Prize for best biography.

a trail to follow. They were not trained but free-running companions of the hunt, who often tired of the long stalk before the final shots and went off on their own pleasure. Soon he could see them, small and wild-looking in a wild, strange light, now that the bush stood trembling on the verge of color, waiting for the sun to paint earth and grass afresh.

The grass stood to his shoulders, and the trees were showering a faint silvery rain. He was soaked; his whole body was clenched in a steady shiver.

Once he bent to the road that was newly scored with animal trails and regretfully straightened, reminding himself that the pleasure of tracking must wait till another day.

He began to run along the edge of a field, noting jerkily how it was filmed over with fresh spiderweb, so that the long reaches of great black clods seemed netted in glistening gray. He was using the steady lope he had learned by watching the natives, the run that is a dropping of the weight of the body from one foot to the next in a slow balancing movement that never tires, nor shortens the breath; and he felt the blood pulsing down his legs and along his arms, and the exultation and pride of body mounted in him till he was shutting his teeth hard against a violent desire to shout his triumph.

What did the boy learn from the natives? What feeling does the boy have as he is running steadily?

Soon he had left the cultivated part of the farm. Behind him the bush was low and black. In front was a long vlei,[5] acres of long, pale grass that sent back a hollowing gleam of light to a satiny sky. Near him thick swaths of grass were bent with the weight of water, and diamond drops sparkled on each frond.

The first bird woke at his feet, and at once a flock of them sprang into the air calling shrilly that day had come; and suddenly, behind him, the bush woke into song, and he could hear the guinea fowl[6] calling far ahead of him. That meant they would now be sailing down from their trees into thick grass, and it was for them he had come: he was too late. But he did not mind. He forgot he had come to shoot. He set his legs wide, and balanced from foot to foot, and swung his gun up and down in both hands horizontally, in a kind of improvised exercise, and let his head sink back till it was pillowed in his neck muscles, and watched how above him small rosy clouds floated in a lake of gold.

For what reason had the boy gone out to the veld? What is it too late to do?

Suddenly it all rose in him: it was unbearable. He leaped up into the air, shouting and yelling wild, unrecognizable noises. Then he began to run, not carefully, as he had before, but madly, like a wild thing. He was clean crazy, yelling mad with the joy of living and a superfluity of youth. He rushed down the vlei under a tumult of crimson and gold, while all the birds of the world sang about him. He ran in great leaping strides and shouted as he ran, feeling his body rise into the crisp rushing air and fall back surely onto sure feet; and he thought briefly, not believing that such a thing could happen to him, that he could break his ankle any moment

What does the boy suddenly do? Why?

5. **vlei.** Swampland
6. **guinea fowl.** Type of African bird with round, dark-feathered bodies and a featherless head

WORDS FOR EVERYDAY USE

lope (lōp) *n.*, a long, easy, swinging stride. *Carla was not a very experienced rider so she guided her horse into an easy lope rather than a full gallop.*

ex • ul • ta • tion (eg' zul tā' shən) *n.*, act of rejoicing; jubilation; triumph. *From the look of exultation on the team's faces, we could tell they had won the state finals.*

frond (fränd) *n.*, a leaf. *The fronds of the palm tree swayed gently in the ocean breeze.*

su • per • flu • i • ty (sʊʊ' pər flʊʊ' ə tē) *n.*, excess; superabundance. *Our cherry tree produced a superfluity of cherries this year—so many that we tired of fresh fruit, pies, and jams and let the birds help themselves to the excess.*

tu • mult (tʊʊ' mult') *n.*, noisy commotion, as of a crowd; uproar. *Even though we were outside the stadium, we knew the home team scored a touchdown because of the tumult of the crowd inside.*

in this thick, tangled grass. He cleared bushes like a duiker,[7] leaped over rocks, and finally came to a dead stop at a place where the ground fell abruptly away below him to the river. It had been a two-mile-long dash through waist-high growth, and he was breathing hoarsely and could no longer sing. But he poised on a rock and looked down at stretches of water that gleamed through stooping trees and thought suddenly, I am fifteen! Fifteen! The words came new to him, so that he kept repeating them wonderingly, with swelling excitement; and he felt the years of his life with his hands, as if he were counting marbles, each one hard and separate and compact, each one a wonderful shining thing. That was what he was: fifteen years of this rich soil, and this slow-moving water, and air that smelled like a challenge whether it was warm and sultry at noon or as brisk as cold water, like it was now.

How old is the boy?

There was nothing he couldn't do, nothing! A vision came to him, as he stood there, like when a child hears the word *eternity* and tries to understand it, and time takes possession of the mind. He felt his life ahead of him as a great and wonderful thing, something that was his; and he said aloud, with the blood rising to his head: "All the great men of the world have been as I am now, and there is nothing I can't become, nothing I can't do; there is no country in the world I cannot make part of myself, if I choose. I contain the world. I can make of it what I want. If I choose, I can change everything that is going to happen: it depends on me and what I decide now."

What are the boy's thoughts about his life and his future?

The urgency, and the truth and the courage of what his voice was saying exulted him, so that he began to sing again, at the top of his voice, and the sound went echoing down the river gorge.[8] He stopped for the echo and sang again: stopped and shouted. That was what he was!—he sang, if he chose; and the world had to answer him.

And for minutes he stood there, shouting and singing and waiting for the lovely eddying[9] sound of the echo, so that his own new strong thoughts came back and washed around his head, as if someone were answering him and encouraging him, till the gorge was full of soft voices clashing back and forth from rock to rock over the river. And then it seemed as if there was a new voice. He listened, puzzled, for it was not his own. Soon he was leaning forward, all his nerves alert, quite still: somewhere close to him there was a noise that was no joyful bird, nor tinkle of falling water, nor ponderous movement of cattle.

There it was again. In the deep morning hush that held his future and his past was a sound of pain, repeated over and over: it was a kind of shortened scream, as if someone, something, had no breath to scream. He came to himself, looked about him, and called for the dogs. They did not appear: they had gone off on their own business, and he was alone. Now he was clean sober, all the madness gone. His heart beating fast, because of that frightened screaming, he stepped carefully off the rock and went towards a belt of trees. He was

What does the boy suddenly hear?

7. **duiker.** Small African antelope common south of the Sahara Desert
8. **gorge.** Deep narrow pass between steep heights
9. **eddying.** Circling like a whirlpool or whirlwind

WORDS FOR EVERYDAY USE

sul • try (sul' trē) *adj.*, oppressively hot and moist. *On a sultry August day, Jerome found himself too exhausted to do anything other than lie in a hammock and sip lemonade.*

ANSWERS TO GUIDED READING QUESTIONS

1. He is fifteen.
2. He thinks that he can do anything at all in life and that his life is a great and wonderful thing stretching ahead of him.
3. He hears a sound of pain as if someone has no breath to scream.

BIOGRAPHICAL NOTE

Lessing's fiction is deeply autobiographical, much of it emerging out of her experiences in Africa. Not only does she draw upon her childhood memories for stories, but she also draws upon the political and social concerns she has for Africa. Lessing has written about the clash of cultures, the gross injustices of racial inequality, the struggle among opposing elements within an individuals own personality, and the conflict between the individual conscience and the collective good. Her stories and novellas set in Africa, published during the fifties and early sixties, decry the dispossession of black Africans by white colonials, and expose the sterility of the white culture in southern Africa. In 1956, in response to Lessing's courageous outspokenness, she was declared a prohibited alien in both Southern Rhodesia and South Africa.

ANSWERS TO GUIDED READING QUESTIONS

1. A buck is making the screams.
2. The black patches are ants.
3. The boy raises his gun to shoot the buck and put it out of its misery. He puts the gun down not only because the buck can no longer feel pain but because he realizes that animals like the buck die in pain everyday, so his interference really changes nothing.
4. The boy tells himself that he can't stop it and that there is nothing he can do.
5. The boy knows fatality, that some things have to be and that you can't do anything about them, for the first time.

moving cautiously, for not so long ago he had seen a leopard in just this spot.

At the edge of the trees he stopped and peered, holding his gun ready; he advanced, looking steadily about him, his eyes narrowed. Then, all at once, in the middle of a step, he faltered, and his face was puzzled. He shook his head impatiently, as if he doubted his own sight.

There, between two trees, against a background of gaunt black rocks, was a figure from a dream, a strange beast that was horned and drunken-legged, but like something he had never even imagined. It seemed to be ragged. It looked like a small buck[10] that had black ragged tufts of fur standing up irregularly all over it, with patches of raw flesh beneath . . . but the patches of rawness were disappearing under moving black and came again elsewhere; and all the time the creature screamed, in small gasping screams, and leaped drunkenly from side to side, as if it were blind.

What is making the strange screams?

Then the boy understood: it *was* a buck. He ran closer and again stood still, stopped by a new fear. Around him the grass was whispering and alive. He looked wildly about and then down. The ground was black with ants, great energetic ants that took no notice of him but hurried and scurried towards the fighting shape, like glistening black water flowing through the grass.

What are the black patches on the buck?

And, as he drew in his breath and pity and terror seized him, the beast fell and the screaming stopped. Now he could hear nothing but one bird singing and the sound of the rustling, whispering ants.

He peered over at the writhing blackness that jerked convulsively with the jerking nerves. It grew quieter. There were small twitches from the mass that still looked vaguely like the shape of a small animal.

It came into his mind that he should shoot it and end its pain, and he raised the gun. Then he lowered it again. The buck could no longer feel; its fighting was a mechanical protest of the nerves. But it was not that which made him put down the gun. It was a swelling feeling of rage and misery and protest that expressed itself in the thought, If I had not come, it would have died like this, so why should I interfere? All over the bush things like this happen; they happen all the time; this is how life goes on, by living things dying in anguish. He gripped the gun between his knees and felt in his own limbs the myriad, swarming pain of the twitching animal that could no longer feel, and set his teeth, and said over and over again under his breath: I can't stop it. I can't stop it. There is nothing I can do.

For what reason does the boy raise his gun? What causes him to put it down again?

He was glad that the buck was unconscious and had gone past suffering so that he did not have to make a decision to kill it even when he was feeling with his whole body, This is what happens, this is how things work.

It was right—that was what he was feeling. *It was right, and nothing could alter it.*

What does the boy tell himself now?

The knowledge of fatality, of what has to be, had gripped him and for the first time in his life; and he was left unable to make any movement of brain or body, except to say: "Yes, yes. That is what living is." It had entered his flesh and his bones and grown into the furthest corners of his brain and would never leave him. And at that moment he

What does the boy know for the first time?

10. **buck.** Male antelope

WORDS FOR EVERYDAY USE

myr • i • ad (mir′ ē əd) *adj.,* of an indefinitely large number; countless. *It is impossible to count the myriad grains of sand on even a small beach.*

fa • tal • i • ty (fā tal′ ə tē) *n.,* fate or necessity. *In Greek dramas, human heroes struggle against fatality only to find that they cannot escape the yoke of necessity.*

could not have performed the smallest action of mercy, knowing as he did, having lived on it all his life, the vast unalterable, cruel veld, where at any moment one might stumble over a skull or crush the skeleton of some small creature.

Suffering, sick, and angry, but also grimly satisfied with his new stoicism, he stood there leaning on his rifle and watched the seething black mound grow smaller. At his feet, now were ants trickling back with pink fragments in their mouths, and there was a fresh acid smell in his nostrils. He sternly controlled the uselessly convulsing muscles of his empty stomach and reminded himself, The ants must eat to! At the same time, he found that the tears were streaming down his face, and his clothes were soaked with the sweat of that other creature's pain.

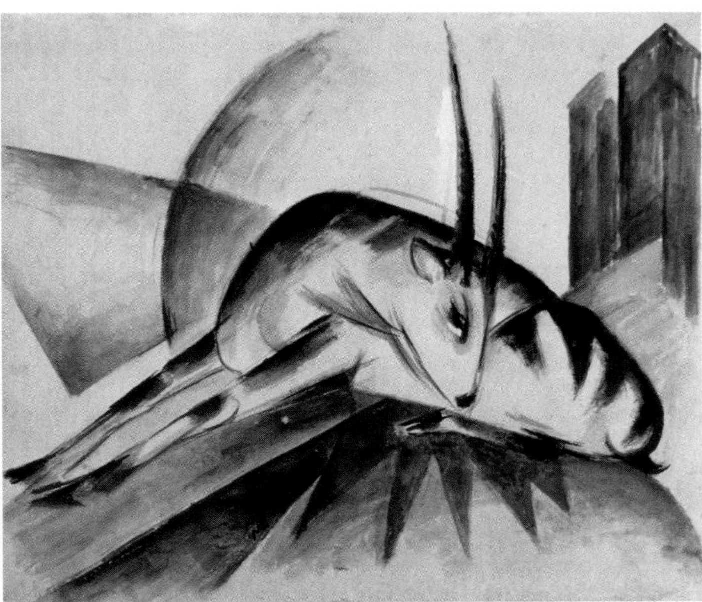

Antelope, 1913. Franz Marc. Rhode Island School of Design Museum.

The shape had grown small. Now it looked like nothing recognizable. He did not know how long it was before he saw the blackness thin, and bits of white showed through, shining in the sun—yes, there was the sun, just up, glowing over the rocks. Why, the whole thing could not have taken longer than a few minutes.

He began to swear, as if the shortness of the time was in itself unbearable, using the words he had heard his father say. He strode forward, crushing ants with each step and brushing them off his clothes, till he stood above the skeleton, which lay sprawled under a small bush. It was clean picked. It might have been lying there years, save that on the white bone were pink fragments of gristle. About the bones, ants were ebbing away, their pincers full of meat.

The boy looked at them, big black ugly insects. A few were standing and gazing up at him with small glittering eyes.

What does the boy tell the ants? What does he imagine they do?

"Go away!" he said to the ants, very coldly. "I am not for you—not just yet, at any rate. Go away." And he fancied that the ants turned and went away.

He bent over the bones and touched the sockets in the skull; that was where the eyes were, he thought incredulously, remembering the liquid

WORDS FOR EVERYDAY USE

sto • i • cism (stō′ ə si zəm) *n.*, indifference to pleasure or pain; impassivity. *Although inwardly she was distraught, Daisy reacted to the horrible news with outward stoicism.*

in • cred • u • lous • ly (in krej′ o͞o ləs lē) *adj.*, in a manner that shows doubt or disbelief. *When the Wright brothers told others about their plans to fly, people must have looked at them incredulously.*

ANSWER TO GUIDED READING QUESTION

1. The boy tells the ants to go away because he is not for them yet, and he imagines the ants heed him and go away.

SELECTION CHECK TEST 4.11.13 WITH ANSWERS

Checking Your Reading

1. Why had the boy stayed awake for three nights? **He wanted to prove he could.**
2. What covers the buck? **Ants cover the buck.**
3. Why doesn't the boy kill the buck? **Responses could include that it is unconscious and past pain, or that he thinks the way it died is natural on the veld.**
4. What does the boy discover when he looks closely at the skeleton? **Its leg is broken.**
5. What does the boy plan to do the next morning? **He plans to think about the buck.**

Vocabulary in Context
Fill each blank with the most appropriate word from the Words for Everyday Use. You may have to change the tense of the word.

lope exultation frond superfluity sultry myriad stoicism

1. Years of harsh life prepared the pioneers to face accept hardship with **stoicism**.
2. Slowly, scientists are mapping the **myriad** heavenly bodies in the universe.
3. When few people showed up, we realized we would have a **superfluity** of food.
4. Early settlers in Florida were called "Skeeter Beaters" because they beat off mosquitoes with palm **fronds**.
5 Jan entered the 5K race just for fun, and **loped** comfortably toward the finish line.

Literary Tools
In each blank below, identify the step in the plot diagram.

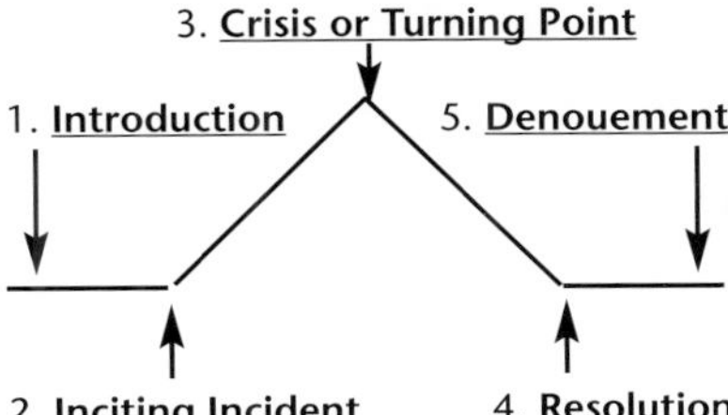

ANSWERS TO GUIDED READING QUESTIONS

1. The boy thinks about how the buck may have been roaming proud, exhilarated, and free and hour ago, just like he was.
2. A broken leg prevented the antelope from escaping the ants.
3. The boy decides that Africans probably threw stones at it to kill it for its meat.
4. The boy realizes that he has taken shots at antelopes, not known if he hit or missed the antelope, decided it was too much bother to track the antelope to find out,. and turned and gone home for breakfast.
5. He feels he must still think out the death of the antelope.

INTERNET RESOURCES

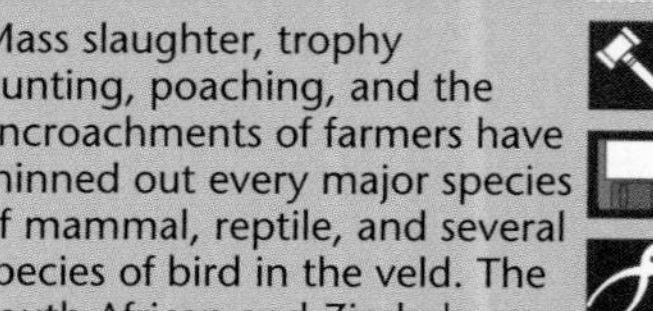

Mass slaughter, trophy hunting, poaching, and the encroachments of farmers have thinned out every major species of mammal, reptile, and several species of bird in the veld. The South African and Zimbabwean governments have, however, tried to conserve areas of veld, such as the Kruger National Park, as wildlife reserves. Here animals such as the lion, leopard, cheetah, elephant, and antelope are protected. What else is Africa doing to conserve and preserve wildlife? Direct students to **WildNet Africa** at http://www.wildnetafrica.com/wildlife/wildlife.html. Assign students into small groups of four. Then have them choose one wildlife conservation organization listed on this website. Have them conduct research on the organization—its mission, goals, accomplishments, and membership information. Then have each group present their information through an extemporaneous speech using visual aids. Refer students to the Language Arts Survey 4.17, "Steps in Preparing an Extemporaneous Speech" and 6.11, "Displaying Effective Visual Information."

RESPOND TO THE SELECTION

What would you have done if you saw the antelope laying in agony? Would you have shot it and put it out of its misery, or would you have acted as the boy did?

dark eyes of a buck. And then he bent the slim foreleg bone, swinging it horizontally in his palm.

That morning, perhaps an hour ago, this small creature had been stepping proud and free through the bush, feeling the chill on its hide even as he himself had done, exhilarated by it. Proudly stepping the earth, tossing its horns, frisking a pretty white tail, it had sniffed the cold morning air. Walking like kings and conquerors, it had moved through this free-held bush, where each blade of grass grew for it alone, and where the river ran pure sparkling water for its slaking.

What similarity does the boy see between himself and the dead buck?

And then—what had happened? Such a swift, sure-footed thing could surely not be trapped by a swarm of ants?

The boy bent curiously to the skeleton. Then he saw that the back leg that lay uppermost and strained out in the tension of death was snapped midway in the thigh, so that broken bones jutted over each other uselessly. So that was it! Limping into the ant masses it could not escape, once it had sensed the danger. Yes, but how had the leg been broken? Had it fallen, perhaps? Impossible, a buck was too light and graceful. Had some jealous rival horned it?

What prevented the antelope from escaping the ants?

What could possibly have happened? Perhaps some Africans had thrown stones at it, as they do, trying to kill it for meat, and had broken its leg. Yes, that must be it.

What does the boy decide must have happened to the buck?

Even as he imagined the crowd of running, shouting natives, and the flying stones, and the leaping buck, another picture came into his mind. He saw himself, on any one of these bright ringing mornings, drunk with excitement, taking a snap shot at some half-seen buck. He saw himself with the gun lowered, wondering whether he had missed or not, and thinking at last that it was late, and he wanted his breakfast, and it was not worthwhile to track miles after an animal that would very likely get away from him in any case.

What does the boy suddenly remember that he has done in the past?

For a moment he would not face it. He was a small boy again, kicking sulkily at the skeleton, hanging his head, refusing to accept the responsibility.

Then he straightened up and looked down at the bones with an odd expression of dismay, all the anger gone out of him. His mind went quite empty: all around him he could see trickles of ants disappearing into the grass. The whispering noise was faint and dry, like the rustling of a cast snakeskin.

At last he picked up his gun and walked homewards. He was telling himself half defiantly that he wanted his breakfast. He was telling himself that it was getting very hot, much too hot to be out roaming the bush.

Really, he was tired. He walked heavily, not looking where he put his feet. When he came within sight of his home, he stopped, knitting his brows. There was something he had to think out. The death of that small animal was a thing that concerned him, and he was by no means finished with it. It lay at the back of his mind uncomfortably.

Soon, the very next morning, he would get clear of everybody and go to the bush and think about it. ■

What does the boy still feel he has to do?

Respond *to the* SELECTION

Imagine that you are a friend of the boy in "A Sunrise on the Veld," and that he comes to you to share the details of his experience with the buck. How would you respond? What might you say to him?

Inquire, Imagine

Recall: Gathering Facts →

1a. What has the boy trained himself to do? What is the boy's reason for going out before dawn each day?

2a. What does the boy do when he his feelings of joy become "unbearable"? What sound suddenly interrupts him as he listens to the echoes of his own voice? What is making this sound? What happens to the creature who makes this sound?

3a. What is the boy about to do to help the antelope before he stops? What does he see when he examines the antelope? What different explanations does the boy come up with for what happened to the antelope?

Interpret: Finding Meaning

1b. How does the boy feel about what he has trained himself to do? How does he feel about what he does every day before dawn? How can you tell?

2b. How does the boy feel about himself, life, and the future before he hears and sees the buck? What makes the writer's description of what the boy sees and hears vivid?

3b. How does what the boy sees happen to the antelope change his mood and feelings? Do you think the boy feels responsible for what happened to the antelope? Why, or why not?

Analyze: Taking Things Apart →

4a. How do the boy's attitudes toward his own abilities, life, and his future change over the course of this story? Support your answer with specific examples from the text.

Synthesize: Bringing Things Together

4b. How do you think the boy's experience on the veld will shape him as a person? What changes might he make in his views and his life as a result of this experience? In what way might the boy's experience be a "sunrise" in his own life?

Evaluate: Making Judgments →

5a. At what points in the story could you most identify with the main character? When was he most likable? least likable? To what extent could you empathize with him throughout the story?

Extend: Connecting Ideas

5b. Explain whether this story has a message about hunting. What are your own views on hunting?

Understanding Literature

Naturalism. Review the definition for **Naturalism** in the Handbook of Literary Terms. Explain what naturalistic ideas are explored in "A Sunrise on the Veld." Would you classify this short story as an example of Naturalism. If so, why? If not, why not?

Plot. Review the definition for **plot** in Literary Tools in the Handbook of Literary Terms. What is the central conflict in this story? Through which specific events in this story is the central conflict brought to light? Is the conflict resolved? Explain.

ANSWERS TO INVESTIGATE, INQUIRE, AND IMAGINE

Recall

1a. The boy has trained himself to wake up at half past four each morning before his alarm clock rings? The boy goes out before dawn each day to hunt.

2a. The boy suddenly begins running "like a wild thing." He then sings and listens to the echoes of his own voice. The "sound of pain, repeated over and over" interrupts him. A buck is making this sound. The buck is eaten alive by ants.

3a. The boy is about to shoot the antelope to put it out of its misery before he stops. He sees nothing but bones and then notices that the antelope couldn't get away because of a broken leg. The boy wonders if the antelope fell. Then he wonders if a jealous rival horned it. Then he decides that Africans probably threw stones at the antelope to kill it for its meat.

Interpret

1b. The boy feels proud and confident, as if he can command sleep at his will. One can tell that he is proud of his own physical prowess when going out to hunt. Because he sneaks out each day to hunt, and because of his confident feeling that he "could walk a hundred miles on feet like these."

2b. The boy feels great joy in being alive and great confidence and pride in himself. Descriptions like "drunken-legged," "the patches of rawness were disappearing under moving black… and all the time the creature screamed" makes what the boy sees and hears vivid.

3b. The boy is now filled with pity and fear; he has lost his confident and proud mood and feels helpless and ineffectual. The boy does feel responsible because he knows he may have injured antelopes in the past and sent them to similar fates.

Analyze

4a. The boy at first is very confident and proud. He is filled with joy in his own abilities and his future. After seeing the antelope die, the boy feels powerless by saying, "I can't stop it. I can't stop it. There is nothing I can do." He feels that sometimes fate is inescapable and that you cannot always bend the world to your will. He feels that he too may die, or be unable to escape his destiny.

Synthesize

4b. Students may suggest that the boy may never feel the same carefree exultation he once did. Students may say that the change in his

ANSWERS TO INVESTIGATE, INQUIRE, AND IMAGINE (cont.)

feelings from wild joy to more thoughtful contemplation of some of the larger issues in life signifies his passing from childhood to adulthood and in this way, his experience is like a "sunrise."

Evaluate

5a. *Responses will vary.*

Extend

5b. Students may say that this story's message may be that people should only hunt for food and do so carefully, without needlessly wounding and abandoning animals to suffer. Students' ideas about hunting will vary.

Answers to Understanding Literature can be found on page 1060.

ANSWER TO UNDERSTANDING LITERATURE

NATURALISM. *Responses will vary.* Students will say that this selection is an example of Naturalism because of the many naturalistic ideas portrayed such as the idea of fate being determined by natural forces and the idea that death and suffering are an inevitable part of nature and necessary for other creatures' continued survival.

PLOT. The central conflict in the story is the boy's struggle to find his place in the cycle of life and death that takes place every day on "the vast unalterable, cruel veld, where at any moment one might stumble over a skull or crush the skeleton of some small creature." This conflict is brought to light when the boy finds the dying buck. He thinks about shooting it to put it out of its misery but then decides he shouldn't interfere. However, the boy reflects again on this internal conflict when thinking about how the buck's leg might've been broken. These reflections cause him to realize that he may have interfered in the lives and deaths of animals on the veld. The boy hasn't resolved this conflict at the end of the story but decides that "Soon, the very next morning, he would get clear of everybody and go to the bush and think about it."

WRITER'S JOURNAL

1. Write an **apology** to the antelope from the point of view of the boy in "A Sunrise on the Veld."
2. Imagine that you write an advice column for a newspaper. The boy in the story writes to you, explaining what he witnessed and his feelings about it. He wants to know what he should do now that he has had this experience. Write an **advice column** in which you write both the letter from the boy, asking for help, and your advice to him.
3. Write a brief **personal essay** about something you experienced that forever altered the way you view the world. Introduce the event and its effect on you to the reader. Describe this event vividly and then explore your reactions to it. Finally, explain how it has affected you.

Integrating *the* LANGUAGE ARTS

Language, Grammar, and Style

DIRECT AND INDIRECT OBJECTS AND COMPLEMENTS. Action verbs often take direct and indirect objects. A **direct object** is the receiver of an action. When a direct object is received by someone or something, this receiver is called the **indirect object**. Unlike action verbs, linking verbs never take direct objects. Instead, linking verbs are often followed by a word that renames the subject, known as a **complement**. Review the Language Arts Survey, 3.22, " Sentence Completers for Action Verbs: Direct and Indirect Objects," and 3.23, "Sentences Completers for Linking Verbs: Predicate Nouns, Pronouns, and Adjectives." Then carefully read each sentence below. Identify any direct objects, indirect objects, or complements used in each sentence.

1. It was half past four to the minute.
2. He slung the shoes over his shoulder.
3. I am fifteen!
4. Would the world give him all that he dreamed?
5. Perhaps some people had thrown stones at it.

Study and Research

TEST-TAKING SKILLS. One type of question that often appears on standardized tests is the sentence completion question. This type of question presents you with a sentence that has two words missing. You must pick the pair of words that best completes the sentence. For each sentence below, choose the pair of words that best completes it.

The ________ of the crops was startling. People expected that it would be a lean year because of the ________.

tumult . . . veld
abundance . . . zephyrs
superfluity . . . drought
dirth . . . exultation

"I can't believe this weather," she said ________. "May is not usually so ________."

incredulously . . . sultry
fatality . . . cold
fastidiously . . . vigilant
vigilantly . . . sultry

He was a ________ dresser, always ________ about making sure his clothes were clean and well-pressed.

stoicism . . . vigilant
myriad . . . fatality
fastidious . . . myriad
fastidious . . .vigilant

Even though she had faced ________ difficulties, she maintained an attitude of ________ rather than despair.

myriad . . . stoicism
superfluity . . .fatality
vigilant . . . stoicism
fatality . . .exultation

ANSWERS TO INTEGRATING THE LANGUAGE ARTS

Language, Grammar, and Style

1. half past four (C—PA)
2. shoes (DO)
3. fifteen (C—PA)
4. all (DO); him (IO)
5. stones (DO); it (IO)

Study and Research

1. c
2. a
3. d
4. a

"RED DRESS—1946"

BY ALICE MUNRO

About the AUTHOR

Alice Munro (1931–) was born in Wingham, Ontario. After attending the University of Western Ontario, Munro moved to Victoria, British Columbia, where she opened a bookstore. In 1968, Munro published her first collection of short stories, *Dance of the Happy Shades,* which won the Governor General's Literary Award. Three years later, Munro's novel, *Lives of Girls and Women,* won the Canadian Booksellers Award. Her other short story collections include *The Beggar Maid* (originally published in North America as *Who Do You Think You Are?*), *Something I've Been Meaning to Tell You, The Moons of Jupiter and Other Stories, The Progress of Love, Friend of My Youth,* and *Open Secrets.* Munro is considered one of the finest of contemporary short fiction writers and has even been acclaimed as "our Chekhov." Today, Munro lives in Clinton, Ontario, near Lake Huron, where she continues to write.

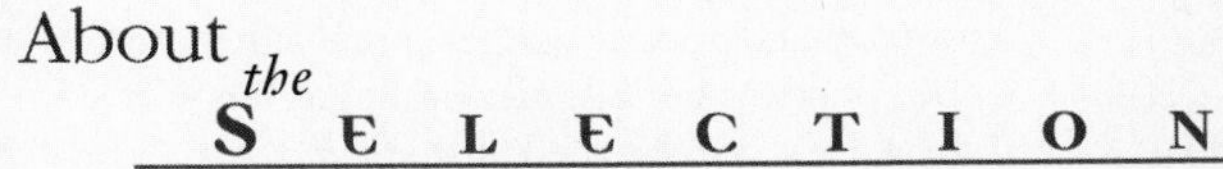

About the SELECTION

"Red Dress—1946" is from Munro's first short story collection, *Dance of the Happy Shades.* Like nearly all of Munro's fiction, this story takes place in semirural southern Ontario, Canada, the landscape of Munro's childhood. The narrator in the selection is a mature woman telling about a pivotal experience, a turning point or epiphany, in her youth. It is a story about a time in life when two paths present themselves and one is chosen, though not without misgiving.

Literary TOOLS

CHARACTERIZATION. **Characterization** is the use of literary techniques to create a character. Writers use three major techniques to create characters: direct description, portrayal of characters' behavior, and representations of characters' internal states. As you read, consider which technique the author relies on most to portray the narrator.

PLOT AND CONFLICT. A **plot** is a series of events related to a central conflict. A **conflict** is a struggle between two forces in a literary work. A struggle that takes place between a character and some outside force is called an *external conflict.* A struggle that takes place within a character is called an *internal conflict.* As you read, take notice of the conflicts the main character faces in the story.

Reader's Journal

Have you ever felt different from your peers in appearance, interests, abilities, desires, or goals for the future? Do you find these differences to be interesting? comfortable? unsettling?

ADDITIONAL RESOURCES

UNIT 11 RESOURCE BOOK
- Selection Worksheet 11.8
- Selection Check Test 4.11.15
- Selection Test 4.11.16

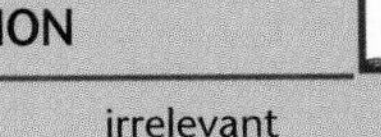

VOCABULARY FROM THE SELECTION

acute	irrelevant
burlesqued	languidly
delirium	nonentity
docility	oppressive
doggedly	organdy
exuberant	palpitation
golliwogs	preoccupied
inanimate	vulnerable

READER'S JOURNAL

In what ways do differences motivate change? Do you think that being different is a positive or negative thing?

GOALS/OBJECTIVES

Studying this lesson will enable students to
- empathize with the protagonist's feelings of exclusion and social discomfort
- describe Alice Munro's literary accomplishments and her style of writing
- define *characterization, plot,* and *conflict* and identify and explain examples of each that they encounter in their reading
- conduct research on world events during 1946

ANSWERS TO GUIDED READING QUESTIONS

1. She took no pride in the fine points of tailoring like the narrator's aunt or grandmother. He mother began her sewing projects with "an inspiration, a brave and dazzling idea."
2. The narrator is embarrassed by the way her mother "crept around" her, her creaking knees, her heavy breathing, and the way she dressed around the house.

INDIVIDUAL LEARNING STRATEGIES

MOTIVATION
Ask a seamstress or a student who is interested in sewing to speak to the class about the sewing process, the things that he or she sews, and what motivated him or her to sew in the first place.

READING PROFICIENCY
Ask students to select portions of the story to read aloud and record. Encourage them to read the chosen portions with the intensity that the words suggest.

ENGLISH LANGUAGE LEARNING
Remind students to use context clues to identify unfamiliar words. For example, students should use the context of sewing to figure out the meaning of *basting, overcasting,* and other unfamiliar words.

SPECIAL NEEDS
If possible, bring in several examples of dresses that were popular during the 1940s and1950s for students to examine and feel.

ENRICHMENT
Have students conduct a class interview project in which class members share experiences that helped them shape their self-identity. Students can videotape, tape record, or take notes during the interviews.

RED DRESS—1946

ALICE MUNRO

My mother was making me a dress. All through the month of November I would come from school and find her in the kitchen, surrounded by cut-up red velvet and scraps of tissue-paper pattern. She worked at an old treadle machine pushed up against the window to get the light, and also to let her look out, past the stubble fields and bare vegetable garden, to see who went by on the road. There was seldom anybody to see.

The red velvet material was hard to work with, it pulled, and the style my mother had chosen was not easy either. She was not really a good sewer. She liked to make things; that is different. Whenever she could she tried to skip basting and pressing and she took no pride in the fine points of tailoring, the finishing of buttonholes and the overcasting of seams as, for instance, my aunt and my grandmother did. Unlike them she started off with an inspiration, a brave and dazzling idea; from that moment on, her pleasure ran downhill. In the first place she could never find a pattern to suit her. It was no wonder; there were no patterns made to match the ideas that blossomed in her head. She had made me, at various times when I was younger, a flowered organdie dress with a high Victorian neckline edged in scratchy lace, with a poke bonnet to match; a Scottish plaid outfit with a velvet jacket and tam; an embroidered peasant blouse worn with a full red skirt and black laced bodice. I had worn these clothes with docility, even pleasure, in the days when I was unaware of the world's opinion. Now, grown wiser, I wished for dresses like those my friend Lonnie had, bought at Beale's store.

In what does the narrator's mother take no pride? With what does the narrator's mother begin her sewing projects?

I had to try it on. Sometimes Lonnie came home from school with me and she would sit on the couch watching. I was embarrassed by the way my mother crept around me, her knees creaking, her breath coming heavily. She muttered to herself. Around the house she wore no corset or stockings, she wore wedge-heeled shoes and ankle socks; her legs were marked with lumps of blue-green veins. I thought her squatting position shameless, even obscene; I tried to keep talking to Lonnie so that her attention would be taken away from my mother as much as possible. Lonnie wore the composed, polite, appreciative expression that was her disguise in the presence of grownups. She laughed at them and was a ferocious mimic, and they never knew.

About what is the narrator embarrassed?

My mother pulled me about, and pricked me with pins. She made me turn around, she made me walk away, she made me stand still. "What do you think of it, Lonnie?" she said around the pins in her mouth.

"It's beautiful," said Lonnie, in her mild, sincere way. Lonnie's own mother was dead. She lived with her father who never noticed her, and this, in my eyes, made her seem both vulnerable and privileged.

WORDS FOR EVERYDAY USE

or • gan • dy or **or • gan • die** (ôr´gən dē) *n.,* sheer fabric. *That organdie dress definitely requires a slip.*

do • cil • i • ty (dō sil´ə tē) *n.,* submissiveness. *The sheepdog's docility is surprising in such a large animal.*

vul • ner • a • ble (vul´nər ə bəl) *adj.,* open to injury or attack; easily hurt. *All the cities along the river were vulnerable to enemy invasions.*

"It *will* be, if I can ever manage the fit," my mother said. "Ah, well," she said theatrically, getting to her feet with a woeful creaking and sighing, "I doubt if she appreciates it." She enraged me, talking like this to Lonnie, as if Lonnie were grown up and I were still a child. "Stand still," she said, hauling the pinned and basted dress over my head. My head was muffled in velvet, my body exposed, in an old cotton school slip. I felt like a great raw lump, clumsy and goose-pimpled. I wished I was like Lonnie, light-boned, pale and thin; she had been a Blue Baby.

Why does the young girl get angry at her mother?

"Well nobody ever made me a dress when I was going to high school," my mother said, "I made my own, or I did without." I was afraid she was going to start again on the story of her walking seven miles to town and finding a job waiting on tables in a boarding-house, so that she could go to high school. All the stories of my mother's life which had once interested me had begun to seem melodramatic, irrelevant, and tiresome.

"One time I had a dress given to me," she said. "It was a cream-coloured cashmere wool with royal blue piping down the front and lovely mother-of-pearl buttons, I wonder what ever became of it?"

When we got free Lonnie and I went upstairs to my room. It was cold, but we stayed there. We talked about the boys in our class, going up and down the rows and saying, "Do you like him? Well, do you half-like him? Do you *hate* him? Would you go out with him if he asked you?" Nobody had asked us. We were thirteen, and we had been going to high school for two months. We did questionnaires in magazines, to find out whether we had personality and whether we would be popular. We read articles on how to make up our faces to accentuate our good points and how to carry on a conversation on the first date and what to do when a boy tried to go too far. Also we read articles on frigidity of the menopause, abortion and why husbands seek satisfaction away from home. When we were not doing school work, we were occupied most of the time with the garnering, passing on and discussing of sexual information. We had made a pact to tell each other everything. But one thing I did not tell was about this dance, the high school Christmas Dance for which my mother was making me a dress. It was that I did not want to go.

What doesn't the narrator want to tell her friend?

At high school I was never comfortable for a minute. I did not know about Lonnie. Before an exam, she got icy hands and palpitations, but I was close to despair at all times. When I was asked a question in class, any simple little question at all, my voice was apt to come out squeaky, or else hoarse and trembling. When I had to go to the blackboard I was sure—even at a time of the month when this could not be true—that I had blood on my skirt. My hands became slippery with sweat when they were required to work the blackboard compass. I could not hit the ball in volleyball; being called upon to perform an action in front of others made all my reflexes come undone. I hated Business Practice because you had to rule pages for an account book, using a straight pen, and when the teacher looked over my shoulder all the delicate lines wobbled and ran together. I hated Science; we perched on stools under harsh lights behind tables of unfamiliar, fragile equipment, and were taught by the principal of the school, a man with a cold, self-relishing voice—he read the Scriptures

WORDS FOR EVERYDAY USE

ir • rel • e • vant (ir rel´ə vənt) *adj.*, not related to the subject. *Because the environmental study focuses on North America, these rain forest statistics are irrelevant.*

pal • pi • ta • tion (pal´pə tā shen) *n.*, rapid heartbeat. *Frequent palpitations could be an indication of a serious heart problem.*

ANSWERS TO GUIDED READING QUESTIONS

1. The girl is angry that her mother talks about her to Lonnie as though Lonnie were a grown-up and she was a child.
2. The young girl doesn't want to tell her friend that she would rather not go to the Christmas Dance.

ADDITIONAL QUESTIONS AND ACTIVITIES

Students can use a chart to compare and contrast the narrator and Lonnie. Refer to the Language Arts Survey, 5.10, "Comparing and Contrasting."

ANSWERS TO GUIDED READING QUESTIONS

1. The girl's primary fear is defeat in the competition for a partner.
2. She tries to make herself sick in various ways.
3. She wants to protect herself from all possible female rituals.

LITERARY NOTE

The Last Days of Pompeii is a book about the destruction of Pompeii. The city was buried in ash and lava as a result of a volcanic eruption. The narrator wishes herself there so she will not have to attend the dance.

every morning—and a great talent for inflicting humiliation. I hated English because the boys played bingo at the back of the room while the teacher, a stout, gentle girl, slightly cross-eyed, read Wordsworth at the front. She threatened them, she begged them, her face red and her voice as unreliable as mine. They offered burlesqued apologies and when she started to read again they took up rapt postures, made swooning faces, crossed their eyes, flung their hands over their hearts. Sometimes she would burst into tears, there was no help for it, she had to run out into the hall. Then the boys made loud mooing noises; our hungry laughter—oh, mine too—pursued her. There was a carnival atmosphere of brutality in the room at such times, scaring weak and suspect people like me.

But what was really going on in the school was not Business Practice and Science and English, there was something else that gave life its urgency and brightness. That old building, with its rock-walled clammy basements and black cloakrooms and pictures of dead royalties and lost explorers, was full of the tension and excitement of sexual competition, and in this, in spite of daydreams of vast successes, I had premonitions of total defeat. Something had to happen, to keep me from that dance.

What is the narrator's primary fear?

With December came snow, and I had an idea. Formerly I had considered falling off my bicycle and spraining my ankle and I had tried to manage this, as I rode home along the hard-frozen, deeply rutted country roads. But it was too difficult. However, my throat and bronchial tubes were supposed to be weak; why not expose them? I started getting out of bed at night and opening my window a little. I knelt down and let the wind, sometimes stinging with snow, rush in around my bared throat. I took off my pajama top. I said to myself the words "blue with cold" and as I knelt there, my eyes shut, I pictured my chest and throat turning blue, the cold, greyed blue of veins under the skin. I stayed until I could not stand it any more, and then I took a handful of snow from the windowsill and smeared it all over my chest, before I buttoned my pajamas. It would melt against the flannelette and I would be sleeping in wet clothes, which was supposed to be the worst thing of all. In the morning, the moment I woke up, I cleared my throat, testing for soreness, coughed experimentally, hopefully, touched my forehead to see if I had fever. It was no good. Every morning, including the day of the dance, I rose defeated, and in perfect health.

What does the narrator do to try to get out of going to the dance?

The day of the dance I did my hair up in steel curlers. I had never done this before, because my hair was naturally curly, but today I wanted the protection of all possible female rituals. I lay on the couch in the kitchen, reading *The Last Days of Pompeii*, and wishing I was there. My mother, never satisfied, was sewing a white lace collar on the dress; she had decided it was too grown-up looking. I watched the hours. It was one of the shortest days of the year. Above the couch, on the wallpaper, were old games of Xs and Os, old drawings and scribblings my brother and I had done when we were sick with bronchitis. I looked at them and longed to be back safe behind the boundaries of childhood.

Why does the narrator put curlers in her hair?

When I took out the curlers my hair, both naturally and artificially stimulated, sprang out in an exuberant glossy bush. I wet it, I combed

WORDS FOR EVERYDAY USE

bur • lesqued (bər leskd´) *part.*, parody, imitate derisively. *The senator was not amused by the manner in which the comedy team burlesqued his scandalous actions.*

ex• u • ber • ant (eg zo͞o´ bər ənt) *adj.*, full of life. *After a few minutes of exuberant applause, the singer returned to the stage for an encore.*

it, beat it with the brush and tugged it down along my cheeks. I applied face powder, which stood out chalkily on my hot face. My mother got out her Ashes of Roses Cologne, which she never used, and let me splash it over my arms. Then she zipped up the dress and turned me around to the mirror. The dress was princess style, very tight in the midriff. I saw how my breasts, in their new stiff brassiere, jutted out surprisingly, with mature authority, under the childish frills of the collar.

"Well I wish I could take a picture," my mother said. "I am really, genuinely proud of that fit. And you might say thank you for it."

"Thank you," I said.

The first thing Lonnie said when I opened the door to her was, "Jesus, what did you do to your hair?"

"I did it up."

"You look like a Zulu. Oh, don't worry. Get me a comb and I'll do the front in a roll. It'll look all right. It'll even make you look older."

I sat in front of the mirror and Lonnie stood behind me, fixing my hair. My mother seemed unable to leave us. I wished she would. She watched the roll take shape and said, "You're a wonder, Lonnie. You should take up hairdressing."

"That's a thought," Lonnie said. She had on a pale blue crepe dress, with a peplum and bow; it was much more grown-up than mine even without the collar. Her hair had come out as sleek as the girl's on the bobby-pin card. I had always thought secretly that Lonnie could not be pretty because she had crooked teeth, but now I saw that crooked teeth or not, her stylish dress and smooth hair made me look a little like a golliwog,[1] stuffed into red velvet, wide-eyed, wild-haired, with a suggestion of <u>delirium</u>.

EVERY MORNING, INCLUDING THE DAY OF THE DANCE, I ROSE DEFEATED, AND IN PERFECT HEALTH.

My mother followed us to the door and called out into the dark, "Au reservoir!" This was a traditional farewell of Lonnie's and mine; it sounded foolish and desolate coming from her, and I was so angry with her for using it that I did not reply. It was only Lonnie who called back cheerfully, encouragingly, "Good night!"

What had the narrator always secretly thought about Lonnie? What does she think now?

The gymnasium smelled of pine and cedar. Red and green bells of fluted paper hung from the basketball hoops; the high, barred windows were hidden by green boughs. Everybody in the upper grades seemed to have come in couples. Some of

1. golliwog. A grotesque black doll

WORDS FOR EVERYDAY USE

de • lir • i • um (di lir´ ē əm) *n.*, wild excitement. *You cannot make a rational decision in such a state of <u>delirium</u>.*

ANSWER TO GUIDED READING QUESTION

1. The narrator thought secretly that Lonnie could never be pretty because of her crooked teeth. She thinks that Lonnie looks stylish and pretty.

ADDITIONAL QUESTIONS AND ACTIVITIES

Students can write about something that they felt compelled to do though they did not want to do it. Ask them to consider what they did to try to avoid the situation and how they felt about the situation after they had gone through it.

ANSWERS TO GUIDED READING QUESTIONS

1. The girl wants to be like the older girls, "aloof and beautiful."
2. He ends the dance by steering her to the floor's edge and saying, "See you."

ADDITIONAL QUESTIONS AND ACTIVITIES

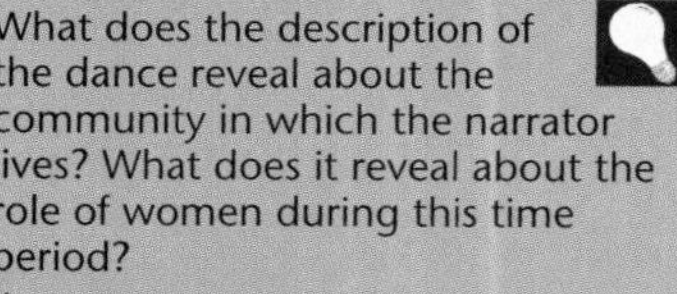

What does the description of the dance reveal about the community in which the narrator lives? What does it reveal about the role of women during this time period?

Answers

The fact that grades nine through thirteen attend the same dance reveals that the school population is small. The fact that the boyfriends of the older girls have graduated from the school and remained in the community indicates that most people probably stayed in the area. The painful description of the narrator waiting to be chosen by a boy reveals that girls were not encouraged to play active roles in courtship.

the Grade Twelve and Thirteen girls had brought boy friends who had already graduated, who were young businessmen around the town. These young men smoked in the gymnasium, nobody could stop them, they were free. The girls stood beside them, resting their hands casually on male sleeves, their faces bored, aloof and beautiful. I longed to be like that. They behaved as if only they—the older ones—were really at the dance, as if the rest of us, whom they moved among and peered around, were, if not invisible, inanimate; when the first dance was announced—a Paul Jones—they moved out languidly, smiling at each other as if they had been asked to take part in some half-forgotten childish game. Holding hands and shivering, crowding up together, Lonnie and I and the other Grade Nine girls followed.

Who does the narrator want to be like?

I didn't dare look at the outer circle as it passed me, for fear I should see some unmannerly hurrying-up. When the music stopped I stayed where I was, and half-raising my eyes I saw a boy named Mason Williams coming reluctantly towards me. Barely touching my waist and my fingers, he began to dance with me. My legs were hollow, my arm trembled from the shoulder, I could not have spoken. This Mason Williams was one of the heroes of the school; he played basketball and hockey and walked the halls with an air of royal sullenness and barbaric contempt. To have to dance with a nonentity like me was as offensive to him as having to memorize Shakespeare. I felt this as keenly as he did, and imagined that he was exchanging looks of dismay with his friends. He steered me, stumbling, to the edge of the floor. He took his hand from my waist and dropped my arm.

"See you," he said. He walked away.

It took me a minute or two to realize what had happened and that he was not coming back. I went and stood by the wall alone. The Physical Education teacher, dancing past energetically in the arms of a Grade Ten boy, gave me an inquisitive look. She was the only teacher in the school who made use of the words social adjustment, and I was afraid that if she had seen, or if she found out, she might make some horribly public attempt to make Mason finish out the dance with me. I myself was not angry or surprised at Mason; I accepted his position, and mine, in the world of school and I saw that what he had done was the realistic thing to do. He was a Natural Hero, not a Student Council type of hero bound for success beyond the school; one of those would have danced with me courteously and patronizingly and left me feeling no better off. Still, I hoped not many people had seen. I hated people seeing. I began to bite the skin on my thumb.

How does Mason Williams end the dance?

When the music stopped I joined the surge of girls to the end of the gymnasium. Pretend it didn't happen, I said to myself. Pretend this is the beginning, now.

The band began to play again. There was movement in the dense crowd at our end of the floor, it thinned rapidly. Boys came over, girls went out to dance. Lonnie went. The girl on the other side of me went. Nobody asked me. I remembered a magazine article Lonnie and I had read, which said *Be gay! Let the boys see your eyes sparkle, let them hear laughter in your voice! Simple, obvious, but how many girls forget!* It was true, I had forgotten. My eyebrows were drawn together with tension, I must look scared and ugly. I took a deep breath and tried to loosen my face. I smiled. But I felt absurd, smiling at no one. And I observed that girls on the dance floor,

WORDS FOR EVERYDAY USE

in • an • i • mate (in an´ə mit) *adj.*, lifeless. *The painter's vivid colors and strong brush strokes seem to instill her inanimate subjects with life.*

lan • guid • ly (laŋ gwid lē) *adv.*, sluggishly; without vigor. *The exhausted patient spoke languidly.*

non • en • ti • ty (nän en´tə tē) *n.*, person of no importance. *The novice reporter felt like a nonentity at the broadcasters' awards banquet.*

popular girls, were not smiling; many of them had sleepy, sulky faces and never smiled at all.

Girls were still going out to the floor. Some, despairing, went with each other. But most went with boys. Fat girls, girls with pimples, a poor girl who didn't own a good dress and had to wear a skirt and sweater to the dance; they were claimed, they danced away. Why take them and not me? Why everybody else and not me? I have a red velvet dress, I did my hair in curlers, I used a deodorant and put on cologne. *Pray*, I thought. I couldn't close my eyes but I said over and over again in my mind, *Please, me, please*, and I locked my fingers behind my back in a sign more potent than crossing, the same secret sign Lonnie and I used not to be sent to the blackboard in Math.

It did not work. What I had been afraid of was true. I was going to be left. There was something mysterious the matter with me, something that could not be put right like bad breath or overlooked like pimples, and everybody knew it, and I knew it; I had known it all along. But I had not known it for sure, I had hoped to be mistaken. Certainty rose inside me like sickness. I hurried past one or two girls who were also left and went into the girls' washroom. I hid myself in a cubicle.

What does the narrator decide about herself?

That was where I stayed. Between dances girls came in and went out quickly. There were plenty of cubicles; nobody noticed that I was not a temporary occupant. During the dances, I listened to the music which I liked but had no part of any more. For I was not going to try any more. I only wanted to hide in here, get out without seeing anybody, get home.

One time after the music started somebody stayed behind. She was taking a long time running the water, washing her hands, combing her hair. She was going to think it funny that I stayed in so long. I had better go out and wash my hands, and maybe while I was washing them she would leave.

It was Mary Fortune. I knew her by name, because she was an officer of the Girls' Athletic Society and she was on the Honour Roll and she was always organizing things. She had something to do with organizing this dance; she had been around to all the classrooms asking for volunteers to do the decorations. She was in Grade Eleven or Twelve.

"Nice and cool in here," she said. "I came in to get cooled off. I get so hot."

She was still combing her hair when I finished my hands. "Do you like the band?" she said.

"It's all right." I didn't really know what to say. I was surprised at her, an older girl, taking this time to talk to me.

"I don't. I can't stand it. I hate dancing when I don't like the band. Listen. They're so choppy. I'd just as soon not dance as dance to that."

I combed my hair. She leaned against a basin, watching me.

"I don't want to dance and don't particularly want to stay in here. Let's go and have a cigarette."

"Where?"

"Come on, I'll show you."

At the end of the washroom there was a door. It was unlocked and led into a dark closet full of mops and pails. She had me hold the door open, to get the washroom light, until she found the knob of another door. This door opened into darkness.

"I can't turn on the light or somebody might see," she said. "It's the janitor's room." I reflected that athletes always seemed to know more than the rest of us about the school as a building; they knew where things were kept and they were always coming out of unauthorized doors with a bold, preoccupied air. "Watch out where you're

WORDS FOR EVERYDAY USE

pre • oc • cu • pied (prē äk´yo͞o pīd) *adj.*, engrossed. *He must be preoccupied because he hasn't responded to anything I've said.*

ANSWER TO GUIDED READING QUESTION

1. Because she is left without a partner, she confirms her fear that "there was something mysterious the matter with her."

LITERARY TECHNIQUE

TAG LINES. Writers use **tag lines** to indicate who is speaking and sometimes the manner in which the speaking is done. In this conversation between the narrator and Mary Fortune, tag lines are used only to indicate who is speaking. Students can discuss why the author might not have included phrases to indicate the manner in which the words are spoken.

ANSWERS TO GUIDED READING QUESTIONS

1. Mary says that most girls are boy-crazy.
2. The narrator feels better after talking to Mary because Mary has felt the same defeat as her, but was full of energy and self-respect.

going," she said. "Over at the far end there's some stairs. They go up to a closet on the second floor. The door's locked at the top, but there's like a partition between the stairs and the room. So if we sit on the steps, even if by chance someone did come in here, they wouldn't see us."

"Wouldn't they smell smoke?" I said.

"Oh, well. Live dangerously."

There was a high window over the stairs which gave us little light. Mary Fortune had cigarettes and matches in her purse. I had not smoked before except the cigarettes Lonnie and I made ourselves, using papers and tobacco stolen from her father; they came apart in the middle. These were much better.

"The only reason I even came to-night," Mary Fortune said, "is because I am responsible for the decorations and I wanted to see, you know, how it looked once people got in there and everything. Otherwise why bother? I'm not boy-crazy."

In the light from the high window I could see her narrow, scornful face, her dark skin pitted with acne, her teeth pushed together at the front, making her look adult and commanding.

What does Mary say about most girls?

"Most girls are. Haven't you noticed that? The greatest collection of boy-crazy girls you could imagine is right here in this school."

I was grateful for her attention, her company and her cigarette. I said I thought so too.

"Like this afternoon. This afternoon I was trying to get them to hang the bells and junk. They just get up on the ladders and fool around with boys. They don't care if it ever gets decorated. It's just an excuse. That's the only aim they have in life, fooling around with boys. As far as I'm concerned, they're idiots."

We talked about teachers, and things at school. She said she wanted to be a physical education teacher and she would have to go to college for that, but her parents did not have enough money. She said she planned to work her own way through, she wanted to be independent anyway, she would work in the cafeteria and in the summer she would do farm work, like picking tobacco. Listening to her, I felt the acute phase of unhappiness passing. Here was someone who had suffered the same defeat as I had—I saw that—but she was full of energy and self respect. She had thought of other things to do. She would pick tobacco.

How does talking to Mary make the narrator feel? Why?

We stayed there talking and smoking during the long pause in the music, when, outside, they were having doughnuts and coffee. When the music started again Mary said, "Look, do we have to hang around here any longer? Let's get our coats and go. We can go down to Lee's and have a hot chocolate and talk in comfort, why not?"

We felt our way across the janitor's room, carrying ashes and cigarette butts in our hands. In the closet, we stopped and listened to make sure there was nobody in the washroom. We came back into the light and threw the ashes into the toilet. We had to go out and cut across the dance-floor to the cloak-room, which was beside the outside door.

A dance was just beginning. "Go round the edge of the floor," Mary said. "Nobody'll notice us."

What does the narrator decide about Lonnie? Why?

I followed her. I didn't look at anybody. I didn't look for Lonnie. Lonnie was probably not going to be my friend any more, not as much as before anyway. She was what Mary would call boy-crazy.

WORDS FOR EVERYDAY USE

a • cute (ə kyo͞ot´) *adj.,* severe and sharp. *An acute, persistent pain on the right side of the body might indicate appendicitis.*

I found that I was not so frightened, now that I had made up my mind to leave the dance behind. I was not waiting for anybody to choose me. I had my own plans. I did not have to smile or make signs for luck. It did not matter to me. I was on my way to have a hot chocolate, with my friend.

A boy said something to me. He was in my way. I thought he must be telling me that I had dropped something or that I couldn't go that way or that the cloakroom was locked. I didn't understand that he was asking me to dance until he said it over again. It was Raymond Bolting from our class, whom I had never talked to in my life. He thought I meant yes. He put his hand on my waist and almost without meaning to, I began to dance.

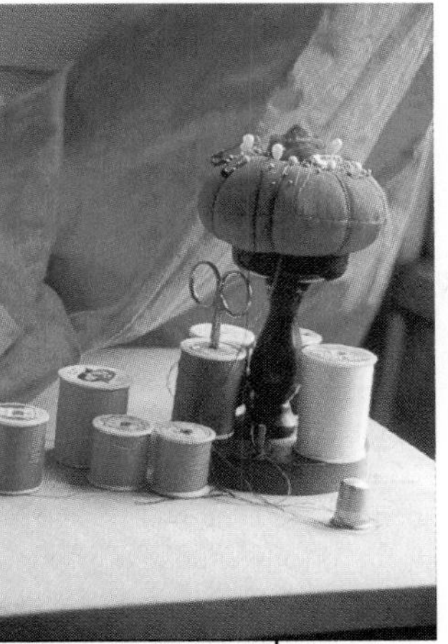

I WAS DANCING WITH A BOY WHO HAD ASKED ME.

We moved to the middle of the floor. I was dancing. My legs had forgotten to tremble and my hands to sweat. I was dancing with a boy who had asked me. Nobody told him to, he didn't have to, he just asked me. Was it possible, could I believe it, was there nothing the matter with me after all?

I thought that I ought to tell him there was a mistake, that I was just leaving, I was going to have a hot chocolate with my girl friend. But I did not say anything. My face was making certain delicate adjustments, achieving with no effort at all the grave absent-minded look of these who were chosen, those who danced. This was the face that Mary Fortune saw, when she looked out of the cloakroom door, her scarf already around her head. I made a weak waving motion with the hand that lay on the boy's shoulder, indicating that I apologized, that I didn't know what had happened and also that it was no use waiting for me. Then I turned my head away, and when I looked again she was gone.

What does Mary Fortune see before she leaves?

Raymond Bolting took me home and Harold Simons took Lonnie home. We all walked together as far as Lonnie's corner. The boys were having an argument about a hockey game, which Lonnie and I could not follow. Then we separated into couples and Raymond continued with me the conversation he had been having with Harold. He did not seem to notice that he was now talking to me instead. Once or twice I said, "Well I don't know I didn't see that game," but after a while decided just to say "H'm hmm," and that seemed to be all that was necessary.

One other thing he said was, "I didn't realize you lived such a long ways out." And he sniffled. The cold was making my nose run a little too, and I worked my fingers through the candy wrappers in my coat pocket until I found a shabby Kleenex. I didn't know whether I ought to offer it to him or not, but he sniffled so loudly that I finally said, "I just have this one Kleenex, it probably isn't even clean, it probably has ink on it. But if I was to tear it in half we'd each have something."

ANSWERS TO GUIDED READING QUESTIONS

1. Lonnie was no longer going to be her friend because she is boy-crazy.
2. Mary Fortune see the narrator dancing with a boy before she leaves.

ADDITIONAL QUESTIONS AND ACTIVITIES

Students may discuss whether they think Mary Fortune understood that the narrator's "weak waving motion" indicated that the narrator "didn't know what had happened and also that it was no use waiting" for her.

ANSWER TO GUIDED READING QUESTION

1. Raymond is the girl's "rescuer" because he saves her from the world of defeat to which she had resigned herself.

SELECTION CHECK TEST 4.11.15 WITH ANSWERS

Checking Your Reading

1. Why did Lonnie seem both "vulnerable and privileged"? **Her mother was dead and her father paid little attention to her.**
2. Why does the narrator want to get sick? **She doesn't want to go to the dance.**
3. What does Mason do when he and the narrator are paired to dance? **He leaves her.**
4. Who offers a cigarette to the narrator? **Mary Fortune does.**
5. What makes the narrator decide that "My life was possible"? **Raymond asks her to dance, walks her home, and kisses her.**

Vocabulary in Context

Fill each blank with the most appropriate word from the Words for Everyday Use. You may have to change the tense of the word.

burlesque, inanimate, vulnerable, irrelevant, doggedly, languidly, exuberant

1. The protestors outside the political convention happily **burlesqued** the candidates.
2. Waking from his nap, our old cat stretched **languidly** in the afternoon sun.
3. The general insisted that the troops' position left them **vulnerable** to an attack.
4. Marcella found it difficult to keep up with her **exuberant** charges.
5. "I hate studying material that seems so **irrelevant**," complained Randy.

Literary Tools

1. What information is shared in the *exposition*? **The exposition sets the mood, introduces setting and characters, and gives background.**

RESPOND TO THE SELECTION

Imagine you are Mary Fortune. How would you feel towards the narrator as you left the dance? How would you feel towards yourself?

"Thanks," he said. "I sure could use it."

It was a good thing, I thought, that I had done that, for at my gate, when I said, "Well, good night," and after he said, "Oh, yeah. Good night," he leaned towards me and kissed me, briefly, with the air of one who knew his job when he saw it, on the corner of my mouth. Then he turned back to town, never knowing he had been my rescuer, that he had brought me from Mary Fortune's territory into the ordinary world.

In what way is Raymond the narrator's rescuer?

I went around the house to the back door, thinking, I have been to a dance and a boy has walked me home and kissed me. It was all true. My life was possible. I went past the kitchen window and I saw my mother. She was sitting with her feet on the open oven door, drinking tea out of a cup without a saucer. She was just sitting and waiting for me to come home and tell her everything that had happened. And I would not do it, I never would. But when I saw the waiting kitchen, and my mother in her faded, fuzzy Paisley kimono, with her sleepy but doggedly expectant face, I understood what a mysterious and oppressive obligation I had, to be happy, and how I had almost failed it, and would be likely to fail it, every time, and she would not know. ■

The Red Dress, c.1900s. Robert Gemmell Hutchison. The Fine Art Society, London.

WORDS FOR EVERYDAY USE

dog • ged • ly (dôg´id lē) *adv.*, persistently. *The team of scientists is doggedly pursuing a cure for the disease.*

op • pres • sive (ə pres´iv) *adj.*, distressing. *Even air conditioners seemed useless against the oppressive summer heat.*

Respond *to the* SELECTION

What might have happened if the girl had gone with Mary for hot chocolate, instead of staying at the dance with Raymond Bolting?

SELECTION CHECK TEST 4.11.15 WITH ANSWERS (CONT.)

2. What is an *inciting incident*? **It is the action that initiates the central conflict.**
3. What happens during a plot's crisis? **The crisis decides the future course of events and the eventual working out of the conflict.**
4. What is the difference between a resolution and a denouement? **The resolution resolves the conflict, and the denouement ties up loose ends.**
5. What is the central conflict of this story? **The narrator is conflicted over the dance, played out in the choice of befriending Mary Fortune or dancing with Raymond.**

INVESTIGATE

Inquire, Imagine

Recall: Gathering Facts →

1a. How does the narrator describe her mother's attitude toward sewing? How did the narrator feel about the outfits her mother made her in the past? How does she feel now?

2a. What does the narrator think of what Mason Williams does?

3a. How does the narrator's mother look when the narrator returns from the dance?

Interpret: Finding Meaning

1b. What insights do these details provide about the narrator's mother and her relationship with her daughter?

2b. What do her thoughts about Mason's actions reveal about how she thinks of herself?

3b. What does this make the narrator understand? Explain.

Analyze: Taking Things Apart →

4a. Look back to the selection and gather details about the uncomfortable experiences the narrator has had in school. What seem to be her biggest fears?

Synthesize: Bringing Things Together

4b. What do the narrator and Mary Fortune have in common? In what ways are they different? What do you think the narrator means when she says that Raymond rescued her from "Mary Fortune's territory" and brought her back into the ordinary world?

Evaluate: Making Judgments →

5a. To what degree do the narrator's insecurities about herself influence the way she interacts with other characters in the story?

Extend: Connecting Ideas

5b. Compare and contrast the qualities of the narrator of "Red Dress—1946" to Laura in "The Garden-Party." Consider how the author uses characterization to present each character, what issues or conflicts concern each character, similarities and differences in the circumstances that surround them, and how each character resolves the conflicts she faces.

Understanding Literature

Characterization. Review the definition for **characterization** in the Handbook of Literary Terms. Which technique of characterization does the author most rely on to portray the narrator? the narrator's mother? Mary Fortune?

Plot and conflict. Review the definitions for **plot** and **conflict** in the Handbook of Literary Terms. What conflicts does the narrator face in this story? Classify these as *internal* or *external conflicts*. What is the *central conflict* in the story? What is the *turning point*, or *crisis*, in the story? Use the model below as a

Answers to Investigate, Inquire, and Imagine

Recall

1a. The narrator says her mother takes no pride in the finer details of sewing like finishing buttonholes or overcasting seams. When the narrator was younger she took pleasure in the outfits her mother made her. Now the narrator wishes for store-bought clothes like those of her friend Lonnie.

2a. The narrator isn't angry or surprised by the way Mason Williams treats her at the dance. She knows that Mason is popular, so dancing with someone like her would be justifiably offensive.

3a. The narrator's mother looks sleepy but doggedly expectant.

Interpret

1b. The fact that her mother continues to sew for her means that she isn't aware that her daughter is embarrassed by the clothes or that she isn't concerned about it. The narrator and her mother experience differences of opinion and generational conflicts.

2b. The narrator's reaction to the way Mason treats her belies that she has little self-confidence and self-worth.

3b. This makes the narrator understand that her mother cares about whether she fits in, wants her to be happy, and wants to take part in what goes on in her life.

Analyze

4a. The narrator has had trouble speaking in class—her voice gets squeaky or hoarse and trembly; she is always uncomfortable if she has to stand up in front of the class; she can't hit the ball in volleyball; at the beginning of the dance, Mason Williams makes it obvious that he doesn't want to dance with her, and no one else asks her to dance either. The narrator's biggest fear is that she won't fit in—that she will do something or say something to embarrass herself in front of the other students at her school.

Synthesize

4b. The narrator and Mary Fortune are both outsiders to some degree; neither girl is popular with boys their age. The narrator is very concerned by what others think of her, especially boys her age; Mary Fortune says she doesn't care about boys; she is independent and not worried about what others think of her. When Raymond asks the narrator to dance, walks her home, and kisses her, he rescues her by

Answers to Investigate, Inquire, and Imagine (cont.)

making her normal, by giving her the typical night at the dance experience.

Evaluate

5a. Some examples include the way she tries to distract Lonnie's attention away from her mother because she is embarrassed of her mother; the way that she is so immediately influenced by Mary, and assumes that she won't be friends with Lonnie anymore because Lonnie is boy-crazy; the way she vows not to let her mother know the difficulties she has at school.

Continued on page 1072

Answers to Understanding Literature can be found on page 1072.

ANSWERS TO INVESTIGATE, INQUIRE, AND IMAGINE (CONT. FROM PAGE 1071)

EXTEND

5b. *Responses will vary.* Although these characters are both young girls, they are very different. Laura in "The Garden-Party" is more self-assured and more focused on those around her than she is on herself. The author of "Red Dress—1946" relies mainly on revealing the narrator's thoughts and feelings to develop her character. The author of "The Garden-Party" creates Laura's character by using direct description and by revealing her thoughts and feelings through a third-person narrator. Both authors use dialogue throughout their stories. The narrator of "Red Dress—1946" wrestles with her insecurities about not fitting in at high school, while Laura in "The Garden-Party" tries to reconcile her feelings about the elaborate party her family is throwing. While Laura's conflict may not be completely resolved at the end of the story, the action she takes toward resolution is to visit the family of the man who was killed. The narrator of "Red Dress—1946 doesn't resolve her conflict, but she does go to the dance, and sighs in relief when it doesn't turn out to be a total disaster.

ANSWERS TO UNDERSTANDING LITERATURE

CHARACTERIZATION. The author relies on revealing the narrator's thoughts and feelings to develop her character. The author also uses dialogue to develop the narrator. The narrator's mother and Mary Fortune are mostly developed by direct description.

PLOT AND CONFLICT. One of the narrator's external conflicts is having to wear yet another of her mother's creations—the red dress. The narrator struggles internally with her unhappiness. The central conflict is the Christmas Dance. For the narrator, the turning point is purely accidental. It occurs just as she is about to leave the dance with Mary, when Raymond Bolting asks her to dance and thinks that she says yes.

Possible answers for Plot Diagram:

Introduction: "My mother was making me a dress. All through the month of November...tissue-paper pattern."

Inciting Incident: Going to the school dance

Rising Action: goes to dance, no one asks her to dance, meets Mary

guide to creating a plot diagram for this selection. Beneath each diagram heading describe events in the story that correspond to that heading.

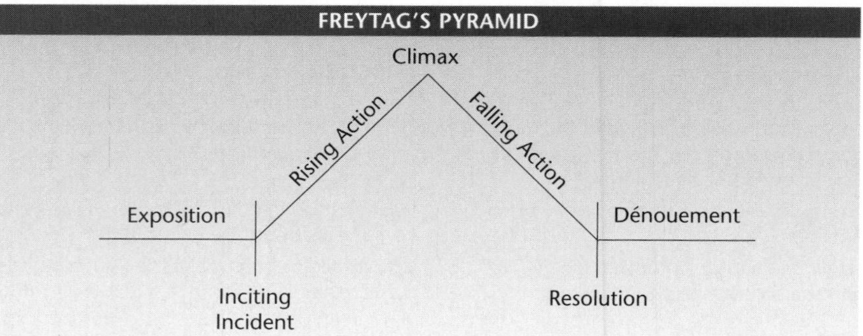

WRITER'S JOURNAL

1. Write Mary Fortune's **journal entry** on the night of the dance.
2. Imagine that the narrator has second thoughts about her decision to stay at the dance with Raymond rather than going with Mary for hot chocolate. Write an **advice-column** response addressing her dilemma.
3. Create a **list of rules of etiquette** on the following topic: " High School Dances, the Unwritten Rules."

Integrating *the* LANGUAGE ARTS

Study and Research & Collaborative Learning

TIME MACHINE. What was happening in the world in 1946? in your state? your town? Form several small groups and assign each group to research the following topics: history and politics, literature and theatre, religion and philosophy, visual arts, music, science and technology, and daily life. After completing the research, each group should create a presentation. You may want to use posters, magazines and newspapers, videos, or tape recorders—whatever you think will best present the information your group has gathered about 1946.

Speaking and Listening

CONDUCTING AN INTERVIEW. Interview someone who would have been in high school in 1946. Prepare for the interview by listing a number of questions, such as: What did you wear? What kind of haircut did you have? In what activities did you participate? How would you describe your personality in high school? What did you want to do when you got out of school? Write a short sketch on school life in the 1940s based on the information from your interview.

ANSWERS TO UNDERSTANDING LITERATURE (CONT.)

Climax/Crisis or Turning Point: agrees to dance with Raymond

Falling Action: narrator, Raymond, Lonnie and her dance partner walk home

Resolution: narrator returns home relieved by the events of the night, glad to have been rescued, determines never to let her mother know how difficult high school is for her.

ANSWERS TO INTEGRATING THE LANGUAGE ARTS

Study and Research & Collaborative Learning

Refer students to the Language Arts Survey 5.19, "How to Locate Library Materials" and 5.26, "Using the Internet" as they conduct their research.

Speaking and Listening

Refer students to the Language Arts Survey 4.14, "Conducting an Interview" to help them prepare for this activity.

from Angela's Ashes

By Frank McCourt

About the Author

Frank McCourt (1930–) was born in Brooklyn, where his parents had recently immigrated, but moved back to Ireland at age four with his parents and brothers. As tough as life had been for the McCourts in New York, it didn't compare to the hardships they encountered in their native country. Penniless and hungry, the McCourts made it to Limerick, where Frank was introduced to a collection of his relatives. Frank's father, Malachy, rarely had a job and when he did, spent his wages in the pubs, leaving Frank's mother, Angela, to beg from churches and charity organizations for food and clothing for the family. Three of McCourt's siblings died from childhood diseases that might have been prevented with the proper medical care and better living conditions. Frank spent several months in quarantine in the hospital, near death from typhoid fever, where he had steady meals, clean sheets, and best of all, books. It is here that he was first introduced to Shakespeare. " I don't know what it means and I don't care because it's Shakespeare and it's like having jewels in my mouth when I say the words," said young Frank in McCourt's memoir.

McCourt lived in Limerick until he saved his money to buy a boat ticket to America at the age of 19. He eventually attended New York University, and was a high school writing teacher for many years in New York City, where he still lives today.

About the Selection

Angela's Ashes is a memoir describing Frank McCourt's life growing up destitute in Ireland. McCourt was quoted to say, "When I look back on my childhood I wonder how I managed to survive at all. It was, of course, a miserable childhood: the happy childhood is hardly worth your while. Worse than the ordinary miserable childhood is the miserable Irish childhood, and worse yet is the miserable Irish Catholic childhood." McCourt was awarded the Pulitzer Prize for *Angela's Ashes* in 1997. He published a sequel in 1999 titled *'Tis: A Memoir,* which tells the story of his journey in America from impoverished immigrant to brilliant teacher and best-selling author.

Literary Tools

Memoir. A **memoir** is a narrative composed from personal experience. A memoir is similar to an autobiography, or the biography or history of a person narrated by himself or herself. As you read, list some facts that you learn about Frank McCourt in this episode from his memoir.

Theme. A **theme** is a central idea in a literary work. One of the themes in *Angela's Ashes* is that humans can overcome adversity. Another theme is that humor has value. As you read, make a chart, listing each theme at the top of the page. Then jot down passages from the excerpt from *Angela's Ashes* that you believe illustrate these themes in the proper columns. A sample chart appears below.

Humans can overcome adversity	Humor has value
Starting first job at fourteen to achieve a goal	

Reader's Journal

When in your own life did you first feel like you had become an adult?

ADDITIONAL RESOURCES

Unit 11 Resource Book
- Selection Worksheet 11.9
- Selection Check Test 4.11.17
- Selection Test 4.11.18
- Language, Grammar, and Style Resource 3.92

GRAPHIC ORGANIZER

Humor has value: Aunt Aggie's remark about Frank's clothes; People's ability to show sympathy and kindness: Mrs. Clohessy feeds Frank bread and jam; Hard work is rewarded: Frank gets his first pound after a week of work which drives his hope of going to America with the money he will earn.

READER'S JOURNAL

Recall back to your first day of work. How did you feel? What was it like to get your first paycheck?

GOALS/OBJECTIVES

Studying this lesson will enable students to
- empathize with the speaker's struggle of growing up in poverty and enjoy Frank McCourt's sense of humor
- describe Frank McCourt's literary accomplishments and explain his contribution to the twentieth-century memoir
- define *memoir* and *theme* and identify and explain examples of each in the selection
- demonstrate the ability to use quotation marks
- create a map of Ireland

ANSWERS TO GUIDED READING QUESTIONS

1. The narrator has a hard time sleeping because the next day he will be fourteen and starting his first job.
2. He bribes him with food—bread and jam.
3. The narrator's aunt tells her to tell his new employers that his aunt is waiting for him and that he will be an hour late.

VOCABULARY FROM THE SELECTION

denounce	laughingstock
frock	squander
galore	wages

Angela's Ashes

Frank McCourt

What makes it hard for the narrator to sleep?

It's hard to sleep when you know the next day you're fourteen and starting your first job as a man. The Abbot[1] wakes at dawn moaning. Would I ever make him some tay[2] and if I do I can have a big cut of bread from the half loaf in his pocket which he was keeping there out of the way of the odd rat and if I look in Grandma's gramophone[3] where she used to keep the records I'll find a jar of jam.

With what does the Abbot bribe the narrator to make him tea?

He can't read, he can't write, but he knows where to hide the jam.

I bring The Abbot his tea and bread and make some for myself. I put on my damp clothes and get into the bed hoping that if I stay there the clothes will dry from my own heat before I go to work. Mam always says it's the damp clothes that give you the consumption and an early grave. The Abbot is sitting up telling me he has a terrible pain in his head from a dream where I was wearing his poor mother's black dress and she flying around screaming, Sin, sin, 'tis a sin.[4] He finishes his tea and falls into a snore sleep and I wait for his clock to say half-past eight, time to get up and be at the post office at nine even if the clothes are still damp on my skin.

On my way out I wonder why Aunt Aggie is coming down the lane. She must be coming to see if The Abbot is dead or needing a doctor. She says, What time do you have to be at that job?[5]

Nine.

All right.

She turns and walks with me to the post office on Henry Street. She doesn't say a word and I wonder if she's going to the post office to denounce me for sleeping in my grandmother's bed and wearing her black dress. She says, Go up and tell them your aunt is down here waiting for you and you'll be an hour late. If they want to argue I'll go up and argue.

What does the narrator's aunt tell the narrator to do?

Why do I have to be an hour late?

Do what you're bloody well told.

1. **The Abbot.** A nickname for the narrator's uncle
2. **tay.** Tea; the author sometimes uses unusual spellings to capture the Irish dialect.
3. **gramophone.** British and Irish term for a phonograph, or record player
4. **damp clothes . . . sin.** Earlier in this memoir the narrator washed his clothes before beginning his first job. Having only one outfit, he had to wear an old dress that belonged to his grandmother while his only clothes dried.
5. **What . . . job.** The author does not use quotation marks to indicate dialogue, so readers must distinguish dialogue from narrative by the context.

Words For Everyday Use

de • nounce (di naünts') *vt.*, accuse publicly; inform against. *Benedict Arnold is now denounced as a traitor during the American Revolution.*

Limerick, Ireland.

There are telegram boys[6] sitting on a bench along a wall. There are two women at a desk, one fat, one thin. The thin one says, Yes?

My name is Frank McCourt, miss, and I'm here to start work.

What kind of work would that be now?

Telegram boy, miss.

The thin one cackles, Oh, God, I thought you were here to clean the lavatories.

No, miss. My mother brought a note from the priest, Dr. Cowpar, and there's supposed to be a job.

Oh, there is, is there? And do you know what day this is?

I do, miss. 'Tis my birthday. I'm fourteen.

Isn't that grand, says the fat woman.

Today is Thursday, says the thin woman. Your job starts on Monday. Go away and wash yourself and come back then.

The telegram boys along the wall are laughing. I don't know why but I feel my face turning hot. I tell the women, Thank you, and on the way out I hear the thin one, Jesus above, Maureen, who dragged in that specimen?[7] and they laugh along with the telegram boys.

Aunt Aggie says, Well? and I tell her I don't start till Monday. She says my clothes are a disgrace and what did I wash them in.

Carbolic soap.[8]

6. **telegram boys.** Boys who delivered telegrams, or messages delivered by telegraph. Before messages were communicated by telephone, they were transmitted using a system of electrical impulses known as Morse code over telegraph wire. These messages had to be decoded, and then delivered on paper to their recipients. The telegraph was still in wide use throughout the early twentieth century even after the invention of the telephone because few people, especially in poor or rural areas had telephones, and using them was often prohibitively expensive.

7. **specimen.** Kind of individual or person; here used derogatorily

8. **carbolic soap.** Very powerful, strong-smelling soap

INDIVIDUAL LEARNING STRATEGIES

Motivation
If possible, ask an Irish immigrant to speak to the class about his or her life in Ireland and the experiences he or she had of traveling to the United States. Students should have at least one question prepared to ask the visitor.

Reading Proficiency
Have students work with a partner to complete the Graphic Organizer on page 1073.

English Language Learning
Because of the large amount of footnotes in this selection, spend time (before they read the selection) going over the footnotes, making sure students comprehend them.

Special Needs
Have students focus on the Guided Reading questions and the Recall questions in the selection.

Enrichment
When Frank McCourt was a child, Ireland's economy was poor and job opportunities were scarce. What is the economic and employment status of Ireland today? Have students make a graph or chart that shows the progress of both the economic and employment rate of Ireland in incriminates of every 10 years. In what ways are the economic status and employment rate related?

ANSWERS TO GUIDED READING QUESTION

1. Aunt Aggie says the narrator is making a laughingstock of the family. She buys him clothes for his new job and gives him money to buy tea and a bun for his birthday.
2. Temporary telegrams boys do not have the same job security as permanent ones and have to leave when they turn sixteen; temporary telegram boys do not get uniforms, holidays, waterproof capes, sick days, or the same pay as permanent ones; and temporary telegram boys can be fired at a moment's notice, unlike permanent ones. The narrator is a temporary telegram boy.

CROSS-CURRICULAR ACTIVITIES

Geography. Ask students to find the River Shannon on a map. Then have them research the River Shannon by finding facts such as the length, the width, and the economic and ecological effects the river has on Ireland. Finally, have them present an oral presentation including pictures of the river both from the 1940s and the present decade.

What does Aunt Aggie say the narrator is doing?

They smell like dead pigeons and you're making a laughingstock of the whole family.

She takes me to Roche's Stores and buys me a shirt, a gansey, a pair of short pants, two pairs of stockings and a pair of summer shoes on sale. She gives me two shillings to have tea and a bun for my birthday. She gets on the bus to go back up O'Connell Street too fat and lazy to walk. Fat and lazy, no son of her own, and still she buys me the clothes for my new job.

I turn toward Arthur's Quay with the package of new clothes under my arm and I have to stand at the edge of the River Shannon so that the whole world won't see the tears of a man the day he's fourteen.

Monday morning I'm up early to wash my face and flatten my hair with water and spit. The Abbot sees me in my new clothes. Jaysus, he says, is it gettin' married you are? and goes back to sleep.

Mrs. O'Connell, the fat woman, says, Well, well, aren't we the height of fashion, and the thin one, Miss Barry, says, Did you rob a bank on the weekend? and there's a great laugh from the telegram boys sitting on the bench along the wall.

I'm told to sit at the end of the bench and wait for my turn to go out with telegrams. Some telegram boys in uniforms are the permanent ones who took the exam. They can stay in the post office forever if they like, take the next exam for postman and then the one for clerk that lets them work inside selling stamps and money orders behind the counter downstairs. The post office gives permanent boys big waterproof capes for the bad weather and they get two weeks holiday every year. Everyone says these are good jobs, steady and pensionable[9] and respectable, and if you get a job like this you never have to worry again in your whole life, so you don't.

Temporary telegram boys are not allowed to stay in the job beyond the age of sixteen. There are no uniforms, no holidays, the pay is less, and if you stay out sick a day you can be fired. No excuses. There are no waterproof capes. Bring your own raincoat or dodge the raindrops.

What is the difference between being a permanent telegram boy and a temporary telegram boy? Which one is the narrator?

Mrs. O'Connell calls me to her desk to give me a black leather belt and pouch. She says there's a great shortage of bicycles so I'll have to walk my first batch of telegrams. I'm to go to the farthest address first, work my way back, and don't take all day. She's long enough in the post office to know how long it takes to deliver six telegrams even by foot. I'm not to be stopping in pubs or bookies[10] or even home for a cup of tea and if I do I'll be found out. I'm not to be stopping in chapels to say a prayer. If I have to pray do it on the hoof[11] or on the bicycle. If it rains pay no attention. Deliver the telegram and don't be a sissy.

One telegram is addressed to Mrs. Clohessy of Arthur's Quay and that couldn't be anyone but Paddy's mother.[12]

Is that you, Frankie McCourt? she says. God, I wouldn't know you you're that big. Come in, will you.

9. **pensionable.** Providing a regular payment to people who have fulfilled a condition of service or reached a certain age
10. **bookies.** Establishment where people, called bookies, take bets, as on horse races
11. **hoof.** Foot
12. **Paddy's mother.** The mother of Paddy (a nickname for Patrick), a friend of the narrator's

Words for Everyday Use

laugh • ing • stock (la' fiŋ stäk) *n.*, a person or thing made the object of ridicule. *Rula hoped to be the school comedian, not its laughingstock—she wanted people laughing at her jokes not at her.*

She's wearing a bright frock with flowers all over and shiny new shoes. There are two children on the floor playing with a toy train. On the table there is a teapot, cups with saucers, a bottle of milk, a loaf of bread, butter, jam. There are two beds over by the window where there were none before. The big bed in the corner is empty and she must know what I'm wondering.[13] He's gone, she says, but he's not dead. Gone t' England with Paddy. Have a cup o' tay an' a bit o' bread. You need it, God help us. You look like one left over from the Famine[14] itself. Ate that bread an' jam an' build yourself up. Paddy always talked about you and Dennis, my poor husband that was in the bed, never got over the day your mother came an' sang the song about the Kerry dancing. He's over in England now making sandwiches in a canteen[15] and sending me a few bob[16] every week. You'd wonder what the English are thinking about when they take a man that has the consumption and give him a job making sandwiches. Paddy has a grand job in a pub in Cricklewood, which is in England. Dennis would still be here if it wasn't for Paddy climbin' the wall for the tongue.

Tongue?

Dennis had the craving, so he did, for a nice sheep's head with a bit of cabbage and a spud[17] so up with me to Barry the butcher with the last few shillings I had. I boiled that head an' sick an' all as he was Dennis couldn't wait for it to be done. He was a demon there in the bed callin' for the head an' when I gave it to him on the plate he was delighted with himself suckin' the marrow outa every inch of that head. Then he finishes an' he says, Mary, where is the tongue?

What did Dennis crave? What is wrong with what he gets?

What tongue? says I.

The tongue of this sheep. Every sheep is born with a tongue that lets him go ba ba ba and there's a great lack of tongue in this head. Go up to Barry the butcher and demand it.

So up with me to Barry the butcher and he said, That bloody[18] sheep came in here bleatin' an' cryin' so much we cut the tongue from her and thrun it to the dog who gobbled it up and ever since ba bas like a sheep and if he doesn't quit I'll cut his tongue and throw it to the cat.

What did the butcher say he did with the tongue?

Back I go to Dennis and he gets frantic in the bed. I want that tongue, he says. All the nourishment is in the tongue. And what do you think happens next but my Paddy, that was your friend, goes up to Barry the butcher after dark, climbs the wall, cuts the tongue of a sheep's head that's on a hook on the wall and brings it back to his poor father in the bed. Of course I have to boil that tongue with salt galore and Dennis, God love him, ates it, lies back in the bed a minute, throws back the blanket and stands out on his two feet announcing to the world that consumption or no consumption, he's not going to die in that bed, if

What does Paddy do for his father? What does his mother do? What does Dennis do after his son and wife do this for him?

13. **big bed . . . wondering.** Formerly, Paddy's father, who has consumption, or tuberculosis of the lungs, a highly infectious disease, spent all his time lying in the big bed, so the narrator is wondering what happened to him.
14. **Famine.** Refers to the Irish Potato Famine (1845–1847), when a potato blight attacked the crop and more than 750,000 Irish people died through starvation and disease
15. **canteen.** Place outside a military camp where refreshments and entertainment are provided
16. **bob.** A shilling
17. **head . . . spud.** The poor in the town described in this memoir cannot afford regular cuts of meat, so they buy for a reasonable price what otherwise would be thrown away—the head of the animal. Spud—potato
18. **bloody.** Vulgar British and Irish slang, meaning cursed

WORDS FOR EVERYDAY USE

frock (fräk) *n.,* girl's or woman's dress. *Alice got grass stains on her new frock from playing in the garden, chasing after rabbits.*

ga • lore (gə lōr') *adj.,* in abundance: used postpositively. *The seafood restaurant served fish and crustaceans galore.*

ANSWERS TO GUIDED READING QUESTIONS

1. Dennis craved a sheep's head. His is missing its tongue.
2. The butcher said he cut it out because the sheep was making too much noise and fed it to his dog, which now makes the noise of a sheep.
3. Paddy steals into the butcher's, cuts the tongue from another sheep's head, and brings it to his father. His mother cooks the tongue for her husband. Dennis announces that despite his illness he is getting out of bed to go earn money for his family.

LITERARY TECHNIQUE

COLLOQUIALISM. Colloquialism is the use of informal language. Writers use colloquialism to represent both time and place. For example, "How y'all doing" represents the language of the southern United States and "We're just chillin'" represents the language of the twentieth-first century generation. McCourt uses colloquialism to help readers imagine themselves in Ireland during the 1940s. Examples from this page include, "Have cup o' tay an' a bit o' bread," "...making sandwiches in a canteen and sending me a few bob every week," "That bloody sheep came in here bleatin' an' cryin'," and "thrun it to the dog."

ANSWERS TO GUIDED READING QUESTIONS

1. She has enough money to buy food and shoes for the rest of her family.
2. She notes that they do not look like they are doing too well.
3. The narrator wants others to know that he too is a workingman with a pound in his pocket. He wants to wave his "pound note at the world so they'll say, There he goes, Frankie McCourt the workingman, with a pound in his pocket."

CROSS-CURRICULAR ACTIVITIES

Field of Medicine. Frank McCourt's brothers died of illnesses that could have been prevented through proper medical care. Find out from what illness each brother died. You may need to find biographical information on McCourt or refer to his book, *Angela's Ashes*. Then research what type of treatment could have been used between the years 1930-1950 to cure those illnesses.

he's going to die at all it might as well be under a German bomb with him making a few pounds for his family instead of whining in the bed there beyond.

She shows me a letter from Paddy. He's working in his uncle Anthony's pub twelve hours a day, twenty-five shillings a week and every day soup and a sandwich. He's delighted when the Germans come over with the bombs so that he can sleep while the pub is closed. At night he sleeps on the floor of the hallway upstairs. He will send his mother two pounds every month and he's saving the rest to bring her and the family to England where they'll be much better off in one room in Cricklewood than ten rooms in Arthur's Quay. She'll be able to get a job no bother. You'd have to be a sad case not to be able to get a job in a country that's at war especially with Yanks pouring in and spending money right and left. Paddy himself is planning to get a job in the middle of London where Yanks leave tips big enough to feed an Irish family of six for a week.

What does Mrs. Clohessy now have enough money to do?

Mrs. Clohessy says, We have enough money for food and shoes at last, thanks be to God and His Blessed Mother. You'll never guess who Paddy met over there in England fourteen years of age an' workin' like a man. Brendan Kiely, the one ye used to call Question. Workin' he is an' savin' so he can go an' join the Mounties[19] an' ride all over Canada like Nelson Eddy singin' I'll be callin' you ooh ooh ooh ooh ooh ooh. If it wasn't for Hitler we'd all be dead[20] an' isn't that a terrible thing to say. And how's your poor mother, Frankie?

She's grand, Mrs. Clohessy.

No, she's not. I seen her in the Dispensary[21] and she looks worse than my Dennis did in the bed. You have to mind your poor mother. You look desperate too, Frankie, with them two red eyes starin' outa your head. Here's a little tip for you. Thruppence.[22] Buy yourself a sweet.

What does Mrs. Clohessy note about the narrator and his mother?

I will, Mrs. Clohessy.

Do.

At the end of the week Mrs. O'Connell hands me the first wages of my life, a pound, my first pound. I run down the stairs and up to O'Connell Street, the main street, where the lights are on and people are going home from work, people like me with wages in their pockets. I want them to know I'm like them, I'm a man, I have a pound. I walk up one side of O'Connell Street and down the other and hope they'll notice me. They don't. I want to wave my pound note at the world so they'll say, There he goes, Frankie McCourt the workingman, with a pound in his pocket.

What does the narrator want others to know? What does he want to do?

It's Friday night and I can do anything I like. I can have fish and chips and go to the Lyric Cinema. No, no more Lyric. I don't have to sit up in the gods[23] anymore with people all around me cheering on the Indians killing General Custer and the Africans chasing Tarzan all over the jungle. I can go to the Savoy Cinema now, pay sixpence for a seat down front

19. **Mounties.** The Royal Canadian Mounted Police
20. **If . . . dead.** Mrs. Clohessy means that if it weren't for World War II, and the Germans attacking England, England would not have the need to hire so many Irish people.
21. **Dispensary.** Place where the poor are given medical attention and charity
22. **Thruppence.** Three pence, or pennies
23. **gods.** The seats up in a high balcony, which are much cheaper

Words for Everyday Use

wage (wāj) *n.,* (often pl.) money paid to an employee for work done, and usually figured on an hourly, daily, or piecework basis. *Almost all of Sheila's wages went straight to her savings account as she was saving for her college education.*

where there's a better class of people eating boxes of chocolates and covering their mouths when they laugh. After the film I can have tea and buns in the restaurant upstairs.

Michael is across the street calling me. He's hungry and wonders if there's any chance he could go to The Abbot's for a bit of bread and stay there for the night instead of going all the way to Laman Griffin's. I tell him he doesn't have to worry about a bit of bread. We'll go to the Coliseum Café and have fish and chips, all he wants, lemonade galore, and then we'll go to see *Yankee Doodle Dandy* with James Cagney[24] and eat two big bars of chocolate. After the film we have tea and buns and we sing and dance like Cagney all the way to The Abbot's. Michael says it must be great to be in America where people have nothing else to do but sing and dance. He's half asleep but he says he's going there some day to sing and dance and would I help him go and when he's asleep I start thinking about America and how I have to save money for my fare instead of squandering it on fish and chips and tea and buns. I'll have to save a few shillings from my pound because if I don't I'll be in Limerick forever. I'm fourteen now and if I save something every week surely I should be able to go to America by the time I'm twenty. ■

What does the narrator decide about himself? Why?

24. **James Cagney.** (1899–1987) American movie actor

Words for Everyday Use

squan • der (skwän′ dər) *vt.*, spend or use wastefully or extravagantly. *Although he made a fortune, he squandered it all through living beyond his means and poor investments.*

Respond to the Selection

How is the narrator's life similar to or different from your own? With what qualities of the narrator can you identify?

ANSWER TO GUIDED READING QUESTION

1. The narrator decides he must save his money so he can but passage to America by the time he is twenty.

SELECTION CHECK TEST 4.11.17 WITH ANSWERS

Checking Your Reading

1. Who asks McCourt for some bread and jam? **His uncle asks him for it.**
2. What does McCourt's aunt buy for him? **She buys him work clothes.**
3. What does McCourt hide as he stands at the River Shannon? **He hides his tears.**
4. Where are Paddy and his father? **They are working in England.**
5. How does McCourt spend his first paycheck? **He buys dinner and a movie.**

Vocabulary in Context

Fill each blank with the most appropriate word from the Words for Everyday Use. You may have to change the tense of the word.

denounce laughingstock frock galore wage

1. Maria had three fittings for her *quinceñeara* **frock** before it was finished.
2. The children's eyes widened at the sight of treats and candies **galore**.
3. The knight **denounced** his former patron and pledged his loyalty to King Arthur.

Literary Tools

1. What is a memoir? **A memoir is a narrative composed from personal experience.**
2. What is unusual about the way McCourt indicates dialogue? **He doesn't use quotation marks.**
3. What is the setting for this memoir? **The setting must note TIME and PLACE: it is set in Ireland during World War II.**
4. What is a possible theme for this selection? **Responses will vary.**
5. Describe the character of Frank McCourt. **Responses will vary.**

RESPOND TO THE SELECTION

How would you describe Frank McCourt based on what you have read? Knowing that he arrived to America at the age of nineteen, what can you deduce about his character?

ANSWERS TO INVESTIGATE, INQUIRE, AND IMAGINE

Recall

1a. The narrator is looking forward to starting his first job. The people at the post office make fun of him because of his shabby clothes and unwashed appearance. Aunt Aggie offers to argue with his employer if the employer gives him a hard time. He reveals that she is "fat and lazy" and has no son of her own. The narrator weeps at the edge of the River Shannon.

2a. The speaker delivers his first telegram to Mrs. Clohessy. She tells him how his friend Paddy is working in a bar in England and is sending home money each month and Dennis Clohessy, her consumptive husband, is working making sandwiches at a canteen in England. She says that she knows that his mother is not doing "grand" because she has seen her in the "Dispensary," looking more ill than her husband used to. She also says that Frank looks famished and that his eyes are too red.

3a. They spend some of his wages on fish and chips, lemonade, a movie and chocolate bars, and tea and buns. Michael thinks that people in America spend all their time singing and dancing. The narrator decides to save his wages so that he can buy passage to America when he is twenty.

Interpret

1b. The narrator seems very impoverished as he only has one set of clothes. He also seems to have no adult figure to take care of him, as he is setting out to support himself at age fourteen. Despite a somewhat gruff and no-nonsense manner, Aunt Aggie is actually very kindhearted and empathetic toward him. The narrator is overcome with feelings of surprise, gratitude, and thankfulness, as evidenced by his tears.

2b. Mrs. Clohessy now has money enough to feed, clothe, and take care of her family, as well as provide them with some simple amusements, such as toys. She feels happy and thankful about her situation. The narrator may also feel happy and thankful that the family was able to make a dramatic recovery. The speaker lies because he is ashamed and too proud to let Mrs. Clohessy think that he is not taking care of his mother or because he does not want her to pity him or his family.

3b. The narrator is very proud of himself and feels grown-up. The fact that they spend most of their money on food and a movie indicates that they have gone hungry and

INVESTIGATE, Inquire, Imagine

Recall: Gathering Facts →

1a. What is the narrator looking forward to doing on his fourteenth birthday? For what reason do the people at the post office make fun of him? What does Aunt Aggie do for the narrator? What details does the narrator provide about Aunt Aggie? What does the narrator do at the edge of the River Shannon?

Interpret: Finding Meaning

1b. Based on people's reaction to the narrator's appearance and what he is setting out to do on his fourteenth birthday, what can you tell about the narrator's life and his financial situation? Based on the details you learn about Aunt Aggie, what type of person is she? How does the narrator feel about what she does for him?

2a. To whom does the narrator deliver his first telegram? What does this person tell him about what has happened to a former friend and his father? What does this person say about how the narrator and his mother are doing?

2b. In what way has what her husband and son have done changed the person who receives the telegram's life? How does this person feel about her situation? How do you think the narrator feels about this news? Why do you think the speaker lies about his mother's condition?

3a. What do the narrator and his brother Michael do with the narrator's wages? What does Michael think of America? What does the narrator decide to do with his wages in the future?

3b. How does the narrator feel about receiving his first wages? What does the way in which the narrator and his brother spend money reveal about their past? In what ways might the narrator be surprised when he comes to America?

Analyze: Taking Things Apart →

4a. Identify some events in this excerpt that reveal details about the narrator's past. What details reveal something about the narrator's character?

Synthesize: Bringing Things Together

4b. What picture does this excerpt paint of the narrator's past and his character? What do you think has happened to the narrator in the past? What type of person does he seem to be?

Evaluate: Making Judgments →

5a. Toward the end of the excerpt, the narrator is proud of himself and thinks of himself as a "workingman." Evaluate how grown up Frank McCourt really is for a fourteen-year-old at this point in the memoir. In what ways is he like an adult? In what ways is he like a child?

Extend: Connecting Ideas

5b. How do you think the narrator's character might grow and change now that he has entered the working world? Explain whether you think the narrator will achieve the goal he sets at the end of the excerpt and how you imagine he will feel if he does achieve it.

Understanding Literature

Memoir. Review the definition for **memoir** in Literary Tools in Prereading. If you had to write a brief biography about Frank McCourt, what basic facts from this memoir might you include? What did you learn about McCourt's character? Write a sentence or two describing McCourt's character, as you see it, in your own words.

ANSWERS TO INVESTIGATE, INQUIRE, AND IMAGINE (cont.)

Continued on page 1081

entertainment is an unusual treat. The narrator might be surprised to discover that movies idealize America and that there is hardship, poverty, and suffering in the United States, too.

Analyze

4a. Students may point to details that reveal that the narrator has a very impoverished past, such as him owning only one set of clothes, his starved appearance and red eyes, and the fact that as soon as he has money he spends it on food. Details that reveal something about his character include his tears when his aunt buys him clothes, the fact that he treats his brother to food and a movie as soon as he has money, and his determination to save money to go to America.

Synthesize

4b. This excerpt reveals that the narrator has known extreme poverty. He is also on his own probably

THEME. Review the definition for **theme** in Literary Tools in Prereading. One of the themes in *Angela's Ashes* is the human ability to overcome adversity. Another theme is the value of humor. Based on what you have read of Angela's Ashes, explain the way in which these two themes might be related.

WRITER'S JOURNAL

1. Imagine that you are fourteen-year-old Frank McCourt, the narrator of *Angela's Ashes.* Write a **personal letter** to your friend Paddy in England. Explain what you are doing now, how your family is doing, and what you hope to do. Use both details from the excerpt and your own imagination as necessary. Try to capture the narrator's voice in your letter.
2. The town in which McCourt lived in Ireland is known as Limerick. A **limerick** is also a type of humorous five-line poem with the rhyme scheme *aabba.* (For more information on limericks, see the Handbook of Literary Terms.) McCourt is able to view his past, even some of the sad aspects of it, with humor. Write a limerick about an event from the excerpt of *Angela's Ashes.*
3. Write an episode that could be part of your own personal **memoir.** Your episode from your memoir should describe an experience you had that helped to shape you into an adult. You may wish to focus on an experience that happened when you were fourteen, the same age as the narrator in *Angela's Ashes.*

Integrating the LANGUAGE ARTS

Language, Grammar, and Style

USING QUOTATION MARKS. Ordinarily, quotation marks indicate the use of dialogue. Review the Language Arts Survey 3.92, "Quotation Marks." Then, punctuate the passages below correctly, using quotation marks.

She must be coming to see if The Abbot is dead or needing a doctor. She says, What time do you have to be at that job?
Nine.
All right.
She turns and walks with me to the post office on Henry Street. . . . She says, Go up and tell them your aunt is down here waiting for you and you'll be an hour late. If they want to argue, I'll go up and argue.
Why do I have to be an hour late?
Do what you're bloody well told.

Study and Research & Collaborative Learning

USING ALMANACS, YEARBOOKS, AND ATLASES. Work in groups of four or five; go to your school or local library, and locate a map of Ireland. Your group should then use this map as a basis for creating your own map of Ireland. Your map should include Limerick, but the other natural features or towns you include are up to you. You should, however, try to include what you see as being some of the more important features of Ireland.

ANSWERS TO INVESTIGATE, INQUIRE, AND IMAGINE (CONT. FROM PAGE 1080)

because he is trying to stop being a burden to his mother. The narrator is portrayed as ambitious and hardworking, kind to his family, and able to set goals for his future. He is also humorous and a little naive.

EVALUATE
5a. *Responses will vary.* Like an adult, Frank is working full time and supporting himself and has set definite goals for his future—to move to America. Nevertheless, Frank is still quite young and displays this sometimes, such as when he immediately spends his wages on immediate pleasures like food and drink rather than saving for his future.

EXTEND
5b. *Responses will vary.* Frank will grow up quickly in the working world and focus on attaining his goal even more. He may achieve his goal of moving to America but may be surprised to find that the United States does not match its depiction in film.

ANSWER TO UNDERSTANDING LITERATURE

MEMOIR. Students might suggest facts such as Frank's going to work at age fourteen, his close relationship with his brother Michael, his poverty, and his determination to go to America.

ANSWERS TO INTEGRATING THE LANGUAGE ARTS

Language, Grammar, and Style
MAKING PASSIVE SENTENCES ACTIVE

1. Mam always says that wearing damp clothes result in consumption and an early grave.
2. I stood at the River Shannon's edge to hide the tears of a fourteen year-old man.
3. The dog ate the sheep's tongue that was thrown to him.
4. He will send two pounds to his mother each month and have the rest to bring her and the rest of the family to England.
5. At the end of the week, Mrs. O'Connell handed me my first wages.

ANSWERS TO INTEGRATING THE LANGUAGE ARTS (CONT.)

Language, Grammar, and Style
USING QUOTATIONS. She must be coming to see if The Abbot is dead or needing a doctor. She says, "What time do you have to be at that job?"
"Nine."
"All right."
She turns and walks with me to the post office on Henry Street. . . . She says, "Go up and tell them your aunt is down here waiting for you and you'll be an hour late. If they want to argue, I'll go up and argue."
"Why do I have to be an hour late?"
"Do what you're bloody well told."

ADDITIONAL RESOURCES

Unit 11 Resource Book
- Selection Worksheet 11.10
- Selection Check Test 4.11.19
- Selection Test 4.11.20
- Language, Grammar, and Style Resource 3.46

VOCABULARY FROM THE SELECTION

abate	pallid
gruel	pervading
impotence	propitious
incessantly	winnow
listlessness	wraithlike

GRAPHIC ORGANIZER

Students should fill in their cluster charts with the following adjectives: resilient, hard-working, observant, and resigned.

READER'S JOURNAL

Have you ever experienced nature to characterize it as a wild animal? If so, what animal would you describe nature and describe your experience. If not, how would you characterize nature? What led you to this characterization?

MULTICULTURAL EXTENSIONS

Literary TOOLS

Simile. A **simile** is a comparison using like or as. As you read the first paragraph, find a simile.

Narrator. A **narrator** is one who tells a story. As you read, make a cluster chart listing the character traits of the narrator.

Reader's Journal

When have you felt the power of nature?

FROM NECTAR IN A SIEVE

BY KAMALA MARKANDAYA

About the AUTHOR

Kamala Markandaya (1923–) was born and educated in India. In her late thirties she moved to England. She went on to become a prolific British novelist. Her early novels illustrate the political and economic struggles India has faced. She also focuses on the pressures of modernization on traditional Indian society. Some of her titles include *The Silence of Desire* (1960), *Possession* (1963), *A Handful of Rice* (1966), *The Coffer Dams* (1969), and *The Nowhere Man* (1972). Some consider *The Golden Honeycomb* (1977), a book about Indian independence, to be her most ambitious piece.

About the SELECTION

This selection comes from Markandaya's first novel, *Nectar in a Sieve,* which tells the story of a woman in a small village in India who, along with her husband, struggles to fulfill the basic needs of her family on a daily basis. This beautiful novel shows how the family changes and adapts when confronted with the challenge of surviving the famine and poverty that gripped India during British colonialism. In the selection you are about to read, the family is picking up the pieces after a devastating natural disaster. Their resources have been depleted by the recent wedding celebration of their daughter Ira, which makes getting on their feet even more difficult. In this excerpt, the character of Kenny appears. Kenny is a supportive and respectful British doctor who lives and works in the community. He encourages the villagers to stand up against Britain's abuses.

GOALS/OBJECTIVES

Studying this lesson will enable students to
- empathize with the narrator's struggle for survival and experience her optimism in the face of adversity
- describe Kamala Markandaya's literary accomplishments and the cultural influences on her writing
- define *simile* and *narrator* and identify and explain examples of each in the selection
- demonstrate the ability to correct misplaced or dangling modifiers
- conduct research on the economic development of India

FROM NECTAR IN A SIEVE

Nature is like a wild animal that you have trained to work for you. So long as you are vigilant and walk warily with thought and care, so long will it give you its aid; but look away for an instant, be heedless or forgetful, and it has you by the throat.

Ira had been given in marriage in the month of June, which is the propitious season for weddings, and what with the preparing for it, and the listlessness that took hold of me in the first days after her departure, nothing was done to make our hut weatherproof or to secure the land from flooding. That year the monsoon broke early with an evil intensity such as none could remember before.

Why had the family not prepared for monsoon season?

It rained so hard, so long and so incessantly that the thought of a period of no rain provoked a mild wonder. It was as if nothing had ever been but rain, and the water pitilessly found every hole in the thatched roof to come in, dripping onto the already damp floor. If we had not built on high ground the very walls would have melted in that moisture. I brought out as many pots and pans as I had and we laid them about to catch the drips, but soon there were more leaks than we had vessels. . . . Fortunately, I had laid in a stock of firewood for Ira's wedding, and the few sticks that remained served at least to cook our rice, and while the fire burnt, hissing at the water in the wood, we huddled round trying to get dry. At first the children were cheerful enough—they had not known such things before, and the lakes and rivulets that formed outside gave them endless delight; but Nathan and I watched with heavy hearts while the waters rose and rose and the tender green of the paddy field sank under and was lost.

"It is a bad season," Nathan said sombrely. "The rains have destroyed much of our work; there will be little eating done this year."

Why did the children cry?

At his words, Arjun broke into doleful sobs and his brother, Thambi, followed suit. They were old enough to understand, but the others, who weren't, burst into tears too, for by now they were

WORDS FOR EVERYDAY USE

pro • pi • tious (prō pish´əs) *adj.*, favorable. *We'll have the picnic on Saturday if the weather is propitious.*

list • less • ness (list' ləs nəs) *n.*, lack of interest, energy, or spirit. *The doctor warned me that with mono I would experience listlessness.*

in • ces • sant • ly (in se' sənt lē) *adv.*, continuing or following without interruption. *Rather than being pleased when Raul raised his hand incessantly, his teacher was perturbed.*

ANSWERS TO GUIDED READING QUESTIONS

1. The family had not prepared for the monsoon season because they were preparing for a family wedding.
2. They rains have destroyed much of the work the family did, so food will be scarce.

INDIVIDUAL LEARNING STRATEGIES

MOTIVATION
Encourage students to share the experiences they have had with storms. First have them name the storm and what happened, how they felt, and if any damage was made by the storm.

READING PROFICIENCY
Encourage students to write down the main ideas of the selection as they read. You may want to give students an outline and have them fill it in as they read the selection.

ENGLISH LANGUAGE LEARNING
Encourage students to use context clues to figure out the meaning of unfamiliar words such as *monsoon, paddy, rupee,* and so on.

SPECIAL NEEDS
Ask advanced students to help special needs students fill out their Graphic Organizer under the Literary Tools section.

ENRICHMENT
Ask students to write about the British colonial rule in India and India's struggle for independence. How and when did they gain independence? Who were the major leaders or groups that helped win India's fight for independence? Students will need to use both library and Internet resources for this activity.

ANSWER TO GUIDED READING QUESTION

1. All the crops were destroyed, Kali's hut was destroyed, six men were killed by lightning, and several people were left homeless due to the monsoon.

CROSS-CURRICULAR ACTIVITIES

Earth Science. Students can create world maps that indicate areas most susceptible to monsoons.

ADDITIONAL QUESTIONS AND ACTIVITIES

Students can discuss other natural disasters they have experienced or learned about through the media. Students may share their personal experiences of loss or rebuilding, or they may discuss relief efforts in such situations. Students may also want to consider how different people react in such situations. Does it become every person for him- or herself or do people pull together?

cramped and out of humour with sitting crouched on the damp floor; and hungry since there was little to eat, for most of the food had gone to make the wedding feast, and the new season's harvesting lay outside ungathered and rotting. I hushed them as best I could, throwing a reproachful glance at my husband for his careless words, but he was unnoticing, sunk in hatred and helplessness.

As night came on—the eighth night of the monsoon—the winds increased, whining and howling around our hut as if seeking to pluck it from the earth. Indoors it was dark—the wick, burning in its shallow saucer of oil, threw only a dim wavering light—but outside the land glimmered, sometimes pale and sometimes vivid, in the flicker of lightning. Towards midnight the storm was at its worst. Lightning kept clawing at the sky almost continuously, thunder shook the earth. I shivered as I looked—for I could not sleep, and even a prayer came with difficulty.

"It cannot last," Nathan said. "The storm will abate by the morning."

Even as he spoke a streak of lightning threw itself down at the earth, there was a tremendous clap of thunder, and when I uncovered my shrinking eyes I saw that our coconut palm had been struck. That, too, the storm had claimed for its own.

In the morning everything was calm. Even the rain had stopped. After the fury of the night before, an unnatural stillness lay on the land. I went out to see if anything could be saved of the vegetables, but the shoots and vines were battered and broken, torn from their supports and bruised; they did not show much sign of surviving. The corn field was lost. Our paddy field lay beneath a placid lake on which the children were already sailing bits of wood.

How much damage did the monsoon cause?

Many of our neighbours fared much worse than we had. Several were homeless, and of a group of men who sheltered under a tree when the storm began six had been killed by lightning.

Kali's hut had been completely destroyed in the last final fury of the storm. The roof had been blown away bodily, the mud walls had crumbled.

"At least it stood until the worst was over," said Kali to me, "and by God's grace we were all spared." She looked worn out; in the many years I had known her I had never seen her so deflated. She had come to ask for some palm leaves to thatch the new hut her husband was building; but I could only point to the blackened tree, its head bitten off and hanging by a few fibres from the withered stump.

"We must thatch our roof before the night," I said. "The rains may come again. We need rice too."

Nathan nodded. "We may be able to buy palm leaves in the village—also rice."

He went to the granary in a corner of which the small cloth bundle of our savings lay buried. It had been heavy once, when we were newly married: now the faded rag in which it was tied was too big and the ends flapped loosely over the knot. Nathan untied it and counted out twelve rupees.

"One will be enough," I said. "Let us go."

"I will take two. We can always put it back."

In the village the storm had left disaster and desolation worse than on our own doorstep. Uprooted trees sprawled their branches in ghastly fashion over streets and houses, flattening them and the bodies of men and women indiscriminately. Sticks and stones lay scattered wildly in angry confusion. The tannery stood, its bricks and cement had held it together

Words for Everyday Use

a • bate (ə bāt´) *vi.,* diminish; terminate. *The dog's barking did not abate until his owner returned.*

despite the raging winds; but the workers' huts, of more flimsy construction, had been demolished. The thatch had been ripped from some, where others stood there was now only a heap of mud with their owners' possessions studding them in a kind of pitiless decoration. The corrugated-iron shacks in which some of the men lived were no more: here and there we could see the iron sheets in unexpected places—suspended from tree tops, or blown and embedded on to the walls of houses still left standing. There was water everywhere, the gutters were overflowing into the streets. Dead dogs, cats and rats cluttered the roadside, or floated starkly on the waters with blown distended bellies.

People were moving about amid this destruction, picking out a rag here, a bundle there, hugging those things that they thought to be theirs, moving haltingly and with a kind of despair about them. People we knew came and spoke to us in low voices, gesturing hopelessly.

"Let us go," I said. "It is no good; we will come back later."

We turned back, the two rupees unspent. Our children came running out to meet us, their faces bright with hope.

"The shops are closed or destroyed," I said. "Go inside. I will get you some gruel presently."

Their faces faded; the two younger ones began crying listlessly from hunger and disappointment. I had no words to comfort them.

At dusk the drums of calamity began; their grave, throbbing rhythm came clearly through the night, throughout the night, each beat, each tattoo, echoing the mighty impotence of our human endeavour. I listened. I could not sleep. In the sound of the drums I understood a vast pervading doom; but in the expectant silences between, my own disaster loomed larger, more consequent and more hurtful.

We ventured out again when the waters had subsided a little, taking with us as before two rupees. This time things were somewhat better; the streets were clear, huts were going up everywhere. My spirits rose.

"To Hanuman first for rice," said Nathan, excited. "The gruel we have been swallowing has been almost plain water these last few days."

I quickened my steps: my stomach began heaving at the thought of food.

Hanuman was standing in the doorway of his shop. He shook his head when he saw us. "You have come for rice," he said. "They all come for rice. I have none to sell, only enough for my wife and children."

"And yet you are a merchant who deals in rice?"

"And what if so? Are you not growers of it? Why then do you come to me? If I have rice I do not choose to sell it now; but I have told you, I have none."

"We ask for only a little. We will pay for what we have—see, here is the money."

"No, no rice, but—wait . . . they say Biswas is selling . . . you can try . . ."

To Biswas. "We come for rice. Look, here is our money."

"Two rupees? How much do you think you can buy with two rupees?"

"We thought—"

"Never mind what you thought! Is this not a time of scarcity? Can you buy rice anywhere else? Am I not entitled to charge more for that? Two ollocks I will let you have and that is charity."

"It is very little for two rupees—"

"Take it or leave it. I can get double that sum from the tanners, but because I know you—"

We take it, we give up the silver coins. Now there is nothing left for the thatching, unless

How are they treated by the two shopkeepers?

WORDS FOR EVERYDAY USE

gru • el (grōō´əl) *n.,* thin porridge made by cooking grain in water or milk. *Mother made gruel with peaches for breakfast.*

im • po • tence (im′ pə təns) *n.,* lacking in power, strength, or vigor. *The Pharoah felt his impotence when a plague of locusts infested Egypt.*

per • vad • ing (pər vād′ iŋ) *part.,* diffused throughout. *The pervading feeling of the team was that we would lose to the Cougars.*

ANSWER TO GUIDED READING QUESTION

1. They are treated with disrespect, cynicism, and sarcasm by the shopkeepers.

CROSS-CURRICULAR ACTIVITIES

SOUTH AFRICAN LITERATURE. The class struggle described by Kamala Markandaya has parallels in the English literature of the twentieth century. Katherine Mansfield's portrait of the increasing disparity between the lower and upper classes in Georgian England echoes Markandaya's description of the poverty among Indian peasants in British-ruled India. Markandaya and South-African writer Nadine Gordimer both witnessed and wrote about the injustices of colonial rule. Ask students to go to the library and find information about Nadine Gordimer. Suggest that they read some of her short stories, and then compare her themes and ideas with those of Mansfield and Markandaya.

ANSWER TO GUIDED READING QUESTION

1. He says that times will not get better, that they should demand and cry out for help, and that their country has nothing to offer.

SELECTION CHECK TEST 4.11.19 WITH ANSWERS

Checking Your Reading

1. What destroys the crops at the beginning of the selection? **The heavy monsoon rains and subsequent flooding destroy the crops.**
2. For what do the people come to Hanuman the shopkeeper? **They come to him for rice.**
3. What does Kenny tell Nathan and the narrator that they should not do? **He tells them that they should not remain silent.**
3. Why do Nathan and the narrator break down the dams? **They break them down in order to capture fish.**
5. What is special about the evening described at the end of the selection? **The family eats a good meal of rice and fish.**

we use a rupee or two from the ten that remain in the granary.

I put the rice in my sari, tuck the precious load securely in at the waist. We turn back. On the outskirts of the village there is Kenny. His face is grim and long, his eyes are burning in his pallid face. He sees us and comes up.

"You too are starving, I suppose."

I tap the roll at my waist—the grains give at my touch.

"We have a little rice—it will last us until times are better."

"Times are better, times are better," he shouts. "Times will not be better for many months. Meanwhile you will suffer and die, you meek suffering fools. Why do you keep this ghastly silence? Why do you not demand—cry out for help—do something? There is nothing in this country, oh God, there is nothing!"

We shrink from his violence. What can we do—what can he mean? The man is raving. We go on our way.

What does Kenny say about the situation?

The paddy was completely destroyed; there would be no rice until the next harvesting. Meanwhile, we lived on what remained of our salted fish, roots and leaves, the fruit of the prickly pear, and on the plantains from our tree. At last the time came for the rice terraces to be drained and got ready for the next sowing. Nathan told me of it with cheer in his voice and I told the children, pleasurably, for the fields were full of fish that would feed us for many a day. Then we waited, spirits lifting, eyes sparkling, bellies pain-ful with anticipation.

At last the day. Nathan went to break the dams and I with him and with me our children, sunken-eyed, noisy as they had not been for many days at the thought of the feast, carrying nets and baskets. First one hole, then another, no bigger than a finger's width, until the water eroded the sides and the outlets grew large enough for two fists to go through. Against them we held our nets, feet firm and braced in the mud while the water rushed away, and the fish came tumbling into them. When the water was all gone, there they were caught in the meshes and among the paddy, shoals of them leaping madly, wet and silver and good to look upon. We gathered them with flying fingers and greedy hearts and bore them away in triumph, with a glow at least as bright as the sun on those shining scales. Then we came and gathered up what remained of the paddy and took it away to thresh and winnow.[1]

Late that night we were still at work, cleaning the fish, hulling the rice, separating the grain from the husk. When we had done, the rice yield was meagre—no more than two measures—all that was left of the year's harvest and the year's labour.

We ate, finding it difficult to believe we did so. The good food lay rich, if uneasy, in our starved bellies. Already the children were looking better, and at the sight of their faces, still pinched but content, a great weight lifted from me. Today we would eat and tomorrow, and for many weeks while the grain lasted. Then there was the fish, cleaned, dried and salted away, and before that was gone we should earn some more money; I would plant more vegetables . . . such dreams, delightful, orderly, satisfying, but of the stuff of dreams, wraithlike. And sleep, such sleep . . . deep and sweet and sound as I had not known for many nights; it claimed me even as I sat amid the rice husks and fish scales and drying salt. ■

1. **winnow.** Remove the unusable portion from the grain

WORDS FOR EVERYDAY USE

pal • lid (pa' ləd) *adj.*, deficient in color. *Because of Rosalind's pallid complexion, she applied blush to her cheeks.*

wraith • like (rāth līk) *adj.*, like a ghost. *Amidst the dense fog, the trees appeared wraithlike.*

Respond to the SELECTION

Think of nature as a character in the selection, and describe her.

INVESTIGATE, Inquire, Imagine

Recall: GATHERING FACTS

1a. On what crop does the family depend?

2a. In what way did nature grab this family "by the throat"?

3a. Why did the woman and Nathan go into the village? How were they treated by the two shopkeepers?

→ **Interpret:** FINDING MEANING

1b. What kind of an economy exists in this village? On what does this economy depend?

2b. What resources, both material and spiritual, did the family have upon which to draw?

3b. Why might the shopkeepers have behaved in this manner?

Analyze: TAKING THINGS APART

4a. Compare and contrast the woman's reaction to the monsoon and its aftermath with Kenny's reaction.

→ **Synthesize:** BRINGING THINGS TOGETHER

4b. Whose viewpoint does Kenny represent?

Evaluate: MAKING JUDGMENTS

5a. Evaluate the woman's effectiveness as a mother.

→ **Extend:** CONNECTING IDEAS

5b. How are the themes of classism and economic disparity dealt with in "The Garden-Party" and *Nectar in a Sieve*? Is there a point at which people have almost too much in the way of material possessions and lose touch with other aspects of life? How does struggling every day to fulfill basic needs prevent people from fulfilling themselves in other ways? Are there advantages to both situations? Think of concrete examples as you prepare your answer.

Understanding Literature

SIMILE. Review the definition for **simile** in Literary Tools on page 1082. To what is nature compared at the beginning of the selection? In what way is nature like this thing? What example of this attitude toward nature is developed in this excerpt?

NARRATOR. Review the definition for **narrator** in the Handbook of Literary Terms and the cluster chart you made for Literary Tools on page 1082. What are the character traits of the narrator? How would the tone of the novel be different if it were told from the viewpoint of Kenny? In what does the narrator find comfort after the monsoon?

RESPOND TO THE SELECTION

To prompt students, you may suggest that they brainstorm a list of adjectives, including *relentless, cruel, severe,* and *indiscriminate.*

ANSWERS TO INVESTIGATE, INQUIRE, AND IMAGINE

RECALL

1a. The family depends on rice.

2a. Nature, in the form of a monsoon, grabbed this family "by the throat" by damaging their home and virtually destroying their livelihood and basic food sources.

3a. The woman and Nathan wanted to buy rice and materials to repair their hut. The two shopkeepers treated them rudely and unfairly. The first did not spare them any rice and the second took advantage of the storm and inflated the price of the rice.

INTERPRET

1b. An agrarian economy exists in the village. It depends heavily on environmental factors.

2b. The family had some money set aside to help them buy food and building materials. They also had the mother's spiritual balance and optimism to sustain them.

3b. The shopkeepers might have behaved this way because they were exhausted by requests from many villagers and by their own attempts to repair their lives after the monsoon. In the case of the second shopkeeper, desperation and greed may have also been motivators.

ANALYZE

4a. The woman feels that her troubles with the monsoon and its aftermath are part of the cycle of life. She does not protest, but instead waits, endures, and struggles. Kenny, on the other hand, is outraged, believing that the villagers' human rights have been trampled. He tells the woman and Nathan to "demand—cry out for help—do something."

SYNTHESIZE

4b. Kenny represents the liberal viewpoint of colonizers who do not want to gain from the labor of the colonized but who want the disparity between the colonizers and the colonized to lessen.

EVALUATE

5a. The woman is sensitive to the feelings of her children and she observes their reactions to the monsoon and hunger with

ANSWERS TO INVESTIGATE, INQUIRE, AND IMAGINE (CONT.)

(Continued on page 1088)

compassion. However, sometimes she is not able to give them the comfort that they need because she herself has been too depleted, as when she and Nathan return from the village the first time without food.

EXTEND

5b. In "The Garden-Party" the disparities between the classes is seen most vividly through descriptive passages. The author details the excesses of an upper-middle-class family and then contrasts them with the bleak living conditions that exist among the poor laborers who "live far too near" the lavish home. In this selection from Nectar in a Sieve, the reader sees only the poverty—inadequate huts with dirt floors, not enough to eat—in which the

Answers to Understanding Literature can be found on page 1088.

ANSWERS TO INVESTIGATE, INQUIRE, AND IMAGINE (CONT. FROM PAGE 1087)

villagers live. In "The Garden-Party" an extravagant afternoon party is given without thought to cost; the family in Nectar in a Sieve spends most of its saving to provide their daughter with a proper wedding. Jose and Mrs. Sheridan in "The Garden-Party" both value the party and their social standing above the suffering of others. The shopkeeper Biswas in Nectar in a Sieve hardens himself against his neighbors' suffering, insisting that he must maintain his business even in the face of hardship. In Nectar in a Sieve the continual struggle to fulfill basic needs prevents the family from comprehending Kenny's plea to "demand" change. However, this struggle also forges a close bond between neighbors and family. This close bond is also visible in the "dark knot of people" who stand outside the workman's cottage in "The Garden-Party."

ANSWERS TO UNDERSTANDING LITERATURE

Simile. Nature is compared to a "wild animal." Although humans may believe they have tamed it, nature will turn on them as soon as they let down their guard. This comparison prepares the reader for the monsoon which devastates the lives of the family and other villagers. The family had let down its guard when it held the wedding for Ira, and nature did not wait to give them time to prepare for the monsoon by repairing their roof.

Narrator. The narrator is resilient, hard-working, observant, and resigned. If the novel were told from the viewpoint of Kenny, it would have a tone of righteous indignation instead of the woman's resignation. The narrator finds comfort in the possibility of life after the monsoon's devastation.

ANSWERS TO INTEGRATING THE LANGUAGE ARTS

Language, Grammar, and Style

1. Having given her daughter in marriage, the narrator was filled with listlessness.
2. The narrator, who understood nature, was still not prepared for the monsoon.
3. To keep from starving, the narrator and her husband paid two rupees for a package of rice.
4. The narrator, wearing a sari, carried the rice back to the hut.
5. Having said careless words in front of the children, the husband made the narrator angry.

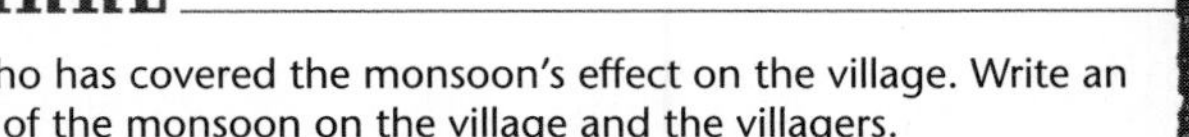

1. Imagine you are a reporter who has covered the monsoon's effect on the village. Write an **article** describing the impact of the monsoon on the village and the villagers.
2. Imagine you are one of the shopkeepers. Write a **journal entry** describing your interactions with the villagers after the monsoon and your motivations for behaving as you did.
3. Imagine you are Kenny. Write a **letter** home indicating your attitude about how the villagers should react to their poverty. Describe what it feels like to be an outsider. What perspective do you feel you have to offer?

Integrating *the* LANGUAGE ARTS

Language, Grammar, and Style

Dangling and Misplaced Modifiers. Read the Language Arts Survey 3.46, "Avoiding Dangling and Misplaced Modifiers." Then, on your own paper, rewrite each sentence, correcting the dangling or misplaced modifiers. You may need to add or delete words to make logical sentences.

1. Having given her daughter in marriage, listlessness filled the narrator.
2. The narrator understood nature who was still not prepared for the monsoon.
3. To keep from starving, two rupees paid for a package of rice.
4. The narrator carried the rice wearing a sari back to the hut.
5. Having said careless words in front of the children, the narrator was angry with her husband.

Media Literacy

Economic Development in India. An Indian peasant's narrative of her difficult life, *Nectar in a Sieve* raises important issues about poverty in India. Access World Bank economic development information about India at http://www.worldbank.org. Then select a topic to research, such as the historical problems of poverty in India, progress thatís been made in poverty reduction since the mid-1970s, or plans for economic development for the twenty-first century. Then report on your findings to the class.

Study and Research

Researching British Colonialism. India was a colony of Britain for two hundred years, only winning its independence in 1949. Research an aspect of the colonization of one of Britain's former colonies. For example, you might be interested to learn more about the penal colonies in Australia, current efforts to redistribute land to natives of Zimbabwe, or American colonists' struggles to gain freedom from Britain. Prepare a presentation using visual aids and give it to the class or a small group.

ANSWERS TO INTEGRATING THE LANGUAGE ARTS (CONT.)

Study and Research

A good representation of British colonialism is shown in the film, "Out of Africa," starring Meryl Streep and Robert Redford. You may want to give students the opportunity to view this film and analyze the role and effects of British colonial rule in Africa. Refer students to the Language Arts Survey 5.32, "How to Evaluate a Film."

Guided Writing

ANALYZING THE MEDIA

The art of advertising has been around forever, depending on logic and emotion to persuade consumers to buy. Knowing they have only seconds to hook consumers before they turn the page or change the channel, advertisers usually rely on emotion to grab attention. They hit at the need to feel attractive and loved, successful, respected, or to be like everyone else.

Advertising is necessary to sell products, but consumers need to be able to separate out fact from opinion or hype to make solid decisions when they buy.

WRITING ASSIGNMENT. In this lesson, you will look closely at an advertisement and write a three-part analysis of its message and how it attempts to persuade the consumer. The three parts of your paper will include 1) a description of the ad, 2) a fictional flashback showing how the ad was designed, and 3) a nonfiction analysis of its persuasive techniques.

> "The image is the most complete technique of all communication."
>
> —*Claes Oldenburg*

Student Model

"The Ad" by Enrique Rollens

Description: The Ad

This print ad for athletic shoes appears in a teen magazine for girls. It covers two pages in high-gloss color, favoring a palette of blues, greens and magentas. The left page of the two-page ad is dominated by the shot of a model's legs. She sits on a wall of a bridge at dusk — relaxed, confident and attractive. Your eye is guided across the page in two arcs, starting with a large picture of shoes in the foreground. Your eye continues down along the bridge model's legs and arcs again over to the faces of a dark-haired girl walking across sea-green tiles. Next, your eye goes to a scowling girl and boy, and then finally to the dramatic sunset shot of a blond girl jumping on the sand with her shoes reflecting light in a band along the soles.

EXAMINING THE MODEL. This three-part analysis begins with a description of an advertisement. What visual techniques and sensory details does it mention? After reading this description, can you picture the ad in your mind?

In the flashback, Enrique imagined the conversation the advertising group had as they created the advertisement. Although this segment of his analysis is fiction, it is still based on the facts of the ad. By carefully examining the elements of the advertisement, he could determine the kinds of decisions the designers made.

continued on page 1090

LESSON OVERVIEW

INDIVIDUAL LEARNING STRATEGIES

MOTIVATION
Ask students to share some of their favorite TV commercials or ads from printed media sources. Hold a class discussion on what qualities and characteristics about ads makes them successful and encourage consumers to buy.

READING PROFICIENCY
Point out the subheads in the Guided Writing lesson and ask students to speculate on what each section will be about.

ENGLISH LANGUAGE LEARNING
Show students various TV commercials. Choose several vocabulary words from the commercial. Then have students define the word based on the way the word is said, the context of it, and the images that are shown as the word is being said. If students are still unable to define the word, have them look it up in the dictionary.

SPECIAL NEEDS
To simplify this lesson, ask students to do a comparison-contrast essay on two commercials—one they think is successful and the other with which they think is unsuccessful. In their essay, have them explain why they think one ad is better than the other.

INDIVIDUAL LEARNING STRATEGIES (CONT.)

ENRICHMENT

Have students create their own advertisement for a product in which they believe. Encourage students to be creative, using graphic aids, actors, music, etc. Then have them submit their ad to a newspaper or magazine company or to a TV or radio company—whichever mode of communication they choose to present their ad.

Prewriting

Finding Your Voice
Ask students to read the Language Arts Survey 2.5, "Finding Your Voice." Encourage students to analyze the voice of Enrique Rollens's student model ad. Then have them write a description of the voice they will be trying to use based on their analysis.

Identifying Your Audience
Since students will be writing for both their teacher and peers, remind them that they will need to use phrases and words that are both formal and informal. Refer students to the Language Arts Survey 3.2, "Formal and Informal English."

Writing with a Plan
Ask students to look for examples of value statements, policy statements, glittering generalities, spin, stereotypes, and other bold-faced words listed in the Language Arts Survey 5.2 and 5.3 as they browse through media advertisements.

GUIDED WRITING *Software*

See the Guided Writing Software for an extended version of this lesson that includes printable graphic organizers, extensive student models and student-friendly checklists, and self-, peer, and teacher evaluation features.

They were looking for attractive, multi-ethnic models to sell their product. What else did the ad designers consider?

In the final analysis, Enrique states in his thesis that the ad uses false arguments to sell its product. What are those arguments? Can you think of other advertisements that use the same techniques?

Analyzing an Ad

Here are several elements to consider when you analyze your advertisement:

Visuals
- photographs
- design & composition
- font
- colors

Appeals to Emotions
- loaded words — words that stir up strong feelings, such as dishonest and lazy, or fresh and new
- snob appeal — appeals to the desire to be beautiful, wealthy, and better than others
- glittering generalities — statements that make something sound more appealing and that are not based on fact
- bandwagon appeal — plays to your desire to be part of a crowd
- transfer — uses famous people to sell products, transferring their glamour to the product

Flashback: The Meeting

It's ten a.m. in the office of the Hoffman, Thiele and Penn Advertising Agency. Three advertising designers for the hot new "Escape" line of running shoes are sipping cafe-lattes and settling in for a meeting. Kevin, the fashion photographer, enters. Trish Thiele appears to be at the center of the meeting. She looks up from her glasses.

"How was the shoot, Kevin?"

"It was cool. I got some great shots of Heather, the blond, jumping on the beach at sunset. I used a flash and the 'escape-glo' was screaming."

"Excellent."

Kevin pulls out a handful of high-gloss photos and spreads them out on the table. The advertising group crowds around.

"Oooh, look at this shot of Kelly!" says Hillary, a thirty-something copywriter.

"Yeah, she's gorgeous, all right," says Kevin.

"She's got the look we want!" Trish says.

"Love the shot of Heather. At least she's being *sort* of athletic," says Chad, another writer.

"Oh, don't start, Chad," says Trish.

Chad smiles and rolls his eyes as Trish and Hillary snicker.

Kevin scratches his head. "What did I miss?"

Trish laughs. "Oh, Chad thinks that we should show more athletic appeal. But this ad is about fashion and lifestyle. We don't want to be *too* athletic."

The Final Analysis

This ad is carefully constructed to emphasize movement, independence, beauty and freedom. It suggests that consumers can have the lifestyle depicted in the photos and that wearing these running shoes might help them attain it. These false arguments are based on emotional appeals.

There are several "glittering generalities" in this ad, though no words state them. The two-page ad says these shoes are worth paying attention to. The photographs say that people who wear these shoes go to interesting places and are beautiful, free, and cool. The models are photographed on a bridge and at the beach and indoors at a mall. One girl is placed beside a handsome young man. The girls have smooth-skin, pouty, red lips and slim, long bodies. Cool blues and greens surround them.

Logically we know that a pair of shoes does not place you in elegant locations or give you a handsome boyfriend. Likewise, we know there is absolutely no connection between a person's face, hair, and figure and a pair of shoes. The ad counts on an emotional response to the layout and models to convince us.

Another false argument in the ad is the "bandwagon appeal" — that is, the ad plays to the desire to be part of a crowd, to be like everyone else and do what everyone else is doing. All the girls are wearing these shoes and no other people appear in the photos.

The ad suggests that teenagers who want to be cool should buy these shoes, but doesn't say anything about the quality of the product. Are the shoes comfortable? Are they well-made? Are they reasonably priced? We are given no facts at all. The only factual information the ad gives is what the shoe looks like and even that piece of information is skewed by fancy photography.

Prewriting

Finding Your Voice. In both the nonfiction and fiction segments, your voice should reflect an even-handed analysis of the advertisement and how its parts work to persuade. Keep in mind that this is a formal assignment, that asks you to show your ability to think critically. Choose straightforward words and sentences that reflect clear thinking.

Identifying Your Audience. You will be writing for your teacher and other students. People want to know how they are being influenced and this assignment gives you a chance to explain and evaluate some of the messages we all receive through the media.

Writing with a Plan. Spend some time flipping through magazines, newspapers, or catalogues to find an advertisement that is rich in images and messages. Once you have chosen an ad, look very closely at how the text, font, color, photographs, and layout work to persuade us to buy. Read the Language Arts Survey 5.2, "Distinguishing Fact from Opinion" and 5.3, "Avoiding False Arguments and Propaganda" to analyze the message in your ad. Look for specific false arguments that the ad makes.

Copy the graphic organizer on page 1092 onto your own paper and write as many responses as you can. Note how Enrique began his graphic organizer.

Language, Grammar, and Style

Dialogue

Identifying Punctuation and Paragraphs in Dialogue. Proper punctuation and paragraph formatting will make your dialogue easy to read and understand. When you are writing dialogue, remember these two general rules: 1) Quotation marks enclose a person's exact words and 2) Commas used to separate the direct quotation from the rest of the sentence always come before the quotation mark.

If you ever forget the following tips, look at the dialogue formatting in a magazine or book to remind yourself how dialogue works.

Punctuating Dialogue

When a sentence begins with a direct quotation, separate the quotation from the rest of the sentence with a comma, question mark, or exclamation point.

EXAMPLES

"Nine windows were broken in the storm," he said.

"Where will you go?" she asked.

"What an awful mistake I've made!" said Sam.

When a sentence does not begin with a direct quotation, separate the quotation from the sentence with a comma before the first quotation mark.

continued on page 1092

Language, Grammar, and Style

Dialogue

In this lesson, students will be asked to do the following:

- Identify Punctuation and Paragraphs in Dialogue
- Revise Punctuation and Paragraph Formatting in Dialogue
- Use Punctuation and Paragraph Formatting in Dialogue

Introducing the Skill

Explain to students that using correct punctuation in dialogue is critical for readers to understand who is speaking. Paragraph formatting also tells the reader when there is a change of speakers or a change of topic.

Previewing the Skill

Encourage students to read the Language Arts Survey 3.9, "Quotation Marks" for examples of correctly punctuated dialogue.

Practicing the Skill

Have students exchange their drafts with another person. Edit their punctuation. Then to check their editing, have them read the draft, changing voice tones for each speaker to represent where the dialogue is in the draft.

STUDENT MODEL—GRAPHIC ORGANIZER

See the Guided Writing Resource for a blackline mast of the of the Graphic Organizer for this lesson.

Drafting

Encourage students to use their completed Graphic Organizer to help them get started on writing their draft. For additional help, refer students to the Language Arts Survey 2.31–2.35, "Drafting."

EXAMPLES

He said, "That's the last time I try to cram for an exam."

Mary asked, "How did the cat get outside?"

When the direct quotation is broken by an expression such as *she said* or *Frank said*, put a comma before the last quotation mark of the first part of the quotation. Then put a comma before the first quotation mark of the second part.

EXAMPLE

"Nobody saw the accident," she said, "until it was over."

If the second part of the quotation is its own sentence, use a period to separate the two sentences.

EXAMPLE

"Nobody saw the accident," she said. "The police are investigating now."

Formatting Paragraphs in Dialogue

Whenever you have two or more people talking, begin a new paragraph every time the speaker changes. This helps your reader follow who is saying what.

EXAMPLE

"How did this car get so battered?" Sydney asked. "I don't remember it looking this bad."

"You don't remember," Miguel replied, "that you backed it into that telephone pole?"

continued on page 1093

Student Model—Graphic Organizer

What: *Advertisement for running shoes*

Who for: *young women between the ages of 13 and 20*

I. Describe the Ad/Nonfiction

Use sensory details and strong verbs to describe what you see in the ad.

- *A brown-skinned girl draped on a bridge/ wearing gray running shoes/ white reflective bands on them.*
- *Asian girl glides across a green tile mall floor/ a pouty girl and boy stare back at the camera/ blond girl jumps on the beach at sunset.*
- *Four shoes- gray, blue, magenta-march across the middle of one page below the photographs.*
- *The bottom of the ad /blue and separated from the photographs by digital dots. Looks like water/ matches the wavy lines on the shoes*

II. The Flashback/Fiction

Imagine a conversation the ad designers had when they met to create the advertisement.

Trish Thiele - at desk/table

Kevin, photographer comes in—they discuss his session and the pictures he took.

Chad — another ad designer—wants a more athletic appeal to ad for athletic shoes. Chad loses.

III. The Final Analysis/Nonfiction

Describe how the message of the ad is conveyed. How does the ad use visuals to persuade the viewer to buy? How does the ad use text? Identify such techniques as generalities, loaded words, or bandwagon appeal to sell a product.

- *The girls are beautiful suggesting that you too can be beautiful too (snob appeal)*
- *Teens in the ad are in interesting locations — like you too could have an exciting life if you only had the shoes (transfer, glittering generalities)*
- *Repetition of photos and shoes across page makes the ad move and seem like shoes are for people on the go*

Drafting

Using your prewriting notes, write a first draft in three parts: 1) a description of the advertisement, 2) the imaginary conversation when the ad was created, and 3) the analysis of the message. Have fun with this draft as you try to discover all the subtle ways that the advertisement persuades.

Self-and Peer Evaluation

Once you have a rough draft, complete a self-evaluation of your analysis. If time allows, have one or two other students give you peer evaluations. Show the advertisement you are analyzing to your peer evaluators. Can they find additional ways the ad persuades?

- Does the description of the advertisement include the target audience and product being sold?
- What elements of the composition or text are described? Are there any places where the description could be more specific or include more examples?
- In the flashback, how does the dialogue reflect the elements discussed in the description of the ad? Are there places where the dialogue needs more references to the ad?
- Are any parts of the dialogue unclear? If so, how could those sections be improved?
- Is the dialogue punctuated correctly? Is there a new paragraph every time the speaker changes?
- What is the main idea for the final analysis? Is it clear and well reasoned? If not, how could it be strengthened?
- Which persuasive devices are discussed and do these need more examples?

Revising and Proofreading

Revise your draft after considering the results of your self-and peer evaluations. Did your peer evaluators come up with some new ideas you hadn't thought about? Try reading your dialogue out loud to see if it makes sense. Add, delete, and move text until you have a draft that says what you want it to say.

Complete a final proofreading of your text.

Publishing and Presenting

Present your final product to your class. This could take the form of oral presentations where you show your ad and read your three pieces aloud. Your class could also design a bulletin board with copies of the ads accompanying the student analyses.

Reflecting

What have you learned about the art of advertising that you didn't know before you analyzed ads? Do you think advertisements have influenced your buying in the past? How might you use the information you learned from your analysis to help you make better purchases in the future?

What do you think about the larger effects of advertising? Do you believe advertisements plant unnecessary or unhealthy desires in consumers? Do you think advertisements cause despair or frustration when people compare their own lives to the images in the ads? Or do they motivate people to improve their lives?

"Sure," Sydney said, laughing, "but I didn't make these other dents."

Miguel pointed to the front of the car. "These are Maria's."

Revising Punctuation and Paragraph Formatting in Dialogue. Read over the following dialogue and find places where it needs punctuation or new paragraphs.

Um, Trish, Hillary said, I spoke with the client last night. I encouraged them to do a *two*-page ad. They're going for it. Oh, Hillary, sweetie you rock, said Trish. Fabulous! Well, in that case I think we should make the shot of Kelley sitting on the wall the centerpiece of the ad. Nice Hillary said. Maybe we can break the next page up into thirds and keep a lot of movement between the shots.

Using Punctuation and Paragraph Formatting in Dialogue. Review your dialogue for punctuation and paragraphing. Have you put quotation marks around all the speaking parts? Do you have punctuation that separates the direct quotation from the rest of the sentence? Have you given each new speaker a new paragraph? Read your dialogue aloud to be sure that the speaker is clear.

Self- and Peer Evaluation

Have students use the questions on this page for self- and peer evaluation. Remind students that comments from classmates can be helpful and can help them to identify weaknesses and strengths in their writing. A blackline master of the checklist is available in the Guided Writing Resource 12.11.

Revising and Proofreading

Remind students that revising includes adding or expanding, cutting or condensing, replacing and moving text. Have students read the Language Arts Survey 2.41, "Revising." Also encourage students to use common proofreader's symbols found in the Language Arts Survey 2.44, "Using Proofreader's Marks."

Publishing and Presenting

To add excitement to the presentation of the ads, organize a contest named "Best Ad Review of the Year." Select a panel of judges that include teachers, students, and other faculty members to analyze the students' presentations. Finally, the winner gets his or her ad analysis aired over the school TV station, radio station, or printed in the school newspaper.

Reflecting

Have students answer the questions listed in the Reflecting section in their journals. Then have them write an essay based on their responses. Finally, have students hand in their essays along with their drafts.

ADDITIONAL RESOURCES

Unit 11 Resource Book
- Vocabulary Worksheet
- Study Guide: Unit 11 Test
- Unit 11 Test

VOCABULARY DEVELOPMENT

Give students the following exercise:

Choose twenty words from the list on page 1094. For each word, write a sentence that relates to something you've read in this unit. The vocabulary word need not have appeared in the selection to which you refer.

EXAMPLE.
Shakespeare's sister would have been vulnerable if she had tried to pursue her writing career.

UNIT 11 REVIEW

Twentieth-Century to Contemporary Prose

Words for Everyday Use

Check your knowledge of the following vocabulary words from the selections in this unit. Write short sentences using these words in context to make the meaning clear. To review the definition or usage of a word, refer to the page number listed or the Glossary of Words for Everyday Use.

abate, 1084
acute, 1068
agog, 994
audacious, 1036
august, 1037
baize, 1022
bethrothed, 994
burlesqued, 1064
conflagration, 1037
crook, 1053
delirium, 1065
denounce, 1073
despotic, 1012
discordant, 1034
docility, 1062
eddies, 1034
enigmatically, 1023
escapade, 994
exuberant, 1064
exultation, 1054
fastidious, 1053
fatality, 1056
festoon, 1035
frock, 1077
frond, 1054
galore, 1077
gruel, 1085
guffaw, 995
haggard, 1021
ignoble, 1037
impotence, 1085
inanimate, 1066
incredulously, 1057
incessantly, 1083
irrelevant, 1063
labyrinth, 1013
lagoon, 1035
languidly, 1066
laughingstock, 1076
listlessness, 1083
lope, 1054
marquee, 1020
myriad, 1056
nonentity, 1066
omnibus, 996
organdy, 1062
pallid, 1086
palpitation, 1063
pervading, 1085
poach, 994
portal, 1034
preoccupied, 1067
pretext, 1016
propitiate, 1035
propitious, 1083
prostrate, 1012
rapturous, 1024
scored, 1013
senility, 1015
sordid, 1026
squander, 1079
stave, 1021
stoicism, 1057
sultry, 1055
superfluity, 1054
tumult, 1054
veld, 1053
veranda, 1022
vigilant, 1052
vulnerable, 1062
wage, 1078
wayfarer, 1035
wraithlike, 1086

Literary Tools

Define the following terms, giving concrete examples of how they are used in the selections in this unit. To review a term, refer to the page number indicated or to the Handbook of Literary Terms.

aim, 993
character, 1033
characterization, 1061
conflict, 1061
essay, 993
image, 1000, 1019, 1033
irony, 1010
memoir, 1073
narrator, 1046, 1082
Naturalism, 1051
objective correlative, 1000, 1019
plot, 1061
point of view, 1046
simile, 1082
stream-of-consciousness writing, 1000
symbol, 1019
theme, 1073
thesis, 1010

Reflecting on Your Reading

Genre Studies

1. **Minimalist Writing.** In the first novels that were ever written, it was common for the narrator and/or protagonist to address the reader directly and comment on his or her feelings about the ongoing action of the book. Modern writers tend toward a more impersonal or minimalist style in which the details of the story are often left to speak for themselves without excessive explanation or commentary by the narrator. How do Alice Munro, Jean Rhys, and Katherine Mansfield allow details to speak for themselves in "Red Dress—1946," "Heat," and "The Garden-Party"? What are the most telling, or powerful details in these three stories?

Thematic Studies

2. **Role of Women.** Look over "The Garden-Party," "Red Dress—1946," and the excerpts from *A Room of One's Own* and *Nectar in a Sieve*. How do the women portrayed in each of these selections differ in age and social class, as well as in the culture and period of history in which they were born? In what ways are their lives still similar? Choose three of the pieces listed above, and compare the main characters of each selection in these ways.

3. **Comparing Themes.** Review "Shooting an Elephant" and "A Sunrise on the Veld." Specify the event around which each story revolves and how theme in each selection originates from this event. Identify and compare the themes expressed in each selection.

Historical and Biographical Studies

4. **Social Commentary.** Many writers in the 20th century have used their writing to make social commentary. The writers in this unit address such issues as education and opportunities of women and the British class system. Choose a selection from this unit that makes social commentary; identify the issue(s) it addresses, and express your opinion on whether the writer effectively conveys his or her position. Support your answer with examples from the selection.

REFLECTING ON YOUR READING

The prompts in "Reflecting on Your Reading" are suitable topics for research papers. Refer to the Language Arts Survey 5.18-5.45, "Research Skills." (To evaluate research papers, see the evaluation forms for writing, revising, and proofreading in the Assessment Resource.)

The prompts in "Reflecting on Your Reading" can also be adapted for use as topics for oral reports or debates. Refer students to the Language Arts Survey 4, Speaking and Listening. (To evaluate these projects, see the evaluation forms in the Assessments Resource.)

UNIT SKILLS OUTLINE

Literary Skills and Concepts
Antihero, 1143, 1149
Blocking, 1131, 1142
Character, 1111, 1130
Climax, 1143, 1149
Dramatic Irony, 1131, 1142
Inciting Incident, 1101, 1110
Myth, 1167, 1169
Narration, 1167, 1169
Resolution, 1150, 1165
Satire, 1111, 1130, 1150, 1165
Spectacle, 1101, 1110

Writing Skills and Concepts
Film or Play Review, 1171

Language, Grammar, and Style
Reducing Wordiness, 1166
Writing Introductory Paragraphs, 1177

England, 1980. Gilbert and George. Tate Gallery, London.

GOALS/OBJECTIVES

Studying this unit will enable students to

- enjoy a twentieth-century drama and understand the motifs and themes that differentiate twentieth-century drama from the work of earlier periods
- describe the literary and social significance of Bernard Shaw's work
- define elements of drama and identify them in a play
- write a film or play review
- demonstrate the ability to write introductory paragraphs

UNIT 12 TWENTIETH-CENTURY TO CONTEMPORARY DRAMA (1900–PRESENT)

The play's the thing.

—William Shakespeare

1097

CROSS-CURRICULAR CONNECTIONS

ARTS AND HUMANITIES
Twentieth-Century Dramas, 1098
Adaptation of a Myth, 1100
Stage Designs, 1112
Advice Columnists, 1126
Interior Decorating, 1132
Shakespearean Comedies, 1158
Ovid's Works, 1168

MATHEMATICS AND SCIENCES
Pre-WW1 Currency, 1114
Careers in Speech, 1119
Counseling, 1163

SOCIAL STUDIES
England Before WW1, 1104
Regional Dialects, 1106
Social Class Systems, 1107
Phonetics, 1109
Pre-WW1 Editorials, 1113
Careers in Speech, 1119
Retirement, 1153
Fabian Society, 1161

APPLIED ARTS
Set Designs and Costumes, 1100
Party Platforms, 1125
Designing an Ideal Person, 1168

TEACHING THE MULTIPLE INTELLIGENCES

LOGICAL-MATHEMATICAL
Pre-WW1 Currency, 1114
Liza's Decision-Making Chart, 1162

SPATIAL
Twentieth-Century Dramas, 1098
Set Designs and Costumes, 1100
Stage Designs, 1112
Interior Decorating, 1132
Compare-and-Contrast Essay, 1152
Liza's Decision-Making Chart, 1162
Designing an Ideal Person, 1168

KINESTHETIC
Set Designs and Costumes, 1100
Interpreting Body Language, 1122
Designing an Ideal Person, 1168

INTERPERSONAL
Social Class Systems, 1107
Manipulation Tactics, 1128
Compare-and-Contrast Essay, 1152
Counseling, 1163

CROSS-CURRICULAR ACTIVITIES

Encourage students to read or view one of the many twentieth-century dramas mentioned on page 1098. Many of the plays mentioned have been made into films such as *Major Barbara, Waiting for Godot* (a twenty-one minute film with no dialogue), *Rosencrantz and Guildenstern are Dead*, and *Amadeus* (which won the 1984 Academy Award for Best Picture). Then have them write a summary paragraph about the themes represented in twentieth-century literature based on the play they read or film they viewed.

The 1978 premier of Tom Stoppard's *Travestian.*

TWENTIETH-CENTURY TO CONTEMPORARY BRITISH DRAMA (1900-PRESENT)

British theater of the early 20th century was dominated by Irish-born writer **Bernard Shaw** (1856–1950). Shaw is considered the most significant British dramatist since Shakespeare. Shaw's comic masterpiece, *Pygmalion* (1913) was also produced many years later as a popular film and as the basis for the musical comedy *My Fair Lady.* By infusing discussions of social problems with wit and paradox in plays such as *Arms and the Man* (1898) and *Major Barbara* (1905), Shaw lent power and success to the 19th-century tradition of realistic drama. **Lady Augusta Gregory's** *The Rising of the Moon* is another example of Realism on stage (Unit 1). During the 1920s **Somerset Maugham** and **Noel Coward** again revived the sophisticated comedy of manners, a longtime British specialty. Coward's *Private Lives* (1930) has been frequently restaged.

In the early 20th century, a number of playwrights attempted to revive poetic drama, which had lost popularity with the rise of realism. The most successful was **T. S. Eliot,** the period's most respected poet, who was born in the United States but became a British citizen. Eliot wrote several poetic dramas of contemporary life and the historical meditation *Murder in the Cathedral* (1935), a verse play that deals with the martyrdom of Thomas à Becket at Canterbury Cathedral.

Around 1950, a new group of playwrights, much influenced by the French philosophers **Albert Camus** and **Jean Paul Sartre,** created a revolution in European drama by bringing the irrational into the motivations, language, and structure, of their plays. Although very different in style, these dramatists rejected traditional cause-and-effect realistic drama, and as a group came to be known as the **absurdists.** The term comes from a 1942 essay by Camus, *The Myth of Sisyphus* (1955), which called the human condition absurd because humans seek order and reason in a universe that was not built on these principles. The first great success of the absurdist movement and probably the best known of all its plays, *Waiting for Godot* (1952), was written in French by Irish-born playwright **Samuel Beckett,** who came to be recognized as one of the major dramatists of the late twentieth century.

The theater of the absurd had limited impact in England, but several playwrights did adopt its approaches and principles. The most important English dramatist with a clear connection to the absurd is **Tom Stoppard,** who began a series of brilliant verbal comedies with *Rosencrantz and Guildenstern are Dead* (1966). Stoppard, with Marc Norman, also wrote the screenplay for the popular film *Shakespeare in Love* (1999), which won seven Academy Awards including Best Original Screenplay. The early plays of **Peter Shaffer,** most notably *The Private Ear* (1962) and *The Public Eye* (1962), also show their debt to absurdist theater in their humorous examinations of a hostile universe. His later and better known works, including *Amadeus* (1979), more closely resemble realism, even though his plays often jump back and forth within space and time. **Harold Pinter,** one of England's leading dramatists during the 1960s, is also associated with absurdist theater in his works such as *The Birthday Party* (1959), *The Caretaker* (1960), and *The Homecoming,* (1965).

Other notable contemporary British dramatists include **John Osborne, John Arden, Arnold Wesker, Edward Bond, Joan Littlewood,** and **Robert Bolt.** British theater continues to make great contributions to the development and appreciation of drama worldwide.

ECHOES ECHOES ECHOES ECHOES ECHOES ECHOES

TWENTIETH-CENTURY TO CONTEMPORY DRAMA

To me the tragedy and comedy of life lie in the consequences, sometimes terrible, sometimes ludicrous, of our persistent attempts to found our institutions on the ideals suggested to our imaginations by our half-satisfied passions, instead of on a genuinely scientific natural history.

—Bernard Shaw, from *Preface to Arms and the Man*

A few hundred scrawls o'chaps with a couple o' guns and Rosary beads, again' a hundhred thousand thrained men with horse, fut an' artillery...an' he wants us to fight fair!

—Sean O'Casey, *The Plough and the Stars*

Will: "You will never age for me, nor fade, nor die."
Viola: "Nor you for me."

—Marc Norman and Tom Stoppard, screenplay of *Shakespeare in Love*

"And maybe one night, after you had been singing, if the other boys had told you some plan they had, some plan to free the country, you might have joined with them . . . and maybe it is you might be in trouble now."

—Lady Augusta Gregory, *The Rising of the Moon*

Don't look.
The world's about to break.

Don't look.
The world's about to chuck out all its light
and stuff us in the chokepit of its dark,
That black and fat suffocated place
Where we will kill or die or dance or weep
Or scream of whine or squeak like mice
To renegotiate our starting price.

—Harold Pinter, *Poem*

my way is in the sand flowing
between the shingle and the dune
the summer rain rains on my life
on me my life harrying fleeing
to its beginning to its end

my peace is there in the receding mist
when I may cease from treading these long shifting
thresholds
and live the space of a door
that opens and shuts

—Samuel Beckett

England [Detail], 1980. Gilbert and George. Tate Gallery, London.

ADDITIONAL QUESTIONS AND ACTIVITIES

Ask students discuss the attitudes and perceptions of the twentieth-century based on the quotes on page 1099. Do artists have positive or negative views of the century? What world events do you think led them to their conclusions about life? Encourage students to back up their opinions using the quotes. Then have students create a poem or saying that reflects their view of life in the twentieth and twenty-first century. Finally, have them share and explain the meaning of their poem or saying.

Pygmalion

BY BERNARD SHAW

About the Author

Born in Dublin into a working-class family, **Bernard Shaw** (1856–1950) confronted poverty throughout his youth. When his parents separated in his teenage years, his mother took him and his two sisters to live in London. There he studied music, art, and literature on his own, interests that were fostered by his mother, who struggled to support the family as a music teacher. Shaw spent his early adulthood trying to become a novelist and failing miserably. Eventually, he took up journalism and began writing book reviews and theater criticism for London periodicals. Not until middle age did he begin writing his own plays, which became more successful than his fiction. At the time, most British plays consisted of fairly simple plots and characters and tended to be overly romantic. Shaw's plays were much more complex. They challenged the social morals and political attitudes of late nineteenth-century England. Since his plays were controversial, they were for a while much more popular in continental Europe than in England. His great range as a writer enabled him to express his political views in highly effective tragedies and comedies. *Pygmalion* is one of Shaw's best-known satires. It combines numerous humorous scenes that comment harshly on the English class system. In 1925, Shaw won the Nobel Prize for literature, perhaps the most prestigious of all literary awards. He kept writing, maintained an active mind, and continued to be a persistent social critic until his death at the age of ninety-four.

About the Selection

Shaw's ***Pygmalion*** is a modernization of the Greek mythical tale of the same name, one version of which was told by the Roman poet Ovid in his *Metamorphoses* of AD 15 (page 1167). In the classical myth, a sculptor falls in love with his own creation. In a sense the same thing happens in Shaw's play. Henry Higgins, a speech professor, bets his friend Colonel Pickering that he can turn a lower-class Cockney girl into a woman of high society within six months. The play's wide appeal resulted in a film version in 1938, for which Shaw wrote the screenplay and won an Academy Award. Later, the musical *My Fair Lady* made the story immensely popular. This transformation shows how a classical myth, through the pen of a gifted author, can become entertaining, popular, and relevant to contemporary audiences.

ADDITIONAL RESOURCES

UNIT 12 RESOURCE BOOK
- Selection Worksheet 12.1
- Selection Check Test 4.12.1
- Selection Test 4.12.2

INDIVIDUAL LEARNING STRATEGIES

MOTIVATION
An important part of a drama is the spectacle. Have students work individually or in groups to design sets, costumes, or sound and lighting effects for *Pygmalion*.

READING PROFICIENCY
Explain to students that Shaw chose not to use an apostrophe to show contractions in his writing. Tell students that the contracted words are pronounced the same way they usually are, though they may not look the same. Give the following examples of spelling and pronunciation: Youre, wont (won't), havnt, wasnt, lets, dont (don't), wouldnt. Remind students that they will still be expected to use the usual apostrophes in their own writing.

Students may have difficulty with the dialect of the Flower Girl in Act I. Assure them that Shaw discontinues writing soley in dialect. Most of the Flower Girl (Liza's) speech should make sense to them.

ENGLISH LANGUAGE LEARNING
Point out the following vocabulary words:
Act 1
oath—vow, promise
subsiding—dying down, lessen
haughtily—arrogantly, disdainfully
detestable—hateful

SPECIAL NEEDS
Students may find it helpful to hear the play read aloud. Other students can take on the different roles. Students should pay close attention to the Guided Reading questions and the Recall questions in the Investigate, Inquire, and Imagine section.

ENRICHMENT
Pygmalion is an adaptation of a classical myth. Have students write their own adaptation of this myth. Or they may choose to write a modern adaptation of a different myth.

GOALS/OBJECTIVES

Studying the lesson will enable students to
- enjoy a twentieth-century adaptation of a classical myth
- describe Bernard Shaw's literary accomplishments and explain the historical significance of his writings
- define the parts of a plot and identify the parts as they relate to their reading
- edit to reduce wordiness
- use formal and informal English appropriately

Pygmalion

BERNARD SHAW

CHARACTERS

Henry Higgins	Mrs. Eynsford Hill
Colonel Pickering	Miss Eynsford Hill
Freddy Eynsford Hill	Mrs. Higgins
Alfred Doolittle	Mrs. Pearce
Bystanders	Parlormaid
Eliza Doolittle	Taximan

ACT ONE

Covent Garden[1] *in London at 11.15 p.m. Torrents of heavy summer rain. Cab whistles blowing frantically in all directions. Pedestrians running for shelter into the market and under the* portico *of St Paul's Church, where there are already several people, among them a lady and her daughter in evening dress. They are all peering out gloomily at the rain, except one man with his back turned to the rest, who seems wholly preoccupied with a notebook in which he is writing busily.*

The church clock strikes the first quarter.

THE DAUGHTER (*in the space between the central pillars, close to the one on her left*). I'm getting chilled to the bone. What can Freddy be doing all this time? He's been gone twenty minutes.

THE MOTHER (*on her daughter's right*). Not so long. But he ought to have got us a cab by this.

A BYSTANDER (*on the lady's right*). He wont[2] get no cab not until half-past eleven, missus, when they come back after dropping their theatre fares.

1. **Covent Garden.** District of London comprised of fruit, vegetable, and flower markets
2. **wont.** Shaw, an advocate of spelling reform, omitted apostrophes in contractions unless the omission was confusing or changed the pronunciation.

WORDS FOR EVERYDAY USE

por • ti • co (pôr′ ti kō) *n.,* porch or covered walk in front of a building. *Many an old southern mansion featured a magnificent* portico *across its pillared front.*

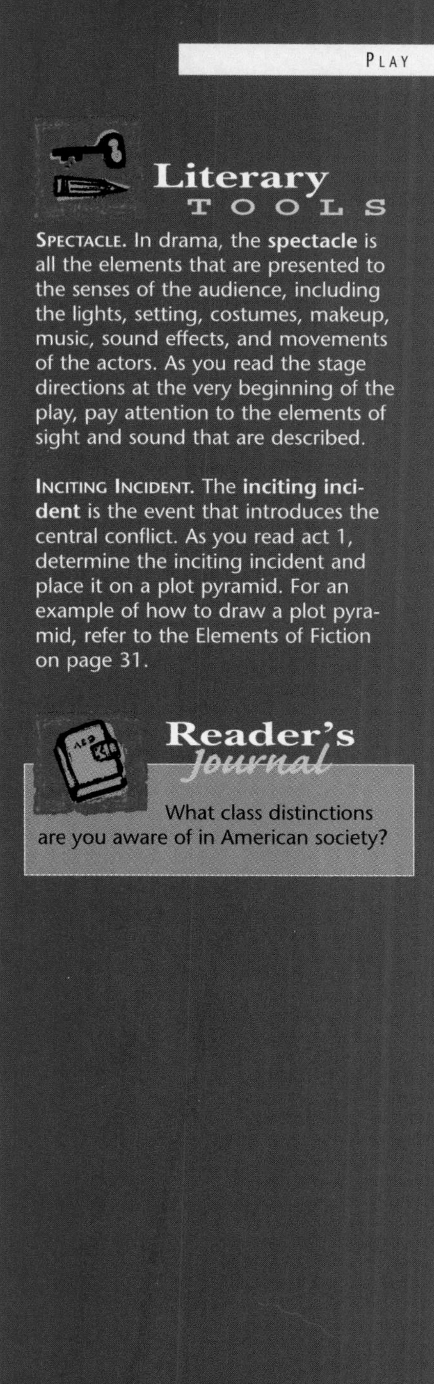

Literary TOOLS

SPECTACLE. In drama, the **spectacle** is all the elements that are presented to the senses of the audience, including the lights, setting, costumes, makeup, music, sound effects, and movements of the actors. As you read the stage directions at the very beginning of the play, pay attention to the elements of sight and sound that are described.

INCITING INCIDENT. The **inciting incident** is the event that introduces the central conflict. As you read act 1, determine the inciting incident and place it on a plot pyramid. For an example of how to draw a plot pyramid, refer to the Elements of Fiction on page 31.

Reader's Journal

What class distinctions are you aware of in American society?

GRAPHIC ORGANIZER

Exposition—the beginning of act I, much of the stage directions because the provide background information

Inciting incident—Higgins bets he could teach Eliza to speak properly and pass her off as a duchess

Rising action—Eliza arrives for lessons. Higgins begins to teach her. Higgins brings Eliza for a test at his mother's.

Climax—Eliza throws the slippers at Higgins and argues with him about the way he treated her.

Falling action—Higgins is looking for Eliza. Doolittle turns up at Mrs. Higgins house.

Resolution—Eliza realizes that she is not dependent on Henry, that she could teach people as he has.

Dénouement—They head off for the wedding and Henry tells Eliza to pick some things up for him at the store.

READER'S JOURNAL

Have students consider the attitudes of one class toward another. They can also discuss whether it is possible to move from one class to another.

VOCABULARY FROM THE SELECTION

amiable	mendacity
bilious	portico
deprecate	proximity
gumption	repudiate
impertinent	staid
melancholy	

ANSWER TO GUIDED READING QUESTION

1. The speech of the mother, the daughter, and Freddy demonstrates that they belong to a social class higher than that of the flower girl. Freddy shows very poor manners in barely apologizing to the flower girl after colliding with her and in not helping her pick up her scattered merchandise. The flower girl shows better manners by remonstrating with him only in a mild way.

LITERARY TECHNIQUE

Satire. Explain to students that Pygmalion is a **satire**—humorous writing intended to point out errors, falsehoods, or failings. The purpose of satire is to reform human behavior or institutions. As they read, students should try to determine what Shaw is satirizing.

The Mother. But we must have a cab. We cant stand here until half-past eleven. It's too bad.

The Bystander. Well, it ain't my fault, missus.

The Daughter. If Freddy had a bit of gumption, he would have got one at the theatre door.

The Mother. What could he have done, poor boy?

The Daughter. Other people got cabs. Why couldnt he?

(FREDDY *rushes in out of the rain from the Southampton Street side, and comes between them closing a dripping umbrella. He is a young man of twenty, in evening dress, very wet round the ankles.*)

The Daughter. Well, havnt you got a cab?

Freddy. Theres not one to be had for love or money.

The Mother. Oh, Freddy, there must be one. You cant have tried.

The Daughter. It's too tiresome. Do you expect us to go and get one ourselves?

Freddy. I tell you theyre all engaged. The rain was so sudden: nobody was prepared; and everybody had to take a cab. Ive been to Charing Cross one way and nearly to Ludgate Circus the other; and they were all engaged.

The Mother. Did you try Trafalgar Square?

Freddy. There wasnt one at Trafalgar Square.

The Daughter. Did you try?

Freddy. I tried as far as Charing Cross Station. Did you expect me to walk to Hammersmith?

The Daughter. You havnt tried at all.

The Mother. You really are very helpless, Freddy. Go again; and dont come back until you have found a cab.

Freddy. I shall simply get soaked for nothing.

The Daughter. And what about us? Are we to stay here all night in this draught,[3] with next to nothing on? You selfish pig—

Freddy. Oh, very well: I'll go, I'll go. (*He opens his umbrella and dashes off Strandwards, but comes into collision with a flower girl, who is hurrying in for shelter, knocking her basket out of her hands. A blinding flash of lightning, followed instantly by a rattling peal of thunder, orchestrates the incident.*)

The Flower Girl. Nah then, Freddy: look wh' y' gowin, deah.

Freddy. Sorry (*he rushes off*).

The Flower Girl (*picking up her scattered flowers and replacing them in the basket*). Theres menners f' yer! Te-oo banches o voylets trod into the mad. (*She sits down on the plinth[4] of the column, sorting her flowers, on the lady's right. She is not at all an attractive person. She is perhaps eighteen, perhaps twenty, hardly older. She wears a little sailor hat of black straw that has long been exposed to the dust and soot of London and has seldom if ever been brushed. Her hair needs washing rather badly: its mousy color can hardly be natural. She wears a shoddy black coat that reaches nearly to her knees and is shaped to her*

What differences in social class are demonstrated in the speech of the flower girl and the other characters introduced so far? What differences in manners are demonstrated by the actions and words of Freddy and the flower girl?

3. **draught.** British spelling of *draft*
4. **plinth.** The square block at the base of a column or pedestal

Words for Everyday Use

gump • tion (gump′ shən) *n.*, courage; boldness. *Because of the savagery of critics, writing a play for the public requires considerable gumption.*

waist. She has a brown skirt with a coarse apron. Her boots are much the worse for wear. She is no doubt as clean as she can afford to be; but compared to the ladies she is very dirty. Her features are no worse than theirs; but their condition leaves something to be desired; and she needs the services of a dentist.)

THE MOTHER. How do you know that my son's name is Freddy, pray?

THE FLOWER GIRL. Ow, eez ye-ooa san, is e? Wal, fewd dan y' de-ooty bawmz a mather should, eed now bettern to spawl a pore gel's flahrzn than ran awy athaht pyin. Will ye-oo py me f' them?[5] (*Here, with apologies, this desperate attempt to represent her dialect without a phonetic alphabet must be abandoned as intelligible outside London.*)

THE DAUGHTER. Do nothing of the sort, mother. The idea!

THE MOTHER. Please allow me, Clara. Have you any pennies?

THE DAUGHTER. No. Ive nothing smaller than sixpence.

THE FLOWER GIRL (*hopefully*). I can give you change for a tanner,[6] kind lady.

THE MOTHER (*to* CLARA). Give it to me. (CLARA *parts reluctantly.*) Now (*to the girl*) this is for your flowers.

THE FLOWER GIRL. Thank you kindly, lady.

THE DAUGHTER. Make her give you the change. These things are only a penny a bunch.

5. **Ow, . . . f' them?** Shaw attempted to spell phonetically the Cockney dialect of London. The passage translates, "Oh, he's your son, is he? Well, if you had done your duty by him as a mother should, he'd know better than to spill a poor girl's flowers and then run away without paying. Will you pay me for them?"

6. **tanner.** British slang for *sixpence* (six pennies)

ADDITIONAL QUESTIONS AND ACTIVITIES

Students can choose an issue in contemporary life that irritates or amuses them and write a one-page dialogue that satirizes it. They should try to make their satires humorous, not simply sarcastic. For more on sarcasm, refer students to the Language Arts Survey, 3.4, "Irony, Sarcasm, and Rudeness."

ANSWERS TO GUIDED READING QUESTIONS

1. The Mother is generous, while the daughter is stingy.
2. The flower girl calls the young man "Freddy" as a general term for a fellow. She happens to hit on his real name. This coincidence helps highlight the fact that many upper-class young men are generally like Freddy.
3. The flower girl is afraid she will be arrested for soliciting.

CROSS-CURRICULAR ACTIVITIES

Social Studies. To better understand Shaw's play and the issues he confronted in it, students should study its social background. They can research and summarize the social situation of London or Great Britain in general before World War I. Good sources of information are histories of Great Britain. Students should look especially for information on the struggle between the classes, the ideas of reformers, and the women's rights movement. The results of researches can be presented in the form of a mini-term paper (two pages) with supporting documentation listed.

THE MOTHER. Do hold your tongue, Clara. (*To the girl*) You can keep the change.

How do the Mother and the Daughter differ?

THE FLOWER GIRL. Oh, thank you, lady.

THE MOTHER. Now tell me how you know that young gentleman's name.

THE FLOWER GIRL. I didnt.

THE MOTHER. I heard you call him by it. Dont try to deceive me.

THE FLOWER GIRL (*protesting*). Who's trying to deceive you? I called him Freddy or Charlie same as you might yourself if you was talking to a stranger and wished to be pleasant. (*She sits down beside her basket.*)

What humorous technique does Shaw use to make the point that upper-class young men, generally, are like Freddy?

THE DAUGHTER. Sixpence thrown away! Really, mamma, you might have spared Freddy that. (*She retreats in disgust behind the pillar.*)

(*An elderly gentleman of the amiable military type rushes into the shelter, and closes a dripping umbrella. He is in the same plight as* FREDDY, *very wet about the ankles. He is in evening dress, with a light overcoat. He takes the place left vacant by the daughter's retirement.*)

THE GENTLEMAN. Phew!

THE MOTHER (*to the gentleman*). Oh, sir, is there any sign of its stopping?

THE GENTLEMAN. I'm afraid not. It started worse than ever about two minutes ago. (*He goes to the plinth beside the flower girl; puts up his foot on it; and stoops to turn down his trouser ends.*)

THE MOTHER. Oh dear! (*She retires sadly and joins her daughter.*)

THE FLOWER GIRL (*taking advantage of the military gentleman's proximity to establish friendly relations with him*). If it's worse, it's a sign it's nearly over. So cheer up, Captain; and buy a flower off a poor girl.

THE GENTLEMAN. I'm sorry. I havnt any change.

THE FLOWER GIRL. I can give you change, Captain.

THE GENTLEMAN. For a sovereign? I've nothing less.

THE FLOWER GIRL. Garn! Oh do buy a flower off me, Captain. I can change half-a-crown. Take this for tuppence.[7]

THE GENTLEMAN. Now dont be troublesome: theres a good girl. (*Trying his pockets*) I really havnt any change—Stop: heres three hapence, if thats any use to you. (*He retreats to the other pillar.*)

THE FLOWER GIRL (*disappointed, but thinking three half-pence better than nothing*). Thank you, sir.

THE BYSTANDER (*to the girl*). You be careful: give him a flower for it. Theres a bloke here behind taking down every blessed word youre saying. (*All turn to the man who is taking notes.*)

THE FLOWER GIRL (*springing up terrified*). I aint done nothing wrong by speaking to the gentleman. Ive a right to sell flowers if I keep off the kerb. (*Hysterically*) I'm a respectable girl: so help me, I never spoke to him except to ask him to buy a flower off me.

Of what is the flower girl afraid?

5. **Ow, . . . f' them?** Shaw attempted to spell phonetically the Cockney dialect of London. The passage translates, "Oh, he's your son, is he? Well, if you had done your duty by him as a mother should, he'd know better than to spill a poor girl's flowers and then run away without paying. Will you pay me for them?"
6. **tanner.** British slang for *sixpence* (six pennies)
7. **tuppence.** Alternate spelling of *twopence*

WORDS FOR EVERYDAY USE

a • mi • a • ble (ā' mē ə bəl) *adj.*, good-natured; friendly. *Jill accepted Josephine as a roommate because she was the most amiable of all those who inquired about the apartment.*

prox • im • i • ty (präks im' ə tē) *n.*, nearness. *The proximity of the bank where Tex kept his money allowed him to sleep better at night.*

(*General hubbub, mostly sympathetic to the* FLOWER GIRL, *but* *deprecating* *her excessive sensibility. Cries of* Dont start hollerin. Who's hurting you? Nobody's going to touch you. Whats the good of fussing? Steady on. Easy, easy, etc., *come from the elderly* *staid* *spectators, who pat her comfortingly. Less patient ones bid her shut her head, or ask her roughly what is wrong with her. A remoter group, not knowing what the matter is, crowd in and increase the noise with question and answer:* What's the row? What she do? Where is he? A tec[8] taking her down. What! him? Yes: him over there: Took money off the gentleman, etc.)

THE FLOWER GIRL (*breaking through them to the* GENTLEMEN, *crying wildly*). Oh, sir, dont let him charge me. You dunno what it means to me. Theyll take away my character and drive me on the streets for speaking to gentlemen. They—

THE NOTE TAKER (*coming forward on her right, the rest crowding after him*). There, there, there, there! who's hurting you, you silly girl? What do you take me for?

THE BYSTANDER. It's all right: he's a gentleman: look at his boots. (*Explaining to the* NOTE TAKER) She thought you was a copper's nark, sir.

THE NOTE TAKER (*with quick interest*). Whats a copper's nark?

THE BYSTANDER (*inapt at definition*). It's a—well, it's a copper's nark, as you might say. What else would you call it? A sort of informer.

THE FLOWER GIRL (*still hysterical*). I take my Bible oath I never said a word—

THE NOTE TAKER (*overbearing but good humored*). Oh, shut up, shut up. Do I look like a policeman?

THE FLOWER GIRL (*far from reassured*). Then what did you take down my words for? How do I know whether you took me down right? You just shew me what youve wrote about me. (*The* NOTE TAKER *opens his book and holds it steadily under her nose, though the pressure of the mob trying to read it over his shoulders would upset a weaker man.*) Whats that? That aint proper writing. I cant read that.

THE NOTE TAKER. I can. (*Reads, reproducing her pronunciation exactly*) "Cheer ap, Keptin; n' baw ya flahr orf a pore gel."

Has the note taker done a good job of recording the flower girl's speech? What seems to interest him?

THE FLOWER GIRL (*much distressed*). It's because I called him Captain. I meant no harm. (*To the* GENTLEMAN) Oh, sir, don't let him lay a charge agen me for a word like that. You—

THE GENTLEMAN. Charge! I make no charge. (*To the* NOTE TAKER) Really, sir, if you are a detective, you need not begin protecting me against molestation by young women until I ask you. Anybody could see that the girl meant no harm.

THE BYSTANDERS GENERALLY (*demonstrating against police espionage*). Course they could. What business is it of yours? You mind your own affairs. He wants promotion, he does. Taking down people's words! Girl never said a word to him. What harm if she did? Nice thing a girl cant shelter from the rain without being insulted, etc., etc., etc. (*She is conducted by the more sympathetic demonstrators back to her plinth, where she resumes her seat and struggles with her emotion.*)

8. **tec.** British slang for detective

WORDS FOR EVERYDAY USE

dep • re • cate (dep′ rə kāt′) *vt.,* belittle; disparage. *Comments that deprecate the contributions of other group members are counterproductive.*

staid (stād) *adj.,* sedate; serious. *The jig was so irresistible that even the most staid couple in the hall had to kick off their shoes and dance.*

ANSWER TO GUIDED READING QUESTION

1. The note-taker has done a good job. He seems to have accurately captured the flower girl's dialect. He seems very interested in the way people speak.

LITERARY TECHNIQUE

MOTIF. A **motif** is any element that recurs in one or more works of literature or art. Consider the following scene: "It's all right: he's a gentleman," says one of the bystanders of the note taker, "look at his boots." Point out to students that the motif of being a gentleman or a lady runs throughout *Pygmalion.* As they read, students can look for ways in which people are defined as gentlemen or ladies. These defining points include their clothes (as in this case), actions, manners, speech, and the way they are treated by others. On the following pages of dialogue, the note taker is accused several times of not being a gentleman because—despite his appearance—his attitude is not genteel.

ANSWER TO GUIDED READING QUESTION

1. The note-taker responds pleasantly to the questions from the gentleman. He apologizes perfunctorally to the daughter.

ADDITIONAL QUESTIONS AND ACTIVITIES

Discuss regional accents with students. Have students suggest words that indicate what region of the United States a person is from. If the class has representatives of different parts of the country, students might be able to perceive among themselves variant pronunciations of the following words: *park, lost, house, Mary, pen, aunt,* and *greasy.* (For more information on American regional dialects, see the article "Dialects of English," in The Language Arts Survey 3.5, "Dialects of English."

THE BYSTANDER. He aint a tec. He's a blooming busybody: thats what he is. I tell you, look at his boots.

THE NOTE TAKER (*turning on him genially*). And how are all your people down at Selsey?

THE BYSTANDER (*suspiciously*). Who told you my people come from Selsey?

THE NOTE TAKER. Never you mind. They did. (*To the girl*) How do you come to be up so far east? You were born in Lisson Grove.

THE FLOWER GIRL (*appalled*). Oh, what harm is there in my leaving Lisson Grove? It wasnt fit for a pig to live in; and I had to pay four-and-six a week. (*In tears*) Oh, boo—hoo—oo—

THE NOTE TAKER. Live where you like; but stop that noise.

THE GENTLEMAN (*to the girl*). Come, come! he cant touch you: you have a right to live where you please.

A SARCASTIC BYSTANDER (*thrusting himself between the* NOTE TAKER *and the* GENTLEMEN). Park Lane, for instance. I'd like to go into the Housing Question with you, I would.

THE FLOWER GIRL (*subsiding into a brooding melancholy over her basket, and talking very low-spiritedly to herself*). I'm a good girl, I am.

THE SARCASTIC BYSTANDER (*not attending to her*). Do you know where *I* come from?

THE NOTE TAKER (*promptly*). Hoxton

(*Titterings. Popular interest in the* NOTE TAKER'*s performance increases.*)

THE SARCASTIC ONE (*amazed*). Well, who said I didnt? Bly me! You know everything, you do.

THE FLOWER GIRL (*still nursing her sense of injury*). Aint no call to meddle with me, he aint.

THE BYSTANDER (*to her*). Of course he aint. Dont you stand it from him. (*To the* NOTE TAKER) See here: what call have you to know about people what never offered to meddle with you? Wheres your warrant?

SEVERAL BYSTANDERS (*encouraged by this seeming point of law*). Yes: wheres your warrant?

THE FLOWER GIRL. Let him say what he likes. I dont want to have no truck with him.

THE BYSTANDER. You take us for dirt under your feet, dont you? Catch you taking liberties with a gentleman!

THE SARCASTIC BYSTANDER. Yes: tell him where he come from if you want to go fortune-telling.

THE NOTE TAKER. Cheltenham, Harrow, Cambridge, and India.

THE GENTLEMAN. Quite right.

(*Great laughter. Reaction in the* NOTE TAKER'*s favor. Exclamations of* He knows all about it. Told him proper. Hear him tell the toff[9] where he come from? etc.)

THE GENTLEMAN. May I ask, sir, do you do this for your living at a music hall?

THE NOTE TAKER. I've thought of that. Perhaps I shall some day.

(*The rain has stopped; and the persons on the outside of the crowd begin to drop off.*)

How does the note taker react to comments from the gentleman? from the daughter?

THE FLOWER GIRL (*resenting the reaction*). He's no gentleman, he aint, to interfere with a poor girl.

THE DAUGHTER (*out of patience, pushing her way rudely to the front and displacing the* GENTLEMAN, *who politely retires to the other side of the*

9. **toff.** British slang for a fashionable, upper-class person

WORDS FOR EVERYDAY USE

mel • an • chol • y (mel′ ən käl′ ē) *n.,* state of sadness or depression. *The seemingly endless series of rainy days contributed to the melancholy I felt when I did not land a part in the play.*

pillar). What on earth is Freddy doing? I shall get pneumonia if I stay in this draught any longer.

THE NOTE TAKER (*to himself, hastily making a note of her pronunciation of "monia"*). Earlscourt.

THE DAUGHTER (*violently*). Will you please keep your impertinent remarks to yourself.

THE NOTE TAKER. Did I say that out loud? I didnt mean to. I beg your pardon. Your mother's Epsom, unmistakably.

THE MOTHER (*advancing between her daughter and the* NOTE TAKER). How very curious! I was brought up in Largelady Park, near Epsom.

THE NOTE TAKER (*uproariously amused*). Ha! ha! What a devil of a name! Excuse me. (*To the* DAUGHTER) You want a cab, do you?

THE DAUGHTER. Dont dare speak to me.

THE MOTHER. Oh please, please, Clara. (*Her daughter repudiates her with an angry shrug and retires haughtily.*) We should be so grateful to you, sir, if you found us a cab. (*The* NOTE TAKER *produces a whistle.*) Oh, thank you. (*She joins her daughter.*)

(*The* NOTE TAKER *blows a piercing blast.*)

THE SARCASTIC BYSTANDER. There! I knowed he was a plainclothes copper.

THE BYSTANDER. That aint a police whistle: thats a sporting whistle.

THE FLOWER GIRL (*still preoccupied with her wounded feelings*). He's no right to take away my character. My character is the same to me as any lady's.

What point does the flower girl make about herself and her rights?

THE NOTE TAKER. I dont know whether youve noticed it; but the rain stopped about two minutes ago.

THE BYSTANDER. So it has. Why didnt you say so before? and us losing our time listening to your silliness! (*He walks off toward the Strand.*)

THE SARCASTIC BYSTANDER. I can tell where you come from. You come from Anwell. Go back there.

THE NOTE TAKER (*helpfully*). Hanwell.

THE SARCASTIC BYSTANDER (*affecting great distinction of speech*). Thenk you, teacher. Haw haw! So long. (*He touches his hat with mock respect and strolls off.*)

THE FLOWER GIRL. Frightening people like that! How would he like it himself?

THE MOTHER. It's quite fine now, Clara. We can walk to a motor bus. Come. (*She gathers her skirts above her ankles and hurries off toward the Strand.*)

THE DAUGHTER. But the cab—(*Her mother is out of hearing.*) Oh, how tiresome! (*She follows angrily.*)

(*All the rest have gone except the* NOTE TAKER, *the* GENTLEMAN, *and the* FLOWER GIRL, *who sits arranging her basket and still pitying herself in murmurs.*)

THE FLOWER GIRL. Poor girl! Hard enough for her to live without being worrited and chivied.[10]

THE GENTLEMAN (*returning to his former place on the* NOTE TAKER'S *left*). How do you do it, if I may ask?

THE NOTE TAKER. Simply phonetics. The science of speech. Thats my profession: also my hobby. Happy is the man

What is the note taker's profession and hobby?

10. **worrited and chivied.** Worried and troubled

WORDS FOR EVERYDAY USE

im • per • ti • nent (im purt´'n ənt) *adj.*, saucy; insolent. *Although I would not classify my sister's child as a brat, several of his remarks to me were highly impertinent.*

re • pu • di • ate (ri pyo͞o´ dē āt´) *vt.*, disown or cast off publicly. *The candidate hastily repudiated the aides who were caught stuffing ballot boxes with forged votes.*

ANSWERS TO GUIDED READING QUESTIONS

1. The flower girl makes the point that she has as much right to her character as a lady or someone of a higher class. She adds that she has enough difficulty making a living without being caused unnecessary trouble.
2. The notetaker's profession is the same as his hobby—phonetics, or the science of speech.

ADDITIONAL QUESTIONS AND ACTIVITIES

Ask students the following questions:

1. To what extent are differences between the classes a problem in the United States?
2. Are class differences and barriers between the classes as great today in the United States as they were in Great Britain before World War I?
3. Could the dialogue and action detailed in Act One ever take place (with allowances for time and place) in the United States?

Answers

1. *Responses will vary,* but students should recognize that significant class differences still exist in the United States, especially between the lower classes and the middle and upper classes.
2. Class differences and barriers between the classes in Great Britain at the time in which the play is set were far greater than similar differences and barriers in the United States today.
3. *Responses will vary.* Some students may feel class conflict is not so sharp in the United States; others may feel the types of conflicts depicted in Act One exist in the United States and would allow such a scene to be played out.

ANSWERS TO GUIDED READING QUESTIONS

1. He is able to make a living because people who never had money are beginning to make money. They want to belong to a different class and they need to speak properly to do so.
2. The note taker claims that the speech of the flower girl is so depressing and disgusting the she has no right to live. This attitude reveals a prejudice against the lower class.
3. The note taker claims to be able to teach the flower girl to speak so well that she could pass as a duchess at an ambassador's garden party.

LITERARY TECHNIQUE

Hyperbole. Remind students that **hyperbole** is exaggeration for emphasis. The note taker tells the flower girl that she has "no right to live" because she utters "depressing and disgusting sounds." Such hyperbole is typical of his extravagant and impulsive responses to other characters. Ask students to keep a list as they read and find at least five examples of hyperbole in the play.

who can make a living by his hobby! You can spot an Irishman or a Yorkshireman by his brogue. *I* can place any man within six miles. I can place him within two miles in London. Sometimes within two streets.

The Flower Girl. Ought to be ashamed of himself, unmanly coward!

The Gentleman. But is there a living in that?

The Note Taker. Oh yes. Quite a fat one. This is an age of upstarts. Men begin in Kentish Town with £80 a year, and end in Park Lane with a hundred thousand. They want to drop Kentish Town; but they give themselves away every time they open their mouths. Now I can teach them—

Why is the note taker able to make a living with his skills at pronunciations?

The Flower Girl. Let him mind his own business and leave a poor girl—

The Note Taker (*explosively*). Woman: cease this detestable boohooing instantly; or else seek the shelter of some other place of worship.

The Flower Girl (*with feeble defiance*). Ive a right to be here if I like, same as you.

The Note Taker. A woman who utters such depressing and disgusting sounds has no right to be anywhere—no right to live. Remember that you are a human being with a soul and the divine gift of articulate speech: that your native language is the language of Shakespear[11] and Milton and The Bible: and dont sit there crooning like a bilious pigeon.

What attitude toward dialectical speech does the note taker have? What does this reveal about him?

The Flower Girl (*quite overwhelmed, looking up at him in mingled wonder and deprecation without daring to raise her head*). Ah-ah-ah-ow-ow-ow-oo!

The Note Taker (*whipping out his book*). Heavens! what a sound! (*He writes; then holds out the book and reads, reproducing her vowels exactly.*) Ah-ah-ah-ow-ow-ow-oo!

The Flower Girl (*tickled by the performance, and laughing in spite of herself*). Garn!

The Note Taker. You see this creature with her kerbstone[12] English: the English that will keep her in the gutter to the end of her days. Well, sir, in three months I could pass that girl off as a duchess at an ambassador's garden party. I could even get her a place as lady's maid or shop assistant, which requires better English. Thats the sort of thing I do for commercial millionaires. And on the profits of it I do genuine scientific work in phonetics, and a little as a poet on Miltonic lines.

What does the note taker claim to be able to do?

The Gentleman. I am myself a student of Indian dialects; and—

The Note Taker (*eagerly*). Are you? Do you know Colonel Pickering, the author of Spoken Sanscrit?

The Gentleman. I am Colonel Pickering. Who are you?

The Note Taker. Henry Higgins, author of Higgins's Universal Alphabet.

Pickering. (*with enthusiasm*). I came from India to meet you.

Higgins. I was going to India to meet you.

Pickering. Where do you live?

Higgins. 27A Wimpole Street. Come and see me tomorrow.

11. **Shakespear**. Shaw spelled names phonetically.
12. **kerbstone.** British spelling of *curbstone*

Words For Everyday Use

bil • ious (bil' yəs) *adj.*, ill-tempered; cranky. *After a hard morning delivering mail, the last thing the letter carrier needed was to be attacked by Mrs. Gramphone's bilious old cat.*

PICKERING. I'm at the Carlton. Come with me now and lets have a jaw over some supper.

HIGGINS. Right you are.

THE FLOWER GIRL (*to* PICKERING, *as he passes her*). Buy a flower, kind gentleman. I'm short for my lodging.

PICKERING. I really havnt any change. I'm sorry. (*He goes away.*)

HIGGINS (*shocked at the girl's mendacity*). Liar. You said you could change half-a-crown.

THE FLOWER GIRL (*rising in desperation*). You ought to be stuffed with nails, you ought. (*Flinging the basket at his feet*) Take the whole blooming basket for sixpence.

(*The church clock strikes the second quarter.*)

HIGGINS (*hearing in it the voice of God, rebuking him for his pharisaic*[13] *want of charity to the poor girl*). A reminder. (*He raises his hat solemnly; then throws a handful of money into the basket and follows* PICKERING.)

THE FLOWER GIRL (*picking up a half-crown*). Ah-ow-ooh! (*Picking up a couple of florins*) Aaah-ow-ooh! (*Picking up several coins*) Aaaaaah-ow-ooh! (*Picking up a half-sovereign*) Aaaaaaaaaaaah-ow-ooh! ! !

FREDDY (*springing out of a taxicab*). Got one at last. Hallo! (*To the* GIRL) Where are the two ladies that were here?

THE FLOWER GIRL They walked to the bus when the rain stopped.

FREDDY. And left me with a cab on my hands! Damnation!

THE FLOWER GIRL (*with grandeur*). Never mind, young man. *I'm* going home in a taxi. (*She sails off to the cab. The driver puts his hand behind him and holds the door firmly shut against her. Quite understanding his mistrust, she shews him her handful of money.*) Eightpence aint no object to me, Charlie. (*He grins and opens the door.*) Angel Court, Drury Lane, round the corner of Micklejohn's oil shop. Lets see how fast you can make her hop it. (*She gets in and pulls the door to with a slam as the taxicab starts.*)

FREDDY. Well, I'm dashed!

13. **pharisaic.** Hypocritical

WORDS FOR EVERYDAY USE

men • dac • i • ty (men das' ə tē) *n.*, lying. *Although the contractor's name was Speaktruth, he was remarkable for his consistent mendacity.*

CROSS-CURRICULAR CONNECTIONS

PHONETICS. Shaw believed that the varying dialects of Great Britain were one of the main obstacles to integrating the classes of society. "The reformer England needs today is an energetic phonetic enthusiast: that is why I have made such a one the hero of a popular play. . . . If the play makes the public aware that there are such people as phoneticians, and that they are among the most important people in England at present, it will serve its turn." In recent decades, the advance of nationwide media such as radio and television has made misunderstandings due to dialect less common both in Great Britain and in the United States.

SELECTION CHECK TEST 4.12.1 WITH ANSWERS

Checking Your Reading

1. Who spills the flower girl's flowers? **Freddy spills them.**
2. What does Clara urge her mother not to do? **She says not to give the girl money.**
3. What does the flower girl mistake the notetaker for? **She thinks he's a policeman.**
4. What is the notetaker's occupation and hobby? **He studies phonetics.**
5. What does Higgins throw in the flower girl's basket? **He throws money in it.**

Vocabulary in Context

Fill each blank with the most appropriate word from the Words for Everyday Use. You may have to change the tense of the word.

amiable bilious portico gumption mendacity proximity repudiate

1. My father grew **bilious** when he had the flu, but he soon was his old self again.
2. Geraldine was shocked and saddened to discover her friend's **mendacity**.
3. Everyone likes Neel for his kind heart and **amiable** personality.
4. Citizens of Salem gathered to **repudiate** the women accused of witchcraft.
5. Clyde pushed the baby's crib in close **proximity** to his parents' big bed.

Literary Tools

A plot in a drama can follow the same pattern as a plot for a novel or short story.

SELECTION CHECK TEST 4.12.1 WITH ANSWERS (CONT.)

Identify the following steps in the plot diagram.

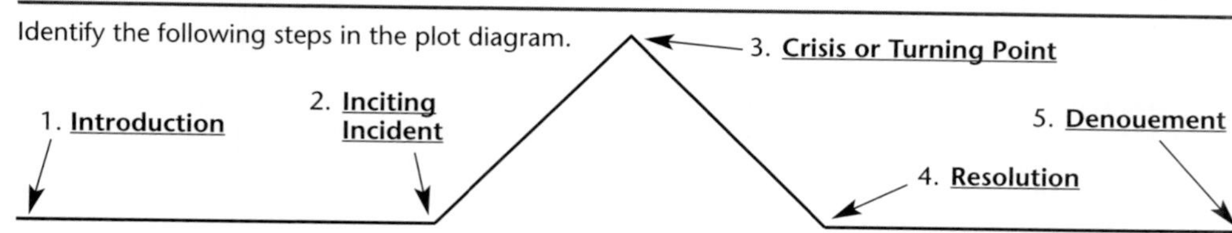

RESPOND TO THE SELECTION

Which of the two characters would you rather be stuck with in an elevator or on a long car ride? Which character do you think would be more interesting or be better company?

ANSWERS FOR INVESTIGATE, INQUIRE, IMAGINE

RECALL

1a. Freddy and the flower girl meet when Freddy collides with her and knocks over her basket.
2a. The flower girl is warned that a man in the crowd is taking notes.
3a. The note taker shows that he is able to identify the places they have lived by the way they speak.

INTERPRET

1b. The flower girl is disturbed but does not seem to be surprised at his lack of manners.
2b. The flower girl believes that the note taker is an undercover policeman who is going to charge her with a crime.
3b. Higgins's ability shows that he is highly intelligent, well educated, and a good observer of details, though not necessarily of larger matters.

ANALYZE

4a. Higgins and Pickering represent the highest class shown. The Eynsford Hills represent another. Some of the bystanders represent a third class that falls below that of the Eynsford Hills. The flower girl is the fourth and lowest class shown.

SYNTHESIZE

4b. *Responses will vary.* The exchanges of the characters show that there was considerable antagonism between the classes in early twentieth-century London.

EVALUATE

5a. *Responses will vary.* Both Higgins and the flower girl are intelligent to the point of being cunning. Both are self-assertive, though the flower girl is apt to collapse when she feels challenged by someone. Higgins is bold and impatient, while the flower girl is more likely to fell frightened and to sulk when she is wronged.

EXTEND

5b. *Responses will vary.* Suggest that students keep their predictions handy as they continue to read the play. Ask them to modify their predictions or make new ones as they learn more.

Respond *to the* SELECTION

At this point, what is your opinion of Higgins? of the flower girl?

INVESTIGATE, Inquire, *Imagine*

Recall: GATHERING FACTS → **Interpret:** FINDING MEANING

1a. How do Freddy and the flower girl meet? → 1b. What is the flower girl's reaction to her "meeting" with Freddy?

2a. What warning does the flower girl get from one of the bystanders? → 2b. Why would the flower girl be frightened of a policeman?

3a. What skill does the note taker display to the bystanders? → 3b. What does Higgins's ability reveal about his character?

Analyze: TAKING THINGS APART → **Synthesize:** BRINGING THINGS TOGETHER

4a. Judging from the information given on the characters in act 1, how many social classes has Shaw portrayed? → 4b. What do the exchanges between the flower girl and the other characters show about the relationships between the classes in twentieth-century London?

Evaluate: MAKING JUDGMENTS → **Extend:** CONNECTING IDEAS

5a. Evaluate whether Higgins or the flower girl shows more self-interest. → 5a. Does a class distinction based on pronunciation work in the United States? How do you judge people who speak differently from you?

Understanding *Literature*

SPECTACLE. Review the definition for **spectacle** in Literary Tools. What elements of sight and sound are described in the stage directions at the very beginning of the play? What about these elements makes them engaging or dramatic?

INCITING INCIDENT. Review the definition for **inciting incident** in the Handbook of Literary Terms and the plot pyramid you made for Literary Tools on page 1101. What is the inciting incident? What consequence might result if Higgins were to carry out his plan?

ANSWERS TO UNDERSTANDING LITERATURE

SPECTACLE. Elements of sight described are the portico of St. Paul's Church, the rainfall, and the pedestrians running for shelter. Elements of sound are the falling rain, cab whistles blowing, and the church clock striking the first quarter. These elements are full of chaotic sound and motion, from which the audience will look for some order or interesting detail to emerge.

INCITING INCIDENT. Higgins boasts that he can pass the flower girl off as a duchess at an ambassador's garden party or get her a place as a lady's maid or shop assistant. He intends to prove his skill as a teacher and phonetician. One consequence of Higgins's plan is that he will give the flower girl, as a member of a very low social class, the ability to pass in superficial respects as a member of a higher class—in effect making her unable to be a part of either class.

ACT TWO

Next day at 11 A.M. HIGGINS*'s laboratory in Wimpole Street. It is a room on the first floor, looking on the street, and was meant for the drawing room. The double doors are in the middle of the back wall; and persons entering find in the corner to their right two tall file cabinets at right angles to one another against the walls. In this corner stands a flat writing-table, on which are a phonograph, a laryngoscope,*[1] *a row of tiny organ pipes with bellows, a set of lamp chimneys for singing flames with burners attached to a gas plug in the wall by an indiarubber tube, several tuning-forks of different sizes, a life-size image of half a human head, shewing*[2] *in section the vocal organs, and a box containing a supply of wax cylinders for the phonograph.*

Further down the room, on the same side, is a fireplace, with a comfortable leather-covered easy-chair at the side of the hearth nearest the door, and a coal-scuttle. There is a clock on the mantel-piece. Between the fireplace and the phonograph table is a stand for newspapers.

On the other side of the central door, to the left of the visitor, is a cabinet of shallow drawers. On it is a telephone and the telephone directory. The corner beyond, and most of the side wall, is occupied by a grand piano, with the keyboard at the end furthest from the door, and a bench for the player extending the full length of the keyboard. On the piano is a dessert dish heaped with fruit and sweets, mostly chocolates.

The middle of the room is clear. Besides the easy-chair, the piano bench, and two chairs at the phonograph table, there is one stray chair. It stands near the fireplace. On the walls, engravings: mostly Piranesis and mezzotint[3] *portraits. No paintings.*

PICKERING *is seated at the table, putting down some cards and a tuning-fork which he has been using.* HIGGINS *is standing up near him, closing two or three file drawers which are hanging out. He appears in the morning light as a robust, vital, appetizing sort of man of forty or thereabouts, dressed in a professional-looking black frock-coat with a white linen collar and black silk tie. He is of the energetic, scientific type, heartily, even violently interested in everything that can be studied as a scientific subject, and careless about himself and other people, including their feelings. He is, in fact, but for his years and size, rather like a very* <u>*impetuous*</u> *baby "taking*

1. **laryngoscope.** A medical instrument used to examine the larynx
2. **shewing.** Archaic spelling of *showing*
3. **Piranesis and mezzotint.** Piranesi was an Italian artist; mezzotint is a method of engraving on metal

Literary TOOLS

SATIRE. Satire is humorous writing or speech intended to point out errors, falsehoods, foibles, or failings. It is written for the purpose of reforming human behavior or human institutions. As you read act 2, think about how Mr. Doolittle's speeches are satiric.

CHARACTER. A **character** is a person who figures in the action of a literary work. As you read, make a chart listing Liza's character traits and an example of how each trait is demonstrated. One example has been done for you.

Character Traits	Examples
whiny	Liza says "Ah-ah-ah-ow-ow-ow-oo" when Higgins says she has no right to live.

Reader's Journal

Have you ever tried to remake part of yourself with a particular purpose in mind?

ADDITIONAL RESOURCES

UNIT 12 RESOURCE BOOK
- Selection Worksheet 12.2
- Selection Check Test 4.12.3
- Selection Test 4.12.4

ENGLISH LANGUAGE LEARNING

Additional Vocabulary for Act 2 is listed below:
robust—strong and healthy
genial—cheerful, friendly
petulance—impatience; instability
follies—foolish action
drudge—person who does hard menial work
disinherit—deprive of rights
idle—not at work
tyrannical—harsh, cruel
prudent—wise; cautious

GRAPHIC ORGANIZER

proud—Liza believes she has the right to be heard since she is ready to pay for services Higgins can offer.

shrewd—offers to pay less for English lessons than for French lesson since she will be learning her own language

emotional—says she has feelings like any one else, claims Higgins has none

suspicious—worries about Higgins' motives

READER'S JOURNAL

Another way to put this question is "Can people change?" Ask students to think about this on both an inward and outward level. For example, is it easier to change one's appearance or one's attitudes? How do other's perceptions shape who we are?

VOCABULARY FROM THE SELECTION

arbitrary
astride
audacity
callous
conscientiously
diffident
disdain
dogmatically
elocutionary
extort
genteel
ginger
impetuous
incensed
jaunt
judicial
magisterially
pauperize
plaint
presumptuous
prudery
remonstrance
resolutely
score
slovenly
snivel
steadfastly
unabashed
unassailable
zephyr

ANSWERS TO GUIDED READING QUESTIONS

1. Higgins is compared to a baby. He takes notice eagerly and loudly. He needs to be watched to be kept out of mischief. He can bully genially or storm petulantly. He is very frank and likable despite often being unreasonable.
2. Mrs. Pearce's comments reveal that the middle class judges and condemns the poor on the basis of the way they speak.

CROSS-CURRICULAR ACTIVITIES

Arts and Humanities. Students may draw pictures of the set of Act Two according to the stage directions given by Shaw. Those whose drawing skills are minimal can represent the set at least in diagram form; others can represent the set in color as if it were a design for a production of the play. You might ask students to sketch costumes as well.

notice" eagerly and loudly, and requiring almost as much watching to keep him out of unintended mischief. His manner varies from genial bullying when he is in a good humor to stormy petulance when anything goes wrong; but he is so entirely frank and void of malice that he remains likeable even in his least reasonable moments.

To what is Higgins compared? What are his main characteristics?

Higgins (*as he shuts the last drawer*). Well, I think thats the whole show.

Pickering. It's really amazing. I havnt taken half of it in, you know.

Higgins. Would you like to go over any of it again?

Pickering (*rising and coming to the fireplace, where he plants himself with his back to the fire*). No, thank you; not now. I'm quite done up for this morning.

Higgins (*following him, and standing beside him on his left*). Tired of listening to sounds?

Pickering. Yes. It's a fearful strain. I rather fancied myself because I can pronounce twenty-four distinct vowel sounds; but your hundred and thirty beat me. I cant hear a bit of difference between most of them.

Higgins (*chuckling, and going over to the piano to eat sweets*). Oh, that comes with practice. You hear no difference at first; but you keep on listening, and presently you find theyre all as different as A from B. (MRS PEARCE *looks in: she is* HIGGINS*'s housekeeper.*) Whats the matter?

Mrs Pearce (*hesitating, evidently perplexed*). A young woman wants to see you sir.

Higgins. A young woman! What does she want?

Mrs Pearce. Well, sir, she says youll be glad to see her when you know what she's come about. She's quite a common girl, sir. Very common indeed. I should have sent her away, only I thought perhaps you wanted her to talk into your machines. I hope Ive not done wrong; but really you see such queer people sometimes—youll excuse me, I'm sure, sir—

What do Mrs. Pearce's comments reveal about middle-class attitudes toward the lower class?

Higgins. Oh, thats all right, Mrs Pearce. Has she an interesting accent?

Mrs Pearce. Oh, something dreadful, sir, really. I dont know how you can take an interest in it.

Higgins (*to* PICKERING). Lets have her up. Shew her up, Mrs Pearce. (*He rushes across to his working table and picks out a cylinder to use on the phonograph.*)

Mrs Pearce (*only half resigned to it*). Very well, sir. It's for you to say. (*She goes downstairs.*)

Higgins. This is rather a bit of luck. I'll shew you how I make records. We'll set her talking; and I'll take it down first in Bell's visible Speech; then in broad Romic; and then we'll get her on the phonograph so that you can turn her on as often as you like with the written transcript before you.

Mrs Pearce (*returning*). This is the young woman, sir.

(*The* FLOWER GIRL *enters in state. She has a hat with three ostrich feathers, orange, sky-blue, and red. She has a nearly clean apron, and the shoddy coat has been tidied a little. The pathos of this deplorable figure, with its innocent vanity and consequential air, touches* PICKERING, *who has already*

Words For Everyday Use

im • pet • u • ous (im pech′ oo əs) *adj.*, acting with little forethought. *When the lion was a cub he was impetuous, but as he grew older, he grew cautious.*

straightened himself in the presence of MRS PEARCE. *But as to* HIGGINS, *the only distinction he makes between men and women is that when he is neither bullying nor exclaiming to the heavens against some feather-weight cross,*[4] *he coaxes women as a child coaxes its nurse when it wants to get anything out of her.*)

HIGGINS (*brusquely, recognizing her with unconcealed disappointment, and at once, babylike, making an intolerable grievance of it*). Why, this is the girl I jotted down last night. She's no use: Ive got all the records I want of the Lisson Grove lingo; and I'm not going to waste another cylinder on it. (*To the* GIRL) Be off with you: I dont want you.

THE FLOWER GIRL. Dont you be so saucy. You aint heard what I come for yet. (*To* MRS. PEARCE, *who is waiting at the door for further instructions*) Did you tell him I come in a taxi ?

Why did Eliza want Mrs. Pearce to tell Higgins she came in a taxi?

MRS PEARCE. Nonsense, girl! what do you think a gentleman like Mr Higgins cares what you came in?

THE FLOWER GIRL. Oh, we are proud! He aint above giving lessons, not him: I heard him say so. Well, I aint come here to ask for any compliment; and if my money's not good enough I can go elsewhere.

HIGGINS. Good enough for what?

THE FLOWER GIRL. Good enough for ye-oo. Now you know, dont you? I'm come to have lessons, I am. And to pay for em too: make no mistake.

HIGGINS (*stupent*).[5] Well!!! (*Recovering his breath with a gasp*) What do you expect me to say to you?

THE FLOWER GIRL. Well, if you was a gentleman, you might ask me to sit down, I think. Dont I tell you I'm bringing you business?

HIGGINS. Pickering: shall we ask this baggage to sit down, or shall we throw her out of the window?

THE FLOWER GIRL (*running away in terror to the piano, where she turns at bay*). Ah-ah-oh-ow-ow-ow-oo! (*Wounded and whimpering*) I wont be called a baggage when Ive offered to pay like any lady.

What actions and comments by the flower girl reveal that she has pride and dignity despite her poverty?

(*Motionless, the two men stare at her from the other side of the room, amazed.*)

PICKERING (*gently*). What is it you want, my girl ?

THE FLOWER GIRL. I want to be a lady in a flower shop stead of selling at the corner of Tottenham Court Road. But they wont take me unless I can talk more genteel. He said he could teach me. Well, here I am ready to pay him—not asking any favor—and he treats me as if I was dirt.

MRS PEARCE. How can you be such a foolish ignorant girl as to think you could afford to pay Mr Higgins?

THE FLOWER GIRL. Why shouldnt I? I know what lessons cost as well as you do; and I'm ready to pay.

HIGGINS. How much?

THE FLOWER GIRL (*coming back to him, triumphant*). Now youre talking! I thought youd come off it when you saw a chance of getting

4. **feather-weight cross.** Trivial problem
5. **stupent.** Astonished

WORDS FOR EVERYDAY USE

gen • teel (gen tēl′) *adj.*, elegant; fashionable. *"Truly genteel manners," said the socialite, "are the outward sign of an inward grace."*

ANSWERS TO GUIDED READING QUESTIONS

1. Liza does not often have the money to spend on a taxi. To her, this is a sign that she has money and should be taken seriously.
2. The flower girl is outraged and hurt when she is called baggage and treated as if she were dirt. She wants to raise her standard of living, and she responds only to Pickering's gentility, not to Higgins's and Mrs. Pearce's bullying.

Quotables

"The worst sin towards our fellow creatures is not to hate them, but to be indifferent to them: That's the essence of inhumanity."

—Bernard Shaw

ADDITIONAL QUESTIONS AND ACTIVITIES

In Great Britain, barriers between one class and the next were extremely rigid until well into this century. A person in Liza's situation had few opportunities to work except as a servant. Because she feels she might never raise her standard of living, she is depicted as highly sensitive to any imputation that she is not a good, decent person.

Students can write an editorial for a newspaper that might have appeared before World War I, in which they call for greater opportunities for women of the lower class and suggest means to bring such opportunities.

ANSWER TO GUIDED READING QUESTION

1. Liza knows how much one woman pays for French lessons. She figures that since English is her native language, she should not have to pay as much.

CROSS-CURRICULAR ACTIVITIES

Mathematics and Sciences
Students can determine the answer to the following problem: "How much money did Liza offer Professor Higgins, in pre–World War I dollars? How much did she earn a day, in pre–World War I dollars?" Give students the following information about British and American currency values before World War I:

1 crown = 5 shillings

1 shilling = 12 pence

20 shillings = 1 pound

1 pound = $4.86

Answer
Liza offered Higgins one shilling, or one-twentieth of a pound, equal to $4.86 divided by twenty, which is .243 dollars, or about twenty-five cents. She earned a half crown, equal to 2.5 shillings, or thirty pence (2.5 x 12); thirty pence is one-eighth of a pound, and therefore one-eighth of $4.86, or about sixty cents.

Point out to students that though the dollar had more buying power before World War I, the amount of Liza's daily income still represents a very small sum.

back a bit of what you chucked at me last night. (*Confidently*) Youd had a drop in, hadnt you?

HIGGINS (*peremptorily*). Sit down.

THE FLOWER GIRL. Oh, if youre going to make a compliment of it—

HIGGINS (*thundering at her*). Sit down.

MRS PEARCE (*severely*). Sit down, girl. Do as youre told. (*She places the stray chair near the hearthrug*[6] *between* HIGGINS *and* PICKERING, *and stands behind it waiting for the girl to sit down.*)

THE FLOWER GIRL. Ah-ah-ah-ow-ow-oo! (*She stands, half rebellious, half bewildered.*)

PICKERING (*very courteous*). Wont you sit down?

THE FLOWER GIRL/LIZA (*coyly*). Dont mind if I do. (*She sits down.* PICKERING *returns to the hearthrug.*)

HIGGINS. Whats your name?

THE FLOWER GIRL. Liza Doolittle.

HIGGINS (*declaiming gravely*).
Eliza, Elizabeth, Betsy and Bess,
They went to the woods to get a bird's nes':

PICKERING. They found a nest with four eggs in it:

HIGGINS. They took one apiece, and left three in it. (*They laugh heartily at their own wit.*)

LIZA. Oh, dont be silly.

MRS PEARCE. You mustnt speak to the gentleman like that.

LIZA. Well, why wont he speak sensible to me?

HIGGINS. Come back to business. How much do you propose to pay me for the lessons?

LIZA. Oh, I know whats right. A lady friend of mine gets French lessons for eighteenpence an hour from a real French gentleman. Well, you wouldnt have the face to ask me the same for teaching me my own language as you would for French; so I wont give more than a shilling.[7] Take it or leave it.

Explain Liza's reasoning for the rate she is willing to pay.

HIGGINS (*walking up and down the room, rattling his keys and his cash in his pockets*). You know, Pickering, if you consider a shilling, not as a simple shilling, but as a percentage of this girl's income, it works out as fully equivalent to sixty or seventy guineas[8] from a millionaire.

PICKERING. How so?

HIGGINS. Figure it out. A millionaire has about £150 a day. She earns about half-a-crown.

LIZA (*haughtily*). Who told you I only—

HIGGINS (*continuing*). She offers me two-fifths of her day's income for a lesson. Two-fifths of a millionaire's income for a day would be somewhere about £60. It's handsome. By George, it's enormous! it's the biggest offer I ever had.

LIZA (*rising, terrified*). Sixty pounds! What are you talking about? I never offered you sixty pounds. Where would I get—

HIGGINS. Hold your tongue.

LIZA (*weeping*). But I aint got sixty pounds. Oh—

MRS PEARCE. Dont cry, you silly girl. Sit down. Nobody is going to touch your money.

HIGGINS. Somebody is going to touch you, with a broomstick, if you dont stop snivelling. Sit down.

---

6. **hearthrug.** A rug placed before a fireplace to protect the floor
7. **shilling.** Former British monetary unit, equal to twelve pence
8. **guineas.** Former British gold coins, equal to twenty-one shillings

WORDS FOR EVERYDAY USE

sniv • el (sniv′ əl) *vi.*, whine, cry, and sniffle. *When the recruit reached Marine boot camp, he discovered to his astonishment that sniveling no longer helped him get what he wanted.*

Liza (*obeying slowly*). Ah-ah-ah-ow-oo-o! One would think you was my father.

Higgins. If I decide to teach you, I'll be worse than two fathers to you. Here! (*He offers her his silk handkerchief.*)

Liza. Whats this for?

Higgins. To wipe your eyes. To wipe any part of your face that feels moist. Remember: thats your handkerchief; and thats your sleeve. Dont mistake the one for the other if you wish to become a lady in a shop.

(Liza, *utterly bewildered, stares helplessly at him.*)

Mrs Pearce. It's no use talking to her like that, Mr Higgins: she doesnt understand you. Besides, youre quite wrong: she doesnt do it that way at all. (*She takes the handkerchief.*)

Liza (*snatching it*). Here! You give me that handkerchief. He give it to me, not to you.

Pickering (*laughing*). He did. I think it must be regarded as her property, Mrs Pearce.

Mrs Pearce (*resigning herself*) . Serve you right, Mr Higgins.

Pickering. Higgins: I'm interested. What about the ambassador's garden party? I'll say youre the greatest teacher alive if you make that good. I'll bet you all the expenses of the experiment you cant do it. And I'll pay for the lessons.

Liza. Oh, you are real good. Thank you, Captain.

Higgins (*tempted, looking at her*). It's almost irresistible. She's so deliciously low—so horribly dirty—

Liza (*protesting extremely*). Ah-ah-ah- ah-ow-ow-oo-oo!!! I aint dirty: I washed my face and hands afore I come, I did.

ADDITIONAL QUESTIONS AND ACTIVITIES

Ask students to consider what each person—Higgins, Pickering, and Liza—gets out of the suggested project. Is it a good prospect for all parties involved?

Answer

Higgins and Pickering have less to lose. They take on the project in fun, as a challenge. In the end, if they tire of the project, they can just drop it. Liza becomes the object of their experiment. While she may seem to have much to gain (acquiring new skills, clothes, etc.), she will also have the least power in this situation. A change in plan or the failure of the project would have the greatest impact on her.

ANSWERS TO GUIDED READING QUESTIONS

1. Liza thinks she is going to be called on to do something immoral. Her reaction reveals that she has high moral standards. Higgins's comment that she has to learn to behave like a duchess is undercut by his instruction to Mrs. Pearce to wallop Liza if need be. He does not seem to be in a good position to teach manners, since he does not have very good manners himself.
2. Higgins has been bullying Liza, but now denies it. He seems to believe that his denial will establish his innocence immediately.

ADDITIONAL QUESTIONS AND ACTIVITIES

Reread to students Higgins's lines on the nature of life: "What is life but a series of inspired follies? The difficulty is to find them to do. Never lose a chance: it doesn't come every day." Students can write in their journal a list of five "follies" they would like to seize on and do—crazy plans like the notion of "making a duchess" out of Liza.

PICKERING. Youre certainly not going to turn her head with flattery, Higgins.

MRS PEARCE (*uneasy*). Oh, dont say that, sir: theres more ways than one of turning a girl's head; and nobody can do it better than Mr Higgins, though he may not always mean it. I do hope, sir, you wont encourage him to do anything foolish.

HIGGINS (*becoming excited as the idea grows on him*). What is life but a series of inspired follies? The difficulty is to find them to do. Never lose a chance: it doesnt come every day. I shall make a duchess of this draggle-tailed guttersnipe.[9]

LIZA (*strongly deprecating this view of her*). Ah-ah-ah-ow-ow-oo!

HIGGINS (*carried away*). Yes: in six months—in three if she has a good ear and a quick tongue—I'll take her anywhere and pass her off as anything. We'll start today: now! this moment! Take her away and clean her, Mrs Pearce. Monkey Brand, if it wont come off any other way. Is there a good fire in the kitchen?

MRS PEARCE (*protesting*). Yes: but—

HIGGINS (*storming on*). Take all her clothes off and burn them. Ring up Whiteley or somebody for new ones. Wrap her up in brown paper til they come.

LIZA. Youre no gentleman, youre not, to talk of such things. I'm a good girl, I am; and I know what the like of you are, I do.

HIGGINS. We want none of your Lisson Grove prudery here, young woman. Youve got to learn to behave like a duchess. Take her away, Mrs Pearce. If she gives you any trouble, wallop her.

What does Liza think is happening? What does her reaction reveal about her? Why is Higgins's comment ironic?

LIZA (*springing up and running between* PICKERING *and* MRS. PEARCE *for protection*). No! I'll call the police, I will.

MRS PEARCE. But Ive no place to put her.

HIGGINS. Put her in the dustbin.[10]

LIZA. Ah-ah-ah-ow-ow-oo!

PICKERING. Oh come, Higgins! be reasonable.

MRS PEARCE (*resolutely*). You must be reasonable, Mr Higgins: really you must. You cant walk over everybody like this.

(HIGGINS, *thus scolded, subsides. The hurricane is succeeded by a zephyr of amiable surprise.*)

HIGGINS (*with professional exquisiteness of modulation*). I walk over everybody! My dear Mrs Pearce, my dear Pickering, I never had the slightest intention of walking over anyone. All I propose is that we should be kind to this poor girl. We must help her to prepare and fit herself for her new station in life. If I did not express myself clearly it was because I did not wish to hurt her delicacy, or yours.

What has Higgins actually been doing? How do his former actions contradict his explanations of his intentions?

(LIZA, *reassured, steals back to her chair.*)

MRS PEARCE (*to* PICKERING). Well, did you ever hear anything like that, sir?

PICKERING (*laughing heartily*). Never, Mrs Pearce: never.

HIGGINS (*patiently*). Whats the matter?

9. **draggle-tailed guttersnipe.** A derogatory term referring to a person of the slums
10. **dustbin.** A rubbish container

WORDS FOR EVERYDAY USE

prud • er • y (prood′ ər ē) *n.*, condition of being overly modest or proper. *Although the Puritans of the 1600s are notorious for prudery, some of their customs would seem scandalous to modern Americans.*

zeph • yr (zef′ ər) *n.*, mild, gentle breeze. *He built his house in a spot warmed by the sun and fanned by the western zephyrs.*

MRS PEARCE. Well, the matter is, sir, that you cant take a girl up like that as if you were picking up a pebble on the beach.

HIGGINS. Why not?

MRS PEARCE. Why not! But you dont know anything about her. What about her parents? She may be married.

LIZA. Garn!

HIGGINS. There! As the girl very properly says, Garn! Married indeed! Dont you know that a woman of that class looks a worn out drudge of fifty a year after she's married?

LIZA. Whood marry me?

HIGGINS (*suddenly resorting to the most thrilling beautiful low tones in his best elocutionary style*). By George, Eliza, the streets will be strewn with the bodies of men shooting themselves for your sake before Ive done with you.

MRS PEARCE. Nonsense, sir. You mustnt talk like that to her.

LIZA (*rising and squaring herself determinedly*). I'm going away. He's off his chump, he is. I dont want no balmies[11] teaching me.

HIGGINS (*wounded in his tenderest point by her insensibility to his elocution*). Oh, indeed! I'm mad, am I? Very well, Mrs Pearce: you neednt order the new clothes for her. Throw her out.

LIZA (*whimpering*). Nah-ow. You got no right to touch me.

MRS PEARCE. You see now what comes of being saucy. (*Indicating the door*) This way, please.

LIZA (*almost in tears*). I didn't want no clothes. I wouldnt have taken them. (*She throws away the handkerchief.*) I can buy my own clothes.

HIGGINS (*deftly retrieving the handkerchief and intercepting her on her reluctant way to the door*). Youre an ungrateful wicked girl. This is my return for offering to take you out of the gutter and dress you beautifully and make a lady of you.

MRS PEARCE. Stop, Mr Higgins I wont allow it. It's you that are wicked. Go home to your parents, girl; and tell them to take better care of you.

LIZA. I aint got no parents. They told me I was big enough to earn my own living and turned me out.

MRS PEARCE. Wheres your mother?

LIZA. I aint got no mother. Her that turned me out was my sixth stepmother. But I done without them. And I'm a good girl, I am.

HIGGINS. Very well, then, what on earth is all this fuss about? The girl doesnt belong to anybody—is no use to anybody but me. (*He goes to* MRS PEARCE *and begins coaxing.*) You can adopt her, Mrs Pearce: I'm sure a daughter would be a great amusement to you. Now dont make any more fuss. Take her downstairs; and—

MRS PEARCE. But whats to become of her? Is she to be paid anything? Do be sensible, sir.

HIGGINS. Oh, pay her whatever is necessary: put it down in the housekeeping book. (*Impatiently*) What on earth will she want with money? She'll have her food and her clothes. She'll only drink if you give her money.

LIZA (*turning on him*). Oh you are a brute. It's a lie: nobody ever saw the sign of liquor on me. (*She goes back to her chair and plants herself there defiantly.*)

---

11. **balmies.** British slang for crazy or foolish people

WORDS FOR EVERYDAY USE

el • o • cu • tion • ar • y (el'ə kyōō´ shən er ē) *adj.*, appropriate for public speaking. *In the late 1800s, professional speakers toured cities giving elocutionary performances of famous poems.*

ADDITIONAL QUESTIONS AND ACTIVITIES

Shaw's dialogue has been compared to a tennis game: as one side seems to be about to score, the other side hits the subject right back over the net. In a class discussion, ask students to summarize each speech on this page and the next. Ask who appears to be "winning" after each speech.

LITERARY TECHNIQUE

POINT OF VIEW. Explain to students that **point of view** is the perspective from which a story is told. In drama, point of view is generally less important than in other forms of fiction. Students can write an account from Liza's point of view of the scene in which Liza first comes to ask for lessons. They should reinterpret Higgins's words and actions as those words and actions would have seemed to Liza, based on her reactions in the play.

ANSWERS TO GUIDED READING QUESTIONS

1. Higgins treats Liza as if she is of no value to anyone and has no feelings worth considering. This attitude reveals that he is self-centered and inconsiderate of others. It is also a reflection of the rigidity of class distinctions.
2. Mrs. Pearce is concerned about what will happen to Liza when Higgins is done with her. She knows that Higgins has not thought his plan through and has not thought of what this might mean to Liza.

ADDITIONAL QUESTIONS AND ACTIVITIES

- Tell students that critics of Shaw have pointed out that the servants in his plays are often more intelligent than their masters. Ask the following question: Is this true of Mrs. Pearce? Explain your answer.
- Ask students: Which character in this scene would you most like to be? Why?
- Students can write one paragraph in support of the following statement: "Higgins is paternalistic toward Liza." Before writing, students should consult a dictionary to clarify in their minds the meaning of the word "paternalistic." Suggest that they concentrate on material on this page of the text in developing their themes.

PICKERING (*in good-humored remonstrance*). Does it occur to you, Higgins, that the girl has some feelings?

HIGGINS (*looking critically at her*). Oh no, I dont think so. Not any feelings that we need bother about. (*Cheerily*) Have you, Eliza?

LIZA. I got my feelings same as anyone else.

How does Higgins treat Liza? What does his treatment of her reveal about him?

HIGGINS (*to* PICKERING, *reflectively*). You see the difficulty?

PICKERING. Eh? What difficulty?

HIGGINS. To get her to talk grammar. The mere pronunciation is easy enough.

LIZA. I dont want to talk grammar. I want to talk like a lady.

MRS PEARCE. Will you please keep to the point, Mr Higgins? I want to know on what terms the girl is to be here. Is she to have any wages? And what is to become of her when youve finished your teaching? You must look ahead a little.

Why is Mrs. Pearce concerned?

HIGGINS (*impatiently*). Whats to become of her if I leave her in the gutter? Tell me that, Mrs Pearce.

MRS PEARCE. Thats her own business, not yours, Mr Higgins.

HIGGINS. Well, when Ive done with her, we can throw her back into the gutter; and then it will be her own business again; so thats all right.

LIZA. Oh, youve no feeling heart in you: you dont care for nothing but yourself. (*She rises and takes the floor resolutely.*) Here! Ive had enough of this. I'm going. (*Making for the door*) You ought to be ashamed of yourself, you ought.

HIGGINS (*snatching a chocolate cream from the piano, his eyes suddenly beginning to twinkle with mischief*). Have some chocolates, Eliza.

LIZA (*halting, tempted*). How do I know what might be in them? I've heard of girls being drugged by the like of you.

(HIGGINS *whips out his penknife; cuts a chocolate in two; puts one half into his mouth and bolts it; and offers her the other half.*)

HIGGINS. Pledge of good faith, Eliza. I eat one half: you eat the other. (LIZA *opens her mouth to retort: he pops the half chocolate into it.*) You shall have boxes of them, barrels of them, every day. You shall live on them. Eh?

LIZA (*who has disposed of the chocolate after being nearly choked by it*). I wouldnt have ate it, only I'm too ladylike to take it out of my mouth.

HIGGINS. Listen, Eliza. I think you said you came in a taxi.

LIZA. Well, what if I did? Ive as good a right to take a taxi as anyone else.

HIGGINS. You have, Eliza; and in future you shall have as many taxis as you want. You shall go up and down and round the town in a taxi every day. Think of that, Eliza.

MRS PEARCE. Mr Higgins: youre tempting the girl. It's not right. She should think of the future.

HIGGINS. At her age! Nonsense! Time enough to think of the future when you havnt any future to think of. No, Eliza: do as this lady does: think of other people's futures; but never think of your own. Think of chocolates, and taxis, and gold, and diamonds.

LIZA. No: I dont want no gold and no diamonds. I'm a good girl, I am. (*She sits down again, with an attempt at dignity.*)

WORDS FOR EVERYDAY USE

re • mon • strance (ri män′ strəns) *n.*, act or instance of protest or complaint. *After the dancers scratched the gym floor with their tap shoes, they received a severe remonstrance from the principal.*

res • o • lute • ly (rez ə loot′ le) *adv.*, with a firm, fixed purpose. *The captain of the ship resolutely held course through the hurricane and reached the harbor.*

HIGGINS. You shall remain so, Eliza, under the care of Mrs Pearce. And you shall marry an officer in the Guards,[12] with a beautiful moustache: the son of a marquis,[13] who will disinherit him for marrying you, but will relent when he sees your beauty and goodness—

PICKERING. Excuse me, Higgins; but I really must interfere. Mrs Pearce is quite right. If this girl is to put herself in your hands for six months for an experiment in teaching, she must understand thoroughly what she's doing.

HIGGINS. How can she? She's incapable of understanding anything. Besides, do any of us understand what we are doing? If we did, would we ever do it?

PICKERING. Very clever, Higgins; but not sound sense. (*To* ELIZA) Miss Doolittle—

LIZA (*overwhelmed*). Ah-ah-ow-oo!

HIGGINS. There! Thats all youll get out of Eliza. Ah-ah-ow-oo! No use explaining. As a military man you ought to know that. Give her her orders: thats what she wants. Eliza: you are to live here for the next six months, learning how to speak beautifully, like a lady in a florist's shop. If youre good and do whatever youre told, you shall sleep in a proper bedroom, and have lots to eat, and money to buy chocolates and take rides in taxis. If youre naughty and idle you will sleep in the back kitchen among the black beetles, and be walloped by Mrs Pearce with a broomstick. At the end of six months you shall go to Buckingham Palace in a carriage, beautifully dressed. If the King finds out youre not a lady, you will be taken by the police to the Tower of London, where your head will be cut off as a warning to other presumptuous flower girls. If you are not found out, you shall have a present of seven-and-sixpence to start life with as a lady in a shop. If you refuse this offer you will be a most ungrateful and wicked girl; and the angels will weep for you. (*To* PICKERING) Now are you satisfied, Pickering? (*To* MRS PEARCE) Can I put it more plainly and fairly, Mrs Pearce?

How does Higgins respond to the suggestion made by Mrs. Pearce and by Pickering that he should explain his plans to Liza so that she can give informed consent to them? Does Higgins's reply meet their objections? Why, or why not?

MRS PEARCE (*patiently*). I think youd better let me speak to the girl properly in private. I dont know that I can take charge of her or consent to the arrangement at all. Of course I know you dont mean her any harm; but when you get what you call interested in people's accents, you never think or care what may happen to them or you. Come with me, Eliza.

What interest makes Higgins lose sight of people?

HIGGINS. Thats all right. Thank you, Mrs Pearce. Bundle her off to the bath-room.

LIZA (*rising reluctantly and suspiciously*). Youre a great bully, you are. I wont stay here if I dont like. I wont let nobody wallop me. I never asked to go to Bucknam Palace, I didnt. I was never in trouble with the police, not me. I'm a good girl—

MRS PEARCE. Dont answer back, girl. You dont understand the gentleman. Come with me. (*She leads the way to the door, and holds open for* ELIZA.)

LIZA (*as she goes out*). Well, what I say is right. I wont go near the King, not if I'm going to

12. **the Guards.** A highly decorated British military unit
13. **marquis.** A European nobleman, ranked above an earl or count and below a duke

WORDS FOR EVERYDAY USE

pre • sump • tu • ous (prē zump′ cho͞o əs) *adj.*, overconfident or arrogant. *Donald was presumptuous enough to ask for a raise on his third day on the job.*

ANSWERS TO GUIDED READING QUESTIONS

1. Higgins maintains that Liza does not have the intelligence to understand what is happening to her. He responds to the protests of Mrs. Pearce and Pickering by giving Liza orders, threatening her with imaginary punishments, and offering her meager rewards, as if she were a child. His response does not meet their objections, because Liza is no better informed about the true consequences of her agreeing to participate in the experiment than she was before he spoke.
2. He loses sight of people when he becomes interested in their accents.

CROSS-CURRICULAR ACTIVITIES

SPEECH. Students can research careers related to speech. They might include speech and language pathologist, speech therapist, voice coach. Students can use the Internet, library or career library resources, and if possible, interviews with people in the profession they are researching. Have students to write assess their interests and abilities in relation to such a career.

ANSWER TO GUIDED READING QUESTION

1. Mrs. Pearce believes the hat should be disinfected, possibly because it may have lice.

ADDITIONAL QUESTIONS AND ACTIVITIES

Ask the following questions:

1. Why, do you suppose, do women seem to Higgins to become "jealous, exacting, suspicious," and turn into "nuisances" when they become involved with him? How is his statement about women ironic?
2. Why does Higgins become "selfish and tyrannical" when he makes friends with a woman?
3. Why would it be likely that Higgins would believe that women are going in the opposite direction from him?

Answers

1. Higgins is so impulsive, bullying, self-absorbed, and capricious that he is likely to make a person exacting and suspicious in response. His statement about women is ironic because it is clear to the audience that he is a difficult person to live with and that the characteristics he describes are only a reaction to him.
2. Higgins is almost always self-absorbed and frequently overbearing and pushy; when he makes friends with a woman, he finds himself in a situation in which he can perceive his own personality and sees himself as acting in a selfish and tyrannical manner.
3. Almost anyone dealing with Higgins in a close relationship would have to resist his bullying and coaxing, and so would be perceived by him as "driving at one thing" while he was "driving at another."

have my head cut off. If I'd known what I was letting myself in for, I wouldnt have come here. I always been a good girl; and I never offered to say a word to him; and I dont owe him nothing; and I dont care; and I wont be put upon; and I have my feelings the same as anyone else—

(MRS PEARCE *shuts the door; and* ELIZA'*s* *plaints* *are no longer audible.* PICKERING *comes from the hearth to the chair and sits* *astride* *it with his arms on the back.*)

PICKERING. Excuse the straight question, Higgins. Are you a man of good character where women are concerned?

HIGGINS (*moodily*). Have you ever met a man of good character where women are concerned?

PICKERING. Yes: very frequently.

HIGGINS (*dogmatically, lifting himself on his hands to the level of the piano, and sitting on it with a bounce*). Well, I havnt. I find that the moment I let a woman make friends with me, she becomes jealous, exacting, suspicious, and a damned nuisance. I find that the moment I let myself make friends with a woman, I become selfish and tyrannical. Women upset everything. When you let them into your life, you find that the woman is driving at one thing and youre driving at another.

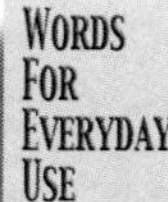

PICKERING. At what, for example?

HIGGINS (*coming off the piano restlessly*). Oh, Lord knows! I suppose the woman wants to live her own life; and the man wants to live his; and each tries to drag the other on to the wrong track. One wants to go north and the other south; and the result is that both have to go east, though they both hate the east wind. (*He sits down on the bench at the keyboard.*) So here I am, a confirmed old bachelor, and likely to remain so.

PICKERING (*rising and standing over him gravely*). Come, Higgins! You know what I mean. If I'm to be in this business I shall feel responsible for that girl. I hope its understood that no advantage is to be taken of her position.

HIGGINS. What! That thing! Sacred, I assure you. (*Rising to explain*) You see, she'll be a pupil; and teaching would be impossible unless pupils were sacred. Ive taught scores of American millionairesses how to speak English: the best looking women in the world. I'm seasoned. They might as well be blocks of wood. *I* might as well be a block of wood. It's—

(MRS PEARCE *opens the door. She has* ELIZA'*s hat in her hand.* PICKERING *retires to the easy-chair at the hearth and sits down.*)

HIGGINS (*eagerly*). Well, Mrs Pearce: is it all right?

MRS PEARCE (*at the door*). I just wish to trouble you with a word, if I may, Mr Higgins.

HIGGINS. Yes, certainly. Come in. (*She comes forward.*) Dont burn that, Mrs Pearce. I'll keep it as a curiosity. (*He takes the hat.*)

Why does Mrs. Pearce feel she must put the hat into the oven?

MRS PEARCE. Handle it carefully, sir, please. I had to promise her not to burn it; but I had better put it in the oven for a while.

HIGGINS (*putting it down hastily on the piano*). Oh! thank you. Well, what have you to say to me?

PICKERING. Am I in the way?

WORDS FOR EVERYDAY USE

plaint (plānt) *n.*, complaint or grievance. *The tenants presented the landlord with a list of four hundred and sixty-five plaints about his tenements.*

a • stride (ə strīd') *adv.*, with legs on either side. *The logger rode down the rapids astride an enormous fir tree.*

dog • mat • i • cal • ly (dôg mat' ik ə lē) *adv.*, stating an opinion in an arrogant manner. *Biff's idea of a discussion was that everyone should listen quietly while he dogmatically asserted his beliefs.*

score (skôr) *n.*, set of twenty persons or things. *"Three score and ten years" is a common expression signifying a life span.*

MRS PEARCE. Not at all, sir. Mr Higgins: will you please be very particular what you say before the girl?

HIGGINS (*sternly*). Of course. I'm always particular about what I say. Why do you say this to me?

MRS PEARCE (*unmoved*). No, sir: youre not at all particular when youve mislaid anything or when you get a little impatient. Now it doesnt matter before me: I'm used to it. But you really must not swear before the girl.

HIGGINS (*indignantly*). *I* swear! (*Most emphatically*) I never swear. I detest the habit. What the devil do you mean?

Is Higgins very self-aware? How do you know?

MRS PEARCE (*stolidly*). Thats what I mean, sir. You swear a great deal too much. I dont mind your damning and blasting, and what the devil and where the devil and who the devil—

HIGGINS. Mrs Pearce: this language from your lips! Really!

MRS PEARCE (*not to be put off*).—but there is a certain word I must ask you not to use. The girl has just used it herself because the bath was too hot. It begins with the same letter as bath. She knows no better: she learnt it at her mother's knee. But she must not hear it from your lips.

HIGGINS (*loftily*). I cannot charge myself with having ever uttered it, Mrs Pearce. (*She looks at him steadfastly. He adds, hiding an uneasy conscience with a judicial air*) Except perhaps in a moment of extreme and justifiable excitement.

MRS PEARCE. Only this morning, sir, you applied it to your boots, to the butter, and to the brown bread.

HIGGINS. Oh, that! Mere alliteration, Mrs Pearce, natural to a poet.

MRS PEARCE. Well, sir, whatever you choose to call it, I beg you not to let the girl hear you repeat it.

HIGGINS. Oh, very well, very well. Is that all?

MRS PEARCE. No, sir. We shall have to be very particular with this girl as to personal cleanliness.

HIGGINS. Certainly. Quite right. Most important.

MRS PEARCE. I mean not to be slovenly about her dress or untidy in leaving things about.

HIGGINS (*going to her solemnly*). Just so. I intended to call your attention to that. (*He passes on to* PICKERING, *who is enjoying the conversation immensely.*) It is these little things that matter, Pickering. Take care of the pence and the pounds will take care of themselves is as true of personal habits as of money. (*He comes to anchor on the hearth-rug, with the air of a man in an unassailable position.*)

MRS PEARCE. Yes, sir. Then might I ask you not to come down to breakfast in your dressing-gown, or at any rate not to use it as a napkin to the extent you do, sir. And if you would be so good as not to eat everything off the same plate, and to remember not to put the porridge saucepan out of your hand on the clean tablecloth, it would be a better example to the girl. You know you nearly choked yourself with a fishbone in the jam only last week.

WORDS FOR EVERYDAY USE

stead • fast • ly (sted′ fast lē) *adv.*, in a firm or established manner. *The boy demonstrated his morals by steadfastly refusing to steal a single piece of candy when dared by his friends.*

ju • di • cial (jo͞o dish′ əl) *adj.*, carefully considering the facts. *The umpire had a judicial manner, but her mask and chest protector did not contribute to a judicial appearance.*

slov • en • ly (sluv′ ən lē) *adj.*, careless in appearance, untidy. *The editor soon found to her horror that the historian's research techniques were as slovenly as his greasy tweed jacket.*

un • as • sail • a • ble (un e sal′ e bel) *adj.*, undeniable. *People who consider their financial know-how unassailable are unwilling to take advice about their investments.*

ANSWER TO GUIDED READING QUESTION

1. Higgins is not self-aware. If he were, he would know that he is very careless in what he says to others.

LITERARY TECHNIQUE

ALLITERATION. Higgins refers to his use of *bloody* in reference to his "boots, to the butter, and to the brown bread" as mere alliteration. Remind students that **alliteration** is the repetition of initial consonant sounds. In this case, the *b* sound is repeated.

ANSWERS TO GUIDED READING QUESTIONS

1. Mrs. Pearce knows that Higgins is an overbearing, bossy person.
2. One might guess that Doolittle is not a hardworking man.
3. Higgins wants to meet Doolittle because he is interested in his accent. This suggests that Mrs. Pearce is right, that Higgins doesn't pay attention to people when he is interested in their accents.

ADDITIONAL QUESTIONS AND ACTIVITIES

Students can take turns attempting to express Alfred Doolittle's body language as he enters the room. In entering and speaking he has to express wounded honor and stern resolution, as well as uncertainty about the identity of the gentlemen before him.

HIGGINS (*routed from the hearthrug and drifting back to the piano*). I may do these things sometimes in absence of mind; but surely I dont do them habitually. (*Angrily*) By the way: my dressing-gown smells most damnably of benzine.

MRS PEARCE. No doubt it does, Mr Higgins. But if you will wipe your fingers—

HIGGINS (*yelling*). Oh very well, very well: I'll wipe them in my hair in future.

MRS PEARCE. I hope youre not offended, Mr Higgins.

HIGGINS (*shocked at finding himself thought capable of an unamiable sentiment*). Not at all, not at all. Youre quite right, Mrs Pearce: I shall be particularly careful before the girl. Is that all?

MRS PEARCE. No, sir. Might she use some of those Japanese dresses you brought from abroad? I really cant put her back into her old things.

HIGGINS. Certainly. Anything you like. Is that all?

MRS PEARCE. Thank you, sir. Thats all. (*She goes out.*)

HIGGINS. You know, Pickering, that woman has the most extraordinary ideas about me. Here I am, a shy, diffident sort of man. Ive never been able to feel really grown-up and tremendous, like other chaps. And yet she's firmly persuaded that I'm an arbitrary overbearing bossing kind of person. I cant account for it.

What does Mrs. Pearce know about Higgins that he doesn't know himself?

(MRS PEARCE *returns.*)

MRS PEARCE. If you please, sir, the trouble's beginning already. Theres a dustman[14] downstairs, Alfred Doolittle, wants to see you. He says you have his daughter here.

What might you be able to predict about Doolittle based on his last name?

PICKERING (*rising*). Phew! I say! (*He retreats to the hearthrug.*)

HIGGINS (*promptly*). Send the blackguard[15] up.

MRS PEARCE. Oh, very well, sir. (*She goes out.*)

PICKERING. He may not be a blackguard, Higgins.

HIGGINS. Nonsense. Of course he's a blackguard.

PICKERING. Whether he is or not, I'm afraid we shall have some trouble with him.

HIGGINS (*confidently*). Oh no: I think not. If theres any trouble he shall have it with me, not I with him. And we are sure to get something interesting out of him.

PICKERING. About the girl?

HIGGINS. No. I mean his dialect.

PICKERING. Oh!

Why does Higgins want to meet Doolittle? What does his reason suggest about Higgins?

MRS PEARCE (*at the door*). Doolittle, sir. (*She admits* DOOLITTLE *and retires.*)

(ALFRED DOOLITTLE *is an elderly but vigorous dustman, clad in the costume of his profession, including a hat with a back brim covering his neck and shoulders. He has well marked and rather interesting features, and seems equally free from fear and conscience. He has a remarkably expressive voice, the result of a habit of giving vent to his feelings without reserve. His present pose is that of wounded honor and stern resolution.*)

14. **dustman.** Garbage or trash collector
15. **blackguard.** Vulgar person of the lower class

WORDS FOR EVERYDAY USE

dif • fi • dent (dif' ə dənt) *adj.*, lacking self-confidence; timid. *Bing was so diffident that I had difficulty maintaining a conversation with him.*

ar • bi • trar • y (är' bə trer' ē) *adj.*, despotic; dictatorial. *When we realized that the team leader had an arbitrary leadership style, we quickly replaced him with a more productive team member.*

DOOLITTLE (*at the door, uncertain which of the two gentlemen is his man*). Professor Higgins?

HIGGINS Here. Good morning. Sit down.

DOOLITTLE. Morning, Governor. (*He sits down magisterially.*) I come about a very serious matter, Governor.

HIGGINS (*to* PICKERING). Brought up in Hounslow. Mother Welsh, I should think. (DOOLITTLE *opens his mouth, amazed.* HIGGINS *continues.*) What do you want, Doolittle?

DOOLITTLE (*menacingly*). I want my daughter: thats what I want. See?

HIGGINS. Of course you do. Youre her father, arnt you? You dont suppose anyone else wants her, do you? I'm glad to see you have some spark of family feeling left. She's upstairs. Take her away at once.

DOOLITTLE (*rising, fearfully taken aback*). What!

HIGGINS. Take her away. Do you suppose I'm going to keep your daughter for you?

DOOLITTLE (*remonstrating*). Now, now, look here, Governor. Is this reasonable? Is it fairity[16] to take advantage of a man like this? The girl belongs to me. You got her. Where do I come in? (*He sits down again.*)

HIGGINS. Your daughter had the audacity to come to my house and ask me to teach her how to speak properly so that she could get a place in a flower-shop. This gentleman and my housekeeper have been here all the time. (*Bullying him*) How dare you come here and attempt to blackmail me? You sent her here on purpose.

DOOLITTLE (*protesting*). No, Governor.

HIGGINS. You must have. How else could you possibly know that she is here?

DOOLITTLE. Dont take a man up like that, Governor.

HIGGINS. The police shall take you up. This is a plant—a plot to extort money by threats. I shall telephone for the police. (*He goes resolutely to the telephone and opens the directory.*)

DOOLITTLE. Have I asked you for a brass farthing? I leave it to the gentleman here: have I said a word about money?

HIGGINS (*throwing the book aside and marching down on* DOOLITTLE *with a poser*). What else did you come for?

DOOLITTLE (*sweetly*). Well, what would a man come for? Be human, Governor.

HIGGINS (*disarmed*). Alfred: did you put her up to it?

Why has Doolittle come? What does he want?

DOOLITTLE. So help me, Governor, I never did. I take my Bible oath I aint seen the girl these two months past.

HIGGINS. Then how did you know she was here?

DOOLITTLE (*"most musical, most melancholy"*). I'll tell you, Governor, if youll only let me get a word in. I'm willing to tell you. I'm wanting to tell you. I'm waiting to tell you.

HIGGINS. Pickering: this chap has a certain natural gift of rhetoric. Observe the rhythm of his native woodnotes wild.[17] "I'm willing to tell you: I'm wanting to tell you: I'm waiting to tell you." Sentimental rhetoric! thats the Welsh strain in him. It also accounts for his mendacity and dishonesty.

16. **fairity.** Just and honest
17. **rhythm . . . wild.** A reference to the sound of a warbling in the forest

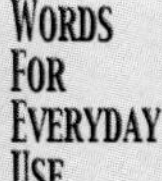

WORDS FOR EVERYDAY USE

mag • is • te • ri • al • ly (maj′ is tir′ ē əl lē) *adv.*, in a domineering or masterful manner. *When someone coughed before the symphony began, the conductor magisterially stared him into silence.*

au • dac • i • ty (ô das′ ə tē) *n.*, boldness; insolence. *The pirate demonstrated his audacity by attacking ships far better armed than his own.*

ex • tort (eks tôrt′) *vt.*, get something from somebody through threats or violence. *A favored tactic of organized crime is to extort money from a business in return for a promise not to disrupt it.*

ANSWER TO GUIDED READING QUESTION

1. Doolittle has come for money. He wants some kind of payment from Higgins.

ADDITIONAL QUESTIONS AND ACTIVITIES

Students can imagine that they are Doolittle trying to obtain money from Higgins, not in person, but by means of a note. They can compose the note as they imagine Doolittle might have written it himself, keeping in mind that he does not want Liza back and that all he is asking for is five pounds.

ANSWERS TO GUIDED READING QUESTIONS

1. Higgins assumes that Doolittle is dishonest because he is from Wales. Pickering protests because is own background is Welsh.
2. Doolittle believes that his daughter is going to become romantically involved with Higgins. His actions reveal he has no objection to that arrangement as long as he profits form it, which demonstrates that he values money more than morality.

LITERARY TECHNIQUE

CHARACTERIZATION. Characterization is the use of literary techniques to create a character. Point out to students that Shaw uses interruptions in and responses to Doolittle's account of events to develop our understanding of his character and to advance the plot. Doolittle is interrupted by Higgins first, who identifies the corner of Long Acre and Endell Street as a pub. Next, Pickering interrupts him with a question that results in Doolittle's disclosing that he is not trusted by Liza's landlady. Pickering finally confronts him with the contradiction between his words and his actions, asking him why he brought Liza's luggage if he was intending to rescue her.

What does Higgins assume about Doolittle? on what basis? Why does Pickering protest?

PICKERING. Oh, please, Higgins: I'm west country myself. (*To* DOOLITTLE) How did you know the girl was here if you didnt send her?

DOOLITTLE. It was like this, Governor. The girl took a boy in the taxi to give him a jaunt. Son of her landlady, he is. He hung about on the chance of her giving him another ride home. Well, she sent him back for her luggage when she heard you was willing for her to stop here. I met the boy at the corner of Long Acre and Endell Street.

HIGGINS. Public house. Yes?

DOOLITTLE. The poor man's club, Governor: why shouldnt I?

PICKERING. Do let him tell his story, Higgins.

DOOLITTLE. He told me what was up. And I ask you, what was my feelings and my duty as a father? I says to the boy, "You bring me the luggage," I says—

PICKERING. Why didn't you go for it yourself?

DOOLITTLE. Landlady wouldnt have trusted me with it, Governor. She's that kind of woman: you know. I had to give the boy a penny afore he trusted me with it, the little swine. I brought it to her just to oblige you like, and make myself agreeable. Thats all.

HIGGINS. How much luggage?

DOOLITTLE. Musical instrument, Governor. A few pictures, a trifle of jewelry, and a bird-cage. She said she didn't want no clothes. What was I to think from that, Governor? I ask you as a parent what was I to think?

HIGGINS. So you came to rescue her from worse than death, eh?

DOOLITTLE (*appreciatively: relieved at being so well understood*). Just so, Governor. Thats right.

PICKERING. But why did you bring her luggage if you intended to take her away?

DOOLITTLE. Have I said a word about taking her away? Have I now?

HIGGINS (*determinedly*). Youre going to take her away, double quick. (*He crosses to the hearth and rings the bell.*)

DOOLITTLE (*rising*). No, Governor. Dont say that. I'm not the man to stand in my girl's light. Heres a career opening for her, as you might say; and—

What does Doolittle think is occurring? What do his actions reveal about him?

(MRS PEARCE *opens the door and awaits orders.*)

HIGGINS. Mrs Pearce: this is Eliza's father. He has come to take her away. Give her to him. (*He goes back to the piano, with an air of washing his hands of the whole affair.*)

DOOLITTLE. No. This is a misunderstanding. Listen here—

MRS PEARCE. He cant take her away, Mr Higgins: how can he? You told me to burn her clothes.

DOOLITTLE. Thats right. I cant carry the girl through the streets like a blooming monkey, can I? I put it to you.

HIGGINS. You have put it to me that you want your daughter. Take your daughter. If she has no clothes go out and buy her some.

DOOLITTLE (*desperate*). Wheres the clothes she come in? Did I burn them or did your missus here?

MRS PEARCE. I am the housekeeper, if you please. I have sent for some clothes for your

WORDS FOR EVERYDAY USE

jaunt (jônt) *n.*, short pleasure trip. *Before beginning his new job plowing snow, Jack took a* jaunt *to a sunny climate.*

girl. When they come you can take her away. You can wait in the kitchen. This way, please.

(DOOLITTLE, *much troubled, accompanies her to the door; then hesitates; finally turns confidentially to* HIGGINS.)

DOOLITTLE. Listen here, Governor. You and me is men of the world, aint we?

HIGGINS. Oh! Men of the world, are we? Youd better go, Mrs Pearce.

MRS PEARCE. I think so, indeed, sir. (*She goes, with dignity.*)

PICKERING. The floor is yours, Mr Doolittle.

DOOLITTLE (*to* PICKERING). I thank you, Governor. (*To* HIGGINS, *who takes refuge on the piano bench, a little overwhelmed by the proximity of his visitor; for* DOOLITTLE *has a professional flavour of dust about him.*) Well, the truth is, Ive taken a sort of fancy to you, Governor; and if you want the girl, I'm not so set on having her back home again but what I might be open to an arrangement. Regarded in the light of a young woman, she's a fine handsome girl. As a daughter she's not worth her keep; and so I tell you straight. All I ask is my rights as a father; and youre the last man alive to expect me to let her go for nothing; for I can see youre one of the straight sort, Governor. Well, whats a five-pound note to you? And whats Eliza to me? (*He returns to his chair and sits down judicially.*)

What deal does Doolittle offer?

PICKERING. I think you ought to know, Doolittle, that Mr Higgins's intentions are entirely honorable.

DOOLITTLE. Course they are, Governor. If I thought they wasnt, I'd ask fifty.

HIGGINS (*revolted*). Do you mean to say, you callous rascal, that you would sell your daughter for £50?

DOOLITTLE. Not in a general way I wouldnt; but to oblige a gentleman like you I'd do a good deal, I do assure you.

PICKERING. Have you no morals, man?

DOOLITTLE (*unabashed*). Cant afford them, Governor. Neither could you if you was as poor as me. Not that I mean any harm, you know. But if Liza is going to have a bit out of this, why not me too?

What does Doolittle offer to do? What serious point is Shaw making about morality in this humorous scene?

HIGGINS (*troubled*). I dont know what to do, Pickering. There can be no question that as a matter of morals it's a positive crime to give this chap a farthing.[18] And yet I feel a sort of rough justice in his claim.

DOOLITTLE. Thats it, Governor. Thats all I say. A father's heart, as it were.

PICKERING. Well, I know the feeling; but really it seems hardly right—

DOOLITTLE. Dont say that, Governor. Dont look at it that way. What am I, Governors both? I ask you, what am I? I'm one of the undeserving poor: thats what I am. Think of what that means to a man. It means that he's up agen[19] middle class morality all the time. If theres anything going, and I put in for a bit of it, it's always the same story: "Youre undeserving; so you cant have it." But my needs is as great as the most deserving widow's that ever

18. **farthing.** Former British coin, equal to one-fourth of a penny
19. **agen.** Against

WORDS FOR EVERYDAY USE

cal • lous (kal′ əs) *adj.*, unfeeling; merciless. *Even the most callous person in the crowd shed a tear when the little ballerina gave her teacher a bouquet.*

un • a • bashed (un ə bashd′) *adv.*, without embarrassment. *Unabashed by the television cameras, George followed the hypnotist's suggestion, gargling and yodeling wildly.*

ANSWERS TO GUIDED READING QUESTIONS

1. Doolittle offers Liza to Higgins for five pounds.
2. Doolittle suggests that he would raise no objections to his daughter's becoming Higgins's mistress as long as he received fifty pounds himself. Shaw is pointing out that it is easier for well-to-do people to maintain moral standards because their poverty does not compel them to compromise what they think is right.

ADDITIONAL QUESTIONS AND ACTIVITIES

Students can imagine Doolittle is running for public office in the United States and write party platforms describing the proposals he might make for governing the nation and changing society.

ANSWER TO GUIDED READING QUESTION

1. Doolittle argues that the others should not be concerned about his making bad use of the money, because he will spend the money promptly on a drinking spree. He challenges middle-class morality by assuming that a spree is the least harmful use he could make of the money given him.

ADDITIONAL QUESTIONS AND ACTIVITIES

Students can imagine they are advice columnists. Higgins has just written to them to ask whether he should marry Liza. Students can write a one-paragraph response, in view of the situation as it stands in Act Two. Before they begin, they should reread Doolittle's opinion of marriage, as expressed on this page.

got money out of six different charities in one week for the death of the same husband. I dont need less than a deserving man: I need more. I dont eat less hearty than him; and I drink a lot more. I want a bit of amusement, cause I'm a thinking man. I want cheerfulness and a song and a band when I feel low. Well, they charge me just the same for everything as they charge the deserving. What is middle class morality? Just an excuse for never giving me anything. Therefore, I ask you, as two gentlemen, not to play that game on me. I'm playing straight with you. I aint pretending to be deserving. I'm undeserving; and I mean to go on being undeserving. I like it; and thats the truth. Will you take advantage of a man's nature to do him out of the price of his own daughter what he's brought up and fed and clothed by the sweat of his brow until she's growed big enough to be interesting to you two gentlemen? Is five pounds unreasonable? I put it to you; and I leave it to you.

HIGGINS (*rising, and going over to* PICKERING). Pickering: if we were to take this man in hand for three months, he could choose between a seat in the Cabinet and a popular pulpit in Wales.

PICKERING. What do you say to that, Doolittle?

DOOLITTLE. Not me, Governor, thank you kindly. Ive heard all the preachers and all the prime ministers—for I'm a thinking man and game for politics or religion or social reform same as all the other amusements—and I tell you it's a dog's life any way you look at it. Undeserving poverty is my line. Taking one station in society with another, it's—it's—well, it's the only one that has any ginger in it, to my taste.

HIGGINS. I suppose we must give him a fiver.[20]

PICKERING. He'll make a bad use of it, I'm afraid.

DOOLITTLE. Not me, Governor, so help me I wont. Dont you be afraid that I'll save it and spare it and live idle on it. There wont be a penny of it left by Monday: I'll have to go to work same as if I'd never had it. It wont pauperize me, you bet. Just one good spree for myself and the missus, giving pleasure to ourselves and employment to others, and satisfaction to you to think it's not been throwed away. You couldnt spend it better.

What unexpected, unusual argument does Doolittle make? How does he challenge "middle-class morality"?

HIGGINS (*taking out his pocket book and coming between* DOOLITTLE *and the piano*). This is irresistible. Lets give him ten. (*He offers two notes to the dustman.*)

DOOLITTLE. No, Governor. She wouldnt have the heart to spend ten; and perhaps I shouldnt neither. Ten pounds is a lot of money: it makes a man feel prudent like; and then goodbye to happiness. You give me what I ask you, Governor: not a penny more, and not a penny less.

PICKERING. Why dont you marry that missus of yours? I rather draw the line at encouraging that sort of immorality.

DOOLITTLE. Tell her so, Governor: tell her so. *I*'m willing. It's me that suffers by it. Ive no hold on her. I got to be agreeable to her. I got to give her presents. I got to buy her clothes something sinful. I'm a slave to that woman, Governor, just because I'm not her

20. **fiver.** British slang for a five-pound note

WORDS FOR EVERYDAY USE

gin • ger (jin′ gər) *n.*, liveliness, spirit. *"Come on, boys and girls," the band leader said. "Put some ginger in it, or this crowd will fall asleep."*

pau • per • ize (pô′ pər īz′) *vt.*, impoverish. *Tolstoy, insisting upon major changes in society, claimed that charity pauperized the lower class.*

lawful husband. And she knows it too. Catch her marrying me! Take my advice, Governor: marry Eliza while she's young and dont know no better. If you dont youll be sorry for it after. If you do, she'll be sorry for it after; but better her than you, because youre a man, and she's only a woman and dont know how to be happy anyhow.

HIGGINS. Pickering if we listen to this man another minute, we shall have no convictions left. (*To* DOOLITTLE) Five pounds I think you said.

DOOLITTLE. Thank you kindly, Governor.

HIGGINS. Youre sure you wont take ten?

DOOLITTLE. Not now. Another time, Governor.

HIGGINS (*handing him a five-pound note*). Here you are.

DOOLITTLE. Thank you, Governor. Good morning. (*He hurries to the door, anxious to get away with his booty. When he opens it he is confronted with a dainty and exquisitely clean young Japanese lady in a simple blue cotton kimono printed cunningly with small white jasmine blossoms.* MRS PEARCE *is with her. He gets out of her way deferentially and apologizes.*) Beg pardon, miss.

THE JAPANESE LADY. Garn! Dont you know your own daughter?

DOOLITTLE (*exclaiming simultaneously*) Bly me! it's Eliza!
HIGGINS Whats that! This!
PICKERING By Jove!

LIZA. Dont I look silly?

HIGGINS. Silly?

MRS PEARCE (*at the door*). Now, Mr Higgins, please dont say anything to make the girl conceited about herself.

HIGGINS (*conscientiously*). Oh! Quite right, Mrs Pearce. (*To* Eliza) Yes: damned silly.

MRS PEARCE. Please, sir.

In what way does Higgins almost immediately violate his promise to Mrs. Pearce?

HIGGINS (*correcting himself*). I mean extremely silly.

LIZA. I should look all right with my hat on. (*She takes up her hat; puts it on; and walks across the room to the fireplace with a fashionable air.*)

HIGGINS. A new fashion, by George! and it ought to look horrible!

DOOLITTLE (*with fatherly pride*). Well, I never thought she'd clean up as good looking as that, Governor. She's a credit to me, aint she ?

LIZA. I tell you, it's easy to clean up here. Hot and cold water on tap, just as much as you like, there is. Woolly towels, there is; and a towel horse[21] so hot, it burns your fingers. Soft brushes to scrub yourself, and a wooden bowl of soap smelling like primroses. Now I know why ladies is so clean. Washing's a treat for them. Wish they saw what it is for the like of me!

What does Liza's speech reveal about the plight of poor people in Shaw's day? How does this passage reveal Shaw's compassion?

HIGGINS. I'm glad the bathroom met with your approval.

LIZA. It didnt: not all of it; and I dont care who hears me say it. Mrs Pearce knows.

HIGGINS. What was wrong, Mrs Pearce?

MRS. PEARCE (*blandly*). Oh, nothing, sir. It doesnt matter.

LIZA. I had a good mind to break it. I didnt

21. **towel horse.** A metal rack with hot water in it to make towels warm

WORDS FOR EVERYDAY USE

con • sci • en • tious • ly (kän′ shē ən shəs lē) *adv.*, in an honest or painstaking manner. *By saving pennies conscientiously for sixty-two years, grandfather was able to retire to Florida.*

ANSWERS TO GUIDED READING QUESTIONS

1. Higgins uses inappropriate language.
2. Shaw points out that the reason the poor in his time were dirty is that they did not have adequate bathing facilities. It seems as if Shaw believes the poor should be provided with these necessities.

ADDITIONAL QUESTIONS AND ACTIVITIES

Explain to students that people have various ways of manipulating others, including bullying, coaxing, crying, and playing the martyr or victim. One technique commonly used by parents of very small children is to offer a reason to defer a proposed activity in the hopes that the desire for the activity will soon be forgotten. Pickering uses this manipulation strategy when he says to Liza that she should wait to confront her old acquaintances "til we get you something really fashionable." Higgins's actions are frequently directed toward controlling others and making them do as he wishes. Have students list other manipulation strategies used in this act of the play.

know which way to look. But I hung a towel over it, I did.

HIGGINS. Over what?

MRS PEARCE. Over the looking-glass, sir.

HIGGINS. Doolittle: you have brought your daughter up too strictly.

DOOLITTLE. Me! I never brought her up at all, except to give her a lick of a strap now and again. Dont put it on me, Governor. She aint accustomed to it, you see: thats all. But she'll soon pick up your free-and-easy ways.

LIZA. I'm a good girl, I am; and I wont pick up no free-and-easy ways.

HIGGINS. Eliza: if you say again that youre a good girl, your father shall take you home.

LIZA. Not him. You dont know my father. All he come here for was to touch you for some money to get drunk on.

DOOLITTLE. Well, what else would I want money for? To put into the plate in church, I suppose. (*She puts out her tongue at him. He is so incensed by this that* PICKERING *presently finds it necessary to step between them.*) Dont you give me none of your lip; and dont let me hear you giving this gentleman any of it neither, or youll hear from me about it. See?

HIGGINS. Have you any further advice to give her before you go, Doolittle? Your blessing, for instance.

DOOLITTLE. No, Governor: I aint such a mug as to put up my children to all I know myself. Hard enough to hold them in without that. If you want Eliza's mind improved, Governor, you do it yourself with a strap. So long, gentlemen. (*He turns to go.*)

HIGGINS (*impressively*). Stop. Youll come regularly to see your daughter. It's your duty, you know. My brother is a clergyman; and he could help you in your talks with her.

DOOLITTLE (*evasively*). Certainly. I'll come, Governor. Not just this week, because I have a job at a distance. But later on you may depend on me. Afternoon, gentlemen. Afternoon, maam. (*He takes off his hat to* MRS PEARCE, *who disdains the salutation and goes out. He winks at* HIGGINS, *thinking him probably a fellow sufferer from* MRS PEARCE*'s difficult disposition, and follows her.*)

LIZA. Dont you believe the old liar. He'd as soon you set a bull-dog on him as a clergyman. You wont see him again in a hurry.

HIGGINS. I dont want to, Eliza. Do you?

LIZA. Not me. I dont want never to see him again, I dont. He's a disgrace to me, he is, collecting dust, instead of working at his trade.

PICKERING. What is his trade, Eliza?

LIZA. Taking money out of other people's pockets into his own. His proper trade's a navvy;[22] and he works at it sometimes too—for exercise—and earns good money at it. Aint you going to call me Miss Doolittle any more?

PICKERING. I beg your pardon, Miss Doolittle. It was a slip of the tongue.

LIZA. Oh, I dont mind; only it sounded so genteel. I should just like to take a taxi to the corner of Tottenham Court Road and get out there and tell it to wait for me, just to put the girls in their place a bit. I wouldnt speak to them, you know.

PICKERING. Better wait til we get you something really fashionable.

22. **navvy.** Common laborer

WORDS FOR EVERYDAY USE

in • censed (in sensd') *adj.*, very angry; enraged. *I was incensed when the dry cleaners tried to charge me separately for the liner and the shell of my coat.*

dis • dain (dis dān') *vt.*, regard with contempt or scorn. *After the defendant had proved his innocence, he strode out of the court, disdaining his accusers.*

HIGGINS. Besides, you shouldnt cut your old friends now that you have risen in the world. Thats what we call snobbery.

LIZA. You dont call the like of them my friends now, I should hope. Theyve took it out of me often enough with their ridicule when they had the chance; and now I mean to get a bit of my own back. But if I'm to have fashionable clothes, I'll wait. I should like to have some. Mrs Pearce says youre going to give me some to wear in bed at night different to what I wear in the daytime; but it do seem a waste of money when you could get something to shew. Besides, I never could fancy changing into cold things on a winter night.

What elements in Liza's speech show that Shaw did not sentimentalize even his sympathetic characters?

MRS PEARCE (*coming back*). Now, Eliza. The new things have come for you to try on.

LIZA. Ah-ow-oo-ooh! (*She rushes out.*)

MRS PEARCE (*following her*). Oh, dont rush about like that, girl. (*She shuts the door behind her.*)

HIGGINS. Pickering: we have taken on a stiff job.

PICKERING (*with conviction*). Higgins: we have.

Respond *to the* SELECTION

Is Higgins motivated by a desire to help Liza or by some other reason?

ANSWER TO GUIDED READING QUESTION

1. By insisting that her old acquaintances are no longer her friends, Liza demonstrates that she is vindictive and ready to abandon those whom she once knew. In other words, Liza shows she has faults.

SELECTION CHECK TEST 4.12.3 WITH ANSWERS

Checking Your Reading

1. What does the flower girl offer to pay Higgins for? **She wants locution lessons.**
2. What bet does Pickering make with Higgins? **They wager on Higgins' ability to pass Liza off as a lady at the ambassador's garden party in six months.**
3. Why does Higgins think it would be easy to take Liza in? **She is alone and, in Higgins' mind, of no use to anyone.**
4. Who gets Liza cleaned up? **Mrs. Pearce gets Liza cleaned up.**
5. What does Doolittle promise to do with the money from Higgins? **Spend it unwisely.**

Vocabulary in Context

Fill each blank with the most appropriate word from the Words for Everyday Use. You may have to change the tense of the word.

callous plaint score astride
resolutely diffident ginger

1. Before hiring the contractor, we checked the Better Business Bureau for **plaints**.
2. A strong showing in the primaries put **ginger** into the tired campaign workers' efforts.
3. Elizabethan ladies tended to have a **diffident** manner and let others speak for them.
4. We lost sight of Ed as he climbed, but then spotted him proudly **astride** the peak.
5. The new FBI recruits **resolutely** stuck out their first day of training in the hot weather.

SELECTION CHECK TEST 4.12.3 WITH ANSWERS (CONT.)

Literary Tools

1. Describe the character of Liza. ***Responses will vary.***
2. What can you deduce about Higgins through his treatment of Liza? **He is dismissive and rude, and does not consider the feelings of other human beings.**
3. Identify a conflict that you see developing in the play. **There will be conflict between Higgins and Liza.**
4. What is satire? **Satire is humorous writing or speech intended to point out errors, falsehoods, foibles, or failings.**
5. What is a writer's purpose when he or she writes satire? **Writers use satire to reform human behavior or human institutions.**

RESPONDING TO THE SELECTION

Students might present their ideas in a role-play. Working in pairs, they can play Higgins and a friend who is assessing Higgins's plan.

ANSWERS FOR INVESTIGATE, INQUIRE, IMAGINE

RECALL

1a. Liza wants to change the way she speaks so that she can obtain a job selling flowers in a shop. Higgins tempts Liza by suggesting that if she learns from him, men will become interested in her and will give her chocolate, taxi rides, and gold and diamonds, and then she shall marry an officer.

2a. Higgins believes that men and women want to live different kinds of lives.

3a. Although Doolittle claims he wants her back, he repeatedly refuses opportunities to take her.

INTERPRET

1b. *Responses will vary.* Liza's desire to better her position indicates that she is not content with being a flower girl. Liza responds by saying that she is a good girl, implying that she cannot be bought by material rewards. Her reaction reveals that she cares for herself and has a strong moral sense.

2b. The relationship between Liza and Higgins reflects the conflict Higgins sees between the genders.

3b. Doolittle is trying to obtain money from Higgins without being accused of impropriety, just as Liza was trying to obtain money from Pickering.

ANALYZE

4a. *Responses will vary.* Doolittle is all for Liza making out well, as long as he gets something out of it. He cares little for her moral condition, though Liza cares a great deal about her moral condition. There is little love between them.

SYNTHESIZE

4b. *Responses will vary.* Pickering believes women should be treated well and with respect by men.

EVALUATE

5a. *Responses will vary.* In many respects Higgins is a misogynist. He treats women with contempt and often finds them silly. But Higgins does not seem to take a great deal of concern for others in general. Also, we have seen him interact mainly with women who are of a lower social class, so his actions are tinged by his classism as well.

EXTEND

5b. *Responses will vary.* The media still often project women as silly, flighty, emotional, and needing to be taken care of. They often show men as strong and unemotional and sometimes violent.

INVESTIGATE, Inquire, Imagine

Recall: GATHERING FACTS → **Interpret:** FINDING MEANING

1a. Why does Liza seek out Higgins? How does Higgins tempt Liza into accepting the lessons and being made into a lady?

1b. What does Liza's request reveal about her? What is revealed about Liza when she is tempted?

2a. According to Higgins, what is the basic trouble between men and women?

2b. In this act, which relationship characterizes the conflict Higgins sees between men and women?

3a. What is the flaw in Doolittle's claim that he wants his daughter back?

3b. Who shows the most concern for Liza's welfare in this act?

Analyze: TAKING THINGS APART → **Synthesize:** BRINGING THINGS TOGETHER

4a. Analyze the relationship between Liza and her father.

4a. Which man in this act has the highest opinion of women?

Evaluate: MAKING JUDGMENTS → **Extend:** CONNECTING IDEAS

5a. Evaluate whether Higgins is a misogynist.

5b. What prejudices about men and women are reflected in the media today?

Understanding Literature

SATIRE. Review the definition for **satire** in Literary Tools on page 1111. How do Doolittle's speeches satirize the upper and lower classes?

CHARACTER. Review the definition for **character** in the Handbook of Literary Terms and the chart you made for Literary Tools on page 1111. Which of Liza's character traits best show that she is a good match for Higgins? Which are signs that she will succeed in being tutored to speak better English and act like a lady?

ANSWERS TO UNDERSTANDING LITERATURE

SATIRE. Doolittle's speeches satirize the hypocrisy of both classes, because he pretends to have high standards only to extort money. He suggests that only the upper-class can afford to have moral standards.

CHARACTER. Liza is shrewd and careful of her character. She will be wary of Higgins taking advantage of her. She is clever and eager to learn, so she is likely to succeed.

ACT THREE

It is MRS HIGGINS'*s at-home day. Nobody has yet arrived. Her drawing room, in a flat*[1] *on Chelsea Embankment, has three windows looking on the river; and the ceiling is not so lofty as it would be in an older house of the same pretension. The windows are open, giving access to a balcony with flowers in pots. If you stand with your face to the windows, you have the fireplace on your left and the door in the right-hand wall close to the corner nearest the windows.*

MRS HIGGINS *was brought up on Morris*[2] *and Burne Jones;*[3] *and her room, which is very unlike her son's room in Wimpole Street, is not crowded with furniture and little tables and nicknacks. In the middle of the room there is a big ottoman;*[4] *and this, with the carpet, the Morris wall-papers, and the Morris chintz*[5] *window curtains and brocade covers of the ottoman and its cushions, supply all the ornament, and are much too handsome to be hidden by odds and ends of useless things. A few good oil-paintings from the exhibitions in the Grosvenor Gallery thirty years ago (the Burne Jones, not the Whistler*[6] *side of them) are on the walls. The only landscape is a Cecil Lawson*[7] *on the scale of a Rubens.*[8] *There is a portrait of Mrs Higgins as she was when she defied fashion in her youth in one of the beautiful Rossettian*[9] *costumes which, when caricatured by people who did not understand, led to the absurdities of popular estheticism in the eighteen-seventies.*

1. **flat.** Apartment or suite of rooms
2. **Morris.** William Morris (1834–1896), English artist and designer
3. **Burne Jones.** Sir Edward Coley Burne-Jones (1833–1898), English painter and designer
4. **ottoman.** Low cushioned seat without back or arms
5. **chintz.** Glazed cotton cloth, often printed with flowers or other colorful patterns
6. **Whistler.** James Abbot McNeill Whistler (1834–1903), U. S. painter and etcher
7. **Cecil Lawson.** English landscape painter (1851–1882)
8. **Rubens.** Peter Paul Rubens (1577–1640), Flemish painter who often painted on very large canvases
9. **Rossettian.** In the style of Dante Gabriel Rossetti (1828–1882), English poet and painter, brother of Christina Rossetti (see page 840)

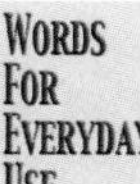

WORDS FOR EVERYDAY USE

pre • ten • sion (prē ten´shən) *n.,* a showy display of wealth. *His expensive car perfectly accorded with his vast house and other indications of pretension.*

bro • cade (brō kād´) *n.,* cloth with a raised design woven into it. *The weaver produced brocade belts on a small hand loom.*

car • i • ca • ture (kar´i kə chər´) *vi.,* depict in a style involving exaggeration for satirical effect. *When caricatured, people's idiosyncrosies are put into relief.*

es • thet • i cism (es thet´ə siz´əm) *n.,* doctrine that artistic principles should underlie values. *People who oppose estheticism deny that art is a means to achieving moral good, believing instead that art is an end in itself.*

Literary TOOLS

DRAMATIC IRONY. In **dramatic irony** something is known by the reader or audience but unknown to the characters. As you read, decide what dramatic irony Shaw provides in act 3.

BLOCKING. Blocking is the act of determining how actors will move on a stage. Blocking is almost always done by the director of the play. As you read, make a sketch of the set for act 3. Then mark where you would block the characters that are present for Liza's story at Mrs. Higgins's "at-home."

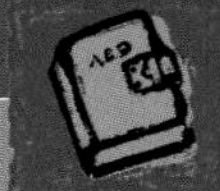

Reader's Journal

What topics do you discuss when you meet someone new in a social situation?

ADDITIONAL RESOURCES

UNIT 12 RESOURCE BOOK
- Selection Worksheet 12.3
- Selection Check Test 4.12.5
- Selection Test 4.12.6

READER'S JOURNAL

Students might brainstorm a list of conventional topics for small talk. Or have them try this activity:
Role play a meeting at a social gathering of people who do not know each other well. One character should be wildly out of place at such a gathering. Unplanned role playing can quickly lead to stereotyping. Remind students that they should not rely on stereotypes, but should try to make their characters original individuals.

VOCABULARY FROM THE SELECTION

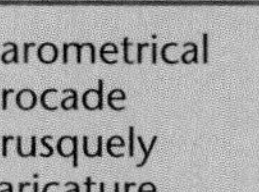

barometrical	imprecation
brocade	infatuated
brusquely	pedantic
caricature	pretension
convulsively	snigger
estheticism	soirée
forecastle	straiten

ANSWERS TO GUIDED READING QUESTIONS

1. Mrs. Higgins is dismayed to see Henry because he promised not to come on her at-home day.
2. Many people are driven away by Henry. He is not socially adept and has no small talk. People often find him annoying, abrasive, or otherwise off-putting.

CROSS-CURRICULAR ACTIVITIES

INTERIOR DECORATING. Students can write an updated, American version of the description of Mrs. Higgins's drawing room. Before they begin, they should consider what qualities of Mrs. Higgins Shaw was trying to convey by the decor of her drawing room and what contemporary art and furnishings would convey the same impression today.

ADDITIONAL QUESTIONS AND ACTIVITIES

Students can write short messages using a phonetic alphabet from a dictionary. After writing their messages, they can pair off, exchange what they have written with their partners, and decipher their partners' messages.

In the corner diagonally opposite the door MRS HIGGINS, *now over sixty and long past taking the trouble to dress out of the fashion, sits writing at an elegantly simple writing table with a bell button within reach of her hand. There is a Chippendale*[10] *chair further back in the room between her and the window nearest her side. At the other side of the room, further forward, is an Elizabethan chair roughly carved in the taste of Inigo Jones.*[11] *On the same side a piano in a decorated case. The corner between the fireplace and the window is occupied by a divan cushioned in Morris chintz.*

It is between four and five in the afternoon.

The door is opened violently; and HIGGINS *enters with his hat on.*

MRS HIGGINS (*dismayed*). Henry (*scolding him*)! What are you doing here today? It is my at-home day: you promised not to come. (*As he bends to kiss her, she takes his hat off, and presents it to him.*)

How does Mrs. Higgins feel about seeing Henry? Why?

HIGGINS. Oh bother! (*He throws the hat down on the table.*)

MRS HIGGINS. Go home at once.

HIGGINS (*kissing her*). I know, mother. I came on purpose.

MRS HIGGINS. But you mustnt. I'm serious, Henry. You offend all my friends: they stop coming whenever they meet you.

HIGGINS. Nonsense! I know I have no small talk; but people dont mind. (*He sits on the settee.*)

How do many people react to Higgins?

MRS HIGGINS. Oh! dont they? Small talk indeed! What about your large talk? Really, dear, you mustnt stay.

HIGGINS. I must. Ive a job for you. A phonetic job.

MRS HIGGINS. No use, dear, I'm sorry; but I cant get round your vowels; and though I like to get pretty postcards in your patent shorthand, I always have to read the copies in ordinary writing you so thoughtfully send me.

HIGGINS. Well, this isnt a phonetic job.

MRS HIGGINS. You said it was.

HIGGINS. Not your part of it. Ive picked up a girl.

MRS HIGGINS. Does that mean that some girl has picked you up?

HIGGINS. Not at all. I dont mean a love affair.

MRS HIGGINS. What a pity!

HIGGINS. Why?

MRS HIGGINS. Well, you never fall in love with anyone under forty-five. When will you discover that there are some rather nice-looking young women about?

HIGGINS. Oh, I cant be bothered with young women. My idea of a lovable woman is something as like you as possible. I shall never get into the way of seriously liking young women: some habits lie too deep to be changed. (*Rising abruptly and walking about, jingling his money and his keys in his trouser pockets*) Besides, theyre all idiots.

MRS HIGGINS. Do you know what you would do if you really loved me, Henry?

HIGGINS. Oh bother! What? Marry, I suppose?

MRS HIGGINS. No. Stop fidgeting and take your hands out of your pockets. (*With a gesture of despair, he obeys and sits down again.*) Thats a good boy. Now tell me about the girl.

HIGGINS. She's coming to see you.

MRS HIGGINS. I dont remember asking her.

HIGGINS. You didnt. *I* asked her. If youd known her you wouldnt have asked her.

MRS HIGGINS. Indeed! Why?

HIGGINS. Well, it's like this. She's a common flower girl. I picked her off the kerbstone.

---

10. **Chippendale.** Thomas Chippendale (1712–1779), English furniture-maker
11. **Inigo Jones.** English architect and stage designer

Mrs Higgins. And invited her to my at-home!

Higgins (*rising and coming to her to coax her*). Oh, thatll be all right. Ive taught her to speak properly; and she has strict orders as to her behavior. She's to keep to two subjects: the weather and everybody's health—Fine day and How do you do, you know—and not to let herself go on things in general. That will be safe.

Why has Higgins invited Liza to his mother's apartment?

Mrs Higgins. Safe! To talk about our health! about our insides! perhaps about our outsides! How could you be so silly, Henry?

Higgins (*impatiently*). Well, she must talk about something. (*He controls himself and sits down again.*) Oh, she'll be all right: dont you fuss. Pickering is in it with me. Ive a sort of bet on that I'll pass her off as a duchess in six months. I started on her some months ago; and she's getting on like a house on fire. I shall win my bet. She has a quick ear; and she's been easier to teach than my middle-class pupils because she's had to learn a complete new language. She talks English almost as you talk French.

Mrs Higgins. Thats satisfactory, at all events.

Higgins. Well, it is and it isnt.

Mrs Higgins. What does that mean?

Higgins. You see, Ive got her pronunciation all right; but you have to consider not only how a girl pronounces, but what she pronounces; and thats where—

(*They are interrupted by the* PARLORMAID *announcing guests.*)

What does Higgins's comment foreshadow?

The parlormaid. Mrs and Miss Eynsford Hill. (*She withdraws.*)

Higgins. Oh Lord! (*He rises; snatches his hat from the table; and makes for the door; but before he reaches it his mother introduces him.*)

(MRS *and* MISS EYNSFORD HILL *are the mother and daughter who sheltered from the rain in Covent Garden. The mother is well bred, quiet, and has the habitual anxiety of straitened means. The daughter has acquired a gay air of being very much at home in society: the bravado of genteel poverty.*)

Mrs Eynsford Hill (*to* MRS HIGGINS). How do you do? (*They shake hands.*)

Miss Eynsford Hill. How d'you do? (*She shakes.*)

Mrs Higgins (*introducing*). My son Henry.

Mrs Eynsford Hill. Your celebrated son! I have so longed to meet you, Professor Higgins.

Higgins (*glumly, making no movement in her direction*). Delighted. (*He backs against the piano and bows brusquely.*)

Miss Eynsford Hill (*going to him with confident familiarity*). How do you do?

Higgins (*staring at her*). Ive seen you before somewhere. I havnt the ghost of a notion where; but Ive heard your voice. (*Drearily*) It doesnt matter. Youd better sit down.

Mrs Higgins. I'm sorry to say that my celebrated son has no manners. You mustnt mind him.

Miss Eynsford Hill (*gaily*). I dont. (*She sits in the Elizabethan chair.*)

Mrs Eynsford Hill (*a little bewildered*). Not at all. (*She sits on the ottoman between her daughter and* MRS HIGGINS, *who has turned her chair away from the writing-table.*)

Words for Everyday Use

strait • ened (strāt´nd) *adj.*, subjected to privation or deficiency, especially of funds. *Although I wanted to go to the concert, I couldn't afford the ticket in my straitened circumstances.*

brusque • ly (brusk´lē) *adv.*, abrupt or curt in manner. *Though Jill spoke brusquely to me at first, when she found I had really not forgotten her birthday, she changed her tune.*

ANSWERS TO GUIDED READING QUESTIONS

1. Evidently Higgins has invited Liza to his mother's apartment as practice and as a test of her manners.
2. His comment foreshadows that Liza is likely to say something that is unconventional or considered out of place or improper.

ADDITIONAL QUESTIONS AND ACTIVITIES

Ask students the following questions:

1. What topics has Higgins permitted Liza to talk about? Are these safe choices?
2. What topics would you consider "safe" topics if you were guiding Liza?
3. How does this situation show that Higgins isn't particularly socially adept?

Answers

1. Higgins has permitted Liza to talk about health and the weather. Higgins thinks they are safe, but his mother does not.
2. *Responses will vary.* Students may find it easier to find topics that are not "safe."
3. Higgins thinks he has the situation under control. He is pretty sure that if Liza follows his rules about what to talk about, things will go fine. He doesn't really know how to make small talk, so he can't teach Liza how to do it.

LITERARY TECHNIQUE

Foreshadowing. Foreshadowing is the act of presenting materials that hint at events to occur later in a story. Have students consider what Higgins's comments might foreshadow. Ask students:

1. What is Higgins's idea of a lovable woman?
2. Does Higgins believe he is the kind of person who could become attached to a younger woman?
3. What significance do these remarks have in the play? Do you think they foreshadow Higgins's eventually falling in love with Liza, or his being unable to fall in love with Liza?

LITERARY TECHNIQUE (CONT.)

Answers

1. Higgins's idea of a lovable woman is someone as much like his mother as possible.
2. Higgins believes he will never seriously like a woman younger than himself.
3. *Responses will vary.* In a way, Higgins's comments foreshadow both of these outcomes: he does grow fond of Liza, but he is unable to view her in romantic terms.

ANSWER TO GUIDED READING QUESTION

1. First, he suggests that their arrival interrupted him. Then, he says they will do as well as anybody. Then, he says with a tone of annoyance or distaste, "another of them" as the last of the Eynsford Hills is introduced.

Quotables

"There is nothing so bad or so good that you will not find Englishmen doing it; but you will never find an Englishman in the wrong. He does everything on principle. He fights you on patriotic principles; he robs you on business principles; he enslaves you on imperial principles."

—Bernard Shaw

INTERNET RESOURCES

Students can learn more about Bernard Shaw at www.almaz.com/nobel/literature/1925a.html. Remind students that Shaw was a Nobel Prize winner. Students might also use the Internet to find other winners of the Nobel Prize for literature.

HIGGINS. Oh, have I been rude? I didnt mean to be.

(He goes to the central window, through which, with his back to the company, he contemplates the river and the flowers in Battersea Park on the opposite bank as if they were a frozen desert.)

(The PARLORMAID *returns, ushering in* PICKERING.*)*

THE PARLORMAID. Colonel Pickering. *(She withdraws.)*

PICKERING. How do you do, Mrs Higgins?

MRS HIGGINS. So glad youve come. Do you know Mrs Eynsford Hill—Miss Eynsford Hill? *(Exchange of bows. The* COLONEL *brings the Chippendale chair a little forward between* MRS HILL *and* MRS HIGGINS, *and sits down.)*

PICKERING. Has Henry told you what weve come for?

HIGGINS *(over his shoulder)*. We were interrupted: damn it!

MRS HIGGINS. Oh Henry, Henry, really!

MRS EYNSFORD HILL *(half rising)*. Are we in the way?

How is Henry rude to the Eynsford Hills?

MRS HIGGINS *(rising and making her sit down again)*. No, no. You couldnt have come more fortunately: we want you to meet a friend of ours.

HIGGINS *(turning hopefully)*. Yes, by George! We want two or three people. Youll do as well as anybody else.

(The PARLORMAID *returns, ushering in* FREDDY.*)*

THE PARLORMAID. Mr Eynsford Hill.

HIGGINS *(almost audibly, past endurance)*. God of Heaven! another of them.

FREDDY *(shaking hands with* MRS HIGGINS*)*. Ahdedo?

MRS HIGGINS. Very good of you to come. *(Introducing)* Colonel Pickering.

FREDDY *(bowing)*. Ahdedo?

MRS HIGGINS. I dont think you know my son, Professor Higgins.

FREDDY *(going to* HIGGINS*)*. Ahdedo?

HIGGINS *(looking at him much as if he were a pickpocket)*. I'll take my oath Ive met you before somewhere. Where was it?

FREDDY. I dont think so.

HIGGINS *(resignedly)*. It dont matter, anyhow. Sit down.

He shakes FREDDY's *hand, and almost slings him on to the ottoman with his face to the windows; then comes round to the other side of it.*

HIGGINS. Well, here we are, anyhow! *(He sits down on the ottoman next to* MRS EYNSFORD HILL, *on her left.)* And now, what the devil are we going to talk about until Eliza comes ?

MRS HIGGINS. Henry: you are the life and soul of the Royal Society's soirées; but really youre rather trying on more commonplace occasions.

HIGGINS. Am I? Very sorry. *(Beaming suddenly)* I suppose I am, you know. *(Uproariously)* Ha, ha!

MISS EYNSFORD HILL *(who considers* HIGGINS *quite eligible matrimonially)*. I sympathize. *I* havnt any small talk. If people would only be frank and say what they really think!

HIGGINS *(relapsing into gloom)*. Lord forbid!

MRS EYNSFORD HILL *(taking up her daughter's cue)*. But why?

HIGGINS. What they think they ought to think is bad enough, Lord knows; but what they

WORDS FOR EVERYDAY USE

soi • rée (swä rā´) *n.,* evening party. *The elegant soirée consisted of cocktails and hors-d'oeuvres followed by a sit-down dinner.*

really think would break up the whole show. Do you suppose it would be really agreeable if I were to come out now with what *I* really think?

MISS EYNSFORD HILL (*gaily*). Is it so very cynical?

HIGGINS. Cynical! Who the dickens said it was cynical? I mean it wouldnt be decent.

MRS EYNSFORD HILL (*seriously*). Oh! I'm sure you dont mean that, Mr Higgins.

HIGGINS. You see, we're all savages, more or less. We're supposed to be civilized and cultured—to know all about poetry and philosophy and art and science, and so on; but how many of us know even the meanings of these names? (*To* MISS HILL) What do you know of poetry? (*To* MRS HILL) What do you know of science? (*Indicating* FREDDY) What does he know of art or science or anything else? What the devil do you imagine I know of philosophy?

Why does Higgins say hypocrisy is necessary? What social function does is serve?

MRS HIGGINS (*warningly*). Or of manners, Henry?

THE PARLORMAID (*opening the door*). Miss Doolittle. (*She withdraws.*)

HIGGINS (*rising hastily and running to* MRS HIGGINS). Here she is, mother. (*He stands on tiptoe and makes signs over his mother's head to* ELIZA *to indicate to her which lady is her hostess.*)

(ELIZA, *who is exquisitely dressed, produces an impression of such remarkable distinction and beauty as she enters that they all rise, quite fluttered. Guided by* HIGGINS*'s signals, she comes to* MRS HIGGINS *with studied grace.*)

LIZA (*speaking with pedantic correctness of pronunciation and great beauty of tone*). How do you do, Mrs Higgins? (*She gasps slightly in making sure of the H in* HIGGINS, *but is quite successful.*) Mr Higgins told me I might come.

MRS HIGGINS (*cordially*). Quite right: I'm very glad indeed to see you.

PICKERING. How do you do, Miss Doolittle?

LIZA (*shaking hands with him*). Colonel Pickering, is it not?

MRS EYNSFORD HILL. I feel sure we have met before, Miss Doolittle. I remember your eyes.

LIZA. How do you do? (*She sits down on the ottoman gracefully in the place just left vacant by* HIGGINS.)

MRS EYNSFORD HILL (*introducing*). My daughter Clara.

LIZA. How do you do?

CLARA (*impulsively*). How do you do? (*She sits down on the ottoman beside* ELIZA, *devouring her with her eyes.*)

FREDDY (*coming to their side of the ottoman*). Ive certainly had the pleasure.

MRS EYNSFORD HILL (*introducing*). My son Freddy.

LIZA. How do you do?

(FREDDY *bows and sits down in the Elizabethan chair, infatuated.*)

HIGGINS (*suddenly*). By George, yes: it all comes back to me! (*They stare at him.*) Covent Garden! (*Lamentably*) What a damned thing!

MRS HIGGINS. Henry, please! (*He is about to sit on the edge of the table.*) Dont sit on my writing-table: youll break it.

HIGGINS (*sulkily*). Sorry.

(*He goes to the divan, stumbling into the fender and over the fire-irons on his way; extricating him-*

WORDS FOR EVERYDAY USE

pe • dan • tic (ped′′nt ik) *adj.*, in a manner stressing minor or trivial points of learning. *Lucia was bored by the professor's pedantic lecutre about different types of fungus.*

in • fat • u • at • ed (in fach′o͞ot′id) *adj.*, completely overcome by love. *The instant I saw Electra, twenty thousand volts leapt between her eyes and mine, and I was infatuated.*

ANSWER TO GUIDED READING QUESTION

1. According to Higgins, hypocrisy conceals the fact that people are really savages with no genuine knowledge of culture.

ADDITIONAL QUESTIONS AND ACTIVITIES

Discuss with students who demonstrates better manners when Liza first arrives, Higgins or Liza. Point out that Higgins was raised in an environment with good manners, as his mother demonstrates. Why, then, does he not behave better? What does this say about what manners really reflect?

Answers

Liza demonstrates better manners upon first arriving. Higgins does not use good manners because his personality interferes with his willingness to treat other people considerately. This suggests that manners sometimes do reflect a person's thoughtfulness toward others.

ADDITIONAL QUESTIONS AND ACTIVITIES

Ask students to evaluate Higgins' ideas about conventions. Ask them to think about things that they sometimes want to say but do not out of politeness. What purpose do such conventions serve? Are they beneficial?

ANSWERS TO GUIDED READING QUESTIONS

1. Liza seems to have derived this comment from a weather report in a newspaper. The answer is too detailed and technical for the situation.
2. Higgins says Liza is using the new "small talk."

ADDITIONAL QUESTIONS AND ACTIVITIES

Students can give examples of the "new small talk" of their own generation—that is, words they use in a special meaning among people their own age. Before citing examples, students should read the Language Arts Survey, 3.2, "Formal and Informal English."

self with muttered imprecations; and finishing his disastrous journey by throwing himself so impatiently on the divan that he almost breaks it. MRS HIGGINS *looks at him, but controls herself and says nothing. A long and painful pause ensues.)*

MRS HIGGINS (*at last, conversationally*). Will it rain, do you think?

LIZA. The shallow depression in the west of these islands is likely to move slowly in an easterly direction. There are no indications of any great change in the barometrical situation.

What is the source of Liza's answer? What makes this answer inappropriate and therefore humorous?

FREDDY. Ha! ha! how awfully funny!

LIZA. What is wrong with that, young man? I bet I got it right.

FREDDY. Killing!

MRS EYNSFORD HILL. I'm sure I hope it wont turn cold. Theres so much influenza about. It runs right through our whole family regularly every spring.

LIZA (*darkly*). My aunt died of influenza: so they said.

MRS EYNSFORD HILL (*clicks her tongue sympathetically*)!!!

LIZA (*in the same tragic tone*). But it's my belief they done the old woman in.

MRS HIGGINS (*puzzled*). Done her in?

LIZA. Y-e-e-e-es, Lord love you! Why should she die of influenza? She come through diphtheria right enough the year before. I saw her with my own eyes. Fairly blue with it, she was. They all thought she was dead; but my father he kept ladling gin down her throat til she came to so sudden that she bit the bowl off the spoon.

MRS EYNSFORD HILL (*startled*). Dear me!

LIZA (*piling up the indictment*). What call would a woman with that strength in her have to die of influenza? What become of her new straw hat that should have come to me? Somebody pinched it; and what I say is, them as pinched it done her in.

MRS EYNSFORD HILL. What does doing her in mean?

HIGGINS. (*hastily*). Oh, thats the new small talk. To do a person in means to kill them.

How does Higgins explain Eliza's use of "doing someone in"?

MRS EYNSFORD HILL (*to* ELIZA, *horrified*). You surely dont believe that your aunt was killed?

LIZA. Do I not! Them she lived with would have killed her for a hat-pin, let alone a hat.

MRS EYNSFORD HILL. But it cant have been right for your father to pour spirits down her throat like that. It might have killed her.

LIZA. Not her. Gin was mother's milk to her. Besides, he'd poured so much down his own throat that he knew the good of it.

MRS EYNSFORD HILL. Do you mean that he drank?

LIZA. Drank! My word! Something chronic.

MRS EYNSFORD HILL. How dreadful for you!

LIZA. Not a bit. It never did him no harm what I could see. But then he did not keep it up regular. (*Cheerfully*) On the burst, as you might say, from time to time. And always more agreeable when he had a drop in. When he was out of work, my mother used to give him fourpence and tell him to go out and not come back until he'd drunk himself cheerful and loving-like. Theres lots of women has to make their husbands drunk to make them fit to live with. (*Now quite at her ease*) You see, it's like this. If a

WORDS FOR EVERYDAY USE

im • pre • ca • tion (im´pri kā´shən) *n.*, obscene language; curse. *The alert bank guard suspected the priest was phony when he saw him stub his toe and mutter a string of imprecations.*

bar • o • met • ri • cal (bar´ə me´trik əl) *adj.*, referring to atmospheric pressure. *A simple container of properly blown glass can be an accurate barometrical instrument.*

man has a bit of a conscience, it always takes him when he's sober; and then it makes him low-spirited. A drop of booze just takes that off and makes him happy. (*To* FREDDY, *who is in convulsions of suppressed laughter*) Here! what are you sniggering at?

FREDDY. The new small talk. You do it so awfully well.

LIZA. If I was doing it proper, what was you laughing at? (*To* HIGGINS) Have I said anything I oughtnt?

MRS HIGGINS (*interposing*). Not at all, Miss Doolittle.

LIZA. Well, thats a mercy, anyhow. (*Expansively*) What I always say is—

HIGGINS (*rising and looking at his watch*). Ahem!

LIZA (*looking round at him; taking the hint; and rising*). Well: I must go. (*They all rise.* FREDDY *goes to the door.*) So pleased to have met you. Goodbye. (*She shakes hands with* MRS HIGGINS.)

MRS HIGGINS. Goodbye.

LIZA. Goodbye, Colonel Pickering.

PICKERING. Goodbye, Miss Doolittle. (*They shake hands.*)

LIZA (*nodding to the others*). Goodbye, all.

FREDDY (*opening the door for her*). Are you walking across the Park, Miss Doolittle? If so—

LIZA. Walk! Not bloody likely. (*Sensation.*) I am going in a taxi. (*She goes out.*)

WORDS FOR EVERYDAY USE

snig • ger • (snig´ər) *vi.,* laugh in a derisive manner. *The maitre d' sniggered at the homeless man when he asked for a table.*

ADDITIONAL QUESTIONS AND ACTIVITIES

Ask students the following questions:

1. Imagine what the conversation would have been like if Liza had not been present. Would it have been more or less interesting? Why?
2. Imagine how Higgins would have answered Liza's question, "Have I said anything I oughtnt" if Mrs. Higgins had not interposed. Does Mrs. Higgins believe what she said? Why did she answer in this way?

Answers

1. The conversation probably would have been very conventional if Liza had not been present. Higgins may have made it less than pleasant with his abrupt manner and lack of conversational skills. But without Liza's freshness, the conversation would likely have followed a genteel pattern and the visitation would have ended pleasantly, but dully.
2. Higgins might have agreed with his mother that Liza has said nothing wrong. However, his response would be based on a belief that she had said nothing wrong, while his mother's response was most likely based on a desire to make her guest feel comfortable.

ANSWERS TO GUIDED READING QUESTIONS

1. Liza's use of the word bloody causes a sensation. Many of her comments are out of place in such a gathering, beginning with her remark that "they done the old woman in," and continuing through her story of her aunt's illness.
2. Freddy and Clara find Liza quite amusing and original. They are pleased to have met her. Mrs. Eynsford Hill is a bit shocked by Liza, but she seems to think it is something wrong with a whole generation. In fact she sees that her own daughter uses expressions that she does not consider proper.

LITERARY NOTE

Some literary critics believe that Shaw paralleled the classical myth of Pygmalion by making Liza pass through three stages: first she was the flower girl (corresponding to the unformed ivory from which the mythic Pygmalion made his statue), then the "triumph" of Higgins's art (corresponding to the statue), and finally a free and independent woman (corresponding to the statue brought to life). Discuss this theory with students. In what sense is Liza like a statue in this scene? In what sense is she simply her constantly irrepressible, lively self? In what sense is Higgins a sculptor?

Answers

Liza is like a statue only in her attempt to live up to the norm established by her "sculptor," Professor Higgins. When she dips into her own life for material for conversation, she is fresh, original, and lively. Higgins tries to "sculpt" or control Liza, treating her like an inanimate object until she is molded in the shape he wants.

(PICKERING *gasps and sits down.* FREDDY *goes out on the balcony to catch another glimpse of* ELIZA.)

What in Liza's response causes a sensation? What comments by her throughout the scene are out of place in a society gathering?

MRS EYNSFORD HILL (*suffering from shock*). Well, I really cant get used to the new ways.

CLARA (*throwing herself discontentedly into the Elizabethan chair*). Oh, it's all right, mamma, quite right. People will think we never go anywhere or see anybody if you are so old-fashioned.

MRS EYNSFORD HILL. I daresay I am very old-fashioned; but I do hope you wont begin using that expression, Clara. I have got accustomed to hear you talking about men as rotters, and calling everything filthy and beastly; though I do think it horrible and unladylike. But this last is really too much. Don't you think so, Colonel Pickering?

PICKERING. Don't ask me. Ive been away in India for several years; and manners have changed so much that I sometimes dont know whether I'm at a respectable dinnertable or in a ship's forecastle.

How have Freddy, Clara, and their mother interpreted Liza's odd comments?

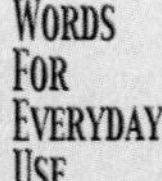

CLARA. It's all a matter of habit. Theres no right or wrong in it. Nobody means anything by it. And it's so quaint, and gives such a smart emphasis to things that are not in themselves very witty. I find the new small talk delightful and quite innocent.

MRS EYNSFORD HILL (*rising*). Well, after that, I think it's time for us to go.

(PICKERING *and* HIGGINS *rise.*)

CLARA (*rising*). Oh yes: we have three at-homes to go to still. Goodbye, Mrs. Higgins. Goodbye, Colonel Pickering. Goodbye, Professor Higgins.

HIGGINS (*coming grimly at her from the divan, and accompanying her to the door*). Goodbye. Be sure you try on that small talk at the three at-homes. Dont be nervous about it. Pitch it in strong.

CLARA (*all smiles*). I will. Goodbye. Such nonsense, all this early Victorian prudery!

HIGGINS (*tempting her*). Such damned nonsense!

CLARA. Such bloody nonsense!

MRS EYNSFORD HILL (*convulsively*). Clara!

CLARA. Ha! ha! (*She goes out radiant, conscious of being thoroughly up to date, and is heard descending the stairs in a stream of silvery laughter.*)

FREDDY (*to the heavens at large*). Well, I ask you—(*He gives it up, and comes to* MRS HIGGINS.) Goodbye.

MRS HIGGINS (*shaking hands*). Goodbye. Would you like to meet Miss Doolittle again?

FREDDY (*eagerly*). Yes, I should, most awfully.

MRS HIGGINS. Well, you know my days.

FREDDY. Yes. Thanks awfully. Goodbye. (*He goes out.*)

MRS EYNSFORD HILL. Goodbye, Mr Higgins.

HIGGINS. Goodbye. Goodbye.

MRS EYNSFORD HILL (*to* PICKERING). It's no use. I shall never be able to bring myself to use that word.

PICKERING. Dont. It's not compulsory, you know. Youll get on quite well without it.

MRS EYNSFORD HILL. Only, Clara is so down on me if I am not positively reeking with the latest slang. Goodbye.

PICKERING. Goodbye. (*They shake hands.*)

WORDS FOR EVERYDAY USE

fore • cas • tle (fōk´s'l) *n.*, crew's quarters in the front of a merchant ship. *Freep, the new communications specialist, found the place that would be his bunk for the next century in the forecastle of the space cruiser.*

con • vul • sive • ly (kən vul´siv lē) *adv.*, in an agitated manner. *Any attempt we made to approach the fence made the guard dog lunge convulsively at the wire mesh.*

MRS EYNSFORD HILL (*to* MRS HIGGINS). You mustnt mind Clara. (PICKERING, *catching from her lowered tone that this is not meant for him to hear, discreetly joins* HIGGINS *at the window.*) We're so poor! and she gets so few parties, poor child! She doesnt quite know. (MRS HIGGINS, *seeing that her eyes are moist, takes her hand sympathetically and goes with her to the door.*) But the boy is nice. Dont you think so?

MRS HIGGINS. Oh, quite nice. I shall always be delighted to see him.

MRS EYNSFORD HILL. Thank you, dear. Goodbye. (*She goes out.*)

HIGGINS (*eagerly*). Well? Is Eliza presentable? (*He swoops on his mother and drags her to the ottoman, where she sits down in* ELIZA's *place with her son on her left.*)

(PICKERING *returns to his chair on her right.*)

MRS HIGGINS. You silly boy, of course she's not presentable. She's a triumph of your art and of her dressmaker's; but if you suppose for a moment that she doesnt give herself away in every sentence she utters, you must be perfectly cracked about her.

What is Mrs. Higgins's assessment of Eliza's progress?

PICKERING. But dont you think something might be done? I mean something to eliminate the sanguinary[12] element from her conversation.

MRS HIGGINS. Not as long as she is in Henry's hands.

HIGGINS (*aggrieved*). Do you mean that my language is improper?

MRS HIGGINS. No, dearest: it would be quite proper—say on a canal barge; but it would not be proper for her at a garden party.

HIGGINS (*deeply injured*). Well I must say—

PICKERING (*interrupting him*). Come, Higgins: you must learn to know yourself. I havnt heard such language as yours since we used to review the volunteers in Hyde Park twenty years ago.

HIGGINS (*sulkily*). Oh, well, if you say so, I suppose I dont always talk like a bishop.

MRS HIGGINS (*quieting* HENRY *with a touch*). Colonel Pickering: will you tell me what is the exact state of things in Wimpole Street?

PICKERING (*cheerfully: as if this completely changed the subject*). Well, I have come to live there with Henry. We work together at my Indian Dialects; and we think it more convenient—

MRS HIGGINS. Quite so. I know all about that: it's an excellent arrangement. But where does this girl live?

HIGGINS. With us, of course. Where should she live?

MRS HIGGINS. But on what terms? Is she a servant? If not, what is she?

PICKERING (*slowly*). I think I know what you mean, Mrs Higgins.

HIGGINS. Well, dash me if *I* do! Ive had to work at the girl every day for months to get her to her present pitch. Besides, she's useful. She knows where my things are, and remembers my appointments and so forth.

What does Higgins like about Eliza?

MRS HIGGINS. How does your housekeeper get on with her?

HIGGINS. Mrs Pearce? Oh, she's jolly glad to get so much taken off her hands; for before Eliza came, she used to have to find things and remind me of my appointments. But she's got some silly bee in her bonnet about Eliza. She keeps saying "You dont think, sir": doesnt she, Pick?

PICKERING. Yes: thats the formula. "You dont think, sir." Thats the end of every conversation about Eliza.

12. **sanguinary.** Realated to blood; a reference to Liza's conversational use of the slang term *bloody*

ANSWERS TO GUIDED READING QUESTIONS

1. Mrs. Higgins does not think that Liza is at all presentable. She is dressed properly and pronounces her words properly, but she does not speak or act naturally in conventional ways for the class Higgins wants her to appear to be from.
2. Higgins thinks Liza is useful. She helps him find his things and remember his appointments.

ADDITIONAL QUESTIONS AND ACTIVITIES

Suggest to students that the basis of personal change is self-awareness. Higgins's character remains constant throughout the play because he never gains any awareness of his own character. "Come, Higgins," says Pickering, "you must learn to know yourself"; yet Higgins never does. Students can write in their journals to explain ways that they can become self-aware and open to personality growth.

ANSWER TO GUIDED READING QUESTION

1. Learning to blend into a new social class requires more than simply changing speech and dress. Higgins does not seem concerned that he is not giving Liza the knowledge and interests that go along with the class she is supposedly entering.

ADDITIONAL QUESTIONS AND ACTIVITIES

Ask students the following questions to explore the material on this page.

1. Why, do you think, are Mrs. Pearce and Mrs. Higgins so sure that Liza's future will be a problem?
2. Why do Higgins and Pickering refuse to face the "problem" of what is to become of Liza when the experiment is over?

Answers

1. Both Mrs. Pearce and Mrs. Higgins are more perceptive and far-seeing than Higgins and Pickering; they also have an innate sympathy for Liza as a woman.
2. *Responses will vary.* One possible reason is that Higgins and Pickering are enjoying Liza's company so much that they are avoiding the thought that the situation will change.

HIGGINS. As if I ever stop thinking about the girl and her confounded vowels and consonants. I'm worn out, thinking about her, and watching her lips and her teeth and her tongue, not to mention her soul, which is the quaintest of the lot.

MRS HIGGINS. You certainly are a pretty pair of babies, playing with your live doll.

HIGGINS. Playing! The hardest job I ever tackled: make no mistake about that, mother. But you have no idea how frightfully interesting it is to take a human being and change her into a quite different human being by creating a new speech for her. It's filling up the deepest gulf that separates class from class and soul from soul.

Can a person's social class be changed simply by a change in speech and dress? What is Higgins failing to understand?

PICKERING (*drawing his chair closer to* MRS HIGGINS *and bending over to her eagerly*). Yes: it's enormously interesting. I assure you, Mrs Higgins, we take Eliza very seriously. Every week—every day almost—there is some new change. (*Closer again*) We keep records of every stage—dozens of gramophone disks[13] and photographs—

HIGGINS (*assailing her at the other ear*). Yes, by George: it's the most absorbing experiment I ever tackled. She regularly fills our lives up: doesnt she, Pick?

PICKERING. We're always talking Eliza.

HIGGINS. Teaching Eliza.

PICKERING. Dressing Eliza.

MRS HIGGINS. What!

HIGGINS. Inventing new Elizas.

HIGGINS. (*speaking together*) You know, she has the most extraordinary quickness of ear:

PICKERING. I assure you, my dear Mrs Higgins, that girl

HIGGINS. just like a parrot. Ive tried her with every—

PICKERING. is a genius. She can play the piano quite beautifully.

HIGGINS. possible sort of sound that a human being can make—

PICKERING. We have taken her to classical concerts and to music

HIGGINS. Continental dialects, African dialects, Hottentot

PICKERING. halls; and it's all the same to her: she plays everything

HIGGINS. clicks, things it took me years to get hold of; and

PICKERING. she hears right off when she comes home, whether it's

HIGGINS. she picks them up like a shot, right away, as if she had

PICKERING. Beethoven and Brahms or Lehar and Lionel Monckton;

HIGGINS. been at it all her life.

PICKERING. though six months ago, she'd never as much as touched a piano—

MRS HIGGINS (*putting her fingers in her ears, as they are by this time shouting one another down with an intolerable noise*). Shsh-sh—sh! (*They stop.*)

PICKERING. I beg your pardon. (*He draws his chair back apologetically.*)

HIGGINS. Sorry. When Pickering starts shouting nobody can get a word in edgeways.

MRS HIGGINS. Be quiet, Henry. Colonel Pickering: dont you realize that when Eliza walked into Wimpole Street, something walked in with her?

PICKERING. Her father did. But Henry soon got rid of him.

MRS HIGGINS. It would have been more to the point if her mother had. But as her mother didnt something else did.

---

13. **gramophone disks.** Phonograph records

PICKERING. But what?

MRS HIGGINS (*unconsciously dating herself by the word*). A problem.

PICKERING. Oh, I see. The problem of how to pass her off as a lady.

HIGGINS. I'll solve that problem. Ive half solved it already.

MRS HIGGINS. No, you two infinitely stupid male creatures: the problem of what is to be done with her afterwards.

HIGGINS. I dont see anything in that. She can go her own way, with all the advantages I have given her.

MRS HIGGINS. The advantages of that poor woman who was here just now! The manners and habits that disqualify a fine lady from earning her own living without giving her a fine lady's income! Is that what you mean?

PICKERING (*indulgently, being rather bored*). Oh, that will be all right, Mrs Higgins. (*He rises to go.*)

HIGGINS (*rising also*). We'll find her some light employment.

PICKERING. She's happy enough. Dont you worry about her. Goodbye. (*He shakes her hands as if he were consoling a frightened child, and makes for the door.*)

HIGGINS. Anyhow, theres no good bothering now. The thing's done. Goodbye, mother. (*He kisses her, and follows* PICKERING.)

PICKERING (*turning for a final consolation*). There are plenty of openings. We'll do whats right. Goodbye.

HIGGINS (*to* PICKERING *as they go out together*). Let's take her to the Shakespear exhibition at Earls Court.

PICKERING. Yes: lets. Her remarks will be delicious.

HIGGINS. She'll mimic all the people for us when we get home.

PICKERING. Ripping.[14] (*Both are heard laughing as they go downstairs.*)

MRS HIGGINS (*rises with an impatient bounce, and returns to her work at the writing-table. She sweeps a litter of disarranged papers out of her way; snatches a sheet of paper from her stationery case; and tries resolutely to write. At the third line she gives it up; flings down her pen; grips the table angrily and exclaims*). Oh, men! men!! men!!!

Why does Mrs. Higgins make this exclamation? What characteristic is she imputing to all men?

14. **ripping.** British slang for splendid, excellent

Respond *to the* SELECTION

At this point, would you call Higgins's experiment with Liza a success or a failure?

ANSWER TO GUIDED READING QUESTION

1. Mrs. Higgins is exasperated, presumably because Higgins and Pickering refuse to take seriously her objection that her new speech and habits will disqualify Liza from any way of making a living. She seems to impute to all men this stubborn refusal to listen to common sense.

SELECTION CHECK TEST 4.12.5 WITH ANSWERS

Checking Your Reading

1. When Henry arrives, what does his mother ask him to do? **She asks him to leave.**
2. Liza is allowed to discuss what two subjects? **She may talk of weather and health.**
3. Where have the Eynsford Hills and Liza met before? **They met at Covent Garden.**
4. What does Higgins encourage Miss Eynsford Hill to do at her next party? **He tells her to use the "new slang."**
5. What extraordinary talent does Liza have? **She has quickness of ear—she can play the piano by ear and can mimic any accent.**

Vocabulary in Context

Fill each blank with the most appropriate word from the Words for Everyday Use. You may have to change the tense of the word.

brusquely pedantic soiree
caricature imprecation straiten
snigger

1. The treasurer's sloppy bookkeeping landed our club in **straitened** circumstances.
2. Elsa had never been to a **soiree** and eagerly opened the invitation.
3. After my awkward presentation, I could hear **sniggers** from the back of the room.
4. The ship's captain **brusquely** asked the passengers to leave the bridge.
5. The character was a thinly veiled **caricature** of a famous politician.

Literary Tools

1. What is irony? **Irony is the difference between appearance and reality.**
2. What does the audience know about Liza that the Eynsford Hills do not? **The audience know that she is from a lower class.**
3. What does Mrs. Higgins understand about Liza that Higgins and

SELECTION CHECK TEST 4.12.5 WITH ANSWERS (CONT.)

Pickering do not? **She understands the difficulty they've created for Liza's future.**

4. Who is generally responsible for blocking a set? **The director blocks the set.**
5. Draw a picture of the set, blocking as it would look in Act 3. **The drawings should follow the description at the beginning of Act 3.**

RESPOND TO THE SELECTION

If students think the experiment is going successfully, what do they think Higgins must to continue with this success? If they think the experiment is a failure, what would Higgins have to do to change the course of the experiment and turn it into a success? Also ask students to consider how the experiment is going for both Higgins and Liza.

ANSWERS FOR INVESTIGATE, INQUIRE, IMAGINE

Recall

1a. Higgins admits that he cannot make small talk.

2a. Henry brings Liza to his mother's house as a test to see what kind of progress he is making with her.

3a. Mrs. Higgins believes that Liza will be given the manners of a fine lady without any way of earning the income necessary to live like a fine lady.

Interpret

1b. Higgins's social skills are very poor. He is rude, stubborn, and thoughtless.

2b. Liza's choice of topics is inappropriate. She also uses language that is too detailed or technical when she first arrives and later uses language that is too colloquial or slang for the situation.

3b. Mrs. Higgins is less impulsive than Higgins. She does not insist on having her own way. She is considerate of others.

Analyze

4a. *Responses will vary.* Mrs. Eynsford Hill is sympathetic but horrified; Freddy and Clara are delighted at Liza's manner of telling the story, and do not seem to object to its subject manner. Their reactions indicate that a situation such a s Liza describes is completely foreign to their experience.

Synthesize

4b. *Responses will vary.* These reactions reveal that the situations Liza describes are foreign to them. Freddy and Clara enjoy a less formal, lively, and fresh conversation. Mrs. Eynsford Hill is conventional but sympathetic to suffering.

Evaluate

5a. *Responses will vary.* Higgins thinks things went quite well. He suspected there might be some problems because Liza would not know what to talk about. She stuck to the subjects he gave her—health and the weather—and, he thought, got along quite nicely. Higgins's perception is clouded by his own inability to interact socially.

Extend

5b. *Responses will vary.* Education is very important. This scene highlights Mrs. Higgins's concern that what Liza is learning will not leave her fit to make a living. This suggests that education must be linked to the goals it is meant to serve.

Investigate, Inquire, Imagine

Recall: Gathering Facts → **Interpret: Finding Meaning**

1a. When he arrives at his mother's, what skill does Higgins admit that he lacks?

2a. Why does Higgins bring Liza to his mother's?

3a. What problem does Mrs. Higgins foresee for Higgins's experiment with Liza?

1b. What does the action of this scene show about Higgins's social skills?

2b. What is inappropriate about Liza's performance?

3b. How does Mrs. Higgins differ from her son?

Analyze: Taking Things Apart → **Synthesize: Bringing Things Together**

4a. Analyze the reactions of the Eynsford Hills to Liza's story.

4b. What do the reactions of the Eynsford Hills reveal about them?

Evaluate: Making Judgments → **Extend: Connecting Ideas**

5a. Evaluate whether the outcome of the at-home day was what Higgins expected.

5b. What idea does *Pygmalion* present about the importance of education in securing equality for women?

Understanding Literature

Dramatic Irony. Review the definition for **dramatic irony** in Literary Tools on page 1131. What does the audience or reader know about Liza that the other guests at the at-home do not know? What makes Liza's telling about her aunt's death humorous? Why is it funny when Freddy becomes infatuated by Liza and her command of "the new small talk"?

Blocking. Review the definition for **blocking** in the Handbook of Literary Terms and the blocking map you made for Literary Tools on page 1131. What did you take into consideration when blocking the scene in which Liza tells her story?

ANSWERS TO UNDERSTANDING LITERATURE

Dramatic Irony. The audience is aware that Liza is from the lower class, while the Eynsford Hills are not. The humor of the story Liza tells lies in the fact that the Eynsford Hills interpret it in terms of their own background, and imagine Liza experiencing it as a member of the middle class. Freddy's infatuation with Liza is ludicrous because he is ignorant of her background and identity. He thinks the words and phrases she chooses are the new small talk, not realizing that they indicate the social class in which she was raised.

Blocking. Students should take into consideration Liza's dramatic story telling, Freddy's interest in Liza, and Higgins's generally restless nature.

ACT FOUR

The Wimpole Street laboratory. Midnight. Nobody in the room. The clock on the mantelpiece strikes twelve. The fire is not alight: it is a summer night.

Presently HIGGINS *and* PICKERING *are heard on the stairs.*

HIGGINS (*calling down to* PICKERING). I say, Pick: lock up, will you? I shant be going out again.

PICKERING. Right. Can Mrs Pearce go to bed? We dont want anything more, do we?

HIGGINS. Lord, no!

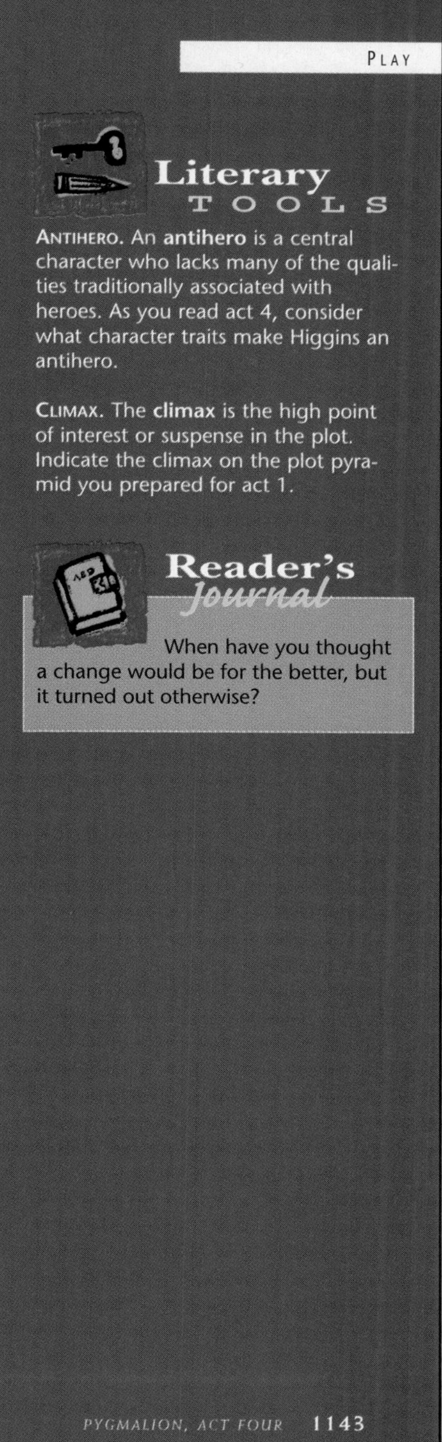

Literary TOOLS

ANTIHERO. An **antihero** is a central character who lacks many of the qualities traditionally associated with heroes. As you read act 4, consider what character traits make Higgins an antihero.

CLIMAX. The **climax** is the high point of interest or suspense in the plot. Indicate the climax on the plot pyramid you prepared for act 1.

Reader's Journal

When have you thought a change would be for the better, but it turned out otherwise?

ADDITIONAL RESOURCES

UNIT 12 RESOURCE BOOK
- Selection Worksheet 12.4
- Selection Check Test 4.12.7
- Selection Test 4.12.8

ENGLISH LANGUAGE LEARNING

Additional Vocabulary for Act 4 is listed below:
flinch—draw back in fear or pain
gorge—stuff, eat a lot
superlatively—better than any other
trivial—unimportant
cant—insincere talk
lavish—spend extravagantly

GRAPHIC ORGANIZER

Climax—Liza throws the slippers at Higgins and argues with him about the way he treated her.

READER'S JOURNAL

Students who have difficulty identifying such a change can consider those points in life when changes usually occur—moving from one place to another or from one grade in school to another, or adopting a new schedule.

VOCABULARY FROM THE SELECTION

condescend, coroneted, dudgeon, millennium, pallor, perfunctorily, purgatory

ANSWERS TO GUIDED READING QUESTIONS

1. Pickering is learning that Mrs. Pearce becomes upset when people act like slobs and leave their clothing lying around.
2. The "love letter" turns out to be a bill from a moneylender. Higgins has no room in his life for romance; he is too self-absorbed.
3. Higgins fails to notice that Liza has brought him his slippers.

LITERARY NOTE

Ask students if they notice the mistake of the playwright in the first stage direction of Act Four.

Answer

In the stage direction, Shaw states that it is a summer night; however, six months have passed since the events of Act One, which (according to the stage direction there) took place during "a heavy summer rain."

Such errors by authors are not uncommon. A famous error, or perhaps intentional misdirection, by Shakespeare sets Scene iii of Act III of *The Winter's Tale* in a region near the sea in Bohemia. (Bohemia is a landlocked region far from the sea.)

(ELIZA *opens the door and is seen on the lighted landing in opera cloak, brilliant evening dress, and diamonds, with fan, flowers, and all accessories. She comes to the hearth and switches on the electric lights there. She is tired: her* pallor *contrasts strongly with her dark eyes and hair; and her expression is almost tragic. She takes off her cloak; puts her fan and flowers on the piano; and sits down on the bench, brooding and silent.* HIGGINS, *in evening dress, with overcoat and hat, comes in, carrying a smoking jacket which he has picked up downstairs. He takes off the hat and overcoat; throws them carelessly on the newspaper stand; disposes of his coat in the same way; puts on the smoking jacket; and throws himself wearily into the easy-chair at the hearth.* PICKERING, *similarly attired, comes in. He also takes off his hat and overcoat, and is about to throw them on* HIGGINS*'s when he hesitates.*)

PICKERING. I say: Mrs Pearce will row if we leave these things lying about in the drawing room.

HIGGINS. Oh, chuck them over the bannisters into the hall. She'll find them there in the morning and put them away all right. She'll think we were drunk.

What is Pickering learning about Mrs. Pearce that Higgins has not learned?

PICKERING. We are, slightly. Are there any letters?

HIGGINS. I didnt look. (PICKERING *takes the overcoats and hats and goes downstairs,* HIGGINS *begins half singing half yawning an air from La Fanciulla del Golden West.*[1] *Suddenly he stops and exclaims*) I wonder where the devil my slippers are!

(ELIZA *looks at him darkly; then rises suddenly and leaves the room.* HIGGINS *yawns again, and resumes his song.* PICKERING *returns, with the contents of the letter-box in his hand.*)

PICKERING. Only circulars, and this coroneted billet-doux[2] for you. (*He throws the circulars into the fender, and posts himself on the hearthrug, with his back to the grate.*)

What is ironic about Pickering's comment and the actual contents of the letter? What isn't a part of Higgins's life? Why might that be so?

HIGGINS (*glancing at the billet-doux*). Moneylender. (*He throws the letter after the circulars.*)

(ELIZA *returns with a pair of large down-at-heel slippers. She places them on the carpet before* HIGGINS, *and sits as before without a word.*)

HIGGINS (*yawning again*). Oh Lord! What an evening! What a crew! What a silly tomfoolery! (*He raises his shoe to unlace it, and catches sight of the slippers. He stops unlacing and looks at them as if they had appeared there of their own accord.*) Oh! theyre there, are they?

What does Higgins fail to notice?

PICKERING (*stretching himself*). Well, I feel a bit tired. It's been a long day. The garden party, a dinner party, and the opera! Rather too much of a good thing. But youve won your bet, Higgins. Eliza did the trick, and something to spare, eh?

HIGGINS (*fervently*). Thank God it's over!

(ELIZA *flinches violently; but they take no notice of her; and she recovers herself and sits stonily as before.*)

PICKERING. Were you nervous at the garden party? *I* was. Eliza didnt seem a bit nervous.

HIGGINS. Oh, she wasnt nervous. I knew she'd be all right. No: it's the strain of putting the job through all these months that has told on me. It was interesting enough at first, while we were at

1. **La Fanciulla del Golden West.** An opera by Puccini, *The Girl of the Golden West*
2. **billet-doux.** French term for a love letter (literally, a "letter sweet")

WORDS FOR EVERYDAY USE

pal • lor (pal´ər) *n.*, unnatural paleness. *A few days in the sun after exams will banish your bookish* pallor.

cor • o • net • ed (kôr´ə net´id) *adj.*, with a band of ornamentation. *The duchess arrived at the ball in a* coroneted *carriage.*

the phonetics; but after that I got deadly sick of it. If I hadnt backed myself to do it I should have chucked the whole thing up two months ago. It was a silly notion: the whole thing has been a bore.

What interested Higgins? In what did he fail to show interest? What does his failure reveal about his character?

PICKERING. Oh come! the garden party was frightfully exciting. My heart began beating like anything.

HIGGINS. Yes, for the first three minutes. But when I saw we were going to win hands down, I felt like a bear in a cage, hanging about doing nothing. The dinner was worse: sitting gorging there for over an hour, with nobody but a damned fool of a fashionable woman to talk to! I tell you, Pickering, never again for me. No more artificial duchesses. The whole thing has been simple purgatory.

PICKERING. Youve never been broken in properly to the social routine. (*Strolling over to the piano*) I rather enjoy dipping into it occasionally myself: it makes me feel young again. Anyhow, it was a great success: an immense success. I was quite frightened once or twice because Eliza was doing it so well. You see, lots of the real people cant do it at all: theyre such fools that they think style comes by nature to people in their position; and so they never learn. Theres always something professional about doing a thing superlatively well.

Why was Pickering frightened? What does he say about style?

HIGGINS. Yes: thats what drives me mad: the silly people dont know their own silly business. (*Rising*) However, it's over and done with; and now I can go to bed at last without dreading tomorrow.

(ELIZA'*s beauty becomes murderous.*)

PICKERING. I think I shall turn in too. Still, it's been a great occasion: a triumph for you. Goodnight. (*He goes.*)

HIGGINS (*following him*). Goodnight. (*Over his shoulder, at the door*) Put out the lights, Eliza; and tell Mrs Pearce not to make coffee for me in the morning; I'll take tea. (*He goes out.*)

(ELIZA *tries to control herself and feel indifferent as she rises and walks across to the hearth to switch off the lights. By the time she gets there she is on the point of screaming. She sits down in* HIGGINS'*s chair and holds on hard to the arms. Finally she gives way and flings herself furiously on the floor, raging.*)

HIGGINS (*in despairing wrath outside*). What the devil have I done with my slippers? (*He appears at the door.*)

LIZA (*snatching up the slippers, and hurling them at him one after the other with all her force*). There are your slippers. And there. Take your slippers; and may you never have a day's luck with them!

HIGGINS (*astounded*). What on earth—! (*He comes to her.*) Whats the matter? Get up. (*He pulls her up.*) Anything wrong?

LIZA (*breathless*). Nothing wrong—with you. Ive won your bet for you, havnt I? Thats enough for you. *I* dont matter, I suppose.

HIGGINS. You won my bet! You! Presumptuous insect! *I* won it. What did you throw those slippers at me for?

What has Higgins done wrong? Why is Liza angry at him?

LIZA. Because I wanted to smash your face. I'd like to kill you, you selfish brute. Why didnt you leave me where you picked me out of—in the gutter? You thank God it's all over, and that now you can throw me back again there, do you? (*She crisps her fingers*[3] *frantically.*)

3. **crisps her fingers.** Clenches and unclenches her hands

WORDS FOR EVERYDAY USE

pur • ga • to • ry (pʉr´gə tôr´ē) *n.*, temporary state of suffering or misery. *Daniel endured purgatory for 15 minutes wondering why the principal had summoned him to the office.*

ANSWERS TO GUIDED READING QUESTIONS

1. Higgins was interested in the phonetic aspects of Liza's transformation, but not the personal aspects. He failed to show interest in Liza as a human being. It shows that he has little compassion or ability to identify with or take interest in others.
2. Pickering was frightened once or twice because Liza was "doing so well." He was afraid she wouldn't appear natural, since so many people don't do it well. He thinks style and mannerisms often aren't learned by the people of the class with which they are associated because people assume they should be born with them.
3. Higgins has talked about his own very negative feelings about the experiment, but he has not considered Liza's feelings. She is hurt that she does not matter to him.

LITERARY TECHNIQUE

ASIDE. Shaw chose not to use a technique students have seen in other works, the aside. An **aside** is a statement made by a character in a play, intended to be heard by the audience but not by other characters on the stage. Students can write asides for Liza that will express the thoughts and emotions she has as she listens in silence to Pickering and Higgins congratulating themselves on her transformation.

Quotables

"There are two tragedies in life. One is not to get your heart's desire. The other is to get it."

—Bernard Shaw

ADDITIONAL QUESTIONS AND ACTIVITIES

Discuss with students why the communication between Higgins and Liza does not work in this scene. Points you may want to raise: Higgins is unable to give Liza credit, to see the situation from her perspective, to hear any remark that impugns his self-respect, or to give up his standard techniques for dealing with others—that is, bullying, evasion, and condescension.

LITERARY TECHNIQUE

ANTIHERO. An **antihero** is a central character who lacks all the qualities traditionally associated with heroes. You might wish to discuss with students which character, if any, is the hero of this drama. Is it Higgins? Is it Liza? To what extent can Higgins be described as an antihero? Can Liza be described as an antihero? What qualities does each possess that differentiates him or her from a typical hero?

HIGGINS (*looking at her in cool wonder*). The creature is nervous, after all.

LIZA (*gives a suffocated scream of fury, and instinctively darts her nails at his face*)!!

HIGGINS (*catching her wrists*). Ah! would you? Claws in, you cat. How dare you shew your temper to me? Sit down and be quiet. (*He throws her roughly into the easy-chair.*)

LIZA (*crushed by superior strength and weight*). Whats to become of me? Whats to become of me?

HIGGINS. How the devil do I know whats to become of you? What does it matter what becomes of you?

LIZA. You dont care. I know you dont care. You wouldnt care if I was dead. I'm nothing to you—not so much as them slippers.

HIGGINS (*thundering*). Those slippers.

LIZA (*with bitter submission*). Those slippers. I didnt think it made any difference now.

(*A pause.* ELIZA *hopeless and crushed.* HIGGINS *a little uneasy.*)

HIGGINS (*in his loftiest manner*). Why have you begun going on like this? May I ask whether you complain of your treatment here?

LIZA. No.

HIGGINS. Has anybody behaved badly to you? Colonel Pickering? Mrs Pearce? Any of the servants?

LIZA. No.

HIGGINS. I presume you dont pretend that *I* have treated you badly?

LIZA. No.

HIGGINS. I am glad to hear it. (*He moderates his tone.*) Perhaps youre tired after the strain of the day. Will you have a glass of champagne? (*He moves towards the door.*)

LIZA. No. (*Recollecting her manners*) Thank you.

HIGGINS (*good-humored again*). This has been coming on you for some days. I suppose it was natural for you to be anxious about the garden party. But thats all over now. (*He pats her kindly on the shoulder. She writhes.*) Theres nothing more to worry about.

LIZA. No. Nothing more for you to worry about. (*She suddenly rises and gets away from him by going to the piano bench, where she sits and hides her face.*) Oh God! I wish I was dead.

HIGGINS (*staring after her in sincere surprise*). Why? In heaven's name, why? (*Reasonably, going to her*) Listen to me, Eliza. All this irritation is purely subjective.

LIZA. I dont understand. I'm too ignorant.

HIGGINS. It's only imagination. Low spirits and nothing else. Nobody's hurting you. Nothing's wrong. You go to bed like a good girl and sleep it off. Have a little cry and say your prayers: that will make you comfortable.

LIZA. I heard your prayers. "Thank God it's all over!"

HIGGINS (*impatiently*). Well, dont you thank God it's all over? Now you are free and can do what you like.

LIZA (*pulling herself together in desperation*). What am I fit for? What have you left me fit for? Where am I to go? What am I to do? Whats to become of me?

HIGGINS (*enlightened, but not at all impressed*). Oh thats whats worrying you, is it? (*He thrusts his hands into his pockets, and walks about in his usual manner, rattling the contents of his pockets, as if condescending to a trivial subject out of pure kindness.*) I shouldnt bother about it if I were

WORDS FOR EVERYDAY USE

con • de • scend (kän´di send´) *vi.*, descend to the level of one considered inferior. *Jim could tell by the way Peg walked onto the dance floor that she was only condescending to dance with him.*

you. I should imagine you wont have much difficulty in settling yourself somewhere or other, though I hadnt quite realized that you were going away. (*She looks quickly at him: he does not look at her, but examines the dessert stand on the piano and decides that he will eat an apple.*) You might marry, you know. (*He bites a large piece out of the apple and munches it noisily.*) You see, Eliza, all men are not confirmed old bachelors like me and the Colonel. Most men are the marrying sort (poor devils!); and youre not bad-looking: it's quite a pleasure to look at you sometimes—not now, of course, because youre crying and looking as ugly as the very devil; but when youre all right and quite yourself, youre what I should call attractive. That is, to the people in the marrying line, you understand. You go to bed and have a good nice rest; and then get up and look at yourself in the glass; and you wont feel so cheap.

(ELIZA *again looks at him, speechless, and does not stir.*
The look is quite lost on him: he eats his apple with a dreamy expression of happiness, as it is quite a good one.)

HIGGINS (*a genial afterthought occurring to him*). I daresay my mother could find some chap or other who would do very well.

What in this passage reveals Liza's moral superiority?

LIZA. We were above that at the corner of Tottenham Court Road.

HIGGINS (*waking up*). What do you mean?

LIZA. I sold flowers. I didn't sell myself. Now youve made a lady of me I'm not fit to sell anything else. I wish youd left me where you found me.

HIGGINS (*slinging the core of the apple decisively into the grate*). Tosh, Eliza. Dont you insult human relations by dragging all this cant about buying and selling into it. You neednt marry the fellow if you dont like him.

LIZA. What else am I to do?

HIGGINS. Oh, lots of things. What about your old idea of a florist's shop? Pickering could set you up in one: he's lots of money. (*Chuckling*) He'll have to pay for all those togs you have been wearing today; and that, with the hire of the jewellery, will make a big hole in two hundred pounds. Why, six months ago you would have thought it the millennium to have a flower shop of your own. Come! youll be all right. I must clear off to bed: I'm devilish sleepy. By the way, I came down for something: I forget what it was.

LIZA. Your slippers.

HIGGINS. Oh yes, of course. You shied[4] them at me. (*He picks them up, and is going out when she rises and speaks to him.*)

LIZA. Before you go, sir—

Why does Liza call him "sir"? Why might Higgins be surprised at this formality?

HIGGINS (*dropping the slippers in his surprise at her calling him Sir*). Eh?

LIZA. Do my clothes belong to me or to Colonel Pickering?

HIGGINS (*coming back into the room as if her question were the very climax of unreason*). What the devil use would they be to Pickering?

LIZA. He might want them for the next girl you pick up to experiment on.

HIGGINS (*shocked and hurt*). Is that the way you feel towards us?

LIZA. I dont want to hear anything more about that. All I want to know is whether

4. **shied.** Threw or flung sideways

WORDS FOR EVERYDAY USE

mil • len • ni • um (mi len´ē əm) *n.,* period of perfection or great prosperity, as in the Golden Age. *When the millennium comes, the lion and the lamb will lie down together.*

ANSWERS TO GUIDED READING QUESTIONS

1. Liza refuses to consider the possibility of a marriage of convenience, equating it with selling herself.
2. Liza is distancing herself from Higgins because she plans to leave. Higgins is surprised because this kind of formality is unusual between them; he may sense that she is distancing herself.

LITERARY TECHNIQUE

MYTH. A **myth** is a story that explains objects or events in the natural world as resulting from the action of some supernatural force or entity, most often a god. Considering that Shaw's play is based on Ovid's *Metamorphoses*, you might have students discuss what mystic elements or themes are present in this play. A common character flaw in the hero of Classical Era literature is *hubris*, or arrogance resulting from excessive pride. Would students describe Higgins's decision to "create" Liza as an act of hubris? Encourage students to note whether or not Higgins falls or suffers as a result of his act of hubris.

SELECTION CHECK TEST 4.12.7 WITH ANSWERS

Checking Your Reading

1. Where have Higgins, Pickering, and Liza been? **They've been the garden party, a dinner party, and the opera.**
2. Why is Higgins glad the experiment is over? **He says it was a bore.**
3. What does Liza throw at Higgins? **She throws the slippers at him.**
4. What does Liza say she is fit to sell now? **She says she can only sell herself.**
5. Why does Liza offer to return her clothes to Pickering? **He may want them for the next girl they pick up to experiment on.**

Vocabulary in Context

Fill each blank with the most appropriate word from the Words for Everyday Use. You may have to change the tense of the word.

perfunctorily dudgeon condescend millennium pallor coroneted purgatory

1. For Bud and Stacy, the first years of marriage were the **millennium**.
2. My older sister **condescended** to take me with her only after our father paid her.
3. The immigration officer **perfunctorily** stamped our passports and waved us through.
4. It took hours for the makeup artist to give the actor the unnatural **pallor** of a vampire.
5. Time spent waiting for the results of medical tests can be **purgatory**.

Literary Tools

1. How has Liza changed since the beginning of the play? **She is cultured and somewhat educated.**
2. How has she not changed? **She is still independent, feisty, and clever.**
3. What is an anti-hero? **An anti-hero is a central character who lacks many qualities traditionally associated with heroes.**
4. What qualities of Higgins define him as an anti-hero? ***Responses will vary.***
5. How is the central conflict advanced in this act? **Liza passes the "test" and hears Higgins claim that he's glad the boring experiment is over. She and Higgins fight.**

RESPOND TO THE SELECTION

Students might respond as if they were an advice columnist counseling Liza on her next move or as a friend offering suggestions.

anything belongs to me. My own clothes were burnt.

HIGGINS. But what does it matter? Why need you start bothering about that in the middle of the night?

LIZA. I want to know what I may take away with me. I dont want to be accused of stealing.

HIGGINS (*now deeply wounded*). Stealing! You shouldnt have said that, Eliza. That shews a want of feeling.

LIZA. I'm sorry. I'm only a common ignorant girl; and in my station I have to be careful. There cant be any feelings between the like of you and the like of me. Please will you tell me what belongs to me and what doesnt ?

HIGGINS (*very sulky*). You may take the whole damned houseful if you like. Except the jewels. Theyre hired. Will that satisfy you? (*He turns on his heel and is about to go in extreme dudgeon.*)

LIZA (*drinking in his emotion like nectar, and nagging him to provoke a further supply*). Stop, please. (*She takes off her jewels.*) Will you take these to your room and keep them safe? I dont want to run the risk of their being missing.

HIGGINS (*furious*). Hand them over. (*She puts them into his hands.*) If these belonged to me instead of to the jeweller, I'd ram them down your ungrateful throat. (*He perfunctorily thrusts them into his pockets, unconsciously decorating himself with the protruding ends of the chains.*)

LIZA (*taking a ring off*). This ring isnt the jeweller's: it's the one you bought me in Brighton. I dont want it now. (HIGGINS *dashes the ring violently into the fireplace, and turns on her so threateningly that she crouches over the piano with her hands over her face, and exclaims*) Dont you hit me.

HIGGINS. Hit you! You infamous creature, how dare you accuse me of such a thing? It is you who have hit me. You have wounded me to the heart.

LIZA (*thrilling with hidden joy*). I'm glad. Ive got a little of my own back, anyhow.

HIGGINS (*with dignity, in his finest professional style*). You have caused me to lose my temper: a thing that has hardly ever happened to me before. I prefer to say nothing more tonight. I am going to bed.

LIZA (*pertly*). Youd better leave a note for Mrs Pearce about the coffee; for she wont be told by me.

HIGGINS (*formally*). Damn Mrs Pearce; and damn the coffee; and damn you; and damn my own folly in having lavished hard-earned knowledge and the treasure of my regard and intimacy on a heartless guttersnipe. (*He goes out with impressive decorum, and spoils it by slamming the door savagely.*)

(ELIZA *smiles for the first time; expresses her feelings by a wild pantomime in which an imitation of* HIGGINS*'s exit is confused with her own triumph; and finally goes down on her knees on the hearthrug to look for the ring.*)

WORDS FOR EVERYDAY USE

dudg • eon (duj´ən) *n.*, anger and resentment. *When his favorite television program was dropped from the schedule, Jeb sat down in high dudgeon and wrote a letter to the network.*

per • func • to • ri • ly (pər fuŋk´tə rē lē) *adv.*, in an indifferent or disinterested manner. *Sasha's housecleaning consisted of a dustcloth perfunctorily applied once or twice a week.*

Respond to the SELECTION

What do you think Eliza will do next?

INVESTIGATE, Inquire, Imagine

Recall: GATHERING FACTS →

1a. What does Higgins look for soon after he enters the room?

2a. Has Higgins won his bet with Colonel Pickering? How do you know?

3a. What options does Higgins offer Eliza for her future?

Interpret: FINDING MEANING

1b. What action illustrates Eliza's finally standing up to Higgins and asserting herself?

2b. How does Higgins feel about the work he has done with Eliza now that the experiment is over? How does Eliza feel after the social events of the day? How can you tell?

3b. Why do the options that Higgins offers Eliza seem distasteful to her?

Analyze: TAKING THINGS APART →

4a. What comments and reactions on Higgins's part show that, unknown even to himself, he has grown fond of Eliza?

Synthesize: BRINGING THINGS TOGETHER

4b. How has Eliza and Higgins's relationship changed since the beginning of the play? What signifies this change?

Evaluate: MAKING JUDGMENTS →

5a. Evaluate Eliza's questions: "What am I fit for? . . . What's to become of me?" Are these real fears, or is she being silly, as Higgins suggests?

Extend: CONNECTING IDEAS

5b. Who else has worried about these questions?

Understanding Literature

ANTIHERO. Review the definition for **antihero** in Literary Tools on page 1143. What character traits make Higgins an antihero? Which is his worst flaw? Why?

CLIMAX. Review the definition for **climax** in the Handbook of Literary Terms and the plot pyramid you filled in for Literary Tools on page 1143. What is the climax of *Pygmalion*?

ANSWERS TO UNDERSTANDING LITERATURE

ANTIHERO. Higgins is the central character in this play, but he is not at all admirable. In fact he is often rude, selfish, childish, and inconsiderate of others. He changes little over the course of the play. His lack of compassion or even consideration for others may be his worst flaw. He is often oblivious to the impact he has on others, especially the terrible way he treated Liza.

CLIMAX. It is arguable that the discussion between Higgins and Liza in Act 4 is the climax of the play, because here Liza first declares her independence from Higgins.

ANSWERS FOR INVESTIGATE, INQUIRE, IMAGINE

RECALL

1a. He looks for his slippers.

2a. Higgins has won the bet. He describes how he knew at the garden party that he was going to win "hands down."

3a. Higgins suggests that Liza might marry someone or that she could run a florist's shop.

INTERPRET

1b. Liza demonstrates that she is standing up to Higgins when she throws the slippers at him.

2b. Higgins describe the work he has done with Liza since the first month as a "silly notion" and "a bore" and says he has been "deadly sick of it." Liza is tired and upset. She realizes that she has been used by Higgins and that he does not care for her at all.

3b. Liza considers the prospect of marrying just to make a living as little better than selling herself. She is offended by his causal offer to set her up in some other way of life.

ANALYZE

4a. *Responses will vary.* Higgins becomes extremely angry, almost violent, when Liza returns the ring he bought for her. He then delivers a formal oration in which he curses her as a "heartless guttersnipe." If he were indifferent to Liza, he would not have responded so passionately.

SYNTHESIZE

4b *Responses will vary.* The relationship between Liza and Higgins has changed in that Liza is no longer afraid of Higgins and has developed strong feelings for him, and Higgins has developed some feelings for her. Higgins reaction to Liza's talk of departure shows that he has feelings for her though the does not want to admit it. Liza's desire to continue to live with Higgins and her anger at her treatment by him show her feelings.

EVALUATE

5a. *Responses will vary.* These are real fears. Liza no longer knows her place in the world. She is no longer fit to sell flowers on the street, but she does not have the means or the social network to be a lady of the upper class.

EXTEND

5b. *Responses will vary.* Mrs. Pearce and Mrs. Higgins were worried about what would become of Liza. They foresaw that she would not really have a place when Henry was done with her.

ADDITIONAL RESOURCES

Unit 12 Resource Book

- Selection Worksheet 12.5
- Selection Check Test 4.12.9
- Selection Test 4.12.10

GRAPHIC ORGANIZER

Resolution—Liza realizes that she is not dependent on Henry, that she could teach people as he has.

READER'S JOURNAL

Point out that people are dependent to others to some extent. It is possible to feel independent despite being dependent on others in some ways. Ask students how to consider how independence is related to freedom.

ENGLISH LANGUAGE LEARNING

Additional Vocabulary for Act 5 is listed below:
vehement—forceful
bequest—something left in a will
rogue—scoundrel
contempt—disrespect, scorn

VOCABULARY FROM THE SELECTION

blasphemy	placidly
consort	proffer
impudence	solicitor
incorrigible	spraddle
magnanimous	toady

Literary TOOLS

Satire. **Satire** is humorous writing or speech intended to point out errors, falsehoods, foibles, or failings. As you consider the meaning of the play, think about what topics Shaw satirizes.

Resolution. The **resolution** is the point at which the central conflict is ended, or resolved. Include the resolution on the plot pyramid you made for act 1.

Reader's Journal

What does *independence* mean to you?

ACT FIVE

MRS HIGGINS*'s drawing room. She is at her writing-table as before. The* PARLORMAID *comes in.*

The parlormaid *(at the door).* Mr Henry, maam, is downstairs with Colonel Pickering.

Mrs Higgins. Well, shew them up.

The parlormaid. Theyre using the telephone, maam. Telephoning to the police, I think.

Mrs Higgins. What!

The parlormaid. *(coming further in and lowering her voice).* Mr Henry is in a state, maam. I thought I'd better tell you.

Mrs Higgins. If you had told me that Mr Henry was not in a state it would have been more surprising. Tell them to come up when theyve finished with the police. I suppose he's lost something.

The parlormaid. Yes, maam *(going).*

Mrs Higgins. Go upstairs and tell Miss Doolittle that Mr Henry and the Colonel are here. Ask her not to come down til I send for her.

The parlormaid. Yes, maam.

(HIGGINS *bursts in. He is, as the* PARLORMAID *has said, in a state.)*

Higgins. Look here, mother: heres a confounded thing!

Mrs Higgins. Yes, dear. Good morning. *(He checks his impatience and kisses her, whilst the* PARLORMAID *goes out.)* What is it?

Higgins. Eliza's bolted.

Mrs Higgins *(calmly continuing her writing).* You must have frightened her.

Higgins. Frightened her! nonsense! She was left last night, as usual, to turn out the lights and all that; and instead of going to bed she changed her clothes and went right off: her bed wasnt slept in. She came in a cab for her things before seven this morning; and that fool Mrs Pearce let her have them without telling me a word about it. What am I to do?

Mrs Higgins. Do without, I'm afraid, Henry. The girl has a perfect right to leave if she chooses.

Higgins *(wandering distractedly across the room).* But I cant find anything. I dont know what appointments Ive got. I'm— (PICKERING *comes in.* MRS HIGGINS *puts down her pen and turns away from the writing-table.)*

PICKERING (*shaking hands*). Good morning, Mrs Higgins. Has Henry told you? (*He sits down on the ottoman.*)

HIGGINS. What does that ass of an inspector say? Have you offered a reward?

MRS HIGGINS (*rising in indignant amazement*). You dont mean to say you have set the police after Eliza.

HIGGINS. Of course. What are the police for? What else could we do? (*He sits in the Elizabethan chair.*)

PICKERING. The inspector made a lot of difficulties. I really think he suspected us of some improper purpose.

MRS HIGGINS. Well, of course he did. What right have you to go to the police and give the girl's name as if she were a thief, or a lost umbrella, or something? Really! (*She sits down again, deeply vexed.*)

What does Mrs. Higgins understand that her son does not?

HIGGINS. But we want to find her.

PICKERING. We cant let her go like this, you know, Mrs Higgins. What were we to do?

MRS HIGGINS. You have no more sense, either of you, than two children. Why—

(*The* PARLORMAID *comes in and breaks off the conversation.*)

THE PARLORMAID. Mr Henry: a gentleman wants to see you very particular. He's been sent on from Wimpole Street.

HIGGINS. Oh, bother! I cant see anyone now. Who is it?

THE PARLORMAID. A Mr Doolittle, sir.

PICKERING. Doolittle! Do you mean the dustman?

THE PARLORMAID. Dustman! Oh no, sir: a gentleman.

HIGGINS (*springing up excitedly*). By George, Pick, it's some relative of hers that she's gone to. Somebody we know nothing about. (*To the* PARLORMAID) Send him up, quick.

THE PARLORMAID. Yes, sir. (*She goes.*)

HIGGINS (*eagerly, going to his mother*). Genteel relatives! now we shall hear something. (*He sits down in the Chippendale chair.*)

MRS HIGGINS. Do you know any of her people?

PICKERING. Only her father: the fellow we told you about.

THE PARLORMAID (*announcing*). Mr. Doolittle. (*She withdraws.*)

(DOOLITTLE *enters. He is brilliantly dressed in a new fashionable frock-coat, with white waistcoat and grey trousers. A flower in his buttonhole, a dazzling silk hat, and patent leather shoes complete the effect. He is too concerned with the business he has come on to notice* MRS HIGGINS. *He walks straight to* HIGGINS, *and accosts him with vehement reproach.*)

DOOLITTLE. (*indicating his own person*). See here! Do you see this? You done this.

HIGGINS. Done what, man?

DOOLITTLE. This, I tell you. Look at it. Look at this hat. Look at this coat.

PICKERING. Has Eliza been buying you clothes?

DOOLITTLE. Eliza! not she. Not half. Why would she buy me clothes?

MRS HIGGINS. Good morning, Mr. Doolittle. Wont you sit down?

DOOLITTLE (*taken aback as he becomes conscious that he has forgotten his hostess*). Asking your pardon, maam. (*He approaches her and shakes her proffered hand.*) Thank you. (*He sits down on the ottoman, on*

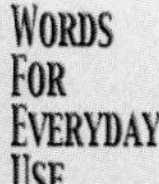

WORDS FOR EVERYDAY USE

prof • fer (präf ´ər) *vt.*, offer; extend. *I proffered the cab fare to the driver, and he grabbed it.*

ANSWER TO GUIDED READING QUESTION

1. Mrs. Higgins understands that Liza is a person in her own right and not a piece of property.

ADDITIONAL QUESTIONS AND ANSWERS

Students can write an essay comparing and contrasting Doolittle's entrance into the middle class with that of Liza. Before writing their essays, students should review Comparison-and-Contrast Order in the Language Arts Survey 2.27, "Choosing a Method of Organization."

ANSWERS TO GUIDED READING QUESTIONS

1. Doolittle objects to being made a gentleman. He feels he has lost his freedom and his right to ask others for money. (Now that he has money, others request it from him.)
2. Doolittle objects to being made a gentleman. He feels he has lost his freedom and his right to ask others for money. (Now that he has money, others request it from him.)

LITERARY NOTE

Despite the fact that Shaw claimed he despised Shakespeare, the two authors share a similar technique—the use of low comic characters to relieve tension. Doolittle, as a proud member of the lower class, a dedicated tavern-goer, and an unwittingly wise orator, bears remarkable resemblance to Shakespearean characters such as Falstaff in *Henry IV*, acts I and II, and the porter in *Macbeth*.

ADDITIONAL QUESTIONS AND ACTIVITIES

Students can write an essay comparing and contrasting Doolittle's entrance into the middle class with that of Liza. Before writing their essays, students should review the Language Arts Survey, 2.27 "Choosing a Method of Organization," and 5.10, "Comparing and Contrasting." Venn diagrams are an excellent way to organize ideas for a comparison and contrast essay. For more information on this organizer, refer students to the Language Arts Survey, 2.16, "Completing Venn Diagrams."

PICKERING's *right*.) I am that full of what has happened to me that I cant think of anything else.

HIGGINS. What the dickens has happened to you?

DOOLITTLE. I shouldnt mind if it had only happened to me: anything might happen to anybody and nobody to blame but Providence, as you might say. But this is something that you done to me: yes, you, Henry Higgins.

HIGGINS. Have you found Eliza? Thats the point.

DOOLITTLE. Have you lost her?

HIGGINS. Yes.

DOOLITTLE. You have all the luck, you have. I aint found her; but she'll find me quick enough now after what you done to me.

MRS HIGGINS. But what has my son done to you, Mr Doolittle?

DOOLITTLE. Done to me! Ruined me. Destroyed my happiness. Tied me up and delivered me into the hands of middle class morality.

HIGGINS (*rising intolerantly and standing over* DOOLITTLE). Youre raving. Youre drunk. Youre mad. I gave you five pounds. After that I had two conversations with you, at half-a-crown an hour. Ive never seen you since.

DOOLITTLE. Oh! Drunk! am I? Mad! am I? Tell me this. Did you or did you not write a letter to an old blighter[1] in America that was giving five millions to found Moral Reform Societies all over the world, and that wanted you to invent a universal language for him?

HIGGINS. What! Ezra D. Wannafeller! He's dead. (*He sits down again carelessly*.)

DOOLITTLE. Yes: he's dead; and I'm done for. Now did you or did you not write a letter to him to say that the most original moralist at present in England, to the best of your knowledge, was Alfred Doolittle, a common dustman.

What joke did Higgins have at Wannafeller's expense? What were the unexpected consequences of Higgins's joke?

HIGGINS. Oh, after your last visit I remember making some silly joke of the kind.

DOOLITTLE. Ah! You may well call it a silly joke. It put the lid on me right enough. Just give him the chance he wanted to shew that Americans is not like us: that they recognize and respect merit in every class of life, however humble. Them words is in his blooming will, in which, Henry Higgins, thanks to your silly joking, he leaves me a share in his Pre-digested Cheese Trust worth three thousand a year on condition that I lecture for his Wannafeller Moral Reform World League as often as they ask me up to six times a year.

HIGGINS. The devil he does! Whew! (*Brightening suddenly*) What a lark!

PICKERING. A safe thing for you, Doolittle. They wont ask you twice.

DOOLITTLE. It aint the lecturing I mind. I'll lecture them blue in the face, I will, and not turn a hair. It's making a gentleman of me that I object to. Who asked him to make a gentleman of me? I was happy. I was free. I touched pretty nigh everybody for money when I wanted it, same as I touched you, Henry Higgins. Now I am worrited;[2] tied neck and heels; and everybody touches me for money. It's a fine thing for you, says my solicitor. Is it? says I. You mean it's a good

To what does Doolittle object? What does he feel he has lost?

1. **old blighter.** British slang for a mean or comtemptible person
2. **worrited.** Worried

WORDS FOR EVERYDAY USE

so • lic • i • tor (sə lis´it ər) *n.*, lawyer. *In Great Britain, a lawyer who advises clients and appears for them in lower courts is called a* solicitor.

thing for you, I says. When I was a poor man and had a solicitor once when they found a pram in the dust cart, he got me off, and got shut of me and got me shut of him as quick as he could. Same with the doctors: used to shove me out of the hospital before I could hardly stand on my legs, and nothing to pay. Now they finds out that I'm not a healthy man and cant live unless they looks after me twice a day. In the house I'm not let do a hand's turn for myself: somebody else must do it and touch me for it. A year ago I hadnt a relative in the world except two or three that wouldnt speak to me. Now Ive fifty, and not a decent week's wages among the lot of them. I have to live for others and not for myself: thats middle class morality. You talk of losing Eliza. Dont you be anxious: I bet she's on my doorstep by this: she that could support herself easy by selling flowers if I wasnt respectable. And the next one to touch me will be you, Henry Higgins. I'll have to learn to speak middle class language from you, instead of speaking proper English. Thats where youll come in; and I daresay thats what you done it for.

What does Doolittle consider to be "proper English"? Why is it funny that he should describe his speech in that way?

Mrs Higgins. But, my dear Mr Doolittle, you need not suffer all this if you are really in earnest. Nobody can force you to accept this bequest. You can repudiate it. Isnt that so, Colonel Pickering?

Pickering. I believe so.

Doolittle (*softening his manner in deference to her sex*). Thats the tragedy of it, maam. It's easy to say chuck it; but I havnt the nerve. Which of us has? We're all intimidated. Intimidated, maam: thats what we are. What is there for me if I chuck it but the workhouse in my old age? I have to dye my hair already to keep my job as a dustman. If I was one of the deserving poor, and had put by a bit, I could chuck it; but then why should I, acause the deserving poor might as well be millionaires for all the happiness they ever has. They dont know what happiness is. But I, as one of the undeserving poor, have nothing between me and the pauper's uniform but this here blasted three thousand a year that shoves me into the middle class. (Excuse the expression, maam: youd use it yourself if you had my provocation.) Theyve got you every way you turn: it's a choice between the Skilly of the workhouse and the Char Bydis[3] of the middle class; and I havnt the nerve for the workhouse. Intimidated: thats what I am. Broke. Bought up. Happier men than me will call for my dust, and touch me for their tip; and I'll look on helpless, and envy them. And thats what your son has brought me to. (*He is overcome by emotion.*)

How does Doolittle differ from Higgins with regard to cursing? What does this say about him?

Mrs Higgins. Well, I'm very glad youre not going to do anything foolish, Mr Doolittle. For this solves the problem of Eliza's future. You can provide for her now.

Doolittle (*with melancholy resignation*). Yes, maam: I'm expected to provide for everyone now, out of three thousand a year.

Higgins (*jumping up*). Nonsense! he cant provide for her. He shant provide for her. She doesn't belong to him. I paid him five pounds for her. Doolittle: either youre an honest man or a rogue.

What does Higgins still not understand about Liza?

Doolittle (*tolerantly*). A little of both, Henry, like the rest of us: a little of both.

Higgins. Well, you took that money for the girl; and you have no right to take her as well.

Mrs Higgins. Henry: dont be absurd. If you want to know where Eliza is, she is upstairs.

Higgins (*amazed*). Upstairs! ! ! Then I shall jolly soon fetch her downstairs. (*He makes resolutely for the door.*)

3. **Skilly . . . Char Bydis.** A reference to Scylla and Charybdis, a dangerous rock and whirlpool in the waters between Sicily and Italy. They present equal dangers regardless of which course an individual follows.

ANSWERS TO GUIDED READING QUESTIONS

1. Doolittle considers the language of the lower class "proper English." His judgment is humorous because Higgins views middle- and upper-class English as the proper and desirable form of English.
2. Doolittle is aware of the effect of his language on others and apologizes for it; Higgins is unaware of the effects of his cursing on others. Doolittle's consciousness suggests that he is more thoughtful toward others than Higgins.
3. Higgins still views Liza as property.

CROSS-CURRICULAR ACTIVITIES

Retirement. Students can research the situation of retired people in the United States today to learn what percentage live in poverty and what the average income of a retired person is. They should write a statement relating their findings in a general way to the position of Alfred Doolittle.

LITERARY TECHNIQUE

Incongruity. Incongruity is the juxtaposition of incompatible things to produce a surprising or humorous effect. Ask students to identify incongruities in the dialogue on this page, or generally in the passage in which Doolittle appears. Examples include Doolittle's appearance versus his claim to be unhappy; Doolittle's lack of morality versus his position as a supposed moralist; Doolittle's "dustman" personality versus his position in the middle class; and the support of the lofty-sounding Moral Reform World League by the ludicrous Pre-digested Cheese Trust.

ANSWERS TO GUIDED READING QUESTIONS

1. Higgins's disregard for Liza's feelings provoked her to throw the slippers. Higgins doesn't realize how his actions affect other people.
2. Higgins is furious at the suggestion that he hurt Liza; he prefers to believe that she has wronged him by running away.

ADDITIONAL QUESTIONS AND ACTIVITIES

Ask students the following questions:

1. What attitudes does Mrs. Higgins take toward Liza? What attitude does she take toward Higgins?
2. What attitude does Higgins have toward seeing Liza?
3. Do you think he will "behave" himself when he sees her? Why or why not?

Answers

1. Mrs. Higgins is sympathetic toward Liza's situation and feelings. She expected this to happen and seems happy to be able to help Liza. She is unsympathetic to Higgins's story and angry, though not surprised, by his treatment of Liza.
2. Higgins is condescending toward seeing Liza. He calls her "this creature we picked out of the mud."
3. It is not likely that Higgins will behave himself. He has not shown much self restraint and generally does not interact well with others. It seems unlikely that he will do so at this time when he is already feeling superior to Liza.

MRS HIGGINS (*rising and following him*). Be quiet, Henry. Sit down.

HIGGINS. I—

MRS HIGGINS. Sit down, dear; and listen to me.

HIGGINS. Oh very well, very well, very well. (*He throws himself ungraciously on the ottoman, with his face towards the windows.*) But I think you might have told us this half an hour ago.

MRS HIGGINS. Eliza came to me this morning. She passed the night partly walking about in a rage, partly trying to throw herself into the river and being afraid to, and partly in the Carlton Hotel. She told me of the brutal way you two treated her.

HIGGINS (*bounding up again*). What!

PICKERING (*rising also*). My dear Mrs Higgins, she's been telling you stories. We didnt treat her brutally. We hardly said a word to her; and we parted on particularly good terms. (*Turning on* HIGGINS) Higgins: did you bully her after I went to bed?

HIGGINS. Just the other way about. She threw my slippers in my face. She behaved in the most outrageous way. I never gave her the slightest provocation. The slippers came bang into my face the moment I entered the room—before I had uttered a word. And used perfectly awful language.

What provocation did Higgins give Liza to throw the slippers? What doesn't he realize about his actions?

PICKERING (*astonished*). But why? What did we do to her?

MRS HIGGINS. I think I know pretty well what you did. The girl is naturally rather affectionate, I think. Isnt she, Mr. Doolittle?

DOOLITTLE. Very tender-hearted, maam. Takes after me.

MRS HIGGINS. Just so. She had become attached to you both. She worked very hard for you, Henry! I dont think you quite realize what anything in the nature of brain work means to a girl like that. Well, it seems that when the great day of trial came, and she did this wonderful thing for you without making a single mistake, you two sat there and never said a word to her, but talked together of how glad you were that it was all over and how you had been bored with the whole thing. And then you were surprised because she threw your slippers at you! *I* should have thrown the fire-irons[4] at you.

HIGGINS. We said nothing except that we were tired and wanted to go to bed. Did we, Pick?

PICKERING (*shrugging his shoulders*). That was all.

MRS HIGGINS (*ironically*). Quite sure?

PICKERING. Absolutely. Really, that was all.

MRS HIGGINS. You didnt thank her, or pet her, or admire her, or tell her how splendid she'd been.

HIGGINS (*impatiently*). But she knew all about that. We didnt make speeches to her, if thats what you mean.

PICKERING (*conscience stricken*). Perhaps we were a little inconsiderate. Is she very angry?

MRS HIGGINS (*returning to her place at the writing-table*). Well, I'm afraid she wont go back to Wimpole Street, especially now that Mr Doolittle is able to keep up the position you have thrust on her; but she says she is quite willing to meet you on friendly terms and to let bygones be bygones.

HIGGINS (*furious*). Is she, by George? Ho!

Why is Higgins furious?

MRS HIGGINS. If you promise to behave yourself, Henry, I'll ask her to come down. If not, go home; for you have taken up quite enough of my time.

HIGGINS. Oh, all right. Very well. Pick: you behave yourself. Let us put on our best Sunday manners for this creature that we picked out of

4. **fire-irons.** Metal tools for tending a fireplace

the mud. (*He flings himself sulkily into the Elizabethan chair.*)

DOOLITTLE (*remonstrating*). Now, now, Henry Higgins! Have some consideration for my feelings as a middle class man.

MRS HIGGINS. Remember your promise, Henry. (*She presses the bell-button on the writing-table.*) Mr. Doolittle: will you be so good as to step out on the balcony for a moment. I dont want Eliza to have the shock of your news until she has made it up with these two gentlemen. Would you mind?

DOOLITTLE. As you wish, lady. Anything to help Henry to keep her off my hands. (*He disappears through the window.*)

(*The* PARLORMAID *answers the bell.* PICKERING *sits down in* DOOLITTLE'*s place.*)

MRS HIGGINS. Ask Miss Doolittle to come down, please.

THE PARLORMAID. Yes, maam. (*She goes out.*)

MRS HIGGINS. Now, Henry: be good.

HIGGINS. I am behaving myself perfectly.

PICKERING. He is doing his best, Mrs Higgins.

(*A pause.* HIGGINS *throws back his head; stretches out his legs; and begins to whistle.*)

MRS HIGGINS. Henry, dearest, you dont look at all nice in that attitude.

HIGGINS (*pulling himself together*). I was not trying to look nice, mother.

MRS HIGGINS. It doesnt matter, dear. I only wanted to make you speak.

HIGGINS. Why?

MRS HIGGINS. Because you cant speak and whistle at the same time.

(HIGGINS *groans. Another very trying pause.*)

HIGGINS (*springing up, out of patience*). Where the devil is that girl? Are we to wait here all day?

(ELIZA *enters, sunny, self-possessed, and giving a staggeringly convincing exhibition of ease of manner. She carries a little workbasket, and is very much at home.* PICKERING *is too much taken aback to rise.*)

LIZA. How do you do, Professor Higgins? Are you quite well?

HIGGINS (*choking*). Am I—(*He can say no more.*)

LIZA. But of course you are: you are never ill. So glad to see you again, Colonel Pickering. (*He rises hastily; and they shake hands.*) Quite chilly this morning, isnt it? (*She sits down on his left. He sits beside her.*)

What is Liza trying to prove with her behavior? Why does Higgins get angry?

HIGGINS. Dont you dare try this game on me. I taught it to you; and it doesnt take me in. Get up and come home; and dont be a fool.

(ELIZA *takes a piece of needlework from her basket, and begins to stitch at it, without taking the least notice of this outburst.*)

MRS HIGGINS. Very nicely put, indeed, Henry. No woman could resist such an invitation.

What is Mrs. Higgins saying to her son?

HIGGINS. You let her alone, mother. Let her speak for herself. You will jolly soon see whether she has an idea that I havnt put into her head or a word that I havnt put into her mouth. I tell you I have created this thing out of the squashed cabbage leaves of Covent Garden; and now she pretends to play the fine lady with me.

MRS HIGGINS (*placidly*). Yes, dear; but youll sit down, wont you?

WORDS FOR EVERYDAY USE

plac • id • ly (plas´id lē) *adv.*, in a tranquil or calm manner. *Little did the canoeists know that the stream carrying them so placidly along led to a raging waterfall.*

ANSWERS TO GUIDED READING QUESTIONS

1. Liza is coolly pretending that nothing unusual is going on in order to demonstrate her independence from Higgins. Higgins gets angry because he thinks she is playing a game with him.
2. Mrs. Higgins is telling her son that he should try to be more considerate and gentle with Liza if he really wants her to return home.

ANSWERS TO GUIDED READING QUESTIONS

1. Higgins was not capable of teaching manners to Liza, because he did not have any himself.
2. The difference between a lady and a flower girl is how she is treated. Pickering always treated Liza as a lady.

ADDITIONAL QUESTIONS AND ACTIVITIES

Ask students the following interpretive question: Why is Liza attracted to Higgins rather than Pickering, though Pickering treats her better than Higgins?

Answer

Responses will vary. A likely explanation is that Liza is attracted to Higgins because he also needs to be changed. In this sense, Liza is as much a "sculptor" as Higgins is; unfortunately, Higgins is utterly intractable. Liza will eventually realize that her efforts are wasted and will abandon her attempt to elicit a different response from Higgins.

ADDITIONAL QUESTIONS AND ACTIVITIES

- Ask students who have lived in another country to discuss their experience learning a new language.
- Have students try to have a conversation without resorting to slang or "fillers" that are often part of our language, for example "um" or "like." The latter example is especially problematic for some people. Practicing speaking without these words may make students more aware of their usage.

(HIGGINS *sits down again, savagely.*)

LIZA (*to* PICKERING, *taking no apparent notice of* HIGGINS, *and working away deftly*). Will you drop me altogether now that the experiment is over, Colonel Pickering?

PICKERING. Oh dont. You mustnt think of it as an experiment. It shocks me, somehow.

LIZA. Oh, I'm only a squashed cabbage leaf—

PICKERING (*impulsively*). No.

LIZA (*continuing quietly*).—but I owe so much to you that I should be very unhappy if you forgot me.

PICKERING. It's very kind of you to say so, Miss Doolittle.

LIZA. It's not because you paid for my dresses. I know you are generous to everybody with money. But it was from you that I learnt really nice manners; and that is what makes one a lady, isnt it? You see it was so very difficult for me with the example of Professor Higgins always before me. I was brought up to be just like him, unable to control myself, and using bad language on the slightest provocation. And I should never have known that ladies and gentlemen didnt behave like that if you hadnt been there.

What wasn't Higgins capable of teaching Liza?

HIGGINS. Well!!

PICKERING. Oh, thats only his way, you know. He doesnt mean it.

LIZA. Oh, *I* didnt mean it either, when I was a flower girl. It was only my way. But you see I did it; and thats what makes the difference after all.

PICKERING. No doubt. Still, he taught you to speak; and I couldnt have done that, you know.

LIZA (*trivially*). Of course: that is his profession.

HIGGINS. Damnation!

LIZA (*continuing*). It was just like learning to dance in the fashionable way: there was nothing more than that in it. But do you know what began my real education?

PICKERING. What?

LIZA (*stopping her work for a moment*). Your calling me Miss Doolittle that day when I first came to Wimpole Street. That was the beginning of self-respect for me. (*She resumes her stitching.*) And there were a hundred little things you never noticed because they came naturally to you. Things about standing up and taking off your hat and opening doors—

PICKERING. Oh, that was nothing.

LIZA. Yes: things that shewed you thought and felt about me as if I were something better than a scullery-maid;[5] though of course I know you would have been just the same to a scullery-maid if she had been let into the drawing room. You never took off your boots in the dining room when I was there.

PICKERING. You mustnt mind that. Higgins takes off his boots all over the place.

LIZA. I know. I am not blaming him. It is his way, isn't it? But it made such a difference to me that you didnt do it. You see, really and truly, apart from the things anyone can pick up (the dressing and the proper way of speaking, and so on), the difference between a lady and a flower girl is not how she behaves, but how she's treated. I shall always be a flower girl to Professor Higgins, because he always treats me as a flower girl, and always will; but I know I can be a lady to you, because you always treat me as a lady, and always will.

What is the difference between a lady and a flower girl? Why was Pickering so important in Liza's transformation?

MRS HIGGINS. Please dont grind your teeth, Henry.

PICKERING. Well, this is really very nice of you, Miss Doolittle.

LIZA. I should like you to call me Eliza, now, if you would.

5. **scullery-maid.** Household help responsible for cleaning pots and pans

PICKERING. Thank you. Eliza, of course.

Why does Eliza wish to be called this way?

LIZA. And I should like Professor Higgins to call me Miss Doolittle.

HIGGINS. I'll see you damned first.

MRS HIGGINS. Henry! Henry!

PICKERING (*laughing*). Why dont you slang back at him? Dont stand it. It would do him a lot of good.

LIZA. I cant. I could have done it once; but now I cant go back to it. Last night, when I was wandering about, a girl spoke to me; and I tried to get back into the old way with her; but it was no use. You told me, you know, that when a child is brought to a foreign country, it picks up the language in a few weeks, and forgets its own. Well, I am a child in your country. I have forgotten my own language, and can speak nothing but yours. Thats the real break-off with the corner of Tottenham Court Road. Leaving Wimpole Street finishes it.

PICKERING (*much alarmed*). Oh! but youre coming back to Wimpole Street, arnt you? Youll forgive Higgins?

HIGGINS (*rising*). Forgive! Will she, by George! Let her go. Let her find out how she can get on without us. She will relapse into the gutter in three weeks without me at her elbow.

(DOOLITTLE *appears at the center window. With a look of dignified reproach at* HIGGINS, *he comes slowly and silently to his daughter, who, with her back to the window, is unconscious of his approach.*)

PICKERING. He's incorrigible, Eliza. You wont relapse, will you?

WORDS FOR EVERYDAY USE

in • cor • ri • gi • ble (in kôr´ə jə bəl) *adj.*, unable to be reformed; unmanageable; unruly. *Paul Morel thought his father was incorrigible because he took his pay to the bar rather than home to his wife.*

ANSWER TO GUIDED READING QUESTION

1. Eliza wants Colonel Pickering to call her by name because she likes and respects him. She suggests that their relationship is such that he can drop the formality of calling her Miss Doolittle. She wants Higgins to call her Miss Doolittle as a sign of respect, something he does not show her. This also shows that she still view Higgins very coolly.

ADDITIONAL QUESTIONS AND ACTIVITIES

Ask students if they think Liza will "relapse into the gutter" with out Higgins. Students should point out characteristics of Liza's that help shape their response.

ANSWER TO GUIDED READING QUESTION

1. Eliza reverts to her old sounds in her surprise at seeing her father.

ADDITIONAL QUESTIONS AND ACTIVITIES

Many couples today write their own wedding vows. Students can imagine they are Doolittle and his bride-to-be and compose vows for their wedding. They should make their vows reflect Doolittle's unique understanding of his situation.

LITERARY NOTE

For centuries, many theatrical comedies produced one or more marriages in its final act. For example, many of Shakespeare's comedies, such as *A Midsummer Night's Dream* and *The Merchant of Venice,* involve young people moving away from child-hood and the parental home toward love and marriage. *Pygmalion*, however, ends with an uncomfortable reversal of this convention—a daughter remains single while a father remarries. Ask students why Shaw may have wished to alter the traditional comic ending. Is Shaw's choice of an ending indicative of any changes in twentieth-century literature?

LIZA. No: not now. Never again. I have learnt my lesson. I dont believe I could utter one of the old sounds if I tried. (DOOLITTLE *touches her on her left shoulder. She drops her work losing her self-possession utterly at the spectacle of her father's splendor*) A-a-a-a-a-ah-ow-ooh!

HIGGINS (*with a crow of triumph*). Aha! Just so. A-a-a-a-ahowooh! A-a-a-aahowooh! A-a-a-a-ahowooh! Victory! Victory! (*He throws himself on the divan, folding his arms, and spraddling arrogantly.*)

What makes Eliza revert to her old sounds?

DOOLITTLE. Can you blame the girl? Dont look at me like that, Eliza. It aint my fault. Ive come into some money.

LIZA. You must have touched a millionaire this time, dad.

DOOLITTLE. I have. But I'm dressed something special today. I'm going to St George's, Hanover Square. Your stepmother is going to marry me.

LIZA (*angrily*). Youre going to let yourself down to marry that low common woman!

PICKERING (*quietly*). He ought to, Eliza (*To* DOOLITTLE) Why has she changed her mind?

DOOLITTLE (*sadly*). Intimidated, Governor. Intimidated. Middle class morality claims its victim. Wont you put on your hat, Liza, and come and see me turned off?[6]

LIZA. If the Colonel says I must, I—I'll (*almost sobbing*) I'll demean myself. And get insulted for my pains, like enough.

DOOLITTLE. Dont be afraid: she never comes to words with anyone now, poor woman! respectability has broke all the spirit out of her.

PICKERING (*squeezing* ELIZA'S *elbow gently*). Be kind to them, Eliza. Make the best of it.

LIZA (*forcing a little smile for him through her vexation*). Oh well, just to shew theres no ill feeling. I'll be back in a moment. (*She goes out.*)

DOOLITTLE (*sitting down beside* PICKERING). I feel uncommon nervous about the ceremony, Colonel. I wish youd come and see me through it.

PICKERING. But youve been through it before, man. You were married to Eliza's mother.

DOOLITTLE. Who told you that, Colonel?

PICKERING. Well, nobody told me. But I concluded—naturally—

DOOLITTLE. No: that aint the natural way, Colonel: it's only the middle class way. My way was always the undeserving way. But dont say nothing to Eliza. She dont know: I always had a delicacy about telling her.

PICKERING. Quite right. We'll leave it so, if you dont mind.

DOOLITTLE. And youll come to the church, Colonel, and put me through straight?

PICKERING. With pleasure. As far as a bachelor can.

MRS HIGGINS. May I come, Mr Doolittle? I should be very sorry to miss your wedding.

DOOLITTLE. I should indeed be honored by your condescension, maam; and my poor old woman would take it as a tremendous compliment. She's been very low, thinking of the happy days that are no more.

MRS HIGGINS (*rising*). I'll order the carriage and get ready. (*The men rise, except* HIGGINS) I shant be more than fifteen minutes. (*As she goes to the door* ELIZA *comes in, hatted and buttoning her gloves.*) I'm going to the church to see your

6. **turned off.** To be joined in marriage

WORDS FOR EVERYDAY USE

sprad • dle (sprad´əl) *part.*, sprawl or straddle. *The young father soon learned how difficult it is to put a diaper on a spraddling baby.*

father married, Eliza. You had better come in the brougham[7] with me. Colonel Pickering can go on with the bridegroom.

(MRS HIGGINS *goes out.* ELIZA *comes to the middle of the room between the centre window and the ottoman.* PICKERING *joins her.*)

DOOLITTLE. Bridegroom! What a word! It makes a man realize his position, somehow. (*He takes up his hat and goes towards the door.*)

PICKERING. Before I go, Eliza, do forgive him and come back to us.

LIZA. I dont think papa would allow me. Would you, dad?

DOOLITTLE (*sad but magnanimous*). They played you off very cunning, Eliza, them two sportsmen. If it had been only one of them, you could have nailed him. But you see, there was two; and one of them chaperoned the other, as you might say. (*To* PICKERING) It was artful of you, Colonel; but I bear no malice: I should have done the same myself. I been the victim of one woman after another all my life; and I dont grudge you two getting the better of Eliza. I shant interfere. It's time for us to go, Colonel. So long, Henry. See you in St George's, Eliza. (*He goes out.*)

PICKERING (*coaxing*). Do stay with us, Eliza. (*He follows* DOOLITTLE).

(ELIZA *goes out on the balcony to avoid being alone with* HIGGINS. *He rises and joins her there. She immediately comes back into the room and makes for the door; but he goes along the balcony quickly and gets his back to the door before she reaches it.*)

HIGGINS. Well, Eliza, youve had a bit of your own back, as you call it. Have you had enough? and are you going to be reasonable? Or do you want any more?

What does Higgins mean when he asks Liza if she is going to "be reasonable"?

LIZA. You want me back only to pick up your slippers and put up with your tempers and fetch and carry for you.

HIGGINS. I havnt said I wanted you back at all.

LIZA. Oh, indeed. Then what are we talking about?

HIGGINS. About you, not about me. If you come back I shall treat you just as I have always treated you. I cant change my nature; and I dont intend to change my manners. My manners are exactly the same as Colonel Pickering's.

LIZA. Thats not true. He treats a flower girl as if she was a duchess.

HIGGINS. And I treat a duchess as if she was a flower girl.

LIZA. I see. (*She turns away composedly, and sits on the ottoman, facing the window.*) The same to everybody.

HIGGINS. Just so.

LIZA. Like father.

HIGGINS (*grinning, a little taken down*). Without accepting the comparison at all points, Eliza, it's quite true that your father is not a snob, and that he will be quite at home in any station of life to which his eccentric destiny may call him. (*Seriously*) The great secret, Eliza, is not having bad manners or good manners or any other particular sort of manners, but having the same manner for all human souls: in short, behaving as if you were in Heaven, where there are no third-class carriages, and one soul is as good as another.

How, according to Higgins, is heaven different from earth?

7. **brougham.** Enclosed four-wheeled carriage

WORDS FOR EVERYDAY USE

mag • nan • i • mous (mag nan´ə məs) *adj.*, gracious and generous. *Magnanimous people forgive their enemies.*

ANSWERS TO GUIDED READING QUESTIONS

1. He means is she going to go back to taking his orders and putting up with his tempers and doing things for him without complaint.
2. In heaven, according to Higgins, there are no social classes.

ADDITIONAL QUESTIONS AND ACTIVITIES

Higgins makes several important statements in his dialogue. Use the following questions to explore these statements with students:

1. "I cant change my nature," says Higgins. Based on what you have seen of Higgins in the play, do you believe this is true, or just a position he is taking?
2. Do you believe that Higgins is correct when he says that what really matters is not the type of manners one has but that one treats all people the same regardless of their social class?

Answers

1. Higgins has repeatedly demonstrated a refusal to change his nature.
2. *Responses will vary.* Students may point out that Higgins is half right: what really matters is that one treats all people, regardless of class, with good manners, as Pickering does.

ANSWER TO GUIDED READING QUESTION

1. Higgins says Eliza's actions, fetching his slippers, etc., were a commercialism of affection.

ADDITIONAL QUESTIONS AND ACTIVITIES

Ask students the following questions:

1. Why will Higgins miss Liza?
2. What does Higgins say he is unable to do? Do you agree?
3. What does Higgins say he cares for? Have his actions supported this assertion?

Answers

1. Higgins says he will miss Liza's voice and appearance.
2. Higgins says he is unable to turn on Liza's soul. Students may say that by arousing strong emotion in Liza, Higgins is turning on her soul. Others may say that Higgins is right that he has nothing to offer Liza that will really touch and affect her.
3. Higgins says he cares for humanity. Higgins may have ideas about how people should treat each other and how they should be. His disregard for individuals goes against his statement that he cares for humanity.

LIZA. Amen. You are a born preacher.

HIGGINS (*irritated*). The question is not whether I treat you rudely, but whether you ever heard me treat anyone else better.

LIZA (*with sudden sincerity*). I dont care how you treat me. I dont mind your swearing at me. I dont mind a black eye: Ive had one before this. But (*standing up and facing him*) I wont be passed over.

HIGGINS. Then get out of my way; for I wont stop for you. You talk about me as if I were a motor bus.

LIZA. So you are a motor bus: all bounce and go, and no consideration for anyone. But I can do without you: dont think I cant.

HIGGINS. I know you can. I told you you could.

LIZA (*wounded, getting away from him to the other side of the ottoman with her face to the hearth*). I know you did, you brute. You wanted to get rid of me.

HIGGINS. Liar.

LIZA. Thank you. (*She sits down with dignity.*)

HIGGINS. You never asked yourself, I suppose, whether I could do without you.

LIZA (*earnestly*). Dont you try to get round me. Youll have to do without me.

HIGGINS (*arrogant*). I can do without anybody. I have my own soul: my own spark of divine fire. But (*with sudden humility*) I shall miss you, Eliza. (*He sits down near her on the ottoman.*) I have learnt something from your idiotic notions: I confess that humbly and gratefully. And I have grown accustomed to your voice and appearance. I like them, rather.

LIZA. Well, you have both of them on your gramophone and in your book of photographs. When you feel lonely without me, you can turn the machine on. It's got no feelings to hurt.

HIGGINS. I cant turn your soul on. Leave me those feelings; and you can take away the voice and the face. They are not you.

LIZA. Oh, you are a devil. You can twist the heart in a girl as easy as some could twist her arms to hurt her. Mrs Pearce warned me. Time and again she has wanted to leave you; and you always got round her at the last minute. And you dont care a bit for her. And you dont care a bit for me.

HIGGINS. I care for life, for humanity; and you are a part of it that has come my way and been built into my house. What more can you or anyone ask?

LIZA. I wont care for anybody that doesnt care for me.

HIGGINS. Commercial principles, Eliza. Like (*reproducing her Covent Garden pronunciation with professional exactness*) s'yollin voylets [selling violets], isn't it?

LIZA. Dont sneer at me. It's mean to sneer at me.

HIGGINS. I have never sneered in my life. Sneering doesnt become either the human face or the human soul. I am expressing my righteous contempt for Commercialism. I dont and wont trade in affection. You call me a brute because you couldnt buy a claim on me by fetching my slippers and finding my spectacles. You were a fool: I think a woman fetching a man's slippers is a disgusting sight: did I ever fetch your slippers? I think a good deal more of you for throwing them in my face. No use slaving for me and then saying you want to be cared for: who cares for a slave? If you come back, come back for the sake of good fellowship; for youll get nothing else. Youve had a thousand times as much out of me as I have out of you; and if you dare to set up your little dog's tricks of fetching and carrying slippers against my creation of a Duchess Eliza, I'll slam the door in your silly face.

What does Higgins say is a commercialism of affection?

LIZA. What did you do it for if you didnt care for me?

HIGGINS (*heartily*). Why, because it was my job.

LIZA. You never thought of the trouble it would make for me.

HIGGINS. Would the world ever have been made if its maker had been afraid of making trouble? Making life means making trouble. Theres only one way of escaping trouble; and thats killing things. Cowards, you notice, are always shrieking to have troublesome people killed.

LIZA. I'm no preacher: I dont notice things like that. I notice that you dont notice me.

HIGGINS (*jumping up and walking about intolerantly*). Eliza: youre an idiot. I waste the treasures of my Miltonic[8] mind by spreading them before you. Once for all, understand that I go my way and do my work without caring twopence what happens to either of us. I am not intimidated, like your father and your stepmother. So you can come back or go to the devil: which you please.

LIZA. What am I to come back for?

HIGGINS (*bouncing up on his knees on the ottoman and leaning over it to her*). For the fun of it. Thats why I took you on.

LIZA (*with averted face*). And you may throw me out tomorrow if I dont do everything you want me to?

HIGGINS. Yes; and you may walk out tomorrow if I dont do everything you want me to.

LIZA. And live with my stepmother?

HIGGINS. Yes, or sell flowers.

LIZA. Oh! if I only could go back to my flower basket! I should be independent of both you and father and all the world! Why did you take my independence from me? Why did I give it up? I'm a slave now, for all my fine clothes.

What does Liza want? What has she wanted from the beginning of act two, when she came to Higgins for lessons?

HIGGINS. Not a bit. I'll adopt you as my daughter and settle money on you if you like. Or would you rather marry Pickering?

LIZA (*looking fiercely round at him*). I wouldnt marry you if you asked me; and youre nearer my age than what he is.

HIGGINS (*gently*). Than he is: not "than what he is."

LIZA (*losing her temper and rising*). I'll talk as I like. Youre not my teacher now.

HIGGINS (*reflectively*). I dont suppose Pickering would, though. He's as confirmed an old bachelor as I am.

LIZA. Thats not what I want; and dont you think it. Ive always had chaps enough wanting me that way. Freddy Hill writes to me twice and three times a day, sheets and sheets.

HIGGINS (*disagreeably surprised*). Damn his impudence! (*He recoils and finds himself sitting on his heels.*)

LIZA. He has a right to if he likes, poor lad. And he does love me.

HIGGINS (*getting off the ottoman*). You have no right to encourage him.

LIZA. Every girl has a right to be loved.

HIGGINS. What! By fools like that?

LIZA. Freddy's not a fool. And if he's weak and poor and wants me, may be he'd make me happier than my betters that bully me and dont want me.

8. **Miltonic.** Like the poet John Milton, that is, brilliant

WORDS FOR EVERYDAY USE

im • pu • dence (im´pyo͞o dəns) *n.*, quality of being shamelessly bold or saucy. *The public finds nothing so unbearable as impudence in a public employee.*

ANSWER TO GUIDED READING QUESTION

1. Liza wants her independence and wants to be respected and treated well as a human being.

BIOGRAPHICAL NOTE

In the dialogue on this page, Higgins exclaims, "Theres only one way of escaping trouble; and thats killing things. Cowards, you notice, are always shrieking to have troublesome people killed." His "preaching," as Liza calls it, has a larger meaning than that called for in the dialogue.

Shaw was a member of the Fabian Society, a group dedicated to changing British society by permeating all levels with its new ideas. When World War I began, Shaw insisted that Britain was as much to blame for hostilities as Germany and its allies—a position that brought him much public censure. In this light, Higgins's statement is typical of the views of the author, who was not afraid to take on trouble in order to improve conditions in society.

ANSWERS FOR GUIDED READING QUESTIONS

1. Such efforts are generally bound to fail and often make one or both people unhappy.
2. Henry doesn't want to have his "masterpiece thrown away on Freddy." He reveals that he still views Liza as an object and his creation.

ADDITIONAL QUESTIONS AND ACTIVITIES

Use the table below to explain the various possibilities for Liza's future that are raised and discarded in the selection on pages 1162–1164.

Possibility	Reason Discarded
Liza could live with her father.	Liza would have to live with her unpleasant stepmother.
Liza could sell flowers for a living.	Liza cannot go back to that life.
Higgins could adopt Liza.	She ignores this suggestion.
Liza could marry Pickering.	She implies that Pickering is too old for her.
Liza could marry Freddy.	This is not discarded by Liza, though Higgins condemns it.
Liza could have seduced Higgins.	Her moral standards are too high.
Liza could continue living at Higgins's under the same terms that she has been living there.	Liza craves the respect and kindliness that Higgins refuses to give her.
Liza could marry someone of higher social standing than Freddy.	Liza insists that she will at least have independence if she cannot have kindness.
Liza could be an assistant to Professor Nepean.	Higgins is outraged by this idea, though it is never discarded by Liza.
Liza could become a teacher of phonetics herself.	This possibility is never discarded by Liza.

HIGGINS. Can he make anything of you? Thats the point.

LIZA. Perhaps I could make something of him. But I never thought of us making anything of one another; and you never think of anything else. I only want to be natural.

Why is it important for romantic partners not to try to remake one another?

HIGGINS. In short, you want me to be as infatuated about you as Freddy? Is that it?

LIZA. No I dont. Thats not the sort of feeling I want from you. And dont you be too sure of yourself or of me. I could have been a bad girl if I'd liked. Ive seen more of some things than you, for all your learning. Girls like me can drag gentlemen down to make love to them easy enough. And they wish each other dead the next minute.

HIGGINS. Of course they do. Then what in thunder are we quarrelling about?

LIZA (*much troubled*). I want a little kindness. I know I'm a common ignorant girl, and you a book-learned gentleman; but I'm not dirt under your feet. What I done (*correcting herself*) what I did was not for the dresses and the taxis: I did it because we were pleasant together and I come—came—to care for you; not to want you to make love to me, and not forgetting the difference between us, but more friendly like.

HIGGINS. Well, of course. Thats just how I feel. And how Pickering feels. Eliza: youre a fool.

LIZA. Thats not a proper answer to give me (*she sinks on the chair at the writing-table in tears*).

HIGGINS. It's all youll get until you stop being a common idiot. If youre going to be a lady, youll have to give up feeling neglected if the men you know dont spend half their time snivelling over you and the other half giving you black eyes. If you cant stand the coldness of my sort of life, and the strain of it, go back to the gutter. Work til you are more a brute than a human being; and then cuddle and squabble and drink til you fall asleep. Oh, it's a fine life, the life of the gutter. It's real: it's warm: it's violent: you can feel it through the thickest skin: you can taste it and smell it without any training or any work. Not like Science and Literature and Classical Music and Philosophy and Art. You find me cold, unfeeling, selfish, dont you? Very well: be off with you to the sort of people you like. Marry some sentimental hog or other with lots of money, and a thick pair of lips to kiss you with and a thick pair of boots to kick you with. If you cant appreciate what youve got, youd better get what you can appreciate.

LIZA (*desperate*). Oh, you are a cruel tyrant. I cant talk to you: you turn everything against me: I'm always in the wrong. But you know very well all the time that youre nothing but a bully. You know I cant go back to the gutter, as you call it, and that I have no real friends in the world but you and the Colonel. You know well I couldn't bear to live with a low common man after you two; and it's wicked and cruel of you to insult me by pretending I could. You think I must go back to Wimpole Street because I have nowhere else to go but father's. But dont you be too sure that you have me under your feet to be trampled on and talked down. I'll marry Freddy, I will, as soon as he's able to support me.

HIGGINS (*sitting down beside her*). Rubbish! you shall marry an ambassador. You shall marry the Governor-General of India or the Lord-Lieutenant of Ireland, or somebody who wants a deputy-queen. I'm not going to have my masterpiece thrown away on Freddy.

Why doesn't Henry want Liza to marry Freddy? What does his statement reveal about the way he views Liza?

LIZA. You think I like you to say that. But I havent forgot what you said a minute ago; and I wont be coaxed round as if I was a baby or a puppy. If I cant have kindness, I'll have independence.

Higgins. Independence? Thats middle class blasphemy. We are all dependent on one another, every soul of us on earth.

Liza (*rising determinedly*). I'll let you see whether I'm dependent on you. If you can preach, I can teach. I'll go and be a teacher.

Higgins. Whatll you teach, in heaven's name?

Liza. What you taught me. I'll teach phonetics.

Higgins. Ha! ha! ha!

Liza. I'll offer myself as an assistant to Professor Nepean.

Higgins (*rising in a fury*). What! That impostor! that humbug! that toadying ignoramus! Teach him my methods! my discoveries! You take one step in his direction and I'll wring your neck. (*He lays hands on her.*) Do you hear?

Liza (*defiantly non-resistant*). Wring away. What do I care? I knew youd strike me some day. (*He lets her go, stamping with rage at having forgotten himself, and recoils so hastily that he stumbles back into his seat on the ottoman.*) Aha! Now I know how to deal with you. What a fool I was not to think of it before! You cant take away the knowledge you gave me. You said I had a finer ear than you. And I can be civil and kind to people, which is more than you can. Aha! Thats done you, Henry Higgins, it has. Now I dont care that (*snapping her fingers*) for your bullying and your big talk. I'll advertize it in the papers that your duchess is only a flower girl that you taught, and that she'll teach anybody to be a duchess just the same in six months for a thousand guineas. Oh, when I think of myself crawling under your feet and being trampled on and called names, when all the time I had only to lift up my finger to be as good as you, I could just kick myself.

What idea does Liza propose? Why would she be a better teacher than Henry?

Higgins (*wondering at her*). You damned impudent slut, you! But it's better than snivelling; better than fetching slippers and finding spectacles, isn't it? (*Rising*) By George, Eliza, I said I'd make a woman of you; and I have. I like you like this.

Liza. Yes: you turn round and make up to me now that I'm not afraid of you, and can do without you.

Higgins. Of course I do, you little fool. Five minutes ago you were like a millstone round my neck. Now youre a tower of strength: a consort battleship. You and I and Pickering will be three old bachelors together instead of only two men and a silly girl.

(MRS HIGGINS *returns, dressed for the wedding.* ELIZA *instantly becomes cool and elegant.*)

Mrs Higgins. The carriage is waiting, Eliza. Are you ready?

Liza. Quite. Is the Professor coming?

Mrs Higgins. Certainly not. He cant behave himself in church. He makes remarks out loud all the time on the clergyman's pronunciation.

Liza. Then I shall not see you again, Professor. Goodbye. (*She goes to the door.*)

Mrs Higgins (*coming to* HIGGINS). Goodbye, dear.

Higgins. Goodbye, mother. (*He is about to kiss her, when he recollects something.*) Oh, by the way, Eliza, order a ham and a Stilton cheese, will you? And buy me a pair of reindeer gloves, number eights, and a tie to match that new suit

Words for Everyday Use

blas • phe • my (blas´ fə mē´) *n.,* irreverent or disrespectful remark or action. *To some people, uttering a negative word about Elvis is blasphemy.*

toad • y • ing (tōd´ ē iŋ) *vt.,* flattering in order to gain favor. *The toadying class president got the principal to approve the dance.*

con • sort (kän´sôrt´) *n.,* ship that travels with other ships; companion. *The flagship of the ill-fated Arctic expedition sinking the minute it left the harbor, and its crew was rescued by the consorts.*

ANSWER TO GUIDED READING QUESTION

1. Liza proposes to teach phonetics. She has a finer ear and can be civil and kind to people.

CROSS-CURRICULAR ACTIVITIES

Psychology. Students can imagine they are career counselors. Liza Doolittle has come to them to ask them what line of work she should pursue. They should list at least three possible careers for her, giving reasons why each would be appropriate for a person of her background and training.

ANSWER TO GUIDED READING QUESTION

1. Higgins thinks that Liza will resume the same role in his household that she has played for the past several months. It seems unlikely that she will do so.

INTERNET RESOURCE

Shaw wrote an afterward for this play. Students can access it online at www.bartleby.com/138. Ask students to discuss the ending Shaw presents in the afterward. Do they like it? How do they feel about Shaw's tone? In what way the afterward illuminate the connection between the afterward and the myth of Pygmalion?

SELECTION CHECK TEST 4.12.9 WITH ANSWERS

Checking Your Reading

1. For what does Higgins want to offer a reward? **He offers a reward for finding Liza.**
2. Who is now a "middle class man"? **Doolittle is now middle class.**
3. Where is Liza hiding? **She is upstairs at Mrs. Higgins' house.**
4. What does Liza say is the difference between a lady and a flower girl? **The difference is how she is treated.**
5. How does Higgins compare the way he treats Liza with the way he treats others? **He says he treats everyone the same way.**

Vocabulary in Context

Fill each blank with the most appropriate word from the Words for Everyday Use. You may have to change the tense of the word.

proffered impudence blasphemy
placidly magnanimous toadying
consort

1. The learned she could get what she wanted by **toadying** to the boss.
2. Our building manager **proffered** extra keys to the new tenants.
3. In our town, it's considered **blasphemy** to not support the local football team.
4. The breeze blew **placidly** across the still lake.
5. As a toddler her bold remarks were cute, but in school they smack of **impudence**.

Literary Tools

Stage of Plot—Events in Pygmalion

Exposition—Setting (Victorian London) and characters (Liza, Higgins, Pickering, the Eynsford Hills family) is introduced.

of mine, at Eale & Binman's. You can choose the color. (*His cheerful, careless, vigorous voice shows that he is incorrigible.*)

What does Higgins think that Liza will do? Will she?

LIZA (*disdainfully*). Buy them yourself. (*She sweeps out.*)

MRS HIGGINS. I'm afraid youve spoiled that girl, Henry. But never mind, dear: I'll buy you the tie and gloves.

HIGGINS (*sunnily*). Oh, dont bother. She'll buy em all right enough. Goodbye.

(*They kiss.* MRS HIGGINS *runs out.* HIGGINS, *left alone, rattles his cash in his pocket; chuckles; and disports himself in a highly self-satisfied manner.*) ■

Respond *to the* SELECTION

Who has the upper hand at the end of the play—Eliza or Higgins? Explain.

SELECTION CHECK TEST 4.12.9 WITH ANSWERS (CONT.)

Evidence of Higgins' interest in phonetics and of class distinctions

Inciting Incident—Liza comes for locution lessons; Higgins and Pickering wager

Rising Action—Higgins and Pickering take Liza in; Doolittle visits; Liza meets Mrs. Higgins and the Eynsford Hills family

Crisis/Turning Point—Liza passes the "test" at the garden party; Higgins declares the experiment over; Liza and Higgins fight

Resolution/Denouement—Liza discovers ways to care for herself and stands up to Higgins; Higgins explains himself; Liza resists his attempts to treat her like a servant

Investigate, Inquire, Imagine

Recall: Gathering Facts →

1a. What does Doolittle look like when he arrives at Mrs. Higgins's? How does Doolittle react to his new status?

2a. What relationship does Eliza not want to have with Higgins and her father?

3a. How does Higgins attempt to justify his bad manners toward Eliza?

Interpret: Finding Meaning

1b. Why does Doolittle blame Higgins for delivering him into the hands of middle-class morality? What fear keeps Doolittle from renouncing his new station in life? For whom does Doolittle feel responsible?

2b. Under what conditions might Eliza have agreed to stay with Higgins? Could Higgins meet those conditions?

3b. How does Higgins continue to treat Eliza?

Analyze: Taking Things Apart →

4a. In act 5, both Eliza and Doolittle claim that rising out of the lower class has taken away their independence. What constraints do Eliza and Doolittle feel as part of the middle class that they did not feel before?

Synthesize: Bringing Things Together

4b. What ideas about class does Shaw present in *Pygmalion?*

Evaluate: Making Judgments →

5a. Evaluate how Higgins sees Eliza.

Extend: Connecting Ideas

5b. Read "The Story of Pygmalion" on page 1168. How is Higgins like Pygmalion?

Understanding Literature

Satire. Review the definition for **satire** in Literary Tools on page 1150. In what ways does Shaw satirize the following in his play?

- male domination of women
- "middle-class morality" and the work ethic
- upper-class attitudes toward the members of the lower classes
- artificial barriers between the classes
- late Victorian prudery
- fads among young people

Resolution. Review the definition for **resolution** in the Handbook of Literary Terms and the plot pyramid you made for Literary Tools. If this play is viewed as being about Eliza's struggle to gain independence, how does the act end, or resolve, that struggle? What idea does Eliza hit upon to make herself independent both of Higgins and of her father?

RESPOND TO THE SELECTION

Students might consider how each of the characters feels about himself or herself at this point. They might also consider where the support of the other characters falls. Students should consider the question from the point of view of Eliza, Higgins, and themselves as the audience. Do all three see the situation the same way?

Answers to Understanding Literature can be found on page 1166.

ANSWERS FOR INVESTIGATE, INQUIRE, IMAGINE

Recall

1a. Doolittle is dressed like a gentleman, wearing a new coat, trousers, a silk hat, patent leather shoes, and a flower in his buttonhole. Doolittle reacts to his new status with a mixture of regret for his past independence and plaintive resignation.

2a. She does not want to be dependent on either her father or Higgins.

3a. Higgins says that he treats all people as badly as he treats her, so she should not object.

Interpret

1b. Higgins was indirectly responsible for Doolittle receiving an income from a trust. Doolittle fears he will be forced to go to the workhouse if he does not accept the money offered him.

2b. Liza wants Higgins to treat her "more friendly like." While Higgins claims he has always felt "friendly like" toward Liza, he follows this claim by suggesting she return to the gutter, thus revealing that he will never be able to meet her conditions.

3b. Higgins is still attempting to treat Liza as a servant he can order about, but Liza is now resolutely refusing to submit to this treatment.

Analyze

4a. Some points students may raise in their discussion are the following: Liza and Doolittle feel the need to conform to the middle-class way of speaking and dressing. Liza feels constrained to do something genteel for a living. Doolittle feels compelled to care for his dependents and relatives.

Synthesize

4b. *Responses will vary.* The play suggests that there is a sharp difference between the classes. It also points out that one can acquire the trappings of a particular class or learn to look like a particular class. It also suggests that it is possible to be from a class but not to have acquired the skills or graces associated with that class.

Evaluate

5a. *Responses will vary.* Henry sees Eliza as his creation. He sees that he has changed her dramatically. He credits himself with any qualities or advantages that she has.

Extend

5b. *Responses will vary.* Higgins is like Pygmalion in that he falls in love with his own creation. Higgins might as well be admiring a statue because he generally objectifies Eliza and does not see her as a real person.

ANSWERS TO UNDERSTANDING LITERATURE

Satire. Shaw satirizes male domination of women by showing that it is counterproductive and ultimately destructive of the relationship between Higgins and Liza. He uses Doolittle as a running satire on" middle-class morality" by having Doolittle continually flaunt his transgressions of the norms of behavior for the middle class. He satirizes upper-class attitudes toward the members of the lower classes by showing Liza and Alfred Doolittle as equally able to act thoughtfully and intelligently and by characterizing Higgins as perfectly able to be ill-mannered and inconsiderate. The rise of Liza and Alfred Doolittle to the middle class satirizes the artificial distinctions between the classes. Higgins's iconoclastic remarks to the Eynsford Hills in Act Three satirize late Victorian prudery. The fascination of Freddy and Clara with "the new small talk," which exists only in their own imaginations, satirizes fads among young people.

Resolution. Act Five resolves Liza's struggle to be independent, because she considers and rejects the various options of dependency open to her (marriage or return to Higgins's or her father's household). Liza speaks of becoming a teacher of speech like Higgins in order to support herself.

ANSWERS TO INTEGRATING THE LANGUAGE ARTS

Language, Grammar, and Style
Responses will vary.

1. Colonel Pickering challenged Professor Higgins to make Liza a lady.
2. George Bernard Shaw clashed with both the political views and social attitudes of the London of his time.
3. Henry Higgins is attached to his mother and, for that reason, tries to avoid attachments to other women.
4. Is Doolittle better off as a member of the middle class, considering that he has lost his independence?
5. Higgins believes that without him Liza would soon return to selling flowers at Covent Garden.

Applied English
Remind students that the cost of ads is often based on number of lines or words. They should try to make their ads as concise as possible why clearly presenting all the relevant information.

Writer's Journal

1. Write a **note** from Colonel Pickering to Eliza apologizing for his and Higgins's behavior.
2. An epilogue is a concluding section or statement, often one that comments on or draws conclusions from the work as a whole. Write a brief prose **epilogue** for *Pygmalion* in which you tell what happens to each of the main characters after this act.

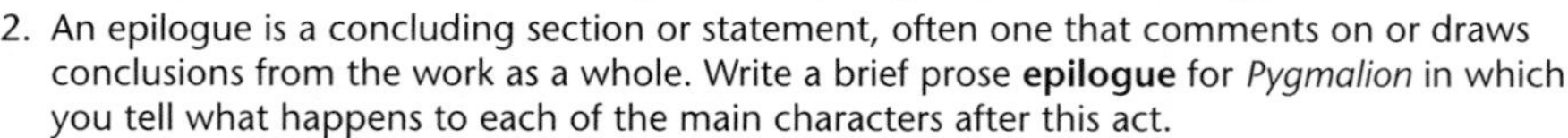

3. A treatment gives the story line for a film. Imagine you are a screenwriter. Write a **treatment** for a contemporary American film based on *Pygmalion* in much the same way as *West Side Story* is a revised *Romeo and Juliet*.

Integrating *the* Language Arts

Language, Grammar, and Style

Reducing Wordiness. Read the Language Arts Survey 3.35, "Correcting Wordy Sentences." Then rewrite the following sentences, eliminating unnecessary words. You may also make other minor revisions, as needed.

1. It was Colonel Pickering who was the one who challenged Professor Higgins to make a lady out of Eliza.
2. Not only the political views, but also the social attitudes of George Bernard Shaw were a cause of conflict with the London of his time.
3. It is in his relationship with his mother that Henry Higgins shows that he is attached to her and tries to avoid attachments to other women.
4. The question of whether or not Doolittle is better off as a middle-class man can be resolved by considering the fact that he has lost his independence.
5. It is Higgins's belief that if it were not for the continuance of his teaching, Eliza would end up returning to selling flowers at Covent Garden.

Applied English

Writing a Newspaper Ad. Imagine you are Eliza and you want to start your teaching business. Write a newspaper ad in which you describe your services, promise specified results, give the cost, and tell how you can be contacted.

Media Literacy & Collaborative Learning

Comparing Genres. Shaw detested the musical theater, considering it trivial and vulgar. During his lifetime, he was offered the opportunity to turn *Pygmalion* into a musical but refused. After he died, however, a musical, *My Fair Lady*, was made of the play. This was followed by a movie. View a videotape of *My Fair Lady* as a class. Then discuss the relative merits of the play and the musical. Was Shaw's play trivialized by making it into a musical? Were its social messages watered down? Do any examples of his biting satire remain? Does the musical take the same ideas to a wider audience? Which do you prefer and why?

ANSWERS TO INTEGRATING THE LANGUAGE ARTS (CONT.)

Speaking and Listening and Collaborative Learning
Before students view the musical, My Fair Lady, encourage them to read the Language Arts Survey 5.32, "How to Evaluate a Film."

PREREADING

"The Story of Pygmalion"

FROM THE METAMORPHOSES

BY OVID, RETOLD BY SARA HYRY

About the AUTHOR

Publius Ovidius Naso (43 BC–AD 17) was born in Sulmo, east of Rome, to a well-to-do family that was able to send him to Athens to finish his education. Originally destined for a law career, he soon turned to poetry and gained some success when his first series of love poems, *Amores,* was written about 15 BC. Ovid's early work showed a casual and witty treatment of love and marriage, and it is as a love poet that he was principally known throughout most of literary history. His fortunes turned drastically in AD 8 when he was banished from Rome by Emperor Augustus for an offense that remains unknown to this day. He was sent to live in Tomis, part of modern-day Romania, then an outpost of the Roman Empire populated by semibarbarous tribes. There Ovid spent the rest of his life, at times depressed and despondent, while his wife back in Rome vainly pleaded his case. The years in exile were still productive, for he continued to write poetry. However, his interest in amorous subjects decreased; during this time he wrote *Metamorphoses,* which is generally considered to be his greatest work.

About the SELECTION

"The Story of Pygmalion" comes from Ovid's ***Metamorphoses.*** This work, whose title means "changing forms," is a vast compendium of the myths of classical Greece and Rome, many of which deal with miraculous transformations—of Midas's daughter into gold, of Ariadne into a spider, and so on. That Ovid, whose life was subject to the buffets of change, should have hit upon this subject is not surprising. The Pygmalion myth is an example of both the early and late interests of Ovid, for love is the story's subject, but its theme is transformation.

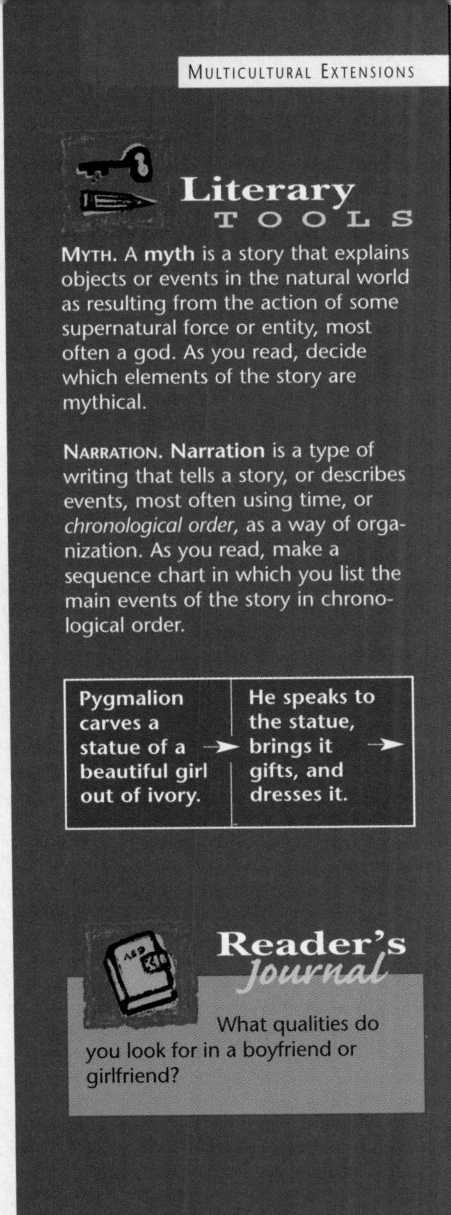

MULTICULTURAL EXTENSIONS

Literary TOOLS

MYTH. A **myth** is a story that explains objects or events in the natural world as resulting from the action of some supernatural force or entity, most often a god. As you read, decide which elements of the story are mythical.

NARRATION. **Narration** is a type of writing that tells a story, or describes events, most often using time, or *chronological order,* as a way of organization. As you read, make a sequence chart in which you list the main events of the story in chronological order.

Pygmalion carves a statue of a beautiful girl out of ivory. →	He speaks to the statue, brings it gifts, and dresses it. →

Reader's Journal

What qualities do you look for in a boyfriend or girlfriend?

ADDITIONAL RESOURCES

UNIT 12 RESOURCE BOOK
- Selection Worksheet 12.6
- Selection Check Test 4.12.11
- Selection Test 4.12.12
- Speaking and Listening Resource 4.20, 4.21

VOCABULARY FROM THE SELECTION

captivate

GRAPHIC ORGANIZER

He made offerings to Venus and asked that his statue be made his wife.
He changes his request and asks for a wife like her.
Pygmalion returned to and spoke to his statue.
He thought he saw her move.
He realized she was alive

READER'S JOURNAL

Ask students why these qualities are important to them.

GOALS/OBJECTIVES

Studying this lesson will enable students to
- enjoy a myth
- compare and contrast Ovid's version of the myth of Pygmalion and Shaw's *Pygmalion*
- define *myth* and *narration* and identify elements of each
- demonstrate the ability to research on a variety of topics
- participate in a debate

ANSWER TO GUIDED READING QUESTION

1. Pygmalion made a statue of a young woman. He fell in love with his creation.

INDIVIDUAL LEARNING STRATEGIES

MOTIVATION
In this selection, the main character sculpts a person he thinks is ideal. Have students create drawing, paintings, sculptures, or collages that demonstrate their ideal.

READING PROFICIENCY
Remind students that Ovid often dealt with the theme of transformation. Have them make a prediction about what will happen in this story.

ENGLISH LANGUAGE LEARNING
Point out the following words:
adorned—decorated
humbly—without pride
petition—request
fluidly—with easy and grace

SPECIAL NEEDS
Students will find it helpful to listen to the selection using the Audio Library. Make sure students focus on the Guided Reading question and the Recall questions in the Investigate, Inquire, and Imagine section.

ENRICHMENT
Ovid's *Metamorphoses* makes entertaining reading and is a tremendous storehouse of Greek and Roman mythology. Students can read one or more stories from Ovid. Ask students to write their own retelling of one of these stories.

SELECTION CHECK TEST 4.12.13 WITH ANSWERS

Checking Your Reading

1. What did Pygmalion carve out of snow-white ivory? **He carved a statue of a girl.**
2. How did Pygmalion begin to act toward this creation? **He treated it as if it were real.**
3. To whom did Pygmalion make an offering? **He made an offering to Venus.**
4. What did Pygmalion ask for? **He asked for a wife like his statue.**
5. What did he find when he returned home? **His statue came alive.**

Literary Tools

1. What is a myth? **A myth is a story that explains objects or events in the natural world, usually with supernatural forces or entities, such as gods.**
2. What elements suggest that this story is a myth? **It explains the creation of an ideal lover through the intervention of the goddess Venus.**
3. What is narration? **Narration is writing that tells a story or describes an event.**
4. What is the most common organizational pattern for narration? **Chronological order is the most common pattern for narration.**
5. What is a possible theme for this selection? **Responses will vary.**

CLASSICAL SOURCES

"THE STORY OF PYGMALION" FROM THE *METAMORPHOSES*

> *What did Pygmalion make? How did he feel about his creation?*

Pygmalion the sculptor lived alone. In his loneliness, he carved from a block of snow-white ivory a statue of a girl more beautiful than any who had ever lived. Pygmalion loved his statue so much that it seemed to him nearly alive. He spoke often to the statue and sometimes almost believed that it (or "she," as he preferred to call her) responded. He began to act as if the statue were indeed a real person: he brought her gifts of delicate shells, colorful flowers, pet birds, painted balls, and bits of amber.[1] He dressed her and adorned her with rings, earrings, and ribbons, all of which were very becoming, but it was her own beauty, the beauty that he had given her, that captivated him.

The holiday of Venus, the goddess of love and beauty, came, and the traditional festivities were held. As was customary, Pygmalion made an offering to Venus and humbly presented a petition. He almost asked that his ivory statue be made his wife, but on second thought, he changed his request and asked only for a wife like her. Venus heard his prayer and the true wish behind it and showed her presence in the leaping flame upon the altar.

After offering his prayer, Pygmalion returned to his snow-white statue and, as was his custom, spoke to her and extended her the same kindness he would offer to a person. He gazed at the white loveliness of her cold limbs and imagined what it would be like to see them flush with color. Alas, he thought, that shall never happen. Consider his amazement, then, when he thought he saw her move! He rubbed his eyes and looked again. Her snow-white skin had taken on a lifelike glow. Her stiff ivory limbs began to move fluidly and gracefully. She was alive! Her eyes opened, and she smiled upon him, and from above, Venus smiled upon him too, happy with the love she had created. ■

1. **amber.** Hard yellowish fossil resin used as a gem

WORDS FOR EVERYDAY USE

cap • ti • vate (kap′ tə vāt) *vt.*, influence and dominate with an irresistible appeal; attract. *Justin's athletic ability captivated Julia.*

Respond *to the* SELECTION

Imagine that you are the statue and you have just come to life. Describe your first sensations—seeing, touching, hearing, tasting, smelling.

INVESTIGATE, Inquire, *Imagine*

Recall: GATHERING FACTS

1a. What is Pygmalion's profession?

2a. To whom does Pygmalion pray? What does he pray for?

3a. What happens as a result of his prayer?

Interpret: FINDING MEANING

1b. What does Pygmalion appreciate about his art?

2b. Why does Venus believe Pygmalion loves the statue?

3b. What kind of relationship does Pygmalion have with his statue at the end of the story?

Analyze: TAKING THINGS APART →

4a. What does Pygmalion believe about Venus?

Synthesize: BRINGING THINGS TOGETHER

4b. What can you infer about the powers of the the Roman gods?

Evaluate: MAKING JUDGMENTS →

5a. Evaluate whether Pygmalion is shallow and egotistical.

Extend: CONNECTING IDEAS

5b. How do the conclusions of the Ovid's story and of Shaw's play differ? How are they alike? What lessons about love and pride does Henry Higgins fail to learn? Why is it presumptuous and unforgivable for Higgins to view Eliza as his creation? What point does Shaw make about love?

Understanding *Literature*

MYTH. Review the definition for **myth** in Literary Tools on page 1167. Which elements of the story are mythical?

NARRATION. Review the definition for **narration** in the Handbook of Literary Terms and the sequence chart you made for Literary Tools on page 1167. Which event in your sequence chart makes this story a myth? How could the story have an ending that is not mythical?

ANSWERS FOR UNDERSTANDING LITERATURE

MYTH. Events that make this story mythical are: the presence of mythical characters—Pygmalion and Venus; a mortal making a request to the goddess, Venus; a man falling in love with an inanimate object—a statue that he created out of ivory; and a goddess bringing life to a statue.

NARRATION. The statue comes to life. If Pygmalion met a real woman, who looked like his statue or who in some other way attracted him, and he fell in love with her, the ending would be more realistic than mythical.

RESPOND TO THE SELECTION

Students might also role play a dialogue between Pygmalion and the statue that has come to life.

ANSWERS TO INVESTIGATE, INQUIRE, IMAGINE

RECALL

1a. Pygmalion is a sculptor

2a. He prays to Venus. First he asks for his statue to become his wife. He changes his request and asks for a wife like his statue.

3a. The statue comes to life.

INTERPRET

1b. He appreciates the beauty of his art.

2b. Venus sees the attention Pygmalion lavishes on his statue and the kind way he talks to her as though she were a person.

3b. Pygmalion and the statue come to life seem to have a loving relationship.

ANALYZE

4a. *Responses will vary.* Pygmalion believes that Venus as the goddess of love can grant his request.

SYNTHESIZE

4b. *Responses will vary.* The Roman gods seem to have the power to grant wishes as they chose and to make things come to life.

EVALUATE

5a. *Responses will vary.* Pygmalion does fall in love based solely on beauty and his own ability to create. He is, however, looking for something outside of himself to love. He is humble in front of the gods.

EXTEND

5b. *Responses will vary.* The myth ends with Pygmalion loving his creation. At the end of Shaw's play, Higgins is unable to love his "creation." Both men have strong feelings about their ability to create. Pygmalion learns to love only what he has created. Higgins fails to learn that his self-absorbed behavior will prevent him from ever having a loving relationship with an equal. Eliza is a person not a thing that Higgins created. He may have taught her a few things, but she picked up many more on her own. She is an independent being, not a creation who can only exist in his shadow. Shaw suggests that any relationship not based on mutual respect is bound to be unsatisfactory and one-sided.

ANSWERS TO INTEGRATING THE LANGUAGE ARTS

Speaking and Listening & Study and Research
Ovid's *Metamorphoses* and Edith Hamilton's *Mythology* are two good sources for myths about Venus. Many children's storybooks have concise stories about different gods and goddesses as well.

Internet Resource
Many of the stories Ovid tells are depicted in works of art. Students can find examples of many of these at www.geocities.com/Athens/Atlantis/8268/index.html. Ask students to examine one or more work of art. Have them find a version of the myth that corresponds to the work they choose. Then have them answer these questions: Does the work of art represent the same attitude toward the story that the literary version does? What discrepancies between the two versions can you find? Students can try to tell the story based on what they see in the work of art.

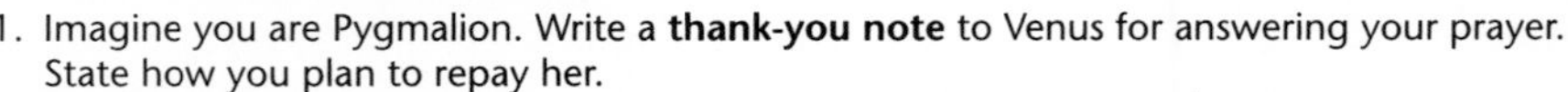

Writer's Journal

1. Imagine you are Pygmalion. Write a **thank-you note** to Venus for answering your prayer. State how you plan to repay her.
2. Ovid has been known through the ages for his poems about love. Write your own **definition** for *love* and for *infatuation*. Then give an example for each.
3. Imagine you are a museum curator. Write a **catalogue entry** for a famous statue, such as Michelangelo's *David* or Rodin's *The Thinker*. A catalogue entry gives the date the statue was completed, some information about the sculptor, and details about the artistic importance of the statue.

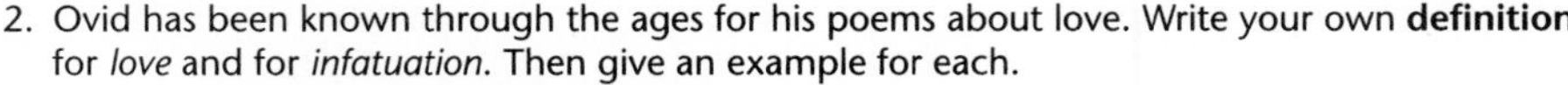

Integrating *the* Language Arts

Speaking and Listening & Study and Research

Researching Venus. Venus was the Roman goddess of love and beauty. Research the elements associated with her such as the pomegranate, several stories in which she plays a part (e.g., the story of her birth), and other interesting facts such as her Greek counterpart. Then tell a story about Venus to a small group of your classmates. You may want to review the Language Arts Survey 4.20, "Telling a Story."

Study and Research & Collaborative Learning

Researching the *Metamorphoses*. The *Metamorphoses* tells transformation stories that the ancient Romans believed in. For example, the first metamorphosis in Ovid's collection tells the story of how the gods changed chaos into order in the universe. Research five of these stories, then make a chart listing what was transformed and what it became. Explain your chart to two classmates, giving a synopsis of each story. Each person in the group should be responsible for five stories.

Speaking and Listening & Collaborative Learning

Participating in a Debate. In small groups, imagine you are the gods on Mount Olympus deciding whether or not to grant Pygmalion his wish. Half the group provides arguments why Venus should change the statue into a live woman, and half the group provides arguments why Venus should not intervene in the affairs of humans. Allow time for both constructive speeches and rebuttal speeches. Before you begin, you may want to review the Language Arts Survey 4.21, "Participating in a Debate."

REVIEWING A FILM OR PLAY

You're already a seasoned critical reviewer. Every time you share your opinions about a video you rented over the weekend or a play you saw with a friend, you're acting the part of a critic. As we know from watching or listening to professional reviewers, opinions can be powerful. But an effective film review cannot rely on opinion alone. A reviewer must be acutely aware of the elements of dramatic performance and how those elements can work harmoniously to make a great theatrical or cinematic experience. Acting, lighting, script, direction, where he or she was sitting in the theater: these are only some of the elements the critic must examine. After being a member of the audience, the reviewer must then take his or her critical perspective and pair it with strong persuasive writing. The combination of critical viewing and persuasion, if done convincingly, can make us run to the theaters on opening night, or patiently "wait until it comes out on video."

WRITING ASSIGNMENT. In this assignment you will write a review of a film or play. In doing so, you will practice your persuasive writing and hone your abilities to convince your audience of your well-reasoned opinion.

"O, it offends me to the soul to hear a robustious periwig-pated fellow tear a passion to tatters, to very rags, to split the ears of the groundlings..."

—William Shakespeare, *Hamlet*

Professional Model

from a film review by James Berardinelli of *My Fair Lady*

Consider this possibility: a romantic comedy with no nudity, no sex, and no kissing. In fact, there aren't even any declarations of love. The closest the female character comes to admitting her feelings is saying that she could have danced all night with the man; the closest he gets is remarking that he's grown accustomed to her face. Could such a project lift off the pad in today's climate? Almost certainly not.... So it's fortunate that circumstances and expectations were different in 1964, when *My Fair Lady* reached the screen.

It could easily be argued that *My Fair Lady* is one of the richest and most intelligent romantic comedies ever

EXAMINING THE MODEL. Any persuasive writer needs to be clear about his or her opinion. Beyond just indicating that he likes *My Fair Lady*, Berardinelli uses concise language to express his opinion about the acting and dialogue, thereby supporting and adding depth to his obviously favorable review. What other elements of filmmaking could Berardinelli examine in his review?

continued on page 1172

LESSON OVERVIEW

GUIDED WRITING *Software*

See the Guided Writing Software for an extended version of this lesson that includes printable graphic organizers, extensive student models and student-friendly checklists, and self-, peer, and teacher evaluation features.

INDIVIDUAL LEARNING STRATEGIES

MOTIVATION
Hold a class discussion on how useful students find film and play reviews. You may also want to show the musical *My Fair Lady* (the basis of the professional model) and ask students if they agree with James Berardinelli's review or not.

READING PROFICIENCY
Refer students to the Language Arts Survey 5.32, "How to Evaluate a Film." By knowing the guidelines by which films are critiqued, students will have a clearer idea of writing a film or play review.

(Continued on page 1172)

INDIVIDUAL LEARNING STRATEGIES

(CONT. FROM PAGE 1171)

ENGLISH LANGUAGE LEARNING
See strategies for Reading Proficiency above that will benefit students who are English language learners. Also refer students to the Language Arts Survey 1.16, "Using Context Clues to Estimate Word Meaning" to help them develop their vocabulary.

SPECIAL NEEDS
Encourage students to use the student model review as a basis for writing their own review. You may want to focus the assignment for them by asking them to provide the plot of the film or play and then to establish who is the most effective character. They can then illustrate this premise with examples from the film or play.

ENRICHMENT
Ask students to submit their film or play review to their school or local newspaper. Remind students that published work needs to be polished, professional, and free of grammatical errors.

Prewriting

FINDING YOUR VOICE
Ask students to read the Language Arts Survey 2.5, "Finding Your Voice." Encourage students to analyze the voice of Karen Arle's revised student model film review on page 1176. Then have them write a description of the voice they will be trying to use in their own review.

IDENTIFYING YOUR AUDIENCE
Review point of view with students. Explain to students that a review told in the first-person is more casual and informal, whereas a review told in the third-person point of view reflects a more formal and academic tone. This information should help students to identify their audience and the type of voice they want to use.

WRITING WITH A PLAN
Have students write out the questions they want to address in their review, using those shown in the Student Model—Graphic Organizer to get them started.

Regardless of how well-informed your audience is, it is always a good idea for a reviewer to provide some basic plot and character information in the review. Your goal is not to provide a complete summary of the movie. Instead, summarize only those details necessary to establish a clear understanding of the basic story and the main characters. By providing a simple frame of reference, you will keep your audience informed enough to understand your comments without giving the story away in the process. What are the essential details of plot and character Berardinelli provides in his review?

A well-supported, persuasive review cannot exist on opinion alone. Look again at Berardinelli's review and notice the words he chooses to express his ideas. Saying an actor is "good" is not as effective as saying, "Rex Harrison was born to play Higgins, and he delivers every line with the snap and zing of one who relishes the chance to speak such delicious dialogue." Such vivid language makes clear the enthusiasm of Berardinelli's opinion and increases the power of his persuasion.

produced. The dialogue...is brilliant: a perfect amalgamation of well-honed wit and barbed satire.

The basic story line concerns Eliza, a poor Cockney from Covent Garden who is transformed into a lady under the tutelage of [Henry] Higgins. When he first encounters her, an unwashed girl with a grating voice selling flowers, he forms an opinion: "A woman who utters such disgusting and depressing noises has...no right to live. Remember that you're a human being with a soul and the divine gift of articulate speech..." The next morning, she shows up at his house, asking him to teach her how to speak properly and be a lady. Higgins…agrees.
Not only does *My Fair Lady* feature an involving story with compelling characters, but there's not a dud to be found on the roster of more than a dozen songs....

Rarely has a movie been as well cast as this one. Rex Harrison was born to play Higgins, and he delivers every line with the snap and zing of one who relishes the chance to speak such delicious dialogue. Audrey Hepburn is luminous as Eliza… Few genres of films are as magical as musicals, and few musicals are as intelligent and lively as *My Fair Lady*. It's a classic... because it has been, and always will be, a pure joy to experience.

Prewriting

FINDING YOUR VOICE. If you've ever seen a film or play reviewed on television or heard one over the radio, then you know how conversational the tone of a review can be. The reviewer wants to convince the audience and he or she certainly can't do so by sounding stilted or arrogant. The voice with which you write your film review should be natural and direct, making clear your opinion with the emphasis necessary to persuade your audience. Avoid being overly dramatic in either direction. Once you state an opinion, make sure you back it up with evidence.

IDENTIFYING YOUR AUDIENCE. Before you begin drafting your review, consider the target audience of the film or play. Is it a comedy meant for a high school crowd? Is it a serious drama? Is it intended for children, but one that parents may want more information about? Keep the movie audience in mind as you draft your review. Consider that you may publish your findings on a school web page that has categories for different genres and audiences.

WRITING WITH A PLAN. Before you write, consider what you want to accomplish. Do you want your audience to be excited by your opinion? Ambivalent about the actors' performance? Do you want your reader to know about the way the film or play was produced, who the stage designer is, who directed the film, or why it is considered controversial? You need to have a specific focus in mind before you start a draft. That means having some questions in mind while you watch the movie or play.

Think about the different elements that make a film or play what it is: the story, the actors and the way each interprets his or her individual character, the way the director uses cameras and lighting, the musical score, the length of the production. Each of these elements contributes to the completed product we see when we sit down in a theater. As you watch your film or play, look for these elements and consider how each makes an impact on the final performance. Remember that just about everything we see on the screen or stage has been scripted, practiced and edited numerous times to create a particular feel or response from the audience. Your job as the reviewer is to be aware of these individual elements and determine their net result on the story.

As you organize your ideas and write your review, realize that you can't write about everything that is a success or failure of the production. Once you've written your lead paragraph stating your general opinion, choose the details that you think had the greatest impact and focus on those. Writing with depth about a few items is usually better than a cursory glance at every minute element. Karyn Arle, a senior English student, began her graphic organizer as follows:

"He hath a heart as sound as a bell and his tongue is the clapper; for what his heart thinks his tongue speaks."
—William Shakespeare, *Much Ado About Nothing*

Student Model—Graphic Organizer

Name of Film/Director: *A Room with a View* Directed by James Ivory
What is the theme of the film and how do the development in plot, character and conflict contribute to it? Central theme: if follow your heart — it will lead you to what you desire most.
Is the theme "modern"? If not, is it relevant to life today, and how? Not modern—still relevant to life and love. Sometimes we may think too hard rather than following our hearts.
Does the setting/time period add anything to the film? If so, what? Yes, in the time of the film everyone was worried about his or her neighbor's opinion and it was imperative for a woman to be proper.

STUDENT MODEL—GRAPHIC ORGANIZER

See the Guided Writing Resource for a blackline master of the Graphic Organizer for this lesson.

Drafting

Encourage students to use their completed Graphic Organizer to help them make sure they have organized the main points of their review carefully. When providing a synopsis, remind students not to reveal the outcome of the film or play. One way to consider their synopsis is to see it as a motivation tool to get their audience to see or not see the film or play. You might want to review documenting sources at the end or their reviews.

Drafting

Once you have gathered your notes in the prewriting stage, begin your draft. The draft is your chance to organize those thoughts into something more cohesive and unified.

The first paragraph is critical since it is where you state your main idea or thesis while hooking the reader's interest. In the professional model, James Berardinelli challenges our expectations of what elements are "necessary" to make a romantic comedy succeed. How you approach your thesis is up to you, but don't forget that what you write in your first sentences will determine whether or not your reader moves on to the second paragraph or puts your review in the recycling bin.

Your notes are your raw materials at this point. You need to form and reshape them numerous times before you will have a finished piece. Your notes should ultimately focus on a limited number of elements. Perhaps the performance from the main character was strong in spite of a weak script. Maybe the lighting caught your attention more than the music. As you organize your comments on these ideas into paragraphs, support them with examples from the performance.

While drafting, remember that you are the critic. Ask yourself what its strengths or weaknesses do to the film or play as a whole. They will serve as evidence for your opinion and give credibility to your review.

continued on page 1175

Are there any notable symbols that contribute to the overall message? *Lucy's brother Freddie: freedom of heart* *Lucy's Aunt Charlotte: someone who worries excessively about what others think. Both: the two sides of the conflict present in the film.*
Possible Thesis Statements *The film is beautifully photographed and the performances are all good, but the strongest element of A Room with a View is character development.* *James Ivory's A Room with a View is a wonderful film about love, honesty and beauty. With strong performances from the entire cast, magnificent cinematography, a humorous but restrained script, and brilliant characterization, A Room with a View is a necessary addition to anyone's film library.* *The main conflict of the film is Lucy versus herself in the matter of love and whether or not she should follow her heart or adhere to what is proper.*

Your prewriting notes should provide you with a few good generalizations from which to start your draft. Let those notes be a guide to your reactions to the film.

Student Model—Rough Draft

Title? excerpted from a review
by Karyn Arle

You need a stronger intro. — This is a love story. Imagine a time when you were not expected to marry for love, but only for money and status. *Are these the best words here?* Sure~~,~~*ly* it sounds very old fashioned and ridiculous but ~~on~~ *after* a quick overview of modern society, the idea does not seem so preposterous. Today we still choose our partners upon ~~qualities~~ *best word? superficialities* such as wealth, beauty, and prestige rather than an intimate knowledge *understanding* of them. "A Room with a View" *italicize title* is a film set in the late 1800s in Europe and encourages the audience to look beyond the exterior and into their hearts, an old theme that still holds relevance in our society today. James Ivory's *A Room with a View* is a wonderful film about love, honesty and beauty. With strong performances from the entire cast, magnificent cinematography, a humorous but restrained script, and brilliant characterization, *A Room with a View* is a necessary addition to anyone's film library.

It is a story of a woman's indecision between doing what her heart desires and what society wished for her to do, personified by her struggle to choose between two suitors. She meets George Emerson in Paris, a modern city that has more tolerance for freedom of ideas. He is strange to her in his lack of restraint she is accustomed to and she finds herself simultaneously drawn and repelled by him. The most intense moment between them is set in a barley field in the country in Paris where she walks over to him after being shooed away by her aunt and is drawn into his arms in a passionate kiss. The scene is

that

You don't mention any of the elements of film—what about acting? camera? directing?

Is "wishes" best word? What about "expects" or "demands"

expects

make it parallel

than what?

awkward–reword

to

be more specific?

Fix run-on sentence

Keep your paragraphs focused on your main idea and conclude with a clear recommendation to your audience. For more information, see the Language Arts Survey 2.24, "Writing Paragraphs," 2.32, "Drafting an Introduction," 2.33, "Drafting Body Paragraphs," and 2.34, "Drafting a Conclusion."

Self- and Peer Evaluation

After you finish your first draft, complete a self-evaluation of your review. If time allows, you may want to get input from one or two other students. As you evaluate your essay, ask yourself the following questions. Take notes to help you with your revision.

- How effectively in the first paragraph does the writer grab the reader's attention?
- What individual elements of the film (like acting, cinematography, and scripting) does the reviewer address in the introduction?
- What facts about the film or play does the first paragraph offer?
- What are the key words in the thesis statement? Are there other possibilities in word choice that would state the opinion with more clarity, confidence, or understanding of the material?

continued on page 1176

Self- and Peer Evaluation

Have students review the Language Arts Survey 2.37, "Self- and Peer Evaluation." Then have students use the checklist on pages 1175 and 1176 for self- and peer evaluation. The checklist is intended to act as a student-friendly rubric that should help students identify specific evidence of writing strengths and areas needing improvement. Make sure they provide concrete suggestions for improvement or specific evidence of why the writing works.

Revising and Proofreading

A handout of the proofreading checklist in the Language Arts Survey is available in the Teacher's Resource Kit, Guided Writing Resource Book 2.45. Students critiquing their classmates' work might be interested in using common proofreader's symbols, which are found in the Language Arts Survey 2.44, "Using Proofreader's Marks."

- Does the reviewer "give away" the film too much? Is there enough detail in the review about directing, acting, and scripting to interest the audience in this film?
- What elements from the play or film does the reviewer choose to comment on? What examples support the commentary?
- How would you describe the voice of the reviewer? Is it confident? derisive? uncertain? well informed? More importantly, is the voice consistent?
- What elements of plot summary and characterization does the reviewer use? Are the details sufficient to form a frame of reference for the uninformed audience?

Revising and Proofreading

Review your self- and peer evaluations. Revise your writing after considering these comments. Keep in mind that revision is just that—re-vision. This means more than adding a comma or fixing capitalization. Be prepared to change, perhaps even remove, entire paragraphs. Consider adding points you omitted in your first draft. Then look at word order, sentence structure, and paragraph organization. Finally, proofread your work for errors in grammar, usage, and mechanics. See the Language Arts Survey 2.45 for a proofreading checklist.

soon broken by the appearance of her excessively proper Aunt Charlotte who demands that they return home as soon as possible.

This first half of the film, shot in Florence, is particulary enjoyable. James Ivory uses the art and archetecture to his advantage as Lucy and the rest of the cast tour the city and learn about its rich past. The ~~passion~~ spirit of the Renaissance lives on as the characters lose themselves in winding alleyways and city-square mayhem, only to emerge as changed individuals on the other side. In the country, where George and Lucy share their moment, the beauty of Tuscany is revealed as the characters picnic in an orchard and view Florence from their distant hilltop.

Good comparison here

yes

Yes, now you're addressing the film!

Student Model—Revised

Matters of the Victorian Heart
by Karyn Arle

Imagine a time when people were forced to marry because of social standing and cultural expectations. Surely, it sounds old-fashioned, but after a quick overview of modern society, the idea does not seem so preposterous. Today we often choose our partners upon superficialities such as wealth, beauty, and prestige rather than on a solid understanding of who they really are. *A Room with a View* is a film set in the late 1800s in Europe that encourages the audience to look beyond the exterior world of custom and manners and look instead into their hearts. Directed by James Ivory, *A Room with a View* is a wonderful film about love, honesty, and beauty. With strong performances from the entire cast, magnificent cinematography, a humorous but restrained script, and brilliant characterization, *A Room with a View* is a necessary addition to anyone's film library.

A Room with a View is the story of Lucy Honeychurch, a young English woman of some means, and her indecision between doing what her heart desires and what society expects. Lucy's struggle is revealed in a choice she must make between two suitors.

She meets George Emerson in Florence, a city full of the passion of the Renaissance and the roughness of urban life. George is strange to her, with a lack of restraint to which she is unaccustomed. She finds herself simultaneously drawn to and repelled by him. The most intense moment between George and Lucy is set in the countryside. Out for a carriage ride with a group of other tourists, Lucy encounters George, alone in a barley field, and is drawn into his arms in a passionate kiss. The scene is soon broken by the arrival of her excessively proper Aunt Charlotte, who demands that she and Lucy return home as soon as possible. Lucy and George don't speak after the kiss and with the vacation over, we presume the same for the couple.

The first half of the film, shot in Florence, is particularly enjoyable. James Ivory uses art and architecture to his advantage as Lucy and the rest

Language, Grammar, and Style

Writing Introductory Paragraphs

IDENTIFYING WELL-WRITTEN INTRODUCTORY PARAGRAPHS. While the first sentence must be an attention-grabbing "headline," the thesis must act as the anchor of the paper. In a review such as the one you are doing for this unit, your thesis is embodied in your opinion. In a persuasive paper, you are writing to persuade or convince your reader to agree with what you have to say or, at least, consider another perspective. Like a good opening sentence, a good thesis grabs attention because it offers a new perspective or makes readers re-evaluate what they thinks they already know. Look at the professional model. Notice how Berardinelli opens his review and moves into his main idea.

> "Consider this possibility: a romantic comedy with no nudity, no sex, and no kissing. In fact, there aren't even any declarations of love. The closest the female character comes to admitting her feelings is saying that she could have danced all night with the man; the closest he gets is remarking that he's grown accustomed to her face. Could such a project lift off the pad in today's

continued on page 1178

Language, Grammar, and Style

WRITING INTRODUCTORY PARAGRAPHS
Lesson Overview
In this lesson, students will be asked to do the following:

- Identify Well-Written Introductory Paragraphs
- Fix Introductory Paragraphs
- Use Well-Written Introductory Paragraphs

INTRODUCING THE SKILL
Explain to students to because a review is based on opinion, the introductory paragraph must be well-written in order to keep the reader's attention. Therefore, the first paragraph must be attention-grabbing, clear, and coherent.

Previewing the Skill
Ask students to analyze the introductory paragraph in the Professional Model. What grabbed their attention? What motivated them to read further? How does the tone or voice the writer uses add to the effectiveness of the first paragraph?

Practicing the Skill
For more information on writing well-written paragraphs, refer students to the Language Arts Survey 2.25, "Writing a Thesis Statement" and 2.32, "Drafting an Introduction"

climate? Almost certainly not... So it's fortunate that circumstances and expectations were different in 1964, when *My Fair Lady* reached the screen. More than three decades later, the movie, which won the Best Picture Oscar, remains a musical favorite."

What technique does Berardinelli use to get his audience's attention?

The thesis, or in this case, the opinion of the writer, follows on the heels of the opening salvo. Berardinelli asks, "Could such a project lift off the pad in today's climate?" The answer is one he feels confident with and one he thinks his audience agrees with. He then states, "So it's fortunate..." It is at this point that we know we're dealing with a favorable review. What, then, is Berardinelli's thesis?

Fixing Introductory Paragraphs. Look at the opening sentence of the rough and final drafts of the student model. See if you can determine why the author settled for the final version over the rough. Do you agree with her changes?

DRAFT

This is a love story.

REVISION

Imagine a time when people were forced to marry because of social standing and cultural expectations.

continued on page 1179

of the characters tour the city and learn about its rich past. The spirit of the Renaissance lives in the characters as they lose themselves down winding alleyways and city-square mayhem and emerge as changed individuals on the other side. In the countryside, where George and Lucy share their moment, the beauty of Tuscany is revealed while the cast picnics in an orchard and views Florence from their distant hilltop.

The beauty of the setting serves the script and characterization well. Lucy and her aunt find themselves out of their element in Florence and tend to follow the lead of others. George and his father, however, fit the city perfectly. They embrace the spirit of its beauty and mystery, and as George shouts his creed and asks his questions, he is doing so with all due respect to the sculptures and buildings around him.

Once home, Lucy is quickly engaged to Cecil Vyse, a man of impeccable standing and social grace. He is what she assumes a husband should be, though he may not be what she really wants. When George shows up, unexpectedly rents a house close by and befriends Lucy's wild brother, she is forced to decide between George's persistent love and the snobbish appeal of Cecil.

The tension that started in Florence continues back home in Britain and it is here the script shines brightest with humor and grace. Cecil, played by Daniel Day Lewis, is fun to hate. Lucy's uncertainty, serious and believable, never succumbs to melodrama. And George, always persistently passionate, is magnetic to both Lucy and the viewing audience. We want him to find love. We want to believe his creed.

Lucy's is a decision that requires knowledge of self, and she only reaches for this knowledge reluctantly. *A Room with a View,* by allowing us to witness this indecision, prompts us to face the humor and frailty behind matters of the heart. With wit and beauty, Ivory reveals this restrained Victorian heart with clarity and kindness. And, of course, Lucy makes the right decision in the end.

Publishing and Presenting

If you're writing a review of a current production of a film or play, submit your review to a local paper or perhaps a public radio station. Guest opinions keep the media connected to the public and a voice from the crowd can be a welcome change from a professional critic.

If the movie or play you're reviewing is an older production, consider publishing your findings on your school website or in the school newspaper.

Finally, film and stage drama are often important reflections of social change. Your review could become part of a research project in a social studies or science class that is examining trends or fads related to a certain historical era or scientific discipline.

Reflecting

Do you remember when you saw your first movie or play? Think of how many you have seen since then and how well you already know this medium. The language of pictures and the power of drama are all around us. How has reviewing the play or film changed the way you viewed it? How will it affect the way you view productions in the future? Many people find that becoming an astute member of the audience can help them enjoy these activities more.

Now find the thesis statement in both models. Is it clear to you, the reader, just what the main point of the review will be? If not, how do you think this student author could sharpen the focus of the thesis?

Using Well-Written Introductory Paragraphs. As you write your own film review, keep a collection of opening sentences that you tried but didn't like. When you print a copy of your final draft, print a separate sheet containing only the first sentences. Compare your evolving sentence with your classmates'. Discuss your final choice and process of selection and ask your peer editor if he or she agrees with your decision.

Revising a thesis can be even more daunting than an opening sentence. Remember that in a review, you are addressing the "why" (your explanation) as much as the "what" (your opinion.) Avoid writing vague thesis statements or statements that are too obvious in nature.

For more information, see the Language Arts Survey 2.25, "Writing a Thesis Statement."

Publishing and Presenting

Students may want to print all their reviews together, with a section for films and a section for plays, and distribute the collection to their friends and teachers. You might also talk to the librarian of your school and see about including the film and play reviews collection to the library.

Reflecting

Encourage students to analyze several reviews of plays and films written by professionals to see how they are judged by professional reviewers. Then have them compare those reviews with the reviews their class wrote.

ADDITIONAL RESOURCES

Unit 12 Resource Book
- Vocabulary Worksheet
- Study Guide: Unit 12 Test
- Unit 12 Test

VOCABULARY DEVELOPMENT

Give students the following exercise: Write a dialogue in which you incorporate 15 words from the list on page 1180. Then with a partner, practice both dialogues aloud, paying attention to correct pronunciation of the new vocabulary words.

UNIT 12 REVIEW
Twentieth-Century to Contemporary Drama

Words for Everyday Use

Check your knowledge of the following vocabulary words from the selections in this unit. Write short sentences using these words in context to make the meaning clear. To review the definition or usage of a word, refer to the page number listed or the Glossary of Words for Everyday Use.

amiable, 1104
arbitrary, 1122
astride, 1120
audacity, 1123
barometrical, 1136
bilious, 1108
blasphemy, 1163
brocade, 1131
brusquely, 1133
callous, 1125
captivate, 1168
caricature, 1131
condescend, 1146
conscientiously, 1127
consort, 1163
convulsively, 1138
coroneted, 1144
deprecate, 1105
diffident, 1122
disdain, 1128
dogmatically, 1120
dudgeon, 1148
elocutionary, 1117
estheticism, 1131
extort, 1123
forecastle, 1138
genteel, 1113
ginger, 1126
gumption, 1102
impertinent, 1107
impetuous, 1112
imprecation, 1136
impudence, 1161
incensed, 1128
incorrigible, 1157
infatuated, 1135
jaunt, 1124
judicial, 1121
magisterially, 1123
magnanimous, 1159
melancholy, 1106
mendacity, 1109
millennium, 1147
pallor, 1144
pauperize, 1126
pedantic, 1135
perfunctorily, 1148
placidly, 1155
plaint, 1120
portico, 1101
presumptuous, 1118
pretension, 1131
proximity, 1104
prudery, 1116
purgatory, 1145
remonstrance, 1118
resolutely, 1118
repudiate, 1107
score, 1120
snigger, 1137
snivel, 1114
soirée, 1134
solicitor, 1152
spraddling, 1158
staid, 1105
steadfastly, 1121
straitened, 1133
toadying, 1163
unabashed, 1125
unassailable, 1121
zephyr, 1116

Literary Tools

Define the following terms, giving concrete examples of how they are used in the selections in this unit. To review a term, refer to the page number indicated or to the Handbook of Literary Terms.

antihero, 1143
blocking, 1131
characterize, 1111
climax, 1143
dramatic irony, 1131
inciting incident, 1101
myth, 1167
narration, 1167
resolution, 1150
satire, 1111, 1150
spectacle, 1101

Reflecting on Your Reading

Genre Studies

1. **Dramatic Irony.** Irony is a difference between appearance and reality. Dramatic irony is a type of irony in which something is known by the reader or audience but not known by the characters. Identify instances of dramatic irony in Shaw's *Pygmalion* and in Shakespeare's *Macbeth.* Discuss any similarities between these instances.

2. **Didacticism.** A didactic work is one in which the artistic values of the work are subordinated to the goal of conveying a moral, social, educational, or political message. Is Shaw's play *Pygmalion* a didactic work in this sense? Explain your answer.

3. **Staging in Modern Theater.** Theater changed a great deal between Shakespeare's day and Shaw's day. Discuss some of these changes and their significance by comparing and contrasting the stage directions given in Shakespeare's *Macbeth* and Shaw's *Pygmalion*. You may wish to review the discussion of Elizabethan staging in the Introduction to Unit 5.

Thematic Studies

4. **Gender.** Shaw's play has much to say about social mores regarding relations between men and women. Compare and contrast the ideas about women's equality expressed in *Pygmalion* with such ideas expressed in one or two of these works: Aemelia Lanyer's "Eve's Apology in Defense of Women," Anne Finch's "The Introduction," Margaret Cavendish's "To All Writing Ladies," or Mary Wollstonecraft's *A Vindication of the Rights of Woman.* In your discussion, point out differences between these speakers' views and techniques and distinguish them from differences between the speakers' respective societies.

Historical/Biographical Studies

5. **Social Class.** Compare and contrast the beliefs and attitudes about class distinctions that are presented in Chaucer's "Prologue" to *The Canterbury Tales* and in Shaw's *Pygmalion*. What virtues and vices does each author associate with the aristocracy and the common person?

Reflecting on Your Reading

The prompts in "Reflecting on Your Reading" are suitable topics for research papers. Refer to the Language Arts Survey 5.18–5.45, "Research Skills." (To evaluate research papers, see the evaluation forms for writing, revising, and proofreading in the Assessment Resource.)

The prompts in "Reflecting on Your Reading" can also be adapted for use as topics for oral reports or debates. Refer students to the Language Arts Survey 4, Speaking and Listening. (To evaluate these projects, see the evaluation forms in the Assessment Resource.)

Fero Ins.
Schetlāt
LEDONIVS
Orcades Ins
Rona
Lewys
S.Kilda
Hebrides sive Hebudes
S.Peter
Stakes of Ara
Dungal
Knockfergus
IBERNIA
Galway
Dublyn
Lmrick
Kork
Wexford
Cape Cler
S.David
Man
Aberden
S.Andres
Barwich
Glasquo
Carliste
Newcast
Lancaster
Yorck
Chester
Stafford
Bristol
Oxfort
London
Exceter
Salesburi
The Lands end
Sorlinges
Portland
OCEANVS BRITA
NOO
zee

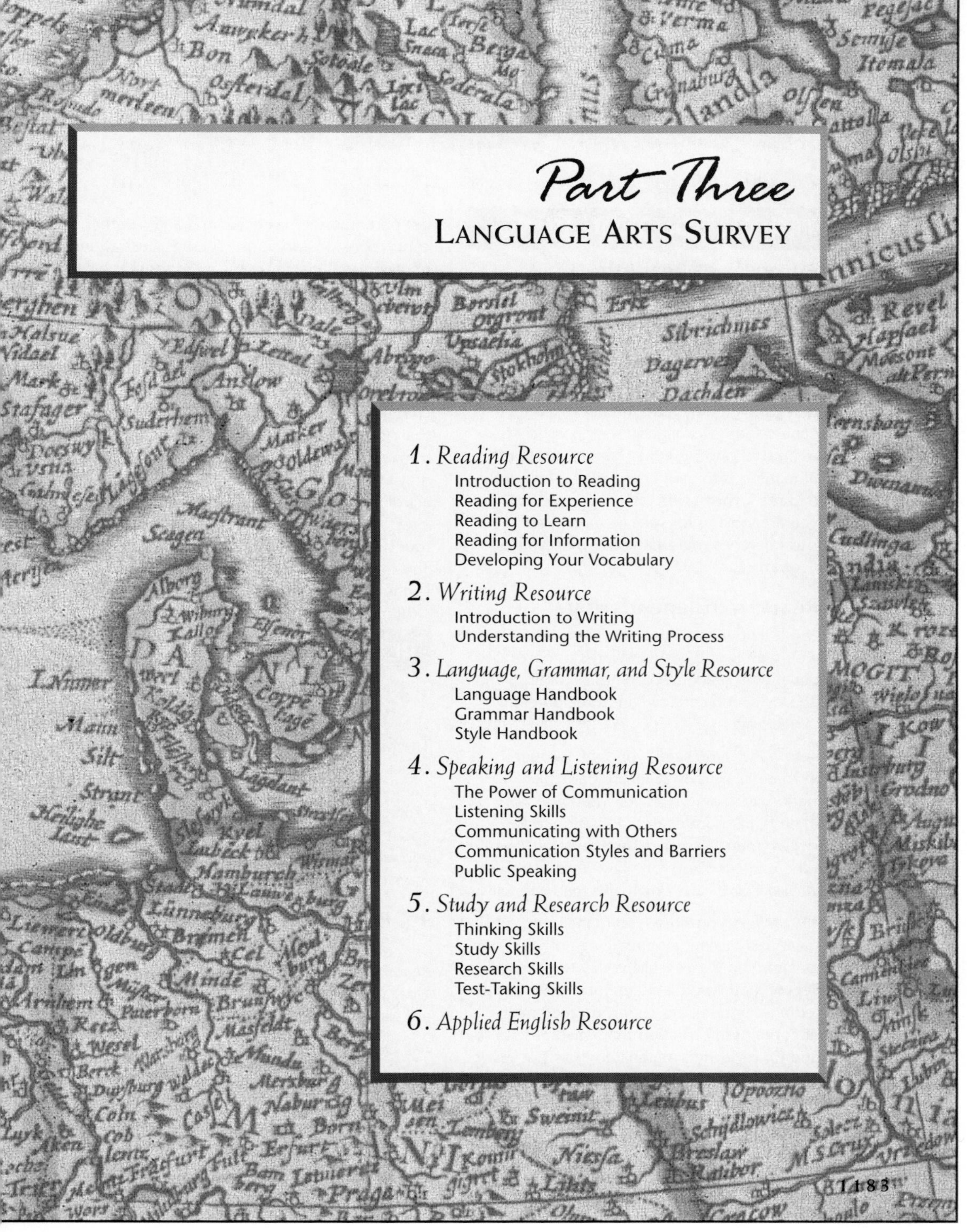

Part Three
Language Arts Survey

INTERNET RESOURCES

Visit the **National Council of Teachers of English Teaching Ideas** page at http://www.ncte.org/teach/read.html for Practical Teaching Ideas on Reading. Here you'll find links to literature teaching ideas selected from NCTE publications or submitted directly by teachers.

For helpful tips for teaching basic reading skills, you can access the article **"Teaching Reading Skills: Tips from the Trenches"** at http://www.midtesol.org/articles/art1.htm. This site features articles published by MIDTESOL (MidAmerica Teachers of English to Speakers of Other Languages.)

RESPOND TO THE SELECTION

The Respond to the Selection questions and critical thinking prompts following each selection provide students with the opportunity to be active readers by asking questions that get the students involved in the literature, like the questions mentioned in section 1.4, "Educating Your Imagination as an Active Reader." See pages 393 and 408 in Unit 5 for examples.

INTRODUCTION TO READING

1.1 Purposes of Reading

You as a reader read for different purposes. You might **read for experience**—for insights into ideas, other people, and the world around you. You can also **read to learn**. This is the kind of reading done most often in school. When you read to learn, you may read textbooks, newspapers and newsmagazines, and visual "texts" such as art and photographs. The purpose of this type of reading is to gain knowledge. Third, you can **read for information**. When you read in this way, you are looking for specific data in such things as reference materials, tables, databases, and diagrams.

1.2 Reading Independently

Learning to know and value your own response to what you read is one of the rewards of becoming an independent reader. Scanning, skimming, and reading slowly and carefully are three different ways of reading.

SCANNING. When you **scan**, you look through written material quickly to locate particular information. Scanning is useful when you want to find an entry in an index or a definition in a textbook chapter. To scan, simply run your eye down the page, looking for a key word. When you find the key word, slow down and read carefully.

SKIMMING. When you **skim**, you glance through material quickly to get a general idea of what it is about. Skimming is an excellent way to get a quick overview of material. It is useful for previewing a chapter in a textbook, for surveying material to see if it contains information that will be useful to you, and for reviewing material for a test or essay. When skimming, look at titles, headings, and words that appear in boldface or colored type. Also read topic sentences of paragraphs, first and last paragraphs of sections, and any summaries or conclusions. In addition, glance at illustrations, photographs, charts, maps, or other graphics.

SLOW AND CAREFUL READING. When you **read slowly and carefully**, you look at each sentence, taking the time to absorb its meaning before going on. Slow and careful reading is appropriate when reading for pleasure or when studying a textbook chapter for the first time. If you encounter words that you do not understand, try to figure them out from context or look them up in a dictionary. You may want to write such words in a notebook. The act of writing a word will help you to remember it later. When reading for school, take notes using a rough outline form. Writing the material will help you to remember it. For more information, see the Language Arts Survey 5.16, "Taking Notes, Outlining, and Summarizing Information."

READING FOR EXPERIENCE

1.3 Reading Literature: Educating Your Imagination

The most important reason to read literature is to educate your imagination. Reading literature will train you to think and feel in new ways. In the process of reading literary works and thinking about your own and others' responses to them, you will exercise your imagination and grow in ways that might otherwise have been impossible.

1.4 Educating Your Imagination as an Active Reader

Reading literature actively means thinking about what you are reading as you are reading it. Here are some important strategies for reading actively.

ASK QUESTIONS AS YOU READ.

- How does what I am reading make me feel?
- What is the setting of this work? How do things look, sound, taste, feel, or smell?

- Do I identify with any of the characters? What would I do if I were in their place?
- Does what I am reading involve a conflict? If so, what is it? How might it be resolved?
- What main images, ideas, symbols, or themes appear in the work?
- What can be learned from the experiences of these characters?

Make Predictions As You Read. While reading, think often about what will come next. Think about how situations might turn out and what characters might do.

Summarize Parts As You Read Them. Especially when reading longer works, it is a good idea to stop, perhaps at the end of each chapter or section, to summarize on paper what you have read so far. Doing so will help you remember complicated literary works.

1.5 Keeping a Reader's Journal

Keeping a reader's journal will help you get the most out of your experience with literature. A reader's journal can first act as a log in which you record the title and author of the work you are reading. You may want to briefly summarize the work. You can write a journal response to questions such as those in the Reader's Journal and Respond to the Selection features of this textbook. Or you might write your own questions and respond to them.

What associations do you have with snakes? How have you been educated to react to them? I associate snakes with sneakiness. I also see them as being cold and inhuman, unlike other creatures like the fox that are easier to humanize. Snakes make me think of the Bible story when Eve was tempted by the snake to eat the fruit of the Tree of Knowledge. I have been educated to be wary of snakes because some of them are poisonous. In school we learned that many snakes are harmless, but I still distrust and am afraid of them. I feel it's safer to distrust them all and keep my distance just in case the one I run into turns out to be poisonous.

1.6 Reading Silently versus Reading Out Loud

At times you will find it best to read silently and at other times to read out loud. When reading independently, you will probably make the most progress by reading silently. However, you may find it most helpful to read difficult passages out loud, even if softly. Hearing the words spoken can help make sense of complex passages. Another good time to read out loud is with poetry. By speaking the lines, you will be able to hear the rhythm and rhyme. Plays are also intended to be performed, and as with poetry, they are best appreciated when they are read out loud. This can be particularly helpful when different people take on the roles of different characters.

1.7 Reading with a Book Club or Literature Circle

No two people are exactly alike. Because of this, the experience that you have when reading a particular story, poem, or play will be different from the experience of each of your classmates. That's what makes discussing literature with other students interesting.

In a classroom literature circle, students get together in a small group to exchange insights, interpretations, and questions about literature they have read independently. Students in a literature circle may gather to discuss a selection and work together to understand it. Or they might read different literary works and meet to compare themes, writing styles of different authors, or different selections by the same author. Personal insights recorded in a reading log or journal can be shared when the literature circle meets.

1.8 Guidelines for Discussing Literature in a Book Club

At first, your literature group might need help from your teacher to get started, but soon your group should be able to conduct its own sessions if you follow these guidelines.

BEFORE THE SESSION

- Finish reading the assignment on time.
- Write down ideas in your reader's journal to help yourself get ready for the discussion.

Reader's Journal. The Reader's Journal questions in the Prereading section of each selection provide students with response questions and writing prompts that they can use to get started writing in their own reading journals. See pages 497 and 500 in Unit 6 for examples.

Book Club. You might have your students read the books suggested in the For Your Reading List section at the end of each unit and have students conduct a book club in small groups. See pages 477 and 551.

- Mark places in the reading that you don't understand or want to discuss with your group. Also mark passages that you like, disagree with, or find especially worth remembering.
- Make sure you bring the literature to school instead of leaving it home on discussion day.

DURING THE SESSION

- Share your ideas and offer suggestions.
- Speak clearly, loudly, and slowly enough.
- Make eye contact with others.
- Answer questions other people ask.
- Ask questions to help other members clarify or expand on their points.
- Help keep the group on track and focused.
- Encourage others to talk.
- Disagree when you find it necessary without hurting others' feelings.
- Summarize and repeat your ideas when necessary.
- Give reasons for your opinions.
- Listen politely and ask follow-up questions.
- Try to understand and carry out other members' suggestions.

AFTER THE SESSION

- Evaluate your contribution to the group.
- Evaluate the overall success of your group.
- List ways to improve the next time.

READING TO LEARN

When you are reading to learn, you have two main goals: to expand your knowledge on a particular topic and to remember the information later. When you read to learn, you will often work with textbooks, nonfiction library books, newspapers, or journals, newsmagazines, and related art and photographs.

1.9 Reading Textbooks and Nonfiction Books

Textbooks provide a broad overview of a course of study. Textbooks should provide as much material as possible in an objective, factual way. Other nonfiction books provide information about actual people, places, things, events, and ideas. Types of nonfiction books include histories, biographies, autobiographies, and memoirs.

The Parts of a Book. When previewing an entire book, you might want to glance at all of its parts. Every book will have some or all of the following parts:

THE PARTS OF A BOOK	
Title page	Gives the title, author, and publisher
Copyright page	Gives information regarding the publication of the book and the copyrights protecting it from being copied or sold illegally
Table of contents	Lists the units, chapters, and/or subjects of the book and the page numbers where they are found
Preface, introduction, or foreword	Introduces the book
Text	Main part of the book
Afterword or epilogue	Gives conclusion or tells what happened later
Appendix	Gives additional information about subjects covered in the book, often in chart or table form
Glossary	Lists key words used in the book and their definitions
Bibliography	Lists sources used in writing the book or sources for further study
Index	Lists in alphabetical order the subjects mentioned in the book and pages where these subjects are treated

Reading Textbooks. Have students locate the parts of this textbook. Students could copy the headings on page 1186 onto their own paper and write the page number for each book part once they have found it.

1.10 Reading Newspapers, Journals, and Newsmagazines

Newspapers, journals, and newsmagazines contain an enormous amount of information. Few people have time to read everything that appears in a newspaper each day. Nonetheless, staying aware of the news is important.

To get an overview of a newspaper, journal, or newsmagazine, skim the headlines and leads (the first sentence in a news story that explains the who, what, where, why, and how of the story). Read any news summaries included in the publication. Then read in depth any stories that seem particularly important or interesting. Also take advantage of the features and entertainment sections, which often reflect contemporary culture or the particular flavor of a community.

When reading news stories and editorials, make sure to distinguish between facts and opinions. **Facts** are statements that can be proved by observation or by consulting a reliable and objective source. **Opinions** are predictions or statements of value or belief. When you encounter opinions in the news, try to determine whether they are sound. Sound opinions are supported by facts. For more information, see the Language Arts Survey 5.2, "Distinguishing Fact from Opinion."

1.11 "Reading" Art and Photographs

In today's visually stimulating world, books and news media rely on art, photographs, and other visuals as well as the printed word to convey ideas. Being able to understand and interpret graphic images is important in today's society. Visual arts offer insights into our world in a different way than print does.

Careful examination of a painting can lead you to discover meaning in it and to compare and contrast the painting's meaning with that of a literary work or other piece of writing. The same thing happens with photographs. Learning to interpret other graphics or images—drawings, diagrams, charts, and maps—will help you to understand more easily how things work, what things mean, and how things compare.

1.12 Seeking Knowledge as an Active Reader

Reading to learn requires you to develop and use key skills to acquire knowledge. Reading actively means thinking about what you are reading as you read it. Slow and careful reading—and sometimes rereading—is necessary when reading to understand new and complex material. There are five key skills required for active reading:

- asking questions
- using your prior knowledge to make inferences and predictions about what you are reading
- recognizing what you do not know
- being able to synthesize information or create summaries, and
- knowing when to adapt your reading approach.

Ask Questions. Questioning allows you to realize what you understand about what you are reading. Before you read, think about your prior knowledge about the subject. When confronted with new information, your mind is doing many things at once. It is trying to figure out what it already knows about the topic and how this information connects to the information already in your brain. During reading, your mind is trying to answer these questions: What is the essential information presented here? How is this new information organized? After reading, you need to examine how your knowledge has grown, and identify the questions you still have about the material.

BEFORE READING

What is this going to be about?
What do I already know about the topic?
What's my purpose for reading this?

DURING READING

What does the author want me to know?
What is the significance of what I am reading?
What do I need to remember from this material?

AFTER READING

What have I learned?
What else do I want to know about this topic?

Seeking Knowledge as an Active Reader. Students are asked to use active reading skills in the Critical Thinking activity on page 313.

MEDIA LITERACY

Art Smart. The Art Smart notes that accompany much of the fine art in this text provide students with an opportunity to critically view and interpret works of art. See the Art Smart notes on pages 683 and 787 for examples.

Use Your Prior Knowledge to Make Inferences and Predictions. While you are reading, you need to use what you already know about the topic to make inferences about what the author is saying. As you read, think about what might come next and try to make predictions about the next section of material.

Know What You Do Not Know. Recognizing when you do not understand something is as important as knowing that you do understand it. Try to form questions about the material you do not understand. Reread the text. Explain the topic to another student. Teaching someone else forces you to work to understand the material in deeper ways.

Summarize or Synthesize Text. Summarizing what you are reading not only helps you identify and understand the main and subordinate points in the text, it is essential for storing and retrieving the information from long-term memory. Write a summary for each major section of the text you read. Create meaningful labels for a list of things or actions.

Adapt Your Reading Approach. If you become aware that you are not comprehending the material, you need to try another approach. Expert readers alter their reading strategies to compensate for any problems they have. You may need to experiment with different tactics like speeding up, slowing down, rereading, standing up and reading, reading the same material from another book, reading with a dictionary in your lap, or generalizing or visualizing what you are reading.

1.13 Strategies for Reading to Learn: SQ3R

A five-step reading strategy called SQ3R can help you reduce your study time and increase your ability to understand the essential information. The main steps of SQ3R are **S**urvey, **Q**uestion, **R**ead, **R**ecite, and **R**eview.

SURVEY

- Preview the organization of material.
- Glance at visuals and assess how they contribute to the meaning of the text.
- Skim headings and introductory paragraphs.
- Notice words in italics, boldface, and other terms that stand out.
- Ask yourself: What is the scope of the reading task? What should I learn from this material?

QUESTION

- Turn chapter titles and headings into questions.
- Ask yourself what the text is offering and what the author is saying.
- Ask yourself what you should know about the material and what you already know about it.
- Question graphics and visual materials. Try to translate the information they offer into your own words.
- Use words like *who, what, when, where, why,* and *how* to retrieve information.

READ

- Read and interact with the text.
- Underline or copy in your journal the main points.
- Make note of unusual or interesting ideas.
- Jot down words you need to define.
- Write your reactions to what you read.

RECALL

- Condense the major points of the text by writing recall cues.
- Summarize the material you have read. Reread any sections you don't clearly remember.
- Use graphic organizers to visualize or map out the material.
- Reread the text aloud if you need help recalling.

REVIEW

- After you have finished the chapter or book, go back and reread main headings and compare them to your notes.
- Review your notes, summaries, and definitions. Answer any questions you wrote.
- Ask yourself: What do I now understand? What is still confusing?

READING FOR INFORMATION

1.14 Reading Internet Materials, Reference Works, Graphic Aids, and Other Visuals

When you are reading for information, you are looking for information that answers a specific,

SQ3R. Ask students to apply the SQ3R reading method to the Guided Writing lessons found at the end of each unit.

immediate question; that helps you learn how to do something; or that will help you make a decision or draw a conclusion about something. One of the most important tasks for you to learn in school is how to access, process, and think about the vast amount of information available to you on the Internet and in online and print reference works, graphic aids, and other visuals.

Skills critical to reading for information include:

- determining your specific purpose for reading or viewing
- determining the creator's or author's purpose
- knowing how to interpret symbols and numeric data, and
- using an appropriate approach for the reading or viewing task.

Determine Your Specific Purpose For Reading or Viewing. Know why you are reading and what information you seek. State your purpose for reading as clearly as you can. Are you searching the Internet for a review of the movie you're unsure whether to see? Are you learning to operate a computer program? Are you researching data to determine if city regulations allow pet ferrets?

Determine the Creator's or Author's Purpose. It is important to interpret the creator's or author's viewpoint. Ask yourself what the writer or illustrator wants the reader to think, believe, or do after reading this piece. Ask yourself if the author has bias on the topic that is affecting his or her views. If you are on the Internet, check for the following: Who is sponsoring the site? What hyperlinks are embedded in the site? Can you contact the website? When was the content on the site developed, and how might that affect the information it provides?

Determine How the Author Uses Symbols and Numeric Data. Work to understand how the creator or author uses symbols, icons, and abbreviated headings on tables. Use any icons as shortcuts for navigating through the text and also for identifying the important from unimportant material.

Use the Search Approach. Although your reading and viewing strategies should vary and relate directly to your purpose, you may find the SEARCH method helpful when you are reading for information. SEARCH stands for **S**can, **E**xamine, **A**ct, **R**eview, **C**onnect, and **H**unt.

SCAN

- Look over the text and determine how the material is structured.
- Look for a table of contents, a glossary, an index, and other helpful sections.
- For an Internet site, look for a site map.

EXAMINE

- Do directions appear in a sequence of steps? Are there diagrams? Do directions reveal exactly what to do, or do you need to experiment a little?
- Is there a pattern in headings or icons?
- Are there any references to other sources of information?
- If you are on the Internet, does the site provide any links?

ACT

- Explore the procedures you are reading and learn by doing.
- If you are seeking data, take notes about the information. Is it exactly what you were looking for, or do you need to keep looking?

REVIEW

- Revisit the steps of a procedure to make sure you have them clear in your head.
- Compare similar resources and read any additional references or links provided.

CONNECT

- Connect the information to what you previously knew about the topic. How did you build on what you knew?
- Connect text with visual aids. How do the visual aids supplement the text? What additional information do they provide?

HUNT

- Look up the meanings of any new words you found.
- Use the help feature on a computer program to find answers to your questions.
- Make a visual diagram of a procedure if it will help you remember it.

Reading Internet Materials, Reference Works, Graphic Aids, and Other Visuals. Students are asked to use these resources in the Study and Research activity on page 817.

USING GRAPHIC AIDS. Students are asked to use graphic aids in the Study and Research activities on pages 52 and 210.

1.15 Using Graphic Aids

Graphic aids are pictures, maps, illustrations, charts, graphs, diagrams, spreadsheets, and other visual materials that present information. Many people, including scientists, sociologists, economists, business analysts, and school administrators use graphic aids to present data in understandable ways. Information presented in tables, charts, and graphs can help you find information, see trends, discover facts, and uncover patterns. Here are some common types of structures for presenting data.

PIE CHARTS. A pie chart is a circle that stands for a whole group or set. The circle is divided into parts to show the divisions of the whole. When you look at a pie chart, you can see the relationships of the parts to one another and to the whole.

BAR GRAPHS. A bar graph compares amounts of something by representing the amounts as bars of different lengths. In the bar graph below, each bar represents the value in dollars of canned goods donated by several communities to a food drive. To read the graph, simply draw in your imagination a line from the edge of the bar to the bottom of the graph. Then read the number. For example, the bar graph below shows that the community of Russell Springs donated $600 worth of goods during the food drive.

MAPS. A map is a representation, usually on a surface such as paper or a sheet of plastic, of a geographic area, showing various significant features of that area.

ARLINGTON HIGH SCHOOL POETRY SURVEY

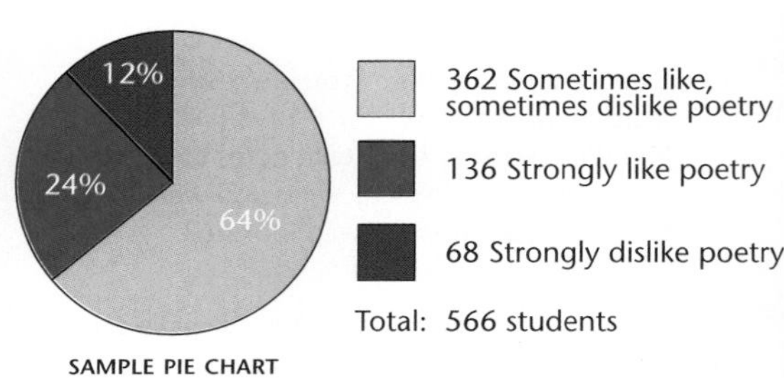

SAMPLE PIE CHART

THE WANDERINGS OF ODYSSEUS

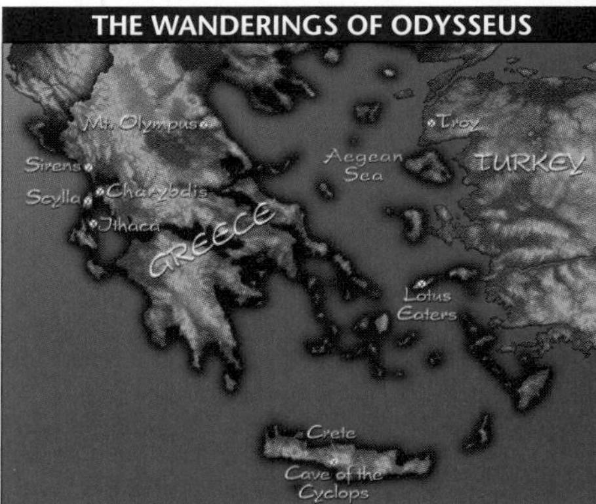

SAMPLE MAP

DOLLAR VALUE OF DONATED GOODS TO CANNED FOOD DRIVE

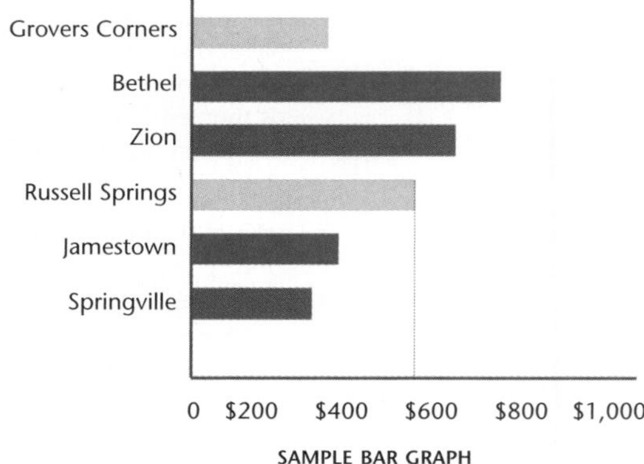

SAMPLE BAR GRAPH

Here are guidelines for working with graphics:

BEFORE READING

- Determine what the subject of the graphic by reading the title, headings, and other textual clues.
- Determine how the data are organized, classified, or divided by reading the labels along rows or columns.
- Ask yourself: Why am I reading this document? What do I need to find? Where in this graphic is that information located?

DURING READING

- Survey the data and look for trends by comparing columns and rows, noting changes among information fields, looking for patterns, or navigating map sections.
- Use legends, keys, and other helpful sections in the graphic.
- Ask yourself: How do the data I need compare to other data on the graphic? What do those comparisons mean to me? What in this graphic can I skim or skip?

AFTER READING

- Check footnotes or references for additional information about the data and its sources.
- Ask yourself: Did this graphic answer my questions? If so, what are the answers? If not, where do I go to find the answers?

DEVELOPING YOUR VOCABULARY

1.16 Using Context Clues to Estimate Word Meaning

If you come across an unfamiliar word in your reading and you can't access a dictionary, you can often figure out the meaning of a word by using context clues.

One type of context clue is **restatement**. The author may tell you the meaning of the word you do not know by using different words to express the same idea in another sentence.

EXAMPLE

The dog snarled at Donald malevolently.
The dog's vicious behavior warned Donald to stay away.

The restatement provides a context clue that malevolently means "maliciously, with intent to do harm."

Another type of context clue is **apposition**. An apposition is renaming something in different words. Look for a word or phrase that has been placed in the sentence to clarify the word you do not know.

EXAMPLE

Evan's conclusion was based on a fallacy, a false idea about how Maggie felt toward him.

Examples given in a sentence can also be used as context clues.

EXAMPLE

The words *dad*, *radar*, *noon*, and *tenet* are all palindromes; so is the phrase "A man, a plan, a canal, Panama!"

1.17 Using a Dictionary

Dictionary entries provide much more information about words than just their spelling and definitions.

The **pronunciation** is given immediately after the entry word. You can find a complete key to pronunciation symbols in the dictionary's table of contents. In some dictionaries, a simplified key is provided at the bottom of each page.

An abbreviation of the **part of speech** usually follows the pronunciation. This label tells the ways in which a word can be used (see the Language Arts Survey 2.1–2.8, "The Parts of Speech"). If a word can be used in more than one way, definitions are grouped by part of speech.

An **etymology** is the history of a word. In the first entry, the word *pole* can be traced back through Middle English (ME) and Old English (OE) to the Latin (L) word *palus*, which means "stake." In the second entry, the word *pole* can be traced back through Middle English to the Latin word *polus*, which comes from the Greek word *polos*, meaning "axis of the sphere."

Each **definition** in the entry gives a different meaning of the word. When a word has more than one meaning, the different definitions are numbered. The first definition in an entry is the most common meaning of the word.

Sometimes the entry will include a list of **synonyms**. The entry may also include an **illustration of usage**, which is an example of how the word is used.

USING A DICTIONARY. Students are asked to use their dictionary skills in the Study and Research activities on pages 626 and 665.

Footnotes. Footnotes at the bottom of the page of the selections define vocabulary words not listed in Words for Everyday Use.

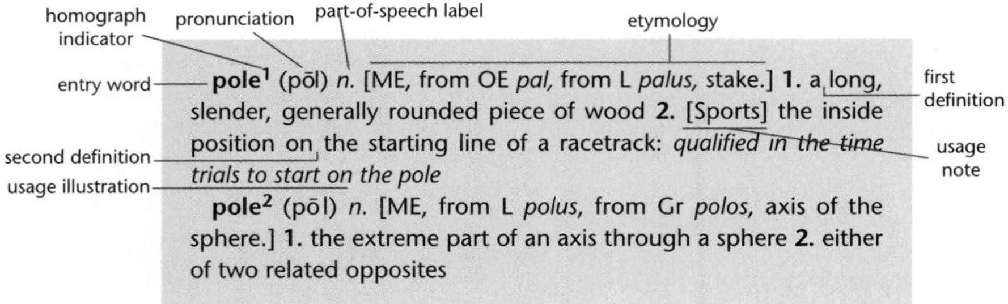

homograph indicator
pronunciation
part-of-speech label
etymology
entry word
first definition
second definition
usage note
usage illustration
pole¹ (pōl) n. [ME, from OE pal, from L palus, stake.] 1. a long, slender, generally rounded piece of wood 2. [Sports] the inside position on the starting line of a racetrack: qualified in the time trials to start on the pole
pole² (pōl) n. [ME, from L polus, from Gr polos, axis of the sphere.] 1. the extreme part of an axis through a sphere 2. either of two related opposites

1.18 Using Glossaries and Footnotes

A **glossary** is an alphabetized list of words that lists and defines text at the end of an article, chapter, or book. **Footnotes** appear at the foot, or bottom, of a page. Sometimes they cite a source of information. Other times they define annotated words in order of appearance.

1.19 Learning Base Words, Prefixes, and Suffixes

Many words are formed by adding prefixes or suffixes to base words. (See the Language Arts Survey 3.95, "Using Spelling Rules I.") If you are unfamiliar with a word that is formed with a prefix or a suffix, check to see if you recognize the meaning of the base word and the meaning of its prefix or the suffix.

PREFIX	MEANING	EXAMPLE	MEANING
anti–	"against"	antibacterial	against bacteria
dis–	"not, opposite"	disagreeable	not agreeable
hyper–	"over, excessively"	hyperactive	excessively active
im–, un–	"not"	unusual	not usual
post–	"after"	postseason	after the season
re–	"again"	reprint	print again

SUFFIX	MEANING	EXAMPLE	MEANING
–er, –or	"one who"	narrator	one who narrates
–ful	"full of"	graceful	full of grace
–ish	"like"	childish	like a child
–ity, –ty	"state of, quality"	captivity	state of being captive
–less	"without"	fearless	without fear
–ment	"act of, state of"	achievement	act of achieving

1.20 Learning Synonyms, Antonyms, and Homonyms

A **synonym** is a word that has the same or nearly the same meaning as another word.

EXAMPLES discover, find, locate, pinpoint

An **antonym** is a word that means the opposite of another word.

EXAMPLES discover, conceal give, take success, defeat

A **homonym** is a word that has the same pronunciation as another word but with a different meaning, origin, and, usually, spelling.

EXAMPLES bight, bite, byte

Learning Synonyms, Antonyms, and Homonyms. Students are asked to identify and use synonyms in the Vocabulary activity on page 523.

1.21 Exploring Word Origins and Word Families

The English language gains new words from many different sources. One source is the names of people and places. Another source of words in the English language is **acronyms**. Acronyms are words formed from the first letter or letters of the major parts of terms.

EXAMPLES
sonar, from sound navigation ranging; NATO, from North Atlantic Treaty Organization; NASA, from National Aeronautic and Space Administration

Some words in the English language are **borrowed** from other languages.

EXAMPLES **deluxe** (French), **Gesundheit** (German), **kayak** (Eskimo)

Many words are formed by **shortening** longer words.

EXAMPLES
ad, from advertisement; auto, from automobile; lab, from laboratory; phone, from telephone; stereo, from stereophonic

Brand names are often taken into the English language. People begin to use these words as common nouns, even though most of them are still brand names.

EXAMPLES Scotch tape, Xerox, Rollerblade

HAMBURGER
Originally known as "Hamburg steak," the hamburger takes its name from the city of Hamburg, Germany.

SPOONERISM
A slip of the tongue whereby the beginning sounds of words are switched; named after Rev. William A. Spooner, who was noted for such slips. For example, after officiating at a wedding, he told the groom, "It is kisstomary to cuss the bride."

1.22 Jargon and Gobbledygook

Jargon is the specialized vocabulary used by members of a profession. It tends to be difficult for people outside the profession to understand. A plumber may speak of a "hubless fitting" or a "street elbow" (kinds of pipe). A computer programmer may talk of "ram cache" (part of computer memory) or a "shell" (a type of operating software for computers).

Jargon is useful to writers who want to describe authentically situations in which jargon would naturally be used. A novel about fighter pilots would probably be full of aviation jargon. A science fiction film might include futuristic jargon about warps in space and energy shields.

Gobbledygook is unclear, wordy jargon used by bureaucrats, government officials, and others. For example, the failure of a program might be called an "incomplete success." A bureaucrat might say, "We are engaged in conducting a study with a view to ascertaining which employees might be assigned to the mobility pool and how we might create revenue enhancement," when he means, "We are planning to cut jobs and increase taxes." Avoid the use of gobbledygook. Effective communication involves using precise language instead of muddy, vague vocabulary.

1.23 Clichés and Euphemisms

A **cliché** is an expression that has been used so often it has been colorless and uninteresting. The use of cliches instantly makes writing dull.

EXAMPLES quick as a wink, pretty as a picture

A **euphemism** is an inoffensive term that substitutes for one considered offensive.

EXAMPLES aerial mishap (for "plane crash")
building engineer (for "janitor")

1.24 Connotation and Denotation

A **denotation** of a word is its dictionary definition. A **connotation** of a word is all the associations it has in addition to its literal meaning. For example, the words *cheap* and *economical* both denote "inexpensive," but *cheap* connotes shoddy and inferior while *economical* connotes a good value for the money. Writers and speakers should be aware of the connotations as well as the denotations of the words they use. Contrast these denotations and connotations:

EXAMPLES
curious: nosy, snoopy, prying, inquisitive, inquiring

Exploring Word Origins and Word Families. Students are asked to explore word origins and word families in the Language, Grammar, and Style activity on page 872.

Clichés and Euphemisms. Students are asked to identify clichés and euphemisms in the Language, Grammar, and Style activities on pages 748 and 798.

Connotation and Denotation. Students are asked to work with connotation and denotation in the Language, Grammar, and Style activity on page 532 and the Vocabulary activity on page 626.

INTERNET RESOURCES

Access the **National Writing Project** web site at http://www.gse.berkeley.edu/Research/NWP/info.html. The mission of the National Writing Project is to improve the teaching of writing and learning in the nation's schools. Through its professional development model, the National Writing Project recognizes the primary importance of teacher knowledge, expertise, and leadership.

Visit the **Austin Writers' League** at http://www.eden.com/~awl/. With over twelve hundred members AWL is the second largest regional writing group in the nation. Members include award winning best sellers as emerging writers, including poets, journalists, novelists, mystery, romance, and science fiction writers.

Inkspot: The Writer's Resource at http://www.inkspot.com/ is a place for student authors to share in the collective conscience of writers, bot published and unpublished. From this site, your students can find information on how to write screenplays, book reports, essays, and poetry. There is also a section for teachers.

THE SEVEN STAGES IN THE WRITING PROCESS are developed thoroughly in each of the Guided Writing lessons that appear at the end of each unit. See pages 756-763 at the end of Unit 8 for an example.

WRITING Resource

INTRODUCTION TO WRITING

2.1 The Writing Process

We live in an information age in which success in most fields requires well-developed writing skills. The most important action that you can take to shape a successful future for yourself is to learn how to write clearly and effectively. Almost anyone can learn to write well by learning the writing process. The writing process is simply the steps that a person takes to compose a piece of writing.

SEVEN STAGES IN THE PROCESS OF WRITING

PREWRITING · DRAFTING · SELF- AND PEER EVALUATION · REVISING · PROOFREADING · PUBLISHING AND PRESENTING · REFLECTING

Stage	Tasks
1. **Prewriting**	Plan your writing: choose a topic, audience, purpose, and form; gather ideas; arrange them logically.
2. **Drafting**	Get your ideas down on paper.
3. **Self- and Peer Evaluation**	Evaluate, or judge, the writing piece and suggest ways to improve it. Judging your own writing is called **self-evaluation**. Judging a classmate's writing is called **peer evaluation**.
4. **Revising**	Work to improve the content, organization, and expression of your ideas.
5. **Proofreading**	Check your writing for errors in spelling, grammar, capitalization, and punctuation. Correct these errors, make a final copy of your paper, and proofread it again.
6. **Publishing and Presenting**	Share your work with an audience.
7. **Reflecting**	Think through the writing process to determine what you learned as a writer, what you accomplished, and what you would like to strengthen the next time you write.

While writing moves through these seven stages, it is also is a continuing cycle. You might need to go back to a previous stage before going on to the next step. Returning to a previous stage will strengthen your final work. Note also that the Reflecting stage can be done between any of the other stages. The more you reflect on your writing, the better your writing will become.

UNDERSTANDING THE WRITING PROCESS

2.2 Prewriting

In the **prewriting** stage of the writing process, you make a writing plan. You decide on a purpose, audience, form, and topic. You also begin to discover your voice and gather and organize ideas.

THE PARTS OF A WRITING PLAN	
Purpose	A **purpose,** or **aim,** is the goal that you want your writing to accomplish.
Audience	An **audience** is the person or group of people intended to read what you write.
Voice	**Voice** is the quality of a work that tells you that one person wrote it.
Form	A **form** is a kind of writing. For example, you might write a paragraph, an essay, a short story, a poem, or a news article.
Topic	A **topic** is simply something to write about. For example, you might write about a sports hero or about a cultural event in your community.

2.3 Identifying Your Purpose. A **purpose**, or aim, is the goal that you want your writing to accomplish. For example, you might write to inform, to entertain, to tell a story, to reflect, or to persuade. Your writing might have more than one purpose. For example, a piece of writing might inform about an important event while persuading the audience to respond in a specific way.

MODES AND PURPOSES OF WRITING

Mode	Purpose	Example
expository/informative writing	to inform	news article, research report
imaginative writing	to entertain, enrich, and enlighten by using a form such as fiction or poetry to share a perspective	poem, short story
narrative writing	to make a point by sharing a story about an event	biography, family history
personal/expressive writing	to reflect	diary entry, personal letter
persuasive/argumentative writing	to persuade readers or listeners to respond in some way, such as to agree with a position, change a view on an issue, reach an agreement, or perform an action	editorial, petition

2.4 Identifying Your Audience. An **audience** is the person or group of people intended to read what you write. For example, you might write for yourself, for a friend, for a relative, or for your classmates. The best writing usually is intended for a specific audience. Choosing a specific

WRITING RESOURCE

Prewriting. The Parts of a Writing Plan: Purpose, Audience, Form, and Topic, are discussed in depth in each of the Guided Writing lessons that appear at the end of each unit. For examples see pages 884–886 and 980–982.

Identifying Your Purpose. Students are asked to identify author's aims in the Reader's Toolbox on pages 66 and 90.

Identifying Your Audience. The Guided Writing lessons at the end of each unit contain instruction about identifying your audience as part of the prewriting process. For examples, see pages 1091 and 1172.

audience beforehand will help you make important decisions about your work. For example, for an audience of young children, you would use simple words and ideas. For an audience of fellow members of a technology club, you would use jargon and other specialized words that they already know. For more information, see the the Language Arts Survey 3.3, "Register, Tone, and Voice."

THINKING ABOUT YOUR AUDIENCE

- What people would be most interested in my topic?
- How much does the audience that I am considering already know about the topic?
- How much background information do I need to provide?
- What words, phrases, or concepts in my writing will my audience not understand? For which ones will I have to provide clear explanations?
- What can I do at the beginning of my writing to capture my audience's interest?

2.5 Finding Your Voice. **Voice** is the quality of a work that tells you that one person in particular wrote it. Voice makes a person's writing unique. Beginning with the prewriting stage and continuing through the rest of the writing process, a writer discovers his or her own unique voice. For more information, see the section about voice in the Language Arts Survey 3.3, "Register, Tone, and Voice."

2.6 Choosing a Form. Another important decision that a writer needs to make is what form his or her writing will take. A form is a kind of writing. For example, you might write a paragraph, an essay, a short story, a poem, or a newspaper article. The following chart lists some forms of writing that you might want to consider.

FORMS OF WRITING

Advertisement	Directions	Letter	Rap
Adventure	Dream report	Magazine article	Recipe
Advice column	Editorial	Memorandum	Recommendation
Agenda	Epitaph	Menu	Research report
Apology	Essay	Minutes	Résumé
Appeal	Eulogy	Movie review	Schedule
Autobiography	Experiment	Mystery	Science fiction
Biography	Fable	Myth	Short story
Book review	Family history	Narrative	Slide show
Brochure	Fantasy	Newspaper article	Slogan
Calendar	Greeting card	Obituary	Song lyric
Caption	Headline	Parable	Speech
Cartoon	History	Paraphrase	Sports story
Character sketch	Human interest story	Petition	Statement of belief
Children's story	Instructions	Play	Summary
Comedy	Interview questions	Police/Accident report	Tall tale
Consumer report	Invitation	Poem	Thank-you note
Debate	Itinerary	Poster	Tour guide
Detective story	Joke	Proposal	Want ad
Dialogue	Journal entry	Radio or TV spot	Wish list

Finding Your Voice. Sections on finding your voice are found in each of the Guided Writing lessons at the end of each unit. See pages 556 and 757 for examples.

Forms of Writing. Students are asked to use various forms of writing in the Writer's Journal found after each selection. For example, students are asked to write an epitaph on page 999 and a police report on page 1018.

2.7 Choosing a Topic. A topic is simply something to write about. For example, you might write about a sports hero or about a cultural event in your community. Here are some ideas that may help you find interesting writing topics:

WAYS TO FIND A WRITING TOPIC	
Check your journal	Search through your journal for ideas that you jotted down in the past. Many professional writers get their ideas from their journals.
Think about your experiences	Think about people, places, or events that affected you strongly. Recall experiences that taught you important lessons or that you felt strongly about.
Look at reference works	Reference works include printed or computerized dictionaries, atlases, almanacs, and encyclopedias.
Browse in a library	Libraries are treasure houses of information and ideas. Simply looking around in the stacks of a library can suggest good ideas for writing.
Use the mass media	Newspapers, magazines, radio, television, and films can suggest good topics for writing. For example, a glance at listings for public television programs might suggest topics related to the arts, to history, or to nature.
Talk to people	Friends, relatives, teachers, and other people you know can be valuable sources for writing.
Do some freewriting	Simply put your pen or pencil down on a piece of paper and write about whatever pops into your mind. Write for two to five minutes without pausing to worry about whether your writing is perfect. Then look back over what you have written to see if you can find any good topics there.
Ask "What if" questions	Ask questions beginning with "What if"to come up with topics for creative writing. For example, you might ask, "What if a kid with a ham radio set received a message from space? Would people believe her?"
Make a cluster chart	Write some general subject such as music or sports in the middle of a piece of paper. Circle this subject. Then, around it, write other ideas that come into your mind as you think about the subject. Circle these and draw lines to connect the outer circles to the inner one.

2.8 Focusing a Topic. Sometimes a topic is too broad to be treated in a short piece of writing. When you have a topic that is too broad, you must **focus**, or limit, the topic.

WAYS TO FOCUS A WRITING TOPIC	
Break the topic into parts	For example, the topic "newspapers" could be broken down into reporting, copyediting, advertising, circulation, and so on.
Ask questions about the topic	Begin your questions with the words *who, what, where, when, why,* and *how.* Then ask what stands out about your topic or what interests you most.
Make a cluster chart or do some freewriting	For information on these techniques, see the Language Arts Survey 1.5, "Finding a Topic."

Choosing a Topic. Students can learn more about freewriting by reading the Language Arts Survey 2.12, "Freewriting." Students can read more about making a cluster chart in the Language Arts Survey 2.13, "Clustering."

GATHERING IDEAS

Once you have made your writing plan by identifying your purpose, form, audience, and topic, the next step in the prewriting stage is to **gather ideas**. There are many ways to gather ideas for writing. This section will introduce you to some of the most useful ones.

2.9 Brainstorming. When you **brainstorm,** you think of as many ideas as you can, as quickly as you can, without stopping to evaluate or criticize the ideas. In brainstorming, anything goes. Sometimes even silly-sounding ideas can lead to productive ones. When you brainstorm in a group, often one person's idea will help another person to build on that concept. It is a good way to come up with creative, new ideas and innovative solutions to problems. Remember that no idea should be rejected in the brainstorming stage. Welcome all ideas with an encouraging response such as, "Great! Any other ideas?" Be sure to get contributions from everyone in your group and to record all ideas so they can be considered and judged later.

2.10 Learning from Professional Models. Professional models are works by published authors. They can be an excellent way to gather your own ideas. For example, one student was impressed by the way Bob Berman wrote about comets in his essay "Best Sky Sights of the Next Century" in Unit 6. He analyzed this informative essay and used it as a model when he wrote his own piece on astronomy for a science fair exhibit. For more examples, see the way Professional Models are used in the Guided Writing lessons at the end of each unit in this textbook.

Learning from Professional Models. The Guided Writing lessons at the end of each unit contain professional or student writing models as the basis for writing instruction. See examples on pages 556 and 884.

2.11 Keeping a Journal. A **journal** is a record of your ideas, dreams, wishes, and experiences. Composition books, spiral notebooks, looseleaf binders, and bound books with blank pages all make excellent journal books. Some people even keep electronic journals on computers.

TYPES OF JOURNALS	
A Diary, or Day-to-day Record of Your Life	August 3, 2003. Today I started keeping a journal. My brother Sean saw me writing and asked me what I was doing. When I told him, he said, "Don't go writing about me in that thing!" I guess he thinks he has all kinds of fascinating secrets! In a family as large as ours ough, it is pretty difficult to have any privacy. . . .
A Reader Response Journal	There have been times when I have joined in doing something that I knew was wrong, just because my friends were doing it. I always felt guilty afterwards and regretted doing it. In "The Monsters are Due on Maple Street" everyone becomes suspicious of their friends and neighbors out of fear. I think that's what motivates the characters to develop into a mob. It's ironic that the aliens have figured out that humans' most dangerous enemy is themselves, and the attitudes and prejudices they have in their own minds.
A Commonplace Book, or Book of Quotations	"Many a thing is despised that is worth more than is supposed." —Chrétien de Troyes, Arthurian Romances "Who knows why people do what they do?" —Barbara Kingsolver, Animal Dreams
A Writer's Lab, or Collection of Ideas for Writing	What if some new supercomputer fell in love with one of its programmers? That could be a very funny or a very sad story. How would it begin? Let's see. One day Randall Meeks, a programmer for the Department of Defense, goes in to work and sits down at a terminal connected to ERICA, a new top secret computer whose name means Efficient Risk-Instruction Computational Automaton. He logs onto the computer. A message appears, reading, "Good morning. You are looking quite handsome today." He thinks that one of the other programmers is playing a joke on him—but he's wrong.

continued

A Learning Log, or Record of What You Have Learned	Science: I read today in my science textbook that at the top of Mt. Everest, the highest point on the planet, there are rocks that were formed when sediment fell to the bottom of an ocean. How could the bottom of an ocean get pushed up to the top of the highest mountain? I'll have to ask in class tomorrow about that. Wow, Earth really is a turbulent thing, constantly changing. I wonder what it will look like millions of years into the future?
A Record of Questions	What causes the sky to glow at sunset? Chandra seems unhappy lately. How could I cheer her up? How does a person get a job as a zookeeper? Do you have to study animal behavior or biology or something like that in college? I think it would be fun to work with animals and to help save endangered species.
A Daily Organizer	Things to do tomorrow: • Go to library for book on Gandhi for social studies report • Go to football practice after school • Call Pete about concert tickets • Turn in overdue math homework

2.12 Freewriting. **Freewriting** is simply taking a pencil and paper and writing whatever comes into your mind. Try to write for several minutes without stopping and without worrying about spelling, grammar, usage, or mechanics. If you get stuck, just repeat the last few words until something new pops into your mind.

I really don't get this freewriting stuff. Just write? About what? Hum. I don't think of myself as a writer. I mean, sure, I can write and all, but . . . OK, I'm stuck . . . OK, I'm stuck. Funny, I was just thinking, what if some character in a short story kept saying that this was just a story that he was stuck in and the other characters thought he was crazy, and maybe he manages to figure out a way to pop in and out of the story that he was in, or maybe he can get into different stories at different times. Weird idea, I know it's like that idea that "maybe this is all just a dream." Dreams are interesting. There's that nursery rhyme, "Life is but a dream." What's that called. Oh, Row, Row, Row Your Boat. We used to sing that on the bus in elementary school.

To gather ideas about a specific topic, you might want to try **focused freewriting**. In a focused freewrite, you still write nonstop for a few minutes, but you stick with one topic and write whatever comes to mind as you think about that topic.

2.13 Clustering. Another good way to tap what you already know is to make a **cluster chart.** To make a cluster chart, draw a circle in the center of your paper. In it write a topic you want to explore. Draw more circles branching out from your center circle, and fill them with subtopics related to your main topic. See the sample cluster chart on page 966.

Clustering. Students often practice clustering in the Prereading stage under the Graphic Organizer on the first page of the selection. For examples, see pages 813 and 846.

SAMPLE CLUSTER CHART

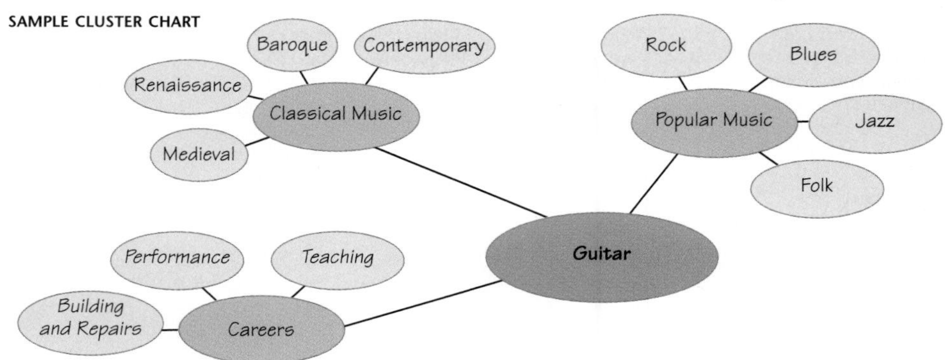

2.14 QUESTIONING: USING THE 5 *WS* AND AN *H*. Using the 5 *Ws* and an *H* means asking the **reporting questions** *who, what, where, when, why,* and *how* about your topic. This questioning strategy is especially useful for gathering information about an event or for planning a story.

USING QUESTIONING (TOPIC: ABBEY THEATRE)	
Who	William Butler Yeats, Lady Gregory, and John Millington Synge
What	Abbey Theatre
Where	Dublin, Ireland
When	1904
Why	To promote Irish plays
How	State subsidies

Sample paragraph using this information:

> In 1904, William Butler Yeats, Lady Gregory, and John Millington Synge founded the Abbey Theater in Dublin, Ireland. With state subsidies the theater has been able to promote Irish plays.

2.15 IMAGINING: ASKING *WHAT IF* QUESTIONS. If you are doing imaginative or creative writing, ask questions that begin with the words *what if.* "What if" questions can spark your imagination and lead you down unexpected and interesting paths. It can also help you see another side of things and strengthen your own when writing a persuasive piece.

EXAMPLES

What if I could run school for a week? What changes would I make?
What if I could go back in time to speak with a historical figure?
What if the greenhouse effect melted the polar icecaps and raised the levels of the oceans around the world? How would people respond?
What if the city council rejects the proposal for a teen center? How will this affect me and the kids I know?

2.16 Completing Venn Diagrams. If you are writing a comparison and contrast essay, one of the best ways to gather ideas is by completing a Venn diagram. A Venn diagram shows two slightly overlapping circles. The outer part of each circle shows what aspects of two things are different from each other. The inner, or shared, part of each circle shows what aspects the two things share.

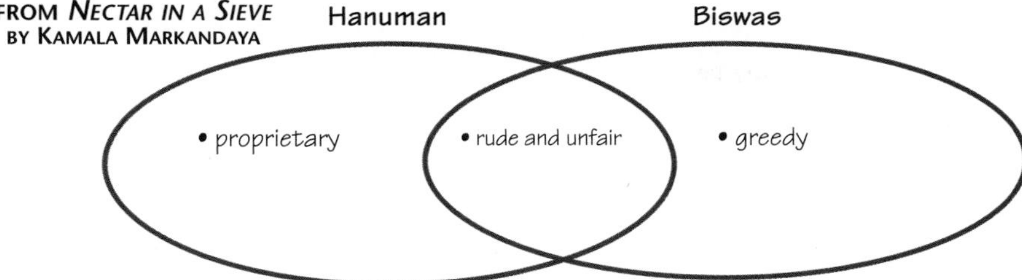

2.17 Analyzing. To **analyze** is to break something down into its parts and then think about how the parts are related. Analyzing is a way to sort out information about a topic. An **analysis chart** can help you to list the parts and to describe each one.

Analysis of "Bread" by Margaret Atwood

Part	Description	Relation of Part to Whole
Section 1	Describes use of bread in middle-class home	Shows how bread is taken for granted
Section 2	Describes bread during a famine	Shows bread as a life and death issue
Section 3	Describes bread in prison	Shows bread used as a political tool
Section 4	Describes bread in a fairy tale	Shows punishment for selfishness
Section 5	Describes hallucination of bread	Shows change in the reader's perception of bread so that it is linked to famine and political oppression and is no longer taken for granted

2.18 Sensory Detail Charts. Most people have the use of five major **senses**: sight, sound, touch, taste, and smell. The larger the number of these senses you use to observe something, the more you will notice about it. A **sensory detail chart** can help you to collect information about something so that you can describe it thoroughly. To make a sensory detail chart, begin by writing your subject at the top of the page. Make a box with a column for each of the five senses. In the column under each heading, list details about the subject that you learn from that sense.

Sensory Details of a Marathon

Sight	Sound	Touch	Taste	Smell
hundreds of runners of all ages	starting gun	hot, sore feet from standing so long	hot dogs and lemonade from vendor carts	hot asphalt
news reporters and onlookers	crowds clapping	stinging face from sun and wind		perspiration
running clothes	running shoes slapping on asphalt			

Sensory Detail Charts. In the Graphic Organizer activity in Unit 8 students are asked to complete a Sensory Detail Chart on page 749.

TIME LINES. Students are asked to make a time line in the Collaborative Learning and Study and Research activity on page 537.

PRO AND CON CHARTS. Students are asked to make pro and con charts in Speaking and Listening activity on page 46.

2.19 TIME LINES. A **time line** can be useful when you are planning to write a story or a historical account. It gives you an overview of the sequence of events during a particular time period. To make a time line, draw a line on a piece of paper and divide it into equal parts. Label each part with a date or a time. Then add key events at the right places along the time line.

Nobel Prizes for Literature (1994–1999)

1994	1995	1996	1997	1998	1999
Kensaburo Oe (Japan)	Seamus Heaney (Ireland)	Wislawa Szymborska (Poland)	Dario Fo (Italy)	José Saramago (Portugal)	Günther Grass (Germany)

2.20 STORY MAPS. A **story map** is a chart that shows the various parts of a fable, myth, tall tale, legend, short story, or other fictional work. Most story maps include the following elements:

ELEMENTS OF A STORY MAP

ELEMENT	DESCRIPTION
Setting	The time and place in which the story occurs
Mood	The emotion created in the reader by the story
Conflict	A struggle between two forces in the story
Plot	The series of events taking place in the story
Characters	The people (or sometimes animals) who play roles in the story
Theme	The main idea of the story

2.21 PRO AND CON CHARTS. A **pro and con chart** shows arguments for and against taking a particular position on some issue. To create a pro and con chart, begin by writing a statement, called a **proposition**, at the top of a piece of paper. Under the proposition, make two columns, one labeled *Pro* and the other, *Con.* In the pro column, list arguments in favor of the proposition. In the con column, list arguments against the proposition.

PRO AND CON CHART

Proposition: All students should take an hour of physical education each day.

Pro	Con
—would keep students in good physical condition	—would take time away from academic studies
—improved health would also improve students' ability to think clearly and work hard	—the same ends might be achieved in less time per day

2.22 INTERVIEWING. In an **interview**, you meet with someone and ask him or her questions. Interviewing experts is an excellent way to gain information about a particular topic. For example, if you are interested in writing about the making of pottery, you might interview an art teacher, a professional potter, or the owner of a ceramics shop. When planning an interview, list the questions you would like to ask, including some about the person's background as well as about your topic. Other questions might occur to you as the interview proceeds. See the Language Arts Survey 4.14, "Conducting an Interview."

2.23 Researching for Ideas. No matter what your subject, you can probably find information about it by doing research in reference works. **Reference works** include encyclopedias, dictionaries, almanacs, atlases, indexes, Internet sites, and more. For additional information about reference materials and how to find them, see the Language Arts Survey 5.20, "Using Reference Works" and 5.36, "Keeping a Research Journal."

Organizing Ideas

2.24 Writing Paragraphs. After you have gathered ideas for a piece of writing, the next step is to organize these ideas in a useful and reader-friendly way. The most basic organization of ideas occurs in forming paragraphs. A good paragraph is a carefully organized unit of writing. It develops a sequence in narrative writing or develops a particular topic in informational or persuasive writing.

Paragraphs with Topic Sentences. Many paragraphs include a topic sentence that presents a main idea. The topic sentence can be placed at the beginning, middle or end of the paragraph. Topic sentences usually appear early on in the paragraph and are commonly followed by one or more supporting sentences. Often these supporting sentences begin with transitions that relate them to the other sentences or to the topic sentence. This type of paragraph may end with a clincher sentence, which sums up what has been said in the paragraph.

EXAMPLE

Topic Sentence	The Cavalier poets were loyal supporters of King Charles I during the English Civil Wars, courtiers and soldiers who incidentally wrote lighthearted verse, often on amorous themes.
Supporting Sentences	Classified among the Cavalier poets are Sir John Suckling, Richard Lovelace, and Robert Herrick. Besides writing love lyrics, the Cavaliers sometimes wrote of war, honor, and their duty to the king. Lovelace's "Lucasta, Going to the Wars" deftly combines all these themes.
Clincher Sentence	The Cavalier poets counted the writing of polished and elegant lyrics as only one of their many accomplishments as soldiers, courtiers, gallants, and wits.

Paragraphs without Topic Sentences. Most paragraphs do not have topic sentences. In a narrative piece of writing, many paragraphs state a series of events, and no sentence in the paragraph sums up the events. In good narrative writing, the sequence of events appears in chronological order. Descriptive writing may contain paragraphs organized spatially—in the order in which the speaker or narrator sees, hears, feels, smells, and tastes things in a given situation.

EXAMPLE

The front door bell pealed, and there sounded the rustle of Sadie's print skirt on the stairs. A man's voice murmured; Sadie answered, careless, "I'm sure I don't know. Wait. I'll ask Mrs. Sheridan."

Katherine Mansfield, "The Garden-Party," Unit 11

Organizing Ideas: Writing with a Plan. For instruction on different types of writing organization, see the Writing with a Plan section of the Guided Writing lessons at the end of each unit. For examples, turn to pages 481 and 557.

PARAGRAPH UNITY. The ideas in a paragraph should be tightly linked, or "together." They should be ordered and linked in a logical and easily understandable way. You can organize a paragraph in the order of time (chronologically), in the order of importance, or in order to achieve a specific purpose, such as describing or comparing and contrasting. To link the ideas in a paragraph, use connective words and phrases. In informational or persuasive paragraphs, *for example, as a result, finally, therefore,* and *in fact* are common connectives. In narrative and descriptive paragraphs, words like *first, then, suddenly, above, beyond, in the distance,* and *there* are common connectives. In comparison-contrast paragraphs, common phrases include *similarly, on the other hand,* and *in contrast.* In cause-and-effect paragraphs, linkers include *one cause, another effect, as a result, consequently, finally,* and *therefore.*

2.25 WRITING A THESIS STATEMENT. One way to start organizing your writing, especially if you are writing an informative or persuasive essay, is to identify the main idea of what you want to say. Present this idea in the form of a sentence or two called a thesis statement. A **thesis statement** is simply a sentence that presents the main idea or the position you will take in your essay.

THESIS FOR A PERSUASIVE ESSAY

> The development at Rice Creek Farm should be stopped because it will destroy one of the best natural areas near the city.

THESIS FOR AN INFORMATIVE ESSAY

> Wilma Rudolph was an athlete who succeeded in the elite sport of tennis before the world was willing to recognize her.

WRITING A THESIS STATEMENT. Students are asked to write a thesis statement in the Guided Writing lessons for Unit 8 on page 757.

2.26 WRITING MAIN IDEAS AND SUPPORTING DETAILS. Once you have a thesis statement, the next step is to select several main ideas to support your thesis statement. Begin by writing your thesis at the top of a piece of paper. Then list the main points that you will use to support your thesis. For each main idea, list several supporting details—statements, facts, examples, quotes, and illustrations that explain or demonstrate your idea.

THESIS: The development at Rice Creek Farm should be stopped because people will be unable to enjoy the area, a considerable amount of wildlife will be harmed, and an important water resource will be lost.

- People will be unable to enjoy the area
  - — Hundreds of people of all ages now bike, run, and swim in the area in the summer and ski in the winter. Last year's recreation survey was completed by 653 people. Eighty-five percent said that they visited Rice Creek Farm at least twice a month.
  - — The development of an industrial park would ban people from using the area. It will become a factory site instead of a wooded recreation area. "The industrial park site would be strictly off limits to the public for their own protection," developer Orrin Q. Smedley said in the *Rice Creek Times*.
- A considerable amount of wildlife will be harmed.
  - — The wooded area will be completely eliminated, destroying habitat.

continued

— The species that will be lost will include deer, fox, racoons, skunks, and wild birds, according to the parks board supervisor.

- An important water resource will be lost.
  — The water resource has many uses, including recreational and agricultural.
  — The quality of our city water supply depends on the preservation of this habitat.

2.27 Choosing a Method of Organization. Writing can be organized in different ways.

METHOD	DESCRIPTION
Chronological Order	Give events in the order in which they happen or should be done; connect events by using transition words such as *first, second, next, then,* and *finally.* Chronological organization would be a good method for relating a narrative, giving a recipe, writing a how-to article on building a bird-feeder, or to describe a process, such as what happens when a volcano erupts.
Spatial Order	Describe parts in order of their location in space, for example, from back to front, left to right, or top to bottom; connect your descriptions with transition words or phrases such as *next to, beside, above, below, beyond,* and *around.* Spatial order would be a useful form for an article describing a kitchen renovation, or a descriptive passage in a science fiction story set in a space station.
Order of Importance	List details from least important to most important or from most important to least important; connect your details with transition phrases such as *more important, less important, most important,* and *least important.* A speech telling voters why they should elect you class president could be organized from the least important reason and build to the most important reason.
Comparison-and-Contrast Order	Details of two subjects are presented in one of two ways. In the first method, the characteristics of one subject are presented, followed by the characteristics of the second subject. This method would be useful to organize an essay that compares and contrasts two fast-food chains. You could use this method to say why one is superior to another. "BurgerWorld has the most restaurants. They broil their hamburgers, and offer a line of low-fat meals. Ma's Burgers has far fewer restaurants, fries their hamburgers, and offers no low-fat choices." In the second method, both subjects are compared and contrasted with regard to one quality, then with regard to a second quality, and so on. An essay organized according to this method could compare the platforms of two political parties, issue by issue: the environment, the economy, and so on. Ideas are connected by transitional words and phrases that indicate similarities or differences, such as *likewise, similarly, in contrast, a different kind,* and *another difference.*
Cause-and-Effect Order	One or more causes are presented followed by one or more effects, or one or more effects are presented followed by one or more causes. A public health announcement warning about the dangers of playing with fire would be usefully organized by cause-and-effect. An essay discussing the outbreak of World War I and the events that led up to it could be organized by effect and causes. Transitional words and phrases that indicate cause and effect include *one cause, another effect, as a result, consequently,* and *therefore.*

continued

Choosing a Method of Organization. Students are asked to use comparison-and-contrast order in the Critical Thinking activity on page 831.

Part-by-Part Order	Ideas are presented according to no *overall* organizational pattern. However, each idea is connected logically to the one that precedes it and/or to the one that follows it. A letter to a friend might be organized part by part. One paragraph might discuss a party the writer just attended and the next could focus on the writer's feelings about a person he or she met there. After chronological order, this is the most common method for organizing ideas in writing. Transitional words or phrases include anything that indicates the relationship or connection between the ideas.

2.28 Outlining. An **outline** is an excellent framework for highlighting main ideas and supporting details. Rough and formal outlines are the two main types of outlines writers commonly use.

2.29 Rough Outlines. To create a **rough outline**, simply list your main ideas in some logical order. Under each main idea, list the supporting details set off by dashes.

What Is Drama?

Definition of Drama
—Tells a story
—Uses actors to play characters
—Uses a stage, properties, lights, costumes, makeup, and special effects

Types of Drama
—Tragedy
  —Definition: A play in which the main character meets a negative fate
  —Examples: Antigone, Romeo and Juliet, Death of a Salesman
—Comedy
  —Definition: A play in which the main character meets a positive fate
  —Examples: A Midsummer Night's Dream, Cyrano de Bergerac, The Odd Couple

2.30 Formal Outlines. A **formal outline** has headings and subheadings identified by numbers and letters. One type of formal outline is the **topic outline**. Such an outline has entries that are words or phrases rather than complete sentences.

What Is a Myth?

I. Definition of *myth*
  A. Ancient story involving gods
    1. Multiple gods in mythology
    2. Gods given human characteristics
  B. Often about origins
    1. Reflect prescientific world view
    2. Gods and humans actively participate
  C. Often about heroes
II. Creation myths
  A. The Greek myth of the origins of the universe
  B. The Greek myth of the origins of human beings
III. Origin myths
  A. Arachne and the origins of spiders
  B. Phaëthon and the origins of deserts
IV. Hero myths
  A. Theseus and the Minotaur
  B. Herakles and the twelve labors

2.31 Drafting

After you have gathered your information and organized it, the next step in writing is to produce a draft. A **draft** is simply an early attempt at writing a paper. When working on a draft, keep in mind that you do not have to get everything just right the first time through. The beauty of a draft is that you can rework it many times until you are satisfied with the final product.

Different writers approach drafting in different ways. Some prefer to work slowly and carefully, perfecting each part as they go. Producing such a **careful draft** can be rewarding because you get to see a finished, polished piece emerging part by part. However, many writers find that perfecting each part as they come to it bogs down the process. These writers prefer to write a discovery draft, getting all their ideas down on paper in rough form and then going back over the paper to work it into shape. When writing a **discovery draft**, you do not focus on spelling, grammar, usage, and mechanics. You can take care of those matters during revision.

2.32 Drafting an Introduction. The purpose of an introduction is to capture your reader's attention and establish what you want to say. An effective introduction can start with a quotation, a question, an anecdote, an intriguing fact, or a description that hooks the reader to keep reading.

An effective introduction can open with:

A QUOTE	"That's one small step for man, one giant leap for mankind." With these words, Neil Armstrong signaled his success as the first man to set foot on the moon...
A QUESTION	What would it be like if all the birds in the world suddenly stopped their singing?
AN ANECDOTE	When my brother was nineteen, he volunteered in a homeless shelter making sure people had a safe place to spend the night. He told me once that he would never forget the time he met...
A FACT	More than a million new web pages appear each day on the Internet...
A DESCRIPTION	Along the murky bottom of the ocean floor, at the deepest part of the ocean, lies the giant squid, a creature so elusive that few people have ever seen it. For hundreds of years, no one knew it really existed—although tales of sea monsters had long hinted of it.

2.33 Drafting Body Paragraphs. When writing the body of an essay, refer to your outline. Each heading in your outline will become the main idea of one of your paragraphs. To move smoothly from one idea to another, use transitional words or phrases. As you draft, include evidence from documented sources to support the ideas that you present. This evidence can be paraphrased, summarized, or quoted directly. For information on documenting sources, see the Language Arts Survey 5.35, "Documenting Sources" and 5.42, "Paraphrasing, Summarizing, and Quoting."

2.34 Drafting a Conclusion. In the conclusion, bring together the main ideas you included in the body of your essay and create a sense of closure to the issue you raised in your thesis. There is no single right way to conclude a piece of writing. Possibilities include:

- Making a generalization
- Restating the thesis and major supporting ideas in different words
- Summarizing the points made in the rest of the essay
- Drawing a lesson or moral
- Calling on the reader to adopt a view or take an action
- Expanding on your thesis or main idea by connecting it to the reader's own interests
- Linking your thesis to a larger issue or concern.

2.35 Using Transitions Effectively. Transitions are words and phrases that help you move smoothly from one idea to the next in your writing. The transition words themselves depend on the method of organization you are using in your paper. For lists of these words and when to use them, see the Language Arts Survey 2.27, "Choosing a Method of Organization."

Drafting. The Guided Writing lessons at the end of each unit allow students the opportunity to go through the drafting process of writing. For examples see pages 483 and 758.

Writing Description, Dialogue, Narrative, and Exposition. Students are to incorporate dialogue in their short stories in the Unit 5 Guided Writing lesson on page 483.

Self- and Peer Evaluation. Self- and peer evaluation is covered in each of the Guided Writing lessons at the end of the units. See pages 559 and 984 for examples.

2.36 Writing Description, Dialogue, Narrative, and Exposition. Some writing purposes do not require a thesis or a formal outline. They rely on other types of writing to present their ideas effectively. These types include description, dialogue, narration, and exposition.

TYPE OF WRITING	DESCRIPTION AND ORGANIZATION
Narration	As with the narrative mode, this method tells a story or presents events using time, or **chronological order**, as a way of organization.
Dialogue	Writing using this method presents words as they were actually spoken by people. Quotation marks are usually used to set off direct speech.
Description	Writing with this method portrays a character, an object, or a scene. Descriptions make use of sensory details—words and phrases that describe how things look, sound, smell, taste, or feel. Descriptive writing frequently uses **spatial order** as a way of organization.
Exposition	Writing using this method presents facts or opinions in an organized manner. There are many ways to organize exposition. Among the most common are the following: **Analysis** breaks something into its parts and shows how the parts are related. **Cause and Effect** identifies and analyzes the causes and effects of something. **Classification** involves placing subjects into categories, or classes, according to their properties or characteristics. These groups are then presented, one-by-one, in some reasonable order. **Comparison and Contrast Order** is a method of organization in which details about the similarities and differences between two subjects are presented in one of two ways. In the first method, characteristics of one subject are presented, followed by the characteristics of a second subject. In the second method, both subjects are compared and contrasted with regard to one characteristic, then with regard to a second characteristic, and so on. **Definition** explains a concept or idea and examines its qualities. **Problem/Solution** writing analyzes a problem and proposes possible solutions. It can be objective or persuasive. **Process/How-to** writing presents the steps in a process or gives the reader directions on how to do something.

2.37 Self- and Peer Evaluation

When you evaluate something, you examine it carefully to find its strengths and weaknesses. Evaluating your own writing is called **self-evaluation**. A **peer evaluation** is an evaluation of a piece of writing done by a classmate, or peer.

2.38 How to Evaluate a Piece of Writing. After producing a rough draft of a piece of writing, the next step is to evaluate that draft to find out what you or the writer you are evaluating should improve.

A good evaluation practice is to read through the piece of writing three times:

- **First, check for content.** If you are evaluating your own writing, make sure that you have said all that you want to say, that you have not left out important details, and that you have not included unimportant or unrelated details. If you are evaluating a peer's writing, make sure the content is clear, that nothing is missing to prevent the work from carrying the reader forward, and that the writer has not included any unrelated details.

- **Second, check for organization.** Make sure that the ideas in the writing are presented in a reasonable order.
- **Third, check the style and language** of the piece. Make sure that the language is appropriately formal or informal, that the tone is appropriate to the message and the audience the piece addresses, and that the writer has defined any key or unfamiliar terms.

As you check the writing piece, make notes about what the writer needs to revise, or change. See the Language Arts Survey 2.42, "A Revision Checklist," for further information on what to look for as you evaluate your or a peer's writing.

2.39 How to Deliver Helpful Criticism

- **Be focused.** Concentrate on content, organization, and style. Do not concentrate at this point on proofreading matters such as spelling and punctuation; they can be fixed later.
- **Be positive.** Let the writer know what he or she has done right. Show how the paper could be improved by making the changes that you are suggesting.
- **Be specific.** Give the writer concrete ideas for improving his or her work. For example, if you think that two ideas seem unconnected, suggest a way in which they might be connected clearly.
- **Be tactful.** Consider the other person's feelings, and use a pleasant tone of voice. Do not criticize the writer. Instead, focus on the writing.

2.40 How to Benefit from Helpful Criticism

- **Tell your evaluator specific concerns.** For example, if you are wondering whether something you have written is clear, ask the evaluator if he or she understands that part of what you have written.
- **Ask questions to clarify comments** that your evaluator makes.
- **Accept your evaluator's comments graciously.** Remember that criticisms can be helpful. They can help you to identify weaknesses and produce a better piece through revision. If, on the other hand, you think that a given suggestion will not truly improve your writing, you do not have to follow it. There are many ways to strengthen writing. By reflecting on reviewer comments and your own self-evaluation, you will be ready to go on to the next step: revision.

2.41 Revising

After identifying weaknesses in a draft through self-evaluation and peer evaluation, the next step is to **revise** the draft. Here are four basic ways to improve meaning and content:

Adding or Expanding. Sometimes writing can be improved by adding details, examples, or transitions to connect ideas. Often a single added adjective, for example, can make a piece of writing clearer or more vivid.

UNREVISED	Wind whistled through the park.
REVISED	A **bone-chilling** wind whistled through the park.

At other times, you will find you will need to add details to back up your main idea.

UNREVISED	Everyone uses the park so its destruction would be a major loss to the community.
REVISED	Of the 653 people who responded to the survey, 85 percent said they would consider the destruction of the park a major loss to the community.

WRITING RESOURCE

Revising. Instruction on revising and proofreading is given in each of the Guided Writing lessons at the end of the units. For examples see pages 759 and 984.

Revision Checklist. A blackline master of the Revision Checklist is provided in the Writing Resource 2.42 of the Teacher's Resource Kit.

Proofreading. Instruction on revising and proofreading is given in each of the Guided Writing lessons at the end of the units. For examples see pages 759 and 984.

Cutting or Condensing. Often writing can be improved by cutting unnecessary or unrelated material.

UNREVISED	Watson was firmly determined to find the structure of the DNA molecule.
REVISED	Watson was determined to find the structure of the DNA molecule.

Replacing. Sometimes weak writing can be made stronger through more concrete, more vivid, or more precise details.

UNREVISED	Several things had been bothering Bill.
REVISED	Several personal problems had been bothering Bill.
UNREVISED	Chandra lived in a house down the street.
REVISED	Chandra lived in a Garrison colonial down Mulberry Street.

Moving. Often you can improve the organization of your writing by moving part of it so that related ideas appear near one another.

UNREVISED	Mince the garlic in very fine pieces. Then heat a tablespoon of olive oil in a small skillet. Stir it with a wooden spoon and saute just until it starts to brown. Then remove it. Oh—before you put it in the skillet, heat some oil. Use about a tablespoon. Olive oil is best. Use medium low heat.
REVISED	Mince the garlic in very fine pieces. Heat a tablespoon of olive oil in a small skillet at a medium low temperature. When the oil is hot, add the garlic. Stir it with a wooden spoon and saute it just until it starts to brown. Then remove the garlic.

When you mark a piece of writing for revision, use the standard proofreading symbols. The symbols for adding, cutting, replacing, and moving are the first four symbols in the Language Arts Survey 2.44, "Using Proofreader's Marks."

2.42 A Revision Checklist. The following chart lists some questions to ask yourself whenever you are revising your writing. If you cannot answer *yes* to any of these questions, then you need to revise your work. Continue revising until you can answer *yes*.

REVISION CHECKLIST	
Content	• Does the writing achieve its purpose? • Are the main ideas clearly stated and supported by details?
Organization	• Are the ideas arranged in a sensible order? • Are the ideas connected to one another within paragraphs and between paragraphs?
Style	• Is the language appropriate to the audience and purpose? • Is the mood appropriate to the purpose of the writing?

2.43 Proofreading

When you proofread your writing, you read it through to look for errors and mark corrections. When you mark corrections to your writing, use the standard proofreading symbols. With just a little practice you'll find them very easy and convenient.

2.44 USING PROOFREADER'S MARKS. Consult the chart below for standard proofreading marks.

PROOFREADER'S SYMBOLS	
Symbol and Example	**Meaning of Symbol**
The very first time	Delete (cut) this material.
cat cradle	Insert (add) something that is missing.
Georze	Replace this letter or word.
All the horses king's	Move this word to where the arrow points.
french toast	Capitalize this letter.
the vice-President	Lowercase this letter.
housse	Take out this letter and close up space.
book keeper	Close up space.
gebril	Change the order of these letters.
end. "Watch out," she yelled.	Begin a new paragraph.
Love conquers all	Put a period here.
Welcome friends.	Put a comma here.
Getthe stopwatch	Put a space here.
Dear Madam	Put a colon here.
She walked he rode.	Put a semicolon here.
name brand products	Put a hyphen here.
cats meow	Put an apostrophe here.
cat's cradle (stet)	Let it stand. (Leave as it is.)

2.45 A PROOFREADING CHECKLIST. After you have revised your draft, make a clean copy of it and proofread it for errors in spelling, grammar, and punctuation. Use the following proofreading checklist.

PROOFREADING CHECKLIST	
Spelling	• Are all words, including names, spelled correctly?
Grammar	• Does each verb agree with its subject? • Are verb tenses consistent and correct? • Are irregular verbs formed correctly? • Are there any sentence fragments or run-ons? • Have double negatives been avoided? • Have frequently confused words, such as *affect* and *effect*, been used correctly?
Punctuation	• Does every sentence end with an end mark? • Are commas used correctly? • Do all proper nouns and proper adjectives begin with capital letters?

USING PROOFREADER'S MARKS. Encourage students to use proofreader's marks when they do peer evaluations. A blackline master of the Proofreader's Symbols is provided in the Writing Resource 2.44 of the Teacher's Resource Kit.

Proper Manuscript Form. Encourage students to read the Language Arts Survey 2.46, "Proper Manuscript Form" after they are done revising and proofreading their written assignments.

Publishing and Presenting. Ideas for publishing and presenting student writing are suggested in each of the Guided Writing lessons at the end of the units. For examples, see pages 763 and 1093.

Maintaining a Writing Portfolio. You might find additional suggestions for helping students maintain a writing portfolio in *Portfolio Keeping: A Guide for Students* by Nedra Reynolds.

2.46 Proper Manuscript Form. After proofreading your draft, you will want to prepare your final manuscript. Follow the guidelines given by your teacher or, if your teacher tells you to do so, the guidelines given here. After preparing a final manuscript according to these guidelines, proofread it one last time for errors.

GUIDELINES FOR PREPARING A MANUSCRIPT

- Keyboard your manuscript using a typewriter or word processor, or write it out neatly using blue or black ink.
- Double-space your paper. Leave one blank line between every line of text.
- Use one side of the paper.
- Leave one-inch margins on all sides of the text.
- Indent the first line of each paragraph.
- In the upper right-hand corner of the first page, put your name, class, and date. On every page after the first, include the page number in this heading, as follows:
  Keanna Pérez
  English 7
  May 3, 1999
  p. 2
- Make a cover sheet listing the title of the work, your name, the date, and the class.

2.47 Publishing and Presenting Your Work

In the **publishing and presenting stage**, you share your work with an audience.

2.48 Maintaining a Writing Portfolio. A **writing portfolio** is a collection of your writing. Usually, a portfolio is a file folder with your name on it and your writing in it. Your teacher may ask you to keep a complete portfolio, one that includes all the pieces that you write. Another possibility is that your teacher will ask you to keep a selected portfolio, one that contains only your very best pieces of writing.

When you put a piece of writing in your portfolio, make sure that your name and the date are on it. Attach any notes or earlier versions of the writing that you have.

From time to time, you and your teacher will evaluate, or examine, your portfolio. You will meet in a student-teacher conference and talk about your pieces of writing. Your teacher will help you to find strengths and weaknesses in your writing. He or she also will help you to make plans for improving your writing in the future.

Keeping a writing portfolio can be exciting. In very little time, you can build a collection of your work. Looking over this work, you can take pride in your accomplishments. You can also reflect on how you are growing as a writer.

2.49 Sharing Your Work with Others. Some writing is done just for one's self. Journal writing usually falls into that category. Most writing, however, is meant to be shared with others. There are many ways in which to share your work. Here are several ways in which you can publish your writing or present it to others:

- Find a local publication that will accept your work. (A school literary magazine, a school newspaper, or a community newspaper are possibilities.)

- Submit the work to a regional or national publication. Check a reference work such as Writer's *Market* to find information on types of manuscripts accepted, manuscript form, and methods and amounts of payment.
- Enter the work in a contest. Your teacher may be able to tell you about writing contests for students. You can also find out about such contests by looking for announcements in writers' magazines and literary magazines.
- Read your work aloud to classmates, friends, or family members.
- Obtain permission to read your work aloud over the school's public address system.
- Work with other students to prepare a publication—a brochure, on-line literary magazine, anthology, or newspaper.
- Prepare a poster or bulletin board, perhaps in collaboration with other students, to display your writing.
- Make your own book by typing or word processing the pages and binding them together. Or copy your work into a blank book.
- Hold a reading or performance of student writing as a class or school-wide project.
- Share your writing with other students in a small writers' group that meets periodically to discuss one or two students' recent work. (Members of the group should receive the work to be discussed beforehand so they can read it and make notes on it.)
- If the work is dramatic in nature, work with other students to present a performance of it, either as straight drama or as readers' theater. If the work is poetry, fiction, or nonfiction, work with others to present it as an oral interpretation.

2.50 Reflecting on Your Writing

In the **reflecting** stage, you think through the writing process to determine what you learned as a writer, what you accomplished, and what skills you would like to strengthen the next time you write. Reflection can be done in a journal, on a self-evaluation form for writing, in small group discussion, or simply in your own thoughts. Here are some questions to ask as you reflect on the writing process and yourself as a writer.

QUESTIONS FOR REFLECTION

- What have I learned in writing about this topic?
- What have I learned in writing for this purpose?
- What have I learned by using this form?
- How do I perceive my audience? What would I like my audience to gain from my writing?
- What kind of voice does my writing have?
- How have I developed as a writer while writing this piece?
- What strengths have I discovered in my work?
- What aspects of my writing do I want to strengthen? What can I do to strengthen them?

WRITING RESOURCE

Reflecting on Your Writing. Students are asked to reflect on their writing at various stages of the writing process in the Guided Writing lessons at the end of each unit. For examples, turn to pages 1093 and 1179.

INTERNET RESOURCES

Elements of Style by William Strunk, Jr. is now available online at http://www.bartleby.com/141/index.html. This popular writing resource guide is intended for classrooms where the practice of composition is combined with the study of literature. In a brief form, it covers the principal requirements of plain English style.

Access Online English Grammar at http://www.edunet.com/english/grammar/index.cfm for a grammar guide and reference tool for students that need to brush up on their English skills.

Take a tour of the Lingua Center Grammar Safari at http://deil.lang.uiuc.edu/web.pages/grammarsafari.html. This site will broaden your students' horizons by exploring grammar as it occurs in its natural surroundings—the jungle out in the real world.

Register, Tone, and Voice. Refer students to the Language Arts survey 3.3, "Register, Tone, and Voice" when they are reading the Finding Your Voice section of each Guided Writing lesson. See pages 1091 and 1172 for examples.

LANGUAGE, GRAMMAR, AND STYLE Resource

LANGUAGE HANDBOOK

3.1 Appropriate Uses of English

Language is a powerful tool for conveying meaning. It is also a complex tool that must be used appropriately if genuine communication is to occur. In deciding how to communicate most effectively, a speaker must make choices concerning use of formal or informal English; what tone to use, the effects of irony, sarcasm, and rudeness; and how dialect affects the communicated message.

3.2 Formal and Informal English

Depending on the situation, you might use either formal English or informal English when you speak or write. Formal English is appropriate for school essays, newspaper and magazine articles, some literary works, oral or written reports, and test answers. Informal English is appropriate when speaking with a friend or writing personal letters or notes; it can also be used in some literary works.

How do you decide whether to use formal or informal English? You will naturally tend to use informal English, so all you need to remember are the situations just described in which formal English may be expected instead. Your audience and purpose help determine whether to use formal or informal English. For example, you would use formal English to discuss a grade with a teacher or to ask for a refund from a store manager. You would use informal English talking with your friends. You might use somewhat formal English in getting to know a new friend, and then relax and use more informal English as the friendship developed.

How do you tell the difference between formal and informal English? Informal English allows grammatical constructions that would not be acceptable in formal English. Many of these constructions are described in the Grammar Handbook on page 1055, where they are labeled "nonstandard." Informal English also uses *colloquialisms* and *slang*.

A **colloquialism** is a word or phrase used in everyday conversation.

COLLOQUIAL ENGLISH

You guys must be **sick of** doing the same thing day after day.
He was **totally turned off** by the movie.

FORMAL ENGLISH

All of you must be **weary** of doing the same thing day after day.
He was completely **displeased** by the movie.

Slang is a form of speech made up of invented words or old words that are given a new meaning.

SLANG

You better **chill out** for a while—you're too angry to talk to him now.

FORMAL ENGLISH

You had better **relax** for a while—you're too angry to talk to him now.

3.3 Register, Tone, and Voice

To understand the concept of register, imagine that all the different kinds of usage in a language—both formal and informal—form one large set. A **register** is a subset of language usage specific to a particular relationship between people. In talking to a friend, for example, you speak in a register that is casual, warm, and open. In speaking to a young child, you speak in a register that is nonthreatening and simple to understand. In speaking to an official such as a police officer or a government clerk, you speak in a register that is polite but forthright—the same register that person should use with you. The words you choose, the grammar you employ to say those words, and your tone of voice will change depending on the register in which you are speaking.

Another way to understand register is to examine its meaning as a musical term. In music, register means the range of notes a singer or instrument is capable of producing. Your speaking and writing, however, are not limited to one range of usage. You can call on any part of a broad scale of usage, ranging from a grunt to a complex and formal declaration of your thought.

One hallmark of people who know how to use the power of language is their ability to choose and use the appropriate register for whatever situation they are in. They do not offend strangers by being too familiar or puzzle their friends by being too formal.

Tone is a writer's or speaker's attitude toward a subject. The tone of a message should reflect the speaker's attitude toward the subject and his or her audience. The speaker shapes the tone of a message by carefully choosing words and phrases. *Diction*, or choice of words, determines much of a speaker's tone. For instance, when writing a letter of complaint, do you want to say, "Your new product is so disgusting that I'll never buy anything you make ever again" or "I am concerned with the danger your new product poses to young children"? The tone you convey will depend greatly upon word choice.

The following examples give two different descriptions of the same scene. In one the scene is described in a tone of fear, and in the other it is described in a tone of awe. If you were telling a story about someone who was afraid of the ocean, you might use the more negative description. If you were writing about someone who enjoyed the ocean, you would probably use the more positive description.

TONE OF FEAR

Menacing black waves rolled in relentlessly, crashing down upon the rocks and threatening to sweep everything in their path out to sea. Mountainous and savage, the waves pounded the shore with a fury that sent a chill of dread through my soul.

TONE OF AWE

Powerful breakers rolled in majestically, splashing against the rocks and sending fountains of spray high into the air. I stood in awe of this force so mighty that nothing could stop it.

Voice is the quality of a work that tells you that one person in particular wrote it—not several, and not just anyone. Voice is one feature that makes a spoken or written work unique. The voice of a work can be difficult to define; it may have to do with the way a writer or speaker views people, events, objects, ideas, the passage of time, even life itself. If this treatment of the subject is consistent throughout, despite variations in tone, register, point of view, and topic, then the writer or speaker has established a voice, a sense of individuality, in the work.

In your own communication, whether in speaking or writing, you should strive to develop your own voice, not to imitate the voices of others. What that voice is, and how it compares to others, are matters no one can decide for you. "To thine own self be true," says Polonius in Shakespeare's *Hamlet*, "and thou canst not then be false to any man." Be true to your own voice, and your experience will speak directly to the experience of others.

3.4 Irony, Sarcasm, and Rudeness

It is easy to mistake the term *rude* to mean anything that is crude, distasteful, or not pleasing to someone. The word *rude* has been adapted and expanded into a general slang term. The standard definition of *rude* means bad-mannered, impolite, or inconsiderate. If someone says something a listener doesn't like, that person is not rude in the original meaning of the word. However, a person who interrupts someone else's conversation, curses, or forgets to say "please," "thank you," or "excuse me" is being selfish and inconsiderate—all characteristics of rude behavior within the original meaning of the word.

Frequently students confuse sarcasm or irony with rudeness. **Verbal irony** is present when someone says or writes the opposite of what he or she means in order to create humor or to make a point. It can be funny or serious. For example, if someone pushes to the front of a line, and someone else says, "What polite behavior," the speaker is expressing verbal irony. **Sarcasm** is a specialized kind of irony; the difference is the speaker's intentions. Sarcastic people say the opposite of what they mean in order to criticize, hurt, or humiliate someone. Sarcasm differs from other forms of irony because it is usually unkind.

Jonathan Swift uses sarcasm in "A Modest Proposal" when he argues that children be eaten in order to curtail the overpopulation of peasants in Ireland:

EXAMPLE

I have been assured by a very knowing American of my acquaintance in London, that a young healthy child well nursed is at a year old a most delicious, nourishing, and wholesome food, whether stewed, roasted, baked, or boiled; and I make no doubt that it will equally serve in a fricassee or a ragout.

3.5 Dialects of English

A **dialect** is a version of a language spoken by people of a particular place, time, or group. Dialects are characterized by differences in pronunciation, word choice, grammar, and accent. They are usually based on social differences (upper class, middle class, and lower class) or on regional differences. In the United States, the major regional dialects are northern, southern, midland, and western.

All dialects are equally capable of expressing thought, which is what language is for. Therefore, no dialect is better than any other dialect. The dialect used by the most powerful social class is usually considered the **standard**, and other dialects are considered **nonstandard**. But standard does not mean "correct" or "better than others." Knowledge of the standard dialect is useful because it is widely understood, and because in many situations, speaking or writing in the standard dialect will ensure that people focus on what you say rather than how you say it. They will understand your meaning, without being distracted by your use of an unfamiliar dialect.

Knowing nonstandard dialect is also useful to writers. Consider the way Robert Burns uses dialect to make his writing more authentic.

EXAMPLE

We twa hae paidled i' the burn,
  From morning sun till dine,
But seas between us braid hae roared,
  Sin' auld lang syne.

Differences in dialect show up especially in the terms speakers use to refer to certain objects in various areas of the country. For example, the generic term for a carbonated beverage is "soda" in Florida and Washington, DC, "pop" in Ohio and Minnesota, "coke" in Georgia and Tennessee, and "tonic" in Boston. Similarly, the grassy strip separating the lanes of an interstate highway is called a "mall" in upstate New York, a "median" in Ohio, a "medial strip" in Pennsylvania, a "meridian" in the upper Midwest, and "neutral ground" in Louisiana.

DIALECTS OF ENGLISH. Students are asked to rewrite and translate dialect in the Language, Grammar, and Style activities on pages 61 and 827.

GRAMMAR HANDBOOK

In English the basic unit of meaning is the sentence. In this integrated approach to grammar you will examine sentences to determine what they mean. This should help you to be a better reader and more skillful writer. This approach may be new to you, so here are a series of charts and references to help you as you begin. Do not memorize these charts. The more you use them, the less you will need them. With time, you will develop a feeling for the way language works so you will not need them at all.

3.6 Identifying the Parts of Speech

Each word in a sentence has one of four basic functions: it **names**, **modifies**, **expresses action or state of being**, or **links**.

A fifth "extra" function is to interrupt for effect; words that **interrupt** will be discussed at the end of this section.

English also has words that can work as more than one part of speech. Words that can take on different parts of speech are called **hybrids**. These words will be explained at the end of this section.

Below is an overview of the parts of speech. For a more detailed description of what each part of speech does, see the "Parts of Speech Summary" on page 1071.

3.7 Grammar Reference Chart—Parts of Speech Overview

PARTS OF SPEECH	EXAMPLE(S)
NAMERS (nouns and pronouns) are subjects and objects.	
Noun. A **noun** names a person, place, thing, or idea.	Adam, journalist, mountain, India, rose, motorcycle, honesty, feeling
Pronoun. A **pronoun** is used in place of a noun to name a person, place, thing, or idea.	**I** bought the bricks and used **them** to build a wall. Take Schuyler to the ice cream shop and buy **him** (used in place of Schuyler) a cone.
EXPRESSERS (verbs) name an action or state of being plus the conditions around it.	
Verb. A **verb** expresses action or state of being.	bake, glance, give, build, compose, think, look, feel, am
MODIFIERS (adjectives and adverbs) make other parts of speech more specific.	
Adjective. An **adjective** modifies, or changes the meaning of, a noun or pronoun.	**gray** skies, **deep** water, **eerie** laughter
Adverb. An **adverb** modifies, or changes the meaning of a verb, an adjective, or another adverb.	Leanne gripped the wheel **nervously**. Elliot thought the exam was **extremely** easy. Giovanni peered over the edge of the cliff **very** cautiously.
LINKERS (prepositions and conjunctions) join all the constructions of the English language.	
Preposition. A **preposition** is used to show how a noun or a pronoun is related to other words in the sentence. Common prepositions are *in, after, among, at, behind, beside, off, through, until, upon,* and *with.*	Pablo enjoyed the concert **at** the Wang Center. Theresa squeezed **through** the opening **of** the cave and crawled **into** the narrow passage.
Conjunction. A **conjunction** joins words or groups of words. Common conjunctions are *and, but, for, nor, or, so,* and *yet.*	Wilhelm plays the guitar, **but** Leonard plays drums. Wilhelm **and** Leonard play loudly.
INTERRUPTERS (interjections and other constructions) interrupt a sentence for emphasis.	
Interjection. An **interjection** is a word used to express emotion. Common interjections are *oh, ah, well, say,* and *wow.*	**Hey!** What are you doing in there? **Oh well,** I didn't expect to win the election anyway.
Appositive. An **appositive** is an interrupter that renames a noun.	My friend **Yang Yardley** did a beautiful project on birds. Mrs. Cokely, **my favorite teacher**, will retire.
Noun of Direct Address. A noun of direct address says the name of the person or group spoken to and is never the subject of the sentence.	Wait until dark, **Audrey**. **Class**, listen to the instructions. (*Class* is a noun of direct address; the subject of the sentence is *you*; the pronoun *you* is understood.)

CONTINUED

Grammar Reference Chart—Parts of Speech Overview. Students are asked to review the Parts of Speech in the Language, Grammar, and Style activities on pages 174 and 317.

PARTS OF SPEECH	EXAMPLE(S)
HYBRIDS (such as possessive nouns, pronouns, verbals) can act as more than one part of speech.	
POSSESSIVE NOUNS AND PRONOUNS. **Possessive nouns** and **pronouns** are nouns and pronouns that function as adjectives.	Angela read **Scott's** essay. (*Scott's* is a possessive noun modifying *essay*.) Angela read **his** essay. (*His* is a possessive pronoun modifying *essay*.)
VERBALS. **Verbals** are verb forms such as participles, gerunds, and infinitives that can function as adjectives, nouns, and adverbs.	I love the **swimming** pool. (*Swimming* is a verbal called a participle and acts as an adjective.) **Swimming** is my favorite sport. (*Swimming* is a verbal called a gerund and acts as a noun.) I like **to swim**. (*To swim* is a verbal called an infinitive.)

To understand how a sentence works, here are other groups of words that you should know about.

3.8 Grammar Reference Chart—Helping Verbs

A **helping verb** helps a main verb to express action or state of being.

HELPING VERBS		
be (am, are, is, was, were, being, and been)	have (has, had)	shall
can	may	should
could	might	will
do (does, did)	must	would

3.9 Grammar Reference Chart—The Verb *To Be*

Most languages use the verb *to be* more than any other verb because its forms have more uses than any other verb form. It can be the main verb of a sentence, used to express existence. It also can be a helping verb used with action verbs. Here are some forms of *to be:*

THE VERB *TO BE*	
Present: am, is, are **Past:** was, were, has been, had been **Future:** will be, shall be, will have been	**Other Expressions and Forms that use *Be*:** being, can be, could be, could have been, may be, may have been, might be, might have been, must be, must have been, would be, would have been

3.10 Grammar Reference Chart—Linking Verbs

A linking verb connects a noun with another noun, a pronoun, or pronoun adjective that describes or defines it. Note that some linking verbs can also be action verbs. For example, *I grow tired* uses *grow* as a linking verb. *I grow flowers* uses *grow* as an action verb. Notice how I am a junior and A junior am I mean exactly the same thing. This is because *am* is a linking, not an action verb. Sentences with action verbs cannot be reversed in the same way: *I made a bookshelf* and *A bookshelf*

GRAMMAR REFERENCE CHART—LINKING VERBS. Students are asked to distinguish action verbs from linking verbs in the Language, Grammar, and Style activity on page 505.

made me do not mean the same thing. Here is a list of common linking verbs. *Be* is the most common of all.

LINKING VERBS		
appear	grow	smell
be (am, is, are, was, were, been)	look	sound
become	remain	stay
feel	seem	taste

3.11 Grammar Reference Chart—Prepositions

These are the most commonly used prepositions. Remember, though, that any word on this list may not always be used as a preposition. If it is a preposition, it will always have an object.

PREPOSITIONS				
aboard	at	concerning	off	until
about	before	down	on	up
above	behind	during	over	upon
across	below	except	past	with
after	beside	for	since	within
against	besides	from	through	without
along	between	in	throughout	
amid	beyond	into	to	
among	but	like	under	
around	by	of	underneath	

3.12 What Is Grammar?

The **grammar** of a language refers to two different language areas. First, grammar is the collection of rules and standards that careful speakers use as they write and speak. Second, a **grammar** is any one of several possible descriptions of a language.

Classical grammar has troubled English students because it was originally designed to fit Latin, an inflected language. In Latin every word has an ending or inflection that defines its sentence function, so word order doesn't matter. About the middle of this century, different English grammars began to appear. The most successful of the new grammars were based upon rules of English word order, but frequently the terms used were too confusing to be widely used.

Consequently, the grammar presented here uses elements of both. It demands that students label words and language groups according to what language is doing (which we know by word order). Many terms are familiar because they come from classical grammar, but their meaning may change to fit the grammar of a syntactic language, English.

3.13 English Is a Syntactic Language

Scholars who study language have classified European languages into two major categories: **inflected languages** and **syntactic languages.** The words of **inflected** languages change their forms to tell speakers how the word is used. Word order isn't all that important to meaning. Some inflected languages are Latin and German. English is a **syntactic language**. Word order **(syntax)** determines meaning for **syntactic languages.**

LANGUAGE, GRAMMAR, AND STYLE

ENGLISH IS A SYNTACTIC LANGUAGE. Students are asked to use proper syntax in the Language, Grammar, and Style activity on page 510.

Functions of Sentences. Students are asked to identify or write declarative, interrogative, imperative, and exclamatory sentences in the Language, Grammar, and Style activities on pages 944 and 951.

3.14 The Importance of Syntax, or Word Order

EXAMPLE The junior class plans the prom each spring.

In English sentences words are arranged in specific patterns. In the most frequently used sentence, the sentence tells who (*The junior class*), and then it tells what that *who* does (*plans the prom each spring*). When word order changes, the sentence changes meaning; if the pattern rules are ignored, the sentence may become awkward, or even meaningless.

EXAMPLES
Class the the prom plans each spring junior.
Plans the junior spring the prom class each.
Class the plans each the prom junior spring.

A change in syntax results in a change in meaning; different sentence positions of the same word results in different meanings.

EXAMPLES
Junior prom plans are finished by March.
Plans for our house were completed last fall.
Our family plans a vacation every summer.

In the first two sentences, *plans* names something. In the first sentence it is used to mean arrangements; in the second it means blueprints. In the third sentence, *plans* is an action. In all sentences the word form is the same, but different positions signal different meanings.

3.15 Inflections in English

English does have some **inflections**, or changes in form, but word order is most important! English verbs, adjectives, and pronouns are inflected. Sometimes we add a suffix (add *-ed* to *work*, *-er* or *-est* to *hard*), other times interior letters or the entire forms change: *drive* becomes *drove*, *my* becomes *mine*, *was* becomes *were*.

EXAMPLES

Inflected verbs
Today I *carry* my lunch. Yesterday I *carried* it, too. (The *y* is replaced by *i*, and the suffix *-ed* is added.)

Today I *have* lots of homework; yesterday I *had* very little. (The entire verb form changes.)

Inflected adjectives
My sister is *wise*; my mother is *wiser*, but my grandmother is the *wisest* woman in the family. (The suffixes *-er* and *-est* are added to indicate higher degrees of quality.)

Kevin's day was *good*; Tua's was *better*, but mine turned out *best*. (The form changes altogether.)

Inflected Pronouns
Most pronouns change forms: *me*, *mine*; *they*, *them*. A specialized group of pronouns, the reflexive and intensive pronouns, add the suffix *-self* to the singular possessive pronoun forms *my*, *him*, *her*, *it*, and *your*; and add *-selves* to the plural forms *them*, *your*; and *our*.

3.16 The Sentence: The Basic Building Block of the English Language

Since first grade you have been encouraged to write and speak in sentences because they are the basic units of meaning. English sentences are organized to tell us whom or what a speaker is talking about and information about that whom or what. Classical grammar defines a sentence as "a group of words that expresses a complete thought."

3.17 Functions of Sentences

English speakers use four kinds of sentences to express four different kinds of complete thoughts:

- A **declarative sentence** informs us. First, it tells whom or what a speaker is writing or speaking about, and second, information about that whom or what.
- An **interrogative sentence** asks a question.
- An **imperative sentence** gives orders or makes requests.
- An **exclamatory sentence** expresses strong feeling.

EXAMPLES
Declarative: I am ready to eat dinner.
Interrogative: Is dinner ready?
Imperative: Give me my food.
Exclamatory: I'm starving to death!

3.18 Subjects and Verbs: The Basic Building Blocks in a Sentence

Good readers and writers analyze meaning by examining the structure of sentences. Finding the parts of a sentence is a basic tool for people who use language well.

3.19 Finding the Complete Subject and Complete Predicate in a Sentence

All simple English sentences can be divided into two parts, the subject and the predicate. In the most common English sentence, the first part of the sentence tells us what it is talking about. This is the **complete subject**. Then it gives us information about the subject; this second part of the sentence is called the **complete predicate**. In the following examples, the complete subject is underlined once and the complete predicate is underlined twice.

EXAMPLES

One of my brothers fixed his own car.
Sharyl and Ken will be presenting Friday's history lesson.
Lala might have been given a wrong classroom number.

Note: Every word in every sentence is a part of the complete subject or the complete predicate.

3.20 Finding the Simple Subject and Simple Predicate in a Sentence

Most people need more specific information than that given by the complete subject and the complete predicate. The basic units of meaning are found in the **simple subject** and the **simple predicate** (more frequently called the **verb)**. The **simple subject** is the **complete subject** without any of its modifiers. The **verb** is the **complete predicate** without any complements or modifiers.

The **simple subject** is the complete subject without any modifiers or linkers—the extra words.

EXAMPLES

Little **kids** like pet kittens and puppies.
Telly's **mother** wants a new car.

The **simple predicate** or **verb** is the complete predicate without any complements, linkers, or modifiers.

EXAMPLES

Little kids **like** pet kittens and puppies.
Telly's mother **wants** a new car.

Note: Verbs may have more than one word—they may have as many as four! Each of the examples is one verb.

EXAMPLES

play (one word)
is playing (two words)
has been playing (3 words)
may have been playing (4 words)

3.21 How to Find the Simple Subject and Verb

The following four-step method will help you to find the simple subject and verb.

SAMPLE SENTENCE

My older sister might not get a motorcycle for high school graduation.

1. Ask, "What is the action of this sentence?" The action is *get*.
2. Using the Language Arts Survey 3.8, "Helping Verbs," check some of the words around the action word. For the sample sentence, you might want to check *might* and *not*. *Might* is on the list; *not* isn't. Only *might* is a helping verb. The verb of the sentence is *might get*.
3. After finding the verb, ask who (what) did the action? Who *might get*? *My older sister*.
4. Finally, what words aren't necessary for simplest meaning? *Older sister* makes sense, so omit *my*; *older* can be left out, too. *Sister* is the simple subject of the sentence.

3.22 Sentence Completers for Action Verbs: Direct and Indirect Objects

A sentence must have a subject and a verb, but sometimes sentences have other parts that complete the meaning. The completers for action verbs are **direct objects** and **indirect objects**.

First, it is important to realize that not all sentences have objects. Here are some examples of sentences without objects. In each of these sentences there is no receiver of the action. The verb expresses the total concept.

EXAMPLES

Birds fly south.

LANGUAGE, GRAMMAR, AND STYLE

Sentence Completers for Action Verbs: Direct and Indirect Objects. Students are asked to identify the direct and indirect object in sentences in the Language, Grammar, and Style activities on pages 752 and 1060.

Work fast.
I have been walking.

Direct Objects. A **direct object** receives the action in the sentence. The following sentences do have receivers of the action, or direct objects. In each case, once the verb is found, the direct object answers the question *what?* about the verb.

EXAMPLES
Birds ate grain. (Birds ate what? *grain*)
Work the problems fast. (Work what? *problems*)
I walked the dog. (Walked what? *dog*)

The last step was to get rid of any modifiers. That tells you what the direct object itself is. Also note: direct object is *never* in a prepositional phrase.

Indirect Objects. Sometimes the direct object is received by someone or something. This receiver is called the **indirect object**. A sentence without a direct object cannot have an indirect object.

EXAMPLE Mike gave me a red pencil.

What is the *action* (the verb)? gave
Who gave? (the subject) *Mike*
What did he give? (the direct object) *pencil*

To find the indirect object, check to see if the direct object had a receiver. Who got the direct object? In this sentence we ask, "Who got the pencil?" The answer is me.

Who received the pencil? (the indirect object) *me*.

3.23 Sentence Completers for Linking Verbs: Predicate Nouns, Pronouns, and Adjectives

Unlike action verbs, **linking verbs** do not describe an *action*. They simply join a subject to another word that describes or identifies it. Since no action is being performed, there are no objects or direct objects. Instead, the first noun, or naming word, is assumed to be the subject while the renaming or describing word is called its **complement.**

Because a linking verb has no object or direct object, the order of the sentence can sometimes be reversed without affecting the meaning. For example, *I am a student* and *A student am I* mean the same thing. *Am* is merely linking the two nouns, no matter what the order. On the other hand, *I made dinner* and *Dinner made me* mean very different things. Because *made* is an action verb, the sentence cannot be reversed. There are three types of sentence completers for linking verbs: predicate nouns, predicate pronouns, and predicate adjectives.

EXAMPLES
predicate noun: Tala is my best friend.
predicate pronoun: We are the ones!
predicate adjectives: Tierre felt ill.

3.24 Predicate Nouns and Pronouns as Sentence Completers

Sentences with predicate nouns and pronouns do not use action verbs: they use forms of the verb *to be*. (Forms of *to be* are listed in 3.9, "Grammar Reference Chart.") To find a **predicate noun** or **predicate pronoun**, ask the same questions asked to find a **direct object**.

EXAMPLE Mary will have been my friend for six years.

To find the predicate noun, ask, "Mary will have been what?" The answer is *friend.*

EXAMPLE The most dangerous criminal was he.

To find the predicate pronoun, ask, "The most dangerous criminal was who?" The answer is *he.*

Note: Direct and indirect objects include *me, her, him*, etc. Predicate pronouns include *I, she, he*, etc., the same forms as subjects.

3.25 Predicate Adjectives as Sentence Completers

A **predicate adjective** modifies, or describes, the subject of a sentence. Sentences with predicate adjectives may use a variety of linking verbs. Consult 3.9, the "Grammar Reference Chart," for a list of linking verbs. Most of these are used just with predicate adjectives, not with predicate nouns or pronouns.

EXAMPLE Della feels blue today.

To find the predicate adjective, ask, "Della feels what?" The answer is *blue. Blue* describes Della.

SUBJECTS AND VERBS: PROBLEM CONSTRUCTIONS

English speakers often rearrange or use different kinds of sentences. Some of these constructions can be challenging!

3.26 Working with Inverted Sentences

A sentence is **inverted** when all or part of the complete predicate comes before the subject. When you ask a question, you automatically invert your sentence. Usually, part of the verb is in front of the subject.

EXAMPLES
(declarative sentence): Sitka did study the math problem.
(interrogative sentence): Did Sitka study the math problem?

In both sentences, the verb is *did study*. Part of the verb comes before the subject.

Other sentences may be inverted so that a modifier comes before the subject.

EXAMPLE Sitka studied the math problem today.
Today Sitka studied the math problem.
Today modifies *studied* in both sentences.

Be sure to find all the words in the verb of an inverted sentence.

3.27 Working with *There* Sentences

The word *there* often appears as the first word or as one of the first few words in a sentence. *There* will never be a basic part of the sentence; it is a modifier. To make finding the subject and verb easier, cross out *there* before determining the basic parts of the sentence.

EXAMPLE
There will be two standardized tests given this week.
Remove *there*:
will be two standardized tests given this week
Rearrange words:
two standardized tests will be given this week

Now the subject and verb are easy to find. The subject is *tests*; the verb is *will be given*.

3.28 Working with Compound Subjects, Verbs, and Sentences

If a sentence has more than one subject, together they are called a **compound subject**.

EXAMPLE
Frank and Jesus work at a carwash.

If a sentence has more than one verb, the verbs together are called a **compound verb**.

EXAMPLE
Helen cooked dinner, washed dishes, and swept the floor.

Notice that each verb has its own direct object.

Sentences can have both a compound subject and a compound verb.

EXAMPLE
Mikka and Juan cut the grass and washed the car.
Subjects: Mikka, Juan; Verbs: cut, washed.

A **compound sentence** refers to two sentences that are either 1) connected by a semicolon *or* 2) connected with a coordinating conjunction and a comma. Each part of the compound sentence has its own subject and verb.

EXAMPLES
Sally wanted a car, but her family wouldn't buy one.
Sally wanted a car; her family wouldn't buy one.

In both sentences, the subjects are *Sally* and *family*; the verbs are *wanted* and *would buy*. (*Not* is not part of the verb; it only modifies the verb.)

For more information, see the Language Arts Survey 3.36, "Combining and Expanding Sentences."

3.29 Working with Negatives and Contractions

Negatives. Negatives such as *not* and *never* frequently affect verbs. They are adverbs, because they add to the meaning of the verb. The verb tells what an action is, and the negative says that the writer or speaker means the opposite of that.

EXAMPLES
I play basketball.
Negative: I do not play basketball.

Make sure to use only one negative in each sentence. Check your writing to be sure that you

Inverted Sentences. Students are asked to work with inverted sentences in the Language, Grammar, and Style activity on page 931.

Identifying Prepositional Phrases. Students are asked to work with prepositional phrases in the Language, Grammar, and Style activity on page 688.

have not used a negative word such *as not, nobody, none, nothing, hardly, barely, can't, doesn't, won't, isn't,* or *aren't* with another negative word.

DOUBLE NEGATIVE (NONSTANDARD)

I hardly never eat my lunch at school.
Didn't Joyce never go to Chicago?
It doesn't make no difference!
Why wasn't Jerry hurt no worse when the car was destroyed?

CORRECTED SENTENCES (STANDARD)

I hardly ever eat my lunch at school.
Didn't Joyce ever go to Chicago?
It doesn't make any difference!
Why wasn't Jerry hurt any worse when the car was destroyed?

Contractions. Contractions combine two words by shortening and joining them with an apostrophe.

EXAMPLES

isn't, aren't, don't, can't

When you are trying to determine subjects and verbs in a sentence, contractions need to be written out into the two words that they represent. After the contraction is written out, each word should be considered separately. Each of the contractions above contains a negative. Remember that a negative is never part of a verb but is an adverb.

CONTRACTION	WORDS CONTRACTED	PARTS OF SPEECH
isn't	is not	is (verb or helping verb), not (negative; adverb)
aren't	are not	are (verb), not (negative; adverb)
don't	do not	do (verb), not (negative; adverb)
can't	can not	can (helping verb), not (negative; adverb)

3.30 Identifying Prepositional Phrases

The simple subject and verb is *never* in a prepositional phrase. If you think a word might be a preposition, check the chart of common prepositions in the Grammar Reference Chart 3.11, "Prepositions." If the word is there, find its object.

The prepositional phrases have been underlined in the example below:

EXAMPLE

One of my brothers is planning a medical career after college.

Note: The simple subject, verb, and complements are NEVER in prepositional phrases, so before determining the subject and verb of a sentence, if you cross out the prepositional phrases, you will have fewer words to consider.

3.31 Using Indefinite Pronouns

You seldom have problems with personal pronouns in sentences because they are easy to recognize. When you encounter an indefinite pronoun (used to replace a person or a group of people not specifically identified), you might make errors in subject and verb agreement. Subjects and objects are particularly tricky when they are followed by a prepositional phrase, as shown below.

EXAMPLES

Some of the students wrote excellent short stories.
Ten from the senior class were chosen for a legislative workshop.
Mr. James gave several of my friends top grades on their papers.

You might want to cross out prepositional phrases in a sentence before you determine subjects and verbs.

3.32 Avoiding Problems Caused by Understood Subjects and Nouns of Direct Address

Understood subjects are sometimes used in sentences that make requests or give commands. The subject is *you*, but it is not written out, because both the speaker/writer and listener/reader understand who is meant.

EXAMPLES

Open your books. Give me your attention.
Run outside; the school is burning down!

In each of these the speaker does not have to say the *you* because it is understood.

If you are not sure that the subject is understood, try using *you* in front of the verb.

Nouns of direct address are never a part of the basic sentence. They name the person talked to, and they are always set off from the rest of the sentence using commas. They can appear at any place in a sentence.

EXAMPLES

Hank, when did you plan to finish your project?
Have you seen the new science lab, Carrie?
I need to know, class, if you had any problems with today's homework.

If you pay attention to the comma clues—that is, the way the noun of direct address is set off from the rest of the sentence—you will realize that these nouns are not actually a part of the basic sentence.

WRITER'S WORKSHOP: BUILDING EFFECTIVE SENTENCES

3.33 Correcting Sentence Fragments

A sentence contains a subject and a verb and should express a complete thought. A **sentence fragment** is a phrase or clause that does not express a complete thought but has been punctuated as though it did.

SENTENCE FRAGMENT

So he could explore the clear waters of the lake.

COMPLETE SENTENCE

Teddy bought a new mask and snorkel so he could explore the clear waters of the lake.

SENTENCE FRAGMENT

Looking for the lost little girl.

COMPLETE SENTENCE

The searchers combed the woods looking for the lost little girl.

3.34 Correcting Sentence Run-ons

A **sentence run-on** is made up of two or more sentences that have been run together as if they were one complete thought. You can fix a run-on by dividing it into two separate sentences. Mark the end of each idea with a period, question mark, or exclamation point. Capitalize the first word of each new sentence.

RUN-ON

Jason tried to jump across the swollen stream he slipped in the mud on the other side.

TWO SENTENCES

Jason tried to jump across the swollen stream. He slipped in the mud on the other side.

RUN-ON

Mr. Strauss refused to reconsider his decision, he had made up his mind and didn't want to be bothered with the facts.

TWO SENTENCES

Mr. Strauss refused to reconsider his decision. He had made up his mind and didn't want to be bothered with the facts.

You can also correct a run-on sentence with a semicolon.

RUN-ON

I went to bed early I got up late.

CORRECTED WITH SEMI-COLONS

I went to bed early; I got up late.

A **sentence string** is a sentence run-on formed of several sentences strung together with conjunctions. Edit sentence strings by breaking them into separate sentences and subordinate clauses.

STRINGY

When I decided to audition for the part, I had no idea how to do it so I asked my friend Eileen who has some acting talent what to do and she said to practice in front of a mirror, but I tried that and it didn't help, so I had Eileen come over instead and when I read my lines to her that really helped.

CORRECTING SENTENCE RUN-ONS. Students are asked to correct sentence run-ons in sentences in the Language, Grammar, and Style activities on page 329 and 542.

CORRECTING SENTENCE FRAGMENTS. Students are asked to correct sentence fragments in the Language, Grammar, and Style activities on pages 329 and 549.

CORRECTING WORDY SENTENCES. In the Language, Grammar, and Style activities on pages 26 and 242, students are asked to reduce wordiness in sentences.

REVISED

When I decided to audition for the part, I had no idea how to do it. I asked my friend Eileen, who has some acting talent, what to do. She said to practice in front of a mirror, but I tried that and it didn't help. I had Eileen come over instead. When I read my lines to her, that really helped.

3.35 Correcting Wordy Sentences

As you write, avoid **wordy sentences**. Use only the words necessary to make your meaning clear to a reader. Edit your sentences so that they are not wordy and complicated. Replace complicated or general words with simple and specific words.

WORDY

Make sure that you are very careful not to forget to lock the door to the house when you leave the house.

CLEAR AND DIRECT

Don't forget to lock the door as you leave.

3.36 Combining and Expanding Sentences

There are many ways to combine and expand sentences to achieve smooth writing and sentence variety.

COMBINING SENTENCES. If you use several short sentences in a paragraph, your writing might sound choppy, and your reader might have trouble understanding how ideas are connected. **Combining sentences** is a good way to bring two sentences together that deal with the same main idea. If you combine short sentences, your writing will sound smooth and clear, and your reader will see how ideas are connected to one another.

One way of combining sentences is to take a word or phrase from one sentence and insert it into another sentence. You might need to change the form of the word.

BORING, SHORT SENTENCES

The cowboys walked into the saloon. Their walk was more like a swagger. They were boisterous.

COMBINED SENTENCE

The boisterous cowboys swaggered into the saloon.

Another way of combining sentences is to merge two related sentences into one sentence that states both ideas. Your two sentences can be combined with a comma and a **conjunction** such as *and, or, for, nor, but, so,* or *yet*.

BORING, SHORT SENTENCES

The storm was fierce. The captain brought the ship to safety.

COMBINED SENTENCE

The storm was fierce, but the captain brought the ship to safety.

EXPANDING SENTENCES. You can expand sentences and achieve sentence variety by knowing how to use different types of clauses and sentences. These include independent clauses, compound sentences, complex sentences, and compound-complex sentences.

An **independent clause** expresses a complete thought and can stand by itself as a sentence.

INDEPENDENT CLAUSES

The geese flew away.
The geese flew away at the sound of the plane.

A **compound sentence** is formed by two or more independent clauses joined by a conjunction and a comma; or by a semicolon followed by a transition word such as *however* or *therefore* and a comma.

COMPOUND SENTENCES

The geese flew away at the sound of the plane, and all was quiet.
The geese flew away at the sound of the plane; however, the crows remained.

You can also expand a sentence that has only one independent clause by adding a subordinate clause. You will then have a **complex sentence**—one formed of an independent clause and at least one subordinate clause. In the following examples, the subordinate clauses are underlined.

COMPLEX SENTENCES

After the geese flew away, the crows remained.
The geese flew away, scared by the noise.

If you combine a compound sentence and a complex sentence, you will have a **compound-complex sentence**. This kind of sentence must have two or more independent clauses and at least one subordinate clause. In the following examples, the subordinate clauses are underlined.

COMPOUND-COMPLEX SENTENCES

Although they were accustomed to loud noises, the geese flew away at the sound of the plane; however, the crows remained.

The geese flew away at the sound of the plane; however, the crows remained, greedily eating the corn in the fields.

3.37 Making Passive Sentences Active

A verb is **active** when the subject of the verb performs the action. It is **passive** when the subject of the verb receives the action.

ACTIVE Caroline delivered a powerful speech.
PASSIVE A powerful speech was delivered by Caroline.

Poor writing uses too many passive verbs. Use active verbs unless you have a good reason for using the passive voice. In the examples that follow, note how the active verbs make the writing more natural and interesting.

WITH PASSIVE VERBS

The school was flooded with requests from students for a longer vacation. It was not decided by the school board until later to give them a hearing. The meeting was begun by the student council. The vote was unanimous to extend spring break an extra week. It was considered an unprecedented move favoring all students suffering spring fever.

WITH ACTIVE VERBS

Students flooded the school with requests for a longer vacation. The school board did not decide until later to give them a hearing. The student council began the meeting. Everyone voted to extend spring break an extra week. The unpredecented move favored all students suffering spring fever.

Note that the writer could still combine, expand, and add variety to these sentences. Making such sentences active instead of passive, however, is a good start toward livelier writing.

3.38 Achieving Parallelism

A sentence has **parallelism** when it uses the same grammatical forms to express ideas of equal, or parallel, importance. When you edit your sentences during revision, check to be sure that your parallelism is not faulty.

FAULTY

The teacher told me to think better and having more focus.

PARALLEL

The teacher told me to think better and to have more focus.

FAULTY

Being too late for the bus and to get something to eat, I decided to walk to the mall.

PARALLEL

Being too late for the bus and wanting to get something to eat, I decided to walk to the mall.

FAULTY

I really like playing chess, walking my dog, and vacations in Florida.

PARALLEL

I really like playing chess, walking my dog, and taking vacations in Florida.

3.39 Adding Colorful Language to Sentences

When you write, use words that tell your reader exactly what you mean. Precise and lively language makes your writing more interesting to your reader.

DULL

The people made noise.

COLORFUL

The mob made an uproar.

Specific verbs also help to create a clear picture in a reader's mind. Use verbs that tell the reader exactly what you mean.

DULL

He took the pitcher and drank the cool water.

COLORFUL

He grabbed the pitcher and gulped the cool water.

A modifier is a word that modifies—that is, changes or explains—the meaning of another word. Adjectives and adverbs are modifiers. Colorful modifiers can turn dull reading into dynamic reading.

DULL

The cold wind blew hard.

MAKING PASSIVE SENTENCES ACTIVE. In the Language, Grammar, and Style activity on page 341 students identify sentences in the active and passive voices and change passive sentences to active ones.

ADDING COLORFUL LANGUAGE TO SENTENCES. Students are asked to work with vivid words in sentences in the Language, Grammar, and Style activities on pages 587 and 1033.

ACHIEVING PARALLELISM. Students are asked to achieve parallelism in sentences in the Language, Grammar, and Style activities on pages 446 and 999.

GETTING SUBJECT AND VERB TO AGREE. In the Language, Grammar, and Style activity on page 583, students are asked to find subject/verb agreement in sentences.

COLORFUL
The frigid wind blew furiously.

EDITING FOR GRAMMAR AND USAGE ERRORS

3.40 Getting Subject and Verb to Agree

A word that describes or stands for *one* person, place, thing, or idea is **singular**. A word that describes or stands for *more than one* person, place, thing, or idea is **plural**.

SINGULAR NOUNS	prize, child, instrument
PLURAL NOUNS	prizes, children, instruments

In a sentence, a verb must be singular if its subject is singular and plural if its subject is plural. **A verb must agree in number with its subject.**

SINGULAR AGREEMENT	Charles needs forty more dollars.
PLURAL AGREEMENT	They need forty more dollars.
SINGULAR AGREEMENT	She exercises every day.
PLURAL AGREEMENT	The girls exercise every day.

The pronouns *I* and *you*, although singular, almost always take the same verb forms as for the plural pronouns *we* and *they*. The only exceptions are the forms *I am* and *I was*.

EXAMPLES
I believe the car industry will continue to rebound.
You sense my uneasiness.

AGREEMENT WITH COMPOUND SUBJECTS. A **compound subject** is formed of two or more nouns or pronouns that are joined by a conjunction and have the same verb. A compound subject joined by the conjunction *and* usually takes a plural verb.

EXAMPLE Salt and acid rain are hard on a car's body.

A compound subject in which the subjects are joined by the conjunction *and* takes a singular verb if the compound subject really names only one person or thing.

EXAMPLE His work and love is writing.

A compound subject formed of two singular subjects joined by the conjunctions *or* or *nor* takes a singular verb.

EXAMPLES
Neither Streep nor Foster is usually guilty of underpreparing.
Either poetry or drama is appropriate for public performance.

A compound subject formed of a singular subject and a plural subject joined by the conjunctions *or* or *nor* takes a verb that agrees in number with the subject nearer the verb.

EXAMPLES
Either Kim or the backup vocalists are responsible for the recording.
Either the backup vocalists or Kim is responsible for the recording.

AGREEMENT WITH INDEFINITE PRONOUNS. These indefinite pronouns are singular and take a singular verb: *anybody, anyone, anything, each, either, everybody, everyone, everything, neither, nobody, no one, nothing, one, somebody, someone,* and *something.*

EXAMPLES
Nobody wants to take the exam on Friday.
Everybody enjoys some kind of music.

These indefinite pronouns are plural and take a plural verb: *both, few, many,* and *several.*

EXAMPLES
Both of these choices are unacceptable.
Several new students are on the honor roll.

The following indefinite pronouns can be singular or plural: *all, any, most, none,* and *some.*

EXAMPLES
All of the cookies were saved. (*All* is plural.)
All of the pie was eaten. (*All* is singular.)

AGREEMENT IN INVERTED SENTENCES. When you invert sentences for emphasis, make sure you maintain agreement in number between subject and verb.

EXAMPLES
For those ghastly performances he takes full credit.
The last straw she took.

AGREEMENT WITH *DOESN'T* AND *DON'T*. The contraction *doesn't* (from *does not*) is third-person singular and should be used only with a third-person singular subject (*he, she,* or *it,* for example). The contraction *don't* (from *do not*) should be used with all other subjects.

EXAMPLES
She doesn't want material things.
They don't understand the procedure.
I don't find the subject boring.

OTHER PROBLEMS IN SUBJECT/VERB AGREEMENT. When a sentence begins with *here, there, when,* or *where,* often the subject follows the verb. In editing your writing, use extra care to check that the subject and verb of such sentences agree in number. Remember that the contractions *here's, there's, when's,* and *where's* contain a singular verb (is) and should only be used with a singular subject.

EXAMPLES
Here's the team.
There is one more exam being given.
When's the test?
When are the band members joining us?
Where's the rub?

Also check to be sure a verb in a sentence with a predicate nominative agrees in number with the subject and not with the predicate nominative.

EXAMPLES
Essays are the hardest part of school.
The hardest part of school is essays.

A collective noun takes a singular verb when the noun refers to the group as a unit, and it takes a plural verb when it refers to the members of the group as individuals.

AS SINGULAR The team runs laps every day.
AS PLURAL The team joke among themselves behind the coach's back.

While editing your work, check for nouns that are plural in form but singular in meaning. They should take singular verbs.

EXAMPLES cryogenics, slacks, measles

The title of a creative work such as a book or song takes a singular verb, as does a group of words used as a unit.

EXAMPLES
The book *Aphorisms* has been on the bestseller list for two weeks.
Sidney and Austen is the smallest firm in Chicago.

An expression stating an amount is singular and takes a singular verb when the amount is considered as one unit. It is plural and takes a plural verb when the amount is considered as something with many parts.

AS SINGULAR
Three eggs is a high-cholesterol breakfast.

AS PLURAL
Three eggs were found splattered across the windshield.

A fraction or a percentage is singular when it refers to a singular word and plural when it refers to a plural word.

AS SINGULAR
One-fourth of the text was footnotes.

AS PLURAL
One-fourth of all the pages were footnotes.

AS SINGULAR
Over 60 percent of the nation is hopeful about the economy.

AS PLURAL
Over 60 percent of all citizens are hopeful about the economy.

Expressions of measurement, such as area, length, volume, and weight, are usually singular.

EXAMPLE
Two quarts is a lot of milk to drink in one sitting.

3.41 Using Irregular Verbs

To write about something that happened in the past, use past tense verbs (tense means *time* in grammar). For regular verbs, add *ed* or *–d* to the present form of the verb. For more information, see the Language Arts Survey 3.62, "Properties of Verbs: Tense."

EXAMPLES
The bandit guarded the hideout.
guard (base form) + ed

Carmen gazed at the distant mountains.
gaze (base form) + d

Avoiding Split Infinitives. In the Language, Grammar, and Style activities on pages 333, 741, and 965, students are asked to avoid split infinitives when writing sentences.

Irregular verbs often have different past tense forms and are formed using a different spelling. The following chart lists some of the most common irregular verbs.

IRREGULAR VERBS			
begin	/ began	grow	/ grew
bring	/ brought	have	/ had
burst	/ burst	hurt	/ hurt
choose	/ chose	know	/ knew
come	/ came	lay	/ laid
cut	/ cut	make	/ made
do	/ did	ride	/ rode
draw	/ drew	run	/ ran
drink	/ drank	see	/ saw
eat	/ ate	sing	/ sang
fall	/ fell	take	/ took
feel	/ felt	teach	/ taught
fly	/ flew	wear	/ wore
give	/ gave	write	/ wrote
go	/ went		

When using irregular verbs in the perfect tense (with *has* or *have*), make sure you do not use the past form instead of the past participle.

NONSTANDARD
I have knew him since I was in middle school.

STANDARD
I have known him since I was in middle school.

Another error to avoid is using the past participle form without a helping verb, or mistaking the past participle for the past.

NONSTANDARD I flown this plane dozens of times.
STANDARD I have flown this plane dozens of times.

NONSTANDARD I done all I could do to convince him.
STANDARD I did all I could do to convince him.

Finally, do not add *-d* or *-ed* to the past form of an irregular verb.

NONSTANDARD I ated an apple.
STANDARD I ate an apple.

3.42 Avoiding Split Infinitives

In the English language, the infinitive is often in the form of two words, *to* and the base word.

EXAMPLES to catch, to succeed, to entertain

Under traditional rules of grammar, the infinitive should not be "split." In other words, adverbs or other sentence components should not come between *to* and the base word.

NONSTANDARD Irving begged me to immediately show him the photos.
STANDARD Irving begged me to show him the photos immediately.

3.43 Using *I* and *Me*

Before you use the words *I* and *me* in a sentence, remember that *I* is always the subject of a verb and *me* is always the object of a verb or of a preposition.

EXAMPLES
I went sailing in Florida.
Amber and I went sailing in Florida.

I is the subject in both of these sentences.

Lester helped me set up for the party.
Lester helped Brianna and me set up for the party.

In both sentences, *me* is the object of the verb *helped.*

If you are not sure which pronoun to use with a compound subject, drop the other part of the subject and use your pronoun separately with the verb.

EXAMPLE
Sam and (I, me) went sledding at the golf course.

After dropping out Sam:
I went sledding at the golf course. OR Me went sledding at the golf course.

Correct: Sam and I went sledding at the golf course.

EXAMPLE
Please apologize for Carol and (I, me).

After dropping out Carol:
Please apologize for me. OR Please apologize for I.

Correct: Please apologize for Carol and me.

3.44 Using *Who* and *Whom*

The pronoun *who* has two different forms. *Who* is used as a subject of a sentence. *Whom* is used as the direct object of a verb or of a preposition.

SUBJECT

Who knows the answer?

Where is the boy who looks after the sheep?

DIRECT OBJECT

Whom did the police arrest?

The plumber whom we called charged a huge fee.

OBJECT OF PREPOSITION

By whom is this painting?

From whom is that gift?

3.45 Getting Pronouns and Antecedents to Agree

Make sure pronouns in your writing agree with their antecedents (the words they refer back to) in number and gender.

Number refers to singular and plural. If the antecedent is singular, the pronoun must also be singular; if the antecedent is plural, the pronoun must also be plural.

INCORRECT NUMBER

One of the boys need tennis shoes.

CORRECT NUMBER

One of the boys needs tennis shoes.

Gender is the form a word takes to show whether it is masculine, feminine, or neutral (neither masculine nor feminine). The pronoun must match its antecedent in terms of gender.

3.46 Avoiding Dangling and Misplaced Modifiers

A **dangling modifier** seems to modify a word it is not intended to modify. If this error occurs when the modifier is too far away from the word it is supposed to modify, it is called a **misplaced modifier**. Edit a dangling or misplaced modifier by rewording the sentence or moving the modifier closer to the phrase it modifies.

DANGLING

Valerie drove to the airport while taking a nap.

WORDS ADDED

Valerie drove to the airport while I was taking a nap.

MISPLACED

Alex walked his dog wearing shorts.

REWORDED

Alex, wearing shorts, walked his dog.

3.47 Recognizing Other Problems with Modifiers

Them is a personal pronoun. *Those* is a demonstrative pronoun, which means it points out a particular person, place, or thing.

NONSTANDARD Them cars have four-wheel drive.

STANDARD Those cars have four-wheel drive.

The words *bad* and *badly* often confuse writers. Use *bad* as an adjective, and *badly* as an adverb. The adjective *bad* should follow a linking verb such as *feel, see, smell, sound,* or *taste.*

NONSTANDARD

Reports of the forest fire sounded badly.

STANDARD

Reports of the forest fire sounded bad.

NONSTANDARD

Ricky behaved bad for the babysitter.

STANDARD

Ricky behaved badly for the babysitter.

The words *good* and *well* also tend to confuse writers. *Good* is an adjective used to modify a person, place, thing, or idea, not an action verb. *Well* is an adverb meaning "successfully" or "skillfully" and an adjective meaning "healthy" or "of a satisfactory condition."

NONSTANDARD

Allen swims good.

STANDARD

Allen swims well.

Allen is a good swimmer.

Allen is well now that he is over his cold.

Each modifier has a **positive, comparative,** and **superlative** form of comparison. Most one-syllable modifiers and some two-syllable modifiers form comparative and superlative degrees by adding *-er* and *-est.* Other two-syllable modifiers, and all modifiers of more than two syllables, use *more* and *most* to form these degrees.

	POSITIVE	COMPARATIVE	SUPERLATIVE
ADJECTIVES	hungry	hungrier	hungriest
	daring	more daring	most daring
ADVERBS	late	later	latest
	fully	more fully	most fully

LANGUAGE, GRAMMAR, AND STYLE

GETTING PRONOUNS AND ANTECEDENTS TO AGREE. In the Language, Grammar, and Style activity on page 325, students are asked to get pronouns and antecedents to agree in sentences.

AVOIDING DANGLING AND MISPLACED MODIFIERS. Students are asked to correct dangling and misplaced modifiers in sentences in the Language, Grammar, and Style activity on page 1088.

To show a decrease in the quality of any modifier, form the comparative and superlative degrees by using *less* and *least.*

EXAMPLES dense, less dense, least dense
skeptically, less skeptically, least skeptically

Some modifiers form comparative and superlative degrees irregularly. Check the dictionary if you are unsure about the comparison of a modifier.

EXAMPLES good, better, best
well, better, best
bad, worse, worst

Use the comparative degree when comparing two things. Use the superlative degree when comparing more than two things.

COMPARATIVE
Santha was the **more easily** intimidated of the two sisters.

SUPERLATIVE
The skin is the **largest** organ of the human body.

3.48 Correcting Common Usage Problems

Watch for these words and learn their correct usage as you edit your own writing.

accept, except. To *accept* is to "welcome something" or to "receive something willingly." To *except* is to "exclude or leave something out." *Except* is also used as a preposition meaning "but."

The Tigers accept our challenge to a rematch.
She excepted Roland from the guest list.
I will eat any vegetable except collard greens.

advice, advise. *Advice* is a noun meaning "guidance or recommendation regarding a decision." To *advise* is to "recommend or inform."

I took your advice about the movie.
I would advise you to avoid that movie.

affect, effect. *Affect* is a verb meaning "have an effect on." *Effect* is a noun meaning "the result of an action."

The short story affected me strangely.
The short story had a strange effect on me.

altogether, all together. *Altogether* is an adverb meaning "thoroughly." Something *done all together* is done as a group or mass.

She was altogether frustrated waiting all day.
We were all together awaiting news of the surgery.

among, between. Use the word *between* when talking about two people or things at a time. Use the word *among* when talking about a group of three or more.

Oscar and Lucas had five dollars between them.
There was disagreement among the team members.

can, may. Use the word *can* to mean "able to do something." Use the word *may* to ask or give permission.

Can you swim across Gull Pond?
May I go swimming? Yes, you may go.

fewer, less. *Fewer* refers to the number of units of something. *Less* refers to bulk quantity.

I have fewer than eight items.
I have less energy when it is very humid.

in, into. The preposition *in* indicates location. The preposition *into* indicates direction from the outside to the inside.

The meeting is being held in the gym.
The students are going into the gym now.

its, it's The word *its* is a possessive pronoun. The word *it's* is a contraction of *it is.*

The turtle dug its nest.
The sun will be up by the time it's over.

lay, lie. *Lay* means to "put" or to "place" and always takes a direct object. *Lie* means to "rest" or to "be in a lying position." *Lie* never takes a direct object. (Note that the past tense of *lie* is *lay.*)

Lay the map on the table.
Gretchen laid the map on the table.
Lie down and keep quiet.
Oliver lay down and kept quiet.

like, as. *Like* is a preposition meaning "similar to." *Like* usually introduces a phrase. *As* should be used as a conjunction. *As* usually introduces a clause that has a subject and a verb.

NONSTANDARD
The sun came out earlier, just like I had hoped.

STANDARD
The sun came out earlier, just as I had hoped.

NONSTANDARD

Rodney has been acting as a spoiled brat.

STANDARD

Rodney has been acting like a spoiled brat.

their, they're, there. These three *homonyms* (words that sound alike but that have different spellings and meanings) sometimes confuse writers. The word *their* is a possessive pronoun. The word *they're* is the contracted form of *they are*. The word *there* refers to a place.

Marsupials carry their young in a pouch.
They're complaining about the noise.
The lamp should go over there.

to, too, two. *To* is a preposition that can mean "in the direction of." *Too* is an adverb that means both "extremely, overly" and "also." *Two* is the spelling for the number 2.

Take the basket to Granny's house.
Ivan has too many fish in his tank.
Sharon is invited, too.
I have two wishes left.

your, you're. *Your* is a possessive pronoun. *You're* is the contracted form of *you are*.

Your mittens are in the dryer.
You're the winner!

PARTS OF SPEECH SUMMARY

As you have seen, the meanings of words depend on their positions in a sentence. As their positions change, both meaning and function change. You have looked at function to determine parts of the sentence.

You can now go one step further. By looking at the relationship of a word to the rest of the words in a sentence, you can determine the parts of speech for individual words. Once again, you will be examining what a word does; then you will label its part of speech.

Remember two important facts: 1) words have four primary functions—they **name**, **express**, **modify**, and **link**. They can also **interrupt**. 2) Groups of words can function as one individual part of speech.

3.49 Namers—Nouns and Pronouns

Namers are **nouns** and **pronouns**, parts of speech that name people, places, ideas, and things or refer to them; you can tell what they are by what they do. Nouns and pronouns are subjects and objects: direct objects, indirect objects, objects of prepositions, and objects of infinitives. Namers:

NAME PEOPLE	Dylan, principal, father, choreographer
NAME PLACES	home, Central Park, Joe's Tacos
NAME IDEAS	love, multiplication, tonality, smell
NAME THINGS	basketball, dance, orbit, trading card

3.50 Specific Kinds of Nouns

There are many kinds of nouns. They include common and proper nouns, concrete and abstract nouns, and collective nouns.

3.51 COMMON NOUNS AND PROPER NOUNS. **Common nouns** are the names given to general objects. **Proper nouns** are names of specific people or things. They are always capitalized.

COMMON NOUNS

girl, monument, government agency

PROPER NOUNS

Michelle, Washington Monument, The United States Supreme Court

Some proper nouns may have more than one word. *Michelle Adams, Central High School,* and the *United States Department of the Interior* are all names of one person or one (place or organization.) These multi-word names are still considered to be one noun because they name only one person or thing.

3.52 CONCRETE NOUNS AND ABSTRACT NOUNS. A **concrete noun** names anything you can physically taste, touch, smell, see or hear. An **abstract noun** names something that cannot be physically sensed.

CONCRETE NOUNS	automobile, textbook, lunchbox
ABSTRACT NOUNS	sadness, suffering, mood

3.53 COLLECTIVE NOUNS. **Collective nouns** name groups—family, committee, class. Collectives are interesting nouns because, in their singular forms, they can be either singular or plural, depending upon how the group acts. When the group acts together as one unit to do something, the group is considered singular.

COMMON NOUNS AND PROPER NOUNS. Students are asked to identify common and proper nouns in sentences in the Language, Grammar, and Style activity on page 537.

COLLECTIVE NOUNS. Students are asked to identify collective nouns in sentences in the Language, Grammar, and Style activity on page 142.

EXAMPLE The committee votes on its agenda.

Because the committee acted as one unit (by everyone doing the same one thing at the same time), the noun is singular and takes a singular verb form. The possessive pronoun *its* also reflects that the noun is collective.

When the group acts as individuals instead of as one unit, the group is considered plural.

EXAMPLE The committee were giving their reports.

Because individual members gave their reports at different times and functioned as individuals, the group is considered plural. Note how the verb *were giving* and the possessive pronoun *their* reflect this.

3.54 Types of Pronouns

Pronouns replace names (nouns) with reference words. Because we use these references in so many situations, there are four different kinds of pronouns and three hybrids. The four kinds of pronouns are **personal pronouns, demonstrative pronouns, indefinite pronouns, interrogative pronouns,** and **reflexive pronouns**.

The three kinds of hybrids are **possessive pronouns**, **relative pronouns**, and **intensifying pronouns**. **Possessive pronouns** are hybrids because they take pronoun forms but act as modifiers; **relative pronouns** are hybrids because they are pronoun forms that act as linkers, and **intensifying pronouns** are hybrids because they use the same forms as reflexive pronouns but act as interrupters. The three hybrids are discussed in the hybrids section (see Language Arts Survey 3.78, "Hybrids").

3.55 PERSONAL PRONOUNS. A personal pronoun is a substitute for the name of a person or thing. The personal pronouns are *I, me, we, us, he, she, it, him, her, you, they,* and *them*. Personal pronouns refer to three groups of speakers: first, second, and third person.

FIRST PERSON: the speaker or speakers talks about themselves: *I, me, we, us*

SECOND PERSON: the speaker talks about the person talked to: *you*

THIRD PERSON: the speaker talks about someone or something else: *he, she, it, they*

All personal pronouns require clear **antecedents**, or nouns that come before the pronoun. That means that the person or thing that the pronoun refers to must be obvious.

EXAMPLE Have you seen Mary? Yes, I saw her yesterday. (Mary is the antecedent of her.)

3.56 DEMONSTRATIVE AND INDEFINITE PRONOUNS. A **demonstrative pronoun** is a pronoun used to point out a particular person, place, or thing. The demonstrative pronouns are *this, that, these,* and *those*.

EXAMPLE Do you hear? That is the silly jingle stuck in my head. These are the times that try peoples souls.

Indefinite pronouns are pronouns used when we may not be sure whom we are talking about. They also include numbers. Frequently they are used when the reference word is in a prepositional phrase. Indefinite pronouns include *somebody, anybody, few, many, some, nobody, each, either, one, other, none, both, no one, someone, something,* and *nothing*.

EXAMPLES

A few in our English class are reviewing a new textbook.

We asked for some of the details about the news story.

Nobody knows where the homecoming decorations were stored.

Three of the swimmers qualified for the state meet.

3.57 INTERROGATIVE PRONOUNS. Interrogative pronouns are the question-askers of the pronoun family. *Who, whom, whose, which,* and *what* are the interrogative pronouns.

EXAMPLES

Which of these buses do I take to reach my school?

Whom do I ask for directions?

What do I do now?

Be careful when identifying interrogative pronouns. The same words are used as relative pronouns (discussed in 3.79), but relative pronouns do not ask a question.

PERSONAL PRONOUNS. In the Language, Grammar, and Style activity on page 291, students are asked to work with personal pronouns.

3.58 Reflexive Pronouns. Reflexive pronouns refer back to a noun previously used and can be recognized because *-self* and *-selves* have been added to other pronoun forms. Some reflexive pronouns include *myself, herself, yourself, themselves,* and *ourselves.*

EXAMPLES

I talk to myself.

Mike and James helped themselves to more food.

Reflexive pronouns are often parts of the basic sentence or objects of prepositions. (Note that **intensifying pronouns**, discussed in 3.78, "Hybrids," use the same forms, but they are interrupters and are neither a part of a basic sentence nor an object of a preposition.)

3.59 Expressers—Verbs

Verbs are the **expressers** of the English language, and they carry more information than any other single part of speech because they have three major properties: *tense, mood,* and *voice.* They reveal the time something happened or will happen, whether the action is finished or continuing, whether the subject is the actor or receiver of the action, and the manner in which the action occurred. English verbs can be from one to four words long.

EXAMPLES runs
has run
has been running
may have been running

Note: The same verb may fit into several of the classes below, depending on its uses in different sentences.

3.60 Action Verbs and State of Being Verbs. The verb of any sentence is either an **action verb** or a **state of being verb**, depending on the message the verb expresses in the sentence. **Action verbs** are all of the words that refer to actions and to things you can do.

EXAMPLES have, get, drive, run, get, sleep

State of being verbs indicate that something exists. These are all the forms of the verb *to be* that are listed on your Grammar Reference Chart in the Language Arts Survey 3.9, "The Verb *To Be.*"

3.61 Transitive and Intransitive Verbs. Transitive verbs are action verbs that have completers. If a verb has a direct object, it is a transitive verb.

EXAMPLE Jamie writes short stories.

(*Short stories* is a direct object, so the verb *writes* is transitive.)

Intransitive verbs are action verbs that do not take objects.

EXAMPLE The sun shines every day in Mexico.

The action *shines* is complete in itself; no extra material is necessary. This makes *shines* an intransitive verb.

3.62 Properties of Verbs: Tense

Verbs carry a concept of time, called **tense**. The simple tenses express simple past, present, and future. The perfect tenses give information about actions that take place over time.

Simple Tenses. Present tense shows that something is happening now. **Past tense** verbs talk about something that happened before now, and **future tense** verbs talk about something that will happen in the future:

SIMPLE TENSES FOR THE VERB *EAT*

PRESENT TENSE	
SINGULAR	PLURAL
Today I eat chocolate ice cream.	Today we do eat chocolate ice cream.
Today I do eat chocolate ice cream.	Today we are eating chocolate ice cream.
Today I am eating chocolate ice cream.	Today you eat chocolate ice cream.
Today you eat chocolate ice cream.	Today you do eat chocolate ice cream.
Today you do eat chocolate ice cream.	Today you are eating chocolate ice cream.
Today you are eating chocolate ice cream.	Today they eat chocolate ice cream.
Today he/she/it eats chocolate ice cream.	Today they do eat chocolate ice cream.

CONTINUED

Action Verbs and State of Being Verbs. On page 505 in the Language, Grammar, and Style activity students are asked to identify action and state of being verbs in each sentence.

PAST TENSE	
SINGULAR	PLURAL
Today he/she/it does eat chocolate ice cream.	Today we eat chocolate ice cream.
Today he/she/it is eating chocolate ice cream.	Today they are eating chocolate ice cream.
Yesterday I ate strawberry ice cream.	Yesterday we ate strawberry ice cream.
Yesterday I did eat strawberry ice cream.	Yesterday we did eat strawberry ice cream.
Yesterday I was eating strawberry ice cream.	Yesterday we were eating strawberry ice cream.
Yesterday you ate strawberry ice cream.	Yesterday you ate strawberry ice cream.
Yesterday you did eat strawberry ice cream.	Yesterday you did eat strawberry ice cream.
Yesterday you were eating strawberry ice cream.	Yesterday you were eating strawberry ice cream.
Yesterday he/she/it ate strawberry ice cream.	Yesterday they ate strawberry ice cream.
Yesterday he/she/it did eat strawberry ice cream.	Yesterday they did eat strawberry ice cream.
Yesterday he/she/it was eating strawberry ice cream.	Yesterday they were eating strawberry ice cream.

FUTURE TENSE	
SINGULAR	
Tomorrow I will eat vanilla ice cream.	Tomorrow he/she/it will be eating vanilla ice cream.
Tomorrow I will be eating vanilla ice cream.	Tomorrow he/she/it will be eating vanilla ice cream.
	PLURAL
Tomorrow you will eat vanilla ice cream.	Tomorrow we will eat vanilla ice cream.
Tomorrow you will be eating vanilla ice cream.	Tomorrow we will be eating vanilla ice cream.
Tomorrow you will eat vanilla ice cream.	Tomorrow they will eat vanilla ice cream.
Tomorrow you will be eating vanilla ice cream.	Tomorrow they will be eating vanilla ice cream.

CONTINUED

Perfect Tenses. The **perfect tenses** express past, present and future, but they add information about actions that continued over a period of time and were completed in the past or will be completed in the present or future. All perfect tenses use some form of the helping verb *to have*.

PERFECT TENSES FOR THE VERB *WEAR*

PRESENT PERFECT TENSE	
SINGULAR	PLURAL
Today I have worn a sweater. Today I have been wearing a sweater.	Today we have worn sweaters. Today we have been wearing sweaters.
Today you have worn a sweater. Today you have been wearing a sweater.	Today you have worn sweaters. Today you have been wearing sweaters.
Today he/she/it has worn a sweater. Today he/she/it has been wearing a sweater.	Today they have worn sweaters. Today they have been wearing sweaters.

PAST PERFECT TENSE	
SINGULAR	PLURAL
Yesterday I had worn jeans. Yesterday I had been wearing jeans.	Yesterday we had worn jeans. Yesterday we had been wearing jeans.
Yesterday you had worn jeans. Yesterday you had been wearing jeans.	Yesterday you had worn jeans. Yesterday you had been wearing jeans.
Yesterday he/she/it had worn jeans. Yesterday he/she/it had been wearing jeans.	Yesterday they had worn jeans. Yesterday they had been wearing jeans.

CONTINUED

FUTURE PERFECT TENSE	
SINGULAR	PLURAL
Tomorrow I will have worn a sweatshirt. I will have been wearing a sweatshirt.	Tomorrow we will have worn sweat shirts. We will have been wearing sweatshirts.
Tomorrow you will have worn a sweatshirt. You will have been wearing a sweatshirt.	Tomorrow you will have worn a sweatshirt. You will have been wearing sweatshirts.
Tomorrow he/she/it will have worn a sweatshirt. He/she/it will have been wearing a sweatshirt.	Tomorrow they will have worn a sweatshirt. They will have been wearing sweatshirts.

3.63 Properties of Verbs: Voice

The **voice** of a verb refers to the relationship between the subject and the action. A verb is in the **active voice** if the subject did the acting. It is in the **passive voice** if someone or something else did the acting and the subject is the receiver of the action.

ACTIVE Mary gave her sister Ronda a new skirt.
PASSIVE Ronda was given a new skirt for her birthday.

If the sentence is in the active voice, the subject of the sentence, Mary, did the acting—she gave a skirt to Rhonda. The first sentence is in the active voice. In the second sentence, Ronda did nothing at all. Someone else, not named, did the acting. The second sentence is in the passive voice.

Writing in the active voice strengthens writing; writing in the passive voice usually weakens it. The passive voice can be very effective in many cases, but it should be used seldomly and carefully. For more information, see the Language Arts Survey 3.37, "Making Passive Sentences Active."

3.64 Properties of Verbs: Mood

The **mood** of a verb is the manner in which the verb relates the action. English uses three moods: the **indicative, the declarative,** and the **subjunctive.**

The **indicative mood** (notice how close this word is to "indicate") is used most frequently. This is the mood used to make a statement or ask a question. Most declarative and interrogative sentences fall into this mood.

INDICATIVE
Gordon and Caley are my two brothers.
Don't you have two brothers, also?

Imperative sentences are in the **imperative mood**. These make requests or give commands.

IMPERATIVE
Please, hand me the salt.
Run before the flood gets you!

The **subjunctive mood** has few uses in English, and is used much less frequently than it is used in other languages. It is used to express a wish, a possible condition, or a condition contrary to a fact.

SUBJUNCTIVE
If I were you, I would dress more warmly in this weather.
If I had a million dollars, I would buy an airplane and fly around the world.
It is necessary that you be on time.
If they were here, they would win the prize.

Notice the verb form in the first sentence. The only verb that has a unique form in the subjunctive is the verb *to be. Were* is used with all pronouns, not just the singular.

3.65 Modifiers—Adverbs and Adjectives

Adjectives and **adverbs**, two kinds of **modifiers,** add meaning to nouns, adjectives, verbs and adverbs. To determine whether the word is an adjective or adverb, follow the following procedure:

1. Look at the word that is modified.
2. Ask yourself, "Is this modified word a noun or a pronoun?"

If the answer is *yes*, the modifier is an adjective. **Adjectives** modify only nouns and pronouns. If the answer is *no*, the modifier is an **adverb**. **Adverbs** modify verbs, adjectives and other adverbs.

3.66 Adjectives. Adjectives modify nouns or pronouns by making them more specific.

GENERAL REFERENCE puppy
A LITTLE MORE SPECIFIC the puppy

LANGUAGE, GRAMMAR, AND STYLE

Properties of Verbs: Mood. In the Language, Grammar, and Style activity on page 975, students are asked to identify subjunctive mood.

MORE SPECIFIC YET	the little puppy
EVEN MORE SPECIFIC	the little, black-spotted puppy
WITH A PREPOSITIONAL PHRASE	the little, black-spotted puppy with the shaggy coat

As each step adds more modifiers (more information), it becomes more possible for the listener or reader to visualize the actual dog.

3.67 Adverbs. Adverbs are the generalists of the modifier family. They modify anything that is not a namer (noun or pronoun)—verbs, adjectives, and other adverbs. Many times they will specify *where* or *when*; nouns and pronouns specify *who* or *what*.

ADVERBS MODIFY VERBS

Katie came home quickly.

Quickly tells how Katie came home.

ADVERBS MODIFY ADJECTIVES

She wore a really new dress.

New modifies *dress*; *really* modifies the modifier, *new*. Since *new* is an **adjective**, not a **noun** or **pronoun**, *really* has to be an **adverb**.

ADVERBS MODIFY OTHER ADVERBS

Katie scurried home really fast.

Fast modifies the verb *scurried*; *really* modifies *fast*. In this sentence, one adverb modifies another.

3.68 Linkers / Joiners

Conjunctions and **prepositions** are the joiners of the English language. These words join everything from individual words to complete sentences to create compound sentences. Because there are many kinds of links that need to be made, there are many kinds of linkers: prepositions, coordinating conjunctions, correlative conjunctions, and subordinating conjunctions.

3.69 Prepositions. Prepositions are easy to identify because they have objects. If the word does not have an object, then it is another part of speech. See the Language Arts Survey 3.11 for a list of prepositions. If you find one of these words in a sentence, find its object. If it has an object, then the preposition and its object(s)—it may have more than one—form a prepositional phrase.

EXAMPLE I went [to the store] [for a loaf] [of sandwich bread].

In this sentence, three words are on the preposition list: *to*, *for*, and *of*. Does *to* have an object? Ask, "*to* what?" The answer is *the store*. *To* has an object, so it is a preposition. *To the store* is a prepositional phrase. After you apply the same test to *for* and *of*, you will find that they are both prepositions and that the sample sentence has three prepositional phrases. These are *to the store*, *for a loaf*, and *of sandwich bread*.

3.70 Coordinating Conjunctions. Coordinating conjunctions join words and groups of words of equal importance. The most common coordinating conjunctions are *and*, *or*, *nor*, *for*, *but*, *yet*, and *so*. The word is not important; what is important is that both words or word groups are equally important.

EXAMPLE

Her morning schedule included math and history and music and home room.

Note that joining a series of words using coordinating conjunctions between them is perfectly acceptable grammar. Most writers use commas, however, and save multiple conjunctions for sentences with special emphasis. (Note: All but the last and could be replaced by commas.)

When a coordinating conjunction plus a comma joins two or more complete thoughts that could be separate sentences, the resulting structure is called a **compound sentence**.

COMPOUND SENTENCE

I wanted to go to a movie, but nothing sounded very good.

Here a comma plus *but* join two short, complete, independent thoughts. Each of the two parts could be a sentence of its own. Since their ideas are closely related, they can be joined using proper punctuation.

3.71 Correlative Conjunctions. Correlative conjunctions travel in pairs that belong together. Some of these pairs are *both...and*, *neither...nor*, *either...or*, and *not only...but also*.

EXAMPLES

Both art and graphic design are electives in our school.

Neither Latin nor Greek languages are studied by

most high school students.
She wanted to study <u>either</u> architecture <u>or</u> industrial design.
He spoke <u>not only</u> German, <u>but also</u> spoke French and Spanish.

3.72 Subordinating Conjunctions. Subordinating conjunctions join two phrases or clauses that are not of equal importance. Subordinating conjunctions are used to establish that one idea in a sentence is more important than the other. Subordinating conjunctions include *after, before, if, than, since, unless, when,* and *while*; there are many more. All of the following examples contain **subordinating conjunctions**.

SUBORDINATING CONJUNCTIONS

We will go on a picnic on Saturday <u>unless</u> it rains.
<u>Whenever</u> the pollen count is high, I start to sneeze and get itchy eyes.
I want to visit my grandmother in Detroit <u>if</u> I can save enough money.
<u>When</u> the deadline arrives, students need to get their projects handed in.

Even though both clauses have subjects and verbs, the parts of the sentence of the most important clause (called the **main clause**) will be the subject and verb of the sentence. The parts of the sentence found in the less important clause (called the **subordinate clause**) can be ignored. These are NOT the main subject and verb of the sentence; they are only the subject and verb of a **dependent clause**.

3.73 Interrupters

Sometimes you will want to interrupt the flow of your sentences and thoughts by adding a word or phrase for emphasis. Most **interrupters** are set off from the rest of the sentences by commas because they are not basic building blocks of meaning. **Interrupters** include **interjections, parenthetical expressions, nouns of direct address,** and **appositives**. Another interrupter, **intensifying pronouns**, is discussed in the Language Arts Survey 3.78, "Hybrids."

Interrupters (with the exception of one-word appositives) are set off from other parts of the sentence using commas. It is important to note that no interrupter is ever a basic part of a sentence.

3.74 Interjections. Interjections are parts of speech that express strong feeling or enhance meaning.

EXAMPLES

<u>Yes</u>, I finished my homework.
<u>Good grief</u>, you did what again?
<u>Wow</u>, Sam got a new car for his birthday.

Note that omitting the interjection does not affect the basic meaning of the sentence. Each interjection is set off from the rest of the sentence by commas.

3.75 Parenthetical Expressions. Parenthetical expressions are those comments (set off by commas) that explain, comment, or qualify the ideas contained in the sentence. Common parenthetical expressions include *by the way, however, on the other hand, incidentally*.

EXAMPLES

I went right home after school; <u>however</u>, my sister went shopping for school supplies.
Mary misplaced her coat. <u>By the way</u>, have you seen a red raincoat in your closet?

3.76 Nouns of Direct Address. A **noun of direct address** says the name of the person or group spoken to. A noun of direct address is *never* the subject of the sentence. This becomes especially tricky when the subject is understood.

EXAMPLE <u>Class</u>, listen to the instructions.

Class is a noun of direct address; the understood subject is *you*.

3.77 Appositives. Appositives rename a noun. Like all interrupters, appositives are enclosed or set off from the rest of the sentence by commas. There is one exception: word names do not require commas.

EXAMPLES

My friend <u>Yang</u> did a beautiful project on birds. (No punctuation is required.)

Mrs. Cokley, <u>my favorite teacher</u>, will retire this year. (Commas are needed.)

LANGUAGE, GRAMMAR, AND STYLE

VERBALS: PARTICIPLES GERUNDS, AND INFINITIVES. Students are asked to identify participles and gerunds in sentences in the Language, Grammar, and Style activities on pages 198 and 936.

3.78 Hybrids

Hybrids are words usually thought of as one part of speech that occasionally function as another. Each word form should be labeled according to what it does in the sentence. Some common hybrids include **possessive nouns and pronouns, relative pronouns**, **intensifying pronouns**, and a group of verb forms called **verbals**.

3.79 POSSESSIVE NOUNS AND PRONOUNS. Possessive nouns and pronouns are namer forms that work as modifiers. To form a possessive noun, an apostrophe plus an *s* is added to a singular; an apostrophe is added to a plural. Notice how the possessive noun uses a noun form, but with the suffix it becomes a modifier.

EXAMPLE Linda proofread Marty's assignment.

Marty's modifies *assignment*. Consequently this construction is a hybrid: it looks like a noun, but it functions as an adjective. When listing parts of the sentence, label a possessive noun as an adjective.

Possessive pronouns act much the same way. Many possessive forms are the same as other pronouns, but a few pronoun forms are uniquely possessive. Some of the unique forms include *mine, your, yours, hers, its, our, their,* and *theirs.* Two other possessive forms, *her* and *him,* are not always possessive.

EXAMPLE I ate my pizza.

My modifies *pizza. My* looks like a pronoun, but here it works as a modifier by telling whom the pizza belongs to. Because we label parts of speech according to what they are doing in the sentence, this word should be considered a modifier—in this case, an adjective.

Relative pronouns are pronoun forms that function like **subordinating conjunctions**. The commonly used relative pronouns are *who, whom, whose, which,* and *that.* These words can connect a subordinate clause to the main clause of the sentence. But they also will function as a subject, object, or predicate pronoun—these are exactly the same functions as naming parts of speech.

EXAMPLE
I want to meet the person who painted that picture.

Who is the **relative pronoun** that connects the subordinate clause (underlined) with the main clause. Also notice that *who* is the subject of the clause; the verb is *painted.*

EXAMPLE
I want to meet the cousin whom you described.

Whom, the **relative pronoun**, is the connection between the two clauses; it also is the direct object of the verb *described.*

EXAMPLE
Kate was the one with whom I designed my art sculpture.

In this sentence, *whom* is the object of the preposition *with*; it also connects the two clauses.

3.80 VERBALS: PARTICIPLES, GERUNDS, AND INFINITIVES. Verbals are verb forms that act as namers or modifiers. There are three different forms of verbals. These include participles (that act as modifiers), gerunds (that act like nouns), and infinitives (that can act like nouns, adjectives and adverbs).

To determine if a verb is used as a verbal, you must be aware of what the word is actually doing in the sentence. Like other verbs, verbals can take objects, modifiers or both. When a verbal has modifiers and/or objects, the group of words is called a participial phrase, a gerund phrase, or an infinitive phrase. Like all phrases, verbal phrases function as one part of speech.

Participles are action adjectives. They have two forms: the present participle and the past participle. Both are used the same way.

The **present participle** uses the –ing form.

EXAMPLES Jana jumped off the diving board.
My uncle has a hearing aid.
I love to listen to that marching band.

The **past participle** uses the *–ed* form.

EXAMPLES A raided cookie jar is not a pretty sight.
The forgotten language will never be recovered.
A watched pot never boils.

Note that you can find the object of a participle by using the same questioning strategy you use to find the verb of a sentence. The participle and its object form a construction called a **participial phrase**. It acts as one part of speech, an adjective.

EXAMPLE The student taking notes got an *A* last semester.

Taking is a participle. If you ask, "*taking* what?", the answer is *notes*. The object of *taking*, the **participle**, is *notes*. Since *taking notes* modifies *student*, the entire construction (called a participial phrase) is working as an adjective.

Gerunds are verb forms used as namers. When you use any action as a name (running, jumping, writing, singing, playing), you use a gerund.

EXAMPLES

Running was her favorite activity.
(The gerund is the subject of the sentence.)

He liked high jumping.
(The gerund is the direct object.)

She wanted a tutor for writing.
(The gerund is the object of a preposition.)

Like participles, gerands can take objects. You can find the object of a gerund just as you find the object of a verb.

EXAMPLE

Buying a prom dress took all of Katy's money.

Buying is a **gerund**. If you ask, "Buying what?", the answer is *a prom dress*. After you eliminate the modifiers, you will see that the object of the gerund *buying* is *dress*.

Gerunds can also take modifiers; since the gerund acts as a noun, the modifiers are adjectives.

EXAMPLE Dan began ice skating.

In this case, *ice* modifies *skating*.

EXAMPLE Senna began complaining to her mother.

Note that the prepositional phrase *to her mother* modifies *complaining*. This makes the modifier a prepositional phrase.

In both of the sentences above, the entire **gerund phrase** (the gerund + objects and/or modifiers) acts as one noun. In both these sentences, the phrases are direct objects.

Infinitives are verbals that use the form *to* + the verb. Each of the examples below illustrates a different use of infinitives. Infinitives can be used as nouns or as modifiers (adjectives and adverbs).

EXAMPLES

Her desire to win dominated her entire life. (Adjective)

The entire family gathered to celebrate my grandmother's birthday. (Adverb)

To attend college is my ultimate goal. (Noun)

When I turned sixteen, my parents allowed me to drive my car to school.

Like other verbals, infinitives can take modifiers and objects. In the second and third sample sentences, the infinitives have objects. *To celebrate* has an object, *my grandmother's birthday*; the object of *to attend* is *college*. The fourth, *to drive*, has an object, *my car*, and a modifier, *to school*.

Infinitives can get tricky because speakers and writers may leave out *to* when it follows some commonly used verbs. Sometimes the *to* is omitted in infinitives that follow *dare, do, feel, hear, help, let, make, need, see, watch*. These constructions, called **bare infinitives**, are usually direct objects that name an action. The *to* is understood.

EXAMPLES

I heard her (to) play the piano.
Help me (to) carry this table.

Be careful. The *to* is not always left out after these verbs, and no dependable rule seems to exist. Native speakers with good ears will have a sense of this, but others may find it difficult. Fortunately, it is never wrong to include the *to* with an infinitive, although it may sound a little awkward.

3.81 Groups of Words That Function as One Part of Speech

Sometimes groups of words function as one part of speech. These groups fall into two categories: **phrases** and **clauses**. **Clauses** have both subjects and verbs; **phrases** do not.

EXAMPLES

I need to get another spiral notebook. (Phrase)

She will be elected to the Student Council. (Phrase)

I will watch television when I finish my homework. (Clause)

LANGUAGE, GRAMMAR, AND STYLE

Do you know who will be our next class president? (Clause)

Most clauses and phrases are named after the functions that they perform.

3.82 Phrases. Phrases are groups of words that do not contain a subject and verb and that function as one part of speech. The following kinds of phrases are used in the English language:
Adjective phrases are prepositional phrases that modify nouns or pronouns.

EXAMPLE Slim wanted a job with good hours.

Adverb phrases are prepositional phrases that modify anything except nouns and pronouns.

EXAMPLE I spoke to the two-headed alien.

Participial phrases are verbal phrases that function as adjectives.

EXAMPLE Their recently remodeled house is the jewel of the neighborhood.

Gerund phrases are verbal phrases that function as nouns.

EXAMPLE Getting good grades is important to many students.

Infinitive phrases are verbal phrases that function as nouns, adjectives, or adverbs.

EXAMPLES To see angels is to believe in them. (Noun)
The ride to go on is the Ferris wheel. (Adjective)
We are ready to go home. (Adverb)

3.83 Clauses within a Sentence. The **clauses** within a sentence are groups of words that 1) contain a subject and verb and that 2) function as one part of speech. The following kinds of clauses are used in the English language:

Adjective clauses are subordinate clauses that function as adjectives; they modify nouns and pronouns.

EXAMPLE
I admired the girl who won the speech contest.

Adverb clauses are subordinate clauses that function as adverbs, modifiying anything except nouns and pronouns.

EXAMPLE
My mother got upset when she learned where I was going.

Noun clauses function as subjects and objects.

EXAMPLE
Whoever gets straight *A*'s in math gets a four year scholarship from the school's foundation.

3.84 The Clauses of a Sentence: Simple, Compound, and Complex Sentences. The independent clauses of a sentence are the parts that contain a subject and verb. Without coordinating and/or subordinating words, they could stand alone. A sentence with only one independent clause is called a simple sentence.

SIMPLE SENTENCE
Mabel made a broccoli pizza.

When sentences have more than one clause, they are called **main clauses** and **subordinate clauses**. The **main clause** is the most important idea in a sentence. When the sentence has two or more ideas of equal importance, it is a **compound sentence**, and each of the clauses is called a **main clause**. Main clauses are separated by a comma and *but*.

COMPOUND SENTENCE
Mabel made a broccoli pizza, but I didn't eat it!

When we use **subordinating conjunctions** or **relative pronouns**, the main clause has one or more **subordinate clauses** (less important clauses). Sentences with one or more subordinate clauses are called **complex sentences**.

COMPLEX SENTENCE
After I returned home, I ate a cheese pizza.

The **main clause** is *I ate a cheese pizza*. The less important idea hooked to it is *I returned home*. *After* is a **subordinating conjunction**.

If a sentence contains both kinds of clauses, it is called a **compound-complex sentence**.

COMPOUND-COMPLEX SENTENCE
After I returned home, I ate a cheese pizza, but Mabel was insulted.

For more information, see the Language Arts Survey 3.36, "Combining and Expanding Sentences."

Editing for Punctuation Errors. Students are asked to edit end marks, commas, and semicolons in the Language, Grammar, and Style activity on page 1050.

3.85 Editing for Punctuation Errors

To avoid punctuation errors, you should know how to use end marks, commas, semicolons, colons, apostrophes, underlining, italics, quotation marks, dashes, and hyphens.

3.86 End Marks. End marks tell the reader where a sentence ends. An end mark also shows the purpose of the sentence. The three end marks are the period, the question mark, and the exclamation point.

A **declarative sentence** ends with a period.

DECLARATIVE

For many years the Empire State Building was the tallest skyscraper in the world.

An **interrogative sentence** ends with a question mark.

INTERROGATIVE

When did World War I begin?
How do you spell your name?

An **exclamatory sentence** ends with an exclamation point.

EXCLAMATORY

The view from the top is breathtaking!
Help! Marvin is choking!

3.87 Commas. A **comma** separates words or groups of words within a sentence. Commas tell the reader to pause at certain spots in the sentence. These pauses help keep the reader from running certain words and phrases together when these phrases should be kept apart for clarity. Following is a list of the most common ways commas should be used.

RULES	EXAMPLES
Use commas to separate **items in a series.** Three or more words make a series.	The primary particles in an atom are protons, neutrons, and electrons. Choices include carrots, green beans, and asparagus.
Use commas when you **combine sentences using *and, but, or, nor, yet, so,*** or ***for.*** Place the comma before these words.	Casey was confident that he could hit a home run. He struck out. Casey was confident that he could hit a home run, but he struck out. Joanna will sing in the talent show. Margaret will accompany her. Joanna will sing in the talent show, and Margaret will accompany her.
Use a comma to **set off words or phrases that interrupt sentences.** Use two commas if the word or phrase falls in the middle of the sentence. Use one comma if the word or phrase comes at the beginning or at the end of a sentence.	Emily's twin brothers, Eric and Derrick, look exactly alike. Hercules, a hero of classical mythology, was said to be the strongest man on earth. After the first quarter, the Knicks dominated the game. How did you solve that problem, Jared?

CONTINUED

RULES	EXAMPLES
Use commas to **separate the parts of a date**. Do not use a comma between the month and the day.	The Germans surrendered on May 8, 1945. My appointment is on Wednesday, January 7.
Use commas to **separate items in addresses**. Do not put a comma between the state and the ZIP code.	Francisco was born in Caracas, Venezuela. They live at 210 Newfield Road, DeWitt, New York 13214.

3.88 Semicolons. You have seen how two related sentences can be combined into one using a conjunction such as *and, but, so,* and *or.* Another way to join two related sentences into one is to use a semicolon. The **semicolon** can be used in place of the comma and the conjunction.

EXAMPLES

A fin was spotted moving through the water, so the bathers scrambled onto the beach.
A fin was spotted moving through the water; the bathers scrambled onto the beach.

Danielle is an exchange student from Paris, and everyone is enjoying getting to know her.
Danielle is an exchange student from Paris; everyone is enjoying getting to know her.

3.89 Colons. Use a **colon** to introduce a list of items.

EXAMPLES

Don't forget the following items for the hike: water bottle, food, first-aid kit, extra sweater, and rain gear.
Make sure you have all your paperwork in order: passport, visa, and tickets.

You should also use a colon between numbers that tell hours and minutes.

1:07 p.m. 6:00 a.m. 9:54 p.m.

A colon is often used after the greeting in a business letter.

Dear Sirs: Dear Ms. Flanagan:

3.90 Apostrophes. An **apostrophe** is used to form the possessive of nouns. To form the possessive of a singular noun, you should add an apostrophe and an s to the end of the word.

EXAMPLES

The Sun's diameter is about 864,000 miles.
(Sun + 's = Sun's)

Isaac's room is plastered with posters of the Pacers.
(Isaac + 's = Isaac's)

The possessive of a plural noun is formed two different ways. If the plural noun does not end in *s,* you add an apostrophe and an *s* to the end of the word. If the plural noun ends with an *s,* add only an apostrophe.

EXAMPLES

The women's volleyball team is undefeated.
(women + 's = women's)

The Vikings' star quarterback is on the injured list.
(Vikings + ' = Vikings')

There are some words that end in *s* and are singular, such as *species* or *Jesus,* that have an irregular possessive form. Form the possessive of these words by adding only an apostrophe.

EXAMPLES

Moses' staff
Euripedes' tragedies

3.91 Underlining and Italics. Italics are a type of slanted printing used to make a word or phrase stand out. In handwritten documents, or in forms of printing in which italics are not available, underlining is used. You should underline or italicize the titles of books, magazines, works of art, movies, and plays.

BOOKS *A Portrait of the Artist as a Young Man, Angela's Ashes* or A Portrait of the Artist as a Young Man, Angela's Ashes

MAGAZINES *The Tattler, Best of British Magazine* or The Tattler, Best of British Magazine

Underlining and Italics. Students are asked to correctly underline and italicize words in the Language, Grammar, and Style activity on page 955.

WORKS OF ART	*The Thinker, Starry Night* or The Thinker, Starry Night
MOVIES	*American Beauty, The Matrix* or American Beauty, The Matrix
PLAYS	*The Tragedy of Macbeth, Pygmalion* or The Tragedy of Macbeth, Pygmalion

3.92 Quotation Marks. When you use a person's exact words in your writing, you are using a **direct quotation**. Enclose the words of a direct quotation in quotation marks.

EXAMPLES

"It looks as if thunderclouds are gathering," Sylvia remarked.
Pietro said, "It's good to be back home."

A direct quotation should always begin with a capital letter. Separate a direct quotation from the rest of the sentence with a comma, question mark, or exclamation point. Do not separate the direct quotation from the rest of the sentence with a period. All punctuation marks that belong to the direct quotation itself should be placed inside the quotation marks.

EXAMPLES

"Your golf game has really improved," Avram remarked.
Victor lamented, "I wish Uncle Don were here."
"Did I turn off the iron?" wondered Mrs. Cameron.
Joy asked, "Have you seen my red blouse?"

Use quotation marks to enclose the titles of short works such as short stories, poems, songs, articles, and parts of books.

SHORT STORIES
"The Lagoon," "Heat"

POEMS
"Ode on a Grecian Urn," "My Last Duchess"

SONGS
"Auld Lang Syne"

ARTICLES, ESSAYS
"Macbeth," "Why I Vouch for Vouchers"

PARTS OF BOOKS
"The Slave Ship," "The Medieval Period"

3.93 Hyphens and Dashes. A **hyphen** is used to make a compound word.

EXAMPLES

four-year-old boy, great-grandmother, run-of-the-mill, seventh-grade student, three-time winner

A **dash** is used to show a sudden break or change in thought.

EXAMPLE

Juan surprised his teacher—and himself—by getting an *A* on the science test.

3.94 Editing for Capitalization Errors

To avoid capitalization errors, you should know how to capitalize proper nouns and adjectives; geographical names, directions and historical names; and titles of art and history books.

3.95 Proper Nouns and Adjectives. Using capital letters is called **capitalization**. Always capitalize proper nouns and adjectives. A proper noun names a specific person, place, or thing. A **proper adjective** is an adjective formed from a proper noun.

PROPER NOUNS
Lebanon, Queen Elizabeth, Democrat

PROPER ADJECTIVES
Lebanese, Elizabethan, Democratic

Capitalize the names of people and pets.

PEOPLE AND PETS
Charles A. Lindbergh, Marie Curie, Smoky

There are many different kinds of proper nouns. The chart below should help you to recognize some of them.

PROPER NOUNS

Titles Used with Names
Dr. Stetson, Ms. Dixon, Mr. Meletiadis
Months, Days, Holidays
January, Wednesday, Labor Day
Religions
Hinduism, Catholicism, Buddhism

CONTINUED

LANGUAGE, GRAMMAR, AND STYLE

Quotation Marks. In the Language, Grammar, and Style activities on pages 955 and 1081, students are asked to use quotation marks.

Editing for Capitalization Errors. Students are asked to edit capitalization errors in sentences in the Language, Grammar, and Style activity on page 613.

PROPER NOUNS

Sacred Beings and Writings
the Great Spirit, the Bible, the Koran

Cities, States, Countries
Seattle, Louisiana, Peru

Nationalities
Danish, Brazilian, Greek

Streets, Bridges
Highland Street, Tappan Zee Bridge

Buildings, Monuments
World Trade Center, Washington Monument

Clubs, Organizations, Businesses
Kiwanis Club, National Audubon Society, Sears Roebuck

3.96 *I* and First Words. Capitalize the first word of every sentence.

EXAMPLES
Did you see that meteor?
The river rose over its banks.

Capitalize the word *I* whenever it appears.

EXAMPLES
Janice and I will buy the present.
Whenever I see horses, I think of Uncle Sherman.

3.97 Family Relationships and Titles of Persons. A word for a family relation such as *Mom, Dad,* or *Grandpa* should be capitalized if it is used as the name or part of the name of a particular person. Do not capitalize a word for a family relation if a modifier such as *the, a, my,* or *your* comes before it.

CAPITALIZED
When they were children, Dad, Aunt Polly, and Uncle Richard went down the Grand Canyon on mules.

NOT CAPITALIZED
My grandma has a cousin who lives in Germany.

Capitalize the official title of a person when it is followed by the person's name or when it is used instead of a name in direct address.

President James Polk, Queen Mary, Sir Winston Churchill, Pope Paul
"I am honored to meet you, Ambassador."

Do not capitalize references to occupations.

the electrician, the doctor, the sergeant, the judge, the chef, the editor

3.98 Geographical Names, Directions, and Historical Names. Capitalize the names of specific places, including terms such as *lake, mountain, river,* or *valley* if they are used as part of a name.

BODIES OF WATER	Colorado River, Black Sea
CITIES AND TOWNS	Kansas City, Fayetteville
COUNTIES	Cayuga County, Kosciusko County
COUNTRIES	Switzerland, Indonesia
ISLANDS	Ellis Island, Isle of Wight
MOUNTAINS	Pike's Peak, Mount Rainier
STATES	Montana, South Carolina
STREETS, HIGHWAYS	Erie Boulevard, Route 71

Do not capitalize general names for places.

EXAMPLES
The still lake beautifully reflected the white-capped mountain.
Follow this road for two more miles and you will reach a small town.

Capitalize geographical directions if they are part of a specific name or a commonly recognized region. Do not capitalize words such as east(ern), west(ern), north(ern), and south(ern) if they are used only to indicate direction.

CAPITALIZED
Western Samoa, East Africa, South Bend, Northern Ireland

NOT CAPITALIZED
west of Denver, eastern face of the mountain, south side of the city, northern regions

Capitalize historical events, special events, and recognized periods of time.

HISTORICAL EVENTS
Continental Congress, Boxer Rebellion

HISTORICAL PERIODS
Paleozoic Era, Industrial Age

SPECIAL EVENTS
Empire State Games, Rose Bowl

3.99 Titles of Art Works and Literary Works. Apply title capitalization to titles of art works and literary works. In title capitalization, capitalize the first word, the last word, and all other words except articles (*a, an,* and *the*) and prepositions.

EXAMPLES
Raphael's *The School of Athens*, Matisse's *Joy of Life*, Jackson Pollock's *Autumn Rhythm*, Shakespeare's *The Taming of the Shrew*, Faulkner's *The Sound and the Fury*, Ray Bradbury's "All Summer in a Day"

3.100 Editing for Spelling Errors

You can improve your spelling by following the rules given here, and by memorizing the list of commonly misspelled words.

3.101 Using Spelling Rules I. Always check your writing for spelling errors, and try to recognize the words that give you more trouble than others. Adding prefixes and suffixes often causes spelling errors. A prefix is a letter or a group of letters added to the beginning of a word to change its meaning. When adding a prefix, do not change the spelling of the word itself.

dis + similar = dissimilar
un + necessary = unnecessary

A **suffix** is a letter or group of letters added to the end of a word to change its meaning. The spelling of most words is not changed when the suffix *–ness* or *–ly* is added.

even + ness = evenness
usual + ly = usually

If you are adding a suffix to a word that ends with *y*, and that *y* follows a vowel, you should usually leave the *y* in place. (**Vowels** are the letters *a, e, i, o,* and *u.*)

employ + ment = employment
stay + ing = staying
destroy + ed = destroyed

If you are adding a suffix to a word that ends with *y*, and that *y* follows a consonant, you should usually change the *y* to *i.* (**Consonants** are all letters that are not vowels.)

silly + est = silliest
sticky + ness = stickiness
cry + ed = cried
cheery + ly = cheerily

If you are adding a suffix that begins with a vowel to a word that ends with a silent *e*, you should usually drop the *e.*

shave + ing = shaving
value + able = valuable
rose + y = rosy
take + ing = taking

If you are adding a suffix that begins with a consonant to a word that ends with a silent *e*, you should usually leave the *e* in place.

tire + less = tireless
sincere + ly = sincerely
fate + ful = fateful
place + ment = placement

3.102 Using Spelling Rules II. When a word is spelled with the letters *i* and *e* and has the long *e* sound, it is spelled *ie* except after the letter *c.*

thief, relieve, yield, pierce
ceiling, conceive, receipt, deceive

The only word in the English language that ends in *–sede* is *supersede.* Only the following three words end in *–ceed*: *exceed, proceed,* and *succeed.* Every other word that ends with the "seed" sound is spelled *–cede.*

precede, recede, concede, accede

Most noun plurals are formed by simply adding *–s* to the end of the word.

stairs, ducklings, kites, rockets

The plurals of nouns that end in *o, s, x, z, ch,* or *sh* should be formed by adding *–es.*

tomatoes, classes, taxes, topazes, beaches, flashes

An exception to the rule above is that musical terms (and certain other words that end in *o*) are usually pluralized by adding *–s.*

pianos, solos, concertos, sopranos, banjos, radios

Form the plurals of nouns that end in *y* following a vowel by adding *–s.*

EXAMPLES toy + s = toys
donkey + s = donkeys
Thursday + s = Thursdays
ray + s = rays

LANGUAGE, GRAMMAR, AND STYLE

Form the plurals of nouns that end in *y* following a consonant by changing the *y* to an *i* and adding –es.

EXAMPLES pony + s = ponies
spy + s = spies
country + s = countries
story + s = stories

3.103 Common Spelling Errors. Some English words are often misspelled. The following box contains a list of 150 commonly misspelled words. If you master this list, you will avoid many errors in your spelling.

COMMONLY MISSPELLED ENGLISH WORDS					
absence	biscuit	enormous	liquefy	parallel	siege
abundant	breathe	enthusiastically	magnificent	pastime	significance
academically	business	environment	manageable	peasant	souvenir
accessible	calendar	exhaust	maneuver	permanent	sponsor
accidentally	camouflage	existence	meadow	persistent	succeed
accommodate	catastrophe	fascinating	mediocre	phenomenon	surprise
accurate	cellar	finally	miniature	physician	symbol
acknowledgment	cemetery	forfeit	mischievous	pneumonia	synonymous
acquaintance	changeable	fulfill	misspell	prestige	temperature
adequately	clothes	guidance	mortgage	privilege	tomorrow
adolescent	colossal	guerrilla	mysterious	procedure	transparent
advantageous	column	hindrance	naive	prophesy	twelfth
advisable	committee	hypocrite	necessity	prove	undoubtedly
ancient	conceivable	independent	nickel	receipt	unmistakable
annihilate	conscientious	influential	niece	referred	unnecessary
anonymous	conscious	ingenious	noticeable	rehearsal	vacuum
answer	consistency	institution	nucleus	relieve	vehicle
apparent	deceitful	interference	nuisance	resistance	vengeance
article	descendant	irrelevant	nutritious	resources	villain
attendance	desirable	irresistible	obedience	responsibility	vinegar
bankruptcy	disastrous	judgment	occasionally	rhythm	weird
beautiful	discipline	league	occurrence	schedule	whistle
beggar	efficiency	leisure	orchestra	seize	withhold
beginning	eighth	license	outrageous	separate	yacht
behavior	embarrass	lightning	pageant	sergeant	yield

SPEAKING AND LISTENING Resource

THE POWER OF COMMUNICATION

Humans are by nature social creatures. **Communication** is a form of behavior that fulfills the basic human need to connect and interact with other individuals in society. Because democratic government requires the free exchange of ideas, communication is also fundamental to the political way of life in the United States.

4.1 Verbal and Nonverbal Communication

Human beings use both verbal and nonverbal communication to convey meaning and exchange ideas. When a person expresses meaning through words, he or she is using **verbal communication**. When a person expresses meaning without using words, for example by standing up straight or shaking his or her head, he or she is using **nonverbal communication**. When we speak to another person, we usually think that the meaning of what we say comes chiefly from the words we use. However, as much as 60% of the meaning of a message may be communicated nonverbally.

ELEMENTS OF VERBAL COMMUNICATION

ELEMENT	DESCRIPTION	GUIDELINES FOR SPEAKERS
Volume	loudness or softness	Vary your volume, but make sure that you can be heard.
Melody, Pitch	highness or lowness	Vary your pitch. Avoid speaking in a monotone (at a single pitch).
Pace	speed	Vary the speed of your delivery to suit what you are saying. Excitement, for example, can be communicated by a fast pace, and seriousness can be communicated by slowing down and saying something forcefully.
Tone	emotional quality	Suit your tone to your message, and vary it appropriately as you speak. For example, you might use a light tone for a happy message and a heavier one for a sad message.
Enunciation	clearness with which words are spoken	When speaking before a group, pronounce your words more precisely than you would in ordinary conversation.

INTERNET RESOURCES

Access Teaching Online's *Confidence in Public Speaking* oral language lesson for middle or high school at http://www.teachingonline.org/publicspeaking.html.

VERBAL AND NONVERBAL COMMUNICATION. Students are asked to use verbal and nonverbal skills in the Speaking and Listening activity on page 174 and the Collaborative Learning activity on page 243.

Active versus Passive Listening. Students are given the opportunity to practice active listening skills in the Speaking and Listening activity on page 1050.

Elements of Nonverbal Communication

Element	Description	Guidelines for Speakers
Eye contact	Looking audience members in the eye	Make eye contact regularly with people in your audience. Try to include all audience members.
Facial expression	Using your face to show your emotions	Use expressions to emphasize your message—raised eyebrows for a question, pursed lips for concentration, eyebrows lowered for anger, and so on.
Gesture	Meaningful motions of the arms and hands	Use gestures to emphasize points. Be careful, however, not to overuse gestures. Too many can be distracting.
Posture	Position of the body	Keep your spine straight and head high, but avoid appearing stiff. Stand with your arms and legs slightly open, except when adopting other postures to express particular emotions.
Proximity	Distance from audience	Keep the right amount of distance between yourself and the audience. You should be a comfortable distance away, but not so far away that the audience cannot hear you.

LISTENING SKILLS

Learning to listen well is essential not only for success in personal life but also for success in school and, later, on the job. It is estimated that high school and college students spend over half their waking time listening to others, yet most people are rather poor listeners.

4.2 Active versus Passive Listening

Effective listening requires skill and concentration. The mind of a good listener is focused on what a speaker is trying to communicate. In other words, an effective listerner is an active listener. Ineffective listeners view listening as a passive activity, something that simply "happens" without any effort on their part. Passive listening is nothing more than hearing sounds. This type of listening can cause misunderstanding and miscommunication.

Different situations require different listening skills. The following suggestions can help you become a better listener in particular situations.

4.3 Listening to a Lecture or Demonstration

- Think of creative reasons to listen. It can be difficult to pay attention to a lecture or demonstration if you do not think the information being presented is important to you. Try to think of reasons why the information is important by asking yourself: How can I use this information?
- As you listen, show the speaker that you are involved. Remember that in a lecture or demonstration, as in a conversation, the speaker depends on you for positive feedback or response. Try to maintain an attentive posture by sitting up straight, making eye contact, and nodding when you understand.
- Listen for major ideas. Try to identify the speaker's main points and the facts or materials that are offered to support them. Check your understanding of what the speaker is saying by putting it into your own words, in your head, as you listen.

- Take notes as you listen. Note the major ideas and related details. Do not try to write down what the speaker says word for word. Use phrases, symbols, and abbreviations such as *w/* for with, *Amer.* for American, and & or + for and. (For more information, see the Language Arts Survey 5.17, "Taking Notes, Summarizing, and Outlining Information.")
- When you do not understand something that the speaker is saying, make a note. Save questions and comments for an appropriate time, usually when the speaker pauses or when he or she invites questions. Then raise your hand before asking your question or making your comment.
- Do not let yourself become distracted. Avoid such things as daydreaming, focusing on the speaker's delivery, or listening to background noise. Giving in to distractions can prevent you from understanding the speaker's message.

4.4 Listening in Conversations

- Do not monopolize the conversation. Give the other person plenty of opportunities to speak.
- When the other person is speaking, pay attention to what he or she is saying. Show through eye contact, body language, and facial expressions that you are interested and attentive.
- Avoid mentally debating the other person while he or she is speaking. This may distract you from truly hearing what the person has to say. Try to withhold judgment until the other person has finished.
- Ask the other person questions. Asking questions is a good way to start a conversation, to keep the conversation going, and to show the other person that you are really listening. The best questions are usually ones that directly relate to what the speaker has been saying.
- When you speak, respond to what the other person has been saying. Relate what you say to what he or she has said.
- Take time to think about what the other speaker has said before responding. Do not be afraid of a lull in the conversation while you think about what has been said and about your response.
- If you find yourself becoming overly emotional during a conversation, stop, take a deep breath, and bring your emotions under control before continuing. If controlling your emotions seems too difficult, consider continuing the conversation at a later time.

4.5 Listening to the Media

- Avoid being a "couch potato." Television, movies, and radio programs can be powerful manipulators. As you watch or listen, think critically about what you are seeing or hearing by evaluating these messages.
- When watching or listening to news programs or commercial advertisements, make sure to distinguish facts from opinions. Facts are statements that can be proved by checking a reference work or making observations. Opinions are statements of value or statements of policy that express personal beliefs. A statement of value expresses positive or negative attitudes toward a person, object, or idea. For example, "Albert Einstein was a great humanitarian" is a statement of value because it expresses a positive attitude toward Einstein. A statement of policy says what should or should not be done. "Congress should spend more money on education" is a statement of policy because it suggests what Congress should do. When you hear an opinion, ask yourself whether it is supported by the facts. For more information, see the Language Arts Survey 5.2, "Distinguishing Fact from Opinion."
- When watching or listening to an entertainment program, think about the quality of the program. Consider the quality of the acting, directing, and writing. Also consider the production qualities of the program—the lighting, sound effects, staging, camera work, costuming, properties, and music.
- Think about what message or messages are being delivered by the program and whether you agree or disagree with them. Do not assume that just because a program is entertaining, it does not communicate a message.

Listening to the Media. Students are encouraged to follow the guidelines for listening to the media in the Media Literacy activity on page 798.

Listening in Conversations. Students are encouraged to follow the guidelines for listening in conversations in the Collaborative Learning & Speaking and Listening activities on pages 329 and 944.

- Set standards about what you will watch or listen to. Learn to turn off a program or to switch to another program when something does not meet your standards.
- Limit the time that you spend watching or listening to the broadcast media. Remember that there is much more that you might be doing with your life such as reading, learning a new hobby or skill, writing in your journal, exercising, interacting with other people, creating works of art, or simply thinking.

4.6 Adapting Listening Skills to Specific Tasks

Just as different situations require different types of listening, different tasks or goals may also require different listening strategies and skills.

Listening for comprehension means listening for information or ideas communicated by other people. For example, you are listening for comprehension when you try to understand directions to a friend's house or your teacher's explanation of how to conduct a classroom debate. When listening for comprehension, your goal is to reach understanding, so it is important to recognize and remember the key information or ideas presented. Concentrate on getting the main points or major ideas of a message rather than all the supporting details. This can prevent you from becoming overwhelmed by the amount of information presented. You might also use a technique called clarifying and confirming to help you better remember and understand information. The technique involves paraphrasing or repeating back to the speaker in your own words the key information presented to make sure that you have understood correctly. If the situation prevents you from using the technique—for instance, if there is no opportunity for you to respond directly to the speaker—it can still be helpful to rephrase the information in your own words in your head to help you remember and understand it.

Listening critically means listening to a message in order to comprehend and evaluate it. When listening for comprehension, you usually assume that the information presented is true. Critical listening, on the other hand, includes comprehending and judging the arguments and appeals in a message in order to decide whether to accept or reject them. Critical listening is most useful when you encounter a persuasive message such as a sales pitch, advertisement, campaign speech, or news editorial. When evaluating a persuasive message, you might consider the following: Is the speaker trustworthy and qualified to speak about this subject? Does the speaker present logical arguments supported by solid facts? Does the speaker use unproven assumptions to make a case? Does the speaker use questionable motivational appeals, such as appeals to fear or to prejudice? These questions can help you decide whether or not to be convinced by a persuasive message.

Listening to learn vocabulary involves a very different kind of listening because the focus is on learning new words and how to use them properly. For instance, if you were to hear a presentation on hip-hop music, the speaker might introduce some of the many slang terms used in this musical style and explain what they mean. Or you might have a conversation with someone who has a more advanced vocabulary and use this as an opportunity to learn new words. The key to listening in order to learn vocabulary is to pay attention to how words are used in context. Sometimes it is possible to figure out what an unfamiliar word means based simply on how the word is used in a sentence. Once you learn a new word, try to use it several times so it becomes more familiar and you become comfortable using it. Also be sure to look up the word in a dictionary to find out whether it has other meanings or connotations of which you are not aware.

Listening for appreciation means listening purely for enjoyment or entertainment. You might listen appreciatively to a singer, a comedian, a storyteller, an acting company, or a humorous speaker. Appreciation is a very individual matter and there are no rules about how to appreciate something. However, as with all forms of listening, listening for appreciation requires attention and concentration.

COMMUNICATING WITH OTHERS

4.7 Communicating with Another Person

The ordinary human interactions that take place in daily life involve a great deal of interpersonal communication, or communication between two individuals. The following guidelines will help you to communicate more effectively in such daily interactions.

- **Make eye contact** and maintain a relaxed posture.
- **Provide feedback as you listen.** Smile or nod to show understanding and/or agreement. Ask questions or make comments when the speaker pauses for feedback. Try not to interrupt or to finish the speaker's sentences for him or her.
- **Reflect back or rephrase what the speaker has said** to make sure that you understand him or her. For example, suppose that the speaker says, "Crazy Horse never allowed anyone to make a likeness of him or take his photograph." You could reflect back, "So, nobody ever made a likeness of Crazy Horse or took his photograph? That's interesting. Why do you think he felt that way?"
- **Control your emotions.** If you become angry while listening to the speaker, take a deep breath and count to ten. Make sure you haven't misunder-stood by rephrasing the statement that angered you. If you can contain your anger, express your objections calmly. If you cannot contain your anger, end your conversation and say that you would like to continue it at another time.
- **Distinguish between facts and opinions.** Facts are statements that can be proven true, whereas opinions are expressions of personal belief that may or may not be true. When presenting factual information in a conversation, it is helpful to explain what the basis for the fact is. When presenting opinions, try to indicate this by introducing these ideas with phrases like "I believe that. . ." or "In my opinion. . ." If you are unsure whether another person is stating a fact or opinion, ask what his or her statement is based on.

4.8 Communicating in a Small Group

Much human activity takes place in small groups. A small group is defined as a group of three to fifteen people, interacting in a face-to-face situation, who have an awareness of a group identity. Everyone is involved in a small group at one point or another in their lives, whether it be a high school clique, an after-school organization, an athletic team, or a family. Although many of the principles of interpersonal communication hold true in small group situations, there are additional factors to consider because of the number of people involved. The following guidelines will help you become a better communicator and participant in small group situations.

- **Respect group norms and culture.** Most groups have norms or rules that govern appropriate behavior for group members. Groups also have their own culture or way of life that may include certain beliefs, rituals, or behaviors. When participating in a small group, be sure to pay attention to and respect the norms and culture of the group.
- **Understand group roles.** Individual members are likely to fulfill particular roles in a group based on what they do best. Constructive roles help the group to achieve its goals. These include the **leader** (directs the work of the group), **secretary** (keeps minutes of group meetings), **gatekeeper** (keeps communication open by encouraging and discouraging participation), and **harmonizer** (helps to resolve conflict or reduce tension between group members). Destructive roles may prevent the group from achieving its goals. These include the **joker** (distracts the group by engaging in horseplay), **dominator** (tries to control the group for his or her own interests), **blocker** (puts down the ideas of others or refuses to cooperate), and **deserter** (withdraws from the group and does not participate). Successful group participants attempt to fulfill positive and constructive roles within the group and encourage others to do so.

Communicating in a Small Group. Examples of Collaborative Learning activities can be found on pages 325 and 1032.

- **Take turns participating**. Good group members make contributions to the discussion, but also allow others to participate. If an overly talkative person seems to dominate the discussion, be willing to take on the role of gatekeeper and gently suggest that others be allowed to contribute. For instance, you might say, "I've been interested in what you have to say, Ed. What do other people think about this issue?"
- **Help to foster a positive group climate**. Group climate refers to the degree of warmth or coldness that group members feel toward each other. You have probably been in a group with a cold climate before, where members constantly bicker and argue and never seem to accomplish anything. Positive or warm group climates are characterized by trust, cooperation, and concern for others. Negative or cold group climates are characterized by suspicion, competition, and selfishness. As a good group member, you can help to create a positive and warm climate by being supportive of others ideas, empathizing with others, treating others as equals, and remaining flexible and open to new ideas and information.
- **Establish group goals**. Some groups have a difficult time accomplishing anything because it is not clear what the goals of the group are. Without goals, a group is like a ship that sets sail with no clear destination. Chances are the ship and the group will drift aimlessly until they run aground. You can help your group stay focused by encouraging its members to establish clear goals at the beginning, and referring to these goals whenever the group seems to run aground or lose its way.

4.9 Communicating in a Large Group

Large groups are those that contain more than fifteen people. Generally the larger the size of the group, the less opportunity there is for each individual to participate. However, there are still principles that can help you become a better communicator in large group situations.

- **Share group roles**. In larger groups, it may be difficult to decide who takes what role as many members may have the skills needed for any one role. Sharing roles and responsibilities can allow everyone to contribute to the group.
- **Focus on key relationships**. It may not be possible to get to know everyone in a large group setting. Identify those key individuals in the group that you will most need to interact with in carrying out your assignments or duties, and focus on getting to know them.
- **Emphasize group identity, norms, and goals**. As groups become larger in size, they are likely to become less cohesive. Cohesiveness refers to the level of commitment and attraction members feel to each other and the group. Groups that experience low cohesion are usually not productive or successful. Try to increase cohesion by reinforcing the identity, norms, and goals of the group at every opportunity.
- **Stand up when speaking**. Make sure that everyone in the room can see and hear you. If there is a microphone available, use it. Speak in a normal tone 4 to 6 inches from the microphone.
- **Avoid the pressure to conform**. In larger groups, individuals are less comfortable speaking out if they disagree with an idea or decision. This can produce "groupthink," where members give in to the pressure to conform and do not critically evaluate information and/or decisions. If you disagree with an expressed idea or decision, do not hesitate to speak out and share your reservations.
- **Foster responsibility**. In large groups, it is relatively easy for individual members to shirk their duties and avoid responsibility. If something goes wrong, there are usually many people to blame so no one feels individually responsible for the outcomes of the group. Take responsibility yourself, and encourage others in the group to carry out their assigned duties.

4.10 Asking and Answering Questions

There are many situations in which you will find it useful to ask questions of a speaker, or in which you will be asked questions about a presentation. Often a formal speech or presentation will be

COMMUNICATING IN A LARGE GROUP. A group project classroom planning activity to create a time capsule is found in the Collaborative Learning & Media Literacy activity on page 597.

followed by a question-and-answer period. Keep the following guidelines in mind when asking or answering questions.

ASKING QUESTIONS

- **Wait to be recognized**. In most cases, it is appropriate to raise your hand if you have a question and to wait for the speaker or moderator to call on you.
- **Make questions clear and direct**. The longer your question, the less chance a speaker will understand it. Make your questions short and to the point.
- **Do not debate or argue**. If you disagree with a speaker, the question-and-answer period is not the time to hash out an argument. Ask to speak with the speaker privately after the presentation is over, or agree on a later time and place to meet.
- **Do not take others' time**. Be courteous to other audience members and allow them time to ask questions. If you have a follow-up question, ask the speaker if you may proceed with your follow up.
- **Do not give a speech**. Sometimes audience members are more interested in expressing their own opinion than in asking the speaker a question. Do not give in to the temptation to present a speech of your own.

ANSWERING QUESTIONS

- **Come prepared** for a question-and-answer period. Although you can never predict the exact questions that people will ask you, you can anticipate many questions that are likley to be asked. Rehearse aloud your answers to the most difficult questions.
- **Be patient**. It may take some time for audience members to formulate questions in response to your speech. Give the audience a moment to do so. Don't run back to your seat the minute your speech is over, or if there is an awkward pause after you invite questions.
- **Be direct and succinct**. Be sure to answer the question directly as it has been asked, and to provide a short but clear answer.
- **Rephrase difficult or ambiguous questions**. If you are not sure what an audience member's question is, repeat the question back to them to clarify. You may also want to repeat the question if not everyone in the audience could hear it.
- **Be courteous**. Sometimes audience members will ask a question you have already answered in your speech. Be tactful in such situations. Briefly repeat the information from your speech in case the audience member did not hear or understand you the first time.
- **Handle difficult audience members gracefully**. Sometimes audience members hog the stage or try to pick a verbal fight with a speaker. In such situations, keep your cool and gently suggest that the audience member talk to you privately after the presentation so you can discuss the issue with him or her more fully.

COMMUNICATION STYLES AND CULTURAL BARRIERS

4.11 Being Considerate of Other Cultures and Communication Styles

Communication styles and behaviors vary greatly between people of different cultures—even those who live and were raised in the same country. There are many possible verbal and nonverbal sources of miscommunication between cultural groups. In some cultures, emotionally intense discussions and insults are expected forms of behavior. In other cultures, such behavior is considered rude. In traditional Asian cultures, a slap on the back is considered insulting and it is not customary to shake hands with people of the opposite sex. In other cultures, a slap on the back expresses friendliness and it is customary to shake hands with anyone you meet for the first time. When listening to someone speak, Native Americans consider a bowed head a sign of respect. In other cultures, lack of eye contact may be seen as a sign of shyness, weakness, or disrespect. In Latino cultures, two speakers in conversation may stand very close and even touch each other. In other cultures, standing close is considered an intrusion on personal space and

BEING CONSIDERATE OF OTHER CULTURES AND COMMUNICATION STYLES. Students are asked to be considerate of other cultures and communication styles as they conduct a survey in the Speaking and Listening and Collaborative Learning activity on page 142.

Collaborative Learning and Communication. Students are asked to use the various guidelines for collaborative learning and communication in the Critical Thinking & Collaborative Learning activity on page 827 and Collaborative Learning & Media Literacy activity on page 931.

thought to be rude, and touching is generally acceptable only with close friends or relatives.

These are only a few of the many communication differences that exist among people of different cultures. When interacting with a person from another culture, it is important to remember that such differences may exist and to respect the other individual's cultural practices and behaviors.

4.12 Overcoming Barriers to Effective Multicultural Communication

The following guidelines and suggestions will help you to overcome some common barriers and stumbling blocks to communicating with people of different cultural backgrounds.

- **Treat people as individuals**. Do not assume that everyone is "the same" as you are, or even that people with similar cultural backgrounds are the same. Avoid relying on preconceptions and stereotypes when interacting with someone from another culture. Regardless of what cultural practices, physical characteristics, or behaviors they might share, human beings are individuals and should always be treated as such.
- **Be sensitive to sources of miscommunication**. Remember that both verbal and nonverbal behaviors send messages to others, and that both can lead to miscommunication and misunderstanding. If you think you have done or said something that has offended someone from another culture, ask if this is the case. It may be uncomfortable to do so at first, but you are more likely to overcome your error and become friends if you show respect and sensitivity to the other person.
- **Seek common ground**. One reason people from different cultures may have difficulty communicating is because they focus on differences rather than similarities. A simple way to overcome this problem is to find some common interest, belief, or activity that you share with the other person and that can help to bridge differences.
- **Accept others as they are**. Avoid the temptation to evaluate or judge the behavior, beliefs, feelings, or experiences of others. Instead, learn to accept differences as valid, even if you personally disagree with what someone else thinks or feels. It is also helpful to remember that the other person is probably doing the best he or she can with whatever resources are available at the time.
- **Avoid provoking language**. Racial, ethnic, or gender slurs have no place in an enlightened society and should never be used. Profanity or swearing is unacceptable, even among close friends, and should be avoided. You-statements ("You are not listening to me," "You should not do that," "You don't know what you're talking about") can feel like an attack, even when they are well-intentioned. People often react to you-statements by becoming defensive or hostile. Try to use I-statements instead ("I feel like you aren't listening to me," "I don't think you should do that," "I'm not sure I agree with you").

4.13 Collaborative Learning and Communication

Collaboration is the act of working with one or more other people to achieve a goal. Many common learning situations involve collaboration.

- Participating in a small-group discussion
- Doing a small-group project
- Tutoring another student or being tutored
- Doing peer evaluation

Guidelines for Discussion

- **Listen actively during the discussion**. Maintain eye contact with the speakers. Make notes on what they say. Mentally translate what they say into your own words. Think critically about whether you agree or disagree with each speaker, and why.
- **Be polite**. Wait for your turn to speak. Do not interrupt others. If your discussion has a group leader, ask to be recognized before speaking by raising your hand.
- **Participate in the discussion**. At appropriate times, make your own comments or ask questions of other speakers.
- **Stick to the discussion topic**. Do not introduce unrelated or irrelevant ideas.
- **For a formal discussion, assign roles**. Choose a group leader to guide the discussion and a secretary to record the minutes (the main ideas

and proposals made by group members). Also draw up an agenda before the discussion, listing items to be discussed.

Guidelines for Projects

- **Choose a group leader** to conduct the meetings of your project group.
- **Set a goal** for the group, some specific outcome or set of outcomes that you want to bring about.
- **Make a list of tasks** that need to be performed.
- **Make a schedule** for completing the tasks, including dates and times for completion of each task.
- **Make an assignment sheet**. Assign certain tasks to particular group members. Be fair in distributing the work to be done.
- **Set times for future meetings**. You might want to schedule meetings to evaluate your progress toward your goal as well as meetings to actually carry out specific tasks.
- **Meet to evaluate your overall success** when the project is completed. Also look at the individual contributions of each group member.

Guidelines for Tutoring

- **Find out what the other student needs to learn**. Help him or her clarify assignments and areas of strength and weakness.
- **Break down your teaching into steps** that can be followed easily. Then help the other student to follow through on each step.
- **Review basic concepts, terms, and processes**. Encourage the other student to explain these to you in his or her own words.
- **Give the other student practice activities or exercises**, and help him or her to complete them.
- **Be patient**. Give the other student time to respond, to make mistakes, and to ask questions.
- **Be encouraging and supportive**. Remember that your job is to help someone else to learn, not to display your own knowledge.

Guidelines for Being Tutored

- **Bring with you all the materials that you need**, such as your textbook, study guides, notes, worksheets, pencils, and paper.
- **Explain as clearly as you can what you need help with**. Prepare questions beforehand.
- **Ask questions about anything that you do not understand.** Remember that no question is silly if it is sincere.
- **Be patient**. Learning takes time.
- **Do not give up if you do not understand immediately**. Practice makes perfect.
- **Be polite** and thank your tutor for his or her help.

Guidelines for Peer Evaluation. For more information on peer evaluation, see the Language Arts Survey 2.37, "Self- and Peer Evaluation, " 2.39, "How to Deliver Helpful Criticism," and 2.40, "How to Benefit from Helpful Criticism."

4.14 Conducting an Interview

In an interview, you meet with someone and ask him or her questions. Interviewing experts is an excellent way to gain information about a particular topic. For example, if you are interested in writing about the art of making pottery, you might interview an art teacher, a professional potter, or the owner of a ceramics shop.

When planning an interview, you should do some background research on your subject and think carefully about questions you would like to ask. Write out a list of questions, including some about the person's background as well as about your topic. Other questions might occur to you as the interview proceeds, but it is best to be prepared. For guidelines on being a good listener, read the Language Arts Survey 4.2, "Active versus Passive Listening," and 4.4, "Listening in Conversations." Here are some more tips for interviewing:

- **Set up a time for the interview in advance**. Don't just try to work questions into a regular conversation. Set aside time to meet in a quiet place where both you and the person you are interviewing can focus on the interview.
- **Explain the purpose of the interview**. Be sure the person you are interviewing knows what you want to find out and why you need to know it. This will help him or her to answer your questions in a way that is more useful and helpful to you.

Conducting an Interview. For practice, see the interviewing activities in Integrating the Language Arts activities on pages 538 and 965.

Conducting an Interview. Additional interviewing activities are found in Integrating the Language Arts activities on pages 309 and 1072.

- **Ask mostly open-ended questions**. These are questions that allow the person you are interviewing to express a personal point of view. They cannot be answered with a simple "yes" or "no" nor a brief statement of fact. The following are all examples of open-ended questions: "Why did you become a professional potter?" "What is the most challenging thing about owning your own ceramics shop?" "What advice would you give to a beginning potter?" One of the most valuable questions to ask at the end of the interview is, "What would you like to add that I haven't asked about?" This can provide some of the most interesting or vital information of all.
- **If possible, tape-record the interview**. Then you can review the interview at your leisure. Be sure to ask the person you are interviewing whether or not you can tape-record the session. If the person refuses, accept his or her decision.
- **Take notes during the interview**, whether or not you are also tape-recording it. Write down the main points and some key words to help you remember details. Record the person's most important statements word for word.
- **Clarify spelling and get permission for quotes**. Be sure to get the correct spelling of the person's name and to ask permission to quote his or her statements.
- **End the interview on time**. Do not extend the interview beyond the time limits of your appointment. The person you are interviewing has been courteous enough to give you his or her time. Return this courtesy by ending the interview on time, thanking the person for his or her help, and leaving.
- **Write up the results of the interview as soon as possible after you conduct it**. Over time, what seemed like a very clear note may become unclear or confusing. If you are unclear of something important that the person said, contact him or her and ask for clarification.

PUBLIC SPEAKING

4.15 Giving a Speech

The fear of speaking in public, although quite common and quite strong in some people, can be overcome by preparing a speech thoroughly and practicing positive thinking and relaxation. Learning how to give a speech is a valuable skill, one that you most likely will find much opportunity to use in the future.

The nature of a speech, whether formal or informal, is usually determined by the situation or context in which it is presented. **Formal speeches** usually call for a greater degree of preparation, might require special attire such as a suit or dress, and are often presented to larger groups who attend specifically to hear the presentation. A formal speech situation might exist when presenting an assigned speech to classmates, giving a presentation to a community group or organization, or presenting a speech at an awards ceremony. **Informal speech** situations are more casual and might include telling a story among friends, giving a pep talk to your team at halftime, or presenting a toast at the dinner table.

4.16 Types of Speeches

The following are the three main types of speeches:

- **Impromptu speech**. This is a speech given without any advance preparation. For example, if you were surprised by a gift or an award, you might be called upon to give a brief speech that was not written or rehearsed.
- **Memorized speech**. This is a speech that has been written out and memorized word for word. Your teacher may ask you to prepare a memorized speech on a topic you are studying at school.
- **Extemporaneous speech**. This is a speech in which the speaker refers to notes occasionally. Most professional speakers prefer to deliver extemporaneous speeches because they combine the liveliness of an impromptu speech with the careful preparation of a memorized or manuscript speech. While the speaker does not plan what he or she will say word for word, the speaker does create an overall plan for the speech, records important points on cards, and rehearses until she or he is comfortable with the material. You might give an extemporaneous speech at a city council meeting about funding for your school.

Giving a Speech. For practice working on and presenting speeches, see the Speaking and Listening activities on pages 305, 613, and 727.

4.17 Steps In Preparing an Extemporaneous Speech

1. **Choose a topic for your speech**. Consider the audience, occasion, and your own strengths and weaknesses as a speaker when choosing a topic.
2. **Do prewriting to identify what you know or think about the topic**. As you write, think about different ways to approach the topic.
3. Do **research on the topic**. Use a variety of source materials, including newspapers, magazines, books, interviews, Internet sources, and personal experience.
4. **Determine your specific purpose in speaking about your topic**. What are you trying to accomplish in speaking to your audience? Are you trying to demonstrate something to them? Compare and contrast two things or ideas? Strengthen their commitment to something? Spur them to take action?
5. **Organize your material into three to five main points**. Use a clear, logical, and interesting organizational strategy that is suited to your specific purpose, the audience, and the occasion. Be sure each point flows logically and smoothly from the one that comes before it. Include transitions between main points, and between the introduction, body, and conclusion of the speech.
6. **Create visual aids**. Some material is too difficult to present orally and is best presented visually. Visual aids should be neat, attractive, visible from a distance, and relevant to your speech. For more information, see the Language Arts Survey 6.11, "Displaying Effective Visual Information."
7. **Prepare note cards**. Notecards should be no larger than 4 x 6 inches and should contain as much information as you need to present your speech, but not so much that you are tempted to read from the cards. Write clearly and legibly so you can read your notes at a distance.
8. **Rehearse with your note cards**. Never attempt to speak at length on a subject without practicing what you will say. If possible, practice a few times in front of a live audience. Otherwise, use a mirror or recording device. Rehearse until you feel comfortable with the material and can present the speech with minimal use of notecards. Be sure to rehearse with visual aids if you are using them.
9. **Deliver your speech**.

4.18 Guidelines for Giving a Speech

A speech should always include a beginning, a middle, and an end. The beginning, or introduction, of your speech should spark the audience's interest, present your central idea, and briefly preview your main points. The middle, or body, of your speech should expand upon each of your main points in order to support the central idea. The end, or conclusion, of your speech should be memorable and should give your audience a sense of completion.

TIPS FOR SUCCESSFUL PUBLIC SPEAKING

- **Be sincere and enthusiastic**. Feel what you are speaking about. Apathy is infectious and will quickly spread to your audience.
- **Maintain good but relaxed posture**. Don't slouch or lean. It's fine to move around a bit; it releases normal nervous tension. Keep your hands free to gesture naturally instead of holding on to notecards, props, or the podium so much that you will "tie up" your hands.
- **Speak slowly**. Oral communication is more difficult than written language and visual images for audiences to process and understand. Practice pausing. Don't be afraid of silence. Focus on communicating with the audience. By looking for feedback from the audience, you will be able to pace yourself appropriately.
- **Maintain genuine eye contact**. Treat the audience as individuals, not as a mass of people. Look at individual faces.
- **Speak in a genuine, relaxed, conversational tone**. Don't act or stiffen up. Just be yourself.
- **Communicate**. Focus on conveying your message, not "getting through" the speech. Focus on communicating with the audience, not speaking at or to it.
- **Use strategic pauses**. Pause briefly before proceeding to the next major point, before

SPEAKING AND LISTENING RESOURCE

Oral Interpretation. For an activity to provide students experience with oral interpretation of poetry see pages 26, 325, and 329.

direct quotations, and to allow important or more complex bits of information to sink in.

- **Remain confident and composed**. Remember that listeners are generally "for you" while you are speaking, and signs of nervousness are usually undetectable. To overcome initial nervousness, take two or three deep breaths as you are stepping up to speak.

4.19 Oral Interpretation

Oral interpretation is the process of presenting a dramatic reading of a literary work or group of works. The presentation should be sufficiently dramatic to convey to the audience a sense of the particular qualities of the work. Here are the steps you need to follow to prepare and present an oral interpretation:

1. **Choose a cutting.** The cutting may be a single piece; a selection from a single piece; or several short, related pieces on a single topic or theme.
2. **Write the introduction and any necessary transitions.** The introduction should mention the name of each piece, the author, and, if appropriate, the translator. It should also present the overall topic or theme of the interpretation. Transitions should introduce and connect the parts of the interpretation.
3. **Rehearse, using appropriate variations in volume, pitch, pace, stress, tone, gestures, facial expressions, and body language.** If your cutting contains different voices (a narrator's voice and characters' voices, for example), distinguish them. Try to make your verbal and nonverbal expression mirror what the piece is saying. However, avoid movement—that's for drama. Practice in front of an audience or mirror or use a video camera or tape recorder.
4. **Present your oral interpretation.** Before actually presenting your interpretation, relax and adopt a confident attitude. If you begin to feel stage fright, try to concentrate on the work you are presenting and the audience, not on yourself.

Interpreting Poetry. Here are some additional considerations as you prepare to interpret a poem. The way you prepare your interpretation of a poem will depend on whether the poem you have chosen is a lyric poem, a narrative poem, or a dramatic poem.

- A **lyric poem** has a single speaker who reports his or her own emotions.
- A **narrative poem** tells a story. Usually a narrative poem has lines belonging to narrator, or person who is telling the story. The narrator may or may not take part in the action.
- A **dramatic poem** contains characters who speak. A dramatic poem may be a lyric, in which characters simply report emotions, or a narrative, which tells a story. A dramatic monologue presents a single speaker at a moment of crisis or self-revelation and may be either lyric or narrative.

Before attempting to dramatize any poem, read through the poem carefully several times. Make sure that you understand it well. To check your understanding, try to paraphrase the poem, or restate its ideas, line by line, in your own words.

Analyzing the Speaker of a Lyric Poem. When dramatizing a lyric or dramatic poem, think about the speaker of the poem. Ask yourself:

- Who is the speaker?
- How old is the speaker?
- Is the speaker male or female?
- What is the situation in which the speaker finds himself or herself?
- What does the speaker think about his or her situation?
- What values, opinions, beliefs, wishes, or needs does the speaker have?
- Is the speaker fully aware of the implications of what he or she is saying, or does the reader know more than the speaker?

Try to form a clear image of the speaker in your mind. Think about how such a person might sound, feeling and thinking as he or she does.

Analyzing the Narrator and Characters of a Narrative or Dramatic Poem. When analyzing a narrative or dramatic poem, ask about the narrator and the characters the same questions that you would ask about the speaker of a lyric poem. How are the narrator and the characters related to one another? In what ways are they different? Is there anything that the narrator understands that one or more of the characters do not?

List the narrator and each of the characters in the poem. After each, list his or her characteristics. Then try to form a clear image of each in your mind. Again, think about how each might sound, feeling and thinking as he or she does. If the poem is narrative, think of how each character reacts to the events in the story that the poem tells.

Using Verbal and Nonverbal Communication to Interpret the Poem. After analyzing the speaker (in a lyric poem) or the narrator and characters (in a narrative or dramatic poem), make a copy of the poem and mark it to show

- the different voices you will use when reading
- the emotions that you will express
- places to increase or decrease your pace
- places to raise or lower your volume
- gestures and facial expressions to use to communicate emotions

Memorizing a Poem. To memorize a poem, work line by line. Look at one line. Look away and repeat it. Then check to see that you got it right. Once you get that line right, add a second line. Look away and repeat both lines. Then check them. Continue in this manner until the entire poem is memorized. You may wish to have someone else look at a copy of the poem while you recite it out loud. This second person can prompt you when you forget a line. Memorize the poem thoroughly before you begin working on the qualities of your reading. If you have not thoroughly memorized the lines, you will not be able to concentrate on how you sound.

4.20 Telling a Story

A story or narrative is a series of events linked together in some meaningful fashion. We use narratives constantly in our daily lives: to make a journal entry, to tell a joke, to report a news story, to recount an historical event, to record a laboratory experiment, and so on. When creating a narrative, consider all of the following elements:

- **Decide on your purpose**. Every story has a point or purpose. It may be simply to entertain or to share a personal experience, but it may have a moral or lesson. Your purpose in telling a story will shape many other parts of the narrative, so it is important to know your purpose before you construct your narrative.
- **Select a focus**. The focus for your narrative will depend largely on your purpose in telling it. For example, if you were telling the story of Abraham Lincoln's life, and your purpose was to show how someone could rise from humble roots to a position of greatness, you would probably choose a broad focus for the story. You might begin with Lincoln's birth in a Kentucky log cabin and end with his eventual rise to the position of President of the United States and his many accomplishments in office. If your purpose was to show that perseverance is an important virtue, you might choose a narrower focus. Your story could ignore Lincoln's early life and instead focus on his long political career and his many defeats on the way to the presidency.
- **Choose your point of view**. The storyteller or narrator determines the point of view from which the story will be told. You can choose to speak in the first person, either as a direct participant in the events or as an observer (real or imagined) who witnessed the events first hand. You can also use the third person voice to achieve greater objectivity. Once again, your purpose in telling the story may affect your decision about what point of view you choose.
- **Determine sequence of events**. The sequence of events refers to the order in which they are presented. Although it might seem obvious that stories should "begin at the beginning," this is not always the best approach. Some narratives begin with the turning point of the story to create a sense of drama and capture the listener's interest. Others begin at the end of the story and present the events leading up to this point in hindsight. Wherever you choose to begin the story, your narrative should present events in a logical fashion and establish a clear sense of direction for your listeners.
- **Determine duration of events**. Duration refers to how long something lasts. Everyone has experienced an event that seemed to last for hours, when in reality it only took minutes to

Telling a Story. Storytelling activities are found in the Speaking and Listening activities on pages 186 and 242.

occur. A good storyteller can likewise manipulate the duration of events in order to affect the way listeners experience them.

- **Select details carefully**. Make them consistent with your focus and make sure they are necessary to your purpose. A well-constructed story should flow smoothly, and should not get bogged down by irrelevant or unnecessary detail. Details can also establish the tone and style of the story and affect how listeners react to the events being described.
- **Choose characters**. All stories include characters, who need to be developed so that they become real for listeners. Try to provide your listeners with vivid, concrete descriptions of the mental and physical qualities of important characters in the story. Remember that listeners need to understand and relate to the characters in order to appreciate their behavior.
- **Create dialogue**. Although it is possible to tell a story in which the characters do not speak directly, conversation and dialogue help to add life to a story. As with detail, dialogue should be used carefully. It is important that dialogue sound authentic, relate to the main action of the story, and advance the narrative. When telling a story, you might choose to enact the characters by creating an individual voice for each one.

Participating in a Debate. For practice debating see Integrating the Language Arts activities on pages 46 and 215.

4.21 Participating in a Debate

A **debate** is a contest in which two people or groups of people defend opposite sides of a proposition in an attempt to convince a judge or audience to agree with their views. **Propositions** are statements of fact, value, or policy that usually begin with the word "resolved." The following are examples of typical propositions for debate:

RESOLVED	That lie detector tests are inaccurate. (proposition of fact)
RESOLVED	That imagination is more important than knowledge. (proposition of value
RESOLVED	That Congress should prohibit the sale of handguns to private citizens. (proposition of policy)

The two sides in a debate are usually called the affirmative and the negative. The **affirmative** takes the "pro" side of the debate and argues in favor of the proposition, while the **negative** takes the "con" side and argues against the proposition. Using a single proposition to focus the debate ensures that the two sides argue or clash over a common topic. This allows the participants in the debate to develop their logic and ability to argue their positions persuasively.

Sometimes you may find that you are defending a side of a proposition that you do not personally agree with. For example, you may be asked to defend gun control in class even though you believe that the Second Amendment to the Constitution prohibits regulations on the sale of guns. Although some people may find this distasteful, there is good reason to play the "devil's advocate." First, defending a position you do not believe in will allow you to better understand the position of those who disagree with you. Although you may not change your stance, you may come to appreciate why others see the issue differently. Second, in a society based on the free and open exchange of ideas, debate is a fundamental method for arriving at just and reasonable decisions. Every idea deserves consideration, even if it is ultimately rejected.

Typically, both sides in a debate are allowed an equal amount of time to prepare for the debate and to state their case for or against the proposition. To ensure fairness, the affirmative and negative teams take turns presenting speeches. Typically there are two types of speeches: **constructive speeches** in which each side states its case for or against the proposition, and **rebuttal speeches** in which each side refutes or attacks its opponent's arguments, while defending its own case. Sometimes debaters are allowed to cross-examine or ask questions of their opponents during the debate. A typical debate might be organized as follows:

AFFIRMATIVE CONSTRUCTIVE	7 minutes
Cross-Examination by Negative	2 minutes
Negative Constructive	7 minutes
Cross-Examination by Affirmative	2 minutes
Affirmative Rebuttal	3 minutes
Negative Rebuttal	5 minutes
Affirmative Rebuttal	2 minutes

In addition, each side might be granted 4 or 5 minutes of preparation time during the debate to prepare its upcoming speeches. Preparation time may only be used between speeches.

Once the debate is finished, the audience or judge is asked to consider the arguments that have been made and to vote for which side made the more persuasive case. Ideally, judges or audience members will try to be objective and make their decision based not on their personal views of the issue but rather based on the arguments made by the debaters in the contest.

SUGGESTIONS FOR PARTICIPATING IN A DEBATE

- **Be prepared.** In a debate, it will never be possible to anticipate all the arguments your opponent might make. However, by conducting careful and through research on both sides of the issue, you should be able to prepare for the most likely arguments you will encounter. You can prepare briefs or notes on particular issues in advance of the debate to save yourself preparation time during the debate.
- **Be organized.** Because a debate involves several speeches that concern the same basic arguments or issues, it is important that you remain organized during the debate. When attacking or refuting an opponent's argument, or when advancing or defending your own argument, be sure to follow a logical organizational pattern to avoid confusing the audience or the other team.
- **Take notes** by turning a long sheet of paper sideways. Draw one column for each speaker, taking notes on each speech going down one column, and recording notes about a particular argument or issue across the page as it is discussed in each successive speech.
- **Be audience-centered.** In the argument with your opponent it is easy to forget the goal of the debate: to persuade your audience that your case is correct.
- **Prepare in advance** for the most likely arguments your opponents will raise. Use time sparingly to organize your materials and think of responses to unanticipated arguments. Save time for the end of the debate, during rebuttal speeches, when it will be more valuable.

4.22 Preparing a Multimedia Presentation

Whether you use a simple overhead projector and transparencies or a PowerPoint presentation that involves graphics, video, and sound, multimedia technology can add an important visual element to a presentation. Consider the following guidelines to create a multimedia presentation:

- **Ensure that audio-visual elements enhance understanding**. The multimedia elements should add to the verbal elements, not distract from them. Be sure the content of the presentation is understandable, and that the amount of information—both verbal and visual—will not overwhelm audience members.
- **Make sure the presentation is clearly audible and visible**. Video clips or graphics may appear blurry on a projection screen, or may not be visible to audience members in the back or on the sides of the room. Audio clips may sound muffled or may echo in a larger room or a room with different acoustics. When creating a multimedia presentation, be sure the presentation can be easily and heard from all parts of the room.
- **Become familiar with the equipment**. Well before the presentation, be sure you know how to operate the equipment you will need, that you know how to troubleshoot if the equipment malfunctions, and that the equipment you will use during the presentation is the same as that which you practiced with.
- **Be sure the room can accommodate your needs**. Once you know where you will make your presentation, be sure the necessary electrical outlets and extension cords are available, that lights can be dimmed or turned off as needed, that the room can accommodate the equipment you will use, etc.
- **Rehearse with the equipment**. Make sure that you can operate the equipment while speaking at the same time. Be sure that the multimedia elements are coordinated with other parts of your presentation. If you will need to turn the lights off in the room, make sure you can operate the equipment in the dark and can still see your notecards.

PREPARING A MULTIMEDIA PRESENTATION. Students are asked to create a multimedia presentation in the Study and Research activity on page 583 and Speaking and Listening activity on page 845.

INTERNET RESOURCES

You can now access **Merriam-Webster Online** at http://www.m-w.com/. Webster's online site in as excellent reference for information about the English language, including basic word definitions, pronunciation, etymology, spelling, and usage. It also includes a Word of the Day feature and transcripts of their *Word for the Wise* radio program.

The **American Library Association** homepage can be accessed at http://www.ala.org/. This site also hosts the online version of *American Libraries: The Magazine of the American Library Association,* and the digital counterpart of the American Library Association's *Booklist* magazine. For more than 90 years, *Booklist* has provided reviews of the latest books and (more recently) electronic media.

School Library Journal Online, the web companion to *School Library Journal,* one of the top print resources for librarians who work with children and young adults, is available at http://www.slj.com/.

Making Decisions and Solving Problems. Students are asked to make decisions and solve problems in the Critical Thinking activity on page 549 and Speaking and Listening activity on page 882.

STUDY AND RESEARCH Resource

THINKING SKILLS

Everyone thinks, but not everyone realizes that thinking—like hitting a baseball or playing the piano—is a skill that you can improve by learning and practicing. This section gives you some tips that can greatly improve your ability to make decisions, to solve problems, and to learn and think critically.

5.1 Making Decisions and Solving Problems

Making Decisions. When you have a decision to make, the best approach is to weigh the alternatives available to you. You can do this by making a **criteria analysis chart**. To make such a chart, list the results that you want to achieve down the left side of the chart. List your choices across the top of the chart. Then assign points from 1 to 5 to each choice, with 1 being the lowest and 5 being the highest. Add up the points for each choice to see which one is best.

CRITERIA ANALYSIS CHART

Purchase of Portable Radio	Brand A	Brand B
1. Low cost	2	3
2. Good warranty	2	1
3. Attractive design	3	1
4. Many features	2	3
total	**9**	**8**

When making a decision, you often must weigh several factors. You can compare your options by making a **pros and cons** chart on paper. First make a list of all your options. For each option list the reasons for choosing it (the pros) and the reasons for not choosing it (the cons). Then compare the lists.

PROS AND CONS

Painting Yearbook Illustration or Drawing It in Pencil

	Painting	Drawing in Pencil
Pros	colorful	easier less expensive
Cons	more expensive more difficult	not colorful

Solving Problems. There are many ways to solve problems. To solve a complex problem, you will probably need to use more than one strategy. Here are two approaches you can try:

Trial and error. Sometimes when you have to solve a problem, you just make a guess and see if it works. In a **trial-and-error approach**, you try one possible solution and if it doesn't work you try another. If you don't know how to solve a particular math problem, you could guess the answer, plug it back into the problem, and then revise your answer as necessary.

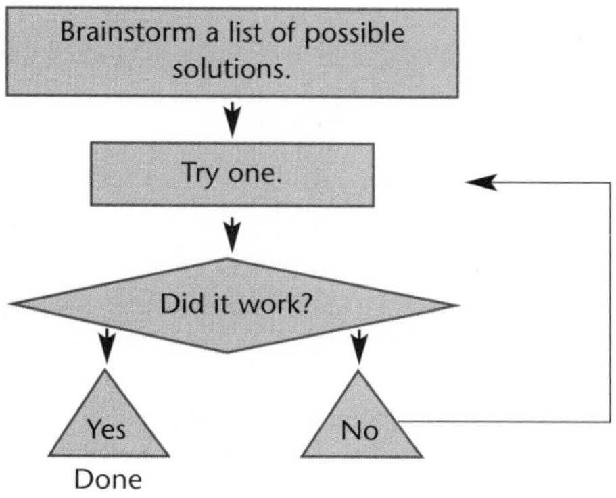

Brainstorm a list of possible solutions.

Try one.

Did it work?

Yes — Done

No — (return to "Try one.")

Divide and conquer. Another strategy for problem solving is to divide the problem into parts and then solve each part one at a time in a logical sequence. Here is an example:

PROBLEM

A friend is coming to stay in your house for a few days and you need to prepare a room for him.

SOLUTION

Break the job down into small, manageable goals:

STRATEGY

(1) Move desk and computer from small downstairs room.
(2) Remove storage boxes from closet and put in basement.
(3) Clean the room.
(4) Put cot in room and make bed.

5.2 Distinguishing Fact from Opinion

What is the difference between the following statements?

The language with the greatest number of speakers, over nine hundred million, is Mandarin Chinese.

Mandarin Chinese is the greatest language in the world.

The first statement expresses a **fact**. You can prove this fact by looking in a reference book. The second statement expresses an **opinion**. This statement can be supported but not proved.

A fact is a statement that, at least in principle, could be proved by direct observation. Every statement of fact is either true or false. The following statement is an example of a fact:

Edgar Allan Poe wrote "The Pit and the Pendulum." (This statement can be proved by getting a published copy of the story to see who the author is.)

An opinion is a statement that expresses not a fact about the world but rather an attitude or desire. Three common types of opinions are value statements, policy statements, and certain types of predictions.

A **value statement** expresses an attitude toward something. Such statements often include judgment words such as the following:

attractive	awesome	beautiful
cheap	dishonest	excellent
good	honest	junk
kind	mean	nice
petty	treasure	ugly
unattractive	valuable	wonderful
worthless	worthwhile	

Ancient Greece produced some beautiful and inspiring myths.
Those violent "action films" are just awful.

A **policy statement** tells not what is but what someone believes should be. Such statements usually include words such as *should, should not, ought to, ought not to, must,* or *must not*. Examples of policy statements include the following:

The president should be reelected.
You must not play your radio during study hall.

Closely related to policy statements are **requests** and **commands**:

Reelect the president.
Do not play your radio during study hall.

A **prediction** makes a statement about the future. Because the future is unpredictable, most predictions can be considered opinions:

People will live longer in the future.
Tomorrow will be partly cloudy.

Evaluating Facts and Opinions. When evaluating a fact, ask yourself whether it can be proved

Distinguishing Fact from Opinion. Encourage students to distinguish fact from opinion in About the Author sections. Students might make a column listing facts and another column listing opinions. Then ask students to assess the section as being objective or subjective in its approach. Students will generally find that there are more facts than opinions in the About the Author sections.

Avoiding False Arguments and Propaganda. Students are asked to avoid false arguments and propaganda in the Critical Thinking activities on pages 295 and 510.

through direct observation or by checking a reliable source such as a reference work or an unbiased expert. An opinion is as good as the facts that support it. The opinion that Mandarin Chinese is the greatest language in the world is supported by such facts as the number of speakers that it has. However, others might argue that English is the greater language because it is spoken more widely around the globe. Of course, no list of facts would conclusively prove or disprove the opinion.

When you write and speak, express opinions sparingly. Usually, you can make a stronger case by substituting related facts for opinions. For example, instead of saying, "This was a wonderful day," you could say something like, "Today the sun was shining, it was 74 degrees outside, and I got an *A* on my math test. That's what made it a great day." When you express an opinion, especially in writing, include facts to back up or support that opinion.

When reading or listening, be critical about the statements that you encounter. Ask yourself, "Is this a fact or an opinion?" If it is a statement of fact, consider whether it can be proved or seems likely. If it is an opinion, consider whether it is supported by facts.

5.3 Avoiding False Arguments and Propaganda

Another very important thinking skill is learning to use good logic. Life is a process of trying to learn what is true and then to live according to what you believe to be true. Not only do you need good facts, but you also need to know how to put those facts together to come up with the right conclusions. Learning how to think clearly will enable you to avoid errors in logic and to arrive at true conclusions. It will also help you to recognize the faulty thinking of others (especially advertisers) who might be trying to persuade you of something. The intentional use of false arguments to persuade others is called **propaganda**. Here are some of the many faulty arguments of which you should be aware:

Glittering Generalities and "Spin." Glittering generalities are statements given to make something sound more appealing. Such statements can be hard to prove, as they appeal to the emotions.

EXAMPLE

These trading cards are the best ever in this limited-time collection!

ANALYSIS

Nothing in this statement tells the listener why the trading cards are the best ever. Adding "limited-time collection" to the statement vaguely implies that the trading cards will be available for only a short while, and that the listener should buy them quickly before they are unavailable.

Spin is a technique used to slant public perception of the news. Public relations firms and advertisers use this technique to create a favorable perception of a product or organization. Unlike more obvious forms of advertising, spin is hard to recognize because it can be invisible. It is important to know how to recognize such manipulative and misleading statements.

EXAMPLE

The accident was a minor incident because only 25 people were injured.

ANALYSIS

The fact is that 25 people were injured. This does not make it a minor incident; someone is merely interpreting the accident as minor.

Stereotypes. An overgeneralization about a group of people is known as a **stereotype**. Stereotypes are one of the most dangerous of all overgeneralizations. Remember that the differences among people within a single race or ethnic background are greater than the average differences between races or ethnic groups as a whole. Stereotyping is always based on lack of knowledge or experience. It is the basis of prejudice and is unacceptable in a civilized society.

Unsound Opinions. A fact is a statement that can be proved. An opinion is a statement that cannot be proved. An opinion is someone's personal idea of what is right and may or may not be true. A sound opinion is one that can be supported by facts. An **unsound opinion** is one that cannot be supported by facts. Always be sure that you make a clear distinction between facts and opinions and that you can back up your opinions with facts.

FACT

Miss Rivers won this year's award for excellence in teaching.

OPINION

Miss Rivers is the best teacher at Jordan High School.

ANALYSIS

The statement that "Miss Rivers is the best teacher at Jordan High School" is someone's personal feeling about her. However, it is probably a sound opinion because it is backed up by the fact that she received the award for excellence in teaching.

Circular Reasoning. **Circular reasoning** is the error of trying to support an opinion by restating it in different words. You can avoid circular reasoning by always backing up your opinions with facts.

EXAMPLE

That adventure book was exciting because it was full of action.

ANALYSIS

The "reason" the speaker gives for saying that the book was exciting is really just another way of saying it was exciting. He or she should mention some specific examples to show what makes the story exciting.

Loaded Words. In trying to argue for or against something, people will often use **loaded words**, or words that stir up strong feelings, whether positive or negative. Be careful not to let your feelings interfere with your understanding of the facts.

EXAMPLE

Congressman Philbert is a lazy, good-for-nothing imbecile.

ANALYSIS

This statement, an emotional attack on the congressman, uses loaded words that will stir up feelings against him. It is not a reasonable evaluation of his policies or actions in office.

Bandwagon Appeal. **Bandwagon appeal** plays to your desire to be part of the crowd—to be like everyone else and to do what everyone else is doing. Beware of advertisements or arguments that try to get you to think or act like everyone else. Just because "everybody" believes or does something does not make it good or right for you.

EXAMPLE

Those who want to be cool wear Star jeans.

ANALYSIS

This statement suggests that you aren't really part of the "in" crowd unless you wear this brand of jeans. It does not prove, or even say, anything about the quality of the clothing.

5.4 Classifying

One of the many higher-level thinking skills you can develop is the ability to classify. To **classify** is to put into classes or categories. Items in the same category should share one or more characteristics. For example, whales are classified by their method of eating as baleen or toothed whales. The key step in classifying is choosing categories that fit your purpose. Make sure you clearly define your categories.

5.5 Generalizing

To **generalize** is to make a broad statement based on one or more particular observations. For example, suppose that you observe that several cats like to stare through windows. You might generalize, based on this discovery, that "cats like to stare through windows." Such generalizations are also called **inferences**. People have learned most of what they know about the world by making generalizations based on their experiences.

Generalizing is therefore an extremely important thinking tool. Unfortunately, it is not a perfect one. Generalizations can be proved false by only one exception. Since generalizations can be proved false by a new experience, avoid making generalizations based on too little evidence. Keep an open mind and be willing to revise your ideas about the world.

CLASSIFYING. Students are asked to use classifying skills in the Critical Thinking activity on page 305 and the Collaborative Learning & Critical Thinking activity on page 523.

ANALYZING AND SYNTHESIZING. The Analyze and Synthesize question pairs in Inquire, Investigate, and Imagine following each selection provide opportunities for students to develop their analyzing and synthesizing skills.

5.6 Making Inferences, Predictions, and Hypotheses

From careful observation, it is possible to make generalizations, or **inferences**, about the world around us. From there it is possible to **predict** what will happen and to form hypotheses. A **hypothesis** is an educated guess about a cause or an effect. A prediction based on a theory is a hypothesis. A possible explanation for an observed event is also a hypothesis. A hypothesis always needs to be tested against experience. You can test hypotheses the following ways:

- Conduct actual experiments to see if your prediction will occur.
- Examine many relevant examples.
- Conduct a "thought experiment" by asking "What if" questions. (See 2.15, "Imagining: Asking *What If* Questions.")

Notice that a hypothesis can be disproved by only one exception. However, a hypothesis cannot be proved merely by gathering examples. Theories and hypotheses can change if a discovery shows them to be inadequate.

5.7 Deductive versus Inductive Reasoning

Deduction and induction are two types of logical reasoning. **Deductive reasoning** starts with a generalization to make a statement or statements about something specific. **Inductive reasoning** examines specific facts or instances to make a generalization.

DEDUCTIVE

All whales live in the sea. **(general)**
The beluga whale must live in the sea. **(specific)**

All students have signed the school policy statement. **(general)**
Tom is a student at the school. Therefore, he has signed the policy statement. **(specific)**

INDUCTIVE

The blue whale, beluga, and orca live in the sea. **(specific)**
Therefore, all whales live in the sea. **(general)**

More than 100 students have signed the school policy statement. **(specific)**
Therefore, all students have signed the policy statement. **(general)**

Note that with inductive reasoning, only one specific example is needed to prove the generalization false. See the Language Arts Survey 5.5, "Generalizing."

5.8 Estimating and Quantifying

To support an argument, you need to provide facts, and often facts are strengthened by numbers or quantities. If you claim, for instance, that too many people are without health insurance, you should **quantify** your claim by stating how many. The numbers you need may be available in reference works. If not, you might be able to **estimate**, or find the approximate quantity. Sometimes you will have only enough knowledge to estimate a range within which the actual number actually falls. If you need to estimate, always make clear that you are doing so.

QUANTIFYING

The science fair had 314 registered participants.

ESTIMATING

The science fair was attended by about 300 students and their parents.

5.9 Analyzing and Synthesizing

When you **analyze** something, you break it down into parts and then think about how the parts are related to each other and to the whole. For example, you might analyze a painting by describing its composition, shapes, lines, colors, and subject. You might analyze a short story by describing its conflict, plot, characters, setting, and theme. You might analyze a movie by describing its acting, directing, writing, settings, and costumes.

When you **synthesize** something, you bring everything that you were considering together into a whole.

5.10 Comparing and Contrasting

Comparing and contrasting are closely related processes. When you **compare** one thing to another, you describe similarities between the two things. When you **contrast** two things, you describe their differences.

To compare and contrast, begin by listing the features of each subject. Then go down both lists and check whether each feature is shared or not. You can also show similarities and differences in a Venn diagram. For more information, see the Language Arts Survey 2.16, "Completing Venn Diagrams" and 2.27, "Choosing a Method of Organization: Comparison-and-Contrast Order."

5.11 Evaluating

When you evaluate, you make a judgment about something. You may be asked to compare two things to determine which is more valuable or effective. Evaluate questions use such words as *evaluate, judge, justify, critique, determine whether, decide the effectiveness of,* and *appraise.*

> Determine whether Hawthorne believably portrays Beatrice in "Rappaccini's Daughter," using evidence from the text to support your response.

5.12 Extending

When you extend your knowledge, you connect one experience to another. In the study of literature, you extend your knowledge by making connections between two pieces of literature, between the literary work and your own experience, or between a literary work and a cultural or current event. Extend questions use such words as *extend your knowledge, connect, relate,* and *apply.*

> In popular culture and throughout history, people have been accused of being poisonous, like Dr. Rappaccini. Name examples of such people and the ways they have influenced the world around them. Then name people who have countered them.

5.13 Perspective, Empathy, and Self-Understanding

When you are asked to use perspective, empathy, and self-understanding to answer a question, you are exercising an important ability to connect the experience of one person or group to your own. Such thinking allows you to see multiple perspectives, generate alternative viewpoints, and understand another person's feelings and worldview. These questions also allow you to understand your own perspective.

> Why do you think Susan B. Anthony was willing to be arrested for her convictions? How would you react if you lost your rights as a citizen? Would you be willing to risk arrest to fight for your rights, as Susan B. Anthony did? Why, or why not?

STUDY SKILLS

5.14 Developing Good Study Habits

Success in a future career depends largely on success in school. No matter what your experience in school so far, you can improve your performance enormously by developing good study habits. Doing so will make learning easier and more enjoyable.

Finding a place to work. Homework is best done in a special study area. Follow these guidelines for picking an appropriate place to study:

- Choose a quiet location, away from distractions such as conversation, television, or loud music.
- Choose a place that is well lit and comfortable. Adequate lighting will help you to avoid eyestrain and headaches.
- Choose a study area that is available at regular times. Set aside a specific time each day for study.
- Have all the tools that you will need, such as paper, pencils, textbooks, handouts, and reference works, ready and at hand.

Making a study plan. Many of your assignments will be due on the following day. Others will be long-term projects. At the end of each school day, make a habit of looking over your assignment notebook. Decide what tasks you need to complete for the following day. Break longer assignments down into specific steps that need to be completed by specific times. Record all of these assignments on a calendar or study plan.

5.15 Keeping an Assignment Notebook

Keeping track of assignments in your head can be dangerous because of the possibility of forgetting important details. Instead, write all your

Evaluating and Extending. The Evaluate and Extend question pairs in Inquire, Investigate, and Imagine following each selection ask students to make judgements about what they have read and to make connections between the selection and other literature, personal experiences, or cultural events.

Developing Good Study Habits. Go over the tips in this section at the beginning of every semester with students.

Perspective and Empathy. The Perspective and Empathy question pairs in Inquire, Investigate, and Imagine help students to develop insight, self-knowledge, and knowledge of others.

assignments down in an assignment notebook. For each assignment, record:

- The name of the subject
- Details of the assignment, including what, precisely, you need to do
- The date of the assignment
- The date when the assignment is due

5.16 Understanding the Assignment

Understanding an assignment depends on your ability to follow directions.

Following Spoken Directions. Often teachers give assignments orally. When listening to spoken assignments,

- Listen carefully. Write down the directions as you hear them.
- Notice what steps are involved in the assignment. Also notice the order of these steps.
- Listen for the key word in each step. A key word is one that tells you what to do. Examples are read, write, organize, and memorize.
- If you do not understand the directions, ask your teacher to explain them.

Following Written Directions. Directions for tests usually are written down. Assignment directions also sometimes appear in written form on the board, overhead transparencies, or handouts. When reading written directions,

- Read all the directions completely before you begin the assignment.
- Ask questions to clarify any points not covered in the directions.
- Divide the assignment into steps. Put these steps in a logical order.
- Decide what materials you will need, and assemble them before you begin.
- Reread each step before you actually do it.

5.17 Taking Notes, Summarizing, and Outlining Information

When **taking notes** in class or while conducting your own research, you may find it helpful to use a **rough outline**, or modified outline, form. Write main ideas, capitalizing the first letter of the first word and all proper nouns and proper adjectives. Beneath the main ideas, write related subordinate ideas, preceded by dashes.

Major Cultures in N. Amer., 1492
–Eastern woodland (incl. Iroquois & Algonquians)
–Southeastern (incl. Cherokee & Chicasaw)
–Plains (incl. Dakota, Pawnee, & Kiowa)
–Southwestern (incl. Navajo, Hopi, & Apache)
–Great Basin (incl. Ute & Paiute)
–Plateau (incl. Nez Perce & Yakima)
–Northwestern (incl. Chinook & Yurok)
–California (incl. Shasta, Pomo, & Chumash)

Origins
–Came to Amer. by land bridge across Bering Strait
– ~ 35,000 bc
–May have followed herds, mammoths, musk oxen, etc.

To review the material, you might find it helpful to read over your notes and outline, and then to **summarize** what you have learned. Writing a summary of the material is more powerful than thinking through your summary or even saying it out loud. The act of writing reinforces your memory of what you have learned.

RESEARCH SKILLS

Learning is a lifelong process, one that extends far beyond school. Both in school and on your own, it is important to remember that your learning and growth are up to you. One good way to become an independent lifelong learner is to master research skills. Research is the process of gathering ideas and information. One of the best resources for research is the library.

5.18 How Library Materials Are Organized

Each book in a library is assigned a unique number, called a **call number.** The call number is printed on the **spine** (edge) of each book. The

Research Skills. For practice applying library research skills, see the Study and Research activities found in the Skill Builders section following each selection.

numbers serve to classify books as well as to help the library keep track of them.

Libraries commonly use one of two systems for classifying books. Most school and public libraries use the **Dewey Decimal System.** Most college libraries use the **Library of Congress Classification System** (known as the LC system).

5.19 How to Locate Library Materials

If you know the call number of a book or the subject classification number you want, you can usually go to the bookshelves, or stacks, to obtain the book. Use the signs at the ends of the rows to locate the section you need. Then find the

THE LIBRARY OF CONGRESS SYSTEM

Call Letters	Subjects
A	Reference and General Works
B–BJ	Philosophy, Psychology
BK–BX	Religion
C–DF	History
G	Geography, Autobiography, Recreation
H	Social Sciences
J	Political Science
K	Law
L	Education
M	Music
N	Fine Arts
P	Language, Literature
Q	Science, Mathematics
R	Medicine
S	Agriculture
T	Technology
U	Military Science
V	Naval Science
Z	Bibliography, Library Science

THE DEWEY DECIMAL SYSTEM

Call Numbers	Subjects
000–099	Reference and General Works
100–199	Philosophy, Psychology
200–299	Religion
300–399	Social Studies
400–499	Language
500–599	Science, Mathematics
600–699	Technology
700–799	Arts
800–899	Literature
900–999	History, Geography, Biography[1]

1. Biographies (920s) are arranged alphabetically by the name of the person whose life is treated in each biography.

STUDY AND RESEARCH RESOURCE

INTERNET RESOURCES

Let your fingers do the walking and visit the **Internet Public Library** at http://www.ipl.org/. The Internet Public Library is the first public library of the Internet. This site provides library services to the Internet community by finding, evaluating, selecting, organizing, describing, and creating quality information resources; teaches what librarians have to contribute in a digital environment; and promotes the importance of libraries.

THE DEWEY DECIMAL SYSTEM. Have students locate a book for each subject and write down its title and call number.

Computerized Catalogs. You might plan to have your school librarian visit your class to explain how to use the computerized catalog in your library. Then give students an assignment sheet and have them use the computerized catalog to list books based on criteria that you provide. For example, students could locate a novel by their favorite author, a book about a topic they are interested in, or a reference book such as a dictionary, thesaurus, or encyclopedia.

particular shelf that contains call numbers close to yours.

Library collections include many other types of publications besides books, such as magazines, newspapers, audio and video recordings, and government documents. Ask a librarian to tell you where to find the materials you need.

To find the call numbers of books that will help you with your research, use the library's catalog. The catalog lists all the books in the library (or a group of libraries if it is part of a larger system).

Computerized Catalogs. Many libraries today use computerized catalogs. Systems differ from library to library, but most involve using a computer terminal to search through the library's collection. You can usually search by author, title, subject, or key word. If your library has a computerized catalog, you will need to learn how to use your library's particular system. A librarian can help you to master the system. Here is a sample book entry screen from a computerized catalog.

Author	Wallace, David Rains, 1945-
Title	The Quetzal and the Macaw: The story of Costa Rica's National Parks
Publication info.	Sierra Club Books, 1992
No. of pages/size	xvi, 222p. : maps : 24 cm.
ISBN	ISBN 0-87156-585-4
Subjects	National Parks and reserves-Costa Rica-History
	Costa Rica. Servicio de Parques Nacionales-History
	Nature conservation-Costa Rica-History
Dewey call number	333.78

COMPUTERIZED CATALOG SEARCHES

Search By	Example	Hints
Author	gould, stephen j	Type last name first. Type as much of the name as you know.
Title	mismeasure of man	Omit articles such as *a, an,* or *the* at the beginning of titles.
Subject	intelligence tests; ability-testing	Use the list of subjects provided by the library.
Key words	darwin; intelligence; craniology	Use related topics if you can't find anything in your subject.

Card Catalogs. Like a computerized catalog, a card catalog contains basic information about each book in the library. In a card catalog the information is typed on paper cards, which are arranged alphabetically in drawers. For each book there is a title card, one author card for each author, and at least one subject card. All of these cards show the book's title, author, and call number, so you can search for a book by title, author, or subject. The following illustration shows a typical title card.

A TITLE CARD

333.78 The Quetzal and the Macaw : the story of
Costa Rica's national parks.
Wallace, David Rains, 1945–
The Quetzal and the Macaw : the story of
Costa Rica's national parks.—San
Francisco: Sierra Club Books, 1992
xvi, 222 p. : maps : 24 cm.
1. National parks and reserves—Costa Rica—
History. 2. Costa Rica. Servicio de
Parques nacionales—History. 3. Nature
conservation—Costa Rica—History. I. Title.
ISBN 0-394-57456-7

When you find the entries for the books you want, write down the call number of each book and then go to the shelves. If you cannot find a particular book you need in the catalog, ask the librarian if your library can request books from another library through an interlibrary loan.

Interlibrary Loans. Many libraries are part of larger library networks. In these libraries, the computerized catalog covers the collections of several libraries. If you want a book from a different library, you will need to request the book at the library's request desk or by using its computer. Ask your librarian to help you if you have questions. He or she will be able to tell you when the book will be shipped to your library.

5.20 Using Reference Works

Most libraries have an assortment of reference works in which knowledge is collected and organized so that you can find it easily. Usually, reference works cannot be checked out of the library.

5.21 Types of Dictionaries. You will find many types of dictionaries in the library reference section. The most common is a dictionary of the English language. Examples include the American Heritage Dictionary, Webster's New World Dictionary, and the multi-volume Oxford English Dictionary. Other word dictionaries focus on slang, abbreviations and acronyms, English/foreign language translation, and spelling. Biographical, historical, scientific, and world language dictionaries are also some of the works you will find in the reference section.

For more information on using a dictionary to look us specific words in English, see the Language Arts Survey 1.17, "Using a Dictionary."

5.22 Using a Thesaurus. A thesaurus is a reference book that groups synonyms, or words with similar meanings. Suppose that you are writing an essay and have a word that means almost but not quite what you want, or perhaps you find yourself using the same word over and over. A thesaurus can give you fresh and precise words to use. For example, if you look up the word *sing* in a thesaurus, you might find the following synonyms listed:

> **sing** (v.) carol, chant, croon, hum, vocalize, warble, yodel

5.23 Using Almanacs, Yearbooks, and Atlases. **Almanacs and yearbooks** are published each year. An almanac provides statistics and lists, often related to recent events. In an almanac you can find facts about current events, countries of the world, famous people, sports, entertainment, and many other subjects. An overview of the events of the year can be found in a yearbook.

Some of the more widely used almanacs and yearbooks are *The Guinness Book of World Records;* the *Information Please, Almanac, Atlas, and Yearbook;* the *World Almanac and Book of Facts;* and the *World Book Yearbook of Events.*

An **atlas** is a collection of maps and other geographical information. Some atlases show natural features such as mountains and rivers; others show political features such as countries and cities. If you need to locate a particular feature on a map in an atlas, refer to the gazetteer, an index that lists every item shown on the map.

Title Cards. Have students make a title card for a book they are interested in.

Using an Almanac. You might want to prepare a list of questions that students could find answers for by using an almanac. Have students work with a partner to find answers for the worksheet.

Using Reference Works. For activities using various reference works, see the Study and Research activities on pages 313 and 317.

Using the Internet. Internet research activities are found in the Study and Research & Media Literacy activities on pages 427 and 678.

Conducting an Internet Search. Students are encouraged to use the search tips in conducting research in Integrating the Language Arts activities on pages 446 and 463.

5.24 Using Biographical References, Encyclopedias, and Periodicals. A **biographical reference** contains information on the lives of famous people. Examples include *Who's Who*, the *Dictionary of American Biography*, and *Contemporary Authors*.

Encyclopedias provide a survey of knowledge. General encyclopedias, such as *World Book*, contain information on many different subjects. Specialized encyclopedias, such as the *LaRousse Encyclopedia of Mythology*, contain information on one particular area of knowledge.

The topics in an encyclopedia are treated in articles, which are usually arranged in alphabetical order. If you look up a topic and do not find it, check the index (usually in the last volume). The index will tell you where in the encyclopedia your topic is covered.

A **periodical** is a publication that comes out regularly, usually once a week, once a month, or four times a year. Magazines and newspapers are periodicals. Because they are published frequently and quickly, periodicals are an excellent source for the latest news and information, but they may not be as accurate as some other sources.

5.25 Using Indexes, Appendices, and Glossaries. An **index** lists in alphabetical order the subjects mentioned in a book or collection of periodicals and pages where these subjects are treated. Indexes help you locate possible sources of information about your topic. An index can be at the back of a book of nonfiction, or it can be a published book itself.

An example of a published index is *The Reader's Guide to Periodic Literature*, a comprehen-sive index to popular magazine and journal articles. Some periodicals, such as the *New York Times* and *National Geographic*, publish their own indexes, listing articles in past issues. Most indexes are published in sequential volumes that are issued yearly or monthly. Indexes are available as bound books, on microfilm, and on-line on the Internet.

An **appendix** provides additional material, often in chart or table form, at the end of a book or other writing.

A **glossary** lists key words in a book and their definitons.

5.26 Using the Internet

The **Internet** is a vast collection of computer networks that can provide you with a great wealth of information from libraries, government agencies, high schools and universities, non-profit and educational organizations, museums, user groups, and individuals around the world. The Internet provides a valuable way to do research--if you know how to use it. Here are some guidelines.

5.27 Browsing versus Searching on the Internet. **Browsing** means sifting through Internet sites by means of an Internet browser, or software that connects you to the Internet. **Searching** means conducting focused research by using an Internet search engine. By both browsing and searching, you can gain access to the information you want. Browsing allows you to navigate through different sites, either before or after you have conducted a search. Searching allows you to narrow and expand your research in a focused way to find the particular information you need.

Internet Search Engines

www.alltheweb.com.
This enormous engine tracks more than 200 million (Universal Resource Locators, or Internet addresses).

www.altavista.digital.com.
This engine claims to index 30 million Web pages.

www.infoseek.com.
This search engine also contains a large database and an associated directory, Infoseek Guide.

www.yahoo.com.
This popular search service is maintained by on-line editors who sift through Internet sites and keep only the valuable ones.

5.28 Conducting an Internet Search

- Access a reliable search engine.
- Browse the search engine's links or do a keyword search.
- Use Boolean search strategies (see the Language Arts Survey 5.29) or other specialized search tools to narrow and expand your search as needed.
- Browse the results of your search.

- Repeat this process using different search engines until you find what you want.

To keep track of your Internet research, see the Language Arts Survey 5.41, "Documenting and Mapping Internet Research."

5.29 Using Boolean Search Strategies. Boolean logic refers to the logical relationship among search terms. It is named for the mathematician George Boole. To conduct a focused search on the Internet, you should know Boolean operators such as AND, OR, NOT, and NEAR. These operators allow you to limit or expand your research. There are several guides to using Boolean search strategies on the Internet. They can be found by searching with the keyword "Boolean."

Boolean Operators

" "	Quote marks help limit your search to just the phrase in quotes. "Hitchhiker's Guide to the Galaxy" will find references to that specific book title. Without the quotes, a search engine might list numerous other sites, including those related to hitchhikers, guide, and galaxy.
AND	This operator lets you join two ideas. "Greece" AND "travel" would provide you with travel information to Greece. The two words by themselves would give you listings too general to be helpful.
OR	This operator gives you sites that carry information about one or the other of two groups. "Rottweilers OR Huskies" will give you sites that include either one of these dog breeds. "Rottweilers AND Huskies" will list only sites that include both dog breeds.
NOT	This command lets you eliminate certain sites. "American food NOT pizza" will find sites on American food but exclude sites related to pizza.

5.30 Evaluating Information and Media Sources

To conduct your research efficiently, you need to evaluate your sources and set priorities among them. Ideally, a source will be:

- **Unbiased.** When an author has a personal stake in what people think about a subject, he or she may withhold or distort information. Investigate the author's background to see if she or he is liable to be biased. Using loaded language and overlooking obvious counter-arguments are signs of author bias.
- **Authoritative.** An authoritative source is reliable and trustworthy. An author's reputation, especially among others who conduct research in the same field, is a sign of authority. Likewise, periodicals and publishers acquire reputations for responsible or poor editing and research.
- **Timely.** Information about many subjects changes rapidly. An astronomy text published last year may already be out of date. In other fields—for instance, algebra—older texts may be perfectly adequate. Consult with your teacher and your librarian to decide how current your sources must be.
- **Available.** Borrowing through interlibrary loan, tracing a book that is missing, or recalling a book that has been checked out to another person takes time. Make sure to allow enough time for these materials.
- **Appropriate for your level.** Find sources that present useful information that you can understand. Materials written for "young people" may be too simple to be helpful. Books written for experts may presume knowledge that you do not have. Struggling with a difficult text is often worth the effort, but if you do so, monitor your time and stay on schedule.

5.31 How to Read a Newspaper or Newsmagazine. Newspapers and news magazines contain an enormous amount of information. Few people who are not professional politicians or news personnel have the time to read all or most of what appears in a newspaper each day. Nonetheless, reading the news is important. Only by doing that can you take

Evaluating Information and Media Sources. For practice evaluating media sources see the Study and Research & Media Literacy activities on pages 626 and 817.

How to Evaluate a Film. For practice in evaluating films, see the Integrating the Language Arts activities on pages 748, 872, and 965.

advantage of democratic freedoms and make informed voting decisions.

An excellent way to approach reading a newspaper is as follows: Skim the headlines and leads for world, national, state, and local news stories. Read any news summaries included in your paper. Then read in depth any stories that seem particularly important or interesting. You may also wish to read the feature or entertainment sections of the newspaper, according to your own interests.

When reading news stories and editorials, make sure to distinguish between facts and opinions. Facts are statements that can be proved by observation or by consulting a reliable and objective source. Opinions are predictions or statements of value or policy. When you encounter opinions in a newspaper, try to determine whether these opinions are sound. Sound opinions are ones supported by facts. For more information on distinguishing between facts and opinions, see the Language Arts Survey 5.2, "Distinguishing Fact from Opinion."

5.32 How to Evaluate a Film. We watch movies for a multitude of reasons, but perhaps the most common is that a movie allows us to escape our own realities for a couple of hours. It lets us visit new places, see and try exciting new things, and experience life in someone else's shoes. A great film gives us insight into the lives of others and so expands our understanding and our sympathies. Some films, however, are created solely for the purpose of making money through exploitating sensational elements or gimmicks. Although you cannot control the types of movies Hollywood decides to make, you can control the types of movies you choose to watch. The following guidelines will enable you to become a more discriminating consumer of films.

- **Plan ahead**. Decide in advance which films you would like to see. Don't settle for just any movie that happens to be playing at your local theater or on television.
- **Listen, watch, and read what the critics have to say.** Take what the critics have to say into consideration to help you decide which movies to see. Once you have seen the movie, decide for yourself whether you agree or disagree with a particular critic. Consider what elements of the movie you liked or disliked, and what could have been altered to make it better. If, after a while, you find one particular critic with whom you tend to agree on a regular basis, use his or her opinion to help you choose which movies to see.
- **Be a critic yourself**. Be critical of dialogue and story lines. Many films recycle conventional story lines and dialogue. Many contain sensational scenes that provoke audiences but forfeit quality in story line, dialogue, and content. When you see a film, ask yourself questions such as the following:
  - Does each scene move the story forward?
  - Do the characters' actions fit their motives? Is their dialogue believable?
  - Are the themes raised in the film fully developed?
  - What effects do lighting, camera angle, and musical background produce?
- **Be aware of previews and coming attractions**. These are designed with the help of the production company's marketing and sales departments to motivate you to see their film. Previews can make a film seem more humorous, exciting, and powerful than it really is by showing only the best dialogue and action.
- **Try something new!** Try viewing a film that is much different from the type and genre that you usually see. Keep an open mind; you might just surprise yourself and enjoy it.
- **Never substitute.** Never see a film adaptation of a literary work as a substitute for reading the work itself. While seeing such an adaptation can be a good introduction to a literary work, do not rely on it to capture all the richness of the original.

5.33 How to Evaluate Radio and Television. Television and radio are other communication media. You may not be able to respond directly to the broadcaster, but you can still control the broadcast message. Follow the guidelines below to effectively control television output:

- **Plan your television and radio time.** Rather

than accepting whatever program happens to be on, look at broadcast listings and choose programs that are of interest to you.

- **Be a critic.** Question what you see and hear. What criticisms do you have about a program: its quality, its message, its originality, the depth and reliability of its coverage?
- **Remember that advertisers pay for most broadcast programs.** They also control the content of the programs they sponsor and pay for your attention because they want to sell you something. Listen to and watch these advertisements and programs critically. Read the Language Arts Survey 5.2, "Distinguishing Fact from Opinion," for tips on evaluating information critically.

5.34 How to Evaluate Advertisements. Advertising messages are everywhere in the media. To sharpen your skills in evaluating them, see the Language Arts Survey 5.2, "Distinguishing Fact from Opinion" and 5.3, "Avoiding False Arguments and Propaganda."

5.35 How to Understand Internet Sites. Most published print materials have been checked carefully before publication. But anyone can publish something on the Internet—without having to verify facts or guarantee quality. When you use the Internet for research, be careful to evaluate your sources. Here are some guidelines.

- **Consider the resource's domain name.** Documents that end with .edu and .gov are generally reliable, since they come from educational and governmental organizations. Commercial sites end in .com. They can be reliable, too, but watch for biases that favor the company's product. Sites ending in .org or .net can be trusted if they are from a reliable organization, but watch for special interest group sites that slant or "spin" information to their advantage.

Key to Internet Domains

.com	commercial entity
.edu	educational institution
.firm	business entity
.gov	government agency or department
.info	organizations that provide information
.mil	military organization
.net	network resource
.org	other type of organization, usually non-profit
.store	on-line stores

Consider the author.

- Is the author's name listed?
- What are this person's credentials?
- What makes him or her qualified to provide this information?
- Does the author provide a way for you to contact him or her?

Evaluate the quality of information.

- How accurate is the information? Does it appear to be reliable and without errors?
- Are there links to other reliable sources? Do the links really work?
- How current is the information? Is the date provided for when the site was authored or revised? Is this the latest information on this topic?
- How clearly does the author provide information?
- How well does the author cover the topic, based on what you know from other sources?
- How does the author support the information—with charts, graphs, a bibliography?

Look for objectivity.

- Is the information given without bias?
- Is the author objective, or does he or she try to influence the way you think?

5.36 Documenting Sources

As you use your research in your writing, you must document your sources of information. Remember to:

- Credit the sources of all ideas and facts that you use.
- Credit original ideas or facts that are expressed in text, tables, charts, and other graphic information.
- Credit all artistic property, including works of literature, song lyrics, and ideas.

Evaluating Advertisements. An activity that provides an opportunity to critically analyze advertisements is found in the Media Literacy activity on page 32.

Documenting Sources. Direct instruction on properly citing sources can be found in the Language, Grammar, and Style section of the Guided Writing lesson at the end of Unit 8, pages 760–762.

5.37 Keeping a Research Journal. Just as a writing journal can help you track your thoughts, experiences, and responses to literature, a research journal can help you track your research. A research journal is a notebook, electronic file, or other means to track the information you find as you conduct research. A research journal can include:

- A list of questions you want to research. (Such questions can be an excellent source of writing topics.)

EXAMPLES

How did the Vietnam Veterans Memorial come to be? Why is it one of the most visited memorials in America?

Where can I find more artwork by Faith Ringgold?

Why was Transcendentalism such an important literary movement in America but not in Europe?

5.38 Using Your Research Journal for Documentation. As you conduct your research, rely on your research journal as a place to take notes on the sources you find and your evaluation of them. Keeping a research journal can be an invaluable way to track your research and to take notes.

5.39 Informal and Formal Note-Taking.
Informal Note-Taking. Take informal notes when you want information for your own use only, and when you will not need to quote or document your sources. You would take informal notes when preparing materials to use in studying, for instance, as you watch a film or listen to a lecture.

QUOTATION "Jerzy Kosinski came to the United States in 1957, and in 1958 he was awarded a Ford Foundation fellowship."

NOTES Jerzy Kosinski
—came to US 1957
—Ford Foundation fellowship 1958

Informal note-taking is much like outlining (see 2.29, "Rough Outlines"). Use important ideas as headings, and write relevant details below. You will not be able to copy every word, nor is there any need to. Write phrases instead of sentences.

You will also want to record information about the event or performance, including the date, time, place, speaker, and title, as applicable. After you are done taking notes, read them over to ensure that they are legible and meaningful. If you have used idiosyncratic shorthand or abbreviations that you may not later recall, write out your notes more fully.

PREPARING NOTE CARDS

1. Identify the source at the top right corner of the card. (Use the source numbers from your bibliography cards.)
2. Identify the subject or topic of the note on the top line of the card. (This will make it easier to organize the cards later.)
3. Use a separate card for each fact or quotation. (This will make it easier to organize the cards later.)
4. Write the pertinent source page number or numbers after the note.

SAMPLE NOTE CARD

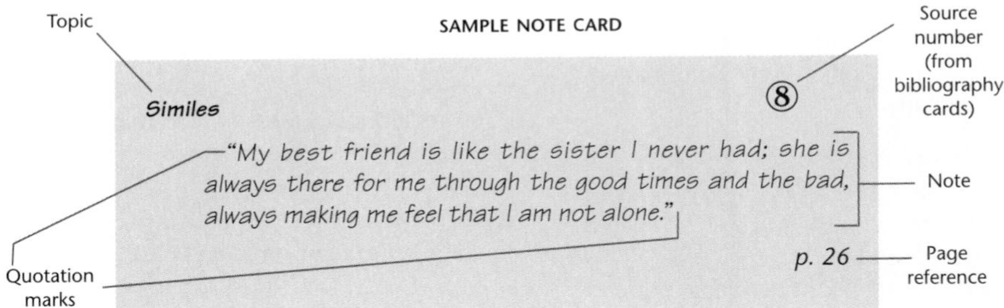
Topic
Source number (from bibliography cards)
Similes
⑧
"My best friend is like the sister I never had; she is always there for me through the good times and the bad, always making me feel that I am not alone."
Note
p. 26
Page reference
Quotation marks

Formal Note-Taking. Take formal notes when you may need to quote or document your sources. When you are keeping formal notes for a project—for instance, for a debate or a research paper—you should use 4" x 6" index cards.

5.40 Making Bibliographies and Bibliography Cards. If you are writing a research paper, your teacher will ask you to include a bibliography to tell where you got your information. A **bibliography** is a list of sources that you used for your writing. A **source** is a book, a magazine, a film, or any other written or audio-visual material that you use to get information. As you work on your paper, you should be writing down on note cards the information for each source that you use. The chart

FORMS FOR BIBLIOGRAPHY ENTRIES

A. A book
Douglass, Frederick. Escape from Slavery: The Boyhood of Frederick Douglass in His Own Words. New York: Alfred A. Knopf, 1994.

B. A magazine article
Reston, James, Jr. "Orion: Where Stars Are Born." National Geographic. December 1995: 90–101.

C. An encyclopedia entry
"Lewis and Clark Expedition." Encyclopedia Americana. Jackson, Donald. 1995 ed.

D. An interview
Campbell, Silas. Personal interview. 6 February 1997.

E. Film
The Big Heat. Dir. Fritz Lang. With Glenn Ford and Gloria Grahame. Writ. Sidney Boehm. Based on the novel of the same title by William P. McGiven. 90 min. Columbia, 1953.

F. Internet
Durham, Dacia. The Charles A. and Anne Morrow Lindbergh Foundation. 24 Oct. 1995, updated 18 June 1999. <http://www.mtn.org/lindfdtn/>

INFORMATION TO INCLUDE ON A BIBLIOGRAPHY CARD

Author(s)	Write the complete name(s) of all author(s), editor(s), and translator(s).
Title	Write the complete title. If the piece is contained in a larger work, include the title of the larger work. (For example, write the name of the encyclopedia as well as the name of the article you used.)
Publisher	Write exactly as it appears on the title page.
Place and date of publication	Copy this information from the title page or copyright page of a book. For a magazine, write the date of the issue that you used.
Location and call number	Note where you found the book. If it is in a library collection, write the call number.
Card number	Give each bibliography card that you prepare a number. Write that number in the top right-hand corner of the card and circle it. When you take notes from the source, include this number on each note card so that you will be able to identify the source of the note later on.

Making Bibliographies and Bibliography Cards. Students are asked to make bibliography cards in the Study and Research activities on pages 261 and 613.

②

Van Lawick-Goodall, Jane.
In the Shadow of Man
Boston: Houghton, 1971.
Peabody Institute Library
599.8

below shows the correct form for different types of bibliography entries.

Bibliography Cards. For each source used, prepare an index card with complete bibliographical information. Include all of the information in the following chart when preparing your cards.

5.41 Documenting and Mapping Internet Research. Your research journal is an excellent tool for tracking how you find information. It can be especially invaluable for documenting and mapping Internet research. As you browse and search on the Internet, it can be easy to jump from one Internet site to the next and to lose track of how you got from place to place. Especially as you conduct research, it is important to map your path. Here is one way to do so.

- Write a brief statement of the topic of your research.
- Write key words or phrases that will help you search for this information.
- Note the search engines that you will use.
- As you conduct a search, note how many "hits" or Internet sites the search engine has accessed. Determine whether you need to narrow or expand your search. Write down new key words accordingly, and the results of each new search.
- When you find promising sites, write them down.
- Access each promising site. Evaluate its information using the guidelines in 5.35, "How to Understand Internet Sites."
- Once you find information to include in your work, document it carefully. For more information on how to document Internet sites, see the Language Arts Survey 5.40, "Making Bibliographies and Bibliography Cards."

5.42 Avoiding Plagiarism. Plagiarism is taking someone else's words or thoughts and pretending that they are your own. Plagiarism is a very serious problem and has been the downfall of many students and even famous people. Whenever you use someone else's writing to help you with a paper or a speech, you must be careful either to put the

FORMAL NOTE-TAKING

Type of Note	When to Use	What to Watch for
Quotation	When the exact wording of a primary source is important to your topic	Copy spelling, capitalization, punctuation, and numbers exactly as in the source.
	When you are providing a definition	Place quotation marks around all direct quotations.
Paraphrase	When the wording of a secondary source is particularly memorable or insightful	Record, when appropriate, explanatory background information about the speaker or the context of a quotation.
	Most of the time	Focus on your main purpose, and note only points related to your topic.
		Place quotation marks around any quoted words or phrases.
Summary	When the point you are making does not require the detail of a paraphrase	Reread the source after writing your summary to be sure that you have not altered the meaning.

ideas in your own words or to use quotation marks. In either case, you must give credit to the person whose ideas you are using. Giving such credit to others is called documenting your sources.

5.43 Paraphrasing, Summarizing, and Quoting. As you do research, your notes will include paraphrases, summaries, and quotations.

5.44 Parenthetical Documentation. Parenthetical documentation is currently the most widely used form of documentation. To use this method to document the source of a quotation or an idea, you place a brief note identifying the source in parentheses immediately after the borrowed material. This type of note is called a **parenthetical citation**, and the act of placing such a note is called **citing a source**.

The first part of a parenthetical citation refers the reader to a source in your List of Works Cited or Works Consulted. For the reader's ease in finding the source in your bibliography, you must cite the work according to how it is listed in the bibliography.

SAMPLE PARENTHETICAL CITATIONS

A. For works listed by title, use an abbreviated title.

Sample bibliographic entry

"History." Encyclopedia Britannica: Macropædia. 1992 ed.

Sample citation

Historians go through three stages in textual criticism ("History" 615).

B. For works listed by author or editor, use the author's or editor's last name.

Sample bibliographic entry

Brown, Dee. Bury My Heart at Wounded Knee: An Indian History of the American West. New York: Holt, 1970.

Sample citation

"Big Eyes Schurz agreed to the arrest" (Brown 364).

C. When the listed name or title is stated in the text, cite only the page number.

Brown avers that Big Eyes Schurz agreed to it (364).

D. For works of multiple volumes, use a colon after the volume number.

Sample bibliographic entry

Pepys, Samuel. The Diary of Samuel Pepys. Ed. Robert Latham and William Matthews. 10 vols. Berkeley: University of California Press, 1972.

Sample citation

On the last day of 1665, Pepys took the occasion of the new year to reflect, but not to celebrate (6: 341-2).

E. For works quoted in secondary sources, use the abbreviation "qtd. in."

Sample citation

According to R. Bentley, "reason and the facts outweigh a hundred manuscripts" (qtd. in "History" 615).

F. For classic works that are available in various editions, give the page number from the edition you are using, followed by a semicolon; then identify the section of the work to help people with other editions find the reference.

STUDY AND RESEARCH RESOURCE

Summarizing. You will find activities that require students to summarize their research in Study and Research on pages 613 and 678.

5.45 Footnotes and Endnotes. Parenthetical documentation, described in 5.44, is the most common of many accepted systems. Footnoting and endnoting are two other accepted methods.

Footnotes. Instead of putting citations in parentheses within the text, you can place them at the bottom or foot of the page; hence the term **footnote**. In this system, a number or symbol is placed in the text where the parenthetical citation would otherwise be, and a matching number or symbol at the bottom of the page identifies the citation. This textbook, for example, uses numbered footnotes in its literature selections to define obscure words and to provide background information.

Endnotes. Many books use endnotes instead of footnotes. Endnotes are like footnotes in that a number or symbol is placed within the text, but the matching citations are compiled at the end of the book, chapter, or article rather than at the foot of the page.

Footnote and endnote entries begin with the author's (or editor's) name in its usual order (first name, then last) and include publication information and a page reference.

SAMPLE FOOTNOTE OR ENDNOTE CITATIONS	
A BOOK WITH ONE AUTHOR	[1]Jean Paul-Sartre, *Being and Nothingness* (New York: The Citadel Press, 1966) 149-151.
A BOOK WITH ONE EDITOR AND NO SINGLE AUTHOR	[2]Shannon Ravenel, ed., *New Stories from the South: The Year's Best, 1992* (Chapel Hill, NC: Algonquin Books, 1992) 305.
A MAGAZINE ARTICLE	[3]Andrew Gore, "Road Test: The Apple Powerbook," *MacUser* December 1996: 72.

TEST-TAKING SKILLS

5.46 Preparing for Tests

Tests are a common part of school life. These guidelines will help you to prepare for and take a test.

Preparing for a Test

- **Know exactly what you will be tested on.** If you have questions, ask your teacher.
- **Make a study plan** to allow yourself time to go over the material. Avoid last-minute cramming.
- **Review the subject matter.** Use your notes, your SQ3R strategy, and any study questions given by your teacher.
- **Make lists** of important names, dates, definitions, or events. Ask a friend or family member to quiz you on them.
- **Try to predict questions** that may be on the test. Make sure you can answer them.
- **Get plenty of sleep** the night before the test. Eat a nutritious breakfast on the morning of the test.

Taking a Test

- **Survey the test** to see how long it is and what types of questions are included.
- **Read all directions and questions** carefully. Make sure that you know exactly what to do.
- **Plan your time.** Answer easy questions first. Allow extra time for complicated questions. If a question seems too difficult, skip it and go back to it later. Work quickly, but do not rush.
- **Save time for review.** Once you have finished, look back over the test. Double-check your answers, but do not change answers too often. Your first ideas are often the correct ones.

5.47 Taking Objective Tests

Objective tests require simple right-or-wrong answers. This chart describes the kinds of questions you may see on objective tests.

Taking Objective Tests. Students are asked to practice taking an objective test in the Study and Research activity on page 678.

QUESTIONS FOUND ON OBJECTIVE TESTS	
Description	**Guidelines**
True/False. You are given a statement and asked to tell whether the statement is true or false.	• If any part of a statement is false, then the statement is false. • Words like *all, always, never,* and *everyone* often appear in false statements. • Words like *some, usually, often,* and *most* often appear in true statements. • If you do not know the answer, guess. You have a 50/50 chance of being right.
Matching. You are asked to match items in one column with items in another column.	• Check the directions. See if each item is used only once. Also check to see if some are not used at all. • Read all items before starting. • Match those you know first. • Cross out items as you match them.
Multiple-choice. You are asked to choose the best answer from a group of answers given.	• Read *all* choices first. • Rule out incorrect answers. • Choose the answer that is most complete or accurate. • Pay particular attention to choices such as *none of the above* or *all of the above.*
Short Answer. You are asked to answer the question with a word, a phrase, or a sentence.	• Read the directions to find out if you are required to answer in complete sentences. • Use correct spelling, grammar, punctuation, and capitalization. • If you cannot think of the answer, move on. Something in another question might remind you of the answer.

5.48 Strategies for Taking Standardized Tests

Standardized tests are given to many students in a school district, a state, or a country. You may already have taken a standardized test, such as the Iowa Test of Basic Skills, and you certainly will take more during your school career. Some standardized tests, such as the Scholastic Aptitude Test, or SAT, are used to help determine entrance to colleges and universities. Others must be passed to enter certain vocations or professions. A standardized test measures overall ability, or achievement over a period of time. Learning how to take standardized tests well can help you to achieve your academic and career goals.

When selecting an answer on a standardized test, remember these points:

- If you do not know the answer, try to rule out some choices and then guess from those remaining.
- If a question seems too difficult, skip it and go back to it later. Be aware, however, that most

True/False Questions. Point out that the word not completely changes the meaning of a sentence. To evaluate a sentence that contains a negative, students should see if its opposite makes sense or is plausible. If it does, the original must be false. Also point out that excessive wordiness might point to a statement's being false. Only one part of the statement needs to be false to make the entire statement false.

INTERNET RESOURCES

An excellent online resource for note-taking and test taking tips (excerpts from *The Confident Student* by Carol Kanar) can be accessed at http://www. mscc.cc.ar.us/ studentserv/notetaki.htm. This site also contains many other links for note-taking and test preparation tips.

Analogy Questions. Students are asked work with analogy questions in the Study and Research activities on pages 142, 329, and 537.

tests allow you to go back to questions only within a section.

- Always follow the instructions of the test monitor.

5.49 Analogy Questions. Analogy questions ask you to find the relationship between a given pair of words and then to recognize a similar relationship between another pair of words. In an analogy question, the symbols : and :: mean "is to" and "as," respectively. The example below would be "Mare is to horse as . . ." when read aloud. To answer an analogy question, examine all of the answers. If more than one answer seems correct, choose the best one.

To answer an analogy question, think of a sentence that relates the two words. For example, you might think of the sentence "A *mare* is a female *horse*." Then look for another pair of words that would make sense in that sentence: "A *doe* is a female *deer*."

EXAMPLE

MARE : HORSE ::
(A) lamb : sheep
(B) man : woman
(C) boy : girl
(D) bee : wasp
(E) doe : deer

The answer is E.

5.50 Synonym and Antonym Questions. Synonym or antonym questions give you a word and ask you to select the word that has the same meaning (for a synonym) or the opposite meaning (for an antonym). You must select the best answer, even if none is exactly correct. For this type of question, you should try all the choices to see which one works best. Always know whether you are looking for a synonym or an antonym, because you will usually find both among the answers.

EXAMPLE

Write the letter of the word that is most nearly the opposite in meaning to the word in capital letters.

1. AMIABLE
(A) capable
(B) friendly
(C) hostile
(D) lovely

The answer is C.

5.51 Sentence Completion Questions. Sentence-completion questions present you with a sentence that has two words missing. You must select the pair of words that best completes the sentence.

EXAMPLE

The expansion of Cedar Hospital was largely____________by the citizens of Minor county, even though it was a major___________for the taxpayers.

(A) needed...contribution
(B) cheered...burden
(C) criticized...expense
(D) welcomed...dilemma

The answer is B.

5.52 Reading Comprehension Questions. Reading comprehension questions give you a short piece of writing and then ask you several questions about it. The questions may ask you to figure out something based on information in the passage. Use the following strategies when answering reading comprehension questions:

STEPS IN ANSWERING READING COMPREHENSION QUESTIONS

1. Read all the questions quickly.
2. Read the passage with the questions in mind.
3. Reread the first question carefully.
4. Scan the passage, looking for key words related to the question. When you find a key word, slow down and read carefully.
5. Answer the first question.
6. Repeat this process to answer the rest of the questions.

Synonym and Antonym Questions. Students are asked to select synonyms for various words in the Study and Research activities on pages 198 and 543.

5.53 Taking Essay Tests

An **essay** is a short piece of writing that expresses the writer's thoughts about a particular subject. To answer an essay question, follow these guidelines.

- **Analyze each question**. Once you understand clearly what you have to do, you will be able to organize and write more effective essays in the time available.

  First, read the *entire* question carefully. Look for key words in the question that tell you what is expected. Underline these words or write them on your own note paper. Then make sure to answer *all* parts of the question.
- **Organize your answer.** Determining how you will spend the time available is an important part of planning an essay. Allow time for planning, writing, and reviewing. Before you begin writing, make a rough outline of the main points you will make. Include main points and key details. Later, if you find yourself running out of time, try at least to state your remaining main points and to add a conclusion.
- **Write a clear introduction.** This will help to keep you on track as you write each paragraph. Your introduction should state the thesis, or main idea, of your essay and should briefly answer the question. In the rest of the essay, you can elaborate on your answer, providing evidence to support it.
- **Review your answer**. Before you turn in your completed essay, take time to review and polish it.

UNDERSTANDING AN ESSAY QUESTION

TYPE OF ESSAY QUESTION	TASKS OF ESSAY
analyze	break into parts and describe the parts and their relationships
compare; compare and contrast	identify and describe similarities and differences
describe; explain	tell the steps in a process; identify causes and effects
define; describe; identify	classify and tell the features of
interpret	tell the meaning and significance of
summarize	retell very briefly, stating only the main points
argue; prove; show	tell and evaluate reasons for believing a statement

QUESTIONS FOR REVIEWING AN ANSWER TO AN ESSAY QUESTION

- Does the essay answer all parts of the question?
- Does the introduction state clearly the main idea of the essay?
- Does the body of the essay provide evidence to support the main idea?
- Does the essay cover all the points in my rough outline?
- Are there any points that could be made more strongly or clearly?
- Is every word in the essay easily readable?
- Is the essay free of errors in grammar, usage, and mechanics?

TAKING ESSAY TESTS. Students are given the opportunity to practice taking an essay test in the Study and Research activity on page 618.

Filling Out Forms. Students are asked to complete an order form off the Internet in the Collaborative Learning & Applied English activity on page 752.

APPLIED ENGLISH Resource

THE IMPORTANCE OF APPLIED ENGLISH

Applied English is English in the world of work, or practical English. When you apply English skills to real-world situations, you are using your reading, writing, speaking, and listening abilities for practical reasons.

6.1 Filling Out Forms

Entering a new school, going to a new doctor, registering computer software, applying for a job—these are but a few of the thousands of activities that involve filling out forms. The following guidelines will help you to complete a form in a way that will make a good impression.

Guidelines for Completing Forms:

- Get an extra copy or make a photocopy of the form so that you can complete a practice form.
- Read through the directions and the form itself before completing it.
- Gather the information you will need to complete the form. This information may include former addresses, dates of events, or a social security number.
- Complete the form neatly. Avoid smudges or cross-outs. Use the writing method requested on the form. Most forms request that you either type or use black or blue ink.
- Do not leave any lines blank. Use N.A. for "not applicable" if a request for information does not apply to you. For example, if you have always lived at the same address, you would write N.A. in the blank following "Previous Addresses."
- Proofread your information for errors in punctuation, spelling, or grammar. Make sure all information is correct.
- Submit the form to the appropriate person or address. Use an envelope or folder to keep the form neat and clean.
- Keep a copy of the form for your own records.

6.2 Following Directions

Every day people all over the world face the challenge of doing something they have never done before. Despite their inexperience, many people are able to succeed because they are able to follow directions. At the same time, someone must be able to give them clear, precise directions. Consider these guidelines before you begin following or giving directions.

Guidelines for Following Directions

- If the directions are being given in written form, read them carefully before beginning the procedure. If they are being given in spoken form, take notes as you listen. Ask for clarification if something is confusing.
- If written directions include any vocabulary or technical words you do not understand, look them up in a dictionary, or see if the materials include footnotes, a glossary, or an appendix. If an instructor uses words you do not understand, ask him or her to rephrase.
- Take your time and make sure you have performed each step carefully and accurately before proceeding to the next step.
- If you get stuck following directions, retrace your steps or reread the step you are on. If they are available, consult diagrams, maps, or illustrations. You might find it helpful to ask someone else to read the directions and see if he or she arrives at the same conclusion as you do. If the directions include a "help hotline" or other contact information, you may want to use it.

6.3 Giving Directions

Guidelines for Giving Directions:

- Think through the directions completely, from start to finish, before you begin.
- Give each step in the order in which it should be taken.
- Include all necessary steps. Do not assume that your reader or listener already knows any part of the directions unless you are absolutely sure that this is the case.
- Do not include any unnecessary steps.
- Use simple language that can be understood easily.
- Use transition words such as *first, second, third, next, then,* and *finally* to connect your ideas.
- When possible, use a parallel or similar sentence structure for each part of the directions.
- When giving directions orally, ask the listener to repeat the directions to you when you have finished. This way you can check to make sure that your directions have been understood.
- If the directions that you are giving are complicated, put them into writing. Number each direction to help you and your reader to keep the steps separate and clear. You may also wish to include a map, diagram, or other illustration to accompany the written directions. For more information, see the Language Arts Survey 6.11, "Displaying Effective Visual Information."

6.4 Writing a Step-by-Step Procedure

A **step-by-step procedure** is a how-to or process piece that uses directions to teach someone something new. Written procedures include textual information and sometimes graphics. Spoken procedures can be given as oral demonstrations. They can include textual and graphic information and other props.

Examples of step-by-step procedures include: an oral demonstration of how to saddle a horse; instructions on how to treat a sprained ankle; a video showing how to do the perfect lay-up in basketball; and an interactive Internet site allowing the user to design and send a bouquet of flowers.

To write a step-by-step procedure, review the Language Arts Survey 6.3, "Giving Directions" and 6.11, "Displaying Effective Visual Information."

Guidelines for Writing a Step-By-Step Procedure

- If you are showing how to make something, create several different samples to show each step of the procedure. For example, if you are showing how to make a wooden basket, you might want to display the raw materials, the started basket, the basket halfway finished, and then the finished product. You might also want to have a sample showing a variation—a different type of weaving, for example, that the finished product may not have.
- Be prepared. The best way to prevent problems is to anticipate and plan for them. Rehearse an oral demonstration several times. If you are preparing the procedure in written form, go through your directions as if you knew nothing about the process. Anticipate what it would be like to learn this procedure for the first time. See if you can follow your own directions, or have a friend work through the procedure and offer suggestions for improvement.
- Acknowledge mistakes. If you are sharing a procedure "live" as an oral demonstration and you can't talk around or correct a mistake, tell your audience what has gone wrong, and why. If you handle the situation in a calm, direct way, the audience may also learn from your mistake.
- Know your topic well. The better you know it, the better you will be able to teach others.

6.5 Writing a Business Letter

A business letter is usually addressed to someone you do not know personally. Therefore, a formal tone is appropriate for such a letter.

Following appropriate form is especially important when writing business letters. If you follow the correct form and avoid errors in spelling, grammar, usage, and mechanics, your letter will sound professional and make a good impression.

Writing a Step-by-Step Procedure. Students are asked to give directions using step-by-step procedure in the Applied English activities on pages 606 and 927.

Writing a Business Letter. Students are asked to write business letters in the Applied English activities on pages 253, 506, and 970.

Above the salutation, a business letter should contain the name and title of the person to whom you are writing and the name and address of that person's company or organization (see the model on the following page).

One common form for a business letter is the block form. In the block form, each part of the letter begins at the left margin. The parts are separated by line spaces.

Begin the salutation with the word *Dear*, followed by the courtesy or professional title used in the inside address, such as Ms., Mr., or Dr., and a colon. If you are not writing to a specific person, you may use a general salutation such as *Dear Sir or Madam*.

In the body of your letter, use a polite, formal tone and standard English. Make your points clearly, in as few words as possible.

End with a standard closing such as *Sincerely, Yours truly,* or *Respectfully yours*. Capitalize only the first word of the closing. Type your full name below the closing, leaving three or four blank lines for your signature. Sign your name below the closing in blue or black ink (never in red or green). Proofread your letter before you send it. Poor spelling, grammar, or punctuation can ruin an otherwise well-written business letter.

Guidelines for Writing a Business Letter:

- Outline your main points before you begin.
- Word process your letter, if at all possible. Type or print it on clean 8 1/2" x 11" white or off-white paper. Use only one side of the paper.
- Use the block form or another standard business letter form.
- Single space, leaving a blank line between each part, including paragraphs.
- Use a standard salutation and a standard closing.
- Stick to the subject. State your main idea clearly at the beginning of the letter. Keep the letter brief and informative.
- Check your spelling, grammar, usage, and punctuation carefully.

Student Model:

Jorge loves snorkeling and wants to get a summer job working part time in a dive shop. This is a copy of the letter that he sent to the owner of the shop.

498 Blue Key Rd.
Charleston, SC 02716

May 3, 1999

Mr. Davy Jones, Owner
Deep Sea Divers, Inc.
73 Ocean St.
Charleston, SC 02716

Dear Mr. Jones:

Please consider me for a position as a part-time clerk in your store for the coming summer. I understand that in the summer your business increases considerably and that you might need a conscientious, hard-working clerk. I can offer you considerable knowledge of snorkeling and diving equipment and experience working in a retail shop.

I will be available for work three days per week between June 1 and August 12. I am enclosing a résumé and references. Please contact me if you wish to set up an interview.

Sincerely,

Jorge Alvarez

Jorge Alvarez

6.6 Writing a Memo

In businesses, schools, and other organizations, employees, students, and others often communicate by means of memoranda, or memos. For example, the director of a school drama club might write a memo to the editor of the student newspaper announcing tryouts for a new play.

Some memos will be more informal than others. If you know the person to whom you are writing well or if the memo has only a social function such as announcing a party, the tone can be fairly informal. Most memos, however, have a fairly formal tone.

A memo begins with a header. Often this header contains the word *memorandum* (the singular form of memoranda) and the following words and abbreviations:

TO:
FR: (from)
DT: (date)
RE: (regarding)
cc: (copy)

STUDENT MODEL:
Jack Hart, the president of the drama club at Wheaton High School, wishes to have the upcoming tryouts for his club's production of *Oklahoma!* announced in the school newspaper. He decides to write a memo to the editor of the paper, Lisa Lowry.

MEMORANDUM

TO: Lisa Lowry
FR: Jack Hart
RE: Tryouts for the spring production of *Oklahoma!*
DT: February 12, 1999
cc: Ms. Wise

Please include the following announcement in the upcoming issue of the *Wheaton Crier*: Tryouts for the Wheaton Drama Club's spring production of *Oklahoma!* will be held on Friday, February 26, at 6:00 p.m. in the Wheaton High School Auditorium. Students interested in performing in this musical should come to the auditorium at that time prepared to deliver a monologue less than two minutes long and to sing one song from the musical. Copies of the music and lyrics can be obtained from the sponsor of the Wheaton Drama Club, Ms. Wise. For additional information, please contact Ms. Wise or any member of the Drama Club.

Thank you.

6.7 Writing a Proposal

A **proposal** outlines a project that a person wants to complete. It presents a summary of an idea, the reasons why the idea is important, and an outline of how the project would be carried out. Because the proposal audience is people who can help carry out the proposal, a proposal is both informative and persuasive.

EXAMPLES

- You want funding for an art project that would benefit your community
- Your student council proposes a clothing drive for disaster relief
- You and a group of your friends want to help organize a summer program for teens your age

WRITING A MEMO. For practice writing a memo, see the Applied English activity on page 641.

APPLIED ENGLISH

Proposal: To host a community arts day at the park behind Jordan High School that would allow high school artists to try new art forms and to exhibit their work.

Rationale: The art students at Jordan High School have shown there is a lot of talent here worth sharing. An Art Day would let everyone interested get involved, and build school and community pride. Art students could lead others through simple art projects, and people could learn new things. At the end, the art could be displayed in an art fair at the community park. Artwork and refreshments could be sold, with all proceeds going to the Jordan High School Art Scholarship.

Schedule/Preparation Outline

Present proposal to School Pride Committee	April 1
Meet with art students to organize event	April 6-15
Contact area businesses for donations	April 6-15
Advertise event and sell tickets	April 16-25
Have practice day to make sure art activities work	April 20
Hold community Arts Day	April 26

BUDGET

Expenses

Posters, mailings, tickets	$30
Art supplies	$200
Refreshments	$75

Note: Expenses will be less if we ask area businesses to help sponsor event

Total estimated expenses	$305

Income

Ticket sales (Estimated 150 tickets sold @ $3 each)	$450
Refreshment sales	$100
Earnings from art sold at exhibit	$200
Total estimated income	$750
Net proceeds	$445

Note: All proceeds will be donated to the Jordan High School Art Scholarship Fund

Guidelines for Writing a Proposal

- Keep the tone positive, courteous, and respectful.
- State your purpose and rationale briefly and clearly.
- Give your audience all necessary information. A proposal with specific details makes it clear what you want approved, and why your audience—often a committee or someone in authority—should approve it.
- Use standard, formal English.
- Format your proposal with headings, lists, and schedules to make your proposed project easy to understand and approve.

6.8 Writing a Résumé

A **résumé** is a summary of a job applicant's career objectives, previous employment experience, and education. Its purpose is to help the applicant obtain the job he or she seeks. A résumé should be accompanied by a cover letter to the employer (see an example in the Language Arts Survey 6.5, "Writing a Business Letter"). Many helpful books and articles are available in libraries and bookstores on writing a résumé. Here are some guidelines.

Guidelines for Writing a Résumé

- Keep your information brief—to one page if possible. The goal of the resume is to give a potential employer a quick snapshot of your skills and abilities.
- Include all vital contact information—name, address, phone number, and e-mail address, if applicable—at the top of the page.
- Use headings to summarize information regarding job or career objective, education, work experience, skills, extracurricular activities, awards (if applicable), and references. Note that work experience should be listed starting with your most recent job and working backward.
- Key or type your résumé on white or cream-colored paper. Proofread it carefully for any errors; all facts must be accurate as well. Make it as neat as possible.
- You may list references, or simply state that they are available on request.

Pat Mizos
5555 Elm Street
Anytown, NY 20111
(212) 555-5555

Objective:
To gain employment working in a summer camp program for children

Education:
Orchard High School, 2001 graduate

Major area of study: College preparatory, with concentration in science and physical education classes

Grade point average: 3.5 (B+)

Work experience:

Summer 1999 Summer youth counselor, Anytown Parks and Recreation Department

Summer 1998 Dishwasher, the Lobster Shack
Anytown, NY

Skills:
Intermediate level Spanish (3 years in high school)
Beginning level American Sign Language (1 semester at Anytown Vocational School)
Certified in CPR

Extracurricular Activities:
Swim team, tennis team, youth hotline crisis volunteer

References:
Available on request.

Writing a Résumé. Students have the opportunity to practice writing a resume in the Applied English activity on pages 111 and 915. Also the Unit 6 Guided Writing lesson focuses on writing a resume on pages 554–561.

Delivering a Press Release. Students can practice writing a press release in the Applied English activities on pages 300 and 341.

Writing a Public Service Announcement. Students are asked to write a public service announcement in the Applied English activities on pages 587, 940, and 955.

6.9 Delivering a Press Release

A **press release** is an informative piece intended for publication in local news media. A press release is usually written to promote an upcoming event or to inform the community of a recent event that promotes, or strengthens, an individual or organization.

EXAMPLES

- a brief notice from the choir director telling the community of the upcoming spring concert
- an informative piece by the district public information officer announcing that your school's art instructor has been named the state Teacher of the Year

Guidelines for Writing a Press Release

- Know your purpose. What do you want your audience to know from reading your piece?
- Use the 5 *Ws* and an *H—who, what, where, why, when,* and *how*—questioning strategy to convey the important information at the beginning of your story. (For more information, see the Language Arts Survey 2.14, "Questioning: Using the 5 *Ws* and an *H*.")
- Keep the press release brief. Local media are more likely to publish or broadcast your piece if it is short and to the point.
- Include contact information such as your name, phone number, and times you can be reached. Make this information available to the media representative or, if applicable, to the reading public.
- Type your press release using conventional manuscript form. Make sure the text is double-spaced and that you leave margins of at least an inch on all sides of the page.
- At the beginning of the press release, key the day's date and the date the information is to be released. (You can type "For immediate release" or designate the date you would like the press release to be printed in the newspaper.)
- At the end of the press release, key the word "END."
- Check a previous newspaper for deadline information or call the newspaper office to make sure you get your material there on time. Address the press release to the editor.

6.10 Writing a Public Service Announcement

A **public service announcement**, or PSA, is a brief, informative article intended to be helpful to the community. PSAs are written by non-profit organizations and concerned citizens for print in local newspapers, for broadcast by television and radio stations, and for publication on the Internet.

EXAMPLES

- an article by the American Cancer Society outlining early warning signs of cancer
- an announcement promoting Safety Week
- an informative piece telling coastal residents what to do during a hurricane

Guidelines for Writing a Public Service Announcement

- Know your purpose. What do you want your audience to know from reading or hearing your piece?
- State your information as objectively as possible.
- As with most informative writing, use the 5 *Ws* and an *H—who, what, where, why, when,* and *how*—questioning strategy to get your important information at the beginning of your story.
- Keep your announcement brief. Local media are more likely to publish or broadcast your piece if it is short and to the point.
- Include contact information in case the media representative has any questions. You might also include contact information in the PSA itself.
- Key or type your PSA in conventional manuscript form. Make sure the text is double-spaced and that you leave margins of at least an inch on all sides of the page.
- At the end of the PSA, key "END" to designate the end of the announcement.
- Be aware of print and broadcast deadlines and make sure your material is sent on time.

6.11 Displaying Effective Visual Information

People frequently learn things best and remember more when information is presented visually. Whenever possible, use charts, tables, pictures, slides, photographs, models, and art to express key points.

Purposes of Visuals

- focus and hold audience attention
- help the audience grasp facts quickly
- clarify something complicated
- show comparisons
- emphasize key points
- summarize main thoughts
- serve as an outline or guide in a presentation

The quality of your visuals will affect your presentation. Depending on their use, visuals can detract from a presentation or enhance it. Before you use a visual, ask yourself:

- Is it attention-grabbing?
- Is it simple and neat?
- Does it serve a real purpose?
- Can I use it easily?
- Does it fit smoothly into the presentation?

The success of your presentation will depend on how you display visual information. Here are some guidelines.

Guidelines for Displaying Visual Information

- Keep visual information simple. Do not clutter visual display with multiple lettering or font styles, too many small images, or too much textual or graphic information.
- Design your visual display in a way that the
- Clearly label your visual display. Make it easy for the viewer to know what you are showing. Include a title or caption, labels for different parts, and simple, main points when needed.
- Make the visual visible. Type or graphics that are too small can make the best visual presentation useless. If the display is on a computer screen, make sure you can read it. If the display is for a speech or exhibit, stand back and see if you can see it from the back of the room or wherever your audience members will be. (A general rule is that one-inch letters can be read at 32 feet, two-inch letters at 64 feet, and three-inch letters at 128 feet.)
- Use bullets or numbering to organize your text. For simple presentations, use either one or the other; don't use both.
- Use color carefully. Color can add visual interest, but it can also be distracting or make a graphic or text area illegible.
- Document all sources of graphic information. The ideas in visual information are someone's intellectual property, just like the ideas in text material. Make sure you give proper credit for all work not your own.

For more information on types of visual presentations, see the Language Arts Survey 1.15, "Using Graphic Aids."

6.12 Working on a Team

Working on a team, or doing collaborative learning, is an essential Applied English skill that depends on a strong ability to communicate. This ability can be strengthened with practice.

Individual members of a team or small group are likely to fulfill particular roles or positions based on what they know or do best. Sometimes a group decides before it starts a project who should take on what role. For instance, a group might choose someone to lead it or to act as secretary. At other times, roles emerge as a group progresses. Often, one person fulfills many roles in a group.

Constructive group roles help the group achieve its goals and objectives. These include:

- **leader:** directs the work of the group by assigning tasks or roles to other group members
- **implementer:** carries out or implements group tasks
- **information seeker:** asks for facts, information, or opinions
- **information giver:** offers facts, information, or opinions
- **coordinator:** pulls ideas together, identifies relationships between ideas

Displaying Effective Visual Information. Students are asked create a visual display in the Collaborative Learning activity on page 333. The Collaborative Learning & Study and Research activities on pages 915 and 1088 encourages students to use visual information in their report.

Working on a Team. Collaborative Learning activities follow many of the selections in the Skill Builders section of the Post Reading. Also refer to the Speaking and Listening Resource 4.7–4.13 for more information on group communication and collaborative learning.

- **summarizer:** summarizes group discussions, calls attention to tasks that need to be fulfilled
- **evaluator:** analyzes data, reasoning, conclusions, or decisions of the group
- **energizer:** motivates the group, stimulates greater productivity and discussion
- **administrator:** keeps meetings on track, makes members aware of time and other constraints
- **secretary:** keeps minutes or a record of what occurs at group meetings
- **encourager:** provides understanding, positive reinforcement, and group solidarity
- **harmonizer:** helps to resolve conflict or misunderstandings between group members; encourages compromise
- **gatekeeper:** keeps communication open by encouraging and discouraging participation
- **tension reliever:** uses humor in a productive way to reduce tension and relax group members

Destructive group roles are counterproductive and prevent the group from achieving its goals or objectives.

- **blocker:** puts down others or their ideas, refuses to cooperate
- **aggressor:** picks fights with other members, is too negative and critical
- **recognition seeker:** uses group to boast about personal accomplishments
- **self-confessor:** unloads personal problems on group members, or otherwise uses the group to gain sympathy
- **joker:** uninvolved in group work, creates distractions, engages in "horseplay"
- **dominator:** tries to control group and monopolize its time in order to advance his or her own interests
- **distractor:** goes off on tangents; offers irrelevant information or ideas
- **deserter:** withdraws from the group; does not participate in group discussions or decisionmaking

Tasks for Being a Productive Team Member

AS A PARTICIPANT

- share personal experience
- contribute relevant ideas
- support statements with evidence
- respond to others with respect
- try to understand others' views
- show willingness to change views when appropriate
- show willingness to clarify and defend views
- allow others to speak
- maintain focus on discussion

AS A LEADER

- help the group keep on track
- help ensure that everyone gets a chance to speak
- help the group achieve its goals

AS A RECORD KEEPER

- keep accurate records of the discussion
- make sure all group members have records useful to the project

For more information, see the Language Arts Survey 4.7–4.9, Speaking and Listening Resource, "Communicating with Others" and 4.13, "Collaborative Learning and Communication."

ABRIDGMENT. An **abridgment** is a shortened version of a work. When doing an abridgment, an editor attempts to preserve the most significant elements of the original. See also *abstract, bowdlerize,* and *paraphrase.*

ABSTRACT. 1. *n.* An **abstract, *précis,*** or **summary** is a brief account of the main ideas or arguments presented in a work. A well-made abstract presents those ideas or arguments in the same order as in the original. Writing an abstract is an excellent way to commit to memory the major ideas of a nonfiction work such as an essay or a chapter in a textbook. See *paraphrase.* 2. *adj.* An **abstract** word or phrase is one that refers to something that cannot be directly perceived by the senses. *Freedom, justice, integrity, dignity,* and *loyalty* are examples of abstract terms. The opposite of *abstract* in this sense is *concrete.* See *concrete.*

ABSURD. See *literature of the absurd.*

ACCENT. See *stress.*

ACRONYM. An **acronym** is a word created from the first, or initial, letters of a series of words. Examples of acronyms include *scuba,* from the words *self-contained underwater breathing apparatus,* and *radar,* from *radio detecting and ranging.*

ACROSTIC. An **acrostic** is a poem organized so that the first or last letters of each line form a word, a phrase, or a regular sequence of letters of the alphabet.

ACT. An **act** is a major division of a drama. The dramas of ancient Rome were generally divided into five acts, as were the plays of Shakespeare and other dramatists of the Elizabethan Age. In modern times, plays are most often divided into three acts, and short plays called "one-acts" are quite common.

ACTION. The **action** is the sequence of events that actually occur in a literary work, as opposed to those that occur off-scene or that precede or follow the events in the work itself. A common literary technique, inherited from the classical *epic,* is to begin a work *in medias res,* in the middle of the action, and to fill in the background details later through flashbacks. See *flashback.*

ACTOR. An **actor** is one who performs the role of a character in a play. The term is now used both for male and female performers.

ADAGE. See *proverb.*

ADAPTATION. An **adaptation** is a rewriting of a literary work in another form. In modern times, adaptations for film are often made of successful novels, musicals, and plays. *My Fair Lady* was an adaptation for the musical theater and later for film of George Bernard Shaw's play *Pygmalion.*

AESTHETICS. **Aesthetics** is the philosophical study of beauty. *Aesthetic principles* are guidelines established for the making and judging of works of art. From age to age, accepted aesthetic principles have differed, and these differences have dramatically influenced the nature of works of art produced in those ages. For example, the ancient Greek philosopher Aristotle propounded an aesthetic of *mimesis,* or *imitation,* believing that the proper function of art was to provide an accurate portrayal of life, an idea perhaps best expressed in Shakespeare's description of dramatic art as "a mirror held up to nature." In sharp contrast to such an aesthetic is the idea, derived from the Greek philosopher Plato, that the function of art is to rise above ordinary nature and to embody ideal, or *sublime,* forms of a kind not found in this material world of the ordinary and transient.

In England and the United States, the dominant aesthetics have been the Neoclassical, dating from the eighteenth century; the Romantic, dating from the nineteenth century; and the Realistic and Naturalistic, dating from the late nineteenth and early twentieth centuries.

The Neoclassical aesthetic values order, ration-ality, and artifice. The Romantic aesthetic values wildness, emotion, imagination, and nature. The Realist aesthetic harkens back to Aristotle and values imitation, but imitation of a modern kind—of the depths as well as the heights of human experience. The Naturalistic aesthetic, like the Realistic, views the purpose of art as the accurate imitation of life, but it also attempts to show how all things, including human actions, thoughts, and feelings, are caused, or determined, by circumstances.

The critic I. A. Richards claimed that a radical shift away from an aesthetic based on beauty to one based on interest occurred in the twentieth century. While beauty, however defined, remains the guiding principle of artistic judgment in lowbrow circles—as for example, in popular judgments made about sentimental novels and verses—interest, both intellectual and emotional, has emerged as the primary standard by which professional critics today judge works of art. See *Naturalism, Neoclassicism, Realism,* and *Romanticism.*

AFFECTIVE FALLACY. The **affective fallacy** is the evaluation of works of art based not on their artistic merit but rather on their emotional effects on the reader, viewer, or listener. A person who holds a didactic or utilitarian view of the function of art would not consider this approach a fallacy. See *didacticism* and *Utilitarianism.*

AFTERWORD. An **afterword** is a statement made at the end of a work, often an analysis, a summary, or a celebration of the preceding work. See *epilogue.*

AGE OF REASON. See *Enlightenment* and *Neoclassicism.*

AIM. A writer's **aim** is his or her purpose, or goal. People may write with the following aims:

- to inform (expository/informational writing)
- to entertain, enrich, enlighten, and/or use an artistic medium, such as fiction or poetry, to share a perspective (imaginative writing)
- to make a point by sharing a story about an event (narrative writing)
- to reflect (personal/expressive writing)
- to persuade readers or listeners to respond in some way, such as to agree with a position, change a view on an issue, reach an agreement, or perform an action (persuasive/ argumentative writing)

Here are examples of writing that reflect these five aims:

expository/informational
news article, research report
imaginative
poem, short story
narrative
biography, family history
personal/expressive
diary entry, personal letter
persuasive/argumentative
editorial, petition

ALEXANDRINE. An **alexandrine,** or **iambic hexameter,** is a verse with six iambic feet. The Spenserian stanza used by Edmund Spenser in *The Færie Queene* (excerpted in Unit 4), contained eight pentameter, or five-foot, lines followed by an alexandrine. See *meter.*

ALLEGORY. An **allegory** is a work in which each element *symbolizes,* or represents, something else. In *naive allegory,* of the kind found in *Everyman* (excerpted in Unit 3) or in *The Pilgrim's Progress* (excerpted in Unit 6), characters, objects, places, and actions are personifications of abstractions such as Good Deeds, Beauty, Vanity, and the journey to the Celestial Kingdom. In more sophisticated allegories, such as Edmund Spenser's *The Færie Queene* (excerpted in Unit 4), the elements of the work make up an *extended metaphor* in which the literal elements are described but their part-by-part interpretation is left up to the reader. In one sense, all literature can be viewed as allegorical in that individual characters, objects, places, and actions are types representing others of their kind. See *concrete universal* and *extended metaphor.*

ALLITERATION. **Alliteration** is the repetition of initial consonant sounds. Some writers also use the term to describe repeated initial vowel sounds. The following line from Thomas Gray's "Elegy Written in a Country Churchyard" (Unit 8) contains three examples of alliteration: the repetition of the *pl* sound in *plowman* and *plods,* the repetition of the *h* sound in *homeward* and *his,* and the repetition of the *w* sound in *weary* and *way.*

The **pl**owman **h**omeward **pl**ods **h**is
weary **w**ay.

Alliteration was the primary organizing principle of Anglo-Saxon verse. See *Anglo-Saxon verse.*

ALLUSION. An **allusion** is a rhetorical technique in which reference is made to a person, event, object, or work from history or literature. W. H. Auden's poem "Musée des Beaux Arts" (Unit

10) alludes, or refers, to a painting of the fall of Icarus by Pieter Brueghel.

AMBIGUITY. An **ambiguity** is a statement that has a double meaning or a meaning that cannot be clearly resolved. In English, the word *cleave* is oddly ambiguous, for it can mean either "to cling together" or "to cut apart." Many literary *figures of speech,* including *metaphors, similes, personifications,* and *symbols*, are examples of intentional ambiguity, speaking of one thing when another is intended. The apparitions' statement to Macbeth (in act 4 of *The Tragedy of Macbeth*, Unit 5) that "no man of woman born" can harm him is an example of ambiguity. It can be taken to mean that no man can harm Macbeth, for it is natural to assume that all men are "of woman born." However, as the play turns out, the statement is actually a reference to Macduff, who was "from his mother's womb untimely ripped," that is, delivered by Cœsarean section and not, therefore, conventionally "born."

AMPLIFICATION. See *elaboration*.

ANACHRONISM. An **anachronism** is a reference to something that did not exist at the time being described. Thus a reference to a watch in a modern retelling of an Arthurian romance would be an anachronism because watches had not been invented in the time of King Arthur.

ANAGRAM. An **anagram** is a word or a phrase created by rearranging the letters of another word or phrase. The title of Samuel Butler's novel *Erewhon* is an anagram for *nowhere*. See *palindrome*.

ANALECTS. **Analects** are collections of passages from the works of one or more authors. A famous example of such a collection is the *Analects* of the Chinese philosopher Confucius (excerpted in Unit 5).

ANALOGY. An **analogy** is a comparison of two things that are alike in some respects. Often an analogy explains or describes something unfamiliar by comparing it to something more familiar. A *simile* is an expressed analogy; a *metaphor* is an implied analogy. See *simile* and *metaphor.*

ANALYSIS. **1. Analysis** is a thinking strategy in which one divides a subject into parts and then examines the relationships among the parts and between individual parts and the whole. An analysis of a short story, for example, might consist of a division of the work into such parts as the exposition, the rising action, the climax, the resolution, and the dénouement, along with an examination of the role played by each of these parts in advancing the plot. An analysis of a line of poetry might consist of a careful examination of its rhythm, its figures of speech, its images, and its meaning or meanings. **2. Analysis** is also a way to organize exposition, a type of nonfiction writing.

ANAPEST. An **anapest** is a poetic foot containing two weakly stressed syllables followed by one strongly stressed syllable, as in the words *unimpressed* and *correlate*. A line of poetry made up of anapests is said to be *anapestic*.

ANAPHORA. An **anaphora**, as that term is used by linguists, is any word or phrase that repeats or refers to something that precedes or follows it. Consider, for example, the opening line of Percy Shelley's "Ode to the West Wind" (Unit 8):

> O Wild West Wind, thou breath of
> Autumn's being

In this line, *thou* and *breath of Autumn's being* are both examples of anaphora because they refer back to, or rename, the West Wind. The simplest form of anaphora is repetition of a word or phrase, as in the repetition of the word *Camelot* in Tennyson's "The Lady of Shalott" (Unit 9).

ANECDOTE. An **anecdote** is a usually short narrative of an interesting, amusing, or biographical incident. Although anecdotes are often the basis for short stories, an anecdote differs from a short story in that it lacks a complicated plot and relates a single episode. Anecdotes are sometimes used in nonfiction writing as examples to help support an idea or opinion. See *exemplum.*

ANGLO-NORMAN LITERATURE. **Anglo-Norman literature** is the literature written in French by the Norman conquerors of England. Anglo-Norman literature, along with literature written in Latin, dominated English literary life for two centuries following the Norman Conquest in 1066. Examples of this literature are the *lais,* or songs, of Marie de France, one of which appears in Unit 3.

Anglo-Saxon. See *Old English.*

Anglo-Saxon Era. The **Anglo-Saxon Era** is the period of English history dating from the Anglo-Saxon invasion of England in the mid-fifth century to the invasion of England by the Normans in 1066. It was during the Anglo-Saxon Era that English literature and the English language were born. See *Old English.*

Anglo-Saxon verse. **Anglo-Saxon verse** is the poetic form used in most Old English poetry. This poetry does not rhyme. It consists of lines that typically have four strong stresses, or beats. In the middle of the line is a pause, or cæsura. Often, the first three stressed words in the line alliterate, or begin with the same sound. An example of Anglo-Saxon verse is "Cædmon's Hymn" on page 97.

antagonist. See *character.*

antihero. An **antihero** is a central character who lacks all the qualities traditionally associated with heroes. An antihero may be lacking in beauty, courage, grace, intelligence, or moral scruples. Antiheroes are common figures in modern fiction and drama.

antithesis. **Antithesis** is a rhetorical technique in which words, phrases, or ideas are strongly contrasted, often by means of a repetition of grammatical structure. An example is Pope's description of the ideal critic in *An Essay on Criticism* (excerpted in Unit 7), who is "Still pleased to praise, yet not afraid to blame."

aphorism. An **aphorism** is a short saying or pointed statement. Examples of aphorisms include Tennyson's "Better to have loved and lost / Than never to have loved at all" and Shakespeare's "All the world's a stage." An aphorism that gains currency and is passed from generation to generation is called a *proverb* or *adage.* See *proverb.*

apocrypha. **Apocrypha** are works that are doubtful in their origin or authorship. The term was first used to describe works from biblical times not considered to be divinely inspired. It is now sometimes used to describe works of doubtful authorship. Examples of Shakespearean apocrypha, works attributed to Shakespeare but on questionable evidence, include "A Lover's Complaint" and "The Passionate Pilgrim."

apology. An **apology** is a literary defense. Famous examples include Plato's *Apology,* which defends Socrates against the charges of impiety brought against him, and Sir Philip Sidney's "The Defence of Poesy," which presents an argument for the value of poetry, claiming that the poet can create a world more beautiful than the real one.

apostrophe. An **apostrophe** is a rhetorical device by which a speaker turns from the audience as a whole to address a single person or thing. John Milton uses apostrophe at the beginning of his work *Paradise Lost* (excerpted in Unit 6) when he addresses the Holy Spirit, calling upon it to be his Muse.

apposition. An **apposition** is a grammatical form in which a thing is renamed, in different words, in a word, phrase, or clause. An example of extended apposition is John of Gaunt's description of his country in Shakespeare's *Richard II.* (Gaunt's speech appears in Unit 5.)

> This royal throne of kings, this scepter'd
>   isle,
> This earth of majesty, this seat of Mars,
> This other Eden, demi-paradise,
> This fortress built by Nature for herself
> Against infection and the hand of war,
> This happy breed of men, this little world,
> This precious stone set in a silver sea . . .
> This blessed plot, this earth, this realm,
>   this England.

archaic language. **Archaic language** consists of old or obsolete words or phrases such as *smote* for *hit.* Spenser uses intentionally archaic language in *The Fœrie Queene* (excerpted in Unit 4) to transport his readers back to the days of chivalry and romance.

archetype. An **archetype** is an inherited, often unconscious ancestral memory or motif that recurs throughout history and literature. The notion of the archetype derives from the psychology of Carl Jung, who wrote of archetypes as making up humanity's "collective unconscious." The term is often used, more generally, to refer to any element that recurs throughout the literature of the world. Thus the story of the journey, in which someone sets out on a path, experiences adventures, and emerges wiser, may be considered archetypal, for it is found in all cultures and in all times. See *motif.*

ARGUMENT. 1. An **argument** is a summary, in prose, of the plot or meaning of a poem or drama. 2. In nonfiction writing, an **argument** is the case for accepting or rejecting a proposition or course of action.

ARGUMENTATION. **Argumentation** is a type of writing that presents reasons or arguments for accepting a position or for adopting a course of action.

ART FOR ART'S SAKE. **Art for art's sake** was the rallying cry of a group of nineteenth-century writers, among them Walter Pater, who believed that art should serve the ends of beauty and beauty alone, rather than some political, social, religious, or moral purpose. Other champions of art for art's sake included Oscar Wilde, Andrew Lang, and the American Edgar Allan Poe. The movement influenced other writers, including a young William Butler Yeats.

ARTHURIAN ROMANCE. **Arthurian romances** are stories of the exploits of the legendary King Arthur and his knights of the Round Table. For more information about these tales, see page 187 and page 199.

ARTICLE. An **article** is a brief work of nonfiction on a specific topic. The term *article* is typically used of encyclopedia entries and short nonfiction works that appear in newspapers and popular magazines. The term is sometimes used as a synonym of *essay,* though the latter term often connotes a more serious, important, or lasting work. See *essay.*

ASIDE. An **aside** is a statement made by a character in a play, intended to be heard by the audience but not by other characters on the stage.

ASSONANCE. **Assonance** is the repetition of vowel sounds in stressed syllables that end with different consonant sounds. An example is the repetition of the long *a* sound in this line from George Crabbe's *The Village:*

The rustic poet pr**ai**sed his n**a**tive pl**ai**ns.

ATMOSPHERE. See *mood.*

AUTOBIOGRAPHY. An **autobiography** is the story of a person's life, written by that person. *The Book of Margery Kempe* (see excerpt in Unit 3), written by a medieval woman, may well be the first full-fledged autobiography in the English language. Some editors and critics distinguish between autobiographies, which focus on personal experiences, and *memoirs,* which focus on public events, though the terms are often used interchangeably.

BACKGROUND INFORMATION. See *flashback, plot,* and *setting.*

BALLAD. A **ballad** is a simple narrative poem in four-line stanzas, usually meant to be sung and usually rhyming *abcb. Folk ballads,* composed orally and passed by word of mouth from generation to generation, have enjoyed enormous popularity throughout English literary history, from the Middle Ages to the present. Examples include "Sir Patrick Spens" and "Bonny Barbara Allan" (Unit 3). *Literary ballads,* written in imitation of folk ballads, have also been very popular. A famous example of the literary ballad is Samuel Taylor Coleridge's "The Rime of the Ancient Mariner." The folk ballad stanza usually alternates between lines of four and three feet. Common techniques used in ballads include repeated lines, or *refrains,* and *incremental repetition,* the repetition of lines with slight, often cumulative, changes throughout the poem. See *refrain.*

BIBLIOGRAPHY. A **bibliography** is a list of works on a given subject or of works consulted by an author. See *List of Works Cited.*

BILDUNGSROMAN. A ***Bildungsroman*** is a novel that tells the story of the growth or development of a person from youth to adulthood. Examples include George Eliot's *The Mill on the Floss,* Charles Dickens's *Great Expectations,* and D. H. Lawrence's *Sons and Lovers.*

BIOGRAPHICAL CRITICISM. See *criticism.*

BIOGRAPHY. A **biography** is the story of a person's life, told by someone other than that person. Perhaps the most famous of all English biographies is James Boswell's *Life of Samuel Johnson, LL. D.* (excerpted in Unit 7).

BLANK VERSE. **Blank verse** is unrhymed poetry written in iambic pentameter. An *iambic pentameter* line consists of five *feet,* each containing two syllables, the first weakly stressed and the second strongly stressed. Blank verse was introduced into English in Surrey's translation of Virgil's *Aeneid.* Marlowe and Shakespeare adopted it as the standard medium for their dramatic works. The form was used to great effect by

Milton, William Wordsworth, Tennyson, Robert Browning, Arnold, Yeats, and T. S. Eliot, among others. For an example of blank verse, see the selection from Shakespeare's *Richard II* on page 478.

BLEND. A **blend,** or **portmanteau,** is a word created by joining together two previously existing words, such as *smoke* and *fog* for *smog* or *whale* and *horse* for *walrus.* In his poem "Jabberwocky," Lewis Carroll coined *slithy* by joining together, or blending, *lithe* and *slimy.*

BLOOMSBURY GROUP. The **Bloomsbury Group** was a circle of English writers and thinkers of the 1920s and 1930s that included Virginia Woolf, John Maynard Keynes, Lytton Strachey, and E. M. Forster.

BOWDLERIZE. To **bowdlerize** a piece of writing is to censor it by deleting material considered offensive. The term comes from the name of Thomas Bowdler, who published a "bowdlerized" edition of Shakespeare's works in the early nineteenth century.

BRETON LAI. A **Breton lai** is a brief medieval romance of the kind produced in Brittany and later in England in imitation of such works. Breton lais dealt with conventional romance themes such as courtly love. Examples of such works include Marie de France's "Chevrefoil" (Unit 3) and the anonymous Middle English poem "Sir Orfeo," a retelling of the Greek myth of Orpheus and Eurydice.

BROADSIDE. A **broadside** was a form of short, printed work common in England after the introduction of printing. Broadsides were printed in columns and on one side only. Many early ballads and short political and religious tracts survive in the form of broadsides.

BUCOLIC. A **bucolic** is a fanciful pastoral poem. See *pastoral poem.*

CACOPHONY. **Cacophony** is harsh or unpleasant sound. Writers sometimes intentionally use cacophony for effect, as when Robert Browning began his poem "Soliloquy of the Spanish Cloister" with a growl spelled "Grr . . . ."

CÆSURA. A **cæsura** is a major pause in a line of poetry, as in the following line from Shakespeare's *A Midsummer Night's Dream:*

I know a bank || where the wild thyme blows

CALVINISM. **Calvinism** is a Protestant theology, or religious philosophy, based on the teachings of John Calvin. It stresses original sin, the inability of people to exercise free will, the preordination of events by God, and the choice (or election) by God of those who will be saved ("the elect") and those who will be condemned. Puritanism was a Calvinist movement. See *Puritanism.*

CANON. A **canon** is a group of literary works considered to be authentic or worthy. The term was originally used for biblical books believed to be divinely inspired. It was later adapted to describe works that can be definitely assigned to a given author (as in *the canonical works of Geoffrey Chaucer*). The term is also used to describe those works in a given literary tradition considered to be classics and thus worthy of inclusion in textbooks, in anthologies, and on the reading lists of courses in schools and universities. In the eighteenth century, there was much debate in France and England concerning whether the canon should include primarily modern or ancient works. In the twentieth century, debates over the canon centered on the inattention given works by non-male, non-European writers. Feminist critics, in particular, noted the tendency of male editors and anthologists to include in their collections works by male writers and to exclude works by female writers. See *feminist criticism* under the entry for *criticism.*

CANTO. A **canto** is a section or part of a long poem. The sections of such long poems as *Beowulf,* Dante's *The Divine Comedy,* and Spenser's *The Fœrie Queene* are called cantos. The word comes from the Latin *cantus,* meaning "song."

CARICATURE. In literature, a **caricature** is a piece of writing that exaggerates certain qualities of a character in order to satirize or ridicule that character or type. See *satire.*

CARMEN FIGURATUM. See *concrete poem.*

CARPE DIEM. ***Carpe diem*** is a Latin term meaning "seize the day." The *carpe diem* theme, telling people not to waste time but rather to enjoy themselves while they have a chance, was common in Renaissance English poetry. The following stanza by Robert Herrick (See Unit 6) is perhaps the most famous expression of this theme in English:

Gather ye rosebuds while ye may,
Old Time is still a-flying;
And this same flower that smiles today,
Tomorrow will be dying.

CATALOG. A **catalog** is a list of people or things. T. S. Eliot's "The Naming of Cats" (Unit 1) contains a sort of catalog of cat's names, some that are for everyday, and some that are quite unusual, such as "Munkustrap, Quaxo, or Coricopat."

CATASTROPHE. The **catastrophe** is a conclusion of a play, particularly of a tragedy, marked by the fall of the central character. In the catastrophe, the central conflict of the play is ended, or resolved. See *plot.*

CATHARSIS. The ancient Greek philosopher Aristotle described tragedy as bringing about a **catharsis,** or purging, of the emotions of fear and pity. Debate has raged around the proper interpretation of Aristotle's description. Some critics take it to mean, simply, that at the end of a tragedy, in the catastrophe or resolution, the emotional equilibrium of the characters is restored. Others take it to mean that viewing a tragedy causes the audience to feel emotions of fear and pity, which are then released at the end of the play, leaving the viewer calm, wiser, and perhaps more thoughtful. This idea of the purgative or cathartic effect of viewing enacted displays of strong emotion is contradicted by recent psychological studies that suggest that people tend to imitate enacted feelings and behaviors that they witness. Much of the current debate over violence on television and in films centers on this question of whether enacted violence has a cathartic or an arousing effect on the viewer.

CAVALIER POETS. The **Cavalier poets** were loyal supporters of the English king Charles I, courtiers and soldiers who incidentally wrote lighthearted verse, often on amorous themes. Classified among the Cavalier poets are Sir John Suckling, Richard Lovelace, and Robert Herrick.

CELTIC. **Celtic** is a term used to refer to the art and culture of the Celts, a people who inhabited ancient Britain and much of Europe. It is also used to refer to the art and culture of descendants of the Celts, including modern Welsh, Cornish, Breton, Irish, Manx, and Scots peoples. The late nineteenth and early twentieth centuries saw in Ireland a Celtic Revival or Celtic Renaissance characterized by the renewed use of the Gaelic language and by an explosion of literary production on Irish themes by authors such as W. B. Yeats, John Millington Synge, and Lady Augusta Gregory.

CENSORSHIP. **Censorship** is the act of examining works to see if they meet predetermined standards of political, social, or moral acceptability. Official censorship is aimed at works that will undermine authority or morals and has often in the past resulted in the suppression of works considered dangerous or licentious. Throughout much of English history, censorship was freely exercised by the church and the state. Milton's *Areopagitica* is an eloquent argument against censorship and in favor of unlicensed printing. Milton's principal argument is that when free expression of ideas is allowed, the truth will prevail, driving out falsehood and error as day drives out night. See *bowdlerize.*

CENTRAL CONFLICT. A **central conflict** is the primary struggle dealt with in the plot of a story or drama. See *conflict* and *plot.*

CHARACTER. A **character** is a person (or sometimes an animal) who figures in the action of a literary work. A *protagonist,* or *main character,* is the central figure in a literary work. An *antagonist* is a character who is pitted against a protagonist. *Major characters* are those who play significant roles in a work. *Minor characters* are those who play lesser roles. A *one-dimensional character, flat character,* or *caricature* is one who exhibits a single dominant quality, or *character trait.* A *three-dimensional, full,* or *rounded character* is one who exhibits the complexity of traits associated with actual human beings. A *static character* is one who does not change during the course of the action. A *dynamic character* is one who does change. A *stock character* is one found again and again in different literary works. Examples of stock characters include the braggart soldier of ancient Roman drama, the Virtues and Vices of medieval allegory, and the mad scientist of nineteenth- and twentieth-century science fiction.

CHARACTERIZATION. **Characterization** is the use of literary techniques to create a character. Writers use three major techniques to create characters: direct description, portrayal of characters' behavior, and representations of characters' internal states. When using direct description, the writer, through a speaker, a narrator, or another character, simply comments on the character, telling the reader about such matters as the character's appearance, habits, dress, background, personality, motivations, and so on. When using portrayal of a character's behavior, the writer presents the actions and speech of the character, allowing the reader to draw his or her own conclusions from what the character says or does. When using representations of internal states, the writer reveals directly the character's private thoughts and emotions, often by means of what is known as the *internal monologue.* See *character* and *internal monologue.*

CHIASMUS. A **chiasmus** is a rhetorical technique in which the order of occurrence of words or phrases is reversed, as in the line "We can weather changes, but we can't change the weather."

CHIVALRY. **Chivalry** was the code of conduct of the medieval knight. The word derives from the French *cheval,* for "horse," indicating the importance of this animal to the knight, who typically traveled and fought on horseback. According to the code of chivalry, a knight was to be a loyal servant to his lord or lady and a perfect exemplar of such virtues as bravery, courage, courtesy, honesty, faith, and gentleness. Medieval romance literature, such as *Sir Gawain and the Green Knight* (excerpted in Unit 3), typically presents a series of tests (trials or quests) of these knightly virtues. See *romance.*

CHRONICLE. A **chronicle** is a record of historical events. The *Anglo-Saxon Chronicle,* begun in the time of King Alfred and covering the period from 60 BC to AD 1154, is one of our major sources of information about the Anglo-Saxon period.

CHRONOLOGICAL ORDER. **Chronological order** is the arrangement of details in order of their occurrence. It is the primary method of organization used in narrative writing. It is also common in nonfiction writing that describes processes, events, and cause-and-effect relationships.

CLASSIC. A **classic** is a work of literature that is widely held to be one of the greatest creations within a given literary tradition. The question of just what works may be considered classic, and thus the question of what constitutes the *canon,* is a much-debated one. See *canon.*

CLASSICAL ERA. The **Classical Era** is the period in European history that saw the flowering of the ancient Greek and Roman cultures. *Classical literature* is the literature of ancient Greece and Rome from the time of Homer and Hesiod to the fall of the Roman Empire in AD 410.

CLASSICISM. **Classicism** is a collection of ideas about literature and about art in general derived from study of works by Greeks and Romans of the *Classical Era.* Definitions of what constitutes the Classical style differ, but most would agree that the Classical aesthetic emphasizes authority, austerity, clarity, conservatism, decorum, imitation, moderation, order, reason, restraint, self-control, simplicity, tradition, and unity. Classicism is most often contrasted with *Romanticism.* See *Classical Era* and *Neoclassicism.*

CLASSIFICATION ORDER. **Classification order** is a method of organization in which subjects are divided into groups, or classes. These groups are then presented, one-by-one, in some reasonable order. Classification order is commonly used in exposition, or expository writing. See *exposition,* #1.

CLICHÉ. A **cliché** is a tired or hackneyed expression such as *quiet as a mouse* or *couch potato.* Most clichés originate as vivid, colorful expressions but soon lose their interest because of overuse. Careful writers and speakers avoid clichés, which are dull and signify lack of originality.

CLIMAX. The **climax** is the point of highest interest and suspense in a literary work. The term also is sometimes used to describe the *turning point* of the action in a story or play, the point at which the rising action ends and the falling action begins. See *crisis* and *plot.*

CLOSED COUPLET. A **closed couplet** is a pair of rhyming lines that present a complete statement.

> True wit is Nature to advantage dressed,
> What oft was thought, but ne'er so well
> expressed.
> —Alexander Pope, *An Essay on Criticism*
> (excerpted in Unit 7)

CLOSET DRAMA. A **closet drama** is one that is meant to be read rather than acted. Examples of the form include Milton's *Samson Agonistes,* Percy Shelley's *The Cenci,* and Robert Browning's *Pippa Passes.*

COHERENCE. **Coherence** is the logical arrangement and progression of ideas in a speech or piece of writing. Writers achieve coherence by presenting their ideas in a logical sequence and by using transitions to show how their ideas are connected to one another. See *transition.*

COINED WORDS. **Coined words** are ones that are intentionally created, often from the raw materials provided by already existing words and word parts. Examples of recently coined words include *spacewalk* and *quark,* the latter taken from James Joyce's *Finnegans Wake.*

COLLAGE. In literature, a **collage** is a work that incorporates or brings together an odd assortment of materials, such as allusions, quotations, bits of song, dialogue, foreign words, mythical or folkloric elements, headlines, and pictures or other graphic devices. Collage is an interesting way to present a portrait of a particular time. In America, John Dos Passos used the technique in sections, called "Newsreels," of his *U.S.A.* trilogy of novels. The technique is used to a lesser degree in much modern poetry and fiction, including James Joyce's *Finnegans Wake* and Ezra Pound's *The Cantos.*

COLLOQUIALISM. **Colloquialism** is the use of informal language. Much modern poetry is characterized by its use of colloquialism, the language of ordinary speech first championed by William Wordsworth in the Preface to *Lyrical Ballads.*

COMEDY. Originally a literary work with a happy ending, a **comedy** is any lighthearted or humorous work, especially one prepared for the stage or the screen. Comedy is often contrasted with tragedy, in which the hero meets an unhappy fate. (It is perhaps only a slight exaggeration to say that comedies end with wedding bells and tragedies with funeral bells.) Comedies typically present less-than-exalted characters who display all-too-human limitations, foibles, faults, and misunderstandings. The typical progression of the action in a comedy is from initial order to a humorous misunderstanding or confusion and back to order again. Stock elements of comedy include mistaken identities, word play, satire, and exaggerated characters and events. See *tragedy.*

COMEDY OF MANNERS. The **comedy of manners** is a type of satirical comedy that originated in the Restoration Period and that deals with the conventions and manners of a highly artificial and sophisticated society. Typical subjects dealt with in the comedy of manners include amorous intrigue, fakery, pomposity, and flattery. Examples of the genre include Congreve's *The Way of the World,* Goldsmith's *She Stoops to Conquer,* and Oscar Wilde's *The Importance of Being Earnest.*

COMIC RELIEF. Writers sometimes insert into a serious work of fiction or drama a humorous scene that is said to provide **comic relief** because it relieves the seriousness or emotional intensity felt by the audience. Paradoxically, a scene introduced for comic relief can sometimes, because of the contrast it provides, increase the perceived intensity or seriousness of the action around it. A famous example of comic relief is the appearance of the drunken porter in act 2, scene 3 of *Macbeth,* right after the murder of Duncan.

commonplace book A **commonplace book** is a collection of quotations gleaned from various sources.

COMPARATIVE LITERATURE. **Comparative literature** is the study of relationships among works of literature written at different times, in different places, or in different languages. A study that showed influences of French revolutionary writing on English *Romanticism* would be an example, as would a study that dealt with the motif of the foundling left in a basket floating upon the waters. The latter motif is found in such widely separated stories as the Babylonian *Epic of Gilgamesh,* the story of Moses in the Hebrew scriptures, and the story of Scyld Scefing told at the beginning of the Old English epic poem *Beowulf.*

COMPARISON-CONTRAST. See *exposition,* #1.

COMPLAINT. A **complaint** is a lyric poem that deals with loss, regret, unrequited love, or some other negative state experienced by the speaker of the poem. Examples include the Old English poem "The Wife's Lament" (Unit 2) and Chaucer's "The Complaint of Chaucer to His Empty Purse."

COMPLICATION. The **complication** is the part of a plot in which the conflict is developed or built to its high point of intensity. See *plot.*

CONCEIT. A **conceit** is an elaborate or extremely fanciful analogy or metaphor. The conceit was a common element of Renaissance English poetry and of the so-called Metaphysical poetry written by such authors as John Donne. The comparison in Shakespeare's Sonnet 73 (Unit 4) of the speaker with nature in the late fall or early winter is an example of conceit, as is Ben Jonson's "Song, to Celia" (Unit 4). In Sonnets 18 and 130, also in Unit 4, Shakespeare mocks the conceits common in poetry of his day.

CONCRETE. A **concrete** word or phrase is one that names or describes something that can be directly perceived by one or more of the five senses. *Rainbow, lark, scorpion,* and *field* are examples of concrete terms. See *abstract* and *concrete universal.*

CONCRETE POEM. A **concrete poem** is one printed or written in a shape that suggests its subject matter. An example of the concrete poem, also known as a *shape poem* or *carmen figuratum,* is George Herbert's "Easter Wings" (Unit 6).

CONCRETE UNIVERSAL. A **concrete universal** is a particular object, person, action, or event that provides an instance or example of a general type. So, for example, Shakespeare's Macbeth can be seen as a concrete example of a man suffering from extreme guilt and Percy Shelley's statue of Ozymandias (see "Ozymandias" in Unit 8) can be seen as a concrete example of the general idea that all worldly pomp and pride is eventually reduced to ruin. During the *Neoclassical Age,* writers tended to disparage concrete particulars and to write, instead, in abstract terms. As a result, modern readers sometimes find Neoclassical literature not to their taste. In our time, literary taste tends toward the particular. In the *minimalist style* championed by writers such as Ezra Pound, T. S. Eliot, and Hilda Doolittle, direct statement of abstract ideas and emotions is avoided. Instead, images are presented as concrete examples to arouse abstract ideas and emotions in the reader. So, for example, instead of saying something abstract like "I feel that some terrible, earth-shattering event is about to take place," the later Yeats, who was influenced greatly by Pound, would write,

"And what rough beast, his hour come
round at last,
Slouches toward Bethlehem to be born."
—W. B. Yeats, "The Second Coming"

The concrete image of the "rough beast" is much more emotionally powerful than the abstract statement. See *abstract, concrete, Neoclassicism,* and *objective correlative.*

CONFESSIONAL POETRY. **Confessional poetry** is verse that describes, sometimes with painful explicitness, the private or personal affairs of the writer. Contemporary confessional poets include Allen Ginsberg, Sylvia Plath, Anne Sexton, and Robert Lowell.

CONFLICT. A **conflict** is a struggle between two forces in a literary work. A *plot* involves the introduction, development, and eventual resolution of a conflict. One side of the *central conflict* in a story or drama is usually taken by the *main character.* That character may struggle against another character, against the forces of nature, against society or social norms, against fate, or against some element within himself or herself. A struggle that takes place between a character and some outside force is called an *external conflict.* A struggle that takes place within a character is called an *internal conflict.* Shakespeare's Macbeth experiences external conflicts with Banquo and Macduff. He experiences an internal conflict between his own ambition and his guilt. See *central conflict* and *plot.*

CONNOTATION. A **connotation** is an emotional association or implication attached to an expression. For example, the word *inexpensive* has positive emotional associations, whereas the word *cheap* has negative ones, even though the two words both *denote,* or refer to, low cost. Good writers choose their words carefully in order to express appropriate connotations. See *denotation.*

CONSONANCE. **Consonance** is a kind of slant rhyme in which the ending consonant sounds of two words match, but the preceding vowel sound does not, as in the words *wind* and *sound.* The final lines of Percy Shelley's "Ode to the West Wind" (Unit 8) provide an example:

The trumpet of a prophecy! O *Wind*
If Winter comes, can Spring be far *behind?*

CONVENTION. A **convention** is an unrealistic element in a literary work that is accepted by readers or viewers because the element is tradition al. One of the conventions of fiction, for example, is that it uses the past tense to describe current or present action. Rhyme schemes and organization into stanzas are among the many commonly employed conventions of poetry. Violation of accepted conventions is one of the hallmarks of *avant garde* or *Modernist* literature. See *dramatic convention.*

CONVENTIONAL SYMBOL. See *symbol.*

COUPLET. A **couplet** is a pair of rhyming lines that expresses a complete thought. These lines from Shakespeare's *Romeo and Juliet* provide an example:

For never was a story of more woe
Than this of Juliet and her Romeo.

A pair of rhyming iambic pentameter lines is called a *heroic couplet.*

COURTLY LOVE. **Courtly love** is a code of romantic love celebrated in songs and romances of the Medieval Period in France and England. According to this code, the male lover knows himself to be truly in love if he is overcome by extreme, transforming emotion. This emotion, felt for an idealized, venerated woman, leads the smitten man sometimes to depths of despair and sometimes to heights of gentleness, courtesy, and heroism to prove his worth to his lady fair. Courtly love was one of the primary themes of medieval *romance* literature. See *romance.*

CRISIS. In the plot of a story or a drama, the **crisis** is that point in the development of the conflict at which a decisive event occurs that causes the main character's situation to become better or worse. See *plot.*

CRITIC. A literary **critic** is a person who evaluates or interprets a work of literature. See *criticism.*

CRITICAL ESSAY. A **critical essay** is a type of informative or persuasive writing that presents an argument in support of a particular interpretation or evaluation of a work of literature. A well-constructed critical essay presents a clear *thesis,* or main idea, supported by ample evidence from the work or works being considered.

CRITICISM. **Criticism** is the act of evaluating or interpreting a work of art or the act of developing general guidelines or principles for such evaluation or interpretation. Over the centuries, many schools, or philosophies, of criticism have been developed. However, most readers and teachers are eclectic critics, drawing consciously or unconsciously upon various shools of critical thought. Common schools of criticism include the following:

Biographical criticism attempts to account for elements of literary works by relating them to events in the lives of their authors. A reading of Yeats's poem "Adam's Curse" (Unit 10) as a reflection on his real-life relationship with actor Maude Gonne would be an example of biographical criticism.

Deconstructionist criticism calls into question the idea that there is one "meaning" behind a literary work by inviting the reader to reverse the binary, or two-part, relations that structure meaning in the work. For example, a deconstructionist analysis might invite the reader to consider, again, the contrast between natural order and supernatural disorder in *Macbeth* (Unit 5). It might claim that the disorder exemplified by Macbeth and Lady Macbeth's madness is, in fact, in the natural order of things. Such a reading deconstructs the conventional reading of the play, which insists that Shakespeare intended to reveal the awful consequences of an unnatural violation of the moral order of the universe. See *structuralist criticism.*

Didactic criticism evaluates works of art in terms of the moral, ethical, or political messages that they convey. Dismissal of a book as dangerous or obscene would be an example of didactic criticism.

Feminist criticism evaluates and interprets works of art with regard to their portrayal of or influence upon gender roles. Many feminist critics and scholars have been working to give women writers—often ignored in the past by male critics, editors, scholars, and teachers—the recognition they deserve. Other feminist critics point out gender bias in literary works by analyzing variations in literary depictions of males and females, and by analyzing the effects of literary works, activities, and movements on cultural norms related to gender. An example of feminist criticism would be an analysis of how women in medieval courtly love and romance literature were idealized and the consequences of that idealization for later Western ideas about femininity and relations between the sexes.

Formal criticism analyzes a work of literature in terms of its genre or type. An explanation of those characteristics of *Paradise Lost* that make it an epic would be an example of formal criticism.

Freudian criticism draws upon the works of the founder of psychoanalysis, Sigmund Freud, and generally views literary works or the parts thereof as expressions of unconscious desires, as wish fulfillments, or as neurotic sublimations of unresolved conflicts from childhood. An example of Freudian criticism would be the interpretation of the ancient Greek Œdipus myth, in which Œdipus unwittingly marries his mother, as an expression of the young male child's competition with his father for his mother's affection.

Historical criticism views the work of art as a product of the period in which it was produced. Examples of historical criticism would be an analysis of the feudal concept of vassalage in Malory's *Le Morte d'Arthur* (excerpted in Unit 3) or a description of the influence of the French and American revolutions on the development of Romanticism in England.

Jungian criticism explores the presence in works of art of *archetypes*—unconscious images, symbols, associations, or concepts presumed to be a common inheritance of all human beings. An analysis of symbols of rebirth in a number of myths or folk tales would be an example of Jungian criticism.

Marxist criticism, based upon the work of the German-born political philosopher Karl Marx, evaluates and interprets works of art with regard to the material, economic forces that shape them or with regard to their origins in or depictions of struggle between the social classes. An example of Marxist criticism would be an explanation of the emergence of Neoclassicism in England in terms of desire for order, authority, and control on the part of the privileged classes during the Restoration Era.

Mimetic criticism, which derives from the teachings of Aristotle, views works of art as imitations of nature or of the real world and evaluates them according to the accuracy of those portrayals. Insisting that a character is poorly drawn because he or she is unrealistic is an example of mimetic criticism.

The ***New Criticism*** championed in the early to mid-twentieth century by such critics as I. A. Richards and Cleanth Brooks insists upon the interpretation and evaluation of literary works based on details found in the works themselves rather than on information gathered from outside the works. It disregards such matters as the life of the author, the period in which the work was written, the literary movement that led to its production, and the emotional effect of the work upon the reader. The New Critics insisted on the importance of close analysis of literary texts and the irreducibility of those texts to generalizations or paraphrases.

Pragmatic or ***rhetorical criticism*** interprets or evaluates a work of art in terms of its effects on an audience. Many critics have claimed that Milton intended to have his readers identify with Satan as described in the opening books of *Paradise Lost* (excerpted in Unit 6) so that he could then have the reader go through the experience of falling into sin only to be redeemed afterward. This is an example of rhetorical criticism.

Reader-response criticism views the meaning of a text as resulting from a relationship between the text itself and the subjective experiences or consciousness of a reader. According to reader-response theory, a literary text has no meaning *per se.* It is, instead, an occasion that the reader has for a participatory experience. That experience may be meaningful or significant to the reader, but its meaning and significance will depend, in part, on what the reader brings to the text.

Romantic or ***expressivist criticism*** views a work of art as primarily an expression of the spirit, ideas, beliefs, values, or emotions of its creator. A reading of "Lines Composed a Few Miles above Tintern Abbey" (Unit 8) as expressive of the moral posture adopted by William Wordsworth would be an example of expressivist criticism.

Structuralist criticism analyzes works of literature and art in terms of binary, or two-part, relationships or structures. A structuralist analysis of Shakespeare's *Macbeth,* for example, might view the central character as caught between supernatural disorder and the natural order, between reality and illusion.

Textual criticism analyzes the various existing manuscript and printed versions of a work in order to construct an original or definitive text for use by readers.

DACTYL. A **dactyl** is a poetic foot made up of a strongly stressed syllable followed by two weakly stressed syllables, as in the word *feverish*. A line of poetry made up of dactyls is said to be *dactylic*.

DEAD METAPHOR. A **dead metaphor** is one that is so familiar that its original metaphorical meaning is rarely thought of when the expression is used. An example would be the word *nightfall,* which describes the coming of darkness as a falling object.

DECONSTRUCTIONIST CRITICISM. See *criticism.*

DEFINITION. A **definition** is an explanation of the meaning of a word or phrase. A dictionary definition typically consists of two parts: the *genus,* or class to which the thing belongs, and the *differentia,* or differences between the thing and other things of its class. Consider, for example, Samuel Johnson's famous tongue-in-cheek definition of *oats:* "A grain, which in England is generally given to horses, but in Scotland supports the people." In this definition, "grain" is the genus. The rest of the definition presents the differentia.

DENOTATION. The **denotation** is the basic meaning or reference of an expression, excluding its emotional associations, or *connotations*. For example, the words *dirt* and *soil* share a single common denotation. However, *dirt* has negative connotations of uncleanliness, whereas *soil* does not. See *connotation.*

DÉNOUEMENT. See *plot.*

DESCRIPTION. **Description** is a type of writing that portrays a character, an object, or a scene. Descriptions make use of *sensory details*—words and phrases that describe how things look, sound, smell, taste, or feel. Effective descriptions contain precise nouns, verbs, adverbs, and adjectives. Descriptions often use *imagery* and *figurative language*.

DIALECT. A **dialect** is a version of a language spoken by the people of a particular place, time, or social group. Writers often use dialect, as in Thomas Hardy's "The Man He Killed" (Unit 9), to give their works a realistic flavor. In his play *Pygmalion* (Unit 12), George Bernard Shaw satirizes the division of English society along class lines differentiated by the dialects spoken by members of each class. A *regional dialect* is one spoken in a particular place. A *social dialect* is one spoken by members of a particular social group or class.

DIALOGUE. 1. **Dialogue** is conversation involving two or more people or characters. Plays are made up of dialogue and stage directions. Fictional works are made up of dialogue, narration, and description. 2. **Dialogue** is also used to describe a type of literary composition in which characters debate or discuss an idea. Many of Plato's philosophical works were presented in the form of dialogues. Dialogues between abstractions such as the body and the soul, or virtue and vice, were common in the poetry of the Middle Ages.

DIARY. A **diary** is a day-to-day record of a person's activities, experiences, thoughts, and feelings. Perhaps the most famous of all English diaries is that kept by Samuel Pepys (see Unit 7). See *journal.*

DICTION. **Diction,** when applied to writing, refers to word choice. Much of a writer's *style* is determined by his or her diction, the types of words that he or she chooses. Diction can be formal or informal, simple or complex, contemporary or archaic, ordinary or unusual, foreign or native, standard or dialectical, euphemistic or blunt. See *style.*

DIDACTIC CRITICISM. See *criticism.*

DIDACTIC POEM. A **didactic poem** is a verse that has a primary purpose of teaching one or more lessons. Alexander Pope's *An Essay on Criticism* (excerpted in Unit 7) is an example. See *didacticism.*

DIDACTICISM. **Didacticism** is the use of works of art to convey moral, social, educational, or political messages. A didactic work is one in which the artistic values of the work are subordinated to the message or meaning. Didacticism was a common element of literature in the Middle Ages and of the *proletarian art* and literature produced in Communist countries in the twentieth century.

DIMETER. See *meter.*

DIRGE. A **dirge** is a funeral song or a poem written in imitation thereof.

DOMINANT IMPRESSION. See *effect.*

DRAMA. A **drama** is a story told through characters played by actors. The script of a drama typically consists of characters' names, *dialogue* spoken by the characters, and *stage directions.* Because it is meant to be performed before an audience, drama can be distinguished from other forms of non-performance-based literary works by the central role played in it by the *spectacle*—the sensory presentation to the audience, which includes such elements as lighting, costumes, make-up, properties, set pieces, music, sound effects, and the movements and expressions of actors. Another important distinguishing feature of drama is that it is *collaborative.* The interpretation of the work depends not only upon the author and his or her audience but also upon the director, the actors, and others involved in mounting a production. Two major types of drama are *comedy* and *tragedy.* George Bernard Shaw's *Pygmalion* (Unit 12) is an example of the former; Shakespeare's *Macbeth* (Unit 5), of the latter. See *comedy, dialogue, spectacle, stage directions,* and *tragedy.*

DRAMATIC CONVENTION. A **dramatic convention** is an unreal element in a drama that is accepted as realistic by the audience because it is traditional. Such conventions include the impersonation of characters by actors, the use of a curtain to open or close an act or a scene, the revelation of a character's thoughts through *asides* and *soliloquies,* and the removal of the so-called *fourth wall* at the front of the stage that allows the audience to see action taking place in an imagined interior. See *convention* and *suspension of disbelief.*

DRAMATIC IRONY. See *irony.*

DRAMATIC MONOLOGUE. A **dramatic monologue** is a poem that presents the speech of a single character in a dramatic situation. The speech is one side of an imagined conversation. Robert Browning is often credited with the creation of the dramatic monologue. He popularized the form in such poems as "My Last Duchess" and "Andrea del Sarto" (both in Unit 9). See *soliloquy.*

DRAMATIC POEM. A **dramatic poem** is a verse that relies heavily on dramatic elements such as monologue or dialogue. Types of dramatic poetry include the *dramatic monologue* and the *soliloquy.* Often dramatic poems are narrative as well—that is, they often tell stories. See *poetry, lyric poem,* and *narrative poem.*

DRAMATIS PERSONÆ. ***Dramatis personæ*** are the characters in a literary work. The term is most often used for the characters in a drama.

DREAM RECORD. A **dream record** is a *diary* or *journal* in which a writer records his or her dreams. See *diary* and *journal.*

DYNAMIC CHARACTER. See *character.*

DYSTOPIA. A **dystopia** is an imaginary, horrible world, the opposite of a *utopia.* Dystopias are common in science fiction. Famous examples of dystopias include the societies described in Aldous Huxley's *Brave New World,* H. G. Wells's *The Time Machine,* and George Orwell's *1984.* See *utopia.*

ECLOGUE. An **eclogue** is a pastoral poem written in imitation of Greek works by Theocritus and Virgil. See *pastoral poem.*

EDITORIAL. An **editorial** is a short persuasive piece that appears in a newspaper, magazine, or other periodical.

EFFECT. The **effect** of a literary work is the general impression or emotional impact that it achieves. Some writers and critics, notably Edgar Allan Poe, have insisted that a successful short story or poem is one in which each detail contributes to the overall effect, or *dominant impression,* produced by the piece.

ELABORATION. **Elaboration**, or **amplification,** is a writing technique in which a subject is introduced and then expanded upon by means of repetition with slight changes, the addition of details, or similar devices.

ELEGIAC LYRIC. An **elegiac lyric** is a poem that expresses a speaker's feelings of loss. The Anglo-Saxon poem "The Wife's Lament" (Unit 2) and William Wordsworth's "She Dwelt among the Untrodden Ways" (Unit 8) are examples.

ELEGY. An **elegy** is a long formal poem about death or loss. Gray's "Elegy Written in a Country Churchyard" (Unit 8) and Tennyson's *In Memoriam* (excerpted in Unit 9) are famous examples. See *elegaic lyric.*

ELIZABETHAN DRAMA. **Elizabethan drama** is the body of plays created during the reign of Queen Elizabeth I of England, from 1558 to

1603. The term is also used to refer to works produced during the reign of James I, which followed that of Elizabeth and lasted until 1625. Famous Elizabethan dramatists included William Shakespeare, Christopher Marlowe, and Ben Jonson.

ELIZABETHAN SONNET. See *sonnet.*

EMPHASIS. **Emphasis** is importance placed on an element in a literary work. Writers achieve emphasis by various means, including repetition, elaboration, stress, restatement in other words, and placement in a strategic position at the beginning or end of a line or a sentence.

END RHYME. **End rhyme** is rhyme that occurs at the ends of lines of verse. See *rhyme.*

END-STOPPED LINE. An **end-stopped line** is a line of verse in which both the sense and the grammar are complete at the end of the line. The opposite of an end-stopped line is a *run-on line.* The following lines are end-stopped:

A little learning is a dangerous thing;
Drink deep, or taste not the Pierian spring.
—Alexander Pope, *An Essay on Criticism*

Excessive use of end-stopped lines gives verse an unnatural, halting quality. See *run-on line.*

ENGLISH SONNET. See *sonnet.*

ENJAMBMENT. See *run-on line.*

ENLIGHTENMENT. The **Enlightenment** was an eighteenth-century philosophical movement characterized by belief in reason, the scientific method, and the perfectibility of people and society. Thinkers of the Enlightenment Era, or Age of Reason, believed that the universe was governed by discoverable, rational principles like the laws of physics discovered by Sir Isaac Newton. By extension, they believed that people could, through application of reason, discover truths relating to the conduct of life or of society. Leading thinkers of the Enlightenment included Diderot, Franklin, Gibbon, Hume, Jefferson, Kant, Montesquieu, Pope, Swift, and Voltaire. See *Neoclassicism.*

EPIC. An **epic** is a long story, often told in verse, involving heroes and gods. Grand in length and scope, an epic provides a portrait of an entire culture, of the legends, beliefs, values, laws, arts, and ways of life of a people. Famous epic poems include Homer's *Iliad* and *Odyssey*, Virgil's *Aeneid*, Dante's *The Divine Comedy,* the anonymous Old English *Beowulf*, and Milton's *Paradise Lost.*

EPIGRAM. An **epigram** is a short, often witty, saying. Pope's "To err is human, to forgive divine" is an example.

EPIGRAPH. An **epigraph** is a quotation or motto used at the beginning of the whole or part of a literary work to help establish the work's theme.

EPILOGUE. An **epilogue** is a concluding section or statement, often one that comments on or draws conclusions from the work as a whole.

EPIPHANY. When applied to literature, the term **epiphany** refers to a moment of sudden insight in which the essence, or nature, of a person, thing, or situation is revealed. The use of the term in this sense was introduced by James Joyce.

EPISODE. An **episode** is a complete action within a literary work.

EPISODIC STRUCTURE. **Episodic structure** is the stringing together of loosely related incidents, or episodes. Many medieval romances have an episodic structure. They tell about the loosely related adventures of a knight or group of knights.

EPISTLE. An **epistle** is a letter, especially one that is highly formal. Letters in verse are sometimes called epistles.

EPISTOLARY FICTION. **Epistolary fiction** is imaginative prose that tells a story through letters, or epistles. Famous epistolary novels include Samuel Richardson's *Pamela* and his *Clarissa,* written in the mid-1700s.

EPITAPH. An **epitaph** is an inscription or verse written to be used on a tomb or written in commemoration of someone who has died. The epitaph on the grave of William Butler Yeats, written by the poet himself, reads, "Cast a cold eye on life, on death. Horseman, pass by!" The following lines are from an epitaph written by the Elizabethan poet Ben Jonson:

Underneath this stone doth lie
As much beauty as could die,
Which in life did harbor give
To more virtue than doth live.

EPITHET. An **epithet** is a characteristic word or phrase used alongside the name of a person, place, or thing. Homer used a traditional epithet when he referred to "rosy-fingered" dawn.

EPONYM. An **eponym** is a person or character from whose name a word or title is derived, or a name that has become synonymous with some general characteristic or idea. Julius Cæsar is the eponym of the medical term *Cesarean section.* England's Queen Victoria is the eponym of Victoria Falls. A reference to *Helen of Troy,* used in place of the more general term *beauty,* or a reference to *an Einstein,* in place of a more general term such as *a smart person,* would be an eponym.

ESSAY. An **essay** is a brief work of prose nonfiction. The original meaning of essay was "a trial or attempt," and the word retains some of this original force. An essay need not be a complete or exhaustive treatment of a subject but rather a tentative exploration of it. A good essay develops a single idea and is characterized by *unity* and *coherence.* See *coherence* and *unity.*

EUPHEMISM. A **euphemism** is an indirect word or phrase used in place of a direct statement that might be considered too offensive. The phrase *passed away,* used instead of *died,* is a euphemism.

EUPHONY. **Euphony** is pleasing sound. Writers achieve euphony by various means, including repetitions of vowel and consonant sounds, rhyme, and parallelism. See *cacophony.*

EXEMPLUM. An **exemplum** is a brief story or *anecdote,* common in the Middle Ages, told to illustrate an idea or a moral. Exempla were often inserted into *homilies,* the sermons included as part of the Roman Catholic mass. See *anecdote* and *parable.*

EXISTENTIALISM. **Existentialism** is a twentieth-century philosophical school that postulates the essential absurdity and meaninglessness of life. Existentialist philosophers such as Albert Camus and Jean-Paul Sartre argued that existence, or being, emerges out of nothingness without any essential, or defining, nature. A human being simply finds himself or herself alive and aware without having any essential defining direction. Any choices that a person makes in order to define himself or herself are made freely and therefore absurdly—one may as well make one choice as another. Freedom of the will is therefore seen by the Existentialist as a terrific burden, one causing anguish to the thinking person, who longs for meaningfulness, not absurd choices. Another significant aspect of Existentialism is its insistence on the essential isolation of each individual consciousness and the consequent anguish of people looking for meaningful connection to others. Though many of the essential tenets of Existentialism have been discredited by contemporary philosophers, the school nonetheless exerted tremendous influence on mid-twentieth-century literature in Europe, Great Britain, and the United States. See *literature of the absurd* and *theater of the absurd.*

EXPOSITION. **1. Exposition** is a type of writing that presents facts or opinions in an organized manner. Among the most common ways to organize exposition are the following: *analysis; classification; comparison-contrast;* and *process* or *how-to* writing. See Purpose and Organization in Nonfiction, pages 64–65, for more information. **2.** In a plot, the **exposition** is that part of a narrative that provides background information, often about the characters, setting, or conflict. See *plot.*

EXPOSITORY WRITING. See *aim.*

EXPRESSIONISM. **Expressionism** is the name given to a twentieth-century movement in literature and art that reacted against Realism in favor of an exaggeration of the elements of the artistic medium itself in an attempt to express ideas or feelings. The use in a play of characters named, simply, Person, Mother, and Character 1 is an example of Expressionism. Modern Expressionist dramatists include Karl Capek, Luigi Pirandello, Elmer Rice, Edward Albee, and to a lesser extent, Tennessee Williams.

EXPRESSIVE WRITING. See *aim.*

EXTENDED METAPHOR. An **extended metaphor** is a point-by-point presentation of one thing as though it were another. The description is meant as an implied comparison, inviting the reader to associate the thing being described with something that is quite different from it. Wyatt's "Whoso List to Hunt" (Unit 4) is an example. In the poem, a woman is described as a deer, the pursuit of the woman as poaching, and the woman's mate as Cæsar, the owner of the property on which the poaching might be done.

EXTERNAL CONFLICT. See *conflict.*

EYE RHYME. See *sight rhyme.*

FABLE. A **fable** is a brief story, often with animal characters, told to express a moral. Famous fables include those of Æsop and La Fontaine. George Orwell's *Animal Farm* is an adaptation of the fable form to political satire.

FABLIAU. A **fabliau** is a brief, humorous tale, often ribald. The form was extremely popular during the Middle Ages. "The Miller's Tale" in Chaucer's *Canterbury Tales* is a famous example. The plural of fabliau is *fabliaux.*

FAIRY TALE. A **fairy tale** is a story that deals with mischievous spirits and other supernatural occurrences, often in medieval settings. The name is generally applied to stories of the kinds collected by Charles Perrault in France and the Brothers Grimm in Germany or told by Hans Christian Andersen of Denmark. "Cinderella," "The White Snake," and "The Little Mermaid" are famous examples.

FALLING ACTION. See *plot.*

FANTASY. A **fantasy** is a literary work that contains highly unrealistic elements. Swift's *Gulliver's Travels* (excerpted in Unit 7) is a fantasy. Fantasy is often contrasted with *science fiction,* in which the unreal elements are given a scientific or pseudo-scientific basis. See *science fiction.*

FARCE. A **farce** is a type of comedy that depends heavily on so-called low humor and on improbable, exaggerated, extreme situations or characters.

FEMINIST CRITICISM. See *criticism.*

FICTION. **Fiction** is prose writing about imagined events or characters. The primary forms of fiction are the *novel* and the *short story.*

FIGURATIVE LANGUAGE. **Figurative language,** also called **figures of speech,** is language meant to understood imaginatively instead of literally. Many writers, especially poets, use figurative language to help readers to see things in new ways. Figurative language includes such literary techniques as *apostrophe, hyperbole, irony, metaphor, metonymy, oxymoron, paradox, personification, simile, synechdoche,* and *understatement.*

FIGURES OF SPEECH. See *figurative language.*

FIRST-PERSON POINT OF VIEW. See *point of view.*

FLASHBACK. A **flashback** is a section of a literary work that presents an event or series of events that occurred earlier than the current time in the work. Writers use flashbacks for many purposes, but most notably to provide *background information,* or exposition. In popular melodramatic works, including modern romance fiction and detective stories, flashbacks are often used to end suspense by revealing key elements of the plot such as a character's true identity or the actual perpetrator of a crime. One common technique is to begin a work with a final event and then to tell the rest of the story as a flashback that explains how that event came about. Another common technique is to begin a story *in medias res* (in the middle of the action) and then to use a flashback to fill in the events that occurred before the opening of the story.

FLASH FICTION. See *short short.*

FLAT CHARACTER. See *character.*

FOIL. A **foil** is a character whose attributes, or characteristics, contrast with and therefore throw into relief the attributes of another character. In Shakespeare's *Hamlet,* for example, Fortinbras, a determined, self-assured person of action, provides a foil for Hamlet, who is plagued with doubts and cannot commit himself to a course of action.

FOLK BALLAD. See *ballad.*

FOLK SONG. A **folk song** is a traditional or composed song typically made up of stanzas, a refrain, and a simple melody. A form of folk literature, folk songs are expressions of commonly shared ideas or feelings and may be narrative or lyric in style. Traditional folk songs are anonymous songs that have been transmitted orally. Examples include the ballad "Bonny Barbara Allan" (Unit 3), the sea chantey "Blow the Man Down," the children's song "Row, Row, Row Your Boat," the spiritual "Go Down, Moses," the railroad song "Casey Jones," and the cowboy song "The Streets of Laredo." Contemporary composers of songs in the folk tradition include Bob Dylan, Paul Simon, Joan Baez, and the Indigo Girls. See *ballad.*

FOLK TALE. A **folk tale** is a brief story passed by word of mouth from generation to generation. Writers often make use of materials from folk tales. Chaucer's "The Pardoner's Tale" (Unit 3) for example, is a retelling of a folk tale, and Yeats's poem "The Stolen Child" is based on Irish folk tales about fairies, called the Sidhe, that steal away children. Famous collections of folk tales include the German *Märchen,* or fairy tales, collected by the Brothers Grimm; Yeats's collection of Irish stories, *Mythologies;* and Zora Neale Hurston's collection of African-American folk tales and other folklore materials, *Their Eyes Were Watching God.* See *fairy tale, folklore,* and *oral tradition.*

FOLKLORE. **Folklore** is a body of orally transmitted beliefs, customs, rituals, traditions, songs, verses, or stories. *Folk tales, fables, fairy tales, tall tales, nursery rhymes, proverbs, legends, myths, parables, riddles, charms, spells,* and *ballads* are all common kinds of folklore, though each of these can be found, as well, in literary forms made in imitation of works from the *oral tradition.*

FOOT. In a poem, a **foot** is a unit of rhythm consisting of strongly and weakly stressed syllables. See *meter* and *scansion.* Also see the specific types of feet: *anapest, dactyl, iamb, spondee,* and *trochee.*

FORESHADOWING. **Foreshadowing** is the act of presenting materials that hint at events to occur later in a story. In Shakespeare's *Macbeth* (Unit 5), the witches' statement that "Fair is foul" and "foul is fair" foreshadows many later events, including Macbeth's confounding of illusion and reality and the several events that occur in the catastrophe of the play that were predicted, but duplicitously, by the witches.

FOREWORD. See *preface.*

FORMAL CRITICISM. See *criticism.*

FOURTEENER. See *meter.*

FOURTH WALL. See *dramatic convention.*

FRAME TALE. A **frame tale** is a story that itself provides a vehicle for the telling of other stories. The *Thousand and One Nights,* Boccaccio's *Decameron,* and Chaucer's *The Canterbury Tales* are frame tales.

FREE VERSE. **Free verse,** or ***vers libre,*** is poetry that avoids use of regular rhyme, rhythm, meter, or division into stanzas. Ted Hughes's "Thistles" and Derek Walcott's "Map of the New World" (both in Unit 10) are examples, though both poems make use of numerous regularities of rhythm. Much of the English and American poetry written in the twentieth century is in free verse.

FREUDIAN CRITICISM. See *criticism.*

FULL CHARACTER. See *character.*

GENRE. A **genre** (zhän´rə) is one of the types or categories into which literary works are divided. Some terms used to name literary genres include *autobiography, biography, comedy, drama, epic, essay, lyric, narrative, novel, pastoral, poetry, short story,* and *tragedy.* Literary works are sometimes classified into genres based on subject matter. Such a classification might describe *detective stories, mysteries, adventure stories, romances, westerns,* and *science fiction* as different genres of fiction.

GHOST STORY. A **ghost story**, or story of the supernatural, includes elements that cannot be explained in a rational or logical way.

GLEEMAN. See *scop.*

GOTHIC NOVEL. A **Gothic novel,** or **Gothic romance,** is a long story containing elements of horror, suspense, mystery, and magic. Gothic novels often contain dark, brooding descriptions of settings and characters. Mary Shelley's *Frankenstein* (excerpted in Unit 8) and Daphne du Maurier's *Rebecca* are examples of the form. Emily Brontë's *Wuthering Heights* contains many Gothic elements.

GOTHIC ROMANCE. See *Gothic novel.*

HAIKU. A **haiku** is a traditional Japanese three-line poem containing five syllables in the first line, seven in the second, and five again in the third. A haiku presents a picture, or image, in order to arouse in the reader a specific emotional and/or spiritual state.

HALF RHYME. See *slant rhyme.*

HEPTAMETER. See *meter.*

HEROIC COUPLET. See *couplet.*

HEROIC EPIC. A **heroic epic** is an epic that has a main purpose of telling the life story of a great hero. Examples of the heroic epic include Homer's *Iliad* and *Odyssey,* Virgil's *Aeneid,* and the Old English poem *Beowulf* (excerpted in Unit 2). See *epic.*

hexameter. See *meter.*

high style. See *style.*

historical criticism. See *criticism.*

how-to writing. See *exposition,* #1.

hymn. A **hymn** is a song or verse of praise, often religious. "Cædmon's Hymn" (in Unit 2) in praise of God the creator is the earliest known poem written in the English language.

hyperbole. A **hyperbole** (hī pur´bə lē) is an exaggeration made for rhetorical effect. Robert Burns uses hyperbole in "To a Red, Red Rose" when he writes,

And I will love you still, my dear,
When all the seas run dry.

iamb. An **iamb** is a poetic foot containing one weakly stressed syllable followed by one strongly stressed syllable, as in the words *afraid* and *release.* A line of poetry made up of iambs is said to be *iambic.*

iambic. See *iamb.*

idiosyncratic symbol. See *symbol.*

image. An **image** is language that creates a representation of an object or experience. An image is also the vivid mental picture created in the reader's mind by that language. The images in a literary work are referred to, collectively, as the work's *imagery.*

imagery. See *image.*

inciting incident. See *plot.*

informational writing. See *aim.*

incremental repetition. See *ballad.*

in medias res. See *action* and *flashback.*

internal conflict. See *conflict.*

internal monologue. An **internal monologue** presents the private sensations, thoughts, and emotions of a character. The reader is allowed to step inside the character's mind and overhear what is going on in there. Which characters' internal states can be revealed in a work of fiction depends on the *point of view* from which the work is told. See *point of view.*

introduction. See *preface.*

inversion. An **inversion** is a poetic technique in which the normal order of words in an utterance is altered. Robert Frost's "Whose woods these are, I think I know" is an inversion of the usual order of expression: "I think I know whose woods these are."

irony. **Irony** is a difference between appearance and reality. Types of irony include the following: *dramatic irony,* in which something is known by the reader or audience but unknown to the characters; *verbal irony,* in which a statement is made that implies its opposite; and *irony of situation,* in which an event occurs that violates the expectations of the characters, the reader, or the audience.

irony of situation. See *irony.*

journal. A **journal,** like a *diary,* is a day-to-day record of a person's activities, experiences, thoughts, and feelings. In contrast to *diary,* the word *journal* connotes an outward rather than an inward focus. However, the two terms are often used interchangeably. See *diary.*

Jungian criticism. See *criticism.*

kenning. A **kenning** is an imaginative compound used in place of an ordinary noun. Examples of kennings from Old English poetry include *whale-road* and *swan's road* for *sea* and *slaughter-wolf* for *Viking.*

limited point of view. See *narrator* and *point of view.*

List of Works Cited. A **List of Works Cited** is a type of bibliography that lists works used or referred to by an author. A standard feature of a research paper, the List of Works Cited appears at the end of the paper and is arranged in alphabetical order.

literary ballad. See *ballad.*

literature of the absurd. **Literature of the absurd** is literature influenced by existentialist philosophy, which represents human life as meaningless or absurd because of the supposed lack of essential connection between human beings and the world around them. In brief, the existentialist philosophers, such as Albert Camus and Jean-Paul Sartre, believed that a person's conscious existence precedes, or comes before, any essential self-definition and that self-definition can occur only as a result of making an absurd, completely free choice to act, think, or believe in certain ways. The literature of the absurd emphasizes the meaninglessness of life and the isolation, or alienation, of individuals. Much of the literature of the absurd is filled with horrors, anguish, random events, and illogical or improbable occurrences. Modern practitioners of the literature of the absurd include the novelists Franz Kafka, Thomas Pynchon, and Kurt Vonnegut, Jr., and the playwrights Eugène Ionesco, Samuel Beckett, Edward Albee, and Harold Pinter. See *Existentialism* and *theater of the absurd.*

LOW STYLE. See *style.*

LYRIC POEM. A **lyric poem** is a highly musical verse that expresses the emotions of a speaker. Shakespeare's sonnets and Byron's "She Walks in Beauty" are examples. Lyric poems are often contrasted with narrative poems, which have telling a story as their main purpose. See *poetry.*

MAIN CHARACTER. See *character.*

MAJOR CHARACTER. See *character.*

MARXIST CRITICISM. See *criticism.*

MEMOIR. A **memoir** is a nonfiction narration that tells a story. A memoir can be autobiographical (about one's life) or biographical (about someone else's life). Memoirs are based on a person's experiences and reactions to historical events.

METAPHOR. A **metaphor** is a figure of speech in which one thing is spoken or written about as if it were another. This figure of speech invites the reader to make a comparison between the two things. The two "things" involved are the writer's actual subject, the *tenor* of the metaphor, and another thing to which the subject is likened, the *vehicle* of the metaphor. When, in Meditation 17 (Unit 6), John Donne writes that "all mankind is of one author and is one volume," he is using two metaphors:

TENOR	VEHICLE
mankind	a volume or book
God	the author of the volume or book

Personifications and similes are types of metaphor. See *dead metaphor, mixed metaphor, personification,* and *simile.*

METER. The **meter** of a poem is its rhythmical pattern. English verse is generally described as being made up of rhythmical units called *feet,* as follows:

TYPE OF FOOT	STRESS PATTERN	EXAMPLE
iamb, or iambic foot	⌣ /	insist
trochee, or trochaic foot	/ ⌣	freedom
anapest, or anapestic foot	⌣ ⌣ /	unimpressed
dactyl, or dactylic foot	/ ⌣ ⌣	feverish
spondee, or spondaic foot	/ /	baseball

Some scholars also use the term *pyrrhic* to describe a foot with two weak stresses. Using this term, the word *unbelievable* might be described as consisting of two feet, an anapest followed by a pyrrhic:

⌣ ⌣ / | ⌣ ⌣
un be liev | a ble

Terms used to describe the number of feet in a line include the following:

monometer for a one-foot line
dimeter for a two-foot line
trimeter for a three-foot line
tetrameter for a four-foot line
pentameter for a five-foot line
hexameter, or *Alexandrine,* for a six-foot line
heptameter for a seven-foot line
octameter for an eight-foot line

A seven-foot line of iambic feet is called a *fourteener.*

A complete description of the meter of a line includes both the term for the type of foot that predominates in the line and the term for the number of feet in the line. The most common English meters are iambic tetrameter and iambic pentameter. The following are examples of each:

IAMBIC TETRAMETER:

⌣ / ⌣ / ⌣ / ⌣ /
O slow | ly, slow | ly rose | she up

IAMBIC PENTAMETER:

⌣ / ⌣ / ⌣ / ⌣ /
The cur | few tolls | the knell | of part |

⌣ /
ing day,

METONYMY. Metonymy is the naming of an object associated with a thing in place of the name of the thing itself. Speaking of *the White House* when one means *the administrative or executive branch of the United States government* is an example of metonymy.

MIDDLE ENGLISH. Middle English is the form of the English language that was used from approximately 1100 to 1500. Middle English grew out of Old English and was heavily influenced by the variety of French spoken by the Normans, who conquered England in 1066. Great writers in Middle English included The Pearl Poet and Geoffrey Chaucer.

MIDDLE STYLE. See *style.*

MIMETIC CRITICISM. See *criticism.*

MINOR CHARACTER. See *character.*

MIRACLE PLAY. A **miracle play** is a type of medieval drama that tells a story from a saint's life.

MIXED METAPHOR. A **mixed metaphor** is an expression or passage that conflates, or garbles together, two or more metaphors. An example of mixed metaphor would be the sentence "The chariot of the sun screamed across the sky," in which the sun is described, inconsistently, as both a chariot and as something that screams. See *metaphor.*

MODE. A **mode** is a form of writing. One common classification system, based on purpose or aim, divides types of writing into five modes: expository/informative, imaginative, narrative, personal/expressive, and persuasive/argumentative. See *aim.*

MODERN ENGLISH. Modern English is the form of the English language used from approximately AD 1500 to the present day. Modern English grew out of Middle English. Major influences on the emergence of Modern English include, first, the Renaissance Era revival of Greek and Latin learning, and, second, increased exploration, colonization, and trade. Both led to extensive borrowings from other languages, especially Latin and French.

MONOMETER. See *meter.*

MOOD. Mood, or **atmosphere,** is the emotion created in the reader by part or all of a literary work. The writer can evoke in the reader an emotional response—such as fear, discomfort, longing, or anticipation—by working carefully with descriptive language and sensory details.

MORAL. A **moral** is a practical or moral lesson, usually relating to the principles of right and wrong, to be drawn from a story or other work of literature.

MORALITY PLAY. A **morality play** is a type of medieval drama in which the characters are abstract caricatures of virtues, vices, and the like. Morality plays are a type of *naive allegory. Everyman* (excerpted in Unit 3), is the most famous example of the morality play. See *allegory.*

MOTIF. A **motif** is any element that recurs in one or more works of literature or art. Examples of common folk tale motifs found in oral traditions throughout the world include grateful animals or the grateful dead, three wishes, the trial or quest, and the magical metamorphosis, or transformation of one thing into another. "Cinderella," "The Ugly Duckling," and the Arthurian "Sword in the Stone" are examples of the transformation motif, in which persons or creatures of humble station are revealed to be exceptional. Much can be revealed about a literary work by studying the motifs within it. In Shakespeare's *Macbeth,* (Unit 5), for example, recurring motifs include ambiguity, disturbances in nature, madness, and blood. At the beginning of the play, the witches, through their double talk, invite Macbeth to violate the moral order. Disturbances in nature, madness, and blood are all consequences of this violation.

MOTIVATION. A **motivation** is a force that moves a character to think, feel, or behave in a certain way. In D. H. Lawrence's "The Rocking-Horse Winner" (Unit 1), the protagonist, Paul, is motivated by a desire to earn money to make life more pleasant for his mother.

MUSE. In ancient Greek and Roman myth, the **Muses**—the nine daughters of Zeus and Mnemosyne, or Memory—were believed to provide the inspiration for the arts and sciences. Calliope was the Muse of epic poetry; Clio, the Muse of history; Erato, the Muse of lyrical poetry; Euterpe, the Muse of music; Melpomene, the Muse of tragedy; Polyhymnia, the Muse of sacred choral poetry; Terpischore, the Muse of choral dance and song; Thalia, the Muse of comedy; and Urania, the Muse of astronomy. The idea of the Muse has often been used by later writers to explain the vagaries and mysteries of literary inspiration. In the opening of *Paradise Lost* (excerpted in Unit 6), Milton calls upon the Holy Spirit, one of the three members of the Christian Trinity, asking that spirit to be his Muse and to inspire his verse. The connection of the Muses with entertainments and the arts survives in our English words *amusing* and *amusement.*

MYSTERY PLAY. A **mystery play** is a type of medieval drama that tells a story from the Bible.

MYTH. A **myth** is a story that explains objects or events in the natural world as resulting from the action of some supernatural force or entity, most often a god. Every early culture around the globe has produced its own myths. A typical example is the Greek myth of the origin of the Narcissus flower. Narcissus was a vain boy who liked to look at his own reflection in pools of water. The punishment for his vanity was to be turned into a flower that grows near water. There he can look at his own reflection for as long as the world lasts. Literature in English often alludes to or makes use of materials from Greek, Roman, Germanic, and Celtic myths. Bernard Shaw's play *Pygmalion* (Unit 12), for example, is a reworking in modern dress of the Greco-Roman myth of Pygmalion. One version of the myth is told in the Roman poet Ovid's collection of myths known as the *Metamorphoses,* or *Book of Changing Forms.*

NARRATION. **Narration** is a type of writing that tells a story, or describes events, most often using time, or *chronological order,* as a way of organization. See *chronological order.*

NARRATIVE POEM. A **narrative poem** is a verse that tells a story. The ballad "Sir Patrick Spens" (Unit 3) and the epic *Paradise Lost* (excerpted in Unit 6) are both examples of narrative poems. See *poetry, ballad,* and *epic.*

NARRATOR. A **narrator** is one who tells a story. In a drama, the narrator may be a character who introduces, concludes, or comments upon the action of the play. However, dramas typically do not have narrators. Works of fiction, on the other hand, always do, unless they consist entirely of dialogue without *tag lines,* in which case they become no longer fictions but *closet dramas,* ones meant to be read but not performed. The narrator in a work of fiction may be a central or minor character or simply someone who witnessed or heard about the events being related. Writers achieve a wide variety of ends by varying the characteristics of the narrator chosen for a particular work. Of primary importance is the choice of the narrator's *point of view.* Will the narrator be *omniscient,* knowing all things, including the internal workings of the minds of the characters in the story, or will the narrator be *limited* in his or her knowledge? Will the narrator participate in the action of the story or stand outside that action and comment on it? Will the narrator be reliable or unreliable? That is, will the reader be able to trust the narrator's statements? These are all questions that a writer must answer when developing a narrator. See *point of view* and *speaker.*

NATURALISM. **Naturalism** was a literary movement of the late nineteenth and early twentieth centuries that saw actions and events as resulting inevitably from biological or natural forces or from forces in the environment. Often these forces were beyond the comprehension or control of the characters subjected to them. Taken to its extreme, Naturalism views all events as mechanically determined by external forces, including the decisions made by people. Much of modern fiction, with its emphasis on social conditions leading to particular consequences for characters, is naturalistic in this sense. The novels of Thomas Hardy, which present characters who are victims of fate, are naturalistic in the sense that the characters' destinies are determined. Great writers of fiction informed by the philosophy of Naturalism include Émile Zola, Stephen Crane, Jack London, and Theodore Dreiser.

NEAR RHYME. See *slant rhyme.*

NEOCLASSICISM. **Neoclassicism** is the term used to describe the revival during the English Enlightenment or Restoration Era of ideals of art and literature derived from the Greek and Roman classics. These ideals included respect for authority and tradition, austerity, clarity, conservatism, decorum, economy, grace, imitation of the natural order, harmony, moderation, proportion, reason, restraint, self-control, simplicity, tradition, wit, and unity. Neoclassical literature was witty and socially astute but tended toward excessive *didacticism* and an excessive distrust of invention and imagination. Popular forms of Neoclassical writing included the essay, the epistle, the satire, the parody, poems in rhymed couplets, and the earliest novels. As if in response to Pope's dictum that "The proper study of man is man," Neoclassical writers wrote primarily about social life and social interactions. Great English Neoclassical writers included Dryden, Swift, Pope, Behn, Johnson, Boswell, Congreve, Addison, Steele, Defoe, Richardson, Fielding, and Smollett. Romanticism can be seen as a reaction against Neoclassical restraint. See *Classicism, didacticism,* and *Romanticism.*

NEW CRITICISM. See *criticism.*

NONFICTION. Nonfiction is writing about real events. Essays, autobiographies, biographies, and news stories are all types of nonfiction. See *prose.*

NONSENSE VERSE. A **nonsense verse** is a kind of light verse that contains elements that are silly, absurd, or meaningless. Sometimes, as is the case with Lewis Carroll's "Jabberwocky," the apparent nonsense of the verse gives way to sense upon closer analysis. Carroll's poem turns out not to be nonsense at all, but rather an ingenious retelling, in a mock heroic ballad, of a stock folk tale story—that of a young person who sets off on a quest, slays a terrible beast, and returns home victorious. A purer example of nonsense can be found in the following lines of a famous nursery rhyme:

> As I was going up the stair,
> I met a man who wasn't there.
> He wasn't there again today.
> I wish, I wish he'd go away.

NOVEL. A **novel** is a long work of prose fiction. Often novels have involved plots; many characters, both major and minor; and numerous settings. Among the first extended works of prose fiction in English were Aphra Behn's *Oroonoko,* written in 1688; John Bunyan's *Pilgrim's Progress,* completed in 1684; and Swift's *Gulliver's Travels,* written in 1726. Excerpts of these three novels can be found in Unit 6. Early novels of note include Defoe's *Robinson Crusoe,* Richardson's *Pamela* and *Clarissa,* Fielding's *Tom Jones,* and Sterne's *Tristram Shandy.* Classic English novels in various genres include Anne Radcliffe's Gothic novel *Mysteries of Udolpho;* Jane Austen's novel of manners *Pride and Prejudice;* Sir Walter Scott's historical novel *Ivanhoe;* and Dickens's *Bildungsroman*, or novel of personal development, *Great Expectations*. Other great British novelists include Emily Brontë, George Eliot, Thomas Hardy, James Joyce, Virginia Woolf, D. H. Lawrence, Henry James, E. M. Forster, Joseph Conrad, Graham Greene, Patrick White, and Doris Lessing.

NOVELLA. A **novella** is a short novel.

NURSERY RHYME. A **nursery rhyme** is a children's verse. Famous English writers of nursery rhymes include Rudyard Kipling and Edward Lear.

OBJECTIVE CORRELATIVE. An **objective correlative** is a group of images that together create a particular emotion in the reader. The term was coined by T. S. Eliot. See *image.*

OCCASIONAL VERSE. An **occasional verse** is one written to celebrate or commemorate some particular event. Auden's "In Memory of W. B. Yeats," written on the death of the great Irish poet, is an example.

OCTAMETER. See *meter.*

OCTAVE. An **octave** is an eight-line stanza. A Petrarchan sonnet begins with an octave. See *meter* and *sonnet.*

ODE. An **ode** is a lofty lyric poem on a serious theme. It may employ alternating stanza patterns, developed from the choral ode of Greek dramatic poetry. These stanza patterns are called the *strophe*, the *antistrophe*, and the *epode*. However, not all odes follow this pattern. Keats's "Ode on a Grecian Urn" (Unit 8) is an example of an ode that does not.

OFF RHYME. See *slant rhyme.*

OLD ENGLISH. Old English, or **Anglo-Saxon,** is the earliest form of the English language. It declined after the Norman invasion of England in 1066. Old English was a highly inflected language, one that used syllables at the ends of words to indicate the words' grammatical functions. It was related to other Germanic languages that gave rise to modern Dutch, German, Icelandic, and Norwegian. For more information on Old English, see page 145.

OMNISCIENT POINT OF VIEW. See *narrator* and *point of view.*

ONE-ACT. See *act.*

ONE-DIMENSIONAL CHARACTER. See *character.*

ONOMATOPOEIA. **Onomatopoeia** is the use of words or phrases that sound like the things to which they refer. Examples of onomatopoeia include words such as *buzz, click,* and *pop.* Poets and other writers often make use of onomatopoeia, as in Tennyson's description of the "murmuring of innumerable bees" in "Come Down, O Maid."

ORAL TRADITION. An **oral tradition** is a work, a motif, an idea, or a custom that is passed by word-of-mouth from generation to generation. Materials transmitted orally may be simplified in the retelling. They also may be sensationalized because of the tendency of retellers to add to or elaborate upon the materials that come down to them. Often, works in an oral tradition contain miraculous or magical elements. Common works found in the oral traditions of peoples around the world include *folk tales, fables, fairy tales, tall tales, nursery rhymes, proverbs, legends, myths, parables, riddles, charms, spells,* and *ballads.* See *folklore.*

OTTAVA RIMA. ***Ottava rima*** is a stanza form made up of eight iambic pentameter lines rhyming *abababcc.* William Butler Yeats used this form in his poem "Among School Children." (See page 19 for a stanza of that poem.)

OXYMORON. An **oxymoron** is a statement that contradicts itself. Words like *bittersweet, tragicomedy,* and *pianoforte* (literally, "soft-loud") are oxymorons that develop a complex meaning from two seemingly contradictory elements. Milton uses an oxymoron in Book I of *Paradise Lost* (excerpted in Unit 6) when he describes the flames of Hell as giving no light but rather being "darkness visible."

PALINDROME. A **palindrome** is a word, a phrase, or a sentence that reads the same backward as forward. Examples include the word *radar* and the sentence *Able was I ere I saw Elba,* which describes Napoleon's condition prior to his exile to the island of Elba.

PARABLE. A **parable** is a very brief story told to teach a moral lesson. The most famous parables are those such as "The Parable of the Prodigal Son" told by Christ in the Bible. The medieval *exemplum* was a kind of parable. See *exemplum.*

PARADOX. A **paradox** is a seemingly contradictory statement, idea, or event. All forms of *irony* involve paradox. An *oxymoron* is a paradoxical statement. William Wordsworth's statement that "the child is father to the man" is an example of a paradox that can be resolved, on analysis, into a coherent, noncontradictory idea. Some paradoxes, however, present unresolvable contradictory ideas. An example of such a paradox is the statement, "This sentence is a lie." If the sentence is true, then it is false; if it is false, then it is true. See *irony* and *oxymoron.*

PARALLELISM. **Parallelism** is a rhetorical technique in which a writer emphasizes the equal value or weight of two or more ideas by expressing them in the same grammatical form. William Blake uses parallelism in these lines from "The Lamb" (Unit 8):

And I made a rural pen,
And I stain'd the water clear,
And I wrote my happy songs
Every child may joy to hear.

PARAPHRASE. A **paraphrase** is a rewriting of a passage in different words. A paraphrase is often distinguished from an *abstract* or *summary* as follows: a summary is shorter than the original, whereas a paraphrase may be as long as or longer than the original. One of the central ideas of the so-called New Criticism was that it is impossible to paraphrase a literary work precisely. Much of the content or meaning of a literary work lies in how it is expressed. Changing the expression therefore inevitably changes the meaning. See *abstract.*

PARODY. A **parody** is a literary work that imitates another work for humorous, often satirical, purposes. The opening lines of Elizabeth Barrett Browning's Sonnet 43 (Unit 9),

How do I love thee? Let me count the ways.
I love thee to the depth and breadth and height
My soul can reach, when feeling out of sight
For the ends of Being and ideal Grace.

have been parodied as follows:

How do I love thee? Let me count the ways.
Gee, there aren't any. Too bad for you.
Toodle-loo.

PASTORAL POEM. A **pastoral poem,** from the Latin *pastor,* meaning "shepherd," is a verse that deals with idealized rural life. Examples of pastoral poems include the song Psalm 23 from the Biblical book Proverbs that begins "The Lord is my shepherd" (Unit 4), Marlowe's "The Passionate Shepherd to His Love" (Unit 4), and Blake's "The Lamb" (Unit 8). Pastoral verse, based on the *Idylls* of Theocritus and the *Eclogues* of Virgil, enjoyed great popularity during the Renaissance Period. Writers of pastoral poems included Spenser, Sidney, and Shakespeare.

PATHETIC FALLACY. The **pathetic fallacy** is the tendency to attribute human emotions to nonhuman things, particularly to things in the natural world. The term was coined by the Victorian critic John Ruskin and has often been used to describe the excesses of sentimental verse.

PENTAMETER. See *meter.*

PERIODICAL. A **periodical** is a newspaper, magazine, journal, newsletter, or other publication that is produced on a regular basis.

PERSONA. A **persona** consists of the qualities of a person or character that are shown through speech or actions.

PERSONAL ESSAY. A **personal essay** is a short work of nonfictional prose on a single topic related to the life or interests of the writer. Personal essays are characterized by an intimate and informal style and tone. They often, but not always, are written in the first person. See *essay.*

PERSONAL SYMBOL. See *symbol.*

PERSONIFICATION. **Personification** is a figure of speech in which an idea, animal, or thing is described as if it were a person. The speaker of Shelley's "Ode to the West Wind" (Unit 8) is using personification when he addresses the wind using the words "thou breath of Autumn's being."

PERSUASIVE WRITING. See *aim.*

PETRARCHAN SONNET. See *sonnet.*

PLAGIARISM. **Plagiarism** is the act of using material gathered from another person or work without crediting the source of the material.

PLOT. A **plot** is a series of events related to a central *conflict,* or struggle. A typical plot involves the introduction of a conflict, its development, and its eventual resolution. Terms used to describe elements of plot include the following:

- The **exposition,** or **introduction,** sets the tone or mood, introduces the characters and the setting, and provides necessary background information.
- The **inciting incident** is the event that introduces the central conflict.
- The **rising action,** or **complication,** develops the conflict to a high point of intensity.
- The **climax** is the high point of interest or suspense in the plot.
- The **crisis,** or **turning point,** often the same event as the climax, is the point in the plot where something decisive happens to determine the future course of events and the eventual working out of the conflict.
- The **falling action** is all of the events that follow the climax.
- The **resolution** is the point at which the central conflict is ended, or resolved.
- The **dénouement** is any material that follows the resolution and that ties up loose ends.
- The **catastrophe,** in tragedy, is the event that marks the ultimate tragic fall of the central character. Often this event is the character's death.

Plots rarely contain all these elements in precisely this order. Elements of exposition may be introduced at any time in the course of a work. A work may begin with a catastrophe and then use flashback to explain it. The exposition or dénouement or even the resolution may be missing. The inciting incident may occur before the beginning of the action actually described in the work. These are but a few of the many possible variations that plots can exhibit. See *conflict.*

POETIC LICENSE. **Poetic license** is the right claimed by writers to change elements of reality to suit the purposes of particular works that they create. Thomas Hardy's use in "Channel Firing" (Unit 9) of characters who rise from their graves and talk is an example of poetic license. Such things do not happen in reality, but they are accepted by readers willing to suspend disbelief in order to have imaginary experiences. See *suspension of disbelief.*

POETRY. **Poetry** is imaginative language carefully chosen and arranged to communicate experiences, thoughts, or emotions. It differs from prose in that it compresses meaning into fewer words, and often uses *meter, rhyme,* and techniques such as *metaphor* and *simile.* Poetry is usually arranged in lines and stanzas as opposed to sentences and paragraphs, and it can be more free in the ordering of words and the use of punctuation. Types of poetry include *narrative, dramatic,* and *lyric.* See *meter* and *rhyme.*

POINT OF VIEW. **Point of view** is the vantage point from which a story is told. Stories are typically written from a *first-person point of view,* in which the narrator uses words such as *I* and *we,* or from a *third-person point of view,* in which the narrator uses words such as *he, she, it,* and *they* and avoids the use of *I* and *we.* Some stories are told from a *second-person point of view,* in which the narrator uses *you,* directly addressing the reader. In stories written from a first-person point of view, the narrator may be a participant or witness of the action. In stories told from a third-person point of view, the narrator generally stands outside the action. In some stories, the narrator's point of view is *limited.* In such stories, the narrator can reveal the private, internal thoughts of himself or herself or of a single character. In other stories, the narrator's point of view is *omniscient.* In such stories the narrator can reveal the private, internal thoughts of any character.

PORTMANTEAU. See *blend.*

POULTER'S MEASURE. **Poulter's measure** is a metrical form that makes use of couplets containing alternating iambic hexameter and iambic heptameter lines. The form is used in Queen Elizabeth I's "Doubt of Future Foes" (Unit 4).

PRAGMATIC CRITICISM. See *criticism.*

PRÉCIS. See *abstract.*

PREFACE. A **preface** is a statement made at the beginning of a literary work, often by way of introduction. The terms *foreword, preface,* and *introduction* are often used interchangeably.

PROCESS WRITING. See *exposition,* #1.

PROLOGUE. A **prologue** is an introduction to a literary work, often one that sets the scene and introduces the conflict or the main characters. "The Prologue" to Chaucer's *The Canterbury Tales* (Unit 3) is an example. In Renaissance times, the use of a prologue spoken by a narrator at the beginning of a drama was quite common.

PROSCENIUM STAGE. See *stage.*

PROSE. **Prose** is the broad term used to describe all writing that is not drama or poetry, including fiction and nonfiction. Types of prose writing include novels, short stories, essays, and news stories. Most biographies, autobiographies, and letters are written in prose. See *fiction.*

PROSE POEM. A **prose poem** is a work of prose, usually a short work, that makes such extensive use of poetic language, such as figures of speech and words that echo their sense, that the line between prose and poetry, never a clear one, becomes blurred. An example of a prose poem is Margaret Atwood's "Bread" (Unit 10).

PROSODY. **Prosody,** or **versification,** is the study of the structure of poetry. In particular, prosodists study meter, rhyme, rhythm, and stanza form. See *meter, rhyme, rhythm,* and *stanza.*

PROTAGONIST. See *character.*

PROVERB. A **proverb,** or **adage,** is a traditional saying, such as "You can lead a horse to water, but you can't make it drink" or the title of Shakespeare's play *All's Well That Ends Well.*

PSALM. A **psalm** is a lyrical hymn of praise, supplication, or thanksgiving. Psalm 23 (Unit 4), attributed to David, that begins with the line "The Lord is my shepherd," is an example.

PSEUDONYM. A **pseudonym** is a name assumed by a writer. Examples of pseudonyms include *George Eliot,* the pseudonym of Mary Ann Evans, and *Lewis Carroll,* the pseudonym of Charles Dodgson.

PSYCHOLOGICAL FICTION. **Psychological fiction** is fiction that emphasizes the interior, subjective experiences of its characters, and especially such fiction when it deals with emotional or mental disturbance or anguish.

PUN. A **pun** is a play on words, one that wittily exploits a double meaning. The porter scene in Shakespeare's *Macbeth* (Unit 5) contains a pun based on an Elizabethan usage. In Elizabethan English, the word *goose* referred both to a type of fowl and to a tailor's pressing iron. Shakespeare has his porter pretend to be the porter of Hell's gate, opening it to let in a tailor guilty of theft: "Who's there? Faith, here's an English tailor come hither for stealing out of a French hose. Come in, tailor. Here you may roast your goose."

PURITANISM. **Puritanism** was a Protestant religious movement that emerged in England in the 1500s and later spread to the colonies of New England. The Puritans objected to the wealth, power, authority, and elaborate ritual of the Catholic Church. They professed a desire to "purify" the Church of England by ridding it of Catholic practices. The English Puritans overthrew the monarchy and, under Oliver Cromwell, governed the country during what is known as the Commonwealth, or Puritan Interregnum, from 1642 to 1646. The Puritans are known for their austerity and acceptance of the basic principles of Calvinism, including the ideas of preordination and original sin. Some important English Puritan writers are John Bunyan and John Milton. Important American Puritan writers include Cotton Mather and Jonathan Edwards. See *Calvinism.*

PURPOSE. See *aim.*

PYRRHIC. See *meter.*

QUATRAIN. A **quatrain** is a stanza containing four lines.

QUINTAIN. A **quintain,** or **quintet**, is a stanza containing five lines.

QUINTET. See *quintain.*

RAP. **Rap** is improvised, rhymed verse that is chanted or sung, often to a musical accompaniment.

READER-RESPONSE CRITICISM. See *criticism.*

REALISM. **Realism** is the attempt to render in art an accurate portrayal of reality. The theory that the purpose of art is to imitate life is at least as old as Aristotle. The eighteenth-century development of the novel, with its attention to details of character, setting, and social life, can be thought of as a step toward increased Realism in writing. However, the term *Realism* is generally applied to literature of the late nineteenth century written in reaction to Romanticism and emphasizing details of ordinary life.

REDUNDANCY. **Redundancy** is needless repetition. The phrase *firmly determined* is redundant because the word *determined* already implies firmness.

REFRAIN. A **refrain** is a line or group of lines repeated in a poem or song. Many *ballads* contain refrains.

REGIONAL DIALECT. See *dialect.*

RENAISSANCE. The **Renaissance** was the period from the fourteenth to the early seventeenth century when Europe was making the transition from the medieval to the modern world. The word *renaissance* means "rebirth." The term refers to the rebirth of interest in ancient Greek and Latin writing that occurred during the period, a rebirth that is known as Humanism. The Renaissance was characterized by a lessening of reliance on authority, by a decline in feudalism and in the universal authority of the church, by increased nationalism, by increasingly active university and city life, by increased opportunities for individual economic attainment and freedom, and by increased belief in the value of this life (as opposed to the afterlife) in and of itself.

REPETITION. **Repetition** is the writer's conscious reuse of a sound, word, phrase, sentence, or other element.

RESOLUTION. See *plot.*

REVERSAL. A **reversal** is a dramatic change in the direction of events in a drama or narrative, especially a change in the fortunes of the protagonist. See *plot.*

REVIEW. A **review** is a written evaluation of a work of art, a performance, or a literary work, especially one that appears in a periodical or on a broadcast news program. Common subjects of reviews include books, films, art exhibitions, restaurants, and performances of all kinds, from rock concerts to ballets.

RHETORIC. **Rhetoric** is the art of speaking or writing effectively. It involves the study of ways in which speech and writing affect or influence audiences. Rhetoric has also been defined as the art of persuasion.

RHETORICAL CRITICISM. See *criticism.*

RHETORICAL QUESTION. A **rhetorical question** is one asked for effect but not meant to be answered because the answer is clear from context, as in Christina Rossetti's lines, "Who has seen the wind? / Neither you nor I."

RHETORICAL TECHNIQUE. A **rhetorical technique** is an extraordinary but literal use of language to achieve a particular effect on an audience. Common rhetorical techniques include *antithesis, apostrophe, catalog, chiasmus, parallelism, repetition,* and *the rhetorical question.*

RHYME. **Rhyme** is the repetition of sounds at the ends of words. Types of rhyme include *end rhyme* (the use of rhyming words at the ends of lines), *internal rhyme* (the use of rhyming words within lines), *exact rhyme* (in which the rhyming words end with the same sound or sounds), and *slant rhyme* (in which the rhyming sounds are similar but not identical). An example of exact rhyme is the word pair *moon/June.* Examples of slant rhyme are the word pairs *rave/rove* and *rot/rock.* See *poetry, slant rhyme,* and *rhyme scheme.*

RHYME SCHEME. A **rhyme scheme** is a pattern of end rhymes, or rhymes at the ends of lines of verse. The rhyme scheme of a poem is designated by letters, with matching letters signifying matching sounds.

RHYTHM. **Rhythm** is the pattern of beats or stresses in a line of verse or prose. See *meter.*

RIDDLE. A **riddle** is a word game in which something is described in an unusual way and the reader or listener must figure out what that something is. Riddles are common in folklore and myth throughout the world. Examples include the Anglo-Saxon riddles collected in the *Exeter Book* (see Unit 2).

RISING ACTION. See *plot.*

ROMANCE. **Romance** is a term used to refer to four types of literature: 1. medieval stories about the adventures and loves of knights; 2. novels and other fictions involving exotic locales and extraordinary or mysterious events and characters; 3. nonrealistic fictions in general; and 4. in popular modern usage, love stories of all kinds. The term originated in the Middle Ages. It was first used to describe stories believed to be based upon Latin originals (stories told by the Romans). It came to be used in Europe and England for stories in prose or poetry about knightly exploits, including those told about such characters as Alexander the Great, Roland, Percival, Tristan and Isolde, and King Arthur and his knights of the Round Table. Because the later medieval romances were for the most part told in prose, the term came to be applied to prose fictions in general, and especially to those that were highly imaginative. In the nineteenth century, the term was commonly used to describe fictional works, such as the novels of Sir Walter Scott, that dealt with adventure in exotic locales. It was used by Nathaniel Hawthorne to describe stories like his *Blithedale Romance* and *House of the Seven Gables* because of their deviations from Realism. Today, the term is quite widely used to refer to love stories, especially popular, sentimental stories of the sort often turned into television movies.

ROMANTIC CRITICISM. See *criticism.*

ROMANTICISM. **Romanticism** was a literary and artistic movement of the eighteenth and nineteenth centuries that placed value on emotion or imagination over reason, the individual over society, nature and wildness over human works, the country over the town, common people over aristocrats, and freedom over control or authority. Major writers of the Romantic Era included William Blake, William Wordsworth, Samuel Taylor Coleridge, Percy Bysshe Shelley, Mary Shelley, and George Gordon, Lord Byron.

ROUNDED CHARACTER. See *character.*

RUN-ON LINE. A **run-on line** is a line of verse in which the sense or the grammatical structure does not end with the end of the line but rather is continued on one or more subsequent lines. The following lines from Byron's "She Walks in Beauty" (Unit 8) form a single sentence:

> She walks in beauty, like the night
>   Of cloudless climes and starry skies;
> And all that's best of dark and bright
>   Meet in her aspect and her eyes:
> Thus mellow'd to that tender light
>   Which heaven to gaudy day denies.

The act of continuing a statement beyond the end of a line is called *enjambment.* See *end-stopped line.*

SATIRE. **Satire** is humorous writing or speech intended to point out errors, falsehoods, foibles, or failings. It is written for the purpose of reforming human behavior or human institutions. Jonathan Swift's *Gulliver's Travels* (excerpted in Unit 7), for example, satirizes political and social institutions.

SCANSION. **Scansion** is the art of analyzing poetry to determine its meter. See *meter.*

SCENE. A **scene** is a short section of a literary work that presents action that occurs in a single place or at a single time. Long divisions of dramas are often divided into scenes.

SCIENCE FICTION. **Science fiction** is highly imaginative fiction containing fantastic elements based on scientific principles, discoveries, or laws. It is similar to *fantasy* in that it deals with imaginary worlds but differs from fantasy in having a scientific basis. Mary Shelley's *Frankenstein* (excerpted in Unit 8) was an early precursor of modern science fiction. She based her idea of the creation of artificial life on nineteenth-century experiments with so-called animal magnetism, the electrical charges believed by some people in those days to be the force motivating living things and distinguishing them from nonliving things. Arthur C. Clarke's short story "History Lesson," which is set on Venus, is an example of science fiction. George Orwell's *Nineteen Eighty-four* has many science fiction elements. Often science fiction deals with the future, the distant past, or with worlds other than our own such as distant planets, parallel universes, and worlds under the ground or the sea. The genre allows writers to suspend or alter certain elements of reality in order to create fascinating and sometimes instructive alternatives. Important writers of science fiction include H. G. Wells, Jules Verne, Ray Bradbury, Arthur C. Clarke, Isaac Asimov, Ursula K. Le Guin, Robert Heinlein, and Kurt Vonnegut, Jr. See *fantasy.*

SCOP. An Anglo-Saxon poet or minstrel was known as a **scop,** or **gleeman.** The scop composed verse orally and recited it to the accompaniment of a harp.

SENSORY DETAIL. See *description.*

SENTIMENTALITY. **Sentimentality** is an excessive expression of emotion. Much popular literature of the nineteenth and twentieth centuries is characterized by sentimentality.

SEPTET. A **septet** is a stanza with seven lines.

SESTET. A **sestet** is a stanza with six lines, such as the second part of a Petrarchan sonnet. See *meter* and *sonnet.*

SET. A **set** is a collection of objects on a stage arranged in such a way as to create a scene.

SETTING. The **setting** of a literary work is the time and place in which it occurs, together with all the details used to create a sense of a particular time and place. Writers create setting by various means. In drama, the setting is often revealed by the stage *set* and the costumes, though it may be revealed through what the characters say about their environs. In fiction, setting is most often revealed by means of description of such elements as landscape, scenery, buildings, furniture, clothing, the weather, and the season. It can also be revealed by how characters talk and behave. In its widest sense, setting includes the general social, political, moral, and psychological conditions in which characters find themselves. See *set.*

SHAKESPEAREAN SONNET. See *sonnet.*

SHAPE POEM. See *concrete poem.*

SHORT SHORT. A **short short,** or **flash fiction,** is an extremely brief short story. This recently recognized genre of the short story is currently enjoying considerable popularity among readers of literary magazines and short story collections published in the United States. Short shorts sometimes take the form of *anecdotes,* or retellings of single incidents. Alternatively, they may attempt to develop an entire plot within the compass of a few paragraphs. Many short shorts are highly poetic and may be considered prose poems. See *anecdote* and *prose poem.*

SIGHT RHYME. A **sight rhyme,** or **eye rhyme,** is a pair of words, generally at the ends of lines of verse, that are spelled similarly but pronounced differently. This couplet from Shakespeare's *A Midsummer Night's Dream* provides an example:

> Or in the night, imagining some *fear,*
> How easy is a bush suppos'd a *bear!*

SIMILE. A **simile** is a comparison using *like* or *as.* Christina Rossetti's "A Birthday" (Unit 9) begins with three similes:

> My heart is like a singing bird
>   Whose nest is in a watered shoot:
> My heart is like an apple tree
>   Whose boughs are bent with thickset fruit;

My heart is like a rainbow shell
That paddles in a halcyon sea.
My heart is gladder than all these
Because my love is come to me.

A simile is a type of *metaphor,* and like any other metaphor, can be analyzed into two parts, the *tenor* (or subject being described), and the *vehicle* (or object being used in the description). In the simile "your locks are like the snow," the tenor is locks of hair and the vehicle is snow. They can be compared because they share some quality, in this case, whiteness. See *metaphor.*

SLANG. **Slang** is extremely colloquial speech not suitable for formal occasions and usually associated with a particular group of people. An example of slang current among young people in the United States in the 1920s is "the bee's knees," for something uniquely attractive or wonderful. Among young people in the northeastern United States, the word *wicked* is now sometimes used as a slang term meaning "extremely," as in "That song is *wicked* good." Writers sometimes use slang in an attempt to render characters and setting vividly.

SLANT RHYME. A **slant rhyme, half rhyme, near rhyme,** or **off rhyme** is substitution of assonance or consonance for true rhyme. The pairs *world/boiled* and *bear/bore* are examples. See *assonance, consonance,* and *rhyme.*

SOCIAL DIALECT. See *dialect.*

SOLILOQUY. A **soliloquy** is a speech delivered by a lone character that reveals the speaker's thoughts and feelings. Macbeth's "Tomorrow and tomorrow and tomorrow" speech (act 5, scene 5) is an example.

SONNET. A **sonnet** is a fourteen-line poem that follows one of a number of different rhyme schemes. The *English, Elizabethan,* or *Shakespearean sonnet* is divided into four parts: three *quatrains* and a final *couplet.* The rhyme scheme of such a sonnet is *abab cdcd efef gg.* The sonnets by Shakespeare in Unit 4 of this book are examples. The *Italian* or *Petrarchan sonnet* is divided into two parts: an *octave* and a *sestet.* The rhyme scheme of the octave is *abbaabba.* The rhyme scheme of the sestet can be *cdecde, cdcdcd,* or *cdedce.* Sir Thomas Wyatt's "Whoso List to Hunt" (Unit 4) is an example of the Petrarchan sonnet.

SONNET CYCLE. See *sonnet sequence.*

SONNET SEQUENCE. A **sonnet sequence** is a group of related sonnets. Famous sonnet sequences in English include the sonnets of William Shakespeare, Sir Philip Sidney's *Astrophil and Stella,* and Edmund Spenser's *Amoretti.* See *sonnet.*

SOURCE. A **source** is a work from which an author takes his or her materials. For example, Shakespeare found the outlines of his story of Macbeth in Ralph Holinshed's *Chronicles.*

SPEAKER. The **speaker** is the character who speaks in, or narrates, a poem—the voice assumed by the writer. The speaker and the writer of a poem are not necessarily the same person. The speaker of Robert Browning's "My Last Duchess" (Unit 9), for example, is an Italian duke of the Renaissance Era. The speaker of Thomas Hardy's "Channel Firing" (Unit 9) is a dead person. The speakers of the Anglo-Saxon riddles in Unit 2 are various objects—mead, a shield, and a book.

SPECTACLE. In drama, the **spectacle** is all the elements that are presented to the senses of the audience, including the lights, setting, costumes, make-up, music, sound effects, and movements of the actors.

SPENSERIAN STANZA. The **Spenserian stanza,** used by Edmund Spenser in *The Færie Queene* (excerpted in Unit 4) contains nine lines, the first eight in iambic pentameter and the ninth in iambic hexameter. The rhyme scheme is *ababbcbcc.*

SPONDEE. A **spondee** is a poetic foot containing two strongly stressed syllables, as in the words *compound* and *roughhouse.* Such a foot is said to be *spondaic.*

SPRUNG RHYTHM. **Sprung rhythm** is the term coined by Gerard Manley Hopkins to describe the unique metrical forms of his verse. Hopkins used a foot consisting of a single stressed syllable and feet containing a stressed syllable followed by one, two, or three weakly stressed syllables. One consequence of Hopkins's use of sprung rhythm was the frequent occurrence in his poetry of several stressed syllables in a row, as in the following line:

/ ‿ / / / / ‿ ‿ ‿
Summer ends now; now, barbarous in

/ ⌣ ⌣ / ⌣ /
beauty, the stoks [sheaves] arise

STAGE. A **stage** is any arena on which the action of a drama is performed. In the Middle Ages, stages often consisted of the beds of wagons, which were wheeled from place to place for performances. From the use of such wagons in innyards, the *thrust stage* developed. This was a platform that extended out into the audience and that was closed at the back. In front of the platform in the first English theaters, such as Shakespeare's Globe Theatre, was an open area, the pit, where common people stood. Around the pit were balconies in imitation of the balconies of inns. The modern *proscenium stage* typically is closed on three sides and open at the front, as though the fourth wall had been removed. Sometimes contemporary plays are performed as *theater in the round,* with the audience seated on all sides of the playing area.

STAGE DIRECTIONS. **Stage directions** are notes included in a play in addition to the dialogue for the purpose of describing how something should be performed on stage. Stage directions describe setting, lighting, music, sound effects, entrances and exits, properties, and the movements of characters. They are usually printed in italics and enclosed in brackets or parentheses.

STANZA. A **stanza** is a recurring pattern of grouped lines in a poem. The following are some types of stanza:

two-line stanza	*couplet*
three-line stanza	*tercet* or *triplet*
four-line stanza	*quatrain*
five-line stanza	*quintain*
six-line stanza	*sestet*
seven-line stanza	*heptastich*
eight-line stanza	*octave*

STATIC CHARACTER. See *character.*

STEREOTYPE. A **stereotype** is an uncritically accepted fixed or conventional idea, particularly such an idea held about whole groups of people. A *stereotypical,* or *stock,* character is one who does not deviate from conventional expectations of such a character. Examples of stereotypical characters include the merciless villain, the mad scientist, and the hard-boiled private eye. See *character.*

STOCK CHARACTER. See *character* and *stereotype.*

STORY. A **story,** or **narrative,** is writing or speech that relates a series of events. When these events are causally connected and related to a conflict, they make up a *plot.* See *plot.*

STREAM-OF-CONSCIOUSNESS WRITING. **Stream-of-consciousness writing** is literary work that attempts to render the flow of feelings, thoughts, and impressions within the minds of characters. Modern masters of stream-of-consciousness writing include Virginia Woolf, James Joyce, and William Faulkner. An example of stream-of-consciousness writing is the opening of James Joyce's *A Portrait of the Artist as a Young Man* (excerpted in unit 11).

STRESS. **Stress,** or **accent,** is the level of emphasis given to a syllable. In English *metrics,* the art of rhythm in written and spoken expression, syllables are generally described as being *strongly* or *weakly stressed,* in other words, *accented* or *unaccented.* A strongly stressed or accented syllable receives a strong emphasis. A weakly stressed or unaccented syllable receives a weak one. In the following line on the beauty of Helen of Troy, the strongly stressed or accented syllables are marked with a slash mark (/).

/ / /
Was this the face that launched a
/ /
thousand ships?

—Christopher Marlowe, *The Tragical History of Doctor Faustus*

STRUCTURALIST CRITICISM. See *criticism.*

STYLE. **Style** is the manner in which something is said or written. Traditionally, critics and scholars have referred to three levels of style: *high style,* for formal occasions or lofty subjects; *middle style,* for ordinary occasions or subjects; and *low style,* for extremely informal occasions or subjects. A writer's style depends upon many things, including his or her *diction* (the words that the writer chooses), selection of grammatical structures (simple versus complex sentences, for example), and preference for abstract or concrete words. Any recurring feature that distinguishes one writer's work from another can be said to be part of that writer's style. See *abstract* and *fiction.*

SUBPLOT. A **subplot** is a subordinate story told in addition to the major story in a work of fiction. Often a subplot mirrors or provides a foil for the primary plot. See *plot* and *story.*

SUMMARY. See *abstract.*

SUSPENSE. **Suspense** is a feeling of expectation, anxiousness, or curiosity created by questions raised in the mind of a reader or viewer.

SUSPENSION OF DISBELIEF. **Suspension of disbelief** is the phrase used by Coleridge in his *Biographia Literaria* to describe the act by which the reader willingly sets aside his or her skepticism in order to participate imaginatively in the work being read. A modern adult reader of *Beowulf,* for example, will most likely not believe in dragons. However, he or she may suspend disbelief in dragons and imagine, while reading, what the world would be like if such creatures did exist. The willingness to suspend disbelief, to participate imaginatively in a story being read, is the most important attribute, beyond literacy, that a person can bring to the act of reading.

SYMBOL. A **symbol** is a thing that stands for or represents both itself and something else. Writers use two types of symbols—conventional, and personal or idiosyncratic. A *conventional symbol* is one with traditional, widely recognized associations. Such symbols include doves for peace; laurel wreaths for heroism or poetic excellence; the color green for jealousy; the color purple for royalty; the color red for anger; morning or spring for youth; winter, evening, or night for old age; wind for change or inspiration; rainbows for hope; roses for beauty; the moon for fickleness or inconstancy; roads or paths for the journey through life; woods or darkness for moral or spiritual confusion; thorns for troubles or pain; stars for unchangeableness or constancy; mirrors for vanity or introspection; snakes for evil or duplicity; and owls for wisdom. A *personal* or *idiosyncratic symbol* is one that assumes its secondary meaning because of the special use to which it is put by a writer. Thus in Ted Hughes's poem "Thistles" (Unit 10), the thistles become a symbol of a certain toughness or tenacity of the human spirit.

SYNAESTHESIA. **Synaesthesia** is a figure of speech that combines in a single expression images related to two or more different senses. William Blake's description in "London" (Unit 8) of the "soldier's cry" that "runs in blood down palace walls" is an example of synaesthesia involving the senses of sound and sight.

SYNECDOCHE. A **synecdoche** (sin ek′ də kē′) is a figure of speech in which the name of part of something is used in place of the name of the whole or *vice versa.* In the command *"All hands on deck!" hands* is a synecdoche in which a part (hands) is used to refer to a whole (people, sailors). Addressing a representative of the country of France as *France* would be a synecdoche in which a whole (France) is used to refer to a part (one French person).

SYNTAX. **Syntax** is the pattern of arrangement of words in a statement. Poets often vary the syntax of ordinary speech or experiment with unusual syntactic arrangements. For example, in "A Refusal to Mourn the Death by Fire of a Child in London," Dylan Thomas begins with a long series of adjectives, delaying until the third line the appearance of the noun that is modified:

> Never until the mankind making,
> Bird, beast, and flower-fathering,
> And all-humbling darkness . . .

See *inversion.*

TAG LINE. A **tag line** is an expression in a work of fiction that indicates who is speaking and sometimes indicates the manner of speaking. Examples include the familiar *she said* as well as more elaborate expressions such as *Raoul retorted angrily.*

TALL TALE. A **tall tale** is a story, often light-hearted or humorous, that contains highly exaggerated, unrealistic elements. The stories told in Swift's *Gulliver's Travels* (excerpted in Unit 7) are examples.

TENOR. See *metaphor.*

TERCET. See *triplet.*

TERZA RIMA. ***Terza rima*** is a three-line stanza of the kind used in Dante's *Divine Comedy,* rhyming *aba, bcb, cdc, ded,* and so on. Percy Shelley's "Ode to the West Wind" (Unit 8) is written in *terza rima.*

TETRAMETER. See *meter.*

TEXTUAL CRITICISM. See *criticism.*

THEATER. **(playing area)** See *stage.*

THEATER IN THE ROUND. See *stage.*

THEATER OF THE ABSURD. The **theater of the absurd** is a kind of twentieth-century drama that presents illogical, absurd, or unrealistic scenes, characters, events, or juxtapositions in an attempt to convey the essential meaninglessness of human life, although playwrights have often used the form to convey significant moral messages. Practitioners of the theater of the absurd, which grew out of the philosophy of *Existentialism,* include Eugène Ionesco, Samuel Becket, Edward Albee, and Harold Pinter. See *Existentialism* and *literature of the absurd.*

THEME. A **theme** is a central idea in a literary work. One reading of Wordsworth's "The World Is Too Much with Us" (Unit 8), for example, would say that the poem's theme is the great spiritual or emotional cost of our modern alienation from the natural world.

THESIS. A **thesis** is a main idea that is supported in a work of nonfictional prose.

THIRD-PERSON POINT OF VIEW. See *point of view.*

THREE-DIMENSIONAL CHARACTER. See *character.*

THRUST STAGE. See *stage.*

TONE. **Tone** is the emotional attitude toward the reader or toward the subject implied by a literary work. Examples of the different tones that a work may have include familiar, ironic, playful, sarcastic, serious, and sincere.

TRAGEDY. A **tragedy** is a drama (or by extension any work of literature) that tells the story of the fall of a person of high status. Tragedy tends to be serious. It celebrates the courage and dignity of a tragic hero in the face of inevitable doom. Sometimes that doom is made inevitable by a *tragic flaw* in the hero, such as the ambition that brings about the fall of Shakespeare's Macbeth. In the twentieth century, writers have extended the definition of *tragedy* to cover works that deal with the fall of any sympathetic character, despite his or her status.

TRAGIC FLAW. A **tragic flaw** is a personal weakness that brings about the fall of a character in a tragedy. In Shakespeare's *Romeo and Juliet,* for example, both Romeo and Juliet suffer from the tragic flaw of impetuousness, a flaw to be forgiven, perhaps, by those familiar with young love, but not one that can be forgiven by the fateful stars that govern the fortunes of these two in the play.

TRANSITION. A **transition** is a word, phrase, sentence, or paragraph used to connect ideas and to show relationships between them. *However, therefore, in addition,* and *in contrast* are common transitions. Repeated nouns, synonyms, and pronouns can also serve as transitions. For more information on transitions, see the Language Arts Survey 2.27, "Choosing a Method of Organization." See *coherence.*

TRANSLATION. **Translation** is the art of rendering speech or writing into another language.

TRIMETER. See *meter.*

TRIPLET. A **triplet,** or **tercet,** is a stanza of three lines.

TROCHEE. A **trochee** is a poetic foot consisting of a strongly stressed syllable followed by a weakly stressed syllable, as in the word *winter.* A line of poetry made up of trochees is said to be *trochaic.*

TROPE. See *figure of speech.*

TURNING POINT. See *plot.*

UNDERSTATEMENT. An **understatement** is an ironic expression in which something of importance is emphasized by being spoken of as though it were not important, as in "He's sort of dead, I think."

UNITY. A work has **unity** when its various parts all contribute to creating an integrated whole. An essay with unity, for example, is one in which all the parts help to support the thesis statement, or main idea. See *essay.*

UNRELIABLE NARRATOR. An **unreliable narrator** is one whom the reader cannot trust. Browning's dramatic monologue "My Last Duchess" (Unit 9) employs an unreliable narrator. See *narrator.*

UTILITARIANISM. **Utilitarianism** was a philosophical movement of the nineteenth century associated with Jeremy Bentham and John Stuart Mill in England and with Charles Peirce and William James in the United States. The primary guiding principle of Utilitarianism was that the truth of an idea or the rightness of an action should be judged not according to some abstract or ideal principle but rather according to its practical consequences. Another tenet of Utilitarianism was that moral and political decisions should be made as a result of considering what course of action would bring about "the greatest good [or happiness] for the greatest number" of people.

UTOPIA. A **utopia** is an imaginary, idealized world. The term comes from the title of Sir Thomas More's *Utopia*, which described what More believed to be an ideal society. More took the word from the Greek roots meaning "no-place." See *dystopia*.

VEHICLE. See *metaphor*.

VERBAL IRONY. See *irony*.

VERNACULAR. The **vernacular** is the speech of the common people. During the Middle Ages, much writing throughout Europe was done in Latin, the official language of the church. Only gradually, during the late Middle Ages and the Renaissance Era, did the vernacular languages of Europe replace Latin for scholarly purposes. The term *vernacular* is often used loosely today to refer to dialogue or to writing in general that uses colloquial, dialectical, or slang expressions.

VERSIFICATION. See *prosody*.

VERS LIBRE. See *free verse*.

VILLANELLE. A **villanelle** is a complex and intricate nineteen-line French verse form. The rhyme scheme is *aba aba aba aba abaa.* The first line is repeated as lines 6, 12, and 18. The third line is repeated as lines 9, 15, and 19. The first and third lines appear as a rhymed couplet at the end of the poem. Dylan Thomas's "Do Not Go Gentle into That Good Night" (Unit 10) is a villanelle.

VOICE. **Voice** is the way a writer uses language to reflect his or her unique personality and attitude toward topic, form, and audience. A writer expresses voice through tone, word choice, and sentence structure.

GLOSSARY
Of Words For Everyday Use

PRONUNCIATION KEY

VOWEL SOUNDS

a	hat	i	sit	o͞o (*or* ü)	blue, stew	ə	extra
ā	play	ī	my	oi (*or* ȯi)	boy		under
ä	star			ou (*or* aù)	wow		civil
		ô	go				honor
e	then	ô (*or* ȯ)	paw, born	u	up		bogus
ē	me	o͝o (*or* u̇)	book, put	ʉ	burn		

CONSONANT SOUNDS

b	but	j	jump	p	pop	th	the
ch	watch	k	brick	r	rod	v	valley
d	do	l	lip	s	see	w	work
f	fudge	m	money	sh	she	y	yell
g	go	n	on	t	sit	z	pleasure
h	hot	ŋ	song, sink	th	with		

a • bate (ə bāt´) *vi.*, diminish; terminate.
ab • hor • rence (ab hôr´ əns) *n.*, loathing.
ab • jure (ab jo͞or′) *vi.*, renounce; give up publicly.
a • bom • i • nate (ə bäm´ə nāt′) *vt.*, dislike very much.
ab • so • lu • tion (ab sə lo͞o′ shən) *n.*, forgiveness.
ab • strus • est (ab stro͞os´ əst) *adj.*, most difficult to understand.
ac • ced • ed (ak sēd′ əd) *vi.*, agreed.
ac • crue (ə kro͞o) *vi.*, accumulate periodically.
a • cute (ə kyo͞ot′) *adj.*, keenly intelligent; sharp.
ad • age (a´ dij) *n.*, old saying that is popularly believed to be true.
a • dieu (ə dyo͞o´) *interj.*, goodbye.
ad • ver • si • ty (ad vʉr´ sə tē) *n.*, misfortune; trouble.
a • gen • cy (ā´jən sē) *n.*, force or power.
ag • i • ta • tion (aj´ə tā´shən) *n.*, violent motion.
a • gog (ə gäg´) *adj.*, eagerly excited.
a • gue (ā´ gyo͞o) *n.*, fever and chills.
am • bling (am′ bliŋ) *part.*, moving with a smooth, easy gait.
a • mends (ə mendz´) *n. pl.*, something done to make up for injury, loss, etc., that one has caused.
a • mi • a • ble (ā′ mē ə bəl) *adj.*, good-natured; friendly.
a • mi • a • bly (ā′ mē ə blē) *adv.*, in a pleasant and friendly manner.
am • pli • fy (am′ plə fī) *vt.*, make stronger; increase.
ap • prise (ə prīz′) *vt.*, inform; notify.
ap • pur • te • nance (ə pʉrt´′n əns) *n.*, thing that belongs to another.
ar • bi • trar • y (är′ bə trer ē) *adj.*, despotic; dictatorial.
ar • bi • trate (är´bə trāt´) *vt.*, settle a dispute.
ar • dent (ärd´′nt) *adj.*, intensely enthusiastic or devoted; zealous.
ar • du • ous (är´ jo͞o əs) *adj.*, extremely difficult.
ar • ti • cu • late (är tik´yo͞o lāt´) *vt.*, express clearly; join or connect.
as • per • i • ty (ə sper´ ə tē) *n.*, harshness.
as • pire (ə spīr´) *vi.*, seek to achieve lofty goals.
as • sev • er • a • tion (ə sev ə rā′ shən) *n.*, act of stating positively; an assertion.
a • stride (ə strīd′) *adv.*, with legs on either side.
a • sun • der (ə sən′ dər) *adv.*, apart or separate.
at • tire (ə tīr′) *n.*, dress; clothing.
au • da • cious (ô dā′ shəs) *adj.*, bold; brave; spirited.
au • dac • i • ty (ô das′ ə tē) *n.*, boldness; insolence.
aug • ment (ôg ment′) *vt.*, add to; supplement.
au • gust (ö gəst′) *adj.*, magnificent; admirable.
au • re • ate (ô´rē it) *adj.*, splendid or brilliant.
a • vail (ə vāl′) *vi.,vt.*, be of use, help.
a • venge (ə venj′) *vt.*, to take vengeance for or on behalf of some-one else.
a • vert (ə vərt′) *vt.*, avoid, keep from happening.
baize (bāz) *n.*, woolen or cotton fabric made to resemble felt.
bale • ful (bāl´fəl) *adj.*, sorrowful; wretched.
bar • o • met • ri • cal (bar´ə me´trik əl) *adj.*, referring to atmos-pheric pressure.
beau • te • ous (byo͞o´ tē əs) *adj.*, beautiful.
be • guile (bē gīl´) *vt.*, mislead by tricking.
be • tide (bē tīd) *vi.*, happen to.
be • trothed (bē trô thd´) *adj.*, engaged to be married.
bil • ious (bil′ yəs) *adj.*, ill-tempered; cranky.
bil • low • ing (bi′ lō wiŋ), *adj.*, rising and rolling in waves or

surges.
black • guard (blag´ərd) *n.,* scoundrel; villain; low person.
blas • pheme (blas' fēm) *vt.,* show contempt or irreverence for something sacred.
blas • phe • my (blas´ fə mē´) *n.,* irreverent or disrespectful remark or action.
blight (blīt) *vt.,* destroy; prevent growth.
blithe (blīth) *adj.,* cheerful; carefree.
bog (bôg) *n.,* wet, spongy ground.
bolt (bōlt) *vt.,* swallow (food) hurriedly; gulp down.
bro • cade (brō kād´) *n.,* cloth with a raised design woven into it.
brood (bro͞od) *n.,* offspring, or a family of offspring, of animals.
brook (brook) *vt.,* put up with.
brusque • ly (brusk´lē) *adv.,* abrupt or curt in manner.
bur • lesqued (bər leskd´) *part.,* parodied; imitated derisively.
bur • nish (bʉr´nish) *vt.,* make smooth and shiny by rubbing.
cai • tiff (kāt´if) *n.,* cowardly person.
ca • jole (kə jōl´) *vt.,* coax with flattery.
ca • la • mi • ty (kə la' mə tē) *n.,* disaster.
cal • lous (kal' əs) *adj.,* unfeeling; merciless.
can • ker (kaŋ' kər) *vt.,* infect with corruption.
ca • price (kə prēs´) *n.,* whim.
cap • ti • vate (kap' tə vāt) *vt.,* influence and dominate with an irresistible appeal; attract.
ca • reer (kə rir´) *vi.,* move at full speed.
car • i • ca • ture (kar´i kə chər´) *vi.,* depict in a style involving exaggeration for satirical effect.
car • ob (kar´ əb) *n.,* leguminous tree of the eastern Mediterranean, bearing long, flat, leathery, brown pods with a sweet pulp.
cav • ern (kav´ ərn) *n.,* cave.
ce • les • tial (sə les´chəl) *adj.,* heavenly; divine.
cer • ti • tude (sʉrt´ə to͞od´) *n.,* absolute sureness.
chasm (kaz´əm) *n.,* a crack in the surface of the earth.
chas • tise (chas tīz´) *vt.,* scold or condemn sharply.
chas • tise • ment (chas' tīz' mənt) *n.,* punishment or censure.
cir • cum • scribe (sʉr 'kəm scrīb) *vt.,* constrict, enclose.
cit • a • del (sit´ə del) *n.,* fortress; safe place.
clem • en • cy (klem´ən sē) *n.,* leniency; mercy.
clois • ter (klois´tər) *n.,* monastery.
cloy'd (klöid) *adj.,* to have had too much; surfeited.
come • li • est (kum´lē est) *adj.,* most attractive.
com • pose (kəm pōz) *vt.,* calm; put in order.
com • pul • sion (kəm pul´ shən) *n.,* coercion, driving force.
con • cil • i • ate (kən sil´ē āt´) *vt.,* win over.
con • cord (kän´ kôrd) *n.,* agreement; harmony.
con • de • scend (kän di send´) *vi.,* descend to the level of one considered inferior.
con • fine • less (kən fīn´ləs) *adj.,* limitless.
con • fla • gra • tion (kän flə grā' shən) *n.,* fire.
con • found • ed (kən found´əd) *adj.,* confused.
con • jure (kôn´ jər) *vt.,* make appear as by magic.
con • sci • en • tious • ly (kän shē ən' shəs lē) *adv.,* in an honest or painstaking manner.
con • sort (kän´sôrt ´) *n.,* ship that travels with other ships; companion.
con • sti • tute (kän´stə to͞ot´) *vt.,* make up; be the components or elements of; form; compose.
con • tem • plate (kän´ təm plāt) *vt.,* think about carefully.
con • temp • tu • ous • ly (kən temp´cho͞o əs lē) *adv.,* scornfully.
con • tin • gen • cy (kən tin´ jən(t) se) *n.,* occurrence that depends upon chance.
con • trive (kən trīv´) *vt.,* scheme.
con • triv • er (kən triv´ər) *n.,* one who plans.
con • vulse (kən vuls´) *vt.,* shake or disturb violently; agitate.
con • vul • sive • ly (kən vul´siv lē) *adv.,* in an agitated manner.
copse (käps) *n.,* thicket of small trees or bushes.
cor • o • net • ed (kôr´ə net´id) *adj.,* with a band of ornamentation.
cor • po • ral (kôr' pə rəl) *adj.,* of the body; bodily.
cor • po • re • al (kôr pôr´ ē əl) *adj.,* of a bodily or physical nature.
co • til • lion (kō til' yən) *n.,* a formal ball.
coun • te • nance (koun´tə nəns) *n.,* appearance; facial features or expression.
cov • e • nant (kuv´ə nənt) *n.,* binding agreement.
cow • er (cou' ər) *vi.,* shrink and tremble, as from fear or cold.
coy (koi) *adj.,* playful or evasive.
coy • ness (koi´nes) *n.,* playful evasiveness; pretense of shyness or bashfulness.
crest • fal • len (krest´ fô lən) *adj.,* dejected; humbled.
crook (kro͝ok) *n.,* hooked, bent, or curved thing or part.
cyn • i • cal (sin´i kəl) *adj.,* believing that people are insincere or selfish; sarcastic or sneering.
da • is (dā´is *or* dī´is) *n.,* raised platform, as for a seat of honor.
dal • li • ance (dal´yəns) *n.,* flirting; toying; trifling.
dam • ask (dam´əsk) *vt.,* make a deep pink or rose.
dan • dle (dan´dəl) *vt.,* swing up and down.
dap • pled (dap´ əld) *adj.,* marked with spots.
daunt (dônt) *vt.,* make afraid or discouraged.
daunt • less (dônt´ləs) *adj.,* fearless.
de • barred (dē bärd') *part.,* kept from some right or privilege; excluded.
de • i • ty (dē´ ə tē) *n.,* god.
de • lir • i • um (di lir´ ē əm) *n.,* wild excitement.
de • mur (dē mʉr') *vi.,* hesitate; object.
de • nounce (di naünts') *vt.,* accuse publicly; inform against.
de • rive (di rīv') *vi.,* come from; get from a source.
dep • re • cate (dep' rə kāt') *vt.,* belittle; disparage.
des • o • la • tion (des´ə lā´shən) *n.,* ruin.
des • pot • ic (des pä' tik) *adj.,* of, relating to, or characteristic of a tyrant.
de • tract (dē trakt') *vi.,* take or draw away.
dif • fi • dent (dif' ə dənt) *adj.,* lacking self-confidence; timid.
dif • fu • sive (di fyo͞o' siv) *adj.,* tending to disperse.
dil • i • gent (dil´ə jənt) *adj.,* hard-working; persevering.
dirge (dʉrj) *n.,* funeral song.
dis • cern • ing (di zʉrn' iŋ) *part.,* showing good judgment.
dis • cor • dant (dis kôr' dənt) *adj.,* quarrelsome; unmelodious.
dis • dain (dis dān') *vt.,* regard with contempt or scorn.
dis • dain • ful (dis dān´ fəl) *adj.,* proud; aloof.
di • shev • eled (di shev´əld) *adj.,* disarranged and untidy.
dis • po • si • tion (dis´ pə zish´ ən) *n.,* tendency; habit.
do • cil • i • ty (dō sil´ə tē) *n.,* submissiveness.
doff (dôf) *vt.,* take off; remove.
dog • ged • ly (dôg´id lē) *adv.,* persistently.
dog • mat • i • cal • ly (dôg mat' ik ə lē) *adv.,* stating an opinion in an arrogant manner.
drear • i • some (drir' ē sum) *adj.,* sad.
drudge (druj) *n.,* person who does tedious work.
dudg • eon (duj´ən) *n.,* anger and resentment.
dupe (do͞op) *vt.,* deceive by trickery.
du • ress (do͞o res´) *n.,* constraint by threat.
ear • nest (ʉr´nist) *n.,* something given or done as an indication or assurance of what is to come.
ec • cle • si • as • ti • cal (e klē´ zē as´ ti kəl) *adj.,* having to do with the church.
ed • dies (e' dēz) *n., pl.,* currents of water or air running contrary to the main current; whirlpools.

ef • faced (e fāsd') *vt.,* eliminated; vanished.
el • o • cu • tion • ar • y (el'ə kyo͞o shən er ē) *adj.,* appropriate for public speaking.
e • lude (ē lo͞od') *vt.,* evade; escape.
em • bar • go (em bär´gō) *n.,* government order prohibiting the entry or departure of ships.
em • i • nent (em´ ə nənt) *adj.,* noteworthy.
em • phat • ic (em fat' ik) *adj.,* forceful; definite.
en • cum • bered (en kum´bərd) *part.,* held back.
en • deav • or (en dev´ ər) *vt.,* attempt; try.
en • ig • mat • i • cal • ly (en ig mat´ik lē) *adv.,* in a perplexed manner.
en • tail (en tāl') *vt.,* require.
en • tice (en tīs') *vt.,* tempt.
en • treat (en trēt´) *vt.,* ask earnestly; beg.
ep • i • thet (ep´ə thet´) *n.,* word or phrase used to characterize a person or thing.
ep • och (ep´ ək) *n.,* period of time.
e • quiv • o • ca • tor (ē kwiv´ə kā tor) *n.,* one who speaks ambiguously.
er • ro • ne • ous (ər rōn´ nē əs) *adj.,* based on error, wrong.
err (ʉr) *vi.,* be wrong.
es • ca • pade (es´kə pād´) *n.,* reckless adventure.
es • thet • i cism (es thet´ə siz´əm) *n.,* doctrine that artistic principles should underlie values.
e • the • re • al (ē thir´ē əl) *adj.,* not earthly; heavenly; celestial.
et • y • mol • o • gy (et ə mäl´ə je) *n.,* origin and development of a word.
ex • alt (eg zôlt´) *vt.,* heighten or intensify the action or effect of.
ex • hort (eg zôrt´) *vt.,* warn, plead with.
ex • hor • ta • tion (eg´ zôr tā´ shən) *n.,* strong urging.
ex • pen • di • ture (ik spen' di chər) *n.,* disbursement of money.
ex • tort (eks tôrt') *vt.,* get something from somebody through threats or violence.
ex • trem • i • ties (ek strem´ə tēz) *n.,* outermost parts.
ex• u • ber • ant (eg zo͞o´ bər ənt) *adj.,* full of life.
ex • ul • ta • tion (eg zul tā' shən) *n.,* act of rejoicing; jubilation; triumph.
fain (fān) *adv.,* with pleasure; gladly.
fas • tid • i • ous (fas tid' ē əs) *adj.,* not easy to please; very critical.
fa • tal • i • ty (fā tal' ə tē) *n.,* fate or necessity.
fe • lic • i • ty (fə lis´i tē) *n.,* happiness; bliss.
fes • toon (fes tün') *vt.,* decorate.
fet • tered (fe' tərd) *part.,* chained or shackled.
fick • le (fik' əl) *adj.,* unstable in affection, loyalty, interest, etc.
fil • ial (fi' lē əl) *adj.,* of, relating to, or befitting a son or daughter.
fir • ma • ment (fʉrm'ə mənt) *n.,* sky.
fis • sure (fish´ ər) *n.,* long, narrow, deep cleft or crack.
flax (flaks) *n.,* pale-yellow plant used to make linen.
flout (flout) *vt.,* show scorn or contempt for.
fore • cas • tle (fōk´s'l) *n.,* crew's quarters in the front of a merchant ship.
for • ti • fied (fôr´ tə fīd) *part.,* strengthened.
frock (fräk) *n.,* girl's or woman's dress.
fru • gal (fro͞o´gəl) *adj.,* thrifty.
fur • row (fʉr´ō) *n.,* groove made in the earth by a plow.
fus • tian (fus´chən) *n.,* coarse cloth.
gall (gôl) *n.,* bitterness.
ga • lore (gə lōr') *adj.,* in abundance: used postpositively.
gape (gāp) *vi.,* open wide.
gaunt (gônt) *adj.,* haggard; emaciated.
gen • teel (gen tēl') *adj.,* elegant; fashionable.
gin • ger (jin' gər) *n.,* liveliness; spirit.
glade (glād) *n.,* open space in a forest.
grav • en (grāv´ ən) *vt.,* engraved.
gris • ly (griz´lē) *adj.,* horrible; terrifying.
gru • el (gro͞o´əl) *n.,* thin porridge made by cooking grain in water or milk.
guf • faw (gu fô´) *vi.,* let out a short burst of laughter.
guile (gīl) *n.,* slyness and cunning in dealing with others; deception.
gump • tion (gump' shən) *n.,* courage; boldness.
gut • ter (gut´ər) *vi.,* gurgle and sputter.
hacked (hakt) *adj.,* cut rudely, roughly, or irregularly.
hag • gard (hag´ərd) *adj.,* worn; gaunt.
hal • cy • on (hal´sē ən) *adj.,* tranquil; happy.
hap • less (hap´lis) *adj.,* unfortunate; unlucky.
har • bin • ger (här´bin jər) *n.,* person or thing that comes before and hints at what is to follow.
har • bor (här´bər) *vt.,* provide protection.
heath (hēth) *n.,* open wasteland.
heav • ing (hē' viŋ) *vt.,* cause to swell or rise; rise and fall rhythmically.
her • maph • ro • dite (hər maf´ro dīt) *adj.,* with both male and female characteristics.
her •mit • age (hʉr´ mi tij) *n.,* secluded retreat.
hith • er • to (hith´ər to͞o) *adv.,* until this time.
hoar • y (hōr' ē), *adj.,* gray or white with age; extremely old; ancient.
hom • age (ä' mij) *n.,* expression of high regard or tribute.
home • ly (hōm' lē) *adj.,* simple; unpretentious.
hos • tel • ry (häs´təl rē) *n.,* lodging place.
hov • el (huv´əl) *n.,* a shed or hut.
hu • mil • i • ty (hyo͞o mil´ ə tē) *n.,* absence of pride or self-assertion.
i • dle (ī' dəl) *adj.,* useless; having no value.
ig • no • ble (ig nō´ bəl) *adj.,* dishonorable; mean; destestable.
ig • no • min • i • ous • ly (ig´nə min´ē əs lē) *adv.,* shamefully; disgracefully.
im • mod • er • ate (im mä' də rət) *adj.,* exceeding just, usual, or suitable bounds.
im • pede (im pēd´) *vt.,* obstruct or delay.
im • ped • i • ment (im ped´ə mənt) *n.,* obstacle.
im • per • ti • nent (im pʉrt´'n ənt) *adj.,* saucy; insolent.
im • pet • u • ous (im pech´o͞o əs) *adj.,* acting on impulse.
im • pi • ous (im´pī əs) *adj.,* lacking respect or dutifulness.
im • plic • it • ly (im plis´it lē) *adv.,* doubtlessly.
im • po • tence (im' pə tənts) *n.,* lacking in power, strength, or vigor.
im • po • tent (im´pə tənt) *adj.,* powerless.
im • pre • ca • tion (im´pri kā´shən) *n.,* obscene language; curse.
im • pu • dence (im´pyo͞o dəns) *n.,* quality of being shamelessly bold or saucy.
in • an • i • mate (in an´ə mit) *adj.,* lifeless.
in • censed (in sensd') *adj.,* very angry; enraged.
in • ces • sant (in ses´ənt) *adj.,* neverending.
in • ces • sant • ly (in se' sənt lē) *adv.,* continuing or following without interruption.
in • con • gru • i • ty (in kən grü' ə tē) *n.,* lack of appropriateness or fitness.
in • cor • ri • gi • ble (in kôr´ə jə bəl) *adj.,* unable to be reformed; unmanageable; unruly.
in • cor • rupt • i • ble (in´kə rup´tə bəl) *adj.,* that cannot be contaminated or debased.
in • cred • u • lous • ly (in krej' o͞o ləs lē) *adj.,* in a manner that shows doubt or disbelief.
in • dig • na • tion (in dig nā' shən) *n.,* anger or scorn.
in • dul • gent (in dəl´ jənt) *adj.,* excessively kind or lenient.
in • ex • pli • ca • ble (i nik spli' kə bəl) *adj.,* that cannot be explained or understood.
in • fal • li • bly (in fal´ə blē) *adv.,* unmistakedly.

in • fa • mous (in′ fə məs) *adj.,* having a very bad reputation; notorious; in disgrace or dishonor.

in • fat • u • at • ed (in fach′o͞ot′id) *adj.,* completely overcome by love.

in • fest (in fest′) *vt.,* overrun in large numbers.

in • gen • u • ous (in jen′ yo͞o əs) *adj.,* artless, naive.

in • gra • ti • ate (in grā′shē āt′) *vt.,* bring into favor.

in • sin • u • ate (in sin′yo͞o āt′) *vt.,* suggest; imply.

in • sip • id (in sip′id) *adj.,* not exciting or interesting.

in • so • lence (in′ sə lens) *n.,* disrespect; contempt.

in • ter (in tur′) *vi.,* bury.

in •trigue (in trēg′) *n.,* plotting or scheming.

in • voke (in vōk′) *vt.,* ask solemnly for; beg for; implore.

ire • ful (īr′fəl) *adj.,* angry.

ir • rel • e • vant (ir rel′ə vənt) *adj.,* not related to the subject.

jaunt (jônt) *n.,* short pleasure trip.

joc • und (jäk′ənd) *adj.,* cheerful; merry; pleasant.

ju • di • cial (jo͞o dish′ əl) *adj.,* carefully considering the facts.

jun • ta (ho͞on′tə) *n.,* council.

kin • dred (kin′ drid) *adj.,* related; similar.

lab • y • rinth (la′ bə rinth) *n.,* a place full of intricate pathways and blind alleys.

la • goon (lə gün′) *n.,* a shallow sound, channel, or pond near a larger body of water.

la • ment (lə ment′) *vt.,* regret.

la • ment • ing (lə ment′iŋ), *vt.,* mourning aloud; wailing; expressing sorrow, mourning, or regret, often in a demonstrative way.

lan • guid • ly (laŋ′ gwid lē) *adv.,* sluggishly; without vigor.

lan • guish (laŋ′ gwish) *vi.,* lose vigor or vitality.

lan • guished (lan′ gwisht) *adj.,* drooping; lacking vitality.

lan • yard (lan′yərd) *n.,* cord worn around the neck.

laugh • ing • stock (la′ fiŋ st äk) *n.,* a person or thing made the object of ridicule.

len • i • ty (len′ə tē) *n.,* leniency; mildness.

list • less • ness (list′ ləs nəs) *n.,* lack of interest, energy, or spirit.

lit • er • al (lit′ ər əl) *adj.,* word-for-word; true to the actual or original meaning.

lope (lōp) *n.,* a long, easy, swinging stride.

mad • ri •gal (má dri gəl) *n.,* song, often in several parts.

mag • is • te • ri • al • ly (maj′ is tir′ ē əl lē) *adv.,* in a domineering or masterful manner.

mag • nan • i • mous (mag nan′ə məs) *adj.,* gracious and generous.

ma • lev • o • lence (mə lev′ə lens) *n.,* malice, spitefulness.

man • a • cle (man′ ə kəl) *n.,* handcuff, shackle.

mar • quee (mär kē′) *n.,* tent with open sides.

mar• tyr • dom (mär′ tər dəm) *n.,* death or suffering for a cause.

mas • quer • ade (mas′kər ād′) *n.,* ball or party at which masks and fancy costumes or disguises are worn.

me • an • der (mē an′ dər) *vi.,* follow a winding course.

mel • an • chol • y (mel′ ən käl ē) *n.,* state of sadness or depression.

men • dac • i • ty (men das′ ə tē) *n.,* lying.

met • a • phy • si • cian (met′ə fə zish′ən) *n.,* one who studies metaphysics, that branch of philosophy that deals with ultimate realities and the nature of being.

met • tle (me′ təl) *n.,* high quality; spirit; courage.

mil • len • ni • um (mi len′ē əm) *n.,* period of perfection or great prosperity, as in the Golden Age.

min • ion (min′ yən) *n.,* favorite.

mire (mīr) *n.,* soggy ground.

mis • cre • ant (mis′ krē ənt) *n.,* evil person.

moor (mo͞or) *n.,* tract of open, rolling wasteland, usually covered with heather and often marshy.

mor • tal (môr′təl) *adj.,* deadly.

mor • ti • fi • ca • tion (môr′tə fi kā′shən) *n.,* shame; humiliation.

mot • ley (mät′lē) *adj.,* multicolored.

mould • ered or **mold • ered** (mōl′ derd) *adj.,* decayed.

mul • ti • tu • di • nous (mul tə to͞od′ nəs) *adj.,* very numerous.

mu • nif • i • cence (myo͞o nif′ ə səns) *n.,* generosity.

muse (myo͞oz) *vi.,* think deeply and at length; meditate.

myr • i • ad (mir′ ē əd) *adj.,* of an indefinitely large number; countless.

na • tiv • i • ty (nə tiv′ ə tē) *n.,* birth.

nec • ro • man • cy (nek′rə man′sē) *n.,* black magic; sorcery.

non • en • ti • ty (nän en′tə tē) *n.,* person of no importance.

non • pa • reil (nän′pə rel′) *n.,* someone unequaled.

o • bei • sance (ō bā′ səns) *n.,* authority; rule.

ob • du •rate (äb′door it) *adj.,* stubborn; obstinate; inflexible.

ob • scure (əb skyo͞or′) *adj.,* faint; undefined; relatively unkown.

o • di • ous (ō′dē əs) *adj.,* arousing disgust; offensive.

of • fi • cious (ə fish′ əs) *adj.,* meddlesome.

om • ni • bus (äm′ni bəs) *n.,* bus.

om • nip • o • tent (äm nip′ə tənt) *n.,* God; one having unlimited power.

op • pres • sive (ə pres′iv) *adj.,* distressing.

or • a • cle (ör′ə kəl) *n.,* person in communication with the gods; person of great knowledge or wisdom.

or • gan • dy or **or • gan • die** (ôr′gən dē) *n.,* sheer fabric.

or • gan • ic (ôr gan′ ik) *adj.,* inherent; inborn.

os • ten • ta • tious (äs′tən tā′shəs) *adj.,* excessively showy.

os • ten • ta • tious • ly (äs′ tən tā′ shəs lē) *adv.,* in a showy display.

pall (pôl) *vt.,* cloak in darkness.

pal • lid (pa′ ləd) *adj.,* deficient in color.

pal • lor (pal′ər) *n.,* unnatural paleness.

pal • pa • ble (pal′pə bəl) *adj.,* tangible.

pal • pi • ta • tion (pal′pə tā shen) *n.,* rapid heartbeat.

pal • try (pôl′ trē) *adj.,* practically worthless; trifling; insignificant; contemptible; petty.

pan • e • gyr • ic (pan′ə jir′ik) *n.,* high praise.

par • ry (par′ē) *vt.,* reply in a clever or evasive way.

pau • per • ize (pô′ pər īz) *vt.,* impoverish.

pe • dan • tic (ped′′nt ik) *adj.,* in a manner stressing minor or trivial points of learning.

per • di • tion (pər dish′ən) *n.,* complete and irreparable loss; ruin.

per • func • to • ri • ly (pər fuŋk′tə rē lē) *adv.,* in an indifferent or disinterested manner.

per • ni • cious (pər nish′əs) *adj.,* wicked; causing ruin and death.

per • pen • dic • u • lar (pur′pən dik′yo͞o lər) *adj.,* exactly upright.

per • pet • u • al (pər pech′ o͞o əl) *adj.,* lasting forever.

per • son • a • ble (pur′sən ə bəl) *adj.,* having a pleasant appearance and personality.

per • vad • ing (pər vād′ iŋ) *part.,* diffused throughout.

per • ver • si • ty (pər vur′ sə tē) *n.,* quality or condition of deviating from what is considered right or good.

pe • ruse (pə rüz′) *vt.,* examine carefully.

per • vert (pər vurt′) *vt.,* distort; misinterpret.

pes • ti • lence (pes′tə ləns) *n.,* virulent or infectious disease of epidemic proportions.

phan • tas • ma • go • ri • a (fan taz′mə gôr′ē ə) *n.,* rapidly changing series of imagined figures or events.

plac • id • ly (plas′id lē) *adv.,* in a tranquil or calm manner.

plaint (plānt) *n.,* complaint or grievance.

plat • i • tude (plat′ ə to͞od′) *n.,* commonplace saying.

poach (pōch) *vt.,* hunt illegally.

por • tal (pōr′ təl) *n.,* door; entrance.

por • ti • co (pôr′ ti kō) *n.,* porch or covered walk in front of a building.

pos • ter • i • ty (päs ter′ə tē) *n.,* succeeding generations.

pos • tern (pōs´tərn) *n.,* private rear entrance.
prat • ing (prāt´iŋ) *ger.,* chattering.
pre • cept (prē' sept) *n.,* commandment or direction meant as a rule of action or conduct.
prel • ate (prel´it) *n.,* high-ranking member of the clergy.
pre • oc • cu • pied (prē äk´yo͞o pīd) *adj.,* engrossed.
pre • sump • tu • ous (prē zump' cho͞o əs) *adj.,* overconfident or arrogant.
pre • ten • sion (prē ten´shən) *n.,* showy display of wealth.
pre • text (prē' tekst) *n.,* an appearance assumed in order to disguise the truth.
pre • vail (prē vāl´) *vi.,* be victorious.
pre • var • i • ca • tion (pri vari kā' shən) *n.,* lie.
prin • ci • pal (prin´ sə pəl) *adj.,* main or chief.
pro • bos • cis (prō bäs´is) *n.,* an elephant's trunk; a long, flexible snout.
pro • cure (prō´kyoor´) *vt.,* obtain.
pro • di • gious (prō dij´əs) *adj.,* amazing; huge.
prod • i • gy (präd´ə jē) *n.,* person with talent or genius.
prof • fer (präf´ər) *vt.,* offer; extend.
pro • fuse • ly (prō fyo͞os' lē) *adv.,* generously; freely.
prog • e • ny (präj´ə nē) *n.,* offspring.
pro • pi • ti • ate (prō pi' shē āt) *vt.,* regain the favor of; pacify.
prom • i • nent (prä' mə nənt) *adj.,* noticeable; obvious.
pro • pi • tious (prō pish´əs) *adj.,* favorable.
pros • trate (prä' strate) *adj.,* completely overcome and lacking the will or power to rise.
prov • i • dence (präv´ə dəns) *n.,* benevolent guidance.
pro • voke (prō vōk´) *vt.,* stir up action or feeling.
prox • im • i • ty (präks im' ə tē) *n.,* nearness.
prud • er • y (prood' ər ē) *n.,* condition of being overly modest or proper.
pu • er • ile (pyo͞o´ər il) *adj.,* childish; immature.
pur • ga • to • ry (pur´gə tôr´ē) *n.,* temporary state of suffering or misery.
purge (pərj) *vt.,* cleanse or rid of impurities, foreign matter, or undesirable elements.
pur • vey • or (pər vā' ər) *n.,* one who supplies or provides.
pyre (pīr'), *n.,* combustible heap for burning a dead body as a funeral rite.
quay (kē) *n.,* wharf.
quell (kwel) *vt.,* subdue.
quick • sil • ver (kwik' sil vər) *adj.,* resembling mercury or its properties.
quill (kwil) *n.,* stiff feather of a bird.
quo • rum (kwôr´əm) *n.,* select group or company.
rai • ment (rā' mənt) *n.,* clothing; garments.
rap • tur • ous (rap´chər əs) *adj.,* full of pleasure.
re • ca • pit • u • late (rē´ kə pich´ə lāt) *vt.,* summarize.
rec • om • pense (rek´ əm pens) *n.,* repayment, reward.
re • dou • bled (rē də' bəld) *adj.,* twice intensified.
re • dress (rē´dres´) *n.,* compensation for wrong done.
reg • i • ment (rej´ə ment) *n.,* unit of soldiers.
re • join (ri jôin') *vi.,* answer.
rel • ish (re' lish) *vt.,* enjoy; like.
re • mon • strance (ri mä¨n' strəns) *n.,* act or instance of protest or complaint.
re • mon • strate (ri män´ strāt) *vt.,* say in protest or object.
re • morse (rē môrs´) *n.,* pity; compassion.
rend (rend) *vt.,* rip apart.
re • pose (rē pōs) *vt.,* rest.
re • pu • di • ate (ri pyo͞o´ dē āt) *vt.,* disown or cast off publicly.
res • o • lute • ly (rez ə loot' le) *adv.,* with a firm, fixed purpose.
res • pite (res´pit) *n.,* short interval of rest or delay.
re • tired (ri tīrd´) *adj.,* withdrawn or apart from; secluded.
rev • er • ent • ly (rev´ər ənt lē) *adv.,* with respect or awe.
rev • er • ie (rev´ər ē) *n.,* dreaming.
re • vile (ri vīl') *vt.,* subject to verbal abuse.
rue • ful (rü' fəl) *adj.,* exciting pity or sympathy; mournful.
ru • mi • nat • ing (ro͞o´mə nāt´ŋ) *part.,* chewing cud, as a cow does; turning something over in the mind.
sanc • ti • tude (saŋk´tə to͞od) *n.,* fact of being sacred or inviolable.
san • guine (saŋ´gwin) *adj.,* ruddy; red; happy.
sans (sänz) *prep.,* without.
sa • ti • at • ed (sā' shē āt' əd) *part.,* to satisfy fully or to excess.
sat • i • rize (sat´ə rīz) *vt.,* attack or ridicule with satire.
sau • cy (sô´ sē) *adj.,* stylish.
score (skôr) *n.,* set of twenty persons or things; *vt.,* mark with lines or notches.
scored (skōrd') *vt.,* marked with lines, grooves, scratches, or notches.
scorn (skôrn) *vt.,* view with contempt.
scourg • er (skurj´ər) *n.,* one who scourges, or flogs.
scru • ple (scro͞o´pəl) *n.,* qualm about something one feels is wrong.
scru • pu • los • i • ty (skro͞o pyo͞o lôs´i tē) *n.,* moral worry or qualm.
scru • pu • lous (skro͞o´ pyə ləs) *adj.,* extremely careful.
scur • ril • i • ty (skə ril´ə tē) *n.,* coarseness or indecency of language.
se• clud • ed (si klo͞od´ id) *adj.,* hidden from public view.
sec • u • lar (sek´yə lər) *adj.,* of the world; not sacred or religious.
se • date • ly (si dāt´lē) *adv.,* in a dignified manner.
seem • ly (sēm´lē) *adv.,* proper.
se • nil • ity (si ni' lə tē) *n.,* the physical and mental infirmity of old age.
sep • ul • chre or **sep • ul • cher** (sep´əl kər) *n.,* burial vault or tomb.
se • rene • ly (sə rēn´lē) *adv.,* peacefully.
shun (shun) *vt.,* keep away from; avoid.
si • new (sin' yü) *n.,* tendon or nerve.
slov • en • ly (sluv' ən lē) *adj.,* careless in appearance; untidy.
smite (smīt) *vt.,* inflict a heavy blow.
snig • ger • (snig´ər) *vi.,* laugh in a derisive manner.
sniv • el (sniv' əl) *vi.,* whine, cry, and sniffle.
so • ber (sō´bər) *adj.,* serious; grave.
soi • rée (swä rā´) *n.,* evening party.
so • lic • it (sə lis´it) *vt.,* ask or seek pleadingly.
so • lic • i • tor (sə lis´it ər) *n.,* lawyer.
so • lic • i • tous (sə lis´ə təs) *adj.,* showing concern.
so • no • rous (sə nôr´əs) *adj.,* having an impressive sound.
sor • did (sôr´ did) *adj.,* ignoble; squalid; wretched.
sov • er • eign (säv´rən) *adj.,* above or superior to all others; greatest; supreme.
spe • cious (spē shəs) *adj.,* seeming sound or logical while not really being so.
splay (splā) *vt.,* spread out.
spoil (spoil) *n.,* arms, money, or goods taken from a defeated foe; plunder.
sprad • dle (sprad´əl) *part.,* sprawl or straddle.
squan • der (skwän' dər) *vt.,* spend or use wastefully or extravagantly.
stag • nate (stag' nāt') *vi.,* become sluggish.
staid (stād) *adj.,* sedate; serious.
stanch • less or **staunch • less** (stônch´ləs) *adj.,* unstoppable.
stat • ure (stach´ər) *n.,* height.
staunch (stônch) *adj.,* strong.
stave (stāv) *n.,* pole.
stead • fast • ly (sted' fast lē) *adv.,* in a firm or established manner.
stealth (stelth) *n.,* act of proceeding secretly or imperceptibly.

GLOSSARY

stealth • y (stel´thē) *adj.*, furtive; sly.
steep (stēp) *adj.*, mounting or falling precipitously; *vt.*, soak; immerse; steps used to climb over a wall.
stip • ple (stip´ əl) *adj.*, flecked.
stip • u • late (stip´ yo͞o lāt) *vi.*, specify conditions of an agreement.
sto • i • cism (stō' ə si zəm) *n.*, indifference to pleasure or pain; impassivity.
strait • ened (strāt´nd) *adj.*, subjected to privation or deficiency, especially of funds.
strand (strand) *n.*, shore.
strat • a • gem (strat´ ə jəm) *n.*, trick or plan.
strife (strīf) *n.*, conflict; struggle.
sub • due (səb dü´) *vt.*, conquer.
sub • lime (sə blīm´) *adj.*, noble; majestic.
sub • lime • ly (sə blīm´ lē) *adv.*, nobly; majestically.
sub • ver • sive (səb vʉr´ siv) *adj.*, with a goal to undermine or corrupt.
sul • ly (sul´ē) *vt.*, soil or stain.
sul • try (sul' trē) *adj.*, oppressively hot and moist.
sun • der (sun´dər) *vt.*, break apart; separate.
su • per • flu • i • ty (so͝o' pər flo͝o' ə tē) *n.*, excess; superabundance.
sur • feit (sʉr´ fit) *n.*, overabundance.
sur • mise (sər mīz´) *n.*, guessing; imagined actions.
swain (swān) *n.*, country youth, especially a shepherd.
sward (swôrd) *n.*, grass-covered soil.
taint (tānt) *vi.*, be infected.
teem (tēm) *vi.*, bring forth.
tem • per • ate (tem´ pər it) *adj.*, moderate.
tem • po • ral (tem´ pə rəl) *adj.*, lasting only for a time, limited; of this world, not spiritual.
ten • ta • tive • ly (ten' tə tiv lē) *adv.*, hesitantly; uncertainly.
till • age (til´ij) *n.*, land that is tilled for farming.
toad • y • ing (tōd´ ē iŋ) *vt.*, flattering in order to gain favor.
tor • por (tōr' pər) *n.*, extreme sluggishness; lethargy.
tran • quil (tran´ kwil) *adj.*, peaceful; calm.
trans • gress (trans gres´) *vi.*, overstep or break a law.
tran • si • to • ry (tran´sə tôr´ē) *adj.*, temporary.
trav • ail (trə vāl´) *n.*, very hard work.
treach • er • ous (trech´ ər əs) *adj.*, traitorous; disloyal; unsafe.
treach • er • y (trech´ər ē) *n.*, betrayal of trust; treason.
trem • u • lous (trem´yo͞o ləs) *adj.*, trembling.
trib • ute (trib´yo͞ot) *n.*, homage; regular payment of money or goods made by one ruler or nation to another as acknowledgment of servitude, for protection from invasion, etc.
tri • fle (trī´fəl) *n.*, something of little value or importance.
tu • mult (to͞o' mult') *n.*, noisy commotion, as of a crowd; uproar.
tur • bid (tʉr´bid) *adj.*, muddled.
un • a • bashed (un ə bashd') *adv.*, without embarrassment.
un • as • sail • a • ble (un e sal' e bel) *adj.*, undeniable.
un • can • ny (ən ka' nē) *adj.*, seeming to have an supernatural or mysterious character or origin.
un • couth (un küth´) *adj.*, uncultured; crude.
un • de • filed (un dē fīld´) *adj.*, uncorrupt; honorable.
un • du • lat • ing (ən' jə lāt iŋ) *part.*, moving in a wavy or flowing manner.
un • gen • i • al (un jēn´yəl) *adj.*, unpleasant.
un • world • ly (un wʉrld´lē) *adj.*, unsophisticated.
u • surp (yo͞o zʉrp´) *vt.*, unlawfully seize a throne.
u • surp • er (yo͞o sʉrp´ər) *n.*, one who assumes power without right.
va • grant (vāg´ rənt) *adj.*, nomadic; wandering.
vain (vān) *adj.*, empty; worthless.
vain • ly (vān 'lē) *adv.*, uselessly.
van • quish (vaŋ´kwish) *vt.*, conquer or defeat in battle.
van • quished (van´ kwisht) *n.*, conquered people.
ve • he • mence (vē' ə mənts) *n.*, great force and strong feeling.
veld (velt) *n.*, in South Africa, open grassy country, with few bushes and almost no trees; grassland.
ven • er • a • tion (ven´ər ā´shən) *n.*, deep respect.
venge • ance (ven´jens) *n.*, revenge; retribution.
ve • ran • da (və ran´də) *n.*, open porch.
ver • i • ty (ver´ə tē) *n.*, truth.
vig • i • lant (vij' ə lənt) *adj.*, staying watchful and alert to danger or trouble.
vis • age (viz´ ij) *n.*, face.
vi • vac • i • ty (vī vas´ə tē) *n.*, liveliness.
vul • ner • a • ble (vul´nər ə bəl) *adj.*, open to injury or attack; easily hurt.
wage (wāj) *n.*, (often pl.) money paid to an employee for work done, and usually figured on an hourly, daily, or piecework basis.
wan (wän) *adj.*, pale; faint.
wane (wān) *vi.*, lose strength.
wan • ton (wän´ tən) *adj.*, undisciplined; unmanageable; luxuriant; extravagant.
war • y (wer´ē) *adj.*, cautious.
wax (waks) *vi.*, grow gradually larger.
way • far • er (wā' far ər) *n.*, traveler, especially one who travels on foot.
whorled (hwôrld) *adj.*, coiled.
wield (wēld) *vt.*, handle and use a weapon or tool.
with • al (with ôl´) *adv.*, besides; nevertheless.
with • er (with´ ər) *vi.*, wilt and shrivel.
wraith • like (rāth līk) *adj.*, like a ghost.
wroth (rôth) *adj.*, angry.
wrought (rôt) *adj.*, shaped by hammering or beating.
yearn (yʉrn') *vi.*, filled with longing.
zeal (zēl) *n.*, passion; fervor.
ze • nith (zē´nith) *n.*, the highest point in the sky.
zeph • yr (zef' ər) *n.*, mild, gentle breeze.

INDEX Of Titles and Authors

INDEX OF TITLES AND AUTHORS

INDEX Of Skills

READING

INDEX OF SKILLS

WRITING

INDEX OF SKILLS

LANGUAGE, GRAMMAR, AND STYLE

INDEX OF SKILLS

SPEAKING AND LISTENING

STUDY AND RESEARCH

INDEX OF SKILLS

APPLIED ENGLISH

INDEX Of Fine Art

ACKNOWLEDGMENTS

ART ACKNOWLEDGMENTS
Cover Bell: Tate Gallery, London/Art Resource, NY; **Cover** Derain: © 2000 Artists Rights Society (ARS), New York / ADAGP, Paris. Museum of Modern Art. Gift of Mr. and Mrs. Charles Zadok.; **Cover** Uccello: Courtesy of the Trustees of the National Gallery, London.; **Cover** William Shakespeare: © Archivo Iconografico, S.A./CORBIS; **1** Grooten Atlas, c.1600s. Joan Blaeu. The Huntington Library, Art Collections and Botanical Gardens, San Marino, CA/Superstock; **2** Bridgeman Art Library; **5** The Pierpont Morgan Library, New York; **15** Bridgeman Art Library; **22** © Bettmann/CORBIS; **24** Derold Page (contemporary artist). Private Collection/Bridgeman Art Library; **28** Courtesy of the Trustees of the Victoria & Albert Museum, London; **32** © Hulton-Deutsch Collection/CORBIS; **33** Collection of the Museum of American Folk Art, New York; **48** Tate Gallery, London/Art Resource, NY; **51** © Hulton-Deutsch Collection/CORBIS; **53** Bridgeman Art Library; **62** National Maritime Museum, Greenwich, England; **66** National Portrait Gallery, London; **80** Grooten Atlas, c.1600s. Joan Blaeu. The Huntington Library, Art Collections and Botanical Gardens, San Marino, CA/Superstock; **82** Norrkoping Art Museum, Sweden; **84** Merseyside Country Museum, Liverpool; **85** Antikensammlung im Pergamonmuseum, Staatliche Museum, Berlin; **86** Helmet: British Museum, London; **86** Horns: The National Museum, Copenhagen.; **87** © Bede's World, Jarrow; **92** Courtesy of the British Library, London; **98** Bridgeman Art Library; **108** The Board of Trinity College, Dublin; **115** The British Museum, London; **117** British Library, London; **122** © Gianni Dagli Orti/CORBIS; **127** Superstock; **132** Bridgeman Art Library; **139** Bridgeman Art Library; **158** Courtesy of the Trustees of the National Gallery, London; **161** By special permission of the city of Bayeux; **165** Birmingham City Museums and Art Gallery/Bridgeman Art Library; **167** Bodleian Library, Oxford; **169** Bridgeman Art Library; **172** Bridgeman Art Library; **176** © National Gallery Collection; By kind permission of the Trustees of the National Gallery, London/CORBIS; **179** Bridgeman Art Library; **183** Wellesley College Library, Special Collections; **188** British Library, London; **201** Wellesley College Library, Special Collections; **212** Bridgeman Art Library; **217** Wellesley College Library, Special Collections; **219** Wellesley College Library, Special Collections; **237** Bridgeman Art Library; **245** In the collection of Corcoran Gallery of Art, Gift of E. Gerald Lamboley; **254** © Bettmann/CORBIS; **256** Wellesley College Library, Special Collections; **278** Bridgeman Art Library; **280** Board of Trustees of the National Museums and Galleries on Mearseyside (Walker Art Gallery, Liverpool); **282** The Granger Collection; **284** National Portrait Gallery, London; **285** National Maritime Museum, Greenwich, England; **288** Archive Photos; **289** Bridgeman Art Library; **292** © Michael Nicholson/CORBIS; **293** Bridgeman Art Library; **296** © Bettmann/CORBIS; **297** Bridgeman Art Library; **301** CORBIS-Bettmann; **302** Manchester City Art Gallery; **306** © Michael Nicholson/CORBIS; **310** Queen Elizabeth I, c.1500s. National Portrait Gallery, London; **311** Bridgeman Art Library; **315** Bridgeman Art Library; **318** © Archivo Iconografico, S.A./CORBIS; **319** Courtesy of the Trustees of the Victoria & Albert Museum, London; **326** © Michael Nicholson/CORBIS; **327** © Ali Meyer/CORBIS; **331** Both: Bridgeman Art Library; **334** Sir Thomas More, 1527. Hans Holbein. The Frick Collection, New York; **335** Bridgeman Art Library; **342** © Archivo Iconografico, S.A./CORBIS; **344** Bridgeman Art Library; **364** Bridgeman Art Library; **369** Bridgeman Art Library; **371** Courtesy the Dean and Chaplaincy, Westminster Abbey; **374** © Archivo Iconografico, S.A./CORBIS; **378** Bridgeman Art Library; **393** © Robbie Jack/CORBIS; **397** Bridgeman Art Library; **411** Bridgeman Art Library; **425** © Hulton-Deutsch Collection/CORBIS; **429** Bridgeman Art Library; **448** Bridgeman Art Library; **456** Bridgeman Art Library; **461** © COR-BIS; **464** Bridgeman Art Library; **465** Bridgeman Art Library; **468** Bridgeman Art Library; **473** Bridgeman Art Library; **488** Bridgeman Art Library; **491** The National Gallery, London; **492** Bridgeman Art Library; **493** Bridgeman Art Library/Art Resource, NY; **494** Bridgeman Art Library; **496** © Michael Nicholson/CORBIS; **497** Planet Art; **500** Bridgeman Art Library; **507** © Michael Nicholson/CORBIS; **511** © CORBIS; **512** Wellesley College Library, Special Collections; **521** Bridgeman Art Library; **524** © CORBIS; **526** Tate Gallery, London/Art Resource, NY; **533** CORBIS-Bettmann; **538** © Michael Nicholson/CORBIS; **539** Bridgeman Art Library; **564** Tate Gallery, London/Art Resource, NY; **567** Giraudon/Art Resource, NY; **568** Popperfoto, Archive Photo; **569** Masters and Fellows, Magdalene College, Cambridge; **570** Bridgeman Art Library; **573** Bridgeman Art Library; **578** © Bettmann/CORBIS; **579** © Board of Trustees, National Gallery of Art, Washington, DC.; **584** Archive Photos; **585** Bridgeman Art Library; **588** Archive Photos; **592** Museum

of London; **598** © Bettmann/CORBIS; **599** Wellesley College Library, Special Collections; **607** Courtesy of the Trustees of the British Museum. Photo by J.R. Freeman & Co. Ltd; **614** © Bettmann/CORBIS; **619** Wellesley College Library, Special Collections; **624** Library of Congress; **627** Archive Photos; **628** Bridgeman Art Library; **629** Bridgeman Art Library; **634** © Archivo Iconografico, S.A./CORBIS; **636** PhotoDisc; **658** Charles H. Bayley Picture and Painting Fund. Museum of Fine Arts, Boston; **660** The Granger Collection; **661** The Granger Collection; **662** Courtesy Westminster Abbey; **663** Charles H. Bayley Picture and Painting Fund. Museum of Fine Arts, Boston; **664** © Michael Nicholson/CORBIS; **665** Bridgeman Art Library; **672** © Michael Nicholson/CORBIS; **674** Virginia Museum of Fine Arts, Richmond. The Adolph D. and Wilkins C. Williams Fund; **676** Bridgeman Art Library; **679** © Bettmann/CORBIS; **683** Yale Center for British Art.; **686** Bridgeman Art Library; **689** Archive Photos; **692** Ashmolean Museum, Oxford; **694** Courtesy of the Fogg Art Museum, Harvard University. Bequest - Collection of Maurice Wertheim, Beq uest of Grenville L. Winthrop Class of 1906; **694** The Granger Collection; **696** Gift of Miss Caroline Newtown, 1974.7. © The Pierpont Morgan Library; **697** Fitzwilliam Museum, Cambridge; **704** © Michael Nicholson/CORBIS; **706** Wellesley College Library, Special Collections; **710** Wellesley College Library, Special Collections; **712** Bridgeman Art Library; **715** Bridgeman Art Library; **720** © Bettmann/CORBIS; **721** Bridgeman Art Library; **725** Bridgeman Art Library; **728** © Bettmann/CORBIS; **729** Bridgeman Art Library; **736** © Bettmann/CORBIS; **738** Bridgeman Art Library; **742** © Bettmann/CORBIS; **745** Bridgeman Art Library; **750** Bridgeman Art Library; **766** Bridgeman Art Library; **769** The Granger Collection; **770** *Portrait of Queen Elizabeth I*, c.1500s. English artist. Uffizi, Florence, Italy. © Archivo Iconografico, S.A./CORBIS; **773** Bridgeman Art Library; **776** Library of Congress; **781** Tate Gallery, London/Art Resource, NY; **785** © Romare Bearden Foundation/Licensed by VAGA, New York. National Museum of American Art, Washington, DC; **789** © 2000 Artists Rights Society (ARS), New York / ADAGP, Paris/Bridgeman Art Library; **800** Bridgeman Art Library; **804** The Metropolitan Museum of Art, Maria DeWitt Jesup Fund; **813** Archive Photos; **815** Bridgeman Art Library; **818** © E.O. Hoppé/CORBIS; **819** Bridgeman Art Library; **821** Archive Photos; **828** © Bettmann/CORBIS; **829** Bridgeman Art Library; **837** Bridgeman Art Library; **843** Bridgeman Art Library; **846** Archive Photos; **847** Bridgeman Art Library; **850** Wellesley College Library, Special Collections; **851** Bridgeman Art Library; **857** Bridgeman Art Library; **864** Humpty Dumpty, 1865. John Tenniel. Wellesley College Library, Special Collections; **873** © Hulton-Deutsch Collection/CORBIS; **892** © Sir Roland Penrose Estate. Tate Gallery, London/Art Resource, NY. Photo by John Webb; **895** Archive Photos; **897** Archive Photos; **898** Archive Photos; **899** Archive Photos; **900** Archive Photos; **901** Archive Photos; **902** Museum of Modern Art, New York; **906** Library of Congress; **907** Bridgeman Art Library; **910** © 2000 Artists Rights Society (ARS), New York / BONO Oslo. © Burstein Collection/CORBIS; **913** Courtesy of Museum of Fine Arts, Boston; **916** © Bettmann/CORBIS; **917** © Lucian Freud. Oil on canvas 91.1 x 61 cm. The Beaverbrook Foundation. Beaverbrook Art Gallery, Fredericton, N.B., Canada; **921** © Hulton-Deutsch Collection/CORBIS; **923** © 2000 Artists Rights Society (ARS), New York / ADAGP, Paris. Sheldon Memorial Art Gallery, UNL-F.M. Hall Collection; **928** © Hulton-Deutsch Collection/CORBIS; **929** Bridgeman Art Library; **932** © Hulton-Deutsch Collection/CORBIS; **933** Bridgeman Art Library; **937** © Hulton-Deutsch Collection/CORBIS; **941** © Hulton-Deutsch Collection/CORBIS; **945** © Jerry Cooke/CORBIS; **949** Musees Royaux des Beaux-Arts, Brussels; **952** © Hulton-Deutsch Collection/CORBIS; **953** Bridgeman Art Library; **956** © AFP/CORBIS; **957** © Bettmann/CORBIS; **960** AP/Irish Independent/Wide World Photos; **961** Bridgeman Art Library; **966** Library of Congress; **967** © The State Russian Museum/CORBIS; **973** Courtesy Freer Gallery of Art, Smithsonian Institution, Washington, DC.; **976** AP/Paula Alye Scully/Wide World Photos; **990** © 2000 Artists Rights Society (ARS), New York / ADAGP, Paris. Museum of Modern Art. Gift of Mr. and Mrs. Charles Zadok; **992** © 2000 Artists Rights Society (ARS), New York / ADAGP, Paris. Museum of Modern Art. Gift of Mr. and Mrs. Charles Zadok; **993** © Hulton-Deutsch Collection/CORBIS; **995** Tate Gallery, London/Art Resource, NY; **1000** © Bettmann/CORBIS; **1001** Bridgeman Art Library; **1010** © Bettmann/CORBIS; **1011** © Michael Maslan Historic Photographs/CORBIS; **1019** The Granger Collection; **1025** Oil on canvas, 21 x 32 in., Louise Jordan Smith Fund; **1033** © Hulton-Deutsch Collection/CORBIS; **1039** Planet Art; **1048** © CORBIS; **1051** AP/World Wide Photos; **1057** © Burstein Collection/CORBIS; **1061** Canapress Photo Service; **1070** Bridgeman Art Library; **1073** © Micheal Gerber/CORBIS; **1075** © Underwood & Underwood/CORBIS; **1096** © Gilbert and George. Tate Gallery, London/Art Resource, NY; **1100** © Bettmann/CORBIS; **1103** © 1995 Michael Romanos; **1115** © 1995 Michael Romanos; **1137** © 1995 Michael Romanos; **1143** © 1995 Michael Romanos; **1157** © 1995 Michael Romanos

LITERARY ACKNOWLEDGMENTS
Jonathan Clowes, Ltd. "A Sunrise on the Veld" from *This Was the Old Chief's Country* by Doris Lessing, copyright © 1951 Doris Lessing.

Reprinted in Canada by kind permission of Jonathan Clowes, Ltd., London, on behalf of Doris Lessing. **Harland Davidson Inc./Forum Press.** Sonnet 1, Sonnet 47, Sonnet 54 from Petrarch, *Selected Sonnets, Odes and Letters*, edited by Thomas G. Bergin (Crofts Classics Series) pp. 19, 40, 41. Copyright © 1966 by Harlan Davidson, Inc. Reprinted by permission. **Dover Publications, Inc.** "Robin Hood and Allen a Dale," Dover Publications, Inc. **ETT Imprint, Australia.** "Naked Girl and Mirror" from *A Human Pattern: Selected Poems* by Judith Wright. Reprinted by permission of ETT Imprint, Sydney, Australia. **Faber and Faber Limited.** "A Call" by Seamus Heaney from *Poems 1966–1996.* Copyright © 1998 by Seamus Heaney. Reprinted in Canada by permission of Faber and Faber, Ltd. "Follower" by Seamus Heaney from *Death of a Naturalist.* Copyright © 1966 by Seamus Heaney. Reprinted in Canada by permission of Faber and Faber, Ltd. "Thistles" from *Wodwo* by Ted Hughes. Copyright © 1961 by Ted Hughes. Reprinted by permission of HarperCollins Publishers [for USA] and Faber and Faber, London [for Canada]. **Farrar, Straus & Giroux, LLC.** "Map of the New World" from *Collected Poems 1948–1984* by Derek Walcott. Copyright © 1986 by Derek Walcott. Reprinted by permission of Farrar, Straus & Giroux, LLC. "A Call" by Seamus Heaney from *Opened Ground.* Copyright © 1998 by Seamus Heaney. Reprinted in the United States by permission of Farrar, Straus & Giroux, Inc. "Follower" by Seamus Heaney from *Poems 1965–1975.* Copyright © 1966, 1980 by Seamus Heaney. Reprinted in the United States by permission of Farrar, Straus & Giroux, Inc. **Garland Publishing, Inc.** "The Book of Margery Kemp" by Margery Kemp, "The Honeysuckle: Chevrefoil" by Marie de France, "The Wife's Lament", "Wulf and Eadwacer." These selections originally appeared in *The Writings of Medieval Women,* Marcelle Thiebaux. Copyright 1994 by Garland Publishing, Inc. Reprinted by permission. **Harcourt, Inc.** From *A Room of One's Own* by Virginia Woolf, copyright 1929 by Harcourt Brace & Company and renewed 1957 by Leonard Woolf, reprinted in the United States by permission of the publisher. "The Naming of Cats" from *Old Possum's Book of Practical Cats* by T.S. Eliot, copyright 1939 by T. S. Eliot and renewed 1967 by Esme Valerie Eliot, reprinted by permission of Harcourt, Inc. "Preludes," from *Collected Poems 1909–1962 by T.S. Eliot*, copyright 1936 by Harcourt Inc., copyright © 1964, 1963 by T.S. Eliot, reprinted by permission of the publisher. "Shooting an Elephant," from *Shooting an Elephant and Other Essays* by George Orwell, copyright © 1950 by Sonia Brownell Orwell; renewed 1978 by Sonia Pitt-Rivers. Reprinted by permission of Harcourt, Inc. and A. M. Heath & Company, Limited. **HarperCollins Publishers. From *The Analects of Confucius,*** Arthur Waley, HarperCollins Publishers Ltd. From *Nectar in a Sieve* by Kamala Markandaya. Copyright 1954 by The John Day Company. Copyright renewed © 1982 by Kamala Markdanaya. HarperCollins Publishers, Inc. "Thistles," from *Wodwo* by Ted Hughes. Copyright © 1961 by Ted Hughes. Reprinted by permission of HarperCollins Publishers, Inc. **A. M. Heath & Company, Limited.** "Shooting an Elephant" from *Shooting an Elephant and Other Essays* by George Orwell, copyright © 1950 by Sonia Brownell Orwell; renewed 1978 by Sonia Pitt-Rivers. Reprinted by permission of Harcourt, Inc. and A. M. Heath & Company, Limited. **David Higham Associates, Ltd.** "Do Not Go Gentle into That Good Night" from *The Poems of Dylan Thomas,* copyright ©1952 by Dylan Thomas. Reprinted in Canada by permission of David Higham Associates, Ltd., London. **Alfred A. Knopf, Inc.** "The Garden-Party" from *The Short Stories of Katherine Mansfield* by Katherine Mansfield. Copyright 1937 and renewed 1965 by Alfred A. Knopf, Inc. Reprinted by permission of the publisher. **Louisiana State University Press.** Sonnet 77 from *The Poems of Lady Mary Wroth,* edited by Josephine Roberts. Copyright © 1983 by Louisiana State University Press. **Macmillan & Company Ltd.** Excerpts *from The Ingenious Hidalgo Don Quixote de La Mancha* by Miguel de Cervantes Saavedra, translation by Walter Starkie. Macmillan & Company, Ltd. London, 1957. Reprinted by permission of the publisher. **McClelland & Stewart Inc.** "Bread" from *Murder in the Dark* by Margaret Atwood. Copyright © 1983, 1997 by O. W. Toad, Ltd. Used by written permission, McClelland & Stewart, Inc. *The Canadian Publishers.* **McGraw-Hill Ryerson.** "Red Dress—1946" from *Dance of the Happy Shades* by Alice Munro. Copyright © 1998 by Alice Munro. Reprinted by permission of McGraw-Hill Ryerson Limited and the The Writers Shop. **New Directions Publishing Corporation.** "Do Not Go Gentle into That Good Night" by Dylan Thomas from *The Poems of Dylan Thomas*, copyright © 1952 by Dylan Thomas. Reprinted by permission of New Directions Publishing Corp. "Dulce et Decorum Est" by Wilfred Owen from *The Collected Poems of Wilfred Owen,* copyright © 1963 by Chatto & Windus, Ltd. Reprinted by permission of New Directions Publishing Corp. "Not Waving but Drowning" by Stevie Smith from *Collected Poems of Stevie Smith,* copyright © 1972 by Stevie Smith. Reprinted by permission of New Directions Publishing Corp. **The New York Times.** From "Generous Memories of a Poor, Painful Childhood" by Michiko Kakutani, *The New York Times,* copyright © 2000 by the New York Times Co. Reprinted by permission. **Penguin Putnam, Inc.** 4 haiku (pp. 63, 68, 82, 87) from *The Narrow Road to*

The Deep North and Other Travel Sketches by Basho, translated by Nobuyuji Uasas (Penguin Classics, 1966), copyright © Nabuyuki Yuasa, 1966. Reprinted by permission of the publisher. From *A Portrait of the Artist as a Young Man*, by James Joyce, copyright 1916 by B. W. Huebsch, Copyright 1944 by Nora Joyce, Copyright © 1964 by the Estate of James Joyce. Used by permission of Viking Penguin, a division of Penguin Putnam Inc. From *Beowulf*, translated by Burton Raffel. Copyright © 1963 by Burton Raffel, renewed. Used by permission of Dutton Signet, a division of Penguin Putnam, Inc. "The Pardoner" from *The Canterbury Tales* by Geoffrey Chaucer, translated by Nevill Coghill (Penguin Classics 1951, Fourth revised edition, 1977), copyright © Nevill Coghill, 1951, 1958, 1960, 1975, 1977: The Pardoner (512 lines; pp. 268–274). "The Prologue" from *The Canterbury Tales* by Geoffrey Chaucer, translated by Nevill Coghill (Penguin Classics 1951, Fourth revised edition, 1977), copyright © Nevill Coghill, 1951, 1958, 1960, 1975, 1977: The Prologue (878 lines; pp. 19–42). "The Rocking-Horse Winner" by D. H. Lawrence, copyright 1933 by the Estate of D. H. Lawrence, renewed © 1961 by Angelo Ravagli and C. M. Weekley, Executors of the Estate of Frieda Lawrence, from *Complete Short Stories of D. H. Lawrence* by D. H. Lawrence. Used by permission of Viking Penguin, a division of Penguin Putnam Inc. "Snake" from *The Complete Poems of D. H. Lawrence* by D. H. Lawrence, edited by V. de Sola Pinto & F. W. Roberts, copyright © 1964, 1971 by Angelo Ravagli and C. M. Weekley, Executors of the Estate of Frieda Lawrence Ravagli. Used by permission of Viking Penguin, a division of Penguin Putnam Inc. **Phoebe Larmore.** "Bread" from the collection *Good Bones and Simple Murders* by Margaret Atwood. © 1983, 1992, 1994 O. W. Toad, Ltd., published in the United States by Doubleday Dell. From the collection *Murder in the Dark* in Canada. © 1983 by O. W. Toad, Ltd., published by McClelland and Stewart, Inc. **Random House, Inc.** "Bread" from *Good Bones and Simple Murders* by Margaret Atwood. Copyright © 1983, 1992, 1994 O.W Toad, Ltd. A Nan A. Talese Book. Used by permission of Doubleday, a division of Random House, Inc. "The Lagoon" by Joseph Conrad. Reprinted by permission of Doubleday, a division of Random House, Inc., 1975. "Musee Des Beaux Arts" from *W. H. Auden: Collected Poems* by W. H. Auden, edited by Edward Mendelsohn. Copyright © 1940 and renewed 1968 by W. H. Auden. Reprinted by permission of Random House, Inc. "Rough " from *Selected Poems* by Stephen Spender. Copyright © 1934 and renewed 1962 by Stephen Spender. Reprinted by permission of Random House, Inc. "Who's Who" from *W. H. Auden: Collected Poems* by W. H. Auden, edited by Edward Mendelsohn. Copyright © 1937 and renewed 1965 by W. H. Auden. Reprinted by permission of Random House, Inc. **Simon & Schuster, Inc.** From *Angela's Ashes: A Memoir* by Frank McCourt. Copyright © 1996 by Frank McCourt. Reprinted by permission of Scribner, a division of Simon & Schuster, Inc. "Channel Firing", "The Darkling Thrush", "The Man He Killed" from *The Complete Poems of Thomas Hardy,* edited by James Gibson. Copyright © 1978 by Macmillan London Ltd. Reprinted by permission of Scribner, a Division of Simon & Schuster, Inc. "Adam's Curse", "The Lake Isle of Innisfree", "The Second Coming" from *The Collected Poems of W. B. Yeats*, Revised Second Edition edited by Richard J. Finneran. Copyright © 1924 by Macmillan Publishing Company, renewed 1952 by Bertha Georgie Yeats. Reprinted with the permission of Scribner, a Division of Simon & Schuster. "A Sunrise on the Veld" from *African Stories* by Doris Lessing. Reprinted with permission of Simon & Schuster. Copyright © 1951, 1953, 1954, 1957, 1958, 1962, 1963 1964, 1965, 1972, 1981 by Doris Lessing. **The Society of Authors.** From *A Room of One's Own* by Virginia Woolf, copyright 1957 by Leonard Woolf, reprinted in Canada by permission of Society of Authors. *Pygmalion* by Bernard Shaw, Copyright 1913, 1914, 1916, 1930, 1941,1944 Bernard Shaw. Copyright 1957 The Public Trustee as Executor of the Estate of Bernard Shaw. The Society of Authors on behalf of the Estate of Bernard Shaw. **A. P. Watts, Ltd.** "Adam's Curse", "The Lake Isle of Innisfree", "The Second Coming" from *The Collected Poems of W. B. Yeats*, Revised Second Edition edited by Richard J. Finneran. Copyright © 1924 by Macmillan Publishing Company, renewed 1952 by Bertha Georgie Yeats. Reprinted with the permission of Scribner, a Division of Simon & Schuster. Reprinted in Canada by permission of A. P. Watts, Ltd. **The Writers Shop.** "Red Dress—1946" originally published *in Dance of the Happy Shades* by Alice Munro, originally published by McGraw Hill Ryerson, copyright 1968. Reprinted by permission of The Writers Shop. All rights reserved. **Wallace Literary Agency, Inc.** "Heat" by Jean Rhys from *The Collected Short Stories* published by W. W. Norton, 1987. Copyright © 1987 by Jean Rhys. Used by permission of the Wallace Literary Agency, Inc.

We have made every effort to trace the ownership of all copyrighted material and to secure permission from copyright holders. In the event of any question arising as to the use of any material, we will be pleased to make the necessary corrections in future printings. Thanks are due to the aforementioned authors, publishers, and agents for permission to use the materials indicated.

Study Guide

for

Carlson

Physiology of Behavior

Ninth Edition

(Revised Printing)

prepared by

Mary Carlson

Neil R. Carlson
University of Massachusetts at Amherst

Boston New York San Francisco
Mexico City Montreal Toronto London Madrid Munich Paris
Hong Kong Singapore Tokyo Cape Town Sydney

Copyright © 2007 Pearson Education, Inc.

All rights reserved. No part of the material protected by this copyright notice may be reproduced or utilized in any form or by any means, electronic or mechanical, including photocopying, recording, or by any information storage and retrieval system, without written permission from the copyright owner.

To obtain permission(s) to use material from this work, please submit a written request to Allyn and Bacon, Permissions Department, 75 Arlington Street, Boston, MA 02116 or fax your request to 617-848-7320.

ISBN-13: 978-0-205-55383-9
ISBN-10: 0-205-55383-4

Printed in the United States of America

10 9 8 7 6 5 4 3 2 11 10 09 08 07

Contents

Preface

Welcome to your textbook and to your study guide. We remember what it was like to be students, and we have tried to write something that will help you learn the information in the text in a way that it will stay with you. Your goal is to learn something interesting and useful, and our goal is to help you accomplish that.

The purpose of a study guide is, as its name suggests, to guide you through the text and make sure you see the important points, think about them, write about them, and, most important, *remember* them. We hope that you will remember what you learn even after the semester is over.

Learning is an active process, not a passive one. It is easy to read a chapter and say to yourself, "Yes, I understand that," but still learn and remember very little. If you do not put some effort into your studying, you are not spending your time very effectively.

Although you already have some well established study habits, we urge you to think about trying something different this semester. Begin by leafing through the chapter so that you can see what it is about. Look at the outline at the beginning of the chapter, then read the chapter. Don't take notes or worry about remembering too many details—you only want to see what the chapter is all about. Do all of this *before your professor lectures about the material.* If you are familiar with the chapter, you will understand the lecture much better, and you will remember much more of what you hear. Your lecture notes will also be much clearer.

Now you are ready to work with the study guide. With the exception of Chapter 1 (which is short) we have divided each chapter into two lessons. Finish the first lesson and take a break. You will find it easier to work if you have a break to look forward to. Take some time off, even if you feel that you could finish the chapter in one sitting. As the semester goes on, you will find it easier to begin studying if the habit of taking a break is well established.

Each lesson in the study guide is broken into learning objectives, which are enclosed in a box. The objective states what you should learn to do. Before the first objective, you will see the following statement: "Read the interim summary on page 000 of your text to re-acquaint yourself with the material in this section." Do just that. The interim summaries will remind you about what you read previously. Then, after the objective, you will find the following statement: "Read pages 000-000 and answer the following questions." Do that, too. Then, begin answering the questions. *Try to answer each question without looking at the book.* If all you do is copy the answer from the book into the study guide, you will learn very little. If the purpose of having a study guide were simply to have a list of answers to a list of questions, we could have written the answers, too. Don't be a scribe, copying from the book to the study guide. That's boring and pointless. If you can't answer a particular question, read the appropriate section in the text again, close the book (or at least push it away so that you can't see it), and then write the answer from memory. *If you cannot remember an answer a short time after reading the information in the book, how can you expect to remember it when you take the exam?* The delay between reading the information and writing it in your own words is crucial to your remembering what you have read.

The study guide contains some features that will help you to study your text. It lists the pages that you should read, and many questions refer to specific figures that contain information that you will need to answer a question. Each chapter ends with crossword puzzles that incorporate some important vocabulary terms introduced in each chapter. We have also included a set of concept cards. These cards contain most of the terms that are listed in the margins of each chapter. Learning these terms will help you acquire the vocabulary of physiological psychology. To use the concept cards effectively, cut them apart, put them in a stack, and test yourself. Obviously, you do not need to learn the definitions word-for-word, because there is more than one way to explain a term. But if you forget something important about a term, put the card into a stack that you will go through again until you are satisfied with your performance.

We have tried to supply you with the tools to change some neural circuits in your brain—after all, that is what learning is all about. Let us know how the study guide works for you. If you have some suggestions for the next edition, please write to us at the address listed in the preface of the textbook.

Good luck!

Mary Carlson
Neil Carlson

Chapter 1
Introduction

Read the interim summary on page 9 of your text to re-acquaint yourself with the material in this section.

Learning Objective 1-1 Describe blindsight, the behavior of people with split brains, and unilateral neglect and explain the contribution of these phenomena to our understanding of self-awareness.

Read pages 3-9 and answer the following questions.

1. How did animists explain the behavior of both living and nonliving objects?

2. Briefly describe the mind-body question.

3. _______________ and _______________ are two different explanations of the relationship between the mind and body.

4. Dualism is the belief that mind and body are _______________ and only the _______________ is ordinary matter.

5. Monism, on the other hand, is the belief the mind and body are not _______________ entities and that the _______________ is a phenomenon of the nervous system.

6. Which approach is favored by modern physiological psychologists?

7. a. What evidence suggests that consciousness is a physiological function?

   b. How might verbal communication be related to consciousness?

8. Study Figure 1.2 in your text. List the two visual systems of the brain (noting which is older), and indicate the behavioral mechanisms controlled by each system.

9. a. If the mammalian visual system on the left side of the brain is damaged, what does the person report seeing in the right half of his or her visual field?

   b. If the person is asked to reach for an object that has been placed in the blind field, will he or she be able to do so?

   c. What is this phenomenon called? (Weiskrantz et al., 1974)

d. What does this phenomenon suggest about the nature of consciousness?

10. Very severe epilepsy that does not respond to medication may be controlled by a split-brain operation. Study Figure 1.3 in your text and explain how the cerebral hemispheres are split. Be sure to refer to the corpus callosum in your answer.

11. Explain why patients recovering from split-brain surgery are surprised to find their left hand putting down a book they were reading with interest.

12. Study Figure 1.4 in your text and describe the responses of a person with a split brain.

    a. Will the patient say "I smell a rose" after sniffing a rose through the left nostril? the right nostril?

    b. The patient sniffs a rose through the right nostril. Will the patient then correctly select the flower from among other objects with the left hand or the right hand?

    c. Explain why the aroma must enter the left nostril in order for the patient to become conscious of the sensation of odor.

13. What does work with patients who have undergone a split-brain operation contribute to an understanding of consciousness?

14. a. Describe the behavior of people with unilateral neglect.

    b. Look more closely at the cortex of the parietal lobe which, when damaged on the right side, causes unilateral neglect. What kind of sensory information does the parietal lobe receive directly? What other information does it receive?

    c. What is the most important function of this part of the brain?

15. How do people with unilateral neglect respond when they are asked

    a. to say whether or not two stimuli are identical? (Volpe et al., 1979)

    b. to draw a picture of a clock or a daisy?

    c. to describe a well-known local landmark? (Bisiach and Luzzatti, 1978)

16. List the two major symptoms of this condition.

    1.

    2.

17. a. Carefully explain how researchers demonstrate the rubber hand illusion in people without brain damage. (See Figure 1.5 in your text. Ehrsson et al., 2004)

    b. As recorded by functional MRI, what brain region became active

    1. at first?

2. when stroking was coordinated and then uncoordinated?

c. What do these results suggest about the role of the parietal cortex?

18. What does the phenomenon of unilateral neglect contribute to an understanding of consciousness?

Read the interim summary on page 14 of your text to re-acquaint yourself with the material in this section.

Learning Objective 1-2 Describe the nature of physiological psychology and the goals of research.

Read pages 9-11 and answer the following questions.

1. _______________ _______________ wrote the first textbook of psychology, which was called _______________ of _______________ _______________.

2. a. What is the ultimate function of the brain?

   b. How do behaviors such as perception and thinking support it?

   c. Why then did the abilities to learn and remember evolve?

3. The two forms of scientific explanation are _______________ and _______________.

4. Decide whether the examples below illustrate generalization (G) or reduction (R). You will find answers at the end of this chapter.

_____ When an acid is poured over a carbonate, a gas is formed.

_____ When some people have coffee after dinner they have trouble falling asleep.

_____ The sky looks blue because particles in the atmosphere scatter light of short-wavelengths.

_____ Because she was stung several times by bees when she was young, Jessica is now afraid of them.

_____ $E=MC^2$.

_____ Lemon juice tastes sour because the hydrogen ions present in citric acid stimulate special receptors in the tongue.

5. State the goal of psychological research.

Learning Objective 1-3 Describe the biological roots of physiological psychology.

Read pages 11-14 and answer the following questions.

1. a. According to many ancient cultures, which organ was responsible for thought and emotions?

   b. Both _______________ and _______________ disagreed, believing instead that thought and emotions originated in the _______________.

2. a. How did Descartes explain the automatic responses of humans, which he named reflexes? (See Figure 1.6 in your text.)

   b. Describe the relationship between the mind and the body hypothesized by Descartes and illustrated in Figure 1.7 in your text. Be sure to explain the role of the pineal body in your answer.

3. a. Descartes's early visits to the Royal Gardens suggested a _______________ to explain how the human body worked.

   b. Define *model* in your own words.

   c. What is an important advantage of using a model?

4. Why did Galvani's experiment with muscular contraction stimulate further research?

5. When Müller first began his career, what two techniques were widely used by natural scientists?

   1. 2.

6. What kind of new research techniques did he propose using?

7. Explain the doctrine of specific nerve energies.

8. How did Flourens extend Müller's advocacy of experimentation? (Be sure to mention experimental ablation in your answer.)

9. How did Broca modify the method of experimental ablation for work with humans? (See Figure 1.9 in your text.)

10. Describe early studies by Fritsch and Hitzig using electrical stimulation of the brain.

11. a. List several important contributions to 19th century science by von Helmholtz.

    b. How did von Helmholtz's views differ from those of his teacher, Müller?

Read the interim summary on pages 22-23 of your text to reacquaint yourself with the material in this section.

Learning Objective 1-4 Describe the role of natural selection in the evolution of behavioral traits.

Read pages 14-17 and answer the following questions.

1. Who proposed the principles of natural selection and evolution?

2. a. Define *functionalism* in your own words and explain its importance in understanding behavior.

   b. Explain the difference between function and purpose. (See Figure 1.11 in your text.)

3. How did Blest (1957) confirm a useful function of eyespots on the wings of certain species of moths and butterflies? (See Figure 1.12 in your text.)

4. Summarize these principles incorporated in Darwin's theory of evolution.

   a. Natural selection

b. Mutation

c. Selective advantage

5. a. What is the effect of most mutations? (See Figure 1.13 in your text.)

   b. What kind of effect do a small percentage of mutations have?

   c. Explain how the selective advantage conferred by beneficial mutations can indirectly affect the behavior of the next generation or of subsequent ones.

   d. Explain how mutations that are not immediately beneficial may eventually benefit the species.

6. Match these scientists with their contributions.

___ Wilhelm Wundt — a. Doctrine of specific nerve energies

___ René Descartes — b. Method of experimental ablation

___ Johannes Müller — c. *Principles of Physiological Psychology*

___ Pierre Flourens — d. Principle of natural selection

___ Fritsch and Hitzig — e. Modified method of experimental ablation to work with humans

___ Paul Broca — f. Used electrical stimulation to study brain

___ H. von Helmholtz — g. Electrical stimulation, not pressurized fluid, caused muscular contraction

___ Charles Darwin — h. Early use of a model

___ Luigi Galvani — i. Measured speed of conduction through nerves

Learning Objective 1-5 Discuss the evolution of the human species and a large brain.

Read pages 17-22 and answer the following questions.

1. Explain the process of evolution in your own words.

2. a. Which species of vertebrates was the first to emerge from the sea, and how does the sea continue to play an integral part in their life cycle?

   b. Approximately how many million years ago did the first reptiles appear?

   c. What advantage did reptiles have over amphibians and how did this advantage contribute to their survival?

3. Reptiles soon divided into three lines. List them and some of the animals which evolved from each division. (The evolution of the vertebrates is illustrated in Figure 1.14 in your text.)

   1.

2.

3.

4. a. What event triggered a mass extinction at the end of the Permian period?

   b. Among the survivors was the _______________, a small _______________, the direct ancestor of the _______________.

5. Briefly explain why the earliest mammals had better hearing than the cynodonts and describe the advantage of this ability. (Study Figure 1.15 in your text.)

6. a. What animal dominated the world for millions of years, forcing mammals to remain inconspicuous?

   b. What led to their extinction, permitting mammals to evolve and become more numerous?

   c. Who were our most direct ancestors and where did they evolve first?

   d. Describe these early primates.

   e. How did the appearance of fruit-bearing trees benefit the evolving primates?

7. a. On which continent and in what kind of environment did the first hominids appear?

   b. What kind of skills did they develop?

   c. Review the four major species of hominids and compare the percentage differences in their DNA. (Study Figures 1.16 and 1.17 in your text.)

8. a. Which species of hominids was the first to leave Africa?

   b. To what regions did they migrate?

   c. Name the human-like species that appears to have evolved from *Homo erectus* and settled in Western Europe.

   d. Where did our own species *Homo sapiens* evolve?

   e. Study the migration routes of *Homo sapiens* shown in Figure 1.18 in your text.

   f. Offer two reasons why *Homo sapiens* replaced the Neanderthals after coexisting for about 10,000 years.

9. List at least four characteristics that enabled mature humans to become the dominant species.

   1. 3.

   2. 4.

10. a. How did an upright posture affect the evolution of the size of a newborn baby's head and brain?

    b. How did the restricted size of the baby's head affect the level of complexity of the brain at birth?

    c. How did, (and still does), an immature infant brain affect the nature and length of parental care?

11. a. If we calculate and compare the percentage of brain weight to body weight for humans and other animals, the comparison will not yield meaningful results. Why?

    b. Study Figure 1.19 in your text and explain a more useful comparison.

12. Define *neoteny* in your own words and explain how this phenomenon contributes to the larger brain size of humans. (See Figure 1.20 in your text.)

Read the interim summary on page 25 of your text to reacquaint yourself with the material in this section.

Learning Objective 1-6 Discuss the value of research with animals and ethical issues concerning their care.

Read pages 23-24 and answer the following questions.

1. List several ways in which the humane care of animals used in scientific research is assured.

2. According to Miller (1983), what are some of the animal care regulations that scientific researchers are required to follow, but pet owners are not?

3. Describe the statistics that indicate that the use of animals in research and teaching is a special target of animal rights activists. (Nicholl and Russell, 1990)

4. Explain the statement that the use of animals in research and education is the only indispensable use of animals.

5. Describe some actual and potential benefits of research with animals.

Learning Objective 1-7 Describe career opportunities in neuroscience.

Read pages 24-25 and answer the following questions.

1. a. In general, what do physiological psychologists study?

   b. In general, what do neuroscientists study?

   c. More specifically, what are some of the research topics in these fields?

2. a. What kind of academic degree do most physiological psychologists and neuroscientists obtain?
   b. What kind of subsequent training do they receive?
   c. Where do most professional physiological psychologists and neuroscientists work?
3. a. What do neurologists and experimental neuropsychologists study?
   b. What kind of degree is appropriate for each of these professions?
4. What kind of careers in neuroscience are open to those without a Ph.D.?

Introduction Self Test

1. A person who argues that the body and mind consist of physical matter and energy believes in
   a. animism.
   b. dualism.
   c. monism.
   d. ethnocentrism.
2. The phenomenon of blindsight confirms that
   a. visual information must enter our consciousness for us to respond appropriately.
   b. consciousness is not a general property of all parts of the brain.
   c. there is no evolutionary advantage to possessing two visual systems.
   d. the mammalian visual system is responsible for consciousness.
3. The right hemisphere of a person who has had a split-brain operation can no longer
   a. perceive sensory information.
   b. understand verbal instructions.
   c. produce speech.
   d. control movements of the right hand.
4. The effects of the split-brain operation suggest that
   a. consciousness developed in the right hemisphere.
   b. the left hemisphere is more adept at analyzing sensory information than the right hemisphere.
   c. all cognitive processes are located in the left hemisphere.
   d. information does not reach consciousness unless it reaches those parts of the brain responsible for verbal communication.
5. A researcher concluded that a drug made animals eat because it altered the insulin level in their blood. What kind of explanation did the researcher provide?
   a. Generalization
   b. Reduction
   c. Rationalization
   d. Deduction
6. Models, first used by Descartes to explain how the body worked,
   a. were the forerunners of the scientific method.
   b. were useful because they could be tested experimentally.
   c. challenged the usefulness of philosophical speculation.
   d. negated the distinction between function and purpose.
7. The work of Müller and many physiologists who followed him is characterized by
   a. experimentation and logical deduction.
   b. observation and classification.
   c. self-report and introspective evidence.
   d. philosophical speculation.
8. Darwin's theory of evolution suggests that all of an organism's characteristics
   a. are given to it by its creator.
   b. confer a selective advantage on the species.
   c. have been naturally selected by its ancestors.
   d. have functional significance.
9. A small _____ survived a mass extinction to become the direct ancestors of the _____.
   a. anapsid; amphibian
   b. diapsid; vertebrate

c. cynodont; mammal
d. therapsid; hominid

10. The human brain

a. at birth is comparable to that of other mammals relative to body weight.
b. contains an abundance of circuits that can be modified through experience.
c. and skull change much less from birth to adulthood than do those of other mammals.
d. following birth grows at a rate proportional to the growth of the body.

11. Which is the only true statement about animal research?

a. Behavior cannot be studied using tissue cultures or computers.
b. The characteristics of tissue cultures are similar enough to living organisms to replace them in research.
c. Computer research can replace animal research if the results are interpreted cautiously.
d. The results of research using tissue cultures can be more reliably replicated than the results of research using animals.

12. Most professional physiological psychologists work in

a. industry.
b. hospitals.
c. colleges and universities.
d. government.

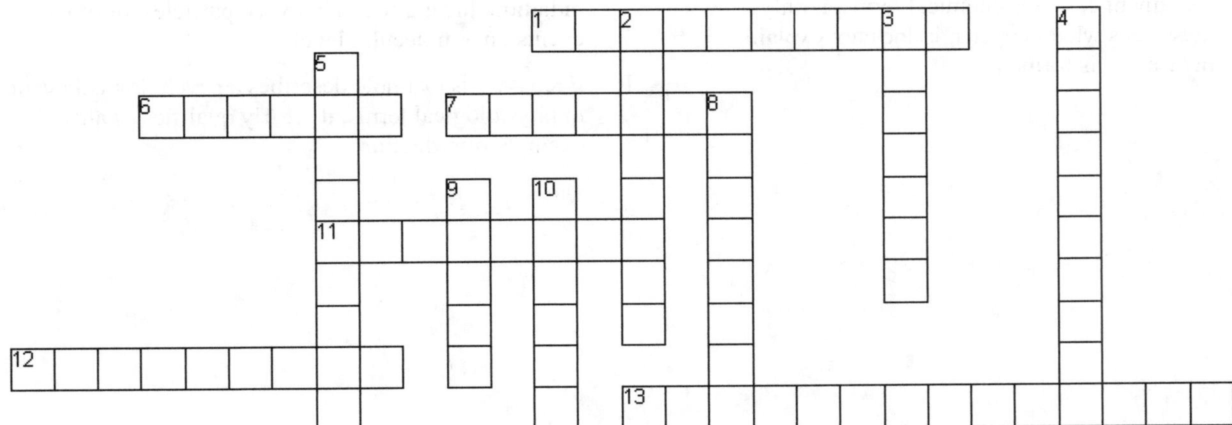

Across
1. First vertebrates to evolve
6. Automatic movement resulting from direct stimulus
7. Belief that the body is physical, but the mind is not
11. Direct ancestor of mammals
12. Gradual change as a result of natural selection
13. Scientific explanation based on many observations of similar phenomena

Down
2. Most direct ancestor of humans
3. Slowing of maturation process
4. Phenomenon that suggests consciousness is not a general property of the brain
5. Scientific explanation of a phenomena in terms of underlying basic processes
8. Change in genetic information in chromosomes of sperms or eggs
9. Mathematical or physical analogy for a physiological process
10. Belief that the mind is a product of the workings of the nervous system

Answers for Self Test

1. c Obj. 1-1
2. b Obj. 1-1
3. c Obj. 1-1
4. d Obj. 1-1
5. b Obj. 1-2
6. b Obj. 1-3
7. a Obj. 1-3
8. d Obj. 1-4
9. c Obj. 1-5
10. b Obj. 1-5
11. a Obj. 1-6
12. c Obj. 1-7

Answers to Learning Objective 1-2, question 4:

G This one is tricky. Even though the statement contains chemical terms, it only describes what happens; it does not explain *why* a gas is formed.

G If the statement had talked about the physiological effects of caffeine, it would have been an example of reduction.

R The perceptual phenomena are explained in terms of physical events.

G A behavioral phenomenon is being explained in terms of environmental events. If the statement had talked about changes that had taken place in her brain, it would have been an example of reduction.

G This one is tricky, too. Even though it is a formula, it relates physical observations (energy = mass multiplied by the speed of light, squared). To be an example of reduction, the statement would have had to talk about the characteristics of electromagnetic radiation, the attraction between particles, or other events on a molecular level.

R Because this example describes a psychological event in physiological terms, it clearly qualifies as an example of reduction

CHAPTER 2
Structure and Functions of Cells of the Nervous System

Lesson I: Cells of the Nervous System and Communication Within a Neuron

Read the interim summary on page 41 of your text to re-acquaint yourself with the material in this section.

Learning Objective 2-1 Name and describe the parts of a neuron and explain their functions.

Read pages 29-36 and answer the following questions.

1. List the three types of neurons that respond to the environment or control the muscles.

   1. 2.

   3.

2. List the two types of interneurons, noting their functions.

   1.

   2.

3. List the two divisions of the nervous system and their principal parts.

   1.

   2.

4. Label the four principal structures of the neuron shown in Figure 1. (See Figure 2.1 in your text and Animation 2.1.)

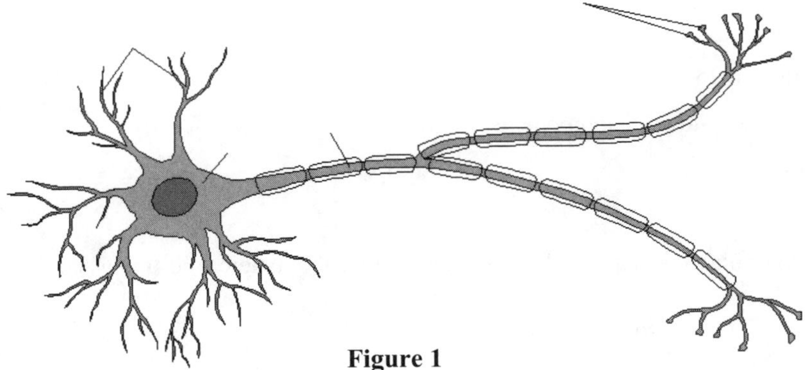

Figure 1

5. Where is the cell nucleus located?

6. a. Communication between neurons occurs across the ______________, which is a junction between the ______________ ______________ of the sending cell and a portion of the ______________ or ______________ ______________ of the receiving cell. In general, communication proceeds in ______________ direction; from the ______________ ______________ to the ______________ of the other cell.

   b. Briefly describe the appearance and explain the role of these structures of the neuron in communication.

      1. Dendrites

      2. Axon (Be sure to refer to the myelin sheath and the action potential.)

7. Study Figures 2.1 and 2.2 in your text and describe the difference between unipolar, bipolar, and multipolar neurons.

8. Study Figure 2.3 in your text and describe the appearance of the nerves.

9. a. Describe the location and appearance of the terminal buttons.

   b. Name the type of chemical secreted by terminal buttons and identify the effects it can have on the receiving cell.

10. Study Figure 2.4 in your text and describe the nature of synaptic connections in your own words.

11. Look at the internal structure of a typical multipolar neuron which is shown in Figure 2.5 in your text.

    a. Describe the composition of the cell membrane.

    b. List some of the functions of the protein molecules that are embedded in the cell membrane.

12. Name the covering which encloses the nucleus of a cell.

13. Describe the function of the following components of the nucleus.

    a. Nucleolus and ribosomes

    b. Chromosomes, deoxyribonucleic acid (DNA), and messenger ribonucleic acid (mRNA). (Study Figure 2.6 in your text.)

14. Briefly describe the role of proteins, including serving as enzymes.

15. Define *genome* in your own words.

16. State a surprising observation revealed by genome research about

    a. genes and organism complexity. (Mattick, 2004)

    b. "junk" DNA. (Be sure to explain what is "junk" DNA. See Figure 2.7 in your text.)

17. a. What did a comparison of the genomes of humans and pufferfish indicate the longevity of non-coding DNA? (Woolfe et al., 2005)

    b. Where are these conserved sequences found?

18. What may be the function of this non-coding DNA? (Be sure to mention spliceosomes in your answer. Szymanski et al., 2003; Storz et al., 2005)

19. What substance fills the cell?

20. Briefly discuss these aspects of mitochondria.

    a. Appearance

    b. Function (Be sure to mention ATP.)

    c. Presumed origin

    d. Reproduction

21. a. List the two forms of endoplasmic reticulum and describe their appearance.

    1. 2.

    b. Explain their functions.

22. a. Name a special form of smooth endoplasmic reticulum and explain its functions.

    b. Briefly summarize the process of exocytosis.

    c. What is the function of the lysosomes?

23. a. What is the name of the matrix that gives the cell its shape?

    b. Describe its composition.

24. a. Why is axoplasmic transport required by the cell?

b. Movement from the soma to the terminal buttons is called ________________ axoplasmic transport and is accomplished by the protein ______________.

c. Explain how this protein transports its cargo. (Study Figure 2.8 in your text.)

d. Movement from the terminal buttons to the soma is known as ________________ axoplasmic transport and is accomplished by the protein ______________.

25. Immediately review the principal internal structures of a multipolar neuron which are shown in Figure 2.5 in your text.

Learning Objective 2-2 Describe the supporting cells of the central and peripheral nervous systems and explain the blood-brain barrier.

Read pages 36-41 and answer the following questions.

1. Why are the supporting cells essential?

2. ______________ are the most important supporting cells in the central nervous system (CNS).

3. List four functions performed by these cells.

   1.
   2.
   3.
   4.

4. List the three most important types of glial cells.

   1.
   2.
   3.

5. a. Describe six general functions of astrocytes.

   1.
   2.
   3.
   4.
   5.
   6,

   b. What did the arrangement of the processes of astrocytes suggest to Golgi (1903)?

   c. What does recent research suggest about Golgi's hypothesis? Explain how the astrocytes provide cells with energy. Be sure to mention lactate and glycogen in your answer. (Study Figure 2.9 in your text. Tsacopoulos and Magistretti, 1996; Magistretti et al., 1999; Brown et al., 2003)

6. Describe how certain kinds of astrocytes clean up the debris from dead neurons through phagocytosis. Be sure to describe how they provide physical support once the dead tissue has been removed.

7. What is the principal function of the oligodendrocytes?

8. a. Study Figures 2.10 and 2.11a in your text and describe how the oligodendroglia form the myelin sheath around an axon. Be sure to mention the nodes of Ranvier in your answer.

   b. Go back to Figure 1 in this study guide and add labels for the myelin sheath and nodes of Ranvier.

9. Summarize the functions of microglia.

10. The _______________ _______________ in the PNS perform the same functions as the _______________ in the CNS.

11. How do the segments of myelin surrounding axons in the PNS differ from those in the CNS? (Study Figure 2.11b in your text.)

12. a. Contrast the restorative roles of astrocytes in the CNS and Schwann cells in the PNS if axons are damaged.

    b. What may account for this difference? (Liuzzi and Lasek, 1987)

13. What is a second difference between these structures?

14. a. What tissue is tinted when dye is injected into an animal's bloodstream?

    b. What tissue is tinted when dye is injected into an animal's brain ventricles? (Bradbury, 1979)

    c. What does this experiment demonstrate about the relationship between the blood and the fluid that surrounds the cells of the brain?

15. a. Look at Figure 2.12 in your text and explain why some substances pass easily through the blood-brain barrier and others do not.

    b. Briefly explain two functions of the blood-brain barrier.

16. Discuss the uniformity of the blood-brain barrier throughout the nervous system and its relationship to the control of vomiting. Be sure to use the term *area postrema* in your answer.

Read the interim summary on pages 52-53 of your text to re-acquaint yourself with the material in this section.

Learning Objective 2-3 Briefly describe the role of neural communication in a simple reflex and its inhibition by brain mechanisms.

Read pages 42-43 answer the following questions.

1. Study Animation 2.2 to learn about the action potential.
2. In a withdrawal reflex, shown in Figure 2.13 in your text, what is the function of the

a. sensory neuron?

b. interneuron?

c. motor neuron?

3. Explain how neural circuits in the brain signal inhibition. (See Figure 2.14 in your text.)

4. Communication received from terminal buttons produces one of two possible effects on the rate of firing of the receiving neurons. Name them.

1. 2.

Learning Objective 2-4 Describe the measurement of the action potential and explain the dynamic equilibrium that is responsible for the membrane potential.

Read pages 43-47 and answer the following questions.

1. What kind of axon do neuroscientists find useful for studying the electrical potentials of axons? Why?

2. In your own words, define

   a. *electrode.*

   b. *microelectrode.*

3. a. Describe how electrodes and microelectrodes are used to measure the membrane potential of an axon shown in Figure 2.15 in your text.

   b. Is the inside of the membrane positively or negatively charged with respect to the outside?

   c. What is the approximate value of the electrical charge across the membrane of the axon?

   d. What is this electrical charge called?

4. a. If we wish to study changes in the membrane potential that occur when a message is conducted down an axon, we will need some equipment more complicated than a voltmeter. Why?

   b. What does an oscilloscope do and what kind of record does it produce?

5. Define *resting potential* in your own words.

6. If we wish to alter the resting potential, what device is necessary? (See Figure 2.16 in your text.)

7. If a positive electrical stimulus is applied to the inside of the membrane, what will be the effect on the membrane potential? What term is used to describe this change?

8. a. What happens to the membrane potential when the membrane receives a very weak depolarizing stimulus? (Study Figure 2.17 in your text.)

b. Describe what happens to the electrical charge across the membrane after it receives a sufficiently large stimulus (number 4 on Figure 2.17).

c. As the membrane returns to normal, it overshoots the resting potential. Name this phenomenon.

d. About how long does the entire process—from the electrical stimulus to the return to a normal resting potential–take?

e. What do we call this phenomenon and the voltage level at which it is triggered?

9. A spoonful of sugar has been poured into a container of water. What eventually happens to the sugar?

10. a. Name the process that you just described.

b. State the rule that describes how molecules will diffuse.

11. _______________ are substances that split into two parts when dissolved in water. The charged particles into which they decompose are called _______________. _____________ have a positive charge and _______________ have a negative charge. The force of attraction or repulsion between these particles is called _______________ _______________.

12. Read the explanation of ionic movements between the intracellular and extracellular fluid and study Figure 2.18 in your text. Without looking back, make the following additions to Figure 2.

a. Minus signs are located both above and below the membrane. Change the appropriate ones to plus signs.

b. Write the names of the four ions in the 7 boxes.

c. Add two arrows, oriented appropriately, to each of the large boxes, indicating the direction of the force of diffusion and electrostatic pressure operating on each ion. (Add just one arrow to the box representing the ion that cannot leave the cell.)

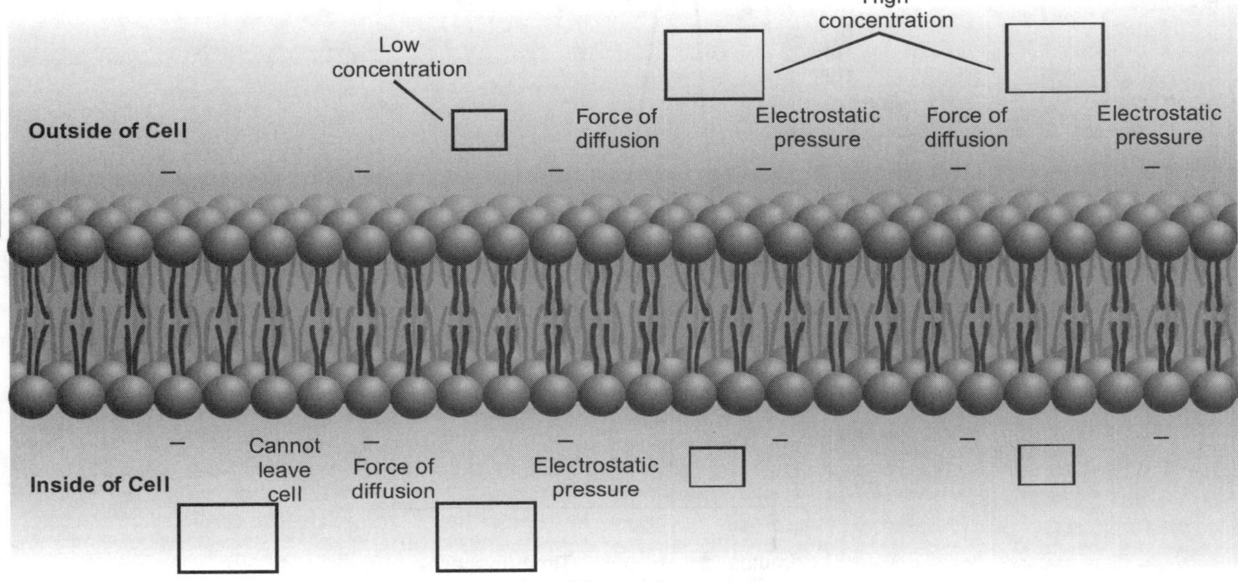

Figure 2

13. a. Explain why sodium stays where it is.

b. Study Figure 2.19 in your text and describe the action of the sodium-potassium transporters that compose the sodium-potassium pump including the

1. source of energy.

2. exchange ratio between sodium and potassium and direction of movement of these ions.

14. What is the relative permeability of the membrane to sodium and potassium?

Learning Objective 2-5 Describe the role of ion channels in action potentials and explain the all-or-none law and the rate law.

Read pages 47-52 and answer the following questions.

1. a. What happens if the membrane suddenly became very permeable to sodium ions?

   b. What forces cause this change?

   c. How is the membrane potential affected?

2. What pathways do ions use to enter and leave a cell? (Study Figure 2.20 in your text.)

3. Read the description and carefully study Figures 2.17 and 2.21 in your text. Then add numbers to Figure 3, below, that indicate the following:

   1. K^+ continues to leave cell, causes membrane potential to return to resting level
   2. Na^+ channels open, and Na^+ begins to enter cell
   3. Extra K^+ outside diffuses away
   4. K^+ channels open, K^+ begins to leave cell
   5. K^+ channels close, Na^+ channels reset
   6. Na^+ channels become refractory, no more Na^+ enters cell
   7. Depolarization
   8. Hyperpolarization

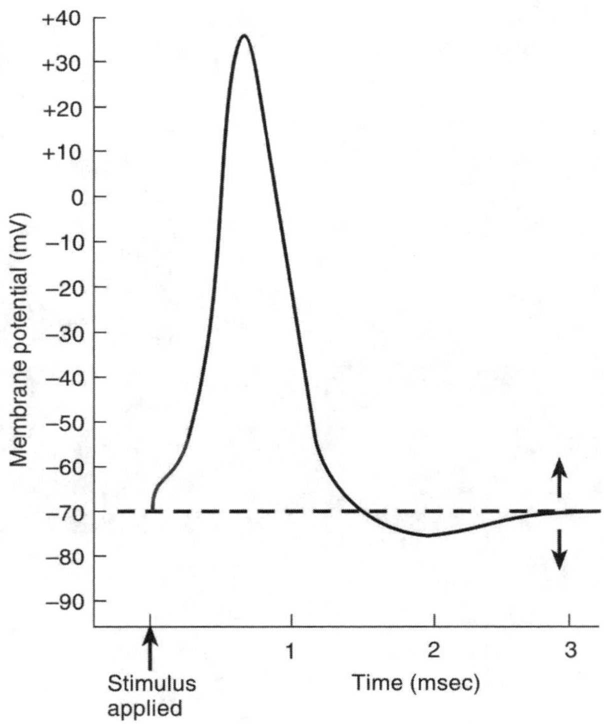

Figure 3

4. During an action potential there is only a slight increase in the concentration of sodium ions in the axoplasm. (Study Figure 2.22 in your text.) Why, then, are sodium-potassium transporters important?

5. Study Figure 2.23 in your text and state the all-or-none law in your own words.

6. Explain how action potentials, which are transmitted according to the all-or-none law, are able to transmit information of varying strength (for example, sensory stimuli of differing intensities). Be sure to use the term *rate law* in your answer. (See Figure 2.24 in your text.)

7. Compare the conduction of an electrical signal along an axon and an underwater cable. Be sure to use the terms *decremental conduction* (illustrated in Figure 2.25 in your text) and *cable properties* in your answer.

8. Study Figure 2.26 in your text and describe the step-by-step conduction of the action potential along a myelinated axon using these terms in this order.

   a. Schwann cells or oligodendroglia
   b. nodes of Ranvier
   c. inward flow of sodium
   d. extracellular sodium
   e. cable properties
   f. decremental conduction
   g. renewed signal strength
   h. saltatory conduction

9. Identify and explain the two advantages of saltatory conduction.

10. The interim summary for this section provides an overview of how action potentials are triggered and transmitted.

Lesson I Self Test

1. What is the correct sequence of structures encountered by neural information as it travels along a neuron?

   a. dendrites to soma to axon to terminal buttons
   b. dendrites to soma to terminal buttons to axon
   c. soma to axon to dendrites to terminal buttons
   d. terminal buttons to axon to soma to dendrites

2. Research to determine genome sequences indicates that the _____ correlates well with the _____ of the organism.

   a. amount of non-coding DNA; complexity
   b. amount of coding DNA; estimated evolutionary age
   c. amount of mRNA; protein lengths
   d. number of genes; complexity

3. Which of the following are the *least* similar in their functions?

   a. lysosomes and mitochondria
   b. axons and dendrites
   c. chromosomes and genes
   d. nucleolus and ribosomes

4. Which of these structures does *not* provide support to neurons?

   a. Oligodendrocytes
   b. Astrocytes
   c. Nodes of Ranvier
   d. Glia

5. When nerves in the PNS are damaged, Schwann cells

   a. dissolve scar tissue.
   b. secrete enzymes that stimulate neurons to divide.
   c. form cylinders to guide the new axon sprouts.
   d. manufacture extra myelin.

6. Some substances in the blood cannot enter the brain because

   a. the area postrema controls vomiting.
   b. the sodium-potassium transporters only pass certain molecules.
   c. capillaries in the brain do not have gaps.
   d. capillaries in the brain have gaps.

7. What role does the inhibitory interneuron play in preventing a withdrawal reflex that would make you drop a hot casserole on the floor?

   a. It signals the neural circuits in the brain of the consequences of the action potential.
   b. It inhibits a sensory neuron.
   c. It inhibits a motor neuron.
   d. It prevents pain signals from entering the spinal cord.

8. If the membrane of an axon receives a sufficiently large depolarization, the resulting rapid reversal of charge is called a(n)

   a. threshold of excitation.
   b. membrane potential.
   c. action potential.
   d. resting potential shift.

9. The membrane potential is the result of two forces:

   a. diffusion and electrostatic pressure.
   b. hyperpolarization and depolarization.
   c. equilibrium and inertia.
   d. the resting potential and the threshold of excitation.

10. Sodium-potassium transporters keep the intracellular concentration of

    a. Na^+ low.
    b. K^+ low.
    c. Na^+ high.
    d. Cl^- high.

11. All of the following are true about conduction of an action potential in a myelinated axon *except:*

    a. Saltatory conduction is more energy efficient than transmission in unmyelinated axons.
    b. Conduction of the message under the myelin segment is via passive cable properties.
    c. Saltatory conduction is slower than conduction in unmyelinated axons.
    d. Action potentials occur only at the nodes of Ranvier.

12. Saltatory conduction is advantageous because

    a. it is unaffected by diseases that damage myelin.
    b. it permits myelinated axons to transmit action potentials almost as fast as unmyelinated axons.
    c. nodes of Ranvier are bypassed.
    d. less energy is required to operate the sodium-potassium transporters.

Lesson II: Communication Between Neurons

Read the interim summary on page 66 of your text to re-acquaint yourself with the material in this section.

Learning Objective 2-6 Describe the structure of synapses, the release of the neurotransmitter, and the activation of postsynaptic receptors.

Read pages 53-59 and answer the following questions.

1. Definitions. In your own words, define

   a. *synaptic transmission*, noting three benefits of neural communication.

   b. *postsynaptic potential,* noting its two possible effects on an axon.

c. *binding site.*

d. *ligand*, giving several different examples.

2. List the three types of synapses illustrated in Figure 2.27 in your text and note where they are found.
   1.
   2.
   3.

3. A synapse is a(n) _______________ between the _______________ _______________ at the ends of axons of one neuron with the _______________ of another neuron. The membrane of the transmitting neuron is called the _______________ membrane, and the message is received by the _______________ membrane. These two membranes are separated by a small gap called the _______________ _______________.
4. On Figure 4 on the next page, label the parts listed in question 3. (See Figures 2.28 and 2.29 in your text.)
5. Look at some of the structures found in the cytoplasm of the terminal button.
   a. What is the function of the microtubules?

   b. What does the presence of mitochondria suggest?
   c. Describe the appearance of a synaptic vesicle. Where are they found?

   d. What chemical do small synaptic vesicles contain?
   e. What chemical do large synaptic vesicles contain?
   f. What kind of proteins do synaptic vesicles contain?

   g. Where are synaptic vesicles found in greatest concentration?
6. Where are large and small synaptic vesicles produced and how are they transported to the terminal buttons?

7. What constitutes the postsynaptic density?
8. Label the rest of the features on Figure 4. (See Figures 2.28 and 2.29 in your text.)
9. Begin an explanation of how neurotransmitter is released from synaptic vesicles when an action potential arrives at the terminal button. (See Figure 2.30 in your text.)
   a. What is the first step in this process? Be sure to mention the term *docking* in your answer. (Study Figure 2.31 in your text.)

   b. What change occurs in the calcium channels of the release zone of the presynaptic membrane?
   c. Calcium now flows into the cell. What evidence shows that the presence of calcium is essential?

   d. Explain the process of fusion shown in Figures 2.31 and 2.32 in your text.

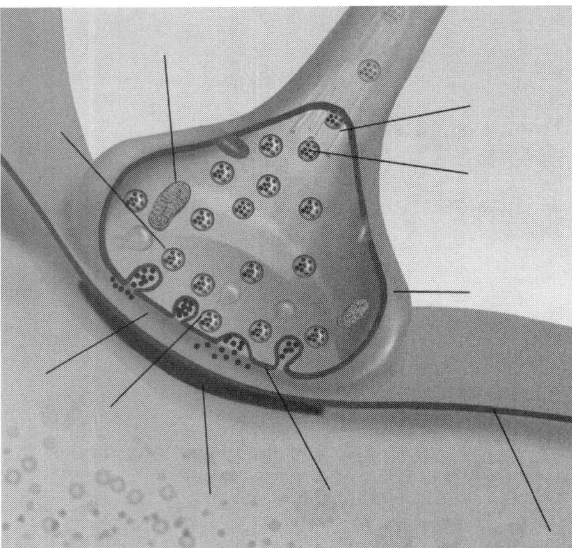

Figure 4

10. Explain the three ways synaptic vesicles release neurotransmitters. (See Figure 2.33 in your text. Aravanis et al., 2003; Gandhi and Stevens, 2003; Sudhof, 2004)

    a. Kiss and stay

    b. Kiss and leave

    c. Merge and recycle

11. How are new synaptic vesicles formed? Be sure to mention the role of endosomes in your answer.

12. When molecules of the neurotransmitter diffuse across the synaptic cleft to the postsynaptic membrane, what structures do they bind with? Once binding occurs, what happens next?

13. a. Neurotransmitters open ion channels in at least two different ways. First explain the direct method involving ionotropic receptors illustrated in Figure 2.34 in your text.

    b. Explain the indirect method involving metabotropic receptors and the G protein illustrated in Figure 2.35 in your text.

    c. What are chemicals that open metabotropic receptors called?

    d. What are some of their other functions?

14. To review what you have just learned, follow Animation 2.3.

Learning Objective 2-7 Describe postsynaptic potentials: the ionic movements that cause them, the processes that terminate them, and their integration.

Read pages 60-63 and answer the following questions.

1. a. To review: What are the two possible effects of postsynaptic potentials?

   b. What determines which effect will occur?

2. List the four major types of neurotransmitter-dependent ion channels in the postsynaptic membrane.

   1. 3.

   2. 4.

3. Describe the movements of sodium and potassium ions during an

   a. EPSP. (See Figure 2.36a in your text.)

   b. IPSP. (See Figure 2.36b.)

4. Describe the movement of

   a. chloride, which neutralizes an EPSP. (See Figure 2.36c.)

   b. calcium, which produces special effects as well as an EPSP. (See Figure 2.36d.)

5. Define *postsynaptic potential* in your own words.

6. Name and describe the mechanism that terminates almost all postsynaptic potentials. (See Figure 2.37 in your text.)

7. Name and describe the mechanism that deactivates the neurotransmitter acetylcholine. Be sure to use the term *acetylcholinesterase (AChE)* in your answer.

8. a. Define *neural integration* in your own words.

   b. Explain what happens to the axon of a neuron when several excitatory synapses or several inhibitory synapses become active at the same time. (Study Figure 2.38 in your text.)

      1. Excitatory synapses

      2. Inhibitory synapses

   c. What controls the rate at which a neuron fires?

9. Explain why neural inhibition or excitation does not always result in behavioral inhibition or excitation.

Learning Objective 2-8 Describe the regulation of the effects of the neurotransmitters by autoreceptors, presynaptic inhibition, presynaptic facilitation and nonsynaptic communication.

Read pages 63-65 and answer the following questions.

1. Many neurons contain _______________, which respond to the neurotransmitter they themselves produce.
   a. Where are they found and what seems to be their function?

   b. What is the usual effect of their activation?

2. Axoaxonic synapses alter the amount of _______________ released by the terminal buttons of the _______________ _______________. If the activity of these synapses decreases the amount of _______________ the effect is called _______________ _______________, but if their activity increases the amount of _______________ the effect is called _______________ _______________. (See Figure 2.39 in your text.)

3. a. What may be the function of dendrodendritic synapses formed by small neurons with short processes?

   b. At electrical synapses the membranes of two neurons meet and almost touch. What do we call the space between them? (See Figure 2.40 in your text.)

   c. Explain how these adjacent neurons influence the activity of each other across this gap.

4 Neuromodulators and hormones play a role in nonsynaptic chemical communication between neurons.
   a. Describe these characteristics of neuromodulators.
      1. The structure that releases them
      2. Their range, especially as compared to neurotransmitters
      3. Their chemical composition Be sure to mention peptides and peptide bonds.

      4. Their general function
   b. Describe these characteristics of hormones.
      1. The structures that release them
      2. How they are distributed
      3. The structures that detect them Be sure to mention target cells in your answer.
      4. Their general function

5. Briefly summarize the means by which peptide and steroid hormones are distributed and their effect on target cells. (See Figure 2.41 in your text.)

6. To review what you have just learned, follow Animation 2.4.

Lesson II Self Test

1. Ligands are chemicals that
   a. are found only at axodendritic synapses.
   b. attach to binding sites.
   c. detect the presence of neurotransmitters in the synaptic cleft.
   d. surround synaptic vesicles and prevent the premature release of the neurotransmitter.

2. Neurotransmitters are released when
   a. the presynaptic and postsynaptic membrane fuse briefly.
   b. synaptic vesicles spill their contents into the synaptic cleft.
   c. a brief electrical charge crosses the synaptic gap.
   d. the release zone is hyperpolarized.

3. Large synaptic vesicles are produced in the __________ and are transported to the __________.
   a. cytoplasm; dendrites
   b. soma; terminal buttons
   c. dendrites; release zone
   d. synapse; extracellular fluid

4. What ion plays a crucial role in propelling synaptic vesicles toward the presynaptic membrane?
   a. Na^+
   b. Cl^-
   c. Ca^{2+}
   d. K^+

5. In the _____ form of neurotransmitter release , the terminal button becomes slightly _____ and pieces of _____ become new synaptic vesicles.
   a. kiss and stay; smaller; endosomes
   b. kiss and leave; larger; spliceosomes
   c. kiss and recycle; smaller; G proteins
   d. merge and recycle; larger; endosomes

6. Postsynaptic receptors bind with molecules of neurotransmitter and
   a. transport them to synaptic vesicles.
   b. open neurotransmitter-dependent ion channels.
   c. release them during an EPSP or IPSP.
   d. deactivate them through reuptake.

7. During an EPSP
   a. Na^+ enters the cell.
   b. K^+ enters the cell.
   c. K^+ leaves the cell.
   d. Cl^- leaves the cell.

8. During an IPSP
   a. Na^+ enters the cell.
   b. K^+ enters the cell.
   c. K^+ leaves the cell.
   d. Cl^- leaves the cell.

9. At most synapses, postsynaptic potentials are terminated by
   a. reuptake.
   b. enzymatic deactivation.
   c. ionic flow.
   d. phagocytosis.

10. A neuron's own neurotransmitter, detected by its presynaptic autoreceptors,
    a. initiates changes in the local membrane potential.
    b. opens the gates of neurotransmitter-dependent ion channels.
    c. facilitates the synthesis of other neurotransmitters.
    d. inhibits the synthesis or release of that neurotransmitter.

11. _____ synapses _____.
    a. Axosomatic; do not contribute directly to neural integration
    b. Axoaxonic; regulate neurotransmitter release
    c. Axodendritic; are found only in the peripheral nervous system
    d. Axosomatic; are more numerous than the other types of synapses

12. Peptide hormones
    a. bind with metabotropic receptors in the membrane.
    b. and neurotransmitters diffuse only a short distance.
    c. are found only in the peripheral nervous system.
    d. attach themselves to receptors in the nucleus of a cell.

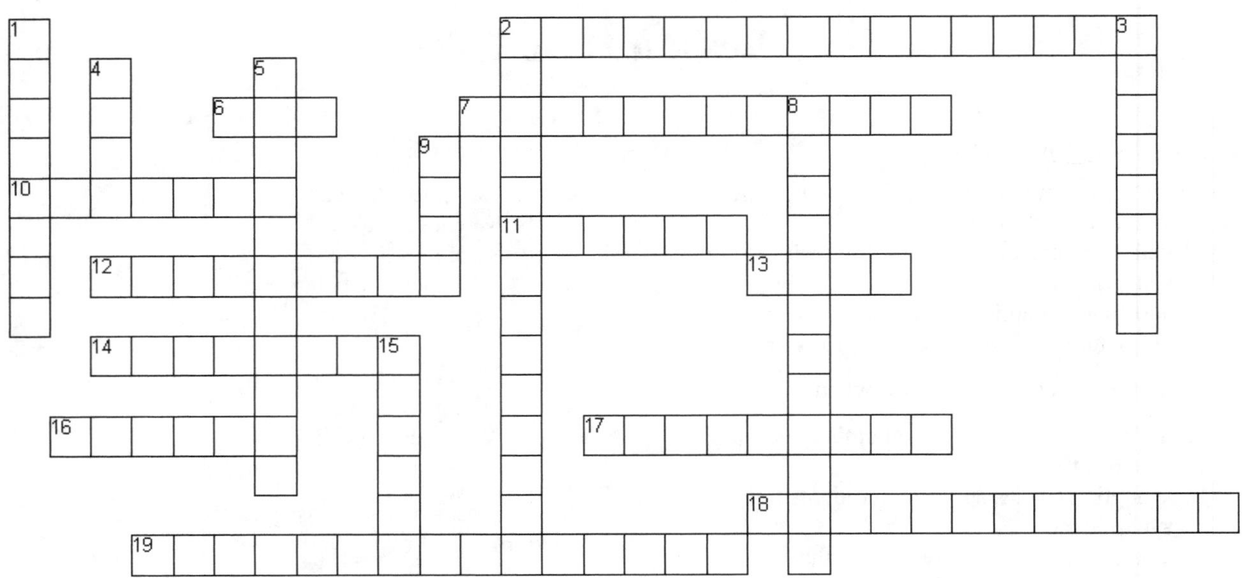

Across
2. Chemical released by terminal button
6. The brain and spinal cord
7. Receptor molecule on neuron that reacts to neuron's own neurotransmitter
10. Junction between terminal buttons of an axon and membrane of another neuron
11. Substance that insulates most axons from one another
12. Glial cell that provides support for neurons of the CNS
13. Cell body of a neuron
14. Treelike structures which receive information from terminal buttons of other neurons
16. Chemical that binds with the binding site of a receptor
17. Structure within nucleus that produces ribosomes
18. Organelles that extracts energy from nutrients
19. Type of glial cell in the CNS that forms myelin sheaths

Down
1. Structure that produces proteins translated from mRNA
2. Substance that acts like neurotransmitter but diffuses through extracellular fluid
3. Reentry of just released neurotransmitter back through its membrane terminating its effects
4. Cylindrical structure conveys information from soma to terminal buttons of a neuron
5. Direction along an axon from the cell body toward the terminal buttons
8. Process of engulfing and digesting other cells or debris
9. Functional unit of the chromosome
15. Molecule that controls a chemical reaction

Answers for Self Tests

Lesson I

1. a Obj. 2-1
2. a Obj. 2-1
3. a Obj. 2-1
4. c Obj. 2-2
5. c Obj. 2-2
6. c Obj. 2-2
7. c Obj. 2-3
8. c Obj. 2-4
9. a Obj. 2-4
10. b Obj. 2-4
11. c Obj. 2-5
12. d Obj. 2-5

Lesson II

1. b Obj. 2-6
2. b Obj. 2-6
3. b Obj. 2-6
4. c Obj. 2-6
5. d Obj. 2-6
6. b Obj. 2-7
7. a Obj. 2-7
8. c Obj. 2-7
9. a Obj. 2-7
10. d Obj. 2-8
11. b Obj. 2-8
12. a Obj. 2-8

CHAPTER 3
Structure of The Nervous System

Lesson I: Basic Features of the Nervous System and Some Structures of the Central Nervous System

Read the interim summary on page 76 of your text to re-acquaint yourself with the material in this section.

Learning Objective 3-1 Explain the origins of the names of brain structures and the terms used to indicate directions and planes of section.

Read pages 69-72 and answer the following questions.

1. Why did early anatomists choose particular names for the brain structures they saw?

2. Draw two pictures of a snake. Make the first a side view and the second a front view. Label your drawings with these terms of anatomical direction: neuraxis, anterior, posterior, rostral, caudal, dorsal, ventral, lateral, and medial. (Study Figure 3.1 in your text.)

3. Repeat this exercise by labeling two stick figure drawings of a human.

4. Define these frequently used terms in your own words.

   a. superior

   b. inferior

c. ipsilateral

d. contralateral

5. To confirm your understanding of the nomenclature for planes of section, try using these terms to describe these pieces of food: *cross* or *frontal, horizontal,* and *sagittal*. You will have to imagine the neuraxis. (Study Figure 3.2 in your text.)

_______________ cutting a hamburger bun into top and bottom halves

_______________ a slice of bread

_______________ slicing a fish into two symmetrical halves

Learning Objective 3-2 Describe the blood supply to the brain, the meninges, the ventricular system, and flow of cerebrospinal fluid through the brain and its production.

Read pages 72-76 and answer the following questions.

1. Name the two major divisions of the nervous system and then list their parts. (See Table 3.1 and Figure 3.3 in your text.)

   a.

   b.

2. a. Briefly explain why the brain is the most protected organ of the body.

   b. Approximately how much blood flow does the brain receive from the heart?

   c. Why is an uninterrupted blood supply essential?

   d. What are the consequences if blood supply is interrupted for 1-second, for 6 seconds, and for a few minutes?

3. a. Study Figure 3.3 in your text and then list and describe the three layers of the meninges that cover the brain and spinal cord beginning with the outer layer.

   1.

   2.

   3.

   b. What area lies between the arachnoid membrane and the pia mater?

   c. What liquid fills this space?

   d. Which two layers of the meninges fuse outside the CNS? What does this sheath cover?

4. Describe how CSF protects the brain.

5 Define *ventricles* in your own words.

6. Study Figure 3.4 a, b, c in your text and describe the major components of the ventricular system:

a. Name the two largest chambers in the brain.

b. What structure

1. crosses the middle of the third ventricle?

2. connects the third and fourth ventricles?

7. Where is CSF produced and how is it reabsorbed? (Study Figures 3.4d and 3.5 in your text.)

8. Write a sentence describing the flow of CSF, using all of the following terms: lateral ventricles, third ventricle, fourth ventricle, blood supply, choroid plexus, arachnoid granulations, small openings, subarachnoid space, cerebral aqueduct, superior sagittal sinus, central nervous system (See Animation 3.1.)

9. What is the cause and treatment of obstructive hydrocephalus? (See Figure 3.6 in your text.)

10. To review: The interim summary presents important anatomical nomenclature, the divisions of the central and peripheral nervous system, and an overview of the ventricular system and cerebrospinal fluid.

Read the interim summary on page 95 of your text to re-acquaint yourself with the material in this section.

Learning Objective 3-3 Outline the development of the central nervous system and the evolution of the human brain.

Read pages 77-83 and answer the following questions.

1. As you begin this section, remember that you will be able to review and test yourself on the anatomy of the brain using Animations 3.2 and 3.3.

2. a. Describe how, between about the eighteenth and twenty-first days after conception, the ectoderm of the back of the embryo develops into the neural tube. (Study Figure 3.7 in your text.)

b. What structures develop from the neural tube? the ridges which break away?

3. Look more closely at the early development of the neural tube illustrated in Figure 3.8 in your text.

a. What change occurs to the rostral end of the neural tube by the twenty-eighth day of development?

b. What structures develop from these chambers and from the surrounding tissue?

c. What change occurs to the rostral chamber?

d. What structure will develop around the lateral ventricles? the third ventricle?

e. How does the chamber inside the midbrain continue to develop? the hindbrain?

f. How does the hindbrain continue to develop?

4. With the help of Figure 3.8, label the portions of the neural tube shown in Figure 1a that become the forebrain, the midbrain, and the hindbrain.
5. On Figure 1b, indicate how the forebrain continues to develop by labeling the telencephalon, the diencephalon, the mesencephalon, and the two parts of the hindbrain—the metencephalon and the myelencephalon.
6. On Figure 1c, indicate the location of the cerebral hemisphere, cerebellum, thalamus, hypothalamus, pituitary gland, midbrain, pons, medulla, brain stem and spinal cord.

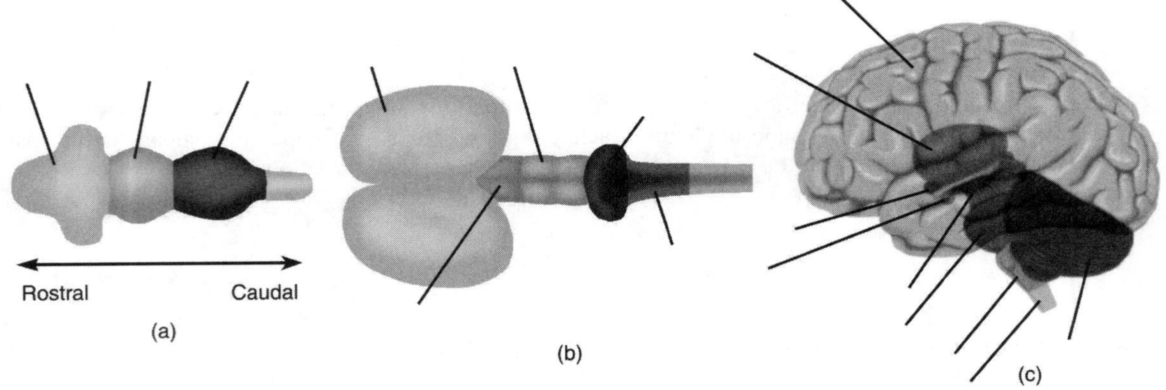

Figure 1

7. Immediately review what you have just learned by studying Table 3.2 in your text. Complete the blank version of that table below.

Anatomical Subdivisions of the Brain			
Major Division	***Ventricle***	***Subdivision***	***Principal Structures***

8. Where are the cells that give rise to the cells of the central nervous system found?

9. a. What tissue is found on the exterior of the cerebral hemispheres, and what are some of its functions?

b. Compare its size with that of other species.

10. a. Explain how researchers use radioactive labeling to study brain development.

 b. What do studies using this technique indicate about the development of the cerebral cortex?

11. By what means do newly formed neurons reach their final destination? (Rakic, 1972, 1988)

12. a. What is the name of the cells in the ventricular zone that give rise to neurons?

 b. Study Figure 3.9 in your text and complete this table summarizing the two periods of division these cells undergo.

Name of Division	*Begins*	*Ends*	*Neural Development*

 c. Approximately how long does it take the first neurons to reach their final destination?

 d. Approximately how long does it take the last neurons to reach their final destination?

 e. Name and describe the event that stops cortical development?

13. a. Describe how neurons continue to develop and form synaptic connections with postsynaptic cells after they reach their final locations. Be sure to mention the vital signal from the postsynaptic cell. (Benson et al., 2001)

 b. What happens to about half of the neurons produced in the neural tube which fail to form synaptic connections?

 c. Outline a possible explanation for this phenomenon.

14. What role may the founder cells play in the specialization of a particular region of cerebral cortex?

15. a. Why did Krubitzer and her colleagues use opossums to study the role of axons in specialization? (Krubitzer, 1998. Study Figure 3.10 in your text.)

 b. Krubitzer and her colleagues removed a portion of the cerebral cortex of an opossum before what kind of brain connections developed?

 c. When brain development ended, Krubitzer and her colleagues examined various regions of cortex. What did their examination reveal and what does it suggest about the role of axons in specialization?

16. What additional influence on brain development was suggested by research on stereoscopic vision? (Poggio and Poggio; 1984; Banks et al., 1975)

17. How was the adult brain affected by

    a. amputation of a person's arm? (Elbert et al., 1994; Kew et al., 1994; Yang et al., 1994)

    b. playing a stringed instrument?

    c. reading Braille? (Elbert et al., 1995; Sadato et al., 1996)

18. a. Summarize the technique used to obtain evidence of neurogenesis in an adult brain. (See Figure 3.11 in your text.)

    b. Which two parts of the adult brain showed evidence of neurogenesis? (Doetsch and Hen, 2005)

    c. What factors can suppress or reinstate neurogenesis?

19. a. Explain genetic duplication in your own words, noting what it contributes to the evolution of a complex brain. (Allman, 1999; Lewis, 1992)

    b. How did duplication influence the development of the vertebrate rhombomeres shown in Figure 3.12 in your text? (Be sure to refer to master genes in your answer.)

20. Summarize Rakic's explanation of how the length of the periods of symmetrical and asymmetrical division may be responsible for the ultimate development of the brain.

Learning Objective 3-4 Describe the telencephalon, one of the two major structures of the forebrain.

Read pages 83-89 and answer the following questions.

1. List the two major components of the forebrain.

   1. 2.

2. The telencephalon includes most of the two _______________ _______________, which are covered by the _______________ _______________.

3. List two subcortical structures of the telencephalon that are found deep within the cerebral hemispheres.

   1. 2.

4. a. Large grooves in the cerebral cortex are called _______________ and small ones are called _______________. The bulges between grooves are called _______________. (See Figure 3.13 in your text.)

   b. To what extent do the convolutions affect the total surface area of the cortex?

   c. What do the following terms apply to, and what is responsible for the colors?

      1. Gray matter

2. White matter

5. Study Figure 3.14 in your text and describe the location of these three areas of cerebral cortex noting nearby fissures or sulci.

   1. Primary visual cortex

   2. Primary auditory cortex

   3. Primary somatosensory cortex

6. What kind of sensory information is not sent to the contralateral side of the brain?

7. Which region of the cerebral cortex is most directly involved in the control of movement?

8. a. In general, what kinds of functions are mediated by the association areas of the cerebral cortex?

   b. Name the structure that divides the rostral and caudal regions of the cerebral cortex.

9. List the four lobes of the cerebral cortex.

   1. 3.

   2. 4.

10. Label the following regions on Figure 2 below: the four lobes; the primary visual, somatosensory, auditory, and motor cortex; and the central sulcus. Indicate rostral, caudal, dorsal, and ventral, making a total of 13 items to label. Study Figures 3.14 and 3.15 in your text.

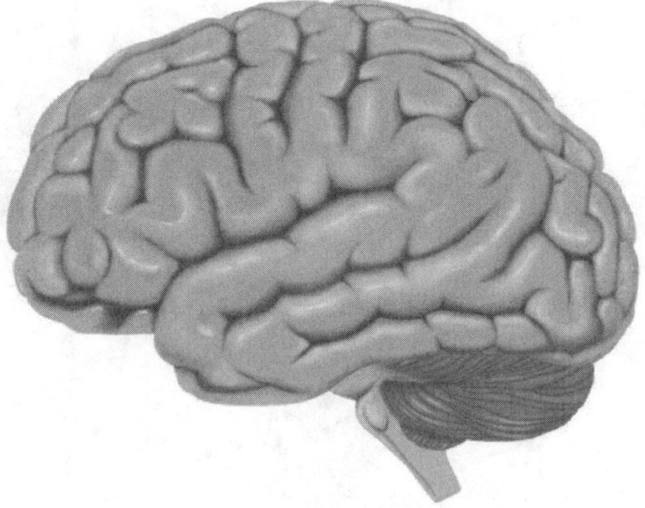

Figure 2

11. a. Where is information from each primary sensory area of the cerebral cortex sent and analyzed?

    b. Which regions of sensory association cortex receive information from only one sensory system?

c. Which regions of sensory association cortex receive information from more than one system? (See Figure 3.15 again.)

12. What are the general functions of

a. sensory association cortex of the posterior part of the brain?

b. frontal association cortex?

c. motor association cortex?

d. prefrontal cortex?

13. The functions of the cerebral hemispheres are _______________. The right hemisphere is involved in the _______________ of information and the left is involved in the _______________ of information.

14. a. What is the location and function of the corpus callosum?

b. Name the portion of cerebral cortex that covers most of the surface of the cerebral hemispheres. (See Figures 3.15 and 3.16 in your text.)

c. Name the portion of cerebral cortex located around the medial edge of the cerebral hemispheres and an important region found there.

15. Label the regions indicated by the lines on Figure 3 with the help of Figures 3.15 and 3.16 in your text.

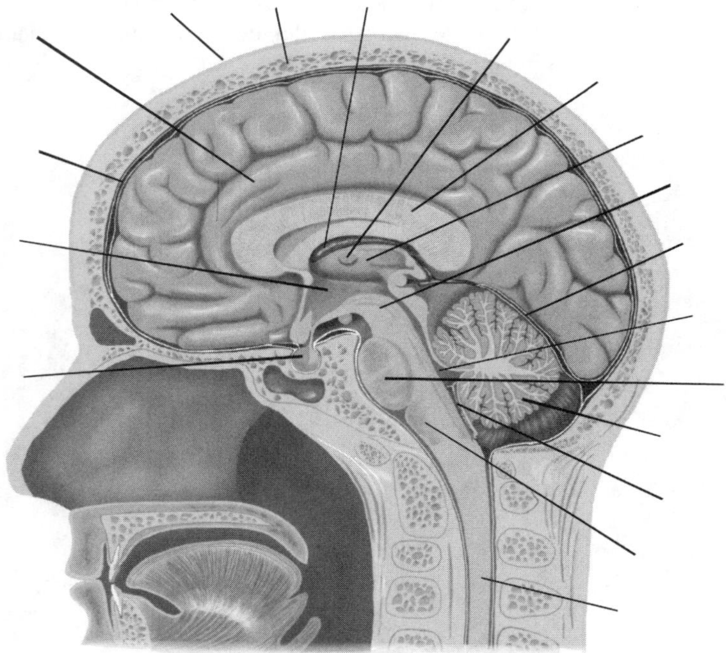

Figure 3

16. Study Figure 3.17 in your text and list the four most important structures that are a part of the limbic system.

1.

2.

3.

4.

17. What kinds of functions are controlled by the limbic system?

18. What structure connects the hippocampus with other parts of the brain, including the mammillary bodies?

19. Define *nuclei* in your own words.

20. a. List the major parts of the basal ganglia. (Figure 3.18 in your text shows their location.)

    1.   3.

    2.

    b. What is the general function of the basal ganglia?

    c. Describe the cause and some of the symptoms of Parkinson's disease.

Lesson I Self Test

1. As you look down on the snake, you see its _____ surface, and it slithers along the ground on its _____surface.

   a. lateral; ventral
   b. ventral; medial
   c. dorsal; ventral
   d. dorsal; lateral

2. Which of the following would not be visible in a midsagittal view of the brain?

   a. the lateral fissure
   b. the cerebral aqueduct
   c. the corpus callosum
   d. the cingulate gyrus

3. The meninges and subarachnoid space surround the brain in the following order, beginning with the outer layer:

   a. dura mater, pia mater, arachnoid membrane, subarachnoid space.
   b. dura mater, arachnoid membrane, subarachnoid space, pia mater.
   c. pia mater, dura mater, subarachnoid space, arachnoid membrane.
   d. pia mater, arachnoid membrane, subarachnoid space, dura mater.

4. Cerebrospinal fluid is produced by the

   a. meninges.
   b. subarachnoid space.
   c. choroid plexus.
   d. ventricles.

5. After cerebrospinal fluid has circulated through the brain and subarachnoid space it is

   a. excreted by the kidneys.
   b. recirculated for the next three hours.
   c. reabsorbed into the blood supply.
   d. transported through the central canal to the abdomen.

6. In the central nervous system neurons develop in the

   a. ventricular zone of the neural tube.
   b. radial glial cells.
   c. chambers that become the ventricles of the brain.
   d. growth cones.

7. The three major parts of the brain are the

   a. telencephalon, the diencephalon, and the metencephalon.
   b. cerebral cortex, the association cortex, and the brain stem.
   c. frontal lobe, the parietal lobe, and the temporal lobe.
   d. forebrain, the midbrain, and the hindbrain.

8. Neurons that do not establish synaptic connections with a postsynaptic cell

   a. migrate to the bone marrow.
   b. are destroyed through apoptosis.
   c. may later become malignant.

d. attract synaptic connections from presynaptic cells.

9. Genetic duplication

a. increases the size of the ventricular zone.
b. preserves important functions even if mutation occurs.
c. ceases when the neural tube closes.
d. is limited to approximately three or four symmetrical divisions.

10. The corpus callosum connects the

a. two hemispheres of the brain.
b. structures of the limbic system.
c. pituitary gland and the hypothalamus.
d. thalamus and the hypothalamus.

11. The most important structures of the limbic system are the limbic cortex, the

a. hippocampus, and the amygdala.
b. basal ganglia, and the thalamus.
c. primary motor cortex, and the primary association cortex.
d. hypothalamus, and the medulla.

12. The limbic system plays a role in

a. planning and execution of movement.
b. visual and auditory functions.
c. control of sleep.
d. emotional behavior, learning, and memory.

Lesson II: Some Structures of the Central Nervous System and The Peripheral Nervous System

Read the interim summary on page 95 of your text to re-acquaint yourself with the material in this section.

Learning Objective 3-5 Describe the two major structures of the diencephalon.

Read pages 89-90 and answer the following questions.

1. a. The diencephalon is the second major division of the _______________ and is located between the _______________ and the _______________. The two most important structures of the diencephalon are the _______________ and the _______________.

b. Study Figures 3.4, 3.16, 3.17, 3.18 and 3.19 in your text and describe the location and appearance of the thalamus and the massa intermedia.

2. Define *projection fibers* in your own words and explain their relation to the function of the thalamus.

3. Where do these thalamic nuclei receive and relay their sensory information?

a. Lateral geniculate nucleus

b. Medial geniculate nucleus

4. a. Describe the location and general functions of the hypothalamus. (Study Figures 3.19 and 3.20 in your text.)

b. What structure is attached to the base of the hypothalamus? What other structure lies just in front of it? (See Figure 3.19 in your text.)

c. The hypothalamus controls the anterior pituitary gland, and through it most of the _______________ system, by secreting the hypothalamic _______________, which are produced by specialized neurons called

_______________ __________, located near the base of the _______________ _______________. (See Figure 3.20 in your text.)

d. To explain why the anterior pituitary gland is often called the “master gland,” briefly summarize the effects of some of the hormones it secretes.

e. Describe the production and secretion of the hormones of the posterior pituitary gland.

f. Summarize the effects of some of the hormones secreted by the posterior pituitary gland

Learning Objective 3-6 Describe the two major structures of the midbrain, the two major structures of the hindbrain, and the spinal cord.

Read pages 91-95 and answer the following questions.

1. List the two major parts of the midbrain or mesencephalon.

   1. 2.

2. Then list the two principal structures of the tectum and the sensory systems they are a part of. (See Figure 3.21 in your text.)

   1. 2.

3. Continue by listing the structures of the brain stem.

   1. 3.

   2.

4. Finally, list the principal structures of the tegmentum shown in Figure 3.21d.

   1. 4.

   2. 5.

   3. 6.

5. a. Briefly describe the location, composition, and appearance of the reticular formation.

   b. List some of its functions.

6. a. What gives the periaqueductal gray matter its name?

   b. List a function of the

      1. periaqueductal gray matter.

      2. red nucleus.

      3. substantia nigra.

7. a. List the two divisions of the hindbrain.

   1. 2.

b. List the two structures of the metencephalon.

1. 2.

8. Briefly describe the location of the

a. cerebellar cortex.

b. deep cerebellar nuclei.

c. cerebellar peduncles. (See Figure 3.21c.)

9. Briefly describe some of the functions of the cerebellum and the kinds of disability resulting from damage to this structure.

10. Describe the location of the pons and the function of several nuclei found there. (Look back at Figures 3.16 and 3.21a in your text.)

11. Describe the location and functions of the medulla oblongata, the major structure of the myelencephalon. (Look back once again at Figures 3.16 and 3.21a.)

12. What is the principal function of the spinal cord?

13. How is the spinal cord protected?

14. Name the passage at the center of each vertebra through which the spinal cord passes. (See Figure 3.22 in your text.)

15. a. Explain why the spinal cord is only about two-thirds as long as the vertebral column.

b. Describe the cauda equina and explain how it is possible to eliminate sensations from the lower part of the body using a caudal block. (Look back at Figure 3.3c in your text.)

c. Study Figure 3.23a in your text and describe the dorsal roots and ventral roots and the axons they contain. Be sure to notice the location of the white matter and gray matter.

16. To review: The interim summary outlines the development of the human brain and its principal divisions and structures.

Read the interim summary on page 100 of your text to re-acquaint yourself with the material in this section.

Learning Objective 3-7 Describe the peripheral nervous system, including the two divisions of the autonomic nervous system.

Read pages 96-100 and answer the following questions.

1. List the two sets of nerves of the peripheral nervous system and describe their general functions:

1.

2.

2. Look back at Figure 3.3 in your text and review the pathways of the spinal nerves throughout the body.

3. The cell bodies of _______________ axons which bring sensory information into the brain and spinal cord are located _______________ the central nervous system with the exception of the _______________ _______________ because the _______________ is a part of the brain. Incoming axons are called _______________ axons and the cell bodies from which they arise are found in the _______________ _______________ _______________. _______________ axons leave the spinal cord through the _______________ _______________ and control the muscles and glands. (See Figure 3.24 in your text.)

4. Study Figure 3.25 in your text and list the names, numbers, and functions of at least four of the twelve pairs of cranial nerves that leave the brain. Begin with the vagus nerve.

   1. Vagus nerve (10)

   2.

   3.

   4.

5. List the two main divisions of the PNS and identify their functions.

   1. 2.

6. The autonomic nervous system is further divided into two parts. List them.

   1. 2.

7. a. Using examples, describe the kinds of activity mediated by the sympathetic division.

   b. Where are the cells bodies of sympathetic motor neurons located?

   c. Study Figure 3.26 in your text and describe how the sympathetic ganglion chain is formed.

   d. Where do preganglionic neurons synapse?

   e. Where do postganglionic neurons synapse?

8. Which hormones are secreted by the cells of the adrenal medulla and what are their effects on the body?

9. Using examples, describe the kinds of activity mediated by the parasympathetic division.

10. Name the two regions that give rise to preganglionic axons of the parasympathetic division.

    1. 2.

11. Name the neurotransmitter secreted by both preganglionic and postganglionic neurons in the parasympathetic nervous system.

12. To review: Study Table 3.3 in your text.

Lesson II Self Test

1. The _____ surrounds the third ventricle and its two most important structures are the _____.
   a. forebrain; the telencephalon and the diencephalon
   b. diencephalon; thalamus and the hypothalamus
   c. limbic system; basal ganglia and the amygdala
   d. diencephalon; hippocampus and the amygdala

2. The thalamus is responsible for
   a. most of the neural input received by the cerebral cortex.
   b. emotional behavior.
   c. movement of a particular part of the body.
   d. behaviors related to survival of the species.

3. Neurons in the hypothalamus
   a. control the autonomic nervous system and the endocrine system.
   b. send projection fibers through the optic chiasm.
   c. are controlled by hormones secreted by the anterior pituitary gland.
   d. are involved in vision and audition.

4. The anterior pituitary gland produces
   a. vasopressin.
   b. oxytocin.
   c. gonadotropic hormones.
   d. estrogen.

5. The principal structures of the tectum are the
   a. superior and inferior colliculi.
   b. hippocampus and amygdala.
   c. thalamus and hypothalamus.
   d. lateral and medial geniculate nuclei.

6. The reticular formation
   a. relays visual information from the retina to the rest of the brain.
   b. appears as four bumps on the brain stem.
   c. is one of two major fiber systems within the brain.
   d. plays a role in sleep and arousal.

7. The periaqueductal gray matter is so called because of its location and an abundance of
   a. fibers.
   b. cell bodies.
   c. synapses.
   d. axons.

8. The spinal cord is _______________ the vertebral column.
   a. fused to
   b. longer than
   c. outside
   d. shorter than

9. _____ axons bring sensory information into the brain and spinal cord and _____ axons leave the spinal cord through the ventral roots.
   a. Unipolar; bipolar
   b. Myelinated; unmyelinated
   c. Afferent; efferent
   d. Motor; sensory

10. The cranial nerve that controls the parasympathetic function of organs in the thoracic and abdominal cavities is called the
    a. preganglionic nerve.
    b. hypoglossal nerve.
    c. vagus nerve.
    d. trigeminal nerve.

11. The two components of the autonomic nervous system are the
    a. brain and the spinal cord.
    b. somatic nervous system and the autonomic nervous system.
    c. sympathetic division and the parasympathetic division.
    d. spinal nerves and the cranial nerves.

12. __________ __________ leave the spinal cord through the ventral root.
    a. Preganglionic axons
    b. Postganglionic axons
    c. Sympathetic ganglia
    d. Cranial nerves

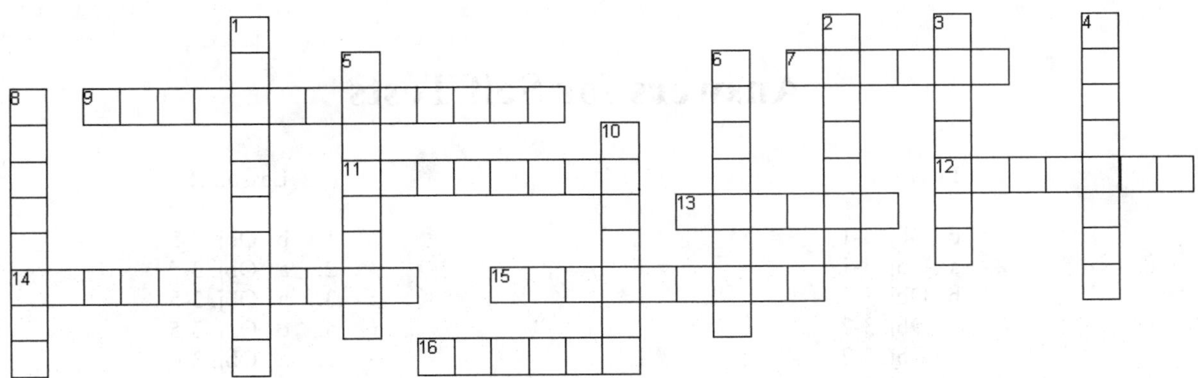

Across

7. Toward the middle of the body, away from the side
9. Located on the opposite side of the body
11. Below
12. Toward the front of the face
13. Away from the front of the face
14. Located on the same side of the body
15. Near or toward the tail
16. Toward the top of the head or back

Down

1. A section through the brain parallel to the ground
2. Toward the bottom of the skull or body
3. Toward the side of the body, away from the middle
4. Above
5. A section through the brain parallel to the neuraxis and perpendicular to the ground
6. Imaginary line from bottom of spinal cord to front of forebrain
8. Near or toward the head
10. A section through the brain parallel to the forehead

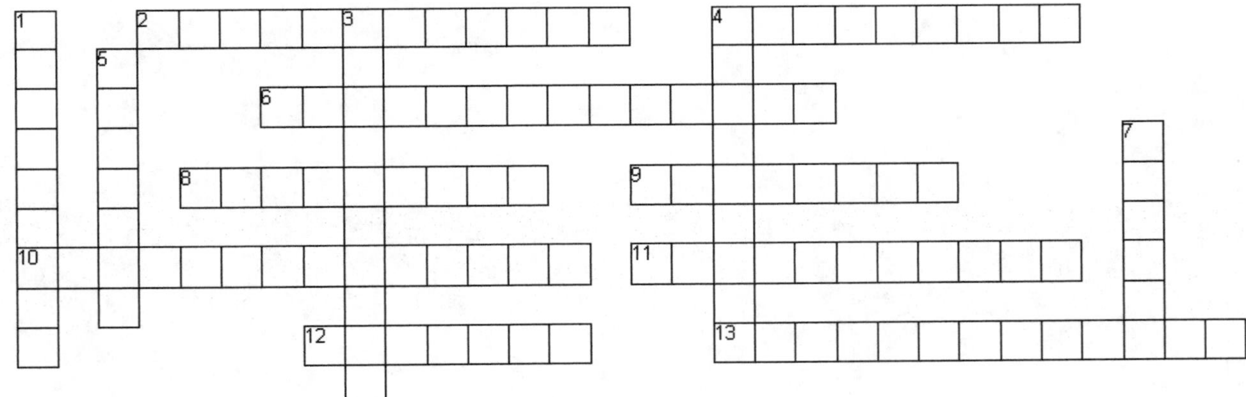

Across

2. Group of brain regions including thalamic nuclei, amygdala, and hippocampus
4. Cell death caused by a chemical signal
6. Outermost layer of gray matter of the cerebral hemispheres
8. Brain division, includes the telencephalon and diencephalon
9. Three tissue layers encasing the CNS
10. Large band of axons connecting association cortex on each side of brain
11. Division of ANS, increases expenditure of energy
12. Group of neural cell bodies in CNS
13. Tissue that produces the cerebrospinal fluid

Down

1. Hollow spaces within the brain
3. Dorsal to pons, important part of motor system
4. Part of the PNS, controls vegetative functions
5. Major groove in the surface of the brain
7. Fiber bundle connecting hippocampus with other parts of brain

Answers for Self Tests

Lesson I

1. c Obj. 3-1
2. a Obj. 3-1
3. b Obj. 3-2
4. c Obj. 3-2
5. c Obj. 3-2
6. a Obj. 3-3
7. d Obj. 3-3
8. b Obj. 3-3
9. b Obj. 3-3
10. a Obj. 3-4
11. a Obj. 3-4
12. d Obj. 3-4

Lesson II

1. b Obj. 3-5
2. a Obj. 3-5
3. a Obj. 3-5
4. c Obj. 3-5
5. a Obj. 3-6
6. d Obj. 3-6
7. b Obj. 3-6
8. d Obj. 3-6
9. c Obj. 3-7
10. c Obj. 3-7
11. c Obj. 3-7
12. a Obj. 3-7

CHAPTER 4
Psychopharmacology

Lesson I: Principles of Psychopharmacology and Sites of Drug Action

Read the interim summary on pages 109-110 of your text to re-acquaint yourself with the material in this section.

Learning Objective 4-1 Describe the routes of administration and the distribution of drugs within the body.

Read pages 103-107 and answer the following questions.

1. Define these terms in your own words.
   a. *Psychopharmacology*

   b. *Drug* (as it will be used in the chapter)

   c. *Drug effects*

   d. *Site of action*

   e. *Pharmacokinetics*

2. The most common route of drug administration for laboratory animals is ______________.
3. Complete this table of the types of injections.

Type	*Injection Site*	*Speed of Absorption*	*Comments*
Intravenous (IV)			
Intraperitoneal (IP)			
Intramuscular (IM)			
Subcutaneous (SC)			
Intracerebral			
Intracerebroventricular (ICV)			

4. a. The most common route for administration of medicinal drugs for humans is _______________

_______________.

   b. What kind of drugs cannot be administered this way?

5. List four other routes of drug administration for humans, noting when each route is most appropriate.

   1.

   2.

   3.

   4.

6. Figure 4.1 in your text illustrates the speed at which cocaine reaches the blood when taken in some of the ways you have just described.

7. a. Let's look at factors that affect how quickly a drug exerts its effects. Why does the lipid solubility of a drug affect the rate at which it reaches sites of action in the brain?

   b. Define *depot binding* in your own words.

   c. Go on to explain how this process can both delay and prolong the effects of a drug. Be sure to mention the role of albumin in your answer. (Study Figure 4.2 in your text.)

   d. In addition to albumin, what are some other sources of depot binding?

8. What eventually happens to all drugs that have been introduced into the body?

Learning Objective 4-2 Describe drug effectiveness, the effects of repeated administration, and the placebo effect.

Read pages 107-109 and answer the following questions.

1. Complete these sentences. (Study Figures 4.3 and 4.4 in your text.)

   a. The best way to measure the effectiveness of a drug is

   b. The most desirable drugs have

   c. One measure of a drug's margin of safety is

   d. The therapeutic index is

   e. The lower the therapeutic index is

2. a. Provide two reasons why drugs vary in their effectiveness.

   1. 2.

   b. How is the dosage of a drug affected by a high affinity for its binding site?

c. How is the dosage of a drug affected by a low affinity for its binding site?

d. What is the most desirable pattern of affinity for a drug?

3. a. Define these two phenomena, which may occur with repeated administration of a drug.

   1. Tolerance

   2. Sensitization

   b. Define *withdrawal symptoms,* a phenomenon which occurs when a person who has reached tolerance suddenly stops taking an opiate.

   c. Carefully explain how the body's compensatory mechanisms are linked to the body's reaction to continued drug use and its sudden cessation.

4. Discuss two types of compensatory mechanisms.

5. a. Using barbiturates as an example, explain how its sites of action are affected differently by continued drug use.

   b. Why is sensitization less common than tolerance?

6. a. Define *placebo* in your own words.

   b. Why is it incorrect to say placebos have no effects?

7. Why must control groups that receive placebos be used in research with animal and human subjects?

Read the interim summary on pages 113-114 of your text to re-acquaint yourself with the material in this section.

Learning Objective 4-3 Describe the effects of drugs on neurotransmitters and presynaptic and postsynaptic receptors.

Read pages 110-113 and answer the following questions.

1. Most drugs that affect behavior do so by affecting _______________ _______________. Those that block or inhibit the postsynaptic effects are called _______________, and those that facilitate them are called _______________.

2. Outline the sequence of synaptic activity that you learned about in Chapter 2.

Figure 1 on the next page illustrates eleven ways that drugs can affect synaptic transmission. As you answer the following questions, fill in the missing information. (Study Figure 4.5 in your text and Animation 4.1.)

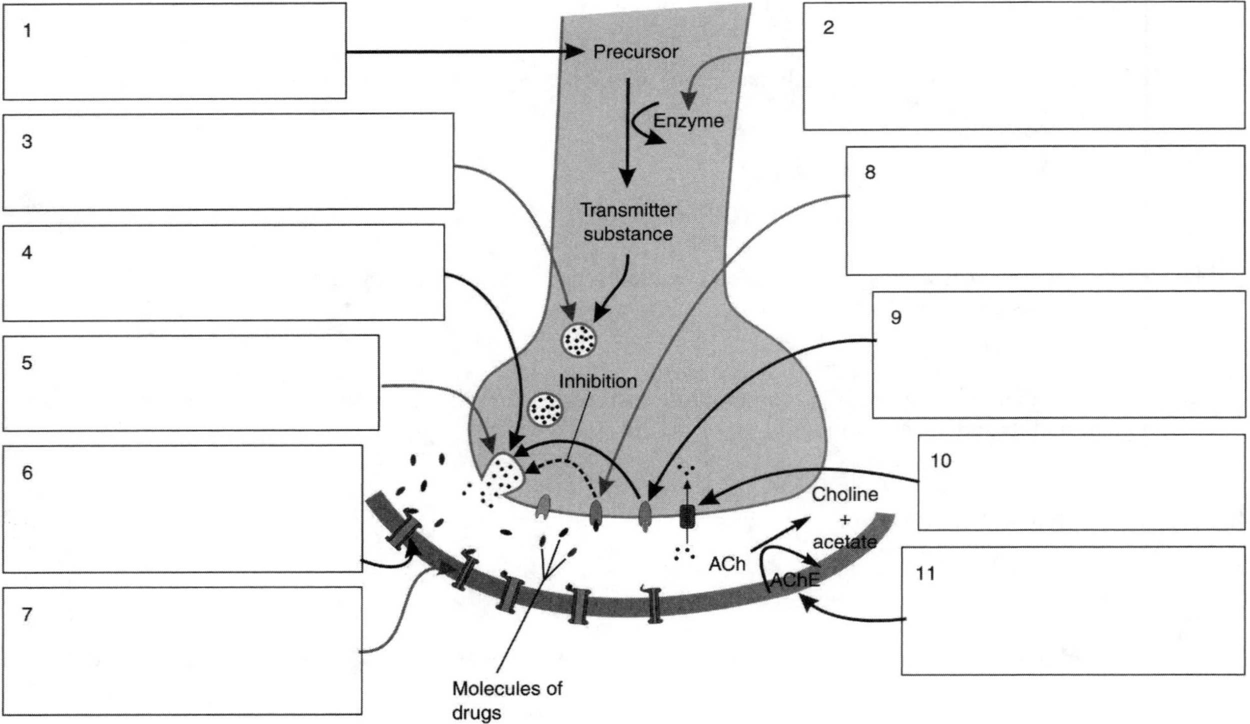

Figure 1

3. Describe the two ways in which drugs can affect the production of a neurotransmitter. Put your answers in boxes 1 and 2 and indicate if the effects are those of an agonist or antagonist.

4. What effect can drugs have on the storage of a neurotransmitter in synaptic vesicles? Explain the process below, write a brief summary in box 3, and indicate if the drug is an agonist or antagonist.

5. What effect can drugs have on the release of a neurotransmitter? Explain the process, and write a summary statement in boxes 4 and 5. Indicate if the drug is an agonist or antagonist.

6. Describe how a drug acts as a direct agonist. Write a summary statement in box 6.

7. How do direct antagonists function? What is another name for drugs with this effect? Write a summary statement in box 7.

8. In contrast, how do indirect agonists function? Be sure to use the term *noncompetitive binding* in your answer. (Study Figure 4.6 in your text.)

9. Drugs can stimulate or block presynaptic autoreceptors. Describe these effects and write summary statements in boxes 8 and 9.

10. a. In an axoaxonic synapse, with what does the terminal button form a synapse?

    b. When the first terminal button is active, how may it affect the second one?

    c. What kind of receptors are found on the second terminal button?

    d. How do these receptors produce presynaptic inhibition? (Study Figure 4.7 in your text.)

    e. How do these receptors produce presynaptic facilitation? (Study Figure 4.7 in your text.)

    f. What effects can drugs have on presynaptic inhibition and facilitation?

11. a. Where are autoreceptors found and how are they affected by the neurotransmitter released by the dendrites?

    b. What is the effect of drugs that bind with and activate dendritic autoreceptors? (Study Figure 4.8 in your text.)

    c. What is the effect of drugs that bind with and block dendritic autoreceptors? (Study Figure 4.8 in your text.)

12. What two processes terminate the postsynaptic potential? How do drugs affect these processes? Write summary statements in boxes 10 and 11.

Lesson I Self Test

1. The fastest way to have a drug reach the brain is to administer it through
   a. an intravenous injection.
   b. an intraperitoneal injection.
   c. an intramuscular injection.
   d. a subcutaneous injection.

2. A(n) _____ is the most common route for administering drugs to small animals and a(n) _____ is never used with small animals.
   a. intramuscular injection; intrarectal administration
   b. intravenous injection; subcutaneous injection
   c. intraperitoneal injection; sublingual administration
   d. intracerebral injection; topical administration

3. Depot binding
   a. can halt the effects of a drug.
   b. can prolong or delay the effects of a drug.
   c. begins when albumin molecules are fully saturated with a drug.
   d. does not usually alter the initial effects of a drug.

4. The therapeutic index of a drug is
   a. derived from the dose-response curve.
   b. the dose that produces desired effects in 50 percent of the animals.
   c. a measure of a drug's margin of safety.
   d. an indication of the drug's affinity for its site of action.

5. Repeated administration of a drug
   a. can produce sensitization.
   b. can inhibit tolerance.
   c. contributes to the uniform effects of a drug over time.
   d. may prevent compensatory mechanisms from engaging.

6. A placebo effect
   a. varies with the strength of the drug.
   b. is always pleasurable.
   c. can have physiological causes.
   d. has no role in neuroscience research.

7. Select the *incorrect* statement.
   a. When a drug acts as a precursor, it increases the production of a neurotransmitter, serving as an agonist.
   b. If a drug inactivates enzymes responsible for the production of a neurotransmitter, it acts as an agonist.
   c. Transporter molecules that fill synaptic vesicles may be blocked by a drug, which then serves as an antagonist.
   d. Some antagonist drugs prevent the release of the neurotransmitter from terminal buttons.

8. A drug that mimics the effects of a neurotransmitter acts as a(n)
   a. receptor blocker.
   b. direct antagonist.
   c. direct agonist.
   d. indirect ligand.

9. All of these statements are true *except*
   a. The terms *receptor blocker* and *direct antagonist* are synonyms.
   b. Receptor blockers can prevent ion channels from opening.
   c. A direct agonist attaches to an alternate binding site and facilitates the opening of the ion channel.
   d. Drugs that block presynaptic autoreceptors increase the release of the neurotransmitter.

10. Some neurons contain presynaptic heteroreceptors that are found in the
   a. nucleus.
   b. synaptic cleft between two neurons.
   c. first terminal button at an axoaxonic synapse.
   d. second terminal button at an axoaxonic synapse.

11. Drugs that bind with and stimulate dendritic autoreceptors
   a. produce an inhibitory hyperpolarization.
   b. prevent noncompetitive binding.
   c. block the nodes of Ranvier.
   d. reduce the production of the neurotransmitter.

12. For most neurotransmitters, termination of the postsynaptic potential occurs when molecules of the neurotransmitter are
   a. encapsulated between branches of dendrites.
   b. destroyed by an enzyme.
   c. surrounded and absorbed by the synaptic vesicles.
   d. taken back into the terminal buttons.

Lesson II: Neurotransmitters and Neuromodulators

Read the interim summary on page 131 of your text to re-acquaint yourself with the material in this section.

Learning Objective 4-4 Review the general role of neurotransmitters and neuromodulators, and describe the acetylcholinergic pathways in the brain and the drugs that affect these neurons.

Read pages 114-118 and answer the following questions.

1. a. List the two neurotransmitters involved in most synaptic activity in the brain and their general effects.

   1. 2.

   b. What, do all the other neurotransmitters do? Provide two examples to support your answer.

2. ______________ is the primary neurotransmitter secreted by the efferent axons of the CNS and it is also found in the ______________ of the ANS and ______________ ______________ of the parasympathetic branch

of the ANS. This neurotransmitter is essential for _______________ _______________.

3. Why was acetylcholine the first neurotransmitter to be discovered?

4. List three sites in the brain with systems of acetylcholinergic neurons and the functions these neurons influence. (See Figure 4.9 in your text.)

Site	*Function*
1.	
2.	
3.	

5. a. Figure 2 illustrates the chemical reactions responsible for the production of acetylcholine. Label each component. (Study Figure 4.10 in your text.)

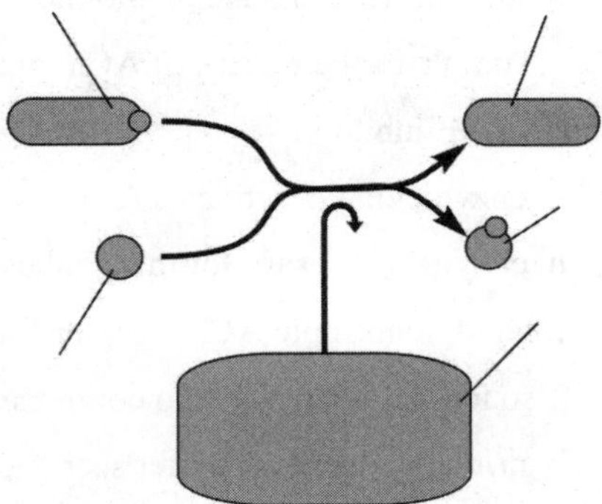

Figure 2

b. Summarize the details of this reaction in your own words.

6. How do these drugs affect the release of acetylcholine?

a. botulinum toxin

b. black widow spider venom

7. Explain why choline released from the destruction of acetylcholine must be recycled. (Study Figure 4.11 in your text.)

8. Explain how choline is affected by the drug hemicholinium.

9. Explain how AChE is affected by

a. insecticides.

b. neostigmine. Be sure to explain the symptoms of the hereditary disorder myasthenia gravis.

10. Name and classify the two types of acetylcholine receptors. Indicate some of the places in the body where they are found and the drugs that stimulate and block them.

    a.

    b.

11. Within minutes of receiving curare, what physical changes occur in the body? Explain how the drug works and describe its use in surgery.

12. To review: Match the term on the left with the correct definition of the right.

_____ acetylcholine	a. prevents the release of ACh by the terminal buttons
_____ acetyl-CoA	b. blocks muscarinic receptors
_____ ChAT	c. metabotropic ACh receptor which predominates in the CNS
_____ AChE	d. inhibits the reuptake of choline
_____ botulinum toxin	e. stimulates the release of ACh by the terminal buttons
_____ black widow spider venom	f. AChE inhibitor
_____ neostigmine	g. enzyme that deactivates ACh
_____hemicholinium	h. enzyme necessary for the synthesis of ACh
_____ nicotinic receptor	i. rapid, ionotropic ACh receptor found of muscles
_____ muscarinic receptor	j. source of one of the two components of ACh
_____ atropine	k. primary neurotransmitter secreted by the efferent axons of the CNS
_____ curare	l. blocks nicotinic receptors

Learning Objective 4-5 Describe the monoaminergic pathways in the brain and the drugs that affect these neurons.

Read pages 118-125 and answer the following questions.

1. List and group by subclass the four transmitter substances that belong to the monoamine family. (See Table 4.1 in your text.)

Subclass:	Subclass:
1.	4.
2.	
3.	

2. Why do the monoamines affect widespread regions of the brain?

3. What are some of the functions in which dopaminergic neurons play a role?

4. Outline the synthesis of the catecholamines. Study Figure 4.12 in your text and name the

    a. precursor of both dopamine and norepinephrine.

b. chemical that results when a hydroxyl group is added to tyrosine.

c. enzyme that facilitates this addition.

d. neurotransmitter that results when L-DOPA then looses a carboxyl group.

e. enzyme that facilitates this change.

f. neurotransmitter that results when a hydroxyl group is added to dopamine.

g. enzyme that facilitates this addition.

5. List the three most important systems of dopaminergic neurons. Note where their axons originate and project and their functions. (Study Figure 4.13 in your text.)

   1.

   2.

   3.

6. Name and describe a serious disorder caused by the degeneration of dopaminergic neurons. What drug is effective in the treatment of this disorder and how does it work?

7. How does the drug AMPT interfere with the synthesis of dopamine?

8. What monoamine antagonist was discovered over three thousand years ago in India? How does it function?

9. Identify the two most common dopamine receptors and briefly describe their characteristics.

   1.

   2.

10. a. How do active dopamine autoreceptors in the dendritic and somatic membrane affect neural firing?

    b. How do presynaptic dopamine autoreceptors affect the supply of neurotransmitter?

11. a. Under what circumstances is apomorphine a dopamine antagonist? (Study Figure 4.14 in your text.)

    b. Under what circumstances is apomorphine a dopamine agonist? (Study Figure 4.14 in your text.)

12. List several drugs that inhibit the reuptake of dopamine and their medical uses.

13. What is the role of monoamine oxidase (MAO) found in

    1. terminal buttons? What is the effect of deprenyl? (See Figure 4.15 in your text.)

    2. blood?

14. Name a drug used in the treatment of schizophrenia and identify the dopamine receptors it affects.

15. a. Briefly explain why researchers investigated MAO inhibitors as a possible treatment for Parkinson's disease. (Langston et al., 1984; Maret et al., 1990)

    b. What treatment evolved and how effective is it? (Tetrud and Langston, 1989; Shoulson et al., 2002)

16. Adrenalin and ______________________ are synonymous, as are noradrenalin and ______________________.

17. a. Where does the final step in the synthesis of norepinephrine take place? Go on to explain how the synthesis occurs and the enzyme that facilitates it.

    b. How is the synthesis of norepinephrine affected by fusaric acid?

    c. Why is moclobemide a noradrenergic agonist?

18. a. The cell bodies of the most important noradrenergic system begin in the ________________ ________________ a nucleus located in the dorsal ________________. (See Figure 4.16 in your text.)

    b. What is the primary behavioral effect of activation of these neurons?

19. Name and describe the appearance of the structures that release norepinephrine.

20. What are the effects of activation of α_1, α_2, and β adrenergic receptors?

21. What are some of the behavioral effects of serotonin which is also called 5-HT, or 5-hydroxytryptamine?

22. Outline the synthesis of serotonin. Study Figure 4.17 in your text and name the

    a. precursor for serotonin.

    b. enzyme that adds a hydroxyl group to tryptophan.

    c. chemical that results from this addition.

    d. enzyme that removes a carboxyl group from 5-HTP resulting in serotonin.

23. How does PCPA affect this synthesis?

24. Of the nine clusters of cell bodies of serotonergic neurons in the body, which are the two most important? (See Figure 4.18 in your text.)

25. What are some of the behavioral functions of the serotonin receptors that have been identified?

26. For each of the following drugs, note which catecholamine(s) they interact with, how they interact, and their clinical effects:

    a. Fluoxetine (Prozac)

b. Fenfluramine

c. LSD

d. MDMA (Ecstasy)

Learning Objective 4-6 Review the role of neurons that release amino acid neurotransmitters and describe drugs that affect these neurons.

Read pages 125-128 and answer the following questions.

1. a. Of the eight amino acids believed to act as neurotransmitters, three are the most common neurotransmitters in the CNS. List them.

   1. 2. 3.

   b. List the two thought to have evolved first.

   1. 2.

   c. Circle the one that is the principal excitatory neurotransmitter in the brain and spinal cord.

2. a. How is glutamate produced?

   b. List the four types of glutamate receptors.

   1. 3.

   2. 4.

   c. Circle the most common glutamate receptor.

3. What is the function of the AMPA receptor and which other receptor has similar effects?

4. a. How many binding sites are found on the NMDA receptor? (See Figure 4.19 in your text.)

   b. When the ion channel controlled by the NMDA receptor is open, sodium and calcium flow into the cell. Why is the entry of calcium so important?

   c. If the drug AP5 blocks the glutamate binding site on the NMDA receptor, what functions are affected?

5. a. Let's look at the conditions that are necessary for the opening of the calcium channel on the NMDA receptor. In addition to a molecule of glutamate attached to its binding site, what other binding site must be occupied?

   b. Which binding site must not be occupied? Why?

6. a. Explain how PCP affects ion channels on the NMDA receptor. (Review the behavioral symptoms of PCP summarized in Table 4.2 in your text.)

   b. What common drug acts as an antagonist of the NMDA receptor: What is a serious consequence of abruptly withdrawing from its use?

7. a. GABA (______________-______________ ______________), the most important ______________ neurotransmitter in the brain, is synthesized from ______________ ______________ by the action of ______________, a(n) ______________. The synthesis of GABA can be halted by ______________.

   Two receptors, ______________ and ______________ have been identified.

   b. What disease may be caused by an abnormality in the biochemistry of GABA-secreting neurons or GABA receptors? What do we call a manifestation of this disease?

8. Look at some of the binding sites on the $GABA_A$ receptor, shown in Figure 4.20 in your text, and some of the substances that bind with them.

   a. The principal binding site is for GABA. Which drug serves as a direct agonist for this site? a direct antagonist?

   b. Which drug(s) or class of drugs binds with the

      1. second site?
      2. third site?
      3. fourth site?
      4. fifth site?

   c. Which site may alcohol bind with?

9. What is a therapeutic effect of taking benzodiazepines?

10. a. What is the effect of low doses of barbiturates?

    b. What is the effect of high doses of barbiturates?

11. Which drug has an effect opposite to that of benzodiazepines and barbiturates?

12. When the $GABA_B$ receptor is activated, what changes occur in the cell?

13. a. Where is glycine found and what is its principal effect?

    b. What are the pharmacological and behavioral effects of the following drugs?

       1. Tetanus toxin

       2. Strychnine

Learning Objective 4-7 Describe the effects of peptides, lipids, nucleosides, and soluble gases released by neurons.

Read pages 128-131 and answer the following questions.

1. Peptides, which are composed of two or more ______________ ______________ linked together by ______________ ______________, are produced in the ______________ from ______________ ______________. ______________ then deliver the peptides to the terminal buttons by ______________ ______________. Once released, peptides are destroyed by ______________. Most peptides serve as ______________, but some act as ______________.

2. Define these terms in your own words:

   a. *Endogenous opioids*

b. *Enkephalins*

3. If opiate receptors are stimulated, what kinds of events are affected?

4. How does naloxone affect these receptors and what are its practical uses?

5. What may be the function of peptides which are released with the neurotransmitter in many terminal buttons? Describe research to support your answer.

6. a. Define *endocannabinoid* in your own words.

   b. Which cannabinoid receptor is found inside the brain?

   c. Which cannabinoid receptor is found outside the brain?

7. a. Identify the active substance in marijuana that simulates cannabinoid receptors in specific regions of the brain. (See Figure 4.21 in your text. Matsuda et al., 1990)

   b. Summarize some of the behavioral effects of THC. (Iversen, 2003)

   c. Why does THC have a low toxicity level inside the brain?

   d. Identify two substances that are natural ligands for THC receptors. (Devane et al., 1992; Mechoulam et al., 1995)

   e. Briefly describe what stimulates the synthesis of anandamide and how it is deactivated.

8. a. List some of the regions of the brain where CB_1 receptors are found.

   b. List some of the kinds of neurons with these receptors.

   c. How do CB_1 receptors regulate neurotransmitter release by these neurons? (Iversen, 2003)

   d. How may these receptors be involved in short-term memory impairment associated with marijuana use?

9. A nucleoside is a compound that consists of a(n) _______________ _______________ bound with a(n) _______________ or _______________ base.

10. One of these compounds is adenosine.

    a. Under what circumstances is it released?

    b. Which structures appear to release it?

    c. In general, how do adenosine and adenosine receptor agonists affect neural activity and behavior?

    d. What common drug blocks adenosine receptors? (See Table 4.3 in your text.)

11. a. List two soluble gases involved in neural communication.

    1. 2.

    b. Which bodily functions are affected by nitric oxide? (Culotta and Koshland, 1992)

c. How and where is nitric oxide produced? Be sure to mention nitric oxide synthase in your answer.

d. How quickly does it diffuse, and how long is it present in nearby cells?

Lesson II Self Test

1. Most neural communication involves the release of either _____, an inhibitory neurotransmitter or _____, an excitatory neurotransmitter.
   a. epinephrine; norepinephrine
   b. GABA; glutamate
   c. glycine; glutamate
   c. acetylcholine; GABA

2. All of the following statements about acetylcholine are true *except*
   a. It was the first neurotransmitter to be discovered.
   b. Muscle movement is stimulated by its release.
   c. It is deactivated by choline acetyltransferase (ChAT) into its components, acetate and choline.
   d. Once it is deactivated, choline is returned to the terminal buttons and recycled.

3. _____ blocks muscarinic receptors and _____ blocks nicotinic receptors.
   a. Curare; atropine
   b. Apomorphine; physostigmine
   c. Atropine; curare
   d. Tyrosine; atropine

4. The four monoamines are
   a. epinephrine, norepinephrine, dopamine, and serotonin.
   b. GABA, glycine, glutamate, and serotonin.
   c. dopamine, L-DOPA, epinephrine, and norepinephrine.
   d. tyrosine, glycine, reserpine, and catecholamine.

5. The precursor of dopamine and norepinephrine is _____, and their synthesis is interrupted by _____.
   a. atropine; reserpine
   b. tryptophan; deprenyl
   c. adenosine; neostigmine
   d. tyrosine; AMPT

6. Axonal varicosities _____ norepinephrine.
   a. synthesize
   b. release
   c. recycle
   d. deactivate

7. The hallucinogenic drug LSD produces its effect by interacting with _____ neurons.
   a. noradrenergic
   b. serotonergic
   c. GABAergic
   d. acetylcholinergic

8. NMDA receptors, AMPA receptors, and kainate receptors all respond to
   a. serotonin.
   b. GABA.
   c. glutamate.
   d. glycine

9. One of the necessary conditions for the NMDA receptor to open is _____.
   a. depolarization of the postsynaptic membrane
   b. the presence of zinc
   c. the binding of calcium with certain enzymes in the cell
   d. the attachment of magnesium to the magnesium binding site

10. Benzodiazepines bind with _____ receptors and _____.
    a. $GABA_A$; have an anxiolytic effect
    b. glycine; and are anticonvulsive drugs
    c. $GABA_B$; have a tranquilizing effect
    d. glycine; are used to treat seizure disorders

11. Many peptides that are released along with a neurotransmitter may serve to regulate the
    a. sensitivity of postsynaptic receptors to the neurotransmitter.
    b. reuptake of the neurotransmitter.
    c. axoplasmic flow to the terminal buttons.
    d. metabolism of the brain.

12. Endogenous opioids are
    a. byproducts of neurotransmitter synthesis.
    b. steroids synthesized from cholesterol.
    c. neuromodulators produced in the brain.
    d. hormones secreted not only by the brain but by many other tissues of the body.

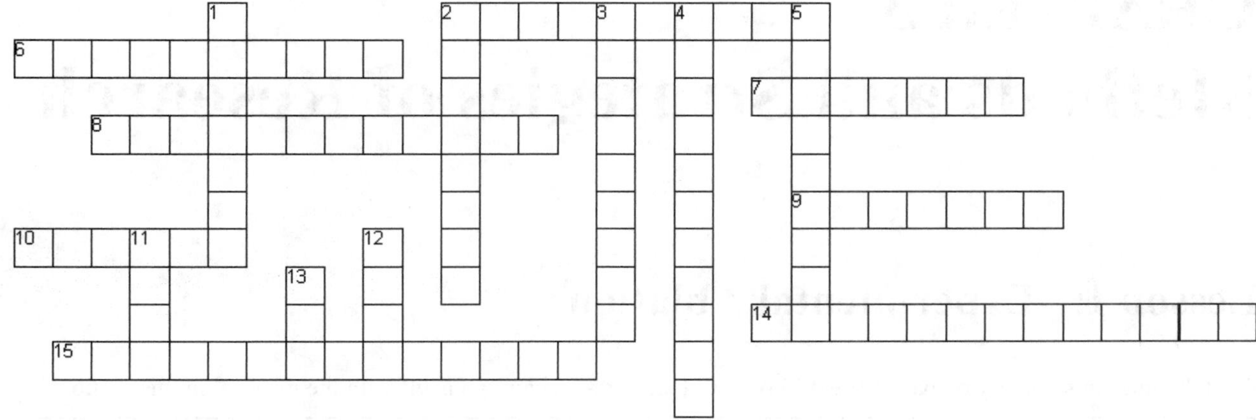

Across
2. Drug that opposes or inhibits the effects of a neurotransmitter
6. An anxiety-reducing effect
7. Inert substance given to control subjects in research
8. Injection under skin
9. Drug that facilitates the effects of a neurotransmitter
10. Drug that blocks nicotinic acetylcholine receptors
14. Increase in effectiveness of drug taken repeatedly
15. Dopamine, norepinephrine, epinephrine

Down
1. Important inhibitory neurotransmitter in lower brain tem and spinal cord
2. Drug that blocks muscarinic acetylcholine receptors
3. Most important excitatory neurotransmitter in brain
4. Gas involved in cell communication
5. Decrease in effectiveness of drug taken repeatedly
11. Drug that blocks tyrosine hydroxylase and therefore catecholamine synthesis
12. Most important inhibitory neurotransmitter in brain
13. Class of enzymes that destroys the monoamines

Answers for Self Tests

Lesson I

1. a Obj. 4-1
2. c Obj. 4-1
3. b Obj. 4-1
4. c Obj. 4-2
5. a Obj. 4-2
6. c Obj. 4-2
7. b Obj. 4-3
8. c Obj. 4-3
9. c Obj. 4-3
10. d Obj. 4-3
11. a Obj. 4-3
12. d Obj. 4-3

Lesson II

1. b Obj. 4-4
2. c Obj. 4-4
3. c Obj. 4-4
4. a Obj. 4-5
5. d Obj. 4-5
6. b Obj. 4-5
7. b Obj. 4-5
8. c Obj. 4-6
9. a Obj. 4-6
10. a Obj. 4-6
11. a Obj. 4-7
12. c Obj. 4-7

CHAPTER 5
Methods and Strategies of Research

Lesson I: Experimental Ablation

Read the interim summary on pages 149-150 of your text to re-acquaint yourself with the material in this section.

> ***Learning Objective 5-1*** Discuss the research method of experimental ablation: the rationale, the evaluation of behavioral effects resulting from brain damage, and the production of brain lesions.

Read pages 135-138 and answer the following questions.

1. Define these terms in your own words.

   a. *experimental ablation*

   b. *lesion studies*

2. Explain the rationale for lesion studies.

3. a. Distinguish between *brain function* and *behavior* and explain why this distinction is important in interpreting research results.

   b. What anatomical difficulty do researchers encounter in interpreting results of lesion studies?

4. Briefly describe and compare research techniques used to produce brain lesions.

   a. Suction

      1. procedure

      2. selectivity

   b. Radio frequency (RF) current (See Figure 5.1 in your text.)

      1. procedure

      2. selectivity

c. Excitatory amino acids such as kainic acid that produce excitotoxic lesions (See Figure 5.2 in your text.)

1. procedure

2. selectivity

d. Drugs such as 6-hydroxydopamine (6-HD)

1. procedure

2. selectivity

5. Whenever subcortical regions are destroyed, what other kind of damage is unavoidable?

6. What procedure do researchers follow to try to determine whether this damage has affected their results? (Be sure to use the term *sham lesion* in your answer.)

7. Briefly describe how brain activity can be temporarily interrupted using local anesthetics.

Learning Objective 5-2 Describe stereotaxic surgery.

Read pages 138-140 and answer the following questions.

1. Name the instrument and the reference book researchers use during stereotaxic surgery.

2. a. Describe the contents and organization of a stereotaxic atlas.

   b. Describe how a researcher uses the atlas to locate a subcortical brain structure. Be sure to use the term *bregma* in your answer. (See Figures 5.3 and 5.4 in your text.)

   c. Why are the locations described in stereotaxic atlases only approximate?

3. Study Figure 5.5 in your text and describe a stereotaxic apparatus.

4. How is an animal prepared and positioned for surgery?

5. List several uses of stereotaxic surgery. (See Figure 5.6 in your text.)

Learning Objective 5-3 Describe research methods for preserving, sectioning, and staining the brain and for studying its parts and interconnections.

Read pages 140-143 and answer the following questions.

1. Why do researchers use histological methods to prepare brain tissue for microscopic examination?

2. After the brain is removed from the skull, it is placed in a _______________ such as _______________, which _______________ the tissue, halts _______________ and kills any _______________ that might destroy it.

3. Why is tissue usually perfused before placing it in a fixative?

4. Study Figure 5.7 in your text and describe a microtome and its function.

5. Follow the preparation of brain tissue for microscopic examination shown in Animation 5.1. Begin by explaining why brain tissue must be stained.

6. If a researcher stains neural tissue with cresyl violet, what kind of material will take up the stain? (See Figure 5.8 in your text.)

7. a. When do researchers use a transmission electron microscope rather than a light microscope?

   b. How do transmission electron microscopes produce images that can be seen on a computer?

   c. What kind of images does a scanning electron microscope produce?

   d. Study Figure 5.9 and 5.10 in your text and compare the images.

8. a. What constraint of conventional microscopy do confocal laser scanning microscopes overcome?

   b. With the help of Figure 5.11 in your text, explain how confocal laser scanning microscopic images are produced.

   c. Study the images shown in Figure 5.12 in your text to see how this procedure is used in research. (Mizrahi et al., 2004)

Learning Objective 5-4 Describe research methods for tracing efferent and afferent axons and for studying the living human brain.

Read pages 143-149 and answer the following questions.

1. Sometimes a researcher may wish to trace pathways of *efferent* axons—that is, those that leave a particular brain structure—in order to learn more about how that structure may ultimately influence behavior. (See Figure 5.13 in your text.)

   a. What is the general name for all techniques used for this purpose?

b. Write a description of the method that uses PHA-L using the following phrases, some of which are shown in Figure 5.14 in your text.

travel by means of fast axoplasmic transport
into the brain structure being studied
examine tissue under the microscope
molecules of PHA-L are taken up by dendrites
to the terminal buttons
transported through the soma to the axon
cells are filled with molecules of PHA-L
slice and mount the brain tissue
use an immunocytochemical method
inject a minute quantity of PHA-L
kill the animal
within a few days

c. Carefully explain how immunocytochemical methods make use of our knowledge of the role of proteins, antibodies, and antigens in the immune system. (See Figure 5.15 in your text.)

2. Researchers must also trace pathways of *afferent* axons; that is, those that lead to a particular brain structure.

   a. What is the general name for all techniques used for this purpose?

   b. Name a chemical used to trace afferent axons and the means by which it is transported to the cell bodies. Some results are shown in Figure 5.16 in your text.

3. Researchers may also wish to identify a series of neurons that form synaptic connections with each other.

   a. What is the general name for all techniques used for this purpose?

   b. Name the most effective chemical used to identify synaptic connections.

   c. Once the virus has been injected into the brain, how does it affect neurons at the injection site and other neurons with which they form synaptic connections?

   d. How did Daniels et al. (1999) use this technique to study synaptic connections in the VMH? (Some of these connections are shown in Figure 5.17 in your text.)

4. How has the development of computerized tomography (CT) and magnetic resonance imaging (MRI) overcome some of the earlier difficulties inherent in studying the living human brain? (See Figures 5.18 in your text.)

5. Compare and contrast the use of CT and MRI in humans. (An example of a CT scan is shown in Figure 5.19 in your text and an example of a MRI scan is shown in Figure 5.20.)

   a. Procedure used to obtain a scan

   b. Details shown in scans

6. To review: All the research methods discussed in this section are summarized in Table 5.1 in your text.

Lesson I Self Test

1. The results of lesion studies are often difficult to interpret because
   a. a particular neural circuit can perform only one behavior.
   b. no one brain region or neural circuit is solely responsible for a behavior.
   c. sometimes there is no clear difference between behavior and function.
   d. the effects of surgical anesthesia cannot be determined.

2. Which of these methods produces the most selective brain lesions?
   a. Suction
   b. Microdialysis
   c. Excitatory amino acids
   d. Radio frequency current

3. To account for incidental brain damage when lesions are produced, researchers
   a. increase the number of animals in the study.
   b. use equal numbers of male and female animals.
   c. produce sham lesions.
   d. repeat the study.

4. Using a stereotaxic apparatus, researchers can
   a. assess loss of function resulting from brain lesions.
   b. slice brains for histological examination.
   c. make subcortical lesions in the brain.
   d. confirm the location of brain lesions.

5. Using a stereotaxic atlas, researchers can
   a. locate bregma.
   b. determine the approximate location of structures deep within the brain.
   c. calculate the correct amount of anesthesia required.
   d. determine which method of making brain lesions to use.

6. A fixative performs all these functions *except*
   a. attaching tissue to a microscope slide.
   b. halting autolysis.
   c. hardening tissue.
   d. killing destructive microorganisms.

7. Using a microtome, researchers can
   a. apply a mounting medium.
   b. dry and heat tissue.
   c. examine and photograph stained and mounted brain sections.
   d. slice tissue into thin sections.

8. Scanning electron microscopes produce
   a. moving images that can be viewed and preserved on a computer.
   b. images of higher magnification than standard transmission electron microscopes.
   c. images in three dimensions.
   d. images of tissue that cannot be exposed to light.

9. An advantage of using confocal laser scanning microscopes is
   a. tissue does not have to be treated first with a dye.
   b. living brain tissue can be examined.
   c. the scanning laser light beam can destroy destructive microorganisms in the tissue.
   d. the scanning laser light beam can produce lesions and then verify the location almost simultaneously.

10. _____ labeling methods are used to trace _____ axons which carry information _____ a brain structure.
    a. Retrograde; afferent; toward
    b. Anterograde; afferent; away from
    c. Retrograde; efferent; away from
    d. Anterograde; afferent; toward

11. Immunocytochemical methods are used to
    a. locate peptides and proteins.
    b. provide a view of a “slice” of the human brain.
    c. selectively destroy axons.
    d. inhibit fast axoplasmic transport.

12. Researchers using CT or MRI
    a. do not have to obtain permission from either the patient or the family.
    b. can study the living brain without operating on the patient.
    c. must first anesthetize the patient.
    d. must first shave the patient’s head.

Lesson II: Recording and Stimulating Neural Activity, Neurochemical Methods, and Genetic Methods

Read the interim summary on pages 159-160 of your text to re-acquaint yourself with the material in this section.

Learning Objective 5-5 Describe how the neural activity of the brain is measured and recorded, both electrically and chemically.

Read pages 150-156 and answer the following questions.

1. To review: List the two types of electrical events in the brain that can be recorded.

   1. 2.

2. Compare the duration and behavioral state of the animal during chronic and acute recordings.

3. Explain what the phrase *single-unit recording* means. Be sure to describe microelectrodes in your answer.

4. Describe the preparation for recording the neural activity of individual neurons in the brain.

   a. How are microelectrodes implanted in the brain? (See Figure 5.21 in your text.)

   b. How are the electrical signals detected by the microelectrodes recorded?

5. How does the preparation change for recording the neural activity of a whole region of the brain? Be sure to describe macroelectrodes in your answer.

6. a. How is the electrical activity of the human brain most often studied?

   b. By studying these records of electrical patterns, called electroencephalograms (EEGs), what can researchers learn? (See Figure 5.22 in your text.)

7. Explain how researchers detect extremely small magnetic fields produced by neural activity in the brain using SQUIDS and magnetoencephalography. (See Figure 5.23 in your text.)

8. a. In addition to the electrical activity of the brain, what other sign of neural activity can be measured?

   b. Explain the role of 2-deoxyglucose (2-DG) in measuring the metabolic activity of the brain.

   c. Explain how autoradiographs are prepared. (See Figure 5.24 in your text and Animation 5.2.)

9. a. How are nuclear proteins produced and what do they indicate?

b. Describe the procedure that detects the presence of Fos and explain what is shown in Figure 5.25 in your text.

10. a. Explain how the metabolic activity of the human brain is measured using positron emission tomography (PET). (See Figure 5.26 in your text.)

b. What is one of the reasons why PET scanners are expensive to use?

11. Explain several advantages of functional magnetic resonance imaging (fMRI). (See Figure 5.27 in your text.)

12. Study Figure 5.28 in your text and then carefully explain how neurochemicals can be detected using microdialysis.

13. How can neurochemicals be measured in the human brain by means of a noninvasive technique? (See Figure 5.29 in your text)

Learning Objective 5-6 Describe how neural activity in the brain is stimulated, both chemically and electrically, and describe the behavioral effects of electrical brain stimulation.

Read pages 156-159 and answer the following questions.

1. List two ways that neurons can be artificially stimulated.

   1. 2.

2. Briefly explain both procedures, mentioning any advantages and disadvantages. (See Figure 5.30 in your text and Animation 5.3.)

3. a. Describe how extremely small quantities of a substance can be discharged into a single neuron using a multibarreled micropipette which is illustrated in Figure 5.31 in your text.

   b. What is this procedure called?

   c. How is neural activity recorded during microiontophoresis?

4. Discuss why it is difficult to interpret any behavioral changes elicited by electrical brain stimulation.

5. a. Study Figure 5.32 in your text and explain how a patient is prepared for transcranial magnetic stimulation (TMS).

   b. The effects of TMS are similar to the effects of what other research method that you have studied?

6. To review: All the research methods discussed in this section are summarized in Table 5.2 in your text.

Read the interim summary on page 164 of your text to re-acquaint yourself with the material in this section.

Learning Objective 5-7 Describe research methods for locating particular neurochemicals, the neurons that produce them, and the receptors that respond to them.

Read pages 160-164 and answer the following questions.

1. Follow the example of the effects of organophosphate insecticides to learn how researchers look for a particular neurochemical and, at the same time, review information about acetylcholine.

   a. State the two hypotheses that could explain why organophosphate insecticides disrupt dreaming.

   b. Which one of these is correct?

   c. Carefully explain how acetylcholinesterase inhibitors such as the organophosphate insecticides affect the brain.

   d. Further research is still needed to determine in which region of the brain the acetylcholinergic synapses are affected. Outline three possible strategies to search for the affected region.

2. Outline three ways to search for a particular neurochemical.

3. a. Briefly explain how brain tissue is prepared using immunocytochemical methods. (See Figure 5.33 in your text.)

   b. Which one of the ways outlined in question 2 can be studied using immunocytochemical methods?

   c. Name the enzyme involved in the synthesis of acetylcholine and explain how it is identified using immunocytochemical methods. (See Figure 5.34 in your text.)

4. a. Which one of the ways outlined in question 2 can be studied using in situ hybridization?

   b. Study Figures 5.35 and 5.36 in your text and briefly explain how in situ hybridization is used to find the location of a particular messenger RNA.

5. List and briefly describe two methods that are used to search for receptors. (See Figure 5.37 in your text.)

   1.

   2.

6. Explain how we can verify that neurons in the VMH contain receptors for ovarian sex hormones by using autoradiography or immunocytochemistry.

7. What kinds of information can be obtained using double labeling? (See Figure 5.38 in your text.)

8. To review: All the research methods discussed in this section are summarized in Table 5.3 in your text.

Read the interim summary on page 166 of your text to re-acquaint yourself with the material in this section.

Learning Objective 5-8 Discuss research techniques to identify genetic factors that may influence behavior.

Read pages 164-166 and answer the following questions.

1. List the two factors that interact to determine behavior.

   1. 2.

2. What method is particularly useful in estimating the role of heredity on a particular trait?

3. What do we mean when we say that a pair of twins is concordant for a trait? discordant for a trait?

4. Explain why monozygotic twins have a higher concordance rate for genetically controlled traits than do dizygotic twins.

5. Look at another method of estimating the influence of heredity on a particular trait. In an adoption study,

   a. which two groups of people are adopted people compared with?

   b. what kinds of information must the researcher obtain in order to use this method?

6. a. What will researchers conclude about the factors that influence a trait if adopted people strongly resemble their biological parents?

   b. What will researchers conclude about the factors that influence a trait if adopted people strongly resemble their adoptive parents?

   c. What will researchers conclude about the factors that influence a trait if adopted people strongly resemble both sets of parents?

7. a. Define *targeted mutations* in your own words.

   b. What other name has been given to targeted mutations?

8. What is the most common type of antisense oligonucleotide and what is its function?

Lesson II Self Test

1. An electroencephalogram is a(n)

   a. microscope slide of radioactivity in the brain.
   b. paper or computerized record of electrical activity in the brain.
   c. x-ray record of normal or abnormal brain tissue.
   d. treated photographic film showing receptor location.

2. The metabolic activity in the brain of a laboratory animal can be measured by giving an injection of _____ and analyzing the results using _____.

   a. Fos; PET scanner
   b. 2-DG; autoradiography
   c. fluorogold; in situ hybridization
   d. saline; electroencephalography

3. SQUIDS are used to detect

   a. magnetic fields.
   b. particular enzymes.
   c. radioactivity.
   d. particular fluorescent dyes.

4. Functional MRI (fMRI)

   a. was the first imaging technique for studying the living brain.
   b. images are more detailed than those obtained using PET scanners, but take longer to achieve.
   c. permits the measuring of regional metabolism.
   d. can be used to locate any radioactive substance.

5. Microdialysis is used to measure the

   a. permeability of the cell membrane.
   b. intracranial pressure.
   c. secretions of the brain.
   d. electrical activity of the brain.

6. An advantage of chemical stimulation over electrical stimulation of the brain is that

   a. it requires less equipment.
   b. stereotaxic surgery is not necessary.
   c. the effects are more localized.
   d. no tissue is destroyed.

7. One of the difficulties in using electrical brain stimulation as a research tool is stimulation

   a. sometimes causes neurotransmitters to be released.
   b. is difficult to localize.
   c. must always be administered during open head procedures.
   d. can never duplicate natural neural processes.

8. To study the effects of chemicals on the activity of a single cells, researchers use _____ methods.

   a. microiontophoresis
   b. anterograde tracing
   c. autoradiographic
   d. retrograde tracing

9. To search for a particular messenger RNA, researchers use

   a. the Fos protein.
   b. autoradiography.
   c. in situ hybridization.
   d. 2-DG.

10. Double labeling techniques permit researchers to determine what chemicals a neuron contains and

    a. their connections with other neurons.
    b. the enzymes that produce them.
    c. the messenger RNA involved in their synthesis.
    d. nearby agonists or antagonists.

11. In adoption studies, the heritability of a particular behavioral trait is determined by comparing adopted people with

    a. other adopted people matched for that trait.
    b. other people matched for that trait, but who were raised by their biological parents.
    c. their biological and adoptive parents.
    d. their biological siblings, but not other children in their adoptive families.

12. Targeted mutations are deliberately mutated genes that

    a. interrupt the immune reaction.
    b. inactivate enzymes.
    c. fail to produce a functional protein.
    d. increase protein synthesis.

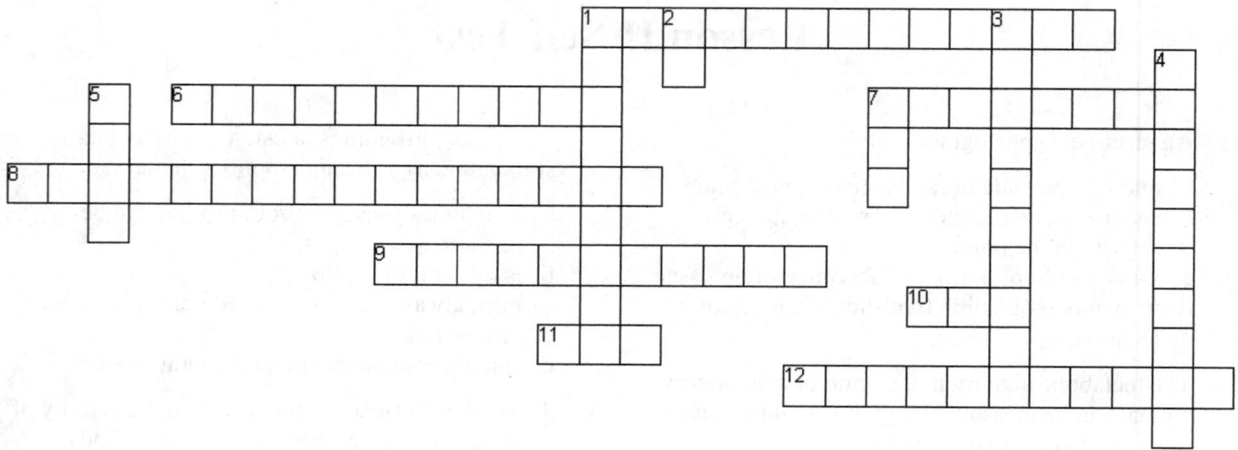

Across
1. Procedure to measure chemicals in interstitial fluid
6. Apparatus used to position electrode or cannula in brain
7. Chemical used to preserve brain tissue
8. A "knockout" of a gene
9. Labeling method to trace pathways followed by efferent axons
10. Device using radio waves and magnetic fields to view interior of body
11. Device that shows location of radioactive tracer in living brain
12. Synonym for experimental ablation

Down
1. Instrument used to cut very thin tissue slices
2. Device using scanning X-ray beam to produce two-dimensional view of body parts
3. Procedure duplicating all experimental steps except actual brain damage
4. Labeling method to trace pathways followed by afferent axons
5. Procedure that measures regional metabolism of brain
7. Protein produced in cell nucleus in response to synaptic stimulation

Answers for Self Tests

Lesson I

1. b Obj. 5-1
2. c Obj. 5-1
3. c Obj. 5-1
4. c Obj. 5-2
5. b Obj. 5-2
6. a Obj. 5-3
7. d Obj. 5-3
8. c Obj. 5-3
9. b Obj. 5-3
10. a Obj. 5-4
11. a Obj. 5-4
12. b Obj. 5-4

Lesson II

1. b Obj. 5-5
2. b Obj. 5-5
3. a Obj. 5-5
4. c Obj. 5-5
5. c Obj. 5-5
6. c Obj. 5-6
7. d Obj. 5-6
8. a Obj. 5-6
9. c Obj. 5-7
10. a Obj. 5-7
11. c Obj. 5-8
12. c Obj. 5-8

CHAPTER 6
Vision

Lesson I: Anatomy of the Visual System, Coding of Visual Information in the Retina, and Analysis of Visual Information in the Striate Cortex

Read the interim summary on page 178 of your text to re-acquaint yourself with the material in this section.

> ***Learning Objective 6-1*** Describe the characteristics of light and color, outline the anatomy of the eye and its connections with the brain, and describe the transduction of visual information.

Read pages 169–177 and answer the following questions.

1. a. We receive information about the environment from sensory receptors. What is the name of the process by which stimuli are detected by these receptors?
   b. What is the name of the electrical change in the cells' membrane?
   c. If these receptors lack axons, how do they form synapses with other neurons?
   d. How do receptor potentials affect the firing of the cells with which they form synapses?

2. _______________ is that portion of the spectrum of electromagnetic radiation that we humans can see. Light travels at a constant speed of _______________ per second and the wavelength of visible light determines one of the perceptual dimensions of color, the _______________. When the intensity of the electromagnetic signal increases, we perceive that the _______________ of the color has increased. The degree of _______________ of a color depends on the purity of the light. (See Figures 6.1 and 6.2 in your text.)

3. Begin a review of the anatomy of the eye by studying Figures 6.3 and 6.4 in your text.
   a. Name the bony pockets in the front of the skull that surround the eyes.
   b. What holds the eyes in place and moves them?
   c. Name the white outer layer of the eye.
   d. Name the mucous membranes that line the eyelid.
   e. Light enters through which layer of the eye?
   f. Describe how the amount of light that enters the eye is regulated.

g. Describe the lens and its location then explain the process of accommodation.

h. Name the substance between the lens and retina that gives the eye its volume.

i. Name the light-sensitive region of the back of the eye.

4. List the three types of movement that eyes make and describe them briefly.

 1.

 2.

 3.

5. List the characteristics of the specialized photoreceptors—the rods and the cones—in Table 1 below. (See Table 6.1 in your text.)

	Cones	Rods
Number		
Location		
Sensitive to what kind of light?		
Role in visual acuity		
Role in color vision		

Table 1

6. Label the parts of the eye in Figure 1 below.

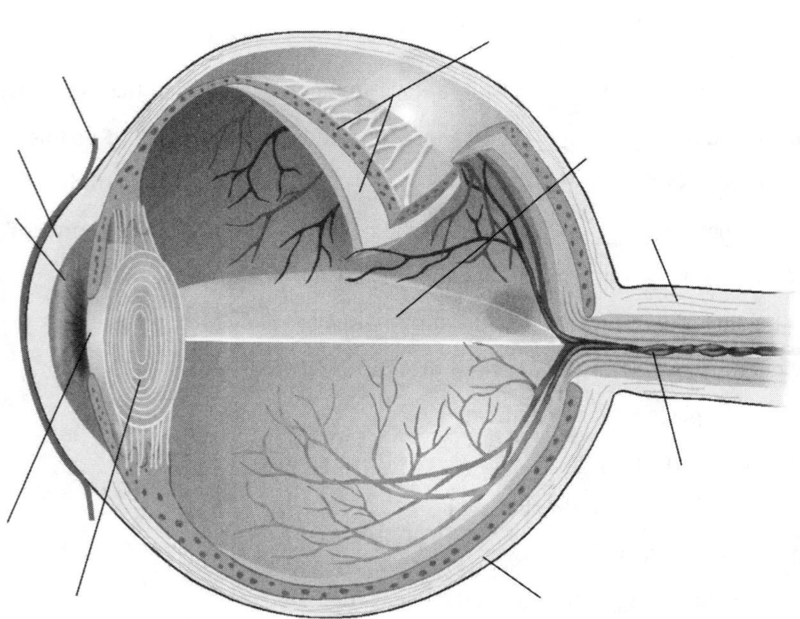

7. Explain why the optic disk is called the blind spot. Be sure to try the demonstration in Figure 6.5 in your text.

8. a. Study Figure 6.6 in your text and list the three primary layers of the retina.

   1. 3.

   2.

   b. Where are the photoreceptors located in relation to these layers and to the direction of entering light?

   c. Photoreceptors form synapses with _________ _________, which form synapses with _________ _________.

   d. Name two other kinds of cells found in the retina.

   1. 2.

9. Study Figure 6.7 in your text for a closer look at the anatomy of photoreceptors. Sketch a rod and a cone and label their parts.

10. Follow the process of visual perception step by step. We will begin with the role of the photopigments.

    a. List the two components of photopigments.

    1. 2.

    b. Indicate on your sketch in question 9 where photopigments are found.

    c. Name the photopigment found in human rods.

    d. Describe how rhodopsin changes when it is exposed to light.

    e. How is the membrane of photoreceptors different from that of other neurons? (Baylor, 1996)

    f. Study Figure 6.8 in your text and carefully explain the changes that occur in the photoreceptor when it is struck by light. Be sure to use the terms *transducin* and *phosphodiesterase* in your answer.

11. Continue by studying the neural circuit from the photoreceptors to the ganglion cells.

    a. Study Figure 6.9 in your text and list the first two types of cells in this circuit.

    1. 2.

    b. Light __________ polarizes the photoreceptors and __________ polarizes the bipolar cells.

    c. Describe how the release of neurotransmitter by photoreceptors and bipolar cells changes and explain why these changes affect the firing rate of the ganglion cells.

12. Axons of the retinal ganglion cell ascend through the optic nerves to which part of the brain?

13. a. What is the name of the inner two layers of neurons in the dorsal lateral geniculate nucleus? (See Figure 6.10 in your text.)

    b. What is the name of the outer four layers of neurons in the dorsal lateral geniculate nucleus? (See Figure 6.10 in your text.)

    c. What do these names indicate about the size of the cells found there?

    d. Name the layer containing a third set of neurons.

14. a. To what region of the cerebral cortex do axons of neurons in the dorsal lateral geniculate nucleus project?

    b. Where is this region located?

    c. Study Figure 6.11 in your text and explain why the primary visual cortex is sometimes called the striate cortex.

15. a. Where do the optic nerves join together? (See Figure 6.12 in your text.)

    b. From the optic chiasm, where do the axons of the ganglion cells serving the inner halves of the retina travel? axons of ganglion cells serving the outer halves of the retina?

16. a. If a person looks straight ahead, the right hemisphere receives information from the ________________ side of the visual field and the left hemisphere receives information from the ________________.

    b. Explain why the previous statement is true. Be sure to explain the role of the lens in your answer.

17. Identify and briefly describe the functions of several other pathways from the retina.

Read the interim summary on pages 184-185 of your text to re-acquaint yourself with the material in this section.

Learning Objective 6-2 Describe the coding of visual information by photoreceptors and ganglion cells in the retina.

Read pages 178-184 and answer the following questions.

1. a. Define the *receptive field* of a neuron in your own words.

   b. Using the term *receptive field*, explain why foveal vision is especially acute. (See Figure 6.13 in your text.)

2. List and describe

   a. the response pattern of ganglion cells in the frog retina, discovered by Hartline. (1938)

   b. the receptive field of ganglion cells in the cat retina, discovered by Kuffler. (1952, 1953) (See Figure 6.14 in your text.)

   c. the connections of ON/OFF cells in the primate retina. (Schiller and Malpeli, 1977)

3. Why can the firing rate of ON and OFF ganglions be described as efficient?

4. a. When monkeys were given an injection of APB, a drug that blocks synaptic transmission in ON bipolar cells, what kind of stimuli did they have difficulty detecting? did not have difficulty detecting? (Schiller et al., 1986)

   b. When monkeys were given an injection of APB, a drug that blocks synaptic transmission in ON bipolar cells, what kind of stimuli did the monkeys not have difficulty detecting? (Schiller et al., 1986)

   c. Explain why we can conclude that rod bipolar cells in the monkey retina must be ON cells. (Dolan and Schiller, 1989)

5. a. Describe a phenomenon that results from the center-surround organization of the receptive fields of ganglion cells. (Look at Figure 6.15 for an example.)

   b. Study Figure 6.16 in your text and explain how this phenomenon works.

6. State two advantages of color vision. (Mollon, 1989; Regan et al., 2001)

7. Briefly state Thomas Young's theory of color vision.

8. Before continuing, study Figure 6.17 in your text and explain the difference between color mixing and pigment mixing.

9. Briefly state Ewald Hering's theory of color vision.

10. What two problems with the Young theory did Hering's theory overcome?

    1.

    2.

11. a. Later research with photoreceptors in the retina proved Young was right. Study Figure 6.18 in your text and explain the relationship between the particular opsins found in retinal photoreceptors and color vision.

    b. List the three types of cones found in the retina and compare their relative numbers.

    1.

    3.

    2.

12. Supply characteristics for the following three genetic defects in color vision:

Defect	Description	Visual Acuity
Protanopia		
Deuteranopia		
Tritanopia		

13. Retinal ganglion cells respond to ______________ of opposing primary colors, thus there are two kinds of color-sensitive cells ______________-______________ and ______________-______________.

14. Describe the typical response pattern of color-sensitive and "black and white" retinal ganglion cells. (Study Figure 6.19 in your text.)

15. Study Figure 6.20 in your text and describe how retinal ganglion cells code different wavelengths of light detected by the cones.

    a. How does red light affect

    1. red cones?

    2. red-green ganglion cells?

    b. How does green light affect

    1. green cones?

    2. red-green ganglion cells?

    c. How does yellow light affect

    1. red and green cones?

    3. red-green ganglion cells?

    2. yellow-blue ganglion cells?

d. How does blue light affect

1. blue cones?

2. yellow-blue ganglion cells?

16. Explain why we can see (and imagine) a yellowish red but not a bluish yellow.

17. Explain why you will see a red and green radish on the right of Figure 6.21 in your text after staring at the left side for thirty seconds. (See Animation 6.1 for another demonstration of this phenomenon.)

Read the interim summary on page 191 of your text to re-acquaint yourself with the material in this section.

Learning Objective 6-3 Discuss the striate cortex and discuss how its neurons respond to orientation and movement, spatial frequency, and texture.

Read pages 185-188 and answer the following questions.

1. Study Figures 6.11 and Figure 6.22 in your text to review the appearance of striate cortex.

2. Approximately what percentage of the striate cortex analyzes information from the fovea?

3. What discovery by Hubel and Wiesel (1977, 1979) revolutionized the study of the physiology of visual perception?

4. Study Figure 6.23 in your text and explain what is meant when we say, "Most neurons in the striate cortex are sensitive to orientation."

5. Study Figure 6.24 in your text and compare the responses of simple, complex, and hypercomplex cells to various line orientations and backgrounds as well as movement.

6. Explain the importance of sine-wave gratings in visual detection. (See Figure 6.25 in your text. De Valois et al., 1978)

7. a. Study Figure 6.26 in your text and explain the concept of visual angle.

   b. Go on to explain its relationship to the spatial frequency of a sine-wave grating.

8. Summarize research on the receptive fields of simple cells by Albrecht (1978).

a. Describe or sketch the stimulus. (Study Figure 6.27 in your text.)

b. How did the cells respond to the moving stimulus?

c. What did the response pattern resemble?

9. Compare the spatial frequencies that indicate small objects or large objects with sharp edges and large areas of light and dark.

10. a. The most important visual information for object recognition is contained in _______________ spatial frequencies.

b. Compare the photographs of Abraham Lincoln in Figure 6.28 in your text and explain how the figure on the left was created. (Harmon and Julesz, 1973) You may want to try the demonstration as you answer this question.

c. Explain how these figures confirm the statement in question 10a.

Learning Objective 6-4 Discuss how neurons in the striate cortex respond to retinal disparity and color; explain the modular organization of striate cortex.

Read pages 188-190 and answer the following questions.

1. a. List some of the cues we can observe using only one eye that help us determine depth.

b. When we use both eyes we receive a vivid perception of depth through the process of stereopsis. When is stereopsis especially useful?

c. Most neurons in the striate cortex are _______________ and respond to visual stimuli from _______________ eye.

d. Explain how the response of these neurons to visual stimuli contributes to depth perception. Be sure to discuss retinal disparity in your answer.

2. a. What observation led Wong-Riley (1978) to discover blobs?

b. Describe the location and organization of the CO blobs in primary visual cortex. (Horton and Hubel, 1980; Humphrey and Hendrickson, 1980; Fitzpatrick et al., 1983; Livingstone and Hubel, 1987)

c. Study Figure 6.29 in your text which shows a portion of the striate cortex of a macaque monkey. Be sure to note the CO blobs and their distribution in thick stripes, thin stripes, and pale strips.

d. How has the role of the parvocellular system in color vision been revised? (Hendry and Yoshioka, 1994; Chatterjee and Callaway, 2003)

3. The brain is most likely organized in _______________. The striate cortex consists of approximately 2500 _______________, each containing about _______________ neurons. These modules consist of two segments each centered around a _______________. Each half of the module receives input from only

_______________ _______________, but the module combines the information from both eyes making most of the neurons _______________.

4. What is the function of neurons
   a. within a CO blob? (Kaas and Collins, 2001)
   b. outside the CO blobs? (Livingstone and Hubel, 1984; Born and Tootell, 1991; Edwards et al. 1995)

5. What have recordings revealed about the
   a. arrangement of the receptive fields of all the neurons of a module?
   b. region of the visual field that all the neurons of a module analyze?
   c. kinds of cells found in the interblob region?
   d. orientation sensitivity of cells in the interblob region?
   e. ocular dominance? (Study Figure 6.30 in your text.)

6. Study Figure 6.31 in your text and explain how the response to spatial frequency by neurons found inside and outside the CO blobs varied. (Edwards et al., 1995)

Lesson I Self Test

1. If a color is fully saturated, the radiation contains
   a. all wavelengths.
   b. one wavelength.
   c. wavelengths beyond the visible spectrum.
   d. a mixture of wavelengths from a specific band of the spectrum.

2. Optic nerves join together at the __________, where half of the axons cross to the opposite side of the brain.
   a. calcarine fissure
   b. optic chiasm
   c. optic disk
   d. striate cortex

3. The first step in visual perception occurs when light
   a. causes a photopigment to split into its two constituents.
   b. enters the sclera.
   c. reaches the brain through the optic chiasm.
   d. causes a change in the receptor potential of the photoreceptor.

4. Foveal vision is more acute than peripheral vision because
   a. the receptor-to-axon relationships are approximately equal in the fovea.
   b. its photoreceptors respond more quickly to changes in illumination.
   c. its receptive field is near the fixation point.
   d. its ganglion cells fire continuously.

5. Kuffler found that the receptive field of cat ganglion cells resembles
   a. a mosaic.
   b. a circle surrounded by a ring.
   c. staggered columns.
   d. a polka-dot pattern of CO blobs.

6. Retinal ganglion cells use a(n) __________ coding system.
   a. trichromatic
   b. relative brightness
   c. opponent-process
   d. black and white

7. Hubel and Wiesel first suggested that orientation-sensitive neurons in the visual cortex respond best to _____ but other research indicates the best stimulus is _____.

   a. lines and edges; spots
   b. low spatial frequencies; high spatial frequencies
   c. lines and edges; sine-wave gratings
   d. sine-wave gratings; spots

8. When low frequency information is removed from an image of an object, it becomes

   a. easier to identify.
   b. more difficult to identify.
   c. easier to identify if it is moved closer.
   d. more difficult to identify if it is moved closer.

9. Retinal disparity helps us to recognize

   a. shapes and patterns.
   b. depth.
   c. density.
   d. right and left.

10. Which cells in striate cortex detect the ends of lines of a particular orientation?

   a. simple cells
   b. complex cells
   c. hypercomplex cells
   d. type 2 complex cells

11. Striate cortex is organized into

   a. modules each surrounding a pair of CO blobs.
   b. magnocellular, parvocellular, and koniocellular layers.
   c. modules of ON/OFF cells.
   d. six parallel layers of uniform thickness.

12. CO blobs of the striate cortex

   a. contain color sensitive neurons.
   b. are found in a polka-dot pattern within columns.
   c. receive input from either the right or left eye, but not both.
   d. do not respond to low spatial frequencies.

Lesson II: Analysis of Visual Information: Role of the Visual Association Cortex

Read the interim summary on pages 206-208 of your text to re-acquaint yourself with the material in this section.

Learning Objective 6-5 Describe the anatomy of the visual association cortex and discuss the location and functions of the two streams of visual analysis that take place there.

Read pages 191-193 and answer the following questions.

1. Where is the visual information from the modules in striate cortex analyzed?

2. Where do neurons in the striate cortex send axons? (Zeki and Shipp, 1988)

3. Briefly describe the organization and specialization within the primate extrastriate cortex.

4. In general, how is visual information transferred through visual association cortex? (Grill-Spector and Malach, 2004)

5. To see the striate and extrastriate cortex of the human brain, study Figure 6.32 in your text.

6. a. Where do most of the outputs of striate cortex (area V1) send information?

   b. Where do neurons in area V1 blobs project? (See Figure 6.33 in your text.)

   c. Where do neurons outside area V1 blobs project? (See Figure 6.33 in your text.)

d. List the two pathways of visual analysis found in visual association cortex and their general function. (See Figure 6.34 in your text. Ungerleider and Mishkin, 1982; Baizer et al., 1991)

1.

2.

7. Summarize the characteristics and functions of the parvocellular, magnocellular, and koniocellular divisions of the visual system by completing the table below. (Study Table 6.2 in your text.)

Property	Magnocellular division	Parvocellular division	Koniocellular division
Color			
Sensitivity to contrast			
Spatial resolution			
Temporal resolution			

8. a. Which systems are found in all mammals? in only primates?

b. Which systems are found only in primates?

Learning Objective 6-6 Discuss the perception of color and the analysis of form by neurons in the ventral stream.

Read pages 193-195 and answer the following questions.

1. Compare the response characteristics to color by neurons in CO blobs with neurons in subarea V4 of extrastriate cortex in the monkey. (Zeki, 1980)

2. Describe the phenomenon of color constancy in your own words.

3. Describe research on color constancy in neurons in subarea V4 in monkey extrastriate cortex. (Schein and Desimone, 1990).

   a. What kinds of stimuli did neurons in the primary receptive field of area V4 respond to?

   b. How did stimuli in the secondary receptive field influence the response to stimuli in the primary receptive field of neurons in subarea V4?

   c. What do these responses suggest about color constancy?

4. a. What did Walsh et al. (1993) conclude after studying the response to color by damaged neurons in area V4?

   b. To see the effects of the color of overall illumination on color perception, see Animation 6.2.

5. a. Describe the location of area TEO.

   b. When area TEO was destroyed, what severe deficit did monkeys exhibit? (Heywood et al., 1995)

c. What, then, may be the function of area TEO?

6. a. Describe *cerebral achromatopsia* in your own words.

   b. What is the location of brain damage that causes this disability? (See again Figure 6.33.)

7. a. What kind of stimuli did and did not activate neurons in area V8? (See Figure 6.35 in your text. Zeki and Marini, 1999)

   b. What do these responses suggest about the function of area V8?

8. Explain why the perception of color and shape is interrelated. Summarize the case of patient P. B. to support your answer.

9. Complete the following sentences:

   a. The analysis of visual information leading to the perception of form by the visual cortex begins with neurons in

   b. These neurons send information to

   c. Analyzed information is then sent to

10. a. Describe the location and the kinds of analyses performed by the inferior temporal cortex.

    b. List the two major regions of the inferior temporal cortex.

    1. 2.

11. a. Compare the size of the receptive fields of area TEO and area TE. (Boussaoud et al., 1991)

    b. List some of the stimuli that provoke a good and a poor response from these neurons. (Rolls and Baylis, 1986; Kovács et al., 1995)

    c. What may be the general function of these neurons?

12. What can we conclude from the complex response patterns of neurons in primate inferior temporal cortex. (Kobatake et al., 1992; Logothetis et al., 1995)

Learning Objective 6-7 Describe the two basic forms of visual agnosia: apperceptive agnosia and associative visual agnosia.

Read pages 195-199 and answer the following questions.

1. a. Define *agnosia* in your own words.

   b. What kind of deficit is associated with apperceptive visual agnosia?

   c. What kind of deficit is associated with associative visual agnosia?

2. Would you expect a person with apperceptive visual agnosia to be able to:

   a. identify the contents of a first aid kit by sight? by touch?

   b. read the list of contents of a first aid kit?

   c. draw a picture of some of the contents of a first aid kit?

3. How successfully did a patient with associative visual agnosia studied by Ratcliff and Newcombe (1982)

   a. copy a picture of an anchor and recognize what it was? (See Figure 6.36 in your text.)

   b. draw a picture of an anchor from memory?

   c. define *anchor*?

4. Which brain connections appear to be disrupted in associative visual agnosia?

5. a. Consider a common symptom of visual agnosia—prosopagnosia. Explain why it would it be inappropriate to give a patient with this symptom the following directions.: "Look for Max. He'll give you a ride home."

   b. What kind of cues do these patients use to identify people? (Buxbaum et al., 1999)

6. a. Name and describe the location of the region that contains the circuits in the brain involved in the specific recognition of facial features. (See Figure 6.37 in your text. Grill-Spector et al., 2004)

   b. How did the man studied by Moscovitch et al., (1997) react to the picture in Figure 6.38 in your text?

   c. What kind of stimuli activated the FFA in a functional imaging study? (Cox et al., 2004)

   d. What do these finding suggest about this region?

7. Outline the discussion that a brain region for facial recognition developed through experience and not natural selection. To support your answer, cite studies of the

   a. disrupted ability of experts to recognize closely related complex stimuli. (Bornstein et al., 1969; Damasio et al., 1982)

   b. stimuli that activated the fusiform face area. (See Figure 6.40 in your text. Gauthier et al., 2000; Xu, 2005; Gauthier et al., 1999; Golby et al., 2001)

   c. ability of autistic people to recognize faces. (Grelotti et al., 2002)

8. a. What kind of stimuli activated the extrastriate body area (EBA)? (Downing et al., 2001)

   b. How did transcranial stimulation of the EBA impair people's ability? (Urgesi et al., 2004)

9. a. What kinds of stimuli does the parahippocampal place area (PPA) respond to?

   b. What does the case of patient D. F. suggest about the function of the PPA and scene recognition? (See Figure 6.41 in your text. Steeves et al., 2004)

Learning Objective 6-8 Describe how neurons in extrastriate cortex respond to movement and location, and discuss the effects of brain damage on perception of these features.

Read pages 199-206 and answer the following questions.

1. a. Name and describe the location of neurons that respond to movement.

   b. List some of the regions that relay information to this area.

   c. Compare the speed and duration of the response to stimuli in the receptive fields of areas V4 and V5 of extrastriate cortex by studying Figure 6.42 in your text. (Petersen et al., 1988)

   d. What anatomical difference may account for the response rate?

   e. What combination of brain damage disrupts sensitivity to movement in area V5? (Rodman et al., 1989, 1990; Seagraves et al., 1987)

2. Area V5 sends information about movement to an adjacent area the _______________ _______________ _______________ (_____). Neurons here respond to _______________ patterns of movement. Analysis of _______________ _______________ appears to take place in the _______________ MST (_____).

3. Briefly explain how we use information from optic flow and the center of expansion to move in our environment.

4. Summarize research on the response of neurons in MSTd using single-unit recording (Bradley et al., 1996) and electrical stimulation. (Britten and van Wezel, 1998)

5. Study the location of MT/MST or MST+ (the motion–sensitive area V5) shown in Figure 6.43 in your text. (Annese et al., 2004)

6. What kind of brain damage did patient L.M. receive and how was her perception of movement affected? (Zihl et al., 1991)

7. a. Describe the procedure Walsh and colleagues used to deactivate MT+ in normal human subjects. (Walsh et al., 1998)

   b. How was the response of subjects to moving stimuli displayed on a computer screen disrupted?

8. For more information on an interesting movement-related phenomenon, see Animation 6.3.

9. a. What region became active when subjects judged their heading while viewing a display showing optic flow? (Peuskens et al., 2001)

   b. How did lesions of this region disrupt subjects' response? (Jornales et al., 1997; Vaina, 1998)

10. a. Describe what actors wore in laboratory movies filmed by Johansson. (1973)

    b. How easily could people watching the movies identify the depicted motion? (See Animation 6.4 which demonstrates this phenomenon.)

c. What is the name of this phenomenon?

11. a. What kind of brain damage did patient R.A. receive? (reported by Vaina, 1998)

    b. Compare what patients L.M. and R.A. reported when they saw moving points of light. (McCleod et al., 1996; Zihl et al., 1991)

    c. What do their differing perceptions suggest about the neural control of the perception of motion and structure from motion?

    d. What area became active when people imagined watching points of light representing form from motion? (See Figure 6.44 in your text. Grossman and Blake, 2001)

    e. What area became active when people viewed a video showing form from motion? (Grossman et al., 2000)

12. a. What kind of brain damage did patient S.B. sustain? (Lê et al., 2002)

    b. What kind of visual analysis was he no longer able to perform? still able to perform?

    c. What does this case suggest about brain mechanisms for recognizing form from motion and normal object perception?

13. How did watching a computer-generated image of a person making hand, eye, or mouth movements affect the subjects' brain activity? (Pelphrey et al., 2005)

14. According to Thier et al., (2001), which brain region may be involved in compensation of image movement caused by head and eye movement? Cite research by Haarmeier et al., (1997) to support your answer.

15. a. What kind of visual analysis is performed by the parietal lobe?

    b. What kind of deficits result from damage to this region?

16. a. People with Balint's syndrome have suffered brain damage to which part of the brain? (Balint, 1909; Damasio, 1985; Rizzo and Vecera, 2002)

    b. List and describe the three major symptoms of this syndrome.

       1.

       2.

       3.

    c. What is the characteristic response when a person with Balint's syndrome is asked to

       1. reach for an object?

2. look around a room and describe its contents and their location? Why?

3. identify several objects held together?

d. What does simultanagnosia suggest about the perception of separate objects?

17. a. Study the anatomy of the posterior parietal cortex shown in Figure 6.45 in your text.

b. List five regions within the intraparietal sulcus (IPS) and the kind of movements they are involved in. (Snyder et al., 2000; Culham and Kanwisher, 2001; Astafiev et al., 2003; Tsao et al., 2003; Frey et al., 2005)

1.

2.

3.

4.

5.

18. a. What terms do Goodale and his colleagues prefer to use to describe the functions of the dorsal and ventral streams of visual cortex? (Goodale and Milner, 1992; Goodale et al., 1994; Goodale and Westwood, 2004)

b. Carefully state their reasons.

c. What kind of movements are impaired and remain intact as a result of brain lesions in this region? (Milner et al., 1991; Goodale et al., 1994; James et al., 2003)

19. Explain why associative visual agnosia may result from disconnection of the ventral stream and verbal mechanisms in the brain. Cite research demonstrating the difference between behavior and function to support your answer. (Sirigu et al., 1991)

20. a. Describe the way young children played first with large toys and then with identical small toys. (See Animation 6.5. DeLoache et al., 2004)

b. What does the behavior of the children suggest about brain development?

21. To review: The anatomy of the visual cortex, its internal organization, its presumed functions, and many of its connections within the brain are outlined in the interim summary, Figure 6.46 in your text, and Table 6.3. The effects of brain damage on visual analysis by humans are covered as well.

Lesson II Self Test

1. The ventral stream of visual association cortex recognizes
   a. the distance of an object from the viewer.
   b. where an object is located.
   c. the identity and color of an object.
   d. the movement of an object.

2. Extrastriate cortex
   a. consists of several regions that each respond to a particular kind of visual information.
   b. receives information directly from the retina.
   c. performs the initial analysis of visual information.
   d. responds best to familiar stimuli.

3. Neurons in subarea V4 of extrastriate cortex
   a. have two independent receptive fields.
   b. respond to a variety of wavelengths of light.
   c. are especially sensitive to changes in illumination.
   d. cannot compensate for the source of illumination.

4. People with cerebral achromatopsia have
   a. difficulty tracking a moving object.
   b. lost some or all of their color vision.
   c. no peripheral vision.
   d. diminished visual acuity.

5. Inferior temporal cortex performs the analysis of
   a. form and function.
   b. figure and background.
   c. location and movement.
   d. form and color.

6. Neurons in area TE
   a. have the smallest receptive fields.
   b. send their primary outputs to area TEO.
   c. respond best to simple stimuli such as spots, lines, or sine-wave gratings.
   d. appear to participate in the recognition of objects.

7. People who cannot recognize common objects by sight have
   a. apperceptive visual agnosia.
   b. akinetopsia.
   c. Balint’s syndrome.
   d. ocular apraxia.

8. People with prosopagnosia
   a. have difficulty with visual accommodation.
   b. do not have binocular vision.
   c. do not recognize faces.
   d. are color blind.

9. Neurons in area V5
   a. appear to analyze optic flow.
   b. are arranged in grids.
   c. appear to perceive structure from motion.
   d. respond to movement and show directional sensitivity.

10. Analysis of optic flow seems to be a function of the
    a. mirror neurons.
    b. MSTd.
    c. superior colliculus.
    d. visual association cortex.

11. Simultanagnosia, one of the symptoms of Balint's syndrome, is the inability to
    a. reach for an object successfully.
    b. scan the contents of a room and perceive object locations.
    c. perceive more than one object in a group.
    d. identify objects by sight alone.

12. The primary function of the dorsal stream of visual association cortex may be
    a. to associate sounds with sights.
    b. to direct visually-guided movements.
    c. to identify fine detail in a visual scene.
    d. to perceive form from motion.

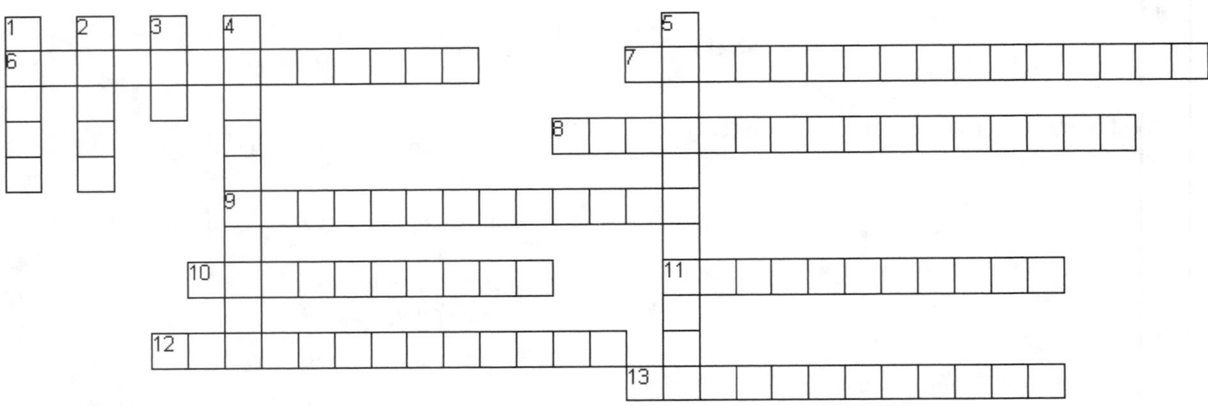

Across

6. Failure to recognize particular people by the sight of their faces
7. The relative width of the bands in a sine-wave grating, measured in cycles per degree of visual angle
8. A region of the extrastriate cortex located at the base of the brain; involved in perception of faces and other complex objects that require expertise to recognize
9. Inability to discriminate among different hues; caused by damage to the visual association cortex
10. An orientation-sensitive neuron in the striate cortex whose receptive field is organized in an opponent fashion
11. Inability to perceive movement, caused by damage to area V5 (also called MST) of the visual association cortex
12. A system of interconnected regions of visual cortex involved in the perception of form
13. A neuron located in the retina that receives visual information from bipolar cells; its axons give rise to the optic nerve

Down

1. A class of protein that, together with retinal, constitutes the photopigments
2. The region of the retina that mediates the most acute vision of birds and higher mammals
3. One of the receptor cells of the retina; sensitive to light of low intensity
4. One of the perceptual dimensions of color; purity
5. Difficulty in reaching for objects under visual guidance

Answers for Self Tests

Lesson I			Lesson II		
1.	b	Obj. 6-1	1.	c	Obj. 6-5
2.	b	Obj. 6-1	2.	a	Obj. 6-5
3.	a	Obj. 6-1	3.	b	Obj. 6-6
4.	a	Obj. 6-2	4.	b	Obj. 6-6
5.	b	Obj. 6-2	5.	d	Obj. 6-6
6.	c	Obj. 6-2	6.	d	Obj. 6-7
7.	c	Obj. 6-3	7.	a	Obj. 6-7
8.	b	Obj. 6-3	8.	c	Obj. 6-7
9.	b	Obj. 6-4	9.	d	Obj. 6-8
10.	c	Obj. 6-4	10.	b	Obj. 6-8
11.	a	Obj. 6-4	11.	c	Obj. 6-8
12.	a	Obj. 6-4	12.	b	Obj. 6-8

CHAPTER 7
Audition, the Body Senses, and the Chemical Senses

Lesson I: Audition and the Vestibular System

Read the interim summary on pages 230-231 of your text to re-acquaint yourself with the material in this section.

Learning Objective 7-1 Describe the parts of the ear and the auditory pathway.

Read pages 211-219 and answer the following questions.

1. a. What makes a sound? (See Figure 7.1 in your text.)

   b. What range of vibrations can humans hear?

2. Explain the following characteristics of sound. (See Figure 7.2 in your text.)

   a. Pitch (Be sure to use the term *hertz* in your answer.)

   b. Loudness

   c. Timbre

3. Explain the difference between an analytic and a synthetic sense organ.

4. Study Figure 7.3 in your text and then describe the path of sound from your outer ear through your middle ear.

   a. When sound enters your external ear and moves through the ear canal what structure begins to vibrate?

   b. Describe the appearance and explain the function of the ossicles of the middle ear.

   c. Where is the oval window located?

5. Name the parts of the ear shown in Figure 1, below.

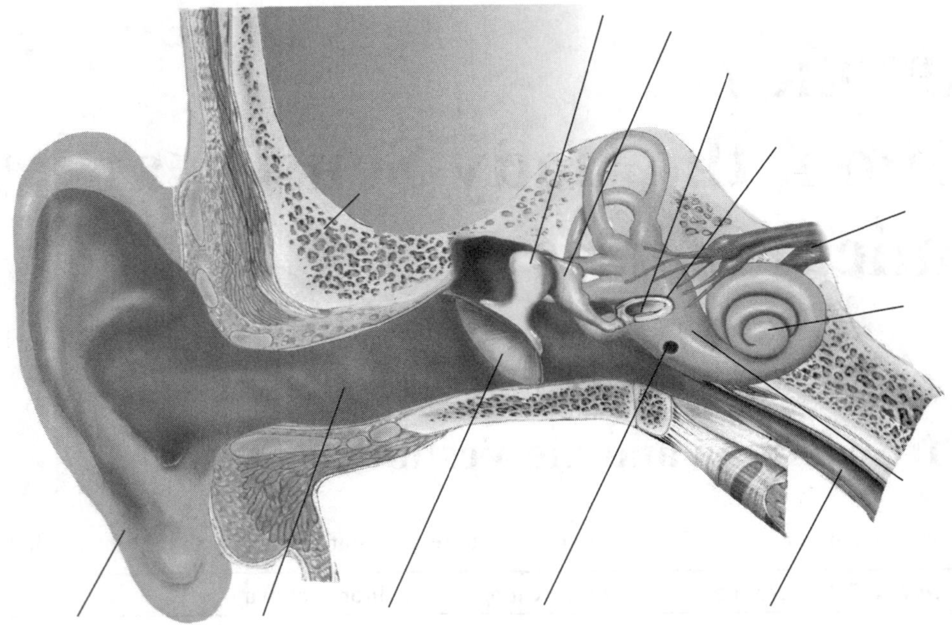

Figure 1

6. Briefly explain how airborne sound is transmitted to the cochlea of the inner ear.

7. a. List the names of the three sections of the cochlea.

   1. 2. 3.

   b. List the three structures that compose the organ of Corti which are shown in Figure 7.4 in your text.

   1. 2. 3.

8. Begin a description of the hair cells.

   a. What is their function?

   b. What is their physical relation to the other structures of the organ of Corti? Be sure to mention Deiters's cells in your answer.

9. a. What causes the basilar membrane to bend and what is the result?

   b. Explain what von Békésy (1960) observed about the relationship between the portion of the basilar membrane that bends and the frequency of the sound.

10. Study Figure 7.5 in your text and explain the role that the round window plays in hearing.

11. Continue with your description of the hair cells.

    a. Where are the inner and outer hair cells found?

b. The hair cells contain cilia. Study Figure 7.6 in your text and describe their

1. appearance.
2. arrangement.
3. composition. (Flock, 1977)

c. When the basilar and tectorial membranes bend in response to sound waves, how do the cilia move in response?

d. How are the basilar and tectorial membranes attached to each other and what are the points of attachment called? Be sure to mention the TRPA1 family of receptors in your answer. (See Figure 7.7 in your text.)

12. Study Figure 7.8 in your text and carefully explain how the direction of movement of the cilia affects their ion channels and results in a receptor potential. (Pickles and Corey, 1992; Hudspeth and Gillespie, 1994; Gillespie, 1995; Jaramillo, 1995)

13. a. Name the cranial nerve that connects the cochlea to the brain. Briefly describe the bipolar neurons that travel through this nerve. (Return to Figure 7.4 in your text.)

b. Where do the vast majority of incoming cochlear nerve axons synapse?

c. Where do the rest of the incoming cochlear nerve axons synapse?

d. What do the connections of the inner hair cells suggest about their function? the outer hair cells?

e. Briefly describe the olivocochlear bundle, noting the neurotransmitters that are secreted.

14. Trace the central auditory pathway with the help of Figure 7.9 in your text. Begin with the axons that enter the cochlear nucleus of the medulla. Where do neurons of the

a. cochlear nucleus send axons?

b. superior olivary complex send axons? Be sure to mention the lateral lemniscus in your answer.

c. inferior colliculus send axons?

d. medial geniculate nucleus send axons?

15. What other parts of the brain receive auditory information?

16. Describe the connections between the basilar membrane and the auditory cortex. How do we refer to the relationship between these two structures? Why?

17. Describe the location and organization of the:

a. primary auditory cortex. (Kaas et al., 1999; Hackett et al., 2001; Poremba et al., 2003)

b. auditory association cortex. (See Figure 7.10 in your text.)

18. What is the function of the dorsal stream of auditory cortex? the ventral stream? (Rauschecker and Tian, 2000)

Learning Objective 7-2 Describe the detection of pitch, loudness, and timbre.

Read pages 219-223 and answer the following questions.

1. Explain the notion that moderate to high frequencies of sound are detected by place coding. Support your answer by referring to

   a. the work of von Békésy. (See Figure 7.11 in your text.)

   b. hearing loss induced by antibiotics. (Stebbins et al., 1969)

   c. cochlear implants. (Figure 7.12 in your text shows a person with a cochlear implant. Copeland and Pillsbury, 2004)

2. a. What discrepancy between the vibrations of the basilar membrane and the frequency of sounds that humans can detect became apparent from early research? Why?

   b. What has more recent research discovered? (Evans. 1992; Ruggero, 1992; Narayan et al., 1998)

   c. Carefully explain how the contraction of the cilia of the outer hair cells of the organ of Corti in response to electrical current or acetylcholine affects the response properties of the inner hair cells. (Brownell et al., 1985; Zenner et al., 1985; Frank et al., 1999; Fridberger et al., 2004)

3. Explain why the results obtained by Kiang (1965) suggested that low frequencies must be detected by some means other than place coding.

4. Describe the experiments by Pijl and Schwartz (1995a, 1995b) that provide evidence for rate coding. (See Animation 7.1.)

5. Explain the means by which axons in the cochlear nerve inform the brain of the loudness of a stimulus.

6. a. What characteristic of sound allows us to distinguish between a clarinet and a violin?

b. Study Figure 7.13 in your text and describe the waveform produced when a clarinet plays a sustained note. Be sure to use the terms *fundamental frequency* and *overtones* in your answer.

Learning Objective 7-3 Discuss the perception of spatial location, the perception of complex sounds, and the perception of music.

Read pages 223-230 and answer the following questions.

1. By what means do we recognize
   a. the location of low frequency sounds?
   b. the location of high frequency sounds?
   c. whether a sound is in front of us or behind us?
2. a. You and a friend have decided to study together at her apartment. When you stop talking and settle down to study, you notice the ticking of the clock. Explain how your eardrums will respond if the clock is
      1. on a table to the left.
      2. straight ahead of you on the mantle.

   b. When someone in the apartment to the right of yours turns on the stereo, the insistent bass notes make it difficult for you to concentrate. You ask your friend if she can ask her neighbors to turn the music down. How did you know the music was coming from the right? Study Figure 7.14 in your text and be sure to use the terms *phase differences* and *out of phase* in your answer.
3. a. Outline Jeffress's (1948) explanation of how the nervous system detects very short delays in the arrival time of two signals. (Study Figure 7.15 in your text.)

   b. Describe anatomical evidence from work with barn owls in support of this explanation. (Compare Figure 7.15 and Figure 7.16 in your text. See Animation 7.2. Carr and Konishi, 1989; 1990)
4. a. Why is it difficult for the auditory system to use binaural phase differences to detect the location of high-frequency sounds?

   b. How then does the auditory system detect the location of these sounds?

   c. Where are neurons that detect binaural differences in loudness found?
5. a. By what means, other than turning our head, does the auditory system determine whether a sound is in front of us or behind us?

b. Explain the role of the external ear (pinna) in this method.

6. a. Describe the experimental procedure used in a study of the effects of elevation on the intensity of sounds by Oertel and Young (2004).

   b. Explain what a transfer function is and then study the graphs of the transfer functions of the cat's ear shown in Figure 7.17 in your text. What does the data indicate about the effects of elevation on the timbre of sound?

7. a. Identify the brain region where the first level of analysis of the information about the elevation of a sound takes place.

   b. If axons that connect this nucleus with the rest of the auditory system are destroyed, what is the effect on localizing sound by elevation differences? (Sutherland et al., 1998)

8. Why is the recognition of the timbre of a sound most likely the result of experience?

9. a. When blind and sighted people were asked to determine the elevation of a sound, which group did better?

   b. Under what circumstances was the ability of blind people as good as that of sighted people?

   c. What is the presumed explanation for these results? (Zwiers et al., 2001)

10. List the three primary functions of hearing. (Heffner and Heffner, 1990; Yost, 1991)

    1. 3.

    2.

11. a. By what means does the auditory system appear to identify the sources of sounds?

    b. Describe some anatomical characteristics of neurons that carry auditory information that enable them to carry this information rapidly and accurately. (Trussel, 1999.)

12. a. Once again, list the two streams of the auditory cortex and their functions.

    1. Stream: Function:

    2. Stream: Function:

    b. Summarize evidence confirming the two streams of auditory cortex. (See Figure 7.18 in your text. Arnott et al., 2004; Alain et al., 2001)

13. a. Compare the regions of the monkey brain which process visual and auditory information shown in Figure 7.19 in your text.

    b. Where do these regions overlap and what is the presumed reason?

14. a. After presenting subjects with recordings of environmental sounds, they then presented these sounds backwards. Why? (Lewis et al., 2004; Animation 7.3)

b. What was the effect on the auditory cortex of all sounds? (See Figure 7.20 in your text.)

c. What was the effect on the auditory cortex of recognized sounds? (See Figure 7.20 in your text.)

d. What elements of music help us with the complex task of musical perception?

15. a. What brain regions were activated when subjects listened to

1. all sounds?

2. sounds that took on pitch and then melody? (See Figure 7.21 in your text. Patterson et al., 2002)

b. List some other brain regions and the kinds of musical stimuli that activate them. (Peretz and Zatorre, 2005)

16. Briefly summarize the abilities that patient I. R. retained and lost as a result of surgery to treat aneurysms. (Peretz et al., 1998; Peretz et al., 2001. See Animation 7.4)

17. a. Compare the response of the auditory cortex of musicians and non-musicians to tones played on a piano. (Pantev et al., 1998)

b. What other difference in the primary auditory cortex of musicians and non-musicians did Schneider et al. (2002) find? (See Figure 7.22 in your text.)

18. The anatomy and complex functions of the auditory system are reviewed in the interim summary.

Read the interim summary on page 234 of your text to re-acquaint yourself with the material in this section.

Learning Objective 7-4 Describe the structures and functions of the vestibular system.

Read pages 231-234 and answer the following questions.

1. a. List the three components of the labyrinths of the inner ear.

1. 2.

b. Which of these labyrinths that comprise the vestibular system?

1. 2.

c. List the functions of the

1. vestibular sacs.

2. semicircular canals

d. List the two vestibular sacs.

1. 2.

e. Finally, list the functions of the vestibular system.

1. 2. 3.

2. Study Figure 7.23 in your text and label the labyrinths of the inner ear shown in Figure 2, on the next page.

3. The semicircular canal consists of a _______________ canal floating within a _______________ one. The membranous canal is filled with _______________. An enlargement called the _______________ contains the organ in which the sensory receptors reside. The cilia of the sensory receptors are embedded in a gelatinous mass called the _______________.

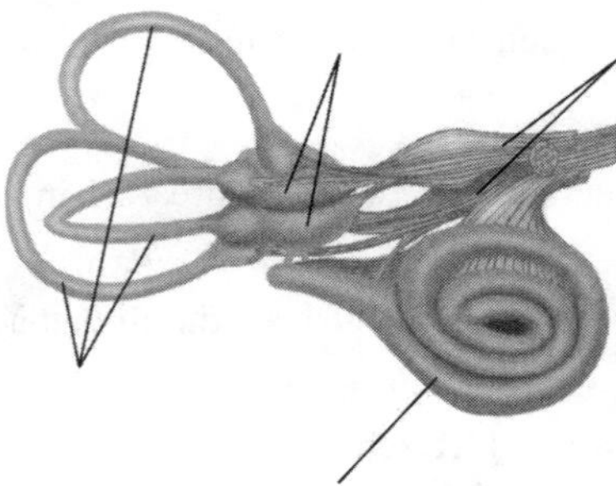

Figure 2

4. Carefully describe how angular acceleration of the head affects the fluid in the semicircular canals.

5. Study Figure 7.24 in your text and explain how the vestibular sacs provide information on the head's orientation. Be sure to mention the otoconia in your answer.

6. Describe the appearance and function of the hair cells of the semicircular canals and the vestibular sacs. Figure 7.25 in your text shows a vestibular hair cell of a bullfrog.

7. Name the two branches of the eighth cranial nerve–the auditory nerve.

   1. 2.

8. a. Where are the bipolar cells that give rise to the afferent axons of the vestibular nerve found?

   b. Where do most of the afferent axons form synapses and send axons?

   c. Where do neurons of the vestibular nuclei send their axons?

9. Explain the importance of the vestibulo-ocular reflex.

Lesson I Self Test

1. The frequency of vibration determines its
   a. pitch.
   b. loudness.
   c. timbre.
   d. complexity.

2. Because the cochlea is filled with fluid,
   a. its shape remains constant because liquids cannot be compressed.

b. the ability to hear high frequencies diminishes with age as this liquid is absorbed by the body.
c. sounds transmitted through air must be transferred to a liquid medium.
d. it is most sensitive to rolling movements; thus we can experience seasickness.

3. Most of the neurons in the cochlear nucleus send axons directly to the

a. auditory cortex.
b. superior olivary complex.
c. thalamus.
d. medial geniculate nucleus.

4. Progressive hair cell damage from the use of certain antibiotics causes a parallel progressive hearing loss, which suggests that perception of the pitch of some sounds is accomplished through

a. place coding.
b. rate coding.
c. synthetic coding.
d. analytic coding.

5. Musical overtones are

a. a series of complex waveforms.
b. repetitions of the fundamental frequency at a constant intensity.
c. multiples of the fundamental frequency.
d. repetitions of the fundamental frequency at varying intensities.

6. The lowest frequencies of sound are detected by means of

a. place coding.
b. rate coding.
c. synthetic coding.
d. analytic coding.

7. To determine the left-right localization of continuous low-pitched sounds, we use *phase differences*, which refers to

a. the time interval between the arrival at each ear of different portions of the oscillating sound wave.
b. the time interval between the arrival at each ear of the same portion of the oscillating sound wave.
c. the simultaneous arrival at each ear of the same portion of an oscillating sound wave.
d. a or c, depending on the frequency of the stimulus.

8. To determine the left-right localization of high-frequency sounds, we use

a. an analysis of arrival time.
b. intensity differences.
c. an analysis of timbre.
d. coincidence detectors.

9. A review of functional imaging studies reported a consistent finding that the _____ stream of auditory cortex is involved in the perception of the _____ and the _____ stream is involved in the perception of the _____.

a. dorsal; identity of sounds; ventral; location of sounds
b. ventral; particular patterns of sounds; dorsal; complexity of sounds
c. dorsal; particular patterns of sounds; ventral; complexity of sounds
d. ventral; identity of sounds; dorsal; location of sounds

10. The _____ contains the sensory receptors of the semicircular canals.

a. utricle
b. saccule
c. ampulla
d. vestibular nerve

11. The semicircular canals

a. respond to gravity.
b. are part of the system of ossicles.
c. are located in the sagittal, transverse, and horizontal planes in the head.
d. respond to steady rotation of the head.

12. The gelatinous mass within the vestibular sacs shifts in response to movement of the

a. cilia.
b. otoconia.
c. fluid in the cupula.
d. fluid in the semicircular canal.

Lesson II: The Somatosenses, Gustation, and Olfaction

Read the interim summary on pages 245-246 of your text to re-acquaint yourself with the material in this section.

Learning Objective 7-5 Describe the cutaneous receptors and their response to touch, temperature, and pain.

Read pages 234-239 and answer the following questions.

1. Identify the kind of information each of the following senses provides:

   a. cutaneous senses

   b. kinesthesia

   c. organic senses

2. List five stimuli to which the cutaneous senses respond.

   1. 4.

   2. 5.

   3.

3. a. List two functions of the skin.

   1. 2.

   b. List the three layers of the skin. (See Figure 7.26 in your text.)

   1. 3.

   2.

   c. Finally, list the two types of skin.

   1. 2.

4. What kind of stimuli are detected by these receptors in hairy skin?

   a. Free nerve endings

   b. Ruffini corpuscles

   c. Pacinian corpuscles

5. In addition to the kinds of receptors found in hairy skin, glabrous skin contains other receptors. What kind of stimuli are detected by

   a. Meissner's corpuscles?

   b. Merkel's disks?

6. What kind of stimuli are detected by the mechanoreceptors in the skin? (Table 7.1 in your text summarizes the categories of mechanoreceptors.)

7. List the three most important categories of cutaneous stimulation.

   1. 3.

   2.

8. a. Identify the mechanoreceptor responsible for the transduction of pressure and vibration. (Maroto et al., 2005)

   b. What causes the ion channel in this receptor to open? (Barritt and Rychkov, 2005)

9. Review the case of paient G. L. and then explain what the sensations she can and cannot experience indicate about the kind of axons that convey information about tactile stimulation. (Olausson et al., 2002)

10. Describe the cooperative roles played by the muscles and cutaneous receptors in detecting the physical characteristics of objects that a person touches.

11. Explain why the right and left corresponding areas of somatosensory cortex that receives information from the four fingers of each hand were different sizes in violin players. (Elbert et al., 1995)

12. Explain what we mean when we say that feelings of warmth and coolness are relative. (You may want to try the demonstration of adaptation to ambient temperature described in your text.)

13. List the two types of thermal receptors.

    1. 2.

14. a. All six known mammalian thermoreceptors belong to the _____ family. _____ of these receptors is sensitive to temperatures close to body temperature and is found in the _______________ _______________. (See Table 7.2 in your text. Voets et al., 2004; Güler et al., 2002)

    b. What is the function of this brain region?

    c. What other kind of stimulus do thermoreceptors respond to?

15. There appear to be at least three types of nociceptors or pain receptors. List them and identify some of the stimuli to which they respond citing relevant research.

    1.

    2. (Be sure to mention the TRPV1 receptor. Kress and Zeilhofer, 1999; Caterina et al., 2000)

    3. (Burnstock and Wood, 1996)

Learning Objective 7-6 Describe the somatosensory pathways and the perception of pain.

Read pages 239-245 and answer the following questions.

1. Trace the somatosensory pathways with the help of Figure 7.27 in your text.

    a. In general, how do most of the somatosensory axons from the skin, muscles, and internal organs enter the central nervous system?

    b. Where do somatosensory axons from the head and face enter the CNS?

    c. Axons carrying precisely localized information ascend the dorsal columns in the white matter of the spinal cord to which brain region?

    d. These axons then cross the brain and ascend to which region? Where do axons from the thalamus project?

    e. Axons carrying poorly localized information follow a different route. What pathway do these axons follow to ascend to the ventral posterior nuclei of the thalamus?

2. Describe the arrangement of cells within the somatosensory cortex and the kind of stimuli that evoke a response. (Mountcastle, 1957).

3. What did Dykes' (1983) review of research conclude about the divisions of primary and secondary somatosensory cortical areas?

4. Briefly describe the location of brain damage and the type of tactile agnosia experienced by
   a. Patient E.C., studied by Reed et al. (1996).
   b. Patient M.T., studied by Nakamura et al. (1998). (See Figure 7.28 in your text.)
   c. A patient studied by Valenza et al. (2001).
5. a. Explain why the perception of pain is beneficial.
   b. Explain why painful inflammation of injured tissue may be beneficial. (Basbaum and Woolf, 1999)
   c. Which receptor may play a role in detecting this type of pain?
   d. Give an example of an environmental event that can alter a person's perception of pain. (Beecher, 1959)
6. a. Describe these components of pain. (Price. 2000)
      1. Sensory component
      2. Immediate emotional component
      3. Long-term emotional component
   b. Study Figure 7.29 in your text and note the pathways that appear to mediate each component.
   c. Which brain regions are activated by painful stimuli?
   d. How are subjects affected if the insular cortex is
      1. electrically stimulated? (Ostrowsky et al., 2002)
      2. damaged? (Berthier et al., 1933)
7. a. How did hypnotized subjects who had plunged their arms into ice water respond when questioned about the intensity of the pain and its unpleasantness?
   b. When the subjects reported the pain was less unpleasant which brain region showed decreased activity? (See Figure 7.30 in your text. Rainville et al., 1997)
   c. When the subjects reported the pain was less unpleasant which brain region showed continued high activity? (See Figure 7.30 in your text. Rainville et al., 1997)
   d. What do these results suggest about the particular aspects of pain?
8. a. In later research with hypnotized subjects, which brain region appeared to be involved in the perceived intensity of pain? (Hofbauer et al., 2001)
   b. Which brain region appeared to be involved in the perceived unpleasantness of pain? (Hofbauer et al., 2001)
9. When subjects heard Japanese words vividly denoting various types of pain, what brain region became active? (Osaka et al., 2004)

10. a. Which brain regions became active when women received a painful electrical shock to the back of their hands?

    b. Which brain regions became active when their partners received a painful shock?

    c. What do these findings suggest about the effects of the emotional component of pain on the brain? (Singer et al., 2004)

11. Which brain region may be involved in the emotional response to chronic pain?

12. a. Describe some of the sensations reported by people who have had a limb amputated—the phantom limb phenomenon. (Melzak, 1992)

    b. Outline the classic explanation and treatment for this phenomenon.

    c. According to Melzak, what may account for phantom limb sensations? Cite the experiences of people with brain lesions or birth defects that support his suggestion.

13. a. List the two brain regions that effectively produce analgesia when electrically stimulated.

    1. 2.

    b. How has electrical stimulation been used to help humans suffering from chronic pain? (Kumar et al., 1990)

14. Study Figure 7.31 in your text and sketch and explain the neural circuit that mediates opiate-induced analgesia proposed by Basbaum and Fields (1978, 1984).

15. Describe two situations in which reduction of pain sensitivity is beneficial, thus suggesting the biological importance of analgesia.

16. Summarize research on reduced sensitivity to pain:

    a. Classically conditioned analgesia (Maier et al., 1982)

    b. Defeat or threat (Kavaliers, 1985; Lester and Fanselow, 1985; Hendrie, 1991)

    c. Blocking the analgesic effects of acupuncture (Mayer et al., 1976) and the role of "belief" in the procedure (Lee and Beitz, 1992) Be sure to note why acupuncture appears to cause analgesia.

    d. Behaviors important to survival (Komisaruk and Larsson, 1971; Komisaruk and Steinman, 1987; Whipple and Komisaruk, 1988)

    e. Blocking the analgesic effects of a placebo (Benedetti et al., 1999)

f. The role of the prefrontal cortex and periaqueductal gray matter. (See Figure 7.32 in your text. Wager et al., 2004)

Read the interim summary on page 251 of your text to re-acquaint yourself with the material in this section.

Learning Objective 7-7 Describe the five taste qualities, the anatomy of the taste buds and how they detect taste, and the gustatory pathway and neural coding of taste.

Read pages 246-251 and answer the following questions.

1. List the five major qualities of taste.

   1.
   2.
   3.
   4.
   5.

2. How does flavor differ from taste?

3. Explain the biological significance of some of the taste qualities.

4. a. The _______________, _______________, _______________, and _______________ all contain taste buds, but most of them are found on the _______________, small protuberances on the _______________. (See Figure 7.33 in your text.)

   b. Where are the cilia found?

   c. What is the function of the tight junctions between taste cells?

   d. What is the life span of a taste bud and why is it so short? (Beidler, 1970)

5. Look at the nature of molecules with a particular taste and the receptors that detect them, beginning with salty molecules and their receptors. (Study Figure 7.34 in your text.)

   a. State the best stimulus for saltiness receptors.

   b. What is the apparent receptor for saltiness and how does it respond to a salty substance? (Avenet and Lindemann, 1989; Kinnamon and Cummings, 1992)

   c. Explain the effect of amiloride on sodium channels and its significance. (Schiffman et al., 1983; Ossebaard et al., 1997)

6. a. Name the stimulus for sourness receptors.

   b. Where is sourness apparently detected and how do these sites respond to a sour substance? (Kinnamon et al., 1988)

7. Name the stimulus for bitterness.

8. Name the stimulus for sweetness.

9. a. Which proteins are receptors sensitive to bitterness and sweetness linked to? Receptors sensitive to umami? (McLaughlin et al., 1993; Wong et al., 1996; He et al., 2004)

   b. Explain what happens when a bitter molecule binds with the receptor sensitive to bitterness.

10. Describe the two families of receptors responsible for the detection of sweet, bitter, and umami tastes. (See Figure 7.35 in your text. Scott, 2004 for a review)

11. List the three cranial nerves that carry gustatory information to the brain and indicate which regions they serve.

    1. 3.

    2.

12. Begin with taste receptors on the tongue and continue to trace the gustatory pathway shown in Figure 7.36 in your text.

    a. Name the first station on this pathway.

    b. Where do the axons go from there?

    c. What other nerve sends information to this nucleus? (Beckstead et al., 1980)

    d. Where do thalamic taste-sensitive neurons project? (Pritchard et al., 1986)

    e. Where do neurons in the primary gustatory cortex project? (Rolls et al., 1990)

    f. Finally, what other brain regions receive gustatory information? (Nauta, 1964; Russchen et al., 1986)

13. Researchers had subjects sip water with different flavors. What did functional imaging indicate about the representation of taste in the gustatory cortex. (See Figure 7.37 in your text. Schoenfeld et al., 2004)

Read the interim summary on page 256 of your text to re-acquaint yourself with the material in this section.

Learning Objective 7-8 Describe the major structures of the olfactory system, explain how odors may be detected, and describe the patterns of neural activity produced by these stimuli.

Read pages 251-256 and answer the following questions.

1. Briefly summarize some of the benefits of a sense of olfaction.

2. Describe the anatomy of the olfactory system and its connections:

   a. Describe the location and size of the mucous membrane that is the olfactory epithelium. (See Figure 7.38 in your text.)

   b. Where are the cell bodies of olfactory receptors located?

   c. How do these receptor cells come in contact with odorous molecules?

   d. What prevents receptor cells from being damaged by these molecules?

e. Describe the location of the olfactory bulbs and their complex connections with olfactory receptor cells, mitral cells, and olfactory glomeruli.

f. The axons of the olfactory tract project to three regions of the brain. List them and the regions to which they, in turn, project. (Buck, 1996; Shipley and Ennis,1996)

1. projects to

2. projects to

3. projects to

g. With regard to olfaction, what may be the function of the

1. orbitofrontal cortex?

2. hypothalamus?

3 a. What changes within the olfactory cell does the G_{olf} protein initiate?(Nakamura and Gold, 1987; Firestein et al., 1991; Menco et al., 1992)

b. What does the discovery of this protein suggest about the anatomy of olfactory cilia? Cite confirming research. (Buck and Axel, 1991)

4. Study Figure 7.39 in your text and review the relationship between the receptors, olfactory neurons, and the glomeruli.

a. The cilia of each olfactory neuron contain _______________ type of receptor. Each glomerulus receives information from approximately _______________ different olfactory receptor cells. (Nef et al., 1992; Vassar et al., 1993)

b. How are these olfactory receptor cells similar? (Ressler et al., 1994b)

c. Explain this statement. There are as many types of glomeruli as there are types of receptor molecules, noting research by Serizawa et al., 2003)

5. By tracing the path of barley lectin from the olfactory receptor cells to olfactory cortex, what did researchers discover about the way olfactory information is transmitted? (Zou et al., 2001)

6. How, then, do we use a relatively small number of receptors to detect so many different odorants? (Study Figures 7.40 and 7.41 in your text which illustrate the process. Malnic et al., 1999; Rubin and Katz, 1999)

7. a. How were rats prepared for microscopic examination in research on masking of odors. (Takahashi et al., 2004)

b. What was the effect on spices such as fennel and clove on the response to bad odors?

Lesson II Self Test

1. The _____ respond to _____ and are the largest sensory end organs in the body.
   a. Pacinian corpuscles; rapid vibrations
   b. Ruffini corpuscles; feelings of warmth and coolness
   c. Meissner's corpuscles; pain
   d. Merkel's disks; stretch

2. Which region of the brain is responsible for maintaining body temperature?
   a. Anterior cingulate cortex
   b. Anterior hypothalamus
   c. Insular cortex
   d. Medial geniculate nucleus

3. TRPV1 receptors are sensitive to
   a. warmth and coolness.
   b. stretch.
   c. ATP.
   d. extremes of heat, acids, and capsaicin.

4. The somatosensory cortex
   a. is divided into four maps of the body surface.
   b. is composed of five layers, each of which makes increasingly complex analyses and responses to stimuli.
   c. is arranged in columns that respond to particular types of stimuli.
   d. is divided into three subareas that respond to the limbs, trunk, and head of the body.

5. The most effective locations for producing analgesia using electrical brain stimulation are the
   a. nucleus of the solitary tract and the nucleus raphe magnus.
   b. trigeminal nerve and the rostroventral medulla.
   c. periaqueductal gray matter and the rostroventral medulla.
   d. nucleus raphe magnus and the posterior nuclei of the thalamus.

6. Electrical brain stimulation apparently produces analgesia by stimulating the release of
   a. prostaglandins.
   b. morphine.
   c. histamines.
   d. endogenous opioids.

7. Sourness receptors respond best to
   a. hydrogen ions.
   b. plant alkaloids.
   c. potassium ions.
   d. glycerol.

8. The first relay station for taste is the
   a. primary gustatory cortex.
   b. basal forebrain.
   c. chorda tympani.
   d. nucleus of the solitary tract.

9. Studies have confirmed that _____ and _____ tastes are detected by receptors bound to _____.
   a. sweet; bitter; gustducin
   b. sweet; umami; hydrophobic residues
   c. sour; salty; cyclic AMP
   d. bitter; salty; potassium

10. Olfactory receptors cells are located in the olfactory _____ that line(s) the _____.
    a. mitral cells; olfactory glomeruli
    b. epithelium; cribriform plate
    c. epithelium; olfactory bulbs
    d. glomeruli; olfactory tracts

11. Select the *incorrect* statement.
    a. The cilia of each olfactory neuron contain only one type of receptor.
    b. There are as many types of glomeruli as there are types of receptor molecules.
    c. A particular odorant binds to only one receptor molecule.
    d. The locations of particular types of glomeruli appear to be the same in each of the olfactory bulbs of a particular animal.

12. Select the *correct* statement.
    a. Olfactory receptor cells are constantly being produced, at about the same rate as gustatory receptor cells.
    b. Olfactory receptor cells are protected from destruction by free nerve endings which mediate pain from irritating chemicals.
    c. Efferent axons of mitral cells modify the activity of olfactory receptor cells.
    d. The axons of olfactory receptor cells project to the amygdala, pyriform cortex, and entorhinal cortex.

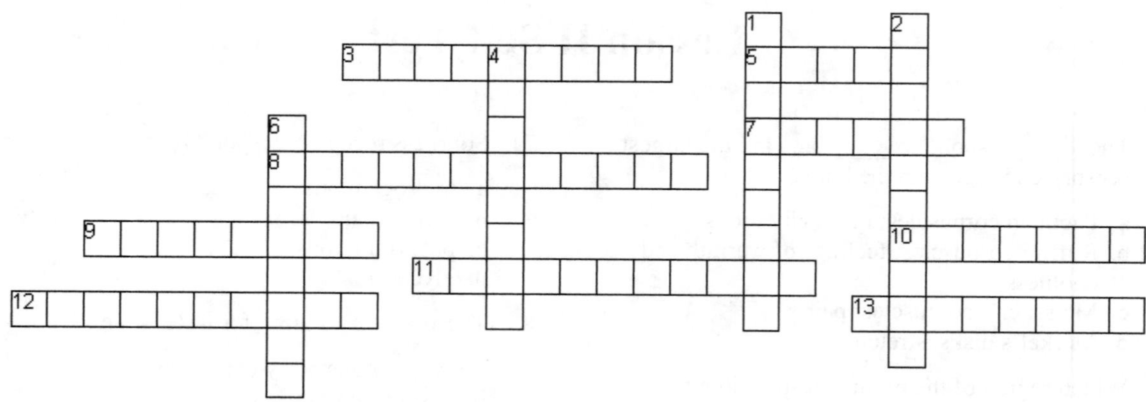

Across
3. Membrane against which cilia of auditory hair cells move
5. Taste sensation produced by glutamate
7. Perceptual dimension of sound corresponding to complexity
8. Canal that detects changes in head rotation
9. Corpuscle that responds to vibration
10. Inner ear structure containing auditory transducing mechanisms
11. Perception of body's own movements
12. Sac that detects changes in tilt of head
13. Skin found on palms and soles of feet

Down
1. G protein vital to transduction of sweetness and bitterness
2. A neuron located in the olfactory bulb that receives information from olfactory receptors
4. Multiple of the fundamental frequency
6. Bones of the middle ear

Answers for Self Tests

Lesson I

1. a Obj. 7-1
2. c Obj. 7-1
3. b Obj. 7-1
4. a Obj. 7-2
5. c Obj. 7-2
6. b Obj. 7-2
7. b Obj. 7-3
8. b Obj. 7-3
9. d Obj. 7-3
10. c Obj. 7-4
11. c Obj. 7-4
12. d Obj. 7-4

Lesson II

1. a Obj. 7-5
2. b Obj. 7-5
3. d Obj. 7-5
4. c Obj. 7-6
5. c Obj. 7-6
6. d Obj. 7-6
7. a Obj. 7-7
8. d Obj. 7-7
9. a Obj. 7-7
10. b Obj. 7-8
11. b Obj. 7-8
12. d Obj. 7-8

CHAPTER 8
Control of Movement

Lesson I: Muscles and the Reflexive Control of Movement

Read the interim summary on pages 263-264 of your text to re-acquaint yourself with the material in this section.

Learning Objective 8-1 Describe the three types of muscles found in the bodies of mammals, and explain the physical basis of muscular contraction.

Read pages 259-263 and answer the following questions.

1. List the three types of muscles found in the bodies of mammals.

   1. 2. 3.

2. How are skeletal muscles attached to the bones?

3. a. Describe flexion and give an example.

   b. Describe extension and give an example.

4. a. Study the portion of a skeletal muscle shown in Figure 8.1 in your text and list the two types of muscle fibers that are pictured and the neurons that synapse on them.

      1.

      2.

   b. Which type of muscle fibers form the muscle spindles?

   c. Which type of muscle fibers are found outside the spindles?

   d. What is the function of the extrafusal muscle fibers?

   e. What is the function of the intrafusal muscle fibers?

5. What is the relationship between precision of movement and the number of muscle fibers served by a single axon of the alpha motor neuron?

6. List the three components of a motor unit.

   1. 2. 3.

7. Immediately review what you have just learned by labeling Figure 1 on the next page.

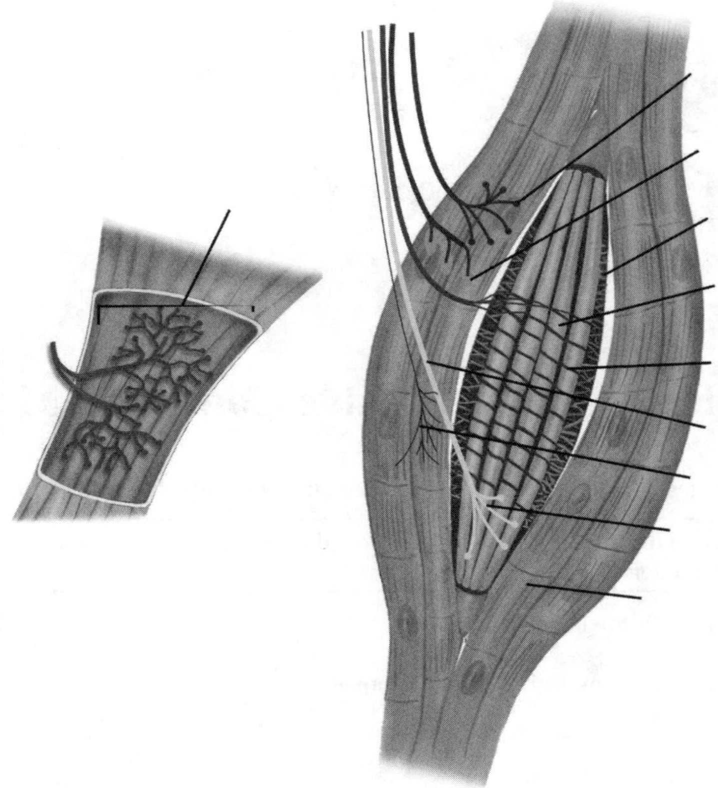

Figure 1

8. a. A single muscle fiber consists of a bundle of myofibrils. Describe their composition. (See Figure 8.1.)

   b. Describe the location of myosin cross bridges and explain their function.

   c. Why is skeletal muscle often called striated muscle?

9. A(n) _______________ _______________ is the synapse between the terminal button of a(n) _______________ _______________ and the membrane of a(n) _______________ _______________. The terminal buttons of the _______________ synapse on _______________ _______________.

10. Identify the following events involved in a muscular contraction.

    a. The neurotransmitter that is released by the terminal buttons when an axon fires

    b. The change in the postsynaptic membrane that is produced by the neurotransmitter

    c. The unalterable effect on the membrane of the muscle fiber by an endplate potential

    d. The effect on calcium channels and ionic movement

    e. The effect of calcium on the myofibrils

11. Study Figure 8.2 in your text and explain how the myosin cross bridges contribute to muscular contraction.

12. Cite two reasons why the physical effects of a muscular contraction last longer than the action potential. (See Figure 8.3 in your text.)

    1.

    2.

13. What determines the strength of a muscular contraction?

14. a. Explain the distinction between the functions of the stretch receptors of the intrafusal muscle fibers and those of the Golgi tendon organ. Label the Golgi tendon organ in Figure 8.1 of this study guide.

    b. To be sure that you understand this distinction, describe the response of the intrafusal muscle fibers and the Golgi tendon organ to various kinds of movement which are illustrated in Figure 8.4 in your text.

    1. Slow, passive lowering of arm

    2. Arm is abruptly dropped

    3. Weight is dropped into hand

15. There are two types of smooth muscle. List some of the places where each is found and note what initiates contractions.

    1. Multiunit smooth muscle

    2. Single-unit smooth muscle

16. a. What factors modulate heart rate?

    b. What initiates the heartbeat?

Read the interim summary on page 268 of your text to re-acquaint yourself with the material in this section.

Learning Objective 8-2 Explain the monosynaptic stretch reflex, the gamma motor system, and the contribution of the Golgi tendon organ.

Read pages 264-267 and answer the following questions.

1. a. Describe the patellar reflex.

   b. How do we know this reflex does not involve the brain?

2. a. Study Figure 8.5 in your text and the arrange the following phrases into two sentences that together describe the neural circuit of a monosynaptic stretch reflex:

in the gray matter of the spinal cord / an α motor neuron / are conducted to / the muscle spindle / terminal buttons / starting at / extrafusal muscle fibers / these terminal buttons / synapse on / that innervates the / afferent impulses / of the same muscle

b. When a weight placed in the hand is increased, what happens to the activity of the muscle spindles? (Continue to study Figure 8.5)

c. Briefly explain how the monosynaptic stretch reflex aides in the control of posture. (See Figure 8.6 in your text.)

3. Explain the relationship between activity of the gamma motor system and the degree of sensitivity to stretch by the intrafusal muscle fibers.

4. When the brain initiates limb movement

   a. what two sets of motor neurons in the spinal cord are activated?

   b. and there is little resistance, how will the extrafusal and the intrafusal muscle fibers respond?

   c. and there is little resistance, how will the afferent axons of the muscle spindle respond?

   d. and unexpected resistance is encountered, how will extrafusal and intrafusal muscle fibers respond?

5. a. Study Figure 8.7 in your text and trace the circuit for the inhibitory Golgi tendon organ reflex.

   b. What possible damage to the body does this circuit detect?

   c. If weight lifters use an anesthetic to deactivate the Golgi tendon organ, what injury may occur?

   d. Why was the discovery of the reflex important?

6. a. Describe the cause and characteristics of decerebrate rigidity in a cat.

   b. Carefully explain why the cat's limbs are first rigid and then suddenly limp when they are flexed. Be sure to mention the clasp-knife reflex.

7. Describe the arrangement of opposing pairs of muscles in a limb.

8. a. A stretch reflex excites the _______________ and inhibits the _______________.

b. Finally, study Figure 8.8 in your text and explain why this occurs.

Read the interim summary on pages 288-289 of your text to re-acquaint yourself with the material in this section.

Learning Objective 8-3 Describe the organization of motor cortex, and the role of the motor cortex in initiating, imitating, and comprehending movements.

Read pages 268-274 and answer the following questions.

1. a. What do we mean when we say that the primary motor cortex shows somatotopic organization?

   b. Study Figure 8.9 in your text and explain why some features of the motor homunculus are exaggerated in size.

2. Find the locations of primary motor cortex, the supplementary motor area (SMA), and the premotor cortex which are shown in Figure 8.9.

3. a. Describe the organization of primary motor cortex.

   b. Name the principal cortical input to the primary motor cortex.

   c. From which regions do the supplementary motor area and the premotor cortex receive sensory information? send information?

4. What is the anatomical and functional relationship between the primary motor cortex and the primary somatosensory cortex? Cite research to support your answer. (Asanuma and Rosén, 1972; Rosén and Asanuma, 1972)

5. a. What tasks did Evarts (1974) teach subject monkeys? (Study Figure 8.10 in your text.)

   b. What did single-unit recordings indicate about

      1. the relationship between lever movement for a squirt of juice and the rate of firing by the cell?

      2. the response of neurons in the motor cortex to visual and tactile stimulation?

   c. What do these results indicate about the control of hand and finger movements?

6. a. What were the results of a functional imaging study by Roth et al. (1996)?

   b. What else does recent evidence suggest about the function of the motor association cortex and what may be its utility?

7. Carefully outline the connections between the parietal, temporal, and frontal lobes to explain how sensory information is integrated with the control of movement. (See Figure 8.11 in your text.)

8. State the functions of

   a. the supplementary motor area (SMA) and a nearby region.

   b. premotor cortex.

9. Look at research with both monkeys and humans on the functions of the SMA.

   a. Briefly describe the task monkeys were taught and how performance was impaired by lesions of the SMA. (See Figure 8.12 in your text. Chen et al., 1995)

   b. Summarize the results of a single-unit study that also indicated the importance of this area in movement. (Mushiake et al., 1991)

   c. When researchers recorded the activity of single neurons in the SMA while monkeys performed particular sequences of movement, what did they observe? (The firing patterns of a single neuron are shown in Figure 8.13 in your text. Shima and Tanji, 2000)

   d. If this region was inactivated, how was a monkey's ability to perform a sequence of movements altered? (Shima and Tanji, 1998)

10. a. Which area in the human brain showed increased activity during performance of a learned sequence of button presses? (Hikosaka et al., 1996)

    b. If the activity of the SMA was disrupted, how and when was performance of a sequence of finger presses altered in humans? (Gerloff et al., 1997)

    c. What do these results suggest about the functions of the SMA?

    d. What do people report wanting to do when the pre-SMA is electrically stimulated? (Fried et al., 1991)

    e. Researchers asked subjects to make random finger movements and when they did, what else did they ask subjects to note? (Lau et al., 2004)

    f. How did the timing of the decision, the movement, and the activity of the pre-SMA all differ?

    g. What do these results suggest about the role of the pre-SMA in the decision to move?

11. a. What did people with parietal lesions report about making a movement and their decision to make that movement? (Sirigu et al., 2004)

    b. What do these results suggest about the function of the inputs from the parietal lobes to the pre-SMA?

    c. What evidence suggests that the prefrontal cortex also plays a role?

12. a. Once again, describe the kind of movement that the premotor cortex is involved in. Be sure to explain the difference between arbitrary and nonarbitrary spatial information.

b. Describe the task monkeys were trained to perform, noting the arbitrary and nonarbitrary spatial signals. (Kurata and Hoffman, 1994)

c. When the premotor cortex was temporarily inactivated, how was task performance altered?

13. How well did people with premotor cortex damage perform on a task involving spatial cues? arbitrary visual cues? (Halsband and Freund, 1990)

14. a. Why did the response of particular neurons in the area F5 of the monkey brain lead researchers to name them mirror neurons? (Gallese et al., 1996; Rizzolatti et al., 2001)

b. What may be their function?

c. What region are they connected with?

15. What kind of stimuli activated human mirror neurons in research by Buccino et al. (2004)?

16. State a possible explanation why mirror neurons also become active when animals hear sounds they recognize. (Kohler et al., 2002)

17. Finally, outline explanations of the function of the mirror neuron circuit proposed by

a. Rizzolatti et al. (2001).

b. Iacoboni et al. (2005) Be sure to describe research in which subjects saw video clips. (See Figure 8.14 in your text.)

Learning Objective 8-4 Describe the four principal motor tracts and the movements they control.

Read pages 275-278 and answer the following questions.

1. a. Neurons in the ______ ______ ______ control movement through two groups of descending tracts located in the ______ ______ of the spinal cord. The ______ group consists of the ______ tract, the ______ tract, and the ______ tract and is principally involved in the control of ______ ______ movements. The ______ group consists of the ______ tract, the ______ tract, the ______ tract, and the ______ ______ tract and controls more ______ movements.

b. Give several examples of independent and automatic movements.

2. Trace these pathways, shown in Figures 8.15 and 8.16 in your text, through which the primary motor cortex controls movement, beginning with the lateral group of descending pathways.

a. Where do axons in the corticospinal tract terminate?

b. Which brain regions send axons through this pathway?

c. Describe the pathway that axons follow to the cerebral peduncles.

d. At what point do the axons of the corticospinal tract form the pyramidal tracts?

e. Most fibers now cross to the other side of the brain to form what tract?

f. The remaining fibers descend to form what other tract?

g. Where do the axons of the lateral corticospinal tract originate? (Study the light blue lines in Figure 8.15.)

h. Where do the axons of the lateral corticospinal tract synapse? (Study the light blue lines in Figure 8.15.)

i. Where do the axons of the ventral corticospinal tract originate? (Study the dark blue lines in Figure 8.15.)

j. Where do the axons of the ventral corticospinal tract synapse? (Study the dark blue lines in Figure 8.15.)

k. What kind of movement does each tract control?

3. Describe the recovery of movement and any difficulties Lawrence and Kuypers (1968a) observed in monkeys whose pyramidal tracts (corticospinal tracts) were cut

   a. six to ten hours after recovery from anesthesia.

   b. the day after surgery.

   c. six weeks later.

4. What do their results indicate about the organization of the control of fingers, posture, and locomotion? the same behavior in different circumstances?

5. a. Where does the corticobulbar tract terminate? (Study the green lines in Figure 8.15.)

   b. What functions does it control?

6. a. Where does the rubrospinal tract originate and terminate? (Study the red lines in Figure 8.15.)

   b. From which region does this tract receive its most important inputs?

   c. Which muscle groups are controlled by this pathway? are not controlled?

7. In another study Lawrence and Kuypers (1968b) destroyed the rubrospinal tract unilaterally in some of the monkeys who had previously received bilateral pyramidal tract lesions.

a. Describe the eating behavior of these monkeys.

b. How well did they grip the cage bars?

c. What do the results suggest about the function of the rubrospinal pathway?

8. Turn to the second set of pathways originating in the brain stem—the ventromedial group of descending pathways. List the three tracts of the ventromedial group which have not already been described. Next to each tract indicate where its cell bodies are located and its function.

   1.

   2.

   3.

9. Lawrence and Kuypers (1968b) also cut the ventromedial fibers of some of the monkeys who had previously received bilateral pyramidal tract lesions.

   a. Describe the posture, locomotion, and eating movements of these monkeys.

   b. What do the results suggest about the function of ventromedial pathways?

10. To review these pathways, their locations, and the muscle groups they control, study Table 8.1 in your text.

Lesson I Self Test

1. The number of muscle fibers that a single axon serves determines
   a. the size of the body part that must be moved.
   b. the precision with which a muscle can be controlled.
   c. whether the axon controls flexion or extension.
   d. the muscle's sensitivity to stretch.

2. The three components of a motor unit are
   a. an alpha motor neuron; its axon; and associated extrafusal muscle fibers.
   b. a gamma motor neuron; its axon; and associated intrafusal muscle fibers.
   c. an alpha motor neuron; its terminal buttons; and associated neurotransmitter.
   d. muscles; tendons; and associated stretch receptors.

3. During a depolarization of the muscle fiber, which event does *not* occur?
   a. Calcium enters the cytoplasm.
   b. The contraction of actin causes the muscle fiber to shorten.
   c. The myosin cross bridges move, shortening the muscle fiber.
   d. Myofibrils extract energy provided by the ATP that is present.

4. The Golgi tendon organ detects
   a. the total amount of stretch exerted by the muscle.
   b. the duration of muscular contraction.
   c. muscle length.
   d. the rate of muscular contraction.

5. The monosynaptic stretch reflex
   a. initiates limb withdrawal in response to pain.

b. helps compensate for changes in weight that cause limb movement.
c. maintains muscles in a constant state of contraction.
d. is the simplest neural pathway and has little utility.

6. One type of polysynaptic reflex

a. can be demonstrated by tapping the patellar tendon.
b. contains no interneurons between the sensory neurons and the motor neurons.
c. simplifies the role of the brain in controlling movement.
d. limits the amount of muscular contraction to prevent injury.

7. The principal cortical input to the primary motor cortex is

a. temporal cortex.
b. parietal cortex.
c. frontal association cortex.
d. posterior association cortex.

8. The supplementary motor area (SMA) is involved in

a. imitating, predicting, and understanding the responses of others.
b. learning and executing complex movements that are guided by arbitrary and nonarbitrary sensory information.
c. inhibiting spontaneous movements.
d. learning and performing behaviors that consist of sequences of movements.

9. The ventral premotor cortex is involved in

a. integrating spatial information with movement.
b. learning and performing behaviors that consist of sequences of movements.
c. imitating, predicting, and understanding the responses of others.
d. controlling the duration of a movement by initiating and stopping it.

10. Mirror neuron circuits

a. respond to either the sight or execution of particular movements.
b. respond to visual, but not auditory information.
c. determine the complexity of a movement and the competency with which it is performed.
d. may be responsible for other responses associated with a particular movement such as a particular facial expression or sound.

11. The fact that monkeys with bilateral pyramidal tract lesions had no trouble opening their hands when climbing but had difficulty opening their hands when eating indicates that

a. these monkeys can still successfully forage for food.
b. damaged neural pathways that mediate large movements can regenerate, but neural pathways that mediate precise movements cannot.
c. the ability to use the hands to flee (climb) conveys a greater selective advantage to the species than feeding.
d. the same behavior can be controlled by different brain mechanisms in different contexts.

12. The reticulospinal tracts control

a. movements of the fingers and hands.
b. several autonomic functions such as respiration, sneezing, coughing, as well as walking.
c. movements of forelimb and hindlimb muscles.
d. reflexive movements of the head and neck.

Lesson II: Control of Movement by the Brain

Read the interim summary on pages 288-289 in your text to re-acquaint yourself with the material in this section.

Learning Objective 8-5 Describe the symptoms and causes of limb apraxia and constructional apraxia.

Read pages 278-280 and answer the following questions.

1. a. Define *apraxia* in your own words and explain the difference between apraxia and paralysis.

b. Why are they studied?

2. List the four kinds of apraxia and the associated deficit.

   1.

   3.

   2.

   4.

3. a. More specifically, list the three kinds of movement difficulties patients with limb apraxia may exhibit.

   1.

   3.

   2.

   b. Describe how a patient with limb apraxia is tested orally, beginning with the easiest task.

   c. If the patient cannot understand speech, how is the apraxia evaluated? (Heilman et al., 1983)

4. Summarize the cause and physical disabilities for each of the following types of limb apraxia.

   a. Callosal apraxia

      1. Lesion site (Study Figure 8.17, lesion A in your text. Watson and Heilman, 1983)

      2. Affected neural circuits

      3. Affected limb

   b. Sympathetic apraxia

      1. Lesion site (Study Figure 8.17, lesion B)

      2. Affected limbs

   c. Left parietal apraxia

      1. Lesion site (Study Figure 8.17, lesion C. Haaland et al., 2000)

      2. Affected limbs

5. a. Describe the procedure and results of research by Chaminade et al. (2005)?

   b. How do these results help to explain apraxias caused by damage to the left and right parietal lobes?

6. Study Figure 8.18 in your text and then explain how the command to reach for an object is processed by the brain. Begin your explanation right after the person hears the request to do something.

7. a. What kind of lesion results in constructional apraxia?

   b. What are some tasks that people with constructional apraxia can and cannot perform successfully? (See Figure 8.19 in your text.)

   c. Why are these tasks difficult?

Learning Objective 8-6 Discuss the anatomy and function of the basal ganglia, and its role in Parkinson's disease and Huntington's disease.

Read pages 280-284 and answer the following questions.

1. a. List the components of the basal ganglia. (Study Figure 8.20a in your text.)

   1. 2. 3.

   b. List some of the nuclei associated with the basal ganglia.

   1. 2. 3.

   c. Finally, list the afferent and efferent connections of the basal ganglia.

   1. Afferent connections

   2. Efferent connections

   d. Which motor systems do the basal ganglia influence?

   1. 2.

2. Trace the connections between the basal ganglia and the cortex—the cortical-basal ganglia loop— with the help of Figure 8.20b.

   a. Where do the frontal, parietal, and temporal cortex send axons?

   b. Where do the caudate nucleus and putamen send axons?

   c. Where does the globus pallidus send axons?

   d. What kinds of information, do the basal ganglia receive and how is it used?

3. What do we mean when we say the information in this circuit is represented somatotopically?

4. What other important structure sends information to the basal ganglia?

5. Look more closely at the nature of the connections in the cortical-basal ganglia loop that you have just traced.

   a. Which neurotransmitter is secreted by the excitatory neurons in this loop?

   b. Which neurotransmitter is secreted by the inhibitory neurons in this loop?

   c. Which region sends excitatory input to the caudate nucleus and the putamen?

   d. Where do they, in turn, send inhibitory axons?

   e. What is the name of the pathway that includes the GP_i?

   f. Where does the GP_i send inhibitory axons?

   g. Where does the VA/VL thalamus send excitatory axons?

   h. Carefully explain why the net effect of this loop is excitatory. (Study the arrows with solid lines in Figure 8.20b.)

   i. Where in this loop does the GP_e send inhibitory axons?

j. Where does the subthalamic nucleus send excitatory input?

k What is the name of this loop and what is it's net effect? (Study the arrows with broken lines in Figure 8.20b.)

l. Where does the globus pallidus send axons? the subthalamic nucleus?

m. Where does the globus pallidus send axons? the subthalamic nucleus?

6. Briefly describe the primary symptoms of Parkinson's disease and explain how such activities as getting up, walking, writing, and maintaining balance are disrupted. (Poizner et al., 2000)

7. Explain how we know that tremor and rigidity are not the cause of slowness of motion.

8. To explain the symptoms of Parkinson's disease, study Figure 8.20b in your text and then add labels to the ovals and the leader lines in Figure 2. Add the missing arrows, indicating excitatory connections with black lines and inhibitory connections with red or broken lines.

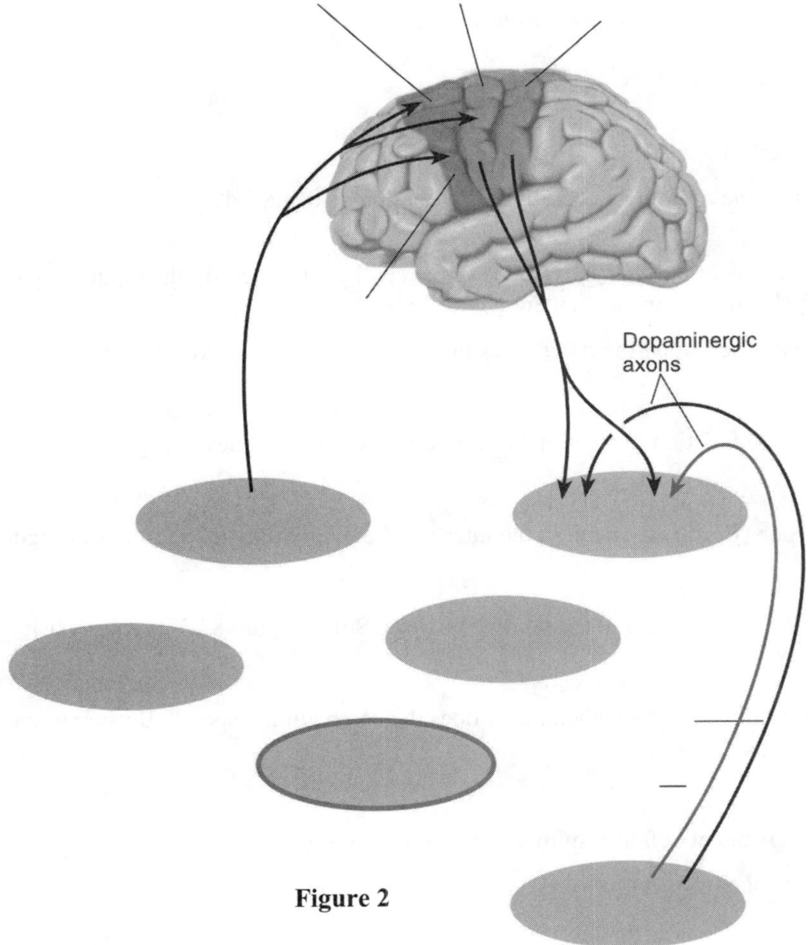

Figure 2

9. a. List two side effects of treatment with L-DOPA.

   1. 2.

   b. Why does this treatment eventually become less effective?

10. a. Where does the neural degeneration that is the cause of Huntington's disease begin and how does it progress? (See Figure 8.21 in your text.)

    b. At what age do the symptoms usually begin?

    c. How does progressive degeneration affect movement?

    d. Briefly describe the location of the gene that causes Huntington's disease and its particular defect. Be sure to mention huntingtin in your answer. (Collaborative Research Group, 1993)

Learning Objective 8-7 Discuss the role of the cerebellum and the reticular formation in the control of movement.

Read pages 284-288 and answer the following questions.

1. a. Describe the appearance of the cerebellum.

   b. Where does it send outputs?

   c. In general, what kind of deficits occur if the cerebellum is damaged?

2. Describe neural circuits found in these regions of the cerebellum. Identify the input(s) and output(s) to each region, and the types of movements that are controlled.

   a. Flocculonodular lobe (Study the green lines in Figure 8.22 in your text.)

   b. Vermis (Be sure to mention the fastigial nucleus. Study the blue lines in Figure 8.22.)

   c. Intermediate zone (Be sure to mention the interposed nuclei. Study the red lines in Figure 8.22.)

   d. Lateral zone (Be sure to mention the pontine nucleus. Study Figure 8.23 in your text.)

3. When motor cortex initiates a movement, how does the cerebellum respond? Be sure to mention the dentate nucleus.

4. List some of the movement deficit resulting from damage to the

   a. flocculonodular lobe or vermis.

   b. intermediate zone.

c. lateral zone. (Be sure to describe decomposition of movement and ballistic movements.)

5. a. According to Kornhuber (1974) what may be a primary function of the cerebellum?

   b. To illustrate this function of the cerebellum, compare the timing of the release of a ball by normal subjects and subjects with cerebellar lesions. (Timmann et al., 1999)

6. Describe research findings (Thach, 1978) that support earlier clinical observations (Holmes, 1939) that the cerebellum appears to integrate successive sequences of movements.

7. Where is the reticular formation located?

8. List some of the functions of the reticular formation.

   1. 3.

   2.

9. Describe the results of the following studies of the reticular formation.

   a. Stimulation of the mesencephalic locomotor region (Shik and Orlovsky, 1976)

   b. Recordings from single neurons in freely moving cats (Siegel and McGinty, 1977)

10. To review the movement of the motor system, follow the description in the interim summary of your text.

Lesson II Self Test

1. Apraxia is the inability to
   a. properly imitate or produce a particular movement.
   b. benefit from practicing a skilled movement.
   c. perceive sequences of skilled movements.
   d. resume performing a skilled movement that has been interrupted.

2. Limb apraxia is assessed by asking a patient to
   a. perform a movement.
   b. describe how he or she would move in a particular situation.
   c. teach someone else a movement.
   d. list components of a motion in sequential order.

3. Patients with callosal apraxia are able to perform a requested movement with their right arm, but not their left because
   a. the lesion has paralyzed the left arm.
   b. most people are right handed and the lesion does not affect "handedness."
   c. the anterior corpus callosum has been damaged and the right and left frontal lobes can no longer communicate.
   d. Wernicke's area has been damaged and requests to perform a movement are only partially understood.

4. Patients with constructional apraxia have difficulty
   a. pantomiming particular actions.
   b. "constructing" the proper sequence of action when shown a series of pictures, in random order, of the components of a motion.
   c. controlling the movements of their hands and arms.
   d. building shapes using toy building blocks.

5. The primary deficit in constructional apraxia appears to involve

   a. motor impairment of the hands and arms.
   b. the ability to perceive and imagine geometric shapes.
   c. difficulty in sequencing of actions.
   d. the inability to follow instructions.

6. The components of the basal ganglia are the

   a. ventrolateral nucleus, the ventral anterior nucleus, and the pontine nucleus.
   b. premotor cortex, the primary motor cortex, and the supplementary motor area.
   c. the globus pallidus, the substantia nigra, and the subthalamic nuclei.
   d. caudate nucleus, the putamen, and the globus pallidus.

7. The _____ pathway of the cortical-basal loop, which includes the _____, has an _____ net effect on the neurons in the motor cortex.

   a. direct; GP_i; inhibitory.
   b. indirect; GP_e and subthalamic nucleus; excitatory.
   c. direct; GP_i; excitatory
   d. indirect; GP_i, inhibitory

8. Parkinson's disease is characterized by _____ movements and Huntington's disease is characterized by _____ movements.

   a. slow; jerky
   b. smooth; slow
   c. rigid; smooth
   d. slow; smooth

9. Huntington's disease is caused by a defective gene that

   a. causes the faulty conversion of MPTP into toxic MPP.
   b. results in abnormally high levels of GADPH.
   c. halts nitric oxide synthesis.
   d. produces a protein with an elongated stretch of glutamine.

10. The cerebellum consists of two _____ with the _____ located on the midline.

    a. lobes; intermediate zone
    b. zones; corpus callosum
    c. sets of nuclei; interposed nuclei
    d. hemispheres; vermis

11. If a patient complains to a physician that he or she has recently been having difficulty maintaining balance, the physician may suspect a lesion in the

    a. basal ganglia.
    b. lateral zone of the cerebellum.
    c. red nucleus.
    d. flocculonodular lobe of the cerebellum or the vermis.

12. Stimulation of the mesencephalic locomotor region of the reticular formation causes cats to

    a. sit down.
    b. tremble.
    c. pace.
    d. stare.

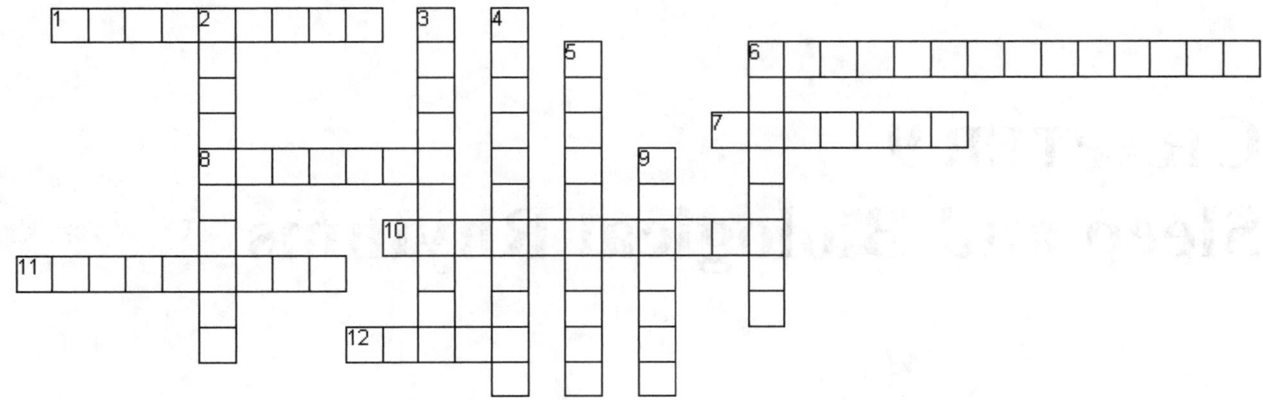

Across

1. Consists of overlapping strands of actin and myosin
6. Type of apraxia with difficulty in drawing or building with blocks
7. Limb movement that tends to bend joints
8. Difficulty in carrying out purposeful movements
10. Disease characterized by uncontrollable movements
11. Limb movement that tends to straighten joints
12. Tendon organ sensitive to stretch

Down

2. Muscle fiber that acts as stretch receptor
3. Muscle fiber responsible for contraction of skeletal muscle
4. Representation of body parts as they are represented in particular brain region
5. Disease characterized by a poverty of movements
6. Type of apraxia of the left hand; caused by damage to anterior corpus callosum
9. A nucleus of the basal ganglia

Answers for Self Tests

Lesson I

1. b Obj. 8-1
2. a Obj. 8-1
3. b Obj. 8-1
4. a Obj. 8-1
5. b Obj. 8-2
6. d Obj. 8-2
7. c Obj. 8-3
8. d Obj. 8-3
9. c Obj. 8-3
10. a Obj. 8-3
11. d Obj. 8-4
12. b Obj. 8-4

Lesson II

1. a Obj. 8-5
2. a Obj. 8-5
3. c Obj. 8-5
4. d Obj. 8-5
5. b Obj. 8-5
6. d Obj. 8-6
7. c Obj. 8-6
8. a Obj. 8-6
9. d Obj. 8-6
10. d Obj. 8-7
11. d Obj. 8-7
12. c Obj. 8-7

CHAPTER 9
Sleep and Biological Rhythms

Lesson I: Sleep and its Functions and Disorders of Sleep

Read the interim summary on pages 295-296 of your text to re-acquaint yourself with the material in this section.

Learning Objective 9-1 Describe the course of a night's sleep: its stages and their characteristics.

Read pages 291-295 and answer the following questions.

1. Explain why sleep is properly considered to be a behavior.

2. Briefly describe the appearance of a sleep laboratory.

3. List the physiological functions that are monitored during a night of sleep in a sleep laboratory and explain how they are measured. (See Figure 9.1 in your text.)

4. Name and describe the two activity patterns that characterize the waking EEG of a normal person and identify the behavioral state that each accompanies. (See Figure 9.2 in your text.)

   1.

   2.

5. Look at some of the characteristics of the stages of sleep of a normal person.

   a. Name and describe the characteristic brain activity of stage 1 sleep—the transition between wakefulness and sleep.

   b. List two characteristics of stage 2 sleep.

      1. 2.

   c. Describe sleep spindles, noting how often they occur.

   d. What may be their function? (Bowersox et al., 1985; Steriade, 1992; Nicholas et al., 2001)

   e. Describe K complexes, which occur during stage 2 sleep, and say what may trigger them.

f. According to Czisch et al. (2004), what function may K complexes triggered by auditory stimuli serve?

g. What characteristic of sleep do K complexes appear to precede? (De Gennaro et al., 2000)

6. If a subject who is sleeping is awakened and asked if he or she was asleep, what is often the response?

7. Name and describe the brain activity characteristic of stage 3 and stage 4 sleep.

8. a. What does the acronym REM stand for?

   b. Summarize the changes that occur during REM sleep in the

      1. EEG. 2. EOG.

      3. EMG.

9. Immediately review what you have just learned by completing the following table. (See Figure 9.2.)

Stage	*Name of EEG pattern*	*Description of EEG pattern*
Resting		
Alert		
Stage 1		
Stage 2		
Stage 3		
Stage 4		
REM sleep		

10. a. Which stages of sleep are called non-REM sleep?

    b. Which stages of sleep are called slow-wave sleep?

    c. Why do most investigators consider slow-wave sleep and REM sleep to be more important than stages 1 and 2 sleep?

    d. What stimuli will cause a sleeper to awaken from stage 4 sleep?

    e. What stimuli will cause a sleeper to awaken from REM sleep?

11. Compare dreams that occur during REM with those that occur during slow-wave sleep.

12. Describe the typical pattern of sleep stages that occurs during a night's sleep. (See Figure 9.3 in your text.)

    a. Normal sleep alternates between what two kinds of sleep?

    b. Approximately how long is each cycle?

    c. How many periods of REM sleep occur each night?

    d. When does most slow-wave sleep occur?

e. Which sleep stage normally precedes a bout of REM sleep?

13. a. What name did Kleitman give to the mechanism that regulates both the alternating pattern of REM and slow-wave sleep and the activity cycle during waking? (Kleitman 1982)

b. What observation of infant behavior first suggested the existence of this 90-minute activity cycle? (Kleitman, 1961)

14. Explain how a response of male subjects that occurs during REM sleep has been used to assess the causes of impotence. (Karacan et al., 1978; Singer and Weiner, 1996)

15. Review by listing the principal characteristics of slow-wave and REM sleep in the table below, and then compare this table with Table 9.1 in your text.

REM Sleep	Slow-Wave Sleep

16. Why is it incorrect to assert that sleep is a state of unconsciousness?

17. a. In which region of the brain is cerebral blood flow during REM sleep high? (Madsen et al., 1991; Braun et al., 1998)

b. In which region of the brain is cerebral blood flow during REM sleep low? (Madsen et al., 1991; Braun et al., 1998)

c. What does this pattern reflect?

d. How may this pattern correlate with the content of dreams during REM sleep? (Hobson, 1988; Melges, 1982)

18. a. After recording eye movements during REM sleep, Roffwarg and colleagues awakened the sleepers and asked them to describe the dreams they had just had. How did their dream descriptions correlate with their recorded eye movements? (Roffwarg et al., 1962)

b. When does a particular EEG wave that accompanies eye movements made during REM sleep also occur? (Miyauchi et al., 1990)

c. When does a particular EEG wave that accompanies eye movements made during REM fail to occur? (Miyauchi et al., 1990)

d. What does this finding suggest about the origin of this wave?

e. What other brain mechanisms may be active during a dream? (McCarley and Hobson, 1979; Hong et al., 1996)

19. During which stage of sleep do the most terrifying nightmares occur? (Fisher et al., 1970)
20. To review: Some of the most important characteristics of the stages of sleep are outlined in the interim summary.

Read the interim summary on page 300 of your text to re-acquaint yourself with the material in this section.

Learning Objective 9-2 Discuss insomnia, sleeping medications, and sleep apnea.

Read pages 296-297 and answer the following questions.

1. Describe insomnia, including its incidence, problems of definition, and most important cause. (Ancoli-Israel and Roth, 1999)

2. Explain how the use of sleeping medication often leads to

   a. drug tolerance and a withdrawal effect. (Weitzman, 1981)

   b. drug dependency insomnia. (Kales et al., 1979)

3. Briefly explain why self-reports of insomnia must be regarded skeptically. (Rosa and Bonnet, 2000; U.S. Institute of Medicine, 1979)

4. What is the appropriate goal of sleeping medication?
5. a. Describe sleep apnea. Carefully explain the change in blood levels of carbon dioxide and its effect.

   b. What is a frequent cause of sleep apnea and how is it corrected? (Sher, 1990; Piccirillo et al., 2000)

Learning Objective 9-3 Discuss narcolepsy and problems associated with REM and slow-wave sleep.

Read pages 297-300 and answer the following questions.

1. Describe the four symptoms of narcolepsy.

   a. Sleep attack

   b. Cataplexy

   c. Sleep paralysis

   d. Hypnagogic hallucination

2. Describe the sleep patterns of people with narcolepsy.

3. a. What is the cause of human narcolepsy? (Mignot, 1998)

   b. Carefully explain how a mutation of a specific gene leads to canine narcolepsy? (See Figure 9.5 in your text. Lin et al., 1999)

4. Summarize research on abnormalities in the hypocretin system that produce narcolepsy in

   a. mice. (Chemelli et al., 1999; Hara et al., 2001)

   b. rats. (Geraschchenko et al., 2001, 2003)

5. Briefly summarize the results of analyses of the cerebrospinal fluid of nine patients with narcolepsy and the presumed cause of their condition. (Nishino et al., 2000)

   a. Seven patients

   b. The other two patients

6. To see videos of narcoleptic dogs, mice, and people watch Animation 9.1.

7. Describe the hypocretin level of a patient who developed narcolepsy

   a. as a child. (Peyron et al., 2000)

   b. after a stroke that damaged the hypothalamus. (Scammell et al., 2001)

8. Which kinds of drugs are used to treat the symptoms of narcolepsy? (For example, Vgontzas and Kales, 1999)

9. a. What happens when people suffering from REM-sleep behavior disorder dream? (Schenck et al., 1986)

   b. What are two causes of this condition? (Schenck et al., 1996; Boeve et al., 2001; Culebras and Moore, 1989)

   c. How is it treated? (Schenck et al., 1996)

10. Describe four maladaptive behaviors that may occur during slow-wave sleep, noting any association with sleep stages, who is most susceptible, and what the best treatments are.

    1.

    2.

3.

4.

Read the interim summary on pages 305-306 of your text to re-acquaint yourself with the material in this section.

Learning Objective 9-4 Review the hypothesis that sleep serves as a period of restoration by discussing the effects of sleep deprivation, exercise, and mental activity and explain the functions of REM sleep.

Read pages 300-305 and answer the following questions.

1. Sleep is a ______________ phenomenon among ______________. However, only warm-blooded vertebrates experience ______________ sleep.
2. Summarize evidence that sleep is more than an adaptive response and may be physiologically necessary.
   a. Describe the sleep patterns of the Indus dolphin. (Pilleri, 1979)

   b. Study Figure 9.6 in your text and describe the sleep patterns of the cerebral hemispheres of the bottlenose dolphin. (Mukhametov, 1984)

3. Explain why these unusual sleep patterns suggest that sleep is more than an adaptive response.

4. Outline the rationale for using sleep deprivation to study the functions of sleep.

5. What did a review of over fifty sleep studies indicate about the effects of sleep deprivation on the ability to perform physical exercise, on physiological stress, and on cognitive abilities? (Horne, 1978)

6. Summarize the experience of a teenager who obtained a place in the *Guinness Book of World Records* by comparing
   a. the total number of hours of his enforced wakefulness with the total number of hours he slept during the three days following his record attempt.
   b. the percentage of recovery of stage 1 and 2 sleep, slow-wave (stage 4), and REM sleep. (Gulevich et al., 1966)

   c. the importance of each sleep stage.

7. Summarize research results that suggest that during stage 4 sleep the body and brain are resting.
   a. Cerebral metabolic rate and cerebral blood flow during stage 4 sleep (Sakai et al., 1979; Buchsbaum et al., 1989; Maquet, 1995)

   b. Amount of activity during waking and the subsequent level of delta waves during stage 4 sleep and what this comparison may indicate

   c. Behavior if awakened from stage 4 sleep
   d. Effect of missing a night's sleep on cognitive abilities (Harrison and Horne, 1998, 1999)

8. a. According to Siegel (2003), what may happen during wakefulness that necessitates a period of rest for the brain? Be sure to refer to oxidative stress in your answer.

   b. What evidence suggests harmful effects of prolonged sleep deprivation? (Ramanathan et al., 2002)

9. a. Fatal familial insomnia, an inherited neurological disorder, results from damage to which part of the brain? Sforza et al., 1995; Gallassi et al., 1996; Montagna et al., 2003)

   b. What are the first symptoms of this disorder? the later symptoms?

10. a. Describe the apparatus, shown in Figure 9.7 in your text, and the procedure developed to keep rats awake and exercising. Be sure to use the term *yoked control* in your answer. (Rechtschaffen et al., 1983; 1989; Rechtschaffen and Bergman, 1995, 2002)

    b. How successful were the experimenters in producing sleep deprivation?

    c. Summarize the effects of sleep deprivation on both the experimental (sleep-deprived) rats and the yoked-control rats.

    d. How could the lives of the experimental animals be extended? (Everson and Wehr, 1993)

    e. What do these results suggest about the need for sleep?

11. Explain the rationale for evaluating a possible restorative function of sleep by studying the effects of daytime activity on nighttime sleep.

12. Summarize changes in slow-wave sleep of

    a. healthy subjects after six weeks of bed rest. (Ryback and Lewis, 1971)

    b. completely immobile quadriplegics and paraplegics. (Adey et al., 1968)

13. a. What is the effect of tasks that demand mental activity and alertness on the brain?

    b. In what part of the brain is the effect most significant? (Roland, 1984)

    c. What do these results suggest about the function of sleep?

    d. Describe other research that supports this interpretation. (Kattler et al., 1994)

14. a. Describe how Horne and Minard (1985) studied the effects on sleep of increased mental activity that did not increase physical activity.

    b. What changes were observed in their slow-wave sleep that night, and what do the results suggest about the function of sleep?

15. Review the physiological changes that occur during REM sleep to
    a. the eyes.
    b. the heart rate.
    c. breathing.
    d. the brain.
16. a. When subjects are deprived of REM sleep, what do researchers observe
        1. as deprivation progresses? (Dement, 1960)
        2. a few days later, when subjects are permitted to sleep normally? Be sure to use the term *rebound phenomenon* in your answer.

    b. What do these results suggest about a necessary amount of REM sleep?
17. Briefly state the hypothesis concerning the function of REM sleep that falls into each of these categories.
    a. Brain development (Roffwarg et al., 1966 ; Petre-Quadens and De Lee, 1974; Inoue et al., 1986))

    b. Learning (Greenberg and Pearlman, 1974; Crick and Mitchison, 1983, 1995)
18. Describe two experimental procedures used to study the effects of REM sleep on learning.
19. What may be the role of REM sleep in learning in studies using the first procedure? Cite research to support your answer. (Smith, 1996)
20. Describe how Bloch et al. (1977), using the second procedure, studied the effect of learning on the REM sleep of rats.
    a. What task were rat subjects taught to perform?
    b. Study Figure 9.8 in your text and describe how subsequent REM sleep was related to
        1. the training experience.
        2. daily performance.
        3. the well-learned task.
21. a. How does REM sleep deprivation affect human learning and remembering, and how does learning affect REM sleep?

    b. Compare the amount of REM sleep of retarded children, gifted children, and normal children. (Dujardin et al., 1990)

    c. How does the amount of REM sleep of college students change during exam week? (Smith and Lapp, 1991)

Read the interim summary on pages 318-319 of your text to re-acquaint yourself with the material in this section.

Learning Objective 9-5 Evaluate evidence that the onset and amount of sleep is chemically controlled, and describe the neural control of arousal.

Read pages 306-311 and answer the following questions.

1. Cite evidence that indicates that sleep is regulated. (Karacan et al., 1970)
2. Briefly explain how sleep might be triggered chemically by either a sleep-promoting substance or a wakefulness-promoting substance. (Study Figure 9.9 in your text.)

3. Look at some chemicals that may regulate sleep.
   a. Review research on the sleep patterns of bottlenose dolphins. (Mukhametov, 1984) What is the effect of depriving the dolphin of sleep in only one hemisphere? (Oleksenko et al., 1992)

   b. If sleep is chemically controlled, what do these results suggest about where the chemicals are produced and where they circulate?

4. a. The primary nutrient of the brain is _______________. If the brain uses it more quickly than it can be supplied in the blood, extra nutrients in the form of _______________ are supplied by the _______________. An increase in the metabolism of this substance causes a rise in the level of _______________, which is a _______________ with _______________ effects.
   b. When the level of adenosine rises, how is the next night's sleep affected?
   c. When the level of adenosine rises, how is the glycogen production affected?

   d. If wakefulness is prolonged, what other changes occur?

   e. What evidence supports the adenosine hypothesis? (Benington et al., 1995)

5. Define *arousal* in your own words.

6. List five neurotransmitters that play a some role in arousal.
   1.
   2.
   3.
   4.
   5.
7. Look at each of these in turn. Where are groups of acetylcholinergic neurons that produce activation located? (Jones, 1990; Steriade, 1996)
   1.
   2.
   3.
8. a. How do acetylcholinergic agonists affect EEG signs of cortical arousal? (Vanderwolf, 1992)

   b. How do acetylcholinergic antagonists affect EEG signs of cortical arousal? (Vanderwolf, 1992)

9. What were the results of a comparison of acetylcholine levels in the striatum, hippocampus and frontal cortex and the level of an animal's arousal? (Day et al., 1991)

10. a. How did electrical stimulation of a region of the dorsal pons affect the level of acetylcholine in the cerebral cortex? (Rasmusson et al., 1994)

    b. Explain how and why this effect can be eliminated.

11. Amphetamine is a _______________ _______________ that produces _______________ and _______________.

12. Explain why the neurons of the locus coeruleus are affected by drugs like amphetamine. (To see the location of the locus coeruleus, study Figure 9.10 in your text.)

13. a. Study Figure 9.11 in your text and either describe or draw the changes in the firing rate of noradrenergic neurons in the locus coeruleus during various stages of sleep and waking. (Aston-Jones and Bloom, 1981a)

    b. What do these differences in firing rate suggest about the control of REM sleep?

14. a. Describe the task Aston-Jones et al. (1994) taught monkeys.

    b. How did their performance correspond to the rate of firing of noradrenergic LC neurons?

    c. What do the differences in firing rate of these neurons suggest about their role?

15. a. Almost all of the brain's serotonergic neurons are found in the _______________ _______________. (See Figure 9.12 in your text.)

    b. Where do their axons project?

16. a. How is cortical arousal affected by stimulation of the raphe nuclei? (Peck and Vanderwolf, 1991)

    b. How is cortical arousal affected by administration of PCPA? (Peck and Vanderwolf, 1991)

    c. Compare the response of noradrenergic and serotonergic neurons to external stimuli that produce pain or induce stress. (Jacobs et al., 1990)

17. According to Jacobs and Fornal (1999), how may serotonergic neurons be involved in an animal's ongoing activities?

18. Study Figure 9.13 in your text and either describe or draw the changes in the firing rate of serotonergic neurons during waking and slow-wave and REM sleep. (Trulson and Jacobs, 1979)

19. a. Where are histaminergic neurons located?

b. Where do they project and how do they influence these regions? (Khateb et al., 1995; Brown et al., 2001)

20. Summarize the effect on waking and sleep of
    a. injections of drugs that prevent the synthesis of histamine or block histamine H_1 receptors. (Lin et al., 1988)

    b. infusions of histamine into the basal forebrain region. (Ramesh et al., 2004)

21 a. When is the activity of histaminergic neurons high? (Steininger et al., 1996)
   b. When is the activity of histaminergic neurons low? (Steininger et al., 1996)

22. Explain why the control of wakefulness is not controlled by histamine alone. (Parmentier et al., 2002)

23. According to Gerashchenko et al. (2004), what is the role of the body's five systems of arousal?

24. a. Where are neurons that secrete hypocretin (orexin) located, and where do they terminate? (Saper et al., 2001)

    b. How does hypocretin affect these regions? (Burlet et al., 2002)

25. a. What may be the general effect of hypocretin on motor activity? (Seigel, 2004; Kiyashchenko et al., 2002)

    b. How did infusion of hypocretin into the locus coeruleus and medial medulla affect muscle tone? (Kiyashchenko et al., 2001; Mileykovskiy et al., 2002)

Lesson I Self Test

1. The waking EEG is characterized by
   a. occasional delta activity.
   b. periods of alpha and beta activity.
   c. regular changes in heart rate, blood pressure and respiration.
   d. bursts of K complexes.

2. A bout of REM sleep
   a. almost always follows a period of slow-wave sleep.
   b. occurs four or five times during an 8-hour sleep and lasts approximately 90 minutes.
   c. contains more than 50 percent delta activity.
   d. is the deepest stage of sleep.

3. Evidence suggests that many of the brain mechanisms that become active during a dream
   a. continue after the dream ends and are responsible for the general inability to recall dreams.
   b. occasionally become overactive, resulting in terrifying dreams.
   c. are those that would become active if the events of the dream were actually occurring.
   d. are related to the duration rather than the content of a dream.

4. The right amount of sleep is
   a. only obtained by infants.
   b. whatever seems to be enough.
   c. assured with sleeping medication.
   d. infrequently obtained by insomniacs.

5. Sleep apnea is
   a. a form of drug dependency insomnia.
   b. a side affect of sleeping medications.
   c. a period of sleep without dreams.
   d. the inability to sleep and breathe at the same time.

6. During a cataplectic attack, the individual
   a. awakens gasping for breath.
   b. tries to act out dreams.
   c. is unconscious.
   d. is overcome by muscular paralysis.

7. A person afflicted with REM-sleep behavior disorder
   a. is not paralyzed during dreaming and acts out the dream.
   b. dreams while lying awake paralyzed.
   c. becomes paralyzed or remains paralyzed for several minutes just before or just after otherwise normal REM sleep.
   d. experiences profound REM sleep paralysis and does not exhibit the characteristic rapid eye movements that accompany dreaming.

8. When sleep-deprived subjects are permitted to sleep normally, they
   a. regain most of the stage 1 sleep they lost.
   b. do not regain all the sleep they lost.
   c. experience a nearly equal percentage of recovery for all stages of sleep.
   d. go directly into REM sleep from waking.

9. The effects of forced exercise using the yoked-control method
   a. increased the needs for REM sleep on recovery nights following the experiment in all subjects.
   b. reduced the total sleep time of experimental and control subjects about the same amount.
   c. did not lead to unusually high levels of stress hormones.
   d. are exaggerated when subjects are fed an enriched diet.

10. A rebound phenomenon
    a. indicates that REM sleep has the same function as slow-wave sleep.
    b. occurs when REM sleep-deprived subjects are permitted to sleep normally.
    c. results when aspects of REM sleep intrude into wakefulness.
    d. suggests that REM sleep deprivation causes physiological harm.

11. The level of adenosine in the brain increases
    a. when glycogen is used to fuel the brain.
    b. when astrocytes renew their stock of glycogen.
    c. if the amount of delta activity during a night's sleep increases.
    d. if the amount of glucose in the blood supply increases.

12. _____ neurons are found in the _____, and _____ neurons are found in the _____.
    a. Noradrenergic; locus coeruleus; serotonergic neurons; tuberomammillary nucleus
    b. Acetylcholinergic; pons; histaminergic; basal forebrain
    c. Acetylcholinergic; locus coeruleus; noradrenergic; raphe nuclei
    d. Serotonergic; raphe nuclei; histaminergic; tuberomammillary nucleus

Lesson II: Physiological Mechanisms of Sleep and Waking and Biological Clocks

Read the interim summary on pages 318-319 to re-acquaint yourself with the material in this section.

Learning Objective 9-6 Discuss the neural control of slow-wave and REM sleep.

Read pages 311-318 and answer the following questions.

1. Summarize research results using a variety of experimental procedures that strongly suggest that the preoptic area just rostral to the hypothalamus is particularly important in the control of sleep.
   a. Begin with lesion studies. How did the destruction of the preoptic area affect the sleep and health of rats? (Nauta, 1946) of cats? (McGinty and Sterman, 1968)

b. Turn to stimulation studies. How did electrical stimulation of this region affect the behavior of freely moving cats? (Sterman and Clemente, 1962a, 1962b)

2. Describe the findings of the following research to determine where these neurons are found.

   a. Fos protein levels in a cluster of neurons in the VLPA in sleeping animals (Sherin et al., 1996)

   b. The effects of excitotoxic lesions in this cluster on sleep (Lu et al., 2000)

   c. The activity of single neurons in the VLPA during sleep, and during and following sleep deprivation (Szymusiak et al., 1998)

   d. Neuron activity during sleep in another location (Gong et al., 2000; Suntsova et al., 2002)

3. a. What did anatomical and histochemical studies indicate about projections and inhibitory secretions of neurons in the VLPA? (Sherin et al., 1998)

   b. Taken together, what do all these results suggest is a necessary condition for sleep to occur?

4. List the regions which send inhibitory inputs to the VLPA as well as the neurotransmitters that also contribute to inhibition. (Chou et al., 2002)

   1.

   2.

   3.

5. a. According to Saper et al. (2001), what may be the role of reciprocal inhibition in the regulation of sleep? (Study Figure 9.14 in your text.)

   b. Discuss an advantage and disadvantage of a sleep/waking flip-flop arrangement.

   c. What important role may hypocretinergic neurons play in the flip-flop arrangement? (Saper et al., 2001)

   d. How is the firing of these neurons affected by enforced wakefulness? (Study Figure 9.15 in your text. Estabrooke et al., 2001)

   e. How is the stability of a flip-flop arrangement affected by a targeted mutation against the hypocretin gene? (Mochizuki et al., 2004)

6. What two factors appear to control a feeling of sleepiness?

   1. 2.

7. a. When does the level of adenosine in the brain increase? (Dunwiddie and Masino, 2001)

   b. What is the behavioral effect of an increase and where may adenosine exert this effect?

c. As measured by microdialysis, how do the levels of adenosine change during wakefulness and sleep, and which brain region is involved? (See Figure 9.16 in your text. Porkka-Heiskanen et al., 1997, Porkka-Heiskanen et al., 2000)

d. What behavioral change occurs if

1. an adenosine agonist is infused into the basal forebrain? (Strecker et al., 2000)
2. adenosine receptors there are disrupted? (Thakkar et al., 2003)

8. Explain why the effect of adenosine on the VLPA must be indirect. Summarize research findings to support your answer. (See Figure 9.17 in your text. Scammell et al., 2001; Chamberlin et al., 2003)

9. a. List some of the changes in the sleep of people as they age.

b. Summarize research results that suggest a cause for these changes. (Murillo-Rodriguez et al., 2004)

10. List again the characteristics of REM sleep that you have already studied.

1.
2.
3.
4.
5.

11. a. What is the earliest component of REM sleep recorded from laboratory animals?

b. Describe PGO waves and explain the name. (See Figure 9.18 in your text.)

c. Why can we only speculate that PGO waves occur in humans?

d. Where is the executive mechanism that turns on the components of REM sleep located and what neurotransmitter is involved?

e. Which regions inhibit REM sleep and what neurotransmitters are involved?

12. a. Why do people who have been exposed to organophosphate insecticides engage in more REM sleep? (Stoyva and Metcalf, 1968)

b. How was the REM sleep of human subjects in a controlled experiment affected by an acetylcholinergic agonist? (Sitaram et al., 1978)

c. How was the REM sleep of human subjects in a controlled experiment affected by an acetylcholinergic antagonist? (Sitaram et al., 1978)

13. a. When are the levels of acetylcholine released by the terminal buttons in the cerebral cortex of the cat highest? (Jasper and Tessier, 1969)

b. When are the levels of acetylcholine released by the terminal buttons in the cerebral cortex of the cat lowest? (Jasper and Tessier, 1969)

c. Use one word to describe the rate of glucose metabolism during REM sleep in brain regions that contain ACh-secreting neurons or receive input from them. (Lydic et al., 1991)

d. What do these results suggest is the role of these neurons in REM sleep?

14. _______________ neurons in the dorsolateral pons play a central role in triggering the onset of REM sleep. Contained primarily in two _______________, this region is referred to as the _____________________ _______________. (Jones and Beaudet, 1987. See Figure 9.19 in your text.)

15. a. At what times, do the neurons in the peribrachial area fire at a high rate? (The firing of a single cell is shown in Figure 9.20 in your text. El Mansari et al., 1989)

b. What event might the increased activity of these acetylcholinergic neurons initiate?

c. How did the amount of destruction caused by lesions of the peribrachial area affect the amount of REM sleep of subjects? (Webster and Jones, 1988)

16. List three regions to which acetylcholinergic neurons of the peribrachial area project. (Cornwall et al., 1990; Bolton et al., 1993)

1.

2.

3.

17. a. What is the pharmacological effect of carbachol? the behavioral effect if it is infused into the MPRF of a cat? (See Figure 9.21 in your text. Katayama et al., 1986; Callaway et al., 1987)

b. What is the behavioral effect if it is infused into the MPRF of a cat? (See Figure 9.21 in your text. Katayama et al., 1986; Callaway et al., 1987)

c.. Why? (Quattrochi et al., 1989)

d. Microdialysis studies have shown an _______________ in acetylcholine levels in this region during REM sleep. (Kodama et al., 1990)

e. What is the effect of lesions of the MPRF on REM sleep? (Siegel, 1989)

18. What parts of the brain are responsible for the following components of REM sleep?

a. Cortical arousal

b. PGO waves (Sakai and Jouvet, 1980; Steriade et al., 1990)

c. Rapid eye movements (Webster and Jones, 1988)

19. a. When Jouvet (1972) made a lesion just caudal to the peribrachial area of the dorsolateral pons of a laboratory cat, what behavioral change did he observe?

b. What, therefore, is the function of these neurons?

c. Describe more precisely the location of the neurons that Jouvet destroyed.

d. Where do their axons project? (Sakai, 1980)

e. Where do axons from the magnocellular nucleus project? What kind of synapses do they form here? (Morales et al., 1987)

20. Review research that supports the role of this pathway in REM sleep paralysis.

a. How do lesions of the subcoerulear region affect REM sleep and its accompanying paralysis? (Shouse and Siegel, 1992)

b. When do single neurons in the magnocellular nucleus become active? (Kanamori et al., 1980)

c. What is the effect on REM sleep paralysis of electrical stimulation of the magnocellular nucleus? (Sakai, 1980) lesions? (Schenkel and Siegel, 1989)

d. Identify the inhibitory neurotransmitter found in the magnocellular nucleus and its likely function. (Fort et al., 1990)

21. What does this presence of this inhibitory mechanism suggest about the importance of the motor components of dreaming?

22. a. Immediately review the neural circuitry of REM sleep shown in Figure 9.22 in your text.

b. The first event preceding REM sleep is the activation of _______________ neurons in the _______________ area of the _______________ _______________.

c. Identify the regions these neurons, either directly or through their projections, affect to produce

1. rapid eye movements.
2. PGO waves.
3. muscular paralysis.
4. genital changes.
5. cortical activation.

23. Briefly explain how the activity of serotonergic neurons in the locus coeruleus and the dorsal raphe nucleus may be involved in REM sleep. (Study Figures 9.23 and 9.24 in your text. Lydic et al., 1983)

24. Finally, summarize research results that suggest that serotonin and norepinephrine inhibit REM sleep. (Portas et al., 1996; Bier and McCarley, 1994)

Read the interim summary on page 326 of your text to re-acquaint yourself with the material in this section.

Learning Objective 9-7 Describe circadian rhythms and discuss research on the role of the suprachiasmatic nucleus in the control of these rhythms.

Read pages 319-322 and answer the following questions.

1. Define *circadian rhythms* in your own words.

2. Study the record of wheel-running activity of a rat under various conditions of illumination presented in Figure 9.25 in your text. Use this example to continue your explanation of daily rhythms.
   a. During which portion of a normal day/night cycle is the rat active?
   b. When the "day" was artificially advanced 6 hours, what happened to the rat's activity cycle?
   c. What effects did constant dim light have on the rat's activity?
   d. Because there were no stimuli in the rat's environment that varied throughout the day, what must have been the source of rhythmicity?
3. a. What term describes the effect of light on daily activity cycles?
   b. How do pulses of light affect the activity cycles of animals kept in constant darkness? (Aschoff, 1979)
4. Describe the circadian rhythm of a modern human and how it changes under constant illumination.
5. Circadian rhythms are controlled by biological clocks. Name the structure that contains the primary biological clock of the rat. (See Figure 9.26 in your text. Moore and Eichler, 1972; Stephan and Zucker, 1972)
6. How do lesions of the SCN affect
   a. running, drinking, and hormonal secretions?
   b. the timing of sleep cycles? (Ibuka and Kawamura, 1975; Stephan and Nuñez, 1977)
   c. total amount of sleep?
7. a. What region sends a direct projection of fibers to the SCN? (Hendrickson et al., 1972; Aronson et al., 1993)
   b. What is the name of the pathway? (Again, look at Figure 9.26.)
8. a. What changes, if any, occurred in the circadian rhythms of mice
      1. with targeted mutations against genes necessary for the production of rods and cones?
      2. whose eyes had been removed? (Freedman et al., 1999)
   b. What do these results suggest about the way diurnal rhythms are synchronized?
   c. What is that mechanism, where is it found, and what is it called? (Provencio et al., 2000)
   d. Where do the axons of these cells terminate? (Berson et al., 2002; Hattar et al., 2002; Gooley et al., 2003)
   e. What response to light may this chemical regulate? (See Figure 9.27 in your text.)
9. a. What protein is produced when light pulses reset an animal's circadian rhythm?
   b. What does the presence of this protein further indicate about the effects of light? (Rusak et al., 1990, 1992)

c. If the glutamate receptors in the connections between the retina and the SCN are blocked by drugs, how are the effects of a period of bright light altered? (Abe et al., 1991; Vindlacheruvu et al., 1992)

10. a. Look briefly at the anatomy of the SCN. List the two regions and then describe their location. (Moore et al., 2002)

    1.

    2.

    b. Carefully describe the flow of information to and through the SCN.

    c. Describe the path of the output of the SCN and list the three nearby regions where shell neurons of the SCN axons terminate.

    1. 3.

    2.

    d. Where do neurons in these three regions further connect? (Deurveilher and Semba, 2005)

11. Describe the connections of the SPZ that suggest its role in the control of sleep and body temperature. (See Figure 9.28 in your text. Lu et al., 2001)

12. How did Lehman et al., (1987) abolish the circadian rhythms of subject animals and then reestablish them?

13. a. After destroying the SCN of hamsters to abolish their circadian rhythms, Silver and her colleagues transplanted SCN tissue in semipermeable capsules in to the subjects. Why did they encapsulate the transplants? (Silver et al., 1996)

    b. What changes, if any, occurred in the subjects' circadian rhythms?

14. What notion about the control of circadian rhythms do these research results support?

Learning Objective 9-8 Discuss the time base of the circadian clock, control of seasonal rhythms, and changes in circadian rhythms caused by work schedules and travel.

Read pages 322-326 and answer the following questions.

1. Before continuing, briefly review evidence that the SCN contains a circadian clock.

2. a. Compare autoradiographs of rats, shown in Figure 9.29 in your text, who were injected with 2-DG either during the day or at night. (Schwartz and Gainer, 1977)

   b. Which rats showed a higher metabolic rate of the SCN and what does that indicate?

3. a. Compare the peak activity periods of individual SCN cells kept alive in a tissue culture shown in Figure 9.30 in your text. (Welsh et al., 1995)

   b. Suggest two locations for the "ticking" of the biological clock, noting which one appears to be accurate.

4. a. If particular neurons in the core region of the SCN containing a calcium-binding protein are destroyed, what is the effect on neurons in the shell region and cycles of behavior and hormone secretion? (See Figure 9.31 in your text. LeSauter and Sliver, 1999; Kriegsfeld et al., 2004)

   b. How can normal functioning of the SCN be restored in animals with SCN lesions?

   c. What do the results suggest about the necessary conditions for the normal control of circadian rhythms within the SCN?

5. a. Outline the long-held explanation for the synchronized activity of SCN neurons which is diagrammed in Figure 9.32 in your text.

   b. Describe the results of confirming research on the interaction between genes and their products that may be responsible for the intracellular ticking in the common fruit fly and mammals. (Shearman et al., 2000; Reppert and Weaver, 2001; Van Gelder et al., 2003)

   c. How do brief periods of bright light affect levels of these proteins? (Yan and Silver, 2004; Aschoff, 1979)

6. a. Why did researchers insert a luciferase reporter gene into a strain of mice? (Yamaguchi et al., 2003)

   b. What did photographs of a slice of the SCN of the treated mice indicate? (See Animation 9.2.)

   c. How was the cycling stopped? restored?

7. a. What were the results of an analysis of the SCN of the brains of deceased humans? (Hoffman, 2003)

   b. What do these results suggest about the control of circadian rhythms in humans and other mammals?

8. a. To illustrate the function of the interlocking feedback loops, describe the symptoms and the cause of advanced sleep phase syndrome. (Toh et al., 2001)

   b. Describe an opposite disorder, delayed sleep phase syndrome. (Ebisawa et al., 2001)

9. Review the physiological control of seasonal rhythms.

   a. What is the relationship between the male hamster's testosterone cycle and the length of day?

   b. What effect do lesions of the SCN have on this cycle? What is a possible explanation for this effect? (Rusak and Morin, 1976)

   c. Identify the gland and the hormone it secretes that control seasonal rhythms. (See Figure 9.33 in your text. Bartness et al., 1993; Moore, 1995)

d. Briefly describe how the SCN and this gland interact to control seasonal rhythms.

e. What kind of procedures can disrupt seasonal rhythms?

f. Explain why transplants of fetal suprachiasmatic nuclei will restore circadian, but not seasonal, rhythms. (Ralph and Lehman, 1991)

10. a. Shift work or travel across several time zones produce a desynchrony between the internal _______________ and the external _______________.

b. In general, what is the best way to ease the transition? (Dijk et al., 1995; Boulos et al., 1995; Horowitz et al., 2001)

11. a. How does melatonin affect receptors in the SCN? (Gillette and McArthur, 1995; Starkey et al., 1995)

b. If melatonin is used to regulate circadian rhythms, what is the best time to administer it? Why? (Arendt et al., 1995; Deacon and Arendt, 1996)

Lesson II Self Test

1. Activation of the VLPA results in

   a. behavioral arousal.
   b. difficulty remaining asleep.
   c. total insomnia.
   d. sleep.

2. An important function of hypocretinergic neurons may be

   a. to keep an animal asleep.
   b. to stabilize the flip-flop circuit that controls sleep and waking.
   c. to maintain alertness during times of increased mental activity.
   d. to increase sleep by regulating the release of adenosine.

3. PGO waves

   a. are the first sign of REM sleep during a night's sleep.
   b. decrease with the onset of REM sleep.
   c. inhibit the muscular paralysis associated with REM sleep.
   d. indicate a change in cerebral metabolism.

4. REM sleep is initiated by a group of neurons in the _____ that secrete _____.

   a. raphe nuclei; serotonin
   b. locus coeruleus; norepinephrine
   c. dorsal pons; acetylcholine
   d. thalamus; adenosine

5. Neurons in the _____ send axons to the spinal cord, and this pathway may be responsible for the muscular paralysis that accompanies REM sleep.

   a. peribrachial area
   b. locus coeruleus
   c. magnocellular nucleus
   d. ventrolateral preoptic area

6. If a small amount of carbachol is infused into the MPRF, an animal will

   a. fail to become paralyzed during REM sleep.
   b. display some or all of the components of REM sleep.
   c. show a decrease in the amount of REM sleep during a night's sleep.

d. enter REM sleep almost immediately upon falling asleep.

7. How did the daily behavior of a rat change with constant dim illumination?

a. Periods of activity increased and periods of sleep decreased.
b. Food consumption increased with activity levels.
c. The biological clock ran slower; activity began about one hour later each day.
d. Body temperature increased slightly with constant light.

8. The primary biological clock of the rat is located in the

a. suprachiasmatic nucleus.
b. reticular formation.
c. locus coeruleus.
d. pons.

9. Researchers transplanted semipermeable capsules containing donor SCN tissue into animals whose SCN had been destroyed and

a. failed to reestablish circadian rhythms because synaptic connections with surrounding tissue were not established.
b. successfully reestablished circadian rhythms even though synaptic connections with surrounding tissue were not established.
c. failed to reestablish circadian rhythms because the donor tissue was rejected even though it had been encapsulated.
d. successfully reestablished circadian rhythms only when transplants were placed in the normal location of the SCN .

10. The "ticking" of the biological clock

a. and the control of sleep and waking cycles are complementary functions of the SCN.
b. occurs in the glial cells that surround the neurons of the SCN.
c. occurs in individual neurons of the SCN.
d. is a characteristic of circuits of neurons, not individual neurons.

11. The control of seasonal rhythms is a function of the

a. locus coeruleus.
b. paraventricular nucleus of the hypothalamus.
c. tuberomammillary nucleus.
d. pineal gland.

12. Taking melatonin _____ may help people adjust to the effects of shift work or jet-lag.

a. in the morning
b. at bedtime
c. beginning several days before a time change
d. whenever drowsiness occurs

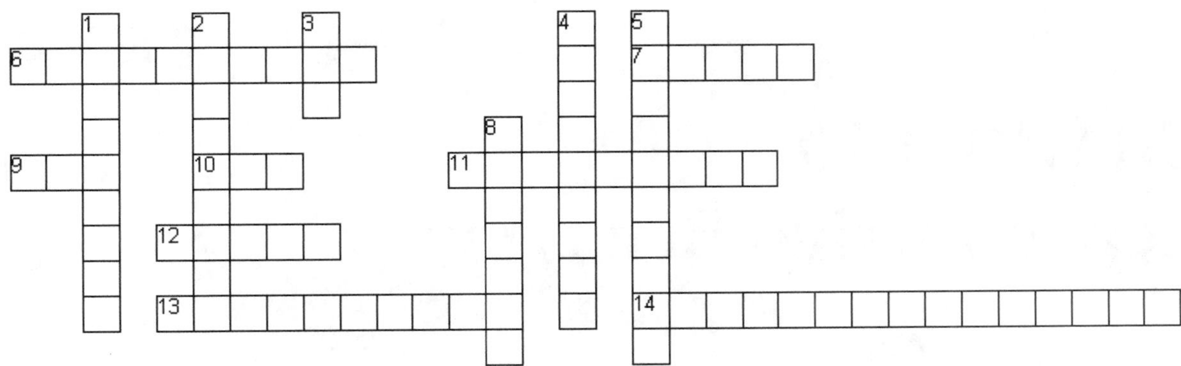

Across

6. Sleep disorder characterized by cessation of breathing while sleeping
7. Electrical brain activity of brain during relaxation
9. Electrical potential recorded from muscle
10. Wave that is first manifestation of REM sleep
11. Hormone that plays a role in circadian and seasonal rhythms
12. Electrical brain activity during deepest stages of slow-wave sleep
13. Peptide produced by neurons in hypothalamus; their destruction causes narcolepsy
14. Nucleus that contains the body's biological clock

Down

1. Stimulus that resets biological clock of daily rhythms
2. Narcolepsy symptom, complete paralysis during waking
3. Sleep characterized by muscular paralysis
4. Daily rhythmical change in behavior or body processes
5. Sleep disorder characterized by irresistible sleep
8. Increased REM sleep after REM sleep deprivation

Answers for Self Tests

Lesson I

1. b Obj. 9-1
2. a Obj. 9-1
3. c Obj. 9-1
4. b Obj. 9-2
5. d Obj. 9-2
6. d Obj. 9-3
7. a Obj. 9-3
8. b Obj. 9-4
9. c Obj. 9-4
10. b Obj. 9-4
11. a Obj. 9-5
12. d Obj. 9-5

Lesson II

1. d Obj. 9-6
2. b Obj. 9-6
3. a Obj. 9-6
4. c Obj. 9-6
5. c Obj. 9-6
6. b Obj. 9-6
7. c Obj. 9-7
8. a Obj. 9-7
9. b Obj. 9-8
10. c Obj. 9-8
11. d Obj. 9-8
12. b Obj. 9-8

CHAPTER 10
Reproductive Behavior

Lesson I: Sexual Development and Hormonal Control of Sexual Behavior

Read the interim summary on page 336 of your text to re-acquaint yourself with the material in this section.

Learning Objective 10-1 Describe mammalian sexual development and explain the factors that control it.

Read pages 329-335 and answer the following questions.

1. Define *sexually dimorphic behavior* in your own words and list several examples.

2. a. How many pairs of chromosomes do cells other than sperms and ova contain?

   b. Explain why gametes contain only one member of each pair of chromosomes.

3. a. How many types of sex chromosomes are there?

   b. What is the sex chromosome pattern for a female?

   c. What is the sex chromosome pattern for a male?

4. a. At what point is the sex of an offspring normally determined?

   b. The gamete from which parent determines the sex of an offspring? (See Figure 10.1 in your text.)

5. What event is responsible for sexual dimorphism?

6. a. List the three categories of sex organs.

   1. 2. 3.

   b. List the gonads.

   1. 2.

   c. What are the dual functions of the gonads?

   1. 2.

   d. What factor determines whether the initially identical gonads become ovaries or testes? (Sinclair et al., 1990; Smith, 1994; Koopman, 2001)

7. Explain the difference between organizational effects and activational effects of sex hormones.

8. Name the precursors of the male and female internal sex organs and the organs that develop from them. (Study Figure 10.2 in your text to see how the precursors of the internal sex organs continue to develop.)

   a. Male

   b. Female

9. a. List the two types of hormones secreted by the testes that determine whether the Müllerian system or the Wolffian system continues to develop and describe their effects.

      1.

      2.

   b. List the specific androgens responsible for masculinization.

      1. 2.

10. Be sure that you understand how hormones exert their effects on the body and then explain the cause and consequences of

    a. androgen insensitivity syndrome. (See Figure 10.3 in your text. Money and Ehrhardt, 1972; MacLean et al., 1995))

    b. persistent Müllerian duct syndrome. (Warne and Zajac, 1998)

11. What do people with Turner's syndrome reveal about the hormones necessary for the development of female internal and external sex organs? Explain your answer. (Knebelmann et al. 1991)

12. Stop to review what you have learned. The development of the external genitalia is shown in Figure 10.4 in your text. The hormonal control of the development of the internal genitalia is shown in Figure 10.5 in your text. Cover the right half of this figure including the triple arrows. Identify the hormones that are secreted by the newly developed testes or ovaries and describe their effect on the development of the internal sex organs and external genitalia.

13. Complete these statements.

    a. The primary sex characteristics include

    b. The secondary sex characteristics include

    c. Puberty begins when cells in the hypothalamus

    d. (See Figure 10.6 in your text.) Gonadotropin-releasing hormones in turn stimulate

    e. The two gonadotropic hormones are

f. Although the gonadotropic hormones are named for the effects they produce in the female,

14. a. What is the presumed reason for the fall in the age of puberty in developed countries? (Foster and Nagatani, 1999)

    b. What characteristic appears to influence whether a young girl experiences puberty earlier than normal? (Frisch, 1990)

    c. What characteristic appears to influence whether a young girl experiences puberty later than normal? (Frisch, 1990)

    d. What tissue secretes the peptide leptin?

    e. In addition to signaling the brain to suppress appetite, what appear to be another function of leptin? Cite research to support your answer. (Chehab et al. 1997)

15. Summarize the changes in the bodies of males and females that are initiated by gonadotropic hormones at puberty.

16. What evidence confirms that the bipotentiality of some secondary sex characteristics is lifelong.

17. To review: Table 10.1 in your text summarizes information about sex steroid hormones.

Read the interim summary on pages 349-350 of your text to re-acquaint yourself with the material in this section.

Learning Objective 10-2 Describe the hormonal control of the female reproductive cycle and of male and female sexual behavior.

Read pages 336-340 and answer the following questions.

1. What are several differences between the human menstrual cycle and the estrous cycle of other female mammals?

2. Study Figure 10.7 in your text and follow Animation 10.1 to see the menstrual cycle from beginning to end.
   a. Name the principal hormone that stimulates the growth of ovarian follicles.
   b. Name the hormone secreted by the maturing ovarian follicle.
   c. What changes begin to occur in the uterus in response to this hormone?
   d. What effect does this hormone have on the anterior pituitary gland?
   e. What does the hormone from the anterior pituitary gland do?
   f. After the ovum is released, what happens to the ruptured follicle?
   g. What hormones does this structure release?
   h. If the ovum is not fertilized or is fertilized too late, what changes occur?

3. List the three features common to all male sexual behavior:

1. 2. 3.

4. What is the refractory period?

5. What is the Coolidge effect and what may be its evolutionary importance?

6. What evidence indicates the importance of testosterone in male sexual behavior? (Bermant and Davidson, 1974)

7. a. Where is oxytocin produced?

   b. How does this hormone facilitate lactation?

   c. During orgasm, what are the effects of its release in females? (Carmichael et al., 1994; Carter, 1992)

   d. During orgasm, what are the effects of its release in males? (Carmichael et al., 1994; Carter, 1992)

8. a. Where is prolactin produced and what are the effects of its release in females?

   b. Where is prolactin produced and what are the effects of its release in males?

   c. What is one of the symptoms of hyperprolactinemia—the oversecretion of prolactin? (Foster et al., 1990)

   d. How is this condition treated? (De Rosa et al., 2004)

   e. What is the effect on male sexual behavior of injecting small amounts of prolactin into the MPA of male rats? (Mas et al., 1995)

9. a. Name the position that receptive females of many four-legged species will assume to facilitate copulation.

   b. List the two hormones required for the sexual response of a female rodent.

   1. 2.

   c. Which hormone "primes" the other? Explain. (Takahashi, 1990)

   d. Describe the response to males of female mice without estrogen receptors. (Rissman et al., 1997) without progesterone receptors. (Lydon et al., 1995)

10. List and briefly explain the effects that the sequence of estradiol followed by progesterone have on the female rat.

   1.

   2.

   3.

11. Define these terms in your own words.

   a. *behavioral defeminization*

   b. *behavioral masculinization*

12. Using these terms, explain the effects of the following treatments on sexual behavior.
    a. a male rat, castrated at birth and given no hormones, then given estradiol and progesterone in adulthood (Blaustein and Olster, 1989)
    b. an adult male, castrated in adulthood, then given estradiol and progesterone in adulthood
    c. an adult female rodent, ovariectomized at birth and given testosterone, then given estradiol and progesterone in adulthood
    d. an adult female, ovariectomized at birth and given testosterone, then given testosterone in adulthood (Breedlove, 1992; Carter, 1992)

13. Check your understanding of the organizational effects of androgens by studying Figure 10.8 in your text and then completing the blanks in the table below. Note that the order of the entries has been changed.
    a. Circle the entry that indicates the activational effect of estradiol and progesterone. Label it AE.
    b. Circle the entry that indicates evidence of behavioral defeminization. Label it BDF.
    c. Circle the entry that indicates evidence of behavioral masculinization. Label it BM.

Hormone Treatment			
Immediately after birth	*When rat is fully grown*	**Resulting Sexual Behavior**	
Testosterone	Testosterone	Female: __________	Male: __________
None	Testosterone	Female: __________	Male: __________
None	Estradiol + progesterone	Female: __________	Male: __________
Testosterone	Estradiol + progesterone	Female: __________	Male: __________

14. a. Circle the group of castrated rats treated with testosterone that showed more male mating behavior? Those castrated before they reached puberty or those castrated afterwards? (Schultz et al., 2004)
    b. When these same rats were later given estradiol and progesterone and tested with another male, how did they behave?
    c. What do these results suggest about the organizational effects of androgens?

Learning Objective 10-3 Describe the role of pheromones in reproductive and sexual behavior.

Read pages 340-342 and answer the following questions.

1. Pheromones transmit chemical messages from one _______________ to another, unlike hormones, which transmit messages from one part of the _______________ to another. Pheromones are usually detected through _______________. They can affect reproductive _______________ or _______________.
2. Describe each of the following phenomena, which affect reproductive physiology.

a. Lee-Boot effect (van der Lee and Boot, 1955)

b. Whitten effect (Whitten, 1959)

c. Vandenbergh effect (Vandenbergh et al., 1975)

d. Bruce effect (Bruce, 1960a, 1960b)

3. a. Name and describe the location of the sensory organ that mediates these four effects that pheromones have on reproductive cycles.

   b. Where do afferent axons from this organ project? (Wysocki, 1979. See Figure 10.9 in your text.)

   c. What kind of compounds does the vomeronasal organ most likely detect? (Brennan and Keverne, 2004) Cite research to support your answer. (Meredith and O'Connell, 1979; Meredith, 1994)

   d. When did the firing rate of neurons in the accessory olfactory bulb of subject mice show increased activity? (Luo et al., 2003. See Animation 10.2.)

   e. What is the effect of removal of the accessory olfactory bulb? (Halpern, 1987)

4. Trace the neural circuit responsible for the effects of these pheromones beginning with the region to which the accessory olfactory bulb projects. (Study Figure 10.10 in your text.)

5. a. By what two means may pheromones that affect male reproductive behavior be detected?

   b. Under what circumstances is this mating behavior abolished? (Powers and Winans, 1975; Winans and Powers, 1977; Lehman and Winans, 1982)

   c. What do these results indicate about the neural control of the effects of pheromones on sexual behavior of male hamsters?

6. If female sows can still detect pheromones in the saliva of boars after the VNO has been destroyed, then what other system must detect the pheromones and elicits behavior? (Dorries et al., 1997)

7. a. Describe the timing of the menstrual cycle of women who spent large amounts of time together. (McClintock, 1971)

   b. Compare the length of menstrual cycle of women who spent time in the presence of men and those who rarely did so.

8. Summarize how menstrual cycles were affected
   a. by daily samples of an underarm extract swabbed on the upper lips of a group of women. (Russell et al., 1980)
   b. by underarm compounds from around the time of ovulation and compounds taken later in the cycle. (Stern and McClintock, 1998)
   c. by extracts of men's sweat. (Preti et al., 2003)
9. How did these compounds found in human sweat affect men and women? (Jacob and McClintock, 2000; Savic et al., 2001)
   a. Androstadienone
   b. Estratetraene
10. a. What kinds of information were correctly determined from the odor of T-shirts? (Russell, 1976)
    b. What do these correct responses suggest about the nature of sexual attraction? the role of pheromones in this situation?
11. Where is the human vomeronasal organ located and does it also detect pheromones? (Garcia-Velasco and Mondragon, 1991.

Learning Objective 10-4 Discuss the activational effects of gonadal hormones on the sexual behavior of women and men.

Read pages 342-344 and answer the following questions.

1. Ovarian hormones control both the ________________ and the ________________ to mate of most estrous female mammals other than primates. (Wallen, 1990)
2. Compare the sexual receptivity of women throughout the menstrual cycle with that of other female mammals throughout the estrous cycle.
3. a. What have most studies of the influence of ovarian hormones on women's sexual interest concluded? (Adams et al., 1978; Morris et al., 1987)
   b. What did Wallen (1990) point out about the sexual interest and sexual activity of women in these studies?
   c. When does sexual activity of lesbian couples tend to increase and what does this pattern suggest about the role of ovarian hormones? (Matteo and Rissman, 1984)
   d. Compare the incidence of sexual activity initiated by men and by women throughout the female menstrual cycle. (See Figure 10.11 in your text. Van Goozen et al., 1997)

4. How may the wish to avoid pregnancy or achieve pregnancy affect a woman's sexual activity in spite of the level of her ovarian hormones? (Wallen, 2001)

5. a. What androgen is produced in the female body by the adrenal glands?

   b. What androgen is produced in the female body by the ovaries?

6. a. What do the results of most studies suggest about the effect of androgens on women's sexual interest and behavior? (Wallen, 2001)

   b. Summarize the effects of testosterone on the sexual behavior of ovariectomized women. (Shifren et al., 2000)

7. a. To study male sexual interest, what treatments did researchers give male volunteers? (Bagatell et al., 1994)

   b. How did these treatments subsequently affect sexual interest?

8. What factor appears to influence the decline in sexual ability after castration? (Money and Ehrhardt, 1972)

9. a. After receiving a GnRH antagonist, which suppresses testosterone secretion, how did the sexual activity of the seven subject monkeys who were part of a larger group change? (Wallen et al., 1991; Wallen, 2001)

   b. What factors appeared to influence their change in behavior?

10. Describe research that confirms that testosterone levels are affected by sexual arousal.

    a. The beard growth of an isolated scientist (Anonymous, 1970)

    b. Watching erotic films (Hellhammer et al., 1985)

Learning Objective 10-5 Discuss sexual orientation, the prenatal androgenization of genetic females, and the failure of androgenization of genetic males.

Read pages 344-349 and answer the following questions.

1. Define *sexual orientation* in your own words.

2. a. What belief concerning the cause of homosexuality was dispelled by a large-scale study by Bell et al. (1981)?

   b. What factor did they find to be the best predictor of homosexuality?

   c. What do these results suggest is a more likely cause for homosexuality than childhood social interactions?

3. a. Compare the levels of sex hormones during adulthood of male and female homosexuals with male and female heterosexuals. (Meyer-Bahlberg, 1984)

   b. What do the results of a few studies indicate about the testosterone levels of about 30 percent of female homosexuals?

c. What, then, can we conclude about the levels of sex hormones as a biological cause of homosexuality?

d. What is a more likely biological cause?

4. a. What is the cause of congenital adrenal hyperplasia (CAH)?

b. How does prenatal masculinization affect males and females fetuses?

c. Once diagnosed, how are human females medically treated?

5. a. What is the sexual orientation of approximately one third of women with CAH? (Cohen-Bendaham et al., 2005)

b. Outline an explanation of how abnormally high levels of androgens may influence the sexual orientation of these women.

c. What does the influence of androgens on female sexual orientation also suggest about male sexual orientation?

6. a. Study the drawings made by young children shown in Figure 10.12 in your text, noting how the drawing made by a young girl with CAH compared to the other two. (Iijima et al., 2001)

b. Summarize the preferences for particular kinds of toys of normal boys and girls and normal young male and female vervet monkeys. (See Figure 10.13 in your text. Alexander, 2003; Connellan et al., 2000; Alexander and Hines, 2002)

c. What kind of toys do girls with CAH prefer and what environmental factor does not account for their preference? (Pasterski et al., 2005)

d. Summarize an explanation that could account for the increased masculine sexual orientation of females with CAH.

7. Briefly discuss some of the concerns about medical treatment for strongly androgenized girls.

8. a. Briefly describe how the internal and external genitalia of males with androgen insensitivity syndrome develop.

b. What is the best treatment of this condition, and how is this confirmed at the time of puberty?

c. What is the sexual orientation and behavior of these adults?

d. Carefully explain what this syndrome suggests about conditions that influence sexual orientation.

9. What can we conclude about the effects of prenatal exposure to androgens on a person's sexual orientation and sexual identity? Be sure to refer to the tragic life of the twin described in your text and another child with a similar experience. (Bradley et al., 1998)

10. Briefly summarize some of the documented differences between men's and women's brains. (Breedlove, 1994; Swaab et al., 1995; Goldstein et al., 2001 for specific references.)
    a. Shared functions of the hemispheres
    b. Overall brain size
    c. Size and shape of particular regions

11. What do most researchers believe accounts for the sexual dimorphism of the human brain? (Schultz et al., 2004)

12. a. Identify and compare the three subregions of the brain that differ in size in heterosexual and homosexual men and heterosexual women. (Swaab and Hofman, 1990; LeVay, 1991; Allen and Gorski, 1992)

    b. Summarize follow-up research by Byne et al. (2002) that questioned these findings.

13. a. Describe the sexual behavior and preference of approximately 8 percent of domestic male rams. (Price et al., 1988)

    b. What anatomical difference did Roselli et al. (2004) discover in the brains of heterosexual and homosexual rams? (See Figure 10.14 in your text.)

14. a. Savic et al. (2005) compared the patterns of brain activation of heterosexual women and heterosexual and homosexual men in response to the odors of AND and EST, chemicals that may be human pheromones. Which group(s) responded to
       1. EST?
       2. AND?

    b. What do these response patterns suggest about the brains of these subjects and their particular sexual orientations?

15 a. Compare the size of the bed nucleus of the stria terminalis (BNST) of
       1. males and females.
       2. male transsexuals and normal females.
       3. male homosexuals and male heterosexuals.

    b. What aspect of sexuality appears to be correlated with the size of the BNST? (Zhou et al., 1995; Study Figure 10.15 in your text.)

    c. What limited conclusions about sexual orientation can we draw from this and later research that replicated these results? (Kruijver et al., 2000)?

16. Why must we be cautious about concluding that differences in brain or body structures are directly involved in determining an individual's sexual orientation? (See Figure 10.16 in your text. Martin and Nguyen, 2004)

17. Before continuing, be sure that you understand how a male transsexual views his body and sexual identity.

18. a. Summarize research findings on the effects of prenatal maternal stress on prenatal brain development. Explain how stress may have affected the
    1. sexual behavior of male rats. (Ward, 1972)
    2. play behavior of juvenile male rats. (Ward and Stehm, 1991)
    3. brain development of laboratory animals. (Anderson, et al., 1986)

    b. What do the results of these studies suggest about a biological cause of male homosexuality?

19. a. What did studies of the siblings of homosexual and heterosexual men and women indicate? (Reviewed by Blanchard, 2001)

    b. What is a possible explanation of the results and how do they contribute to an understanding of sexual orientation?

20. What were the results of twin studies to determine the role of heredity in male and female homosexuality? (Bailey and Pillard, 1991; Bailey et al., 1993; Pattatucci and Hamer, 1995)

21. To review: List the two biological factors that research indicates may affect sexual orientation.

    1. 2.

Lesson I Self Test

1. Which example illustrates the activational effects of sex hormones?
    a. Development of ovaries and uterus
    b. Production of sperm
    c. Differentiation of the primordial gonads
    d. Changes in brain development caused by androgens

2. The precursor of the _____ sex organs is the _____ system which develops _____.
    a. female; Wolffian; without any hormonal stimuli
    b. male; Wolffian; only if the testes secrete the appropriate hormones
    c. male; Müllerian; without any hormonal stimuli
    d. female; Müllerian; only if the ovaries secrete the appropriate hormones

3. Which event first marks the beginning of puberty?
    a. release of gonadotropic hormones by anterior pituitary gland
    b. secretion of gonadotropin-releasing hormones by hypothalamus
    c. appearance of secondary sex characteristics
    d. production of estrogens by ovaries or androgens by testes

4. The LH surge causes
    a. estrus.
    b. the refractory period.
    c. the release of milk.
    d. ovulation.

5. The sequence of _____ followed by _____ facilitates the sexual behavior of female rodents.

a. progesterone; prolactin
b. estradiol; oxytocin
c. progesterone; estradiol
d. estradiol; progesterone

6. Lordosis is

a. a posture assumed by some female mammals during copulation that exposes her genitals to a male.
b. the pelvic thrusting by a male during copulation.
c. decreasing sexual interest from repeated copulation with the same female.
d. active rebuffing of a male's attempts at copulation by a female not in estrus.

7. The acceleration of the onset of puberty in a female rodent caused by the odor of a male is known as the _____ effect.

a. Whitten
b. Bruce
c. Vandenbergh
d. Lee-Boot

8. Removal of the _____ disrupts the Lee-Boot, Bruce, Vandenbergh, and Whitten effects.

a. pituitary gland
b. ventromedial nucleus of the hypothalamus
c. accessory olfactory bulb
d. adrenal glands

9. Sexual activity initiated by a woman shows a distinct peak when levels of _____ are highest.

a. testosterone
b. progesterone
c. estradiol
d. oxytocin

10. Male rhesus monkeys, who had previously received injections of a GnRH antagonist, were returned to the larger group of monkeys with whom they lived. Their decline in sexual behavior was related to

a. age at the time of injection.
b. social rank and sexual experience.
c. physical size.
d. levels of residual testosterone in their bodies.

11. A large-scale study of male and female homosexuals found that

a. homosexuality results from unhappy parent-child relationships.
b. self-report was the best predictor of adult homosexuality.
c. only children were more likely to be homosexual than children with siblings.
d. homosexuality is often the result of poor interpersonal relationships with peers.

12. The biological basis of homosexuality may be differences in the

a. organizational affects of prenatal hormones.
b. activational affects of prenatal hormones.
c. degree of sexual dimorphism of the prenatal brain.
d. hormone levels during adulthood.

Lesson II: Neural Control of Sexual Behavior and Parental Behavior

Read the interim summary on pages 356-357 of your text to re-acquaint yourself with the material in this section.

Learning Objective 10-6 Discuss the neural control of male sexual behavior.

Read pages 350-353 and answer the following questions.

1. a. Explain how men with spinal cord damage may still become fathers. (Hart, 1978)

   b. Summarize research results that suggest that circuits that control erection and ejaculation appear to be located

      1. below the 10th thoracic segment of the spinal cord? (Brackett et al., 1998)

   2. in a group of neurons in the lumbar region of the rat spinal cord. Be sure to use the term *spinal ejaculation generator* in your answer. (Coolen et al., 2004)

   c. What two findings indicate that erection and ejaculation, but not other components of male sexual behavior, activate these neurons?

2. Turn from spinal cord mechanisms that play a role in male sexual behavior to brain mechanisms that play a role. Name and describe the location of the forebrain region most important for male sexual behavior.

3. a. If the medial preoptic area (MPA) is electrically stimulated, what kind of behavior occurs? (Malsbury, 1971)

   b. How does sexual activity affect the

      1. electrical activity of the neurons in the MPA? (Shimura et al., 1994; Mas, 1995)

      2. metabolic activity of a male's MPA and Fos production? (Oaknin et al., 1989; Robertson et al., 1991; Wood and Newman, 1993)

   c. What profound effect does the destruction of the MPA have on male sexual behavior? (Heimer and Larsson, 1966/1967)

4. a. Where is the sexually-dimorphic nucleus (SDN) located? Compare its size in males and females rats. (See Figure 10.17 in your text. Gorski et al., 1978)

   b. During fetal development, what determines the size of the SDN?

   c. How do lesions of the SDN affect male sexual activity? (De Jonge et al., 1989)

5. a. Both ______________ ______________ ______________, the ______________ ______________ is sexually dimorphic in rats.

   b. Why may one region within this structure be much bigger in male rats than in female rats? (Hines et al., 1992)

6. a. How does destruction of the medial amygdala alter the sexual behavior of male rats? (De Jonge et al., 1992)

   b. How does mating affect chemical secretions of the medial amygdala? (Wood and Newman, 1993)

7. Explain how the MPA receives chemosensory information and sensory information. (See Figure 10.18 in your text.)

8. How can the sexual behavior of a male rodent castrated in adulthood be restored? (Sipos and Nyby, 1996; Coolen and Wood, 1999)

9. a. Trace some of the anatomical connections important for male sexual behavior. Through which regions are the most important connections between the MPA and the spinal ejaculation generator in the spinal cord found? (See Murphy and Hoffman, 2001 for references.)

      1. 2.

   b. Which pathway has inhibitory effects on spinal cord sexual reflexes?

   c. What, then, is one of the functions of the pathway from the MPA to the spinal cord? (Marson and McKenna, 1996)

d. Which region sends excitatory input from the MPA to spinal cord mechanism?

e. Which neurotransmitter is involved in the inhibitory connections between the PGi and the lumbar spinothalamic neurons?

f. Explain why SSRIs taken for treatment of depression alter male sexual behavior.

10. During ejaculation, which brain region showed

a. increased neural activity?

b. decreased neural activity? (Holstege et al., 2003b)

11. Immediately review what you have learned by studying Figure 10.19 in your text.

Learning Objective 10-7 Discuss the neural control of female sexual behavior and the formation of pair bonds.

Read pages 353-356 and answer the following questions.

1. a. The most important forebrain region for male sexual behavior is the _______________ _______________ _______________ and the most important forebrain region for female sexual behavior is the _______________ _______________ of the _______________. (The location is shown in Figure 10.20 in your text.)

b. Trace the connections for chemosensory and somatosensory information between this structure involved in female sexual behavior and the rest of the brain.

2. How does production of Fos protein in the VMH change with copulation or mechanical stimulation of the genitals or flanks? (Pfaus et al., 1993; Tetel et al., 1993)

3. a. How is female sexual behavior affected by injections of

1. estradiol, followed by progesterone, in females whose ovaries were removed? (Rubin and Barfield, 1980; Pleim and Barfield, 1988)

2. a chemical that blocks the production of progesterone receptors? (Ogawa et al., 1994)

b. What do these results confirm about the control of female sexual behavior?

4. a. When female hamsters are given injections of progesterone after treatment with estradiol, what neural change occurs? (Rose, 1990)

b. Where are neurons that show an increase in Fos production in response to genital stimulation found? (Tetel et al., 1994)

c. Explain how estradiol increases the effectiveness of progesterone. Cite research to support your answer. (Study Figure 10.21 in your text. Blaustein and Feder, 1979)

5. a. Where do axons of neurons in the VMH project?

   b. Summarize changes in female sexual behavior resulting from

      1. electrical stimulation of the PAG and lesions of the PAG. (Sakuma and Pfaff, 1979a, 1979b)

      2. lesions that disconnect the VMH from the PAG. (Hennessey et al., 1990)

      3. estradiol treatment or electrical stimulation of the VMH. (Sakuma and Pfaff, 1980a, 1980b)

6. Complete the diagram below to show the neural pathway that innervates the muscles responsible for the lordosis response of female rats. (Daniels et al., 1999)

   ______________ → ______________ → ______________ → ______________

7. Explain why it is likely that erections of the penis and clitoris are controlled by similar brain mechanism. Cite research to support your answer. (Marson, 1995)

8. Immediately review what you have just learned by studying Figure 10.22 in your text.

9. During orgasm in women, which brain regions showed increased neural activity? (Holstege et al., 2003a)

10. a. Which two peptides which play a role in monogamy.

    b. Which two brain regions release them?

    c. Which one appears to play the more important role in females?

    d. Which one appears to play the more important role in males?

11. a. Compare the number of V1a receptors in monogamous male prairie voles and promiscuous male meadow voles. (Insel et al., 1994) If male prairie voles are given an injection of a drug that blocks V1a receptors, how is the formation of pair bonds affected? (Lim and Young, 2004)

    b. What physical and behavioral changes occurred after normally polygamous male voles were injected with a modified virus that contained the gene for the V1a receptor? (Lim et al., 2004)

12. Summarize research that confirms the importance of oxytocin in pair bonding in females. (Williams et al., 1994; Cho et al., 1999)

13. a. What were the rules of the investment game subjects played? (Kosfeld et al., 2005)

    b. Some subjects received pre-game injections of oxytocin and other subjects did not. Compare the way these groups of subjects played the game.

    c. What do the results suggest is one of the effects oxytocin has on humans?

    d. How did the results of a second study confirm that “trust” rather than “confidence” was affected by oxytocin?

Read the interim summary on page 361 of your text to re-acquaint yourself with the material in this section.

> ***Learning Objective 10-8*** Describe the maternal behavior of rodents including how it is elicited and maintained, and explain the hormonal and neural mechanisms that control maternal behavior and the neural control of paternal behavior.

Read pages 357-360 and answer the following questions.

1. Why is the attentive maternal behavior of a female rodent necessary for the survival of her offspring?

2. Describe the maternal behavior of a female rodent
   a. during pregnancy. (See Figure 10.23 in your text.)
   b. at the time of parturition.

3. Following birth, how does the mother
   a. assist elimination? Be sure to explain the procedure Friedman and Bruno (1976) used to determine the mutually beneficial nature of this behavior.
   b. retrieve pups outside the nest? (See Figure 10.24 in your text.)

4. In addition to prenatal hormones, what physical sensations at the time of parturition also plays an important role in inducing maternal behavior? Cite research to support your answer (Graber and Kristal, 1977; Yeo and Keverne, 1986)

5. a. In what two ways does maternal behavior differ from other sexually dimorphic behaviors?
      1.
      2.
   b. Explain how young virgin rats are sensitized to care for young pups. (Wiesner and Sheard, 1933)

6. a. Identify the hormones that facilitate nest building.
   b. Which hormone plays a role during pregnancy and after parturition? (Lisk et al., 1969)
   c. Which hormone facilitates nest building in virgin female mice? (Voci and Carlson, 1973)

7. Explain how the blood levels of these three hormones change with insemination, pregnancy, and parturition. (Study Figure 10.25 in your text.)
   a. Estradiol
   b. Progesterone
   c. Prolactin

8. If ovariectomized virgin rats are given estradiol and progesterone in the pattern that duplicates the normal sequence, what behavioral change occurs? (Moltz et al., 1970; Bridges, 1984)

9. Summarize some research results on the importance of lactogenic hormones for maternal behavior.
   a. Explain the sequence of hormone treatments that caused virgin rats to begin caring for young pups. (Bridges et al., 1990)

b. What does this research suggest about the hormonal control of maternal behavior?

c. Describe the maternal behavior of mice with a targeted mutation against the gene for the prolactin receptor. (Lucas et al., 1998)

10. a. Which hormone was injected into the cerebral ventricles of rats when they began to give birth? (Van Leengoed et al., 1987)

b. Their pups were removed from the nest as they were born and returned 40 minutes later. How did these mothers react to their pups?

c. How did mothers, who had not received hormone injections, react when their pups, who had also been removed, were returned?

d. What do the results suggest about the effect of oxytocin on bonding between mother and offspring?

11. a. Name the brain region critical for the expression of maternal behavior by female rodents.

b. What behavior that you have already studied depends on this region?

c. How do lesions of the MPA affect maternal behavior and female sexual behavior? (Numan, 1974)

d. What change occurs in the MPA as a result of

1. parturition? (Del Cerro et al., 1995)
2. exposure to pups?

e. List the two regions of the midbrain where axons of the MPA that are activated by maternal behavior send axons. (Numan and Numan, 1997)

1. 2.

f. Where do some of these axons continue to project?

g. What procedure abolishes maternal behavior? (Numan and Smith, 1984)

12. a. What kind of hormone receptors are found in the medial preoptic area? (Pfaff and Keiner, 1973)

b. How does pregnancy affect these receptors? (Giordano et al., 1989)

c. What is the effect on maternal behavior of

1. estradiol implants in the MPA? (Numan et al., 1977)

2. antiestrogen chemical injections in the MPA? (Adieh et al., 1987)

3. prolactin infusions into the MPA of virgin female rats primed with estradiol and progesterone? (Bridges et al., 1990)

13. a. How are reinforcement mechanisms altered in females with pups and virgin females? (Ferris et al., 2005)

b. What hormone may play a role in the behavior of lactating females?

14. a. When human mothers looked at pictures of their infants, which brain regions showed increased activity? (Bartels and Zeki, 2004)

b. When human mothers looked at pictures of their infants, which brain regions showed decreased activity? (Bartels and Zeki, 2004)

c. When human mothers looked at pictures of their infants, which brain regions became active? (Bartels and Zeki, 2004)

15. Look at some research on the neural control of paternal behavior.

a. Does the MPA shows less sexual dimorphism in monogamous voles or promiscuous voles. (Shapiro et al., 1991)

b. If male prairie voles are exposed to pups, what change occurs in the MPA? (Kirkpatrick et al., 1994)

c. How is the paternal behavior of male rats affected by

1. lesions of the MPA? (Rosenblatt et al., 1996; Sturgis and Bridges, 1997)

2. implants of estradiol into the MPA of male rats?

d. What do these research results suggest about the neural control of the maternal and paternal behavior of rodents?

Lesson II Self Test

1. The lumbar region of the spinal cord plays a critical role in

a. mounting.
b. erection.
c. intromission.
d. ejaculation.

2. The size of the sexually dimorphic nucleus of the _____ is _____.

a. medial amygdala; reduced in pups whose mother was prenatally sensitized
b. ventral horn of the spinal cord lumbar region; directly related to level of prenatal stress
c. preoptic area; controlled by the amount of androgens present during fetal development
d. ventral tegmental area; directly related to fertility

3. The _____ connections between the _____ and the lumbar spinothalamic neurons involve _____.

a. excitatory; PGi; glutamate
b. inhibitory; PAG; serotonin
c. excitatory; PAG; glutamate
d. inhibitory; PGi; serotonin

4. If a male rat is castrated in adulthood, sexual activity

a. will not be affected, but the rat will be infertile.
b. will continue to be attempted, but not always successfully.
c. will cease, but can be restored by testosterone implants in the MPA.
d. sexual activity will cease and cannot be restored.

5. The brain region most critical for female sexual behavior is the _____ and the brain region most critical for male sexual behavior is the _____.

a. ventromedial nucleus of the hypothalamus; ventral tegmental area
b. medial preoptic area; sexually dimorphic nucleus
c. ventromedial nucleus of the hypothalamus; medial preoptic area
d. medial amygdala, medial preoptic area

6. The priming effect of estradiol is caused by

a. the LH surge.
b. an increase in progesterone receptors.
c. increased release of norepinephrine in the hypothalamus.
d. an increase in the firing rate of neurons in the periaqueductal gray matter.

7. Electrical stimulation of the periaqueductal gray matter facilitates

a. ovulation.
b. lordosis.

c. hormonal priming.
d. lactation.

8. _____ plays a major role in pair bonding in _____.

a. Vasopressin; males
b. Oxytocin; males
c. Progesterone; females
d. Testosterone; males

9. Virgin female rats can be made to care for infants if they are

a. caged with an experienced mother.
b. allowed to observe pups through a glass partition.
c. given injections of progesterone.
d. placed with young pups for several days.

10. If virgin female rats, primed with estradiol and progesterone, receive infusions of prolactin in the lateral ventricles or MPA, they will

a. begin to build brood nests.
b. begin to lactate.
c. not retrieve pups.
d. be sensitized to care for young quickly.

11. Just before parturition the level of estradiol

a. rises; the level of progesterone begins to fall; and the level of prolactin rises.
b. and progesterone begin to fall and the level of prolactin rises.
c. falls, the level of progesterone rises, and the level of prolactin falls.
d. rises, the level of prolactin falls, and then the level of progesterone rises.

12. When monogamous species of voles in which the male and female both care for the offspring are compared to promiscuous species that do not share parental responsibility

a. there are fewer connections between the MPA and the ventral tegmental area in monogamous males.
b. Fos production in the MPA of monogamous males is lower.
c. the sexual dimorphism of the MPA is less pronounced in the monogamous species.
d. the vasopressin levels in the MPA of monogamous males are lower.

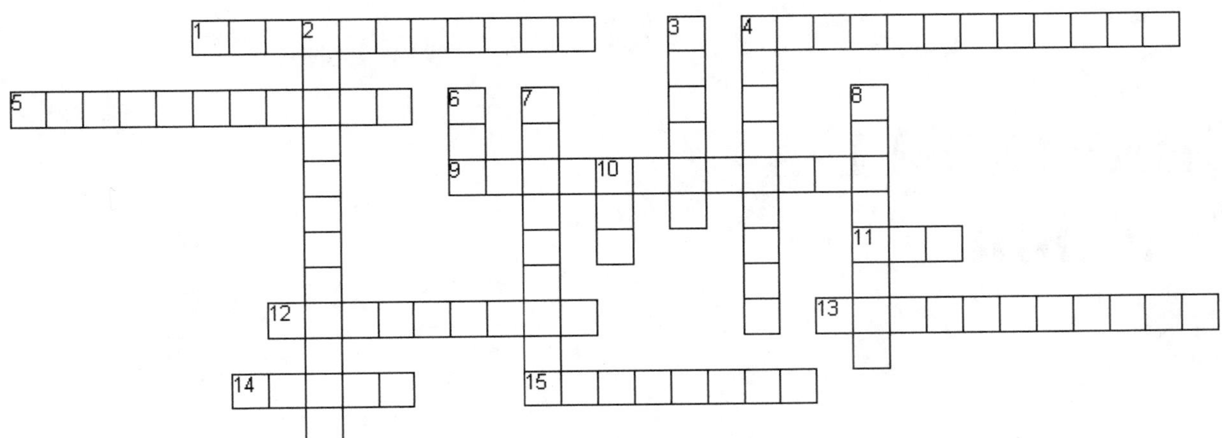

Across
1. Act of giving birth
4. Hormone that, along with estradiol, promotes sexual receptivity in female mammals with estrous cycles
5. Sensory organ that mediates effects of some pheromones
9. Effect of a hormone in fully developed organism
11. Hormone that causes development of ovarian follicle and maturation of ovum
12. Hormone necessary for milk production
13. Pheromone effect: early onset of puberty in female housed with males
14. An ovary or testis
15. Position of four-legged female mammals that permits copulation

Down
2. Principal androgen found in males
3. A sperm or ovum
4. Chemical of one animal that affects behavior of another
6. Nucleus in brain; plays essential role in male sexual behavior and parental behavior
7. Principal estrogen of many mammals, including humans
8. Embryonic precursors of the male internal sex organs
10. Nucleus in brain; plays an essential role in female sexual behavior

Answers for Self Tests

Lesson I

1. b Obj. 10-1
2. b Obj. 10-1
3. b Obj. 10-1
4. d Obj. 10-2
5. d Obj. 10-2
6. a Obj. 10-2
7. c Obj. 10-3
8. c Obj. 10-3
9. c Obj. 10-4
10. b Obj. 10-4
11. b Obj. 10-5
12. a Obj. 10-5

Lesson II

1. d Obj. 10-6
2. c Obj. 10-6
3. d Obj. 10-6
4. c Obj. 10-6
5. c Obj. 10-7
6. b Obj. 10-7
7. b Obj. 10-7
8. a Obj. 10-7
9. d Obj. 10-8
10. d Obj. 10-8
11. a Obj. 10-8
12. c Obj. 10-8

CHAPTER 11
Emotion

Lesson I: Emotions as Response Patterns

Read the interim summary on pages 379-380 of your text to re-acquaint yourself with the material in this section.

Learning Objective 11-1 Discuss the behavioral, autonomic, and hormonal components of an emotional response and the role of the amygdala in controlling them.

Read pages 363-368 and answer the following questions.

1. List and define the three components of an emotional response in your own words.

   1.

   2.

   3.

2. In general, what is the role of the amygdala in the neural control of the components of fear?

3. List the five major nuclei of the amygdala and their connections. (Study Figure 11.1 in your text.)

Nucleus/Nuclei	*Receives information from*	*Sends information to*

4. Underline the nucleus that is most important for expressing emotional responses provoked by aversive stimuli.

5. What behavioral and/or physiological changes occur

   a. in the central nucleus in the presence of aversive stimuli? (Pascoe and Kapp, 1985; Campeau et al., 1991)

b. if the central nucleus is destroyed? (Coover et al., 1992; Davis, 1992b; LeDoux, 1992)

c. from short-term and long-term stimulation of the central nucleus? (Davis, 1992b; Henke, 1982)

6. What do these research findings suggest about the relationship between the central nucleus and long-term stress?

7. List several other regions which receive information from the central nucleus and the responses they control, which are summarized in Figure 11.2 in your text.

8. A classically conditioned response is produced when a(n) _______________ stimulus is regularly paired with a stimulus that _______________ produces a response and a conditioned emotional response is produced by a(n) _______________ stimulus that is paired with a(n) _______________-_______________ stimulus. The first or _______________ response elicited by a painful stimulus is aimed at _______________ the stimulus and the second or _______________ response involves physiological changes controlled by the autonomic nervous system.

9. a. In the example in your text, what was the specific defensive response you made when you received a shock?

b. What was the nonspecific response you made?

c. What did you do on your next visit when the mixer made the sputtering noise, and what is this response called?

10. a. Study Figure 11.3 in your text, which diagrams how LeDoux and his colleagues classically conditioned an emotional withdrawal response in rats, and identify the warning stimulus and the emotion-producing stimulus. (reviewed by LeDoux, 2000)

b. On the day following conditioning, how did the rats respond when they heard the warning tone? What additional response did they make? Be sure to use the term *freezing* in your answer.

c. What brain region appears to be necessary for a conditioned emotional response to occur? (Paré et al., 2004)

11. a. Once again, explain how a conditioned emotional response develops. Be sure to use the terms *CS*, *CR* and *aversive* stimulus in your answer.

b. Explain how this response can be extinguished.

c. Why are learning to make a conditioned response and extinction of that response both useful behaviors?

d. When a conditioned response has been extinguished, has the animal learned not to respond or simply forgotten to respond? Support your explanation with research results. (Quirk et al., 2000; Milad et al., 2004; Santini et al., 2004)

12. Summarize evidence suggesting the amygdala plays a role in human emotional responses.

   a. Under what circumstances did seizure disorder patients report feeling afraid? (White, 1940; Halgren et al., 1978; Gloor et al., 1982)

   b. How do lesions of the amygdala affect a person's

      1. acquisition of a conditioned emotional response? (LaBar et al., 1995; Bechara et al., 1995)

      2. startle response? (Angrilli et al., 1996)

   c. Compare the memories of normal subjects and people with amygdala damage for emotional story details (Cahill et al., 1995) or a devastating earthquake (Mori et al., 1999).

   d. Compare the reaction to particular aspects of music of Patient I. R. and patients with damage to the amygdala. (Peretz et al., 2001; Gosselin et al., 2005)

   e. Compare the PET scans of people when they recalled neutral films vs. their scans taken during emotionally arousing films. (Cahill et al., 1996)

   f. Compare the PET scans of normal subjects when they saw threatening words vs. scans taken while they were viewing neutral words. (See Figure 11.4 in your text. Isenberg et al., 1999)

Learning Objective 11-2 Discuss the nature, functions, and neural control of aggressive behavior.

Read pages 368-370 and answer the following questions.

1. Complete these statements.

   a. Aggressive behaviors are species-typical; that is

   b. Many aggressive behaviors are related to

2. Define these types of aggressive behavior and the responses they evoke.

   a. Threat behaviors

   b. Defensive behaviors

   c. Submissive behaviors

3. Why are threat behaviors, which are much more frequent than actual attacks, useful responses?

4. a. Define *predation* in your own words.

   b. Compare the level of arousal and activity of the autonomic nervous system of animals engaged in offensive or defensive behaviors and predatory behaviors.

5. a. The neural control of aggressive behavior is _______________. Explain this statement.

   b. Which parts of the brain may control brain stem circuits?

   c. Which parts of the brain may control the limbic system?

6. a. List two forms of aggressive behavior in cats that can be elicited by electrical or chemical stimulation of the periaqueductal gray matter (PAG).

      1. 2.

   b. Study Figure 11.5 in your text and note the connections between the PAG, the amygdala, and the hypothalamus that are involved in these behaviors. (Reviewed by Siegel et al., 1999)

7. a. According to strong evidence, what is the effect of the activity of serotonergic synapses on aggression?

   b. If serotonergic axons in the forebrain are destroyed, how is aggressive attack affected? (Vergnes et al., 1988)

8. a. How did researchers assess the level of serotonergic activity in the brains of monkeys living in a free-ranging colony? (Mehlman et al., 1995; Higley et al., 1996a, 1996b.)

   b. To be sure that you understand what happens when serotonin (5-HT) is released in the brain, explain the relationship between the level of 5-HIAA in cerebrospinal fluid and the level of 5-HT.

   c. What kinds of activities did young male monkeys with the lowest levels of 5-HIAA engage in?

   d. What was their survival rate? (Study Figure 11.6 in your text.)

   e. What do these results suggest about the role of serotonin in aggressive behavior and risk taking?

9. a. In targeted mutation studies with mice, how did mice lacking receptors for 5-HT_{1B} and normal mice react to an intruder? (Saudou et al., 1994; Bouwknecht et al., 2001)

   b. What do the results confirm about the effect of serotonin on aggression?

10. a. How does a depressed rate of serotonin release in humans affect

      1. aggression and other forms of antisocial behavior? (Lidberg et al., 1984, 1985; Virkkunen et al., 1989)

      2. behavioral problems among other close relatives of affected people? (Coccaro et al., 1994)

    b. In humans, then, what is the relationship between serotonergic activity and aggression?

c. What is the effect of Prozac, a serotonin agonist, on human aggressive behavior? (Coccaro and Kavoussi, 1997)

11. a. In general, how may the behavior of a person with at least one short allele for the serotonin transporter be affected? (Lesch and Mossner, 1998)

b. What task were subjects asked to perform by Hariri and his colleagues? (See Figure 11.7a in your text. Hariri et al., 2005)

c. Compare the activity of the amygdala of normal subjects with that of subjects with the short allele for the serotonin transporter. (See Figure 11.7b.)

Learning Objective 11-3 Discuss the role of the ventral prefrontal cortex in the analysis of social situations and the effects of damage to this region.

Read pages 370-375 and answer the following questions.

1. a. List the two regions of the ventral prefrontal cortex.

   1. 2.

   b. Study Figure 11.8 in your text and describe their locations.

2. List the direct inputs and the outputs from the ventral prefrontal cortex.

Direct Inputs	**Outputs**
1.	1.
2.	2.
3.	3.
4.	4.
5.	5.

3. a. What kind of information is received through the inputs?

   b. What kinds of activities are influenced through the outputs?

4. Summarize the case of Phineas Gage which first suggested the importance of the orbitofrontal cortex in emotional behavior. Study Figure 11.9 in your text and describe his injury and how it affected his subsequent behavior. (Damasio et al., 1994)

5. What role does the ventral prefrontal cortex appear to play in regulating emotional responses?

6. a. Look at other case studies of people with ventral prefrontal damage caused by accident or disease. How well did a patient with bilateral ventral prefrontal cortex damage assess hypothetical social situations? (Eslinger and Damasio, 1985)

   b. How well did this same patient conduct his personal affairs following surgery?

   c. What does this clinical evidence suggest about the role of the ventral prefrontal cortex in making judgments and conclusions?

7. a. Briefly describe the card game that normal subjects, subjects with ventromedial prefrontal lesions and subjects with amygdala lesions were taught. (Bechara et al., 1997, 1999)

   b. How did normal subjects react just before choosing a card from the "bad" deck? How did their emotional response change their strategy?

   c. In contrast, how did subjects with prefrontal lesions react to cards from the "bad" deck? subjects with lesions of the amygdala?

   d. What, then, may emotional responses contribute to the process of making appropriate decisions?

8. a. When subjects were involved in decision-making during gambling games, what part of the brain, as indicated by functional imaging studies, became active? (Rogers et al., 1999; Erst et al., 2002)

   b. When subjects were losing money gambling and not simply making an error, what part of the brain became active? (Gehring and Willoughby, 2002)

   c. What brain regions became active when people were anticipating seeing pictures with negative emotional content? (Ueda et al., 2003)

   d. What do these findings suggest about the role of the ventral prefrontal cortex and the amygdala in assessing a situation?

9. a. How well did boys with psychopathic tendencies play the card gambling game used by Bechara and colleagues? (Blair et al, 2001)

   b. Outline a possible explanation of their performance.

   c. What brain abnormality has been found in 11 percent of people with antisocial personality disorder? (Raine et al., 2000)

10. a. How did researchers try to establish a conditioned emotional response in normal men and psychopathic men with criminal records? (Birbaumer et al., 2005)

    b. How successful were they with normal subjects?

    c. How successful were they with psychopathic subjects?

d. What did the fMRI scans, shown in Figure 11.10 in your text, indicate?

11. a. Retell the story of the runaway trolley and the two ways the passengers can be saved. Which action do most people choose? Which action do most people refuse?

    b. What does this story suggest about the way we make moral judgments?

    c. When people consider moral dilemmas, which parts of the brain become active? (Greene et al., 2001)

    d. What does this finding suggest about the reluctance to push the man in the runaway trolley story to his death?

12. a. What kind of expected and unexpected deficits did adults who had sustained damage to the prefrontal cortex during infancy show? (Anderson et al., 1999)

    b. What explanation do the researchers suggest?

13. a. What kind of changes in the brain have been documented

       1. when subjects thought again, and became angry again, about personal situations that had made them angry in the past? (Dougherty et al., 1999)
       2. in impulsive, emotional murderers? (Raine et al., 1998)
       3. cold-blooded, calculating murderers?

    b. Outline an explanation for these different reactions.

14. a. Before viewing erotic films, each group of normal subjects was given a different set of instructions. What were they?

    b. As they watched the films, what kind of changes were recorded in the brains of each group of subjects?

    c. What is the presumed explanation? (Beauregard et al., 2001)

15. When women were asked to suppress their sadness aroused by watching sad video excerpts, which brain regions became active? (Levèsque et al., 2003)

16. Explain why a decrease in the activity of serotonergic neurons may result in the decreased activity of the prefrontal cortex. What kind of behaviors are associated with the activity of these parts of the brain? (Mann et al., 1996)

17. Summarize research on serotonin levels and activity of the medial prefrontal cortex.

    a. How did a serotonin-releasing drug affect activity in the medial prefrontal cortex in normal subjects? (New et al., 2002)

b. How did a serotonin-releasing drug affect activity in the medial prefrontal cortex in subjects with a history of impulsive aggression? (New et al., 2002)

c. How is the level of serotonin transporters in the medial prefrontal cortex of people with impulsive aggression different? (Frankle et al., 2005)

d. What do these results suggest about how drugs such as Prozac affect the activity of the orbitofrontal cortex and aggressive behavior? (New et al., 2004)

Learning Objective 11-4 Discuss the hormonal control of aggression in males and aggression in females.

Read pages 375-377 and answer the following questions.

1. a. Explain what the emergence of intermale aggressiveness at puberty suggests about the control mechanism of aggressive behaviors. Cite research to support your answer. (Beeman, 1947)

   b. Briefly review the organizational and activational effects of early androgenization, shown in Figure 11.11 in your text, that influence both intermale aggression and male sexual behavior.

   c. Early androgenization _______________ neural circuits, and the earlier the androgenization the _______________ effective the _______________.

2. a. What treatment restores intermale aggression in castrated cats? (Bean and Conner, 1978)

   b. What is the presumed reason for its effectiveness?

3. a. Male aggressive behavior is usually directed only against other males. How does a male determine the sex of an intruder?

   b. How is intermale aggression affected by

      1. cutting the vomeronasal organ? (Bean, 1982)
      2. painting female mouse urine on a male mouse before it is placed in another male's cage? (Dixon and Mackintosh, 1971; Dixon, 1973)
      3. using a targeted mutation against a protein essential for the detection of pheromones by the vomeronasal organ? (See Animation 11.1. Stowers et al., 2002)

4. a. Look at the activational and organizational effects of testosterone on interfemale aggression. Study Figure 11.12 in your text and state how ovariectomized female rats responded to injections of testosterone, estradiol, and a placebo. (Van de Poll et al., 1988)

   b. What do these results suggest about the activational effects of testosterone on interfemale aggression?

   c. Study Figure 11.13 in your text and be sure you understand the difference between 0M, 1M, and 2M females.

   d. Which of these females had the highest levels of prenatal testosterone and later exhibited the most interfemale aggression? (Vom Saal and Bronson, 1980)

e. What do these results suggest about the organizational effects of prenatal testosterone on interfemale aggression?

5. At what times in the estrous cycle are some female primates more likely to engage in aggressive behavior with males? (Carpenter, 1942; Saayman, 1971) with females? (Sassenrath et al., 1973; Mallow, 1979)

Learning Objective 11-5 Discuss the effects of androgens on human aggressive behavior.

Read pages 377-379 and answer the following questions.

1. Explain why the study of human male aggression must consider the effects of both socialization and androgenization.

2. a. What were the results of a comparison of proneness to aggression in 13-year-old female dizygotic twins who shared the uterus with a brother with those who shared it with a sister? (Cohen-Bendahan et al., 2005)

   b. Offer a physiological and a social explanation for the observed differences in behavior.

3. Be sure you understand congenital adrenal hyperplasia and then explain how CAH affects the behavior of affected females

   a. as children?

   b. as adolescents and adults? (Berenbaum and Resnick, 1997)

4. a. Briefly describe the effects of castration of convicted male sex offenders. (Hawke, 1951; Sturup, 1961; Laschet, 1973)

   b. In what way were these studies flawed?

5. a. What alternative treatment for human sexual aggression is preferable and how effective is it? (Walker and Meyer, 1981)

   b. How did one of these drugs affect aggressive behavior and sexual activity of male monkeys toward other males? (Zumpe et al., 1991)

   c. How did one of these drugs affect aggressive behavior and sexual activity of male monkeys toward females? (Zumpe et al., 1991)

6. a. What was the general conclusion of a literature review concerning the relationship between men's testosterone levels and the level of aggression? (Archer, 1994)

   b. What were the results of a study of nearly 4500 US military veterans? (Dabbs and Morris, 1990)

   c. According to Mazur and Booth (1998), what may be the primary social effect of androgens?

7. Carefully explain why we cannot conclude that high testosterone levels cause increased aggression. Cite research to support your explanation. (Mazur and Lamb, 1980; Elias, 1981; McCaul et al., 1992; Bernhardt et al., 1998)

8. a. How did anabolic steroids affect the aggressive behavior of male weight lifters? (Yates et al., 1992)

   b. Why is it incorrect to conclude that steroids are responsible for increased aggressiveness?

9. a. Study Figure 11.14 in your text and summarize how and when alcohol affected intermale aggression in dominant male squirrel monkeys? (Winslow and Miczek, 1985, 1988)

   b. Summarize the results of later, confirming research. (Winslow et al., 1988)

   c. What do these results suggest about the influence of alcohol on behavior?

Lesson I Self Test

1. An emotional response consists of three components:

   a. offensive, defensive, and social.
   b. positive, negative, and neutral.
   c. behavioral, autonomic, and hormonal.
   d. conditioned, unconditioned, and species-typical.

2. Classical conditioning occurs when a neutral stimulus is regularly _____ by a stimulus that _____ evokes a response.

   a. preceded; consistently
   b. followed; automatically
   c. preceded; usually
   d. followed; rarely

3. Research indicates neural changes leading to a conditioned emotional response take place in the _____ and that inhibition of the conditioned response takes place in the _____.

   a. lateral nucleus of the amygdala; periaqueductal gray area (PAG)
   b. central nucleus of the amygdale; medial nucleus of the amygdala
   c. central nucleus, lateral hypothalamus
   d. lateral nucleus of the amygdala; medial prefrontal cortex

4. Antidepressant drugs that act as serotonin _____ _____ irritability and aggressiveness.

   a. antagonists; increase
   b. agonists; decrease
   c. antagonists; decrease
   d. agonists; increase

5. In a free-ranging colony, monkeys with the lowest levels of a metabolite of serotonin

   a. showed increased risk-taking behavior.
   b. had the longest survival rates.
   c. usually became the dominant monkeys.
   d. had the highest levels of social competency.

6. People who have sustained damage to the ventral prefrontal cortex

   a. exhibit compulsive behaviors.
   b. do not exhibit normal timidity in strange situations.
   c. respond appropriately to hypothetical social situations, but not when these situations apply to them.
   d. show a tendency to express emotional feelings using gestures and facial expressions rather than verbally.

7. Subjects with ventromedial prefrontal lesions continued to draw cards from a "bad" deck because their lesions may have

   a. increased their preference for the riskier behavior of drawing from the "bad" deck.

b. increased the tendency to continue on a particular course such as drawing from the "bad" deck.
c. prevented normal gratification derived from making correct choices.
d. prevented emotional warnings from changing their playing strategy.

8. What may be the function of the prefrontal cortex?

a. to control voluntary activity
b. to organize hormonal responses to emotional stimuli
c. to make judgments and conclusions
d. to transmit information on emotional states and the consequences of actions to other brain regions.

9. Cutting the vomeronasal nerve in male mice _____ intermale aggression.

a. increases
b. decreases
c. abolishes
d. has no effect

10. Females of some primate species are more likely to engage in fights

a. during interruptions of menstruation caused by events such as pregnancy or low food supply.
b. just before and just after menstruation.
c. around the time of ovulation and just before menstruation.
d. following ovulation if pregnancy does not occur.

11. Select the *incorrect* statement about aggression and men's testosterone levels.

a. Testosterone levels are genetically determined, and are not modified by environmental factors.
b. The primary effect of testosterone might not be on aggression, but on dominance.
c. The relation between testosterone and aggression can vary with socioeconomic status.
d. Correlation does not prove causation.

12. Alcohol increases intermale aggression among

a. all male squirrel monkeys.
b. dominant male squirrel monkeys but only during the mating season.
c. subordinate male squirrel monkeys only.
d. subordinate male squirrel monkeys only when they were engaged in defensive behaviors.

Lesson II: Communication of Emotions and Feelings of Emotions

Read the interim summary on page 390 in your text to re-acquaint yourself with the material in this section.

Learning Objective 11-6 Discuss cross-cultural studies on the expression and comprehension of emotions.

Read pages 380-381 and answer the following questions.

1. Why is the expression and recognition of emotions a beneficial social behavior?

2. a. State Darwin's hypothesis concerning the origin of human facial expression of emotion. (Darwin, 1872/1965)

   b. What evidence did he obtain to support his conclusions?

3. Describe modern research that tends to confirm Darwin's hypothesis. (Ekman and Friesen, 1971; Ekman, 1980)

   a. Who were the subjects?

b. How easily did they recognize the facial expression of Westerners?

c. How easily did Westerners recognize the facial expressions of a man from this tribe shown in Figure 11.15 in your text?

4. Explain the rationale for and the results of research comparing the facial expressions of young blind and sighted children, but not of blind and sighted adults. (Woodworth and Schlosberg, 1954; Izard, 1971)

5. Under what circumstances might we choose to modify our seemingly innate facial expressions?

Learning Objective 11-7 Describe the neural control of the recognition of emotional expression in normal people and people with brain damage.

Read pages 381-386 and answer the following questions.

1. a. What were some of the situations in which Kraut and Johnston (1979) observed the emotional expressions of subjects?

   b. When did the subjects show the greatest reaction?

   c. What does this study suggest about emotional expression and communication?

2. Which hemisphere, the right or left, plays the more important role in the comprehension of emotion?

3. a. Which recognition tasks did patients with right-hemisphere lesions find difficult? (Bowers et al., 1991)

   b. Which recognition tasks did patients with right-hemisphere lesions not find difficult? (Bowers et al., 1991)

   c. What do these responses suggest about the role of the right-hemisphere in imaging or producing emotions?

4. a. Describe the three situations George et al. (1996) used to test comprehension of emotion.

   b. As recorded by functional imaging, when did the right and left hemispheres of the brain show increased activity? (See Figure 11.16 in your text.)

5. What kind of stimuli increased blood flow, presumably indicating activation of the right hemisphere, of a chimpanzee? (Parr and Hopkins, 2000)

6. a. How accurately did a man with pure word deafness identify the emotional content of speech through comprehension of the spoken word? (Heilman et al., 1983)

   b. How accurately did a man with pure word deafness identify the emotional content of speech through the recognition of tone of voice? (Heilman et al., 1983)

c. What do these studies suggest about the components of comprehension of emotion?

7. Summarize evidence that the amygdala may play an important role in the recognition of emotion.

   a. How do lesions of the amygdala affect the ability to recognize facial expressions of emotion? (For example, Adolphs et al., 1999)

   b. Compare the activity of the amygdala when normal people viewed photographs of sad and happy faces. (Morris et al., 1996; Whalen et al., 1998)

   c. What means of emotional recognition apparently remains unaffected by lesions of the amygdala? (Anderson and Phelps, 1998; Adolphs and Tranel, 1999)

   d. Which structures provide important visual information for recognition of facial expressions of emotion to the amygdala? Cite research to support your answer. (Adolphs, 2002; de Gelder et al., 1999)

   e. Morris et al., (2001) studied a patient with blindness caused by damage to the visual association cortex. Which brain regions became active when he viewed faces with fearful expressions?

   f. What do these findings suggest about the function of this subcortical pathway?

8. a. Briefly review neural input to the visual cortex in order to better to understand the role of the amygdala in recognition of emotion. Note the kinds of sensory information relayed to the visual system by the

      1. magnocellular system.

      2. parvocellular system.

   b. Which system is found only in some primates and humans?

   c. Which system sends information about face recognition to the visual association cortex? sends information to the amygdala?

9. a. Describe the two kinds of stimuli, shown in Figure 11.17 in your text that Vuilleumier et al. (2003) presented to subjects.

   b. Which stimulus primarily activated the magnocellular system? the parvocellular system?

   c. What kind of information does the fusiform face area primarily use to recognize faces?

   d. What kind of information does the amygdala primarily use to recognize fear?

10. a. For research conducted by Krolak-Salmon et al. (2004), describe the

      1. subjects.

      2. task.

    b. Which facial expression produced the greatest response?

    c. Recordings indicated that the amygdala showed activity before the visual cortex did. Carefully explain what this finding confirms about neural input to this region and its function. (See Figure 11.18 in your text.)

11. a. What kind of brain damage did patient S. M. sustain? (Adolphs et al., 2005)

b. What was different about the way patient S. M. and a normal control subject looked at photographs of faces? (See Figure 11.19 in your text.)

c. What emotion was she unable to recognize and what may explain her behavior? (See Figure 11.20 in your text. Whalen et al., 2004)

d. What instructions helped her recognition? (Adolphs et al., 2005)

e. What do these results suggest about how the brain recognizes the expression of fear?

12. a. When did a single neuron in the cortex lining the superior temporal sulcus (STS) of a monkey's brain fire most vigorously? (See Figure 11.20 in your text and Perrett et al., 1992)

b. Explain why gaze is important for recognition of emotion.

c. When did people most easily recognize anger? (Adams and Kleck, 2005)

d. When did people most easily recognize fear? (Adams and Kleck, 2005)

e. How do lesions of the STS affect monkeys' ability to discriminate the direction of another animal's gaze? to recognize another animal's face? (Campbell et al., 1990; Heywood and Cowey, 1992)

f. When the direction of the gaze of an animated cartoon of a face that subjects were watching changed, which brain regions became active? (Pelphrey et al., 2003)

g. What do these results suggest about the role of these regions?

13. a. What kind of brain damage appeared to cause the most severe impairment in the ability to recognize and identify facial expressions of emotion? (See Figure 11.21 in your text. Adolphs et al., 2000)

b. Summarize a possible explanation of these results.

14. Explain how the mirror-neuron system may help us understand how other people feel. (Carr et al., 2003)

15. a. Briefly describe Moebius syndrome, noting its cause, and effects on the movement of the eyes and face. (Cole, 2001)

b. How may this syndrome further our understanding of the recognition facial expression of emotion?

16. a. Finally, what kind of brain damage impairs people's ability to recognize facial expressions of disgust? (Sprengelmeyer et al., 1996, 1997; Calder et al., 2000)

b. What kind of stimuli activate the insular cortex? (Wicker et al., 2003)

c. What were the results of an online survey on disgust conducted by the British Broadcasting System? (See Figure 11.22 in your text.)

d. What is a possible explanation of those results?

Learning Objective 11-8 Discuss the neural control of emotional expression in normal people and people with brain damage.

Read pages 386-389 and answer the following questions.

1. What does it mean to say that it is impossible to voluntarily produce a genuine smile? (See Figure 11.23 in your text. Duchenne, 1862/1990)

2. a. What kind of voluntary and involuntary facial movements can patients with
    1. volitional facial paresis make?
    2. emotional facial paresis make? (Representative facial movements are shown in Figure 11.24 in your text. Hopf et al., 1992; Topper et al., 1995; Urban et al., 1998)

   b. What kind of brain damage causes each of these syndromes?

   c. What do these syndromes indicate about the movement of facial muscles and the genuine expression of emotion?

3. Summarize research on a more intense emotion—laughter.
   a. How did seizures affect the behavior of a patient studied by Arroyo et al. (1993)?

   b. Where did the seizures begin? Following surgery to remove a nearby noncancerous tumor, how did the patient's behavior change?

   c. Which brain region may be involved in the muscular movements that produce laughter?
   d. What kind of brain damage alters a person's ability to understand and laugh at a joke? (Shammi and Stuss, 1999)
   e. In a functional imaging study, which brain region was activated by all of the jokes subjects heard? (Goel and Dolan, 2001)

4. The _______________ hemisphere appears to be specialized for both the _______________ of emotion and the _______________ of emotion.

5. a. How are the chimerical faces, shown in Figure 11.25 in your text, created?

   b. When researchers studied chimerical faces , what did they note and what do their findings suggest? (Sackeim and Gur, 1978)

   c. What more natural observations confirmed this? (Moscovitch and Olds, 1982; Borod et al., 1998)

   d. When the chimerical faces technique was used with rhesus monkeys, what did the analysis of the videotapes indicate about hemispheric specialization:

1. of emotional expression? (Study Figure 11.26 in your text.)

2. in the evolution of emotional expression? (Hauser, 1993)

6. Compare the effects of left- and right-hemisphere lesions on expressions of emotion using tone of voice.

7. a. Summarize the results of surgery to treat a serious seizure disorder in S. P? (Study Figure 11.27 in your text. Anderson and Phelps, 2000)

   b. What does this case suggest about the role of the amygdala?

Read the interim summary on page 393 in your text to re-acquaint yourself with the information in this section.

Learning Objective 11-9 Discuss the James-Lange theory of feelings of emotion and evaluate relevant research.

Read pages 390-393 and answer the following questions.

1. Outline the James-Lange theory in your own words. (James, 1884; Lange, 1887)

2. Carefully study Figure 11.28 in your text that diagrams the James-Lange theory. Check your understanding by describing the process.

3. According to the theory, in what order do these events produce feelings of emotion?

   "I'm more nervous than I thought I was." / Her stomach felt queasy as she waited to be interviewed a second time for the job.

4. In what way does the James-Lange theory appear to contradict personal experience?

5. a. Explain two of Cannon's objections to the James-Lange theory. (Cannon, 1927)

   b. Refute his objections.

6. Why is the theory difficult to verify?

7. a. Describe the subjects interviewed by Hohman (1966).

   b. Explain how he tested the James-Lange theory by studying these subjects.

   c. What was the relationship between the level of injury and the intensity of feelings of emotion? Explain.

8. a. Why did Ekman and his colleagues ask subjects to move particular facial muscles, but gave them no further information? (Ekman et al., 1983; Levenson et al., 1990)

b. What, according to physiological monitoring, happened to the subjects while they made these movements?

c. Suggest two explanations for the results you have just described.

9. Study Figure 11.29 in your text to see the facial expressions posed by adults in front of infants and the infants' responses. What do their responses suggest about the tendency to imitate? (Field et al., 1982)

Lesson II Self Test

1. Accurate identification of the facial expressions of Westerners by members of an isolated New Guinea tribe tends to confirm Darwin's hypothesis that emotional expressions

   a. are innate, unlearned responses.
   b. consist of four responses: fear, anger, sorrow, and surprise.
   c. are immune to the effects of socialization.
   d. are identical, whether posed or spontaneous.

2. The _____ hemisphere plays a more important role in comprehension of emotion from _____.

   a. right; word meaning
   b. left; tone of voice
   c. right; facial expression
   d. left; facial imitation

3. In monkeys, where are the neurons involved in recognition of the direction of another monkey's gaze found?

   a. pulvinar
   b. superior temporal sulcus
   c. basal ganglia
   d. thalamus

4. The _____ receives information from the _____ system permitting it to recognize the facial expression of _____.

   a. visual cortex; parvocellular; fear
   b. insular cortex; magnocellular; disgust
   c. superior colliculus; parvocellular; disgust
   d. amygdala; magnocellular; fear

5. The mirror-neuron system may be involved in our ability

   a. to recognize whether the expression of an emotion is directed toward us or someone else.
   b. to empathize with the emotions of other people.
   c. to modify our own facial expressions of emotion.
   d. to assess whether our own facial expressions of emotion are understood by others.

6. A person with _____ cannot make an emotional expression when asked to do so, but can express a genuine emotion.

   a. emotional facial paresis.
   b. volitional facial paresis.
   c. Moebius syndrome.
   d. Duchenne's syndrome.

7 Research results using the chimerical faces technique suggest that the _____ half of the _____ is _____ expressive.

   a. left; brain; more
   b. left; face; more
   c. right; brain; less
   d. right; face; more

8. Which brain region may be involved in the muscular movements that produce laughter?

   a. basal ganglia
   b. right primary motor cortex
   c. anterior cingulate cortex
   d. right ventromedial prefrontal cortex

9. The case of S. P., a woman with bilateral amygdala damage, suggests that the amygdala

   a. is involved in the production of facial expressions of emotion.
   b. is not involved in the recognition of facial expression of emotion.
   c. is involved in the recognition of emotion from tone of voice.
   d. is involved only in the recognition of positive emotions from tone of voice.

10. According to the James-Lange theory, emotional feelings
    a. result from sensory feedback from the responses a person makes in emotion-producing situations.
    b. are a direct response to emotion-producing situations.
    c. are a product of both sensory feedback and acquired social behavior.
    d. result in emotional behavior.

11. The James-Lange theory is difficult to verify experimentally because
    a. it is difficult to produce real emotions in experimental settings.
    b. it attempts to explain private events.
    c. genuine expression of emotion is often affected by a person's cultural background.
    d. there is little consensus on what constitutes a typical emotional reaction to a particular situation.

12. The results of research on patients with spinal cord injuries suggests that the intensity of their emotional states is related to the
    a. frequency of social contact.
    b. location of injury to the spinal cord.
    c. length of time following injury.
    d. perception of self-worth.

Across

1. Activity of synapses that secrete this neurotransmitter inhibits aggression
5. Facial paresis; difficulty moving facial muscles voluntarily
7. The region of the prefrontal cortex at the base of the anterior frontal lobes, adjacent to the midline
8. Response to threat behavior of another animal that tends to prevent an attack
10. Cortex involved in control of emotional reactions to social situations
11. Attack on member of another species on which animal normally preys

Down

2. Facial paresis, difficulty moving facial muscles in response to emotions
3. A nucleus of the amygdala that receives sensory information from the neocortex, thalamus, and hippocampus and send projections to the basal, accessory basal, and central nucleus of the amygdala
4. Emotion theory; feelings of emotion result from feedback from emotional responses
6. Nucleus of amygdala that sends projections to many regions; involved in emotional responses
9. A group of subnuclei of the amygdala that receives sensory input, including information about the presence of odors and pheromones, and relays it to the medial basal forebrain and hypothalamus

Answers for Self Tests

Lesson I

1. c Obj. 11-1
2. b Obj. 11-1
3. d Obj. 11-1
4. b Obj. 11-2
5. a Obj. 11-2
6. c Obj. 11-3
7. d Obj. 11-3
8. d Obj. 11-3
9. c Obj. 11-4
10. c Obj. 11-4
11. a Obj. 11-5
12. b Obj. 11-5

Lesson II

1. a Obj. 11-6
2. c Obj. 11-7
3. b Obj. 11-7
4. d Obj. 11-7
5. b Obj. 11-7
6. b Obj. 11-8
7. b Obj. 11-8
8. c Obj. 11-8
9. b Obj. 11-8
10. a Obj. 11-9
11. b Obj. 11-9
12. b Obj. 11-9

CHAPTER 12
Ingestive Behavior

Lesson I: Drinking, Eating and Metabolism, What Starts a Meal, and What Stops a Meal

Read the interim summary on page 403 of your text to re-acquaint yourself with the material in this section.

Learning Objective 12-1 Explain the characteristics of a regulatory mechanism.

Read pages 395-396 and answer the following questions.

1. Define and explain the importance of
   a. homeostasis.

   b. ingestive behavior.

2. List and explain the functions of the four essential features of a regulatory mechanism. (See Figure 12.1 in your text.)

   1.
   2.
   3.
   4.

4. Using the example of the room thermostat, explain the process of negative feedback.

5. a. What role do ingestive behaviors play in homeostasis?

   b. Study Figure 12.2 in your text and explain the relation of the satiety mechanism to the correctional mechanism in the control of drinking.

Learning Objective 12-2 Describe the fluid compartments of the body and explain the control of osmometric and volumetric thirst.

Read pages 397-402 and answer the following questions.

1. There are _____ major fluid compartments in the body—one for _______________ fluid and _____ for _______________ fluid. The intracellular fluid is the fluid portion of the _______________ of cells and contains approximately _____ percent of the body's water. The extracellular fluid includes the _______________ fluid or blood plasma, the _______________ fluid of the brain, and the _______________ fluid between our cells. (Study Figure 12.3 in your text.)

2. Use the terms *isotonic, hypertonic,* and *hypotonic* to explain why the concentration of the interstitial fluid must remain constant. (Study Figure 12.4 in your text.)

3. a. Explain why the volume of blood plasma must be closely regulated by describing the consequences of hypovolemia.

   b. What limited correctional mechanism does the body use when blood volume is too low?

4. Why are the solute concentration of the intracellular fluid and the volume of the blood monitored by two different sets of receptors?

5. With the help of Figure 12.5 in your text, explain how our bodies loose water from three fluid compartments through evaporation, and the accompanying changes that occur.

6. a. _______________ thirst occurs when the tonicity, that is the _______________ _______________ of the interstitial fluid _______________.

   b. What stimulus do these thirst detectors respond to?

7. Study Figure 12.6 in your text and explain how the size and firing rate of an osmoreceptor changes as the surrounding interstitial fluid becomes more concentrated. Be sure that you understand the movement of water in osmosis. (Verney, 1947)

8. Describe what happens, step by step, to the fluid compartments of the body when we eat a salty meal.

9. a. Name and describe the location of the part of the brain where the osmoreceptors are located.

b. What other specialized structures are found there? (Figure 12.7 in your text shows the circumventricular organs of a rat.)

c. What circumventricular organ have you already studied?

d. Which of the two circumventricular organs of the lamina terminalis is thought to contain most of the osmoreceptors? (McKinley et al., 2004)

10. Name and describe the characteristics of the receptor in the membrane of osmoreceptors. (Liedtke et al., 2000)

11. a. While their brains were being scanned, what kind of injections did researchers give normal human subjects? (Egan et al., 2003)

b. Which brain regions then showed strong activation?

c. When the thirsty subjects were permitted to drink water to satisfy their thirst, the activity of which brain region returned to normal? continued to show high activity?

d. Carefully explain what the activity level of the anterior cingulate cortex indicated? the activity level of the lamina terminalis? (See Figure 12.8 in your text.)

12. _______________ thirst occurs when the volume of blood plasma _______________.

13. a. Why does evaporation produce both osmometric and volumetric thirst?

b. Identify three conditions that cause volumetric thirst.

1. 2. 3.

14. Where are the two sets of detectors for initiating volumetric thirst and a salt appetite located?

15. a. What is the primary cause of a reduced flow of blood to the kidneys?

b. How do the cells in the kidneys that detect a reduction respond?

c. Briefly explain how angiotensin II (AII) is produced.

16. a. List three physiological effects of AII.

1.

2.

3.

b. List two behavioral effects of AII.

1.

2.

17. Review what you have just learned by studying Figure 12.9 in your text and completing Figure 1, on the next page.

18. Briefly explain how atrial baroreceptors in the heart detect changes in blood volume.

19. a. How did Fitzsimons and Moore-Gillon (1980) restrict the flow of blood to the hearts of subject dogs?

    b. In response to the reduced blood volume, what did the dogs begin to do?

20. When, after cutting the nerves connecting the atrial baroreceptors with the brain, the blood flow to the heart was temporarily reduced, what did the subject dogs do? (Quillen et al. 1990)

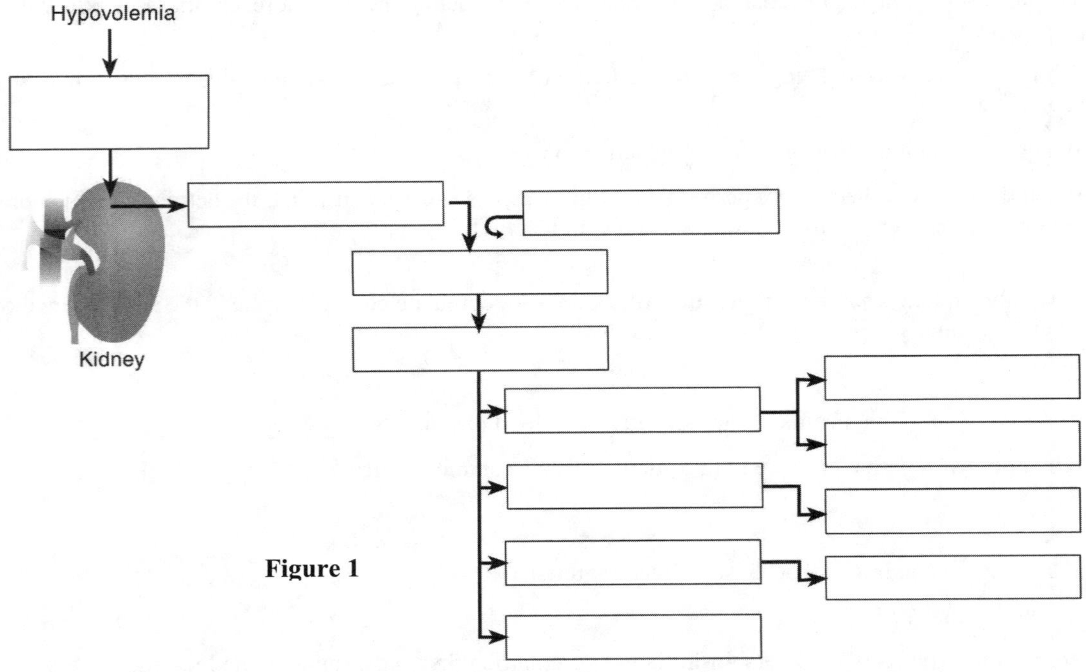

Figure 1

Learning Objective 12-3 Discuss the neural control of thirst.

Read page 402 and answer the following questions.

1. To review what you have just learned, complete these sentences.
    a. Osmometric thirst occurs when
    b. Volumetric thirst occurs when
    c. Osmometric receptors that initiate drinking are located in the
    d. The lamina terminalis appears to be the where
    e. Sensory information from baroreceptors of the heart is sent to

2. a. What physical property of angiotensin II suggests that it may produce thirst through one of the circumventricular organs?

    b. Which circumventricular organ is the site of action of blood angiotensin? (See Figure 12.7 in your text.)

3. How is drinking affected by
    a. very low doses of angiotensin injected directly into the SFO?

b. destruction of the SFO?

c. injection of a drug that blocks angiotensin receptors? (Simpson et al., 1978)

4. How did Phillips and Felix (1976) demonstrate the presence of angiotensin receptors in the SFO?

5. Where do neurons in the SFO project? (Return to Figure 12.7.)

6. Outline the explanation suggested by Thrasher and his colleagues of the role the median preoptic nucleus plays in osmometric and volumetric thirst. (See Figure 12.10 in your text. Thrasher, 1989)

7. What is the cause of adipsia and how is this condition managed? (McIver et al., 1991)

8. For a concise explanation of the regulation of drinking, consult the interim summary.

Read the interim summary on page 406 in your text to re-acquaint yourself with the material in this section.

Learning Objective 12-4 Describe the characteristics of the two nutrient reservoirs and the absorptive and fasting phases of metabolism.

Read pages 403-405 and answer the following questions.

1. a. Why do we eat?

   1. 2.

   b. How do our bodies use most of the food we eat?

2. What is the location of the short-term nutrient reservoir and what is stored there?

3. Explain how glycogen is produced and the mechanism that stimulates its release.

   a. Cells in the ________________ are stimulated by ________________, produced in the ________________, to convert ________________ into glycogen and store it.

   b. What causes the level of glucose in the blood to fall and where is it detected?

   c. List the two changes that occur in the pancreas in response to a fall in glucose?

   1. 2.

   d. What is the effect of glucagon release?

   e. Review what you have just learned by studying Figure 12.11 in your text and completing Figure 2.

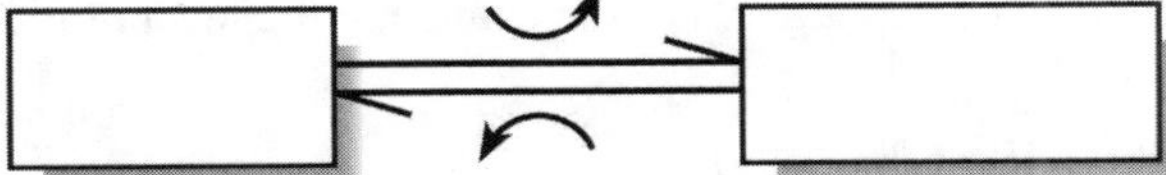

Figure 2

4. a. The short-term carbohydrate reservoir in the liver is the principal fuel supply for what part of the body?

   b. If the short-term reservoir is depleted, what is its next source of reserved fuel?

5. a. The long-term reservoir of _______________ tissue is found beneath the _______________ and in the _______________ _______________. It is filled with _______________, complex molecules that contain _______________ combined with three _______________ _______________.

   b. Briefly describe the cells of adipose tissue.

6. When the digestive tract is empty, what three factors initiate the breakdown of triglycerides into glycerol and fatty acids?

7. Describe the mechanism that saves glucose for the brain during the fasting phase of metabolism. Be sure to mention the role of glucose transporters.

8. To review the fasting phase of metabolism study Figure 12.12 in your text. Continue your review by summarizing the effects of

   a. a fall in the blood glucose level on the pancreas.

   b. the absence of insulin on the cells of the body.

   c. the presence of glucagon and the absence of insulin on the liver.

   d. and the presence of glucagon, the absence of insulin, and the increased activity of the sympathetic nervous system on fat cells.

   e. prolonged fasting.

9. When does the absorptive phase of metabolism begin?

10. List the three nutrients that are supplied by a well-balanced meal.

    1. 2. 3.

11. Describe the changes that occur as each of these nutrients is absorbed.

    a. As carbohydrates break down, what change occurs in the level of glucose in the blood, and how is this change detected?

    b. What change occurs in the pancreas as a result of the change in the level of glucose?

    c. How does insulin affect the cells of the body?

    d. What happens to any extra glucose?

    e. As proteins break down, how are the amino acids used?

    f. How are fats used?

12. To review the absorptive phase of metabolism again study Figure 12.12.

Read the interim summary on pages 409-410 of your text to re-acquaint yourself with the material in this section.

Learning Objective 12-5 Discuss environmental, gastric, and metabolic factors that begin a meal.

Read pages 406-409 and answer the following questions.

1. To maintain a fairly stable body weight, what two
   a. factors must balance?
      1. 2.
   b. mechanisms are necessary if energy expenditure is constant?
      1. 2.
2. a. Briefly explain how cycles of abundant food and little food influenced the behavior of our ancestors.
   b. Therefore, what kind of regulatory mechanisms evolved?
   c. What do people probably mean when they say they eat because they get hungry?
   d. What factors may account for and maintain our custom of eating three meals a day?
3. Look at what starts a meal beginning with the role of the peptide hormone ghrelin.
   a. Where is ghrelin released? (Kojima et al., 1999)
   b. What does the name indicate about its function?
   c. When do blood levels of this hormone rise? fall? (Study Figure 12.13 in your text.)
   d. What is the effect of subcutaneous injections or infusions of ghrelin into the cerebral ventricles? (Tschöp et al., 2000; Ariyasu et al., 2001)
   e. What may be the reason why gastric bypass surgery is successful in treating obesity?
   f. What is the probable cause of Prader-Willi syndrome described in the opening to Chapter 12?
4. What procedures suppress ghrelin secretion? do not suppress secretion? (Schaller et al., 2003)
5. a. When a cuff placed around the pylorus of subject rat is inflated, what happens to food in the rat's stomach?
   b. What happened to ghrelin secretion, when food was infused into the stomach and the cuff was
      1. inflated? (Williams et al., 2003)
      2. not inflated?
6. How was ghrelin secretion affected if food was infused directly into the small intestine, bypassing the stomach? (Overduin et al., 2004)
7. What do all these results suggest about the control of ghrelin secretion?
8. Cite evidence that indicates there are multiple short-term hunger signals from
   a. people who have had gastric bypass surgery.
   b. mice with targeted mutations against the ghrelin gene or receptor. (Sun et al., 2003; Sun et al., 2004)
9. Look at metabolic factors that signal hunger.

a. Define *hypoglycemia* in your own words.

b. Explain two ways hypoglycemia can be produced experimentally.

c. Define *glucoprivation* in your own words.

d. What is the result of this condition?

e. Define *lipoprivation* in your own words.

f. List the two drugs which, when injected, cause lipoprivation.

1. 2.

10. There appear to be two sets of detectors for metabolic fuels. Where are they located and what do they monitor?

11. a. How was glucoprivic hunger induced and then abolished? (Study Figure 12.14 in your text. Novin et al., 1973)

b. How was eating affected by injections of 5-TG into two regions of the brain? (Be sure you understand the effects of 5-TG. Ritter et al., 2000)

c. How was lipoprivic hunger induced and then abolished? (Ritter and Taylor, 1990)

d. What do these experiments suggest about the location of detectors for glucoprivation and lipoprivation and how information from them is transmitted to the brain? (Friedman et al., 2005)

12. Complete this table by labeling the detectors found on each side of the blood-brain barrier.

Inside the blood–brain barrier	***Outside the blood–brain barrier***
Detectors for ______________ are located in the ____________.	Detectors for ______________ or ________________ are located in the ____________.

13. To review the stimuli for hunger study Figure 12.15 in your text.

14. Summarize research that suggests that no single set or receptors controls eating.

a. Tordoff et al. (1982)

b. Ritter et al.(1992)

Read the interim summary on page 413 of your text to re-acquaint yourself with the material in this section.

Learning Objective 12-6 Discuss the head, gastric, and intestinal factors responsible for stopping a meal.

Read pages 410-413 and answer the following questions:

1. a. Where in the body should we look for the source of short-term and long-term satiety signals?

b. What effect does this information have on the brain?

2. a. List factors that encourage us to eat a

1. large meal.
2. small meal. (reviewed by De Castro, 2004)

b. Compare the length of your lists and explain what that indicates about the strength of satiety signals.

3. Define *head factors* in your own words, including the kind of information they detect.

4. a. Use one word to describe how long a rat with a gastric fistula will continue to eat.

   b. Which group of subjects were more satisfied with their meal—those who ate high-fat soup or those whose had the soup infused into their stomachs? (Cecil et al., 1998)

   c. What do these findings indicate about the role of head factors in satiety?

5. a. Once a rat had eaten all it wanted, researchers removed the food from its stomach. What did they observe? (Davis and Campbell, 1973)

   b. In later research the food was replaced with a nonnutritive saline solution, how much did the rats then eat? (Deutsch and Gonzalez, 1980)

   c. What can we conclude from the results about the role of the stomach in short-term satiety?

   d. What conclusion is not justified?

6. Afferent axons in the duodenum are sensitive to what kind of stimuli? (Ritter et al., 1992)

7. a. What did human subjects report when an inflatable bag in their stomachs was inflated and their stomachs

      1. were empty?
      2. were being infused with fats or carbohydrates?

   b. What do the results suggest about stomach and intestinal satiety figures? (Feinle et al., 1997)

8. Before studying the role of cholecystokinin (CCK) in satiety, note some information about this hormone.

   a. Where and when is CCK secreted?

   b. What effect does CCK have on the gallbladder?

   c. What effect does CCK have on the pylorus?

   d. Why has CCK been studied as a satiety signal?

   e. How do injections of CCK affect eating? (Gibbs et al., 1973; Smith et al., 1982)

   f. How does a genetic mutation that prevents the production of CCK receptors alter eating in affected rats? What is the presumed reason? (Moran et al., 1998)

   g. Where is the site of action of CCK? (Moran et al., 1998)

   h. How can the suppressive effect of CCK be overcome and what does this finding indicate about how the effects of CCK are transmitted to the brain? (South and Ritter, 1988)

9. a. The vagus nerve transmits information between the _______________ _______________ and the _______________.

   b. How does damage to the vagus nerve alter the effects of ghrelin on eating in both humans and rats? (le Roux et al., 2005)

   c. How is the firing rate of the vagus nerve affected by injections of ghrelin? (Date et al., 2002)

   d. How is the firing rate of the vagus nerve affected by injections of CCK? (Date et al., 2002)

   e. What effect does capsaicin have on the effects of ghrelin and CCK?

   f. What do these findings suggest about the location of the receptors that ghrelin and CCK bind with?

10. PYY, a peptide released in the _______________ _______________, may serve as a satiety signal. The amount of PPY released after a _______________ is proportional to the amount of calories that were just ingested. Nonnutritive substances have _______________ effect on its secretion. Injections of PYY significantly _______________ the amount of food hungry rats eat. (Pedersen-Bjergaard et al., 1996; Batterham et al., 2002)

11. Summarize research that suggests that PYY may not play an important role in satiety. (Moran et al., 2005)

12. a. When, after a meal, do internal system variables that control hunger, return to normal?

    b. Where does this last stage of satiety appear to take place?

13. a. How did infusion of small amounts of glucose and fructose into the hepatic portal vein affect rats' appetites for food? (Tordoff and Friedman, 1988)

    b. Why did they conclude that it is the liver that signals continued satiety to the brain?

14. Carefully explain why insulin may serve as a satiety signal. Cite research to support your answer. (Unger et al., 1989; Woods et al., 1979; Brüning et al., 2000)

15. Finally, review research on the mechanisms of long-term body fat regulation.

    a. If an animal gains weight through forced feeding and is later permitted to choose its food, how is subsequent food intake affected? (See Figure 12.16 in your text. Wilson et al., 1990)

    b. If an animal loses weight through enforced dieting, how are satiety factors affected? (Cabanac and Lafrance, 1991)

16. Explain why the system variable that permits us to maintain a relatively stable body weight arises not from body weight itself but, more likely, from body fat.

17. a. What are some of the characteristics of the ob mouse? Be sure to mention leptin in your answer.

    b. What is the cause of obesity in the ob mouse? (Campfield et al., 1995; Halaas et al., 1995; Pelleymounter et al., 1995)

    c. If ob mice are given injections of leptin, what physical changes occur? (See Figure 12.17 in your text.)

18. To review what you have learned, match the term with the correct definition.

_____ glycogen	a. adipose tissue
_____ glucagon	b. orexigen secreted in the brain
_____ glucose	c. principal fuel of the brain
_____ glycerol	d. promotes entry of glucose into cells
_____ ghrelin	e. insoluble carbohydrate found in the short-term reservoir
_____ insulin	f. peptide hormone whose effects oppose those of insulin
_____ long-term reservoir	g. converted by the liver to glucose
_____ CCK	h. anorexigen secreted in the brain
_____ MCH	i. duodenal hormone that inhibits eating
_____ CART	j. anorexigen secreted by the intestines
_____ PYY	k. orexigen secreted by the stomach

Lesson I Self Test

1. Satiety mechanisms
   a. monitor system variables.
   b. replenish depleted stores of food, fluid, or nutrients.
   c. are a second correctional mechanism if detectors fail to work properly.
   d. monitor the activity of correctional mechanisms.
2. Osmometric thirst occurs when the
   a. tonicity of the interstitial fluid increases.
   b. volume of the intravascular fluid decreases.
   c. blood flow to the kidneys decreases.
   d. blood level of renin increases.
3. Detectors responsible for initiating volumetric thirst are located in the
   a. circumventricular organs and the duodenum.
   b. duodenum and the kidneys.
   c. kidneys and in the heart and large blood vessels.
   d. heart and brain.
4. Most or all of the signals for osmometric and volumetric thirst appear to be integrated in the
   a. nucleus of the solitary tract of the medulla.
   b. lamina terminalis.
   c. subfornical organ.
   d. OVLT.
5. The short-term fuel reservoir is located in the _____ and is filled with _____.
   a. adipose tissue; triglycerides
   b. digestive tract; amino acids
   c. pancreas; glucose
   d. cells of the liver and the muscles; glycogen
6. During the absorptive phase of metabolism
   a. the blood level of glucose rises.
   b. the pancreas ceases to secrete insulin.
   c. proteins, carbohydrates, and fats are used to fuel the cells of the body.
   d. glucose dissolves in fats and is stored in adipose tissue.
7. During the fasting phase of metabolism
   a. supplies of glucose are abundant.
   b. most cells live on fatty acids.
   c. all cells of the body use glucose as a fuel.
   d. excess nutrients are stored in the liver, muscles, and adipose tissue.
8. Ghrelin secretion
   a. can be suppressed by injections of nutrients into the blood.
   b. appears to be controlled by receptors in the liver.
   c. decreases with fasting and increases with food intake.
   d. is a potent stimulator of food intake.
9. Detectors that monitor the availability of nutrients outside the blood-brain barrier are located in the
   a. liver.
   b. pancreas.
   c. stomach.
   d. circumventricular organs.
10. Injections of cholecystokinin (CCK)
    a. activate stretch receptors in the stomach.
    b. promote stomach emptying.
    c. inhibit the contraction of the gallbladder.
    d. suppress eating.
11. By injecting glucose and fructose into the hepatic portal vein, researchers confirmed that the liver
    a. contains receptors that respond when the liver receives nutrients from the intestines.
    b. metabolizes sugars.
    c. is the first organ to signal satiety.
    d. breaks down fatty acids.

12. If ob mice are given daily injections of leptin
    a. they lose weight rapidly because they develop diabetes and cannot metabolize glucose.
    b. they eat even greater quantities of food.
    c. their weight returns to normal.
    d. eating behavior is not affected.

Lesson II: Brain Mechanisms and Eating Disorders

Read the interim summary on page 420 of your text to re-acquaint yourself with the material in this section.

Learning Objective 12-7 Describe research on the role of the brain stem and hypothalamus in hunger.

Read pages 414-418 and answer the following questions.

1. a. Briefly explain the surgical procedure of decerebration shown in Figure 12.18 in your text.

   b. What are the consequences of this procedure?

   c. Describe research results that demonstrate even decerebrate animals perform ingestive behaviors. How do decerebrate rats respond to

      1. food in their mouths?
      2. different tastes?
      3. hunger and satiety signals?

   d. What do these studies indicate about the functions of the brain stem?

2. a. What kind of sensory information does the AP/NST receive?

   b. Where is this information then transmitted?

   c. What kind of stimuli increase the activity of neurons in this region?

   d. How is lipoprivic hunger and glucoprivic hunger affected by lesions of AP/NST? (See Figure 12.19 in your text. Ritter and Taylor, 1990; Ritter et al., 1994)

3. Briefly summarize conclusions that prevailed for a long time about the role of the lateral and ventromedial hypothalamus in hunger and satiety. (See Figure 12.20 in your text. Anand and Brobeck, 1951; Teitelbaum and Stellar, 1954; Hetherington and Ranson, 1942)

4. a. Melanin-concentrating hormone (MCH) and orexin are both secreted by the lateral hypothalamus. Explain their general role in the control of hunger. (Be sure to use the term *orexigens* . See Figure 12.21 in your text.)

   b. What is another function of MCH? (Kawauchi et al., 1983)

   c. What is another name and function of orexin that you have already studied?

   d. What is the behavioral effect of injections of MCH or orexin into the lateral ventricles or various other regions of the brain?

   e. If rats are deprived of food, how are messenger RNA levels for MCH and orexin affected? (Qu et al., 1996; Sakurai et al., 1998; Dube et al., 1999)

   f. Which of these peptide neurotransmitters, MCH or orexin, appears to play a more important role in feeding?

   g. How are mice with a targeted mutation against the MCH gene affected? (Shimada et al., 1998)

   h. How are mice with a targeted mutation against the orexin gene affected? (Hara et al., 2001)

i. How are genetically-engineered mice with increased production of MCH in the hypothalamus affected? (Ludwig et al., 2001)

5. a. Compare the locomotor activity and level of wakefulness of normal mice and mice with a targeted mutation against the orexin gene just before their single daily meal. (Mieda et al., 2004)

   b. What do these results suggest about the role of orexin in hunger and sleep? (Yamanaka et al., 2003)

6. Trace the connections between MCH and orexin neurons and other brain structures shown in Figure 12.22 in your text. (Sawchenko, 1998; Nambu et al., 1999)

7. Review more research on the role of the lateral hypothalamus in eating, this time involving the neurotransmitter, neuropeptide Y (NPY).

   a. How does NPY affect food intake? (Clark et al., 1984)

   b. How do infusions of this neuropeptide into the hypothalamus affect eating? Be sure to mention the kinds of behaviors that rats will engage in to obtain food. (Flood and Morley, 1991; Jewett et al., 1992)

   c. Where are the cell bodies of most of the neurons that secrete NPY found? (Look back at Figure 12.20.)

   d. Hypothalamic levels of NPY are increased by _______________ _______________ and decreased by _______________. (Sahu et al., 1988)

   e. If NPY receptors are blocked, how is feeding caused by food deprivation affected? (Myers et al., 1995)

   f. What is the response of

      1. normal mice to induced glucoprivation? (Sindelar et al., 2004)

      2. mice with a targeted mutation against the gene for NPY to glucoprivation?

8. a. Trace the neural circuits for the effects of NPY on feeding. Where are neurons that release NPY located and where do the terminals of these neurons project?

   b. How does the arcuate nucleus respond to glucoprivation? (Li and Ritter, 2004)

   c. If a toxin is injected into the arcuate nucleus, how is the medulla affected and then glucoprivic eating?

   d. What do these findings suggest about the pathways involved in glucoprivic eating?

9. Look at some research on ghrelin.

   a. How is the weight of rats without hypothalamic ghrelin receptors affected? (Shuto et al., 2002)

   b. Where may ghrelin produce its effect on appetite and metabolism? (Willesen et al, 1999; Nakazato et al., 2001)

   c. What was the result of application of ghrelin to living brain tissue? (Van den Top et al., 2004)

   d. Which hunger signals, therefore, affect orexigenic NPY neurons?

10. Describe the possible route through which ghrelin signals reach the arcuate nucleus. (Williams and Cummings, 2005)

11. a. Where do these NPY-secreting neurons send a projection of axons? (Broberger et al., 1998; Elias et al., 1998a)

    b. What is the presumed function of this connection?

    c. What other region receives a projection of axons from NPY neurons? (Bai et al., 1985)

    d. In addition to NPY, what other peptide do these hypothalamic neurons secrete? (Hahn et al., 1998)

    e. If a very small amount of it is infused into the third ventricle of a rat, what behavioral effect occurs? (Lu et al., 2001)

12. Endocannabinoids may stimulate _______________ by increasing the release of _____ and _______________. THC, the active ingredient in _______________, mimics their effect. Levels of the endocannabinoids are highest during _______________ and lowest during _______________.

13. Describe a medical use of cannabinoid agonists and agonists.

14. To review what you have just learned, study Figure 12.23 in your text.

Learning Objective 12-8 Describe research on the role of the hypothalamus in satiety.

Read pages 418-419 and answer the following questions.

1. a. Where is leptin secreted, and what are its behavioral and metabolic effects?

   b. Which receptors does leptin bind with to produce these effects?

   c. Summarize some of the effects of activating leptin receptors on NPY/AGRP-secreting neurons of the arcuate nucleus on the release of orexin and MCH. (Glaum et al., 1996; Jobst et al., 2004)

2. Explain why leptin supplements have not been a successful treatment for obesity.

3. What does the acronym CART stand for? (Douglas et al., 1995)

4. a. Where are CART neurons found and where do they send axons? (Koylu et al., 1998)

   b. Which are most important for the study of satiety?

   c. What is the presumed function of CART neurons?

   d. How does the level of CART in an animal change with

      1. administration of cocaine or amphetamine?

      2. food deprivation?

   e. What changes occurs in ob mice

      1. if leptin is injected into their cerebral ventricles?

      2. if CART is injected into their cerebral ventricles?

   f. How does an infusion of a CART antibody affect feeding? (Kristensen et al., 1998)

5. a. Through which connections may CART neurons increase metabolic rate?

   b. Through which connections may CART neurons suppress eating?

   c. Why is it likely that CART neurons interact with leptin to signal satiety? (Elias et al., 1998b)

6. a. A second anorexigen is _____-__________________ ___________________ (_____). It binds with the __________________-____ _________________ receptor (_____) and acts as an ________________.

   b. What other chemical, that you have already studied, binds with this receptor and stimulates eating?

   c. How does leptin affect CART/α-MSH neurons? NPY/AGRP neurons? (Elmquist et al., 1999; Wynne et al., 2005 for specific references.)

7. a. What is the presumed primary effect on eating of the MC4 receptor?

   b. Use one word to describe the weight of mice with a targeted mutation against the gene for the MC4 receptor.

   c. How do agonists for the MC4 receptor affect metabolic rate?

   d. How then does the MC4 receptor appear to reduce body weight? (Hwa et al., 2001)

8. Summarize evidence that PYY may be an important short-term satiety signal. (Batterham et al., 2002)

9. Immediately review some of the connections of CART neurons of the arcuate nucleus and the behavioral effects of leptin that are summarized in Figure 12.24in your text. Complete Figure 3.

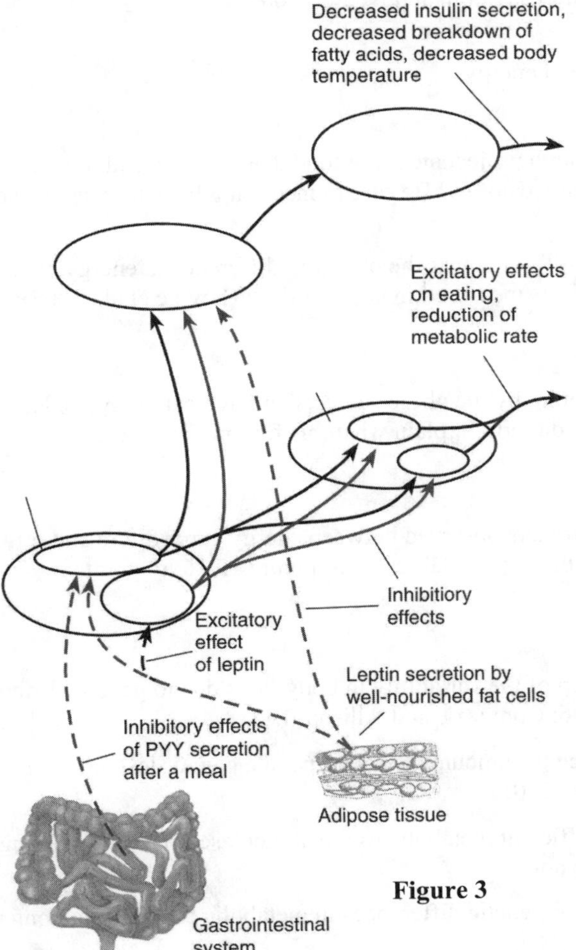

Figure 3

Read the interim summary on pages 427-428 of your text to re-acquaint yourself with the material in this section.

Learning Objective 12-9 Discuss the physiological factors that may contribute to obesity.

Read pages 420-423 and answer the following questions.

1. To underscore the growing problem of obesity, note several relevant statistics.
   a. The percentage of men and women in the United States who are overweight, as defined by a BMI of over 25
   b. The increase in the incidence of obesity over the past 20 years, as defined by a BMI of over 30 (Ogden et al., 2003)
   c. The prevalence of obesity and type 2 diabetes in the United States. (See Figure 12.25 in your text.)
2. What is the probable cause of extreme obesity?
3. Briefly explain how eating patterns and thus body weight are affected by these environmental factors.
   a. Fast-food restaurants
   b. Snack food, their availability and nutritional content (Bray et al., 2004)
   c. Energy expenditure patterns (Booth and Neufer, 2005)
4. List the two ways we expend energy.
   1. 2.
5. Nonobese people in a research project ate more food than they needed to maintain their weight. How did their bodies use about these excess calories? Be sure to mention NEAT in your answer. (Levine et al., 1999)
6. a. In later research on NEAT, what was the observed difference in energy expenditure between lean and moderately obese people as measured in kcal per day? (Levine et al., 2005)
   b. After two months of dieting by the obese subjects and overeating by the lean subjects, their weights changed but their level of NEAT did not. Explain what this finding indicates.
7. State the relationship researchers observed between energy expenditure and infusions of orexin into the paraventricular nucleus of the hypothalamus. (See Figure 12.26 in your text. Kiwaki et al., 2004)
8. According to twin studies,
   a. approximately how much of the variability in body fat is due to genetic differences? (Price and Gottesman, 1991; Allison et al., 1996; Comuzzie and Allison, 1998)
   b. what appears to influence the amount of weight people gain or lose on high- or low-calorie diets? (Bouchard et al., 1990; Hainer et al., 2001)
9. Explain why people with efficient metabolisms are at increased risk of becoming obese whereas people with inefficient metabolisms are not.
10. a. Outline an explanation for genetic differences in metabolic efficiency among people.
    b. Summarize the conclusions of research with two groups of Pima Indians (Ravussin et al., 1994) that support this explanation.

11. Look again at the role of leptin in human obesity.
    a. List two causes of hereditary leptin deficiency—a very rare cause of human obesity.
       1. 2.
    b. How do injections of leptin affect the body weight people who lack sufficient leptin? (See Figure 12.27 in your text.)

12. a. What evidence suggests that obese people may be leptin resistant?
    b. Explain why differences in the transport of leptin molecules across the blood-brain barrier may be one cause of obesity. (Banks et al., 1996; Golden et al., 1997; Caro et al., 1996)
    c. Carefully explain why a fall in blood levels of leptin should be regarded as a hunger signal. Be sure to note how people with efficient and inefficient metabolisms should respond. (Flier, 1998)

13. What two physical changes associated with leptin were observed in aged obese rats? (Scarpace et al., 2001)
    1. 2.

14. What may be the most common genetic cause of severe obesity and approximately how many such people are affected? Cite research to support your answer. (Farooqi and O'Rahilly, 2005)

15. a. Where is uncoupling protein (UCP) found?
    b. What may be its function?
    c. There are three different uncoupling proteins. Which one may play the most important role in determining metabolic efficiency and where is it found?
    d. How does leptin affect UCP3? (Scarpace et al., 2000)
    e. Describe the appetites, body weight, and amount of body fat of mice with abnormally high levels of UCP3 in their skeletal muscles. (Clapham et al., 2000)
    f. What effect did high levels of UPC3 have on the metabolic efficiency of Pima Indians? (Schrauwen et al., 1999)

Learning Objective 12-10	Discuss some surgical, pharmacological, and behavioral treatments of obesity.

Read pages 423-426 and answer the following questions.

1. a. Describe gastroplasty, a bariatric surgical treatment for obesity.
   b. Following surgery, how should patients feel after eating a small amount of food? Unfortunately, how do they often feel? (Be sure to mention *nimiety* in your answer.)

2. Briefly summarize some of the common side effects of intestinal bypass surgery.

3. a. Briefly describe the surgical procedure RYGB, shown in Figure 12.28 in your text.

   b. What is the average post-surgical weight loss of obese patients? (Brolin, 2002)

   c. What unexpected information on the mortality rate of people who have undergone bariatric surgery has recently been reported? (Flum et al., 2005)

   d. What hunger signal is almost entirely suppressed by this surgery?

   e. Which group of rats who had undergone RYBG surgery had the best post-operative results? (Stylopoulos et al., 2005)

4. Regular exercise appears to be beneficial in the treatment of obesity. Describe how exercise programs benefited middle-aged men (Bunyard et al., 1998) and children (Gurin et al., 1999).

5. a. Explain why fenfluramine was used to treat obesity. (Bray, 1992)

   b. Although effective, why was the drug withdrawn from the market in the United States? (Blundell and Halford, 1998)

   c. What other drug has similar benefits without serious side effects?

6. Explain how orlistat alters food absorption and its effectiveness in maintaining weight loss. (Hill et al., 1999)

7. a. What are the pharmacological and behavioral effects of rimonabant?

   b. Summarize the results of clinical trials of this drug. (Di Marzo and Matias, 2005)

   c. What is another beneficial effect of this drug?

Learning Objective 12-11 Discuss the physiological factors that may contribute to anorexia nervosa and bulimia nervosa.

Read pages 426-427 and answer the following questions.

1. Describe the symptoms of anorexia nervosa.

2. Describe the symptoms of bulimia nervosa and its aftermath.

3. What is the incidence of anorexia nervosa and bulimia nervosa

   a. in the general population?

   b. between the sexes?

4. a. To combat their intense fear of becoming obese, what do many anorexics do?

   b. What do studies with food-deprived animals suggest may be a reason for increased exercise? (Smith, 1989)

5. a. Which explanation for anorexia nervosa—biological or social— is favored by most psychologists? Why?

   b. What is another possible explanation?

6. a. What percentage of patients treated for anorexia nervosa make a full recovery?

   b. What had happens to between 5 and 10 percent of them?

7. How does anorexia affect

   a. bone density?

   b. menstruation?

   c. the brain? (Artmann et al., 1985; Herholz, 1996; Kingston et al., 1996; Katzman et al., 2001)

8. a. What behaviors suggest that anorexia nervosa may be linked to obsessive-compulsive disorder?

   b. Compare the incidence of obsessive-compulsive disorder among first-degree relatives of females with anorexia nervosa and normal control females. (Bellodi et al., 2001)

   c. Researchers showed women with anorexia nervosa and bulimia nervosa and women who did not suffer from eating disorders pictures of fattening food and neutral images. How did each group of women react to the pictures?

   d. What brain region showed increased activity in the women with eating disorders? (See Figure 12.29 in your text. Uher et al., 2004)

   e. What other groups of people showed the same increased activity?

   f. What do these results suggest about eating disorders and compulsive behavior?

9. a. Approximately how much of the variability in the occurrence of anorexia nervosa appears to be under the control of genetic factors? (Klein and Walsh, 2004)

   b. What other difficulties increase the incidence? (Cnattingius et al., 1999)

10. a. Why are changes in endocrine levels probably not a cause of this disorder?

    b. Describe the levels of NPY in the cerebrospinal fluid of patients with severe anorexia and the same patients after they have regained their normal weight. (Kaye et al., 1990; Kaye, 1996)

    c. What symptoms of anorexia may be affected by this neuropeptide?

    d. Describe the blood levels of leptin in underweight anorexics and the same patients when they begin eating again but before their weight returns to normal. (Mantzoros et al., 1997)

    e. What aspect of recovery may be affected by this hormone?

    f. Describe the blood levels of ghrelin in anorexics and its possible effect on neuropeptide Y secretion. (Misra et al., 2005)

11. Which classes of drugs have been found to be

    a. ineffective in treating anorexia? (Mitchell, 1989; Attia et al., 1998)

    b. useful in treating bulimia nervosa? (Advokat and Kutlesic, 1995; Kaye et al., 2001)

12. To review the many peptide neurotransmitters that influence eating and metabolism, study Table 12.1 in your text.

Lesson II Self Test

1. Lesions of the area postrema and nucleus of the solitary tract (AP/NST)
   a. stimulate a carbohydrate appetite.
   b. reduce the ability to distinguish between flavors.
   c. stimulate Fos production.
   d. abolish both glucoprivic and lipoprivic feeding.

2. Lesions of the _____ produce _____ and lesions of the _____ produce _____.
   a. lateral hypothalamus; hunger; ventromedial hypothalamus; satiety
   b. ventromedial hypothalamus; overeating; lateral hypothalamus; undereating
   c. paraventricular nucleus; overeating; ventromedial hypothalamus; undereating
   d. ventromedial hypothalamus; satiety; paraventricular nucleus; obesity

3. Neuropeptide Y (NPY), which is secreted by neurons whose cell bodies are located in the _____, _____.
   a. area postrema; controls hormones that regulate the fasting phase of metabolism
   b. paraventricular nucleus; causes a rapid decline in blood glucose levels
   c. arcuate nucleus; stimulates ravenous eating
   d. ventromedial hypothalamus; abolishes eating

4. CART
   a. levels decrease if animals are deprived of food.
   b. infusions into the cerebral ventricles stimulate eating.
   c. neurons do not contain leptin receptors.
   d. production can be stimulated by injections of NPY into the cerebral ventricles.

5. Appetite can be suppressed by the activation of receptors for
   a. CCK, serotonin, and MCH.
   b. NPY, leptin, and MC4.
   c. leptin, serotonin, and CART.
   d. CCK, NPY, and CART.

6. People with an efficient or thrifty metabolism
   a. must eat more food to maintain their body weight.
   b. have difficulty losing weight even on a reduced calorie diet.
   c. have difficulty matching food intake to physical activity.
   d. do not have any calories left over for deposit in long-term nutrient reservoirs.

7. Leptin levels
   a. in obese people are higher than those of lean people, thus obese people show leptin resistance.
   b. in the brains of lean and obese people are approximately the same, thus a leptin deficiency cannot be considered a cause of obesity.
   c. and sensitivity to leptin remain constant throughout a person's life and thus cannot account for weight gain in older people.
   d. appear to remain constant even during periods of famine thus favoring the survival of people with efficient metabolisms.

8. Uncoupling protein may be one of the factors in determining
   a. metabolic efficiency.
   b. sensitivity to leptin.
   c. sensitivity to long-term satiety signals.
   d. weight gain in middle age.

9. Successful bariatric surgery
   a. appears to disrupt the secretion of CCK.
   b. appears to disrupt the secretion of ghrelin.
   c. does not reduce overall food intake, but does reduce the amount of time food is in contact with the intestines.
   d. may change an inefficient metabolism into an efficient one, resulting in weight loss.

10. Fenfluramine and sibutramine, a similar but safer replacement drug, stimulate the release of
    a. NPY.
    b. insulin.
    c. serotonin.
    d. leptin.

11. Anorexics
    a. are unresponsive to the effects of food.
    b. do not experience hunger.
    c. have an intense fear of becoming obese.
    d. attempt to reduce their need for calories by reducing physical activity.

12. The cerebrospinal fluid of anorexics contains elevated levels of
    a. NPY.
    b. cholecystokinin (CCK).
    c. fenfluramine.
    d. leptin.

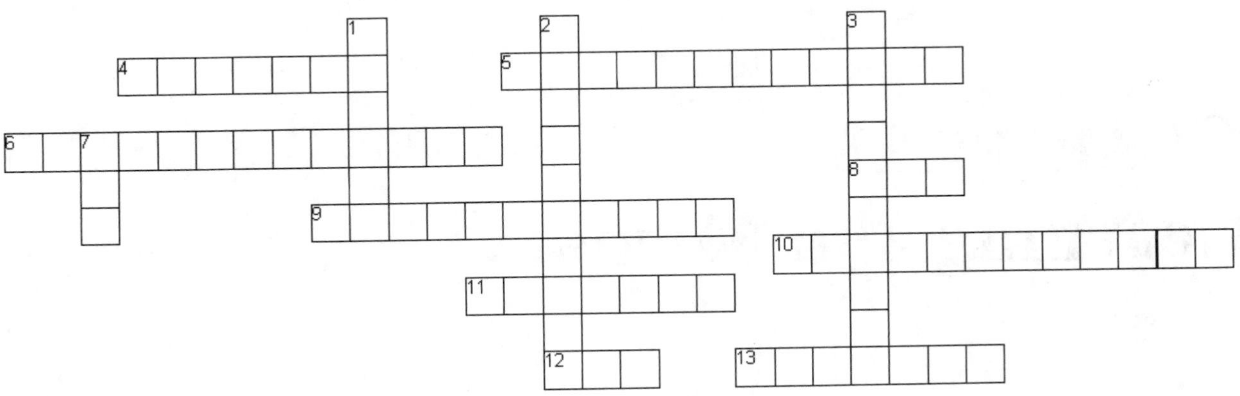

Across

4. Fatty tissue
5. Process that keeps bodily substances and characteristics at optimal level
6. Dramatic fall in level of availability of fatty acids
8. A peptide neurotransmitter found in a system of lateral hypothalamic neurons that stimulate appetite and reduce metabolic rate
9. Peptide hormone that produces thirst and salt appetite
10. Fluid that bathes the cells
11. A peptide hormone released by the stomach that increases eating; also produced by neurons in the brain
12. Hormone secreted by duodenum; may provide satiety signal
13. Principal fuel of the brain

Down

1. Hormone secreted by adipose tissue; decreases food intake
2. Thirst produced by hypovolemia
3. Thirst that occurs when tonicity of interstitial fluid increases
7. Peptide produced after a meal in amounts proportional to size of meal

Answers for Self Tests

Lesson I

1. d Obj. 12-1
2. a Obj. 12-2
3. c Obj. 12-2
4. b Obj. 12-3
5. d Obj. 12-4
6. a Obj. 12-4
7. b Obj. 12-4
8. d Obj. 12-5
9. a Obj. 12-5
10. d Obj. 12-6
11. a Obj. 12-6
12. c Obj. 12-6

Lesson II

1. d Obj. 12-7
2. b Obj. 12-7
3. c Obj. 12-7
4. a Obj. 12-8
5. c Obj. 12-8
6. b Obj. 12-9
7. a Obj. 12-9
8. a Obj. 12-9
9. b Obj. 12-10
10. c Obj. 12-10
11. c Obj. 12-11
12. a Obj. 12-11

CHAPTER 13
Learning and Memory

Lesson I: The Nature of Learning, Synaptic Plasticity, Perceptual Learning, Classical Conditioning, and Instrumental Conditioning

Read the interim summary on pages 434-435 of your text to re-acquaint yourself with the material in this section.

> ***Learning Objective 13-1*** Describe the four basic forms of learning: perceptual learning, stimulus-response learning, motor learning, and relational learning.

Read pages 431-434 and answer the following questions.

1. _______________ physically change the structure of our _______________ _______________ and thereby change our _______________. This process is called _______________ and these changes are called _______________.

2. List four of the basic forms of learning.

   1.　　　　　　　　　　3.

   2.　　　　　　　　　　4.

3. a. Define *perceptual learning* in your own words.

   b. State its primary function.

4. a. Use one word to indicate how many of our sensory systems are capable of perceptual learning.

   b. Where does perceptual learning appear to take place?

5. Define *stimulus-response learning* in your own words, noting its two major categories.

6. Which neural circuits are presumably involved?

7. In your own words, briefly explain what happens during classical conditioning.

8. Let's examine how the species-typical defensive eyeblink response of a rabbit can be conditioned to a tone. Identify the

   a. unconditional stimulus (US).　　　　b. conditional stimulus (CS).

c. unconditional response (UR).

d. conditional response (CR).

9. Study Figure 13.1 in your text and then complete Figure 1, which illustrates the kinds of changes that may take place in the brain during classical conditioning.

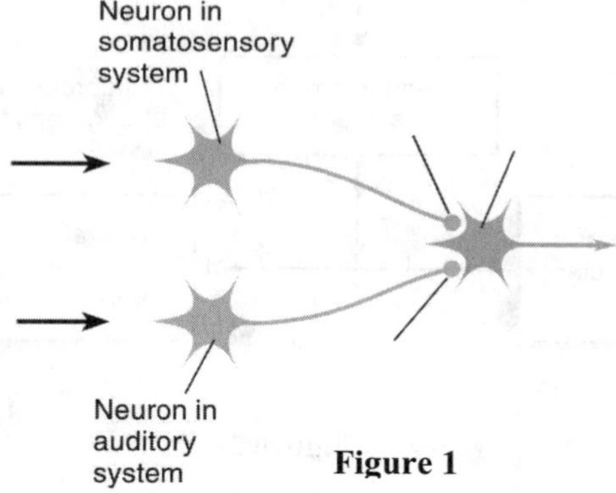

Figure 1

10. State the Hebb rule in your own words. (Hebb, 1949)

11. a. Briefly explain what happens during instrumental conditioning. Be sure to use the terms *reinforcing stimuli* and *punishing stimuli* in your answer.

    b. Define *reinforcement* in your own words.

    c. Explain why it is incorrect to say that reinforcement causes a particular behavior to become more frequent.

12. Study Figure 13.2 in your text and then complete Figure 2 on the next page, which illustrates the kinds of changes that may take place in the brain during instrumental conditioning.

13. Why is instrumental conditioning a more flexible form of learning than classical conditioning?

14. Define *motor learning* in your own words, and explain why it is considered a form of stimulus-response learning. (Study Figure 13.3 in your text.)

15. Define *relational learning* in your own words.

16. Briefly describe these forms of relational learning.

    a. spatial learning

    b. episodic learning

17. To review the definitions of the different kinds of learning that you have just studied, return to the interim summary for this section.

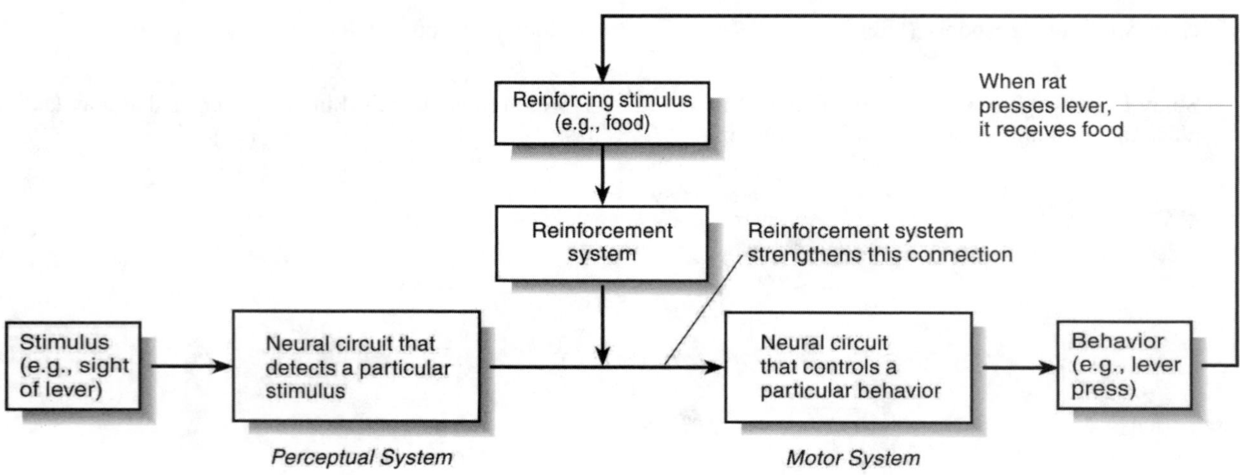

Figure 2

Read the interim summary on pages 445-446 of your text to re-acquaint yourself with the material in this section.

Learning Objective 13-2 Discuss research on the induction of long-term potentiation, and the role of NMDA receptors.

Read pages 435-439 and answer the following questions.

1. Define *synaptic plasticity* in your own words.
2. a. Which axons did Lømo (1966) electrically stimulate? What was the result?

   b. What is this increase called?
3. a. Return to Figure 3.17 in your text and review the location of the hippocampus in the human brain.

   b. List the structures that comprise the hippocampal formation.

      1. 3.

      2.
4. Trace the pathway of incoming information through the hippocampal formation with the help of Figure 13.4 in your text.

   a. Through which structure are the major neocortical inputs and outputs of the hippocampal formation channeled?

   b. Where, in turn, do the neurons of this structure send axons? Be sure to mention the pathway they follow.

   c. Where do these neurons send axons?

   d. What are the two major divisions of the hippocampus? Which one of these receives axons from the dentate gyrus?

   e. Name the cells of field CA3 with which the axons of the dentate gyrus synapse.

   f. Describe these cells, noting why their dendritic spines are important for long-term potentiation.

   g. Briefly describe the axonal connections of field CA3 pyramidal cells with other parts of the brain.

   h. What is the function of CA1 pyramidal cells?

5. Study Figures 13.4 and 13.5 in your text and explain a typical procedure for producing long-term potentiation (LTP).
   a. Where is a stimulating electrode placed?
   b. Where is a recording electrode placed?
   c. Define *population EPSP* in your own words.
   d. What event triggers a population EPSP and what does the size of the first one indicate?
   e. How is long-term potentiation induced?
   f. What evidence confirms that LTP has occurred?

6. a. Briefly describe how long-term potentiation is induced in isolated slices of the hippocampal formation.
   b. What are some of the advantages of this procedure?

7. a. Define *associative long-term potentiation* in your own words. (Study Figure 13.6 in your text.)
   b. How does this phenomenon appear to confirm the Hebb rule?

8. Explain why long-term potentiation occurs if
   a. a series of pulses is given at a high rate all in one burst, but not if the same number of pulses are delivered at a slow rate. (See Figure 13.7 in your text.)
   b. artificially depolarized axons are stimulated, but not if depolarization and stimulation occurred at different times. (See Figure 13.8 in your text. Kelso et al., 1986)

9. To review: What two events are necessary if long-term potentiation is to occur?
   1. 2.

10. Study Figure 13.9 in your text and Animation 13.1 and explain the role of NMDA receptors in long-term potentiation.
    a. Where are NMDA receptors found?
    b. What kind of ion channel does an NMDA receptor control?
    c. Carefully explain what two conditions must occur in order for calcium to enter cells through the ion channels controlled by NMDA receptors.
    d. Therefore, the NMDA receptor is a ______________- and ______________-dependent channel. The entry of calcium through the ion channels controlled by the NMDA receptor appears to be essential for ______________ ________________ ________________ to occur. (Lynch et al., 1984)

11. What is the effect of the drug AP5 on
    a. NMDA receptors?
    b. the establishment of LTP? (Brown et al., 1989)

12. Let's look at the role of dendritic spikes that occur in some kinds of pyramidal cells during long-term potentiation. Carefully explain:

    a. what appears to trigger dendritic spikes.

    b. what happens to all the dendritic spines on the trunk of the dendrite of the axon of the cell.

13. Using TTX, which prevents the formation of dendritic spikes, what did researchers confirm about the necessary conditions for long-term potentiation? (Magee and Johnston, 1997)

14. Finally, study Figure 13.10 in your text and Animation 13.2 and carefully explain why both weak and strong synapses on a dendritic spine must be active at the same time in order for ion channels controlled by NMDA receptors in the weak synapse to open and for associative long-term potentiation to occur.

Learning Objective 13-3 Discuss the mechanisms responsible for the increase in synaptic strength that occurs during long-term potentiation.

Read pages 440-444 and answer the following questions.

1. What change occurs in the postsynaptic membrane of the dendritic spine that may be responsible for synaptic strengthening?

2. a. What kind of ion channels do AMPA receptors control?

   b. When activated by glutamate, what kind of postsynaptic potentials do they produce in the membrane of the dendritic spine?

   c. When the number of AMPA receptors increases, how are the effects of glutamate released by the terminal button changed?

3. a. Using a two-photon laser scanning microscope, researchers studied the movement of AMPA receptors on the dendritic spines of CA1 neurons during long-term potentiation. Where were these receptors found

      1. before long-term potentiation was induced?

      2. fifteen minutes afterwards? (Study Figure 13.11 in your text. Shi et al., 1999)

   b. How can this movement be prevented?

4. a. Let's look at the CAM-KII enzyme, it's characteristics, and its importance in the induction of long-term potentiation. Begin by describing the location, dependence on calcium, and role in LTP of this enzyme.

   b. After researchers introduced a targeted mutation of a gene responsible for the production of CaM-KII into normal mice, how successful were they in inducing LTP in hippocampal slices from these animals? (Silva et al., 1992a)

   c. When Lledo et al. (1995) injected activated CaM-KII into CA1 pyramidal cells, what did they observe?

   d. What do these findings suggest about the mechanisms involved in inducing long-term potentiation?

5. a. What is the name given to the dark band seen just inside the postsynaptic membrane and what kinds of structures are found there?

   b. When researchers induced LTP in cultured hippocampal neurons, what kind of structures concentrated in these postsynaptic densities? (See Figure 13.12 in your text. Allison et al., 2000; Shen and Meyer, 1999)

6. a. Explain *autophosphorylation* in your own words. (Malenka and Nicoll, 1999)

   b. How does this process change the effects of calcium on the dendritic spines?

   c. If autophosphorylation is prevented, how is LTP affected? (See Figure 13.13 in your text. Giese et al., 1998)

7. a. What is a second structural change that appears to accompany LTP and what name did Geinisman et al. (1991, 1996) give to it?

   b. Study Figure 13.14 in your text and Animation 13.3 and then draw a dendritic spine before and after LTP occurred.

   c. What structures appear in the postsynaptic densities of all perforated synapses within 15-30 minutes after LTP has occurred? (Ganeshina et al., 2004)

   d. What eventually happens to these structures and what is a possible explanation?

8. What is a third change that may accompany LTP?

9. a. If nitric oxide were produced in the dendritic spines of the hippocampal formation, why would nearby terminal buttons be the structures that were affected?

   b. What may be the role of nitric oxide in long-term potentiation? Be sure to use the term *retrograde messenger* in your answer.

   c. How do drugs that block the production of nitric oxide affect the establishment of LTP in field CA1? (Haley et al., 1992)

   d. In what other brain regions is a calcium-activated NO synthase found? (Endoh et al., 1994)

   e. Why is it likely that NO is not the only communication signal dendritic spines use?

10. a. How is long-lasting LTP affected if a drug that blocks protein synthesis, is administered

      1. before, during, or immediately after a burst of stimulation?

      2. one hour after stimulation? (Frey et al., 1988)

    b. What, then, is a necessary condition if long-lasting long-term potentiation is to occur?

11. How may the new proteins that result from LTP be delivered to the appropriate dendritic spines? (See Figure 13.15 in your text. Frey and Morris, 1998)

12. The biochemical changes that occur during long-term potentiation are illustrated in Figure 13.16 in your text and Animation 13.4.

Learning Objective 13-4 Discuss long-term depression and other forms of long-term potentiation.

Read pages 444–445 and answer the following questions.

1. a. How does low frequency electrical stimulation affect the strength of the synaptic inputs to a cell?

   b. What is the name of this phenomenon?

   c. What may be the role of long-term depression in memory formation?

   d. How can the establishment of both long-term depression and LTP be prevented? (See Figure 13.17 in your text. Dudek and Bear, 1992)

   e. How is associative long-term depression produced? (Debanne et al., 1994; Thiels et al., 1996)

2. a. How is the number of AMPA receptors affected by long-term potentiation? (Carroll et al., 1999; Lüscher et al., 1999)

   b. How is the number of AMPA receptors affected by long-term depression? (Carroll et al., 1999; Lüscher et al., 1999)

3. a. Outline a possible explanation of why activation of NMDA receptors can produce such different, opposite effects. Be sure to note the role of calcium. (Lisman, 1989)

   b. Before reviewing supporting research, describe two forms of the NMDA receptor.

   c. Carefully explain the presumed reason why researchers were able to block LTP and LTD in NMDA receptors using drugs. (Lui et al., 2004)

4. a. Are NMDA receptors essential for long-term potentiation to occur? Explain. (Monaghan and Cotman, 1985; Lynch et al., 1991)

   b. In what two ways do the neurons in field CA3 differ from those in field CA1 with respect to the establishment of LTP? (Reid et al., 2004)

Read the interim summary on page 450 in your text to re-acquaint yourself with the material in this section.

Learning Objective 13-5 Describe research on the role of the visual cortex in visual perceptual learning.

Read pages 446-448 and answer the following questions.

1. What kinds of stimuli do we recognize through perceptual learning? Cite research to support your answer. (Standing, 1973; Rolls, 1995b)

2. a. Sensory information from the lateral geniculate nucleus of the thalamus is sent to the _______________ _______________ _______________. After a first level of analysis, the information is sent on to the _______________ _______________ which surrounds the _______________ _______________ _______________.

   b. After a second level of analysis by the extrastriate cortex, where is the information then sent?

   c. List the two divisions of the next level of visual association cortex. (See Figure 13.18 in your text.)

   1. 2.

d. What is their common beginning?

e. Where does each end?

f. What is the function of each in visual perception?

3. When the inferior temporal cortex (part of the ventral stream) is damaged, what kind of deficits occur?

4. a. Briefly describe the task Yang and Maunsell (2004) taught monkey subjects.

   b. During testing, when did the monkeys recognize and fail to recognize small differences in visual stimuli?

   c. What did recordings of single neurons in the visual association cortex confirm?

   d. What do these results indicate about the role of the visual association cortex in perceptual learning?

5. When the visual and auditory association cortex of patients undergoing seizure surgery were stimulated, what did patients report? (Penfield and Perot, 1963)

6. a. Describe both pairs of stimuli that subjects learned before testing and the stimuli they saw during testing.

   b. During testing, how was their regional brain activity measured, and what kinds of stimuli activated visual association cortex? (See Figure 13.19 in your text. Wheeler et al., 2000)

   c. During testing, how was their regional brain activity measured, and what kinds of stimuli activated visual auditory association cortex? (See Figure 13.19 in your text. Wheeler et al., 2000)

7. a. What kind of stimuli activated area MT/MST in research subjects? What kind of stimuli did not?

   b. What is the presumed explanation? (See Figure 13.20 in your text. Kourtzi and Kanwisher, 2000)

Learning Objective 13-6 Describe research on perceptual short-term memory.

Read pages 448-450 and answer the following questions.

1. a. Define *short-term memory* in your own words.

   b. Define *recognition* in your own words.

2. Before continuing, explain just what is a delayed matching-to-sample task, noting what happens to the stimulus during the delay interval.

3. a. When short-term memory is tested using a delayed matching-to-sample task, which neurons remain active during the delay interval? (Fuster and Jervey, 1981)

   b. What does the continued response of these neurons suggest about the location of short-term memory for these stimuli?

c. Which brain areas are associated with short-term memories for faces? (See Figure 13.21 in your text. Ranganath et al., 2004)

d. Which brain areas are associated with short-term memories for places? (See Figure 13.21 in your text. Ranganath et al., 2004)

4. a. Briefly describe the matching-to-sample task researchers taught human subjects.(Oliveri et al., 2001)

   b. During testing, what happened when the researchers applied transcranial magnetic stimulation (TMS) to the association cortex of the ventral stream of subjects? (Be sure to explain how TMS affects the brain.)

   c. During testing, what happened when the researchers applied transcranial magnetic stimulation (TMS) to the association cortex of the dorsal stream of subjects? (Be sure to explain how TMS affects the brain.)

   d. What do these results suggest about the location of neurons involved in short-term memory for visual patterns and location?

5. a. Look at other brain regions that are involved in short-term memory. Where do both major regions of visual association cortex form connections with prefrontal cortex in the monkey brain? (See Figure 13.22 in your text. Wilson et al., 1993)

   b. If the activity of the prefrontal cortex is disrupted by damage or temporary deactivation, recognition of what kinds of stimuli are affected? (For example, Bodner et al., 1996)

   c. When monkeys trained in a visual delayed matching-to-sample task were tested, what kind of neural activity occurred when they made a correct response? (Funahashi et al., 1989)

   d. When monkeys trained in a visual delayed matching-to-sample task were tested, what kind of neural activity occurred when they made an error? (Funahashi et al., 1989)

   e. Which regions of human prefrontal cortex became active during the delay interval in a delayed matching-to-sample task in which the stimuli were visual patterns? (Courtney et al., 1998)

   f. Which regions of human prefrontal cortex became active during the delay interval in a delayed matching-to-sample in which the stimuli were specific spatial locations? (Courtney et al., 1998)

6. In addition to encoding information about a stimulus, what other kind of information may be encoded in the prefrontal cortex? (Quintana and Fuster, 1992)

Read the interim summary on pages 452-453 in your text to re-acquaint yourself with the material in this section.

Learning Objective 13-7 Discuss the physiology of the classically conditioned emotional response to aversive stimuli.

Read pages 450-452 and answer the following questions.

1. A hypothetical neural circuit of the changes in synaptic strength resulting from a classically conditioned emotional response is diagrammed in Figure 13.23 in your text.

   a. In this example, what is the CS? the US?

   b. To what location is information about the CS and US sent?

   c. What does the convergence of information suggest about where synaptic changes responsible for this kind of learning may take place?

d. When a rat encounters a painful stimulus, where are the strong synapses that become active located?

e. Where is the next set of neurons that are activated located?

f. According to the Hebb rule, if a tone is paired with the painful stimulus, which neurons are strengthened?

2. a. Look at experimental support that the lateral nucleus of the amygdala is involved in learning a conditioned emotional response. How do lesions of this nucleus affect a conditioned emotional responses established with a tone (CS) followed by a foot shock (US)? (Kapp et al., 1979; Nader et al., 2001)

   b. Summarize the changes in the firing rate of neurons in the lateral nucleus of the amygdala recorded before during, and after pairings of a tone with a footshock. (Study Figure 13.24 in your text. Quirk et al., 1995)

   c. When they repeatedly presented the tone without the foot shock, how did the rate of firing of the neurons then change?

   d. Summarize the results of confirming evidence from (Maren, 2000).

   e. Before attempting to establish a conditioned emotional response, how did researchers temporarily inactivate the lateral amygdala? (Wilensky et al., 1999)

   f. With the lateral amygdala temporarily inactivated, how successful was training?

3. a. Look at experimental support that the changes in the lateral amygdala from a conditioned emotional response involve long-term potentiation. If the medial geniculate nucleus is electrically stimulated, what change then occurs in the lateral amygdala? (Clugnet and LeDoux, 1990)

   b. When LTP is produced in the lateral nucleus of the amygdala, what change is observed in the response of neurons in this nucleus to auditory stimuli? (Rogan and LeDoux, 1995)

   c. If the NR2B subunit of the NMDA receptor is chemically blocked, how is the establishment of a conditioned emotional response affected? (Rodrigues et al. 2001)

   d. If the number of NR2B receptors in the mouse forebrain is increased through genetic manipulation, how are LTP and the acquisition of a conditioned emotional response affected? (Tang et al., 1999)

4. a. How did researchers mark a subunit of AMPA receptors in the lateral amygdala of rats before establishing a conditioned emotional response? (Rumple et al., 2005)

   b. Where were these marked receptors found after learning was established?

   c. What steps did the researchers take which prevented AMPA receptors from being driven into the dendritic spines? What was the effect on conditioning?

   d. When autophosphorylation of the CaM-K11 enzyme in the lateral amygdala was prevented, what other events were altered? (Rodrigues et al., 2004)

   e. What do these research results suggest about the relationship between LTP and conditioned emotional responses in the lateral amygdala?

5. a. Explain the procedure for training an animal on a differential conditioned emotional response.

   b. Study Figure 13.25 in your text and explain the results obtained by Collins and Paré (2000) using this procedure.

6. a. If protein synthesis in the lateral amygdala is blocked using a drug, how is long-lasting LTP affected? long-term retention of a conditioned emotional response? (Schafe and LeDoux, 2000)

   b. What do these results suggest about the importance of protein synthesis for the induction of longlasting LTP?

Read the interim summary on page 458 to re-acquaint yourself with the material in this section.

Learning Objective 13-8 Describe the role of the basal ganglia in instrumental conditioning.

Read pages 453-454 and answer the following questions.

1. To review: Instrumental conditioning involves the strengthening of connections between _______________ _______________ that detect a particular _______________ and those that produce a particular _______________. These _______________ _______________ begin in various regions of _______________ association cortex and end in _______________ association cortex. The two major pathways between them are direct _______________ connections and connections through the _______________ _______________ and the _______________.
2. In general, what kind of learning are both of these pathways involved in?

3. Discuss how we learn a complex behavior through instrumental conditioning and the effects of practice on the basal ganglia and transcortical circuits.

4. a. List the nuclei that comprise the neostriatum, another part of the basal ganglia.

   1. 2.

   b. Complete this table of connections between the basal ganglia and the rest of the brain with the help of Figure 13.26 in your text.

Neostriatum	**Globus Pallidus**
Inputs:	Inputs:
Outputs:	Outputs:

5. a. What kind of learning is disrupted by lesions of the basal ganglia? is not disrupted? (Divac et al., 1967)

   b. What kind of learning is disrupted by cutting visual association cortex and frontal cortex connections (sparing connections via the basal ganglia)? (Gaffan and Harrison, 1987; Gaffan and Eacott, 1995)

   c. What region is therefore necessary for acquisition of instrumental conditioning tasks?

6. During testing, monkeys were required to remember either the _______________ or the _______________ of visual stimuli. Remembering the _______________ of the stimuli increased activity of the neurons in the _______________ of the caudate nucleus, which receives information from the _______________ _______________ of visual information, and remembering information about the _______________ of the stimulus increased the activity in the _______________ of the caudate nucleus, which receives information from the _______________ _______________. (Levy et al., 1997)
7. a. Describe the location of brain lesions in laboratory monkeys. (Fernandez-Ruiz et al., 2001)

b. What kind of tasks were impaired?

c. What kind of tasks were unimpaired?

d. What do the results suggest about the role of the damaged brain region?

8. What kind of tasks are impaired if NMDA receptors in the basal ganglia are blocked by AP5? (Packard and Teather, 1997)

Learning Objective 13-9 Discuss how the reinforcement system may detect reinforcing stimuli and strengthen synaptic connections.

Read pages 454-458 and answer the following questions.

1. Briefly recount the discovery of reinforcing brain stimulation by Olds and Milner (1954).

2. a. The most reliable location for producing reinforcing brain stimulation is the _______________

_______________ _______________ (_____) which is a bundle of _______________ that travels from the

_______________ to the _______________ _______________ _______________.

b. Where do most researchers place the tips of their electrodes?

3. a. List the three major systems of dopaminergic neurons.

1. 3.

2.

b. What is the primary function of the nigrostriatal system?

4. With the help of Figure 13.27 in your text, complete the following table of the projections of the mesolimbic system and the mesocortical system.

Mesolimbic System	Mesocortical System
Begins in:	Begins in:
Projections	*Projections*
1.	1.
2.	2.
3.	3.

5. a. If you do not remember the microdialysis technique, review the description in Chapter 5.

b. Which neurotransmitter, verified using this technique, is released at the time of reinforcing electrical brain stimulation? (Moghadam and Bunney, 1989; Nakahara et al., 1989; Phillips et al., 1992. See Figure 13.28 in your text.)

c. What other kinds of stimuli trigger this release?

6. a. Under what circumstances did the activity of the human nucleus accumbens increase? (Knutson et al., 2001; Aharon et al., 2001)

b. What neurotransmitter was presumably released?

c. What other kinds of stimuli trigger this release? (Salamone, 1992)

d. What, then, does research indicate about the functions of dopamine neurons and multiple mechanisms of reinforcement in the brain?

7. What two functions must be performed by the reinforcement system if a stimulus is to become reinforcing? (Return to Figure 13.2.)

   1. 2.

8. Nick, having taken advantage of a special offer at the DVD store, watched three movies in two days. When a friend called to see if he wanted to get together and rent a movie, Nick suggested they go out for pizza instead. Use this example to explain one of the difficulties in determining what is a reinforcing event.

9. a. The reinforcement system appears to be activated by _______________ reinforcing stimuli.

   b. Describe the operant task laboratory monkeys were taught, noting the reinforcing stimulus.

   c. When, during training, did neurons in the ventral tegmental area (VTA) become active?

   d. How did this response change once the task was learned?

   e. Carefully explain why this change illustrates unexpected reinforcement. (Mirenowicz and Schultz, 1994; 1996)

   f. Study Figure 13.29 in your text and summarize the results of similar research with humans. (Berns et al., 2001)

   g. What do Schultz and his colleagues suggest happens when dopaminergic neurons of the VTA become active?

10. a. Describe both parts of the task that human subjects learned. (Schott et al., 2004)

    b. Which part of the task activated the ventral tegmentum and increased recall by the subjects?

11. a. How did exposing rats to a novel situation affect the establishment of LTP in field CA1? (Li et al.,2003)

    b. How could this response be blocked?

    c. Under what conditions did the activity of the ventral tegmentum of human subjects (and later recall) increase? (Knudson and Adcock, 2005)

12. a. How does glutamate secreted by the terminal buttons of axons that connect the prefrontal cortex and the ventral tegmental area affect the secretion of dopamine in the ventral tegmental area and the nucleus accumbens? (Gariano and Groves, 1988)

    b. What are some of the functions of the prefrontal cortex? (Mesulam, 1986) How may the role of the prefrontal cortex in reinforcement compliment these functions?

13. Keeping the three elements essential for instrumental conditioning to occur in mind, explain when and how dopamine (and perhaps other neurotransmitters) may strengthen synaptic connections during instrumental conditioning. (Wise, 2004)

14. What two conditions appear necessary for successful instrumental conditioning? (Smith-Roe and Kelley, 2000)

15. a. Describe the different treatments two groups of subjects received before beginning a vocabulary task. (Knecht et al. 2004)

    b. Which group of subjects learned the artificial vocabulary better?

    c. What do these results suggest about the importance of dopamine in instrumental conditioning?

16. Describe evidence that suggests that the prefrontal cortex may be involved in the reinforcing effects of dopamine on behavior. (Stein and Belluzzi, 1989; Duvauchelle and Ettenberg, 1991; Hernandez and Hoebel, 1990)

17. Describe evidence that suggests that dopamine may play a modulating role in LTP in parts of the brain involved in reinforcement. (Gurden et al., 1999; Gurden et al., 2000; Bissière et al., 2003)

Lesson I Self Test

1. Instrumental conditioning results from an association between

    a. motivation and a reinforcing stimulus.
    b. a stimulus and a response.
    c. a conditional and an unconditional stimulus.
    d. two responses.

2. The Hebb rule states that a synapse will be strengthened if it repeatedly becomes active _____ the _____ neuron fires.

    a. at the same time that; presynaptic
    b. soon after; presynaptic
    c. about the same time that; postsynaptic
    d. before; postsynaptic

3. In order for long-term potentiation to occur

    a. the presynaptic membrane must be depolarized at the same time that the synapses are active.
    b. the postsynaptic membrane must be depolarized at the same time that the synapses are active.
    c. the postsynaptic membrane must be hyperpolarized at the same time that the synapses are active.
    d. a series of electrical pulses must be delivered at a slow rate.

4. One of the effects of long-term potentiation is a(n)

    a. inhibition of calcium-dependent enzymes.
    b. decrease in the amount of postsynaptic thickening of neurons in the hippocampal formation.
    c. decrease in protein synthesis in the cell body.
    d. increase in the number of postsynaptic AMPA receptors.

5. Long-term depression may result from

    a. sustained increases in protein synthesis in the cell body.
    b. the gradual atrophy of the dendrites that transmit chemical messages to the cell.
    c. low-frequency stimulation of the synaptic inputs to a cell.
    d. increased sensitivity of protein kinases to calcium.

6. Lesions that damage inferior temporal cortex disrupt the ability

    a. to remember the location of particular stimuli.
    b. to discriminate between different visual stimuli.
    c. to detect tactile stimulation.
    d. to recognize particular sounds.

7. In a delayed matching-to-sample task, the "delay" is the interval

    a. between teaching the subject the task and testing to see whether it has learned it.
    b. between the sample stimulus and the choices.
    c. between successive trials.
    d. a subject must pause before responding.

8. When an animal is trained to make a classically conditioned emotional response by pairing a tone and a foot shock, the tone is the

    a. US.
    b. CS.
    c. US.
    d. UR.

9. The synaptic changes that produce a classically conditioned emotional response occur in the
   a. substantia nigra and the ventral tegmental area.
   b. auditory cortex and the nucleus accumbens.
   c. nucleus of the lateral amygdala.
   d. medial forebrain bundle.

10. Lesions of the _____ disrupt instrumental conditioning.
    a. parietal lobe
    b. basal ganglia
    c. prefrontal cortex
    d. cingulate cortex

11. If you wished to have the best chance of training an animal to press a lever that delivers brain stimulation, where would you place an electrode?
    a. medial forebrain bundle
    b. neostriatum
    c. nucleus accumbens
    d. premotor cortex

12. When a(n) _____ reinforcing stimulus occurs, neurons in the nucleus accumbens become active.
    a. arbitrary
    b. nonarbitrary
    c. unexpected
    d. expected

Lesson II: Relational Learning

Read the interim summary on pages 477-479 of your text to re-acquaint yourself with the material in this section.

Learning Objective 13-10 Describe the nature of human anterograde amnesia and the type of brain damage that causes it.

Read pages 359-462 and answer the following questions.

1. Explain the difference between anterograde amnesia and retrograde amnesia in your own words or draw a time line to illustrate the difference. (See Figure 13.30 in your text.)

2. If you are asked to describe Korsakoff's syndrome, how will you respond to the following questions?
   a. What is the most important symptom?
   b. Is speech affected in Korsakoff's syndrome?
   c. What is the usual cause of Korsakoff's syndrome?
   d. When patients with Korsakoff's syndrome are asked about recent events, what tactic do they take?
   e. What is the formal name for this behavior?

3. a. Why did patient H.M. undergo bilateral removal of the medial temporal lobe? (Corkin et al., 1997)

   b. Although the operation was successful in treating his condition, what unexpected side effect became apparent?

   c. How has the procedure been modified to lessen the side effects?

4. Briefly describe the case of patient H. M. following surgery which is described in the opening of the chapter in your text.
   a. Place an *N* or an *I* in each blank to indicate whether H. M.'s ability in the following areas remains *normal* or has been *impaired* by his surgery.

      _____ intellectual ability

      _____ memory for older events

      _____ memory of events a few years before surgery

      _____ immediate verbal memory for numbers

_____ memory for events after surgery _____ immediate verbal memory for words

_____ personality _____ mental arithmetic computation

b. What has H. M. said that indicates that he is aware of his condition?

c. Under what conditions, and for how long, can H. M. remember small amounts of verbal information?

d. Why does H. M. work well at repetitive tasks?

5. After studying H. M., what conclusions did Milner and her colleagues make about the role of the hippocampus in memory formation? (Milner et al., 1968; Milner, 1970; Corkin et al., 1981)

   1.

   2.

   3.

6. a. What is the capacity and duration of short-term memory?

   b. What is the capacity and duration of long-term memory?

   c. What is the role in memory formation of rehearsal? (See Figure 13.31 in your text.)

   d. What is the role in memory formation of consolidation? (See Figure 13.31 in your text.)

   e. For patients with anterograde amnesia such as H.M., what does not appear to occur?

7. H. M. and other people with anterograde amnesia are not completely unable to learn. What categories of learning have they demonstrated under careful testing conditions? (Spiers et al., 2001)

   1. 2. 3.

8. Describe how Milner (1970) demonstrated that H. M. still has the ability to form perceptual memories. (See Figure 13.32 in your text and Animation 13.5.)

9. a. How did researchers demonstrate that patients with anterograde amnesia can learn to recognize melodies? (Johnson et al., 1985)

   b. How did researchers demonstrate that patients with anterograde amnesia can learn to recognize faces? (Johnson et al., 1985)

10. Describe some of the stimulus-response tasks associated with sensory-response learning that amnesic subjects including H. M. have been taught. (Woodruff-Pak, 1993; Sidman et al., 1968)

11. a. Describe the button-pressing task, shown in Figure 13.33 in your text, that Reber and Squire (1998) used to demonstrate motor learning in people with anterograde amnesia.

    b. Compare the performance of amnesic subjects with that of normal subjects.

    c. What are some other kinds of motor learning that amnesic patients are capable of? (Cavaco et al., 2004)

> ***Learning Objective 13-11*** Discuss the distinction between declarative memories and nondeclarative memories and their relation to anterograde amnesia.

Read pages 462-463 and answer the following questions.

1. When H.M. and other amnesic subjects are asked if they remember anything about experiments they have participated in, how do they respond?

2. Researchers who study anterograde amnesia distinguish between two kinds of memories. Identify and define each. (Eichenbaum et al., 1992; Squire, 1992; Squire et al., 1989)

   a.

   b.

3. Classify these kinds of memories as declarative (D) or nondeclarative (ND).

   _____ catching a ball

   _____ swinging a golf club

   _____ listing all the places you have lived

   _____ programming a VCR

   _____ reminiscing at a high school reunion

   _____ getting up on water skis

4. a. Summarize the task patient E. P. learned over a period of weeks. (Bayley and Squire, 2002)

   b. During testing, which stimulus evoked an incorrect response from patient E.P.?

   c. During testing, which stimulus evoked a correct response from patient E.P.?

   d. Summarize a second task patient E.P. later learned. (Bayley et al., 2005)

   e. How did he attempt to explain why he made a particular response?

   f. What kinds of memories are people with anterograde amnesia capable and incapable of forming?

5. To review these memory tasks study Table 13.1 in your text.

> ***Learning Objective 13-12*** Review the connections of the hippocampal formation with the rest of the brain and describe evidence that damage to the hippocampal formation and related structures causes anterograde amnesia.

Read pages 463-467 and answer the following questions.

1. Complete these sentences.

   a. Anterograde amnesia is the result of damage to

   b. The hippocampal formation consists of

   c. The most important input to the hippocampal formation is

   d. The entorhinal cortex receives its inputs from

   e. The three regions of limbic cortex of the medial temporal lobe are (See Figure 13.34 in your text.)

   f. The outputs of the hippocampal formation are primarily from

g. Most of the outputs of the hippocampal formation are relayed back through

2. Immediately review what you have just learned by completing Figure 1.

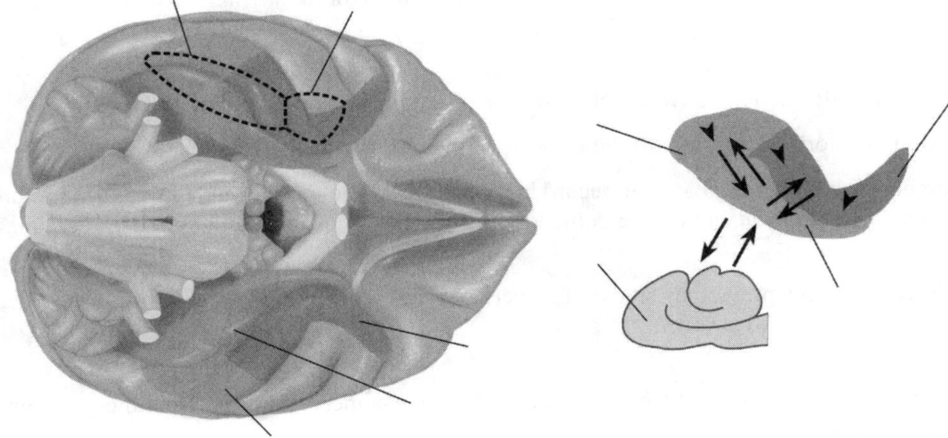

Figure 1

3. a. Which brain region sends visual information to the
   1. perirhinal cortex?
   2. parahippocampal cortex? (Suzuki and Amaral, 2004)

   b. Which brain region is more active and less active when people are learning a declarative task involving learning
   1. particular colored patterns?
   2. the locations of objects?

   c. Which brain region is active during both learning tasks? (Buffalo et al., 2004)

4. a. Name the region through which the hippocampal formation receives input from subcortical regions.

   b. What may be the effect of their input?

   c. List the neurotransmitters that are involved.

   d. What other brain region is connected to the hippocampal formation through the fornix?

   e. What syndrome that you have already studied results from degeneration of this region? (See Figure 13.35 in your text.)

5. a. A temporary interruption in blood flow caused by cardiac arrest left patient R.B. with permanent anterograde amnesia. Following his death, a histological examination of his brain indicated which region of the brain was damaged? (Zola-Morgan et al., 1986)

   b. Damage to field CA1 from anoxia is shown in Figure 13.36 in your text. (Rempel-Clower et al., 1996)

   c. In addition to humans, what other species suffer anterograde amnesia when field CA1 is damaged? (Auer et al., 1989; Zola-Morgan et al., 1992)

6. a. What kind of receptors are found in abundance in field CA1?

   b. What kinds of disturbances stimulate glutamatergic terminal buttons to release high levels of glutamate?

   c. Carefully describe how a high level of glutamate affects NMDA receptors and thus explains why field CA1 is so sensitive to a lack of oxygen.

d. How can the damaging effects of a lack of oxygen be reduced? (Rothman and Olney, 1987)

7. Briefly explain the role that the hippocampal formation is thought to play in forming declarative memories.

8. a. What kind of information activates the right side of the hippocampal formation?

   b. What kind of information activates the left side of the hippocampal formation?

   c. Researchers used functional MRI to record brain activity while normal subjects studied pictures for the first time. Which pictures did subjects remember best during later testing and why? (Brewer et al., 1998)

   d. Which words from a previously studied list were subjects most likely to remember? (See Figure 13.37 in your text. Alkire et al., 1998)

9. Summarize research from several laboratories on retrograde amnesia when it sometimes accompanies anterograde amnesia.

   a. If brain damage was limited to _______________, the patient did not suffer retrograde amnesia as well as anterograde amnesia. (Rempel-Clower et al.,1996)

   b. Describe the brain damage of patients with anterograde amnesia and

      1. limited retrograde amnesia.

      2. profound retrograde amnesia.

   c. What kind of memories are not affected by medial temporal lobe damage? (Reed and Squire, 1998)

10. Outline the possible transformation process accomplished by the structures of the medial temporal lobe for stabilizing long-term memories. (See Figure 13.38 in your text.)

Learning Objective 13-13 Discuss the role of the hippocampal formation in episodic, semantic, and spatial memories and the role of the prefrontal cortex in evaluating the accuracy of memories.

Read pages 467-471 and answer the following questions.

1. a. Researchers studied three human patients who received brain damage at an early age. (Vargha-Khadem et al., 1997) In each patient, which area was damaged? Which area was undamaged?

   b. Provide some examples of the spatial, temporal, and episodic memory deficits these patients suffered.

   c. Memory for what kind of information remained good? (See Table 13.2 in your text.)

2. In your own words, define

   a. *episodic memory.*

   b. *semantic memory.*

3. a. Which form of memory is less specific?

   b. Which form of memory can be acquired gradually over time?

4. a. According to Vargha-Khadem et al.,(1997) what kind of memory is affected by destruction of the hippocampus alone? Why?

b. What kind of brain damage affects all types of declarative memory?

c. Why should this suggestion be viewed cautiously? (Zola et al., 2000)

d. How did damage limited to the hippocampus that occurred in adulthood affect two major categories of declarative memories in five patients? (Manns et al., 2003)

5. Where are perceptual and episodic memories thought to be located in the brain?

6. Describe semantic dementia including

a. the cause.

b. brain regions spared during the early stages of the disease.

c. the symptoms of patient A.M., noting the kind of memory that was severely damaged and that which remained relatively good.

d. how his symptoms differed from those of anterograde amnesia. (Murre et al., 2001)

7. Review the case of patient R.S. and explain what his memories illustrate about the nature of autobiographical information. (Kitchener et al., 1998)

8. a. What kind of brain damage produces the most profound impairment of spatial memory?

b. What kind of brain damage produces the most significant impairment of spatial memory?

9. Look at evidence that these structures are critical in the formation of spatial memory. As recorded by a PET scanner, which brain region became active when

a. London taxi drivers described their routes? (Maguire et al., 1997)

b. subjects played a familiar virtual reality navigation game on a computer? (See Figure 13.39 in your text. Maguire et al., 1998)

10. If you are asked to describe confabulation, how will you reply to the following questions?

a. When patients resort to confabulation, is everything they say untrue?

b. Do the patients themselves actually believe what they say and act on their beliefs? Cite the cases of a 58-year-old woman and an accountant. (Schnider, 2003)

c. What kind of difficulty may patients experience which leads them to confabulate?

d. What strategy works best when these patients insist that what they are saying is real?

e. What clinical observation suggests that confabulation does not result from damage to the medial temporal lobe?

11. a. Summarize the results of a series of PET scans of a patient with Korsakoff's syndrome that suggest the physiological cause of confabulation. (Benson et al., 1996)

b. What kind of brain damage did a patient with amnesia who suddenly began confabulating suffer? (O'Connor et al., 1996)

12. When information is uncertain, what may be the function of the frontal lobes? (Johnson and Raye, 1998)

Learning Objective 13-14 Describe the role of the hippocampus in relational learning including spatial learning and the role of hippocampal place cells.

Read pages 471-474 and answer the following questions.

1. Describe research on the effect of hippocampal lesions on spatial abilities.
   a. Describe the Morris water maze. (Morris et al., 1982)
   b. To test relational learning, how are rat subjects trained in the maze?
   c. To test nonrelational, stimulus-response learning, how are rats trained in the maze?
   d. What is the only kind of information rats can use to find the submerged platform in the nonrelational, stimulus-response task? (Eichenbaum et al., 1990)
   e. How successfully do rats with hippocampal lesions maneuver through the maze if they are
      1. always released from the same position?
      2. released from a new position on each trial? (See Figure 13.40 in your text.)
   f. What do the results suggest about the importance of the hippocampal formation in relational learning?
2. Summarize research on other species that confirms the importance of the hippocampus in spatial learning.
   a. Specifically, how do hippocampal lesions affect the navigation skills of homing pigeons? (Gagliardo et al., 1999)
   b. Compare the size of the hippocampus of birds and rodents that store food with those who do not. (Sherry et al., 1992)
3. a. As revealed in structural MRI scans, how did the brains of London taxi drivers differ from those of normal subjects? (Maguire et al., 2000)
   b. How did these structural changes correlate with length of time spent in the occupation?
4. a. In general, how did single pyramidal cells in the hippocampus respond as rats moved around their environment? (Be sure to mention spatial receptive fields in your answer. O'Keefe and Dostrovsky, 1971)
   b. What were these neurons named?
5. a. In a symmetrical chamber, what kind of cues do rats use to orient themselves?
   b. How do place cells respond when these cues are moved as a group?
   c. How do place cells respond when these cues interchanged?
6. a. How is information about location thought to be organized in the hippocampal formation?

b. Where in the rodent hippocampus are most place cells found, and how does this location correspond to the human brain? (Best et al., 2001)

7. a. Draw or describe the apparatus shown in Figure 13.41 in your text, and explain how Skaggs and McNaughton (1998) used it to study the firing of hippocampal place cells in rats.

b. Each day when a rat was placed in its customary chamber, how did some of its hippocampal place cells respond?

c. How did other hippocampal cells respond?

d. What did these patterns seem to indicate?

e. On the last day of the experiment what change occurred?

f. What evidence indicates that a rat "realized" it had made a mistake?

g. What, then, may the firing patterns of hippocampal place cells indicate?

8. a. The hippocampus appears to receive its spatial information through the ______________ ______________.

b. What property do neurons in entorhinal cortex and hippocampal pyramidal cells share to varying degrees? (Quirk et al., 1992)

c. If the entorhinal cortex is damaged, what deficits are seen? (Miller and Best, 1980)

9. a. Describe or draw the experimental apparatus, shown in Figure 13.42 in your text, to learn what kinds of information hippocampal neurons encode. (Wood et al., 2000)

b. Summarize the responses of field CA1 pyramidal cells.

c. What do these response patterns suggest about the nature of encoded information?

10. a. Although some neurons in the hippocampus of monkeys respond to location, most of them respond to a different cue. Name it.

b. What name do Rolls and his colleagues use to refer to these neurons and why do they think they are present? (Rolls, 1996; Georges-François et al., 1999)

c. Compare the amount of place cells in the hippocampus of primates and rodents. (O'Mara et al., 1994)

Learning Objective 13-15 Outline a possible explanation for the role of the hippocampal formation in learning and memory.

Read pages 474-477 and answer the following questions.

1. Animals were taught a spatial learning task and were later tested on their memory for that task.

a. When the animals were tested five days after learning the task, which brain regions showed increased activity, and how did the level of activity correlate with task performance?

b. Twenty-five days later, what changes were noted in both brain activity and the correlation with performance?

c. How do the researchers interpret these results? (Bontempi et al., 1999)

2. a. Rats were trained in a Morris water maze to locate a platform. One day after training, and before testing, researchers deactivated specific regions of the animals' brains. How well did these animals do during testing?

   b. If the hippocampus was deactivated 30 days after training, how well did the animals do during testing?

   c. What do these results suggest about the role of the hippocampus and the cerebral cortex in consolidation and retrieval of new and old spatial memories? (See Figure 13.43 in your text. Maviel et al., 2004)

3. Define *reconsolidation* in your own words.

4. a. Summarize the effects of electroconvulsive shock (ECS), which is used to treat severe cases of depression, on memory. Begin by stating a well-known side effect of ECS treatment and why it occurs.

   b. If, prior to ECS, the person is reminded of a previous experience, how is the memory of that experience affected by treatment?

   c. How does ECS affect a learning experience that takes place

      1. just before treatment?
      2. the day before treatment?
      3. the day before treatment and followed by a "reminder" stimulus the next day before treatment?

   d. Carefully explain why ECS treatment disrupted retention under some testing conditions, but not others. (Study Figure 13.44 in your text. Misanin et al., 1968)

5. In addition to the stimulus-response learning in the previous study, what other kind of learning appears vulnerable to reconsolidation? (Nader, 2003)

6. a. What kind of task did researchers teach subject rats?

   b. How was consolidation affected if a drug that interfered with protein synthesis was infused into the hippocampus

      1. immediately after training?
      2. 45 days after training?
      3. 45 days after the original training and reactivated by presenting the CS? (Study Figure 13.45 in your text. Debiec et al. 2002)

   c. What is the presumed explanation for these results?

7. a. What physical changes were observed in the hippocampal formation of rats that learned a radial-arm maze? (Mitsuno et al., 1994)

   b. Changes in the hippocampal formation resemble what phenomenon that you have already studied?

8. Summarize the results of research using a method that interferes with long-term potentiation and affects learning. How do targeted mutations of the NMDA receptor gene affecting only CA1 pyramidal cells affect

   a. NMDA receptor development in this part of the brain? other parts of the brain? (See Figure 13.46 in your text. McHugh et al., 1996, Tsien et al., 1996)

   b. the establishment of long-term potentiation in field CA1 of the knockout mice?

c. the spatial receptive fields of affected CA1 pyramidal cells?

d. learning the Morris water maze by the knockout mice?

9. Researchers used genetic manipulation to increase the production of a particular subunit of the NMDA receptor in mice. (Tang et al., 1999)

   a. How were the EPSPs produced by the altered NMDA receptor different from those of unaltered receptors?

   b. Describe how the changed EPSPs affected long-term potentiation observed in hippocampal slices from subject mice.

   c. Compare the speed with which subject mice and normal mice learned the Morris water maze, and then explain what these differing rates indicate about the importance of the hippocampus in relational learning.

10. Why is it inadvisable to attempt to use this technique to produce smarter animals or people?

11. How do targeted mutations of genes responsible for the production of CaM-KII affect long-term potentiation? The ability to learn the Morris water maze? (Grant et al., 1992; Silva et al., 1992b; Giese et al., 1998)

12. a. What did an examination of field CA1 reveal about synaptic density in

      1. of young rats?

      2. old rats with normal spatial learning ability?

      3. old rats with impaired spatial learning ability?

    b. What do these results suggest about the causes of age-related learning decline? (Nicolson et al., 2004)

13. What do all these results suggest about the role of the hippocampal formation in long-term potentiation?

14. Look at evidence for neurogenesis and enhanced learning in the brain.

    a. What kind of learning tasks in the Morris water maze do and do not increase the number of new neurons in the dentate gyrus? (Gould et al., 1999)

    b. The newly formed neurons in the dentate gyrus of rats in another study who had also been trained in a relational learning task in the Morris water maze showed an increase in fos protein. What does an increase in this protein suggest about neuronal activity? (Jessberger and Kempermann, 2003)

    c. Why may neurogenesis facilitate synaptic plasticity? (Schmidt-Hieber et al., 2004)

    d. Why may the benefits of enhanced neurogenesis only be of a long-term nature? (Kempermann et al., 2004)

Lesson II Self Test

1. Anterograde amnesia can best be described as

   a. a failure of short-term memory.
   b. a failure to establish new nondeclarative memories.
   c. the loss of relational learning ability.
   d. a diminished sense of time.

2. Patient H.M. is

   a. bored by repetitive tasks.
   b. aware of his disorder.
   c. unable to learn any new information.
   d. frustrated by his difficulty in following a conversation.

3. Nondeclarative memories

   a. are a form of perceptual memory.
   b. are usually expressed in writing.
   c. fade more quickly than declarative memories.

d. do not require deliberate efforts to memorize something.

4. The most important input of information to the hippocampal formation comes from the

a. anterior thalamus.
b. locus coeruleus.
c. entorhinal cortex.
d. subiculum.

5. Neurons in field CA1 of the hippocampus are easily damaged when metabolic disturbances set off a series of events that include the

a. rapid proliferation of NMDA receptors.
b. desynchronized firing of presynaptic axons.
c. entry of calcium into the neurons.
d. release of abnormally high levels of serotonin.

6. Semantic memories

a. are forms of perceptual memories.
b. involve facts, but not the context in which they are learned.
c. are usually expressed in writing.
d. must be acquired deliberately.

7. When a person is remembering or performing a navigational task, the _____ becomes active.

a. right hippocampal formation
b. left hippocampal formation
c. limbic cortex
d. mammillary bodies

8. Confabulation, a symptom of Korsakoff's syndrome, may be caused by damage to the

a. prefrontal cortex.
b. mammillary bodies.
c. perirhinal cortex.
d. caudate nucleus.

9. Rats are trained in a Morris water maze

a. to reduce the effects of tactile stimulation.
b. to test their spatial perception and memory.
c. to avoid using food as a reinforcing stimulus.
d. to assess their stimulus-response learning.

10. On the last day of testing, rats were switched from one nearly identical chamber to another. While inside the chamber, the firing of hippocampal place cells indicated that _____, but once outside the chamber _____.

a. some rats "thought" they were in the usual chamber; the response pattern changed appropriately as if to correct a mistake
b. rats "thought" they were in the usual chamber; the response pattern became erratic and only stabilized when rats returned to the chamber
c. some rats "recognized" they were in a different chamber; the response pattern did not change and rats could not find their former chamber
d. rats "recognized" they were in a different chamber; the response pattern of only about half the rats made the appropriate change

11. A targeted mutation that increased the production of NMDA receptors with a particular subunit _____ leading to enhanced long-term potentiation.

a. caused production of slightly larger EPSPs,
b. caused development of an increased number of calcium channels,
c. decreased the likelihood of damage from seizures or anoxia,
d. decreased postsynaptic levels of CaM-KII,

12. Long-term memories can be modified during a process known as

a. consolidation.
b. reconsolidation.
c. reactivation.
d. confabulation.

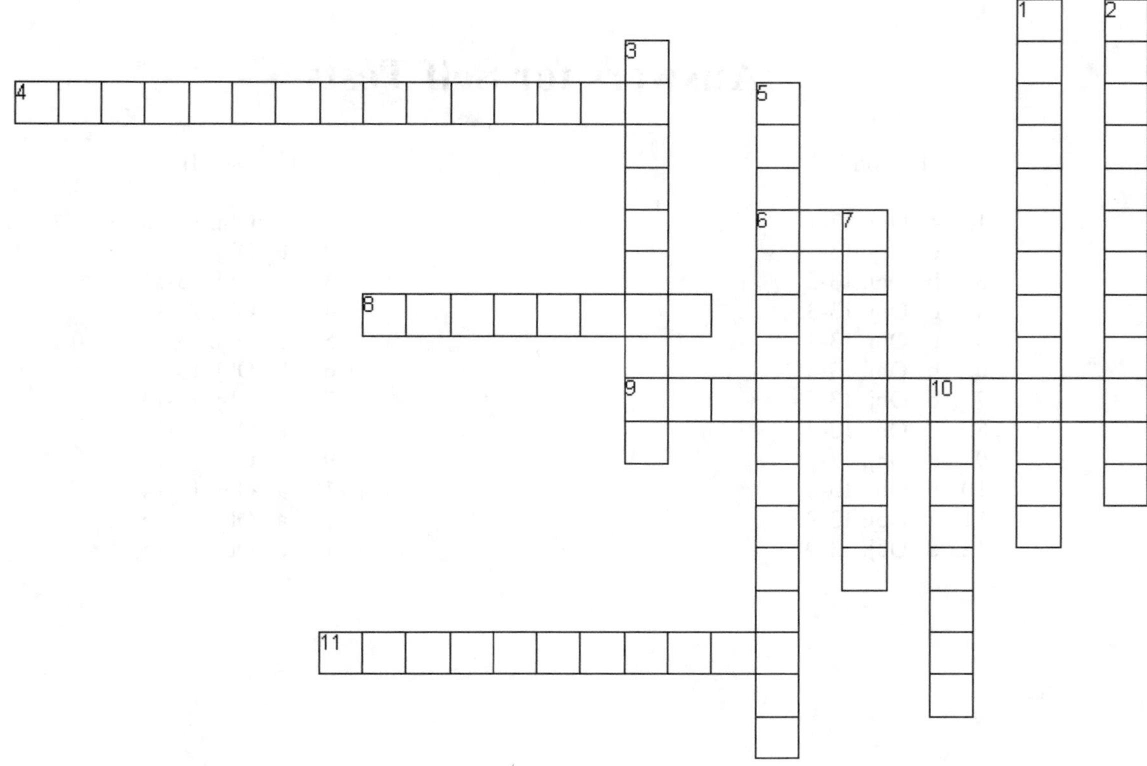

Across

4. A process of memory consolidation that can be triggered by a reminder of the original stimulus
6. A long-term increase in the excitability of a neuron to a particular synaptic input caused by repeated high-frequency activity of that input
8. A memory of facts and general information
9. An ionotropic glutamate receptor that controls a sodium channel; when open, it produces EPSPs
11. Memory that can be verbally expressed, such as memory for events in a person's past.

Down

1. The reporting of memories of events that did not take place without the intention to deceive; seen in people with Korsakoff's syndrome
2. Part of the hippocampal formation; receives inputs from the entorhinal cortex and projects to the field CA3 of the hippocampus
3. A region of the limbic cortex that provides the major source of input to the hippocampal formation
5. A nucleus of the basal forebrain that receives dopamine-secreting terminal buttons from neurons of the VTA; involved in reinforcement
7. A neuron that becomes active when the animal is in a particular location in the environment
10. Memory of a collection of perceptions of events organized in time and identified by a particular context

Answers for Self Tests

Lesson I

1. c Obj. 13-1
2. c Obj. 13-1
3. b Obj. 13-2
4. d Obj. 13-3
5. c Obj. 13-4
6. b Obj. 13-5
7. b Obj. 13-6
8. b Obj. 13-7
9. c Obj. 13-7
10. b Obj. 13-8
11. a Obj. 13-9
12. c Obj. 13-9

Lesson II

1. c Obj. 13-10
2. b Obj. 13-10
3. d Obj. 13-11
4. c Obj. 13-12
5. c Obj. 13-12
6. b Obj. 13-13
7. a Obj. 13-13
8. a Obj. 13-13
9. b Obj. 13-14
10. a Obj. 13-14
11. a Obj. 13-15
12. b Obj. 13-15

CHAPTER 14
Human Communication

Lesson I: Speech Production and Comprehension: Brain Mechanisms

Read the interim summary on pages 502-503 of your text to re-acquaint yourself with the material in this section.

> ***Learning Objective 14-1*** Describe the use of subjects with brain damage in the study of language and explain the concept of lateralization.

Read pages 481-482 and answer the following questions.

1. a. List some of the medical conditions that researchers often study to learn more about the effects that physical damage to the brain has on speech.

   b. Underline the most frequently studied of these conditions.
2. Identify another source of information about verbal communication.
3. Name and describe the most important category of speech disorders.

4. Verbal behavior is a _______________ function. The _______________ hemisphere is dominant for speech in approximately _____ percent of the population. However, if the _______________ hemisphere is malformed or damaged early in life language dominance is very likely to pass to the _______________ hemisphere. (Vikingstad et al., 2000) Most language disturbances follow damage to the _______________ hemisphere whether people are _______________-_______________ or _______________-_______________.
5. Carefully explain why the left hemisphere is specialized for speech.

6. Explain how the right hemisphere contributes to speech. (Gardner et al., 1983)

> ***Learning Objective 14-2*** Describe Broca's aphasia and the three major speech deficits that result from damage to Broca's area: agrammatism, anomia, and articulation difficulties.

Read pages 482-486 and answer the following questions.
1. Describe how Broca's aphasia affect:

   a. speech production.

b. production of meaningful speech.

c. grammar, especially the use of function words and content words. (See Figure 14.1 in your text.)

d. comprehension.

2. a. Broca's aphasia, named for Paul Broca, appears to result from damage to what region of the brain? (See Figure 14.2 in your text. Broca, 1861)

   b. Describe more precisely the areas in the vicinity of Broca's area that, when damaged, do and do not produce Broca's aphasia. (H. Damasio, 1989; Naeser et al., 1989)

   c. What other region if damaged produces a Broca-like aphasia? (Damasio et al., 1984)

   d. Describe the severe speech deficit that afflicts some members of the KE family. (Watkins et al., 2002a, 2002b)

   e. Which brain regions develop abnormally as a result of a mutation of a single gene on chromosome 7?

3. What did Wernicke (1874) suggest is the speech function of Broca's area?

4. List the three deficits that are characteristic of Broca's aphasia, suggesting that the disorder is not a simple one. (See Animation 14.1.)

   1.

   2.

   3.

5. Look at each of these more closely, as well as speech comprehension. Begin by explaining how agrammatism affects the speech of patients with Broca's aphasia.

6. a. Describe the task and the cards, one of which is shown in Figure 14.3 in your text, that Schwartz and her colleagues used to test the speech comprehension skills of people with Broca's aphasia. (Schwartz et al., 1980)

   b. How well did their subjects do?

   c. What do these results suggest about the ability of Broca's aphasics to use grammatical information?

7. How is the speech of patients with Broca's aphasia affected by

   a. anomia?

   b. difficulty with articulation?

8. Rank the deficits you have just described from the most elementary to the least.

9. a. What critical location for control of speech articulation did Dronkers (1996) find? (See Figure 14.4 in your text.)

   b. How did she locate it? Be sure to mention apraxia of speech in your answer. Cite research that supports Dronkers's conclusions. (See Figure 14.5 in your text. Kuriki et al. 1999; Wise et al., 1999)

   c. Cite research that suggests Broca's area is also involved in articulation. How did subjects respond when transcranial magnetic stimulation activated neurons in

      1. Broca's area?

      2. the primary motor cortex adjacent to Broca's area? (Stewart, 2001)

10. a. What is another region of the brain that seems to be involved in speech production?

    b. How is speech production in a number of species affected if this region is damaged?

    c. How does chemical or electrical stimulation affect the firing rate of neurons in this region and vocalization? (Jürgens, 2000)

    d. Summarize the effects of PAG lesions in a woman studied by Esposito et al. (1999).

11. a. Normal speech and whispering involve the same movements with one exception—the vocal cords do not vibrate when a person whispers. However, some brain regions become active only during normal speech. Name them. (Schulz et al., 2005)

    b. According to the researchers, what may be the function of the auditory cortex of the temporal lobes?

12. a. The agrammatism and anomia characteristic of Broca's aphasia are normally caused by damage to what area of the brain?

    b. Describe how Stromswold et al. (1996) confirmed this location.

Learning Objective 14-3 Describe the symptoms of Wernicke's aphasia, pure word deafness, and transcortical sensory aphasia and explain how they are related.

Read pages 486-492 and answer the following questions.

1. Return to Figure 14.2 and describe the location of Wernicke's area. What is its presumed function?

2. List the two primary characteristics of Wernicke's aphasia.

   1. 2.

3. a. Describe how Wernicke's aphasia affects

      1. speech production.

      2. production of meaningful speech.

3. grammar, especially the use of content and function words.

4. comprehension.

5. observing social conventions of speech.

b. How is the speech comprehension of people with Wernicke's aphasia tested? Why?

c. What do the results of comprehension tests indicate?

4. Describe the reaction of patients with Wernicke's aphasia to their own speech difficulties. (See Animation 14.1.)

5. a. What did Wernicke himself suggest is the function of the region that bears his name?

b. What anatomical evidence appears to confirm the role of Wernicke's area in learning? (Jacobs et al., 1993)

6. List three characteristic deficits resulting from damage to Wernicke's area.

1.

2.

3.

7. Explain the distinction between recognizing and comprehending a word. (See Figure 14.6 in your text.)

8. a. Describe how pure word deafness affects

1. the ability to hear.

2. comprehension of speech.

3. comprehension of nonspeech sounds.

4. comprehension of emotion expressed through intonation.

5. speech production.

6. reading and writing.

b. How do people with this disorder communicate with other people?

9. Where does perception of speech sounds occur?

10. Describe the procedure and results of research on the functions of the superior temporal lobe. (See Figure 14.7 in your text and Animation 14.2. Scott et al., 2000)

11. Compare Figures 14.7 and 14.8 in your text, noting where brain damage that affected speech comprehension or speech production overlapped. (Sharp et al., 2004)

12. Concerning the analysis of sounds, what do most researchers believe is the function of the auditory association cortex of the

    a. left hemisphere?

    b. right hemisphere?

13. a. What aspect of speech is important for the identification of

        1. individual words?

        2. prosody (emphasis and emotion)?

    b. Which of these speech aspects is of longer duration than the other?

    c. Which hemisphere seems to be specialized for recognition of acoustical events of long duration? short duration?

    d. Describe the speech recognition deficits of patients with pure word deafness to support your answer. (Phillips and Farmer, 1990; Stefanatos et al., 2005)

14. Study Figure 14.9 in your text and then list the two types of brain damage that cause pure word deafness. (Poeppel, 2001; Stefanatos et al., 2005)

    1.

    2.

15. In general, when do the circuits of mirror neurons in our brains become active, and how do we use the feedback we receive from them?

16. Summarize evidence that suggests the brain mechanisms that control speech also contain mirror neurons.

    a. What distinguished the two groups of words that researchers had Italian-speaking subjects listen to?

    b. Which group of words excited the subjects' tongue muscles the most? (See Figure 14.10 in your text. Fadiga et al., 2002)

    c. What kind of speech strongly activates the human auditory cortex? (Schultz et al., 2005)

17. What does the case of Mr. S. illustrate about the mechanisms that contribute to accurate speech pronunciation?

18. a. Study Figure 14.11 in your text and describe the location of the posterior language area, noting its proximity to Wernicke's area.

    b. What is the presumed function of this area?

    c. What symptoms of Wernicke's aphasia appear to be produced by damage to this area?

    d. Damage to this area alone results in the disorder ________________ ________________ ________________.

19. Compare Wernicke's aphasia and transcortical sensory aphasia by describing how transcortical sensory aphasia affects

    a. speech recognition and repetition.

b. speech comprehension.

c. production of meaningful speech.

20. Because patients can repeat what they hear, what kind of connection must exist within the brain? (Return to Figure 14.11.)

21. Which brain areas, when stimulated, produced the symptoms of transcortical sensory aphasia? (See Figure 14.12 in your text. Boatman et al., 2000)

22. a. Describe how extensive brain damage resulting from carbon monoxide affected a patient's speech recognition, comprehension and production. (Geschwind et al., 1968)

b. What does this case confirm about the brain mechanisms of speech?

Learning Objective 14-4 Discuss the brain mechanisms that underlie our ability to understand the meaning of words and to express our own thoughts and perceptions in words.

Read pages 492-494 and answer the following questions.

1. Words have meaning for us because they evoke particular _______________, which are not stored in primary _______________ _______________, but in other parts of the brain.

2. a. Study Figure 14.13 in your text and follow the pathway responsible for recognizing and comprehending a spoken word.

   b. Use the concept of cell assemblies to explain how we learn words and their meanings according to the Hebb rule.

   c. How does the process work when we want to describe our thoughts or perceptions in words?

3. Look at some evidence that supports the notion of cell assemblies.

   a. Following a stroke that damaged part of the right parietal lobe, which plays a role in spatial perception, what kind of difficulty did a patient have in describing spatial relationships?

   b. She could understand some meanings of particular words, but not other meanings. Explain and give examples.

4. Name and describe the specific comprehension difficulties associated with damage to the

   a. association cortex of the left parietal lobe. Be sure to use the term *autotopagnosia* in your answer.

   b. lateral temporal lobe. (Semenza and Zettin, 1989)

   c. temporal pole or inferior temporal cortex. (Damasio et al., 1991; Proverbio et al., 2001)

5. According to Damasio and his colleagues, what distinction between proper and common nouns is useful in understanding brain function? Cite supporting evidence. (Grabowski et al., 2001)

6. What hemisphere is involved in the comprehension of abstract aspects of speech? Briefly summarize confirming research, noting the kinds of analyses subjects were asked to make.

   a. Brownell et al. (1983,1990)

   b. Bottini et al. (1994)

   c. Nichelli et al. (1995)

   d. Sotillo et al. (2005) (See Figure 14.14 in your text.)

Learning Objective 14-5 Describe the symptoms of conduction aphasia and anomic aphasia, including aphasia in deaf people.

Read pages 494-499 and answer the following questions.

1. a. The ________________ ________________ is a direct connection between Wernicke's area and Broca's area.

   b. What kind of information does it presumably convey?

2. a. Describe the brain damage that causes conduction aphasia. (Study Figure 14.15 in your text. Damasio and Damasio, 1980)

   b. How does conduction aphasia affect these aspects of speech? Refer to specific examples from patients. (See Animation 14.1. Margolin and Walker, 1981)

      1. Speech production

      2. Speech comprehension

      3. Repetition

   c. What is the essential difference between the words such patients can and cannot repeat?

3. Study Figure 14.16 in your text and carefully describe the direct and indirect pathways that may connect the speech mechanisms of the temporal and frontal lobes suggested by the communication deficits of patients with transcortical sensory aphasia or conduction aphasia.

   a. Direct pathways

   b. Indirect pathways

4. Next to each pathway, note its presumed function.

5. a. Briefly describe the kind of equipment that researchers used to study the presumed pathways between Wernicke's area and Broca's area. (Catani et al., 2005)

   b. Describe their results:

1. Direct deep pathway

2. Indirect shallower pathway, including both segments (See Figure 14.17 in your text.)

c. What kind of damage results from damage to the direct pathway?

d. What kind of damage results from damage to the indirect pathway?

6. To review what you have learned, draw in and label the following regions in Figure 1: Broca's area, Wernicke's area, posterior language area, primary auditory cortex, the arcuate fasciculus, and the location of perceptions and memories. Draw in and label arrows for the repetition of a perceived word and the translation of perceptions and thoughts into words. The information needed to complete the figure is found in Figures 14.2, 14.9, 14.11, and 14.16.

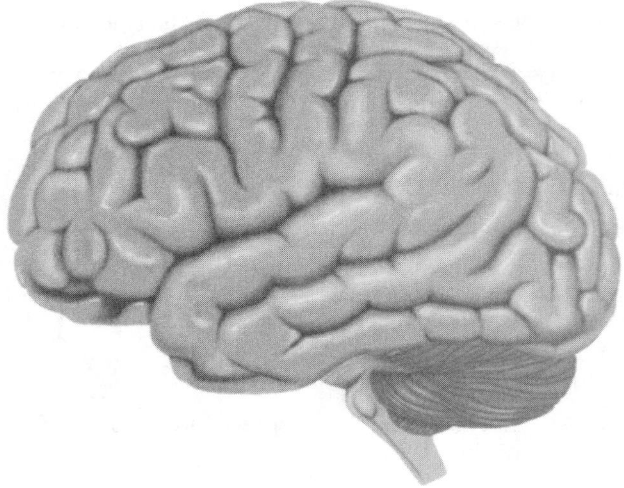

Figure 1

7. a. What do the symptoms of conduction aphasia suggest is the function of the connection between Wernicke's area and Broca's area?

   b. Describe the circuit that Baddeley (1993) refers to as the phonological loop. Be sure to refer to the *arcuate fasciculus* in your answer.

   c. Summarize research that supports this hypothesis. (See Figure 14.18 in your text. Paulesu et al., 1993; Fiez et al., 1996)

8. Read over the description of the picture in Figure 14.1 in your text given by the woman with anomic aphasia reported by Margolin and his colleagues. (See Animation 14.1. Margolin et al., 1985)

   a. How did anomic aphasia affect her speech production, production of meaningful speech, and comprehension?

b. When did she use circumlocutions?

c. Which area of this woman's brain had been damaged?

d. Which area of this woman's brain was spared?

e. In follow-up informal testing, what word-finding difficulty became more apparent?

9. a. Some patients have anomia for verbs which results from damage to the frontal cortex in and around Broca's area. Explain why this finding is consistent with our knowledge of the functions of the frontal lobes. (Damasio and Tranel, 1993; Daniele et al., 1994; Bak et al., 2001)

b. Study Figure 14.19 in your text and briefly describe research that confirms the importance of Broca's area and the surrounding region in the production of verbs. (Petersen et al., 1988; Wise et al., 1991; McCarthy et al., 1993; Fiez et al., 1996)

c. In general, how did the region of motor cortex that became active when subjects thought about a particular verb correlate with its function? (Pulvermüller et al., 2000; Buccino et al., 2005)

10. Describe the presumed flow of information through the brain for the

a. comprehension of speech.

b. production of spontaneous speech.

c. thinking in words.

11. a. What anatomical evidence supports the notion that our ancestors may have first communicated using hand gestures?

b. What were the results of a functional imagining study that further supported this notion? (Figure 14.20 in your text. Iacoboni et al., 1999)

c. How did subjects respond when they watched a researcher grasp a large object? (Gentilucci 2003)

d. How did subjects respond when they watched a researcher grasp a small object? (Gentilucci 2003)

e. What do the subjects' responses suggest about the development of spoken language? (See Figure 14.21 in your text.)

f. Explain the presumed function of this region in communication.

12. a. In which hemisphere might we expect to find damage in deaf people with aphasia for signs? Why?

    b. All reported cases of deaf people who are aphasic for signs have suffered lesions on the left side of the brain. (Hickok et al., 1996) Summarize research to learn more about the functions of the right and left hemispheres of deaf people:

       1. a. Which brain region became active when deaf signers made meaningful signs? (Pettito et al., 2000)

          b. Which brain region became active when deaf signers viewed signs made by others? (Pettito et al., 2000)

       2. What do these results suggest about the similarity between sign language, auditory, and written language?

       3. Which brain region was damaged in deaf signers who had problems using sign language? (Hickok et al., 1999)

Learning Objective 14-6 Summarize some research on the location of cell assemblies that encode different languages in the bilingual brain and describe the use of prosody in communication, including the effects of stuttering.

Read pages 499-502 and answer the following questions.

1. a. What percentage of bilingual patients who had suffered a severe stroke resulting in aphasia showed recovery in both languages? (Fabbro, 2001a)

   b. What percentage of bilingual patients who had suffered a severe stroke resulting in aphasia showed a greater improvement in their first language? (Fabbro, 2001a)

   c. What percentage of bilingual patients who had suffered a severe stroke resulting in aphasia showed their second language? (Fabbro, 2001a)

   d. What do these results suggest about which language is more vulnerable to brain damage?

2. How does the organization of cell assemblies for the neural representations of words in people's first and second languages differ from that of the cell assemblies for grammar rules? (Fabbro, 2001b)

3. When bilingual subjects listened to and read abstract nouns in their two languages, what did researchers observe about active brain regions? (See Figure 14.22 in your text. Simos et al., 2001)

4. a. Outline the experimental procedure used to teach bilingual subjects two kinds of mathematical problems. (Dehaene et al., 1999)

      1. Approximate method

      2. Exact method

   b. Explain how the language of training and testing affected success on the approximate method and the exact method.

   c. During testing, which brain regions became active as subjects attempted to solve the problems using the approximate method?

d. During testing, which brain regions became active as subjects attempted to solve the problems using the exact method?

5. Define *prosody* in your own words.

6. How do we indicate some of the elements of prosody when we write?

7. Contrast the prosody of the speech of people with fluent aphasia, Wernicke's aphasia, and Broca's aphasia.

8. a. Which hemisphere plays the most important role in prosody?

   b. Name some of the other functions of this hemisphere that are probably related to prosody.

9. a. Describe the testing procedure Weintraub and her colleagues (Weintraub et al., 1981) used to test the use of prosody by subjects with right-hemisphere damage.

   b. What did researchers notice about the way subjects correctly answered the questions?

   c. What do the results suggest about the role of the right hemisphere in the use of prosody?

10. a. Explain how stuttering disrupts normal speech.

    b. What is the incidence of stuttering

       1. in the population?

       2. between men and women? (Brown et al., 2005)

    c. How is the speech of a person who stutters changed by activities such as singing or reading aloud with another person who does not stutter?

    d. In general, what kind of brain abnormalities are not a cause of this speech disorder?

    e. In general, what kind of brain abnormalities may be a cause of this speech disorder?

11. a. List the brain regions that tend to show excessive activity in speakers who stutter when compared to those of fluent speakers. (See Figure 14.24 in your text. Brown et al., 2005)

       1. 3.

       2. 4.

    b. Which brain region shows an absence of activation?

    c. What do the researchers suggest may cause stuttering? Be sure to mention supporting research by Salmelin et al. (2000) which they cited.

12. a. Explain the delayed auditory feedback procedure.

    b. How does using this kind of equipment affect the speech of fluent speakers? (Foundas et al., 2004a)

    c. How does using this kind of equipment affect the speech of speakers who stutter? (Foundas et al., 2004a)

    d. Following a course in fluency shaping therapy, how did the activity of the temporal cortex of people who stutter change? (See Figure 14.25 in your text. Neumann et al., 2005)

    e. What do these results support is the cause of stuttering?

13. To review your understanding of the deficits associated with each of the disorders covered in this lesson, fill in the blanks in the table on the next page. Compare your answers with the information in Table 14.1 in your text.

Disorder	Area of lesion	Spontaneous speech	Comprehension	Repetition	Naming
Wernicke's aphasia					
Pure word deafness					
Broca's aphasia					
Conduction aphasia					
Anomic aphasia					
Transcortical sensory aphasia					

Lesson I Self Test

1. Most conclusions about the physiology of language have been made through work with subjects who have sustained
   a. head injuries.
   b. cerebrovascular accidents.
   c. brain tumors.
   d. infections.

2. When we say that verbal behavior is a lateralized function, we mean that
   a. both hemispheres of the brain are equally important for speech.
   b. both hemispheres of the brain have the capacity to perform all aspects of speech.
   c. one hemisphere is dominant for speech and the other hemisphere plays no role.
   d. one hemisphere is dominant for speech and the other hemisphere plays a smaller role.

3. People with Broca's aphasia
   a. speak fluently, but have anomia.

b. speak fluently, but have poor comprehension.
c. speak slowly, with difficulty, but grammatically.
d. speak slowly, with difficulty, but with meaning.

4. Anomia is a difficulty in

a. finding the correct word to describe an object, action, or situation.
b. pronouncing abstract, but not concrete, words.
c. repeating sequences longer than three words.
d. using function and content words.

5. People with Wernicke's aphasia

a. speak fluently but without meaning and have poor comprehension.
b. speak haltingly but with meaning and have excellent comprehension.
c. can no longer speak but still comprehend the speech of others.
d. speak sporadically but to the point.

6. Research with people who have transcortical sensory aphasia suggests that

a. the ability to understand is necessary for accurate memorization.
b. recognition, repetition, and rhythm are inseparable aspects of speech production.
c. the ability to speak spontaneously is necessary in order to repeat what is heard.
d. brain mechanisms needed for recognition and comprehension of speech are different.

7. The fact that damage to particular regions of the sensory association cortex causes specific deficits suggests that

a. redundancy in function is an important characteristic of the brain.
b. localization of function within some brain regions is more specific than was previously thought.
c. the meaning of words are stored in cell assemblies in various regions of association cortex.
d. the importance of a function and the size of the brain region devoted to it are positively correlated.

8. Damage to the posterior language area disrupts the ability to

a. recognize spoken words.
b. repeat spoken words.
c. understand words and produce meaningful speech.
d. understand particular categories of words.

9. Which is *not* true of the arcuate fasciculus?

a. It conveys meanings of words but not sounds.
b. It conveys sounds of words but not meanings.
c. It is an arch-shaped bundle that connects Wernicke's area and Broca's area.
d. Damage results in conduction aphasia.

10. Researchers suggest that people with conduction aphasia can repeat words only if they

a. are spelled regularly.
b. have meaning.
c. have no threatening emotional content.
d. are short.

11. In the bilingual brain, the neural representations of _____ of a person's first and second languages appear to be _____.

a. the spelling rules; are intermingled based on similarity
b. the pronunciation rules; stored separately
c. grammar rules; intermingled to a limited extent depending on complexity
d. words; intermingled

12. Which of the following disorders is characterized by poor prosody?

a. Wernicke's aphasia
b. Broca's aphasia
c. anomic aphasia
d. conduction aphasia

Lesson II: Disorders of Reading and Writing

Read the interim summary on page 515-516 of your text to re-acquaint yourself with the material in this section.

Learning Objective 14-7 Describe pure alexia and explain why this disorder is caused by damage to two specific parts of the brain.

Read pages 504-507 and answer the following questions.

1. Make a general statement about the relationship between the speaking and understanding skills and the reading and writing skills of people with aphasia.

2. Briefly describe the abilities of a patient with severe fluent aphasia studied by Semenza et al. (1992) and explain what these rare exceptions suggest about neural organization.

3. Describe how pure alexia affects

   a. reading.

   b. writing. (For an example, see Figure 14.26 in your text.)

   c. recognition of orally spelled words.

4. a. If a patient suffered damage limited to the left primary visual cortex, how would reading ability be affected? Trace the flow of visual information paying special attention to the role of the corpus callosum.(Study Figure 14.27a in your text.)

   b. If, however, a patient suffers damage to both the left primary visual cortex and the posterior corpus callosum, how is reading ability affected? (Study Figure 14.27b. See Animation 14.3.)

5. Discuss the forms of human communication that appear to have been influenced by natural selection. (Patterson and Ralph, 1999)

6. How may recognition of real objects differ from recognition of written words? (Behrmann et al., 1998)

7. a. What other perceptual deficit did musicians with pure alexia suffer as a result of brain damage? (Horikoshi et al., 1997; Beversdorf and Heilman, 1998)

   b. Outline a possible explanation.

8. a. As a result of a stroke, what kind of brain damage did a deaf woman sustain? (Hickok et al., 1993)

   b. Which of her communication abilities were spared and which were damaged as a result of the brain damage?

Learning Objective 14-8 Describe whole-word and phonetic reading and discuss five categories of acquired dyslexias.

Read pages 507-511 and answer the following questions.

1. a. Explain the distinction between whole-word reading and phonetic reading.

b. What kind of words do we usually read using the whole-word method? the phonetic methods?

2. a. Define *dyslexia* in your own words.

   b. Contrast acquired dyslexia with developmental dyslexia.

3. Before we study dyslexia, follow the simplified model of the reading process shown in Figure 14.28 in your text.

4. Look at some of the reading disorders resulting from acquired dyslexia, beginning with surface dyslexia.

   a. Surface dyslexia is usually caused by damage to the _______________ _______________ _______________ lobe. (Marshall and Newcombe, 1973; McCarthy and Warrington, 1990; Patterson and Ralph, 1999)

   b. Why is this deficit called surface dyslexia?

   c. Provide some examples of the kinds of words surface dyslexics can read :

      1. easily.
      2. with difficulty.
      3. only in context. (Gurd and Marshall, 1993)

   d. If people with surface dyslexia cannot recognize words by their appearance, how then do they understand what they have read? (See Figure 14.29 in your text.)

5. a. By what method do people with phonological dyslexia read?

   b. Provide some examples of the kinds of words phonological dyslexics can read

      1. easily.
      2. with difficulty. (Beauvois and Dérouesné, 1979; Dérouesné and Beauvois, 1979)

   c. Explain how the study of phonological dyslexia contributes to an understanding of whole-word and phonological reading. (See Figure 14.30 in your text.)

6. a. Explain the kana and kanji symbols of the Japanese language.

   b. What form of reading is used for kana symbols?

   c. What form of reading is used for kanji symbols?

   d. What condition that you have already studied is analogous to difficulty reading kana symbols? kanji symbols?

7. a. Whether someone is reading using the whole-word or the phonological method, what common pathway is activated?

   b. The circuits begin to diverge. Where do the circuits for whole-word reading lead?

   c. What other kinds of stimuli are recognized by this region?

   d. Where do the circuits for phonological reading lead?

   e. What does the involvement of a region near Broca's area suggest about phonological reading?

f. In order to understand what is being read, where do both of these circuits converge? (See Figure 14.31 in your text.)

8. a. Trace the circuit of neural activation responsible for the analysis of the spoken word.

b. Trace the circuit of neural activation responsible for the analysis of the printed word. (See Figure 14.32 in your text. See Animation 14.4. Marinkovic et al., 2003)

c. What brain regions are activated by reading kanji and kana words? (Thuy et al., 2004)

d. What additional regions are activated by kanji words?

e. What additional regions are activated by kana words?

9. a. What reading methods appear to be lost in word-form or spelling dyslexia?

b. Explain how people with word-form dyslexia read by describing their ability to recognize words if

1. permitted to spell the word.
2. someone else spells the word aloud.
3. they spell the word incorrectly due to the severity of their deficit. (Patterson and Kay, 1980. See Figure 14.33 in your text.)

10. Explain why direct dyslexia resembles transcortical sensory aphasia. (Schwartz et al., 1979; Lytton and Brust, 1989; Gerhand, 2001)

11. Describe how direct dyslexia affects the ability to read aloud and to understand what is read. Be sure to mention which reading method is lost.

12. a. Summarize how a stroke that damaged his left frontal and temporal lobes affected a patient studied by Lytton and Brust (1989).

b. What do his deficits indicate about neural circuits in the brain?

13. Describe how brain injury resulting from an automobile accident affected patient R.F.'s ability to

a. speak and repeat.

b. name most common objects.

c. read most words.

d. match pictures of words and objects she could not read or name. (See Figure 14.34 in your text. Margolin et al., 1985)

14. a. What reading method appears to be lost?

b. What reading method is still partially intact?

c. What observation about spelling did R.F. make that confirms this assessment?

Learning Objective 14-9 Explain the relation between speaking and writing and describe the symptoms of phonological dysgraphia, orthographic dysgraphia and semantic (direct) dysgraphia.

Read pages 511-514 answer the following questions.

1. Explain why people with speech difficulties usually have writing difficulties as well.

2. Describe some of the remarkably specific writing deficits related to difficulties in motor control. (Cubelli, 1991; Alexander et al., 1992; Margolin and Goodman-Schulman, 1992; Silveri, 1996)

3. a. Which regions of the brain are involved in the motor aspects of writing and when they are damaged how is writing affected? (Otsuki et al., 1999; Katanoda et al., 2001; Menon and Desmond, 2001)

   b. What region of the brain became active when people signed their name with either their index finger or their big toe? (Rijntjes et al., 1999)

   c. What does this finding suggest about the organization of the brain?

   d. What side of the brain became active when right-handed people looked at alphabetical characters? Left-handed people? (See Figure 14.35 in your text. Longcamp et al., 2005)

4. Look at a second type of writing disorder involving the ability to spell words. Begin by describing four presumed ways of spelling or writing words.

   a. Explain the progression of skills from hearing words to spelling them that children experience.

   b. If you have not already tried the antidisestablishmentarianism experiment, try it now. Use you own experience to describe any difficulties that you had when you wrote the word

      1. without saying it softly to yourself.

      2. while softly singing a song at the same time.

   c. What kind of sensory memories do people use when they spell a word by imagining what it looks like?

   d. Explain the process of spelling words by memorizing letter sequences.

   e. Explain the process of spelling words through motor memories.

5. Describe how phonological dysgraphia affects the ability to write familiar and unfamiliar words.

6. Describe how orthographic dysgraphia affects the ability to write

   a. regular words and pronounceable nonsense words.

   b. irregular words. (Beauvois and Dérouesné, 1981)

7. Phonological dysgraphia then is impaired _____________ writing resulting from damage to the _____________ _____________ lobe and orthographic dysgraphia is impaired _____________ writing resulting from damage to the _____________ _____________ lobe. (Benson and Geschwind, 1985)

8. a. How successfully did a patient who had suffered a left hemisphere stroke recognize words that were spelled aloud to him when he was permitted to make writing movements with his hands? (Cipolotti and Warrington, 1996)

   b. How successfully did a patient who had suffered a left hemisphere stroke recognize words that were spelled aloud to him when he was asked not to make writing movements with his hands? (Cipolotti and Warrington, 1996)

9. a. Which brain region is involved in both phonological and whole-word reading?

   b. Cite evidence that this region is also involved in writing as well. (Nakamura et al., 2000; Rapszak and Beeson, 2004)

10. a. Explain how damage to the middle part of the corpus callosum affected the ability of a Japanese patient to write kana and kanji symbols with his right and left hand? An example of his writing is shown in Figure 14.36 in your text. (Kawamura et al., 1989)

    b. What do these results suggest about the organization of writing in the brain? (Study Figure 14.37 in your text.)

11. What is the characteristic symptom of semantic agraphia? (Roeltgen et al, 1986; Lesser, 1989)

Learning Objective 14-10 Describe research on the neurological basis of developmental dyslexias.

Read pages 514-515 and answer the following questions.

1. a. Compare the concordance rate of monozygotic and dizygotic twins for developmental dyslexias. (Demonet et al., 2004)

   b. What does this comparison suggest about an important cause of these disorders?

2. Describe the nature of the deficit by summarizing the results of a study of fifty-six dyslexia boys. (Castles and Coltheart, 1993)

3. a. Explain why we should not be surprised to find that developmental dyslexia is more than a reading deficit.

   b. List three different language deficits that people with developmental dyslexia may also have. (Eden and Zeffiro, 1998; Helenius et al., 1999; Habib, 2000)

      1.

      2.

      3.

c. Of these deficits, which one is the most common? Cite research to support your answer. (Ramus et al., 2003)

4. a. Describe the two groups of subjects and the experimental task researchers used to study the way dyslexics process written information. (Shaywitz et al., 2002)

   b. Which brain regions of proficient readers became active as they read?

   c. Reading skill was positively correlated with activity in which brain regions?

5. a. Researchers studied developmental dyslexia in a group of subjects who spoke English, French, or Italian. Which language did people who had the lowest incidence of dyslexia speak? less severe disorders? (Paulesu et al., 2001)

   b. Which language did people who had the lowest incidence of less severe disorders speak? (Paulesu et al., 2001)

   c. All three groups of people were asked to read while their heads were in PET scanner. Which region showed decreased activity in all subjects?

   d. How did these results compare with results obtained by Shaywitz et al. (2002) with dyslexic children?

   e. How did the researchers explain their results?

6. To review the reading and writing disorders you have just learned about, study Table 15.2 in your text.

Lesson II Self Test

1. Pure alexia is a(n) _______________ disorder and patients __________.
   a. perceptual; can no longer read, but can still write
   b. motor; can no longer read or write
   c. sensory; can read but no longer write
   d. auditory; can read and write silently but cannot read or spell aloud
2. Pure alexia is the result of brain damage to the
   a. right primary visual cortex and extrastriate cortex.
   b. extrastriate cortex and arcuate fasciculus.
   c. left primary visual cortex and posterior corpus callosum.
   d. right and left primary visual cortex.
3. People with surface dyslexia can only read
   a. using the whole-word method.
   b. using the phonetic method.
   c. if they were good readers before they suffered brain damage.
   d. real words with regular spellings.
4. People with phonological dyslexia will have difficulty reading
   a. function words.
   b. abstract words.
   c. pronounceable nonwords.
   d. content words.
5. In which form of dyslexia do people fail to comprehend what they read?
   a. word-form dyslexia
   b. phonological dyslexia
   c. direct dyslexia
   d. surface dyslexia
6. Studies of Japanese people with localized brain damage who have difficulty reading kana or kanji symbols provide evidence
   a. for reading forms based on the type of alphabet used in the language.

b. for a universal reading form that involves brain mechanisms that existed before the invention of writing.
c. that the brain contains redundant neural circuits involved in reading.
d. for two different forms of reading that involve different brain mechanisms.

7. The fact that it is more difficult to write the word *antidisestablishmentarianism* while singing suggests that

a. the "auditory image" of words expressed in music is stronger than the image of words expressed in speech.
b. the ability to write some words depends on being able to articulate them subvocally.
c. it is more difficult to understand the spoken (or sung) word than the written word.
d. the ability to write words depends on the strength of the "visual image" that is evoked.

8. People with phonological dysgraphia _____ words and then write them.

a. visually imagine
b. sound out
c. finger-spell
d. rehearse

9. People with orthographic dysgraphia have difficulty spelling and writing

a. compound words.
b. nonwords.
c. regular words.
d. irregular words.

10. Which brain region is involved in both whole-word and phonological reading?

a. motor association cortex.
b. posterior inferior temporal cortex.
c. anterior occipital lobe.
d. fusiform gyrus.

11. In a study of the pattern of brain activity when dyslexic and nondyslexic children read words and pronounceable nonwords, a child's reading skill was positively correlated with activation of the

a. magnocellular layers of the lateral geniculate nucleus.
b. gray matter of the left temporal lobe.
c. the left occipitotemporal cortex.
d. left basal posterior temporal lobe.

12. Researchers have noted a relationship between developmental dyslexias, and

a. the spelling of words in a person's native language.
b. the age at which a child starts to learn to read.
c. whether a very young child is taught two languages simultaneously.
d. whether reading education emphasizes the whole word or phonetic method of reading.

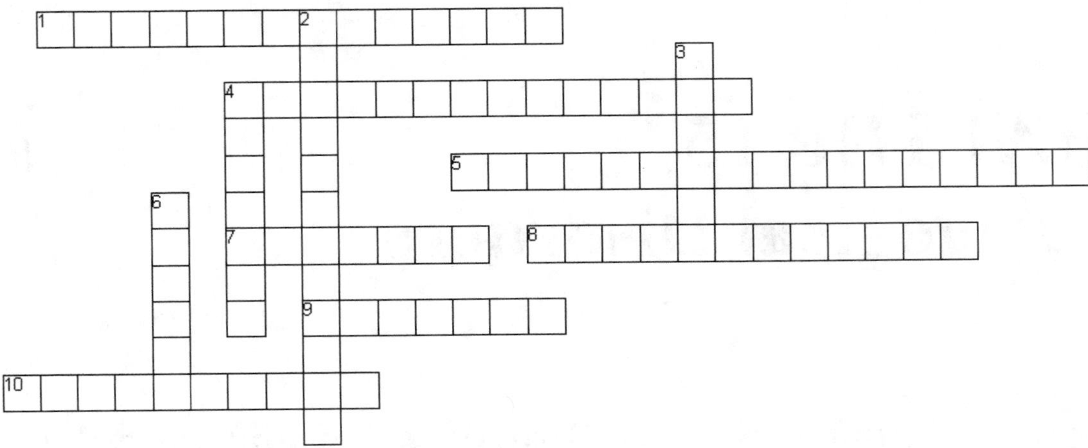

Across

1. Strategy by which people with anomia find alternative ways to say something when they are unable to think of the most appropriate word
4. Inability to name body parts or to identify body parts that another person names
5. Bundle of axons that connects Wernicke's area with Broca's area; damage causes conduction aphasia
7. Dyslexia in which a person can read words phonetically but has difficulty reading irregularly spelled words by the whole-word method
8. Preposition, article, or other word that conveys little of the meaning of a sentence but is important in specifying its grammatical structure
9. Use of changes in intonation and emphasis to convey meaning in speech besides that specified by the particular words
10. Loss of the ability to read without loss of the ability to write; produced by brain damage

Down

2. Dysgraphia in which the person can spell regularly spelled words but not irregularly spelled ones
3. Dyslexia caused by brain damage in which the person can read words aloud without understanding them
4. Difficulty in producing or comprehending speech not produced by deafness or a simple motor deficit; caused by brain damage
6. Difficulty in finding (remembering) the appropriate word to describe an object, action, or attribute

Answers for Self Tests

Lesson I

1. b Obj. 14-1
2. d Obj. 14-1
3. d Obj. 14-2
4. a Obj. 14-2
5. a Obj. 14-3
6. d Obj. 14-3
7. b Obj. 14-4
8. c Obj. 14-4
9. a Obj. 14-5
10. b Obj. 14-5
11. d Obj. 14-6
12. b Obj. 14-6

Lesson II

1. a Obj. 14-7
2. c Obj. 14-7
3. b Obj. 14-8
4. c Obj. 14-8
5. c Obj. 14-8
6. d Obj. 14-8
7. b Obj. 14-9
8. a Obj. 14-9
9. d Obj. 14-9
10. b Obj. 14-9
11. c Obj. 14-10
12. a Obj. 14-10

CHAPTER 15
Neurological Disorders

Lesson I: Tumors, Seizure Disorders, Cerebrovascular Accidents, and Disorders of Development

Read the interim summary on page 528 of your text to re-acquaint yourself with the material in this section.

Learning Objective 15-1 Discuss the causes, symptoms, and treatment of brain tumors, seizure disorders and cerebrovascular accidents.

Read pages 519-528 and answer the following questions.

1. a. What is a tumor?

   b. Distinguish between a malignant and a benign tumor and explain the major distinction between the two types.

   c. What is a metastasis?

2. Explain the two means by which tumors can cause brain damage. (See Figure 15.1 in your text for an example.)

   1. 2.

3. a. Explain why tumors do not begin in nerve cells.

   b. What kinds of tissue gives rise to tumors? (See Table 15.1 in your text for some examples.)

   c. What kinds of tumors are the most serious? (See Figures 15.2, 15.3, and 15.4 in your text to see what several different kinds of tumors look like.)

   d. Explain the two-step procedure used to treat tumors sensitive to radiation.

   e. Study Figure 15.5 in your text and identify and describe the type of tumor that developed in the brain of Mrs. R., the woman in the prologue.

4. a. Distinguish between a seizure and a convulsion.

   b. Explain the difference between a:

1. partial seizure and a generalized seizure. Be sure to use the term *focus* in your answer.

2. simple partial seizure and a complex partial seizure. Be sure to note how consciousness is affected. (See Table 15.2 in your text for a summary.)

5. a. Describe a grand mal seizure. Begin by explaining what an aura is in your own words.

   b. Name and describe the beginning phase of a grand mal seizure, paying special attention to posture and consciousness.

   c. Name and describe the next phase of a grand mal seizure paying special attention to muscular activity and breathing.

   d. How does the patient behave immediately following the seizure? for a few hours afterwards?

   e. Describe the neural firing that accompanies the progression of symptoms during a grand mal seizure.

   1. Where and when does neural firing begin? (Adams and Victor, 1981)
   2. What other regions start firing as the seizure progresses?
   3. At what point do the first symptoms appear?
   4. What triggers the tonic phase?
   5. What triggers the clonic phase?
   6. What brings the seizure to an end?

6. Study Figure 15.6 in your text and reread the prologue and then briefly describe Mrs. R.'s complex partial seizure and explain what was happening in her brain.

7. a. What population is especially susceptible to seizures?

   b. Describe the characteristics and consequences of an absence, or petit mal, seizure.

8. a. In approximately half of patients with seizure disorders which brain region shows evidence of damage?

   b. Explain what occurs during an episode of status epilepticus and its serious consequences.

   c. What is a possible explanation for this brain damage? (Thompson et al., 1996)

9. List some frequent causes of seizures. Indicate which is the most common cause.

   1.

   2.

   3.

10. a. Explain the cause of seizures following withdrawal from prolonged intake of alcohol or barbiturates.

    b. If medical help is not immediately obtained what may occur?

11. a. To explain the hypothesized role of NMDA receptors, list again the two conditions which must occur in order for these receptors to open which was discussed in Chapter 12.

    1. 2.

    b. How does alcohol affect NMDA receptors? (Gonzales, 1990)

    c. When an alcoholic suddenly stops drinking, what change occurs in the receptors that may trigger a seizure?

12. a. What is the preferred treatment for seizures?

    b. What more invasive treatment is sometimes required?

13. Carefully explain this seemingly contradictory statement: A patient's performance on tests of neuropsychological functioning usually improves following seizure surgery.

14. Define these terms in your own words. (See Figure 15.7 in your text.)

    a. *hemorrhagic stroke*

    b. *obstructive stroke*

    c. *ischemia*

    d. *thrombus*

    e. *embolus*

15. a. Describe treatment for hemorrhagic strokes caused by

       1. high blood pressure.

       2. weak or malformed blood vessels.

    b. Describe treatment for obstructive strokes caused by

       1. a thrombus.

       2. an embolus caused by bacterial debris.

16. During a stroke, what change occurs that is the immediate cause of neuron death? (For a review, see Koroshetz and Moskowitz, 1996)

17. Look more closely at how permanent brain damage occurs. When blood supply to a region of the brain is abruptly cut off, what happens to
    a. oxygen and glucose levels?
    b. sodium-potassium transporters?
    c. neural membranes?
    d. release of glutamate?
    e. glutamate receptors?
    f. sodium and calcium levels within cells?
18. a. How does an excessive amount of sodium affect absorption of water by the cell?
    b. How does the resulting swelling affect the cell?
    c. What types of cells are then attracted to the cell?
       1. 2.
    d. What do they begin to do?
19. a. How does an excessive amount of calcium affect calcium-dependent enzymes?
    b. What do these enzymes then do?
20. a. Define *free radicals* in your own words.
    b. How do they affect a cell?
21. a. What kind of drug, especially when given within three hours following a stroke, appears to reduce the brain damage resulting from ischemia? (NINDS, 1995)
    b. Carefully explain how drugs such as tPA affect the brain.
    c. Under what circumstances can drugs, such as tPA, cause further brain damage? (Benchenane et al., 2004; Klaur et al., 2004)
    d. Name the drug that has the same benefits of tPA without the damaging side effects. (See Figure 15.8 in your text. Reddrop et al., 2005; Hacke et al., 2005)
22. a. Explain *atherosclerosis* in your own words.
    b. Where do atherosclerotic plaques most often form?
    c. How is blood flow to the brain then affected?
    d. As a result, what is likely to occur?
    e. How are atherosclerotic plaques detected and treated to prevent the patient from suffering a massive stroke? Be sure to use the terms *angiogram* and *carotid endarterectomy* in your answer. (See Figure 15.9 in your text.)
    f. How effective is this treatment?

23. a. Describe a stent in your own words.

    b. Describe how a stent is inserted to improve blood flow through a narrowed carotid artery. (See Figure 15.10 in your text.)

24. When researchers forced stroke patients to use their affected arm exclusively, what were the results? What is this type of therapy called? (See Figure15.11 in your text. Taub et al., 1993)

25. What changes caused by constraint-induced movement therapy did Liepert et al. (2000) document using TMS?

Read the interim summary on page 531 of your text to re-acquaint yourself with the material in this section.

Learning Objective 15-2 Discuss developmental disorders resulting from toxic chemicals, inherited metabolic disorders, and Down syndrome.

Read pages 528-531 and answer the following questions.

1. List two causes of mental retardation that sometimes occur during pregnancy.

   1. 2.

2. a. Describe several abnormalities resulting from fetal alcohol syndrome. (See Figure 15.12 in your text.)

   b. How may alcohol damage the developing brain? Be sure to mention neural adhesion protein in your answer. (Braun, 1996; Sutherland et al., 1997)

3. How much alcohol can a pregnant woman safely drink without risking the health of her fetus? Explain.

4. When we use the phrase "error of metabolism" what, precisely, do we mean?

5. Describe the cause and treatment of the metabolic disorder phenylketonuria (PKU).

   a. What is the cause of PKU?

   b. What is the role of the enzyme missing in the patients with PKU?

   c. If an infant with undetected PKU eats food containing phenylalanine, what changes will occur in the central nervous system?

   d. What is the obvious treatment of this disorder?

   e. Why is it important that a pregnant woman with PKU receive good prenatal care?

   f. To reduce mental retardation from PKU, what legislation has been passed by many governments?

6. Two other less well-known metabolic disorders can also be controlled by diet. For each of these disorders, describe the treatment and the kind of neural damage that results if the disorder is not treated.

   a. Pyridoxine dependency

   b. Galactosemia

7. a. Describe Tay-Sachs disease. What population is most likely to inherit the faulty gene for this disease?

   b. What are some of the early symptoms? At what age do they first appear?

   c. Explain the physiological cause of this disorder. Be sure to use the term *lysosomes* in your answer.

8. Although there is currently no effective treatment or cure for diseases like Tay-Sachs, what kind of research may lead to one?

9. a. Describe Down syndrome. Explain the genetic cause of this disease. Be sure to distinguish between congenital and hereditary causes of disorders.

   b. What is the incidence of Down syndrome?

   c. Describe the physical and neurological differences between a Down victim and a normal person.

   d. What important neurological change have researchers observed in the brains of older Down victims?

Lesson I Self Test

1. A mass of cells whose growth is uncontrolled and which serves no useful function is a

   a. cyst.
   b. tumor.
   c. embolus.
   d. thrombus.

2. Benign tumors

   a. do not require surgery.
   b. do not cause brain damage.
   c. spread through infiltration.
   d. have a distinct border.

3. In which kind of seizure is consciousness not lost?

   a. simple partial seizure
   b. complex partial seizure
   c. generalized seizure
   d. absence seizure

4. The tonic phase of a grand mal seizure begins when

   a. motor cortex neurons fire continuously.
   b. diencephalic structures send inhibitory messages to the cortex.
   c. bursts of inhibition from diencephalic structures predominate.
   d. neurons in the focus begin to fire.

5. Hemorrhagic strokes cause brain damage by

   a. increasing the production of cerebrospinal fluid.
   b. spreading infection throughout the brain.
   c. exerting pressure on surrounding tissue.
   d. producing hydrocephalus.

6. The immediate cause of neuron death following a stroke is the presence of

   a. phagocytic microglia.
   b. unabsorbed calcium.
   c. excessive amounts of glutamate.
   d. too much intracellular sodium.

7. Fetal alcohol syndrome results

a. from as little as a single drinking binge.
b. only from chronic maternal alcoholism.
c. from chronic paternal alcoholism.
d. from the combined effects of alcohol and other drugs.

8. Treatment for phenylketonuria (PKU) consists of early diagnosis and

a. a complete blood transfusion at birth.
b. a diet low in phenylalanine.
c. life-long supplemental phenylalanine.
d. injections of the precursor of phenylalanine.

9. Children with Tay-Sachs disease

a. have brains that are approximately ten percent lighter than normal.
b. can be treated if diagnosed immediately after birth.
c. are missing a vital enzyme, so their lysosomes cannot remove certain waste products.
d. are unable to metabolize milk sugar.

10. Down syndrome

a. is an hereditary disorder.
b. results from an extra 21st chromosome.
c. is a metabolic storage disorder.
d. is especially frequent among children of older fathers.

11. The same abnormal microscopic structures develop in the brains of patients with Down's syndrome and

a. Parkinson's disease.
b. Alzheimer's disease.
c. Korsakoff's syndrome.
d. Tay-Sachs disease.

12. If untreated, inherited metabolic disorders such as pyridoxine dependency and galactosemia damage

a. synaptic vesicles.
b. the lining of the stomach.
c. the meninges.
d. cerebral white matter.

Lesson II: Degenerative Disorders and Disorders Caused by Infectious Diseases

Read the interim summary on pages 546-547 of your text to re-acquaint yourself with the material in this section.

Learning Objective 15-3 Discuss research on the role of misfolded prion proteins in the transmissible spongiform encephalopathies.

Read pages 531-532 and answer the following questions.

1. What is the cause of transmissible spongiform encephalopathies (TSE) such as bovine spongiform encephalopathy (BSE) or Creutzfeldt-Jakob disease? (Prusiner, 1982)

2. a. Look more closely at these infectious agents. Where are prion proteins primarily found and what is their presumed function?

   b. Prions are resistant to both _______________ _______________ and _______________.

   c. Compare the sequence of amino acids in normal prion protein (PrPc) and infectious prion protein (PrPSc).

   d. Why, then, do these two proteins have such different and tragic effects? (Hetz et al., 2003 for a review)

3. a. In what two ways can prion protein diseases be transmitted making them unique?

   b. What is the cause of

      1. familial Creutzfeldt-Jacob disease?

      2. sporadic prion protein diseases?

c. Circle the more common method of transmission.

4. Summarize research with mice that suggests that normal PrPc is not essential for the life of the cell. (Bueler et al., 1993)

5. a. According to some researchers, what is a possible function of a prionlike mechanism in the brain? (For example, Bailey et al., 2004)

   b. What kind of deficits did mice with a targeted mutation against the PRNP gene show? (Criado et al., 2005)

   c. Compare the information retention performance of people with different normal alleles? (Papassotiropoulos et al., 2005)

6. a. Describe the genetic modification of mice used in research by Mallucci et al. (2003).

   b. When the mice were infected with misfolded mouse scrapie prions at a few weeks of age, what changes began to appear in their brains?

   c. Then at 12 weeks of age as a result of genetic modification, how did the course of the disease change? (See Figure 15.13 in your text.)

   d. How long did these mice live?

   e. How long did mice without the special enzyme live?

   f. What did the researchers conclude about the cause of prion protein diseases?

7. Cell death, a process called _______________, can be triggered _______________ by a chemical signal or _______________ by biochemical processes that disrupt _______________ cell functioning. Abnormal _______________ _______________ might provide such a signal.

8. Define *caspases* in your own words and go onto explain how they might be part of a treatment for TSEs. (Mallucci et al., 2003)

Learning Objective 15-4 Discuss the causes, symptoms, and available treatments for the degeneration of the basal ganglia that occurs in Parkinson's disease and Huntington's disease.

Read pages 532-538 and answer the following questions.

1. Complete these sentences.

   a. Parkinson's disease is caused by

   b. The incidence of Parkinson's disease is

   c. Some of the primary symptoms of this disease are

2. a. What kind of neurons have almost completely disappeared in the brains of Parkinson's patients?

b. Identify and describe the abnormal structures found on many of these neurons which still remain. (See Figure 15.14 in your text. Forno, 1996)

3. a. Parkinson's disease is sometimes caused by a genetic mutation on a particular gene on chromosome 4. (Polymeropoulos et al., 1996) What protein does this gene produce, where is it normally found, and what may be its function? (Moore et al., 2005)

   b. How does the mutation alter protein function? Be sure to use the phrase *toxic gain of function* in your answer.

   c. How is the physical structure of this protein also changed? (Goedert, 2001)

   d. Are mutations that cause toxic gain of function normally dominant or recessive?

4. a. Parkinson's disease is also caused by a mutation of a gene on chromosome 6. What is this gene called? (Kitada et al., 1998)

   b. In general, what is the effect of this mutation?

   c. Are genes that cause loss of function normally dominant or recessive?

   d. Carefully explain how normal parkin, the proteasomes, and ubiquitin work cooperatively to destroy abnormal proteins. (Moore et al., 2005)

   e. How does this kind of mutation alter the normal functioning of parkin? (See Figure 15.15 in your text.)

5. Immediately review what you have just learned by summarizing what happens if, because of a mutation,

   a. parkin is defective.

   b. α-synuclein is defective.

6. Briefly, what other aspects of normal brain function leading to Parkinson's disease are disrupted by mutations of

   a. UCH-L1?

   b. DJ-1?

   c. PINK1? (Vila and Przedborski, 2004)

   d. mitochondrial DNA?(Swerdlow et al., 1998)

7. a. What do we mean when we say that the overwhelming majority of cases of Parkinson's disease are sporadic?

   b. List three possible causes of sporadic Parkinson's disease.

   1. 2. 3.

   c. How do toxic chemicals affect the brain leading to Parkinson's disease? (Dawson and Dawson, 2003)

8. a. Explain why treatment with L-DOPA does not work indefinitely.

b. What is an additional side effect of long-term use of this drug?

9. a. What is the pharmacological effect of deprenyl?

b. Explain the original rationale for giving this drug to Parkinson's patients.

c. How may age-related increases in MAO-B levels affect the brain and thus is a beneficial effect of MAO-B inhibitors? (Kumar and Andersen, 2004)

10. What have functional imaging studies shown is the cause of

a. akinesia?

b. tremors? Grafton, 2004)

11. a. How does akinetic hemiparkinsonism affect movement?

b. When patients were asked to touch their finger to their thumb, which brain regions showed decreased activity? (Buhmann et al., 2003)

c. What treatment improved their performance?

12. An experimental procedure, the transplantation of fetal tissue through stereotaxically guided needles, has shown good results in patients who no longer respond to L-DOPA.

a. What do surgeons hope to achieve by transplanting fetal tissue?

b. Where is the fetal tissue obtained?

c. In which regions of patients' brains is it implanted?

d. According to Freed et al. (2002) which patients were most likely to benefit? Why?

e. Why is this kind of surgery no longer recommended? Be sure to mention dyskinesias in your answer. (Olanow et al., 2003)

13. a. Explain what stem cells are in your own words.

b. How can they be used to treat Parkinson's disease and what is an advantage of using them? (Snyder and Olanow, 2005)

14. Study Figure 15.16 in your text and carefully explain why damage to GP_i might relieve the symptoms of Parkinson's disease.

15. a. Define *pallidotomies* in your own words.

b. What were the results of these early surgeries? (Svennilson et al., 1960; Laitinen et al., 1992)

c. Why was this surgery first abandoned and then resumed?

d. What have been the results using improved surgical techniques in young patients and patients with advanced disease? Be sure to describe what changes occur in the frontal lobes. (Grafton et al., 1995)

16. a. Carefully explain why damage to the subthalamus might be expected to improve movement in Parkinson patients. (See Figure 15.16.)

    b. How successful has this kind of surgery been? (Guridi and Obeso, 2001)

17. a. Study Figure 15.17 in your text and describe a third treatment procedure.

    b. What are some of its presumed advantages? (Simuni et al., 2002; Speelman et al. 2002; Funkiewiez et al., 2004)

18. Construct a profile of Huntington's disease.

    a. Describe the characteristic brain degeneration.

    b. How is movement affected?

    c. When do symptoms usually begin?

    d. Where do the first signs of neural degeneration begin?

19. Huntington's disease results from a hereditary defect in a dominant gene on chromosome 4.

    a. In what way is the gene defective? (Collaborative Research Group, 1993)

    b. How does abnormal huntingtin (htt) change shape to affect the nuclei of the cells?

    c. What eventually leads to cell death?

    d. What treatment increased the life expectancy of mice with Huntington's disease? (Li et al., 2000)

    e. Explain why abnormal htt may trigger apoptosis. (Hague et al., 2005)

20. a. Look at the role of normal htt in the body. Which cells contain especially high levels of this protein?

    b. Summarize research on the function of normal htt using mice as subjects. What happens to mouse fetuses with a knockout gene for htt? (O'Kusky et al., 1999)

    c. What happens to heterozygous knockout mice with a knockout gene for htt who survive to adulthood? (O'Kusky et al., 1999)

    d. What do these results suggest about the effect of normal htt on physical development and abnormal htt on the development of Huntington's disease?

    e. What is one of the most important functions of normal htt during adulthood? Be sure to mention BDNF in your answer.

    f. How does abnormal htt affect BDNF? (Zuccato et al., 2001, 2003; Gauthier et al., 2004)

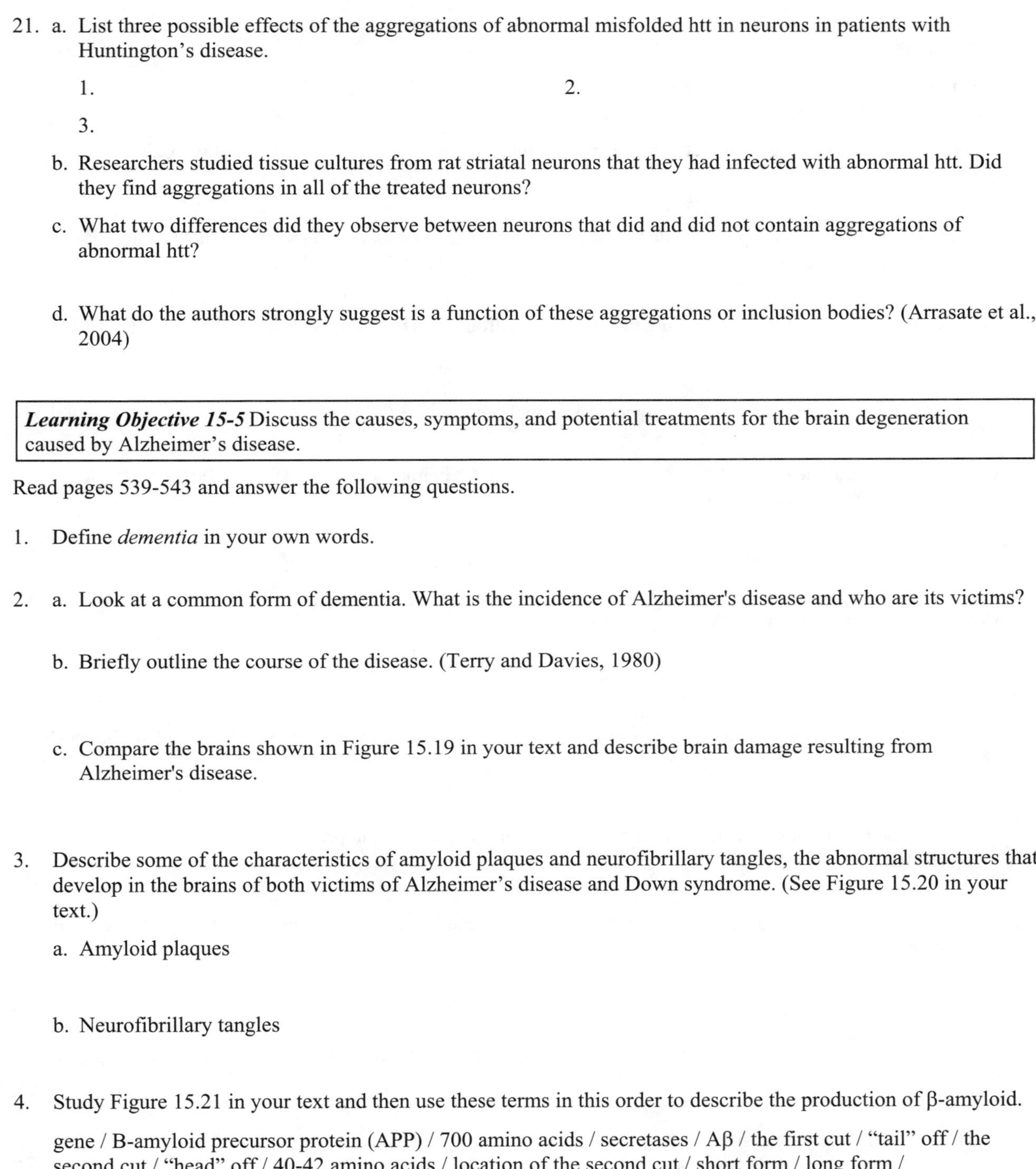

21. a. List three possible effects of the aggregations of abnormal misfolded htt in neurons in patients with Huntington's disease.

    1. 2.

    3.

    b. Researchers studied tissue cultures from rat striatal neurons that they had infected with abnormal htt. Did they find aggregations in all of the treated neurons?

    c. What two differences did they observe between neurons that did and did not contain aggregations of abnormal htt?

    d. What do the authors strongly suggest is a function of these aggregations or inclusion bodies? (Arrasate et al., 2004)

Learning Objective 15-5 Discuss the causes, symptoms, and potential treatments for the brain degeneration caused by Alzheimer's disease.

Read pages 539-543 and answer the following questions.

1. Define *dementia* in your own words.

2. a. Look at a common form of dementia. What is the incidence of Alzheimer's disease and who are its victims?

   b. Briefly outline the course of the disease. (Terry and Davies, 1980)

   c. Compare the brains shown in Figure 15.19 in your text and describe brain damage resulting from Alzheimer's disease.

3. Describe some of the characteristics of amyloid plaques and neurofibrillary tangles, the abnormal structures that develop in the brains of both victims of Alzheimer's disease and Down syndrome. (See Figure 15.20 in your text.)

   a. Amyloid plaques

   b. Neurofibrillary tangles

4. Study Figure 15.21 in your text and then use these terms in this order to describe the production of β-amyloid.

   gene / B-amyloid precursor protein (APP) / 700 amino acids / secretases / Aβ / the first cut / "tail" off / the second cut / "head" off / 40-42 amino acids / location of the second cut / short form / long form /

5. a. Compare the approximate percentage of the long form of Aβ found in the normal brain and Alzheimer brain.

   b. How are small amounts of the long form of Aβ cleared from the normal brain?

c. What happens to large amounts of the long form which cannot be cleared from the brain quickly enough before they cause harm?

6. What is the action of the drug that Klunk and his colleagues (Klunk et al., 2003; Mathis et al., 2005) developed and how will it advance research on Alzheimer's disease? (See Figure 15.22 in your text.)

7. a. What observation suggested that chromosome 21 may be involved in the development of Alzheimer's disease?

   b Explain the function of a gene located on the twenty-first chromosome and its involvement in familial Alzheimer's disease. (St George-Hyslop et al., 1987; Martinez et al., 1993; Farlow et al., 1994)

   c. How do mutations of the presenilin genes found on chromosomes 1 and 14 cause this disease? (Hardy, 1997)

8. a. What is the normal function of the glycoprotein apolipoprotein E (ApoE)?

   b. How may one allele on the ApoE gene cause late-onset Alzheimer's disease? (Roses, 1997; Price and Sisodia, 1998; Mahley and Rall, 2000)

   c. What may be the function of the ApoE2 allele? (Wilhelmus et al.. 2005)

9. What is yet another serious risk factor for Alzheimer's disease? What other factor further increases this existing risk? (Lesné et al., 2005; Luukinen et al., 2005)

10. a. Carefully explain why abnormal forms of B-amyloid and not tau protein are thought to cause Alzheimer's disease.

    b. Identify and describe dementia caused by mutations in the gene for tau protein. (Goate, 1998; Goedert and Spillantini, 2000)

11. a. What is the presumed cause of the neural degeneration seen in Alzheimer's disease? (Bossy-Wetzel et al., 2004)

    b. Describe Aβ oligomers.

    c. Look at how the Aβ oligomers affect the brain. Begin with their effect on the microglia and the response the microglia trigger.

    d. How does the immune system then respond?

    e. What is a second effect of Aβ oligomers in the brain?

    f. What kind of damage then results?

    g. Name several additional harmful effects of these structures.

12. In which regions of the brain are increases in destructive Aβ first seen? Be sure to use the phrase *default activity* in your answer. (See Figure 15.23 in your text. Buckner et al., 2005)

13. a. Summarize the results of the Religious Orders Study. Who are the subjects and how are they studied in life and after death?

    b. What factor appears to influence the incidence of Alzheimer's disease even in people whose brains have a significant number of amyloid plaques? (Bennett et al., 2003)

    c. What do these results suggest people can do that may prevent Alzheimer's disease in old age?

14. a. What observation led Rogers and colleagues (Rogers et al., 1993) to study the effects of anti-inflammatory drugs on the progression of Alzheimer's disease?

    b. Describe the treatment received by two groups of patients with mild to moderate Alzheimer's disease.

    c. How did the cognitive performance of each group change during the six-month trial? (Schnabel, 1993)

    d. What may be some of the benefits of NSAIDs? (Sastre et al., 2003; Weggen et al., 2003; Klegeris and McGeer, 2005)

15. List and discuss the limited beneficial physiological effects of the two types of medication that have been approved for treatment of this disease.

    a.

    b. (Rogawski and Wenk, 2003)

16. a. Describe the animal subjects in a study of a vaccine to prevent Alzheimer's' disease. (Schenk et al., 1999)

    b. How did the researcher hope the vaccine would affect the subjects' brains?

    c. How successful was vaccination when given at an early age?

    d. How successful was vaccination when given later in life?

17. How successful in treating Alzheimer's disease was

    a. a drug that reduced the level of Aβ in the brains of AD mice? (Dovey et al., 2001)

    b. a targeted mutation against genes responsible for γ-secretase? (Saura et al., 2004)

    c. What do the results of this later study suggest about the importance of γ-secretase in normal brain function?

18. a. How did Monsonego and Weiner (2003) hope their treatment would change the brains of Alzheimer patients?

    b. Summarize the results that are shown in Figure 15.24 in your text. (Hock et al., 2003)

    c. Unfortunately, what happened to approximately five percent of the patients?

    d. What two possible solutions did the researchers suggest?

19. Finally, what were the results of passive immunization of AD mice with an anti-Aβ antibody? (See Figure 15-25 in your text. Hartman et al., 2005)

Learning Objective 15-6 Discuss the causes, symptoms and treatments of the brain degeneration caused by amyotrophic lateral sclerosis (ALS), multiple sclerosis, and Korsakoff's syndrome.

Read pages 543-546 and answer the following questions.

1. Construct a patient profile for amyotrophic lateral sclerosis (ALS).
   a. What tissue is attacked by this degenerative disease? spared by this disease? (Bruijn et al., 2004)
   b. What are the early and later symptoms?
   c. Approximately how long do patients live after the onset of the disease?
   d. What usually causes their death?
   e. How are cognitive abilities affected?
   f. What is the incidence of this disease in the general population?
   g. Approximately how many of these cases are hereditary?
   h. Approximately how many of these cases are sporadic?
2. Describe the many changes caused by a mutation of a gene on chromosome 21 that lead to approximately 10-20 percent of the hereditary cases of ALS. (Bossy-Wetzel et al.,2004)
3. What seems to be the cause of sporadic ALS?
   a. To understand faulty RNA editing, first look at how the process normally occurs. Describe the two-step process by which proteins are produced in the body.
   b. When during this process can an error occur and what causes it?
   c. Describe the specific error that occurs which produces cell death in ALS.
   d. What did an examination of the spinal cords and brains of five deceased ALS patients reveal? (Kawahara et al., 2004)
4. a. What kind of genetic mutation did researchers produce in subject mice? (Kuner et al., 2005)
   b. What symptoms did the mice later develop?
5. a. How did researchers produce an animal model of ALS?

b. What did an examination of the degenerating motor neurons of these animals reveal?

c. What do these results suggest about the cause of hereditary and sporadic ALS? (Kawahara et al., 2005)

6. a. What is the physiological effect of the only drug treatment for this disease and how effective is it? (Bensimon et al., 1994)

b. Briefly describe the physiological effect of a more effective treatment that is being developed. (See Figure 15.26 in your text. Kaspar et al., 2003)

7. Discuss the formation of the sclerotic plaques characteristic of multiple sclerosis and the resulting widespread disabilities. (See Figure 15.27 in your text.)

8. Construct a patient profile of multiple sclerosis (MS), by noting the

a. incidence between the sexes.

b. age at onset of symptoms.

c. season of a patient's birth.

d. general location of a patient's childhood residence.

e. rate of progression of the illness.

9. What does the patient profile suggest about possible causes for multiple sclerosis?

10. Discuss two treatments have been shown to be of some benefit to patients?

a. interferon β (Arnason, 1999)

b. glatiramer acetate (Farina et al., 2005; Sormani et al., 2005)

11. Why is it unwise to assess the effectiveness of treatments for MS by relying solely on reports from patients and their families?

12. a. Korsakoff's syndrome usually, but not always, results from what behavior?

b. What two serious consequences of chronic alcoholism lead to this syndrome?

c. What other condition sometimes causes Korsakoff's syndrome?

d. In these cases, what is standard medical treatment?

e. Which region of the brain is most seriously damaged and what is the behavioral consequence? (See Figure 15.28 in your text.)

Read the interim summary on page 549 of your text to re-acquaint yourself with the material in this section.

Learning Objective 15-7 Discuss the causes, symptoms, and available treatments for encephalitis, dementia caused by the AIDS virus, and meningitis.

Read pages 547-549 and answer the following questions.

1. List the two most common neurological disorders caused by infectious diseases.

   1. 2.

2. Look more closely at viral encephalitis.

   a. What is the most common cause?

   b. List some of the symptoms of an attack.

   c. How is the disease treated?

   d. What is the prognosis?

   e. How can the herpes simplex virus cause encephalitis?

3. List two other forms of viral encephalitis.

   1. 2.

4. a. What kind of neurons are attacked by the virus that causes acute anterior poliomyelitis?

   b. How may the virus damage these neurons?

5. a. Explain how the virus that causes rabies is transmitted and identify the areas of the brain that are especially vulnerable.

   b. Briefly describe the symptoms and prognosis for the disease if it is not treated.

   c. Explain the treatment and time span in which the treatment is effective.

6. a. What is the incidence of brain damage among people who have died from AIDS? (Levy and Bredesen, 1989)

   b. Briefly describe the symptoms and progression of AIDS dementia. (Maj, 1990)

   c. What may be the cause of AIDS dementia and which brain structures may be involved? (Lipton et al., 1990; Lipton 1996, 1997)

   d. What is the affect of nimodipine, a drug that may be effective in treating the neurological symptoms of AIDS? (Navia et al., 1998)

7. Look at meningitis.

   a. What tissue is affected by meningitis?

   b. List the two causes of infection.

      1. 2.

   c. Describe the symptoms of all forms of the disease and explain the significance of a stiff neck.

d. How likely is brain damage from viral meningitis?

e. How likely is brain damage from bacterial meningitis?

f. List three causes of infection in bacterial meningitis.

1.

2.

3.

g. If untreated, how does bacterial meningitis cause brain damage?

h. How is bacterial meningitis treated?

Lesson II Self Test

1. The difference between normal prion protein and infectious prion is
   a. normal prion protein is essential for life.
   b. the sequence of amino acids.
   c. the way the protein is folded.
   d. the way amino acids are bonded together.
2. When normal prion protein began to be destroyed at 12 weeks of age in genetically modified mice,
   a. the mice began to die.
   b. the brain degeneration ceased.
   c. cells in the brain compensated by increasing production of normal prion protein.
   d. the mice developed antibodies against infectious proteins.
3. Caspase is a(n) _____ that plays a role in _____.
   a. amino acid; cell metabolism
   b. virus; transmissible spongiform encephalopathy
   c. catalyst; cell division
   d. enzyme; apoptosis
4. The dense core of Lewy bodies found in the brains of people with _____ contain_____.
   a. transmissible spongiform encephalopathy; misfolded prions
   b. Parkinson's disease; aggregations of misfolded α-synuclein
   c. Alzheimer's disease; β-amyloid
   d. multiple sclerosis; sclerotic plaques
5. Mutation of the parkin gene permits the formation of toxic levels of
   a. proteasomes.
   b. dopamine.
   c. α-synuclein.
   d. presenilin.
6. Fetal tissue transplants into the brains of Parkinson patients are an attempt to
   a. increase the sensitivity of remaining dopamine receptors.
   b. reduce the reuptake of dopamine.
   c. reestablish connections between the substantia nigra and the basal ganglia.
   d. reestablish the secretion of dopamine in the neostriatum.
7. Secretases are
   a. enzymes that cut the β-amyloid precursor molecule in pieces.
   b. a component of microtubules.
   c. filaments of tau protein.
   d. degenerating axons.
8. Mutations of the presenilin gene _____ of the long form of β-amyloid.
   a. interfere with the removal
   b. interfere with the production
   c. cause the removal
   d. cause the production
9. Multiple sclerosis is more likely to strike
   a. men than women.
   b. people whose childhood was spent far from the equator.
   c. people born in late summer and fall.
   d. people with a low birth weight.
10. The most common cause of encephalitis is a virus
   a. found in untreated drinking water.
   b. found in bird droppings.
   c. transmitted by sexual intercourse.

d. transmitted by mosquitoes.

11. Rabies vaccine is only effective if

a. administered when the neurological symptoms first appear.
b. administered during the incubation period.
c. the bite was not on the neck or head.
d. injected through the abdominal wall.

12. AIDS dementia appears to be caused by

a. excitotoxic lesions caused by excessive amounts of GABA.
b. the death of axons and dendrites.
c. entry of excessive amounts of calcium into neurons.
d. separation of the meninges.

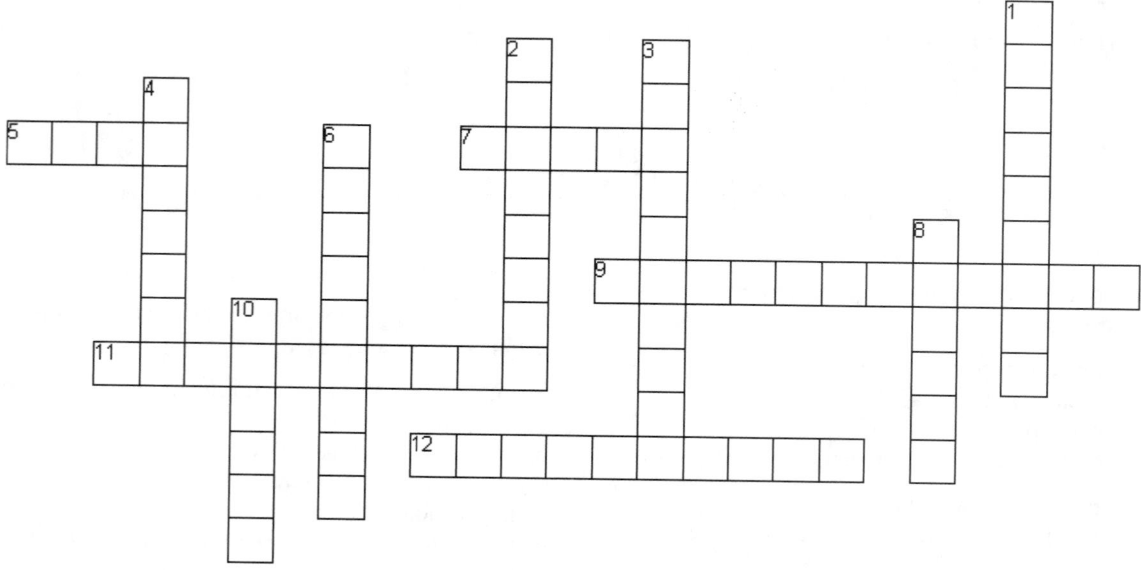

Across

5. A sensation that precedes a seizure; its exact nature depends on the location of the seizure focus
7. A protein that can exist in two forms that differ only in their three-dimensional shape; accumulation of the misfolded form is responsible for transmissible spongiform encephalopathies
9. An inflammation of the brain; caused by bacteria, viruses, or toxic chemicals
11. The process by which cells break off of a tumor, travel through the vascular system, and grow elsewhere in the body
12. A protein produced by a faulty gene that causes β-amyloid precursor protein to be converted to the abnormal short form; may be a cause of Alzheimer's disease

Down

1. A protein that attaches itself to faulty or misfolded proteins and thus targets them for destruction by proteasomes
2. A blood clot that forms within a blood vessel, which may occlude it
3. A protein that may serve to facilitate the production and transport of brain-derived neurotrophic factor. An abnormal form is the cause of Huntington's disease
4. A "killer enzyme" that plays a role in apoptosis, or programmed cell death
6. A class of enzymes that cut the β-amyloid precursor protein into smaller fragments, including β-amyloid
8. The phase of a grand mal seizure in which the patient shows rhythmic jerking movements
10. A protein that plays a role in ferrying defective or misfolded proteins to the proteasomes; an abnormal form is a cause of familial Parkinson's disease

Answers for Self Test

Lesson I

1. b Obj. 15-1
2. d Obj. 15-1
3. a Obj. 15-1
4. a Obj. 15-1
5. c Obj. 15-1
6. c Obj. 15-1
7. a Obj. 15-2
8. b Obj. 15-2
9. c Obj. 15-2
10. b Obj. 15-2
11. b Obj. 15-2
12. d Obi. 15-2

Lesson II

1. c Obj. 15-3
2. b Obj. 15-3
3. d Obj. 15-4
4. b Obj. 15-4
5. c Obj. 15-4
6. d Obj. 15-5
7. a Obj. 15-5
8. d Obj. 15-5
9. b Obj. 15-6
10. d Obj. 15-6
11. b Obj. 15-7
12. c Obj. 15-7

CHAPTER 16
Schizophrenia and the Affective Disorders

Lesson I: Schizophrenia

Read the interim summary on pages 567-568 of your text to re-acquaint yourself with the material in this section.

Learning Objective 16-1 Describe the symptoms of schizophrenia and discuss the evidence that some forms of schizophrenia are heritable.

Read pages 551-554 and answer the following questions.

1. Schizophrenia affects what percent of the world's population?
2. Who first used the term *schizophrenia*? What does the term mean? What did he intend the term to signify?
3. a. List the three categories of symptoms common to schizophrenia. (Mueser and McGurk, 2004)

   1.   2.   3.

   b. Explain the general difference between the positive and negative symptoms of schizophrenia.
4. Describe these positive symptoms of schizophrenia.

   a. Thought disorders

   b. Delusions of persecution, grandeur, and control

   c. Hallucinations
5. Describe some of the negative symptoms of schizophrenia.
6. Describe the cognitive symptoms of schizophrenia.
7. Immediately review these symptoms by studying Table 16.1 in your text.

8. What appears to be the cause of the positive symptoms of schizophrenia? the negative and cognitive symptoms of schizophrenia?

9. Over what period of time do the symptoms of schizophrenia develop, and which symptoms are the first to appear?

10. State the conclusion of both twin studies and adoption studies concerning the heritability of schizophrenia. (Kety et al., 1968, 1994; Gottesman and Shields, 1982; Tsuang et al., 1991).

11. a. If schizophrenia is a simple trait produced by a single dominant gene, what percentage of the offspring of two schizophrenic parents would be schizophrenic?

    b. If schizophrenia is a recessive trait, what percentage of the offspring of two schizophrenic parents would be schizophrenic?

    c. What is the actual incidence of this disease among children who have two schizophrenic parents?

    d. What does the incidence suggest about the transmission of schizophrenia?

12. a. If a susceptibility to schizophrenia is inherited, name one group of people who may carry the "schizophrenia gene" but not express it.

    b. Study Figure 16.1 in your text and compare the incidence of schizophrenia in the offspring of monozygotic and dizygotic twins both discordant for the disease. (Gottesman and Bertelsen, 1989)

    c. What do the incidence rates suggest about the heritability of schizophrenia and the inevitability of developing the disease?

13. a. What other contributing genetic factor was recently discovered? (Malaspina et al., 2001; Brown et al., 2002; Sipos et al., 2004)

    b. According to most researchers, what may account for this finding?

14. a. In the search for a "schizophrenia gene," how many genes have so far been implicated? (Shastry, 2002)

    b. Explain what non-coding RNA (ncRNA) is and how it may be involved in the development of schizophrenia. (Szymanski et al., 2005; Petronis, 2004; Perkins et al., 2005)

Learning Objective 16-2 Discuss drugs that alleviate or produce the positive symptoms of schizophrenia; discuss research into the nature of a possible dopamine abnormality in the brains of schizophrenics.

Read pages 554-556 and answer the following questions.

1. State the dopamine hypothesis of schizophrenia in your own words.

2. Briefly retell how chlorpromazine was developed, and how its use completely changed the treatment of schizophrenia. (Delay and Deniker, 1952a; Snyder, 1974; Baldessarini, 1977; Gilbert et al., 1955)

3. a. What is the common pharmacological effect of all antipsychotic drugs that *relieve* the positive symptoms of schizophrenia? (Creese et al., 1976; Tamminga et al., 1988)

   b. What is the common pharmacological effect of all antipsychotic drugs that *produce* the positive symptoms of schizophrenia?

4. a. List four drugs that produce the positive symptoms of schizophrenia.

   1. 3

   2. 4.

   b. How can the symptoms that these drugs produce be alleviated?

5. The most important systems of dopaminergic neurons begin in two midbrain nuclei: the ______________ ______________ and the ______________ ______________ ______________. Most researchers believe that the ______________ pathway which begins in the ______________ ______________ ______________ and ends in the ______________ ______________ and the ______________ is more likely to be involved in the symptoms of schizophrenia.

6. a. In order to explain how the overactivity of dopaminergic synapses in the mesolimbic pathway might produce the symptoms of schizophrenia, explain the behavioral effect of drugs such as cocaine and amphetamine on these synapses.

   b. Explain why the positive symptoms of schizophrenia might eventually appear if neural reinforcement occurs at inappropriate times.

   c. How might these hyperactive dopaminergic synapses cause the euphoria that is often present before the beginning of a schizophrenic episode and the disordered thinking that is also characteristic of schizophrenia? (Snyder, 1974; Fibiger, 1991)

7. a. How did an intravenous injection of amphetamine alter dopamine release in the striatum of schizophrenic patients? (Laruelle et al., 1996; Breier et al., 1997)

   b. What was the relationship between dopamine release and changes in the positive symptoms these patients experienced? (See Figure 16.2 in your text.)

8. a. Describe research to investigate another possibility—that there is an overabundance of dopamine receptors in the brain. What research methods have been used to study this possibility?

   b. Briefly summarize the inconclusive results of studies using these methods. (Kestler et al., 2001)

9. a. Up to one third of schizophrenic patients who take "classic" antipsychotic drugs develop tardive dyskinesia. Describe the symptoms of this serious side effect.

   b. Using the concepts of compensatory mechanisms and supersensitivity, explain why tardive dyskinesia develops.

10. State two benefits of newer atypical antipsychotic medications.

 a.

 b.

Learning Objective 16-3 Discuss evidence based on population studies that the negative symptoms of schizophrenia may result from brain damage.

Read pages 556-559 and answer the following questions.

1. Describe some of the neurological symptoms of schizophrenia that suggest the disease may result from brain damage. (Stevens, 1982)

2. a. By examining CT scans, what did Weinberger and Wyatt (1982) discover about the relative ventricle size of chronic schizophrenics and normal control subjects of the same age? (Study Figure 16.3 in your text.)

 b. What is the best explanation for the difference in size?

3. Compare the rate of loss of cerebral gray matter that results from aging in schizophrenic people to that of non-schizophrenics. (See Figure 16.4 in your text. Hulshoff-Pol et al., 2002)

4. a. Define e*pidemiology* in your own words.

 b. List five environmental factors that have been associated with the incidence of schizophrenia.

 1. 4.

 2. 5.

 3.

5. a. Some people, who were born in the Northern Hemisphere and whose birthdays fall during the late _______________ and early _______________ months, are more likely to develop schizophrenia later in life—a relationship called the _______________ _______________. (See Figure 16.5 in your text. Kendell and Adams, 1991; Davies et al., 2003)

 b. What have been the mixed results of similar research in the Southern Hemisphere? (McGrath and Welham, 1999)

 c. Which trimester of pregnancy coincides with these winter months, and what threat to a pregnant woman's health rises at this time? (Pallast et al., 1994)

 d. If winter temperatures are lower than normal, how is the incidence of schizophrenia affected? Why? (Kendell and Adams, 1991)

6. What is the prenatal and postnatal relationship between population density and the incidence of schizophrenia? (Eaton et al., 2000; Pedersen and Mortensen, 2001)

7. a. In general, how is the incidence of schizophrenia affected by influenza epidemics?
   b. Summarize the results of research on the seasonality effect conducted in
      1. Finland. (Mednick et al., 1990)
      2. England and Wales. (See Figure 16.6 in your text. Sham et al., 1992)
   c. What substance was found in the stored samples of blood serum of pregnant women whose children later developed schizophrenia? (Brown et al., 2004)
   d. What do these results confirm about a seasonality effect in the development of schizophrenia?

8. Turn to the role of prenatal malnutrition in the development of schizophrenia. What did researchers (Susser and Lin, 1992; Susser et al., 1996) find when they studied the offspring of women who were pregnant during the Hunger Winter? Explain the role of a thiamine deficiency in your answer. (Davis and Bracha, 1996)

9. What other nutrition-related conditions are likely to lead to an increased incidence of schizophrenia? (Kunugi et al., 2001; Wahlbeck et al., 2001)

10. Finally, what might explain a higher incidence of schizophrenia among the children of women who learned that their husbands had been killed in combat in World War II? (Huttunen and Niskanen, 1978)

11. Particular kinds of medical situations at or around childbirth can cause schizophrenia. Provide some examples of these kinds of obstetric complications. (Cannon et al., 2002)
    a. complications of pregnancy
    b. abnormal fetal development
    c. complications of labor and delivery (Boksa, 2004)

12. a. How did researchers affect the blood supply to the developing offspring of guinea pigs? (Rehn et al., 2004)
    b. What brain abnormalities were present when the offspring reached adolescence?
    c. What do the results suggest about the effects of obstetric complications on brain development?

Learning Objective 16-4 Discuss direct evidence that schizophrenia is associated with brain damage.

Read pages 560-563 and answer the following questions.

1. In two different studies with different subjects, independent observers watched the behavior of children who later became schizophrenic. What were their conclusions after seeing
   a. them in family home movies? (Walker et al., 1994; Walker et al., 1996)
   b. brief videotapes of them having lunch with other Danish children, aged 11-13 years? (Schiffman et al., 2004)

2. What did Cannon et al. (1997) conclude about the social adjustment and school work of children who later became schizophrenic?

3. What do the results of these studies suggest about the early brain development of children who later develop schizophrenia?

4. a. Identify several minor physical abnormalities that have been shown to be associated with the incidence of schizophrenia. (See Table 16.2. Schiffman et al., 2002)

   b. How does the risk of developing schizophrenia change in a person who has both schizophrenic relatives and minor physical abnormalities?

   c. What do these findings suggest about the relationship between minor physical abnormalities and genetic factors associated with schizophrenia?

5. a. List the anatomical differences in the MRI scans, shown in Figure 16.7 in your text, of the brains of monozygotic twins discordant for schizophrenia. (Suddath et al., 1990)

   1. 3.

   2.

   b. Summarize the long-held explanation for why these differences and schizophrenia developed in one twin and not the other.

6. a. Study Figure 16.8 in your text and then explain why the prenatal environment of monozygotic twins is not always identical. Be sure to use the terms *monochorionic* and *dichorionic* in your answer.

   b. How do researchers try to determine whether a pair of twins is monochorionic or dichorionic?

   c. The concordance rate for schizophrenia is _____ percent for _______________ monozygotic twins and _____ percent for _______________ monozygotic twins. (Davis et al., 1995)

7. a. Figure 16.9 in your text shows the ages at which the first signs of mental disorder appeared in schizophrenia patients. Discuss how a prenatal viral infection might affect the developing brain and lead to schizophrenia later in life. (Squires, 1977)

   b. Discuss how prenatal deficiencies in the brain might affect early childhood and then progress during puberty and early adulthood. (Woods, 1998)

   c. What kind of anatomical loss appears to take place? (Lewis and Levitt, 2002)

8. a. Explain the procedure Thompson et al. (2001) used to track the loss of cortical gray matter during adolescence of early-onset schizophrenics.

   b. In these adolescents, where did the degeneration begin?

   c. In what direction did degeneration progress and which regions were affected?

d. Study Figure 16.10 in your text to see which regions underwent the greatest loss.

e. How did symptoms correspond to regional degeneration?

f. In general, how did tissue loss in adolescent schizophrenics compare to that of non-schizophrenics?

9. In a later comparison of the brains of twins discordant for schizophrenia, which twin had greater changes in the brain and which region was strongly affected by genetic influences? (Cannon et al., 2002)

10. If schizophrenia does not result from genetic factors, what nongenetic factor may be responsible? (See Figure 16.9 again.)

Learning Objective 16-5 Discuss the relationship between the prefrontal cortex in the positive and negative symptoms of schizophrenia.

Read pages 563-567 and answer the following questions.

1. a. According to Weinberger (1988), what kind of brain damage appears to cause the negative symptoms of schizophrenia?

   b. What did a literature review by Taylor (1996) confirm?

   c. What kind of task were subjects with schizophrenia and normal comparison subjects working on when fMRI scans of their brains were being made? (MacDonald et al., 2005)

   d. Which brain region was not activated in the schizophrenic subjects? (See Figure 16.11 in your text.)

2. Provide a possible explanation for the widely observed hypofrontality in schizophrenics by noting the behavioral effects of

   a. destruction of the dopaminergic input to the prefrontal cortex of monkeys. (Brozowski et al., 1979)

   b. an injection of dopamine antagonists into the prefrontal cortex. (Sawaguchi and Goldman-Rakic, 1994)

3. What is the rationale for studying phencyclidine (PCP, also know as "angel dust") and ketamine (Special K) to understand schizophrenia?

4. How does chronic abuse of PCP appear to alter the brain to produce the negative symptoms of schizophrenia? (Hertzmann et al., 1990; Wu et al., 1991)

5. a. To study chronic PCP abuse, how often were subject monkeys injected with the drug? (Jentsch et al., 1997)

   b. Describe the task the animals learned to perform one week later.

   c. Why was this particular task chosen?

d. How successfully did normal monkeys perform when the box was rotated? How successful were subject monkeys? (See Figure 16.12 in your text.)

e. What were the physiological effects of PCP on the brain?

f. What treatment improved the task performance of subject monkeys?

6. In later research, what was the correlation between changes in level of dopamine transmission caused by PCP and behavioral impairment? (Jentsch et al., 1999)

7. a. Once again, explain the relationship between the activation of NMDA receptors and dopamine receptors. (Scott et al., 2002; Chen et al., 2004; Pei et a., 2004)

   b. How may PCP and ketamine suppress the activity of the prefrontal cortex?

8. Begin an explanation of the presumed link between hypoactivity of NMDA receptors in the prefrontal cortex and the hyperactivity of dopaminergic neurons in the nucleus accumbens by describing the neural connections between these regions. (Carr and Sesack, 2000)

   a. If the prefrontal cortex is electrically stimulated, how is dopamine release in the nucleus accumbens affected? (Study Figure 16.13 in your text. Jackson et al., 2001)

   b. However, how do infusions of PCP into the prefrontal cortex affect dopamine release in the nucleus accumbens? (Jentsch et al., 1998)

   c. Go on to explain why the positive symptoms of schizophrenia then occur.

9. How does clozapine affect:

   a. the positive, negative, and cognitive symptoms of schizophrenia?

   b. the psychotic symptoms triggered by ketamine? (Malhotra et al., 1997)

   c. dopamine release in the prefrontal cortex and the nucleus accumbens? (Youngren et al., 1999)

10. Dopaminergic neurons in two different regions of the _______________ _______________ _______________ project to two different brain regions. One group, which projects to the _______________ _______________, is activated by the administration of NMDA antagonists; and the other group, which projects to the _______________ _______________, is inhibited by NMDA antagonists. NMDA antagonists _______________ the release of dopamine in the nucleus accumbens and cause the _______________ symptoms of schizophrenia, and they _______________ the release of dopamine in the prefrontal cortex and cause the _______________ and _______________ symptoms of this disease. (Svensson, 2000)

11. To review what you have just learned, explain the presumed role of hypofrontality in the appearance and progression of the symptoms of schizophrenia as shown in Figure 16.14 in your text.

12. a. Explain a possible cause of hypofrontality that occurs around the time of adolescence.

    b. Explain why direct NMDA agonists cannot be used to treat the symptoms caused by hypofrontality.

    c. Why have researchers used glycine agonists to study the role of the NMDA receptor in schizophrenia? (Review the anatomy of the NMDA receptor described in Chapter 4.)

    d. What were the results of a double-blind study using glycine agonists with atypical antischizophrenic drugs to reduce patients' symptoms? Be sure to note why large doses of glycine were used. (See Figure 16.15 in your text. Heresco-Levy et al., 2004)

    e. Why do the "classic" antischizophrenic drugs fail to reduce the negative and cognitive symptoms of this disease?

13. a. Before explaining the action of the atypical antischizophrenic drugs, define *partial agonist* in your own words.

    b. How does aripiprazole, an atypical drug, affect regions such as the nucleus accumbens and the prefrontal cortex? (Winans, 2003; Lieberman, 2004)

    c. How does aripiprazole affect serotonin receptors?

    d. Which symptoms of schizophrenia are relieved by aripiprazole? (See Figure 16.16 in your text.)

14. What is the significance to research on schizophrenia of :

    a. the failure of ketamine and probably, PCP, to affect the brains of prepubertal children? (Marshall and Longnecker, 1990)

    b. the failure of MK-801 to produce brain abnormalities in prepubertal rats, but not adult rats? (Farber et al., 1995)

Lesson I Self Test

1. Schizophrenia, which _____, may be caused by _____.

    a. develops in all children with two schizophrenic parents; a recessive gene or genes.
    b. is more likely in children with older fathers; a DNA copying errors.
    c. is more likely to develop in first-born children; environmental factors that trigger an inherited susceptibility to the disease.
    d. develops more often in males than females; defects that affect the Y chromosome more than the X chromosome.

2. The _____ symptoms of schizophrenia are characterized by _____.

    a. positive; their presence and may include delusions and hallucinations.
    b. negative; their absence and may include poor abstract thinking
    c. cognitive; their similarity to the positive symptoms and may include feelings of unworthiness
    d. atypical; their presence and may be seen in other neurological disorders as well.

3. Drugs that relieve the _____ symptoms of schizophrenia have one property in common, they all _____.

    a. positive; stimulate dopamine receptors.
    b. negative and cognitive ; block dopamine receptors.

c. positive; block dopamine receptors.
d. negative and cognitive; retard dopamine re-uptake.

4. Tardive dyskinesia

a. is relieved by decreasing the amount of antipsychotic medication.
b. is most common after treatment with atypical antipsychotic medications.
c. is a Parkinsonian side effect of all antipsychotic medications.
d. may develop when previously blocked dopamine receptors become supersensitive.

5. Many studies of CT and MRI scans indicate that schizophrenics have

a. enlarged ventricles.
b. fewer convolutions in the cerebellum.
c. atrophy of the neostriatum.
d. a thicker corpus callosum.

6. The "seasonality effect" in schizophrenia refers to

a. the increased likelihood that people born in the summer months will develop schizophrenia.
b. the increased likelihood that people born in the late winter and early spring months will develop schizophrenia.
c. the intensification of schizophrenic symptoms in the winter months.
d. the increased incidence of schizophrenia in countries farther from the equator.

7. Monozygotic twins are most likely to be concordant for schizophrenia if they

a. are monochorionic.
b. are dichorionic.
c. have had unequal exposure to the maternal hormones of pregnancy.
d. have been exposed to the same predisposing environmental factors after birth.

8. Brain abnormalities associated with schizophrenia

a. result from a degenerative process similar to Parkinson's disease or Alzheimer's disease.
b. begin with a rapid loss of brain volume that usually begins during young adulthood.
c. begin prenatally and become worse during puberty.
d. result when dying neurons are replaced by glial cells.

9. _____ cause both negative and positive symptoms.

a. PCP and ketamine
b. Clozapine and dopamine antagonists
c. PCP and clozapine
d. Ketamine and amphetamines

10. The cause of hypofrontality suggested by studies with monkeys, may be a(n) _____ in the release of dopamine in the prefrontal cortex which _____.

a. increase; creates a toxic environment leads to the death of neurons
b. decrease; lowers its metabolic rate
c. increase; stimulates even greater loss of neurons at puberty
d. decrease; causes greater pressure within the ventricles

11. How is the nucleus accumbens affected by decreased activity of the prefrontal cortex?

a. GABA release increases.
b. GABA release decreases.
c. Dopamine release increases.
d. Dopamine release decreases.

12. NMDA receptor activity can be increased to reduce schizophrenic symptoms by administering drugs

a. that act like dopamine agonists.
b. that act as direct antagonists to all NMDA receptor site except that for dopamine.
c. supply the precursors for dopamine.
d. such as glycine that act as indirect agonists at the NMDA receptor.

Lesson II: The Major Affective Disorders

Read the interim summary on pages 581-582 of your text to re-acquaint yourself with the material in this section.

Learning Objective 16-6 Describe the two major affective disorders, the heritability of these diseases, and their physiological treatments.

Read pages 568-572 and answer the following questions.

1. a. The primary symptom of schizophrenia is ______________ ______________ and the primary symptom of the major affective disorders is ______________ ______________.

   b. List the two principal types of major affective disorders:

   1. 2.

2. Describe bipolar disorder.

   a. Name and describe the two alternating moods.

   b. Approximately how long is each episode?

   c. What is the incidence of bipolar disorder in men and women?

3. Describe unipolar depression, including its incidence in men and women.

4. Present a profile of patients suffering from affective disorders by describing the effect of the disease on

   a. self-esteem.

   b. personal safety. (Chen and Dilsaver, 1996; Schneider et al., 2001))

   c. energy level.

   d. appetite.

   e. sex drive.

   f. sleep patterns.

   g. body functions.

5. Explain the differences between mania and a normal enthusiasm for life.

6. State the results of these studies tracing the heritability of the affective disorders.

   a. Incidence among close relatives of patients (Rosenthal, 1971)

   b. Incidence in sets of monozygotic and dizygotic twins (Gershon et al., 1976) reared together or apart (Price, 1968)

   c. The existence of a gene responsible for susceptibility to bipolar disorder (Spence et al., 1995; MacKinnon et al., 1997; Berrettini, 1998; Garner et al., 2001)

7. a. List five effective biological treatments of unipolar depression.

   1. 4.

   2. 5.

   3.

   b. List two effective biological treatments for bipolar disorder.

   1. 2.

   c. What does the efficacy of drug therapy suggest about the cause of the affective disorders?

d. Why are bipolar disorder and unipolar depression thought to be different illnesses? (Soares and Gershon, 1998)

8. a. Explain how an early antidepressant drug, iproniazid, affects the brain. Be sure to state the function of monoamine oxidase (MAO).

   b. Administration of iproniazid causes which neurotransmitters to be released in greater amounts?

9. a. Explain the pharmacological effects of the tricyclic antidepressant drugs.

   b. In other words, both MAO inhibitors and the tricyclic antidepressant drugs are _______________ _______________.

10. a. State what these acronyms stand for and in doing so you will also explain their action.

    1. SSRI

    2. SNRI

    b. Name several widely prescribed SSRIs and the conditions they treat.

    c. What is an advantage of antidepressant SNRI drugs?

11. Briefly describe the process of electroconvulsive therapy (ECT) and the history of its development. (See Figure 16.17 in your text. Cerletti, 1956))

12. a. Compare the speed with which antidepressant drugs and ECT relieve depression.

    b. State a serious side effect of the excessive use of ECT. (Squire, 1974)

    c. State the results of a study to determine the side effects of a typical course of ECT. (Ende et al., 2000)

    d. State two reasons why the occasional use of ECT is justified. (Bolwig, 2003)

13. Explain how ECT relieves depression.

14. a. What treatment may provide some of the benefits of ECT without the risk of its side effects? (Padberg and Moller, 2003; Fitzgerald, 2004)

    b. Although beneficial, why are some patients reluctant to repeat this treatment?

15. a. Explain how electrical stimulation of the vagus nerve is administered to a patient.

    b. How effective is this treatment in improving depression, and what are several advantages of its use over TMS? (Grovesand Brown, 2005; Rush et al., 2005)

16. a. Which phase of bipolar disorder is effectively treated with lithium? (Gerbino et al., 1978; Soares and Gershon, 1998)

    b. What are some of the significant advantages of treating bipolar disorder with lithium? (Fieve, 1979)

    c. Between _____ percent and _____ percent of people suffering from bipolar disorder show a positive response to lithium within a _______________ or _______________. (Price and Heninger, 1994)

    d. Lithium is not without side effects. List some.

    e. Why are patients' blood levels of lithium tested regularly?

17. Why do some patients eventually stop taking this highly effective drug, and what risk do they run? (Suppes et al., 1991; Post et al., 1992)

18. Although the pharmacological effect of lithium that eliminates mania has not been determined, researchers have discovered many of its physiological effects. (Phiel and Klein, 2001) How may lithium affect

    a. certain classes of neurotransmitters and second messengers? (Atack et al., 1995; Jope et al., 1996; Manji and Lenox, 1999)

    b. neuroprotective proteins? (Manji et al., 2001; Moore et al., 2000)

    c. neural and glial growth? (Moore et al., 2000)

19. What are two advantages of the use of carbamazepine to treat bipolar disorder? (See Figure 16.18 in your text. Post et al., 1984)

Learning Objective 16-7 Summarize the monoamine hypothesis of depression, evidence for brain abnormalities, and the role of the 5-HT transporter in depression.

Read pages 572-578 and answer the following questions.

1. Briefly explain the monoamine hypothesis of depression.

2. When reserpine was first used to treat high blood pressure, what side effect did physicians notice in about 15 percent of their patients? (Sachar and Baron, 1979)

3. What effect of reserpine makes it a potent antagonist for norepinephrine, dopamine, and serotonin?

4. Explain how the pharmacological and behavioral effects of reserpine complement those of MAO inhibitors.

5. a. Why and how did Delgado et al. (1990) lower the tryptophan level in subjects' brains?

b. What was the effect of very low levels of tryptophan on subjects' depression?

c. What happened when subjects began eating a normal diet again?

d. How, then, may some drugs successfully relieve depression?

6. a. In addition, how does tryptophan depletion affect the mood of
   1. healthy people?
   2. people with a family history of depression? (Young and Leyton, 2002; Neumeister et al., 2004)
   3. depressed people being treated with serotonin reuptake inhibitors? norepinephrine reuptake inhibitors?

   b. What happens if patients whose depression is successfully being treated with norepinephrine reuptake inhibitors are given AMPT? (See Figure 16.19 in your text. Heninger et al., 1996)

7. What aspects of the drug treatments for depression that you have just studied, suggest that the monoamine hypothesis is not a complete explanation for depression?

8. a. What were the results of a comparison of the ventricle size of healthy subjects and subjects who had just experienced their first episode of bipolar disorder? (See Figure 16.20 in your text. Strakowski et al., 2002)

   b. How did repeated episodes of depression and mania affect ventricle size?

9. a. List some of the brain regions that have been documented to show abnormalities in depressed people. (Soares and Mann, 1997; Kumar et al., 2004)

   b. What did a meta-analysis indicate is the average decrease in hippocampal volume in depressed people? (Videnbech and Ravnkilde, 2004)

   c. Which two treatments for depression improve BDNF gene expression and why is this important? (Altar et al., 2004; Hayler et al., 2005; Martinez-Turrillas et al., 2005)

10. a. Review evidence obtained from animal studies that depression suppresses hippocampal neurogenesis and antidepressant drug treatments increases it. (See Malberg and Schechter, 2005, for a review.)

    b. Why is it as yet incorrect to conclude that hippocampal damage plays a role in depression?

11. Look at evidence that the amygdala and several regions of the prefrontal cortex may play a role in the development of an affective disorder.

    a. The amygdala plays a critical role in the expression of _______________ _______________.

    b. Summarize the results of research on the metabolic activity and blood flow of the amygdala in normal and depressed subjects.

       1. What did functional imaging indicate about the blood flow and metabolism of the amygdala of depressed subjects? (Drevets et al., 1992; Links et al., 1996)

2. What is the correlation between activity of the amygdala and the severity of depression of subjects? (Abercrombie et al., 1998)

3. What kind of stimuli increased metabolic activity in the amygdala of depressed subjects? What kind of stimuli increased metabolic activity in the amygdala of non-depressed subjects? (Drevets, 2000b; Liotti et al., 2002)

12. a. Circle the group with a generally higher level of activity in the orbitofrontal cortex (Drevets 2000a).

healthy people depressed people

b. When the orbitofrontal cortex is damaged, what kind of behaviors are disrupted? (Bechara et al., 1998)

c. Why, according to Drevets (2001) may the orbitofrontal cortex be more active in depressed people? (See Figure 16.21 in your text.)

13. a. Describe the location of the subgenual anterior cingulated cortex (subgenual ACC).

b. What is its role in emotion?

c. Compare the subgenual ACC 's level of activation in depressed and non-depressed people. (Drevets et al., 1997)

d. How does damage to the medial prefrontal cortex, including the subgenual ACC, affect the extinction of conditioned emotional responses?

e. When the activity of this region increases in patients with bipolar disorder, what kind of episode are they said to be experiencing? (See Figure 16.22 in your text. Quirk et al., 1997)

14 a. Define *silent cerebral infarctions (SCI)* in your own words, noting their relationship to late-onset depression.

b. What are some of the other risk factors? (Howard et al., 1998)

c. If late-onset depression is not caused by SCIs, what, then, is the likely cause? (Fujikawa et al., 1994)

d. How does the cause of late-onset depression affect treatment success? (Yamashita et al., 2001)

15. a. Begin an explanation of the possible role of the 5-HT transporter (5-HTT) in depression, by first describing the two forms of the premotor region on the 5-HT transporter gene.

b. How does having a short allele on one or both chromosomes affect the

1. amounts of the 5-HTT?

2. activity of the amygdala when seeing photographs of angry or sad faces?

3. response to tryptophan depletion? (Neumeister et al., 2002)

16. a. What kind of events did researchers note as they followed 847 people over more than twenty years? (Caspi et al., 2005)

b. In general, how was the probability of developing major depression and suicidality affected by the number of stressful events a person experienced?

c. More specifically, how did having one or two copies of the short alleles affect this probability? (See Figure 16.23 in your text.)

d. What interaction do these results confirm?

17. Explain the effects on depression of having two long alleles for this gene, by explaining how they affect

    a. a positive response to antidepressant drugs or a placebo. (Rausch et al., 2002)

    b. a positive long-term outcome of treatment. (Lee et al., 2004)

18. In which regions of the developing fetal brain may serotonin play a role?

19. a. Carefully describe the results of a structural and functional imaging study of the brains of healthy subjects without a history of depression, but who had one or more short alleles of the promoter region. (Pezawas et al., 2005)

    b. In which region was the greatest change observed? (See Figure 16.24 in your text.)

    c. What kind of pictures did researchers have subjects view while their neural activity was being recorded?

    d. Study Figure 16.25 in your text and carefully explain both the positive and negative correlations in neural activity researchers observed in the brains of people who had either two long alleles or one or two short alleles.

    e. What do these results suggest about functional connections between the amygdala and the subgenual ACC?

    f. How did scores on a standardized psychological test measuring susceptibility to developing depression correlate with functional connectivity in these subjects?

20. Study Figure 16.26 in your text and trace the hypothesized feedback loop suggested by these findings that may play a role in susceptibility to depression.

Learning Objective 16-8 Explain the role of circadian and seasonal rhythms in affective disorders: the effects of REM sleep deprivation and total sleep deprivation, and seasonal affective disorder.

Read pages 578-581 and answer the following questions.

1. Describe how the sleep of people with depression is disrupted with reference to

    a. amounts of slow-wave delta sleep and stage 1 sleep

    b. fragmentation of sleep

    c. changes in REM sleep patterns (See Figure 16.27 in your text. Kupfer, 1976; Vogel et al., 1980)

2. a. What is the effect on depression of selective deprivation of REM sleep? (Vogel et al., 1975, Vogel et al., 1990)

    b. Approximately how long does it take for relief from depression to occur?

c. Following treatment, how long do patients continue to show improvement?

3. a. How did twenty antidepressant drugs affect the sleep cycle of cats? (Scherschlicht et al., 1982)

   b All drugs that _______________ REM sleep act as _______________. (Vogel et al., 1990)

   c. How long do the changes in sleep patterns caused by treatment with antidepressant drugs persist? (Kupfer et al., 1994)

4. If depression is successfully treated by ECT or psychotherapy, what change in sleep occurs? (Grunhaus et al., 1997; Thase et al., 2000)

5. What evidence suggests that some antidepressant drugs may have a different pharmacological effect on sleep? (Mayers and Baldwin, 2005)

6. a. Describe research on the antidepressant effect of total sleep deprivation. How quickly does total sleep deprivation relieve depression? (See Figure 16.28 in your text. Wu and Bunney, 1990)

   b. According to Wu and Bunney (1990), why may sleep trigger depression in susceptible people? (See Figure 16.29 in your text.)

   c. Approximately what percent of people with major depression improve with total sleep deprivation?

   d. What characteristics of a depressed patient predict a good response to total sleep deprivation? (Look again at Figure 16.25 and note how the mood of people who responded to sleep deprivation treatment changed during the day. Riemann et al., 1991; Haug, 1992; Wirz-Justice and Van den Hoofdakker, 1999)

7. Although total sleep deprivation is impossible and impractical, what patterns of partial sleep deprivation are practical and effective? (Szuba et al., 1991; Leibenluft and Wehr, 1992; Papadimitriou et al., 1993)

8. Cite research results that suggest the best sleep pattern for people who suffer from depression. (Riemann et al., 1999; Reimann et al., 2001)

9. a. Describe the symptoms of seasonal affective disorder, noting how they differ from the symptoms of major depression.

   b. Compare the symptoms of seasonal affective disorder and summer depression. (Wehr et al., 1987; Wehr et al., 1991)

   c. What evidence suggests a genetic basis for seasonal affective disorder? (Madden et al., 1996)

10. a. How is seasonal affective disorder best treated? (Rosentahal et al., 1985; Stinson and Thompson, 1990)

    b. Outline a possible explanation why phototherapy is effective against seasonal affective disorder. Be sure to use the term *zeitgeber* in your answer.

c. Summarize research results that conflicts with this explanation. (Wirz-Justice et al., 1993; Meesters et al., 1995; Lewy et al., 1998; Terman et al., 1998)

11. a. What other form of depression improves with phototherapy?
    b. What treatment plan
        1. led to an improvement in symptoms?
        2. caused a relapse? (Neumeister et al., 1996)
        3. led to greater benefits than phototherapy alone? (Martiny et al., 2005)

12. Patients with bipolar disorder responded better to a combination of phototherapy and sleep deprivation if they had two _____________ alleles for the 5HTT promoter. (Benedetti et al., 2003)

13. a. What are the "winter blahs" and what is an effective treatment? (Kasper et al., 1989b)
    b. What is an alternative to phototherapy? (Wirz-Justice, 1996)
    c. What is the effect of exercise on depression? (Singh et al., 1997)

Lesson II Self Test

1. Bipolar disorder is characterized by
    a. unremitting or episodic depression without periods of mania and afflicts more women than men.
    b. mania without periods of depression and afflicts more women than men.
    c. alternating bouts of depression followed by periods of normal affect and afflicts more men than women.
    d. alternating bouts of mania and depression and afflicts men and women about equally.

2. Studies of the genetic basis of affective disorders have shown that
    a. there is little evidence in favor of a genetic component in these disorders.
    b. concordance rates for monozygotic twins are considerably higher than concordance rates for dizygotic twins.
    c. there is a genetic basis for unipolar depression but not bipolar disorder.
    d. the responsible dominant gene is located on chromosome 11.

3. A serious problem of frequent electroconvulsive therapy is _____, and a possible complication of transcranial magnetic stimulation is _____.
    a. suppression of normal feelings of emotion; sexual dysfunction.
    b. disturbances in most biological rhythms; weight gain
    c. elevated blood pressure; increased sensitivity to pain
    d. long-lasting memory impairments; seizures

4. Lithium
    a. is most effective in treating the manic phase of bipolar disorder.
    b. has a harmful side effect referred to as the cheese effect.
    c. has a high therapeutic index, reducing the risk of accidental overdose.
    d. works relatively quickly and very effectively so compliance is not a problem.

5. The monoamine hypothesis suggests that depression is a result of _____ of monoaminergic neurons.
    a. insufficient activity
    b. excessive numbers
    c. overactivity
    d. the proliferation

6. Depressed individuals fed a diet low in tryptophan and a "cocktail" high in other amino acids

a. become manic.
b. relapse into depression.
c. show changes in cognition but not affect.
d. have elevated levels of serotonin metabolites.

7. When people with two long alleles of the 5-HTT promoter see angry or fearful faces, the activity of the subgenual ACC _____ and that of the _____ increases.

a. increases; dorsal ACC
b. decreases; dorsal ACC
c. increases; orbitofrontal cortex
d. decreases; orbitofrontal cortex

8. A hypothesized feedback loop that may play a role in susceptibility to major depression runs from the

a. amygdala to the hippocampus to the cingulate cortex and back to the amygdala.
b. hippocampus to the subgenual ACC to the dorsal ACC and back to the amygdala.
c. parietal lobes to the temporal lobes to the dorsolateral prefrontal cortex and back to the parietal lobes.
d. amygdala to the subgenual ACC to the dorsal ACC and back to the amygdala.

9. People whose depression is relieved by total sleep deprivation

a. gradually feel better over the course of several weeks.
b. feel better in the morning than in the evening.
c. must limit their sleep to brief naps.
d. begin to feel better immediately.

10. Wu and Bunney suggested that sleep deprivation causes an improvement in depressive symptoms because

a. during sleep a depressogenic substance is produced that needs to be metabolized during waking hours.
b. waking produces a substance with antidepressant effects.
c. REM sleep allows a person to actively rehearse the life events that may be causing depression.
d. it causes memory loss.

11. Seasonal affective disorder

a. appears to have a geographical rather than a genetic basis.
b. does not affect people who work indoors as often as it affects people who work outdoors.
c. develops about the time the temperature drops below freezing in the fall.
d. involves weight gain whereas major depression involves weight loss.

12. An effective treatment for seasonal affective disorder is

a. avoidance of temperature changes, especially at night.
b. infrequent naps to regulate the amount of REM sleep.
c. a fixed meal schedule to minimize changes in metabolic rate.
d. exposure to several hours of bright light each day.

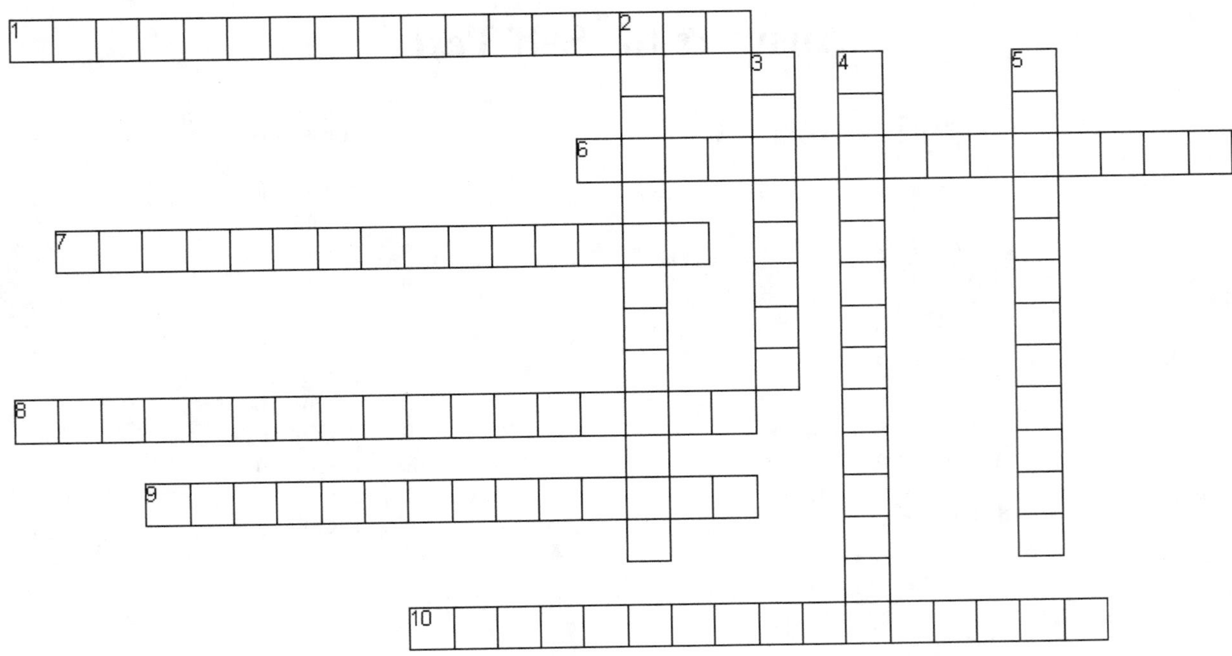

Across

1. Movement disorder that can occur after prolonged treatment with antipsychotic medication, characterized by involuntary movements of the face and neck
6. Serious mood disorder characterized by cyclical periods of mania and depression
7. Symptom of schizophrenia evident by its presence: delusions, hallucinations, or thought disorders
8. Increased incidence of schizophrenia in people born during late winter and early spring
9. Decreased activity of the prefrontal cortex; believed to be responsible for the negative symptoms of schizophrenia
10. Increased sensitivity of neurotransmitter receptors; caused by damage to the afferent axons or long-term blockage of neurotransmitter release

Down

2. Serious mental disorder characterized by disordered thoughts, delusions, hallucinations, and often bizarre behaviors
3. Belief that is clearly in contradiction to reality
4. A drug that has a very high affinity for a particular receptor but activates that receptor less than the normal ligand does
5. Treatment of seasonal affective disorder by daily exposure to bright light

Answers for Self Tests

Lesson I	Lesson II
1. b Obj. 16-1	1. d Obj. 16-6
2. a Obj. 16-1	2. b Obj. 16-6
3. c Obj. 16-2	3. c Obj. 16-6
4. d Obj. 16-2	4. a Obj. 16-6
5. a Obj. 16-3	5. a Obj. 16-7
6. b Obj. 16-3	6. b Obj. 16-7
7. a Obj. 16-3	7. a Obj. 16-7
8. c Obj. 16-4	8. d Obj. 16-7
9. a Obj. 16-4	9. d Obj. 16-8
10. b Obj. 16-5	10. a Obj. 16-8
11. c Obj. 16-5	11. d Obj. 16-8
12. d Obj. 16-5	12. d Obj. 16-8

CHAPTER 17
Anxiety Disorders, Autistic Disorder, Attention-Deficit/Hyperactivity Disorder, and Stress Disorders

Lesson I: Anxiety Disorders and Autistic Disorder

Read the interim summary on pages 593-594 of your text to re-acquaint yourself with the material in this section.

Learning Objective 17-1 Describe the symptoms and possible causes of panic disorder.

Read pages 585-588 and answer the following questions.

1. In general, what is the primary symptom of the anxiety disorders?

2. a. Define *panic disorder* in your own words.

   b. Which sex is more likely to be afflicted by panic disorder, and at what age does this disorder most commonly begin? (See Figure 17.1 in your text. Eaton et al., 1994)

3. a. List some of the universal symptoms of a panic attack.

   b. Explain the relationship between panic attacks, anticipatory anxiety, and agoraphobia.

4. Why are many people who suffer from panic attacks convinced that it is a medical, rather than a mental, condition?

5. Summarize the results of a literature review to determine possible hereditary origins of panic disorder. (Hettema et al., 2001)

6. a. Briefly describe some of the situations that activate the autonomic nervous system and induce a panic attack in people with a history of panic disorder. (Stein et al., 1994)

   b. After receiving an injection of sodium lactate, what percentage of a group of normal subjects experienced a panic attack? (Balon et al., 1989)

c. What percentage of the relatives of the subjects who experienced an induced panic attack had a history of anxiety disorders?

7. a. How do benzodiazepines agonists and antagonists affect the sensitivity of GABA binding sites?

   b. What possible causes of anxiety disorders are suggested by the effects of these drugs on GABA receptors?

   c. What is the effect of the benzodiazepine antagonist flumazenil on control subjects and subjects with panic disorder? (Nutt et al., 1990)

   d. What did a functional imaging study reveal about structural changes in the brains of people with panic disorder? (Malizia et al., 1998)

8. a. What is the preferred treatment for panic disorder? (See Figure 17.2 in your text. American Psychiatric Association, 1998; Asnis et al., 2001)

   b. What neurotransmitter appears to play a role in anxiety disorders just as it does in depression?

9. a. Describe the anatomical difference between the two groups of subject mice used in research on the effectiveness of SSRIs in treating anxiety disorders. (Santarelli et al., 2003)

   b. After four weeks of treatment with an SSRI, which mice would and would not retrieve food from an open chamber?

   c. Therefore, what physical characteristic appears to determine the efficacy of SSRIs in treating anxiety?

10. a. Explain how researchers manipulated a gene for the 5-HT1A receptor in two groups of mice. (Gross et al., 2002)

    b. Which group of mice showed anxious behavior in adulthood?

11. Why may serotonin have different effects at different times during an animal's life? (D'Amato et al., 1987)

12. How does having one or two short alleles of the promoter region of the serotonin transporter affect

    a. anxiety levels in very young infants? (Auerbach et al., 1999)

    b. anxiety in adults with social phobia when they anticipated speaking before an audience? (Furmark et al., 2004)

    c. activation of the amygdala in these same adults? (See Figure 17. 3 in your text.)

13. a. What changes occurred in the brain(s) of

       1. a woman who had an unexpected panic attack while undergoing a PET scan? (Fischer et al., 1998)

       2. women with severe spider phobias who did and did not panic when they saw spider videos? (Johanson et al., 1998)

    b. According to the researchers, why may some women have been able to successfully suppress their panic attacks?

c. Which brain areas showed increased activity in people with panic disorder who imagined situations that caused them anxiety? (Bystritsky et al., 2001)

Learning Objective 17-2 Describe the symptoms and possible causes of obsessive-compulsive disorder.

Read pages 588-593 and answer the following questions.

1. a. In your own words, define *obsessions* and *compulsions*.

   b. Unlike schizophrenics, what insight into their behavior do people with obsessive-compulsive have?

2. a. What is the incidence of obsessive-compulsive disorder (OCD)

      1. in the general population?

      2. among men and women?

   b. At what age does this disorder commonly begin? (Robbins et al., 1984)

   c. What does a comparison of symptoms in various racial and ethnic groups reveal? (Akhtar et al., 1975; Khanna and Channabasavanna, 1987; Hinjo et al., 1989)

   d. How does this disorder disrupt normal social contact? (Turner et al., 1985)

3. List the four categories of compulsions and give an example of each. (Study Table 17.1 in your text.)

   1.

   2.

   3.

   4.

4. Discuss the possible relationship between compulsive behaviors and species-typical behaviors. (Wise and Rapoport, 1988)

5. Fiske and Haslam (1997) propose a particular explanation for the origins of OCD. Summarize their hypothesis.

6. Review research on the possible causes of hereditary OCD.

   a. Summarize the findings of several studies of obsessions and compulsions in monozygotic and dizygotic twins. (Hettema et al., 2001)

   b. What have family studies revealed about the incidence of OCD and Tourette's syndrome? (Pauls and Leckman, 1986; Pauls et al., 1986)

   c. Briefly describe Tourette's syndrome, its treatment, and note any similarities with OCD. (Swerdlow, 2001; Leonard et al., 1992a, 1992c; Grados et al., 2001)

d. What may be the cause of both of these disorders?

7. Review research on the possible causes of nonhereditary OCD.
   a. What injuries or diseases may contribute to this disorder? (Berthier et al., 1996; Hollander et al., 1990)

   b. Which brain regions appear to be damaged or dysfunctional? (Giedd et al., 1995; Robinson et al., 1995)

   c. Retell the experience of 5 ½ year old Frances following a viral infection, noting how her symptoms coincided with an active infection. (See Figure 17.4 in your text. Perlmutter et al., 1998)

8. a. Symptoms of OCD appear to be caused by damage to which brain region? (Bodner et al., 2001)

   b. Which brain regions show increased activity in patients with OCD? (Saxena et al., 1998)

   c. Which brain regions show decreased activity following successful behavior therapy or drug therapy?

   d. Why are these results surprising?

9. a. What interesting technique did Breiter et al. (1996) use to investigate the brain functions of people with OCD?

   b. Which brain regions became active during testing?

10. a. What kind of surgery is often a successful treatment for OCD? (Ballantine et al., 1987; Mindus et al., 1994; Baer et al., 1995)

    b. Under what circumstances is surgery justified?

    c. Summarize the success rates for this type of surgery. (Baer et al., 1995; Dougherty et al., 2002; Sachdev and Hay, 1995)

11. How successful is deep brain stimulation in treating OCD? (Nuttin et al., 2003; Abelson et al., 2005; Fontaine et al., 2004)

12. According to Saxena et al. (1998), what may be the cause of obsessive-compulsive disorder? (Refer back to Figure 8.20 in your text.)

13. a. Outline the drug treatment schedule OCD research subjects followed in the study by Leonard et al., 1989.

    b. Study Figure 17.5 in your text and compare the effectiveness of clomipramine and the antidepressant drug desipramine in relieving their symptoms.

c. When patients were switched from CMI to DMI, what happened to their symptoms?

14. How do all effective antiobsessional drugs affect the brain? Cite supporting research. (Hollander et al., 1992)

15. Which brain regions have been implicated in OCD? (Lavoie and Parent, 1990; El Mansari and Blier, 1997)

16. a. Briefly describe several other compulsive behaviors which afflict people and how they are successfully treated. (Rapoport, 1991; Leonard et al., 1992b)

    b. Describe a compulsive behavior seen in some breeds of large dogs and how it can be successfully treated. (Rapoport et al., 1992)

Read the interim summary on page 598 of your text to re-acquaint yourself with the material in this section.

Learning Objective 17-3 Describe the symptoms and possible causes of autistic disorder.

Read pages 594-598 and answer the following questions.

1. a. What is the incidence of autism in the general population?

   b. What is the incidence of autism between boys and girls?

2. List some characteristic abnormalities of autistic disorder that fall into each of these categories.

   a. Affective

   b. Cognitive

   c. Behavioral

3. List and briefly describe three other pervasive developmental disorders.

   1.

   2.

   3.

4. When autistic children with mental retardation reach puberty, what additional condition do many develop and what does its occurrence suggest about brain development? (Rapin, 1995)

5. What is the incidence of all forms of pervasive developmental disorders in the general population? (Fombonne, 1999)

6. Outline the explanation of the cause and social consequences of autism proposed by Frith and her colleagues. (Frith et al., 1991)

7. a. Describe the animations that researchers asked normal subjects and autistic subjects to watch. (Castelli et al., 2002)

   b. How accurately did autistic subjects describe the goal-directed interactions of the triangles?

   c. How accurately did autistic subjects describe the "intentions" of the triangles?

   d. Which brain regions of the autistic subjects showed normal activation and lower activation while they watched the animations? (See Figure 17.6 in your text.)

8. What appears to be an important role of the superior temporal sulcus? (Allison et al., 2000)

9. a. Compare the activity in the fusiform face area (FFA) of normal subjects and autistic subjects who were looking at pictures of human faces, shown in Figure 17.7 in your text. (Pierce et al., 2001)

   b. Why may autistic people be poor at recognizing facial expressions?

   c. Compare the activity of the FFA of an autistic boy in two different situations, when he watched "Digimon" cartoon characters and when he watched photos of faces. (Grelotti et al., 2005)

   d. What do these results suggest about the functioning of the FFA of autistic people?

10. a. When autistic subjects are asked to determine the emotions expressed in photographs of faces, which part of the face to they avoid looking at? (See Figure 17.8 in your text.)

    b. How does their behavior contribute to their impaired social abilities?

11. Explain two approaches to understanding the basis of autism—one incorrect (Bettelheim, 1967) and one widely accepted. (Cox et al., 1975)

12. a. Cite evidence from family studies, especially of autism in siblings, that supports the role of genetics in this disorder. (Folstein and Piven, 1991; Bailey, 1993)

    b. Compare the concordance rates for autism in monozygotic and dizygotic twins. (Folstein and Rosen-Scheidley, 2001)

    c. What deficits do most of the nonautistic members of a pair of monozygotic twins discordant for autism exhibit? (Bailey et al., 1995)

    d. What do their deficits suggest about the causes of this disorder?

13. a. Approximately what percent of all cases of autism have definable biological causes?

    b. List some of these biological causes. (De Long, 1999; Rapin, 1999; Hollander et al., 1999)

14. What drug has been shown to have some benefit in treating stereotyped behaviors of autistic children? (See Figure 17.9 in your text. McDougle et al., 2005)

15. a. In which brain regions of autistic people have researchers documented abnormalities? (Courchesne et al., 2005)

    b. What are some of the general functions of these areas?

    c. How did hearing speech and nonspeech sounds affect the activity of the brains of autistic people with speech abilities? (Gervais et al., 2004)

16. a. Explain the general pattern of growth of the brain from birth through adolescence.

    b. Which brain regions that are involved in autism grow more quickly early in life and more slowly later on?

    c. What kind of specific abnormalities have been found in the "higher-order" regions of autistics? (Casanova et al., 2003; Levitt et al., 2003)

    d. What kind of specific abnormalities have been found in the white matter of autistics? (Herbert et al., 2004)

    e. What kind of abnormality may account for the exceptional skills of some autistic people? (Courchesne et al., 2005)

17. Finally, has any link been found between autism and childhood immunizations? (Andrews et al., 2004; Chen et al., 2004)

Lesson I Self Test

1. People with panic disorder suffer from anticipatory anxiety, which is

   a. a brief interval of unrealistic fear that precedes a panic attack.
   b. the first stage of a panic attack.
   c. often sufficient to trigger a panic attack.
   d. the fear that another panic attack will strike.

2. Studies concerning the genetic basis of panic disorder have found

   a. a significant genetic factor.
   b. that over 50 percent of the relatives of a person with panic disorder also had a history of anxiety disorders.
   c. that panic disorder may be caused by a single, dominant gene.
   d. that environmental factors outweigh genetic factors.

3. An injection of _____ may cause a panic attack in susceptible people.

   a. alcohol
   b. lactic acid
   c. benzodiazepine
   d. lithium carbonate

4. Drugs that are _____ have been used to successfully treat panic disorder and obsessive-compulsive disorder.

   a. serotonin agonists

b. serotonin antagonists
c. benzodiazepine receptor antagonists
d. dopamine antagonists

5. People suffering from obsessive-compulsive disorder

a. discuss their behavior openly.
b. have periodic episodes of mania.
c. recognize that their thoughts and behaviors are senseless.
d. are often insomniacs.

6. The tics, obsessions, and compulsions that young Frances experienced appear to have been caused by

a. activation of the basal ganglia.
b. phenylketonuria.
c. antibiotics used to treat a chronic viral infection.
d. a group A β-hemolytic streptococcal infection.

7. All effective antiobsessional drugs

a. block dopamine receptors.
b. are MAO antagonists.
c. increases the sensitivity of the GABA binding site.
d. are specific blockers of the reuptake of 5-HT.

8. People whose OCD is being treated with drugs begin to show improvement with a reduction in the activity of the

a. basal ganglia and amygdala.
b. caudate nucleus and orbitofrontal cortex.
c. cingulate cortex.
d. basal ganglia and cingulate gyrus.

9. Children with autistic disorder

a. are usually of normal intelligence and sometimes have advanced isolated skills.
b. have abnormal language development and usually interpret other people's speech literally.
c. have an impaired private imagination and, therefore, appreciate fantasy stories.
d. try very hard to please others even though they do not like or seek physical contact.

10. The best evidence for a genetic basis of autistic disorder is from studies of twins and siblings and indicates that

a. all offspring of parents who carry the faulty genes will be autistic.
b. the concordance rate for dizygotic twins is extremely low.
c. if a pair of monozygotic twins is discordant for autism the autistic member of the pair is a male.
d. if a pair of monozygotic twins is discordant for autism the nonautistic member of the pair develops normally.

11. An explanation for the deficits associated with autistic disorder, proposed by Frith and colleagues, suggests their lack of interest in other people is due

a. to abnormalities in the fusiform face area of their brains.
b. to a decreased connectivity between the visual system and other sensory systems leading autistic people to avoid looking at the eyes and mouths of other people.
c. to an inability to infer and predict the thoughts and feelings of other people from normal social cues due to brain abnormalities.
d. to an autoimmune reaction that causes rapid brain development early in life and decreased brain development from early childhood to adolescence.

12. Which of these structural abnormalities has been documented in the brains of people with autistic disorder?

a. a decrease in the volume of white matter containing long-range axons
b. a slightly larger than normal size brain at birth which then begins to shrink as result of a process still not understood
c. fewer connections through the corpus callosum connecting the right and left hemispheres of the brain
d. incomplete development of the meninges covering the brain

Lesson II: Attention-Deficit/Hyperactivity Disorder and Stress Disorders

Read the interim summary on page 601 in your text to re-acquaint yourself with the material in this section.

Learning Objective 17-4 Describe the symptoms and possible causes of attention-deficit/hyperactivity disorder.

Read pages 598-601 and answer the following questions.

1. Usually first discovered in the _______________, attention-deficit/hyperactivity disorder (ADHD) is the _______________ _______________ disorder that appears in childhood.

2. a. How is ADHD diagnosed and why is diagnosis difficult?

   b. What is the incidence of ADHD

      1. in grade school children?

      2. between the sexes both in childhood and adulthood?

   c. What does this shift indicate?

   d. Approximately what percent of children with ADHD continue to experience symptoms as adults?

   e. As adults, what other serious difficulties do they develop? (Ernst et al., 1998; Seidman et al., 1998)

3. What is the most common treatment for ADHD and what is its pharmacological effect?

4. What is the estimated heritability of ADHD?

5. a. Who were the subjects in research on ADHD by Schachar et al. (2005)?

   b. Describe the stop signal task researchers taught them.

   c. Compare the task performances of all of the research subjects.

   d. What do the results suggest about a possible cause of ADHD?

6. Sagvolden and his colleagues suggest that physiological differences in the brains of children with ADHD may cause them to have a steeper delay of reinforcement gradient than normal children. Carefully explain how immediate and delayed reinforcement may contribute to the development of inappropriate behavior in these children. (Study Figure 17.10 in your text. Sagvolden and Sargent, 1998; Savolden et al., 2005)

7. a. Describe the instrumental conditioning task Sagvolden and his colleagues taught normal boys and boys with ADHD. (Sagvolden et al., 1998)

   b. Describe the response of both groups of subjects to the two experimental conditions.

   c. How did the researchers interpret the results?

8. a. Explain how the successful treatment of the symptoms of ADHD with methylphenidate suggested a cause of this disorder. Be sure to mention the pharmacological effect of methylphenidate on the brain.

b. What have several studies indicated about

1. the number of dopamine transporters in the brains of people with ADHD? (Spencer et al., 2005)
2. associations between particular alleles for the dopamine transporter and ADHD? (Mazei-Robinson et al., 2005)

c. What cause of ADHD is suggested by these structural protein differences and symptom improvement following treatment with methylphenidate?

d. What other drug has also been used to improve performance on tasks that are usually difficult for people with ADHD and what is its pharmacological effect? (Turner et al., 2004)

9. a. How did researchers increase the levels of extracellular dopamine in subject mice? Be sure you understand the difference between a knockout gene and a knock-down gene. (Zhuang et al., 2001)

b. In what ways did their behavior resemble that of ADHD?

c. When treated with amphetamine, how did the behavior of the mice change?

d. Why do these results appear to contradict the suggestion that an excessive number of dopamine transporters plays a role in the development of the symptoms of ADHD?

e. How do the researchers interpret their results?

10. What have studies of the brain structure of people with ADHD reveal about

a. total volume of their brains? (Castellanos et al., 2002)

b. localized decreases in volume? (See Figure 17.11 in your text. Seidman et al., 2005; Castellanos et al., 2003)

c. activation of the caudate nucleus or medial prefrontal cortex while subjects with ADHD performed particular kinds of tasks? (Rubia et al., 1999; Durston et al., 2003; Vaidya et al., 2005; Tamm et al., 2004)

11. According to many researchers, where may the abnormalities leading to ADHD be located in the brain?

Read the interim summary on pages 611-612 of your text to re-acquaint yourself with the material in this section.

Learning Objective 17-5 Describe the physiological responses to stress and their effects on health.

Read pages 601-606 and answer the following questions.

1. In your own words, define

a. *stress*

b. *fight-or-flight response.*

2. The _______________ and _______________ responses to an emotion can have harmful effects on health. These responses are _______________ and ready the body's _______________ _______________.

3. a. Where are epinephrine, norepinephrine, and steroid stress hormones secreted?

   b. What are some of the effects of epinephrine? Which effect of epinephrine and norepinephrine together contributes to cardiovascular disease?

   c. In stressful situations, what change occurs in the secretion of norepinephrine in the brain? (Yokoo et al., 1990; Cenci et al., 1992)

   d. If noradrenergic axons from the brain stem to the forebrain are destroyed, how is the response to social isolation stress affected? (Montero et al., 1990)

   e. Trace the brain circuit that appears to produce the release of norepinephrine. (Van Bockstaele et al., 2001)

4. a. What is the other stress-related hormone and where is it secreted?

   b. List some of its effects.

      1. 4.

      2. 5.

      3. 6.

   c. What is the significance of the fact that nearly every cell of the body has glucocorticoid receptors?

   d. The secretion of glucocorticoids is controlled by neurons of the ________________ ________________ of the ________________ which secrete a peptide called ________________-________________ ________________, which, in turn, stimulates the anterior pituitary gland to secrete ________________ ________________. The ________________ ________________ secretes glucocorticoids in response to ACTH. (See Figure 17.12 in your text.)

5. a. In which brain region does CRH serve as a neuromodulator/neurotransmitter?

   b. What are the effects of an intracerebroventricular injection of CRH? (Britton et al., 1982; Cole and Koob, 1988; Swerdlow et al., 1986) of a CRF antagonist? (Kalin et al., 1988; Heinrichs et al., 1994; Skutella et al., 1994)

6. a. What are the effects of stress on rats who have had their adrenal glands removed?

   b. What medical treatment do adrenalectomized human patients receive in times of stress? (Tyrell and Baxter, 1981)

7. What have many studies on the effects of long-term stress on health concluded? (See Figure 17.13 in your text. (Cobb and Rose, 1973; Cohen, 1953; Theorell et al., 1992)

8. a. According to Selye (1976), what causes most of the harmful effects of stress?

   b. List some of the effects on health of

      1. prolonged stress.

2. long-term administration of steroids for medical reasons. (Lewis and Smith, 1983)

c. How were the effects of stress on healing demonstrated in subjects who cared for relatives with Alzheimer's disease? What were the results? (See Figure 17.14 in your text. Kiecold-Glaser et al., 1995)

9. a. What changes produced by long-term exposure to glucocorticoids appear to cause the death of neurons located in field CA1 of the hippocampal formation? (Sapolsky, 1992, 1995; McEwen and Sapolsky, 1995)

b. What cognitive change may then develop in old age? Cite research to support your answer. (Lupien et al., 1996)

10. a. How did researchers create a stressful situation for newborn rat pups? (Brunson et al., 2005)

b. Although the pups' behavior was normal at 4-5 months of age, what kind of deficits were observed when they were tested at 12 months of age?

c. What do these results suggest about the long-term effects of stress that occurs early in life?

11. How did acute stress resulting from the sight and smell of a cat affect the functioning of the hippocampus in subject rats? (See Figure 17.15 in your text. Diamond et al., 1999; Mesches et al., 1999)

12. a. What kind of brain damage appears to abolish the effects of stress on rats' performance in a Morris water maze?

b. What physiological effect of stress was not abolished by this damage?

c. What do these results suggest about the mechanisms through which short-term stress affects hippocampal memory functions? (Kim et al., 2001)

13. a. How did researchers subject pregnant rats to stress and how did prenatal stress affect the brain development of their pups? (See Figure 17.16 in your text. Salm et al., 2004)

b. What is the presumed explanation for the increased fearfulness in novel situations shown by animals who were stressed prenatally that has been demonstrated in other studies? (Ward et al., 2000)

14. a. How was glucocorticoid secretion in adult rats affected if they had been

1. prenatally stressed?
2. prenatally-stressed, but the adrenal glands of their mothers had previously been removed? (See Figure 17.17 in your text. Barbazanges et al., 1996)

b. What do these results suggest about how the effects of prenatal stress occur?

15. a. Briefly describe the social structure of vervet monkey colonies.

b. What changes were documented in the brains of monkeys who were subjected to constant stress and died? (See Figure 17.18 in your text. Uno et al., 1989)

c. Cite evidence that stress-induced brain degeneration occurs in humans as well. (Jensen et al., 1982)

16. How did severe chronic back pain affect the brain year by year? (Apkarian et al., 2004b)

Learning Objective 17-6 Discuss posttraumatic stress disorder.

Read pages 606-607 and answer the following questions.

1. Describe posttraumatic stress disorder (PTSD) noting

   a. the cause.

   b. the symptoms.

   c. the onset of symptoms.

   d. their effects on mental and physical health. (Zayfert et al., 2002)

   e. the vulnerability to this disorder of men and women. (Fullerton et al., 2001)

   f. the special symptoms of children.

2. List two genetic factors that may influence susceptibility to PTSD. (Stein et al., 2002)

   1. 2.

3. List three factors that increased risk of being exposed to traumatic events gathered from a Vietnam Era Twin Registry. (Koenen et al., 2002)

   1. 3.

   2.

4. List five factors that predict the risk of developing PTSD following exposure to a traumatic event.

   1. 4.

   2. 5.

   3.

5. a. What do MRI studies reveal about the effects of posttraumatic stress disorder on the hippocampus of combat veterans (Bremner et al., 1995; Gurvits et al., 1996)?

   b. What do MRI studies reveal about the effects of posttraumatic stress disorder on the hippocampus of adults who experienced severe childhood abuse (Bremner, 1999)?

6. a. What was an unexpected finding in a study of the incidence of PTSD in pairs of monozygotic male twins? (See Figure 17.19 in your text. Gilbertson et al., 2002)

b. What do these results suggest about a predisposition to PTSD?

7. a. Why did researchers believe that one of the causes of PTSD was high levels of cortisol?

   b. What did the evidence indicate about the level of cortisol in people with PTSD and the level of cortisol in people at the time they experienced trauma and who later developed PTSD?

   c. What did blood samples obtained in the emergency room from female rape victims who had been previously assaulted reveal? What was the likelihood that these women would develop PTSD? (Resnick et al., 1995)

8. According to Yehuda (2001), why may people who have been subjected to traumatic events show decreased cortisol production?

9. a. Summarize the results of an analysis of the CRH and cortisol levels in the cerebrospinal fluid of normal volunteers and combat veterans with PTSD as measured over a six-hour period. (Baker et al., 1999)

   b. How did CRH levels correlate with the severity of PTSD symptoms?

   c. Which of these substances, then, may be the more important factor than in the development of these symptoms? (See Figures 17.20 and 17.21 in your text.)

Learning Objective 17-7 Discuss psychoneuroimmunology and the interactions between the immune system and stress.

Read pages 607-611 and answer the following questions.

1. Define *psychoneuroimmunology* in your own words.

2. a. Construct an overview of the functions of the immune system.

   The white blood cells of the immune system develop in the ______________ ______________ and the ______________ ______________. Some of these cells circulate in the ______________ or ______________ ______________ and others reside permanently in one ______________.

   b. What triggers an immune reaction? What are the two types of reactions?

   c. Briefly describe a specific immune reaction—the chemically mediated reaction—by explaining the relationship between

      1. antigens and antibodies.

      2. B-lymphocytes and immunoglobulins.

      3. immunoglobulins and antigens. (Study Figure 17.22a in your text.)

d. Briefly describe a second specific immune reaction—the cell-mediated reaction. Be sure to mention T-lymphocytes in your answer. (See Figure 17.22b.)

e. Explain the role of cytokines in both of these immune reactions.

f. Finally, how do glucocorticoids suppress this immune response? (Sapolsky, 1992)

3. What is the most important mechanism by which stress impairs the immune system?

4. State the general conclusion of research on stress and the immune system based on studies of the caregivers of family members with Alzheimer's disease (See Figure 17.23 in your text. Kiecolt-Glaser et al., 1987; Glaser et al., 2000), of husbands who lost their wives to breast cancer (Schleifer et al., 1983), and of healthy subjects imagining past unpleasant situations (Knapp et al., 1992).

5. a. Explain why the brain is responsible for the suppressing effect of glucocorticoids on the immune system.

b. More specifically, what role does the central nucleus of the amygdala seem to play in immunosuppression? (Sharp et al., 1991; Imaki et al., 1992)

c. What other parts of the body may play a role in stress-induced immunosuppression not involving glucocorticoids?

d. List two effects of inescapable intermittent shock.

1. 2.

e. Which brain chemicals appear to mediate these effects and how can they be abolished in the laboratory? (Shavit et al., 1984)

6. What stress-related responses sometimes occur to

a. a surviving spouse?

b. medical students during final examinations? (Glaser et al., 1987)

c. patients with rheumatoid arthritis? (Feigenbaum et al., 1979)

d. rats who are handled or exposed to a cat? (Rogers et al., 1980)

e. rats predisposed to diabetes and subjected to moderate chronic stress? (Lehman et al., 1991)

7. a. Explain the hypothesis of research on stress and upper respiratory illness. (Stone et al., 1987)

b. Summarize the results of records kept by volunteers who developed upper respiratory illness which are shown in Figure 17.18 in your text.

c. How did the researchers account for the effect? Be sure to refer to IgA in your answer.

d. Briefly describe research by Cohen et al. (1991) that confirmed this study. (See Figure 17.25 in your text.)

Lesson II Self Test

1. Select the *incorrect* statement about the incidence of attention-deficit/hyperactivity disorder (ADHD).

   a. In childhood, boys are about ten times more likely than girls to receive a diagnosis of ADHD.
   b. In adulthood, men are about twice as likely than women to receive a diagnosis of ADHD.
   c. Approximately 60 percent of children with ADHD will continue to display symptoms into adulthood.
   d. Approximately 50 percent of children with a diagnosis of ADHD have been misdiagnosed.

2. _____, the most common treatment of ADHD, is a _____ and _____.

   a. Amphetamine; dopamine agonist; increases the sensitivity of the postsynaptic membrane
   b. Methylphenidate; dopamine agonist; blocks dopamine transporters
   c. Fluoxetine; serotonin agonist; decreases the reuptake of serotonin
   d. Methylphenidate; dopamine antagonist; blocks dopamine receptors

3. If ADHD results from a steeper than normal delay of reinforcement gradient, then for children with ADHD

   a. constant reinforcement is the only effective reinforcement.
   b. delayed reinforcement is the only effective reinforcement.
   c. immediate reinforcement is even more effective than for normal children.
   d. slightly delayed reinforcement heightens symptoms.

4. The secretion of glucocorticoids is controlled by neurons in the _____ and glucocorticoid receptors are _____.

   a. paraventricular nucleus of the hypothalamus; contained in almost every cell of the body
   b. central nucleus of the amygdala; found in highest concentration in the adrenal glands
   c. hippocampal formation; especially susceptible to the effects of stress
   d. hypothalamus; the first to signal a rise in blood pressure

5. Long-term stress increases the secretion of _____ which may be responsible for _____.

   a. aldosterone; cardiovascular disease
   b. epinephrine; learning and memory deficits
   c. glucocorticoids; the harmful effects of stress
   d. antigens; autoimmune diseases

6. Young vervet monkeys near the bottom of the social hierarchy who experienced almost constant stress

   a. failed to learn normal group coping responses.
   b. engaged in more fight-or-flight responses than other young monkeys who were not subjected to stress.
   c. later showed the highest rates of coronary artery disease.
   d. sustained severe damage to the hippocampal formation.

7. Posttraumatic stress disorder

   a. is associated with decreased size of the hippocampal formation, but the decrease may be a precipitating factor rather than a consequence.
   b. occurs only after the onset of adolescence.
   c. occurs more often in persons from secure backgrounds with little previous experience with stress and how to manage it.
   d. is more likely to occur in men than women, given exposure to similarly traumatic events.

8. Posttraumatic stress disorder may result from high levels of

   a. corticotrophin-releasing hormone (CRH).
   b. ACTH.
   c. norepinephrine and epinephrine.

d. cortisol.

9. The immune system develops _____ through exposure to _____.

a. antibodies; antigens
b. interferon; antibodies
c. antigens; antibodies
d. antibodies; B-lymphocytes

10. Cytokines

a. are the body's first defense against malignant tumors.
b. stimulate cell division.
c. develop in the bone marrow.
d. are unique proteins on the surface of infectious microorganisms.

11. The records of volunteers in a study of the effects of stress on the immune system indicated that

a. people who felt they had more control over the events in their lives had fewer illnesses.
b. people with the strongest peer support had fewer illnesses.
c. people who lived alone, but had a pet, had fewer illnesses.
d. a few days before showing symptoms of an upper respiratory infection, the volunteers experienced more undesirable than desirable events in their lives.

12. Select the *correct* statement about immunoglobulin, IgA.

a. High levels of IgA are associated with an unhappy mood in the subject.
b. IgA blood levels are severely decreased in people with autoimmune diseases.
c. IgA is secreted in the nose, mouth, throat, and lungs, and it acts as a defense against infection.
d. Stress stimulates the production of IgA.

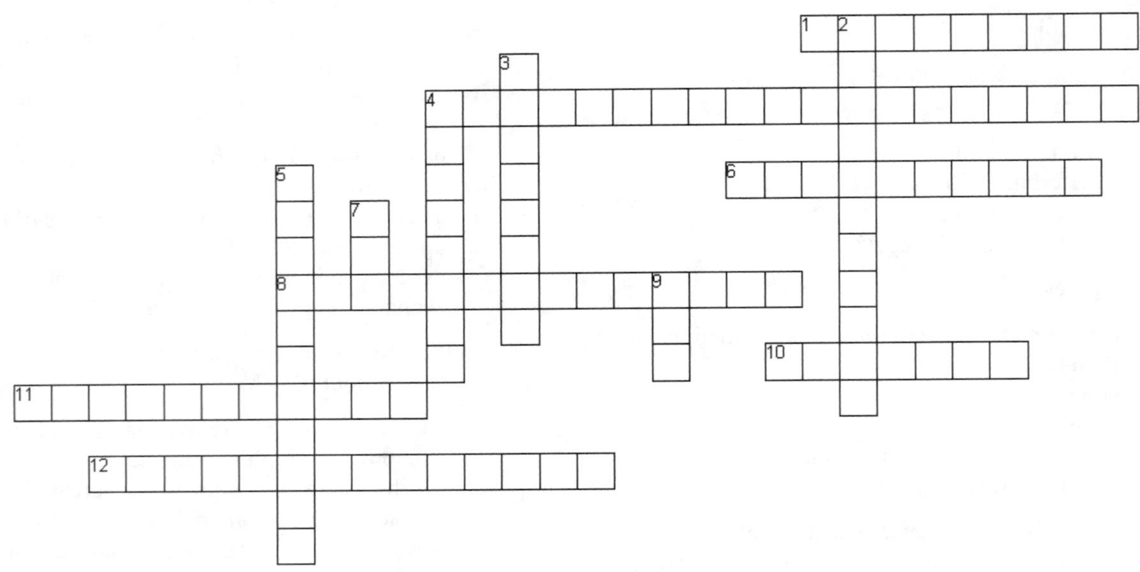

Across

1. Unwanted thought or idea with which a person is preoccupied
4. Fear of having a panic attack; may lead to the development of agoraphobia
6. Feeling that one is obliged to perform a behavior, even if one prefers not to do so
8. One of a group of hormones of the adrenal cortex that are important in protein and carbohydrate metabolism, secreted especially in times of stress
10. Protein present on a microorganism that permits the immune system to recognize the microorganism as an invader
11. Fear of being away from home or other protected places
12. Antibody released by B-lymphocytes that binds with antigens and helps to destroy invading microorganisms

Down

2. White blood cell that originates in the bone marrow; part of the immune system
3. Stimulus (or situation) that produces a stress response
4. Protein produced by a cell of the immune system that recognizes antigens present on invading microorganisms
5. Surgical destruction of the cingulum bundle, which connects the prefrontal cortex with the limbic system; helps to reduce intense anxiety and the symptoms of obsessive-compulsive disorder
7. Hereditary disorder caused by the absence of an enzyme that converts the amino acid phenylalanine to tyrosine
9. Hypothalamic hormone that stimulates the anterior pituitary gland to secrete ACTH

Answers for Self Tests

Lesson I

1. d Obj. 17-1
2. a Obj. 17-1
3. b Obj. 17-1
4. a Obj. 17-1
5. c Obj. 17-2
6. d Obj. 17-2
7. d Obj. 17-2
8. b Obj. 17-2
9. b Obj. 17-3
10. b Obj. 17-3
11. c Obj. 17-3
12. a Obj. 17-3

Lesson II

1. d Obj. 17-4
2. d Obj. 17-4
3. c Obj. 17-4
4. a Obj. 17-5
5. c Obj. 17-5
6. d Obj. 17-5
7. a Obj. 17-6
8. a Obj. 17-6
9. a Obj. 17-7
10. b Obj. 17-7
11. d Obj. 17-7
12. c Obj. 17-7

CHAPTER 18
Drug Abuse

Lesson I: Common Features of Addiction and Some Commonly Abused Drugs

Read the interim summary on pages 623-624 in your text to re-acquaint yourself with the material in this section.

Learning Objective 18-1 Describe two common features of addiction: positive and negative reinforcement.

Read pages 615-618 and answer the following questions.

1. Describe some of the adverse effects of the following addictive substances.
   a. Alcohol

   b. Smoking

   c. Cocaine

   d. Designer drugs

2. Table 18. 1 in your text lists the most important addictive drugs and their sites of action.
3. Drugs that lead to dependency must first reinforce _______________ _________________.
4. a. If, in a particular situation, the behavior of an animal or a person is regularly followed by an appetitive stimulus, how is their behavior subsequently affected?

   b. How are appetitive stimuli thought to affect the brain?

   c. When is the effectiveness of reinforcing stimuli the greatest?

5. To better understand drug addiction, look more closely at the role of immediate reinforcement.
   a. Why did hungry rats prefer the corridor in the maze that delivered less food to the corridor that delivered more food? (Logan, 1965)

   b. How do these results explain why some drugs are more addictive than others?

c. Explain why someone willingly takes an addictive drug with powerful, long-term, aversive effects.

d. Why are nonhuman animals unlikely to become addicted to drugs administered in the form of a pill?

6. What physiological effect is common to all natural reinforcers? (White, 1996)

7. a. Define *negative reinforcement* in your own words.

   b. How does it differ from punishment?

8. Carefully explain how an addictive drug provides both positive and negative reinforcement.

9. Define

   a. *tolerance.*

   b. *withdrawal symptoms.*

10. a. Carefully explain how the body's compensatory mechanisms to re-establish homeostasis may account for both tolerance and the accompanying withdrawal symptoms.

    b. How may withdrawal symptoms play a role in maintaining addiction?

    c. How may negative reinforcement account for drug addiction in some circumstances?

Learning Objective 18-2 Describe the neural mechanisms responsible for craving and relapse.

Read pages 618-623 and answer the following questions.

1. Why may a person with a history of drug addiction experience craving when seeing or thinking about drug-related stimuli? Be sure to refer to incentive salience in your answer. (Robinson and Berridge, 1993)

2. As a result of drug addiction, what changes may take place in the reinforcement system of the brain and increase the likelihood of craving and relapse? Be sure to refer to allostasis in your answer. (Koob and Le Moal, 2002)

3. Explain how stimuli that have been associated with drug use in the past can elicit cravings.

4. a. Explain the training procedure and results of research with animals to illustrate the reinstatement model of drug seeking. (Shalev et al., 2002)

   b. Why is the reinstatement model useful in studying craving?

5. a. List two procedures that prevent an unexpected shot of cocaine from causing relapse.

1. Grimm and See (2002)

2. McFarland and Kalivas (2001)

b. What procedure reinstates cocaine seeking in rats? (Park et al., 2002)

6. a. Which brain regions are activated by addictive drugs and their associated cues? (Dackis and O'Brien, 2005) Cite research results shown in Figure 18.1 in your text to support your answer. (David et al., 2005)

b. When smokers were treated with bupropion, what changes occurred when they saw smoking-related cues? (Brody et al., 2004)

c. What evidence suggests that the medial prefrontal cortex is related to craving for both addictive and typical reinforcers ? (Wang et al., 2004)

7. a. Before continuing, review

1. the role of the prefrontal cortex.
2. the gambling task.
3. how lesions of the medial prefrontal cortex affect performance on this task.

b. Explain why it is valid to compare the behavior of subjects during the gambling task with that of people addicted to drugs.

8. a. Under what conditions is the activity of the medial prefrontal cortex increased? Under what conditions is the activity of the medial prefrontal cortex decreased? (See Figure 18.2 in your text). (Volkow et al., 1992; Bolla et al., 2004; Garavan and Stout, 2005)

b. How are the activity of the medial prefrontal cortex and the amount of cocaine an addict uses correlated? (Bolla et al., 2004)

c. In addition to behavioral performance deficits similar to those of people with lesions of the prefrontal cortex, what physical changes were observed in the brains of addicts? (See Figure 18.4 in your text. Franklin et al., 2002; Thompson et al., 2004)

9. a. Summarize some similarities between people with long-term drug abuse and schizophrenia, particularly regarding

1. the use of alcohol or illicit drugs.
2. nicotine dependency. (Dani and Harris, 2005)
3. volume of prefrontal gray matter. (See Figure 18.5 in your text. Mathalon et al., 2003)
4. hospitalization for schizophrenia in smokers. (See Figure 18.6 in your text. Weiser et al., 2004)

b. What do all these results suggest about the involvement of the prefrontal cortex in both diseases?

10. a. Explain why adolescents are more vulnerable to drug addiction than adults.

b. How is early onset of drug-taking associated with later drug abuse? (Chambers et al., 2003)

11. Turn to the role stress may play in drug addiction in both animals and humans. When former drug addicts are subjected to stress, what often happens? What is the presumed explanation?

12. a. How did researchers induce stress in subject rats? (Covington and Miczek, 2001)

 b. How did the stress affect the behavior of the defeated rats?

 c. How did researchers induce stress in infant subject rats? (Kosten et al., 2000)

 d. Summarize the effects of stress, shown in Figure 18.7 in your text, on the later behavior of these rats.

13. a. Which animals, among those in small groups of rhesus monkeys that had established a pattern of social dominance,

  1. had a greater number of D2 receptors?

  2. self-administered less cocaine? (See Figure 18.8 in your text. Morgan et al., 2002)

 b. What do these results suggest about the role of positive social satisfaction in susceptibility to drug addiction?

14. a. Outline the training procedure for rats before they were given a brief foot shock. (Erb and Stewart, 1999)

 b. How did rats respond after receiving the shock and how could this response be prevented?

 c. Which neurons, as determined by later research, are responsible for this effect? (Erb et al., 2001)

Read the interim summary on page 635 in your text to re-acquaint yourself with the material in this section.

Learning Objective 18-3 Review the neural basis of the reinforcing effects and withdrawal effects of opiates.

Read pages 624-626 and answer the following questions.

1. To review: Why are endogenous opioids important for the survival of species?

2. When opiate receptors are stimulated by an injection of an opiate, they produce different effects in the body. List four locations of opiate receptors and the effects they are responsible for.

 1. 3.

 2. 4.

3. a. List the three major types of opiate receptors and the effects they produce when stimulated.

  1.

  2.

3.

b. How did animals without μ opiate receptors respond to morphine or withdrawal from morphine? (Study Figure 18.9 in your text. Matthes et al., 1996)

4. a. What is the general behavioral effect of injections of opiates into both ends of the mesolimbic dopaminergic system? (Wise et al., 1995; Devine and Wise, 1994; Goeders et al., 1984)

b. Why may this effect occur? (Johnson and North, 1992)

5. a. How did destruction of dopaminergic axons and terminals in the nucleus accumbens affect lever pressing by rats for intravenous cocaine? intravenous heroin? (Gerrits and Vanree, 1996)

b. Activation of which brain region, then, is sufficient to produce the reinforcing effects of opiates?

6. a. Using the conditioned place preference procedure, what did Agmo et al., (1993) find about the physiology of reinforcement produced by natural reinforcers? Be sure to mention the pharmacological effect of naloxone and how it was used in this study.

b. What evidence suggests that endogenous opioids may also play a role in the reinforcing effects of addictive drugs?

7. a. Explain how antagonist-precipitated withdrawal is produced in the laboratory.

b. Summarize results from research using this and a similar technique to study brain locations involved in withdrawal symptoms.

1. (Maldonado et al., 1992)

2. (Bozarth, 1994)

8. a. How is the firing rate of neurons in the locus coeruleus affected by

1. a single dose of an opiate?

2. chronically administered opiate?

3. administration of an opiate antagonist after addiction has been established? What chemical is released? (Hyman, 1996b; Koob, 1996; Nestler, 1996)

b. How do lesions of the locus coeruleus affect the severity of withdrawal symptoms? (Maldonado and Koob, 1993)

c. How does withdrawal affect the level of excitatory neurotransmitters in the locus coeruleus? (Aghajanian et al., 1994)

9. a. Which neuropeptide, involved in the stimulation of drug craving caused by stress, may also be involved in the aversive effects of withdrawal from cocaine, opiates, alcohol and marijuana? (Rodriguez de Fonseca et al., 1997; Koob, 1999; Richter and Weiss, 1999; Service, 1999.)

   b. What treatment produced a conditioned place aversion in rats that had previously been chronically treated with morphine? (Stinus et al., 2005)

   c. What treatment, given just before precipitating withdrawal, prevented a conditioned place aversion in the rats?

   d. What do these results suggest about the role of CRH in the aversive effects of opiate withdrawal?

Learning Objective 18-4 Describe the behavioral and physical effects of cocaine and amphetamine.

Read pages 626-628 and answer the following questions.

1. Complete these sentences.

   a. Cocaine and amphetamine have similar behavioral effects because

   b. Cocaine binds with

   c. In addition to inhibiting the reuptake of dopamine, amphetamines directly stimulate

   d. Of all available drugs, probably the most effective reinforcer is

2. a. Describe the behavior of 1) people and 2) animals after taking cocaine. (Geary, 1987)

   b. Compare the death rate between rats who are given continuous access to self-administered cocaine with those who are given continuous access to self-administered heroin. (Study Figure 18.10 in your text. Bozarth and Wise, 1985)

3. a. How did dopamine levels in the nucleus accumbens change with the number of self-injections of amphetamine or cocaine in rats? (See Figure 18.11 in your text. Di Ciano et al., 1995)

   b. What treatment blocks the reinforcing effects of

      1. cocaine? (McGregor and Roberts, 1993; Caine et al., 1995)

      2. cocaine and amphetamines? (Caine and Koob, 1994)

4. a. Describe the psychotic behavior that usually results from the regular abuse of cocaine and amphetamines.

   b. Once a person stops taking the drug(s), what happens to these symptoms?

5. Look at some of the physical and behavioral effects of the long-term use of stimulant drugs.

   a. Almost three years after drug abuse ceased, what change was observed in the caudate nucleus and putamen of users? (Study Figure 18.12 in your text. McCann et al., 1998)

   b. What possible long-term health risk do these people face?

   c. What serious damage to the brain resulting from injections of methamphetamine was seen in laboratory animals? (Cadet et al., 2003)

6. What physical characteristic determined whether people without a history of drug abuse found the effects of methylphenidate to be pleasant? (See Figure 18.13 in your text. Volkow et al., 1999)

7. a. How does chronic abuse of stimulant drugs appear to affect the number of dopamine D_2 receptors in the striatum? (Volkow et al., 2001; Martinez et al., 2004)

   b. How may the level of D2 receptors affect the activity of the orbitofrontal cortex? (See Figure 18.14 in your text. Volkow et al., 2001)

   c. State two possible explanations of these results.

Lesson I Self Test

1. Withdrawal symptoms
   a. are caused by sensitization to the effects of drugs.
   b. are often more severe if the drug user has also developed a psychological dependency on drugs.
   c. result when drug users attempt to stop using any addictive drug.
   d. are primarily the opposite of the effects of the drug itself.

2. Drug tolerance is the _____ that results from its continued use.
   a. ability to delay a drug dose
   b. decreased sensitivity to a drug
   c. ability to accept the unpleasant side effects when a drug dose is not available
   d. increased sensitivity to a drug after a period of abstinence

3. When rats were given the choice between a small amount of food delivered immediately and a larger amount of food delivered after a delay, they
   a. eventually learned to wait for the larger amount of food.
   b. showed signs of stress.
   c. preferred the immediate reward to the greater reward.
   d. chose the small amount of food when they were sated and the larger amount of food when they were hungry.

4. Long-term drug use appears to
   a. decrease the incentive salience of drug-related stimuli.
   b. increase both the pleasure of the craving for the drug and the rush produced by the drug itself.
   c. produce a long-term change in the set point of the brain's reinforcement mechanisms.
   d. be more difficult to study in humans than in animals with the reinstatement model.

5. When people with a history of drug abuse see stimuli associated with drug use, the activation of the _____ increases.
   a. orbitofrontal cortex
   b. basolateral amygdala and the bed nucleus of the stria terminalis.
   c. nucleus accumbens and prefrontal cortex
   d. ventral tegmental area

6. Choose the correct statement.
   a. Stress does not increase sensitivity to the effects of drugs because the pharmacological effects of drugs are constant.
   b. Stress that occurs in infancy has no effect on susceptibility to drugs in adult rats.
   c. Susceptibility to drug craving is decreased if the animal experiences some social satisfaction.
   d. Stress has a greater effect on the probability of acquiring a drug habit than on the probability of relapsing after recovery.

7. Animals with a knockout gene for the μ opiate receptor are _____ to the _____ effects of morphine.
   a. somewhat more sensitive; analgesic
   b. completely insensitive; analgesic
   c. somewhat less sensitive; reinforcing
   d. somewhat more sensitive; reinforcing

8. Several studies suggest that unlike other addictive drugs, the reinforcing effects of the opiates

a. occur only when dopamine is released in the mesolimbic system.
b. cannot be blocked by injections of naloxone.
c. can result from activation of the opiate receptors in the nucleus accumbens alone.
d. usually cause the release of endogenous opioids as well.

9. Results from research using the antagonist-precipitated withdrawal procedure indicate that opiate receptors in the _____ are responsible for withdrawal symptoms.

a. locus coeruleus and the periaqueductal gray matter
b. nucleus accumbens and prefrontal cortex
c. locus coeruleus and the amygdala
d. bed nucleus of the stria terminalis and central nucleus of the amygdala

10. Cocaine _____ and amphetamine _____.

a. stimulates the reuptake of dopamine; inhibits the reuptake of dopamine
b. stimulates dopamine synthesis; does the same, but for a shorter period of time
c. stimulates the release of dopamine before synaptic vesicles reach the presynaptic membrane; blocks postsynaptic receptors
d. deactivates dopamine transporter molecules; stimulates dopamine release by terminal buttons

11. The most effective reinforcer of all available drugs is probably

a. heroin.
b. cocaine.
c. methamphetamine.
d. PCP.

12. Subjects who found the effect of methylphenidate pleasing were more likely

a. to have lower levels of D_2 receptors in the striatum.
b. to have damage to the terminals of serotonergic axons.
c. to show reduced metabolic activity in the orbitofrontal cortex.
d. to show volume reductions in the caudate nucleus and putamen.

Lesson II: Heredity and Drug Abuse, and Therapy for Drug Abuse

Read the interim summary on page 635 in your text to re-acquaint yourself with the material in this section.

Learning Objective 18-5 Describe the behavioral and physical effects of nicotine.

Read pages 628-631 and answer the following questions.

1. To underscore the serious consequences of smoking, complete these sentences.

a. Nicotine accounts for more deaths than

b. The WHO estimates that 50 percent of the people who begin to smoke as adolescents

c. The leading cause of preventable death in developing countries is (Dani and Harris, 2005)

d. By the year 2020, tobacco use

e. Although nicotine has negative effects on developing fetuses, approximately 25 percent of pregnant women

f. Growing evidence suggests that compulsive tobacco use is not merely a habit, but

2. How does nicotine affect

a. acetylcholine receptors?

b. dopaminergic neurons of the mesolimbic system? (Mereu et al., 1987)

c. the nucleus accumbens? (Study Figure 18.15 in your text. Damsma et al., 1989)

3. The reinforcing effects of nicotine appear to be caused by activation of nicotinic receptors in the

______________ ______________ ______________.

4. If a nicotinic agonist is injected directly into the ventral tegmental area, how is a conditioned place preference affected? (Museo and Wise, 1994)

5. If a nicotinic antagonist is

   a. injected into the VTA, how are the effects of an intravenous injection of nicotine affected? (Corrigall et al., 1994)

   b. injected into the nucleus accumbens, how is reinforcement affected?

   c. infused into the VTA, but not the nucleus accumbens, how are the effects of an intravenous injection of nicotine affected? (See Figure 18.16 in your text. Nisell et al., 1994)

6. a. What is the pharmacological effect of rimonabant on CB1 receptors, which detect the presence of the endogenous opioids?

   b. How do injections of this drug affect

      1. a conditioned place preference in rats? (Forget et al., 2005)

      2. self-administration of nicotine and nicotine-seeking behavior? (Cohen et al., 2005)

   c. How may rimonabant alter the effects of nicotine? (De Vries and Schoffelmeer, 2005)

7. a. Explain the effects of acetylcholine on nicotinic ACh receptors during the few milliseconds from its release to its destruction.

   b. After the neurotransmitter is destroyed, what is the state of a few ACh receptors?

   c. When a person smokes and the level of nicotine slowly rises, how do ACh receptors respond?

   d. What, then, are the two effects of nicotine on ACh receptors?

   e. How may desensitization affect the number of these receptors? (Dani and De Biasi, 2001)

8. a. Using the concept of desensitization, explain why the first cigarette of the day is the most pleasurable.

   b. Why, according to smokers, do they smoke later in the day?

9. a. Why is it likely nicotine causes other changes in the brain?

   b. What may be one of these changes? (Mansvelder and McGehee, 2000)

10. What are some of the symptoms of nicotine withdrawal? Explain why they contribute to a resumption of smoking, but not to addiction. (Hughes et al., 1989; Fung et al., 1996)

11. a. When a person stops smoking, what often happens to their weight?

    b. Carefully explain how the absence of nicotine affects the secretion of MCH and appetite. (Jo et al., 2005)

Learning Objective 18-6 Describe the behavioral and physical effects of alcohol and cannabis.

Read pages 631-635 and answer the following questions.

1. To establish the importance of understanding the behavioral and physiological effects of this drug, summarize some of the social costs of alcohol use, especially its effect on brain development.

2. When during pregnancy and how long after birth does alcohol have the most serious effects on brain development?

3. What did the study of immature rats exposed to alcohol indicate is the cause of fetal brain damage? (See Figure 18.17 in your text. Ikonomidou et al., 2000.)

4. How did exposure to alcohol somewhat later in life affect behavior? (Siciliano and Smith, 2001)

5. Define *anxiolytic* in your own words.

6. Explain how the anxiolytic effects of low doses of alcohol influence the behavior of both laboratory animals and people. (Koob et al., 1984)

7. a. What behavior reflects the positive reinforcement of alcohol? the negative reinforcement?

   b. Explain why the negative reinforcement provided by alcohol alone does not explain its addictive potential.

8. Explain why laboratory animals will not ingest enough alcohol to experience its reinforcing effects unless the alcohol solution is sweetened. (Reid, 1996)

9. a. How does alcohol affect the mesolimbic system? the nucleus accumbens? (Gessa et al., 1985; Imperato and Di Chiara, 1986)

   b. How can the reinforcing effects of alcohol and alcohol intake be reduced? Why? (Samson et al., 1993; Hodge et al., 1993; Enggasser and de Wit, 2001)

10. a. Alcohol acts as an indirect antagonist at _______________ receptors and it acts as an indirect agonist at _______________ receptors. (Chandler et al., 1998)

    b. In other words, how does alcohol affect the neurotransmitters glutamate and GABA?

11. a. Compare the effects of alcohol with those of other NMDA antagonists. (Tabakoff and Hoffman, 1996; Imperato et al., 1990; Loscher et al., 1991)

    b. How may alcohol affect NMDA receptors and cognitive function? (Givens and McMahon et al., 1995; Matthews et al., 1996)

12. a. Carefully explain what happens to NMDA receptors when an alcoholic suddenly stops drinking. (Diana et al., 1993)

    b. How is this medical emergency treated? Why?

13. a. Two strains of mice have been used to study sudden alcohol withdrawal. How did the brains of withdrawal-seizure-prone mice differ from those of resistant mice? (Valverius et al., 1990)

    b. What treatment prevented seizures, and what does its effectiveness suggest about the role of NMDA receptors in producing seizures? (Liljequist, 1991)

14. a. Explain what happens when alcohol binds with the $GABA_A$ receptor.

    b. In the presence of alcohol, how is the IPSP produced by GABA altered? (Proctor et al., 1992)

    c. Therefore, what action of alcohol may produce its anxiolytic effect?

15. a. Where may the sedative effects of alcohol occur?

    b. How can these effects be blocked?

    c. What would be the tragic consequences of the use of this drug? (See Figure 18.17 in your text. Suzdak et al., 1986)

16. a. What were the results of a PET scan to study the effects of alcohol on dopamine D2 receptors? (Volkow et al., 1996)

    b. Researchers used a harmless virus to increase the D2 receptor genes in the nucleus accumbens of rats who had been trained to drink alcohol. How was alcohol intake affected at first and then later? (Thanos et al., 2001)

17. Why do opiate receptor blockers such as naloxone block the reinforcing effects of alcohol? (Altschuler et al., 1980; Davidson et al., 1996; Reid, 1996)

18. Explain how endogenous opioids may contribute to a craving for alcohol in people who have stopped drinking. (See Figure 18.19 in your text. Heinz et al., 2005)

19. a. Identify the active ingredient in marijuana and its receptor.

    b. How is dopamine release in the nucleus accumbens affected by low doses of THC injected into the

       1. bodies of rats? (See Figure 18.20 in your text. Chen et al., 1990)

       2. ventral tegmental area?

       3. nucleus accumbens itself? (Chen et al., 1993)

    c. Therefore, where in the brain does THC appear to act?

20. The reinforcing effects of which addictive drugs were blocked by a targeted mutation that prevents the production of the CB1 receptor? Which ones were not? (Cossu et al., 2001; Houchi et al., 2005; Soria et al., 2005)

21. a. How does THC use affect the ability of users to converse?

    b. How is the drug thought to disrupt the normal functioning of the hippocampus and interfere with memory and long-term potentiation? (Kunos and Batkai, 2001; Hampson and Deadwyler, 2000)

Read the interim summary on page 637 in your text to re-acquaint yourself with the material in this section.

Learning Objective 18-7 Describe research on the role that heredity plays in addiction.

Read pages 636-637 and answer the following questions.

1. _______________ and _______________ are the only two possible sources of individual differences in any characteristic.

2. Summarize the results of a study of over 3,000 male twin pairs to assess genetic contributions to drug abuse. (Tsuang et al., 1998)
   a. How was the abuse of any category of drugs associated with the abuse of all other categories?
   b. Abuse of which drug was especially influenced by family environmental factors?
   c. Abuse of which drug was especially influenced by unique genetic factors?

3. What did a different study of male twin pairs conclude about the influence of genetics and environment on 1) trying a drug, 2) using it recreationally, and 3) becoming addicted to a drug? (Kendler et al., 2003)

4. What were the results of another twin study to attempt to measure the heritability of various classes of addictive drugs? (See Figure 18.21 in your text. Goldman et al., 2005)

5. a. Approximately what percent of the population of the United States drinks 50 percent of the alcohol? (Heckler, 1983)
   b. What is the primary reason for this imbalance?

6. Describe the two principal types of alcoholics—binge drinkers and steady drinkers. (Cloninger, 1987)

7. Steady drinking, which is associated with _______________ _______________ _______________, is strongly influenced by _______________, and binge drinking, which is associated with _______________ _______________, is strongly influenced by both _______________ and _______________. Steady drinkers usually begin drinking _______________ in life, but binge drinkers begin much _______________.

8. How did having a steady drinking biological father affect the sons? the daughters? Be sure to use the term *somatization disorder* in your answer.

9. Offer two possible explanations for a susceptibility to alcoholism.
   a.
   b.

10. a. What aspect of metabolism could play a part in alcohol addiction? Be sure to mention alcohol dehydrogenase.

    b. How do people with a particular variant of the gene for this enzyme, which is prevalent in eastern Asia, react to alcohol? (Goldman et al., 2005)

11. a. Describe some of the personality characteristics of

        1. steady drinkers.

        2. binge drinkers.

    b. What does Cloninger suggest may account for these differences?

12. a. Explain how undersensitive punishment and/or reinforcement systems may contribute to steady drinking. Heath et al., 1999)

    b. If binge drinkers do have oversensitive punishment systems, how may they overcome them to drink excessively?

13. How may differences in specific neurotransmitters systems contribute to a susceptibility to addiction? (Edenberg et al., 2004; Wang et al., 2004; Bart et al., 2005)

Read the interim summary on page 641 in your text to re-acquaint yourself with the material in this section.

Learning Objective 18-8 Discuss different methods of therapy for drug abuse.

Read pages 639-640 and answer the following questions.

1. Describe the most common treatment for opiate addiction. Be sure to explain why treatment is given orally.

2. a. Name a promising new drug for the treatment of opiate addiction. (Vocci et al., 2005)

   b. How does this drug affect the brain to block the effects of opiates? Be sure to explain how partial agonists affect receptors and how their effects differ from those of normal ligands.

3. a. Describe the two different drug treatments recovering opiate addicts received in a study of the effectiveness of buprenorphine and naloxone in treating drug addiction. (Fudala et al., 2003)

   b. Which drug therapy was more effective after one month?

   c. For the next eleven months, what treatment did all subjects receive?

d. What was the range of the abstinence rate for these subjects over the eleven month period?

e. What is an administrative advantage of buprenorphine?

4. a. Emergency rooms treat patients who have taken an overdose of heroin with drugs that act as ________________ ________________ ________________.

   b. Why are drugs that either block or stimulate dopamine receptors not used to treat addiction?

5. a. Describe how Carrera et al. (1996) managed to "immunize" rats to cocaine.

   b. What further research have these results suggested? (Kosten and Owens, 2005)

6. a. Describe how Dewey et al., (1997) reduced the reinforcing effects of cocaine in baboons. Be sure to mention GVG in your answer.

   b. What other addictive drug is affected by GVG? (Dewey et al., 1999)

7. Describe nicotine maintenance as a treatment for withdrawal from cigarette smoking. (See Figure 18.23 in your text.)

8. a. What other type of addiction has rimonabant successfully treated? (Henningfield et al., 2005)

   b. What undesirable side effect of stopping smoking does not occur using rimonabant? Why not?

9. What is the pharmacological action of bupropion, an antidepressant drug, that is being used to treat nicotine addiction? (Brody et al., 2004)

10. How do serotonin agonists help treat addiction to alcohol? (Naranjo et al., 1992)

11. College students who participated in research on social drinking took either naltrexone or a placebo. How did these procedures affect their behavior when they were given alcoholic beverages during test sessions? (Davidson et al., 1996)

12. Describe the effectiveness of programs using naltrexone to treat alcohol abuse. (See Figure 18.24 in your text. O'Brien et al., 1996)

13. a. What other drug appears to be a promising treatment for alcoholism? What may be its site of action? (Wickelgren, 1998)

    b. How has the effectiveness of this drug been further improved? (Soyke and Chick, 2003)

Lesson II Self Test

1. The reinforcing effects of nicotine appear to occur in the

   a. locus coeruleus.
   b. striate nucleus.
   c. ventral tegmental area.
   d. periaqueductal gray matter.

2. The first cigarette of the day brings the most pleasure because after a night's abstinence

   a. the airways into the lungs are less irritated.
   b. nicotinic receptors are in the closed state.
   c. dopamine levels have risen after a night's sleep.
   d. the effects of nicotine are augmented by the caffeine in morning coffee.

3. One of the leading cause of mental retardation in the Western world today results from _____ by pregnant women.

   a. cocaine and heroin use
   b. alcohol consumption
   c. sudden unsupervised drug cessation and withdrawal symptoms
   d. the combined effects of the use of caffeine and nicotine

4. The anxiolytic effect of alcohol

   a. reduces the discomfort of anxiety.
   b. forces the drinker to consume more and more to feel the same effects.
   c. reinforces social controls on behavior.
   d. provides positive reinforcement.

5. Alcohol appears to act on the following receptor(s):

   a. D_2 and D_3 receptors.
   b. THC receptors.
   c. NMDA receptors and $GABA_A$ receptors.
   d. CB1 receptors and ACh receptors.

6. THC may affect memory by disrupting the normal function of

   a. acetylcholine receptors.
   b. $GABA_A$ receptors.
   c. the nucleus accumbens.
   d. the hippocampus.

7. The reinforcing effects of smoking marijuana can be abolished by administering a drug that

   a. blocks CB1 receptors.
   b. stimulates hippocampal pyramidal cells.
   c. stimulates the release of endogenous cannabinoids.
   d. increases dopamine release in the nucleus accumbens.

8. Steady drinkers are most likely to

   a. be male; have a biological parent who is a steady drinker; begin drinking late in life.
   b. be male; have a father who is a steady drinker; begin drinking early in life.
   c. be female; have two biological parents who are alcoholic; drink secretly.
   d. be either male or female; be exposed to a family environment of heavy drinking; begin drinking early in life.

9. Twin studies of the genetic and environmental factors of drug use and addiction concluded that

   a. marijuana abuse is particularly influenced by heredity, and heroin abuse is particularly influenced by family environmental factors.
   b. environmental factors play a stronger role in influencing a person to try a drug, and heredity plays a stronger role in determining whether a person becomes addicted.
   c. heredity plays a stronger role in drug addiction by males than by females.
   d. drug abuse is a specific addiction, that is, people who abuse a particular drug are no more likely to abuse other drugs.

10. Methadone

    a. has short-acting effects on the brain, thus necessitating frequent doses to treat addiction.
    b. blocks opiate receptors so successfully that even a large dose of heroin has little effect.
    c. is administered orally to opiate addicts, which increases the opiate level in the brain slowly.
    d. maintenance for opiate addiction is successful because methadone is not an addictive drug.

11. A life-saving treatment for heroin overdose is

    a. naloxone or naltrexone.
    b. methadone.
    c. gamma-vinyl GABA (GVG).
    d. acamprosate.

12. Work with "cocaine-immunized" rats suggests a treatment for addiction based on developing

a. enzymes to destroy the chemical precursors of dopamine.
b. a means to prevent the reinforcing effects of all pleasurable stimuli.
c. antibodies to the drug.
d. a vaccine to prevent dopamine from reaching the nucleus accumbens.

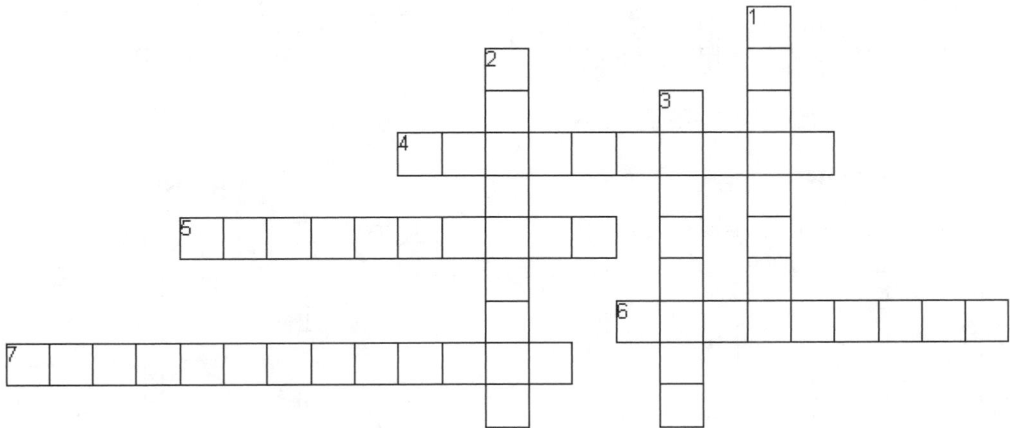

Across

4. Symptoms opposite to those produced by a drug when the drug is suddenly no longer taken; caused by the presence of compensatory mechanisms
5. A drug that blocks cannabinoid CB1 receptors
6. The fact that increasingly large doses of drugs must be taken to achieve a particular effect; caused by compensatory mechanisms that oppose the effect of the drug
7. A drug that serves as a partial agonist for the μ opioid receptor; reduces craving for opiates

Down

1. A form of reinforcement caused by the removal or reduction of an aversive stimulus that is contingent on a particular response
2. An opiate given in oral form; used to treat heroin addicts
3. A drug that blocks μ opiate receptors; antagonizes the reinforcing and sedative effects of opiates

Answers for Self Tests

Lesson I

1. d Obj. 18-1
2. b Obj. 18-1
3. c Obj. 18-1
4. c Obj. 18-2
5. c Obj. 18-2
6. c Obj. 18-2
7. b Obj. 18-3
8. c Obj. 18-3
9. a Obj. 18-3
10. d Obj. 18-4
11. b Obj. 18-4
12. a Obj. 18-4

Lesson II

1. c Obj. 18-5
2. b Obj. 18-5
3. b Obj. 18-6
4. a Obj. 18-6
5. c Obj. 18-6
6. d Obj. 18-6
7. a Obj. 18-6
8. b Obj. 18-7
9. b Obj. 18-7
10. c Obj. 18-8
11. a Obj. 18-8
12. c Obj. 18-8

Chapter 1

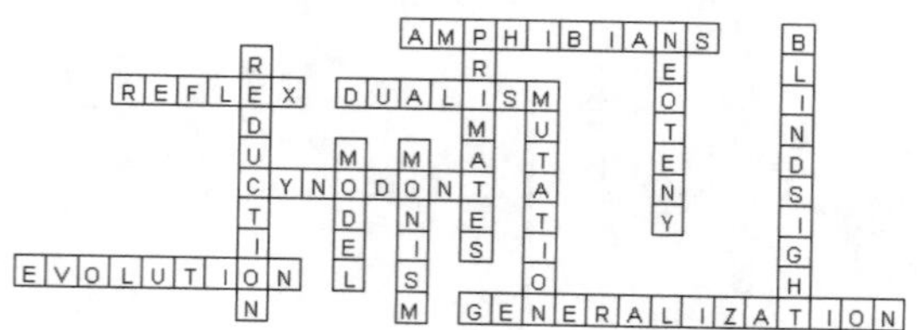

Chapter 2

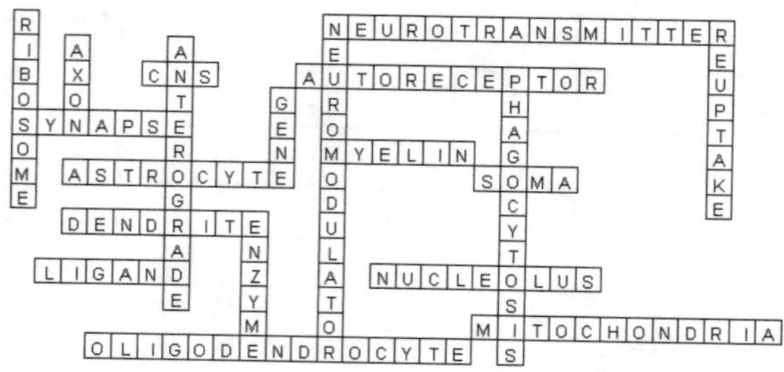

Chapter 3, Puzzle 1

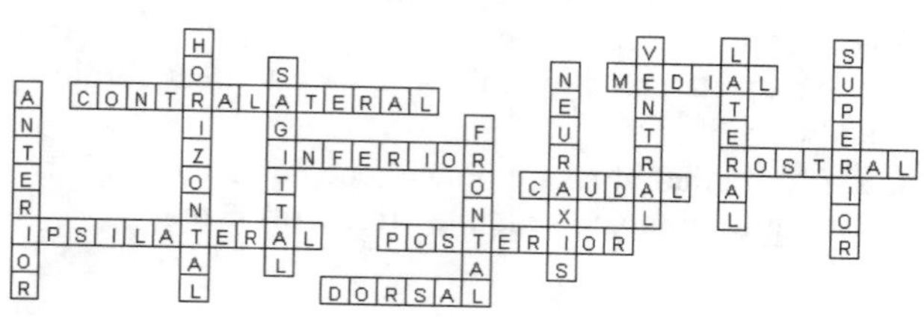

Chapter 3, Puzzle 2

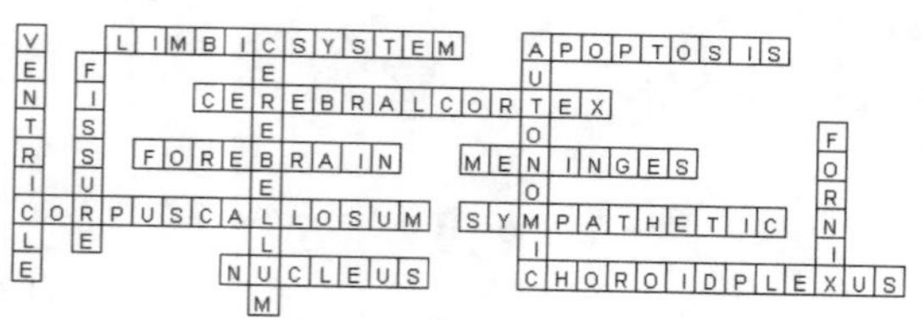

Chapter 4

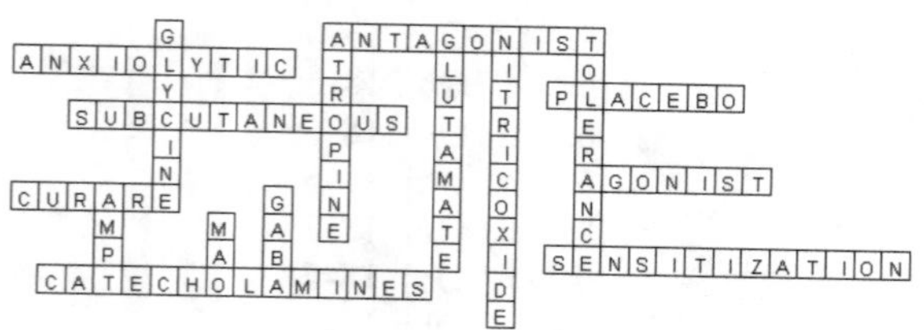

Chapter 5

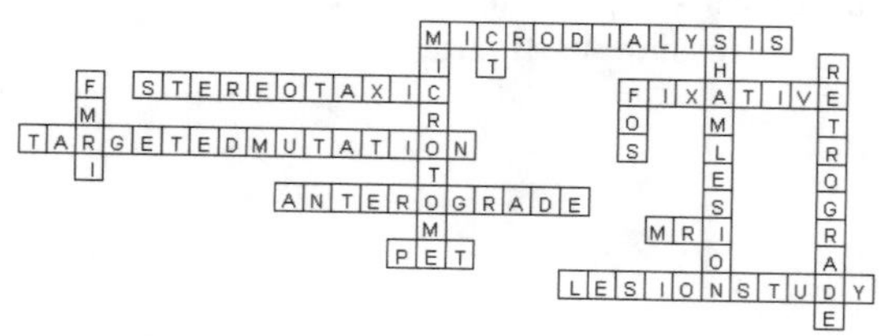

Chapter 6

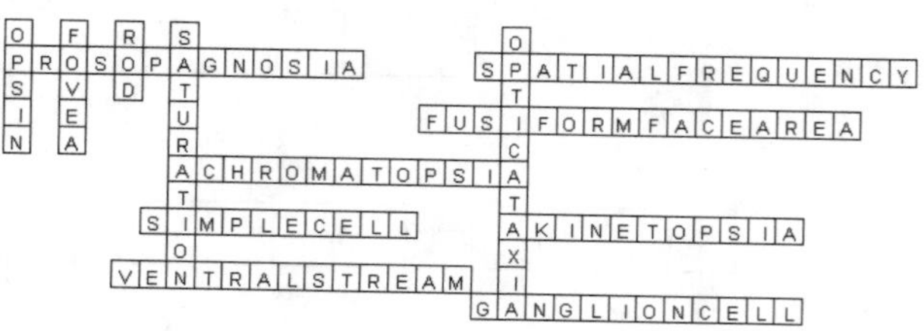

Chapter 7

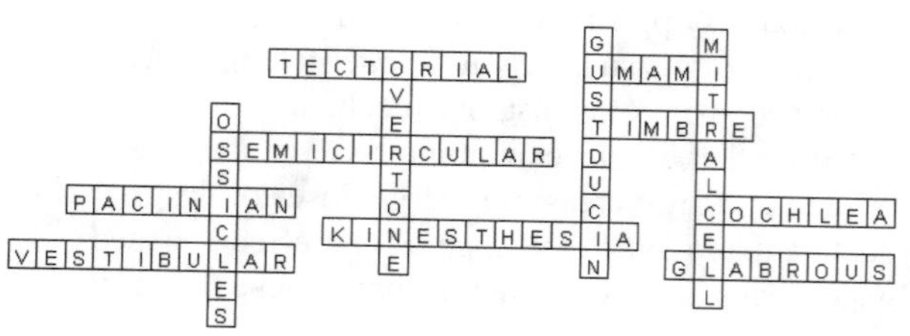

Chapter 8

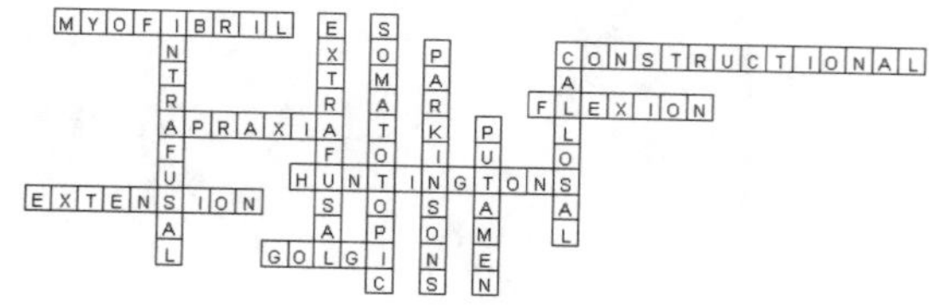

Chapter 9

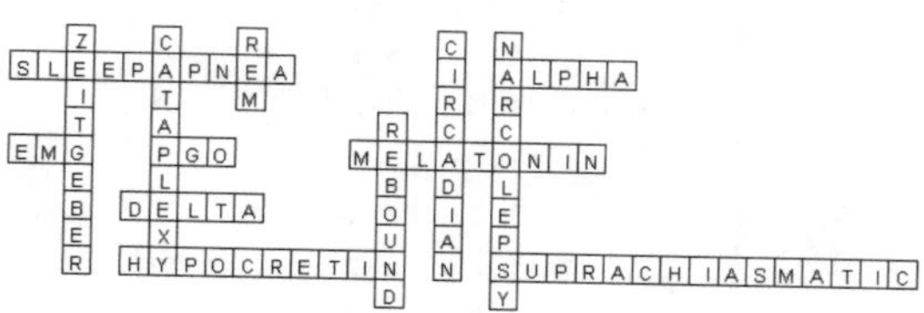

Chapter 10

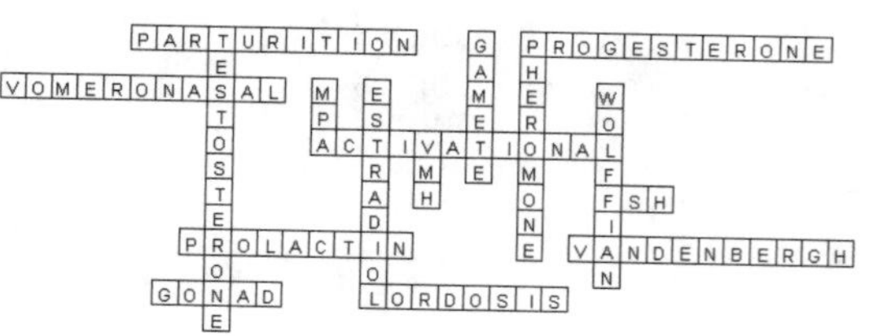

Chapter 11

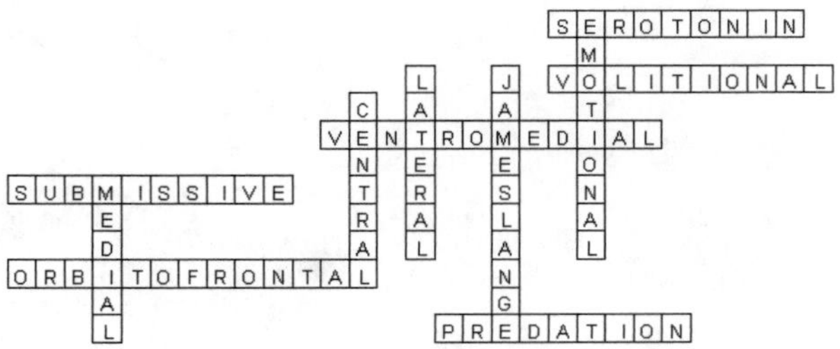

Chapter 12

Chapter 13

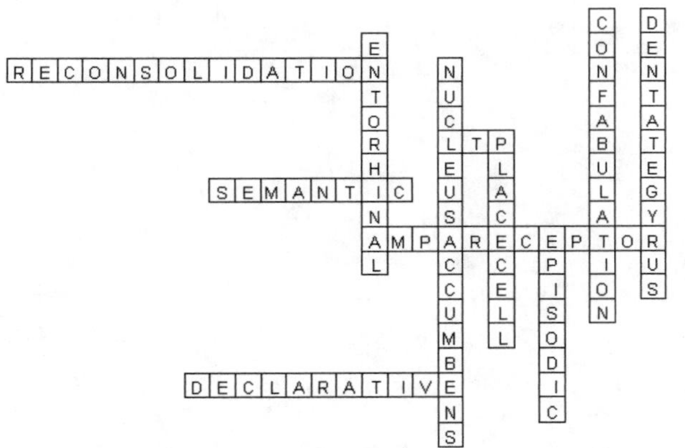

Chapter 14

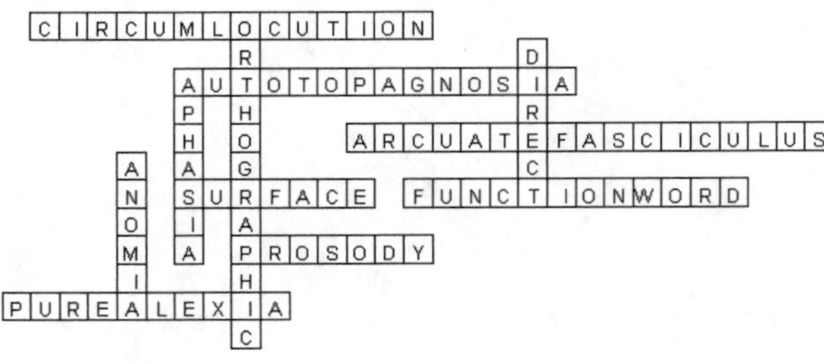

Chapter 15

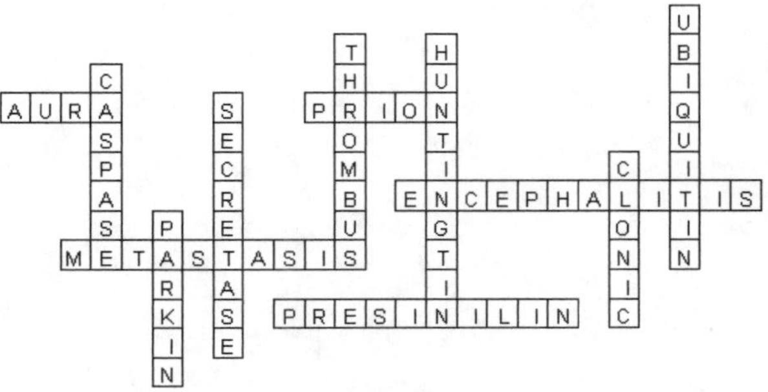

Chapter 16

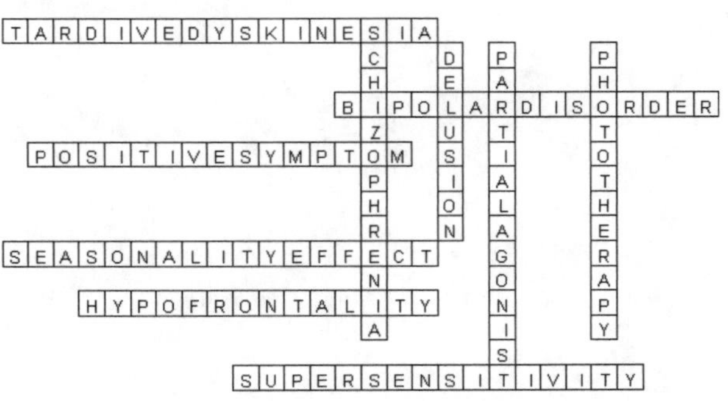

Chapter 17

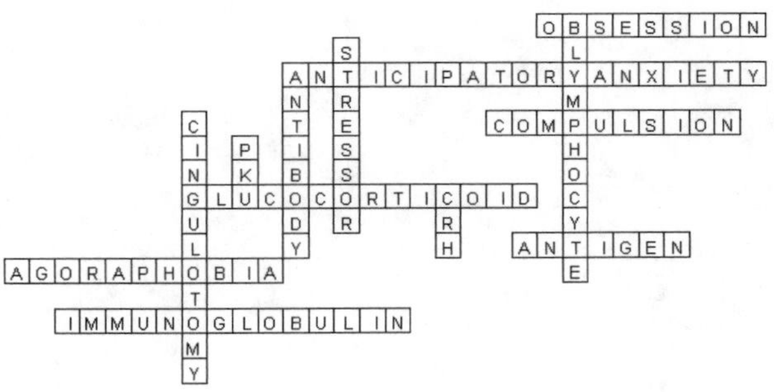

Chapter 18

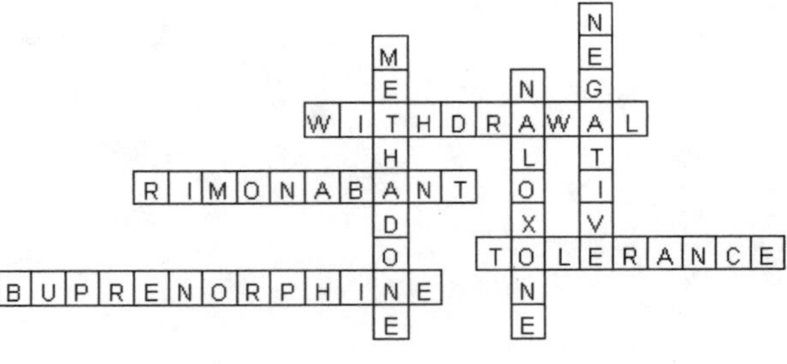

1.1 dualism	1.10 reflex
1.2 monism	1.11 model
1.3 blindsight	1.12 doctrine of specific nerve energies
1.4 corpus callosum	1.13 experimental ablation
1.5 split-brain operation	1.14 functionalism
1.6 cerebral hemispheres	1.15 natural selection
1.7 unilateral neglect	1.16 mutation
1.8 generalization	1.17 selective advantage
1.9 reduction	1.18 evolution

1.10 An automatic, stereotyped movement that is produced as the direct result of a stimulus.	1.1 The belief that the body is physical but the mind (or soul) is not.
1.11 A mathematical or physical analogy for a physiological process; for example, computers have been used as models for various functions of the brain.	1.2 The belief that the world consists only of matter and energy and that the mind is a phenomenon produced by the workings of the nervous system.
1.12 Müller's conclusion that because all nerve fibers carry the same type of message, sensory information must be specified by the particular nerve fibers that are active.	1.3 The ability of a person who cannot see objects in his or her blind field to accurately reach for them while remaining unconscious of perceiving them; caused by damage to the "mammalian" visual system of the brain.
1.13 The research method in which the function of a part of the brain is inferred by observing the behaviors an animal can no longer perform after that part is damaged.	1.4 The largest commissure of the brain, interconnecting the areas of neocortex on each side of the brain.
1.14 The principle that the best way to understand a biological phenomenon (a behavior or a physiological structure) is to try to understand its useful functions for the organism.	1.5 Brain surgery that is occasionally performed to treat a form of epilepsy; the surgeon cuts the corpus callosum, which connects the two hemispheres of the brain.
1.15 The process by which inherited traits that confer a selective advantage (increase an animal's likelihood to live and reproduce) become more prevalent in a population.	1.6 The two symmetrical halves of the brain; constitute the major part of the brain.
1.16 A change in the genetic information contained in the chromosomes of sperms or eggs, which can be passed on to an organism's offspring; provides genetic variability.	1.7 A syndrome in which people ignore objects located toward their left and the left sides of objects located anywhere; most often caused by damage to the right parietal lobe.
1.17 A characteristic of an organism that permits it to produce more than the average number of offspring of its species.	1.8 A type of scientific explanation; a general conclusion based on many observations of similar phenomena.
1.18 A gradual change in the structure and physiology of plant and animal species—generally producing more complex organisms—as a result of natural selection.	1.9 A type of scientific explanation; a phenomenon is described in terms of the more elementary processes that underlie it.

1.19 neoteny	2.8 synapse
1.20 physiological psychologist	2.9 axon
2.1 sensory neuron	2.10 multipolar neuron
2.2 motor neuron	2.11 bipolar neuron
2.3 interneuron	2.12 unipolar neuron
2.4 central nervous system (CNS)	2.13 terminal button
2.5 peripheral nervous system (PNS)	2.14 neurotransmitter
2.6 soma	2.15 membrane
2.7 dendrite	2.16 nucleus

2.8 A junction between the terminal button of an axon and the membrane of another neuron.	1.19 A slowing of the process of maturation, allowing more time for growth; an important factor in the development of large brains.
2.9 The long, thin, cylindrical structure that conveys information from the soma of a neuron to its terminal buttons.	1.20 A scientist who studies the physiology of behavior, primarily by performing physiological and behavioral experiments with laboratory animals.
2.10 A neuron with one axon and many dendrites attached to its soma.	2.1 A neuron that detects changes in the external or internal environment and sends information about these changes to the central nervous system.
2.11 A neuron with one axon and one dendrite attached to its soma.	2.2 A neuron located within the central nervous system that controls the contraction of a muscle or the secretion of a gland.
2.12 A neuron with one axon attached to its soma; the axon divides, with one branch receiving sensory information and the other sending the information into the central nervous system.	2.3 A neuron located entirely within the central nervous system.
2.13 The bud at the end of a branch of an axon; forms synapses with another neuron; sends information to that neuron.	2.4 The brain and spinal cord.
2.14 A chemical that is released by a terminal button; has an excitatory or inhibitory effect on another neuron.	2.5 The part of the nervous system outside the brain and spinal cord, including the nerves attached to the brain and spinal cord.
2.15 A structure consisting principally of lipid molecules that defines the outer boundaries of a cell and also constitutes many of the cell organelles, such as the Golgi apparatus.	2.6 The cell body of a neuron, which contains the nucleus.
2.16 A structure in the central region of a cell, containing the nucleolus and chromosomes.	2.7 A branched, treelike structure attached to the soma of a neuron; receives information from the terminal buttons of other neurons.

2.17 nucleolus	2.26 mitochondrion
2.18 ribosome	2.27 adenosine triphosphate (ATP)
2.19 chromosome	2.28 endoplasmic reticulum
2.20 deoxyribonucleic acid (DNA)	2.29 Golgi apparatus
2.21 gene	2.30 exocytosis
2.22 messenger ribonucleic acid (mRNA)	2.31 lysosome
2.23 enzyme	2.32 cytoskeleton
2.24 non-coding RNA (ncRNA)	2.33 microtubule
2.25 cytoplasm	2.34 axoplasmic transport

2.26 An organelle that is responsible for extracting energy from nutrients.	2.17 A structure within the nucleus of a cell that produces the ribosomes.
2.27 A molecule of prime importance to cellular energy metabolism; its breakdown liberates energy.	2.18 A cytoplasmic structure, made of protein, that serves as the site of production of proteins translated from mRNA.
2.28 Parallel layers of membrane found within the cytoplasm of a cell. The rough kind contains ribosomes and is involved with production of proteins that are secreted by the cell. The smooth kind is the site of lipid synthesis and provides channels for the segregation of molecules involved in various cellular processes.	2.19 A strand of DNA, with associated proteins, found in the nucleus; carries genetic information.
2.29 A complex of parallel membranes in the cytoplasm that wraps the products of a secretory cell.	2.20 A long, complex macromolecule consisting of two interconnected helical strands; along with associated proteins, strands of DNA constitute the chromosomes.
2.30 The secretion of a substance by a cell through means of vesicles; the process by which neurotransmitters are secreted.	2.21 The functional unit of the chromosome, which directs synthesis of one or more proteins.
2.31 An organelle surrounded by membrane; contains enzymes that break down waste products.	2.22 A macromolecule that delivers genetic information concerning the synthesis of a protein from a portion of a chromosome to a ribosome.
2.32 Formed of microtubules and other protein fibers, linked to each other and forming a cohesive mass that gives a cell its shape.	2.23 A molecule that controls a chemical reaction, combining two substances or breaking a substance into two parts.
2.33 A long strand of bundles of protein filaments arranged around a hollow core; part of the cytoskeleton and involved in transporting substances from place to place within the cell.	2.24 A form of RNA that does not encode for protein, but has functions of its own.
2.34 An active process by which substances are propelled along microtubules that run the length of the axon.	2.25 The viscous, semiliquid substance contained in the interior of a cell.

2.35 anterograde	2.44 Schwann cell
2.36 retrograde	2.45 blood–brain barrier
2.37 glia	2.46 area postrema
2.38 astrocyte	2.47 electrode
2.39 phagocytosis	2.48 microelectrode
2.40 oligodendrocyte	2.49 membrane potential
2.41 myelin sheath	2.50 oscilloscope
2.42 node of Ranvier	2.51 resting potential
2.43 microglia	2.52 depolarization

2.44 A cell in the peripheral nervous system that is wrapped around a myelinated axon, providing one segment of its myelin sheath.	2.35 In a direction along an axon from the cell body toward the terminal buttons.
2.45 A semipermeable barrier between the blood and the brain produced by the cells in the walls of the brain's capillaries.	2.36 In a direction along an axon from the terminal buttons toward the cell body.
2.46 A region of the medulla where the blood-brain barrier is weak; poisons can be detected there and can initiate vomiting.	2.37 The supporting cells of the central nervous system.
2.47 A conductive medium that can be used to apply electrical stimulation or to record electrical potentials.	2.38 A glial cell that provides support for neurons of the central nervous system, provides nutrients and other substances, and regulates the chemical composition of the extracellular fluid.
2.48 A very fine electrode, generally used to record activity of individual neurons.	2.39 The process by which cells engulf and digest other cells or debris caused by cellular degeneration.
2.49 The electrical charge across a cell membrane; the difference in electrical potential inside and outside the cell.	2.40 A type of glial cell in the central nervous system that forms myelin sheaths.
2.50 A laboratory instrument that is capable of displaying a graph of voltage as a function of time on the face of a cathode ray tube.	2.41 A sheath that surrounds axons and insulates them, preventing messages from spreading between adjacent axons.
2.51 The membrane potential of a neuron when it is not being altered by excitatory or inhibitory postsynaptic potentials; approximately -70 mV in the giant squid axon.	2.42 A naked portion of a myelinated axon, between adjacent oligodendroglia or Schwann cells.
2.52 Reduction (toward zero) of the membrane potential of a cell from its normal resting potential.	2.43 The smallest of glial cells; act as phagocytes and protect the brain from invading microorganisms.

2.53 hyperpolarization	2.62 sodium-potassium transporter
2.54 action potential	2.63 ion channel
2.55 threshold of excitation	2.64 voltage-dependent ion channel
2.56 diffusion	2.65 all-or-none law
2.57 electrolyte	2.66 rate law
2.58 ion	2.67 cable properties
2.59 electrostatic pressure	2.68 saltatory conduction
2.60 intracellular fluid	2.69 postsynaptic potential
2.61 extracellular fluid	2.70 binding site

2.62 A protein found in the membrane of all cells that extrudes sodium ions from and transports potassium ions into the cell.	2.53 An increase in the membrane potential of a cell, relative to the normal resting potential.
2.63 A specialized protein molecule that permits specific ions to enter or leave cells.	2.54 The brief electrical impulse that provides the basis for conduction of information along an axon.
2.64 An ion channel that opens or closes according to the value of the membrane potential.	2.55 The value of the membrane potential that must be reached to produce an action potential.
2.65 The principle that once an action potential is triggered in an axon, it is propagated, without decrement, to the end of the fiber.	2.56 Movement of molecules from regions of high concentration to regions of low concentration.
2.66 The principle that variations in the intensity of a stimulus or other information being transmitted in an axon are represented by variations in the rate at which that axon fires.	2.57 An aqueous solution of a material that ionizes—namely, a soluble acid, base, or salt.
2.67 The passive conduction of electrical current, in a decremental fashion, down the length of an axon.	2.58 A charged molecule. Cations are positively charged, and anions are negatively charged.
2.68 Conduction of action potentials by myelinated axons. The action potential appears to jump from one node of Ranvier to the next.	2.59 The attractive force between atomic particles charged with opposite signs or the repulsive force between atomic particles charged with the same sign.
2.69 Alterations in the membrane potential of a postsynaptic neuron, produced by liberation of neurotransmitter at the synapse.	2.60 The fluid contained within cells.
2.70 The location on a receptor protein to which a ligand binds.	2.61 Body fluids located outside of cells.

2.71 ligand	2.80 ionotropic receptor
2.72 dendritic spine	2.81 metabotropic receptor
2.73 presynaptic membrane	2.82 G protein
2.74 postsynaptic membrane	2.83 second messenger
2.75 synaptic cleft	2.84 excitatory postsynaptic potential (EPSP)
2.76 synaptic vesicle	2.85 inhibitory postsynaptic potential (IPSP)
2.77 release zone	2.86 reuptake
2.78 postsynaptic receptor	2.87 enzymatic deactivation
2.79 neurotransmitter-dependent ion channel	2.88 acetylcholine (ACh)

2.80
A receptor that contains a binding site for a neurotransmitter and an ion channel that opens when a molecule of the neurotransmitter attaches to the binding site.

2.81
A receptor that contains a binding site for a neurotransmitter; activates an enzyme that begins a series of events that opens an ion channel elsewhere in the membrane of the cell when a molecule of the neurotransmitter attaches to the binding site.

2.82
A protein coupled to a metabotropic receptor; conveys messages to other molecules when a ligand binds with and activates the receptor.

2.83
A chemical produced when a G protein activates an enzyme; carries a signal that results in the opening of the ion channel or causes other events to occur in the cell.

2.84
An excitatory depolarization of the postsynaptic membrane of a synapse caused by the liberation of a neurotransmitter by the terminal button.

2.85
An inhibitory hyperpolarization of the postsynaptic membrane of a synapse caused by the liberation of a neurotransmitter by the terminal button.

2.86
The reentry of a neurotransmitter just liberated by a terminal button back through its membrane, thus terminating the postsynaptic potential.

2.87
The destruction of a neurotransmitter by an enzyme after its release—for example, the destruction of acetylcholine by acetylcholinesterase.

2.88
A neurotransmitter found in the brain, spinal cord, and parts of the peripheral nervous system; responsible for muscular contraction.

2.71
A chemical that binds with the binding site of a receptor.

2.72
A small bud on the surface of a dendrite, with which a terminal button of another neuron forms a synapse.

2.73
The membrane of a terminal button that lies adjacent to the postsynaptic membrane and through which the neurotransmitter is released.

2.74
The cell membrane opposite the terminal button in a synapse; the membrane of the cell that receives the message.

2.75
The space between the presynaptic membrane and the postsynaptic membrane.

2.76
A small, hollow, beadlike structure found in terminal buttons; contains molecules of a neurotransmitter.

2.77
A region of the interior of the presynaptic membrane of a synapse to which synaptic vesicles attach and release their neurotransmitter into the synaptic cleft.

2.78
A receptor molecule in the postsynaptic membrane of a synapse that contains a binding site for a neurotransmitter.

2.79
An ion channel that opens when a molecule of a neurotransmitter binds with a postsynaptic receptor.

2.89 acetylcholinesterase (AChE)	2.98 endocrine gland
2.90 neural integration	2.99 target cell
2.91 autoreceptor	2.100 steroid
2.92 presynaptic inhibition	3.1 neuraxis
2.93 presynaptic facilitation	3.2 anterior
2.94 gap junction	3.3 posterior
2.95 neuromodulator	3.4 rostral
2.96 peptide	3.5 caudal
2.97 hormone	3.6 dorsal

2.98
A gland that liberates its secretions into the extracellular fluid around capillaries and hence into the bloodstream.

2.99
The type of cell that is directly affected by a hormone or other chemical signal.

2.100
A chemical of low molecular weight, derived from cholesterol. Steroid hormones affect their target cells by attaching to receptors found within the nucleus.

3.1
An imaginary line drawn through the center of the length of the central nervous system, from the bottom of the spinal cord to the front of the forebrain.

3.2
With respect to the central nervous system, located near or toward the head.

3.3
With respect to the central nervous system, located near or toward the tail.

3.4
"Toward the beak"; with respect to the central nervous system, in a direction along the neuraxis toward the front of the face.

3.5
"Toward the tail"; with respect to the central nervous system, in a direction along the neuraxis away from the front of the face.

3.6
"Toward the back"; with respect to the central nervous system, in a direction perpendicular to the neuraxis toward the top of the head or the back.

2.89
The enzyme that destroys acetylcholine soon after it is liberated by the terminal buttons, thus terminating the postsynaptic potential.

2.90
The process by which inhibitory and excitatory postsynaptic potentials summate and control the rate of firing of a neuron.

2.91
A receptor molecule located on a neuron that responds to the neurotransmitter released by that neuron.

2.92
The action of a presynaptic terminal button in an axoaxonic synapse; reduces the amount of neurotransmitter released by the postsynaptic terminal button.

2.93
The action of a presynaptic terminal button in an axoaxonic synapse; increases the amount of neurotransmitter released by the postsynaptic terminal button.

2.94
A special junction between cells that permits direct communication by means of electrical coupling.

2.95
A naturally secreted substance that acts like a neurotransmitter except that it is not restricted to the synaptic cleft but diffuses through the extracellular fluid.

2.96
A chain of amino acids joined together by peptide bonds. Most neuromodulators, and some hormones, consist of peptide molecules.

2.97
A chemical substance that is released by an endocrine gland that has effects on target cells in other organs.

3.7 **ventral**	3.16 **midsagittal plane**
3.8 **lateral**	3.17 **meninges (singular: meninx)**
3.9 **medial**	3.18 **dura mater**
3.10 **ipsilateral**	3.19 **arachnoid membrane**
3.11 **contralateral**	3.20 **pia mater**
3.12 **cross section**	3.21 **subarachnoid space**
3.13 **frontal section**	3.22 **cerebrospinal fluid (CSF)**
3.14 **horizontal section**	3.23 **ventricle**
3.15 **sagittal section**	3.24 **lateral ventricle**

3.16 The plane through the neuraxis perpendicular to the ground; divides the brain into two symmetrical halves.	3.7 "Toward the belly"; with respect to the central nervous system, in a direction perpendicular to the neuraxis toward the bottom of the skull or the front surface of the body.
3.17 The three layers of tissue that encase the central nervous system: the dura mater, arachnoid membrane, and pia mater.	3.8 Toward the side of the body, away from the middle.
3.18 The outermost of the meninges; tough and flexible.	3.9 Toward the middle of the body, away from the side.
3.19 The middle layer of the meninges, located between the outer dura mater and inner pia mater.	3.10 Located on the same side of the body.
3.20 The layer of the meninges that clings to the surface of the brain; thin and delicate.	3.11 Located on the opposite side of the body.
3.21 The fluid-filled space that cushions the brain; located between the arachnoid membrane and the pia mater.	3.12 With respect to the central nervous system, a slice taken at right angles to the neuraxis.
3.22 A clear fluid, similar to blood plasma, that fills the ventricular system of the brain and the subarachnoid space surrounding the brain and spinal cord.	3.13 A slice through the brain parallel to the forehead.
3.23 One of the hollow spaces within the brain, filled with cerebrospinal fluid.	3.14 A slice through the brain parallel to the ground.
3.24 One of the two ventricles located in the center of the telencephalon.	3.15 A slice through the brain parallel to the neuraxis and perpendicular to the ground.

3.25 third ventricle	3.34 cerebral cortex
3.26 cerebral aqueduct	3.35 radial glia
3.27 fourth ventricle	3.36 founder cells
3.28 choroid plexus	3.37 symmetrical division
3.29 arachnoid granulation	3.38 asymmetrical division
3.30 superior sagittal sinus	3.39 apoptosis
3.31 obstructive hydrocephalus	3.40 forebrain
3.32 neural tube	3.41 cerebral hemisphere
3.33 ventricular zone	3.42 subcortical region

3.34
The outermost layer of gray matter of the cerebral hemispheres.

3.35
Special glia with fibers that grow radially outward from the ventricular zone to the surface of the cortex; provide guidance for neurons migrating outward during brain development.

3.36
Cells of the ventricular zone that divide and give rise to cells of the central nervous system.

3.37
Division of a founder cell that gives rise to two identical founder cells; increases the size of the ventricular zone and hence the brain that develops from it.

3.38
Division of a founder cell that gives rise to another founder cell and a neuron, which migrates away from the ventricular zone toward its final resting place in the brain.

3.39
Death of a cell caused by a chemical signal that activates a genetic mechanism inside the cell.

3.40
The most rostral of the three major divisions of the brain; includes the telencephalon and diencephalon.

3.41
One of the two major portions of the forebrain, covered by the cerebral cortex.

3.42
The region located within the brain, beneath the cortical surface.

3.25
The ventricle located in the center of the diencephalon.

3.26
A narrow tube interconnecting the third and fourth ventricles of the brain, located in the center of the mesencephalon.

3.27
The ventricle located between the cerebellum and the dorsal pons, in the center of the metencephalon.

3.28
The highly vascular tissue that protrudes into the ventricles and produces cerebrospinal fluid.

3.29
Small projections of the arachnoid membrane through the dura mater into the superior sagittal sinus; CSF flows through them to be reabsorbed into the blood supply.

3.30
A venous sinus located in the midline just dorsal to the corpus callosum, between the two cerebral hemispheres.

3.31
A condition in which all or some of the brain's ventricles are enlarged; caused by an obstruction that impedes the normal flow of CSF.

3.32
A hollow tube, closed at the rostral end, that forms from ectodermal tissue early in embryonic development; serves as the origin of the central nervous system.

3.33
A layer of cells that line the inside of the neural tube; contains founder cells that divide and give rise to cells of the central nervous system.

3.43 sulcus (plural: sulci)	3.52 insular cortex
3.44 fissure	3.53 primary motor cortex
3.45 gyrus (plural: gyri)	3.54 frontal lobe
3.46 primary visual cortex	3.55 parietal lobe
3.47 calcarine fissure	3.56 temporal lobe
3.48 primary auditory cortex	3.57 occipital lobe
3.49 lateral fissure	3.58 sensory association cortex
3.50 primary somatosensory cortex	3.59 motor association cortex
3.51 central sulcus	3.60 prefrontal cortex

3.52 A sunken region of the cerebral cortex that is normally covered by the rostral superior temporal lobe and caudal inferior frontal lobe.	3.43 A groove in the surface of the cerebral hemisphere, smaller than a fissure.
3.53 The region of the posterior frontal lobe that contains neurons that control movements of skeletal muscles.	3.44 A major groove in the surface of the brain, larger than a sulcus.
3.54 The anterior portion of the cerebral cortex, rostral to the parietal lobe and dorsal to the temporal lobe.	3.45 A convolution of the cortex of the cerebral hemispheres, separated by sulci or fissures.
3.55 The region of the cerebral cortex caudal to the frontal lobe and dorsal to the temporal lobe.	3.46 The region of the posterior occipital lobe whose primary input is from the visual system.
3.56 The region of the cerebral cortex rostral to the occipital lobe and ventral to the parietal and frontal lobes.	3.47 A fissure located in the occipital lobe on the medial surface of the brain; most of the primary visual cortex is located along its upper and lower banks.
3.57 The region of the cerebral cortex caudal to the parietal and temporal lobes.	3.48 The region of the superior temporal lobe whose primary input is from the auditory system.
3.58 Those regions of the cerebral cortex that receive information from the regions of primary sensory cortex.	3.49 The fissure that separates the temporal lobe from the overlying frontal and parietal lobes.
3.59 The region of the frontal lobe rostral to the primary motor cortex; also known as the premotor cortex.	3.50 The region of the anterior parietal lobe whose primary input is from the somatosensory system.
3.60 The region of the frontal lobe rostral to the motor association cortex.	3.51 The sulcus that separates the frontal lobe from the parietal lobe.

3.61 corpus callosum	3.70 basal ganglia
3.62 neocortex	3.71 nucleus (plural: nuclei)
3.63 limbic cortex	3.72 diencephalon
3.64 cingulate gyrus	3.73 thalamus
3.65 limbic system	3.74 projection fiber
3.66 hippocampus	3.75 lateral geniculate nucleus
3.67 amygdala	3.76 medial geniculate nucleus
3.68 fornix	3.77 ventrolateral nucleus
3.69 mammillary bodies	3.78 hypothalamus

3.70 A group of subcortical nuclei in the telencephalon, the caudate nucleus, the globus pallidus, and the putamen; important parts of the motor system.	3.61 A large bundle of axons that interconnects corresponding regions of the association cortex on each side of the brain.
3.71 An identifiable group of neural cell bodies in the central nervous system.	3.62 The phylogenetically newest cortex, including the primary sensory cortex, primary motor cortex, and association cortex.
3.72 A region of the forebrain surrounding the third ventricle; includes the thalamus and the hypothalamus.	3.63 Phylogenetically old cortex, located at the medial edge ("limbus") of the cerebral hemispheres; part of the limbic system.
3.73 The largest portion of the diencephalon, located above the hypothalamus; contains nuclei that project information to specific regions of the cerebral cortex and receive information from it.	3.64 A strip of limbic cortex lying along the lateral walls of the groove separating the cerebral hemispheres, just above the corpus callosum.
3.74 An axon of a neuron in one region of the brain whose terminals form synapses with neurons in another region.	3.65 A group of brain regions including the anterior thalamic nuclei, amygdala, hippocampus, limbic cortex, and parts of the hypothalamus, as well as their interconnecting fiber bundles.
3.75 A group of cell bodies within the lateral geniculate body of the thalamus that receives fibers from the retina and projects fibers to the primary visual cortex.	3.66 A forebrain structure of the temporal lobe, constituting an important part of the limbic system; includes the hippocampus proper (Ammon's horn), dentate gyrus, and subiculum.
3.76 A group of cell bodies within the medial geniculate body of the thalamus; receives fibers from the auditory system and projects fibers to the primary auditory cortex.	3.67 A structure in the interior of the rostral temporal lobe, containing a set of nuclei; part of the limbic system.
3.77 A nucleus of the thalamus that receives inputs from the cerebellum and sends axons to the primary motor cortex.	3.68 A fiber bundle that connects the hippocampus with other parts of the brain, including the mammillary bodies of the hypothalamus; part of the limbic system.
3.78 The group of nuclei of the diencephalon situated beneath the thalamus; involved in regulation of the autonomic nervous system, control of the anterior and posterior pituitary glands, and integration of species-typical behaviors.	3.69 A protrusion of the bottom of the brain at the posterior end of the hypothalamus, containing some hypothalamic nuclei; part of the limbic system.

3.79 **optic chiasm**	3.88 **brain stem**
3.80 **anterior pituitary gland**	3.89 **tegmentum**
3.81 **neurosecretory cell**	3.90 **reticular formation**
3.82 **posterior pituitary gland**	3.91 **periaqueductal gray matter**
3.83 **midbrain**	3.92 **red nucleus**
3.84 **mesencephalon**	3.93 **substantia nigra**
3.85 **tectum**	3.94 **hindbrain**
3.86 **superior colliculi**	3.95 **cerebellum**
3.87 **inferior colliculi**	3.96 **cerebellar cortex**

3.88 The "stem" of the brain, from the medulla to the diencephalon, excluding the cerebellum.	3.79 An X-shaped connection between the optic nerves, located below the base of the brain, just anterior to the pituitary gland.
3.89 The ventral part of the midbrain; includes the periaqueductal gray matter, reticular formation, red nucleus, and substantia nigra.	3.80 The anterior part of the pituitary gland; an endocrine gland whose secretions are controlled by the hypothalamic hormones.
3.90 A large network of neural tissue located in the central region of the brain stem, from the medulla to the diencephalon.	3.81 A neuron that secretes a hormone or hormonelike substance.
3.91 The region of the midbrain surrounding the cerebral aqueduct; contains neural circuits involved in species-typical behaviors.	3.82 The posterior part of the pituitary gland; an endocrine gland that contains hormone-secreting terminal buttons of axons whose cell bodies lie within the hypothalamus.
3.92 A large nucleus of the midbrain that receives inputs from the cerebellum and motor cortex and sends axons to motor neurons in the spinal cord.	3.83 The mesencephalon; the central of the three major divisions of the brain.
3.93 A darkly stained region of the tegmentum that contains neurons that communicate with the caudate nucleus and putamen in the basal ganglia.	3.84 The midbrain; a region of the brain that surrounds the cerebral aqueduct; includes the tectum and the tegmentum.
3.94 The most caudal of the three major divisions of the brain; includes the metencephalon and myelencephalon.	3.85 The dorsal part of the midbrain; includes the superior and inferior colliculi.
3.95 A major part of the brain located dorsal to the pons, containing the two cerebellar hemispheres, covered with the cerebellar cortex; an important component of the motor system.	3.86 Protrusions on top of the midbrain; part of the visual system.
3.96 The cortex that covers the surface of the cerebellum.	3.87 Protrusions on top of the midbrain; part of the auditory system.

3.97 deep cerebellar nuclei	3.106 ventral root
3.98 cerebellar peduncle	3.107 spinal nerve
3.99 pons	3.108 afferent axon
3.100 medulla oblongata	3.109 dorsal root ganglion
3.101 spinal cord	3.110 efferent axon
3.102 spinal root	3.111 cranial nerve
3.103 cauda equina	3.112 vagus nerve
3.104 caudal block	3.113 olfactory bulb
3.105 dorsal root	3.114 somatic nervous system

3.106 The spinal root that contains outgoing (efferent) motor fibers.	3.97 Nuclei located within the cerebellar hemispheres; receive projections from the cerebellar cortex and send projections out of the cerebellum to other parts of the brain.
3.107 A peripheral nerve attached to the spinal cord.	3.98 One of three bundles of axons that attach each cerebellar hemisphere to the dorsal pons.
3.108 An axon directed toward the central nervous system, conveying sensory information.	3.99 The region of the metencephalon rostral to the medulla, caudal to the midbrain, and ventral to the cerebellum.
3.109 A nodule on a dorsal root that contains cell bodies of afferent spinal nerve neurons.	3.100 The most caudal portion of the brain; located in the myelencephalon, immediately rostral to the spinal cord.
3.110 An axon directed away from the central nervous system, conveying motor commands to muscles and glands.	3.101 The cord of nervous tissue that extends caudally from the medulla.
3.111 A peripheral nerve attached directly to the brain.	3.102 A bundle of axons surrounded by connective tissue that occurs in pairs, which fuse and form a spinal nerve.
3.112 The largest of the cranial nerves, conveying efferent fibers of the parasympathetic division of the autonomic nervous system to organs of the thoracic and abdominal cavities.	3.103 A bundle of spinal roots located caudal to the end of the spinal cord.
3.113 The protrusion at the end of the olfactory nerve; receives input from the olfactory receptors.	3.104 The anesthesia and paralysis of the lower part of the body produced by injection of a local anesthetic into the cerebrospinal fluid surrounding the cauda equina.
3.114 The part of the peripheral nervous system that controls the movement of skeletal muscles or transmits somatosensory information to the central nervous system.	3.105 The spinal root that contains incoming (afferent) sensory fibers.

3.115 autonomic nervous system (ANS)	4.2 drug effect
3.116 sympathetic division	4.3 sites of action
3.117 sympathetic ganglia	4.4 pharmacokinetics
3.118 sympathetic ganglion chain	4.5 intravenous (IV) injection
3.119 preganglionic neuron	4.6 intraperitoneal (IP) injection
3.120 postganglionic neuron	4.7 intramuscular (IM) injection
3.121 adrenal medulla	4.8 subcutaneous (SC) injection
3.122 parasympathetic division	4.9 oral administration
4.1 psychopharmacology	4.10 sublingual administration

4.2 The changes a drug produces in an animal's physiological processes and behavior.	3.115 The portion of the peripheral nervous system that controls the body's vegetative functions.
4.3 The locations at which molecules of drugs interact with molecules located on or in cells of the body, thus affecting some biochemical processes of these cells.	3.116 The portion of the autonomic nervous system that controls functions that accompany arousal and expenditure of energy.
4.4 The process by which drugs are absorbed, distributed within the body, metabolized, and excreted.	3.117 Nodules that contain synapses between preganglionic and postganglionic neurons of the sympathetic nervous system.
4.5 Injection of a substance directly into a vein.	3.118 One of a pair of groups of sympathetic ganglia that lie ventrolateral to the vertebral column.
4.6 Injection of a substance into the peritoneal cavity—the space that surrounds the stomach, intestines, liver, and other abdominal organs.	3.119 The efferent neuron of the autonomic nervous system whose cell body is located in a cranial nerve nucleus or in the intermediate horn of the spinal gray matter and whose terminal buttons synapse upon postganglionic neurons in the autonomic ganglia.
4.7 Injection of a substance into a muscle.	3.120 Neurons of the autonomic nervous system that form synapses directly with their target organ.
4.8 Injection of a substance into the space beneath the skin.	3.121 The inner portion of the adrenal gland, located atop the kidney, controlled by sympathetic nerve fibers; secretes epinephrine and norepinephrine.
4.9 Administration of a substance into the mouth, so that it is swallowed.	3.122 The portion of the autonomic nervous system that controls functions that occur during a relaxed state.
4.10 Administration of a substance by placing it beneath the tongue.	4.1 The study of the effects of drugs on the nervous system and on behavior.

4.11 intrarectal administration	4.20 affinity
4.12 inhalation	4.21 tolerance
4.13 topical administration	4.22 sensitization
4.14 intracerebral administration	4.23 withdrawal symptom
4.15 intracerebroventricular (ICV) administration	4.24 placebo
4.16 depot binding	4.25 antagonist
4.17 albumin	4.26 agonist
4.18 dose-response curve	4.27 direct agonist
4.19 therapeutic index	4.28 receptor blocker

4.20
The readiness with which two molecules join together.

4.11
Administration of a substance into the rectum.

4.21
A decrease in the effectiveness of a drug that is administered repeatedly.

4.12
Administration of a vaporous substance into the lungs.

4.22
An increase in the effectiveness of a drug that is administered repeatedly.

4.13
Administration of a substance directly onto the skin or mucous membrane.

4.23
The appearance of symptoms opposite to those produced by a drug when the drug is administered repeatedly and then suddenly no longer taken.

4.14
Administration of a substance directly into the brain.

4.24
An inert substance that is given to an organism in lieu of a physiologically active drug; used experimentally to control for the effects of mere administration of a drug.

4.15
Administration of a substance into one of the cerebral ventricles.

4.25
A drug that opposes or inhibits the effects of a particular neurotransmitter on the postsynaptic cell.

4.16
Binding of a drug with various tissues of the body or with proteins in the blood.

4.26
A drug that facilitates the effects of a particular neurotransmitter on the postsynaptic cell.

4.17
A protein found in the blood; serves to transport free fatty acids and can bind with some lipid-soluble drugs.

4.27
A drug that binds with and activates a receptor.

4.18
A graph of the magnitude of an effect of a drug as a function of the amount of drug administered.

4.28
A drug that binds with a receptor but does not activate it; prevents the natural ligand from binding with the receptor.

4.19
The ratio between the dose that produces the desired effect in 50 percent of the animals and the dose that produces toxic effects in 50 percent of the animals.

4.29 direct antagonist	4.38 hemicholinium
4.30 noncompetitive binding	4.39 neostigmine
4.31 indirect antagonist	4.40 nicotinic receptor
4.32 indirect agonist	4.41 muscarinic receptor
4.33 presynaptic heteroreceptor	4.42 atropine
4.34 acetyl-CoA	4.43 curare
4.35 choline acetyltransferase (ChAT)	4.44 monoamine
4.36 botulinum toxin	4.45 catecholamine
4.37 black widow spider venom	4.46 dopamine (DA)

4.38 A drug that inhibits the uptake of choline.	4.29 A synonym for receptor blocker.
4.39 A drug that inhibits the activity of acetylcholinesterase.	4.30 Binding of a drug to a site on a receptor; does not interfere with the binding site for the principal ligand.
4.40 An ionotropic acetylcholine receptor that is stimulated by nicotine and blocked by curare.	4.31 A drug that attaches to a binding site on a receptor and interferes with the action of the receptor; does not interfere with the binding site for the principal ligand.
4.41 A metabotropic acetylcholine receptor that is stimulated by muscarine and blocked by atropine.	4.32 A drug that attaches to a binding site on a receptor and facilitates the action of the receptor; does not interfere with the binding site for the principal ligand.
4.42 A drug that blocks muscarinic acetylcholine receptors.	4.33 A receptor located in the membrane of a terminal button that receives input from another terminal button by means of an axoaxonic synapse; binds with the neurotransmitter released by the presynaptic terminal button.
4.43 A drug that blocks nicotinic acetylcholine receptors.	4.34 A cofactor that supplies acetate for the synthesis of acetylcholine.
4.44 A class of amines that includes indolamines such as serotonin and catecholamines such as dopamine, norepinephrine, and epinephrine.	4.35 The enzyme that transfers the acetate ion from acetyl coenzyme A to choline, producing the neurotransmitter acetylcholine.
4.45 A class of amines that includes the neurotransmitters dopamine, norepinephrine, and epinephrine.	4.36 An acetylcholine antagonist; prevents release by terminal buttons.
4.46 A neurotransmitter; one of the catecholamines.	4.37 A poison produced by the black widow spider that triggers the release of acetylcholine.

4.47 L-DOPA	4.56 monoamine oxidase (MAO)
4.48 nigrostriatal system	4.57 deprenyl
4.49 mesolimbic system	4.58 chlorpromazine
4.50 mesocortical system	4.59 norepinephrine (NE)
4.51 Parkinson's disease	4.60 epinephrine
4.52 AMPT	4.61 fusaric acid
4.53 reserpine	4.62 moclobemide
4.54 apomorphine	4.63 locus coeruleus
4.55 methylphenidate	4.64 axonal varicosity

4.56 A class of enzymes that destroy the monoamines: dopamine, norepinephrine, and serotonin.	4.47 The levorotatory form of DOPA; the precursor of the catecholamines; often used to treat Parkinson's disease because of its effect as a dopamine agonist.
4.57 A drug that blocks the activity of MAO-B; acts as a dopamine agonist.	4.48 A system of neurons originating in the substantia nigra and terminating in the neostriatum (caudate nucleus and putamen).
4.58 A drug that reduces the symptoms of schizophrenia by blocking dopamine D2 receptors.	4.49 A system of dopaminergic neurons originating in the ventral tegmental area and terminating in the nucleus accumbens, amygdala, and hippocampus.
4.59 One of the catecholamines; a neurotransmitter found in the brain and in the sympathetic division of the autonomic nervous system.	4.50 A system of dopaminergic neurons originating in the ventral tegmental area and terminating in the prefrontal cortex.
4.60 One of the catecholamines; a hormone secreted by the adrenal medulla; serves also as a neurotransmitter in the brain.	4.51 A neurological disease characterized by tremors, rigidity of the limbs, poor balance, and difficulty in initiating movements; caused by degeneration of the nigrostriatal system.
4.61 A drug that inhibits the activity of the enzyme dopamine-β-hydroxylase and thus blocks the production of norepinephrine.	4.52 A drug that blocks the activity of tyrosine hydroxylase and thus interferes with the synthesis of the catecholamines.
4.62 A drug that blocks the activity of MAO-A; acts as a noradrenergic agonist.	4.53 A drug that interferes with the storage of monoamines in synaptic vesicles.
4.63 A dark-colored group of noradrenergic cell bodies located in the pons near the rostral end of the floor of the fourth ventricle.	4.54 A drug that blocks dopamine autoreceptors at low doses; at higher doses, blocks postsynaptic receptors as well.
4.64 An enlarged region along the length of an axon that contains synaptic vesicles and releases a neurotransmitter or neuromodulator.	4.55 A drug that inhibits the reuptake of dopamine.

4.65 idazoxan	4.74 AMPA receptor
4.66 serotonin (5-HT)	4.75 kainate receptor
4.67 PCPA	4.76 metabotropic glutamate receptor
4.68 fluoxetine	4.77 AP5 (2-amino-5-phosphonopentanoate)
4.69 fenfluramine	4.78 PCP
4.70 LSD	4.79 GABA
4.71 MDMA	4.80 allylglycine
4.72 glutamate	4.81 muscimol
4.73 NMDA receptor	4.82 bicuculline

4.74 An ionotropic glutamate receptor that controls a sodium channel; stimulated by AMPA.	4.65 A drug that blocks presynaptic noradrenergic α2 receptors and hence acts as an agonist, facilitating the synthesis and release of NE.
4.75 An ionotropic glutamate receptor that controls a sodium channel; stimulated by kainic acid.	4.66 An indolamine neurotransmitter; also called 5-hydroxytryptamine.
4.76 A category of metabotropic receptors that are sensitive to glutamate.	4.67 A drug that inhibits the activity of tryptophan hydroxylase and thus interferes with the synthesis of 5-HT.
4.77 A drug that blocks the glutamate binding site on NMDA receptors.	4.68 A drug that inhibits the reuptake of 5-HT.
4.78 Phencyclidine; a drug that binds with the PCP binding site of the NMDA receptor and serves as an indirect antagonist.	4.69 A drug that stimulates the release of 5-HT.
4.79 An amino acid; the most important inhibitory neurotransmitter in the brain.	4.70 A drug that stimulates 5-HT2A receptors.
4.80 A drug that inhibits the activity of GAD and thus blocks the synthesis of GABA.	4.71 A drug that serves as a noradrenergic and serotonergic agonist, also known as "ecstasy"; has excitatory and hallucinogenic effects.
4.81 A direct agonist for the GABA binding site on the GABAA receptor.	4.72 An amino acid; the most important excitatory neurotransmitter in the brain.
4.82 A direct antagonist for the GABA binding site on the GABAA receptor.	4.73 A specialized ionotropic glutamate receptor that controls a calcium channel that is normally blocked by Mg^{2+} ions; has several other binding sites.

4.83 benzodiazepine	4.92 anandamide
4.84 anxiolytic	4.93 FAAH
4.85 glycine	4.94 rimonabant
4.86 strychnine	4.95 MAFP
4.87 endogenous opioid	4.96 AM1172
4.88 enkephalin	4.97 adenosine
4.89 naloxone	4.98 caffeine
4.90 endocannabinoid	4.99 nitric oxide (NO)
4.91 THC	5.1 experimental ablation

4.92 The first cannabinoid to be discovered and probably the most important one.	4.83 A category of anxiolytic drugs; an indirect agonist for the GABAA receptor.
4.93 Fatty acid amide hydrolase, the enzyme that destroys anandamide after it is brought back into the cell by anandamide transporters.	4.84 An anxiety-reducing effect.
4.94 A drug that blocks CB1 receptors.	4.85 An amino acid; an important inhibitory neurotransmitter in the lower brain stem and spinal cord.
4.95 A drug that inhibits FAAH; prevents the breakdown of anandamide.	4.86 A direct antagonist for the glycine receptor.
4.96 A drug that inhibits the reuptake of anandamide.	4.87 A class of peptides secreted by the brain that act as opiates.
4.97 A nucleoside; a combination of ribose and adenine; serves as a neuromodulator in the brain.	4.88 One of the endogenous opioids.
4.98 A drug that blocks adenosine receptors.	4.89 A drug that blocks opiate receptors.
4.99 A gas produced by cells in the nervous system; used as a means of communication between cells.	4.90 A lipid; an endogenous ligand for cannabinoid receptors, which also bind with THC, the active ingredient of marijuana.
5.1 The removal or destruction of a portion of the brain of a laboratory animal; presumably, the functions that can no longer be performed are the ones the region previously controlled.	4.91 The active ingredient in marijuana; activates CB1 receptors in the brain.

5.2 lesion study	5.11 formalin
5.3 excitotoxic lesion	5.12 perfusion
5.4 6-hydroxydopamine (6-HD)	5.13 microtome
5.5 sham lesion	5.14 transmission electron microscope
5.6 stereotaxic surgery	5.15 scanning electron microscope
5.7 bregma	5.16 confocal laser scanning microscope
5.8 stereotaxic atlas	5.17 anterograde labeling method
5.9 stereotaxic apparatus	5.18 PHA-L
5.10 fixative	5.19 immunocytochemical method

5.11
The aqueous solution of formaldehyde gas; the most commonly used tissue fixative.

5.2
A synonym for experimental ablation.

5.12
The process by which an animal's blood is replaced by a fluid such as a saline solution or a fixative in preparing the brain for histological examination.

5.3
A brain lesion produced by intracerebral injection of an excitatory amino acid, such as kainic acid.

5.13
An instrument that produces very thin slices of body tissues.

5.4
A chemical that is selectively taken up by axons and terminal buttons of noradrenergic or dopaminergic neurons and acts as a poison, damaging or killing them.

5.14
A microscope that passes a focused beam of electrons through thin slices of tissue to reveal extremely small details.

5.5
A placebo procedure that duplicates all the steps of producing a brain lesion except for the one that actually causes the brain damage.

5.15
A microscope that provides three-dimensional information about the shape of the surface of a small object by scanning the object with a thin beam of electrons.

5.6
Brain surgery using a stereotaxic apparatus to position an electrode or cannula in a specified position of the brain.

5.16
A microscope that provides high-resolution images of various depths of thick tissue that contains fluorescent molecules by scanning the tissue with light from a laser beam.

5.7
The junction of the sagittal and coronal sutures of the skull; often used as a reference point for stereotaxic brain surgery.

5.17
A histological method that labels the axons and terminal buttons of neurons whose cell bodies are located in a particular region.

5.8
A collection of drawings of sections of the brain of a particular animal with measurements that provide coordinates for stereotaxic surgery.

5.18
Phaseolus vulgaris leukoagglutinin; a protein derived from kidney beans and used as an anterograde tracer; taken up by dendrites and cell bodies and carried to the ends of the axons.

5.9
A device that permits a surgeon to position an electrode or cannula into a specific part of the brain.

5.19
A histological method that uses radioactive antibodies or antibodies bound with a dye molecule to indicate the presence of particular proteins of peptides.

5.10
A chemical such as formalin; used to prepare and preserve body tissue.

5.20 retrograde labeling method	5.29 magnetoencephalography
5.21 fluorogold	5.30 2-deoxyglucose (2-DG)
5.22 pseudorabies virus	5.31 autoradiography
5.23 computerized tomography (CT)	5.32 Fos
5.24 magnetic resonance imaging (MRI)	5.33 positron emission tomography (PET)
5.25 microelectrode	5.34 functional MRI (fMRI)
5.26 single-unit recording	5.35 microdialysis
5.27 macroelectrode	5.36 multibarreled micropipette
5.28 electroencephalogram (EEG)	5.37 microiontophoresis

5.29 A procedure that detects groups of synchronously activated neurons by means of the magnetic field induced by their electrical activity; uses an array of superconducting quantum interference devices, or SQUIDs.	5.20 A histological method that labels cell bodies that give rise to the terminal buttons that form synapses with cells in a particular region.
5.30 A sugar that enters cells along with glucose but is not metabolized.	5.21 A dye that serves as a retrograde label; taken up by terminal buttons and carried back to the cell bodies.
5.31 A procedure that locates radioactive substances in a slice of tissue; the radiation exposes a photographic emulsion or a piece of film that covers the tissue.	5.22 A weakened form of a pig herpes virus; used for transneuronal tracing, which labels a series of neurons that are interconnected synaptically.
5.32 A protein produced in the nucleus of a neuron in response to synaptic stimulation.	5.23 The use of a device that employs a computer to analyze data obtained by a scanning beam of X-rays to produce a two-dimensional picture of a "slice" through the body.
5.33 The use of a device that reveals the localization of a radioactive tracer in a living brain.	5.24 A technique whereby the interior of the body can be accurately imaged; involves the interaction between radio waves and a strong magnetic field.
5.34 A modification of the MRI procedure that permits the measurement of regional metabolism in the brain.	5.25 A very fine electrode, generally used to record activity of individual neurons.
5.35 A procedure for analyzing chemicals present in the interstitial fluid through a small piece of tubing made of a semipermeable membrane that is implanted in the brain.	5.26 Recording of the electrical activity of a single neuron.
5.36 A group of micropipettes attached together, used to infuse several different substances by means of iontophoresis while recording from a single neuron.	5.27 An electrode used to record the electrical activity of large numbers of neurons in a particular region of the brain; much larger than a microelectrode.
5.37 A procedure that uses electricity to eject a chemical from a micropipette to determine the effects of the chemical on the electrical activity of a cell.	5.28 An electrical brain potential recorded by placing electrodes on in the scalp.

5.38 transcranial magnetic stimulation	6.6 saturation
5.39 in situ hybridization	6.7 vergence movement
5.40 double labeling	6.8 saccadic movement
5.41 targeted mutation	6.9 pursuit movement
6.1 sensory receptor	6.10 accommodation
6.2 sensory transduction	6.11 retina
6.3 receptor potential	6.12 rod
6.4 hue	6.13 cone
6.5 brightness	6.14 photoreceptor

6.6 One of the perceptual dimensions of color; purity.	5.38 Stimulation of the cerebral cortex by means of magnetic fields produced by passing pulses of electricity through a coil of wire placed next to the skull; interferes with the functions of the brain region that is stimulated.
6.7 The cooperative movement of the eyes, which ensures that the image of an object falls on identical portions of both retinas.	5.39 The production of DNA complementary to a particular messenger RNA in order to detect the presence of the RNA.
6.8 The rapid, jerky movement of the eyes used in scanning a visual scene.	5.40 Labeling neurons in a particular region by two different means, for example, by using an anterograde tracer and a label for a particular enzyme.
6.9 The movement that the eyes make to maintain an image of a moving object on the fovea.	5.41 A mutated gene (also called a "knockout gene") produced in the laboratory and inserted into the chromosomes of mice; fails to produce a functional protein.
6.10 Changes in the thickness of the lens of the eye, accomplished by the ciliary muscles, that focus images of near or distant objects on the retina.	6.1 A specialized neuron that detects a particular category of physical events.
6.11 The neural tissue and photoreceptive cells located on the inner surface of the posterior portion of the eye.	6.2 The process by which sensory stimuli are transduced into slow, graded receptor potentials.
6.12 One of the receptor cells of the retina; sensitive to light of low intensity.	6.3 A slow, graded electrical potential produced by a receptor cell in response to a physical stimulus.
6.13 One of the receptor cells of the retina; maximally sensitive to one of three different wavelengths of light and hence encodes color vision.	6.4 One of the perceptual dimensions of color; the dominant wavelength.
6.14 One of the receptor cells of the retina; transduces photic energy into electrical potentials.	6.5 One of the perceptual dimensions of color; intensity.

6.15 fovea	6.24 retinal
6.16 optic disk	6.25 rhodopsin
6.17 bipolar cell	6.26 dorsal lateral geniculate nucleus
6.18 ganglion cell	6.27 magnocellular layer
6.19 horizontal cell	6.28 parvocellular layer
6.20 amacrine cell	6.29 koniocellular sublayer
6.21 lamella	6.30 calcarine fissure
6.22 photopigment	6.31 striate cortex
6.23 opsin	6.32 optic chiasm

6.24
A chemical synthesized from vitamin A; joins with an opsin to form a photopigment.

6.25
A particular opsin found in rods.

6.26
A group of cell bodies within the lateral geniculate body of the thalamus; receives inputs from the retina and projects to the primary visual cortex.

6.27
One of the inner two layers of neurons in the dorsal lateral geniculate nucleus; transmits information necessary for the perception of form, movement, depth, and small differences in brightness to the primary visual cortex.

6.28
One of the four outer layers of neurons in the dorsal lateral geniculate nucleus; transmits information necessary for perception of color and fine details to the primary visual cortex.

6.29
One of the sublayers of neurons in the dorsal lateral geniculate nucleus found ventral to each of the magnocellular and parvocellular layers; transmits information from short-wavelength ("blue") cones to the primary visual cortex.

6.30
A horizontal fissure on the inner surface of the posterior cerebral cortex; the location of the primary visual cortex.

6.31
The primary visual cortex.

6.32
A cross-shaped connection between the optic nerves, located below the base of the brain, just anterior to the pituitary gland.

6.15
The region of the retina that mediates the most acute vision of birds and higher mammals. Color-sensitive cones constitute the only type of photoreceptor found in the fovea.

6.16
The location of the exit point from the retina of the fibers of the ganglion cells that form the optic nerve; responsible for the blind spot.

6.17
A bipolar neuron located in the middle layer of the retina, conveying information from the photoreceptors to the ganglion cells.

6.18
A neuron located in the retina that receives visual information from bipolar cells; its axons give rise to the optic nerve.

6.19
A neuron in the retina that interconnects adjacent photoreceptors and the outer processes of the bipolar cells.

6.20
A neuron in the retina that interconnects adjacent ganglion cells and the inner processes of the bipolar cells.

6.21
A layer of membrane containing photopigments; found in rods and cones of the retina.

6.22
A protein dye bonded to retinal, a substance derived from vitamin A; responsible for transduction of visual information.

6.23
A class of protein that, together with retinal, constitutes the photopigments.

6.33 receptive field	6.42 sine-wave grating
6.34 protanopia	6.43 spatial frequency
6.35 deuteranopia	6.44 retinal disparity
6.36 tritanopia	6.45 cytochrome oxidase (CO) blob
6.37 negative afterimage	6.46 ocular dominance
6.38 complementary colors	6.47 extrastriate cortex
6.39 simple cell	6.48 dorsal stream
6.40 complex cell	6.49 ventral stream
6.41 hypercomplex cell	6.50 inferior temporal cortex

6.42 A series of straight parallel bands varying continuously in brightness according to a sine-wave function, along a line perpendicular to their lengths.	6.33 That portion of the visual field in which the presentation of visual stimuli will produce an alteration in the firing rate of a particular neuron.
6.43 The relative width of the bands in a sine-wave grating, measured in cycles per degree of visual angle.	6.34 An inherited form of defective color vision in which red and green hues are confused; "red" cones are filled with "green" cone opsin.
6.44 The fact that points on objects located at different distances from the observer will fall on slightly different locations on the two retinas; provides the basis for stereopsis.	6.35 An inherited form of defective color vision in which red and green hues are confused; "green" cones are filled with "red" cone opsin.
6.45 The central region of a module of the primary visual cortex, revealed by a stain for cytochrome oxidase; contains wavelength-sensitive neurons; part of the parvocellular system.	6.36 An inherited form of defective color vision in which hues with short wavelengths are confused; "blue" cones are either lacking or faulty.
6.46 The extent to which a particular neuron receives more input from one eye than from the other.	6.37 The image seen after a portion of the retina is exposed to an intense visual stimulus; consists of colors complementary to those of the physical stimulus.
6.47 A region of visual association cortex; receives fibers from the striate cortex and from the superior colliculi and projects to the inferior temporal cortex.	6.38 Colors that make white or gray when mixed together.
6.48 A system of interconnected regions of visual cortex involved in the perception of spatial location, beginning with the striate cortex and ending with the posterior parietal cortex.	6.39 An orientation-sensitive neuron in the striate cortex whose receptive field is organized in an opponent fashion.
6.49 A system of interconnected regions of visual cortex involved in the perception of form, beginning with the striate cortex and ending with the inferior temporal cortex.	6.40 A neuron in the visual cortex that responds to the presence of a line segment with a particular orientation located within its receptive field, especially when the line moves perpendicularly to its orientation.
6.50 In primates the highest level of the ventral stream of the visual association cortex; located on the inferior portion of the temporal lobe.	6.41 A neuron in the visual cortex that responds to the presence of a line segment with a particular orientation that ends at a particular point within the cell's receptive field.

6.51 color constancy	6.60 optic flow
6.52 cerebral achromatopsia	6.61 akinetopsia
6.53 visual agnosia	6.62 Balint's syndrome
6.54 apperceptive visual agnosia	6.63 optic ataxia
6.55 associative visual agnosia	6.64 ocular apraxia
6.56 prosopagnosia	6.65 simultanagnosia
6.57 fusiform face area (FFA)	6.66 intraparietal sulcus (IPS)
6.58 extrastriate body area (EBA)	7.1 pitch
6.59 parahippocampal place area (PPA)	7.2 hertz (Hz)

6.60 The complex motion of points in the visual field caused by relative movement between the observer and environment; provides information about the relative distance of objects from the observer and of the relative direction of movement.	6.51 The relatively constant appearance of the colors of objects viewed under varying lighting conditions.
6.61 Inability to perceive movement, caused by damage to area V5 (also called MST) of the visual association cortex.	6.52 Inability to discriminate among different hues; caused by damage to area V8 of the visual association cortex.
6.62 A syndrome caused by bilateral damage to the parieto-occipital region; includes optic ataxia, ocular apraxia, and simultanagnosia	6.53 Deficits in visual perception in the absence of blindness; caused by brain damage.
6.63 Difficulty in reaching for objects under visual guidance.	6.54 Failure to perceive objects, even though visual acuity is relatively normal.
6.64 Difficulty in visual scanning.	6.55 Inability to identify objects that are perceived visually, even though the form of the perceived object can be drawn or matched with similar objects.
6.65 Difficulty in perceiving more than one object at a time.	6.56 Failure to recognize particular people by the sight of their faces.
6.66 The end of the dorsal stream of the visual association cortex; involved in perception of location, visual attention, and control of eye and hand movements.	6.57 A region of the visual association cortex located in the inferior temporal; involved in perception of faces and other complex objects that require expertise to recognize.
7.1 A perceptual dimension of sound; corresponds to the fundamental frequency.	6.58 A region of the visual association cortex located in the lateral occipitotemporal cortex; involved in perception of the human body and body parts other than faces.
7.2 Cycles per second.	6.59 A region of the medial temporal cortex; involved in perception of particular places (“scenes”).

7.3

loudness

7.4

timbre

7.5

tympanic membrane

7.6

ossicle

7.7

malleus

7.8

incus

7.9

stapes

7.10

cochlea

7.11

oval window

7.12

organ of Corti

7.13

hair cell

7.14

Deiters's cell

7.15

basilar membrane

7.16

tectorial membrane

7.17

round window

7.18

cilium

7.19

tip link

7.20

insertional plaque

7.12 The sensory organ on the basilar membrane that contains the auditory hair cells.	7.3 A perceptual dimension of sound; corresponds to intensity.
7.13 The receptive cell of the auditory apparatus.	7.4 A perceptual dimension of sound; corresponds to complexity.
7.14 A supporting cell found in the organ of Corti; sustains the auditory hair cells.	7.5 The eardrum.
7.15 A membrane in the cochlea of the inner ear; contains the organ of Corti.	7.6 One of the three bones of the middle ear.
7.16 A membrane located above the basilar membrane; serves as a shelf against which the cilia of the auditory hair cells move.	7.7 The "hammer"; the first of the three ossicles.
7.17 An opening in the bone surrounding the cochlea of the inner ear that permits vibrations to be transmitted, via the oval window, into the fluid in the cochlea.	7.8 The "anvil"; the second of the three ossicles.
7.18 A hairlike appendage of a cell involved in movement or in transducing sensory information; found on the receptors in the auditory and vestibular system.	7.9 The "stirrup"; the last of the three ossicles.
7.19 An elastic filament that attaches the tip of one cilium to the side of the adjacent cilium.	7.10 The snail-shaped structure of the inner ear that contains the auditory transducing mechanisms.
7.20 The point of attachment of a tip link to a cilium.	7.11 An opening in the bone surrounding the cochlea that reveals a membrane, against which the baseplate of the stapes presses, transmitting sound vibrations into the fluid within the cochlea.

7.21 cochlear nerve	7.30 place code
7.22 olivocochlear bundle	7.31 cochlear implant
7.23 cochlear nucleus	7.32 rate code
7.24 superior olivary complex	7.33 fundamental frequency
7.25 lateral lemniscus	7.34 overtone
7.26 tonotopic representation	7.35 phase difference
7.27 core region	7.36 amusia
7.28 belt region	7.37 vestibular sac
7.29 parabelt region	7.38 semicircular canal

7.30
The system by which information about different frequencies is coded by different locations on the basilar membrane.

7.21
The branch of the auditory nerve that transmits auditory information from the cochlea to the brain.

7.31
An electronic device surgically implanted in the inner ear that can enable a deaf person to hear.

7.22
A bundle of efferent axons that travel from the olivary complex of the medulla to the auditory hair cells on the cochlea.

7.32
The system by which information about different frequencies is coded by the rate of firing of neurons in the auditory system.

7.23
One of a group of nuclei in the medulla that receive auditory information from the cochlea.

7.33
The lowest, and usually most intense, frequency of a complex sound; most often perceived as the sound's basic pitch.

7.24
A group of nuclei in the medulla; involved with auditory functions, including localization of the source of sounds.

7.34
The frequency of complex tones that occurs at multiples of the fundamental frequency.

7.25
A band of fibers running rostrally through the medulla and pons; carries fibers of the auditory system.

7.35
The difference in arrival times of sound waves at each of the eardrums.

7.26
A topographically organized mapping of different frequencies of sound that are represented in a particular region of the brain.

7.36
Loss or impairment of musical abilities, produced by hereditary factors or brain damage.

7.27
The primary auditory cortex, located on a gyrus on the dorsal surface of the temporal lobe.

7.37
One of a set of two receptor organs in each inner ear that detect changes in the tilt of the head.

7.28
The first level of auditory association cortex; surrounds the primary auditory cortex.

7.38
One of the three ringlike structures of the vestibular apparatus that detect changes in head rotation.

7.29
The second level of auditory association cortex; surrounds the belt region.

7.39 utricle	7.48 Ruffini corpuscle
7.40 saccule	7.49 Pacinian corpuscle
7.41 ampulla	7.50 Meissner's corpuscle
7.42 cupula	7.51 Merkel's disk
7.43 vestibular ganglion	7.52 phantom limb
7.44 cutaneous sense	7.53 nucleus raphe magnus
7.45 kinesthesia	7.54 umami
7.46 organic sense	7.55 chorda tympani
7.47 glabrous skin	7.56 nucleus of the solitary tract

7.48 A vibration-sensitive organ located in hairy skin.	7.39 One of the vestibular sacs.
7.49 A specialized, encapsulated somatosensory nerve ending that detects mechanical stimuli, especially vibrations.	7.40 One of the vestibular sacs.
7.50 The touch-sensitive end organs located in the papillae, small elevations of the dermis that project up into the epidermis.	7.41 An enlargement in a semicircular canal; contains the cupula and the crista.
7.51 The touch-sensitive end organs found at the base of the epidermis, adjacent to sweat ducts.	7.42 A gelatinous mass found in the ampulla of the semicircular canals; moves in response to the flow of the fluid in the canals.
7.52 Sensations that appear to originate in a limb that has been amputated.	7.43 A nodule on the vestibular nerve that contains the cell bodies of the bipolar neurons that convey vestibular information to the brain.
7.53 A nucleus of the raphe that contains serotonin-secreting neurons that project to the dorsal gray matter of the spinal cord and is involved in analgesia produced by opiates.	7.44 One of the somatosenses; includes sensitivity to stimuli that involve the skin.
7.54 The taste sensation produced by glutamate.	7.45 Perception of the body's own movements.
7.55 A branch of the facial nerve that passes beneath the eardrum; conveys taste information from the anterior part of the tongue and controls the secretion of some salivary glands.	7.46 A sense modality that arises from receptors located within the inner organs of the body.
7.56 A nucleus of the medulla that receives information from visceral organs and from the gustatory system.	7.47 Skin that does not contain hair; found on the palms and the soles of the feet.

7.57 olfactory epithelium	8.6 intrafusal muscle fiber
7.58 olfactory bulb	8.7 gamma motor neuron
7.59 mitral cell	8.8 motor unit
7.60 olfactory glomerulus	8.9 myofibril
8.1 skeletal muscle	8.10 actin
8.2 flexion	8.11 myosin
8.3 extension	8.12 striated muscle
8.4 extrafusal muscle fiber	8.13 neuromuscular junction
8.5 α motor neuron	8.14 motor endplate

8.6 A muscle fiber that functions as a stretch receptor, arranged parallel to the extrafusal muscle fibers, thus detecting changes in muscle length.	7.57 The epithelial tissue of the nasal sinus that covers the cribriform plate; contains the cilia of the olfactory receptors.
8.7 A neuron whose axons form synapses with intrafusal muscle fibers.	7.58 The protrusion at the end of the olfactory tract; receives input from the olfactory receptors.
8.8 A motor neuron and its associated muscle fibers.	7.59 A neuron located in the olfactory bulb that receives information from olfactory receptors; axons of mitral cells bring information to the rest of the brain.
8.9 An element of muscle fibers that consists of overlapping strands of actin and myosin; responsible for muscular contractions.	7.60 A bundle of dendrites of mitral cells and the associated terminal buttons of the axons of olfactory receptors.
8.10 One of the proteins (with myosin) that provide the physical basis for muscular contraction.	8.1 One of the striated muscles attached to bones.
8.11 One of the proteins (with actin) that provide the physical basis for muscular contraction.	8.2 A movement of a limb that tends to bend its joints; the opposite of extension.
8.12 Skeletal muscle; muscle that contains striations.	8.3 A movement of a limb that tends to straighten its joints; the opposite of flexion.
8.13 The synapse between the terminal buttons of an axon and a muscle fiber.	8.4 One of the muscle fibers that are responsible for the force exerted by contraction of a skeletal muscle.
8.14 The postsynaptic membrane of a neuromuscular junction.	8.5 A neuron whose axon forms synapses with extrafusal muscle fibers of a skeletal muscle; activation contracts the muscle fibers.

8.15 endplate potential	8.24 antagonist
8.16 Golgi tendon organ	8.25 somatotopic organization
8.17 smooth muscle	8.26 supplementary motor area (SMA)
8.18 cardiac muscle	8.27 premotor cortex
8.19 monosynaptic stretch reflex	8.28 mirror neurons
8.20 decerebrate	8.29 lateral group
8.21 decerebrate rigidity	8.30 ventromedial group
8.22 clasp-knife reflex	8.31 corticospinal tract
8.23 agonist	8.32 pyramidal tract

8.24 A muscle whose contraction resists or reverses a particular movement.	8.15 The postsynaptic potential that occurs in the motor endplate in response to release of acetylcholine by the terminal button.
8.25 A topographically organized mapping of parts of the body that are represented in a particular region of the brain.	8.16 The receptor organ at the junction of the tendon and muscle that is sensitive to stretch.
8.26 A region of motor association cortex of the dorsal and dorsomedial frontal lobe, rostral to the primary motor cortex.	8.17 Nonstriated muscle innervated by the autonomic nervous system, found in the walls of blood vessels, in the reproductive tracts, in sphincters, within the eye, in the digestive system, and around hair follicles.
8.27 A region of motor association cortex of the lateral frontal lobe, rostral to the primary motor cortex.	8.18 The muscle responsible for the contraction of the heart.
8.28 Neurons located in the ventral premotor cortex and inferior parietal lobule that respond when the individual makes a particular movement or sees another individual making that movement.	8.19 A reflex in which a muscle contracts in response to its being quickly stretched; involves a sensory neuron and a motor neuron, with one synapse between them.
8.29 The corticospinal tract, the corticobulbar tract, and the rubrospinal tract.	8.20 Describes an animal whose brain stem has been transected.
8.30 The vestibulospinal tract, the tectospinal tract, the reticulospinal tract, and the ventral corticospinal tract.	8.21 Simultaneous contraction of agonistic and antagonistic muscles; caused by decerebration or damage to the reticular formation.
8.31 The system of axons that originates in the motor cortex and terminates in the ventral gray matter of the spinal cord.	8.22 A reflex that occurs when force is applied to flex or extend the limb of an animal showing decerebrate rigidity; resistance is replaced by sudden relaxation.
8.32 The portion of the corticospinal tract on the ventral border of the medulla.	8.23 A muscle whose contraction produces or facilitates a particular movement.

8.33 lateral corticospinal tract	8.42 callosal apraxia
8.34 ventral corticospinal tract	8.43 sympathetic apraxia
8.35 corticobulbar tract	8.44 left parietal apraxia
8.36 rubrospinal tract	8.45 constructional apraxia
8.37 corticorubral tract	8.46 caudate nucleus
8.38 vestibulospinal tract	8.47 putamen
8.39 tectospinal tract	8.48 globus pallidus
8.40 reticulospinal tract	8.49 ventral anterior nucleus (of thalamus)
8.41 apraxia	8.50 ventrolateral nucleus (of thalamus)

8.42 An apraxia of the left hand caused by damage to the anterior corpus callosum.	8.33 The system of axons that originates in the motor cortex and terminates in the contralateral ventral gray matter of the spinal cord; controls movements of the distal limbs.
8.43 A movement disorder of the left hand caused by damage to the left frontal lobe; similar to callosal apraxia.	8.34 The system of axons that originates in the motor cortex and terminates in the ipsilateral ventral gray matter of the spinal cord; controls movements of the upper legs and trunk.
8.44 An apraxia caused by damage to the left parietal lobe; characterized by difficulty in producing sequences of movements by verbal request or in imitation of movements made by someone else.	8.35 A bundle of axons from the motor cortex to the fifth, seventh, ninth, tenth, eleventh, and twelfth cranial nerves; controls movements of the face, neck, tongue, and parts of the extraocular eye muscles.
8.45 Difficulty in drawing pictures or diagrams or in making geometrical constructions of elements such as building blocks or sticks; caused by damage to the right parietal lobe.	8.36 The system of axons that travels from the red nucleus to the spinal cord; controls independent limb movements.
8.46 A telencephalic nucleus, one of the input nuclei of basal ganglia; involved with control of voluntary movement.	8.37 The system of axons that travels from the motor cortex to the red nucleus.
8.47 A telencephalic nucleus; one of the input nuclei of the basal ganglia; involved with control of voluntary movement.	8.38 A bundle of axons that travels from the vestibular nuclei to the gray matter of the spinal cord; controls postural movements in response to information from the vestibular system.
8.48 A telencephalic nucleus; the primary output nucleus of the basal ganglia; involved with control of voluntary movement.	8.39 A bundle of axons that travels from the tectum to the spinal cord; coordinates head and trunk movements with eye movements.
8.49 A thalamic nucleus that receives projections from the basal ganglia and sends projections to the motor cortex.	8.40 A bundle of axons that travels from the reticular formation to the gray matter of the spinal cord; controls the muscles responsible for postural movements.
8.50 A thalamic nucleus that receives projections from the basal ganglia and sends projections to the motor cortex.	8.41 Difficulty in carrying out purposeful movements, in the absence of paralysis or muscular weakness.

8.51 direct pathway (in basal ganglia)	8.60 mesencephalic locomotor region
8.52 indirect pathway (in basal ganglia)	9.1 electromyogram (EMG)
8.53 Huntington's disease	9.2 electro-oculogram (EOG)
8.54 flocculonodular lobe	9.3 • activity
8.55 vermis	9.4 β activity
8.56 fastigial nucleus	9.5 theta activity
8.57 interposed nuclei	9.6 delta activity
8.58 pontine nucleus	9.7 REM sleep
8.59 dentate nucleus	9.8 non-REM sleep

8.60 A region of the reticular formation of the midbrain whose stimulation causes alternating movements of the limbs normally seen during locomotion.	8.51 The pathway that includes the caudate nucleus and putamen, the external division of the globus pallidus, the subthalamic nucleus, the internal division of the globus pallidus, and the ventral anterior/ventrolateral thalamic nuclei; has an inhibitory effect on movement.
9.1 An electrical potential recorded from an electrode placed on or in a muscle.	8.52 The pathway that includes the caudate nucleus and putamen, the internal division of the globus pallidus, and the ventral anterior/ventrolateral thalamic nuclei; has an excitatory effect on movement.
9.2 An electrical potential from the eyes, recorded by means of electrodes placed on the skin around them; detects eye movements.	8.53 A fatal inherited disorder that causes degeneration of the caudate nucleus and putamen; characterized by uncontrollable jerking movements, writhing movements, and dementia.
9.3 Smooth electrical activity of 8-12 Hz recorded from the brain; generally associated with a state of relaxation.	8.54 A region of the cerebellum; involved in control of postural reflexes.
9.4 Irregular electrical activity of 13-30 Hz recorded from the brain; generally associated with a state of arousal.	8.55 The portion of the cerebellum located at the midline; receives somatosensory information and helps to control the vestibulospinal and reticulospinal tracts through its connections with the fastigial nucleus.
9.5 EEG activity of 3.5-7.5 Hz that occurs intermittently during early stages of slow-wave sleep and REM sleep.	8.56 A deep cerebellar nucleus; involved in the control of movement by the reticulospinal and vestibulospinal tracts.
9.6 Regular, synchronous electrical activity of less than 4 Hz recorded from the brain; occurs during the deepest stages of slow-wave sleep.	8.57 A set of deep cerebellar nuclei; involved in the control of the rubrospinal system.
9.7 A period of desynchronized EEG activity during sleep, at which time dreaming, rapid eye movements, and muscular paralysis occur; also called paradoxical sleep.	8.58 A large nucleus in the pons that serves as an important source of input to the cerebellum.
9.8 All stages of sleep except REM sleep.	8.59 A deep cerebellar nucleus; involved in the control of rapid, skilled movements by the corticospinal and rubrospinal systems.

9.9 slow-wave sleep	9.18 hypocretin
9.10 basic rest-activity cycle	9.19 REM sleep behavior disorder
9.11 drug dependency insomnia	9.20 sleep-related eating disorder
9.12 sleep apnea	9.21 fatal familial insomnia
9.13 narcolepsy	9.22 rebound phenomenon
9.14 sleep attack	9.23 locus coeruleus
9.15 cataplexy	9.24 raphe nuclei
9.16 sleep paralysis	9.25 tuberomammillary nucleus (TMN)
9.17 hypnagogic hallucination	9.26 ventrolateral preoptic area (VLPA)

9.18 A peptide, also known as orexin, produced by neurons whose cell bodies are located in the hypothalamus; their destruction causes narcolepsy.	9.9 Non-REM sleep, characterized by synchronized EEG activity during its deeper stages.
9.19 A neurological disorder in which the person does not become paralyzed during REM sleep and thus acts out dreams.	9.10 A 90-minute cycle (in humans) of waxing and waning alertness, controlled by a biological clock in the caudal brain stem; controls cycles of REM sleep and slow-wave sleep.
9.20 A disorder in which the person leaves his or her bed and seeks out and eats food while sleepwalking, usually without a memory for the episode the next day.	9.11 An insomnia caused by the side effects of ever-increasing doses of sleeping medications.
9.21 A fatal inherited disorder characterized by progressive insomnia.	9.12 Cessation of breathing while sleeping.
9.22 The increased frequency or intensity of a phenomenon after it has been temporarily suppressed; for example, the increase in REM sleep seen after a period of REM sleep deprivation.	9.13 A sleep disorder characterized by periods of irresistible sleep, attacks of cataplexy, sleep paralysis, and hypnagogic hallucinations.
9.23 A dark-colored group of noradrenergic cell bodies located in the pons near the rostral end of the floor of the fourth ventricle; involved in arousal and vigilance.	9.14 A symptom of narcolepsy; an irresistible urge to sleep during the day, after which the person awakens feeling refreshed.
9.24 A group of nuclei located in the reticular formation of the medulla, pons, and midbrain, situated along the midline; contain serotonergic neurons.	9.15 A symptom of narcolepsy; complete paralysis that occurs during waking.
9.25 A nucleus in the ventral posterior hypothalamus, just rostral to the mammillary bodies; contains histaminergic neurons involved in cortical activation and behavioral arousal.	9.16 A symptom of narcolepsy; paralysis occurring just before a person falls asleep.
9.26 A group of GABAergic neurons in the preoptic area whose activity suppresses alertness and behavioral arousal and promotes sleep.	9.17 A symptom of narcolepsy; vivid dreams that occur just before a person falls asleep; accompanied by sleep paralysis.

9.27 PGO wave	9.36 advanced sleep phase syndrome
9.28 peribrachial area	9.37 delayed sleep phase syndrome
9.29 carbachol	9.38 pineal gland
9.30 medial pontine reticular formation (MPRF)	9.39 melatonin
9.31 magnocellular nucleus	10.1 sexually dimorphic behavior
9.32 circadian rhythm	10.2 gamete
9.33 zeitgeber	10.3 sex chromosome
9.34 suprachiasmatic nucleus (SCN)	10.4 gonad
9.35 melanopsin	10.5 Sry

9.36 A 4-hour advance in rhythms of sleep and temperature cycles, apparently caused by a mutation of a gene (per2) involved in the rhythmicity of neurons of the SCN.	9.27 Bursts of phasic electrical activity originating in the pons, followed by activity in the lateral geniculate nucleus and visual cortex; a characteristic of REM sleep.
9.37 A 4-hour delay in rhythms of sleep and temperature cycles, possibly caused by a mutation of a gene (per3) involved in the rhythmicity of neurons of the SCN.	9.28 The region around the brachium conjunctivum, located in the dorsolateral pons; contains acetylcholinergic neurons involved in the initiation of REM sleep.
9.38 A gland attached to the dorsal tectum; produces melatonin and plays a role in circadian and seasonal rhythms.	9.29 A drug that stimulates acetylcholine receptors.
9.39 A hormone secreted during the night by the pineal body; plays a role in circadian and seasonal rhythms.	9.30 A region that contains neurons involved in the initiation of REM sleep; activated by acetylcholinergic neurons of the peribrachial area.
10.1 A behavior that has different forms or that occurs with different probabilities or under different circumstances in males and females.	9.31 A nucleus in the medulla; involved in the muscular paralysis that accompanies REM sleep.
10.2 A mature reproductive cell; a sperm or ovum.	9.32 A daily rhythmical change in behavior or physiological process.
10.3 The X and Y chromosomes, which determine an organism's gender. Normally, XX individuals are female, and XY individuals are male.	9.33 A stimulus (usually the light of dawn) that resets the biological clock that is responsible for circadian rhythms.
10.4 An ovary or testis.	9.34 A nucleus situated atop the optic chiasm. It contains a biological clock that is responsible for organizing many of the body's circadian rhythms.
10.5 The gene on the Y chromosome whose product instructs the undifferentiated fetal gonads to develop into testes.	9.35 A photopigment present in ganglion cells in the retina whose axons transmit information to the SCN, the thalamus, and the olivary pretectal nuclei.

10.6 organizational effect (of hormone)	10.15 dihydrotestosterone
10.7 activational effect (of hormone)	10.16 androgen insensitivity syndrome
10.8 Müllerian system	10.17 persistent Müllerian duct syndrome
10.9 Wolffian system	10.18 Turner's syndrome
10.10 anti-Müllerian hormone	10.19 gonadotropin releasing hormone
10.11 defeminizing effect	10.20 gonadotropic hormone
10.12 androgen	10.21 follicle-stimulating hormone (FSH)
10.13 masculinizing effect	10.22 luteinizing hormone (LH)
10.14 testosterone	10.23 estradiol

10.15 An androgen, produced from testosterone through the action of the enzyme 5-α reductase.	10.6 The effect of a hormone on tissue differentiation and development.
10.16 A condition caused by a congenital lack of functioning androgen receptors; in a person with XY sex chromosomes, causes the development of a female with testes but no internal sex organs.	10.7 The effect of a hormone that occurs in the fully developed organism; may depend on the organism's prior exposure to the organizational effects of hormones.
10.17 A condition caused by a congenital lack of anti-Müllerian hormone or receptors for this hormone; in a male, causes development of both male and female internal sex organs.	10.8 The embryonic precursors of the female internal sex organs.
10.18 The presence of only one sex chromosome (an X chromosome); characterized by lack of ovaries but otherwise normal female sex organs and genitalia.	10.9 The embryonic precursors of the male internal sex organs.
10.19 A hypothalamic hormone that stimulates the anterior pituitary gland to secrete gonadotropic hormone.	10.10 A peptide secreted by the fetal testes that inhibits the development of the Müllerian system, which would otherwise become the female internal sex organs.
10.20 A hormone of the anterior pituitary gland that has a stimulating effect on cells of the gonads.	10.11 An effect of a hormone present early in development that reduces or prevents the later development of anatomical or behavioral characteristics typical of females.
10.21 The hormone of the anterior pituitary gland that causes development of an ovarian follicle and the maturation of an ovum.	10.12 A male sex steroid hormone. Testosterone is the principal mammalian androgen.
10.22 A hormone of the anterior pituitary gland that causes ovulation and development of the ovarian follicle into a corpus luteum.	10.13 An effect of a hormone present early in development that promotes the later development of anatomical or behavioral characteristics typical of males.
10.23 The principal estrogen of many mammals, including humans.	10.14 The principal androgen found in males.

10.24 estrogen	10.33 prolactin
10.25 menstrual cycle	10.34 lordosis
10.26 estrous cycle	10.35 pheromone
10.27 ovarian follicle	10.36 Lee-Boot effect
10.28 corpus luteum	10.37 Whitten effect
10.29 progesterone	10.38 Vandenbergh effect
10.30 refractory period	10.39 Bruce effect
10.31 Coolidge effect	10.40 vomeronasal organ (VNO)
10.32 oxytocin	10.41 accessory olfactory bulb

10.33 A hormone of the anterior pituitary gland, necessary for production of milk; has an inhibitory effect on male sexual behavior.	10.24 A class of sex hormones that cause maturation of the female genitalia, growth of breast tissue, and development of other physical features characteristic of females.
10.34 A spinal sexual reflex seen in many four-legged female mammals; arching of the back in response to approach of a male or to touching the flanks, which elevates the hindquarters.	10.25 The female reproductive cycle of most primates, including humans; characterized by growth of the lining of the uterus, ovulation, development of a corpus luteum, and (if pregnancy does not occur), menstruation.
10.35 A chemical released by one animal that affects the behavior or physiology of another animal; usually smelled or tasted.	10.26 The female reproductive cycle of mammals other than primates.
10.36 The slowing and eventual cessation of estrous cycles in groups of female animals that are housed together; caused by a pheromone in the animals' urine; first observed in mice.	10.27 A cluster of epithelial cells surrounding an oocyte, which develops into an ovum.
10.37 The synchronization of the menstrual or estrous cycles of a group of females, which occurs only in the presence of a pheromone in a male's urine.	10.28 A cluster of cells that develops from the ovarian follicle after ovulation; secretes estradiol and progesterone.
10.38 The earlier onset of puberty seen in female animals that are housed with males; caused by a pheromone in the male's urine; first observed in mice.	10.29 A steroid hormone produced by the ovary that maintains the endometrial lining of the uterus during the later part of the menstrual cycle and during pregnancy; along with estradiol it promotes receptivity in female mammals with estrous cycles.
10.39 Termination of pregnancy caused by the odor of a pheromone in the urine of a male other than the one that impregnated the female; first identified in mice.	10.30 A period of time after a particular action (for example, an ejaculation by a male) during which that action cannot occur again.
10.40 A sensory organ that detects the presence of certain chemicals, especially when a liquid is actively sniffed; mediates the effects of some pheromones.	10.31 The restorative effect of introducing a new female sex partner to a male that has apparently become "exhausted" by sexual activity.
10.41 A neural structure located in the main olfactory bulb that receives information from the vomeronasal organ.	10.32 A hormone secreted by the posterior pituitary gland; causes contraction of the smooth muscle of the milk ducts, the uterus, and the male ejaculatory system; also serves as a neurotransmitter in the brain.

10.42 medial nucleus of the amygdala	11.2 lateral nucleus (LA)
10.43 congenital adrenal hyperplasia (CAH)	11.3 central nucleus (CE)
10.44 medial preoptic area (MPA)	11.4 conditioned emotional response
10.45 sexually dimorphic nucleus	11.5 threat behavior
10.46 periaqueductal gray matter (PAG)	11.6 defensive behavior
10.47 nucleus paragigantocellularis (PGi)	11.7 submissive behavior
10.48 ventromedial nucleus of the hypothalamus (VMH)	11.8 predation
10.49 parturition	11.9 orbitofrontal cortex
11.1 medial nucleus	11.10 ventromedial prefrontal cortex

11.2 A nucleus of the amygdala that receives sensory information from the neocortex, thalamus, and hippocampus and send projections to the basal, accessory basal, and central nucleus of the amygdala.	10.42 A nucleus that receives olfactory information from the olfactory bulb and accessory olfactory bulb; involved in the effects of odors and pheromones on reproductive behavior.
11.3 The region of the amygdala that receives information from the basal, lateral, and accessory basal nuclei and sends projections to a wide variety of regions in the brain; involved in emotional responses.	10.43 A condition characterized by hypersecretion of androgens by the adrenal cortex; in females, causes masculinization of the external genitalia.
11.4 A classically conditioned response that occurs when a neutral stimulus is followed by an aversive stimulus; usually includes autonomic, behavioral, and endocrine components such as changes in heart rate, freezing, and secretion of stress-related hormones.	10.44 An area of cell bodies just rostral to the hypothalamus; plays an essential role in male sexual behavior.
11.5 A stereotypical species-typical behavior that warns another animal that it may be attacked if it does not flee or show a submissive behavior.	10.45 A nucleus in the preoptic area that is much larger in males than in females; first observed in rats; plays a role in male sexual behavior.
11.6 A species-typical behavior by which an animal defends itself against the threat of another animal.	10.46 The region of the midbrain that surrounds the cerebral aqueduct; plays an essential role in various species-typical behaviors, including female sexual behavior.
11.7 A stereotyped behavior shown by an animal in response to threat behavior by another animal; serves to prevent an attack.	10.47 A nucleus of the medulla that receives input from the medial preoptic area and contains neurons whose axons form synapses with motor neurons in the spinal cord that participate in sexual reflexes in males.
11.8 Attack of one animal directed at an individual of another species on which the attacking animal normally preys.	10.48 A large nucleus of the hypothalamus located near the walls of the third ventricle; plays an essential role in female sexual behavior.
11.9 The region of the prefrontal cortex at the base of the anterior frontal lobes, just above the orbits of the eyes.	10.49 The act of giving birth.
11.10 The region of the prefrontal cortex at the base of the anterior frontal lobes, adjacent to the midline.	11.1 A group of subnuclei of the amygdala that receives sensory input, including information about the presence of odors and pheromones, and relays it to the medial basal forebrain and hypothalamus.

11.11 volitional facial paresis	12.7 negative feedback
11.12 emotional facial paresis	12.8 satiety mechanism
11.13 James-Lange theory	12.9 intracellular fluid
12.1 homeostasis	12.10 extracellular fluid
12.2 ingestive behavior	12.11 intravascular fluid
12.3 system variable	12.12 interstitial fluid
12.4 set point	12.13 isotonic
12.5 detector	12.14 hypertonic
12.6 correctional mechanism	12.15 hypotonic

12.7 A process whereby the effect produced by an action serves to diminish or terminate that action; a characteristic of regulatory systems.	11.11 Difficulty in moving the facial muscles voluntarily; caused by damage to the face region of the primary motor cortex or its subcortical connections.
12.8 A brain mechanism that causes cessation of hunger or thirst, produced by adequate and available supplies of nutrients or water.	11.12 Lack of movement of facial muscles in response to emotions in people who have no difficulty moving these muscles voluntarily; caused by damage to the insular prefrontal cortex, subcortical white matter of the frontal lobe, or parts of the thalamus.
12.9 The fluid contained within cells.	11.13 A theory of emotion that suggests that behaviors and physiological responses are directly elicited by situations and that feelings of emotions are produced by feedback from these behaviors and responses.
12.10 All body fluids outside cells: interstitial fluid, blood plasma, and cerebrospinal fluid.	12.1 The process by which the body's substances and characteristics (such as temperature and glucose level) are maintained at their optimal level.
12.11 The fluid found within the blood vessels.	12.2 Eating or drinking.
12.12 The fluid that bathes the cells, filling the space between the cells of the body (the "interstices").	12.3 A variable that is controlled by a regulatory mechanism, for example, temperature in a heating system.
12.13 Equal in osmotic pressure to the contents of a cell. A cell placed in an isotonic solution neither gains nor loses water.	12.4 The optimal value of the system variable in a regulatory mechanism.
12.14 The characteristic of a solution that contains enough solute that it will draw water out of a cell placed in it, through the process of osmosis.	12.5 In a regulatory process, a mechanism that signals when the system variable deviates from its set point.
12.15 The characteristic of a solution that contains so little solute that a cell placed in it will absorb water, through the process of osmosis.	12.6 In a regulatory process, the mechanism that is capable of changing the value of the system variable.

12.16 hypovolemia	12.25 **median preoptic nucleus**
12.17 osmometric thirst	12.26 **glycogen**
12.18 osmoreceptor	12.27 **insulin**
12.19 OVLT (organum vasculosum of the lamina terminalis)	12.28 **glucagon**
12.20 subfornical organ (SFO)	12.29 **triglyceride**
12.21 volumetric thirst	12.30 **glycerol**
12.22 renin	12.31 **fatty acid**
12.23 angiotensin	12.32 **fasting phase**
12.24 nucleus of the solitary tract	12.33 **absorptive phase**

12.25
A small nucleus situated around the decussation of the anterior commissure; plays a role in thirst stimulated by angiotensin.

12.26
A polysaccharide often referred to as animal starch; stored in liver and muscle; constitutes the short-term store of nutrients.

12.27
A pancreatic hormone that facilitates entry of glucose and amino acids into the cell, conversion of glucose into glycogen, and transport of fats into adipose tissue.

12.28
A pancreatic hormone that promotes the conversion of liver glycogen into glucose.

12.29
The form of fat storage in adipose cells; consists of a molecule of glycerol joined with three fatty acids.

12.30
A substance (also called glycerine) derived from the breakdown of triglycerides, along with fatty acids; can be converted by the liver into glucose.

12.31
A substance derived from the breakdown of triglycerides, along with glycerol; can be metabolized by most cells of the body except for the brain.

12.32
The phase of metabolism during which nutrients are not available from the digestive system; glucose, amino acids, and fatty acids are derived from glycogen, protein, and adipose tissue during this phase.

12.33
The phase of metabolism during which nutrients are absorbed from the digestive system; glucose and amino acids constitute the principal source of energy for cells during this phase, and excess nutrients are stored in adipose tissue in the form of triglycerides.

12.16
Reduction in the volume of the intravascular fluid.

12.17
Thirst produced by an increase in the osmotic pressure of the interstitial fluid relative to the intracellular fluid, thus producing cellular dehydration.

12.18
A neuron that detects changes in the solute concentration of the interstitial fluid that surrounds it.

12.19
A circumventricular organ located anterior to the anteroventral portion of the third ventricle; served by fenestrated capillaries and thus lacks a blood-brain barrier.

12.20
A small organ located in the confluence of the lateral ventricles, attached to the underside of the fornix; contains neurons that detect the presence of angiotensin in the blood and excite neural circuits that initiate drinking.

12.21
Thirst produced by hypovolemia.

12.22
A hormone secreted by the kidneys that causes the conversion of angiotensinogen in the blood into angiotensin.

12.23
A peptide hormone that constricts blood vessels, causes the retention of sodium and water, and produces thirst and a salt appetite.

12.24
A nucleus of the medulla that receives information from visceral organs and from the gustatory system.

12.34 **ghrelin**	12.43 **peptide YY3-36 (PYY)**
12.35 **duodenum**	12.44 **ob mouse**
12.36 **glucoprivation**	12.45 **leptin**
12.37 **lipoprivation**	12.46 **decerebration**
12.38 **methyl palmoxirate (MP)**	12.47 **melanin-concentrating hormone (MCH)**
12.39 **mercaptoacetate (MA)**	12.48 **orexin**
12.40 **hepatic portal vein**	12.49 **neuropeptide Y (NPY)**
12.41 **gastric fistula**	12.50 **arcuate nucleus**
12.42 **cholecystokinin (CCK)**	12.51 **paraventricular nucleus (PVN)**

12.43 A peptide released by the gastrointestinal system after a meal in amounts proportional to the size of the meal.	12.34 A peptide hormone released by the stomach that increases eating; also produced by neurons in the brain.
12.44 A strain of mice whose obesity and low metabolic rate are caused by a mutation that prevents the production of leptin.	12.35 The first portion of the small intestine, attached directly to the stomach.
12.45 A hormone secreted by adipose tissue; decreases food intake and increases metabolic rate, primarily by inhibiting NPY-secreting neurons in the arcuate nucleus.	12.36 A dramatic fall in the level of glucose available to cells; can be caused by a fall in the blood level of glucose or by drugs that inhibit glucose metabolism.
12.46 A surgical procedure that severs the brain stem, disconnecting the hindbrain from the forebrain.	12.37 A dramatic fall in the level of fatty acids available to cells; usually caused by drugs that inhibit fatty acid metabolism.
12.47 A peptide neurotransmitter found in a system of lateral hypothalamic neurons that stimulate appetite and reduce metabolic rate.	12.38 A drug that inhibits fatty acid metabolism and produces lipoprivic hunger.
12.48 A peptide neurotransmitter found in a system of lateral hypothalamic neurons that stimulate appetite and reduce metabolic rate.	12.39 A drug that inhibits fatty acid metabolism and produces lipoprivic hunger.
12.49 A peptide neurotransmitter found in a system of neurons of the arcuate nucleus that stimulate feeding, insulin and glucocorticoid secretion, decrease the breakdown of triglycerides, and decrease body temperature.	12.40 The vein that transports blood from the digestive system to the liver.
12.50 A nucleus in the base of the hypothalamus that controls secretions of the anterior pituitary gland; contains NPY-secreting neurons involved in feeding and control of metabolism.	12.41 A tube that drains out the contents of the stomach.
12.51 A nucleus of the hypothalamus located adjacent to the dorsal third ventricle; contains neurons involved in control of the autonomic nervous system and the posterior pituitary gland.	12.42 A hormone secreted by the duodenum that regulates gastric motility and causes the gallbladder (cholecyst) to contract; appears to provide a satiety signal transmitted to the brain through the vagus nerve.

12.52 agouti-related protein (AGRP)	13.3 classical conditioning
12.53 CART	13.4 Hebb rule
12.54 α-melanocyte-stimulating hormone (α-MSH)	13.5 instrumental conditioning
12.55 melanocortin-4 receptor (MC-4R)	13.6 reinforcing stimulus
12.56 uncoupling protein (UCP)	13.7 punishing stimulus
12.57 anorexia nervosa	13.8 motor learning
12.58 bulimia nervosa	13.9 long-term potentiation (LTP)
13.1 perceptual learning	13.10 hippocampal formation
13.2 stimulus-response learning	13.11 entorhinal cortex

13.3 A learning procedure; when a stimulus that initially produces no particular response is followed several times by an unconditional stimulus that produces a defensive or appetitive response (the unconditional response), the first stimulus (now called a conditional stimulus) itself evokes the response (now called a conditional response).	12.52 A neuropeptide that acts as an antagonist at MC-4 receptors and increases eating.
13.4 The hypothesis proposed by Donald Hebb that the cellular basis of learning involves strengthening of a synapse that is repeatedly active when the postsynaptic neuron fires.	12.53 Cocaine- and amphetamine-regulated transcript; a peptide neurotransmitter found in a system of neurons of the arcuate nucleus that inhibit feeding.
13.5 A learning procedure whereby the effects of a particular behavior in a particular situation increase (reinforce) or decrease (punish) the probability of the behavior; also called operant conditioning.	12.54 A neuropeptide that acts as an agonist at MC-4 receptors and inhibits eating.
13.6 An appetitive stimulus that follows a particular behavior and thus makes the behavior become more frequent.	12.55 A receptor found in the brain that binds with α-MSH and agouti-related protein; plays a role in control of appetite.
13.7 An aversive stimulus that follows a particular behavior and thus makes the behavior become less frequent.	12.56 A mitochondrial protein that facilitates the conversion of nutrients into heat.
13.8 Learning to make a new response.	12.57 A disorder that most frequently afflicts young women; exaggerated concern with overweight that leads to excessive dieting and often compulsive exercising; can lead to starvation.
13.9 A long-term increase in the excitability of a neuron to a particular synaptic input caused by repeated high-frequency activity of that input.	12.58 Bouts of excessive hunger and eating, often followed by forced vomiting or purging with laxatives; sometimes seen in people with anorexia nervosa.
13.10 A forebrain structure of the temporal lobe, constituting an important part of the limbic system; includes the hippocampus proper (Ammon's horn), dentate gyrus, and subiculum.	13.1 Learning to recognize a particular stimulus.
13.11 A region of the limbic cortex that provides the major source of input to the hippocampal formation.	13.2 Learning to automatically make a particular response in the presence of a particular stimulus; includes classical and instrumental conditioning.

13.12 granule cell	13.21 AP5
13.13 dentate gyrus	13.22 dendritic spike
13.14 perforant path	13.23 AMPA receptor
13.15 field CA3	13.24 CaM-KII
13.16 pyramidal cell	13.25 nitric oxide synthase
13.17 field CA1	13.26 long-term depression (LTD)
13.18 population EPSP	13.27 short-term memory
13.19 associative long-term potentiation	13.28 delayed matching-to-sample task
13.20 NMDA receptor	13.29 medial forebrain bundle (MFB)

13.21 2-Amino-5-phosphonopentanoate; a drug that blocks NMDA receptors.	13.12 A small, granular cell; those found in the dentate gyrus send axons to the field CA3 of the hippocampus.
13.22 An action potential that occurs in the dendrite of some types of pyramidal cells.	13.13 Part of the hippocampal formation; receives inputs from the entorhinal cortex and projects to the field CA3 of the hippocampus.
13.23 An ionotropic glutamate receptor that controls a sodium channel; when open, it produces EPSPs.	13.14 The system of axons that travel from cells in the entorhinal cortex to the dentate gyrus of the hippocampal formation.
13.24 Type II calcium-calmodulin kinase, an enzyme that must be activated by calcium; may play a role in the establishment of long-term potentiation.	13.15 Part of the hippocampus; receives inputs from the dentate gyrus and projects to field CA1.
13.25 An enzyme responsible for the production of nitric oxide.	13.16 A category of large neurons with a pyramid shape; found in the cerebral cortex and Ammon's horn of the hippocampal formation.
13.26 A long-term decrease in the excitability of a neuron to a particular synaptic input caused by stimulation of the terminal button while the postsynaptic membrane is hyperpolarized or only slightly depolarized.	13.17 Part of the hippocampus; receives inputs from field CA3 and projects out of the hippocampal formation via the subiculum.
13.27 Memory for a stimulus or an event that lasts for a short while.	13.18 An evoked potential that represents the EPSPs of a population of neurons.
13.28 A task that requires the subject to indicate which of several stimuli has just been perceived.	13.19 A long-term potentiation in which concurrent stimulation of weak and strong synapses to a given neuron strengthens the weak ones.
13.29 A fiber bundle that runs in a rostral-caudal direction through the basal forebrain and lateral hypothalamus; electrical stimulation of these axons is reinforcing.	13.20 A specialized ionotropic glutamate receptor that controls a calcium channel that is normally blocked by Mg^{2+} ions; involved in long-term potentiation.

13.30 ventral tegmental area (VTA)	13.39 perirhinal cortex
13.31 nucleus accumbens	13.40 parahippocampal cortex
13.32 anterograde amnesia	13.41 episodic memory
13.33 retrograde amnesia	13.42 semantic memory
13.34 Korsakoff's syndrome	13.43 semantic dementia
13.35 confabulation	13.44 place cell
13.36 consolidation	13.45 reconsolidation
13.37 declarative memory	14.1 cerebrovascular accident
13.38 nondeclarative memory	14.2 aphasia

13.39 A region of limbic cortex adjacent to the hippocampal formation that, along with the parahippocampal cortex, relays information between the entorhinal cortex and other regions of the brain.	13.30 A group of dopaminergic neurons in the ventral midbrain whose axons form the mesolimbic and mesocortical systems; plays a critical role in reinforcement.
13.40 A region of limbic cortex adjacent to the hippocampal formation that, along with the perirhinal cortex, relays information between the entorhinal cortex and other regions of the brain.	13.31 A nucleus of the basal forebrain near the septum; receives dopamine-secreting terminal buttons from neurons of the ventral tegmental area and is thought to be involved in reinforcement and attention.
13.41 Memory of a collection of perceptions of events organized in time and identified by a particular context.	13.32 Amnesia for events that occur after some disturbance to the brain, such as head injury or certain degenerative brain diseases.
13.42 A memory of facts and general information.	13.33 Amnesia for events that preceded some disturbance to the brain, such as a head injury or electroconvulsive shock.
13.43 Loss of semantic memories caused by progressive degeneration of the neocortex of the lateral temporal lobes.	13.34 Permanent anterograde amnesia caused by brain damage resulting from chronic alcoholism or malnutrition.
13.44 A neuron that becomes active when the animal is in a particular location in the environment; most typically found in the hippocampal formation.	13.35 The reporting of memories of events that did not take place without the intention to deceive; seen in people with Korsakoff's syndrome.
13.45 A process of consolidation of a memory that occurs subsequent to the original consolidation that can be triggered by a reminder of the original stimulus; thought to provide the means for modifying existing memories.	13.36 The process by which short-term memories are converted into long-term memories.
14.1 A "stroke"; brain damage caused by occlusion or rupture of a blood vessel in the brain.	13.37 Memory that can be verbally expressed, such as memory for events in a person's past.
14.2 Difficulty in producing or comprehending speech not produced by deafness or a simple motor deficit; caused by brain damage.	13.38 Memory whose formation does not depend on the hippocampal formation; a collective term for perceptual, stimulus-response, and motor memory.

14.3 Broca's aphasia	14.12 pure word deafness
14.4 function word	14.13 transcortical sensory aphasia
14.5 content word	14.14 autotopagnosia
14.6 Broca's area	14.15 arcuate fasciculus
14.7 agrammatism	14.16 conduction aphasia
14.8 anomia	14.17 circumlocution
14.9 apraxia of speech	14.18 prosody
14.10 Wernicke's area	14.19 pure alexia
14.11 Wernicke's aphasia	14.20 whole-word reading

14.12 The ability to hear, to speak, and (usually) to read and write without being able to comprehend the meaning of speech; caused by damage to Wernicke's area or disruption of auditory input to this region.	14.3 A form of aphasia characterized by agrammatism, anomia, and extreme difficulty in speech articulation.
14.13 A speech disorder in which a person has difficulty comprehending speech and producing meaningful spontaneous speech but can repeat speech; caused by damage to the region of the brain posterior to Wernicke's area.	14.4 A preposition, article, or other word that conveys little of the meaning of a sentence but is important in specifying its grammatical structure.
14.14 Inability to name body parts or to identify body parts that another person names.	14.5 A noun, verb, adjective, or adverb that conveys meaning.
14.15 A bundle of axons that connects Wernicke's area with Broca's area; damage causes conduction aphasia.	14.6 A region of frontal cortex, located just rostral to the base of the left primary motor cortex, that is necessary for normal speech production.
14.16 An aphasia characterized by inability to repeat words that are heard but the ability to speak normally and comprehend the speech of others.	14.7 One of the usual symptoms of Broca's aphasia; a difficulty in comprehending or properly employing grammatical devices, such as verb endings and word order.
14.17 A strategy by which people with anomia find alternative ways to say something when they are unable to think of the most appropriate word.	14.8 Difficulty in finding (remembering) the appropriate word to describe an object, action, or attribute; one of the symptoms of aphasia.
14.18 The use of changes in intonation and emphasis to convey meaning in speech besides that specified by the particular words; an important means of communication of emotion.	14.9 Impairment in the ability to program movements of the tongue, lips, and throat required to produce the proper sequence of speech sounds.
14.19 Loss of the ability to read without loss of the ability to write; produced by brain damage.	14.10 A region of auditory association cortex on the left temporal lobe of humans, which is important in the comprehension of words and the production of meaningful speech.
14.20 Reading by recognizing a word as a whole; "sight reading."	14.11 A form of aphasia characterized by poor speech comprehension and fluent but meaningless speech.

14.21 phonetic reading	15.1 tumor
14.22 surface dyslexia	15.2 malignant tumor
14.23 phonological dyslexia	15.3 benign tumor
14.24 word-form dyslexia	15.4 metastasis
14.25 spelling dyslexia	15.5 glioma
14.26 direct dyslexia	15.6 meningioma
14.27 phonological dysgraphia	15.7 seizure disorder
14.28 orthographic dysgraphia	15.8 convulsion
14.29 developmental dyslexia	15.9 partial seizure

15.1 A mass of cells whose growth is uncontrolled and that serves no useful function.	14.21 Reading by decoding the phonetic significance of letter strings; "sound reading."
15.2 A cancerous (literally, "harm-producing") tumor; lacks a distinct border and may metastasize.	14.22 A reading disorder in which a person can read words phonetically but has difficulty reading irregularly spelled words by the whole-word method.
15.3 A noncancerous (literally, "harmless") tumor; has a distinct border and cannot metastasize.	14.23 A reading disorder in which a person can read familiar words but has difficulty reading unfamiliar words or pronounceable nonwords.
15.4 The process by which cells break off of a tumor, travel through the vascular system, and grow elsewhere in the body.	14.24 A disorder in which a person can read a word only after spelling out the individual letters.
15.5 A cancerous brain tumor composed of one of several types of glial cells.	14.25 An alternative name for word-form dyslexia.
15.6 A benign brain tumor composed of the cells that constitute the meninges.	14.26 A language disorder caused by brain damage in which the person can read words aloud without understanding them.
15.7 The preferred term for epilepsy.	14.27 A writing disorder in which the person cannot sound out words and write them phonetically.
15.8 A violent sequence of uncontrollable muscular movements caused by a seizure.	14.28 A writing disorder in which the person can spell regularly spelled words but not irregularly spelled ones.
15.9 A seizure that begins at a focus and remains localized, not generalizing to the rest of the brain.	14.29 A reading difficulty in a person of normal intelligence and perceptual ability; of genetic origin or caused by prenatal or perinatal factors.

15.10 generalized seizure	15.19 hemorrhagic stroke
15.11 simple partial seizure	15.20 obstructive stroke
15.12 complex partial seizure	15.21 ischemia
15.13 grand mal seizure	15.22 thrombus
15.14 aura	15.23 embolus
15.15 tonic phase	15.24 free radical
15.16 clonic phase	15.25 fetal alcohol syndrome
15.17 absence	15.26 neural adhesion protein
15.18 status epilepticus	15.27 phenylketonuria (PKU)

15.19 A cerebrovascular accident caused by the rupture of a cerebral blood vessel.	15.10 A seizure that involves most of the brain, as contrasted with a partial seizure, which remains localized.
15.20 A cerebrovascular accident caused by occlusion of a blood vessel.	15.11 A partial seizure, starting from a focus and remaining localized, that does not produce loss of consciousness.
15.21 The interruption of the blood supply to a region of the body.	15.12 A partial seizure, starting from a focus and remaining localized, that produces loss of consciousness.
15.22 A blood clot that forms within a blood vessel, which may occlude it.	15.13 A generalized, tonic-clonic seizure, which results in a convulsion.
15.23 A piece of matter (such as a blood clot, fat, or bacterial debris) that dislodges from its site of origin and occludes an artery; in the brain an embolus can lead to a stroke.	15.14 A sensation that precedes a seizure; its exact nature depends on the location of the seizure focus.
15.24 A molecule with unpaired electrons; acts as a powerful oxidizing agent; toxic to cells.	15.15 The first phase of a grand mal seizure, in which all of the patient's skeletal muscles are contracted.
15.25 A birth defect caused by ingestion of alcohol by a pregnant woman; includes characteristic facial anomalies and faulty brain development.	15.16 The phase of a grand mal seizure in which the patient shows rhythmic jerking movements.
15.26 A protein that plays a role in brain development; helps to guide the growth of neurons.	15.17 A type of seizure disorder often seen in children; characterized by periods of inattention, which are not subsequently remembered; also called petit mal seizure.
15.27 A hereditary disorder caused by the absence of an enzyme that converts the amino acid phenylalanine to tyrosine; the accumulation of phenylalanine causes brain damage unless a special diet is implemented soon after birth.	15.18 A condition in which a patient undergoes a series of seizures without regaining consciousness.

15.28 pyridoxine dependency	15.37 α-synuclein
15.29 galactosemia	15.38 toxic gain of function
15.30 Tay-Sachs disease	15.39 parkin
15.31 Down syndrome	15.40 loss of function
15.32 transmissible spongiform encephalopathy	15.41 proteasome
15.33 prion	15.42 ubiquitin
15.34 sporadic disease	15.43 internal division of the globus pallidus (GPi)
15.35 caspase	15.44 Huntington's disease
15.36 Lewy body	15.45 huntingtin (htt)

15.37 A protein normally found in the presynaptic membrane, where it is apparently involved in synaptic plasticity. Abnormal accumulations are apparently the cause of neural degeneration in Parkinson's disease.	15.28 A metabolic disorder in which an infant requires larger-than-normal amounts of pyridoxine (vitamin B6) to avoid neurological symptoms.
15.38 Said of a genetic disorder caused by a dominant mutation that involves a faulty gene that produces a protein with toxic effects.	15.29 An inherited metabolic disorder in which galactose (milk sugar) cannot easily be metabolized.
15.39 A protein that plays a role in ferrying defective or misfolded proteins to the proteasomes; mutated parkin is a cause of familial Parkinson's disease.	15.30 A heritable, fatal, metabolic storage disorder; lack of enzymes in lysosomes causes accumulation of waste produces and swelling of cells of the brain.
15.40 Said of a genetic disorder caused by a recessive gene that fails to produce a protein that is necessary for good health.	15.31 A disorder caused by the presence of an extra twenty-first chromosome, characterized by moderate to severe mental retardation and often by physical abnormalities.
15.41 An organelle responsible for destroying defective or degraded proteins within the cell.	15.32 A contagious brain disease whose degenerative process gives the brain a spongelike appearance; caused by accumulation of misfolded prion protein.
15.42 A protein that attaches itself to faulty or misfolded proteins and thus targets them for destruction by proteasomes.	15.33 A protein that can exist in two forms that differ only in their three-dimensional shape; accumulation of misfolded prion protein is responsible for transmissible spongiform encephalopathies.
15.43 A division of the globus pallidus that provides inhibitory input to the motor cortex via the thalamus; sometimes stereotaxically lesioned to treat the symptoms of Parkinson's disease.	15.34 A disease that occurs rarely and is not obviously caused by heredity or an infectious agent.
15.44 An inherited disorder that causes degeneration of the basal ganglia; characterized by progressively more severe uncontrollable jerking movements, writhing movements, dementia, and finally death.	15.35 A "killer enzyme" that plays a role in apoptosis, or programmed cell death.
15.45 A protein that may serve to facilitate the production and transport of brain-derived neurotrophic factor. Abnormal huntingtin is the cause of Huntington's disease.	15.36 Abnormal circular structures with a dense core consisting of α-synuclein protein; found in the cytoplasm of nigrostriatal neurons in people with Parkinson's disease.

15.46 dementia	15.55 apolipoprotein E (ApoE)
15.47 Alzheimer's disease	15.56 amyotrophic lateral sclerosis (ALS)
15.48 amyloid plaque	15.57 encephalitis
15.49 β-amyloid (Aβ)	15.58 herpes simplex virus
15.50 neurofibrillary tangle	15.59 acute anterior poliomyelitis
15.51 tau protein	15.60 rabies
15.52 β-amyloid precursor protein (APP)	15.61 meningitis
15.53 secretase	16.1 schizophrenia
15.54 presenilin	16.2 positive symptom

15.55 A glycoprotein that transports cholesterol in the blood and plays a role in cellular repair; presence of the E4 allele of the apoE gene increases the risk of late-onset Alzheimer's disease.	15.46 A loss of cognitive abilities such as memory, perception, verbal ability, and judgment; common causes are multiple strokes and Alzheimer's disease.
15.56 A degenerative disorder that attacks the spinal cord and cranial nerve motor neurons.	15.47 A degenerative brain disorder of unknown origin; causes progressive memory loss, motor deficits, and eventual death.
15.57 An inflammation of the brain; caused by bacteria, viruses, or toxic chemicals.	15.48 An extracellular deposit containing a dense core of β-amyloid protein surrounded by degenerating axons and dendrites and activated microglia and reactive astrocytes.
15.58 A virus that normally causes cold sores near the lips but that can also cause brain damage.	15.49 A protein found in excessive amounts in the brains of patients with Alzheimer's disease.
15.59 A viral disease that destroys motor neurons of the brain and spinal cord.	15.50 A dying neuron containing intracellular accumulations of β-amyloid and twisted protein filaments that formerly served as the cell's internal skeleton.
15.60 A fatal viral disease that causes brain damage; usually transmitted through the bite of an infected animal.	15.51 A protein that normally serves as a component of microtubules, which provide the cell's transport mechanism.
15.61 An inflammation of the meninges; can be caused by viruses or bacteria.	15.52 A protein produced and secreted by cells that serves as the precursor for β-amyloid protein.
16.1 A serious mental disorder characterized by disordered thoughts, delusions, hallucinations, and often bizarre behaviors.	15.53 A class of enzymes that cut the β-amyloid precursor protein into smaller fragments, including β-amyloid.
16.2 A symptom of schizophrenia evident by its presence: delusions, hallucinations, or thought disorders.	15.54 A protein produced by a faulty gene that causes β-amyloid precursor protein to be converted to the abnormal short form; may be a cause of Alzheimer's disease.

16.3 thought disorder	16.12 seasonality effect
16.4 delusion	16.13 hypofrontality
16.5 hallucination	16.14 partial agonist
16.6 negative symptom	16.15 major affective disorder
16.7 chlorpromazine	16.16 bipolar disorder
16.8 clozapine	16.17 unipolar depression
16.9 tardive dyskinesia	16.18 tricyclic antidepressant
16.10 supersensitivity	16.19 specific serotonin reuptake inhibitor (SSRI)
16.11 epidemiology	16.20 norepinephrine and serotonin reuptake inhibitor (SNRI)

16.12 The increased incidence of schizophrenia in people born during late winter and early spring.	16.3 Disorganized, irrational thinking.
16.13 Decreased activity of the prefrontal cortex; believed to be responsible for the negative symptoms of schizophrenia.	16.4 A belief that is clearly in contradiction to reality.
16.14 A drug that has a very high affinity for a particular receptor but activates that receptor less than the normal ligand does; serves as an agonist in regions of low concentration of the normal ligand and as an antagonist in regions of high concentrations.	16.5 Perception of a nonexistent object or event.
16.15 A serious mood disorder; includes unipolar depression and bipolar disorder.	16.6 A symptom of schizophrenia characterized by the absence of behaviors that are normally present: social withdrawal, lack of affect, and reduced motivation.
16.16 A serious mood disorder characterized by cyclical periods of mania and depression.	16.7 A dopamine receptor blocker; a commonly prescribed antischizophrenic drug.
16.17 A serious mood disorder that consists of unremitting depression or periods of depression that do not alternate with periods of mania.	16.8 An atypical antipsychotic drug; blocks D4 receptors in the nucleus accumbens.
16.18 A class of drugs used to treat depression; inhibits the reuptake of norepinephrine and serotonin but also affects other neurotransmitters; named for the molecular structure.	16.9 A movement disorder that can occur after prolonged treatment with antipsychotic medication, characterized by involuntary movements of the face and neck.
16.19 An antidepressant drug that specifically inhibits the reuptake of serotonin without affecting the reuptake of other neurotransmitters.	16.10 The increased sensitivity of neurotransmitter receptors; caused by damage to the afferent axons or long-term blockage of neurotransmitter release.
16.20 An antidepressant drug that specifically inhibits the reuptake of norepinephrine and serotonin without affecting the reuptake of other neurotransmitters.	16.11 The study of the distribution and causes of diseases in populations.

16.21 electroconvulsive therapy (ECT)	17.2 panic disorder
16.22 lithium	17.3 anticipatory anxiety
16.23 monoamine hypothesis	17.4 agoraphobia
16.24 tryptophan depletion procedure	17.5 obsessive-compulsive disorder (OCD)
16.25 silent cerebral infarction (SCI)	17.6 obsession
16.26 seasonal affective disorder	17.7 compulsion
16.27 summer depression	17.8 Tourette's syndrome
16.28 phototherapy	17.9 cingulotomy
17.1 anxiety disorder	17.10 autistic disorder

17.2 A disorder characterized by episodic periods of symptoms such as shortness of breath, irregularities in heartbeat, and other autonomic symptoms, accompanied by intense fear.	16.21 A brief electrical shock, applied to the head, that results in an electrical seizure; used therapeutically to alleviate severe depression.
17.3 A fear of having a panic attack; may lead to the development of agoraphobia.	16.22 A chemical element; lithium carbonate is used to treat bipolar disorder.
17.4 A fear of being away from home or other protected places.	16.23 A hypothesis that states that depression is caused by a low level of activity of one or more monoaminergic synapses.
17.5 A mental disorder characterized by obsessions and compulsions.	16.24 A procedure involving a low-tryptophan diet and a tryptophan-free amino acid "cocktail" that lowers brain tryptophan and consequently decreases the synthesis of 5-HT.
17.6 An unwanted thought or idea with which a person is preoccupied.	16.25 A small cerebrovascular accident (stroke) that causes minor brain damage without producing obvious neurological symptoms.
17.7 The feeling that one is obliged to perform a behavior, even if one prefers not to do so.	16.26 A mood disorder characterized by depression, lethargy, sleep disturbances, and craving for carbohydrates during the winter season when days are short.
17.8 A neurological disorder characterized by tics and involuntary vocalizations and sometimes by compulsive uttering of obscenities and repetition of the utterances of others.	16.27 A mood disorder that occurs specifically in the summer; characterized by depression, sleep disturbances, and loss of appetite.
17.9 The surgical destruction of the cingulum bundle, which connects the prefrontal cortex with the limbic system; helps to reduce intense anxiety and the symptoms of obsessive-compulsive disorder.	16.28 Treatment of seasonal affective disorder by daily exposure to bright light.
17.10 A chronic disorder whose symptoms include failure to develop normal social relations with other people, impaired development of communicative ability, lack of imaginative ability, and repetitive, stereotyped movements.	17.1 A psychological disorder characterized by tension, overactivity of the autonomic nervous system, expectation of an impending disaster, and continuous vigilance for danger.

17.11 attention-deficit/hyperactivity disorder (ADHD)	17.20 psychoneuroimmunology
17.12 stress	17.21 antigen
17.13 stressor	17.22 antibody
17.14 stress response	17.23 B-lymphocyte
17.15 fight-or-flight response	17.24 immunoglobulin
17.16 glucocorticoid	17.25 T-lymphocyte
17.17 corticotropin-releasing hormone (CRH)	17.26 cytokine
17.18 adrenocorticotropic hormone (ACTH)	18.1 negative reinforcement
17.19 posttraumatic stress disorder (PTSD)	18.2 tolerance

17.20
The branch of neuroscience involved with interactions between environmental stimuli, the nervous system, and the immune system.

17.21
A protein present on a microorganism that permits the immune system to recognize the microorganism as an invader.

17.22
A protein produced by a cell of the immune system that recognizes antigens present on invading microorganisms.

17.23
A white blood cell that originates in the bone marrow; part of the immune system.

17.24
An antibody released by B-lymphocytes that bind with antigens and help to destroy invading microorganisms.

17.25
A white blood cell that originates in the thymus gland; part of the immune system.

17.26
A category of chemicals released by certain white blood cells when they detect the presence of an invading microorganism; causes other white blood cells to proliferate and mount an attack against the invader.

18.1
The removal or reduction of an aversive stimulus that is contingent on a particular response, with an attendant increase in the frequency of that response.

18.2
The fact that increasingly large doses of drugs must be taken to achieve a particular effect; caused by compensatory mechanisms that oppose the effect of the drug.

17.11
A disorder characterized by uninhibited responses, lack of sustained attention, and hyperactivity; first shows itself in childhood.

17.12
A general, imprecise term that can refer either to a stress response or to a stressor (stressful situation).

17.13
A stimulus (or situation) that produces a stress response.

17.14
A physiological reaction caused by the perception of aversive or threatening situations.

17.15
A species-typical response preparatory to fighting or fleeing; thought to be responsible for some of the deleterious effects of stressful situations on health.

17.16
One of a group of hormones of the adrenal cortex that are important in protein and carbohydrate metabolism, secreted especially in times of stress.

17.17
A hypothalamic hormone that stimulates the anterior pituitary gland to secrete ACTH (adrenocorticotropic hormone).

17.18
A hormone released by the anterior pituitary gland in response to CRH; stimulates the adrenal cortex to produce glucocorticoids.

17.19
A psychological disorder caused by exposure to a situation of extreme danger and stress; symptoms include recurrent dreams or recollections; can interfere with social activities and cause a feeling of hopelessness.

18.3 withdrawal symptoms	
18.4 naloxone	
18.5 antagonist-precipitated withdrawal	

	18.3 The appearance of symptoms opposite to those produced by a drug when the drug is suddenly no longer taken; caused by the presence of compensatory mechanisms.
	18.4 A drug that blocks μ opiate receptors; antagonizes the reinforcing and sedative effects of opiates.
	18.5 Sudden withdrawal from long-term administration of a drug caused by cessation of the drug and administration of an antagonistic drug.

NOTES

NOTES

NOTES

NOTES

NOTES

NOTES

NOTES